Handbook of Mental Health Administration and Management

HANDBOOK OF MENTAL HEALTH ADMINISTRATION AND MANAGEMENT

Edited by

William H. Reid, MD, MPH
Stuart B. Silver, MD

Brunner-Routledge
New York • Hove

Published in 2003 by
Brunner-Routledge
29 West 35th Street
New York, NY 10001
www.brunner-routledge.com

Published in Great Britain by
Brunner-Routledge
27 Church Road
Hove, East Sussex
BN3 2FA
www.brunner-routledge.co.uk

10 9 8 7 6 5 4 3 2 1

Library of Congress Cataloging-in-Publication Data
Reid, William H.
    Handbook of mental health administration and management / William H. Reid and Stuart B. Silver.
      p. cm.
    Includes bibliographical references and index.
    ISBN 1–58391–002–6
    1. Mental health services—Administration. I. Silver, Stuart B. II. Title.

  RA790.5 .R45 2002
  362.2'068—dc21   2002018498

Contents

Foreword

Organizational leadership is a challenging task, but it can be extremely gratifying. Such a leadership position provides an opportunity to extend the scope and impact of one's efforts to make the world a better place. It also represents an opportunity to increase one's influence, stature, and compensation. Of course, greater responsibility is a two-edged sword. It can offer both positive and negative experiences—successes and failures.

Much of the delivery of mental health care takes place in the context of an organization—a hospital, clinic, mental health center, or group practice. Clinicians serving in these organizations are initially hired to provide the clinical services that they were trained to provide. Inevitably, some clinicians will gravitate into a position of organizational leadership, challenged by the opportunity to extend their good works through the supervision and direction of others. However, most professional education does not include training in administration and supervision, to say nothing of the many facets of organizational function—business, finance, information technology, human resource issues, etc.

How does the clinician-administrator/manager compensate for this lack of education? When one assumes a supervisory role as the first step on the ladder of organizational leadership, a primary source of education is one's experience. However, every young administrator inevitably is confronted with the reality of one of the corollaries of Murphy's Law known as Higdon's Law: "Good judgment comes from experience. Experience comes from bad judgment!"

Many young practitioners compensate for their limited experience through the support and direction of a mentor, an experienced colleague who has been in a leadership role and learned lessons over many years. Some complement their clinical expertise through formal education in administration and management, ranging from brief workshops to courses in executive education at universities like Harvard and Stanford. Some make the commitment to an advanced academic degree in business administration.

In today's health care climate, the administrator must be versed not only in the principles of management in general, but in many specific matters directly related to health care delivery. These specifics are outlined by organizations and agencies charged with oversight of our work, including the Joint Commission on the Accreditation of Healthcare Organizations and a number of local, state, and federal governmental agencies.

In addition to having a personality comfortable in a leadership role, an individual engaged in administration should have a solid knowledge base in the many facets of organizational functioning. Few persons really know it all. This text is an effort to provide that solid base of knowledge. It is a collective product of experienced mental health administrators, who share their knowledge and wisdom. Drawing on their experience in administration and management and their understanding of present-day issues in the field of mental health practice, they provide extensive theoretical, factual, and practical information. In so doing, they have created an excellent overview of the topic and a solid resource for colleagues who seek to become, or are already functioning as, organization leaders.

As outlined in the editors' introduction, this work articulates some basic principles about mental health management and then addresses significant areas of the field. The work is thorough, well organized, and presented in terms that are readily understood. It is a valuable resource to any practitioner responsible for managing an organization committed to delivery of mental health services.

Finally, here are some suggestions I presented in the 1992 Administrative Psychiatry Award Lecture at the Annual Meeting of the American Psychiatric Association, which addressed concerns about hope and morale as critical elements in organization function:

1. Articulate a clear statement of the mission and values of your organization, one with which the staff can comfortably agree and identify. At the same time, make explicit the role of the staff in achieving that mission and validate their self-esteem. Consistency of purpose is particularly important in times of uncertainty.
2. Educate the staff:
   - To help them keep in perspective the challenges facing the organization, particularly relative to trends in the outside world;
   - To help them achieve greater mastery in coping with changing situations, such as dealing with utilization reviewers or applying continuous quality improvement principles to enhance patient care and job performance; and
   - To support individual and professional growth.
3. Keep communication lines open and promptly address any instances of significant staff conflict or disagreement in basic values.
4. Allow adequate time for staff to process and work through change. Engage staff in the process of achieving new solutions, to give them some control over their destinies.
5. Be alert to evidence of deteriorating morale, and listen empathically. Empathy may be more critical than taking action. Bitching and verbal discontent are not necessarily bad. Staff members may need to verbalize resentment about change, and it is better that this discontent be reflected upward to management and administration than downward toward patients.
6. Maintain a sense of history and a sense of humor:
   - In all likelihood, any troubling crisis is not the first faced by the institution, nor will it be the last. It, too, shall pass. If one has access to some of the history of the institution, he or she may be able to put today's crisis in an historical perspective.
   - Everyone is subject to Murphy's Law. Murphy's Law and all of its corollaries bewail the propensity for our lives to be undone, ostensibly by some external force. Through that humorous perspective, we safely vent frustration and aggression. In the face of adversity (things going wrong), we no longer have to feel guilty, either about the adverse event—which is Murphy's fault, not our

own—or about our feelings of anger and frustration over what has happened. In the process, we regain some sense of mastery and control, if only over our own mental state relative to the world around us.

7. Finally, attend to your own personal needs. Unless you, the administrator, care adequately for yourself, you will have difficulty caring for your staff and your organization.

—Walter W. Menninger, MD

About the Editors

William H. Reid, MD, MPH, has held positions at many levels of mental health administration and leadership in the public, private, and academic sectors, including that of Medical Director of the Texas Department of Mental Health and Mental Retardation. He has mentored mid-level and senior health care managers, developed an administrative mental health fellowship, taught graduate courses in health care administration, and directed the American Psychiatric Association certification process in psychiatric administration and management. His consultation resume includes public and private mental health systems in several U.S. states, China, and Europe. Dr. Reid is a clinical or adjunct professor at three Texas medical schools, has authored more than 150 professional publications and published 14 textbooks, and is listed in Who's Who in Medicine and Healthcare and Who's Who in the World. He lives with his wife in Horseshoe Bay, Texas, where he maintains an active clinical, administrative, and forensic consultation practice.

Stuart B. Silver, MD, has directed individual diagnostic and treatment programs, a large psychiatric hospital, and the Maryland State Mental Hygiene Administration (1988–1997). He is past president of the National Association of State Mental Health Program Directors (NASMHPD), has consulted to governments and private organizations on topics ranging from hospital design to system administration, and has served on a number of government committees and task forces involving mental health care and funding. The Stuart B. Silver wing of Maryland's Clifton T. Perkins Hospital Center was named in his honor. He received the 1997 American Psychiatric Association Award for Administrative Psychiatry, and currently directs the APA certification process in psychiatric administration and management. Currently, Dr. Silver is clinical professor of psychiatry at the University of Maryland School of Medicine and chairman of the board of directors of Clinical Associates, a Maryland-based multi-specialty medical group.

Contributors

John Baggett, PhD,
Assistant Hospital Director, Dorothea Dix Hospital, Raleigh, North Carolina,
Former Director of the North Carolina Division of Mental Health, Developmental Disabilities, and Substance Abuse Services

Lenore B. Behar, PhD,
Associate Director, National Center for Child Traumatic Stress,
Department of Psychiatry and Behavioral Sciences,
Duke University Medical Center

Matthew J. Blusewicz, PhD,
Associate Chief of Staff for Mental Health,
Veterans Administration Northern California Health Care System,
Clinical Professor of Psychiatry and Neurology, School of Medicine,
University of California, Davis

Harold Carmel, MD,
Clinical Director, John Umstead Hospital, Butner, North Carolina,
Associate Consulting Professor of Psychiatry, Duke University

Patricia L. Christian, PhD, RN,
Chief Executive Officer, John Umstead Hospital, Butner, North Carolina,
Adjunct Assistant Professor, University of North Carolina at Chapel Hill School of Nursing

Carroll A. Cradock, PhD,
Director, Behavioral Health Services,
Advocate Illinois Masonic Medical Center,
Associate Professor of Psychology in Psychiatry,
University of Illinois, Chicago

Peter W. Demuth, PsyD,
Associate Chief Psychologist (Forensics),
Elgin Mental Health Center,
Elgin, Illinois

Stephen H. Dinwiddie, MD,
Professor of Psychiatry,
Finch University of Health Sciences/The Chicago Medical School,
Chicago

Anne B. Fleischer, MPH, OTR/L,
Occupational Therapy Supervisor,
North Carolina Baptist Hospitals, Inc.

Mary E. Fraser, MPA, DSW,
Project Manager for the North Carolina Joint
Legislative Oversight Committee on MH/DD/SAS,
Senior Clinical Instructor at the UNC-CH School of Social Work,
Former Deputy Director of the Utah State Division of Mental Health

Jon E. Gudeman, MD,
Professor of Psychiatry and Behavioral Sciences, Medical College of Wisconsin,
Medical Director, Milwaukee County Mental Health Division,
Milwaukee

Richard C. W. Hall, MD,
Courtesy Clinical Professor of Psychiatry,
University of Florida, Gainesville

Ryan Chaloner Winton Hall, BA,
Fourth-year medical student,
Georgetown University School of Medicine

Ardis Hanson, MLS,
Library Director, Louis de la Parte Florida Mental Health Institute,
Adjunct Faculty,
College of Public Health and School of Library and Information Science,
University of South Florida, Tampa

Thomas W. Hester, MD, MPH,
Clinical-Medical Director, Adult Mental Health Division,
State Department of Health, Honolulu, Hawaii

Ted W. Hirsch, MEd, CHE,
Chief Operating Officer,
Northwest Healthcare/Kalispell Regional Medical Center,
CEO, Pathways Treatment Center, Kalispell, Montana

Leigh W. Jerome, PhD,
Clinical Psychologist,
Chief, Research & Development investigating novel technologies for distance education,
wellness, and clinical care,
Pacific Telehealth and Technology, Hui, Hawaii

Sara A. Kuppin, MSPH,
Research Assistant, Social Psychiatry Research Unit,
Doctoral candidate, Department of Sociomedical Sciences,
Columbia University, New York

Bruce Lubotsky Levin, DrPH, FABHM,
Associate Professor and Head,
Graduate Studies in Behavioral Health,

Louis de la Parte Mental Health Institute and College of Public Health,
University of South Florida, Tampa,
Editor, *Journal of Behavioral Health Services and Research*

Anne M. Mahalik, MPA, RHIA,
Chief Health Information Officer,
Mental Health and Developmental Disabilities,
State of Illinois, Department of Human Services

Michael T. McGuire, MD,
Professor Emeritus,
Department of Psychiatry and Biobehavioral Sciences,
University of California at Los Angeles

Diana J. Meyers, MA,
Director of Quality Strategies, Elgin Mental Health Center,
Elgin, Illinois

Gary E. Miller, MD,
Clinical Professor of Psychiatry, University of Texas Health Science Center, Houston
Medical Director, Cyprus Creek Hospital, Houston
President, Alternative Services Network, Houston

John Petrila, JD, LLM,
Chair and Professor, Department of Mental Health Law and Policy,
Louis de la Parte Florida Mental Health Institute,
University of South Florida, Tampa

James J. Picano, PhD,
Director of Training, Clinical Psychology Internship Program,
VA Northern California Health Care System
Assistant Professor, Department of Psychiatry
University of California, Davis, School of Medicine

Daniel J. Reid, MBA, DPP,
Managing Director, Paladin International, LLC,
International Business and Negotiations Consultants

William H. Reid, MD, MPH,
Clinical Professor of Psychiatry, University of Texas Health Science Center, San Antonio,
Adjunct Professor, Texas A&M College of Medicine and Texas Tech Medical School

Peter B. Rosenquist, MD,
Associate Professor, Department of Psychiatry and Behavioral Medicine,
Wake Forest University School of Medicine

L. Mark Russakoff, MD,
Director of Psychiatry,
Phelps Memorial Hospital, Sleepy Hollow, New York

Stuart B. Silver, MD,
Clinical Professor of Psychiatry, University of Maryland School of Medicine,
Chairman, Clinical Associates, PA, a multispecialty medical group

Thomas A. Simpatico, MD,
Chicago Bureau Chief, Illinois Department of Human Services/Office of Mental Health,
Assistant Professor of Psychiatry, Northwestern University Medical School

Nancy Staples, MS, MBA, RN,
Coordinator for Nursing Services,
Illinois Department of Human Services/Office of Mental Health,
Chicago

Chris E. Stout, PsyD, MBA,
Associate Professor (adj.), Northwestern University Medical School,
Chief of Psychological Services,
Illinois Department of Human Services/Office of Mental Health, Chicago

Sharon Topping, PhD,
Associate Professor of Management, University of Southern Mississippi,
System Evaluator, Division of Youth and Children, Mississippi Department of Mental Health

Philip E. Veenhuis, MD, MPH, LFAPA, FACPM,
Medical Director, North Carolina Division of Mental Health,
Developmental Disabilities, and Substance Abuse Services,
Clinical Professor of Psychiatry, University of North Carolina at Chapel Hill

Daria Zvetina, MEd,
Program and Research Development Consultant,
Bureau of Chicago Network Operations,
Illinois Department of Human Services/Office of Mental Health, Chicago

To our wives,
Elise P. Reid
and
Ann-Louise Silver,
and our families, whose
encouragement and support
sustained us in this work

Introduction

Health care management is fundamentally different from clinical practice. The most successful mental health organizations require their leaders and managers to understand both. People who can accomplish that understanding have a great advantage in working within such organizations, influencing their patient care, and helping them survive and thrive in competitive environments. On a personal level, clinicians who understand mental health care administration in addition to their clinical fields are likely to be valuable to the organizations in which they work, enhance their career opportunities, and feel comfortable in a management environment that contains many nonclinical concepts and colleagues.

Readers from primarily clinical backgrounds will find in this book all the information they need to make sense of the mysteries of health care administration, and to understand the role of their administrative tasks in the overall care of each patient, or a thousand. Those with little administrative experience need not feel overwhelmed: The three chapters in "A Primer for new Clinician-Managers" are especially designed to ease them—painlessly, and with a bit of humor—into important concepts of management, leadership, and negotiation.

Readers who already come from a management background will find in these chapters a broad introduction to the clinical issues that affect mental health organizations. They should not venture far into a mental health management career without understanding them.

The book has 37 authors, each from the interface of mental health and health care administration and all with broad experience in their fields. Most have graduate training in both mental health and management. Many have a management-related graduate degree, such as an MBA, MPA, MPH, or DrPH, in addition to clinical credentials. The author list is not top-heavy with psychiatrists, but includes experts from virtually every field of mental health care and its administration: psychiatrists, psychologists, nurses, social workers, hospital administrators, agency heads, medical records professionals, and even a prominent mental health attorney. The various authors and coauthors have managed—and led—all kinds of mental health organizations, from huge companies and public agencies, to mid-sized departments and centers, to individual units and outreach clinics. They have, as a group, experienced virtually all levels of the public sector, private clinical enterprise, managed care organizations, academia, and Veterans Administration and military health systems.

The section on **Mental Health Management Principles** (Bruce Lubotsky Levin, DrPH, Part Editor) forms the foundation for the more practical chapters to follow. Its chapters deal with the critical principles of mental health management, leadership, administrative theory, and care delivery.

The next section, **Mental Health Care Management** (Philip E. Veenhuis, MD, MPH, Part Editor), provides the administrative "meat" of many different mental health environments (general hospital units, community mental health centers, state hospitals, children's services, managed care organizations) and disciplines (psychiatry, psychology, psychiatric nursing, social work, activities therapies), as well as a discussion of important relationships with outside organizations and ethics.

Stuart B. Silver, MD, wrote and edited the section on **Business, Finance, and the Funding of Care**. His backgrounds as hospital superintendent, state mental health agency director, president of the National Association of Mental Health Program Directors, and head of a large private multispecialty group all come to bear as he discusses the technical and pragmatic aspects of the section topics, as well as some of the values that belong in every clinical organization.

Information and Information Technology, edited by Chris E. Stout, PsyD, MBA, brings today's (and some of tommorow's) technology into focus as indispensible to managing increasing knowledge, data, regulation, patient loads, and patient/public expectations. If information overload is a problem, this section holds the beginning of the answer.

People are at once the largest investment and the most important resource of any organization. Hospital administrator Ted W. Hirsch, MEd, has put together a valuable section on **Human Resources**. The chapters address organization needs, policies, and procedures related to recruitment, termination, and everything in between, as well as employee management, motivation, discipline, harassment, disability, privacy, and other important topics.

John Petrila, JD, LLM, a name familiar to many as former chief counsel to the New York Department of Mental Health, edited the **Legal Issues** section, with its chapters on evolution of mental health law, working with lawyers, and specific topics such as confidentiality and malpractice and related negligence. The section also contains a striking description of the effect of class action lawsuits on mental health agency employees and patients.

The last section is **A Primer for New Clinician-Managers** with chapters by William H. Reid, MD, MPH, and his brother, Daniel J. Reid, an international management consultant and negotiator. The overwhelmed or faint of heart may wish to start here.

The **Appendix** contains a health care information technology glossary.

You are reading the product of years of work by some three dozen authors and section editors. Their words summarize enormous—and enormously useful—experience. We hope and believe that the result will be what *you* need in your mental health management undertaking.

William H. Reid, MD, MPH
Horseshoe Bay, Texas

Stuart B. Silver, MD
Columbia, Maryland

Part One

MENTAL HEALTH MANAGEMENT PRINCIPLES

INTRODUCTION

Bruce Lubotsky Levin

C linicians and administrators have a significant interest in the successful operation of mental health care facilities. Furthermore, social accountability demands that attention be paid to the measuring and reporting of the efficiency, effectiveness, and quality of their operation. In the first chapter of this section, "Critical Issues in Mental Health Administration and Leadership," Ardis Hanson and Bruce Lubotsky Levin examine some of the fundamental issues facing the mental health administration and management field, including evidence-based practice, diversity, comorbidity, insurance and financing, informatics, and policy.

The leadership function within mental health organizations continues to demand that professionals must understand and deal with current multidimensional problems within the internal and external organizational environment. In chapter 2, "Leadership and Training in Mental Health," Levin, Hanson, and Sara Kuppin discuss the obstacles and challenges that leaders face within mental health organizations. They also examine the importance of curriculum changes in graduate and continuing education programs that prepare both clinical and administrative mental health practitioners.

The current conglomerate of mental health providers, agencies, services, institutions, and managed care/insurance entities, operating rather independently of one another, creates complex problems in the organization, financing, and delivery of mental health services. In chapter 3 of this section, "Mental Health Services Delivery," Levin and Hanson emphasize the need for mental health administrators to understand the external health care environment and the resulting impact environmental changes have on the functioning of their mental health organization.

In chapter 4, "Administrative Theory," L. Mark Russakoff suggests that different kinds of leaders may be needed during differing phases of a mental health organization's development. He emphasizes that there is no one complete, satisfactory model of administrative theory for mental health organizations. The complexity of human behavior in mental health organizations requires a model that integrates the individual, group, contextual, hierarchical, social, political, and economic parameters.

In the last chapter of this section, "The Dynamics of Organizational Change in Mental Health Administration," Sharon Topping explores change and its many consequences for mental health organizations. Strategies designed to achieve new forms of management need to be developed with an awareness of existing organizational culture, particularly within public-sector mental health organizations. She briefly reviews the history, nature, and implementation of change, identifying forces that resist and promote organizational change within mental health facilities.

Chapter One

Critical Issues in Mental Health Administration and Leadership

Ardis Hanson

Bruce Lubotsky Levin

In 1999, the first Surgeon General's report on mental health was published by the U.S. Department of Health and Human Services. This landmark report summarized the epidemiology, treatment, financing, and service delivery issues in mental health. Organizationally, it also presented an in-depth examination of populations at risk, that is, children with severe emotional disorders, adults with severe mental disorders, and older adults with co-occurring disorders, as well as individuals with addiction disorders. Even though the report did not make formal policy recommendations, it focused primarily toward overcoming the gaps in what is known, discussed removing the barriers that keep people from seeking and obtaining mental health treatment, and offered a vision that may provide the basis for future policy development.

Although the report focused on the major issues in the organization, financing, and provision of mental health services, there remain additional issues of importance for mental health administrators. This chapter discusses issues critical to mental health administrators at all levels of management, including evidence-based practice, policy impact on treatment, diversity, immigrant populations, comorbidity, financing of care, parity, stigma, and information technology. Several of these are addressed in more detail in other chapters of this book.

It is crucial for all mental health administrators to keep pace with issues, trends, and continuing changes within their internal and external organizational environments. Ideally, while this process should start in graduate school, continuing education has become a vital component for mental health administrators. This chapter introduces the reader to selected issues of importance, including evidence-based practice, policy's impact on treatment, diversity, comorbidity, financing, policy, and informatics.

FROM RESEARCH TO PRACTICE

There have been over 50 years of research on mental illness. The field has made great strides over the years in psychopharmacology and the integration of biological, and behavioral sciences. New medications and psychosocial interven- ... ovided new treatment opportunities for mental disorders, requiring ... hes in evaluating their effectiveness. Some of these new approaches ... come from the evaluation of somatic health care interventions. As somatic delivery systems have evolved, there has been a historical tendency to overlay these organization, financing, and delivery models on mental health care. These changes have not been successfully adapted to the unique characteristics of mental health care. Therefore, mental health administrators must carefully examine the impact of the somatic health care models on services delivery, as well as any additional impacts on organizational effectiveness (Schlesinger & Gray, 1999; Wolfe, 1999) (also see chapter 5 on organizational change, this volume).

Evidence-Based Practice

What it is it —
How to do it
why you do it

Evidence-based practice distinguishes between research that is of direct clinical significance and that which is not. Using a set of simple rules for evaluating research evidence, it provides a framework for making clinical decisions on the basis of research findings and for applying research findings to individual patients. It consists of five explicit steps: (1) The clinician constructs a specific clinical question concerning the care of a patient or group of patients; (2) the clinician finds the best evidence to answer the question; (3) the clinician evaluates the evidence for validity and usefulness; (4) the results are applied to the specific patient or group of patients; and (5) the outcome of the intervention is evaluated (Reynolds, 2000). Evidence-based practice increases accountability and also increases access to resources and dissemination.

There has been much discussion of the role of evidence-based practice in mental health. Barkham and Mellor-Clark (2000) suggested that practice-based evidence should help determine evidence-based practice, along with the contributions of random clinical trials and qualitative methods. Practice research networks should collaborate to collect and analyze large bodies of effectiveness data rather than efficacy data, particularly because observational or audit data may be more clinically relevant than data gathered under experimental conditions.

Cost-effectiveness data differ from cost-efficacy data. Cost-effectiveness studies evaluate a heterogeneous population, patients who are often less compliant with their treatment, and protocols where the researchers have less control over specific treatment interventions. Cost-effectiveness analyses show the relationship between the resources used (costs) and the health benefits achieved (effects) for an intervention compared with alternative strategies. These studies focus on specific treatments, specific dosages or units of service, and duration of treatment. Cost-effectiveness data can support the inclusion of mental health services such as the appropriateness of antipsychotic drug therapy, assertive community treatment, home-based therapies, partial hospitalization, or residential treatment (Goldman, 1996).

Cost-efficacy studies evaluate the impact of treatment on a very selective, homogeneous population using a specific study protocol. These studies often examine patient functioning, patient compliance with the treatment regimen, outcomes, relapse rates, and symptoms. Barkham and Mellor-Clark (2000) further suggested that there should be a greater emphasis on the interface between efficacy and effectiveness studies.

Beutler (2000) observed that the contemporary practice of psychotherapy is not strongly guided by empirical evidence but is moving in that direction. In his opinion, empirically informed change principles are an optimal way of proceeding toward evidence-based practice. As managed mental/behavioral health care systems continue to call for evidence-based interventions, there will be a discernible impact on clinical practice (Goldman, McCulloch, Cuffel, & Kozma, 1999). Because the goal of evidence-based medicine is to improve the quality of clinical judgments, it encourages decisions based on clinically relevant research and minimizes decisions based on outdated information, local practice patterns, product marketing literature, or subjective and conflicting opinions of medical experts (Bilsker, 2000; Sullivan, 2000). If evidence-based treatments are to be effective in clinical practice, administrators must start with the assumption that these treatments have much to offer practitioners in clinical settings. This would lead to qualitative and quantitative research questions involving all parties with an interest in evidence-based practice (Addis, Wade, & Hatgis, 1999).

Rubenstein et al. (1999) predicted three basic directions that administrators will follow as they move toward evidence-based practice. First, they will increasingly rely on external expert intervention design, based on previously tested strategies and premarket assessment of potential service delivery organizations. Second, these interventions will be disseminated to managed care organizations, including but not restricted to clinical care, through marketing, negotiation, and training. Finally, continuing education for staff at all levels will be critical, not only in the implementation of the interventions by trained clinical staff but also for administrators to determine outcomes and impacts (see chapter 2 on leadership and training, this volume).

Policy's Impact on Treatment

One of the main areas of emphasis in the Surgeon General's report was in the area of prevention (U.S. Department of Health and Human Services, 1999). Coupled with the release of prevention goals in *Healthy People 2010* (U.S. Department of Health and Human Services, 2000), prevention is becoming a predominant theme when discussing the costs and treatment of mental illness. Unfortunately, prevention often appears contradictory to the current trend in managed care toward cost reduction. Despite evidence of effective preventive measures in mental health, funding is often inadequate. Preventive measures carry a cost, reflected in the budget and revenues, which in turn may create difficulties in their approval and application (Eisenberg, 1999), even though they may actually reduce costs within a managed care environment. If managed care organizations experience frequent enrollee turnover, they may need the incentive of short-term savings to provide preventive mental health care. However, when managed care organizations offer fewer mental health promotion options, they do experience higher voluntary disenrollment rates. The availability of prevention and promotion options may increase enrollee satisfaction and retention, as well as effective marketing tools to consumers (Dorfman, 2000).

The possibility that managing mental health care might reduce the use of other medical care services and thus lower total health care costs has important implications. Cuffel, Goldman, and Schlesinger (1999); Huskamp (1998); and Goldman, McCulloch, and Sturm (1998) indicated that managing mental health care reduced other medical (somatic) care costs and eased access to these services. If subsequent research supports these findings, health care purchasers and national and state legislators should take into account the influence of mental health care on the cost and utilization of general medical care services.

In the absence of empirical data, public-sector planners have little basis for understanding the economic consequences of managed care for mental health and substance abuse programs (Cuffel et al., 1999). Public-sector administrators need to be informed about the relationship between the organization and financing of mental health programs in the private sector and the cost of publicly funded medical care.

Partnerships between health care organizations and researchers can have successful impacts on health care. A study on depression suggests that support for increased care will require either new resources or shifting of resources (Rubenstein et al., 1999). Because primary care clinics typically do not provide the type of service reviewed in their study, the authors suggested that managed care organizations would find it easier to shift resources toward improved depression care if their competitors were doing the same. In addition, they suggested that resource shifts were more likely to improve care with careful design and evaluation. Achieving this depends on researchers, health care organizations, and other players in mental health service systems fostering collaborations among each other. There are a number of policy incentives that could aid these collaborations: financial, educational, and mandated (Rubenstein et al., 1999). Among financing incentives are tax breaks for implementing mental health–oriented primary care improvements and funding opportunities that encourage the collaboration of health services researchers and health care organizations. Increased public education on treatment of mental disorders and, more importantly, the success of treatment, through the use of national media campaigns would destigmatize mental illness. Finally, legislative mandates for states to more effectively track rates of detection, care, and outcomes for mental illness and substance abuse disorders should be considered.

A review of managed mental health care by the National Institute of Medicine (1997) called for reforms in public and private systems that provide reimbursement for the full and effective treatment of substance abuse and mental disorders. For example, an independent panel convened by the National Institutes of Health called only for broadened access and insurance coverage for methadone treatment (National Institute on Drug Abuse, 1998). However, with movement toward the use of evidence-based studies, all scientifically proven treatment methods should be included in insurance coverage.

The National Institute of Medicine (1997) also focused on accreditation issues, including mechanisms to ensure valid and reliable measures of outcome and quality improvement and the use of evidence-based clinical practice guidelines. The report also emphasized the need for cultural competency and targeted programs for women.

Diversity

America is a country of many languages and cultures, and with each passing year the challenge of caring for persons from diverse backgrounds becomes more compelling. Mental health care professionals and managers should have a basic understanding of the impact of language and culture on mental health services delivery. This will allow them to more efficiently organize services that meet the needs of both service delivery organizations and diverse populations at risk for mental health problems.

Although the Surgeon General's report uses the term *culture* to denote a common heritage and set of beliefs, norms, and values, it adopts Cooper and Denner's (1998) definition for the phrase *cultural identity*, which specifies a reference group that is "an identifiable social entity with whom a person identifies and to whom he or she looks for standards of behavior." Of course, within any given group, an individual's cultural identity may also involve language, country of origin, acculturation, gender, age, class, religious/spiritual beliefs, sexual orientation, and physical disabilities (Lu, Lim, & Mezzich, 1995). In addition, many people have multiple ethnic or cultural identities.

Linguistic and cultural diversity is an inescapable fact of modern American society. According to the U.S. Bureau of the Census (1990a, 1990b), nearly 32 million residents of the United States (or 14% of the total population) spoke a language other than English at home. It is estimated that by the year 2050 half of the U.S. population will be people of color. Further, according to the 1990 census, there were approximately 34 million African Americans in the United States, 10 million Americans of Asian and Pacific Islander origin, 30 million people of Hispanic origin, and 2 million persons of Native American and Alaskan native origin. The foreign-born population in the United States numbered nearly 26 million persons (approximately 9.7% of the total population). It was estimated that 40% of the United States population would be immigrants or first-generation Americans by the year 2001.

Immigrant Populations

Migration has a significant impact on psychological well-being (Lin, 1986). While research indicates that migration per se was not a determinant of excess psychiatric morbidity, particular combinations of circumstances surrounding an individual migration experience increased the likelihood of any given individual experiencing a mental illness (Silove, 1999). Twenty years of studies on refugee populations underscore the extremely high rates of psychiatric sequelae and the prevalence of posttraumatic stress disorder (PTSD) among refugees, particularly survivors of torture and trauma (Allodi, 1990; Hynes & Cardozo, 2000).

In *World Mental Health: Problems and Priorities in Low-Income Countries,* Desjarlais, Eisenberg, Good, and Kleinman (1995) identified a range of mental health and behavioral problems in the world, particularly among low-income countries in Africa, Asia, Latin America, and the Pacific. According to the report, mental illness and related problems exacted a significant toll on the health and well-being of people worldwide, and produced a greater burden (based on a "disability-adjusted life years" index) than cancer, heart disease, or tuberculosis. A second observation was that mental disorders and substance abuse were intertwined with the social world (e.g., social disruption, culture shock, the lack of social supports, and unemployment). A third observation was that the research on substance abuse and women's mental health illustrated that psychopathology was as much pathology of the social world as pathology of the mind or body.

Women

Patterns of mental illness vary considerably by gender, with women and men showing vulnerability to different conditions (Rhodes & Goering, 1998; Office of Research
on Women's Health, 1999). For example, depression occurs at twice the rate in women
as it does in men (U.S. Department of Health and Human Services, 1999). According
to the Commission on Women's Health (Glied & Kofman, 1995), women have used
the health care system more than men do, especially for conditions that do not meet
the diagnostic thresholds for mental disorder but were associated with significant
distress and functional impairment.

Many mental health problems affect women during their childbearing years.
Untreated mental illness in mothers may increase the risk that their children will
have mental health problems. Women were more likely to use outpatient services
and primary care providers, while men were more likely to use inpatient care and
specialists (Glied & Kofman, 1995). In addition, Newmann, Greenley, Sweeney, and
Van Dien (1998) found increased costs of mental health care for women with serious
mental illness who also experienced sexual abuse.

COMORBIDITY

The co-occurrence of somatic and mental disorders has also been a major problem in
America. Depression and anxiety disorders often coexist with other mental, behavioral, and/or somatic disorders. For example, approximately one-half of individuals
with major depression also have an anxiety disorder (Barbee, 1998). In addition,
from 24 to 40% of individuals with a substance disorder also have a mood disorder
(U.S. Department of Health and Human Services, 1999).

One large-scale study on co-occurring disorders was the National Comorbidity
Survey (NCS) (Kessler et al., 1994). The NCS was designed to determine the
comorbidity of psychiatric disorders (Blazer et al., 1994). Individuals with comorbid
disorders included persons diagnosed with more than one physical, mental, or substance disorder. Over 8,000 persons between the ages of 15 and 54 years who lived
in the continental United States were interviewed between 1990 and 1992.

Results from the NCS reported a prevalence of 3.2% for individuals with severe
mental illness. The lifetime prevalence was 48% for any disorder (mental disorder
or substance abuse), and 29% of the respondents reported at least one mental disorder during the previous 12-month period. Approximately 40% of those who reported
at least one mental disorder during their lifetime sought treatment in the mental
health specialty sector.

The National Institute of Mental Health (U.S. Department of Health and Human
Services, 1999) estimated that 1.8 million people have severe mental illness and a
co-occurring substance disorder. More than 15% of 166 million Americans (25.6
million people) over the age of 18 years met the criteria for at least one alcohol, drug,
or mental disorder (Regier, 1988). Persons who suffered from a mental illness were
more likely to abuse drugs and alcohol. The NCS and follow-up reports also found
that 83.5% of those with lifetime comorbidity said that their first mental disorder
preceded their first addictive disorder, and co-occurring disorders tended to be more
chronic than mental disorders.

Kessler et al. (1996) used data from the NCS to study the prevalence of co-occurring addictive and mental disorders. They found that the total number of persons with co-occurring disorders (anyone with both a substance disorder and any mental disorder as described in the *DSM* classification system) was between 7 million and 9.9 million people, depending on the definition of alcohol abuse.

Space does not permit a more extensive review of the results of mental health epidemiologic studies; the reader is referred to Dew (1998) for a review of the relationship between physical illnesses and mental disorders.

FINANCING

Managed Care

Health insurance benefit design has been based on an acute care model and confined to traditional medical services. Generally, it has not been defined within a long-term care treatment environment. The largest unmet needs of persons with severe mental illness have involved community rehabilitation and long-term services that typically have not been covered under private health insurance policies (Mechanic, 1998).

The concept of "managing" health care can be traced to the early part of the 20th century and the evolution of prepaid health plans in the United States (Levin, 1992). Today, managed care has dominated health and mental health coverage for individuals with private insurance. This continued growth of managed care "has (increasingly) blurred the distinction between organizations bearing financial risk for health care (insurers), organizations managing care (health maintenance and utilization management organizations), and organizations making clinical treatment decisions (provider groups or individual clinicians)" (Sturm, 1999, p. 362). At the same time, the rapid growth of managed care in America has raised concerns that reduction in health and mental health care costs may have resulted in cost shifting to public programs and/or patients themselves.

Managed care now provides insurance coverage for 75 to 80% of all U.S. employees (Jensen et al., 1997). The Hay/Huggins Benefits Reports documented trends from 1992 to 1997 in primary health benefit plans for over 1,000 medium- to large-size employers. During this period, fee-for-service (FFS) plans dropped from being the most prevalent primary medical plan (62%) in 1992 to being the least prevalent (20%) in 1997. Preferred-provider organizations (PPOs) increased from 13% to 34% of primary medical plans, with a similar rapid rise in health maintenance organizations (HMOs) from 9% to 24%. Point-of-service (POS) plans increased more slowly as a principal medical plan, from 16% in 1992 to 22% in 1997.

Managed care organizations have expanded into the public sector. Public mental health systems have increasingly shifted their priorities from providing mental health and substance abuse services to purchasing these services. They have begun to use a systems-of-care approach rather than primarily maintaining institutions and other stand-alone services (Essock & Goldman, 1995).

During the past 15 years, an increasing number of employers and government programs have "carved out" or separated mental health service benefits from general health care benefits through contractual arrangements with specialized vendors that may assume some level of financial risk. Specialty managed mental health organizations have subsequently emerged under the rubric of "managed behavioral health care organizations" (MBHOs). MBHOs have attempted to reduce the costs of mental health care through the utilization of mental health practitioners at discounted fees, through the reduction in the length of mental health treatment, through the decreased use of hospital treatment, and through the increased use of ambulatory mental health care treatment. Results of studies have demonstrated significant declines in the costs of mental health care under a broad variety of MBHOs (Cuffel et al., 1999; Goldman et al., 1998; Grazier et al., 1999; Ma & McGuire, 1998).

Nearly all states have implemented managed mental/behavioral health programs. In recent years, public-sector enrollment in managed care plans has increased dramatically, accounting for approximately 13% of the 38 million Medicare beneficiaries, and approximately 54% of the 31 million Medicaid beneficiaries (Health Care Financing Administration, 2000).

The complexity of the contractual arrangements between state and local governments and MBHOs has varied considerably (Findlay, 1999). Some states have contracted directly with MBHOs or subcontract with HMOs, paying a capitated fee to provide mental health services, with the MBHO or HMO assuming the risk. However, other states have preferred to retain at full risk and contract with MBHOs (or subcontract with HMOs or other managed care plans) to manage mental health benefits. Other MBHOs have been contracted only to conduct utilization review and case management services.

Managed care arrangements have proven successful in managing service utilization and plan expense (Congressional Budget Office, 1995; National Advisory Mental Health Council, 1998). A study by the Hay Group (1998) indicated that health care costs increased by only 0.7% per year from 1994 to 1997 under managed care. Prior to the implementation of managed care (1988 to 1993), health care costs increased by 16.8% per year. Studies from Peat Marwick (Jensen, Morrisey, Gafney, & Liston, 1997), William M. Mercer (1997), two by the Rand Corporation (Sturm, 1997; Goldman et al., 1998), and the Lewin Group[1] have provided support regarding the success of these arrangements.

For example, a study by the Rand Corporation (Sturm, 1997) examined claims from 24 managed care carve-out plans that offered unlimited mental health benefits with minimal copayments. Results of the study indicated that companies that complied with the federal mental health parity law by removing an annual limit of $25,000 for mental health care would incur an approximately $1 per enrollee per year increase in mental health care costs. In addition, removal of more costly limitations (i.e., 30 inpatient days and 20 outpatient visits) would translate into a cost increase of less than $7 per enrollee per year. The Rand study also found that access to mental health services increased in these managed care carve-out plans. A second Rand study (Goldman et al., 1998) tracked access, utilization, and costs for mental health care for one large employer in California during a period in which mental health care benefits were carved out of the medical plan and managed care was increased. Prior to the carve-out, costs increased by 20% annually. Post-carve-out costs decreased by 40%. Cost reduction was not due to decreased access.

---

1. *Insurance Carrier/Health Plan Views on Impact of New Hampshire Parity Legislation, 1997* [available online at http://www.nami.org/update/lewinst9704.html].

Entitlement Programs

Over the past 30 years, Medicaid, Medicare, Social Security Disability Insurance (SSDI)/Supplemental Security Income (SSI), and other programs have significantly influenced the ways in which public-sector treatment for mental illness is funded (Mechanic, 1999). In 1998, 36 states operated 46 Medicaid waivers to provide innovative approaches to organize and finance mental health services through various mental health carve-out strategies. Eight states ran voluntary Medicaid HMOs and 26 states had managed care programs in place in related state systems (National Conference of State Legislatures, 1999). The most common approach was to offer acute but limited mental health benefits to all Medicaid recipients, but to carve out persons with more severe mental illness and treatment needs (Ridgley & Goldman, 1996).

Established in 1965 as Title XIX of the Social Security Act, Medicaid programs have been required by law to provide eligible individuals with certain short- and long-term benefits. The Health Care Financing Administration (HCFA) administers this program. In 1996, public spending for Medicaid totaled $121 billion. Two years later, total Medicaid spending was $170.6 billion in 1998, an increase of 6.6% over the 1997 level. Medicaid paid for 15% of all health spending in 1998.[2]

Of the 31,117,679 persons enrolled nationally in Medicaid programs, 16,834,390 (54%) were enrolled in a managed care program,[3] compared to 10% in 1991 (HCFA, 1995). Fiscal pressures have been the main impetus for states to adopt managed care for their Medicaid populations, with the loss of federal "matching dollars" and the move to Medicaid waivers (Ridgley & Goldman, 1996).

The aged, blind, and disabled recipients of Medicaid together consume the lion's share of Medicaid resources. Nationally, disabled individuals comprised about 15% of the Medicaid population and accounted for 39% of Medicaid expenditures, including long-term care (General Accounting Office [GAO], 1996). The Medicaid annual expenditures (per person) for individuals with disabilities averaged $2,072 for inpatient services; $443 for physician, lab, and x-ray services; $773 for outpatient services; $1,183 for prescription drugs, case management, therapy, and other practitioner care; and $3,485 for long-term care, for a total of $7,956 for all services. Unfortunately, no information on breakout by type of mental disability (or updated figures) was available (GAO, 1996).

POLICY

Stigma

Since the 1950s, there has been a significant amount of literature on public attitudes toward and understanding of mental disorders. The literature showed that attitudes toward persons with mental disorders generally have been negative (Nunnally, 1961; Joint Commission on Mental Health and Illness, 1961), even when the individual

---

2. *Highlights: National Health Expenditures, 1998*, last updated 10 January 2000 [http:// www.hcfa.gov/stats/nhe-oact/hilites.htm].

3. *Managed Care*, last updated November 2000 [http://www.hcfa.gov/medicare/mgdcar.htm].

surveyed was educated about the "facts" of mental disorders (Freeman & Kassebaum, 1960). A 1966 study examined the attitudes of college students toward persons with mental illness by asking students to indicate whether they preferred ex-convicts to ex–mental patients to work with on specific tasks (Larry, 1966). According to Larry, the data appeared to indicate that an individual who had been hospitalized for mental illness suffered "a depreciation of social esteem in a wide variety of social roles" (p. 454). Larry further concluded, "It is predicted that the discharged mental patient will find the social community non-hostile, but unaccepting" (pp. 454–455).

Thirty-five years later, stigma is still an issue in the United States when it comes to persons with mental disorders. In an ethnographic study of persons with mental disorders in the community, the study participants felt that mental disorders still carried a public stigma in the dominant culture and, although persons with mental disorders desired normalcy, they still feared rejection by the "dominant" culture (George, 2000).

Public education about mental illness and alcohol and drug abuse is also needed to reduce stigma, ignorance about treatment, and denial, which are pervasive and pose significant barriers to treatment (Grant, 1997). Current efforts include screening and educational programs to boost public awareness, programs aimed at helping providers improve their training, dissemination of information about these disorders, and a push for equity and flexibility in coverage of mental health benefits in corporate benefits plans.

On June 7, 1999, the White House sponsored its first Conference on Mental Health to help end discrimination against those who have mental disorders. The President mandated that all health insurance plans used by federal employees provide equal coverage of both physical and mental illnesses. The President expressed hope that the government's example would eventually become the model for the private sector, encouraging employers to end discriminatory practices and actively seek help for persons with mental disorders (Dunn, 1999).

The Surgeon General's report on mental health stated that mental disorders were the second highest cause of disability in major market economies such as the United States, and that mental disorders collectively comprised more than 15% of all disabilities. Over half of those with severe mental illness do not seek treatment, largely due to two very real barriers to access: first, the stigma people attached to mental disorders; and second, the lack of parity between insurance coverage for mental health services and other health care services. Over the past 25 years, there has been a scientific revolution in the areas of mental health and mental disorders that has helped remove the stigma, so that we now know not only that the workings of the brain affect behavior, emotions, and memory, but that experience, emotion, and behavior have an impact upon the workings of the brain (U.S. Department of Health and Human Services, 1999).

One must then ask how best to change attitudes and inform persons about mental disorders and the most effective treatments. Several have broached the idea of "mental health literacy" to aid the public in better understanding the information that has been made available via the Internet, broadcast media, and print (Christensen & Griffiths, 2000; Jorm, 2000; Jorm et al., 1997). If the public's mental health literacy is not improved, this may hinder public acceptance of evidence-based mental health care.

Parity

Mental health parity has been geared to overcoming discrimination and reducing stigma toward individuals with mental disorders; assuring selected health plans do not suffer financial disadvantages from the adverse selection of treating individuals with the most serious mental disorders; reducing out-of-pocket expenses for individuals with mental disorders; reducing disability through improved access to effective treatment; and increasing the productivity to society of individuals with mental disorders (Levin, Hanson, Coe, & Kuppin, 2000).

There is considerable variability in how states define, determine eligibility standards, and set service limitations for mental health and substance-abuse parity legislation throughout the United States. Thus, although parity in Maryland means coverage for all mental disorders and substance-abuse treatment vis-à-vis coverage for physical illnesses, parity in New Hampshire refers to treatment coverage for specific, biologically based, severe mental disorders.

Furthermore, current exemptions in state insurance regulations potentially further limit the number of companies (and thus individuals) forced to comply with state mental health parity laws and other (mental health and substance abuse) insurance coverage mandates. For example, in Maryland, companies with fewer than 50 employees have been exempt from the parity law, along with self-insured companies, and for those with individual health policies, parity is optional.

Finally, the federal parity law permits states that have passed more comprehensive or a greater level of mental health parity legislation to be exempt from federal law. The rules for a health plan will differ depending on whether the health insurance is self-purchased, employer purchased, or the insurance is part of something called a self-funded ERISA plan. If a health plan is part of an ERISA plan, then the health plan has to comply only with a few minimal federal regulations because of a law passed decades ago that exempts self-funded ERISA plans from state regulation. Mid-size to larger-sized employers will sometimes choose to fund their own health benefits plans for their employees—those are ERISA plans. But if an employer buys health insurance from an insurance company, or if a consumer purchases his or her own private plan, then additional state regulations apply.

Although a handful of states have passed parity provisions, their full impact on the insurance market cannot be assessed because a majority of the plans are preempted from compliance with many state insurance mandates by ERISA (Employee Retirement Income Security Act of 1974). Self-insured plans, including both risk retention plans sponsored by employers and multiemployer trusts developed by unions through collective bargaining, have grown significantly since the passage of ERISA. States are prevented from regulating self-insured employee benefit plans through ERISA's "preemption," "savings," and "deemer" clauses (Ridgley & Goldman, 1996).

Preemption was prompted by the recognition that it is much easier to oversee complex benefit programs by ensuring that all administrative practices of a benefit plan are governed by a single set of regulations (Simmons, 1997). State experimentation with large-scale health reform will be limited because ERISA hinders state government ability to regulate all employers. Although Congress can grant state-by-state exemptions, it has not been inclined to do so (Ridgley & Goldman, 1996). Any legislation or sponsors of legislation supporting funding of mental health or substance-abuse services should make the case of the state's role in providing the mental health safety net and demonstrate the extensive public need (Ridgley & Goldman, 1996). For a full discussion of ERISA and its impact on health care reform, see Stio (1994).

Do these state parity laws have any impact on the organization, financing, and delivery of mental health and substance abuse services? At the present time, because most state parity laws have been recently enacted, relatively few states have sufficient experience to evaluate the impact parity has on service costs. Nevertheless, there have been several cases documented in the literature that highlight the experience of selected public- and private-sector organizational health costs since parity has been implemented (National Advisory Mental Health Council, 1997; Shore, 1994; Sturm & McCulloch, 1998; Sturm, Zhang, & Schoenbaum, 1999).

Others have suggested that savings of about 5% may not result in drastic service cuts or significant underfunding of the delivery system post parity implementation (Frank, McGuire, & Goldman, 1996). As Congress continues to review legislation to broaden parity to children's mental health services and for those persons who have substance-abuse disorders, administrators should consider possible impacts on their individual organizations as well as their larger service delivery system in which they are involved. For example, a number of states are examining and reexamining parity legislation. Rhode Island recently reviewed expanding its 1994 law with intent to eliminate definitions and restrictions that might limit the legislation's effectiveness (Fitzpatrick, 2001). Expansion of mental health parity legislation might substantially reduce the degree to which financial responsibility for the treatment of mental disorders has been shifted to government, especially to state and local government.

Stigma, confusing and exclusionary insurance regulations, and restrictive mental health center policies have both limited and discouraged treatment interventions. However, there have been innovative programming and funding arrangements. One program, the Senior Outreach Program of Park Ridge Mental Health in Rochester, NY, has proven effective in identifying and providing outreach mental health services to elderly individuals (Russell, 1999).

Given the major issues just discussed regarding the structure, provision, and financing of mental health services (also see chapter 3 on mental health services delivery), one component stands out as a common thread: information. One tool to assist in the sharing and management of information lies in the field of informatics.

INFORMATICS

Informatics is found in all disciplines. It deals with resources, devices, and formalized methods for optimizing the storage, retrieval, and management of information for problem solving and decision making. Informatics is an interdisciplinary field based on computer and information sciences, the cognitive and decision sciences, epidemiology, and telecommunications. Researchers in informatics have discovered new methods and techniques to enhance health care, scientific and applied research, and education through information technology.

The emergence of informatics can be attributed to three major factors: (1) technology, (2) information management, and (3) decision support systems. The changes in computing and communications technology are now viewed through the media. For example, e-business is seen as a high-profile commodity in daily advertisements. It is now apparent that traditional paper-based methods for handling patient information and biomedical knowledge have become unmanageable (and expensive), particularly with the continued demand for technology within managed care. Finally, it is important to realize that other information bases are as important to current mental health management decision making as the traditional clinical and research information bases.

Although mental health informatics has emerged as a specialty area, it is not totally new. In 1970, the National Institute of Mental Health published *An Administrator's Handbook on the Application of Operations Research to the Management of Mental Health Systems* (Halpert, Horvath, & Young, 1970). As early as 1974, administrators examined the role of management information systems for mental health facilities (Crawford, Morgan, & Gianturco, 1974). *Mental Health in the 21st Century* (Williams & Johnson, 1979) discussed automated psychological tests, treatment decision makers, community systems simulators, and situational simulators. Sidowski, Johnson, and Williams (1980) wrote *Technology in Mental Health Care Delivery Systems* with an emphasis on the human factors aspect, important in today's computerized environment.

The role of information sciences in mental health has continued to grow. The past few years have seen informatics begin to move into the mainstream of clinical practice. The scope of this field remains enormous. Informatics has found application in the design of decision support systems for practitioners, in the development of computer tools for research, and in the study of a discipline's corpus of knowledge (Trabin, 1996). Medical image transfers, videoconferencing consultations, multidisciplinary and specialist support, records management and transfer, and continuing education all have been aspects of informatics.

Why should administrators care about informatics? First, the quality and efficiency of mental health services could be enhanced, including increased access to health services, especially in rural and remote areas and for linguistically diverse populations. Second, informatics could become part of mainstream service delivery with appropriate funding models. With the continued evolution of managed mental health care, the use of technology plays an increasingly important role. Current standards pertinent to mental health services delivery will be applied to informatics in a variety of ways and through a number of organizations.

Services delivery standards, for example, are used as a blueprint for the development of new services, as a guide to service enhancement and continuous quality improvement, to inform patients and providers about what to expect from a mental health service, and as a checklist for service quality. They also help patients and providers to participate in a service's planning, development, and evaluation processes. These standards will be applied to the delivery of services and resources via electronic formats.

In addition, there are a number of organizations currently working on standards to measure services. Nationally, the Center for Mental Health Services, a division of the Substance Abuse and Mental Health Administration, is field testing the Mental Health Statistics Improvement Project (MHSIP) Report Card, a patient/consumer-centered managed care report card covering the general "domains" of access, quality and appropriateness, promotion/prevention and outcomes. The MHSIP Report Card measures systems performance such as speed and access to a full range of services, affordability, parity of coverage, patient/consumer access to information, and absence of cultural barriers.

The American Managed Behavioral Healthcare Association is field testing PERMS 1.0 (Performance Measures for Managed Behavioral Healthcare Programs). The National Association of County Behavioral Healthcare Directors (NACBHD) contracted with the Evaluation Center at the Human Services Research Institute (HRSI) to develop Candidate Indicators for County Performance Outcomes. The Health Plan Employer Data and Information Set (HEDIS 3.0) developed by the National Association for Quality Assurance includes performance measures of effectiveness, access, availability, patient choice/satisfaction, and cost. Even the Joint Commission on the Accreditation of Healthcare Organizations (JCAHO) has integrated a group of acceptable existing measures into its accreditation process under a single performance measurement umbrella.

Evolving performance measurement technologies are contributing significantly to the dialogue regarding the need to balance cost and quality of care, particularly in the traditional services delivery model. As managed mental health care moves into a more "electronic" environment, the challenge will be to construct performance measurement systems that integrate the needs of purchaser, provider, and recipients within a variety of delivery formats.

Third, with the continued use of electronic and/or digital systems, professional staff will be able to increase their knowledge and skills using these systems. Administrative skills and knowledge of management techniques will change with the use of decision support systems. Professional isolation will also be reduced. Finally, participation of stakeholders in decision making will continue to increase through use of informatics for advisory groups, collaborating organizations, and budget meetings.

Several key issues are apparent. First, clinical practice already revolves around communication. Capturing the informal information currently lost in mental health care's communication channels may soon become an important issue for those developing the formal electronic client record. Deciding what information is important and how that information is made available is essential. It will require not only the resolution of issues of confidentiality and security, but also consideration of the technology of storage and retrieval of voice recordings and electronic mail. Electronic information and storage of client information have required more sophisticated software and hardware solutions (Laske, 1994).

Second, people's understanding of the effects of technology on communication is still in its infancy. Researchers in human–computer interaction believe that before these technologies can be successfully introduced, the way in which people communicate needs to be understood. Professionals and clients will need to understand that the computer is just a tool, that is, that interaction should be between people, not with the machine. Dynamics of the relationships between professionals and in collaborations in case management will change.

Third, there will be a shift in focus in informatics such that the application of communication technologies rather than their development will be emphasized. Many see the development of protocol-based treatment as the essential cultural change in clinical practice that will permit the design of useful clinical information systems. However, the transfer of electronic medical records across state lines raises legal issues (Gobis, 1997). For more information on liability, licensing and accreditation, hardware and software vendors and telecommunications carriers in liability cases, and informed consent as consultations now cross state (and international) borders, see Magenau (1997), Laske (1997), and the Physicians Insurers Association of America (1998).

Finally, with the growth of informatics and technology in the workplace, computer and information literacy will become essential competencies. It will be up to mental health administrators who are concerned with staff members' professional development and ability, to respond to change by providing training and education to use these new information services effectively (Cheuk, 1998). The ongoing expense of time and money for staff training should be incorporated into the payment structure so that training will not be viewed as a "one-time" expense as the infrastructure changes over time. In addition, long-term and/or startup monies will be necessary for financial and/or technical support in the development of provider networks.

KEY ISSUES FOR ADMINISTRATORS

Understanding key issues in mental health services is critical for the continued success of mental health administrators in the current managed mental health care environment. Identification of persons in need of services, cost, and delivery issues represent only a few of the areas that have created enormous challenges for mental health administrators. The topics covered in this chapter—evidence-based mental health practice, diversity, comorbidity, financing, policy, and informatics—represent just a snapshot of mental health issues at this point in time. Although the specific issues will continue to change, administrators need to acquire a knowledge base that will enable them to more successfully manage mental health services within continuously changing internal and external organizational environments.

REFERENCES

Addis, M. E., Wade, W. A., & Hatgis, C. D. (1999). Barriers to dissemination of evidence-based practices: Addressing practitioners' concerns about manual-based psychotherapies. *Clinical Psychology—Science & Practice, 6*(4), 430–441.

Allodi, F. D. (1990). Refugees as victims of torture and trauma. In W. H. Holtzman, & T. H. Bornemann (Eds.), *Mental health of immigrants and refugees* (pp. 245–252). Austin, TX: Hogg Foundation for Mental Health.

Barbee, J. G. (1998). Mixed symptoms and syndromes of anxiety and depression: Diagnostic, prognostic, and etiologic issues. *Annals of Clinical Psychiatry, 10*, 15–29.

Barkham, M. D., & Mellor-Clark, J. D. (2000). Rigour and relevance: The role of practice-based evidence in the psychological therapies. In N. Rowland & S. Goss (Eds.), *Evidence-based counselling and psychological therapies: Research and applications* (pp. 127–144). London, England: Routledge.

Beutler, L. E. (2000). David and Goliath—When empirical and clinical standards of practice meet. *American Psychologist, 55*(9), 997–1007.

Bilsker, D. D. (2000). Teaching evidence-based practice in mental health. *Research on Social Work Practice, 10*(5), 664–669.

Blazer, D. G., Kessler, R. C., McGonable, K. A., & Swartz, M. S. (1994). The prevalence and distribution of major depression in a national comorbidity sample: The National Comorbidity Survey. *American Journal of Psychiatry, 151*(7), 979–986.

Cheuk, B. (1998). An experienced based information literacy model in the workplace: case studies from Singapore. In D. Booker (Ed.), *Information literacy: The professional issue. Proceedings of the 3rd Australian National Information Literacy Conference*, Canberra, Australia (pp. 74–82). Adelaide: University of South Australia Library.

Christensen, H., & Griffiths, K. (2000). The Internet and mental health literacy. *Australian & New Zealand Journal of Psychiatry, 34*(6), 975–979.

Congressional Budget Office. (1995). *Effects of managed care and managed competition* [Memorandum]. Washington, DC: CBO.

Cooper, C. R., & Denner, J. (1998). Theories linking culture and psychopathology: Universal and community-specific processes. *Annual Review of Psychology, 49*, 559–584.

Cuffel, B. J., Goldman, W., & Schlesinger, H. (1999). Does managing behavioral health care services increase the cost of providing medical care? *Journal of Behavioral Health Services & Research, 26*(4), 372–380.

Desjarlais, R., Eisenberg, L., Good, B., & Kleinman, A. (1995). *World mental health: Problems and priorities in low-income countries.* Oxford: Oxford University Press.

Dew, M. A. (1998). Psychiatric disorder in the context of physical illness. In B. P. Dohrenwend (Ed.), *Adversity, stress, and psychopathology* (pp. 177–218). New York: Oxford University Press.

Dorfman, S. (2000). Preventive interventions under managed care: Mental health and substance abuse services (DHHS publication number [SMA] 00-3437). Rockville, MD: Center for Mental Health Services.

Dunn, K. (1999). White House conference addresses mental health. *Workforce, 78*(8), 20–21.

Eisenberg, L (1999). Evidence based health promotion and disease prevention in psychiatry. *Psychiatriki, 10*(1), 15–24.

Essock, S. M., & Goldman, H. H. (1995). States' embrace of managed mental health care. *Health Affairs, 14*(3), 34–44.

Findlay, S. (1999). Managed behavioral health care in 1999: An industry at a crossroads. *Health Affairs, 18*(5), 116–124.

Fitzpatrick, E. (2001, January 19). Blue Cross expands mental health coverage. *Providence Journal*, p. B-1.

Frank, R. G., McGuire, T. G., & Goldman, W. (1996). *Buying in the public interest: A primer for purchasers of managed care in the public sector.* Washington, DC: Bazelon Center for Mental Health Law.

Freeman, H., & Kassebaum, G. (1960). Relationship of education and knowledge to opinions about mental illness. *Mental Hygiene, 44*, 43–47.

General Accounting Office. (1996). *Medicaid managed care: Serving the disabled challenges state programs.* Washington, DC: GAO.

George, T. B. (2000). Defining care in the culture of the chronically mentally ill living in the community. *Journal of Transcultural Nursing, 11*(2), 102–110.

Glied, S., & Kofman, S. (1995). *Women and mental health: Issues for health reform.* New York: Commonwealth Fund, Commission on Women's Health.

Gobis, L. (1997). An overview of state laws and approaches to minimize licensure barriers. *Telemedicine Today, 5*(6), 14–15, 18.

Goldman, H. H. (1996). Using cost-effectiveness data in benefit design. *Psychiatric Annals, 26*(8), 528–530.

Goldman, W., McCulloch, J., Cuffel, B., & Kozma, D. (1999). More evidence for the insurability of managed behavioral health care. *Health Affairs, 18*(5), 172–181.

Goldman, W., McCulloch, J., & Sturm, R. (1998). Cost and use of mental health services before and after managed care. *Health Affairs, 17*, 40–52.

Grant, B. E. (1997). Barriers to alcoholism treatment: Reasons for not seeking treatment in a general population sample. *Journal of the Studies on Alcohol, 58*, 365–371.

Grazier, K. L., Eselius, L. L., Hu, T.-W., Shore, K. K., & G'Sell, W. A. (1999). Effects of a mental health carve-out on use, costs, and payers: A four-year study. *Journal of Behavioral Health Services & Research, 26*(4), 381–389.

Halpert, H. P., Horvath, W. J., & Young, J. P. (1970). *An administrator's handbook on the application of operations research to the management of mental health systems.* Chevy Chase, MD: National Clearinghouse for Mental Health Information.

Hay Group. (1998). *Health care plan design and cost trends—1988 through 1997.* Washington, DC: National Association of Psychiatric Health Systems.

Health Care Financing Administration, Medicaid Bureau. (1995). Medicaid managed care enrollment report. In D. A. Freund & R. E. Hurley (Eds.), *Medicaid managed care: Contribution to issues of health reform* [Special issue]. *Annual Review of Public Health, 16.*

Health Care Financing Administration (2000). *Chartbook 2000: A profile of Medicaid.* Washington, DC: Health Care Financing Administration.

Hukamp, H. A. (1998). How a managed behavioral health care carve-out plan affected spending for episodes of treatment. *Psychiatric Services, 49*, 1559–1562.

Hynes, M. D., & Cardozo, B. L. (2000). Sexual violence against refugee women. *Journal of Women's Health & Gender-Based Medicine, 9*(8), 819–823.

Jensen, G. A., Morrisey, M. A., Gafney, S., & Liston, D. K. (1997). The new dominance of managed care: Insurance trends in the 1990s. *Health Affairs, 16*(1), 125–136.

Joint Commission on Mental Health and Illness. (1961). *Action for mental health.* New York: John Wiley.

Jorm, A. F. (2000). Mental health literacy: Public knowledge and beliefs about mental disorders. *British Journal of Psychiatry, 177*, 396–401.

Jorm, A. F., Korten, A. E., Jacomb, P. A., Christensen, H., Rodgers, B., & Pollit, B. (1997). Public beliefs about causes and risk factors for depression and schizophrenia. *Social Psychiatry & Psychiatric Epidemiology, 32*(3), 143–148.

Kessler, R. C., McGonagle, K. A., & Zhao, S., Nelson, C. B., Hughes, M., Eshleman, S., et al. (1994). Lifetime and 12 month prevalence of *DSM–III–R* psychiatric disorders in the United States: Results from the National Comorbidity Study. *Archives of General Psychiatry, 51*, 8–19.

Kessler, R. C., Nelson, C. B., McGonagle, K. A., Edlund, M. J., Frank, R. G., & Leaf, P. J. (1996). The epidemiology of co-occurring addictive and mental disorders: Implications for prevention and service utilization. *American Journal of Orthopsychiatry, 66*(10), 17–31.

Larry, R. E. (1966). Social consequences of mental illness. *Journal of Consulting Psychology, 30*, 450–455.

Laske, C. (1994). Legal aspects of digital image management and communication. *Medical Informatics, 19*(2), 189–196.

Laske, C. (1997). Health care telematics: Who is liable? *Computer Methods and Programs in Biomedicine, 54*(1–2), 1–6.

Levin, B. L. (1992). Managed mental health care: A national perspective. In R. W. Manderscheid & M. A. Sonnenschein (Eds.), *Mental health United States, 1992* (pp. 208–218). Rockville, MD: Center for Mental Health Services.

Levin, B. L., Hanson, A., Coe, R. D, & Kuppin, S. A. (2000). *Mental health parity: National and state perspectives 2000: A report to the Florida legislature.* Tampa, FL: Louis de la Parte Florida Mental Health Institute. [Copy available from the institute]

Lin, K. M. (1986). Psychopathology and social disruption in refugees. In C. L. Williams & J. Westermeyer (Eds.), *Refugee mental health in resettlement countries* (pp. 61–73). Series in Clinical and Community Psychology. Washington, DC: Hemisphere.

Lu, F. G., Lim, R. F., & Mezzich, J. E. (1995). Issues in the assessment and diagnosis of culturally diverse individuals. In J. Oldham & M. Riba (Eds.), *Review of psychiatry* (vol. 14, pp.

477–510). Washington, DC: American Psychiatric Press.

Ma, C. A., & McGuire, T. G. (1998). Costs and incentives in a behavioral health carve-out. *Health Affairs, 17*(2), 63–69.

Magenau, J. L. (1997). Digital diagnosis: Liability concerns and state licensing issues are inhibiting the progress of telemedicine. *Communications and the Law, 19*(4), 25–43.

Mechanic, D. (1998). Emerging trends in mental health policy and practice. *Health Affairs, 17*(6), 82–98.

Mechanic, D. (1999). *Mental health and social policy: The emergence of managed care* (4th ed.). Boston: Allyn and Bacon.

Mercer, W. M. (1997). *Case studies: A guide to implementing parity for mental illness.* New York: William M. Mercer.

National Advisory Mental Health Council. (1997). *Parity in coverage of mental health services in an era of managed care: An interim report to Congress.* Rockville, MD: Author.

National Advisory Mental Health Council. (1998). *Parity in financing mental health services: Managed care, effects on cost, access, and quality: An interim report to Congress.* Rockville, MD: Author.

National Conference of State Legislatures. (1999). Behavioral health news. *State Health Notes, 20*(292), 2.

National Institute of Medicine. (1997). *Managing managed care: Quality improvement in behavioral health.* Washington, DC: National Academy Press.

National Institute on Drug Abuse. (1998, December 8). *Panel urges broadened access, insurance coverage for methadone treatment nationwide* [press release]. Bethesda, MD: Author.

Newmann, J. P., Greenley, D., Sweeney, J. K., & Van Dien, G. (1998). Abuse histories, severe mental illness, and the cost of care. In B. L. Levin, A. Blanch, & A. Jennings (Eds.), *Women's mental health services: A public health perspective* (pp. 279–308). Thousand Oaks, CA: Sage.

Nunnally, J. (1961). *Popular conceptions of mental health: Their development and change.* New York: Holt, Rinehart and Winston.

Office of Research on Women's Health. (1999). *Strategic plan to address health disparities among diverse populations of women.* Bethesda, MD: National Institutes of Health.

Physicians Insurers Association of America. (1998). *Telemedicine: A medical liability white paper.* Rockville, MD: Author.

Pollack, E. S., Windle, C. D., & Wurster, C. R. (1974). Psychiatric information systems: An historical perspective. In J. L. Crawford, D. W. Morgan, & D. T. Gianturco (Eds.), *Progress in mental health information systems: Computer applications* (pp. 319–332). Cambridge, MA: Ballinger.

Regier, D. A. (1988). One month prevalence disorders in the United States. *Archives of General Psychiatry, 45,* 977–986.

Reynolds, S. (2000). Evidence based practice and psychotherapy research. *Journal of Mental Health, 9*(3), 257–266.

Rhodes, A., & Goering, P. (1998). Gender differences in the use of outpatient mental health services. In B. L. Levin, A. K. Blanch, & A. Jennings (Eds.), *Women's mental health services: A public health perspective* (pp. 19–33). Thousand Oaks, CA: Sage.

Ridgely, M. S., & Goldman, H. H. (1996). Health law symposium: Putting the failure of national health care reform in perspective: Mental health benefits and the "benefit" of incrementalism. *Saint Louis University Law Journal, 40*(2), 407–435.

Rubenstein, L. V., Jackson-Triche, M., Unutzer, J., Miranda, J., Minnium, K., Pearson, M. L., et al. (1999). Evidence-based care for depression in managed primary care practices. *Health Affairs, 18*(5), 89–105.

Russell, R. (1999). The Senior Outreach Program of Park Ridge Mental Health: An innovative approach to mental health and aging. *Abstracts in Social Gerontology, 42*(3).

Schlesinger, M., & Gray, B. (1999). Institutional change and its consequences for the delivery of mental health services. In A. V. Horwitz & T. L. Scheid (Eds.), *A handbook for the study of mental health: Social contexts, theories, and systems* (pp. 427–448). New York: Cambridge University Press.

Shore, M. F. (1994). An overview of managed behavioral health care. In M. F. Shore (Ed.), *Managed care, the private sector, and Medicaid mental health and substance abuse services. New Directions in Mental Health Services, 72*(Winter), 3–12.

Sidowski, J. B., Johnson, J. H., & Williams, T. A. (1980). *Technology in mental health care delivery systems.* Norwood, NJ: Ablex.

Silove, D. D. (1999). The psychosocial effects of torture, mass human rights violations, and refugee trauma: Toward an integrated conceptual framework. *Journal of Nervous & Mental Disease, 187*(4), 200–207.

Simmons, P. (1997, June). ERISA preemption and its impact on behavioral health services. *Behavioral Healthcare Tomorrow,* pp. 67–69.

Stio, A. A. (1994). State government: The laboratory for national health care reform. *Seton Hall Legislative Journal, 322*(19), III, Note.

Sturm, R. (1997). How expensive is unlimited mental health care coverage under managed care? *Journal of the American Medical Association, 278*(18), 1533–1537.

Sturm, R. (1999). Tracking changes in behavioral health services: How have carve-outs changed care? *Journal of Behavioral Health Services & Research, 26*(4), 360–371.

Sturm, R., & McCulloch, J. (1998). Mental health and substance abuse benefits in carve-out plans and the Mental Health Parity Act of 1996. *Journal of Health Care Finance, 24*(3), 82–92.

Sturm, R., Zhang, W., & Schoenbaum, M. (1999). How expensive are unlimited substance abuse benefits under managed care? *Journal of Behavioral Health Services & Research, 26*(2), 203–210.

Sullivan, E. (2000). Healthy resources for evidence based medicine. *Econtent, 23*(6), 42–51.

Trabin, T. (1996). *The computerization of behavioral healthcare: How to enhance clinical practice, management, and communications.* San Francisco: Jossey-Bass.

U.S. Bureau of the Census. (1990a). *1990 Census of population* (CPHL-133). Washington, DC: Author.

U.S. Bureau of the Census (1990b). *1990 Census of population* (CPHL-96.) Washington, DC: Author.

U.S. Department of Health and Human Services. (1999). *Mental health: A report of the Surgeon General—Executive summary.* Rockville, MD: U.S. Department of Health and Human Services, Substance Abuse and Mental Health Services Administration, Center for Mental Health Services, National Institutes of Health, National Institute of Mental Health.

U.S. Department of Health and Human Services. (2000). *Healthy people 2010.* Washington, DC: Author.

Williams, T. A., & Johnson, J. H. (1979). *Mental health in the 21st century.* Lexington, MA: Lexington Books.

Wolfe, J. D. (1999). Overcoming barriers to evidence-based practice: Lessons from medical practitioners. *Clinical Psychology—Science & Practice, 6*(4), 445–448.

Chapter Two

Leadership and Training in Mental Health

Bruce Lubotsky Levin
Ardis Hanson
Sara A. Kuppin

In American society, the growth and success (vs. stagnation and failure) of an organization often have been attributed to the presence of effective leadership. This has been particularly evident through the economic, technologic, and health services delivery changes of the past few decades. Although leadership has been highly valued in organizations, leadership emerges because of certain skills, talents, expertise, and the consent of specific groups under given circumstances (Levinson, 1968).

The leadership function within mental health organizations continues to demand that professionals must understand and deal with current multidimensional problems in the managed behavioral health care industry. Furthermore, the responsibility for preparing these professionals rests within universities to better educate these leaders in public health issues and in basic health and mental health administrative, policy, and services delivery issues. In addition, the responsibility also rests with professional societies to better equip leaders within mental health organizations for the diverse challenges that lie ahead in a changing managed behavioral health care environment.

This chapter examines leadership issues in mental health, discussing the obstacles and challenges that leaders face within mental health organizations. The chapter also discusses the importance of curriculum changes in graduate programs that prepare both clinical and administrative mental health practitioners and emphasizes the critical nature of continuing education in the development of mental health professionals who must function within changing behavioral health services delivery systems.

DEFINITIONS

Leadership has been defined in a variety of ways. Bennis and Nanus (1985) estimated that over 350 definitions of leadership existed in the research literature. Nevertheless, Northouse (1977) identified four basic components common to defining leadership: (1) Leadership is a process; (2) leadership involves influence; (3) leadership occurs within a group; and (4) leadership involves goal attainment. Gabel (1998) suggested that a leader must be able to provide clear direction and a clear vision about his or her organization's future, whereas Bennis and Nanus (1985) emphasized that leaders possess excellent communication skills. DePree (1989) suggested that leadership develops over time through performance and through reflection on performance, where feedback (from others) contributes to that reflection.

THEORIES OF LEADERSHIP

There have been numerous theories of leadership postulated in the research literature. Northouse (1997) reviewed and analyzed the literature on leadership and has summarized nine basic approaches and theories of leadership: (1) the trait approach; (2) the style approach; (3) the situational approach; (4) contingency theory; (5) path–goal theory; (6) leader–member exchange theory; (7) transformational leadership; (8) team leadership theory; and (9) the psychodynamic approach to leadership. Basically, these theories and approaches have focused on leadership traits, behaviors, and processes, as well as the basic personality of the leader and what works best within certain organizational environments or with certain groups of workers.

In addition to the postulation of the nine basic theories and approaches to leadership, Bennis (1993) suggested that leaders possessed four basic competencies: (1) Leaders had vision; (2) leaders communicated the meaning of that vision to workers; (3) leaders displayed trust or consistency in their values and vision; and (4) leaders were aware of their own skills, attitudes, and limitations. Although space restrictions here do not permit an in-depth discussion of approaches and theories of leadership, DuBrin (2001) provided an excellent discussion of these issues.

LEADERSHIP BARRIERS

Despite possessing special skills, knowledge, abilities, and competencies, leaders must learn to function in an environment full of various personal, professional, and organizational barriers. Within the field of public health, Coye (1994) divided barriers to leadership into two basic types: internal barriers to public health, and barriers that are external to the field of public health. External barriers to leadership in public health include the ever-changing ideology of government (i.e., in regulating behavior and in providing health and mental health services), resource constraints (diminished local, state, and federal government resources for public health), special economic interest groups (e.g., lobbies), and conflicting values (e.g., social goods and economic interests).

Within the field of public health, Coye (1994) suggested that there remained a number of internal barriers to leadership and success, including a culture of entitlement; resistance to accountability; scorn for cost-effectiveness considerations; suspicion of the private sector; and ignorance and hostility toward the medical care sector.

Coye (1994) also noted those aspects of government that have created barriers to progress in pubic health, including the inability and slow response time to change in the environment; the categorical approach to program design and implementation; the inability to collaborate across programs and agencies; the inability to focus and prioritize efforts; the erosion of public confidence in government; and the elaborate investment in current structures and systems. These barriers also exist in mental health services.

LEADERSHIP CHALLENGES

What makes these barriers to leadership so challenging? Roper (1994) suggested that leadership in public health (as well as mental health) has suffered from problems of low morale. In addition, public health and behavioral health services have been viewed by society as an underfunded yet overworked profession, particularly in comparison to professionals working within specialty medical care settings. There also has been the need to retool the skills of health and behavioral health professionals. The relatively low pay and minimum benefits have added to the difficulty in recruiting and retaining effective public heath and behavioral health leaders. In addition, with the lack of substantial progress in obtaining empirical evidence in the cost effectiveness of behavioral health preventive interventions, federal and state behavioral health prevention expenditures have been largely discretionary vis-à-vis medical care expenditures, which have (minimum) guaranteed expenditures (through federal/state entitlement benefits).

Roper (1994) suggested that education in the health sciences alone has been insufficient preparation for a career in public health. Communications skills within the workplace as well as within the community have been important when educating the public. Furthermore, an understanding of cultural diversity, health policymaking, and the political process has become a critical skill for leaders in health and behavioral health organizations.

Finally, there has been a continued existence of outdated bureaucracies in public health and behavioral health service delivery systems. All too often, public institutions have represented bureaucracies with outdated civil service systems and/or inflexible personnel systems (Roper, 1994).

LEADERSHIP IN MENTAL HEALTH

In 1955, a symposium on responsibility for leadership in mental health examined the pressing issues of the times (Greenwood, Reid, Novick, & Stubblefield, 1956). These issues included changing patterns of at-risk populations, inadequate aid to the uninsured and working poor, increasing convergence of mental health interests and activities of governmental and voluntary agencies, how to secure the most effective use of lay people as leaders in the mental health field, and contradictions between the expressed goals of training and actual experience. With the exception of the evolution of managed behavioral health care and the necessity for the development of new competencies for effective leadership in managed behavioral health care, seemingly little has changed in the challenges that leaders face in the organization, financing, and delivery of mental health services.

Those taking on responsibility for leadership functions in mental health organizations can no longer survive without recognizing and supporting a system based largely on financial feasibility and increasing productivity (Gabel, 1998; Schreter & Schreter, 1996). Recognizing the reality of an organization and the place that the organization has within a larger context requires a leader to set and achieve goals, be able to set priorities, and establish and move toward these goals.

However, throughout the research literature, these activities also have been found in discussions in competencies for administrators. The primary difference between a mental health administrator and a mental health leader is that the former examines issues as if they were predominately structural, organizational, and authority oriented, and the latter provides vision, direction, and change, skills that cannot be taught (Talbott, 1987). However, others believe that individuals can be nurtured and trained in the diverse elements that comprise leadership, such as engaging and empowering others, appraising and taking risks, and strategic planning, all in conjunction with political savvy (DuBrin, 2001; Northouse, 1997). Furthermore, leadership is the effort of a leader, who may hold (but does not necessarily hold) a formal position of authority, to engage followers in the joint pursuit of mutually agreed-on goals: goals that represent significant change (Kellerman, 1999).

If psychiatrists are to assume these positions, to reclaim the administrative and leadership positions outside of academic psychiatry, a few issues must be addressed. Many authors still address the question of whether or not management and administrative duties are compatible with the clinical practice of psychiatric medicine and have urged psychiatrists to maintain their commitment to the humanistic tradition of psychiatry (Faulkner, Scully, & Shore, 1998; Grusky, Thompson, & Tillman, 1991; Shore, 1997). No doubt, this concern has resulted from the belief that cost will outweigh quality as the most important factor when treating a patient in a managed care environment.

Lazarus (1996) discussed the myth that psychiatric clinicians who enter the management field do so because of incompetence in clinical ability. He suggested that physicians seeking management posts were often high achievers, very skilled at the activities that make for both a good clinician, and a mental health administrator. Rather than pointing out valued qualities of clinical practice that conflicted with administrative expectations, Lazarus (1996) focused on the qualities that were necessary for success in both realms: excellent interpersonal skills, the ability to interact with a variety of people, and the ability to negotiate with and influence others.

The ambivalence of many psychiatrists and their students about accepting managed care principles puts their leadership capabilities in jeopardy, rendering them unable to develop and communicate a clear vision and to motivate and involve other members of the organization (Gabel, 1998). Psychiatrists may have to be convinced earlier in their careers to participate in administrative positions, to maintain the place of psychiatrists in the leadership of mental health organizations. As stated earlier, psychiatric faculty have the power to instill negative attitudes toward managed care, which, when coupled with a historic view of administration as a secondary yet necessary chore, may influence possible leaders in residency training to shy away from taking an administrative and/or leadership route (Cozza & Hales, 1992).

What qualities does a mental health administrator need to successfully lead a mental health organization today? Skills typically associated with good leaders include the ability to set goals, create an environment of trust and open communication, make decisions constructively, resolve conflict effectively, and use power productively (Cozza & Hales, 1992). Mental health administrators in today's constantly changing delivery systems must have flexibility, interdisciplinary teamwork, and an understanding of group and system dynamics as well (Faulkner et al., 1998). These latter qualities have become especially important in light of the demand for integrated somatic and behavioral health services delivery.

There also has been a question of whether or not leaders can be trained (Kellerman, 1999), or whether these (exceptional) qualities are instinctive (Greenblatt, 1992). Although many articles supported the creation of additional training programs to teach leadership as well as administrative and management skills, time has shown that good leaders in mental health have, up until now, developed their skills through years of experience (Greenblatt, 1991; Rodenhauser & Bashook, 1991). These mental health leaders cited the importance of experience in obtaining the ability to lead effectively; however, they believed there was a need going unfilled, particularly in departments of psychiatry, for training programs and experiential opportunities to develop and hone leadership skills (Greenblatt, 1991; Schreter, 1997).

TRAINING IN MENTAL HEALTH

Whether or not psychiatrists or other mental health professionals assume leadership roles in mental health, the trend has increasingly been toward an interdisciplinary approach to patient care. All professional graduate programs, whether they are in psychiatry, clinical/counseling psychology, psychiatric nursing, or social work, need to include training in management, leadership, and behavioral health services at both the master's and doctoral level.

Another model adopted in certain behavioral health care delivery systems has been the psychiatrist, nurse, or social worker assuming clinical leadership roles, while a professional mental health administrator takes the helm in all other areas. This calls for partnerships between the clinical and administrative areas within mental health organizations. It also calls for specialized training for those professional administrators wanting to work in mental health.

In the past several decades, psychiatrists have been less likely to take on administrative leadership roles, leaving other professionals trained in the fields of social work, nursing, and psychology to take on these responsibilities (Barton, 1991a; Greenblatt, 1992). However, psychiatry does not seem satisfied with this situation, believing that the best leadership in a mental health organization comes from someone with the clinical experience and expertise of a psychiatrist (Lipton & Loutsch, 1985). But many psychiatrists have been ill-prepared to take on the role of administrator and lead their organizations administratively as well as clinically, because most psychiatrists rarely (initially) plan to assume administrative leadership roles early in their professional careers (Borus, 1992; Rodenhauser & Bashook, 1991).

Sullivan (1997) and Mayberg (1997), two prominent psychologists and leaders of large mental health organizations, write of their paths to administrative and leadership positions as unplanned, yet successful due to a wide variety of experiences both as clinicians and program developers, administrators, policy analysts, and consultants. These opportunities, allotted to them throughout their graduate and postgraduate careers, provided the variety of experiences each feels was necessary to produce successful leaders. If psychiatrists are to take on administrative leadership roles, how and when should they be trained to acquire the skills to do so successfully? Leaders past and present may have reached their positions through natural leadership skills coupled with the unforeseen opportunity to gain valuable administrative and leadership experience.

Training

Now more than ever, strong effective leadership is essential to successful mental health organizations. Academic departments of psychiatry and health science centers have been especially important in recruiting and training administrators and leaders in mental health. The survival of academic psychiatry depends partially on its ability to produce effective clinician-administrators, knowledgeable and skilled according to the demands of today's managed behavioral health environment, for it is their job to lead both public and private facilities, as well as take on responsibility for their own departments in the future.

Leaders can benefit from critically selected training opportunities, whether a graduate internship or postdoctoral program in psychology or a continuing education program for seasoned professionals, that reflect their professional objectives. The number of postdoctoral training opportunities in psychology has been increasing over the past 10 years, as has interest in executive track (often MBA) programs intended for mental health care professionals interested in receiving additional training while maintaining their current practice (Manley & DeLeon, 1997). These kinds of programs have provided the opportunity for administrative training that has historically been scarce in graduate and professional education.

There remain a number of critical issues in training future mental health professionals. First, the continual shift of mental health services into managed care settings and the impact it is having on the organization and leadership of mental health service delivery systems are significant. A good portion of the pressing concerns with graduate and postgraduate psychiatric education, for example, is closely tied to reform in health care economics (Riba & Carli, 1996).

Another important issue is that although there were too few training opportunities for mental health professionals before managed care, the need for additional training programs has become critical, especially for psychiatrists interested in taking management and clinical administrative positions.

Shore (1997) maintained that academic programs as well as mental health professionals must stay current in the training and/or retraining of psychiatrists and other mental health professionals in their work within today's ever-changing behavioral health care delivery systems.

The dramatic shift toward managed care has had a profound influence on the mental health care organization (Van Dyke & Schlesinger, 1997). This initiated an evaluation of how well mental health professionals have been prepared to operate in this collection of hybrid delivery system environments, and a reevaluation of existing training programs (or lack thereof) that attempt to prepare individuals to work within the mental health field. Riba and Carli (1996) referred to Gabbard's (1992) concept of "the big chill" as characteristic of psychiatric residents who are thrust upon graduation into delivery systems that are unfamiliar due to training experiences that were irrelevant for today's mental health delivery systems. Critics denounce many academic treatment centers as reluctant to follow the move toward managed behavioral health care and unresponsive to the demands of these new types of organizations. Managed care has required new and different skills, including a requirement that mental health professionals reach a level of information literacy.

Information Literacy

Persons working in mental health have found that their environments have been subjected to rapid technological change. Today public- as well as private-sector mental health organizations need to operate in a fast-moving health care marketplace with knowledgeable stakeholders, in which the relationships between provider and patient change equally fast. Public-sector mental health organizations recognized that they faced competition for funding or from alternative services. Academic institutions have had to integrate the online delivery of coursework and digital library resources to provide educational opportunities for local and distant learners. Capability in mental health services often has been predicated on the ability to implement and use the latest technology for services delivery, training, and continuing education.

In 1989, it was postulated that the amount of information created doubled every 5 years (Wurman, 1989). The Secretary's Commission on Achieving Necessary Skills (1992) identified eight areas essential for further education or to enter the job market. These skills consisted of a set of five competencies in the areas of resources, interpersonal skills, information, systems, and technology. If these prognostications were accurate—and the increase in print and electronic resources appears to have substantiated both predictions—then mental health organizations and mental health professionals require information literacy skills identified by the commission report.

Mental health organizations need values that focus on creating and using intellectual assets, and individuals need the ability to navigate and use information to learn new skills and to feel comfortable in ambiguous work situations (Abell, 2000). Academic coursework now requires individuals to find, acquire, manage, and apply information and knowledge.

The term *information literacy* is a derivative of the older term *computer literacy*. Computer literacy, by definition, restricts itself to learning how to understand and use computers.[1] In 1989, the American Library Association defined information literacy as the effective use of technology as well as the ability to recognize when an individual needs information and to locate, evaluate, and use the information found. Bruce (1997) considered information literacy an important generic skill that allows a person to engage in effective decision making, problem solving, research, and continued learning. In today's mental health workplace environments, Bruce's version of information literacy also includes desktop access, the Internet, e-mail, client information systems, and corporate networks.

According to its most popular definition, information literacy may be under-

---

1. From the *American Heritage Dictionary of the English Language*, 4th ed., 2000: "The ability to operate a computer and to understand the language used in working with a specific system or systems."

stood as the ability to recognize when information is needed and the ability to locate, evaluate, and use effectively the needed information (Bruce, 1997). It has become increasingly clear over the past decade that health and mental health educators consider information literacy a critical educational issue in contemporary society.

The research on information literacy is based on a range of user- or people-oriented theoretical frameworks that make possible outcomes highly relevant to professional practice (Bruce, 2000). Some of these studies used existing disciplinary bases, such as information-seeking, and use research or educational research. Overall, information literacy research has become a significant source of knowledge for management and educators in the health and mental health fields.

Information literacy is but one of a number of dimensions involved in successful work practices (Mutch, 1996), and it may be helpful to consider more of these dimensions simultaneously. Creating linkages between higher education institutions and workplaces led Bruce (1997) to propose elements of an information literate organization that act as enablers to individuals and groups interacting with information. These elements (e.g., environmental scanning, information processing, corporate memory, and research and development) raise the importance of the quality of the information environment in supporting information literacy within mental health organizations.

Within the education sector, examining students' abilities across multiple institutions reveals not only that personal characteristics (such as self-confidence) influence capabilities, but also that levels of information literacy have been influenced by gender, race, disciplinary domain, and (potentially) year level (Catts & Appleton, 1999; Castro et al., 1999). These student characteristics have been accompanied by other significant shifts in the patterns of students' academic careers, as well as in the experiences and expectations students bring to the university (Roth, 1999).

Current enrollment patterns in higher education vary dramatically from those of previous generations. Students are more diverse and are older. The university-to-career path is also very different. Many students work part-time or full-time. This, coupled with the fact that many are likely to periodically leave academia to deal with family or work issues, means that students may attend two or more different institutions during the course of their college careers and may take more than 4 years to obtain a degree. It is also evident that after earning a baccalaureate, they are likely to engage in continuing education opportunities, and many of them will change careers three or four times.

The relationships between information seeking and use are critical, with particular ways of seeing the information seeking and use process leading to qualitatively different learning outcomes. Focusing on finding facts or "the right answer" leads to diminished and fragmentary learning outcomes (Klaus, 2000). Experiencing information seeking as an aid to understanding the provision of different perspectives on the topic leads to more powerful learning outcomes for students (Bruce, 2000). Evaluation of new scientific findings is an important skill for a scientifically literate citizenry (Zimmerman, Bisanz, & Bisanz, 1998). For students interested in a mental health professional career, information literacy in an academic setting requires a series of discrete skills. For example, mental health practitioners need to be conversant with the databases used within the academic or research environment.

A questionnaire designed by Verhey (1999) for the San Francisco State University School of Nursing measured six primary content areas: (1) information resources used to complete assignments, (2) the use of bibliographic databases, (3) the use of libraries and the school's learning resource center, (4) comfort level in accessing information resources, (5) barriers encountered in accessing information resources, and (6) plans for accessing current information after graduation. Item 6 has an impact on life as a professional. Both cohorts surveyed listed subscribing to journals and attending educational programs as their first and second most preferred ways of obtaining professional information after graduation. The question then becomes how to expand their options to the universe of professional information that they may not subscribe to or attend. It will be critical for mental health practitioners at all levels to gain a more comprehensive view of information as it relates to a particular administrative, clinical, or research question and how to access that information in a timely fashion.

Once the graduate has moved into the professional arena, information literacy also involves the professional, the patient, and his or her health education. In 1996, patient education took on a new perspective when the Joint Commission on Accreditation of Healthcare Organizations (JCAHO) identified patient and family education as an important function necessary to overall patient care. Education became required in all JCAHO-accredited organizations, and all members of an interdisciplinary treatment team were required to provide education with consideration for literacy (Weiss, Hart, & Pust, 1991), educational level, and language of the patient. This emphasis by the Joint Commission prompted many health care agencies to take a new look at both staff (Brownson, 1998) and patient education materials (Davidhizar & Brownson, 1999). It also prompted health care agencies to examine the literacy levels of their staffs in providing patient information as well as in developing training protocols, many via a computer network or the Internet.

Although job applicant testing has been most common in the retail, manufacturing, and transportation sectors, service and health care organizational settings have begun to turn to preemployment testing as well. Traditionally, tests were used to screen out; now they're being used to screen in. Many agencies use the components from these preemployment tests as a component of professional development. If a person's clinical skills are good but computer skills are weak, the agency can focus on training the individual in basic computer skills while enhancing existing research skills. Training is an increasing imperative in 21st-century working America.

According to Cheuk (1998), there are three groups of people who would be the most interested in ensuring information literacy in the workplace: managers with a concern for staff members' professional development and ability to respond to change; information managers with an interest in training and educating their clientele to effectively use the organization's information services; and trainers and educators who wish to prepare "learners" for their chosen professions.

A recent study concerning Internet connections and information technology skills of public health workers in the Midwest was conducted with 343 local health departments in the 10 states of the Greater Midwest Region (Hollander & Martin, 1999). Overall, half provided Internet access to some or all staff. Two-thirds allowed use of e-mail and half searched the Web. Half were linked to the State Health Department, and 30% were linked to other local health departments. Over half used CDC-Wonder, while less than 20% searched MEDLINE. Two-thirds of the respondents expressed an interest in MEDLINE training, and three-fourths were interested in learning more about the Internet. Sixty-nine percent of respondents planned to enhance electronic communication capacity within the next year. Thus, public health practitioners need timely, convenient access to information to aid them in improving the health of the American public. The survey clearly indicated an expressed desire by public health agencies to have workers become information literate.

The survival of health and mental health care organizations requires their members to develop new work skills and flexibility. Competitive requirements justify genuine study and research for best practices, innovative programs and financing, and use of technology. Mental health administrators will be unable to make good decisions about how to respond to emerging situations in mental health unless they have developed a high level of information literacy to explore the issues facing their organization, much less their service delivery systems. Developing this literacy is a responsibility of leadership, and nowhere is this more critical than in mental health care (Beckham, 1995).

Managing the new technocracy and information resources of this new millennium will be challenging but also exciting. Twenty years ago, mental health administrators were not held accountable for the level of knowledge now required in behavioral health. With electronic medical records, innovations in clinical and community treatment systems, and the impact of the information and technologic revolution, the interface between technology assessment, operationalizing technology, and continually upgrading staff to know the implications of the technology revolution will be imperative for success (Kerfoot, 2000).

Mental health professionals will need to communicate their needs for trained and qualified staff to university programs to include information literacy in their curriculum and core competencies. Universities are important partners in the preparation of upcoming generations of health and mental health leaders to effectively manage the continued complexities in managed mental health care. The success of future mental health leaders will be measured by those individuals' ability to integrate the very complex issues of patient care and technology in a way that makes sense for patients, the mental health organization, and the staff who will be working in that treatment environment.

Training and Academia

Although managed care has focused on providing mental health services primarily within ambulatory settings, within limited referral mechanisms, and through defined insurance benefits, academic health science centers have traditionally provided care in an opposite manner, with much of the care provided in an inpatient setting over a longer period of time. There have been many who criticized a perceived reluctance of academic departments to adapt to managed behavioral health care practice, viewing academic psychiatry as incompatible with the demands of managed behavioral health care (Van Dyke & Schlesinger, 1997). Hoge (1997) noted impediments to change for academic psychiatry, including a culture valuing faculty independence, research, and teaching above services delivery and rewards for faculty unrelated to clinical productivity. England (1997) cited a locus of power shift from these academic health science centers to other stakeholders as one reason for the reluctance of academic centers to change to a model more compatible with managed care. Schreter and Schreter (1996) noted the personal experiences by many psychiatrists in reaction to what they perceived as challenges to their identity as well as the reduced income that comes with managed care.

This negative perception of managed care has made it difficult for academic psychiatry departments and their associated clinics to survive in the current marketplace. Future students of mental health practice and administration should be given opportunities to learn the workings of managed behavioral health care, and be given experiences in situations outside of academe in order to be the innovators needed to create and maintain competent systems of behavioral health care in this country. Aggravating an already fragile relationship, residents and managed care companies may conflict on issues of psychiatric resident training costs. Managed care companies tend to believe that more residents add to the cost of care, although there has been little evidence to support this theory (Ross, 1997). This issue needs to be addressed if residents are to be indoctrinated with a value system compatible with managed care practices.

Held primarily responsible for training new psychiatrists, these academic centers provide students not only with knowledge, but with values as well (Hoge, 1997). As Ross wrote, "There is no substitute for dedicated mentors and supervisors who have thoroughly identified with these values" (1997, p. 304). The values Ross referred to were: (1) quality patient care, (2) sound economic policies and decisions, (3) academic integrity, and (4) the humanistic tradition of psychiatry toward treating patients and training students. Ross's words illustrated the importance of the exchange of consistent values from trainer to trainee, suggesting as well that managed care, with its emphasis on cost, should not be treated as incompatible with quality care, solid academic practice, and the humanistic tradition. What managed care systems intended to accomplish, a collective mission for both providers and payers, as well as intermediaries, will be impossible without clinicians who work within managed care, if only to mold it into something more innovative and functional.

According to the Surgeon General of the United States (U.S. DHHS, 1999), there has been a lack of properly trained mental health professionals, particularly in rural areas and in the treatment of children and older adults with mental disorders. In addressing the need for training and trainers versed in the ways of today's behavioral health care delivery systems, mental health professionals need to be trained to work in multidisciplinary teams and in interdisciplinary health and mental health work settings. Managed care calls for integrated, coordinated patient care, provided by multidisciplinary teams (Faulkner et al., 1998; U.S. DHHS, 1999). Mental health consumer "peer-specialists" have been increasingly included in multidisciplinary case management teams, and studies have shown that clients under this type of team had better outcomes than clients with more traditional case management teams (U.S. DHHS, 1999). Training programs need to provide their trainees with the opportunity to develop these skills if they are to produce competent and competitive mental health professionals (Warwick, 1997).

Historically, inadequate and disjointed mental health care in the public sector, particularly for children and older adults, has given way to efforts to provide more comprehensive and coordinated care through new financing systems and training mental health providers to be more culturally competent (U.S. DHHS, 1999). In looking for solutions to the lack of relevant training opportunities, the literature addressed the selection of trainers where the training opportunities have been located, and what support has been given to these efforts by academic departments and professional associations. If the trainers are unfamiliar with the managed care systems and unwilling to be retrained themselves, their students are less likely to come out with the appropriate skills and will lack role models and mentors to help them succeed both as mental health clinicians and mental health administrators and leaders.

The location of mental health training opportunities is important as well. For psychiatry students, residency and internship opportunities ideally should be available in interdisciplinary settings so trainees get experience in dealing with service system and group issues. Opportunities to train in the public mental health sector are necessary for new clinicians and future administrators to understand the complexities of reaching underserved populations (England, 1997; Warwick, 1997).

Interdisciplinary training is necessary for the multidisciplinary collaboration called for in today's managed behavioral health care settings (U.S. DHHS, 1999). This includes the need for multidiscipline professional educators who will appreciate value for the interdisciplinary approach to behavioral health care. The values inherent in an interdisciplinary curriculum are similar to those values expressed by programs supporting the training of professionals in the provision of culturally competent mental health services. Essentially, a fundamental assumption for supporters of interdisciplinary treatment teams as well as cultural competence has been that there are multiple ways to perceive and approach any situation, all of which may be valid (Dana, 1998; Nissani, 1997). Dana (1998) criticized managed care as being incompatible with culturally competent care, something he perceived as opposite the trend in psychology and society: to recognize and respect self-definition and self-identification by cultural groups.

Culturally appropriate mental health care requires providers who can identify, understand, and utilize natural support systems within families and communities (U.S. DHHS, 1999). The need for training programs valuing interdisciplinary research and practice, as well as cultural competency and the skills necessary to work with underserved populations, was detailed by Dana (1998) and Drotar (1998).

In order for these opportunities to become available to trainees, and eventually part of the required curricula, these types of training initiatives need to be supported by academic departments of psychiatry, psychology, and social work, as well as professional organizations (Austin, 1991). Requirements for psychiatric residency training, as outlined by the Residency Review Committee for Graduate Medical Education, acknowledge the need for training in issues of financing and regulation of psychiatric practice, the structure of both public and private organizations, and group dynamics of interdisciplinary teams (Borus & Sledge, 1996). However, these words mean little if not supported by the endorsement of postdoctoral traineeships and residencies that reflect the value of training mental health professionals in these areas (Warwick, 1997).

Barton (1991b) detailed the components of a model mental health administration curriculum. At the University of South Florida (USF) College of Public Health, graduate students have the opportunity to focus their studies in behavioral health services within both the master's of science in public health and the doctor of philosophy degree programs. Furthermore, this focus in behavioral health services provides the opportunity for graduate students at USF in clinical mental health programs (e.g., psychiatry, clinical psychology, psychiatric social work, educational psychology, counseling psychology, and psychiatric nursing) the opportunity to enroll in behavioral health services courses during their graduate mental health training, thus providing opportunities for future mental health clinicians to integrate principles and key issues of mental health services delivery into their clinical programs.

Continuing Education

Continuing professional education has remained critical in training persons to assume mental health administrative roles, because many candidates for these positions have not received specific training in mental health administration within their formal graduate programs. Continuing education has remained important for the training and/or retraining of mental health administrative practitioners or for (clinically trained) mental health professionals looking to serve in an administrative capacity to address rapidly changing service delivery systems (Schreter & Schreter, 1996). Mental health administrators need a variety of managerial, political, and leadership skills (Cohen, Shore, & Mazade, 1991). Administrators will often need assistance as well in learning new skills as they move between a variety of roles throughout their careers, especially the transition from clinician to supervisor (Austin, 1991). Austin (1991) called for national action to address the need for a framework for meeting the need for appropriate and adequate training, and specifically asked the National Institute of Mental Health to design and maintain a national academy to meet mental health administrative training needs. Unfortunately, this did not occur.

Nevertheless, this need for adequate training of mental health administrators was not completely ignored. State mental health directors received special attention in terms of their skills and training needs when a high turnover rate suggested problems for people in filling this type of position. Studies by Cohen et al. (1991) and Sluyter (1995) indicated a lack of continuing education for state mental health directors.

Cohen et al. (1991) provided an example of a successful continuing education program, the Harvard/NASMHPD Director Training Program, instituted in 1986 by the Harvard Department of Psychiatry. The feedback from the first 90 directors and senior managers who completed the program was positive. Since then, several state mental health directors, having participated in this program, went on to develop similar training opportunities in their other states (Cohen et al., 1991).

Yet Sluyter (1995) subsequently cited the continuing lack of training opportunities in management and leadership for state mental health directors. After a study of the Training Center for Excellence, a partnership between the Missouri Department of Mental Health and the Missouri Institute of Mental Health, Sluyter suggested a multi-level, multi-site, and multi-perspective training institute for mental health administrators, tailored to address the unique problems faced by administrators in the field. In this study, Sluyter (1995) found that the partnership aspect provided a wider range of possibilities for training staff and providers, including those in management and leadership positions. As with the Harvard program, one of the Training Center's goals was to provide a pool of staff, as well as trained and experienced managers and leaders, to fill key positions in mental health organizations. Again, the Training Center's management training program was "well-received," indicating a need for programs to fill a gap in training for mental health administrative professionals (Cohen et al., 1991; Sluyter, 1994).

In addition to continuing education initiatives, certification examinations have been another tool used to ensure that mental health administrators were equipped with the skills needed (Barton, 1991a). Historically, these educational and credentialing programs have been offered by professional associations, and often create an option for those who feel the graduate programs in public health or business administration would be too costly and distracting to their clinical practice. For example, the American Psychiatric Association (APA) offers a certification in administrative psychiatry. In addition, the Association of Behavioral Healthcare Management, in conjunction with the American College of Healthcare Executives, offers a certification for behavioral health care executives.

Blum, Feldman, and Heller (1991) stated that well-planned and strategically designed programs can radically improve the training of mental health administrators who have historically been given responsibility for managing extremely complex organizations that they were ill-prepared to lead. Increasingly, both traditional academic graduate degree programs and continuing education and training programs have offered programs through various distance-learning methodologies.

Distance Learning

The rapid developments in computers and information technology over the past decade have had an impact on health and mental health services, in particular psychology and psychiatry, which has moved in this context from local computer applications to network applications that take advantage of the Internet. Psychological and psychiatric Internet applications have included (1) information resources and self-help guides; (2) testing and assessment; (3) help in deciding to undergo therapy; (4) information about specific mental health services; (5) personal counseling and therapy through e-mail, real-time counseling (through chat, web telephony, and videoconferencing), synchronous and asynchronous support groups, discussion groups, and group counseling; and (6) psychological and social research (Barak, 1999). As information management becomes a greater part of the definition of psychiatric practice, it becomes critical that an understanding of informatics and literacy objectives should be incorporated into all training programs (Huang & Alessi, 1998). Such a curriculum should include basic tasks of patient care, communication, education, and practice management. Mental health administrators will need to deal with the use of these technologies and the allocation of resources to ongoing staff training and technology upgrades.

Mental health administrators should continue to develop analytical and technical skills to anticipate and meet the changing requirements of the managed behavioral health care industry. Lifelong learning, then, becomes a necessity. More than 15 years ago, researchers suggested that distance education programs be built on identified competencies, greater use of distance-learning facilities, convenience, and inclusion of self-assessment indices, and have relevance for practitioners (Dunn & Hamilton, 1985).

As the structure and knowledge of the mental health service systems change, investment in continued education to update strategic thinking and the analytical competency of mental health executives and managers is imperative (Clement & Wan, 1997). Lopez and Prosser (1999) recommended changes to graduate education in psychology to aid the preparation of psychologists for dealing with the emergence of organized systems for mental health services.

Another example has been the transition of psychotherapy to a more neurobiological orientation. Because the supervisory relationship has been the basic method by which trainees develop their identity as psychotherapists, a supervisor's development of knowledge and skills has been critical to his or her role as mentor (Riess & Fishel, 2000). To participate in treatment programs within today's managed behavioral health care delivery, Riess and Fishel (2000) suggested that training of psychologists include: (1) concrete recommendations for fostering a behavioral scientific approach, (2) the development of training communities that could assist in the expansion of the roles and functions of psychologists, and (3) the implementation of management training focusing on managing managed health care.

Academic and continuing professional educational programs need to be able to respond to the educational needs of mental health administrators using cutting-edge computer technology for distance learning. On a recent search of the Internet for "online continuing education for mental health professionals" on Northern Light, 29,417 results were retrieved. Sites ranged in complexity, including viewing a PowerPoint demonstration or journal article and taking an online posttest to receive a 1-hour continuing education credit, an audio-based continuing education online source for mental health professionals (audioPsych!), and online knowledge assessment tools offered by Tufts Managed Care Institute. The following outcomes for online training are common across distance-learning sites: (1) fundamental knowledge, (2) basic learning techniques, (3) clinical skills, and (4) methods for critical appraisal and the effective use of the research literature.

Academic courses offered as continuing education classes, online certificate programs, and online degree-granting programs also emphasize these skills, which often overlap information literacy, discussed earlier in this chapter. Entwined with these literacy skills have been technology skills, such as the ability to use e-mail, send and open attachments, and download plug-ins to read, view, or listen to media applications.

For urban mental health professionals, opportunities to gain information and computer literacy skills have been more plentiful. Telecommunications infrastructure development in urban areas has supported multimedia web-based learning, rapid transmission of text and data, and Internet access via cable. Classes also have been available at university, community college, and technical center settings, where opportunities have been more common for mental health professionals to interact with colleagues and to create informal support networks.

For rural mental health professionals, however, there are numerous problems and obstacles, including the lack of telecommunications infrastructure, professional isolation, and/or the lack of peer support from other mental health colleagues (Levin & Hanson, 2001). This potential "isolation" has also included a lack of access to continuing education, as well as the potential to lose "specialty skills" because of functioning as a health and/or mental health "generalist" (Levin & Hanson, 2001).

Thus, the use of technology, such as interactive television, audio and audio/video telephone conferencing, facsimile, and electronic mail, to teach can create challenging and exciting environments for professionals and staff in the delivery of mental health services. Allowing flexible participation can also enhance the impact of a continuing education program designed for paraprofessional mental health staff.

Increasing the number of professional staff members who experience only a portion of a training has implications for the instructional design and the evaluation of the training provided, as well as true enhancement of staff knowledge. Recommendations to improve accommodation of staff and enhance dissemination of training were offered, as well as appropriate evaluation techniques. Self-contained short units of instruction allowed those with minimal time to benefit from the training.

ISSUES FOR THE FUTURE

Although much of the leadership literature suggests that leadership cannot be taught, there remain differing opinions. Kellerman (1999) suggested that because the elements of leadership can be taught, mentoring would be one way that leadership skills and knowledge can be passed on to others. Walsh and Borkowski (1999) suggested that mentoring in mental health administration would play a critical role during the 21st century in creating opportunities for executive development and to increase the likelihood of promotion opportunities.

Despite Barton's (1991b) suggested curriculum for mental health administration, relatively few graduate degree programs currently exist in mental health administration, policy, and services delivery in the United States. Selected mental health professional societies, through certification exams and continuing education programs, have taken the lead in addressing needs of mental health professionals within managed behavioral health care systems. Continuing education and training opportunities appear further along than formal graduate degree programs regarding the preparation of mental health professionals to adapt to continuing changes in managed behavioral health care. Despite the assertion that no one discipline, professional association, or university can develop a comprehensive framework for the education and training of mental health administrators, perhaps a graduate curriculum model within a college of public health would be most appropriate. A comprehensive approach to the study of managed behavioral health care might naturally rest within a college of public health where epidemiology, biostatistics, environmental health, and community and family health issues, including behavioral health services, could be examined in a more comprehensive, integrated manner (Levin, Beauchamp, & Henry-Beauchamp, 1997).

REFERENCES

Abell, A. (2000). Skills for knowledge environments. *Information Management Journal, 34*(3), 33–41.

Austin, M. J. (1991). Educating the future mental health administrator. *Administration & Policy in Mental Health, 18*(4), 227–236.

Barak, A. (1999). Psychological applications on the Internet: A discipline on the threshold of a new millennium. *Applied & Preventive Psychology, 8*(4), 231–245.

Barton, G. (1991a). Education and certification of mental health administrators: The role of professional associations. *Administration & Policy in Mental Health, 18*(4), 279–283.

Barton, W. E. (1991b). Toward a model curriculum in mental health administration. *Administration & Policy in Mental Health, 18*(4), 237–246.

Beckham, J. D. (1995). The death of management. *Healthcare Forum Journal, 38*(4), 14–21.

Bennis, W. (1993). *An invented life: Reflections on leadership and change.* Reading, MA: Addison-Wesley.

Bennis, W., & Nanus, B. (1985). *Leaders: The strategies for taking charge.* New York: Harper & Row.

Blum, S., Feldman, S., & Heller, K. (1991). Responsibilities and training needs of mental health administrators. *Administration & Policy in Mental Health, 18*(4), 257–270.

Borus, J. (1992). Training. In J. Talbott, R. Hales, & S. Keill (Eds.), *Textbook of administrative psychiatry* (pp. 179–206). Washington, DC: American Psychiatric Press.

Borus, J., & Sledge, W. H. (1996). Psychiatric education. In R. E. Hales & S. C. Yudofsky (Eds.), *The American Psychiatric Press synopsis of psychiatry* (pp. 1357–1370). Washington, DC: American Psychiatric Press.

Brownson, K. (1998). Literacy: A challenge for the health care supervisor. *Health Care Supervisor, 17*(2), 45–54.

Bruce, C. (1997). *Seven faces of information literacy.* Adelaide, South Australia: AUSLIB Press.

Bruce, C. (2000). Information literacy research: Dimensions of the emerging collective consciousness. *Australian Academic & Research Libraries, 31*(2), 91–109.

Castro, G. A., Bouldin, P. A., Farver, D. W., Maugans, L. A., Sanders, L. C., & Booker, J. (1999). The InterCon network: A program for education partnerships at the University of Texas–Houston Health Science Center. *Academic Medicine, 74*(4), 363–365.

Catts, R. M., & Appleton, M. (1999). Assessing models of information literacy. In J. A. Chambers (Ed.), *Selected papers from the 10th International Conference on College Teaching and Learning* (pp. 23–32). Jacksonville, FL: Florida Community College at Jacksonville.

Cheuk, B. (1998). An experienced based information literacy model in the workplace: Case studies from Singapore. In D. Booker (Ed.), *Information literacy: The professional issue* (pp. 74–82). Proceedings of the 3rd Australian National Information Literacy Conference, Canberra, 1997. Adelaide: University of South Australia Library.

Clement, D. G., & Wan, T. T. (1997). Mastering health care executive education: Creating transformational competence. *Journal of Health Administration Education, 15*(4), 265–274.

Cohen, M., Shore, M., & Mazade, N. (1991). Development of a management training program for state mental health program directors. *Administration & Policy in Mental Health, 18*(4), 247–256.

Coye, M. J. (1994). *Our own worst enemy: Obstacles to improving the health of the public.* Available at http://www.milbank.org/mrlead.html, accessed 1/5/01.

Cozza, S., & Hales, R. (1992). Leadership. In J. Talbott, R. Hales, & S. Keill (Eds.), *Textbook of administrative psychiatry* (pp. 31–58). Washington, DC: American Psychiatric Press.

Dana, R. (1998). Problems with managed mental health care for multicultural populations. *Psychological Reports, 83,* 283–294.

Davidhizar, R. E., & Brownson, K. (1999). Literacy, cultural diversity, and client education. *Health Care Manager, 18*(10), 39–47.

Depree, M. (1989). *Leadership is an art.* New York: Doubleday.

Drotar, D. (1998). Training students for careers in medical settings: A graduate program in pediatric psychology. *Professional Psychology: Research and Practice, 29*(4), 402–404.

DuBrin, A. J. (2001). *Leadership: Research findings, practice, and skills.* Boston: Houghton Mifflin.

Dunn, W. R., & Hamilton, D. D. (1985). Competence-based education and distance learning: A tandem for professional continuing education? *Studies in Higher Education, 10*(3), 277–287.

England, M. J. (1997). Training the existing workforce. Discussion. *Administration & Policy in Mental Health, 25*(1), 23–26.

Faulkner, L., Scully, J., & Shore, J. (1998). A strategic approach to the psychiatric workforce dilemma. *Psychiatric Services, 49*(4), 493–497.

Gabbard, G. (1992). The big chill: The transition from residency to managed care nightmare. *Academic Psychiatry, 16*(3), 119–126.

Gabel, S. (1998). Leadership in the managed care era: Challenges, conflict, ambivalence. *Administration & Policy in Mental Health, 26*(1), 3–19.

Greenblatt, M. (1991). Commentary on education and training for mental health administration. *Administration & Policy in Mental Health, 18*(4), 299–309.

Greenblatt, M. (1992). *Anatomy of psychiatric administration: The organization of health and disease.* New York: Plenum Press.

Greenwood, E. D., Reid, J. H., Novick, R. G., & Stubblefield, R. L. (1956). Responsibility for leadership in mental health. *American Journal of Orthopsychiatry, 26,* 1–34.

Grusky, O., Thompson, W., & Tillipman, H. (1991). Clinical vs. administrative background for mental health administrators. *Administration & Policy in Mental Health, 18*(4), 271–278.

Hoge, M. (1997). Training the existing workforce. *Administration & Policy in Mental Health, 25*(1), 17–22.

Hollander, S. M., & Martin, E. R. (1999). Public health professionals in the Midwest: a profile of connectivity and information technology skills. *Bulletin of the Medical Library Association, 87*(3), 329–36.

Huang, M. P., & Alessi, N. E. (1998). An informatics curriculum for psychiatry. *Academic Psychiatry, 22*(2), 77–91.

Kellerman, B. (1999). *Reinventing leadership: Making the connection between politics and business.* Albany, NY: State University of New York Press.

Kerfoot, K. (2000). TIQ (Technical IQ)—A survival skill for the new millennium. *Nursing Economics, 18*(1), 29–31.

Klaus, H. (2000). Understanding scholarly and professional communication: Thesauri and database searching. In C. Bruce, C. P. Candy, & H. Klaus (Eds.), *Information literacy around the world: Advances in programs and research* (pp. 209–222). Wagga Wagga, New South Wales: Centre for Information Studies, Charles Stuart University.

Lazarus, A. (1996). Can psychiatrists become efficient managers? In A. Lazarus (Ed.), *Controversies in managed mental health care* (pp. 319–336). Washington, DC: American Psychiatric Press.

Levin, B. L., Beauchamp, B. T., & Henry-Beauchamp, L. A. (1997). Education and training of children's mental health professionals: The existing and potential role of schools of public health. *Journal of Child and Family Studies, 6*(1), 131–136.

Levin, B. L., & Hanson, A. (2001). Mental health services. In S. Loue & B. E. Quill (Eds.), *Handbook of rural health* (pp. 241–255). New York: Plenum Press.

Levinson, H. (1968). *The exceptional executive: A psychological conception.* Cambridge, MA: Harvard University Press.

Lipton, A. A., & Loutsch, E. (1985). A reconsideration of power in psychiatric administration. *Hospital & Community Psychiatry, 36*(5), 497–503.

Lopez, S. J., & Prosser, E. (1999). Preparing psychologists: More focus on training psychologists for a future in evolving health-care delivery systems. *Journal of Clinical Psychology in Medical Settings, 6*(3), 295–301.

Manley, F. W., & DeLeon, P. H. (1997). Expanding psychology's vision—Bridges for the 21st century. *Professional Psychology: Research & Practice, 2,* 99–100.

Mayberg, S. W. (1997). Insight, assessment, and clinical skills: Do they have a role in the bureaucracy? *Professional Psychology: Research & Practice, 28*(4), 323–325.

Mutch, A. (1996). No such thing as information resource management. *Management Decision, 34*(7), 58–63.

Nissani, M. (1997). Ten cheers for interdisciplinarity: The case for interdisciplinary knowledge and research. *Social Science Journal, 34*(2), 201–216.

Northouse, P. G. (1997). *Leadership: Theory and practice.* Thousand Oaks, CA: Sage.

Riba, M., & Carli, T. (1996). Will academic psychiatry survive managed care? In A. Lazarus (Ed.), *Controversies in managed mental health care* (pp. 81–98). Washington, DC: American Psychiatric Press.

Riess, H., & Fishel, A. K. (2000). The necessity of continuing education for psychotherapy supervisors. *Academic Psychiatry, 24*(3), 147–155.

Rodenhauser, P., & Bashook, P. (1991). On education in administrative psychiatry. *Administration & Policy in Mental Health, 18*(4), 285–298.

Roper, W. L. (1994). *Why the problem of leadership in public health?* Available at http://www.milbank.org/mrlead.html, accessed 1/5/01.

Ross, D. (1997). Training residents in the era of managed care. In R. Schreter, S. Sharfstein, & C. Schreter (Eds.), *Managing care not dollars: The continuum of mental health care* (pp. 299–318). Washington, DC: American Psychiatric Press.

Roth, L. (1999). Educating the cut-and-paste generation. *Library Journal, 124*(18), 42–44.

Schreter, R. K. (1997). Coping with the crisis in psychiatric training. *Psychiatry: Interpersonal & biological processes, 60*(1), 51–59.

Schreter, R., & Schreter, C. (1996). Can psychiatrists be retrained for the future? In A. Lazarus (Ed.), *Controversies in managed mental health care* (pp. 255–268). Washington, DC: American Psychiatric Press.

Secretary's Commission on Achieving Necessary Skills (SCANS). (1992). *What work requires of schools: A SCANS report for America 2000.* Washington, DC: U.S. Department of Labor.

Shore, M. R. (1997). Training the existing workforce. *Administration & Policy in Mental Health, 25*(1), 11–16.

Sluyter, G. (1994). Training of mental health administrators: A state agency and university partnership. *Administration & Policy in Mental Health, 22*(2), 175–179.

Sluyter, G. (1995). Mental health leadership training: A survey of state directors. *Journal of Mental Health Administration, 22*(2), 201–204.

Sullivan, F. J. (1997). Psychologist by training, bureaucrat by practice. *Professional Psychology: Research & Practice, 28*(4), 329–334.

Talbott, J. A. (1987). Management, administration, leadership. What's in a name? *Psychiatric Quarterly, 58*(4), 229–242.

U.S. Department of Health and Human Services. (1999). *Mental health: A report of the Surgeon General.* Rockville, MD: Substance Abuse and Mental Health Services Administration, Center for Mental Health Services, National Institute of Mental Health.

Van Dyke, C., & Schlesinger, H. (1997). Training the trainers. *Administration & Policy in Mental Health, 25*(1), 47–59.

Verhey, M. P. (1999). Information literacy in an undergraduate nursing curriculum: Development, implementation, and evaluation. *Journal of Nursing Education, 38*(6), 252–259.

Walsh, A. M., & Borkowski, S. C. (1999). Mentoring in health administration: The critical link in executive development. *Journal of Healthcare Management, 44*(4), 269–280.

Warwick, T. (1997). Training the trainees: The new imperatives. *Administration & Policy in Mental Health, 25*(1), 27–46.

Weiss, B., Hart, G., & Pust, R. (1991). The relationship between literacy and health. *Journal of Health Care for the Poor and Underserved, 1,* 351–363.

Wurman, R. S. (1989). *Information anxiety: What to do when the information doesn't tell you what you need to know.* New York: Bantam.

Zimmerman, C., Bisanz, G. L., & Bisanz, J. (1998). Everyday scientific literacy: Do students use information about the social context and methods of research to evaluate new briefs about science? *Alberta Journal of Educational Research, 44*(2), 188–207.

Chapter Three

Mental Health Services Delivery

Bruce Lubotsky Levin
Ardis Hanson

Health and mental health care in the United States have come under increasing scrutiny during the last half of the 20th century from a vast array of stakeholders, including patients, providers, employers, administrators, and researchers, as well as policymakers in state and federal government. Proposals for health care (including managed health care) reform have been prompted, in part, by the need to control the rising costs of health and mental health care and to address the obstacles and inequities in accessing health and mental health services. Although the U.S. Congress did not pass major comprehensive health care reform legislation in the final decade of the 20th century, significant health care initiatives (e.g., in managed care and in association with entitlement programs) were proposed and implemented by various individual states.

At the beginning of the 21st century, mental disorders remain significant public health problems. According to the U.S. Surgeon General (U.S. Department of Health and Human Services, 1999), mental disorders comprise 4 of the 10 leading causes of disability for individuals who are 5 years old and older, with depression the leading cause of disability, and suicide one of the leading preventable causes of death. In the United States, mental disorders are also significant contributors to the burden of disease, ranking second only to cardiovascular diseases.

Meanwhile, the organization, financing, and provision of mental health and substance-abuse services in the United States represent a complex and confusing assortment of uncoordinated public and private delivery systems, that is, the "de facto" mental health service delivery system (Regier, Goldberg, & Taube, 1978). In 1999, the "de facto" mental health service delivery system remained fragmented, and consisted of (a) the specialty behavioral (mental health, alcohol, and drug abuse) health sector (including mental health practitioners and public and private mental health facilities), (b) the primary medical care sector (including primary medical care practitioners and health care facilities), (c) the human services sector (including social services, school-based counseling services, rehabilitation services, criminal justice services, and the clergy), and (d) the voluntary support network sector (including self-help groups) (U.S. Department of Health and Human Services, 1999).

Thus, the delivery and financing of mental health services remained generally separated rather than integrated with general (somatic) health services. This lack of integration between health and mental health services contributed to the development of a number of dubious public health policies, including insurance providers' unequal coverage of mental health services vis-à-vis somatic health services (Levin, Hanson, Coe, & Kuppin, 2000).

In addition, the historical reliance on the public sector for long-term mental health care and on the private sector for acute mental health care has contributed to the limited overall continuity of care for mental health services (Elpers & Levin, 1996). Mental health services increasingly have been financed through multiple (public and private) payors as well as numerous (public and private) providers of mental health care (Frank & McGuire, 1996). In 1997, total national expenditures were $73.4 billion for mental disorders and $11.9 billion for the treatment of substance abuse, representing 7.8% of total health care expenditures in the United States (Coffey et al., 2000). These costs have been conservative, because of the 20% of Americans who have a diagnosable mental disorder, only about 15% have utilized mental health services in any of the four "de facto" sectors during any given year.

Given the variety of gatekeeping and referral mechanisms available for organizing, financing, and delivering mental health care in this managed care environment, how do mental health administrators keep current with important trends in health and mental health services delivery? It remains very difficult to obtain this information through traditional graduate school education, because there is a dearth of graduate degree programs in mental health/behavioral health services administration. Continuing education programs appear to be one possible alternative; however, these programs need to emphasize the impact of the entire external health care environment upon behavioral health services, particularly in the continuing metamorphosis of managed care and managed behavioral health care.

To help conceptualize the impact of the total external health care environment upon the organization of mental health delivery systems nationally, Katzper and Manderscheid (1984) applied systems analysis to mental health service delivery systems (see Fig. 3.1). Their conceptualization reemphasized that mental health delivery systems are comprised of interrelated and independent parts that potentially could form a complex whole (but usually don't), with each individual component viewed as a subsystem with its own set of interrelated and interdependent parts. Mental health systems may be open, with internal and external interactions that affect the entire delivery system. On the other hand, closed or self-contained mental health systems often attempt to operate independently from their external environments. Nevertheless, a change in external environmental factors (e.g., federal or state legislation) will affect mental health service delivery components (e.g., mental health facilities, mental health practitioners, training for mental health professionals, and/or the financing of mental health services).

This chapter examines the organization and delivery of mental health services in the United States from a public health perspective. It emphasizes the need for mental health administrators to understand the external health care environment and the resulting impact changes in that environment have upon the functioning of their mental health agency. Because of the complex and continuous changes taking place in the field of mental health administration and behavioral health services, the management of mental health organizations should include the study of health policy and health services delivery issues in the external as well as internal organizational environment.

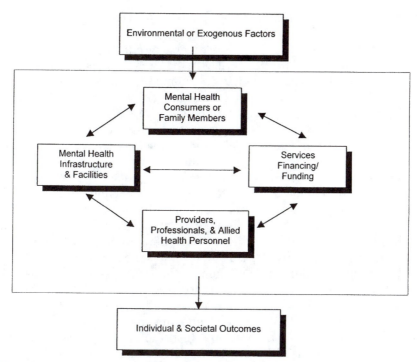

FIGURE 3.1. Systems framework of mental health delivery systems. Adapted from Katzper and Manderscheid (1984), with permission.

CHARACTERISTICS OF MENTAL HEALTH DELIVERY SYSTEMS

During the past 40 years, there have been major shifts in the focus of mental health care. First, there was a gradual shift from the provision of long-term mental health care in state psychiatric hospitals to short-term care in various community settings (including community mental health centers and a variety of health and mental health ambulatory care settings). Second, there was a shift from direct federal funding of mental health services to increased state funding for mental health services. Third, there was a significant change in the patterns of payment for mental health services, from public versus private financing to a more blended array of mixed financing arrangements (e.g., managed behavioral health service contracts with state Medicaid programs). Fourth, there was growing recognition that accountability systems that assess the benefits and impact of mental health services should include a variety of mental health stakeholders, including patients and their families.

Service Delivery Components

For many individuals with mental disorders, there has been a significant absence of a single gatekeeper for mental health services. This is due, in part, to the significant variety of services and treatment regimens available for these individuals. In addition, it is important to acknowledge that a majority of people with a diagnosable mental disorder choose not to seek treatment. For those who do seek treatment, the majority access services within the general health care sector, vis-à-vis the specialty mental health care delivery sector.

As mentioned earlier, an increasingly diverse number of systems, facilities, and practitioners provide mental health services in the United States. For example, mental health services have been available within general hospital emergency rooms, psychiatric units in general hospitals, long-term care facilities, the criminal justice system, the Veterans Administration (VA) medical care system, educational (school) systems, places of employment (via employee assistance programs), managed health care settings, and places of worship. Within the specialty mental health care sector, mental health services have been available through numerous delivery systems and settings, including (but not limited to) state/county psychiatric hospitals, private psychiatric hospitals, community mental health centers, ambulatory mental health facilities, and an assortment of mental health practitioners.

Historically, state governments funded mental health services through state/county psychiatric hospitals. The federal government funded mental health services initially (rather indirectly through consultation to states) through the 1946 legislation[1] for the 10 public health regions. Then, in the 1960s, community mental health centers (CMHCs) provided mental health services through CMHC catchment areas. Densely populated locales such as New York City had many CMHCs, whereas selected states (e.g., North Dakota, New Hampshire) had only a few CMHCs in the entire state. During this time, the National Institute of Mental Health (NIMH) also awarded grants for mental health services and research in selected regions in the United States. Then, in the early 1980s, federal block grants left mental health funding decisions in the hands of the individual states. These multiple state legislative initiatives established separate mental health delivery systems, with virtually no integration of mental health services with other existing mental health delivery systems or other general health care delivery systems. This has culminated in many disjointed mental health delivery systems in both for-profit and nonprofit sectors throughout the country.

SERVICE DELIVERY SYSTEM DESCRIPTORS

When describing, examining, or analyzing mental health service delivery systems, it is often helpful to define the delivery system by a number of *system descriptors,* including (1) disease *prevalence* of mental disorders, (2) *availability* of mental health organizations and service settings, (3) *capacity* and *volume* of mental health services, (4) mental health *staffing,* (5) *funding* of mental health services, and (6) *outcomes/quality* of mental health services.

Prevalence

The most comprehensive mental health epidemiologic study conducted in the United States was the Epidemiologic Catchment Area (ECA) Study (Robins & Regier, 1991).

---

1. Hill–Burton Act: Public Law 79-725 (the Hospital Survey and Construction Act of 1946). This program provided federal support for the construction and modernization of hospitals and other health facilities.

Two elements of the study made it unique: (1) The ECA study was a very large initiative, with more than 20,000 respondents over five catchment areas (New Haven, Durham, Baltimore, Los Angeles, and St. Louis); and (2) the study examined the prevalence and incidence of mental disorders in the community as well as in institutional settings.

The major objective of the ECA study was to obtain prevalence rates of specific mental disorders rather than overall prevalence rates of mental disorders. The results showed that 20% of the people interviewed had an active mental disorder during a given year, with anxiety disorders (e.g., phobias, panic disorder, and post-traumatic stress disorder, among others) found to be the most prevalent mental disorders in adults. The lifetime prevalence was 32% for a mental illness and/or substance-abuse disorder. In addition, the ECA estimated the prevalence rate for severe mental illness at 2.8% of the population.

Nevertheless, less than 15% of the adult population received any treatment for their behavioral disorder. Of the individuals who received mental health treatment, only 6% were treated by specialty behavioral health sector providers, 6% were treated by primary medical care sector providers, 5% sought treatment in the human services sector, and 3% sought treatment in the voluntary support network sector (Kessler, Berglund et al., 1996; Regier et al., 1993).

Approximately one in five children and adolescents (ages 9 to 17 years) was found to have a diagnosable mental disorder during any given year, with 11% of children experiencing significant functional impairment, and 5% of children experiencing extreme functional impairment. In addition, at any given time, between 10 and 15% of children and adolescents have symptoms of depression.

Depression is very prevalent among older Americans, affecting 8 to 20% of older adults in the community and affecting approximately one-third of older adults who utilize primary health care settings. Depression in older adults often leads to impairments in physical, social, and mental functioning.

Another important study on serious mental illness and co-occurring disorders was the National Comorbidity Survey (NCS) (Kessler et al., 1994). The NCS was designed to: (1) improve on the ECA efforts by incorporating revised nomenclature from the *Diagnostic and Statistical Manual of Mental Disorders (DSM)*, third edition (American Psychiatric Association, 1987); (2) more extensively examine risk factors that affected particular mental disorders; and (3) determine the comorbidity of psychiatric disorders in the United States (Blazer, Kessler, McGonagle, & Swartz, 1994). Individuals with comorbid disorders included people diagnosed with more than one physical, mental, or substance disorder. Over 8,000 persons between the ages of 15 and 54 who lived in the continental United States were interviewed between 1990 and 1992.

Results from the NCS indicated a higher lifetime prevalence for mental disorders than the ECA found, particularly for depression, alcohol dependence, and phobia. The NCS reported a prevalence of 3.2% compared with the ECA report of 2.8% for individuals with severe mental illness. The lifetime prevalence was 48% for any disorder (mental illness or substance abuse), and 29% of the respondents reported at least one mental disorder during the previous 12-month period. Approximately 40% of those who reported at least one mental disorder during their lifetime sought treatment in the specialty behavioral health sector.

The National Institute of Mental Health (NIMH) estimated that 1.8 million people have severe mental illness and a co-occurring substance abuse disorder. More than

15% of 166 million Americans (25.6 million people) over the age of 18 years met the criteria for at least one alcohol, drug, or mental disorder (Regier, 1988). Persons who suffered from a mental illness were more likely to abuse drugs and alcohol. The NCS and follow-up reports also found that 83.5% of those with lifetime comorbidity said that their first mental disorder preceded their first addictive disorder, and co-occurring disorders tended to be more chronic than mental disorders.

Kessler, Nelson et al. (1996) used data from the NCS to study the prevalence of co-occurring addictive and mental disorders. They found that the total number of persons with co-occurring disorders (anyone with both a substance-abuse disorder and any mental disorder as described in the *DSM* classification system) was between 7 million and 9.9 million, depending on the definition of alcohol abuse.

Space does not permit a more extensive review of the results of psychiatric epidemiologic studies. The reader is referred to *Mental Health: A Report of the Surgeon General* (U.S. Department of Health and Human Services, 1999) and to Levin and Petrila (1996) for further information about the epidemiology of mental disorders in selected at-risk populations.

Availability

According to the 1998 biennial report of *Mental Health*, the number of mental health organizations has steadily grown over the past thirty-plus years, from 3,005 in 1970 to 3,727 in 1980, and from 5,284 in 1990 to 5,392 in 1994 (Witkin et al., 1998). The number of organizations providing inpatient and residential treatment care settings decreased, whereas the number of outpatient/partial care mental health care settings increased from 1990 to 1994. Unfortunately, 1994 was the most recent year for which data were available.

Capacity/Volume

The number of hospital and residential treatment additions has been one measure of the utilization of mental health services. Although the variety of mental health organizations increased in recent years, the number of beds in mental hospitals and residential facilities has decreased by nearly half, from 524,878 in 1970 to 261,903 in 1998 (Manderscheid et al., 2001). Surveys of the overall number of hospital beds per 100,000 population from 1969 through 1998 indicate a proportionate decrease in free-standing facility mental health beds overall, and an increase in beds in psychiatric units of general hospitals and residential facilities for children. The relative number of patient care episodes in 24-hour-care facilities decreased markedly between 1955 and 1994 compared with care episodes in all settings (e.g., inpatient, outpatient, and emergency clinics). In 1955 the inpatient proportion was 77%; in 1994 it was 24% (Manderscheid et al., 2001).

Trends also indicate that hospital use in the primary medical care sector is significantly higher for persons with coexisting physical and mental health conditions than for those with no mental disorders. For a wide range of medical conditions, the predicted number of hospital admissions and the length of a hospital stay increase substantially when the physical illness is accompanied by a mental disorder (Savoca,

1999). Obviously, these patterns and trends vary throughout the United States, as demographics, financial resources, specific populations at risk, mental health needs and priorities, history, and politics of each community within each state all play important roles in the composition and evolution of state and county mental health delivery systems.

Staffing

There has been a corresponding increase in the staffing (as measured in the number of full-time equivalent or FTE staff) of mental health organizations, from 375,984 in 1972 to 577,669 in 1994 (Witkin et al., 1998). With the exception of psychologists and nurses, all professional staff disciplines comprised a smaller proportion of total mental health staff in 1994 compared to 1990. Other allied mental health workers also decreased as inpatient units (particularly in state and county mental hospitals) consolidated or closed.

Funding/Cost of Care

One way to examine the financing of mental health services has been through total expenditures by mental health organizations and revenues of mental health organizations by funding source. Total expenditures (in current dollars) by mental health organizations increased from $28.4 billion in 1990 to $33.1 billion in 1994. Expenditures per capita also increased, from $116.39 in 1990 to $127.86 in 1994. However, total expenditures in constant dollars (adjusted by the medical care component of the consumer price index) experienced a 10% decrease, from $5.6 billion in 1990 to $5 billion in 1994. State and county psychiatric hospitals, private psychiatric hospitals, and VA medical centers, all part of a group with decreasing numbers of patient days and shorter lengths of stay, comprised a smaller proportion of total mental health expenditures in 1994 compared to 1990 (see Table 3.1).

Where do mental health organizations obtain most of their revenues? Local, state, and federal governments, client fees, and other funding generated revenues for mental health organizations totaling in excess of $36 billion in 1994, up from almost $28 billion in 1990. Unexpectedly, client fees through 1994 did not rise dramatically, and there were similar declines in sources of revenue derived from client fees for private psychiatric hospitals and for non-federal general hospitals (see Table 3.2).

Estimates of national expenditures for mental health and substance abuse treatment are difficult to compare with the estimates of national health expenditures

TABLE 3.1. Percent Distribution of Mental Health Expenditures, Various Years

Type of organization	1969	1979	1990	1994
State/county hospitals	55%	43%	27%	24%
VA medical centers	14%	10%	10%	4%
Private hospitals	7%	9%	22%	20%

Note. Adapted from U.S. Department of Health and Human Services (1999), with permission.

TABLE 3.2. Distribution of Revenue Sources for MH Organizations

Sources	1990	1992	1994
State government	36%	34%	30%
Client fees	22%	20%	18%
Federal government	29%	36%	39%
Local government	8%	7%	8%
Other	5%	3%	5%

Note. Adapted from U.S. Department of Health and Human Services (1999), with permission.

produced annually by the Health Care Financing Administration (HCFA/CMS). HCFA/CMS estimates show health expenditures by major payment source and type of service. To be most useful, estimates of mental health and substance-abuse spending should allow direct comparisons with these figures. Previous mental health and substance-abuse estimates used categories and/or methods that prevented direct comparisons with HCFA/CMS figures. McKusick et al. (1998) presented estimates of national mental health and substance-abuse expenditures for 1996 by payment source and type of service, derived from the most recently available data sources. The authors also estimated trends from 1986 using the same categories, data sources, and methodologies adjusted to allow for direct comparisons with the figures for national health care spending produced by HCFA/CMS.

Outcomes/Quality

The changing locus of care for mental health services is shown in a decline in state/ county psychiatric beds and in the number of hospital and residential patient care episodes in state/county psychiatric hospitals. Many questions emerge. How has managed care influenced the trends presented so far? Is there a continued need for state/county psychiatric hospitals? What is a "good" and "reasonable" balance among hospital, residential, and ambulatory mental health services? Can we improve the gatekeeping and referral into the specialty behavioral health services sector? Can (or should) mental health services be more integrated into primary medical care? And finally, how will all of these issues affect the cost and effectiveness of mental health care?

To answer these and other questions, there have been recent attempts to develop outcomes management initiatives throughout the United States. Mental health performance indicators have been developed across selected domains (including service access, quality/appropriateness, outcome, structure/plan management, and prevention/early intervention) in an attempt to measure performance in public mental health systems. National organizations have developed report cards to measure outcomes for behavioral health care organizations and their respective mental health services "products" (Gemignani, 2000; Hibbard, Harris-Kojetin, Mullin, Lubalin, & Garfinkel, 2000).

Patient-oriented report cards and profiling systems are also being developed to define outcome domains and create outcome indicators in such areas as self-help, well-being and personhood, empowerment, recovery, iatrogenic effects and negative outcomes, and measures of satisfaction and dissatisfaction (Robinson & Brodie, 1997; Scanlon, Chernew, & Lave, 1997). Patients do more than choose their health plans. They make choices about health behavior, when to seek information for a specific health problem, when and whether to seek care and with which provider, how involved they will be in treatment decisions, and finally whether to comply with treatment recommendations. The interaction of these domains is far more complex than can be currently captured in assessing the choice of a health plan, yet it would be hard to argue that some or all of these domains are irrelevant to that choice (Clancy, 1999).

Pelletier and Beaudin (1999) presented a useful discussion on examples of performance standards and principles for the provision of mental health services in managed care organizations. Taylor (1999) recognized the potential for assessing patients' preferences and experiences along a continuum of participation in health and health care as a stimulus and roadmap for improvements in health care policy and services delivery.

One example, the National Outcomes Management Project, examined the use of benchmarking in managed ambulatory behavioral health care and its application in a model collaborative outcome management project at more than 16 sites in nine states in the United States (Dewan, Daniels, Zieman, & Kraner, 2000). Project data indicated that benchmarking was a vital and cost-effective means for demonstrating and improving the value of behavioral health care. As public and private partnerships develop between community mental health centers and private entities, standardizing benchmarks will become an increasingly important task.

The current conglomerate of mental health providers, agencies, services, institutions, and managed care/insurance entities (operating independently of one another) will continue to create challenges for the organization, financing, and delivery of mental health services in the 21st century. How can we improve the integration of service systems among mental health systems and between health and mental health systems? Is the answer to hold providers accountable for costs (risk sharing) in an effort to increase the efficiency of mental health care? Can we improve clinical decision making through case management, provider profiles, risk sharing, and treatment guidelines?

MANAGED CARE

America's health and mental health care delivery systems continue to be in a tumultuous state, with ever-increasing "industry" growth and diversification as well as consolidation and service integration (through the development of integrated delivery systems). The continual flux in supply and demand in recent years has encouraged the development of a wide variety of managed health care plans, which finance and deliver health and mental health services to specific (usually workplace-specific) populations.

The demand for lower prices and for monitoring of treatment outcome has continued to accelerate the growth of managed care organizations (MCOs) and managed behavioral health organizations (MBHOs). In the 1990s, managed care emerged as the dominant mode of health care delivery in the United States. For example, in 1995, three specific managed care models (preferred provider organizations or PPOs, point-of-service or POS health plans, and health maintenance organizations or HMOs) accounted for nearly three-quarters of the insured population in the United States. Furthermore, in 1999, nearly three-quarters (177 million people) of an estimated 244 million Americans with health insurance were enrolled in some type of MBHO. This represents more than a 9% increase over 1998 enrollment in MBHOs (Findlay, 1999).

In recent years, state Medicaid plans and the federal Medicare program have experienced rapid growth of individuals enrolled in MCOs. Increasingly, these programs have utilized the creation of purchasing alliances between public agencies and private MCOs as well as private MBHOs.

Definitions

We have heard the terms *managed care, managed care industry,* and *managed care environment* for many years. However, just what do they mean? That is a really good question, because these are among terms (another example would be the term *mental health*) that have been used in a variety of ways with various meanings. The Institute of Medicine (1997) has defined managed care as "Arrangements for health [and mental health] care delivery and financing that are designed to provide appropriate, effective, and efficient health care through organized relationships with providers. [This] includes formal programs for ongoing quality assurance and utilization review, financial incentives for covered members to use the plan's providers, and financial incentives for providers to contain costs" (pp. 257–258).

Another definition (Levin, 1992) described managed care as an evolving array of health care review and service coordination mechanisms that ultimately attempts to control (i.e., reduce) health and mental health service utilization and costs, improve efficiency and coordination, increase access to preventive services, and improve the quality of care. The utilization management mechanisms used to control service utilization have included prior authorization review for hospitalization and ambulatory treatment, concurrent utilization review encompassing discharge planning and aftercare management, retrospective utilization review, case management, provider profiling, on-site audits, and second-opinion programs. Mechanisms used for cost control typically have included *capitation financing, prospective payment, negotiated fee-for-service* payments, various *cost-sharing* strategies, and the use of *alternative settings and service delivery providers*. The predominant managed care systems over the last 40 years have included HMOs, preferred provider organizations (PPOs), various hybrid models (e.g., point-of-service plans or POS), and specialized health care organizations, including managed behavioral health care carve-out organizations.

Traditionally, patients, providers, and third-party payers (i.e., insurance companies) have been viewed as being the principal interacting parties involved in the various health and mental health care delivery systems in America. Managed care has basically altered the delivery of health and mental health services through the introduction of various mechanisms (described earlier) to control the service utilization and costs through reducing unnecessary or inappropriate treatment. One particular strategy used by MCOs to achieve utilization and cost savings has been through the development of a network of selected health and mental health care providers, including health care facilities (e.g., hospitals and ambulatory care centers), residential programs, and health care practitioners. In addition, the contractual relationship between the third-party payer (i.e., purchaser of health services) and the MCO as well as between the MCO and its health and mental health practitioners has been crucial in terms of risk sharing and other utilization and cost controls for the MCO.

At this point, let us look at the cycles of growth for managed care organizations, their historical development, and several implications for mental health policy and services delivery in America. In addition, what are some of the critical issues in the field of managed mental health services research?

Evolution

Managed care originated in the 1920s in California with the development of a prepaid group practice called the Kaiser Permanente Medical Care Program. Eventually, the Kaiser program would be divided into three separate organizational components: the Permanente Medical Care Group (groups of physicians from a specified geographical region); the Kaiser Foundation Health Plan (the organizational entity); and the Kaiser Hospitals, Clinics, and Ambulatory Care Centers (the actual health care facilities).

The first major growth cycle for managed care organizations occurred between the early 20th century and the late 1960s with the growth in the number of prepaid group practice plans across the United States. Some of the major health plans that emerged during this period of time included Group Health Cooperative of Puget Sound (Seattle, WA), Health Insurance Plan of Greater New York, and Group Health Association (Washington, DC).

The second major growth cycle for managed care organizations occurred in the early 1970s with the growth of individual or independent practice associations (IPAs). IPAs were often more flexible than group or staff HMOs from the consumer perspective, because patients had considerably more choice in selecting their physicians in an IPA-model HMO. The 1970s also marked the emergence of the term *HMO*, "coined" by Paul Ellwood during the preparation (and subsequent passage) of federal HMO legislation passed in 1973.

The rise in popularity of for-profit HMOs occurred in the 1980s during the third major growth cycle of managed health care. During this growth cycle, the term *managed care* became the all-encompassing term that included all types and organizational models of HMOs, POS plans, and PPOs. It was during this initial period that organizations attempted to manage insurance benefits for health and mental health care through specialty utilization review organizations.

Also during this period of time, Levin and colleagues (Levin, Glasser, & Roberts, 1984; Levin, Glasser, & Jaffee, 1988; Levin, Hanson, Coe, & Kuppin, 1992) reported the results from three national surveys of mental health services within HMOs. Most notably, there was near-universal coverage of mental health services within HMOs nationally, with a noted convergence toward a standard mental health benefits structure of 30 days of hospital coverage and 20 ambulatory visits per member per year. However, in comparison to physical health services, significant heterogeneity in mental health benefit structures was found, including a variety of benefit limitations for HMO mental health services (including limitations through copayments, deductibles, specific coverage exclusions, annual lifetime limitations, mandatory waiting periods, and restricted access to specialty mental health providers as well as to specialty mental health facilities) that further restricted mental health insurance coverage within HMOs nationally vis-à-vis somatic health services. Furthermore, the specific mental health benefits offered by individual HMOs did not always represent the actual mental health services that were eventually provided to health plan members. Although near-universal coverage was found for mental health services within HMOs across the United States, substance-abuse benefits (other than detoxification services) were provided by about two-thirds of HMOs nationally.

A fourth generation of MCOs evolved in the 1990s, with the continued growth of for-profit organizations, the divestment of HMO-owned hospitals, mergers and general consolidation in the managed care industry, and the growth and development of more integrated delivery systems. There was an emphasis in outcomes management and the development of specialty service delivery networks for selected health services, including the growth of managed behavioral health organizations (MBHOs) as well as the continuation of the movement to "carve out" the organization, financing, and delivery of mental health and substance-abuse services from other somatic health services.

Managed Behavioral Health Organizations

"Managed behavioral health care" (referring to substance abuse and mental health) care exploded in terms of growth in the 1990s. In 1999, the three largest MBHOs (Magellan, ValueOptions, and United Behavioral Health) collectively managed behavioral health care for 100 million people. In addition, 1998 annual revenues in the managed behavioral health industry alone reached $4.4 billion (Findlay, 1999).

With the increasing exploration of hybrid models of "managing" mental health services, behavioral health purchasers, providers, and consumers have become increasingly concerned with both access to mental health care and the quality of treatment for individuals with mental disorders and substance abuse. Thus, information on evaluating the quality of MBHOs has become important to both the public and private managed care industry as well as to consumers of mental health care.

In the current managed care environment, MBHOs have been increasingly competing for the right to serve selected populations. This has taken two forms: (1) MBHOs have been chosen by individuals within a certain at-risk population from a number of competing health plans; and (2) the purchaser (e.g., state government) selects from a number of "bidding" organizations a single MBHO to provide mental health services to the specific population, often including a risk-sharing arrangement.

The initial results of implementing managed behavioral health care have been mixed. In many cases, it has been demonstrated that significant reductions have been made in overall behavioral health care spending (Mechanic, Schlesinger, & McAlpine, 1995). On the other hand, there have been strong incentives for MBHOs to compete for individuals who are "good risks," or less likely to utilize mental health services. This, of course, is partially dependent on the organizational and financial arrangements involved in the selection of MBHOs by the purchaser.

Mental Health Carve-Outs

In the 1990s, MCOs developed specialty networks or separate systems that "carve out" the organization, financing, treatment, and management of financial risk for selected disorders, including cancer, vision, dental, and mental health and substance-abuse (i.e., behavioral health) services. As previously discussed, MBHOs have been among the fastest-growing companies in the managed care industry.

Carve-out companies vary in their organizational structure, from specialized units within larger MCOs to independently functioning organizations. They have been more common among larger employers vis-à-vis smaller employers. Although some may view carve-out strategies as cost-control mechanisms within MBHOs, carve-out programs may add administrative costs anywhere from 8% to 20% of behavioral benefit costs.

Public mental health systems have also entered into contractual arrangements with MBHOs. In fact, in the past several years, 49 states have implemented or are in the process of implementing managed care programs. Nevertheless, despite this dramatic enrollment shift being undertaken by states and counties of "moving" individuals with severe mental disorders into managed care, how will this privatization of public mental health systems affect consumers with more serious mental disorders? For example, care for individuals with severe mental disorders often must address housing, income support, rehabilitation/vocational training, and social support, as well as many other issues generally not within the experience of many private MBHOs. This may partially explain the heterogeneity of outcomes reported thus far for various cities and states experimenting with private MBHOs for the management of their health care reform initiatives affecting individuals with serious mental disorders (Sturm, 1999).

Numerous articles and volumes have been written on the organizational structures, strategies, performance, regulation, and ethics of managed health and mental health care. Space limitations do not permit a more complete discussion of critical issues in mental health services and managed care; additional articles regarding mental health carve-outs may be found in a special issue (volume 26, number 4, 1999) of the *Journal of Behavioral Health Services & Research* entitled "Tracking Changes in Behavioral Health Services: The Role of Carve-Outs."

Certainly MBHOs and carve-out strategies have advantages and disadvantages related to selection and implementation of behavioral health services. One controversial question relates to the issue of the integration of mental health and substance-abuse services with general health services. Conceptually, integrated health care was the innovative feature of the early prepaid group practice plans, where, in theory, primary and secondary prevention was "utilized" for cost-saving measures. The integration of health and mental health services was viewed as an improvement over the organization of health and mental health care as separate, individual delivery systems. Nevertheless, the carved-out nature of mental health services has a number of advantages. The majority of individuals with diagnosable mental disorders (who seek treatment) present themselves for treatment to primary care physicians. These physicians have not been trained to treat individuals with mental disorders, nor are they interested in treating individuals with mental disorders. Furthermore, primary care physicians have tended to overlook mental illness diagnoses in their patients, and when these illnesses are diagnosed, fail to provide appropriate treatment and/or referral (Wells, Sturm, Sherbourne, & Meredith, 1996).

There are a number of ethical issues that have intensified as MBHOs have expanded into alliances with state and county public mental health systems. Managed care has often increased the necessity for sharing confidential medical information, which raises the concern about confidentiality related to mental health and substance abuse treatment under MBHOs.

Another ethical concern is patient autonomy: whether the restriction of practitioner choice and restriction of access to specialized mental health treatment inherent in managed care result in limitations that potentially affect consumer compliance as well as the outcome of mental health care.

Finally (but certainly not the only other ethical issue related to managed mental health care), what impact has managed care had on the mental health practitioner–patient relationship? To what degree does the disruption of maintaining a primary care physician who coordinates medical care for his/her patients affect the effectiveness of care? What responsibility do managed care purchasers and providers have to minimize the distancing effect of the patient from his or her physician? For additional reading on ethics and managed behavioral health care, see Petrila (1996).

There continues to be a relative absence of reliable information on the quality of care and health outcomes within MBHOs. In addition, there continues to be an absence of regulatory initiatives or a regulatory framework to ensure and maintain some level of quality of mental health care. The major challenge will be for purchasers, providers, consumers, researchers, and MCOs to increase their collaborative efforts in monitoring the quality of care and treatment outcomes of managed behavioral health services.

SERVICE DELIVERY IMPLICATIONS

The landscape of the organization, financing, and provision of mental health services in the United States continues to change, evolve, and become more complex, particularly in the current managed care environment. One example of this complexity is that despite the continued use of carve-out approaches in managed behavioral health services for adults, there continues to be a significant movement toward a more integrated approach in mental health services for children (Holden, Friedman, & Santiago, 2001).

Regardless of future trends in carve-in versus carve-out structures for mental health services, mental health administrators will need to more fully understand the financing and delivery of care in specialty behavioral health, primary medical care, human services, and voluntary support network sectors of the de facto mental health service delivery system. Administrators will also need to increase their understanding of how legislation and policy affect the external environment as well as the impacts on the internal operations of mental health organizations and systems. Therefore, continuing education in health and mental health services becomes critical, not only for chief executives but also for middle-level management within mental health organizations.

REFERENCES

American Psychiatric Association. (1987). *Diagnostic and statistical manual of mental disorders* (3rd ed., rev.). Washington, DC: American Psychiatric Press.

Blazer, D. G., Kessler, R. C., McGonagle, K. A., & Swartz, M. S. (1994). The prevalence and distribution of major depression in a national comorbidity sample: The National Comorbidity Survey. *American Journal of Psychiatry, 151*(7), 979–986.

Clancy, C.M. (1999). Consumer preferences: Path to improvement? *Health Services Research, 34*(4), 807–811.

Coffey, R. M., Mark, T., King, E., Harwood, H., McKusick, D., Genuardi, J., Dilonardo, J., & Buck, J. (2000). *National estimates of expenditures for mental health and substance abuse treatment, 1997* (SAMHSA Publication No. SMA-00-3499). Rockville, MD: Center for Substance Abuse Treatment and Center for Mental Health Services, Substance Abuse and Mental Health Services Administration.

Dewan, N. A., Daniels, A., Zieman, G., & Kraner, T. (2000). The National Outcomes Management Project: A benchmarking collaborative. *Journal of Behavioral Health Services & Research, 27*(4), 431–436.

Elpers, J. R., & Levin, B. L. (1996). Mental health services: Epidemiology, prevention, and service delivery systems. In B. L. Levin & J. Petrila (Eds.), *Mental health services: A public health perspective* (pp. 5–22). New York: Oxford University Press.

Findlay, S. (1999). Managed behavioral health care in 1999: An industry at a crossroads. *Health Affairs, 18*(5), 116–124.

Frank, R. G., & McGuire, T. G. (1996). Introduction to the economics of mental health payment systems. In B. L. Levin & J. Petrila (Eds.), *Mental health services: A public health perspective* (pp. 23–37). New York: Oxford University Press.

Gemignani, J. (2000). NCQA's most usable survey yet. *Business and Health, 18*(9), 10–12.

Hibbard, J. H., Harris-Kojetin, L., Mullin, P., Lubalin, J., & Garfinkel, S. (2000). Increasing the impact of health plan report cards by addressing consumers' concerns. *Health Affairs, 19*(5), 138–143.

Holden, E. W., Friedman, R. M., & Santiago, R. L. (2001). Special issue: The national evaluation of the comprehensive community mental health services for children and their families program. *Journal of Emotional and Behavioral Disorders, 9*(1), 2–76.

Institute of Medicine. (1997). *Managing managed care quality improvements in behavioral health.* Washington, DC: National Academy Press.

Katzper, M., & Manderscheid, R. W. (1984). Applications of systems analysis to national data on the mental health service delivery system. *Psychiatric Annals, 14*(8), 596–607.

Kessler, R. C., Berglund, P. A., Zhao, S., Leaf, P. J., Kouzis, A. C., Bruce, M. L., Friedman, R. M., Grosser, R. C., Kennedy, C., Narrow, W. E., Kuehnel, T. G., Laska, E. M., Manderscheid, R. W., Rosenheck, R. A., Santoni, T. W., & Schneier, M. (1996). The 12-month prevalence and correlates of serious mental illness (SMI). In R. W. Manderscheid & M. J. Sonnenschein (Eds.), *Mental health, United States, 1996* (DHHS Publication No. [SMA] 96-3098). (pp. 59–70). Rockville, MD: Center for Mental Health Services.

Kessler, R. C., McGonagle, K. A., Zhao, S., Nelson, C. B., Hughes, M., Eshleman, S., Wittchen, H. U., & Kendler, K. S. (1994). Lifetime and 12 month prevalence of *DSM–III–R* psychiatric disorders in the United States: Results from the national comorbidity study. *Archives of General Psychiatry, 51*, 8–19.

Kessler, R. C., Nelson, C. B., McGonagle, K. A., Edlund, M. J., Frank, R. G., & Leaf, P. J. (1996). The epidemiology of co-occurring addictive and mental disorders: Implications for prevention and service utilization. *American Journal of Orthopsychiatry, 66*(10), 17–31.

Levin, B. L. (1992). Managed mental health care: a national perspective. In R. W. Manderscheid & M. A. Sonnenschein (Eds.), *Mental health, United States, 1992* (pp. 208–218). Rockville, MD: Center for Mental Health Services.

Levin, B. L., Glasser, J. H., & Roberts, R. E. (1984). Changing patterns in mental health service coverage within health maintenance organizations. *American Journal of Public Health, 74*, 453–458.

Levin, B. L., Glasser, J. H., & Jaffee, C. L. (1988). National trends in coverage and utilization of mental health, alcohol, and substance abuse services within managed health care systems. *American Journal of Public Health, 78*, 1222–1223.

Levin, B. L., Hanson, A., Coe, R., & Kuppin, S. (2000). *Mental health parity: National and state perspectives.* Tampa, FL: Louis de la Parte Florida Mental Health Institute, University of South Florida.

Levin, B. L., & Petrila, J. (Eds.). (1996). *Mental health services: A public health perspective.* New York: Oxford University Press.

Manderscheid, R. W., Atay, J. E., Hernandez-Cartagena, M. D. R., Edmond, P. Y., Male, A., Parker, A. C. E., et al. (2001). Key elements of the national statistical picture. In R. W. Manderscheid & M. J. Henderson (Eds.), *Mental Health United States, 2000. Rockville,* MD: Center for Mental Health Services.

McKusick, D., Mark, T. L., King, E., Harwood, R., Buck, J. A., Dilonardo, J., & Genuardi, J. S. (1998). Spending for mental health and substance abuse treatment, 1996. *Health Affairs, 17*(5), 147–157.

Mechanic, D., Schlesinger, M., & McAlpine, D. (1995). Management of mental health and substance abuse services: State of the art and early results. *Milbank Quarterly, 73*(1), 19–55.

Pelletier, L. R., & Beaudin, C. L. (1999). Mental health services delivery and managed care. In C. A. Shea, L. R. Pelletier, E. C. Poster, G. W. Stuart, & M. P. Verhey (Eds.). *Advanced practice nursing in psychiatric and mental health care* (pp. 37–71). St. Louis, MO: C. V. Mosby.

Petrila, J. (1996). Ethics, money, and the problem of coercion in managed behavioral health care. *Saint Louis University Law Journal, 40,* 359–405.

Regier, D., Goldberg, I., & Taube, C. (1978). The de facto U.S. mental health services system: A public health perspective. *Archives of General Psychiatry, 35,* 685–693.

Regier, D. A. (1988). One month prevalence disorders in the United States. *Archives of General Psychiatry, 45,* 977–986.

Regier, D. A., Narrow, W., Rae, D. S., Manderscheid, R. W., Locke, B. Z., & Goodwin, F. K. (1993). The de facto U.S. mental health and addictive disorders service system. Epidemiologic Catchment Area prospective 1-year prevalence rates of disorders and services. *Archives of General Psychiatry, 50,* 85–94.

Robins, L. N., & Regier, D. A. (Eds.). (1991). *Psychiatric disorders in America: The epidemiologic catchment area study.* New York: Free Press.

Robinson, S., & Brodie, M. (1997). Understanding the quality challenge for health consumers: The Kaiser/AHCPR Survey. *Joint Commission Journal of Quality Improvement, 23*(5), 239–244.

Savoca, E. (1999). Psychiatric co-morbidity and hospital utilization in the general medical sector. *Psychological Medicine, 29*(2), 457–464.

Scanlon, D. P., Chernew, M., & Lave, R. (1997). Consumer health plan choice: Current knowledge and future directions. *Annual Review of Public Health, 18,* 507–528.

Sturm, R. (1999). Tracking changes in behavioral health services: How have carve-outs changed care. *Journal of Behavioral Health Services & Research, 26*(4), 359–370.

Taylor, R. (1999). Commentary on health care consumers: Choices and constraints. *Medical Care Research and Review, 56*(Suppl. 1), 60–66.

U.S. Department of Health and Human Services. (1999). *Mental health: A report of the Surgeon General.* Rockville, MD: Substance Abuse and Mental Health Services Administration, Center for Mental Health Services, National Institute of Mental Health.

Wells, K. B., Sturm, R., Sherbourne, C. D., & Meredith, L. S. (1996). *Caring for depression.* Cambridge, MA: Harvard University Press.

Witkin, M. J., Atay, J. E., Manderscheid, R. W., DeLozier, J., Male, A., & Gillespie, R. (1998). Highlights of organized mental health services in 1994 and major national and state trends. In R. W. Manderscheid & M. J. Henderson (Eds.), *Mental health, United States, 1998* (DHHS Publication No. [SMA] 99-3285) (pp. 143–175). Rockville, MD: Center for Mental Health Services.

Chapter Four

Administrative Theory

L. Mark Russakoff

Some discussants make a distinction between administration and management. Often the distinction resides in whether the emphasis is on dealing with objects or abstract decisions ("administration") or with people ("management"). For the most part, in this chapter I use these terms interchangeably, choosing one over the other for emphasis or variety.

The tasks of an administrator or manager have frequently been described. A classification from before World War II included planning, organizing, staffing, directing, coordinating, reporting, and budgeting (POSDCORB). This chapter focuses on the functions that relate to the management of people. The fact that there are multiple and diverse tasks that are the responsibility of an administrator naturally leads to conflicts. Administrators must manage several types of conflict that arise from different sources: structural (inherent); functional (episodic, phasic, that derive from processes); and idiosyncratic (stemming from individual problems). The first two types of conflict are unavoidable because no system is perfect; the last is inevitable because of the nature of managers and employees as people. In mental health care, more than any other part of health care, personnel are critical. There is no fancy equipment that will entice people to obtain services at a psychiatric hospital or clinic if the staff are not welcoming to the patients. The correlate of the importance of staff in mental health settings is that when there are organizational problems, they often have to do with the staff and how they are managed.

The function of an administrative theory is to inform the practice of management. In the performance of psychotherapy, the knowledge of a model of therapy helps the therapist prioritize issues and delineate appropriate and effective interventions. A mental health worker promoted into a cotherapist's position would be provided with supervision in psychotherapy. Knowledge of administrative theory informs the decisions of managers in order that their actions be comprehensible and effective. However, psychiatrists are typically promoted into managerial positions without concomitant education in administrative theory. The approach in this chapter is from the perspective of the kinds of information I think a new mental health administrator would need to know in order to function effectively.

Paralleling the diversity and contradictory nature of theories of personality and psychological treatments, there are diverse administrative theories that have been proposed to assist managers. Just as in psychiatry, many of the theories proposed offered themselves as being complete, and their authors were evangelical in the promotion of their model to the exclusion (and sometimes derision) of other models.

There is no complete, satisfactory model of administrative theory. The complexity of human behavior in organizations requires a model that integrates the individual, group, contextual, hierarchical, social, political, and economic parameters. No single model comes close to assisting one with the multiple points of view that must be taken into consideration to fully appreciate a given situation. Various administrative theories focus on some of the dimensions. For this reason, it is the thesis of this chapter that familiarity with the works of several theorists is necessary but will never be complete. As the work situation changes, newer models will evolve, focusing on the specific parameters and issues that are critical for the times. Newer models are likely to focus on domains not previously considered or on a previously considered dimension but at a more extreme level.

Continued familiarity with new contributions to administrative theory is necessary because all theories are products of their time. What was important and worked in the 19th century needed revision in the early 20th century. Administrative theories have blossomed since the middle of the 20th century, each in accommodation to differing stressors in the business environment. This evolution in administrative theory is visible in the language and metaphors that are chosen to describe the processes. There is a long and tortuous path from *Scientific Management* (Taylor, 1911/ 1998) to *The Age of Unreason* (Handy, 1990) and *The Fifth Discipline: The Art & Practice of the Learning Organization* (Senge, 1990), as well as from difficult tomes on the executives and organizations (Barnard, 1968) to "One-Minute Managers."

There does seem to be a recent trend to idealize technology and declare some form of it to be the answer to the manager's prayers. Whether the technology is electronic charting, intranets, or the Internet, the functions that can be facilitated by technology are touted as replaced. While there is no question that technology has been enormously helpful—this chapter was written on a word processor—there is much in administration that requires personal contact. As Frederick Winslow Taylor stated: "This close, intimate, personal cooperation between the management and the men is of the essence of modern scientific or task management" (Taylor, 1911/ 1998, p. 10).

TAYLOR'S SCIENTIFIC MANAGEMENT

The literature on management often starts with Frederick Winslow Taylor and his *Principles of Scientific Management*, originally published in 1911. Taylor's work evolved in the late 19th century during the time in which the industrial revolution and science were the rising stars. The industrial revolution had put new demands on managers. No longer were workers responsible for a complete task; workers now did a piece of a task. Previously a cobbler made the entire shoe, whereas now the worker did a limited number of tasks involved in the manufacture of the shoe. Governments had prior experience in organizing people to perform complex tasks—such as going to war—but business had not had such needs. For governments, the authority (see later for discussion of authority and power) to direct people in the performance of the task was understood, as was the obligation to obey. The industrial revolution led to the need for managers who were not owners, and those managers had to have means to direct their workers. The literature of the 19th century clearly indicates that managers were often not successful.

Taylor proposed that scientific principles could be applied to the work environment. He noted that workplaces were characterized by worker inefficiency, avoidance of work ("soldiering"), and fears of job insecurity. Business owners lamented that they could not find qualified and motivated employees. Management was characterized as "rule of thumb," as opposed to scientific. Utilizing the techniques of industrial engineering—time and motion studies—Taylor reported that productivity and worker satisfaction were enhanced. His model presumed that there would be a right way of performing a work function, and that this right way would be discovered through objective analysis of the task. His classic work on shoveling coal is a tribute to his model. He delineated the best shape and size of the shovel, and more. He believed that his model of scientific management was exportable to most areas of work, including surgery. (We have here the model for "best practices," a concept to which we have come full circle.)

Taylor (1911/1998) articulated the principles of scientific management as it would apply to bricklaying as follows:

> *First.* The development (by management, not the workman) of the science of bricklaying, with rigid rules for each motion of very man, and the perfection and standardization of all implements and working conditions.
> *Second.* The careful selection and subsequent training of the bricklayers into first-class men, and the elimination of all men who refuse to or are unable to adopt the best methods.
> *Third.* Bringing the first-class bricklayer and the science of bricklaying together, through the constant help and watchfulness of the management, and through paying each man a large daily bonus for working fast and doing what he is told to do.
> *Fourth.* An almost equal division of the work and responsibility between the workman and the management. All day long the management work almost side by side with the men, helping, encouraging, and smoothing the way for them, while in the past they stood to one side, gave the men but little help, and threw on to them almost the entire responsibility as to methods, implements, speed, and harmonious cooperation. (pp. 42–43)

He articulated these principles as follows:

> *First.* The development of a true science.
> *Second.* The scientific selection of the workman.
> *Third.* His scientific education and development.
> *Fourth.* Intimate friendly cooperation between the management and the men. (p. 68)

It is clear from Taylor's principles that he appreciated that there were efficient and inefficient ways of completing tasks. He characterized the traditional workman as using an idiosyncratic method to approach his work tasks and did not believe that even as a skilled workman the individual had the capacity to conceptualize and implement the most efficient methods. Second, not all persons were suitable to the task of working at high efficiency; thus there was a need to find "first-class workmen." Third, there had to be means to motivate the workman to perform the tasks as the managers desired, usually through substantially higher pay. Taylor noted:

> A reward, if it is to be effective in stimulating men to do their best work, must come soon after the work has been done. But few men are able to look forward for more than a week or perhaps at most a month, and work hard for a reward which they are to receive at the end of this time. (p. 48)

And finally, the role of the manager changes from a peripheral watchdog to someone close by the worker, there to ensure that the workers function efficiently. The key points of focus for Taylor were the task itself, the reward or bonus, and the changed role of the manager. Versions of this approach were adopted, but the alteration in the role of the manager often did not occur. It was against this background, with the results of Elton Mayo's studies, that the human relations approach evolved in the 1950s.

Taylor's model is described by others as focused on the task itself and the objective parameters of the work. Modern industrial psychology with its time and efficiency studies evolved from it. Culture, context of work, motivational states of the employee, interactions between and among the supervisor and employee, and the nature of the task itself are not fully addressed.

This impression is a superficial reading of Taylor. In his classic text he specifically noted the need to *change the role of the manager from the classic taskmaster to a new relationship of manager to employee*. The manager will need to change behaviors no less dramatically than the employee. Taylor noted the different kinds of attention that different groups of people might require in order to be effectively managed. The manager must be available to the worker to help the worker act most efficiently; here is early "management by walking around." He is careful to select workers who will thrive in this new model; there is pay for performance that is substantially higher than before.

Taylor anticipated misapplication of his model. He noted that if his techniques were used to increase productivity without proper training of the workers or bonuses, there would likely be strikes and other labor and production troubles. Taylor's model would predict the troubles that managed care has had with psychiatrists in that the managed care companies mandated the use of short-term therapies and reduced fees, rather than training the clinicians in these short-term treatments and raising the fees for those who were most efficient and effective.

ELTON MAYO:
THE WESTERN ELECTRIC HAWTHORNE PLANT STUDIES

Mayo's studies in the 1920s and 1930s were attempts to extend results from industrial psychology and scientific management to find the optimum work conditions at an electrical components manufacturing plant. The particular concerns that the company was struggling with were fatigue and monotony. For those who like details, it is of note that these experiments—widely quoted in the management literature—were performed on six highly selected workers; two of them dropped out within the first year and were replaced. Another left for a period but then returned (Mayo, 1933, p. 58). The study lasted about 5 years. Despite careful variations in lighting level, rest periods, and so on, Mayo found that productivity of the work group increased. In the process, he delineated the importance of the social needs of the workers as superseding effects such as lighting level. He placed great emphasis on the group of workers, not simply a collectivity of individuals. His findings were captured in what is now referred to as the "Hawthorne effect," in which *attention to the worker and the cohesiveness of the work group supersede many other parameters in effect on productivity.* Mayo (1933) noted:

> The most significant change that the Western Electric Company introduced into its "test room" bore only a casual relation to the experimental changes. What the Company actually did for the group was to reconstruct entirely its whole industrial situation. . . . The consequence was that there was a period during which the individual workers and the group had to re-adapt themselves to a new industrial milieu, a milieu in which their own self-determination and their social well-being ranked first and the work was incidental. (p. 73)

He concluded his work with ideas that are prescient and relevant today in the era of managed care:

> The urgent problem of the present is that our administrative *elite* has become addict of a few specialist studies and has unduly discounted the human and social aspects of industrial organization. The immediate need is to restore effective human collaboration; as a prerequisite of this, extension of the type of research I have reported is the major requirement. An administrator in these days should be qualified as a "listener"; many of our *elite* are so qualified, but are not able to relate the various "echoes" they catch in conversation to anything beyond their own experience. (p. 183)

Here Mayo reacted to the bureaucratization of the work site (mental health care under managed care), through its arrogant assumption of scientific management (best practices established as the only reimbursable practices). He anticipated the limitations of "management by walking around" for the administrator who cannot appreciate what he or she sees or hears.

DRUCKER: MANAGEMENT BY OBJECTIVES

Peter Drucker (1954) provided one of the first systematic attempts at the development of a comprehensive model of management theory. He focused on the economic performance of the organization as a central organizing concept: "The first definition of management is therefore that it is an economic organ, indeed the specifically economic organ of an industrial society. Every act, every decision, every deliberation of management has as its first dimension an economic dimension" (Drucker, 1954, p. 7).

He also understood the central role of the consumer:

> What the customer thinks he is buying, what he considers "value," is decisive—it determines what a business is, what it produces and whether it will prosper (Drucker, 1954 p. 36). . . . What is our business is not determined by the producer but by the consumer. It is not defined by the company's name, statutes or articles of incorporation but by the want the consumer satisfies when he buys a product or service. (Drucker, 1954, p. 50)

Drucker promoted the approach known as "management by objectives" in contrast to the use of intuition. Specification of the objectives provides guidance for all regarding the success (or failure) of the employee, management, and the organization. The selection of objectives follows this precept: "Objectives are needed in every area where performance and results directly and virtually affect the survival and prosperity of the business" (Drucker, 1954, p. 63).

The purpose of operating an enterprise on the principles of management by objectives is:

> To organize and explain the whole range of business phenomenon in a small number of general statements; to test these statements in actual experience; to predict behavior; to appraise the soundness of decisions when they are still being made; and to enable practicing businessmen to analyze their own experience and, as a result, improve their performance. (Drucker, 1954, p. 63)

Drucker was keenly aware of the importance of integrating managers into the *mission* of the organization: "The first requirement in managing managers is therefore that the vision of the individual managers be directed toward the goals of the business, and that their wills and efforts be bent toward reaching these goals. The first requirement in managing managers is management by objectives and self-control" (Drucker, 1954, p. 119).

The application of the model of management by objectives did not remain limited to business enterprises. This model is at the core of the Multidisciplinary Treatment Plan that was mandated under the JCAHO Consolidated Standards, and was adopted by many state mental health departments. In place of "economic performance" for a business, the goal of inpatient treatment is the discharge of the patient from the hospital. Goals and objectives that are linked to the overarching goal of discharge are then described with the means of achieving the objectives specified and the time to obtain the objective indicated. Responsibility for each task is assigned and recorded. At each treatment planning session, the success or failure of the team in achieving its objectives is recorded and the treatment plan revised with new goals and objectives.

Models regarding individual human functioning—psychodynamic, behavioral, cognitive—have been organized through the lens of the development of the person. Gedo and Goldberg (1973) presented an interesting model integrating many disparate models of mental functioning. Theories regarding management do not lend themselves to such neat organization, in part because there is no simple structure within which one can place them (other than chronological). Systems theory (Bercalanffy, 1968) permits the hierarchical organization of models as they aspire to greater breadth, but does not help organize thinking regarding models that compete at the same level of the organization or assist with true integration of the models. Thus, one remains with an agglomeration of models, from which one must pick and choose as the moment seems to direct one. There is no substitute for experience in selecting the model to utilize to guide one's decisions here.

Most models of administration and management stem from the business world. It is important to recognize that there are distinct differences in managing unskilled, skilled, or professional employees. Much of the earlier business literature did not address dealing with the professional employee. In the current market, professional employees abound. Professional employees will be driven by the values of their professions, which may, at times, conflict with organizational needs. There may be professional rewards unavailable to unskilled workers (e.g., recognition of expertise by professional societies). Alternatively, with services previously provided by employees now being contracted to outside agencies, relationships become more complex and less stable.

When one supervises a team, constituted of an amalgam of employees from different groups, resentments will naturally spring forth when one group sees that it doesn't have the prerogatives of the other. For example, in inpatient treatment teams, psychiatrists may be resented by therapy aides for their seeming independence of action, whereas the psychiatrists may be angry with the seeming lack of dedication of the hourly employees who leave on schedule (or get paid time-and-a-half for remaining).

Sometimes there is reference to management as a science. Although administration and management should take into account scientific information, the fact that people seek meaning in what they do and what occurs around them puts severe limitations on the science of management. Meaning evolves in the crucible of personal development and interpersonal experience; it will never be reducible to a set of principles. Administration, as in the practice of medicine, is predicated on certain scientific principles and external conditions, but must be informed by an appreciation of humanistic and symbolic elements. Administration and management are, in substantial part, art, honed by experience. We believe that administrators can learn much of the relevant information from reading or formal didactics. This information, supplemented by practical (and preferably supervised) experience, can help a person become an effective mental health administrator and manager. We believe there is a parallel between the growth of an individual as a psychotherapist and the growth of an individual as an administrator.

The remainder of the chapter is divided into key concepts necessary for mental health administrators.

CONCEPT 1: THE HEALTH CARE ENVIRONMENT IS RAPIDLY CHANGING AND ORGANIZATIONS MUST BE PREPARED TO ACCOMMODATE THOSE CHANGES

Over the past 30 to 40 years there have been major changes in the health care environment. These changes are easily seen in the evolution of various payment systems and how they have been fiscally driven. The change from fee-for-service to capitated systems within managed care has been a discontinuous change. Long-term planning does not usually take into account such discontinuous change. Organizations have evolved or been consumed in the process of accommodating (or failing to accommodate) these fiscal changes. For-profit systems rapidly expanded under fee for service. When managed care began to expand into the market, many of these systems imploded. Classic organizations by their nature have much inertia. Modern health care organizations must be sufficiently flexible to accommodate to the changes. Appreciation of who the customers are—patients, businesses, and insurance companies—permits the organization to know what has to be changed; the art of leadership and administration is in knowing when and how.

The concept of the "learning organization" incorporates the observation that organizations cannot be static in the current environment (Senge, 1990). The organization must build into its culture and functions the inevitability of change. One can never rest on one's laurels, content with the structure that one has created. There is an ongoing tension—stable yet flexible, future-oriented yet retaining positive aspects from the past. There must be a recognition that the organization as currently conceived may not be adaptable to a radically altered environment, and all assumptions must be open to question. Imbuing the organization with the sense that it is viable, responsive, and creative in response to challenges fosters a sense of security and excitement. The alteration of the culture of an organization from cherishing stability at all costs to the learning organization perspective requires enormous effort at all levels.

Organizations often respond to challenges by functional changes where concomitant structural changes are also indicated. Structural change is often even more disquieting to employees than functional changes. Planned radical structural and functional change has been framed as reengineering the organization (Hammer & Champy, 1993). Administrators with a clear and accurate grasp of the customers' needs have effected successful reengineering endeavors, transforming organizations that were conceived of and built in the heyday of intensive psychodynamic treatment to modern and effective facilities. Administrators following the fad of reengineering, who have not carefully analyzed their customers' needs, have failed in the process, merely disrupting their organizations.

CONCEPT 2: THE CONTEXT OF WORK IS CRUCIAL TO UNDERSTANDING ADMINISTRATIVE PROCESSES AND FUNCTIONING

The sociocultural aspects of the work setting are important but largely beyond the scope of this chapter. It would be negligent not to mention them. Cultural expectations regarding work, relationships to one's supervisors and one's peers, and relationships between the sexes can profoundly affect what will occur at the work site. The process of enculturation cannot be assumed to have fully occurred merely because a new immigrant has been hired. Appreciation of various cultural values and how they differ from American ones may facilitate management of staff.

Cultural competence should not be targeted toward dealing with patients alone. The American workforce is multicultural; effective and efficient utilization of staff requires appreciation of cultural factors affecting staff performance. Psychiatrists who come from cultures in which doctors are not questioned by patients need assistance in dealing with Americans. All mental health therapy aides, regardless of their cultural background, need assistance in speaking up in team meetings to inform professional staff as to how patients are acting on the unit. Some cultures have sanctions against all evidence of disagreement or conflict, particularly from a person of lower status to one of higher status. Additionally, all staff need training in dealing with provocative and abusive patients, because the common response of retaliation against the abuser is not therapeutic and is unprofessional.

Many work sites are constrained by rules and regulations that have not accommodated to the realities of recent decades; one such reality is single mothers. Rigid and mindless implementation of policies can do more damage to morale and organizational functioning than deliberate malfeasance. It is as important to understand the intent of rules as it is to understand the ramification of deviation from rules. Flexibility can often be a virtue; on the other hand, capriciousness is disastrous.

CONCEPT 3: THE ARTICULATION OF THE PURPOSE OF AN ORGANIZATION IS CRITICAL TO DIRECTING IT

To the extent that an organization has a meaningful and carefully conceived mission statement, review of such a statement can facilitate an appreciation of the organization and help guide decisions. Until recently, mission statements were given short shrift. More recent administrative theories have focused more sharply on the mission statement, the importance of education of staff members about the mission statement, and its use as an organizational compass (Deming, 1986). In recent years, mission statements for health care organizations have added concepts of "cost-effective" or "efficient" care to statements of "highest quality." As increasing economic pressures have affected both organizations and practitioners, altering the practices of all involved, conflicts between organizational goals and practitioner needs have emerged in sharper focus. Managing such conflicts has become the everyday task of administrators.

Absence of an understanding of the mission statement can lead to a narrowing of the scope of an employee and resistance to necessary changes. "That's not my job" is more likely to be heard by someone who understands the job solely from the job description and not in relationship to the mission of the organization. A mission statement that is not translated into the everyday activities of a worker is meaningless. Part of good management is helping staff understand how activities come together to help in the care of patients. The mission statement must contain transcendent values that will help orient the employees at all levels of the organization. What at the moment may feel like "scut work" can then be appreciated as an appropriate contribution—however small—to the care of the patients.

The mission statement is a starting point for discussions of administration, but it must be coupled with a willingness to accommodate to new realities. Senge's (1990) learning organization concept reappears here. Understanding this mission, members of the organization are in a better position to plan for and respond to changes that will impact it. Members cannot be complacent, as the health care environment is constantly changing. Planning is an ongoing process; not a five-year plan on the shelf.

CONCEPT 4: ORGANIZATIONS HAVE STRUCTURE, AND STRUCTURE IS LINKED TO FUNCTION

A conscious appreciation of the organization and hierarchy at work lays the groundwork for understanding work situations. Weber (1947) articulated the concept of the *ideal bureaucracy*, devoid of the emotional needs of workers and of group processes that evolve. An appreciation of the original concepts is helpful to put real and modern organizations in perspective. The *table of organization* (TO) graphically presents one's *position* in the hierarchy, as well as the *lines of authority* and reporting. Solid lines indicate that the person under a position is accountable to the person above. Dotted lines indicate that there is communication between the positions but authority resides with those with solid lines. A review of a TO can sometimes clarify conflicts. The problems with a "silo mentality" can become clearest when discussed in the context of a TO, as one sees structures laid out on the table of organization with extensive hierarchies and no lines that cross from one column to the next. This problem has also been referred to as the "white space"—no communication between two groups who ought to be working together, but engage more in parallel play than in an integrated and common effort.

Civil service structures are often characterized (or caricatured) as emphasizing organization and structure at the expense of functionality. On the positive side, there is typically little left to the imagination about where one fits into the organization: The table of organization is literally written into law and union contracts. Likewise, the job descriptions are fixed by law, and are often constrained by union contracts. In concept, the specification of the organizational structure and job description prevents the abuse of civil service workers by political appointees. In practice, these same protections may serve to undermine flexible and creative responses to new situations.

Many mental health managers are uncomfortable with the fact of a hierarchy and the associated concepts of power and authority. Max Weber (1947) defined *power* as follows: "Power' (*Macht*) is the probability that one actor within a social relationship will be in a position to carry out his own will despite resistance, regardless of the basis on which this probability rests" (p. 152). *Authority* is the right to effect a decision, or command. Authority is not a singular concept, and may stem from several sources. Authority may be established by organizational or societal rules, by informal organizational rules, or by the possession of special knowledge. Physicians in particular often are puzzled when their authority is challenged, even if in the administrative (as opposed to clinical) sphere. Physicians often feel entitled to a substantial amount of authority by virtue of possession of the medical degree, societal attitudes toward physicians, and their specialty training.

Power and authority do not necessarily reside in expected positions. The informal organization may invest enormous power in particular individuals, such as the elder statesman of the nurses or mental health workers. This person may not be the head nurse or the senior mental health worker. A unit chief who attempts to alter the structure of a unit without getting this person to buy in to the new program will meet extraordinary resistance. On the other hand, co-opting the process by inviting such a person into the planning process can ensure the program's success.

Matrix management structures are commonly found in health care organizations. They violate Weber's ideal model in that although there is a basic hierarchical structure, a matrix is created that undermines that structure. Matrix management can contribute to a lack of clarity regarding authority, accountability, and power. Matrix management structures typically have separate lines of responsibility and reporting for different functions, that is, budget through a nonclinical staff member and clinical issues through physicians. For matrix management to work, there must be cooperation between the line and staff personnel and supervisors. It is possible for a matrix organization to become hopelessly complex. For a relatively simple example, on an inpatient unit, the social worker may report to the physician unit chief for clinical activities but report to the director of social work for issues of appropriateness of the kinds of work being assigned by the unit chief. It must be clear that administration within a matrix structure is markedly different from administration within a clear and simple hierarchy. Authority will be sharply curtailed in the former, relative to the latter, structure.

People must know to whom they report and for what issues. It is not uncommon for psychiatrist administrators to report to a nonphysician for "administrative" issues and to a physician (chair of department, medical director) for "clinical" issues. It is not the eleventh commandment that the distinction will be clear; one may need to have both one's administrative and clinical supervisors in the room to resolve an issue effectively.

Although a person's position should be clear from review of the table of organization, the role of the individual is defined in many ways. Formally, one's role would be described in one's job description. However, most job descriptions are generic and do not include many other functions in sufficient detail. There must be a balance, between the specificity of the job description and actual activities performed in the position, that leaves some room for creativity and flexibility. Additionally, there are the aspects of the role that are ascribed to the individual ("role sent") and the role as the individual understands it ("role received"). The senders of the role include all those who interact in some fashion with the individual. There is nothing simple about this conceptualization. Roles sent may be in conflict with one another. There is typically a discrepancy between role sent and role received, paralleling the failures in dyadic communication when there are differences in what was said and what was heard. The various roles sent and received are often conflicting—for example, the message from the chief executive officer (CEO) to fill beds to maximum capacity versus the message from the inpatient staff to screen out the difficult or otherwise undesirable cases.

For example, as lengths of stay have continued to decrease as a result of managed care, inpatient clinical staffs often complain about workloads and staffing levels. Concomitantly, as reimbursement has decreased, either through reductions in per diem charges or through case-rated contracts, administration has carefully scrutinized staffing levels and often reduced staffing. The "sicker–quicker" problem— sicker patients needing to be treated in a quicker time frame with fewer resources—emerges. Staff members are likely to have their job descriptions changed in terms of what they do as well as when and how they must do it.

No one in the system is likely to be pleased with the changes. Issues of position, role, power, and authority often arise as these changes occur. Staffs regularly see the answer to questions as being to hire more staff, rather than to reengineer processes and reduce costs. The staff typically will have the viewpoint that "previously, we were staffed at a certain level for a given level of patient acuity; since the acuity level has become higher, there should be more staff."

Reducing costs in psychiatry almost always means reducing personnel or personnel utilization. Mental health care models are quite labor-intensive. Third-party payers are not impressed with the nature of the milieu when the length of stay is a couple of days. As the hospital is putting in a new million-dollar imaging system in a radiology suite, the psychiatric staff will not easily comprehend the need to cut labor costs in psychiatry. Mental health managers who are unfamiliar with their role within the organization may be perceived as part of the problem if they permit themselves to be transparent, simply transmitting the complaints of staff up the hierarchy.

In such a scenario, the manager needs to have a full grasp of the hospital's finances, as well as a sense of how to objectively assess staffing needs. Managers who are clueless as to the organization and financing of services will not be effective in helping the staff either argue their point or adjust to current realities. Education of senior administration, or of the staff, may permit an appreciation of the legitimacy of what is requested or done. Recently, it has been possible to objectify the need for higher staffing levels on some clinical services as the level of dangerousness of the patients has continued to increase.

CONCEPT 5: GROUP DYNAMICS APPLY TO WORK GROUPS

Psychiatrists know that the placement of individuals in enduring groups of various sizes induces the development of various group dynamic forces (Parker, 1997). The size of the group makes a difference, as does the composition of the group. Small groups are more likely to foster positive feelings amongst the members (if they are not participating in the group as representatives of other groups) than large groups. Participation in large groups—there is no clear cut-off but somewhere between 15 and 25—and small groups constituted of representatives of other groups often leaves one unsatisfied. It is rare for the positive feelings that may develop in small groups to develop in large groups for a sustained period. Large group dynamics are more fragmented; people typically feel unappreciated. Large groups conduce to feelings of unimportance; small groups often lead people to feel better about themselves. It is easier to lead a small group; large groups typically break into subgroups, resisting singular leadership. All groups can organize against a real or imagined threat, a simple trick of leadership to create at least the illusion of cohesion.

Psychiatrists can use their knowledge of group dynamics to their advantage in understanding processes in organizations. Office romances often enact basic-assumption pairing fantasies. Vilification of the leader is often a result of basic-assumption dependency group dynamics. Vilification of managed care can often be part of the basic-assumption fight/flight group. An appreciation of these dynamics can help the mental health administrator avoid getting caught in processes that distract from the work task.

CONCEPT 6: ESTABLISHING AND MAINTAINING HIGH MORALE AND HIGH MOTIVATION AMONG EMPLOYEES IS A CRITICAL MANAGEMENT FUNCTION

The problem of how to motivate employees is a vexing one. Much work in the 1950s and 1960s focused on the interpersonal aspects of this problem, and the theories took the form of statements about the nature of mankind. Maslow (1987) suggested a *hierarchy of needs*. Lower level needs had to be met before one could go on to higher level needs. Lower level needs were ones that could be satisfied. These are appetitive or consummatory needs that seek to be satisfied, but must be continuously satiated. However, *a satisfied need of this nature does not motivate*. The highest level need was one that led to growth and activity; it would not lead to satiation.

The lowest level needs are *physiological*; a person who is hungry or homeless will be distracted from work. *Safety* concerns are the next level. Administrators of facilities in which aggressive, involuntary patients are seen must be able to appreciate the reality of these concerns, as well as understand irrational distortions. *Security* needs are easily frustrated in an environment that is in constant flux. Hospital administrators often spend much time informing staff of how decisions are made, particularly as fiscal pressures force difficult and painful decisions. The next level of need is that of *self-esteem*. People need to feel respected and worthwhile. The final level, a growth need, is that of *self-actualization*, becoming who one hopes to be. This need is not to be confused with passing a test or achieving a position; it is a process of feeling that one is accomplishing what one would hope to accomplish. It may involve needs to be creative, resourceful, or inspired. Other theorists of the 1950s and 1960s incorporated an appreciation of these differing needs in their formulations of worker motivation.

McGregor: Theory X and Theory Y

McGregor (1960) focused on the attitudes—conscious and unconscious—of the manager and the worker toward work. He understood the problem of motivation of employees as stemming from an incorrect view of the values and needs of employees as harbored by managers. He characterized the then-current view held by managers, which for shorthand he referred to as *Theory X*, as follows:

1. "The average human being has an inherent dislike of work and will avoid it if he can" (p. 33).
2. "Because of this human characteristic of dislike of work, most people must be coerced, controlled, directed, (or) threatened with punishment to get them to put forth adequate effort toward the achievement of organizational objectives" (p. 34).
3. "The average human being prefers to be directed, wishes to avoid responsibility, has relatively little ambition, and wants security above all" (p. 34).

In systems that have been petrified by inattention, his focus may still illuminate the implicit view of the individual as incorporated into company policy and procedure. Alternatively, there are required tasks that most do not like to perform, and people seem to act as if these tasks are escapable. In such situations, a Type X approach may be warranted and necessary.

McGregor believed that the perceived attitudes of employees as articulated in Theory X are in fact the *consequences of management strategy,* not inherent in the employees (p. 42). Alternatively, he proposed a different set of assumptions, which he labeled *Theory Y*:

1. *The expenditure of physical and mental effort in work is as natural as play or rest* [italics added for emphasis]. The average human being does not inherently dislike work. Depending upon controllable conditions, work may be a source of satisfaction (and will be voluntarily performed) or a source of punishment (and will be avoided if possible).
2. *External control and the threat of punishment are not the only means for bring-*

ing about effort toward organizational objectives. Man will exercise self-direction and self-control in the service of objectives to which he is committed.

3. *Commitment to objectives is a function of the rewards associated with their achievement.* The most significant of such rewards, for example, the satisfaction of ego and self-actualization needs, can be direct products of effort directed toward organizational objectives.

4. *The average human being learns, under proper conditions, not only to accept but to seek responsibility.* Avoidance of responsibility, lack of ambition, and emphasis on security are generally consequences of experience, not inherent human characteristics.

5. *The capacity to exercise a relatively high degree of imagination, ingenuity, and creativity in the solution of organizational problems is widely, not narrowly distributed in the population.*

6. Under the conditions of modern industrial life, the intellectual potentialities of the average human being are only partially utilized. (pp. 47–48)

Thus McGregor laid the problem of the poorly motivated employee at the feet of the manager, not the employee. He suggested that managers often harbor Theory X-like assumptions about employees and thus create the problem that they rail against. By examining one's assumptions about employees and shifting to Theory Y-like assumptions, McGregor suggests that there will be higher productivity and morale.

Herzberg: Motivation–Hygiene Theory

Herzberg (1966) explored the relationship between factors that people related to feelings of satisfaction and dissatisfaction at work. He discovered that the factors were not bipolar ones, such that high on the variable is satisfaction and low is dissatisfaction. Instead, he found that it was most efficient to group the factors into two distinct groups: *satisfiers* and *dissatisfiers*. These are two distinct groups: The *satisfiers* are the motivators, the growth factors:

> Achievement and recognition for achievement—opportunity to increase knowledge;
> Responsibility—opportunity to increase understanding;
> Possibility of growth—opportunity for creativity;
> Advancement—opportunity to experience ambiguity in decision making;
> Interest—opportunity to individuate and seek real growth. (p. 177)

The presence of these factors in the experience of a worker led to high ratings of satisfaction with work. This finding was true for a multitude of workers. These were the factors that were effective in motivating workers. The absence of these factors led to *no job satisfaction*, not *job dissatisfaction*.

The *dissatisfiers*—the work environment or hygiene factors—were

> company policy and administration
> supervision
> salary
> interpersonal relations, and
> working conditions. (p. 74)

These factors served to cause dissatisfaction if they were not met, but meeting the needs did not lead to satisfaction. *The opposite of job dissatisfaction is not job satisfaction—it is no job dissatisfaction.* It is interesting to note that most of the hygiene items are the kinds of items that become negotiated in traditional union contracts.

Blake and Mouton: The Managerial Grid

Blake and Mouton (1994) directed attention to the balance between attention to the needs of people and concern for production, described graphically as a *managerial grid.* They characterized administrators with regard to the degree that attention was paid to each dimension. Country-club leaders, laissez-faire leaders, middle of the roaders, and autocratic and team leaders were described. As noted already, the tasks of an administrator are multiple and at times competing. How the administrator balances task orientation and human needs is a critical element in how successful the manager will be. A psychiatrist newly promoted to a managerial position will need to think through issues in a very different fashion than before.

CONCEPT 7: SYSTEMS PROBLEMS OFTEN CAUSE EMPLOYEES TO APPEAR TO BE INEFFECTIVE

When an employee is found to be functioning ineffectively, it behooves the supervisor to investigate in what way the system is structured to impede the proper functioning of the employee. There are many more poorly designed work situations than there are poor employees. Deming (1986) wrote that 80% of the problems were generated by system defects, not bad employees. One cannot depend on an employee to know what the system problem is that impedes his or her performance. More likely than not, the employee will blame the supervisor's attitude or a fellow employee for the problems. The administrator must learn what the tasks are to be performed and then observe him- or herself just what impacts the achievement of those tasks. Here, Taylor's scientific management is quite appropriate in the analysis of the tasks and discerning how the tasks might be accomplished most effectively.

What on the surface may appear to be an inefficient secretary often is a person who has not been provided adequate supervision and direction. Secretaries in clinical offices must be instructed in how to prioritize work, handle inquiries, and deal with distraught patients. Frequently I have seen people with "good secretarial skills"—can type accurately and rapidly, familiar with basic software application packages—seem to fail at a job because they were not trained to perform the other tasks involved. Particularly in a matrix management arrangement—where the secretary reports to an administrator while working for the clinical director—the secretary can founder from lack of supervision regarding the details of work.

It behooves the administrator to recall what McGregor espoused, that the poorly performing employee might be performing poorly because of poor management, that is, responding to messages received from above. It is a too-common event that a "poor employee" who had been successful for several years becomes successful again with a new manager. Sometimes this change occurs through a process of burnout of the employee; sometimes it is when a new manager comes in who wants to exercise more control and thus creates a Theory X environment.

CONCEPT 8: THE LEADERSHIP FUNCTION IS DYNAMIC, AND LEADERSHIP MUST BE RESPONSIVE TO INTERNAL AS WELL AS EXTERNAL CHANGES

In order for there to be a leader, there must be followers. Being a leader may say as much about the leader as it does about those whom the leader leads. There are situations in which no one is willing to accept leadership; the result is anarchy. Leaders ultimately receive their power from their followers. Managers would do well to contemplate the fact that they derive their authority, power, and ability to lead largely through the voluntary compliance of their supervisees. The privilege of leadership is often thrust on managers and usually (at least initially) acquiesced to by supervisees. Ultimately, that privilege must be earned.

It is not meaningful to talk of a "good leader" without talking about the context. The requirements for leadership vary with situations. One must note what the purpose or goal of the leader should be in a particular situation. Again, the issue of the mission of the organization surfaces. The mission statement should embody the core values of the organization. Sometimes leadership involves underscoring the mission and how the particular unit contributes to the mission. At other times, the challenge to leadership is presented when the orientation afforded by the mission provides no guidance as to how to proceed. Here, creativity and the ability to develop a novel solution, combined with the ability to communicate an idea (perhaps an unpalatable one) and to develop a commitment from one's supervisees, are critical. Leadership involves getting people to support a common goal. Different kinds of leaders may be needed during differing phases of an organization's development. There are many ways to classify types of leadership, none of which is completely satisfactory.

A *charismatic* leader may be more successful in the early stages of a program or organization's development. During a period of stability, such a leader may drift off into other directions when the organization needs someone to stay the course. A *consultative* management style is effective when the participants can be relied on to initiate action and accept feedback. It tends not to be sufficiently quick and decisive when crises occur. *Authoritative* leadership may be appreciated in crisis, but is stifling for ordinary decision making. *Participative* management requires obtaining feedback from the various sentient groups and working with the group members to come to decisions. This style can be very effective when there is sufficient time to fully discuss issues with other staff, particularly in group settings.

Participative management does not necessarily mean democracy; it does require that persons participating in the process feel that their points of view are heard. Authoritative or decisive management or leadership is often comforting to staff but can facilitate the creation of a staff totally dependent on the leader; it can infantilize subordinates, interfering with their professional growth. As an ongoing style, it can lead to resentment and poor morale as staff feel too constrained.

Administrators must have an eye toward the future to be effective in the long term. Anticipating trends and then proactively responding to those trends in a timely fashion is the hallmark of an effective leader. Knowing what trends to track is part of fully understanding the nature of one's profession or business. In recent years, these trends have been both fiscal and clinical. Organizations that failed to prepare for the rapid development of managed care suffered. Organizations that sought to capitalize on managed care rapidly expanded, but many failed, having focused almost entirely on the fiscal side. Many clinicians who have obtained training in shorter-term treatments that are demonstrably effective and acceptable to both patients and managed care have been successful, particularly as they organized themselves into groups.

REFERENCES

Barnard, C. I. (1968). *The functions of the executive.* Cambridge, MA: Harvard University Press.

Bercalanffy, L. V. (1968). *General system theory: Foundations, development, applications.* New York: George Braziller.

Blake, R. R., & Mouton, J. S. (1994). *Managerial grid: Leadership styles for achieving production through people.* Woburn, MA: Butterworth-Heinemann.

Deming, W. E. (1986). *Out of the crisis.* Cambridge, MA: MIT Press.

Drucker, P. F. (1954). *The practice of management.* New York: Harper.

Gedo, J. E., & Goldberg, A. (1973). *Models of the mind: A psychoanalytic theory.* Chicago: University of Chicago Press.

Hammer, M., & Champy, J. (1993). *Reengineering the corporation: A manifesto for business revolution.* New York: HarperCollins.

Handy, C. (1990). *The age of unreason.* Boston: Harvard Business School Press.

Herzberg, F. (1966). *Work and the nature of man.* New York: World.

Maslow, A. H. (1987). *Motivation and personality* (3rd ed.). New York: Harper & Row.

Mayo, E. (1933). *The human problems of an industrial civilization.* New York: Macmillan.

McGregor, D. (1960). *The human side of enterprise.* New York: McGraw-Hill.

Parker, I. (1997). Group identity and individuality in times of crisis: Psychoanalytic reflections on social psychological knowledge. *Human Relations, 50*(2), 183–196.

Senge, P. M. (1990). *The fifth discipline: The art & practice of the learning organization.* New York: Doubleday.

Taylor, F. W. (1998). *The principles of scientific management.* Mineola, NY: Dover. (Original work published 1911)

Weber, M. (1947). *The theory of social and economic organization.* New York: Oxford University Press.

Chapter Five

The Dynamics of Organizational Change in Mental Health Administration

Sharon Topping

Some 20 years ago, mental health administrators identified change as the greatest problem they had to face in their roles as managers and decision makers (Davis & Salasin, 1980). Today their answer is the same, for change has become a way of life in most mental health organizations. With this change have come major transformations shaping organizations for the future. Many believe that to withstand profound change, especially that predicted during the new millennium, organizations must be flexible, with loose boundaries and the ability to adapt and respond to the environment and its many stakeholders (Kanter, Stein, & Jick, 1992; Nadler & Tushman, 1997; Sherman & Schultz, 1998; Sifonis & Goldberg, 1996). This chapter explores change and its many consequences for mental health organizations, including: (1) historical perspectives of change, (2) the process of change and its ongoing nature, (3) the forces that resist and promote organizational change, (4) implementation of a change agenda, and (5) special challenges for the future.

Certain words carry with them different connotations depending on a person's experience. *Change* is one of those words. When most mental health administrators are asked the question "what is organizational change?" they generally think of deliberate or intentional change. That is, they imagine organizations going through a transition from one state to another. Kurt Lewin in the 1960s graphically depicted change as a transition that occurs in stages of unfreezing, changing, and refreezing. This perspective may be too simplistic, however, leaving one with the notion that change is a planned, linear process with a discrete beginning and end. In reality, change is best characterized as an ongoing dynamic journey in which a sequence of events unfolds over time. This view allows administrators to understand the continuous nature of change, thereby learning how to better manage their organization in times of turmoil and crisis.

Of course, a person's view of change often depends on whether he or she is creating the change or is on the receiving end. To better understand and manage change, mental health administrators need to look at it from both perspectives. Often, change is forced on organizations, such as when state Medicaid offices secure approval from the federal government for statewide managed care demonstrations. Because of this state-level decision, community mental health centers (CMHC) may be forced to partner with a for-profit managed care organization (MCO) or compete for managed care contracts. On the other hand, CMHC directors are just as likely to act as change agents themselves; thus, it is important that they not only concern themselves with the implementation but also the perspective of the clinical and administrative staffs who are affected as well. There are many in the organization who will view change as an opportunity, but at the same time, others will see it as a disruption and even a threat. Both viewpoints are valid and should be understood as part of the change process.

Given that perspectives on change are rooted in past experiences, the next section of this chapter examines the changing mental health environment over four decades. Mark Twain once said, "If history doesn't repeat itself, it certainly rhymes." Similarly, George Santayana observed that "Those who do not remember the past are condemned to repeat it." Both quotations recognize the value of history in understanding events of today; therefore, this section presents a brief examination of some of the historical factors that have influenced the mental health sector today. Please note that this section is not meant to be a comprehensive history of the mental health movement in the United States; rather, it will provide insights into current changes.

THE ROOTS OF CHANGE IN THE MENTAL HEALTH ENVIRONMENT

Although change is an integral part of the environment today, it is important to note that major transformations in mental health care delivery have occurred in the past as well. Before World War II, states took responsibility for mental health policy, and the federal role was limited. The state psychiatric hospitals were the cornerstone of public policy. However, after the war, many journalists and mental health professionals started publishing critical accounts of mental health treatment in this country (Grob, 1992). At this time, community care began to emerge as a viable alternative. Psychiatrists, once associated primarily with hospitals, began to set up private and community practices. States began establishing outpatient clinics with federal grants and expanding services to schools, courts, and social agencies.

In 1955, the Joint Commission on Mental Illness and Health was created; in 1961, the final report of the Joint Commission was published; and in 1963, the Community Mental Health Centers Act was passed (Grob, 1992). These events resulted in a public policy emphasis on a decentralized system of services linking the federal government and local communities while reducing the role of the states (Starr, 1982). In addition, Medicare and Medicaid expanded the number of persons receiving care and brought the community hospital in as a player in providing mental health services (Hadley, 1996). The result was a profound change in location of services, and because of this, a new group of clients—those not seriously mentally ill—had access to community mental health treatment. Yet few of the deinstitutionalized individuals with serious mental disorders were receiving adequate care in the manner originally envisioned by community advocates (Mechanic & Surles, 1992). The President's

Commission on Mental Health in 1977 described services at both the national and state levels as a "largely unorganized de facto system characterized by extreme fragmentation" (Yank, Hargrove, & Davis, 1992).

The deinstitutionalization of mental health had a profound impact on the structure and organization of mental health services. The state psychiatric hospital moved from center stage; community services expanded along with the client base; and community hospitals assumed a growing role in delivery of care to individuals with serious mental disorders. Nonetheless, the 1980s and President Reagan's "New Federalism" brought another transformation to the system (Mechanic & Surles, 1992). The decision to provide states with reduced block grant funding shifted the direct relationship away from the federal level to the state mental health authorities (SMHAs). This change caused CMHCs to focus their effort on programs mandated by SMHAs and away from those defined by the local communities. The initial shift resulted in a 25% reduction in federal support for mental health services, thereby enhancing the need for fee-generating services (Hargrove & Melton, 1987).

What was the impact of such dramatic change on the mental health system? According to Hadley (1996), by the 1990s, "the public mental health system was an enormously fragmented, large, financially complex structure with multiple providers providing different services, sometimes in the same geographic area and sometimes in direct (or at least indirect) competition with one another" (p. 402). Hence, this environmental context spawned a variety of future challenges for those in the present mental health system. For instance, considerable concern about continuing increases in costs paved the way for managed care reform. With the reduction of long-term psychiatric hospitals, dependence on general hospitals increased, making alliances and partnerships a viable option (Sederer & Bennett, 1996). Taken together, these changes led to an increase in the number of organizations responsible for mental health care, thereby making stakeholder management an important administrative function. These challenges are explored in more detail later in this chapter, along with the skills and strategies necessary to adopt to the kind of change that will follow such challenges.

ENVIRONMENTAL SCANNING

As the preceding section demonstrates, the mental health environment has been changing rapidly for many years. While mental health administrators have been busy working to set goals, develop operational strategies, and make sure that services are provided in their agencies, the external environment has been pushing for more and more change. Managers interested in responding to and guiding this change need more fully to understand the major forces propelling and compelling the change in the environment. They must continually scan the environment, monitor emergent change, and evaluate the appropriateness of their actions against groups both outside and inside the mental health organization.

The scanning function acts much like the organization's window or lens to the external environment. The lens is moved continuously across an array of external organizations (e.g., regulatory, political, economic) in search of current and emerging trends (Ginter, Swayne, & Duncan, 1998). Much of the information when first encountered is diverse and unorganized, so a mental health organization must continuously categorize and organize, while also monitoring and evaluating. During much of this process, the information is subject to human judgment and subjectivity. Thus, it is important for a mental health administrator to understand how to recognize and interpret change in the environment. To do this, he or she must develop a conceptual model to guide the scanning process. In this chapter, an action-oriented, open systems model is used.

OPEN SYSTEMS MODEL AS A MANAGERIAL TOOL

There is a growing tendency to replace the static model of organizations with a more dynamic and open version. One perspective is to view organizations as a system and is based on the assumption that organizations share many of the same basic characteristics as mechanical and living systems (Nadler & Tushman, 1997). A simple way of envisioning an organization as a system is to think of an input–output system (see Fig. 5.1). An open system is one that interacts with the environment, drawing inputs from external sources and transforming them into outputs that are returned to the environment. So, it has the capacity to adapt to changes in the environment. Moreover, an organization—as an open system—is defined as a set of interrelated parts in which change in one part affects the others.

For example, when you think of your mental health agency, ask yourself several questions:

1. Is the environment in which you operate the same as it was 5 years ago?
2. Is your organization structured and managed as it was 5 years ago?
3. Do the employees have the same training and use the same skills?
4. Have client/consumer demands changed in terms of value, quality, delivery, and service?

If the answers are yes, then most elements of your organization have changed or adapted to the external environment over the past 5 years. As each of these changes has occurred, other parts of the organization have changed as well. This fits the definition of an open, dynamic system.

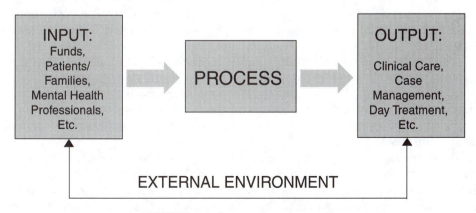

FIGURE 5.1. Input–output system.

In viewing mental health organizations as open systems, it makes sense given the changing environment today to take an action perspective as well. Rosabeth Moss Kanter and her colleagues (Kanter et al., 1992) described the action view in *The Challenge of Organizational Change*:

> Organizations are always in motion. There is some central thrust or directional tendency that results from a combination of the trajectory of past events, pushes arising from the environment, and pulls arising from the strategies embraced by the organization's dominant coalition, all within the context of the organization's character. Of course, the activity clusters (task units, divisions, projects, interest groups, alliances, etc.) themselves are also in motion, and their movements at any time may or may not be in step with each other or with the overall direction. (p. 12)

In essence, change of one sort or the other is always happening in mental health organizations. Stability, then, is nothing more than action that is so smooth and involves so little conflict that it appears that nothing is changing (Kanter et al., 1992). This happens when resources are abundant and easily obtained, stakeholder interests are in accord, and disasters and drastic changes are few—a picture that certainly does not describe the current mental health environment. Consider the situation today. Critics of the existing mental health system are common. Relationships with diverse stakeholders, such as consumers, politicians, psychiatrists, and federal and state governments, are fragile. The political landscape is shifting and diverging, whereas resources are scarce and obtained with much difficulty. As a result, mental health organizations are thought of more realistically as systems made up of interrelated bundles of activities and coalitions of various interests that develop momentum in specific parts and as a whole.

Using an action-oriented, open system model as a guide, it is interesting to consider the changes that have taken place in boundary permeability, for it is difficult today to know where the mental health organization starts and stops. If organizations are viewed as open, dynamic systems, then one recognizes that boundary changes can have unanticipated consequences throughout the organization. A strategic alliance between a CMHC and a rural health clinic in which several CMCH staff members are colocated at the clinic may result in a blurring of boundaries. Contracting between private-sector behavioral managed care companies and public-sector agencies can create changes in internal processes. With the increased dependency on community general hospitals for acute psychiatric care, boundaries between hospitals and mental health organizations can become obscure, leading to identity changes.

The model of an organization as an open, dynamic system is presented in this chapter as an intellectual tool that mental health administrators can use in understanding change and its impact on organizations. The selection of a model is important, for it serves as a guide for analysis and action. Problem solving in organizations involves the collection, analysis, and interpretation of information in order to identify specific problems—in this case the need for change—and the appropriate action (Nadler & Tushman, 1997). A model, such as the one presented here, influences the interpretation and analysis while ultimately shaping the decision. Most persons familiar with organizations already have certain models in mind, but generally they are vague and unspoken, at best. The model presented in this chapter provides a way of conceptualizing a mental health organization and the impact of the environment on that organization.

RECOGNIZING AND INTERPRETING CHANGE

"There are no facts, only interpretations." This quote from Friedrich Nietzsche is certainly relevant to this chapter, because recognizing the need for change in the environment is related to cognitive processes; therefore, interpretation depends on who is doing the interpreting. Of course, interpretation varies depending on the biases and experience of mental health administrators. The significance, however, is that the interpretation determines the response or organizational actions that will be undertaken. Thus it is important to understand the interpretation process and know what affects it. Fahey and Narayanan (1986) described this challenge:

> Analysts have to infuse meaning into data; they have to make the connections among discordant data such that signals of future events are created. This involves acts of perception and intuition on the analysts' parts. It requires the capacity to suspend beliefs, preconceptions, and judgments that may inhibit connections being made among ambiguous and disconnected data. (p. 39)

One factor that has considerable impact on the mental health administrator's perception of change is the organizational context itself. Organizations that have high levels of information-processing capacity—that is, high levels of staff interaction and participation—generally process more information about the environment, which, in turn, can be used in the decision-making process. Thomas and McDaniel (1990) studied how hospital chief executive officers (CEOs) interpreted opportunities and threats in the environment. CEOs in hospitals oriented toward high levels of information processing were more likely to interpret an environmental change as positive, viewing it as an opportunity for hospital gain. From their findings, Thomas and McDaniel recommended that if administrators want to alter their interpretation, they may wish to examine their organization's information-processing capacity to find out how information is collected, processed, and conveyed.

One of the most difficult situations in which to make valid interpretations is when events are extremely unfamiliar, like the passage of Medicare prospective payment legislation for hospitals in 1983 (Barr, 1998). In such a situation, the administrator will make vague interpretations initially, looking for patterns that can be connected to something familiar. Actually, managers overall do not have a very good record at interpreting the environment and recognizing the need for change. They tend to make erroneous assumptions about the magnitude and effect of change. For example, Fombrun (1992) illustrates how U.S. energy companies after the 1973 OPEC oil embargo invested millions of dollars in developing synthetic fuels based on an erroneous assumption about future oil prices. Topping and Ginter (1998) described how Columbia/HCA based its overall marketing strategy on the false assumption that the health care industry was a national market. Mechanic and Rosenthal (1999) discussed how medical directors in MCOs do not view trust-building programs as strategic tools even in the face of a public increasingly distrustful of and hostile to managed care.

Administrators, like most people, frequently have a vested interest in maintaining the status quo, and therefore may be blinded to reality. Sometimes they are able to block out the change, perceiving no threat from the environment. One of the most interesting cases of this was after deregulation of the savings and loan (S&L) industry, when CEOs were asked what strategic change had occurred in response to the new environment (Javidan, 1984). Most answered that no changes had occurred, explaining that deregulation was only temporary, and the industry would be back to its old regulated self in a couple of years. This example can be easily extrapolated to mental health administrators and their reaction to managed care. Some CMHC administrators interpreted managed care as a threat and lobbied legislators to limit MCO activity in their states. Others believed that managed care would go away if they ignored it, whereas some viewed it as an opportunity and aligned their CMHC with behavioral managed care health organizations. From Fig. 5.2, it is easy to see how this can happen. External forces in the environment act to trigger change, whereas inertial forces, often inside the organizations, act to retard change. If the inertial forces influence the interpretation, then those in the organization will see no need to change and resist. This type of resistance to change and how it operates are discussed in more detail in the following sections.

THE PROCESS OF CHANGE

According to Kanter and colleagues (1992), change is messy, it is difficult, and it does not happen in isolation. Nadler and Tushman (1997) described change as involving multiple and often incomplete transactions and uncertain futures. Hence, the process is more like a continual journey toward some elusive, flickering goal, with some right turns and some wrong ones. Sometimes there is a sense of just "muddling through" with small incremental steps, and at other times it feels as if giant transformations are happening all around. This section describes these different types of organizational change and how they fit into the process. Moreover, Chris Argyris (1985) said, "almost any action that disturbs the status quo or represents a threat to the usual way of doing things will invoke resistance or a defensive reaction." This section discusses those roadblocks erected in organizations while offering advice on how to facilitate change.

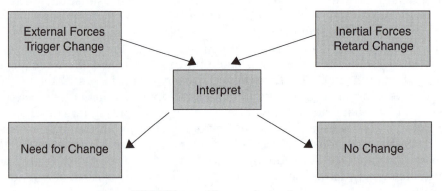

FIGURE 5.2. Change dynamics.

The Pace of Change: Incremental Versus Revolutionary

There are many different kinds of organizational change. One that many mental health administrators are familiar with is deliberate or planned change. This is usually thought of as a consciously intended course of action resulting from a formalized, step-by-step process. Note that this conceptualization is the typical way of visualizing change, yet it excludes both dynamic and unplanned elements. It also excludes the notion of planned change as either realized or unrealized. That is, the plan may be successfully implemented and change occurs, or on the other hand, it may conclude in failure with little or no change occurring.

One type of change that is often overlooked is emergent change. Opportunistic change, as it is better known, gives rise to unplanned change—change that emerges over time. Initially, many public-sector mental health directors viewed managed care as a threat; nevertheless, over time many have realized the opportunities inherent in the new environment and have aligned their agencies accordingly. This is emergent change. It was not intended originally, but with time, it emerges as a viable strategy. Emergent change can be very disruptive in an organization because it may supersede intended plans. Nevertheless, mental health administrators cannot let opportunities pass, so they have to be prepared to take advantage of emergent change.

In conceptualizing change as a process, it is important to understand how organizational change actually occurs. Change is typically described in terms of "waves" or "spurts and pauses." In this context, it may result in a complete reversal—a revolution—of an organization's direction, similar to "drastic leaps forward." A public-sector mental health organization entering into a partnership with a for-profit MCO may experience revolutionary change when efficiency standards and cost reductions become an important priority. To truly be revolutionary, organizational change must involve transformation of structure, culture, and strategy—a "frame-breaking" kind of change. This type of change can pose major complications for mental health organizations and, as a result, must be thought through very carefully. Because of the inherent difficulties, mental health organizations seldom implement revolutionary change. Even when drastic changes occur in the environment, most mental health administrators do not respond by transforming the direction of the organization.

Many times organizations, like public mental health agencies, are constrained by state and federal rules and regulations that preclude major change without legislative action. A number of public academic health centers (AHCs), for example, have lobbied their respective state legislatures to create new public authorities or private nonprofit corporations that allow the teaching hospitals to function without state personnel and purchasing restrictions (Topping, Hyde, Barker, & Woodrell, 1999). The AHCs argue that this major change will allow them to become more efficient and thereby compete more effectively in the managed care environment. Administrators often exhibit common sense when they do not respond immediately to environmental upheavals. It is generally believed that in every industry, sector, or profession, a body of knowledge (i.e., what everyone who knows the industry, sector, or profession understands) exists that serves as a road map describing "how to do business" (Spender, 1989). Those running substance-abuse organizations, for instance, share among themselves the recipe for funding success, staff hiring, and advocacy activities. In the face of major change, directors of substance-abuse organizations will fall back on familiar tactics, not something new and unknown.

When major change occurs in the external environment, mental health administrators face a "catch-22" situation. Launching a revolution in your mental health organization is like charting new waters. Typically, the recipe has changed (e.g., the operational rules under fee-for-service [FFS] vs. managed care), and no one knows what is the best course of action. Changing the direction of the mental health organization is very risky at this point, and what may make more sense is a piecemeal, "testing the waters" type of strategy. On the other hand, most administrators are aware of the "first mover" advantage. Pioneering moves that are successful are generally implemented well in advance of crises and result from careful scrutiny and interpretation of the environment. It appears that the most effective mental health administrators tend to be those who foresee the need for major change and implement the change strategy (Tushman, Newman, & Romanelli, 1997). Often, it is best to act before one is forced to, thereby allowing more time to plan the transition.

Still, in reality, few mental health organizations change willingly. Unfortunately, most organizations implement major change when a crisis threatens survival and drastic action is necessary. Remember the previous section described some mental health administrators as being committed to the status quo, successfully blocking out the changing environment and misinterpreting the cues. As a result, pressure from external stakeholders is generally the reason for change—not influence from inside the organization. What is also interesting about a transformation is that it generally takes an outsider to set change in motion. Many times the inside administrator lacks the energy, leadership ability, or commitment to carry through with an internal revolution. It generally takes a new administrative team that is not linked to the status quo to bring excitement and a fresh set of assumptions and strategies to the organization.

Although revolutionary change is important, change also occurs incrementally or in a series of small steps. Findings from change research indicate that this type of change predominates in most organizations. Incremental change is less disruptive, giving the organization time to adjust to the change process. It also allows for fine-tuning that is very useful when implementing change, especially in a new environment. Furthermore, incremental change can be tied in with the strategic planning process and used to evaluate progress. Still, it is not very useful in times of crisis. When survival is the goal, revolutionary change is needed. Mental health administrators have to be careful about waiting until a crisis to implement change. Although times of adversity and crisis may generate innovation, these are usually the times when successful implementation is less likely. Resources are scarce and time is a luxury. For example, one state's division of mental health waited to fix a badly broken system until it came under attack by the press for a number of questionable deaths. With legislators, press, and consumers breathing down their necks, it was no time for the mental health administrators to be attempting quick repairs.

Change as Transition: A Continuous Process

Revolutionary change represents a dramatic and sharp shift of organizational direction, whereas incremental change involves small steps that represent adjustments to environmental changes or fine-tuning of the direction of the mental health organization. The former can be disruptive; the latter generally is not, resulting in long periods of calm and relatively smooth adjustments. Actually, strategic shifts in organizations can take years if not decades to accomplish, and the change is typically a combination of both revolutionary and incremental change. Consider IBM and its recent success in the marketplace. A new CEO was hired in the early 1990s to re-shape the mission and direction of IBM, and over time, using revolutionary and incremental change, he has accomplished that objective.

Figure 5.3 depicts the continual nature of the organizational change process. This model of change is based on Tushman and Romanelli's (1985) punctuated equilibrium model of change that posits that organizations proceed through long periods of incremental change interrupted by revolutions. To summarize this model, given a major environmental change like the advent of managed care in the public sector, responses are generally crude and experimental because stability and certainty are diminished by the impact of this environmental jolt. This leads to a period of ferment in which the mental health organization attempts to make sense out of the change. During the period of ferment, incremental change predominates. For example, a mental health organization might test a few cost-cutting measures while investigating a short-term alliance with a local MCO. Simultaneously, several forces of change begin to build until one eventually triggers revolutionary change within the mental health organization. It is at this time that a dominant new strategy is recognized (e.g., formal partnerships between public-sector organizations and private for-profit behavioral health MCOs). This new strategy or recipe may be pioneered by the mental health organization itself (being the first mover) or copied from other first-mover organizations. A good example of this is the continuous quality improvement (CQI) programs that many mental health organizations have implemented in an attempt to decrease cost and improve quality. However, after the dominant strategy (revolutionary change) is accepted and implementation begins, it is followed by a period of adjustment or incremental change in which the managerial innovation has to be refined and readjusted to fit the particular agency.

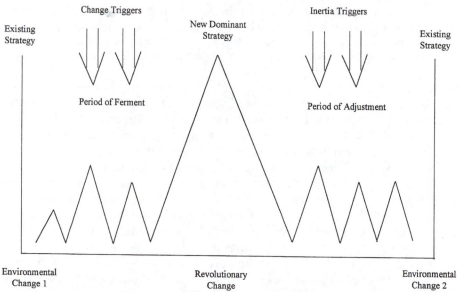

FIGURE 5.3. The dynamics of strategic change.

In all phases, there will be resistance to change, but during the period of adjustment or implementation the triggers of inertia begin in earnest. These are powerful forces that obscure threats and create resistance in organizations and can lead to failure if not managed correctly. One study (Hambrick & D'Aveni, 1988), investigating 57 large bankruptcies occurring between 1972 and 1982, found that few happened suddenly. Most of the bankruptcies had a 10-year decline in accounting performance, but forces of inertia built up a powerful momentum to block change. One of the best safeguards against failure is a leader who knows where the roadblocks are in a mental health organization. Are the forces of inertia in this mental health organization powerful enough to block change? What political strategies can be implemented to prevent this from happening? Roadblocks to change are discussed in more detail in the next section.

Roadblocks to Change

Change is a difficult and complex phenomenon, probably more so than most mental health administrators realize. The failure of organizations to implement change is legendary. This is particularly true when pioneering revolutionary change. Any situation involving change can generate a great deal of tension between those initiating change and those implementing change, as well as between those implementing it and those on the receiving end. Why does this conflict happen? Mostly, people fear uncertainty, and change brings with it surprise and confusion. Because of this, staff members in a mental health organization may view change as a loss of control and a threat to current jobs. They may see it as an infringement on their turf, or a way of requiring more effort and work from them.

Peter Senge in *The Dance of Change* (1999) observed:

> Self-proclaimed "change agents" often complain that "people resist change." But the people or groups typecast as resistant rarely see themselves that way. Often, instead, they believe themselves to be quite open. From a systems viewpoint, it is not the people "who are resisting"—rather, it is a system functioning to maintain its internal balances, as all living systems function. (p. 558)

It seems that many times mental health administrators fight against this balancing process, rather than trying to understand what is happening. They push harder; the system pushes back just as hard. Regardless of the reason, resistance is inherent in the change process. It cannot be eradicated, so it is very important that mental health administrators understand where resistance arises and why.

Some of the roadblocks that serve as barriers to organizational change are presented in Table 5.1. The bureaucracy of an organization can serve as a strong barrier to change. Generally, organizations develop specific competencies or areas in which they excel. The Kaleidoscope Program in Chicago is known for its work with troubled youth and families; consequently, it has built its competencies around the provision of unconditional, individual care in providing in-home family support services and therapeutic foster care to this population (VanDenBerg, 1999). In order to capitalize on these competencies, it has put into place certain routines and rules, such as a team structure, decision-making rules, and treatment procedures, that act to comple-

TABLE 5.1. Roadblocks to Change

Bureaucracy and administrative controls
   Rules and routines
Organizational culture
Organization's history
   Past performance
   Strong leader
Size/age
Lack of resources
People and politics

ment competencies. Once these administrative systems and bureaucratic hierarchies are in place, they reinforce the status quo and act as a barrier to change. In addition to controls, the organizational culture plays a major role in resistance. Culture is a set of beliefs, norms, and values that are shared by the organizational members and serve as a basis for behavior. In this role, the culture of the mental health organization can be a very effective barrier to change.

Another roadblock to change is past performance. If a mental health organization has been successful in the past, the tendency is to continue the status quo. When a particular strategy is successful over a long period of time, the inclination is to continue down that road regardless of environmental jolts to the contrary. Who wants to change something that has been so effective for so long? Consider how slowly assertive community treatment (ACT) programs replaced traditional hospital and aftercare programs, despite the potential cost savings associated with ACT. Related to this is the successful, longtime mental health administrator. Called the "founding effect," a strong leader in a mental health agency puts his or her imprint on the organization, making change challenging. Size and age of a mental health organization are also factors that influence ease of change, because resistance increases as the mental health organization becomes larger and older. With age and size come rules and routines that make it difficult to implement change.

Many organizations put off change until a crisis, and frequently the crisis is financial. Mental health organizations find themselves without the necessary resources to implement change. This lack of resources can create a big barrier to change. Lastly, staff members can be a source of resistance because they may not understand the need for change. Change is a disruption that people may resist because they don't want to alter what they have been doing for years. Consider academic health centers and the resistance to policy recommendations to increase medical training in primary care, or mental health agencies and the resistance to consumer involvement in the design and implementation of mental health services. Of course, where there are people, politics exist, and when change becomes part of the agenda, politics intensify. Remember—the motivation to preserve the mental health organization can serve to entrench current leaders who are antichange.

Resistance to change should be seen as a management challenge. When faced with resistance from staff, many mental health administrators react forcefully. Resistance cannot be controlled, stopped, or made to go away. Therefore, a wiser approach utilizes resistance to change rather than combating it. Change agents have to deal with resistance if they are going to implement change in their mental health organization. Mental health administrators need to accept the fact that every change creates resistance and, consequently, the forces of resistance must be explored willingly for causes. Others in the organization have different points of view, so their understanding of the need to change will be different. The next section describes the implementation process and various strategies that can be used to facilitate change.

IMPLEMENTATION OF CHANGE

A common mistake made by mental health administrators is to view the formulation of a change strategy and the implementation of the strategy as two distinct phases. They are both part of one continuous process and should be approached as such. It is extremely important that the "how to bring about change" is integrated with the "content of change."

Guiding the Transition: Strategies for Change

Management and implementation of change are probably two of the most troublesome and challenging tasks. How do you keep regular operations going while also trying to implement the change agenda? There are many things that can be done to help improve the implementation process, but many mental health managers believe that they do not have time. Senge (1999) considers the "not enough time" excuse as one of the greatest challenges to change—one that signals a lack of flexibility and ability to prioritize. Yet, by automatically anticipating resistance to change, a mental health administrator can develop strategies ahead of time that will lead to successful implementation. What are some of the other forces that can be used to promote change? See Table 5.2 for a listing of the forces that facilitate change in a mental health organization.

Encouraging Open Communication. One of the most important strategies in facilitating change is to encourage open communication. Early on in the process, administrative and clinical staff must feel that they can express different opinions without repercussions. Everyone participates in the discussion of the issues, providing opportunity for a common definition of the problem to develop.

TABLE 5.2. **Strategies That Promote Change**

Open communication
Champions
Stakeholder coalitions
Outside consultants
Change teams
Internal systems
   Shared culture and incentive systems
Partnerships

Another tactic to enhance communication is discussion forums. Here, questions are asked, ideas are contributed, and confrontation of each other's underlying assumptions can occur. Listening and responding to concerns will help members understand what is happening in all parts of the mental health organization. This takes time and effort, but the results are worth it according to Jack Welch, CEO of General Electric. Welch is probably one of the most successful change agents in the world, and he described the process as labor intensive yet invaluable. Welch even recommended administrators walk the halls and share lunch with staff as he does to facilitate open communication.

Winning Over Stakeholders. Stakeholders are those individuals, groups, and organizations that have a stake in the decisions and actions of the organization and attempt to influence those decisions and actions (Blair & Fottler, 1990). Mental health administrators must realize that there are limitations to how much they can accomplish alone. This is particularly true in the environment today, where multiple stakeholders exist and conflicts of interest are becoming more and more apparent. A critical mass of support for change is needed, accomplished by winning over key power groups, such as state legislators, consumer groups, and federal agencies. Thus, it is important that mental health administrators, when implementing change, consider various strategies to influence and win over these stakeholders.

When considering various stakeholder groups, one of the significant forces of change is the use of champions. Studies looking at diffusion of practice protocols to physicians in the field have found that adoption takes a champion, typically someone visible and of prominent status in the medical community, to promote changes. Topping and Hartwig (1997) found that the development of an HIV/AIDS clinic in a very conservative rural community was enhanced by a series of respected, high-status champions.

Rogers (1983) suggested that along with the champions, administrators identify opinion leaders in the organization and elicit their help in supporting the change agenda. That is, a change agent, such as a CMHC administrator, should identify persons in the organization (e.g., a psychiatrist, psychiatric nurse, or social worker) who are able to influence the attitudes and behaviors of other individuals in the mental health organization. The administrator seeks the support of these opinion leaders, thereby working to initiate change through them. However, in using opinion leaders, the mental health administrator must be careful to include them in the initial planning phases of the change process and keep the channels of communication open throughout the process. In this way, there is less chance that they will become part of the opposition.

There are multiple stakeholders at all levels of the mental health organization involved in making change happen, and their assumptions, perspectives, and agendas do not always converge. Although administrators cannot control some of the environmental forces discussed earlier in this chapter, they can influence the way staff members interact. If all of those affected by the change share an understanding of what change is needed, why it is needed, and how they will be affected, there is a far better chance of it succeeding. Nevertheless, the question remains of who should be involved in implementing change.

In attempting to answer this question, many would argue that the entire mental health organization should be involved. Yet because each person will view the change differently, it is probably not wise to treat everyone the same. Rosabeth Kanter and her colleagues (1992) believed that three groups should be considered in the change process:

> *Strategists*—The Strategists lay the foundation for change and craft the vision. They identify the need for change, while also paying attention to selling the plan to all constituencies. Strategists are important to the change process because without them, change generally would not occur. Although formulation is important, they must start thinking about implementation early in the development.
>
> *Implementers*—The Implementers not only develop and institute the steps necessary to enact the change plan but also manage the coordination among all parts of the organization and the relationships between the people involved. These are the persons that make it happen by managing the day-to-day operational process of change. The Implementers need strategies for overcoming resistance, such as communication tools; transition structures, such as teams, training, and development; and reward systems.
>
> *Recipients*—The Recipients either adopt or fail to adopt the change plan; therefore, they give the desired change its ultimate shape. Although Recipients can be a major source of resistance, it is useful to understand how they perceive the change and how they experience it.

Each of these three groups has a specific role in the process of change, and strategies must be devised that enhance the participation of each. One thing that Strategists should remember is that they need allies in the change process. Allies should be brought in ahead of time—before the plan is made public. Often this can result in improvements to the original change agenda. Another strategy that can be used is bringing in outsiders to help set the stage for change and guide the implementation. Many mental health organizations use outside consultants for this very purpose. Not only do they bring new ideas and excitement to a change agenda, but also they bring a sense of independence, thereby giving the need for change more validity. Many mental health administrators bring in outside experts in team-building, for instance, when introducing new clinical interventions requiring team-oriented care.

Using Teams for Innovation. One of the most crucial times for mental health administrators is that of crisis. The challenge is to solve the problem while simultaneously stopping it from interfering with the operation of the mental health organization. The tendency at a time like this is to centralize control—to manage with tighter reins. Although the need for fast decision making may necessitate doing that, centralizing control is risky. Leaders need help facing crises. They need teams that are of manageable size to allow for efficient, rapid communication (Fried, Topping, & Rundall, 1999). They need teams composed of stakeholders in the organization who can contribute to the solution of the problem while also influencing others positively in the change process. At the same time, by using teams, staff members are involved in the change process, allowing them time to prepare psychologically for the change.

Nadler and Tushman (1997) described how Kaiser Permanente's northern California region Hospitals and Health Plan responded to the changing health care environment in the early 1990s. After careful consideration, it was decided to adopt a customer focus in all operations. In order to implement this major change in orientation, a new organizational design was required that removed walls between departments and functions while opening up the flow of information and coordination. This structural change was accomplished using a strategic design team to fully assess the need and to recommend a full-scale plan for reorganization.

Motivating Constructive Behavior Internally. A shared culture is an additional force that can be used to support and motivate change. It is very important that members of the organization share the same explicit set of values about where the organization is going and why. Shared values inspire commitment and cooperation because everyone has the same vision of the future. In addition, if change occurs, the staff must be reoriented and redirected. This requires education and training. Another important element is the development of a structure and a process to implement change. It is surprising how many mental health organizations start full-scale change programs with no idea of how coordination is to be accomplished and who is accountable for various tasks. Many wraparound programs, for instance, have been implemented with little thought as to how individualized, community-based services to children with serious emotional disturbance would be coordinated among the various agencies involved in their care.

Another aspect of the internal operations to be considered is the provision of signals indicating change is important. A reward system that recognizes the extra work that change requires is crucial. Often it is necessary to use symbolic words, acts, and physical representations to enhance the perception of support of change, while being careful not to give conflicting or incorrect signals. For instance, as part of a major General Motors reorganization, officials selected a special day to remove the Buick sign from the plant and replace it with the new one. Unfortunately, they selected the same day that fourth-generation Buick workers and families were gathered in Flint, Michigan, for a formal recognition dinner (Nadler, Tushman, & Nadler, 1998). In this case, management's actions did send the message intended by setting aside the special day for replacing the sign, that all Buick workers are significant, but served to separate and alienate workers who were unable to attend due to the scheduling conflict.

Building Networks and Alliances. Often, available resources are a major factor in the process of change. A good way to increase availability of resources is to build relationships with other organizations. An example of a successful alliance is the Health Care for the Homeless (HCH) program set up to take care of the homeless in Jacksonville, Florida (Bogue & Hall, 1997). This alliance involves not only an on-site medical clinic, but also, due to the high incidence of mental illness, an on-site program with the Mental Health Resources Center. Three full-time mental health counselors work with the clinic staff to provide case management. Because many homeless persons have comorbid disorders, mental health care includes on-site drug and alcohol rehabilitation programs, support groups, and referrals to permanent housing facilities.

Successful collaboration requires hard work and care. For alliances to be successful, mental health administrators must view the relationships as strategically important. There must be adequate resources, management attention and commitment, and sponsorship of the alliance. Compatible cultures, clear objectives, and an understanding of mutual benefits between alliance members are necessary for successful collaboration to occur. Managers must work to integrate the organizations to maintain communication and control. Furthermore, in order for these relationships to endure, trust must exist between organizations. Partnerships have to be built on ethical values that are clearly articulated, communicated, and enforced (Sifonis & Goldberg, 1996). The Alaska Youth Initiative Demonstration Project was a 5-year effort to improve services to children with severe emotional disturbance and their families using interdisciplinary teams to provide individualized services (Burchard, Burchard, Sewell, & VanDenBerg, 1993). This project demonstrated that successful teams involved providers from agencies who believed in the same philosophy of care and basic values.

In addition, mental health organizations have to change internally in order to accommodate an alliance. The reward structure must take collaboration into consideration. Training and education are necessary as well. Thus, change in the boundaries of the organization can only happen successfully if changes occur internally, encouraging everyone to buy into the notion that collaboration is important to the whole mental health organization.

LOOKING AHEAD AS A MENTAL HEALTH ADMINISTRATOR: SOME SPECIAL CHALLENGES

This section identifies some of the challenges facing mental health organizations in the future and how these influence the perspective of change. These special challenges include the further penetration of managed care into the public sector, stakeholder diversity and empowerment, and the changing role of state psychiatric hospitals. The final challenge is to the mental health administrator, who must come to terms with change and use it opportunistically.

The Special Challenge of Managed Care and the Public Sector

Although managed care has entered American medicine with remarkable speed, there is considerable debate as to its effectiveness and future role (Sederer & Bennett, 1996). What is the magnitude of costs savings achieved by managed care? What managed care mechanism is the most effective in reducing costs? Will managed care be able to improve access, satisfy consumers, and develop linkages between fragmented providers? Lastly, will managed care represent a permanent or temporary presence? Gold (1999), for example, showed that health care costs started to stabilize in the early 1990s but recently have begun to increase again. Coincidentally, health maintenance organization (HMO) operating margins began to decline, while premiums began to rise.

One issue to consider is the rapid move of the public sector to adapt managed care (Cutler, McFarland, & Winthrop, 1998). This means that state- and community-based organizations must develop sophistication in contract development, implementation, and monitoring. Administrators and clinical staff, in turn, have to acquire new skills to operate more effectively in that environment. Another side to this issue is the entrance of private, and often for-profit, MCOs into the public arena for both general health and mental health sectors. Private, for-profit, managed behavioral health firms are recognizing that the private-sector market is stabilizing, so they are turning to the public sector for growth (Feldman, Baler, & Penner, 1997). For example, public-sector contracts with private behavioral health MCOs exist at the state level in Massachusetts, Hawaii, Iowa, Colorado, Utah, and Ohio and at the local level in California, New York, and Washington (Feldman et al., 1997; Libby, 1997). In some contracts, mental health services are part of a larger health care program, most notably in HMOs (Hodgkin, Horgan, & Garnick, 1997). These service delivery arrangements typically emphasize acute-care mental health problems and are criticized as being too limited to serve effectively persons who are severely mentally ill (Mechanic, Schlesinger, & McAlpine, 1995).

Often, mental health benefits are managed separately from general health services in a carve-out arrangement. Here, the specialty MCO will contract with providers. This arrangement, at times, may develop into partnerships between traditional public-sector service providers and private, for-profit MCOs. For example, in Tidewater Virginia the MCO that was awarded a Medicaid contract subcapitated with the local CMHC to provide nonhospital care to individuals with severe mental disorders (Fried et al., 2000). In essence, the MCO and CMHC formed a partnership that involved risk sharing for both parties.

The increase in private firms offering mental health coverage in the public sector has come with considerable resistance. Many critics argue that people on Medicaid differ from the employed population with regard to ethnicity, acuity, health care seeking behavior, and social problems (Feldman et al., 1997). They believe that the private not-for-profit MCO does not have the expertise and sense of commitment required to serve this population. For example, one of the basic concerns involves the accessibility and availability of nontraditional services, such as assertive community training (ACT), rehabilitation, housing, and employment support in a managed care environment. Furthermore, consumers have to learn new rules to operate in the managed care environment. This may lead to confusion and resistance. Extending the argument, Snowden (1998) questioned the impact on ethnic minority populations:

> Little has been written about the impact of managed care on ethnic minority populations. Financial and sociocultural barriers, although receding, continue to prevent minority persons from making timely and productive use of mental health treatment. Careful attention must be given to whether managed care will reduce existing problems facing minorities, have no effect, or create new problems of its own. (p. 581)

Other major problems center on the difference in cultures between private and public organizations. For that matter, it is possible that a serious clash of attitudes and perceptions may occur between the two. For instance, many in the public sector view all private-sector MCOs as having ulterior motives for taking over the role of the public sector (Egnew & Baler, 1998). These critics automatically assume that anything having to do with profit is dirty work. Often this leads to problems integrating public-sector behavioral health services with private-sector health plans. This happened with the implementation of the Oregon Health Plan begun in 1994 (Cutler et al., 1998). Although capitation and an expansion of Medicaid enrollment to include the working poor have been achieved throughout Oregon, there are still basic questions about the long-term integration of public, private not-for-profit, and private for-profit entities into a nonfragmented whole to adequately serve individuals with severe mental illness.

The Challenge of Stakeholder Diversity and Empowerment

In her latest book, Herzlinger (1997) discussed the forces of change that have reshaped massive parts of the American economy (e.g., retailing, information, automotive, and manufacturing) and are now at work on health care. Herzlinger believed that this force comes in the form of well-educated consumers who are empowered by information and are assertive in their demands to take part in their treatment. Examples of this phenomenon abound in the mental health sector, including consumer and family advocacy initiatives (Briggs, 1996). The assumption is that people with serious mental illness (i.e., psychiatric survivors) should have increased voice and choice (e.g., democratic participation and self-determination) in treatment decisions. Thus, in the traditional relationship between consumers and mental health professionals, the professionals change from experts and technicians to resources and collaborators (Nelson, Walsh-Bowers, & Hall, 1998). The consumers, of course, move from a position of dependency to developing their own autonomous organization or otherwise influencing the policies and practices of the mental health agency.

As part of the empowerment movement and the changing environment, mental health organizations have had to face increasingly diverse stakeholders. Of course, all organizations have stakeholders. Nonetheless, Blair and Fottler (1998) believed that the health care environment is becoming so complex that managers should be looking at stakeholder relationships in terms of a strategic web. In doing this, mental health administrators are able in visualize a complex set of interrelated strategic relationships and develop skills in strategic navigation or in finding the way through a complex set of informal and formal relationships.

Given the complexity of the mental health environment today, think about the number and diversity of the stakeholders that impact an organization. How would the strategic web look? Potential stakeholders may include but are not limited to state legislators, state agencies (e.g., mental health, public health, human/social services), Medicaid, federal agencies, and community and state psychiatric hospitals. It is important to note that the relevance of a particular stakeholder may increase or decrease, depending on changes in the environment. For instance, the importance of the relationship between mental health and criminal justice is presently high because almost 7% of the total persons incarcerated have a severe mental illness while approximately 13% have significant psychiatric problems that require intermittent care (Emery, Glover, & Mazade, 1998). Hence, the criminal justice system should play an important role in the strategic web of most mental health organizations. Other trends that need to be considered in determining relevant stakeholders are:

- Nearly 10 million individuals are believed to have both a substance-abuse and a mental health disorder (Emery et al., 1998);

- Women are becoming an important consumer group, especially when considering the relationship between violence and sexual abuse and mental health problems (Newmann, Greenley, Sweeney, & Van Dien, 1998);
- With increasing awareness of child mental health needs, pressure is mounting to decrease out-of-state placements and provide community-based services to children with serious emotional disorders (SEDs) (Stroul et al., 1997);
- A major demographic shift is occurring that involves the aging population, in general, and the mental health needs of aging women, in particular (Padgett, Burns, & Grau, 1998).
- As performance outcomes are tied increasingly to financial incentives, more national organizations and accrediting entities are attempting to assume a role in the development and monitoring of these measures (e.g., American Managed Behavioral Healthcare Association [AMBHA], National Alliance for the Mentally Ill [NAMI], National Commission on Quality Assurance [NCQA]) (Emery et al., 1998; Granello, Granello, Lee, et al., 1999).

Figure 5.4 represents the strategic web of a typical rural CMHC. The complexity of the relationships is a function of the interdependence between the various organizations. In this case, the rural location may decrease the number and diversity of relationships. An urban CMHC would have more stakeholders because more mental health and social service organizations exist in cities; however, Fig. 5.4 demonstrates the complexity of stakeholder management for a rural CMHC.

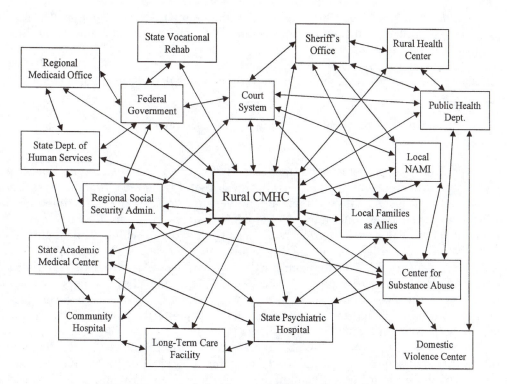

FIGURE 5.4. Stakeholder strategic web for rural CMHC.

The Changing Role of State Psychiatric Hospitals

Many state psychiatric hospitals are closing, whereas others are being downsized or reorganized. From 1990 to 1996, 37 out of 263 were closed, with an additional 8 to be closed in the next 2 years (Emery et al., 1998). In some states, the operation and management of these hospitals are being outsourced or "privatized." As a result, community hospital inpatient psychiatry units are being repositioned to fulfill the role of state psychiatric hospitals. This shift in service is putting tremendous pressure on these units, and, in the long run, may have considerable impact on the quality of inpatient mental health care. Druss and colleagues (Druss, Bruce, Jacobs, & Hoff, 1998), in their study of community hospital inpatient psychiatry units, found four trends that are problematic:

1. A poorer, sicker, and more chronic group of patients is being treated.
2. Length of stay (LOS) is decreasing, whereas readmissions are increasing.
3. Medicaid admissions show a more rapid decline in LOS.
4. Medicaid patients with psychotic diagnoses are more at risk for readmission.

This pattern may reflect the trend of more brief, crisis-oriented admissions replacing fewer, longer hospitalizations, with this effect being stronger for Medicaid admissions and those with psychotic diagnoses than for those admitted otherwise. How this will affect the quality of mental health care can only be answered over time.

Belcher and DeForge (1997) argued that persons with severe mental illnesses need long-term care, but the community hospitals, geared to short-term stays, are inappropriate for this role:

> One of the most glaring problems that has arisen as a result of dismantling the state hospital is that people who do not quickly respond to community-based treatments and are in need of structured care are often left without a place to receive appropriate treatment. This problem was identified in the 1970s and unfortunately persists in the 1990s. (p. 67)

Added to the problem of treatment and patient care, downsizing and closure also create human resource problems. In the case of downsizing, morale decreases substantially as a sense of guilt rises among the survivors. At the same time, those laid off experience considerable psychological distress in the form of depression, feelings of betrayal, and sometimes violence. The degree to which clinical and administrative staff is affected is a function of how the downsizing is handled (Whetten, Keiser, & Urban, 1995). Take for example the downsizing of Middletown Psychiatric Center located in New York state (Citrome, 1997). Using an orderly process, management was able to share information ahead of rumors, notifying staff as to the targeted positions, and providing employee assistance in resumé-writing services and in contacting potential employers.

Regardless of the challenge, the mental health administrators face a changing future that will require certain skills to negotiate changes for themselves and for their clinical and administrative staff. Those in managed care environments, particularly those in the public sector, will have to hone their negotiation and contracting skills while also dealing with the problem of changing perceptions and beliefs. New skills are needed not only for meeting the demands of managed care but also for the management of diverse, often empowered, stakeholders. Lastly, the relationships with state psychiatric and community hospitals have to change, while administrators are left, in some cases, with staff shell-shocked from downsizing, retrenchment, and closures.

Meeting the Final Challenge: Coming to Terms With Change

Although Emery et al. (1998) focused on SMHAs, their advice is applicable to all mental health administrators:

> The intensity, diversity, and rapidity of changes that have buffeted state mental health agencies will continue into the foreseeable future. To survive such a turbulent environment, it is incumbent upon SMHAs to acquire the adaptive skills and organizational capacities that permit them to anticipate and proactively respond to change. (p. 346)

This chapter has attempted to provide an understanding of organizational change and the change process, and, in so doing, identify some of the skills needed to implement a change agenda in mental health organizations.

The future challenge for mental health managers is to be able to interpret the environment so as to respond effectively to the inevitable changes that will transpire. The move of managed care into the public domain brings with it many threats and opportunities. Yet in order to take advantage of the latter, the mental health administrator must think in terms of fresh and innovative approaches to the new environment, such as partnerships and alliances with organizations different in culture and goals. Along with these changes, however, come problems. Administrators of both for-profit behavioral health MCOs and public mental health organizations must realize that inherent in the different cultures are different perceptions and criticisms that have to be managed.

At the same time, stakeholder diversity and empowerment have created and will continue to cause upheavals in mental health organizations. The treatment role has changed; the potential for stakeholder influence has intensified; and the role of stakeholder management has taken on added significance. The mental health administrator who doesn't realize this and act accordingly will not survive. The roles of other organizations that are interdependent with mental health are also changing. Examples of this phenomenon include the role community hospitals are beginning to play in treating individuals with serious mental disorders, and the impact MCOs and HMOs are having on the mental health sector. Again, new relationships and structures, such as joint ventures and partnerships, are inevitable. Often these kinds of changes lead to problems in gaining the acceptance of such a change agenda.

Obviously, change is something that mental health managers cannot avoid. As a result, they need to think in terms of the process. Proper planning of a change agenda is important, especially the inclusion of influential stakeholders and the integration of formulation and implementation. Resistance is inevitable, so it should be part of the plans as well. As this chapter has demonstrated, strategies can be developed that decrease resistance, while enhancing acceptance of change. The effective mental health administrator must devote time to develop a proper change agenda if he or she wants to see change accomplished. As Peter Senge (1999) implied with his book title, change agents must learn the "dance of change."

ACKNOWLEDGMENT

This chapter was completed, in part, while the author was a postdoctoral fellow in the Mental Health Services and Systems Research Training Program at the Cecil G. Sheps Center for Health Services Research at the University of North Carolina at Chapel Hill and Duke University Medical Center.

REFERENCES

Argyris, C. (1985). *Strategy, change, and defensive routines.* Cambridge, MA: Ballinger.

Barr, P. S. (1998). Adapting to unfamiliar environmental events: A look at the evolution of interpretation and its role in strategic change. *Organization Science, 9*(6), 644–669.

Belcher, J. R., & DeForge, B. R. (1997). The appropriate role for the state hospital. *Journal of Mental Health Administration, 24*(1), 64–71.

Blair, J. D., & Fottler, M. D. (1990). *Challenges in health care management: Strategic perspectives for managing key stakeholders.* San Francisco: Jossey-Bass.

Blair, J. D., & Fottler, M. D. (1998). *Strategic leadership for medical groups: Navigating your strategic web.* San Francisco: Jossey-Bass.

Bogue, R., & Hall, C. H. (1997). *Health network innovations: How 20 communities are improving their systems through collaboration.* Chicago: American Hospital Publishing.

Briggs, H. E. (1996). Creating independent voices: The emergence of statewide family advocacy networks. *Journal of Mental Health Administration, 23*(4), 447–457.

Burchard, J. D., Burchard, S. N., Sewell, R., & VanDenBerg, J. (1993). *One kid at a time: Evaluative case studies and description of the Alaska Youth Initiative demonstration project.* Washington, DC: Georgetown University Child Development Center.

Citrome, L. (1997). Layoffs, reductions-in-force, downsizing, rightsizing: The case of a state psychiatric hospital. *Administration and Policy in Mental Health, 24*(6), 523–533.

Cutler, D. L., McFarland, B. H., & Winthrop, K. (1998). Mental health in the Oregon health plan: Fragmentation or integration? *Administration and Policy in Mental Health, 25*(4), 361–368.

Davis, H. R., & Salasin, S. E. 1980. Change: Decisions and their implementation. *Administration of mental health services* (2nd ed.). Springfield, IL: Charles C. Thomas.

Druss, B. G., Bruce, M. L., Jacobs, S. C., & Hoff, R. A. (1998). Trends over a decade for a general hospital psychiatry unit. *Administration and Policy in Mental Health, 25*(4), 427–435.

Egnew, R. C., & Baler, S. G. (1998). Developing principles, goals, and models for public/private partnerships. *Administration and Policy in Mental Health, 25*(6), 571–580.

Emery, B. D., Glover, R. W., & Mazade, N. A. (1998). The environmental trends facing state mental health agencies. *Administration and Policy in Mental Health, 25*(3), 337–347.

Fahey, L., & Narayanan, V. K. (1986). *Macroenvironmental analysis for strategic management.* St. Paul, MN: West.

Feldman, S., Baler, S., & Penner, S. (1997). The role of private-for-profit managed behavioral health in the public sector. *Administration and Policy in Mental Health, 24*(5), 379–389.

Fombrun, C. J. (1992). *Turning points: Creating strategic change in corporations.* New York: McGraw-Hill.

Fried, B. J., Topping, S., Morrissey, J. P., Ellis, A. R., Stroup, S., & Blank, M. (2000). Comparing provider perceptions of access and utilization management in full-risk and no-risk Medicaid programs for adults with serious mental illness. *Journal of Behavioral Health Services & Research, 27*(1), 29–46.

Fried, B., Topping, S., & Rundall, T. G. (1999). Groups and teams in health services organizations. In S. Shortell & A. Kaluzny. *Health care management: Organization, design, and behavior* (4th ed., pp. 154–190). Albany, NY: Delmar.

Ginter, P. M., Swayne, L. E., & Duncan, W. J. (1998). *Strategic management of health care organizations.* Malden, MA: Blackwell.

Gold, M. (1999). The changing US health care system: Challenges for responsible public policy. *Milbank Quarterly, 77*(1), 3–37.

Granello, D. H., Granello, P. F., & Lee, F. (1999). Client satisfaction in a partial hospitalization program. *Journal of Behavioral Health Services & Research, 26*(1), 50–61.

Grob, G. N. (1992, Fall). Mental health policy in America: Myths and realities. *Health Affairs,* pp. 7–21.

Hadley, T. R. (1996). Financing changes and their impact on the organization of the public mental health system. *Administration and Policy in Mental Health, 23*(5), 393–405.

Hambrick, D. C., & D'Aveni, R. A. (1988). Large corporate failures as downward spirals. *Administrative Science Quarterly, 33,* 1–23.

Hargrove, D. S., & Melton, G. B. (1987). Block grants and rural mental health services. *Journal of Rural Community Psychology, 4*(1), 4–11.

Herzlinger, R. E. (1997). *Market-driven health care: Who wins, who loses in the transformation of America's largest service industry.* Reading, MA: Addison-Wesley.

Hodgkin, D., Horgan, C. M., & Garnick, D. W. (1997). Make or buy: HMOs' contracting arrangements for mental health care. *Administration and Policy in Mental Health, 24*(4), 359–376.

Javidan, M. (1984). The impact of environmental uncertainty on long-range planning practices of the U.S. saving and loan industry. *Strategic Management Journal, 5,* 381–392.

Kanter, R. M., Stein, B. A., & Jick, T. D. (1992). *The challenge of organizational change.* New York: Free Press.

Libby, A. M. (1997). Contracting between public and private providers: A survey of mental health services in California. *Administration and Policy in Mental Health, 24*(4), 323–331.

Mechanic, D., & Rosenthal, M. (1999). Responses of HMO medical directors to trust building in managed care. *Milbank Quarterly, 77*(3), 283–303.

Mechanic, D., Schlesinger, M., & McAlpine, D. D. (1995). Management of mental health and substance abuse services: State of the art and early results. *Milbank Quarterly, 73*(1), 19–55.

Mechanic, D., & Surles, R. C. (1992, Fall). Challenges in state mental health policy and administration. *Health Affairs,* pp. 34–50.

Nadler, D. A., Tushman, M. L., & Nadler, M. B. (1997). *Competing by design: The power of organizational architecture.* New York: Oxford University Press.

Nelson, G., Walsh-Bowers, R., & Hall, G. B. (1998). Housing for psychiatric survivors: Values, policy, and research. *Administration and Policy in Mental Health, 25*(4), 455–462.

Newmann, J. P., Greenley, D., Sweeney, J. K., & Van Dien, G. (1998). Abuse histories, severe mental illness, and the cost of care. In B. L. Levin, A. K. Blanch, & A. Jennings (Eds.), *Women's mental health services: A public health perspective* (pp. 279–308). Thousand Oaks, CA: Sage.

Padgett, D. K., Burns, B. J., & Grau, L. A. (1998). Risk factors and resilience: Mental health needs and services use of older women. In B. L. Levin, A. K. Blanch, & A. Jennings (Eds.), *Women's mental health services: A public health perspective* (pp. 390–413). Thousand Oaks, CA: Sage.

Rogers, E. M. (1983). *Diffusion of innovations* (3rd ed.). New York: Free Press.

Sederer, L. I., & Bennett, M. J. (1996). Managed mental health care in the United States: A status report. *Administration and Policy in Mental Health, 23*(4), 289–306.

Senge, P. (1999). *The dance of change: The challenges of sustaining momentum in learning organizations.* New York: Doubleday.

Sherman, H., & Schultz, R. (1998). *Open boundaries: Creating business innovation through complexity.* Reading, MA: Perseus Books.

Sifonis, J. G., & Goldberg, B. (1996). *Corporation on a tightrope: Balancing leadership, governance, and technology in an age of complexity.* New York: Oxford University Press.

Snowden, L. R. (1998). Managed care and ethnic minority populations. *Administration and Policy in Mental Health, 25*(6), 581–590.

Spender, J.-C. (1989). *Industry recipes: An enquiry into the nature and sources of managerial judgement.* Oxford, England: Basil Blackwell.

Starr, P. (1982). *The social transformation of American medicine.* New York: Basic Books.

Stroul, B. A., Pires, S. A., Roebuck, L., Friedman, R. M., Barrett, B., Chambers, K. L., & Kershaw, M. A. (1997). State health care reforms: How they affect children and adolescents with emotional disorders and their families. *Journal of Mental Health Administration, 24*(4), 386–399.

Thomas, J. B., & McDaniel, R. R. (1990). Interpreting strategic issues: Effects of strategy and the information-processing structure of top management teams. *Academy of Management Journal, 33*(2), 286–306.

Topping, S., & Ginter, P. (1998). Columbia/HCA Healthcare Corporation: A growth and acquisition strategy. In P. M. Ginter, L. E. Swayne, & W. J. Duncan (Eds.), *Strategic management of health care organizations* (3rd ed., pp. 811–824). Malden, MA: Blackwell Business.

Topping, S., & Hartwig, L. (1997). Delivering care to rural HIV/AIDS patients. *Journal of Rural Health, 13*(3), 226–236.

Topping, S., Hyde, J., Barker, J., & Woodrell, F. (1999). Academic health centers in turbulent times: An examination for survival. *Health Care Management Review, 24*(2), 7–18.

Tushman, M. L., Newman, W. H., & Romanelli, E. (1997). Convergence and upheaval: Managing the unsteady pace of organizational evolution. In M. L. Tushman & P. Anderson (Eds.), *Managing strategic innovation and change* (pp. 583–594). New York: Oxford University Press.

Tushman, M. L., & Romanelli, E. (1985). Organizational evolution: A metamorphosis model of convergence and reorientation. In B. M. Staw & L. L. Cummings (Eds.), *Research in organizational behavior* (pp. 171–222). Greenwich, CT: JAI Press.

VanDenBerg, J. (1999). History of the wraparound process. In B. J. Burns, & S. K. Goldman (Eds.), *Promising practices in wraparound for children with serious emotional disturbance and their families* (pp. 1–8). Washington, DC: Georgetown University, National Technical Assistance Center for Children's Mental Health.

Whetten, D. A., Keiser, J. D., & Urban, T. (1995). Implications of organizational downsizing for the human resource management function. In F. R. Ferris, S. D. Rosen, & D. T. Barnum (Eds.), *Handbook of human resource management* (pp. 282–296). Cambridge, MA: Blackwell Publishers.

Yank, G. R., Hargrove, D. S., & Davis, K. E. (1992). Toward the financial integration of public mental health services. *Community Mental Health Journal, 28*(2), 97–109.

Part Two

MENTAL HEALTH CARE MANAGEMENT

INTRODUCTION

Philip E. Veenhuis

Health care organizations require effective management and leadership if they are to be, and remain, productive and competitive. During the first seven decades of the 20th century, leadership in mental health organizations was provided by physicians, usually psychiatrists. The medical profession no longer dominates the leadership of organized health care systems; management and administrative roles are shared with other mental health professions and with management professionals.

Clinicians and professional administrators enter health care management for different reasons, and from different backgrounds. Clinicians have the advantage of knowing their profession, but often lack management skills. Nonclinician administrators have valuable management skills, but are faced with a "business" that, more than most, requires special understanding of its products, services, operations, and "customers." There is little consensus about the extent to which each kind of leader/manager must master the other's field (e.g., how much administrative knowledge a clinician must learn in order to manage a health care organization effectively, or how much clinical knowledge a professional manager must accrue to do the same). In some organizations, management at some or many levels is shared between the two (usually within a hierarchical, rather than equal, relationship).

There are at least three common models, each of which may be found at upper, middle, or lower management levels:

- Shared leadership (e.g., business manager and senior clinician operating as some form of management team).
- Clinician leadership (with one or more nonclinicians in a subordinate role, such as administrator or business manager).
- Business leadership (with a clinician in some important but subordinate role, such as medical director).

Organization size, mission, funding, governance, oversight, and other factors play some role in the management strategy. On the other hand, many organizations appear to have developed their business models more through historical happenstance than rational process.

The chapters in this part provide some familiarity with basic management concepts in health care organizations and some common mental health service settings, and a basic discussion of various mental health professions (including training, scope of practice, and entry into management roles), managed care in mental health organizations, and ethics.

BEYOND THIS BOOK

There is little consensus about the extent of management training required for one to assume a substantial management role in a mental health system. Most clinician-managers, particularly at the unit or clinic level, have had only on-the-job experience. Increasingly, however, clinicians who anticipate careers beyond direct patient care seek formal management and leadership training, whether in brief seminars, longer "certificate" programs, or graduate schools. Continuing education programs in health care management or administration are useful and sometimes comprehensive, often including such topics as budget and finance, human resources, administrative principles, and leadership.

Senior management is a profession in itself. Large organizations are unlikely to entrust substantial management or executive responsibility to people who have not demonstrated considerable depth of knowledge and experience in both the health care field and "generic" management. Clinicians anxious to fill such positions often pursue graduate degrees in business administration (e.g., MBA), health administration (MHA), or public health (MPH, with an administrative rather than clinical focus), either during clinical training or early in their careers. Such comprehensive business education is available part-time for practicing clinicians (in so-called "executive MBA programs," for example), but all require considerable time and effort. Many clinicians who have sought advanced management degrees have trained in schools of public health. Lately, however, the cachet of an MBA has become more and more attractive.

Readers with primarily clinical backgrounds will find in this section several descriptions of, and guides to, management roles in clinical settings. For more comprehensive knowledge of management and leadership per se, they should read the other sections as well. Those new to management or seriously contemplating a career in health care administration should perhaps go to the back of the book first, and read "A Primer for New Clinician-Managers."

Readers with primarily business or management backgrounds will find descriptions of the various professional disciplines that work in mental health. This should provide some familiarity with the training and scope of practice of these professions, and describe how the training and background of each prepares a person for management roles. One should not assume, however, that this book conveys a deep understanding of how doctors and allied mental health professionals view their patients and their jobs, nor of how patients and their families—a very special kind of "customers"—choose, receive, use, and respond to the clinical services the organization provides.

Chapter Six

Essential Management Functions

Philip E. Veenhuis

Mental health organizations are professional service organizations. Unlike manufacturing companies, there are no products. The professions involved, by and large, require lengthy training, state licensure, and often certification by a professional organization. They often include psychiatry, other medical specialties, psychology, psychiatric nursing, social work, occupational therapy, and other allied health professions. The management of mental health organizations (and other clinical settings) is partially shaped by the professional nature of the critical revenue-generating staff; that is, the profession controls entry into the clinical field and sets the standards for practice (services delivered).

Services differ from most products in that they are intangible, produced and used immediately, and cannot be saved or stored. It is more difficult to measure the quality of a service than that of a product. A professional service generally involves some interpersonal process in which the professional uses his or her knowledge and skill to meet the need of the patient or client. In mental health care, the services include diagnosis, any of several kinds of treatment, and sometimes protection or other care that might be thought of as patient "management." The clinical activities may take place in a variety of settings, from home, to office, to day treatment setting, to residential or inpatient facility. Ancillary service and business activities are very important to the quality of care and healthy survival of the organization. This creates a need for good organization management, without which the professional activities would be reduced to a rather chaotic collection of individual interactions.

Mental health organizations usually have one or more administrators and various support personnel. Management functions may be divided into several broad clinical and nonclinical activities (such as various forms of patient care, budget and finance, human resources, and marketing), and are often subdivided. In very small organizations, one person may perform both business and clinical administration.

For some time, health care professionals tended to look down on managers and management as not understanding clinical priorities, unimportant to patient care, or "bean counters." To the uninitiated, management was merely an organizing or enumerating activity. Management roles were rarely sought by clinicians. In fact, management is a profession in itself, with aspects of both art and science. It is much more widely recognized today as indispensable to organizational success, and thus necessary to patient care. Incidentally, there is no hard-and-fast distinction between "administration" and "management," although some consider management a relatively more active and broader activity than more routine "administration."

HISTORICAL BACKGROUND AND PERSPECTIVE

There was a time when delivery of mental health care was uncomplicated, at least in the private sector. Inpatient facilities were less complicated, reimbursement avenues were simpler, and the regulatory and risk environments were far easier to negotiate. Many clinicians, perhaps most, were in solo practice, where management functions were even less complicated and often absent. Practices were built informally, with little marketing. Even group practices were generally undifferentiated. There was considerable overlap of the activities of the various mental health professions.

In private hospital settings, what now seem to have been generous insurance benefits permitted a situation in which little administration was required beyond determining the scope of those benefits (now utilization management), delivering a relatively short menu of services, billing, and collecting. Public-sector mental hospitals were largely supported by appropriations, just as today, but the operating environment was far less complex. For the most part, the clinician reigned supreme.

The situation changed dramatically during and shortly before the 1980s, with more complex understanding and treatments of mental illness, increased attention to its prevalence, widespread entitlement to care, and growing concern about the cost from both the government and the private sector. By that time, the federal government had assumed a broad payer role through Medicare and Medicaid; state agencies continued to fund care of the indigent severely and chronically mentally ill. By the 1980s, many industries developed a prevailing belief that health care costs were getting out of control and took the position—now largely discounted—that mental health coverage could "break the bank." This led to a massive expansion of managed care in the private sector, and later use of similar principles (and sometimes private managed care organizations) by the public sector as well. By one definition:

> Managed care is a system that integrates financing and delivery of appropriate medical care by means of the following features: contracts with selected physicians and hospitals that furnish comprehensive services to enrolled members, usually for a predetermined premium; utilization and quality controls that contracting providers agree to accept; financial incentives to use providers and facilities associated with the plan; [and] assumptions of some financial risks by doctors, thus fundamentally altering their roles from serving as an agent for the patient's needs against the need for cost control—or moving from advocacy to allocation. (Inglehart, 1993, p. 742)

When the attempt to control costs began, mental health care was (and arguably still is) underfunded, relative to other types of health care. Insurance benefits for mental health care have never been at parity with those for so-called "physical" health. Attempts to legislate parity of insurance benefits for mental illness or substance abuse have been marginal at best.

Since the 1960s, mental health services to severely ill or dangerous patients has depended substantially on federal and state government funding, and has more recently been affected by the managed care movement. Further, the dearth of adequate private-sector coverage has led to increased utilization of public-sector services (and funds), at a time when the public sector is highly constrained by cost concerns. Public mental health care is the safety net for uninsured persons with serious mental illness (and those whose illness has caused them to become uninsured). The safety net function is stretched woefully thin in many states.

A complete discussion of the impact of managed care is beyond the scope of this chapter. It is, however, important to identify two related effects central to this section: (1) Business management principles have become more and more important to the success of mental health care endeavors, and (2) the application of these principles has come to dominate care delivery.

All organizations that depend on revenue need managerial processes and functions to thrive. Although organizations differ, there are generic principles and processes called *management*.

MANAGERS AND MANAGEMENT FUNCTIONS

Management is a fairly new profession, and even newer in mental health care. However, unlike other professions, management only can be practiced in an organization. Organizations are the raison d'être of management. Modern business organizations, as we know them, are products of the 20th century, and management grew with them. Management is a coherent field. Many observers feel, however, that there is no genuine theory of business and no integrated discipline of business management. Much of the work of the managerial professional is like that of a clinician who bases some of his or her work on knowledge but must sometimes solve problems intuitively. Nevertheless, management has developed into a substantial field of endeavor.

The practice of management is in essence leading, planning, organizing, and maintaining operations; monitoring results; and making corrections as necessary. For clinicians moving into managerial roles, failing to appreciate the active stance required can make the difference between those who succeed and those who fail. Good clinical practice alone is not enough. An absence of active, competent management places the health care organization in a perilous economic position.

The manager is the figurative and literal personification of the organization or one subunit. Management is defined by its functions (Drucker, 1993). Some managers, particularly in small systems or lower levels of large ones, can function without formally understanding administrative principles; however, the days of "intuitive" management seem numbered in all but the smallest business systems. It is important, then, to understand the roles and functions of management.

Managers are leaders. Not all leadership roles are obvious, and the sphere of influence may be small or large, but fundamentally, managers lead the organization.

Managers are planners. Future orientation is one difference between managers and workers (even very sophisticated ones). Whether looking forward a few days to create a work schedule or preparing for community needs over the next several years, managers must have a future orientation in addition to their concern for the present. The more senior the manager, the further he or she plans into the future, sometimes informally and sometimes as a specific organizational exercise (see later discussion, and various chapters and sections on planning in this book).

Managers implement work toward the organization's mission and goals, and its objectives. Managers, perhaps more than others, are responsible for keeping the organization on mission and on goals. Managers are also responsible for strategic and tactical revision of mission and goals.

Managers are responsible for performance. Although they give great credit to employees, managers take responsibility for the performance of the organization and its parts. They accomplish this with judicious exercise of authority, and by figuring out how to get the most both from people (through motivation) and production (through planning, strategy, setting goals, measuring, monitoring, and/or analysis). This is a *leadership* function as much as a coordinating one.

Managers keep the organization organized. Untended, organizations move toward chaos. One of management's main tasks is keeping the system and its parts organized and coordinated. The level of structure and accountability in management systems varies from highly rigid (cf. military units) to rather loose (cf. some software companies, with their casual dress and irregular hours). Almost any reasonable point along this spectrum can be effective, given an appropriate management style (see later discussion) and corporate environment. Some successful organizations use a "loose–tight" principle, in which the level of structure or control is tailored to the needs of individual projects or sections.

Managers shepherd resources. Employees, dollars, materials, time, and even service quality and patient/customer goodwill are not to be squandered. Efficient use of resources involves all levels or management and can easily make the difference between a thriving organization and one that struggles to meet its objectives.

Managers communicate, often as part of a team. The best managers are those who convey what they (and the organization) need accurately, efficiently, and in such a way that the task will be accomplished. Communication to subordinates is only one facet of that activity. Reporting to one's own superiors and sharing useful information with the rest of one's work group, team, and/or system are routine organization activities.

Managers manage people. Management is the process that gets an organization to its goals, largely by coordinating and motivating *people.* For long-term or short-range goals, managers are the ones who organize the group's work, and the activities of those who will carry it out, and evaluate its quality. In a professional service organization, the people are usually of two broad types, professional staff and support personnel, and the work that needs to be done is either revenue generating or not revenue generating.

Managers are experts in the principles and procedures crucial to the organization's survival. Sometimes their expertise is quite limited, but it goes beyond the production skills of subordinate employees (which may be substantial and highly specialized but are not directly focused on the needs of those higher in the administrative hierarchy). Fundamentally, managers lead the organization.

Managers are part of a hierarchy of management and leadership. One person's manager or supervisor is another's employee. At some point, usually low in the table of organization, the manager's work product ceases to be a customer[1] service or product, and becomes an *organizational* service in support of organization objectives. This may take place close to the patient service "front line" (e.g., charge nurses, supervising psychologists) or far from it (e.g., budget directors, hospital or clinic administrators). Managers whose position is in the administrative path between the overall organization leadership and those employees who perform direct services to patients are sometimes said to have "line" positions (from the military analogy). Those whose role is more advisory to senior management may be described as "staff" managers. The latter, which include most managers of such things as quality improvement, risk management, budget and finance, marketing, and many other areas, are nevertheless very important to the organization. Of course, members of the quality improvement section of a mental health system are in the "line" of the quality improvement director, even though that person is probably outside the "line" between the CEO and direct care personnel.

Management Styles

There are several ways to carry out one's management responsibilities, commonly referred to as *management style.* In a classic work, Blake and Mouton (1968) described a two-dimensional "grid" on which various styles may be located on two axes in terms of their relative concern for workers as people and for organization production. Managers who focused strongly on production with low concern for people are said to be autocratic; those who rely entirely on meeting employees' needs and expect production to take care of itself are said to practice "country club" management. Many different styles can be made to work, with the outcome often depending on the manager's comfort and expertise with his or her way of doing things. Most contain some balance of attention to production and people. Nevertheless, there are styles that are much less likely to foster organization success (e.g., one in which the manager is focused neither on production levels nor employee needs, so-called "impoverished" management).

Particular projects, organization needs, products or services, and employee types suggest particular management styles, either temporary or permanent. In a crisis, an authoritative model is almost always preferred. In tight job markets, when workers have fewer employment choices, autocratic managers may be more successful; when employees can choose from many jobs, the work environment becomes more important to retention, and thus to production. Methods of reward and attention to employee needs vary greatly, but one should remember that even relatively

---

1. In this context, *customer* refers to the recipient of services (patient) or user of a product. Broader concepts of *customer*, as those who interact with or are important to the organization, are discussed elsewhere in this book.

unsophisticated, lower level employees often respond well to something more than union standards and a simple paycheck.

Clinical professionals and other highly educated workers are likely to be highly self-motivated, to respond to nontangible rewards, and to be vocationally mobile. They may or may not be directly salaried, even when the organization's mission and success depend on their work. Management that stresses "people support," creating a pleasant and rewarding work environment, is more likely than a production-focused model to attract and retain them, encourage quality and efficient care, and foster organizational loyalty.

MANAGEMENT KNOWLEDGE AND SKILLS

This book is written for at least two kinds of people: clinicians who are (or will become) administrators, and professional administrators/managers who are (or will become) responsible for some form of clinical mental health organization.

Clinicians Who Become Administrators or Managers

In theory, mental health professionals should make good managers. Their training in human motivation and behavior would seem to make them admirably suited for the task. The management functions just described, however, extend far beyond therapeutic skills (and those who treat associates or subordinates as patients or clients rarely succeed). Although there is some overlap between the skills and knowledge of management and those of the mental health professions, a lot of additional information and experience are needed, as well as a shift in viewpoint that often seems counter to the "helping professional." Some very good clinical professionals simply do not make the transition well, whether for reasons of personal style, job preference, or cognitive mismatch. Those who have already chosen administrative activities on their own, rather than being thrust into them, are usually more comfortable with it. This self-selection process is not necessary for managerial success, but it decreases some of the conflict one is apt to feel between the roles of clinician and administrator.

Professional Administrators/Managers Who Enter Mental Health Organizations

Readers in this category—and those engaged in joint clinical–management training programs—are likely to be more familiar with the concepts in this book and to find less conflict between clinical and administrative roles.

Whether one is the organization director (CEO, president, chairperson, administrator) or not, those in administrative positions should have some knowledge and skill in a number of basic managerial topics. As one's career evolves and changes, the different skills and experience will expand and contract. No one is expected to be expert in more than a few. Nevertheless, one must understand the concepts and the organization's reliance on them; be able to share and communicate with and benefit from managers in other parts of the system; and be able to apply the concepts in one's own management environment even when support from management subspecialists is available (e.g., using appropriate budget principles to create one's section budget, developing job descriptions and recruiting for vacancies on a clinical unit, dealing with risk management in clinical settings).

ORGANIZATIONS

A health care organization is a group of professionals, support staff, and mechanisms assembled to provide clinical care. It may be as simple as a small clinic or inpatient unit, or as large and complex as a multistate system. Mental health organizations include hospitals and in-hospital units, many kinds of ambulatory care settings, nonhospital residential care facilities, and broad systems that may include them all. Professional staffing varies from a few clinicians to large numbers of general and specialized clinicians. Patients/clients may receive a wide variety of medical/biological, psychological, management, and social/support services. Sometimes the organization's clients or "customers" include families, advocacy/interest groups, other organizations (such as employers), and entire communities or "covered populations." Revenue may be retrospective, prospective, or both, from individual, group, private, or public sources.

An organization's structure is its musculoskeletal system; internal processes are its physiology. After a brief discussion of organizational structure, we discuss processes, and within them some general elements of planning and operations. In larger systems, planning and operations functions are organized into separate departments, with managerial and support subspecialists. In smaller ones, they are less formal, sometimes carried out by only a few people. More extensive coverage of each of these topics is found elsewhere in this book.

Organizational Structure

"Structure" in this context defines the people, positions, functional groups, and lines of authority and accountability designed to accomplish the organization's mission, goals, and objectives. Whether formal or informal, the structure must be maintained (although it may be changed to meet new needs) if the organization is to survive. One representation of the structure is the organizational chart or "table of organization."

Some organizations, particularly large ones, have a pyramidal, hierarchical arrangement with multiple levels. Other organizations are "flat," with relatively few levels. The higher the "pyramid," the smaller is the immediate "span of control" for each manager and department. That is, they are not "spread thinly" and can easily interact with (oversee and respond to) their directly reporting subordinates. (The optimal number of directly reporting subordinates varies, but is usually under 10; managerial *responsibility*, on the other hand, may extend to hundreds or thousands of people.)

Managers and departments in "flatter" organizations have broader, more diffuse responsibility, but there are fewer layers of administration between direct service providers and senior management. There is less "middle management" in such systems; the perceived increase in empowerment at lower levels, and their potential to be closer to upper level setting of mission and goals, suggest to some that "flatter is better."

Structure includes governance. Different kinds of governance may be chosen for reasons that are legal (such as requirements for public-sector clinics or to qualify for a license to operate a particular kind of facility), financial (e.g., to qualify for tax or revenue-handling benefits, or to make the system more efficient), convenient (e.g., to make operations simpler or easier), or merely traditional. The top decision-making group, or "governing body," may be internal or, in most large systems, external to the operating staff. In public-sector systems (including academic systems), authority for organization *policy* extends—technically at least—upward to the top level of a city, county, state, or federal government, although there is always an intermediate level at which important operating decisions are made. In the private sector, both policy and operating decisions rest with some nongovernment body, such as an owner or board of directors.

The governing body is ultimately responsible for the organization's activities and results. In either format (public or private), the governing body routinely delegates decision-making authority downward, retaining oversight and control through appropriate communication and its ability to appoint or remove even very senior operating staff (such as the system administrator, director, or officers). External (e.g., legal or regulatory) entities interact with the organization through the governing body or its delegates, as do shareholders in private systems.

Some mental health care organizations, such as small clinics or practice groups, exist as sole proprietorships or very small corporations with only informal governance. These rarely require the specialized management contemplated by this book.

Structures of mental health organizations vary to some extent, but function, legal and funding requirements, and organizational evolution have brought common elements and internal structures that can be understood and generalized throughout most of the field. For systems of comparable size, most structural variations are related to special organization function (e.g., outpatient, residential, acute care, multiservice), broad governance (e.g., proprietary, stockholder, governmental), or regulation (e.g., requirements for licensure, funding certification, risk management). Once a modest "critical mass" is reached, size per se does not affect the *kind* of organization structure very much, only its quantity.

Organizational Processes

Processes take the manager, and the system, from one point to another. They are the essence of running a business. Organizational processes are the "physiology" of the organization's "body." This subsection provides a broad overview of two kinds of business processes: planning and operations. Further discussion is largely left to other parts of this book.

In smaller professional organizations, planning and operations are implicit. At some point along the spectrum of size and complexity, however, an organization must make them formal and explicit in order to achieve function effectively and proactively. Even relatively small groups benefit from an orderly approach to their missions and objectives.

Planning.   Because change is one of the most important characteristics of the market environment, good planning often makes the difference between an organization's success or failure. Managers need to be aware of a need to change and beware of not changing. Failure to address external change (e.g., marketplace, risk and regulatory environments, scientific advances) and internal change (e.g., staff turnover, aging equipment and facilities) will defeat even the highest-quality professional services. Virtually all managers participate in short- and long-term planning in some way, as initiators, participants, and/or facilitators. The larger and more complex an organization and its services, the more sophisticated are its planning process; many systems have planning departments that continuously update several kinds of strategic, financial, and operations plans.

Strategic planning takes a long view, usually several years. It includes predicting and analyzing future internal and external factors in order to make present entrepreneurial decisions. The planning process includes arrangements to implement decisions, regular monitoring for mid-course corrections, and preparation for the next planning cycle. Strategic planning does not eliminate risk; it is designed to reduce it and improve performance. Other common forms of planning—such as operations, tactical, budgetary, and financial—are not discussed here.

Operations.   Operations is the business of the organization being done. It includes what most people think of as the actual work of the company—in mental health care organizations, the activity at the interface of clinician and patient/client—as well as the processes and procedures that support its mission.

Service delivery is the primary operations task in mental health care systems. Service delivery operations are affected by many things, including type and quantity of service needed, availability of service providers, range of services offered, acceptability of services to patients and others, environmental limitations, regulatory conditions, scheduling and logistics, task efficiency, and general and specific costs.

Unlike many other organizations, clinical systems must be aware that their service provider disciplines are partially controlled or influenced by external standards, certification, and/or licensure. Many professional functions are controlled by the organization, and large health care systems often develop clinical policies and protocols that might be viewed by some as standards in themselves. Nevertheless, most clinical professionals adhere to external standards and ethical guidelines set by the professions themselves (in addition to government licensing agencies or scope-of-practice statutes). The organization may require various things of a clinical employee, but much of his or her work remains "discretionary" in that he or she is expected to meet reasonable professional standards regardless of organization rules or limitations, and those rules and limitations must not unduly and adversely influence patient care. Review of a clinician's professional activities is usually best done by another professional who is qualified in a similar or identical field.

Modern Clinical Service Delivery.   Mental health services can be planned, managed, and assessed more effectively than in the past, particularly when providing care for large groups of people. This makes the business of planning for and providing that care more efficient and better suited to the application of ordinary administrative principles. Relatively standardized protocols for assessment, locus of care decisions, and even treatment itself have been welcomed by system managers and payers, and are becoming accepted by many clinicians. Carefully developed, appropriately flexible protocols or clinical guidelines, although not usually setting a "standard," enhance overall patient care, offer ways to monitor and evaluate clinicians, and allow more rational decisions regarding resource allocation, productivity, costs, and revenues.

Treatment Protocols. Treatment protocols based on research and clinical pathways are common in some medical specialties (e.g., surgery, oncology), but their use in the broad field of mental health is often problematic. Most organizations and clinicians and organizations favor *evidence-based clinical guidelines* over strict protocols, leaving appropriate latitude for clinicians. Although this raises concerns about resource overutilization, patients (and their doctors) often fear that rigid protocols will limit their access to quality care.

QUALITY CONTROL AND QUALITY IMPROVEMENT

Quality can be defined in many ways, including the well-known formula of *perceived quality* divided by *perceived cost*. For the organization, two of the most important (sometimes overlapping) kinds of quality are (1) "customer satisfaction" (e.g., promptness of being seen, perceived accuracy and completeness of care, comfort, billing accuracy, fairness of charges, facility appearance, staff appearance and demeanor)[2] and (2) service outcome.

Organized health care is expected to provide flawless clinical service but, whether deservedly or not, carries a connotation of egregious patient support (e.g., waiting lists, confusing or inaccurate billing, impersonal care, inadequate follow-up, poor communication with referring community clinicians). Failure to separate customer satisfaction issues from clinical service outcome issues can lead to friction between the managers and clinical staff, even when the latter understand the value of promptness, friendliness, cleanliness, and eagerness to serve.[3] Most clinicians hold themselves to a high standard; a few become defensive when their efforts are questioned.

REFERENCES

Blake, R. R., & Mouton, J. S. (1968). *Corporate excellence through grid organization development*. Houston, TX: Gulf.
Drucker, P. (1993). *The practice of management*. New York: HarperCollins.
Inglehart, J. K. (1993). The American health care system, managed care. *New England Journal of Medicine, 327*(10), 742.

---

2. Note that "customer" satisfaction can also refer to patients' families, their employers and payers, shareholders, other external groups, internal "customers" such as organization employees, and even governing bodies and shareholders.

3. One use for senior clinician-manager positions (e.g., medical director, clinical director) is the buffer they create for explaining and clarifying each group's—clinicians' and non–clinician-managers'—needs and concerns.

Chapter Seven

Mental Health Management Environments: General Hospital Psychiatric Units

L. Mark Russakoff

Psychiatric hospitals are almost as old as our country, but psychiatric units in general hospitals date to 1902, in the Albany Hospital. It was not until the 1920s, under the influence of Adolph Meyer, that there were psychiatric units in general hospitals akin to what we would recognize as such today (Kaufman, 1965). Initially, many of the general hospital units were like small private psychiatric hospitals, with lengths of stay measured in months and even years. There were several developments that occurred in close temporal proximity that profoundly affected the practice of psychiatry: World War II; academic psychiatry's embracing of psychoanalysis; the therapeutic community/social psychiatry/community psychiatry model and movement; the introduction of modern psychopharmacological agents; and the expansion of health insurance, both public and private. We review some of these factors.

During World War II a large number of individuals were screened out as psychiatrically unsuitable for service. This led to a greater consciousness of the prevalence of mental disorders in the public. Additionally, therapeutic interventions with soldiers who had suffered traumatic neuroses were deemed to be successful, leading many to be optimistic about the course of illness if treated early (Grinker & Spiegel, 1945). The importance of the group and group cohesion for psychological health became apparent.

A large literature appeared regarding the intensive, psychoanalytically oriented inpatient treatment of an array of psychiatric disorders. There was great excitement, enthusiasm, and hope that these treatment modalites would effectively treat patients with schizophrenia and severe depression. Programs at the Menninger Clinic, Yale Psychiatric Institute, Chestnut Lodge, Austin Riggs, and Sheppard & Enoch Pratt were the envy of all. Psychiatrists who were psychoanalysts were held in the highest regard, often as chairs of academic departments of psychiatry. From a narrow psychoanalytic perspective, somatic treatments (medications or electroconvulsive therapy [ECT]) interfered with the process of therapy. The centerpiece of treatment was the doctor–patient relationship as explored in the psychoanalytic situation. Into the 1950s, psychiatric care was largely inpatient, located in institutions—state and private psychiatric hospitals. Outpatient treatment was mostly restricted to those of means; private health insurance was limited. For a long time, the gold standard of care was what was provided at the private institutions—intensive psychoanalytic treatment in a hospital that lasted upward of a year or so.

Into the 1950s, psychiatric units in general hospitals as well as in private hospitals often were modeled after medical units: Doctors wore white coats; nurses took orders from the doctors; psychotherapy, sedatives, and ECT were prescribed. After World War II, the concept of the "therapeutic community" took hold on American psychiatric practice (Jones, 1953, 1968; Rapoport, 1960). Jones's book was originally published in England under the title of *Social Psychiatry*. The concepts in the book contributed to the community mental health movement. There was an evolving awareness of the impact of the social milieu on the patients and the staff. Several studies in long-term psychiatric hospitals were performed that analyzed the relationships between staff and patients' behaviors and milieu variables (Caudill, 1958; Rubinstein & Lasswell, 1966; Stanton & Schwartz, 1954). It became axiomatic that to treat the patients you needed to understand and deal with the patient–staff dynamics.

Many of the psychiatric units in general hospitals adopted principles from Maxwell Jones's therapeutic community: democratization, permissiveness, communalism, and reality confrontation. Lengths of stay were in the weeks to months range. Under the influence of this model, the traditional medical hierarchy was radically altered if not discarded; there were apocryphal stories of patients and staff voting on whether or not a patient should get ECT. In its best incarnation, the "therapeutic community" empowered patients, made staff aware of the negative ramifications of some of their benignly motivated actions vis-à-vis patients, and fostered a sense of collegiality among staff that was conducive to professional growth (Almond, 1974; Cumming & Cumming, 1962; Edelson, 1964, 1970a, 1970b; Maxmen, Tucker, & LeBow, 1974; Wessen, 1964). Alternative sites of treatment were sought, with the intention of demedicalizing treatment and empowering the community. Unfortunately, there was a tendency in some areas to treat the models with a mindset that suggested religious zealotry.

The "psychopharmacological revolution," initiated by the introduction of chlorpromazine and quickly followed by the introductions of imipramine and chlordiazepoxide, made possible the effective shorter-term treatment of a wide range of psychiatric disorders (Russakoff, 1999). The introduction of these psychotropic medications changed the equation regarding private care versus public care. A patient admitted to a state psychiatric hospital (which could not afford to provide intensive psychotherapy) for the treatment of acute schizophrenia in the early 1960s was likely to be administered chlorpromazine and discharged in a much improved state within 2 months. A similar, although wealthier, individual admitted to a private psychiatric hospital would likely be treated with intensive psychoanalytic therapy with minimal to no chlorpromazine, and remain for years—or until the person's insurance ran out. When the latter occurred, and if continued inpatient care seemed necessary, that person would be transferred to the state hospital, treated with chlorpromazine, and discharged markedly improved within 2 months!

This discrepancy led some to pursue studies that were to delineated the efficacy of the new medications vis-à-vis intensive therapies (Glick & Hargreaves, 1979; May, 1968). The results of those studies indicated in part that shorter hospitalizations were as efficacious as longer ones in almost all circumstances, with acute violence and suicidal states being the untested exceptions. Because the antipsychotics were rapidly effective in quelling agitation, the social problems of treating individuals in various degrees of behavioral dyscontrol were minimized. State psychiatric hospitals began to empty and downsize; psychiatric units in general hospitals blossomed. The era of deinstitutionalization had begun.

The fifth factor that influenced general hospital psychiatry was the change in the financing of care. Private health insurance was relatively uncommon until after World War II. There was an expansion of private health insurance, primarily through Blue Cross and Blue Shield plans. The introduction of a "limited" psychiatric benefit by the Blue Cross insurance programs, typically 4 to 12 weeks, gave an incentive to general hospitals to create "short-term" alternatives to the extended stays typical of the private and state facilities.

Medicaid and Medicare laws were not passed until the mid-1960s. Medicare made available acute care psychiatric benefits for the elderly and the disabled. Medicaid, a plan at least half funded through the federal government and the remainder through matched funds from the state and local governments, made psychiatric benefits available to the medically indigent. Congress, not wanting to put the burden of the cost of the state psychiatric hospitals into the federal budget, specifically excluded psychiatric coverage through Medicaid for individuals between the ages of 21 through 64 years who were treated in independent mental disease facilities—private and public psychiatric hospitals.

It became apparent to state planners that they could reduce the burden on the state budget by diverting admissions from the state psychiatric hospitals to those facilities that were Medicaid eligible. The state psychiatric hospitals were emptying, due in part to more effective psychiatric treatments. Medicaid and Medicare made treatment available on a widespread basis. No longer were medically indigent people a financial burden to hospitals. Reimbursement methodologies utilized by both programs passed on the actual costs of running the hospital to the government programs. (The reimbursement methodologies have changed over time, from fee for service, to prospective payment based on diagnostic-related groups, to capitated managed care. Federal legislation passed in the late 1990s geared to balance the federal budget further reduced fee-for-service payments to hospitals. See other chapters for further discussion.)

The culmination of the above factors led to a large expansion of psychiatric units in general hospitals, where treatments typically lasted 21 to 28 days, depending often on the insurance benefit.

Potent psychopharmacological agents were introduced into the practice of psychiatry at about the same time as the therapeutic community movement was taking hold. A polarization of opinions took place, that is, the "religious beliefs," with some advocating one treatment to the exclusion of others. Programs were established that eschewed the use of alternative treatments. Units for the psychosocial treatment of schizophrenia were created in exclusive environments. Studies by Philip R. A. May and colleagues had a powerful effect in directing the profession away from a sole reliance on psychosocial interventions in schizophrenia.

This was followed into the 1980s with a rapid expansion of for-profit psychiatric hospitals. With the more sophisticated use of psychotropic medications being widely adopted, and limited insurance benefits for inpatient psychiatric care, the model of treatment in the 1970s through the 1980s became an integration of the medical model (now constituted of psychotherapy and the judicious use of psycho-tropic agents and ECT) with the therapeutic community (acknowledgment of the importance of sociotherapy) (Oldham & Russakoff, 1987).

As can be seen in Table 7.1, the results of the converging forces have been a large decrease in the state and county hospitals with concomitant explosion of growth in the general hospital units and private psychiatric hospitals. The state and county hospitals no longer provide the bulk of psychiatric admissions. Managed care has stopped the explosion of growth.

This integrated model of treatment has recently yielded under the pressures of managed care, with its emphasis on biomedical interventions (if you do not change the dose or kind of medication, then discharge the patient) and lengths of stay mea-sured in days, not weeks or months. Although there are substantial data from re-search studies indicating that patients can be treated as effectively in the community as in a hospital, those studies utilized subsidized services that were not—and often still are not—readily available in the community. Additionally, the patients studied were highly screened and accepted into a research project, often with the agreement of their families. Because the bulk of cost of care is linked to the site of care—inpa-tient care is highly expensive—shortened lengths of stay lead to marked reductions in the cost of care.

Managed care, driven by the financial imperative, now insists that these brief treatment models be utilized, regardless of family burden, consent, or ease of access to services. A direct derivative of the much briefer lengths of stay under managed care has been to render impossible the types of social structures that were the main-stay of therapeutic communities.

TABLE 7.1. 24-Hour Hospital and Residential Treatment Services: Facilities, Beds, and Admissions

Type of facility and parameter	1970	1980	1990	1994
State and county mental hospitals				
Number of facilities	310	280	273	256
Number of beds	413,066	156,482	98,789	81,911
Number of admissions	486,661	383,323	276,231	238,431
Private psychiatric hospitals				
Number of facilities	150	184	462	430
Number of beds	14,295	17,157	44,871	42,399
Number of admissions	92,056	140,831	406,522	485,001
Nonfederal general hospitals with separate psychiatric services				
Number of facilities	664	843	1,571	1,531
Number of beds	22,394	29,384	53,479	52,948
Number of admissions	478,000	551,190	959,893	1,066,547
Total of organizations with 24-hour hospital and residential treatment services				
Number of facilities	1,734	2,526	3,430	3,827
Number of beds	524,878	274,713	272,253	290,604
Number of admissions	1,282,698	1,541,659	2,035,245	2,266,600

(Witkin, Atay, Manderscheid, Delozier, Male, & Gillespie, 1999)

The model of treatment under managed care has turned full circle to the medical model. Many of Jones's principles of the therapeutic community are inapplicable and incomprehensible in a 4-day hospitalization. Patients are now admitted sicker and discharged "sicker and quicker," with more signs and symptoms of their illnesses apparent as they leave the hospital than were present when many were admitted in a previous generation. Previously when a patient was ready for discharge they were often ready to assume household or vocational obligations, whereas now when patients are discharged they are still psychologically, socially, and vocationally disabled by their conditions. The burden this puts on the patient and family is substantial; the benefits are economic (to the insurance company) and may accrue to the patient and family if they are strongly desirous of and prepared to have the individual home.

The change in reimbursement model from fee for service to managed care in the Medicaid and Medicare programs has altered the financial equations. Federal and state laws regulated how the reimbursement rates were to be determined. Typically, commercial insurance rates were the highest, and thus the most profitable for the hospital. Next was the Medicare rate and lowest was the Medicaid rate. The Medicaid rate paid the basic costs of running the hospital, without frills. Thus, with unmanaged Medicaid, a hospital was financially better off with a filled Medicaid bed than an empty bed; the basic costs were covered.

When commercial insurance companies began to dispute payments to hospitals and utilization review procedures were implemented, resulting in the denial of days of hospital care, hospitals came under increasing fiscal pressure. Medicaid patients started to look attractive to even the more exclusive hospitals. As the government embraced managed care and capitated approaches to health care insurance, Medicaid rates became negotiable like any other rate, with the proverbial "race to the bottom." No longer can administrators be confident that the basic costs are covered. The fiscal pressure under which hospital administrators now operate is intense and unrelenting. As this chapter is being written, there is much discussion regarding the financial health of the Medicare program; managed care has not been a panacea. Teaching hospitals in particular have been adversely affected by recent changes in reimbursement; it seems unlikely that the pressures will lessen in the near future.

CLINICAL ISSUES

When the primary model of psychiatric care was inpatient care, many of the patients admitted to psychiatric services were suffering from uncomplicated depression, anxiety disorders, or, less commonly, exacerbations of chronic psychoses. Patients with uncomplicated depressions and anxiety disorders are no longer routinely admitted to inpatient services; they are treated as outpatients. Under managed care, the threshold for admission has been dangerousness or serious medical or psychiatric complications. Thus, the patients admitted typically have comorbidities—significant medical illness and substance abuse—or have had serious complications from their outpatient medication treatment. Substance abuse increases the risk for violence. When the substance abuse involves illicit substances, antisocial behaviors are more frequent.

Patients are discharged when the acute risk for dangerousness has lessened, and those patients are replaced with others who are deemed at imminent risk or who suffer from complicating conditions. The burden on nursing staff is enormous. Unfortunately, the reimbursement for inpatient psychiatric units has been reduced, putting great pressure on administrators to limit staffing. The problem of how to assess the adequacy of nursing staffing levels is complex. Although the Health Care Financing Administration (HCFA) has rules that it applies, there is no universally accepted way to decide on the adequacy of staffing, and nursing staff infrequently seem fully satisfied.

Disturbed substance-abusing patients, and individuals suffering from developmental disorders with concomitant behavioral abnormalities, are two subgroups of patients, sometimes referred to as MICA patients (mentally ill chemical abusers) or "dual diagnosed patients" (used to refer either to MICA patients or mentally ill, developmentally disabled patients), who are often underserved. States typically have separate agencies or departments, paralleling federal grants, to deal with each patient group: mentally ill; alcohol and substance abuse; developmentally disabled. Because therapeutic approaches traditionally differed significantly among the three groups—permissiveness, confrontation, and direct guidance, respectively—the integration of the treatment of patients with comorbid disorders trailed advances in the fields separately. Within psychiatric units, patients themselves have expressed dismay about being housed with the other patients on the unit, feeling that they have little in common with them, adding to the tensions.

Models of integrated treatment of dually diagnosed individuals have been developed. As the market has tightened for psychiatric patients, some hospitals have developed specialty programs to serve MICA patients; some psychiatric hospitals have developed programs for dually diagnosed mentally ill, developmentally disabled patients. Funding streams for the three groups of individuals remain separate and distinct.

The clinical centerpiece in discussions that relate to managed care is that of "medical necessity." This amorphous concept, which in a puzzling fashion varies from company to company, allegedly drives decision making by the managed care companies. One can conceptualize a continuum, with "medically essential" at one extreme, the situation in which all would agree that a specific intervention must occur. The failure to provide that which was medically essential would be unethical and malpractice. At the other end would be "medically beneficial," an intervention that is likely to provide benefit with an acceptable level of risk, but that one could do without—perhaps an example might be magnetic resonance imaging (MRI) in someone with a first episode of what clearly appears to be major depression in the context of serious interpersonal stress (death of a loved one) and whose physical examination and screening laboratory tests are unremarkable. The dollar cost of the procedure would not be a central focus.

Somewhere in between, although many would say too close to "medically essential," is the point of "medical necessity." Medical necessity requires a calculus in which the therapeutic benefits are deemed to justify the medical risks as well as the costs of the procedure. As the determination of medical necessity edges toward the medically essential—that is, the limits of malpractice—many physicians feel the safety margin for the care of patients is too thin. Although some definitions of "medical necessity" in managed care contracts sound like our definition of medically beneficial, they are implemented closer to the medically essential. At the practitioner level, this seems like an unethical marketing ploy. The lack of public access to the criteria for the determination of medical necessity keeps the problem obfuscated.

The aging of America is also visible on the inpatient services. With the aware-ness that it is not "normal" to be depressed merely because you have aged, and that the signs and symptoms of depression may be occult or masked in the geriatric age group, depressed geriatric patients constitute a growing number of admissions. These patients have often either failed an outpatient trial of a selective serotonin reuptake inhibitor (SSRI) or cannot tolerate them. For hospitals with single psychiatric inpa-tient units, this leads to the housing of a wide array of individuals—adolescents who are depressed and suicidal, psychotic young adults who abuse substances, and elderly individuals who are depressed. The challenge to the patients is as great as it is to the staff! A nursing staff member may need to sit one-on-one with a suicidal adolescent while another nurse is checking the intravenous line on a geriatric pa-tient who was severely dehydrated. Other staff need to be prepared to intervene with a psychotic patient who is irritable and threatening. Adolescent patients may be housed with someone old enough to be their parent. There may be advantages to such arrangements—exploration of current life issues, such as conflicts with family members, without the emotional overlay of the particular individual. At other times, such arrangements are difficult—for example, playing of loud music in public areas, choice of TV shows, group therapy discussions of no relevance to the individual. The staff is challenged to create a milieu that can meet the needs of the array of patients the unit serves.

Inpatient psychiatric services with modal lengths of stay of less than a week must be modified from the structures of the 1970s and 1980s. For one thing, there need to be staff members who can be in communication with the managed care companies. These staff members must be sufficiently knowledgeable and skilled clinically to be able to present the clinical information in a fashion that is most likely to obtain the authorizations requested. Social workers—or whoever is desig-nated to work on disposition planning—must be available seven days a week. The close working relationships that used to be formed on inpatient units between pa-tients and specific nursing staff and between patients and their doctors no longer develop, with the team taking on the responsibilities and functions. In place of at-tempts at mutative individual psychotherapy, medication management and crisis intervention are the likely modes. Daily group therapy is conceptualized in a psychoeducational model in which the focus is on the group work of the day, with little to no attention paid to the group dynamics. Most units hold an ongoing series of meetings regarding medications, illnesses, and treatment options as central com-ponents of the group treatment program. With rapid turnover, enculturation into the unit milieu becomes a Sisyphean task.

Nevertheless, there needs to be attention to the milieu as a whole. Although the group psychotherapists may ignore the intragroup and group-session-to-group-ses-sion dynamics, the unit director would be wise to keep a watchful eye on those dynamics. Community meetings in which the patients and staff discuss practical issues that impact on living on the unit are useful to resolve simple administrative grievances as well as to give one a sense of the concerns of the community as a whole. Staff and patients will frequently complain about specific patients; it would be from qualitative shifts in the dynamics of the unit that the director might decide to forgo an admission for the sake of the unit. Absent a means to obtain this informa-tion, the unit director will be faced with a flurry of resignations from staff or re-quests of patients to sign out against medical advice.

MULTIDISCIPLINARY TREATMENT TEAM

Psychiatric units differ from surgical and medical units in that there is more of a focus on team functioning, particularly the multidisciplinary team. Federal and state regulations require the development of a multidisciplinary treatment plan, predicated on a documented, comprehensive psychiatric evaluation of the patient and culminating in a substantiated diagnosis. Linked to this assessment is an inventory of assets and liabilities (problems) predicated on a rehabilitative model. In theory, knowledge of the assets of the individual permits the development of a treatment plan that capitalizes on the individual's assets to intervene in the specific problems. The multidisciplinary treatment plan should serve as a "table of contents" or "menu" to the treatment notes, indicating what problems are being addressed and in what sequence (the treatment notes then are the "book" or the "meal and itemized bill of sale," to complete the metaphors). One should be able to go from the multidisciplinary assessments to the problem (liability) list, to the goals and objectives of treatment, then to the documentation of the treatment and outcome, in a fashion that makes sense.

The medical and surgical services are staffed with nurses, nursing technicians, and social workers. Psychiatric units usually have therapeutic activities personnel and psychologist(s), in addition. When lengths of stay were longer, there might be a vocational rehabilitation counselor on staff, too. The HCFA (Health Care Financing Administration, now the Centers for Medicare and Medicaid Services [CMS]), the parent of Medicare, has specific staffing requirements for units that are reviewed when the JCAHO (Joint Commission on Accreditation of Healthcare Organizations) surveys the hospital. In contrast to the other hospital services, the psychiatric treatment team actually meets together, typically part of the time with the patient, to discuss the treatment plan in detail. An overall goal or limited number of goals are identified and the steps need to achieve that (those) goal(s) spelled out as objectives, in observable, measurable terms, with the time to achieve those objectives specified. (This approach is an adaptation of Drucker's management by objectives, applied to treatment planning. See chapter 4 on administrative theory.) Input from each of the disciplines regarding the degree to which the patient has accomplished the goals and objectives of the treatment plan is noted in the treatment plan updates, and the treatment plan is revised as needed.

The use of multidisciplinary treatment is predicated on the concept that the treatment of psychiatric illnesses is not reducible to simple biomedical interventions in which the patient may be passive. It incorporates the concept that the most effective and humane treatment brings the patient in as a partner, and that a multimodal approach will likely be necessary—that is, medications, psychological interventions, behavioral programs, and family counseling.

As noted earlier, when psychiatry embraced and was consumed by the therapeutic community movement, psychiatric leadership retreated; democracy ruled. With the explosive growth of an array of effective psychotropic agents, and mind-numbing growth of data on their efficacy, combined with the pressures of managed care, psychiatrists have resumed their positions of leadership of psychiatric units. This leadership was always present in regulations that required the psychiatrist's approval of the multidisciplinary treatment plan as evidenced by a signature, but was sometimes implemented in services in an officious fashion. The signature does indicate that the psychiatrist has reviewed and approved of the plan; psychiatrists are obliged to take their signatures seriously.

Effective leadership of a multidisciplinary team requires an understanding and appreciation of group and organizational dynamics, in addition to the requisite clinical skills. The leader must truly value the contributions of the various team members and be able to communicate that appreciation. It is easy to value the contributions if the leader is familiar with the different domains of knowledge and skills that the disciplines bring to the discourse. These skills can be learned, but the leader must know that possession of a graduate degree did not necessarily bestow such knowledge and skills on him or her. Often psychiatrists are placed into positions of leadership without a clue as to what is entailed and how to be an effective—or ineffective—leader (see chapter 4 on administrative theory).

If a general hospital offers psychiatric services, they are likely to include emergency room services and an inpatient adult psychiatric unit. Some hospitals offer psychiatric outpatient clinic services, whereas few non-tertiary-care hospitals can offer even some of the full array of psychiatric services: partial and long-term day programs; case management; psychiatric rehabilitation; crisis intervention; 23-hour beds; residential services; vocational rehabilitation.

RELATIONSHIP TO OTHER HOSPITAL CLINICAL SERVICES

The psychiatrist and the inpatient psychiatric service are likely to interact with the emergency room and the other inpatient clinical services. The emergency room will call for those patients who present with psychiatric emergencies. It is also likely to call for disruptive patients, and for the determination of capacity in persons who refuse medical care, when the decision of the person is suspect. Sometimes the psychiatrist is called to see someone who does not seem to be in crisis but who wants a place to stay. Not infrequently, especially in urban areas, such individuals are severely psychiatrically ill and unable to care for themselves, thus warranting admission for restabilization of their medication regimens.

Medical and surgical units of the hospital are likely to call on psychiatry to take care of "problem patients," including agitated, demented elderly individuals and substance abusers. State regulations may limit the diagnostic categories of who may be treated for what conditions in which sites. For instance, in New York State a patient admitted to the psychiatric service must have a primary psychiatric and not substance-abuse or dementia diagnosis. If the request is for the patient to be whisked away onto the psychiatric service, there are likely to be tensions. If the request is for assistance with managing the situation, psychiatry often can be helpful. Nevertheless, the patient with dementia who tends to wander, yet has completed parenteral antibiotic therapy and is now awaiting nursing-home placement, taxes the system.

As in the emergency room situation, the medical and surgical services will call for opinions regarding capacity. It is probable that psychiatrists are called less often than they ought to be; as long as patients make the "right" decision, that is, agree with the recommended treatment, then they are deemed to have capacity. Many physicians are still uncomfortable with patients making the "wrong" choices. Psychiatrists doing consultations need to educate those physicians through their consultations, as well as to educate members of the nursing staff, who may suffer from feelings of helplessness.

The psychiatrist should participate in the educational conferences that occur within the hospital. Psychiatrists should update their colleagues in the current issues of differential diagnosis, office treatment of common psychiatric disorders, and the new medications. Similarly, it behooves psychiatrists to attend updates on medical and surgical treatments so they can understand the challenges and questions that the patients are confronting.

ECONOMIC ISSUES

Many general hospitals have empty medical–surgical beds, and the development of specialty services, including psychiatric and substance-abuse services, may seem to be a potential source of revenue. Although the profit margins from such services may be thin, certainly thinner than before managed care and managed Medicaid, such services may be attractive compared to unfilled beds and spaces. The reverse of this process is the situation in which there is a potential market for more medical and surgical beds, and the source of them must be current psychiatric beds. Psychiatric beds can generate sizable revenues, and indirect costs can be loaded onto them in circumstances in which payers will cover indirect costs. However, psychiatric beds do not generate the other charges—laboratory tests, procedures, operating room, and so on—that add to the profitability of hospital services. Thus, in environments in which medical or surgical activities can be increased, hospital administrators are likely to convert psychiatric or substance-abuse beds.

If the bed occupancy of the psychiatric service is low, and its size is fairly large, some downsizing may make the most sense for the hospital and psychiatric service as a whole. It behooves the psychiatric administrator to understand the finances of the unit: whether or not it contributes to the bottom line, to what extent that it does, whether or not the size is optimal, and so on. Additionally, the psychiatric administrator must understand the finances of the competing services if the administrator is to be able to defend the service against unwise encroachments. Politically, the rest of the hospital must have an awareness of the direct and indirect benefits that accrue as a result of the presence of the service.

Managed care has been accused of a "race to the bottom," that is, to the lowest possible rates and the least amount of care. Where the bottom seems near, the viability of inpatient services is threatened. Because many hospitals no longer stand alone but are in networks, as the ink turns red economies of scale must be considered by administrators, although no one should anticipate that a decision to consolidate services among cooperating hospitals will be appreciated by the line staff, including doctors, regardless of whether their jobs are preserved. The disruption to their lives will be substantial. Creation of alternatives to inpatient care may be considered, but recent CMS (HCFA) pursuit of partial hospitalization programs for fraudulent billing makes such an alternative fraught with potential trouble.

Another effect of managed care has been on the pattern of referrals. Although previously patients might come from the community to the hospital, or from private practitioners to the hospital, managed care companies often have contracted exclusively with certain hospitals. Patients who present to the local emergency room may need to be transferred to specific hospitals or else be liable for all, or a substantial part, of their bill. Some managed care companies will negotiate an out-of-network rate for a particular patient, but that rate is likely to be punishingly low. Obtaining the exclusive contract oneself may put oneself in the position of accepting too little reimbursement with the delusion that one will make up for the loss by more volume at the inadequate rate.

The development of alternatives to inpatient psychiatric care by general hospitals is limited in part by the potential revenues of such services. Many such services will be provided to chronically mentally ill individuals who are likely to have their care paid for by Medicaid. As managed Medicaid has grown, the financial rewards to the hospital for developing the services is limited. Alternatively, such services keep the patients in the hospital system, and because they are likely to need readmission at some point, they serve as a source of inpatient referrals. In a capitated insurance program in which the hospital is an equity partner, owning an array of services, particularly less expensive ones, is an advantage. Unfortunately, many of the Medicaid contracts have been underfunded, making them financially disadvantageous to health care systems and disadvantageous to patients.

UNIT STRUCTURE

Psychiatric inpatient services in general hospitals must be directed by a psychiatrist; the director must work collaboratively with the head nurse/nurse manager of the unit. There is a healthy tension that will occur between the nursing staff and medical staff. Typically the nursing staff will complain that the psychiatrists are admitting inappropriate patients to the service. Older nursing staff will recall how it was under the previous, beloved director, who admitted "good" cases, not these poorly motivated, substance-abusing psychotic individuals or these medically ill, frail elderly individuals who require so much basic nursing care and who are admitted now. Much work still needs to be done to make comprehensible to the nursing staff what is occurring and why. This education is a process, not an event. To the extent that the director and head nurse can make the staff feel valuable and proud of what they do, morale will be reasonably high and treatment will move smoothly. To the extent that the staff feel abused by administration, morale will be low and patient care will suffer.

The same structural and dynamic issues described in the classic studies of psychiatric hospitals—Goffman's *Asylums* (1962), Stanton and Schwartz's *The Mental Hospital* (1954), Caudill's *The Psychiatric Hospital as a Small Society* (1958)—play out in microcosm in the general hospital units. When staff members are in sharp disagreement regarding a patient or policy issue, there is likely to be acting out by patients. Conversely, when the patients are acting out on the unit—frequent against medical advice (AMA) discharges, incidents—it behooves the unit administrators to explore the unit dynamics to see how these dynamics may contribute to the disturbances.

For example, one area in which clinical staff members often hold very strong and often opposing points of view regards substance abuse. Some staff members are likely to take a hard line and be unforgiving of any transgressions. Other staff members assume that the substance abuser's behaviors are not "bad" but are symptomatic of their illnesses, and require the careful balancing of limits and compassion. Substance-abusing patients, admitted for their psychiatric comorbidities, then find themselves in power struggles with the hard liners. The staff then find themselves in a covert conflict, a situation ripe for acting out of patients and staff. Driven by the covert conflict, the two staff groups polarize their views, pitting the hard liners against the marshmallows. The patients often act out by some (what in other circumstances would be considered minor) violation of a unit rule. The staff argue over whether the patient should be administratively discharged. The staff act out by excessive scrutiny or confrontation of the patient, or by the failure to set reasonable limits, leading to a precipitous request to leave the hospital against medical advice or a major incident. These kinds of conflicts can only be contained or avoided by open staff discussions of all the relevant issues in which all staff feel able to participate and be heard. It is important to hear from all levels of staff in the discussion. In current times it is difficult to effect such meetings because of the pressures on staff for productivity. Directors need to balance the need for such discussions against the other demands on staff time.

MEDICAL STAFF ISSUES

There are several models for psychiatric—or general medical—staffing of a hospital. One model for the hospital is whether or not the staff is open or closed. Closed staffing means that private community practitioners cannot practice at the hospital. Only those individuals who are part of the hospital physician group may practice at the hospital. This hospital physician group may have an exclusive contract with the hospital; alternatively, the physicians may all be employees of the hospital. If the staff is closed, a nonmember cannot obtain privileges to treat a patient at the hospital. In the open staff model, community practitioners are permitted to join the staff, provided that they meet the standards set forth by the medical staff of the hospital. Typically there are responsibilities that occur with joining the medical staff, such as on-call service to the emergency room, work on medical staff committees (such as medical records, utilization review), and accepting "service" cases to treat.

There are other ways to limit who may join the staff of a hospital. One method is by establishing a table of organization (see chapter 4 on administrative theory) that clearly defines the number of clinical positions that the hospital can support. Once those positions are filled, the credentialing and privileging committee may deny applications to the medical staff.

Psychiatric staff may be salaried or voluntary. In recent times, hospitals often have a mix of staff, some salaried and some voluntary. The mixture has been a result of pressure on hospitals to care for the uninsured and for Medicaid patients, for whom the remuneration is low, which is a disincentive for private practitioners to continue their clinical privileges at the hospital. The salaried psychiatrist is expected to assume the care of the uninsured and Medicaid patients who were admitted by the private practitioner while on call. By this mechanism, the hospital retains unpaid psychiatrists to serve on call (the private practitioners) for the cost of the salaried psychiatrist.

Managed care companies may insist that their patients be treated by members of their panels of psychiatrists. When the hospital negotiates a contract with the managed care company, this issue may be negotiated with the rates. Alternatively, the hospital may be able to facilitate the addition of the psychiatrists to the managed care company's panel. There is at least a theoretical risk of the hospital being paid but the psychiatrist's fees being denied if the psychiatrist is not an in-network provider. Whether the psychiatrist could bill the patient directly may be addressed in the contract between the managed care company and the hospital. If the hospital reimbursement is sufficient, it may be cost-effective for the hospital to absorb the physicians' fees.

In the heyday of inpatient psychiatry, the unit medical director position was often purely one of clinical administrative oversight; there were no direct patient care responsibilities. In general it is now too costly to pay for such a position without patient billings linked to it. It is rare for there to be more than one position in a general hospital psychiatric service that does not have direct care responsibilities; in a hospital with a small inpatient service only, the unit medical director is typically the director of the department.

REFERENCES

Almond, R. (1974). *The healing community: Dynamics of the therapeutic milieu*. New York: Jason Aronson.

Caudill, W. (1958). *The psychiatric hospital as a small society*. New York: Commonwealth Fund, Harvard University Press.

Cumming, J., & Cumming, E. (1962). *Ego & milieu: Theory and practice of environmental therapy*. New York: Atherton Press.

Edelson, M. (1964). *Ego psychology, group dynamics and the therapeutic community*. New York: Grune & Stratton.

Edelson, M. (1970a). *Sociotherapy and psychotherapy*. Chicago: University of Chicago Press.

Edelson, M. (1970b). *The practice of sociotherapy: A case study*. New Haven, CT: Yale University Press.

Glick, I. D., & Hargreaves, W. A. (1979). *Psychiatric hospital treatment for the 1980s: A controlled study of short versus long hospitalization*. Lexington, MA: Lexington Books, D.C. Heath.

Goffman, E. (1962). *Asylums: Essays on the social situation of mental patients and other inmates*. Chicago: Aldine. (original 1961)

Grinker, R. R., & Spiegel, J. P. (1945). *Men under stress*. Philadelphia: Blakiston.

Jones, M. (1953). *The therapeutic community: A new treatment method in psychiatry*. New York: Basic Books.

Jones, M. (1968). *Beyond the therapeutic community: Social learning and social psychiatry*. New Haven, CT: Yale University Press.

Kaufman, M. R. (Ed.). (1965). *The psychiatric unit in a general hospital: Its current and future role*. New York: International Universities Press.

Maxmen, J. S., Tucker, G. J., & LeBow, M. (1974). *Rational hospital psychiatry*. New York: Brunner/Mazel.

May, P. R. A. (1968). *Treatment of schizophrenia: A comparative study of five treatment methods*. New York: Science House.

Oldham, J. M., & Russakoff, L. M. (1987). *Dynamic therapy for brief hospitalization*. Northvale, NJ: Jason Aronson.

Rapoport, R. N. (1960). *Community as doctor: New perspectives on a therapeutic community*. Springfield, IL: Charles C. Thomas.

Rubenstein, R., & Lasswell, H. D. (1966). *The sharing of power in a psychiatric hospital.* New Haven, CT: Yale University Press.

Russakoff, L. M. (1999). Psychopharmacology. In J. L. Cutler & E. R. Marcus (Eds.), *Psychiatry* (pp. 308–331). Philadelphia: W. B. Saunders.

Stanton, A. H., & Schwartz, M. S. (1954). *The mental hospital: A study of institutional participation in psychiatric illness and treatment.* New York: Basic Books.

Wessen, A. F. (Ed.). (1964). *The psychiatric hospital as a social system.* Springfield, IL: Charles C. Thomas.

Witkin, M. J., Atay, J. E., Manderscheid, R. W., Delozier, J., Male, A., & Gillespie, R. (1999). Highlights of organized mental health services in 1994 and major national and state trends. In R. W. Manderscheid & M. J. Henderson (Eds.), *Mental health, United States, 1998* (pp. 143–175). Center for Mental Health Services DHHS Pub. No. (SMA)99-3285. Rockville, MD: SAMHSA, U.S. Government Printing Office.

Chapter Eight

Mental Health Management Environments: Management and Leadership in the State Hospital

Harold Carmel

The state hospital can be a rewarding workplace for a clinical manager. Certainly there are many problems. There are never enough resources to meet the need, the clinical problems of the patients can be intractable, the state system can be frustrating, and there are always pressures to cut back. But the work is important to people with severe mental illness, and it is generally fascinating. It can be very rewarding to see how skillful management can make a real difference in the lives of patients and employees.

The clinical manager in a state hospital should be familiar with the history and general structure of state hospitals, because successful leadership needs to accommodate to the particular structure and dynamic of a state hospital. In this chapter, we discuss the background and history of state hospitals in America, their position in contemporary public mental health, and issues the clinical manager in a state hospital needs to successfully address.

WHEN STATE HOSPITALS RULED MENTAL HEALTH

For well over a century, the American public mental health system centered on state hospitals (Deutsch, 1937; Grob, 1991, 1994). Debates over how best to care for people with mental illnesses were played out in institutions. And the development of American state hospitals was a dynamic process, responding to and reflecting broad social trends.

The first American hospital settings to care for people with mental illnesses emerged in the last half of the 18th century. Benjamin Franklin and Benjamin Rush were leaders in establishing in 1751 a general hospital in Philadelphia that included facilities for psychiatric patients. A similar hospital in New York City was delayed by the American Revolution and did not open until 1791 (Grob, 1994, pp. 18–21). The first state hospital opened in 1773 at Williamsburg, VA (Hurd et al., 1916, p. 709). The second state hospital was not established until 1824, when the Eastern

Lunatic Asylum in Lexington, KY, opened. This was followed by the South Carolina State Asylum in Columbia, which opened in 1828 (Hurd et al., 1916, pp. 587–593).

At the same time, the principles of moral treatment (from the French *traitement moral*, "moral" in this case connoting psychologically oriented treatment [Grob, 1994, p. 26 et seq.]) were being developed by Tuke at the York Retreat in England and by Pinel in France (Jimenez, 1987). Moral treatment called for a calm treatment setting where humane vigilance could be brought to bear on the mentally disturbed. It implied respect for the individual and optimism about the course of the disease (Caplan, 1969). A private facility operated by Quakers, the Friends Asylum in Pennsylvania, opened in 1817 (Hurd et al., 1916, pp. 439–443). Others quickly followed and helped disseminate principles of moral treatment over the next few decades (Deutsch, 1937, p. 89 et seq.).

For persons with mental illness who could not be tolerated at large in society, the dominant placement was in the poorhouses or workhouses. These dated from colonial times and would last until the early 20th century. Although poorhouses were brutal environments for anyone, they were particularly barbaric for persons with mental illness (Deutsch, 1937, pp. 114–131). In reaction to this, the reformers of the day worked to establish state hospitals (Jimenez, 1987, pp. 104–105). In the decade before 1843, nine additional state hospitals were built.

Dorothea Dix (1802–1887) became prominent in the 1840s, campaigning tirelessly to improve conditions in state hospitals and to build state hospitals where there were none. Dix was active in all the states east of the Rockies, in Nova Scotia and Newfoundland, and even, in the 1850s, in Europe (Deutsch, 1937, pp. 158–185).

Dix's political efforts climaxed with a six-year campaign to set aside federal land to support the care of people with mental illnesses. In 1854, a bill to set aside 10 million acres for this purpose was passed by both houses of Congress. But what would have been an interesting turn in the history of American state hospitals was not to be. Franklin Pierce, one of the undistinguished presidents in office before the Civil War, vetoed the bill. He did not want to set a precedent that might transfer to the federal government the charge of all the poor in all the states (special message of President Pierce to the Senate of the U.S., May 1854, cited in Deutsch, 1937, p. 178).

The establishment of state hospitals was encouraged by what Grob has called "the cult of curability" (claims of extraordinarily high rates of recovery). Shortly after the Hartford Retreat opened in Connecticut in 1827, it claimed that 21 of its first 23 patients recovered, a cure rate of 91.3% (Caplan, 1969, p. 90). Hospitals competed with each other in announcing high rates of recovery, and claims of cure rates of 90 to 100% were common. These claims fueled the public policy debate by promoting the impression that insanity is largely curable, and that therefore building specialized hospital settings was a worthy government activity. The statistics were meaningless, with poor record-keeping (in many instances, the same patient would be issued a new patient number and not be counted as a readmission), small numbers, and suspicious practices such as sampling only discharged patients or counting as cured patients who died (Caplan, 1969, pp. 88–97). But by the mid-19th century, as wards became chronically overcrowded, as more immigrants and paupers filled asylums, and as public laws obliged superintendents to accept alcoholics, criminals, and other "undesirable" patients (Caplan, 1969, p. 143), the excessive optimism was replaced by profound therapeutic pessimism. The care of patients deteriorated (Caplan, 1969, p. 143–168).

There is no better evidence of the central role of the state hospital in American psychiatry than the establishment, in 1844, of the Association of Medical Superintendents of American Institutions for the Insane (Caplan, 1969, pp. 99–125; Deutsch, 1937, pp. 186–212; Grob, 1994, pp. 74–77). This, of course, is the organization that would become the American Psychiatric Association. The *American Journal of Insanity,* which would become the *American Journal of Psychiatry,* was founded at the Utica (New York) State Asylum, which would publish it until the 1890s (Hurd et al., 1916, pp. 153–156). For this half-century, the deliberations of the Association and in the *Journal* were dominated by the preoccupations of those who ran the hospitals.

But this domination would pass. After the Civil War, with its legacy of head injury, neurology flourished as a scientific specialty. By the 1890s more American doctors, becoming interested in neuropsychiatry, became dissatisfied with the state hospital–oriented psychiatric establishment (Caplan, 1969, pp. 199–232). Reformers increasingly criticized state hospitals (Caplan, 1969, pp. 199–243). Psychiatric research began to develop in state psychopathic hospitals, where scientifically oriented leaders, like Adolf Meyer, could flourish (Kolb & Roizin, 1993). The mental hygiene movement was sparked by the 1908 publication of Clifford Beers's *A Mind That Found Itself.* Mental hygiene called for better institutional conditions, efforts to cure psychiatric illness, and efforts to prevent psychiatric illness (Grob, 1983). The focus of mental health began to shift away from state hospitals.

Subsequent developments are very familiar to contemporary clinicians and administrators. State hospitals were hit hard by the collapse of public funding during the Great Depression. By the late 1940s, conditions in state hospitals were scandalous (Sareyan, 1994). Public exposés followed. One of the consequences of the creation of the National Institute of Mental Health (NIMH) in 1949 was to encourage the community mental health movement (Grob, 1991). This coincided with the introduction of the neuroleptics. The population and number of state hospitals reached its peak in 1954–1955 and has been declining ever since (Witkin et al., 1996).

THE 20TH-CENTURY STATE HOSPITAL

In the past half-century, the state hospital's role has continued to evolve. Although the rate of decline has slowed, the number of hospitals and patients continues to drop. As Bachrach has observed, state mental hospitals in the past were very diverse facilities that varied greatly in their milieus, their treatment offerings, and the competence of their personnel, and they continue to be so to this day (Bachrach, 1996). This diversity extends to the role of a state hospital in its state's public mental health system. Each state system is different and uses its hospitals differently.

A number of factors affect the flow of patients to hospitals. These include the population of people with mental illness in the catchment area, the relevant laws and regulations, the alternative services which are available, and the public mental health system's goals for its state hospital (Bachrach, 1996). Commonly, state hospitals have minimal control over the inflow of patients (Applebaum, 1991). State hospitals are at a natural disadvantage in debates on mental health policy (Lamb & Shaner, 1993). The politically correct position is that state hospitals are inherently undesirable (Bachrach, 1996), and perhaps the most closely watched outcome measure is the decline in the use of state hospital beds (Geller, 1997). This derives from attitudes dating back to the birth of the community mental health movement. These include the conviction that institutions produce, rather than relieve, psychopathology (Goffman, 1961) and the belief that the patient, once discharged from the state hospital, would be well received in a "warm community" (Peele, 1992, p. 479). In addition, important legal doctrines have moved into clinical practice, such as the concept of the "least restrictive alternative" (*Lake v. Cameron,* 364, F.2d 657) and "dangerousness to self and others," without which, in many states, one cannot be admitted to a public psychiatric hospital.

And in this era of smaller government, privatization and capitation is appealing to many policymakers. Replacing public beds with private ones relieves government of the overhead, and capitating state hospital beds can lead to remarkable reductions in census.

Yet state hospitals continue to have important roles:

The state hospital may be the only psychiatric hospital serving a region. It may be the only organization that can assemble the staff and resources to treat patients with specialized needs or needs which can be met nowhere else. The state hospital may be the best choice for services that must be provided, such as emergency and acute psychiatric care. State hospital forensic units are still needed. Often, the state hospital is the last resort for people who have intractable illness, who are repeatedly violent, who do not fit well in any other placement but must be placed somewhere, or who are without financial resources. In many places, the state hospital has the best expertise and experience in treating severe psychiatric illnesses. State hospitals can be valuable sites for training and research, as well as for clinical care.

State hospitals currently have an important role in training and research. A survey done in 1990 (Douglas, Faulkner, Talbott, Robinowitz, Eaton, & Rankin, 1994) reported that 71% of academic departments of psychiatry had a relationship with a state hospital, 40% of which had been established in the preceding decade. Most commonly, the relationship involved the state hospital serving as a residency training rotation site, although other kinds of relationships occur, such as consultation services, provided by 16% of the departments of psychiatry. In North Carolina, for example, the University of North Carolina and Duke University each base major research enterprises, as well as important training sites, in a state hospital. In Colorado, the medical staff of the two state hospitals are full-time faculty of the University of Colorado (Neligh et al., 1991).

THE ORGANIZATION OF THE MODERN STATE HOSPITAL

The challenges faced by a state hospital clinical manager will depend on the particular circumstances of the state hospital. The design of each state's public mental health system defines the role of the hospital, by determining, for example, the commitment laws, the nature of the relationship with community mental health centers, and the clinical mission of the hospital (Bachrach, 1996). But although every state hospital is different, there are common features. For example, that the hospital will be underfunded goes without saying; this has been a defining characteristic from the start.

Most state hospitals are JCAHO-accredited and HCFA (now CMS) certified (data from NAMHSPD web site, http://www.nasmhpd.org/nri/keyword.htm, accessed

March 2000). These are important incentives for state governments to support basic standards of quality in clinical care. There is a constant danger that political leaders, seeing JCAHO accreditation as an unnecessary expense, will attempt to take a hospital out of JCAHO accreditation. Whether openly stated or not, the motivation is to save money. This is generally disastrous for the clinical operations of the hospital. And, even in its own terms, this strategy can lose money for the state in the long run, as litigation resulting from inevitable poor care forces the state to spend money for trials, judgments, and consent decrees.

Leadership in a state hospital requires coordinating the different functional areas—central administration, clinical services, the medical staff, and support services. All employees must understand that the paramount mission of the hospital is patient care and all the nonclinical activities are in support of patient care.

Clinical care is provided by a variety of categories of staff, with varying levels of training and experience. The largest number of clinical staff are psychiatric technicians. These employees, along with registered nurses and licensed practical nurses, have the greatest contact with patients, with responsibility for patient care every hour of every day. These employees are usually organized into a nursing department led by registered nurses.

The medical staff is usually organized along JCAHO lines. Past JCAHO medical staff models, oriented toward private hospitals with medical staffs consisting of private independent practitioners, have been grafted onto state hospitals, with state-employed physicians, with varying results. Each hospital will have its own solution to the question of how much autonomy within the hospital the medical staff has and how much influence on clinical operations it exerts.

The other clinical disciplines—psychology, social work, the rehabilitation therapies, and others—are usually organized along departmental lines.

The lines of authority and supervision for clinical staff can be organized through either a program-based system or a department-based system. In the program-based system, all staff in a clinical program report to the program director. Thus, staff members in many disciplines will be responsible to a supervisor who is not of their professional discipline. This model has the advantage of ensuring that administrative responsibility and decision making governing a clinical program are based in the program. Its disadvantage is that discipline-based professional supervision is diluted.

In a department-based line of authority, all members of a clinical discipline report through clinical supervisors of that discipline to a hospital head of the discipline. The advantage of this system is that it ensures a focus on adherence to professional standards of performance. The disadvantage is that at the clinical program level, lines of authority do not converge on a program manager. As a result, clinical leadership on the program level often can be exercised only through negotiation, which can be protracted, ineffective, and frustrating.

There is no textbook way to organize clinical services. In an ideal world, either system would work, because all the involved supervisors would be excellent at coordinating and communicating with their colleagues. Because such an ideal workplace is uncommon, the choice made in a given hospital probably depends more on the personalities involved and their skills and capabilities than on any given theory of management.

Many organizations seek to finesse this problem through a *matrix* system of management. Here, the direct ("solid line") reporting relationship is via one line of authority; a second line of authority has an indirect, advisory ("dotted line") reporting relationship. Matrix systems are justifiably dreaded in many workplaces, because these systems can breed ambiguity, work against clear leadership, and foster ineffective management.

Clinical leadership and supervision in a state hospital are dominated by the fact that, as a state agency, the hospital is subject to state rules and regulations. These are generally not designed to promote speedy, decisive action. Civil service rules, although valuable in protecting employees from political firings, also protect employees who are not functioning well. The burden of proof in civil service disciplinary processes is generally placed on the supervisor. This becomes a fact of life to which the skilled supervisor adapts. As a result, personnel changes that in the private sector might occur swiftly and with relatively little extra effort can, in the public system, become long-lasting, high-investment projects. Thus, understanding the particular rules of a state system becomes very important to a clinical manager, who must always keep these rules in mind when planning changes in operations.

Just as state regulations dominate personnel matters, they dominate budgeting and purchasing in ways that often seem designed to frustrate. Hospital decisions such as computer purchases and creating clinical positions can be required to go through several layers in the state bureaucracy, often in a far-away state capital. Each layer usually has different priorities, rules, and timetables. Negotiating these successfully is an essential part of the work of the hospital administrators. But this is a time-consuming process, which does not foster a quick response to changing needs. As most clinical operations depend on personnel, budget, and purchasing, the state processes often seem unnecessarily burdensome to clinical managers who are focused on patient care.

THE CLINICAL MANAGER IN THE STATE HOSPITAL

Clinical leadership of the hospital is usually vested in a medical director,[1] although there may be a separate clinical director responsible for nonmedical clinical activities. In a minority of state hospitals (24 in 1996, 9.5% of 252 hospitals),[2] the hospital director is a physician; in smaller hospitals, this can permit the same manager to be both hospital director and medical director.

Many factors contribute to the strength of the clinical leadership of a hospital. Most important are the skills and personal attributes of the medical director. The medical director should be a board-certified psychiatrist with sufficient clinical skills to command the respect of the clinical staff. Managerial and supervisory experience, especially experience in a state hospital setting, is particularly useful. The medical director should be able to perceive how the state hospital needs to function within the state public mental health system and from this should be able to identify how the hospital needs to develop to be of greater service to that system.

The more that all the clinical services ultimately report to the medical director,

---

1. This chapter uses *medical director* somewhat generically. In some organizations, a similar position may be titled *clinical director*, *chief medical officer*, or something else.

2. NASMHPD website, http://www.nasmhpd.org/hlsthtml.htm, accessed March 2000.

the more the medical director is able to organize and coordinate the clinical activities of the hospital. In many hospitals, all clinical services do report to the medical director. Sometimes the nursing service reports directly to the hospital director or another manager, and there are many permutations of how the clinical lines of authority can be structured.

The work of the medical director includes recruiting and retaining capable staff. Often in state hospitals the medical director has less control over salary than he or she has over less tangible aspects of the workplace. If a university or medical school has needs that can be met by the state hospital, this can result in collaborations that enrich the workplace experience for professional staff. This can be easier to negotiate than it might appear. Contemporary departments of psychiatry are under financial pressures that are, if anything, more excruciating than state hospitals face, and mutually beneficial relationships can be negotiated, providing the medical school department with crucial revenue and the state hospital with critical services or staff.

The effective use of clinical staff requires that sufficient numbers of staff are on duty, that the staff are properly trained in what they are supposed to do, and that the staff are properly supervised and led. There is never enough staff. But a hospital's clinical leadership can have an impact on the training and policy and on the supervision and leadership provided staff. Thus, even though deficiencies in clinical operations are usually ascribed to understaffing, often this is not the complete story.

Thus, striving for continual improvement of performance is very important. Although certainly quality improvement is subject to one fad or another, for the clinical leader, whatever the quality of the hospital's current performance, improvement is always possible. The hallmark of excellent clinical leadership is continual striving for improvement, whatever tools and slogans are used.

The best work of a state hospital clinical manager is done by identifying and resolving problems long before they erupt as public scandals. Although undramatic, this is necessary work. In a sense, it can be characterized as preventive maintenance. This work includes attracting and retaining talented managers, supervisors, physicians, and other staff; assuring that proper policies are in place and enforced; fairly allocating available resources within the hospital; improving staff training, which sets the tone of the workplace; and identifying needed plant improvements (such as removing hanging hazards).

The clinical manager needs to stay focused on issues that are within his or her control. At any level, it is tempting to focus on why organizational problems are the fault of other levels in the organization; many times this is true. However, this distracts from trying to improve, as much as possible, the conditions under the manager's control. A manager should try not to justify inaction because of problems in areas over which he or she has no control.

Similarly, the clinical manager's responsibility is to stay focused on patient care, whatever the provocation. Political and budgetary struggles at higher levels should interfere with patient care as little as possible. Pressures from the central office may seem as if they come from a different world (and they do); the wise clinical manager does what he or she can to shield the clinicians in the organization from any disruption these might cause. At the same time, the clinical manager should never yield to the temptation to degrade patient care in order to make a political point or maneuver for budgetary advantage.

A medical director needs to pay attention to the actual experience of patients and staff at the hospital. Knowledge provided indirectly, through the reports of others, can easily prove to be distorted, misleading, or inaccurate. Direct knowledge is an important adjunct to the reports of subordinates. This can come in the form of meetings with patients and staff and of visits to treatment settings. Visits that are unannounced and that occur at times other than the 8-hour/5-day work week can be particularly valuable. The more the medical director has direct knowledge of hospital operations, the better his or her decisions will be.

In the end, the medical director's role is to organize the clinical work of the hospital so that competent professionals can take the best possible care of patients. And the work needs to be organized so that it supports the needs of the larger public mental health system. Doing this effectively requires understanding the structure of the hospital and working through that structure to provide good patient care.

THE STATE HOSPITAL DIRECTOR

The relationship between the hospital director and the medical director is critical. In the best situation, each has identical aspirations for the clinical operations of the hospital. To the extent that both the hospital director and the medical director share philosophies of care and of management, the hospital will operate more smoothly and patient care and staff working conditions will be better. It is very helpful when both share a common focus on the hospital's clinical mission.

The hospital director sets the priorities of the organization, whether explicitly or implicitly. The work of the hospital director is to organize the hospital's resources, staff allocations, and budget in support of the hospital's clinical mission. In the best case, providing the best possible patient care is the central organizing principle controlling the hospital's activities. When this is the case, the priorities and activities even of areas such as housekeeping, plant maintenance, dietary, and communications are focused on supporting the clinical mission of the hospital.

Hospital directors vary in the degree to which they involve themselves with clinical matters. Much depends on the hospital director's own clinical background and skills. Depending on the specific circumstance, a hospital director by being relatively uninvolved can permit a capable medical director to provide unchallenged clinical leadership that is consistent with the hospital director's vision for the hospital. Or, a hospital director can be involved in ways that support the medical director's activities, or that ensure that hospital operations are functioning properly. There are also less beneficial ways the hospital director and medical director can work together, which result in poor patient care. One example is when the two collude in maintaining malfunctioning clinical operations. Conflicts between the two can disrupt a hospital and are not in the medical director's interest, because these tend to be resolved in favor of the hospital director. Much of the work of the hospital director is to identify, recruit, and retain the leadership and clinical staff who can promote good patient care, a good workplace environment, and continual improvement. Without managers and supervisors throughout the hospital who support these goals, the hospital director's effectiveness will be blocked. It can be a process of years for a director to win over or recruit managers and supervisors who promote such goals. This is essential work that needs continual attention.

The state hospital is a venerable type of organization, dating back more than two centuries. Throughout the years, state hospitals have dramatically changed, and changed again and again. At the turn of this century, the state hospital is still a robust organization, capable, within all its limitations, of providing good patient care, of serving the public interest, and of providing satisfying professional careers.

REFERENCES

Applebaum, P. S. (1991). Law and psychiatry: Barring the state hospital door. *Psychiatric Services, 42,* 351–352.

Bachrach, L. (1996). The state of the state hospital. *Psychiatric Services, 47,* 1071–1078.

Caplan, R. B. (1969). *Psychiatry and the community in nineteenth-century America.* New York: Basic Books.

Deutsch, A. (1937). *The mentally ill in America.* New York: Doubleday.

Douglas, E. J., Faulkner, L. R., Talbott, J. A., Robinowitz, C. B., Eaton, J. S., Jr., & Rankin, R. M. (1994). A ten-year update of administrative relationships between hospitals and academic psychiatry departments. *Hospital & Community Psychiatry, 45*(11), 1113–1116.

Geller, J. L. (1997). We still count beds. *Psychiatric Services, 48,* 1233.

Goffman, E. (1961). *Asylums: Essays on the social situation on mental patents and other inmates.* New York: Doubleday.

Grob, G. N. (1983). *Mental illness and American society, 1875–1940.* Princeton, NJ: Princeton University Press.

Grob, G. N. (1991). *From asylum to community: Mental health policy on modern America.* Princeton, NJ: Princeton University Press.

Grob, G. N. (1994). *The mad among us: A history of the care of America's mentally ill.* New York: Free Press.

Hurd, H. H., Drewry, W. F., Dewey, R., Pilgrim, C. W., Blumer, G. A., & Burgess, T. J. W. (1916). *The institutional care of the insane in the United States and Canada* (vol. 3). Baltimore, MD: Johns Hopkins University Pres.

Jimenez, M. A. (1987). *Changing faces of madness: Early American attitudes and treatment of the insane.* Hanover, NH: University Press of New England.

Kolb, L. C., & Roizin, L. (1993). *The first psychiatric institute: How research and education changed practice.* Washington, DC: American Psychiatric Press.

Lamb, H. R., & Shaner, R. (1993). When there are almost no state hospitals left. *Hospital and Community Psychiatry, 44,* 973–976.

Neligh, G., Shore, J. H., Scully, J., Kort, H., Willet, B., Harding, C., & Kawamura, G. (1991). The program for public psychiatry: State–university collaboration in Colorado. *Hospital and Community Psychiatry, 42,* 44–48.

Peele, R. (1992). Ethical issues. In J. A. Talbott, R. E. Hales, & S. L. Keill (Eds.), *Textbook of administrative psychiatry* (2nd ed., pp. 471–491). Washington, DC: American Psychiatric Press.

Sareyan, A. (1994). *The turning point: How men of conscience brought about major change in the care of America's mentally ill.* Washington, DC: American Psychiatric Press.

Witkin, M. J., Atay, J., & Manderscheid, R. (1996). Trends in state and county mental hospitals in the U.S. from 1970 to 1992. *Psychiatric Services, 47,* 1079–1081.

Chapter Nine

Mental Health Management Environments: The Community Mental Health Center Medical Director

Jon E. Gudeman

Describing the typical community mental health center (CMHC) is not an easy task. Many different types of organizations or systems of care may identify themselves as mental health centers, from outpatient clinics to large, complex systems of care serving a variety of patient groups with a broad array of services, including inpatient and long-term care. The role of the medical director depends on many factors, including the size, scope, and overall purpose of the center.

CHARACTERISTICS OF CMHCS

The Joint Commission on Mental Illness in a major planning effort in its 1961 report, *Action for Mental Health,* promoted deinstitutionalization by recommending that hospitals be limited to 1,000 beds and that most persons with serious mental illness be cared for in the community (Joint Commission on Mental Illness and Health, 1961). Then, in the first message a U.S. President ever directed to Congress regarding the needs of the mentally ill, John F. Kennedy asked the legislature to establish "community mental health centers" (CMHCs). He said, "We need a new type of health facility, one which will return mental health care to the mainstream of American medicine and at the same time upgrade mental health services" (Kennedy, 1963). He recommended that the community mental health center become an alternative to state hospitalization and called for federal seed money to construct CMHCs and project grants to cover initial staffing costs. In October 1963, Congress enacted the CMHC construction grants program (Public Law 88-164, 1963), and 2 years later staffing grants were made available to communities.

This chapter uses *medical director* somewhat generically. In some organizations, a similar position may be titled *clinical director*, *chief medical officer*, or something else.

The initial program required that to qualify for funds a center must develop five essential services: inpatient, emergency, partial hospitalization, outpatient, and consultation and education. Five additional services were recommended but not mandated: diagnostic services, rehabilitation services, community precare and aftercare (including foster home placement, home visits, and halfway houses), training, and research and education. In 1975, funding was added for children and adolescents, transitional services for mentally ill persons, and alcohol or substance abuse. It was anticipated that continued funding for CMHCs would come from fees for service, individual and group insurance, voluntary and private contributions, and local and state taxes. Federal support was to "prime the pump," with success depending on development of appropriate arrangements for health insurance.

The operating auspices for a center could vary from state hospitals, to units in general hospital settings, to freestanding programs, to private nonprofit or for-profit psychiatric hospitals. The grant recipient was to be a single agency that would assume responsibility for a designated geographic catchment area with a population of 75,000 to 200,000.

The role of the CMHC relative to the mental health deinstitutionalization movement is complex. As early as 1971, the failure of some CMHCs to work with seriously ill patients in the community was noted (Glasscote & Gudeman, 1971). CMHCs often focused on the care of the less seriously ill. Soon, more emphasis was placed on the care of deinstitutionalized patients, and by 1977 the CMHC legislation was modified to incorporate services for those with serious or persistent mental illness. After several federal administrations tried to decrease centralized national funding, President Reagan finally ceased the federal portion of the CMHC program in January 1981.

COMMUNITY MENTAL HEALTH

It is useful to distinguish three dimensions of community mental health.

- A theory and practice that includes the study of mental illness from a sociocultural perspective, the study of diversity of patients, the role of social class in mental illness, the delivery of services to a community, such as within homes, schools, churches, and so on, and the prevention of mental illness (adapted from the Group for the Advancement of Psychiatry, 1983).
- Broad public health principles, including *primary prevention* (reduction of the incidence of mental disorders in the community), *secondary prevention* (reduction of the duration, intensity, or severity of disorders by early and appropriate intervention), and *tertiary prevention* (reduction of impairment from the ongoing disorder) (Caplan, 1964). The community mental health approach uses consultation and education to intervene as early as feasible with a broad range of people, not just those with serious mental illness.
- Broad service delivery systems with multiple levels of care for specific populations, often through some type of risk sharing. A community service system can be a managed care operation providing services to a defined population, or it can function as the gatekeeper for a managed heath care plan.

Although there is no single description of all community mental health center services, one might begin with the following:

Community mental health centers provide immediately available, readily accessible, local care and treatment, by a multidisciplinary professional staff, to people with a broad range of mental disorders and illnesses.

THE MEDICAL DIRECTOR

Background, Training, and Qualifications

A medical director of a CMHC should be a fully trained psychiatrist, preferably certified by the American Board of Medical Specialties (or its osteopathic or Canadian equivalent, which may be required by some third-party payers). He or she should qualify for privileges as an active member of the medical staff, with appropriate licensure and several years of clinical experience.

The roles of a medical director are foreign to many psychiatrists and other professionals (Feldman, 1981). Psychiatrists are generally trained to diagnose and treat individual patients. Although they are often part of a treatment team or clinical group, their clinical roles are separate from thoughts of (or expertise in) organizations and systems of care. Before one can assume a medical director role in a CMHC, he or she must learn about such things as reporting relationships, rules and regulations, policies and procedures, division of labor, and planning, not as a caregiver but as a manager and leader. In community programs there are multiple demands, especially regarding staffing, funding, and community support.

It is thus useful, although not required, for the medical director to have advanced training in medical or mental health administration, such as a graduate degree in administration or public health. American Psychiatric Association (APA) certification in psychiatric administration and management is evidence of such training and experience, and of successful completion of a rigorous examination. Some professional organizations, such as the APA, the American College of Physician Executives, and the American Association of Psychiatric Administrators (AAPA), offer or support extensive post-MD continuing education programs.

Role, Authority, and Responsibility

Most mental health programs, state departments of mental health, and community mental health centers are directed by administrators who are not physicians, and may or may not have a clinical background. There are both advantages and disadvantages to separation of clinical and overall administrative authority and roles. The roles of the chief executive officer (who may be called an administrator or executive director) and the medical director, when they are separate positions, can be complementary, parallel, independent, or (at times) conflicting, depending on definitions of authority and responsibility and on the working relationship.

Unless the chief executive officer (CEO) is trained and qualified to provide medical direction, the medical director usually has responsibility for the organization's medical/psychiatric services. That responsibility may be carried out in a context of direct authority over clinical services, or through a primarily monitoring and oversight role. In either event, the medical director must have sufficient authority to meet the organization's—and patients'—needs.

In some CMHCs and other mental health organizations, the medical director has *broad and direct* authority, under which all professional staff report ultimately to him or her. In such a setting, regardless of organizational format, doctors, nursing staff and allied health professionals, and nonmedical clinicians know that the "clinical enterprise" is ultimately overseen by a psychiatrist, who is, in turn, very near the top of the organization.

In others, the medical director has *broad but indirect* authority, such as responsibility for policy and procedure decisions but no "line" authority over clinicians. In this setting, the medical director is often seen as a powerful member of the organization's executive team, influential in upper administration, and able to affect clinical care broadly and positively without exerting direct or "chain-of-command" authority. The regard with which he or she is viewed by both the chief executive officer (CEO) and the clinical staff is very important to administrative success.

In still other CMHCs and mental health organizations, the medical director has only *narrow and/or indirect* authority. For example, he or she may be the titular leader of a small staff of physicians but have no real influence over other clinical staff and activities, or may have only some limited level of clinical oversight. Such positions are often created merely to fill some regulatory or payor contract requirement, or simply to offer a flattering title to a doctor. They are often part-time, and may have little real influence on organization policy or patient care.

Some common medical director roles and responsibilities in mental health organizations are outlined next. Note that the list is not all-inclusive, nor is it necessary that each CMHC medical director assume all of the responsibilities. Some topics are highlighted in subsequent sections.

Selected Medical Director Roles

- *Assist, be a partner to, and collaborate with the organization CEO.*
- *Assure that all clinical functions meet the appropriate standard of care, regardless of fiscal or staffing limitations.* When clinically, ethically, and legally adequate standards cannot be met, move rapidly to assess and correct the deficiency, and/or to curtail services that cannot be provided competently.
- *Assure adequate clinical staffing* to provide diagnosis, evaluation, and treatment of people with mental disorders. Be responsible for the clinical competence, ethical behavior, and professional standards of all clinical staff.
- *Oversee the organization's clinical care*, including quality improvement, peer review, utilization review, pharmacy and therapeutics, and other organization functions that monitor and ensure quality.
- *Recruit, supervise, evaluate, and retain clinicians.* Assure appropriate credentialing, privileging, performance appraisal, and chart reviews. Develop clinical job descriptions that include direct patient care and time for collaboration, multidisciplinary planning, training and continuing education, teaching, and record-keeping. Perform direct supervision as per the medical director's role in the organization.
- *Interact administratively with, participate in, and/or support internal CMHC groups and resources*, such as the clinical staff, executive committee, medical staff organization, and board of directors.
- *Define and develop interaction and communication with others who are responsible for critical CMHC functions,* including leaders of the different clinical and

allied disciplines and managers of nonclinical departments (e.g., budget and finance, plant services, policy and planning, public information, legal counsel,
marketing).

- *Work with all levels of the CMHC in the planning function,* including long- and
  short-term planning, strategic planning, budgeting, and implementation.
- *Interact with external organizations and agencies,* such as community groups and
  agencies, clinical partners and referral organizations, community social services,
  jails, regulatory bodies, and payors.
- *Develop appropriate standards of clinical practice.*
- *Develop appropriate continuing medical/professional education for all clinical
  and allied staff.*
- *Develop and participate in program evaluation.*
- *Develop and participate in clinical research and teaching,* including relationships
  with academic institutions.
- *Provide direct patient care.* If the medical director has direct patient care respon-
  sibility, he or she should practice as a model for other clinicians.

After considering these roles and responsibilities, the medical director's job
description should carefully delineate his or her purpose, duties and functions, expectations for direct clinical care, reporting requirements, horizontal and vertical
working relationships, authority for nonmedical clinicians and direct-care staff, program responsibility, salary and benefits, and so on. The position may be full-time or
part-time, employed or contractual, depending on the organization, job description
and size of the CMHC.

Program Development

Development of new programs, maintenance of existing programs, and changing
outmoded programs to meet new needs can be among the most gratifying components of a medical director's position. The first step in the process is usually identification of a need. The need may have been identified by staff observations, some
external source (such as a new grant program), consumer input, quality improvement studies, budget constraints, payer changes, or scientific advances in the field.
Examples might include a new mandate to treat dual-diagnosis patients, or to set up
programs for posttraumatic stress disorders, eating disorders, or dementia. It may be
necessary to develop new alternatives to hospitalization, either to decrease admissions (the "front door" to the center) or to shorten inpatient stay by means of "step-
down" community programs that can accept patients before they are ready for fully
independent living (the discharge or "back door"). These might include mobile crisis teams, crisis respite homes, walk-in services, or continuing care programs such
as case management, assertive community treatment, community support, housing,
and programs for the homeless and jail populations.

Meeting identified needs and developing new programs are multidisciplinary
processes, often involving not only the CMHC itself but outside resources and stakeholders. After a plan has been developed and approved, the medical director may
oversee its implementation. He or she is likely to be involved in the program evaluation that becomes necessary from the beginning of the new project. Based on the
evaluation, comparing effectiveness and efficiency with previous programs or con-

trol groups, feedback can be provided to the program and appropriate adjustments made.

STAFFING AND REPORTING RELATIONSHIPS

Center staffing should reflect overall clinical and social goals and objectives, and be in accord with the needs of the board of directors, outside regulatory bodies, and funding sources. Staffing patterns may also be related to the operating authority. For example, academic mental health centers may have a variety of professional trainees, whereas general-hospital-based centers have a heavier focus on medical personnel. Community-based services, in turn, have proportionately more multidisciplinary staffing.

Reporting Formats

There are three basic reporting formats for professional employees. In a "matrix" organization, each clinician reports both to the head of his or her professional discipline (for professional matters) and to the chief of his or her clinical service (such as an outpatient clinic or hospital ward), who may not be of the same discipline, or may be simply an administrator. Such "two-boss" systems require considerable maturity and professionalism of staff. Accountability and reporting responsibility must be carefully delineated, but have the advantage of maintaining strong professional integrity within each discipline. This system works well in academic environments.

In a "pure" *program* model, all professionals, regardless of background and training, report to the director of their programs or units (e.g., all professionals working on an inpatient service reporting to the director/administrator of that unit, or of some group of units). Employee-physicians may be excepted from such a model, in part because of their independent responsibility for patient care, the "discretionary" nature of their employment (i.e., much of what they do is determined by their own decisions rather than those of a nonphysician or administrative procedure), and laws in some states that prohibit a physician from being directly supervised by a nonphysician.

The third possibility, that of having all professionals report only to professional discipline supervisors outside their work areas (such as academic department heads), creates such a weak work-site environment and administration that it is rarely employed for nonphysicians. Systems which have reporting relationships only to supervisors in one's own discipline (medicine to medicine, nursing to nursing, social work to social work) can create isolated, self-protective disciplines and poorly functioning multidisciplinary teams. With regard to psychiatrists, the medical director should be careful not to develop an elite medical team that excludes the medical staff from multidisciplinary work.

Team and "Medical" Models

The medical director, in collaboration with other professional disciplines, defines the necessary staffing patterns which will permit assessment, diagnosis, medical screening, and medical evaluation, treatment, and case management. There are two main models for clinical service delivery: the so-called "medical" model associated with inpatient units (which we call, more accurately, the *inpatient* model), and the *outpatient team* model sometimes associated primarily with outpatient care. (Note the potential for misunderstanding the connotation of *team*. Both models use a multidisciplinary team approach.)

The *inpatient* model consists largely of physicians who have primary responsibility for diagnosis and treatment orders; nursing and nursing assistants who care for the patient 24 hours a day, carry out orders, observe, and react; social workers who work with families and social and vocational issues (including continuing-care placement and living situations); counseling/therapy staff; other allied professionals, such as occupational and activity therapists; and ancillary professionals, such as psychologists or neurologists, who provide specialized assessments and procedures. There is a great deal of communication in modern versions of this model (e.g., in treatment and discharge planning), as well as significant interchangeability and sharing of functions.

In the *outpatient team* model, the clinical roles are more delineated but the psychiatrist should retain overall diagnostic authority, approval of the treatment plan, and responsibility for at least the biological aspects of treatment (e.g., medications). Community support programs for people with severe and persistent illness rely on a multidisciplinary team approach with interchangeability of many of the management functions. Communication within the treatment team is at once more difficult and more important in multidisciplinary outpatient work with the chronically mentally ill; calls, crisis plans, meetings, and good charting knit the pieces of the patient's care together so that each clinician can see how his or her observations and work affect the whole. Assertive community treatment (ACT, PACT) programs improve treatment further, in part by increasing intensity of care and interdisciplinary communication.

In one version to be avoided of the outpatient team model, the psychiatrist is fairly isolated from the overall care of the patient, providing only medication visits and symptom management. A counselor or therapist may provide some kind of therapy without very much communication with either the psychiatrist or the case manager. The potential for problems is obvious.

MEDICAL STAFF FUNCTIONS

In most CMHCs, the medical director's office is responsible for the recruitment, retention, and performance of the medical staff. In large centers the medical staff is usually organized in accord with external regulatory bodies such as the Joint Commission on Accreditation of Healthcare Organizations (JCAHO), the Health Care Financing Administration (HCFA, now the Centers for Medicare & Medicaid [CMS]), and/or the National Committee for Quality Assurance (NCQA). An officially constituted medical staff organization must be independent of the medical director and center administration. The medical staff organization has bylaws, rules and regulations, and policies and procedures. In smaller centers, many of the functions of the medical staff are subsumed under another agency that has a medical staff organization, such as a hospital.

The medical staff organization reviews virtually all aspects of care and provides recommendations to the medical director, chief executive officer, and governing body. This is often accomplished in a formal meeting with the center's executive committee or governing body. The medical staff organization's work is implemented by the CMHC executive committee and others, such as credentialing and privileging, peer review, pharmacy and therapeutics (drug use evaluation), medical records, utilization review, and others. The medical director's office provides professional input into these committees, often develops appropriate policies and procedures, and may represent the medical staff to external accrediting bodies.

The medical director administratively oversees the work of all physicians, including employees, contracting physicians, volunteer medical staff, and trainees. This includes assessing professional judgment, quantity and quality of work, communication skills, reliability, knowledge, initiative, and cooperation. It also includes monitoring malpractice actions, drug or alcohol abuse, denial of privileges, and other actions against the professional. Repriviliging is done at least biennially; performance evaluations by supervisors should be carried out annually.

Pertinence and performance reviews form a significant component of the ongoing evaluation of medical staff. The medical records department performs quantitative analysis of charting compliance for individual physicians. Physicians perform qualitative reviews of the records and provide confidential peer review to their colleagues. The pharmacy and therapeutics committee monitors medication protocols, adverse drug reactions, and medication errors and, when indicated, carries out a critical incident or sentinel event analysis on adverse outcomes. Formulary restrictions and monitoring of prescribing practices may be implemented when fiscally necessary, but exceptions must be allowed when clinically indicated.

EDUCATION AND TRAINING

The medical director may be responsible for developing appropriate clinical staff training and education (or for working with the human resources department to do so). In some situations, training includes programs with academic centers. All medical/psychiatric staff should receive continuing medical education (CME), much of which should be related directly to their areas of work; 12 to 20 "category I" hours are required in most states. Accredited CME may be provided at the center (with appropriate sponsorship) or elsewhere; attendance at outside educational functions may be funded as a perquisite of employment. Peer review and pertinence reviews can identify areas for additional training.

QUALITY IMPROVEMENT

The medical director should work with the director of quality assurance (total quality management, performance improvement) and with the various program, unit, and department heads. A performance improvement plan should include indicators, expectations, and plans to manage processes to improve and maintain quality of services. The medical leadership, in collaboration with disciplines and programs, establishes measurable objectives for improving organization performance, for example, in areas such as seclusion and restraint, untoward incidents, accidents and injuries, medication errors, adverse drug reactions, or patient satisfaction. The JCAHO plan–do–check–act cycle of performance improvement from Stewart and Deming (Scherkenbach, 1990) is one process for performance improvement. Conclusions, evaluations, and ongoing new initiatives are created to keep the process relevant (Juran, 1989; Senge, 1990). The medical director participates in the quality improvement meetings, reviews all quality improvement (QI) projects, and assists in their implementation. Various questions can be asked of medical leadership:

- Does the medical staff use performance reviews to provide feedback to improve their effectiveness?
- Does the medical staff implement key practices to address requirements arising from rules, regulations, laws, and accountability?
- Does the medical leadership seek input from staff members and their supervisors on education and training needs, expectations, and design?
- Does the medical staff address key needs, including cultural diversity, new staff orientation, and safety?
- Does the organization include patient preferences and decisions in the delivery of patient care?

CLINICAL CARE

The medical director has the professional identity of clinician. The responsibilities just enumerated can easily take all of his or her professional time. The medical director must decide (with the chief executive officer) how much time should be devoted to direct patient care.

Regardless of the amount of direct clinical care, one of the most important aspects of the medical director role is to provide clinical leadership. Not only must one's professional identity be retained, but the medical director's influence on the professional staff is greatly enhanced by clinical competence. Not all medical directors have an extraordinary level of expertise, but when it exists it adds an important dimension to the work.

An understanding of biological, psychological, sociocultural, rehabilitation, and existential dimensions is necessary; no single approach to clinical care is sufficient. The medical director should be familiar with basic neuroscience, old and new medications, medication protocols, practice guidelines and algorithms for care, and legal issues regarding treatment (such as consent and standards of care). He or she should be familiar with (but not necessarily expert in) every kind of psychotherapy or counseling, rehabilitation, and social intervention used in the center, as well as others that might reasonably be useful for its patients. Diagnostic ability is important, and he or she should be able to provide a model for patient evaluation and the clinician–patient relationship.

The medical director's sensitivity to the existential components of work with patients is essential. An appreciation of the personal struggles patients have with their illness contributes to successful work with families and outside agencies. The next subsection provides a framework for the principles of care.

Philosophy of Care

The medical director must be continually guided by, and must lead his or her staff with, the following principles:

- The person with mental illness (patient, client, resident, customer, consumer, case) comes first. Practice must be with dignity and respect for the fragility of the human condition. The Hippocratic Oath to do no harm is as sound today as it was 2,000 years ago.
- It is our job to help each person acknowledge the pain that he or she cannot voice. Then we must help the patient bear the intolerable pain and put it in perspective.
- To the maximum extent possible, the principle "Once your patient, always your patient" should be a principle toward which we strive. Continuity in the care of patients is an essential of good treatment.
- The sociopolitical and economic condition, as well as a historical perspective, is essential to an understanding of the individual. The family must always be appropriately considered in establishing working relationships with an individual.
- As we begin work with every person, we must ask whether there is some biological or medical condition which can explain the person's condition. Medical conditions may present as psychological events, and the reverse holds true as well. Therapeutic intervention always includes a consideration of the medical aspects of illness.
- We must pursue the details of a person's actual experience, helping him or her put into words the painful thoughts, feelings, and actions. Our unique skill is to help an individual learn from experience. We are special teachers.
- To be given the permission to listen to a patient in a therapeutic situation is a privilege that we must never abuse. Neglect, physical or sexual abuse, excessive fraternization, or sexual involvement with a patient is absolutely prohibited. A clinician must understand transference and countertransference as they relate to action in the therapeutic session.
- Ethical principles articulated by each of the professional societies must be strictly adhered to by the professional.
- The pleasure of helping another individual must always be set within the perspective that this is our job. Avarice, greed, and self-aggrandizement have no place in our work.
- Mental illness can be approached from a variety of perspectives—biologic, psychologic, social, political, economic, religious, aesthetic, intellectual. At this time, no one approach holds all the answers to the human condition. We must recognize that all other people are similar in some ways, some other people are similar in some ways, and each person is unique in some ways.

MANAGED CARE AND COMMUNITY MENTAL HEALTH SERVICES

Managed care is difficult to define. In its broadest sense, it is simply management of the system of care to deliver cost-effective and efficient care, and includes service and funding models under which CMHCs have operated for decades. From an insurer's perspective, it is an attempt to provide adequate care while decreasing or limiting the cost of services. From a provider (physician or clinical organization) viewpoint, managed care usually involves coverage of a defined population, with some financial risk for the provider. For a patient, a managed care plan makes some kinds of care available, a usually limited but sometimes comprehensive range of health care services performed by providers who participate in the plan, when approved by the payor. A more comprehensive discussion of managed mental health care is provided elsewhere in this book.

Mental health centers often assume responsibility either as primary providers of managed care for persons with mental illness or mental retardation, or as gatekeepers for other providers. Usually the center contracts with the managed care entity to provide mental health services to insured persons or subscribers of managed care organizations as a "carve-out" for mental health (i.e., as the mental health [and perhaps substance abuse] part of a broader health care plan).

The relationship between a managed care organization (MCO) and a patient is one in which an administrative entity is placed between the patient and the physician or other caregiver. To some extent, any third-party payor affects care. "Managed care" programs affect access, type, and (often) quality of care more directly in that the payor has an influential role (sometimes a controlling role, in the case of health maintenance organizations [HMOs]) in access and clinical decisions themselves. The concept is not new, and CMHCs have long been funded largely through prepayment or capitation schemes (e.g., with tax dollars allocated according to population or case load). There are many variants, including HMOs, preferred provider organizations (PPOs), and independent practice associations (IPAs), some with "point of service" options, options for participants to seek care outside the plan, ways for insurers to "disenroll" consumers, and the like. Some managed health plans have recently begun to focus on monitoring the quality of care rather than managing access to care. Most states require MCOs to offer grievance procedures, access standards, continuity of care, court-ordered services, coverage for dependents, and quality assurance.

The medical director and staff must find providers (clinicians and others) within the CMHC system and outside it who can offer acceptable clinical, rehabilitative, and psychosocial services in a cost-effective manner. Each person who offers clinical services must be credentialed and privileged, and nonclinical providers must be reviewed for appropriate licenses, backgrounds, procedures, and the like. Providers should be educated about the center's goals and purposes, including those of the managed care plan. The medical director is generally involved in assuring that each employee, CMHC unit, contract clinician or service, and referral agency provides appropriate assessment, treatment, confidentiality, quality monitoring, and evaluation (including attention to patient satisfaction).

Staff Model, Carve-Out

In one managed care iteration (the *staff* model, similar to many HMOs), center-employed clinicians provide virtually all the mental health services for a designated population of enrollees in return for a lump-sum payment. This is an attractive approach for a large, comprehensive mental health center because most of the necessary services are in place, collections (although routinely quite discounted) are guaranteed, and large patient populations or catchment areas make service use somewhat predictable. It requires very careful management, however, in order to budget for unexpected usage and cost, survive in a competitive market, and deal with future contract negotiations (which may decrease payment after the center has committed itself to care for the patient population).

"Carve-Ins"

The center's mental health component of overall health care may also be integrated (or "carved in") with other medical care. In this model, the CMHC and its clinicians work more collaboratively with primary care providers, allowing better breadth of care, early intervention, easy consultation and liaison, and sometimes economies of scale. The mental health component (in this case a mental health center) is in a position both to control costs with appropriate "gatekeeping" and to provide more comprehensive care through its affiliation with general medical settings. However, in some situations "carve-ins" allow the health agency to use potential mental health allocations for other purposes.

Less Restrictive Models

Many insurers, purchasers of services, and patients themselves prefer not to restrict care to a specific staff model mental health center, but want a broader choice of providers. In these models, the center generally establishes a network of psychiatrists and other clinicians (providers) who agree to see the center's patients at a particular prearranged rate, under the center's (and the ultimate payer's) particular funding and utilization rules. The center usually receives a lump-sum payment from the MCO for care of the entire covered population, and then budgets payments to the external clinicians (sometimes by service rendered and sometimes in a lump-sum contract amount). Such models spread (or share) the risk of capitation-based funding.

Once again, readers may note that these models of payment and arrangement for care are similar to the public-sector capitation and budgeting used for state- and local-government-funded mental health care. The differences are seen largely in the for-profit nature of most private MCOs and funding plans, a hope of greater efficiency and flexibility in the private sector, less social and political accountability (and arguably less dedication to patient need) in the private sector compared to the public sector, and relative instability of private-sector MCO funding (e.g., a likelihood of contract changes and decreased funding based on company needs, or changes from one MCO to another), even considering the political vicissitudes of public funding.

Medical Necessity

"Medical necessity" is a crucial aspect of managed care, because its primary means of reducing costs is by limiting care while, one hopes, retaining the services patients need and have contracted for. The medical director's office is routinely involved in authorization of services, often by trying to define what care is necessary (both as a matter of center policy and for individual patients whose needs and requests fall outside the norm). There is no universally accepted definition of medical necessity, but Moffic, in his excellent book *The Ethical Way* (Moffic, 1997), suggested that one apply the Sabin and Daniels (1994) definition:

- A diagnosed *DSM (IV)* Axis I or II disorder with the required symptoms documented on the treatment plan.
- Impaired social function as a presumed consequence of the disorder.
- Treatment available that can be justified by professional literature.

Clinical practice guidelines, available from many sources (notably the American Psychiatric Association, 2000), are very helpful for the medical director, care managers, and the providers of service. Properly researched and expounded guidelines often approximate the legal concept of a "standard of care." We strongly recommend that such guidelines come from sources independent of managed care rather than from representatives of the industry (or any specific company) itself.

The role of the medical director is broadened with the advent of managed care, with benefits as well as liabilities accruing. In good-case situations, acceptable care is maintained and the medical director participates with others in cost containment and medical necessity; fees can be based on perceived value rather than tradition; poor treatment can be reduced; treatment-plan guidelines can lead the way and sometimes mental health professionals can spend more time doing what they do best. In worse-case situations, however, managed care can become money saved for profit, clinicians can become overregulated and (especially psychiatrists) undervalued, patients can receive less than adequate (and certainly less than optimal) care, treatment can be unfairly denied, and some treatments (such as psychodynamic psychotherapy) can be unreasonably excluded. The medical director must strive for quality services in an environment of cost containment.

LAW, LIABILITY, AND THE MENTAL HEALTH CENTER

The medical director has a leading role in keeping the CMHC services within what the civil law calls the "standard of care," and in reducing the probability of litigation alleging malpractice or other kinds of negligence. The keys to reducing litigation are quality care, good communication with patients and staff, and appropriate risk management. Some areas that should be addressed and/or monitored are outlined in Table 9.1.

The medical director often has some role in non-patient-related legal issues as well, such as employment- and contract-related issues among the clinical staff. Legal issues in mental health management are addressed more completely in a separate section of this book.

The medical director should have a close working relationship with the organization's legal counsel. The attorney(s) may be employees in some large centers, but are more often either retained from the private sector or employees of a larger entity (such as a state or regional agency or a consortium of mental health centers). Preventive consultations are recommended—for example, when develop-

Table 9.1. Selected Patient-Related Legal Issues

Crisis and admission processes	Availability of emergency and crisis services, involuntary detention and treatment, civil commitment, outpatient commitment, other court-ordered treatment, consent for voluntary admission, right to access services
Assessment and diagnosis	Adequacy of evaluation, seeking and corroboration of important clinical information, access to necessary range of assessment services, completeness of assessment, diagnosis and misdiagnosis
Clinical care and treatment	Appropriateness of treatment, availability of necessary or desirable treatment, consent and refusal, involuntary treatment, appropriateness of treatment environment, least restrictive clinically appropriate setting, side and adverse effects, monitoring for treatment response, communication between and among clinicians and clinical staff, communication to patient and family, appropriate duration of (especially inpatient) care
Safety during treatment	Protection from harm, safety of the treatment environment, recognition of dangers associated with diagnosis and symptoms, potential dangers of treatment, monitoring for self-harm or harm to others, monitoring for abuse or neglect
Safety of third parties	Recognition of danger to staff, family, others; opportunities to protect third parties; obligations to protect third parties
Confidentiality and privilege	Obligation of confidentiality, important exceptions to that obligation
Other patients' rights	
Discharge procedures	Planning for decreased intensity of care, patient needs and stability, appropriate referral, transition to next level of care, abandonment, safety and appropriateness of community psychosocial resources

ing organization policies and procedures or contemplating a new contract. It is much more important to know how and where to obtain legal advice than to try to understand the nuances of the law oneself.

LEADERSHIP

One of the most critical roles the medical director of a community program must fill is leadership of the center's clinical enterprise. The medical director represents both patients and clinical staff in many important fora. Staff should see him or her as a strong supporter of what they need to do their jobs and pursue their careers. Patients need a dedicated person to represent their needs within upper management. External viewers often see the medical director as the personification of the organization's purpose, and the most visible member of the management team. In order to carry out these roles, to lead, the medical director must have knowledge of everything we have discussed and more, but knowledge is not enough.

The medical director must be able to make difficult decisions, listen attentively to staff, provide support, lead by example, and listen for opportunity. Skill-based knowledge must be enhanced by an ability to tolerate ambiguity, establish respect, and perform with dignity and trust.

Each medical director has his or her own unique style. There is no single right way to lead. Some principles of leadership are discussed elsewhere in this book, and we encourage readers who aspire to such positions to seek out resources—and mentors—who can help them move from mental health management to clinical leadership.

REFERENCES

American Psychiatric Association. (2000). *Practice guidelines for the treatment of psychiatric disorders compendium 2000*. Washington, DC: American Psychiatric Press.

Caplan, G. (1964). *Principles of preventive psychiatry*. New York: Basic Books.

Feldman, S. (1981). Leadership in mental health: Changing the guard for the 1980s. *American Journal of Psychiatry, 138*(9), 1147–1153.

Glasscote, R., & Gudeman, J. (1971). *Halfway houses for the mentally ill*. Washington, DC: Joint Information Service of the American Psychiatric Association.

Group for the Advancement of Psychiatry. (1983). *Community psychiatry: A reappraisal*. New York: Mental Health Materials Center.

Joint Commission on Mental Illness and Health. (1961). *Action for mental health, first report*. New York: Basic Books.

Juran, J. M. (1989). *Juran on leadership for quality*. New York: Free Press.

Kennedy, J. F. (1963). *Message from the President of the United States relative to mental illness and mental retardation*. House of Rep. Doc. No. 58, 88th Congress., First Session, 5 February.

Moffic, H. S. (1997). *The ethical way*. San Francisco: Jossey-Bass.

Public Law 88-164. (1963). *Mental retardation facilities and community mental health centers construction act of 1963*. 88th Congress.

Sabin, J., & Daniels, D. N. (1994). Determining medical necessity in mental health practice. *Hastings Center Report, 24*(6), 5–13.

Scherkenbach, W. (1990). *The Deming route to quality and productivity*. Milwaukee, WI: Ceep Press.

Senge, P. (1990). *The fifth discipline: The art and practice of the learning organization*. New York: Doubleday.

Chapter Ten

Mental Health Managment Environments: Children's Mental Health Services—The Challenge of Changing Policy and Practice

Lenore B. Behar

BACKGROUND OF CHILD MENTAL HEALTH SERVICES

Over this past century, services to children with mental health/behavioral health disorders evolved from both the child welfare system and the juvenile court system into a separate and major part of the network of public-sector services designed to address the problems of children.[1] This separate diagnostic and treatment system emerged during the first part of the century, and the specialty professions of child psychiatry, child psychology, and child-oriented social work grew in numbers. Despite this growth, when the White House Conference on Mental Health met in 1961 it included no discussions of children with mental health disorders, and the child mental health professionals raised concerns about this omission. To remedy this oversight, Congress commissioned the Joint Commission on Mental Health of Children in 1966–1968. This commission took the form of a panel of experts who held nationwide public forums and visited settings where professional treatment was offered. The result of this 2-year study was a series of recommendations that were published in a report entitled *Crisis in Child Mental Health: Challenge for the 1970s* (Joint Commission on Mental Health of Children, 1969).

---

1. The term *children* refers to those who are considered to be minors, usually those from birth to the age of 18 years. However, for purposes of mental health services, some states include those up to the age of 21, as this parallels the Medicaid definition. Others include those up to the age of 22, as this parallels the definition for special education, for those children who do not complete their public school education prior to that age. For mental health/juvenile justice/social services, the term *children* also varies from state to state, depending on the state's legal age cutoff for each agency. The age of majority in all states is 18; thus, many states use this age point as the separation between childhood and adulthood for mental health/social services. Juvenile justice services may terminate at 15, 16, or 18, depending on state law.

These recommendations became the blueprint for the next 30 years, being some-what augmented or reshaped over that time period, but having far-reaching implica-tions nonetheless. The major recommendations were that:

1. Despite the growth of the child-oriented professions, there was a large unmet need for diagnostic and treatment services.
2. The services needed by children with a wide range of problems and differing severity of problems should be organized within a continuum of care, so that services would range from the least intensive to the most intensive.
3. The provision of mental health services to children should be a state responsibil-ity because this was too big an order for the federal government, given the need to tailor services by region or geography.
4. There should be a strong advocacy movement to ensure the development of ser-vices to this hidden population of children.

Although all of the recommendations had an impact on the field, the recom-mendation that brought about the biggest change in the delivery of services was the one that addressed the need for a continuum of mental health services ranging from the least restrictive to the most restrictive. The concept of the continuum of care served a twofold purpose: (1) to allow children to move from more restrictive to less restrictive as they demonstrated improvement in their conditions; and (2) to provide a range of services that could meet the varying needs of the population. Prior to the report of the Joint Commission, outpatient therapy and treatment in inpatient set-tings were the services likely to be available in most communities, despite the belief of professionals that a wider range of services was needed.

Opinions may differ on the relative importance of the following events in carv-ing a new role for children's mental health, but there is no doubt that these events pushed ahead the agenda set forth by the Joint Commission on Mental Health of Children.

1. In 1979, a lawsuit was filed against officials of the State of North Carolina on behalf of assaultive children deprived of their rights to treatment and education under a series of state and federal laws. In 1980, in an unprecedented move, the state officials agreed to settle the lawsuit and build a continuum of care for this population and the state legislature provided the needed funding to do so. The Willie M. lawsuit provided "proof" that very difficult children could be treated within a continuum of community-based services, becoming the first real ex-ample of a large-scale response to children's mental health needs (*Willie M. et al. v. James B. Hunt, Jr., et al.*, 1980).
2. In 1982, Jane Knitzer published the results of a national study of children's men-tal health services, entitled *Unclaimed Children* (1982). This publication high-lighted the unmet mental health needs of children across the country, attributing this state of affairs to the failings of states to take on the mandate of the Joint Commission and the failings of the federal government to provide leadership.
3. Within 2 years of Knitzer's publication, Congress funded the National Institute of Mental Health (NIMH) to establish a national agenda for child mental health, called the Child and Adolescent Service System Program (CASSP). Initially, the CASSP program, with small amounts of money per state (approximately $250,000

each), developed a state-level presence for a child mental health office, supported a needs assessment, increased the visibility of this neglected population of children, fostered interagency collaboration, emphasized the importance of a continuum of care, and elevated the roles of parents. Over the next 6 years, funds were provided to all the states to develop this administrative infrastructure and to get them ready for the next phase of organizing the delivery systems.

4. Stroul and Friedman (1986), using the *Willie M.* program in North Carolina as one example, articulated the thinking of those who pioneered the continuum of care and described a more highly evolved model of service delivery, called a system of care. The major advances in this conceptualization included (1) the importance of linkages to other child-serving systems with which the child/family was involved, and (2) the changing role of parents to become partners in the design and delivery of services for their children.

5. In 1992, the Center for Mental Health Services began funding states to develop service demonstration programs through the Comprehensive Community Mental Health Services for Children and Their Families Program. By 1999, using approximately $460,000, 67 local systems of care had been developed and over 40,000 children had been served across the country.

6. During the 1990s, other service demonstrations were funded as major initiatives of the Robert Wood Johnson Foundation and the Annie E. Casey Foundation. These demonstration projects fostered collaboration across the child-serving community agencies to avoid out-of-home placements.

7. During this same time period, 1989–1995, the North Carolina Child Mental Health Office implemented the largest service demonstration project thus far through a contract with the Department of Defense. This project provided a comprehensive array of mental health services for all of the children of the military at Fort Bragg, North Carolina, and demonstrated what was possible with adequate funding.

As the efforts just listed above emerged and expanded, a philosophy of service delivery was shaped that built on the recommendations of the Joint Commission but included new concepts that were derived from the experiences of actually putting a continuum of care/a system of services in place. According to this evolving philosophy, the hallmark of systems of care has been that:

- Children with or at risk for serious emotional disturbance and their families receive timely, effective care in communities where services and community supports, including medical services, are integrated into one system of care.
- A unified effort of child-serving agencies and practitioners provides an integrated approach to service planning and a blended funding plan applicable to all public child-serving agencies.
- Services to children and families are individualized, comprehensive, community based, and are integrated with informal resources.
- Full, sustained family partnerships add value and improve the development and implementation of systems of care.
- Care is responsive to the cultural differences of the child and family.

As demonstration projects were developed and then evaluated, it also started to become clear that although program philosophy and the organization of services were essential to good outcomes, attention to the practice level was seriously needed. Such changes were considered essential but not sufficient to effect positive changes in children.

PRACTICAL APPLICATIONS OF THE NEW MODELS OF SERVICE DELIVERY

Policymakers have embraced the philosophy of service delivery that emerged over the past two decades, and this philosophy became the foundation on which state-level policy was built. Further support for the concept of serving a child in the least restrictive setting was derived from education law, appearing first in the 1960s as a mandate in Public Law 94-142, the Education of All Handicapped People, now called the Individuals with Disabilities Education Act (IDEA). During the same time period, similar philosophy prevailed in the community mental health movement and "deinstitutionalization" encouraged the use of less restrictive community settings as better alternatives to long-term hospitalization. As noted earlier, this concept was further supported by the report of the Joint Commission on Mental Health of Children at the end of the 1960s, which placed a priority on developing community-based continua of care.

The demonstration programs funded though the Center for Mental Health Services, the private foundations, and the Department of Defense have been able, to some degree, to turn philosophy into reality. However, in the day-to-day challenges of delivering services to children with complex disorders and to their families, providers face many practical decisions and many barriers to meeting these lofty goals. The description that follows of a child in need of services and the choices facing the service planning team exemplifies these challenges.

Joey W

Joey is a 14-year-old boy who has had four placements in psychiatric inpatient treatment facilities over the past 3 years. He has experienced increasing behavior difficulties, including fire-setting, self-injurious behavior, suicide attempts, physical aggression, substance use, and periodic rage.

Joey lives with his mother, stepfather, and two sisters. His maternal grandmother raised him the first 4 years of his life, as his mother was unmarried and in training to be a nurse when he was born. He began living with his mother when she married her current husband, an officer in the Navy. Over the past 10 years, since the marriage, two sisters were born. The household has been alternatively peaceful and supportive to chaotic and violent. The positive periods tend to be when his stepfather is at sea, and the negative periods, when his stepfather is struggling with problems of alcoholism. Joey gets along well with his sisters and has a loving relationship with his mother, except when the stepfather is in the home. At those times, there seems to be constant arguing, punishment of the children, and general resentment among the family members.

Joey has had ongoing difficulty with his behavior and has not progressed academically because of his of his erratic attendance in school. When he is in school, he seems to be learning but does not get along with his classmates. He spends time with older boys who accept him as a "mascot" and for whom he runs errands. He has admitted to substance use, primarily marijuana and alcohol, from about the age of 9, usually with the older boys. Joey has progressively become more impulsive and destructive, repeatedly exhibiting ragelike episodes.

Joey has received counseling at school, referred by his teacher, primarily because of his problems in attendance and in getting along with children his own age. His teacher and his counselor have thought he "is headed for disaster" but could improve, if he could establish a good relationship with a male, to provide a positive role model. Mother agrees that Joey has serious problems but believes they reflect larger family problems, which she wants to "work on" but her husband does not. The school counselor is now recommending a comprehensive evaluation of Joey to consider the possibility of long-term residential placement or therapeutic foster care to give him a more positive and therapeutic environment.

There are complex issues to be considered in a diagnostic assessment and subsequent treatment planning for Joey. The suggestion of long-term, residential treatment as a remedy to his problems is, of course, premature to understanding more about him and his family. Also, removal from his home to therapeutic foster care has other serious implications. The suggestion of these two very different treatment settings perhaps reflects more of what is known to the counselor or what appears to be available than reflecting settings that could be responsive to his needs. In a community where a range of treatment options are available and can be combined into a comprehensive package for a child and family with complex needs, like Joey and his family, the recommendations might be considerably different.

Expanding the Array of Services

To implement the most fundamental aspect of the new model of service delivery, a full range of mental health and other support services must be available to provide individualized services in keeping with each child's needs. As noted in the case example of Joey, lack of intermediate-type services leaves professionals with the belief or option of moving the child to a more intensive and restrictive setting for treatment, just to be sure he or she gets intensive treatment. To be able to provide services of varying intensity, the range of services should include the traditional outpatient services for child and family, to include individual and group services, day treatment, partial hospitalization, family-style and group residential treatment, larger residential settings and hospital settings, and case management services as needed. In addition to the traditional services, other supportive services are required to provide a wraparound approach, and these include school services, mentoring and coaching, therapeutic aides, and other individualized services.

Without such an array of services, those designing service plans have to use the services that most nearly meet the children's needs. Given the paucity and the unevenness of child mental health services in many geographic areas, service plans might stray considerably from what professionals determine is most desirable. To deal with this problem, public agencies have worked to obtain state funding for the services and to expand their state's Medicaid Plan and Child Health Insurance Plan (CHIP) to include a wide array of services. Although private insurance surely has a role in supporting the services needed by this young population, few private insurers provide sufficient coverage to address the needed range of program options (see further discussion of funding issues later in this chapter).

A major problem that has emerged as new program types are developed is ensuring the quality of these programs. Most states, or national accrediting bodies, do not have program standards in place for the full range of services, particularly for the "nontraditional" services necessary for a wraparound service. Thus there may be little in the way of requirements or guidance about staffing patterns, qualifications of staff, and program activities, and little indication, based on program evaluation, of program effectiveness. Thus, those developing service plans are faced with the dilemma of wanting to use the most appropriate services, including those newly created within the array, and being uncertain about the quality and effectiveness of these new programs/services. On-site inspection and monitoring are difficult for busy providers. The use of case managers to oversee the services for children in these settings is an option, but this expectation requires good training and support for case managers assuming the role of keeping the services organized for the children, as well as overseeing the quality and effectiveness of the services, at least in terms of meeting the goals of the service plans. If the providers developing the service plans are positioned to be purchasing services for their clients, then a privileging and credentialing process could be used.

Another problem of using the less traditional services in the service array is gaining acceptance and confidence of the families and/or members of the service planing team. Although there has been broad acceptance of the concept of "least restrictive setting," some professionals have been reluctant to use this approach, even with the plan of providing case management using a wraparound approach to cover as much of the child's waking hours as needed to deliver intensive enough services. Despite the paucity of evidence that residential services in large group settings are effective, there continues to be considerable acceptance of this treatment approach. In some communities, residential services are more greatly respected than less restrictive options, singly or combined with wraparound services, such as day treatment, intensive outpatient services (delivered in the clinic, the school, or the home), or therapeutic living situations on a smaller scale, such as those services based in therapeutic (alternative) family settings or group homes. To some, it has seemed that "community-based" means "makeshift," and that not using residential treatment centers is denying the child of the best opportunity. Additionally, the restrictiveness of residential treatment centers has been viewed as a good way to protect the child and the community; there is also a belief that such settings provide a total milieu for treatment to occur. As "nontraditional" community-based interventions have developed and have begun to prove their worth, this image is changing, bringing more acceptance to case management, home-based services, and wraparound approaches, perhaps in combination with the other described services.

Identifying Stable Funding

Prior to the community mental health movement of the 1960s, the majority of child mental health services were delivered through child guidance clinics. Services were paid for by families, resulting in the obvious problem of services being available only to those with means to pay. A limited amount of services to families without means to pay were, for the most part, delivered through nonprofit organizations that were backed by religious organizations or other charitable organizations that raised funds for this purpose. Health insurance provided a limited amount of coverage.

The awareness of need increased at a more rapid rate than funding has been available. Expectations in the 1970s, the early years of the community mental health movement, were that such services would be funded with a combination of federal, state, and local dollars. However, none of the three partners were able to fulfill the expectations and fund needed services either for children or adults. At about the same time, the passage of the law addressing the Education of All Handicapped People (now called the Individuals with Disabilities Education Act or IDEA) held out hope that children would get funding for their mental health needs through special education, as a related service. As a federal mandate, without sufficient state or federal funding, the education system has similarly failed to deliver as the law promised. Lawsuits on behalf of children have been built on this federal entitlement over the past 25 years. Such litigation against states through education law has had an impact on the funding of mental health services, most notably *Willie M. v. James B. Hunt, Jr.,* in North Carolina and *Felix v. Waihae* in Hawaii. Both lawsuits brought sufficient state funding to provide a complete array of needed education and treatment services, the former for a narrow group of children who were violent and assaultive, and the latter for all children with educational and mental health problems.

More recently, particularly during the end of the 1980s and the beginning of the 1990s, state agency managers have sought support for child mental health services through Medicaid. Although Medicaid is a federal entitlement to those who qualify based on income and other categories of need, such as those in foster care or those who are severely disabled, the Medicaid program in each state is governed by a state plan. The state plan can be as broad as the federal plan or, in some categories, has been narrowed considerably. Presumably, the advantage to states to develop a narrow plan is that the required state matching portion is kept smaller. Efforts have been strong, with the help of specialized consultants, to broaden state plans to expand coverage for mental health services to children. In states where a broad Medicaid plan is in place, services have expanded for children with mental health/behavioral health disorders.

However, the results of such efforts have, in many states, led to an unbalanced, wide array of mental health service options for poor children, for those in foster care, and for those who are severely disabled, with little available for those with private health insurance or no insurance. Depending on how states have chosen to implement the newer Child Health Insurance Plan (CHIP), a larger group of children may have access to needed services, through a very broad service array and/or through extension to a higher level of income insufficiency.

As state child mental health directors have become aware of funding sources available to other state agencies, they have worked with their government partners to jointly fund services for those children under the responsibility of multiple agencies. There are many federal and state agencies that have responsibility for providing services to this population of children. Stated another way, children with mental health disorders appear in a variety of public systems and agencies for a variety of reasons, from needing foster care to being adjudicated delinquent, and they have simultaneous mental health needs.

States have organized and funded services for this population differently. In some states, the mental health system provides the majority of mental health treatment services, and the funding for those services is usually a combination of state appropriations, federal funds, and local allocations. In other states, either the child welfare agency or the juvenile justice agency may have the largest budget for mental health treatment services, using the same combination of state, federal, and local public funds. It would not be unusual for some local school systems, child welfare agencies, or juvenile courts to employ or contract for psychiatrists, psychologists, or social workers for the purpose of diagnosing and treating children with mental health/ behavioral health disorders.

In most states, the federal funding for treatment of mental health/behavioral health disorders includes Medicaid, the mental health and substance-abuse block grants, IDEA Part B funds for children with disabilities ages 3–21 years; IDEA Part B funds for the birth-to-3 years groups, maternal and child health funds, Head Start, and other, more specific demonstration grant funds. Given this disparity of agency responsibilities and funding sources, the provision of treatment services and the funding of services for this population are certainly difficult to track. Thus, it is difficult to know what is being spent for mental health diagnosis and treatment, far more difficult than identifying what is being spent for juvenile corrections, foster care, or the education of children. A comparison of expenditures across states would yield only some approximation of the degree of underfunding, as all states fall short of meeting the needs of those children and families that seek treatment, to say nothing of meeting the projected need.

The federal Center for Mental Health Services has provided estimates for all the states of the population in need of treatment for mental health disorders (Department of Health and Human Services, 1998). A recent analysis of seven states (Behar, 1999) indicates that the treatment costs for children at three levels of intensity of services vary little across the states. Based on average costs, reasonable estimates can be made of "appropriate" state budgets for the treatment of the population in need. This same survey provided data to indicate that the major sources of funding, regardless of which agencies managed these funds, were state appropriations and Medicaid funds, with the latter equaling or exceeding the state funds. For almost all states, the projected budget needs represent three to four times the current budgets, compiled as much as possible across agencies. And for all states, no matter how the "funding pie" for children's services is divided, the resources do not exist within one agency alone. Thus, it is essential to coordinate of planning, delivering, and paying for services for children with complex needs to make the best use of professional talents and fiscal resources.

Developing Local Interagency Teams or Other Collaborative Structures

The case of Joey is a good example of the need for several agencies or professionals to come together in a coordinated way to do an assessment of the child and family needs and then to design a service plan that addresses the family's problems and those of its members. There is little disagreement about the value of coordinated assessment, service planning, and delivery once the issues of confidentiality are handled. Partnering with the parents, seeking their agreement to share information on a "need-to-know" basis, and then handling the information in a respectful and judicious manner easily handle these issues. Although "confidentiality" jumps out as the biggest issue to many professionals, it is more easily overcome than other barriers. Probably the most serious impediment to coordinated planning is the sheer lack of time that professionals have. The employees of public agencies, which provide services such as mental health diagnosis and treatment, child protective services, foster care, juvenile court services and aftercare, health care, education, and special education in most communities, are seriously overcommitted. They have high case loads or many children and families for whom they are responsible, and meetings to coordinate services around the needs of one of their cases may be a luxury. At the same time, such meetings are a necessity, to make sure the assessment of the child and family's needs and the subsequent service plan address the multiple and complex needs of the child and family, an effort that should yield the best outcomes. For those in the private sector, the issues are similar; there are few funding sources that will pay for "coordination time," and these unsalaried providers can do a modest amount of free work. Other barriers are more negative in foundation. These include lack of trust among agencies, lack of understanding of the capacity of other agencies, competitiveness, fear of sharing resources, and other negative features, sometimes based on bad experiences, real or perceived.

The remedies to these problems are multidimensional, but the most likely to succeed in breaking through such a community logjam seem to be (1) placing an agency priority on such activity and (2) providing funding to pay for these services. Coordination of services is simply not something that can "come out of the hides" of existing services. Case loads have to be reduced to allow coordination to happen; funding for coordination essentially provides money to an agency to hire more staff and to give time to staff to meet and plan with professionals and with the family. Although the negative barriers that are derived from bad history, bad interactions, and bad attitudes present difficulties, surmounting these barriers becomes an issue of agency leadership, priority setting, and modeling good practice. The other impetus for changing practices comes from experiencing success, so it seems that if this "good" practice can get started, virtue may become its own reward. It should be noted however, that this road might not be without its potholes and pitfalls, as not all cases yield successful results, and good feelings among coordinating professionals may not be always forthcoming. The challenges lie in the difficult cases, in the child and/or family setbacks, which may offer the tendency to cast blame among the coordinating team members. In situations where barriers have been decreased or eliminated, case managers can be effective in bringing together the relevant service providers and the family, and they can, with sufficient background and training, deal with the problems that arise in the interactions of the coordinating team.

Involving Parents

The stigma of having a child with mental health problems has been a significant barrier for parents. The belief that they or the family environment has caused the problems prevents many from seeking help. This concern may be coupled with their view that professionals have related or will relate to them in demeaning ways. Further, as some professionals have regarded parents as the source of their children's problems, parents joining forces with professionals to work together on behalf of the children has been problematic on both sides. The issue of blame has been difficult to overcome for families, and professionals have also had a hard time relinquishing attitudes that foster guilt rather than team building with parents. Parents participating in treatment conferences, as equal partners, has been hard to effect.

Ways of softening these barriers include:

- Education/training of those preparing for the child-serving professions to understand the complexities of child raising, the stresses of parenting in the context of other life stresses, the challenges of having a child with emotional disturbance, and recognition that parents don't do harm intentionally to their children.
- Training of community professionals, focusing on the above, and how to use the strengths of parents in the treatment situation, particularly when done by parents or jointly by parents and professionals.
- Having parents available to serve as supports for "new" parents in treatment conferences or school conferences.
- Having parent-run organizations in the community to participate in education and training, and to advocate for the role of parents in services for their own children, as well as in community planning and priority setting. In some places, formalized parent organizations have organized parent support groups and parents as supports for others, exemplified by their accompanying parents to diagnostic and treatment conferences.

In North Carolina, through the leadership and funding by the state child mental health office, nine of the state university campuses have developed graduate programs with parents as faculty. The "parents in residence" participate as faculty in courses to educate professionals to understand the issues of parents of children with emotional disturbances and to understand how a partnership with parents can augment the treatment process. These same "parents in residence" also provide in-service training to those already in the field.

Culturally Competent Services

As the diversity of racial and ethnic backgrounds of people in the country has increased, the helping professions have been challenged to make their services "culturally competent"—that is, respectful of and responsive to the backgrounds of the people they serve. Such efforts are essential, as minority groups appear to be underserved, in general (Center for Mental Health Services, 1998), and questions have been raised about the appropriateness of the services to those who do access the system. Data from the Great Smoky Mountain Study (Costello & Angold, 2000) indicate that although minority children need mental health services at the same rate as nonminority children, they do not access services. The most common reasons given by parents are that (1) they don't understand how to access services and (2) they don't trust the professionals.

There is no argument with the logic and the importance of cultural competence, but the application of such in the child mental health field has broad implications. Understanding culture in relation to child mental health issues means understanding the cultural approaches to child rearing, what is considered "normal" or "acceptable," and tolerance of differences from those norms, as well as the traditions, beliefs, and patterns of family interactions. Further, the whole issue of intellectual functioning and social–emotional development must be related to cultural patterns and expectations. Understanding culture in relation to service delivery means understanding how people recognize that they need help, how they ask for it, and how they accept it. In practice, efforts to provide culturally competent services have started with trying to hire professional staff that represents the diversity of the community. This effort has been modestly successful, but the common response is that there are not sufficient numbers of minority professionals to hire. Other approaches include training of staff to understand the cultures with which they work, and partnering with community leaders, natural helpers, and agencies within the minority. Materials should be published in the language of the minority population, translators should be available, and physical settings should be appropriate.

CHALLENGES FOR THE FUTURE

There is general agreement on the conceptual framework for the development of quality child mental health services and even of the methods that can be used to implement such a system. Other challenges remain, as follows.

Measuring the Effectiveness of the System of Care

Efforts to measure the effectiveness of this model of service delivery have had uneven results. In recent years, several studies (Attkisson et al., 1997; Bruns, Burchard, & Yoe, 1995; Illback, Nelson, & Sanders, 1998; Rosenblatt, 1998; Santarcangeleo, Bruns, & Yoe, 1998; Stroul, 1993a, 1993b) yielded encouraging findings. Studies by Bickman and his colleagues (Bickman, 1996a, 1996b; Bickman, Guthrie, & Foster, 1995; Bickman, Noser, & Summerfelt, 1999; Bickman, Summerfelt, & Noser, 1997) yielded less positive findings. All of these studies generally indicate that by having a range of community-based services available: (1) The use of hospital or residential treatment settings is reduced; (2) the use of out-of-state placements is reduced; (3) clinical outcomes for children are improved; and (4) child or family satisfaction is high. However, most of these studies with positive findings used a pre–post control method and none used a clear control group. Bickman's studies, using comparison groups, indicated a more questionable finding—that is, although the listed improvements occurred, they came at considerably more cost than the traditional methods of service delivery, which had similar outcomes. Thus, clearly there is a need for more and better formal evaluation of the effectiveness of comprehensive systems of care that address issues such as:

- Whether the clinical changes measured result from treatment within a system of care or result from other variables, such as the passage of time.
- Whether or not the changes are sufficient and derived clearly enough from the "systemness" to warrant increased costs, if such costs can be documented.
- Whether the impact is short or long term.

Developing Manpower

Professional training in the mental health fields, regardless of discipline, has tended to prepare students for independent practice focusing on individual, group, or family treatment (see, e.g., American Academy of Child Psychiatry, 1983). There has historically been less emphasis on training for collaborative work across the agencies that serve children and families, and less emphasis overall on the principles described here as the underpinnings of service delivery. More recently, following conferences and study sessions on the issues of manpower development, states have invested in training programs. These programs have developed through separate training institutes, as has been done in Pennsylvania, or though cultivation and restructuring of university graduate training programs, as has been done in North Carolina. One goal of these programs is to provide needed in-service training to sharpen skills and bring new approaches to the field. A second goal is to impact on preservice training to improve the preparation of professionals so that they enter the field with more of the vision and skills to support that vision.

Both types of training endeavors are based on the recognition that the mental health of children is the province of many, including parents, teachers, welfare workers, primary health care providers, and juvenile court workers. Thus training across these disciplines and agencies in universities and in communities can lay a broader foundation of understanding and an avenue for collaboration around the complicated children that use the services of multiple agencies at the same time.

Improving Practice

During the past two decades, there has been a major emphasis on improving the organization of services. Other foci have been (1) bringing parents into the diagnostic and treatment planning process as equal partners with professionals and (2) emphasizing the importance of understanding the culture of the clients to be served. Although all of these elements are thought to improve clinical practice, there has been an assumption that well-trained professionals have the needed expertise to provide treatment and work toward improvement in the status of the child. Professional standards as set by professional certification organizations have guided clinical practice. Those professionals that achieve certification have been thought to qualify to deliver services without further oversight.

An emphasis from the professional organizations is evolving to develop practice guidelines as a way of standardizing the responses to children and families, rather than relying on the individual judgment of practitioners. These guidelines are to the extent possible "evidence based"—that is, they are developed based on validated treatment techniques. Unfortunately, the research and evaluation side of the equation is in need of further work, leaving practice guidelines and standards to be based on "best judgment," awaiting further validation. However, such standardization at least provides for a consistent pattern of clinical responses, which improves the possibilities of comparative research. The fields of child mental health are no further along than the field of mental health in general. As the emphasis on practice guidelines and standards pushes professionals to refine their treatment techniques, it is important that those who serve children be present to understand and clarify when the guidelines and standards can be applied across age ranges and when specific approaches are needed for children.

The desired outcome of clinical treatment is improvement in the client, at the very least. Some outcome measures, like practice guidelines and standards, can be developed to be applicable to the range of ages of the client population. Others need to be specific to children, emphasizing improvements in the life work of the child, which is school, interaction with peers and adults, development of self-esteem, and feelings of self-worth and competence. As with guidelines, the child mental health professional needs to be cautious about generic measures that do not take into consideration the differences between children and adults.

REFERENCES

American Academy of Child Psychiatry. (1983). *Child psychiatry: A plan for the coming decades.* Washington, DC: Author.

Attkisson, C. C., Rosenblatt, A., Dresser, K. L., Baize, H. R., Clausen, J. M., & Lind, S. L. (1997). Effectiveness of the California system of care model for children and youth with severe emotional disorder. In C. T. Nixon & C. A. Northrup (Eds.), *Evaluating mental health services: How do programs for children "work" in the real world?* (pp. 146–208). Thousand Oaks, CA: Sage.

Behar, L. B. (1999). *A comparison of the costs of mental health services to children across six states.* Raleigh, NC: North Carolina Division of Mental Health, Developmental Disabilities and Substance Abuse Services.

Bickman, L. (1996a). Implications of a children's mental health managed care demonstration project. *Journal of Mental Health Administration, 23,* 107–117.

Bickman, L. (1996b). Reinterpreting the Fort Bragg evaluation findings: The message does not change. *Journal of Mental Health Administration, 23,* 137–145.

Bickman, L., Guthrie, P. R., & Foster, E. M. (1995). *Evaluating managed mental health care: The Fort Bragg experiment.* New York: Plenum Press.

Bickman, L., Noser, K., & Summerfelt, W. T. (1999). Long-term effects of a system of care on children and adolescents. *Journal of Behavioral Health Services & Research, 26,* 185–202.

Bickman, L., Summerfelt, W. T., & Noser, K. (1997). Comparative outcomes of emotionally disturbed children and adolescents in a system of services and usual care. *Psychiatric Services, 48,* 1543–1548.

Bruns, E. J., Burchard, J. D., & Yoe, J. T. (1995). Evaluating the Vermont system of care: Outcomes associated with community-based wraparound services. *Journal of Child and Family Studies, 4,* 321–329.

Center for Mental Health Services. (1998). *Cultural competence standards in managed care mental health services for four underserved/underrepresented racial/ethnic groups.* Rockville, MD: Author.

Costello, E. J., & Angold, A. (2000, July). *Barriers in mental health care among African American and American Indian children and adolescents.* Presented at NIMH Services Conference, Bethesda, MD.

Department of Health and Human Services. (1998). Children with serious emotional disturbance; estimation methodology. *Federal Register, 63*(137), 38661–38665.

Illback, R. J., Nelson, C. M., & Sanders, D. (1998). Community-based services in Kentucky: Description and 5-year evaluation of Kentucky IMPACT. In M. H. Epstein, K. Kutash, & A. Duchnowski (Eds.), *Outcomes for children and youth with behavioral and emotional disorders and their families* (pp. 141–172). Austin, TX: Pro-Ed.

Joint Commission on Mental Health of Children. (1969). *Crisis in child mental health: A challenge for the 1970s.* New York: Harper & Row.

Knitzer, J. (1982). U*nclaimed children: The failure of public responsibility to children and adolescents in need of mental health services.* Washington, DC: Children's Defense Fund.

Rosenblatt, A. (1998). Assessing the child and family outcomes of systems of care youth with serious emotional disturbance. In M. H. Epstein, K. Kutash, & A. Duchnowski (Eds.), *Outcomes for children and youth with behavioral and emotional disorders and their families* (pp. 329–362). Austin, TX: Pro-Ed.

Santarcangeleo, S., Bruns, E. J., & Yoe, J. T, (1998). New directions: Evaluating Vermont's statewide model of individualized care. In M. H. Epstein, K. Kutash, & A. Duchnowski (Eds.), *Outcomes for children and youth with behavioral and emotional disorders and their families* (pp. 117–140). Austin, TX: Pro-Ed.

Stroul, B. (1993a). *Children's mental health: Creating systems of care in a changing society.* Baltimore, MD: Paul H. Brookes.

Stroul, B. (1993b). *Systems of care for children and adolescents with severe emotional disturbances: What are the results?* Washington, DC: CASSP Technical Assistance Center, Georgetown University Child Development Center.

Stroul, B., & Friedman, R. M. (1986). *A system of care for severely emotionally disturbed youth.* Washington, DC: CASSP Technical Assistance Center, Georgetown University Child Development Center.

Chapter Eleven

Mental Health Management Environments: Managed Mental Health Care—From Cottage Industry to System of Care

Peter B. Rosenquist

Among men, . . . the most dissimilar geniuses are of use to one another; the different produces of their respective talents, by the general disposition to truck, barter, and exchange, being brought, as it were, into a common stock, where every man may purchase whatever part of the produce of other men's talents he has occasion for.
—*Adam Smith*, The Wealth of Nations, *1937*

WHY MANAGE CARE?

Economically speaking, there is perhaps no greater testament of the value of the healing arts to American society than that they be gradually redefined as the "health care industry" and come under the same economic scrutiny as any other business. This transition has not been easily achieved. In the manner of a cottage industry, the patient traditionally entered into a direct contract with the doctor or therapist. To varying degrees, the patient delegated responsibility for the *management* of care to the health care provider. However, this basic contractual arrangement belies the reality of how health care is financed today.

For quite some time the patient has not been the sole payer, as payments for services have been reimbursed, or made on behalf of the patient by insurance or government entitlement programs. Insulated from true costs, neither patients nor providers have any incentive to manage costs. Inevitably, under real conditions of increasing demand and rising costs, payers—in particular corporations offering health care insurance as a benefit—have sought the means to define limits of liability and enact constraints. Thus, *managed care* is that segment of the health care industry that has become subject to the full range of market forces. In a market economy, value is established in a dynamic interaction between all participants in the process. By extension, the term is inclusive of the process by which the contractual interests of all the parties are adjudicated, be they patient, provider, or payer. To illustrate, in exchange for labor and a portion of the premium, the employee receives health care benefits, obtained through a group contract between the employer and a health maintenance organization (HMO). When the employee goes to the doctor, the doctor bills the HMO and is paid according to a prearranged fee schedule.

In a purely technical sense, *managed care* also refers to the panoply of regulatory mechanisms and economic incentives used to influence the behavior of all parties. A clear example of direct, regulatory control is the obligation to obtain prior approval for treatment. The provider is required to submit a treatment plan prior to delivering care. Only after reviewing the plan according to specific guidelines does the insurance company authorize payment for the proposed treatment. An example of economic incentives being used to control demand as well as price would be when the doctor accepts a lower fee schedule in exchange for status as an "in-network" provider. All other things being equal, the patient goes to the in-network provider because the benefit specifies a lower copayment, or "out-of-pocket" cost, for this option.

The process of rewriting the rules governing health care in the name of managed care over the past two decades has been arduous and is nowhere near completion. From a managerial perspective, the problems are many. First, the industry is of mammoth proportions, in terms of dollars, personnel, and assets. It is also widely distributed, poorly consolidated, and inescapably linked to a broad range of related industries, including pharmaceutical, technological, and scientific, to name just a few. Furthermore, the existing managerial infrastructure is by and large facility based and locally developed, and not designed to serve a managed-care agenda. The professional workforce has been trained to value and exercise autonomy, and continues to resist many of the changes that have been implemented.

Corporate models of management and control honed principally in the manufacturing sector are relatively new to the service industry, and the assumptions are particularly difficult to generalize across the many divisions and specialties of health care—no more so than in the field of mental health, where a uniquely broad and ill-defined set of treatment alternatives and expectations has necessitated the creation of an entirely new management infrastructure. Any number of very different services offered under the term "counseling" may be provided by psychologist, social worker, physician, minister, or psychic friend. The managed behavioral health care organization (MBHO) has emerged to accept responsibility for delivering a defined set of mental health benefits to a defined population.

Several factors contribute to a growing complexity within organizations serving individuals with mental health needs. As methods of health care financing have become more complex, organizations have in response evolved roles to manage these various objectives. Although these are infinitely differentiable based on specific perspectives, for the purposes of this chapter we focus upon three operational objectives consonant with a managed care agenda. These are access, quality, and accountability. Table 11.1 offers some basic definitions of these objectives.

It is necessary to understand who and what is being managed, in order to understand how care is managed. But like the proverbial blind men describing the el-

TABLE 11.1. Managed Care Objectives

Objective	Definition
Access	A full range of appropriate services is available and delivered in a timely fashion.
Quality	Services meet standards of effectiveness and acceptability to recipients; includes expectation of continuous improvement.
Accountability	Observable mechanisms exist for control of behavior of all components of the network, including costs.

ephant, one receives divergent answers to questions about managed care, depending on who is asked. Care delivery is effected through a variety of mechanisms and organizations, each of which assigns different priorities to the spectrum of objectives. One admittedly crude manner of assessing the resources that a given organization has committed to particular processes of care delivery is to look at the allocation of personnel resources. To a certain extent, function follows form. The form of an organization can be abstracted from its organizational chart, understanding the potential for omission from job descriptions of some elements that are deemed secondary. Using the organizational chart as a starting point, we attempt to provide a "snapshot" view of several mental health care organizations existing side by side in metropolitan North Carolina: a small group practice, a local mental health center, and a locally owned managed mental health care organization. Formally or informally, each has evolved strategic and operational plans that in turn are reflected in the roles and responsibilities emerging to respond to an evolving health care system.

HOW DID MANAGED CARE COME ABOUT?

In his now-classic history of American medicine, Paul Starr (1982) predicted the coming of modern managed care as an inevitable outgrowth of social transformation. In Starr's view, care has always been managed, with the only question being, "Who has been managing?" Early on, physicians gained control by a process of licensing, thereby restricting competition, and establishing authority to define and interpret standards that govern health care. By forming strong political organizations, MDs and to a certain extent other professions were able to limit regulation by both government and private organizations.

Originally, health care providers gave care according to their perception of needs of patient, and charged according to ability to pay. This arrangement did not guarantee economic security for either patient or provider. Medical societies including the American Medical Association (AMA) fought to maintain this state of affairs, from the earliest prepaid experiments.

However, the growth of hospitals as centers for more sophisticated and costly care led to an increased vulnerability in costs to patients. Therefore, some form of insurance to guard against catastrophe made sense. National health insurance has never come to fruition in the United States for a number of reasons, both political and ideological. The medical profession has viewed government regulation as the worst-case scenario. The alternative to government regulation turned out to be commercial insurance, with traditional indemnity plans predominating.

Post–World War II expansion of budgets and facilities occurred at a rapid rate. This included the numbers of hospitals, beds, local health centers, mental health centers, medical schools, and specialties. Medicare and Medicaid funding emerged during this period of history. Growing public acceptance of mental health treatments and unregulated retrospective payment were incentives to provide more and more care. Rising costs and inflation in the health care sector opened the door for multiple regulatory efforts, including professional standards review organizations (PSROs), health planning boards, and the Joint Commission on the Accreditation of Healthcare Organizations (JCAHO). Corporations responded to tightening economic conditions by attempting to cut costs, and health benefits were fair game. In this environment, the health maintenance organization (HMO) was introduced and achieved greater political acceptance.

As a consequence, managed care in its present form began to emerge. The health care system as a whole, including the mental health sector, has been transformed by three fundamental changes. First, there has been a major change in ownership and control. During the 1980s and 1990s for-profit companies increasingly shaped the managed care agenda, as compared with nonprofit and governmental agencies. A great number of previously smaller, freestanding institutions merged into fewer, much larger health care systems, so-called "horizontal integration." "Vertical integration" also ensued, as health care organizations embraced various phases and levels of care in order to preserve market share.

Managed care in its modern form continued to evolve. Geraty (1995) distinguished a series of stages, reflecting the growth and sophistication of managed care. The first of these he termed *managed access*, by which managed care organizations (MCOs) marketed benefit plans, often with reduced coverage for mental health services. This stage focuses on cost control as primary objective; by defining the limits of coverage in terms of dollars visits, days in the hospital, and so on, the insurer can stop its losses beyond a certain maximum. However, this mechanism does not allow for any direct control of utilization. The addition of centralized utilization review functions marked the stage of *managed benefits*. In this iteration, to the objective of cost control is added the need for some accountability.

Even greater accountability is brought about with the next phase, which Geraty termed *managed care* proper. This phase emerged when payers began to contract directly with groups of providers who accepted fee schedules and administrative rules in exchange for referrals. A fourth stage, *managed outcome,* is now emerging as regulatory and market forces combine to demand new standards of quality as well as further cost reduction.

THE STRUCTURE AND FUNCTION
OF MENTAL HEALTH CARE DELIVERY

In this section, we describe and evaluate four separate organizations engaged in the management and provision of mental health care in the same general locale. Armed with a basic understanding of the operational elements comprising each organization, the reader should be able to think about how the basic management objectives of *access, quality,* and *accountability* are achieved.

Outpatient Mental Health Group Practice

We begin by examining a relatively small mental health group practice. Formed in 1987, New Directions employs a clinical staff consisting of three full-time psychiatrists and one part-time psychiatrist, one psychologist, three clinical social workers, one nurse, and one part-time licensed professional counselor. The practice is incorporated, and profits are shared by the participating clinicians. The support staff is divided into reception/medical records, and business/billing office. This organization is quite small, and therefore conforms well to a "simple structure," with very little hierarchy (Robbins, 1992, p. 227). One clinician has assumed responsibility to act as business manager for the practice, while continuing also to see patients. The business manager is uniquely responsible for paying the bills, payroll, and has signature authority for the practice in managed care contracts. Supervision of master's-level clinicians, as well as of support staff, is distributed among the doctoral-level clinicians.

This organization is designed to address the primary mission of providing outpatient care to patients, and to generate revenue for salaries and practice overhead expense. New Directions believes that the current organizational structure is attractive to individual patients, and to payers, including managed care entities. The clinicians work "as a team" providing a range of mental health evaluations, psychotherapy, and psychotropic medication management services. Tasks are divided efficiently among personnel. A nurse handles telephonic "intake," and new patients are first seen by one of two clinicians specializing in making initial evaluations; patients are then referred internally to other clinicians in the practice for subsequent care. The organization is small enough that essentially all clinical staff can meet weekly to discuss clinical or procedural issues.

The practice has been successful in maintaining a sufficient volume of patient contacts to stay in business. A small number of managed care contracts furnishes the majority of referrals. Both the fee schedule and the amount of required paperwork factor into the decision by the practice to participate in a managed care network. In some instances, only some of the clinicians have received status as in-network providers, creating additional logistical inconvenience. With the advent of managed care, the practice has incurred additional administrative burden, in the form of more exacting requirements for documentation, and in monitoring to ensure that visits are authorized by the managed care organization prior to the patients being seen.

Although some clinicians affiliated with New Directions have privileges to treat patients in area hospitals, the focus of the practice is on outpatient psychiatric services for adults with insurance. There are limits to the number of patients the practice can absorb, and there are services the practice does not offer. Therefore, the managed care objective of maintaining access for a large population, as, for example, the employees of a regional corporation, cannot be ensured by the practice alone. Neither is the practice financially able to accept risk in the form of a capitation agreement, or in a position to subcontract services from other practitioners. The clinicians receive payment on a "fee-for-service" basis. Private practitioners in the present environment can be seen as subcontractors, insulated to some degree but also lightening the administrative burden for large populations borne by larger entities in the health care market. For this reason, there are still smaller groups and even some solo practitioners at work today, although working with managed care under these configurations would be difficult, to say the least. Because it has developed internal mechanisms to contract and communicate effectively with managed care organizations, New Directions makes itself accountable to those organizations.

All MBHOs employ a network of professionals to provide direct care to members of that patient population. Mintzberg termed this arrangement a "professional bureaucracy" in which duly trained specialists are hired and given considerable control over their own work. The professional works relatively independently of his or her colleagues, but closely with the clients he or she serves (Mintzberg, 1979, p. 349). Quality of care is measured largely on a case-by-case basis and is maintained by hiring well-trained clinicians. The reputation of the group hinges on clinicians acting individually and in concert in accordance with professional and community standards. Master's-level clinicians are supervised by doctoral clinicians, and consultation with peers is encouraged. To this time-honored method of quality management are added methods of formal oversight initiated by the managed care organization (see later discussion).

Facility-Based Service Continua

We next profile two different facility-based mental health providers offering a continuum of services to the community. First, we will examine a full-service hospital that expanded on a psychiatric inpatient unit to include partial hospital and intensive outpatient services for mental illness and also substance abuse treatment. Then we focus on a local community mental health center and its efforts to provide "wrap-around" services to a number of challenging patient populations.

Community Hospital Diversified. Hospitalization is by far the single most costly unit of care in mental health. Hospitals must employ a highly trained staff, 24 hours a day and 7 days a week. Managed care has successfully reduced costs associated with the most severe forms of mental illness and substance abuse treatment in three basic ways. First and foremost, MBHOs have been able to shift patients toward alternatives to hospitalization, utilizing the requirement of preauthorization of care prior to its provision. The second technique used by MBHOs is to encourage hospitals to be more efficient, thereby reducing the length of stay, accomplished in part through the mechanism of concurrent review during the hospital stay. Finally, MBHOs have negotiated with hospitals to reduce the cost of each day in the hospital (the per diem). In order to compete in this environment, psychiatric hospitals and units have evolved substantially. High Point Regional is a prime example of how "vertical integration" can diversify and expand the role of a single health care entity in the delivery of mental health services.

In order to address the high cost of inpatient care, there need to be alternatives to this "most restrictive" level of care. The so-called continuum of care is made up of a number of different services that may be seen as levels addressing particular needs of patients. Table 11.2 lists the levels of care comprising the continuum. In a well-managed system, patients are triaged to, and move efficiently and appropriately between, different levels of care on this continuum, such that they receive services in the "least restrictive" (and most cost-effective) setting. Besides inpatient care (IP), many hospitals offer ultrashort-stay crisis intervention services providing intensive

TABLE 11.2. A Continuum of Mental Health Care

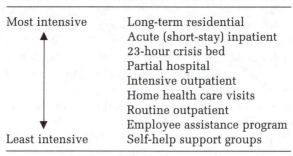

Most intensive	Long-term residential
	Acute (short-stay) inpatient
	23-hour crisis bed
	Partial hospital
	Intensive outpatient
	Home health care visits
	Routine outpatient
	Employee assistance program
Least intensive	Self-help support groups

evaluation, monitoring, and treatment for up to 23 hours. This is a useful option for the patient in crisis for whom the treatment team is uncertain about what services will ultimately be required. Often, a very short time is sufficient to stabilize the patient and effect an appropriate disposition.

A step below inpatient care is partial or day hospital care (PH), where patients attend during the day but return home in the evening. This is useful as a stepdown from the 24-hour inpatient setting, for patients who continue to need intensive treatment and regular monitoring of their status but who have adequate support in the evening hours so as not to need to remain in a hospital. Intensive outpatient (IOP) services are ideal for patients who need the structure of an intensive treatment program (often in a group setting) while at the same time maintaining a regular work schedule. IOP programs can be as often as daily, depending on the needs of the patient. Substance-abuse treatment services are often offered in this setting.

In-home treatment options have also evolved as part of the continuum of care for patients who are "homebound" or unlikely to attend a facility- or office-based program. A home health nurse with psychiatric training can administer medications to a noncompliant patient and can even offer some limited psychotherapy. Family preservation and assertive community treatment (ACT) programs are based on the notion that often the most effective way to treat patients is to bring the appropriate services into the home environment. We have already discussed so-called routine outpatient services, still the highest volume treatment option, appropriate for patients needing only intermittent contact with professionals. Residential services are sometimes included, although long-term residential treatment programs are quite costly and are reserved for the most intractable patients.

High Point Regional now offers IP, PH, and IOP services for both chemical dependency (CD) and psychiatric problems. At the heart of the system are two assessment centers set up to triage all patients and refer them to the appropriate level of care. These assessment centers are in neighboring counties and function as the single "portal of entry" for all patients. Screening up to 400 clients monthly, assessment centers operate 24 hours a day and 7 days a week. Assessments are offered "free of charge." Once in the system, patients move between levels of care on the basis of need, as determined by clinicians and utilization review specialists meeting on a daily basis. In this fashion, the management of access can be fine-tuned. All patients passing through the assessment centers receive a uniform evaluation, and administrative procedures have been developed to respond to the requirements of a variety of payers.

Accountability at the boundary of treatment is ensured by a database recording the insurance vendors for various area employers, including numbers to call for obtaining preauthorization. Similarly, a utilization review staff (two full-time equivalents, 2 FTE) is responsible for coordinating any requested communication between clinical staff and managed care companies once the patient is enrolled in a program (concurrent review). In this way, contractual obligations are routinely honored, and a regular dialogue between utilization managers employed by payers and health systems staff is encouraged. High Point Regional has sought to acquire a reputation for "partnering" with managed care entities. In the words of one manager, "We don't waste time arguing with managed care organizations—we learn how best to work with them." In keeping with this philosophy, High Point Regional also offers an employee assistance program (EAP) targeting mental health problems in the workplace. Mental health professionals are available to employees and supervisors at the work site, for counseling, training, and prevention of violence and drug and alcohol use in the workplace. For some employers, EAP offers greater accountability to the needs of the organization, and a more direct focus on workplace productivity.

High Point Regional began the process of diversification in 1991. At that time, the mental health continuum was limited to an inpatient psychiatric service. A national consulting partner, Parkside, was hired to provide management services. The executive director and several key staff came from Parkside and helped High Point Regional to develop additional services. In 1997, programs had matured sufficiently to discontinue the management services contract, and from that time forward, High Point Regional has been on its own. A current organizational chart is shown in Fig. 11.1.

In comparison with the New Directions outpatient group practice, this organization is considerably more complex, and the organizational chart reflects this. The

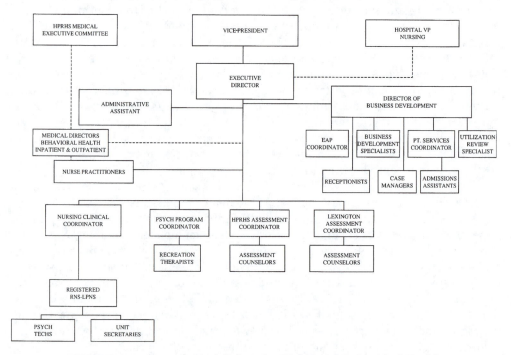

FIGURE 11.1. Organizational chart for High Point Behavioral Health.

executive director reports to a hospital vice-president and directly supervises a series of managers, including a director of business development, and five other clinician-managers, who in turn administer nine separate "cost centers" corresponding
to the various clinical programs. Each cost center is a line item in the overall budget
for mental health, so individual managers have accountability to the overall bottom
line. However, this structure also allows for cross-subsidization within the organization. For example, because initial assessments are made "free of charge," the assessment centers are not expected to be profit centers. Without these operations, none of
the other units would receive an adequate volume of patients to generate revenues.
Similarly, there is an extensive array of secondary inputs to each clinical program
(laboratory, x-ray), which are in turn cost managed in order to meet a contract price
per diem. In terms of organizational design, this arrangement would be called a
matrix structure, where product lines (e.g., chemical dependency services) are su-
perimposed over functional units (e.g., inpatient care, partial hospital, laboratory)
in order to facilitate coordination (Robbins, 1992, p. 229).

Quality improvement activities are generally more systematic in facility-based
programs, due to greater regulation. High Point Regional adheres to standards promulgated by the Joint Commission for Accreditation of Healthcare Organizations
(JCAHO). JCAHO developed initially as a "self-policing" review mechanism for the
hospital industry, but has to some degree modified criteria reflecting the influence
of managed care. Standards are evolving, both in terms of specificity and
generalizabilty, and focus more keenly on the demonstration of well-developed internal mechanisms of quality management. But because mental health standards
represent a small subset of the overall facility-based criteria, many mental health
quality issues are not assessed under JCAHO. Quality improvement monitors at High
Point Regional are administered through the Department of Nursing, and patient
satisfaction is assessed "periodically." Within the organizational chart for High Point
Behavioral Health, however, there is no job title reflecting specifically these activities.

Community Mental Health Center Reorganized. Community mental health centers
(CMHCs) were conceived during the period of expansion of all health services in the
postwar era. With the help of state and federal support, CMHCs are charged with the
responsibility to serve the mental health needs of all residents in the local "catchment" area who cannot otherwise obtain services. Traditionally, these individuals
fall into two main categories: those who meet state Medicaid eligibility requirements, and those "indigent" persons who have no source of health care insurance
whatsoever. Working within a specific budget, and with a defined population, CMHCs
may be seen as the first managed mental health care organizations. Furthermore, a
well-established association between poverty and mental illness means that CMHCs
face a higher rate of illness, and a population with problems that tend to be severe
and persistent.

In 1997, Forsyth County Mental Health Center officially became Centerpoint
Services, capping a major expansion and reorganization touched off by a change in
the way mental health care services were financed by the state. The state Medicaid
waiver program allowed CMHCs to bypass regulatory restrictions concerning services eligible for funding, provided that all those services were made accountable to
the CMHC. Just as High Point Regional needed to evolve a continuum of care, due to
pressure from private payers, Centerpoint responded to a similar demand in the

public sector. The continuum of services offered by this CMHC in the early 1990s consisted of an emergency walk-in clinic, an inpatient unit (actually a rarity for CMHCs), and a largely unspecialized array of outpatient services. Problems with this system included long waiting times for outpatient appointments, and consequent overuse of emergency and inpatient services for less severe problems, as well as escalation of routine problems into emergent problems as a result of delayed treatment. Underlying these problems, there were insufficient means to coordinate the activities of departmental units, characteristic of what organizational design theorists term a *functional structure*. Each clinical program scheduled patients independently, and attempted to meet all the needs of patients within the program, due in part to an expectation of referral barriers with sister programs. For example, a patient with a combination of mental illness and substance abuse in this system would likely receive treatment for only one of these problems.

Therefore, Centerpoint has taken an evolutionary path similar to that followed by High Point Regional, marked by the creation of centralized and specialized gatekeeping functions coupled with a marked expansion of service options. The organizational chart for Centerpoint is shown in Fig. 11.2. It seems clear that without proper coordination between services, expansion of the continuum of services would only lead to more fragmented care. This is the core rationale for management of access to care. Both of these health care entities also have distributed access points across several counties, reflecting their role as a regional provider and the needs of patients in those areas. Centerpoint also employs a number of bachelor's-level case managers who serve as referral agents, whose job is to usher clients through what has become a large and complex organization. Three full-time utilization managers and a part-time medical director oversee decisions made by the assessment unit and often act in the role of "super case managers," particularly as regards more expensive services.

Despite these similarities, there are some noteworthy differences between these two systems of care. One point of divergence between Centerpoint and High Point is in the types of services making up the continuum, dictated by the different patient populations they serve. Centerpoint has evolved quite specialized services designed for treatment-resistant and noncompliant patients, such as assertive community treatment (ACT), as well as residential treatment options, and a host of services for children and their families and also for individuals with developmental disabilities.

Consonant with the scope of treatment and the added responsibilities of a three-county catchment area, Centerpoint has grown substantially in the past 5 years from 200 to over 450 employees. Over the same period, the number of subcontracts for services from other agencies grew from 6 to 250. Centerpoint's budget has grown, but perhaps not as much as might be expected with this growth in personnel. The Medicaid waiver has allowed Centerpoint to employ nonprofessionals to deliver many of its services, and to offer a number of nontraditional services through contract agencies. Access to a broader continuum and better coordination of care have resulted in decreased utilization of more costly inpatient services and, at least in the area of services to children and adolescents, decreased utilization of outpatient services, partially offset by an increase in residential and case management services.

Another major difference in these facility-based continua stemming from their different funding mechanisms relates to the managed care objective of accountabil-

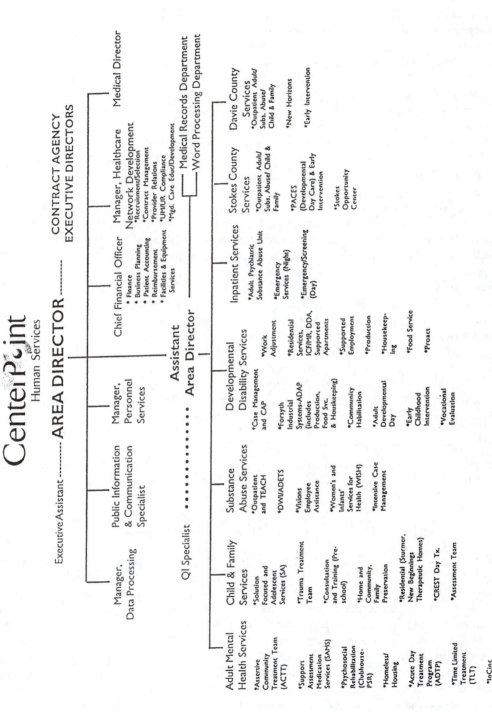

CenterPoint Human Services

FIGURE 11.2.

173

ity. Centerpoint is ultimately responsible to the state government, and each CMHC is monitored by a "performance agreement" defining expectations both financial and clinical. Less formal but no less real expectations also derive from the county political community. The CMHC is subject to audits by the Health Care Financing Administration (HCFA, now CMS), as well as by Medicaid and Medicare. Because inpatient care is part of the continuum (a rarity among CMHCs in the state), Centerpoint, like High Point, is accredited by JCAHO. CMHCs are generally not well configured to compete for enrollees with private insurance, particularly if managed by an MBHO. Besides the administrative burden of communicating with the MBHO, CMHC clinical staff often does not meet credentialing requirements. However, there are some specialized services particularly attractive to MBHOs, and in rural areas often the CMHC may be the only option for enrollees. Finally, Medicaid services are increasingly being managed, prompting further evolution of CMHCs toward the model of efficiency seen in the private sector.

Quality management at Centerpoint has elements of both process outcomes and clinical outcomes. *Process outcomes* focus on the providers of the service or the manner that care is delivered. For example, the medical records department periodically reviews clinical charts to make certain that paperwork is properly completed. Each clinical program is monitored as to the mean number of days from when clients are referred to when they actually receive an appointment with a clinical service. State guidelines set a standard of 14 calendar days. This is a "benchmark" that each program and the CMHC as a whole must attempt to meet. Process outcomes are generally easier to define and to measure.

Clinical outcomes are defined as those measures based on the symptoms or functioning of the persons who receive services. Each of the 41 clinical programs identifies a primary clinical outcome measure and then gathers data to report on a quarterly basis to an agencywide clinical activities committee. Often a standardized rating scale is used, such as the Global Assessment of Functioning (GAF). Goals are set periodically in order to provide incentive for improvement. The degree of success in meeting planned goals is reflected in a team score. The team score can be used as one element of the individual performance evaluation, used to figure bonuses. Oversight of quality improvement efforts is the responsibility of the agency executive team.

MANAGED MENTAL HEALTH ORGANIZATIONS

We turn finally to the MBHO—in the eyes of many, the primary agent of managed care for mental health. Indeed, the MBHO has the greatest concentration of managerial assets and functions, in comparison to the health care entities thus far described. With the exception of the staff model HMO, which employs its own clinicians who in turn provide direct patient care, MCOs and MBHOs are primarily brokers of health care services. Like an insurance company, MCOs and MBHOs charge a premium on a per capita basis from which they pay claims for a defined set of health care benefits for a defined population of persons enrolled in the plan. The prepaid nature of this mechanism of financing places a premium on efficient management of overall costs. The percentage of the annual budget used to pay claims is termed the *medical loss ratio*. The remainder constitutes central administrative expense or profit.

Management of mental health utilization is sufficiently different from that of general medical health that the MBHO has emerged as a specialized subcontract agency for the MCO. When management of mental health services is part of the parent MCO, they are said to be "carved in," whereas the subcontract model is called a "carve-out" (Frank, Huskamp, McGuire, & Newhouse, 1996). There are several important variations upon the types of contracts between the MCO and the MBHO. The MBHO may assume all risk for medical loss, in what is called *full capitation.* Alternatively, the MBHO may receive a smaller fee to provide management without any risk for the cost of the care delivered, and this agreement is called *administrative services only* (ASO). Finally, there are contracts defining "risk pools" shared between the MCO and MBHO. One example of the latter is when a portion of fees are withheld until and unless certain utilization targets are met.

In this section we discuss the inner workings of a small, regional MBHO, which nonetheless interacts regularly with the three health care entities already described. Carolina Behavioral Health Alliance (CBHA) is a "carve-out" MBHO that currently maintains contracts with two MCOs in North Carolina, covering approximately 80,000 lives. This organization was formed in 1999 as a joint venture between three medical schools (East Carolina University, University of North Carolina at Chapel Hill, and Wake Forest University). Prior to this, the organization was called Wake Forest Behavioral Health Services, established in 1996 as it grew out of that institution's Department of Psychiatry (Reifler et al., 2000). Academic departments of psychiatry are not commonly a part of the development of MBHOs, but there have been other successful examples (Wetzler, Schwartz, Sanderson, & Karasu, 1997).

The legal structure for CBHA is a limited liability corporation (LLC) allowing each of the medical-school partners to share equally in ownership. All profits accrue not to CBHA but to the partners, to further improve patient care through support of teaching and research. This differs from the core mission of for-profit MBHOs, which must return on equity from stockholders. Another major aim of the strategic plan for CBHA is to help each partner develop and maintain a referral base. This is furthered by growth in enrollment, and by making medical-school clinicians part of the network. In this sense, CBHA is considered a "provider-sponsored" MBHO. Although risk is not passed directly to clinicians, those physicians and therapists working in the medical school have an incentive to constrain costs. The entire provider panel benefits from a more favorable fee schedule and target medical loss ratio.

The organizational chart for CBHA is depicted in Fig. 11.3. The Board of Directors draws three representatives from each of the three medical schools. This body meets at least quarterly, and more frequently as needed, to discuss major issues affecting the strategic and business plans. The chief executive officer (CEO) reports to the board and has the ultimate authority with regard to running the company. The CEO delegates considerable responsibility to a management team drawn from the managers who report to him or her concerning the activities of health services, quality management, and finance divisions. Currently CBHA employs two part-time medical directors, who have roles in both the health services and quality management divisions. This allows the CEO to focus on business development and contracting issues.

CBHA is a growing entity, but its core operations are now well established. The division of Finance Administration differs little from any other corporation in its

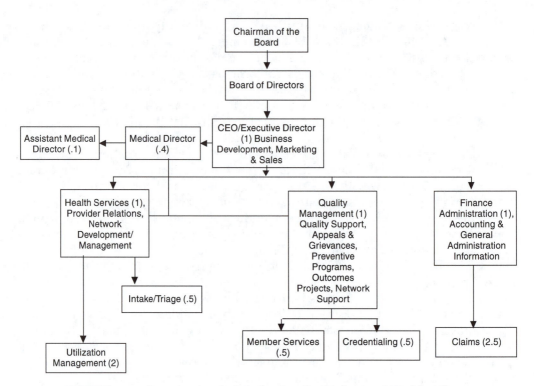

FIGURE 11.3. Organizational chart for Carolina Behavioral Health Alliance.

responsibility for maintaining a budget and the appropriate accounting of the financial activities of the organization. Like all MBHOs, CBHA receives monthly capitation payments, and pays out claims as they are received. The lag time between when the prospective payment is received and when claims pay out creates the operating margin on which the organization depends for its financial health. Claims payment is a painstaking and technical activity subject to intense scrutiny for both its accuracy and its timeliness. Only those services that are properly authorized will be approved for claims payment. Therefore, the information system must be integrated between departments and provide for sophisticated reporting on each phase of operations. The ability to forecast using actuarial techniques the liability incurred but not yet reported is crucial in a business with fixed revenues.

The division of Health Services is comprised of intake/triage and utilization management functions. Broadly speaking, this division is responsible for access: arranging and coordinating care for enrollees accessing their mental health benefits. It is analogous to the assessment units previously discussed for High Point Regional and Centerpoint, with some important distinctions. Once the enrollee makes the decision to get help for a mental health problem, there are several ways to access services. First, the enrollee may call the 800 phone number on his or her enrollment card and speak directly to an intake specialist at CBHA. Alternatively, he or she may see his or her primary care physician for a referral or call an in-network mental health provider directly for an appointment. Finally, if the enrollee's insurance plan has a *point of service* (POS) option, he or she may directly access services from any provider outside the network without any initial contact with CBHA. Generally the POS option is more costly to the employer and also has higher out-of-pocket costs for the enrollee. For some enrollees who wish to have complete freedom of choice, this is an important option, worth paying for. However, the benefit is still likely to have limits on number of days, visits, and dollars.

If the enrollee calls the 800 phone number directly, the intake specialist will request basic information about the nature of the problem and will conduct a risk assessment to make certain that the situation is not an emergency in terms of potential for harm to the enrollee or others. If these concerns exist, then the call is transferred to a care coordinator for further evaluation. Intake specialists have only a bachelor's degree, whereas care coordinators are either master's-level clinicians or nurses. Emergency cases are scheduled for an evaluation with a network provider that same day. If the case is routine, then the intake specialist will proceed to verify the active status of the enrollee by finding the identification (ID) number within the database. A record of each contact is maintained. The database also contains a listing of physicians and therapists by specialty, along with location, office hours, and so on. The enrollee is given the names of several in-network providers who might be appropriate, based on these characteristics. Upon making that choice, an authorization is generated and recorded in the system. A letter confirming this goes out to the provider and the enrollee that day.

At any time an enrollee contacts an in-network provider for initial treatment, it is that provider's contractual duty to obtain preauthorization, again through the 800 phone number. The default number of visits authorized initially is six. This allows the provider an opportunity to evaluate and treat the individual, and in many cases this number may be sufficient. When additional visits are deemed necessary, the provider must obtain further authorization by submitting a treatment plan by mail or fax. A standardized treatment plan is required (Fig. 11.4), with a number of required data elements. These include diagnoses, a list of medications, an account of the results of treatment already rendered, and an indication of what specific goals are planned for the next period of treatment.

The treatment plan is the primary mode of communication between providers and clinical care coordinators, who review the forms and authorize payment for additional services as part of the utilization management plan. This is termed *concurrent review*. When the enrollee is a patient in a more intensive level of care, concurrent review is conducted usually by telephonic interview with utilization managers affiliated with the facility.

Clinical care coordinators at CBHA have the authority to extend authorizations for all levels of care, with their decisions being guided by a set of *medical necessity criteria* specified for each level of care. A generic definition of medical necessity includes the following elements:

- Consistent with the symptoms or diagnosis and treatment of the patient's condition.
- Appropriate with regard to standards of good medical practice.
- Not solely for the convenience of the patient, his or her physician, hospital, or other health care provider.
- The most appropriate supply or level of service that can be safely provided to the patient.

Carolina Behavioral Health Alliance, LLC
Treatment Plan Update and Services Request Form
Fax: (336)-499-4006   Mail: P.O. Box 571137 Winston-Salem, NC 27157-1137

Enrollee ID Number

Enrollee Name

Provider ID Number

Provider Name and Signature

Clinical Communications
- ○ Primary Physician
- ○ Other Behavior Health Provider
- ○ No Communication at enrollee's request

Date First Seen   **Date Last Seen**

Patient/Guardian Participation in Treatment Planning:
I have participated in this treatment plan and agree with the information
○ Yes   ○ No   Patient Guardian Signature _____

Axial Assessments *(List DSM - IV Codes and Conditions)*

Axis I and II Codes   **Axis I and II Condition**

Principal Diagnosis Code

Axis III Diagnoses (list)

Other Diagnosis Code

Global Medical Status ○ Stable   ○ Unstable

Axis IV (Check all applicable)
- ○ Economic   ○ Health Care Access   *Comments*
- ○ Legal   ○ Housing

Other Diagnosis Code
- ○ Educational   ○ Social Environment
- ○ Support   ○ Occupational

Other Diagnosis Code

GAF Scores   Current   Presenting   Highest in Past Year

Outcomes

Does patient report improvement from treatment?
- ○ Yes
- ○ No

Current Family Disruption
○ None ○ Mild ○ Severe

Severity of Psychiatric Symptoms
- ○ In remission
- ○ Mild level of symptoms
- ○ Moderate level of symptoms
- ○ Extreme level of symptoms

Vocational Difficulties
○ None ○ Mild ○ Chronic

Suicide Potential
- ○ None ever
- ○ History of Ideation
- ○ Current Ideation
- ○ Recent Attempt

Self Care Difficulties
○ None ○ Mild-moderate ○ Extreme

Danger to Others
- ○ None ever
- ○ Current verbal aggression or h/o physical
- ○ Current physical threat
- ○ Homicidal

Medication Management Requests
(MDs Only Complete this Section)

NOTE: *If providing psychotherapy, MDs must complete psychotherapy request section on page 2*

Number of medications prescribed by you:
○ 1   ○ 2   ○ 3   ○ 4 or more
List Meds

Current and Anticipated Complications
- ○ Incomplete Response
- ○ Side Effects
- ○ Medication non-compliance
- ○ Abuse Prescribed Medications
- ○ Abuse Street Drugs or Alcohol
- ○ Unreliable attendance
- ○ Other

Comments

Plan for Managing Complications

Prognosis and Plan
- ○ Discontinue medications & discharge
- ○ Transfer to primary MD
- ○ Provide Ongoing Medication Management
- ○ Other

Visits Requested for Next Year of Treatment

90862 Medication Management

(A new authorization will supersede all outstanding authorizations.)

For optimum accuracy, please print carefully and avoid contact with the edges of the box. The following will serve as an example:

0 1 2 3 4 5 6 7 8 9

Shade circles like this: ●
Not like this: ⊗ ✓

20838

FIGURE 11.4.

Medical necessity is based on matching the severity of illness with the intensity of service. These criteria are stratified by level of care, and according to whether the determination is made at the onset of treatment (*initial*) or after a period of treatment (*continuation*). Criteria are further differentiated by age (children and adolescents

TABLE 11.3. Medical Necessity Criteria for Continuation of Adult Inpatient Psychiatric Care

- Documentation of signs and symptoms consistent with *DSM–IV* diagnosis
- Documentation of ongoing disordered behavior in the milieu that, unmonitored, would endanger the welfare of the patient or others or would interfere with activities of daily living
- Documentation of need for ongoing specialized care such as complex medication monitoring, multiple diagnostic procedures, or special risk management
- Evidence of the patient's incapacity for reliable attendance within a partial hospital program
- Documentation of active and realistic psychiatric evaluation, treatment, and discharge planning under way within the shortest possible time frame

vs. adults) and by the benefit being used (mental health vs. chemical dependency). An example of criteria for continuation of adult inpatient care is seen in Table 11.3.

When, in the judgment of the clinical care coordinator, the care being rendered or requested does not meet the criteria, the clinical care coordinator must consult the medical director in order to deny payment. The medical director will conduct an interview directly with the clinician, reviewing medical necessity criteria in what is called a *peer-to-peer* assessment. The medical director may elect to authorize payment for additional services, or may formally deny the request. At this point, the clinician or facility may initiate an appeal, and the case is turned over to the quality management division for further adjudication. There are several levels of appeal, including an independent review by an agency unaffiliated with CBHA.

Although each aspect of the utilization plan is detailed in a policy or procedure, the decisions made by medical directors and clinical care coordinators are subject to the same sources of error and bias that affect clinical judgment (Rosenquist, Colenda, Briggs, Kramer, & Lancaster, 2000). Nevertheless, the potential exists for both overutilization and underutilization of services, and the review and appeal processes hold both clinicians and the MBHO accountable. With an experienced network of clinicians, and a relatively enlightened MBHO such as CBHA, the discussions are less polarized. Increasingly, the discussions are about optimizing outcome within a limited benefit. Equally challenging is the observation that a minority of patients consume the majority of services. Often there is agreement that the patient is quite ill, and although the patient is quite attached to a particular provider, there is little progress being made. One management strategy holding promise for this situation is the second opinion. CBHA offers a premium fee to a handful of skillful network providers who see the patient for a few sessions to develop suggestions for improving care.

Network development is the process of recruiting a sufficient number of providers to serve the needs of the enrollees. CBHA is in the midst of a statewide expansion consonant with its strategic plan to develop additional business in the areas surrounding the three medical schools. An effective network has a mix of providers with different training backgrounds and interests who are located in proximity to enrollees.

The director of network development and provider relations is responsible for the identification, contracting, and verification of the credentials of all providers selected to be in the network. The verification of credentials, called credentialing, is a process that is currently conducted by a contract agency that checks on the education, licensing, malpractice history, and reported ethics violations of each provider, prior to their acceptance into the network, and at 2-year intervals thereafter. A site review is conducted at the time of recredentialing for all providers seeing a high volume of enrollees. In this review, the office physical plant is assessed, and charts are reviewed for clarity and specific process outcomes similar to that discussed earlier for Centerpoint. A credentialing committee made up of network providers reviews all applications and votes to accept or reject each new provider. This same body oversees the quality improvement program. Providers are surveyed regularly as to their satisfaction with the activities of the MBHO.

Although quality management is identified as a separate division, these activities are distributed throughout the organization. Continuous quality improvement (QI) for the internal processes at CBHA is basically no different than that previously discussed for the provider organizations. The various divisions and subdivisions identify areas of potential improvement, a monitor is established and tracked, improvement is specified, and the cycle begins again. Where quality management for the MBHO becomes unique is in the responsibility of monitoring the health of the enrollee population, and the activities of the network of providers.

But where does one begin with such a mammoth undertaking? If quality measures are ever to become sufficiently developed to guide the process of comparing one MBHO with another, there needs to be some standardization of the areas under observation. One indicator of the growth and consolidation of managed care has been the emergence of a national accrediting agency, the National Committee for Quality Assurance (NCQA). This organization was formed in 1991 with input from a number of stakeholders, including the insurance industry, large corporations, and representatives of provider groups. The NCQA has emerged as the primary accrediting agency, and MBHOs wishing to compete must increasingly modify their organization and develop procedures in order to meet the NCQA requirements. Other regulatory bodies include state departments of insurance, and the Health Care Financing Administration (HCFA; now Centers for Medicare & Medicaid Services [CMS]). CBHA fashions its quality management program after the NCQA requirements. Some of these are listed in Table 11.4, grouped according to the primary managed care agenda items.

QI activities have the potential to bring out the best in managed care. It is here that the managed care agenda items come together. With increasing accountability, there can be more accurate measurement of quality issues. Access can be defined and measured explicitly as a quality issue. A focus on outcomes of care has the potential to supplant nearsighted attention to policies and procedures. The unique needs of the population being served can be defined and addressed more completely. As the field develops more effective management strategies, QI mechanisms are in place to help disseminate practice guidelines throughout the network. These potential benefits are balanced by the understanding that QI can be labor-intensive and costly.

The field of managed care is young and rapidly changing. Techniques of management are diverse and are differentially implemented across the country. The perspectives of the individual patient, provider, business community, and society are

TABLE 11.4. NCQA Standards

Accountability: The MBHO can delegate responsibility, but always retains accountability for standards.

- Contracts are worded such that providers and practitioners cooperate with QI activities and standards.
- Procedures for complaints, appeals, and assessment of member satisfaction.

Access: Standards include specific performance goals for access to care and telephone response.

- Explicit qualifications for MBHO referral and triage staff.
- Assessment of the members' cultural needs and preferences is required to ensure network adequacy and acceptability.

Quality: Development of coordinated QI plan.

- Continuity and coordination of mental health with medical care.
- Development of programs for prevention and early intervention in mental health.
- Preservation of patient confidentiality.
- Development and promulgation of practice guidelines.

---

not easily reconciled. This chapter was written with the goal of providing the reader with a view from the trenches. The health care organizations profiled here seem to be doing their best to balance competing values and to evolve with the demands of the present environment.

ACKNOWLEDGMENTS

The author acknowledges the assistance of the following individuals: Lynette McDowell and Cindy Crater (CBHA); Julia Gallardi and Judy Arthofer (Centerpoint); Keith Cottle (High Point Regional); and Rich Cook (New Directions).

REFERENCES

Frank, R., Huskamp, H. A., McGuire, T. G., & Newhouse, J. P. (1996). Some economics of mental health "carve outs." *Archives of General Psychiatry, 53,* 933–937.

Geraty, R. D. (1995). General hospital psychiatry and the new mental health care delivery system. *General Hospital Psychiatry, 17,* 245–250.

Mintzberg, H. (1979). *The structuring of organizations: A synthesis of the research.* Englewood Cliff, NJ: Prentice-Hall.

Reifler, B., Briggs, J., Rosenquist P., Uncapher, H., Colenda, C., Teeter, W., Yates, K., & Reboussin, B. A. (2000). Case report of a managed mental health organization operated by an academic psychiatry department. *Psychiatric Services, 51,* 1273–1277.

Robbins, S. P. (1992). *Essentials of organizational behavior.* Englewood Cliffs, New Jersey: Simon and Schuster.

Rosenquist, P. B., Colenda C. C., Briggs, J., Kramer, S. I., & Lancaster, M. (2000). Using case vignettes to train clinicians and utilization reviewers to make level of care decisions. *Psychiatric Services, 51,* 1363–1365.

Smith, A. (1937). *An inquiry into the nature and causes of the wealth of nations.* New York: Modern Library. (Original work published 1776)

Starr, P. (1982). *The social transformation of American medicine.* New York: Basic Books.

Wetzler, S., Schwartz, B. J., Sanderson, W., & Karasu, T. B. (1997). Academic psychiatry and managed care: A case study. *Psychiatric Services, 48,* 1019–1026.

Chapter Twelve

Disciplinary Foundations: Psychiatry

Philip E. Veenhuis

HISTORICAL PERSPECTIVE

At one time, as stated in the overview portion of this section, mental health management was almost exclusively dominated by psychiatry. Indeed, the founders of what has become the American Psychiatric Association were all superintendents of state insane asylums. Interestingly enough, early papers emanating from this group could more clearly be classed as papers on administration/management rather than on treatment. Understanding of the nature of mental disease, or more exactly, ignorance of the nature of mental disease, shaped the organization of care in the 19th century. The serious mental disorders, such as schizophrenia and major affective disorders, tended to be treated in large state hospitals if at all. There was a prevalent belief that mental disorders were dementias, that is, brain diseases, and were incurable. Illnesses, less debilitating, received little attention. Sigmund Freud's synthesis of mental disorders as intelligible and treatable led in the 1930s to the development of a modest amount of office practice, at least for the affluent. Also in the 1930s there appeared what were perceived to be effective somatic therapies, electroconvulsive therapy (ECT) and insulin coma.

The office practice of psychiatry evolved very slowly. A number of European physicians trained in Freudian psychoanalysis had immigrated to the United States during the 1930s to escape Nazi persecution. This group, along with a smaller group of American-born psychiatrists, who had trained in Europe, founded the American Psychoanalytical Association and training institutes for psychoanalytic training. Office practice of psychiatry involving psychoanalysis, its derivative of psychoanalytically oriented therapy, remained very small until after World War II.

During World War II, an unexpectedly high number of draftees were rejected for neuropsychiatric reasons. In addition, a large number of general physicians (also draftees) were required to provide psychiatric treatment because of the small number of psychiatrists available. An epiphany of sorts took place when it was found that an unexpected number of members of the military, presumed to be "normal" mentally, under the stress of combat suffered "mental breakdowns." As a result, after World War II a large number of physicians who had served in the military became interested in psychiatry, entered training postservice, and the demand for psychoanalytic training escalated.

The 1950s saw the advent of effective medications for the treatment of mental disorders. Psychiatric treatment came out of the state hospitals and became more mainstream. General hospitals opened psychiatric wards. The private practice of psychiatry started to flourish.

The 1960s saw federal legislation that established community mental health centers. In the halcyon days of that time, there was an unsubstantiated belief that social factors were largely the cause of mental disease. Amelioration of these factors, such as poverty and social inequality, could reduce mental disease. Psychiatrists were at first among the leaders of this movement. Psychiatrists led many if not most of the original community mental health centers. Significant numbers of psychiatrists were in management positions. This did not last. A variety of factors served to lead to the withdrawal of psychiatrists from leadership in the community mental health centers. Perhaps the most significant was challenge of the medical model by the other professions. Psychiatrists seem, perhaps, to have been ill equipped for their leadership role.

PROFESSIONAL TRAINING OF A PSYCHIATRIST: COLLEGE AND MEDICAL SCHOOL, STATE LICENSURE

A psychiatrist is a medical doctor who has taken specialty training. To become a psychiatrist, one attends college for 3–4 years. This generally results in a baccalaureate degree. During this time, certain premedical courses are required with an emphasis on science and mathematics. Medical school requires 4 years after that. To that point, all physicians have had more or less the same training. A doctor at some point after completion of the first year of specialty training is eligible to obtain a state license to practice medicine. This may be delayed but is a prerequisite to practice any medical specialty. In the United States, physician licensing is the prerogative of the 50 states. All physicians, regardless of specialty, take the same written examination for state licensure in each state. Most states utilize a standardized national examination.

SPECIALTY TRAINING

Specialty training comes next, called residency. This involves 4 years, with the first year emphasizing primary medical care. This first year formerly was called "internship." The following 3 years are training in the specialty of psychiatry. Residency training involves supervised experience in the treatment of the diseases that are the domain of the respective specialty. Generally, residency programs are based in medical schools. In the instance of psychiatry, patients are treated in various settings, such as inpatient, outpatient, and partial hospital. There is extensive training in the use of the various therapeutic modalities: psychopharmacology (drug treatment of the various disorders), electroconvulsive therapy, and the various psychotherapies. Following completion of this, a physician can practice psychiatry. Essentially, these are practice years with experienced faculty available for supervision and guidance.

BOARD CERTIFICATION

After completion of residency training, certification by the respective medical specialty board is achieved by completion of a certification examination of one of the American Boards of Medical Specialties. In psychiatry, that board is the American Board of Psychiatry and Neurology. Certification depends on the passing both a written and oral examination. The American Board of Psychiatry and Neurology is a member of the American Board of Medical Specialties. Separate boards are possible in addiction medicine, offered by the American Society of Addiction Medicine (ASAM). Certification by ASAM is open to physicians certified by boards other than the American Board of Psychiatry and Neurology, reflecting the fact that other specialists besides psychiatrists work in the field of addiction.

The American Board of Psychiatry and Neurology (ABPN) examination for general psychiatry, the basic board certificate required before taking other APBN examinations, requires first a written examination, passage of which gains the psychiatrist admission into the oral examination. The written examination covers the basic fund of knowledge expected of psychiatrists. The oral examination basically looks at the capacity of the psychiatrist to interact with a patient to elicit data, form a diagnostic impression, and prescribe a treatment plan. Successful completion of both written and oral examinations is necessary for certification. Prior to 1996, permanent certificates were issued. Since that time, certificates are now time limited to 10 years, after which time reexamination is necessary to keep certification in force. At the time of this writing the process to be used for recertification for the basic certificate has not been decided. Recertification for the basic certificate will purportedly involve only a written examination, more in the order of self-study.

"Boards," as they are informally known, are not required to legally practice psychiatry in any of the United States, but increasingly this credential is required for hospital staff privileges and to be enrolled in many managed care panels. Perforce, they have economic importance as well as their traditional prestige.

SUBSPECIALTY TRAINING

It is also possible to take additional training in various subspecialties of psychiatry. The oldest of these is child and adolescent psychiatry. This requires an additional 2 years of training. In recent times there has also been the development of subspecialties in geriatric psychiatry, addiction psychiatry (diagnosis and treatment of alcohol and drug abuse), forensic psychiatry, and neurophysiology (use of electroencephalography [EEG] and other tools for diagnosis).

Each of these carries requirements for additional training. Certification is also possible for all these subspecialties, but the basic board in psychiatry is required for admittance into the subspecialty examination. These subspecialty certificates are now also limited to 10 years. The recertification process in the subspecialties will apparently involve a written examination.

PRACTICE OF PSYCHIATRY

Psychiatrists practice medicine but limit themselves to the diagnosis and treatment of mental diseases and disorders. As with all medical practice, diagnosis is accomplished by taking a history and performing an examination. Examination in psychiatry focuses on the mental status of the patient. This examination is performed with interaction with the patient, observing and evaluating his or her responses. Sometimes mental symptoms in a person are due to a medical illness not in the domain of psychiatry, such as thyroid disease causing depression. Sorting out the cause of a given disease may require a physical examination, if such has not been done by the referring physician. Like many specialists, psychiatrists generally prefer that physical examinations be done by general physicians such as family practitioners or internists. The diagnostic process may also involve such diagnostic procedures as laboratory tests and various imaging techniques. In some cases structured psychological tests, generally performed by a psychologist, may be ordered.

Having established a diagnostic impression, the psychiatrist next develops a treatment plan. As needed, this plan will include biological elements (medications), psychological elements (some form of psychotherapy), and social elements (addressing the patient's relationships, vocation, and living arrangements). This regimen may well involve the use of psychotropic medication (in common use are antipsychotic drugs, antidepressant drugs, mood stabilizers, and antianxiety drugs). Frequency of treatment, drug dosage, and timing of outpatient visits are also prescribed. These drugs, depending on diagnosis, are almost always used in conjunction with some form of psychotherapy. Psychotherapy may be individual, group, couples, family, or some combination of these. The psychiatrist also determines if the patient should be hospitalized or treated as an outpatient. A psychiatrist is expected not only to be capable of diagnosing and developing a treatment plan but also is expected to be an expert in the treatment modalities mentioned above.

The psychiatrist, as a physician, is the only mental health professional who may obtain full medical staff privileges in hospitals. Accordingly, they are the only professionals who can write admission and discharge orders. In hospital environments, the physician is charged with writing orders for all diagnostic tests, medications, and, in general, all aspects of care. Psychiatrists (along with doctoral-level psychologists in some jurisdictions) are the only mental health professionals permitted to make recommendations for commitment for involuntary treatment.

PSYCHIATRISTS' ROLES IN HEALTH ORGANIZATIONS

Psychiatrists practice in solo practice, groups with only other psychiatrists, groups with other mental health professionals, medical school faculties, and multispecialty medical groups. Psychiatrists work in health maintenance organizations, hospitals (private and public, general and psychiatric), and community mental health centers. They may participate in teaching medical students or residents in psychiatry or other fields either on the full-time faculty of a school of medicine or as part-time or voluntary faculty. Teaching may involve lectures or reviewing the psychotherapy work of residents in psychiatry (called psychotherapy supervision).

Hospitals are medical institutions. Psychiatrists may be employed by hospitals and/or work as attending staff (independent contractors). In either of these instances, psychiatrists will be part of a medical or professional staff. The physicians will constitute an autonomous medical staff that will guide the conditions of care. Particularly in hospitals, psychiatrists as physicians will have a leadership role, generally paramount to other mental health professionals. In other settings, the role of the psychiatrist may be less dominant, but given their status as licensed physicians, they play a critical role in all organizations treating persons with mental illnesses serious enough to require certain diagnostic and treatment procedures that only a licensed physician may order.

Regulatory agencies such as the Joint Commission on the Accreditation of Healthcare Organizations (JCAHO) and the federal Health Care Financing Administration (HCFA, now CMS) specify the functions of the medical staff. These also describe the process of credentialing and privileging staff physicians. Nonhospital settings that are not regulated by these agencies generally still are governed by state laws pertaining to health agency licensure and the medical practice acts. In general, certain activities are permitted only to physicians licensed by the state in which the health agency is located. Diagnosing diseases (including mental diseases), ordering of diagnostic tests such as x-rays or laboratory tests, performance of physical examinations, and the prescription of medication are activities limited largely to licensed physicians.

MANAGING PSYCHIATRISTS

In general, managing the work of psychiatrists, as with managing the work of most professionals, involves two separate domains. There is the domain of performance standards expected of all employees such as coming to the office on time and working assigned hours. The other domain is that of professional practice. Psychiatrists are licensed physicians and as such have an independent right to practice their profession in accordance with the medical practice act of the respective state. They are controlled by the respective state medical practice act and the ethical standards of the specialty. No organization can be licensed to practice, nor can the physician delegate any of his or her functions to his employer. The result of this duality is that most organizations need to appoint a psychiatrist as the clinical leader, with such titles as medical director or chairman. This leader is charged with maintaining the professional standards by reviewing the work of the other physicians.

In hospital settings, professional standards are formally organized (as required by accrediting agencies). This is done by an initial credentialing process, which involves verifying a physician's credentials such as medical school graduation, completion of residency, and medical licensure. Privileging is a parallel process, which outlines the specific professional activities that the physician is qualified to perform. Privileging is reviewed at time of appointment and reappointment. When concerns develop regarding a physician's performance in the professional domain, either because of outcome and/or untoward incident or other concern, generally the medical leader is first to review the physician's performance. Following that, some designated body of the medical/professional staff (determined in the staff bylaws), will review the issues in question and, if appropriate, recommend sanctions. The work of a physician is complex. Considerable independence of practice must be granted. There are areas that seem to be at the interface of the domains of performance and professional practice. Managed care has required a focus on productivity. Physicians work at different paces, requiring different times to perform the same tasks. This has made the work of the clinical manager both more important and more challenging.

Outside of hospital settings the management of psychiatrists tends to be a less formalized process. However, there remain the same issues of domains of performance and practice, again generally requiring clinical leadership to assess professional issues.

PSYCHIATRISTS IN MANAGEMENT

Psychiatrists serve in management positions, including high-profile management positions. For example, several medical school deans are psychiatrists. In addition, there are numerous positions open to psychiatrists both in general health care and in mental health. A partial listing of these is vice-president of medical affairs in a general hospital, and chairman or medical director of a department of psychiatry in a general hospital or psychiatric specialty hospital. In a hospital with many subunits, each may have a medical director or chairman. For example, there may be a head child psychiatrist or head of a substance abuse service or consultation/liaison division. HCFA/CMS requires that all psychiatric hospitals receiving federal funds have experienced psychiatrists as medical directors. These physicians are held responsible for all aspects of the clinical care. Psychiatrists may serve as medical directors of community mental health centers. Psychiatrists may have leadership positions in academic departments of psychiatry in schools of medicine.

Psychiatrists, having the entire biopsychosocial spectrum in their scope of practice for diagnosis and treatment, are very well equipped by training to manage mental health organizations. However, not all psychiatrists have the temperament for leadership positions. In medical school, future physicians are inculcated in what some have called the "Aesculapian authority." They learn to establish a relationship with patients characterized by the tenet that if the patients wish to recover they must do as the doctor directs. During psychiatric training, on the other hand, future psychiatrists learn to tolerate deviations in behavior and to accept that patients may not always wish to change symptomatic behaviors. The appropriate authoritarian stance of managerial leadership is probably somewhere between these two extremes. Further, the putative organizational leader must identify primarily with the organizational goals and only secondarily with the human issues of employees.

Probably most psychiatrists currently in management have acquired their administrative knowledge without benefit of formal training or mentoring. In this day and age, however, additional training will soon be expected for most managerial/administrative posts, especially those of health organizations outside of traditional mental health. The American Psychiatric Association through its Committee on Psychiatric Administration and Management has a certification process in psychiatric administration and management. This is a self-study program followed by a written and oral examination of persons who meet certain eligibility requirements. There are also available certification programs through such organizations as the American College of Physician Executives and the American Board of Quality Assurance and Utilization Review Physicians.

There has been a rapid growth in formal training programs in management. Some physicians continue to obtain the traditional degree in health services administration, master of public health (MPH). Some schools of public health, traditional training sites in health care administration (formerly hospital administration), offer part-time programs for physicians (and other professionals) interested in formal management training. The degree of master of business administration (MBA) has acquired a cachet in the 1990s. Physicians, including psychiatrists, are acquiring this degree in greater numbers. MBA degrees are offered with and without a concentration on health care. There are also variations on these traditional degrees, such as master of health administration (MHA) and so forth. It must be said, however, that practically no school or program offers, as yet, an emphasis on mental health. Many continuing medical education courses in psychiatric education and administration have come and gone. There has always been a small number of fellowships in administrative psychiatry, usually elective for residents in their final year of training. These positions have not been popular.

At least one organization, the American Association of Psychiatric Administrators (AAPA), continues to work to encourage the development of training in management for psychiatrists.

FUTURE DIRECTIONS IN PSYCHIATRY

There are major differences of opinion in the specialty of psychiatry as to what should constitute the work of a psychiatrist. Many psychiatrists now in practice, perhaps most, entered with the intention of being psychotherapists. Much of the work of private psychiatry was the model of a psychiatrist providing combinations of psychotherapy and pharmacotherapy. Residency emphasized training in what was called "long-term psychotherapy." The past decade has seen this model seriously challenged. Challenges are essentially from two sources, external and internal, and are interrelated.

The external challenge has been and is from managed care (Detre & McDonald, 1997). All health care is seeing routine activities being assigned to professionals with lesser training, with consequent perceived lowering of costs. So, for example, various physician extenders not uncommonly perform tasks such as routine physical examinations in primary care. Every medical specialty is seeing physician extenders performing routine office services. Psychiatry has always had competition from a number of other professionals that perform psychotherapy, namely, psychologists (doctoral level and master's level), social workers, and various counselors.

Before the advent of managed care, generally there were differential pricing structures for psychotherapy, based loosely on training and implied increased effectiveness. The past decade has largely seen this pricing structure eroded. Psychotherapy will increasingly only be paid at one level, a level generally consistent with the marketplace value of the time and effort of the lowest trained provider. No doubt psychiatrists have different costs—for example, malpractice insurance is generally much higher for the psychiatrist than for non-medically trained psychotherapists—and not infrequently higher debts incurred from longer and more expensive training. However, the industrialization of health care has meant, among other things, that unless there can be shown to be some difference in outcome between the performance of a procedure, like psychotherapy, by a psychiatrist, and by another type of provider, payment would be the same for all professionals. This has significantly altered the private practice of psychiatry and probably recruitment into the field.

If psychotherapy is not to be a significant activity for the specialists in psychiatry, what then is to be the focus of the work of the specialty? Clearly psychiatry has always been the only mental health profession that could use medications to treat patients. This has meant that psychiatrists have always had a clear role in the treatment of the more serious psychiatric diseases. At the present time the largely unchallenged role of psychiatry is in the performance of psychiatric evaluations for diagnosing patients, the prescription and management of the somatic therapies (largely medication), the admission and management of patients to hospitals, and the civil commitment evaluations.

This brings us to the second, internal challenge regarding the work of a psychiatrist. It is impossible to totally separate this challenge from the real and threatened inroads on the economic well-being of the specialty, but some members of the specialty have felt that the time was approaching when psychiatry should focus more on the biological aspects of psychiatric disease (Lieberman & Rush, 1996). There is a belief that diagnosis and somatic treatment of mental disease are already or likely to become much more advanced due to better imaging techniques, better understanding of genetics, and better medications (Cowan & Kandel, 2001). Psychiatrists in training would focus more on those disorders that more clearly have a biological (usually genetic) diathesis, that could be diagnosed by signs as well as symptoms, and that could be treated with medication or other somatic therapy. This would make the field of psychiatry more like neurology. There would be increased overlap between these two specialties, but the disorders currently the province of psychiatry, such as schizophrenia, affective disorder, panic disorder, and obsessive–compulsive disorder, would continue to be the focus of psychiatry. There would still be a psychosocial aspect to psychiatry in evaluation and treatment, but formal psychotherapy would cease to be a major professional activity of psychiatry. While it is estimated that only portion of persons with these disorders receive treatment and only a portion of that group receive treatment from a psychiatrist, it is likely that the number of psychiatrists needed would be much less than historic projections and smaller than the current number of psychiatrists in the United States.

However, many—perhaps most—psychiatrists in practice are committed to the practice of psychotherapy as a significant professional activity and, indeed, were attracted to psychiatry by the intellectual challenge of that activity. This intellectual challenge has tended to be a major recruitment incentive into psychiatry for many of the graduates of American medical schools—however, never in sufficient numbers to fill the available training positions. In fact, for a number of medical students a disincentive to recruitment into psychiatry has always been an identity issue. Professionals in the mental health field besides psychiatrists have performed psychotherapy for several decades now. Entry into medical school and the acquisition of the identity of a physician is a highly competitive affair. If, indeed, the work done by a psychiatrist is the same as that done by a nonphysician, why should any physician with other challenging opportunities go into psychiatry? Seemingly, these challenges, external and internal, will continue to shape the specialty. The traditional draw to those medical students who want to be psychotherapists may diminish; the attraction of the projected "new psychiatry" to medical students is unknown. Finally, as stated before, almost certainly the numbers of psychiatrists in the United States will diminish.

Adding still further to the problems of the specialty is that psychiatric residency programs by and large have not altered their training programs to the context of managed care (Hoge, Jacobs, & Belitsky, 2000). That is to say, the skills necessary to succeed in the practice sector are not being effectively taught in training programs. Psychiatry is not unique in that regard among medical specialties; few— perhaps none—of other mental health professional training programs have significantly addressed this issue.

As alluded to earlier, some leaders in the specialty feel that training programs in psychiatry should alter their training programs not only to better prepare graduates to work in the managed care environment, but more significantly to reemphasize the medical aspects of training, with more emphasis on general medical care and neurology, including the accelerating pace of advances in the neurosciences. There would be a reduction in the amount of training in psychotherapy. The psychiatrist would work with the sickest patients and be prepared still to consult with other physicians and mental health professionals.

Clearly at least two things are proposed in psychiatric training programs. First, training programs should train residents in real-world settings that are shaped by issues controlled by managed care. Second, at the present time there is every reason to believe that fewer and fewer psychiatrists (or any profession, for that matter) will be doing long-term psychotherapy. Accordingly, although principles of psychotherapeutics should be taught, there should be greater emphasis in training programs on the neurosciences and psychopharmacology. Predictably, these changes will take place. The only question is whether the changes will be evolutionary or revolutionary.

Predictably, psychiatry will become a smaller specialty as in the rest of health care, where routine care devolves to professionals with lesser training (and lower income expectations). It is also likely that more psychiatrists will seek management positions.

REFERENCES

Cowan, W. M., & Kandel, E. R. (2001). Prospects for neurology and psychiatry. *Journal of the American Medical Association, 285*(5), 594–600.

Detre, T., & McDonald, M. C. (1997). Managed care and the future of psychiatry. *Archives of General Psychiatry, 54*(3), 201–204.

Hoge, M., Jacobs, S., & Belitsky, R. (2000). Psychiatric residency training, managed care, and contemporary clinical practice. *Psychiatric Services, 51*(8), 1001–1005.

Lieberman, J., & Rush, J. (1996). Redefining the role of psychiatry in medicine. *American Journal of Psychiatry, 153*(11), 1338–1397.

Chapter Thirteen

Disciplinary Foundations: Organization and Adminstration of Psychology Services

James Picano
Matthew Blusewicz

Our task seemed simple enough: Describe the functional organization and administration of clinical services provided by psychologists in health care settings. Between the two of us we have over 35 years of clinical, training, and administrative experience in academic and government agencies. We have developed, managed, reorganized, and administered psychology services and psychology training programs in medical centers, community hospitals, and outpatient clinics. Experience should have provided us with a clear vision of our goal. But as we considered the breadth and nature of the services provided by psychologists in health care settings, it became apparent to us that the task was far more complex than we had initially anticipated. To complicate matters further, we found the published literature to be of little help. That is not to say that material is not available to guide us. In fact, two relatively recent books have been published that describe the practice of psychology in clinical health care settings and hospitals (American Psychological Association, 1998b; Sweet, Rozensky, & Tovian, 1991b). Yet nowhere in either of these two works does one find a discussion of models for organizing and managing the delivery of psychological services.

Although our initial professional development as psychologists took place in different government agencies, our organizational experience was similar. We worked with other psychologists in a section or service, sometimes within a larger division or department, usually psychiatry. This is the traditional model for organizing and administering psychology services in medical settings and is consistent with the identification of psychologists as mental health providers. However, we hold appointments in two departments of our affiliated medical school, and know psychologists in five other departments.

The roles of clinical psychologists in medical settings have broadened considerably over the past 50 or so years, beyond those in the traditional mental health arena. No longer are psychological services available only for mental health patients and problems. Psychologists now practice in such areas as neuropsychology, behavioral medicine or health psychology and the more contemporary primary care psychology (American Psychological Association, 1998a; Levy, Pollak, & Walsh, 1994), and rehabilitation psychology. The practice of psychology has evolved to the point that some propose that psychologists now be considered *health* care providers rather than mental health care providers (American Psychological Association, 1998a; Frank, 1997). The effective and efficient organization and management of psychological services have been complicated considerably by these expanded roles and responsibilities. Our more modest goals for this chapter are to elucidate the roles of psychologists in health care delivery, and to describe some models for organizing and managing the delivery of psychological services. In addition, we touch on issues regarding psychologists as managers in the modern health care environment.

THE EVOLUTION OF CLINICAL PSYCHOLOGY IN HEALTH CARE

Resnick (1997) presented a history of clinical practice in psychology emphasizing major events that have shaped its direction and focus. Clinical psychology began in the late 1890s. Parenthetically, according to Resnick (1997), the term *clinical* was borrowed from medicine to refer to the method of dealing with patients, as opposed to the setting in which the services were delivered. In fact, much of early clinical psychology was essentially child school psychology, and most clinical practice involved intelligence testing. World War I and the wholesale adoption of intelligence testing for induction into the armed services marked a major transition for psychologists: They moved out of academia and into the clinical practice of psychological assessment (Resnick, 1997).

Psychological assessment, and mental abilities testing more specifically, were to dominate the clinical practice of psychologists for the next 50 years. World War II brought renewed vigor to military induction testing. However, the war also produced large numbers of psychiatric casualties in Veterans Administration (VA) hospitals across the country, creating demand for properly trained therapists. The VA worked with the American Psychological Association (APA) to expand training for psychologists. Shortly after World War II, and largely as a function of training within the VA, psychotherapy became a legitimate aspect of psychological practice (Resnick, 1997).

As clinical psychology moved into this new era, pressure rose from within the professional psychology community to develop more stringent standards and certification procedures. In 1949, the APA adopted the scientist-practitioner model for training in clinical psychology, recognizing that the roles for clinical psychologists involved the skills and abilities of both the scientist and professional clinician (Cranston, 1986). Along with this came the endorsement of the doctorate as the entry-level degree for professional practice in clinical psychology.

Licensure and certification of psychologists soon followed, and psychologists became independent practitioners of psychological services. Dependence on the federal government for employment waned, and psychologists found employment in hospitals and clinics, where they began to focus more on psychotherapeutic intervention. Legislative decisions over the past three decades have served to further define psychological practice and opened doors for psychologists to practice independently in hospitals and clinics as members of medical staffs and to receive third-party reimbursement (Resnick, 1997).

Although initial employment opportunities for psychologists in health care were in departments of psychiatry, psychologists have moved beyond their traditional mental health roles, largely capitalizing on deeper understandings regarding the contributions of behavior to health outcomes (Frank, 1997). Since the 1970s the presence of clinical psychologists in health care settings has grown rapidly, with "specialization" emerging in areas such as behavioral medicine or health psychology and neuropsychology, in addition to the slightly more mature area of rehabilitation psychology (Sweet, Rozensky, & Tovian, 1991a). Psychologists now find themselves in a variety of roles in clinical and health care settings, such as educating and training physicians and other health care professionals, providing assessment and psychological or behavioral interventions in the prevention and treatment of nonpsychiatric medical conditions, and providing neuropsychological services—all in addition to the provision of traditional psychological services in mental health (American Psychological Association, 1998a; Frank & Ross, 1995).

Although this diversification of practice has generally been positive for clinical psychology as a profession, psychologists are now frequently scattered throughout the various settings and departments of health care agencies (Frank, 1997). The independent department of psychology or psychology service, with its own organization, management structure, budget, and clinical programs, is the exception rather than the rule, especially in academic medical centers. This lack of coherence and integration makes effective organization, management, program development, and evaluation of clinical programs difficult at best. Even in government and other public-sector institutions, where we have the bulk of our administrative and clinical experience, the trend is away from independent psychology (and psychiatry departments) and toward integrated mental health service systems (American Psychological Association, 1998a; Gilles, Shortell, & Young, 1997). Such an organizational structure potentially facilitates effective organization and management of psychological services, a point to which we return later. First we would like to characterize the training and education of psychologists and highlight some of the core roles and responsibilities of psychologists in health care. In doing so, we hope to enlighten nonpsychologist managers who are charged with effectively deploying psychological resources, overseeing the credentialing and privileging of psychologists, and assuring the quality of psychological services.

EDUCATION AND TRAINING OF CLINICAL PSYCHOLOGISTS

For the health services manager or administrator unfamiliar with the education, training, and clinical roles and responsibilities of psychologists in health care systems, the organization and management of psychological services can seem quite formidable, owing in large part to the diversity in clinical competencies he or she is likely to encounter among psychologists. Effective management of psychological services becomes even more difficult the further one moves away from mental health settings. To clarify, we wish to outline the educational preparation of psychologists to assume roles in health care delivery. More detailed discussion of these issues can be found in Sheridan and Choca (1991).

Academic psychology adopted the scientist-practitioner model to develop the diversity and depth of knowledge required for practice in health care settings. Such programs emphasize, more or less equally, the education and development of skills necessary for both research and clinical practice. Completion of such a program results in the awarding of the doctor of philosophy (PhD) degree. This is sometimes referred to as the "traditional" model of psychological education (Sheridan & Choca, 1991).

New models for training have evolved over the past 30 years that have shifted the emphasis away from research training toward clinical practice. Such models are termed the scientist-professional or scholar-practitioner model, or more simply the "professional" model. Education and training within this model normally culminates in the awarding of the doctor of psychology (PsyD) degree, although some programs with slightly more emphasis on research training continue to award the PhD degree. Debate continues regarding the most appropriate education and training model for clinical practice, with some arguing that the professional models better reflect the reality that the majority of clinical psychologists devote most of their professional time to practice and little if any to research. What has become more salient in recent years, regardless of the training model, is whether or not the American Psychological Association accredits the graduate program. This process assures that graduates have completed the variety of coursework relevant to the practice of psychology in health care settings, and ensures some degree of "quality control" in the education and training of psychologists. Although graduation from an institution accredited by the APA is not a requirement for licensure in most states, there are some agencies (such as VA) that cannot hire psychologists who are graduates of unaccredited programs.

Unlike medical training, the internship in psychology is the capstone experience to a psychologist's professional education. Prior to internship training, an intensive year-long clinical training experience, psychology graduate students will have spent many hours in supervised delivery of psychological services (anywhere from 500 to 1500 hours or more in practica or clerkships, depending on the training model of the program). Psychology internships typically provide general training and experience in the diagnosis, treatment, and management of diverse medical and psychiatric patients and problems in both outpatient and inpatient settings. Quality internships generally permit a broad range of clinical experiences under the supervision of experienced psychologists. As with graduate education, accredited internship programs must also meet stringent standards set forth by the APA.

It is now more common for psychologists to complete formal postdoctoral training beyond internship further qualifying them to work in more specialized areas of clinical psychology. Most commonly, these experiences are in areas of behavioral medicine and related health psychology specialties, and in neuropsychology. It should be noted that although most states require supervised clinical experience beyond the awarding of the doctorate to qualify for licensure as a psychologist, formal intensive postdoctoral training is a relatively recent development. So too is the review and accreditation of such programs. The most recent revision of the guidelines and principles for accreditation of programs in professional psychology (American Psychological Association, 2000) now includes criteria for accreditation of postdoctoral training programs, and the first programs were accredited in 1999. Given the growing importance of APA accreditation in the education and training of psychologists, we anticipate that employment in health care settings will become increasingly tied to APA-approved postdoctoral training.

Again, unlike medical education and training, there is not widespread consensus on the need for board certification for practice in any of the specialty areas of clinical psychology. Additionally, there is no one certifying authority, although the diploma awarded in a number of content areas by the American Board of Professional Psychology (ABPP) is generally recognized as the professional standard. However, we predict that the importance of board certification will grow in the future, driven largely in response to market factors in the managed care environment rather than by the need for standards defining advanced clinical competence.

Health care agencies generally set their own criteria for clinical privileges in psychology, although these are obviously informed by national and state standards where they exist. Factors internal to each agency influence the credentialing, privileging, and professional status of psychologists.

ROLES AND RESPONSIBILITIES OF CLINICAL PSYCHOLOGISTS IN HEALTH CARE SETTINGS

Services provided by psychologists do vary somewhat according to the mission of a particular health care agency and the needs of its patients. However, psychologists engage in a common variety of activities in health care settings. These include psychological assessment, interventions and treatment planning, teaching and scientific research, and management and administration (American Psychological Association, 1998b). In this section, we briefly address each of these activities.

Psychological Assessment

Probably no other function performed by psychologists is as highly associated with the professional identity of a psychologist as psychological assessment. It continues to be the activity that most distinguishes psychologists from other mental health specialists. Yet surveys of the amount of time that psychologists spend in various clinical activities indicate that assessment now ranks second to psychotherapy, occupying on average only about 15% of a psychologist's time in professional practice (American Psychological Association, 1996). Still, the vast majority of psychologists engage in psychological assessment as a routine part of their practice (Norcross, Karg, & Prochaska, 1997), and psychological assessment continues to be practiced across a variety of clinical settings, in all psychology specialties, and with diverse patient populations and problems. Given that psychological assessment is a core and unique element of psychological practice, we provide a relatively more comprehensive discussion of this activity, compared to some others we review.

Psychological assessment involves the integration of information derived from multiple test methods with referral information, historical data obtained from interview, and behavioral observations made during testing and interview, to arrive at a comprehensive understanding of the person and his or her problems (Meyer et al., 1998). It is distinguished from psychological testing in that the latter is a relatively straightforward, technical process involving the administration and scoring of a test or battery of tests. Nevertheless, in practice *psychological assessment* and *psychological testing* are often used synonymously.

Traditionally, the goal of psychological assessment has been to assist in the differential diagnosis of psychiatric and cognitive disorders. Although psychological tests are useful for differentiating among some clinical diagnoses (e.g., intelligence testing in the case of mental retardation, and neuropsychological tests in the determination of dementia), psychiatric diagnosis over the past 20 years (since *DSM–III*) has increasingly relied more on behavioral and historical criteria and less upon test-derived conceptualizations. Consequently, the utility of psychological assessment solely for diagnosis is declining and, not surprisingly, so too are authorization and reimbursement by managed care companies for psychological assessment (Eisman et al., 1998). Our own experience suggests that many clinical psychologists continue to narrowly focus on the diagnostic function of psychological assessment. With its lessening value in the current health care environment, they are devoting increasingly less of their time to assessment.

There are other very important functions of psychological assessment beyond diagnosis that have traditionally been underemphasized. For example, psychological tests can be extremely useful in directing interventions (e.g., determining treatment needs and goals, and the most appropriate treatments based on psychological characteristics) and monitoring the effectiveness of treatments (outcome assessment). These applications have been the subjects of more contemporary texts on psychological assessment (Maruish, 1994). Psychological tests also serve as quality assurance and risk management tools because the standardization and psychometric properties of psychological tests provide objective reference points to serve as checks against the biases and errors limiting interviews or other more informal and subjective methods (Meyer et al., 1998). Interestingly, attention has also recently shifted to the evaluation of psychological assessment as a therapeutic intervention in and of itself, with symptom decline and increased self-esteem demonstrated in patients who have been provided assessment feedback by a psychologist (Finn & Tonsager, 1992).

Although there are clear benefits to the psychological assessment services provided by psychologists, there are also very significant costs. Psychological assessment is a time-consuming and therefore expensive clinical activity, requiring the psychologist to administer, score, analyze, and communicate assessment findings, usually in a comprehensive written report. To date, no data directly demonstrate the cost-effectiveness of psychological assessment. However, there is substantial evidence assembled by a working group on psychological assessment for the APA demonstrating the clear utility and value of psychological assessment in the health care environment (Meyer et al., 1998).

Intervention and Team Treatment Planning

Psychologists now spend the greatest proportion of their clinical time in the delivery of psychological interventions and psychotherapy (Norcross et al., 1997). More traditional forms of interventions typically include individual, group, marital, and family therapy and are usually delivered in the context of mental health service delivery. However, psychotherapy is not a skill unique to psychologists, and psychologists often provide a much wider variety of behavioral interventions for health-related problems, often outside of the mental health arena. Such interventions include programmatic, multicomponent treatments oriented for pain management (Turk, Meichenbaum, & Genest, 1983), smoking cessation (Cinciripini et al., 1994), and bulimia and binge-eating (Fairburn, Jones, Peveler, Hope, & O'Connor, 1993), as well as for a host of other health problems (Sweet et al., 1991b).

Changes in the health care system ushered in by managed care have noticeably influenced the delivery of psychological interventions. Increased emphasis on demonstrated efficacy of psychological interventions is resulting in the expanding use of treatment practice guidelines and therapies having demonstrated efficacy. There have been a number of "empirically validated therapies" developed by psychologists that have met the criteria of being well established, researched, and efficacious. A listing of these therapies has been compiled by a working group on psychological interventions assembled by the Division of Clinical Psychology of the APA (Chambliss et al., 1998). Many of these approaches are detailed in treatment manuals that help to ensure replication of the treatment approach across practitioners and settings (Woody & Sanderson, 1998).

We expect that the intervention roles of psychologists will continue to develop in the direction of delivering such services, as well as those emphasizing short-term problem resolution. However, it is likely that psychologists will move more and more away from the direct provision of intervention services and toward the planning and supervision of interventions delivered by others members of the treatment teams (Spruill, Kohout, & Gehlmann, 1997).

Teaching and Research

Traditionally, psychologists have had significant teaching responsibilities in health care settings consistent with their education and training. Psychologists routinely participate in the education of medical residents in a number of specialty areas. Larger health care organizations often have an identified education and training mission in psychology and conduct formal predoctoral or postdoctoral training. In these agencies, psychologists regularly supervise interns, postdoctoral fellows, and other trainees in clinical psychology. Increasingly, psychologists are now also asked to supervise other nonmedical mental health service providers. It has been speculated that health care psychologists of the future will spend a greater portion of their time training and supervising other mental health professionals in the provision of service than in service delivery itself (Spruill et al., 1997).

As a group, psychologists are specifically trained for roles in scientific research. Training and education experiences prepare psychologists for a variety of research activities, including treatment efficacy and outcome studies, case studies, program evaluations, and intramural or extramural funded clinical research. It is perhaps an unfortunate reality that few psychologists outside of academic medical settings engage in research to any great degree.

Administration and Management

Psychologists are increasingly found at all levels of administration and management of health care agencies (Spruill et al., 1997). As managers, psychologists apply their education and training to the business of organizing and maintaining psychological services, and to the management of multidisciplinary clinical and support personnel. The modern health care environment demands managers that are compassionate and inspiring, but who also possess sound business skills. Administration and management are traditionally not areas of formal education and training in the professional psychology curriculum. In addition, like all professionals, psychologists vary in their aptitude for leadership roles. We have more to say about psychologists as managers later. Now we turn our attention to the organization of psychological services in the health care delivery system.

MODELS FOR ORGANIZING PSYCHOLOGY SERVICES

Although the manner in which psychological services are embedded in a larger health care organization can take many forms, we believe that three organizational models describe the overwhelming majority of instances. These are (a) the service matrix model, (b) the integrated service model, and (c) the point of service model. It is useful to elaborate on these three models and to indicate some of their strengths and weaknesses.

Service Matrix Model

In the service matrix model, there is an independent psychology department or service that is led by a chair or a chief psychologist. All psychologists in the organization ultimately report to the chair or chief of psychology. Under this model, psychology is a coequal department with medicine, surgery, psychiatry, and the other health care professions. The chair or chief of psychology reports to a chief of staff (or some type of chief health care officer) on the same basis as the chairs or chiefs of the other departments and has the same authority and responsibility for the utilization of staff and resources, performance improvement, and so on.

Under this model, psychology organizes, conducts, and leads its own subprograms independently (e.g., health psychology; neuropsychology). If other programs need psychological services and staff, these needs are negotiated between the chair or chief of psychology and the chair or chief of the other departments or services. Although psychologists can be members of another department's or service's programs (e.g., an inpatient psychiatry unit), the ultimate line of authority for them runs to the chair or chief of psychology. Programs function as a result of the cooperation of a matrix of services that contribute staff and resources to the programs.

The service matrix model promotes a strong professional identity for psychologists (as well as members of other professions) in a larger organization. It facilitates relevant peer review as well as performance appraisal and improvement. It also has an advantage in representing a "critical mass" of psychologists that can support predoctoral and postdoctoral training (required by accrediting agencies) and collaborative research. It reflects the professional independence that organized psychology devoted decades to achieve.

The service matrix model can create confusion about authority and responsibility among program staff. This confusion can exacerbate some of the traditional interprofessional conflicts and "turf battles." For example, a psychologist can be assigned from the psychology department or service to function as a diagnostician and group therapist on an inpatient program that is the responsibility of the psychiatry department. The program manager, a psychiatrist, may have his or her professional or personal vision about how psychological testing and group therapy fit into the overall goals and objectives of the program. This vision may conflict with the program psychologist's concept of his or her professional responsibilities or personal preferences. The chiefs of psychology and psychiatry are often drawn into this conflict and, depending on their relationship, the conflict may either be resolved quickly or (too often) never satisfactorily resolved, impairing the efficiency of service delivery to patients and staff morale.

Integrated Service Model

Under the integrated service model, there is an independent mental health department or service (sometimes referred to as product lines or service lines), again led by a chair or chief. The professional members of the mental health department or service almost always include all psychologists and psychiatrists in the organization and may also include social workers, nurses, and technical staff working in mental health programs. These staff members all ultimately report to the chair or chief of mental health. The chair or chief of mental health reports to a chief of staff on the same basis, and has the same authority and responsibilities, as the other product line or service line chiefs in the organization. This model is increasingly found in public-sector health care systems and managed care/health maintenance organizations. It is also becoming more common in the Veterans Health Administration health care system.

Under this model, programs typically are organized and conducted as interprofessional units led by a manager from one of the professions in the mental health department or service. This manager functions as a first-line supervisor for all professional staff in his or her program, with the mental health chair or chief usually serving as a first-line supervisor to the managers and a second-line supervisor to program staff. Programs function as integrated interprofessional units with relatively simple lines of authority and responsibility.

In many ways the benefits and liabilities of the integrated service model are the obverse of those for the service matrix model. Because all mental health staff work within one line of authority, the frequency of interprofessional conflicts (although not necessarily personal conflicts) and other "turf battles" impairing patient care is decreased. However, there is inevitably some weakening of professional identity under this model, as well as more serious problems of professional performance being evaluated by someone other than a member of one's profession. Psychology, as is true of other professional disciplines, has its own history, culture, and standards. A supervisor who is a member of another profession may not have sufficient knowledge to do meaningful evaluation of the critical aspects of a psychologist's performance. Some organizations that are structured by the integrated service model attempt to compensate for this difficulty by appointing senior or lead psychologists, psychiatrists, social workers, and so on, whom program managers must consult when dealing with profession-specific issues.

Point of Service Model

Under the point of service model, psychologists are dispersed throughout a health care organization and work in a variety of departments or services. There is typically no psychology department or service as a formal organizational unit. Thus, departments of psychiatry, medicine, neurology and surgery, and others all independently assess their needs for psychological services and independently hire psychologists to function in their programs (e.g., mental health clinics, primary care medical clinics, dementia centers, dialysis units). The psychologists working under this model report directly to their program managers and ultimately to the department or service chiefs. Thus, psychologists function at the specific points of service to support the diagnostic and treatment needs at these points. This model is most frequently encountered in university health care systems and some health maintenance organizations.

It may seem at first inspection that the point of service model has nothing but liabilities. There is no organized psychology department or service (there may not even be a mental health department or service), and psychologists under this model may report to an individual who has no mental health background at all. This model appears to completely disregard professional identity support for psychologists or opportunities for them to assume professional leadership. At its best, this model of functional organization complicates the coordinated implementation of clinical and training programs. At its worst, this model engenders *intraprofessional* turf battles and conflicts. However, this model can allow and even encourage psychologists' creativity and "thinking outside the box" by positioning them in nontraditional roles where the rules are yet to be written. In addition, it is our experience that psychologists who function outside of traditional programs and venues often have fewer interprofessional conflicts with colleagues and supervisors who are more willing to accept them as equals, and even *the* experts, on their own "turf."

PSYCHOLOGISTS AS MANAGERS: PREPARATION AND ISSUES

There is little, if any, formal didactic training in management or leadership within degree-granting psychology programs. This is certainly understandable, as the clinical and research skills that must be mastered in these programs represent a full plate. Most predoctoral or postdoctoral trainees feel that they must focus on these areas despite the fact that they may have a professional interest in management and leadership. After graduation, the immediate tasks of becoming licensed and otherwise establishing one's professional credentials easily overshadow interests in management and leadership. Added to this is the fact that positions of organizational responsibility are rarely offered to individuals who are just out of training.

As a practical result, most psychologist-managers and psychologist-leaders are individuals with a significant number of years of professional experience. Some of these individuals have acquired additional formal training in management (e.g., MBA degrees) and/or pursued management training and certification through organizations such as the American College of Health Care Executives. However, for the most part we believe it is fair to say that the majority of these individuals learned what they know about management and leadership "on the job," perhaps by working with a mentor, and often assumed positions of responsibility as a result of serendipitous circumstances. It is not unusual for psychologists to receive their first formal training in management and leadership well after they have occupied positions of this nature. (Incidentally, most of these observations are equally true of other clinical professionals who are in positions of management and leadership.)

Despite the absence of formal training in many cases, most psychologists who are managers and organizational leaders perform these roles well. This raises the question of whether being trained to become a psychologist actually imparts at least some of the knowledge and skills required by these roles. In the past 15 or 20 years, an extensive literature on management and leadership has been created. It is of interest to examine some of the characteristics of good managers and leaders and compare them to the (at least aspirational) goals of psychological training.

One model of management and leadership competency is the high performance development model (HPDM) (Department of Veterans Affairs, 1997). This model identifies and defines a number of dimensions that are essential for optimal management and leadership, including personal mastery, interpersonal effectiveness, flexibility/adaptability, creative thinking, systems thinking, organizational stewardship, and technical skills.

For the most part, the meaning of each of the dimensions is evident in its label, and it is of interest to note how many of the dimensions relate to clinical concepts that psychologists encounter on a daily basis as part of their roles as diagnosticians, therapists, supervisors, and researchers. All are ingrained in functioning as an effective psychologist.

The HPDM holds, however, that in most cases one's performance can be improved along any of the defined domains through training and guided experiences; this is the model used by a number of organizations as a basis for mentoring programs. The HPDM also holds that successful performance on *all* of its dimensions is essential for effective management and leadership. Are any of its dimensions either somewhat alien or problematic for psychologists qua psychologists, and therefore a potential obstacle to effective management and leadership?

Technical skill is the most obvious potential candidate for this characterization, because of the earlier noted lack of formal training. A psychologist who wishes to be an effective manager or leader must be willing to acquire the skills related to human resources management, labor relations, and fiscal oversight, as well as a host of other general skills and technical skills related to the particular organizational culture within which he or she works. These areas often have little relationship to the interests and motivations that lead an individual to choose psychology as a career, and there may be some resistance to acquiring these new skills.

Customer service may become an obstacle for some psychologists (as well as other clinicians), not because we do not want those who come to us for help to be satisfied, but because our training has been based on the concept of these individuals being our patients or clients, not our customers. The business-based concept of a customer, and what an organization may consider an appropriate response to customer complaints, may conflict with the responses to such complaints that we consider professionally appropriate.

This last point is related to a more general potential difficulty with the organizational stewardship dimension. In an ideal world, there will not be conflicts between professional standards and ethics and the standards and ethics of the organizations in which we work. There will be no conflicts between what we are expected to do as psychologist-managers and psychologist-leaders and what our organizations expect of us, and no conflicts between supporting our organizations and assuming stewardship while managing high-quality care consistent with our ethical principles.

However, in the past several years the emergence of managed care has raised issues of confidentiality, rationing of care, and so on, that often place clinical managers in dilemmas for which there are no easy solutions. The effective psychologist-manager and psychologist-leader in this situation may find it difficult to be both a good psychologist and a good organizational steward. Further, psychologist-managers will continue to be challenged to ensure that all psychological services are relevant, cost-effective, and of high quality. Newer models for developing and monitoring service delivery may be required. Recently, the Canadian Council on Health Facilities Accreditation funded a task force to develop a prototypical model of quality improvement for psychology services in health care settings. The environmental scan model (Cyr, King, & Ritchie, 1995) is a quality management model that incorporates multiple quality improvement and quality management methods and processes for evaluating the effectiveness and quality of psychological services in health care settings.

FUTURE TRENDS

The first 100 or so years of clinical psychology have seen enormous expansion of the clinical roles and responsibilities of psychologists in health care. The dominant organizational structure that has supported, nurtured, and indeed facilitated this growth, the independent psychology service, with its consolidation of resources and professional solidarity, seems unnecessary and even anachronistic in the modern health care environment. Health care service delivery now favors integration and coordination of service over fragmentation and centralization. The emphasis is on seamless rather than boundary-oriented service delivery. Newer models for organizing and managing psychological services that recognize and support psychologists as members of the broader health care team, dispersed throughout the various departments of health care agencies, are required. Such models must recognize the diversity of services and settings comprising the scope of psychological services, ensure coordinated and efficient service delivery, and assure high standards of quality throughout the agency, all the while fostering the development of a unique and coherent psychology culture and identity. The integrated service model that we described comes close to achieving this, but it has been applied primarily for psychologists working in mental health service delivery. What about other psychologists who work in primary care or neurology and who are likely to find themselves in other product or service lines? As currently implemented, the point of service model falls far short of the challenge of serving as an effective model, largely sacrificing coordination, coherence, and consistency for the sake of integration of care. This model encourages a fragmentation among psychologists that works against efficient and effective management of psychological service delivery, and leads to difficulty establishing and pursuing common professional goals (Frank, 1997). Some degree of management consolidation seems necessary in order to achieve the "critical mass" of psychologists necessary to articulate a common agenda for continued professional growth, minimize intraprofessional turf battles, and attend to more routine issues such as overseeing and managing psychology training and clinical programs, and monitoring performance and quality. Effective and efficient management of psychologists and psychological services in the modern health care environment will require the evolution of new organizational structures that permit psychologists to continue to function as autonomous, integrated members of the health care team while advancing their shared identity, culture, and professional vision.

REFERENCES

American Psychological Association. (1996). *The Committee for the Advancement of Professional Practice (CAPP) practitioner survey.* Washington, DC: American Psychological Association.

American Psychological Association. (1998a). *Interprofessional health care services in primary care settings: Implications for the education and training of psychologists.* Washington, DC: American Psychological Association.

American Psychological Association. (1998b). *Practicing psychology in hospitals and other health care facilities.* Washington, DC: American Psychological Association.

American Psychological Association. (2000). *Guidelines and principles for accreditation of programs in professional psychology.* Washington, DC: American Psychological Association.

Chambliss, D. L., Baker, M. J., Baucom, D. H., Beutler, L. E., Calhoun, K. S., Crits-Christoph, P., Daiuto, A., DeRubeis, R., Detweiler, J., Haaga, D. A. F., Johnson, S. B., McCurry, S., Mueser, K. T., Pope, K. S., Sanderson, W. C., Shoham, V., Stickle, T., Williams, D. A., & Woody, S. R. (1998). Update on empirically validated therapies II. *Clinical Psychologist, 51*(1), 3–16.

Cinciripini, P. M., Lapitsky, L. G., Wallfisch, A., Mace, R., Nezami, E., & van Vunakis, H. (1994). An evaluation of a multicomponent treatment program involving scheduled smoking and relapse prevention procedures: Initial findings. *Addictive Behaviors, 19,* 13–22.

Cranston, A. (1986). Psychology in the Veterans Administration: A storied history, a vital future. *American Psychologist, 41*(9), 990–995.

Cyr, F., King, M. C., & Ritchie, P. L. (1995). Quality management for psychology services in health care facilities. *Canadian Psychology, 36*(3), 202–212.

Department of Veterans Affairs. (1997). *VHA employee development report: High performance development model.* Cleveland, OH: Author.

Eisman, E. J., Dies, R. R., Finn, S. E., Eyde, L. D., Kay, G. G., Kubiszen, T. W., Meyer, G. J., & Moreland, K. L. (1998). *Problems and limitations in the use of psychological assessment in contemporary healthcare delivery: report of the Board of Professional Affairs Psychological Assessment Work Group, Part II.* Washington, DC: American Psychological Association.

Fairburn, C. G., Jones, R., Peveler, R. C., Hope, R. A., & O'Connor, M. (1993). Psychotherapy and bulimia nervosa: Longer-term effects of interpersonal psychotherapy, behavior therapy, and cognitive behavior therapy. *Archives of General Psychiatry, 50,* 419–428.

Finn, S. E., & Tonsager, M. E. (1992). The therapeutic effect of providing MMPI-2 test feedback to college students awaiting psychotherapy. *Psychological Assessment, 4,* 278–287.

Frank, R. G. (1997). Marketing psychology at academic health centers. *Journal of Clinical Psychology in Medical Settings, 4,* 41–49.

Frank, R. G., & Ross, M. J. (1995). The changing workforce: The role of health psychology. *Health Psychology, 14,* 519–525.

Gilles, R. R., Shortell, S. M., & Young, G. J. (1997). Best practices in managing organized delivery systems. *Hospital and Health Services Administration, 42*(3), 299–321.

Levy, S., Pollak, J., & Walsh, M. (1994). Primary care psychology: Current status and future prospects. *Annals of Behavioral Sciences and Medical Education, 1,* 43–48.

Maruish, M. E. (1994). *The use of psychological testing for treatment planning and outcome assessment.* Mahwah, NJ: Lawrence Erlbaum Associates.

Meyer, G. J., Finn, S. E., Eyde, L., Kay, G. G., Kubiszyn, T., Moreland, K., Eisman, E., & Dies, R. (1998). *Benefits and costs of psychological assessment in healthcare delivery: Report of the Board of Professional Affairs Psychological Assessment Work Group, Part I.* Washington, DC: American Psychological Association.

Norcross, J. C., Karg, R. S., & Prochaska, J. O. (1997). Clinical psychologists in the 1990's. *Clinical Psychologist, 50,* 4–11.

Resnick, R. J. (1997). A brief history of practice—Expanded. *American Psychologist, 52*(4), 463–468.

Sheridan, E. P., & Choca, J. P. (1991) Educational preparation and clinical training within a medical setting. In J. J. Sweet, R. H. Rozensky, & S. M. Tovian, (Eds.), *Handbook of clinical psychology in medical settings* (pp. 11–25). New York: Plenum Press.

Spruill, J., Kohout, J., & Gehlmann, S. (1997). *Final report of the American Psychological Association working group on the implications of changes in the health care delivery system for the education, training, and continuing professional education of psychologists.* Washington, DC: American Psychological Association.

Sweet, J. J., Rozensky, R. H., & Tovian, S. M. (1991a). Clinical psychology in medical setttings: Past and present. In J. J. Sweet, R. H. Rozensky, & S. M. Tovian, (Eds.), *Handbook of clinical psychology in medical settings* (pp. 11–25). New York: Plenum Press.

Sweet, J. J., Rozensky, R. H., & Tovian, S. M. (1991b). *Handbook of clinical psychology in medical settings.* New York: Plenum Press.

Turk, D. C., Meichenbaum, D., & Genest, M. (1983). *Pain and behavioral medicine: A cognitive-behavioral perspective.* New York: Guilford Press.

Woody, S. R., & Sanderson, W. C. (1998). Manuals for empirically validated treatments—1998 Update. *Clinical Psychologist, 51*(1), 17–21.

Chapter Fourteen

Disciplinary Foundations: Psychiatric Nursing Administration

Patricia Christian

HISTORICAL DEVELOPMENTS

In the late nineteenth century, nursing began to emerge as a profession. The first school to prepare psychiatric nurses opened in 1882 at McLean Hospital in Waverly, Massachusetts. Although this 2-year program was an attempt to provide mental hospitals with better educated workers, the curriculum was little more than a modified medical–surgical curriculum which focused little on the psychological needs of the patients. Its main thrust was to provide skill in the physical care of psychiatric patients. Nurses were taught, not to treat the mentally ill, but to be kind and tolerant of them. The focus remained on custodial care.

It was not until 1893, when Linda Richards graduated from the New England Hospital for Women and Children in Boston, that psychiatric nursing had its real beginning. Following her graduation, she spent years organizing nursing services in state hospitals in Illinois. Her dedication to improving nursing care in psychiatric hospitals, primarily through education, earned her a place in history as the first American psychiatric nurse. Although the level of psychiatric nursing care in the hospital was improving, the educational system was slow to respond. Well into the early part of the 20th century, educational programs continued to focus on the physical needs of patients and to offer the nursing student little in the way of psychological knowledge. This was true even though the curriculum was seen as distinctly different from general nursing, with training centered on either a general hospital or a psychiatric hospital.

In 1913, Johns Hopkins School of Nursing was the first to include a complete course of psychiatric nursing in its curriculum. Other schools followed suit with programs integrating general and psychiatric nursing. It took about 25 additional years before nursing education actually started emphasizing the importance of psychiatric principles in treating all mental and physical illnesses.

After World War II, psychiatric nursing's importance greatly expanded. Because of the large number of soldiers and veterans with service-related psychiatric conditions, the overall numbers of psychiatric patients increased. As more Veterans Administration hospitals were built, the need for better trained and more extensively prepared nurses became clear. The National Mental Health Act, passed by Congress in 1946, provided for federal funding of nursing programs. Just one year after the act took effect, eight graduate programs in nursing had been established.

The role of the specialized psychiatric nurse continued to develop, becoming well known and credible to the health care community and the general public. But the actual role of the psychiatric nurse continued to be ill-defined and vague. With the publication of Hildegard Peplau's *Interpersonal Relations in Nursing* (1952), actual theory-based psychiatric nursing came into being. Peplau defined nursing as a "significant, therapeutic process" and for the first time defined the phases of the nurse-patient relationship. Ten years later, she distinguished between nurses who worked on psychiatric units and psychiatric nurses who were specialists with graduate degrees in psychiatric nursing. In less than 70 years, psychiatric nursing had moved from an undefined specialty to a well-defined clinical role based on interpersonal techniques.

NURSE PRACTICE ACTS AND BOARDS OF NURSING

Anyone managing members of the nursing team must be familiar with the state's Nurse Practice Act. Each state has an act regulating nursing practice, education, and licensure. The Nurse Practice Act ensures that the practice of nursing is done by qualified individuals and, by so doing, protects the public interest. Most Nurse Practice Acts identify the components of practice, setting parameters within which individuals may practice. Practicing outside the legally approved level of care places any organization, institution, and/or individual at significant risk.

Nearly 100 years ago, boards of nursing were established to protect the public by overseeing the safe practice of nursing. Each state has a board of nursing (five states—California, Georgia, Louisiana, Texas, and West Virginia—have two boards of nursing, one for registered nurses and one for licensed practical nurses). Boards of nursing issue licenses to nurses and establish the standards for safe nursing practice, which the board continues to monitor. Licensure includes the examination of new graduates and other applicants, the approval of licenses, the renewal of licenses, and the reinstatement of licenses. The boards are also responsible for the discipline of persons who violate the Nurse Practice Act. This responsibility includes the ability to deny, revoke, suspend, limit, or otherwise restrict licenses. In addition, the boards conduct hearings and refer cases for criminal prosecution.

MEMBERS OF THE NURSING TEAM

The nursing team in a psychiatric setting is most often composed of a registered nurse, a licensed practical/vocational nurse, and a psychiatric technician/mental health aide. This team works with other disciplines in planning and carrying out the treatment plans for individual patients. A majority of staff time is spent working collaboratively, within their team, to meet the nursing needs of the psychiatric patient. Each member of the nursing team has specific, educationally based job responsibilities. The registered nurse is the head of the nursing team and is responsible for the delivery of care given by the licensed practical nurse and the psychiatric technician.

In general, members of the nursing team work either in a community psychiatric setting or an inpatient setting. The community settings can be in a variety of places including day treatment programs, outpatient community mental health programs, and ambulatory care centers affiliated with general hospitals. The roles are more easily identifiable in an inpatient setting, where patients are all within one area and remain there for at least a brief period of time. For purposes of this chapter, the emphasis is on the role of mental health nursing staff within inpatient units. The majority of inpatient units, whether private or public, have many similarities in the day-to-day operational procedures. Although not always specifically referenced, many of the same concepts can be applied to an outpatient area.

It is extremely important for any manager responsible for nursing to understand the dynamics of the nursing team. Although a team in name, the nursing team does not always function with a team spirit. Differences in educational backgrounds and pay scales can create feelings from "I'm in charge here and not you" from the registered nurse to "I do all the work and you get all the pay" from the psychiatric technician. Even within the registered nurse group one can observe conflicts stemming from different educational levels and perceived "quantity" of work. In some organizations, problems are magnified when the psychiatric technician is not supervised by nursing.

Members of the nursing team usually make up the vast majority of total staff positions. In a large state hospital, this group numbers in the hundreds of positions. This group also has the highest turnover rate of hospital employees, especially among the psychiatric technicians. Organizations with a high turnover of technician staff sustain high costs. This is especially true in inpatient settings, where the cost of technician training can range from $5,000 to $10,000 per technician. Not all hospital patient/residential/partial settings have licensed practical/vocational nurses on staff. When they do, this position is often used to administer medications and at times, within the boundaries of the state Nurse Practice Act, to supervise the nonlicensed personnel.

Although in some patient care areas the psychiatric technician reports to disciplines other than nursing, most inpatient units are organized in such a way that both the licensed practical nurse and psychiatric technician report to the registered nurse. Because nursing is the only discipline that works three shifts a day, seven days a week, it makes sense, organizationally, to have the psychiatric technician report directly to the registered nurse. The nursing supervisory hierarchy is arranged so that the registered nurse is responsible for the care delivered by the licensed practical nurse and the psychiatric technician. When the registered nurse delegates selected tasks or nursing functions, the accountability and responsibility for the safe delivery of the care remains with the registered nurse.

REGISTERED NURSE

The term *registered nurse* refers to an individual who has graduated from an accredited nursing program and passed a national licensing examination to obtain a nursing license. Nurses must be licensed in the state where they are practicing. When managing a nursing department, it is extremely important to verify licensure at the time of employment and also at time of renewal. States differ on renewal processes, so it is imperative to find out the procedure for your state. Allowing a registered nurse to practice without a current license places the manager and the organization in a precarious legal position.

Registered nurses make up the largest health care occupation in the United States. Over 1.9 million jobs were available for registered nurses in 1996 (Bureau of Labor Statistics, 1999). The term *registered nurse* encompasses several different levels of education and practice. These levels define, to a large degree, the parameters within which the nurse is prepared to practice. The common saying, "A nurse is a nurse," is far from true.

There are three basic educational paths that can be taken to become a registered nurse: associate degree in nursing (ADN), "diploma," and bachelor of science in nursing (BSN).

The majority of ADN programs are affiliated with community and junior colleges and take about 2 years to complete. These programs include a clinical course in psychiatric–mental health nursing. Graduates of these programs are prepared for entry-level clinical nursing positions in a structured care setting. These graduates are not prepared for leadership or administrative roles. In spite of this, many ADN graduates quickly find themselves thrust into leadership situations, especially in rural areas. It is important for the ADN and the manager to realize that additional educational opportunities are needed in order to assist the ADN to develop a leadership role. The associate degree programs are currently producing the largest number of registered nurse graduates, with over 55% of the RN graduates in 1996 (National Council of State Boards of Nursing, 1996).

The hospital-based diploma nursing programs, once the most common, now produce the smallest number of graduates (5.6% in 1996) (National Council of State Boards of Nursing, 1996). A diploma program lasts 3 academic or calendar years and provides patient contact very early in the educational process. The diploma obtained on completion is not an academic degree. Academic credit is not awarded for course work unless the diploma program is affiliated with a junior or senior college for the general education component of the curriculum. Students do receive clinical course work in psychiatric–mental health nursing and are most often employed in hospitals and long-term care facilities.

The baccalaureate degree program is affiliated with senior colleges and universities and lasts 4 years. Students not only take clinical nursing courses, but also courses in community health, leadership, and research, and are prepared to work in institutional or community settings. Graduates are prepared to assume beginning leadership positions, such as a ward/shift charge nurse position.

Graduation from any of the three types of programs qualifies the student to take the National Council Licensure Examination for Registered Nurses (NCLEX-RN). Historically, most nurse graduates take early career positions in medical–surgical settings in order to "get experience." Recently, with the closure of many hospital medical–surgical beds, more new graduates are taking their first positions in the areas of community mental health and inpatient psychiatric nursing. It is important that these new graduates, regardless of educational background, be given an intensive orientation with ongoing support from a senior-level registered nurse.

THE ROLE OF THE REGISTERED NURSE

Individual nurses are responsible for identifying their practice parameters. Decisions regarding practice boundaries are based on the state Nursing Practice Act, professional codes, professional practice standards, and the competency of the individual to perform certain nursing activities and functions. Registered nurses are responsible for their own nursing practice but have a professional responsibility to collaborate and coordinate care with other disciplines who are working with the same patients.

Differences in education and experience help to define the various practice parameters of the registered nurse, both in psychiatric ambulatory settings and inpatient settings. The hospital-based staff nurse is the person who provides, either directly or indirectly, the majority of patient care. In general, the role of the staff nurse can be assumed by nurses prepared at the ADN, BSN, or diploma level. Nurses with a basic education (ADN, BSN, or diploma) can be expected to assess patient needs, formulate a nursing diagnosis, develop a nursing care plan, contribute to the comprehensive treatment plan, implement the nursing care plan and the nursing-assigned areas of the treatment plan, and evaluate the delivery of nursing care. In addition, job expectations can include referrals to other professionals, coordination of patient care with other professionals, scheduling of patient activities, arranging and participating in specific groups (i.e., medication education, ward government, resocialization, exercise, stress reduction, etc.), and maintaining a safe and therapeutic milieu.

The baccalaureate-prepared nurse has received greater preparation in skills that are specific to the role of the psychiatric–mental health nurse, specifically patient teaching and the promotion of mental health. In addition, the baccalaureate nurse has greater educational experience in building those skills necessary to function as a member of the treatment team.

In community settings, the nurse's role is slightly different, with more emphasis placed on health teaching and disease prevention. Instead of operating within a defined milieu, the community mental health nurse may provide care in the home, outpatient clinic, school, halfway house, and sometimes on the street. When the role of the community mental health nurse requires autonomous action, it is important that the nurse be prepared at a more advanced clinical nursing level than the basic educational program provides.

The American Nurses Association recognizes psychiatric nurses' abilities through the certification process. Nurses are qualified for specialty practice at two levels—basic (psychiatric–mental health registered nurse) and advanced (psychiatric–mental health advanced practice registered nurse). This is the profession's way of formally validating the nurse's clinical competency. The psychiatric–mental health nurse is a nurse prepared at the baccalaureate level who has demonstrated clinical psychiatric skills that exceed those of a beginning RN or a novice in the specialty. The title psychiatric–mental health nurse applies to those nurses who pass a certifying examination, thus meeting the profession's standards of knowledge and experience. Interventions that are basic-level functions for the psychiatric–mental health nurse include health promotion and maintenance, case management, screening and evaluation, milieu therapy, physical/biological interventions, health teaching, home visits, crisis intervention, and counseling. Basic-level certification is designated by the letter "C" placed after the RN (i.e., RN, C).

The psychiatric–mental health advanced practice registered nurse (APRN) is a licensed RN who is at least master's prepared and is nationally certified as a clinical specialist in psychiatric and mental health nursing. This nurse has obtained a depth of knowledge of theory and practice and exhibited competence in advanced clinical nursing skills. The psychiatric–mental health APRN has the ability to apply this theory and practice autonomously, addressing complex mental health problems.

The APRN generally works in one of two clinical areas: (a) in a structured, organized setting that offers a full array of care services, and where nurses are paid/reimbursed on a salaried, fee-for-service or contractual basis, and (b) in a self-employed practice where the nurse offers services directly to the patient and is reimbursed on a fee-for-service basis or through a third-party payer such as an insurance or managed care company.

Many state legislatures and Congress have recognized the unique role of the advanced practice psychiatric nurse. This recognition has made it possible in some states for the advanced practice nurse to write prescriptions, have admission privileges, and qualify for third-party reimbursement. This applies to those advanced practice nurses within the community who are in private or group practice.

In the past, the advanced practice nurse in psychiatric–mental health nursing was called a clinical nurse specialist (CNS). In order to have more uniform titling, the term *advanced practice nurse* has taken the place of CNS and includes other titles such as nurse anesthetist, nurse midwife, and nurse practitioner. Advanced level functions include psychotherapy, consultation, clinical supervision, and physical/biological interventions. Certification at the advanced level is recognizable by the letters CS (certified specialist) after the RN (RN, CS) The psychiatric–mental health advanced practice nurse is referred to as a certified specialist, although the term *clinical specialist* is still commonly used.

DELEGATION BY THE REGISTERED NURSE

It is important to distinguish the difference between delegation of tasks and assignment of tasks. Delegation by a nurse involves giving to another a task that is within the nurse's practice. Assignment by a nurse involves giving to another a task that is within that person's authorized practice.

The scope of nursing practice is defined and legally regulated by each state's Nurse Practice Act. Although Practice Acts differ from state to state, all have language that speaks to the delegation of nursing tasks to unlicensed persons. There are universal guidelines that must be met prior to the nurse delegating to LPNs/LVNs or to unlicensed staff. The nurse must be assured that:

1. The person has been trained for the task.
2. The person has demonstrated that the task has been learned and that they can safely perform the task in a given situation.
3. The patient is stable enough to have the task delegated to someone other than a registered nurse.
4. Appropriate supervision is available to the person carrying out the delegated task.

In general, Nurse Practice Acts instruct the registered nurse to avoid delegating the essential components of nursing practice, which include the analysis phase of patient assessment, developing a plan of nursing care, evaluating the nursing care, and making nursing judgments. The delegated task must not require that an unlicensed person practice nursing assessment, judgment, evaluation, or teaching skills. Unlicensed staff may collect, report, and document simple patient data such as vital signs and intake/output. In addition, unlicensed staff can be delegated those tasks that are considered basic human needs such as mobility, hygiene, nutrition, elimination, and socialization.

CMS and JCAHO monitor the registered nurses' role in the delegation of nursing tasks. Both organizations hold the RN accountable for the quality and quantity of nursing care provided to patients by self and others being supervised. Nurse managers must ensure that the organization establishes policies that are consistent with the law and with the standards set forth by accrediting and certifying agencies. While budget concerns and/or nursing vacancies may tempt administrators to suggest which nursing acts can be delegated, it is the registered nurse who ultimately decides and is accountable for the outcome of such delegation.

THE ROLE OF THE DIRECTOR OF NURSING

The role of the senior nurse in a psychiatric hospital has undergone major changes in the past few decades. This can be seen where the traditional title *director of nursing* (DON) has been changed to *vice-president for clinical services* or *assistant director for professional services,* which reflect additional roles and responsibilities. It is not unusual to see the traditional DON position now responsible for a variety of clinical services, such as rehabilitation therapy, social work, and in many settings, quality improvement and staff development.

In state psychiatric hospitals, the DON is usually an active participant in the executive leadership group. This makes sense given the DON's 24-hour responsibility for nursing care and for the bulk of clinical employees. Excluding the DON from executive deliberation results in a marginalized nursing department, which is not in the hospital's best interest.

Responsibility for the 24-hour operation of the state hospital often falls on the shoulders of the DON. Most departments of nursing have a "house" supervisor or coordinator who serves as the DON's representative on the off shifts and weekends. These positions provide stable leadership to staff working on weekends and second/third shifts, helping to ensure that policies and procedures are consistently followed. Depending on the specific organizational structure of the hospital, the DON may be the person responsible for keeping the CEO/COO/clinical director informed of events occurring after normal business hours.

HCFA (CMS) regulations and JCAHO standards specify certain DON requirements and responsibilities. These specifications include the DON's qualifications, the DON's role in ensuring adequate numbers of prepared nursing staff, the DON's responsibility for delivery of nursing care, and his or her involvement in overall decision making. When hospital administrators are forced to cut budgets, reallocate positions, or reduce the workforce, the nursing department is usually the first department to come under scrutiny. This is somewhat understandable because the largest numbers of hospital employees are assigned to nursing services. It is the responsibility of the DON to ensure that hospital administration understands the impact of decreasing nursing service positions. Having a collegial working relationship with other senior hospital administrators is essential for the DON when participating in these types of discussions.

THE ROLE OF THE LICENSED PRACTICAL NURSE

The licensed practical nurse (or licensed vocational nurse [LVN]) is often employed in psychiatric inpatient, residential, and partial treatment programs as well as community out-patient programs. The educational preparation of the LPN usually takes about 1 year. Most of the approved programs are in technical schools, with a smaller number offered in community colleges. The graduate of a LPN program is required to pass a state licensing examination in order to practice. Licenses must be renewed based on a time frame set by each state, usually every 2 years. It is extremely important that managers responsible for LPNs ensure that no one practices without a current license.

Unlike the registered nurse, the licensed practical nurse is not an independent practitioner. The LPN practices under the direction of a physician or registered nurse. Although the scope of practice for the LPN is specifically defined by each state in the Nurse Practice Act, the role generally includes: (a) participating in the physical and mental health assessment process; (b) recording/reporting the results of the nursing assessment, including the patient's reaction to illness and treatment; (c) participating in the implementation of a plan of care that has been developed by a registered nurse, physician, or treatment team; (d) reinforcing the teaching and counseling of the registered nurse or physician; and (e) reporting and recording the nursing care rendered, including the patient's response to the care.

The LPN is an entry-level health care provider who is responsible for the delivery of basic nursing care. In mental health, this most often translates to medication administration (some states limit this practice), assisting patients with activities of daily living, and monitoring basic physical functions such as blood pressure. LPNs observe patients and report adverse reactions to medications or treatments. LPNs have input into the comprehensive treatment plan and are responsible for assigned interventions.

In times of registered nurse shortages, some managers of inpatient/outpatient units have assigned RN functions to LPNs, thinking, "a license is a license." This type of reasoning places LPNs in situations beyond the scope of their training and licensure, which is unsafe for patients and very risky for organizations.

PSYCHIATRIC TECHNICIANS/AIDES

Psychiatric technicians (often called mental health aides or by other titles), although the least educated/prepared members of the nursing team, actually spend the most time interacting with patients. This is especially true in psychiatric hospitals and residential treatment centers where care occurs 24 hours a day. Although the laws are different from state to state, most psychiatric technicians need only a high school diploma to apply for a position.

Psychiatric technicians are listed by various job titles. Some of the titles that are used around the country include behavioral science aide, client support assistant, clinical associate, habilitation clerk, health care counselor, milieu practitioner, therapy worker, and residential care trainee. Regardless of the title, the role of the psychiatric technician is similar from state to state. Under the direction of nursing and/or medical staff, the psychiatric-technician-specific patient functions can include assisting with bathing, dressing, and grooming; escorting patients to and from wards for exams and treatments; performing routine nursing procedures such as collecting laboratory specimens, drawing blood, and recording information in the patient's record; assisting the patient in becoming oriented to surroundings; interviewing patient on admission and recording data obtained; escorting patients off grounds; monitoring patients on special precautions; and participating in rehabilitation and treatment programs.

A few states currently license psychiatric technicians. These licensed psychiatric technicians attend an educational program, usually affiliated with a vocational program/community college, and then must pass a state licensing examination. The length of the programs can vary, but in general, the program is very similar to LPN programs. Licensed psychiatric technicians most often work in psychiatric hospitals, usually state hospitals, and have expanded practice rights that can include medication administration. Licensed psychiatric technicians are supervised by registered nurses.

The Omnibus Reconciliation Act of 1987 (1989) required that nurse aides employed in long-term care facilities, acute-care hospitals, and home health care agencies be certified as nursing assistants (CNAs). CNA certification requires that a specific curriculum be taught to all nursing assistants. This move was in an effort to ensure uniform competencies of aides. In addition, the law required states to set up nurse aide registries to list all certified aides and keep a record of all aides involved in patient abuse, neglect, or exploitation.

Psychiatric technicians were not included in the federally mandated legislation. Some states have decided to require psychiatric technicians to be certified. From an organizational perspective, requiring that psychiatric technicians be certified can create challenges to those responsible for hiring. The pool of available applicants is sharply reduced when a CNA requirement is added to the job description, especially if the state only requires that state hospital technicians be certified. Requiring certification does increase the competency expectation level of technicians. This additional knowledge can be applied to improving patient care.

Some individual hospitals, within states requiring certification, have elected to provide their own specialized courses to certify technicians. These courses have to meet the content of the federally mandated curriculum and have to be approved by the appropriate state agency responsible for ensuring uniform curriculums. Having an in-house course increases the pool of available applicants, but creates its own set of problems. The implementation of such a course is time-consuming and expensive for the organization. In addition, some psychiatric technicians who are hired and put through the course before being assigned to patient care are unable to pass the final examination and have to be terminated from the organization. This increases the cost of training to the facility and creates vacancy problems, often leading to additional overtime cost.

STAFFING ISSUES

Although recruiting and retaining nursing staff can be difficult in an outpatient, community mental health setting, it can quickly become a crisis situation in an inpatient psychiatric hospital. When there is a national registered nursing shortage, psychiatric hospitals, especially state hospitals, feel a tremendous impact. This is true for several reasons:

1. The pool of nurses with interest and preparation in working with the mentally ill is not extremely large in comparison with those who focus on medical–surgical nursing.
2. The working conditions and scheduling opportunities at state psychiatric hospitals tend to be less appealing than those at other public, private, or community mental health settings.
3. The salaries at state hospitals are often less than those at other inpatient settings.

During times of shortages of registered nurses and licensed practical nurses, there are predictable pressures to deregulate nursing and substitute staff with lower qualifications for RNs and LPNs. In psychiatric settings, particularly inpatient settings, inappropriate delegation to psychiatric technicians can occur during times of nursing shortages. Substitution of unlicensed personnel for licensed nurses clearly violates state Nurse Practice Acts and places patients and organizations at risk.

Inpatient units and freestanding psychiatric hospitals have staffing plans that dictate minimum numbers of licensed and unlicensed staff needed to safely and therapeutically deliver care to the patient population. When RN numbers fall below safe minimums, staff must be found to maintain the numbers. This can be accomplished in a number of different ways, from overtime to employing temporary nurses.

LPNs are difficult to recruit in many parts of the country. Many LPNs find it more profitable and rewarding to continue school for 1 additional year and become a registered nurse. Practicing LPNs are much in demand in the long-term health industry. This demand is only expected to increase based on the large numbers of persons currently over age 50. Upgrading LPN positions to RN positions is sometimes the most efficient way to deal with a shortage of LPNs. Although more expensive than hiring LPNs, the RN position does offer the organization more flexibility in staffing. The RN can perform the duties carried out by the LPN and can also supervise the psychiatric technicians.

Psychiatric technicians, especially those in states requiring the additional nursing assistant certification (CNA), are difficult to recruit and retain. Low salaries and limited opportunities for advancement are cited as reasons for high turnover in this health care classification. In areas where unemployment is low, the recruitment problem is intensified.

STAFFING RATIOS

One of the most frustrating responsibilities of the nurse manager is determining the staffing numbers needed to deliver safe and appropriate nursing care. Hospital administrators and governing bodies often believe that there is a "magic" number of nursing staff needed to care for any given population. This leads to a quest to find the right answers so that care can be appropriately given and the accrediting or certifying requirements can be satisfied.

Patient classification systems are one method used to quantify patient acuity in a way that can be translated into staffing numbers. The patient assessment instrument usually divides the care needed into categories such as "degree of independence in caring for self," "number of medicines given daily and route of administration," " level of consciousness/awareness," and "ability to ambulate." By assigning values to each care category and totaling those values, the nurse manager can then translate that total number to a level of care needed for the individual patient. The level of care then translates into either number of staff needed to care for an individual patient or, more often, into numbers of staff needed to care for a group of patients (levels added together).

Classification systems have been successfully applied in acute-care medical–surgical settings but have been less successful in mental health settings. Using a patient care assessment to objectively quantify staffing needs for patients receiving intravenous fluids is much more straightforward than quantifying the acuity of psychosis and the risk of patient assault. Mental health needs are more difficult to quantify than are physical needs of patients. Very few instruments have been designed specifically for psychiatric inpatients, and even fewer are appropriate for use in state psychiatric facilities where some patients stay for long periods of time and the layout of obsolete buildings strongly affects staffing needs. Even those instruments that can be used do not quantify how many of which categories (RN, LPN, HCT) of staff are needed to care for groups of patients.

Although number and acuity of patients are the most important deciding factors in determining staffing levels, the geography of the nursing unit must be considered. Locked units with a 15-bed capacity must often be staffed with numbers not significantly lower than those needed to staff a 20- to 25-bed unit. This has to do with minimum numbers of staff needed for active, safe care within a confined setting. In addition, older units or units converted into psychiatric units often have "blind spots" and/or long corridors that make it extremely difficult to observe patients without additional staff.

The director of nursing, along with other nursing managers in the psychiatric setting, is responsible for ensuring that adequate numbers of staff are available to meet the nursing needs of patients. The required "minimum" number of nursing staff is always identified for every unit and shift. As patient census increases, the staffing needs must be reevaluated. In addition, the dynamic nature of inpatient psychiatric units requires that nurse staffing needs be reassessed frequently based on factors such as total number of patients, number of patients on precautions (suicide, homicide, assault, fall, etc.), number of patients attending appointments off grounds, planned programming, volume of medication administration, frequency and duration of treatment team meetings, "atmosphere" of the milieu created by the patient population mix, physical needs of patients, and staff training needs.

ACCREDITATION AND CERTIFICATION

The Joint Commission on Accreditation of Healthcare Organizations (JCAHO) and the Health Care Financing Administration (CMS; now the Centers for Medicare & Medicaid Services [CMS]) are two organizations that evaluate the nursing care given to patients within psychiatric hospitals. It is vital to organizational success that a manager in charge of nursing services be very familiar with the current requirements of these agencies. Deficiencies can have a negative financial and service delivery impact on the hospital.

Many hospitals and some community mental health centers are accredited by the Joint Commission on Accreditation of Healthcare Organizations. JCAHO sets standards for nursing services but does not specify the number of staff needed to provide care to a group of patients. The standards are extensive in nature and require that nursing work collaboratively with other disciplines in the planning, delivery, and evaluation of care. The manager responsible for nursing must be familiar with JCAHO standards and make certain that sufficient numbers of registered nurses and support nursing staff are available to care for the patient population.

Hospitals that bill for Medicare/Medicaid must maintain certified beds. The Health Care Financing Administration (HCFA/CMS) is responsible for ensuring that hospitals belonging to the Medicare program are in compliance with the two special conditions for participation in the program. The two conditions are within the areas of staffing and medical records. The United States is divided into 10 regional HCFA/CMS offices. These offices make decisions regarding survey scheduling for hospitals in their areas. Surveys may be routine or in response to a complaint and can be assigned to the state office or HCFA/CMS central office. HCFA/CMS standards do not specify the number of nursing staff needed in order to be in compliance. The standards and interpretive guidelines speak to nursing functions and requirements and are available through state Medicare/Medicaid program offices.

REFERENCES

Bureau of Labor Statistics, U.S. Department of Labor. (1999). *Occupational outlook handbook,* 1998–1999 edition. Superintendent of Documents, U.S. Government Printing Office, Washington, DC: Author.

National Council of State Boards of Nursing. (1996). *Job analysis of newly registered nurses: Executive summary.* Chicago, IL: Author.

Peplau, H. (1952). *Interpersonal relations in nursing.* New York: G. P. Putnam's Sons.

Chapter Fifteen

Disciplinary Foundations: Social Workers in Mental Health Administration

Mary Fraser

HISTORY OF SOCIAL WORK IN ADMINISTRATION

Social work is a profession committed to the enhancement of human well-being, the alleviation of poverty and oppression, and the promotion of social justice (Council of Social Work Education [CSWE], 1994). Social work professionals practice in a wide variety of settings, including child welfare, family services, and corrections agencies, private and public hospitals, and community-based psychiatric and substance abuse treatment centers. Offering a 2-year professional degree, social work is a growing profession. The U.S. Labor Department projects that there will be close to 650,000 practicing social workers by the year 2005, more than a 30% increase over 1995 (O'Neill, 1999).

Social workers have a long history of working with persons with mental illnesses. Elizabeth Horton opened up this field of social work when she was appointed to the staff of the New York City hospital system as a psychiatric social worker in 1907. Many other hospitals quickly followed suit, concretizing a growing collaboration between the professions of psychiatry and social work (Barker, 1995).

Since those early days of psychiatric social work, social workers have played an increasingly larger role in serving persons with mental illnesses in a variety of settings and in a variety of service capacities. According to recent statistics collected by the U.S. Substance Abuse and Mental Health Services Administration (U.S. SAMHSA, 1998), social work is the largest occupational group staffing mental health facilities in this country. There are at least 192,814 clinically trained social workers; this is more than the combined totals of the other three major mental health professions—33,486 psychiatrists, 73,018 psychologists, and 17,318 psychiatric nurses. This fact is not too surprising, however, when one realizes that schools of social work graduate more students each year than the other professional schools (U.S. SAMHSA, 1998) and that the majority of social work students choose to specialize in mental health services over other options provided during their course of study (Lin, 1995).

The social work profession began in the mid- to late 1800s as volunteers, who served as "friendly visitors" to poor families, and who were formally organized by charity organization societies and associations for improving the condition of the poor. The need for a standardized training program became quickly apparent, and social work education developed soon after. In 1998, the profession celebrated its 100-year anniversary, commemorating the first official class in social work taught at New York University in 1898.

Twenty years later, in 1918, Smith College established the first training program for psychiatric social workers, thus creating a mental health specialization within the field of social work. Psychiatric social work was built on traditional casework, taking into account individuals' social environments, as well as emphasizing the importance of insight into emotions and psychic life.

Over the years, the social work profession has incorporated various theories and practices from allied fields, such as sociology, psychiatry, psychology, and anthropology. However, social work's commitment to an ecological, person-in-environment approach has set it apart from the other professions. Social workers, imbued with this unique perspective and skill base, have been able to supplement and complement the skills and roles traditionally provided by other professionals found practicing in the mental health field.

CLINICAL ROLES

In their clinical work, social workers focus on psychosocial factors including family relationships, living arrangements, and economic and cultural factors as they relate to the understanding and treatment of psychiatric disorders. They are always in tune with changing environmental and cultural factors. Because of their person-in-environment perspective, social workers have been quick to develop family-centered practices, take on case management roles, and embrace goal-directed, empowerment strategies with clients.

Social workers can and do provide a wide variety of services to persons with mental illnesses, in a variety of settings. A psychiatric social worker is trained to conduct mental status exams and intake assessments, and to provide both individual and group psychotherapy. These traditional mental health services are provided by social workers in hospitals, by community mental health centers, and through private practices. In addition to these traditional psychiatric services, social workers are also trained to provide a variety of less traditional services, such as case management, skill and support-group facilitation, and interagency collaboration functions.

Many social workers are found working in inpatient psychiatric facilities. In addition to providing a variety of direct treatment interventions to patients, the jobs of intake assessment and discharge and transition planning are almost always provided by someone with a social work degree. In hospital settings, social workers are usually organized into a single administrative unit where they are accountable to a professional social worker in charge. The director of the social work department is responsible for the supervision of hospital-based social workers and, in part, defines what roles social workers play in patient care within the hospital.

In community settings, social workers are not always supervised by other social workers, but may be supervised by a psychiatrist or another mental health professional with a master's or doctorate degree. In rural areas, where psychiatrist availability is lean, social workers with advanced clinical degrees not only provide direct services to patients but are frequently asked to provide clinical supervision to other employees and often serve as clinical directors in small agencies.

ADMINISTRATIVE ROLES

Social workers are also found in various administrative positions in both community and hospital settings. Social workers can be found holding administrative positions all up and down the organizational ladder. The executive directors of many community mental health centers come from social work backgrounds. Unit or team management positions are widely held by social workers. And master's-level social workers often provide clinical supervision to other social workers, as well as to professionals from other disciplines. Many federal-, state-, and county-level administrative positions are held by persons with a master's or doctorate degree in social work.

GRADUATE SOCIAL WORK EDUCATION

Social workers have held administrative positions within human service organizations since the beginning of the profession. Early charity organizations and social service agencies looked to social workers for leadership. In turn, these organizational leaders helped shape the social work profession and its educational mission. As public social service agencies grew in number and size throughout the 20th century, social work education responded by providing relevant course work on and field experience in administrative functions.

Although the need for administrative content in the graduate social work curriculum has been recognized for many years, the way to organize it has come into considerable and repeated controversy. Over the years, some educators have argued that administrative content should be purely elective, others want some to be required for all students, and still others have wanted to make it a major study specialization. Because individual schools of social work maintain autonomy about most of the content and organization of their coursework, widely varying arrangements have been developed. Unfortunately, despite the attention, not many schools have yet provided the level of administrative content needed by social workers practicing in the field.

In the early 1970s, due to the large numbers of social workers employed as administrators within its many public social service agencies, the U.S. Department of Health, Education, and Welfare (HEW) funded a study to review the administration curricula in schools of social work. The study found that only 5% of enrolled students in the nation's 45 graduate schools of social work were specializing in administration, or even had chosen a "macro-practice" concentration (Kazmerski & Macarov, 1976). Macro-practice concentrations often combine administration coursework with classes in community organization, planning, policy analysis, program development, and program evaluation (Gilbert, Miller, & Specht, 1980). Following this study, many schools attempted to increase coursework offerings, but interest waned as students tended to select more direct service options.

Although nearly 50% of social workers move into management/supervisory positions within a few years after receiving their master's in social work (MSW) degree, only a small number of students enter social work education with the primary objective of preparing for management roles (Permultter, 1990; Raymond, Teare, & Atherton, 1996). The highest enrollment in macro-practice concentrations was 16% of students in 1977; however, macro concentrations generally attract only about 10% of MSW students (Raymond, Teare, & Atherton, 1996).

This disparity between student curriculum choices/academic offerings and later employment requirements is clearly demonstrated by two studies conducted in the early 1990s. Although a 1991 study (Gibelman & Schervish, 1993) found that 16% of employed National Association of Social Work (NASW) members reported that their primary work function was management, a 1992 study (CSWE, 1993) found that only 5.5% of MSW students were enrolled in administration–management specializations or in macro-practice concentrations that included administrative content.

Clearly, graduate schools of social work need to provide course work in administration to their students, as many will need it, even if they may not recognize this fact as students. MSWs with a specialization in mental health services are quickly and regularly promoted into supervisory and management positions within private and public mental health agencies. Many receive no training in management principles or practices.

Where specializations in social administration are provided, students are generally exposed to a fairly wide range of management skills. Table 15.1 shows the frequency at which various administrative skills were covered in social work social administration specialization courses in 1995.

Analyses indicate that more offerings focus on interpersonal skills, such as communication and participatory management skills, than on technical ones, such as using information systems and financial and personnel management. Less than 50% of the schools offered skills in the areas of general or cost accounting and compensation management (McNutt, 1995). This emphasis on interpersonal skills may be what distinguishes social work administrative course work from that offered by schools of business and public administration.

Social workers currently practicing administration in the field and their supervisors have recognized the need for more management training. Recent surveys of MSWs in administrative roles confirm that they have needed and now want more knowledge about management to function effectively in their jobs (Menefee & Thompson, 1994). When surveyed, 75% of state-level mental health and mental retardation administrators said that they desired more management and leadership training for their employees (Sluyter, 1995). "The highest priorities appeared to be for training of supervisors of direct care staff, followed by advanced [management] training for senior managers and people at the mid-management level" (p. 203).

CURRENT CHALLENGES IN MENTAL HEALTH ADMINISTRATION

It is not easy to manage mental health programs in today's economic and political environment. All across the country, health care systems are being reconstructed. Public and private mental health systems alike are in the process of reinventing themselves. Acquisitions, mergers, conversions of not-for-profit organizations to for-

Table 15.1. Frequency of Schools Reporting Skills in Administration in Macro-Practice Concentrations

Skill	n	%
Budgeting	42	95.5
Working with boards	38	86.4
Participatory management	36	81.8
Organizational assessment and diagnosis	36	81.8
Group process and supervision	35	79.5
Computer information systems	33	75.0
Financial management	31	70.5
Personnel supervision	31	70.5
Management systems analysis	30	68.2
Organizational design	30	68.2
Training/staff development	30	68.2
Organizational development	29	65.9
Career management—women and minorities	28	63.6
Personnel selection	27	61.4
Affirmative action principles	27	61.4
Marketing management techniques	24	54.5
Networking	23	52.3
General accounting	20	45.5
Media relationship	20	45.5
Contract management	19	43.2
Career management	18	40.9
Cutback and retrenchment management	16	40.9
Cost accounting	15	34.1
Employee assistance programs	14	31.8
Employee unionization	14	31.8
Compensation management	13	29.5
Physical facilities planning	2	4.5

(McNutt, 1995)

profit ones, acceptance of financial risk for outcomes, and so on are all part of the new behavioral health care landscape. Mental health policies at the national, state, and local levels are in a state of flux as policymakers grapple with the contingencies of health care reform. Traditional financing structures are drastically changing, as are traditional service structures.

Fine-tuned management skills have never been more necessary. Managers of enduring agencies and structures will need to be able to combine their clinical concern for consumers with clear business savvy. They will need to successfully negotiate clinically ethical contracts and financially solvable payment methods. They will need to utilize sophisticated new data technologies to manage resources to survive.

Behavioral health care managers are also increasingly challenged by changing patient profiles and needs, and the growing diversity of their work force. Due to the downsizing of psychiatric hospitals and the increased reliance on outpatient methods to treat consumers with mental illnesses, hospitals, community mental health centers, and residential facilities are all serving consumers with more severe problems than they did a decade or two ago.

The increasing reliance on public insurance programs, such and Medicaid and Medicare, to cover the costs of treatment has kept many consumers with less severe problems from receiving service. Consumers dealing with dual and sometimes triple diagnoses of mental illness, mental retardation, and substance abuse are becoming a larger patient population and are taking up increasing amounts of clinical and financial resources. Greater numbers of persons not speaking English or for whom it is a second language are requesting services.

In addition to the growing diversity of patient populations, America's workforce is also changing. Most administrators are aware of the increasing numbers of women and people of color in today's workplace. Workforce 2000 (Johnson & Packer, 1987) projected that by the year 2000, women and people of color would constitute 85% of the growth in the workforce. Nearly 66% of new workers would be women, and 43% would be people of color, many of whom would be immigrants. Schools of social work, alone, are showing that 23.7% of full-time MSW students are now people of color (O'Neill, 1999).

Women continue to dominate the mental health workforce, and in increasing numbers. Data from 1995–1996 show that 83% of MSW students were female, and 1996 NASW membership data show women comprising 77% of clinically trained social workers, up from 72% just 6 years earlier (O'Neill, 1999). The profession of psychology, once dominated by males, is also moving toward female domination. Women comprised 47% of clinically trained psychologists in 1997, up from 38% in 1989 (U.S. SAMHSA, 1998).

In addition to this growing gender and ethnic diversity, the work force is also growing increasingly older. By the turn of the century, the average age of workers is expected to increase to 39 years (from 36). Workers between the ages of 16 and 24 years will drop by 8%.

To successfully manage tomorrow's behavioral health care industry, mental health administrators will need to be sensitive to the varying types of work styles and benefit needs of its changing workforce. They will have to provide culturally competent services to their diverse patient populations. Organizational success will depend on the degrees of productivity, growth, and satisfaction experienced by all individuals involved in the system.

Staff members of all types and degrees will need to be helped to adjust to the high level of organizational and policy change going on in today's mental health environment. Many staff will have been trained in ineffective methods of clinical practice or will not be used to integrating mental health with other needed services. Defining and measuring treatment outcomes is difficult, controversial, and sometimes threatening. Disagreements among professional staff over when and how services should be provided are common. Mental health administrators need to create environments where professional discourse is encouraged and evidence-based practice supported. Clinical staff need to be provided opportunities to learn and change as required by a rapidly evolving field of practice.

Maintaining professional ethics, in the midst of financial and political upheavals, will be critical for all administrators, no matter their educational background. It will be important to emphasize ethical values while hiring and supervising all staff members to minimize potential for fraud and abuse. Accountability needs to be a way of life.

In addition to maintaining strong professional ethics, some social work administrators may find holding on to typical social work values a challenge in today's increasingly competitive behavioral health care environment. Social workers have been imbued with strong values of social justice and patient self-determinism. Sometimes these values are challenged by political and financial circumstances. Many social worker administrators can be expected to be especially sensitive to such issues as fair access to services and patient rights. The following common decisions may highlight some of these possible value dilemmas for social work administrators:

- When and whether to ask clinicians to restrict treatment choices based primarily on the patient's ability to pay or insurance coverage, rather than on individual need.
- When to permit access to patients' clinical records (to insurers, researchers, etc.).
- Whether or when to accept the agency role as social control agent for the community (favoring community protection over patient choice of treatment).
- Whether or when (or how hard) to challenge local politics when patients are being discriminated against due to the stigma of mental illness or their race/color, or income level.

CONCLUSIONS AND RECOMMENDATIONS

In today's changing mental health environment, managers of mental health programs and services need, more than ever, to be knowledgeable, skilled, and ethical and wise. Graduate schools in social work may not always be able to make their students ethical or wise, but they should provide them with requisite knowledge and skills to fulfill their employment responsibilities. Although most students come to the social work profession with an interest in working directly with clients, they need to be informed, early on, that they will likely end up in management positions. They need to understand that they may be required to make sensitive decisions based on both clinical and administrative knowledge.

Preparation for this likely event can come in various forms. The MSW degree generally requires 2 years of study. The first year focuses on a generalist foundation in social work principles and knowledge and the second year permits specialization.

This second year of advanced practice or specialization is often organized by field of study (mental health, child welfare, aging, delinquency, etc.) or by intervention method (casework, group work, community organization, research, social administration). Sometimes a macro-practice concentration is offered, usually combining content on social administration with other courses on policy development, community organization, and planning.

During the first year of study, general foundation course work must provide a large body of content, including social work values and ethics, diversity, social and economic justice, populations at risk, human behavior and social environment, social welfare policy and services, and research. Although freestanding courses in administration are not likely to be offered in the first year of social work study, relevant administrative issues should be highlighted and discussed whenever possible.

During the second year of advanced practice study, students should learn about human service management theories and practices. Management content should be included in all specialization concentrations. For instance, if concentrations are organized by fields of study, such as mental health, then a course (or at least a section) in mental health administration should be required, along with practice, theory, and policy course work. Administrative content should cover, at a minimum, management issues relevant to the field, an overview of management theory, and an exploration of skills needed to manage both product and human resource systems.

Where macro-practice specializations are offered, increased and in-depth content should be provided in such critical yet sparsely covered areas as financial, personnel, and change management. Courses providing technical skill instruction, such as fund-raising and grant writing, budgeting, and data management, should be at least offered on an elective basis in all macro-practice specializations.

Although management content provided by schools of social work is not unlike that provided by most schools of business and public administration (Crow, 1994), the focus of each of these programs is different. Simply put, schools of business generally focus on the for-profit environment, schools of social work focus on managing nonprofit and public agencies, and schools of public administration prepare students to work in government settings. For students who want to combine a people-centered orientation, so inherent in social work education, with a focus on administration in government or for-profit competitive environments, a joint degree program would best serve their needs.

As students have desired this combining of curricula, various joint degree programs have been developed. In 1992, 5 schools of social work offered a joint degree program with schools of public administration or public affairs; 8 offered a joint degree program with schools of business administration; and 10 offered joint programs with public health graduate schools (CSWE, 1992). As more joint degree programs are being developed all the time, students' skills and knowledge will be strengthened by the similarities among the programs and enriched by the differences.

Another prime opportunity to provide increased offerings in administrative course content is through schools of social work continuing education departments. Courses in management theory should be offered, as well as skill-based courses in such areas as supervision, leadership, fundraising, grant writing, budgeting, and information system management. As reported in numerous surveys, practicing social workers and their supervisors are calling for these training opportunities. Schools of social work should respond.

Some state chapters of NASW have developed mentoring programs for social workers feeling unprepared for newly assigned management and supervisory tasks. These programs pair social workers new to management/supervisory roles with practicing or retired social workers with substantial management/supervisory experience, over a 1-year period. This relationship is voluntary and is, of course, supplemental to any formal supervision provided by the employing agency. NASW chapters should be applauded and encouraged in these efforts. A mentoring program is a great idea. It can help fill an increasing void that academic social work programs have had a major role in creating.

In conclusion, social work graduates continue to explode into the mental health field. Most are trained in clinical specialties. However, the majority of these graduates find themselves quickly promoted from clinical positions into supervisory and administrative ones. Persons with MSW degrees are increasingly expected to manage rather than to provide services.

Schools of social work need to address the growing gap between the percentage of MSW students who prepare for management and supervisory positions within behavioral health care agencies and those who move into these positions within a few years after completing their degree program. In an effort to respond, schools of social work should:

- Increase administrative course content in both first- and second-year curricula.
- Solicit the development of joint degree programs with other management professions.
- Offer continuing education courses in management theory and skill areas to graduates working in management positions on a wide and frequent basis.

The social work profession has an opportunity to make a great contribution to tomorrow's behavioral health care environment by preparing its graduates to lead it. Professional social workers have the ability to combine the values of a people-centered practice with the leadership expertise of a skilled administrator. The field is challenging, but social workers have never run from a challenge!

REFERENCES

Barker, R. L. (Ed.). (1995). *Social work dictionary* (3rd ed.). Washington, DC: NASW Press.

Crow, R. T. (1995). Planning and management positions. In R. L. Edwards (Ed.), *Encyclopedia of social work* (pp. 1837–1843). Washington, DC: NASW Press.

Council of Social Work Education. (1992). *Summary information on master of social work programs: 1991–1992*. Washington, DC: Author.

Council on Social Work Education. (1993). *Statistics of social work education in the United States, 1992*. Alexandria, VA: Author.

Council on Social Work Education. (1994). *Curriculum policy statement for masters degree programs in social work education*. Alexandria, VA: Author.

Gibilman, M., & Schervish, P. H. (1993). *Who we are: The social work labor force as reflected in the NASW membership*. Washington, DC: NASW Press.

Gilbert, N., Miller, H., & Specht, H. (1980). *An introduction to social work practice*. Englewood Cliffs, NJ: Prentice Hall.

Kazmerski, K., & Maracov, D. (1976). *Administration in the social work curriculum*. New York: Council of Social Work Education.

Lin, A. (1995). Mental health overview. In R. L. Edwards (Ed.), *Social work encyclopedia* (pp. 1705–1711). Washington, DC: NASW Press.

McNutt, J. G. (1995). The macro practice curriculum in graduate social work education: Results of a national study. *Administration in Social Work, 19*(3), 59–74.

Menefee, D. T., & Thompson, J. T. (1994). Identifying and comparing competencies for social work management: A practice-driven approach. *Administration in Social Work, 48*(3), 1–25.

O'Neill, J. V. (1999, June). Women gain in clinical fields. *NASW NEWS*, http://www.NASWPRESS.org/publications/news/0699/women.html

Permultter, F. D. (1990). *Changing hats: From social work practice to administration*. Silver Spring, MD: NASW Press.

Raymond, G., Teare, R., & Atherton, C. (1996). Do management tasks differ by field of practice? *Administration in Social Work, 20*(1), 17–30.

Sluyter, G. (1995). Mental health leadership training: A survey of state directors. *Journal of Mental Health Administration, 22*(2), 201–204.

U.S. Substance Abuse and Mental Health Services Administration. (1998). *Mental Health, United States, 1998*. Rockville, MD: Author.

Chapter Sixteen

Disciplinary Foundations: Activities Therapies

Anne B. Fleischer

This chapter examines the various skill sets of activity therapists, their role in a variety of clinical settings, and some issues in the management of expressive, rehabilitative, vocational, and prevocational services. Let us start by reviewing the major divisions in the field and their contribution to the treatment effort. The sequence is in alphabetical order and does not reflect relative importance of the particular discipline.

ACTIVITIES THERAPY DISCIPLINES

Art Therapy

Art therapists utilize art media, images, creative art process, and patient responses to the created art productions as reflections of an individual's development, abilities, personality, interests, concerns, and conflicts. Art therapists use art media as a means of reconciling emotional conflicts, fostering self-awareness, developing social skills, managing behavior, solving problems, reducing anxiety, aiding reality orientation, and increasing self-esteem. Art therapists are trained to work with developmentally, medically, educationally, socially, or psychologically impaired patients. They are frequently employed in mental health, rehabilitation, medical, educational, and forensic institutions.

Registration. The designation ATR (art therapist registered) is granted by the Art Therapy Credentials Board (ATCB) to individuals who have successfully completed the required educational and professional experience.

Board Certification. The designation BC (board certified) is granted by the ATCB to individuals who have successfully passed the independently administered, national certification examination. Recertification is provided every five years by re-examination or by documentation of continuing education, publication, presentation, exhibition, and other activities which demonstrate continuing professional competence.

Educational Requirements.   One must complete the required core curriculum as outlined in the American Art Therapy Association Education Standards to qualify as a professional art therapist. Entry into the profession of art therapy is at the master's level. Avenues of completion offered by graduate-level art therapy programs include receiving one of the following curricula:

- Master's degree in art therapy.
- Master's degree with an emphasis in art therapy.
- Twenty-one semester units in art therapy with a master's degree in a related field.

Dance and Performing Arts Therapy

Dance/movement therapists use movement as a process to further the emotional, cognitive, social, and physical integration of the individual. Dance/movement therapists work with individuals who have social, emotional, cognitive, and/or physical problems.

They are employed in psychiatric hospitals, clinics, day care, community mental health centers, developmental centers, correctional facilities, special schools, and rehabilitation facilities. Not only do dance/movement therapists work with people of all ages in both groups and individually, but also they act as consultants and engage in research.

Registration.   DTR (dance therapist registered) professionals have a master's degree and are fully qualified to work in a professional treatment system. Therapists with an ADTR (Academy of Dance Therapists registered) have met additional requirements and are fully qualified to teach, provide supervision, and engage in private practice.

Education.   Dance/movement therapists have extensive dance experience and a liberal arts background with coursework in psychology. Professional training is on the graduate level. Graduates receive a master's degree in dance/movement therapy. Graduates from an "approved" dance/movement therapy program are eligible for the DTR (dance therapist registered).

Horticulture Therapy

Horticultural therapists use gardening to enhance self-esteem; alleviate depression; improve motor skills; provide opportunities in problem solving; encourage work adjustment, social interaction, and communication; and teach certain marketable horticultural and business skills. They will involve the patient in all phases of gardening, as well as the activity of selling the produce and plants grown. This flows toward the goal of integrating an individual into the everyday community life stream.

These therapists work in hospitals and institutions, vocational training facilities, nursing homes and halfway houses, rehabilitation facilities, older adult centers, correctional facilities, schools, arboreta and botanical gardens, parks and recreational settings, farms and horticultural businesses, and community gardens.

Horticulture therapists provide therapy to people who are physically disabled, mentally ill, or developmentally disabled, and to the elderly, substance abusers, public offenders, and the socially disadvantaged.

Registration. The HTT (horticultural therapist technician) level is intended for persons making the transition into the field. Individuals applying for this initial level of registration will be credited for HT volunteer work, HT employment, employment in related fields, and various educational and professional experiences. HTR (horticultural therapist registered) is the primary level of registration within AHTA's system. Persons registered at this level must have HT employment experience. The level of HTM (horticultural therapist master) is for individuals who have extensive educational and professional backgrounds.

Education. One can attain registration status in horticulture therapy without having a degree but having completed an equivalency point system that awards points for employment in HT and related fields, volunteer work, and various educational and professional experiences.

Many people combine semester hours from various colleges/universities over time to equal a horticulture therapy degree. For example, a student can graduate with a degree in horticulture and earn the rest of the semester hours required in the core curriculum as nondegreed coursework. Individuals who are seeking a horticulture therapy degree must complete an internship (1,000 hours); otherwise, internships are entirely optional but encouraged.

A registered horticulture therapist must complete the core curriculum used by the American Horticultural Therapy Association (AHTA) Registration Review Board. The board assigns point values to the various educational experiences of applicants for professional registration, and may guide the student in a course of study in horticultural therapy. Applicants must complete courses in the following areas: horticultural therapy specialization courses, horticultural science and related courses, therapy/human science courses, and management courses. There is a minimum total semester credits of 78 credits plus an internship.

Music Therapy

Music therapists assess emotional well-being, physical health, social functioning, communication abilities, and cognitive skills through musical responses. They design music sessions for individuals and groups based on patient needs using music improvisation, receptive music listening, song writing, lyric discussion, music and imagery, music performance, and learning through music.

Music therapists provide services to children, adolescents, adults, and the elderly. These individuals may have mental health needs, developmental and learning disabilities, Alzheimer's disease and other aging-related conditions, substance-abuse problems, brain injuries, physical disabilities, and acute and chronic pain, including mothers in labor.

Music therapists work in psychiatric hospitals, rehabilitative facilities, medical hospitals, outpatient clinics, day-care treatment centers, agencies serving developmentally disabled persons, community mental health centers, drug and alcohol programs, senior centers, nursing homes, hospice programs, correctional facilities, halfway houses, schools, and private practice.

Board Certification. At the completion of American Music Therapy Association (AMTA) approved academic training and internship, the student is eligible for admission to the certification exam administered by the Certification Board for Music Therapists, Inc. (CBMT). Upon passing the national examination administered by the CBMT, the student acquires the credential music therapist–board certified (MT–BC).

Education. The undergraduate curriculum includes coursework in music therapy, psychology, music, biological, social and behavioral sciences, disabilities, and general studies. Entry-level study includes practical application of music therapy procedures and techniques learned in the classroom through required fieldwork in facilities serving individuals with disabilities in the community and/or on-campus clinics. Students learn to assess the needs of patients, develop and implement treatment plans, and evaluate and document clinical changes. Individuals who have earned a baccalaureate degree in an area other than music therapy may elect to complete the degree equivalency program in music therapy offered by most AMTA-approved universities.

Under this program, the student completes only the required coursework without necessarily earning a second baccalaureate degree. Graduate programs in music therapy examine, with greater breadth and depth, issues relevant to the clinical, professional, and academic preparation of music therapists, usually in combination with established methods of research inquiry. Candidates for the master's degree in music therapy must hold a baccalaureate degree. Some schools require either a bachelor's degree in music therapy, the equivalency in music therapy, or that the candidate be working concurrently toward fulfilling degree equivalency requirements.

Occupational Therapy

Occupational therapists provide treatment that helps individuals achieve independence in all facets of their lives. Occupational therapists develop treatment programs aimed at improving an individual's abilities to complete daily living activities in home and at work. This may include a comprehensive evaluation of home and job environments along with recommendations for necessary adaptations. In addition, the therapist may provide assessments and treatment for performance skills and provide recommendations and training in the use of adaptive equipment to replace lost function. Furthermore, therapists provide guidance to family members and attendants in safe and effective methods of caring for individuals. Occupational therapists work with individuals from infancy to older adulthood to correct or ameliorate physical, social, cognitive, and/or emotional impairments.

Registration. Practitioners must complete supervised clinical internships in a variety of health care settings, and pass a national examination. Most states also regulate occupational therapy practice either through licensure, certification, or regulation of titles.

Education. Occupational therapy practitioners are skilled professionals whose education includes the study of human growth and development with specific emphasis on the social, emotional, and physiological effects of illness and injury. The occupational therapist enters the field with a bachelor's, master's, or doctoral degree. The occupational therapy assistant generally earns an associate's degree.

Recreational Therapy

Therapeutic recreation specialists are often referred to as recreational therapists. These therapists use activity to treat or maintain the physical, mental, and emotional well-being of consumers served. These interventions help individuals remediate the effects of illness or disability and achieve an optimal level of personal independence. The goals of interventions include improving physical, cognitive, and social functioning.

Therapeutic recreation specialists work with individuals who have mental, physical, or emotional disabilities. Individual treatment plans and programs are developed consistent with patient need, abilities, and interests. For instance, a recreational therapist may utilize a recreational activity, such as fishing, to aid a patient with right-side paralysis learn to use the left side and thus continue a lifetime activity. In a psychiatric setting the recreational therapist may prescribe an assertiveness program to help the depressed patient achieve greater self-confidence and independence.

Registration. National certification is available through the National Council for Therapeutic Recreation Certification (NCTRC). Many employers insist on hiring those individuals who have the NCTRC certification. A few states regulate this profession through either licensure, certification, or regulation of titles.

Education. A degree in therapeutic recreation (or in recreation with an emphasis in therapeutic recreation) is required for jobs in clinical settings such as hospitals or community mental health facilities.

Academic programs in therapeutic recreation emphasize coursework in the physical, biological, and behavioral sciences and recreation and leisure theory. They also require a minimum of 360 hours of internship under the supervision of a certified therapeutic recreation specialist. Newly graduated recreational therapists generally begin as staff therapists.

MANAGING ACTIVITIES WITHIN THE CONTINUUM OF CARE

Acute Care

In acute-care patients and settings, the primary focus is to develop a system in which the professional can evaluate the patient's current functional skills on the day that the physician has ordered the therapy. By developing this system, one will be able to provide feedback to the team expediently.

In order to complete these missions, a process must be developed so that new orders and current patient treatments can be appropriately triaged into one of three categories: (a) discharged in the next 24 hours, (b) daily therapy, and (c) therapy a few days a week. To develop this process, one would need to answer the following questions: What are the indicators of the patients who move through the treatment plan quickly? What are the indicators of patients who do not progress with their treatment? Who could be discharged more quickly if they received more intense therapy?

The answers to these questions have become increasingly more challenging due to shorter lengths of stay. According to Earhart (1999), in 1997, her patients were referred for the functional assessment on day 7 of a 12-day stay; today, the average referral is made on day 3 of an 8-day stay. Shorter lengths of stay mean that medications have not reached peak effectiveness at the time of discharge, and the cognitive level may continue to improve with medication titration. Because the professional does not know how stable the disability is at discharge, he or she must deal with real ambiguities when making recommendations.

McAnanama et al. (1999) found that mean Allen Cognitive Level Test–90 (ACL–90) scores do not change much over the month after discharge. However, how long study participants had been in the hospital and whether they had reached maximum benefits from prescribed medication were not specified. Kohlman's Evaluation of Living Skills has a great deal of face validity but its predictive ability has not been adequately demonstrated, particularly for the increasing number of referrals of individuals with dementia and depression. Discharge recommendations must also factor in further improvements anticipated from medication effects. More serious effort of follow-up to evaluate function post acute care should be made in order to maximize independence of the patients.

State Hospital Inpatient Facilities

One level of care builds on the next level; therefore, the concepts discussed within acute care will also work for inpatient/state facilities. Within these facilities, numbers of patients staying over 180 days are increasing, but not at the same rate as those staying less than 30 days in acute-care settings. Nevertheless, these patients are persistently mentally ill. Therapy for these patients must be directed toward improving the level of independence. Due to the greater length of stay, group treatment is more realistic and can be organized according to specific needs of the patients.

Groups in an acute-care setting should be directed toward immediate discharge needs, and many times care will need to be more individualized. As a result, the majority of treatment/evaluation in the acute-care setting will be one-on-one. In the inpatient/state facilities, more of the treatment will be performed within groups. Groups should be directed toward specific life skills and presented at the patient's current cognitive skill level. Evaluation should be directed toward determining which of these groups the patient should attend (Hays & Baxley, 1998). An example of this tailoring of intensity is reflected in activities of daily living (ADL) groups.

A group aimed at assisting patients functioning at a lower cognitive level might include basic ADL (one-on-one treatment), and instrumental ADL (IADL) activities in which the focus is to sequence activities, demonstrate awareness of safety, and increase attention. In contrast, a group for patients functioning at the middle cognitive level will expect that the patient will have the responsibility to complete basic ADLs at a certain time each day. This group will include planning an instrumental activity of daily living and carrying it out under the supervision of the professional. For those functioning at a higher cognitive level, plan and implement daily activities needed post discharge.

In addition to having group and individual treatments that are patient specific and skill-based to prepare for discharge, the professional will need to work closely with the rest of the team to plan for the patient's discharge into the community.

Outpatient/Community Mental Health

A distinct difference of management within this area, compared to inpatient or residential settings, is that the out patient professional is usually his or her own manager. He or she usually has developed a contract with an agency to provide a service for a particular patient group.

The contract should specify a direct or indirect model of service. In a direct model, treatment is provided to restore function for particular skills that require the expertise of a licensed therapy practitioner. Treatment may be provided in a group or one-on-one. In the indirect model, the professionals provide recommendations to a treatment team. These patients do not require treatment by a licensed professional. Instead, the professional educates the patient, family, and caregiver about specific functional needs. Within the contractual model, the professional may provide recommendations only, recommendations and monitoring, or direct treatment that commonly has an extensive evaluation component (Burson, 1998).

Community interventions should be practical and facilitate return to higher levels of function. Examples may include:

Community-Based Programs.   The goal of this approach is to assist persons in identifying and developing the prerequisite skills necessary for engaging in various social roles that maintain a balance among work, leisure, and rest. Services include individual evaluation and goal planning, skill instruction and practice, on-site teaching and training, community and home-based skill instruction, and transition planning and referral to community services or settings of choice. Program components may consist of a learning center, skills center, outreach services, and prevocational development. All components of the program assist persons in their efforts to be successful, productive members of their community (Flaherty, 1999).

Learning Center.   Activities to develop the cognitive skills crucial to learning; that is, attention, concentration, and memory are the primary initial emphasis. Once these basic skills are mastered, higher order cognitive skills, such as problem solving, organizational skills, judgment, and reasoning, are put into the treatment plan. Furthermore, the learning center could provide classroom instruction for basic academic development, development of study skills, and introduction to computer technology (Flaherty, 1999).

Prevocational Services.   This can mean work-for-pay experience with an emphasis on responsibility and productivity, as well as improved functioning in the following areas: hygiene and grooming, attention span, task completion, money management, self-esteem and a sense of self-worth, time management, socialization, the development of work-related skills, and a work role identity (Flaherty, 1999).

Skill Center and Outreach Services.   Staff work one-on-one with patients in identifying recreational activities of interest that are available within the community. The supports and skills needed to successfully participate in the chosen activity were identified and a goal for community integration is developed. Interventions should be individualized and diverse. These may include hygiene and grooming, money management, problem solving, use of public transportation, initiating conversations, asking for directions for help, and other skills as defined by the patient. In the outreach services program, patients participate in a functional assessment relevant to their environment, public transportation, grocery stores, banks, and other environments relevant to the person's daily routine and skill needs (Flaherty, 1999).

Home Health

This service is distinctly different from community-based programs due to the fact that it is provided within the patient's home. Reasons for being home-bound may include severe anxiety, immobilizing depression, memory impairment, agoraphobia, impaired judgment, impaired safety awareness, or paranoid delusions.

As in all the other areas, therapy evaluation and treatment will focus on function. The evaluation may be more comprehensive due to the complexity of the patient and the need to incorporate the treatment with family and/or caregivers. According to Azok and Tomlinson (1994), therapy should focus on the following areas:

- The patient's ability to identify problems in basic ADLs, home management, work, and leisure performance. The patient will perform activities and/or recommendations that address the identified problems.
- Patient will identify and follow through with adaptive coping strategies.
- Patient will develop and follow through with a plan to maintain a balance of basic ADLs, home management, and work and leisure tasks.
- Patient will concentrate on and pay attention to tasks.
- Patient will use compensatory strategies for cognitive impairment.
- Patient will initiate and follow through with activities to prepare for community reintegration.

As with acute and inpatient admissions, the treatment team will want to focus on moving the patient to less expensive and more functional setting of a community program.

ACTIVITY THERAPIES AND MANAGED CARE

Among occupational, recreational, and the many other activities therapists, the subject of managed care stimulates emotional discussions. Topics include short lengths of stay, challenges of providing effective treatment, hassles of paperwork, bureaucracy, and loss of control over professional decision making. Anger, frustration, loss, and grief are the dominant feelings about a changing health care system that no longer looks familiar (VanLeit, 1996). Changing times require innovation and creativity; this is innate for therapists. Activity therapy programs can contribute to restoring patient function effectively and efficiently even within an environment of decreased budgets and increased demands.

Productivity

Once the programs are organized and a system for moving patients from one level of care to the next has been developed, staffing the programs will be the next challenge. The goal is to hire the most competent person for the job, but not to hire someone over- or underskilled. In addition, understanding the state licensure laws for each profession is a must. What are the specific job responsibilities? What is the vision for the future of the program? The answers to these questions will assist in determining whom to hire.

When developing the productivity standard for a unit, remember that productivity standards should vary according to setting and population served as well as by discipline. To develop a productivity standard, a manager must determine units of productivity. There are two major approaches to this process. One is based on the amount of time spent by the professionals. The other is an attempt to quantify additional factors, such as staff expertise and specialized equipment, into an index known as a relative value unit (RVU). The examples discussed in this chapter are the first approach (Schell & Schell, 1996).

Treatment units (TUs) represent a given amount of treatment of patients and are frequently based on professionals' time, such as 15 minutes of treatment. For instance, a professional who spent 6 hours in treatment in 1 day would record 24 TUs (1 hour = 4 TUs; 6 hours × 4 TUs/hour = 24 TUs). Visits represent occasions of service, regardless of the length of time spent. If the same professional saw 3 patients for 2 hours each, he or she would record 3 visits. If he or she saw 6 patients in the same amount of time, he or she would record 6 visits. TUs and visits are less sensitive than RVUs because they do not account for the skill and the experience level of the professionals. Also, their definitions may vary from setting to setting, so it is important for managers to clarify them in the local context. Whatever important unit of measure an organization uses, it should be meaningful to both staff and administration (Schell & Schell, 1996).

Task groups that are interdepartmental should be developed to reduce consistent barriers to productivity when possible. For example, mental health technicians may be dressing and bathing patients who are going to participate in basic ADL training. Occupational therapy staff then lose productivity because the treatment will need to be deferred to the next day or to develop another activity. As another example, the nursing staff may be inconsistent on the timing of medication administration; therefore, patients arrive at art therapy 30 to 45 minutes late. Non-therapy-related events lead to decreasing productivity.

Task groups are only effective if there is administrative support and if there is an environment of collaboration, openness, flexibility, and creativity between departments. Human resources may help facilitate team building between departments, as needed. This is essential for productivity to increase and for higher quality patient care.

From this information, the manager may determine that another recreational therapist is not needed but a recreational therapy technician is required. The manager may see that the loss productivity of the recreational therapist is due to delivering craft supplies to the patients' rooms. By hiring a technician, each therapist is able to do one more group. The analysis of productivity is not black and white. Trends, volumes, patient, skill mix, budgets, facility philosophy, and goals of the program must all be considered along with the productivity.

Interviewing

When hiring an activities therapist, the manager must keep in mind that the personal traits of the employee are frequently more important than the technical skills. Empathy is vital for the professional to be able to understand and tune into the patients' needs and offer appropriate guidance. These professionals understand the need to respect the therapeutic relationship, are able to demonstrate genuineness to the patient, and are able to engage in spontaneous play. Creative analysis and synthesis of problems are also important skills. Furthermore, these professionals are skilled at choosing activities that generate a sense of meaning and aliveness for the patient.

A manager must develop an organized interview process in order to present a favorable impression to the applicant. The candidate should be informed in advance of what to expect in the interview process, including how long it will take and who will be involved (Schell & Schell, 1996). Adequate time should be allowed for the candidate to tour the facility, obtain an overview of the unit's functions, and be informed about the general conditions of employment. One or more people may participate in the interviews, depending on time constraints, the setting, and the manager's leadership style. Some evidence suggests that interviews become more valid predictors of job success when multiple interviewers are used along with a semistructured interview format.

After the interview is completed, the candidates' references must be checked. These references should be individuals who have seen the candidate perform the job duties required for this current position. There are various methods for performing this. Within some institutions, human resources will perform the reference check either by mail or by telephone. In other institutions, the manager will perform this duty. Having the manager check the reference by telephone has the added benefit of hearing the tone of voice and the quality of the responses to the questions. Again, be consistent with each reference. Each reference should be asked the same questions in order to have comparable information (Schell & Schell, 1996).

Outcomes

Measuring outcomes is an integral part of any program. Although therapy professionals have known for years that outcome measures are the only way to evaluate the impact of treatment and improve the quality of services provided (Stoffel & Cunningham, 1991), the economic incentive to become more cost-effective is what is driving the widespread measurement of outcomes. There are numerous ways to measure outcome. Patient satisfaction surveys are used frequently. Consumers want to know if other consumers were satisfied with the services provided. There are numerous standardized tools that will allow one facility to compare themselves with other facilities, such as the Parkside and the Press Ganey. Many facilities will develop their own tools. When developing a questionnaire, consult professionals who have expertise in writing questionnaires. In addition to measuring patient satisfaction, safety may be measured. An example may include counting the number of patient incidents, such as assaultive behaviors toward others, or falls. Furthermore, patients' functional outcomes could be measured. Determine the number of patients who returned to either the same level of care or a higher one after receiving treatment.

This data should be gathered at predetermined times, such as quarterly. A report should be developed that summarizes the results, discusses the interventions implemented during the last quarter to improve outcomes, and discusses the plans for the next quarter to further improve the outcomes.

The process of developing and implementing these interventions will have multiple positive benefits for the program. If this process is used appropriately, patients should become increasingly more functional as a result of the therapy programs. This process frequently has the additional benefit of giving the employee a sense of empowerment. In order for this to be effective, the employees must be part of the development of the intervention as well as carrying it out. Whether outcomes improve or become worse, the employee will feel a sense of responsibility. Over the long run, patient outcomes should improve.

The International Association for Psychosocial Rehabilitation Services (IAPSRS) has identified a number of domains of outcome measurement: frequency of rehospitalization, employment status, independent living status, educational status, income, program of attendance, and accomplishment of rehabilitation goals (IAPSRS, 1995). In addition, IAPSRS has identified that more research is needed on complex outcome domains, including social activities and skills, level of functioning, quality of life, and patient satisfaction with services.

Measuring effectiveness of care will allow professionals to determine clinical guidelines or protocols that outline appropriate clinical decision making. Refusing to identify treatment guidelines for your team will put your team at great risk. By continuing to demonstrate wide variability in clinical decision making, teams appear subjective and lacking in professional expertise. In response to lack of identified protocols, managed care companies have taken the lead, announcing that if professionals cannot identify dimensions for cost-effective care, then the insurers will.

Because outcome measurement is complex, there is the danger that cost-effectiveness may be evaluated from a perspective that focuses exclusively on cost as opposed to one that addresses effectiveness. In evaluating the effects of managed care, it is necessary to describe specifically which managed care mechanisms were used and what outcomes were measured. Generally, researchers have found that there were cost savings through decreased use of inpatient days. However, the decreased inpatient length of stay was not always accompanied by an increase in outpatient or partial hospitalization use. This suggests that cost containment merely reflects more unmet need or a shifting of the burden of care to the family and community. Community programs should develop tools to assist with this burden and should provide therapy as needed.

Therapy may be in particular danger of being lost in the turmoil of mental health care system changes. Therapy professionals need to be visible, proactive, and accountable in the process of defining and developing a cost-effective continuum of programs and services that emphasizes the community over the inpatient setting as appropriate, identifies effective methods to measure outcomes, and develops clinically reasonable and flexible guidelines and protocols.

As outcome measurements occur, managers will be able to identify which types of mental health and substance-abuse practices are best. Currently, in the private sector, managed care emphasizes brief, focused therapies for persons with mild to moderate psychological difficulties. Budman (1992) characterized the dominant values of brief and long-term therapists.

Brief therapists prefer pragmatic solutions, emphasize patient strengths and resources, and see being in the world as more important than being in therapy. Long-term therapists focus on seeking changes in the patient's basic character, assume that presenting problems are always indicative of underlying pathology, and view being in therapy as the most important part of the patient's life. It is this author's impression that most occupational and recreational therapists would actually agree with many of the values espoused by the brief therapist and already apply them in practice.

More research is needed to determine when brief therapies are appropriate (VanLeit, 1996). As managers and therapy professionals, we need more empirical studies demonstrating the cost-effectiveness of comprehensive, intensive, community-based practice.

Ethics

Sabin (1994) suggested that clinicians must learn how to care for patients while acting as stewards of society's resources; must recommend the least costly treatments, unless there is strong evidence that a more expensive intervention is clearly superior; and must advocate for justice in the health care system. At the same time, professionals must advocate for their patients and work toward a change.

CONCLUSION

Lazarus (1994) described a number of reasons why psychiatrists may dislike managed care. Many of those reasons probably also apply to therapists, including underfunding for services, new practice patterns, turf wars, demand for proof of value of services, bureaucratic hassles, and moral dilemmas. But therapy professionals cannot ignore the evolving mental health care system or pretend that the past few decades have been a golden era. Empirical support for alternatives to inpatient hospitalization (e.g., partial hospitalization, community-based programs) has existed for years, but recommended programs were never implemented because they were not reimbursed by traditional indemnity insurance. Therapy professionals must vigorously advocate for appropriate mental health services and assist in moving beyond the most negative attributes of managed care that emphasize cutting costs and care. At its best, managed care may actually support innovations and diversity of the treatment approaches as long as empirical evidence supports the effectiveness and efficiency of those approaches. It is even possible that mental health and substance-abuse practices and outcomes may be improved (VanLeit, 1996).

REFERENCES

Azok, S. D., & Tomlinson, J. (1994). Occupational therapy in a multidisciplinary psychiatric home health care service. *Mental Health Special Interest Quarterly, 17*(2), 1–3.

Budman, S. H. (1992). Models of brief individual and group psychotherapy. In J. Feldman & R. J. Fitzpatrick (Eds.), *Managed mental health care: Administrative and clinical issues* (pp. 231–248). Washington, DC: American Psychiatric Press.

Burson, K. A. (1998). Reestablishing occupational therapy in a state mental health system. *Mental Health Special Interest Quarterly, 21*(1), 1–2.

Earhart, C. (1999). Clinical interpretation of "Discharge planning in mental health: The relevance of cognition to community living." *American Journal of Occupational Therapy, 53*(2), 139–137.

Flaherty, J. (1999). Community-based psychiatric services: A focus on function. *Mental Health Special Interest Quarterly, 22*(1), 1–4.

Hays, C., & Baxley, S. (1998). The roles of the state psychiatric hospital and the occupational therapy practitioner. *Mental Health Special Interest Quarterly, 21*(1), 1–2.

International Association for Psychosocial Rehabilitation Services (IAPSRS) (1995). *Toolkit for measuring psychosocial outcomes.* Available from IAPSRS, 10025 Governor Warfield Parkway, #301, Columbia, MD 21044.

Lazarus, A. (1994). Ten reasons why psychiatrists may dislike managed competition. *Hospital and Community Psychiatry, 45,* 496–498.

McAnanama, E. P., Rogosin-Rose, M. L., Scott, E. A., Jaffe, R. T., & Kelner, M. (1999). Discharge planning in mental health: The relevance of cognition to community living. *American Journal of Occupational Therapy, 53,* 129–135.

Sabin, J. E. (1994). Caring about patients and caring about money: The American Psychiatric Association Code of Ethics meets managed care. *Behavioral Sciences & the Law, 12*(4), 317–330.

Schell, B. A., & Schell, J. W. (1996). Personnel management. In J. Bair & M. Gray (Eds.), *The occupational therapy manager* (2nd ed., pp. 253–325). Bethesda, MD: American Occupational Therapy Association.

Stoffel, V., & Cunningham, S. (1991). Continuous quality improvement: An innovative approach applied to mental health programs in occupational therapy. *Occupational Therapy Practice, 2*(2), 52–60.

VanLeit, B. (1996). Managed mental health care: Reflections in a time of turmoil. *American Journal of Occupational Therapy, 50*(6), 428–433.

Chapter Seventeen

Extraorganization Relationships

Thomas Hester

All mental health organizations (MHOs), from large state mental health authorities to private and public community providers, have relationships with external organizations. The external organizations most critical to the success of MHOs can be divided into four major groups with examples at national, state, and local levels (Table 17.1). Some are more relevant to public-sector organizations than for-profit ones, but all should be understood by mental health administrators.

The first group is composed of funding, policy, and regulatory organizations that provide operating funds along with policy and regulatory mandates. Examples are national organizations like the Federal Health Care Financing Administration (HCFA; now the Centers for Medicare & Medicaid Services [CMS]), the Joint Commission on Accreditation of Healthcare Organizations (JCAHO), and state agencies, including departments of Medicaid and regulatory offices, and local governments and their affiliated licensing offices.

The second group includes health, education, and social services agencies that provide the services needed by most persons with serious mental illness. Examples are the federal Department of Health and Human Services (HHS) and Department of Housing and Urban Development (HUD), state colleges, departments of education, local schools, and substance-abuse care providers.

The third includes support and advocacy groups that provide community-based recovery supports for patients and their families (e.g., National Alliance for the Mentally Ill [NAMI], the national and state Depressive and Manic Depressive Association [DMDA], patient/consumer networks, and community service and religious service groups).

The fourth group includes criminal justice entities that are increasingly being challenged to meet the needs of persons with serious mental illness who are arrested, tried, incarcerated, and released from jails and prisons. Examples include the Federal Bureau of Prisons, state departments of corrections, and local police and courts. These four groups represent the "*de facto* mental health system" (Regier et al., 1993). It is an often uncoordinated patchwork of national, state, and local agencies and community providers, which has led mental health leaders of state and community provider organizations to emphasize the need for linkage of mental health services with health, social, and criminal justice agencies to create an integrated

TABLE 17.1. Outside Organizations Critical to Mental Health Services

Outside Organizational Groups	Primary Operational Levels		
Functional Goups	National	State	Local
Funding/Policy/ Regulatory Insurance	HCFA/CMS SAMHSA SMHA Companies Foundations JCAHO CARF	State Medicaid Departments Fire Marshal State Regulatory Offices	County, City Governments Business License Offices
Health, Education, & Social Service Agencies	HHS HUD DOE DOL SSA	State Departments of Housing State Departments of Education State Departments of Labor	Schools Colleges/ Universities
Natural Support & Advocacy Groups	NAMI MDMA National Consumer Network	State Advocacy Affiliates	Families Businesses Civic & Religious Service Groups Peer Support Groups
Criminal Justice Entities	Department of Justice FBI Secret Service Federal Bureau of Prisons Federal Courts	State Departments of Corrections State Departments of Pardons & Paroles State Departments of Juvenile Justice State Courts	Sheriffs Police Jails Courts

mental health system (National Association of State Mental Health Program Directors, 2000; National Council for Community Behavioral Healthcare, 2000).

In order to develop a truly integrated system, it is critical to understand the types of relationships that exist between mental health organizations and external organizations. These interorganizational relationships can be classified on the basis of frequency (rare to regular), formality (casual to written contract or memorandum of understanding), degree of conflict (cooperative to antagonistic), or reciprocity (one-sided to balanced and mutually rewarding) (Hall, 1982). Merely classifying interorganizational relationship types, however, is not sufficient for the cohesive vision needed to achieve a working and integrated mental health system. To develop such a system, one must have a sound interorganizational framework.

The conceptual framework of interorganizational relationships has evolved from the early *interorganized set model* (Figure 17.1) in which a series of dyadic interorganizational relationships are viewed as the spokes of a wheel, with the MHO being the hub (Hall, 1982). This framework does not address the vital relationships

FIGURE 17.1. Mental health system as an organizational set.

among all the organizations on the circumference of the wheel (Greenblatt & Rodenhauser, 1992).

A second, more comprehensive model is the *interorganizational network* (Figure 17.2) (Hall, 1982). It depicts the mental health organization as part of an interwoven system with relationships among and between all interacting organizations. It fails, however, to show the relationships of the networking organizations to the patient or other mental health consumer.

If the *patient* is the central hub of this wheel, with interactive relations identified between him or her and each of the organizations (Figure 17.3), then a model emerges of a service system consistent with the goals of rehabilitation, recovery, natural support, and community integration. The patient is seen as a part of the community who may benefit from specialized mental health clinical services, but who has coordinated access to other service agencies. These service agencies provide assistance with housing, employment, income support, social relationships, and recreation to patients in the same manner as they would to community members without psychiatric disabilities.

Understanding of the interorganizational network is enhanced if the administrator completes a detailed, consumer-centered network diagram for each of the

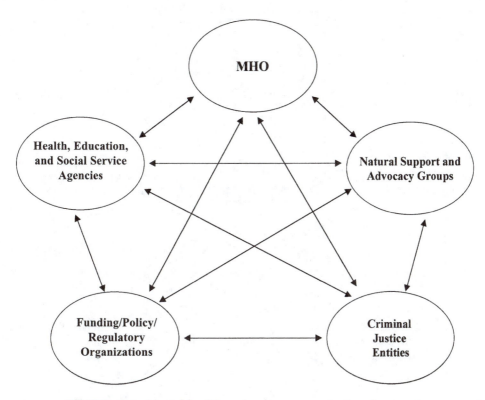

FIGURE 17.2. Mental health system as an organizational network.

organization's important business practices and priority objectives. The network diagram in Figure 17.3 can be used as a framework, and the external organizations can be derived from Table 17.1 based on whether the MHO operates primarily at a national, state, or local level. In developing a network diagram, administrators should include the names of the actual organizations with which they have relationships. Then the relationship between each of the groups and the MHO should be classified based on frequency, formality, degree of conflict, and reciprocity. Finally, specific strategies and tactics should be designed to enhance the effectiveness of the interorganizational network as recommended in this chapter. This chapter is intended to serve as a guide for mental health organizations to develop successful networks. Specific, detailed descriptions for every MHO are beyond the scope of this chapter.

Rather than focusing on the dynamics of all relationships between MHOs and each of the four major groups of external organizations, this chapter highlights the importance of key extraorganizational relationships needed for any MHO to achieve two fundamental requirements: sound business practice and mission-priority issues. All mental health organizations must have effective working relationships with external entities for sound business practices such as fiscal solvency, regulatory compliance, and workforce development. Extraorganizational relationships are also essential to the primarily public-sector mission priorities of ensuring necessary supports for such things as housing, employment, substance-abuse treatment, and improved services in the criminal justice system.

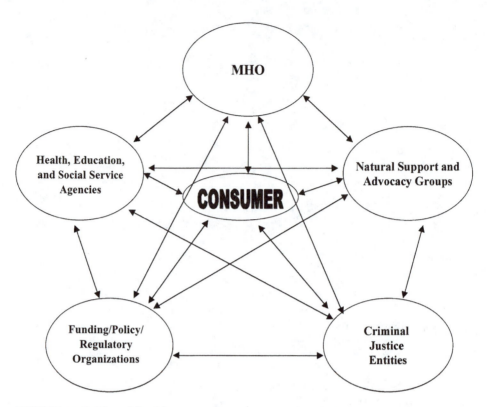

FIGURE 17.3. Mental health system as a consumer-focused organizational network.

FUNDING RELATIONSHIPS

To achieve and maintain fiscal solvency, every MHO must have sound relationships with outside funding entities. The funding structure of the mental health system in the United States makes these relationships especially challenging because of the number of fund sources and their varying expectations and requirements. This section briefly reviews national and state mental health funding, focusing on the importance of associated extraorganizational relationships for state mental health agencies (SMHAs) and local providers.

Basic Funding Facts

In 1996, the United States spent $69 billion (7% of total health spending) for mental health services. Of this amount, $32 billion (47%) was expended by private sources, with $18 billion coming from insurance and the remainder largely from copayment or self-pay. Public payers accounted for $37 billion (53%). Expenditures by public payers included Medicaid ($13 billion), state/local monies ($12.4 billion), Medicare ($9.8 billion), and other federal sources ($1.5 billion) (Mark, McKusick, King, Harwood, & Genuardi, 1998).

It is important to note two major trends that have recently affected U.S. mental health expenditures. First, private-sector expenditures, although growing, have not increased as much as those of the public sector. Private-sector expenditures increased only 6% between 1986 and 1996, whereas public-sector spending increased 8%. Second, the growth in public funding is mainly due to increased Medicaid funding. Thus, "the role of direct state funding has been reduced whereas Medicaid funding of mental health care has grown in relative importance" (U.S. Department of Health & Human Services, 1999). However, much of the public mental health spending is controlled by SMHAs.

In fiscal year (FY) 1997, SMHAs reported that they controlled or expended over $16.35 billion for mental health services (Figure 17.4). This amount included $11.4 billion (69%) state revenue, $4 billion (25%) federal contributions, $822 million (5%) first- and third-party payment, and over $95 million (1%) county and city government funds. The state government contribution included $8.6 billion in general funds and $1.5 billion in state Medicaid funds used to match federal Medicaid program funds. The $3.26 billion supplied by the Medicaid program is by far the largest source of federal funds controlled by SMHAs. Notably, SMHAs do not administratively control an additional $850 million of Medicaid funds that goes directly to community mental health programs. Other federal sources (including Community Mental Health Services Block Grants) make up just 5% of SMHA-controlled funds (National Association of State Mental Health Program Directors Research Institute, 1999).

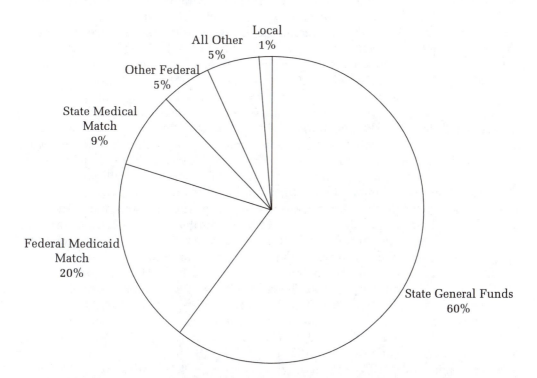

FIGURE 17.4. Fiscal year 1997 SMHA-controlled revenues for mental health services. From National Association of State Mental Health Program Directors Research Institute (NRI), 1999.

In FY 97, SMHAs spent $9.1 billion on community-based mental health services and $6.6 billion on state psychiatric hospitals. Downsizing and closed state institutions resulted in a 17.5% reduction (inflation controlled) in SMHA hospital expenditures during the period FY 93 through FY 97. During the same period, SMHA expenditures for community services increased 31.1%. SMHA-controlled expenditures overall decreased 2.0% (National Association of State Mental Health Program Directors Research Institute, 2000).

This review of funding supports several important conclusions, at least as of the end of FY 1997:

- Public-sector-source funding was greater, and was growing faster, than private-source funds.
- Medicaid was the fastest-growing public mental health payer.
- State funds were the largest portion of SMHA expenditures, with only 25% of state expenditures being from federal funds.
- A sizable amount of Medicaid funding lies outside SMHA control.
- SMHAs have shifted funds from state psychiatric hospitals to community settings.

Importance of Fiscally Oriented Extraorganizational Relationships

In light of these funding issues, three sets of fiscal extraorganizational relationships are most important to SMHAs. The first are relations with payers to ensure the mental health funding that the SMHA controls. The second are linkages used to influence other organizations that fund mental health services within the state. The third are relationships with providers who receive mental health funding from the SMHA.

In order to ensure mental health funding, SMHAs must maintain good relationships with their primary federal and state funding organizations. Because the largest federal payer is Medicaid, SMHAs must work well with the Centers for Medicare & Medicaid Services (CMS; formerly the Health Care Financing Administration [HCFA]), its associated state departments of Medicaid, and its affiliated state regulatory agencies. This working relationship should not be limited simply to meeting federal regulations and associated licensing requirements. SMHAs can help shape federal regulation by responding individually, and in collaboration with other SMHAs, to CMS (HCFA)-proposed regulations. More significantly, SMHAs can work at a state level to craft Medicaid waivers that expand the impact of state revenue funds by using them as a match for federal Medicaid funds. These waivers can also be used to promote a shift from institutional and clinic-based services to more comprehensive, integrated community-based services that focus on rehabilitation and recovery.

Other sources of federal funds that are controlled by SMHAs are provided by the federal Center for Mental Health Services (CMHS). These include the Community Mental Health Block Grant (MHBG), community support programs, the PATH program for people with mental illness who are homeless, the Knowledge Development and Application Program, and the Comprehensive Community Mental Health Services for Children and their Families Programs (U.S. DHHS, 1999). The largest of these programs is the MHBG, which provides significant, flexible funding to SMHAs. Because the inflation-adjusted MHBG dollars have decreased by 49% from FY 83 to FY 97, the MHBG has decreased from an average 10.7% of SMHA community expenditures in FY 83 to 2.8% in FY 97. Congress appropriated an additional $13.4 billion to the MHBG in FY 99 (National Association of State Mental Health Program Directors Research Institute, 1999).

The MHBG promotes extraorganizational relationships because of the range of participants required in states' federally mandated Mental Health Planning Councils. The Mental Health Planning Council's duties include reviewing the state plan for Mental Health Block Grant expenditures, advocating for adults with serious mental illness and children with severe emotional disorders, and conducting an annual adequacy review of state mental health services. Its members must include representatives of state agencies (mental health, education, vocational rehabilitation, housing, criminal justice, and social services) and adults with serious mental illness and their family members (Public Law 102-321, July 1992).

The largest source of SMHA-controlled funds remains, however, state-generated funds. SMHAs need to develop and maintain good relationships with the executive and legislative branches of state governments in order to advocate for inclusion in the governor's proposed budget and legislative appropriations. Because budget promotion by SMHAs is often viewed as motivated by self-interest, SMHA relationships with advocacy groups like the Alliance for the Mentally Ill, Mental Health Association, and Consumer Network are often very helpful; their approach to state politics is earnest and puts a "face" on the need for mental health services.

The second set of highly important funding-related relationships involves linkages to other organizations that fund mental health services. They include state departments of adult and juvenile corrections, welfare departments, and departments of education. These collaborative interagency relations offer the opportunity to pool funding streams and improve continuity across service systems.

The SMHA's relationships with state Medicaid departments are becoming increasingly important, as Medicaid is a major, growing source of federal funding. Many state Medicaid authorities have implemented managed care programs, which are often administered by private companies. If the SMHA is not included in the Medicaid mental health benefits design, access criteria, and utilization management, it is much more difficult to shape the development of community mental health services that focus on rehabilitation, recovery, and community integration. In such cases, the SMHA may be reduced to merely providing state Medicaid match dollars from refinancing state-funded services.

SMHA Funding of Care by Others

It is also vital that SMHAs have effective working relationships with the hospitals and community providers they fund. Without this, there is no way to assure that services directly funded by the SMHA will be used for the purposes intended, and influence over patient care, support, and rehabilitation will diminish. SMHAs directly fund and operate state psychiatric hospitals. States have dramatically downsized and closed hospitals, and moved funding to community-based services; 44 U.S. state psychiatric hospitals were closed between 1990 and 1997 (National Association of State Mental Health Program Directors Research Institute, 2000), and at least 10 states are currently attempting to contract out the operation and management of some 28 more inpatient facilities. One key to maintaining high-quality services in new care environments is to involve hospital staff at all levels in planning for the transition of hospital resources to the community. Resistance to change and fears of job loss can be reduced if employees can participate in the development and operation of new community-based services.

SMHAs usually provide community mental health services by directly funding local providers, or by funding local government mental health authorities, who either operate or contract for mental health services. A variety of contracting mechanisms are used, including fee-for-service reimbursement, grants, and performance contracting. Each requires some form of utilization management, which, in turn, requires communication.

Relationships between SMHAs and community providers are being tested by the implementation of managed care in over half the states (National Association of State Mental Health Program Directors Research Institute, 2000). Although a private company is often responsible for administering the program, it is important for community providers to participate in the service design and evaluation process. Without the involvement of community providers in the development of access criteria and utilization management techniques, the chance for program success dwindles. Controlling entry into state psychiatric hospitals is often a key utilization management role for community providers.

In summary, the mosaic of federal, state, and private funding sources requires all MHOs to develop working extraorganizational relationships with many entities. Provider contractors and agencies, whether public or private, must have sound relationships with their many pay sources: SMHA contracts and grants, federal and private grants, Medicaid and Medicare payments, and private insurance. Recent trends in mental health funding (e.g., proportionately lower private insurance expenditures and increased Medicaid share) reinforce the need to collaborate with other funding sources such as charitable organizations and other state and local government agencies. Although initially designed to increase revenue, this collaboration may also lead to improved mental health service access and continuity across agencies, and may encourage local communities to be more actively involved in meeting the needs of persons with mental illness.

REGULATORY RELATIONSHIPS

Developing extraorganizational relationships to maintain regulatory compliance (e.g., accreditation, licensure) is a second essential business practice. Joint Commission on the Accreditation of Healthcare Organizations (JCAHO) accreditation, for example, has become an interactive process that requires providers to maintain an active relationship with JCAHO.

In general, major accrediting bodies rate standards compliance via triennial on-site surveys. In 1993, however, the JCAHO began augmenting its triennial surveys with random, unannounced surveys of 5% of JCAHO-accredited organizations in between regular surveys. In 1996, increasing public demand for oversight and accountability led JCAHO to establish its "sentinel event" policy, which requires provider self-reporting of significant incidents such as suicides in 24-hour settings and deaths associated with patient restraint. In addition to reporting, provider agencies and facilities must submit a comprehensive analysis of sentinel events and, if problems are discovered, a plan of correction.

In 1997, JCAHO initiated the Oryx program. It requires psychiatric hospitals to report outcome measures on a quarterly basis and provide a regular flow of information to JCAHO regarding hospital performance. JCAHO plans to incorporate its other programs into Oryx in the future.

At least two other relationships may come into play as part of the SMHA's role as a purchaser or monitor of mental health services. In many states, the SMHA functions as the licensing or certifying agency for other public (and sometimes private) service providers. It promulgates regulations, rules, or standards and conducts compliance surveys and investigations of other mental health providers. The SMHA may also serve as an agent of CMS (HCFA) or the state department of medical assistance to certify Medicaid- and Medicare-eligible providers.

Second, the SMHA may contractually obligate its funded providers to meet certain regulatory and accreditation requirements. When requiring accreditation, the SMHA is responsible for determining which accrediting bodies are officially recognized, and may choose to provide full or partial relief from state licensure requirements for agencies accredited by approved bodies ("deemed status").[1]

WORKFORCE DEVELOPMENT RELATIONSHIPS

Workforce development is the final business practice considered in this chapter. The business foundation of a mental health organization will not be sound unless it recruits and retains competent and compassionate professional staff and volunteers who are committed to the agency's vision and mission priorities.

Challenges

Extraorganization relationships and communication can help with five basic challenges:

- Many colleges and universities do not provide the education and training experience required to prepare one to work in the current mental health system. Curriculums are often deficient regarding out-of-clinic services, recovery/rehabilitation models, natural supports, and treatment of co-occurring disorders. Students may have limited experience in providing family education, promoting patient/client self-determination, and/or maximizing nonclinical community supports.
- Potential employees may be discouraged from working in a mental health organization because of stigma of mental illness or beliefs that mentally ill persons are either not really sick, or not capable of significant recovery. The message is that serving the mentally ill is futile.

---

1. That is, certain state licensing or survey requirements are waived—deemed to be met—because the facility or other provider has already met another acceptable standard, such as JCAHO accreditation.

- Staff access to continuing-education activities and expert case consultation is often limited.
- Many staff members enjoy teaching, and teaching others stimulates one's own continuing education. Many mental health employment settings have very limited opportunities to teach or supervise clinical trainees.
- Geography, such as rural or inner-city locations, is not highly desired by most mental health professionals.

These workforce issues can be successfully addressed by SMHAs and community providers through effective relationships with universities, vocational/technical schools, professional organizations, advocacy groups, and large health care employers. In addition, government agencies may provide recruitment and retention assistance for shortage professions and geographic areas.

Public/Academic Collaboration

Collaborations between public MHOs and universities may influence training of clinical graduates who will later work with the mentally ill, particularly in the public mental health system (Bray & Bevilacqua, 1993). In the study cited, evaluation of on-site training that focused on state psychiatric hospital multidisciplinary teams revealed that students valued the experience, hospital staff enjoyed working with students, and recruitment efforts were enhanced (Addleton, Tratnack, & Donat, 1991). In another study, a rural residency rotation was found to help recruit psychiatrists to rural mental health settings (Bridges, 1994).

Since 1989, the collaboration between SMHAs and academia has been aided by the State/University Interdisciplinary Collaboration Project (SUICP), an effort funded by the federal Center for Mental Health Services and administered by the American Psychiatric Association. The project is directed by a committee of representatives from the American Academy of Child and Adolescent Psychiatry, the American Nurses Association, the American Psychiatric Association, the National Alliance for the Mentally Ill, the National Association of Social Workers, and the National Association of State Mental Health Program Directors. The SUICP sponsored regional workshops that brought public agencies and academic representatives together to address problems in the mental health field. One result was a program of SUICP site visits from teams of state mental health agency (SMHA) and university psychiatrists to help build public/academic collaborations.

A state/university collaboration must benefit both parties. SMHAs may, for example, fund undergraduate and postgraduate training slots, then expect some degree of service provision and/or improved clinician recruitment. In another example, academic departments of psychiatry receive fees for consultation delivered by telemedicine, whereas rural MHOs benefit from access to expert evaluation and treatment recommendations.

Advocacy Groups

Mental health advocacy groups can have significant impact on staff development and retention. The groups' assertive support for family inclusion, patient self-determination, recovery, and evidence-based treatment and rehabilitation influences the training and continuing education of provider employees. In addition, advocacy groups work to reduce the stigma attached to serious mental illness and can inspire hope for successful treatment outcomes. Working relationships between SMHAs and advocacy groups can buoy the spirits of a demoralized clinical staff.

Federal Training and Recruitment Incentives

Mental health organizations can link with the Federal Health Resources and Services Administration and the National Health Service Corps (NHSC), which help underserved communities through recruitment incentives for psychiatrists, primary care clinicians, and nonmedical mental health professionals. In order to be eligible for NHSC recruitment assistance, an area must be designated a Health Professional Shortage Area (HPSA). NHSC provides incentives for health care professionals to serve in an HPSA through scholarship and loan repayment programs. For example, general psychiatrists, clinical psychologists, clinical social workers, psychiatric nurse specialists, and marriage and family therapists who agree to serve in an HPSA can have up to $25,000 per year of qualified educational loans repaid in return for 2 years of employment.

MISSION PRIORITY: HOUSING

Housing for persons with mental illness has been a mission priority since the inception of organized mental health services in the United States. A brief review of the history of the mental health system, however, reveals that the way housing and other support services have been provided to patients has profoundly changed (U.S. DHHS, 1999) and now requires more attention to extraorganizational relationships by all mental health organizations.

In the mid-18th century, states began construction and operation of asylums to house persons with mental illness. These asylums and their descendant mental hospitals provided shelter and treatment, often in remote, isolated locations. The development of effective medications such as chlorpromazine, amitriptyline, and lithium paved the way for the community mental health movement in the mid-20th century and a wave of deinstitutionalization. But the promise of new medications for schizophrenia and major mood disorders, as well as community-based mental health centers and residential programs, did not keep persons with serious mental illness from being separated from their communities, returned to unprepared families, incarcerated, or left homeless.

By 1975, a new phase of mental health reform moved beyond the delivery of professional services in contained clinical settings, and attempted to address the social problems of individuals with mental illness. The community support movement was based on the belief that persons with serious mental illness could become accepted, fully integrated members of their communities. This change in vision was largely reinforced by developing family and patient advocacy. Deinstitutionalization forced families who often felt blamed by mental health professionals to reassume care for their adult children.

Help came from the formation of the National Alliance for the Mentally Ill (NAMI) in 1979; it now has members in all 50 states, over 200,000 in all. The Surgeon General's Report on Mental Health cites NAMI as "a powerful voice for the expansion of community-based services to fulfill the vision of the community support reform movement" (U.S. DHHS, 1999). NAMI also promotes family education, so that relatives can provide informed support for patients. By the 1980s, consumers of mental health services began organizing and writing about a recovery concept of hope and productive, meaningful lives for persons with serious mental illness (U.S. DHHS, 1999).

NASMHPD underscored the importance of housing for mentally disabled persons in a 1996 position statement that emphasized that "all people with psychiatric disabilities [should] . . . have the option to live in decent, stable, affordable and safe housing that reflects patient choice [and maximizes] . . . opportunities for participation in the life of the community and promotes self-care, wellness and citizenship" (National Association of State Mental Health Program Directors, 1996b, p. 1). To achieve these housing objectives, SMHAs and local mental health providers need to work with other organizations to assure home financing, combat not-in-my-backyard ("NIMBY") attitudes, provide patient housing and related community supports, and deliver home-based clinical services.

There are several ways in which SMHAs and local providers can develop partnerships with state and local housing agencies to secure financial support for patient housing. At the state level, SMHAs should participate in (or help develop) the creation of the state housing agency's Consolidated Plan (ConPlan).

In 1995, the U.S. Department of Housing and Urban Development (HUD) implemented the ConPlan concept to encourage comprehensive planning by requiring housing agencies to consult with human services agencies about the housing needs of the people they serve (Turner, 1996). The SMHA's impact in the ConPlan is strengthened if it has a state housing plan. Such plans are best guided by work groups that involve key representatives of families, patients, housing finance agencies, housing advocates, and local mental health providers. The group helps ensure public participation, analyzes the housing market and capacity, describes patients' housing needs, reviews past successful approaches, and finally develops the SMHA action plan.

The SMHA's housing action plan can marshal efforts to

- Establish an ongoing interagency housing partnership.
- Require providers to collect and report data on patient housing needs.
- Provide technical assistance to local mental health agencies regarding how to use federal, state, and local housing resources.
- Apply for federal discretionary housing funds.

MHOs cannot confine their efforts to creating access to housing funds. Money alone will not provide integrated community housing in the face of NIMBY attitudes and discrimination. The primary federal laws that address patient housing rights are the Fair Housing Act Amendment of 1998, the Americans With Disabilities Act (ADA) (to the extent that the housing can be deemed a public service under Title II), and the Rehabilitation Act of 1973 (Section 504 covers providers that receive federal funds) (Allen, 1996, p. 82).

It is clear that persons with mental disabilities have a right to housing, and MHOs should join with family and patient advocacy groups to promote open zoning. MHOs can strengthen the support for integrated community housing for patients by educating advocacy groups about fair housing laws and regulations. The MHO leadership must also collaborate with these groups to promote better understanding of mental illness and recovery and decrease stigma in the press, among political leaders, and in the general population.

But perhaps most important, mental health organizations should enlist input from advocacy groups on whether or not service-based housing such as group homes and congregate care settings meet patient needs for housing choice and privacy, and mandate treatment compliance as a condition for housing. The MHO must recognize that "housing is where a person lives, not a residential treatment setting and that acceptance of mental health services cannot and should not be a condition for remaining in one's home" (Allen, 1996, p. 81).

In addition to ensuring financing for housing, combating NIMBY attitudes, and combating any policy that makes adequate housing contingent on patient compliance with service directives, mental health organizations must, either by policy or contract, require that providers deliver an array of support services consistent with the goals of recovery and community integration that

- Actively involve patients in the design, implementation, and evaluation of services.
- Provide service where the patient is found (e.g., home, work, or school).
- Incorporate natural supports (e.g., family, friends, schools, church, public transportation).

MISSION PRIORITY: PATIENT EMPLOYMENT

A second mission priority for MHOs is promoting patient employment. The National Association of State Mental Health Program Directors (NASMHPD) formally "recognizes the fundamental importance of competitive, integrated, paid, and meaningful employment to the quality of life for persons with severe psychiatric disabilities" (National Association of State Mental Health Program Directors, 1996a). In 1992, the National Institute of Mental Health and the Agency for Health Policy and Research funded the Schizophrenia Patient Outcomes Research Team (PORT) to identify evidenced-based recommendations for the treatment of schizophrenia. After extensive reviews of treatment outcome literature, PORT specifically cited the supported employment model as part of its vocational rehabilitation treatment recommendations (Lehman & Steinwachs, 1998). The Rehabilitation Act Amendment of 1986 (revised in 1992) defines the formal features of supported employment as clients working for pay (preferably at prevailing rates) in integrated settings, with ongoing support and regular contact with nondisabled employees. Although there is no universally agreed on principle of supported employment, key elements include:

- Direct assistance in finding and keeping paying jobs, rather than skills training or case management without a clear goal of employment.

- Focus on placement and on-the-job training rather than gradual movement through prevocational training.
- Integration of vocational and clinical services rather than a brokered approach.

A review of six supported employment research studies revealed that 32% to 70% of persons with serious mental illness who were engaged in supported work programs achieved successful, competitive employment (mean 58%), while nonparticipating control group employment was 6% to 48% (mean 21%) (Bond, Drake, Mueser, & Becker, 1997).

Barriers to the successful development, implementation, and maintenance of supported employment programs, in mental health organizations can be overcome through work with other agencies. These barriers include:

- Absence of linkage and integration between vocational and mental health clinical services. This leads to reliance on brokered employment services in which patients are referred to vocational rehabilitation service vendors, which has not demonstrated good results (Bond et al., 1997). Assertive community treatment (ACT), which integrates clinical and employment services within an interdisciplinary team, is often successful (Bond et al., 1997).
- Fear of losing government entitlements. Flaws in the benefit structures of SSI and SSDI programs and potential loss of Medicaid benefits create disincentives for many patients who could enter the workforce. State mental health agencies should advocate for the elimination of these work disincentives with state Medicaid departments.
- Lack of meaningful, competitive jobs. MHOs at all levels should work with state and local chambers of commerce as well as private businesses to expand the number of competitive job opportunities for persons with serious mental illness. Most job placements are in unskilled, entry-level jobs often in group or "enclave" settings. Career opportunities that provide regular contact with nondisabled workers are preferable.
- Focus on prevocational training. State mental health agencies need to establish clear policies, service definitions, and standards that promote the principles of supported employment. They should deemphasize "gradual" prevocational training and focus on direct placement and on-the-job training for such things as career planning, job placement, job application and interview, job skills, transportation, clothing and demeanor, relationships with coworkers and supervisors, and even changing jobs.

With successful interagency collaboration, MHOs can reduce chronic unemployment and its accompanying isolation, poverty, and perpetuation of homelessness. They can be leaders in promoting employment as a critical pathway to economic empowerment and recovery.

MISSION PRIORITY: SUBSTANCE-ABUSE SERVICES

A third mission priority for MHOs is their link with substance-abuse organizations to create services for persons with co-occurring mental health and substance-abuse disorders (one form of "dual diagnosis"). The Epidemiologic Catchment Area study established that about 50% of individuals with severe mental illness develop alcohol or drug-abuse problems during their lives (Regier et al., 1990). In addition, co-occurring substance abuse is associated with symptom exacerbation, increased hospitalization, and medication noncompliance (RachBeisel, Scott, & Dixon, 1999), increased risk for community violence (Steadman et al., 1998), homelessness (Bebout, Drake, Xie, MeHugo, & Harris, 1997), and HIV infection (RachBeisel et al., 1999).

The Surgeon General's Report on Mental Illness highlighted the failure of "decades of treating comorbidity through separate mental health and substance abuse service systems" and concluded that "research amassed over the past 10 years supports a shift to treatment that combines interventions directed simultaneously to both conditions—that is, severe mental illness and substance abuse—by the same group of providers, but access to such treatment remains limited" (U.S. DHHS, 1999, p. 288).

NASMHPD and the National Association of State Alcohol and Drug Abuse Directors (NASADAD) agree that "a comprehensive, coordinated system of care for people with co-occurring disorders must be the expectation, not the exception" but "traditional barriers between the mental health and substance abuse systems have too often prevented them from working together" (NASMHPD & NASADAD, 1999, p. ii) (Substance Abuse and Mental Health Administration, 1999). These "traditional barriers" result from the two systems' different and usually separate governmental oversight, funding streams, and service delivery traditions.

To reduce these barriers, mental health organizations should collaborate productively with substance-abuse organizations. At a national level, NASMHPD and NASADAD have established a joint Task Force on Co-Occurring Mental Health and Substance Abuse Disorders that has had some success in closing the gaps between mental health and substance-abuse governmental agencies. Together, they have created a conceptual framework that provides a common language and promotes a comprehensive continuum of services for those with these dual diagnoses. This framework was endorsed by the federal Substance Abuse and Mental Health Services Administration (SAMHSA) (Substance Abuse and Mental Health Services Administration, 1999), which funds both the Community Mental Health Services (CMHS) and Substance Abuse Prevention and Treatment (SAPT) block grants. In addition, NASMHPD and NASADAD support (with certain stipulations) the use of CMHS and SAPT block grant funds for people with co-occurring disorders.

Administrative and funding relationships often make it difficult to translate the success of federal collaboration to a state level. In some states, mental health and substance-abuse agencies are organizationally separate; in others, they are combined. Whether SMHAs and substance-abuse agencies are separate, or different units within a department, they can often work together for a common purpose.

Massachusetts provides a notable example. Its two state departments collaborate to create a joint mental health and substance-abuse service delivery system in both the public and private sectors. This initiative established a statewide leadership council with regional work groups that include major stakeholders, families and clients, administrators and clinicians, and state and local officials. The work groups identify needs, evaluate funding streams, review legal and regulatory issues, and eventually develop consensus regarding models of care to meet the mental health and substance-abuse service needs in their state (Barreira, Espey, Fishbein, Moran, & Flannery, 2000).

At the community level, MHOs and substance-abuse providers have developed a number of successful programs to serve those who have both psychiatric and substance-abuse disorders. A recent evaluation of some of these programs found five common elements associated with success (Bixler & Emery, 2000):

- Successful programs were customized to meet particular needs identified within the community. Local understanding of needs and resources lead to innovative approaches.
- High-quality clinical leadership was important. Clinical leaders moved beyond program design and were able to deliver the new expectations for organizational cultural change needed to integrate mental health and substance-abuse services. They also made important program modifications as they gained experience during implementation.
- All successful programs were fully integrated, with staff who were competent in both mental health and substance-abuse services. They did not rely on outside consultation or separated treatment (e.g., completion of one program prior to entering the other).
- They developed a referral network for less intense, step-down services to provide ongoing, integrated services.
- They had support from state and county governments for funding and regulatory flexibility, as necessary for innovation.

If significant improvement is to be made in meeting the critical needs of persons with co-occurring substance-abuse and mental health disorders, MHOs at all levels must collaborate with corresponding substance-abuse agencies. The barriers of organizational separation, funding rigidity, and clinical culture differences can only be overcome through interorganizational efforts.

MISSION PRIORITY: CRIMINAL JUSTICE SYSTEM

The criminal justice system consists of an array of federal, state, and local agencies representing law enforcement officials, jail and prison staff, judges, prosecuting and defense attorneys, and probation and parole officers. Directors of SMHAs have stressed the importance of relationships with the criminal justice system in order to "prevent the further stigmatization of people with mental illness and to improve mental health service delivery to those people in the criminal justice system who have mental health needs" (Mazade, Glover, & Hutchings, 2000, p. 171). Relationships with MHOs can reduce jail and prison overcrowding by providing treatment for persons with mental illness, thus reducing the likelihood of re-offense and incarceration (Dvoskin & Steadman, 1994).

Prevalence rates demonstrate that the populations served by mental health and criminal justice are increasingly overlapping. Between 40% and 50% of persons in the public mental health system have a prior arrest (Solomon, 1999). Viewed from the criminal justice system, about 700,000 of the 10 million people that enter the criminal justice system have serious mental disorders (7%), and 75% of those 700,000 have a co-occurring substance-abuse disorder (Steadman et al., 1999). This suggests that programs aimed at improving services for the mentally ill in jails, prisons, and probation/parole populations must include substance-abuse agencies and providers.

Reports noting the increasing number of mentally ill persons in jails and prisons date to the 1970s (Lamb & Weinberger, 1998). Some factors that have been linked to this increase are "deinstitutionalization, more rigid criteria for civil commitment, lack of adequate community support for persons with mental illness, mentally ill offenders' difficulty gaining access to community mental health treatment, violence at the time of arrest, and the attitudes of police and society" (Lamb, Weinberger, & Gross, 1999, p. 907). Regardless of etiology, MHOs and the criminal justice system have begun to join forces to improve and, when appropriate, integrate their services.

Collaboration between MHOs and the criminal justice system has led to three major approaches to the interaction of mentally ill persons with criminal justice entities:

- Reducing the entry of mentally ill persons into the criminal justice system.
- Improving mental health services for incarcerated persons with mental illness.
- Enhancing mental health follow-up for patients after release.

Collaborative efforts most frequently focus on jail diversion programs. These programs seek to redirect mentally ill persons from jail before formal adjudication or sentencing.

Prebooking diversion programs seek to avoid the unnecessary arrest of mentally ill persons who commit nonviolent misdemeanors. These approaches generally use specially trained officers or officers augmented with mental health workers. The goal is to enhance the ability of police to identify persons with mental illness and attempt to resolve problems through on-the-scene crisis management or referral and transport to mental health service facilities. Prebooking programs have greatly reduced arrest rates (Steadman et al., 1999).

Postbooking diversion programs can be either court or jail based. Detainees are usually screened for mental illness and evaluated by a mental health professional. If indicated, the results, or further evaluations, are used to support community-based mental health disposition as an alternative to prosecution or a condition for a reduced charge or probation. Court-based programs, in which a judge monitors treatment, often appear to have better outcomes than jail-based ones (Steadman et al., 1999).

Steadman et al. (1999) described five key elements for successful jail diversion programs:

- Strong endorsement at top levels of the mental health and criminal justice leadership and their continual support.
- Joint participation of mental health, substance-abuse, and criminal justice agencies from the beginning of the program.
- Regular meetings between participating agencies.
- Enhanced service integration across agencies, with a designated liaison.
- Case management that relies less on professional credentials than on successful experience in working across the mental health, substance-abuse, and criminal justice systems.

Even with effective diversion programs, some mentally ill persons receive jail or prison sentences. Incarcerated persons with severe mental illness need access to sound mental health services. MHOs in the various states have different relationships with jails and prisons, ranging from operational management units to contracted services to, in some states and communities, no relationship at all (e.g., when the correctional system operated its own mental health services).

There has been increasing interest in programs for paroled or otherwise released offenders with mental illness (Roskes, Feldman, Arrington, & Leisher, 1999). These programs try to reduce the number of released offenders who return to jail or prison by establishing some link to mental health and substance-abuse services (and other needed services, like housing and income support). Strong relationships between clinicians (sometimes case managers) and probation/parole officers are essential. This relationship should be based on regular, accurate communication, and an effort to see that the role of mental illness is considered and adequate treatment effort applied (or at least considered) before incarcerating mentally ill offenders for minor violations.

Through working partnerships with criminal justice entities, MHOs substantially improve the lives of persons with serious mental illness who are involved with the criminal justice system. With continued efforts, the number of mentally ill persons entering the criminal justice system inappropriately can be reduced, those incarcerated will receive better mental health services, and those released from jails and prisons will be less likely to return.

CONCLUSIONS

All MHOs must have effective working relationships with external organizations in order to meet two fundamental sets of requirements. The first is maintenance of a sound operational foundation based on successful business practices such as, fiscal solvency, regulatory compliance, and workforce development. The second is the meeting of mission priorities that promote recovery and community integration, such as safe community housing, satisfying employment, access to integrated substance abuse services, and decreasing unnecessary involvement with the criminal justice system.

Mental health managers and administrators must recognize the need for an organizational and communication network that relates to each of the above business practices and mission priorities. Understanding, creating, and participating in that network greatly increases the organization's chances for success. The reader should strive to analyze the organization's unique set of relationships (and potential relationships), with their types, strengths, and derivatives, then help the MHO identify tactics for improving them.

The most important parts of the extraorganizational network, and the overall analysis of all relationships, should be centered on the people they serve. MHOs that can focus on their service populations—including patients, other consumers, and their families—create positive changes in the way communities and agencies support people with mental illness. These MHOs are taking the steps needed to realize the driving vision of the community support and recovery movements: people leading satisfying, productive, and meaningful lives as welcome and valued members of the community.

REFERENCES

Addleton, R. L., Tratnack, S. A., & Donat, D. C. (1991). Hospital-based multidisciplinary training in the care of seriously mentally ill patients. *Hospital and Community Psychiatry, 42*(1) 60–61.

Allen, M. (1996). Rights and roles: The law and community-based housing opportunities for mental health consumers. In G. P. Hutchings, B. D. Emery, & L. P. Aronson (Eds.), *The role of the state mental health authority in housing for persons with psychiatric disabilities: Best practices for a changing environment* (p. 82). Alexandria, VA: National Technical Assistance Center for State Mental Health Planning.

Barreira, P., Espey, B., Fishbein, R., Moran, D., & Flannery, R. B. (2000). Linking substance abuse and serious mental illness delivery systems: Initiating a statewide collaborative. *Journal of Behavioral Health Services and Research, 27*(1), 107–113.

Bebout, R. R., Drake, R. E., Xie, H., MeHugo, G. J., & Harris, M. (1997). Housing status among formerly homeless dually diagnosed adults. *Psychiatric Services, 48,* 936–941.

Bixler, J. B., & Emery, B. D. (2000). *Successful programs for individuals with co-occurring mental health and substance abuse disorders: Examples from five states.* Alexandria, VA: Joint NASMHPD–NASADAD Task Force on Co-Occurring Mental Health and Substance Abuse Disorders.

Bond, G. R., Drake, R. E., Mueser, K. T., & Becker, D. R. (1997). An update on supported employment for people with severe mental illness. *Psychiatric Services, 40*(3), 335–346.

Bray, D. J., & Bevilacqua, J. J. (1993). A multidisciplinary public–academic liaison to improve public mental health services in South Carolina. *Hospital and Community Psychiatry, 44*(10), 985–990.

Bridges, D. (1994). A public–academic partnership to train psychiatric residents in a rural mental health program. *Hospital and Community Psychiatry, 45*(1), 66–69.

Dvoskin, J. A., & Steadman, H. J. (1994). Using intensive case management to reduce violence by mentally ill persons in the community. *Hospital and Community Psychiatry, 45*(7), 679–684.

Greenblatt, M., & Rodenhauser, P. (1992). *Anatomy of psychiatric administration: The organization in health and disease.* New York: Plenum Press.

Hall, R. H. (1982). *Organizations: Structure and process.* Englewood Cliffs, NJ: Prentice Hall.

Lamb, R. H., & Weinberger, L. E. (1998). Persons with mental illness in jails and prisons: A review. *Psychiatric Services, 49*(4), 483–492.

Lamb, R. H., Weinberger, L. E., & Gross, B. H. (1999). Community treatment of severely mentally ill offenders under the jurisdiction of the criminal justice system: A review. *Psychiatric Services, 50*(7), 907–913.

Lehman, A. F., & Steinwachs, D. M. (1998). At issue: Translating research into practice: The schizophrenia patient outcome research team (PORT) treatment recommendations. *Schizophrenia Bulletin, 24*(1), 1–10.

Mark, T., McKusick, D., King, E., Harwood, H., & Genuardi, J. (1998). *National expenditures for mental health, alcohol, and other drug treatment, 1996.* Rockville, MD: Substance Abuse and Mental Health Services Administration.

Mazade, N. A., Glover, R. W., & Hutchings, G. P. (2000). Environmental Scan 2000: Issues facing state mental health agencies. *Administration and Policy in Mental Health, 27*(4), 167–181.

National Association of State Mental Health Program Directors. (1996a). *Position statement on employment and rehabilitation for persons with severe psychiatric disabilities.* Alexandria, VA: Author.

National Association of State Mental Health Program Directors. (1996b). *Position statement on housing and supports for people with psychiatric disabilities.* Alexandria, VA: Author.

National Association of State Mental Health Program Directors Research Institute. (NRI) (1999).

Funding sources and expenditures of state mental health agencies FY97. Alexandria, VA: Author.

National Association of State Mental Health Program Directors Research Institute. (2000). *Closing and reorganizing state psychiatric hospitals: 2000. State profile highlights.* Alexandria, VA: Author.

National Association of State Mental Health Program Directors & National Association of State Alcohol and Drug Abuse Directors. (1999). *Financing and marketing the new conceptual framework for co-occurring mental health and substance abuse disorders: A blueprint for systems change.* Final report of the Second National Dialogue of the Joint NASMHPD–NASADAD Task Force on Co-Occurring Disorders. Alexandria, VA: Author.

National Council for Community Behavioral Healthcare. (2000). *Principles for behavioral healthcare delivery* (p. 33). Rockville, MD: Author.

RachBeisel, J., Scott, J., & Dixon, L. (1999). Co-occurring severe mental illness and substance use disorders: A review of recent research. *Psychiatric Services, 50*(11), 1427–1434.

Regier, D. A., Farmer, M. E., Rae, D. S., Locke, B. Z., Keith, S. J., Judd, L. L., & Goodwin, F. K. (1990). Comorbidity of mental disorders with alcohol and drug use. *Journal of the American Medical Association, 264,* 2511–2518.

Regier, D. A., Narrow, W. E., Rae, D. S., Manderscheid, R. W., Locke, B. Z., & Goodwin, F. K. (1993). The *de facto* US mental and addictive disorders service system. Epidemiologic Catchment Area prospective 1-year prevalence rates of disorders and services. *Archives of General Psychiatry, 50,* 85–94.

Roskes, E., Feldman, R., Arrington, S., & Leisher, M. (1999). A model program for the treatment of mentally ill offenders in the community. *Community Mental Health Journal, 35*(5), 461–472.

Solomon, P. (1999). A model program for the treatment of mentally ill offenders in the community. *Community Mental Health Journal, 35*(5), 473–475.

Steadman, H. J., Mulvey, E. P., Monahan, J., Robbins, P. C., Applebaum, P. S., Grisso, T., Roth, L. H., & Silver, E. (1998). Violence by people discharged from acute psychiatric facilities and by others in the same neighborhoods. *Archives of General Psychiatry, 55,* 393–401.

Steadman, H. J., Deane, M. W., Morrissey, J. P., Westcott, M. L., Salasin, S., & Shapiro, S. (1999). A SAMSHA research initiative assessing the effectiveness of jail diversion programs for mentally ill persons. *Psychiatric Services, 50*(12), 1620–1623.

Substance Abuse and Mental Health Services Administration. (1999). *Position on treatment for individuals with co-occurring addictive and mental disorders.* Rockville, MD: Author.

Turner, L. (1996). Supported housing planning. In G. P. Hutchings, B. D. Emery, & L. P. Aronson (Eds.), *The role of the state mental health authority in housing for persons with psychiatric disabilities: Best practices for a changing environment* (p. 10). Alexandria, VA: National Technical Assistance Center for State Mental Health Planning.

U.S. Department of Health and Human Services. (U.S. DHHS) (1999). *Mental health: A report of the Surgeon General.* Washington, DC: U.S. Government Printing Office.

Chapter Eighteen

Ethical Issues in Mental Health Systems Leadership

John F. Baggett

Ethical reflection in the field of mental health in recent years has been focused on clinical issues. Much less attention has been paid to the ethical dilemmas inherent in mental health system leadership roles.

Clinicians have been particularly interested in client rights issues such as informed consent, treatment refusal, involuntary commitment, and, more recently, forced community treatment. These issues have been closely related in the literature to the tensions between treatment professionals and legal rights advocates. Professional boundary issues have also been hot topics. Issues such as sexual relations with patients have been associated in the literature with the civil liabilities of behaviors that deviate from professional practice.

There have been some useful discussions of the ethical choices facing mental health clinicians and administrators associated with the dramatic impact of managed care on mental health practice. But overall, very little attention has been paid to the ethical dilemmas facing mental health system leaders.

ETHICAL CHALLENGES FOR MENTAL HEALTH SYSTEM LEADERS

Those in mental health system administrative leadership roles encounter a wide range of ethical challenges. For heuristic purposes, three fictional mental health system leaders faced with typical ethical challenges are introduced here for the purpose of clarifying the ethical challenges confronting similar leaders and the ethical concepts important to the resolution of such challenges.

Doug's Dilemma: Administrators Must Also Deal with the Ethics of Clinical Issues

Doug is a clinical director at a state psychiatric hospital. The nurse manager on an acute admissions unit has requested that one of her nurses be allowed to file criminal charges against a patient who assaulted and injured her. The treatment team is sharply divided. Some members argue that the patient was psychotic at the time, that risk of injury is a part of the job on an acute care unit, and that the patient's treatment progress will be harmed by involving him in legal charges. Other members of the team argue that the patient, while psychotic, had enough moral awareness to know that the assault was wrong, and that legal charges are important in order to reinforce the point that the patient is responsible for his behavior and that assaulting others will not go unpunished. They also argue that not filing charges sends the wrong signal to staff and makes it more difficult to keep good staff in a time when there is a significant nursing shortage. Doug will need to make the decision for the team.

After hearing both sides and reviewing the patient's chart, Doug is still undecided. He is not yet clear on what is in either the best interest of the patient or of the unit. The context of Doug's dilemma includes the fact that if the patient goes to jail he will likely decompensate further. On the other hand, local judges frequently dismiss these cases and return the patient to the ward, thereby rendering the pressing of charges to a meaningless exercise. If, however, the nurse is not allowed to press charges, will the patient fail to learn an important social lesson? Will staff become more cynical about their work and less therapeutic in their style? Will the ward become a more dangerous work environment? Should these types of situations be decided on a case by case basis or does the hospital need a policy? What should Doug do?

Doug's challenge illustrates the fact that the ethical dilemmas confronting clinical practitioners also represent ethical policy challenges to those in administrative roles. This is true even for those not concerned with direct clinical oversight. Confidentiality, for example, is an area of substantial discussion in the light of the evolving court interpretations of the therapist's duty to warn. But mental health systems leaders must also struggle with the correct balance of these duties in proposed legislation and rules, and the protocols for investigating complaints. Furthermore, the procedures for assuring that the various agencies and significant others involved in the consumer's treatment and habilitation have the needed information to assure continuity of care and maximum support for recovery must be managed, while keeping faith with the consumer's legal right to confidentiality protection.

Likewise, the actual ethical choices confronting treating professionals with regard to involuntary commitment take place within a legal and policy framework created by mental health leaders and legislators seeking to provide protection to society, family members, and consumers themselves, within the parameters set out by the courts. Despite the courts' guidance on these issues, considerable latitude for interpretation and practice remains for those developing policy and procedures for the operation of public mental health systems. The discussions following the Capitol Building shootings concerning forced outpatient treatment has generated a significant number of suggested ways to force community treatment within current court interpretations. Each of these is fraught with ethical complexity.

Rachel and Mark: Systems Leaders Manage Services With Inadequate Resources

Perhaps the greatest ethical challenge facing leaders of mental health systems is presented by the perpetual reality of inadequate resources compared with the demand for services. This issue goes far beyond the choices associated with managed care in the general health care world where there is a reasonable correspondence in this country between resources and need.

> Rachel is director of a community mental health center. She has just received word that the state Medicaid agency has reduced rates for mental health services. In addition, the County Commissioners, facing a budget crisis and not willing to raise taxes, have cut the county support for the program in half. Because past financial crises have already caused severe belt tightening in the agency, Rachel sees no way to balance her budget except by cutting services to clients. Rachel wants to know the right course of action. What process should be used? What principles should guide her in making the difficult decisions about which clients and which services should be cut?
>
> Mark is a state director of mental health services. He has spent many years carefully building his professional career so that he would be in a position to make a positive difference for consumers of mental health services. He has been ordered by his supervisor, a member of the Governor's Cabinet, to close down a multi-million-dollar program for violent and assaultive children, and to transfer those resources to the public health agency for an AIDS education program, a priority of the current administration. The result will be that several hundred seriously emotionally disturbed children will no longer receive treatment that has proven to be effective in reducing involvement of these youth in the criminal justice system. The closing of the program will result in most of the children ending up in juvenile detention centers where their mental health needs will go largely unmet. Mark feels strongly that the order is wrong.

Each of these scenarios involves an ethical dilemma familiar to mental health administrators.

Rachel's choices have been created and limited by forces beyond her control. She cannot change the decisions of her funding sources, she can only respond to them. The decision will inevitably negatively effect some clients, some families, some staff, and one or more private providers. Does she cut psychosocial services to the severely and persistently mentally ill? Does she eliminate a prevention program for children and youth? Whatever decision Rachel makes is likely to anger an advocacy group. She will consult with representatives of each of these constituents. She knows, however, that the final decision will be hers. Although the decision will be made formally by her board of directors, she knows, based on past experience, that they will likely do what she recommends.

Rachel can construct a number of scenarios that allow her to meet her budget objectives. For each scenario, a strong case can be made that it is wrong based on the harm that will result. Rachel must discern which wrong is the right wrong.

Mark's situation, while also involving the cutting of vital services, represents a different ethical dilemma. Mark has received from a superior an order that he strongly believes is wrong. He has felt for several years that the attention AIDS has received from government resources has been substantial, whereas funds for mental illness have been sorely lacking. He sees this inequity as a continuation of the politics of stigma that has resulted in decades of inadequate research and service dollars to significantly impact mental diseases. Is this a line in the sand for Mark? Does he offer his resignation in lieu of carrying out this order? Of course, that would mean that he would no longer be able to be in the position of managing the state mental health system and would no longer be able to do other beneficial things for persons with mental illness. Someone else would be appointed director who would likely carry out the order.

If he carries out the order, perhaps he can manage it in a way so as to lessen the negative impact. But is that the right thing to do? If he does not challenge this decision, how many more raids on mental health resources will follow? Certainly, the publicity following his resignation would make it difficult to close the program or at least to continue to bleed the mental health system for other causes. But, what about his career, his family, the retirement he and his wife have planned? A resignation in protest will almost certainly negatively affect those personal domains permanently.

What is the right thing to do? Obviously, to obey the order would have benefit for prevention and treatment of HIV and AIDS. It would also mean Mark could stay and be there to fight another day for those with mental health needs, and his family goals could stay on track as well. It would also mean, however, according to research, that over half of the children currently served in the mental health program, and hundreds more that would be served in the future, will likely spend most of their lives in prison, a fate that could be avoided if the program continues. What about the fact that there are likely to be potential victims of their future crimes? Mark has a difficult decision to make, either way.

The decisions confronting both Rachel and Mark are also indicative of the ethical choices that confront systems leaders even when budget cuts are not being forced on them. The long-standing stigmatization of persons with mental illness and the reluctance of insurance and business interests to recognize the legitimacy of parity in coverage have resulted in chronically underfunded systems of care. Mental health systems leaders are inevitably faced with the task of rationing care, whether through formal managed care systems or by tacit participation in the inevitable cost shifting to criminal justice and community burden. The latter occurs when treatment is limited by inadequate service availability, and when systems, by default, use the limited resources available to serve only those who are highly motivated and persistently show up for care.

Unwillingness to design a system that rations rationally, out of a mistaken belief that rationing can be avoided, results in an irrational rationing with a variety of unintended negative consequences. Yet designing a system that intentionally limits and denies needed mental health care places mental health systems leaders squarely in the midst of ethical ambiguities.

These ethical dilemmas are compounded for systems leaders by the reality that mental health systems function in highly visible political environments. Ethical conflicts, as Mark's case illustrates, are inevitable between one's personal commitment to the principle of loyalty to one's bosses, who may have agendas that compete with mental health for scarce resources, and one's own personal and professional commitment to the agency's mission to address consumer needs. This reality and pressures from competing stakeholders, each with strong political influence, place leaders squarely in the middle of battles over policy and resources that can easily and suddenly jeopardize careers of a lifetime.

The external health care environment, including major trend shifts in Medicaid, requires that mental health leaders address major systems change. Redesigning the ways in which mental health systems do business carries with it a complex of ethical dilemmas. Major political and cultural changes are not easily achieved. They inevitably mean great risks for the persons served by the systems. Few choices in the design and implementation of intentional change are unambiguous or do not carry the risk of significant unintended consequences.

Although many of the decisions that mental health system leaders make daily are ethical challenges, few mental health system leaders have received formal training in ethics. It is probable that most intuitively engage in a number of strategies designed to assure that the decisions they make daily, and that have profound repercussions for other persons, are ethically sound. It is the presupposition of this chapter that a basic knowledge of the development of ethical reflection would be useful for Doug, Rachel, Mark, and other mental health system leaders. The following discussion is intended to provide a brief outline of ethical foundations in Western culture, and to illustrate the manner in which some fundamental ethical concepts apply to typical decisions facing mental health system leaders.

ETHICAL FOUNDATIONS

Ethical reflection has struggled from early times within the broader philosophical discussions of the problems of *knowing, doing,* and *being.* In order to act in an ethical manner, one must first know what behavior is ethically correct in a given situation. Knowledge of the good is not, however, as easy as having been taught by our parents to know the difference between right and wrong. This is illustrated by the deep-seated problem of the indoctrination of racial and ethnic prejudice. The victims of such prejudice bear witness that ethical knowledge, like all forms of knowledge, can be false. How, then, can one distinguish between true ethical knowledge and the evil that often disguises itself as the good?

Classical Ethics: Reason and the Good

Arising in prominence during the twilight of the Greek pantheon, the classical philosophers shaping Western civilization—Socrates, Plato, and Aristotle—believed that knowledge of the good could be arrived at through the rigorous use of the human capacity to reason. Socrates sought to build a system of morality that was not dependent on religious traditions. The core belief of that effort was the notion that man could be taught to use his powers of thought to predict the distant implications of his deeds.

Plato, building on the foundations of his beloved teacher, posited that in order to act justly it is necessary to envision a just state. Such a vision goes beyond the contemplation of a state of harmonious interaction, but includes identification of the ideas, the ideals and laws that underlie it. Within this framework Plato concluded that a just man will be one who finds his right role or fit in society, and will be able to do his best and give back to the state the full equivalent of what he receives. The key to the enlightened self-interest of the ethical man, which contributes to the harmony of the whole and the benefit of the common good, to put it in more contemporary terms, is an adequate understanding of the context of his deeds. According to Plato, then, by predicting with reasonable accuracy the consequences and implications of his actions, and by envisioning the ideal sociopolitical state in which every man acts on behalf of the common good, the ethical man is able to discern and therefore accomplish the good.

One cannot know the good, however, unless reason prevails over the blinding forces of emotion. The anger that Rachel and Mark are likely to feel when faced with the mandate to cut mental health services is, in Platonic thought, an obstacle to rational consideration of the implications of various courses of action. Anger could lead to blind rash behavior with tragic outcomes. Likewise, Doug is likely to need to set aside his personal feelings based on friendship toward or lack of support from members of the treatment team in order to weigh the choice of whether to allow charges to be filed against the patient. The Platonic problem our three system leaders have is to be able to rationally identify the right action without interference from their emotions.

Aristotle's ethics, although also focused on knowledge of the good, were based on a more mundane notion than the vision of an ideal state. For Aristotle, emotions are not in themselves enemies of reason, for they are a part of that human nature that is driven to seek the good. Aristotle taught that the aim of life is not goodness for its own sake, but happiness. We choose the good when we understand that to do so will bring happiness. Aristotle believed that when logic is brought to bear on ethical problems, happiness becomes the outcome. The use of logic assures that one will avoid extremes and pendulum swings between opposite vices, and will discover the right "fit" that works best and gives the best result. This "golden mean" could be achieved by using logic to successfully identify the extremes that would lead to an unhappy outcome.

If Mark, our state mental health director, uses his logical abilities well, the Aristotelian view would be that he could avoid extreme choices that lead to unhappy outcomes by finding a middle ground. If it is assumed that the extreme choices in Mark's situation consist of either resigning in dramatic protest or enthusiastic and sycophantic implementation of the order to dismantle the program, then it can be discerned that there are other less extreme choices available with somewhat better outcomes. Resignation in protest might be a heroic act, and it might even cause Mark to feel virtuous, but it is not likely to change the outcome for the children in the program, and it has severe consequences for Mark and his family. Enthusiastic implementation of the order might win him a few personal points with his boss, but it would destroy his credibility as a leader in the mental health community along with the children's program.

Instead of choosing between these extremes, Mark could try to find a middle way. Such a way might consist of offering his boss an alternative. With the assumption that his boss is not as interested in where the money is to be found as in finding it, Mark can try to come up with another plan to help his boss achieve the goal. This could be in the form of a set of budget cuts that would produce the necessary funds for the AIDS initiative, but would distribute the pain more widely across all the programs over which he presides. This plan would likely have much less severe consequences than either of the extreme choices. Many programs would lose some resources, but all would likely to be able to continue to operate. Or, Mark might decide to use this as an opportunity to close programs that research demonstrates do not produce beneficial outcomes the way the violent and assaultive children's program does.

This Aristotelian search for a middle ground has so permeated our culture that it is often a second-nature response to ethical dilemmas. Although not always embracing Aristotle's anthropology or the correctness of the logic that led him to various conclusions, subsequent ethical reflection has been profoundly indebted to him. This includes not only the concept of the golden mean, but the notion that the authentic life is one devoted to being true to our nature as human beings, and the notion that sound logic is essential to discerning appropriate ethical behavior.

Modern Ethics: Skepticism and Duty

Although the contributions of the classical philosophers have been substantial, not everyone has shared their optimism regarding human ability to arrive at correct knowledge of right behavior, and their presupposition that once one knows the good, one will do it. Francis Bacon (1561–1626), the great proponent of inductive reason, elucidated the "idols of the mind" that prevent a correct grasp of reality. Thomas Hobbes (1588–1679) wrote passionately about a mechanical mind deceived by false perceptions. Hobbes was so convinced that reason is not trustworthy, he concluded that people cannot be trusted to govern their own behaviors. He espoused a political philosophy that said that people could not be trusted to get along with each other without a strong ruler to make them do the right thing. The history of ethical thought underscores the importance of a healthy skepticism about one's ability to know the right thing.

Doug, our hospital clinical director, having been schooled in the scientific tradition espoused by Bacon, may approach his administrative decision regarding criminal charges against a patient with skepticism concerning the beliefs of both parties. Having been further trained in the Freudian tradition that the philosopher Paul Ricoeur called "the hermeneutics of suspicion," he may develop a hypothesis with regard to staff motivations reflective of the philosophy of Hobbes's view of human nature and self-preservation. One or both parties may not be genuinely concerned about the welfare of the patient. One party may be fearful of retaliation and find it safer not to antagonize the patient by pressing charges. The other party may believe that without punishment that sends a signal to all the patients, the ward will become an unsafe place to work. Doug may well decide to do further investigation of the facts and consider not only the welfare of the patient, but the need to impose his authority as clinical director on the conflict in order to restore peace on the ward. Experience has taught him that such exercise of authority is seldom exercised with any degree of certainty concerning the rightness of one's decision.

Philosophical ethics, however, were not satisfied for long with a negative view of ethical knowledge. Newtonian science with its elucidation of laws of physics provided for much of modern thought the conceptual model for overcoming epistemological skepticism. Immanuel Kant (1724–1804) reminded the world that conscience is a universal and essential human trait. We know, not by our reason, but by inescapable intuitive feeling, that we must avoid behavior that, if adopted by all people, would make social life impossible. Kant believed that all are born imprinted with this "categorical imperative." We may will to lie, for example, but we know in our bowels that lying is wrong, and we cannot will that lying become a universal law of human behavior. Are there not, then, some universal laws governing human behavior, to be discovered and articulated, much as one discovers and articulates the laws of the physical universe? They are not to be derived from the natural world, but are to be discovered by the rational mind. As such, they are the articulation of our duty and are not to be seen as the means to some end, such as happiness, but are commandments to be obeyed. Much of modern Western philosophical thought is indebted to Kant for this focus on the notion of duty.

It is the notion of duty to the well-being of her clients that may well drive Rachel, the community mental health director, to go through an agonizing process in examining each program in order to reduce the potential for harm to her clients when she finalizes her new budget. Furthermore, Rachel will be consciously aware of a set of principles or rules that will guide her in her difficult task. She will, for example, look for as many places in her budget to cut as possible that do not affect direct care of consumers. Once she has reduced her total by that amount, she will then apply other principles to the task of cutting line items in her budget that do affect consumers. One principle that she is likely to use is that seriously disabled clients should have priority over mildly disabled ones. Another principle might be that early intervention programs with emotionally disturbed children should not be cut, due to the assumption that they prevent future severity of disability. Yet a third might be that a distinction can be made for all populations between required core services and desirable services. Seldom are decisions like those facing Rachel made without reference to such principles as justification for the consequences.

But even if Kant is correct and we are born with a basic ethical understanding, questions remain. Do such principles guarantee right actions? When does our ethical thinking reflect the good of humankind, and when is it a rationalization of our darker desires? How are we to know the difference? Even when we have a high degree of confidence that we know our duty correctly, how do we deal with the reality that we frequently are unwilling to do the necessary deed?

St. Paul described the natural condition of humankind as a fierce battle between the knowledge of good and the impulse to evil. The Eastern philosophies, along with some Western thinkers who were influenced by them, such as Schopenhauer (1788–1860), believed that the human problem is primarily a matter of desire or will. They were much more pessimistic than the classical Greeks and most late Western philosophers. From the Eastern perspective, knowledge of the good simply contributes to human suffering, for such knowledge is either a mere reflection of the desire that disappoints, or an ideal that desire prevents from becoming reality.

Mark, the state mental health director struggling with whether to obey an order contrary to his conscience, probably knows what is right, according to those who see the problem to be one of *will* rather than *knowledge*. His problem is not the lack of knowledge of the good, but a deficiency of will to do what is right. Let us say, for the sake of argument, that Mark believes in his heart of hearts that he should resign in protest, yet he does not have the courage to choose the personal consequences of such an act. His knowledge of the good in this case increases the pain he feels about the choice of obeying his superior. If he were the product of an Eastern culture, he might begin to learn from this concerning his need to detach from desire and embark on the path to enlightenment. Being a Westerner, he is more likely to suffer from his guilt, and feel despair over his powerlessness to do what he believes is right.

The Freudian notion that our subconscious will is not controlled by us but in fact controls our thinking and acting, and that our conscious beliefs and morals are projections of our hidden desires and dark impulses, is a Western 20th-century form of a similar fundamental suspicion concerning human knowing and doing.

All three of our mental health systems leaders probably have enough training in clinical dynamics to question their own knowledge and choices as well as those of people around them. Because they are postmodern persons, they probably know at a profound level of self-understanding that they can never be certain that their decisions are the right ones, or that their actions are pure.

Postmodern Ethics: Ontology and Freedom

We live in a world shaped by such suspicion and skepticism. It is taken for granted in our time that we can never have certitude with regard to either the knowing or the doing of right behavior. Such skepticism tends to permit a kind of ethical anarchy in which one person's ethical belief and behavior is considered as good as another's.

The existentialists and some 20th-century theologians, aware of this tendency, reframed the ethical discussion as an ontological question—a question of *being*. *Being* is not so much a separate category from knowing and doing as it is the intensification or embodiment of knowing and doing. I only know and act as a "being in the world." That "being in the world," our human existence, requires by its nature decisions at each moment, concerning not only what actions to take, but also what relationship to take to our situations. The fundamental reality in human existence is this ontological freedom. It is not an option to make no decision. Not to decide is to decide.

This freedom presupposes responsibility. I am responsible for my own choices. The fundamental problem I face as human being, however, is, as Søren Kierkegaard (1813–1855) pointed out, my unwillingness to be the responsible self that I am. I prefer to be a victim of circumstances. I prefer to pretend that people and principles outside myself are responsible and to surrender my decisions to conventional authorities. In doing so, according to the existentialists, I surrender my humanity and the meaning of my life.

Free responsibility, as the theologian Dietrich Bonhoeffer (1906–1945) pointed out, always acts within the domain of relativity—the twilight that the historical circumstances spread over good and evil. We do not decide simply between right and wrong, and between good and evil, but between right and right, and between wrong and wrong. We may have the benefit of moral principles to guide us, such as the Golden Rule, but these decisions do not justify our decisions or guarantee their validity. It is we ourselves who must decide what it means to apply the principle to the present context without any guarantees that our application is the best or even that we have chosen the right principles to apply. When I hide behind my rationalizations and self-justifications, I am estranged from the free responsible being that I am.

The fact that nothing can justify my actions is not tantamount to surrender to an empty relativism. Such a notion is just one more self-justification. To justify selfish and irresponsible actions on the basis that I cannot justify choices arrived at through the exercise of all my ethical capacities is to abandon the struggle to be a free responsible person. My freedom is realized when my ethical choices are exercised with profound conscientiousness, knowing that that conscientiousness is not a justification. I, and I alone, am responsible for my ethical life. In my willingness to be the responsible one that I am, I embrace life as it is, and experience the authenticity of my free existence.

Rachel's task of cutting the mental health center's budget is not an easy one. An almost infinite number of scenarios can be envisioned, each with different sets of those held unharmed and those chosen to lose. As the responsible self that Rachel is, she will accept the reality of her task and be thorough in her gathering of facts, in her analysis of those facts, and in her evaluation of her options. She will be aware of the relevant ethical principles and will take them seriously in her considerations. But Rachel knows that none of her efforts and none of the principles she considers can justify her action or absolve her from the responsibility of her act. Once Rachel has decided which things to cut, she understands that she alone is responsible for the outcome. Rachel does not waste energy, however, struggling with guilt and remorse regarding her decision. As a responsible self, she makes her decision in the midst of ambiguity and moves on to the next set of decisions facing her.

Contemporary Ethics: Communities and Norms

Existential ethics may provide a useful way for contemporary persons to understand the personal responsibility involved in decision making in a time of ethical relativity, but this individualized thinking may obscure the fact that all ethical decisions are made in particular social contexts. Our decisions involve family and work, community, nation, and world. We may not be able to achieve certitude in our ethical behaviors, but we may attain confidence in our decisions if we are conscientious in our examination of the context and the consequences of our behaviors. Conscientiousness in contemporary terms demands, along with the humility of a healthy personal skepticism, that for the most part, wherever possible, ethical leadership will be a corporate activity, an agreed-upon direction in which those who have relevant expertise and those with a stake in the decisions participate meaningfully in the decision-making process.

The reality is that all ethical decisions are made, whether in free responsibility or not, within communities with ethical traditions. We may exercise our ethical freedom as a fierce defender of those traditions because we believe them to be wise and just, and necessary to the happy survival of the species. Or, we may exercise our ethical freedom as an agent of change, one who challenges those traditions, because we believe them to be corrupt, unjust, and destructive to the civilizing process. Either way, the better our understanding of the relevant ethical community in which we find ourselves, the better we are able to exercise our ethical responsibility.

Professional organizations have implicit and explicit norms of ethical behavior. Ethics committees and published statements of ethical practice are common, for these organizations have a profound interest in establishing and maintaining these norms. Health care organizations have also benefited significantly in recent years from the use of ethics committees. These committees not only provide a resource for clinical and administrative decisions that affect patients, but they provide a moral and sometimes legal defense when those decisions are questioned.

Doug, the clinical director of the hospital, has been presented with another problem. The treatment team has requested that he support its decision to restrict the access to snacks of a psychiatric patient with diabetes. This patient uses very poor judgment about her eating habits. She frequently spends her personal funds on sugary foods that cause her insulin levels to be risky. Although the staff members believe she should not be allowed to have such foods, the patient advocate argues that the community has many diabetics who also engage in such risky behavior. These are individuals without mental illness. The advocate asks, "Is it right to attribute this patient's behavior to her mental illness, deprive her of her liberty to spend her own resources on these unhealthy foods, because staff believe she would make different decisions if she were not mentally ill?"

Doug understands that this decision is one he could argue either way. Although he would be willing to make a decision based on his own careful and thoughtful reflection, Doug believes that a wiser decision can be made if he takes the problem to the hospital ethics committee. He knows that the ethics committee cannot make the decision for him, and that he may not do what the committee recommends, but he believes he will benefit from the wisdom of the committee in arriving at a decision. Because the committee is a multidisciplinary group, a number of perspectives based on a wide range of training and experience will be available when the problem is discussed. The committee will consider the circumstances, and relevant values such as autonomy, beneficence, justice, and dignity. It will weigh concerns about coercion, competence, manipulation, paternalism, and decisional capacity. If it functions well, it will, after thorough debate and discussion, arrive at a group consensus resulting in a recommendation to the clinical director.

If Doug agrees with the recommendation, then his confidence level will be high. He may, of course, disagree and choose to go against the committee's recommendation, but he will probably do so only after careful consideration of the committee's arguments. Either way, Doug continues to be the responsible self that makes the choice without ultimate certitude or justification. The use of an ethics committee has not absolved him of that obligation. It has, however, widened the circle of observing, judging, weighing up, and deciding from that of an individual to a group representative of the larger community in which the decision will take place.

Contextual Ethics: Beyond Ethical Reaction to Ethical Construction

Another movement within contemporary ethics is that of contextual ethics. Contextual ethics contributes to the broader ethical discussion by addressing the fundamental problem in short-term decision making—the problem of *reductionism*. In contextual ethics, ethical reflection has come full circle. Similar to the way in which Plato declared that ethical behavior was only possible in the context of the ideal state, contemporary contextual ethics holds that ethical decisions can only be made in a comprehensive context. From this perspective, most ethical decisions are made in a reductionistic context that obscures the relationship of this ethical decision to other ethical decisions. The comprehensive context includes a vision, goals, strategies, and objectives for the future, developed by an ethically oriented community with reference to guiding principles. Contextual ethics is reflected in much of current business management ethics, which is oriented toward constructive change in the form of a vision and plan usually enhanced by a continuous quality improvement (CQI) process.

Most mental health system leaders will attest to the difficulty of addressing long-term systemic issues in the midst of short-term political realities. Administrators in positions similar to those of Doug, Rachel, and Mark usually spend the vast majority of their work time reacting to a series of never-ending problems that require immediate attention. It is difficult to find time and political support for standing back, reexamining the system, and developing long-range plans. Yet failure to do so is, according to contextual ethics, unethical. Any decision, such as the one facing Rachel concerning budget cuts, must be placed in the context of comprehensive plans for the future. It is not simply the immediate impact of her budget decisions that must be considered, but also the impact of those decisions on the long-range plans for community mental health services in the region she serves.

The development and periodic updating of such long-range plans go hand in hand with continuous quality improvement efforts. The institutionalizing of CQI means that problems in current system processes are continually being identified and the root causes of those problems discovered. These in turn lead to the recognition of needed fundamental system changes that become a part of the comprehensive planning process.

The construction of comprehensive system plans for the future, with community stakeholder participation, and built on shared values and principles, is itself a major ethical undertaking. Such efforts provide the essential framework, however, for an improved understanding of the consequences of daily decisions made by the responsible selves in mental health leadership roles.

CONCLUSION

The ethical dilemmas confronting mental health system leaders are challenges involving profound consequences for mental health consumers. Whether faced with policy issues of clinical practice in a legal environment, the rationing of inadequate resources in a political context, or day-to-day management decisions, system leaders encounter these dilemmas today without formal ethical guidance. Part of this deficit can be addressed by the use of ethics committees that can assist with clarification of the ethical concepts and issues involved in decisions. More formal discussion of ethical issues confronting mental health administrators in the literature is also desirable in order to move toward a professional ethical standard for system leadership. A working knowledge of ethical foundations is important to this effort. Ethical leadership involves daily practice in the domains of reason and skepticism, ambiguity and freedom, and the exercise of social responsibility not only in the context of personal, professional, and community norms, but also in the context of a shared vision and plan for the future.

REFERENCES

Barnes, J. (Ed.). (1983). *Complete works of Aristotle. The revised Oxford translation.* Princeton, NJ: Princeton University Press.

Bacon, F. (1995). *The essays.* London: Viking Press. (Original work published 1601)

Bonhoeffer, D. (1995). *Ethics.* E. Bethge (Ed.), N. H. Smith (Trans.). New York: Simon and Schuster, 1995. (Original work published 1949)

Christensen, R. C. (1997). Ethical issues in community mental health: Cases and conflicts. *Community Mental Health Journal, 33*(1), 5–11.

Cooper, J. M., & Hutchinson, D. S. (Eds.). (1997). *Complete works by Plato.* Indianapolis: Hacket. (Original work published 5th century B.C.)

Hobbs, T. (1977). *The leviathan.* C. B. Macpherson (Ed.). London: Penguin Group. (Original work published 1651)

Kant, I. (1990). *Critique of pure reason.* J. M. Meiklejohn (Trans.). Amherst, NY: Prometheus Books. (Original work published 1781)

Kant, I. (1996). *Critique of practical reason. Great books in philosophy.* T. K. Abbot (Trans.). Amherst, NY: Prometheus Books. (Original work published 1786)

Kierkegaard, S. (1983). *The sickness unto death: A Christian psychological exposition for upbuilding and awakening.* H. V. Hong & E. H. Hong (Trans.). Princeton: Princeton University Press. (Original work published 1849)

Ross, J., Glaser, J., Rasinski-Gregory, D., Gibson, J., & Bayley, C. (1993). *Health care ethics committees: The next generation.* Chicago: American Hospital Association Publishing.

Schopenhauer, A. (1966). *World as will and representation.* E. F. Payne (Trans.). Dover, DE: Dover Publishing. (Original work published 1818)

Part Three

BUSINESS, FINANCE, AND THE FUNDING OF CARE

INTRODUCTION

Stuart B. Silver

This section will develop the tools a mental health manager will need to manage the fiscal and planning aspects of a business. Whether the fictitious "Maple Manor" in our vignettes, or the reader's own venture, the following chapters will explore the fundamentals using examples from the field of mental health services.

MODELING OF A BUSINESS AND DEVELOPING A BUSINESS PLAN

The business plan represents the full set of blueprints upon which the successful construction of any new enterprise rests. Just as the construction documents for a building include details of all aspects of the project, from site preparation, to architectural conceptualization, to mechanical details, to a full listing of all the hardware, windows, appliances, and so forth, the business plan must embody all the details outlining a new business, whether charitable or for profit. An experienced manager should be able to visualize the operations of the new service from the details supplied in the business plan. Any such plan, being prospective, will incorporate many assumptions about, for example, cash flow, number of customers, and so forth. The plan should specify the foundation for such assumptions, whether based upon the operations of similar entities, or some other methodology. These two chapters explore many details of business planning, and subsequent chapters examine financial underpinnings of both planning and operations.

BUDGETING

Budgeting is the process of expressing the ideas and visions of a new enterprise in financial terms. The forward-looking business plan is expressed in terms of expected expenditures and revenues in the budget. The budget serves thereby as both a planning exercise in its preparation and a management tool for plotting the activity of the business against the budget expectations. Often the process of budgeting can highlight unanticipated problems in the business plan. Obviously, the more experience one has in the type of business being structured, or the more budget cycles the business has weathered, the more accurately the budget will reflect the likely exigencies of the business during the term of the budget cycle (usually one year, although some governments budget biennially). Most entities think about operations for multi-year plans, but formal budgeting generally looks forward only twelve months. We will examine the intricacies of the budget cycle and processes in the fourth chapter.

FINANCIAL ANALYSIS AND MANAGEMENT

While the budget expresses anticipated results, there are several ways of conceptualizing the health and success of an enterprise. Such accounting methods provide a consistent way to conceptualize the status of a business for a given time interval. They are reflective of actual experience rather than planned-for results and include the balance sheet, income statement, cash flow statement, and reconciliation of net worth. Consideration of the structure, meaning, and use of these documents forms part of the content of this chapter.

We will also explore cash management, a function essential to the health and security of a business. There are two basic elements to this function: cash accounting and cash controls. The first has to do with the mechanics of keeping track of the actual cash receipts and expenditures and views accounts receivable as a cash shortfall and accounts payable as cash available, in contrast to usual accounting, for example, which views accounts receivable as assets and accounts payable as liabilities. The balance sheet will not tell you whether recently issued checks will bounce, but cash accounting may. Internal cash controls maintain the security of money and other negotiable instruments received by the enterprise. These controls are the mechanics of minimizing pilferage and embezzlement. Techniques usually involve having more than one trusted person handling and recording cash transactions, sequentially numbering receipts, and separating functions in the cash management and accounting operations among several departments or individuals depending on the size of the organization. Attention to cash control provides an avenue for untangling cash errors and prevents corruption of individual staff members, who may be tempted by handling relatively large amounts of cash.

FINANCING STARTUP AND OPERATIONS

Usually a new business requires an investment of capital to finance startup costs and operations until such time as revenue is sufficient to meet the obligations of the enterprise. Established businesses may also, at times, require infusions of money to pay for unusual initiatives, such as a new building, kicking off a new program, or opening a new site. There are many potential sources of money available to finance such ventures, including banks, donors, investors, the employees of the business, bond issues, stock issues, grants, endowments, and so forth. Chapter 23 looks at financing and the pros and cons of some of the various sources of capital.

SOURCES OF REVENUE

In chapter 24 we will explore the universe of payers for mental health services, from individuals to corporations to governments. Additionally, we will examine the universe of vendors from a business operator's perspective.

VALUES ISSUES

Virtually all decisions in the planning and operations of a mental health program from a business perspective are founded on the values and ethics of the participants. While a business manager expresses the enterprise in business plans, accounting sheets, and budgets, these materials are only the blueprints. Fundamental questions relate to what kind of building one wishes to create. Time spent conceptualizing the underlying goals and values of the enterprise provides future guidance to the management team when tough business decisions have to be made. Each time a price tag is entered into the budget to accomplish a given priority, it is possible that some other opportunity will no longer fit into the spending plan. For example, rent can be lessened if office sizes are smaller, thus enabling an organization to offer a sliding scale fee schedule to clients without income. If the offices are too small, will staff members become less willing to work in such an environment, thus interfering with recruitment and retention? What is the *right* size for the offices? Obviously, there may be no universally correct answer, but the example illustrates how each management decision may have other programmatic ramifications, such as whether to subsidize the fees paid by patients who have constricted means. The last chapter of this section explores these considerations for mental health ventures in more detail.

Chapter Nineteen

The Modeling of a Business

Stuart B. Silver

L et us consider the development of a hypothetical new mental health entity called "Maple Manor." The imaginary venture originated in response to the changing environment of mental health services in which long-term hospital care was no longer reimbursable by health insurers.

Dr. Hickory, who had worked for decades in an established hospital specializing in long-term care, articulated the idea for this new service. The hospital was in a downsizing phase. The staff members wished to develop a residential setting for patients with serious mental illness in which patients maintained their own apartments, participated in several therapeutic activities, and received individual psychotherapy. This program would operate at a much lower cost than a hospital inpatient unit, as most staff might be available on call rather than on premises. The program, nonetheless, would offer a rich mix of therapeutic endeavors geared to fostering increased self-sufficiency of the patient participants. A central feature of the therapeutic approach would be efforts to mitigate the effects of the illness through gradual increase in insight about underlying dynamics.

The originator of the idea of Maple Manor had a vision of what she would like to accomplish, but the task of converting the vision to a detailed plan required her to think through a number of questions. The overarching question had to do with how to conceptualize the project not simply as a bright idea, but as an ongoing entity in the real world. To do this required her to think about the questions of how, what, who, when, where, and how much will it cost. These are the typical questions asked by a news reporter trying to present information to the public. Their answers provide an avenue for others to come to some approximation of what Maple Manor is all about. The effort to respond to these questions in detail constitutes a business plan. No matter how altruistic the motivation of the founders, no matter what the sources of support, Maple Manor will have to operate in a businesslike way in order to survive and accomplish its goals.

One of the most difficult hurdles for this visionary founder of Maple Manor in converting her thinking from a program model in her mind to a business model on paper was to begin expressing her thoughts in monetary equivalents, that is, dollars. For civilization in general, money is the medium of exchange and valuation. Even in the most primitive societies and in our early records of human activity, the use of a medium of exchange between individuals is the norm. Direct bartering of goods and services is an extremely limited mechanism for societal function. Bartering, or direct trading of one item or service for another, requires prompt transaction and trust between the individuals. Money can store resources for later use and requires general trust within the society where circulated. Whether wampum, grain, cattle, coins, scrip, or gold, the use of a symbol to represent value has permitted social development. To be useful, money must be broadly accepted within the culture and have relatively consistent value over time. It must be hard to obtain privately and difficult to counterfeit. Money has sometimes been called the root of all evil. It might more appropriately be considered the route to civilization (Neal & Eisler, 1996; Weatherford, 1997). For business, as well, money is a medium of exchange and valuation. This section, "Business, Finance, and the Funding of Care," considers how a business works with money in both abstract and concrete terms.

Because Dr. Hickory now was thinking about a new business called Maple Manor, she had to answer the questions of who would be the customers, and would they pay for service or would someone else pay? What would be the deliverables or products? What would be her decisions about marketing, sales, warranties, liabilities, risks, and opportunities for Maple Manor in a business context? What would be the nature of the "managed care" environment for this new program?

Dr. Hickory initially visualized that she would set up this new entity herself, recruiting staff and patients, obtaining accommodations, and building its reputation. She imagined herself as the leader, policymaker, and inspiration for Maple Manor's development. In business terms, she was imagining a sole proprietorship. She would own and operate the store and decide how to invest the proceeds from Maple Manor's operations. A problem that she quickly realized was that a principal payer might be government, which might not offer grant funding to a private for-profit entity. Furthermore, there was a need for money to pay staff and rent space until there might be revenues from the program's billing or fund-raising activities. Dr. Hickory did not wish to remortgage her house to provide this financing. She had to consider alternative modalities of governance and ownership.

A business is typically organized as a sole proprietorship, a partnership, or a corporation (Costales & Szurovy, 1994). Dr. Hickory had already recognized the problems of a becoming the sole proprietor of Maple Manor, although the idea appealed to her entrepreneurial spirit. First, she did not wish to be personally liable for all the debts and obligations of the new entity. Second, she did not wish to have the financial results of Maple Manor's operations pass through to her own personal income taxes.

She thought about structuring the program as a partnership, but soon realized that she would be saddled with the same issues as in a sole proprietorship. She knew of no one whose talents would enhance the ownership of the program or with whom she wished to share management responsibility. If she used the partnership vehicle simply to provide additional financial participants, she might consider a limited partnership. In this structure, she would retain management authority and full ultimate liability for partnership obligations. Also, in thinking about the future, she was concerned about the fact that a partnership dissolves on the death of one of the partners. For that matter, a sole proprietorship ends upon the death of the owner and its contracts are also ended.

A corporation, in contrast, exists as an entity in perpetuity, distinct from any individual. It is separately taxed and its governance is specified in bylaws approved by its owners and by the state government that grants the corporate charter. Ownership is apportioned among stockholders, who own shares in the corporation according to their investment. One major advantage of incorporating is that liability for the business activities of a corporation does not extend to the shareholders' personal lives. Their liability is limited to the value of their stake in the corporation.

A corporation is governed by a board of directors elected by the shareholders and is operated by executive officers hired by the board. Profits may be distributed to the owners through the payment of dividends to shareholders. Shareholders must pay tax on dividend income. Thus, one of the disadvantages of a corporate structure is double taxation on profits. In so-called Subchapter S corporations, profits are distributed to shareholders and no corporate tax is due, thereby eliminating that disadvantage while preserving the liability protections. Other limits restrict the utility of the Subchapter S structure, however.

Corporations may be privately owned by a limited group of investors, with restrictions placed on who is eligible for stock ownership. Such privately owned corporations are called closely held. The requirements for public disclosure about their workings and financial parameters are far less comprehensive than the requirements of corporations whose shares are publicly traded. These so-called "widely held" corporations are subject to strict requirements by the Securities and Exchange Commission in order to protect the public.

Finally, a corporation may be set up as a not-for-profit entity (U.S. Code Title 26, Internal Revenue Code, Subtitle A, Chap. 1, Subchap., F, Part I, Section 501). Many organizations that provide health, mental health, educational, and other charitable or public service activities are organized as nonprofit corporations and are not subject to federal or state tax. Their boards of directors often represent civic leaders, beneficiaries of the program's mission, and relevant professionals, all of whom carry fiduciary responsibility for the performance of the program and who ultimately govern the corporation. Operating surpluses are reinvested in pursuit of the core mission of the corporation and no dividends are paid to any financial contributors. There are no formal shareholders, although many citizens may have a stake in the corporation's success.

In developing her ideas, Dr. Hickory realized that she hadn't investigated whether or not any program like Maple Manor already existed in the area. She had to think about what, in fact, the area was: the town, the state, the region, the country, the hemisphere, the world. Visiting mental health programs, she soon found out that there were a number of entities in the state that served a population of patients similar to the one she had envisioned. None of these programs operated along the theoretical axis of long-term psychotherapy combined with housing supports, although many provided housing and rehabilitative services.

Would Maple Manor be competitive or complementary to existing programs? Should it be independent of existing programs or operate in a joint venture of some sort? Would the combination of payers for the rehabilitation programs be interested in paying for Maple Manor's services or not? Each exploration opened more questions, the answers to which were necessary in writing a business plan or, for that matter, in developing confidence that an entity like Maple Manor was feasible.

Dr. Hickory discovered that most patients for whom the services of Maple Manor might be appropriate were not wealthy. At first she had thought to serve only those who could pay out of pocket, but then she looked at her potential customers. She realized that they needed to draw on their insurance to pay for health services, and many, in fact, were receiving government assistance to pay for their rent. Even if these payers would consider Maple Manor an alternative option to hospital care, insurance benefit managers ("care managers") representing them would scrutinize obsessively all services rendered at the program. There would be prospective consideration of whether placement in Maple Manor was "medically necessary," review concurrent with the patient's stay, and retrospective review of the services rendered.

At any of these reviews, payment could be denied. Dealing with the paper documentation requirements of these new intermediaries would entail more than a therapist staff. Dr. Hickory would need a clerical staff as well. Maple Manor was rapidly becoming a more complex venture than the doctor had initially imagined.

Increasingly, ventures that in the past have been seen as charitable or community service have had to operate in a more entrepreneurial fashion. Not only must Maple Manor and other mental health organizations construe themselves in business terms, but consider this example of how public museums are reinventing themselves as businesses:

> On National Public Radio's *Morning Edition* (1999), David D'Arcy reported that a new museum is opening in Nagoya, Japan. The museum will feature a collection of Western and Japanese art on loan from the Boston Museum of Fine Arts in Massachusetts. According to Malcolm Rogers, director of the museum, "the answer to one museum's problems lies in another museum's stores." In the late 1980s, economic contraction in the Boston area required the museum to think entrepreneurially. Rogers laid off dozens of employees, increased the endowment, and put the museum in the black. D'Arcy noted that "Critics foresee a system of traveling shows and a threat of mergers and consolidations that will make museums seem more like corporations."
>
> "Museums are in many ways like corporations. If they are not changing or improving then they're stagnant," was Rogers' response. The Nagoya museum anticipates 600,000 visitors in its first year of operations. The Boston museum has contracted to supply the exhibitions and expects to realize $50 million in lease payments for the art over the next 20 years.

REFERENCES

Costales, S. B., & Szurovy, G. (1994). *The guide to understanding financial statements* (2nd ed.). New York: McGraw-Hill.

National Public Radio. (1999, June 1). *Morning edition.* Archives: http://www.npr.org.

Neal, T. L., & Eisler, G. K. (1996). *Barter & the future of money.* New York: MasterMedia.

Weatherford, J. M. (1997). *The history of money.* New York: Three Rivers Press.

Chapter Twenty

The Business Plan

Stuart B. Silver

One person can compose a business plan in the privacy of his or her own study. A committee can create a plan. Sections of the plan can be delegated to experts in particular areas. Consultants may be retained. The first step is to decide who should be involved in designing the new venture. For example, it might be useful for Dr. Hickory (chapter 19) to ask potential residents of her new program to assist in the writing of sections of the business plan. Their perspective would foster a program that is customer-friendly.

At the federal level, the Center for Mental Health Services requires each state to submit a mental health plan describing how the public mental health business will be conducted (42 USC 300x-2, Section 1912, a). The center requires that a variety of stakeholders participate actively and meaningfully in drafting the plan. Stakeholders include "consumers," family members, representatives of various provider agencies, advocates, representatives of core mental health disciplines, public health officials, and representatives of allied agencies. Public hearings are also required. Such a large task requires a staff and a director of plan writing to insure that the product will be delivered according to federal guidelines and schedules.

The best choice of individuals to write a particular business plan typically lies between these extremes. Many enterprises involve a program planner, a financial planner, and legal counsel in drafting the business plan. Often it is wise to invite potential antagonists to participate. For example, if you are planning a program that will require siting in a particular location, it might be wise to ask community representatives to participate. This strategy may backfire politically, but at least it should be weighed.

The key is that the first step for the developer of a new program is to decide who should be part of the creative process. Axes of decision making are necessary expertise, complexity of the venture, political considerations, and available resources.

After assembling, those who will have responsibility for creating the business plan will focus on defining the mission of the new entity. The mission is usually articulated as a set of global aims of the organization. For Maple Manor, the drafters might express the mission to:

- Assist persons with severe mental illness toward recovery.
- Minimize the secondary disability caused by mental illness.

- Provide interpersonal dialogue directed at ameliorating underlying illness.
- Foster safe and normalizing housing opportunities.
- Combat stigma against those with mental illness.

Goals express the more specific objectives of the organization in fulfilling the mission. Examples of goals for the hypothetical Maple Manor program might be:

- To develop and maintain program capacity to serve at least 50% of the identified need.
- To develop housing opportunities varied in size and setting.
- To conduct periodic public seminars and other educational programs.
- To have competent staff members available on call 24 hours a day.
- To serve people on a sliding scale according to their ability to pay.
- To develop or associate with various rehabilitation programs.
- To provide specialized supervision for therapists working in the program.

Values are the ethical and professional principles that will guide decision making within the organization. A thoughtful compilation of values early in the planning phase facilitates the choice of operating strategies later. Some values are generally accepted by most organizations, such as operating within the law and within the scope of accepted professional practice. Others may be more enterprise specific, such as a mental health organization always seeking patient participation in fundamental decision making. Maple Manor may have program-specific values such as a commitment to emphasizing excellent community relations and a "good neighbor" policy with regard to residential sites.

The choice of values formally articulated, and thereby prioritized, informs later decisions. For example, when in a given year Maple Manor, according to budget limits, must decide whether to repaint the interior of certain dwellings or provide exterior maintenance, the "good neighbor" value may direct the resource allocation. Clearly, thoughtful statements of values are needed. Often, as the planning process unfolds, values questions may occur and rise to the level of significance where the planners may wish to add them to the organization's statement of basic values.

Early in the business plan document there is a statement of who owns and operates the program. Each owner's business and professional resumé is summarized. If the parent of the program is an umbrella agency, its governance structure should be detailed and its principal owners identified. In the case of a corporate entity, ownership of the stock is detailed. Each member of the board of directors or trustees and each of the principal operating officials is identified with accompanying summaries of their resumés. The business plan clearly shows who is responsible for the overall health and mission of the new enterprise and who is responsible for day-to-day operational decisions.

In addition to clearly identifying those responsible for the program, the business plan will identify the elements of the regulatory environment in which the program will operate. Is a certificate of need necessary and obtainable? What are the steps and schedule? The program may need an operating license. Professional staff will need licenses to practice. Will the program need to obtain a license to handle controlled substances? There may be a need for inspection by the fire marshal. Each of these permits and licenses may take time to obtain, and delays could adversely affect projections. In the case of certain programs, delays in receiving accreditation from relevant bodies may affect third-party payments for service. The planners must attend to these issues in developing the start-up timetable for operations and ultimately in planning for initial financing. Sources of information include similar programs, local and state health authorities, the federal Center for Mental Health Services, and the local chamber of commerce. For certificates of need, the program may wish to consult an attorney experienced in navigating these waters.

A next section of the business plan considers the scope of services to be provided. The classic method is a "needs" analysis. Traditionally, a needs analysis tries to estimate, by some methodology, the number of persons to be served and then considers the particular treatment needs of the population. Once these parameters are developed, program planning can be fleshed out. Often the needs analysis process results in a statement of program needs without the fundamental analysis of the customer population being thoroughly explored. For example, an inpatient program designer may automatically decide that a treatment team consists of a psychiatrist, psychologist, social worker, and occupational therapist. The nature of the illnesses prevalent in the community and the acuity of illness to be treated on the unit may argue for a different mix of professional staff.

Estimating the prevalence of the illness in the community is often a first step in needs analysis. Most new programs lack the resources to mount such a study. Fortunately several large-scale studies have been performed in recent years that may provide a basis for estimate, providing that the catchments studied bear some resemblance to the community of the proposed new program (Bassett, Chase, Folstein, & Regier, 1998; Narrow et al., 2000; Regier et al., 1984). Sampling techniques are difficult, as most random inhabitants of an area don't appreciate surveyors inquiring about their emotional life or mental health treatment history. Other methodologies include examining the needs of persons already in service (Kales et al., 2000) in a program at another site or at a similar agency, or surveying emergency rooms to find out the numbers and types of mental health problems previously untreated patients present.

Whatever the counting method, planners are then confronted with elaborating on the treatment needs of the proposed patients. Here planners should combine professional standards with patients' own ideas of their needs. For example, Maple Manor's planners might pay careful attention to Beth Tanzman's recent report (Tanzman, 1993) on national surveys of mental health service recipients solicited through state and local mental health agencies and residential service providers. She was able to summarize data from 26 of these studies that permitted comparability of data. This overview reported that consumers consistently preferred to live in their own house or apartment, to live alone or with a spouse or romantic partner, and not to live with other mental health consumers. They sought typical social roles and did not wish to be grouped on the basis of disability. Consumers had a strong preference for outreach staff support available on call; few respondents wanted to live with staff. Material supports such as money, rent subsidies, telephone service, and transportation were deemed to be important for community living to be successful (Tanzman, 1993).

In a subsequent article in the same journal, Marty Knisley, reporting on her experience in implementing a revised system of care more responsive to the preferences just described, noted that financing of housing and supports was less difficult than securing the staff, developing procedures, and keeping the project viable. In

Ohio, each community mental health board was asked to develop a plan for residential services and housing options that incorporated the element of choice for consumers plus community treatment and flexible supports. They were encouraged to create housing development corporations that were committed to finding scattered-site housing integrated in the community (Knisley & Fleming, 1993).

Finally, planners must estimate the proportion of those for whom services are appropriate who will utilize the new program. This estimate involves consideration of alternative provider capacity, transportation issues, costs of service in the new program, potential payers, and so on. The ensuing business plan rests on a cogent and adequate needs analysis. This parallels the market analysis business conducts before introducing a new product and is fundamental to decisions about whether to proceed.

In the course of the planning process, the visionaries may wish to christen the new venture. It is not necessary to do so in the business plan. A lawyerly term of art such as "Newco" will suffice for all the planning documents. Naming, however, offers the opportunity to garner publicity, for example, by seeking public input into the name. A contest among potential participants may spark some interest. A name offers the early planners a route to identifying with the new program and helps build some loyalty and motivation even in the planning process. Should the name conjure up a sense of the program's goals, its desired image, or its location? The planners will agonize over these sorts of considerations. Not when, but how naming takes place determines whether the morale and success enhancing opportunity is fully realized.

Even when a proposed venture encompasses novel professional strategies, it is likely that there are other vendors of either similar services or different efforts to serve similar patients. These programs may operate in direct competition, may be complementary, or may not have relevance to the proposed venture. Cataloguing the other community programs in the area proposed for the enterprise's operations is a critical part of the business plan. This recitation of vendors will consider their capacities, whether they serve similar, overlapping, or different target populations, their occupancy or portion of capacity currently utilized, their growth or downsizing trajectories, their payer mix, and recruitment issues. How has the community received such programs? What rates have purchasers been willing to pay? The planners must draw on this experience and analyze its significance for the new venture. Often all these blanks may be difficult to fill in, as programs regard some of this material as confidential. Nonetheless, most mental health program operators welcome expansion of service capacity in the community and will try to be helpful if an effort is made to seek their guidance.

Furthermore, the process of visiting and learning about the vicissitudes of potential sister agencies can be helpful in amplifying issues in the local business environment. What are the neighbors' reactions? How supportive have local politicians been? Do they serve on any governing boards? Have the media been cordial or belligerent? Is there an organized association of mental health service agencies? What is the regulatory environment? These are but a few of the questions that can be explored with existing provider agencies even if there is little direct overlap of their program design or goals. Consideration of these issues in narrative form not only reflects a thorough and conscientious approach to business planning, but also will reassure potential financial backers that they are dealing with competent operators and a well-considered plan.

Finally, any consideration of the business environment for a new mental health program must explore the current expectations of the intermediaries of third-party payers, that is, "managed care." What is the penetrance of managed care in the community? Which firms are acting as intermediaries and what is the status of their provider panels? Will they be willing to include the new services in their benefit structures and what rules will be applied? Do self-contained prepaid plans like "health maintenance organizations" exist in the area, and if so, are mental health services included in their obligations or are such services "carved out" to mental health contractors? Are such contractors open to inclusion of the new program and what will they pay for the service? Will they prefer prepayment on a capitated basis? The insurance environment is rapidly changing and providers are scrambling to maintain a grasp of new expectations. The business plan will recognize this aspect of doing business and anticipate how the new enterprise will fit (Mechanic, 1999).

The section on methods of carrying out mission and organizational structure constitutes the "meat" of the business plan. Here the visionaries must describe in a manner that even a layperson can understand how the mission and goals will be accomplished. How will staff members spend their day? Who will supervise them? How will the activity of the program bring about the desired mental health objectives? Part of the description of the program's activity consists of references to the professional literature and experience that supports the validity of the approach. The proposed organizational structure should support the mission. For example, the military has evolved a rigid, hierarchically structured chain-of-command organization. Other organizations reject this pyramidal configuration in favor of a flatter structure with multiple pods relating to the leadership. Various matrix structures have been prominent in mental health service organizations. Typically there are multidisciplinary service teams forming coherent organizational units, and there is administrative supervision through a set of discipline-based service chiefs.

No ideal organizational pattern fits all, but an experienced administrator can often spot trouble areas that may erupt in day-to-day operations by comparing the structure with the proposed program's goals and methods. Some of the critical questions include: How is the executive function carried out? What is the relationship of financial managers to the professional operations? What is the relationship of governance to the professional staff? How are requests from professionals for administrative support trafficked and prioritized within the organization? For smaller programs these issues may be relatively condensed and simpler than for a large multiservice agency. In any case, the more carefully the program's operations and administrative organization are detailed, the stronger the business plan.

The plan will list all proposed full- and part-time staff positions. It will also describe the functions to be contractually provided, buildings and/or rented sites with their square footage, mechanical requirements, and program capacities, as well as furniture and equipment, expected consumables and their rate of utilization, vehicles, pharmaceuticals to be stocked, and any other items that may be program specific. This enumeration will be important in calculating start-up and operating budget. Generally the planners will include brief explanations of the relevance of each of the major resources sought for specific parts of the program plan.

The most often thought-about siting issue for a mental health program is the receptivity of the neighbors. This is especially true for a residential program to be located in a quiet residential neighborhood. Proximity to public transportation, basic shopping, cinema, and recreational facilities is especially desirable. Depending on the nature of the services and design, other considerations may arise, such as availability of adequate medical care and job opportunities nearby, local emergency rooms' psychiatric capability, and availability in the local community of professional staff who might be willing to work in the new program.

Not only is a welcoming community desirable, but also a welcoming physical plant. Whether an outpatient office or a residential treatment program, the structure should not be intimidating or overly pretentious. Generally, the more homelike and the less institutional the structure, the more likely it is that a patient will feel comfortable and open to the work. A particular consideration is whether the premises are accessible to those in wheelchairs or using crutches or other mobility devices. Federal law and the requirements of most jurisdictions for public accommodations now require compliance in this area, particularly for new construction.

Fire and life safety issues must be addressed in the plan. Some special considerations include visible fire alarms for the deaf and hard of hearing; automated linkages to the local fire station for residential programs; doors that can always be opened from the inside of the building; smoke detectors and fire extinguishers; and so on. Programs serving the public must be aware of and comply with local fire and life safety codes.

Finally, planners will describe the internal "environment of care." What sort of ambience does the service wish to project? Color scheme, furnishings, and wall hangings all contribute to this image. Sometimes ease of maintenance is weighed against the desires of the program's professional staff, as in the decision of whether to carpet or use washable resilient flooring, or whether to use upholstered or vinyl furniture. Notwithstanding final administrative decisions on these specifics, the business plan should at least address the desired environmental ambience.

After the planning group has laid out the mission, outlined the administrative structure, and listed the resources needed, a very worthwhile exercise is to draft a description of how the program will run on a day-to-day basis. Who will do what, and how will their activities interface with the activities of others? How will staff be supervised and operational variances be managed? What about privileging, credentialing, and due process issues related to staff management? How will customers move through the program? How will the different arms of the agency interact with each other, the clients, and the public? The operational description is a different focus than the structural considerations so far developed in the plan. The effort to articulate the operational plan may suggest changes in the administrative structure or in the resource list.

In addition, planners may wish to consider which services should be cemented by formal interagency agreements. Often an extraorganizational agreement is obtained with the local hospital to provide backup health and mental health services. The program may wish to have a specified protocol with local police to assist with elopement or other untoward situations that may arise in the context of ongoing operations. Other such agreements may be worthwhile according to the nature of the service program. To the extent that planners are able to identify the areas where interagency cooperation should be formally specified in writing, these agreements should be included in the business plan.

The business plan should address three important aspects of the financial plan. Where is the cash coming from for start-up and for ongoing operations? How will the operating funds be stored? What will be done with cash excesses that may accumulate? Financing for the initiation of a mental health business is typically supplied by granting agencies, banks, donors, or other sources. Usually fees or prepayments by customers should be sufficient to finance ongoing operations. Finally, the business plan should give some indication of the proposed management of excess funds. For example, will the business permit such funds to be invested in equities or will such funds be limited to insured accounts? What will be the steps to access reserved or investment funds? Although some of these decisions may await experience in operations, the planner may wish to develop some preliminary financial guidance for the future and also to reassure potential funding resources that such matters have been thought through.

If the ongoing health of the enterprise depends on receipts from customers, how will the program inform the public of its existence and mission? The planners will develop an initial and ongoing plan for "marketing" or advertising the program. An initial step, as we noted, might be accomplished in the assembly of a group of planners, surveys of potential clients and related agencies, and public mission planning meetings. The first formal marketing vehicle is the business plan itself. This document markets to potential funding, licensing, granting, and advocacy groups by elaborating on the program's goals, ownership, and operational plans. The business plan may be excerpted for promotional pamphlets and other literature. The initiation of operations may occasion special marketing activities such as open house and media public service announcements. Ongoing marketing activities may be episodic, such as during mental health month and employee open enrollment periods, or may be continuous such as weekly newspaper advertisements or regular sponsorship of community activities such as Little League, advocacy group meetings, and so on. Whatever the sort of marketing effort, the objectives of the campaign should be identified and the choice of medium should be appropriate to the goals. Media consultants usually recommend some sort of survey before and after marketing efforts to discover whether objectives have been met. Whether for profit or not for profit, the success of any service venture depends on customers finding out about it. The marketing plans detail how the new program will make sure that it is widely known, at least within its service area. Sometimes mental health programs are in a conflicted situation with regard to marketing, as they wish to let potential customers know of the program, but may not wish broad publicity to the general public, especially for residential settings such as Maple Manor.

The business plan will contain a summary of performance expectations for the enterprise. These are usually expressed in both programmatic and fiscal terms. The programmatic measures may be volumetric, such as number of patients served or number of hours of therapy delivered. These measures may also be expressed in terms of outcomes for customers. Such measures may include reduction in symptoms, days of gainful employment, minimization of inpatient hospitalization and emergency-room utilization, days of clients maintaining independent living situations, or other program-specific parameters. Measures of success or failure in pursuit of the mission provide program incentives for staff and participants, and for funding sources a vision of the reasons to provide continued support (Manderscheid, 2000; Smith et al., 1997).

Generally the business plan will contain a listing of needed personnel and include some proposed personnel hiring procedures as well as some vision of a proposed pay plan. Will the program be an equal opportunity employer? Will disabled citizens or military veterans be given hiring preference? Will there be a health insurance plan with choices of options? Will there be profit sharing? Will pay increments be based on changes in cost of living or merit based or both? Will pay for professional work be on a straight salary basis or based on productivity? These are some of the questions that the planners may wish to address proactively in the business plan. The full detail of personnel procedures will await operations. A thorough discussion of personnel policy may be found in another section of this book.

We live in a "computer age." A contemporary business plan does not rely on handwritten or typed general ledgers. Most professional practices keep their patient records in handwritten charts, their client lists in computer databases, and their financial general ledgers in computer spreadsheets. There are many off-the-shelf software programs that offer practice management or small business management capabilities. Some specialized mental health packages include evaluation, diagnosis, prescription, and progress note capabilities. Once a business starts down a particular management information system approach, it is hard to change. Data from one application rarely translate easily to another. Furthermore, electronic data systems are rapidly evolving. Because payers often expect electronic claims submission from vendors, firms providing data intermediary services have developed that translate your claims into data submissions that are appropriate to the particular payer. Please refer to the extensive section in this handbook on data management and technology for further discussion.

Beyond accounts receivable and payable, management information systems have the capacity to generate composite and sorted information that may have strategic planning value for an organization. The practice may garner, for example, instant readout of diagnostic mix of recipients of service, types of medications used, productivity per staff member, and outcomes data cross-matched against individual practitioner or program components. The difficulty is in figuring out what questions the organization wants asked regularly, what questions might be asked occasionally or ad hoc, and what questions might be asked in the future. Knowing the answers to this will direct the staff in capturing data elements from the inception of the program. Rather than simplifying the planning task, the "computer age" has enormously complicated it. Nonetheless, the process of thinking through the data challenges will strengthen the business plan and the competitiveness of the organization in the marketplace. Clearly, one of the most likely components of a modern business plan will be the inclusion in the personnel list of a management information specialist and/or programmer and an ongoing group or committee to attend to the data needs of the enterprise.

Most standard procedures for an organization are constructed during operations rather than as part of the business plan. The planners may wish to suggest how the new program contemplates assembling its policy and procedure manuals. Will the writing of procedures be the responsibility of the medical director or will there be a committee? Who will chair and who will sit on it? What will be the review schedule and publication procedure? Although such issues may be more significant for a large and complex organization such as a hospital, the planners of the new program will want to think about the format for communication of expected behaviors and responses to the entire staff. It will also be necessary to describe the linkage between policy and procedure documents and new employee orientation.

Every mental health organization is concerned about the quality and consistency of the services delivered. Approaches can include audits, ad hoc studies, and quality circles, prospective monitoring, retrospective reviews, and quality monitors, to name a few. A consideration of the various techniques is beyond the scope of this section, but there are many sources that explore quality control techniques and theory. The business plan will outline some of the planned approaches to quality control both structurally and operationally, but anticipate considerable flexibility in evolving the overall program. Key elements in any successful quality management system are active involvement of staff at all levels and consistent support, interest, and follow-through on the part of the administrators.

No matter the success of quality control or business planning, the program will need to anticipate unexpected risks. These may come in the form of accidental injuries, patient elopements, lawsuits secondary to poor outcomes, disgruntled employees, property damage, or other hazards. In addition to a formal risk management program directed at keeping staff members tuned to good standards of practice, the program will need liability insurance and access to legal counsel. Choosing legal counsel is discussed in the legal section of this handbook. Although good documentation and attention to following the program's procedures will minimize exposure, the likelihood of damage claims is high. Anyone reviewing the business plan with an eye toward providing financial support will expect to see attention to insurance and protection against catastrophic losses. Often the business plan will list the names and credentials of the proposed insurance firm, lawyers, accountants, and other business consultants who will provide ongoing professional consultation.

Finally, the planners must consider any other areas of concern that apply to this new program in particular. These additions to the business plan may include protocols for records management and the maintenance of confidentiality. Generally, states have enacted statutes governing the confidentiality of health and especially mental health records. These laws usually deal with the conditions under which such records may be released or disclosed. There are also mandatory disclosures required in certain criminal matters, such as when the insanity defense is introduced and, in some cases, when there is allegation of child sexual abuse. In addition to the business plan addressing how the program will comply with applicable law in this area, the planners should describe how the members of the workforce will be sensitized to the issue and the program's policies on privacy. It may be appropriate to expand on the general issue of records management and storage, including how long inactive records will be retained.

In addition to confidentiality issues, planners should address data security issues. These include designation of who has access to which records, the lock status of records, and provisions for reconstruction of records in the event of fire or other calamity. Such concerns are often considered separately for client medical/psychiatric records and for general business and financial records. Electronic data have the potential for greater security and recoverability than do paper-based records. Electronic media offer many off-site mechanisms for backing up critical records, whether web-based security boxes or transportable media. It is unwieldy to duplicate and cart off patient charts nightly or even weekly. Most professional offices do not store patient records even in fireproof files. Paper-based client records are also subject to unauthorized scrutiny if they are not properly secured except during active staff use. Charts in a pile waiting to be filed are vulnerable. Electronic charts can be password protected or subject to even higher-level identification, such a the recognition of personal attributes of authorized users (fingerprints, voiceprints, facial recognition software, etc.). However, there is no system that cannot be breached by persistent snoops or as a result of carelessness. Most programs have computerized their business records and maintain manual client records. The planners will seek a compromise solution that responsibly balances practical access with adequate safeguards against privacy violation and data loss.

It may also be useful for the planners to seek legal review to make sure that the program's business plan does not contain any unwanted expressed or implied warranties to the public or to the clients. Although community safety and patient recovery are goals, there should be no guarantees contained in the documents that these outcomes will be achieved.

REFERENCES

Bassett, S. S., Chase, G. A., Folstein, M. F., & Regier, D. A. (1998). Disability and psychiatric disorders in an urban community: Measurement, prevalence and outcomes. *Psychological Medicine, 28*(3), 509–517.

Kales, H. C., Blow, F. C., Bingham, C. R. Roberts, J. S., Copeland, L. A., & Mellow, A. M. (2000). Race, psychiatric diagnosis, and mental health care utilization in older patients. *American Journal of Geriatric Psychiatry, 8*(4), 301–309.

Knisley, M. B., & Fleming, M. (1993). Implementing supported housing in state and local mental health systems. *Hospital and Community Psychiatry, 44*(5), 456–461.

Manderscheid, R. W. (2000). The measurement and management of clinical outcomes in mental health. *American Journal of Psychiatry, 157*(11), 1903–1904.

Mechanic, D. (1999). *Mental health and social policy: The emergence of managed care.* Needham Heights, MA: Allyn and Bacon.

Narrow, W. E., Regier, D. A., Norquist, G., Rae, D. S., Kennedy, C., & Arons, B. (2000). Mental health service use by Americans with severe mental illnesses. *Social Psychiatry and Psychiatric Epidemiology, 35*(4), 147–155.

Regier, D. A., et al (1984). The NIMH Epidemiologic Catchment Area Program: historical context, major objectives, and study population characteristics. *Archives of General Psychiatry, 41,* 934–941.

Smith, G. R., Jr., Manderscheid, R. W., Flynn, L. M., & Steinwachs, D. M. (1997). Principles for assessment of patient outcomes in mental health care. *Psychiatric Services, 48*(8), 1033–1036.

Tanzman, B. (1993). An overview of surveys of mental health consumers' preferences for housing and support services. *Hospital and Community Psychiatry, 44*(5), 450–455.

Chapter Twenty-One

Budget

Stuart B. Silver

Many people think that the budget process is about conserving dollars. Many families despise the budget as a straitjacket in which their lives are bound. This chapter considers the budget process to be about ideas. The budget breathes life into abstraction; it is the crucible from which ideas can take form. Yet the budget is in itself an abstraction that reflects the values and creativity of all the participants in the enterprise. Budgeting is not a task for the accountants and fiscal managers alone. It is the responsibility of each member of the organization. The budget is both a plan and a management tool. How closely the actual experience of an organization tracks the budget reflects the care, professional experience, and diligence of the entire organization in budget preparation (Dropkin & LaTouche, 1998).

Budgeting is called a process because it is an ongoing task. Often the process is called the *budget cycle.* In many organizations there are set dates for the various tasks of budgeting to be completed. The cycle typically consists of long-range economic forecasting, assembling long-term requests and unfulfilled priorities, short-range economic forecasting, constructing the first draft of the projected spending plan and revenue forecast, review and refinement, finished draft, review and submission to the governing body, final revisions, adoption by the governing body, and implementation. Clearly, these steps may require more than a whole year to complete. If the organization runs on an annual budget, there may be several budgets being monitored simultaneously. For example, there may be long-range planning for 2 years hence, detailed budget construction for next year, management of the current year's budget, and review of last year's budget and experience. Thus, four budgets are alive for the fiscal managers in any given year. Some of the tasks, such as economic forecasting, may appear beyond the scope of the average staff member, but if individual staff members notice, for example, the income trends among recipients of service, that information may materially contribute to the job of economic forecasting.

Various management experts have described many methodologies of budget preparation. The most usual approach is one that draws on prior years' experience and then incorporates new initiatives, deletes discontinued activities, and adjusts for inflation and projected revenue changes. The "experience-based" budget is relatively straightforward and the process is not difficult to understand. Some have advocated for a "zero-based" budget. This method takes the approach that each annual budget is constructed from the ground up. Each area of expenditure must be scrutinized and justified each year; nothing continues automatically. This process encourages careful review of all activities, but it is very time-consuming and requires a heavy commitment of managerial time. It is the approach of a new organization, but because of its unwieldiness, it has not found favor with established businesses.

The budget may be expressed as a "line item" or "program" budget. In the former, each significant item of expenditure is enumerated. In the latter, broad categories of expenditure within certain defined programs are specified, but the managers of these programs are afforded considerable flexibility in spending within the overall budgeted limits (Babigian, 1983).

The overall complexity of the budgeting process depends on the size and complexity of the organization. It can be relatively simple for a sole proprietor of a small office, or require a separate staff, or in the case of state government, an entire executive branch agency. Whatever the complexity, all members of the staff should be oriented to the budget cycle and their role in it. Ideally there is an ongoing exchange between those entrusted with preparing the budget and those required to operate within it. Nothing is more frustrating for a budgeteer than to have omitted an important item of new expenditure that was not requested by the relevant managers during budget preparation. Similarly, it is equally frustrating for a front-line manager to find a significant request omitted from the budget without a dialogue with fiscal management and leadership about the reasons for the deletion and the alternatives available. As in any complex relationship, accurate and honest communication is critical in preserving teamwork. A vignette taken from a recent presentation by the author may illustrate the dangers of neglecting this principle:

Boundary Setting and the Maryland Psychiatric Research Center

When Dr. Will Carpenter came to the University of Maryland, he revitalized the Maryland Psychiatric Research Center. Located on the grounds of Spring Grove State Hospital, the Research Center has evolved into a major site of basic and treatment-oriented scientific research on schizophrenia. It provides clinical services as well, including a clinic for the evaluation and treatment of neuroleptic induced motor disorders, an outpatient service, and an inpatient unit focusing on patients whose illnesses do not respond to standard treatments. The Mental Hygiene Administration provides the infrastructure; the University provides faculty appointments, staff direction, and the base for attaining grants to support research. Under an agreement developed when Dr. Carpenter arrived from NIMH, state funding for the Research Center came into Mental Hygiene Administration's budget and was pegged at 1% of the budget for mental health services, at that time about $2.5 million.

Each year, the budget director of the Department of Health and Mental Hygiene would question why research was in the budget at all, as he attempted to fit all the department's obligations within the spending levels assigned by the governor's budget bureau. Research belonged, in his judgment, in the University's budget, not the budget of an underfunded service department.

Early in my tenure as Director of the Mental Hygiene Administration, the department's budget director struck. Without discussion with me, he placed the entire budget of the Research Center on the cut list. His private reasoning was that the University of Maryland would somehow pick up the cost to preserve the facility and the Department would be rid of that obligation. If such a transfer had been properly negotiated, the Department would have had to transfer resources to the University system, but a surprise last-minute cut would have either crippled the facility or forced the University to have created the necessary funding by reducing other expenditures.

Needless to say, this was hardball politics between the Health Department and the University. The Secretary of Health had apparently been burned in the Medicaid program. The federal Health Care Financing Administration had, on audit, disallowed University Hospital Medicaid charges. The University had never reimbursed the Secretary for the lost federal funds, thereby creating a shortfall in the Department's budget. She was pleased at the revenge anticipated by sticking the University with the Maryland Psychiatric Research Center and no cash.

Even the State's Department of Budget felt the Secretary had gone too far with this gambit, but in deference to her wishes, the Research Center's budget was halved. I first learned of this cut when the budget bill crossed my desk. The Governor would be requesting from the legislative appropriations process only half the funds needed to operate the Center. Maryland is an executive budget state; the General Assembly can only reduce the Governor's request; they cannot add to it. My job was to explain the mental health budget to the legislature and to minimize any further cutting.

Let me put some of this in perspective. The Research Center cost had grown with our increasing budget to about $3 million in state funds and brought in about $1.5 million in grants from outside sources. The mental health budget was then about $300 million in state funds and $50 million in other funds. The budget of the Health Department was $2 billion. The Research Center was an operation of the Department of Psychiatry at the medical school. The medical school interests are dominated by surgery and medicine. The medical school is part of what is called the University of Maryland at Baltimore (UMAB). UMAB is one of many campuses that make up the University of Maryland System. In short, the head bureaucrats who run the University are farther removed from and less invested in the overall success of the Maryland Psychiatric Research Center than are the leaders of the health department. The notion that the University would bail out the Research Center was, to my mind, fatuous.

I also considered it unacceptable that the Secretary, on the advice of her budget director, would decide where to cut the mental health budget without substantial discussions with myself as Administration Director. When I confronted the offending budgeteer, his response was, "We knew you'd never agree to it and we needed to find the money!"

I was furious. Setting mental health priorities is the job of the Mental Hygiene Administration in collaboration with many stakeholders and the Secretary. If this kind of budget action could be taken without consultation, who needed a director of mental health? It wasn't the size of the cut as a percentage of our budget; it was the process.

I gathered my emotional responses, set them aside, and at my meeting with the Secretary, gently told her that she and we would need to part ways as I could not support the Governor's budget proposal as presented to the legislature. When she protested that the cut was necessary to fit within the department's overall spending limits, I indicated that I was not at all interested in resigning over $1.5 million of cuts, but rather over the process and the fact that with the publication of the budget, there was no turning back. She asked me to think it over for a week and indicated she would do the same.

This confrontational approach may seem to be a very dangerous strategy on my part, if I really relished keeping the job of Director. Ordinarily, that might be right, but these events occurred rather close in time to the firing of the previous Director, which had cost her a lot of political points. I didn't think she would risk driving off another Director so soon.

Hardball begets hardball. But please notice that I was very careful not to question the Secretary's request for the Administration to pitch $1.5 million into the Department's budget plan. I wasn't happy about it, but was not willing to challenge a decision she had made that was appropriately within her discretion. I, therefore, did not risk being seen as not a "team player." In fact, I had carefully shifted that onus onto the Secretary herself for not properly using the team.

Toward the end of the week, the Department's budget director came to my office. The Secretary had sent him to see if I could be persuaded to change my mind about leaving. What could be done? My response was that there were three requirements to make it right. The first was that I would be given full discretion over where to find the $1.5 million in the mental health budget. The second was that the Governor and Secretary would issue a joint statement to be presented at the mental health budget hearing indicating their full support of the Maryland Psychiatric Research Center and expressing their regret that in the pressure of final budget formulation a mistake was made and that the funds would be restored from within the Department's resources. The third was that changes in mental health budget priorities would not again happen without full consultation with the Mental Hygiene Administration.

These terms were accepted. The resolution had the effect of reestablishing teamwork among the Budget Bureau, the Governor, the Secretary, and the Administration. We were asked to draft a statement for the Governor and Secretary to issue. I remained on the job, and the Maryland Psychiatric Research Center budget has been stable ever since. (Silver, 1997)

Although the business plan is a narrative of the vision for the enterprise and the mechanics of realizing that vision, the budget is the financial outline of the vision. It represents a plan of a different sort, but one that is equally challenging to construct. This chapter considers the task of converting the business plan into dollar equivalencies, arranging the business assumptions expressed in this manner in a logical sequence, analyzing the result, and using the analysis to revise the business plan. The goal is a viable financial plan to accompany the vision of the business plan. One works back and forth between the documents much as one solves a crossword puzzle, sometimes being sure of the definitions and at other times using the context clues in the grid to figure out the possible correct entries (Dickey, 1992).

The first step of the process is to estimate the income that may accrue to the business by month from all sources. The business plan for Maple Manor anticipated a certain volume of services per month and possible grant funding. A starting venture may have growing income as the year progresses. An established business has prior history of income and monthly variations. After the income has been estimated by what the planners consider to be reasonable assumptions of volume and pricing, the second task is to convert the various requirements of the business plan into items of expense. In a new venture, these may increase monthly, whereas in an established business, prior history is useful. Some of the expenses may be fixed, such as rent, whereas others may be variable, based on numbers of services provided, such as certain salaries, chart materials, supplies, and so on. At a certain volume of sales, the income will equal the fixed costs and associated variable costs, the "break-even point," beyond which additional revenue should exceed variable expenses and a surplus or profit may be generated. Although the preceding general formulation seems simple and self-evident, getting to the numbers is complex and difficult.

In the business plan, the planners estimated the proportion of those for whom services were appropriate who would utilize the program. The process paralleled a market analysis and was considered fundamental to decisions about whether to proceed. The budget process converts the best estimate of numbers of customers and their needs to various service patterns and their projected price tags. The products might include, in the Maple Manor example, psychotherapy, management of medications, emergency visits, in-home support staff, and vocational services. For a new business to estimate what proportion of the potential customer base would purchase which of the available services requires a substantial extrapolation. The more detailed the business planning process, and the more careful the needs estimating methods, the more believable will be this estimate of service volumes to be delivered in the given budget cycle.

The next step obviously involves converting sales into dollars by establishing the price of each item sold. Price can be derived in several different ways. These strategies may each be employed and then reconciled one with the other. For example, the budget maker may save pricing for the end and, after adding all the cost and capacities, compute an actual cost for each service and set the price accordingly. Alternatively, the program director may know the competitive costs for similar services in the community and instruct the budget maker to make a competitive pricing strategy work by fitting the program variables into the total revenue that may be generated at those prices. There may be external forces, notably insurers, which set prices independent of any specific program's operations. If there are preset prices, then the program budget must fit within that pricing structure. Overhead costs such as rent, marketing, and administrative costs may be equally applied as a percentage increment to all services. Alternatively, a cost-finding methodology may attribute to each service those overhead components that the service actually uses (Brice, 1987). Thus, the in-home support team's rates may include very little rental of space costs, but might include substantial transportation costs. The group psychotherapy, in contrast, may include more floor space and housekeeping charges in its rate. The decision of which methodology to use may depend on the requirements of funding agencies, or it may be driven by which produces the most competitive prices for most services. Thus the various pricing strategies may each need to be tried, and some unique formula-based derivative method may ultimately be adopted to serve the program's needs.

As already discussed, a component of pricing examines the sources of funds, their payment schedules, and their requirements. The most widespread template for pricing services is *Current Procedural Terminology* (American Medical Association, 2001), a compendium of generally accepted medical and psychiatric services and accompanying codes that are generally recognized by third-party payers. Although pricing by "CPT codes" may serve a traditional inpatient or outpatient psychiatric service, many innovative services have not yet made their way into the manual. Furthermore, certain composite services may not readily parse into CPT nomenclature. This approach has widest applicability in fee-for-service settings. In programs funded by large grants or by capitation payments, the use of procedural codes may be required for record-keeping by the funding agency, may be useful to the program for internal management record-keeping and analysis, or may be irrelevant.

A program funded by only one type of payer is vulnerable to the vicissitudes of that payer's existence but has a simple analysis of fund source. Play by the payer's rules. Most mental health programs receive funds from a variety of payers, each with different billing and accounting requirements, payment methodologies, and data-keeping requirements. This is explored in a later chapter, "Payers and Players."

For budgeting purposes, the mix of patients and their source of payment may provide guidance on the costs of collecting payments, the likely contribution of different service packages offered by the program to the total bottom line, the timing of receipts, and a reasonable projection of fund balances at different points in time. An accurate forecast of revenues is a critical component of the budget and should be conservative in its assumptions. This means, for example, that allowances are made for pro bono work and bad debt, for delays due to poor entry of data, to wrong insurance numbers, to payer tardiness, and to disallowance due to fee changes or disagreements about medical necessity. There are many ways in which payers stall, no matter how well-intentioned or ethical they are. Many states have enacted "prompt payment" laws governing public agencies, requiring payment of invoices within 30 days, because of vendor complaints about bureaucratic inertia. Therefore, analysis of sources of funds should also take into account their payment history to other vendors, including average age of accounts when paid, use of electronic fund transfers, frequency of disputes, and average percent of dollars billed to the payer that are ultimately collected. In developing this analysis for a new program, information from sister programs with parallel experiences is invaluable. This includes learning the results of their fund-raising activities (those not connected with payment for services) in order not to overproject charitable receipts.

Ultimately, most revenues will be contingent on services provided. The budget draws on the business plan for types of services, estimates of number of people to be served, projected physical plant size, and total staff. These projections are then translated into capacities. How many of what types of services can the program's components as budgeted deliver? Getting to program capacity will require calculations of workload of individual staff members, accrediting body expectations of space per patient, expectations of appointments not kept ("no-show rates"), and infrastructure reserve. These computations yield a check and balance on the revenue forecast, which should not anticipate receipts, based on billings or grant expectations that would exceed the program's capacity to deliver the services. Although it is a simple concept, its application requires that the revenue analysis and the program capacity analysis be independently constructed as much as possible.

Fundamental to the determination of program capacity is the assessment of workload per staff member. For the professional staff, this may mean how many appointments they can schedule per day or week. Because appointment times may vary by type of service, this is usually expressed as "billable hours." How much preparation time is needed for each billable hour? How much allowance should be made for wasted time? Are some billable hours' activities more valuable in the marketplace than other hours? Are payments to the professional staff based on billings or are they straight salary or some combination? Do some services require more time overhead than others do? For example, child psychiatric consultations often necessitate time interacting with parents, schools and teachers, and other child-serving agencies. In-home services require travel time by the staff members. Workload determination requires close collaboration between management and workers to avoid expectations that are beyond the ability of either supervisor to deliver or staff to produce (Finney, 1995).

Part of this exercise requires building in assumptions about total available employee time. How many days will be lost to vacations, holiday leave, sick leave, personal leave, and so on? Thus, personnel policy contributes to this phase of budgeting. Furthermore, some positions may require 24-hour coverage 7 days per week. Usually, 1.5 to 1.8 employees are required for 7-day-a-week coverage, depending on the benefit package. Therefore, as many as 5.4 full-time-equivalent employees may be needed to cover one duty station around the clock. All these issues coalesce to yield an estimate of the efficiency of the program, the ratio of revenue-generating time produced to total staff hours purchased by the program.

For most organizations that produce mental health services, the largest single item of budgeted cost consists of payment to personnel. In a hospital program, with its staff-intensive 24-hour care requirement, 60% to 80% of the annual budget may be payroll. For an outpatient program, 30% to 60% of the budget is typically salary and benefits. Thus, personnel policy is one of the most important parts of the budgeting and administrative requirement of the enterprise. An entire section of this book is therefore directed toward personnel issues.

When there are few employees, the pay plan may be relatively idiosyncratic and ad hoc; when there are many employees, the pay plan will need to be carefully constructed and durable. Forces affecting pay include the current salaries in the local market for the various skills needed, the need to provide some salary advancement potential without having longer-term employees price themselves out of a competitive range, the realities of program revenue potential, the relative pay offered to employees in different classifications, and so on. A balance must be struck between the program's desire to offer reasonable remuneration to its employees and its need to live within its means. An often-small change in pay for one group of employees provides a ripple effect through the workforce, rapidly escalating total personnel costs. Decisions about length of the work week, overtime eligibility, and holidays observed translate into costs that the program must meet in its budget process. Part of unavoidable annual budget escalation is "structural" inflation resulting from employee raises contained in the salary plan, which may provide for increment at various anniversaries of employment, merit raises, and reclassifications leading to higher pay. Furthermore, the cost of employee-based employer-paid taxes, such as FICA, state, and local levies (for injured workers' compensation, for example), must be added to the budget for employees (Newman & Sorensen, 1985).

Additional adjustments of the budget take into account other personnel costs. These include the lost revenue cost or computed payroll cost of providing coverage during employee vacations as well as during other occasions such as personal, compassionate, and sickness leave. The organization may permit accrual of leave from year to year and may increase rates of leave accrual with seniority or length of employment. There also may be direct costs of the employer's contribution to health, disability, life insurance, and retirement plans. Other administrative costs may attach to employee benefits such as those cited, as well as deferred spending accounts and expense accounts. The program may incur additional costs related to time lost due to employee injury and costs associated with workers' compensation. All of these costs must be recognized and provided for in the budget.

Ancillary services such as housekeeping, security, professional consultants, and food and laundry, where applicable, are often provided by independent contractors, rather than though the salaried workforce. Often these services are procured through a process of "competitive bidding." At the level of government, procurement rules are usually complex and highly structured to preserve fair and open access to any qualified vendor who seeks to render publicly funded services. A small business may simply pick someone in the telephone book to fix a broken piece of office equipment. The choice may be based on proximity, convenience of hours, or simply friendship with the repairman. Public enterprises and large organizations tend to structure such transactions in procurement rules or regulations. Often for emergency small items, three solicited bids may suffice. For larger ventures, a request for proposals is published in a number of locations. These "RFPs" require vendors to supply qualifications, offer written bids, and often post bonds. A well-constructed budget will anticipate the actual costs of such activities and avoid cost overruns.

The salary costs that do not directly produce revenue as well as other costs of doing business are often collectively referred to as *overhead*. The use of this term is often an idiosyncratic construct of a particular business entity, but in general it refers to the costs incurred that are necessary to support the provision of reimbursable service. The term *salary overhead* refers to the tax and benefits attached to payroll. General overhead includes rent, supplies, ancillaries, insurance, advertising, and so on. Businesses strive to maintain "overhead" expenditures at a low level, if possible. The utility of the concept of overhead varies depending on the nature of the business and its products. A professional provider is very concerned with "overhead" in the outpatient office budget, as it eats into the proportion of overall revenue headed for the provider's pocket. In looking at the overall costs of surgical care, a hospital's budget may be entirely considered as overhead to surgeons' fees. This way of analyzing budgets has contributed, for example, to the growth of ambulatory "surgi-centers" costing far less than hospitals.

The gradual loss of value of equipment through age, usage, and obsolescence is known as *depreciation* (Costales & Szurovy, 1994). Items depreciate at different rates. For example, the useful life of a vehicle may be 8 years or 100,000 miles, whereas a computer may no longer meet business needs after 4 years. A building may depreciate over 20 or 30 years. A later chapter will consider this concept as addressed in corporate balance sheets. The budget implications, however, are also important. When a budget is constructed based on prior spending patterns, major one-time purchases may not be reflected. Furthermore, impending major expenses may be overlooked. These needs can show up in the middle of the budget cycle as unanticipated crises.

One technique of avoiding these surprises is to budget for the entire life cycle of major equipment and buildings. At the time of acquisition, one schedules the period of useful ownership, plugs in the times of maintenance and costs, and anticipates the time of disposal and residual value. Life-cycle budgeting preplans the budgetary implications of ownership over many years, and the projected costs are simply inserted into each periodic budget. By setting up the ownership timetable in advance and referring to it in budget preparation, the budget constructor minimizes the likelihood of forgetting to include expectable costs.

Part of life-cycle budgeting schedules replacement of vehicles, carpeting, furnishings, and other large items at appropriate intervals. A good budget plan staggers these expenses so that no part of the program's assets become overworn and also so that the program doesn't face overwhelming costs of replacement in a single year.

Sometimes programs try to squeeze extra years out of equipment in order to liberate budgeted funds for a special need or to reduce the expenditure load in a given year. This practice may provoke problems in subsequent years unless all replacements can be similarly rescheduled. Some programs engage in delaying to a sufficient extent that a deferred maintenance account is set aside in each year's budget to provide for the most pressing needs in a given year.

Equipment obsolescence cannot always be predicted, but is becoming a substantial concern for many businesses that rely heavily on computers. The speed of technology advance leads to data-processing equipment often being dated within month of its acquisition. The program may wish to lease or rent items of this nature, thereby assuring modernity and a predictable budget line. Larger businesses, however, incur costs in transitioning programs and staff to newer data applications and are caught between the desire to stay current and the complexity of change. Delays, for example, in getting bills to payers could put the entire enterprise at risk. Yet rarely does a program change its business software without incurring problems and delays.

A major "depreciation"-related cost often omitted in budget preparation is the continuing education of staff members. Whether they must learn a new computer program, take mandatory training in cardiopulmonary resuscitation, learn about new pharmaceuticals, develop skills in a new therapeutic technique, or simply maintain existing professional skills, staff members are often off duty, attending meetings, classes, and seminars. Sometimes the program, as "direct" educational costs in the budget, pays for these educational activities. Sometimes the staff members pay their own way for independently sponsored activities or are reimbursed. In addition, there are the "indirect" costs of lost time and lost billing due to staff absence during training. These costs can be significant if coverage of the employee's duty station is mandatory and the station must be covered by paying someone else overtime or if the employee's billing generates revenue. Although not typically considered as depreciation, the failure of a program to maintain the skills of its workforce can be the most damaging loss of value of all. Careful attention to maintenance in this part of the budget is often overlooked, expensive if done properly, and overwhelmingly costly if bungled.

When the budget planners have entered all projected income and all projected costs into the budget draft, managers can get their first glimpse the financial result of operations. Typically, revenue forecasts are somewhat conservative and needs as expressed in spending plans are somewhat grand. As a result, often the first draft of the budget shows desired expenditures exceeding income. Fortunately, the first draft of a budget is a "planning" vehicle. Rarely does the first draft of the budget show a substantial surplus of income over expense. Regardless of the projected bottom line, now is the time to share the draft with as broad a swath of staff as is practicable. What has been forgotten? Are prices set too high or too low? Are the workload expectations extreme? After that input is analyzed and the budget is edited, program leadership examines the refined first draft. If the budget balances, the leaders may submit the refined first draft to the governing body for approval. Often, however, there remains significant overexpenditure even after refinement of the assumptions. At this point, decisions must be made about either increasing revenues or decreasing the scope of plans. Optimally, managers will cooperate in constructing alternative scenarios to achieve balance. They may include combinations of revenue strategies and service reductions or changes in the proposed conditions of operating the program or changes in personnel policy. These alternatives should receive broad staff consideration. Again, input from staff members and managers leads to a final decision on program modification. Sometimes a few options are submitted to the governing body for policy guidance on direction, but often the program leadership chooses the most workable alternative and submits it for approval.

There are a number of other tasks associated with budget preparation. One of the most important is the projection of the budget plan on a monthly and quarterly basis, and annually if the budget is multiyear. Budget viability rests on resource flow as well as on ultimate bottom line. For example, if major funding from a grant is expected late in the year, but startup costs are heavy early in the year, and staff and other expenses mount on a monthly basis, the program may operate in midyear at a substantial deficit. In the end, an infusion of cash from the grant will balance the bank account. Cash flow analysis is an important part of management and will be considered in another chapter. For budgetary purposes, an anticipated cash flow plan is constructed to estimate the need for a line of credit, or a rescheduling of grant payments if possible, and to estimate financing costs. A program cannot effectively meet the needs of patients with mental illness if its leadership is overwhelmed with worry over whether it will have sufficient cash in the bank to meet payroll.

In addition to assessing the cash flow patterns expectable under the proposed budget, managers will consider the effects of possible deviations from the basic assumptions underlying the budget. Under the most favorable likely conditions, how much surplus will be generated? What is the lowest volume of services that the program can deliver and remain solvent? What are the margins for error built into the budget? Need there be triggers for programmatic modification if certain goals aren't met at certain points in time?

One question that flows from this analysis is whether the program is projecting adequate working capital reserves to cope with underachievement or cash flow difficulties. The budget may not include a line directed at building such reserves, particularly if the program is older and has developed an adequate reserve fund already. Sometimes a portion of startup capital may be set aside as a reserve fund. Often programs use a line of credit, using assets as collateral, to substitute for a reserve fund.

At this stage of budget development, managers will derive various statistics about proposed operations under the new spending plan. They will often compare these statistics with last year's operations or with nationally published data, if available. Typical items in such analyses include an estimate of the total volume of services to be delivered, the volume of services per category, number of services per patient served, and so on. Other parameters often considered include cost per unit of service, surplus generated per unit of service, and services delivered per professional staff member. Each program will define such statistics according to the nature of its services and how they are financed. Often such statistics are included in the formal budget presentation.

An additional way to analyze the budget is to look at data on a per hour of operations basis. Managers will look at each professional staff member's per-hour billing against the person's per-hour cost in salary, benefits, and overhead. Composite data such as cash generated per employee hour for the entire program may be compared from year to year against inflation in the general economy or against some expected increases in efficiency in operations. When these data are developed for different programs within an agency, a comparison of the productivity per unit of effort will be produced. Such comparisons can serve as a basis for creativity in retooling approaches to a desired outcome. A management conference on developing such composite indicators for the particular program is a very useful way of involving the general staff in the intricacies of the budget and business management process.

The final step in budget preparation is reconnecting and reconciling the economic plan resulting from this process to the organization's values, missions, and goals. Often the finished budget reflects many compromises between the original visions of the business plan and its final articulation in the spending plan. All the participants in the enterprise must then reexamine the vision, mission statement, and general goals of the program to see if they or the budget needs further modification. Have prices been set too high to be consistent with a vision of serving patients with limited resources? Has a significant but seemingly not cost-effective service been dropped, thereby violating a principle in the mission statement? Do expected volumes of service per professional exceed the boundaries of quality care? Should the business plan be modified to fit the budget? Perhaps the original business plan was too exuberant in its expectations. Maybe the phasing plans need to be extended. Ultimately, there should be a general level of comfort among all staff, managers, and the governing body that the budget supports and advances the business plan, that it is realistic, and that it does not violate the vision of the program or any principles of care (Mozena et al., 1999).

THE BUDGET AS A MANAGEMENT INSTRUMENT

All have been convinced that the budget represents a sound plan. The governing body has approved it. Now it is turned over to management for implementation. The budget has shifted from a planning instrument to a template for carrying out the enterprise. Each month, the actual fiscal parameters of operations will be compared to the budget's expectations. This comparison will be drawn quarterly and annually. To the extent that the budget has been detailed according to monthly expected performance, direct comparisons are made. These comparisons are also examined cumulatively through the year. If the budget is annual, without monthly detail, then managers analyze the percentages actually experienced against the percentage of weeks of the budget cycle used. Thus, for a program without significant month-to-month variability in business volume, at the end of the sixth month of the cycle, 50% of budgeted revenue should have been received and 50% of total planned expenditure should be reflected on each line of budgeted expense. Management documents are typically prepared at least quarterly showing actual fiscal experience and the budgeted plan.

The management examines deviations carefully. Simple percentage deviations are insufficient for this analysis; dollar amounts of deviation are also needed. For example, a 1% overexpenditure of the personnel budget may represent a far more significant problem in total dollars then a 10% overexpenditure of the communications budget.

Often deviations reflect the timing of certain receipts or expenses, particularly if the budget does not give monthly detail. For example, if the program is grant funded, it may receive funds quarterly or semiannually. At those times there will be a bulge of revenue over budget expectations. As the months go by, the cumulative receipts will gradually reapproach the budget. Similarly, bills for insurance premiums are often rendered annually or semiannually, leading to a seeming surplus (underexpenditure) in those expense lines that accumulates until the invoice arrives and is paid. Then the actual experience and budget again should agree.

Differences may be the result of operational problems, but still need not require reprogramming of funds. For example, at the end of the fourth month of operations, the management team notes that receipts have only reached 25% of budget, rather than the 33% expected. Using the budget as a management tool opens the door to a review of the program's billing operations. The managers discover that over the course of these months, the program has received a high number of rejections of bills by third-party payers. Further analysis indicates that during the prior quarter, a large number of patients went through open enrollment at their businesses and had changed insurance companies. Management institutes a new protocol in which the insurance information is put online to be reviewed at each scheduled appointment and receptionists are instructed to check the patient's current insurance card against the program's database. Thereafter, insurance changes are promptly entered. The agency, in fact, had a problem with receipts, but it was not a budget problem. It was a problem with operations that was correctable by management initiative. Deviations from the budget "template" alerted managers to the issue.

Many times, overexpenditures do not require rebudgeting. As always, the management team closely examines deviations. Often businesses find that expenses for telecommunications run ahead of budget. Managers frequently find, on analysis, that long-distance charges are the culprit and cure the problem by requiring personal codes given only to authorized staff members. Telephone companies can provide detailed analysis of telephone use, delays in answering, number of busy signals, and so on, which enable a business to optimize its telecommunications package, rate structure, and staff numbers to meet its current volume of calls. These management strategies can often reduce costs sufficiently that by year's end, the actual expenditures will be comparable to budget.

Clearly, the later in the budget period these deviations are noticed, the more difficult they will be to correct without rebudgeting. In contrast, the earlier in the budget period deviations are noticed, the less sure managers are about their validity. For this reason, the time of most intense budget analysis starts after first quarter and trends should be clear and on the road to solution by second quarter. By third quarter, deviations will typically require rebudgeting to properly manage.

A well-run business develops, in advance, a management strategy to guide using the budget to identify operational problems (Tracy, 1996), sometimes called an "expenditure management plan." Typically, at preset intervals, managers are asked to project their final expenditures for each budget line. The methodology for deriving these projections from each quarter's actual results is developed by the management team, and special instructions are promulgated periodically as contingencies warrant. Such contingencies may be, for example, a change in the price of heating fuel for a residential program or the introduction of a new pharmaceutical. This formalizes the task of comparing actual and budgeted results by asking program administrators to anticipate costs not yet reflected in actual expenditures and combine them with a forecast based on activity to date. Each manager provides a narrative outlining the sources of deviation, offering alternative methods of addressing overexpenditure, and discussing underexpenditure. Similar methodology is applied to revenue attainment. This lays the groundwork for decisions about whether discrepancies can be dealt with by management initiatives or by rebudgeting. Although the formalized expenditure management process is more appropriate for large organizations, the technique of periodically projecting closing revenues and expenditures can assist the operator of a small enterprise to keep a global view of progress and problems during the course of the business year.

Rebudgeting is the process of using resources designated in the budget for one purpose to cover overexpenditure for another purpose. Typically, this involves diverting money budgeted for staff salaries into another category of expense. These resources may help cover unexpected increased costs for medications, replacement of the transmission in the program's van, legal bills incurred in responding to an employee's complaint of discrimination, and so on. The salary line is often tapped because it is rarely fully expended. The reasons for this lie in a variety of vicissitudes related to personnel management. Recruiting takes longer than expected. Employees quit or retire unexpectedly. Sometimes a manager will delay filling positions in order to rebudget the money set aside for those salaries. In short, when a budgeted position is vacant, the money earmarked for the position is unexpended.

In larger organizations, these unused resources can be substantial. In fact, managers expect a certain percentage of the total salary line and associated budgeted funds to be unspent due to the phenomenon of "turnover" in the workforce. Budget planners often deduct a small percentage from the personnel budget in anticipation of turnover. For example, if a program employs 100 staff members at an average cost (including salary overhead) of $35,000, the total budget for this line will be $3.5 million. If at any given time four jobs are unfilled, the program's turnover is 4%. This means that the program will project a closing surplus of $140,000 in the salary line. To provide rebudgeting flexibility, the budget may assign a turnover adjustment that is less than the program's actual experience. In a lean budget, the planners may assign a turnover adjustment that is slightly higher than the program's actual experience, thereby requiring some delays in filling positions.

It is incumbent on the governing body, with the assistance of senior administration, to provide guidance on rebudgeting policy. Often managers are permitted to make certain substitutions, but are precluded from others. For example, the board of directors may decide that resources may not be transferred among different services in the program without their approval. There may be restrictions placed on using salary resources for equipment purchases or other nonpersonnel expenses. By setting policy on how the budget may be manipulated by the management team without special approval, the governing body maintains oversight and fulfills its fiduciary obligations. Often values and principles that are derived from the program's business statement guide these restrictions. They may be geared to insure that the board of directors reviews any rebudgeting that takes away direct patient care resources for some other purpose. For example, the board may not permit management on its own to abolish a nursing position in order to provide two fiscal clerks. The board may require that, without its approval, the CEO does not spend resources budgeted for pharmaceuticals to fix that van's transmission. In contrast, the governing body may have no objection to rebudgeting projected office equipment purchases for the purpose of refurbishing the patient waiting room. Thus, creating in advance a set of values and policies to guide rebudgeting provides a framework for using the budget as a management tool.

The governance structure of larger organizations requires the delegation of considerable authority from the governing body to the chief executive officer (CEO) of the entity. There is further delegation of authority from the CEO to senior managers, and depending on the organizational structure of the entity there may be other tiers of management. For example, the governing body may limit its role in personnel procurement to the hiring of the CEO. All other hiring authority is delegated to the CEO, who may further delegate the ability to hire staff to service chiefs, for example. Similarly, budgetary authority is delegated. As described earlier, certain policies on rebudgeting are set by the governing body. Typically these restrictions are drawn to offer broad discretion to the CEO to make most decisions in this area. The CEO may further delegate this authority to members of the management team. Generally, there will be checks and balances, as by requiring the chief financial officer (CFO) to countersign a manager's request to rebudget funds. Sometimes dollar limits are set above which the CEO or even governance must be involved. Thus, the board of directors makes clear that a resource budgeted for patient care is used that way. In implementing, the CEO directs that funds budgeted for nurse positions may not be rebudgeted without the CEO's signature. Authority to rebudget equipment purchases is delegated to the service manager, with the signature of the CFO. The choice of copier machine to purchase with budgeted funds may be at the manager's discretion without the need for additional approval. Even when expending budgeted funds, managers may be subject to a consultation requirement if the purchase is above a certain dollar value. It is important that there is clarity within the organization about the rules for each management level's role in implementing the budget and altering the use of budgeted funds.

Imagine the concern of members of the management team when at second quarter they discover that revenue projections are substantially below budget expectations. Inexperienced managers often resort quickly to expenditure reduction schemes such as curtailing major purchases or instituting a hiring "freeze" or both. These approaches may ultimately be necessary, but are extremely disruptive and demoralizing. First, if the problem is insufficient revenue, address the income side of the budget. This requires managers to analyze why revenues are sluggish. The causes could be insufficient services being provided, problems in billing, delays in receiving grant funds, reductions in fees paid by insurers, failures to meet the paperwork requirements of managed care, changes in patient demographics with increased bad debt write-off, and so on. Many of these problems can be addressed as management initiatives. The rebudgeting required may be less severe if new assumptions are plugged in. For example, if the issue, discovered at first quarter, is managed care paperwork, redirecting clerical priorities may fix it. Even if the time lag in recovering revenues is projected at 2 or 3 months, the revenue forecast can be increased by an assumption of normal collections in third and fourth quarter. Therefore the needed expense reduction requires saving only one-half of the amount originally projected. If services are down, is it due to too few customers, or employee vacations, or some other issue? If the first quarter is July through September, it is possible that the revenue shortfall is an artifact of the summer vacation season and is built into the budget already. In both cases cited, a hiring freeze might have made the problem worse. In the first example, a reduction in clerical resources would have delayed paperwork further. In the second example, a nonproblem would have become a problem if retiring professionals were not replaced with new hires, thereby operationally extending the vacation season. The key is to make every effort to fully analyze the revenue problem before taking administrative action that may, through expenditure reduction, exacerbate the situation. Governmental agencies receive appropriated budgets, have little control over the revenue side, and generally do not retain collected funds. They are often limited to expenditure strategies to deal with budget problems. This dilemma leaves them prone to service limitations, equipment breakdowns, and thin staffing when faced with budget contingencies.

An organization needs to maintain some resources in the "savings bank." These funds are typically not considered for spending in budget preparation, but are held in reserve in accounts bearing higher rates interest than typical bank accounts. Therefore, reserve funds may require some time to access. Although governments maintain large financial reserve capabilities, it is very difficult for an individual agency of government to gain access to these resources to solve operating shortfalls. Governors and legislatures instruct agencies to live within their budget allocations, and it requires substantial political effort to obtain authorization for extra spending. Private agencies tend to have less reserve depth of resources than government, but more streamlined methods of using reserve funds. Often the board of directors will grant broad discretion to the CEO to utilize reserves. The key is to find a policy on the use of contingency funds that promotes discipline in adhering to the budget and finding solutions within allocated funds, but does not unduly restrict the organization's ability to meet unexpected contingencies. The governing structure often will outline the types of situations in which reserves may be used, and mandate prompt reporting of such access at the next board of directors meeting. If the board meets frequently or has a responsive committee structure, it may choose to directly authorize use of reserves. An organization must decide on the appropriate level of reserves, because it is not desirable to set aside too much money. Often the goal is to set aside sufficient resources to sustain 3 months of essential or core operations.

If the ongoing operation of the enterprise generates revenue that continues to exceed expenses, a surplus of cash may accumulate. The board of directors will probably wish to prioritize the application of surplus. For example, the first goal may be to replenish reserve funds to their authorized level. A second priority may be the resolution of any deferred maintenance projects. A third priority may be reviewing the salary plan for competitiveness. Although the board spells out the general prioritization of surplus management, if there is a pressing need for a new activity, surplus may first be directed to this activity.

Clearly, the governing body should keep close watch on both the fiscal performance of the organization and on the emerging programmatic needs. This is usually accomplished through an "executive committee" composed of the officers of the board of directors and the key operating leaders of the program such as the CEO, the CFO, and the clinical or medical director. This group will digest management reports for presentation and decision making at the full board meetings. Usually, the board delegates contingency management authority within defined limits to the executive committee. The executive committee reconciles internal management data with the reports provided by external auditors or the organization's accountants.

Typically, the full board receives periodic audit reports, meets with the accountants, and reconciles its perception of the financial status of the organization with the external auditor's view. If there are significant discrepancies, the board may institute stricter control systems.

The management function of the budget includes the gathering of experience with which to plan future budgets. This is not simply plugging last year's numbers into next year, but rather analyzing significant year-to-year trends in both components of the revenue stream and items of expense. With each passing year, the accuracy of forecasts and the budget plan should increase. In the mental health arena, however, the rapidly changing environment of managed care, governmental expectations, and service opportunities makes predictions less reliable than in other businesses. Still, the program will gain considerable experience in estimating its costs for providing certain services. This accumulated budget knowledge will enable established programs to deal effectively with prospective payment systems and capitated systems that are becoming more common. Newer programs are at a disadvantage in making the necessary estimates.

Just as most homebuyers seek a mortgage loan, businesses finance construction projects through borrowed money. The "capital budget" details planning, development, building, and equipment cost for major construction projects. The operating budget contains provision for the amortization payment and interest charges, as well as all other expenditures connected with operations. The capital budget plan bears a relationship to the financial strength and assets of the organization, as lenders will look toward program assets as collateral for lending. In smaller businesses, lenders may seek personal guarantees from principal owners or participants in the business to secure the loan. Governments and larger business may finance major projects through the issuance of bonds for general sale to the public. Financing options are considered in a later chapter.

Certain reserve funds, usually generated from operating revenues, rather than borrowing, are earmarked for maintenance projects that have been postponed from prior years or that have arisen unexpectedly. Such accounts may be flexible in strength from year to year, but receive some resources to insure that maintenance of structures and equipment is not overlooked. If these funds are not spent on maintenance, they will roll into the next year's account or be rebudgeted in next year's plan. Therefore, managers are given an incentive to keep up with their maintenance needs or lose access to these funds.

In sum, budgeting is both a planning and management exercise. An organization does not exist, however, merely to provide an opportunity to work on its budgeting. The scope and effort invested in the budget process should be commensurate with the size and complexity of the organization. This chapter explored many views of the budget cycle and its elements. Not all are germane to every organization. A program relies on the common sense of each of its leaders to devote the proper level of resource to each management task. Budgeting is a tool for success. It should not become so onerous that managers dread the cycle's rhythms.

REFERENCES

American Medical Association. (2001). *Current procedural terminology: CPT 2002*. Chicago: Author.

Babigian, H. M. (1983). Budgeting. In J. A. Talbott & S. R. Kaplan (Eds.), *Psychiatric administration* (pp. 339–356). Orlando, FL: Grune & Stratton.

Brice, R. C. (1983). Financing of psychiatric services. In J. A. Talbott & S. R. Kaplan (Eds.), *Psychiatric administration* (pp. 357–366). Orlando, FL: Grune & Stratton.

Costales, S. B., & Szurovy, G. (1994). *The guide to understanding financial statements* (2nd ed.). New York: McGraw- Hill.

Dickey, T. (1992). *The basics of budgeting*. Menlo Park, CA: Crisp.

Dropkin, M., & LaTouche, B. (1998). *The budget building book for nonprofits*. San Francisco, CA: Jossey-Bass.

Finney, R. G. (1995). *Essentials of business budgeting*. New York: American Management Association.

Mozena, J. P., Emerick, C. E., & Black, S. C. (1999). *Stop managing costs: Designing healthcare organizations around core business systems*. Milwaukee, WI: American Society for Quality.

Newman, F. L., & Sorensen, J. E. (1985). *Integrated clinical and fiscal management in mental health: A guidebook*. Norwood, NJ: Ablex.

Silver, S. B. (1997, May). *The psychiatrist as director in the public mental health system*. Administrative Psychiatry Award Lecture, American Psychiatry Association Annual Meeting, San Diego, CA.

Tracy, J. A. (1996). *Budgeting à la carte: Essential tools for harried business managers*. New York: John Wiley & Sons.

Chapter Twenty-Two

Financial Analysis and Management

Stuart B. Silver

his chapter provides an overview of basic financial reports, their analysis, accounting fundamentals, and cash management principles. The purpose is to introduce concepts as they are applied in the United States and consider their application to the business of providing mental health services. General introductory texts on business financial statements and basic accounting are readily available; this text focuses on the service sector (Costales & Szurovy, 1994; Zelman et al., 1998).

Businesses have maintained some form of financial records since the dawn of recorded history. The sophistication of methods increased during the Renaissance as global trading expanded. A major impetus for formalized accounting rules in the United States was the passage of the Sixteenth Amendment to the Constitution in 1913, authorizing federal taxation. Then there was a need for standardized approaches to calculating taxes due to the government. The stock market crash of 1929 and its sequelae stimulated the creation in 1934 of the Securities and Exchange Commission (SEC), which mandated further specifications for financial reporting of public corporate entities. Through the authority of the SEC delegated to an entity known as the Federal Accounting Standards Board (FASB), generally accepted accounting principles (GAAPs) are defined and periodically refined (Label, 1998).

GAAPs are the rules that accountants follow in preparing financial reports. These principles promote financial reports that accurately portray the state of a business at a given point in time or over a specific term. They assume that the business has an ongoing life. All reports are prepared using conservative estimates of value and realistic assumptions of the realizable value of assets. They require that the currency units used are not adjusted for inflation and values are therefore expressed in costs actually paid. GAAPs require that underlying data elements be reliable, verifiable, and relatively straightforward to obtain. Business financial reports should be quantifiable in currency units and readily understandable. Narrative notes supplied by the accountant are considered an integral part of the particular statement. These accompanying notes should clearly elucidate unique aspects of the dealings of a particular business. Only facts that are germane to an adequate understanding of the financial aspects of the business are to be included in formal reports. Currently, formal business reporting consists of four accounting documents: the balance sheet, the income statement, the cash flow statement, and the reconciliation of net worth.

BALANCE SHEET

The balance sheet presents the value of a business entity at a specific point in time. Its form follows the basic accounting equation, stating that what is owned by an entity equals what is owed plus the value of the owners' investment. This is usually expressed as

$$\text{Assets} = \text{liabilities} + \text{owners' equity}$$

The two sides of the equations must balance—hence the name *balance sheet*. Obviously, the basic accounting formula might also be seen as assets minus liabilities equal owners' equity. The balance sheet is often called the statement of "financial condition" of a business.

Assets consist of so-called "current" assets, including cash on hand, in the bank, or in other revenue-bearing investments, payments due from customers (accounts receivable), prepaid expenses, and inventory of supplies, as well as "noncurrent" assets, including buildings, equipment, and old accounts receivable, all of which would take time to convert to cash. These are so-called tangible assets. A business may own other items of value, such as patents or copyrights, that are intangible, but still real and amenable to valuation. The staff and professionals of a mental health program, for example, are not economic assets of the business by GAAP, because personnel are not owned. In some instance, such as for movie stars working for a studio, contracts may be counted as assets.

Liabilities, in contrast, represent what is owed by the business. These obligations may be considered as resources provided to the business in exchange for the promise of payment in the future. Liabilities include payments due to vendors (accounts payable), payments due to retire loans or mortgages, unpaid taxes, and expenses incurred for which invoices have not yet been received (accrued expenses). These liabilities are similarly divided into short- and long-term obligations. GAAPs consider short-term to be less than 1 year for these purposes. The balance sheet sequence lists both assets and liabilities from the most liquid to the least liquid categories.

Owners' equity represents the value of the owners' investment in the business entity. It consists of the amounts paid into the business by the owners and retained earnings from operations that have not been paid out to the owners in the form of dividends.

The balance sheet gives a snapshot of the business's value at a given point in time, usually the end of the fiscal year. The balance sheet may be drawn up quarterly for some entities. Looking at this report over several years portrays the growth or decline in the value of the business over time. The balance sheet does not show the productive activity of the business over time, however. For this information, one consults the income statement.

INCOME STATEMENT

The income statement presents the activities of the business in financial terms over a finite time period, such as a year. It is structured differently from the balance sheet, looking at services and their costs rather than at static values. Thus, the income statement starts with *total sales* (or, in the case of a professional practice, *total billing*) and subtracts the *cost* of the goods or services sold, yielding a *gross income*. From the gross income, other operating and depreciation expenses are deducted, yielding an *operating income*. Other operating expenses include, for example, administrative salaries, commissions, advertising, utilities, sales taxes, Social Security taxes, and more. The "net" income results when interest, income taxes, and any proceeds or losses that are exceptional (such as the sale of a building or the loss of an asset through uninsured accident) are deducted from the operating income.

CASH FLOW STATEMENT

The net income derived from the income statement forms the basis for the third basic accounting document, the *cash flow statement*. It is important to recognize that the income statement deals with sales and expenses that are incurred during the reporting period, whether or not any cash payments have been made or received. Thus, an entity may report $100,000 in net income on the income statement, yet have no money in the bank. If the net income is a negative number, it is referred to as a net loss. The net income represents the *profit* realized from the operation of the business for the reported time period. Therefore, the income statement is sometimes called the statement of *earnings,* or for nonprofits the *statement of operations.*

The statement of cash flow represents the changes in cash position of the company typically over the same time period as the income statement. It gives a picture of the ability of the business to meet its bills with internal resources. For medical and mental health service operations, in which there are little inventory and relatively few accounts payable relative to the volume, and in which the billing often deviates markedly from the receipts due to write-offs by third-party payers, cash accounting may be the preferred vehicle. In this case, the income statement's data are only entered at the time cash changes hands, rather than at the time financial events occur. For example, when the doctor sees the patient for a psychotherapy hour, a bill is rendered and accounts receivable are created, but the income statement does not record the sale of services until payment is received. Similarly, expenses are not recorded in the income statement until payment is made. Thus there is little need for a cash flow statement. Most businesses utilize *accrual accounting,* which recognizes financial events when they occur, rather than when cash changes hands, thus giving a more complete picture of all the current and pending obligations and assets of the business.

In the cash flow statement, increases in noncash assets are seen as cash losses, and conversely, increases in liabilities are recorded as cash gains. For example, when the accounts receivable increase, the clinic has expended cash in salary, rent, and supplies to produce a service, but the cash payment has not yet been received. Thus the cash account has been depleted. Conversely, when the clinic has purchased paper supplies for record-keeping, it incurred a liability in accounts payable to the paper vendor. Because the clinic may not transfer the cash for 30 days, the cash account has not yet been depleted whereas the asset of the paper is on hand. Thus, the liability represents retained cash. For the purposes of the cash flow statement, *cash* refers to all immediately liquid assets, including bank accounts, certificates of deposit, treasury bills, and actual petty cash on hand.

The cash flow statement starts with net income from the income statement and then records the elements in the current balance sheet in accordance with their effect on cash flows, asset increases subtracted, and liability increases added. Dividend payments to shareholders may not be reflected in the balance sheet or income statement, but are recorded on the cash flow statement as reductions in cash. The sum of all these entries reflects the change in cash position of the business. This method of calculating the cash flows is called *indirect*. The *direct* format draws the cash changes from the income statement rather than the balance sheet. In this method, entries are derived from the logic of business operations. For example, cash from sales is computed by subtracting the accounts receivable from the gross sales. Similarly, cash for income tax is computed by subtracting from the amounts paid during the reporting period the amounts still due. Both methods of preparing the cash flow statement yield the same result, and the format chosen is a matter of accounting preference for the particular business. The normal sequence of the cash flow statement is net income plus cash flows from operations, plus investing, plus financing, yielding net change in cash (Tracy, 1996).

RECONCILIATION OF NET WORTH

The *reconciliation of net worth statement* or statement of *changes in stockholders' equity* combines data from the balance sheet, the income statement, and the cash flow statement to show how profits or losses were allocated to the owners (shareholders). In the case of a corporation that produced a profit, dividends will reduce the stockholders' equity. The form of the statement is the beginning balance plus net income minus dividends, yielding an ending balance. For complex corporations, this statement may be relatively complicated, not only tracking the net value changes, but also attributing value to different classes of stock and indicating changes in stock in circulation.

Large corporations that have a number of wholly owned subsidiary companies often issue *consolidated statements*. The assets and liabilities of each of the owned corporations are included, or "consolidated," into the balance sheet of the parent corporation rather than listed as separate balance sheets for each of the subsidiaries. These corporate relationships are spelled out in detail in the notes accompanying the financial statements.

An offering of an investment vehicle to investors is described by a document known as a *prospectus*. In the prospectus, the entity seeking investment capital lays out the summary of its business plan, ownership, structure of the proposed fundraising vehicle, and as much financial detail about the entity as is available.

In the case of a new venture, this data may consist largely of projections about the future. A statement projecting the financial performance of a business venture looking forward in time is often referred to as a *pro forma*. Such a statement is largely hypothetical and makes many assumptions about the economy, inflation, tax policy, commodity costs, and the state of the particular industry, often looking many years into the future (Zelman et al., 1998). Sometimes projections are offered in more than one version, showing conservative, moderate, and optimistic assumption sets about future parameters. Clearly, the more forward-looking the projections are, the less reliable they are. There is no guarantee of business results, but often the projected returns are an indication of the degree of risk. Higher projected returns suggest greater uncertainty and higher risks. For a publicly offered investment, the prospectus follows specifications of the SEC, including appropriate warnings to the potential buyer about the risks involved, and the externally audited financial statements of the entity are publicly posted, including on the Internet.

DEPRECIATION

The concept of depreciation was discussed in the chapter on budget. Depreciation appears on the income statement, reflecting the decline in value of an asset over the reporting period. In the balance sheet, the term *accumulated* or *cumulative depreciation* refers to the total of the depreciation taken since acquisition of the asset. The rate at which various assets may be depreciated is specified in federal tax instructions. As noted in the preceding chapter, the book value of an asset less its accumulated depreciation may under- or overestimate its liquidation value. The value of land is not subject to depreciation.

Clearly, a potential creditor may examine the net value of assets, such as manufacturing equipment, and see little liquidation value if the borrower cannot pay the debt, therefore concluding that the assests are overvalued on the books. A potential buyer who intends to continue operating the business, in contrast, may see well-functioning equipment with a long potential productive life ahead (in spite of substantial reduction of value through the depreciation schedule) and conclude that the assets are undervalued. A potential vendor, who is considering whether to extend 30-day credit to the business, or require cash payment in advance of shipping goods, may not be as concerned with depreciated assets as with the age of the accounts receivable. Those examining the financial statements of a business assess items of inventory, buildings, accounts payable, and depreciated assets with values that differ from the values laid out by accounting principles (which tend to set values for the owners of the original and presumed ongoing business). Their own interests relative to their relationship to that business instead guide their valuations.

ACCOUNTING SYSTEMS

The accounting systems of a business serve many functions in addition to the production of the four standard statements (balance sheet and statements of income, cash flow, and reconciliation of net worth) (Anthony, 1996). Summaries providing data unique to the particular business are produced, usually monthly, that give managers a view of performance toward meeting specific objectives, an analysis of costs and profits, and information about budget compliance. In general, the accounting system enables the management team to keep track of the unfolding of the business plan and its budgetary translation in contemporaneous financial terms.

The standard financial statements often form a template for management reporting, but more detail may be supplied on the management versions. For example, the income statement includes a line showing the costs of producing goods or services. The management report may detail which of those costs are *fixed* and which are *variable. Fixed costs* represent basic expense lines such as staff salaries, which do not vary with total sales within a normal range of operations.

Variable costs include two components. The first are costs that vary in direct proportion to sales value, such as commissions or raw materials. The second component of variable costs varies in proportion to volume of product, such as shipping and storage costs. "Sunk costs" are those that have already been expended, have no relation to sales, and cannot be recovered. Such costs include startup costs, development of initial accounting systems, office setup, and so on. Clearly in analyzing profitability, the business must generate sufficient net income to cover fixed costs and the continuously escalating variable costs. There is a sales level at which the generated net income will achieve this goal, the so-called "break-even point."

In addition to generating this basic information, the accounting system should enable the management team to estimate the costs of each of the organization's programs. This may be accomplished by examining each component of the program: the staff hours, supplies and equipment, floor space, percent of utilities, and percent of administrative service. These are translated into total dollar cost, a figure then divided by the number of service provided to yield a cost per service. Cost finding has been extremely important in computation of hospital rates for the different services, leading to, for example, very high rates for beds in the neonatal intensive care unit, versus more moderate rates for general medical–surgical beds, rather than a unitary rate for all the beds in the hospital (Brice, 1983).

The accounting system additionally provides the basic information for budget preparation as well as tracking cash flow and estimating cash resources at various projected points in the future. The use of the budget in management is described in the budget chapter, but unless the accounting system can promptly produce the information about current performance, the management team will be hamstrung in responding to deviations. The job of the leadership is to produce the business plan. The job of the accounting system is to produce an accurate financial picture of the plan in the budget and to produce accurate, usable data quickly. The job of management is to digest these data and pilot the organization's direction to produce the outcomes envisioned in the business plan.

In addition to producing management data, the accounting system must support operations. Among these functions are billing and posting receipts, providing accurate claims forms to third-party payers, determining when accounts are delinquent and providing an orderly collections protocol, reconciling invoices received with approved purchases, preparing tax returns, producing employee payroll, and more.

Another important area of accounting support involves developing a system of internal controls to minimize loss of assets through mistakes, fraud, or other criminal activity. Such systems include simple mechanisms of numbering checks and receipts, the use of locked boxes or depository safes to hold cash, requiring more than one employee to perform functions related to each cash transaction to create checks and balances ("separation of functions"), and so on. Separation of functions generally requires that the decision-making and executive functions are independent of the accounting and record-keeping related to that decision. The accounting function will also insert "edits" into the automated records systems to pick up data inconsistencies, and will perform audits ("internal audits") by reviewing past transactions and by creating test transactions in order to trace their progress through operations (Tracy, 1996).

Audits, often performed on a surprise basis, serve the purpose of picking up inconsistencies, errors, and financial misbehavior within the business structure. Internal auditors typically report to the highest management levels within the agency.

A mental health service program develops procedures to make sure that all billable work is properly recorded, that bills and insurance forms are generated promptly, that payments are reconciled with invoices, and that revenues and cash are properly managed. Usually these procedures rely on paper forms that uniquely meet the needs of the particular program. As data-processing networks proliferate through agencies, some of these forms may be displayed on monitors and data may be directly entered without the need for paper. Setting up these forms and data-capturing programs can be costly, and once set up, systems are difficult to change. Therefore, thinking through the data challenges in advance is critical to the competitiveness of the organization in the marketplace.

The principle of *separation of functions* may be illustrated for a mental health provider: The reception staff sets and records appointments. When the service is completed, the provider fills out a billing form or charge ticket. Accounting will reconcile the appointments against the billing forms and investigate appointments for which charge tickets were not created. When cash is paid for service, the receptionist provides a numbered receipt to the client and to the accounting department, which checks the cash received against both the receipts and the charge tickets. A similar system is created to track purchases and payment for operating supplies.

Accounting staff works with management to develop systems to maintain a documented chain of accountability for cash from receipt to final deposit in the bank. Locked bags or boxes transport deposits to the bank; deposit receipts are reconciled with internal accounting records of the deposit. Thus, the records of three independent functions must agree—operations, accounting, and the bank. This is a simple example of how separation of functions creates checks and balances.

COLLECTIONS

Collections is another area of financial management that requires careful planning and sensitive execution. Whether the services are fee-for-service, grant funded, or prepaid, it is essential to follow crisply a process that leads to receipt of funds without delay. In addition, collections policies and procedures must anticipate reluctance on the part of customers to part with their money and have an orderly and uniform approach to this dilemma.

Accounting systems track how often full payment of copayments or full fees is made at the time of the office visit, how reliably dunning notices are sent and the management of third-party obligations, how and when write-off of uncollected bills occurs, when accounts are turned over to lawyers or collection agencies, and how subsequent recoveries are recorded.

Program leaders must decide under what circumstances delinquent accounts will be pursued, whether missed appointments will be billed, the content and style of dunning notices, who will ask customers for payment and how they will do it, whether credit cards will be accepted, and many other business practice issues that affect the image the organization projects in the community. It is difficult to find the right balance of flexibility and firmness, as well as to make sure that all employees involved in the collection effort approach payers consistently.

ACCOUNTS RECEIVABLE

Accounts receivable represent credit the program extends to its clients. The volume and terms of such credit vary, but the term is typically 30 days without interest in the United States. In health care practice, interest is not generally added even after that period of time because insurance issues often delay full payment. Thus, large accounts receivable are a significant cost to the program in terms of lost interest on the money were it all paid at the time of service, or even larger interest payments on lines of credit from banks to provide the missing cash on a short-term basis. Some health care providers pursue ("work") the accounts receivable more vigorously when cash is low. In a well-managed organization, little additional yield would be realized by this strategy as all possible collection avenues are worked continually as a matter of course.

FINANCIAL RATIOS

An important way that managers and investors keep track of business performance is through analysis of certain financial ratios. For example, the relationship of current receivables to annual income from sales gives a picture of the performance of the collections function. This *receivables turnover* ratio can further be considered in terms of time. If, in this example, accounts receivable are 10% of annual income, the average age of the receivables is 35.7 days or a little over a month. If the goal is to keep receivables at no more than 30 days, management attention will focus on this area of activity. In health services, however, collections typically require more than 30 days due to the complexities of third-party payment.

Other accounting ratios have been identified that enable investors to compare the performance of several companies doing similar work. The *current ratio* compares current assets to current liabilities, and suggests whether a firm's current assets are sufficient to meet its financial obligations. The *quick ratio* compares relatively liquid assets to liabilities, indicating whether there is sufficient cash and easily retrieved cash to meet current liabilities. Although these and other ratios give a picture of a firm's "liquidity," additional ratios give indication of financial leverage, operating performance, and return on investment.

Leverage (or *financial leverage*) is the ratio of an entity's liabilities to its tangible net worth. A firm whose leverage is greater than 1.0 may find borrowing from a bank difficult, although other considerations such as past history and overall cash flow through the firm may affect a lender's decision. The relationship of a firm's income to its sales, the so-called *profit margin*, offers insight into overall operating performance and may be calculated based on gross income, operating income, or net income.

The usual measures of return are based on comparing net income with either owner's equity or total assets, yielding a *return on assets* or *return on investment*

(ROA, ROI). Businesses develop and monitor those business ratios that they find particularly useful in their domain of operations. For example, an interstate trucking firm may be concerned with the ratio of trucks returning empty to total truckloads carried. The automotive industry monitors inventory closely; excessive inventories may place auto companies and dealers at significant competitive disadvantage (Tracy, 1996). A mental health organization, on the other hand, is not particularly interested in ratios related to inventory management but may be very interested in filled versus unfilled beds, or billable versus nonbillable clinician work hours.

PRACTICAL FINANCIAL MANAGEMENT

Accounting strategies, systems, and ratios are tools for strategic business management. Often, however, the leaders of a small mental health program are more immediately concerned simply with meeting their payroll. Because accounts receivable are delayed by insurance payment, a new venture must have adequate financing from other sources than sales in order to meet financial obligations. In planning the level of financing needed, managers take into account delays in third-party payments, rate of hiring and payroll development, and construction and other starting costs. There should also be a provision for unforeseen contingencies.

The program will anticipate earning some interest on unspent funds during operations and also will anticipate early receipts through cash payments, grants, and other sources. Assuming a correct calculation of break-even point and accurate projections, there will come a time when startup capitalization is largely utilized and revenues are sufficient to meet expenses.

Cash Flow Imbalance

Transient fluctuations in business may lead to cash flow imbalance and a need for short-term cash infusion, to meet payroll, for example. Managing the cash one has committed, but not yet paid (the "float"), is a way of providing this operating cash without formal borrowing. The float may include customer overpayments, cash received from granting agencies, cash retained by delayed payment of vendors, and so on. The larger the business, the larger is the float. A 1- or 2-week manipulation of the sequence of fulfilling these cash obligations may make the difference between weathering a transient fluctuation or needing to draw on a loan. This technique should not be used to address a chronic imbalance.

Contingency Funds

A business creates special accounts in which savings or retained earnings are placed. These accounts are invested in order to produce a yield of interest and in some cases even the potential for capital gains. Such accounts may be called "discretionary funds" or "investment funds" or "reserve funds" or "capital funds," depending on how the business conceptualizes their use. Although too large an amount of investment funds suggests that the firm is not putting its resources to work properly, an absence of or limited reserves places the firm too much at risk of short-term business volatility and make it difficult for the firm to respond to unexpected opportunity.

Some advisors recommend that there be sufficient funds in reserve for the business to operate for up to 6 months without new receipts before running out of cash. It is often difficult, especially for charitable organizations, to retain this level of resources; such organizations typically aim for a 3-month contingency fund.

The board of directors, in consultation with the agency's accountants and managers, will set policies governing how retained resources are managed. The board may require that these funds may only be invested in government securities. On the other hand, the board may direct that cash reserves be maintained in several accounts, some of which must be conservatively invested, or placed only in insured accounts. In addition to rules governing placement of reserve funds, additional policies will spell out the contingencies for use of these funds, and management checks and balances on access to them.

REFERENCES

Anthony, R. N. (1996). *Essentials of accounting.* Boston, MA: Addison-Wesley.

Brice, R. C. (1983). Financing of psychiatric services. In J. A. Talbott & S. R. Kaplan (Eds.), *Psychiatric administration* (pp. 357–366). Orlando, FL: Grune & Stratton.

Costales, S. B., & Szurovy, G. (1994). *The guide to understanding financial statements* (2nd ed.). New York: McGraw-Hill.

Label, W. A. (1998). *Accounting for non-accountants.* New York: Macmillan Spectrum/Alpha Books.

Tracy, J. A. (1996). *Budgeting à la carte: Essential tools for harried business managers.* New York: John Wiley & Sons.

Zelman, W. N., McCue, M. J., & Millikan, A. R. (1998). *Financial management of healthcare organizations: An introduction to fundamental tools, concepts, and applications.* Malden, MA: Blackwell.

Chapter Twenty-Three

Financing

Stuart B. Silver

The most common mechanism for obtaining the use of a substantial sum of money for a defined period of time is to rent the use of the money by paying a premium called *interest*. The money is said to be *borrowed*. The vehicle for such a transaction is a *loan*. The typical source of loans for both personal and business use is a commercial bank. A contract is signed between the lender of funds and the borrower setting forth the terms of repayment and interest. Such contracts are often called *promissory notes*. The agency's balance sheet will reflect the loan as a *note payable*. The terms of the loan may call for regular monthly or quarterly payments until interest and principal are fully paid, or there may be smaller initial payments and a larger "balloon" payment later in the life of the loan. Interest may be compounded daily, monthly, or annually according to the agreement between lender and borrower. There may be added penalties for late payments and there may or may not be penalties for early payment.

The lender of funds, whether a bank or an individual, is concerned about whether or not the borrower will repay the loan properly. In order to *secure* the loan, the lender will examine the financial statements of the business and its conduct of prior loans as reflected in *credit reports*. The lender may require guarantees from owners and may examine their individual income tax returns, or may place a lien against certain assets of the business including inventory, accounts receivable, or some other valuable. If the business is in a strong financial position and has a good record of management of prior loans, the lender may offer an "unsecured" loan or may extend a "line of credit" indicating the maximum unsecured loan balance that the lender can comfortably permit.

Loans for periods of time longer than a year place more risk on the lender than do short-term loans. The economy can change over many years, or the borrower's solvency can weaken, for example. Often the rate of interest is higher for a long-term commitment. Lenders may apply additional stipulations to long-term loans to provide additional assurance that the terms will be met. These may include a variety of expectations of business performance as reflected in the financial statements and their derived ratios.

Just as accounts receivable reflect credit extended by the business to its customers, accounts payable represent a short-term loan of cash from the vendors who have sold goods or services to the business. Typically this loan is interest free for 30 days, after which some percentage penalty for late payment may be applied. Often the penalty for late payment may represent a substantial rate of interest. Some vendors offer a discount to encourage prompt payment, such as within 10 days. In managing cash flow fluctuations, a business may choose to delay payment of accounts payable, thereby taking a loan, often at unfavorable terms, but that requires no application or proof of collateral value. Needless to add, this practice is only useful to meet very transient cash shortages.

Rather than renting cash to purchase equipment, a business may rent equipment rather than buying it. Functionally, a lease resembles a loan in that there are both a contractual repayments schedule and interest charges. The difference, however, is that the ownership of the equipment remains with the leasing company and when the term of the lease expires, the leasing company has access to the residual value of the equipment. From the perspective of the business that leases rather than buys, the lease may be a way to avoid accumulating ownership of obsolete equipment. The leasing company may offer easy access to maintenance. There also may be tax advantages. With leases, collateral is provided by the residual value of the leased equipment, thereby eliminating the need for liens against the company's assets. These considerations are weighed against the interest contained in the lease, which may be higher than a bank's loan charges. In addition to leasing, a business may also enter into a "lease–purchase" arrangement. In this type of contract, the business agrees to take ownership of the leased equipment at the conclusion of the lease and the terms of the lease fully finance the cost of sale.

Large and well-established firms sometimes make use of their reserve funds by selling promissory notes to other business firms, insurance companies, pension funds, and banks. Also known as "commercial paper," such contracts are issued for periods typically varying from 2 to 6 months.

Business entities may raise resources to be used over the long term through the issuance of stock or borrowing by the issuance of bonds, promissory notes obligating regular interest payments. Bondholders do not participate in the success of the business enterprise through the potential for capital gains or dividends; however, in the event of reversals, they receive repayment before stockholders. If a bond or preferred stock issue was sold when interest rates were higher than they are at present, it may be profitable to call the old issue and refund it with a new, lower-cost issue. This depends on how the immediate costs and premiums that must be paid compare with the annual savings that can be obtained. Various other forms of long-term loans exist in the business world, including *debentures* (unsecured bonds issued by corporations) and *mortgage bonds* (loans secured by liens on buildings or major items of equipment). Detailed discussions of the advantages of different loan vehicles may be found in the business literature on corporate financing.

If a business chooses to raise funding by the issuance of stock, it is essentially distributing ownership to a larger number of people or requiring the current owner to put up more funds to retain ownership. Stock offering requires compliance with Securities and Exchange Commission (SEC) requirements for the publication of business documents and accounting records. The vicissitudes of stock offering are beyond the scope of this section, but in coming years many smaller mental health businesses may be approached by large corporate entities that seek to purchase them by an offering of cash and stock in the corporation. Such tenders will require the mental health program to consult closely with its accountants, attorneys, and business consultants before proceeding very far with negotiations. A careful reading of the business plan of the corporation seeking to purchase is a critical first step for the operators of the mental health program in deciding whether there is even a basis for further discussion.

Large health care providers may enter into prepaid *capitated* contracts for health services. For a fixed lump sum, the provider agrees to provide a defined set of services to a defined group of patients. This type of contract fixes the liability of the payer. The risk is borne by the provider, for if the defined panel of patients requires more care than was anticipated in computing the value of the contract, the provider's reimbursement for services will be eroded. However, if the group of patients remains healthier than expected, the provider will reap economic bonuses. The fixed sum per patient, the *capitation payment,* is usually paid monthly by the insurer to the provider for each beneficiary covered during that month regardless of whether any services were delivered to the beneficiary.

From the provider's perspective, a loan has been received because the capitation payments are made in advance. This money can be invested, earn interest, and be used to meet current obligations, just as can any other receipts. Capitation contracts are often advantageous initially to the provider, as it takes a while for a group of patients to begin utilizing the new services. As time passes, however, the situation may reverse, particularly over years as the patients age and their health care needs intensify. Because mental illnesses make their first appearance in young adults, capitated contracts for mental health services may be less desirable for providers to enter into than similar contracts for medical–surgical services. Most working-age insured persons are in the young adult group, less prone to chronic medical illness. Because the provider may ultimately be accepting considerable financial risk that would otherwise be held by the insurer, capitated contracts have come under the supervision of state insurance regulators. Often, provider agencies must demonstrate considerable financial reserve and organizational stability in order to be authorized to enter into such contracts within the state regulatory environment.

Larger nonprofit agencies rely heavily on donations to support their charitable efforts. Smaller organizations often solicit gifts on a somewhat informal basis to support specific projects. Professional fund-raising can be both costly and elaborate, involving strategies from large-scale phone calling to mass mailing to media advertising. Often, professional fund-raisers work on a commission, taking a percentage of the results of their collections after expenses. In order to launch a successful fund-raising campaign, the enterprise should promulgate a completed, written, board-approved plan. The goals of the fund-raising efforts should be clearly stated. The organization should be well managed and the accounting documents should reflect sound fiscal management. The leadership should be prepared to commit time, resources, and energy to the project, and there should be a reasonable plan, including the identification of potential donors. Respected volunteer leadership and adequately oriented volunteer support are helpful, as are well-edited and clear support documents including pamphlets and mailings.

Generally, mental health service providers do targeted solicitation of the families of service recipients and community leaders, and sometimes solicit through open houses, sales, and silent auctions, for example. The program managers decide what proportion of receipts should appropriately result from charitable collections, in contrast to fees, grants, and other contracts. Often the nature of the enterprise directs the mix of funding sources. On some occasions, fund drives are used to finance new services or equipment or facilities. Universities and hospitals actively solicit contributions to support new construction activities on their campuses.

Similarly, institutions try to promote bequests. Tax laws on inheritance currently favor charitable disposition of large portions of large estates. Sometimes foundations are created that offer grant funding to service agencies. One problem with bequests is that their availability may be unpredictable and therefore the funds may not arrive at the moment of need. Large organizations work with individuals seeking to make such gifts to arrange for orderly transition. For example, the bequest may include real property transfer, with the donor retaining open access to the property during the remainder of his or her life. Smaller organizations may receive such gifts from founders, or other individuals with close connections, but these organizations rarely have the resources to promote an active program soliciting legacy contributions.

Many mental health programs receive lump sum commitments from government to provide for indigent populations or other specified groups. Resources are transferred from the public coffers to these programs pursuant to purchase of service contracts between the state mental health agency and the participating program. Over the course of the past 15 years, state mental health authorities have increasingly contracted for community-based services and in some cases have contracted for inpatient services. These contracts have often been loosely identified as "grants."

Grants may also be awarded by private foundations, usually in response to some bidding process following the issuance of a request for proposals. Agencies that wish to embark on a specialized service mission may also approach charitable organizations or foundations seeking financial support through start-up grants and other subsidies. Generally, these sorts of grants are not for purchase of services on behalf of a specified population. Rather, they require the development of an agreed-upon type of program and periodic reports on its accomplishments. Typically, the granting charitable entity will conduct site visits and require careful financial accounting. Often, scholarly publications about the project are expected.

Finally, all organizations receive some interest on deposited funds. Generally the amount is insufficient to be applied for specific financing purposes, however. Nonetheless, interest income can seed other fund-raising efforts, rather than be included in operating income. This illustrates the utility of earmarking certain revenue flows toward special accounts rather than placing all revenues into budgeted operations.

REFERENCES

Costales, S. B., & Szurovy, G. (1994). *The guide to understanding financial statements* (2nd ed.). New York: McGraw-Hill.

Tracy, J. A. (1996). *Budgeting à la carte: Essential tools for harried business managers.* New York: John Wiley & Sons.

Zelman, W. N., McCue, M. J., & Millikan, A. R. (1998). *Financial management of healthcare organizations: An introduction to fundamental tools, concepts, and applications.* Malden, MA: Blackwell.

Chapter Twenty-Four

Payers and Players

Stuart B. Silver

A long time ago, people with illness paid for medical services either with cash or barter. Those who were indigent sometimes received charitably financed services or some care through governmentally sponsored programs. After the Civil War, state governments developed hospitals for the confinement and care of persons suffering from mental disease. Often the financer of medical care was the doctor, who might see poorer patients at a discounted fee.

During World War II, with wages frozen, health insurance developed as an employee benefit. The concept blossomed and in the ensuing years the financing of health care transferred from out-of-pocket payments by the recipient of care to payments for providers by insurance companies for services received by their policyholders. In time, most physicians signed contracts with insurers under which they would be paid directly by the insurer. When the doctor "participated" in this way, the patient soon lost interest in the bill as well as the payment.

Today, "third-party" payments are the principal engine of health care financing. Increasingly, however, recipients of care are required to contribute a small amount, "copayment," to the cost of their care. These copayments are becoming more significant as a percentage of care costs and in total dollars. Furthermore, with the cost of medical care escalating, premiums for health insurance are rising. Many employers no longer offer to subsidize health insurance premiums as an employee benefit. Those that do expect more and better coverage for their employees while keeping costs as low as possible.

Many Americans cannot afford even the premiums as an out-of-pocket expense; the number of uninsured or underinsured persons in the United States is becoming substantial. A need for "cost containment" has spawned the *managed care* industry, in which a "fourth party" monitors claims for the "third-party" payer to determine if such claims must be paid (often according to a contract definition of "medical necessity"). Questions are proliferating about the cost of so much administrative oversight, not only in dollars, but also in terms of interference with the care process.

Although a full examination of the evolution of health care financing is beyond the scope of this chapter, one can say that we have reentered a time where patient self-payment is an important source of private health care organization (and clinician) revenue. Office systems must efficiently capture and account for fees and copayments. Many providers are becoming more rigid in requiring patients to pay out-of-pocket for services and expecting the patient to seek whatever reimbursement is allowed from their insurer or other third-party payer.

In the face of this ferment, President Clinton attempted sweeping, legislatively driven reform of the health care system. A large task force of experts and stakeholders was assembled and an extremely complex document came forth. It was promptly shredded in the political process that followed. Health care finance reform is proceeding incrementally, but one result of the turmoil is that people throughout the country are more involved in the financing of their health care and, because they are paying for themselves, expecting more customer satisfaction.

THIRD-PARTY PAYERS

Insurance Companies

The most commonly thought-of third-party payer is an insurance company. The initial market for health insurance in the 1950s and 1960s was dominated by the "Blues," Blue Cross and Blue Shield. These organizations were developed in most states to provide a form of health insurance in which physicians were involved in the corporate governance, and ordinary clinicians "participated" by agreeing to certain payment rules and accepting direct reimbursement for their services. Blue Cross paid for hospital bills, and Blue Shield covered physician and other eligible provider bills. The premiums were generally paid by employers, and in the 1970s began to escalate.

Other insurers soon entered the marketplace, and by the 1980s, new kinds of coverage, primarily to contain costs, became common. An alphabet soup of health insurance terms proliferated in the 1980s and 1990s (e.g., CPT, DRG, HMO, PPO, IPA, MCO, BHMCO, RBRVS). All relate to some approach to defining and limiting medical practice and costs (Mechanic, 1999; Rodenhauser, 2000).

Other Third-Party Payers

In addition to insurance companies, other third-party players include government care systems (e.g., state mental health departments, the U.S. Veterans Administration, workers' compensation systems, military and correctional systems), family estates and trusts, and the legal system (e.g., through civil litigation judgments).

FEDERAL FUNDS

The federal government, through a variety of direct and indirect programs, is probably the largest single purchaser of health care in the United States (Dorwart, Chartock, & Epstein, 1992).

Medicare

After John F. Kennedy was assassinated in 1963, Lyndon Johnson's administration led a series of liberal government initiatives directed at eliminating the worst consequences of poverty. Called the "Great Society," this set of programs included Title XVIII and Title XIX of the Social Security Act. The former defines Medicare and set in motion a system of medical insurance for persons over 65 years of age (who are eligible for Social Security benefits) and certain disabled citizens, to be funded under the Social Security system. Although initially opposed by the medical profession, Medicare has become one of the largest funding engines of health care in the country.

Medicare was one of the few initiatives of the Great Society that remained politically "bulletproof" at the close of the 20th century. It is financed entirely with federal funds, administered in the Department of Health and Human Services (DHHS) under the Centers for Medicare & Medicaid Services (CMS; formerly the Health Care Financing Administration [HCFA]), and operated at the state level through contractual arrangements with private insurers. "Part A" of Medicare pays hospital bills retrospectively.

The Medicare claims form, "HCFA form 1500," has become the standard health insurance vehicle not only for federal programs but also for private insurers. Medicare fee schedules have been a benchmark for other payers' fees as well. Some multispecialty medical groups base their compensation formulas on Medicare rate methodology. A substantial number of persons with serious and persistent mental disease come to be supported under the Social Security Disability Insurance program (SSDI). The Medicare program pays for many of their medical expenses (but not prescription drugs).

Medicare's "Part B," which covers some physician bills, does not pay in full. Although Medicare sets allowable physician charges for given procedures, the retiree must pay a percentage of the fee. Part B is an optional enhancement for which beneficiaries are charged monthly premiums.

Some health maintenance organizations (HMOs) have developed under the Medicare program. They may offer coverage for prescriptions, dental benefits, and possibly lower copayments in exchange for the policyholders' agreement to receive nonemergency care only from participating physicians and facilities.

Medicaid: A Combined Federal and State Program

Title XIX of the Social Security Act created Medicaid, a program of health insurance for certain classes of indigent people. The program provides a comprehensive benefit package for women and children receiving "Aid for Dependent Children" (welfare), certain people with disabilities, and people over 64 years of age who meet certain levels of impoverishment.

Medicaid programs are administered by the states under federal regulation. The federal government, through CMS (formerly HCFA), reimburses the state government for a portion of the expenses (from 50% to 83% depending on the state's economic status). Medicaid regulations require that states construct benefit programs that include ambulatory care, hospital care, and laboratory and pharmacy.

One of the compromises in the creation of Medicaid was that because the states were already operating state mental hospitals, there was no need for additional federal participation. Thus the program does not provide federal reimbursement for care provided to persons between ages 21 and 64 years in institutions for the treatment of mental diseases (the "IMD" rule).

State are given options on whether to provide certain coverage packages, but in general Medicaid services must be uniformly available statewide, be free to beneficiaries, provide beneficiaries the freedom to choose their provider, and use practitioners who also serve patients with other types of insurance.

In recent years, states have sought innovations under Medicaid rules in order to maximize the federal funding drawn in to support the state's health care efforts and to minimize uncompensated care. Early in President Clinton's term, Medicaid liberalized its requirements regarding "demonstration" waivers of basic Medicaid rules; a number of states instituted managed care approaches and other innovations under these waivers.

The author was intimately involved in Maryland's approach to the waiver process and, in a presentation to the American Psychiatric Association, summarized the story as follows:

During the 1990s, Maryland experienced rapid growth in Medicaid costs, and especially in Medicaid mental health and substance-abuse costs. At the same time, Maryland, like many states, had a fragmented behavioral health delivery system, in part driven by a complex array of funding sources. This fragmentation reduced coordination of care, frustrated patients and administrators, and increased the administrative costs of the system. In addition, many people in need of mental health care remained uninsured or underinsured. Existing Medicaid prepaid capitated contracts were loosely articulated and difficult to enforce. The prepaid plans accepting these early contracts delivered little in the way of mental health service, particularly to persons with severe mental illnesses, people not targeted for marketing. Such patients were disenrolled readily.

The Mental Hygiene Administration and Medicaid sought consultation in anticipation of likely Medicaid reform. We funded a project to evaluate the advisability, feasibility, and alternative models of initiating community-based mental health managed care systems. We looked at other states; at analyses of Maryland Medicaid's mental health utilization patterns; and at the potential for Core Service Agencies to be involved in managing care.

Our consultants found that the Medicaid programs in some states had reported success, through use of managed care, in controlling costs, in steering patients to appropriate settings, and in maintaining quality and access. However, lack of comparison groups, inadequate data on utilization, and lack of controls for outcomes flawed these assessments. Studies focusing particularly on *mental health* managed care in Medicaid were few. Among these, some problems had been identified, particularly the low rate of diagnosis and treatment of mentally ill patients within health maintenance organizations. Despite an extensive body of research, few studies had disentangled the effects of different managed care mechanisms. Consequently, little was known about which of many approaches was best or what the costs or savings would be.

Demonstration projects in which a risk-adjusted or fixed daily prepaid rate was set for the care of *severely* mentally ill patients had generally improved continuity of care, although the impacts on cost and quality were mixed. Several states had Medicaid programs wherein mental health services were delivered through health maintenance organizations, but little concrete data about utilization or outcomes were available. Anecdotal evidence indicated that treatment of persons with severe mental illness in HMO settings might be inappropriate. It was difficult, based on what was known in 1995 when the study was done, to predict either the cost savings or clinical effects that might be achievable for large public-sector programs. Policymakers expected managed care to reduce Medicaid costs, cover additional populations, and also improve quality of care. These hopes were probably unrealistic.

While "fully integrated" services including both physical and mental health seemed theoretically optimal, achieving such integration for indigent populations and particularly those with disabilities had not succeeded. There was underdiagnosis of mental disease by primary care physicians, the need for a broader range of behavioral services than most health plans were willing to mount, and the difficulty private plans had in linking to nonmedical community support services. Carving out only populations with severe mental illness also seemed to present significant problems, including definition, identification, and tracking; the stigma attached to such labeling; developing actuarial assumptions and rates; and managing selection bias ("dumping" of patients into the carved-out system to avoid high-cost cases).

Due in part to these factors, most states have either excluded the disabled population from their Medicaid reforms or have developed specialty mental health service systems for all categories of Medicaid eligible people. Two states that attempted to include all populations in "fully integrated" managed care programs—Tennessee and Massachusetts—switched to a specialty mental health system approach because of problems they experienced with continuity of care, underservice, and fragmentation of their public mental health systems.

At the time we did this study, at least 16 states had implemented or were planning specialty mental health service systems rather than carving out selected populations. In determining how to structure their systems, states tended to build on strengths. States with strong county-based mental health systems often built on these systems. States in which community mental health centers were dominant often used these as their anchor for managed mental health. Two of the three states that developed statewide contracts with managed behavioral health companies (Iowa and Nebraska) were primarily rural.

Community or county-based managed mental health entities have supplemented their capabilities through purchased services from, or joint ventures with, behavioral managed care organizations. Most recently, states have begun to consider consolidating funding streams as an additional means to eliminate service fragmentation and inefficiency. Maryland has become one of those states.

During the 1990s, our Maryland Administration pursued a variety of initiatives to broaden the continuum of care and to create linkages with critical social and residential services for indigent persons suffering from mental illness. Maryland's public mental health system served an overlapping but different population than the Medicaid system. It included indigent, uninsured, and underinsured individuals with mental health problems. Only some had Medicaid. If the public mental health programs were not structured into the proposed Medicaid reform, the state would continue to bear the fixed costs of operating the public system for those in need of these services but not insured by Medicaid.

The Secretary of Health was mobilized by certain members of the Maryland General Assembly to seek comprehensive Medicaid reform. He made this decision while still very new in office and not very familiar with initiatives undertaken by the prior Secretary to manage escalating Medicaid costs. His vision was to place all beneficiaries into full-service prepaid health plans and ensure quality through health department oversight. By expecting more accountability from the existing Medicaid HMOs and soliciting new plans while reducing their capitation rates, he hoped to contain costs and wring increased efficiency out of the system. The Department would do the marketing, enrollment, and ombudsman functions, thereby saving the plans money over their existing operations. This in part justified the lower fees. Any plan that met the insurance commissioner's solvency requirements and various performance requirements would be eligible to contract for patients. There were to be no population or service carve-outs.

There were dangers in integrating medical–surgical services with the public mental health system. People with serious and persistent mental illness were at risk for being dumped from the HMO rolls back into what was left of the public mental health system. We also were concerned about dividing mental health care activities between providers serving the Medicaid HMOs and those serving the public mental health system. Mental health system provider organizations needed a minimal number of patients to be viable. Splitting the patients among many HMOs would mean that none would have enough mental health specialty clients to keep complex services available.

We therefore were concerned about whether or not adequate services would be provided to HMO patients with severe mental illness and whether or not we could force HMOs to provide an array of aftercare services to minimize lengths of stay in state hospitals. The experiences in other states suggested that solutions in which mental health services were separately administered from the physical health system would be safest.

The Secretary, on the contrary, believed firmly that if we were to write the expectations properly into the HMO contracts, the Department could then hold these organizations accountable for their performance. The Administration doubted that mental health would occupy a sufficiently central priority in the overall physical health scheme to ensure enforcement of any contract provisions that were mental health only. We additionally doubted the health department bureaucracy's ability to regulate a new $2 billion industry. After all, the HMOs were already politically powerful, were not constrained from lobbying, had deep pockets and an inclination toward political contributions. The prior record of the HMOs in providing mental health service was spotty at best. The health department, which had to operate within politically controlled regulations, was, by comparison, a puny watchdog. It was clear to all stakeholders in the mental health community that throwing all Medicaid-related mental health resources into the control of the HMOs was too dangerous, no matter how the contract was written.

Our years of hard work building support and agreement among mental health constituencies now were paying dividends. The Mental Health Association, which had taken the lead in the fight for Maryland's parity law, working with the Alliance for the Mentally Ill, formed a coalition of stakeholders to shepherd the reform. Fortunately, the Secretary had embarked on one of the most open processes that any state had used in changing its Medicaid program. He was extremely chagrined at the unanimity and forcefulness of the mental health community in questioning his plan. He and I conversed at length about how to reconcile his position with what was emerging in the public process. Our concern about splitting the provider base between the state subsidized safety net for the uninsured and many mini–mental health systems in HMOs serving the Medicaid program, he found hard to understand. Our concern about dumping he understood, but believed he could control.

The Secretary believed in the concept of a "medical home" responsible for all aspects of a person's health care. He wanted very much not to relieve these newly constituted HMOs from overall responsibility for psychiatric as well as medical aspects of care. He believed he could "hold their feet to the fire." He feared one exception begetting others. Yet he also knew that his plan could not go forward unless the major advocacy organizations were satisfied. Even the local public health officers from whose ranks the Secretary had come and whose cause he tended to champion, most of whom operated community mental health clinics—even *they* had serious reservations.

One evening, at an employee recognition ceremony at one of the state hospitals, the Secretary and I were side by side at the head table. We began chatting about how to end the impasse. I agreed that we should expect the managed care organization to render primary care mental health services. These were the sort of services that family practitioners, pediatricians, and internists usually offer their patients prior to referral to specialists. Not all upper respiratory illnesses are sent to pulmonologists; not all diabetes is treated by an endocrinologist; not all childhood misbehavior is immediately referred to child psychiatry. Ordinary primary care would include the *psyche* as well as the *soma*.

We would expect competent referral and initial mental status assessments from the managed care organizations. All specialty mental health care would be the province of the Administration, which would operate the Medicaid Specialty Mental Health System. This would be called the "integrated mental health system," meaning that all publicly subsidized services would be provided by one system. The word *carve-out* would not be used. The Secretary of Health smiled. A resolution was found that *night* which he could embrace in the morning. It was not, to his way of thinking, a typical exception; the HMOs would have to deliver primary mental health care; the mental health community would have its system preserved. We both believed it was doable and acceptable to most factions, and that evening a deal was struck between us.

Little did we know, as on stage we sipped coffee, what a battle we were about to initiate. The compromise worked well with virtually all the stakeholders involved in the public planning process. The only opponent to the proposal was one lobbyist, who argued forcefully that the mental health services should be delivered by the HMOs and that the public mental health system should remain only as a safety net for any Medicaid beneficiaries needing state hospital services. She wasn't worried about dumping or about the extraction of one-third of the public mental health system's dollars to be given to private for-profit corporations with very poor history in the mental health field. In spite of her assertive testimony, the plan was ultimately drafted consistent with the dinner deal between the Secretary and me.

However, the HMOs did not receive the news about the specialty mental health system with enthusiasm. They also didn't tell anyone of their opposition during the planning phase.

When the reform proposal, drafted as legislation, went to the General Assembly, the HMO industry struck. Not only did they oppose the mental health provisions, they also opposed aspects of every part of the bill. The Secretary was receiving a graduate education in the difficulty he would have in policing this industry. The industry's alligator shoes were at the legislative committees morning and night. The lobbyist had made killing the mental health compromises her personal battle and seemed to be personally orchestrating the HMO lobbying effort. The fate of the waiver began looking very grim.

All might have been lost had not a new Deputy Secretary for Medicaid been recruited. She was a savvy ex-legislator from California who arrived during a snowstorm that covered the East, oriented herself to the dilemma rapidly, and skillfully led the legislative counterattack. The mental health coalition hired an ex-gubernatorial candidate as a lobbyist for our shared position.

The HMOs desperately wished to keep the mental health dollars in their capitation payment. We later learned that, despite all their pleas that their version of integrated care included broad mental health benefits, only 1% of the 19% of capitation earmarked for mental health was actually spent. *The mental health dollars were their profit line.*

In negotiations, I indicated that if the HMOs wished to continue providing mental health services, their providers could participate in the publicly managed mental health system on a fee-for-service basis. They would also have to accept referrals of uninsured and forensic patients, just as does any other public provider. They were tempted by the offer of funding their mental health providers at the public system's expense, but they didn't want anything to do with these add-on populations. They continued to fight the mental health services carve-out altogether.

The tensest moment came during my testimony in the final hearing before the Environmental Matters Committee:

"Doctor, do you mean that if an HMO wanted to offer mental health services as part of the public mental health system it would also have to accept the care of uninsured and forensic patients who were not part of its panel of patients?" I responded "yes." The hearing room buzzed. The HMOs postured as if it were the first time they had heard this, even though this requirement had always been cited in discussions. The Secretary started to waver.

The committee chairman politely inquired whether I was considering my future employment and repeated the question.

The answer did not change, and, with some trepidation, I began to repeat it. The Deputy Secretary weighed in loudly, "He's already told you the answer. They have got to accept the same responsibility as any other provider in the public mental health system. They've been told that; they just don't like it."

The Secretary relaxed. Most members of the committee, who didn't trust the HMO industry very much, broke into smiles. The legislative committee added language enabling the Department to penalize the HMOs for improper referrals to the mental health system. It was 2 a.m.; the committee vote was favorable; the chairman reached under his desk and produced a bottle of Scotch. We celebrated. The real victory party was in April 1996, when the full legislature, in the closing hour of the session, passed the bill.

The year after that was intense as we moved from winning the legislative endorsement to making the changes happen. Some of the major tasks were writing the regulations describing the detailed functioning of the new Medicaid program and the new public mental health system, developing the procurement for the administrative services organization, contracting with the successful bidder, working out the balance of responsibility between the Administration and the Core Service Agencies, corresponding with the Health Care Financing Administration to obtain the federal government's approval of the reform, setting the rates for mental health services, fighting with the provider community over the adequacy of the rates, and publishing the managed care review criteria. Each of these tasks spawned many subtasks. Each required consultation and consensus building at every step along the way. We moved forward.

On July 1, 1997, Medicaid beneficiaries began to be enrolled in new HMO-like entities called managed care organizations (MCOs) for their medical care. The enrollment process was arranged by the Department. The public mental health system began to provide specialty mental health services to Medicaid enrollees and to uninsured or underinsured patients. Then-current state hospital patients, if Medicaid eligible, joined MCOs upon discharge from the hospital.

The reform plan permitted Medicaid to pay for private psychiatric and state hospital care, affording hospital care at a lower cost. The Administration required discharge of psychiatric inpatients to community alternatives whenever inpatient care was no longer clinically indicated or when appropriate clinical services could be delivered by a community-based system.

Most specialty mental health services are delivered on a fee-for-service basis. The public mental health system and the new MCOs collaborate on interface issues of continuity of care, referral process, information sharing, treatment of dually diagnosed patients, consultation, pharmacy, and other issues. All mental health services require preauthorization by the public system through the services of a private mental health managed care firm contracted to the Administration on an "administrative services only" basis. The firm was recruited through public procurement, answers to the Administration and county-based Core Service Agencies, and is paid a fixed fee minus penalties for poor performance. The Mental Hygiene Administration and the Core Service Agencies must approve all administrative and clinical protocols.

From my perspective, the entire transformation of the Medicaid system posed unique dangers for patients with mental illness served by the public sector. While we are driven by many bosses in the public sector (taxpayers, politicians, providers, advocates), we tried to plan a new approach that was client-centered. By moving to fee-for-service and subsidizing the uninsured on a sliding copayment schedule, we linked resources to the patient rather than the provider. In what may be a first for Medicaid, we became able to pay providers promptly and easily.

We also created, through the deliverables in the contract with the managed care administrative services partner, robust data, outcome analysis, and system planning capabilities. Now decisions about care will involve the client, the care manager, and the provider. Funding will follow the patient, who is afforded considerably more choice than under the old paradigm. (Silver, 1997)

Federal Public-Sector Block Grants

The federal government also contributes to mental health care and substance abuse services through "block grants" to the states. Original federal support for such care was given directly to local nonprofit agencies under the Community Mental Health Centers Act of 1963. This program bypassed the state mental health authorities and provided gradually declining levels of support for individual programs. Later they were supplanted by a consolidated formula-driven grant from the appropriate administrations of DHHS. These block grants came to foster the development of community-based services and catalyze broad-based planning and innovation in state-operated mental health systems. They also provided direct support for the bulk of the national effort in publicly subsidized treatment for substance abusers.

Indirect Federal Funding: Tax Subsidies for Private Employers

The federal government also subsidizes most employer-paid health insurance premiums by permitting the employer to include these costs as legitimate business expenses and thus not seen as corporate profits subject to tax. The employer-paid benefit is not identified as income to the employee and is not subject to individual income tax. Thus, the federal tax methodology contributes about one-quarter of the cost of the private health insurance system by accepting the loss of revenue to the federal coffers and leaving it in private hands. Those who protest the federal government's increasing involvement in the area of private health insurance often do not recognize this fact.

Ancillary Funding: Federal Research Grants

A variety of federal grants, primarily through the National Institute of Mental Health (NIMH), are available for mental health research. Other relevant grants, particularly for services research, come from the Center for Mental Health Services (CMHS), a division of the Substance Abuse and Mental Health Services Administration (SAMHSA). These grants are usually competitive and support a variety of research efforts across the country. Their protocols often contain a substantial service component. One, for example, supported a study of a mobile assertive treatment model in the management of homeless substance abusers with mental illness. While structured as a stringent research protocol, the project nevertheless provided significant service in downtown Baltimore. Provider agencies may work with academic departments to facilitate their project development and participation.

STATE FUNDS

In the middle of the 19th century, state governments across the United States, catalyzed by the efforts of Dorothea Dix, began constructing public mental hospitals. Over the next hundred years those institutions gradually became larger and increasingly dreary. Usually overcrowded, understaffed, and ill-maintained, and with an increasingly diffuse mission, the state hospital systems were discouraging places by the end of World War II.

During the last 50 years, propelled by a variety of forces, states have been reducing the size of the state hospitals and closing many of them. As a result, where state funds in the past mainly paid for state hospital costs, states currently pay for a variety of community-based and ambulatory services designed to minimize use of state hospital beds.

State expenditures for both inpatient and outpatient mental health care exceed the amounts contributed for Medicaid match. Thus, the states remain a major source of payment not only for traditional services, but also for some of the more innovative services such as in-home crisis intervention, assertive community treatment, and therapeutic nurseries.

States typically fund mental health services either through line-item budgeting of state-run programs or through awarding of grants to programs to perform specified services for specific targeted populations. State publicly funded mental health efforts are administered by mental health departments, which in some states are cabinet-level agencies and in others are embedded in health or social service departments. A recent study found that the states spend more than $100 billion each year on purchase-of-service contracts for social services. In 1996, Bachman reported on a study of mental health services procurement in six states. She found that there were a variety of contractual funding arrangements, but that states were reluctant to change established arrangements unless a provider demonstrated egregious behavior. She further reported that these states have begun to contract for specialized or geographically based services based on state planning processes. These contracts were often provided by competitive bidding. Standard monitoring methods included licensure, review of provider budgets, populations served, and Medicaid audits. Recently, states have begun to include consumer participation in site visits and provider reviews. State mental health authorities have become increasingly interested in outcome measures to assess program performance. Included among these were hospital length of stay, recidivism, and evidence of goal-oriented treatment (Bachman, 1996).

LOCAL FUNDS

Cities, counties, and regional multigovernment groups also provide funding for mental health services. The health departments of larger cities like New York and Los Angeles administer larger and more complex programs than those of many states. Usually, local departments of health or social services have a mental health component which receives a composite funding stream from local, state, and federal sources and administers these funds in a manner consistent with the funding agency directives (but tailored to local needs). Some states require local match of state mental health funds, while others depend on voluntary local funding.

Local funds are often earmarked for particular local priorities that are not on the state's list of funding objectives. They are typically awarded as grants or contracts for programs, rather than on a fee-for-service basis. Occasionally, local departments contract with specific providers to see publicly funded patients on a fee basis at the time of service.

In some states, local jurisdictional purchase of services is a major common pathway for funding mental health service. The Robert Wood Johnson Foundation recently awarded large competitive grants to nine cities to establish "local mental health authorities" to better administer local systems of care. Such projects reflect the dispersion of persons with severe mental illness out of state hospitals and into communities, and the complexity of reproducing and administering comprehensive service systems in local jurisdictions.

CLINICIAN/ORGANIZATION RISK-ACCEPTANCE

Because of rapidly increasing costs of health insurance, some business organizations are retaining some of the risk themselves. Visits to practitioners may be funded directly by the patient's employer, or the employer may reimburse the employee for such bills. Insurance is reserved for hospital, pharmacy, and laboratory costs. Employers may retain a care management firm to enroll providers and review care for appropriateness and necessity.

FAMILY PAYERS

When one thinks of third-party payers, one typically thinks of health insurance companies. Often, however, members of the patient's family accept financial responsibility for a patient's treatment. This routinely occurs in the care of children, but sometimes happens with ill or disabled adults as well. This type of arrangement, particularly for psychiatric or other mental health care, introduces several new parameters with regard to such matters as confidentiality, consequences of delayed payment or nonpayment, the psychological meaning attached to such support in psychotherapy, and the like. Although the therapist and the clinical program cannot anticipate all possible contingencies, providers too often enter into this type of "third-party payment" without appreciating that it is often more complex and potentially difficult than dealing with an insurer.

REFERENCES

Bachman, S. S. (1996). Monitoring mental health service contracts: Six states' experiences. *Psychiatric Services, 47*(8), 837–841.

Dorwart, R. A., Chartock, L. R., & Epstein, S. S. (1992). Financing of services. In J. A. Talbott et al. (Eds.), *Textbook of administrative psychiatry* (pp. 313–346). Washington, DC: American Psychiatric Press.

Mechanic, D. (1999). *Mental health and social policy: The emergence of managed care.* Needham Heights, MA: Allyn and Bacon.

Silver, S. B. (1997, May). *The psychiatrist as director in the public mental health system.* Administrative Psychiatry Award Lecture, American Psychiatry Association Annual Meeting, San Diego, CA.

SUGGESTED READING

Rodenhauser, P. (2000). *Mental health care administration.* Ann Arbor, MI: University of Michigan Press.

Talbott, J. A., & Hales, R. E. (Eds.). (2001). *Textbook of administrative psychiatry: New concepts for a changing behavioral health system* (2nd ed.). Washington, DC: American Psychiatric Press.

Chapter Twenty-Five

Values Issues in Fiscal Management

Stuart B. Silver

Most business decisions in the planning and operations of a mental health program are founded on the values and ethics of the participants. One may conceptualize such decisions arising in both budgeting and in operational management. Following this framework, let us explore some examples of these issues at the level of mental health system administration and at the level of the leadership of an individual program.

The state mental health authority operates at the system level. Its leaders are responsible for allocating large sums of money to provide services for large numbers of people, many of whom are indigent. A fundamental question in budgeting is whether public funds only subsidize care of the indigent or are publicly funded services provided to those with some means. Does the presence of a publicly subsidized mental health program in a rural area chill the development of a private practice alternative? Would any services be developed in that rural area without government sponsorship? The state mental health authority aims to foster the availability of adequate services in all regions while providing each consumer several choices of provider and without stifling competition. Is priority given to those suffering the most severe disability and distress, or to those most likely to recover? Is the care of children favored over care for the elderly? What is the basis for regional allocation of resources? Is it based on total population, or indigent population, or the availability of providers, or political considerations unrelated to mental health needs? The owners and managers of the system remain responsible for these calls, not the accountants who prepare the budgets.

Other avenues through which the system's values are expressed in budgeting include copayments policy, the rationale for discontinuing programs deemed inefficient, the level of funding for quality control efforts, and the flexibility of the system to add resources to meet additional needs. These issues are usually interrelated.

A classic example in state government is the decision about whether or not to support the application of state hospitals for survey by the Joint Commission on the Accreditation of Healthcare Organizations (JCAHO). In the private sector, hospitals must be JCAHO-accredited in order to qualify for most sources of third-party payment. Because state hospitals largely serve indigent populations and, in most cases, are precluded by law from reimbursement by the Medicaid program, it is not mandatory for their survival that they be accredited. The cost of maintaining accreditation is high, extending beyond the immediate cost of survey to additional staffing and training costs. Because these costs will not be recovered by higher collections, maintaining hospital accreditation may come at the expense of other needed mental health services.

Mental health professionals know that the process of maintaining accreditation, although at times frustrating and wasteful, pays off in more accountable and thoughtful inpatient care. What mental health service trade-offs are made elsewhere in the mental health system to maintain accreditation at the state hospitals? If no trade-offs are made in the mental health system, are they made in other agencies of government, or are taxes raised?

Values and ethics of the managers also express themselves in decisions about day-to-day operations. The leaders of a mental health system will have to consider such questions as whether to fund individual patients or to offer general grants to programs, whether to require competitive procurement, and how to re-deploy funds. Should the system extend or restrict hours of operation? What kind of patient satisfaction and outcome reporting should be mandated? Should "managed care" be instituted? Each of these decisions may be largely fiscally driven, or the financial planning along these axes may be values driven. In some cases the financial and ethical direction are complementary, whereas in others there may be a tension between service values and financial limits.

At the program level as well, values drive budgeting strategy. An example of such a decisional axis is determination of the proportion of a provider's time to be spent in billable activities. One of the toughest areas for management is computing what volume of service reasonably to expect from professional staff members. This is especially true if these providers are salaried. Incentives drive performance. Typically, providers whose income is based on their collected fees have higher billings than do providers on a fixed salary. Probably the correct level of productivity is between these two values. It is the task of managers to make sure that consultation and charting time are adequate for fee-driven providers and that the salaried types don't spend too much time at coffee break. It is an easier management task to slow down the fee-driven providers than to increase the efficiency of those on salary. Does the budget reflect a realistic allocation of time between revenue-generating activities and other important but not billable activities related to patient care and program support? Additional issues whose dimensions are value laden include the plans for the use of surplus revenues, what kind of severance package is offered to employees, what proportion of budgeted expenditures go for administration, and what portion pays for direct service provision. Does the program provide for clinical supervision of provider staff members, and what other quality control systems are budgeted? Does the program accept prepaid capitated funding?

At the program level, values may be reflected in operational policies such as collections strategies and whether to offer care to indigents. Does the particular agency treat involuntary or otherwise coerced patients? How does the program deal with noncompliant patients? An important operational question for programs that accept capitated funding of care revolves around safeguards against underservice. Does the program provide for patient advocates, an orderly grievance process, and a peer review structure? Operationally, does the program give each patient the opportunity to feel valued and respected, no matter the source and mechanism of funding of that person's care?

At each level, choices that are related to one agenda, such as quality management, affect the level of resources for other priorities, such as hours of service or sliding scale fee schedule. Given this dilemma, the process of weighing alternative decisions and defining the values that guide them may be far more important than the direction of the decisions themselves. The same principles that guided the construction of the business plan are relevant to the process of weighing financial and business strategies. Thus, this section has come full circle from business ideas and their associated vision and mission statements to the development of formal business plans, budgets, financial management tools and financing strategies, and back to the relevance of underlying values to financial management decisions.

Part Four

INFORMATION AND INFORMATION TECHNOLOGY

INTRODUCTION

Chris E. Stout

Clinical leadership has become much more complex and sophisticated than it was even 5 years ago. There are many new challenges that face us all, from regulatory standards to marketplace demands, from consumer advocacy and involvement to evidence-based practice models that focus on manifold outcomes. Thankfully, our tools and models have evolved as well. Today it is incumbent on the competent clinical leader to be able to walk seamlessly between the worlds of clinical science, theory, and practice, as well as business models, organizational postulates, and technological advances—all within a framework of ethical behavior, finite resources, and dynamic systems interplay.

The chapters in this section incorporate those issues in such a way as to provide a practical set of tools, ideas, and models. We have tried to provide a measured balance of what is currently possible, future directions, and a dash here and there of what *may* be.

This section begins with a discussion of the issues of postmodern leadership in a context of informatics, and provides examples of web-based application services and a model of data-driven, integrated clinical decision making enabled by artificial neural network technology. (If some of these terms aren't familiar, the glossary in the appendix will help with the new information technology vocabulary.)

Jerome's work advises us that leaders must keep pace with the transformations occurring in many areas: novel technology applications, new directions in service provision, emerging skill sets, shifts in consumer characteristics, fundamental changes in interpersonal relationships, ethics, and the interface between human beings and machines. Mahalik tackles the vast and important issues involved with technologies and medical records administration, clinical data/knowledge management, and associated regulatory and legal considerations.

Devoting an entire chapter to videoconferencing may at first seem a bit dispro-portionate; however, it is commensurate with the fact that such technologies are likely to be a foundation of future deployment of care services. Cradock and Simpatico provide a powerful examination of the issues and considerations involved. Dinwiddie, Staples, and Meyers offer a virtual "how-to" in their analysis of informed decision making's pivotal role in changing the clinical culture and practice of large inpatient facilities. Their work serves as a model for information technology's powerful role as an instrument for change, and as an enabling tool for what may be a paradigm shift in clinical operations.

For community-based care, Simpatico, Cradock, McGuire, and Zvetina provide a real-world model that uses information technology to integrate many previously disconnected service providers, facilities, and agencies. Their work is an exemplar of how broad-based thinking, combined with sophisticated understanding of sys-tems operations and enabled by technological solutions, can greatly improve patient outcomes. Such is the cornerstone of mental health care leadership. The application of ethical principles plays a crucial role not only in clinical practice, but also in clinical leadership and decision making. Demuth's chapter discusses integrating ethics with technology in clinical decision making, and offers several helpful resources.

The authors in this section have tried to balance the wide-ranging, foundational aspects of information, technology, decision making, and clinical leadership where they come together in mental health management. They offer examples, models, and demonstrations that the clinical administrator can generalize across various disci-plines, settings, and circumstances. We hope that readers will have their assump-tions challenged and their concepts of what could be, broadened.

Chapter Twenty-Six

Informatics, Technology, and the Clinical Leader

Chris E. Stout

P rogressive clinical leadership in an era of postmodern management is based on the ability to relinquish obsolete thinking before such supposed "tried-and-true" ideas become sacrosanct or mistaken for truths (Sherman & Schultz, 1998). Postmodern clinical leadership considers the complex interplay of various, diverse, and seemingly unrelated causal aspects over the more traditional modern approach of linear cause-and-effect relationships. Although this may seem an obvious and easy task for the intelligentsia of clinical leaders, it is often very difficult. In fact, many find that the practice of clinical leadership involves daily battling of illogical bureaucracies, coping with glacial timelines (or lags), constant evangelizing of one's perspective, fostering the systemic adoption of change as a value, and proffering of nonlinear, complex examinations of multiply causal business and clinical considerations. All this plays against a backdrop of perhaps years of preestablished, centrally organized, bureaucratic policies, clichés, and inertia that tend to maintain the often irrational status quo of an organization.

The wise use of knowledge is one of the best means of combating the gravitational pull of organizational mediocrity. Access to such knowledge comes from information, and information is begat by data. Robust informatics (generally defined herein as some form of automated information system) is an indispensable part of organization infrastructures that work to avoid the failures just mentioned. That is, although questioning of assumptions plays a fundamental part in postmodern management, there must be a means of directing the "interrogation." Part of the clinical leader's role involves developing an "understanding of both the nature of how we create what we know—our epistemology—and of [the] practical conduct" of the health care organization (Sherman & Schultz, 1998, p. 28). Informatics is the tool-in-aid for that process.

Such information-based decision making has its roots in data processing. The phrase *data processing* has evolved into *data management*. This fostered the premise that if greater meaning could be added to the representation of the data, we could somehow have *information* that would be more useful to our tasks in managing. This was often achieved by graphical representations and elemental (typically only descriptive) statistical analyses being applied to the data in an aggregated database—heady stuff at the time, but surely better than hunches and bias-prone guessing.

Knowledge management has now evolved as the current in-vogue term. This represents yet another enhanced development of even more sophisticated analysis as well as cross-analysis of various data sources (that are often discrete and nonaggregated), improved statistical analysis beyond just descriptive statistics (to include inferential and predictive modeling methods), improved ease of use at the desktop, and broad availability of access across different levels of users (e.g., from line staff to administration). Some systems now can also provide for scenario planning simulations via one's *notions* in combination with one's *real data*, as well as self-organizing—organic, if you will—emulations based on "what if" experiments. In nonmedical fields, knowledge management will likely beneficially mutate into another even more descriptive term and model as the technology and thinking continue to evolve. A possible future direction that health care leaders may see is a hybrid of knowledge management and disease management in the form of an increasingly rich, evidence-based, technology-enhanced system for care.

Quality information makes informed decision making possible; it is indispensable for organization managers and leaders. What factors create good information? For some, the source is largely free of digital technology (cf. "managing by walking around"). Nothing in this chapter really opposes such an elegant "technology," or other "low-tech" approaches such as observation, trial and error, or "thought experiments." Each has its role, and none should be dismissed out of hand.

No health system manager or clinician, however, should ignore the many other resources that can increase the quality and quantity of important information (and simpler resources aren't always feasible or available). The balance of this chapter focuses on technologically based aids to management decisions in mental health settings.

WHAT ARE WE ALREADY DOING?

The use of technology in managing a practice or an organized system of care is nothing novel. There are hundreds of companies marketing impressive products and services to clinicians clinics, mental health centers, hospitals, multiservice organizations, and government mental health agencies. The fundamental point for the senior manager or clinical leader, however, is that adding technology (such as computers) to a process, or upgrading current equipment, will not by itself improve clinical care, management capabilities, or the financial bottom line. Blindly adding computers to solve problems or improve systems is pure fantasy. Technological enhancement of bad systems usually makes them worse (but faster!). *The positive impact of technology on business is based on careful planning to match the technological investment with need, feasibility, and budget.*

Clinicians and facilities with technology needs often cite the mantra of a "paperless office." Sometimes this is a reasonable goal and a desired outcome, but "service businesses have doubled their investments in computer technology during the last 10 years [before 1996]; yet productivity has grown only 0.1 percent per year in these businesses" (Holtman, 1996, p. 101). Mental health managers must first examine current business processes and clinical practices, and only then consider technology's offerings. Technology is

> a necessary but insufficient tool in practice or facility management. Second, they must examine and evaluate processes of operation—work and information flow—in order to exploit technology most successfully. "Technologizing" a practice or facility does not permit management to abdicate its responsibility for operational design-improved efficiency." (Stout, 1999, p. 53)

How Are Others Using Technology?

In a recent survey of 809 physician group executives conducted by *Modern Physician* and PricewaterhouseCoopers (Scott, 2000), the most frequent use of a computer-based system was for billing, followed by scheduling. Such programs have long been in the market, are easy for staff to use, and provide direct and quantifiable payback in terms of accounts deliverable, efficient aging of accounts, and increased clean claims submitted. When this group was asked about their motivations for investing in information technology, the top three answers were, in order, improved business performance, clinical quality improvement, and managed practice performance. It would thus appear that clinical leaders are indeed using informatics to aid in their management.

In *Business at the Speed of Thought*, Bill Gates devotes a chapter to health care technology and notes that "a five-physician clinic in Hammond, Louisiana, invested about $50,000 in PC patent systems that made data entry easy for the doctors; the clinic saved $60,000 the first year in transcription costs alone" (1999, p. 355). The *Modern Physician*/PricewaterhouseCoopers study noted that most respondents spend less than 2% of their total operating expenses on their information technology budget. The same study found that over half the respondents currently use the Internet; a third responded "sometimes." The primary reason physician executives gave for not using the Internet was that their office staff did so instead. Reasons of slow speed, security concerns, mistrust of information, or fear of being flooded with e-mail were all around 5% or less.

Cost

Cost is a common concern in health care technology decisions. Managed care has deflated the revenues of most private providers and facilities, and expenses related to laboratory and equipment costs may be broadly budgeted under "technology," but "most experts estimate that 20 to 30 percent of the annual trillion-dollar cost of the U.S. healthcare system is tied up in paperwork . . . compounding the cost, about 13 percent of the one to two billion claims filed each year in the United States are returned for errors" (Gates, 1999, p. 335). Health care organizations typically apply 2% to 3% of their revenues to information technology; banking, albeit not a perfect comparison, spends about 15%.

Clinical leaders and managers have faced enormous transitions and increasing practice and administrative demands over the last two decades. Practitioners have had to keep up with changes in treatment approaches, increasing external management of care, extensive regulation, and escalating vulnerability to litigation. During these transitions, the thought of going further into debt (in a time of decreased income and cash flow) to purchase modern information technology made it seem unaffordable, even though most recognized it as critical to economic survival (Stout, 1999). One of the problems was indecision about software, and the hardware needed to run it effectively. The question used to be, "do we build our own custom system, or buy one, or both?" Today, there may be a third, better choice.

Internet-Based Solutions

One of the best solutions for streamlining many mental health organizations is Internet-deployed application service providers (ASPs). These companies keep frequently updated software on *their* computers, and allow others to use it (from a distance, online) for a fee that is usually much less than the cost of purchase, development, and maintenance on one's own system. Access to practice management and clinical decision support software through the Internet on a rental basis provides organizations and practices with the power and efficiency of very sophisticated software without the steep initial costs or ongoing maintenance hassles and costs (Stout & Alter, 2000; Stout & Giolas, 2000). Health care ASPs can combine the power of the Internet with a deep and growing knowledge base, efficient and effective management tools, and broad connectivity to contracted payors and clinical resources. An ASP can unite most or all of the organization's clinical and administrative functions through one seamless interface, making the system available—with appropriate authorizations and safeguards—to every department and staff person that needs it. When this is done well, the organization may deal with only one vendor and one seamless "platform" (rather than several potentially incompatible brands and products).

There are inherent risks involved, however, with using an ASP vendor. The fact that one's ASP could conceivably cease business operations or initiate exorbitant rate increases is cause for very real concern. In mitigating such risks, it is incumbent upon the contracting provider to incorporate contractual language obligating the ASP to rapidly and securely transfer data to another ASP vendor on demand, as well as setting reasonable limits on subsequent fee increases. But even with data transfer between ASPs there can exist translation or "cross-walking" problems that can often require additional and significant costs and time delays in creating translation or "patch" programs. Thus, it is optimal to select an ASP that has a stable financial base and a high likelihood for longevity.

Affordability and accessibility will draw many organizations and their leaders to ASPs. The ASP uses the ubiquitous accessibility of the Web to deliver affordable software applications over the Internet, using one's already familiar browser (e.g., Internet Explorer, Netscape) as the interface with the software. Powerful and expandable functionality, such as with entire practice management systems, can be provided by an ASP as "rentware," eliminating large capital expenditure. The integration function can support and assist clinical decisions and automatically communicate care-related information to payors along with appropriate claims and billing information. Payor denials often decrease, bringing improved cash flow.

Internal Integration and Collaboration

The Internet also offers collaborative mechanisms never before realized in health care practice. An ASP can create and help implement an information management and communication system with staff and patients who may never have even sent an e-mail. Integrating scheduling and billing for geographically separate offices is one of the clearest advantages. E-mail to and from anywhere joins business and clinical processes in a way that marries the convenience of the Internet with the immediate needs of clinicians and staff. The ability to work from home (or a distant hotel room), simply using a familiar browser, adds convenience—and productivity—to busy lives (and supports employee benefits such as job sharing and ADA accommodation).

Connectivity within an organization enables real-time access to pivotal information and data. A process as basic as automated scheduling, for example, can reduce time, error, and frustration when many professionals and staff can access the same schedule from anywhere, at any time. An application service provider can serve as an intranet for an organization without the investment in hardware, software, or maintenance associated with freestanding intranets. Each staff person needs only a Web browser and Internet access to share data and information, and to make changes as they are authorized. Treatment guidelines and evidence-based clinical information can be available to doctors throughout the organization, including the point of care, increasing compliance with treatment protocols and formularies. Critical patient information can be communicated throughout relevant parts of the practice, and appropriate coding and billing information can be quickly transmitted to clerks or payors.

Critical data about the clinical and administrative functioning of an organization are often difficult to assemble. An ASP can provide real-time reports to the clinical leadership, enabling them to keep up with the organization's time management, finances, and practice patterns. This is an important support for continuous quality improvement programs.

It would be difficult to discuss every function an application service provider can provide, but some that are currently available, and that can be made as private and secure as necessary, include:

- Eligibility, benefits, and authorizations, accessed instantly online and automatically entered into a customized patient database.
- Integrating assessments and outcomes with treatment planning and progress tracking.
- Direct and efficient online payor authorizations.
- Online electronic claim submission, electronic payment, and direct deposit.
- Point-of-care database availability for patient records, current clinical information, clinical literature, drug interactions, patient education materials, and other resources (which can also be available to the patient).
- Electronic prescribing and prescription refill.
- Access to a comprehensive database of treatment planning approaches for difficult or ambiguous clinical situations.
- Virtual consultation with other clinicians, even very distant ones.
- Integrating comprehensive practice management solutions that combine different

aspects of the organization (billing, receivables tracking, scheduling, space allocation, and credentialing).
- Distributing payor-mandated measures and documentation throughout the organization, even to remote locations.
- Developing an entire "virtual private network" that is safe and confidential for these and other applications.
- Customizing the applications and network(s) to individual clinical and business needs.

Security

Medical and mental health practitioners and organizations have struggled with privacy, confidentiality, and security issues for decades. Each advance in information processing, storage, and communication—whether photocopiers, facsimile transmission, word processors, computer files, wireless telephones, e-mail, or web-based applications—has brought new challenges. Part of the public's new awareness and concern is related to the unprecedented opportunity for broad loss of privacy (e.g., unauthorized access to or unauthorized distribution of large numbers of records), the huge number of potential points of access (e.g., computers all over the world), and the perception of hidden or intangible threats (e.g., a computerized monitoring program or hacker that uses methods we don't readily understand), as contrasted with an unscrupulous clinic employee snooping through paper files.

The use of technology's offerings, including the Internet, makes it crucial that satisfactory protections be developed, and their presence communicated to consumers and patients. The Health Insurance Portability and Accountability Act (HIPAA) of 1996 deals specifically with health-related data in electronic formats. It provides a minimum level of regulation, including standards, for privacy protection, and allows for stricter state regulations in some areas. Any contract with an ASP should include written assurances that the ASP complies with HIPAA and other relevant privacy-related regulations, *and with the organization's own policies and procedures regarding security and confidentiality.* There should also be a reliable way for the health care organization to verify ASP compliance independently whenever necessary. The software, and sometimes patient data, reside on an ASP computer outside the organization, sometimes very far away, where the organization has little or no control over security or access.

> Any contract with an ASP should include written assurances that the ASP complies with HIPAA and other relevant privacy-related regulations, and with the organization's own policies and procedures regarding security and confidentiality. There should also be a reliable way for the health care organization to verify ASP compliance independently whenever necessary.

Among many other things, HIPAA mandates:

- Compliance with uniform standards of information transaction and data elements.
- A unique identifier for each patient, employer, health plan, and health care provider.

- Standardized code sets for the data elements used in electronic data interchange.
- Compliance with security, electronic signature, and privacy standards.

It is important to understand that *no patient authorization is required when the information is provided for the following purposes:*

- Treatment or payment.
- Management functions to support treatment or payment.
- Providing information to the person to whom protected health information pertains or that person's designee.
- Providing information to the Secretary of HHS for oversight activities or to public health, law enforcement, health oversight, judicial, and administrative proceedings.
- Reporting suspected health care fraud.
- Research (within strict requirements).
- Certain emergencies and military purposes.
- Providing information to a health plan by a health care provider for audit and related purposes.

Additional information and updates can be found at the following websites:

www.himss.org
www.privacysecuritynetwork.com/healthcare/
aspe.os.dhhs.gov/admnsimp/

WHERE MAY WE GO?

The Future Is Wireless

I believe that the next step from desktop Internet-based tools will be widespread use of Internet-based tools in the shirt pocket or palm. Current problems of bandwidth and standards adoption will likely be solved in the near future. "Hybrid" personal digital assistants (PDAs) and mobile telephones (i.e., units that perform more than one function) will soon be able to use broadband networks, as are cellular phones capable of transmitting up to 200 times as fast as today's average of 9,600 bits per second (www.ChiefExecutive.net, special issue 158).

Wireless Internet growth is outpacing that of "wired." In North America and Western Europe, local telephone access has been hard-wired for decades, creating a stable infrastructure that wireless marketing must overcome. In more remote areas, and huge parts of the "Third World," the absence of telephone "land lines" has given wireless communication a great infrastructure advantage. Governments and private enterprise can skip telephone lines altogether and go directly to wireless for a fraction of the cost. The leap to wireless voice, video, data, and Internet applications may be easier in those settings than in the urban United States, where the organization must be motivated to evolve away from an apparently adequate wired system.

According to IDC research (cited in www.ChiefExecutive.net, special issue 158), the number of wireless Internet users in the United States will grow from 7.4 million in 1999 to 61.5 million by 2003, whereas home Internet use in the United States will grow from 67 million to 101 million subscribers during the same period. A currently popular PDA, the 3Com Palm VII with a built-in wireless modem, had sold more than 100,000 units as of early 2001, each to a potential wireless Internet customer (www.ChiefExecutive.net, special issue 158). During the first quarter of 2000, America Online (AOL) announced alliances with Nokia and Ericsson to allow AOL subscribers access to their accounts through their mobile handsets (www.ChiefExecutive.net, special issue 158).

Even Newer Ideas

Our leadership is only as good as our ideas. Ideas that emanate from mechanistic, linear models of thinking often obscure the advantages of other systems. Health care and its management have progressed in a largely mechanical, logical fashion. What if Einstein had been a physician or a health care executive? Would he have handled the complex interplay of health care sophistication, marketplace dynamics, and clinical rigor differently, perhaps as a nonlinear system?

CLINICA

What follows is a conceptual model for readers to ponder, not so much as a suggestion to mimic or apply, but as a structure from which to consider the complex interplay of one's own work in the identification, development, and/or procurement of informatic tools to enhance one's effectiveness as a health care manager, leader, or executive.

I call this model CLINICA. It is a system concept that would have a dramatic impact on the way clinical, operational, and cost aspects of private health care are managed.

The problems in health care are manifold and complex:

- High health care costs.
- Increased liability risks to:
   Doctors and other providers.
   Hospitals.
   Clinics.
   Managed care organizations and insurers.
- Poor relationships between payors and providers, especially in managed care.
- The average phone contact between an MCO/HMO and a provider costs the MCO/HMO about $85.00 (M. Oss, personal communication, February 2001). That cost must be either recouped by the payor or passed to the subscriber.
- Managed care cost savings tend not to continue after initial managed care initiatives are implemented. Annual increases in health care costs and subscriber fees are similar to those in fee-for-service and other payor mechanisms.
- Clinicians and clinical managers continuously struggle to weigh managed care

mandates against patient need, and to provide care within clinical and ethical standards when payors may deny reimbursement.

The Paradox.   How can the health care organization maximize clinical outcome while not alienating the clinician, the patient, or the payor, and do so cost-effectively?

The Method.   The CLINICA solution is based on a "genetic" algorithm used for clinical decision making. Genetic algorithms are the "DNA" that powers artificial intelligence software programs. They enable a complex set of decision rules to be applied to a variety of situations, and they "learn" from the results and incorporate such learning in subsequent responses. This would develop an artificial neural network (ANN)—a diverse group of nonlinear statistical tools whose strengths lie in their ability to process many variables in a parallel fashion. This network would make probabilistic assumptions about the doctor, the patient, the facility (if applicable, such as a hospital), the diagnosis, and symptom presentation variables and would suggest the need for and type of (and perhaps level, frequency, or aggressiveness of) active case management. Patients who need more, get more; those that don't, don't, all without nearly as much expensive, error-prone human review. There are cost savings for both the provider and the payor (e.g., the facility need not draw blood if it is not necessary, and the payor need not pay for it). Decision support that is fast, dispassionate, and more likely to be accurate than humans would mean fewer and briefer payor reviews, and more efficient clinician and provider staff activity. Costs would be decreased, animosities diminished, quality improved, and liability risk reduced.

The algorithms provide guidance to *both* doctors and the MCO/HMO, creating benefits such as:

- Reduced time spent on phone calls, denials, appeals, reversing denials, and so on, which yields tangible savings for the MCO/HMO without the fear that utilization will spiral out of control. The MCO/HMO would likely reduce case management staff, telephony costs, and stress levels for staff dealing with doctors.
- Reduced friction and frustration between MCO/HMO and its case managers and doctors and hospitals.
- Leading knowledge bases would be the basis for treatment decisions, reducing liability risks to the doctors, the hospitals and clinics, and payors.
- Improved clinical outcomes, which could provide a secondary market advantage to those using the algorithm; many people may *want* to have their care managed with such a system.
- Treatment choices could be made vis-à-vis the benefit provided by the patient's plan in tandem with the facility or practice's capabilities while informing the patient as to the benefits and risks of noncovered alternatives.
- Health care costs could be controlled with less risk of poor-quality treatment.

The Technology.   The programs needed to build such a system would initially utilize artificial neural networks (ANNs), a diverse group of nonlinear statistical tools whose strengths lie in their ability to process many variables in a parallel fashion. These tools recognize patterns in complex systems, and perform better than more conventional statistical tools, especially when dealing with many interdependent variables.

The process of training the ANN requires presenting information to the input layer and associating the pattern of inputs with a known output. The ANN "learns" by adjusting the weight matrix of the intermediate and output layers so that a given input pattern will result in the correct output result. The process of doing this is called *supervised learning* in the "back-propagation neural network" (BPNN) paradigm used here. Minor changes in input data can produce substantial changes in output, sometimes called *discontinuities*, but this effect can be minimized by increasing the number of neurodes in the intermediate layer and by a variety of techniques using "simulated annealing" and genetic algorithms.

Thanks to faster, more widely available personal computers and the need for parallel processing methods to analyze complex problems, ANNs are finally gaining momentum in many fields of research, including health care. With proper precautions, for example, ANN sensitivity to input changes can give early warnings of changing patterns of care in health care systems.

The CLINICA technology is the easy part; such a system could literally be built tomorrow. Our challenge lies in developing the leadership to advocate and coordinate various stakeholders into a shared vision. Technology will likely never be a limiting factor in our becoming better clinical leaders and providing better care; the greater problems lie in overcoming parochial, linear models, and the resulting self-imposed boundaries to our imaginations.

REFERENCES

Gates, B. (1999). *Business at the speed of thought*. New York: Warner Books.

Holtman, J. A. (1996). *Re-engineering the medical practice*. Reston, VA: Anthony.

Scott, L. (2000, October). Point of contact. *Modern Physician,* pp. 39–54.

Sherman, H., & Schultz, R. (1998). *Open boundaries*. Reading, MA: Perseus Books.

Stout, C. E. (1999, February). Negotiating the technology maze. *Behavioral Healthcare Tomorrow,* pp. 58–64.

Stout, C. E., & Alter, G. (2000). *ASPs and the group practice*. www.LifescapePro.com (further information available from the author).

Stout, C. E., & Giolas, D. (2000). *ASPs and the solo practitioner*. www.LifescapePro.com (further information available from the author).

Chapter Twenty-Seven

Emerging Health Information Technology

Anne M. Mahalik

I s your organization prepared for 2001 and beyond? Information technologies (ITs) dominate some of the newest breakthroughs in health care. Computer-based patient records (CPRs), wireless systems, the World Wide Web, virtual patient records (VPRs), telemedicine, and ehealth were all unknown to the health care industry a mere 20 years ago. Until very recently, information management consisted of processing a paper-based patient record, gleaning information, and communicating it in arduous, time-consuming, and labor-intensive ways. Is emerging information technology really necessary to be competitive in the health care industry? What factors determine health care ITs' current and future directions?

In some cases, a plethora of new laws mandate how we are to protect and distribute patient information. The loftiest of these is the Health Insurance Portability and Accountability Act (HIPAA) of 1996. This U.S. Department of Health and Human Services regulation contains 24 distinct standards, including those that address administrative safeguards to protect data integrity, confidentiality, and availability; physical safeguards to protect access to hardware and software; technical security services for the application environment; and technical security mechanisms for the network environment. It also addresses individual privacy, individually identifiable health information, how persons can exercise their privacy rights, organization responsibilities to individuals regarding their privacy, and the use and disclosure of health and demographic information. In some contexts, security extends to the integrity and availability of health information that is not individually identifiable.

Accreditation and regulation are another source of IT emphasis. State regulators, federal agencies such as the Health Care Financing Administration (HCFA) (now the Centers for Medicare & Medicaid Services [CMS]), and quasi-"voluntary" accrediting bodies such as the Joint Commission on Accreditation of Healthcare Organizations (JCAHO) have forced health care organizations to look to emerging technologies to help meet licensing, certification, and accreditation standards. During the last decade, JCAHO has placed particular emphasis on information management and the basing of organization and treatment decisions on careful analysis of many kinds of information.

In addition to clinical functions, business and organizational needs spur the use of technology-based processes and solutions. In order to meet and sustain its patient care responsibilities, every organization must find effective, efficient ways to deal with staffing and human resources, costs and cost control, marketing and market understanding, internal communication and integration, many kinds of planning, program development and implementation, and other functions.

Even the smallest mental health organization cannot accomplish its objectives with old-style methods and instruments and hope to remain competitive. Larger systems cannot even meet basic clinical and administrative requirements without modern technology, and there is every indication that the need will increase. With this in mind, the remainder of this chapter will provide an introduction to many information technologies important to mental health organizations, and briefly discuss their relevance and impact.

COMPUTER-BASED PATIENT RECORDS

In 1991, the Institute of Medicine (IOM), an independent research organization, outlined recommended architecture and functionality for a *computer-based patient record* (CPR) (Dick & Steen, 1991). Some 6 years later, despite further definition and interpretation of the concept, the IOM stated that "a universal understanding of the concepts embodied in a CPR still does not exist" (Dick, Steen, & Detmer, 1997). Some confusion still remains. Over the years, a number of new, related terms (such as *electronic patient record* [EPR]) have been used interchangeably.

The CPR was defined by the Computer-based Patient Record Institute (1996) as "electronically maintained information about an individual's lifetime of health status and health care." Using this definition, most organizations can claim some steps taken toward the implementation of a CPR. Simply put, if your system uses computers such as laptops or wireless systems at the point-of-care (POC), and if the information entered is placed into a database which allows for things like registration, billing, physician order entry, or appointment scheduling, then it has the foundation for a CPR.

This does not yet imply an "electronic medical record." The industry, with few exceptions, is still far from retiring paper record-keeping systems, but that day seems to be approaching. The 1996 HIPAA legislation requires standardization and simplification of clinical and financial transactions by 2002. Managed care and affiliated health care networks, system mergers, and contracted ancillary services will further push health care providers and organizations toward computerization of their patient records.

Implementation of a CPR

One logical model for implementing a CPR begins with integration of key applications such as scheduling, billing, master patient index, laboratory, and pharmacy systems. Bringing information from these often "stand-alone" activities into one database creates a comprehensive, integrated picture of many patient-related and business activities. The initial design phase for such a system should address data design, identification of data elements, identification of data values, who is allowed to enter data, where data are entered, and data accuracy, integrity, and validity. Such a system lends itself to a clinical data repository in which data sets are merged in compatible formats, with appropriate access and confidentiality safeguards, for use in many organization applications. The ideal CPR has an extensive technical infrastructure compatible with all the data and functions required within the organization, and allows transfer of data, again with appropriate safeguards, to other health care providers, insurance and remittance centers, governmental agencies, and even patients themselves.

Safeguarding Access to Information

The CPR promises to address communication, billing, risk management, outcomes management, quality improvement, clinical decision support, and research; however, access to the CPR presents many challenges. Authorization and authentication of persons seeking access are at the center of security processes. Once the information is stored electronically (or digitally), the core of the access/security issue becomes electronic as well. The security process should start with patient understanding of the privacy issues, patient knowledge of the way his or her information is stored and the uses to which it may be put, and patient consent. After that, the organization is responsible for limiting access and data use as it has promised. The mechanism required for keeping that promise is a complex but extremely reliable system of information policies, procedures, training, credentialing, passwords, and encryption.

Public key infrastructure (PKI) is the use of two "keys" (strings of keyboard letters and/or symbols), one of which is made public while the other is kept private, to lock (encrypt) information being moved from one computer to another. PKI is one of the few methods of protecting electronic information that currently meets HIPAA requirements.

WIRELESS SYSTEMS

Wireless technology is on the cutting edge of health care IT, but for more than 7 years, aggressive IT departments and solution providers have devoted valuable time to solving the more mundane problems of transmitting patient information to untethered computers. Wireless systems must have dedicated access points and portable transmitting attachments that maintain an always-accessible link to network data via low-frequency radio waves rather than physical (e.g., Ethernet) cabling.

Early wireless systems were costly, but as all IT, they have become more affordable as IT's applications became more reliable and widespread. Wireless point-of-care systems (POCs) put data entry and retrieval mechanisms directly at the point of care, saving time, improving accuracy, and tightening the slack in organization workflow. They have been integrated into many daily routines of health care providers, most often (thus far) for charting and access to patient records, order entry or remote prescribing, consulting clinical guidelines and protocols, and compliance with routine business practices and regulations.

Handheld POCs pose a host of special problems in addition to their benefits, notably battery life, network performance, and signal reliability. With some, data can be lost if the user fails to remember to suspend the operating system without accidentally turning the computer off and to place rechargeable units in a charging station. Depending on transmission modality, performance may be affected by proximity of transmitters and obstacles such as walls and equipment.

The greatest risk of security and privacy violation with wireless systems appears to be from loss or unauthorized use of the ever smaller hand-held devices, rather than through interception of transmissions or unauthorized access to storage files.

The accelerating move to POC systems parallels the explosion in the features and miniaturization of handheld devices, including personal digital assistants (PDAs), as well as modern modem and transmission technology. Their applications have now gone well beyond scheduling and billing, to data entry and sharing of all kinds. The flexibility of wireless data entry and retrieval has made a dramatic difference in workflow and patient care in the health care organizations that have embraced this technology.

VIRTUAL PATIENT RECORDS

Virtual patient records (VPRs) are electronically stored patient data that can be configured differently for different locations (e.g., nursing station, doctor's office, payer/HMO). When required, they can be presented in a common format.

VPRs are one of the few infrastructure-based applications poised to make full use of the World Wide Web. VPRs can be thought of as the web-compliant infrastructure components of the CPR (i.e., they are created and stored in such a way that they can be communicated via the Internet). VPRs integrate data from hospitals, clinics, insurers, and ancillary service providers. They are intended to create a single view of patient data from many—perhaps hundreds of—disparate health care sources. VPRs are also intended to gather transactions from these sources and pass the information to the web interface.

Each user of the VPR has a "filtered" view of the patient record data on which he or she is working. That is the information that is accessible is adjusted and censored to allow the immediate user to do the task at hand (e.g., billing, payment authorization, quality review), with unnecessary or sensitive information omitted. For example, the VPR allows a physician to determine if a patient is filling his or her prescriptions, based on VPR pharmaceutical records. Likewise, the VPR allows a health care administrator to view reimbursement rates and gather data for cost analysis.

Integrating patient data from multiple systems is neither easy nor inexpensive. HIPAA's requirement of standard "transactions" (e.g., patient encounters, status changes, claims) and "code sets" (e.g., groups of codes that represent diagnoses or treatment services, such as those used in the *Diagnostic and Statistical Manual of Mental Disorders* [DSM], *International Classification of Diseases* [ICD], or *Current Procedural Terminology* [CPT]), must be met by the year 2002; that may be the driving force for standardization and commonplace use of VPRs. Implementing web-based patient record systems requires organizational support, good technology management, and a great deal of planning.

Privacy

IT solutions companies (companies that help other companies and organizations with information technology) often assure their clients that patient-identifiable information is confidential and secure, yet breaches in confidentiality can and do occur. But the benefits are many. For the health care manager, these systems provide quick access to vital patient health information during a medical emergency or when the patient is traveling. They provide efficient exchange of data necessary for participation in health plans and for information flow between provider and payer. Other possible benefits can include better clinician-patient or system-patient communication (e.g., through ehealth sites, patient access to his or her own data, or e-mail communication; see later section on ehealth).

Benefits and problems aside, the development of VPRs parallels the consumer-centric approach already evident in some other industries (e.g., banking), in which the customer can access his or her account in a very secure electronic environment 24 hours a day.

TELEMEDICINE

For more detailed information on telemedicine, see other chapters in this section. Telemedicine is

> the use of medical information exchanged from one site to another via electronic communications for the health and education of the patient or healthcare provider and for the purpose of improving patient care. (American Telemedicine Association, 1997)

According to a recent report to Congress by the U.S. Department of Commerce and Departments of Health and Human Services,

> Telemedicine has the potential to make a difference in the lives of many Americans. In remote rural areas, where a patient and the closest health professional can be hundreds of miles apart, telemedicine can mean access to healthcare where little had been available before. In emergency cases, this access can mean the difference between life and death. In particular, in those cases where fast medical response time and specialty care are needed, telemedicine can be critical. (American Telemedicine Association, 1997)

Advances in this technology—which may involve facsimile, telephone, still images, and full-motion video—allow many of today's patients to receive diagnosis, treatment, and care monitoring at home or in a remote site such as a satellite clinic, school-based health center, or jail, services that previously were available only by coming to a central clinic or hospital. The care costs less, recovery time is often shorter, and disruptions for families and caregivers are reduced. Related benefits often include improved access to both primary and specialty care, easier consultation and second opinions, patient and family education and nonclinical communication, improved continuity of care (e.g., reduced travel time for providers, better access in underserved areas), consumer access to medical information, convenient continuing education for professionals, improved access to specialty services, and better attraction and retention of health care professionals in rural and underserved areas.

Privacy Issues

As is the case for computer and web-based applications, the health care system is responsible for patients' privacy and confidentiality. Confidentiality or nondisclosure agreements must be signed by all contract and vendor personnel; appropriate policies, procedures, and training must be in place; data that may be intercepted by unauthorized people should be well encrypted; and conferencing systems should record or monitor activities so that both the referring and consulting facilities have originals of the media and content. Only authorized person(s) should receive and transmit data, and information security maintenance procedures in clinical sites must comply with HIPAA regulations for privacy and security. Home installations (such as PC-based videocams or videophones used for clinical services) are vulnerable to breaches of privacy, which should be discussed with the patient and/or family.

HEALTH CARE ORGANIZATIONS AND THE WORLD WIDE WEB

Health care managers and leaders must understand the fundamental changes the web has brought, ways to conduct business in and around the Internet environment, and at least some of its future potential. The World Wide Web offers health care organizations an enormous range and amount of health care information (and misinformation), as well as the ability to disseminate information and facilitate communication. At a basic management level, Web-based computer applications, whether developed in-house, purchased from third-party vendors, or owned and administered by third-party "solutions" companies, offer highly flexible and easily upgradable software for a variety of critical clinical and management tasks.

"Legacy" and client-server-based systems (i.e., those that store patient information on local computers) installed even 5 years ago cannot reap all the benefits of the World Wide Web without upgrades. Upgrades can be expensive, but they are important to ensure the organization's place in the health care industry. Most IT solution companies are moving to less expensive "browser-based" architectures by "web-enabling" their existing systems and products. This means that an individual sees and accesses programs (e.g., applications such as billing or database software) through a web connection rather than on the local computer system. The authorized software user logs onto the system and is presented with a web page from which the organization's software applications are launched. Most such programs run more rapidly and are more versatile than local ones.

Organizations just starting to consider IT solutions for compliance with HIPAA may wish to consider a health care software company that has utilized web-based programming language in developing its systems. Such companies usually cost more than in-house software development initially, but they create direct access to data and document repositories, queries are completed at very high speed, and they reduce the expenses of network administration and workstation maintenance.

Available Systems and Products

Paper-based: No/few equipment costs, simplicity, real (as contrasted with symbolic) storage format; personnel costs generally higher.

PC-network-based: Equipment and software costs vary, but average $2,000 per desk-based computer; personnel costs for record entry and retrieval lower than for paper-based; fast record retrieval, but clinicians must spend time at both the computer and the point of care.

Wireless: Equipment and software costs vary (need one wireless unit per clinician and one desktop/server per several clinicians); lower personnel costs, fast record retrieval; point-of-care record entry and retrieval; supports remote or point-of-care decision making.

Virtual: Requires more specialized equipment and usually services of an IT support company to "manage" the Web-based functions; lower personnel costs, fast record retrieval, documentation at point of care, then uploaded to desktop or directly to Web; particularly useful in systems with multiple sites or mobile patients

ehealth: Requires web access for all computers, including POC units; fast record retrieval and documentation at POC; supports remote or POC decision making; particularly useful in remote areas; disadvantages include variable reliability of ehealth web sites.

Privacy

HIPAA mandates that all health plans, health care clearinghouses, and health care providers who transmit or store information (electronically or paper-based) must comply with safeguard standards to ensure the confidentiality and integrity of the information, protect against potential threats to its security, and prevent unauthorized uses or disclosures of the information. HIPAA protects demographic data, such as that used in an organization's web-based or otherwise transmitted clinical and management databases. If the health care provider uses other companies or services (e.g., electronic or web-based ones), HIPAA standards must still be met.

Most professional and clerical staff already have some level of familiarity with the web and its derived technologies. Basing IT systems on web technologies may increase employee understanding, compared to non-web systems. However, in order for the web and its derived technologies to continue to evolve and become a foundation for best practices, the technologies must support a viable business model. In health care, that model must result in identifying means of saving costs for health care services. The key to successful cost savings is implementing web-based IT solutions and achieving benefits realized from web-based IT investments.

Under HIPAA, privacy rules apply to providers, payers, and information clearinghouses. Its application to ehealth companies depends on the ehealth clients and the business they transact. If an entity charges for health services, it must comply. websites that offer only "content" (information without interaction) are not required to comply. Other ehealth companies fall into a category called "business associate," defined by HIPAA as not directly covered by its requirements but linked to companies that are covered. There must be a confidentiality contract between a covered entity and a "business associate" if protected information passes between them. HIPAA does not address information that an ehealth web site may obtain from a patient or other consumer through membership registration, surveys, signing up for interest groups or e-mail lists, chat rooms, "cookies" (information sent automatically from a user's computer to a web site), and the like.

eHEALTH FOR PATIENTS AND CONSUMERS

Each day, the number of health-related web sites multiplies and the range of functions they offer expands. As many as 100 million people in the United States have access to the Internet, and that number is expected to grow by 50% within a few years after 2000 (National Center for Policy Analysis, 2000). Some health-related web sites enable consumers to search large medical databases for clinical and diagnostic information, consult with health care professionals, complete health status self-assessments, create and maintain personalized health records, and purchase health-related products and services. According to a recent Harris poll, 70 million Americans used the Internet to search for health information in a single year during the late 1990s (National Center for Policy Analysis, 2000).

Although these sites have empowered consumers to assume increased responsibility for their health, there is substantial and growing concern about the accuracy of Internet-obtained information and about how little power consumers have to control access to their private information on health-related sites (information patients and consumers themselves have provided to a web site, separate from concerns about data from clinical or insurance databases). A recent report from the California Healthcare Foundation suggests reasons for this concern. Issued in January 2000, the report characterized health web sites as not having "matured enough to ensure the quality of information, protect consumers from product fraud or inappropriate prescribing, or guarantee the privacy of individuals' information" (California Healthcare Foundation, 2000).

Consumer Preferences

Many consumers (particularly younger ones) want to take more control of their health care, and ehealth sites allow them to do so. It is important to know why many turn to the Internet.

Patients want to know that they are receiving the best or most appropriate treatment available. In traditional doctor–patient relationships, patients rely on physicians and nurses for most of their information, sometimes supplemented with office pamphlets or personal reading. Many patients are finding that Internet searches provide them with information conveniently, in privacy, and with time to "digest" it.

According to the National Center for Policy Analysis (2000), web access can provide more financial leverage for some patients. In the past, most hospitals and clinics opposed posting of prices or fees for medical services. When the posting of prices for services becomes more prevalent on the Internet, price competition may become more common. Health care providers once hesitant to discuss prices may lose patients if they don't.

Those patients who have a choice (largely the minority who seek fee-for-service care) may go online in the future to look for competing providers, then select the one(s) they believe have the lowest prices and/or highest quality. The Internet may transform patients into financial partners by providing them with the tools they need to consume medical goods and services with more knowledge.

E-Mail

E-mail presents challenges as well as benefits. One of the newest uses for this technology is as a communication tool among clinicians, and between clinicians and their patients. By one estimate, more than 40% of U.S. patients use e-mail to contact health professionals (Kohn, 1999). It is increasingly taking the place of phone calls to reach patients who have Internet access. The availability and compatibility (its "asynchronous" nature) of e-mail on different computer systems make it ideal for managing care through multidisciplinary teams (Mandl, Kohane, & Brandt, 1998).

Despite the advantages of e-mail over telephone or postal communication in many situations, security and reliability are important issues, particularly in mental health:

- Nonencrypted e-mail is often read by third parties, and many encryption programs still allow unexpected perusal (e.g., by Internet service provider technicians). The law in this area is often unclear.
- The sender has little control over who receives or opens the e-mail. Even electronic "receipts" that verify that the message has been opened do not verify that the patient himself read the message, or that he or she understood it.
- Patients may not use e-mail correctly, especially when their symptoms are severe.
- The ease and speed of creating and sending e-mail messages may create sending errors (e.g., a confidential message may be addressed to the wrong person, or a message may be composed and sent too hastily). Once the "Send" button is clicked, it is virtually impossible to retrieve the message.

Inaccurate and Fraudulent Information

The democracy of the Internet—and sometimes its anonymity—creates an enormous opportunity for misinformation, disinformation, and fraud. Patients and other consumers who search for information on a topic are deluged with links to web sites and information they *don't* need, and that may be harmful to their health. Those who visit even legitimate and reliable web sites often find themselves the target of e-mail marketing for disinformation and health care hucksters. Chat rooms and "listservs" (special-interest e-mail groups) sometimes hold useful information and support, but most lack any real control over truth or accuracy, and many are rife with bias, or even fraud.

Patients and their families can be provided with lists of legitimate health care web sites that are likely to address their information needs, and with ways to assess the accuracy of others they may encounter on the Web. They should be warned about the probability of inaccuracy, and given tools with which to sift the material they find or receive.

Privacy

Several organizations have formed within the past few years in response to growing concern with the lack of Internet standards and ethical conduct, including user privacy. These organizations advocate education of consumers, professionals, media, marketers, legislators, and others as a conduit to quality improvement of Internet health resources. The organizations generally favor self-regulation of the industry through the creation of voluntary standards and guidelines. Several of these organizations convened in February 2000 for the *e*Health Ethics Summit in Washington, DC. Industry leaders adopted an International Code of Ethics for the Internet at the summit. The Code of Ethics addresses the need for health care providers and organizations that accept or provide health care information on the Internet to safeguard users' privacy and to obtain informed consent when gathering personal information. It can be viewed at www.ihealthcoalition.org.

Other Concerns

Privacy is a pressing issue for administrators of health websites, but there are many more. Financial integrity and licensing rules are two of the many other issues raised as ehealth sites proliferate. HIPAA will address some of these in short order; however, the lack of regulation thus far has allowed unprecedented opportunities and access to both good and bad health care information. HIPAA calls for detailed attention to security issues, including e-mail protection. Regulations still pending will probably mandate both high standards for data privacy and extensive patient access.

SUMMARY

Mental health managers and leaders continually consider how environmental factors affect their organizations and roles. Vast and rapid changes in the way we collect, process, and manage both patient and organizational information necessitate continuous review of emergent technology. In the end, we must embrace the computerization of health information in order to remain competitive, decrease certain kinds of information and documentation errors, enhance employee satisfaction, improve staff recruitment, deal with managed care, and comply with information management standards promulgated by licensing and regulating bodies, accreditation bodies, and payors.

REFERENCES

American Telemedicine Association. (1997, January 31). *Telemedicine report to Congress by the US Departments of Commerce and Health and Human Services.* Washington, DC: Author.

California Healthcare Foundation. (2000). *Privacy: Report on the privacy policies and practices of health web sites.* Oakland: California Healthcare Foundation.

Computer-based Patient Record Institute. (1996). *Mission and goals.* Bethesda, MD: Author.

Dick, R. S., & Steen, E. B. (Eds.). (1991). *The computer-based patient record: An essential technology.* Washington, DC: National Academy Press.

Dick, R. S., Steen, E. B., & Detmer, D. E. (Eds.). (1997). *The computer-based patient record: An essential technology* (rev. ed.). Washington, DC: National Academy Press.

Kohn, D. (1999). Preparing the environment for Internet-driven technologies. In G. F. Murphy, M. A. Hanken, & K. A. Waters (Eds.), *Electronic health records: Changing the vision* (pp. 143–156). Philadelphia: W. B. Saunders.

Mandl, K. D., Kohane, I. S., & Brandt, A. M. (1998). Electronic patient–physician communication: Problems and promises. *Annals of Internal Medicine, 129,* 495–500.

National Center for Policy Analysis. (2000, March). *Patient power and the Internet* (Brief Analysis No. 317). Dallas, TX: Author.

Chapter Twenty-Eight

Information Trends
for the Clinical Leader

Leigh W. Jerome

The scope and impact of the current technology revolution are enormous. Changes in science and telecommunications are not progressing with a gentle linear slope. The rate of technology development is exponential. The sharp ascent of new information, along with its ready availability, forecasts technological progress with far-reaching impact on the health care delivery system. Increased access to information is fundamentally altering the way that people communicate, work, establish communities, do business, and even experience the world. The Internet and the synthesis of science and technology are changing the rules in health care and the ways in which health care services are provided.

In the field of mental health, successful managers and leaders must keep pace with these rapid developments and identify fledgling changes as they emerge. Evolving transformations are found in recent technologies and novel technology applications, new directions in service provision, emerging sets of skills, shifts in patient/consumer characteristics, and fundamental changes in interpersonal relationships, ethics, and the interface between human beings and machines.

As technology continues to evolve, more and more tools will be generated, promoting better, more efficient, and more widely available clinical practice and education. It is important for leaders and managers to learn something about these new technologies as the tools emerge, and be informed about their relevance to the organization. Knowing some of the language and viewpoints used by information technology professionals helps the mental health manager to call on them before technology needs become critical, and use them effectively. This chapter outlines developing information trends in mental health care and discusses their relevance for leadership and management.

NEW TECHNOLOGIES

Innovative technologies are providing new tools for clinical services. One segment of this innovation, *telehealth,* is "the use of telecommunications and information technology to provide access to health assessment, intervention, consultation, supervision, education and information across distance" (Nickelson, 1998, p. 527). The term emerged when technological solutions were novel. Today, just a few years later, telehealth as a separate term is almost archaic.

Telehealth is really nothing more than the communication of data and information. Put simply, it is the use of technology and telecommunications to accomplish health care. For many, the term has become equated with interactive videoconferencing, but it is broader than that. The telephone and facsimile (fax) machines have long been used for consultations, billing, information transmission, and clerical tasks. E-mail and the Internet are telehealth tools that are becoming increasingly common in health care services. Electronic medical records (EMRs), interactive videoconferencing, biosensors, teleproctoring, distance learning, and many forms of implants are all representative of the rapidly evolving telehealth field.

It is difficult to overestimate the importance of the Internet in the development of modern health care services. There are roughly 387 people for every physician in the United States, but this ratio is 4,361 per physician in Thailand and 6,786 in Indonesia (Risser, 1998). Remote health care through Internet applications is beginning to have a profound impact on health care delivery. One estimate suggests that the global telehealth industry will grow 40% annually for the next 10 years. The World Wide Web already supports two new health care solutions that are exerting enormous impact: distance education and "store and forward" capabilities.

Distance Education (Distance Learning)

Distance education refers to provision of instruction, information, and education from a remote site. It provides alternative and adjunctive, and sometimes primary, curricula for individuals for whom time, resources, or geographical distance limits educational opportunities.

Correspondence courses are an early form of distance education. Public school classes have been available to rural or shut-in students by telephone and radio since the middle of the last century. Accredited courses have been widely distributed by public television, usually without two-way telephone communication, for at least 30 years, and private educational videoconferences (e.g., sponsored by educational consortia or private industry) have been common for almost as long. The Internet is very well suited for distance education. It is inexpensive, easy to use, reasonably accessible; it spans great distances, and is increasingly reliable and educationally sophisticed (Mittman & Cain, 1999). In the current century, online learning will increase dramatically.

Patients go online to acquire and compare health information, to learn particular health practices, and to be monitored and tutored in some health care routines (e.g., self-care for asthma or diabetes). The growing numbers of health sites on the Internet often provide the information that patients and consumers seek, or help them find it, although accuracy and reliability are often lacking, particularly on some mental health websites. Mental health is one of the most popular areas of health and health care researched on the web, and those seeking help are often among the most vulnerable to misinformation or fraud. This enormous access to information requires a certain amount of guidance for maximum usefulness and minimizing risk, but it is already contributing to measurable shifts in patient and potential patient characteristics (discussed later).

Health professionals use the Internet for continuing education, clinical information and research, patient-related information, organization information, professional and educational fora, and interactive projects such as collaborative research and writing, as well as online management tools and databases (see later discussion and elsewhere in this section). Online learning curricula offer convenience and state-of-the-art training opportunities that may be combined with simulations, multisite resource leveraging, and links to images and clinical practice guidelines. Online textbooks and journal articles can be updated or corrected far faster than paper or compact disc (CD) versions. Many standard texts provide new editions and revisions via the web incrementally, a few chapters at a time.

Store and Forward

Store and forward refers to technologies that provide the electronic delivery of information from one location to another. E-mail is the best known and utilized store-and-forward technology (but it is not limited to Internet applications). Information is not delivered in "real time," but is saved (sometimes for less than a second, sometimes much longer) and then forwarded to the desired location. Store-and-forward information can include images, text, Internet links, or other data.

Electronic transmission provides a fast, inexpensive vehicle for transfer of many health-care-related materials, including clerical and reimbursement information, test results, consultation results, medical images, and even entire patient records or groups of records. Thus, for example, important patient information can be immediately provided to a remote professional when and where it is needed. Transmittal of reimbursement and eligibility information is even more common, routinely used to determine, for example, whether or not a patient's insurer or managed care organization will approve services.

Advancements in imaging and store-and-forward technology have substantial application for cases requiring transfer of visual images. Digital images such as digitized radiographs ("x-rays"), tomographs (CT scans), and MRI results are inexpensive and maintain consistent image quality, regardless of duplication. When the images are digitally created in the first place, there is no processing time required and the image need not even be seen at the point of origin. Transmission time is virtually nil; viewing and organization can be better and faster than that for paper or film items (assuming the remote site has the appropriate equipment); forwarding to additional consultants is easily and quickly accomplished, and filing and storage require very little space. Images are moved instead of people, virtually whenever and wherever the need demands them (Tabor, 2000).

The consistent quality and almost immediate availability of digital images provide significant value for emergency and remote care situations. Although some applications require highly specialized equipment and software, useful text and images are often simply attached to an e-mail and sent across town or around the world.

Store-and-forward techniques are by no means limited to static images. Video clips can provide high-resolution, full-motion video (although lower resolution and motion quality is more common on personal computers). Affect and mood can be vividly conveyed from a mental status exam, or abnormal gait diagnosed or demonstrated.

Format and Storage Problems

There are problems to overcome with store-and-forward technology, and with data storage itself (including the electronic medical record described below). Some equipment, although decreasing in price, can be very expensive if it is not compatible with mass-produced (e.g., personal computer) technology. Format changes also create costs and delays associated with staff retraining.

Because no "real" image (such as one finds in paper, film, or microfiche) is preserved in digital storage, format is a substantial issue for images and documents that must be saved for some time ("archived"). Will current retrieval equipment and software be obsolete in a few years? After a couple of decades or more, will data stored in a current format be as difficult to retrieve and read as data stored in, for example, the old CP/M, Commodore PET, or Amiga formats are today? Each of those formats was part of the state of the art in its time, less than 20 years ago, and was used for text and image storage. Technology is evolving far more rapidly now, and one should prepare for the probability that in a few years, today's storage media and formats will be at least as hard to decipher as wire recordings from the 1940s (and probably harder, because wire recordings were "analog" rather than digital, and thus had only one "format").

Finally, digital storage media have not proved their stability over more than a few years. CD-ROM data may deteriorate beyond recovery after a decade or so; magnetic media such as diskettes and Zip or JAZZ disks may not support data integrity much longer. Fixed-disk ("hard-disk") storage has deterioration liabilities as well.

Electronic Medical Records

Health care providers are at the beginning of a slow, but certain, transition to electronic medical records (Mittman & Cain, 1999). The patient's health care record has historically been a collecting place for clinical notes, reports, consultations, and laboratory or procedure results. The record has traditionally been somewhat centralized, but inpatient and outpatient records are often separately housed, and separate diagnostic or treatment sites keep separate files (although often sending copies to each other). The electronic medical record (EMR) implies a transformation from fixed storage to a dynamic, interactive record, which can include alerts and reminders, point-and-click orders, templates for documentation, and even "hyperlinks" to internal and external (e.g., Internet website) resources.

Electronic medical records promise access to historical information, current medications, course of illness, known allergies, digital images, results of tests, and specialist consultations (Paperny, 2000). The EMR provides a means for an automated support system, and makes the information available to authorized users and providers at any time and anywhere computer access is found. The EMR can generate reminders and prompts to the clinician at the time of the clinical encounter (e.g., requests for clinical information, diagnostic alerts, medication renewal reminders, future appointments, clinical practice guidelines, and patient-specific recommendations), a powerful tool in clinical computing.

The EMR helps clinicians provide comprehensive clinical care. Mental health records and services can be integrated with general medical care when appropriate, and seamlessly documented. Specialty care of all kinds, including mental health care, can be accomplished from primary care settings more easily, and the records made accessible (with proper authorization) from the primary care office. Widespread use of EMRs and expansion of telehealth networks will promote fundamental integration of mental health care into the comprehensive health care system.

The "hub-and-spokes" model provides a common telehealth network adopted by many medical and mental health centers and facilitated by EMRs. The "hub" is a central (usually large) clinical organization connected, via telecommunications technology, to numerous "spokes," such as remote clinics or community health centers. The connections may be by telephone, fax, store-and-forward technology, and/or videoconferencing, reducing the need for care at the "hub" site and increasing opportunities for comprehensive and specialized patient care at remote locations. The role of a single, interconnected, broadly accessible medical record (the EMR) is obvious.

The consistency and portability of a patient's care from one neighborhood to another (or, in large systems, from one region to another) is an added benefit of hub-and-spoke networks. In addition, the diversity of clinical work and ability to follow more patients on site, rather than referring them to distant clinics or hospitals, makes local clinical staff jobs more interesting and rewarding. The technological costs of such networks have decreased sufficiently during the past several years that small hospitals and clinics can often afford either ready-made or custom systems with a variety of features.

Several essential features define an effective electronic medical record. It must:

- Capture and code complex data from multiple entry points.
- Share medical information across multiple sites.
- Provide timely, efficient access to medical data and related information.
- Protect patient privacy.

In addition, a well-designed system should allow patients to become more engaged in their own health care.

Two forces are currently driving development of EMRs: (a) miniaturization and the advent of personal digital assistants (PDAs), which offer great advantages in information availability and point-of-care communication, and (b) the Health Insurance Portability and Accountability Act (HIPPA), which, among other things, mandates standardization, security, and rigorously guarded privacy of patient data stored or transmitted on the Internet.

Before EMRs are pervasively implemented, however, organizations must tackle the enormous task of translating existing paper-based records into a searchable, addressable electronic format. In addition, transition to electronic formats must be completed while maintaining the flow of clinical care and, even more important in the view of many, resolving security and privacy concerns. Despite these challenges, EMRs are becoming routine in some settings. Their potential efficiencies and improvements in patient care will eventually make them the norm for mainstream health and mental health care.

Direct Treatment by Remote Means

Telehealth in mental health has moved well beyond simple e-mail communication. In addition to the now common focus on assessment and consultation, referral linking systems, informational services, and online self-help forums are becoming commonplace. Practitioners no longer communicate only with other clinicians (e.g., for consultations or referrals), but may rely on electronic technology to take histories, monitor progress, and maintain therapeutic contact with patients who have access to the necessary technology (or whose families or community clinics can use it).

Direct treatments, such as online counseling, coaching, and psychotherapy, are becoming more common on the Internet. Videoconferencing offers a developing technology for real-time, online services. Bandwidth and infrastructure requirements, platform incompatibilities, and unresolved ethical, legal, and regulatory concerns currently limit widespread use of video and Internet-based treatment. Video or online patients should be chosen carefully. Issues of patient protection, therapist qualifications and licensing, meeting the applicable standard of care, and fraud must all be resolved before the mainstream mental health professions are likely to embrace these alternative treatment methods, although some problems can be overcome by a combination of in-person assessment and online follow-up.

Remote Clinical Monitoring

Many remote monitoring devices, some web-based, are now available and hold some early promise of decreased cost, more active patient involvement, and improved remote diagnoses and assessment (Balas & Iakovidis, 1999). An electronic stethoscope enables a physician or nurse to listen to the heart and lungs of remote patients. Pulse oximetry and respiratory flow data can be electronically transmitted by simple computer modem to help manage patients with chronic obstructive pulmonary disease. Electrocardiography and electroencephalography lend themselves to both remote recording for later interpretation and radiotelemetry for real-time monitoring of cardiac and seizure patients. Blood pressure and fetal heart telemetry can help some preeclamptic obstetrical patients to avoid inconvenient and costly hospitalization, yet remain safely monitored for early signs of an emergency. Remote biofeedback has been successfully used to treat migraine headaches, nausea and vomiting, and chronic pain.

The Immediate Horizon

To health care administrators, the most ubiquitous information technology improvements on the immediate horizon are streamlining paper procedures, including automated patient scheduling; more efficient data entry, organization, and storage; reminder systems; personal health improvement plans with electronic monitoring;

and fingertip access to electronic medical records. Wireless technology and wireless biosensors may eliminate many patients' tethers to their computers or telephones. Medications are often prescribed and cross-checked for interactions and drug sensitivities by computer, sometimes through web-based prescription services (e.g., InfoScriber). Streaming video (one-way video transfer) is likely to move beyond its present applications in distance learning, transmitting moving clinical images such as those generated by ultrasound or continuous electroencephalograph (EEG), and full-motion video of tremors or gait abnormalities. Neurosurgical and electrophysiological procedures already take advantage of advances in microelectronics, membrane technology, and other high-tech fields to create practical electronic and chemical implants to relieve some severe physical conditions, including brain deficits in stroke and epilepsy. The potential for future applications is enormous.

TRENDS IN SERVICE PROVISION

Remote Access to a Range of Health Services: Teletriage

A recent survey found that 77% of patients entering the health system would give up a personal visit with a physician if they could get credible, prompt information by telephone or the Internet (Barr, Laufenberg, & Sieckman, 1998). Triage activities provide immediate care at the point of need, or a first level of care when direct care is not available.

Teletriage services range from simple telephone advice regarding treatment for common illnesses to emergency, on-site response during a disaster or wartime. Call centers, help desks or lines, and customer service are common forms of teletriage. Health care call centers answer patient questions and requests for advice. In most legitimate call centers, the person delivering services is a specially trained nurse or counselor who offers advice based on clinical practice guidelines and standardized protocols. Many traditional call centers are expanding to include e-mail communications, fax, Internet, interactive video kiosks, and videoconferencing for triage and consultations (Angaran, 1999).

Teletriage is further expanding to include management of patients through home monitoring, care management, and data tracking. Home monitoring systems link patients to primary care facilities through computerized stations that transmit such things as weight, vital signs, blood glucose, arterial oxygen saturation, and electrocardiographic information, depending on patient need (Lathan, Kinsella, Rosen, Winters, & Trepagnier, 1999). They are especially useful for elderly patients and those with chronic conditions such as asthma, diabetes, and heart failure, as well as individuals taking medications with small "therapeutic windows." Two-way communication also offers opportunities for rehabilitation and mental health interventions for people recovering from trauma or emotional distress.

Teletriage can improve disaster outcomes. A portable telemedicine instrumentation pack (TIP) was developed in 1996 to provide a briefcase-sized, integrated suite of tools to collect and transmit diagnostic data for ear, nose, throat, and skin imaging, electrocardiography, blood oxygen saturation, and heart and lung sounds (Garshnek & Burkle, 1999). It allows on-site telemedical examinations to capture and transmit patient audio, video, and laboratory data for remote interpretation and consultation.

Specialized PDAs

Computer miniaturization has enabled pocket-sized personal digital assistants (PDAs) that support keyboard, pen, touch, and voice inputs and provide information management, portability, and connectivity. The U.S. military is developing PDAs and videotransmission applications that can read patients' medical histories (digitally imprinted on a new form of "dog tag") and transmit information about wounds or illness via a medic's compact video camera and (e.g., throat) microphone to physicians, who can then assess the casualty and guide the immediate field intervention and care.

Miniaturization also supports development of another military application, the personnel status monitor (PSM). The PSM is a combination of environmental and physiologic sensors and global positioning satellite receiver that is integrated into a soldier's field uniform to continuously monitor vital signs and other information. If the data depart significantly from normal values, the PSM could transmit health and location information to a medic or other person, enhancing triage and field treatment (Garshnek & Burkle, 1999). Mental health applications of telemedicine in disaster and wartime situations include immediate critical incident management and crisis intervention to alleviate symptoms, preserve functioning, and decrease the likelihood of posttraumatic syndromes.

Home Health Care

Home health care is one of the fastest growing segments of the health care industry, particularly as the definition of "home" often includes nursing homes, assisted living facilities, and other nonacute care settings (Lathan et al., 1999). As both community infrastructure (e.g., availability of high-speed transmission capability) and health care infrastructure continue to develop, telehealth options will become available to more and more people, some of whom now find it difficult to obtain primary and specialty services.

Individuals are often discharged from hospitals to their homes while still in the early stages of recovery (Trepagnier & Rosen, 1999). Pressure to reduce hospital stays supports consideration of home care technology such as emergency alerting and ambulatory monitoring in discharge plans. Some remote monitoring devices allow clinicians or health monitoring personnel to see and interact with the patient; others record and/or transmit clinical data. Audio or video counseling to and from home helps the patient understand his or her care, follow treatment recommendations, and maintain person-to-person contact with a real person, objectives that fit psychiatric patients and their families as well as general medical ones.

Sometimes the home health interaction is best accomplished through videoconferencing or other sophisticated technology, but often a "low-tech" approach such as the telephone is all that is needed. The point is not to place the newest technology in every home, but rather to use technology, at whatever level best meets the patient's needs, to improve and maintain communication between patient and clinician or clinical staff. Even the most modern clinicians and health care managers should not forget that realizing the need and seizing the opportunity to meet it are more important than dwelling on the technology itself.

NEW SKILLS AND TRAINING

Technology Awareness and Acceptance

As new technologies continue to evolve and telehealth solutions are integrated into clinical practice, new skills and skill sets will emerge and require training and credentialing. This is a transitional time in health care information technology. On one hand, new tools are rapidly emerging; on the other, telehealth utilization is still low compared to the overall health/mental health arena (Lathan et al., 1999). Over 50% of doctors and medical staff were "computer illiterate" in 1999 (Nakajima, Sawada, Ashihara, & Takashima, 1999). Simply installing telehealth equipment and providing a user manual doesn't encourage use or ensure competence. A comprehensive, continuous program of technology awareness and training for clinicians, educators, and managers is essential if the benefits of modern information technology are to be realized (Blignault & Kennedy, 1999).

Getting clinicians interested in new technology, helping them adapt it to their work, and changing their practices is not always an easy task. System design must allow for ease of use, convenience, and existing practice patterns (Puskin, Morris, Hassol, Gaumer, & Mintzer, 1997). Schneider and Eisenberg (1998) described six management tools that can be employed to change clinician practice or behavior: **education, feedback, clinician participation** in the change, **rule enforcement, financial incentives,** and **financial penalties**. The different tools may or may not apply in particular situations, but each should be considered as new health care technologies and systems are planned.

As patients and consumers incorporate electronic solutions into their health care repertoire, mental health professionals tend to underutilize telecommunications and the Internet in their clinical work (Allen, 2000). One of the biggest barriers to professional acceptance of telemedicine, for example, is lack of reliable or systematic reimbursement (Chin, 2000). Other barriers include cost, questions about clinical effectiveness, lack of technical and associated training, and concerns about security, privacy, ethics, competence, and training time (Puskin et al., 1997). It is increasingly obvious that clinical training must include, at its core, knowledge, skills, and attitudes that support information literacy and applied clinical informatics (McGowan et al., 1998). As Stamm and Perednia (2000) noted, "the best equipment in the world will not function well if the people using it are not trained and willing to use it." (p. 186).

Data Acquisition and Information Overload

The available knowledge base has been exploding exponentially for years, and individual knowledge acquisition struggles to keep pace. There are approximately 550 billion documents online (albeit not just in health fields), growing at the rate of 7.3 million pages a day (Weise, 2000). The vast number, variety, and sources of information is a spiraling problem among health care professionals (Noone, Warran, & Brittain, 1998). Subspecialization is one way doctors and scientists have handled the volume, but we are rapidly approaching a point at which extreme subspecialization makes clinicians into technicians, and important generalist and primary care roles become very difficult indeed. Information "filtering" is another, technological, method for dealing with the volume of information and the huge task of discarding inaccurate or extraneous material. Defining human information-processing limitations and helping clinical and management professionals to use filtering methods and algorithms with large volumes of information without ignoring important data is an important IT task.

CHANGING PATIENT CHARACTERISTICS AND EXPECTATIONS

Access to Health Information

Millions of people go online every year to search the thousands of good and bad health care websites for information. The Internet enables patients to find mental health literature of all kinds, and to communicate with people who may have similar problems. This is rapidly creating a new kind of patient, one who is better informed, is aware of a broader range resources (accurate or not), develops higher expectations for care, and takes a more active role in his or her care than the "traditional" patient. The fact that patients have access to some of the same databases as clinicians will have a significant impact on many patients' knowledge and expectations.

Technology and Health Care Options

I believe that patients and consumers will eventually want more than simple access to health information. Research suggests that videoconferencing is acceptable to patients in a variety of clinical circumstances (Mair & Whitten, 2000). As they become more accustomed to electronic communication, some patients may demand electronic health care options. They will expect more choices, greater control, customer service, better interaction with their health care providers, and access to information (Mittman & Cain, 1999). Telehealth options are driven by a technological push and a strong consumer pull (Eysenbach, Sa, & Diepgen, 1999). Assessing public acceptance, including acceptance of or desire for better information technology, should be an important part of the mental health system's overall program evaluation.

Technology, Self-Help, and Wellness

Computer-assisted self-help, in-home therapeutic interventions, and even virtual reality programs are being offered by both legitimate and more questionable sources as alternatives to traditional therapies (Andrade, 2000). Both direct and online psychiatric and behavioral telehealth services are available in myriad contexts, including community mental health centers, hospitals, schools, and correctional facilities (Jerome et al., 2000). Patient-to-patient or peer interchanges are becoming an important part of health care for some, and may redefine the traditional model of preventive medicine and health promotion for a large portion of the population (Eysenbach et al., 1999). Consumer technology enables those with the motivation and access to increase their control over many determinants of their health, and sometimes to prevent or mitigate disease. As opportunities for computer and telecommunications connectedness increase, so will self-help options, "open global networks," and the positive impact of social interaction. The eventual results may include fundamental shifts in what large populations need from health and mental health systems, and in the ways those systems interact with patients and consumers.

CHALLENGES FOR MENTAL HEALTH MANAGEMENT

Optimal use of modern technology and telecommunciations in health care requires concentrated organizational planning that targets not only markets but changes in care delivery (Birch, Rigby, & Roberts, 2000). Patients expect individualized, confidential, ethical, and personal clinical services that incorporate scientific and technological changes as they occur. Practitioners often recognize the importance of information and information access, but are less likely to have the skills necessary to keep up with advances in information technology, in part because they must spend the bulk of their time seeing patients and continuing their clinical study, and perhaps because their interests lie more in patient care than in computers or information management.

This means that clinical managers and administrators must take the lead, and make it easy for the clinical enterprise to take advantage of information technology. From an organizational perspective, communication and information are central to the speed, quality, availability, and cost control of mental health care—*and thus central to the organization's competitive position as well.*

Internet Use

Although access to and business uses of the Internet are growing steadily, Internet utilization by health care organizations has trailed that of many comparable industries. Barriers to utilization by mental health organizations and systems include security issues, higher priority of other projects, immaturity of technologies, platform incompatibilities, lack of confidence in business benefit, cost, complexity, and/or lack of industry-wide standards (Angaran, 1999).

Public education offers a simpler, less expensive use of the Web that can add value for patients and families, and for the larger community. Mental health organizations can direct patients and their families to credible websites. The quality of information on the Internet varies tremendously (Eysenbach et al., 1999), and is often impossible for a layperson to evaluate. Helping people avoid websites that are inaccurate, unreliable, biased, or even dangerous is a valuable, yet inexpensive, service. An organization's own web site is a flexible, inexpensive tool for information, communication (e.g., through e-mail to clinicians or scheduling centers), and marketing, and can include links to reliable information and resources for patients.

IT Planning and Sustainability

Although the outward goal for mental health organizations is quality care, they cannot provide that care without remaining organizationally and financially stable. Those in the private sector must earn their way and keep a competitive edge. Some in the public sector must do the same, and all must at least demonstrate administrative and fiscal wisdom to legislatures and funding agencies. Good IT planning must foresee most of the impact and imposition that new information technology will have on the overall organization, and should include at least the following three components:

- A *technology plan* that defines how the integrated delivery system is going to utilize the technology.
- A *tactical plan* that states the projects and initiatives to be undertaken, the priorities, the people who will be involved and responsible, and the cost.
- A *fundamental structure* for making decisions about IT and the enterprise, such as those associated with implementation, processes, policies, and standards to be met (McGregor & Nimtz, 1998).

New technology is rarely perpetual; it has a finite life cycle. Sheng, Hu, Wei, and Ma (1999) posited a life-cycle-based technology management model consisting of six management phases that collectively depict technology evolution:

- Technology *planning*.
- Technology *adoption*.
- Technology *customization*.
- *Change management*.
- Technology *maintenance*.
- Technology *abandonment*.

New technologies and telecommunication solutions must be managed from the vantage point of sustainability. Implementation plans should include continuous evaluation indicators that measure utilization, cost, performance standards, and patient and clinician satisfaction. When introducing new technologies, it is essential that quality assurance go beyond a simple determination of whether a particular piece of equipment is suitable for a particular purpose. Management must assess the quality of the technology, the quality of the information created or obtained, the quality of both clinical and data-handling processes, and the quality of patient and organization outcomes (Birch et al., 2000).

REFERENCES

Note: Dates in parentheses at end of online references are the current dates of access. Some websites may move or become unavailable.

Allen, A. (2000). They love it, they love it not. *Telemedicine Today, 8*(3), 12.

Andrade, C. (2000, September 1). Can the computer help with mental problems? *Computers at Home.* http://computersathome.com/content/comp_at_work/comp_health/100090101.asp

Angaran, D. M. (1999). Telemedicine and telepharmacy: Current status and future implications. *American Journal of Health-System Pharmacists, 56,* 1405–1426.

Balas, E. A., & Iakovidis, I. (1999). Distance technologies for patient monitoring. *British Medical Journal* (electronic edition), *319*(7220), 1309. http://www.bmj.com (02/01/00).

Barr, J. L., Laufenberg, S., & Sieckman, B. L. (1998). Creating a vision for your medical call center. *Healthcare Information Management, 12*(2), 71–85.

Birch, K., Rigby, M., & Roberts, R. (2000). Putting the "tele" into health-care effectively. *Journal of Telemedicine and Telecare, 6*(1), 113–115.

Blignault, I., & Kennedy, C. (1999). Training for telemedicine. *Journal of Telemedicine and Telecare, 5,* suppl. 1, S112–114.

Eysenback, G., Sa, E. R., & Diepgen, T. L. (1999). Shopping around the internet today and tomorrow: Towards the millennium of cybermedicine. *British Medical Journal* (electronic edition), *319,* 1294.

Garshnek, V., & Burkle, F. M. (1999). Applications of telemedicine and telecommunications to disaster medicine: Historical and future perspectives. *Journal of the American Informatics Association, 6*(1), 26–37.

Jerome, L. W., DeLeon, P. H., James, L. C., Folen, R., Earles, J., & Gedney, J. J. (2000). The coming age of telecommunications in psychological research and practice. *American Psychologist, 55*(4), 407–421.

Lathan, C. E., Kinsella, M. A., Rosen, M. J., Winters, J., & Trepagnier, C. (1999). Aspects of human factors engineering in home telemedicine and telerehabilitation systems. *Telemedicine Journal, 5*(2), 169–175.

Mair, F., & Whitten, P. (2000). Systematic review of studies of patient satisfaction with telemedicine. *British Medical Journal* (electronic edition), *320,* 1517–1520. http://www.bmj.com (02/01/00).

McGowan, J., Raszka, W., Light, J., Magrane, D., O'Malley, D., & Bertsch, T. (1998). A vertical curriculum to teach the knowledge, skills and attitudes of medical informatics. *Proceedings of the American Medical Informatics Association Symposium,* pp. 457–461.

McGregor, J., & Nimtz, P. (1998). Health information network planning: Key steps, critical processes. *Healthcare Technology Management, 9*(4), 26–29.

Mittman, R., & Cain, M. (1999). *The future of the Internet in health care.* Report by the California Health Care Foundation. Menlo Park, CA: Institute for the Future.

Nakajima, I., Sawada, Y., Ashihara, T., & Takashima, Y. (1999). Problems and our solutions for implementing telemedicine systems. *Journal of Medical Systems, 23*(6), 425–435.

Nickelson, D. W. (1998). Telehealth and the evolving health care system: Strategic opportunities for professional psychology. *Professional Psychology: Research and Practice, 29,* 527–535.

Noone, J., Warren, J., & Brittain, M. (1998). Information overload: Opportunities and challenges for the GP's desktop. *Medinfo, 9*(2), 287–291.

Paperny, D. M. N. (2000). Computers and information technology: Implications for the 21st century. *Adolescent Medicine, 11*(1), 183–201.

Puskin, D. S., Morris, T., Hassol, A., Gaumer, G., & Mintzer, C. L. (1997). Patient and provider acceptance of telemedicine. *New Medicine, 1,* 55–59.

Risser, J. (1998). Telemedicine: The up side, and . . . *Distance Education Report, 2*(2), 1–3.

Schneider, E. C., & Eisenberg, J. M. (1998). Strategies and methods for aligning current and best medical practices. The role of information technologies. *Western Journal of Medicine, 168*(5), 311–318.

Sheng, O. R. L., Hu, P. J. H., Wei, C. P., & Ma, P. C. (1999). Organizational management of telemedicine technology: Conquering time and space boundaries in health care services. *IEEE Transactions on Engineering Management, 46*(3), 265–278.

Stamm, B. H., & Perednia, D. A. (2000). Evaluating psychosocial aspects of telemedicine and telehealth systems. *Professional Psychology: Research and Practice, 31*(2), 1684–1689.

Tabor, P. (2000). Got images? The skinny on teleradiology. *Healthcare Informatics,* 16–17 (cited on www.healthcare-informatics.com).

Trepagnier, C., & Rosen, M. J. (1999). Research and development in telerehabilitation. In C. Buhler & H. Knops (Eds.), *Assistive technology on the threshold of the new millennium* (pp. 102–105). Washington, DC: IOS Press.

Weise, E. (2000, August 8). One click starts the avalanche. *USA Today,* p. 3-D.

Chapter Twenty-Nine

Using Technology to "Defragment" a Mental Health Service System

Thomas A. Simpatico

Carroll A. Cradock

Michael McGuire

Daria Zvetina

The [quality control] issue has more to do with people and motivation and less to do with capital and equipment than one would think. It involves a cultural change.
—Michael Beer, Harvard Business School

Suppose someone claimed to have a microscopically exact replica of Michelangelo's David in his home. When you go to see this marvel, you find a twenty-five foot tall, roughly rectilinear hunk of pure white marble standing in his living room. "I haven't gotten around to unpacking it yet," he says, "but I know it's in there."
—Douglas Hofstadter

It has been nearly 40 years since President Kennedy called for a "bold new approach" to the delivery of mental health services, a community-based strategy that would offer an array of services responsive to different levels of disability and need, located close to where consumers live, and involving a new partnership among local, state, and federal funding sources (Kennedy, 1963). In the decades that have followed, prospects for the severely and persistently mentally ill, as well as others who rely on public-sector mental health services, have certainly improved. Advances in programs and staffing ratios in the state hospital system have supported the goals of active treatment and a return to the community for the severely disabled. The availability of community-based services has also increased dramatically through the development of the community mental health center system. In addition, psychotropic medications have continued to improve, the field of community psychiatry has come into its own, and the consumer movement has helped to establish the patient as a legitimate partner in the design and implementation of treatment plans.

However, the evolution of care since the advent of deinstitutionalization has not been problem-free. The number of homeless Americans continues to rise, and it is estimated that 30% to 50% of all long-term homeless adults have a major mental illness, and up to 80% have either a major mental illness or a severe substance-use disorder, or both (Baum & Burnes, 1993). Since the 1970s, much concern has been expressed about the number of mentally ill persons in jails and prisons (Stelovich, 1979; Swank & Winer, 1976; Torrey, 1997). A portion of our criminal justice system population resembles, in many respects, those who used to be long-term patients in state hospitals (Lamb & Grant, 1982; Teplin, 1983, 1990).

The mental health care system has grown in a haphazard, reactive fashion, with little coordinated planning or consistent vision (Regier et al., 1993). Coordination of efforts among community mental health centers, state and private hospitals, and local agencies has left much to be desired. A 1988 report to Congress from the Committee on Government Operations described the mental health care system as "fragmented, uncoordinated, and disorganized" (Brooks, 1988). The 1999 Surgeon General's report described the U.S. mental health service system as having been determined by many heterogeneous factors rather than by a single guiding set of organized principles (U.S. Department of Health and Human Services, 1999). Although there have been gallant and innovative attempts to "defragment" the mental health care system over the years, it remains an often impenetrable morass. This is perhaps nowhere as evident as in metropolitan centers, which are characterized by large concentrations of persons in need, labyrinthine systems of care, and quite finite resources.

METROPOLITAN CHICAGO AS CONTEXT

The service challenges confronting metropolitan Chicago are in many ways typical of those of other large urban centers. The Office of Mental Health of the Illinois Department of Human Services (IDHS) serves approximately 6 million people and maintains three adult psychiatric hospitals with a combined inpatient capacity of about 500 beds. The Office of Mental Health also funds approximately 80 Chicagoland community mental health centers, serving an estimated 12,000 open cases on any given day (Bureau of Chicago Network Operations, Office of Mental Health, IDHS, 2000) (see Fig. 29.1). Although this system alone is complex enough, Fig. 29.2 illustrates the even more complicated *functional system of care*[1] for persons with major mental illness, a huge matrix of diverse public service systems, a much larger machine with many more gears and cogs than one might presume. Table 29.1 lists some of the components.

Persons served through Chicago's mental health system and those who care for them are struggling to navigate these multiple, poorly connected systems. Without coordinated planning, a substantial number of persons receiving mental health services fall through the cracks and chasms that exist within and between the organiza-

---

1. The "functional system of care" is the (often *dys*functional) group of organizations that patients and their families must negotiate to obtain care and services.

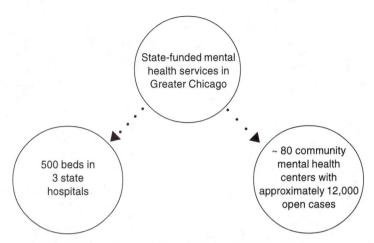

FIGURE 29.1. Metropolitan Chicago OMH-funded services.

tional bureaucracies and provider networks that make up their service safety net (Hansen, Collins, & Malotte, 1985). This discontinuity in care is one likely culprit in higher rates of recidivism and other problems that are costly in both humanitarian and economic terms.

TRACKING MARGINAL POPULATIONS

Human service agencies and systems are increasingly looking to information technologies for tools to improve service access, coordination and continuity, and for evaluating program effectiveness. Information management systems are being employed to document client characteristics, track and coordinate service delivery, and monitor client and program outcomes. In line with this movement, several years ago the Illinois mental health authority began to develop a "real-time" case-tracking and clinical information system, dubbed "Bridger." The objective was to create a mechanism for integrating case information across the various arms of the metropolitan Chicago mental health system to enhance the continuity of patient care and better inform clinical and administrative decision making. Another purpose was to create an information system shared by key components of the functional system of care that would serve as a template on which a common clinical and system culture would be built.

The balance of this chapter describes the components and evolution of this information management system and the key aspects most relevant to clinical leaders.

THE BRIDGER SYSTEM

In a recent review of the service tracking literature, 10 elements were identified as critical to working longitudinally with members of marginalized populations (McKenzie, Tulsky, Long, Chesney, & Moss, 1999). The crucial elements are:

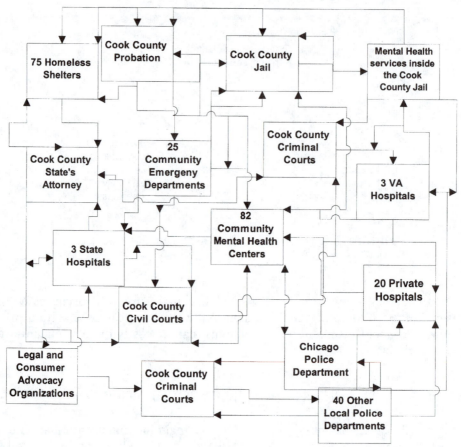

FIGURE 29.2. A simplified map of the metropolitan Chicago functional system of mental health services.

1. Collection of contact information.
2. Thorough organization of tracking efforts.
3. Attention to staff training and support.
4. Use of phone and mail follow-up.
5. Use of incentives.
6. Establishment of rapport with participants.
7. Assurance of confidentiality.
8. Use of agency tracking.
9. Use of field tracking.
10. Attention to safety concerns.

The information and tracking system under development in metropolitan Chicago has taken these basic principles and applied them to the functional system of care in the following phases.

**Table 29.1. Some Components of the Greater Chicago
"Functional System" of Mental Health Care**

Hospitals
- 4 State hospitals
- 25 Private hospitals
- 3 Federal VA hospitals
- County jail inpatient services

Outpatient services
- 80 CMHCs
- 25 Private emergency rooms

Human service agencies
- Illinois Office of Public Aid (IOPA)
- Office of Developmental Disabilities/IDHS
- Office of Rehabilitation Services/IDHS
- Office of Alcohol and Substance Abuse/IDHS

Criminal justice system
- County jails
- State prison system
- Federal prison system
- County criminal courts
- Chicago police department
- More than 40 local police departments

Legal services
- State's attorney
- Public defender
- County civil courts

Advocacy services
- Alliance for the Mentally Ill
- Federal Guardianship and Advocacy
- Equip for Equality
- Mental Health Association

Phase I: Getting Started

At the project's inception, assessments were conducted in one of the three state
psychiatric hospitals serving metropolitan Chicago to determine whether any of the
individual data fields from old databases was valuable enough to retain in the new
system. The old databases generally existed on archaic software and were used idiosyncratically by isolated pockets of staff (Fig. 29.3). Information was inconsistently
entered, and the databases were both redundant and incompatible with each other.
Thus, ironically, the initial presence of information technology served to perpetuate
a hospital culture of noncommunication.

All of the databases being used in the hospital were collected and reduced to
their constituent fields. Duplicate fields were eliminated, and a flow chart was created to illustrate where in the patient care process the field was to be completed, by
whom, and within what time frame. In addition, the flow chart identified the department that had editorial control over each field. Once the chart had been devised,

FIGURE 29.3. Multiple idiosyncratic competing databases.

a new array of interactive databases was constructed, which became the first components of the Bridger system. These databases made it possible for key hospital sub-
systems to work from a single data set that was generated in the natural course of
patient care (Fig. 29.4). After an initial training period, both staff workload and data
errors decreased as successive forms utilized in the hospitalization process built on
data derived from work that had been done upstream. Staff then spent less time
creating the medical record and more time engaged in direct patient care.

By the end of Phase I, there was evidence that Bridger had begun to induce a
transformation in the worldview of hospital staff. Screens that were now being seen
each day by hundreds of employees presented consistent diagnostic terminology
and treatment and provider options. As a result of daily interaction with Bridger, a
common clinical lexicon began to emerge among staff, and confidence in the data
and reports generated through the system began to grow.

Phase II: "Connecting the Dots"

In Phase II, Bridger connected the now internally integrated state hospital to 27
community mental health centers (CMHCs). This was a critical development because it dramatically ended the provincial "black box" mentality that pervaded these
two components—hospitals and CMHCs—of the mental health system.

Bridger now provided the rudiments of a virtual medical record that was *shared*
by the state hospitals and CMHCs. It also provided functions that did not recognize
the distinction between hospital and community, and therefore could be initiated
and/or completed in either setting. For example, an algorithm that led staff through
the process of obtaining entitlements for someone could be started in the hospital

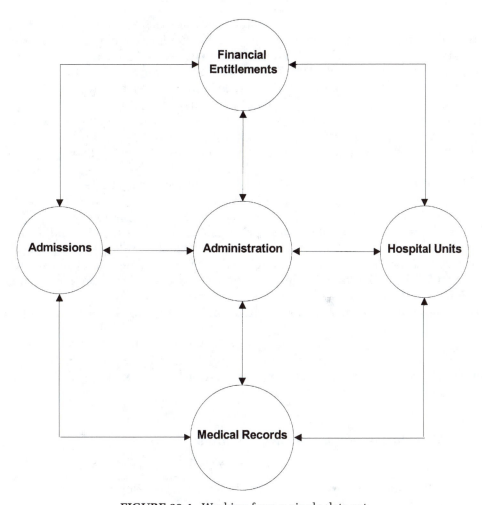

FIGURE 29.4. Working from a single data set.

and completed in the community. The existence of computers connecting hospital and community staff created didactic interfaces that standardized documentation procedures and clinical and operational terms and criteria across systems. Virtual protocols with drop-down lists and prompts replaced slow, vulnerable, and redundant paper forms. As a result, clinicians and service providers who had seemed to be on opposite sides of a "wall" learned they could understand the world in much the same way.

Phase III: Go Directly to Jail

The next developmental milestone in Bridger's evolution was its extension to Cermak Mental Health Services, the mental health provider quartered in the large Cook County Jail. This was crucially important for two reasons. First, there are significant numbers of current and potential psychiatric patients in Cook County Jail. About 10% to

15% of the 12,000 or more detainees the jail houses each day have a serious and persistent mental illness, a psychiatric population double that of the Chicago area's three state hospitals. Second, the extension of Bridger to Cermak signaled the joining of two large bureaucracies. Once established, the connection signified a radical departure from the status quo of day-to-day operations in each institution.

Initially, batch files of the jail's general census data were downloaded to disk and walked to Bridger, where they were cross-matched with mental health files. Soon the process was automated. At this writing, a daily automated cross-match is about to begin that will channel important reports to clinical staff working in the jail, the three metropolitan state hospitals, and the 80 greater Chicago community mental health centers. At first, confidentiality requirements mandated that a release be completed for each record requested by Cermak staff at the jail. This severely limited Bridger's utility, because it prevented automatic information exchange. New Illinois legislation, a result of the Bridger project, created an exception to the confidentiality statute, allowing jails and the Office of Mental Health to exchange mental health records without each individual's authorization for release of information. This enabled reports to flow in both directions: Cermak staff can more easily identify inmates with previously diagnosed mental illness, and community mental health centers can locate their incarcerated clients (and facilitate timely treatment and discharge planning).

We are now collecting baseline data for a scientific study of this part of the Bridger project. Preliminary data strongly suggest that Bridger greatly facilitates coordinated discharge planning between Cermak Health Services at the Cook County Jail and community mental health centers.

Phase IV: Inclusion of the Homeless Shelters

Encouraged by what we were able to accomplish in collaboration with the Cook County Departments of Health and Corrections, we next extended the Bridger system to the Chicago homeless shelter system.

The initial focus of this phase of the Bridger system evolution was simply to make the 75 homeless shelters funded through the Chicago Department of Human Services part of the system. A pilot study with 6 of the 75 shelters was established to develop and test a simple interface that would require little staff training, decrease staff workload, and permit reciprocal information flow between the shelters and mental health service providers. In order to accomplish these objectives, we chose to "virtualize" the standard intake form. An authorization form for release of information was embedded in the virtual intake form, which, once signed, allowed the name and birth date of shelter clients to be sent to the Office of Mental Health.

The intake process is generally completed by 9:00 p.m. in each of the six pilot shelters. At that time, a batch download is performed which transfers the names and birth dates of shelter clients to the Office of Mental Health so that a cross-match can be performed to identify persons who have been receiving mental health services. The next morning, "hits" are provided to a mental health mobile assessment unit. The mobile assessment unit then visits identified persons before they leave the shelter and attempts to engage them so that they don't fall away from treatment (Fig. 29.5).

As the pilot study proceeded, the system quickly became efficient and reliable.

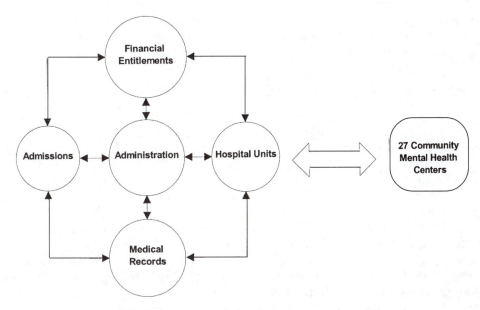

FIGURE 29.5. Initial "Bridger" system concept.

Only an extremely small portion of shelter clients refused to sign the release, so that virtually all patients served by the 6 pilot shelters are cross-matched each day with Office of Mental Health records. At this writing, the Bridger system is being deployed in an additional 21 shelters. We project that all 75 Chicago shelters will be part of the system by the summer of 2003.

INFORMATION SYSTEM AS AN AGENT OF CHANGE AND LEADER'S TOOLBOX

One way to think about the aftermath of the deinstitutionalization movement is that the fix for a large social problem (how to care for, and to some extent what to do with, so many seriously mentally ill people) was moved from one governmental bureaucracy (the state hospital system) to an array of other bureaucratic organizations and systems, each of which was interested in the seriously mentally ill person from a different perspective.

Many of the organizations that make up the functional system of care are city, county, or state bureaucracies. As such, they tend to rely on rigid, hierarchical organizational structures and define their work as a function of that structure. The nature of such bureaucracies provides a certain institutional stability at the expense of organizational plasticity; the "square peg" of the task at hand generally must fit into the "round hole" provided by the organization.

Such organizational inertia is often a desirable (if sometimes frustrating) quality for governmental institutions to have; we benefit by having a stable and predictable societal infrastructure that ultimately reflects the will of the people. However, the very qualities that promote this stability make it difficult for governmental organizations to collaborate with one another around a shared task (e.g., caring for large numbers of mentally ill). The information technology represented by the Bridger system improves both intra- and interorganization collaboration without threatening the infrastructure, to the considerable benefit of all.

CONCLUSION

As the reader may have surmised, we named our information system "Bridger" in recognition of its boundary-spanning capacity. By customizing the interface to the likes and styles of each participating organization, Bridger is experienced as a natural extension of that organization rather than an external imposition. This promotes user "buy-in" and increases the accuracy of the information captured about each organization's work product.

One should not infer that clinical leaders can simply "plug in" and use software solutions as a cure-all for bureaucratic ills. Neither Bridger nor any other information system can magically transform complex, inertia-laden organizations. However, when the leaders of respective organizations create a top-down climate of intra- and interorganization collaboration, information systems like Bridger can serve as relatively simple templates for the cultural convergence required for health care networks to work as true systems.

REFERENCES

Baum, A. S., & Burnes, D. W. (1993). *A nation in denial: The truth about homelessness.* Boulder, CO: Westview.

Brooks, J. (1988). *From back wards to back streets: The failure of the federal government in providing services for the mentally ill.* Forty-First Report by the Committee on Government Operations, 100th Congress, 2nd Session, House Report 100–541. Washington, DC: U.S. Government Printing Office.

Bureau of Chicago Network Operations. (1999). Data from Springfield, IL, Office of Mental Health, Illinois Department of Human Services.

Hansen, W. B., Collins, L. M., & Malotte, C. K. (1985). Attrition in prevention research. *Journal of Behavioral Medicine, 8*(3), 261–275.

Kennedy, J. F. (1963). *A Message from the President of the United States relative to mental illness and mental retardation* (88th Congress, First Session, U.S. House of Representatives Doc. No. 58). Washington, DC: U.S. Government Printing Office.

Lamb, H. R., & Grant, R. W. (1982). The mentally ill in an urban county jail. *Archives of General Psychiatry, 39,* 17–22.

McKenzie, M., Tulsky, J. P., Long, H. L., Chesney, M., & Moss, A. (1999). Tracking and follow-up of marginalized populations: A review. *Journal of Health Care for the Poor and Underserved, 10,* 409–429.

Regier, D. A., Narrow, W. E., Rae, D. S., Manderscheid, R. W., Locke, B. Z., & Goodwin F. K. (1993). The de facto US mental and addictive disorders service system. Epidemiologic Catchment Area prospective 1-year prevalence rates of disorders and services. *Archives of General Psychiatry, 50,* 85–94.

Stelovich, S. (1979). From the hospital to the prison: A step forward in deinstitutionalization? *Hospital and Community Psychiatry, 30,* 618–620.

Swank, G. E., & Winer, D. (1976). Occurrence of psychiatric disorder in a county jail population. *American Journal of Psychiatry, 133,* 1331–1333.

Teplin, L. A. (1983). The criminalization of the mentally ill: Speculation in search of data. *Psychological Bulletin, 94,* 54–67.

Teplin, L. A. (1990). The prevalence of severe mental disorder among male urban jail detainees: Comparison with the Epidemiologic Catchment Area Program. *American Journal of Public Health, 80,* 663–669.

Torrey, E. F. (1997). *Out of the shadows: Confronting America's mental illness crisis.* New York: Wiley.

U.S. Department of Health and Human Services. (1999). *Mental health: A report of the Surgeon General.* Rockville, MD: U.S. Department of Health and Human Services, Substance Abuse and Mental Health Services Administration, Center for Mental Health Services, National Institutes of Health, National Institute of Mental Health.

Chapter Thirty

Videoconferencing in Mental Health Care: Barriers, Opportunities, and Principles for Program Development

Carroll A. Cradock

Thomas A. Simpatico

If you build it, they will come.

Not always—or, they may not stay.

The 30-year history of videoconferencing in U.S. mental health care demonstrates the limitations of the preceding axiom. Quality of care compared to face-to-face encounters was the initial challenge. Many people believed that encounters via videoconferencing could not provide adequate clinical care. In fact, most of these (grant-funded) demonstration projects confirmed that a wide variety of health care services could be delivered competently using videoconferencing technology. Unfortunately, almost all of these early programs closed when their grant funding ended (Bashshur, 1997; Crump & Pfeil, 1995).

The last 10 years have witnessed a renewal of interest in telemedicine and increasing use of telemedicine technology. This is particularly true in the specialties of radiology, mental health, and dermatology. Between 1994 and 1999, total clinical consultations provided by telemedicine services in the United States increased from about 2,000 to 74,000 (Association of Telehealth Providers, 1999). Mental health is second only to radiology in clinical use of telemedicine in the United States (Association of Telehealth Providers, 1999). These programs have often delivered high-quality clinical care (Smith & Allison, 1998).

Videoconferencing is among the oldest electronic tools in mental health. Its potential in mental health care is often obvious to nonprofessionals, because their experience with both television and mental health treatment includes "talking heads." In addition, preliminary data indicate that telehealth services may offer some advantages that traditional office visits do not, such as improved accessibility, attendance, involvement of family members, and efficiency (Zaylor, 1999).

Videoconferenced mental health care involves real-time, simultaneous, video-mediated interaction of a clinician and patient(s) who are located at different sites. There are three types of interactive video equipment that lend themselves to clinical practice: "wide bandwidth" videoconferencing setups, personal-computer-based (PC-based) equipment, and video telephones ("videophones"). Each has advantages and disadvantages for mental health.

Videoconferencing equipment is the most expensive. It offers the highest degree of visual resolution (picture clarity). One of the benefits of the more expensive videoconferencing equipment is that clinicians can zoom in to examine part of a patient's body (such as pupil, mouth) for drug side effects or other physical symptoms without calling attention to this activity or invading the patient's space. Simultaneous communication between people at several locations requires "bridging" capacity and is more expensive than two-way communication for both equipment and operation. Most research on clinical effectiveness of real-time video-mediated clinical care has used this type of equipment.

PC-based (desktop or laptop) video-mediated communications are feasible using computers equipped with inexpensive cameras and speakers. PC-based equipment is far less expensive than standard videoconferencing setups, but it has lower visual resolution and movement is often poorly transmitted (producing a coarse, jerky appearance that is particularly noticeable with low-speed or "dial-up" modem connections). Patients who are familiar with home computers require little additional training and may quickly feel at home with this kind of equipment.

Videophones are smaller and cheaper still, often costing a few hundred dollars. Some types are connected to the patient's and clinician's telephone and television, then operated by simply pressing a button on the telephone keypad; any phone call can become a videophone call if the other party also has a videophone. Other types have integral screens, and still others are PC-based, with the "telephone" and video picture in a window on the PC monitor. Although videophones lack both high visual resolution and smooth transmission of movement, they have some advantages. Both PC-based videoconferencing and videophones provide a "social" or "personal" presence not found in ordinary telephone conversations, but may lack the capacity to transmit subtleties such as eyeblinks and blushes (Cukor et al., 1998). Dedicated (non-Internet-based) videophones provide greater security from "hackers" than most PC-based videoconferencing. The videophone can be loaned or rented to patients (who can usually install it themselves).

In the remainder of this chapter, terms such as *videoconferencing* or *videoconferenced* care refer to use of any of these kinds of equipment, unless otherwise noted.

BARRIERS TO ACCEPTING VIDEOCONFERENCED TELEHEALTH

Broad acceptance, by clinicians, administrators, payers, and some patients, is the biggest current challenge for videoconferenced mental health. Despite current interest in and enthusiasm for videoconferenced mental health services in some quarters, sound business and administrative strategies must guide their further development. The remainder of this chapter discusses barriers to acceptance and sustainability, trends and opportunities for adoption of videoconferenced services, and principles for development of sustainable mental health services via videoconferencing. In order to be sustainable, services must be integrated into the mission and goals of mental health organizations, actively supported by stakeholders such as patients, advocacy groups, governing boards, and clinical staff. In addition, videoconferenced mental health services must be cost-effective (Siwicki, 1998).

Despite consistently high patient satisfaction ratings (Grigsby, 1997; Gustke, Bach, West, & Rogers, 2000), professionals, accrediting bodies, and payers typically express distrust of videoconferencing for psychiatric consultations, psychotherapy, and counseling. Barriers to acceptance arise for several reasons. First, although there are some promising studies, empirical research demonstrating that videoconferenced mental health care is as effective as face-to-face visits is still lacking. Published reports to date, however, suggest equivalent outcomes for several paradigms of diagnosis and follow-up psychiatric care, and no serious adverse findings (Zaylor, 1999).

Second, many psychiatrists, clinical psychologists, and counselors fear mechanization of an intimate, sensitive, interpersonal process. Some clinicians express discomfort about how they "come across on TV," in addition to fears of losing control of the treatment process. Third, in the authors' experience, public and commercial payers have been reluctant to authorize reimbursement for videoconferenced mental health services, in part because it is difficult to project the impact of increased access and utilization on costs. Fourth, regulatory and accreditation bodies have avoided creating guidelines for videoconferenced mental health care because of inadequate empirical data and "best practice" models on which to base them. Effective in 2001, the Joint Commission on Accreditation of Healthcare Organizations (JCAHO) published guidelines for credentialing and privileging telemedicine practitioners and for defining the scope of an organization's authorized telemedicine services (Joint Commission on Accreditation of Healthcare Organizations [JCAHO], 2001).

Fifth, many clinicians regard videoconferenced care as an economic threat to the structure of their current practices. Psychologists, psychiatrists, clinical social workers, counselors, and their respective state professional organizations have sometimes expressed concern that widespread use of telepsychiatry and telecounseling may lead to a relaxing of state licensure. More liberal state licensing or adoption of federal licensing could create a nationwide mental heath care market for clinicians that would undermine the professional and financial autonomy of practitioners (Jacobson & Selvin, 2000, e.g., p. 436). Sixth, there are few current financing models that can guide videoconferencing program planning, which creates a budgetary consideration for administrators (Whitten, Zaylor, & Kingsley, 2000).

TRENDS FOR ADOPTING VIDEOCONFERENCING IN MENTAL HEALTH CARE

Several technological, economic, demographic, cultural, and paradigmatic changes support more widespread adoption of videoconferencing in mental health care delivery. U.S. video visits increased 314% between 1996 and 1998, the most rapid rate of growth of any clinical specialty (Association of Telehealth Service Providers, 1999). The impact of e-commerce on patient expectations and evidence of patient satisfaction with telemedicine were major contributing factors to the increase.

Public Experience With Technology

The accessibility of a widening array of services by telephone (e.g., keypad and/or automated voice response systems) and Internet-based companies, plus the availability of real-time computer interaction with people at great distances (not just by letter or e-mail), is creating a demand for home-based medical services. Computer-literate, Internet-experienced potential patients can obtain an enormous number of products and services on the Web, from real estate to education to travel plans. The question arises: "Why can't I get (therapy, counseling, psychiatric care) without having to leave my home?" (Bauer & Ringel, 1999).

One study conducted prior to the electronic revolution found that some people were unwilling to travel even short distances (such as two miles) for mental health care (Baer, Cukor, & Coyle, 1997). Some patients or potential patients find videophone technology simpler and easier to set up than other home electronic equipment. Electronic services that use keypads are routine for a growing number of people, for such services as retrieving phone messages, activating home alarms, accessing financial balances, and ordering event tickets. These skills are transferable to keypad-operated video equipment, and soon many keypads may be replaced by simpler, voice- and touch-activated systems.

Lower Startup Costs

Equipment costs were once a major obstacle to adoption of videoconferencing in health care. Until recently, the technology required was very expensive, stationary, cumbersome, and unfamiliar to most clinical staff and patients. Early projects generally required an expensive engineering staff to operate the complicated, studio-type equipment. As this book goes to press, "high-end," portable, state-of-the-art videoconferencing workstations with bandwidth suitable for medical care cost as little as $4,000, and equipment has become smaller and more user-friendly for clinicians and patients alike.

The technology is now as easy to operate as cable TV or a VCR. Limitations would apply to individuals who lack sufficiently private telephone or television access. In addition, this technology is not yet "user-friendly" for those patients who suffer from cognitive and/or motor impairments that limit their ability to use comparable home communication or entertainment systems. In some cases, family or office staff can be recruited to help such patients with the equipment.

Telephone line costs, however, can still be substantial. Dedicated, "point-to-point" systems carry high fixed costs regardless of utilization. In many cases, integrated services digital network (ISDN) based systems (one form of Internet access) are less expensive than point-to-point dedicated lines because costs are correlated with usage. Local circumstances also affect costs, particularly in regions in which one or more local telephone companies control rates between the place where health care service originates (the "hub" site) and where it is received by the patient ("spoke" site). The U.S. Telecommunications Act of 1996, which provides subsidies for telephone and telecommunications infrastructure in rural areas, may help lower costs for some providers.

Need for Broader Mental Health Access, Especially in Primary Health Care Settings

Mental health specialists see fewer than 30% of all patients with well-defined mental illness; the others are seen in primary care settings (Miranda, Hohmann, & Attkinsson, 1994). The evidence for competent assessment and treatment of mental illness and addictions provided by primary care physicians is discomfiting. Studies conducted both in the United States and Great Britain indicate that primary care practitioners may fail to detect psychiatric conditions in over half of their patients with mental illness (Borus, Howes, Devins, Rosenberg, & Livingston, 1988; Vazquez-Barquero et al., 1997). Approximately 19 million health maintenance organization (HMO)–enrolled Americans receive their mental health and substance abuse services under a "carve-in" contract arrangement (Findlay, 1999). This number may increase if/as the value of integrating primary medical and mental health care achieves wider acceptance (Johnson & Kuraitis, 1999). Approximately 70% of patients with severe and chronic mental illness (SCMI; e.g., schizophrenia, bipolar disorder) also have chronic medical conditions and addictions (Lewis, Lurigio, & Riger, 1994).

Family practitioners, internists, and pediatricians commonly make referrals to mental health specialists, yet between one-third and one-half of patients do not follow up on these referrals (Fischer & Ransom, 1997). Stigma and inconvenience are two of the many barriers patients face in making and keeping referral appointments. A number of people simply don't want to call or visit a mental health office, either on-site or elsewhere. The volume or uneven rate of referrals may not warrant a staff mental health professional. Videoconferenced mental health consultations can add value to primary health care by transcending barriers that include distance, time, stigma, and costs.

School-based health centers (SBHCs), most of which are primary care centers established to offer a combination of triage, urgent care, health education, preventive services, and treatment of sexually transmitted diseases, offer another opportunity for videoconferencing. According to Marchetti (2000), the number of SBHCs in the United States increased from 31 to over 1,300 between 1984 and 1999, with at least 21 states maintaining special offices to provide technical assistance.

A disproportionate number of visits to SBHCs are for mental health or substance abuse care: 30% to 60% of total encounters (Anglin, Naylor, & Kaplan, 1996; Pastore, Juszcak, Fisher, & Friedman, 1998). The emotional problems and/or substance abuse are often complicated by medical problems such as asthma, diabetes, or sexually transmitted disease. Mental health care offered in SBHCs has been linked to reduced depression and dropout rates (Kisker & Brown, 1996; McCord, Klein, Joy, & Fothergill, 1993; Weist, Paskewitz, Warner, & Flaherty, 1996).

Videoconferencing can increase accessibility, convenience, and privacy, and decrease stigma and cost. Primary care physicians and nurse practitioners that staff SBHCs can benefit from easy video consultation with psychiatrists.

Similar benefits of increased access apply to many other settings, including worksites, adult and juvenile detention facilities, residential treatment centers, half-way houses, and group homes. As the population ages, more nursing-home patients and home-bound elderly persons will need mental health care; these patients' complicated medical conditions often require psychiatric evaluation.

Accommodating Language and Culture

Cultural and linguistic values influence clinical practice (American Psychological Association, 1990; Joint Commission on Accreditation of Healthcare Organizations, 2000). Several studies support the importance of providing care in the patient's primary or preferred language (Clauss, 1998; Flaskerud & Liu, 1991; Gomez, 1992; Oquendo, 1996). In addition to improving access to clinical skills, videoconferencing can make it easier and more cost-effective to match patients with clinicians who understand their culture and speak their preferred language.

Patient and Family Education and Communication

Patient and family education and nontherapy communication are often the first components of a clinical videoconferencing system. They are simpler and more straightforward than diagnostic and treatment programs, and can play an important role in treatment compliance and relapse prevention (Falloon & Optimal Treatment Project Collaborators, 1999).

Videoconferencing can also help bring family members and other important participants together in "virtual" family conferences, team meetings, or clinician-to-clinician consultations. A recent study of family consultation to treat teenagers with epilepsy demonstrated easy and effective use of videophones in this way (Glueckauf & Whitton, 1998). Attendance at videoconferenced and telephone visits was higher than at in-person visits, and satisfaction with videoconferenced visits equaled or exceeded that with in-person visits. In western Virginia, the Appalink Mental Health Program has successfully used videoconferencing to create family support groups in remote, mountainous areas (Smith & Allison, 1998).

LESSONS FOR ADMINISTRATORS

There is no question that videoconferencing technology can open new opportunities and markets for mental health organizations. Recent societal, technological, and economic changes make "virtual" services more feasible. There are, however, lessons to be learned from previous generations of telemedicine programs, and a few principles for successful current program development.

Anecdotes abound about urban medical centers that purchased expensive, sophisticated equipment to provide care in rural areas, disregarding the fact that less expensive equipment would have accomplished the same task. In some cases, purchasers were insensitive to the possibility that "outsider" services would be seen as competitive by local providers. In others, "hub site" links to rural patient care "spoke sites" overlooked the fact that a trip to the city for care might provide added benefits to the patient and his or her family, such as an opportunity to travel to the city or time off from work (Stamm, 1998). In the past, proponents of tele-mental-health often purchased the most sophisticated technology, implemented programs without adequate needs assessments, failed to address financial sustainability, and set up telehealth programs without securing support from local clinicians and building on their practice and referral patterns.

Given these considerations, the following principles of program development are recommended for administrators who are considering videoconferenced mental health programs.

1. *Use technology to solve existing problems, address existing needs, and add value to as many user groups as possible.* The simple availability of impressive and sophisticated technology will not convince people to use it regularly. Despite their initial enthusiasm, everyone resists change, particularly when it involves learning new skills, real or imagined role changes, reallocation of resources, and a threat to the status quo. If the project is to succeed, it must be obvious to many stakeholders that it solves some key problem in their daily lives.

2. *Conduct a needs assessment with input from all user groups.* "All user groups" includes agency clinical staff, local clinicians, patients, their families, administrative support staff, technical support staff, advocacy groups, referral sources, and even local telephone companies. Identify what the groups want, can offer, and are prepared to lose (if anything); what new demands will be placed on them; and what resources will be required to provide as much benefit to as many user groups as possible. The needs assessment should include face-to-face group meetings, in which members can present their respective concerns and conflicts in goals and objectives can be resolved.

3. *Design operations to build on the needs assessment and on existing relationships, referral patterns, routines, and locations.* Use telehealth to solve problems that potential users identify, and not to address assumed needs or the priorities of those who fund grants. Although videoconferenced services are intended to transcend boundaries, don't forget that economic factors, like politics, are local. Locate "spoke" videoconference units in places where people are accustomed to going for health care services. Colocation is important. For example, locate "hub" equipment where physicians already work on a daily or weekly basis.

   Centralizing equipment in a "telepsychiatry" suite may deter utilization, even if the building is just next door. The equipment must be as convenient as any other that the doctor uses regularly.

   Add value to local referral patterns rather than disrupting them. Importing specialized expertise from another location through videoconferencing can be regarded as competition for local clinicians and patients, both of whom have long-term relationships to protect. An excellent model of combining colocation with sensitivity to local clinician relationships is used at the University of Kentucky, where telepsychiatry services are located within the offices of rural primary care physicians, who control access and referrals (Blackmon, Kaak, & Ranseen, 1997).

4. *Select equipment that is both appropriate to its intended function and as user-friendly as possible.* Do not "over-purchase," and resist the temptation to listen to vendors' "puffery" about their latest technical breakthrough. Keep the equipment simple to learn, simple to use, and simple to connect with other equipment. Repeat users, critical to the success and sustainability of the program, will be those who find it easy to operate and effective for the task at hand.

   Many mental health procedures do not require expensive, high-quality visual resolution; basic telemonitoring, clinical support, and (in some cases) counseling can be adequate. Still other services can be provided just as well on an ordinary telephone or interactive voice response system as on a videophone (Hall & Huber, 2000). On the other hand, procedures such as diagnostic interviews or fitness-for-duty assessments require more expensive, higher-resolution equipment. Consider carefully what added value is provided to the patient, family, and/or clinician through a real-time audiovisual interaction, as contrasted with other communication modes (e.g., telephone, phone, e-mail), and how sophisticated the images must be to achieve one's objectives.

   Be aware that different parties in a clinical process need different things. The clinician may only need to hear how the patient is doing, but the patient may respond better to seeing his or her doctor's face (or vice versa).

5. *Initial applications should add value to as many user groups as possible.* In the early stages, every user is a new "customer," and that person's experience may either recruit or deter other potential users. If most user groups receive added value early in the project, the project becomes more securely anchored in the user community. The impact of informal patient evaluations is much greater in institutional settings such as schools and workplaces than in home-based services. Avoid selecting initial applications that appeal to only one user group (e.g., families, school administrators, employers, patients, payers, or clinicians).

6. *Provide comprehensive, hands-on training for clinicians, especially if they are providing services in an institutional setting.* Clinicians, technology "pioneers" in a sense, must be at ease in this new medium. In addition, they must sometimes handle technical questions from new patient users. If clinicians don't feel competent and at ease with clinical videoconferencing, they will avoid using the service and program development will stall.

7. *Design accountability and outcome assessment systems before implementing the telehealth services.* Program developers often focus on the challenges of equipment selection, program design, training, and marketing at the expense of identifying quality benchmarks against which the program will be evaluated. The outcome and accountability instruments must be directly linked to the problems and goals identified at the needs assessment. Otherwise, even stellar accomplishments may be irrelevant to constituents whose support is critical for program sustainability.

8. *Plan for financial sustainability at the outset.* Excellent, worthwhile projects don't survive their early years of "startup" or grant funding simply because of some inherent value. Fiscal sustainability must be addressed with respect to each organization's needs. Videoconferenced services must also be able to demonstrate sufficient revenues and/or cost savings, and improve the organization's performance on objective measures (Siwicki, 1998). For example, reduction of

absenteeism and increased productivity matter in workplaces and school districts. Reduced inpatient episodes matter in capitated health care systems. Identify and track the variables that matter most in your organization.

9. *To minimize the effects of unanticipated consequences, try to build in added value for the telehealth patient.* Home and rural telehealth programs often bring care and resources directly to the patient or family location. Interestingly, although the benefits of immediate, on-site consultation are appealing to business, they may not be attractive to the worker or his or her family (e.g., removing subtle benefits of traveling to the doctor or clinic). In those settings where the use of tele-mental-health may remove benefits the patient previously received (such as time off work, or postponing deadlines or school exams), create added value to discourage the belief that telemedicine users are being penalized.

10. *Include accreditation and regulatory groups in the needs assessment and program planning.* As noted previously, the manuals and guidelines of many accreditation organizations do not yet address services provided through videoconferencing. This will, no doubt, change during the next few years as other groups follow the lead of the JCAHO. In the interim, policies and procedures developed for new tele-mental-health programs should parallel the intent of existing standards as closely as possible. Programs should carefully follow existing guidelines and consider consulting with specialists in the relevant regulatory and accreditation requirements. Consultation with professional societies such as the American Telemedicine Association and the American Society for Telemedicine is strongly advised.

THE FUTURE OF REIMBURSEMENT

Fiscal reimbursement is expected to be a short-term problem, because public and commercial payers are beginning to include telehealth in their payment systems. At present, 17 states authorize Medicaid payment for telemedicine (Tavener & Zelinger, 2000), as does Medicare, although the Medicare requirements for reimbursement are generally viewed as so restrictive that they are virtually prohibitive. Patient and professional advocates of telemedicine expect some relief from these restrictions as a result of legislation due to take effect toward the end of 2001 (Medicare, Medicaid and SCHIP Benefits Improvement and Protection Act, P.L. 106-1033, Section 223, 2000; Health Care Financing Administration, 2001). In the near term, until changes like these are implemented broadly and commercial payers routinely support telemedicine, the greatest expansions are expected to occur in health care environments that are not dependent on a fee-for-service reimbursement: school-based health, occupational health, capitated "carve-in" systems, the criminal justice system, and the military services.

Cost-benefit analyses must be built into new telemedicine programs from the beginning. Both startup and operational costs are a fraction of what they once were, and significant cost savings can be achieved in, for example, occupational health, school health, and prison settings. This must be demonstrated to corporate offices, payers, regulatory bodies, and administrators, however, to insure the sustainability of these programs. Failure to attend to these matters, and the belief that some inherent value of these exciting services will justify continued funding, has resulted in the demise of many programs, and will no doubt do so in the future. We must give administrators and executives solid, practical reasons to pursue videoconferenced mental health services.

REFERENCES

American Psychological Association. (1990). Ethical principles of psychologists. (Amended June 2, 1989). *American Psychologist, 45,* 390–395.

Association of Telehealth Service Providers (1999). *1999 Telemedicine report.* www.atsp.prg/survey.

Anglin, R. M., Naylor, K. E., & Kaplan, D. W. (1996). Comprehensive school-based health care: High school students' use of medical, mental health, and substance abuse services. *Pediatrics, 97*(3), 318–329.

Baer, L., Cukor, P., & Coyle, J. T. (1997). Telepsychiatry: Application of telemedicine to psychiatry. In R. L. Bashshur, J. H. Sanders, & G. W. Shannon (Eds.), *Telemedicine: Theory and practice* (pp. 265–288). Springfield, IL: Charles C. Thomas.

Bashshur, R. L. (1997). Telemedicine and the health care system. In R. L. Bashshur, J. H. Sanders, & G. W. Shannon (Eds.), *Telemedicine: Theory and practice* (pp. 5–36). Springfield, IL: Charles C. Thomas.

Bauer, J. C., & Ringel, M. A. (1999). *Telemedicine and the reinvention of healthcare.* New York: McGraw-Hill.

Blackmon, L. A., Kaak, H. O., & Ranseen, J. (1997). Consumer satisfaction with telemedicine child psychiatry consultation in rural Kentucky. *Psychiatric Services, 48*(11), 464.

Borus, J. F., Howes, M. J., Devins, N. P., Rosenberg, R., & Livingston, W. W. (1988). Primary health care providers' recognition and diagnosis of mental disorders in their patients. *General Hospital Psychiatry, 10*(5), 317–321.

Clauss, C. S. (1998). Language: The unspoken variable in psychotherapy practice. *Psychotherapy, 35*(2), 188–196.

Crump, W. J., & Pfeil, T. A. (1995). Telemedicine primer: An introduction to the technology and an overview of the literature. *Archives of Family Medicine, 9,* 796–803.

Cukor, P., Baer, L., Willis, B. S., Leahy, L., O'Laughlen, J., Murphy, M. E., Withers, M., & Martin, E. (1998). Use of videophones and low-cost standard telephone lines to provide a social presence in psychiatry. *Telemedicine Journal, 4*(4), 313.

Falloon, I., & Optimal Treatment Project Collaborators. (1999). Optimal treatment for psychosis in an international multisite demonstration project. *Psychiatric Services, 50*(5), 615–618.

Findlay, S. (1999). *Managed behavioral health care in 1999: An industry at a crossroads.* Washington, DC: National Coalition on Health Care.

Fischer, L., & Ransom, D. C. (1997). Developing a strategy for managing behavioral healthcare within the context of primary care. *Archives of Internal Medicine, 6,* 324–333.

Flaskerud, J. H., & Liu, P. Y. (1991). Effects of an Asian client-therapist language, ethnicity and gender match on utilization and outcome of therapy. *Community Mental Health Journal, 27*(1), 31–42.

Glueckauf, R., & Whitton, J. (1998). Home-based videocounseling for rural teens with epilepsy: Initial outcomes, costs and implementation lag times. *Telehealth News, 2*(2). Available online: http://www.cybertowers.com.

Gomez, M. (1989). *A projectile study of the affective expression of bilinguals.* (Doctoral dissertation, Northwestern University, 1989). *Dissertation Abstracts International, 49*(7-B), 2854.

Grigsby, B. (1997). Fourth annual telemedicine program review. *Telemedicine Today, 5*(4), 30–38, 42.

Gustke, S. S., Bach, M. A., West, R. L., & Rogers, L. O. (2000). Patient satisfaction with telemedicine. *Telemedicine Journal, 6*(1), 5–13.

Hall, J. A., & Huber, D. L. (2000). Telephone management in substance abuse treatment. *Telemedicine Journal and e-Health, 6*(4), 401.

Health Care Financing Administration. (2001). *Program Memorandum: Revision of Medicare Reimbursement for Telehealth Services.* (Publication 60-AB, May 1). Washington, DC: Author.

Jacobson, P. Y., & Selvin, E. (2000) Licensing telemedicine: The need for a national system. *Telemedicine Journal and e-Health, 6*(4), 429.

Joint Commission on Accreditation of Healthcare Organizations. (2000). *Hospital accreditation standards for psychiatric hospitals and psychiatric units: A functional approach.* Oakbrook Terrace, IL: Author.

Joint Commission on Accreditation of Healthcare Organizations. (2001). *Comprehensive accreditation manual for hospitals.* Oakbrook Terrace, IL: Author.

Kisker, E. E., & Brown, R. S. (1996). Do school-based health centers improve adolescents' access to health care, health status, and risk-taking behavior? *Journal of Adolescent Health, 18,* 335–343.

Lewis, D., Lurigio, A. J., & Riger, S. (1994). *The state mental patient and urban life: Moving in and out of the institution.* Springfield, IL: Charles C. Thomas.

Marchetti, A. (2000, July). *Illinois Coalition for School Health Centers.* Illinois Maternal and Child Health Coalition website, http://www.hmhb.org/ilmaternal/sblhcindex.htm.

McCord, M. T., Klein, J. D., Joy, J. M., & Fothergill, K. (1993). School-based clinic use and school performance. *Journal of Adolescent Health, 19*(4), 267–275.

Miranda, J., Hohmann, A. A., & Attkinsson, C. C. (1994). Epidemiology of mental disorders in primary care. In J. Miranda, A. A. Hohmann, C. C. Attkinsson, & D. P. Larson (Eds.), *Mental disorders in primary care* (pp. 3–15). San Francisco: Jossey-Bass.

Oquendo, M. (1996). Psychiatric evaluation and psychotherapy in the patient's second language. *Psychiatric Services, 47*(6), 614–618.

Pastore, D. R., Juszczak, L., Fisher, M. M., & Friedman, S. B. (1998). School based health center utilization: A survey of users and nonusers. *Archives of Pediatric and Adolescent Medicine, 162*(8), 763–767.

Siwicki, B. (1998, April). Telemedicine providers ponder the profitability issue. *Health Data Management,* p. 85.

Smith, H. A., & Allison, R. A. (1998). *Telemental health: Delivering mental health care at a distance* (unpublished). Washington, DC: USDHHS, SAMHSA, CMS.

Stamm, B. H. (1998). Clinical applications of telehealth in mental health care. *Professional Psychology: Research and Practice, 29*(6), 536–543.

Tavener, L., & Zelinger, J. (2000, June). *Medicaid and telemedicine.* Available online: Health Care Financing Administration, Department of Health and Human Services information page, http://www.hcfa.gov/medicaid/telemed.htm

Vazquez-Barquero, J. L., Garcia, J., Simon, J. A., Iglesias, C., Montejo, J., Herran, A., & Dunn, G. (1997). Mental health in primary care: An epidemiological study of morbidity and use of health resources. *British Journal of Psychiatry, 170,* 529–535.

Weist, M. D., Paskewitz, D. A., Warner, B., & Flaherty, L. T. (1996). Treatment outcome of school-based mental health services for urban teenagers. *Community Mental Health Journal, 32*(2), 149–157.

Whitten, P., Zaylor, C., & Kingsley, C. (2000). An analysis of telepsychiatry programs from an organizational perspective. *Cyberpsychology and Behavior, 3*(6), 911.

Zaylor, C. (1999). Clinical outcomes in telepsychiatry. *Journal of Telemedicine and Telecare, 5*(Suppl. 1), S59–60.

Chapter Thirty-One

Using Information to Manage Cultural Change: Establishing the Medical Model for Inpatient Care

Stephen H. Dinwiddie
Nancy Staples
Diana Meyers

Things have their due measure; there are ultimately fixed limits, beyond which, or short of which, something must be wrong.

—Horace

The information revolution is, at the least, well underway, if not effectively over. It is now possible to measure with ease virtually whatever we wish, and to apply highly sophisticated statistical methods to analyze the information gathered. All too often, however, the awesome number-crunching ability now accessible to almost anyone is not matched with comparable critical thinking about what to measure, when to measure it, and to what ends the data should be applied.

This is perhaps most strikingly true at the interface of medicine and administration. The task of medical leadership in such an environment should be to go beyond tweaking and fine-tuning the current structure of the organization without questioning its goals and methods. Senior leaders and managers should anticipate the evolution of the field and position the organization to influence, rather than respond to, change.

We believe that leadership at this level should use quantitative measures to gauge progress toward identified ends, but goals should be informed by values and/ or philosophical position. Quantitative methods may be useful in determining whether a given strategic goal can be reached using a specific methodology, but cannot determine whether the goal is consistent with the organization's mission or with appropriate clinical ends. For that, a different kind of judgment is necessary.

PSYCHIATRISTS AND THE MEDICAL MODEL

In 1996, our hospital, a state public-sector facility located just outside a major metropolitan area, had a total of 590 beds (approximately 290 civil beds and 300 in a forensic program), employed a staff of 1,147 full-time equivalent (FTE) persons, and had an annual budget of about $55 million. The guiding paradigm for treatment was psychosocial rehabilitation, but because of markedly different interpretations of its implications by different units and programs, its unifying role and impact on planning were limited.

Leadership at the individual unit level was vested in the unit director, a mental health professional (typically a psychologist or social worker) who not only assumed administrative responsibilities but also functioned as the "lead clinician," responsible for coordinating treatment team efforts. The treatment team consisted of a psychiatrist, psychologist, nurses, and social work staff (clinical social workers or mental health specialists). Although most staff psychiatrists had formal residency training, state statute at the time allowed credentialing as a psychiatrist as long as the physician had at least 3 years of mental disorder treatment experience, even without any psychiatry residency training. Primary care physicians were assigned to units (typically one per 30 to 40 patients) and were expected to handle all nonpsychiatric medical care. Case coordination was divided relatively equally among psychologists and social workers; programming varied widely by unit. The organizational culture at the unit level was characterized by a generalist approach, led by a mental health professional who had achieved an administrative position by virtue of good performance as a clinician, and who was expected to meld, at the unit level, administrative and clinical leadership.

The culture of the state Office of Mental Health (OMH), responsible for administration of state hospitals and oversight of numerous grant-in-aid agencies, was, at this time, undergoing considerable transformation. The provision of care had been reorganized into geographically organized "networks" consisting of a state-operated hospital providing inpatient care and a number of affiliated agencies charged with delivering outpatient care to the indigent population. The network system was developed, in part, in response to criticisms and challenges during the preceding few years.

The requirement of fairly strict hospital operations guidelines applicable to a variety of facilities led, not surprisingly, to emergence of a reactive and somewhat risk-averse culture that valued the security of following central policies and procedures over innovation. In the latter half of the 1990s, this culture was challenged by new psychiatric leadership within the OMH.

Psychiatrist Recruitment

During 1997, the mix of short- and long-stay patients at our facility, psychiatric staffing (one psychiatrist per 29 beds; Table 31.1) was not strikingly out of line with that in comparable centers (Pelonero, Elliott, Barber, & Best, 1996). Justification for recruiting additional staff purely on the basis of some ideal ratio described in the professional literature is not, by itself, very persuasive. Nor could it plausibly be based on allegations of ineffective or inappropriate treatment, because overall care appeared to be acceptable.

On the other hand, a fairly coherent set of staffing needs and expectations for clinical care could be based on a "medical model" treatment philosophy, which has subsequently developed into a treatment approach at our facility that we called "assertive psychiatric treatment."

It is important to note that the medical model outlined here is not a narrow, pharmacologically based treatment approach, but rather is one derived from Guze's conceptualization, which

> views the illness as the hub of the clinical problem. It is concerned with the individual's past life, special circumstances, personality, etc. primarily as these bear upon the nature and development of the illness. The basic feature of the medical model is concern for the symptoms and signs of illness. . . . The medical model does not require ignoring the patient's psychosocial context. On the contrary, the medical model suggests that the social and psychologic environments of the individual may be very important, but their role in illness cannot be assessed correctly if the medical model is ignored. (Guze, 1978, pp. 295–296)

Guze further emphasized the latter point by noting that

> Good medicine and good psychiatry involve much more than simply prescribing medicine. Any physician or any psychiatrist who believes that such prescribing is all that is required is failing his or her patients. . . . There need be no inherent conflict between biological psychiatry and the practice of psychotherapy. (Guze, 1989, p. 320)

The medical model as outlined here is thus less concerned with any particular school of therapy or theory of disease etiology (except insofar as it provides clues to more effective treatments), but is instead a clinical–administrative approach that emphasizes the medical tradition of the centrality of the physician–patient relationship. It also views diagnosis as central to relieving suffering by optimally matching symptoms with effective remedies. Choice of therapy and prediction of likely response and course of illness are based on diagnosis, and diagnosis is seen as primarily the physician's province.

This orientation has a number of implications. One is that treatment should be, insofar as possible, evidence based, rather than provided primarily because of the practitioner's adherence to a specific school of therapy or theoretical orientation. It may be broadly characterized, therefore, as more "scientific" than "humanistic" in orientation (because it implicitly requires adherence to scientific method as a means by which to judge success of therapy), and is thus compatible with rigorous examination of well-defined clinical outcomes as a measure of success.

One implication of this orientation is that by virtue of training and expertise, overall clinical responsibility and authority should be explicitly vested in the treating psychiatrist, who should be held accountable for effectively carrying out that responsibility. Part of the psychiatrist's role with respect to the treatment team, therefore, is to provide clinical team leadership. That leadership includes soliciting the expertise of team members, synthesizing the contributions of the various profes-

Table 31.1. Inpatient Beds per Psychiatrist

1997	28.6
1998	26.6
1999	25.9
2000	20.1

sionals, and working to assure that the clinical care rendered by all team members is appropriate, coordinated, and effective.

Hospital- and unit-level administration are vital to facilitating the efforts of caregivers, but responsibility for clinical care and (at the hospital level in particular) setting clinical priorities is the province of clinical leadership. In this model, administration ensures that the trains run on time, but clinical leadership sets the direction of clinical travel. Awareness of this distinction prevents role diffusion and promotes individual care decisions that are based on patient need rather than institutional ends.

It should be emphasized that initial adoption of this approach was not based primarily on data. Other, competing, models exist, each with its own advantages or disadvantages. The decision to follow a medical model approach was a values-driven one, the adoption of one specific vision over competing models of how care should be delivered. Although we believe that it is effective on a variety of practical grounds, it is at least as important that, regardless of orientation, *some* coherent, unifying theme or approach be adopted and shared by the organization's leadership.

Over the past 4 years, our medical model philosophy has evolved in a variety of ways. For example, reassessing the psychiatrist's role within the treatment team had implications for staffing. The role is clearly more comprehensive. It involves clinical leadership functions as well as direct care, and thus requires additional skills and a higher psychiatrist-to-patient ratio.

It spurred reevaluation of the primary care physicians' role as well. As in most psychiatric hospitals, when a psychiatrist is the patient's primary physician, primary care roles are consultative (with the attending psychiatrist taking *responsibility* for overall health care but relying on actions and/or recommendations by a primary care doctor). As proportionately more residency-trained psychiatrists were credentialed (Table 31.1), and fewer primary care physicians functioned as psychiatrists, primary care consultation became the norm and primary care physicians took on attending roles only when patients were unstable or particularly medically complex. Patient care thus became generally better integrated and simplified, with fewer doctors writing orders for each patient. Eventually, the facility was able to develop a policy of credentialing only fully trained psychiatrists to provide psychiatric care.

Our reconceptualization of medical roles and models led to a reexamination of (and emphasis on) role definitions among other treatment team members as well. We moved from a largely "generalist" approach to one in which a team member's responsibility for aspects of clinical care is based more heavily on his or her training and expertise.

ASSESSMENT OF STAFF COMPETENCIES

Core Expectations and Monitoring

The reconceptualization of role definitions led to a major initiative within the facility to create definitions of, and assess, staff competencies. During the first phase of the initiative, clinical leadership in psychiatry, primary care, psychology, social work, rehabilitation, and nursing developed lists of "core" expectations in the general areas of assessment, treatment, and aftercare. Next, performance measures for each discipline were established for the purpose of assessing the quality of service provided within each of these general areas, as measured by documentation in the clinical record. Finally (an ongoing strategy), as specific indicators achieve acceptable thresholds of achievement, they are removed from review and replaced by other areas identified as needing examination.

Identification of an expectation may occur via critical case review or sentinel event review (which can highlight significant process variance), or may be specified by clinical leadership as a means of furthering strategic goals (facility-wide or at a lower level). This cycle of assessment is crucial in determining the effect of educational or policy interventions, particularly for case identification via critical case review.

The nature of the data to be collected on staff competencies was initially determined by expert consensus, collected by each discipline, with results reported to clinical leadership. The need for a more organized venue for interpretation of results, selection of new indicators, and explicit consideration of how such indicators fit the hospital's strategic plan led to the creation of a Treatment, Evaluation, and Competency Committee, composed of medical administrators; quality strategy heads from psychology, social work, rehabilitation, and nursing; and representatives from the medical records and information services departments. The committee meets monthly, and disciplines report on their progress (as determined by percentage of charts meeting documentation standards) toward specific performance goals within the general areas of assessment, treatment, and aftercare. Committee findings are then conveyed via discipline heads to the various disciplines and, if necessary, plans of correction are instituted.

Peer Review

The process also led to a reconceptualization of the role of peer review among medical staff. It is now seen as contributing to two distinct but vital systems: assessment of clinical competence related to credentialing, continuing training, and job preparation, and annual performance evaluation in an environment in which physicians are directly employed by the hospital. Peer review is one means of identifying poor performance on the part of a single physician and planning corrective action taken at the individual level if necessary. In addition, by using aggregate peer review data, systemic physician/clinician problems can be identified and procedural corrections instituted and assessed. Information compiled from peer review is based on the informed clinical judgment of the reviewers. It is more likely to be a valid reflection of clinicians' actual performance than relying on rote indicators or simple chart documentation.

Peer review can thus be used in at least three ways for the organization: generic reprivileging review and individual monitoring, aggregate monitoring of the physician/clinician portion of the overall medical care system (using both routine reviews and those triggered by untoward and high-risk events, or strategic needs), and monitoring the effects of clinical policy changes.

At the hospital level, the information derived from peer review is aggregated not by physician but by scores to allow estimation of performance overall in the general areas of assessment, treatment, or aftercare, with the reviewing body able if desired to "drill down" to more specific items to determine if results are satisfactory and in line with the hospital's strategic goals. Similarly, if progress toward resolving a problem identified in a critical case review is desired, information on a specific item (or several items), aggregated across physicians, can be examined.

Finally, discussions among peer reviewers and between reviewers and colleagues (but keeping the strict confidentiality of the peer review system) are important to performance improvement. Because choice of items to review is influenced by clinicians' input, the results are given credence and legitimacy. Substantial (and sustained) improvement can often be seen with no intervention other than the knowledge that a topic is being reviewed (Patel, Black, Thompson, Giffort, & O'Brien, 2000), a kind of "halo" effect.

These aspects are summarized in Fig. 31.1.

REDUCING RISKS OF CARE AND TREATMENT

One of the difficulties in designing hospital-based risk reduction strategies lies in the fact that, although psychiatric inpatients are at elevated risk for adverse outcomes such as suicide attempts, assault, and so on, relative to most (but not all) less disordered populations who are not hospitalized, the base rate of such events in the hospital is still quite low. As the transition to more systematic use of data was occurring, analysis of performance improvement projects, review of relevant clinical literature, and sentinel event data indicated that this low base rate, combined with the nonspecificity of clinical risk indicators, would cause traditional monitors to miss many patients and staff who are at risk for clinical problems or care-related injury (e.g., suicide, injury during restraint or seclusion, harm from other patients, staff injury), while at the same time misidentifying as being at elevated risk many others who were in fact not. That is, a strategy that relies primarily on identifying high-risk patients for special observation or high-intensity intervention would both miss important needs and create many "false-positives" (Fawcett, Clark, & Busch, 1993; Goldstein, Black, Nasrallah, & Winokur, 1991; Mossman, 2000; Rice & Harris, 1995; Silberberg, Shanoff, Brakel, & Yee, 1999). To make matters more difficult, such risk is not stable, but varies with symptom level.

In order to achieve meaningful risk reduction in a population whose average risk is relatively high, but in which many individuals cannot be classified with sufficient accuracy, we concluded that risk reduction would be best achieved by minimizing the time during which patients remain at elevated risk, largely by treating *all*

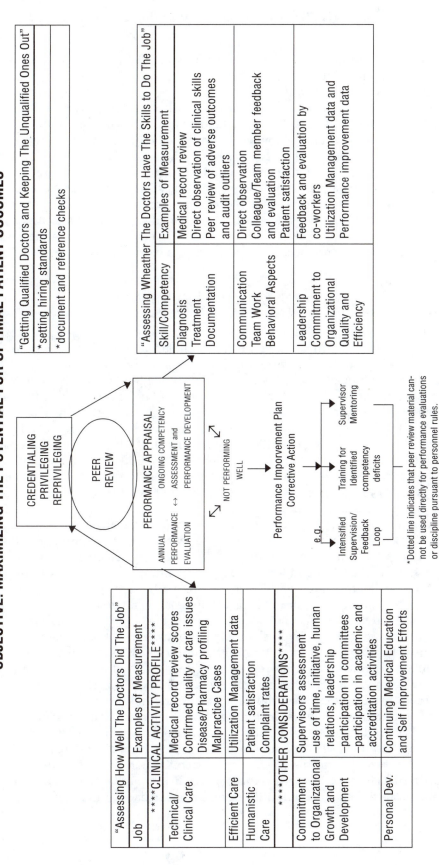

FIGURE 31.1. Proposed model: physician performance assessment and management.

patients as quickly and effectively as feasible, rather than by relying solely on identifying specific individuals upon whom to concentrate resources. The focus of care was "decentered" from identified high-risk *patients* to putting systems into place to monitor and deal with patients' *problems* as rapidly and effectively as we could. This approach has the added advantage of vigorously treating those whose suffering is significant but not posing an imminent risk, while reducing risk for those who need it.

As the system benchmarking process got underway during the mid-1990s, we soon moved from internal data and limited focus (e.g., on restraint use) to broader data sets and comparators. Statewide information sharing made it possible to relate our performance to other hospitals, and eventually compare our findings and progress to similar facilities nationwide. We have extended our benchmarking to include other risk-management-related data sets. Such expansion of information resources should help identify variances not readily visible in our single clinical setting.

UTILIZATION REVIEW

Many of the changes just described in philosophy and activity suggested a reconsideration of the role of utilization review (UR). In our facility, UR has became a clinically oriented tool rather than primarily an economically oriented function. UR staff are trained by clinicians to review charts for documentation of treatment efforts and response, thus monitoring both clinical practice and documentation as tools for improvement. We chose 14 days after admission as a fairly arbitrary, but clinically generous, threshold by which time most patients should have symptomatically improved enough to allow safe discharge (i.e., their risk of adverse clinical outcomes— discussed earlier—should have been reduced to baseline level). It should be noted that the actual decision to discharge is not made at this point of "clinical stabilization," because appropriate arrangements for housing, aftercare, and so forth may not be in place. The determination is, rather, whether or not further hospitalization as based on psychiatric symptoms, as contrasted with other needs, is justified. If the point of "clinical stabilization" has not been reached by the beginning of the third week of hospitalization, the attending psychiatrist must document the patient's current status, plan of treatment (including consideration of clinically appropriate alternative treatments, such as electroconvulsive therapy [ECT] or nonstandard medications), and whether or not consultation has been requested.

This process serves as a mechanism to encourage timely, comprehensive clinical review without overriding the clinician's control of treatment. Patients who are still unstable after 4 weeks are identified and their care is reviewed by a medical (physician) administrator. That review is couched as a clinical consultation by a senior colleague, but also allows some assessment of clinician competence, citing and promptly addressing potential deficiencies or other problems.

Instituting these changes, including emphasizing clinically driven utilization review, has produced several results. The average daily census on the civil side of the hospital declined substantially (from 245 in 1997 to 149 in 2000). In addition, by monitoring discrepancies between clinical stabilization and actual discharge, and collecting data on specific barriers to discharge in our public-sector setting, it is now possible to feed data on community resource needs back to the mental health and social services network and, ultimately, to shift resources within the network to address them.

At present, UR data, aggregated by unit and program, are regularly reported to the medical executive staff and to the hospital's executive committee, so that both medical and administrative leaders can review trends in things like overall bed utilization, unit-specific performance, discrepancies between length of stay and clinical stability, barriers to discharge, and community care. We are also beginning to use these data to compare performance between similar units and between psychiatrists with similar patients and workloads, as a way of assessing staffing needs at the unit level.

INFORMATION GATHERING AFFECTING TREATMENT CHOICE

Systematically gathering information on patient improvement and stabilization soon showed that some patients received aggressive pharmacotherapy without sufficient response, but also without a change in the therapy. A patient with schizophrenia, for example, might not be offered an atypical antispychotic medication (even though our rate of using atypical antipsychotics is comparable to national figures), or electroconvulsive therapy (ECT) might not be considered for a patient with a severe and refractory mood disorder. Further chart review indicated that clozapine or a similar medication was indeed considered for most refractory schizophrenic patients, but that ECT was rarely used.

An effort to revise the policies guiding provision of ECT and educate clinicians on this treatment was made, with rapid results. Before 1996, our hospital, like others in our state system, provided ECT to about two patients per year (C. Fitchtner, personal communication, 2000). With staff education through grand rounds and clinical consultations, and after revision of policies and procedures allowed greater patient access to this therapy, ECT use grew to between 30 and 40 patients per year as of late 2000. The change has proved quite successful, with preliminary review of 80 patients who received ECT between 1996 and 2000 indicating good clinical response in 86%, often allowing discharge of patients who had been continuously hospitalized for lengthy periods before receiving ECT.

Refusing Treatment; Court-Ordered Treatment

Another result of focusing on the risks of patients' remaining clinically unstable was reassessment of court-ordered treatment (Patel & Hardy, 2001). Initially, monthly feedback to the treating psychiatrists simply gave the number of patients on each unit who had been refusing medication for a week or more. We provided additional education for psychiatrists, including a workshop on courtroom testimony skills, and encouraged them to identify patients who were refusing treatment early in their hospital stays and to petition the court for involuntary admission and/or treatment when clinically indicated. The message was strong that although going to court is unpleasant, it is the patient who suffers most.

Individual psychiatrist performance is assessed by a forensic psychiatrist who

TABLE 31.2. Petitions Filed for Court-Ordered
Treatment (per 12 Months, July–June)

1996–1997	97
1997–1998	133
1998–1999	153
1999–2000	192

observes the courtroom testimony and "coaches" the testifying psychiatrists periodically. The assessment is not based on success or failure of the petition, but simply on the psychiatrist's willingness to file a petition when clinically appropriate. This approach has led to a significant increase in number of petitions filed and, presumably, better patient care (see Table 31.2.)

MULTIDISCIPLINARY SAFETY REVIEW

We believe the interventions described have contributed to a dramatic decrease in average daily inpatient census, despite an increase in admissions of about 100 patients per year (from 988 in FY 1997 to 1,092 in FY 2000). However, some patients remained unstable despite vigorous treatment. This led to creation of a multidisciplinary "clinical safety committee" composed of medical and nursing administrators, program managers, UR staff, and senior psychologists. Their responsibility is to review cases that trip specific clinical triggers, such as a suicide attempt or orders for one-to-one observation.

During these reviews, the emphasis remains on determining which symptoms remain unimproved despite vigorous treatment (not specifically on identification of higher vs. lower risk patients, because those remaining clinically unstable are at elevated risk), and on examining clinical options to address those symptoms so that the risk they convey to the patient can be mitigated. Including senior clinicians from a variety of disciplines ensures a multidisciplinary conceptualization, whereas blending administrative staff with clinicians ensures that both groups are "on the same page" and that programmatic implications can be identified and promptly addressed when necessary. The number and duration of special precautions orders (e.g., one-to-one observation) has decreased substantially with this higher level of scrutiny (apparently as a result of it), with a roughly 50% decrease in nursing overtime costs related to special observations noted in FY 2000 compared to the prior 2 years.

ASSAULTS BY PATIENTS

Another "second-generation" outcome was development of a protocol by which selected patients might be prosecuted for alleged criminal acts (typically assault) committed in the hospital. We realized that violence, although not predictable overall, was not random. Reviews indicated that while some violent behavior was a symptom of psychiatric illness, in many situations it appeared clearly purposeful and "instrumental." In those cases, somatic and psychosocial treatments tended not to affect the patient's behavior very much, but were still employed, often to the exclusion of other potentially effective interventions.

Before 1996, unit staff viewed the option of pressing charges as countertherapeutic and, perhaps more limiting, impractical. Prosecutors were not eager to bring charges against someone who, from their viewpoint, was not a threat to the community and had a presumptive insanity defense, both simply by virtue of being a psychiatric inpatient.

Much of the success of our new policy of legal intervention of this sort is related to recognizing "spikes" in unit utilization of violent behavior indicators (such as use of PRN medications, number of restraint/seclusion episodes, or hours of restraint/ seclusion) that upon investigation are traced to specific individuals. Success of the intervention itself can be measured through data trends on indicators of continuing violent behavior in either the individual or the unit as a whole, because experience suggests that employing legal intervention may have a deterrent effect on others.

SUMMARY

We demonstrated that significant change can occur in an institutional culture—change that fosters more efficient and effective patient care—through examining data on clinical indicators and feeding information back to the treatment team. Between FY 1996 and 2000, at our hospital, budgeted beds decreased from 590 to 500, average daily census shrank by nearly 100 patients, and staffing was increased from 1,147 to 1,237 full-time equivalents, with approximately a 25% increase in number of psychiatrists and a corresponding decrease in nonpsychiatrically trained physicians on staff. We believe that using information to lead cultural change contributed substantially to positive alterations in the way our facility treats patients and pursues the "business" of public-sector mental health care.

Our approach was based on a specific philosophy of treatment, a specially defined "medical model" (described earlier) that has clear implications for staffing, programs, and a number of institutional processes. It is important to keep in mind that although this philosophy guided our information priorities, the initial choice was driven by organization values. It informed policy (by clarifying staffing needs, for example) and was dependent in its implementation on tracking of a variety of indicators (such as staffing levels and staff competencies). Needs identified by these exercises, in turn, led to significant conceptual changes (e.g., in the roles of peer review and utilization review processes).

Feeding back information derived from these processes to clinical personnel helped to establish the legitimacy of the model among staff, and also allowed staff to act on the information in a way that enhanced patient care (either directly or indirectly [e.g., by identification of unstable patients and emphasizing areas of relative weakness, respectively]). Feedback to administration, conversely, allowed for systematic evaluation of the needs and progress of the institution, which could be used to modify training processes and gauge progress toward reaching strategic goals.

The intertwined support of the Quality Strategies Department, the Information Systems Department, and the facility medical leadership were fundamental to this approach. Each of the three groups must, of necessity, understand the others' languages. Medical leadership must explain goals in a way that can be meaningfully measured. Quality Strategies must identify relevant indicators that will yield useful information when analyzed, and Information Systems must design ways of collecting, managing, and disseminating the information needed.

Each of the three has an impact on the others' processes. Clinical activities such as peer review and utilization review, for example, have become key tools for measuring progress toward strategic goals. Conversely, the hospital's strategic plan drives such processes as recruitment and training, based in part on clinically derived information.

We believe that to successfully change the culture of a health care organization, one must first identify and champion a specific philosophy of treatment, and both clinical and administrative leadership must share a commitment to that vision. Collaboration must occur at all levels to work out the implications of the model for care delivery, and for the administrative processes supporting care delivery. Finally, information derived from those processes must be shared in a useful way with both clinicians (who will value information which improves treatment) and administrators (who will value aggregate information on important processes), keeping in mind the needs of both groups. Our experience suggests that substantial change can occur relatively rapidly when these elements are present.

REFERENCES

Fawcett, J., Clark, D. C., & Busch, K. A. (1993). Assessing and treating the patient at risk for suicide. *Psychiatric Annals, 23*(5), 244–254.

Goldstein, R. B., Black, D. W., Nasrallah, A., & Winokur, G. (1991). The prediction of suicide. Sensitivity, specificity, and predictive value of a multivariate model applied to suicide among 1906 patients with affective disorders. *Archives of General Psychiatry, 48*(5), 418–422.

Guze, S. B. (1978). Nature of psychiatric illness: Why psychiatry is a branch of medicine. *Comprehensive Psychiatry, 29*(4), 295–307.

Guze, S. B. (1989). Biological psychiatry: Is there any other kind? *Psychological Medicine, 19,* 315–323.

Mossman, D. (2000). Assessing the risk of violence: Are "accurate" predictions useful? *Journal of the American Academy of Psychiatry and the Law, 28*(3), 272–281.

Patel, M., Black, C., Thompson, R., Giffort, D., & O'Brien, T. (2000). *Report of the Physician Performance Workgroup.* Unpublished document commissioned by the Clinical Services Division, Illinois Department of Human Services, Chicago.

Patel, M., & Hardy, D. (2001). Encouraging pursuit of court-ordered treatment in a state hospital. *Psychiatric Services, 52*(12), 1656–1657.

Pelonero, A. L., Elliott, R. L., Barber, J. W., & Best, A. (1996). Physician caseloads at public mental hospitals. *American Journal of Psychiatry, 133*(3), 429–431.

Rice, M. E., & Harris, G. T. (1995). Violent recidivism: Assessing predictive validity. *Journal of Consulting and Clinical Psychology, 63*(5), 737–748.

Silberberg, J., Shanoff, K. M., Brakel, S. J., & Yee, E. G. (1999, October). *Prediction of violence in a public-sector hospital.* Poster session, American Academy of Psychiatry and the Law Annual Meeting, Baltimore, MD.

Chapter Thirty-Two

Technology, Practice, and Ethics

Peter W. Demuth

How do administrators and leaders in mental health management make their decisions? Intuition? Experience? Or do skilled leaders carefully collect information, weigh its veracity and relevance, and then exercise their best judgment in tandem with intuition and experience? In this era of increasing technology and fast-paced competition, those in decision-making positions face a plethora of ethical challenges. These challenges make it incumbent on leaders to use as many guiding resources and principles as possible. To paraphrase Henry Ford, it may not be important to know everything, but it is important to know where to get the correct information when you need it. Ethics is an important consideration in decision making, particularly in today's environment of technology and information.

Ethics has been defined as "the body of moral principles or values held by or governing a culture, a group, or an individual" (*Webster's*, 1998). *Values* can be defined as the shared and agreed-to standards on which an individual and/or group base their decisions and actions. In any activity, there is a need to define the "rules of engagement."

In the workplace, there are hiring rules, firing rules, and rules that address professional issues. Structured systems provide guidelines on which the participants in a given situation can base their behavior and decisions. The structure, which can be either formal or informal, written or unwritten, serves as the foundation for the organization's culture.

The rules can be further divided into formal laws and formal ethics. Laws apply to all members of society and have the weight of governmental authority behind them. Ethical principles generally apply to individuals who choose to belong to a particular group, such as a professional association, that promulgates them. In some cases, administrative rules or regulations, such as licensure rules, adopt part or all of a professional organization's ethical guidelines. Then the "ethics" (now a matter of law) apply not just to members of the professional group, but to anyone whose practice is governed by the regulations.

THE IMPORTANCE OF ETHICS IN AN ERA OF INCREASING TECHNOLOGY

In this age of increasing technology, new ideas and techniques create ethical considerations—and not a few dilemmas—not contemplated just a few years ago. Conventional ethics are still with us, and deserve a place in clinical and organizational decision making, but modern management opportunities and environments, and the breadth and speed of their influence, have brought both quantitative and qualitative changes. Should an expensive but highly effective treatment be made available to anyone in a system if it cannot be provided to everyone? Should individual privacy be curtailed in favor of efficiency or economic needs? Should standards of care be reduced to meet the demands of for-profit managed care organizations or limited public-sector resources?

Perhaps most important, will such decisions be based on a lack of facts, ignorance, impulsiveness, political sway, public opinion, unpreparedness, or bias? Or will they be derived instead from some set of guiding principles? The latter principles can attenuate some of the inherent pressures and anxieties that leaders feel when making the decisions just described. One such pressure occurs when a problem has two or more "right" answers. Ethical codes may not supply a simple answer, but they can provide a structure through which administrators and clinicians can build a consensus on how to deal with complex and difficult situations.

Seglin (2000, p. 9) said that managers must be able to understand the context in which they operate and to make decisions fully informed, with a clear sense of right and wrong, if they are to weigh difficult choices and stay honed for competition. He suggested that in order to make good business judgments, the decision maker should consider three spheres: people, money, and the common good. When all three are considered, decisions are more likely to be balanced and fair, and to include all relevant aspects of the situation. As pressures mount and situations become more complicated, such a structure minimizes shortsighted and self-serving choices, and tends to orchestrate sound conclusions.

ETHICAL CONSIDERATIONS IN LEADING OTHERS

Evans (2000) examined leadership issues in an ethical context, as a process in which one may follow policies, procedures, and rules without examining one's ideologies. On the other hand, one may create meaning without being locked into rigid ideologies, by engaging in both collaboration and debate, and by resolving differences without necessarily establishing one as true and the other as false. The latter method requires give and take by participants, and suggests that leaders encourage an atmosphere of "win–win" (Fisher & Ury, 1991) whenever feasible. Such a concept allows participants to feel their views are not only heard, but also incorporated into the final plan when appropriate. When all is said and done, some of the best decisions lead to all parties feeling they have shared in a successful undertaking. There are often losers, of course, but the negotiations inherent in leadership need not leave them embarrassed or bereft.

TECHNOLOGY: COST REDUCTION
AND IMPROVING PATIENT CARE

Technology often reduces cost. Cost reduction, however, doesn't always benefit individual patients or their families. Leaders and administrators have a responsibility to understand the potential impact of their cost-reduction efforts, and to make judicious decisions.

Wendel (2000) addressed the issue of medication errors and presented a strong case for how storing medical records on the Internet can help to reduce errors and increase the effectiveness of decision making. For example, when a physician enters a medication order into an electronic medical record, the computer program can identify possible drug interactions and allergy sensitivity for that patient. In a study by Bates et al. (1998), medication errors were reduced 55% when such a system was in place. However, the issue of how to protect the confidentiality of the patient's record seems of paramount importance when such technology is employed.

CONCLUSION

Mental health leaders and managers face many decisions that involve technology and its potential impact on the patients and others who trust them. If clinical leaders simply want a rule to follow, an objective ethical position will serve them nicely. It is straightforward and unambiguous. It is also dogmatic and not open to argument or critical debate. It can be implemented without much judgment or thought.

If, however, leaders and senior managers want the option of exercising real judgment, applying a fixed rule, even an ethical one, often will not suffice. Instead, all the facts of a situation must be considered dispassionately and without bias, and there has to be a desire to make decisions that benefit the group and not simply the individual. Such decisions can be based on a predetermined but flexible heuristic ethical structure, provided clinical leaders have both the ability to think critically and the desire to act collectively.

REFERENCES

Bates, D. W., Leape, L. L., Cullen, D. J., Laird, N., Petersen, L. A., Teich, J. M., Burdick, E., Hickey, M., Kleefield, S., Shea, B., Vander Vliet, M., & Seger, D. L. (1998). Effects of computerized physician order entry and a team intervention on prevention of serious medication errors. *Journal of the American Medical Association, 280*(15), 1311–1316.

Evans, M. (2000). The significance of ethical sophistication. *Journal of Psychosocial Nursing, 38*(4), 11.

Fisher, R., & Ury, W. (1991). *Getting to yes.* New York: Penguin Books.

Seglin, J. L. (2000). *The good, the bad and your business: Choosing right when ethical dilemmas pull you apart.* New York: John Wiley & Sons.

Webster's American college dictionary. (1998). New York: Random House.

Wendel, S. (2000, February). Medical errors. *Healthcare Informatics Online.* www.healthcare-informatics.com

BIBLIOGRAPHY

Internet Websites

American Psychological Association (www.apa.org)
Georgetown Journal of Legal Ethics (www.law.georgetown.edu/journals/ethics)
Health Internet Ethics (www.hiethics.com)
Institute for Jewish Medical Ethics (www.ijme.org)
Medscape (www.medscape.com/home/cmecenter/cmecenter.html)
National Center for Ethics, Veterans Health Administration (www.va.gov/vhaethics/spotlight.cfm)
The Ethics Center–Links (www.taknosys.com/ethics/links.htm)
WebMD (www.WebMD.com)

Books

Beauchamp, T. L., & Childress, J. F. (1994). *Principles of biomedical ethics* (5th ed.). New York: Oxford University Press.
Bersoff, D. N. (1999). *Ethical conflicts in psychology* (2nd ed.). Washington, DC: American Psychological Association Press.
Lowman, R. L. (1998). *The ethical practice of psychology organizations.* Washington, DC: American Psychological Association Press.
McMinn, M. R. (1998). *Technology in practice.* In M. Herson, A. S. Bellack (Series Eds.), & A. N. Wiens (Vol. Ed.), *Comprehensive clinical psychology* (Vol. 2): Professional issues (pp. 363–375). Oxford: Elsevier Sciences.
Small, R. F., & Barnhill, L. R. (1998). *Practicing in the new mental health marketplace: Ethical, legal, and moral issues.* Washington, DC: American Psychological Association Press.
Werhane, P., & Freeman, E. (1998). *Blackwell encyclopedic dictionary of business ethics.* New York: Blackwell.

Part Five

HUMAN RESOURCES

INTRODUCTION

William H. Reid

T he people who work in and for a health care organization are the heart of almost everything it does. They are its most important asset, the source of its mission, and, not surprisingly, its most expensive resource. Every aspect of successful management and leadership depends on, and is often defined by, excellence in locating, hiring, motivating, guiding, retaining, and satisfying the organization's employees and contracting staff.

It is not enough to do all these things for only half the staff, or even three-quarters of the workforce. Human resources skills are aimed toward serving the organization by filling every position with the right person, meeting the individual and group needs of many different kinds of people, and being certain that the organization adheres to a morass of employment laws, regulations, and policies that must be followed in order to act fairly and remain in business.

This short section focuses first, in the chapter by Ted W. Hirsch and William H. Reid, on a comprehensive set of human resources functions and issues that must be managed in both small and large health care organizations: recruiting, hiring, compensation, motivation, performance evaluation, discipline, reductions in force, diversity, legal issues, harassment, employee relations, training and education, policies and procedures, and several special topics. Then Richard C. W. Hall and Ryan C. W. Hall discuss a particularly important kind of recruiting, that of physicians.

Chapter Thirty-Three

Principles of Human Resource Management

Ted W. Hirsch
William H. Reid

Human resources represent the largest single operating expense in any mental health care organization, largely because of salary and benefit costs. Human resource management has undergone dynamic transition over the past decade or so, due largely to great changes in the health care environment, increased competition for funding and resources, shortages of qualified employees, and increasingly complex employment laws. The role of human resource management in the organization has expanded dramatically.

Executives, owners, and other organization leadership must understand human resource functions and their role in the facility's mission and day-to-day operations. In turn, human resource professionals and their departments must understand the broad objectives and challenges of the organization as they assume greater and more varied responsibilities within it.

If the last 5 to 10 years are representative of what the future holds, human resource professionals face continued change in all areas of the helping professions. "Traditional" freestanding psychiatric hospitals are very rare. Managed care and other pressures, some good and some unfortunate, have caused facilities that offered typical adult and adolescent inpatient psychiatric services and short-term chemical dependency stabilization to evolve, create new product lines, and change some management strategies in order to survive. Acute treatment units are often closed in favor of residential programs, offender treatment units, partial hospitalization, and other programs in order to meet both community and financial demands. Mental health care "business" is done differently today, and the organization's management and staff must meet those new challenges.

Human resource departments and leaders must be integrated with the entire organizational process in order to motivate facility employees to accept change and achieve organizational objectives. Human resource professionals must work at all levels on both tangible elements (such as staffing) and, particularly, less tangible ones (e.g., communication, negotiation, contracting, and organizational value sharing). Information technology management must be developed, and delivery processes reengineered, to cope with change (Carignani, 2000).

This chapter addresses such issues and challenges of the human resource function as: '

- Recruiting, interviewing, and selecting employees.
- Hiring.
- Compensation (including benefits and benefit plans).
- Motivation and rewards.
- Performance evaluation and productivity.
- Employee discipline, and termination.
- Reductions in force (RIFs).
- Workforce diversity.
- Employee-related legal issues.
- Sexual and other harassment.
- Employee relations.
- Orientation, training, and in-service education.
- Policies and procedures.
- Special workforce issues.

RECRUITING, INTERVIEWING, AND SELECTING EMPLOYEES

The human resource division must plan effectively *before* implementing recruitment activities. Detailed job descriptions must be developed for every position in the organization, each based on the criteria required to perform the job. When a position becomes available and recruitment is anticipated, a human resources representative should meet with management to determine whether or not the job description is up to date and lists all job criteria. A work-site analysis should be prepared which reviews the working environment, coworkers, and other characteristics of the position.[1] The process may be routine or complex, depending on the level and position being filled, but the principles are similar for all.

The human resource division should be responsible for all recruitment activities, including advertising and other means of collecting job applicants for review by the person or group that makes the hiring decision. Records should be kept of all advertising, placement, and other recruitment activities, including all responses to the effort. All applications and resumés should be kept according to federal and organization record-keeping requirements, even those for unsuccessful applicants.

It is a good policy to have the human resource division carry out an early review of the applications to determine whether or not they meet the requirements of the job description, then perform initial screening interviews on behalf of management. This preliminary interviewing process should include a structured, fairly standardized question technique that follows the requirements of the job and complies strictly with relevant employment law (see following discussion and the section on mental health law elsewhere in this text).

---

1. Note that such if such reviews and work-site analyses are done and updated periodically for commonly filled positions, they need not be repeated for each new vacancy.

The preemployment screening procedure includes any tests that are necessary to assess the applicant's competence or other specific job qualifications. Preemployment testing has advantages and disadvantages, and should be limited to subjects which are clearly relevant to the position. Personality inventories may be acceptable in that light, as are more specifically task-oriented tests such as those for typing, computer literacy, and other job-related skills.

It is important to gain authorization from the applicant to gather job-relevant information about him or her. Information and references may be required from previous employers, personal contacts, and other sources (such as licensing or law enforcement agencies). Although many previous employers will have a policy of releasing only employment confirmation (dates of employment and perhaps salary), it is very important to ask about the employee's previous work performance and behavior. Some positions require special background checks, such as verification of licensure, criminal background checks, or malpractice insurance coverage.

Failure to carry out a diligent background and reference check may result in danger to patients and liability for the organization. There have been lawsuits in which an employee whom the organization should have known had serious problems harmed patients or staff. Sometimes following up a simple reference check would have been sufficient. Although there is no guarantee that a previous employer, for example, will reveal all the information requested, a documented effort can go a long way toward providing evidence of due diligence in hiring.

Once the prescreening process is completed, a list of qualified candidates should be reviewed with the hiring manager and interviews scheduled with (at least) the person who supervises the position. Human resources staff should monitor the review and hiring process carried out by organization managers and supervisors. Many are not experienced in such things as interview techniques, selection principles, and (especially) the legal requirements that must be followed when interviewing and choosing new employees. This can be ameliorated by meeting with the supervisor beforehand to discuss the process, by sitting in on the process itself, by providing written guidelines for the hiring person, and/or by offering in-house training sessions in recruitment, interviewing, and selection procedures.

HIRING

Once the best candidate has been found, the offer of employment is made by whomever the organization chooses. Many organizations delegate this responsibility (for all except the highest positions) to the human resources department, in part to assure consistency, compliance with federal and state laws, and compliance with internal policy and procedures (e.g., those related to compensation).

An offer of employment may be contingent on satisfactory completion of some parts of the review process (such as return of satisfactory references). Employment per se does not necessarily imply that the new employee will begin all duties until the requirements for those duties have been met (e.g., reference checks, orientation, required training, and skills testing).

Once an individual is employed, it is important for human resources to coordinate an organizational orientation program that includes introduction to the organization's mission, vision, and philosophy, along with specific requirements for the position. Please see the separate section on "Employee Orientation, Inservice Education, Training, and Development."

COMPENSATION (INCLUDING BENEFITS AND BENEFIT PLANS)

Compensation

Compensation is the basic motivation for employees (although not the only one, and sometimes not the most important one). Employee motivation through compensation and benefits systems implies that there will be a positive impact on recruitment, retention, and promotion of individuals in the organization through those systems. They should be viewed as a quid pro quo, an exchange of one thing (satisfactory work) for another (salary and benefits), each of which is expected for the other. Sometimes one speaks of a "compensation package" as including things like bonuses; however, the bonuses are actually opportunities for additional reward (not usually an entitlement) based on special effort, achievement, or organization success (see the "Motivation and Rewards" section, below).

Compensation systems should be established in such a way that individuals are attracted to come to work at the organization in exchange for what is considered to be a fair and competitive wage within the marketplace. The wage and salary program should provide opportunities for increases based on time, position, and job performance. Wage scales should be established for each position which allow for upward mobility over time. The organization should establish a compensation policy and procedures that include a statement of the organization's intent to pay employees fairly and equitably based on the skills and experience they bring to employment, job performance, job conditions, and the prevailing rate for similar work in the employment marketplace.

Each position within the organization should have an established pay range with an entry point, midpoint, and top. These ranges may be established using competitive salary survey information (easily available for most mental health fields). Employees who work inconvenient or unusual shifts (e.g., nurses and aides on evening or night shifts; weekend coverage) may be provided an incentive increase, often called a "shift differential."

The pay scale and compensation system should meet federal and state guidelines (and must meet relevant laws), such as those requiring equal pay for equal work. Organizations wishing to remain competitive in the job market should consult both local and national wage scales information and regularly update their wage and benefit practices.

Employee Benefits

Compensation packages routinely include some level of benefits to which employees are entitled. The benefit plan(s) are largely developed by the human resources division, which (with appropriate review and approval) chooses insurance carriers and creates opportunities for other benefits in recognition of the employee's relationship with the organization.

The benefits that organizations provide vary significantly, sometimes by employer choice and sometimes by state or federal regulation. Very small organizations may opt for few benefits (which may, however, put them at a recruiting and retention disadvantage), but those they provide are governed by strict regulations about consistency, protection, and contribution. Larger organizations may have little choice in the categories of benefits they must make available (e.g., health care premiums, other insurance, retirement plans), but considerable latitude in the specific programs they choose to make available. Private employers have a bit more flexibility than those in the public sector, and those private employers that are privately held generally have more options than those that are publicly held.

In mental health organizations, the benefit package is typically a significant portion of the employee's total compensation and thus a significant part of the organization's budget. Some organizations choose to provide these benefits almost exclusively in cash, giving the employee the ability to purchase things like insurance for him- or herself and downplaying benefits paid directly by the company to a third party. Employees often view cash as of higher value than employer- sponsored medical and dental programs or retirement contributions. More commonly, especially in larger or public-sector organizations, the employer (through the human resources division) chooses third-party vendors[2] and offers their products (insurance, mutual funds, etc.) to its employees.

Employee perception of company-provided benefits is a major issue. Employees should be provided with a detailed list of benefit options as well as the dollar amount that the company contributes to each item. They may also be told that certain benefits can best be obtained through the organization's group purchase plan (if there is one), and that individuals cannot purchase them for the same price (or perhaps not get them at all) without being part of the organization.

Cafeteria Plans.   Many companies provide employees with considerable opportunity for personal choice through a flexible or "cafeteria-style" benefit program. In cafeteria programs, each employee chooses from an approved list an individual benefit package to suit his or her individual and family needs. The organization provides a certain cash contribution to each employee and allows him or her to allocate the employer's contribution among the various available benefit options as he sees fit. In such programs, the human resources division should periodically review each employee's choices and the available health, dental, optical, pharmaceutical, and other benefits in order to help the employee receive the most benefit for his or her choice, and to ensure that the organization is buying the most cost-effective plan.

Employee Assistance Programs (EAPs).   Many mental health organization employees are clinical professionals themselves, yet it is important to keep in mind that they need personal support at times. EAPs provide independent, confidential assessment and support services on a range of personal matters, including mental health, financial, and family issues. EAPs typically provide assessment, short-term intervention, and referral; however, some offer comprehensive services that may be of-

---

2. A few very large employers create internal health care pools (becoming "self-insured") instead of contracting with insurance companies or brokers. A very few also provide the health care itself (e.g., large health care organizations, large government organizations).

fered both on and off the work site. All maintain considerable confidentiality and distance between the (EAP) client and organization management; communication with an employee's supervisor or more senior management may be negotiated (e.g., to recommend workplace changes or in matters of potential danger to others). A few EAPs are operated by (usually large) employers themselves.

MOTIVATION AND REWARDS

The subject of motivation at work has received considerable attention in management organizational research, as well as from concerned leadership in mental health facilities and organizations. It can be one of the more challenging areas of human resource management, because what may be considered highly satisfying by one employee may not be as motivating for another. For a more complete discussion of theories and research related to employee reward (such as Mazlow's "hierarchy of needs"), please see the chapters in the "Mental Health Management Principles" section of this book.

Rewards and similar motivation methods are different from salary and benefit compensation in that they are generally extra items to which the employee is not routinely entitled and that he or she receives in return for doing something special (i.e., beyond basic expectations). The "something special" may be as simple as staying on the job for several years or not using sick leave, or it may be related to an unusual effort or achievement, but it is not (or should not be) based on merely adequate meeting of job requirements. Sometimes motivational items are given before additional work is done, in order to increase productivity. More often, there is some promise of reward (or the potential for reward), with the actual item (e.g., a bonus) given after the special effort.

Large organizations should have a consistent, centrally moderated reward system that allows similar opportunities for every employee. Individual managers may be allowed some latitude in recognizing hard work and excellence, but overall fairness to employees suggests that substantial reward processes be reviewed by the human resources division and often the management team.

Tangible Rewards

Tangible rewards are generally something of immediate value, such as money, stock (or stock options), leisure travel, tickets to an event, or "perks" such as a company car or expense account. They are usually one-time, temporary items which are noticeable and motivating but (a) do not obligate the organization in the future and (b) do not allow the employee to rest on his or her laurels for very long. Remember that the reward is almost always for past performance. One hopes that future behavior will be positively affected (as should the behavior of other employees), but future reward depends on future performance.

Raises and promotions might be considered part of compensation, especially if they are related solely to time with the company or an external factor such as increases in cost of living. Those that come with achievement, however, and are not given to all employees of similar rank, are rewards. Raises and promotions are a complex form of reward, quite different from one-time bonuses or gifts. They are permanent "bonuses," permanent increases in the organization budget, and set a new "floor" for the employee's compensation and performance. They also represent some loss of opportunity for future reward, because most positions have a salary limit. Use them judiciously.

Intangible, Nonfinancial Motivation

There are a great many ways to reward employees without spending very much money. As a corollary, many employees (especially professionals and mid- to upper-level managers) seek and respond better to some nontangible rewards.

The most obvious is praise, and the most effective praise, in general, is that which is genuine and unexpected in both schedule and amount.[3] Management style is related to the employee's perception of praise. Positive comments from a stoic or taciturn boss may be keenly appreciated, whereas the same words from someone who says "good job" every day, to everyone, are not very valuable to most employees.

Other forms of recognition, often available at the supervisor level, include being singled out as an example to others (e.g., as the section's "resident expert," teacher for new employees, or employee of the month), being recommended for broader reward (such as a promotion or organization-wide employee of the month), and being supported in some personal or career effort (such as forwarding an employee's suggestion to a higher level).

"Line" supervisors (i.e., those supervising lower-level employees such as direct-care workers) and "middle managers" may not have the authority to reward employees with things like an office (or a larger one, with a window), but they can support the employee's efforts to get them (e.g., through supportive memos, addenda to performance evaluations, and opportunities to serve on committees or otherwise expand their visibility in the organization). Support for training or educational opportunities (e.g., with time and sometimes tuition costs) is an excellent motivator for many, often leading to a more loyal and productive employee. The organization's overall policy regarding such programs is a human resources matter, but the procedures can often allow approval (for small amounts of time, if not money) at the individual supervisor level. Examples range from a few hours for a job-related workshop, to continuing professional education courses, to full-time college classes.

Privacy and independence in performing work assignments are valued commodities in many organizations, especially with the current trend toward open offices and inexpensive cubicles. Walls that actually go to the ceiling and a door that can be closed help many employees and managers to do their best. Some others, however, prefer the interaction of an open-desk arrangement. Some "modern" organization cultures may mitigate against walls and doors, but the pendulum is swinging back a little.

Titles make great rewards for some employees. Being "Director of Recreational Services" feels good, even if one is the only recreational therapist on the unit. The employee's job description should clearly indicate whether or not the title carries more than recognition, however (such as new responsibility and/or new authority).

---

3. Familiar to behavioral psychologists as "variable schedule reinforcement," and distressingly similar to rewards from a casino slot machine.

Ironically, one of the best rewards and motivators for some employees, particularly those with the highest individual productivity, is more work. The work, and form of work, must be chosen carefully, using principles discussed elsewhere in this book as *job enhancement*. That is, the work must be meaningful to the employee, offering a feeling of pride or other reward. Some examples include leadership positions, responsibility for more important tasks, and opportunity to demonstrate special skills.

PERFORMANCE EVALUATION AND PRODUCTIVITY

Performance evaluation is an important part of employment. In some organizations, employees are entitled to be evaluated at regular intervals. Properly designed evaluation helps form the basis of the performance record, establishes benchmarks for advancement or criticism, helps the employee stay aware of how he or she is doing in the organization, and documents all of the foregoing. The human resources division should establish or recommend policies and procedures for performance appraisals, and provide training or other guidance to supervisors so that the evaluations are carried out in an appropriate and timely fashion.

Formal evaluation is usually carried out annually, in a structured format. Periodic additional evaluations and feedback are useful, and should also be carefully documented in the employee's record. Negative evaluations, especially, should be supported with specific examples and requirements or suggestions for improvement. There should be an opportunity for the employee's own comments or feedback, which should also be documented in the record.

The evaluation format should contain some very objective ratings (ranging, say, from "unsatisfactory" to "outstanding," with very specific guidelines for using the scale) along with ample opportunity for more subjective comments (which should still be supported with specific examples). The format should follow each employee's job description closely, but may contain space for extra or relatively less tangible tasks and behaviors.

Performance evaluations are ordinarily carried out by one's immediate superior. It is important that every supervisor and manager be trained in the organization's evaluation procedures and techniques and be given guidance in the sometimes difficult task of objective evaluation. Many find it uncomfortable to criticize their subordinates, with whom they must work every day. A smaller number of supervisors and managers are overly critical, and need guidance to keep their evaluations objective and job related.

Ratings Creep. "Ratings creep" is one of the biggest issues in creating useful performance evaluations. It seems superficially logical that most "average" employees should get an "average" rating (although this is not always true; see later discussion). Unfortunately, there is a strong temptation to rate even marginal employees as "very good," because few people view themselves as "average" and such a rating may prevent the employee from being considered for a bonus, raise, or promotion.

Evaluating Versus Comparing Employees. Evaluating performance is not the same as comparing quality or performance. Supervisors/evaluators should understand this, whether they are rating individuals independently or creating a hierarchy of employees. Rating systems that demand a comparison rather than an individual rating are arguably less useful for most (but not all) organization purposes. Physician or psychotherapist employees, for example, may all be expected to maintain "very good" or "excellent" performance, as may the senior managers. Thus, an "average" staff doctor or division chief may deserve an "excellent" rating, at least in most parts of the evaluation.

Be Objective.   The need for honesty and objectivity in evaluations is perhaps most clearly seen when a marginal employee must be disciplined or terminated (see the Employee "Discipline and Termination" section, below). It is difficult to justify serious action if a reticent supervisor has taken the "easy" path, given the person passing marks for job performance, and failed to document performance or behavior problems. Consistency is also important. It is difficult to terminate an employee who has garnered several complaints but recently received an "average" or "above average" performance evaluation.

Communicate with the Employee.   Performance evaluations and their content should not be a surprise to the employee. Management should provide feedback to the employee concerning his or her work performance throughout the year. When the time comes for the annual performance evaluation, it is helpful for the employee to have an opportunity to submit a self-evaluation prior to the formal meeting with the supervisor or manager. This often helps the employee feel that the evaluation is based on a more fair and equitable review, and may provide helpful insight to the supervisor. (The employee's self-evaluation is often more critical than that of the manager or supervisor.)

EMPLOYEE DISCIPLINE AND TERMINATION

Discipline

Most organizations employ a practice of "progressive counseling" or "progressive discipline" for routine disciplinary matters. This practice strives to be fair to the employee and conserve, when feasible, good workers for the organization. Progressive discipline is a hierarchical series of actions, usually starting with verbal, carefully documented communication and progressing as necessary through steps that may result in termination of employment (discussed later). Progressive counseling/discipline should provide the employee with:

- *Notice* that he or she is doing something wrong, the possible employment consequences, and the progressive discipline procedures.
- *Information* about the correct way to do things.
- *Opportunity* to correct the problem.
- Clear *expectation* that the employee will change (and clear consequences for not changing).
- *Guidance*, when appropriate, for correcting the problem and returning to his or her former good employment standing.

Progressive discipline or counseling sessions should focus on the specific work behavior that the employee needs to improve. The employee should be provided with written documentation, generally expressed in terms of work behavior, which includes a detailed statement of how the employee is not currently meeting the standard, a clear statement that the performance needs to improve, and an expectation of performance for the employee. It may be noted that *correction* is not the same as *improvement*. If the need is for complete correction of a problem, it should be made clear that mere "improvement" is not sufficient.

The responsibility for correction or improvement is placed squarely on the employee, not the manager. Management should only be responsible for providing adequate notice, information, and opportunity (e.g., a specific length of time within which correction is expected), communicating expectations, and offering guidance when appropriate (e.g., specific advice or referral to training or educational materials). Whatever the organization's disciplinary system, it should be applied consistently across employees and positions, and followed carefully in individual situations. The human relations division should work with the legal department as necessary.

Seriousness of Infraction or Performance Problem.   Note that serious infractions, dangerous behavior, or behavior that affects significant rights of others may cause the progressive counseling process to be abridged, or eliminated altogether. The organization should have a policy that outlines the kinds of behaviors that cannot be even briefly tolerated and that are likely to lead to summary punishment or termination (e.g., patient abuse or neglect, intoxication, certain threats, weapons in the workplace). Various employee problems or infractions may be categorized as minor, major, or critical, and the categories may or may not be assigned specific levels of disciplinary actions or some sort of "point system."

Clarity and Documentation.   Two management errors in the progressive discipline process stand out as causing enormous problems in some organizations: (a) lack of clarity of communication and (b) lack of documentation of the process. The manager or supervisor must be absolutely clear with the employee, often putting a description of the problem(s) in writing, in painfully objective terms. It is not fair to either the employee or the organization to minimize the problem or describe it in vague terms. And if (or when) the required correction does not occur, the employee may assert that the manager didn't tell him or her what the real problem was in the first place. Be fair, but be very clear.

Document everything that is done, by both the supervisor (who represents the organization) and the employee. If every disciplinary or performance counseling session led to successful corrections, everyone would be happy; however, one cannot predict which employees will improve and which will not. Human resources division guidelines for progressive counseling must allow for the possibility that each disciplinary or performance matter will escalate in the future and may come to termination proceedings. Supervisors/managers must understand the need to follow those guidelines, which should include instructions for clear documentation of every step as well as filing, forwarding, and maintenance of the materials generated.

Once again, clinical managers and supervisors may consider themselves more "clinicians" than "managers." They may balk at routine administrative procedures that are easily understood and accepted by nonclinicians. The human resources division and upper organization management must emphasize the importance of administrative concepts and provide guidance, training, and, if necessary, reassignment for those clinician-managers who do not accept the rules under which the organization must operate to protect itself and its mission.

Separating "Support" from Discipline in Mental Health Organizations. Mental health organization supervisors who are also "helping professionals," particularly, may need management training to confront employees with their areas of need and perform the necessary management task of disciplinary counseling rather than a misguided (from the organization's perspective) "therapeutic" task. Confusing "support" with discipline can cause significant practical and legal problems. Employees may be short-changed and the discipline rendered useless (e.g., by being challenged as being outside company policy or union contract requirements). In any event, the organization is likely to suffer. The human resources division should help managers and supervisors understand the importance of structured, objective disciplinary counseling that follows organization guidelines.

Termination for Cause

At times it is necessary to terminate employment. We focus here on "termination for cause," that is, firing an employee because he or she has done something (or failed to do something) that is inconsistent with further employment in the organization. There are other forms of termination that do not reflect as badly on the employee, or may not suggest problems at all (e.g., budget-related layoffs and reductions in force, termination because the position has been eliminated for strategic or other nonbudget reasons, or closing of the company). Some of those are discussed separately.

The legal issues in termination (and in disciplinary actions; see earlier discussion) should be clarified in organization policy and clarified with organization counsel as necessary. The human resources division must stay abreast of employment law and acceptable organization procedures and provide reliable guidance to management in discipline and termination matters.

The ease with which an organization can terminate an employee for cause (and the employee's rights under the concept of "due process"—his or her entitlement to be treated fairly and within appropriate procedures, which may or may not apply to a particular organization) generally varies with three things: the "cause," the type of organization, and its size and location. Although there are always circumstances under which bad employees can be fired, some situations are more complex than others.

The "Cause." Most terminations for cause do not happen quickly, but are the end-point of a long period of progressive counseling, job rehabilitation, and/or poor performance. As already pointed out, documentation of the process should be clear and complete from the beginning of every disciplinary action or counseling event, because one cannot predict which situations will end in uneventful correction and which will deteriorate into a need for serious disciplinary measures or termination.

Some problems or allegations are so serious that employees may be suspended pending investigation or even terminated on the spot. It is usually best to opt for suspension, because this accomplishes the objective of removing the employee and leaves time for human resources and legal consultation at management's leisure. Salary may or may not be continued while investigation proceeds. Although employees often have rights or entitlements that protect them from unfair termination, a clearly ineffective, or potentially dangerous or destructive, employee need not be allowed to remain in the workplace. Employees who routinely come into contact with patients, especially, should be reassigned or removed from the workplace if patient abuse or neglect is at issue, with or without pay.

Employees on job probation (e.g., new employees, who are often routinely on probation for several months) are usually not given the same entitlements as those who have completed their probation periods. They may often be summarily terminated without the employer's having to show any cause.

Organization Type and Governance.   Government and other public-sector employers usually have less flexibility than those in the private sector, although organizations that are regulated through licensure or certification (such as clinical facilities) operate within strict parameters as well. Federal employment law applies to all organizations (but may have exceptions based on size and/or governance). Very small organizations (those with, say, fewer than 25 employees) may be exempt from many employment laws and regulations, but one should consult an attorney before assuming that termination and other employment actions can be approached with impunity.

Employees who provide patient/client care (or who merely come into contact with patients) often enjoy less job security than others, by virtue of patients' vulnerability to incompetent or unscrupulous behavior. Organizations have much more "employment" flexibility with contract staff than with employees. Volunteer medical/clinical staffing is often even easier to manage (administratively at least), with a separate medical staff organization that takes over some of the procedure and liability. External or outside staffing—that is, arrangements in which staff are hired through an outside agency rather than the organization itself—simplifies administration in some ways, but the organization should retain some ability to prevent unsatisfactory employees from remaining in the workplace. This is not addressed in this chapter.

Location.   We have already alluded to several state laws and regulations. Two other functions of location are (a) the presence or absence in different states of so-called "at will" employment, and (b) union penetrance into mental health organizations (often a function of geographic location or absence of state "right-to-work" laws).

In some states, employees may be terminated "at (the employer's) will" under certain circumstances and by certain kinds of employers. In these, employees have fewer entitlements and opportunities for redress under state law (but may retain important rights under federal law).

When employees are heavily unionized, the union contract usually creates an additional layer of complexity for many employment issues, especially discipline and termination. Sometimes this makes management's task harder; however, a clear union contract and good relationship between the organization and the union that represents the employee can also clarify the procedures for all concerned.

The Termination Decision and Process.   The employer should consider many basic issues before deciding to fire an employee, and the process should be handled within an approved organization protocol. The human resources division should be a repository of knowledge and experience for many of these topics, and should be involved in their development.

1. Review all documentation and other company records for sufficient support and consistency. It is often wise to interview all involved managers for their input.
2. Be satisfied that the decision was made for the correct reasons. Is the termination for cause truly based on job performance, job expectations, and/or inappropriate behavior (and not on some idiosyncracy which is not reasonably related to his or her job duties)? Has the organization discharged other employees for the same or similar reasons or behaviors? Is the reason for discharge based on a recent issue or is this an old offense?
3. Be satisfied that the employee knew (and documentation shows) that the employee knew that if the performance or behavior issue was not corrected, further disciplinary action, including termination, was likely.
4. Except in situations of danger or destructive behavior, be certain the employee was given an opportunity to correct the problem(s).
5. Be sure that Equal Employment Opportunity Commission (EEOC), Americans with Disabilities Act (ADA), and other antidiscrimination issues (e.g., race, age, gender, national origin, handicap, religion) have been adequately addressed.
6. Try to meet with the employee personally. Do not discharge an employee by telephone or letter unless absolutely necessary (but do provide documentation of the termination, entitlements, rights to redress, etc., in writing). All important postal communication should be by registered mail or courier, with proof of delivery and appropriate safeguards for the employee's privacy.
7. Have an objective management witness at the termination meeting (e.g., a human resources representative). An organization attorney may or may not be a good choice, depending on circumstances.
8. Prepare adequately for the termination meeting, and have all necessary communications and paperwork ready for the employee.
9. Conduct the meeting in a private area.
10. Both the terminating manager and the witness should document (independently) what transpires during the termination meeting.
11. Be sure the employee knows the reason for discharge. This should be prepared in advance and given to the employee in writing, and may be further explained orally.
12. Keep the conversation fairly formal. Although the employee's tone may become emotional, the manager should maintain a businesslike decorum and strictly limit extraneous comments. This is not the time or place to make unplanned promises, respond to threats the employee may make, and so on.
13. Discuss relevant employee benefits and entitlements, including COBRA health insurance continuation, severance pay, and disposition of other insurance benefits (life, disability, etc.), retirement/pension/profit-sharing options, and so on. These should be prepared in advance and provided in writing.
14. Discuss the organization's policy regarding job references, communication with potential future employers, reporting to licensing boards or reporting agencies (such as, in the case of physicians, the National Practitioner Data Bank), and so on, as applicable.

15. Discuss the organization's policy regarding reemployment, as it applies to the employee.
16. Discuss the organization's requirements or policies regarding keys, passwords, credit cards, equipment and other organization property, ownership of stored computer data, confidentiality, business and proprietary information, noncompetition issues, and access to the organization premises, as applicable.
17. Monitor the employee after the termination meeting until he or she has left the premises, as necessary, to be certain that he or she complies with the requirements mentioned in item 16.

REDUCTIONS IN FORCE (RIFs)

Organization needs sometimes require significant reductions in the workforce that are not directly related to employees' individual qualifications. Terminations or layoffs for such reasons are different from termination for cause, and are governed by different rules and procedures. They may be precipitated by shifts in the business plan, changes in mission or major objectives, loss of business, or financial problems. Sometimes reductions in one area are associated with hiring in another, but most reductions in force (RIFs) result in fewer employees overall.

Because many reasons for reduction in force affect the health (and perhaps even survival) of the overall organization, some RIFs (such as closure of an entire unit or department) allow the organization to bypass some employee job protections (such as tenure). Other protections and benefits remain in force; human resources managers or organization counsel may clarify the policies, laws, and regulations that apply in each RIF situation. In any event, such decisions should be made with care. Most organizations try to preserve as many jobs as feasible, encourage or reward voluntary leaving or retirement, and reduce the workforce as much as possible by attrition. When layoffs cannot be avoided, they should be based on broad, generic criteria (such as seniority) rather than individual ones (such as performance ratings or supervisor choice). Most organizations try to help displaced employees to relocate and offer some compensation for the transition.

RIFs should not be viewed as an opportunity to get rid of problem employees. They are across-the-board cuts for organizational administrative reasons, and should not connote bias against the affected employees.

DIVERSITY IN THE WORKFORCE AND COMMUNITY

Diversity in the Workplace

Cultural diversity is an important part of the health care workplace. Mental health organizations should be aware of diversity in both staff and patients, and its potential impact on employee relations, individual and team performance, and quality of care. Human resource divisions should help the organization to identify and assess the many issues of race, culture, age, and gender that exist in the organization and the community, as well as to recognize any absence of diversity that should be corrected.

The organization leadership should establish policies and procedures that explain the organization's position on workplace diversity and specify the expected behavior of all employees, including management, regarding any problems that may arise.

Cultural Sensitivity and Program Needs: An Example

Montana's Pathways Treatment Center, a freestanding, not-for-profit inpatient psychiatric and chemical dependency facility, serves at least two separate Indian nations, as well as an immediate vicinity that is largely populated by Anglos. During a revision of marketing and program strategies, the staff determined that they needed to develop chemical dependency services sensitive to the Native American culture. They quickly realized that none of the staff was of Native American heritage, although some doctors and employees had experience with these populations. They rapidly set about creating programs and special activities that included Native American customs; however, they did not consult with key referral sources from the nearby reservations.

During a later program evaluation, the staff visited with Native American health care leaders and were told (rather bluntly) that they should not try to recreate Native American customs in the treatment program, but that the facility should continue to offer a traditional chemical dependency recovery program. The program managers quickly learned that the first step to successful program integration is to listen to the needs and desires of the special population.

EMPLOYEE-RELATED LEGAL ISSUES

Mental health care organizations must be able to comply with employment laws and have an effective way of updating the organization's policies, procedures, and practices. The organization must be aware of the most important of these laws, summarized in Table 33.1, in establishing employment procedures. The federal Equal Employment Opportunity Commission (EEOC) enforces all of these laws. The EEOC also provides oversight in coordination of all federal equal employment opportunity regulations, practices, and policies. In most organizations, the human resources staff develops specific policies and procedures to deal with the various federal and state laws regarding recruitment, hiring, and employment, including structured interviewing and job selection criteria to be followed by all managers in order to assure compliance while meeting the needs of the organization.

Discrimination in an employment context refers to exclusion or differential treatment based on something other than a bona fide occupational qualification. The EEOC does not protect employees or applicants who cannot meet reasonable job requirements; however, the organization is not always allowed to define those job requirements as it sees fit, and it is illegal to define them in such a way that covered classes of people are arbitrarily excluded from employment or other applicable considerations (e.g., equal salary, promotion, job conditions). Job qualifications that specify abilities (such as to lift a certain weight, perform a certain activity, or be available during certain hours), for example, are much more likely to meet EEOC

TABLE 33.1. Federal Equal Employment Opportunity (EEO) Laws

Equal Pay Act of 1963	Protects men and women who perform substantially equal work in the same setting
Title VII of the Civil Rights Act of 1964 ("Title VII")	Prohibits employment discrimination based on race, color, religion, sex, or national origin
Age Discrimination and Employment Act of 1967 (ADEA)	Protects individuals 40 years of age or older
Section 501, Rehabilitation Act of 1973 ("Section 501")	Prohibits discrimination against qualified federal government employees with disabilities
Title I, Americans with Disabilities Act of 1990 (ADA)	Prohibits employment discrimination against qualified individuals with disabilities in the private sector, and in state and local governments
Civil Rights Act of 1991	Provides money damages in cases of intentional employment discrimination

requirements than those that specify or exclude a particular size, age, gender, or the like.

Covered persons (see later discussion) refers to classes of individuals covered by the statute. There are limitations and exceptions to the applicability of EEO statutes; however, the laws themselves apply to a very broad range of people and situations. It is important that organizations understand them well, have access to reliable legal interpretation, and not assume that an exception applies without careful examination of the law and its context.

Under Title VII, the ADEA, and the ADA, it is illegal to discriminate against covered persons, in covered situations, in any aspect of employment. Topics addressed in these statutes include:

- Hiring and firing.
- Compensation, assignment, or classification of employees.
- Transfer, promotion, layoff, or recall.
- Job advertisements.
- Recruitment.
- Testing.
- Use of company facilities.
- Training and apprenticeship programs.
- Fringe benefits.
- Pay, retirement plans, and disability leave.
- Other terms and conditions of employment.

Discriminatory practices under these laws also include, for covered persons:

- Harassment on the basis of race, color, religion, sex, national origin, disability, or age.
- Retaliation against an individual for filing a good-faith charge of discrimination, participating in an investigation, or opposing discriminatory practices.

- Employment decisions based on stereotypes or unwarranted assumptions about the abilities, traits, or performance of individuals of a particular sex, race, age, religion, or ethnic group, or individuals with disabilities.
- Denying employment opportunities to a person because of marriage to, or association with, an individual of a particular race, religion, or national origin, or an individual with a disability.

Title VII prohibits not only intentional discrimination, but also practices that have the *effect* of discriminating against individuals because of their race, color, national origin, religion, or sex. It is generally illegal to discriminate against an individual because of linguistic characteristics common to a specific ethnic group. For example, a rule requiring that employees speak only English on the job may violate Title VII unless an employer shows the requirement is necessary for conducting business. Title VII also prohibits discrimination because of participation in schools or places of worship associated with a particular racial, ethnic, or religious group. Employers are required to post notices to all employees advising them of their rights under the laws that EEOC enforces and their right to be free from retaliation. Such notices must be accessible, as needed, to persons with visual or other disabilities that affect reading. An employer is also required to reasonably accommodate the religious beliefs of an employee or prospective employee, unless doing so would impose an undue hardship.

There is a broad ban against age discrimination that specifically prohibits statements or specifications of age preference or limitations in job notices or advertisements. An age limit may only be specified when age is a bona fide occupational qualification, and not merely for the employer's convenience.

The Equal Pay Act (EPA) requires that men and women who perform substantially similar work be paid equally. However, employers may not achieve that parity by reducing the wages of either gender. Violation of the EPA may also occur if a different wage is paid to a person who works in the same job before or after an employee of the opposite sex. Employers should be cautious to avoid pay differentials when labor unions cause wage adjustments; the organization, not the union, is responsible for adhering to the law.

Title I of the Americans with Disabilities Act (ADA) prohibits employment discrimination on the basis of disability. The ADA defines disability as a physical or mental impairment that substantially limits one or more "major life activities,"[4] a record of such an impairment, or simply being regarded as having such an impairment. The employer must not discriminate against a potential or active employee if he or she satisfies the skill, experience, and education requirements for the position and can perform the essential functions of the position (with or without what the ADA describes as "reasonable accommodation"). An employer is not required to lower production standards to make an accommodation, or undergo undue difficulty or expense (but those are often difficult to define).

Employers are prohibited from asking job applicants about the existence, nature, or severity of a disability, but they can (and should) ask about their ability to perform job functions. A job offer may be conditioned on the results of the medical

---

4. "Major life activity," like many other important terms in employment law, is specifically defined in the statute. One should not assume that one's own definition is a "legal" one.

examination, but only if the examination is required for all entering employees in the same job category. Medical examinations of employees must be job-relevant and consistent with business necessity.

Drug and alcohol use are especially important in the mental health professions. Employees and applicants currently engaging in illegal use of drugs are not protected by the ADA when an employer acts on the basis of such use. Testing for illegal use of drugs is not considered a "medical examination" and thus is not subject to ADA restrictions on medical examinations. Although current use is not protected, substance dependence may be considered a disability, particularly under federal law.

Genetic discrimination is an emerging issue in preemployment physicals and employment suitability. Our developing ability to predict genetic health risk (Rosen, 1999) may, in concept at least, lead to social stigmatization and genetic discrimination. In 2000, President Clinton signed an executive order prohibiting federal departments and agencies from making employment decisions based on protected genetic information. The U.S. Equal Employment Opportunity Commission has been given the responsibility for coordinating this policy with federal departments and agencies.

SEXUAL AND OTHER HARASSMENT

Sexual harassment includes practices ranging from direct requests for sexual favors, to less obvious verbal or physical actions, to workplace conditions that create a hostile work environment for persons of either gender. The EEOC has federal legal oversight over the area of sexual and other forms of harassment, but it is a practical and ethical issue as well. Harassment can arise in virtually any employment setting, and may involve actions by both employees and other individuals who may come into contact with employees in the workplace. Employers should keep in mind that much of the definition of sexual harassment in particular (especially in terms of an actionable offense) may rest with the perceptions of the recipient.

A significant number of mental health professionals experience unwanted sexual contact from patients and clients, such as deliberate touching, inappropriate closeness or "cornering," or communications containing sexual material. Employees should be aware that such behaviors are possible and should have some training in prevention, handling, and personal safety. Even though the behavior may be explained as part of a mental illness, organizations should take such incidents seriously, communicate their inappropriateness to patients, encourage reporting, investigate as appropriate, and take reasonable steps to protect staff and other patients from harm. Aggressive and intrusive conduct aside, even relatively nonthreatening sexual behaviors, including those obviously arising from severe mental illness, can have a psychological impact on the recipient.

E-mail, computer networks, and Internet access offer new ways to pursue sexual and other forms of harassment. Organizations have some responsibility to be aware of the opportunity for misuse and work with management information professionals to creating policies and procedures regarding use of computers and e-mail. Such policies routinely stress that all e-mail is the property of the employer and may be retrieved at any time. Information transmitted should be for organization purposes, and personal use is subject to organization policy and scrutiny. The policy should state that no e-mail messages that contain material reasonably known to be offensive should be created, sent, forwarded, or knowingly received. It may also reiterate classifications of offensive material from which employees may be legally protected (e.g., race, color, religion, sex, age, national origin, and disability). Using networks and e-mail to express political views, solicit donations, or pursue other nonorganization endeavors is usually inappropriate in the workplace, and may sometimes be considered harassment.

Organizations should take a proactive approach to preventing, detecting, and correcting instances of harassment. Policies and procedures should clearly define harassment, outline the organization's position (often "zero tolerance" for some things, such as sexual harassment), and outline the investigative process triggered by harassment claims. The policy should identify a responsible department and individual to which complaints should be reported, typically the human resources director or a designated member of his or her staff.

Investigation should be swift, with a definitive outcome whenever possible and communication back to the complainant. Confidentiality for both the complainant and the alleged perpetrator is important, to an extent consistent with adequate investigation and, when indicated, appropriate corrective action. Corrective action may include training, referral to counseling, and/or disciplinary actions such as warning, reprimand, withholding of a promotion or pay increase, reassignment, suspension, or termination. As in other investigative and disciplinary situations, due process, including an appeals process, is required.

EMPLOYEE RELATIONS

Good employee relations can create an environment in which employees feel that they have both power and responsibility, and contribute at the highest feasible level. But how does the organization come to understand the needs of its employees? In addition to creating and examining standard human resource statistical reports on absenteeism, accident rates, sick days, and number of employee breaks, the human resources department should find ways to assess employee perceptions and gather information about how they feel about the organization.

Employee surveys are one method, but are often overdone. Employees become tired of merely providing information, particularly when they believe the organization doesn't respond very well to the needs they identify. Other ways of gathering employee feedback should be pursued, such as interactive feedback groups, conducting "exit interviews" with employees who leave the organization, regular community forums, and simply having managers walk about in the workplace. One should create an atmosphere in which honest feedback is appreciated and never punished (good-faith "feedback" should not be confused with insubordination by either the employee or the manager). One should find ways to ask whether employees feel listened to, and understood, when talking to their managers and supervisors.

Communication to employees, informally and by newsletter, meeting, memo, and (especially) participation in organization planning and problem solving, is crucial to good employee relations. Benefits fairs showcase job perquisites and explain benefits. Strategic planning can involve employees at all levels, which strengthens the planning process and makes it clear that employees' ideas and needs help shape the future of the organization. Most employees can be part of a process improvement team. The result is usually a more effective process and employees who feel respect, empowerment, and loyalty.

Communication from management should be accurate, and not false reassurance or "lip service." Executive memos that promise employee participation but never deliver only create suspicion and resentment. Similarly, a senior manager who tells workers that their jobs are secure (or by omission implies it) a few months before a reduction in force risks a great deal of valuable personal and organizational credibility.

Sheppard (2000) suggested that managers first determine the goals and objectives of the organization, then go to the target audiences (usually employees or stakeholders of some kind) and ask, through focus groups and interviews, where they are vis-à-vis those goals and objectives. What perceptions and views do they have? What do they see as their role in the organization's mission and goals? Are there gaps between where organization leaders want employees to be and where the employees are (or believe they are)? How can those gaps be narrowed? Shephard and others believe that basic principles of communication and determining employee needs apply to all organizations, from very large to very small, although size and structure may affect ease of access to employees and the ability to engage them.

Unions and Employee Relations

Health care employee unions are common—even ubiquitous—in some states and rare in others. An effective human resource program with adequate policies and procedures and proactive employee relations programs creates an environment in which employees feel recognized and rewarded for the work they provide to the organization, but mental health systems are not immune from unionization. In a few states, clinical professionals may be unionized as well.

Labor laws deal primarily with the relationship between employers and unions, attempting to equalize the bargaining power between employers and employees. They grant employees the right to unionize and allow or prohibit certain activities by employees and employers seeking to have their demands met (such as strikes, picketing, lock-outs, and injunctions). Organizations that aggressively develop good employee–employer communication, multilevel planning and problem solving, compensation practices, performance evaluations, and other elements of solid employee relations have gone a long way toward providing a positive and balanced relationship with employees.

Grievances

Human resource policies and procedures should include specific steps for employees to express differences and grievances concerning another employee, supervisors, or policy. A grievance policy and procedure typically includes specific steps that the employee should follow to air his or her concern. Most employers encourage employees to deal directly with the individual with whom the problem exists and, if unsuccessful, to go to an immediate supervisor. Human resources staff may advise either party about organization policy, and avenues of employee appeal if the grievance resolution is unacceptable to him or her.

The appeals procedure should specify a time period within which the supervisor or manager should respond to the employee (in writing), as well as any right to further appeal to the manager's superior. Human resources staff should be available to advise and assist the employee through the process to its ultimate resolution. The grievance and appeals procedure should establish an environment in which a reasonable employee feels his or her concerns have been fairly heard, by someone with the authority to act on them if appropriate.

Alternative Dispute Resolution

Serious grievances, such as contested termination, that cannot be resolved within the organization may go to an alternative form of dispute resolution specified in, for example, an employment contract. In some jurisdictions, alternative dispute resolution (ADR) programs are voluntary on the part of the contestants; in others, a valid contract may obligate the parties to use some form of ADR before—or instead of—a court procedure (such as a lawsuit).

The two most common forms of ADR are arbitration and mediation. The two terms are sometimes loosely defined and used interchangeably, but there are some commonly accepted distinctions between them.

In *arbitration*, the parties work together to come to an agreement between themselves, generally with the help of a mutually agreed-upon neutral arbiter (arbitrator). Labor-management negotiations are a common example. Strictly defined, an arbiter has the authority to decide the matter; however, in common practice arbitration may be "binding" or "nonbinding," with the former requiring the parties to abide by the result.

In *mediation*, the parties present their cases to a neutral third party, often assigned by a judge, who then decides the matter for them (as contrasted with the mutual agreement goal of arbitration). Mediation is sometimes imposed by a court or contract when parties fail to reach agreement during arbitration (e.g., stalemated labor negotiations). The mediator usually has special training in dispute resolution and is often licensed or certified by a state or other body; many are lawyers or retired judges. The process is formal but much more flexible, less expensive, and usually more efficient than a court procedure.

EMPLOYEE ORIENTATION, IN-SERVICE EDUCATION, TRAINING, AND DEVELOPMENT

New Employee Orientation

Once a person has been employed, the organization should provide him or her with an orientation program that includes a comprehensive introduction to the organization's mission and philosophy, goals and objectives, structure, and the characteristics and requirements of his or her position. The specific content and time spent on orientation vary with the position and type and size of the organization. Common topics include facility orientation, safety, risk management, job policies and procedures, and personnel policies and procedures (including employee rights, expectations, and benefits). Mental health organizations often include additional topics mandated or recommended by licensing, funding, insuring, and/or accrediting organizations (e.g., state government, Health Care Financing Administration [HCFA], liability insurers, or Joint Commission on Accreditation of Healthcare Organizations [JCAHO], respectively).

It is not uncommon for orientation to require two to four weeks during which the employee may or may not be allowed to work in his or her position under supervision. The orientation period should not be confused with a commonly imposed introductory "probation" period, which typically lasts much longer.

In-Service Education

In-service education implies job-related training that (a) takes place at or near the work site, (b) is held during working (or paid) hours, and (c) is required of all relevant employees. It is typically provided to introduce new policies and procedures, cover new laws or regulations, or keep important (e.g., clinical or safety) knowledge and skills up to date.

Some forms and topics of in-service training are recommended or required by licensing, funding, insuring, and/or accrediting organizations. Others are determined by individual organization or employee need, as ascertained through some form of needs assessment (e.g., an employee survey or review of quality improvement data patterns). Training and educational programs should be coordinated with by the human resource division, which should have experience in such things as needs assessment, continuing education requirements, training methods, access to training materials, staff communication and coordination, pre- and post-training assessments, and program evaluation.

Other Training and Development

Many health care organizations support employees' personal development (e.g., with time and/or funding for high school equivalency diplomas and college courses), training for job-related advancement, and (for professionals) continuing education. These educational opportunities usually occur outside working hours and away from the work site, although larger organizations (particularly government agencies) often offer internal continuing education and job-related training. This kind of investment in the organization's human resources leads to a better-trained, more sophisticated, more loyal, and more satisfied workforce, with concomitant increases in productivity and decreases in employee grievance and turnover.

POLICIES AND PROCEDURES

Why have formal policies and procedures? Some very small organizations, such as some small sole proprietorships, operate well without a formalized policy and procedure book. As the organization grows, however, things get more complicated.

Additional employees are hired; more supervisors and managers are added; more state and federal regulations and guidelines begin to apply to the organization. With more employees, and more tasks and services being performed with more patients or clients, consistency among workers and job activities becomes an important part of service quality. Each employee must know expected behaviors, rules, procedures, and management goals that heretofore had to be explained to only one or two. Each employee must be supervised and fairly evaluated. With the larger workforce, employee interactions increase exponentially, and with them opportunities for misunderstandings, miscommunications, and conflict. The executives' (e.g., owners') span of control broadens, requiring more delegation of authority and layers of supervision. A change in leadership or absence of key managers creates inconsistency, if not chaos. A policy and procedure manual that addresses key areas of expected consistency in day-to-day work becomes an important asset.

The policy and procedure manual should be easily accessible to every employee, and each should be expected to read and understand the parts relevant to his or her work. The manual documents expected procedures and behaviors, clarifies lines of authority, and promotes consistent and impartial administration of organization policy. It also allows the organization to maintain and control the ways in which it complies with external regulations and guidelines (e.g., those promulgated or suggested by federal and state licensing, certifying, monitoring, insuring, and funding agencies). It becomes the "one source" of consistent, reliable information on many topics in the workplace, and documents management's effort to meet or exceed the standards required of the organization.[5]

It takes time to develop good, effective policies and procedures. They routinely evolve with the organization, and should be reviewed and updated periodically. Sometimes mature policies and procedures are borrowed, in part at least, from another, similar organization where they have been successfully implemented. If so, they should be reviewed by relevant organization staff and/or committees (and perhaps outside consultants), often including representatives of those to whom they will apply. New policies and procedures should often be reassessed a few weeks or months after they are implemented. Good ones are rarely created de novo, from the mind of a single manager or executive. The road to "unintended consequences" is paved with good intentions.

SPECIAL WORKFORCE TOPICS

Succession Planning

Succession planning is a process of identifying people who could move into key positions if and when they are vacated, or who could fill new positions that may be created by organization growth or change. Succession planning does not usually

---

5. Note that organization policies and procedures manuals do not create a legal or external professional standard for the organization. They do not, in themselves, establish any legal standard (e.g., a "standard of care") that must be met. Rather, some may mirror an outside guideline, regulation, or standard; others may set a goal that exceeds external standards or requirements; and still others may provide rules or guidelines that have only internal relevance.

specify people certain to be promoted, but rather helps prepare (or "groom") eligible managers and executives for new roles well before the need is critical. It is an important element of smooth transition from the present to the future of the organization. Although the details of succession planning are appropriately assigned to human resource professionals, it is important that the chief executive officer (CEO) or administrator of the organization be supportive of the process.

The succession planning process identifies highly qualified people in the organization and takes a consistent approach to assembling, analyzing, and retaining information about potential leaders and planning their further development. Policies and procedures should be established that make employees aware that the organization is actively planning for its overall health and survival, and that it cares about their career development and opportunity to progress within the organization.

Job Sharing and Special Shifts

Recruiting and retaining good employees sometimes requires employers to adjust work sites, shifts, and hours to meet their needs. Progressive organizations have found ways to create unique work shifts outside standard work times. Given the opportunity, and perhaps some support from the employer (e.g., funding home workstations for transcriptionists), many employees find ways to work efficiently from home. Policies and procedures should be established that deal with such situations, particularly in the areas of attendance and work time/productivity tracking.

Many mental health care organizations have mobile or outreach staff that do not visit the main facility on a day-to-day basis. New technology, such as cell phones, laptop computers, wireless communication, and other means of linkage to the main facility, make such point-of-service arrangements much easier than in the past (see chapters on information technology). Productive employees who cannot work full-time may be able to share a position ("job sharing"), providing service to the organization while also meeting personal or family needs.

SUMMARY

Recruiting, employing, supervising, evaluating, and retaining the right people is an extremely challenging task. An effective human resource function in mental health organizations can create an environment in which employees and job seekers choose to work with your organization over another.

> It is not about bragging rights or battles or even the accumulation of wealth; it's about connecting and engaging at multiple levels. It's about challenging minds and capturing hearts. . . . Leaders can no longer view strategy and execution as abstract concepts but must realize that both elements are ultimately about people. [We must realize that] the most magical and tangible and ultimately the most important ingredient in a transformed landscape is people. (Fiorina, 2000)

REFERENCES

Carignani, V. (2000). Management of change in health care organizations and human resource role. *European Journal of Radiology, 33*(1), 8–13.

Fiorina, C. (2000). Commencement address, Massachusetts Institute of Technology, Cambridge, MA.

Rosen, E. (1999). Genetic information and genetic discrimination: How medical records vitiate legal protection. A comparative analysis of international legislation and policies. *Scandanavian Journal of Public Health, 27*(3), 166–172.

Sheppard, D. (2000). Large vs. small companies: Is there a difference? *HR Magazine, 45*(2). Available online at www.shrm.org/hrmagazine/articles/default.asp?page-0200cova.htm

BIBLIOGRAPHY

Epting, L. A., Glover, S. H., & Boyd, S. D. (1994). Managing diversity. *Health Care Supervisor, 12*(4), 73–83.

Koonin, S. (2000). Talk to me: Monitoring and measures. *HR Magazine, 45*(3). Available online at www.shrm.org/hrmagazine/articles/default.asp?page-0198cov.htm

Chapter Thirty-Four

Principles of Physician Recruiting

Richard C. W. Hall
Ryan C. W. Hall

RECRUITMENT

Recruitment of well-trained, highly motivated, stable, and productive individuals is one of the most important functions a department chairman or program administrator can discharge. The ability to recruit, train, and maintain a team of highly qualified professionals is critical to organizations that work smoothly and meet their performance goals and obligations. The process is particularly complicated during times of budgetary constraint, high patient demand, constant regulatory scrutiny, and an adversarial system that pits providers against one another, as well as the "suppliers of services" (health maintenance organizations [HMOs], large insurance companies, etc.) in a financially fluid and constantly shifting managerial environment (Burda, 1995).

Although many managed care organizations (MCOs) and large bureaucratic institutions regard physicians as "service units," seasoned administrators understand that recruiting the wrong physician or misrepresenting the position is likely to produce dissatisfaction and, in the long run, undermine the harmonious and efficient operation of the organization (Montague, 1994a). To recruit successfully, one needs to carefully define the role and function of the individual being hired and understand the type of personality structure that the organization needs in each position (Burda, 1994; Cejka, 1993; Lowes, 1999; Pulde, 1997).

> A high-quality researcher was hired by a VA section chief to fill a high-demand service billet because no other funding slot was available within the departmental research budget. Although an excellent research physician, he became an immediate source of tension and controversy within the organization. He regarded his role as "research executive," seeing himself as overseeing the research product of his junior associates, and directing grant development that would "ennoble" his department and "bring favorable credit to the university." His colleagues and subordinates saw him as a dilettante with poor clinical skills who thought of himself as "too good to work in the trenches." This disastrous mismatch pitted the individual physician against the organization and produced considerable tension between the program in which he was hired and the university, which provided support to it.

This vignette illustrates the danger of using billets inappropriately, particularly when a patient-related work product is desired.

In hiring, one must know the specific traits one wishes to see in place within the organization. One might recruit one kind of individual to start a new program with a tight budget and skeletal staff, and a very different person to develop the same program if good funding and extensive staff support were available. Similarly, the person selected to manage a smooth-running large outpatient department should be different from one chosen to reorganize and repair a failing program.

> Robert Oppenheimer was a brilliant leader of physicists at Los Alamos. He inspired confidence and got the most out of his team's varied personalities. Edward Teller, on the other hand, was a brilliant physicist, but was rejected in his bid to become Los Alamos leader for the development of the "Super" (the hydrogen bomb), a project to which he had dedicated his career. He was "passed over" not because of his lack of knowledge, but because of his confrontational leadership style. (Rhodes, 1995)

When hiring people for positions of importance and responsibility, such as physicians, one must consider the important needs of the individual being hired, and not merely immediate the needs of the organization. Is the person a good work "fit"? Will the new team member feel comfortable? Is the job a good long-term fit for the family's needs? If the job is transitional, does it meet the organizational requirements as well as those of the physician? These issues should be discussed carefully at the times of interview and hiring. It is also wise to have other members of the work team involved in the interview process, so that as much information as possible can be provided to the candidate. Similarly, if the team is uncomfortable with the new member, that person's success may be compromised.

Honesty, even if sometimes bordering on the painful, is essential in defining both the assets and liabilities of the program. The individual being considered should have a clear and accurate picture of his or her potential role and work tasks, problems to be solved, and the degree of support to be expected.

> Several years ago, one of the authors hired a brilliant physician, who was a perfect fit with the programs that he was to run and develop. The organization promised office and secretarial services, placement of residents in the program, and a budget and support structure that would permit the job to be done well. Some of the promised support did not materialize. After six months, the physician resigned, observing that if the organization could not provide him with an office during his first six months on the job, it would not be likely to honor any of the other promises made to him.

This vignette illustrates another key factor in physician recruitment: the ability of the administrator or physician who is doing the recruiting or hiring to describe the job realistically and provide (or accurately estimate) the resources promised. Inability to deliver anticipated work conditions is a serious disservice to the organization and its physicians, as well as to other members of the team, who become dispirited and demoralized by cavalier, unmet promises.

Managed care cost reductions have altered both the nature and scope of physicians' roles and practices within organizations. These factors have to be carefully evaluated before hiring physicians. The physician's workplace must be designed to remain intellectually challenging and personally gratifying. It is essential that demands are reasonable, realistic, and can be accomplished over time (Hawkins, 1994). Repetitive short-term crises, which burn out physician members of the team, ensure that the task of recruiting physicians is never finished. Conversely, if recruited physicians have a reasonably productive and high-quality work environment, they will stay and grow, and the organization will prosper.

The rapidly changing nature of health care systems makes it crucial that clinical administrators define the specific role, responsibility, and risks for new physicians. Their power relationships, reporting hierarchies, autonomy, and the demands made on them to practice within a particular economic environment must be carefully defined and understood, as do their relative roles and relationships with other members of the treatment team (Dismuke, 1989; Garofolo, 1984). Human resource professionals should evaluate each job and ascertain its clinical, gatekeeping, and fiduciary roles. They should clarify whether or not the physician will be expected to subordinate clinical decisions to financial and/or utilization management controls or to the expectations of contracted external programs (e.g., those that impose limits on procedures, consultations, or length of stay). Physicians should be advised at the time of hiring if formularies are restrictive, what medical role functions are authorized by the administration, and what treatment functions will be divided among physician and nonphysician "providers." The administration should also define any nonclinical roles or expectations (e.g., marketing, program development, quality improvement, performance standards, risk management, conflict resolution) (Couvillon, 1999).

Finally, professional, medical, and business ethics are not just about "doing the right thing"; they are critical to long-term success in the health care marketplace. The organization administration should remember that quality physicians and other clinicians consider the ethical quality of the work environment more important than dollars paid.

Physician Recruitment Incentives

A number of factors affect an individual's initial engagement with a hiring body:

- *Geography*: People apply for jobs in regions of the country in which they would like to live or in areas that have specific appeal (e.g., a hometown or proximity to an ill parent or a spouse's job or schooling). Geography is the most crucial initial factor in a physician's search.
- *Direct pay*: Several recent studies indicate that straight compensation packages with a bonus possibility are preferred over incentive hiring plans (Cotter & Bonds, 1995; McCullough, Dodge, & Moeller, 1999). This is particularly true as managed care develops a greater presence in the marketplace. Compensation should be competitive for the type of work and geographic region.
- *Schedule, hours*: Physicians, on average, work 50 to 60 hours a week. They are not usually accustomed to punching a clock. However, most employed doctors now prefer improved on-call coverage, some part-time scheduling for call, and staggered shifts. Reasonable work hours, well-defined responsibilities, continuing education opportunities, and time to spend with their families are often deter-

mining factors in accepting employment. For single female physicians, availability of free time and a structured work week are the most critical factors in surveys of job preference (Cejka, 1993; Dismuke, 1989; Hawkins, 1994).

- *Benefit package*: A carefully constituted package of health, life, disability, and malpractice insurance, vacation time, personal days, and sick leave is very attractive, particularly to young physicians beginning practice. Older and more senior-level physicians are often more interested in longer-term contracts and guarantees (Cotter & Bonds, 1995).
- *Staff, equipment*: As the vicissitudes of work become greater, office space, computers, quality support staff, reasonableness of work setting, availability of a library, quality lab and x-ray support, and pleasant, well-trained colleagues become important recruitment factors.
- *Peer group*: The value of competent colleagues has become increasingly important in physician recruitment. Maturity, competence, and collegiality are valued recruitment variables. Most physicians fear isolation, a loss of autonomy, and humiliation in settings that do not recognize them as individuals or do not provide adequate peer support.
- *Positive program history*: It is very difficult to recruit and retain physicians for programs that have a history of chaos, ruthless or vindictive administration, or interdisciplinary conflict (Dismuke, 1989; Garofolo, 1984; Hawkins, 1994; Lowes, 1999; McCullough et al., 1999).
- *Quality of life*: Physicians are looking for a good quality of life for their children and spouses, as well as themselves. Pointing out those things that make the community livable and arranging for spouse visits and support during interviews are helpful recruitment tools (Montague, 1994b).

Changes in Recruitment Incentives

Once financial requirements have been met, doctors look for security. Many young doctors are afraid of solo, or even small-group, practices. The majority of physicians leaving training programs today gravitate toward some form of group or large organization practice. These environments are safer both for sharing their expertise and for helping them develop administrative and clinical skills. Many look for systems that will handle billing, office logistics, and in-service education, and provide collegial stimulation. They are anxious for time off and such less tangible factors as educational and loan assistance, legal support should they be sued, and a work environment that provides a sense of dignity and decorum (Montague, 1994b).

Female physicians are particularly impressed by organizations that provide them with longer-term security and better lifestyles. More than 50% of undergraduates entering medical school are female. Many of these young women hope to find positions that will permit them to be not only doctors, but mothers as well. Most female physicians defer having children until the end of residency, and look for early-career jobs that will permit an opportunity to start a family. They want stable, pleasant, productive employment, not troubled, controlling, angry, or humiliating professional environments (Burda, 1994; Cejka, 1993; McCullough et al., 1999; Montague, 1994b; Pulde, 1997).

All of this means that physicians look at both the day-to-day quality and the long-term health of the organizations that recruit them. Those that physicians rate as having the highest employment appeal are established practices, groups, or organizations that have a substantial financial reserve; are physician-driven; have a history of service in the community; and have a reputation for physician loyalty and high-quality clinical service. Things that are adverse to physician recruitment include settings with a reputation for physician animosity, organizations run by venture capital firms, and the more aggressive managed care organizations and insurance companies that use physicians as "provider units."

Legal Issues in Recruitment and Credentialing

Recruiting. West (1995) noted that the general public has not accepted physicians' routine level of compensation, and are thus often critical when they discover how much doctors make. In addition, the Internal Revenue Service (IRS) and the federal Department of Health and Human Services have criticized administrative packages that offer financial incentives they believe are illegal. The Stark Law of 1992 limits the type and amount of recruitment incentives hospitals can offer to physicians. It also makes it clear that doctors cannot refer Medicare patients to laboratories or radiological facilities in which they have a financial interest. In 1995, this list of prohibited services was extended to "all business services" (West, 1995).

When group practices, hospitals, or medical organizations violate these Stark Law standards, they are subject to a loss of tax-exempt status, loss of Medicare/ Medicaid provider status, civil fines, and criminal penalties (Hawkins, 1994). The IRS has also noted, specifically in its Announcement 95-25, that if any organization violates recruitment incentive standards, its tax-exempt status can and will be removed.

Credentialing. The judge's decision in *Elam v. College Park Hospital* (183 Calif. Rptr. 156, 1982) states, "as a general principle, a hospital's failure to insure the competence of its medical staff through careful selection and review creates an unreasonable risk of harm to its patients." Although this decision is directly binding only in its California jurisdiction, it reflects the standard of care expected of hospitals and other health care entities that employ clinicians, contract with them, or (in the case of "volunteer" medical staffs) allow them to diagnose or treat the entity's patients. Administrators should note that it is the institution, not the clinician, that is liable for improper credentialing.

Credentialing activities should be undertaken at the time candidates are assessed for hiring or contracting. They should follow a standardized, well-defined process that is carefully pursued both initially and during reappointment throughout the physician's relationship with the organization. Inadequately credentialed clinicians markedly increase the risk to patients and the probability of financial loss through complaint or lawsuit. In addition, inadequate credentialing threatens facility accreditation, reimbursement certificates, and operating licenses.

The basic tenet of credentialing is ensuring that the physician being hired is qualified to perform his or her designated duties. To do so, the organization must have a specific, reliable system in place. The credentialing process should generally ensure, insofar as feasible, that the appointment is appropriate and that:

1. The individual being considered actually possesses the training, licensure, and experience listed on his or her application.
2. The requested privileges fall within the scope of his or her competence.
3. He or she has no impairment or other characteristic (including criminal behavior) likely to adversely affect patient care or effective operation of the health care organization.
4. He or she has not been reprimanded, sued, or the recipient of some action that reasonably suggests a threat to patients or effective operation of the organization.
5. He or she is clinically competent, as determined by training history, documented experience, and/or personal observation during a probationary period.
6. The application is free of false or deliberately misleading information.

Other issues, including the legal concept of *respondeat superior*, corporate practice of medicine, and the ethics of working in a corporate managed care environment (Hall, 1994, 1997), are discussed elsewhere in this volume.

The New Realities of Physician Recruitment Strategy

As recently as 1980, few physicians would seriously consider employment in multispecialty clinics, health maintenance organizations, hospitals, and other health care organizations (Cotter & Bonds, 1995). Today, many doctors and other clinicians actively seek salaried positions and full-time contracts. Three different studies described next agree on the principles that should guide organizations in successful physician recruiting.

Cotter and Bonds (1995) noted that many young physicians bypass private practice altogether and embark on what they hope will be long-term careers with health care organizations. These doctors are interested in trading the traditional long physician practice hours for a known financial reward and fixed quantity of work. Women are especially attracted to these systems, and are highly motivated to join organizations that may pay less but provide flexible work schedules. According to Cotter and Bonds, the most common elements offered in a benefit package designed to recruit physicians are:

- Moving expenses (80% of organizations).
- Fixed salaries or income guarantees (70%).
- Malpractice insurance (54%).
- Management services (45%).
- Loan forgiveness over time (45%).
- Quality office space (44%).
- Signing bonus (40%).
- Control over that physician's office personnel (40%).
- Computer systems and services (33%).
- Appropriate office and medical equipment (30%).
- Loan guarantees for housing (30%).
- Staff support and clinical and administrative roles (30%).
- Paid malpractice "tail" coverage (24%).
- Joint venture partnership (12%) (West, 1995).

McCullough et al. (1999), in an excellent study, found that two compensation systems compete to attract today's physician. In the first, the organization pays a fixed salary. In the second, the salary floor is set low with multiple incentive and bonus features. Incentive and bonus plans sometimes reward physicians in (inverse) proportion to the cost of the treatments and procedures they provide to patients (managed care), or peg compensation to their performance in taking care of a specified group of patients assigned to them.

The same study suggested that recruiting in the new millennium is governed by rules that are different from those of the past. Although salary remains critical in candidates' choices between acceptable organizations, it is not the primary factor in the physician's ultimate choice. The recruiting incentives most valued by physicians were, in order of significance:

- Quality of the working environment and staff support.
- Location.
- Total potential earnings.
- Flexibility of scheduling.
- Total salary (contrasted with total potential salary).
- Good retirement plans.
- Guaranteed minimum income.
- Adequate salary plus profit sharing.
- Good insurance plans (life, dental, disability, supplemental, retirement).
- Time and reimbursement for attending professional meetings.
- Straight salary (as contrasted with incentive-related compensation).
- Signing bonus.

Among female physicians overall, the quality of staff support, pleasantness of work environment, location, and scheduling flexibility were more important than salary. Women physicians were willing to accept considerably lower salaries in exchange for these benefits. They also felt that a guaranteed minimum salary was more important than performance-driven maximum compensation. There were no significant group differences between married and single physicians in incentive priorities, nor were there differences for physicians with or without children. Physicians working in health maintenance organization (HMO) settings placed a high value on life, disability, medical, dental, and malpractice insurance plans, but no other differences emerged among those affiliated with HMOs, physician hospital organizations (PHOs), and physician-run group practices. The McCullough et al. study suggested that recruiters should identify doctors likely to be attracted to the specific type of practice offered. They should be aware that females are more concerned with guaranteed minimum wages and flexible schedules than are males.

Montague (1994b) found five similar major lifestyle priorities for young physicians leaving training:

- They tend to choose positions related to specific geography. Many want to live in urban areas near their families or former training sites.
- Compensation that provides set salaries or guaranteed compensation is deemed more desirable than performance clauses or compensation that requires independent motivation.

- Less on-call time, staggered shifts, and more ability to work part-time are major recruiting factors for young physicians. This is particularly true for female doctors, who, on average, look for better working hours and more time off than their male colleagues.
- A benefit package that reflects lifestyle needs is important, including health care and life insurance benefits, but also dental insurance, malpractice insurance, travel reimbursement, retirement plans, and subsidized education for the physician and/or the physician's children.
- Young physicians look for facilities with collegiality and the opportunity to work with a well-trained staff and state-of-the-art equipment.

Physician-Run Group Practices Versus Other Administrative Structures

Administrators in physician-run group practices must realize that in order to compete with broader private- and public-sector health care systems for new physicians, they should strongly consider developing a compensation package with high potential total earnings and, at the same time, a guaranteed minimum income. Physicians who join physician-run groups tend to be motivated by salary and profit incentive plans, whereas physicians joining the public-sector and HMO-like systems (assuming they have an employment choice) tend to be fearful of such plans. HMO and public-sector administrators find recruiting female physicians advantageous, because they are less likely to be driven by profit; are more interested in stability, flexible scheduling, and management services; and are statistically more willing than many of their male counterparts to work in systems with lots of rules and restrictions. Female doctors also appear to be proportionately more motivated by loan opportunities than are males (McCullough et al., 1999).

ACKNOWLEDGMENT

The authors wish to thank Marcia J. Chapman for her able administrative assistance in preparing this chapter.

REFERENCES

Burda, D. (1994). Physician recruiting changing with the times. *Modern Healthcare, 47*(6), 49–50.

Burda, D. (1995). Legal fears force some changes in recruiting tactics. *Modern Healthcare, 25*(34), 88, 90.

Cejka, S. (1993). Recruiting women physicians requires hospitals to offer benefits, flexibility. *Modern Healthcare, 23*(8), 34.

Cotter, T. J., & Bonds, R. B. (1995, December). Structuring competitive physician compensation programs. Physician issues. *Healthcare Financial Management,* pp. 52–55.

Couvillon, J. (1999). How to select and motivate physicians in managed care. *Medical Group Management Journal, 46*(4), 50–56.

Dismuke, B. J. (1989). Maximizing physician recruitment efforts in today's competitive environment. *Medical Staff Counselor, 3*(3), 43–48.

Garofolo, F. (1984). What medical staffs need to know about recruiting physicians. *Hospital Medical Staff, 13*(9), 18–24.

Hall, R. C. W. (1994). Social and legal implications of managed care in psychiatry. *Psychosomatics, 35*(2), 150–158.

Hall, R. C. W. (1997). Ethical and legal implications of managed care. *General Hospital Psychiatry, 19,* 200–208.

Hawkins, J. (1994). A guide to physician recruitment. *Trustee, 47*(5), 22–23.

Lowes, R. (1999). Recruiting doctors who'll stay. *Medical Economics, 76*(5), 160–176.

McCullough, T., Dodge, H. R., & Moeller, S. (1999). Physician recruitment: Understanding what physicians want. *Health Marketing Quarterly, 16*(2), 55–64.

Montague, J. (1994a). What do new physicians want? *Trustee, 24*(37), 12–13.

Montague, J. (1994b, May 5). Safe and sound: Security, improved lifestyles are driving physician recruiting. *Hospitals and Health Networks,* pp. 48–50.

Pulde, M. F. (1997). Preserving the quality of physician work life. *Physician Executive, 23*(5), 40–41.

Rhodes, R. (1995). *Dark sun: The making of the hydrogen bomb.* New York: Simon & Schuster.

West, D. J. (1995, June). Strategic issues requiring public accountability: Food for thought. *Physician Executive,* p. 3.

Part Six

LEGAL ISSUES

INTRODUCTION

Stuart B. Silver

T he contemporary evolution of mental health law is rooted in the civil rights movement. A seminal event in the civil rights movement was the decision by the United States Supreme Court in *Brown v. Board of Education*. In *Brown*, the Supreme Court ruled unanimously that the equal protection clause of the 14th Amendment prohibited "separate but equal" educational facilities based on race. The civil rights movement, combined with other social changes in the 1960s, also had an impact on law schools. Legal aid societies were formed, classes in "rights" were added or increased, and at least some law students began choosing public interest law as a career. Litigation was filed on behalf of a number of groups claiming violations of constitutional rights, including prisoners, women, people with nontraditional sexual orientation, and people with mental illnesses. These lawsuits sought a variety of remedies, from improvement in institutional conditions for those who were confined to release from confinement, better conditions of care, monetary damages, and so forth. To address these issues, plaintiffs' lawyers conceptualized their claims as civil rights claims rather than medical malpractice. Instead of endorsing the view that the restrictions placed on mental patients were primarily a medical issue, these lawyers argued that they fundamentally restricted personal liberty. As a result, the review of commitment statutes was placed in a constitutional framework. The first chapter in this section reviews the transformations in practice that have resulted from these conceptual changes.

The second chapter explores the challenges for an administrator in working with an attorney. Everyone in an executive capacity will require the advice of an attorney at some point. An attorney can play a variety of roles, including but not limited to advisor, litigator, writer of contracts, reviewer of policies, and risk manager. Legal training can be very helpful to counsel in structuring discussions and assuring that the client has fully explored various options and their potential consequences before acting. The chapter also considers the question of how the client should act in working with counsel. The client, as much as the attorney, can maximize the advantages of having legal advice. The best attorney–client relationships, like most relationships, are based on trust. Examples of instances when a lawyer should always be consulted are explored. The chapter also considers the issue of finding competent counsel.

Confidentiality is a core ethical and legal principle in health care. Research suggests that people who believe that details of their health care relationships will be kept private are more likely to seek health care. As confidentiality protections diminish, the willingness of individuals to engage in help-seeking behavior may diminish as well. The third chapter of the legal section examines the issue of confidentiality and privilege. Confidentiality refers to the ethical and legal principles that protect from unauthorized disclosure material that is gathered about the client during treatment. In contrast, privilege refers to the legal rule that protects from disclosure in judicial proceedings material that is confidential but would be disclosed absent the application of a privilege. The ramifications of these legal constructs for administrators in a variety of situations form the substance of this chapter.

The best defense against malpractice litigation is good clinical and administrative practice. The significant areas of vulnerability to malpractice suits and how to manage them form the content of the fourth chapter in this section. However, in practice there are probably fewer cases brought, and certainly fewer awards granted, than many practitioners and administrators imagine. The chapter discusses the elements of malpractice, describes areas of vulnerability in mental health, and suggests ways of lessening the risk of a lawsuit in those areas. The discussion of liability in the context of managed care that ends the chapter looks at these administrative issues from a fresh perspective.

Finally, in chapter 39, Dr. Gary Miller provides a clear and accurate perspective on the effect of class-action lawsuits against state mental health and developmental disability agencies. His personal account, and his efforts to protect and encourage thousands of clinicians and other staff, each working to help severely and chronically ill and disabled persons, is unique in the mental management literature.

Chapter Thirty-Five

The Evolution
of Mental Health Law

John Petrila

M ental health law, as a discrete body of law, has its roots in the civil rights movement. A seminal event in the civil rights movement was the decision by the United States Supreme Court in *Brown v. Board of Education*. In *Brown*, the Supreme Court ruled unanimously that the equal protection clause of the 14th Amendment prohibited "separate but equal" educational facilities based on race.

This decision was important for many reasons. The most obvious was that it reified the principle that discrimination based on race, even when the discrimination was theoretically ameliorated by the provision of "equal" facilities or services, violated constitutional guarantees. In reaching its conclusion, the Court found explicitly that social sciences research then available suggested that segregation was inherently harmful to children. The notion that harm caused by state action could support a constitutional challenge to the relevant statutes led to attacks on civil commitment by patients' rights advocates. They eventually suggested that civil commitment laws should be narrowed because they resulted in state hospital confinements that were often more harmful than beneficial to the individual.

The Court's ruling in *Brown* was also important because it suggested that the federal courts would be a good forum for the adjudication of claims that individual rights had been violated. The Supreme Court historically had not always been open to rights claims. In fact, the Supreme Court at the end of the 19th century had ruled that the doctrine of "separate but equal" had sound legal footing, a ruling that created an underpinning for the Jim Crow laws present in a number of states at the time *Brown* was decided. However, the *Brown* decision was the opening chapter in what ultimately resulted in a broad judicial redefinition of constitutional rights and the role of the courts in a number of areas. By the end of the 1960s, the "Warren Court" (so titled for its Chief Judge, Earl Warren) had expanded the rights of criminal defendants and upheld the authority of Congress to legislate broadly in the field of civil rights. It had made the federal courts the preferred venue for individuals and groups challenging disparate and inappropriate treatment.

The civil rights movement, combined with other social changes in the 1960s, also had an impact on law schools. Legal aid societies were formed, classes in "rights" were added or increased, and at least some law students began choosing public interest law as a career. Litigation was filed on behalf of a number of groups claiming violations of constitutional rights: These included prisoners, women, people with nontraditional sexual orientation, and people with mental illnesses. These lawsuits sought a variety of remedies, from improvement in institutional conditions for those who were confined to release from confinement, better conditions of care, monetary damages, and so on.

CORE ISSUES IN THE CONSTITUTIONAL ERA

Plaintiffs' lawyers confronted a mental health system in which many people with serious mental illness were treated in state psychiatric facilities, often confined there under broadly written civil commitment statutes. Most civil commitment statutes explicitly adopted a medical model, permitting a single physician to certify that a person had a mental illness. This often resulted in confinement of indefinite length. Although court review was available at some point in the process, such hearings were generally cursory and courts routinely adopted the findings of the examining physician. In addition, conditions in the state hospitals to which most people were committed were often horrendous.

To address these issues, plaintiffs' lawyers conceptualized their claims as civil rights claims rather than medical malpractice. Instead of endorsing the view that civil commitment was primarily a medical issue, these lawyers argued that it fundamentally was a matter of personal liberty. This placed review of commitment statutes in a constitutional framework. The U.S. Constitution prohibits the denial of liberty without "due process of law," and if civil commitment was a matter of liberty more than medicine, then the constitutional framework that had developed to give people "due process" became relevant. Once that framework became available, medical decision making as the primary vehicle for civil commitment became suspect, because to most judges and lawyers "due process" requires judicial hearings, a higher standard of proof, and the right to counsel and other procedural elements most commonly associated with criminal law.

The challenge to state civil commitment laws also rested on a strong challenge to clinical decision making. Diagnostic nomenclature was relatively less clearly defined than it is today, and mental health professionals were considered unable to predict dangerousness with any degree of accuracy. Because commitment rested primarily on evidence produced by mental health professionals (principally psychiatrists in the 1960s and 1970s), discrediting of the basis of that evidence also suggested to mental health lawyers the need for judicial hearings rather than medical certification. In addition, if a mental health professional was unable to accurately predict dangerousness, then something more was required as a basis for confinement. This gave rise to the demand that commitment laws be based on behavior (often called an "overt act") in order to minimize the possibility that someone would be confined simply because of a speculative opinion about their possible future dangerousness.

Federal courts almost without exception accepted these arguments. As a result, by the end of the 1970s, a medical model of commitment largely had been abandoned by state legislatures, replaced by judicial hearings. There were exceptions to the principle that a court must make a commitment decision. For example, all states allow some period of emergency confinement without prior judicial authorization. However, in general, judicial decision making became the norm. The process was changed in other ways. The person subject to the hearing was provided with counsel, the right to present evidence, the right to cross-examine adverse witnesses, and a right to jury trial. In addition, the standard of proof was required to be "clear and convincing evidence," the intermediate standard of proof, rather than preponderance of evidence, the lowest.

The other two core issues in mental disability law at its inception were the right to treatment and the right to refuse treatment, both based on constitutional principles. The *right to treatment* was grounded initially on what advocates labeled the "quid pro quo" theory. The argument was that if the state involuntarily confined someone, it was obligated at a minimum to provide treatment and to minimize the time of involuntary confinement. This theory was never endorsed by the U.S. Supreme Court, and then–Chief Justice Warren Burger went out of his way to note that historically a government could involuntarily confine someone for a number of reasons other than treatment.

Although the Supreme Court never endorsed a "right to treatment," other federal courts were very receptive to lawsuits seeking improvements in the conditions of state hospitals. The seminal case of *Wyatt v. Stickney* set the pattern. In 1971 a federal district judge set explicit conditions for the operation of state facilities in Alabama, in a detailed order that set staffing standards, physical plant standards, safety standards, and other rules governing institutional conditions. By the mid-1980s, many state facilities for people with mental illness and people with developmental disabilities were under federal court order. Some of the litigation was collusive, in the sense that state executive officials viewed the litigation as an opportunity to gain funding increases for facilities that were in many cases poorly staffed, in deteriorating condition physically, overcrowded and unsafe.

The *right to refuse treatment* was based on the constitutional principle of liberty that informed much of the litigation challenging state civil commitment laws. The controversy in this area was almost exclusively about the use of antipsychotic medication. Advocates successfully characterized medications available in the 1970s and 1980s as likely to do more harm than good. Judicial opinions finding that people who had been involuntarily civilly committed had a constitutional right to refuse medication in most situations are replete with references to tardive dyskinesia and other side effects that often developed with people who had been medicated. In general, courts (and eventually legislatures) decoupled civil commitment and incompetency. Historically, people who had been involuntarily committed were presumptively viewed as incompetent to make a variety of decisions, including treatment decisions, as well. One of the effects of the mental health law movement was to separate the two issues conceptually. As a result, people with mental illness, including those subject to involuntary confinement, were viewed as competent to refuse treatment (typically the administration of psychotropic medication) unless presenting an emergency situation (typically defined as an immediate risk to self or others that could only be addressed by medication) or until found to be incompetent.

The question of who could determine that a person was incompetent for the purpose of refusing treatment was one that split the courts. Some courts ruled that a judge had to make the decision, because the adjudication of incompetence was fundamentally a legal decision. Other courts ruled that an administrative proceeding could be used to make the decision. As time evolved, state courts tended to find that judicial decision making was necessary, whereas the federal courts often found that administrative decision making would suffice.

Although medication was the primary focus of this debate, other types of treatment became regulated as well. Two specific examples were the use of electroconvulsive therapy (ECT) and aversive treatments. Electroconvulsive therapy was regulated because of its perceived dangers, a perception fueled by the movie *One Flew Over the Cuckoo's Nest*. Aversive treatments—for example, the use of substances that would cause a patient to vomit in an effort to control behavior—were barred in most instances because of their perceived inhumanity and lack of connection to treatment. Over time, a regulatory structure also emerged for the use of restraint and seclusion.

In short, by the end of the 1970s, a conceptual framework, based on the constitutional principles of liberty and due process, had emerged and was being widely used by the federal courts in particular to articulate rights for people with mental illness. The major focus was on the public mental health system and the state inpatient institutions in particular. The cause of advocates for people with mental illness was aided by the substandard care often provided people in state facilities, as well as documented problems with the medications that were in many instances the most available treatment. However, the U.S. Supreme Court had taken a more conservative approach to mental disability law questions than had many of the lower federal courts, and the Supreme Court gradually placed significant limits on the doctrines just discussed.

SUPREME COURT RETRENCHMENT

The U.S. Supreme Court decided a number of cases involving mental disability law in the 1970s and 1980s. Ironically, the Supreme Court to some degree had invited the creation of the mental disability law movement in its seminal ruling in *Jackson v. Indiana*. In *Jackson*, decided in 1972, the Court placed limits on the confinement of criminal defendants found incompetent to stand trial by requiring that at some point such defendants be confined, if at all, under a state civil commitment statute. This would enable the person to challenge the commitment, in contrast to the permanent confinement to which defendants found incompetent had generally been subject. In writing for the Court, Justice Blackmun observed that "considering the number of persons affected [by civil commitment] it is perhaps remarkable that the substantive constitutional limitations on this power have not been more frequently litigated." Blackmun went on to note that "at the least, due process requires that the nature and duration of commitment bear some reasonable relation to the purpose for which the individual is committed."

Once Blackmun's invitation was accepted, however, the Court turned out to be more conservative than some had anticipated. In 1975, in *O'Connor v. Donaldson*, the Court was presented with a lower court ruling that the Constitution created a right to treatment (based on the "quid pro quo" theory noted earlier). The case involved the long-term confinement of an individual in a Florida state hospital simply on the ground that he had a mental illness. During the person's confinement he had received little or no treatment. The Supreme Court decided to not rule on the question of whether the Constitution created a right to treatment. The Court instead found that "a State cannot constitutionally confine without more a non-dangerous individual who is capable of surviving safely in freedom by himself or with the help of willing and responsible family members or friends." Justice Burger, in a long concurring opinion, argued that it was unclear that the Constitution permitted confinement of a person with a mental illness only for the purpose of providing treatment.

This early opinion had two effects. First, the language from the majority opinion just noted led a number of observers to conclude that the Court in fact had limited the state's civil commitment authority. The eventual result was the adoption of "grave disability" statutes that permitted the commitment of people who were unable to care for themselves with or without the help of others; the Court's ruling also seemed to make it clear that mental illness alone was an insufficient predicate for commitment. Second, Justice Burger's concurrence sparked a debate that is active today, that is, whether treatment, and to what end, is a necessary condition of involuntary confinement.

In 1979, the Court, this time with Chief Justice Burger writing the majority opinion, ruled in *Parham v. J.L. and J.R.* that a child could be admitted to a state hospital by his or her custodian without a judicial hearing. The plaintiff had argued that under the principles governing state civil commitment hearings, a judge should have to make such a decision when it involved a child. However, the Court, noting the long legal tradition of parental control of medical decision making involving children, found it reasonable to assume that the parent would act in the child's best interest in cases of psychiatric hospitalization. The Court also noted that in its view due process "has never been thought to require that the neutral and detached trier of fact be law-trained or a judicial or administrative officer. Surely, this is the case as to medical decisions for 'neither judges nor administrative hearing officers are better qualified than psychiatrists to render psychiatric judgments.'" Therefore, a staff physician could decide on the appropriateness of hospitalization, as long as the physician could make an independent judgment.

Parham revealed a Court majority willing to retreat from the principle that had been advanced in the lower federal courts that judicial decision making was presumptively required in civil commitment cases. Although *Parham* is grounded in large measure on presumptions about the manner in which parents make decisions regarding their children, the Court's willingness to characterize the decision at stake as medical rather than legal ran contrary to the conceptual anchor of the civil commitment litigation that preceded it—that is, that commitment was first a deprivation of legally protected liberty.

The Court also in 1979, again under Chief Justice Burger's leadership, undercut another core tenet of the mental health law movement in its decision in *Addington v. Texas.* In this case, a lower court had ruled that because civil commitment had consequences for the individual that were as detrimental for the individual as being convicted of a crime, a state was constitutionally required to prove that a person met civil commitment standards by the "beyond a reasonable doubt" standard used in criminal cases. The Supreme Court ruled that this standard was not required, and that the intermediate standard of "clear and convincing" evidence would suffice. As important, the Court rejected the analogy between civil commitment and the criminal law, noting that "in a civil commitment state power is not exercised in a punitive sense." The Court also turned the attacks on psychiatric decision making that had fueled challenges to civil commitment on their head: Rather than warranting stricter processes for civil commitment proceedings, Chief Justice Burger concluded that the "subjective analysis" that was at the heart of psychiatry could not meet the standards used in criminal law. In his view, the resulting reduction in the use of commitment would result in "'freedom' for a mentally ill person . . . purchased at a high price."

Finally, in 1982, in its decision in *Youngberg v. Romeo*, the Supreme Court signaled clearly that the constitutional era of mental disability law had reached its limits conceptually. The case arose from the care of an individual who was profoundly retarded in a Pennsylvania facility for people with developmental disabilities. The plaintiff argued that he had a constitutional liberty interest in safety, freedom of movement, and training within the institution. The Court agreed, as it had earlier, that people who are involuntarily confined retained a right to safety and a right to be free from unwarranted bodily restraint.

The Court characterized as "more troubling" the claim to a constitutional right to minimally adequate habilitation. The Court did agree that a person had a right to the "training" necessary to ensure safety and freedom from undue restraint. At the same time, in determining what was reasonable in implementing this right, the Court said:

> We emphasize that courts must show deference to the judgment exercised by a qualified professional. By so limiting judicial review of challenges to conditions in state institutions, interference by the federal judiciary with the internal operations of these institutions should be minimized. Moreover, there certainly is no reason to think judges or juries are better qualified than appropriate professionals in making such decisions. For these reasons, the decision, if made by a professional, is presumptively valid; liability may be imposed only when the decision by the professional is such a substantial departure from accepted professional judgment, practice, or standards as to demonstrate that the person responsible actually did not base the decision on such a judgment . . . decisions made by the appropriate professional are entitled to a presumption of correctness. Such a presumption is necessary to enable institutions of this type—often, unfortunately, overcrowded and understaffed—to continue to function.

The *Youngberg* decision marks a turning point in mental disability law in its constitutional phase. The Supreme Court, although recognizing that people in institutions had certain rights, also made clear that the federal courts had to limit the exercise of their authority over such institutions, and that certain conditions—for example, overcrowding—although undesirable, were part of the public mental health system. The principle that the courts were to defer to the professional judgment of state administrative and clinical staff became one of the most important principles of the next phase of mental health law, a phase that saw a diminution of the importance of constitutional litigation and the emergence of a number of issues that reflected changes in the public mental health system.

THE POST-CONSTITUTIONAL ERA

The federal courts continued to hear litigation regarding conditions in state facilities in the 1980s and even into the 1990s. In part, this was the result of litigation brought by the U.S. Department of Justice (DOJ) under the Civil Rights for Institutionalized Persons Act (CRIPA), providing DOJ with independent authority to act on behalf of people confined in state institutions. The Justice Department brought a number of lawsuits against states after enactment of the statute. In part, there was continuing litigation over the implementation of consent decrees (agreed-on settlements) that many states had entered into rather than go through litigation.

At the same time, the limits of constitutional litigation manifested themselves in a number of significant ways. First, the Supreme Court's admonition to defer to the professional judgment of state officials began to have an impact on the way in which federal courts approached institutional litigation. Second, such litigation did not result in the creation of a right to *community* treatment; most courts were unwilling to rule that the federal Constitution created rights beyond the walls of the state institution. Although there were modest exceptions to this, in general the Constitution tended to end at the gate of the institution. This was important because the downsizing of state hospitals continued in the 1980s (as it continues to some degree today), so many people with serious mental illness spent little time in state hospitals. Instead, community stays punctuated with sometimes frequent acute hospital admissions became the rule. Furthermore, because of changes in federal financing of the Medicaid program, even those admissions increasingly occurred in community-based hospitals rather than state hospitals.

Because many people with mental illness were in the community (whether they were receiving adequate treatment or not was a separate question), and because the courts had refused generally to extend constitutional protections to community care issues, advocates had to rely on different theories. In particular, the 1980s were dominated by continuing debate over civil commitment (this time, however, outpatient commitment came to the fore) and litigation over access to community-based care based on state statutory rather than federal constitutional law claims.

LITIGATION OVER ACCESS TO COMMUNITY CARE

One of the core policy issues in the 1980s was the emergence of homelessness. The number of people who were homeless, their characteristics, and the causes for homelessness were all subject to great debate. One argument posited that the deinstitutionalization of state hospitals, unaccompanied by adequate community resources, had resulted in large numbers of homeless persons with mental illness. Proposed solutions included broadening civil commitment criteria and creating a legal right of access to community care, including housing. Another theory assumed that the primary cause of homelessness was a lack of affordable housing, and that tax policies tilted toward the redevelopment of lower-income housing stock had resulted in the depletion of the supply of such housing.

Litigation resulted in a number of places, most prominently New York City. The litigation argued that the state mental health discharge statute created a right to housing as part of discharge from a psychiatric hospital. In Arizona, plaintiffs argued that approximately 4,000 individuals with mental illness in Maricopa County had a right to a community care system, including adequate treatment, social supports, and residences. This case was based on the Arizona mental health statute. In both cases, courts created rights for plaintiffs based on state law: In New York, a state court agreed that individuals discharged from either a state or city hospital had a right to an adequate residence and prohibited discharges to homeless shelters. In Arizona, the state Supreme Court ruled that the Arizona mental health statute created a duty on the part of the state to create a community care system for the plaintiffs.

These cases were important, but ultimately had a comparatively limited effect nationally. They were important in part because state courts decided them. This reflected a larger trend by litigants to pursue claims of rights violations in state rather than federal court, because of the increasingly conservative reading given the federal Constitution by those courts. Also, state laws had become rather more specific in language setting forth the rights of people with mental illness. However, such litigation was infrequently brought. One might speculate that this was in part because the publicly funded lawyers that represented people with mental illness (the civil rights division of the Department of Justice; the protection and advocacy offices) had missions that by statute focused on institutions. Therefore, simply finding counsel willing to pursue complex community-based claims was often difficult. In addition, many state courts are reticent to impose large financial obligations on state or local government, for a variety of reasons. This may have also played a role in the comparative paucity of such litigation.

THE CONTINUING DEBATE OVER CIVIL COMMITMENT

The debate regarding civil commitment has continued through the 1980s and today, but its tenor has changed somewhat. Much of the debate has focused on whether and how to expand the reach of commitment laws. There are three issues that have been most debated.

The first is the *broadening of criteria* for inpatient commitment. States have added criteria permitting commitment on the ground that someone is gravely disabled (i.e., unable to meet basic needs), and lately some states have added a criterion permitting commitment if the person is found likely to deteriorate in the absence of treatment.

The second has been a continuing debate regarding *outpatient commitment*. A number of states have moved to permit the commitment of an individual to outpatient treatment. Although the criteria and processes for doing so vary, the theory (to date not completely substantiated) is that ordering such treatment will improve the individual's prospects for continued community tenure.

The third has been debate regarding the *commitment of special groups*. The prime example is the adoption by some states of violent sexual predator statutes. Such laws permit the indefinite confinement in an inpatient psychiatric unit of an individual found to present a continuing risk of sexual offending upon the end of a prison term. These statutes have been controversial, though the U.S. Supreme Court upheld their constitutionality in 1997.

EMERGENCE OF HEALTH LAW ISSUES IN MENTAL HEALTH LAW

Another trend in the 1980s and 1990s that affected mental health law was the emergence of managed care. As states turned to managed care in their Medicaid programs, and as employers turned to managed care to administer private health insurance plans, mental health and substance-abuse benefits provided a ready target. A general assumption in both publicly and privately financed plans was that expenditures for behavioral health (the common term that emerged to describe mental health and substance abuse) had increased much too rapidly and that the rate of inflation needed to be controlled. The strategies adopted to achieve this (gatekeeping, preferred providers, capitated payment schemes, prospective approval for services) were controversial, and led to court challenges as well as calls for legislative reform.

However, both litigation and legislation had their limitations in this context. Litigation on behalf of Medicaid enrollees (and in some cases Medicare enrollees) tended to focus on procedural issues—for example, the creation of grievance processes to handle complaints from plan enrollees. However, the benefit that was available to plan enrollees was generally beyond the reach of litigation, because Medicaid and Medicare are fundamentally the products of legislation and administrative regulation, and the courts generally will not superimpose their own ideas of what should be available under the program. Some courts in the 1990s have concluded that states have an obligation to make benefits available with "reasonable promptness" once it is decided that a person enrolled in Medicaid requires a particular benefit, but at the time of writing another federal district court had ruled that the states could not be sued by Medicaid beneficiaries, a ruling that if upheld will dramatically reduce litigation on behalf of Medicaid recipients.

In the private sector, litigation designed to create additional benefits for individuals with mental illness was also generally unsuccessful. First, the authority to design benefits within an employer-sponsored health care plan, including mental health benefits, rests almost exclusively with the employer. The supposition is that because most health insurance is purchased through employer-sponsored plans, labor negotiations are the best place in which such discussions should occur. In addition, the Employee Retirement Income Security Act (ERISA), enacted in 1974 to create a uniform standard nationally for qualifying plans, has been interpreted to give the courts virtually no authority to intervene in a dispute about the benefits available under a plan.

Second, some litigants argued that the Americans with Disabilities Act (ADA) required equity in the benefits made available to cover mental health services with those made available to cover physical ailments. The courts have rejected this position repeatedly, and at this point the ADA appears to be an unlikely tool for redressing differences in benefits between mental health and physical health benefits.

The inability to achieve benefit reform in the courts has led to legislative efforts to achieve parity in benefits. This has become a rallying cry for advocacy groups, particularly the National Alliance for the Mentally Ill. As a result, a number of states have enacted legislation requiring parity. Congress has also enacted limited parity legislation at the federal level, although not without controversy.

Parity legislation itself does not lead automatically to increased expenditures on mental health. In fact, the most important question in health care in the last decade has been the manner in which benefits are managed: Even the most generous benefit on paper may provide little in the way of services if the benefit is managed aggressively to control costs. As a result, Congress and state legislatures have attempted to provide a variety of legislative protections to people enrolled in private health plans (an effort that has some corollary in publicly financed plans such as

Medicaid and Medicare). Such efforts have resulted in statutes providing for liability of managed care plans in some states in state court; various patient rights protections, including various grievance procedures; and some efforts to expand the availability to providers of slots in managed care plans.

MENTAL HEALTH LAW IN THE 21ST CENTURY

Mental health law is interrelated with the service system—when most people with serious mental illness were treated in state facilities, advocates necessarily focused their attention there. Because the state was custodian and deprived people of their liberty, the federal Constitution was implicated, so the first era of mental health law had its roots in the civil rights movement. As the use of state hospitals declined, and most people with mental illness spent most of their time in other settings, other types of law were implicated. The Constitution did not reach community-based care. Therefore, as the issue became one of access to services, other legal provisions—for example, state statutes and Medicaid law—assumed more importance. In the future, one may anticipate that much mental health law will exist as a part of general health care law. The same legal issues that exist in general health law will apply to mental health systems, with the primary difference not one of legality but of defining characteristics of the population at issue.

At the same time, a number of issues that dominated mental health law in its original era continue to resonate today, primarily because of the continuing use of coercion. For example, civil commitment continues to be debated, as noted earlier. At the same time, a perspective is emerging that coercion and perceived coercion must be viewed in a broader context: Work is developing that will consider the potentially coercive effects not only of civil commitment, but of other vehicles commonly used in providing treatment in the community—for example, the rules governing housing for people with mental illness, the use of representative payee status to control the use of money, and specialty courts designed to divert people from the criminal justice system into treatment. This more expansive focus also considers whether coercion can be minimized through maximizing client choice, for example, through the use of advance directives. Finally, alternatives to judicial or medical decision making such as mediation are being considered in the context of treatment as well.

Discrimination also continues to be a core legal issue. As mental health law was developing, there was much discussion about the issue of stigma and its effect on people with a mental illness. Although stigma continues to be discussed today, its manifestation as discrimination presents a more important issue for many people with mental illness. The Americans with Disabilities Act (ADA) and the Fair Housing Amendments Act of 1988 represent congressional efforts to address the problem of discrimination. The ADA in particular has been a useful tool in addressing some types of discrimination, for example, in the workplace (although mental illness claims in general are less successful than physical disability claims).

The question of risk to others continues to be of concern as well, as a legal and clinical issue. There have been significant advances in knowledge regarding the clinical assessment of risk since the early days of the mental health law movement. At the same time, people who may present a risk to others are no longer primarily treated in state psychiatric facilities. This means that many treatment agencies may treat individuals with some history of violent or threatening behavior to others. In addition, the issue of risk continues to drive much of the debate regarding the use of civil commitment as well. For example, it is the perception that people convicted of sexual offenses are likely to recidivate that underlies the enactment of violent sexual predator statutes.

Another issue that will continue to be of interest is what happens to individuals with mental illnesses who are brought into the criminal justice system. The prevalence rate for mental illness and substance abuse among arrested and incarcerated populations runs as high as 60% in the adult system and 80% in the juvenile system. One of the most interesting developments in the 1990s was the development of drug courts, special-jurisdiction courts designed to divert people charged with comparatively low-level substance abuse felonies into treatment. Spurred by reports that such courts had been successful in reducing recidivism and in obtaining treatment for defendants, some jurisdictions have developed mental health courts as well. These courts typically accept nonviolent misdemeanor cases when the defendant has or may have a mental illness. The court is designed to divert people into treatment. Although it is too early to judge the success of such courts, their development reflects an interest on the part of the criminal justice system in stemming the flow of people with mental illness into the criminal justice system. There have been other developments designed to accomplish the same goal, for example, providing specialized training for police officers.

Finally, that part of mental health law that concerns itself with general health law questions will continue to thrive as well. Questions of confidentiality, informed consent, the rights of patients relative to payers, and the regulatory structures that emerge to govern the provision and payment of all affect the general health system, but that also apply to people being treated for mental illness.

CASES CITED

Addington v. Texas, 441 US 418, 99 S.Ct. 1804 (1979).
Brown v. Board of Education, 347 US 483 (1954).
Jackson v. Indiana, 406 US 715, 729 (1972).
O'Connor v. Donaldson, 422 US 563, 93 S.Ct. 2486 (1975).
Parham v. J.L. and J.R., 99 S.Ct. 2493 (1979).
Wyatt v. Stickney, 325 F.Supp. 781 (M.D. Ala. 1971).
Youngberg v. Romeo, 457 US 307 (1982).

Chapter Thirty-Six

Working with an Attorney

John Petrila

WHAT DOES AN ATTORNEY DO?

An administrator invariably will require the advice of an attorney at some point. An attorney can play a variety of roles, including but not limited to advisor, litigator, writer of contracts, reviewer of policies, and risk manager. Some, although not many, lawyers are comfortable in each of these roles. Most, however, because of training, experience, or temperament, prefer some of these roles to others. In addition, it is difficult as a practical matter to play each of these roles: An in-house counsel who advises management and treatment staff on day-to-day issues will be unlikely to have the time to handle a complex piece of litigation.

The best lawyers first seek to ascertain what the client wishes to do. Effective attorneys often can assist their clients in defining clear and reasonable goals of action. Acting as "counsel" should include participating in discussions that are less about "the law" and more about understanding what the client wishes as well as the consequences of a particular course of action. For example, if the organization is exploring purchasing a private practice, the attorney for the organization obviously will have to make sure that the purchase is in accordance with tax laws, that the contract for the purchase is negotiated in a way that is clear and accomplishes the organization's agenda, and that any other state or federal regulatory requirements are met. However, an attorney can also help in framing the discussion before contract negotiations are begun. Legal training can be very helpful to counsel in structuring discussions and assuring that the client has fully explored various options and their potential consequences before acting.

HOW SHOULD AN ATTORNEY ACT?

In providing "counsel" an attorney's first response to a question from a client should not be "you can't do that" (unless of course the action the client wishes to take is prohibited by law). In most situations, an administrator or clinician has a great deal of discretion in deciding what to do and how to do it. As discussed in the section on negligence and malpractice, the legal standard for assessing a defendant's actions is whether the defendant exercised professional judgment and acted in accordance with accepted professional norms. The exercise of professional judgment necessarily implies the use of discretion. There is seldom a single way to do something, just as comparatively few actions are outlawed. Of course, there are exceptions. A clinician who routinely prescribes medications far in excess of the guidelines articulated in the *Physicians' Desk Reference* or the pharmaceutical inserts is creating a serious legal issue unless all of his or her patients meet the criteria for an exception. Similarly, an administrator who wishes to create a physician reimbursement package that clearly contravenes IRS guidelines invites legal trouble. However, most of the time an administrator or clinician has discretion, and an attorney whose instinctive first response is to say "no" is usually not the right attorney for a health or mental health care organization.

An attorney should also be courteous, and keep his or her ego in check. As noted later, attorneys increasingly have been exposed to health care if not mental health care law, so substantive knowledge may be easier to find than it was in the past. However, it is important for the attorney to present well externally (because he or she may be representing the organization externally, for example, in contract negotiations) as well as internally (because those running the organization, as well as clinical staff, will need to rely on the attorney's judgment in their own work).

The attorney's temperament should also be a good match for his or her principal organizational clients. An attorney, if used properly, will be called on in most of the difficult decisions that the organization must make, whether clinical or administrative. As with any other core advisor, personal comfort is an important attribute in such decision making.

At the same time, the attorney must be an individual who can say "no." The attorney, at times, must tell a strong-willed administrator or clinician clearly (although respectfully) that what is being proposed is simply untenable legally. It is important for the attorney to be clear that his or her advice with reference to a proposed course of action is based on legal grounds. An attorney's disagreement with a proposed course of action should not be masked as legal advice if the disagreement is based on other grounds. It is as important for the client to listen carefully if the attorney advises that a particular course of action is legally problematic or prohibited.

HOW SHOULD THE CLIENT ACT?

The client, as much as the attorney, can maximize the advantages of having legal advice. Some administrators and clinicians do not know or have never learned how to use an attorney. They might call after the fact and then advise the attorney that "we sent those records over to the newspaper, and thought you'd want to know in case there is trouble over it." Or they might simply neglect to tell the attorney anything. The attorney learns about the action only after it has resulted in a threatened lawsuit, a contract has not worked out, or one of the myriad problems that can arise in the course of organizational life has emerged.

The best attorney–client relationships, like most relationships, are based on trust. Ideally, the client will involve the attorney from the beginning of difficult decisions. This is not because the lawyer is going to make those decisions. However, as noted earlier, a good lawyer can help structure conversations so that the risks and benefits of various courses of action are explored. Being involved from the beginning also helps the attorney anticipate legal problems that a proposed action might present, as well as better handle legal issues if they do develop later.

The client should also never hesitate to ask the lawyer to explain his or her reasoning. Lawyers are used to asking clients "why?" Some lawyers may be less comfortable answering the same question, but it is important for the client to know why his or her lawyer has reached a particular conclusion. If the lawyer's advice is that the law prohibits a particular action, it is entirely reasonable for the client to ask the lawyer to reveal the section of law that creates the prohibition. It is important as a client to not permit "the law" to remain an entirely mysterious realm where one cannot reasonably go. It is exceedingly useful to have a guide when entering that realm. However, a guide whose advice is essentially "you'll have to trust me because it's simply too complex for those without my training" is not generally the best guide available.

A client can also strengthen the attorney–client relationship by offering to explain the operation to the lawyer outside the context of a formal consultation. Some lawyers (a minority) are quite knowledgeable about health and mental health care and understand clearly organizational and clinical issues. Most do not. Offering to enable the lawyer to gain more information about the client's work informally may greatly benefit the relationship by making the client's work less abstract to the attorney.

WHEN IS LEGAL ADVICE ESSENTIAL?

There are certain types of issues in which a lawyer should always be consulted. Examples include the following:

- *When a lawsuit is brought or threatened.* When a lawsuit is filed, a response must be prepared, filing deadlines must be met, and an organizational strategy for dealing with the litigation must be prepared. Obviously, in such situations, a lawyer must be involved from the beginning. Similarly, a lawyer should be consulted if a lawsuit is threatened. A lawsuit may or may not materialize from a threat but the lawyer should be advised. It is also possible that steps may be taken to address the issue that gave rise to the threat, even if litigation does not ensue.
- *When a subpoena or court order is issued* for records or for a staff member to appear in a legal proceeding. Medical records personnel may acquire great skill in responding appropriately to routine requests for information. However, when a court orders production of records or personnel, a lawyer should be consulted to determine the appropriate response. An organization may also wish to consult a lawyer when a lawyer's subpoena is received, unless the medical records office is competent to handle such subpoenas without legal advice. Preferably, the organization's lawyer will determine whether the office has the appropriate competence.
- *When contracts are being negotiated and written.* Some organizations do not involve lawyers in the negotiation and preparation of contracts. In general, this is a mistake in all but the most routine circumstances. It is important for the lawyer to be involved before the contract is written, as the contract itself simply memorializes any agreements that have been reached. Contracts have to be drafted carefully; however, involving the lawyer in discussions and negotiation before the

contract is written should help assure that the contract captures the intent of the client and the agreement that has been reached. In addition, new federal laws governing Medicare and Medicaid prohibit referrals for services in which the provider has a financial interest (Stark I and Stark II—named for their sponsor, Representative Peter Stark (Democrat–California). Almost all medical service contracts will require analysis with a view towards whether they violate these new rules, which are to this date being reinterpreted by regulations (Social Security Act, Title 18; Federal Register).

- *When complex transactions are proposed.* Health care and mental health care have been marked in the last two decades by the emergence of for-profit companies, the increased horizontal and vertical integration of providers through acquisitions and mergers, the formation of large physician groups, and increased competition among providers. The involvement of a lawyer is essential not only in deciding to engage in such transactions and in the negotiation and preparation of contracts, but in assuring that other legal rules, for example, antitrust principles, are not violated. For example, a group of community mental health providers may wish to set a minimum price for its services when negotiating with an insurer; such discussions may violate antitrust rules prohibiting price fixing. Having competent legal advice is critical in such circumstances, before they progress too far.
- *In advising staff on the rights of patients and employees.* The legal landscape has gotten more complex in recent years. Patients have more rights and health care organizations have more legal obligations, not only to patients but to employees (e.g., those rights created by the Americans with Disabilities Act). A lawyer should be consulted to assure that organizational policies comply with applicable law in the various roles (caregiver, employer) that the organization plays.

WHERE CAN A COMPETENT LAWYER BE FOUND?

Mental health law as a discrete body of law is only three decades old. It is only in the last 20 years that many law schools have offered even a single course in mental health law; it continues to be seen in most schools as a boutique course. Health care law emerged in the 1990s as an important mainstream specialty area of law, but law schools have also lagged behind the market in preparing law students to practice in this area. However, there are certainly more lawyers today who know at least something about mental health law and health law than was the case even a decade ago.

A lawyer ideally will have at least some acquaintance either with mental health or health care law. How important this is will vary depending on the role of the lawyer: If advice is primarily going to be given to clinicians, then a knowledge of mental health law and some knowledge of mental illness may be very important. However, if the lawyer is going to perform primarily corporate law—for example, negotiating complex transactions—then knowledge of contract law, corporate law, and tax law may be more important.

As with most professions, word of mouth is often an important factor in finding a good lawyer. The Yellow Pages in most cities list lawyers by specialty; a law firm advertising itself as specializing in health law may or may not have a good reputation among a city's health care providers. Individual lawyers within a particular firm may also have quite different reputations. One factor to be considered in retaining a lawyer is how experienced the person is. For a complex contract, a client ordinarily would not want a junior associate (lawyers who have not yet made partner are usually referred to as associates) but may want a partner. In other situations, an associate may do the bulk of the work but the client may reasonably ask whether a partner reviews the associate's work and whether a partner is available for consultation as appropriate.

If a lawyer is to be hired as "in-house" counsel (i.e., be employed by the organization, generally on a full-time basis), the type of lawyer most appropriate for the organization will depend on the work that the organization would like the lawyer to do as well as prevailing market conditions. If the organization is hiring a lawyer for the first time, asking local law firms about salary schedules, or asking the placement office of a law school, if one is nearby, may assist in establishing a salary range for the position. A lawyer who will be joining the organization in a senior position, and who will be involved in the most important organizational decisions, will usually be more senior and command a higher salary than a lawyer hired to advise clinical staff on patient care decisions that have legal ramifications. This is not to suggest that the latter is less important than the former, but only that salaries for in-house counsel have often been skewed in that direction.

HOW MUCH WILL IT COST?

Lawyer salaries and fees vary around the country. Although lawyers are prohibited from fixing prices, fees and salaries generally fall within a particular range in each location. One decision an organization will have to make is whether its work can be accomplished by an in-house counsel rather than by retaining a law firm on an as-needed basis. Given that the hourly fees of partners in well-known firms may range from $200 (in comparatively small markets) to three and four times that in the biggest markets, an organization may decide that it is more cost-effective to hire a lawyer on salary. However, even if a lawyer is hired on salary, certain types of work, for example, litigation, may be contracted out.

One can also anticipate paying associates, who are less experienced, less than partners. If negotiating a retainer with a law firm, it is important to know whether associates or partners will be performing the work, and at what rate the work will be billed.

It may be that the organization does not have enough legal work to warrant hiring a lawyer on salary, and that it also finds it unnecessary to retain a firm on a regular basis. In such a case, it is useful to identify for contingency purposes one or more lawyers who can provide advice to the organization if required, so that such a decision does not have to be made in the middle of a crisis.

REFERENCES

Federal Register No. 166, No. 232., pp. 60154–60156. December 3, 2001 Rules and Regulations.
U.S. Code, Social Security Act, Title 18, Section 1877 ("Stark I, Stark II").

Chapter Thirty-Seven

Confidentiality and Privilege

John Petrila

C onfidentiality is a core ethical and legal principle in health care. Research suggests that people who believe that their health care relationship will be kept private are more likely to seek health care. As confidentiality protections diminish, the willingness of individuals to engage in help-seeking behavior may diminish as well.

The U.S. Supreme Court emphasized the importance of confidentiality in mental health treatment in a 1996 decision creating a psychotherapeutic privilege in federal court. The Court wrote that "Effective psychotherapy depends upon an atmosphere of confidence and trust in which the patient is willing to make a frank and complete disclosure of facts, emotions, memories, and fears. Because of the sensitive nature of the problems for which individuals consult psychotherapists, disclosure of confidential communications made during counseling sessions may cause embarrassment or disgrace. For this reason, the mere possibility of disclosure may impede development of the confidential relationship necessary for successful treatment" (*Jaffe v. Redmond*, 1996).

Confidentiality, however, is not absolute. As this chapter discusses, there are many exceptions to confidentiality. Some depend on the consent of the client; others do not. Confidentiality in mental health and substance abuse is a mixture of state and federal law, with the former governing the confidentiality of mental health information while the latter controls the confidentiality of substance and alcohol abuse information. This split in law sometimes complicates the application of confidentiality principles. In addition, many state laws were enacted before the emergence of managed care, interprovider networks, and the increased demands for information from health care payers. This means that confidentiality statutes may not reliably address questions that arise in practice.

Confidentiality as used in this section refers to the ethical and legal principles that protect from unauthorized disclosure material that is gathered about the client during treatment. The chapter also discusses privilege. In this context, privilege refers to the legal rule that protects from disclosure in judicial proceedings material that is confidential but would be disclosed absent the application of a privilege. For example, if a court issues an order requiring the production in a court proceeding of a mental health record, the court order may constitute an exception to the general legal rule protecting the confidentiality of that record. However, a party may assert, even in the face of the court order, that the material is "privileged" and should not be disclosed in court. This topic is discussed in more detail later.

Finally, the federal government, at the time of writing, has proposed regulations that would create federal rules protecting the confidentiality of health care information. Those rules would not replace state laws that provide more protection for confidentiality than the federal regulations; however, the federal regulations would create the standard where state law either does not address a particular topic or provides less protection than the federal rule. These proposed regulations are discussed briefly as well.

CONFIDENTIALITY AS AN ETHICAL PRINCIPLE; VALUES UNDERLYING CONFIDENTIALITY

Each of the health and mental health professions embraces confidentiality as an ethical matter. For example, the Ethical Principles of Psychologists note that psychologists have a primary obligation to take reasonable precautions to respect confidentiality rights (American Psychological Association, 1992).

Confidentiality as a principle rests on four core values. First, confidentiality is designed to *reduce the stigma and discrimination* often suffered by people suffering from mental disorders. As recently as the early 1970s, people lost legal rights if they acknowledged or were treated for mental illness. State statutes, for example, often stripped individuals of the right to vote, the right to contract, the right to receive a driver's license, and other rights if a person received treatment for mental illness. Although these legal penalties largely have been abolished, and replaced by federal law (the Americans with Disabilities Act; see chapter 33 on human resources) that prohibits discrimination on the basis of disability, individuals may still encounter prejudice and discrimination if their mental disorder is disclosed.

Second, confidentiality rests on the value of *fostering trust* in the clinical relationship. The assumption, buttressed by recent research, is that mental health care is most likely to succeed if the patient or client trusts the caregiver. The assumption is that trust is more likely to develop if the patient or client can assume that the caregiver will not disclose information gained during treatment.

Third, health care law in the last three decades has given increasing weight to the notion that people are *entitled to privacy* in seeking health care. Although privacy has been discussed most frequently in the context of reproductive rights, it is an important value in other health care decision making as well, including the decision to seek or forgo treatment.

Finally, confidentiality is designed *to further autonomy* in health care decision making. During congressional debates on creating a federal confidentiality standard, Congress heard testimony that individuals have decided either to pay for treatment privately or not to seek treatment, to avoid having health care information created that might become available to others. The most famous example is that of Michael Eisner, chief executive officer of the Disney Corporation, who reportedly paid for heart surgery privately rather than have Disney pay for his care.

CONFIDENTIALITY PROTECTIONS AND EXCEPTIONS

Although few dispute the importance of keeping health and mental health records confidential, there are many exceptions to confidentiality that sometimes threaten to overwhelm the principle itself. All states have laws that protect information that is gathered about an individual during treatment. A typical statute provides for the confidentiality of information regarding admission to treatment, material disclosed by the patient/client during treatment, written records regarding the client, and any other material (e.g., laboratory results) gathered during treatment. The federal definition is somewhat more expansive than many state statutes, and defines health care information as

> Any information, whether oral or recorded in any form or medium, that is created or received by a health care provider, health plan, public health authority, employer, life insurer, school or university, or health care clearinghouse; and that relates to the past, present, or future physical or mental health or condition of an individual, the provision of health care to an individual, or the past, present, or future payment for the provision of health care to an individual. (Health Insurance Portability and Accountability Act, 1996)

Federal law governing the confidentiality of alcohol and substance-abuse information protects information if it would identify an individual as receiving treatment services from an alcohol or substance-abuse program (42 USC 290dd-2; 42 CFR 2.1 et seq.). This is a somewhat different approach than that taken by many state mental health laws; the latter focus on information gathered during treatment, whereas the federal law focuses on the disclosure of any information that might identify an individual as receiving substance-use treatment.

EXCEPTIONS TO CONFIDENTIALITY

All states, as well as the proposed federal regulations, provide for exceptions to confidentiality. The most common exceptions are discussed here.

Consent of the Patient/Client

The right to confidentiality belongs to the individual in treatment, not to the organization or provider. The latter may have an obligation to keep information confidential, but the right to confidentiality exists for the benefit of the patient. Therefore, a patient/client may consent to the release of information that otherwise is to be kept confidential. In some circumstances, another party may exercise rights on behalf of the patient/client. For example, if a guardian has been appointed, the guardian may provide consent to disclosure. In the case of children, the law is sometimes unclear regarding whether the parent or child may consent to disclosure. Absent a specific statutory provision addressing this topic, a general principle that can be followed is that a parent has the authority to consent to a waiver of confidentiality unless state law provides a minor with an independent right to seek treatment. For example, in some states, minors aged 14 and older may seek outpatient mental health treatment in some circumstances. In such a situation, presumably the minor is the appropriate party to consent to disclosure, because the legislation explicitly permits the minor to make treatment decisions in such circumstances. However, if the same state law permits voluntary inpatient hospitalization only for individuals aged 18 and older, then authority to consent to disclose inpatient records of an individual younger than 18 presumably would rest with the parent or legal guardian.

Some state laws provide quite detailed information regarding what constitutes a legally adequate consent to disclosure, whereas many do not. The proposed federal regulations (as well as the federal alcohol and substance-abuse regulations) provide explicit criteria that a consent form must meet. These include a requirement that consent be in writing, the name of the individual or entity to which disclosure is to be made, the purpose for the disclosure, the type of information to be disclosed, and the period for which consent is effective. Consent forms are discussed in more detail later, in the section providing recommendations for administrators in dealing with confidentiality.

Child and Elder Abuse

There are a number of situations in which confidentiality must be breached, whether or not the patient has consented. For example, in cases of suspected child abuse (and today, in many states, elder abuse), reporting to the responsible state agency is mandatory, not discretionary. The program administrator should also be aware of other abuse-reporting requirements—for example, state law mandating the report of suspected abuse in institutional settings such as hospitals or nursing homes.

Access by the Patient/Client

Increasingly, state law provides for a right of access by the patient or client to his or her record. Some states condition access by permitting treatment staff to excise information considered potentially harmful to the patient or provided in confidence by third parties. However, these limiting provisions are subject to increasing challenge on the ground that they are paternalistic. The proposed federal regulations provide a right of patient access to health care information, based on the assumption that an individual is entitled to assure that information is accurate and it is subject to correction if inadequate.

Access by Other Providers

Most state confidentiality laws were written before the emergence of multiprovider networks. Therefore, many state mental health confidentiality provisions provide little guidance on the disclosure of information to other providers, or limit such disclosure to circumstances in which the client has provided consent. Other state statutes permit the disclosure of information to another provider that is going to provide treatment without consent. The proposed federal regulations presume patient/client consent to disclosure to another provider, giving the individual the right to deny disclosure to particular providers. Ideally, forms consenting to disclosure contemplate disclosure to a variety of providers, something that is perhaps easier to do in an environment where many providers operate within the context of a provider system.

Access by Payers

One of the stimulants to congressional debate regarding confidentiality was the growth of managed care. Most state laws permit the disclosure without client consent of information necessary to obtain reimbursement for services. However, such statutes generally were written long before the emergence of managed care and the increased demands for information from payers of care. As a result, providers often have found themselves in the position of having to release large quantities of information, some quite revealing about the individual, in order to obtain reimbursement.

Because of this, some states have taken steps to reduce the amount of information that a payer may request in making reimbursement decisions. For example, New Jersey permits disclosure of information obtained by a psychologist to a payer only if the client consents, and disclosure is limited to administrative information, diagnostic information, the legal status of the patient, the reason for continuing psychological services, assessment of the client's current level of functioning and level of distress, and a prognosis, limited to the time that treatment might continue.

Federal standards for privacy of individual health information provide for regulated disclosure of information to payers without consent, although as with information disclosed to other providers, the individual may decide to withhold consent. If the individual withholds consent, the payer is not obligated to pay for services: The practical effect is to create a strong incentive to permit disclosure. What is more useful from the perspective of protecting confidentiality is that the proposed federal regulations exempt notes defined in statute as "psychotherapy notes" from disclosure. These are defined in the following manner:

> Psychotherapy notes means notes recorded (in any medium) by a health care provider who is a mental health professional documenting or analyzing the contents of conversation during a private counseling session or a group, joint, or family counseling session and that are separated from the rest of the individual's medical record. Psychotherapy notes excludes medication prescription and monitoring, counseling session start and stop times, the modalities and frequencies of treatment furnished, results of clinical tests, and any summary of the following items: diagnosis, functional status, the treatment plan, symptoms, prognosis, and progress to date. (45 CFR Subtitle A, Subchapter C, §164.501)

Oversight, Research, and Public Health

All states have provisions making health and behavioral health information accessible to regulators providing oversight for state agencies such as the state health or mental health department. Client consent is typically not required in such circumstances. In addition, certain types of information might have to be reported to public health officials, for example, the prescription of certain types of medication or particular types of infectious diseases.

State law also often provides for access by researchers to medical records when the research has been approved by an Institutional Review Board (IRB) and obtaining consent from the clients whose records are to be reviewed would be impractical. In other circumstances, however, client consent is required before records can be accessed for research purposes.

Access by Families

Some states provide that families may have access to certain types of information regarding the care of a family member. Such information is usually limited to diagnosis, prognosis, and information regarding treatment, particularly medications; a further limitation is that this information is typically available only to families who are acting in a caregiver role. The proposed federal regulation (which, as noted, deals with health care information in general, not only mental health information) provides for access by next of kin to limited information regarding the current status of the patient.

Access by Law Enforcement

Many state mental health statutes limit law enforcement access to situations in which a patient has left a hospital without authorization, or to situations of crime on facility grounds. A handful of state laws permit law enforcement access without consent to investigate health care fraud. In other circumstances, law enforcement typically must obtain a court order for access.

The proposed federal regulation, in contrast, provides for virtually unlimited access to health care information by law enforcement officials. The rationale is that government requires broad access to combat health care fraud. If these regulations become law, the more protective state standards would continue to apply, because of the provision in the proposed federal regulations that more protective state laws may continue to be applied in lieu of the federal rules.

Disclosure to Protect Third Parties: The So-Called "Tarasoff Rule"

In 1976, the California Supreme Court ruled that mental health professionals (MHPs) have a duty to protect third parties when the MHP concludes that his or her client presented a risk to an identified third party (*Tarasoff v. Regents*, 1976); in its initial ruling the Court had held that an MHP had a duty to warn a third party of potential harm.

The California court's ruling has been followed by many other jurisdictions, and has resulted in statutory language in many states. In most states that have adopted statutory language, the legislature provides that a mental health provider may take steps to protect an identified third party that might be endangered by a patient.

However, most states do not require steps to be taken, leaving resolution of the issue to the discretion of the treatment provider. On the other hand, a handful of states provide for a mandatory duty: The Ohio Supreme Court, for example, ruled that a mental health professional who reasonably concludes that his or her client may present a danger to the public (not simply an identifiable third party) had an obligation to take steps to protect the public (*Estates of Morgan v. Fairfield Family Counseling Ctr.*, 1997). Soon thereafter, the Ohio legislature adopted language to define a duty to third parties, but restricted it to certain settings and identifiable potential victims (Ohio Rev. Code §2305.51). Finally, in at least some states, most notably Texas (*Van Horn v. Chambers*, 1998; *Praesel v. Johnson*, 1998; *Thapar v. Zezulka*, 1999), courts have ruled that mental health professionals have no obligation to third parties that might be endangered by a person in treatment.

This is an issue where it is essential that the mental health administrator receive competent legal advice regarding the state of the law in the particular jurisdiction in which the administrator works. There is much misapprehension among mental health professionals concerning the Tarasoff rule, and because it involves the safety of third parties, it is critical that the precise state of the law be understood before policies for handling such situations are established.

FEDERAL LAW GOVERNING ALCOHOL
AND SUBSTANCE-ABUSE INFORMATION

As noted earlier, federal law controls the confidentiality of alcohol and substance-abuse treatment information. The law protects "patient identifying information," which is defined as the name, address, social security number, fingerprints, photograph, or similar information by which the identity of a patient can be determined with reasonable accuracy and speed either directly or by reference to other publicly available information (42 CFR 2.11 [b]). The statute and implementing regulations apply to a federally assisted alcohol or drug abuse program.

The rules for disclosure of this type of information are very strict, primarily because when the statute was enacted and regulations adopted nearly all involvement with controlled substances was a crime. The underlying premise of these rules is that strict protection of confidentiality would create an incentive for people abusing substances to seek treatment; the absence of confidentiality, in contrast, would be a disincentive because of the criminalization of substance-abuse-related behaviors.

The federal rules permit disclosure in a number of situations, but are much stricter than most comparable state laws. Consent by the client must be in writing; must name the client, the program making the disclosure, and the party that will receive the information; must state the purpose of the disclosure as well as specify the information to be disclosed; must be signed by the client or legal representative; and must indicate the duration of the consent.

Disclosures may be made without consent in specifically delineated situations, such as within the treatment program when necessary to provide services; to other providers, pursuant to a qualified service agreement; to report a crime on the premises of the treatment program; and in response to a court order that complies with the elements specified in federal law.

The major problem that may arise in implementing the federal law is in programs that are treating co-occurring disorders (both mental illness and substance abuse). If there is a problem in such circumstances, it stems from the fact that the state law governing mental health information and the federal law governing substance-abuse information will usually not be identical. In general, the federal law is stricter than most state laws. Providers have a variety of options, none particularly attractive. These include separating in the chart material related to mental health treatment from material related to substance-abuse or alcohol treatment, or, if the material is integrated, applying the federal standard to all requests for disclosure.

PRIVILEGE

Information regarding a person's mental health status or treatment may be sought in a variety of legal proceedings. For example, mental state is often relevant in criminal proceedings examining a person's competence to stand trial or responsibility at the time of the alleged offense (the insanity defense). A person's mental state is obviously relevant in civil commitment proceedings, or in a proceeding contesting an individual's competency to execute a will. Mental health records and mental health practitioners may also be ordered to court in other contexts in which a party has put another party's mental state at issue. An example is in a custody dispute, when one party argues that he or she is the better custodian for the children because his or her former spouse has a mental illness that affects his or her ability to parent.

However, the fact that a person's mental state may be at issue does not mean that otherwise confidential information necessarily must be disclosed in the legal proceeding. The information may be privileged and therefore unavailable. Privilege is the law's way of preserving the confidentiality of material that might otherwise be made available in a legal proceeding, based on the assumption that the preservation of confidentiality has a higher value than providing the information in a legal proceeding.

There are a number of well-known privileges. These include the attorney–client privilege (an attorney cannot be compelled to divulge conversations with his or her client); the marital privilege (a spouse cannot be compelled to testify against another spouse); and the penitential privilege (a priest or minister cannot be compelled to provide testimony about material divulged in the confessional). Health care information in general, and information about mental health and substance abuse treatment in particular, is also privileged, although the privilege is not absolute.

The reason for the privilege is a judgment by courts and legislatures that compelling a mental health therapist to testify about materials gathered during treatment would do grave harm to the therapeutic relationship. As noted earlier, the U.S. Supreme Court, creating a federal psychotherapeutic privilege, discussed the need for privacy and trust within the clinical relationship. The Court also found that the psychotherapeutic privilege serves the public interest by facilitating the provision of appropriate treatment for individuals suffering the effects of a mental or emotional problem. The mental health of our citizenry, no less than its physical health, is a public good of transcendent importance (*Jaffe v. Redmond*, 1996).

State laws also recognize a variety of privileges. Common privileges include the physician–patient privilege, the psychologist–patient privilege, the psychotherapist privilege, and in many states privileges applicable to social workers, marital counselors, and others.

These privileges are not absolute, and a court, after hearing a claim of privilege, can rule that the material at issue must be disclosed. In some situations the privilege is waived automatically. For example, in a civil commitment proceeding, because the person's mental state is directly relevant to the decision whether or not to commit, the privilege generally does not apply and a practitioner will be expected to provide testimony based on information that otherwise would be confidential. Privilege is also waived when a patient sues a practitioner; the practitioner, to stage a defense, must be able to rely on material from treatment. The privilege is also waived when an individual makes his or her mental state an issue. For example, a defendant in a criminal case who pleads the insanity defense has made his or her mental state the core of the defense. Therefore, privilege is automatically waived, and the defendant cannot later object to the production of mental health information that otherwise would be confidential. In another common situation, privilege is waived when a court orders a mental health exam.

MAINTAINING CONFIDENTIALITY IN PRACTICE

There are a number of commonsense principles that administrators can adopt in addressing confidentiality.

First, *information must be kept physically secure*. Many breaches of confidentiality occur when records are left out, when confidential information is faxed to a location where it is accessible to individuals who do not require it in their jobs, and when file cabinets are unlocked. Sensitivity to internal security is important. As records become increasingly computerized, the organization must comply with emerging federal guidelines. In addition, other steps must be taken—for example, assuring that access is limited and requires special passwords.

Second, *consent forms used for client-authorized disclosure should be reviewed*. Those providing for disclosure of substance- or alcohol-use treatment information must comply with the federal rules. For mental health information, if state law does not provide guidance, the proposed federal regulations are useful in their specificity. In addition, use of a consent form that permits the patient to consent to disclosure to a variety of providers is useful. If the provider is part of a multi-provider group, it is useful for the group to adopt a uniform consent form for the purpose of facilitating disclosure within the group.

Third, *a subpoena from an attorney is different from a court order directing the disclosure of information*. In most states, an attorney subpoena does not have to be complied with; most states require a court order before confidential mental health information must be disclosed. Having an in-house expert on such matters will help in assuring a consistent response to subpoenas and orders and also will assure that material is not released inappropriately.

Fourth, *even if a court order is issued for material, privilege can still be asserted*. For example, if a court demands the production of material that treatment staff members believe should not be introduced into a court proceeding, staff can raise the issue with the judge (e.g., in a letter). Alternatively, the lawyer for the patient can be notified that staff members have a question regarding the application of privilege.

Privilege can also be asserted by clinical staff on the witness stand. For example, a clinician, called to testify, can address the court after being sworn in, indicating respectfully that the clinician wishes to be certain before testifying that privilege does not apply. This is an area in which discussion with an attorney beforehand is recommended.

REFERENCES

American Psychological Association. (1992). *Ethical principles of psychologists and code of conduct*. Washington, DC: Author.

LEGISLATION AND CASES CITED

42 USC 290dd-2; 42 CFR 2.1, et seq., on confidentiality of information related to alcohol or drug abuse treatment.

45 CFR Subtitle A, Subchapter C, § 164.501, on definitions, including "psychotherapy notes." Federal Register, December 28, 2000 (volume 65, number 250).

Estates of Morgan v. Fairfield Family Counseling Ctr., 77 Ohio St. 3d 284 (1997).

Health Insurance Portability and Accountability Act of 1996 (HIPAA). P.L. 104, Part C (Administrative Simplification), Sec. 1171 (Definitions).

Jaffe v. Redmond, 515 U.S. 1 (1996).

Ohio Rev. Code §2305.51 (1999), on duties of psychotherapists to protect third parties.

Praesel v. Johnson, 967 SW. 2d 391 (Tex. 1998).

Tarasoff v. Regents of the University of California, 551 P. 2d 334, 345–47 (1976) (also 131 Cal. Rptr. 14, 551 p. 2d 334 [1976]).

Thapar v. Zezulka, 994 SW. 2d 635(Tex. 1999).

Van Horn v. Chambers, 970 SW. 2d 542, 544 (Tex. 1998).

Chapter Thirty-Eight

Malpractice and Other Negligence

John Petrila

alpractice is a topic of major concern to many mental health administrators and practitioners. Stories about the "malpractice crisis" or news accounts of cases resulting in multi-million-dollar verdicts lead many to conclude that lawsuits are inevitable. Although it is true that lawsuits against mental health practitioners have increased in recent years, such litigation is not inevitable. More important, the best defense against malpractice litigation is good clinical and administrative practice.

According to Dr. Robert Simon, one of the leading experts in the United States on law and psychiatry issues, the annual incidence of claims against psychiatrists in 1975 was about 1 in 45, or approximately 2.25%. The chance of a psychiatrist being sued doubled in the 1980s to 1 in 25, but claims filed against psychiatrists remained lower than claims against most other medical specialties. In addition, only 2 or 3 of every 10 claims filed resulted in a judgment (Simon, 1998).

Lawsuits arose from a variety of clinical practices and were distributed in the following manner:

- Incorrect treatment (33%).
- Suicide or attempted suicide (20%).
- Incorrect diagnosis (11%).
- Improper commitment (5%).
- Breach of confidentiality (4%).
- Undue familiarity (3%).
- Libel/slander (2%).
- Other (abandonment, etc.) (4%).

A study conducted in Texas, examining malpractice claims and licensing complaints filed against psychologists, found few lawsuits filed. Those that had been filed included claims for false imprisonment (filed in the context of civil commitment), child custody hearings, issues arising in therapy, supervisory issues (involving the supervision of students or more junior psychologists), and billing practices (Montgomery, Cupit, & Wimberley, 1999). When asked to describe their perceptions of vulnerability to litigation and licensing inquiries, psychologists indicated that sexual misconduct, failure to warn endangered third parties, child custody issues, and client suicide caused the greatest anxiety. However, the actual lawsuits filed against them tended, with the exception of child custody issues, to focus on other types of issues.

The author's review of Florida cases resulting in judgments against mental health practitioners revealed fewer than a dozen judgments. In many of the cases in which liability was found or a settlement reached, the practitioner's conduct appeared to present obvious concerns. One case, for example, resulting in a settlement of several hundred thousand dollars, involved a practitioner who berated and occasionally struck his patients. It requires little imagination to understand how such practice resulted in a lawsuit and eventual financial award to the plaintiffs.

This is not to suggest that malpractice concerns are not real. There are significant areas of vulnerability, as the discussion that follows suggests. However, in practice there are probably fewer cases brought, and certainly fewer awards, than many practitioners and administrators imagine.

The sections that follow discuss the elements of malpractice, describe areas of vulnerability in mental health, and suggest ways of lessening the risk of a lawsuit in those areas. A discussion of liability in the context of managed care follows.

ELEMENTS OF MALPRACTICE

A plaintiff in a malpractice or negligence claim must prove four elements to be successful.

1. The defendant must have a *duty to the plaintiff.*
2. The defendant must have *breached that duty.*
3. The plaintiff must have suffered *damages.*
4. The defendant's *breach must have caused those damages.*

Duty

Duty refers to the obligation of a provider to exercise "reasonable care" in providing treatment. A provider does *not* have an obligation to provide the best care imaginable. Rather, the practitioner's general obligation is to exercise his or her best judgment in providing "ordinary and reasonable" care. What constitutes "ordinary and reasonable" care will be determined by the standards of the profession.

There are also specific duties that may arise in the course of treatment. For example, the exercise of "ordinary and reasonable" care in prescribing medications may be governed by various sources of information about how particular medications should be prescribed.

In other instances, courts may create new duties. An example is the California Supreme Court's decision in the Tarasoff case (discussed in the chapter on confidentiality and privilege) creating a duty, in California, to protect third parties who might be at risk of harm from a patient. Before the Court's decision, there was no such duty.

It is worth noting that a provider has no duty until a person becomes a patient or client. In other words, with the exception of emergency rooms (which are obligated under federal law to assess, stabilize, and treat or transfer any individual who presents in the emergency room), providers are not obligated to treat anyone who walks through their doors. Generally, duties do not arise until a therapeutic relationship is established. However, in managed care settings, providers may assume through contract obligations that otherwise would not exist. For example, if a provider signs a contract agreeing to provide mental health screens to all individuals enrolled in an employer's health plan, the provider must provide assessments to any enrollee who presents for an assessment. Absent such a contract, there is no duty to provide assessments to anyone presenting for care.

Breach of the Duty

Once an obligation is established, the plaintiff must prove that the defendant breached his or her duty. In a malpractice case, this will usually be shown through testimony of an expert witness. The expert will attempt to demonstrate that the applicable standard of care has been violated—that is, that the defendant's care did not constitute the exercise of professional judgment as measured by the standards of the applicable profession.

The expert of course is supposed to be able to articulate the basis of his or her opinion. As discussed later in more detail, the expert will have reviewed the case record and other pertinent documents (e.g., incident reports, mortality review reports, and other internal documents if they are available through discovery). The larger question is how one determines what constitutes "professional standards" in a particular area.

There are a variety of sources for determining the standard of care in a particular case. These include the following:

The Expert's Own Experience.   An expert may have vast clinical experience in the relevant area. For example, if the subject of the lawsuit is medication practice, the plaintiff may call an expert who has extensive practice experience and who can testify, based on personal experience in treating patients similar to the plaintiff, about what is "ordinary" practice in such a case. In a case addressing institutional conditions (e.g., a lawsuit by the Department of Justice alleging civil rights violations), the expert may have either administered a similar facility, or surveyed similar facilities in other cases or as an organizational surveyor, for example, for the Joint Commission on Accreditation of Healthcare Organizations (JCAHO).

Standard Texts and Articles.   Textbooks and articles may also provide a basis for determining professional standards in a particular area. For example, the *Diagnostic and Statistical Manual* (*DSM–IV*) of the American Psychiatric Association is used frequently in examining diagnoses. Recent works on risk assessment reporting studies of the MacArthur Foundation's Mental Disability Law Network (Appelbaum, Robbins, & Monahan, 2000; Silver, Mulvey, & Monahar, 1999; Skeem & Mulvey, 2001) may be used in providing testimony on prevailing standards in assessing risk among people with mental illness. A textbook or article does not automatically establish the standard of care in a particular area; it may, however, be very helpful in providing evidence as to what the standard might be.

Statutes and Regulations.   A state law may create a standard of care. For example, if a state office of mental health promulgates a regulation mandating that all mental health units licensed by the state must have one nurse per ward per shift, that effectively becomes the standard of care for such units in providing nursing coverage. A failure to have such coverage will provide compelling evidence that the provider was negligent in staffing, because the state law has created a precise standard.

Organizational Policies.   Another source frequently used in litigation to establish the applicable standard is policies established by the defendant organization. All provider organizations have policy manuals; what administrators occasionally fail to appreciate is that those policy manuals may establish a standard of care for that organization. For example, if the policy manual requires an incident to be reported and investigated in a particular way, and that is not done, then the failure to do so will probably be viewed as negligence, because the organization's policies were not followed. In an outpatient setting, if the policy requires any outpatient who has not been compliant with prescribed medication to be seen within 2 days of the report of noncompliance, a failure to follow that policy could be legally devastating in a case in which an outpatient killed another person after stopping his or her medication.

Accreditation Standards.   The standards established by the JCAHO or by the Commission on Accreditation of Rehabilitation Facilities (CARF) do not automatically establish a binding standard of care. However, a plaintiff may rely on deficiencies in relevant standards to assist in establishing a case that the defendant did not act according to prevailing professional norms. In addition, compliance with accrediting standards may assist a defendant in demonstrating that it provides ordinary and reasonable care.

Contractual Obligations.   As noted earlier, a provider by contract may assume obligations that it would not otherwise have. If a provider contracts with another provider or payer to provide care in a certain manner, or to provide care to a designated group, and does not do so, a plaintiff and its expert will look to the contractual provision as establishing the applicable standard of care.

There are myriad sources for establishing the standard of care in a malpractice lawsuit. The administrator and clinician should be aware of these sources, and should be particularly attentive to assuring that they can meet obligations assumed through contracts, policies, and other sources within their control.

Damages

A plaintiff must show that he or she has been injured in order to recover in litigation. Many states, in an effort to control malpractice litigation, have imposed limits on certain types of damages. There are various damages a plaintiff might claim. These include lost wages because of time spent away from work due to the defendant's negligence, damages for pain and suffering (a difficult type of damage to quantify and one that some states have attempted to cap), the costs of past and future medical care made necessary by the injury suffered as a result of the defendant's negligence, and punitive damages if the defendant's conduct has been egregious.

A plaintiff will show damages in a variety of ways. If the case proceeds to trial, an expert may be called to testify about the prospective earnings that the plaintiff likely would have earned but for his or her injury. Receipts from medical expenses will be produced, and medical testimony may be introduced describing the prospective medical care that the plaintiff will require.

Causation

Finally, the defendant's conduct must have directly caused the plaintiff's injury. This is a concept that is sometimes applied loosely. For example, in a handful of states liability has been imposed when a former patient is involved in an automobile accident, injuring another party. The theory of one type of case arising from such an event is that the clinician should be found liable for having released the patient from inpatient care sometime previously. There are often many intervening events that occur between the release of the patient and the accident: The release "caused" the accident only in the most general sense that had the patient been hospitalized he or she would not have been able to become involved in an automobile accident.

This suggests that the law may use a more primitive assessment of causation than others might use. A malpractice case attempts to identify conduct or a failure to act on the part of the defendant that "but for" that conduct the injury in question may not have occurred. Because the analysis is retrospective (malpractice litigation often occurring years after the event in question), the importance of the defendant's conduct as causative may be magnified in the eyes of the decision maker.

SOME AREAS OF POTENTIAL VULNERABILITY IN MALPRACTICE/NEGLIGENCE LITIGATION

Claims arising from mental health care constitute a comparatively small portion of malpractice and negligence claims in U.S. health care and related fields. There are, however, several areas in which mental health organizations, facilities, and clinicians (such as psychiatrists, psychologists, social workers, and other independent or contracting providers) may have considerable vulnerability. Some are unique to the mental health field; others are common to both mental health and general medical settings.

Harm to Self or Others

One area of significant vulnerability occurs when a patient harms himself or others. The legal analysis, and degree of vulnerability, may vary depending on whether the patient is an inpatient or outpatient.

Some states, for example, Florida, impose different standards based on the patient's status. Inpatient providers are held to a higher standard, because they have the ability to physically control the patient—for example, by keeping him or her on a locked ward. Outpatient providers, in contrast, because they lack physical control of the patient, are held to a lesser standard. In Florida, because of this lack of physical control, it is virtually impossible to hold an outpatient provider liable for harm caused by an outpatient.

In other states, inpatient and outpatient providers are held to the same standard, and it is expected that outpatient providers will take steps to protect third parties (in the case of harm to others) or the patient who may be at risk for suicide or self-injury.

If a patient harms another or himself, a plaintiff will focus on two general areas. One will be the manner in which the assessment of risk was performed. For example, at the time of the decision to release the patient from inpatient care, does the discharge summary reflect organizational awareness of those factors that initially caused the patient to be admitted in the first place? Is there evidence that treatment was designed to address risk factors? Is there evidence that risk factors have been ameliorated? What provisions were made for the patient upon discharge in terms of living place, assuring that financial supports were available, referrals for additional treatment, particularly alcohol or substance-abuse treatment, and staff awareness of the potential availability of weapons? There are various resources available today on risk assessment, and these should be available to staff.

The second area of focus, particularly in an outpatient setting, will be on how staff members responded when they knew, or should have known, that the patient's status might be problematic. Did the patient attend appointments as scheduled? Was the patient taking prescribed medication? Was there evidence that the patient's mental state was deteriorating? Had the patient made threats to harm self or others? What was staff's response to evidence of problems? Was the patient telephoned if he missed appointments? If the patient did not respond, did staff visit the patient? Were efforts made to enlist others, for example, family, in persuading the patient to take prescribed medication? Was a change in medication considered? Were the potential targets of threats notified? Was civil commitment considered?

A provider can take steps to minimize the risk of a successful lawsuit in this area. First, the provider should provide the training and resources necessary to assure that staff members are familiar with the latest research on the relationship between mental illness and risk, as well as the latest techniques for assessing risk to self and to others. This is a literature that has changed quite markedly in the last three decades, and the professional consensus that used to hold that clinicians could predict dangerousness no better than chance has been replaced by a professional consensus that a properly trained clinician can provide useful assessments of the probabilities that an individual will present a risk in the future.

Second, the provider should encourage, if not require consultations, either from other staff or from outside the organization, on difficult cases. A clinician who seeks a second opinion has taken what remains the most useful step in legal risk management. Some providers have institutionalized the practice, by creating in-house panels to review the status of patients deemed to constitute a risk, particularly when treatment staff propose a change in status. Whether or not the practice is institutionalized, obtaining second opinions from well-trained colleagues is important.

Third, treatment and risk reduction must be integrated whenever possible. Traditionally, providers viewed treatment and risk as somewhat separate issues. Today, most agree that treatment must be focused on the reduction and management of risk, whether in inpatient or outpatient settings. If a patient is placed in anger management counseling, it should be because the patient has a documented problem with anger management that in the past has been implicated in behaviors that are problematic. Too often, treatment goals are written in the most general terms ("patient will learn self-control"), that have little to do with the reason the patient was brought into treatment in the first place. In many instances, risky behavior precipitated the decision by the patient or someone else to initiate treatment; if treatment is not geared toward identifying and addressing the causes of this behavior, the provider's legal position if the patient later causes harm will be compromised.

Fourth, the patient's chart should be written with legal risk management in mind. There are certain decisions in both inpatient and outpatient settings that have importance beyond the treatment of the patient. For example, a decision to release an inpatient to the community is significant because it places the patient at increased liberty. Conversely, a decision *not* to rehospitalize an outpatient who appears to be deteriorating and who has missed two appointments is a major decision. Each should be charted in a way that captures not only the clinical decision, but *why* the clinical decision was made. What is often missing from patient charts is "why" something happened—a medication may be changed, but there may be no explanation as to why the change occurred. Yet a change in medication is a potentially significant event, not only clinically but legally. Given this, insisting that the reasons for important clinical decisions are noted briefly in the chart is an excellent legal risk management tool.

Sexual Misconduct

There are no circumstances in which sexual contact or sexual behavior between patient and staff is appropriate. Allegations of sexual misconduct must be investigated swiftly and thoroughly. As with any allegation of abuse, patient claims cannot be dismissed on the ground that the patient is mentally ill and therefore must surely be incompetent or exaggerating.

Insurance companies providing malpractice insurance generally view sexual misconduct as conduct that is not covered. Therefore, an individual charged with sexual misconduct may have to bear the cost of his or her defense as well as pay any damages out of personal funds.

Child Custody Evaluations and Child Treatment

There have been a number of cases in recent years in which clinicians who perform evaluations in child custody cases have been severely punished by licensing boards or lost negligence claims. An administrator of a program providing family services should be aware that this is a legally problematic area.

The primary problem in cases in which clinicians have been judged to have acted inappropriately is one of role. Ethical principles of all the mental health professions (including both psychiatry and psychology) prohibit (or strongly recommend against) a clinician's providing a legal evaluation and opinion on which parent should receive custody when the clinician is providing treatment in the same case. Similarly, a clinician is generally ethically barred from providing an opinion about the fitness of a person to be a parent if the clinician has not evaluated the person. Failure to follow this ethical norm may subject the clinician to exclusion from the case, censure by his or her professional organization, or licensure sanctions (*Loomis v. Board of Psychologist Examiners*, 1998). Persons who testify or otherwise provide opinions to a court must openly acknowledge their roles, methods, and allegiances, and must provide disclaimers when important parts of an evaluation, for example, have not been done (e.g., when one has not personally evaluated all members of the family in a custody battle).

In addressing these issues, the administrator should assure that staff working with families are aware of the ethical principles governing practice. If these ethical precepts are followed, vulnerability in this area will be reduced significantly.

Medication Practices

Much mental health care relies on medication. Potential liability may arise for a number of reasons. These include use of the "wrong" medication, use of too much (or too little) medication, a failure to consider alternative medications, polypharmacy, and a failure to monitor the course of a medication.

The best legal risk management tool in dealing with medication issues is to hire or retain well-trained psychiatrists who are sophisticated about mental illness. It is critical that clinicians talk with their patients in some detail about the rationale for proposed medications and alternatives available. They must be careful in dosing, regularly consider how the patient is doing with a particular medication, and assure the performance of necessary monitoring (e.g., the blood draws required when a patient is taking clozapine). However, even in an ideal world, the administrator can take other steps to reduce potential liability.

First, the administrator can insist that those prescribing medications talk to their patients. For example, as Appelbaum and Gutheil (1991) pointed out years ago, patients refuse medication for a variety of reasons. The best way to learn *why* a patient doesn't take a medication that may help, or whether or not he or she is experiencing adverse effects, is by talking with the patient. Such conversations may increase patients' participation in treatment and decrease the probability of a medication-related mishap.

Second, organizational quality assurance review regarding medication practices is particularly important. If the organization has a pharmacy committee, it is essential that the committee be capable of quickly identifying and responding to prescription practices that might signal a problem, as well as any reported issues of adverse patient response. If the organization lacks this capacity, then periodic reviews of medication practices by outside consultants should prove helpful in identifying potential problems. In spite of all efforts, medication practices can be a major source of potential liability. A combination of good clinical work, careful discussions with patients, and a capacity to identify and respond to problems should dramatically reduce legal risk.

Seclusion and Restraint

The use of seclusion and restraint has drawn increased and often critical attention in the 1990s, including congressional examination of abuses. In addition, the U.S. Supreme Court ruled in *Youngberg v. Romeo* (1982) that inappropriate restraint may compromise a person's constitutionally protected liberty.

Practices that are particularly legally risky include the use of seclusion or restraints without a physician order; failing to monitor the condition of someone in restraints or seclusion as prescribed by institutional policies; the use of excessive or inappropriate force in restraining someone; the use of outdated or dangerous equipment, or the placement of individuals in a room in which they can injure themselves; and the use of seclusion or restraint as punishment or for the convenience of staff.

It is important that the use of seclusion and restraint be monitored. Physicians must adhere to organizational policies on writing, reviewing, and renewing orders, and the rooms and equipment used in these practices must not create additional risk of harm. In addition, the standards of the JCAHO should be met, and the appropriate committees and executive staff should regularly review the use of seclusion and restraint. Finally, it is often the case that a small group of patients are placed in seclusion and restraint frequently, compared to all other patients. When that type of pattern begins to emerge, a case review may be useful in attempting to determine why restraint and/or seclusion are being used so frequently, and whether there are alternative strategies that can be used.

Supervisory Practices

A final area of vulnerability arises in situations where clinicians are providing supervision of students or less experienced clinicians. If harm occurs to a patient in such a setting, a plaintiff may question the adequacy of the supervision, as well as raise questions regarding which party was ultimately responsible for care.

Two things are particularly important in minimizing liability in a supervisory arrangement. First, the person being supervised cannot exceed the limits of his or her authority in providing care. If state law requires licensure to perform a particular service and the individual under supervision lacks that license, then the service must be provided by a person meeting statutory standards.

Second, it is critical that the role of the person being supervised and the person providing supervision be clear, in writing if necessary. This is particularly true of treatment decisions; if a lawsuit is brought, the defendant does not want to be in a position of having ambiguous or contradictory testimony presented on who ultimately was responsible for the patient's care.

Liability in Managed Care Settings

A core issue in the debate regarding managed care has been whether payers services can be held liable for injuries suffered by individuals. The most common situation in which this issue has been argued is when care is denied or cut short of what the practitioner might have believed appropriate.

Traditionally, the primary ground on which a payer for services (e.g., an insurance company) might be found liable was breach of contract. If an insurance contract promised to pay for three visits to a mental health counselor and the company simply refused to pay, the beneficiary would be able to pursue a claim arguing that the insurance company breached its contractual obligation under the plan.

Since the advent of managed care, contracts have assumed even greater importance in defining the terms under which health and mental health care is provided. For example, a mental health center may have a variety of contracts with employers, with insurance companies, with managed care companies, and with others, each defining the conditions under which individuals covered by a particular plan might receive services from the center. These contracts, often premised on reducing utilization of care, may create conflicts with the perceived clinical needs of a patient, creating ethical and legal issues quite different from those presented in a traditional fee-for-service environment. For example, in a fee-for-service setting, a common criticism was that clinicians had incentives to provide more or more expensive treatment than warranted, simply because it would generally be paid for. However, the underlying incentive in most managed care plans, whether publicly or privately financed, is to reduce utilization, particularly of more expensive services such as hospitalization. This meant that in many cases a clinician (or the company for which he or she worked) potentially had an incentive to underserve a patient. This was true particularly in the case of capitated contracts, in which the provider receives a fixed amount of money to provide identified services to a group of individuals entitled to services under the plan. When the provider went at risk fiscally, it created a direct conflict between potential financial risk and obligations to individual patients.

This clash with ethical values lies at the heart of much of the debate over managed care. Clinicians have an ethical obligation to provide the care needed by the individual whose needs are being addressed at a particular time. As James Sabin (1994) pointed out, the fiduciary obligations of health care professionals are seldom read to include balancing individual needs against group needs. This makes it ethically problematic to ration resources within the context of individual treatment. Whether managed care plans should be liable for practitioner conduct affected by payment decisions, or whether practitioners should legally be assumed able to hold themselves free of economic pressures when prescribing treatment, has been at the heart of some of the most heated debates regarding managed care.

Most early decisions considering the potential liability of insurance companies or other payers of services emphasized that a health care provider could not excuse substandard care by blaming such care on inadequate financial resources. The comment by a court considering a challenge to the decision by General Motors to have its mental health benefit "managed" by a managed care company is typical:

> The purpose of the Pilot Program is to determine in advance whether the GM plan will pay for the proposed treatment. Whether or not the proposed treatment is approved, the physician retains the right and indeed the ethical and legal obligation to provide appropriate treatment to the patient. . . . The most persuasive argument against the plaintiffs . . . is the argument plaintiffs themselves assert. Plaintiffs say, in effect, "irrespective of any obligations I have to my patients and to my

profession, my judgment as to what is in the best interests of my patients will not be determined by the exercise of my medical judgment, but by how much I will be paid for my services." Plaintiffs are saying in effect, "Since I am weak in my resolve to afford proper treatment, [the] preauthorization program would induce me to breach my ethical and legal duties, and the Court must protect me from my own weakness." In other words, protect me from my own misconduct. This is strange stuff indeed from which to fashion a legal argument. (*Varol v. Blue* Cross, 1989)

Other courts suggested that in some circumstances, a payer (in the early cases, typically an insurance company) could be found liable (see, e.g., *Wilson v. Blue Cross,* 1990), but in general the courts were not sympathetic to arguments that a lack of financial resources caused a practitioner or mental health provider to provide substandard care.

The issue of liability has been complicated by a federal statute originally designed to strengthen protection of employee benefits. The Employee Retirement Income Security Act (ERISA) was enacted in 1974 and created a set of fiduciary obligations for administrators of employee benefit plans. In exchange, employers that created ERISA-qualified health care plans enjoyed exemption from most state insurance regulations. In addition, lawsuits arising from those plans would be heard only in federal court (i.e., states would be "preempted" from hearing such suits) and damages were limited. For example, in contrast to state malpractice claims, financial recovery in a lawsuit against an ERISA-qualified plan is generally limited to the amount of the contractual provision in dispute, and punitive and similar damages are not available to plaintiffs. This made lawsuits against ERISA-qualified plans financially unattractive to lawyers engaged in malpractice work, because the potential recovery (and subsequent attorneys' fees) were quite small compared to the potential recovery from a malpractice claim.

Because most major employer-sponsored health care plans in the United States are ERISA qualified, the practical effect was to limit significantly the number of claims brought against managed care companies administering such health care plans through the 1990s. As a result, it appeared at least through the mid-1990s that managed care plans, at least those administering ERISA-qualified plans, as a practical matter were virtually immune from litigation designed to hold them responsible for inadequate care arguably caused, at least in part, by their financial decisions.

This situation has changed to some degree since the mid-1990s, as the federal courts have showed more willingness to find managed care companies liable in some circumstances. In general, if a managed care plan (e.g., a health maintenance organization [HMO]) is involved, or appears to a plan enrollee to be involved, in providing care or arranging for the provision of care, then that plan may be sued in state court under a malpractice theory.

For example, in a seminal case in this area (*Dukes v. U.S. Healthcare, Inc.,* 1995), a 1995 federal court of appeals ruled that a malpractice claim in which an HMO was defendant could proceed in state court. One plaintiff's spouse had died shortly after seeking treatment for an unspecified blood ailment; in another case considered by the court of appeals at the same time, plaintiffs had lost a daughter during the wife's pregnancy when the wife developed symptoms typical of preeclampsia. Both plaintiffs had received their care from an ERISA-qualified HMO organized by the defendant U.S. Healthcare.

The defendant removed the claims to federal court, on the ground that the state courts were preempted from hearing claims involving an ERISA-qualified plan. However, the federal court of appeals ruled that the claims could proceed in state court. The court said that the plaintiffs' cases were not based on the failure of the HMO to provide benefits due under the plan (something that would have been preempted by ERISA and therefore the state courts would have lacked jurisdiction). Rather, each case before the court dealt with the quality of care, something the court said it was "confident" was not covered by ERISA. Therefore, under the court's ruling, if an HMO played not only a utilization review role, but arranged for the actual care the quality of which was disputed, the HMO could be sued in state court based on this latter role. At the same time, an entity that simply administers a plan—for example, deciding whether a benefit will be available in a particular case—cannot be sued in state court. In that case, the litigation must be brought in federal court, and the restrictions on damages noted earlier apply.

The exception to the application of ERISA created in the *Dukes* case is one that other federal and state courts have followed in both health and mental health cases (*Dukes v. U.S. Healthcare, Inc.,* 1995). In addition, a number of state legislatures have enacted statutes that permit lawsuits to be brought in state court against insurers, including ERISA-qualified managed care plans, over the quality of care provided to individuals enrolled in managed care plans. The Texas statute, which was the first of its type in the country, was upheld against a challenge that it violated ERISA (*Corporate Health Insurance Inc. v. Texas Department of Insurance*, 2000). Congress has debated similar attempts to formally amend ERISA to permit state court lawsuits against such plans, but has been unable at this point to reach agreement on how that would be done.

Other Fiduciary Duties in Managed Care Settings

Another legal theory employed in litigation against managed care plans and practitioners is that there is an obligation on the part of each to disclose the financial incentives that govern the provision of care to the particular patient. For example, in *Neade v. Portes* (2000), the defendant allegedly denied further inpatient care to a 37-year-old man with an extensive history of treatment for heart disease, including a previous hospitalization. The defendant did not examine the patient himself, but despite this overturned the recommendations of physicians who worked for him that the patient be hospitalized for an angiogram. After the patient's death, his wife brought suit against Dr. Portes on two grounds. First, she brought a traditional malpractice claim, alleging a variety of inadequacies in his treatment of her husband. The second sought to establish as an independent legal claim an obligation on Dr. Portes's part to disclose to the patient that Dr. Portes had a contract with the patient's HMO that created incentives to minimize diagnostic tests and specialist referrals.

The trial court dismissed that part of her complaint seeking to impose a fiduciary duty to disclose the contractual relationship between the defendant physician and the HMO in which the patient was enrolled. However, an Illinois appellate court reversed, agreeing that this disclosure was mandated legally. The plaintiff argued that the contract, in rewarding physicians for minimizing referrals to specialists, placed the physician's financial well-being in conflict with the patient's health. The court noted several Illinois statutory provisions prohibiting a health care provider from referring patients to services in which the provider was an investor, absent disclosure to the patient. The court said, "it follows, then, that there is a potential conflict of interest, which the physician should disclose, where, incompatibly with the patient's interest, he has a financial interest in minimizing referrals or tests" (*Neade v. Portes,* pp. 426–427). The court also noted in support of its ruling this language from the American Medical Association Council on Ethical and Judicial Affairs (2000):

> Physicians must not deny their patients access to appropriate medical services based upon the promise of personal financial reward, or the avoidance of financial penalties. Because patients must have the necessary information to make informed decisions about their care, physicians have an obligation to assure the disclosure of medically appropriate treatment alternatives, regardless of cost. (pp. 181–182)

This notion that financial incentives should be disclosed has been called "economic informed consent." Although it is a comparatively new construct, and not all courts agree such disclosures must be made, approximately one-half of state legislatures have enacted this duty into law (Stauffer & Levy, 1999).

Other litigation has addressed the issue of financial incentives. In a recent decision (*Pegram et al. v. Herdrich,* 2000), the U.S. Supreme Court overturned a federal court of appeals decision that certain types of incentives in managed care plans were illegal because of their potential impact on health care practitioners. In *Herdrich,* the plaintiff alleged that physicians employed by an HMO failed to diagnose her appendicitis before her appendix ruptured. She recovered $35,000 in an award in a malpractice case brought in state court, but also sued alleging fraud by the defendants in administering the insurance plan under which her care was covered. The defendants, under ERISA, removed to federal court the claims dealing with fraud. A federal court of appeals ruled that the defendants (the primary defendant being a physician-owned HMO) had breached their fiduciary responsibilities under ERISA by creating incentives that could cause physicians to use fewer services for patients. The court of appeals concluded that these incentives created dual loyalties on the part of a physician, jeopardizing the ability of a patient to receive adequate care. The U.S. Supreme Court, in a unanimous decision, reversed the court of appeals.

The Supreme Court ruled that it was for Congress, not the courts, to determine whether some types of financial incentives should be illegal. The Court noted that to do otherwise would inject the federal courts into the process of judging incentives on a case-by-case basis, something the Supreme Court believed was an inappropriate role for the courts. In addition, the Court observed that any reimbursement plan, whether fee-for-service or managed care, included incentives designed to affect the behavior of health care professionals and that it was not possible to create a judicially drawn line sorting those incentives that were legal from those that were not.

The Court's ruling does not mean that managed care plans, including those that provide or arrange for care, can no longer be sued. In fact, it has been suggested that the Court's ruling implicitly accepts that such suits can be brought over quality of care in state court, an issue as noted earlier that was closely contested through the 1990s. However, the Court's ruling does make clear that significant amendments to ERISA, particularly those that address the substantive fiduciary responsibilities of health plan administrators, will have to come from Congress, rather than the courts.

In summary, malpractice litigation continues to be a topic of concern for mental health providers. As noted in the first section of this chapter, there are a number of substantive areas that may present more potential vulnerability than others. Good legal risk management plans, combined with up-to-date clinical practice, should ameliorate the risk of adverse judgments in the vast majority of such cases. The question of liability against managed care plans has been one of the most controversial issues in the managed care era. As the latter section of this chapter suggests, the courts have been more willing since the mid-1990s to entertain lawsuits alleging that a managed care plan may be liable under a malpractice theory, when the managed care plan provides care as well as provides plan administration. However, cases against ERISA-qualified plans over the availability of a particular benefit—for example, a denial of care on the ground of medical necessity or other applications of utilization review—must continue to be brought in federal court, where the potential recovery is much less than that available in a state malpractice claim. In addition, state legislatures continue to consider legislation that would explicitly permit lawsuits against managed care plans in state court, although Congress continues to be split on whether and how to amend ERISA and create a national standard for such litigation.

REFERENCES

American Medical Association Council on Ethical and Judicial Affairs. (2000). Code of Medical Ethics (Current Opinions). Section 8.132 of Current Opinions (pp. 181–182).

Appelbaum, P. S., & Gutheil, T. G. (1991). *Clinical handbook of psychiatry and the law* (2nd ed.). Baltimore, MD: Williams & Wilkins.

Appelbaum, P. S., Robbins, P. C., & Monahan, J. (2000). Violence and delusions: Data from the MacArthur Violence Risk Assessment Study. *American Journal of Psychiatry, 157*(4), 566–572.

Corporate Health Insurance Inc. v. Texas Department of Insurance, 215 F. 3d 526 (5th Cir. 2000).

Dukes v. U.S. Healthcare, Inc., 57 F. 3d 350 (3rd Cir. 1995).

Loomis v. Board of Psychologist Examiners, 954 P. 2d 839 (Ore. App. 1998).

Montgomery, L. M., Cupit, B. E., & Wimberley, T. K. (1999). Complaints, malpractice, and risk management. *Professional Psychology: Research & Practice, 30,* 402–410.

Neade v. Portes et al., Ill. Supreme Ct. No. 87445 (2000).

Pegram et al. v. Herdrich (98-1949), 154 F. 3d 362 (2000).

Sabin, J. E. (1994). A credo for ethical managed care in mental health practice. *Hospital and Community Psychiatry, 45,* 389.

Silver, E., Mulvey, E. P., & Monahan, J. (1999). Assessing violence risk among discharged psychiatric patients: Toward an ecological approach. *Law and Human Behavior, 23*(2), 237–255.

Simon, R. I. (1998). *Concise guide to psychiatry and law for clinicians.* Washington, DC: American Psychiatric Press.

Skeem, J. L., & Mulvey, E. P. (2001). Psychopathy and community violence among civil psychiatric patients: Results from the MacArthur Violence Risk Assessment Study. *Journal of Consulting and Clinical Psychology, 69*(3), 358–374.

Stauffer, M., & Levy, D. R. (1999). *1999 State by state guide to managed care law.* New York: Panel.

Tarasoff v. Regents of the University of California, 551 P. 2d 334, 345-47 (1976) (also 131 Cal Rptr 14, 551 p2d 334 [1976]).

Varol v. Blue Cross, 708 F. Supp. 826, 831-833 (E.D. Mich. 1989).

Wilson v. Blue Cross of So. California, 271 Cal Rptr 876 (1990).

Youngberg v. Romeo, 457 US 307 (1982).

Chapter Thirty-Nine

Living Under Class Action Lawsuits: Their Effect on Mental Health Agency Staff and Patients

Gary E. Miller

EDITOR'S NOTE

"Class action" lawsuits involve large groups of plaintiffs (many of whom may not realize that they are plaintiffs) who seek broad redress for alleged wrongs against the group as a whole. In mental health, and particularly in the public sector, class action litigation, usually brought in federal court, has for decades been viewed by some as a legitimate mechanism for social change. Others see great potential for unintended damage to the very people it is supposed to help.

The process often goes something like this:

- A group of people, spurred by attorneys and/or executives of organizations such as advocacy groups, the American Civil Liberties Union, the U.S. Department of Justice, or federally funded protection and advocacy bodies (called "Advocacy, Inc." or "Protection & Advocacy" in many states), find or solicit complaints about a mental health agency's care. Next, using a few patients as examples, they file suit on behalf of all people receiving certain services or with a certain status (the "class," e.g., all patients of the mental health agency). The suit routinely covers the entire system or agency.
- Once the suit is filed, lawyers for both sides start the process of preparing their cases, beginning with a long search to uncover information that might support their views. For the plaintiffs, this "discovery" process includes requesting huge volumes of records and other data kept by the agency. Because public service agencies operate largely in the public domain, records are relatively easy to obtain (although expensive for the agency to provide). Even confidential patient records are reviewed, in a process that takes many months, and often years. The legal rules for the discovery process require that the agency provide virtually all of the requested data, at considerable cost in time and resources.
- Most such suits are settled or otherwise resolved in such a way that the agency

agrees to make changes under the broad, long-lasting control of a court (through complex rules enumerated in documents often called "consent decrees" or "settlement agreements" in which the agency consents to those changes and control). The court appoints a group of people, led by a "master" of some kind who reports solely to the court. The master has no responsibility to the agency, its government or legislature, or patients themselves. The master thus has enormous authority as long as the consent decree or settlement agreement is in place. (It is important to note that, for a number of largely practical and political reasons, *mental health agencies rarely take class action lawsuits all the way to trial,* even when the allegations are unlikely to be substantiated. Thus there is no final determination of liability or negligence, only the agreement between the sides.)

- Most consent decrees and settlement agreements contain a long list of requirements that the agency must meet, after which the lawsuit is ended. This is not as simple as it appears, however. The requirements are usually extremely complex, and in large suits require millions (occasionally billions) of taxpayer dollars and years of work, followed by years of court (master) monitoring to see that the required changes are maintained. During this period, resources must be diverted from things the *agency* needs or wants for patients, to things the *master* (representing the court) believes are more important. The single master's view of what is more important is extremely influential, subject only to the court's approval. This condition, in which the court, through its master, controls the agency and its priorities and resources, may last for decades.

Public-sector mental health agencies are a fairly easy target. Unlike private businesses and companies, they operate almost entirely in the public view, sometimes described as a "in a fishbowl." It is easy to muster public opinion against government agencies, in part because they are so visible and rarely "fight back" against media attacks by, for example, the lawyers who sue them. Public agencies, more than most private ones, must carefully balance their relationships with patients/clients, legislators and government executives, employees and clinical providers, other organizations, and the media. Plaintiffs' attorneys and clients in class actions have far fewer constraints.

Are class action lawsuits good or bad? No one wants bad or abusive care. The availability of lawsuits to potential plaintiffs as a "remedy" for negligent and damaging actions is an important right. The civil courts exist to help plaintiffs seek reasonable redress for wrongs against them, and to create a "level playing field" for the battles that can ensue.

Some public-sector mental health managers and executives used to view lawsuits as one way to force legislators and governments to provide better funding for care. Indeed, this is often the purported goal of class action litigation. A number of recent lawsuits, however, have shown just how costly such litigation can be, and strongly imply that the lawsuits themselves can bring damage to agencies, their employees, *and their patients* that is worse than the problems they were designed to address.

Here is how the head of one of the largest state agencies in the country explained the effects of two class action suits to thousands of beleaguered employees who had labored under them for several years. The message came in the form of a memo from Commissioner Gary E. Miller to the staff of the Texas Department of Mental Health and Mental Retardation (TXMHMR).

MEMO

From: The Commissioner, Gary E. Miller, M.D.
To: ALL TXMHMR Employees
Date: July 1, 1987

This is a difficult time for TXMHMR employees. Almost daily the public is told by television, radio, and newspapers that our department is doing a poor job in caring for people with mental illness and mental retardation.

I have no doubt that these media reports have led some people to think that TXMHMR employees do not care about their clients or that they lack the knowledge and skills necessary to provide quality services for them.

But what I fear most is that some of you may come to doubt the value of your work or of your services to our clients. The continuing publicity about allegedly poor care in our state hospitals and state schools cannot help but undermine the morale of the people who work for our department. The bad publicity and some other problems I will discuss later are what prompted me to write this special message to you.

The first point I want to make is that the stories in the press about poor care are either untrue or gross exaggerations. Except for isolated instances of abuse or neglect—which occur in every health care setting—the services you provide are not just "adequate"; they are exceptional. If objective measures were used to compare our MHMR programs to programs in other states and even some of those in the private sector, the Texas system would be ranked near the top. Our state facilities and community programs are at least the equal of most others; in many cases, they are much better. I am not arguing that our system is perfect or that it could not use more money and more staff. I am saying only that we do an excellent job with the money we have—in fact, a better job than a lot of other states that spend more money.

Some of the newspaper accounts of TXMHMR facilities must seem incredible to those of you who work daily on the dormitories and wards of those facilities—as they must seem incredible to the hundreds of visitors and volunteers who have intimate knowledge of the care you give to our clients. Unfortunately, less knowledgeable members of the general public may conclude from the media stories that our hospitals and schools are bad places. They may worry about what could happen if a family member is admitted to a TXMHMR facility; they may even fear for the safety of a relative or friend who resides in a facility.

Although the bad publicity is a serious problem for our department, our clients, and the people of Texas, I believe we will eventually be able to tell the public about the fine job that you do. I am committed to using all available departmental resources to get that message across.

My second point is that most of the bad publicity can be traced to the two class-action lawsuits against the department (*R.A.J. v. Miller* and *Lelsz v. Kavanagh*). Although often sensational in tone, inaccurate and misleading, the publicity is not the fault of the press. The journalists who produce it are just doing their jobs. And as I have said, it is not your fault. You and your fellow employees do a good job under what are sometimes less than ideal conditions.

Why is it then that the professional judgments of our clinicians are assailed in public merely because some other "expert" has a different opinion? Why is it that our state hospitals are attacked in the press as substandard when (unlike those of most other large states) they meet the only nationally recognized standard—accreditation by the Joint Commission on Accreditation of Hospitals? Why is it that we are subjected to media claims that the programs of our state schools are inadequate when they all comply with stringent federal Medicaid standards?

The answer, as I have suggested, lies with the two class-action lawsuits. The issue is not whether the plaintiffs were justified in filing the lawsuits in 1974 or even whether the lawsuits are, on balance, good or bad for the people we serve.

It is just that the lawsuits permit—or encourage—actions on the part of the participants that complicate our already formidable task of serving the state's mentally retarded and mentally ill. The bad publicity is one of those complications, but there are others just as serious. Here are some detrimental effects of the lawsuits, which, as you will see, include but extend beyond the problem of bad publicity.

The lawsuits violate basic management principles. The present structure of the lawsuits directly affects the administration of our department. It is easy to forget—because we usually think of lawsuits in terms of lawyers, courtrooms, and black-robed judges—that lawsuits can take a managerial role, intruding into the agency's policymaking authority and directing the work of its employees. That is what has been happening to TXMHMR since the *R.A.J.* and *Lelsz* lawsuits were settled in 1981 and 1983. (I use the word "settled" advisedly. Although technically the cases were settled when the parties negotiated Settlement Agreements that were later approved by the courts, the settlements marked the beginning rather than the end of intense adversarial activity.)

Let me explain how the lawsuits result in management decisions that violate basic management principles. Today, court-appointed monitors (an expert consultant in *Lelsz*, a review panel in *R.A.J.*) inspect our department programs (often with the help of other experts they hire), form conclusions about the job we are doing, and pass those conclusions on to the court and—as we have seen—to the media.

The monitors and their consultants are not the only experts who make pronouncements about the department. Other parties in the lawsuits (the plaintiffs who file the suits and several organizational intervenors) also send their experts to review our programs and announce their conclusions to the court and the public.

Sometimes these experts offer suggestions that can help us do a better job. Most of the time, their reports are critical of our work. Minor problems are exaggerated; isolated incidents are portrayed as typical of an entire state hospital or state school, or of all state hospitals or state schools; opinions of outside professionals, which are usually no better than and sometimes not as good as those of our own TXMHMR professionals, are presented to the courts and the public as the only "correct" or "acceptable" way of doing things.

Thus, we read in the newspaper that our programs are unacceptable, our professionals inadequately trained, and our clients systematically abused and neglected.

All of this is frustrating to me as I know it is to you. We rarely have the opportunity to challenge or question the accuracy of the conclusions of these court monitors and experts. And on those rare occasions when we do have that opportunity, we are automatically on the defensive. Unlike the criminal justice system where one is presumed innocent until proven guilty, we are assumed to be guilty and must struggle to defend the care we provide to our clients.

Federal judges do not simply think about or study accusations made by our adversaries and our defenses against them; they act. The enormous power of the federal court is exercised in the form of court orders. We have been told in exquisite detail how many mentally retarded people from certain categories we are required to place from state schools into community programs in a year's time; we have been told how many mental health workers must be present on every ward of every state hospital; we have been told that community MHMR centers are now to be known as department facilities; we have been told that there is "too much" violence in our state hospitals, even though there was not a shred of evidence to support that conclusion. If we are told by a district court that red is blue, we have no choice but to accept the court's decision unless and until an appellate court reminds the district court that the color is really red.

Court orders thus affect the department's management of personnel, finances, and treatment programs. Unlike normal management practices, these management decisions represent the exercise of power without accountability. You and I have superiors. We are given direction about what sort of work and accomplishments are expected of us. Our supervisors look at how we perform and hold us accountable for the results. Beyond those basics, as state employees we are responsible ultimately to the people of Texas. The elected representatives of the people—the governor, lieutenant governor, and legislators—make state policy, write the laws, and select the members of our state board who, in turn, direct my activities and yours.

This political constituency to which we in TXMHMR are accountable, and the accountability that we all have within our agency, are almost entirely lacking in the control of our department by the federal courts.

Anyone who is the least bit familiar with management principles knows that authority and responsibility must go together. That is clearly not the case in management by court order. The department is always the fall guy. If something goes wrong in our facilities, it is our fault; whatever progress is made is of course to the credit of the lawsuits and the court monitors. The court monitors can do no wrong; they do not have to account directly or indirectly to the people of Texas for the correctness of their conclusions about TXMHMR facilities or for the accuracy of their statements to the press.

The lawsuits violate another basic management principle: that decisions should be based on the best available information. A federal judge may not be motivated to "reform" a state institution, but the structure of the lawsuits guarantees that the judge will have neither the information necessary to make good management decisions (that is, issue court orders) nor reliable information about how his decisions affect the state institution. Private conversations with court monitors, briefs filed by lawyers, and legal rhetoric in the courtroom are simply not the equivalent of the comprehensive flow of accurate information and feedback that a manager would need in order to make important decisions about a complex program like a state hospital or state school.

For example, a manager with the authority to make decisions about such things as staffing and treatment programs in our facilities would normally not exercise that authority without first spending some time at the facilities and becoming familiar with your work by talking to you and your clients, learning something about what people with mental illness and mental retardation are like, and learning as much as possible about treatment methods and their limitations. Obviously, none of this is possible under the peculiar management structure dictated by the lawsuits.

The real responsibility for care of the patients and clients rests with you and me, the employees of TXMHMR. Our job is not made any easier by the bad management practices that result from the lawsuits.

The Public Is Being Misled

This is where the bad publicity comes in. Let me begin by describing how I believe our adversaries view their role in the lawsuits. They are the good guys, out to reform an antiquated and inadequate system of care. We, on the other hand, are the defenders of the old and bad way of doing things. They are the people who really care about our clients; we are merely bureaucrats collecting our paychecks. It is they, not we, who are "concerned" about client abuse, good treatment planning, and habilitation programs.

It is ironic that people like you who take on some of the most challenging and difficult jobs in government for relatively low pay are viewed as the problem by monitors and outside experts. Not only do you care, not only are you concerned about our patients and clients, it is you who have shown your willingness to do something about it. You made a personal commitment to help the patients and clients of this department by taking on a care and treatment or management and support role. Your role is vital to the well-being of our clients—and a lot tougher then standing on the sidelines and criticizing our facilities.

I began this section with a description of how I believe our adversaries view their role and ours. It is the structure of the lawsuits and the resulting poor management practices that permit these views of the monitors, plaintiffs, and intervenors to be broadcast to the public as though they were proven facts. As we have seen, when there is no accountability—no reason to be accurate, to explain or to defend one's opinions—we have what is in effect an invitation to distort the facts.

Will the Lawsuits Ever Go Away?

TXMHMR employees must wonder whether our agency can ever do enough or be good enough to be released from the jurisdiction of the federal court.

I wish that getting out from under these lawsuits were simply a matter of doing everything the department said it would do in the Settlement Agreements in *Lelsz* and *R.A.J.* Unfortunately, our experience in Texas and our knowledge of similar lawsuits in other states tells us that won't happen.

Both *Lelsz* and *R.A.J.* have demonstrated a tendency to create new issues on a regular basis, that is, to find new things wrong about what we do, thus expanding the scope of the lawsuits and the number of areas that must be monitored by the court. This serves, of course, to perpetuate the lawsuits, to keep them moving along from year to year like a runaway train.

It is not difficult to figure out the motivation of various parties for those activities that expand and continue the lawsuits. People seldom give up power voluntarily, especially when the power is exercised without accountability. There must be a good deal of gratification in exercising power over a state agency, summoning up vast quantities of indignation and concern about conditions in our facilities for the benefit of the press, and having no need to defend one's actions or take any political heat.

Economic forces are also at work. A lot of people make a lot of money as long as the lawsuits continue. There are attorneys' fees, expensive outside experts, and of course the money that pays the salaries of the monitors and members of their organizations.

Although the court monitors are doubtless motivated by a desire to reform a state system they perceive as requiring reform, they also do this for a living. Their job depends on there being enough work for them to justify their continued employment. Thus, they have little motivation to find our department in compliance with various provisions of the Settlement Agreements and a lot of motivation to read new meanings into the language of those agreements and to discover new "problems" that raise compliance issues and require more monitoring.

The lawsuits seem as though they will drag on forever, but there are some things we can do to make them "go away."

What Can We Do?

We are not helpless. There are actions we are taking and can take that will ultimately lead to our vindication in the eyes of the public and to resolution of the lawsuits.

First, it is important that you continue to do the good job you are doing. It is easy to become distracted or discouraged because of the bad publicity and other pressures of the lawsuits. Nevertheless, we must work as hard as we can at our various jobs to keep the quality of care we give to our patients and clients and to efficiently administer our agency and its facilities.

Second, we must continually improve our delivery system and the treatment of people in our care. This means, among other things, working with the governor and the legislature to increase our funding (already being done), keeping up to date with modern techniques through training and continuing education, improving the individual program and treatment planning for our clients and patients, and striving to improve our management of personnel and other resources of the Department.

Third, we must get the message to the people of Texas that we do a good job in serving the mentally retarded and mentally ill, and that our treatment programs are constantly improving. The Department will initiate an intensified public information program which will involve Central Office and all of our facilities. You will hear more about this later.

Finally, we must deal with the lawsuits on their own terms—that is, we must vigorously defend the interests of our agency and the state of Texas in the federal courts. I am extremely pleased with the staff of the Attorney General's Office who represent our agency. They have done a superb job not only as articulate legal advocates for our department, but also as colleagues, supporters, and even as advisors on ways to improve our programs.

The Department won a decisive victory in January when the Fifth Circuit Court of Appeals overturned an order of the District Court and prohibited court-ordered quotas for community placement of mentally retarded people. The language of the Fifth Circuit opinion offers us hope that the lawsuits may eventually be resolved. For example, in discussing the plaintiffs' argument that a District Court judge has the right to interpret a settlement agreement in any way he wants so long as the judge's orders are consistent with the spirit of the agreement, the Fifth Circuit said: "If, as appellees (plaintiffs) argue, a federal court may take almost any action against a state to enforce a consent decree (settlement agreement) so long as it is 'consistent with' the 'spirit' of the applicable constitutional law and the decree itself, there is no limitation on the scope of the court's power. Lack of restraint on an organ of government (even the judiciary) is the antithesis of law."

Let me end this message by reminding you how much I appreciate the contribution that each of you makes to this department. I am confident that the problems created by the lawsuits will eventually be a thing of the past. Our efforts can do a lot toward achieving that end.

Editor's Note: Final resolution of both lawsuits did not occur for may more years.

Part Seven

A PRIMER FOR NEW CLINICIAN-MANAGERS

INTRODUCTION

William H. Reid

The following three chapters are designed for clinicians who want to succeed in health care administration. You may be enthusiastic about moving from a primarily clinical base to a management career, or you may be stuck in a frustrating management environment and want to do something about it. These chapters ("Management and the Management Environment," "Leadership," and "Negotiation") are purposely informal and practical, even simplistic, compared to other chapters and sections in this book. They are a guide, not a scholarly reference. We hope you find them useful, and even fun at times.

Chapter Forty

Management and the Management Environment

William H. Reid
Daniel J. Reid

Over 2000 years ago, a Chinese general named Sun Tzu[1] wrote *The Art of War*. Since then, every study of strategy, including those in the vast array of "power books" in bookstores and airport book stalls, has begun with the same idea: Understand where you are and where you want to be.

> *Understand where you are and where you want to be.*

One must also know the "enemy." History is full of generals who won battles by knowing both their own armies and the enemy's strategy and capabilities. Custer knew the former, but had a serious problem with the latter. The process of moving you into the management arena begins with understanding that arena and its functions.

Sounds like we're talking about a war, doesn't it? With some important exceptions, pursuing what is best for you or your organization is often a highly aggressive activity. We strongly suggest that you accept and practice a certain amount of aggression in your pursuit of the management ranks.[2]

Finally, we want you to *identify with the people whose positions you would like to attain.* If you want to be taken seriously—by yourself as well as by senior management—start thinking of yourself as something more than a clinical professional. Show others that you think and feel like a manager, even an executive. Learn and *use* the vocabulary and principles you'll find in this book; don't keep them to yourself like some bit of scholarly knowledge or cocktail-party information.

Dress the part. Identify with that which you want to become, not just with your

---

1, No one is completely sure who Sun Tzu was. Some scholars think the real general was his grandfather, or even his grandson. A minority are convinced "Sun Tzu" actually referred to a popular pre-Confucian beer.

2. Dan calls it our "balls to the wall" approach to management, a reference not to things sexist or genital, but to WWII fighter pilots who got maximum power by pushing their throttle controls (often levers with spheres at the top) all the way forward, toward the firewall.

professional peers. We're sorry to have to break this to you, but most of your peers aren't good managers or leaders. We'll have lots of suggestions about this later.

Identify with that which you want to become,

Please note that we did not say your peers are bad or unimportant people. We're not asking you to be mean or unethical, or to shun your friends and patients. We just want you to see some things that other clinicians don't see. We want you to be ambitious, not "cutthroat." Believe it or not, business and management have some pretty strong ethics, to which this book devotes considerable space.

MANAGERS AND EXECUTIVES—THERE IS A DIFFERENCE

The management environment has a hierarchy of people whose function is to design and execute the goals of the organization. If this sounds simple, that's because it is. Let's start with *managers.*

Managers manage, right? Well, yes and no. Most people believe that the function of a manager (aside from getting in your hair) is simply to ensure that certain goals and/or tasks are completed. Although this is generally true as far as it goes, only the lowest level managers have so simple a job description.

Herein lies a fundamental flaw in many clinicians' perception of management. It goes like this: "I'm a professional. I know my job and do it well. Why do I need a manager, as long as I complete my tasks on my own?"

First of all, if you perform a professional function with little or no direct supervision, then you are by definition already a manager of sorts. Add a few more tasks and a few more people and you are still a manager, but now you have a few more tasks and a few more people. Add some time constraints, quality constraints, and budgetary constraints, and you have become a middle manager with more people and tasks, working within a lot of constraints. Although an important step, this isn't where you ultimately want to be, managing ever-larger tasks and more people, under ever more complex constraints. Does this sound like the freedom and control you seek?

Whether they manage a little or a lot, managers carry out assignments. They are measured and compensated on the basis of how well they perform a directed function, whether that function is greater output, reduced cost, or higher quality. The key is that, as a rule, managers do not make major policy; they carry it out.

Managers don't make major policy; they carry it out.

Here's the catch, and the reason you should want to be a manager, at least for a while: Managers, as contrasted with many other employees, have added *flexibility* in how they accomplish their assignments; the more senior the manager, the more flexibility. In a progressive organization, they are allowed—and encouraged—to be very creative. Since most management centers on people, this means choosing from a variety of *management tools* for motivating, rewarding, and controlling others. You already know that you do your best work when your boss recognizes your abilities and lets you use them. Successful managers know lots of ways to do that.

Policy refers to decisions about how and why things are done in the organization. Some policy affects the entire organization, but some is as simple as adhering to a particular job procedure. If you have influence over such procedures, that's a start. We don't want you to use your professional training and experience just to carry out others' directives, however. We want you to be able to influence major policy decisions.

The logical hierarchy of management levels is where most of us "pay our dues" and learn about the organization, its various functions, and its culture. Clinicians, by virtue of their college degrees, skills, and special importance to the organization's mission, often enter that hierarchy at a level that is beyond their management skills, or are promoted into professional management positions early in their careers. This is especially common in rural areas, professional shortage specialties, and organizations in which the pay for senior clinician-manager positions is so low that it doesn't attract highly experienced candidates (e.g., some public-sector mental health facilities and agencies).

That sounds good for your career, but it's actually bad. Think about it. Should a recently graduated psychologist be expected to manage a treatment program? Does nursing school alone prepare one to be a hospital unit chief or director of nursing? Do psychiatrists have any business being state mental hospital superintendents?

Not without management skills and attitudes, they don't.

The newly anointed clinician-manager often does a mediocre job, and sometimes fails completely. "Mediocre" and "fail" are not in the lexicon of most physicians and other clinicians. They don't feel good. They can crush your self-image, sour you on management in general, contribute to early burnout, and, of course, destroy any hope of your being recognized and promoted for your management success.

The new clinician-manager, the person who has just been promoted to section chief or program director (or who wants to be), is thus at a critical crossroads in his or her career. The crucial question is: "Are you sure you want to be one of Them?"

If you just answered "Yes," you must address a second question: "Do you understand that your potential for success does not rest with your professional skills and experience?"

> *Your management success does not rely on*
> *your professional skills and experience.*

We believe that, in the long run, the skills required of policymakers and senior management staff need not require years in the trenches of the organization. It is the skills and attitudes of management, not the types[3] nor durations of management jobs, that are important. The particular management skills and knowledge that we consider vital for you are explained elsewhere in our three chapters and the remainder of the book.

> *Executive and senior management qualities are not the result of time*
> *spent in the trenches; your management skills and attitudes*
> *are more important than where you have worked.*

---

3. Corporation CEOs, for example, may come from careers in marketing, finance, operations, or research and development, but they *always* have excellent management and executive skills.

We want you to think of "middle" managerial positions as *steps*, important but interim in nature. Think of management positions as a training ground. In general, the better you do and the more you learn, the better are your chances of becoming a senior manager or executive. Management positions are your first steps toward influencing policy and weaning yourself from being solely a clinician.

Executives are an interesting breed. They come in all flavors, from Lee Iacocca, to RJR Nabisco's flamboyant Ross Johnson, to the back-room types who move and shake from obscurity. Some are the true leaders, whereas some are more like senior managers than archetypal executives. The line is fuzzy at times. The important point, and one we stress, is that executives in large organizations spend most of their time developing and fostering major policy, not implementing it. It is here that your biggest great ideas can see some action.

That's the good news.

The bad news is that with the executive's power to create comes the responsibility for his or her creations. A failed managerial *task* affects your job and a small part of the organization's mission. Failed major *policy* can affect everyone's job, and the entire system. That's why organizations are so particular about who becomes a senior manager or executive. Even in small organizations, the executive/senior management arena is no place for amateurs. Organizations simply can't afford to put much power in the hands of clinicians (even highly competent ones) who don't deeply understand broad management, executive, and leadership issues.

> *Organizations can't afford to give power to people who don't understand broad management, executive, and leadership issues.*

This also applies to small groups such as mental health practice partnerships. Although management problems may be hidden for a while by the ability of the individuals to make money, office and business management—by a real manager—can make the difference between failure and success of the group enterprise.

Again, there is no magic to all of this. Whether you work for a large mental health agency or a small clinical practice, whether you have a Harvard MBA or can't spell businiss, executives and senior managers must succeed at three functions: defining the goals of the organization, developing strategies for reaching those goals, and implementing the strategies. They devote most or all of their working hours to these three functions. Everything else is detail.

> *Executives and senior managers do only three things: define organization goals, develop goal-oriented strategies, and implement those strategies.*

AN INTRODUCTION TO ORGANIZATION STRUCTURE

Managing well is essential, but let's broaden our scope for a moment. The more you understand about the overall structure of the organization, its culture, and what it needs, the more you will succeed and the more you will be rewarded.

Clinicians work in far more organizations than we can specifically describe. Mental health organizations can be public or private, for-profit or nonprofit. They can be as large as a huge government agency with many subdivisions or as small as a private office or rural outreach center. You may work in a mental health clinic, a hospital, a managed care organization, or a public agency.

In every case, your organization has a *structure* that both supports and is a result of its *function*. Understanding the structure tells you more about where you are (remember Sun Tzu). It also provides valuable information about goals, strategies, and organization culture. In ailing or struggling organizations, the structure is a good place to look for areas of mismatch between what is there and what is needed for success (managerial "diagnostic and treatment" suggestions).

Knowledge of *goals* and *strategies* is another key to understanding any organization. All the reasoning behind the organization's structure is related to these two concepts. Change either and the structure should change as well. If it doesn't, the organization will begin to fail.

For example, the motto, or "mission statement," of a once very successful company was, "We Make the Finest Available Carriages and Related Equestrian Tack." Then along came Henry Ford and his Model T. Horses stayed in style, but carriages were out. The mission statement had to become, "We Make the Finest Equestrian Tack." (Note: "Tack" is bridles, saddles, etc. We're from Texas.)

That organization had to change a peripheral portion of the business into the core of the business. It then had to create demand, expand the line, change the sales emphasis, and deal with a lot of displaced workers. It no longer needed a carriage division, with its wheelwrights, upholsterers, salespeople, testing facility (with a wind tunnel for really fast carriages), or even the executives that planned new ways to increase carriage production. Had they been allowed to stay—had the old structure remained—the company's future would have been more like that of the Mortimer & Fitz Carriage Company (bet you've never heard of them).

We're sneaking in another concept here, so subtly that you probably haven't noticed it: the constancy, the inevitability, of *change*.

CHANGE

If you are a professor whose speciality is Cold War politics, you have two choices: You could (a) find a *niche* that lets you study and teach about a topic whose relevance is rapidly decreasing (a job strategy we might call "entrenchment"), or (b) find some way to turn the change in academic and political relevance to your advantage in your organization's environment. You might, for example, learn more about the goals and strategies of your department and college, then plan the next few years of your career accordingly.

Guess which we recommend.

Knowing the "Big Picture"

Knowledge of the current mission and goals of the mental health organization leads to an understanding of its structure (and vice versa). If you see that the structure is inefficient or doesn't fit the goals, *and* you have placed yourself in a position visible to upper management, your input (assuming you understand the mission and therefore the structure) is more likely to be heard. If you are heard, you are more likely to be heeded. If heeded, you are influencing policy. And that's where you want to be.

The same applies to strategy. You are more likely to be heard if your idea is clearly related to accomplishing *organization* goals than if your ideas seem limited to your profession. If you don't know the "big picture," you are less likely to be heard.

Smaller Parts of the Big Picture

This doesn't mean that suggestions about an individual job always fall on deaf ears. Progressive organizations pay attention to employee comments, suggestions, and feelings. After all, increasing the effectiveness of, say, a particular treatment procedure may save money and increase service quality.

Let's examine how such an idea might be presented.

- A state mental health center clinician tells his or her unit chief how to improve a particular procedure.
- The unit chief tells his or her program director how the department can do a better, more cost-effective job.
- The program director says "Let's do it," and puts the change in his or her next report to the CMHC director. The report says something like, "This process contributes to a 12% increase in our overall clinic productivity, with a 3% reduction in costs and a significant decrease in patient readmissions."
- The CMHC director makes darn sure the appropriate senior manager in the state agency central office knows that his or her CMHC is supporting the agency's mission, which happens to be "Higher Quality and Greater Efficiency Working Hand-in-hand for Patient Care."

Now, who benefits from the treatment procedure suggestion? (Keep an eye on how the local clinician makes out.)

- The statewide senior agency manager's position is strengthened because payer costs went down and quality went up.
- The CMHC director (a local "CEO") gets recognized for contributing to the agency mission and to the strength of upper management. He or she wonders when the statewide senior manager is due to retire.
- The program director is recognized as a good local manager, one who supports organization goals and gets the job done.
- The unit chief (who may also be a direct-care clinician) gets a raise and recognition for his or her managerial success. If he or she is able to translate this talent to broader CMHC/agency issues (broader than the local unit), and has the attitude and initiative necessary for broader responsibility, he or she may be ready to move out of this specific niche and into general management.
- The unit clinician gets a pat on the back and the satisfaction of seeing others take his or her idea and run with it.

If that's happened to you, keep reading.

ORGANIZATIONAL CULTURE

It may seem strange to talk about "culture" in a mental health organization. It's a real thing, however, and a concept that can be of great use both to you and to the organization. It might be described as "personality," how things get done, the expected atmosphere and traditional modus operandi. It is important to realize the importance of culture to the organization and its people.

For example, many systems have very strict service and billing specifications. The specifications and their strictness are *policy*. The way clinical employees are motivated to meet those specifications is one (and only one) reflection of the organization's *culture*. One clinic or system may do it by punishing noncompliance. Another may accomplish the same goal by creating an atmosphere of dedication and teamwork.

Like "personality" in people, the organizational culture may not always seem logical. It may actually work against the corporate mission. In the carriage factory example mentioned earlier, even seemingly business-oriented executives may find it difficult to move from carriages to mere accessories. Why? Because "We've always made carriages." "I've devoted my career to carriages." "The equestrian tack division has always been second-class around here." "When people see our name, they think of carriages." "Everybody admires a fine carriage."

Never mind that no one *buys* them anymore.

As you study the culture of your organization, think about the following.

1. *Culture evolves from the needs and personalities of the people who shape (or shaped) the organization.* Study the personalities and look for the relationships.
2. *Culture can be healthy or unhealthy.* The sweatshop culture common to early industrialization was unhealthy. Companies that abolished the sweatshop mentality tended to prosper. The innovations and evolving ideas of Herman Miller, Inc., is one of the better examples of a healthy culture. CEO Max DePree summed it up as follows:

   Corporations, like the people who compose them, are always in a state of becoming. Covenants bind people together and enable them to meet their corporate needs by meeting the needs of one another.

3. *Mission, strategy, leadership, and structure should be in harmony.* Should a new CEO take the reins at Herman Miller, Inc. (described earlier), there would be conflict until the new leadership conforms to the culture,[4] the culture changes, or the leadership changes again.
4. *Examine your compatibility with your organization's culture.* Do the mission and culture of your organization reflect ideals with which you can agree and identify? *This is one of the fundamental things you must know about yourself and your employer before you can set a course for the future.* One might think that few people would seek employment in a culture that is counter to their personalities or ideals. The fact is, they do it every day.

---

4. There is a historical adage that "the religion of the king is the religion of the people." This doesn't mean the people conform to the king, as most readers assume, but that the king—if he knows what's good for him—will conform to the needs of the people.

A good example can be found in the conflict among environmentalists, the logging industry, and the National Forest Service. Environmentalists want to protect virgin timber stands. Loggers want to make a living. The Forest Service has a duty to serve the needs of both. Many people join the Forest Service because of an interest in preserving forests, but soon come to believe that they cannot fairly serve both environmentalists and the logging industry. As the mission and policies of the U.S. Department of Agriculture change, can the individuals change as well? If so, the culture will gradually shift. If not, either the workers will be replaced or a dysfunctional culture will evolve.

What happens if your beliefs are fundamentally different from those of your organization? Should you hang on, hoping for change? Quit and look for another job? Even if you quit, where can you find the compatibility you seek?

For some, there is little choice. You're dedicated to patient care and perfect jobs are pretty rare. Hanging on may be frustrating, but security and retirement vesting may be important to you. The best answer may be to hone your management skills, work with the organization, and prepare to become a shaper of your job and company policy rather than a victim of both.

HANDS-ON WORK

We've looked at organizational missions and goals, strategy, the corporate structure that follows those concepts, and the people who staff them. Now it's your turn to do some work.[5]

Mission Statement

Your organization has a mission, and probably a published *mission statement*. Mission statements are short, a few lines at most. They describe the business the company is in and why. Write down what you think is the mission of your organization.

Next, write down what you think the mission of your organization *should be*. Think only in terms of your perception, including what you see in the way of organizational culture.

---

5. It's for your own good. Honest.

Finally, write down your organization's actual mission statement. It may be found in a policy manual, a formal document issued by the head of your organization, or even on the letterhead.

Compare the things you've written here. They are almost never the same. Set them aside for the time being and let's look at strategy.

Strategy

Strategy within an organization is the current and future plan to accomplish the goals outlined in the mission statement. This can get complex; there are often many strategies, constantly changing as old ideas become obsolete and new ones take their places.

An organization's strategies are often not available to the general workforce. They may or may not be written, and they may be disguised as something else. A strategy to increase market share may appear to the public and most employees as an offer of superior products or services at a lower price. To the marketing department, however, the real purpose may be to increase market share by ruining the competition's market.

Write down what you think are your organization's primary strategies, what you think they *should* be, and whatever you can find out about what they actually are.

I think our main strategies are:

I think they *should* be:

When I looked into it, I found they are:

Organization Structure

You guessed it. Same exercise.

Outline the structure of your organization. The result should be similar to the proverbial "table of organization." Be as complete as you can. It will take some time, but it will also encourage some new kinds of thought.

For readers in large, diversified organizations, keep it simple by entering the senior executive positions and then cutting to your division. The point is to include enough positions that you can see the effect of structure on the mission, strategies, and activities of the organization.

Here's the way I think we're organized:

Here's the way we *should* be organized:

Here's the official organizational chart:

Culture

Cultural features are tough to put on paper. In an ideal situation, many cultural aspects of the organization are reflected in its stated mission and goals. In reality, they may be quite different. Cultural features may be small and localized, and may not appear to have anything to do with the overall organization. If you think certain common feelings and actions reflect "the way things are done around here," write them down.

I think our culture highlights the following:

Next, write what you think the culture should be. How *should* things be done around here? Let yourself go on this one. If you could pick the organization's methods and attitudes, what would you try to change?

Our culture *should* emphasize:

After some research, I've found that our culture is reflected in:

Now that you have three mission statements, three sets of strategies, three organizational charts, and some cultural features, what do you have besides an exercise that was probably a pain? *You now have the foundation for getting where you want to go, either in your present organization or in another one.*

Study the differences within each category. Next, study ways in which they fit together. Could you mix and match different items from each category to make the "perfect" organization? Are there similarities among your perceptions, your recommendations, and the realities of your organization and the environment in which it functions?

There are no right answers, only awareness. For instance, if there were very few similarities, is it because of you or because of the organization? Are your ideas better or worse than the realities? Is it as simple as being in an organization that doesn't fit your ideals? Or are you in the right place but either you or your organization has some serious problems?

Chapter Forty-One

Leadership

William H. Reid
Daniel J. Reid

People are hired for their technical competence, fired for their technical incompetence, and promoted for their leadership skills.
—Jack Zenger

Leadership is the art of getting someone else to do something you want done because he wants to do it.
—Dwight D. Eisenhower

L et's go back to the carriage manufacturer in the last chapter. Henry Ford has just developed a practical automobile (and production lines) and the carriage business is in deep *kimchee*. The company CEO is nearing retirement and wants to choose a successor who will get the company through these trying, changing times. He calls Ted and Bob,[1] his two top vice-presidents:

"I know you two don't see eye to eye," he says, "but one of you has got to carry on after I'm gone."

(Insert sad violins here.)

He continues: "The violins are nice, but what I really care about is this company's survival. You've each got 30 days to come up with a plan. The winner becomes the new CEO."

(Close-up of calendar pages flying away; a month passes.)

The CEO opens the discussion. "Today's the day. You first, Ted."

"Well, Dad . . . er, Chief, the automobile's here to stay. That's bad news; but there is some good news. First, it's 1908 and cars aren't very sturdy. Sales are confined mainly to cities, where roads are pretty good. The rural areas will remain a market for our carriages for years. Second, Ford is looking for manufacturing space and warehouses to hold his inventory. We have lots of both in the cities.

---

1. We wanted to make one of the vice-presidents a woman, but this is 1908.

"I say we close down most of our manufacturing plants in the cities and sell our plant and warehouse space to Henry for top dollar. Then we concentrate our sales in the rural areas to fill continuing rural customer need. We'll lower our overhead and operating expense and reduce our debt. The balance sheet will look good and our stockholders will continue to receive dividends for the foreseeable future."

The CEO grunted, and seemed to be thinking of Tahiti. "Your turn, Bob."

"Chief, I agree with Ted that the automobile is here to stay. I also agree that the automobile is currently manufactured and used in cities. My plan, however, is different.

"I'd retain most of our existing plants and personnel and concentrate on retooling and retraining to take advantage of this new automotive industry. Henry Ford knows engines, but we make great coaches and we know how to create a smooth ride on bumpy roads. I think Henry would be interested in a joint venture to furnish leather seats, good wheels, and maybe even frames for 'horseless' carriages. At the same time, I'd like to take some of our more entrenched personnel, nonconvertible equipment, and sizeable inventory and do exactly what Ted wants to do: Go to the rural population, although for the short term.

"I know we'll have to raise lots of capital, and there will be some risk. Our debt and overhead will increase in the short term, and we'll have to stop paying dividends for a couple of years to plow profits back into the company."

Pop quiz. Both plans were worthwhile, but who is the better leader and who is more a manager? Who ended up heading the rural division (not a bad job either)?

All levels of successful management require leadership. Unfortunately, not all managers are good leaders. In a lot of ways, management is not even the same as leadership, and may sometimes conflict with it. That's why we tend to separate the two concepts. Peter Drucker has said that the requirements for leadership are identical to those for being an effective manager.[2] We're in awe of the man, but we live far enough from him to come right out and disagree. Warren Bennis's concept, that managers and leaders are different in both thinking and temperament, seems closer to the truth.

The fact remains, however, that if you can't lead the people who are important to your organization—who may or may not report to you—you will have trouble getting where you want to be.

As much as we'd like for you to believe that this chapter can teach you everything you need to know about leadership, we must, in all conscience, tell you that book learning can take you only part of the way. We do *not* believe that good leaders are "born that way," nor do we feel that natural charisma is always helpful; much of what is important can be taught, and can be learned. You'll have to work at it, though, and practice whenever you can.

We recommend that you carefully observe some real-life models of leadership (better yet, try to secure a *mentor*). Age, sex, situation, and century are unimportant (remember Napoleon). You may not even like the person, because the qualities you are learning about aren't all part of your daily life yet. But be certain (a) that he or she has a track record of successful leadership and (b) that his or her characteristics can reasonably be translated to your own situation.

---

2. *Wall Street Journal,* January 6, 1988.

POWER

Some authors say leadership depends on power or authority for its effectiveness. If you are new to management, however, *it is important that you not focus your leadership style on power and authority right now*, for several reasons.

First, it is unlikely that you have direct authority over very many people at the moment. Your ability to reward others, or coerce them, is probably limited; most of your power is "inferred" (i.e., related to attributes such as being well liked, having useful knowledge, or possessing special training or experience, rather than to direct authority). Second, and more important, many of the people you will want to lead at various times don't report directly to you (e.g., members of a committee or task force, or people outside the organization). Finally, reliance on power is simply not the most effective way to lead.

> *Power is not the most*
> *important part of leadership.*

Here's why. Of all the quotations about leadership that we have seen, these two come closest to summarizing what you have to know:

> The best leadership situation is one in which the led want the same thing as the leader. (Russell Fershleiser)

> Find a great parade and get in front of it. (Somebody we wish we could remember)

Most leading is really the artful taking advantage of an *opportunity* to lead, not dragging other people kicking and screaming toward what you want them to do. Those being led sometimes complain, to be sure. But if you are successful, the complaints will be about the conditions of the journey, not about the destination.

> During the Battle of the Bulge in World War II, the 101st Airborne Division was surrounded by enemy troops at the town of Bastogne, and faced with near-certain defeat. In one of the most incredible feats of the war, General George Patton marched his exhausted Third Army over 100 miles to the rescue, in the dead of winter, in less than three days.[3]

Cold, hunger, and exhaustion are not the best motivators for any group. What got them there? Patton knew how to make *his* vision into his *troops'* vision. They responded as much to the goal as to the leader. Patton had power—but the rescue would almost surely have failed if the troops had not responded willingly.

Soldiers sometimes seem to hate good leaders, but they'll follow them anywhere.

Martin Luther King, Jr.,[4] in his "I Have a Dream" speech, summarized four things one has to do to "move people."

1. Move them toward a vision they feel is positive.
2. Draw upon values they feel are important.

---

3. To this day, the 101st Airborne maintains it didn't really need rescuing.
4. We can't recall a more effective leader, and none of his followers *had* to do anything he asked.

3. Give them something they want.
4. Present it in a compelling, inspiring way.

Note that three of the four are related to the desires of the follower.

LEADERSHIP REQUIREMENTS

Ask yourself, "Why should people want to follow me?" "How will they benefit from following me?" If people feel you are doing something that has value to them, they will pay attention. If the value you tap is an important one, their attentiveness increases.

All leadership experts are required to outline the things leaders have to do. Here's our list, with some critical items starred:

- Have a clear vision of what you want others to achieve.*
- Make your vision their vision (better still, make their vision yours).*
- Realize that others usually *want* to act on their/your vision.
- Convert the vision into attainable goals.
- Motivate others to move toward the goals.*
- Bring people together to work toward the goals.
- Engender their trust.*
- Guide their actions.
- Empower them to act without you.*
- Oversee progress toward the goals.
- Realize that change is likely, and invite it to occur.
- Be (or be closely associated with) a symbol for your vision.
- Give visible credit for success.
- Take visible responsibility for failure.*
- Be absolutely credible to your followers.*

Sounds like a lot of work, doesn't it? Let's take a look at the most critical (starred) items.

- *Clarity of vision* is critical both to the mission and to the follower's view of the leader. The vision should be realistic, not Pollyanna-like or overly grandiose. Manageable goals and priorities can be successfully developed only if the vision is clear.
- *Melding the visions of leader and followers* provides the initial energy for group action. If the leader's view remains separate from that of the followers, there can be no coordination of expectation or purpose.
- *Continuously motivating others to pursue the vision* is the leader's way of replenishing the energy just mentioned. Sometimes the common vision is enough. Often, though, you'll have to figure out what else the follower wants. Money drives some people, but in the long run most clinical employees have other, stronger values. The need to produce something worthwhile is an important one. Others include helping the organization (provided one feels positively about it), helping other people, feeling good about oneself, being associated with a successful project,

and securing a favorable position with the leader or the organization. Look for values you can tap in those you want to lead or influence. Become aware of values that may be related to, for example, a person's age, social situation, background, culture, or position in the organization. Stereotyping is not the answer, but different things motivate different people.

- *Trust* is a big part of loyalty and commitment. Trust has little to do with being liked, but everything to do with being reliable. It has little to do with the mission at hand, but everything to do with the leader's consistent belief in that mission.
- *Empowering followers to act without you is one* of the hardest things for some people to do, but it is critical to long-range success. Stop thinking that unless *you* do something, you won't get credit for it. We know you're ambitious, and that's good, but we want you to realize that your followers can multiply your effectiveness manyfold. Stop being afraid that others' strengths and successes imply that you are a failure. Your followers' successes are truly yours as well. In fact, your superiors are more likely to judge you by your followers' accomplishments than by the things you do alone. Ask any executive who has been promoted—or fired—for the actions of his subordinates. Upper management is less upset by bad performance than by bad leadership.

> *You will be judged by your*
> *followers' accomplishments.*

"Empowerment" is the placing of control over a situation into the hands of the people who are affected by it. It is the opposite of paternalism and autocracy. Empowerment shows faith in subordinates' ideas and talents.

> *Empowerment shows your faith*
> *in subordinates' talents.*

In an organization, empowerment implies an opportunity for individuals or groups to do things their own way. It allows employees and groups to make decisions on their own, and to focus their strengths and experience on goals without undue restraint or fear of reprisal from the boss. It means they may try new things and if they fail, they will be recognized—perhaps even celebrated—for trying.

To take advantage of empowerment, the manager or leader must give up some "ownership" of the group or project. (Readers who are into control will have to work on this.) By empowering employees or followers, you almost always increase your chances for success and create very loyal workers.

- *Good leaders take responsibility seriously.* They know they will be given credit for success, and they take responsibility for failure. Their followers trust that the leader won't let them down, and won't steal the spotlight when the job is over. Followers don't become deeply dedicated to leaders who are primarily in the game for their own profit.
- *Followers can smell lack of credibility a mile away.* Enough said.

You may have noticed that "charisma" isn't on our Mandatory List of leaders' qualities. It's fun to think about dashing exploits and fodder for legends and movies, but a lot of very effective leaders seem to have been fairly boring folks. Drucker cites a couple of presidents (no, not Gerald Ford) in this regard. He also notes that charisma can disguise inflexibility, or even incompetence.

It is good to enumerate the tasks of leadership, but what we really want you to understand is that you usually have to do *all* of the above to be an effective leader. Fortunately, your followers will help if you let them.

LEADERSHIP BEHAVIOR AND STYLE

Leadership Behavior

Leadership behavior is basically related to two things: the job to be done, and the people who are to do it. You must consider both, and balance them, to most effectively accomplish any goal.

Your view of those you would lead is crucial to your success. Douglas McGregor's "Theory Y"[5] says people want to do a good job. They also want to be led by good leaders.

People want to do a good job.

Some situations require great emphasis on treating people with extra care and respect, in an effort to let their talent, human nature, and cooperativeness produce the necessary results. Others demand that you be much more directive. Learn to vary your attention to the group's needs to fit the situation at hand. Your followers are your most important resource.

Workers may be motivated by money or security, or by accomplishment, recognition, or self-actualization. Giving the people (workers) what they want is a very good way to motivate them to do what *you* want (there are exceptions). In short, satisfying the follower is an important part of leadership. This takes time and energy from the immediate task, but it is often worthwhile. It may even make it possible to achieve goals that are otherwise not attainable. Dissatisfied followers, even those over whom you have direct authority, make life tough for everyone.[6]

Satisfy the follower.

Let people have some influence over what you want them to do. When people are empowered and participate in the conception, planning, implementation, and evaluation of their work, they become invested. In modern factories, for example, productivity increases when line employees are allowed to organize their own tasks, measure their own quality, and arrange their own work schedules. Participation and investment are especially important when the project at hand is unpleasant, or when it involves any kind of organizational change.

Sometimes, however, time is short. You are handed a job that simply has to be done by next week—no arguments, no flexibility. Or maybe the job is so stressful that your followers really need to be told what to do. When one of these happens, those you lead must follow your autocratic demands without question or input. Unless you already have lots of power, the best way to ensure this is to have built a prior foundation of trust and respect for your leadership. What kind of person were you before the new project was assigned? Can you run on your reputation for a few

---

5. The opposite of McGregor's "Theory X." Really.
6. Look in the dictionary under "sabotage."

weeks? Will your followers go out of their way to help *you*, or will you have to rely on their wish to help the organization?

Leadership Style

If you've been listening, you have already learned a lot about leadership style. You may also have thought about how you lead.

The real *autocrat* is concerned only with production. He (most seem to be "he") is also pretty passé. We suppose Attila was one, but his followers probably had few alternatives. One still finds the autocrats in small organizations, but they don't get very far in larger ones. Their superiors recognize their shortcomings and stifle their progress. If they happen to own the company, the company is headed for a fall.

We did *not* say that firm leadership is a thing of the past. It is alive and well, has a place in most organizations, and attracts employees and managers who work well in such a system. It suffers from an intolerance of new ideas from the ranks, however, which can be a problem.

The *benevolent dictator* recalls everyone's fantasy that "if I had the power, I could really set things right." Organizations led by benevolent dictators tend to stagnate because, as with the autocrat, there is limited opportunity for change from below.[7] If market competition is a factor, they eventually lose.

What we are saying about an organization's fate may be generalized to your own fate. If your style is primarily autocratic or dictatorial, it may work for a leadership project once or twice, especially if you get the job done. But if you insist on doing everything your way, people (including your bosses) will see that you are ignoring opportunities for valuable follower participation and not planting the seeds of follower investment in your work.

At the other end of the spectrum,[8] one finds leaders and managers who are so concerned with people that all they want to do, in one consultant's words, is "grow humans." They have trouble focusing leadership on the present task, and rely almost completely on the goodness of the follower to get the job done. As one can imagine, projects that rely on this "country-club" management style often take a long time. Success is a hit-or-miss proposition unless one's followers are extremely committed to their work (as is the case in some medical settings).

One can develop the people in an organization without entirely abandoning productivity. People are the key to most worthwhile organization endeavors. Leaders willing to allow some followers, or even a project, to fail while pursuing lofty goals are often rewarded with extraordinary loyalty and commitment from all employees. The more skillful, experienced, and ready for responsibility the followers are, the better this leadership style will work. It may also be the style to use when employees and followers *expect* to be allowed meaningful participation (e.g., when it is an important part of the organization's culture).

Although one may try for *both* the highest possible "relationship quotient" and the highest possible level of production, opportunities for such an ideal match of

---

7. "Below" is a great source of positive organizational change.

8. There really is a spectrum that summarizes much of this, called the Blake–Mouton Grid. See elsewhere in this text.

Table 41.1. Mandatory (Abbreviated) Chart of Leadership Styles

Authoritative (autocratic, dictatorial)
  Values production over people.
  Advantages: Gets things done fast. Decisive. Can overcome follower anxiety in stressful situations.
  Disadvantages: Quashes follower talent and initiative. Quickly uses up leader charisma.

"Country-club," superdemocratic
  Values people and consensus over production.
  Advantages: (We can't think of any, unless all the followers are expert and committed, as in some medical settings.)
  Disadvantages: Inefficient. Time-consuming. Leader looks weak.

Participative
  Allows input but leader retains veto power. Participation of followers may range from simple input to delegated authority for major parts of the task.
  Advantages: Taps the potential of followers. Empowers them. Builds commitment and teams.
  Disadvantages: Slows decision making. May make leader appear a little indecisive or weak.

people and production are few. Delaying action while waiting for the perfect balance can be a waste of everyone's time. A good leader is adept at analyzing the needs of the situation and the organization, then choosing the leadership style that will produce the best overall result.[9] See Table 41.1 for a summary.

The late, great Gene Roddenberry gave us some fine illustrations of leadership style. *Enterprise* Captains Kirk and Picard, and their officers, seem to do it all. The crew knows the mission and is empowered to act. The captain listens to his people and takes decisive action. When they win, they all win. The captain takes full responsibility for failures. There are times when the captain is authoritative and times when he is superdemocratic. Kirk and Picard "walk the talk" (see later discussion), although the captain and first officer shouldn't be on so many "away teams."[10]

Take a look at some of the subordinate officers:

Spock and "Data." Brilliant. They lack people skills, but each is aware of that deficit and compensates for it.

Scotty and Worf. Totally linear thinkers (see later discussion). Very competent, but they'll never make Starship Captain.

Geordi. Seems smarter than Scotty, not so linear a thinker, and probably has a healthier liver. Good bet for advancement if he wants to expand his horizons.[11]

Bones, Dr. Crusher, Counselor Troi. Very democratic; not fully organization oriented. They'll never lead the ship, but they're indispensable to the team.

Picard's #1. Getting there, but lacks authoritative skills. Picard allows him to make mistakes. Sometimes *big* mistakes.

---

9. Pay attention to your CEO's style. It is likely to be both successful and consistent with the prevailing organizational culture.

10. *Homework assignment*: Watch a lot of *Star Trek* reruns and identify different leadership styles. Pay no attention to others' ridicule. Tell them you're on a mission.

11. A model for technically oriented readers.

If your leadership style limits your options for either people or tasks, we encourage you to broaden it. If you believe you will always be able to choose people and projects to fit your favorite style, either you are very powerful or you're watching too much television.

Your leadership style should be
flexible enough to fit different situations.

LINEAR THINKING

Your ability to focus on a task and think it through to the end has helped you make a good living for years. You developed that talent early, and it served you well in clinical training. Too bad it may be keeping you from being the leader you could be.

The ability to focus, consolidate, and follow a train of thought is good, but it's not enough to lead a group or organization through a complex world. The best minds in management are "geometric," not "linear." They can focus when necessary, but unlike the average manager, they know when to relax their mental constrictions and invite innovation. In the carriage factory example at the beginning of this chapter, the executives agreed on their research results, but only one saw ways to enter a new arena and to use new technology to service an existing market.

You don't need Eastern mysticism to learn to open yourself to new ways of seeing problems. Don't try too hard; most solutions involve simplifying the issues, not complicating them.

LEADING YOUR PROFESSIONAL PEERS

You will probably treat followers who share your professional background differently from those who do not. If you are a former outpatient psychiatrist or psychologist recently promoted to facility clinical director, you will be tempted to spend lots of time with the outpatient clinicians, and with the Outpatient Department in general. On the other hand, you may consciously or unconsciously slight your former peers.[12] The same principle applies to people like academic chairpersons and hospital nursing directors.

Remember, your role in the organization has become much less clinical (with less or no direct care). You now have a responsibility to focus on *organizational* issues and goals. Your friends in the Outpatient Department may not like this, but they should be able to understand it.

You may not always like it either, but it's part of the reason the organization gave you a shot at management. Some professionals in management positions continue to see patients or keep a little laboratory space. It works for some, but for others it confuses the management role and limits the way one is viewed by superiors and subordinates alike. Leadership is a little like parenting in that respect: When the chips are down, both kids and coworkers need leaders, not peers.

---

12. We don't mean to imply that you are no longer any kind of peer to your professional colleagues. They are, however, no longer your organizational peers—remember, "Identify with that which you want to become."

LEADERSHIP IN BUREAUCRACIES AND THE PUBLIC SECTOR

This deserves some special mention. We have been speaking of leadership as if it had only to do with the leader, the followers, and the goal. In almost every organization, however, a project of any size involves the interests of many departments, and often those of people outside the organization. If you are asked to expand a partial hospitalization program, for example, space and staffing resources aren't the only things you have to worry about. Clinicians and staff in other areas, such as inpatient and outpatient units, advocacy groups, and local practitioners are likely to speak up (and if not, you should query them). Budget people may complain about how you're spending their money.

The complaints may not come directly to you, but to your boss, to a powerful person in another part of your organization, or to an influential outsider (such as a legislator). You will be expected to respond to them, and to deal with both the people and the management issues necessary to get the job done.

As in many touchy management situations, broadening the base of input and participation usually helps. Interdepartmental meetings and public hearings can be used to your advantage, but the real answer is participation from the very beginning. Appoint both outsiders and section employees to a planning team. Better yet, let organized groups (such as other departments and outside groups) send their own appointees. *Give those with a stake in the outcome a chance to be heard.*

Listen hard. You will have to live with them during the entire project. They may even have some great ideas. And if you aren't honest in your attention to them, they will know it very soon.

> *Consider the broadest effects of your project,*
> *then listen to those who will be affected.*

Dr. Rodney M. was head of a large hospital psychiatry department, part of a major medical complex. He was well known for quality care, up-to-date medical knowledge, and getting along with his clinical peers. The physicians in his department looked to him for leadership and representation to the hospital administrator. They did not depend on him for income, because each was a partner in the hospital's group practice plan. Rodney became aware of changes in the mental health practice environment, with lowered reimbursement and increasing constraints on clinical work. He knew evolution is inevitable, and he was looking for ways to expand his career horizons.

The hospital felt the pinch of changing health care reimbursement patterns, too. The Hospital Director asked Rodney to chair a committee to recommend changes in the hospital's clinical focus, payer mix, and marketing. She appointed four other committee members—the marketing director, a staff physician with a large surgical practice, the assistant administrator for planning and strategy, and an outside business consultant. Rodney was to select three or four others.

This was Rodney's chance to help lead the hospital into a new era, to show his value to the larger organization, and to multiply his career options. All he had to do was make sure his team provided the results the hospital needed.

Picking the Team

Rodney decided to appoint four more people to his committee: the medical director of a successful health maintenance organization (HMO) that contracted with the hospital, an entrepreneurial physical therapist who represented several non-MD clinicians who used the hospital, a regional telephone company benefits manager, and a local banker whose husband had recently endured a lengthy hospital stay.

Criticism from Peers

Several clinical colleagues, mostly fellow psychiatrists, wanted to be on the committee. They were miffed at not being appointed, but most figured Rodney would represent their interests. Some were also irritated that some of the committee members came from backgrounds they felt were "anti-medicine" (in this case, the physical therapist and the HMO director) or insensitive to mental health (the surgeon).

Using the Team Members

As the committee began its work, Rodney listened to the other team members. He wasn't quite sure why the marketing director wanted to ask local employers what they wanted in a hospital, but he went along with it. He had always thought HMOs practice poor care, but when the assistant administrator told him that HMO contributions to hospital revenues had increased fivefold during the past decade, he listened. In spite of "turf" battles between physicians and non-MD professionals, he realized that the latter refer patients to doctors and to the hospital, that employers and payers see them as cost-effective caregivers, and that they represent "value added" to the hospital's traditional clinical "products."

Rodney was tempted to steer the committee toward the kinds of issues that affect physicians' practices. Instead, however, he decided to let the other doctors on the committee present most of the physician-related points. Sometimes he was surprised to find that the nonphysicians could hold their own in the deliberations, and had some pretty good ideas.

Input from Internal and External Customers

The committee surveyed a number of professional staff members, employees, community physicians and health care professionals, local employers, and even local citizens and families. They invited several groups, including physicians in various hospital departments, to speak to the committee in person.

Today, both Rodney and the hospital are thriving in the modern health care environment.

LEADERSHIP TIDBITS—SOME THINGS TO KEEP IN MIND

"Walk the Talk"

People pay a lot more attention to what you do than to what you say. You must set the example for those whom you would lead. If you want your subordinates or project participants to come to work early, then be the first one there. If you want them to participate in some kind of training, go through it yourself. If you promise something, keep your promise. Your behavior must embody what you say, including your vision, your advice, and your ethics.

Robert L. Dilenschneider, CEO of the giant public relations firm of Hill & Knowlton, once had to choose between two lucrative projects, one of which seemed to contradict his personal standards. He chose the other, and wrote to company employees:

> The only conduct we can control is our own, and it is imperative that it be—and be seen to be—always in the high end of the ethical scale. And it is our responsibility to urge the same conduct of our clients.

Meetings

Sometimes it is good to exert your power or leadership in meetings. At other times, you will want to draw others out and see what they have to say. The quickest way to establish a leadership position in a meeting is to ask the opening question. The person who asks the first good question—and gets someone to answer it—is immediately seen as a leader.

If you want to play down your role, to keep other people thinking and contributing, keep your mouth shut. Don't sit at the head of the table. Don't even open the meeting.

Close That Open Door

Every management applicant we interview says the same thing: "I'll have an open-door policy. I want to be available when my people need me."

Peachy keen, but not very realistic. An open door is not the moral equivalent of accessibility and fair play. The farther you move up the managerial ladder, the more you are paid to think, not merely to be available to other people. Of course you should be approachable and supportive, even available at times. But you also need privacy and a chance to work uninterrupted when you want to. If others see your closed door as unusual or ominous (like "I'll bet she's chewing somebody out" or "he's probably talking to his girlfriend"), try opening and closing it randomly for awhile.

Delegation

Delegation is one of the most important skills of management, and is very often a part of leadership. You can't do everything. If you try, you may drop all the balls you've been juggling. If a follower or subordinate can do something, it is often poor use of your (and organization) time to do it yourself.[13] This way of looking at delegation is associated with several other concepts we discuss in this chapter, such as empowerment and expectations.

Expectations

What you *expect* is almost as important as what you do. When you are a legitimately appointed leader, you should act and feel the part. You have a right, even an obligation, to expect respect for your position and for the goals of the group and the organization. You also have a right, and an obligation, to expect *performance* from the group and its members. Those expectations can lead to a self-fulfilling prophecy for success. If you stop expecting either performance or respect, both will abandon you.

Expect performance and respect from your followers.

This is confusing for many first-time leaders and managers. Picture the classic movie stereotype of the new lieutenant, fresh from officer training and trying to establish himself. He tries an authoritarian approach and fails. Then he learns, usually from that old sergeant played by what's-his-name, that he doesn't have to be so nervous; his subordinates expect to be led; he can rely on them more than he thought; rank really does command respect; and it's O.K. to listen to subordinates' ideas. Try it.

Stewardship

Camille Barnett, an experienced city manager, speaks of organization leadership as "stewardship." The leader doesn't merely succeed; he or she takes custody of the organization, does work of significance, and brings the organization (or part of it) to the next phase of its existence. This concept is especially applicable to leadership in the public sector. Take your position seriously.

FOLLOWERS

Robert Kelley wrote a nice paean to followers in the *Harvard Business Review*.[14] They are important, and they deserve to be treated well. Good ones take care of their own job needs, are committed to the organization and to important things beyond themselves, try to do a good job, build their competence as they go along, and are

---

13. One of Dan's mottos is, "Do everything you have to do and nothing you don't." Bill has always been aware of Dan's innate laziness, but acknowledges that it has contributed greatly to his success.

14. November/December 1988.

pretty honest and forthright folks. A good leader, by the way, turns "subordinates" into "followers."[15]

In spite of that advice, we'd better talk about some problems one can encounter, and what to do about them.

Problem Followers

People who like to work are easy to manage and lead. People who don't are a real pain. The simplest solution is to avoid putting them on your team. Give them an opportunity for input, but don't give them a chance to slow things down or sabotage them. These are often the same people who passively obstruct projects and progress, and they strongly resist being told that they're doing it. The old "80:20 Rule" suggests that 80% of the problems will be caused by 20% of your followers.

Judith Bardwick is an expert on employees like that, who feel "entitled" to their jobs but don't do very much to deserve them. She says entitlement behavior has little to do with intelligence or experience, and everything to do with motivation and fear. Leadership should not be delegated to "entitled" people. They don't make very good team members, either, although they may work acceptably in groups. And there is a difference between teams and groups.

Deep down, many people who feel entitled are very concerned about security and anxious about change.[16] Being overly firm with them probably won't help. The best approach is simply to require performance. Focus on getting the job done, and on their peers' expectation that the job will get done. It's harder for them to hide from peers than from the boss.

When you can, use different rewards for problem employees than for other workers. In some organizations, it is almost impossible to treat some people differently from others, but do your best. Consider rewarding problem workers or followers as individuals rather than as part of a group (but reward teamwork). Don't be afraid to let your pressure create losers as well as winners. Increasing morale, with incentives for example, doesn't work with these folks. In Bardwick's words, "The best morale enhancer is increased productivity."

CONCLUSIONS

Managers do things right.
Leaders do the right thing.

This clever *bon mot* was coined by Warren Bennis, a man who is concerned about the stifling of crucial leadership roles by a national culture that is fearful of others' accomplishments and bent on protecting its mediocre position.

We're not so sure this is really the end of American leadership. We think there are lots of people like you ready to take the reins, and—just as important—lots of health care executives and senior managers who see your value to their organiza-

---

15. Russell Fershleiser again.
16. Bill said that. He's a psychiatrist; he has to talk that way.—Dan

tions. We *don't* think you are doomed to suppression if you show leadership skills. Those skills and the good things they bring are simply too important for the facility, company, or agency to ignore. We admit that some clinicians can't exercise much leadership in their current roles. You may have to consider a "lateral" move to start your climb out of the clinician bailiwick. We told you earlier that such a change is scary, and we never said it would be easy.

HANDS-ON WORK

List the four most important people in your organization:

List the four best leaders you can think of in your organization:

List the four highest-paid people in your organization:

Do your lists overlap? What characteristics define the leaders? What do you make of the areas in which the lists *don't* overlap?

Chapter Forty-Two

Negotiation

Daniel J. Reid
William H. Reid

Some people hate the thought of negotiating anything. They get sweaty palms when it's time to buy a new car. They turn down free trips to any country with street vendors and open-air markets. These people equate negotiation with confrontation. We're not going to tell you that there isn't some confrontation in negotiation. Far from it. But serious, successful negotiating in the management environment is much more than haggling.

Negotiation is a big part of successful management. This chapter will help you to get more than what you *need* from other people. It will introduce you to the principles of getting what you *want* from them. It will show you that getting the best deal for yourself or your organization is not always tantamount to defeating the other party, nor is it mutually exclusive.[1] It will discuss multiparty negotiations, coalitions, optimizing, negotiating your own salary and perks, and, of course, hostage situations.

Hostage situations?

What better place to start our discussion than with life-or-death scenarios, bristling with weapons and tension: "I want a helicopter and five million dollars or the old lady gets it in the belly!"

A New York man who had just committed armed robbery ran from police and barricaded himself in a small apartment with a woman, threatening to kill her. He demanded a number of things, including safe passage from the scene. Reinforcements were called, and soon the building was surrounded.

Instead of rushing in with guns blazing, the police called a specially trained negotiator. He began to talk with the perpetrator, gaining his confidence and even promising him a ride through Central Park in a patrol car. No shots were fired, and after several hours, the man surrendered.

Although the local officers wanted to take him directly to jail, the negotiator insisted that the perpetrator be given his ride through the park. When asked why the city should give in and waste good gasoline on a criminal, the negotiator replied that he had made a promise, in the name of the city, and that it should be kept.

---

1. Getting what you want can actually benefit the other side, and often should.

The criminal must have talked about the episode in jail, because several months later, another hostage situation arose, with the same negotiator. The new perpetrator recognized the negotiator's name and, after some acceptable compromise, gave himself up. He later told the negotiator, "I knew I could trust you; you kept your promise about the ride through the park."

This vignette is based on a true story. The negotiator was then-detective Frank Bolz of the New York Police Department, who developed many of the hostage negotiation techniques now used by law enforcement agencies. Those techniques are based on the premise that the best way to get what you want is not just to flex your muscles, but to *understand the opponent's interests and be sure everyone comes out alive*. Let's take a look at what happened.

First, law enforcement agencies have learned the hard way that aggression should usually take a back seat in situations in which the other person has something you really want. Wading in with guns blazing can hurt a lot of innocent people, and almost always hurts the agency's reputation.[2] The order of the day is, "Calm down and examine the situation."

Second, the negotiator is specially trained and usually *not* empowered to make big decisions (such as ordering a helicopter and $5 million). This person is responsible for the negotiating process, and will try to develop an outcome that will be *both* optimal for his organization (in this case law enforcement and local citizens) and acceptable for the other party. In the hostage example, that means everyone comes out unhurt and the perpetrator ends up in custody. The idea that everyone can come out of the situation unhurt is communicated to the perpetrator, while keeping in mind (but not usually revealing) the things the police are willing—and not willing—to offer as bargaining chips. (They will not, for example, trade weapons for hostages, and it is very unusual for a policeman to take the place of a hostage, no matter what you see in the movies.)

Third, *honesty is surprisingly important in negotiation*. Credibility can go a long way if one should have to restart failed negotiations, deal with the same person at some future time, or deal later with someone who has heard about the current negotiation.

Finally, the negotiator is aware of his or her organization's absolute limits for negotiation, the "choke point" beyond which he or she will not go. If the choke point is reached, negotiations cease (one way or another). Many law enforcement agencies have a policy that "deadly force" will be strongly considered if the perpetrator injures a hostage after negotiations begin. In the world of health care organizations, the offended party usually just leaves the table.

Nonlethal Applications

You have probably already guessed that we will use the preceding example to illustrate some tenets of successful business negotiation.

---

2. A decade or so ago, Philadelphia police confronted members of a radical militant group who had barricaded themselves in a row house. In a tragic mistake of negotiation and confrontation, the city used its heavy artillery. The resulting conflagration, seen on nationwide television, turned public opinion away from the police and caused far more damage—physical and political—than it was worth.

First, a little fear can be a good motivator, but regularly flexing your (or your organization's) muscles is a poor way to get what you want. It may work if you're the only game in town, but it irritates and sometimes frightens the other players. You probably will have to work with those people in the near future. Why would you want them irritated or frightened?

If a health care organization can purchase supplies or rent office space from any of several local vendors, for example, it may be tempting to say to one of them, "Shave your profit to the bone to please us, or we'll take our huge order to your competition." But business relationships built on cutthroat tactics don't last long. The vendor may desert you at the first opportunity, or join your competition. Don't be a tyrant.

Second, the negotiator should be experienced. In fact, if the deal is really important, organizations often use professional negotiators. Sometimes they are internal (such as buyers or lawyers) and sometimes they are hired for a specific arbitration (such as those chosen for major labor contract negotiations).[3] The professional takes his or her basic orders from the organization, including specifics about what is or is not acceptable and where the choke point lies. The negotiator should not usually be empowered to change these basic policies on his or her own, nor to accept any unplanned agreement on behalf of the organization.

Third, the negotiator should look for areas of *optimization*, often by learning what is important to the other party or parties. Let's consider a classic labor–management situation:

> The members of Texas Widget Makers' Local 102 have had it up to here with management that doesn't respect their skills and compensate them accordingly. Furthermore, a number of the members are worried about the dangers of widget making and fear disability and medical bills. There's not much call for widgets in Texas at the moment, and management has threatened either to train its own, nonunion widget makers or to move the factory to Florida. The national union is supporting Local 102 in its demands for salary increases of 50% over three years, special disability insurance, and a guarantee that all widget makers hired will be union members.
>
> Management has been having a tough time selling widgets. There's not much market in Texas, and shipping costs to that great Florida market are so high that manufacturing costs simply must be controlled. The company is the main employer in Niederwald, Texas,[4] and it would be a shame to relocate. They can't afford more than a 10% salary increase right now, but there are good indications that Texas business will pick up during the next two or three years (another reason not to relocate to Florida). They have just discovered that if they can keep a workforce of over 100 people, they are eligible for an excellent, cost-effective medical benefit plan. If they have to close a widget division because of the threatened strike, the number of employees will dip below 100. To make matters worse, Niederwald just raised its city corporate taxes in order to finance subdivision utilities.

---

3. In a 1992 national railroad strike, as in several similar major conflicts, accord was reached by having each side choose a lead negotiator, then the lead negotiators jointly chose a single arbitrator. Finally, when at an impasse, each side submitted its "final" offer and the arbitrator was empowered to bind both parties to either of them.

4. Actually, the largest business in Niederwald, as far as we know, is the Linnaeus Medicine Ball Company. Honest.

What are some of the issues relevant to the negotiation, and what is their relative importance to each side? Let's outline a few and assign some priorities.

For the union, salary is important but the critical thing is keeping the company (and thus jobs) in Niederwald. Union strength is also a priority in this small town, where some feel that labor is at the mercy of management. Health care isn't an overriding concern to the relatively young workforce, and takes a back seat to workplace safety.

Management has to place its highest priorities on operating costs and proximity to a good widget market. Moving would be a lot of trouble, but could be readily accomplished if local costs threaten to drive the company out of business. Safety and health care expenses are moderate concerns, and the company wants to do the right thing for workers and their families. Union strength is a factor, but the company is fairly mobile and is not worried about labor having a stranglehold on operations.

A chart of the relative priorities might look something like this:

	Labor	Management	City
Top priority	Jobs Union strength Location (local)	Salaries Market	Tax base Jobs
Midpriority	Salaries Safety	Health care costs Local taxes Safety	
Low Priority	Health care	Location Union strength	

The chart suggests two things. First, there are areas in which the two sides' priorities are different, which invite compromise. Later, we'll refer to this as optimization of the system at the expense of some of its parts. Second, there aren't just two sides: At least one outside party (the City of Niederwald) has a stake in the outcome.

What happened? The company and the union realized their mutual interdependence. The union, faced with a glut of members with little other employment opportunity, accepted a one-time 10% salary increase along with a guarantee that if the Texas market indeed improves, salaries will be renegotiated. This allowed the workforce to remain above 100 and medical benefits to be improved. Management agreed to 100% union employment in the widget division, because training is expensive and there are plenty of good union workers. Management and labor agreed to develop a joint injury-prevention program, with funding and consultants to come from the national union.

Because company employees were the main prospects for the new subdivision, and company relocation to Florida would cripple the town's growth, the City of Niederwald agreed to delay any tax increase that would affect the company for at least two years.

Good negotiators look for areas of optimization,
in which all parties can realize some benefit.

Incidentally, who did the negotiating in this example? Local 102 hired a professional recommended by the national union. The company decided against an outside negotiator, in part because it wanted to convey a friendly, local image, and chose a team consisting of one of its lawyers and a personnel manager with negotiating experience.

CAN YOU NEGOTIATE EVERYTHING?

Some people (and one popular book) say you can; a few even say you should. We recently heard a speaker boast that she negotiated the price of her dry cleaning. The cleaners, a small mom-and-pop operation, wanted a consistent customer and she wanted a single, reliable supplier. She firmly reminded them that she could take her business elsewhere, and believes she got a real deal.

This example raises other issues as well. On the one hand, it is a microexample of a single-supplier economy (see another case later in the chapter). On the other, it is kind of silly unless the customer considers services, not just price. Neighborhood businesses usually can't beat chain-store prices, but may be able to offer special amenities. One might also question the ethics of pushing a neighborhood business (and thus a neighbor) toward insolvency by forcing it to set its prices below those of larger organizations.

Large purchasers, like managed care organizations, medical centers, and government agencies, routinely negotiate deep discounts.

WHY A RELATIONSHIP IS IMPORTANT

The "single-supplier" concept is a good example of balancing priorities and working together for common goals and mutual benefit, rather than simple immediate gain. This concept is not necessarily "win–win" (a vastly overused term that makes little sense in many negotiating situations) or compromise. It is an exercise in efficiency and maximizing long-term gains for your organization. Benefit for the other guy is necessary but irrelevant, in the sense that your (and your organization's) interests are what count. That sounds tough, and politically incorrect, but negotiation is not about being nice for nice's sake. We advocate helping your opponent to the extent that it somehow benefits *you* in the long run (and good will often has significant value), or is at least irrelevant to your success. If the other side gets a lot from the deal—even if they get more than you—you should not care. The point is not to compare benefits, but to get as much as possible of what you want.

> Okra Delite, a profitable fast-food chain with about $20 million in annual sales, had reached a plateau in its growth. For some reason, none of the big investors on Wall Street wanted to capitalize the expansion of the company at acceptable interest rates. The owners decided to talk with their suppliers about discounts, based on their prediction that the chain would expand and the suppliers would enjoy bigger and bigger orders for raw okra, okra fixin's, alcoholic beverages,[5] and the like. (We'll use one supplier as an example.)
>
> Sweet Home Okra Farms saw an opportunity to stabilize its own market as well. Okra Delite generally purchased about 20% of the Sweet Home crop, but in

---

5. It is very hard to enjoy okra in any form without an alcoholic beverage.

some years Sweet Home was outbid by other farms and had lots of okra left over. Moreover, Okra Delite was the only customer that paid Sweet Home close to top dollar (some 80% of the crop usually going to animal feed companies in the Outer Hebrides at great discounts, with attendant shipping costs and export hassles).

Sweet Home agreed to sell okra to Okra Delite at half their current U.S. price, provided the price would be allowed to rise and fall with the consumer price index and provided Okra Delite promised to buy at least 75% of its crop or 100,000 bushels per year, whichever was less, for 20 years. Sweet Home would guarantee safe delivery of high-quality raw okra to all Okra Delite processing plants. If Sweet Home could not grow enough raw okra for Okra Delite's needs, it would locate and deliver additional product, anywhere it could, at the agreed price plus reasonable shipping costs.

What happened? Okra Delite got a heck of a deal on okra, a dedicated and reliable supplier, and a partner in its future. Sweet Home Okra Farms gained a guaranteed market for its product, a steady stream of revenue, and a partner in its future. The okra industry in general got a boost and help with price stability without government price supports.

A few years later, when okra became one of our most popular vegetables, seed prices skyrocketed. At Sweet Home's request, Okra Delite agreed to help Sweet Home by paying a bit more per bushel than was originally promised. Some time after that, Okra Delite suffered a bad year because of rumors of okra-related baldness. Sweet Home, investing in their long-term, mutually beneficial relationship, allowed Okra Delite to purchase only half of the agreed-upon amount.

This kind of negotiation can have many advantages. A buyer who is willing to guarantee purchases of goods or services for many years can often negotiate excellent long-term discounts, dictate product and service specifications, lower inventory and warehousing expenses, predict costs far into the future, and expect priority treatment in time of need. Another advantage: The buyer has fewer suppliers to deal with and worry about.

The long-range success of the negotiated arrangement depends on the relationship that forms between purchaser and supplier. If the relationship is built on mutual needs, trust, and respect, either party will probably be willing to change the agreement a bit if necessary. Each knows that the enduring benefits of the business relationship often transcend short-term gains or losses. Such a relationship helps an agreement to last because it fosters good communication, and therefore allows flexibility, or even renegotiation, when needed.

ONE-SIDED NEGOTIATIONS

Before going any further, we need to warn you: We'll stress mutual satisfaction in negotiation, but don't be so naive that you believe every negotiation can have mutually optimal (we dislike the term "win–win") results. However, if the parties don't create a relationship for future dealings, the chances of the deal falling through or not remaining optimized increase greatly. If the playing field isn't level, the other guy may not do you any favors, but he doesn't have to. He only has to better your bottom line and meet his own. Consider the hapless automobile buyer next (and apply the following to health care, as appropriate).

One reason most of us don't like to negotiate automobile purchases is that losing isn't any fun. We are in the dealer's and salesperson's arena. They negotiate car sales every day. Only they know the real price of the car, and only they know the dealer's choke point (the lowest acceptable price). You may be satisfied with the deal you get (which is, of course, a measure of success), but unless you are an excellent negotiator, the probability is overwhelming that you won't get the best price the dealer could allow.

Can one make it more nearly optimal? Probably not by very much, unless you're buying a fleet of cars. But there may be some things in the negotiating process that can make the outcome better for the buyer.

Certain parts of the deal, such as selling price, accessory markup, inventory cost, and (often) local reputation, are more important to the dealership than others. For example, the dealer would rather sell a car from stock, where it is devouring finance and storage dollars, than order one from the factory. The salesperson's priorities, on the other hand, are often limited to a quickly consummated sale and an acceptable commission.

By the same token, certain parts of the deal are more important than others to you, the buyer. Perhaps you are very interested in service after the sale, with a loaner car for every tuneup and a promise that if the transmission falls out, they'll take the whole car back. Maybe you need the car delivered to a special place on a special day, with a big sign that reads "Welcome Home, Shirley."

The point is to try to learn the other person's priorities, then work on those areas in which you don't mind attending to his priorities and vice versa. In this example, try telling the dealer that you're willing to take a car from existing stock, provided you pay less for it and get a special deal on service. The dealer might go for it, because his service costs will not change much in any event, to get you to sign on the dotted line.

Some people buy new cars by soliciting written bids for a very specific model from several area dealerships. This can be a good strategy when one sticks to the original game plan, but it falls apart if one allows the model to change, accessories to be added, or salespeople to call.

Here's a critical point for all negotiations: *If you are not prepared to establish your choke point and "deal breakers," and then walk away if your terms aren't met, your "negotiation" is probably a waste of time.* It is pointless to tell the salesperson you won't budge if you really will; any experienced negotiator (or salesperson) will sense your lack of commitment. That's why car dealers invented those magic words, "This special price is only good if you buy right now."

> *The ease with which you can walk away*
> *and not look back is one of your biggest assets.*
> *The absence of that asset is a serious liability.*

As in the Niederwald example, it is often useful to actually list the issues to be negotiated and their respective priorities. Is price your first priority? Location a distant third? How much would one priority item have to change, positively or negatively, before it offset other considerations of the deal? Where do you think the other side's priorities lie? How might you get information that could help level the playing field? In some negotiations, one can literally run the numbers and priorities by formula, and thus be prepared to respond quickly to the other party's offers.

WHAT DOES YOUR SIDE HAVE TO OFFER?

To succeed in any negotiation, one must have something to offer and must be able to describe it convincingly.

Successful negotiation depends on having something to offer.

You or your organization may have more to offer than you think. In the car-buying scenario just given, you have money and little else. Not much clout. But in other negotiations the things you bring to the table can be significant.

> Nancy never thought much about asking for a raise until she turned 40 and real-ized her retirement plan was woefully underfunded. She had been a psychologist with the same managed behavioral care organization for years and, given the prob-lems in the managed care industry, felt lucky just to have a job. Nevertheless, it was clear that she had to do something if she expected to support herself and her husband in the years ahead. She talked with Fred, another psychologist, just after the boss turned down his request for a similar raise. "Psychologists are a dime a dozen," Fred had reflected, "and the company knows it."
>
> A couple of months later, Nancy got her raise, along with a promotion to a supervisory position. She had successfully convinced her boss to go to bat for her with upper management by reminding him that she was not only an excellent psychologist, but that she made him (her immediate superior) look good as well. Her professional track record was very good, and she helped others to perform at their best. She showcased her skills as a team player, letting management know she had studied the company goals and objectives and was ready to do what it took for both the company and herself to succeed. She did not threaten to quit, but *she* knew that *they* knew she was serious about advancement, and that training an-other person with her qualifications would be expensive. She showed manage-ment that she had much more to offer than her clinical skills.[6]

TRY TO REACH THE PERSON WHO CAN SAY YES

Many interactions that sound like negotiations are really mere discussions. Lots of people are authorized to turn down requests, suggestions, and offers of negotiation; few are empowered to say "yes." Most of the former don't know what you want or what you have to offer, can't act on anything without someone else's permission, and, no matter what they tell you, won't take your offer or idea to upper manage-ment. You may feel you are getting somewhere when talking with peers or middle managers about some conflict or concept, but that alone does not often lead to a decision in your favor. Similarly, an important-sounding committee may have a worthy topic to explore, but unless the result goes to someone who is authorized to act, its time has largely been wasted. Lots of ideas that are important to you never reach the real decision makers.

What can you do? We suggest you respect your organization's chain of com-mand, but try to do your negotiating with people who have the power to act.

---

6. She had also read this chapter, but putting that into the example would be tawdry and self-serving.

> *Communicate with the person who can say "yes."*
> *Don't spend too much energy on those*
> *who have only enough authority to say "no."*

COMPLEX NEGOTIATIONS AND COALITIONS

Complex Projects

Many projects that must be negotiated involve several important parties or groups directly, and many more that are less important but should be considered. Public agency projects, for example, usually require approval by many people and entities before they may proceed. Similarly, starting or changing a complex service line often means negotiating with new suppliers, staff candidates, and financing resources, all of whom must arrive at acceptable agreements at about the same time.

The negotiating principles are similar to the concepts we've discussed, but the complexity of the process increases almost exponentially with the number of parties to be satisfied. Recruited clinicians want job and salary guarantees. Existing staff need interim plans for patient referral and care (as well as reassurance about their jobs). Unions want a fair balance of compensation and job security. In really big projects, suppliers want purchase guarantees before tooling up to provide bulk materials. The community wants to increase its tax base, maintain service levels, and keep new traffic to a minimum. Venture capitalists want control over the business plan. The list goes on, depending on the undertaking.

Some of the interest groups will collaborate; others will play off each other. City government, for example, may not be able to offer local tax relief because federal loan guarantees are linked to a certain level of taxation. The unions may be torn between local jobs and the competition the new project will mean for other health care employers. Bankers and other capitalists may use fears of labor unrest to demand higher interest or a greater voice in organization affairs.

Coalitions

Smaller groups can get pushed around in the struggle. Their best bet is often to try to align themselves, in official or unofficial "coalitions," with one or more other groups with whom they can find some common ground. Thus a small advocacy group, in an effort to gain support from the regional chapter of the National Alliance for the Mentally Ill (NAMI), may loudly proclaim that the new clinical service will discriminate against some people with mental illness. The NAMI chapter, on the other hand, may not wish such a coalition (or may unexpectedly dissolve it later in the negotiations) if it perceives a conflict between the small group's concerns and those of NAMI constituents.

Some coalitions are more effective than others, and all are targets for efforts to split them apart. In the long run, small groups benefit most from coalitions with other small groups. They are usually not very valuable to larger groups, and are thus vulnerable to being sacrificed when the going gets tough. Large, influential groups need good reasons before they will go to the trouble of allying themselves with disparate small groups.

Let's pause a moment and apply what we've just described to the structure of a single organization, such as your own. Do you see different internal factions? Conflict among strong and weak interests? Compromise and coalition? As you recognize these and try to get what you want, you should slowly become aware that resolution of conflict and *optimizing overall system interests and resources* is one of the organization's overriding goals. Senior management must not allow any part of the system to flourish at the expense of the whole (i.e., the organization mission and goals).

> *When negotiating within your organization,*
> *be able to demonstrate that your position helps*
> *optimize the system, not merely a part of it.*

NEGOTIATING EMOTIONAL ISSUES

In the real world, the heat of conflict often ignites even cool business heads; polite demeanor can go south in a hurry. Dr. John Sheridan, L. R. Jordan Professor of Health Services Administration at the University of Alabama, listed a number of "conflict management" principles that are particularly applicable to negotiations in which the parties are highly sensitive or emotionally involved:

- **Separate the *people* from the *problem*.** A negotiation is not about friendship, but it is about relationship. Liking or disliking the other people is irrelevant, but you will probably have to work with them in the future. Listen actively to the other person. When you do speak, express regard for him or her and keep the topic on the issues. Avoid wording that is likely to worsen the conflict.

- **Focus on the interests being negotiated, not on "position" or "posturing."** The word "position" implies something stationary. Negotiation is *fluid*. Stationary people have to defend their positions. Even worse, you may end up becoming an attacker. Optimization and interests are often lost. When someone states a position, look for the needs that lie behind it. Search for common ground, perhaps even rewording the issue being negotiated in a way that lends itself to optimization for all parties.

  Try taking the word "position" out of your vocabulary for a week and see what happens. Look for other ways to describe where you are and what you want. If someone uses the p-word, tell him or her that it implies a rigid, take-it-or-leave-it attitude that creates a barrier to getting the deal consummated.

- **Generate several options before pronouncing what you want to do.** Divide the issue into workable problems and develop propositions to which most parties can say "yes." Make it easier for the other parties to come to a decision.

> *Try to make it easier for the other*
> *parties to come to a decision.*

- **Strive to have all parties use fair and reasonable criteria in the negotiation.** Be practical and open to others' interpretations of the criteria—but yield to principle, not pressure.

WHO SHOULD NEGOTIATE AND HOW MUCH SHOULD HE OR SHE CARE ABOUT THE OUTCOME?

Here's one last principle to put in your hat until you need it. It is difficult to negotiate matters that are crucially important to your own interests. That sounds odd, but a bit of reflection will bear it out. After all, the best lawyers don't defend their own families. The company CEO doesn't lead the negotiating team for government contracts. The chief of police doesn't negotiate directly with hostage takers or terrorists.

One reason is obvious: When it really matters, or is out of your league, one should use the best negotiator around (and sometimes hire an outsider). Few CEOs, and almost none of the readers of this book, meet that test. You know health care. You probably know enough to help set the parameters and choke points for some negotiations. But you aren't a professional negotiator.

Does this mean you should avoid negotiation? Of course not. But use good judgment and protect the resources with which you are entrusted. Know when to call for help.

Know when the negotiation
requires a professional.

Finally, a professional negotiator once told us one of his secrets. He was flying to Europe with an organization CEO to negotiate a huge deal, one that could literally make or break either company. The CEO, noting his relaxed demeanor, said, "I'm paying you a king's ransom to get us what we need at the table tomorrow. You're going up against the best they have to offer. Why are you laughing at the in-flight movie while I'm doing all the worrying?"

The professional replied, in essence, "I take you and your company very seriously. You've coached me, and I've done my homework. My reputation is on the line. But it's your company, not mine. I can do what has to be done all the more effectively, all the more confidently, because *I care, but not too much.*"

The person charged with negotiating should
care about the outcome, "but not too much."

HANDS-ON WORK

What characteristics of your current position are negotiated, even in a broad sense?

Name at least four things your organization must negotiate with outside parties:

Assuming a professional negotiator were not available, what kind of person would you choose to carry out important negotiations for your organization?

Why?

If you were head of a health care group that wanted to build a facility in downtown Cleveland, with whom would you expect to have to negotiate?

Who else?

What bargaining power does each of the above groups bring to the table?

Appendix

Medical Information Technology Glossary

Anne M. Mahalik

Chris E. Stout

William H. Reid

algorithm. In medicine, a series of steps in diagnosis or treatment that, when followed exactly, addresses every possibility and leads the user to a correct diagnosis or activity. In computer programming, a series of steps that, when followed exactly, leads the computer or user to a correct outcome.

apple. A small application (q.v.) program. On the World Wide Web, it is a small program that can be sent to a viewer/user along with a web page.

application. A software program that allows a computer user to perform some task (including simply interacting with the computer).

application service provider. A company that provides software products and services on an outsourced, subscription basis.

architecture. Referring to computers, a basic internal software structure on which other programs are placed (e.g., an operating system).

ASP. See "application service provider."

bandwidth. In digital systems, the speed at which data is transmitted over the system, measured in bits per second (bps). Greater "bandwidth" allows more, and more complex, data transmission.

batch. Organize multiple files into a single group for transmitting or processing.

biosensor. A device that monitors and transmits information about a biological function.

broadband. Referring to a communication system whose bandwidth exceeds a given minimum.

browser. A computer program used for access to and manipulation of the World Wide Web (e.g., Netscape Navigator/Communicator, Microsoft Internet Explorer).

client. In computing, a program or computer that is able to share the resources of another program or computer called a server.

code sets. Commonly accepted representations for clinical diagnoses, procedures, treatments, and so on. (cf., numeric coding used in reference publications such as *Current Procedural Terminology* [*CPT*], *International Classification of Diseases* [*ICD*], or *Diagnostic and Statistical Manual of Mental Disorders* [*DSM*]).

computer-based patient record (CPR). Defined by the Computer-based Patient Record Institute as "electronically maintained information about an individual's . . . health status and health care."

cookie. A small amount of information stored on one's computer by a distant computer, which automatically provides identifying, access, and/or user information about the local to the distant computer (e.g., via a website).

cyber-, cyberspace. Referring to the Internet and/or "virtual" (as contrasted with real) data or environments.

data field. See "field."

digital. Referring to data or other information expressed symbolically as combinations of zeros and ones. Differentiated from "analog," which involves true (not symbolic) representation. Computers and the Internet create and store information in digital form.

digital subscriber line (DSL). A broadband technology capable of transmitting digital information at high bandwidths on existing phone lines.

distance education (distance learning). Referring to provision of instruction, information, and education from a remote site.

domain name. A user-friendly name that identifies a website rather than its actual URL address (q.v.). Also used in the terms "domain name system," DNS.

DNS. See "domain name."

DSL. See "digital subscriber line."

EDI. See "electronic data interchange."

emr. See "electronic medical record."

electronic data interchange (EDI). A generic name for digital e-commerce data.

electronic medical record (EMR). A medical record kept in computer memory, whether stored on-site or elsewhere, and generally accessed using an electronic device rather than a printed page. Contrast with "paper" charts and records.

field, data field. In a database, the space in which a piece of data is entered. Also, a specific type of information field in a database (e.g., name, age, diagnosis).

File Transfer Protocol. The primary Internet protocol for transferring files from one computer to another. Also FTP, File Transport Protocol.

filtered. Referring to abridged (censored) data presented to a user or observer (e.g., which has some parts deleted because they are irrelevant or because the user lacks authorization to see it).

firewall. A program or system designed to prevent unauthorized access to or from a private computer or network.

FTP. See "File Transfer Protocol."

gateway. Hardware or software that acts as a bridge between two applications or networks so that data can be transferred between a number of computers.

gigabyte. One billion bytes (referring to bytes of digital data).

Health Insurance Portability and Accountability Act (HIPAA). Federal legislation enacted in 1996 that affects the privacy, security, and standardization of electronic and paper-based transactions in the health care industry. The act also provides for the portability of insurance.

HIPAA. Health Insurance Portability and Accountability Act (q.v.).

HL7. See "Hospital Layer 7."

Hospital Layer 7. A standard used to exchange admission and billing information among hospitals and billing agencies.

Host. The computer on which a website is physically located, usually quite remote from the client (q.v.; local) computer.

HTML. See "Hypertext Markup Language."

http. See "Hypertext Transfer Protocol."

hub and spokes. A model of communications technology in which a central organization (e.g., an academic or medical setting, the "hub") is connected via telecommunication to remote sites (e.g., clinics or health centers ["spokes"]). In computers, the "hub" is a central connection for all the computers in a network.

hyperlink, link. Point in a website or computer file that, when "clicked" with the mouse, moves the cursor or user computer to another site (within the same file, or elsewhere in the computer or on the Internet).

Hypertext Markup Language (HTML). The computer language in which most web pages are written.

Hypertext Transfer Protocol (http). An Internet-wide protocol that tells the server (remote) computer what to send to the client (q.v.; local) computer.

Identifier Protocol Address. The code of numbers that electronically identifies a particular computer or device on the Internet or a network.

interactive video, interactive televideo. See "videoconferencing."

Integrated Services Digital Network (ISDN). One suite of standards used to support digital telephony.

Internet Protocol (IP). An international protocol that allows data to be transferred between systems over the Internet.

Internet service provider (ISP). Technology or a contract provider that connects subscribers' computers to the Internet.

intranet. An internal network based on TCP/IP protocols (q.v.) usually found within a corporation. Allows employees and others access to share files and information while keeping out unauthorized users with a secure firewall.

IP. See "Internet Protocol."

IP address. See "Identifier Protocol Address."

ISDN. See "Integrated Services Digital Network."

ISP. See "Internet service provider."

IT. Information technology. The broad subject concerned with all aspects of managing and processing information.

IT solutions company. A company that specializes in information technology. (See also "web solutions company.")

Java. A computer language used to write small applets that are uploaded onto Web pages and run within them.

JAZZ disk. A proprietary type of computer storage diskette.

LAN. See "local area network."

legacy (legacy system or application). A system or application in which an organization has already invested considerable time and money in the past. Typically database systems running on older mainframes or minicomputers.

link. See "hyperlink."

list server (listserv). A software program used to set up and maintain online (often e-mail) discussion groups.

local area network (LAN). A system of connecting computers and other digital equipment that allows sharing of files and/or equipment within an organization.

MIME. See "Multipurpose Internet Mail Extension."

mirror monitor. In videoconferencing, a video monitor that shows what one is transmitting to the other party.

Multipurpose Internet Mail Extension. A way of converting certain incompatible files, such as e-mail attachments, into files that can be carried within the body of an e-mail.

OCR. See "optical character recognition." Converts characters on a paper page into a text document that the computer can read.

optical character recognition (OCR). Process or software that converts characters (e.g., on a paper page) into text that can be manipulated by a software program. For example, paper documents may be scanned into a computer as pictures or the document characters may be recognized and converted to a word-processing file format. Also used for computer "reading" of labels.

PDA. See "personal digital assistant."

PDF. See "Portable Document Format."

personal digital assistant (PDA). A handheld computer that may include computing, telephone/fax, networking, and/or voice and handwriting recognition features.

personnel status monitor (PSM). In military computing, a system of physiological and environmental sensors integrated into the basic combat uniform to transmit information, generally to global positioning satellites, for example, to monitor the soldier's vital signs.

PGP. See "Pretty Good Privacy."

point of care. Where the patient is actually seen, often referring to "point-of-care" technologies and their communication with central files, computers, or telehealth equipment.

Portable Document Format. A file format that captures all the elements of a printed document as an electronic image and can present it to the viewer just as originally printed.

Pretty Good Privacy. A widely used but not formally standardized data encryption method.

PSM. See "personnel status monitor."

public key infrastructure (PKI). The use of two "keys" (strings of keyboard letters and/or symbols), one of which is made public while the other is kept private, to lock (encrypt) information being moved from one computer to another. PKI is one of the few methods of protecting electronic information that currently meets HIPAA requirements.

real time. In computer or media applications, refers to activities happening currently ("live") and at their actual speed, as contrasted with slowed or accelerated activity.

rich text format (RTF). A universal file format that allows one to save and transmit text files while preserving their formatting, fonts, text color, and so on.

RTF. See "rich text format."

search engine. An Internet program or service that allows one to search the Internet (or a particular website) for specific topics.

secure socket layer (SSL). A standard way to transfer secure information, such as payment data, over the World Wide Web.

server. A computer that provides ("serves") information to other computers connected to it. Often the "hub" (q.v.) in a hub-and-spoke system/network, or a central computer on which web pages are kept on the Internet.

SMTP. See "Simple Mail Transfer Protocol."

Simple Mail Transfer Protocol (SMTP). The Internet's e-mail protocol.

solutions company. See "web solutions company" or "Internet solutions company."

spam. Junk e-mail.

SQL. See "Structured Query Language."

Structured Query Language (SQL). A standard language used to formulate queries posted to computer databases.

SSL. See "secure socket layer."

store-and-forward. Refers to technologies that provide the electronic delivery of information from one location to another. E-mail is the best known and utilized store- and-forward technology (but it is not limited to Internet applications).

streaming. A data transfer method that allows the data to be processed as a steady and continuous stream (cf., streaming video).

TCP/IP. See "Transmission Control Protocol/Internet Protocol."

telehealth, telepsychiatry. Use of technology and telecommunications to accomplish health care or health care activities at remote sites.

telemedicine. "The use of medical information exchanged from one site to another via electronic communications for the health and education of the patient or healthcare provider and for the purpose of improving patient care" (American Telemedicine Association, 1997).

tele-triage. Using telehealth technology (e.g., remote conferencing) for triage.

Transmission Control Protocol/Internet Protocol (TCP/IP). Also "Transport" or "Transfer" Control Protocol. The key transport and addressing protocol for the Internet.

uniform resource locator (URL). Also "universal resource locator." The unique Internet address of a website or website content page, expressed either as a set of numbers or a wordlike description (e.g., www.reidpsychiatry.com or www.psych.org)

virtual. In computers, refers to storing or viewing data conceptually or symbolically (e.g., digitally), as contrasted with physically.

virtual patient record (VPR). Patient data stored electronically in symbolic (e.g., digital, as contrasted with physical) form. The information can be configured differently for different locations (e.g., nursing station, doctor's office, payer/HMO) or, when required, it can be presented in a common format.

Web-based. Refers to files, records, or computer programs which are kept, and used, on the Internet rather than on a personal computer or local network (LAN).

Web solutions company. An information technology company that specializes in helping organizations use the Internet for information storage, data processing, and communication, often maintaining World-Wide-Web–based applications that can be leased to clients.

wireless. Referring to computers, communication from one device or unit (such as a modem or handheld data-entry device) to another (such a stationary computer or printer) without physical connections (e.g., using radio frequencies or infrared technology). Also refers to microwave transmission for Internet access.

Zip disk. A proprietary type of computer storage diskette.

REFERENCES

(All web sites were available as of this printing.)

Centrax, glossary available at www.centrax.com.

Lifescape Pro, Practice Management Center, glossary available at www.lifescapepro.com.

NetAction, glossary of telecommunication and technology terms, available at
www.netaction.org

Sharpening Your Knowledge of Computers and the Internet, glossary available at
www.sharpened.net

Webopedia, The #1 online encyclopedia dedicated to computer technology, available at
www.webopedia.com

Author Index

Subject Index

INTERVIEWING STRATEGIES
FOR HELPERS
Fundamental Skills and Cognitive Behavioral Interventions

**THIRD
EDITION**

INTERVIEWING STRATEGIES FOR HELPERS
Fundamental Skills and Cognitive Behavioral Interventions

THIRD EDITION

WILLIAM H. CORMIER
West Virginia University

L. SHERILYN CORMIER
West Virginia University

Brooks/Cole Publishing Company
Pacific Grove, California

To our parents,
Edith and Bill,
and Leona and Doc
with grateful appreciation
and affection

 ™
The trademark ITP is used under license.

Brooks/Cole Publishing Company
A Division of Wadsworth, Inc.

Printed in the United States of America
10 9 8 7 6 5

Library of Congress Cataloging-in-Publication Data

Cormier, William H. (William Henry), [date]
  Interviewing strategies for helpers: fundamental skills
and cognitive behavioral interventions / William H.
Cormier, L. Sherilyn Cormier.—3rd ed.
    p.   cm.
  Includes bibliographical references.
  ISBN 0-534-13824-1
  1. Counseling. 2. Helping behavior. 3. Interviewing.
4. Cognitive therapy. 5. Behavior therapy. I. Cormier, L.
Sherilyn (Louise Sherilyn), [date]. II. Title.
BF637.C6C584   1990
158'.3—dc20   90-30196
                                                        CIP

Sponsoring Editor: *Claire Verduin*
Editorial Assistant: *Gay C. Bond*
Production Editor: *Ben Greensfelder*
Manuscript Editor: *Barbara Kimmel*
Permissions Editor: *Marie DuBois*
Interior and Cover Design: *Sharon L. Kinghan*
Art Coordinator: *Lisa Torri*
Interior Illustration: *Precision Graphics*
Typesetting: *Progressive Typographers*
Cover Printing: *Lehigh Press Lithographers*
Printing and Binding: *R. R. Donnelley & Sons Company*

PREFACE

Counseling and therapy have been likened to a "craft" (Goldfried & Padawer, 1982). A skilled counselor is like a master craftsperson— someone who has acquired and mastered the basic "knowhow" of his or her craft, coupled with individualized expression that gives the craft a unique form. Extremely skilled craftspersons have mastered the basic skills of their craft and also its more technical or complex features. *Interviewing Strategies for Helpers* is designed to help students and practitioners develop and refine the "craft" of counseling by acquiring and using various fundamental skills associated with helping and by acquiring and refining some of the more complex and comprehensive intervention strategies.

The skills and strategies selected for inclusion in this book are representative of those found in four major stages of the helping process: relationship, assessment and goal setting, strategy selection and implementation, and evaluation and termination. Chapters Two through Six describe relationship variables, nonverbal behavior, and verbal responses which are fundamental to any helping interaction, which are essential for developing an effective therapeutic relationship, and which seem to cut across varying theoretical orientations. In Chapters Seven through Twenty our focus shifts from rather basic skills considered important for a variety of theoretical orientations to a framework that is more cognitive-behavioral in orientation. Chapters Seven through Nine describe and model ways to help clients assess problems and define goals, or outcomes, in an interview setting. Chapter Ten describes a variety of ways in which helpers can, in rather practical ways, evaluate the effects of interventions and monitor client progress. Chapters Eleven through Twenty describe guidelines for selecting and implementing strategies, as well as a variety of intervention strategies, including ways to manage resistance, or "being stuck."

In part, the usefulness of this book may lie in its comprehensive coverage of skills and strategies associated with all the major phases of effective helpgiving in counseling with individuals. It should be noted that although some of the material in this book is relevant to relationship, group, or systems interventions, the book focuses primarily on the "one to one" interaction.

Another feature of the book is its emphasis on practical application. The content of the book is designed to help developing counselors and therapists acquire and refine a repertory of effective helpgiving behaviors. Coverage of theoretical concepts or research associated with the skills and strategies is limited because these areas are covered adequately in other texts.

The format of the book also emphasizes skill acquisition and application. Each chapter includes a brief introduction, chapter objectives, content material sprinkled with model examples, learning activities and feedback, a post-evaluation, and a role-play interview assessment. The book can be completed by individuals on a self-instructional basis or within an organized course or in-service training. Identifying some ways to use this format may enhance the acquisition of the content. Chapter One describes the content and format of the book, recognizing that a variety of people — counselors, psychotherapists, social workers, nurses, and so on — engage in helping-oriented interactions with other persons. In this edition of the book, we have used the words *counselor* and *therapist* interchangeably. This is not meant to confuse anyone but simply to recognize the various kinds of practitioners and students who are covered under the broad term *helpers* and are readers of this book.

If you are familiar with the second edition, you might be interested in knowing about the few changes included in the third edition. In addition to updated material and references on all skills and strategies, we have made the following few changes:

- Deleted the material associated with neurolinguistic programming (NLP)
- Deleted the thought-stopping strategy
- Added a new section on the problem-solving strategy
- Included material about mindful meditation

As you can see, very few changes were made in this third edition. Our rationale for the limited number of changes is reflected in what one reviewer said of this edition, "If it isn't broken, why try to fix it?"

We appreciate the helpful comments and suggestions of all those persons who served as reviewers for the third edition: Alan Basham, Seattle Pacific University, Seattle; Robert W. Brown, Oakland University, Rochester, Michigan; Ben Cohen, State University of New York at Buffalo; Arthur M. Nezu, Hahneman University, Philadelphia, Pennsylvania; Warren F. Shaffer, University of Minnesota; Fred Stickle, Western Kentucky University, Bowling Green; and Donald E. Ward, Pittsburg State University, Pittsburg, Kansas.

We are also grateful to three of our colleagues at West Virginia University: Robert Marinelli, David Srebalus, and Roy Tunick, who have used the second edition in their sections of our Counseling Techniques course and have provided us with many helpful suggestions for this edition. We also wish to acknowledge the contribution of Wayne Coombs, who reviewed material, learning activities, and the checklist for the problem-solving strategy. We are grateful for the instructive feedback provided by our own students. Finally, we acknowledge the support of our project editor, Claire Verduin.

William H. Cormier
L. Sherilyn Cormier

CONTENTS

LEARNING ACTIVITIES AND FEEDBACKS

ABOUT THIS BOOK

Imagine yourself as the helper in the following four situations. Try to see, hear, and sense what is happening to you.

A 14-year-old boy who is accused of setting fire to his family home walks in defiantly to see you. He has been "mandated" to see you by the judge. He sits down, crosses his arms and legs in front of him, and stares at the ceiling. He is silent after your initial greeting.

An 8-year-old girl walks in and can't hold back the tears and the sobs. After a while, she talks about how confused and upset she's been feeling. As she continues to talk almost without stopping, you discover that in the last year three of her very close relatives and friends have died and her parents have divorced. She can almost not get the words out fast enough.

An older, now retired gentleman appears at your door. He walks slowly with quite stooped shoulders. His face reflects resignation and discouragement and also a hint of pride. He speaks to you in a halting fashion and in a slow, soft voice. He seems to have difficulty concentrating and cannot always remember what you're saying to him.

A middle-aged woman comes in. She has been escorted to your facility by her husband. She is so afraid to go out of her house that she does not drive anymore. In talking with her, you discover that she has confined herself to her home almost exclusively for the last year because of incapacitating anxiety attacks. Her husband has recently turned down a lucrative job offer in order not to have to move her into a new environment.

Now try to process exactly what it is like for you to imagine helping or counseling each of these four clients. How were you feeling? What thoughts were running through your head? How did you see or hear yourself responding? What things about yourself were you aware of that helped you in the interaction; what things that hindered you? What skills did you utilize to deal with the client? What skills were you lacking? What did you observe about the client, and how did your observations affect your helpgiving? How did you know whether what you were doing was helpful?

Although it may be difficult for you to respond to these kinds of questions now, it will probably become easier as you go through the book and as you also acquire greater experience and more feedback. Specific purposes of the book are described in the following section.

☐ PURPOSES OF THE BOOK

We hope that, in this book, you will find training experiences that facilitate personal growth, develop your counseling skills, and provide ways for you to evaluate your effectiveness. Personal growth is the most elusive and the most difficult to define of these three areas. Although it is beyond the scope of this book to focus primarily on self-development, you may engage in self-exploration as you go through certain parts of the book, particularly Chapters 2 and 3. We also encourage you to seek out additional experiences in which you can receive feedback from others about yourself, your strengths, and some behaviors that may interfere with counseling. These experiences might consist in individual or classroom activities and feedback, growth groups, and personal counseling. It is well documented that a counselor's warmth, empathy, and positive regard can contribute to client change. We feel that your demonstration of these relationship conditions will enhance the way you perform the skills and strategies presented in this book.

We created the book with three specific purposes. First, we think it will help you acquire a repertory of counseling interview skills and strategies. The book focuses on *interview* skills and strategies as used in a helping relationship. It is directed (but not restricted) to applying skills within a counselor/client dyadic relationship. Although some of the skills and strategies may be used appropriately in group counseling, organizational interventions, or marriage and family counseling, the major focus of this book is on the application of these skills with individuals.

In the first six chapters of this book, we present what we call "fundamental skills." These include relationship conditions, nonverbal behavior, and verbal responses that are useful for practitioners of varying theoretical orientations. In the remaining chapters, our selection of models and strategies reflects a cognitive-behavioral framework. The in-

tervention strategies we have chosen to include have some supporting data base, although many of the existing research studies are analog ones (that is, conducted in simulated counseling settings) and the results may not always generalize to actual counseling situations.

In addition to the cognitive-behavioral "flavor" of the strategies, reference to skills and strategies based on other theoretical orientations is often mentioned throughout the book. This is because cognitive-behavioral therapies are increasingly broad-based in nature and focus (Goldfried, 1982) and also because of our own belief that skilled counselors are at least knowledgeable about, if not proficient in, more than one approach to working with client problems. For your benefit if you are not yet familiar with the concepts associated with various theoretical approaches to counseling and therapy, Table 1-1 presents a synopsis of eleven major counseling theories.

Our second purpose is to assist you in identifying the potential applicability of many counseling strategies for different client problems. As Krumboltz and Thoresen (1976) point out, a variety of useful counseling methods are available for different problem areas. When you have finished the book, we hope you will be able to select and use appropriate counseling strategies when confronted with a depressed client, an anxious client, a nonassertive client, and so forth. We also hope you will be aware of cases in which approaches and strategies included in this book may not be very useful.

Thus, we hope to provide you with some ways to monitor and evaluate your behavior and the client's behavior during counseling. The recent emphasis on accountability requires each of us to explore the results of our helping activities more closely. Evaluation of counseling also assesses the extent to which the therapeutic goals are achieved.

Above all, we want to convey that the book is about *practical application* of selected skills and strategies. Our coverage of theoretical and research concepts is very limited because they are covered adequately in other texts.

☐ AN OVERVIEW OF HELPING

A helping professional is someone who facilitates the exploration and resolution of issues and problems presented by a helpee or a client. Helping interactions have four recognized components: (1) someone seeking help, (2) someone willing to give

TABLE 1-1. Synopsis of theoretical approaches to counseling and psychotherapy

General approach	Chapter and theoretical system	Personality theory base and founder or major contributors	Key characteristics
Psychodynamic	2. Psychoanalytic therapy	*Psychoanalysis* Founder: Sigmund Freud	Deterministic, topographic, dynamic, genetic, analytic, developmental, historical, insightful, unconscious-motivational
Social-psychological	3. Adlerian therapy	*Individual psychology* Founder: Alfred Adler	Holistic, phenomenological, socially oriented, teleological, field-theoretical, functionalistic
Humanistic, experiential, existential	4. Person-centered counseling	*Person-centered theory* Founder: Carl Rogers	Humanistic, experiential, existential, organismic, self-theoretical, phenomenological, person-centered, here-and-now-oriented
	5. Gestalt therapy	*Gestalt therapy theory* Founder: Frederick Perls	Existential, experiential, humanistic, organismic, awareness-evocative, here-and-now-oriented, client-centered, confrontive
Cognitive, behavioral, action-oriented	6. Transactional Analysis (TA)	*Transactional Analysis theory* Founder: Eric Berne	Cognitive, analytic, redecisional, contractual, interpretational, confrontational, action-oriented, awareness-evocative, social-interactive
	7. Behavioral counseling, therapy, and modification	*Behavior theory and conditioning theory* Major contributors: B. F. Skinner J. Wolpe	Behavioristic, pragmatic, scientific, learning-theoretical, cognitive, action-oriented, experimental, goal-oriented, contractual
	8. Rational-emotive therapy (RET)	*Rational-emotive theory* Founder: Albert Ellis	Rational, cognitive, scientific, philosophic, action-oriented, relativistic, didactic, here-and-now-oriented, decisional, contractual, humanistic
	9. Reality therapy	*Reality theory* Founder: William Glasser	Reality-based, rational, anti-deterministic, cognitive, action-oriented, scientific, directive, didactic, contractual, supportive, nonpunitive, positivistic, here-and-now-oriented
	10. Cognitive-behavior therapy	*Cognitive theory* Major contributors: A. Beck A. Ellis D. Meichenbaum A. Lazarus J. Wolpe	Cognitive, rational, scientific, goal-directed, systematic, logical, mental and emotive, imaginal, perceptual, stress-, thought-, and belief-managerial
Trait, factor, decisional	11. Trait-factor counseling	*Trait-factor theory* Contributors: E. G. Williamson D. Paterson J. Darley D. Biggs	Scientific, empirical, decisional, informational, educational, vocational, evaluative, data-based, past-present-future-oriented, action-oriented, technological, person-environment-interactive, problem-solving, objective, systematic, didactic, interpretative
Integrative	12. Eclectic counseling and psychotherapy	*Eclecticism* Contributors: F. C. Thorne S. Garfield J. Palmer A. Ivey R. Carkhuff	Integrative, systematic, scientific, comprehensive, organismic-environmental, cognitive, past-present-future-oriented, behavioral, educational, developmental, humanistic, analytic, decisional

From Gilliland/James/Bowman, *Theories and Strategies in Counseling and Psychotherapy* (2nd ed.). © 1989, pp. 2–3. Reprinted by permission of Prentice-Hall, Inc., Englewood Cliffs, N.J.

help who is also (3) capable of or trained to help (4) in a setting that permits help to be given and received (Hackney & Cormier, 1988, p. 2).

Most helping or therapeutic interactions also involve certain stages or processes. In this book, we describe skills and strategies associated with four primary stages in helping:

1. Relationship
2. Assessment and goal setting
3. Strategy selection and implementation
4. Evaluation and termination

The first stage of the helping process involves *establishing an effective therapeutic relationship* with the client. This part of the process is based primarily on client- or person-centered therapy (Rogers, 1951) and more recently on social influence theory (Strong & Claiborn, 1982). The potential value of a sound relationship base cannot be overlooked, because the relationship is the specific part of the process that conveys the counselor's interest in and acceptance of the client as a unique and worthwhile person and builds sufficient trust for eventual self-disclosure and self-revelation to occur. For some clients, working with a counselor who stays primarily in this stage may be useful and sufficient. For example, as we mention in Chapter 11, for some clients who are troubled by generalized anxiety or low self-esteem, relationship-oriented therapy is often the first treatment of choice. For other clients, the relationship part of therapy is necessary but not sufficient to help them with the kinds of choices and changes they seek to make. These clients need additional kinds of action or intervention strategies.

The second phase of helping, assessment and goal setting, often begins concurrently with or shortly after relationship building. In both stages, the counselor is interested mainly in helping clients *explore* themselves and their concerns. Assessment is designed to help both the counselor and the client obtain a better picture, idea, or grasp of what is happening with the client and what prompted the client to seek the services of a helper at this time. The information gleaned during the assessment phase is extremely valuable in planning strategies and also can be used to manage resistance. After the problems and issues are identified and defined, the counselor and client together work through the process of developing outcome goals. Outcome goals refer to the specific results the client would like to occur as a result of

counseling. Outcome goals also provide useful information for planning action strategies.

In the third phase of helping, strategy selection and implementation, the counselor's task is to facilitate client *understanding and related action.* Insight can be useful, but insight alone is far less useful than insight accompanied by a supporting plan that helps the client translate new or different understandings into observable and specific actions or behaviors. Toward this end, the counselor and client select and sequence a plan of action or intervention strategies that are based on the assessment data and are designed to help the client achieve the designated goals. In developing action plans, it is important to select ones that relate to the identified problems and goals and also ones that are not in conflict with the client's primary beliefs and values.

The last major phase of helping, evaluation, involves *assessing the effectiveness* of your interventions and the progress the client has made toward the desired goals. This kind of evaluation assists you in knowing when to terminate or when your action plans need revamping. Additionally, observable and concrete signs of progress are often quite reinforcing to clients, who can easily get discouraged during the change process.

Table 1-2 presents an overview of the helping process as described in the remaining chapters of this book. In reviewing this table, you may note some flow and interrelationship among the four major stages of the helping process.

☐ FORMAT OF THE BOOK

We have used a learning format designed to help you to demonstrate and measure your use of the counseling competencies presented in this book. Each chapter includes a brief introduction, chapter objectives, content material interspersed with model examples, activities, and feedback, a post-evaluation, and a role-play interview assessment. People who have participated in field-testing this book have found that using these activities has helped them to get involved and to interact with the content material. You can complete the chapters by yourself or in a class. If you feel you need to go over an exercise several times, do so! If part of the material is familiar, jump ahead. Throughout each chapter, your performance on the learning activities and self-evaluations will be a clue to the pace at which you can work through the chapter.

TABLE 1-2. Four stages of helping and the chapters presenting related skills

Fundamental skills (relationship conditions, nonverbal behavior, verbal responses)	Assessment and goal-setting	Evaluation	Strategy selection and implementation
2—"Ingredients of an Effective Helping Relationship" 3—"Relationship Enhancement Variables and Interpersonal Influence" 4—"Nonverbal Behavior" 5—"Listening Responses" 6—"Action Responses"	7—"Conceptualizing Client Problems" 8—"Defining Client Problems with an Interview Assessment" 9—"Selecting and Defining Outcome Goals"	10—"Evaluating Processes and Outcomes in Helping"	11—"Selecting Strategies" 12—"Common Elements of Strategy Implementation" 13—"Symbolic Modeling, Self-as-a-Model, and Participant Modeling" 14—"Emotive Imagery and Covert Modeling" 15—"Cognitive Modeling and Problem Solving" 16—"Cognitive Restructuring, Reframing, and Stress Inoculation" 17—"Meditation and Muscle Relaxation" 18—"Systematic Desensitization" 19—"Self-Management Strategies: Self-Monitoring, Stimulus Control, and Self-Reward" 20—"Strategies for Managing Resistance"

To help you use the book's format to your advantage, we will explain each of its components briefly.

Objectives

As we developed each chapter, we had certain goals in mind for the chapter and for you. For each major topic, there are certain concepts and skills to be learned. We feel the best way to communicate this is to make our intentions explicit. After a short chapter introduction, you will find a section called "Objectives." The list of objectives describes the kinds of things that can be learned from the chapter. Using objectives for learning is similar to using goals in counseling. The objectives provide cues for your "end results" and serve as benchmarks for

you to assess your progress. As you will see in Chapter 9, an objective or goal contains three parts:

1. The behavior, or what is to be learned or performed.
2. The level of performance, or how much or how often to demonstrate the behavior.
3. The conditions of performance, or the circumstances or situations under which the behavior can be performed.

Part 1 of an objective refers to what you should learn or demonstrate. Parts 2 and 3 are concerned with evaluation of performance. The evaluative parts of an objective, such as the suggested level of performance, may seem a bit hard-nosed. However, there is evidence that setting objectives with a fairly high mastery level results in more-improved performance (Johnston & O'Neill, 1973; Semb, Hopkins, & Hursh, 1973). In this book, the objectives are stated at the beginning of each chapter so you know what to look for and how to assess your performance in the activities and self-evaluations. If you feel it would be helpful to see some objectives now, take a look at the beginning of Chapter 2.

Learning Activities

Learning activities that reflect the chapter objectives are interspersed throughout each chapter. These learning activities, which are intended to provide both practice and feedback, consist of model examples, exercises, and feedback. There are several ways you can use the learning activities. Many of the exercises suggest that you write your responses. Your written responses may help you or your instructor check the accuracy and specificity of your work. Take a piece of paper and actually write the responses down. Or you may prefer to work through an activity covertly and just think about your responses.

Some exercises instruct you to respond covertly by imagining yourself in a certain situation, doing certain things. We feel that this form of mental rehearsal can help you prepare for the kinds of counseling responses you might use in a particular situation. Covert responding does not require any written responses. However, if it would help you to jot down some notes after the activity is over, go ahead. You are the best person to determine how to use these exercises to your advantage.

Many of the exercises, particularly in the first six chapters, are based on cognitive self-instruction. The objective of this type of activity is to help you not only to acquire the skill in a "rote" manner but also to internalize it. Some research suggests that this may be an important addition to the more common elements of microtraining (modeling, rehearsal, feedback) found to be so helpful in skill acquisition (Richardson & Stone, 1981). The cognitive learning strategy is designed specifically to help you develop your own way to think about the skill or to "put it together" in a way that makes sense to you.

Another kind of learning activity involves a more direct rehearsal than the written or covert exercises. These "overt rehearsal" exercises are de-signed to help you apply your skills in simulated counseling sessions with a role-play interview. The role-play activities involve three persons or roles: a counselor, a client, and an observer. Each group should trade roles so that each person can experience the role-play from these different perspectives. One person's task is to serve as the counselor and practice the skills specified in the instructions. The counselor role provides an opportunity to try out the skills in simulated counseling situations. A second person, the client, will be counseled during the role play.

We give one word of caution to whoever takes the client role. Assuming that "counselor" and "client" are classmates, or at least not close friends or relatives, each of you will benefit more when in the counselor's seat if the "client" shares a real concern. These concerns do not have to be issues of life or death. Often someone will say "I won't be a good client because I don't have a problem." It is hard to imagine a person who has no concerns. Maybe your role-play concern will be about a decision to be made, a relationship conflict, some uneasiness about a new situation, or feeling sorry for or angry with yourself or someone else. Taking the part of a client in these role-play exercises may require that you first get in touch with yourself.

The third person in the role-play exercise is the "observer." This is a very important role because it develops and sharpens observational skills that are an important part of effective counseling. The observer has three tasks to accomplish. First, this person should observe the process and identify what the client does and how the counselor responds. When the counselor is rehearsing a particular skill or strategy, the observer can also determine the strengths and limitations of the counselor's approach. Second, the observer can provide consultation at any point during the role play if it might facilitate the experience. Such consultation may occur if the counselor gets stuck or if the observer perceives that the counselor is practicing too many nonhelpful behaviors. In this capacity, we have often found it helpful for the observer to serve as a sort of "alter ego" for the counselor. The observer can then become involved in the role play to help give the counselor more options or better focus. It is important, however, not to take over for the counselor in such instances. The third and most important task of the observer is to provide feedback to the counselor about his or her performance following the role play. The person who role-played the client may also wish to provide feedback.

Giving helpful feedback is itself a skill that is used in some counseling strategies (see Chapter 12). The feedback that occurs following the role play should be considered just as important as the role play itself. Although everyone involved in the role play will receive feedback after serving as the counselor, it is still sometimes difficult to "hear" negative feedback. Sometimes receptiveness to feedback will depend on the way the observer presents it. We encourage you to make use of these opportunities to practice giving feedback to another person in a constructive, useful manner. Try to make your feedback specific and concise. Remember, the feedback is to help the counselor learn more about the role play; it should not be construed as the time to analyze the counselor's personality or lifestyle.

Another learning activity involves having people learn the strategies as partners or in small groups by teaching one another. We suggest that you trade off teaching a strategy to your partner or the group. Person A might teach covert modeling to Person B, and then Person B will teach Person A muscle relaxation. The "student" can be checked out in role play. Person B would check out on covert modeling (taught by A), and Person A would demonstrate the strategy learned from Person B. This method helps the teacher learn and teach at the same time. If the "student" does not master the skills, additional sessions with the "teacher" can be scheduled.

The role of feedback in learning activities. Most of the chapter learning activities are followed by some form of feedback. For example, if a learning activity involves identifying positive and negative examples of a counseling conversational style, the feedback will indicate which examples are positive and which are negative. We also have attempted in most of our feedback to give some rationale for the responses. In many of the feedback sections, several possible responses are included. Our purpose in including feedback is not for you to find out how many "right" and "wrong" answers you have given in a particular activity. The responses listed in the feedback sections should serve as a guideline for you to code and judge your own responses. With this in mind, we would like you to view the feedback sections as sources of information and alternatives. We hope you are not put off or dis-

couraged if your responses are different from the ones in the feedback. We don't expect you to come up with identical responses; some of your responses may be just as good as or better than the ones given in the feedback. Space does not permit us to list a plethora of possibly useful responses in the feedback for each learning activity.

Locating learning activities and feedback sections in the text. As we have indicated, each chapter contains a variety of learning activities and feedback. Usually a learning activity directly follows the related content section. We have placed learning activities in this way (rather than at the end of a chapter) to give you an immediate opportunity to work with and apply that content area before moving ahead to new material. Feedback for each learning activity is usually given on the *following* page. This is done in order to encourage you to work through the learning activity on your own without concurrently scanning the same page to see how we have responded. We believe this helps you work more independently and encourages you to develop and rely more on your own knowledge base and skills. A potential problem with this format is difficulty in finding a particular learning activity or its corresponding feedback section. To minimize this problem, we have done two things: (1) Each learning activity and its corresponding feedback section are numbered. For example, the first learning activity in the book is found on page 15; it is numbered #1. Its corresponding feedback section, found on page 19, is also labeled #1. (2) An index to all learning activities and feedback sections can be found in the front of the book.

Postevaluation

A postevaluation can be found at the end of each chapter. It consists of questions and activities related to the knowledge and skills to be acquired in the chapter. Because you respond to the questions after completing a chapter, this evaluation is called *post;* that is, it assesses your level of performance *after* receiving instruction. The evaluation questions and activities reflect the conditions specified in the objectives. When the conditions ask you to identify a response in a written statement or case, take some paper and write down your responses to these activities. However, if the objective calls for demonstrating a response in a role play, the evaluation will suggest how you can assess your performance level by setting up a role-play assessment. Other evaluation activities may suggest that you do something or experience something to heighten your awareness of or information about the idea or skill to be learned.

The primary purpose of the postevaluation is to help you assess your competencies after completing the chapter. One way to do this is to check your responses against those provided in the feedback at the end of each postevaluation. If there is a great discrepancy, the postevaluation can shed light on those areas still troublesome for you. You may wish to improve in these areas by reviewing parts of the chapter, redoing the learning activities, or asking for additional help from your instructor or a colleague.

Role-Play Evaluation

In actual counseling, you must demonstrate your skills orally—not write about them. To help you determine the extent to which you can apply and evaluate your skills, role-play evaluations are provided at the end of most chapters. Each role-play evaluation consists of a structured situation in which you are asked to demonstrate certain skills as a counselor with a role-play client. Your performance on the role-play interview can be assessed by using the role-play checklist at the end of the chapter. These checklists consist of steps and possible responses associated with a particular strategy. The checklist should be used only as a guideline. You should always adapt any helping strategy to the client and to the particular demands of the situation.

There are two ways to assess your role-play performance. You can ask your instructor, a colleague, or another person to observe your performance, using the checklist. Your instructor may even schedule you periodically to do a role-play "checkout" individually or in a small group. If you do not have anyone to observe you, assess yourself. Audiotape your interview and rate your performance on the checklist. Also ask your "client" for feedback. If you don't reach the criterion level of the objective on the first try, you may need some extra work. The following section explains the need for additional practice.

Additional Practice

You may find some skills more difficult to acquire the first time around than others. Often people are chagrined and disappointed when they do not demonstrate the strategy as well as they would like

on their first attempt. We ask these individuals whether they hold similar expectation levels for their clients! You cannot quickly and simply let go of behaviors you don't find useful in counseling and acquire others that are more helpful. It may be unrealistic to assume you will always demonstrate an adequate level of performance on *all* the evaluations on the first go-round. Much covert and overt rehearsal may be necessary before you feel comfortable with skill demonstration in the evaluations. On some occasions, it may be necessary for you to work through the learning activities and postevaluations more than once.

Some Cautions about Using This Format

Although we believe the format of this book will promote learning, we want you to consider several cautions about using it. As you will see, we have defined the skills and strategies in precise and systematic ways to make it easier for you to acquire and develop the skills. However, we do not intend that our definitions and guidelines be used like cookbook instructions. Perhaps our definitions and categories will give you some methodology and helping. But do not be restrained by this, particularly in applying your skills in the interview process. As you come to feel more comfortable with a strategy, we hope you will use the procedure creatively. Technical skills are not sufficient in counseling unless accompanied by inventiveness (Frey, 1975, p. 23), and "therapeutic guidelines cannot substitute for the clinical sensitivity and ingenuity of the therapist" (Goldfried & Goldfried, 1980, p. 125).

One of the most difficult parts of learning counseling skills seems to be trusting the skills to work and not being preoccupied with your own performance. We are reminded of a story in *Time* (November 29, 1976) about the conductor of the Berlin Philharmonic, Herbert Von Karajan. When asked why he didn't rely more on entry and cutoff cues in conducting a large orchestra, he replied "My hands do their job because they have learned what to do. In the performance I forget about them" (p. 82).

Preoccupation with yourself, your skills, or a particular procedure reduces your ability to relate to and be involved with another person. At first, it is natural to focus on the skill or strategy because it is new and feels a little awkward or cumbersome. But once you have learned a particular skill or strategy, the skills will be there when you need them. Gradually, as you acquire your repertory of skills and strategies, you should be able to change your focus from the procedure to the person.

Remember, also, that counseling is a complex process composed of many interrelated parts. Although different counseling stages, skills, and strategies are presented in this book in separate chapters, in practice there is a meshing of all these components. As an example, the relationship does not stop or diminish in importance when a counselor and client begin to assess problems, establish goals, or implement strategies. Nor is evaluation something that occurs only when counseling is terminated. Evaluation involves continual monitoring throughout the counseling interaction. Even obtaining a client's commitment to use strategies consistently and to monitor their effects may be aided or hindered by the quality of the relationship and the degree to which client problems and goals have been defined clearly. In the same vein, keep in mind that most client problems are complex and multifaceted. Successful counseling may involve changes in the client's feelings, observable behavior, beliefs, and cognitions. To model some of the skills and procedures you will learn, we have included cases and model dialogues in most chapters. These are intended to illustrate one example of a way in which a particular procedure can be used with a client. However, the cases and dialogues have been simplified for demonstration purposes, and the printed words may not communicate the sense of flow and direction that is normally present in counselor/client interchanges. Again, with actual clients, you will probably encounter more dimensions to the relationship and to the client's concerns than are reflected in the chapter examples.

Our third concern involves the way you approach the examples and practice opportunities in this book. Obviously, reading an example or doing a role-play interview is not as real as seeing an actual client or engaging in a live counseling interaction. However, some practice is necessary in any new learning program. Even if the exercises seem artificial, they probably will help you learn counseling skills. The structured practice opportunities in the book may require a great deal of discipline on your part, but the degree to which you can generalize your skills from practice to an actual counseling interview may depend on how much you invest in the practice opportunities.

One more word on such practice: Our Western culture regards practice as useful because "practice makes perfect." We prefer the Eastern concept—"practice makes different." Practice does not make perfect, because people are not intended to be perfect. However, practice may result in a change within ourselves, in our ideas, attitudes, beliefs, and actions. Practice can help all of us transform ourselves into more competent helpers.

Options for Using the Book

We have written this book in its particular format because each component seems to play a unique role in the learning process. But we are also committed to the idea that each person must determine the most suitable individual method of learning. With this in mind, we suggest a number of ways to use this book. First, you can go through the book and use the entire format in the way it is described in this chapter. If you do this, we suggest you familiarize yourself carefully with the format as described here. If you want to use this format but do not understand it, it is not likely to be helpful. Another way to use the book is to use only certain parts of the format in any combination you choose. You may want to experiment initially to determine which components seem especially useful. For example, you might use the postevaluation but not complete the chapter learning activities. Finally, if you prefer a "straight" textbook format, you can read only the content of the book and ignore the special format. Our intent is for you to use the book in whatever way is most suitable for your learning strategies.

☐ ONE FINAL THOUGHT

As you go through the book, you undoubtedly will get some feel for the particular ways to use each strategy. However, we caution you against using this book as a prescriptive device, like medicine handed over a counter automatically and without thought or imagination. We are discovering that no one method of learning is equally useful for all people (McKeachie, 1976; Snow, 1974). Similarly, one counseling strategy may not work well for all clients. As your counseling experience accumulates, you will find that one client does not use a strategy in the same way, at the same pace, or with similar results as another client. In selecting counseling strategies, it is helpful to be guided by the documentation concerning the ways in which the strategy has been used. But it is just as important to remember that each client may respond in an idiosyncratic manner to any particular approach. Mahoney and Mahoney (1976) emphasize that counseling is a "personalized science, in which each client's problems are given due recognition for their uniqueness and potential complexity" (p. 100). Finally, remember that almost anybody can learn and perform a skill in a rote and mechanistic manner. But not everyone shows the qualities of sensitivity and ingenuity to give the skills his or her own unique touch.

INGREDIENTS OF AN EFFECTIVE HELPING RELATIONSHIP

TWO

It is widely accepted today by persons of various theoretical orientations to counseling that the therapeutic relationship is an important part of the total helping process. According to Brammer, Shostrom, and Abrego (1989), the relationship is important not only because "it constitutes the principal medium for eliciting and handling significant feelings and ideas which are aimed at changing client behavior" but also because it often determines "whether counseling will continue at all" (pp. 74–75). Without an effective therapeutic relationship, client change is unlikely to occur. An effective relationship provides the impetus and groundwork for more direct intervention strategies "to yield their intended effects" (Goldstein, 1980, p. 20).

☐ OBJECTIVES

After completing this chapter, you will be able to—

1. Identify attitudes and behaviors about yourself that might facilitate or interfere with establishing a positive helping relationship, given a written self-assessment checklist.
2. Identify issues related to values, ethics, and emotional objectivity that might affect the development of a therapeutic relationship, given six written case descriptions.
3. Communicate the three facilitative relationship conditions (empathy, genuineness, positive regard) to a client, given a role-play situation.

☐ CHARACTERISTICS OF EFFECTIVE HELPERS

The counselor's attitudes and skills are important determinants of the quality of the therapeutic relationship. (Client attitudes and behaviors also shape the relationship, since it is interactive and reciprocal.) The most effective helper is one who has successfully integrated the personal and scientific parts of himself or herself—in other words, who has achieved a balance of interpersonal and technical competence. In this section we examine the qualities and behaviors present in very effective counselors and therapists.

Intellectual Competence

Counseling is an intellectually demanding process. In addition to being a "warm fuzzy," counseling and therapy require that one have a thorough and adequate knowledge base of many diverse areas. Counselors need to be knowledgeable and also to have a desire to learn, to be curious enough to want to check things out and know what is happening to clients. Intellectual competence also involves searching for data to make informed decisions about client treatment choice and progress (see also Chapter 10).

Energy

Counseling and therapy are emotionally demanding as well. Counselors who see several clients every day are likely to feel emotionally drained and physically fatigued at day's end—or sometimes even before! Passive, nonenergetic helpers are not likely to inspire much trust and confidence from their clients. Dynamism and intensity are more likely to produce client confidence and to encourage clients to work and to be active themselves during the session.

Flexibility

Effective therapists are also flexible—that is, they are not tied to a single ideology or methodology that they use for all clients. Flexible counselors adapt methods and technologies to clients rather than pushing clients and their problems to fit the use of a particular theoretical orientation or strategy. The flexible therapist's behavior is always mediated by the covert question posed by Kiesler (1966): Which technique will work best for this particular client with this set of problems?

Support

Effective therapists are supporting to clients. Support has a number of functions in the therapeutic relationship, including engendering hope, reducing client anxiety, and giving emotional security (Brammer, Shostrom, & Abrego, 1989). Giving support does not mean encouraging the client to lean on you, however, or taking responsibility away from the client. As Rogers (1951) notes, the counseling relationship "is experienced as basically supporting, but in no way supportive. The

client does not feel that someone is behind him, that someone approves of him. He does experience the fact that here is someone who respects him *as he is,* and is willing for him to take any direction which he chooses" (p. 209). (An exception would be in crisis intervention, where very direct supportive techniques are often the recommended treatment.) The counselor must maintain a careful balance between being supporting and being supportive in order to avoid promoting client dependence and to avoid "rescuing" the client, thus robbing clients of their own self-support system.

Good Will

Counselors who have good will work on behalf of their clients, not themselves. Their desire to help is not thwarted because of their own unmet needs. All of us who counsel get certain needs met through doing so. If we have "good will," however, we are not dependent on our counseling relationships as our *primary* source for meeting our own needs. Good will also implies that our motives and intentions are positive and constructive rather than negative and destructive. For example, we seek information about a client's sexual history because it is critical to the assessment of the particular problem, not because we are voyeuristic, curious, or in need of vicarious sexual reinforcement ourselves. Good will also suggests that we behave in ethical and responsible ways with clients (see also "Ethical Issues," later in this chapter).

Self-Awareness

The ability to be involved in an effective interpersonal interaction is influenced by our feelings and attitudes about ourselves. If we lack awareness about ourselves, we may be unable to establish the type of counseling relationship that is best for the client.

Our attitudes about ourselves can significantly influence the way we behave. People who have negative views of themselves will "put themselves down" and will either seek out or avoid types of interactions with others that confirm their negative self-image. This has serious implications for counselors. If we don't feel competent or valuable as people, we may communicate this attitude to the client. Or if we don't feel confident about our ability to counsel, we may inadvertently structure the counseling process to meet our own self-image problems or to confirm our negative self-pictures.

All our feelings and thoughts influence the way we handle certain things in the counseling relationship. Very strong feelings and attitudes about ourselves may significantly influence our behavior with clients. For instance a counselor who is very sensitive to rejection may be unduly careful not to offend a client or may avoid confronting a client when confrontation could be helpful. A counselor who has trouble dealing with negative feelings may structure the counseling interaction so that negative feelings are never "on the agenda."

In addition to skillful use of intervention strategies to produce client change, we need to be aware of our own strengths and limitations or "blind spots." In other words, it is just as important to keep track of our own personal growth as it is to keep track of which technique or change program we are using with a client. Otherwise, we run the risk of behaving incongruently in our relationships with clients. There are three areas that most counselors need to examine closely about themselves because they can have a significant impact on the quality of the relationship and the kind of service they give to clients: competence, power, and intimacy. These three areas and the possible feelings, attitudes, and behaviors associated with them are depicted in Table 2-1. We describe them in more detail in the next three sections.

TABLE 2-1. Effects of counselor's self-image on counseling interaction

Potential problem area and unresolved feelings and needs	Attitude about self	Possible counseling behaviors
Competence Incompetence Inadequacy	1. Pollyanna; overly positive — fearful of failing	Structures counseling to maintain Pollyanna attitude, avoiding conflicts by— 1. discounting negative feedback 2. giving "fake" feedback 3. avoiding or smoothing over "heavy stuff"
Fear of failure Fear of success	2. Negative; overly self-critical — fearful of succeeding	Structures counseling to maintain negative self-image by— 1. avoiding positive interactions 2. discounting positive feedback 3. giving self overly negative feedback 4. making goals and expectations too high 5. making self-deprecating or apologetic comments
	3. Not masculine enough or not feminine enough	Structures counseling to make self feel more secure as a male or female by— 1. overidentifying with or rejecting very masculine or very feminine clients 2. seducing clients of opposite sex 3. overreacting to or misinterpreting both positive and negative reactions from male and female clients
Power Impotence Control Passivity Dependence	1. Omnipotent — fearful of losing control	Structures counseling to get and stay in control by— 1. persuading clients to do whatever counselor wants 2. subtly informing client how good or right counselor is 3. dominating content and direction of interview 4. getting upset or irritated if client is resistant or reluctant

(continued)

TABLE 2-1. Effects of counselor's self-image on counseling interaction (continued)

Potential problem area and unresolved feelings and needs	Attitude about self	Possible counseling behaviors
Power		
Independence Counterdependence	2. Weak and unresourceful—fearful of control	Structures counseling to avoid taking control by— 1. being overly silent and nonparticipatory 2. allowing client too much direction, as in constant client rambling 3. frequently asking client for permission to do or say something 4. not expressing opinion; always referring back to client 5. avoiding any other risks
	3. Lifestyle converter	Structures counseling to convert client to counselor's beliefs or lifestyle by— 1. promoting ideology 2. getting in a power struggle 3. rejecting clients who are too different or who don't respond 4. "preaching"
Intimacy Affection Rejection	1. Needing warmth and acceptance—fearful of being rejected	Structures counseling to make self liked by— 1. eliciting positive feelings from client 2. avoiding use of confrontation 3. ignoring negative client cues 4. doing things for client—favors and so on
	2. Needing distance—fearful of closeness, affection	Structures counseling to maintain distance and avoid emotional intimacy by— 1. ignoring client's positive feelings 2. acting overly gruff or distant 3. maintaining professional role as "expert"

Competence. Your feelings of personal adequacy and professional competence can influence your covert and overt behavior in counseling interactions. Feelings of incompetence and inadequacy can be described as either fear of failure or fear of success. A counselor who is afraid of failure may approach counseling with an overly positive "Pollyanna" attitude. The fear of failure can be interfering if the counselor structures counseling to avoid conflicts. The counseling interaction may remain superficial because issues and negative topics are pushed under the table.

Other people may maintain a negative picture of themselves by being afraid of success and by avoiding successful situations and interactions. A counselor who fears success may structure counseling to maintain or confirm such a negative self-concept. This counselor tends to discount positive feedback and to have expectations that are out of reach.

Concerns about one's adequacy as a male or a female can also enter into the counseling relationship. Counselors who do not feel comfortable with themselves as men or women may behave in ways that add to their security in this area. For example, a counselor could promote his or her masculinity or femininity by overidentifying with or rejecting clients of the same sex, seducing clients of the opposite sex, and overreacting to or misinterpreting some client cues.

Power. Unresolved feelings about oneself in relation to power and control may include impotence, passivity, dependence. There are several ways that power can be misused in counseling. First, a counselor who fears being impotent or weak or who is afraid to give up control may try to be omnipotent. For this person, counseling is manageable only when it is controllable. Such a counselor may use a variety of maneuvers to stay in control, including persuading the client to do what the counselor wants, getting upset or defensive if a client is resistant or hesitant, and dominating the content and direction of the interview. The counselor who needs to control the interview may be more likely to engage in a power struggle with a client.

In contrast, a counselor may be afraid of power and control. This counselor may attempt to escape from as much responsibility and participation in counseling as possible. Such a counselor avoids taking control by allowing the client too much direction and by not expressing opinions. In other words, risks are avoided or ignored.

Another way that unresolved power needs can influence counseling is seen in the "lifestyle converter." This person has very strong feelings about the value of one particular lifestyle. Such a counselor may take unwarranted advantage of the influence processes in a helping relationship by using counseling to convert the client to that lifestyle or ideology. Counseling, in this case, turns into a forum for the counselor's views and pet peeves.

Intimacy. A counselor's unresolved intimacy needs can also significantly alter the direction and course of counseling. Generally, a counselor who has trouble with intimacy may fear rejection or be threatened by closeness and affection. A counselor who is afraid of rejection may behave in ways that meet the need to be accepted and liked by the client. For example, the counselor may avoid challenging or confronting the client for fear the client may be "turned off." Or the counselor may subtly seek positive client feedback as a reassurance of being valued and liked. Negative client cues also may be ignored because the counselor does not want to hear expressions of client dissatisfaction.

A counselor who is afraid of intimacy and affection may create excessive distance in the relationship. The counselor may avoid emotional intimacy in the relationship by ignoring expressions of positive feelings from the client or by behaving in a gruff, distant, or aloof manner and relating to the client through the "professional role."

LEARNING ACTIVITY #1: SELF-IMAGE

The following learning activity may help you explore some of your feelings and attitudes about yourself and possible effects on your counseling interactions. The activity consists of a Self-Rating Checklist divided into the three areas of competence, power, and intimacy. We suggest you work through each section separately. As you read the items listed for each section, think about the extent to which the item accurately describes your behavior *most* of the time (there are always exceptions to our consistent behaviors). If an item asks about you in relation to a client and you haven't had much counseling experience, try to project yourself into the counselor's role. Check the items that are most descriptive of you. Try to be as honest with yourself as possible. After completing the checklist, refer to the feedback that follows.

SELF-RATING CHECKLIST
Check the items that are most descriptive of you.

I. Competence Assessment
_____ 1. Constructive negative feedback about myself doesn't make me feel incompetent or uncertain of myself.

_____ 2. I tend to put myself down frequently.

_____ 3. I feel fairly confident about myself as a helper.

_____ 4. I am often preoccupied with thinking that I'm not going to be a competent counselor.

_____ 5. When I am involved in a conflict, I don't go out of my way to ignore or avoid it.

_____ 6. When I get positive feedback about myself, I often don't believe it's true.

_____ 7. I set realistic goals for myself as a helper that are within reach.

✓ 8. I believe that a confronting, hostile client could make me feel uneasy or incompetent.

_____ 9. I often find myself apologizing for myself or my behavior.

_____10. I'm fairly confident I can or will be a successful counselor.

_____11. I find myself worrying a lot about "not making it" as a counselor.

✓12. I'm likely to be a little scared by clients who would idealize me.

_____13. A lot of times I will set standards or goals for myself that are too tough to attain.

_____14. I tend to avoid negative feedback when I can.

(continued)

LEARNING ACTIVITY #1: SELF-IMAGE (continued)

✓ 15. Doing well or being successful does not make me feel uneasy.

II. Power Assessment

___ 1. If I'm really honest, I think my counseling methods are a little superior to other people's.

___ 2. A lot of times I try to get people to do what I want. I might get pretty defensive or upset if the client disagreed with what I wanted to do or did not follow my direction in the interview.

___ 3. I believe there is (or will be) a balance in the interviews between my participation and the client's.

✓ 4. I could feel angry when working with a resistant or stubborn client.

✓ 5. I can see that I might be tempted to get some of my own ideology across to the client.

___ 6. As a counselor, "preaching" is not likely to be a problem for me.

✓ 7. Sometimes I feel impatient with clients who have a different way of looking at the world than I do.

___ 8. I know there are times when I would be reluctant to refer my client to someone else, especially if the other counselor's style differed from mine.

✓ 9. Sometimes I feel rejecting or intolerant of clients whose values and lifestyles are very different from mine.

✓ 10. It is hard for me to avoid getting into a power struggle with some clients.

III. Intimacy Assessment

___ 1. There are times when I act more gruff than I really feel.

___ 2. It's hard for me to express positive feelings to a client.

___ 3. There are some clients I would really like to be my friends more than my clients.

✓ 4. It would upset me if a client didn't like me.

___ 5. If I sense a client has some negative feelings toward me, I try to talk about it rather than avoid it.

✓ 6. Many times I go out of my way to avoid offending clients.

✓ 7. I feel more comfortable maintaining a professional distance between myself and the client.

___ 8. Being close to people is something that does not make me feel uncomfortable.

✓ 9. I am more comfortable when I am a little aloof.

✓ 10. I am very sensitive to how clients feel about me, especially if it's negative.

___ 11. I can accept positive feedback from clients fairly easily.

___ 12. It is difficult for me to confront a client.

☐ ISSUES AFFECTING THE THERAPEUTIC RELATIONSHIP

Although each therapeutic relationship is always defined somewhat idiosyncratically by each therapeutic dyad, there are certain issues that will affect many of the therapeutic relationships you will encounter. These include (but are not limited to) values, ethics, and emotional objectivity.

Values

The word *value* denotes something we prize, regard highly, or prefer. Values are our feelings or attitudes about something and our preferred actions or behaviors. As an example, take a few minutes to think of (and perhaps list) five things you love to do. Now look over your list to determine how frequently and consistently you actually engage in each of these five actions. Your values are indicated by your frequent and consistent actions (Raths, Harmin, & Simon, 1966). If you say you value spending time with friends but you hardly ever do this, then other activities and actions probably have more value for you.

In interactions with clients, it is impossible to be "value-free." Values permeate every interaction. Counselors cannot be "scrupulously neutral" in their interactions with clients (Corey, Corey, & Callanan, 1988, p. 67). Okun (1987) asserts that "in recent years, we have recognized that in any interpersonal relationship, whether a helping relationship or not, values are transmitted either directly or indirectly between the participants" (p. 229). Interviewers may unintentionally influence a patient to embrace their values in subtle ways by what they pay attention to or by nonverbal cues of approval and disapproval (Corey et al., 1988). If clients feel they need the counselor's approval, they may act in ways they think will please the counselor instead of making choices independently according to their own value system.

Obviously, not all of our values have an impact on the helping process. For example, the counselor who values sailing can probably work with a client who values being a landlubber without any problem. However, values that reflect our ideas about "the good life," morality, ethics, lifestyle, roles, interpersonal living, and so forth have a greater chance of entering into the helping process. The very fact that we have entered a helping profession suggests some of our values. As discussed in Chapter 9, there may be times when a referral is necessary because of an unresolved and interfering value conflict with a client. For example, a counselor who views rape as the most terrible and sexist act a person can perform might have difficulty counseling someone accused of rape. This counselor might tend to identify more with the rape victim than with the client. From an ethical viewpoint, if a counselor is unable to promote and respect the welfare of a client, a referral may be necessary (American Association for Counseling and Development, 1981; American Psychological Association, 1981).

There are other times in the counseling process when our values affect helping, not because they conflict with the client's values, but because they restrict or limit the client. In these instances, our values are getting in the way of helping the person reach her or his potential. Restricting or delimiting values are reflected in such areas as our expectations for different clients, our beliefs about change, and our values about an "ism" such as sexism, racism, culturism, or ageism. One of *our* values is the need for counselors to be aware of values that might prevent the client from developing his or her potential. We have acted on this value by including in Learning Activity #2 some ways to help you examine your values about a number of "isms" and about your expectations for client change.

Stereotypical values.   There is a legitimate concern about the possible limiting effects of counselor stereotyping in the helping process. Maslin and Davis (1975, p. 87) define *stereotyping* as ascribing characteristics to a person on the basis of presumed knowledge about a group to which the person belongs. E. J. Smith (1977) asserts that stereotypes "are the conventions that people use for refusing to deal with one another on an individual

basis" (p. 390). Stereotyping in counseling may occur when the counselor projects his or her biases on the client or applies cultural and sociological characteristics of a particular cultural group "indiscriminately to all members" of that group (p. 391).

The most damaging kinds of stereotyping have to do with sex roles and ethnicity. For example, there is some evidence that, during the helping process, many counselors communicate the stereotypical attitudes toward sex roles of our Western culture (Broverman, Broverman, Clarkson, Rosenkrantz, & Vogel, 1970). In other words, some counselors may try to influence male and female clients to behave according to stereotypical concepts of masculinity and femininity portrayed in our culture. Male clients may be reinforced for being strong, independent, and unemotional, whereas female clients are told it is more "healthy" to be less assertive and more passive, dependent, and "soft." Our sex-role values also may be used inappropriately in counseling even when our biases do not reflect the traditional male and female roles. Using nontraditional sex-role values to urge a nonworking mother to work is another example of limiting the client's choices. Okun (1987) suggests that sexist counseling occurs whenever the counselor employs her or his own sex-role ideology as a basis for helping.

Sexism is not the only area in which our values may dominate the helping process. Our biases can interfere when counseling people with handicaps and disabilities, people of limited abilities, and people of different cultures, races, and socioeconomic levels. E. J. Smith (1977) points out that stereotypical counseling treatment of Blacks occurs whenever the counselor applies assumptions and research findings about Black clients in a general, nonidiosyncratic manner. Smith adds that many of the proverbial conclusions about counseling Black clients—such as that Blacks have poor self-concepts, Black clients are nonverbal, or Black clients profit only from counseling that is highly structured and action-oriented—may be more myths than realities and may reflect White Anglo-Saxon interpretations and values. Okun (1987) observes that another common form of stereotypical counseling involves ageism, when we convey "our own beliefs and values about what can or should be done at different ages" (p. 256). A counselor who becomes aware that his or her limiting expectations or stereotypical values are interfering with the helping process has the responsibility to modify the stereotypes or refer the client to another helper.

In some cases, a counselor may be unaware of tendencies toward "ism" counseling because of lack of opportunities to counsel different kinds of clients. For example, if you have never worked with an older person, a handicapped person, or a person of another culture, perhaps you have never confronted your values about such clients. Learning Activity #2 may give you a chance to simulate doing so.

LEARNING ACTIVITY #2: PERSONAL VALUES

This learning activity presents descriptions of six clients. If you work through this activity by yourself, we suggest that you imagine yourself counseling each of these clients. Try to generate a very vivid picture of yourself and the client in your mind. If you do this activity with a partner, you can role-play the counselor while your partner assumes the part of each client as described in the six examples. As you imagine or role-play the counselor, try to notice your feelings, attitudes, values, and behavior during the visualization or role-play process. After *each* example, stop to think about or discuss these questions:

1. What attitudes and beliefs did you have about the client?
2. Were your beliefs and attitudes based on actual or presumed information about the client?
3. How did you behave with the client?
4. What values are portrayed by your behavior?
5. Could you work with this person effectively?

There are no right or wrong answers. A reaction to this learning activity can be found after the client descriptions in the feedback section.

Client 1

This client is a young woman who is having financial problems. She is the sole supporter of three young children. She earns her living by prostitution and pushing drugs. She states that she is concerned about her financial problems but can't make enough money from welfare or from an unskilled job to support her kids.

Client 2

The client is an older man (age 60) who is approaching retirement. He has been working most of his life as a furniture salesperson. He has a high school diploma and has not been in school since he was 18 years old. Now he feels that he wants to go to college and earn a degree.

Client 3

You have been assigned a client who is charged with rape and sexual assault. The client, a man, tells you that he is not to blame for the incident because the victim, a woman, "asked for it."

Client 4

This client is concerned about general feelings of depression. Overweight and unkempt, the client is in poor physical condition and smokes constantly during the interview.

Client 5

The client is a middle-aged woman on welfare. She says she was raped and as a result gave birth to a child. She is torn between trying to keep this baby and giving it up.

Client 6

The client is a 12-year-old boy who recently lost a leg in an automobile accident. He was a strong swimmer before the accident; he wants to continue his swimming now so he can eventually make the high school swimming team. He wants to know your opinion about this decision.

Ethical Issues

The therapeutic relationship needs to be handled in such a way as to promote and protect the client's welfare. Indeed, as Brammer, Shostrom, and Abrego (1989, p. 81) observe, ethical handling of client relationships is a "distinctive mark" of the professional counselor/therapist. All professional groups of helpers have a code of ethics adopted by their profession, such as the ethical standards of the American Association for Counseling and Development (1981), the American Psychological Association (1981), and the National Association of Social Workers (1979) (see Appendixes A, B, C, and D). Marriage and family therapists, rehabilitation counselors, and health professionals also have their own sets of corresponding ethical standards.

FEEDBACK #1: SELF-IMAGE

1. For each of the three assessment areas you can look over your responses and determine the areas that seem to be OK and the areas that may be a problem for you or something to watch out for. You may find more problems in one area than another.
2. Do your "trouble spots" seem to occur with almost everyone or just with certain types of people? In all situations or some situations?
3. Compare yourself now with where you might have been four years ago or where you may be four years from now.
4. Identify any areas you feel you could use some help with, from a colleague, a supervisor, or a counselor.

The counselor's value system is an important factor in determining ethical behavior. Behaving unethically can have consequences such as loss of membership in professional organizations and malpractice lawsuits. Of most consequence is the detrimental effect that unethical behavior can have on clients and on the therapeutic relationship.

All student and practicing counselors and therapists should be familiar with the ethical codes of their profession. The following discussion highlights a few of the more critical issues and in no way is intended to be a substitute for careful scrutiny of existing ethical codes of behavior.

Client welfare. Counselors are obligated to protect the welfare of their clients. In most instances, this means putting the client's needs first. It also means ensuring that you are intellectually and emotionally ready to give the best that you can to each client—or to see that the client has a referral option if seeing you is not in the client's best interests.

Confidentiality. Closely related to protecting client well-being is the issue of confidentiality. Counselors who breach client confidences can do serious and often irreparable harm to the therapeutic relationship. Counselors are generally not free to reveal or disclose information about clients unless they have first received written permission from the client. An exception can be in instances in which the counselor believes the client poses a serious threat of harm to self or others and in states where the helping professional can be subpoenaed because of lack of a legal statute protecting counselor disclosure about the therapeutic relationship in a court of law (known as "privileged communication").

Dual relationships. A dual relationship is one in which the counselor is in a therapeutic relationship with the client and simultaneously also has another kind of relationship with that same person, such as an administrative, instructional, supervisory, social, or sexual relationship. Dual relationships are problematic because they reduce the counselor's objectivity, confuse the issue, and often put the client in a position of diminished consent. Counselors should avoid becoming involved in dual relationships. If such involvement is unavoidable, make use of the referral option so that two relationships are not carried on simultaneously.

Client rights. Establishing an effective therapeutic relationship entails being open with clients about their rights and options during the course of therapy. Nothing can be more damaging to trust and rapport than to have the client discover in midstream that the therapist is not qualified to help with a particular issue or that the financial costs of therapy are high or that therapy involves certain limitations or nonguarantees of outcomes. At the outset, the therapist should provide the client with enough information about therapy to help the client make informed choices (also called "informed consent"). Usually this means discussing four general aspects of counseling with clients: (1) confidentiality and its limitations, (2) the procedures and goals of therapy and any possible side effects of change (such as anxiety, pain, or disruption of the status quo), (3) the qualifications and practices of the therapist, and (4) other available resources and sources of help other than oneself and other than traditional therapy (for example, self-help groups) (Hare-Mustin, Maracek, Kaplan, & Liss-Levinson, 1979; see also "Structuring," in Chapter 3 and Informed Consent Checklist in Chapter 11).

Referral. It is important for counselors to handle referral effectively and responsibly. Referring a client to another therapist may be necessary when, for one reason or another, you are not able to provide the service or care that the client requires. Careful referral, however, involves more than just

FEEDBACK #2: PERSONAL VALUES

Perhaps your visualizations or role plays revealed to you that you may have certain biases and values about sex roles, age, cultures, race, physical appearance, and rape. Some of your biases may reflect your past experiences with a person or an incident. Most people in the helping professions agree that some of our values are communicated to clients, even unintentionally. Try to identify any values or biases you hold now that could communicate disapproval to a client or could keep you from "promoting the welfare" of your client. With yourself, a peer, or an instructor, work out a plan to reevaluate your biases or to help you prevent yourself from imposing your values on clients.

giving the client the name of another counselor. The client should be given a choice among therapists who are competent and are qualified to deal with the client's problems. The counselor must obtain written client permission before discussing the case with the new therapist. And to protect against abandonment, the counselor should follow up on the referral to determine whether the appropriate contact was made.

Emotional Objectivity

The therapeutic relationship has the capacity to invoke great emotional intensity, often experienced by both the counselor and the client. To some extent, counselors need to become emotionally involved in the relationship. If they are too aloof or distant, clients will feel that the counselor is cold, mechanical, and noncaring. However, if counselors are too involved, they may scare the client away or may lose all objectivity and cloud their judgment.

The degree of emotional objectivity and intensity felt by counselors can affect two relationship issues: transference and countertransference. *Transference* is the

> process whereby clients project onto their therapists past feelings or attitudes toward significant people in their lives. . . . In transference, a client's unfinished business produces a distortion in the way he or she perceives the therapist. The feelings that are experienced in transference may be positive or negative. . . . They are connected with the past but are now directed toward the therapist [Corey et al., 1988, p. 47].

Transference can occur very easily with counselors of all theoretical orientations when the emotional intensity has become so great that the client loses his or her objectivity and starts to relate to the counselor as if he or she were some significant other person in the client's life.

It is important for counselors to be clearly aware of their own needs, motivations, and personal reactions. If they are unaware of their own dynamics, they will be less effective with their clients. They will avoid important therapeutic issues instead of focusing on challenging their clients to understand and resolve the feelings they are bringing into the present from their past [Corey et al.; 1988, p. 48].

Countertransference occurs when counselors lose their objectivity and develop a strong emotional reaction to the client. According to Corey et al. (1988, pp. 50–52), countertransference may be manifested in a number of ways, including—

1. Being overprotective with clients manifests itself in an oversolicitous attitude.
2. Treating clients in benign ways may stem from the counselor's fears of the clients' anger.
3. Rejection of clients may be based on perceiving them as needy and dependent.
4. The need for constant reinforcement and approval from your clients.
5. Seeing yourself in your clients.
6. Development of sexual or romantic feelings toward your clients.
7. Compulsive advice giving with your clients.
8. A desire to develop social relationships with your clients.

To handle transference and countertransference effectively, the counselor needs, first of all, to be aware of when these dynamics occur. Clues to transference and countertransference include a sudden eruption of strong emotions (by either client or counselor) that seems inappropriate in timing or intensity, given the context in which the feelings arise (Reiser & Schroder, 1980, p. 150). The counselor who fails to recognize transference or countertransference may respond inappropriately to the client.

Second, counselors must be constantly aware of the various levels of impact that they have on clients and clients have on them (Brammer, Shostrom, & Abrego, 1989, p. 77). Either end of the continuum—too little impact or too intense an impact—can adversely affect the therapeutic relationship.

Finally, one must seek a level of emotional involvement that is sufficient to generate client involvement without clouding one's own objectivity about the client (Brammer & Shostrom, 1982).

□ FUNDAMENTAL HELPING SKILLS AND PERSON-CENTERED THERAPY

In the remainder of this chapter, as well as in Chapters 3–6, we describe a number of fundamental, or *core*, skills of helping. Relationship, responding, and listening skills are parts of most current helping approaches. These skills have roots in a counseling theory developed by Rogers (1951), called "client-centered" or "person-centered" therapy. Because this theory is the basis of these fundamental skills, we will describe it briefly in this section.

The first stage of this theory (Rogers, 1942) was known as the *nondirective* period. The counselor essentially attended and listened to the client for the purpose of mirroring the client's communication. The second stage of this theory (Rogers, 1951) was known as the *client-centered* period. In this phase, the therapist not only mirrored the client's communication but also reflected underlying or implicit affect or feelings. (This is the basis of current concepts of the skill of empathy, discussed in the next section.)

In the most recent stage, known as *person-centered therapy* (Meador & Rogers, 1984), therapy is construed as an active partnership between two persons. In this current stage, emphasis is on client growth through *experiencing* of oneself and of the other person in the relationship.

Although client-centered therapy has evolved and changed, certain fundamental tenets have remained the same. One of these is that all people have an inherent tendency to strive toward growth, self-actualization, and self-direction. This tendency is realized when individuals have access to conditions (both within and outside therapy) that nurture growth. In the context of therapy, client growth is associated with high levels of three core, or facilitative, relationship conditions: *empathy* (accurate understanding), *respect* (positive regard), and *genuineness* (congruence) (Rogers, Gendlin, Kiesler, & Truax, 1967). If these conditions are absent from the therapeutic relationship, clients may not only fail to grow, they may deteriorate (Berenson & Mitchell, 1974; Carkhuff, 1969a, 1969b; Truax & Mitchell, 1971). Presumably, in order for these conditions to enhance the thera-

peutic relationship, they must be communicated by the counselor *and* perceived by the client (Rogers, 1951, 1957).

Gazda, Asbury, Balzer, Childers, and Walters (1984, p. 131) summarize a number of important purposes of facilitative conditions, including the following:

1. The use of facilitative conditions establishes a relationship of mutual trust and caring in which clients feel secure and able to express themselves in any way or form necessary.
2. The facilitative conditions help to define the counselor or therapist role; counselors utilize effective therapeutic behaviors and try to avoid ineffective skills and behaviors.
3. The use of facilitative conditions helps clients to obtain a more complete and concrete self-image, or self-picture, allowing them to see or understand things that formerly may have been hidden or only partly understood.
4. Facilitative responding is a concrete way to show clients they have your full attention without personal or environmental distractions.

Although Rogerian-based strategies for helping "are devoid of techniques that involve *doing* something to or for the client" (Gilliland, James, Roberts, & Bowman, 1984), in current writings Rogers (1977) asserts that these three core conditions represent a set of skills as well as an attitude on the part of the therapist. In recent years, a variety of persons have developed concrete skills associated with these three core conditions; much of this development is based on accumulating research evidence (Carkhuff, 1969a, 1969b; Egan, 1990; Gazda et al., 1984; Ivey, 1988). This delineation of the core conditions into teachable skills has made it possible for people to learn how to communicate these core conditions to clients. In the following three sections, we describe these three important relationship conditions and associated skills in more detail.

□ EMPATHY, OR ACCURATE UNDERSTANDING

Empathy may be described as the ability to understand people from their frame of reference rather than your own. Responding to a client empathically may be "an attempt to think *with,* rather than *for* or *about* the client" (Brammer, Shostrom, & Abrego, 1989, p. 92). For example, if a client says "I've tried to get along with my father, but it doesn't work out. He's too hard on me," an empathic response would be something like "You feel discouraged about your unsuccessful attempts to get along with your father." In contrast, if you say something like "You ought to try harder," you are responding from your frame of reference, not the client's.

Empathy has received a great deal of attention from both researchers and practitioners over the years. Current concepts emphasize that empathy is far more than a single concept or skill. Empathy is believed to be a multistage process consisting of multiple elements (Barrett-Lennard, 1981; Gladstein, 1983).

Current research has abandoned the "uniformity myth" (Kiesler, 1966) with respect to empathy and seeks to determine when empathic understanding is most useful for particular clients and problems and at particular stages in the counseling process. As Gladstein (1983, p. 178) observes, "in counseling/psychotherapy, affective and cognitive empathy can be helpful in certain stages, with certain clients, and for certain goals. However, at other times, they can interfere with positive outcomes." Generally, empathy is useful in influencing the quality and effectiveness of the therapeutic relationship. Empathy helps to build rapport and elicit information from clients by showing understanding, demonstrating civility (Egan, 1990), conveying that both counselor and client are working "from the same side" (Krumboltz &

Thoresen, 1976), and fostering client goals related to self-exploration (Gladstein, 1983) (see also Table 2-2).

Empathy is conveyed to clients by reflective and additive verbal messages (Carkhuff, 1969a; Carkhuff & Pierce, 1975; Egan, 1990), by nonverbal behavior (Maurer & Tindall, 1983; Smith-Hanen, 1977), and by the use of selected words or predicates that match clients' sensory systems (Lankton, 1980; Hammer, 1983).

Verbal Means of Conveying Empathy

Consider the following specific tools for conveying empathy:

- *Show desire to comprehend.* It is necessary not only to convey an accurate understanding from the client's perspective but also to convey your *desire* to comprehend from the client's frame of reference. This is evidenced by statements indicating your attempts to make sense of the client's world and by clarification and questions about the client's experiences and feelings.
- *Discuss what is important to the client.* Show by your questions and statements that you are aware of what is most important to the client. Respond in ways that relate to the client's basic problem or complaint. This should be a brief statement that captures the thoughts and feelings of the client and one that is directly related to the client's concerns.

TABLE 2-2. Components and purposes of facilitative, or core, relationship conditions (empathy, genuineness, positive regard)

Condition	Components	Purposes
Empathy (accurate understanding)	Desire to comprehend Reflection of implicit client messages Reference to client feelings Discussion of what is most important to client Pacing of client's experience	1. To build rapport 2. To elicit information by showing understanding 3. To foster client self-exploration
Genuineness (congruence)	Appropriate role behavior Congruence Spontaneity Openness and self-disclosure Supporting nonverbal behaviors	1. To reduce the emotional distance between client and counselor 2. To increase identification between client and counselor, thereby contributing to trust and rapport
Positive regard (respect)	Commitment Effort to understand Nonjudgmental behavior Warmth and immediacy	1. To communicate a willingness to work with the client 2. To show interest in the client as a person 3. To convey acceptance of the client

- Use verbal responses that *refer to client feelings.* One way to define empathy is through verbal statements that reflect the client's feelings (Uhlemann, Lea, & Stone, 1976). Use responses that convey your awareness of the client's feelings. Focus on the client's feelings by naming or labeling them. This is sometimes called "interchangeable" (Carkhuff, 1969a) or "primary" (Egan, 1990) empathy.
- Use verbal responses that bridge or *add on to implicit client messages.* Empathy also involves comprehension of the client's innermost thoughts and perspectives even when these are unspoken and implicit. According to Rogers (1977), "The therapist is so much inside the private world of the other that she can clarify not only the messages of which the client is aware but even those just below the level of awareness" (p. 11). The counselor bridges or adds on to client messages by conveying understanding of what the client implies or infers in order to add to the client's frame of reference or to draw out implications of the issue. This is sometimes called "additive empathy" (Carkhuff, 1969a) or "advanced empathy" (Egan, 1990).

Carkhuff and Pierce (1975) have developed a Discrimination Inventory that presents a scale for assessing both primary and additive empathy messages. On this scale, counselor responses are rated according to one of five levels; Level 3 is considered the *minimally* acceptable response. Level 3 responses on this scale correspond to Carkhuff and Pierce's concept of interchangeable empathy and Egan's (1975) concept of primary-level empathy; Level 4 corresponds to additive empathy (Carkhuff, 1969a) or advanced empathy (Egan); and Level 5 represents facilitating action. The scale can be used either to discriminate among levels of responses or to rate levels of counselor communication. Here is an example of a verbal empathic response at each level of Carkhuff and Pierce's Discrimination Inventory.

Client: I've tried to get along with my father, but it doesn't work out. He's too hard on me.
Counselor at Level 1: I'm sure it will all work out in time [reassurance and denial].
or
    You ought to try harder to see his point of view [advice].
or
    Why can't you two get along? [question].

Level 1 is a question, reassurance, denial, or advice.

Counselor at Level 2: You're having a hard time getting along with your father.

Level 2 is a response to only the *content,* or cognitive portion, of the message; feelings are ignored.

Counselor at Level 3: You feel discouraged because your attempts to get along with your father have not been very successful.

Level 3 has understanding but no direction; it is a reflection of feeling and meaning based on the client's explicit message. In other words, a Level 3 response reflects both the feeling and the situation. In this response, "You feel discouraged" is the reflection of the feeling, and "because of not getting along" is the reflection of the situation.

Counselor at Level 4: You feel discouraged because you can't seem to reach your father. You want him to let up on you.

Level 4 has understanding and some direction. A Level 4 response identifies not only the client's feelings but also the client's deficit that is implied. In a Level 4 response, the client's deficit is personalized, meaning the client owns or accepts responsibility for the deficit, as in "You can't reach" in this response.

Counselor at Level 5: You feel discouraged because you can't seem to reach your father. You want him to let up on you. One step could be to express your feelings about this to your father.

A Level 5 response contains all of a Level 4 response plus at least one action step the person can take to master the deficit and attain the goal. In this example, the action step is "One step could be to express your feelings about this to your father."

Nonverbal Means of Conveying Empathy

In addition to the use of selected verbal messages, empathy is conveyed by attentive nonverbal behaviors such as direct eye contact, a forward-leaning body position, facing the client (Haase & Tepper, 1972), and an open-arm position (Smith-Hanen, 1977). These nonverbal behaviors are particularly useful when they match (or pace) the client's nonverbal behavior. Pacing means simply moving as the client moves or matching the client's nonverbal behavior without mimicking the client or doing it so deliberately that the client becomes aware of it. For example, when the counselor's and client's body postures are similar, the client is likely to perceive the counselor as more empathic (Maurer & Tindall, 1983).

■

LEARNING ACTIVITIES #3: EMPATHY

Activity One: Empathy Discrimination Exercise

Using the description of Carkhuff and Pierce's (1975) Discrimination Inventory on page 23, decide whether each of the following counselor responses belongs in:

Level 1—No understanding, no direction. Counselor response is a question, a denial or reassurance, or advice.

Level 2—No understanding, some direction. Counselor response highlights only *content* of client's message; feelings are ignored.

Level 3—Understanding present; direction absent. Counselor responds to both *content* or meaning and *feelings*.

Level 4—Both understanding and direction present. Helper responds to client *feelings* and identifies *deficit*.

Level 5—Understanding, direction, and action present. Counselor response includes all of Level 4 plus one *action* step.

After rating each response, explain your choice. An example is provided at the beginning of the activity. Feedback can be found after the learning activities.

Example

Client: I've become burned out with teaching. I've thought about changing jobs, but you know it's hard to find a good job now.

Counselor response: Teaching is no longer too satisfying to you.
This response is: *Level 2.* Because: *Response is only to the content or the situation of teaching. Client's feelings are ignored.*

Practice Statements

1. *Client:* I've always wanted to be a doctor, but I've been discouraged from this.
   Counselor: Oh, I'm sure this is something you could do if you really wanted to.
   This response is:
   Because:

2. *Client:* I've had such a rough semester. I don't know what I got myself into. I'm not sure where to go from here.
   Counselor: You feel perturbed about the way your semester turned out and confused because of this.
   This response is:
   Because:

3. *Client:* My teacher always picks on me.
   Counselor: Why do you suppose she picks on you?
   This response is:
   Because:

4. *Client:* I'm bored with my job. It's getting to be the same old thing. But what else is there to do?
   Counselor: You feel dissatisfied with your job because of the routine. You can't find anything in it that really turns you on. You want to find some more appealing work. One step is to list the most important needs a job meets for you and to identify how those needs could be met by certain jobs.
   This response is:
   Because:

5. *Client:* I don't understand why this accident happened to me; I've always led a good life; now this.
   Counselor: You feel resentful because you can't explain why this sudden accident happened to you. You want to at least figure out some reason that might make it seem more fair.
   This response is:
   Because:

6. *Client:* My parents are getting a divorce. I wish they wouldn't.
   Counselor: You feel upset because your parents are divorcing.
   This response is:
   Because:

7. *Client:* It just seems like each year goes by without our being able to have children.
   Counselor: You feel discouraged because you can't seem to get pregnant. You want to have a child very much.
   This response is:
   Because:

8. *Client:* I'm caught in the middle. I'm not able to move into public housing unless my husband leaves for good. But I'd also want my husband to continue to come and live with me at least some of the time.
   Counselor: Moving into public housing might prevent you and your husband from living together.
   This response is:
   Because:

(continued)

9. *Client:* It's been hard for me to adjust since I've retired. The days seem so empty.
Counselor: You feel useless because of all the time on your hands now. You can't find a way to fill up your days. You want to find some meaningful things to do. One step is to think of some ways you can continue using your work interests even though you are no longer employed.
This response is:
Because:

□ GENUINENESS

Genuineness means being oneself without being phony or playing a role. Although most counselors are trained to be "professionals," a counselor can convey genuineness by being human and by collaborating with the client. Genuineness contributes to an effective therapeutic relationship by reducing the emotional distance between the counselor and client and by helping the client to identify with the counselor, to perceive the counselor as another person similar to oneself. Genuineness has at least five components, summarized in Table 2-2: supporting nonverbal behaviors, role behavior, congruence, spontaneity, and openness (see also Egan, 1990).

Supporting Nonverbal Behaviors

Genuineness is communicated by the therapist's use of appropriate, or supporting, nonverbal behaviors. Nonverbal behaviors that convey genuineness include eye contact, smiling, and leaning toward the client while sitting (Seay & Altekruse, 1979). These two nonverbal behaviors, however, should be used discreetly and gracefully. For example, direct yet intermittent eye contact is perceived as more indicative of genuineness than is persistent gazing, which clients may interpret as staring. Similarly, continual smiling or leaning forward may be viewed as phony and artificial rather than genuine and sincere. As we mentioned during our discussion of empathy, when establishing rapport, the counselor should display nonverbal behaviors that parallel or match those of the client.

Role Behavior

Counselors who do not overemphasize their role, authority, or status are likely to be perceived as more genuine by clients. Too much emphasis on one's role and position can create excessive and unnecessary emotional distance in the relationship. Clients can feel intimidated or even resentful.

The genuine counselor also is someone who is comfortable with himself or herself and with a variety of persons and situations and does not need to "put on" new or different roles to feel or behave comfortably and effectively. As Egan (1990, p. 69) observes, genuine counselors "do not take refuge in the role of counselor. Relating deeply to others and helping are part of their lifestyle, not roles they put on or take off at will."*

Congruence

Congruence means simply that the counselor's words, actions, and feelings match — they are consistent. For example, when a therapist becomes uncomfortable because of a client's constant verbal assault, she acknowledges this feeling of discomfort, at least to herself, and does not try to cover up or feign comfort when it does not exist. Counselors who are not aware of their feelings or of discrepancies between their feelings, words, and actions may send mixed, or incongruent, messages to clients — for example, saying "Sure, go ahead and tell me how you feel about me" while fidgeting or tapping feet or fingers. Such messages are likely to be very confusing and even irritating to clients.

Spontaneity

Spontaneity is the capacity to express oneself naturally without contrived or artificial behaviors. Spontaneity also means being tactful without deliberating about everything you say or do. Spontaneity, however, does not mean that counselors need to verbalize every passing thought or feeling to clients, particularly negative feelings. Rogers (1957) suggests that counselors express negative feelings to clients only if the feelings are constant and persistent or if they interfere with the counselor's ability to convey empathy and positive regard.

---

* This and all other quotations from this source are from *The Skilled Helper* by G. Egan (4th ed.). Copyright © 1990 by Brooks/Cole. Reprinted by permission.

FEEDBACK #3: EMPATHY

Activity One

Counselor response 1 is at Level 1—no understanding and no direction. The response is a denial of client's concern and a form of advice.

Counselor response 2 is at Level 3—understanding is present; direction is absent. Responds to client's feelings (you feel perturbed) and to content or situation (about the semester).

Counselor response 3 is at Level 1—no understanding, no direction. Response is a question and ignores both the content and feelings of client's message.

Counselor response 4 is at Level 5—understanding, direction, and action are all present. Response tunes in to client's feelings, identifies client's deficit, and identifies one action step (to list the important needs a job meets).

Counselor response 5 is at Level 4—understanding and direction. Both client's feelings (you feel resentful) and client's deficit (you can't explain why) are included in counselor's response.

Counselor response 6 is at Level 3—understanding is there; no direction. Counselor responds to client's feelings (you feel upset) and to the content or situation (your parents are divorcing).

Counselor response 7 is at Level 4—understanding and direction. Response reflects client's feelings (you feel discouraged) and identifies her deficit (you can't seem to get pregnant).

Counselor response 8 is at Level 2—some direction but no understanding. Response is only to content of client's message; feelings are ignored.

Counselor response 9 is at Level 5—understanding, direction, and action are all there. Response picks up client's feelings and deficit and identifies one possible action step (to think of some ways).

Openness and Self-Disclosure

Part of genuineness involves the ability to be open, to share yourself, to self-disclose. Because self-disclosure is a complex skill and should not be used indiscriminately, we will discuss it in some detail in this section.

Self-disclosure. Self-disclosure may be defined as any information counselors convey about themselves to their clients (Cozby, 1973). Typically, counselors may choose to reveal something about themselves through verbal sharing of such information. Self-disclosure is not confined to verbal behavior, of course. As Egan (1976, p. 55) points out, we always disclose information about ourselves through nonverbal channels and by our actions even when we don't intend to. This section, however, will focus on the purposeful use of verbal disclosure as a way to convey genuineness.

Although all self-disclosures reveal information about oneself, the type of information disclosed may vary. As shown in Figure 2-1, the content of a self-disclosure can be categorized as demographic or personal (Simonson, 1976) and as positive or negative (Hoffman-Graff, 1977).

In demographic disclosures, the counselor talks about nonintimate events. In personal disclosures, or self-involving statements (McCarthy & Betz, 1978), the counselor reveals more private, personal events and also refers directly to a feeling or feelings that the counselor believes will parallel the client's implicit feeling (McCarthy, 1982). Examples of demographic self-disclosure would be "I had some discouraging times during my schoolwork also" or "At first I had thought I didn't want children; then I changed my mind, so we had them." A personal self-disclosure could mean saying something like "Well, I don't always feel loving toward my children. There are times when I feel pretty angry with them and just want some peace and quiet" or "I think it's pretty natural to have very warm feelings for your close friends. There are times when I've been a little scared of my deep feelings for my friends, too."

In addition, a counselor's self-disclosure may be positive or negative. Positive self-disclosure re-

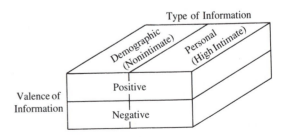

Figure 2-1. *Possible content of self-disclosive information*

veals personal strengths, successful experiences, and experiences similar to the client's. Negative self-disclosure provides information about personal limitations, unsuccessful or inappropriate behaviors and situations, and experiences dissimilar to the client's. Some examples of positive self-disclosure are—

"I'm pretty honest with other people. If I have something to say, I usually try to tell them in a tactful way."

"Sticking with my wife for 20 years has been a great experience. Sure, we've had our ups and downs, but overall we've had a really good relationship, and the stability makes me feel super."

"I also had troubles in college, so I can relate to what you're experiencing now. I did a lot of partying, but in the long run I did settle down and finally made decent grades."

Examples of negative self-disclosure are—

"I, too, have a really hard time making decisions on my own without the advice of others to depend on."

"I, too, am divorced. My marriage was very rocky and just didn't work out."

There are several purposes for using self-disclosure with a client. Counselor self-disclosure may generate an open and facilitative counseling atmosphere. In some instances, a disclosive counselor may be perceived as more sensitive and warm than a nondisclosive counselor (Nilsson, Strassberg, & Bannon, 1979). Counselor disclosure can reduce the role distance between a counselor and client (Egan, 1990). Counselor self-disclosure can also be used to increase the disclosure level of clients (Nilsson et al., 1979), to bring about changes in clients' perceptions of their behavior (Hoffman-Graff, 1977), and to increase client expression of feelings (McCarthy, 1982). Counselor self-disclosure may also help clients develop new perspectives needed for goal setting and action (Egan, 1990).

Ground rules.   There are several ground rules that may help a counselor decide what, when, and how much to disclose. As Nilsson et al. (1979, p. 399) observe, "The issue is far more complex than whether a counselor should or should not disclose. . . . Content, timing, and client expectation, are critical mediating variables determining the influence of counselor disclosure." One ground rule relates to the "breadth," the cumulative amount of information disclosed (Cozby, 1973, p. 75). Most of the evidence indicates that a moderate amount of disclosure has more positive effects than a high or low level (Banikiotes, Kubinski, & Pursell, 1981). Some self-disclosure may indicate a desire for a close relationship and may increase the client's estimate of the helper's trustworthiness (Levin & Gergen, 1969). Counselors who disclose very little could add to the role distance between themselves and their clients. At the other extreme, too much disclosure may be counterproductive. The counselor who discloses too much may be perceived as lacking in discretion, being untrustworthy (Levin & Gergen), seeming self-preoccupied (Cozby), or needing assistance. A real danger in overdisclosing is the risk of being perceived as needing therapy as much as the client. This could undermine the client's confidence in the counselor's ability to be helpful.

Another ground rule concerns the duration of self-disclosure—the amount of time used to give information about yourself. Extended periods of counselor disclosure will consume time that could be spent in client disclosure. As one person reveals more, the other person will necessarily reveal less (Levin & Gergen, 1969). From this perspective, some conciseness in the length of self-disclosive statements seems warranted. Another consideration in duration of self-disclosure involves the capacity of the client to utilize and benefit from the information shared. As Egan (1990, p. 223) observes, counselors should avoid self-disclosing to the point of adding a burden to an already overwhelmed client.

A third ground rule to consider in using self-disclosure concerns the depth, or intimacy, of the information revealed (Cozby, 1973, p. 75). You should try to make your statements similar in content and mood to the client's messages. Ivey and Gluckstern (1976, p. 86) refer to this similarity as "parallelism," meaning that the counselor's self-disclosure is closely linked to the client's statements. For example:

Client: I just feel so down on myself. My husband is so critical of me, and often I think he's right. I really can't do much of anything well.

Counselor (parallel): There have been times when I've also felt down on myself, so I can sense how discouraged you are. Sometimes, too, criticism from a male has made me feel even worse, although I'm learning how to value myself regardless of critical comments from my husband or a male friend.

Counselor (nonparallel): I've felt bummed out, too. Sometimes the day just doesn't go well.

A counselor can alter the depth of a self-disclosure by adapting the content of the information revealed. For instance, if a client discloses about a nonintimate event, a demographic counselor disclosure may be more appropriate than a personal disclosure. Or if the client is discussing a negative experience, a negative counselor disclosure will be more similar than a positive disclosure. In fact, a positive counselor disclosure following client expression of negative feelings (or vice versa) can inhibit, rather than expand, the client's communication. Imagine how insensitive it would sound if a counselor said "I'm very happy today. Of course, I consider myself to be a very optimistic person" after a client had just revealed feelings of sadness or depression. Generally, the counselor can achieve the desired impact of self-disclosure as long as the depth or content of the information is not grossly discrepant from the client's messages and behavior.

The depth, or degree of intimacy, of your self-disclosure is also affected by the timing of the interaction. Demographic (nonintimate) disclosure may be very useful in initial phases because it informs the client that disclosure is part of the treatment process. Starting off with nonintimate disclosure is less threatening, and the client is not surprised later on by more intimate disclosures. Personal, or high-intimate, self-disclosures are more effective than demographic, or low-intimate, self-disclosures in eliciting client affect and in increasing client self-references and "present-tense talk" (McCarthy, 1982; McCarthy & Betz, 1978). Additionally, "high self-disclosure is 'additive' because it identifies previously unstated client feelings, thus adding to an understanding of the client's concern" (McCarthy, 1982, p. 130). Thus, personal, or highly intimate, disclosures may be more useful in subsequent sessions, after disclosure has already been made a part of the treatment contract in less threatening form.

In using self-disclosure, a counselor should be very aware of the effects it produces in the interview. There is always a danger of accelerating self-disclosure to the point where the counselor and client spend time swapping stories about themselves or playing "I've got one to top that." This effect does not reflect the intended purposes of self-disclosure.

In addition to being cognizant of the actual effects of self-disclosure, counselors should be aware of their motivation for using the response in the first place. Self-disclosure is appropriate only when you can explain how it may benefit the client. Counselors who are unaware of their own biases and vulnerabilities may self-disclose because they identify too much with a client or a topic area. Other helpers may self-disclose simply to reduce their anxiety level in the interview. As with all other counselor behavior, self-disclosure should be structured to meet the client's needs.

LEARNING ACTIVITIES #4: SELF-DISCLOSURE

I. Respond to the following three client situations with a self-disclosing response. Make sure you reveal something about yourself. It might help you to start your statements with "I." Also try to make your statements similar in content and depth to the client messages and situations. An example is given first, and feedback is provided on page 30.

Example

The client is having a hard time stating specific reasons for seeking counseling. Your self-disclosing statement: "I'm reluctant at times to share something that is personal about myself with someone I don't know; I know it takes time to get started."

Now use your self-disclosure responses:
1. The client is feeling like a failure because "nothing seems to be going well."
Your self-disclosure:
2. The client is hinting that he or she has some concerns about sexual performance but does not seem to know how to introduce this concern in the session.
Your self-disclosure:

(continued)

3. The client has started to become aware of feelings of anger for the first time and is questioning whether such feelings are legitimate or whether something is wrong with him or her.
Your self-disclosure:

II. In a conversation with a friend or in a group, use the skill of self-disclosure. You may wish to use the questions below as "starters." Consider the criteria listed in the feedback to assess your use of this response.

Preference Survey

1. What things or activities do you enjoy doing most?
2. What things or activities do you dislike?
3. What things or activities do you try to avoid?
4. When you're feeling down in the dumps, what do you do to get out of it?
5. What things or people do you think about most?
6. What things or people do you avoid thinking about?

☐ POSITIVE REGARD

Positive regard, also called "respect," means the ability to prize or value the client as a person with worth and dignity (Rogers, 1957). Communication of positive regard has a number of important functions in establishing an effective therapeutic relationship, including the communication of willingness to work with the client, interest in the client as a person, and acceptance of the client. Raush and Bordin (1957) and Egan (1990) have identified four components of positive regard: having a sense of commitment to the client, making an effort to understand the client, suspending critical judgment, and expressing a reasonable amount of warmth (see also Table 2-2).

Commitment

Commitment means you are willing to work with the client and interested in doing so. It is translated into such actions as being on time for appointments, reserving time for the client's exclusive use, ensuring privacy during sessions, maintaining confidentiality, and applying skills to help the client. Lack of time and lack of concern are two major barriers to communicating a sense of commitment.

Understanding

Clients will feel respected to the degree that they *feel* the counselor is trying to understand them and to treat their problems with concern. Counselors can demonstrate their efforts to understand by being empathic, by asking questions designed to elicit information important to the client, and by indicating with comments or actions their interest in understanding the client (Raush & Bordin,

1957, p. 352). Counselors also convey understanding with the use of specific listening responses such as paraphrasing and reflecting client messages (see also Chapter 5).

Nonjudgmental Attitude

A nonjudgmental attitude is the counselor's capacity to suspend judgment of the client's actions or motives and to avoid condemning or condoning the client's thoughts, feelings, or actions. It may also be described as the counselor's acceptance of the client without conditions or reservations, although it does not mean that the counselor supports or agrees with all the client says or does. A counselor conveys a nonjudgmental attitude by warmly accepting the client's expressions and experiences without expressing disapproval or criticism. For example, suppose a client states "I can't help cheating on my wife. I love her, but I've got this need to be with other women." The counselor who responds with regard and respect might say something like "You feel pulled between your feelings for your wife and your need for other women." This response neither condones nor criticizes the client's feelings and behaviors. In contrast, a counselor who states "What a mess! You got married because you love your wife. Now you're fooling around with other women" conveys criticism and lack of respect for the client as a unique human being. The experience of having positive regard for clients can also be identified by the presence of certain (covert) thoughts and feelings such as "I feel good when I'm with this person" or "I don't feel bothered or uncomfortable with what this person is telling me."

A question that counselors frequently face is how they can overcome personal and cultural biases to deal effectively with an individual who is

FEEDBACK #4: SELF-DISCLOSURE

I. Here are some possible examples of counselor self-disclosure for these three client situations. See whether your responses are *similar;* your statements will probably reflect more of your own feelings and experiences. Are your statements fairly concise? Are they similar to the client messages in content and intensity?

1. "I, too, have felt down and out about myself at times."
   or
   "I can remember, especially when I was younger, feeling very depressed if things didn't turn out the way I wanted."
2. "For myself, I have sometimes questioned the adequacy of my sexual performance."
   or
   "I find it hard sometimes to start talking about really personal topics like sex."
3. "I can remember when I used to feel pretty afraid of admitting I felt angry. I always used to control it by telling myself I really wasn't angry."
   or
   "I know of times when some of my thoughts or feelings have seemed hard for me to accept."

II. Self-Disclosure Assessment

1. What was the amount of your self-disclosure in relation to the amount of the other person's — low, medium, or high?
2. What was the *total* amount of time you spent in self-disclosure?
3. Were your self-disclosure statements similar in content and depth to those expressed by the other person?
4. Did your self-disclosure detract from or overwhelm the other person?

---

perceived as unlikable, worthless, or offensive by society at large—for example, a convicted rapist or a child abuser. George and Cristiani (1981) observe that the answer to this question lies partly in the fact that the nature of the relationship is a helping one. Counselors can create an atmosphere in which the client feels safe and behaves nondefensively and may be more responsive to the counselor than to people with whom he or she interacts in the course of ordinary life. In other words, the helping relationship can be the impetus for such clients "to move beyond behaviors, defenses, and facades that others (would) find offensive" (George & Cristiani, 1981, p. 152).

Warmth

According to Goldstein (1986), without the expression of warmth, particular strategies and helping interventions may be "technically correct but therapeutically impotent" (p. 43). Warmth reduces the impersonal nature or sterility of a given intervention or treatment procedure. In addition, warmth begets warmth. As Truax and Carkhuff (1967) observe, most clients respond to warmth with warmth. In interactions with hostile or reluctant clients, warmth and caring can disarm and diminish the intensity of the clients' angry feelings.

Nonverbal cues of warmth. A primary way in which warmth is communicated is with supporting nonverbal behaviors such as voice tone, eye contact, facial animation and expressions, gestures, and touch. Johnson (1986) describes some nonverbal cues that express warmth or coldness (see Table 2-3). Remember that these behaviors may be interpreted as warm or cold by clients from Western cultures. Clients from other cultures may perceive these nonverbal aspects of warmth and cold differently. Even clients from Western cul-

TABLE 2-3. Nonverbal cues of warmth and coldness

Nonverbal cue	Warmth	Coldness
Tone of voice	Soft, soothing	Callous, reserved, hard
Facial expression	Smiling, interested	Poker-faced, frowning, disinterested
Posture	Relaxed, leaning toward the other person	Tense, leaning away from the other person
Eye contact	Looking directly into the other person's eyes	Avoiding eye contact
Touching	Touching the other softly and discreetly	Avoiding all touch
Gestures	Open, welcoming	Closed, as if guarding oneself
Physical proximity	Close	Distant

From *Reaching Out: Interpersonal Effectiveness and Self-Actualization* (3rd ed.), by D. W. Johnson. Copyright © 1986 by Prentice-Hall. Reprinted by permission.

tures may vary in the amount of warmth they need or can handle.

An important aspect of the nonverbal dimension of warmth is touch (see also Chapter 4). In times of emotional stress, many clients welcome a well-intentioned touch. The difficulty with touch is that it may have a different meaning to the client than the meaning you intended to convey. In deciding whether to use touch, it is important to consider the level of trust between you and the client, whether or not the *client* may perceive the touch as sexual, and the client's past history associated with touch (occasionally a client will associate touch with punishment and will say "I can't stand to be touched"). To help you assess the probable impact of touch on the client, Gazda et al. (1984, p. 111) recommend asking yourself the following questions:

1. How does the other person perceive this? Is it seen as genuine or as a superficial technique?
2. Is the other person uncomfortable? (If the other person draws back from being touched, adjust your behavior accordingly.)
3. Am I interested in the person or in touching the person? Whom is it for — me, the other person, or to impress those who observe?

Verbal responses associated with warmth and immediacy. Warmth can also be expressed to clients through selected verbal responses. One way to express warmth is to use enhancing statements (Ivey, Ivey, & Simek-Downing, 1987) that portray some positive aspect or attribute about the client, such as "It's great to see how well you're handling this situation," "You're really expressing yourself well," or "You've done a super job on this action plan." Enhancing statements offer positive reinforcement to clients and must be sincere, deserved, and accurate in order to be effective.

Another verbal response used to express warmth is immediacy. Immediacy is a characteristic of a counselor verbal response describing something *as it occurs* within a session. Immediacy involves self-disclosure but is limited to self-disclosure of *current* feelings or what is occurring at the present time in the relationship or the session. When persons avoid being immediate with each other over the course of a developing relationship, distance sets in and coldness can quickly evaporate any warmth formerly established. Egan (1990, p. 227) describes the potential impact on a relationship when immediacy is absent:

People often fail to be immediate with one another in their interactions. For instance, a husband feels slighted by something his wife says. He says nothing and "swallows" his feelings. But he becomes a little bit distant from her the next couple of days, a bit more quiet. She notices this, wonders what is happening, but says nothing. Soon little things in their relationship that would ordinarily be ignored become irritating. Things become more and more tense, but still they do not engage in direct, mutual talk about what is happening. The whole thing ends as a game of "uproar" (see Berne, 1964) — that is, a huge argument over something quite small. Once they've vented their emotions, they feel both relieved because they've dealt with their emotions and guilty because they've done so in a somewhat childish way.

In using immediacy in counseling, the therapist reflects on a current aspect of (1) some thought, feeling, or behavior of the *counselor,* (2) some thought, feeling, or behavior of the *client,* or (3) some aspect of the *relationship.* Here are some examples of these three categories of immediacy.

1. *Counselor immediacy:* The counselor reveals his or her own thoughts or feelings in the counseling process as they occur "in the moment."
"I'm glad to see you today."
"I'm sorry, I am having difficulty focusing. Let's go over that again."
2. *Client immediacy:* The counselor provides feedback to the client about some client behavior or feeling as it occurs in the interview.
"You're fidgeting and seem uncomfortable here right now."
"You're really smiling now — you must be very pleased about it."
3. *Relationship immediacy:* The counselor reveals feelings or thoughts about how he or she experiences the relationship.
"I'm glad that you're able to share that with me."
"It makes me feel good that we're getting somewhere today."

Relationship immediacy may include references to specific "here and now" transactions or to the overall pattern or development of the relationship (Egan, 1990). For example, "I'm aware that right now as I'm talking again, you are looking away and tapping your feet and fingers. I'm wondering if you're feeling impatient with me or if I'm talking too much" (specific transaction). Consider another example in which immediacy is used to focus on the development and pattern of the relationship: "This session feels so good to me. I remember when we first started a few months ago and it seemed we were both being very careful and having trouble expressing what was on our minds. Today, I'm aware we're not measuring our words so carefully. It feels like there's more comfort between us."

Immediacy is not an end in and of itself but, rather, a means of helping the counselor and client work together better. If allowed to become a goal in and of itself, it can be distracting rather than helpful (Egan, 1990). Examples of instances in which immediacy might be useful include the following:

1. Hesitancy or "carefulness" in speech or behavior ("Mary, I'm aware that you [or I] seem to be choosing words very carefully right now—as if you [or I] might say something wrong").
2. Hostility, anger, resentment, irritation ("Joe, I'm feeling pretty irritated now because you're indicating you want me to keep this time slot open for you but you may not be able to make it next week. Since this has happened the last two weeks, I'm concerned about what might be happening in our relationship").
3. Attraction ("At first it seemed great that we liked each other so much. Now I'm wondering if we're so comfortable that we may be holding back a little and not sharing what's really on our minds").
4. Feeling of being "stuck"—lack of focus or direction ("Right now I feel like our session is sort of a broken record. We're just like a needle tracking in the same groove without really making any music or going anywhere").
5. Tension ("I'm aware there's some discomfort and tension we're both feeling now—about who we are as people and where this is going and what's going to happen").

Immediacy can also be used to deal with the issues of transference and countertransference described earlier in this chapter.

Immediacy has three purposes. One purpose is to bring out in the open something that you feel about yourself, the client, or the relationship that has not been expressed directly. Generally, it is assumed that covert, or unexpressed, feelings about the relationship may inhibit effective communication or may prevent further development of the relationship unless the counselor recognizes and responds to these feelings. This may be especially important for negative feelings. As Eisenberg and Delaney (1977) note, "when stress occurs in the relationship between the client and counselor, it is generally more adaptive to deal openly with the stress than to avoid dealing with it" (p. 203). In this way, immediacy may reduce the distance that overshadows the relationship because of unacknowledged underlying issues.

A second purpose of immediacy is to generate discussion or to provide feedback about some aspects of the relationship or the interactions as they occur. This feedback may include verbal sharing of the counselor's feelings or of something the counselor sees going on in the interactive process. Immediacy is not used to describe every passing counselor feeling or observation to the client. But when something happens in the counseling process that influences the client's feelings toward counseling, then dealing openly with this issue has high priority. Usually it is up to the counselor to initiate discussion of unresolved feelings or issues (Eisenberg & Delaney, 1977, p. 202). Immediacy can be a way to begin such discussion and, if used properly, can strengthen the counselor/client relationship and help the counselor and client work together more effectively.

Finally, immediacy is useful to facilitate client self-exploration and to maintain the focus of the interaction on the client or the relationship rather than on the counselor (McCarthy, 1982; McCarthy & Betz, 1978).

Steps in immediacy. Immediacy is a complex set of skills. The first part of immediacy—and an important prerequisite of the actual verbal response—is awareness, or the ability to sense what is happening in the interaction (Egan, 1990; Turock, 1980). To do this, it is important to monitor the flow of the interaction in order to process what is happening to you, to the client, and to your developing relationship. Awareness also implies that you can read the clues without a great deal of decoding errors and without projecting your own biases and "blind spots" into the interaction. After awareness, the next step is to formulate a verbal response that somehow shares your sense or picture of the process with the client. The actual form of the response may vary and can include some of the listening or action responses we describe in Chapters 5 and 6. Regardless of the form, the critical feature of immediacy is its emphasis on the "here and now"—the present.

Turock (1980, p. 170) suggests some useful sentence stems for immediacy:

1. "Right now I'm feeling _____" (counselor immediacy).
2. "Even right now you're feeling _____ (feelings toward counselor) because _____" (client immediacy).
3. "When I see (hear, grasp) you _____ (client's behavior or feelings), I _____" (counselor's behavior or feelings).

Ground rules. There are several rules to consider in using immediacy effectively. First, the counselor should describe what she or he sees *as it happens.* If the counselor waits until later in the session or until the next interview to describe a feeling or experience, the impact is lost. In addition, feelings about the relationship that are discounted or ignored may build up and eventually be expressed in more intense or distorted ways. The counselor who puts off using immediacy to initiate a needed discussion runs the risk of having unresolved feelings or issues damage the relationship.

Second, to reflect the "here-and-nowness" of the experience, any immediacy statement should be in the present tense—"I'm feeling uncomfortable now," rather than "I just felt uncomfortable." This models expression of current rather than past feelings for the client.

Further, when referring to your feelings and perceptions, own them—take responsibility for them—by using the personal pronoun *I, me,* or *mine,* as in "I'm feeling concerned about you now" instead of "You're making me feel concerned." Expressing your current feelings with "I" language communicates that you are responsible for your feelings and observations, and this may increase the client's receptivity to your immediacy expressions.

Finally, as in using all other responses, the counselor should consider timing. Using a lot of immediacy in an early session may be overwhelming for some clients and can elicit anxiety in either counselor or client. As Gazda et al. (1984, p. 191) observe, "High level communication of immediacy of relationship involves talking about persons who are present and feelings that exist at that particular moment. Thus . . . it is desirable that a strong base relationship exist before using the dimension of immediacy." If a counselor uses immediacy and senses that this has threatened or scared the client, then the counselor should decide that the client is not yet ready to handle these feelings or issues. And not every feeling or observation a counselor has needs to be verbalized to a client. The session does not need to turn into a "heavy" discussion, nor should it resemble a confessional. Generally, immediacy is reserved for initiating exploration of the most significant or most influential feelings or issues. Of course, a counselor who never expresses immediacy may be avoiding issues that have a significant effect on the relationship.

There is some evidence that counselors tend to avoid immediacy issues even when raised directly by clients (Turock, 1980). Counselors who are not comfortable with their own self-image or who are struggling with intimacy issues in their own life (see "Characteristics of Effective Helpers," earlier in this chapter) are likely to have trouble with this skill or to try to avoid the use of it altogether. Unfortunately, this may result in the continuation of an unhealthy or somewhat stagnant therapeutic relationship (Turock, 1980).

LEARNING ACTIVITIES #5: IMMEDIACY

I. For each of the following client stimuli, write an example of a counselor immediacy response. An example has been completed below, and feedback can be found on p. 39.

Example

The client has come in late for the third time, and you have some concern about this.

Immediacy response: "I'm aware that you're having difficulty getting here on time, and I'm feeling uncomfortable about this."

Now use immediacy in the following five situations:

1. Tears begin to well up in the client's eyes as he or she describes the loss of a close friend.
   Your immediacy response:
2. The client stops talking whenever you bring up the subject of his or her academic performance.
   Your immediacy response:
3. The client has asked you several questions about your competence and qualifications.
   Your immediacy response:

(continued)

LEARNING ACTIVITIES #5: IMMEDIACY (continued)

4. You experience a great deal of tension and caution between yourself and the client; the two of you seem to be treating each other with "kid gloves." You notice physical sensations of tension in your body, and signs of tension are also apparent in looking at the client.
Your immediacy response:

5. You and the client like each other a great deal and have a lot in common; lately you've been spending more time swapping life stories than focusing on or dealing with the client's presented concern of career indecision and dissatisfaction.
Your immediacy response:

II. In a conversation with a close friend or in a group, use the sharing skill of immediacy. If possible, tape the conversation for feedback—or ask for feedback from the friend or the group. You should consider the criteria listed in the feedback in assessing your use of immediacy. You may wish to use the topics listed in the following Relationship Assessment Inventory as topics for discussion using immediacy.

Relationship Assessment Inventory
1. To what extent do we really know each other?

2. How do I feel in your presence?
3. How do you feel in my presence?
4. What areas do I have trouble sharing with you?
5. What is it about our relationship that makes it hard to share some things?
6. Do we both have a fairly equal role in maintaining our relationship, or is one of us dominant and the other passive?
7. How do we handle power and conflict in the relationship? Is one of us consistently "top dog" or "underdog"?
8. Do we express or avoid feelings of warmth and affection for each other?
9. How do our concepts of our sex roles affect the way we relate to each other?
10. How often do we give feedback to each other—and in what manner is it given?
11. How do we hurt each other?
12. How do we help each other?
13. Where do we want our relationship to go from here?

☐ SUMMARY

It is important to remember that the three core or facilitative conditions described in this chapter—empathy, genuineness, and positive regard—are mutually reinforcing and, in practice, work "hand in hand." The three core conditions are synergistic—the overall effect of all three is greater than the effect of any one alone.

The ability to communicate the core conditions to clients is a function not only of learned skills but also of your own biases and unresolved issues which could prevent you from adopting the client's frame of reference, could make you rely excessively on artificial or mechanistic roles and could interfere with your capacity to convey respect and warmth for your clients. Being in a relationship, thus, requires an awareness, scrutiny, and resolution of your own needs and behaviors before you can effectively relate to clients.

POSTEVALUATION

I. According to Chapter Objective One, you will be able to identify attitudes and behaviors about yourself that could facilitate or interfere with establishing a positive helping relationship. In this activity, we present a Checklist for Effective Helpers. This checklist refers to characteristics of effective helpers. Your task is to use the checklist to assess yourself *now* with respect to these attitudes and behaviors. If you haven't yet had any or much contact with actual clients, try to use this checklist to assess how you believe you would be in actual interactions. Identify any issues or areas you may need to work on in your development as a counselor. Discuss your assessment in small groups or with an instructor, colleague, or supervisor. There is no written feedback for this part of the postevaluation. (continued)

CHECKLIST FOR EFFECTIVE HELPERS

Instructions: Rate yourself on each item by circling the number and word that best describe you *now*. If an item represents a behavior or situation you have not yet encountered, rate yourself the way you *think* you would be or would handle the situation.

Intellectual Competence

1. I feel knowledgeable about counseling/psychotherapy theories and techniques and other counseling-related issues.

1	2	3	4	5
Not at all	A little	Somewhat	Quite a bit	Almost always

2. I feel curious about areas of knowledge related to counseling and try to seek information about areas in which I am uninformed.

1	2	3	4	5
Not at all	A little	Somewhat	Quite a bit	Almost always

3. It is important to me to monitor progress of clients throughout therapy in order to keep track of process and outcomes.

1	2	3	4	5
Not at all	A little	Somewhat	Quite a bit	Almost always

Energy

4. I have enough physical stamina to see several clients daily.

1	2	3	4	5
Not at all	A little	Somewhat	Quite a bit	Almost always

5. Even after seeing several clients in a row, I don't feel emotionally depleted.

1	2	3	4	5
Not at all	A little	Somewhat	Quite a bit	Almost always

6. I convey intensity and dynamism to my clients.

1	2	3	4	5
Not at all	A little	Somewhat	Quite a bit	Almost always

Flexibility

7. I adapt my counseling and therapy techniques to each client rather than having the client fit the technique or therapy.

1	2	3	4	5
Not at all	A little	Somewhat	Quite a bit	Almost always

8. I do not use a single methodology or theoretical orientation with all clients.

1	2	3	4	5
Not at all	A little	Somewhat	Quite a bit	Almost always

Support

9. I am supporting of a client's efforts to engage in self-directed choices and behaviors.

1	2	3	4	5
Not at all	A little	Somewhat	Quite a bit	Almost always

(continued)

POSTEVALUATION (continued)

10. I provide support to clients without rescuing them or taking more than my share of responsibility for therapy process and outcomes.

1	2	3	4	5
Not at all	A little	Somewhat	Quite a bit	Almost always

Good Will

11. I have other people and activities (outside my counseling relationship) where I get many of my own needs met.

1	2	3	4	5
Not at all	A little	Somewhat	Quite a bit	Almost always

12. I am clear about my motives for wanting to be a counselor.

1	2	3	4	5
Not at all	A little	Somewhat	Quite a bit	Almost always

13. I try to behave in ethical ways which meet the client's needs and which protect the client's welfare.

1	2	3	4	5
Not at all	A little	Somewhat	Quite a bit	Almost always

Self-Awareness

14. I am aware of my own unique strengths that I have to offer to clients.

1	2	3	4	5
Not at all	A little	Somewhat	Quite a bit	Almost always

15. I am aware of my limitations or self-defeating behaviors that may interfere with effective therapy.

1	2	3	4	5
Not at all	A little	Somewhat	Quite a bit	Almost always

16. I am aware of any unfinished or unresolved issues in my life right now.

1	2	3	4	5
Not at all	A little	Somewhat	Quite a bit	Almost always

II. According to Chapter Objective Two, you will be able to identify issues related to values, ethics, and emotional objectivity that could affect the development of a therapeutic relationship, given six written case descriptions. In this activity, read each case description carefully; then identify in writing the major kind of issue reflected in the case by matching the type of issue with the case descriptions listed below. Feedback follows the postevaluation (p. 42).

Type of Issue
A. Values conflict
B. Values stereotyping
C. Ethics—breach of confidentiality
D. Ethics—client welfare and rights
E. Ethics—referral
F. Transference
G. Countertransference

Case Description
____1. You are counseling a client who is almost flunking out of high school. The client states that he feels like a failure because all the other students are so smart. In an effort to make him feel better, you tell him about one of your former clients who also almost flunked out.

____2. A 58-year-old man who is having difficulty getting it together since his wife died comes to you for counseling. He has difficulty in discussing his concern or problem with you, and he is not clear about your role as a counselor and what counseling might do for him. He seems to feel that you can give him a tranquilizer. You tell him that you are not able to prescribe medication, and you suggest that he seek the services of a physician.

(continued)

_____3. You are leading a problem-solving group in a high school. The members are spending a lot of time talking about the flak they get from their parents. After a while, they start to "get the leader" and complain about all the flak they get from you.

_____4. A fourth-grade girl is referred to you by her teacher. The teacher states that the girl is doing poorly in class yet seems motivated to learn. After working with the girl for several weeks, including giving a battery of tests, you conclude that she has a severe learning disability. After obtaining her permission to talk to her teacher, you inform her teacher of this and state that the teacher might as well not spend too much more time working on what you believe is a "useless case."

_____5. You are counseling a person of the other sex who is the same age as yourself. After several weeks of seeing the client, you feel extremely disappointed and let down when the client postpones the next session.

_____6. You are counseling a couple who are considering a trial separation because of constant marital problems. You tell them you don't believe separation or divorce is the answer to their problems.

III. According to the third objective of this chapter, you will be able to communicate the three facilitative conditions to a client, given a role-play situation. Complete this activity in triads, one person assuming the role of the counselor, another the role of client, and the third acting as the observer. The counselor's task is to communicate the behavioral aspects of empathy, genuineness, and positive regard to the client. The client can share a concern with the counselor. The observer will monitor the interaction, using the accompanying Checklist for Facilitative Conditions as a guide, and provide feedback after completion of the session. Each role play can last about 10–15 minutes. Switch roles so each person has an opportunity to be in each of the three roles. If you do not have access to another person to serve as an observer, find someone with whom you can engage in a role-played helping interaction. Tape-record your interaction and use the accompanying checklist as a guide to reviewing your tape.

CHECKLIST FOR FACILITATIVE CONDITIONS

Counselor _____ Observer _____ Date _____ Instructions: Assess the counselor's communication of the three facilitative conditions by circling the number and word that best represent the counselor's overall behavior during this session.

Empathy

1. Did the counselor use verbal responses indicating a desire to comprehend the client?

1	2	3	4
A little	Somewhat	A great deal	Almost always

2. Did the counselor reflect *implicit,* or hidden, client messages?

1	2	3	4
A little	Somewhat	A great deal	Almost always

3. Did the counselor refer to the client's feelings?

1	2	3	4
A little	Somewhat	A great deal	Almost always

4. Did the counselor discuss what appeared to be important to the client?

1	2	3	4
A little	Somewhat	A great deal	Almost always

5. Did the counselor pace (match) the client's nonverbal behavior?

1	2	3	4
A little	Somewhat	A great deal	Almost always
			(continued)

POSTEVALUATION (continued)

6. Did the counselor match the client's predicates and phrases?

1	2	3	4
A little	Somewhat	A great deal	Almost always

Genuineness

7. Did the counselor avoid overemphasizing her or his role, position, and status?

1	2	3	4
A little	Somewhat	A great deal	Almost always

8. Did the counselor exhibit congruence, or consistency, among feelings, words, nonverbal behavior, and actions?

1	2	3	4
A little	Somewhat	A great deal	Almost always

9. Was the counselor appropriately spontaneous (for example, also tactful)?

1	2	3	4
A little	Somewhat	A great deal	Almost always

10. Did the counselor self-disclose, or share similar feelings and experiences?

1	2	3	4
A little	Somewhat	A great deal	Almost always

11. Did the counselor demonstrate supporting nonverbal behaviors such as eye contact, smiling, and leaning toward the client?

1	2	3	4
A little	Somewhat	A great deal	Almost always

Positive Regard

12. Did the counselor demonstrate behaviors related to commitment and willingness to see the client (for example, starting on time, responding with intensity)?

1	2	3	4
A little	Somewhat	A great deal	Almost always

13. Did the counselor respond verbally and nonverbally to the client without judging or evaluating the client?

1	2	3	4
A little	Somewhat	A great deal	Almost always

14. Did the counselor convey warmth to the client with supporting nonverbal behaviors (soft voice tone, smiling, eye contact, touch) and verbal responses (enhancing statements and/or immediacy)?

1	2	3	4
A little	Somewhat	A great deal	Almost always

Observer comments:_____

_____

_____

_____

FEEDBACK #5: IMMEDIACY

I. Here are some expressions of immediacy. See how these compare with yours.

1. "At this moment you seem to be experiencing this loss very intensely."
or
"I'm sensing now that it is very painful for you to talk about this."
2. "Every time I mention academic performance, like now, you seem to back off from this topic."
or
"I'm aware that, during this session, you stop talking when the topic of your grades comes up."
3. "You seem to be questioning now how qualified I am to help you."
or
"I'm wondering if it's difficult right now for you to trust me."
4. "I'm aware of how physically tight I feel now and how tense you look to me. I'm sensing that we're just not too comfortable with each other yet. We seem to be treating each other in a very fragile and cautious way right now."
5. "I'm aware of how well we get along and, because we have so much in common, how easy it is right now just to share stories and events instead of exploring your career concerns."

Are your immediacy responses in the present tense? Do you "own" your feelings and perceptions by using "I feel" rather than "You're making me feel"?

II. Immediacy Assessment

1. Did you express something personal about your feelings, the other person's feelings, or the relationship?
2. Were your immediacy statements in the present tense?
3. Did you use *I*, *me*, or *mine* when referring to *your* feelings and perceptions?
4. Did you express immediacy as your feelings occurred within the conversation?

FEEDBACK: POSTEVALUATION

1. C: Ethics—breach of confidentiality. The counselor broke the confidence of a former client by revealing his grade difficulties without his consent.
2. E: Ethics—referral. The counselor did not refer in an ethical or responsible way, because of failure to give the client names of at least several physicians

or psychiatrists who might be competent to see the client.
3. F: Transference. The group members seem to be transferring their angry feelings toward their parents onto you.
4. B: Values stereotyping. The counselor is obviously stereotyping all kids with learning disabilities as useless and hopeless (the "label" is also not helpful or in the client's best interest).
5. G: Countertransference. You are having a more than usually intense emotional reaction to this client (disappointment), which suggests that you are developing some affectionate feelings for the client and countertransference is occurring.
6. A: Values conflict. Your values are showing: Although separation and divorce may not be your solution, be careful of persuading clients to pursue your views and answers to issues.

☐ SUGGESTED READINGS

Barrett-Lennard, G. T. (1981). The empathy cycle: Refinement of a nuclear concept. *Journal of Counseling Psychology, 28,* 91–100.

Cavanaugh, M. E. (1982). *The counseling experience.* Pacific Grove, CA: Brooks/Cole. Chapter 4, "The Person of the Counselor"; Chapter 11, "Problems That Counselors Face."

Corey, G., Corey, M., & Callanan, P. (1988). *Issues and ethics in the helping professions* (3rd ed.). Pacific Grove, CA: Brooks/Cole.

D'Augelli, A., D'Augelli, J., & Danish, S. (1981). *Helping others.* Pacific Grove, CA: Brooks/Cole. Chapter 2, "Helpers Are People Too."

Doster, J. A., & Nesbitt, J. G. (1979). Psychotherapy and self-disclosure. In G. J. Chelune (Ed.), *Self-disclosure: Origins, patterns, and implications of openness in interpersonal relationships.* San Francisco: Jossey-Bass.

Egan, G. (1990). *The skilled helper* (4th ed.). Pacific Grove, CA: Brooks/Cole.

Gazda, G. M., Asbury, F. S., Balzer, F. J., Childers, W. C., & Walters, R. P. (1984). *Human relations development: A manual for educators* (3rd ed.). Boston: Allyn & Bacon. Chapter 11, "Perceiving and Responding with Warmth."

Gladstein, G. (1983). Understanding empathy: Integrating counseling, developmental, and social psychology perspectives. *Journal of Counseling Psychology, 30,* 467–482.

Johnson, D. W. (1986). *Reaching out: Interpersonal effectiveness and self-actualization* (3rd ed.). Englewood Cliffs, NJ: Prentice-Hall, Chapter 2, "Self-Disclosure."

Laborde, G. (1984). *Influencing with integrity.* Palo Alto: Science & Behavior Books.

Maurer, R. E., & Tindall, J. H. (1983). Effect of postural congruence on client's perception of counselor empathy. *Journal of Counseling Psychology, 30,* 158–163.

McCarthy, P. (1982). Differential effects of counselor self-referent responses and counselor status. *Journal of Counseling Psychology, 29,* 125–131.

Nilsson, D., Strassberg, D., & Bannon, J. (1979). Perceptions of counselor self-disclosure: An analogue study. *Journal of Counseling Psychology, 26,* 399–404.

Okun, B. F. (1987). *Effective helping* (3rd ed.). Pacific Grove, CA: Brooks/Cole. Chapter 9, "Issues Affecting Helping."

Schutz, B. (1982). *Legal liability in psychotherapy.* San Francisco: Jossey-Bass.

Seay, T. A., & Altekruse, M. K. (1979). Verbal and nonverbal behavior in judgments of facilitative conditions. *Journal of Counseling Psychology, 26,* 108–119.

Turock, A. (1980). Immediacy in counseling: Recognizing clients' unspoken messages. *Personnel and Guidance Journal, 59,* 168–172.

Watkins, C. E., Jr. (1983). Transference phenomena in the counseling situation. *Personnel and Guidance Journal, 62,* 206–210.

RELATIONSHIP ENHANCEMENT VARIABLES AND INTERPERSONAL INFLUENCE

THREE

In all human relationships, persons try to influence one another. The counseling relationship is no exception. The fact that counselors do influence clients is inescapable and, according to Senour (1982, p. 346), the desire to avoid influence is "patently absurd [since] there would be no point to counseling if we had no influence on those with whom we work." Moreover, the influence process that operates in counseling is a two-way street. Clients also seek to influence their counselors. As Dorn (1984b, p. 343) observes, "Although the client has sought counseling because of dissatisfaction with personal circumstances, this same client will attempt to influence the counselor's behavior."

Thus, the influence process in counseling and therapy is interpersonal—that is, between two persons—and reciprocal, or mutual. Some recent research (Heppner & Heesacker, 1982) provided a good illustration of the reciprocal and interpersonal influence exchanges. At the beginning of counseling, the highly motivated clients perceived their counselors to be attractive and likable. The counselors of these same clients also perceived their clients to be quite interpersonally attractive. These counselors also were the ones who believed they had the greatest impact or influence on their clients.

The interpersonal and reciprocal nature of this influence process makes for "very intricate dynamics" during counseling (Dorn, 1984b, p. 344). Dorn provides a useful example of how the influence process between the two parties occurs:

Person A exhibits verbal and nonverbal behavior in an effort to have Person B respond in a specific manner. Person B responds, again with verbal and nonverbal behavior, and this behavior is immediate feedback to Person A about how successful his or her initial influence attempts were. Person A then assesses this feedback and compares it with his or her initial expectations. Person A then decides what behavior to exhibit next. Of course, Person B is simultaneously involved in the same process [p. 344].

41

□ OBJECTIVES

1. Given a role-play interaction, identify and challenge any deletions, distortions, and generalizations in the client's verbal messages in order to obtain specificity and concreteness.
2. Given written descriptions of six clients, match the client description with the corresponding client "test of trust."
3. Given a role-play interaction, conduct a 30-minute initial interview in which you demonstrate both descriptive and behavioral aspects of attractiveness.
4. Given a role-play interaction, conduct a 30-minute problem identification interview in which you demonstrate verbal and nonverbal behaviors of expertness and trustworthiness.

□ STRONG'S MODEL OF COUNSELING AS INTERPERSONAL INFLUENCE

In 1968 Strong published what is now regarded as a landmark paper on counseling as a social influence process. He hypothesized that counselors' attempts to change clients precipitate dissonance in clients because of the inconsistency, or discrepancy, between the counselor's and the client's attitudes. This dissonance feels uncomfortable to clients, and they try to reduce this discomfort in a variety of ways, including discrediting the counselor, rationalizing about the importance of their problem, seeking out information or opinions that contradict the counselor, attempting to change the counselor's opinion, or accepting the opinion of the counselor. Strong (1968) asserted that clients would be more likely to accept the counselor's opinions and less likely to discredit or refute the counselor if the clients perceive the counselor as expert, attractive, and trustworthy. These three helper characteristics (expertness, attractiveness, and trustworthiness) can also be called "relationship enhancers" (Goldstein, 1986) because they have been identified as ways of making the therapeutic relationship more positive.

Strong (1968) suggested a two-stage model of counseling:

1. The counselor establishes a power base, or influence base, with the client through the three relationship enhancers of expertness, attractiveness, and trustworthiness. This influence base enhances the quality of the relationship and also encourages client involvement in counseling. This stage of the model (drawing from social-psychology literature) assumes that counselors establish this influence base by drawing on power bases that can effect attitude change. Common power bases used by counselors include these:

• *Legitimate power:* power that occurs as a result of the counselor's role—a form that society at large views as acceptable and helpful.
• *Expert power:* power that results from descriptive and behavioral cues of expertness and competence.
• *Referent power:* power that results from descriptive and behavioral cues of interpersonal attractiveness, friendliness, and similarity between counselor and client (such as is found in "indigenous" helpers, for example).

2. The counselor actively uses this influence base to effect attitudinal and behavioral change in clients. In this second stage of the model, it is important that clients perceive the counselor as expert, attractive, and trustworthy, since it is the *client's* perception of these counselor characteristics that determines, at least in part, how much influence counselors will have with their clients.

During the last decade, an increasing number of research studies on Strong's social influence model have appeared, although much of the existing research consists of analogue (not "in the field") studies limited to one or two contacts between persons (Corrigan, Dell, Lewis, & Schmidt, 1980). The influence base that we describe above seems to have the most effect on clients during initial contacts, since that is when clients formulate their first impressions of counselors.

□ THE INTERACTIONAL NATURE OF THE INFLUENCE PROCESS

As we noted at the beginning of this chapter, counselor and client influence attempts are interdependent and interrelated. In considering counselor attributes and behaviors (expertness, attractiveness, and trustworthiness) that contribute to influence, it is also important to consider client variables that may enhance or mediate counselor influence effects.

Although most of this chapter will focus on the three counselor characteristics that contribute most to the influence process in counseling, remember that certain client characteristics may also enhance or mediate the counselor's influence attempts. In other words, some clients may be more susceptible or less susceptible to counselor influence, depending on such things as

- Gender, race, cultural background
- Attractiveness and social competence
- Conceptual level and cognitive style
- "Myths," beliefs, and expectations about counseling
- Motivation
- Satisfaction with outcomes of counseling
- Level of commitment required to change target behaviors

Additionally, since counseling is a *process* and involves distinctly different phases or stages, such as the ones mentioned in Chapter 1 (that is, relationship, assessment and goal setting, intervention and action, and evaluation and termination), it is also imperative to consider what kind of influence might be best suited for different phases of the process. For example, the descriptive aspects of expertness, such as role, reputation, education, and setting, are most useful and influential during the first part of counseling, in which you are trying to encourage the client to continue counseling by demonstrating your credibility. Yet, as counseling ensues, these external trappings are *not* sufficient unless accompanied by behavioral demonstrations of expertness or competence that indicate the counselor is skilled enough to handle the client's concerns successfully. The relationship of various aspects of counselor expertness, attractiveness, and trustworthiness to stages of counseling is depicted in summary form in Table 3-1. *Descriptive* cues associated with these three relationship enhancers refer to nonbehavioral aspects of the counselor such as demeanor, attire, and appearance, to situational aspects such as the office setting, and to the counselor's reputation inferred from introductions, prior knowledge, and the display of diplomas and certificates. *Behavioral* aspects of these three variables refer to the counselor's verbal and nonverbal behaviors or specific things the counselor says and does. In the remainder of the chapter, we describe the behavioral components of these three variables and provide examples.

TABLE 3-1. Relationship of counselor expertness, attractiveness, and trustworthiness to stages of counseling

Stage of counseling	*Purposes of influence efforts*
Rapport and relationship (Stage 1)	
Descriptive aspects of *expertness:* education, role, reputation, setting	"Hook" client to continue counseling by communicating credibility
Physical demeanor and *attractiveness*	Create initial favorable impression
Interpersonal attractiveness conveyed by structuring	Reduce client anxiety, "check out" client expectations
Descriptive aspects of *trust*—role and reputation	Encourage client openness and self-expression
Assessment and goal setting (Stage 2)	
Behavioral aspects of *expertness:*	
Verbal and nonverbal attentiveness	Contribute to client understanding of self and of issues
Concreteness	Challenge client's language errors and omissions
Relevant and thought-provoking questions	Obtain specificity
Behavioral aspects of *attractiveness:*	
Responsive nonverbal behavior	Encourage relevant client self-disclosure and self-exploration
Self-disclosure	Convey likability and perceived similarity to client
Behavioral aspects of *trustworthiness:* nonverbal acceptance of client disclosures, maintaining of confidentiality, accurate paraphrasing, nondefensive reactions to client "tests of trust"	Convey yourself as trustworthy of client communications so client will feel comfortable "opening up" and self-disclosing

(continued)

TABLE 3-1. Relationship of counselor expertness, attractiveness, and trustworthiness to stages of counseling (continued)

Stage of counseling	Purposes of influence efforts
Intervention strategies and action steps (Stage 3)	
Behavioral aspects of *expertness:* directness, fluency, confidence in presentation, and delivery; interpretations	Use of selected skills and strategies and display of confidence to demonstrate ability to help client resolve problems and take necessary action
Behavioral aspects of *trustworthiness:* nonverbal dynamism, dependability and consistency of talk and actions, accurate and reliable information giving	Demonstrate dynamism, congruence, and reliability to encourage client to trust your suggestions and ideas for action; also to diffuse any resistance to action, especially if target behaviors require high level of commitment or change
Evaluation, termination, and follow-up (Stage 4)	
Behavioral areas of *expertness:*	
Relevant questions	Assess client progress and readiness for termination
Directness and confidence in presentation	Contribute to client confidence in maintenance of change through self-directed efforts
Interpersonal attractiveness: structuring	Reduce client anxiety about termination and dissolution of therapeutic relationship
Trustworthiness: reputation or demonstrated lack of ulterior motives or personal gain, honesty and openness	Increase client openness to dissolve relationship when appropriate and necessary

☐ COUNSELOR CHARACTERISTICS OR RELATIONSHIP ENHANCERS

Earlier we described the importance of three counselor characteristics for establishing and using an influence base with clients: expertness, attractiveness, and trustworthiness. These three characteristics are also related and, in fact, intercorrelated (Zamostny, Corrigan, & Eggert, 1981) to the extent that counselors who are perceived by clients as competent are also likely to be viewed as interpersonally attractive and trustworthy. Additionally, of the three variables, expertness, or competence, seems to be the most important to client satisfaction (Zamostny et al., 1981) and client goal-related outcomes (LaCrosse, 1980). Expertness has also received the most attention in the research, followed by attractiveness. Very few studies have explored parameters of trustworthiness, despite its acknowledged importance to the developing therapeutic relationship.

☐ EXPERTNESS

Expertness, also known as "competence" (Egan, 1990), is the client's perception that the counselor will be helpful in resolving the client's concerns. Clients develop this perception from such things as the counselor's apparent level of skill, relevant education, specialized training or experience, certificates or licenses, seniority, status, type of setting in which the counselor works, history of success in solving problems of others, and the counselor's ascribed role as a helper. Clients appear to formulate these perceptions from aspects of the counselor (language, attire, sex, and so on) and of the setting (display of diplomas, certificates, professional literature, title) that are *immediately* evident to a client — that is, in initial contacts. Thus, in the initial stage of counseling, in which the main goal is to establish an effective relationship and build rapport, descriptive cues such as those mentioned above (see also Table 3-2) associated with expertness play a predominant part in helping the counselor to establish an influence base with the client.

Initially, the *role* of counselor also contributes to client perceptions of counselor competence. In our society, a "helper" role is viewed as socially acceptable and valuable. Counselors convey legitimate power or influence simply by the role they hold. Thus, the "counselor role carries considerable initial influence regardless of its occupant" (Corrigan et al., 1980, p. 425). These authors believe that the legitimate power of our role is, in fact, so strong that demonstrated or behavioral cues of counselor expertness are masked in the initial stage of counseling because sufficient inher-

TABLE 3-2. Descriptive and behavioral cues of expertness, attractiveness, and trustworthiness

Expertness	Attractiveness	Trustworthiness
Descriptive cues		
Relevant education (diplomas)	Physical attractiveness	Role as helper (regarded as trustworthy by society)
Specialized training or experience		
Certificates or licenses		Reputation for honesty and "straightness," lack of ulterior motives
Seniority		
Status		
Type of setting		
Display of professional literature		
Attire		
Reputation (past history of success in resolving problems of others)		
Socially validated role of helper		
Behavioral cues		
Nonverbal behaviors	*Nonverbal behaviors (responsive)*	*Nonverbal behaviors*
Eye contact	Eye contact	Nonverbal congruence
Forward body lean	Direct body orientation facing client	Nonverbal acceptance of client disclosures
Fluent speech delivery	Forward body lean	
	Smiling	Nonverbal responsiveness/dynamism
	Head nodding	
Verbal behaviors	*Verbal behaviors*	*Verbal behaviors*
Relevant and thought-provoking questions	Structuring	Accurate and reliable information giving
Verbal attentiveness	Moderate level of self-disclosure	Accurate paraphrasing
Directness and confidence in presentation	Content of self-disclosure similar to client experiences and opinions	Dependability and consistency of talk and actions
Interpretations		Confidentiality
Concreteness		Openness, honesty
		Reflection of "tests of trust" nondefensively

ent power is ascribed to the role of a helper (Corrigan et al., 1980).

As shown in Table 3-1, in the initial stage of counseling, the counselor wants to create a favorable initial impression and also to encourage the client into counseling by communicating credibility. To some extent, such credibility will be conveyed for counselors by the inherent "power" of our roles as helpers. Additionally, counselors can seek to enhance evident and readily accessible descriptive cues associated with expertness by displaying diplomas, certificates, professional literature, titles, and so on. The helper's initial credibility is also enhanced when the counselor

has acquired a positive reputation (based on past history of helping others to resolve their problems) and the client is aware of this reputation.

Role, reputation, and external or office "trappings," however, are insufficient to carry the counselor through anything but the initial phase of counseling. In subsequent phases, the counselor must show actual evidence of competence by his or her behavior. Behavioral expertness is measured by the extent to which the counselor actually helps clients achieve their goals (Egan, 1990). Behavioral demonstrations of expertness are particularly crucial in the second and third stages of counseling (assessment, goal setting, and intervention).

These stages require great skill or actual technical competence in order to make a thorough and accurate assessment of the client's problem, help the client set realistic and worthwhile goals, and help the client take suitable action to reach those goals. This is extremely important because having charisma or being a "good guy" or a "good gal" will not get you through successive interactions with clients. As Corrigan et al. note, "In longer term counseling . . . continued evidence of a lack of expertise might negate the power conferred on a counselor by virtue of his/her role" (1980, p. 425).

Perceived expertness does not seem to be equivalent to counselor experience—that is, experienced counselors are not automatically perceived as more competent or expert than less experienced or even paraprofessional helpers (Heppner & Heesacker, 1982). Instead, expertness is enhanced by the presence or absence of selected nonverbal *and* verbal counselor behaviors that, together, interact to convey behavioral manifestations of competence (Barak, Patkin, & Dell, 1982). *Nonverbal* behaviors associated with the communication of expertness include these:

1. Eye contact
2. Forward body lean
3. Fluent speech delivery (see also Chapter 4)

These nonverbal behaviors appear to contribute to perceived expertness by conveying counselor attentiveness and spontaneity and lack of hesitancy in speech and presentation (see also Table 3-2).

Certain *verbal* behaviors seem to contribute to perceived expertness by establishing the counselor as a source of knowledge and skill and by promoting counselor credibility. These include the following:

1. Use of relevant and thought-provoking questions (see Chapter 6)
2. Verbal indications of attentiveness, such as verbal following, lack of interruptions, listening responses (see Chapter 5)
3. Directness and confidence in presentation
4. Interpretations (see Chapter 6)
5. Concreteness

Concreteness

Because the skill of concreteness is not presented in any other part of the book, we will describe it in some detail in this section. What clients say to you is often an incomplete representation of their experience. Their words and language (sometimes called "surface structure") do not really represent their experience or the meaning of their communication (sometimes called "deep structure"). Not only is the language of clients an incomplete representation of their experience, it also is full of various sorts of "gaps"—three in particular:

Deletions—when things are left out, omitted.
Distortions—when things are not as they seem or are misconstrued.
Generalization—when a whole class of things or people is associated with one feeling or with the same meaning or when conclusions are reached without supporting data.

Because of these gaps, it is important for the counselor to use some linguistic tools to make meaning of the client's words and to fill in these gaps. The most efficient linguistic tool for achieving these two objectives is questions—not just any questions, but particular questions designed to extract exactness and concreteness from clients. These questions also help to ensure that you do not project your own sense of meaning onto the client, because your meaning may be irrelevant or inaccurate.

Consider the following example: A client says "I'm depressed." Therapist A responds by asking "About what, specifically?" Therapist B responds with "Depressed? Oh, yes, I know what that's like. How depressed?" The first therapist is likely to get a response from the client that leads to what depression is like for this client and eventually client responses that recover many missing pieces to the problem, since the client's initial statement is full of deletions, or omissions. The second therapist assumes that her sensory experience or meaning of the word *depressed* is the same as the client's and fails to determine how the client's model of reality (or depression) may differ from her own and even from those of other clients.

Concreteness is a way to ensure that general and common experiences and feelings such as depression, anxiety, anger, and so on are defined idiosyncratically for each client. Further, by requesting specific information from clients, you are relieved of having to search for your own equivalent meanings and interpretations. According to Lankton (1980, p. 52), "To translate a client's words into your own subjective experience, at best, results in valuable time and attention lost from the therapy session. At worst, the meaning you make of a client's experience may be wholly inaccurate."

Asking specific questions designed to elicit concreteness from clients is useful for assessing the client's current problems and also desired outcomes. Consequently, it is a facet of expertness that is particularly critical in the data-gathering and self-exploratory and understanding process characterized by the second stage of counseling — assessment and goal setting. Moreover, it helps you to identify client limitations and resources that could contribute to or militate against effective solutions to problems. Thus, it is also an important part of expertness in the third phase of counseling, in which action plans and intervention strategies are selected and applied.

As we mentioned earlier, client language contains linguistic errors known as deletions, distortions, and generalizations. Table 3-3 describes common categories of client incomplete linguistic communications and sample counselor responses designed to extract exactness and concreteness.

TABLE 3-3. Categories and examples of client linguistic errors and sample counselor responses designed to elicit concreteness

Category	Description	Examples	Sample therapist responses
Deletions			
Simple deletion	Some object, person, or event is left out	"I am going" "I'm scared"	"Going where?" "Of what?"
Comparative deletion	Basis for using a comparative or superlative is deleted	"She is the best" "My brother is better than me"	"Best compared with whom?" "Best when (or where)?" "Better when (or how or where)"?
Referential index, lack of	Object or person being referred to is left out or is unspecified	"They're always in my way" "It makes me sick"	"Who, specifically, is always in your way?" "What, specifically, makes you sick?
Unspecified verb	Parts of the action are missing — for example, verb is introduced but not clarified	"He frustrates me" "I'm stymied"	"Specifically, how does he frustrate you?" "How, specifically, are you stymied?"
Modal operator of *necessity*	Assumption of no choice — "have to," "can't," "impossible," "necessary"	"I can't make sense of this list" "It's impossible to think straight"	"What stops you?" "What prevents you from thinking straight?"
Modal operator of *possibility*	Assumption of no choice — "should, "must not," "ought to"	"I should learn this list" "I must not neglect my studies"	"What would happen if you did not?" "What would happen if you did?"
Lost performative	Who is making a judgment or evaluation is omitted	"It is bad to neglect studying" "People should do better by each other"	"For whom it is bad?" "Bad in whose opinion?" "Who, specifically, should do better?" "Should do better in whose opinion?"
Distortions			
Nominalization	Action (verb) made into a thing (noun) — tends to delete person's responsibility for the action	"I do not have freedom" "I want security"	"How, specifically, do you not feel free? When, where, with whom?" "How do you want to be secure?"

(continued)

TABLE 3-3. Categories and examples of client linguistic errors and sample counselor responses designed to elicit concreteness (continued)

Category	Description	Examples	Sample therapist responses
Cause/effect	Assumption that one event *causes* another	"Your frowning makes me mad"	"Specifically, how does my frowning cause you to be mad?"
		"As long as my teacher is around, I feel happy"	"How, specifically, does the presence of your teacher cause you to be happy?"
Mind reading	Assumption of how the other person thinks or feels (inside) without specific evidence	"When you frown, I know you hate me"	"How, specifically, do you know that my frowning means I hate you?"
		"I know he doesn't love me"	"How, specifically, do you know this?"
Presuppositions	Some experience must be assumed for the statement to make sense	"You know I suffer" (Assumes that you know I suffer)	"How, specifically, do you suffer?"
		"My daughter is as stubborn as my husband" (Assumes husband is stubborn)	"How, specifically, does your husband seem stubborn to you?"
Generalizations			
Universal quantifiers	Generalization to whole class; "always," "never," "none," "all," "every"	"I always have trouble learning this kind of material"	"You *never* have learned any kind of material like this before, ever?"
		"I always lose arguments"	"Was there ever a time when you didn't lose an argument?"
Complex equivalence	Assuming that one experience means another (implied cause/effect)	"When he frowns, I know he hates me"	"Was there ever a time when he frowned and he loved you?" "Have you ever frowned at someone you love?"
		"My wife wants to work. She doesn't love me"	"Do you love your wife? And do you also work?"

Adapted from list compiled by R. Rittenhouse (personal communication, June 1982) and Bandler and Grinder (1975). The authors appreciate their contribution to this table.

Expertness Is Not "One Up"

It is extremely important to remember that expertness is not in any way the same as being dogmatic, authoritarian, or "one up." Expert helpers are those perceived as confident, attentive, and, because of background and behavior, capable of helping the client resolve problems and work toward goals. Helpers misuse this important variable when they come across as "the expert" or in a one-up position with clients. This may intimidate clients, who might then decide not to return for more counseling. In fact, particularly in initial sessions, helpers must do just the opposite: convey friendliness, equality, and likability. In later sessions, it is also important to deemphasize your influence efforts or make them inconspicuous in order to avoid engendering client resistance (see also Chapter 20). In the next section, we describe how helpers exercise likability and friendliness through the variable of attractiveness.

LEARNING ACTIVITIES #6: EXPERTNESS

I. Counselor Competence

A. With a partner or in small groups, describe the ideal counseling setting that would enhance most clients' initial impressions of counselor competence. Be very specific in your descriptions.

B. With your partner or in small groups, discuss any clients who might not view your ideal setting described above as indicative of counselor competence. Discuss the limitations of setting, role, and reputation as a means of enhancing the competence variable with these clients.

C. With your partner or in small groups, identify what you believe are the *three most important* things you can do behaviorally to enhance client perceptions of your competence. When you finish this part of the learning activity, you may want to share your descriptions of all three parts with another dyad or group, and vice versa.

II. Concreteness and Linguistic Errors

Twelve client statements are listed in this learning activity. Identify the category of the linguistic error contained in each statement (deletion, distortion, or generalization) and then write a sample counselor response that recovers the omission or challenges the distortion or generalization. An example is given. You may want to refer to Table 3-3 if you have difficulty. Feedback follows.

Example

1. a. Client statement: "I hate them."
   b. __✔__ Deletion   _____ Distortion
      _____ Generalization
   c. Counselor response: "Whom, specifically, do you hate?"

2. a. Client statement: "She upsets me."
   b. _____ Deletion   _____ Distortion
      _____ Generalization
   c. Counselor response:

3. a. Client statement: "I can't do this."
   b. _____ Deletion   _____ Distortion
      _____ Generalization
   c. Counselor response:

4. a. Client statement: "I know he thinks I'm dumb."
   b. _____ Deletion   _____ Distortion
      _____ Generalization
   c. Counselor response:

5. a. Client statement: "I always lose my cool in front of large groups."
   b. _____ Deletion   _____ Distortion
      _____ Generalization
   c. Counselor response:

6. a. Client statement: "The way you look makes me scared."
   b. _____ Deletion   _____ Distortion
      _____ Generalization
   c. Counselor response:

7. a. Client statement: "I'm sad."
   b. _____ Deletion   _____ Distortion
      _____ Generalization
   c. Counselor response:

8. a. Client statement: "I do not have independence."
   b. _____ Deletion   _____ Distortion
      _____ Generalization
   c. Counselor response:

9. a. Client statement: "My daughter wants to move out. I guess that means she doesn't like it here."
   b. _____ Deletion   _____ Distortion
      _____ Generalization
   c. Counselor response:

10. a. Client statement: "It is bad not to exercise."
    b. _____ Deletion   _____ Distortion
       _____ Generalization
    c. Counselor response:

11. a. Client statement: "It blows my top off."
    b. _____ Deletion   _____ Distortion
       _____ Generalization
    c. Counselor response:

12. a. Client statement: "I should do more work."
    b. _____ Deletion   _____ Distortion
       _____ Generalization
    c. Counselor response:

■
FEEDBACK #6: EXPERTNESS

II. Concreteness and Linguistic Errors

2. b. Deletion (unspecified verb)
   c. "Specifically, how does she upset you?"
3. b. Deletion (modal operator of necessity)
   c. "What is stopping you?"
4. b. Distortion (mind reading)
   c. "How, specifically, do you know this?"
5. b. Generalization (universal quantifier "always")
   c. "You *never* have kept it together in front of a large group?"
6. b. Distortion (cause/effect)
   c. "How, specifically, does the way I look cause you to feel afraid?"
7. b. Deletion (simple omission)
   c. "About what?"
8. b. Distortion (nominalization)
   c. "How, specifically, do you not act (or behave) independently?"
9. b. Generalization (complex equivalence)
   c. "Have you ever left a place or a person you liked or loved?"
10. b. Deletion (lost performative)
    c. "For whom is it bad?"
11. b. Deletion (lack of referential index)
    c. "What, specifically, blows your top off?"
12. b. Deletion (modal operator of possibility)
    c. "What would happen if you didn't do more work?"

■

☐ ATTRACTIVENESS

Attractiveness is inferred by clients from the counselor's apparent friendliness, likability, and similarity to the client. As we mentioned earlier, the counselor who is perceived as attractive by clients becomes an important source of referent power. The effects of attractiveness are apparently greatest when it is mutual—when the client likes the helper and the helper likes to work with the client (Heppner & Heesacker, 1982).

Attractiveness consists of both physical and interpersonal dimensions. Physical attractiveness is the primary descriptive cue associated with this relationship enhancer and, like the descriptive cues of expertness, appears to exert most influence in the *initial* stage of counseling—during relationship and rapport building, when impression formation by clients is based on relatively apparent and accessible cues (Cash & Salzbach, 1978). Dur-

ing later stages of counseling, the skills and competence, or behavioral manifestations, of expertness seem to outweigh the effects of physical attractiveness. In one study, clients did not want to return for counseling with counselors having poor skills even if the counselors were perceived as physically attractive (Vargas & Borkowski, 1982). Zlotlow and Allen (1981, p. 201) conclude that "although the physically attractive counselor may have a head start in developing rapport with clients as a result of widely held stereotypes about good-looking people, this advantage clearly is not an adequate substitute for technical skill or social competence."

In the initial stage of counseling, counselors can utilize the potential benefit from the attractiveness stereotype by trying to maximize their physical attractiveness, appearance, and demeanor. Although there is obviously little we can do to alter certain aspects of our appearance short of plastic surgery, other aspects of our appearance, such as attire, weight, personal hygiene, and grooming, are under our control and can be used to enhance, rather than detract from, initial impressions that clients formulate of us.

Selected nonverbal and verbal behaviors convey interpersonal attractiveness and also are quite important during the first two stages of counseling—relationship/rapport and assessment and goal setting. Interpersonal attractiveness helps clients to open up and self-disclose by reducing client anxiety (through structuring and self-disclosure) and by creating the belief that this counselor is someone with whom the client wants to work.

Nonverbal behaviors that contribute to attractiveness include eye contact, body orientation (facing client), forward body lean, smiling, and head nodding (Barak, Patkin, & Dell, 1982; see also Table 3-2). These and other aspects of counselor nonverbal behavior are discussed more extensively in Chapter 4.

Verbal behaviors that contribute to attractiveness include self-disclosure and structuring, discussed below. These behaviors appear to enhance the relationship by creating positive expectations, reducing unnecessary anxiety, and increasing the perceived similarity between client and counselor.

Self-Disclosure

With respect to attractiveness, three factors related to self-disclosure are worth reemphasizing:

1. Perceived attractiveness is related to a *mod-*

erate level of helper self-disclosure (Banikiotes, Kubinski, & Pursell, 1981). Too much or too little disclosure detracts from the client's perception of the helper as attractive.

2. The depth of intimacy reflected in self-disclosure statements needs to be adapted to the stage of counseling and the degree of the therapeutic relationship. In early sessions, self-disclosure of a factual, nonintimate nature is more useful; in later sessions, more personal or self-involving disclosures are more helpful (McCarthy, 1982).

3. Attractiveness is enhanced when helpers self-disclose problems and concerns previously experienced that are *similar* to the client's present problem. Similarity of self-disclosure may also promote the credibility and competence of the helper by suggesting that the counselor knows about and can understand the client's concern (Corrigan et al., 1980). Accordingly, "disclosure of any prior problem (now successfully resolved) may confer on the counselor some 'expertise in problem resolution' or credibility accorded to 'one who has also suffered'" (Corrigan et al., 1980, p. 425).

Structuring

Another way to maximize perceived similarity between counselor and client is by the use of direct structuring. *Structuring* refers to an interactional process between counselors and clients in which they arrive at similar perceptions of the role of the counselor, an understanding of what occurs in the counseling process, and an agreement on which outcome goals will be achieved (Brammer, Shostrom, and Abrego, 1989; Day & Sparacio, 1980). Structuring enhances perceived counselor/client similarity and interpersonal attractiveness (Goldstein, 1971) and also fulfills an ethical obligation that requires counselors to inform clients of such things as the purposes, goals, techniques, and limitations of counseling (American Association for Counseling and Development, 1981).

Direct structuring means that the counselor actively and directly provides structure to the clients concerning the elements mentioned above. Direct structuring contributes to attractiveness by enhancing helper/helpee agreement on basic information and issues, thereby establishing some security in the relationship. Insecurity results from excessive ambiguity and anxiety. Direct structuring is most important sometime in the first stage of counseling (relationship and rapport), in which ambiguity and anxiety and lack of information

about counseling are likely to be greatest and the need to promote helper/helpee similarity is critical. An example of the use of direct structuring with a new client in an initial interview follows:

Counselor: Mary, I understand this is the first time you have ever been to see a counselor. Is that accurate or not?

Client: Yes, it is. I've thought about seeing someone for a while, but I finally got the courage to actually do it just recently.

Counselor: I noticed you used the word *courage* as if perhaps you're feeling relieved you're here and also still somewhat uneasy about what happens in counseling.

Client: That's true. I'm glad I came, but I guess I'm also still a little unsure.

Counselor: One thing that might help with the uncertainty is to talk for a few minutes about what goes on in counseling, what my role and your role is, and the kinds of things you may want to talk about or work on. How does that sound?

Client: Great. I think that would help.

Counselor: OK. Many people come into counseling with something they need to get "off their chest" —at first sometimes they just need to talk and think about it. Later on it is usually important to also do something about the issue. My role is to help you identify, talk about, and understand issues of concern to you and then to help you take any action that seems important to resolve the issue or to take your life in a different direction. This process can take several months or longer. At first, it usually is a little hard to open up and share some personal things with someone you don't know, but one thing that might help you do this is to know that, short of feeling strongly like you are going to harm yourself or someone else, whatever you tell me is kept in this room between us. Now —what are your questions or reactions?

Direct structuring is also very useful during the last stage of counseling to ensure a smooth termination, to reduce client anxiety about dissolution of the therapeutic relationship, and to convey action expectations and information about what may happen after counseling terminates. Consider the following example as a counselor and client approach termination:

Counselor: Jim, we started seeing each other every week six months ago; the last two months you've been coming in every other week. Several times you've mentioned recently how good you feel and how your relationships with women are now starting to take off in a direction you want. It seems to me that after about one or two more contacts we will be ready to stop seeing each other because you are able to handle these issues on your own now. What is your reaction to this?

Client: That sounds about right. I do feel a lot more confident in the way my relationships are going. I guess it does seem a little strange to think of not coming in here.

Counselor: Yes. After you've been working together like we have, sometimes there's a little bit of strangeness or apprehension that accompanies the idea of finishing with counseling. However, I wouldn't suggest it at this time if I didn't feel very sure that you are ready to do this. It might help you to know that I'll be calling you several times after we finish to see how things are going, and of course, if anything comes up in the future you want to talk over, just give me a call.

According to Day and Sparacio (1980), structure is also helpful at major transition points in counseling, such as moving from one stage to another. This also reduces ambiguity, informs the client about any role and process changes in a different stage of therapy, and increases the likelihood that both counselor and client will approach the forthcoming stage with similar rather than highly discrepant perceptions.

To provide structure effectively with clients, consider the following ten guidelines for structuring suggested by Day and Sparacio (1980, pp. 248–249):

1. Structure should be negotiated or requested, not coerced. Clients should be given the opportunity to respond and react to structure as well as to be able to modify it.

2. Structure, particularly restrictions and limitations, should not be applied for punitive reasons or in a punitive manner (Bixler, 1949).

3. The counselor should be aware of his or her rationale for structuring and should explain the reasons at the time of structuring or be prepared to provide rationale in response to the client's request for explanation.

4. The counselor should be guided by the client's readiness for structure and by the context of the relationship and process.

5. Too much or a too-rigid structure can be constraining for both the client and the counselor (Pietrofesa, Hoffman, Splete, & Pinto, 1978).

6. Ill-timed, lengthy, or insensitive structuring can result in client frustration or resistance (Benjamin, 1974), and can interrupt the continuity of the therapeutic process (Pietrofesa et al., 1978).

7. Unnecessary and purposeless recitation of rules and guidelines can imply that the counselor is more concerned with procedure than with helpfulness. In fact, a compulsive approach to structuring can be indicative of low levels of counselor self-assurance (Hansen, Stevic, & Warner, 1977).

8. The counselor must relate structure to the client's emotional, cognitive, and behavioral predisposition. For example, the highly independent individual or the isolate may be expected to resist what she or he interprets as personal threats or infringements. In such cases, structuring must be accomplished by sensitivity, tentativeness, and flexibility.

9. Structuring can "imply that the relationship will continue with this particular client. It may turn out that the counselor will decide not to work with this client, or that the client may not be suitable for this counselor. Hence, the client or counselor may feel too committed to the relationship if it has been overstructured" (Brammer, Shostrom, and Abrego, 1989, p. 121).

10. Structure cannot replace or substitute for therapeutic competence. Structure is not a panacea. It is not the total solution to building a productive therapeutic relationship. Structure is complementary and supplementary to human relations, communications, diagnostic, and intervention skills.*

* From "Structuring the counseling process." by R. W. Day & R. T. Sparacio. *The Personnel and Guidance Journal,* (1981), *59,* 246–249. Copyright AACD. Reprinted with permission. No further reproduction authorized without permission from AACD.

LEARNING ACTIVITIES #7: ATTRACTIVENESS

I. Attributes of Attractive Persons

In a dyad or a small group, discuss the attributes of persons you know and consider to be "attractive" persons. Compile a written list of their attributes. Review your list to determine which attributes are descriptive ones, such as appearance and demeanor, and which attributes are behavioral—that is, things the person does. To what extent do the attributes of attractive people listed in your compilation generalize to effective helpers?

II. Structuring

In this activity, write an example of the use of direct structuring for each of the following four examples. Feedback follows.

(continued)

1. Write an example of structuring in an initial interview with a client who has never seen a counselor before.
2. Write an example of structuring in an initial interview with a client who is new to you but has seen three other counselors before.
3. Write an example of structuring prior to starting the termination phase with a client who has never been in counseling before.
4. Write an example of structuring prior to starting the termination phase with a client who has been in counseling several times before.

☐ TRUSTWORTHINESS

"Trust is the client's perception and belief that the counselor will not mislead or injure the client in any way"* (Fong & Cox, 1983, p. 163). According to the interpersonal influence model, trustworthiness is perceived by clients from such things as the counselor's role, reputation for honesty, demonstrated sincerity and openness, and lack of ulterior motives (Strong, 1968).

Establishing Trust

In the initial stage of counseling (relationship and rapport), clients are also dependent on readily accessible descriptive cues to judge the trustworthiness of counselors. For example, many clients are likely to find counselors trustworthy, at least initially, because of the status of their role in society. According to Egan (1975, p. 111), "In our society, people who have certain roles are usually considered trustworthy until the opposite is demonstrated. . . . When exceptions do occur (as when a dentist is convicted of molesting a patient), the scandal is greater because it is unexpected." Clients also are more likely to perceive a counselor as trustworthy if she or he has acquired a reputation for honesty and for ethical and professional behavior. Likewise, a negative reputation can erode initial trust in a helper. Thus, many clients may put their faith in the helper initially on the basis of role and reputation and, over the course of counseling, continue to trust the counselor unless the trust is in some way abused. This is particularly true for majority-group clients.

For clients who are members of minority groups, it may be the other way around. As LaFromboise and Dixon (1981, p. 135) observe, "A member of the minority group frequently enters the relationship suspending trust until the person

proves that he/she is worthy of being trusted." For these and some other clients, counselors may have to earn initial trust. This is especially true as counseling progresses. Trust can be difficult to establish yet easily destroyed. Trust between counselor and client involves a series of "relationship interchanges" (Fong & Cox, 1983), takes time to develop fully, and is not a fixed phenomenon but changes constantly depending on the actions of both persons (Johnson, 1986). Initial trust based on external factors such as the counselor's role and reputation must be solidified with appropriate actions and behaviors of helpers that occur during successive interactions (see also Table 3-2).

During the second stage of counseling, assessment and goal setting, trust is essential in order for the client to be open and revealing of very personal problems and concerns. Clients' self-exploration of problems during this phase can be limited by the amount of trust that has developed in the relationship prior to this time. Trust is also critical during the third and fourth stages of counseling. In the third stage (action/intervention), the client often has to set in motion the difficult and vulnerable process of change. Trust can provide the impetus necessary for the client to do so. Trust is also critical to the fourth stage of counseling (evaluation and termination). Effective termination ensues when the client trusts the counselor's decision to terminate, trusts that it is not too early (leaving the client hanging) or too prolonged (creating excessive dependency for the client), and trusts that the counselor is reliable and concerned enough to check in with the client on a periodic basis as a follow-up to therapy.

The behaviors that contribute most importantly to trustworthiness include counselor congruence, or consistency, of verbal and nonverbal behavior, nonverbal acceptance of client disclosures, and nonverbal responsiveness and dynamism (see also Chapter 4). Incongruence, judgmental or evaluative reactions, and passivity quickly erode any initial trust.

Important verbal behaviors (see also Table 3-2) contributing to trust include accurate paraphras-

* This and all other quotations from this source are from "Trust as an underlying dynamic in the counseling process: How clients test trust." by M. L. Fong and B. G. Cox. *The Personnel and Guidance Journal, 62,* 163–166. Copyright AACD. Reprinted with permission. No further reproduction authorized without permission of AACD.

FEEDBACK #7: ATTRACTIVENESS

II. Structuring

1. "You're probably feeling uncertain about what to expect. It might help if we talked a little about what happens in counseling. You may have one or more things on your mind you want to talk about and work through. I'm here to help you do that and to do it in a safe and confidential place."

2. "You probably know what goes on in counseling generally. What I do might vary a little bit from the other counselors you've seen. I believe I'm here to listen to you, to help you understand some of your concerns, and to assist you in taking a course of action best for you to resolve these issues."

3. "I have the sense that you have really accomplished what you wanted to do. Let's take a few minutes to see . . . [reviews client's progress toward desired goals]. Since you also feel our work's about done, it seems like after two more sessions it will be time to close out our relationship for now. You may feel a little apprehensive about this, but I'll be calling you shortly after we finish to see how things are going. I imagine things will go quite smoothly for you. Once in a while, people find it's hard to start out on their own, but soon things start to fall into place. During these last three sessions, we'll also be working specifically on how you can take the things you've learned and done in our sessions out into your own world so things do fall into place for you out there."

4. "I believe after one or two more sessions, we're ready to finish. Since you've been through this before, do you have the same or a different opinion? [Time for client to respond.] One thing I want you to know about myself is that I'll call you once or twice after we stop to see how things are going, and of course, you can feel free to call me, too, if something comes up you need to discuss.

ing (see also Chapter 5), dependability and consistency between talk and actions, confidentiality, openness and honesty, accurate and reliable information giving (see also Chapter 6), and nondefensive reflections/interpretations of clients' "tests of trusts." This latter behavior is discussed in greater depth in the following section.

Client Tests of Counselor Trustworthiness

According to Johnson (1986), trust between counselors and clients does not always develop automatically. Clients need to be assured that counsel-

ing will be structured to meet their needs and that the counselor will not take advantage of their vulnerability (Johnson, 1986). Often clients do not ask about these issues directly. Instead, they engage in subtle maneuvers to obtain data about the counselor's trustworthiness. Fong and Cox (1983) call these maneuvers "tests of trust" and liken them to trial balloons sent up to "see how they fly" before the client decides whether to send up the big one or the real one.

Counselors may be insensitive to such "tests of trust" and fail to identify that trust is the real concern of the client. Instead of responding to the trust issue, counselors may respond just to the content, the surface level of the message. Or the counselor may view the client as "defensive, resistant, or hostile" and respond negatively (Fong & Cox, 1983, p. 163). If the trust issue is unresolved, the relationship may deteriorate or even terminate with the counselor unaware that "the real issue was lack of trust" (Fong & Cox, 1983, p. 163).

Fong and Cox observe that some client statements and behaviors are used repeatedly by many clients as "tests of trust." They state that "the specific content of clients' questions and statements is unique to individual clients, but the general form that tests of trust take—for example, requesting information or telling a secret—are relatively predictable" (p. 164). These authors have identified six common types of client "tests of trust," which we describe as follows.

Requesting information (or "Can you understand and help me?"). Counselors need to be alert to whether client questions are searches for factual information or for counselor opinions and beliefs. Clients who ask questions like "Do you have children?" or "How long have you been married?" are probably looking for something in addition to the factual response. Most often they are seeking verification from you that you will be able to understand, to accept, and to help them with their particular set of concerns. In responding to such client questions, it is important to convey your understanding and acceptance of the clients' concerns and of their need to feel understood. For example, a counselor might say "Yes, I do have two children. I'm also wondering whether you believe that the fact that I have children means I can better understand your concerns."

Telling a secret (or "Can I be vulnerable or take risks with you?"). Clients share secrets—very personal aspects of their lives—to test whether they can trust the counselor to accept them as they really are, to keep their communications confidential, and to avoid exploiting their vulnerability after they have disclosed very personal concerns. Usually, this secret is not even relevant to the client's presenting problem but, rather, is related to something the client does that has "embarrassment or shame attached to it" (Fong & Cox, 1983, p. 164). And "if the counselor becomes perceptively defensive in reaction to the client's revelation or makes some statement that seems to be judgmental, the client is almost certain to decide that it is unsafe to be vulnerable with this person. The level of trust drops. And further self-disclosure of any depth may not be forthcoming, at least for a very long time" (p. 164).

Counselors need to remember that clients who share secrets are really testing the waters to see how safe it is to self-disclose personal issues with you. Responding with nonverbal and verbal acceptance and listening assure clients that their private thoughts, feelings, and behaviors are safe with you. For example, suppose a client blurts out: "I had an affair several years ago. No one knows about this, not even my husband." The counselor must respond to the entire message, especially acknowledging the "risk" involved. "That is your way of saying to me that this is secret between you and me."

Asking a favor (or "Are you reliable?"). Clients may ask counselors to perform favors that may or may not be appropriate. According to Fong and Cox (1983, p. 165), "all requests of clients for a favor should be viewed, especially initially, as potential tests of trust." When clients ask you to lend them a book, see them at their home, or call their boss for them, whether you grant or deny the favor is not as important as how you handle the request and how reliably you follow through with your stated intentions. It is crucial to follow through on reasonable favors you have promised to do. For unreasonable favors, it is important to state tactfully but directly your reason for not granting the favor. Efforts to camouflage the real reason with an excuse or to grant an unreasonable favor grudgingly are just as damaging to trust as is failure to follow through on a favor (Fong & Cox, 1983, p. 165). For instance, if a client asks you to see her at her home in order to save her time and gas money, you might tactfully deny her favor by saying "Jane, I can certainly appreciate your need to save time and money. I would much prefer to continue to see you in the office, however, because it is easier for me to concentrate and listen to you without any distractions I'm not used to." Asking favors is generally an indication that the client is testing your reliability, dependability, honesty, and directness. A good rule of thumb to follow is "Don't promise more than you can deliver, and be sure to deliver what you have promised as promised."

Putting oneself down (or "Can you accept me?"). Clients put themselves down to test the counselor's level of acceptance. This test of trust is designed to help clients determine whether the counselor will continue to be accepting even of parts of themselves that clients view as bad, negative, or dirty. Often this test of trust is conveyed by statements or behaviors designed to shock the counselor, followed by a careful scrutiny of the counselor's verbal and nonverbal reactions. Counselors need to respond neutrally to client self-putdowns rather than condoning or evaluating the client's statements and actions. As Fong and Cox note,

> In responding to the client's self-putdowns, the counselor reflects to the client what the counselor has heard and then responds with statements of interest and acceptance. If the counselor makes the mistake of reacting either positively or negatively to the client's descriptions of their "bad" behavior early in the relationship, trust is unlikely to be built. Clients will see the counselor as potentially judgmental or opinionated [1983, p. 165].

A client may say "Did you know I've had three abortions in the last three years? It's my own fault. I just get carried away and keep forgetting to use birth control." The counselor needs to respond with nonverbal acceptance and may say something like "You've found yourself with several unwanted pregnancies."

Inconveniencing the counselor (or "Do you have consistent limits?"). Clients often test trust by creating inconveniences to the counselor such as changing appointment times, canceling at the last minute, changing the location of sessions, or asking to make a phone call during the session. Counselors need to respond directly and openly to the inconvenience, especially if it occurs more than once or twice. When the counselor sets limits, clients may begin feeling secure and assured that the counselor is dependable and consistent. Setting limits often serves a reciprocal purpose: the clients realize they also can set limits in the relationship. As an example of this test of trust, consider the client who is repeatedly late to sessions. After three consecutive late starts, the counselor mentions "You know, Gary, I've realized that the last three weeks we've got off to quite a late start. This creates problems for me because if we have a full session, it throws the rest of my schedule off. Or if I stop at the designated time, you end up getting shortchanged of time. Can we start on time, or do we need to reschedule the appointment time?"

Questioning the counselor's motives (or "Is your caring real?"). As we mentioned earlier, one aspect of trustworthiness is sincerity. Clients test this aspect of trust by statements and questions designed to answer the question "Do you really care about me, or is it just your job?" Clients may ask about the number of other clients the counselor sees or how the counselor distinguishes and

remembers all his clients or whether the counselor thinks about the client during the week (Fong & Cox, 1983). Fong and Cox observe that "unless counselors are alert to the fact that this is a form of testing trust, they may fail to respond adequately to the crucial issue; that is, the client's need to be seen as a worthwhile human being in the counselor's eyes and not just as a source of income for the counselor" (p. 166). For instance, suppose a client says to her counselor "I bet you get tired of listening to people like me all the time." The counselor may respond with something that affirms her interest in the client, such as "You're feeling unsure about your place here, wondering whether I really care about you when I see so many other persons. Suzanne, from you I've learned . . ." (follow through with a personal statement directly related to this client).

Table 3-4 presents a summary of these six tests of trust with sample client statements and helpful and nonhelpful counselor responses.

TABLE 3-4. Examples of client tests of trust and helpful and nonhelpful counselor responses

Test of trust	Client statement	Examples of nonhelpful responses	Example of helpful response
Requesting information (can you understand and help me?)	"Have you ever worked with anyone else who seems as mixed up as I am?"	"Yes, all the time" "No, not too often" "Once in a while" "Oh, you're not *that* mixed up"	"Many people I work with often come in feeling confused and over-whelmed. I'm also wondering whether you want to know that I have the experience to help you"
Telling a secret (can I be vulnerable with you?)	"I've never been able to tell anyone about this— not even my husband or my priest. But I did have an abortion several years ago. I just was not ready to be a good and loving mother"	"Oh, an abortion— really?" "You haven't even told your husband even though it might be his child too?"	"What you're sharing with me now is our secret, something between you and me"
Asking a favor (are you reliable?)	"Could you bring this information (or book) in for me next week?"	Promises to do it but forgets altogether or does not do it when specified	Promises to do it and does it when promised
Putting oneself down (can you accept me?)	"I just couldn't take all the pressure from the constant travel, the competition, the need to always win and be number one. When they offered me the uppers, it seemed like the easiest thing to cope with all this. Now I need more and more of the stuff"	"Don't you know you could hurt yourself if you keep going like this?" "You'll get hurt from this — is it really a smart thing to do?"	"The pressure has gotten so intense it's hard to find a way out from under it"

(continued)

TABLE 3-4. Examples of client tests of trust and helpful and nonhelpful counselor responses (continued)

Test of trust	Client statement	Examples of nonhelpful responses	Example of helpful response
Inconveniencing the counselor (do you have consistent limits?)	"Can I use your phone again before we get started?"	"Of course, go ahead—feel free any time" "Absolutely not"	"Marc, the last two times I've seen you, you have started the session by asking to use my phone. When this happens, you and I don't have the full time to use for counseling. Would it be possible for you to make these calls before our session starts, or do we need to change our appointment time?"
Questioning the counselor's motives (is your caring real?)	"I don't see how you have the energy to see me at the end of the day like this. You must be exhausted after seeing all the other people with problems, too"	"Oh, no, I'm really not" "Yes, I'm pretty tired"	"You're probably feeling unsure about how much energy I have left for you after seeing other people first. One thing about you that helps me keep my energy up is . . ."

LEARNING ACTIVITIES #8: TRUSTWORTHINESS

I. Identification of Trust-Related Issues

With a partner or in a small group, develop responses to the following questions:

A. For clients belonging to majority groups or from racial/cultural backgrounds similar to your own:

1. How does trust develop during therapeutic interactions?
2. How is trust during therapeutic interactions violated?
3. How does it feel to have your trust in someone else violated?
4. What are ten things a counselor can do (or ten behaviors to engage in) to build trust? Of the ten, select five that are most important and rank-order these from 1 (most critical, top priority to establish trust) to 5 (least critical or least priority to establish trust).

B. Complete the same four questions above for clients belonging to minority groups or from a racial/cultural background distinctly different from your own.

II. Client Tests of Trust

Listed below are six client descriptions. For each description, (a) identify the content and process reflected in the test of trust, and (b) write an example of a counselor response that could be used appropri-

ately with this type of trust test. You may wish to refer to Table 3-4. An example is completed. Feedback follows.

Example

1. The client asks whether you have seen other people before who have attempted suicide.

   a. Test of trust (content): request for information (process): can you understand and help me?

   b. Example of counselor response: "Yes, I have worked with other persons before you who have thought life wasn't worth living. Perhaps this will help you know that I will try to understand what this experience is like for you and will help you try to resolve it in your own best way."

2. The client's phone has been disconnected, and the client wants to know whether he can come ten minutes early to use your phone.

   a. Test of trust (content): _____

   (process): _____

   b. Example of counselor response: _____

(continued)

LEARNING ACTIVITIES #8:   TRUSTWORTHINESS (continued)

3. The client wonders aloud whether you make enough money as a counselor that you would choose this occupation if you had to do it over again.

   a. Test of trust (content): _____

   _____

          (process): _____

   _____

   b. Example of counselor response: _____

   _____

4. The client states that she must be kind of stupid because she now has to repeat third grade when all the other kids in her class are going on to fourth grade.

   a. Test of trust (content): _____

   _____

          (process): _____

   _____

   b. Example of counselor response: _____

5. The client has changed the appointment time at the last minute four times in the last several weeks.

   a. Test of trust (content): _____

   _____

          (process): _____

   b. Example of counselor response: _____

6. The client states that she is pregnant and doesn't know for sure whether the father is her husband or her husband's brother and doesn't know what to do and hasn't told anyone else about this.

   a. Test of trust (content): _____

   _____

          (process): _____

   b. Example of counselor response: _____

   _____

   _____

   _____

☐ SUMMARY

In this chapter, we examined the social influence model of counseling. In this model, the counselor establishes an influence base with the client through the three relationship enhancers of expertness, attractiveness, and trustworthiness. The counselor then uses this influence base to effect client change.

Counselor characteristics contributing most to the influence process include expertness (or competence), attractiveness, and trustworthiness. Components of expertness include descriptive cues such as education and training, certificates and licenses, title and status, setting, reputation, and role. Behavioral cues associated with expertness include responsive nonverbal behaviors such as fluent speech delivery, nonverbal and verbal attentiveness, relevant and thought-provoking questions, interpretations, and concreteness.

Descriptive cues associated with attractiveness include physical attractiveness and demeanor. Behavioral cues of attractiveness are responsive nonverbal behavior, moderate level of counselor self-disclosure, similarity of the content of self-disclosure, and structuring.

Trustworthiness is based on one's role and reputation for honesty as well as nonverbal congruence, dynamism, and acceptance of client disclosures. Trustworthiness is also associated with accurate and reliable information giving, accurate paraphrasing, maintaining of confidentiality, openness and honesty, and nondefensive reactions to clients' "tests of trust."

Physical and interpersonal attractiveness and the role, reputation, and setting of the counselor contribute to early impressions of clients that the counselor is attractive, competent, and trustworthy. These aspects are most useful during the early sessions, in which the counselor strives to establish rapport and to motivate the client to continue with counseling. As therapy progresses, these aspects become less influential and must be substantiated by actual skills that demonstrate the counselor's competence and resourcefulness toward resolving client problems. Behavioral expressions of expertness and trustworthiness are particularly critical during all the remaining phases of counseling— assessment and goal setting, intervention and action, and evaluation and termination.

Clients also contribute to the influence process in counseling. Client variables that enhance or mediate the counselor's influence efforts include motivation; expectations; satisfaction and success of outcomes; conceptual level; sex, race, and gender; and degree of commitment required to make target behavior changes.

POSTEVALUATION

PART ONE

Complete this activity in triads, with one person assuming the role of client, another the counselor, and the third the observer. Engage in a ten-minute role-play interview *or* a ten-minute conversation. The client may present a problem *or* discuss a topic of interest to the client. The counselor's task is to listen for any deletions, distortions, and generalizations in the client's verbal messages. Once you identify these, challenge them. Challenge deletions to help the client recover or add the missing pieces; challenge distortions to help the client determine how the event is misconstrued; and challenge generalizations to help the client determine whether there are sufficient data to support his or her conclusion (Chapter Objective One). The observer should keep track of the interaction by jotting down instances of client deletions, distortions, and generalizations and by noting the subsequent counselor response. After the interaction is over, the observer can give feedback and you can trade roles so that each person has an opportunity to try out each of the three roles once.

PART TWO

Listed below are six written client descriptions. Your task is to match each description with the corresponding "test of trust" (Chapter Objective Two). Feedback for this part follows on p. 62.

Test of Trust
a. Information request
b. Telling a secret
c. Asking a favor
d. Putting oneself down
e. Inconveniencing the counselor
f. Questioning the counselor's motives

Client Situation
1. The client asks you whether you get "burned out" or fatigued talking to people with problems all day.
2. The client says she has been sexually abused by her stepfather.
3. The client asks to borrow a book she sees on your desk.
4. The client wants to know whether you have been married before.
5. The client wants you to see him on the weekend.
6. The client says some people consider her a whore because she sleeps around a lot.

PART THREE

This part of the postevaluation is to be completed in triads; the first person assumes the role of counselor, another takes the role of client, and the third assumes the role of observer. Trade roles so that each person has an opportunity to try out each of the three roles once. If triads are not available, an instructor can also observe you, or you can audiotape or videotape your interview for additional assessment.

Instructions to Counselors

Your task is to conduct a 30-minute *initial interview* with a client in which you demonstrate descriptive and behavioral aspects of attractiveness listed in the "Attractiveness Checklist" that follows (Chapter Objective Three). Remember, too, the purposes of trying to enhance your perceived attractiveness in initial interviews: to reduce client anxiety, to be perceived as likeable and friendly and similar to the client, and to increase the probability of client disclosure.

Instructions to Clients

Present a real or hypothetical concern to the counselor. Try to assume the role of a typical "new" client in an initial interview — somewhat apprehensive and a little reticent.

Instructions to Observers

Watch, listen, and assess the use of the counselor's physical and interpersonal cues associated with attractiveness. Use the Attractiveness Checklist that follows as a guide for your observation and feedback.

ATTRACTIVENESS CHECKLIST

I. Descriptive Cues

Instructions: Assess the counselor's degree of perceived attractiveness on these three items, using the following scale for rating: 1, not at all attractive; 2, minimally attractive; 3, somewhat attractive; 4, quite attractive; 5, very attractive.

1. Appearance

| 1 | 2 | 3 | 4 | 5 |

2. Demeanor

| 1 | 2 | 2 | 4 | 5 |

3. Grooming, hygiene

| 1 | 2 | 3 | 4 | 5 |

(continued)

POSTEVALUATION   (continued)

II. Behavioral Cues

Instructions: Check "Yes" if the counselor demonstrated the following skills and behaviors; "No" if they were not demonstrated.

4. Use of structure
   Yes _____ No _____
5. Moderate level of self-disclosure
   Yes _____ No _____
6. Content of self-disclosure similar to client's concerns and experiences
   Yes _____ No _____
7. Disclosure of factual, nonintimate material (since this is an initial session)
   Yes _____ No _____
8. Responsive nonverbal behaviors
   a. Eye contact
   Yes _____ No _____
   b. Direct body orientation facing client
   Yes _____ No _____
   c. Smiling (intermittent, not constant)
   Yes _____ No _____

Observer comments: _____
_____

PART FOUR

This part of the post evaluation will also be conducted in triads so that each person can assume the roles of counselor, client, and observer. For continuity, you may wish to stay in the same triads you used in Part Three of the postevaluation and trade roles in the same sequence.

Instructions to Counselors

You will be conducting a 30-minute *problem identification interview* — one in which you assess or explore the client's primary problems or concerns. During this interview, your task is to demonstrate behaviors associated with expertness and trustworthiness listed on the "Expertness and Trustworthiness Checklist" that follows (Chapter Objective Four). Remember, too, that the purposes of trying to enhance your perceived expertness and trustworthiness during this stage of counseling are to contribute to the client's exploration and understanding of self and of issues, to work toward specificity and concreteness, and to encourage the client to share personal and relevant information with you.

Instructions to Clients

Be sure to have a particular "presenting problem" in mind to discuss with the counselor during this role play. It will be helpful if the problem is something real for you, although it doesn't have to be "heavy." In addition to discussing your "presenting problem" try also to ask several questions related to at least one of the following "tests of trust" — requesting information, telling a secret, asking a favor, putting yourself down, inconveniencing the counselor, or questioning the counselor's motives.

Instructions to Observers

Watch, listen, and assess the use of the counselor's behaviors associated with competence and trustworthiness. Use the "Expertness and Trustworthiness Checklist" that follows as a guide for your observation and feedback.

EXPERTNESS AND TRUSTWORTHINESS CHECKLIST

I. Expertness

Instructions to observer: Check "Yes" if the counselor demonstrated the behavior; "No" if the counselor did not.

1. Did the counselor maintain eye contact with the client?
   Yes _____ No _____
2. Did the counselor lean toward the client during the interaction?
   Yes _____ No _____
3. Did the counselor talk fluently and without hesitation?
   Yes _____ No _____
4. Did the counselor use relevant and thought-provoking questions?
   Yes _____ No _____
5. Was the counselor attentive to the client?
   Yes _____ No _____
6. Was the counselor's presentation direct and confident?
   Yes _____ No _____
7. Did the counselor accurately interpret any implicit client messages?
   Yes _____ No _____
8. Did the counselor challenge any deletions, distortions, or generalizations apparent in the client's messages?
   Yes _____ No _____

(continued)

II. Trustworthiness

9. Did the counselor convey nonverbal and verbal acceptance of the client's disclosures?
   Yes   No
10. Was the counselor's nonverbal behavior responsive and dynamic?
   Yes   No
11. Did the counselor engage in accurate paraphrasing of the client's messages?
   Yes   No
12. Did the counselor appear to safeguard and respect confidentiality of the client's communication?
   Yes   No

13. Did the counselor seem open, honest, and direct with the client?
   Yes   No
14. Was the information the counselor gave "checked out" (or promised to be checked out) for accuracy and reliability?
   Yes   No
15. Were the counselor's verbal messages consistent with overt actions or behaviors?
   Yes   No
16. Did the counselor respond to any client "tests of trust" appropriately and nondefensively?
   Yes   No

Observer comments: _____

FEEDBACK #8: TRUSTWORTHINESS

II. Client Tests of Trust

2. a. Test of Trust (content): asking a favor
   (process): are you reliable and open with me?
   b. Example response: "I know how difficult it can be to manage without a telephone. Unfortunately, I see someone almost up until the minute you arrive for your session, and so my office is occupied. There's a pay phone in the outer lobby of the building if you find you need to make a call on a particular day or time."

3. a. Test of trust (content): questioning your motives
   (process): do you really care, or are you just going through the motions?
   b. Example response: "Perhaps, Bill, you're feeling unsure about whether I see people like yourself for the money or because I'm sincerely interested in you. One way in which I really enjoy [value] working with you is. . . ."

4. a. Test of trust (content): putting oneself down
   (process): can you accept me even though I'm not too accepting of myself right now?
   b. Example response: "You're feeling pretty upset right now that you're going to be back in the third grade again. I wonder if you're concerned, too, about losing friends or making new ones?"

5. a. Test of trust (content): inconveniencing you
   (process): do you have consistent limits?
   b. Example response: "Mary, I'm not really sure anymore when to expect you. I noticed you've

changed your appointment time several times in the last few weeks at the last minute. I want to be sure I'm here or available when you do come in, so it would help if you could decide on one time that suits you and then just one back-up time in case the first time doesn't work out. If you can give some advance notice of a need to change times, then I won't have to postpone or cancel out on you because of my schedule conflicts."

6. a. Test of trust (content): telling you a secret
   (process): how much is it safe to disclose with you?
   b. Example response: "You're in a quandary right now about this pregnancy. It's probably hard enough just to tell me about it. You're also saying it's something you want to keep secret between the two of us."

☐ SUGGESTED READINGS

Bandler, R., & Grinder, J. (1975). *The structure of magic: A book about language and therapy* (Vol. 1). Palo Alto, CA: Science & Behavior Books.

Barak, A., Patkin, J., & Dell, D. M. (1982). Effects of certain counselor behaviors on perceived expertness and attractiveness. *Journal of Counseling Psychology, 29,* 261–267.

Corrigan, J. D., Dell, D. M., Lewis, K. N., & Schmidt, L. D. (1980). Counseling as a social influence process: A review. *Journal of Counseling Psychology, 27,* 395–441.

Day, R. W., & Sparacio, R. T. (1980). Structuring the counseling process. *Personnel and Guidance Journal, 59,* 246–250.

Dorn, F. J. (1984a). *Counseling as applied social psychology: An introduction to the social influence model.* Springfield, IL: Charles C Thomas.

Dorn, F. J. (1984b). The social influence model: A social psychological approach to counseling. *Personnel and Guidance Journal, 62,* 342–345.

Fong, M. L., & Cox, B. G. (1983). Trust as an underlying dynamic in the counseling process: How clients test trust. *Personnel and Guidance Journal, 62,* 163–166.

Goldstein, A. P. (1986). Relationship-enhancement methods. In F. H. Kanfer & A. P. Goldstein (Eds.), *Helping people change* (3rd ed.) (pp. 19–65). New York: Pergamon Press.

Goodyear, R., & Robyak, J. (1981). Counseling as an interpersonal influence process: A perspective for counseling practice. *Personnel and Guidance Journal, 60,* 654–657.

Heppner, P. P., & Heesacker, M. (1982). Interpersonal influence process in real-life counseling: Investigating client perceptions, counselor experience level, and counselor power over time. *Journal of Counseling Psychology, 29,* 215–223.

Heppner, P. P., & Heesacker, M. (1983). Perceived counselor attractiveness, client expectations, and client satisfaction with counseling. *Journal of Counseling Psychology, 30,* 31–39.

Johnson, D. W. (1986). *Reaching out: Interpersonal effectiveness and self-actualization* (3rd ed.). Englewood Cliffs, NJ: Prentice-Hall, Chapter 3, "Developing and Maintaining Trust."

LaCrosse, M. B. (1980). Perceived counselor social influence and counseling outcomes: Validity of the Counselor Rating Form. *Journal of Counseling Psychology, 27,* 320–327.

LaFromboise, T. D., & Dixon, D. N. (1981). American Indian perception of trustworthiness in a counseling interview. *Journal of Counseling Psychology, 28,* 135–139.

Rothmeier, R. C., & Dixon, D. N. (1980). Trustworthiness and influence: A reexamination in an extended counseling analogue. *Journal of Counseling Psychology, 27,* 315–319.

Senour, M. (1982). How counselors influence clients. *Personnel and Guidance Journal, 60,* 345–350.

Siegel, J. C. (1980). Effects of objective evidence of expertness, nonverbal behavior, and subject sex on client-perceived expertness. *Journal of Counseling Psychology, 27,* 117–121.

Strong, S. R., & Claiborn, C. (1982). *Change through interaction: Social psychological processes of counseling and psychotherapy.* New York: Wiley-Interscience.

Vargas, A. M., & Borkowski, J. G. (1982). Physical attractiveness and counseling skills. *Journal of Counseling Psychology, 29,* 246–255.

FEEDBACK: POSTEVALUATION

PART TWO

1. f. Questioning your motives to see whether you really care

2. b. Telling you a secret, something she perhaps feels embarrassed about

3. c. Asking you a favor; in this case, it is probably a reasonable one

4. a. Requesting information overtly — but covertly wondering whether your personal life is together enough to help the client or whether you have enough significant life experiences similar to his own to help him

5. e. Trying to inconvenience you to see whether you have limits and how you set them and follow through on them

6. d. Putting herself down by revealing some part of herself she feels is "bad" and also something that will test your reaction to her

NONVERBAL BEHAVIOR

FOUR

Nonverbal behavior plays an important role in our communication and relationships with others. In communicating, we tend to emphasize the spoken word. Yet much of the meaning of a message, 65% or more, is conveyed by our nonverbal behavior (Birdwhistell, 1970). Knapp (1978, p. 38) defines nonverbal behavior as "all human communication events which transcend spoken or written words." Of course, many nonverbal behaviors are interpreted by verbal symbols. Nonverbal behavior is an important part of counseling because of the tremendous amount of information it communicates.

Counselors can learn much about a client by becoming sensitized to the client's nonverbal cues. Moreover, the counselor's nonverbal behavior has a great deal of impact on the client. One of the primary kinds of client verbal messages dealt with in counseling—the affective message—is highly dependent on nonverbal means of communication. Ekman and Friesen (1969a, p. 88) have noted that much of the information that can be gleaned from words of clients is derived from their nonverbal behavior. Schutz (1967), in his book *Joy: Expanding Human Awareness,* has stated that the "close connection between the emotional and the physical is evident in the verbal idioms that have developed in social interaction. Feelings and behavior are expressed in terms of all parts of the body, of body movement, and of bodily functions" (pp. 25–26). Schutz provided a list of some of these terms that associate the physical with the emotional: "lost your head, chin up, hair-raising, get it off your chest, no backbone, tight-fisted, hard-nosed, butterflies in the stomach, brokenhearted, stiff upper lip, eyebrow lifting, sweat of your brow, stand on your own feet, tight ass, choke up, and shrug it off"—to name a few (pp. 25–26).

Five dimensions of nonverbal behavior with significant effects on communication are *kinesics, paralinguistics, proxemics, environmental factors,* and *time.* Body motion, or kinesic behavior, includes gestures, body movements, facial expressions, eye behavior, and posture (Knapp, 1972,

p. 5). Associated with the work of Birdwhistell (1970), kinesics also involves physical characteristics that remain relatively unchanged during a conversation, such as body physique, height, weight, and general appearance. In addition to observing body motion, counseling involves identifying nonverbal vocal cues called paralanguage—the "how" of the message. Paralanguage includes voice qualities and vocalizations (Trager, 1958). Silent pauses and speech errors can also be considered part of paralanguage (Knapp, 1978, p. 19). Also of interest to counselors is the area of proxemics (Hall, 1966)—that is, one's use of social and personal space. As it affects the counseling relationship, proxemics involves the size of the room, seating arrangements, touch, and distance between counselor and client.

Perception of one's environment is another important part of nonverbal behavior because people react emotionally to their surroundings. Environments can produce effects on clients such as arousal or boredom and comfort or stress depending on the degree to which an individual tunes into or screens out relevant parts of the surroundings. A fifth aspect of nonverbal behavior involves perception and use of time. Time can be a significant factor in counseling. Time factors include promptness or delay in starting and ending sessions as well as the amount of time spent in communicating with a client about particular topics or events.

☐ OBJECTIVES

1. From a list of client descriptions and nonverbal client behaviors, describe one possible meaning associated with each nonverbal behavior.
2. In an interview situation, identify as many nonverbal behaviors of the person with whom you are communicating as possible. Describe the possible meanings associated with these behaviors. The nonverbal behaviors you identify may come from any one or all of the categories of kinesics, or body motion; paralinguistics, or voice qualities; proxemics, or room space and distance; and the person's general appearance.
3. Demonstrate effective use of counselor nonverbal behaviors in a role-play interview.
4. Identify at least four out of five occasions for responding to client nonverbal behavior in an interview.

☐ CLIENT NONVERBAL BEHAVIOR

An important part of a counselor's repertory is the capacity to discriminate various nonverbal behaviors of clients and their possible meanings. Recognizing and exploring client nonverbal cues is important in counseling for several reasons. First of all, clients' nonverbal behaviors are clues about their emotions. Even more generally, nonverbal behaviors are part of clients' expressions of themselves. As Perls states, "Everything the patient does, obvious or concealed, is an expression of the self" (1973, p. 75). Much of a client's nonverbal behavior may be obvious to you but hidden to the client. Passons (1975, p. 102) points out that most clients are more aware of their words than of their nonverbal behavior. Exploring nonverbal communication may give clients a more complete understanding of their behavior.

Nonverbal client cues may represent more "leakage" than client verbal messages do (Ekman & Friesen, 1969a). Leakage is the communication of messages that are valid yet are not sent intentionally. Passons (1975) suggests that, because of this leakage, client nonverbal behavior may portray the client more accurately than verbal messages (p. 102). He notes that "nonverbal behaviors are generally more spontaneous than verbal behaviors. Words can be selected and monitored prior to being emitted. . . . Nonverbal behaviors, on the other hand, are not as easily subject to control" (p. 102). A client may come in and *tell* you one story and in nonverbal language convey a completely different story (Erickson, Rossi, & Rossi, 1976).

Knapp (1978, p. 20) points out that nonverbal and verbal behavior are interrelated. It is helpful to recognize the ways nonverbal cues support verbal messages. Knapp identifies six such ways:

1. *Repetition:* The verbal message is to "come in and sit down"; the hand gesture pointing to the room and chair is a nonverbal repeater.
2. *Contradiction:* The verbal message is "I like you," communicated with a frown and an angry tone of voice. Some evidence suggests that when we receive contradictory verbal and nonverbal messages, we tend to believe the nonverbal one.
3. *Substitution:* Often a nonverbal message is used in lieu of a verbal one. For example, if you ask someone "How are you?" and you get

a smile, the smile substitutes for a "Very good today."

4. *Complementation:* A nonverbal message can complement a verbal message by modifying or elaborating the message. For example, if someone is talking about feeling uncomfortable and begins talking faster with more speech errors, these nonverbal messages add to the verbal one of discomfort.

5. *Accent:* Nonverbal messages can emphasize verbal ones and often heighten the impact of a verbal message. For example, if you are communicating verbal concern, your message may come through stronger with nonverbal cues such as furrow of the brows, frown, or tears. The kind of emotion one conveys is detected best by facial expressions. The body conveys a better description of the intensity of the emotion (Ekman, 1964; Ekman & Friesen, 1967).

6. *Regulation:* Nonverbal communication helps to regulate the flow of conversation. Have you ever noticed that when you nod your head at someone after he or she speaks, the person tends to keep talking? But if you look away and shift in body position, the person may stop talking, at least momentarily. Whether or not we realize it, we rely on certain nonverbal cues as feedback for starting or stopping a conversation and for indicating whether the other person is listening [pp. 21–24].*

Identifying the relation between the client's verbal and nonverbal communication may yield a more accurate picture of the client, the client's feelings, and the concerns that have led the client to seek help. In addition, the counselor can detect the extent to which the client's nonverbal behavior and verbal behavior match or are congruent. Frequent discrepancies between the client's expressions may indicate lack of integration or some conflict (Passons, 1975).

Nonverbal behavior has received a great deal of attention in recent years in newspapers, magazine articles, and popular books. These publications may have value in increasing awareness of nonverbal behaviors. However, the meanings that have been attached to a particular behavior may have become oversimplified. It is important to note that the meaning of nonverbal behavior will vary with people and situations (contexts). For example, water in the eyes may be a sign of happiness and glee for one person; for another, it may mean anger, frustration, or trouble with contact lenses. A person who has a lisp may be dependent; another may have a speech impediment. Twisting, rocking, or squirming in a seat might mean anxiety for one person and a stomach cramp for someone else. Further, nonverbal behaviors of one culture may have different or even opposite meanings in another culture. Watson (1970) reports significant differences among cultures in contact and noncontact nonverbal behaviors (distance, touch, eye contact, and so on). As an example, in some cultures, avoidance of eye contact is regarded as an indication of respect. We simply caution you to be careful not to assume that nonverbal behavior has the same meaning or effect for all. It is important to remember that much of what we know about client nonverbal behavior is extrapolated from research on "typical populations" or from analog studies, thus limiting the generalizability of the results.

Our Inventory of Nonverbal Behavior (Table 4-1) presents some possible categories of nonverbal behavior in kinesics, paralinguistics, proxemics, environment, and time and the *probable* or *possible* meanings associated with each nonverbal behavior. Remember, the effect or meaning of each nonverbal behavior we have presented is very tentative; these meanings will vary with people, context, and culture. We present some possible meanings only to help increase your awareness about different behaviors, not to make you an expert on client feelings by using an inventory to generalize meanings applicable to all clients. Any client nonverbal behavior must be interpreted with respect to both the antecedents of the behavior and the counselor's reaction that follows the behavior. To show you the importance of interpreting the meaning of nonverbal behavior within a given context, we present various counselor/client interaction descriptions to accompany the nonverbal cues and possible meanings in this inventory.

*Excerpt adapted from *Nonverbal Communication in Human Interaction,* 2nd Ed., by Mark L. Knapp. Copyright © 1978 by Holt, Rinehart and Winston, Inc. Reprinted by permission of the publisher.

Kinesics

Kinesics involves eyes, face, head, gestures, body expressions, and movements.

TABLE 4-1. Inventory of nonverbal behavior

Nonverbal dimension	Observed behavior	Example of counselor/client interaction (context)	Possible effect or meaning
I. Kinesics			
Eyes			
____	Direct eye contact	Client has just shared concern with counselor. Counselor responds; client maintains eye contact.	Readiness or willingness for interpersonal communication or exchange; attentiveness
____	Lack of sustained eye contact	Each time counselor brings up the topic of client's family, client looks away.	Withdrawal or avoidance of interpersonal exchange; or respect or deference
		Client demonstrates intermittent breaks in eye contact while conversing with counselor.	Respect or deference
		Client mentions sexual concerns, then abruptly looks away. When counselor initiates this topic, client looks away again.	Withdrawal from topic of conversation; discomfort or embarrassment; or preoccupation
____	Lowering eyes—looking down or away	Client talks at some length about alternatives to present job situation; pauses briefly and looks down; then resumes speaking and eye contact with counselor.	Preoccupation
____	Staring or fixation on person or object	Counselor has just asked client to consider consequences of a certain decision. Client is silent and gazes at a picture on the wall.	Preoccupation; possibly rigidity or uptightness
____	Darting eyes or blinking rapidly—rapid eye movements; twitching brow	Client indicates desire to discuss a topic yet is hesitant. As counselor probes, client's eyes move around the room rapidly.	Excitation or anxiety; or wearing contact lenses
____	Squinting or furrow on brow	Client has just asked counselor for advice. Counselor explains role, and client squints and furrows appear in client's brow.	Thought or perplexity; or avoidance of person or topic
		Counselor suggests possible things for client to explore in difficulties with parents. Client doesn't respond verbally; furrow in brow appears.	Avoidance of person or topic
____	Moisture or tears	Client has just reported recent death of father; tears well up in client's eyes.	Sadness; frustration; sensitive areas of concern
		Client reports real progress during past week in marital communication; eyes get moist.	Happiness
____	Eye shifts	Counselor has just asked client to remember significant events in week; client pauses and looks away, then responds and looks back.	Processing or recalling material; or keen interest; satisfaction
____	Pupil dilation	Client discusses spouse's sudden disinterest and pupils dilate.	Alarm; or keen interest
		Client leans forward while counselor talks and pupils dilate.	Keen interest; satisfaction
Mouth			
____	Smiles	Counselor has just asked client to report positive events of the week. Client smiles, then recounts some of these instances.	Positive thought, feeling, or action in content of conversation
		Client responds with a smile to counselor's verbal greeting at beginning of interview.	Greeting

(continued)

TABLE 4-1. Inventory of nonverbal behavior (continued)

Nonverbal dimension	Observed behavior	Example of counselor/client interaction (context)	Possible effect or meaning

I. Kinesics (continued)

Mouth

____	Tight lips (pursed together)	Client has just described efforts at sticking to a difficult living arrangement. Pauses and purses lips together.	Stress or determination; anger or hostility
		Client just expressed irritation at counselor's lateness. Client sits with lips pursed together while counselor explains the reasons.	Anger or hostility
____	Lower lip quivers or biting lip	Client starts to describe her recent experience of being raped. As client continues to talk, her lower lip quivers; occasionally she bites her lip.	Anxiety or sadness
		Client discusses loss of parental support after a recent divorce. Client bites her lip after discussing this.	Sadness
____	Open mouth without speaking	Counselor has just expressed feelings about a block in the relationship. Client's mouth drops open; client says he was not aware of it.	Surprise; or suppression of yawn — fatigue
		It has been a long session. As counselor talks, client's mouth parts slightly.	Suppression of yawn — fatigue

Facial Expressions

____	Eye contact with smiles	Client talks very easily and smoothly, occasionally smiling; maintains eye contact for most of session.	Happiness or comfortableness
____	Eyes strained; furrow on brow; mouth tight	Client has just reported strained situation with a child. Then client sits with lips pursed together and a frown.	Anger; or concern; sadness
____	Eyes rigid, mouth rigid (unanimated)	Client states she or he has nothing to say; there is no evident expression or alertness on client's face.	Preoccupation; anxiety; fear
____	Face flushes, red blotches appear on neck	Client has started to discuss a sexual concern.	Anxiety, discomfort, embarrassment

Head

____	Nodding head up and down	Client just expressed concern over the status of her health; counselor reflects client's feelings. Client nods head and says "That's right."	Confirmation; agreement; or listening, attending
		Client nods head during counselor explanation.	Listening; attending
____	Shaking head from left to right	Counselor has just suggested that client's continual lateness to sessions may be an issue that needs to be discussed. Client responds with "No" and shakes head from left to right.	Disagreement; or disapproval
____	Hanging head down, jaw down toward chest	Counselor initiates topic of termination. Client lowers head toward chest, then says he is not ready to stop the counseling sessions.	Sadness; concern

(continued)

TABLE 4-1. Inventory of nonverbal behavior (continued)

Nonverbal dimension	Observed behavior	Example of counselor/client interaction (context)	Possible effect or meaning

I. *Kinesics (continued)*

Shoulders

	—— Shrugging	Client reports that spouse just walked out with no explanation. Client shrugs shoulders while describing this.	Uncertainty; or ambivalence
	—— Leaning forward	Client has been sitting back in the chair. Counselor discloses something about herself; client leans forward and asks counselor a question about the experience.	Eagerness; attentiveness, openness to communication
	—— Slouched, stooped, rounded, or turned away from person	Client reports feeling inadequate and defeated because of poor grades; slouches in chair after saying this.	Sadness or ambivalence; or lack of receptivity to interpersonal exchange
		Client reports difficulty in talking. As counselor pursues this, client slouches in chair and turns shoulders away from counselor.	Lack of receptivity to interpersonal exchange

Arms and hands

	—— Arms folded across chest	Counselor has just initiated conversation. Client doesn't respond verbally; sits back in chair with arms crossed against chest.	Avoidance of interpersonal exchange or dislike
	—— Trembling and fidgety hands	Client expresses fear of suicide; hands tremble while talking about this.	Anxiety or anger
		In a loud voice, client expresses resentment; client's hands shake while talking.	Anger
	—— Fist clenching to objects or holding hands tightly	Client has just come in for initial interview. Says that he or she feels uncomfortable; hands are clasped together tightly.	Anxiety or anger
		Client expresses hostility toward boss; clenches fists while talking.	Anger
	—— Arms unfolded — arms and hands gesturing in conversation	Counselor has just asked a question; client replies and gestures during reply.	Accenting or emphasizing point in conversation; or openness to interpersonal exchange
		Counselor initiates new topic. Client readily responds; arms are unfolded at this time.	Openness to interpersonal exchange
	—— Rarely gesturing, hands and arms stiff	Client arrives for initial session. Responds to counselor's questions with short answers. Arms are kept down at side.	Tension or anger
		Client has been referred; sits with arms down at side while explaining reasons for referral and irritation at being here.	Anger

Legs and feet

	—— Legs and feet appear comfortable and relaxed	Client's legs and feet are relaxed without excessive movement while client freely discusses personal concerns.	Openness to interpersonal exchange; relaxation
	—— Crossing and uncrossing legs repeatedly	Client is talking rapidly in spurts about problems; continually crosses and uncrosses legs while doing so.	Anxiety; depression

(continued)

TABLE 4-1. Inventory of nonverbal behavior (continued)

Nonverbal dimension	Observed behavior	Example of counselor/client interaction (context)	Possible effect or meaning
Legs and feet			
——	Foot tapping	Client is tapping feet during a lengthy counselor summary; client interrupts counselor to make a point.	Anxiety; impatience—wanting to make a point
——	Legs and feet appear stiff and controlled	Client is open and relaxed while talking about job. When counselor introduces topic of marriage, client's legs become more rigid.	Uptightness or anxiety; closed to extensive interpersonal exchange
Total body			
——	Facing other person squarely or leaning forward	Client shares a concern and faces counselor directly while talking; continues to face counselor while counselor responds.	Openness to interpersonal communication and exchange
——	Turning of body orientation at an angle, not directly facing person, or slouching in seat	Client indicates some difficulty in "getting into" interview. Counselor probes for reasons; client turns body away.	Less openness to interpersonal exchange
——	Rocking back and forth in chair or squirming in seat	Client indicates a lot of nervousness about an approaching conflict situation. Client rocks as this is discussed.	Concern; worry; anxiety
——	Stiff—sitting erect and rigidly on edge of chair	Client indicates some uncertainty about direction of interview; sits very stiff and erect at this time.	Tension; anxiety; concern
——	Repetitive twisting of hair, tapping of fingers	Client responds with short, minimal, non-self-revealing responses.	Feeling distracted, bored, or uncomfortable —or indication of some unexpressed emotion
——	Breathing becomes slower and deeper	Client begins to settle back in chair and relate a positive event that occurred during the week.	Client is feeling more comfortable and relaxed; breathing changes reflect the decreased arousal

II. Paralinguistics

Voice level and pitch			
——	Whispering or inaudibility	Client has been silent for a long time. Counselor probes; client responds, but in a barely audible voice.	Difficulty in disclosing
——	Pitch changes	Client is speaking at a moderate voice level while discussing job. Then client begins to talk about boss, and voice pitch rises considerably.	Topics of conversation have different emotional meanings
Fluency in speech			
——	Stuttering, hesitations, speech errors	Client is talking rapidly about feeling uptight in certain social situations; client stutters and makes some speech errors while doing so.	Sensitivity about topic in conversation; or anxiety and discomfort

(continued)

TABLE 4-1. Inventory of nonverbal behavior (continued)

Nonverbal dimension	Observed behavior	Example of counselor/client interaction (context)	Possible effect or meaning
II. *Paralinguistics (continued)*			
Fluency in speech			
	____ Whining or lisp	Client is complaining about having a hard time losing weight; voice goes up like a whine.	Dependency or emotional emphasis
	____ Rate of speech slow, rapid, or jerky	Client begins interview talking slowly about a bad weekend. As topic shifts to client's feelings about himself, client talks more rapidly.	Sensitivity to topics of conversation; or topics have different emotional meanings
	____ Silence	Client comes in and counselor invites client to talk; client remains silent.	Reluctance to talk; or preoccupation
		Counselor has just asked client a question. Client pauses and thinks over a response.	Preoccupation; or desire to continue speaking after making a point
III. *Proxemics*			
Distance			
	____ Moves away	Counselor has just confronted client; client moves back before responding verbally.	Signal that space has been invaded; increased arousal, discomfort
	____ Moves closer	Midway through session, client moves chair toward helper.	Seeking closer interaction, more intimacy
Position in room			
	____ Sits behind or next to an object in the room, such as table or desk	A new client comes in and sits in a chair that is distant from counselor.	Seeking protection or more space
	____ Sits near counselor without any intervening objects	Client who has been to see counselor before chooses chair closest to counselor.	Expression of adequate comfort level
Touch			
	____ Handshake accompanied by smile and verbal greeting	Client greets counselor and returns counselor's outstretched arm for handshake.	Desire to initiate interaction nonverbally
	____ Touch on client arm	Counselor touches client's arm when client is expressing concern over her extremely ill child.	Desire to convey support and comfort
IV. *Environment*			
	____ Counseling room is small, has subdued colors and soft lights	Client states he feels lethargic. Lack of self-disclosure is also evident.	So little arousal associated with counseling environment that client is too comfortable to "work"
V. *Time*			
	____ Client discusses many unrelated topics during session	Counselor starts to terminate session. Client then states she has a "big problem" to bring up.	Anxiety about bringing up problem or manipulation to get counselor to spend more time with her

TABLE 4-1. Inventory of nonverbal behavior (continued)

Nonverbal dimension	Observed behavior	Example of counselor/client interaction (context)	Possible effect or meaning
V. *Time (continued)*			
_____	Repeated delays by client in responding to counselor	After counselor makes a statement or asks a question, client waits for a while before responding verbally.	Hesitation in responding to counselor or discomfort in relationship

Eyes. In our culture, we show a great deal of interest in one another's eyes. Western culture particularly emphasizes the importance of visual contact in interpersonal interactions. Therapists who are sensitive to the eye area of clients may detect various client emotions, such as the following:

Surprise: Eyebrows are raised so that they appear curved and high.
Fear: Brows are raised and drawn together.
Anger: Brows are lowered and drawn together. Vertical lines show up between the brows. The eyes may appear to have a "cold stare."
Sadness: Inner corners of the eyebrows are drawn up until the inner corners of the upper eyelids are raised.

Also significant to counselor/client interactions is eye contact (also called "direct mutual gaze"). Eye contact may indicate expressions of feeling, willingness for interpersonal exchange, or a desire to continue or stop talking. Lack of eye contact or looking away may signal withdrawal, embarrassment, or discomfort (Exline & Winters, 1965). Contrary to popular opinion, lack of eye contact does not seem to suggest deception or lack of truthfulness (Sitton & Griffin, 1981). People who generally avoid eye contact may nevertheless make eye contact when they seek feedback. Eye contact may also signal a desire to pause in the conversation or to say something (Knapp, 1978). The more shared glances there are between two persons, the higher the level of emotional involvement and comfort. An averted gaze may serve to hide shame over expressing a particular feeling that is seen as culturally or socially taboo (Exline & Winters, 1965). Any kind of reduced eye movement, such as staring or fixated eyes, may signal rigidity or preoccupation in thought (Singer, 1975). Darting or rapid eye movement may mean excitation, anger, or poorly fitting contact lenses.

Excessive blinking (normal = 6 to 10 times per minute in adults) may be related to anxiety. During periods of attentiveness and concentration, blinking usually decreases in frequency. Moisture or tears in the eyes may have contrasting emotional meanings for different people. Eye shifts — away from the counselor to a wall, for example — may indicate that the client is processing or recalling material (Singer, 1975). Pupil dilation, which is an autonomic (involuntary) response, may indicate emotional arousal, attentiveness, and interest (Hess, 1975). Although pupil dilation seems to occur under conditions that represent positive interpersonal attitudes, little or no evidence supports the belief that the opposite (pupil constriction) is associated with negative attitudes toward people (Knapp, 1978).

In counseling, *more mutual gazing,* or eye contact, seems to occur when —

1. Greater physical distance exists between the counselor and client.
2. Comfortable, less personal topics are discussed.
3. Interpersonal involvement exists between the counselor and client.
4. You are listening rather than talking.
5. You are female.
6. You are from a culture that emphasizes visual contact in interaction.

Less gazing occurs when —

1. The counselor and client are physically close.
2. Difficult, intimate topics are being discussed.
3. Either the counselor or the client is not interested in the other's reactions.
4. You are talking rather than listening.
5. You are embarrassed, ashamed, or trying to hide something.
6. You are from a culture that has sanctions on visual contact during some kinds of interpersonal interactions.

Some behaviors of the eyes and their conjectured meanings are presented in Table 4-1; however, these meanings must be viewed idiosyncratically for each client, depending on the context and culture.

Mouth. Smiles are associated with the emotions of happiness and joy. Tight lips may mean stress, frustration, hostility, or anger. Lower-lip quivering or biting lips may connote anxiety or sadness. An open mouth without speaking may indicate surprise or difficulty in talking (see Table 4-1).

Facial expressions. The face of the other person may be the most important stimulus in an interaction, because it is the primary communicator of emotional information (Ekman, Friesen, & Ellsworth, 1972). Facial expressions are used to initiate or terminate conversation, provide feedback on the comments of others, underline or support verbal communication, and convey emotions. Most of the time, the face conveys multiple emotions (Ekman & Friesen, 1969b). For example, one emotion may be conveyed in one part of the face and another in a different area. It is rare for one's face to express only a single emotion at a time. More often than not, the face depicts a blend of varying emotions.

Different facial areas express different emotions. Happiness, surprise, and disgust may be conveyed through the lower face (mouth and jaw region) and the eye area, whereas sadness is conveyed with the eyes. The lower face and brows express anger; fear is usually indicated by the eyes (Ekman, Friesen, & Tomkins, 1971). Although it is hard to "read" someone by facial cues alone, these cues may support other nonverbal indexes of emotion within the context of an interview. The facial expressions listed in Table 4-1 are combinations of the mouth and eye regions.

Facial expressions conveying the basic emotions described above do *not* seem to vary much among cultures. According to Harper, Wiens, and Matarazzo (1978, p. 99), "There is considerable evidence that facial expressions of emotion themselves are 'universal' or not 'culture bound.'" In other words, primary or basic emotions such as anger, disgust, fear, sadness, and happiness do seem to be represented by the same facial expressions across cultures, although individual cultural norms may influence how and when such emotions are expressed.

Head. The movements of the head can be a rich source for interpreting a person's emotional or affective state. The head held erect, facing the other person in a relaxed way, indicates receptivity to interpersonal communication. Nodding the head up and down implies confirmation or agreement. Shaking the head from left to right may signal disapproval or disagreement. Shaking the head with accompanying leg movements may connote anger. Holding the head rigidly may mean anxiety or anger, and hanging the head down toward the chest may reflect disapproval or sadness. See Table 4-1 for an outline of these five behaviors and their associated meanings.

Shoulders. The orientation of the shoulders may give clues to a person's attitude about interpersonal exchanges. Shoulders leaning forward may indicate eagerness, attentiveness, or receptivity to interpersonal communication. Slouched, stooped, rounded, or turned-away shoulders may mean that the person is not receptive to interpersonal exchanges. This posture also may reflect sadness or ambivalence. Shrugging shoulders may mean uncertainty, puzzlement, ambivalence, or frustration.

Arms and hands. The arms and hands can be very expressive of an individual's emotional state. Arms folded across the chest may signal avoidance of interpersonal exchange or reluctance to disclose. Anxiety or anger may be reflected in trembling and fidgety hands or clenching fists. Arms and hands that rarely gesture and are stiffly positioned may mean tension, anxiety, or anger. Relaxed, unfolded arms and hands gesturing during conversation can signal openness to interpersonal involvement or accentuation of points in conversation. The autonomic response of perspiration of the palms may reflect anxiety or arousal.

Legs and feet. If the legs and feet appear comfortable and relaxed, the person may be signaling openness to interpersonal exchange. Shuffling feet or a tapping foot may mean that the person is experiencing some anxiety or impatience or wants to make a point. Repeatedly crossing and uncrossing legs may indicate anxiety, depression, or impatience. A person who appears to be very "controlled" or to have "stiff" legs and feet may be uptight, anxious, or closed to an extensive interpersonal exchange (see Table 4-1).

Total body and body movements. Most body movements do not have precise social meanings. Body movements are learned and culture-specific.

The body movements discussed in this section are derived from analyses of (and therefore most applicable to) White adults from middle and upper socioeconomic classes in the United States.

Body movements are not produced randomly. Instead, they appear to be linked to human speech. From birth, there seems to be an effort to synchronize body movements and speech sounds. In adults, lack of synchrony may be a sign of pathology. Lack of synchrony in body movements and speech between two persons may indicate an absence of listening behavior on the part of both (Condon & Ogston, 1966).

One of the most important functions of body movements is *regulation.* Various body movements regulate or maintain an interpersonal interaction. For example, important body movements that accompany the counselor's verbal greeting of a client include eye gaze, smiling, use of hand gestures, and a vertical or sideways motion of the head (Krivonos & Knapp, 1975). Body movements are also useful to terminate an interaction, as at the end of a counseling interview. Nonverbal exit or leave-taking behaviors accompanying a verbal summary statement include decreased eye gaze and positioning of your body near the exit. In terminating an interaction, particularly a therapeutic one, it is also important to display nonverbal behaviors that signify support, such as smiling, shaking the client's hand, touching the client on the arm or shoulder, and nodding your head. As Knapp (1978, p. 213) explains, "Supportiveness tends to offset any negativity which might arise from encounter termination signals while simultaneously setting a positive mood for the next encounter—that is, our conversation has terminated but our relationship hasn't."

Another way that body movements regulate an interaction involves *turn taking*—the exchange of speaker and listener roles within a conversation. Most of the time we take turns rather automatically. "Without much awareness for what we are doing, we use body movements, vocalizations, and some verbal behavior which often seems to accomplish this turn-taking with surprising efficiency" (Knapp, 1978, p. 213). Effective turn taking is important in a counseling interaction because it contributes to the perception that you and the client have a good relationship and that, as the counselor, you are a competent communicator. Conversely, ineffective turn taking may mean that a client perceives you as rude (too many inter-ruptions) or as dominating (not enough talk time for the client).

Duncan (1972, 1974) has found a variety of nonverbal behaviors, called *turn signals,* that regulate the exchange of speaking and listening roles. These turn signals are described in this section. *Turn yielding* occurs when the therapist (as speaker) wants to stop talking and expects a response from the client (as listener). To engage in effective turn yielding, the counselor can ask a question and talk more slowly, slow down the rate of speech, drawl on the last syllable of the last word, utter a "trailer" such as "you know," or use silence. Terminating body movements and gazing at the client will also indicate that it is now the client's turn to talk. If, after a lengthy silence, the client does not respond, more explicit turn-yielding cues may be used, such as touching the client or raising and holding your eyebrows in expectation. Use of these more explicit nonverbal cues may be particularly important with a quiet, nontalkative client.

Turn maintaining occurs when the therapist (or client) wants to keep talking and not yield a turn to the other person, probably because an important idea is being expressed. Signals that indicate turn maintaining include talking louder and continuing or even increasing the gestures and other body movements accompanying your words. Counselors do not want to maintain their turns too often, or the client is likely to feel frustrated and unable to make a point. Conversely, overtalkative clients may try to take control of the interview by maintaining rather than yielding turns.

Turn requesting occurs when either the therapist or the client is listening and wants to talk. Turn requesting may be signified by an upraised index finger, often accompanied by an audible inspiration of breath and straightening or tightening of one's posture. The counselor can use turn-requesting signals more frequently with an overtalkative, rambling client who tends to hang on rather than give up his or her turn as speaker. In fact, to encourage a client to finish more quickly, the counselor can use rapid head nods accompanied by verbalizations of pseudoagreement such as "Yes," "Mm-hmm," and "I see" (Knapp, 1978).

Turn denying occurs when we get a turn-yielding cue from the speaker but don't want to talk. For example, if the client is nontalkative or if the counselor wants the client to take more responsibility for the interaction, the counselor may choose to deny or give up a turn in order to prompt the client to continue talking. Turn-denying signals include a relaxed body posture, silence, and eye gaze. The counselor will also want to exhibit behaviors that show continuing involvement in the ideas expressed by the client by smiling, nodding, or using minimal verbal prompts such as "Mm-hmm."

In addition to regulation, body movements also serve the function of *adaptors.* Adaptors may include such behaviors as picking, scratching, rubbing, and tapping. In counseling, it is important to note the frequency with which a client uses nonverbal adaptors, because these behaviors seem to be associated with emotional arousal and psychological discomfort (Dittmann, 1962; Ekman & Friesen, 1972). Body touching may reflect preoccupation with oneself and withdrawal from the interaction at hand (Freedman, 1972). A client who uses adaptors frequently may be uncomfortable with the counselor or with the topic of discussion. The counselor can use the frequency of client adaptors as an index of the client's overall comfort level during counseling.

Another important aspect of a client's total body is his or her breathing. Changes in breathing rate (slower, faster) or depth (shallower, deeper) provide clues about comfort level, feelings, and significant issues. As clients relax, for example, their breathing usually becomes slower and deeper. Faster, more shallow breathing is more often associated with arousal, distress, discomfort, and anxiety.

Paralinguistics

Paralinguistics includes such extralinguistic variables as voice level (volume), pitch (intonation), rate of speech, and fluency of speech. Pauses and silence also belong in this category. Paralinguistic cues are those pertaining to *how* a message is delivered, although occasionally these vocal cues represent what is said as well.

Vocal cues are important in counseling interactions for several reasons. First, they help to manage the interaction by playing an important role in the exchange of speaker and listener roles—that is, turn taking. As you may recall from the discussion of body movements, certain vocalizations are used to yield, maintain, request, or deny turns. For example, decreased pitch is associated with turn yielding, whereas increased volume and rate of speech are associated with turn maintaining. Second, vocal characteristics convey data about a client's emotional states. You can identify the presence of basic emotions from a client's vocal cues if you are able to make auditory discriminations. In recognizing emotions from vocal cues, it is also important to be knowledgeable about various vocal characteristics of basic emotions. For example, a client who speaks slowly and softly may be feeling sad or may be reluctant to discuss a sensitive topic. Increased volume and rate of speech are usually signs of anger or happiness (see also Table 4-1). Changes in voice level and pitch should be interpreted along with accompanying changes in topics of conversation and changes in other nonverbal behaviors.

Voice level may vary among cultures. Sue and Sue (1977) point out that some Americans have louder voice levels than people of other cultures. In counseling a client from a different cultural background, an American counselor should not automatically conclude that the client's lower voice volume indicates weakness or shyness (Sue & Sue, p. 427).

Vocal cues in the form of speech disturbances or aspects of *fluency* in speech also convey important information for therapists, since client anxiety or discomfort is often detected by identifying the type and frequency of client speech errors. Most speech errors become more frequent as anxiety and discomfort increase (Knapp, 1978).

Pauses and silence are another part of paralinguistics that can give the counselor clues about the level of arousal and anxiety experienced by the client. There are two types of pauses—filled and unfilled.

Filled pauses are those filled simply with some type of phonation such as "uh," or stutters, false starts, repetitions, and slips of the tongue (Knapp, 1978, p. 356). Filled pauses are associated with emotional arousal and anxiety (Knapp, 1978). A client may be more likely to make a false start or a slip of the tongue when anxious or uncomfortable.

Unfilled pauses are those in which no sound occurs. Unfilled pauses occur to give the person time to interpret a message and to make a decision about past, present, or future responses. Unfilled pauses, or periods of silence, serve various functions in a counseling interview. The purpose of an unfilled pause often depends on whether the pause is initiated by the counselor or client. Clients use silence to express emotions, to reflect about an issue, to recall an idea or feeling, to avoid a topic, or to catch up on the progress of the moment. Counselor-initiated silences are most effective when used with a particular purpose in mind, such as reducing the counselor's level of activity, slowing down the pace of the session, giving the *client* time to think, or transferring some responsibility to the client through turn yielding or turn denying. When therapists pause to meet their own needs, as, for example, because they are at a loss for words, the effects of silence may or may not be so therapeutic. As Hackney and Cormier (1988, p. 44) observe, in such instances, when the effect is therapeutic, the counselor is apt to feel lucky rather than competent.

Proxemics

Proxemics concerns the concept of environmental and personal space (Hall, 1966). As it applies to a counseling interaction, proxemics includes use of space relative to the counseling room, arrangement of the furniture, seating arrangements, and distance between counselor and client. Proxemics also includes a variable that seems to be very important to any human interaction — territoriality. Many people are possessive not only of their belongings but of the space around them. It is important for therapists to communicate nonverbal sensitivity to a client's need for space. A client who feels that his or her space or territory has been encroached on may behave in ways intended to restore the proper distance. Such behaviors may include looking away, changing the topic to a less personal one, or crossing one's arms to provide a "frontal barrier" (Knapp, 1978, p. 119).

In counseling, a distance of three to four feet between counselor and client seems to be the least anxiety-producing and most productive, at least for adult, middle-class Americans (Lecomte, Bernstein, & Dumont, 1981). For these Americans, closer distances may inhibit verbal productivity (Schulz & Barefoot, 1974), although females in Western cultures are generally more tolerant of less personal space than males, especially when interacting with other females (Harper et al., 1978). Disturbed clients also seem to require greater interaction distance (Harper et al., 1978). These spatial limits (three to four feet) may be inappropriate for clients of varying ages or cultures. The very young and very old seem to elicit interaction at closer distances. People from "contact" cultures (cultures where interactants face one another more directly, interact closer to one another, and use more touch and direct eye contact) may use different distances for interpersonal interactions than people from "noncontact" cultures (Watson, 1970). In short, unlike facial expressions, distance setting has no universals.

An important use of proxemics in counseling is to note proxemic *shifts* such as increasing or decreasing space or moving forward or backward. Some evidence suggests that proxemic shifts signal important segments or hiatus points of an interaction, such as the beginning or ending of a topic or a shift to a different subject (Erickson, 1975). Proxemic shifts can give counselors clues about when the client is initiating a new topic, is finishing with a topic, or is avoiding a topic by changing the subject.

Another aspect of proxemics involves seating and furniture arrangement. In Western cultures, most therapists prefer a seating arrangement with no intervening desk or objects, although many clients like to have the protective space or "body buffer" of a desk corner (Harper et al., 1978).

Seating and spatial arrangements are an important part of family therapy as well. Successful family therapists pay attention to family proxemics such as the following: How far apart do family members sit from each other? Who sits next to whom? Who stays closest to the therapist? Answers to these questions about family proxemics provide information about family rules, relationships, boundaries, alliances, roles, and so on.

A final aspect of proxemics has to do with touch. Although touch can be a powerful nonverbal stimulus, its effects in the counseling interaction have rarely been examined. A counselor-initiated touch may be perceived by the client as positive or negative, depending on the type of touch (expression of caring versus intimate gesture) and the context, or situation (supportive versus evaluative). In two recent studies, counseling touch consisting of handshakes and touches to the arm and back had a significant positive effect on the client's evaluation of counseling (Alagna, Whitcher, Fisher, & Wicas, 1979) and on the client's perceptions of the counselor's expertness (Hubble, Noble, & Robinson, 1981). According to Alagna et al. (1979, p. 471), these results

> point up the possibility of setting aside some of the reservations that practitioners experience when they think about physically contacting a client, since under no conditions did communication by touch lead to negative reactions. However, while the effect of touch in this experiment was consistently positive, it is obvious that under certain conditions (e.g. overtly sexual intent), touch in counseling could have negative effects.

Counselors should also be aware that ethical standards such as those adopted by the American Association for Counseling and Development (1981) and the American Psychological Association (1981) state that any form of sexual intimacy with clients, including sexuality in touch, is unethical.

Environment

Counseling and therapy take place in some surroundings, or environment—typically an office, although other indoor and outdoor environments can be used. The same surroundings can affect clients in different ways. Surroundings are perceived as arousing or nonarousing (Mehrabian, 1976). If a client reacts to an environment with low arousal and mild pleasure, the client will feel comfortable and relaxed. Environments need to be moderately arousing so that the client feels relaxed enough to explore her or his problems and to self-disclose. If the client feels so comfortable that the desire to work on a problem is inhibited, the therapist might consider increasing the arousal cues associated with the surroundings by moving the furniture around, using brighter colors, using more light, or even increasing vocal expressiveness. Therapists who talk louder and faster and use more expressive intonation patterns are greater sources of arousal for those around them (Mehrabian, 1976).

An important concept for considering the effects of environmental arousal on clients is *stimulus screening*—the extent to which a person characteristically screens out the less relevant parts of the environment and thereby effectively reduces the environmental load and the person's own arousal level (Mehrabian, 1976). This concept is useful for understanding different reactions of clients to the same room or office. Individuals who screen their environment well, or "screeners," select various parts of their surroundings to which they respond. As a result, they are more focused on key aspects of their surroundings because they screen out less relevant components. Nonscreeners, in contrast, are less selective in what they respond to in any environment. Consequently, nonscreeners experience places as more complex and loaded, which may result in too much arousal and even stress (Mehrabian, 1976). Overall, nonscreeners are more sensitive to the emotional reactions of others and to subtle changes in their environment and tend to react more strongly to such changes.

Time

Time has several dimensions that can affect a therapeutic interaction. One aspect has to do with the counselor's and client's perception of time and promptness or delays in initiating or terminating topics and sessions. Many clients will feel put off by delays or rescheduled appointments and, conversely, feel appreciated and valued when extra time is spent with them. Clients may communicate anxiety or resistance by being late or by waiting until the end of a session to bring up a significant topic. Perceptions of time also vary. Some persons have a highly structured view of time, so that being "on time" or ready to see the counselor (or client) is important. Others have a more casual view of time and do not feel offended or put off if the counselor is late for the appointment and do not expect the counselor to be upset when they arrive later than the designated time.

LEARNING ACTIVITIES #9: CLIENT NONVERBAL COMMUNICATION

I. The purpose of this activity is to have you sample some nonverbal behaviors associated with varying emotions for different regions of the body. You can do this in dyads or in a small group. Act out each of the five emotions listed below, using your face, body, arms, legs, and voice.

1. Sadness, depression
2. Pleasure, satisfaction
3. Anxiety, agitation
4. Anger
5. Confusion, uncertainty

As an example, if the emotion to be portrayed were "surprise," you would show how your eyes, mouth, face, arms, hands, legs and feet, and total body might behave in terms of movement or posture, and you would indicate what your voice level and pitch would be like and how fluent your speech might be. After someone portrays one emotion, other members of the group can share how their nonverbal behaviors associated with the same emotion might differ.

II. This activity will help you develop greater sensitivity to nonverbal behaviors of clients. It can be done

(continued)

in dyads or triads. Select one person to assume the role of the communicator and another to assume the role of the listener. A third person can act as observer. As the communicator, recall a recent time when you felt either (1) very happy, (2) very sad, and (3) very angry. Your task is to retrieve that experience *nonverbally*. Do *not say* anything to the listener, and do *not* tell the listener in advance which of the three emotions you are going to recall. Simply decide which of the three you will recall and tell the listener when to begin. The listener's task is to *observe* the communicator, to *note* nonverbal behaviors and changes during the recall, and, from these, to *guess* which of the three emotional experiences the person was retrieving. After about three to four minutes, stop the interaction to process it. Observers can add behaviors and changes they noted at this time. After the communicator has retrieved one of the emotions, switch roles.

☐ HOW TO WORK WITH CLIENT NONVERBAL BEHAVIOR

Many theoretical approaches emphasize the importance of working with client nonverbal behavior. For example, behavioral counselors may recognize and point out particular nonverbal behaviors of a client that constitute effective or ineffective social skills (Eisler & Frederiksen, 1980). A client who consistently mumbles and avoids eye contact may find such behaviors detrimental to establishing effective interpersonal relationships. Use of effective nonverbal behaviors also forms a portion of assertion training programs (Otter & Guerra, 1976). In Transactional Analysis (TA), nonverbal behaviors are used to assess "ego states," or parts of one's personality used to communicate and relate to others. For example, the "critical" or controlling parent may be associated with a condescending and blaming voice tone, pointing fingers, frowning, hands on hips, and so forth (Woollams & Brown, 1979). TA therapists also note how a client's nonverbal behavior may keep communication going (complementary transactions) or break communication down (crossed transactions). Client-centered therapists use client nonverbal behaviors as indicators of client feelings and emotions. Gestalt therapists help clients recognize their nonverbal behaviors in order to increase awareness of themselves and of conflicts or discrepancies. For example, a client may say "Yes, I want to get my degree" and at the same time shake his head no and lower his voice tone and eyes. Body-oriented therapists actively use body language as a tool for understanding hidden and unresolved "business," conflicts, and personality. Adlerian counselors use nonverbal reactions of clients as an aid to discovering purposes (often hidden) of behavior and mistaken logic. Family therapists are concerned with a family's nonverbal (analogic) communication as well as verbal (digital) communication. A tool based on family nonverbal communication is known as "family sculpture" (Duhl, Kantor, & Duhl, 1973). Family sculpture is a nonverbal arrangement of people placed in various physical positions in space to represent their relationship to one another. In an extension of this technique, family *choreography* (Papp, 1976), the sculptures or spatial arrangements are purposely moved to realign existing relationships and create new patterns.

Passons (1975) has described five ways of responding to client nonverbal behavior in an interview. His suggestions are useful because they represent ways of working with clients nonverbally that are consistent with various theoretical orientations. These five ways are the following:

1. Ascertain the congruence between the client's verbal and nonverbal behavior.
2. Note or respond to discrepancies, or mixed verbal and nonverbal messages.
3. Respond to or note nonverbal behaviors when the client is silent or not speaking.
4. Focus on nonverbal behaviors to change the content of the interview.
5. Note changes in client nonverbal behavior that have occurred in an interview or over a series of sessions.

Congruence between Behaviors

The counselor can determine whether the client's verbal message is congruent with his or her nonverbal behavior. An example of congruence is when the client expresses confusion about a situation accompanied by squinting of the eyes or furrowing of the brow. Another client may say "I'm really happy with the way things have been working since I've been coming to see you," which is correlated with eye contact, relaxed body posture, and a smile. The counselor can respond in one of two ways to congruence between the client's verbal and nonverbal behaviors. A counselor might make a *mental* note of the congruence in behaviors. Or the counselor could ask the client to explain the meaning of the nonverbal behaviors. For example, the counselor could ask: "While you were saying this is a difficult topic for you, your eyes were moist, your head was lowered, and your hands were fidgety. I wonder what that means?"

Mixed Messages

The counselor can observe the client and see whether what the client is saying and the client's nonverbal behavior are mixed messages. Contradictory verbal and nonverbal behavior would be apparent with a client who says "I feel really [pause] excited about the relationship. I've never [pause] experienced anything like this before" while looking down and leaning away. The counselor has at least three options for dealing with a verbal/nonverbal discrepancy. The first is to note mentally the discrepancies between what the client says and the nonverbal body and paralinguistic cues with which the client delivers the message. The second option is to describe the discrepancy to the client, as in this example: "You say you are excited about the relationship, but your head was hanging down while you were talking, and you spoke with a lot of hesitation." (Other examples of confronting the client with discrepancies can be found in Chapter 6.) The third option is to ask the client, "I noticed you looked away and paused as you said that. What does that mean?"

Nonverbal Behavior during Silence

The third way a counselor can respond to the nonverbal behavior of the client is during periods of silence in the interview. Silence does not mean that nothing is happening! Also remember that silence has different meanings from one culture to another. In some cultures, silence is a sign of respect, not an indication that the client does not wish to talk more (Sue & Sue, 1977). The counselor can focus on client nonverbal behavior during silence by noting the silence mentally, by describing the silence to the client, or by asking the client about the meaning of the silence.

Changing the Content of the Interview

It may be necessary with some clients to change the flow of the interview, because to continue on the same topic may be unproductive. Changing the flow may also be useful when the client is delivering a lot of information or is rambling. In such instances, the counselor can distract the client from the verbal content by redirecting the focus to the client's nonverbal behavior.

For "unproductive" content in the client's messages, the counselor might say "Our conversation so far has been dwelling on the death of your brother and your relationship with your parents. Right now, I would like you to focus on what we have been doing while we have been talking. Are you aware of what you have been doing with your hands?"

Such counselor distractions can be either productive or detrimental to the progress of therapy. Passons (1975) suggests that these distractions will be useful if they bring the client in touch with "present behavior." If they take the client away from the current flow of feelings, the distractions will be unproductive (p. 105). Passons also states that "experience, knowledge of the counselor, and intuition" all contribute to the counselor's decision to change the content of the interview by focusing on client nonverbal behavior.

Changes in Client Nonverbal Behavior

For some clients, nonverbal behaviors may be indexes of therapeutic change. For example, at the beginning of counseling, a client's arms may be folded across the chest. Later, the client may be more relaxed, with arms unfolded and hands gesturing during conversation. At the initial stages of counseling, the client may blush, perspire, and exhibit frequent body movement during the interview when certain topics are discussed. Later in counseling, these nonverbal behaviors may disappear and be replaced with a more comfortable and relaxed posture. Again, depending on the timing, the counselor can respond to nonverbal changes covertly or overtly.

This decision to respond to client nonverbal behavior covertly (with a mental note) or overtly depends not only on your purpose in focusing on nonverbal behavior but also on timing. Passons (1975) believes that counselors need to make overt responses such as immediacy (see Chapter 2) to client nonverbal behavior early in the therapeutic process. Otherwise, when you call attention to something the client is doing nonverbally after the tenth session or so, the client is likely to feel confused and bewildered by what is seen as a change in your approach. Another aspect of timing involves discriminating the likely effects of responding to the nonverbal behavior with immediacy. If the immediacy is likely to contribute to increased understanding and continuity of the session, it may be helpful. If, however, the timing of your response interrupts the client's flow of exploration, your response may be distracting and interfering.

When responding to client nonverbal behavior with immediacy, it is helpful to be descriptive rather than evaluative and to phrase your responses in a tentative way. For example, saying something like "Are you aware that as you're talking with Gene, your neck and face are getting red splotches of color?" is likely to be more useful than evaluative and dogmatic comments such as "Why is your face getting red?", "You sure do have a red face," or "You're getting so red—you must feel very embarrassed about this."

LEARNING ACTIVITIES #10: RESPONDING TO CLIENT NONVERBAL BEHAVIOR

I. The purpose of this activity is to practice verbal responses to client nonverbal behaviors. One person portrays a client (1) giving congruent messages between verbal and nonverbal behavior; (2) giving mixed messages, (3) being silent, (4) rambling and delivering a lot of information, and (5) portraying a rather obvious change from the beginning of the interview to the end of the interview in nonverbal behavior. The person playing the counselor responds verbally to each of these five portrayals. After going through all these portrayals with an opportunity for the role-play counselor to respond to each, switch roles. During these role plays, try to focus primarily on your responses to the other person's nonverbal behavior.

II. With yourself and several colleagues or members of your class to help you, use spatial arrangements to portray your role in your family and to depict your perceptions of your relationship to the other members of your family. Position yourself in a room and tell the other participants where to position themselves in relation to you and one another. (If you are short one or two participants, an object can fill a gap.) After the arrangement is complete, look around you. What can you learn about your own family from this aspect of nonverbal behavior? Do you like what you see and feel? If you could change your position in the family, where would you move? What effect would this have on you and on other family members?

III. In a role-play interaction or counseling session in which you function as the therapist, watch for some significant nonverbal behavior of the client, such as change in breathing, shifts in eye contact, voice tone, and proxemics. (Do not focus on a small nonverbal behavior out of context with the spoken words.) Focus on this behavior by asking the client whether she or he is aware of what is happening to her or his voice, body posture, eyes, or whatever. Do not interpret or assign meaning to the behavior for the client. Notice where your focus takes the client.

☐ COUNSELOR NONVERBAL BEHAVIOR

As a counselor, it is important for you to pay attention to your nonverbal behavior for several reasons. First, some kinds of counselor nonverbal behavior seem to contribute to a facilitative relationship; other nonverbal behaviors may detract from the relationship. For example, "high," or facilitative, levels of such nonverbal behaviors as direct eye contact and body orientation and relaxed body posture can contribute to positive client ratings of counselor empathy even in the presence of a low-level, or detracting, verbal message (Fretz, Corn, Tuemmler, & Bellet, 1979). In addition, the degree to which clients perceive you as interpersonally attractive and as having some expertise is associated with effective nonverbal skills (Claiborn, 1979).

Because much of the research on counselor nonverbal behavior has been done with ratings of videotapes and photographs, it is difficult to specify precisely what counselor nonverbal behaviors are related to counseling effectiveness. Table 4-2 lists presumed effective and ineffective uses of counselor nonverbal behaviors. In assessing this list, it is also important to remember that the effects of various counselor nonverbal behaviors are related to contextual variables in counseling, such as type of client, verbal content, timing in session, and client's perceptual style (Hill, Siegelman, Gronsky, Sturniolo, & Fretz, 1981; Seay & Altekruse, 1979). Thus, clients who subjectively have a favorable impression of the therapist may not be adversely affected by an ineffective, or "low-level," nonverbal behavior such as tapping your finger or fiddling with your pen or hair (we still recommend you avoid such distracting mannerisms). Similarly, just engaging in effective use of

TABLE 4-2. Effective and ineffective counselor nonverbal behavior

Ineffective use	Nonverbal mode of communication	Effective use
Doing any of these things will probably close off or slow down the conversation		These behaviors encourage talk because they show acceptance and respect for the other person
Distant or very close	Space	Approximately arm's length
Away	Movement	Toward
Slouching; rigid; seated leaning away	Posture	Relaxed but attentive; seated leaning slightly toward
Absent; defiant; jittery	Eye contact	Regular
You continue with what you are doing before responding; in a hurry	Time	Respond at first opportunity; share time with the client
Used to keep distance between the persons	Feet and legs (in sitting)	Unobtrusive
Used as a barrier	Furniture	Used to draw persons together
Does not match feelings; scowl; blank look	Facial expression	Matches your own or other's feelings; smile
Compete for attention with your words	Gestures	Highlight your words; unobtrusive; smooth
Obvious; distracting	Mannerisms	None or unobtrusive
Very loud or very soft	Voice: volume	Clearly audible
Impatient or staccato; very slow or hesitant	Voice: rate	Average or a bit slower
Apathetic; sleepy; jumpy; pushy	Energy level	Alert; stays alert throughout a long conversation

From *Amity: Friendship in action, Part 1: Basic friendship skills.* Copyright © 1980 by Richard P. Walters, Boulder, Colo.: Christian Helpers, Inc. Reproduced by permission.

nonverbal behaviors such as those listed in Table 4-2 may not be sufficient to alter the negative impressions of a particular client about yourself.

In addition to the use of effective nonverbal behaviors such as those listed in Table 4-2, there are three other important aspects of a therapist's nonverbal demeanor: sensitivity, congruence, and synchrony.

Sensitivity

Presumably, skilled interviewers are better able to send effective nonverbal messages (encoding) and are more aware of client nonverbal messages (decoding) than ineffective interviewers. There is some evidence that females of various cultures are better decoders—that is, more sensitive to other persons' nonverbal cues—than males (Sweeney, Cottle, & Kobayashi, 1980). Male therapists may need to ensure that they are not overlooking important client cues. Nonverbal sensitivity is also related to representational systems. Since most of us may rely on one representational system (vi-

sual, auditory, kinesthetic) more than another, we can increase our nonverbal sensitivity by opening up all our sensory channels. For example, people who tend to process information through auditory channels can learn to pay closer attention to visual cues, and those who process visually can sensitize themselves to voice cues.

Congruence

Counselor nonverbal behaviors in conjunction with verbal messages also have some consequences in the relationship, particularly if these messages are mixed, or incongruent. Mixed messages can be confusing to the client. For example, suppose that a counselor says to a client "I am really interested in how you feel about your parents," while the counselor's body is turned away from the client with arms folded across the chest. The effect of this inconsistent message on the client could be quite potent. In fact, a *negative nonverbal* message mixed with a *positive verbal* one may have greater effects than the opposite (positive nonverbal and negative verbal). As Gazda et al. (1977, p. 93) point out, "When verbal and nonverbal messages are in contradiction, the helpee will usually believe the nonverbal message." Negative nonverbal messages are communicated by infrequent eye contact, body position rotated 45° away from the client, backward body lean (from waist up leaning back), legs crossed away from the client, and arms folded across the chest (Graves & Robinson, 1976; Smith-Hanen, 1977). The client may respond to inconsistent counselor messages by increasing interpersonal distance and may view such messages as indicators of counselor deception (Graves & Robinson, 1976). Further, mixed messages may reduce the extent to which the client feels psychologically close to the counselor and perceives the counselor as genuine.

In contrast, congruence between counselor verbal and nonverbal messages is related to both client and counselor ratings of counselor facilitativeness (Hill et al., 1981; Reade & Smouse, 1980). The importance of counselor congruence, or consistency, among various verbal, kinesic, and paralinguistic behaviors cannot be overemphasized. Congruence between verbal and nonverbal channels seems especially critical when confronting clients (see Chapter 6) or when discussing personal, sensitive, or stressful issues (Reade & Smouse, 1980). A useful aspect of counselor congruence involves learning to match the *intensity* of your nonverbal behaviors with those of the client. For example, if you are asking the client to recall a time when she or he felt strong, resourceful, or powerful, it is helpful to convey these feelings by your own nonverbal behaviors. Become more animated, speak louder, and emphasize key words such as "strong" and "powerful." Many of us

overlook one of our most significant tools in achieving congruence — our voice. Changes in pitch, volume, rate of speech, and voice emphasis are particularly useful ways of matching our experience with the experience of clients.

Synchrony

Synchrony is the degree of harmony between the counselor's and client's nonverbal behavior. In helping interactions, especially initial ones, it is important to match, or pace, the client's nonverbal behaviors. Pacing of body posture and other client nonverbal behaviors contributes to rapport and builds empathy (Maurer & Tindall, 1983). Synchrony does not mean that the counselor mimics every move or sound the client makes. It does mean that the counselor's overall nonverbal demeanor is closely aligned with or very similar to the client's. For example, if the client is sitting back in a relaxed position with crossed legs, the counselor matches and displays similar body posture and leg movements. Dissynchrony, or lack of pacing, is evident when, for example, a client is leaning back, very relaxed, and the counselor is leaning foward, very intently, or when the client has a very sad look on her face and the counselor smiles, or when the client speaks in a low, soft voice and the counselor responds in a strong, powerful voice. The more nonverbal patterns you can pace, the more powerful the effect will be. However, when learning this skill, it is too overwhelming to try to match many aspects of a client's nonverbal behavior simultaneously. Find an aspect of the client's demeanor, such as voice, body posture, or gestures, that feels natural and comfortable for you to match, and concentrate on synchronizing this one aspect at a time.

LEARNING ACTIVITY #11: COUNSELOR NONVERBAL BEHAVIOR

The purpose of this activity is to have you experience the effects of different kinds of nonverbal behavior. You can do this in dyads or groups or outside a classroom setting.

1. Observe the response of a person you are talking with when—
   a. You look at the person or have relaxed eye contact.
   b. You don't look at the person consistently; you avert your eyes with only occasional glances.
   c. You stare at the person.
   Obtain a reaction from the other person about your behavior.
2. With other people, observe the effects of varying conversational distance. Talk with someone at a distance of (a) 3 feet (about 1 meter), (b) 6 feet (2 meters), and (c) 9 feet (3 meters).
   Observe the effect these distances have on the person.

(continued)

LEARNING ACTIVITY #11: COUNSELOR NONVERBAL BEHAVIOR (continued)

3. You can also do the same kind of experimenting with your body posture. For example, contrast the effects of two body positions in conversation: (a) slouching in seat, leaning back, and turning away from the person, compared with (b) facing the person, with a slight lean forward toward the person (from waist up) and with body relaxed.

LEARNING ACTIVITY #12: OBSERVATION OF COUNSELOR AND CLIENT NONVERBAL BEHAVIOR

The purpose of this activity is to apply the material presented in this chapter in an interview setting. Using the Nonverbal Behavior Checklist at the end of the chapter, observe a counselor and determine how many behaviors listed on the checklist she or he demonstrates. In addition, in the role play, see how much you can identify about the client's nonverbal behaviors. Finally, look for evidence of synchrony (pacing) or dissynchrony between the two persons and congruence or incongruence for each person.

☐ SUMMARY

The focus of this chapter has been on counselor and client nonverbal behavior. The importance of nonverbal communication in counseling is illustrated by the trust that both counselor and client place in each other's nonverbal messages. Nonverbal behavior may be a more accurate portrayal of our real selves. Most nonverbal behaviors are very spontaneous and cannot easily be faked. Nonverbal behavior adds significantly to our interpretation of verbal messages.

Five significant dimensions of nonverbal behavior were discussed in this chapter: kinesics (face and body expressions), paralinguistics (vocal cues), proxemics (space and distance), environment, and time. Although much popular literature has speculated on the meanings of "body lan-guage," in counseling interactions it is important to remember that the meaning of nonverbal behavior varies with people, situations, and cultures and, further, cannot be easily interpreted without supporting verbal messages.

These categories of nonverbal behavior also apply to the counselor's use of effective nonverbal behavior in the interview. In addition to using nonverbal behaviors that communicate interest and attentiveness, counselors must ensure that their own verbal and nonverbal messages are congruent and that their nonverbal behavior is synchronized with, or matches, the client's nonverbal behavior. Congruence and synchrony are important ways of contributing to rapport and building empathy within the developing relationship.

POSTEVALUATION

PART ONE

Describe briefly one possible effect or meaning associated with each of the following ten client nonverbal behaviors (Chapter Objective One). Speculate on the meaning of the client nonverbal behavior from the client description and context presented. If you wish, write your answers on a piece of paper. Feedback follows the evaluation.

Observed Client Nonverbal Behavior	Client Description (Context)
1. Lowering eyes—looking down or away	Client has just described incestuous relationship with father. She looks away after recounting the episode.
2. Pupil dilation	Client has just been informed that she will be committed to the state hospital. Her pupils dilate as she sits back and listens.

(continued)

3. Lower lip quivers or biting lip

Client has just reported a recent abortion to the counselor. As she's finishing, her lip quivers and she bites it.

4. Nodding head up and down

Counselor has just described reasons for client to stop drinking. Client responds by nodding and saying "I know that."

5. Shrugging of shoulders

Counselor has just informed client that he is not eligible for services at that agency. Client shrugs shoulders while listening.

6. Fist clenching to objects or holding hands tightly.

Client is describing recent argument with spouse. Fists are clenched while relating incident.

7. Crossing and uncrossing legs repeatedly

Counselor has just asked client whether he has been taking his medicine as prescribed. Client crosses and uncrosses legs while responding.

8. Stuttering, hesitations, speech errors

Client hesitates when counselor inquires about marital fidelity. Starts to stutter and makes speech errors when describing extramarital affairs.

9. Moves closer

As counselor self-discloses an episode similar to client's, client moves chair toward helper.

10. Flushing of face and appearance of sweat beads

Counselor has just confronted client about provocative clothing and posture. Client's face turns red and sweat appears on the forehead.

PART TWO

Conduct a short interview as a helper and see how many client nonverbal behaviors of kinesics (body motion), paralinguistics (voice qualities), and proxemics (space) you can identify by debriefing with an observer after the session (Chapter Objective Two). Describe the possible effects or meanings associated with each behavior you identify. Confer with the observer about which nonverbal client behaviors you identified and which you missed.

PART THREE

In a role-play interview in which you are the counselor, demonstrate effective use of your face and body, your voice, and distance/space/touch (Objective Three). Be aware of the degree to which your nonverbal behavior matches your words. Also attempt to pace at least one aspect of the client's nonverbal behavior, such as body posture or breathing rate and depth. Use the Nonverbal Behavior Checklist at the end of the chapter to assess your performance from a videotape or have an observer rate you during your session.

PART FOUR

Recall that there are five occasions for responding to client nonverbal behavior:

a. Evidence of congruence between the client's verbal and nonverbal behavior
b. A client's "mixed" (discrepant) verbal and nonverbal message
c. Client's use of silence
d. Changes in client's nonverbal cues
e. Focusing on client's nonverbal behavior to change or redirect the interview

Identify four of the five occasions presented in the following client descriptions, according to Chapter Objective Four.

1. The client says that your feedback doesn't bother him; yet he frowns, looks away, and turns away.
2. The client has paused for a long time after your last question.
3. The client has flooded you with a great deal of information for the last five minutes.
4. The client says she feels angry about having to stay in the hospital. As she says this, her voice pitch gets louder, she clasps her hands together, and she frowns.
5. The client's face was very animated for the first part of the interview; now the client's face has a very serious look.

☐ SUGGESTED READINGS

Duhl, F. J., Kantor, D., & Duhl, B. S. (1973). Learning, space, and action in family therapy: A primer of sculpture. In D. A. Bloch (Ed.), *Techniques of family psychotherapy.* New York: Grune & Stratton.

Eisler, R. M., & Frederiksen, L. W. (1980). *Perfecting social skills.* New York: Plenum Press.

Ekman, P., & Friesen, W. V. (1975). *Unmasking the face.* Englewood Cliffs, NJ: Prentice-Hall.

Gazda, G. M., Asbury, F. S., Balzer, F. J., Childers, W. C., & Walters, R. P. (1984). *Human relations development* (3rd ed.). Boston: Allyn & Bacon. Chapter 6, "Awareness of Nonverbal Behaviors in Helping."

Harper, R. G., Wiens, A. N., & Matarazzo, J. D. (1978). *Nonverbal communication: The state of the art.* New York: Wiley.

Hess, E. H. (1975). *The tell-tale eye.* New York: Van Nostrand Reinhold.

Hill, C. E., Siegelman, L., Gronsky, B. R., Sturniolo, F., & Fretz, B. R. (1981). Nonverbal communication and counseling outcome. *Journal of Counseling Psychology, 28,* 203–212.

Hubble, M. A., Noble, F. C., & Robinson, S. E. (1981). The effect of counselor touch in an initial counseling session. *Journal of Counseling Psychology, 28,* 533–535.

King, M., Novik, L., & Citrenbaum, C. (1983). *Irresistible communication.* Philadelphia: Saunders.

Knapp, M. L. (1978). *Nonverbal communication in human interaction* (2nd ed.). New York: Holt, Rinehart and Winston.

Lecomte, C., Bernstein, B. L., & Dumont, F. (1981). Counseling interactions as a function of spatial-environmental conditions. *Journal of Counseling Psychology, 28,* 536–539.

Lee, D. Y., Hallberg, E. T., Kocsis, M., & Haase, R. F. (1980). Decoding skills in nonverbal communication and perceived interviewer effectiveness. *Journal of Counseling Psychology, 27,* 89–92.

Maurer, R. E., & Tindall, J. H. (1983). Effect of postural congruence on client's perception of counselor empathy. *Journal of Counseling Psychology, 30,* 158–163.

Mehrabian, A. (1976). *Public places and private spaces.* New York: Basic Books.

Otter, S. B., & Guerra, J. J. (1976). *Assertion training.* Champaign, IL: Resource Press.

Passons, W. R. (1975). *Gestalt approaches in counseling.* New York: Holt, Rinehart and Winston.

Reade, M. N., & Smouse, A. D. (1980). Effect of inconsistent verbal-nonverbal communication and counselor response mode on client estimate of counselor regard and effectiveness. *Journal of Counseling Psychology, 27,* 546–553.

Saha, G. B., Palchoudhury, S., & Mandal, M. K. (1982). A study on facial expression of emotion. *Psychologia, 25,* 255–259.

Sherer, M., & Rogers, R. (1980). Effects of therapist's nonverbal communication on rated skill and effectiveness. *Journal of Clinical Psychology, 26,* 696–700.

Sweeney, M. A., Cottle, W. C., & Kobayashi, M. J. (1980). Nonverbal communication: A cross-cultural comparison of American and Japanese counseling students. *Journal of Counseling Psychology, 27,* 150–156.

Young, D. W. (1980). Meanings of counselor nonverbal gestures: Fixed or interpretive? *Journal of Counseling Psychology, 27,* 447–452.

FEEDBACK: POSTEVALUATION

PART ONE

Some of the possible meanings of these client nonverbal behaviors are as follows:

1. This client's lowering of her eyes and looking away probably indicates her *embarrassment* and *discomfort* in discussing this particular problem.

2. Dilation of this client's pupils probably signifies *arousal* and *fear* of being committed.

3. In this example, the quivering of the client's lower lip and biting of the lip probably denote *ambivalence* and *sorrow* over her actions.

4. The client's head nodding indicates *agreement* with the counselor's rationale for remaining sober.

5. The client's shrugging of the shoulders may indicate *uncertainty* or *reconcilement*.

6. In this case, the client's fist clenching probably connotes *anger* with the spouse.

7. The client's crossing and uncrossing of his legs may signify *anxiety* or *discomfort*.

8. The client's hesitation in responding and subsequent stuttering and speech errors may indicate *sensitivity* to this topic, as well as *discomfort* in discussing it.

9. In this case, the client's moving closer to the counselor probably indicates *intrigue* and *identification* with what the counselor is revealing.

10. The client's sweating and blushing may be signs of *negative arousal* — that is, *anxiety* and/or *embarrassment* with the counselor's confrontation about suggestive dress and pose.

PART TWO

Have the observer debrief you for feedback or use the Nonverbal Behavior Checklist to recall which nonverbal behaviors you identified.

PART THREE

You or your observer can determine which desirable nonverbal behaviors you exhibited as a counselor, using the Nonverbal Behavior Checklist.

(continued)

PART FOUR

The five possible occasions for responding to client nonverbal cues as reflected in the postevaluation examples are these:

1. b. Responding to a client's mixed message; in this case the client's frown, break in eye contact, and shift in body position contradict the client's verbal message.
2. c. Responding to client silence; in this example the client's pause indicates silence.
3. e. Responding to client nonverbal behaviors to redirect the interview focus—in this example, to "break up" the flood of client information.
4. a. Responding to congruence in client verbal and nonverbal messages; in this case, the client's nonverbal behaviors "match" her verbal report of feeling angry.
5. d. Responding to changes in client nonverbal cues—in this example, responding to the change in the client's facial expression.

NONVERBAL BEHAVIOR CHECKLIST

Name of Counselor _____
Name of Observer _____

Instructions: Using a videotaped or live interview, use the categories below as guides for observing nonverbal behavior. The checklist can be used to observe the counselor, the client, or both. The left-hand column lists a number of behaviors to be observed. The right-hand column has spaces to record a √ when the behavior is observed and to fill in any descriptive comments about it—for example, "Blinking—*excessive*" or "Colors in room—*high arousal*."

I. Kinesics	(√)	Comments
1. *Eyes*		
Eyebrows raised, lowered, or drawn together	___	_____
Staring or "glazed" quality	___	_____
Blinking—excessive, moderate, or slight	___	_____
Moisture, tears	___	_____
Pupil dilation	___	_____
2. *Face, mouth, head*		
Continuity or changes in facial expression	___	_____
Appropriate or inappropriate smiling	___	_____
Swelling, tightening, or quivering lips	___	_____

(continued)

	(√)	Comments
Changes in skin color	___	_____
Flushing, rashes on upper neck, face	___	_____
Appearance of sweat beads	___	_____
Head nodding	___	_____
3. *Body movements, posture, and gestures*		
Body posture—rigid or relaxed	___	_____
Continuity or shifts in body posture	___	_____
Frequency of body movements—excessive, moderate, or slight	___	_____
Gestures—open or closed	___	_____
Frequency of nonverbal adaptors (distracting mannerisms)—excessive, moderate, or slight	___	_____
Body orientation: direct (facing each other) or sideways	___	_____
Breathing—shallow or deep, fast or slow	___	_____
Continuity or changes in breathing depth and rate	___	_____
Crossed arms or legs	___	_____

II. Paralinguistics

	(√)	Comments
Continuity or changes in voice level, pitch, rate of speech	___	_____
Verbal underlining—voice emphasis of particular words/phrases	___	_____
Whispering, inaudibility	___	_____
Directness or lack of directness in speech	___	_____
Speech errors—excessive, moderate, or slight	___	_____
Pauses initiated by counselor	___	_____
Pauses initiated by client	___	_____

III. Proxemics

	(√)	Comments
Continuity or shifts in distance (closer, farther away)	___	_____
Use of touch (handshake, shoulder pat, back pat, and so on)	___	_____

(continued)

FEEDBACK: POSTEVALUATION (continued)

Position in room—behind
or next to object or person   _____ _____

IV. Environment

Arousal (high or low)
associated with:

Furniture arrangement   _____ _____
Colors   _____ _____
Light   _____ _____
Voice   _____ _____
Overall room   _____ _____

V. Time

Session started promptly or
late   _____ _____

Promptness or delay in
responding to other's
communication   _____ _____

Amount of time spent on
primary and secondary
problems—excessive,
moderate, or slight   _____ _____

Continuity or changes in
pace of session   _____ _____

Session terminated
promptly or late   _____ _____

VI. Synchrony and Pacing

Synchrony or dissynchrony
between nonverbal
behaviors and words   _____ _____

Pacing or lack of pacing
between counselor and
client nonverbal behavior   _____ _____

VII. Congruence

Congruence or
discrepancies:

Nonverbal—between
various parts of the
body   _____ _____

Nonverbal/verbal—
between nonverbal
behavior and words   _____ _____

VIII. Summary

Using your observations of nonverbal behavior and
the cultural/contextual variables of the interaction,
what conclusions can you make about the therapist?
The client? The counseling relationship? Consider
such things as emotions, comfort level, deception,
desire for more exchange, and liking/attraction.

FIVE

Communication is ever two-way. Listening is the other half of talking. Listening well is no less important than speaking well and it is probably more difficult. Could you listen to a 45-minute discourse without once allowing your thoughts to wander? Good listening is an art that demands the concentration of all your mental facilities. In general, people in the western world talk better than they listen [Potter, 1965, p. 6].

Listening is a prerequisite for all other counseling responses and strategies. Listening should precede whatever else is done in counseling. When a counselor fails to listen, the client may be discouraged from self-exploring, the wrong problem may be discussed, or a strategy may be proposed prematurely.

We define listening as involving three processes: receiving a message, processing a message, and sending a message. These three processes are illustrated in Figure 5-1.

Each client message (verbal or nonverbal) is a stimulus to be received and processed by the counselor. When a client sends a message, the counselor receives it. Reception of a message is a covert process; that is, we cannot see how or what the counselor receives. Failure to receive all of the message may occur when the counselor stops attending.

Once a message is received, it must be processed in some way. Processing, like reception, is covert, because it goes on within the counselor's mind and is not visible to the outside world—except, perhaps, from the counselor's nonverbal cues. Processing includes thinking about the message and pondering its meaning. Processing is important because a counselor's cognitions, self-talk, and mental (covert) preparation and visualization set the stage for overt responding (Richardson & Stone, 1981). Errors in processing a message accurately often occur when counselors' biases or blind spots prevent them from acknowledging parts of a message or from interpreting a message without distortion. Counselors may hear what they want to hear instead of the actual message sent.

The third process of listening involves the verbal and nonverbal messages sent by a counselor.

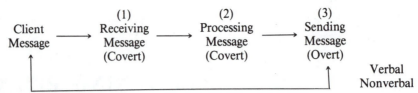

Figure 5-1. Three processes of listening.

Sometimes a counselor may receive and process a message accurately but have difficulty sending a message because of lack of skills. Fortunately, you can learn to use listening responses to send messages. Problems in sending messages can be more easily corrected than errors in the covert processes of receiving and processing messages. We hope that you are already able to receive and process a message without difficulty. Of course, this is a big assumption! If you think your own covert processes in listening are in need of further development, this may be an area you will need to work on by yourself or with someone else.

This chapter is designed to help you acquire four verbal listening responses that you can use to send messages to a client: clarification, paraphrase, reflection, and summarization.

□ OBJECTIVES

1. Using a written list of counselor responses, accurately identify at least nine of the twelve different types of counselor listening responses (clarification, paraphrase, reflection, summarization).
2. From a written list, match each of the four listening responses with its intended purposes.
3. From a list of three client statements, write an example of each of the four listening responses for each client statement.
4. In a 15-minute counseling interview in which you function as an observer, listen for and record five key aspects of client messages that form the basis of effective listening.
5. In a 15-minute role-play interview or a conversation in which you function as a listener, demonstrate at least two accurate examples of each of the four listening responses.

□ LISTENING IS A PREREQUISITE

We consider listening responses to be the foundation of the entire counseling process. If you conceptualize counseling and each interview as having a beginning, a middle, and an end, then attending and listening are the predominant counselor behaviors for the beginning part, or the first stage, of counseling. Listening also plays a major role in the beginning part of every interview.

One of the difficulties encountered in listening is to achieve a reasonable balance between too much and too little listening. If listening is the only tool used in counseling, the sessions will probably lack direction. However, if the counselor fails to listen, the sessions may be overly structured—at the client's expense. Egan (1990) points out that counselors who move into facilitating action too quickly are satisfying more of their own needs than those of the client.

□ LISTENING AND SENSORY MODALITIES

Effective listening involves all three major sensory modalities: sight (visual), sound (auditory), and experiencing/touch (kinesthetic). Recall from Chapter 2 that some clients use predominantly sensory words that are visual (such as *clear, look, appears, seems*), auditory *(hear, tell, sounds, listen),* or kinesthetic *(feel, sense, grasp, touch).* Others use a variety of words, or mixed modalities, in describing their experience, and occasionally a client may not use sensory-based words in a particular message.

Since listening responses are one way to communicate empathy and attentiveness, it is important to try to match the client's choice of sensory words in your listening response. If the client uses visually oriented words, you can select a sentence stem that matches these words—for example, "It looks as if . . ." or "I can see that. . . ." (The same matching can occur for auditory or kinesthetic words.) If the client selects words from mixed sensory modalities or does not include any words from sensory modalities, it is wise to use words in your response from two or three of the sensory channels rather than just one. Remember that clients will usually feel listened to and understood most when you let them know you have *seen* things from their frame of reference, *heard* what they have said, and *felt* or *grasped* their feelings and experiences.

☐ FOUR LISTENING RESPONSES

This chapter will present four kinds of listening responses: clarification, paraphrase, reflection, and summarization. *Clarification* is a question, often used after an ambiguous client message. It starts with "Do you mean that . . ." or "Are you saying that . . ." along with a repetition or rephrasing of all or part of the client's previous message. Similar to a clarification is the *paraphrase,* defined as a rephrasing of the content part of the message, which describes a situation, event, person, or idea. In contrast, *reflection* is a rephrasing of the client's feelings, or the affect part of the message. Usually the affect part of the message reveals the client's feelings about the content; for example, a client may feel discouraged (affect) about not doing well in a class (content). *Summarization* is an extension of the paraphrase and reflection responses that involves tying together and rephrasing two or more different parts of a message or messages.

To illustrate these four responses, we present a client message with an example of each:

Client, a 35-year-old widow, mother of two young children: My whole life fell apart when my husband died. I keep feeling so unsure about my ability to make it on my own and to support my kids. My husband always made all the decisions for me. Now I haven't slept well for so long, and I'm drinking more heavily—I can't even think straight. Besides, I've put on 15 pounds. I look like a witch. Who would even want to think of hiring me the way I am now?

Counselor clarification: Are you saying that one of the hardest things facing you now is to have enough confidence in your ability to make the decisions alone?

Counselor paraphrase: Since your husband's death you have all the responsibilities and decisions on your shoulders.

Counselor reflection: You feel concerned about your ability to shoulder all the family responsibilities now.

Counselor summarization: Now that your husband has died, you're facing a few things that are very difficult for you right now . . . handling the family responsibilities, making the decisions, and trying to take better care of yourself.

Table 5-1 presents the definitions and the *intended* or hypothesized purposes of the four counselor listening responses of clarification, paraphrase, reflection, and summarization. The counselor responses may not have the same results

TABLE 5-1. Definitions and intended purposes of counselor listening responses

Response	Definition	Intended purpose
Clarification	A question beginning with, for example, "Do you mean that" or "Are you saying that" plus a rephrasing of the client's message	1. To encourage more client elaboration 2. To check out the accuracy of what you heard the client say 3. To clear up vague, confusing messages
Paraphrase (responding to content)	A rephrasing of the content of the client's message	1. To help the client focus on the content of his or her message 2. To highlight content when attention to feelings is premature or self-defeating
Reflection (responding to feelings)	A rephrasing of the affective part of the client's message	1. To encourage the client to express more of his or her feelings 2. To have the client experience feelings more intensely 3. To help the client become more aware of the feelings that dominate him or her 4. To help the client acknowledge and manage feelings 5. To help the client discriminate accurately among feelings
Summarization	Two or more paraphrases or reflections that condense the client's messages or the session	1. To tie together multiple elements of client messages 2. To identify a common theme or pattern 3. To interrupt excessive rambling 4. To review progress

for all clients. For example, a counselor may find that reflecting feelings prompts some clients to discuss feelings, whereas other clients may not even acknowledge the counselor's statements (Highlen & Baccus, 1977; Hill & Gormally, 1977). The point is that we are presenting some "modal" intentions for each counselor listening response; there are exceptions. The counselor responses will achieve their intended purposes most of the time. However, other dynamics within an interview may yield different client outcomes. Moreover, the effects of these verbal messages may vary depending on the nonverbal cues sent along with the message. It is helpful to have some rationale in mind for using a response. Keep in mind, however, that the influence a response has on the client may not be what you intended to achieve by selecting it. The guidelines in Table 5-1 should be used tentatively, *subject to modification by particular client reactions.*

The next three sections will describe the listening responses and will present model examples of each skill. Opportunities to practice each skill and receive feedback follow the examples.

Listening for Accuracy: The Clarification Response

Because most messages are expressed from the speaker's internal frame of reference, they may be vague or confusing. Messages that may be particularly confusing are those that include inclusive terms *(they* and *them),* ambiguous phrases *(you know),* and words with a double meaning *(stoned, trip)* (Hein, 1980, p. 35). When you aren't sure of the meaning of a message, it is helpful to clarify it.

According to Hein (1980, p. 56), a clarification asks the client to elaborate on "a vague, ambiguous, or implied statement." The request for clarification is usually expressed in the form of a question and may begin with phrases such as "Are you saying this . . ." or "Could you try to describe that . . ." or "Can you clarify that. . . ."

Purposes of clarification. A clarification may be used to make the client's previous message explicit and to confirm the accuracy of your perceptions about the message. A clarification is appropriate for any occasion when you aren't sure whether you understand the client's message and you need more elaboration. A second purpose of clarification is to check out what you heard of the client's message. Ivey and Gluckstern (1974, p. 26) point out that too often counselors "charge ahead without stopping to check out whether or not they have

really heard what the helpee has to say." In this case, the counselor often makes assumptions and draws conclusions about the client that are somewhat distorted or premature. Particularly in the beginning stages of counseling, it is important to verify client messages before jumping to quick conclusions. The following example may help you see the value of the clarification response.

Client: Sometimes I just want to get away from it all.
Counselor: It sounds like you have to split and be on your own.
Client: No, it's not that. I don't want to be alone. It's just that I wish I could get out from under all this work I have to do.

In this example, the counselor drew a quick conclusion about the initial client message that turned out to be inaccurate. The session might have gone more smoothly if the counselor had requested clarification before assuming something about the client, as in the next example:

Client: Sometimes I just want to get away from it all.
Counselor: Could you describe for me what you mean by getting away from it all?
Client: Well, I just have so much work to do—I'm always feeling behind and overloaded. I'd like to get out from under that miserable feeling.

In this case, the clarification helped both persons to establish exactly what was being said and felt. Neither the client nor the counselor had to rely on assumptions and inferences that were not explored and confirmed. The skilled counselor uses clarification responses to determine the accuracy of messages as they are received and processed. Otherwise, inaccurate information may not be corrected and distorted assumptions may remain untested.

Steps in clarifying. There are four steps in clarifying for accuracy. First, identify the content of the client's verbal and nonverbal messages—what has the client told you? Second, identify whether there are any vague or confusing parts to the message that you need to check out for accuracy or elaboration. Third, decide on an appropriate beginning, or sentence stem, for your clarification, such as "Could you describe," "Could you clarify," or "Are you saying." In addition, use your voice to deliver the clarification as a question rather than a statement. Finally, remember to assess the effectiveness of your clarification by listening and observing the client's response. If your clarification is useful, the client will elaborate on the ambiguous or confusing part of the message. If it is not useful, the client will clam up, ignore your request for clarification, and/or continue to make deletions or omissions. At this point, you can attempt a subsequent clarification or switch to an alternative response.

To help you formulate a clarification, decide when to use it, and assess its effectiveness, consider the following cognitive learning strategy:

1. What has this client told me?
2. Are there any vague parts or missing pictures to the message that I need to check out? If so, what? If not, decide on another, more suitable response.
3. How can I hear, see, or grasp a way to start this response?
4. How will I know whether my clarification is useful?

Notice how a counselor applies this cognitive learning strategy in clarifying the client's message given in the previous example:

Client: Sometimes I just want to get away from it all.
Counselor: 1. What has this client told me? That she wants to get away from something. [Asked and answered covertly]
2. Are there any vague parts or missing pictures in her message? If so, what? (If not, I'll decide on a more suitable response.)

Yes—I need to check out what she means by "getting away from it all."
3. Now, how can I begin a clarification response? I can see the start of it, hear the start of it, or grasp the start of it. Something like "Well, could you tell me, or could you describe. . . ."
4. Now, how will I know that the response will be helpful? I'll have to see, hear, and grasp whether she elaborates or not. Let's try it . . . .

Suppose that, at this juncture, the counselor's covert visualization or self-talk ends, and the following actual dialogue occurs:

Counselor clarification: Could you describe what you mean by "getting away from it all"?
Client response: Well, I just have so much work to do—I'm always feeling behind and overloaded. I'd like to get out from under that miserable feeling.

From the client's response, the counselor can determine that the clarification was effective because the client elaborated and added the missing parts or pictures from her previous message. The counselor can covertly congratulate himself or herself for not jumping ahead too quickly and for taking the time to check out the client's deletion and the resulting ambiguity.

The following learning activity gives you an opportunity to try out this cognitive learning strategy in order to develop the skill of clarification.

LEARNING ACTIVITY #13: CLARIFICATION

In this learning activity, you are presented with three client practice messages. For each client message, develop an example of a clarification response, using the cognitive learning strategy described earlier and outlined in the following example. In order to internalize this learning strategy, you may wish to talk through these self-questions overtly (aloud) and then covertly (silently to yourself). The end product will be a clarification response that you can say aloud or write down or both. An example precedes the practice messages. Feedback follows on page 94.

Example

Client, a 15-year-old high school student: My grades have really slipped. I don't know why; I just feel so down about everything:

Self-question 1: What has this client told me? That she feels down and rather discouraged.
Self-question 2: Are there any vague parts or missing pictures to the message that I need to check out—

if so, what? (If not, decide on a different response.)
Yes, several—one is what she feels so down about. Another is what this feeling of being down is like for her.
Self-question 3: How can I hear, see, or grasp a way to start this response?
Well, "Are you saying there's something specific?" or "Can you describe this feeling . . . ?"
Self-question 4: Say aloud or write an actual clarification response:
"Are you saying there is something specific you feel down about?" or "Could you describe what this feeling of being down is like for you?"

Client Practice Messages

Client 1, a fourth-grader: I don't want to do this dumb homework anyway. I don't care about learning these math problems. Girls don't need to know this anyway.

Self-question 1: What has this client told me?

(continued)

LEARNING ACTIVITY #13: CLARIFICATION (continued)

Self-question 2: Are there any vague parts or missing pictures I need to check out—if so, what?
Self-question 3: How can I hear, see, or grasp a way to start my response?
Actual clarification response: _____

_____

Client 2, a middle-aged man: I'm really discouraged with this physical disability now. I feel like I can't do anything the way I used to. Not only has it affected me in my job, but at home. I just don't feel like I have anything good to offer anyone.

Self-question 1: What has this client told me?
Self-question 2: Are there any vague parts or missing pictures I need to check out—if so, what?
Self-question 3: How can I hear, see, or grasp a way to start my response?

Actual clarification response: _____

_____

Client 3, an older person: The company is going to make me retire even though I don't want to. What will I do with myself then? I find myself just thinking over the good times of the past, not wanting to face the future at all. Sometimes retirement makes me so nervous I can't sleep or eat. My family suggested I see someone about this.

Self-question 1: What has this client told me?
Self-question 2: Are there any vague parts or missing pictures I need to check out—if so, what?
Self-question 3: How can I hear, see, or grasp a way to start my response?
Actual clarification response: _____

_____

Listening for Content and Affect: Paraphrasing and Reflecting

In addition to clarifying the accuracy of client messages, the counselor needs to listen for information revealed in messages about significant situations and events in the client's life—and the client's feelings about these events. Each client message will express (directly or indirectly) some information about client situations or concerns and about client feelings. The portion of the message that expresses information or describes a situation or event is called the *content,* or the cognitive part, of the message. The cognitive part of a message includes references to a situation or event, people, objects, or ideas. Another portion of the message may reveal how the client feels about the content; expression of feelings or an emotional tone is called the *affective* part of the message (Hackney & Cormier, 1988). Generally, the affect part of the verbal message is distinguished by the client's use of an affect or feeling word, such as *happy, angry,* or *sad.* However, clients may also express their feelings in less obvious ways, particularly through various nonverbal behaviors.

The following illustrations may help you distinguish between the content and affective parts of a client's verbal message.

Client, a 6-year-old first-grader: I don't like school. It isn't much fun.

The first sentence ("I don't like school") is the affect part of the message. The client's feelings are suggested by the words "don't like." The second sentence ("It isn't much fun") is the content part of the message because it refers to a situation or an event in this child's life—not having fun at school.

Here is another example:

Client, a 20-year-old woman: How can I tell my boyfriend I want to break off our relationship? He will be very upset. I guess I'm afraid to tell him.

In this example, the first two sentences are the content because they describe the situation of wanting to break off a relationship. The third sentence, the affect part, indicates the client's feelings about this situation—being *afraid* to tell the boyfriend of her intentions.

See whether you can discriminate between the content and affective parts of the following two client messages:

Client 1, a young man: I just can't satisfy my wife sexually. It's very frustrating for me.

In this example, the content part is "I can't satisfy my wife sexually." The affect part, or the client's feelings about the content, is "It's very *frustrating* for me."

Client 2, an institutionalized man: This place is a trap. It seems like I've been here forever. I'd feel much better if I weren't here.

In the second example, the statements referring to the institution as a trap and being there forever are the content parts of the message. The statement of "feeling better" is the affect part.

The skilled counselor tries to listen for both content and affect parts of client messages because it is important to deal with significant situations or relationships *and* with the client's feelings about the situations. Responding to cognitive or affective messages will direct the focus of the session in different ways. At some points, the counselor will respond to content by focusing on events, objects, people, or ideas. At other times, the counselor will respond to affect by focusing on the client's feelings and emotions. Generally, the counselor can respond to content by using a paraphrase and can respond to affect with a reflection.

Paraphrase. A paraphrase is a rephrasing of the client's primary words and thoughts. Paraphrasing involves selective attention given to the cognitive part of the message—with the client's key ideas translated into *your own words.* Thus, an effective paraphrase is more than just "parroting" the words of the client. The rephrasal should be carefully worded to lead to further discussion or increased understanding on the part of the client. It is helpful to stress the most important words and ideas expressed by the client. Consider the following example:

Client: I know it doesn't help my depression to sit around or stay in bed all day.
Counselor: You know you need to avoid staying in bed or sitting around all day to help your depression.

In this example, the counselor merely "parroted" the client's message. The likely outcome is that the client may respond with a minimal answer such as "I agree" or "That's right" and not elaborate further or that the client may feel ridiculed by what seems to be an obvious or mimicking response. A more effective paraphrase would be "You are aware that you need to get up and move around in order to minimize being depressed."

Purposes of paraphrasing. There are several purposes in using the paraphrase at selected times n client interactions. First, use of the paraphrase tells clients that you have understood their communication. If your understanding is complete, clients can expand or clarify their ideas. Second, paraphrasing can encourage client elaboration of a key idea or thought. Clients may talk about an important topic in greater depth. A third reason for use of paraphrases is to help the client focus on a particular situation or event, idea, or behavior. Sometimes, by increasing focus, paraphrasing can help get a client "on track." For example, ac-

curate paraphrasing can help stop a client from merely repeating a "story" (Ivey, 1988).

A fourth use of paraphrase is to help clients who need to make decisions. As Ivey, Ivey, and Simek-Downing (1987, p. 73) observe, "Paraphrasing is often helpful to clients who have a decision to make, for the repetition of key ideas and phrases clarifies the essence of the problem." Paraphrasing is also useful when emphasizing content if attention to affect is premature or counterproductive.

Steps in paraphrasing. There are five steps in paraphrasing content. First, attend to and recall the message by restating it to yourself covertly—what has the client told you? Second, identify the content part of the message by asking yourself "What situation, person, object, or idea is discussed in this message?" Third, select an appropriate beginning, or sentence stem, for your paraphrase. Paraphrases can begin with many possible sentence stems. Try to select one that is likely to match the client's choice of sensory words. Table 5-2 provides examples of typical sensory words that clients may use and corresponding counselor phrases. Next, using the sentence stem you se-

TABLE 5-2. Examples of client sensory words and corresponding counselor phrases

Client sensory words		Corresponding counselor phrases
Visual		
see	bright	It seems like
clear	show	It appears as though
focus	colorful	From my perspective
picture	glimpse	As I see it
view	"now look"	I see what you mean
perspective		It looks like
Auditory		
listen	discuss	Sounds like
yell	should	As I hear it
tell	loud	What you're saying is
told	noisy	I hear you saying
talk	call	Something tells you
hear	"now listen"	You're telling me that
ears		
Kinesthetic		
feel	relaxed	You feel
touch	sense	From my standpoint
pressure	experience	I sense that
hurt	firm	I have the feeling that
pushy	"you know"	
grasp		

Adapted from Lankton (1980).

FEEDBACK #13: CLARIFICATION

Client 1

1. What did the client say?

   That she doesn't want to do her math homework —that she thinks it's not important for girls.

2. Are there any vague parts or missing pictures?

   Yes—whether she really doesn't care about math or whether she's had a bad experience with it and is denying her concern.

3. Examples of clarification responses: "Are you saying that you really dislike math or that it's not going as well for you as you would like?"

   "Are you saying that math is not too important for you or that it is hard for you?"

Client 2

1. What did the client say?

   That he feels useless to himself and others.

2. Are there any vague parts or missing pictures?

   Yes—it's not clear exactly how things are different for him now and also whether it's the disability itself that's bothering him or its effects (inability to get around, reactions of others, and so on).

3. Examples of clarification responses: "Could you clarify exactly how things are different for you now than the way they used to be?"

   "Are you saying you feel discouraged about having the disability—or about the effects and constraints from it?"

   "Are you saying you feel differently about yourself now than the way you used to?"

Client 3

1. What did the client say?

   He is going to have to retire because of company policy. He doesn't want to retire now and feels upset about this. He's here at his family's suggestion.

2. Are there any vague parts or missing pictures?

   Yes—he says he feels nervous, although from his description of not eating and sleeping it may be sadness or depression. Also, is he here only because his family sent him or because he feels a need too? Finally, what specifically bothers him about retirement?

3. Examples of clarification responses: "Would you say you're feeling more nervous or more depressed about your upcoming retirement?"

   "Are you saying you're here just because of your family's feelings or because of your feelings too?"

   "Could you describe what it is about retiring that worries you?"

lected, translate the key content or constructs into your own words and verbalize this into a paraphrase. Remember to use your voice as you deliver the paraphrase so it sounds like a statement instead of a question. Finally, assess the effectiveness of your paraphrase by listening to and observing the client's response. If your paraphrase is accurate, the client will in some way—verbally and/or nonverbally—confirm its accuracy and usefulness. Consider the following example of the way a counselor uses the cognitive learning strategy to formulate a paraphrase:

Client, a 40-year-old woman: How can I tell my husband I want a divorce? He'll think I'm crazy. I guess I'm just afraid to tell him. [Said in a level, monotone voice]

1. What has this client told me?

   That she wants a divorce and she's afraid to tell her husband, as he will think she's crazy.

2. What is the content of this message—what person, object, idea, or situation is the client discussing?

   Wants divorce but hasn't told husband because husband will think she's crazy.

3. What is an appropriate sentence stem (one that matches the sensory words used by the client)?

   Client uses the verb *tell* two times and *think* once, so I'll go with a stem such as "You think," "I hear you saying," or "It sounds like."

4. How can I translate the client's key content into my own words?

   Want a divorce = break off, terminate the relationship, split.

5. How will I know whether my paraphrase is helpful?

   Listen and notice whether the client confirms its accuracy.

Suppose that at this point the counselor's self-talk stopped and the following dialogue ensued:

Counselor paraphrase: It sounds like you haven't found a way to tell your husband you want to end the relationship because of his possible reaction. Is that right?

Client: Yeah—I've decided—I've even been to see a lawyer. But I just don't know how to approach him with this. He thinks things are wonderful.

At this point, the counselor can congratulate herself or himself for having formulated a paraphrase that has encouraged client elaboration and focus on a main issue.

Learning Activity #14 gives you an opportunity to develop your own paraphrase responses.

LEARNING ACTIVITY #14: PARAPHRASE

In this learning activity, you are presented with three client practice messages. For each client message, develop an example of a paraphrase response, using the cognitive learning strategy outlined in the example below. In order to internalize this learning strategy, you may wish to talk through these self-questions overtly (aloud) and then covertly (silently to yourself). The end product will be a paraphrase response that you can say aloud or write down or both. Feedback is given on page 96.

Example

Client, a middle-aged graduate student: It's just a rough time for me—trying to work, keeping up with graduate school, and spending time with my family. I keep telling myself it will slow down someday. [Said in a level, monotone voice]

Self-question 1: What has this client told me?
That it's hard to keep up with everything he has to do.
Self-question 2: What is the content of this message —what person, object, idea, or situation is the client discussing?
Trying to keep up with work, school, and family.
Self-question 3: What is an appropriate sentence stem?
I'll try a stem like "It sounds like" or "There are."
Actual paraphrase response: It sounds like you're having a tough time balancing all your commitments *or* There are a lot of demands on your time right now.

Client Practice Statements

Client 1, a 30-year-old woman: My husband and I argue all the time about how to manage our kids. He says I always interfere with his discipline—I

think he is too harsh with them. [Said in a level voice tone without much variation in pitch or tempo]

Self-question 1: What has this client told me?
Self-question 2: What is the content of this message —what person, object, idea, or situation is the client discussing?
Self-question 3: What is a useful sentence stem?
Actual paraphrase response: _____

_____

Client 2, a 6-year-old boy: I wish I didn't have a little sister. I know my parents love her more than me. [Said in slow, soft voice with downcast eyes]

Self-question 1: What has this client told me?
Self-question 2: What is the content of this message —what person, object, idea, or situation is this client discussing?
Self-question 3: What is a useful sentence stem?
Actual paraphrase response: _____

_____

Client 3, a college student: I've said to my family before, I just can't compete with the other students who aren't blind. There's no way I can keep up with this kind of handicap. I've told them it's natural to be behind and do more poorly. [Said in level, measured words with little pitch and inflection change]

Self-question 1: What has this client told me?
Self-question 2: What is the content of this message —what person, object, idea, or situation is the client discussing?
Self-question 3: What is a useful sentence stem?
Actual paraphrase response: _____

_____

Reflection of feeling. We have just seen that the paraphrase is used to restate the cognitive part of the message. Although the paraphrase and the reflection of feeling are not mutually exclusive responses, the reflection of feeling is used to rephrase the *affective* part of the message, the client's emotional tone. A reflection is similar to a paraphrase but different in that a reflection adds an emotional tone or component to the message that is lacking in a paraphrase. Here are two examples that may illustrate the difference between a paraphrase and a reflection of feeling.

Client: Everything is humdrum. There's nothing new going on, nothing exciting. All my friends are away. I wish I had some money to do something different.
Counselor paraphrase: With your friends gone and no money around, there is nothing for you to do right now.
Counselor reflection: You feel bored with the way things are for you right now.

Note the counselor's use of the affect word *bored* in the reflection response to turn into the feelings of the client created by the particular situation.

FEEDBACK #14: PARAPHRASE

Client 1

Question 1. What has the client said?
  That she and her husband argue over child rearing.
Question 2. What is the content of her message?
  As a couple, they have different ideas on who should discipline their kids and how.
Question 3. What is a useful sentence stem?
  Try "It sounds like" or "Your ideas about discipline are."
Actual paraphrase response: Here are examples; see whether yours are similar.
  It sounds like you and your husband disagree a great deal on which one of you should discipline your kids and how it should be done *or* Your ideas about discipline for your kids are really different from your husband's, and this creates disagreements between the two of you.

Client 2

Question 1. What has this client said?
  He believes his little sister is loved more by his folks than he is, and he wishes she weren't around.
Question 2. What is the content of his message?
  Client feels "dethroned"—wishes the new "queen" would go away.
Question 3. What is a useful sentence stem?
  I'll try "It seems that" or "I sense that."
Actual paraphrase response: Here are examples. What are yours like?
  It seems that you'd like to be "number one" again in your family *or* I sense you are not sure of your place in your family since your little sister arrived.

Client 3

Question 1. What has this client said?
  He is behind in school and is not doing as well as his peers because he is blind—a point he has emphasized to his family.
Question 2. What is the content of his message?
  Client wants to impress on his family that his blindness is a handicap that interferes with his doing as much or as well as other students.
Question 3. What is a useful sentence stem?
  "It sounds like," "I hear you saying," or "You'd like."
Actual paraphrase response: Here are some examples.
  It sounds like it's very important to you that your family realize how tough it is for you to do well in your studies here *or* You'd like your family to realize how difficult it is for you to keep up academically with people who don't have the added problem of being blind.

Purposes of reflection. Reflecting feelings has five intended purposes. First, this response, if used effectively and accurately, helps clients to feel understood. Clients tend to communicate more freely with persons whom they feel try to understand them. As Buggs (1975, p. 293) notes, "Understanding never makes feelings worse; it only gives them permission to be revealed."

Reflection is also used to encourage clients to express more of their feelings (both positive and negative) about a particular situation, person, or whatever. Some clients do not readily reveal feelings because they have never learned to do so, and other clients hold back feelings until the therapist gives permission to focus on them. Expression of feelings is not usually an end in itself; rather, it is a means of helping clients and counselors understand the scope of the problem or situation. Most if not all of the concerns presented by clients involve underlying emotional factors to be resolved (Ivey, Ivey, & Simek-Downing, 1987, p. 73). For example, in focusing on feelings, the client may become more aware of lingering feelings about an unfinished situation or of intense feelings that seem to dominate his or her reaction to a situation. Clients may also become aware of mixed, or conflicting, feelings. Ambivalence is a common way that clients express feelings about problematic issues.

A third purpose of reflection is to help clients manage feelings. Learning to deal with feelings is especially important when a client experiences intense feelings such as fear, dependency, or anger. Strong emotions can interfere with a client's ability to make a rational response (cognitive or behavioral) to pressure.

A fourth use of reflection is with clients who express negative feelings about therapy or about the counselor. When a client becomes angry or upset with you or with the help you are offering, there is a tendency to take the client's remarks personally and become defensive. Using reflection in these instances "lessens the possibility of an emotional conflict, which often arises simply because two people are trying to make themselves heard and neither is trying to listen" (Long & Prophit, 1981, p. 89). The use of reflection in these situations lets clients know that the counselor understands their feelings in such a way that the intensity of the anger is usually diminished. As anger subsides, the client may become more receptive, and the counselor can again initiate action-oriented responses or intervention strategies.

Finally, reflection helps clients discriminate accurately among various feelings. Clients often use feeling words like *anxious* or *nervous* that, on occasion, mask deeper or more intense feelings (Ivey, 1988). Clients may also use an affect word that does not really portray their emotional state accurately. It is common, for instance, for a client to say "It's my nerves" or "I'm nervous" to depict other feelings, such as resentment and depression. Accurate reflections of feeling help clients to refine their understanding of various emotional moods.

Steps in reflecting feelings.   Reflecting feelings can be a difficult skill to learn because often feelings are ignored or misunderstood (Long & Prophit, 1981). Reflection of feelings involves six steps that include identifying the emotional tone

of the communication and verbally reflecting the client's feelings, using your own words.

The first step is to listen for the presence of feeling words, or affect words, in the client's messages. Positive, negative, and ambivalent feelings are expressed by one or more affect words falling into one of seven major categories: anger, fear, uncertainty, sadness, happiness, strength, and weakness. Table 5-3 presents a list of commonly used affect words. Becoming acquainted with such words may help you recognize them in client communications and expand your vocabulary for describing emotions.

A second way to identify the client's feelings is to watch the nonverbal behavior while the verbal message is being delivered. As you may remember

TABLE 5-3. Commonly used affect words

Level of Intensity	Category of feeling						
	Happiness	Sadness	Fear	Uncertainty	Anger	Strength, potency	Weakness, inadequacy
Strong	Excited Thrilled Delighted Overjoyed Ecstatic Elated Jubilant	Despairing Hopeless Depressed Crushed Miserable Abandoned Defeated Desolate	Panicked Terrified Afraid Frightened Scared Overwhelmed	Bewildered Disoriented Mistrustful Confused	Outraged Hostile Furious Angry Harsh Hateful Mean Vindictive	Powerful Authoritative Forceful Potent	Ashamed Powerless Vulnerable Cowardly Exhausted Impotent
Moderate	"Up" Good Happy Optimistic Cheerful Enthusiastic Joyful "Turned on"	Dejected Dismayed Disillusioned Lonely Bad Unhappy Pessimistic Sad Hurt Lost	Worried Shaky Tense Anxious Threatened Agitated	Doubtful Mixed up Insecure Skeptical Puzzled	Aggravated Irritated Offended Mad Frustrated Resentful "Sore" Upset Impatient Obstinate	Tough Important Confident Fearless Energetic Brave Courageous Daring Assured Adequate Self-confident Skillful	Embarrassed Useless Demoralized Helpless Worn out Inept Incapable Incompetent Inadequate Shaken
Weak	Pleased Glad Content Relaxed Satisfied Calm	"Down" Discouraged Disappointed "Blue" Alone Left out	Jittery Jumpy Nervous Uncomfortable Uptight Uneasy Defensive Apprehensive Hesitant Edgy	Unsure Surprised Uncertain Undecided Bothered	Perturbed Annoyed Grouchy Hassled Bothered Disagreeable	Determined Firm Able Strong	Frail Meek Unable Weak

Adapted from *The Skills of Helping* by R. R. Carkhuff and W. A. Anthony. Copyright © 1979 by Human Resource Development Press, Inc., Amherst, Massachusetts. Reprinted by permission. All rights reserved.

from Chapter 4, nonverbal cues such as body posture, facial expression, and voice quality are important indicators of client emotion. In fact, nonverbal behavior is often a more reliable clue to client emotions because nonverbal behaviors are less easily controlled than words. Observing nonverbal behavior is particularly important when the client's feelings are implied or expressed very subtly.

After the feelings reflected by the client's words and nonverbal behavior have been identified, the next step involves verbally reflecting the feelings back to the client, using different words. The choice of words to reflect feelings is critical to the effectiveness of this skill. For example, if a client expresses feeling annoyed, interchangeable affect words would be *bothered, irritated,* and *hassled.* Words such as *angry, mad,* or *outraged,* however, probably go beyond the intensity expressed by the client. It is important to select affect words that accurately match not only the type of feeling but also its intensity — otherwise, the counselor makes an understatement, which can make a client feel ridiculed, or an overstatement, which can make a client feel put off or intimidated. Note the three major levels of intensity of affect words in Table 5-3 — weak, moderate, and strong. You can also control the intensity of the expressed affect by the type of preceding adverb used — for example, *somewhat* (weak), *quite* (moderate), or *very* (strong) *upset.* Study Table 5-3 carefully so that you can develop an extensive affect-word vocabulary. Overuse of a few common affect words misses the varied nuances of the client's emotional experience.

The next step in reflecting is to start the reflection statement with an appropriate sentence stem — if possible, one that matches the client's choice of sensory words. These are some sample reflections to match the visual modality:

"It *appears* that you are *angry* now."
"It *looks* like you are *angry* now."
"It is *clear* to me that you are *angry* now."

Sample reflections to match the auditory modality:

"It *sounds* like you are *angry* now."
"I *hear* you saying you are *angry* now."
"My *ears tell* me that you are *angry* now."

Sample reflections to match kinesthetic words:

"I can *grasp* your *anger.*"

"You are *feeling angry* now."
"Let's get in *touch* with your *anger.*"

If you don't know how the client processes information, or if the client uses visual, auditory, and kinesthetic words interchangeably, you can do the same by varying the sentence stems you select (refer also to Table 5-2).

The next step in reflecting is to add on the context, or situation, around which the feelings occur. This takes the form of a brief paraphrase. Usually the context can be determined from the cognitive part of the client's message. For example, a client might say "I just can't take tests. I get so anxious I just never do well even though I study a lot." In this message, the affect is anxiety; the context is test taking. The counselor reflects the affect ("You feel uptight") *and* the context ("whenever you have to take a test").

The final step in reflecting feelings is to assess the effectiveness of your reflection after delivering it. Usually, if your reflection accurately identifies the client's feelings, the client will confirm your response by saying something like "Yes, that's right" or "Yes, that's exactly how I feel." If your response is off target, the client may reply with "Well, it's not quite like that" or "I don't feel exactly that way" or "No, I don't feel that way." When the client responds by denying feelings, it may mean your reflection was inaccurate or ill-timed. It is very important for counselors to decide when to respond to emotions. Reflection of feelings may be too powerful to be used *frequently* in the very early stage of counseling. At that time, overuse of this response may make the client feel uncomfortable, which can result in denial rather than acknowledgment of emotions. But do not ignore the potential impact or usefulness of reflection later on, when focusing on the client's feelings would promote the goals of the session. In the following example, notice the way a therapist uses a cognitive learning strategy (adapted from Richardson & Stone, 1981) to formulate a reflection of client feelings:

Client, a middle-aged man: You can't imagine what it was like when I found out my wife was cheating on me. I saw red! What should I do — get even — leave her — I'm not sure. [Said in loud, shrill, high-pitched voice, clenched fists]

1. What overt feeling words has this client used? None — except for the suggested affect phrase "saw red."

2. What feelings are implied in the client's voice and nonverbal behavior?
   Anger, outrage, hostility?
3. What is a good choice of affect words that accurately describe this client's feelings at a similar level of intensity?
   Furious, angry, vindictive, outraged.
4. What is an appropriate sentence stem that matches the sensory words used by the client?
   From the client's use of words like "imagine" and "saw red," I'll try visual sentence stems like "It seems," "It appears," "It looks like."
5. What is the context, or situation, surrounding his feelings that I'll paraphrase?
   Finding out wife was cheating on him.
6. How will I know whether my reflection is accurate and helpful?
   Watch and listen for the client's response—whether he confirms or denies the feeling of being angry and vindictive.

Actual examples of reflection:
   It looks like you're very angry now about your wife's going out on you.

It appears that you're furious with your wife's actions.
It seems like you're both angry and vindictive now that you've discovered your wife has been going out with other men.

Suppose that, following the reflection, the client said "Yes, I'm very angry, for sure—I don't know about vindictive, though I guess I'd like to make her feel as crappy as I do." The client has confirmed the counselor's reflection of the feelings of anger and vindictiveness but has also given a clue that the word *vindictive* was too strong for the client to accept *at this time.* The counselor can congratulate himself or herself for having picked up on the feelings, noting that the word *vindictive* might be used again later, after the client has sorted through his mixed feelings about his wife's behavior.

Learning Activity #15 will give you an opportunity to try out the reflection-of-feeling response.

LEARNING ACTIVITY #15: REFLECTION OF FEELINGS

In this learning activity, you are presented with three client practice messages. For each message, develop an example of a reflection-of-feeling response, using the cognitive learning strategy (Richardson & Stone, 1981) described earlier and outlined below. To internalize this learning strategy, you may wish to talk through these self-questions overtly (aloud) and then covertly (silently to yourself). The end product will be a reflection-of-feeling response that you can say aloud or write down or both. An example precedes the practice messages. Feedback is given after the learning activity (on page 102).

Example
Client, a 50-year-old steelworker now laid off: Now look, what can I do? I've been laid off over a year now, I've got no money, no job, and a family to take care of. It's also clear to me that my mind and skills are just wasting away. [Said in a loud, critical voice, staring at the ceiling, brow furrowed, eyes squinting]

Self-question 1: What overt feeling words has the client used?
None.
Self-question 2: What feelings are implied in the client's nonverbal behavior?

Disgust, angry, upset, frustrated, resentful, disillusioned, discouraged.
Self-question 3: What is a good choice of affect words that accurately describes the client's feelings at a similar level of intensity?
Seem to be two feelings—anger and discouragement. Anger seems to be the stronger emotion of the two.
Self-question 4: What is an appropriate sentence stem that matches the sensory words used by the client?
Use stems like "I see you" or "It's clear to me that you" or "From where I'm looking, you" to match the client phrases "now look" and "it's clear."
Self-question 5: What is the context, or situation, surrounding his feelings that I'll paraphrase?
Loss of job, no resources, no job prospects in sight.
Reflection-of-feeling response: I can see you're angry about being out of work and discouraged about the future *or* It looks like you're very upset about having your job and stability taken away from you.

Client Practice Statements
Client 1, an 8-year-old girl: I'm telling you I don't like living at home anymore. I wish I could live with my friend and her parents. I told my mommy that one day I'm going to run away, but she doesn't listen
(continued)

LEARNING ACTIVITY #15: REFLECTION OF FEELINGS (continued)

to me. [Said in level, measured words, glancing from side to side, lips drawn tightly together, flushed face]

Self-question 1: What overt feeling words has the client used?
Self-question 2: What feelings are implied in the client's nonverbal behavior?
Self-question 3: What are accurate and similar interchangeable affect words?
Self-question 4: What is a useful sentence stem that matches the sensory words used by the client?
Self-question 5: What is the context, or situation, concerning her feelings that I'll paraphrase?
Actual reflection response: _____

Client 2, a middle-aged man in marital therapy: As far as I'm concerned, our marriage turned sour last year when my wife went back to work. She's more in touch with her work than with me. [Said in soft voice tone with downcast eyes]

Self-question 1: What overt feeling words did the client use?
Self-question 2: What feelings are implied in the client's nonverbal behavior?

Self-question 3: What are accurate and similar interchangeable affect words?
Self-question 4: What is a useful sentence stem that matches the sensory words used by the client?
Self-question 5: What is the context, or situation, surrounding his feelings that I'll paraphrase?
Actual reflection response: _____

Client 3, an adolescent: Now look, we have too damn many rules around this school. I'm getting the hell out of here. As far as I can see, this place is a dump. [Said in loud, harsh voice]

Self-question 1: What overt feeling words has this client used?
Self-question 2: What feelings are implied in the client's nonverbal behavior?
Self-question 3: What are accurate and similar interchangeable affect words?
Self-question 4: What is a useful sentence stem that matches the sensory words used by the client?
Self-question 5: What is the context, or situation, surrounding his feelings that I'll paraphrase?
Actual reflection response: _____

Listening for Themes: Summarization

Usually, after a client has expressed several messages or has talked for a while, her or his messages will suggest certain consistencies or patterns that we refer to as *themes*. Themes in client messages are expressed in topics that the client continually refers to or brings up in some way. The counselor can identify themes by listening to what the client repeats "over and over and with the most intensity" (Carkhuff, Pierce, & Cannon, 1977). The themes indicate what the client is trying to tell us and what the client needs to focus on in the counseling sessions. The counselor can respond to client themes by using a summarization response. For example, suppose you have been counseling a young man who, during the last three sessions, has made repeated references to homosexual relationships yet has not really identified this issue intentionally. You could use a summarization to identify the theme from these repeated references by saying something like "I'm aware that during our last few sessions you've spoken consistently about homosexual relationships. Perhaps this is an issue for you we might want to focus on."

As another example, suppose that in one session a client has given you several descriptions of different situations in which she feels concerned about how other people perceive her. You might discern that the one theme common to all these situations is the client's need for approval from others, or "other-directedness." You could use a summarization such as this to identify this theme: "One thing I see in all three of the situations you've described, Jane, is that you seem quite concerned about having the approval of the other people. Is this accurate?"

Purposes of summarization. One purpose of summarization is to tie together multiple elements of client messages. In this case, summarization can serve as a good feedback tool for the client by extracting meaning from vague and ambiguous messages. A second purpose of summarization is to identify a common theme or pattern that becomes apparent after several messages or sometimes after several sessions. Occasionally, a counselor may summarize to interrupt a client's incessant rambling or "storytelling." At such times, summarization is an important focusing tool that brings direction to the interview.

A fourth use of summarization is to moderate the pace of a session that is moving too quickly. In such instances, summaries provide psychological breathing space during the session. A final purpose of a summary is to review progress that has been made during one or more interviews.

A summarization can be defined as a collection of two or more paraphrases or reflections that condenses the client's messages or the session. In using a summarization, "a helper attends to the helpee's verbal and nonverbal statements over a period of time (e.g., three minutes to a complete session or even several sessions). The helper then selects out critical dimensions of the helpee's statements and behavior and restates them for the helpee as accurately as possible" (Ivey & Gluckstern, 1974, p. 48).

A summarization may represent collective rephrasings of either cognitive or affective data. Many summarization responses will include references to both cognitive and affective messages, as in the following four examples:

1. Example of summarization to *tie together multiple elements* of a client message:

Client, a college student: All my life I thought I wanted to be a teacher. Now I'm not sure. I always thought it was the ideal career for a woman. I don't know now if that's such a good reason. Maybe there's a career out there I'm more interested in.
Summarization: You are questioning whether being a teacher is what you really want or what you think as a woman you're supposed to be.

2. Example of summarization to *identify a theme:*

Client, a 35-year-old male: One of the reasons we divorced was because she always pushed me. I could never say no to her; I always gave in. I guess it's hard for me just to say no to requests people make.
Summarization: You're discovering that you tend to give in or not do what you want in many of your significant relationships, not just with your ex-wife.

3. Example of summarization *to regulate pace of session and to give focus:*

Client, a young woman: What a terrible week I had! The water heater broke, the dog got lost, someone stole my wallet, my car ran out of gas, and to top it all off, I gained five pounds. I can't stand myself. It seems like it shows all over me.

Summarization: Let's stop for just a minute before we go on. It seems like you've encountered an unending series of bad events this week.

4. Example of summarization *to review progress* (often used as termination strategy near end of session):

Client summary: Jane, we've got about five minutes left today. Could you summarize the key things we've been working on today?
Counselor summary: Jane, we've got about five minutes left today. It seems like most of the time we've been working on the ways you find to sabotage yourself from doing things you want to do but yet feel are out of your control. This week I'd like you to work on the following homework before our next session. . . .

Steps in summarizing. Summarizing requires careful attention to and concentration on the client's verbal and nonverbal messages. Accurate use of this response involves good recall of client behavior, not only within a session but over time —across several sessions or even several months of therapy. Developing a summarization involves the following five steps:

1. Attend to and recall the message or series of messages by restating these to yourself covertly — what has the client been telling you, focusing on, working on? This is a key and difficult part of effective summaries because it requires you to be aware of many, varying verbal and nonverbal messages you have processed *over time.*
2. Identify any apparent patterns, themes, or multiple elements of these messages by asking yourself questions like "What has the client repeated over and over" or "What are the different parts of this puzzle?"
3. Select an appropriate beginning (sentence stem) for your summarization that uses the personal pronoun *you* or the client's name and matches one or more of the client's sensory words. (See Table 5-2.)
4. Next, using the sentence stem you've selected, select words to describe the theme or tie together multiple elements, and verbalize this as the summarization response. Remember to use your voice so that the summarization sounds like a statement instead of a question.
5. Assess the effectiveness of your summarization by listening for and observing whether the client confirms or denies the theme or whether the summary adds to or detracts from the focus of the session.

FEEDBACK #15: REFLECTION OF FEELINGS

Client 1

Question 1: What overt feeling words did the client use?
"Don't like."

Question 2: What feelings are implied in the client's nonverbal behavior?
Upset, irritation, resentment.

Question 3: What are interchangeable affect words?
Bothered, perturbed, irritated, upset.

Question 4: What sentence stem matches the client's sensory words?
"Seems like," "It sounds like," "I hear you saying that" match her words "tell" and "listen."

Question 5: What is the context, or situation, surrounding her feelings?
Living at home with her parents.

Actual examples of reflection: It sounds like you're upset about some things going on at your home now *or* I hear you saying you're bothered about your parents.

Client 2

Question 1: What overt feeling words did the client use?
No obvious ones except for phrases "turned sour" and "in touch with."

Question 2: What feelings are implied in the client's nonverbal behavior?
Sadness, loneliness, hurt.

Question 3: What are interchangeable affect words?
Hurt, lonely, left out, unhappy.

Question 4: What sentence stem matches the client's choice of sensory words?
"I sense," "You feel" match his phrases "turned sour" and "in touch with."

Question 5: What is the context, or situation, surrounding his feelings?
Wife's return to work.

Actual examples of reflection: You're feeling left out and lonely since your wife's gone back to work *or* I sense you're feeling hurt and unhappy because your wife seems so interested in her work.

Client 3

Question 1: What overt feeling words did the client use?
No obvious ones, but words like "damn," "hell," and "dump" suggest intensity of emotions.

Question 2: What feelings are implied in the client's nonverbal behavior?
Anger, frustration.

Question 3: What are interchangeable affect words?
Angry, offended, disgusted.

Question 4: What sentence stem matches the client's sensory words?
Stems such as "It seems," "It appears," "It looks like," "I can see" match his words "now look" and "I can see."

Question 5: What is the context surrounding the feelings?
School rules.

Actual examples of reflection: It looks like you're pretty disgusted now because you see these rules restricting you *or* It seems like you're very angry about having all these rules here at school.

To help you formulate a summarization, consider the following cognitive learning strategy:

1. What was this client telling me and working on today and over time? That is, what are the *key content* and *key affect?*
2. What has the client repeated over and over today and over time? That is, what is the *pattern* or *theme?*
3. What is a useful sentence stem that matches the client's sensory words?
4. How will I know whether my summarization is useful?

Notice how a counselor applies this cognitive learning strategy in developing a summarization in the following example:

Client, a middle-aged male fighting alcoholism who has told you for the last three sessions that his drinking is ruining his family life but he can't stop because it makes him feel better and helps him to handle job stress: I know drinking doesn't really help me in the long run. And it sure doesn't help my family. My wife keeps threatening to leave. I know all this. It's hard to stay away from the booze. Having a drink makes me feel relieved. [Said in low, soft voice, downcast eyes, stooped shoulders]

Self-question 1: What has this client been telling me today and over time?
Key content: results of drinking aren't good for him or his family.
Key affect: drinking makes him feel better, less anxious.

Self-question 2: What has this client repeated over and over today and over time—pattern or theme?
That despite adverse effects and family deterioration, he continues to drink for stress reduction;

that is, stress reduction through alcohol seems worth losing his family.

Self-question 3: What sentence stem matches the client's sensory words?

I'll try "You're feeling," "My sense of it," and so on to match his words "know" and "feel."

Suppose that at this time the counselor delivered one of the following summarizations to the client:

"Jerry, I sense that you feel it's worth having the hassle of family problems because of the good, calm feelings you get whenever you drink."

"Jerry, you feel that your persistent drinking is creating a lot of difficulties for you in your family, and I sense your reluctance to stop drinking in spite of these adverse effects."

"Jerry, I sense that, despite everything, alcohol feels more satisfying (rewarding) to you than your own family."

If Jerry confirms the theme that alcohol is more important now than his family, the counselor can conclude that the summarization was useful. If Jerry denies the theme or issue summarized by the counselor, the counselor can ask Jerry to clarify how the summarization was inaccurate, remembering that the summary may indeed be inaccurate or that Jerry may not be ready to acknowledge the issue at this time.

LEARNING ACTIVITY #16: SUMMARIZATION

In this learning activity, you are presented with three client practice messages. For each message, develop a summarization response, using the cognitive learning strategy described earlier and outlined below. To internalize this learning strategy, you may wish to talk through these self-questions overtly (aloud) and then covertly — that is, silently to yourself. The end product will be a summarization response that you can say aloud or write down or both. An example precedes the practice messages. Feedback is given on pages 108–109.

Example

Client, a 10-year-old girl:

At beginning of the session: I don't understand why my parents can't live together anymore. I'm not blaming anybody, but it just feels very confusing to me. [Said in low, soft voice with lowered, moist eyes]

Near the middle of the same session: I wish they could keep it together. I guess I feel like they can't because they fight about me so much. Maybe I'm the reason they don't want to live together anymore.

Self-question 1: What has this client been telling me and looking at today in terms of key *content* and key *affect?*

Key content: wants parents to stay together.

Key affect: feels sad, upset, responsible.

Self-question 2: What has the client repeated over and over today or over time — that is, pattern or theme?

She's the one who's responsible for her parents' breakup.

Self-question 3: What is a useful sentence stem that matches the client's sensory words?

Try "I sense" or "You're feeling," to match her words such as "don't understand" and "feels."

Examples of summarization response: Joan, at the start of our talk today, you were feeling like no one person was responsible for your parents' separation. Now I sense you're saying that you feel responsible *or* Joan, earlier today you indicated you didn't feel like blaming anyone for what's happening to your folks. Now I'm sensing that you are feeling like you are responsible for their breakup.

Client Practice Messages

Client 1, a 30-year-old man who has been blaming himself for his wife's unhappiness: I really feel guilty about marrying her in the first place. It wasn't really for love. It was just a convenient thing to do. I feel like I've messed up her life really badly. I also feel obliged to her. [Said in low, soft voice tone with lowered eyes]

Self-question 1: What has this client been telling me and working on today?

Key content:

Key affect:

Self-question 2: What has this client repeated over and over today or over time in terms of patterns and themes?

Self-question 3: What is a sentence stem that matches the client's sensory words?

Summarization response: _____

_____

Client 2, a 35-year-old woman who focused on how her life has improved since having children: I never thought I would feel this great. I always thought being a parent would be boring and terri-

(continued)

LEARNING ACTIVITY #16: SUMMARIZATION (continued)

bly difficult. It's not, for me. It's fascinating and easy. It makes everything worthwhile. [Said with alertness and animation]

Self-question 1: What has this client been telling me and working on today?
Key content:
Key affect:
Self-question 2: What has this client repeated over and over today or over time in terms of patterns and themes?
Self-question 3: What is a sentence stem that uses the client's sensory words?
Summarization response: _____
_____

Client 3, a 27-year-old woman who has continually focused on her relationships with men and her needs for excitement and stability:
First session: I've been dating lots and lots of men for

the last few years. Most of them have been married. That's great because there are no demands on me. [Bright eyes, facial animation, high-pitched voice]
Fourth session: It doesn't feel so good anymore. It's not so much fun. Now I guess I miss having some commitment and stability in my life. [Soft voice, lowered eyes]

Self-question 1: What has this client been telling me and working on today?
Key content:
Key affect:
Self-question 2: What has this client repeated over and over today or over time in terms of patterns and themes?
Self-question 3: What is a sentence stem that matches the client's sensory words?
Summarization response: _____
_____

☐ SUMMARY

We often hear these questions: "What good does all this listening do? How does just rephrasing client messages really help?" In response, we will reiterate the rationale for using listening responses in counseling.

1. Listening to clients is a very powerful reinforcer and may strengthen clients' desire to talk about themselves and their concerns. Not listening may prevent clients from sharing relevant information (Morganstern, 1986, p. 102).

2. Listening to a client first may mean a greater chance of responding accurately to the client in later stages of counseling, such as problem solving (Carkhuff et al., 1977). By jumping to quick solutions without laying a foundation of listening, you may inadvertently ignore the primary problem or propose inadequate and ill-timed action steps.

3. Listening encourages the client to assume responsibility for selecting the topic and focus of an interview. Not listening may meet your needs to find information or to solve problems. In doing so, you may portray yourself as an expert rather than a collaborator. Simply asking a series of questions or proposing a series of action steps in the initial phase of helping can cause the client to perceive you as the expert and can hinder proper development of client self-responsibility in the interview.

4. Good listening and attending skills model socially appropriate behavior for clients (Gazda et al., 1984). Many clients have not yet learned to use the art of listening in their own relationship and social contacts. They are more likely to incorporate these skills to improve their interpersonal relationships when they experience them firsthand through their contact with a significant other, such as a therapist.

Some counselors can articulate a clear rationale for listening but nevertheless cannot listen in an interview because of blocks that inhibit effective listening. Some of the most common blocks to listening are these:

1. The tendency to judge and evaluate the client's messages.
2. The tendency to stop attending because of distractions such as noise, the time of day, or the topic.
3. The temptation to respond to missing pieces of information by asking questions.
4. The temptation or the pressure put on yourself to solve problems or find answers.
5. The preoccupation with yourself as you try to practice the skills. This preoccupation shifts the focus from the client to you and actually reduces, rather than increases, your potential for listening.

Effective use of listening responses requires you to

confront these blocks head-on. Too often a counselor will simply get discouraged and not listen because it is too difficult. Start slowly and work with each listening response until you feel comfortable with it. As you accumulate counseling experience and confidence, you can listen with greater ease and facility. As you go through the remainder of this book and add to your repertory of skills, we hope that you will treat listening responses as a permanent fixture.

POSTEVALUATION

PART ONE

This part is designed for you to assess your performance on Chapter Objective One. On a sheet of paper, classify each of the counselor listening responses in the following list as a clarification, paraphrase, reflection of feelings, or summarization. If you identify 9 out of 12 responses correctly, you have met this objective. You can check your answers against those provided in the feedback that follows on pages 109–110.

1. Client, an older, retired person: "How do they expect me to live on this little bit of Social Security? I've worked hard all my life. Now I have so little to show for it—I've got to choose between heat and food."
   a. "Can you tell me who exactly expects you to be able to manage on this amount of money?"
   b. "All your life you've worked hard, hoping to give yourself a secure future. Now it's very upsetting to have only a little bit of money that can't possibly cover your basic needs."
2. Client: "I don't like taking this medication. It makes me feel worse. I can't see how it can possibly help. I know I asked you to give me something to help calm me down, but I didn't imagine it would have these effects."
   a. "Can you clarify exactly what effects these pills have seemed to have on you?"
   b. "Originally you seemed to want very much to be given some medication to rely on to help calm your nerves. Now that you're taking it, it's hard for you to see whether it's been helping or hurting."
3. Client: "I feel so nervous when I have to give a speech in front of lots of people."
   a. "You feel anxious when you have to talk to a group of people."
   b. "You would rather not have to talk in front of large groups."
4. Client: "I always have a drink when I'm under pressure.
   a. "Are you saying that you use alcohol to calm you down?"

   b. "You think alcohol has a calming effect on you."
5. Client: "I don't know whether I've ever experienced orgasm. My husband thinks I have, though."
   a. "Are you saying that you've been trying to have your husband believe you do experience orgasm?"
   b. "You feel uncertain about whether you've ever really had an orgasm, even though your husband senses that you have."
6. Client: "I haven't left my house in years. I'm even afraid to hang out the clothes."
   a. "You feel panicked and uneasy when you go outside the security of your house."
   b. "Because of this fear, you've stayed inside your house for a long time."

PART TWO

Match the four listening responses listed in the right column with the intended purposes of these responses listed in the left column (Chapter Objective Two). Feedback follows the postevaluation.

Intended Purpose of Response	Listening Response
____1. To encourage greater expression of feeling	a. Clarification
____2. To confirm the accuracy of what you heard, saw, or grasped	b. Paraphrase
____3. To highlight the content part of a message	c. Reflection of feelings
____4. To interrupt rambling and provide focus to the session	d. Summarization
____5. To clear up vague or confusing client messages	
____6. To help the client discriminate accurately among feelings	

(continued)

POSTEVALUATION (continued)

_____7. To identify a common theme from client messages

_____8. To tie together multiple elements of a client message

PART THREE

Three client statements are presented. Objective Three asks you to verbalize or write an example of each of the four listening responses for each client statement.* In developing these responses, it may be helpful to use the cognitive learning strategy you practiced earlier for each response. Feedback follows the evaluation.

Client 1, a 28-year-old woman: My life is a shambles. I lost my job, my friends never come around anymore. It's been months now, but I still can't seem to cut down. I can't see clearly. It seems hopeless. [Said in high-pitched voice, with crossed legs, lots of nervous "twitching" in hands and face]
Clarification:
Paraphrase:
Reflection:
Summarization:

Client 2, a sophomore in high school: I can't seem to get along with my parents. They're always harassing me, telling me what to do. Sometimes I get so mad I feel like hitting them, but I don't, because it would only make the situation worse.
Clarification:
Paraphrase:
Reflection:
Summarization:

Client 3, a 54-year-old man: Ever since my wife died four months ago, I can't get interested in anything. I don't want to eat or sleep. I'm losing weight. Sometimes I just tell myself I'd be better off if I were dead, too.
Clarification:
Paraphrase:
Reflection:
Summarization:

PART FOUR

This part of the evaluation gives you an opportunity to develop your observation skills of key aspects of

* These three client messages can be put on audiotape with pauses between statements. Instead of reading the message, you can listen to the message and write or verbalize your responses during the pause.

client behavior that must be attended to in order to listen effectively:

1. Vague or confusing phrases and messages
2. Key content expressed
3. Use of affect words
4. Nonverbal behavior illustrative of feeling or mood states
5. Presence of themes or patterns

Objective Four asks you to observe these five aspects of a client's behavior during a 15-minute interview conducted by someone else. Record your observations on the Client Observation Checklist that follows. You can obtain feedback for this activity by having two or more persons observe and rate the same session—then compare your responses.

CLIENT OBSERVATION CHECKLIST

Name of counselor _____

Name of observer(s) _____

_____

Instructions: Given the five categories of client behavior to observe (left column), use the right column to record separate occurrences of behaviors within these categories as they occur during a short counseling interview.*

Observed category of behavior	Selected key client words and nonverbal behavior
1. Vague, confusing, ambiguous phrases, messages	1. _____ 2. _____ 3. _____ 4. _____ 5. _____
2. Key content (situation, event, idea, person)	1. _____ 2. _____ 3. _____ 4. _____ 5. _____
3. Affect words used	1. _____ 2. _____ 3. _____ 4. _____ 5. _____

(continued)

* If observers are not available, audiotape or videotape your sessions and complete the checklist while reviewing the tape.

4. Nonverbal behavior indicative of certain feelings

1. _____
2. _____
3. _____
4. _____
5. _____

5. Themes, patterns

1. _____
2. _____
3. _____
4. _____
5. _____

Observer impressions and comments _____
_____
_____

PART FIVE

This part of the evaluation gives you a chance to demonstrate the four listening responses. Objective Five asks you to conduct a 15-minute role-play interview in which you use at least two examples of each of the four listening responses. Someone can observe your performance, or you can assess yourself from an audiotape of the interview. You or the observer can classify your responses and judge their effectiveness using the Listening Checklist that follows. Try to select a listening response to use when you have a particular purpose in mind. Remember, in order to listen, it is helpful to—

1. refrain from making judgments
2. resist distractions
3. avoid asking questions
4. avoid giving advice
5. stay focused on the client

Obtain feedback for this activity by noting the categories of responses on the Listening Checklist and their judged effectiveness.

LISTENING CHECKLIST

Name of counselor _____
Name of observer _____

Instructions: In the far left column, "Counselor response," summarize a few key words of each counselor statement, followed by a brief notation of the client's verbal and nonverbal response in the next column, "Client response." Then classify the message as a clarification, paraphrase, reflection of feeling, summarization, or other under the corresponding column. Rate the *effectiveness* of each counselor response in the far right column, "Effectiveness of response," on the following 1–3 scale.

1 = not effective. Client ignored counselor message or gave indication that counselor message was inaccurate and "off target."

2 = somewhat effective. Client gave some verbal or nonverbal indication that counselor message was partly right, accurate, "on target."

3 = very effective. Client's verbal and nonverbal behavior confirmed that counselor response was very accurate, "on target," or "fit."

Remember to watch and listen for the *client's* reaction to the response for your effectiveness rating.

(continued)

POSTEVALUATION (continued)

Counselor response (key words)	Client Response (key words)	Type of counselor response					Effectiveness of response (determined by client response) Rate from 1 to 3 (3 = high)
		Clarification	Paraphrase	Reflection of feelings	Summarization	Other	
1.							
2.							
3.							
4.							
5.							
6.							
7.							
8.							
9.							
10.							
11.							
12.							
13.							
14.							
15.							
16.							
17.							
18.							
19.							
20.							

Observer comments and general observations _____

_____

FEEDBACK #16: SUMMARIZATION

Client 1

Question 1: What has the client told me?

Key content: He married for convenience, not love.

Key affect: Now he feels both guilty and indebted.

Question 2: What has the client repeated over and over now and before in terms of patterns and themes?

Conflicting feelings—feels a strong desire to get out of the marriage yet feels a need to keep relationship going because he feels responsible for his wife's unhappiness.

Question 3: What is an appropriate sentence stem that matches the client's sensory words?

Use stems such as "You're feeling," "My grasp of it is," "I sense that" to match his constant use of the verb "feel."

Examples of summarization response: I sense you're feeling pulled in two different directions. For yourself, you want out of the relationship. For her sake, you feel you should stay in the relationship" *or* You're feeling like you've used her for your convenience and because of this you think you owe it to her to keep the relationship going *or* I can grasp how very much you want to pull yourself out of the marriage and also how responsible you feel for your wife's present unhappiness.

(continued)

Client 2

Question 1: What has the client told me?
Key content: Children have made her life better, more worthwhile.
Key affect: Surprise and pleasure.
Question 2: What has the client said over and over in terms of patterns and themes?
Being a parent is uplifting and rewarding even though she didn't expect it to be. In addition, her children are very important to her. To some extent, they define her worth and value as a person.
Question 3: What is an appropriate sentence stem that matches the client's sensory words?
There are no real clear-cut sensory words exhibited in this message, so I may want to emphasize several in my response—for example, "It *seems* like you're *feeling*" or "I *hear* feelings of."
Examples of summarization response: It seems like you're feeling surprise, satisfaction, and relief about finding parenting so much easier and more rewarding than you had expected it would be *or* I hear feelings of surprise and pleasure in your voice as you reveal how great it is to be a parent and how important your children are to you *or* You seem so happy about the way your life is going since you've had children—as if they make you and your life more worthwhile.

Client 3

Question 1: What has the client told me?
Key content: She has been dating lots of men who have their own commitments.
Key affect: It used to feel great; now she feels a sense of loss and emptiness.
Question 2: What has she repeated over and over in terms of patterns and themes?
At first—feelings of pleasure, relief not to have demands in close relationships. Now, feelings are changing, feels less satisfied, wants more stability in close relationships.
Question 3: What is an appropriate sentence stem that matches the client's sensory words?
There are no clear-cut sensory words except for "feel" in the fourth session, so I'll vary my own words in my response and also include the word "feel."
Examples of summarization response: Lee Ann, originally you said it was great to be going out with a lot of different men who didn't ask much of you. Now you're also feeling it's not so great—it's keeping you from finding some purpose and stability in your life *or* In our first session, you were feeling "up" about all those relationships with noncommittal men. Now you're feeling like this is

interfering with the stability you need and haven't yet found *or* At first it was great to have all this excitement and few demands. Now you're feeling some loss from lack of a more stable, involved relationship.

☐ SUGGESTED READINGS

Brammer, L. M., Shostrom, E. L., & Abrego, P. J. (1989). *Therapeutic psychology* (5th ed.). Englewood Cliffs, NJ: Prentice-Hall.
Carkhuff, R. R., & Anthony, W. A. (1979). *The skills of helping.* Amherst, MA: Human Resource Development Press.
Hackney, H., & Cormier, L. S. (1988). *Counseling strategies and interventions* (3rd ed.). Englewood Cliffs, NJ: Prentice-Hall.
Ivey, A. E. (1988). *Intentional interviewing and counseling* (2nd ed.). Pacific Grove, CA: Brooks/Cole.
Richardson, B., & Stone, G. L. (1981). Effects of a cognitive adjunct procedure within a microtraining situation. *Journal of Counseling Psychology, 28,* 168–175.

FEEDBACK: POSTEVALUATION

PART ONE
1. a. Clarification
   b. Summarization
2. a. Clarification
   b. Summarization
3. a. Reflection
   b. Paraphrase
4. a. Clarification
   b. Paraphrase
5. a. Clarification
   b. Reflection
6. a. Reflection
   b. Paraphrase

PART TWO
1. c. Reflection
2. a. Clarification
3. b. Paraphrase
4. d. Summarization
5. a. Clarification
6. c. Reflection
7. d. Summarization
8. d. Summarization

(continued)

FEEDBACK: POSTEVALUATION (continued)

PART THREE

Here are some examples of listening responses. See whether yours are similar:

Client statement 1

1. Clarification: "Can you describe what you mean by 'cutting down'?"
2. Paraphrase: "You seem to realize that your life is not going the way you want it to."
3. Reflection: "You appear frightened about the chaos in your life, and you seem uncertain of what you can do to straighten it out."
4. Summarization: "Your whole life seems to be falling apart. Your friends are avoiding you, and now you don't even have a job to go to. Even though you've tried to solve the problem, you can't seem to handle it alone. Coming here to talk is a useful first step in 'clearing up the water' for you."

Client statement 2

1. Clarification: "Can you describe what it's like when you don't get along with them?"
2. Paraphrase: "It appears that your relationship with your parents is deteriorating to the point where you feel you may lose control of yourself."
3. Reflection: "You feel frustrated and angry with your parents because they're always giving you orders."
4. Summarization: "It seems like the situation at home with your parents has become intolerable. You can't stand their badgering, and you feel afraid that you might do something you would later regret."

Client statement 3

1. Clarification: "Are you saying that since the death of your wife, life has become so miserable that you occasionally contemplate taking your own life?"
2. Paraphrase: "Your life has lost much of its meaning since your wife's recent death."
3. Reflection: "It sounds like you're very lonely and depressed since your wife died."
4. Summarization: "Since your wife died, you've lost interest in living. There's no fun or excitement anymore, and further, you're telling yourself that it's not going to get any better."

ACTION RESPONSES

SIX

TABLE on PAGE 113

Listening responses involve responding to client messages primarily from the client's point of view, or frame of reference. There are times in the counseling process when it is legitimate to move beyond the client's frame of reference and to use responses that include more counselor-generated data and perceptions. These responses, which we have labeled *action responses,* are active rather than passive and reflect a counselor-directed more than a client-centered style. Whereas listening responses influence the client indirectly, action responses exert a more direct influence on the client (Ivey, 1988). Action responses are based as much on the counselor's perceptions and hypotheses as on the client's messages and behavior. We have selected four such action responses: probes, confrontation, interpretation, and information giving. The general purpose of action responses, according to Egan (1990), is to help clients see the need for change and action through a more objective frame of reference.

□ OBJECTIVES

1. Given a written list of counselor responses, be able to identify accurately at least six out of eight examples of the four counselor action responses.
2. Using a written list, match the four action responses with the intended purpose of each response.
3. With a written list of three client statements, write an example of each of the four action responses for each client statement.
4. In a 30-minute counseling interview in which you are an observer, listen for and record five key aspects of client behavior that form the basis for action responding.
5. Conduct at least one 20-minute counseling interview in which you integrate relationship variables (Chapters 2 and 3), nonverbal behavior (Chapter 4), listening responses (Chapter 5), and action responses (Chapter 6).

111

☐ ACTION RESPONSES AND TIMING

The most difficult part of using action responses is the timing, the point at which these responses are used in the interview. As you recall from Chapter 5, some helpers tend to jump into action responses before listening and establishing rapport with the client. Listening responses generally reflect clients' understanding of themselves. In contrast, action responses reflect the *counselor's* understanding of the client. Action responses can be used a great deal in the interview as long as the counselor is careful to lay the foundation with attending and listening. The listening base can heighten the client's receptivity to a counselor action message. If the counselor "lays on" his or her opinions and perceptions too quickly, the client may respond with denial, with defensiveness, or even with dropping out of counseling. When this happens, the counselor needs to "drop back" to a less obtrusive level of influence and do more listening, at least until a strong base of client trust and confidence has been developed.

☐ FOUR ACTION RESPONSES

We have selected four action responses to describe in this chapter: the probe, confrontation, interpretation, and information giving. A *probe* is an open or closed question or inquiry. A *confrontation* is a description of a client discrepancy. An *interpretation* is a possible explanation for the client's behavior. *Information giving* is the communication of data or facts about experiences, events, alternatives, or people.

Look at the way these four action responses differ in this illustration:

Client, a 35-year-old widow, mother of two young children: My whole life fell apart when my husband died. I keep feeling so unsure about my ability to make it on my own and to support my kids. My husband always made all the decisions for me. Now I haven't slept well for so long, and I'm drinking more heavily—I can't even think straight. Besides, I've put on 15 pounds. I look like a witch. Who would even want to think of hiring me the way I am now?

Counselor probe: What makes you think of yourself as not being able to make it on your own?
or
How do you think you could handle the situation?

Counselor confrontation: It seems that you're saying two things—first, that you aren't sure of your ability to work and support your family, but also that you're almost making it hard for someone else to see you as employable by some of the things you're doing, such as drinking and putting on weight.

Counselor interpretation: It's possible that your drinking heavily and not sleeping well are ways to continue to avoid accepting the responsibility of making decisions for yourself.

Counselor information giving: Perhaps you are still not over the grief process. It might help to acknowledge your feelings of loss and to take a look at where you are with respect to the different stages of grieving. For example, . . .

Table 6-1 describes the definitions and intended purposes of these four action responses. Remember, these intended purposes are presented only as tentative guidelines, not as "the truth." The remainder of the chapter will describe and present model examples of these four skills. You will have an opportunity to practice each skill and receive feedback about your responses.

Probes

Probes, or questions, are an indispensable part of the interview process. Their effectiveness depends on the type of question and the frequency of their use. Questions have the potential for establishing a desirable or undesirable pattern of interpersonal exchange, depending on the skill of the therapist (Long, Paradise, & Long, 1981). Beginning interviewers err by assuming that a helping interview is a series of questions and answers or by asking the wrong kind of question at a particular time. These practices are likely to make the client feel interrogated rather than understood. Research has shown that even more experienced counselors overuse this potentially valuable verbal response (Spooner & Stone, 1977). Unfortunately, asking a question is all too easy to do during silence or when you are at a loss for words. Questions should not be asked unless you have a particular purpose for the question in mind. For example, if you are using a question as an open invitation to talk, realize that you are in fact asking the client to initiate a dialogue and allow the client to respond in this way (Long et al., 1981).

Open and closed probes. Most effective questions are worded in an open-ended fashion, beginning

TABLE 6-1. Definitions and intended purposes of counselor action responses

Response	Definition	Intended purpose
Probe	Open-ended or closed question or inquiry	*Open-ended questions* 1. To begin an interview 2. To encourage client elaboration or to obtain information 3. To elicit specific examples of client's behaviors, feelings or thoughts 4. To motivate client to communicate *Closed questions* 1. To narrow the topic of discussion 2. To obtain specific information 3. To identify parameters of a problem or issue 4. To interrupt an overtalkative client—for example, to give focus to the session
Confrontation	Description of client discrepancy	1. To identify client's mixed (incongruent) messages 2. To explore other ways of perceiving client's self or situation
Interpretation	Possible explanation of or association among various client behaviors	1. To identify the relation between client's implicit messages and behaviors 2. To examine client behavior from alternative view or with different explanation 3. To add to client's self-understanding as a basis for client action
Information giving	Verbal communication of data or facts	1. To identify alternatives 2. To evaluate alternatives 3. To dispel myths 4. To motivate clients to examine issues they may have been avoiding

with words such as *what, how, when, where,* or *who.* According to Ivey, Ivey, and Simek-Downing (1987, p. 71), "Open questions will predictably result in a rather specific client response, thus providing you with important data about the problem." The particular word used to begin an open-ended question is important. Research has shown that "what" questions tend to solicit facts and information, "how" questions are associated with sequence and process or emotions, and "why" questions produce reasons and "intellectualizing" (Ivey, Ivey, & Simek-Downing, 1987). Similarly, "when" and "where" questions solicit information about time and place, and "who" questions are associated with information about people. The importance of using *different* words in formulating open-ended questions is critical.

Open-ended probes have a number of purposes in different counseling situations (Hackney & Cormier, 1988; Ivey, 1988; Long et al., 1981).

1. Beginning an interview ("What would you like to discuss today?").

2. Encouraging the client to express more information ("What else can you tell me about this?").

3. Eliciting examples of particular behaviors, thoughts, or feelings so that the counselor can better understand the conditions contributing to the client's problem ("What are you doing in this situation? What are you thinking in this situation? How are you feeling about this?").

4. Developing client commitment to communicate by inviting the client to talk and guiding the client along a focused interaction.

In contrast to open-ended questions, closed, or focused, questions can be useful if the counselor needs a particular fact or seeks a particular bit of information. These questions begin with words such as *are, do, can, is, did* and can be answered with a yes, a no, or a very short response. As we will see in Chapter 8, questions are a major tool for obtaining information during the assessment process.

These are examples of closed questions:

1. "Of all the problems we discussed, which bothers you the most?"
2. "Is there a history of depression in your family?"
3. "Are you planning to look for a job in the next few months?"

The purposes of closed questions include the following:

1. Narrowing the area of discussion by asking the client for a specific response ("Is there a history of depression in your family?").
2. Gathering specific information ("Is your daughter still living at home?").
3. Identifying parameters of problems ("Have you noticed anything that makes the depression worse?").
4. Interrupting an overtalkative client who rambles or "storytells" ("Do you want to focus now on the family situation you mentioned earlier?").

Closed questions must be used sparingly within an interview. Too many closed questions may discourage discussion and may subtly give the client permission to avoid sensitive or important topics.

Guidelines in the use of probes. Probes will be used more effectively and efficiently if you remember some important guidelines for their use.

First, develop questions that center on the concerns of the client. Effective questions arise from what the client has already said, not from the counselor's curiosity or need for closure.

Second, after a question, use a pause to give the client sufficient time to respond. Remember that the client may not have a ready response. The feeling of having to supply a quick answer may be threatening and may encourage the client to give a response that pleases the therapist.

Third, ask only one question at a time. Some interviewers tend to ask multiple questions (two or more) before allowing the client time to respond. We call this "stacking questions." It confuses the client, who may respond only to the least important of your series of questions.

Fourth, avoid accusatory or antagonistic questions. These are questions that reflect antagonism either because of the counselor's voice tone or because of use of the word *why.* You can obtain the same information by asking "what" instead of "why." Accusatory questions can make a client feel defensive.

Finally, avoid relying on questions as a primary response mode during an interview (an exception would be when doing an intake, a history, or an assessment session). Remember that in some non-Western cultures questions may seem offensive and intrusive. In any culture, consistent overuse of questions can create a number of problems in the therapeutic relationship, including creating dependency, promoting yourself as an expert, reducing responsibility and involvement by the client, and creating resentment (Gazda et al., 1984). The feeling of being interrogated may be especially harmful with "reluctant" clients. Questions are most effective when they provoke new insights and yield new information. To determine whether it is really necessary to use a question at any particular time during a session, ask the question covertly to yourself and see whether you can answer it for the client. If you can, the question is probably unnecessary, and a different response would be more productive (D'Augelli, D'Augelli, & Danish, 1981).

Steps in the use of probes. There are four steps in formulating effective probes. First, determine the purpose of your probe—is it legitimate and therapeutically useful? Often, before probing for information, it is therapeutically useful to demonstrate first that you have heard the client's message. Listening before probing is particularly important when clients reveal strong emotions. It also helps clients to feel understood rather than interrogated. For this reason, before each of our example probes, we use a paraphrase or reflection response. In actual practice, this "bridging" of listening and action responses is very important. Second, depending on the purpose, decide what type of question would be most helpful. Remember that open-ended probes foster client exploration, while closed or focused questions should be reserved for times when you want specific information or you need to narrow the area of discussion. Make sure your question centers on concerns of the client, not issues of interest only to you. Finally, remember to assess the effectiveness of your questioning by determining whether its purpose was achieved. A question is not useful simply because the client answered or responded to it. Additionally, examine how the client responded and the overall explanation, inquiry, and dialogue that ensued as a result of particular questions (Long et al., 1981).

These steps are summarized in the following cognitive learning strategy:

1. What is the purpose of my probe, and is it therapeutically useful?
2. Can I anticipate the client's answer?
3. Given the purpose, how can I start the wording of my probe to be most effective?
4. How will I know whether my probe is effective?

Notice how the counselor applies this cognitive learning strategy in the following example:

Client: I just don't know where to start. My marriage is falling apart. My mom recently died. And I've been having some difficulties at work.
Counselor:
1. What is the purpose of my probe—and is it therapeutically useful?
   To get the client to focus more specifically on an issue of most concern to her.
2. Can I anticipate the client's answer?
   No.
3. Given the purpose, how can I start the wording of my probe to be most effective?
   "Which one of these?"
   "Do you want to discuss _____?"
4. How will I know whether my probe is effective?

Examine the client's verbal and nonverbal response and resulting dialogue, as well as whether the purpose was achieved (whether client starts to focus on the specific concern).

Suppose that at this time the counselor's covert visualization or self-talk ends and the following dialogue ensues:

Counselor question: Things must feel overwhelming to you right now. [reflection] Of the three concerns you just mentioned, which one is of most concern to you now? [probe]
Client response: My marriage. I want to keep it together, but I don't think my husband does. [accompanied by direct eye contact; body posture, which had been tense, now starts to relax]

From the client's verbal and nonverbal response, the therapist can conclude the question was effective because the client focused on a specific concern and did not appear to be threatened by the question. The therapist can now covertly congratulate herself or himself for formulating an effective question with this client.

Learning Activity #17 gives you an opportunity to try out this cognitive learning strategy in order to develop effective probes.

LEARNING ACTIVITY #17: PROBES

In this learning activity, you are given three client practice statements. For each client message, develop an example of a probe, using the cognitive learning strategy described earlier and outlined below. To internalize this learning strategy, you may wish to talk through these self-questions overtly (aloud) and then covertly (silently to yourself). The end product will be a probe that you can say aloud or write down or both. An example precedes the practice messages. Feedback is at the end of the learning activity on page 119).

Example

Client 1, a middle-aged woman: I just get so nervous. I'm just a bunch of nerves.

Self-question 1: What is the purpose of my probe—and is it therapeutically useful?
To ask for examples of times when she is nervous. This is therapeutically useful because it contributes to increased understanding of the problem.
Self-question 2: Can I anticipate the client's answer?
No.
Self-question 3: Given the purpose, how can I start

the wording of my probe to be most effective?
"When" or "what."
Actual probes: You say you're feeling pretty upset. [reflection] When do you feel this way? [probe] *or* What are some times when you get this feeling? [probe]

Client Practice Messages

The purpose of the probe is given to you for each message. Try to develop probes that relate to the stated purposes. Remember too, to precede your probe with a listening response such as paraphrase or reflection.

Client 1, a retired woman: To be frank about it, it's been pure hell around my house the last year.

Self-question 1: What is the purpose of my probe?
To encourage client to elaborate on how and what has been hell for her.
Self-question 2: Can I anticipate the client's answer?
Self-question 3: Given the purpose, how can I start the wording of my probe to be most effective?
Actual probe(s): _____

(continued)

Client 2, a 40-year-old man: Sometimes I just feel kind of blue. It goes on for a while. Not every day but sometimes.

Self-question 1: What is the purpose of my probe? To find out whether client has noticed anything that makes the "blueness" better.
Self-question 2: Can I anticipate the client's answer?
Self-question 3: Given the purpose, how can I start the wording of my probe to be most effective?
Actual probe(s): _____

_____

Client 3, a 35-year-old woman: I just feel over-whelmed right now. Too many kids underfoot. Not enough time for *me.*

Self-question 1: What is the purpose of my probe? To find out how many kids are underfoot and in what capacity client is responsible for them.
Self-question 2: Can I anticipate the client's answer?
Self-question 3: Given the purpose, how can I start the wording of my probe to be most effective?
Actual probe(s): _____

_____

Confrontation

A confrontation is a verbal response in which the counselor describes discrepancies, conflicts, and mixed messages apparent in the client's feelings, thoughts, and actions. Patterson and Eisenberg (1983) believe that confrontation is a tool to focus "the client's attention on some aspect of his or her behavior that, if changed, would lead to more effective functioning" (p. 75). Confrontation has several purposes. One purpose is to help clients explore other ways of perceiving themselves or an issue, leading ultimately to different actions or behaviors. A second and major purpose of confrontation is to help the client become more aware of discrepancies or incongruities in thoughts, feelings, and actions. There are many instances within an interview in which a client says or does something that is inconsistent. For example, a client may say she doesn't want to talk to you because you are a male but then goes ahead and talks to you. In this case, the client's verbal message is inconsistent with her actual behavior. This is an example of an inconsistent, or mixed, message. The purpose of using a confrontation to deal with a mixed message is to describe the discrepancy or contradiction to the client. Often the client is unaware or only vaguely aware of the conflict before the counselor points it out. In describing the discrepancy, it is often most helpful to use a confrontation that presents or connects *both* parts of the discrepancy.

Six major types of mixed messages and accompanying descriptions of counselor confrontations are presented as examples (see also Egan, 1990; Ivey, 1988).

1. *Verbal and nonverbal behavior*
   a. The client says "I feel comfortable" (verbal message) and at the same time is fidgeting and twisting her hands (nonverbal message).
   Counselor confrontation: You say you feel comfortable, and you're also fidgeting and twisting your hands.
   b. Client says "I feel happy about the relationship being over—it's better this way" (verbal message) and is talking in a slow, low-pitched voice (nonverbal message).
   Counselor confrontation: You say you're happy it's over, and at the same time your voice suggests you have some other feelings, too.
2. *Verbal messages and action steps or behaviors*
   a. Client says "I'm going to call her" (verbal message) but reports the next week that he did not make the call (action step).
   Counselor confrontation: You said you would call her, and as of now you haven't done so.
   b. Client says "Counseling is very important to me" (verbal message) but calls off the next two sessions (behavior).
   Counselor confrontation: Several weeks ago you said how important counseling is to you; now I'm also aware that you called off our last two meetings.
3. *Two verbal messages* (stated inconsistencies)
   a. Client says "He's sleeping around with other people. I don't feel bothered [verbal message 1], but I think our relationship should mean more to him than it does" [verbal message 2].
   Counselor confrontation: First you say you feel OK about his behavior; now you're feeling upset that your relationship is not as important to him as it is to you.

b. Client says "I really do love little Georgie [verbal message 1], although he often bugs the hell out of me" [verbal message 2].
Counselor confrontation: You seem to be aware that much of the time you love him, and at other times you feel very irritated toward him, too.

4. *Two nonverbal messages* (apparent inconsistencies)

a. Client is smiling (nonverbal message 1) and crying (nonverbal message 2) at the same time.
Counselor confrontation: You're smiling and also crying at the same time.

b. Client is looking directly at counselor (nonverbal message 1) and has just moved chair back from counselor (nonverbal message 2).
Counselor confrontation: You're looking at me while you say this, and at the same time, you also just moved away.

5. *Two persons* (counselor/client, parent/child, teacher/student, spouse/spouse, and so on)

a. Client's husband lost his job two years ago. Client wants to move; husband wants to stick around near his family.
Counselor confrontation: Edie, you'd like to move. Marshall, you're feeling family ties and want to stick around.

b. A woman presents anxiety, depression, and memory loss. You suggest a medical workup to rule out any organic dysfunction, and the client refuses.
Counselor confrontation: Irene, I feel it's very important for us to have a medical workup so we know what to do that will be most helpful for you. You seem to feel very reluctant to have the workup done. How can we work this out?

6. *Verbal message and context or situation*

a. A young child deplores her parents' divorce and states that she wants to help her parents get back together.
Counselor confrontation: Juanita, you say you want to help your parents get back together. At the same time, you had no role in their breakup. How do you put these two things together?

b. A young married couple have had severe conflicts for the past three years, and still they want to have a baby to improve their marriage.
Counselor confrontation: The two of you have separated three times since I've been seeing you in therapy. Now you're saying you want to use a child to improve your relationship. Many couples indicate that having a child and being parents increases, rather than relieves, stress. How do you put this together?

LEARNING ACTIVITY #18: MIXED MESSAGES

An important part of developing effective confrontations is learning to identify accurately various client discrepancies and incongruities. In this learning activity, we present four client messages. For each message, use the list below to identify the type of mixed message you observe from the client's message, and identify concrete verbal/nonverbal cues that indicate the discrepancy. An example precedes the practice messages. Feedback is given after the learning activity (on page 120).

Types of mixed messages

1. Verbal and nonverbal behavior
2. Verbal messages and actions or behaviors
3. Two verbal messages
4. Two nonverbal messages
5. Two persons
6. Verbal messages and context

Example

Client: I'm very happy. [Said with lowered, moist eyes, stooped shoulders, impassive facial expression]

1. Identify the type of mixed message: #1 — verbal and nonverbal behavior.
2. Identify any cues that are indicative of the mixed message: Client *says* she's happy, but eyes, shoulders, and face suggest sadness.

Client Practice Messages

Client 1, a teenage girl with an obvious limp: I'd like to start ballet or gymnastics. I'd like to be a star gymnast or ballerina.

1. Identify the type of mixed message: _____

_____

(continued)

2. Identify any cues that are indicative of the mixed message: _____
_____

Client 2, a young man who has been talking very openly with you about some sexual concerns: A big part of the problem is that I can't talk to her about our sex life. I've just never been able to talk about sex.

1. Identify the type of mixed message: _____
_____

2. Identify any cues that are indicative of the mixed message: _____
_____

Client 3: My husband and I are thinking about having a baby. It would be a good way to fill this void we feel; to keep busy with someone who needs

you all the time. It will be great as long as it isn't too confining. I don't want to be too tied down.

1. Identify the type of mixed message: _____
_____

2. Identify any cues that are indicative of the mixed message: _____
_____

Client 4: My wife is always interested in sex. She could just wear me out. She wants it two or three times a night. I've told her I think that's a little much, especially for two persons who have been married as long as we have.

1. Identify the type of mixed message: _____
_____

2. Identify any cues that are indicative of the mixed message: _____
_____

Ground rules for confronting. Confrontation needs to be offered in a way that helps clients to examine the consequences of their behavior rather than defending their actions (Johnson, 1981). In other words, confrontation must be used carefully in order not to increase the very behavior or pattern that the therapist feels may need to be diminished or modified. The following ground rules may assist you in using this response to help rather than to harm. First, be aware of your own motives for confronting at any particular time. Although the word itself has a punitive or emotionally charged sound, confrontation in the helping process is not an attack on the client or an opportunity to badger the client (Patterson & Eisenberg, 1983). Confrontation is also not to be used as a way to ventilate or "dump" your frustration onto the client. It is a means of offering constructive, "growth-directed" feedback that is positive in context and intent, not disapproving or critical (Patterson & Eisenberg, 1983, p. 75). To avoid blame, focus on the incongruity as the problem, not on the person, and "allow your nonjudgmental stance to be reflected in your tone of voice and body language" (Ivey, 1988, p. 175). In describing the distortion or discrepancy, the confrontation should cite a *specific example* of the behavior rather than make a vague inference. A poor confrontation might be "You want people to like you, but your personality turns them off." In this case, the counselor is making a general inference about the client's personality

and also is implying that the client must undergo a major "overhaul" in order to get along with others. A more helpful confrontation would be "You want people to like you, and at the same time you make frequent remarks about yourself that seem to get in the way and turn people off."

Moreover, before a counselor tries to confront a client, rapport and trust should be established. Confrontation probably should not be used unless you, the counselor, are willing to maintain or increase your involvement in or commitment to the counseling relationship (Johnson, 1986). Some counselors, regardless of the status of the counseling relationship, sprinkle their counseling style with liberal doses of critical, negative messages. Egan (1975, p. 171) suggests that someone who specializes in confrontation may be a destructive person who isn't too adept at her or his chosen specialty. At the other extreme, some counselors may be so uncomfortable with anything other than positive communication, or "good news," that they totally avoid using confrontation even with long-term clients. The primary consideration is to judge what your level of involvement seems to be with each client and adapt accordingly. The stronger the relationship, the more receptive the client may be to a confrontation.

The *timing* of a confrontation is very important. Since the purpose is to help the person engage in self-examination, try to offer the confrontation at a time when the client is likely to use it. The per-

FEEDBACK #17: PROBES

Client 1

Sample probes based on defined purpose: It sounds like things have gotten out of hand. [paraphrase] What exactly has been going on that's been so bad for you? [probe] or How has it been like hell for you? [probe]

Client 2

Sample probes based on defined purpose: Now and then you feel kind of down. [reflection] What have you noticed that makes this feeling go away? [probe] or Have you noticed anything in particular that makes you feel better? [probe]

Client 3

Sample probes based on defined purpose: With everyone else to take care of, there's not much time left for you. [paraphrase] Exactly how many kids are underfoot? [probe] or How many kids are you responsible for? [probe]

ceived ability of the client to act on the confrontation should be a major guideline in deciding when to confront (Johnson, 1986). In other words, before you jump in and confront, determine the person's attention level, anxiety level, desire to change, and ability to listen.

Appropriate use of timing also means that the helper does not confront on a "hit and run" basis (Johnson, 1986). Ample time should be given after the confrontation to allow the client to react to and discuss the effects of this response. For this reason, counselors should avoid confronting near the end of a therapy session.

It is also a good idea not to overload the client with confrontations that make heavy demands in a short time. The rule of "successive approximations" suggests that people learn small steps of behaviors gradually more easily than trying to make big changes overnight. Initially, you may want to confront the person with something that can be managed fairly easily and with some success. Carkhuff (1987) suggests that two successive confrontations may be too intense and should be avoided.

Finally, acknowledge the limits of confrontation. Confrontation usually brings about client awareness of a discrepancy or conflict. Awareness of discrepancies is an initial step in resolving conflicts. Confrontation, as a single response, may not always bring about resolution of the discrepancy without additional discussion or intervention strategies such as role playing, role reversal, Gestalt dialoguing, and TA redecision work.

Client reactions. Sometimes counselors are afraid to confront because they are uncertain how to handle the client's reactions to the confrontation. Even clients who hear and acknowledge the confrontation may be anxious or upset about the implications. Generally, a counselor can expect four types of client reaction to a confrontation: denial, confusion, false acceptance, or genuine acceptance.

In a denial of the confrontation, the client does not want to acknowledge or agree to the counselor's message. A denial may indicate that the client is not ready or tolerant enough to face the discrepant or distorted behavior. Egan (1990, pp. 206–207) lists some specific ways the client might deny the confrontation:

1. Discredit the counselor (for example, "How do you know when you don't even have kids?").
2. Persuade the counselor that his or her views are wrong or misinterpreted ("I didn't mean it that way").
3. Devalue the importance of the topic ("This isn't worth all this time anyway").
4. Seek support elsewhere ("I told my friends about your comment last week and none of them had ever noticed that").
5. Agree with the challenger but don't act on the challenge ("I think you're right. I should speak up and tell how I feel but I'm not sure I can do that").

At other times, the client may indicate confusion or uncertainty about the meaning of the confrontation. In some cases, the client may be genuinely confused about what the counselor is saying. This may indicate that your confrontation was not concise and specific. At other times, the client may use a lack of understanding as a smokescreen— that is, as a way to avoid dealing with the impact of the confrontation.

Sometimes the client may seem to accept the confrontation. Acceptance is usually genuine if the client responds with a sincere desire to examine her or his behavior. Eventually such clients may be able to catch their own discrepancies and confront themselves. But Egan (1990) cautions that false acceptance also can occur, which is an-

FEEDBACK #18: MIXED MESSAGES

Client 1

1. #6—verbal messages and context.
2. Client says she wants to be a star in two sports that require considerable leg work and muscle dexterity; contraindicated by her obvious limp.

Client 2

1. #2—verbal message and behavior.
2. Client says he's never been able to talk about sex but has been talking about it openly with you.

Client 3

1. #3—two verbal messages.
2. Client says she wants to have a child to fill a void by keeping busy and also that she doesn't want to be too tied down or confined by a child.

Client 4

1. #5—two persons.
2. Client's wife wants frequent sex; client does not.

other client game. In this case, the client verbally agrees with the counselor. However, instead of pursuing the confrontation, the client agrees only to get the counselor to leave well enough alone.

There is no set way of dealing with client reactions to confrontation. However, a general rule of thumb is to go back to the client-oriented listening responses of paraphrase and reflection and to continue to pace, or match, the client's primary representational system (predicates). A counselor can use these responses to lay the foundation before the confrontation and return to this foundation after the confrontation. The sequence might go something like this:

Counselor: You seem to feel concerned about your parents' divorce. [reflection]
Client: Actually, I feel pretty happy—I'm glad for their sake they got a divorce. [said with low, sad voice—mixed message]
Counselor: You say you're happy, and at the same time, from your voice I sense that you feel unhappy. [confrontation]
Client: I don't know what you're talking about, really. [denial]
Counselor: I feel that what I just said has upset you. [reflection]

Steps in confronting. There are four steps in developing effective confrontations. First, observe the client carefully to identify the type of discrepancy, or mixed message, that the client presents. Note the specific verbal cues, nonverbal cues, and behaviors that support the type of discrepancy. Second, summarize the different elements of the discrepancy. In doing so, use a statement that *connects* the parts of the conflict rather than disputes any one part, since the overall aim of confrontation is to resolve conflicts and to achieve integration. A useful summary is "On the one hand, you _____, *and* on the other hand, _____." Note that the elements are connected with the word *and* rather than *but* or *yet*. Third, be sure to include words in your summary that reflect the client's choice of sensory words, or predicates, so that the confrontation paces the client's experience. Finally, remember to assess the effectiveness of your confrontation. A confrontation is effective whenever the client acknowledges the existence of the incongruity or conflict.

To help you formulate a confrontation, consider the following cognitive learning strategy:

1. What discrepancy, or mixed message, do I see, hear, or grasp in this client's communication?
2. How can I summarize the various elements of the discrepancy?
3. What words can I include in my response that match the client's sensory words?
4. How will I know whether my confrontation is effective?

Notice how a therapist uses this cognitive learning strategy for confrontation in the following example:

Client: It's hard for me to discipline my son. I know I'm too indulgent. I know he needs limits. But I just don't give him any. I let him do basically whatever he feels like doing. [Said in low, soft voice]
Counselor: 1. What discrepancy do I see, hear, or grasp in this client's communication?
   A discrepancy between two verbal messages and between verbal cues and behavior: client knows son needs limits but doesn't give him any.
2. How can I summarize the various elements of the discrepancy?
   Client believes limits would help son; at the same time, client doesn't follow through.
3. What words can I include in my response that match the client's sensory words?
   I'll use words in my response like "sense" and

"feel" that match client's words "know" and "feel."

4. How will I know whether my confrontation is effective?
Observe the client's response and see whether he acknowledges the discrepancy.

Suppose that at this point the therapist's self-talk or covert visualization ends and the following dialogue occurs:

Counselor confrontation: William, on the one hand, you feel like having limits would really help your son, and at the same time, he can do whatever he pleases with you. How do you put this together?

Client response: Well, I guess that's right. I do feel strongly he would benefit from having limits. He gets away with a lot. He's going to become very spoiled, I know. But I just can't seem to "put my foot down" or make him do something.

From the client's response, which confirmed the discrepancy, the counselor can conclude that the confrontation was initially useful (further discussion of the discrepancy seems necessary in order to help the client resolve the conflict between feelings and actions).

Learning Activity #19 gives you an opportunity to apply this cognitive learning strategy to develop the skill of confrontation.

LEARNING ACTIVITY #19: CONFRONTATION

We give you three client practice statements in this learning activity. For each message, develop an example of a confrontation, using the cognitive learning strategy described earlier and outlined below. To internalize this learning strategy, you may wish to talk through these self-questions overtly (aloud) and then covertly (silently to yourself). The end product will be a confrontation that you can say aloud or write down or both. An example precedes the practice messages. Feedback follows the learning activity (on page 124).

Example

Client, a college student: I'd like to get through nursing school with a flourish. I want to be at the top of my class and achieve a lot. All this partying is getting in my way and preventing me from doing my best work.

Counselor:

Self-question 1: What discrepancy do I see, hear, or grasp in this client's communication?
A discrepancy between verbal message and behavior; he says he wants to be at the top of his class and at the same time is doing a lot of partying.
Self-question 2: How can I summarize the various elements of the discrepancy?
He wants to be at the top of his class and at the same time is doing a lot of partying, which is interfering with his goal.
Self-question 3: What words can I include in my response that match the client's sensory words?
There are no clear-cut sensory words reflected in this example; so use words of varying modalities ("see," "hear," "feel").
Actual confrontation response: You're saying that you feel like achieving a lot and being at the top of your class and also that you're doing a lot of partying, which appears to be interfering with this goal
or
Juan, you're saying that doing well in nursing school is very important to you. You have also indicated you are partying instead of studying. How important is being at the top for you?

Client Practice Messages

Client 1, a graduate student: My wife and child are very important to me. They make me feel it's all worth it. It's just that I know I have to work all the time if I want to make it in my field, and right now I can't be with them too much.

Self-question 1: What discrepancy do I see, hear, or grasp in this client's communication?
Self-question 2: How can I summarize the various elements of the discrepancy?
Self-question 3: What words can I include in my response that match the client's sensory words?
Actual confrontation response: _____

Client 2, a 10-year-old girl: Sure, it would be nice to have mom at home when I get there after school. I don't feel lonely. It's just that it would feel so good to have someone close to me there and not to have to spend a couple of hours every day by myself.

Self question 1: What discrepancy do I see, hear, or grasp in this client's communication?

(continued)

LEARNING ACTIVITY #19: CONFRONTATION (continued)

Self-question 2: How can I summarize the various elements of the discrepancy?

Self-question 3: What words can I include in my response that match the client's sensory words?

Actual confrontation response: _____

_____

Client 3, a high school student: My dad thinks it's terribly important for me to get all As. He thinks I'm not working up to my potential if I get a B. I told him I'd much rather be well rounded and get a few Bs and also have time to talk to my friends and play basketball.

Self-question 1: What discrepancy do I see, hear, or grasp in this client's communication?

Self-question 2: How can I summarize the various elements of the discrepancy?

Self-question 3: What words can I include in my response that match the client's sensory words?

Actual confrontation response: _____

_____

Interpretation

Interpretation is a skill that involves understanding and communicating the meaning of a client's messages. In making interpretive statements, the counselor provides clients with a fresh look at themselves or with another explanation for their attitudes or behaviors (Ivey & Gluckstern, 1976). According to Brammer, Shostrom, and Abrego (1989, p. 175), interpretation involves "presenting the client with a *hypothesis* about *relationships* or *meanings* among his or her behaviors." Johnson (1986, p. 154) observes that interpretation is useful for clients because it leads to insight, and insight is a key to better psychological living and a precursor to effective behavior change.

Interpretive responses can be defined in a variety of ways (Brammer, Shostrom, & Abrego, 1989; Ivey & Gluckstern, 1976; Levy, 1963). An interpretation may vary to some degree according to your own perspective, your theoretical orientation, and what you decide is causing or contributing to the client's problems and behaviors (Johnson, 1986). We define an interpretation as a counselor statement that makes an association or a causal connection among various client behaviors, events, or ideas or presents a possible explanation of a client's behavior (including the client's feelings, thoughts, and observable actions). An interpretation differs from the listening responses (paraphrase, clarification, reflection, summarization) in that it deals with the *implicit* part of a message—the part the client does not talk about explicitly or directly. As Brammer, Shostrom, and Abrego (1989) note, when interpreting, a counselor will often verbalize issues that the client may have felt only vaguely. Our concept of interpretation is similar to what Egan (1990) calls "advanced accurate empathy," which is a tool to help the client "move from the less to the more" (p. 220). In other words, "If clients are not clear about some issue or if they speak guardedly, then the helper speaks directly, clearly, and openly."

There are many benefits and purposes for which interpretation can be used appropriately in a helping interview. First, effective interpretations can contribute to the development of a positive therapeutic relationship by reinforcing client self-disclosure, enhancing the credibility of the therapist, and communicating therapeutic attitudes to the client (Claiborn, 1982, p. 415). Another purpose of interpretation is to identify causal relations or patterns between clients' explicit and implicit messages and behaviors. A third purpose is to help clients examine their behavior from a different frame of reference or with a different explanation in order to achieve a better understanding of the problem. A final and most important reason for using interpretation is to motivate the client to replace self-defeating or ineffective behaviors with more functional ones.

The frame of reference selected for an interpretation should be consistent with one's preferred theoretical orientation(s) to counseling: a psychodynamic therapist might interpret unresolved anxiety or conflicts; an Adlerian therapist might highlight the client's mistaken logic; a Transactional Analysis interviewer may interpret client games and ego states; a cognitive therapist might emphasize irrational and rational thinking; and a behavioral counselor may emphasize self-defeating or maladaptive behavior patterns. *Traditional* (or "old guard") client-centered counselors often refrained from interpreting, but recent client-centered therapists do interpret and often emphasize such themes as self-image and intimacy in their interpretations (Egan, 1990). Gestalt therapists consider interpretation a "therapeutic mistake" because it takes responsibility away from the client.

Here is an example that may help you understand the nature of the interpretation response more clearly. Note how the frame of reference or content varies with the counselor's theoretical orientation.

Client 1, a young woman: Everything is humdrum. There's nothing new going on, nothing exciting. All my friends are away. I wish I had some money to do something different.

1. *Interpretation from Adlerian orientation:* It seems as if you believe you need friends, money, and lots of excitement in order to make your life worthwhile and to feel good about yourself.
2. *Interpretation from TA perspective:* It seems as if you function best only when you can play and have a lot of fun. Your "Child" seems in control of so much of your life.
3. *Interpretation from cognitive or rational-emotive perspective:* It sounds as if you're catastrophizing —because you have no friends around now and no money, things are going to be terrible. Yet where is the proof or data for this? I suspect your feelings of boredom would change if you could draw a different and more logical conclusion about not having friends and money right now.
4. *Interpretation from behavioral orientation:* You seem to be saying that you don't know how to get along or have fun without having other people around. Perhaps recognizing this will help you learn to behave in more self-reliant ways.

In all the above examples, the counselors use interpretation to point out that the client is more dependent on things or other people than on herself for making her life meaningful. In other words, the counselor is describing a possible association, or relationship, between the client's explicit feelings of being bored and her explicit behavior of depending on others to alleviate the boredom. The counselor hopes that this explanation will give the client an increased understanding of herself that she can use to create meaning and enjoyment in her life.

Content and wording of effective interpretations. During the last several years, a variety of research studies have explored different parameters of interpretation (Beck & Strong, 1982; Claiborn, Ward, & Strong, 1981; Forsyth & Forsyth, 1982; Milne & Dowd, 1983; Strong, Wambach, Lopez, & Cooper, 1979). The results of these studies suggest three parameters that affect the content and wording of an effective interpretation: (1) depth, (2) focus, and (3) connotation. Depth is the degree of discrepancy between the viewpoint expressed

by the counselor and the client's beliefs. Presenting clients with a viewpoint discrepant from their own is believed to facilitate change by providing clients with a reconceptualization of the problem (Claiborn et al., 1981). An important question is to what extent the counselor's communicated conceptualization of the problem should differ from the client's beliefs. A study by Claiborn et al. (1981) addressed this question. The results supported the general assumption that highly discrepant (that is, very deep) interpretations are more likely to be rejected by the client, possibly because they are unacceptable, seem too preposterous, or evoke resistance. In contrast, interpretations that are either congruent with or only slightly discrepant from the client's viewpoint are most likely to facilitate change, possibly because these are "more immediately understandable and useful to the clients" (Claiborn et al., p. 108).

A second factor affecting the content and wording of interpretations has to do with the focus, or direction, of the interpretation. Research now suggests that interpretations that focus on control by highlighting causes the client can control are more effective than those that draw attention to causes the client cannot change (Strong et al., 1979). Focusing on controllable causes appears especially useful with clients who report a higher internal, as opposed to external, locus of control (Forsyth & Forsyth, 1982).

The third parameter that influences the content and wording of an interpretation is the connotation of the interpretation—that is, whether the counselor reframes or relabels the client's behavior and beliefs in a positive or a negative fashion. For example, an interpretation with a negative connotation would be "Harry, you seem to be saying it's too difficult for you to share your father with his new wife because you've been used to having him to yourself for the last ten years. I'm wondering if you're demanding that you be number one with him or else you won't 'play ball' [relate, cooperate]. It's almost as if you're coming across like a small child, begging for attention and then sulking if you don't get it." In contrast, an interpretation with a positive connotation goes like this: "Harry, you seem to be saying it's too difficult for you to share your father with his new wife because you've been used to having him to yourself for the past ten years. Perhaps the fact that you're recognizing that you feel shut out now will help you behave in ways that actually increase your chances of being included rather than excluded." Although both types of interpretation may produce some imme-

FEEDBACK #19: CONFRONTATION

Client 1

Question 1: There is a discrepancy between the client's verbal message that his wife and child are very important and his behavior, which suggests he doesn't spend much time with them.

Question 2: He feels that his family is very valuable, while he also feels he must continually spend more time on his career than with his family.

Question 3: Use words like "sense" and "feel" to match the client's words "feel" and "know."

Examples of confrontation responses: Jerry, on the one hand, you feel your family is very important, and at the same time, you feel your work takes priority over them. How do you put this together? *or* Jerry, you're saying that your family makes things feel worthwhile for you. At the same time you're indicating you must make it in your field in order to feel worthwhile.

Client 2

Question 1: There is a discrepancy between two verbal messages—one denying she is lonely and the other indicating she doesn't want to be left alone.

Question 2: She doesn't feel lonely—and at the same time she wishes someone could be with her.

Question 3: Use "feel" to match client's repeated use of the word "feel."

Examples of confrontation responses: Shelley, you're saying that you don't feel lonely and also that you wish someone like your mom could be home with you. How do you put this together? *or* Shelley, it seems like you're trying to accept your mom's absence and at the same time still feeling like you'd rather have her home with you. I wonder if it does feel kind of lonely sometimes?

Client 3

Question 1: There is a discrepancy between two persons' views on this issue—the client and his father. A second discrepancy might be between the client's desire to please his father and to be well-rounded.

Question 2: The client feels getting all As is not as important as being well rounded, while his father values very high grades. Also, for discrep-

ancy #2, the client may want to please both his father and himself.

Question 3: Use words such as "saying," "believes," "tells," "hear" to match client words such as "told," "think," "talk."

Examples of confrontation responses: Gary, you're saying that doing a variety of things is more important than getting all As, while your father believes that all As should be your top priority.

or

Gary, you're saying you value variety and balance in your life; your father believes high grades come first.

or

Gary, you want to please your father and make good grades and, at the same time, you want to spend time according to your priorities and values.

(Note: Do not attempt to confront both discrepancies at once!)

diate change, structuring interpretations to reflect a positive connotation seems to promote more enduring change (Beck & Strong, 1982).

To summarize, in constructing an interpretation, be sure that the viewpoint expressed in your statement is only slightly discrepant from the client's beliefs. Second, focus on causes that the client can control and modify, if desired. Finally, cast the new or different frame of reference into a positive, rather than negative, connotation.

Client reactions to interpretation. Client reactions to interpretation may range from expression of greater self-understanding and release of emotions to less verbal expression and more silence. Although research suggests that interpretations can contribute to self-exploration and behavior change (Auerswald, 1974; Beck & Strong, 1982; Claiborn et al., 1981; Elliott, Barker, Caskey, & Pistrang, 1982; Strong et al., 1979), clients can also react to interpretations with defensiveness and decreased disclosure. As Pope (1979) observes, interpretations often delve into material or experiences the client has resisted learning about because of the anxiety aroused by the particular situation.

If interpretation is met initially with defensiveness or hostility, it may be best to drop the issue temporarily and introduce it again later. Repetition is an important concept in the use of interpretations. As Brammer, Shostrom, & Abrego observe, "Since a useful and valid interpretation may be resisted, it may be necessary for the counselor to repeat the interpretation at appropriate times, in different forms, and with additional supporting evidence" (1989, p. 182). However, don't push an interpretation on a resistant client without first reexamining the accuracy of your response (Brammer, Shostrom, & Abrego, 1989). Another way to manage client resistance to a seemingly valid interpretation is to use a metaphor—that is, to tell the client a parable, story, or myth that serves as a mirror onto which the client can project his or her own life situation (Gordon, 1978; see also Chapter 20).

Ground rules for interpreting. Interpretation may be the one counselor activity that helps a client to face, rather than defend or avoid, a conflict or problem. However, the potential contribution of an interpretation depends somewhat on the counselor's ability to use this response effectively and at an advantageous time. There are several ground rules to consider in deciding to use interpretation. First, be careful about timing. The client should show some degree of readiness to explore or examine himself or herself before you use an interpretation. Generally, an interpretation response is reserved for later, rather than initial, sessions, because some data must be gathered as a basis for an interpretive response and because the typical client requires several sessions to become accustomed to the type of material discussed in counseling. The client may be more receptive to your interpretation if she or he is comfortable with the topics being explored and shows some readiness to accept the interpretive response. As Brammer, Shostrom, and Abrego (1989, p. 180) note, a counselor usually does not interpret until the time when the client can almost formulate the interpretation for herself or himself.

Timing of an interpretation within a session is also important. Generally, an interpretation is more helpful in the initial or middle phase of an interview, so that the counselor and client have sufficient time to work through the client's reaction. If the counselor suspects that the interpretation may produce anxiety or resistance or break the client's "emotional dam," it may be a good idea to postpone it until the beginning of the next session (Brammer, Shostrom, & Abrego, 1989).

A second ground rule is to make sure your interpretation is based on the client's actual message rather than your own biases and values projected onto the client. This requires that you be aware of your own blind spots. As an example, if you have had a bad experience with marriage and are biased against people's getting or staying married, be aware of how this could affect the way you interpret client statements about marriage. If you aren't careful with your values, you could easily advise all marital-counseling clients away from marriage, which might not be in the best interests of some of them. As Ivey and Gluckstern (1976, p. 135) state, "psychological imperialism" must be avoided—especially in the use of an interpretation. Try to be aware of whether you are interpreting to present helpful data to the client or only to show off your expertise. Make sure your interpretation is based on sufficient data, and offer the interpretation in a collaborative spirit, making the client an active participant.

A third ground rule in using interpretation effectively concerns the way the counselor phrases the statement and offers it to the client. Although preliminary research suggests there is no difference between interpretations offered with absolute and with tentative phrasing (Milne & Dowd, 1983), we believe that in most cases the interpretation should be phrased tentatively, using phrases such as "perhaps," "I wonder whether," "it's possible that," or "it appears as though." Using tentative rather than absolute phrasing helps to avoid putting the counselor in a one-up position and engendering client resistance or defensiveness to the interpretation. Jones and Gelso (1988) support the use of tentative interpretations (versus absolute or questioning interpretations), at least in the early stages of counseling. After an interpretation, check out the accuracy of your interpretive response by asking the client whether your message fits. Returning to a clarification is always a useful way to determine whether you have interpreted the message accurately.

Steps in interpreting. There are five steps in formulating effective interpretations. First, listen for and identify the *implicit* meaning of the client's communication—what the client conveys subtly and indirectly. Second, formulate an interpretation that provides the client with a *slightly* different way to view the problem or issue. This alternative frame of reference should be consistent with your theoretical orientation and not too discrepant from the client's beliefs. Third, make sure your view of the issue, your frame of reference, emphasizes positive factors rather than negative factors or things the client can't change or modify. Next, select words in the interpretation that match the client's sensory words, or predicates. Finally, examine the effectiveness of your interpretation by assessing the client's reaction to it. Look for nonverbal "recognition" signs such as a smile or contemplative look as well as verbal and behavioral cues that indicate the client is considering the issue from a different frame of reference.

To help you formulate an effective interpretation and assess its usefulness, consider the following cognitive learning strategy:

1. What is the implicit part of the client's message?
2. What is a slightly different way to view this problem or issue that is consistent with the theoretical orientation I am using with this client?
3. What are positive aspects of the problem that are under the client's control?
4. What words can I use that will match the client's sensory words, or predicates?
5. How will I know whether my interpretation is useful?

Notice how a therapist applies this cognitive learning strategy in the following example:

Client: I really don't understand it myself. I can always have good sex whenever we're not at home —even in the car. But at home it's never too good.

Counselor: 1. What is the implicit part of the client's message? That sex is not good or fulfilling unless it occurs in special, out-of-the-ordinary circumstances or places.
2. What is a slightly different way to view this problem or issue consistent with the theoretical orientation I am using with this client?
Behavioral—Adaptive response learned in special places, hasn't generalized to home setting, perhaps because of different "setting events" there (for example, fatigue, lack of novelty).
Cognitive—Client is catastrophizing about "no good" sex when it occurs at home; continued reindoctrination prevents spontaneity, increases preoccupation with himself.
Psychodynamic—Problem with sex at home is

indicative of unresolved anxiety or possible unresolved oedipal issue.
Transactional Analysis—Sex is good in places that are novel and exciting, where the "Child" ego state can be predominant; not as good at home, where Child ego state is probably excluded.
Adlerian—Client has developed a lifestyle and accompanying mistaken logic that emphasizes novelty, excitement, out-of-the-ordinary events in order for things (like sex) to be good or great.
3. What are positive aspects of the problem that are under the client's control?
That client does experience sex as good some of the time; has potential for good sex more of the time.
4. What words can I use that will match the client's primary representational system?
There are no clear-cut sensory words in this example, so vary the words used in the actual interpretation that reflect all three major sensory modalities.

Suppose that at this point the counselor's covert visualization or self-talk ends and the following dialogue ensues:

Counselor interpretation: Shawn, I might be wrong about this—it seems that you get psyched up for sex only when it occurs in out-of-the-ordinary places where you feel there's a lot of novelty and excitement. Is that possible? [Note: This is an interpretation that could be consistent with a behavioral, Adlerian, or eclectic orientation.]

Client: [Lips part, slight smile, eyes widen] Well, I never thought about it quite that way. I guess I do need to feel like there's some thrills around when I do have sex—maybe it's that I find unusual places like the elevator a challenge.

At this point, the counselor can conclude that the interpretation was effective because of the client's nonverbal "recognition" behavior and because of the client's verbal response suggesting the interpretation was "on target." The therapist might continue to help the client explore whether he needs thrills and challenge to function satisfactorily in other areas of his life as well.

Learning activity #20 gives you an opportunity to try out the interpretation response.

LEARNING ACTIVITY #20: INTERPRETATION

Three client practice statements are given in this learning activity. For each message, develop an example of an interpretation, using the cognitive learn-

ing strategy described earlier and outlined below. To internalize this learning strategy, you may want to
(continued)

talk through these self-questions overtly (aloud) and then covertly (silently to yourself). The end product will be an interpretation that you can say aloud or write down or both. An example precedes the practice messages. Feedback follows the learning activity (on page 132).

Example

Client, a young woman: I don't know what to do. I guess I just never thought I'd ever be asked to be a supervisor. I feel so content just being an assistant. But my husband says I'd be foolish to pass up this opportunity.

Self-question 1: What is the implicit part of the client's message?
That the client feels afraid to achieve more than she's presently doing.
Self-question 2: What is a slightly different way to view this problem or issue consistent with the theoretical orientation I am using with this client?
Behavioral—Client has acquired anxiety about job success, possibly because of lack of exposure to other successful female models and also because of lack of reinforcement from significant others for job achievement. It is also possible that she has been punished for being successful or achieving in the past, which is maintaining her present avoidance behavior on this issue.
Cognitive—Client is indoctrinating herself with irrational or self-defeating thoughts of possible failure or loss of friends if she moves up the job ladder.
Psychodynamic—Client has anxiety about a job situation; suggests possible unresolved conflict and also identity issue.
Transactional Analysis—Client is confronted with a decision that her Adapted Child ego state is afraid to make, possibly because in the role of supervisor she would have to function in more of her Parent ego state, which is probably excluded from her personality to some degree.
Adlerian—Client's lifestyle and family background haven't accommodated personal achievement; possibly client has relied on others, such as husband, to take care of her rather than putting herself in roles where she is responsible for others.
Self-question 3: What are positive aspects of the problem that are under the client's control?
She has a job she feels satisfied with; further, that she was given an opportunity for a promotion suggests she is doing good work.
Self-question 4: What words can I use that will match the client's sensory words?
Use words like "feel," "sense" to match client words "don't know," "guess," "feel."
Actual interpretation responses: Despite your husband's encouragement and your obvious success at your present position, you seem to feel like holding back. I wonder whether you're afraid to move up for fear that someone close to you will be upset with you or won't like you if you're more successful? [This interpretation is consistent with the behavioral and cognitive frameworks.] or I wonder whether a big part of you feels more comfortable in situations where others can take care of you? So it feels scary to think of being in a situation where you are in charge and responsible for other people. [This interpretation is consistent with the TA and Adlerian frameworks.]

Client Practice Statements

Client 1, a 35-year-old male factory worker: I know I don't get along very well with my buddies [coworkers], but they tease me all the time because I'm very religious, especially compared with them.

Self-question 1: What is the implicit part of the client's message?
Self-question 2: What is a slightly different way to view this problem or issue consistent with my theoretical orientation?*
Self-question 3: What are positive aspects of the problem that are under the client's control?
Self-question 4: What words can I use that will match the client's sensory words?
Actual interpretation response: _____

_____

Client 2, a 50-year-old man: Sure, I seemed upset when I got laid off several years ago. After all, I'd been an industrial engineer for almost 23 years. At least I didn't have to put myself on welfare. I have a clear conscience about that, and I can support my family with my job supervising these custodial workers. So I should be very thankful. Then why do I seem so depressed?

Self-question 1: What is the implicit part of this message?
Self-question 2: What is a slightly different way to view this problem or issue consistent with my theoretical orientation?*
Self-question 3: What are positive aspects of the problem that are under the client's control?
Self-question 4: What words can I use that will match the client's sensory words?
Actual interpretation response: _____

_____

(continued)

* If you have not yet had much exposure to counseling theories, you may find it useful just to reframe the client statement in a slightly different manner without trying to conceptualize it according to a counseling theory.

LEARNING ACTIVITY #20: INTERPRETATION (continued)

Client 3: I have a great time with Susie [his girl-friend], but I've told her I don't want to settle down. She's always so bossy and tries to tell me what to do. She always decides what we're going to do and when and where and so on. I get real upset at her.

Self-question 1: What is the implicit part of the client's message?

Self-question 2: What is a slightly different way to view this problem or issue consistent with my theoretical orientation?*

Self-question 3: What are positive aspects of the problem that are under the client's control?

Self-question 4: What words can I use that will match the client's sensory words?

Actual interpretation response: _____
_____

* If you have not yet had much exposure to counseling theories, you may find it useful just to reframe the client statement in a slightly different manner without trying to conceptualize it according to a counseling theory.

Information Giving

There are many times in the counseling interview when a client may have a legitimate need for information. For instance, a client who reports being abused by her husband may need information about her legal rights and alternatives. A client who has recently become physically disabled may need some information about employment and about lifestyle adaptations such as carrying out domestic chores or engaging in sexual relationships. According to Selby and Calhoun (1980, p. 236), "Conveying information about the psychological and social changes accompanying a particular problem situation (. . . such as divorce) may be a highly effective addition to any therapeutic strategy." Selby and Calhoun assert that information giving has been neglected as an explicit and important part of treatment "in spite of evidence indicating the therapeutic value of information about the client's problem situation" (p. 236).

We define information giving as the verbal communication of data or facts about experiences, events, alternatives, or people. As summarized in Table 6-1, there are four intended purposes of information giving in counseling. First, information is necessary when the client does not know her or his options. Giving information is a way to help the client identify possible alternatives. As Gelatt, Varenhorst, Carey, and Miller (1973, p. 6) suggest, a "person's choices are increased if he can create new alternatives based on information." For example, you may be counseling a pregnant client who says she is going to get an abortion because it is her only choice. Although she may eventually decide to pursue this choice, she should be aware of other options before making a final decision. Information giving is also helpful when a client is not aware of the possible outcomes of a particular choice or plan of action. Giving information can help the client evaluate different choices and actions. For example, if the client is a minor and is not aware that she may need her parents' consent for an abortion, this information may influence her choice. In the preceding kinds of situations, information is given to counteract ignorance. According to Egan (1990, p. 212), this is especially critical "when ignorance is either one of the principal causes of a problem situation or it is making an existing problem worse." Information giving can also be useful to correct invalid or unreliable data or to dispel a myth. In other words, information giving may be necessary when the client is misinformed about something. For example, a pregnant client may decide to have an abortion on the erroneous assumption that an abortion is also a means of subsequent birth control.

A final purpose of information giving is to help clients examine issues or problems they have been successfully avoiding (Egan, 1990). For example, a client who hasn't felt physically well for a year may be prompted to explore this problem when confronted with information about possible effects of neglected treatment for various illnesses.

Differences between information giving and advice. It is important to note that information giving differs from advice. In giving advice, a person usually recommends or prescribes a particular solution or course of action for the listener to follow. In contrast, information giving consists in presenting relevant information about the issue or problem, and the decision concerning the final course of action—if any—is made by the client. Consider the differences between the following two responses:

Client, a young mother: I just find it so difficult to refuse requests made by my child—to say no to her—even when I know they are unreasonable requests or could even be dangerous to her.

Counselor (advice giving): Why don't you start by saying no to her just on one request a day for now —anything that you feel comfortable with refusing—and then see what happens?

Counselor (information giving): I think there are two things we could discuss that may be affecting the way you are handling this situation. First, we could talk about what you feel might happen if you say no. We also need to examine how your requests were handled in your own family when you were a child. Very often as parents we repeat with our children the way we were parented—in such an automatic way we don't even realize it's happening.

In the first example, the counselor has recommended action that may or may not be successful. If it works, the client may feel elated and expect the counselor to have other magical solutions. If it fails, the client may feel even more discouraged and question whether counseling can really help her resolve this problem. Appropriate and effective information giving is presented as what the client *could* ponder or do, not what the client *should* do, and what the client *might* consider, not *must* consider (D'Augelli et al., 1981, p. 80).

Several dangers are associated with advice giving that make it a potential trap for counselors. First, the client may reject not only this piece of advice but any other ideas presented by the therapist in an effort to establish independence and thwart any conspicuous efforts by the counselor to influence or coerce. Second, if the client accepts the advice and the advice leads to an unsatisfactory action, the client is likely to blame the counselor and may terminate therapy prematurely. Third, if the client follows the advice and is pleased with the action, the client may become overly dependent on the counselor and expect, if not demand, more "advice" in subsequent sessions. Finally, there is always the possibility that an occasional client may misinterpret the advice and may cause injury to self or others in trying to comply with it.

Ground rules for giving information. Lewis (1970) observes that information should be a tool for counseling, not an end in itself. Information giving is generally considered appropriate when the need for information is directly related to the client's concerns and goals and when the presentation and discussion of information are used to help the client achieve these goals (p. 135).

To use information giving appropriately, a counselor should consider three major guidelines. These cover when to give information, what information is needed, and how the information should be delivered. Table 6-2 summarizes the "when,"

TABLE 6-2. The "when," "what," and "how" of information giving in helping

When—recognizing client's need for information	*What—identifying type of information*	*How—delivery of information in interview*
1. Identify information presently available to client.	1. Identify kind of information useful to client.	1. Avoid jargon.
2. Evaluate client's present information—is it valid? data-based? sufficient?	2. Identify reliable sources of information to validate accuracy of information.	2. Present all the relevant facts; don't protect client from negative information.
3. Wait for client cues of readiness to avoid giving information prematurely.	3. Identify any sequencing of information (option A before option B).	3. Limit amount of information given at one time; don't overload.
		4. Ask for and discuss client's feelings and biases about information.
		5. Know when to stop giving information so action isn't avoided.
		6. Use paper and pencil to highlight key ideas or facts.

FEEDBACK #20: INTERPRETATION

Client 1

Question 1: The implicit part of the client's message is "I'm better than they [buddies] are."

Question 2: Different ways to view this issue, depending on your theoretical orientation, include the following:

Behavioral—Client and buddies have set up a relationship based on negative and reciprocal contingencies; each punishes rather than reinforces the other.

Cognitive—Client is "awfulizing" about how terrible it is not to be liked by his buddies and also is imposing his religious "shoulds" on them.

Psychodynamic—Client has unresolved sexual identity issue that surfaces when in competition with other males.

Transactional Analysis—Communication between client and co-workers has broken down because of crossed transactions in which they are communicating with each other from different and noncomplementary ego states. Additionally, they seem to be playing games with each other. Client may be playing games such as "They'll be glad they knew me" or "I'm only trying to help."

Adlerian—Client has not learned much "social interest"; lifestyle is based on acting superior to others while actually feeling inferior.

Question 3: Client's values or religion can be reframed to help him get along rather than compete or fight with his buddies.

Question 4: No one sensory modality seems predominant in this example, so use words in interpretation that emphasize all modalities.

Examples of interpretations:

1. Could there be something you are doing or saying that makes your buddies feel threatened or irritated—perhaps you seem better or more religious or perhaps because they feel you are telling them how they should live? [This is consistent with the Adlerian and cognitive frameworks.]

2. Could you be using your religiousness to avoid having to get along with them and work things out? [Eclectic framework.]

3. It seems that you and your buddies have got off on the wrong track and good communication is sort of stymied. Perhaps you sort of tear each other down instead of building each other up, so no one feels like a winner. [Behavioral and TA frameworks.]

Client 2

Question 1: Implicit part of this client's message is that he's sort of an independent, self-made man whose independence, masculinity, and pride have been damaged by being laid off and by doing "menial" work.

Question 2: Alternative ways to view this issue, depending on your theoretical orientation, include the following:

Behavioral: Depression was precipitated and is maintained by loss of powerful positive, or reinforcing, contingencies (job loss, lack of satisfying current employment).

Cognitive: Depression is maintained by client's negative and irrational thoughts or self-statements about his lack of human worth due to job loss and subsequent type of employment.

Psychodynamic: Depression is the result of his loss of masculinity.

Transactional Analysis: Depressed feelings are the result of the adapted child ego state, which probably became a greater part of his personality after the job loss, while other ego states formerly functional, such as nurturing parent, are being somewhat excluded now from his personality.

Adlerian: Client has developed lifestyle and image of self in which he is independent, intelligent, strong, and masculine. Self-image is now challenged by job loss and menial work, resulting in depression.

Question 3: Positive aspects of the problem include the fact that he has a job that is economically sufficient. In this way, he continues to be independent, self-reliant, and resourceful.

Question 4: Use words like "seems," "appears," "looks like" to match client's visual words "should," "seem," "clear."

Examples of interpretations:

1. It seems like when you lost your job as an engineer, you let your masculinity and strength go out the window, too. [Consistent with psychodynamic and Adlerian frameworks.]

2. Probably at some level you keep picturing yourself as worthless and weak because of the type of work you're doing. The more of these pictures you keep flashing in your head, the worse you feel. [Consistent with cognitive framework, but "pictures" is used instead of "ideas" or "self-statements" to match the visual sensory modality.]

3. The depression is probably the result of having to give up a big part of your life—a part of yourself

(continued)

— that was very important and rewarding to you. What you're doing instead hasn't seemed to fill the void for you even though you appear to be behaving in an independent, self-reliant, and resourceful manner. [Consistent with behavioral framework.]

Client 3

Question 1: Implicit part of this message is that client doesn't want to settle down with a controlling woman; he's also upset with himself for giving her so much control.

Question 2: Different ways to view this issue, depending on your theoretical orientation:

Behavioral: Client uses a relationship with a controlling female to maintain avoidance behavior against settling down.

Cognitive: Client allows himself to get upset with Susie because of all the negative things he tells himself about her and her need to control his life.

Psychodynamic: Client's need to be controlled by a domineering female suggests unresolved oedipal issue.

Transactional Analysis: Client is both attracted to and repelled by Susie; he is hooked because he relates to her out of his Child ego state, which hooks or maintains her Parent ego state. At the same time, he dislikes feeling so "trapped" or controlled by her. He needs to find ways of relating to her from other ego states.

Adlerian: Client has developed lifestyle in which he feels adequate by giving up control to others. He may also have been parented by a controlling mother who made all his decisions for him.

Question 3: Client enjoys being with Susie; her bossiness can be reframed as her need to take care of him and his letting her do so.

Question 4: Use words like "feel," "say," "hear" to match client words "tell," "say," "hear."

Examples of interpretations:

1. You say you have great times with Susie although you told her you don't want to settle down. I may be wrong—I'm wondering whether you've got yourself hooked up with a controlling woman as a way to avoid settling down. [Consistent with behavioral framework.]
2. You seem to be both attracted to and turned off to Susie. I wonder what your relationship with your mother was like and whether you see any similarities between that relationship and the present one? [Consistent with psychodynamic and Adlerian frameworks.]

3. You seem to be blaming Susie for being so controlling and nurturing. Perhaps you haven't thought about how what you say to her might encourage her to be this way. Could it be that you relate to her as a child might relate to a parent? [Consistent with Transactional Analysis framework.]

"what," and "how" guidelines for information giving in counseling. The first guideline, the "when," involves recognizing the client's need for information. If the client does not have all the data or has invalid data, a need exists.

To be effective, information must also be well timed. The client should indicate receptivity to the information before it is delivered. As Lewis (1970, p. 135) observes, a client may ignore information if it is introduced too early in the interaction.

The counselor also needs to determine what information is useful and relevant to the client. Generally, information is useful if it is something the client is not likely to find on her or his own and if the client has the resources to act on the information. The counselor also needs to determine whether the information must be presented sequentially in order to make most sense to the client. Since clients may remember initial information best, presenting the most significant information *first* may be a good rule of thumb in sequencing information. Finally, in selecting information to give, be careful not to impose information on the client, who is ultimately responsible for deciding what information to use and act on (Lewis, 1970). In other words, information giving should not be used as a forum for the counselor to subtly push his or her own values on the client (Egan, 1990).

In the interview itself, the actual delivery of information, the "how" of information giving, is crucial. The information should be discussed in a way that makes it "usable" to the client and encourages the client to "hear and apply" the information (Gazda et al., 1984). Moreover, information should be presented objectively. Don't leave out facts simply because they aren't pleasant. Watch out, too, for information overload. Most people are not "bionic" and cannot assimilate a great deal of information in "one shot." Limit the amount of information presented at any one time. Usually, the more information you give the clients, the less they remember. Clients recall information best when you give no more than several pieces of information at one time (Ley, 1976).

Be aware that information differs in depth and may have an emotional impact on clients. Clients may not react emotionally to relatively simple or factual information such as information about a counseling procedure or an occupation or a résumé. However, clients may react with anger, anxiety, or relief to information that has more depth or far-reaching consequences, such as the results of a test. Ask about and discuss the client's reactions to the information you give. In addition, make an effort to promote client understanding of the information. Avoid jargon in offering explanations. Use paper and pencil as you're giving information to draw a picture or diagram highlighting the most important points, or give clients paper and pencil so they can get down key ideas. Remember to ask clients to verify their impression of your information either by summarizing it or by repeating it back to you. Try to determine, too, when it's time to stop dealing with information. Continued information giving may reinforce a client's tendency to avoid taking action (Gelatt et al., 1973).

Steps in information giving. There are six steps in formulating the what, when, and how of presenting information to clients. First, assess what information the client lacks about the issue or problem. Second, determine the most important parts to include in your presentation. Third, decide how the information can be sequenced in a way that facilitates client comprehension and retention. Fourth, consider how you can deliver the information in such a way that the client is likely to comprehend it. Fifth, assess the emotional impact the information is likely to have on the client. Finally, determine whether your information giving was effective. Note client reactions to it and follow up on client use of the information in a subsequent session. Remember, too, that some clients may "store" information and act on it at a much later date—often even after therapy has terminated.

To facilitate your use of information giving, we have put these six steps in the form of questions that you can use as a cognitive learning strategy:

1. What information does this client lack about the problem or issue?
2. What are the most important parts of this information to include in my presentation?
3. How can I best sequence this information?

4. How can I deliver this information so that the client is likely to comprehend it?
5. What emotional impact is this information likely to have on this client?
6. How will I know whether my information giving has been effective?

Consider the way a therapist uses this cognitive learning strategy in the following example. The therapist is counseling with a woman who has been advised by three physicians to have a mastectomy because of a breast carcinoma (cancer). Although the client admits she realizes that her decision not to have surgery could have negative health consequences, she expresses reluctance to undergo surgery because of possible public reactions to her "deformity" after the operation.

1. What information does this client lack about this problem or issue?
   The client seems to lack information about a prosthesis and about special clothing designed to make her look as "typical" as she did prior to surgery. (Note—in this particular situation, because of this type of problem, it would be important to check out whether she has all the necessary medical and health-related information as well.)
2. What are the most important parts of this information to include in my presentation?
   a. That if this is the only concern she has about surgery, it is potentially remedied with a prosthesis and good choices of clothing.
   b. That other women in a Reach for Recovery group who have dealt with this concern after similar surgery are available to share their insights with her.
3. How can I best sequence this information?
   Mention the prosthesis first, since it may be most important to her, and how it is fitted especially for her, followed by information about clothing and then about the Reach for Recovery group.
4. How can I deliver this information so that the client is likely to comprehend it?
   Make sure she knows what I mean by the term *prosthesis;* show her one or pictures of one so she can see how it really looks and feels.
5. What emotional impact is this information likely to have on the client?
   May be relieved to know these options exist or anxious because the options remove her reason

for avoiding the operation.

6. How will I know whether my information giving has been effective?

Watch and listen to her reactions to it; follow up in subsequent session to determine what she did with the information—whether she acted on it and, if so, in what ways.

Suppose that at this point the counselor responds to the client with the following information:

Sheila, I'm aware of your reluctance to have this operation. One of the major reasons for your reluctance seems to be your concern about how you will look to yourself and to others after the surgery is over. I'd like to share some information with you that you may not be aware of. I'm not giving this information to persuade you to have the surgery. That's a decision only you can make. This infor-mation is something you can use to decide the best possible course of action for you under the circum-stances. Now you mentioned the word *deformity*. Did you know you can get a prosthesis that is made especially for you and your body? I have one here [or can get one] to show you. When this is properly fitted, your body will look just as it does now. In fact, you can even wear any type of bathing suit that you choose and feel comfortable with. It also might be helpful for you to talk with some of the women in the "Reach for Recovery" group. These women have all had some type of mastectomy and would be happy to talk with you about your feelings con-cerning your body image. After you've thought about this, maybe you could share your reactions to this information with me.

Learning Activity #21 gives you an opportunity to try out the skill of information giving.

LEARNING ACTIVITY #21: INFORMATION GIVING

In this learning activity, three client situations are pre-sented. For each situation, determine what informa-tion the client lacks and develop a suitable informa-tion-giving response, using the cognitive learning strategy described earlier and outlined below. To in-ternalize this learning strategy, you may want to talk through these self-questions overtly (aloud) and then covertly (silently to yourself). The end product will be an information-giving response that you can say aloud or write down or both. An example precedes the practice situations. Feedback follows the learning activity (on pages 140–141).

Example

The clients are a married couple in their thirties who disagree about the way to handle their 4-year-old son. The father believes he is a "spoiled brat" and states that he thinks the best way to keep him in line is to give him a spanking. The mother believes that her son is just a "typical boy" and the best way to handle him is to be understanding and loving. The couple admit that there is little consistency in the way the two of them deal with their son. The typical pattern is for the father to reprimand him and swat him while the mother stands, watches, comforts him, and often intercedes on the child's behalf.

Self-question 1: What information do these clients lack about this problem or issue?

Information about effective parenting and child-rearing skills.

Self-question 2: What are the most important parts of this information to include in my presentation?

a. All children need discipline.

b. Discipline involves setting and enforcing limits, not spanking, getting revenge, or giving in to a child.

c. All disciplining should occur in a manner that en-hances rather than destroys a child's self-esteem.

d. There is a hierarchy in parent/child relationships: parents are there to be in charge and to take care of children, not the other way around.

e. Kids behave better and feel better and more secure when their parents work together rather than argue on how to handle and respond to them.

All five of these things are too much to emphasize at one time, so for today, I'll concentrate on a, b, and c only.

Self-question 3: How can I best sequence this infor-mation?

Discuss children's need for discipline first, fol-lowed by what discipline is and then how it should help rather than hurt a child's self-esteem.

Self-question 4: How can I deliver this information so that the clients are likely to comprehend it?

Define what I mean by *discipline* and define it in such a way that it appeals to the values of both parents. The mother values understanding, sup-port, and nurturing, while the father values author-ity, respect, and control.

Self-question 5: What emotional impact is this infor-mation likely to have on these clients?

(continued)

LEARNING ACTIVITY #21: INFORMATION GIVING (continued)

If I frame the information positively, it will appeal to both parents. I have to be careful not to take sides or cause one parent to feel relieved while the other feels anxious, guilty, or put down.

Self-question 6: How will I know whether my information giving has been effective?

I'll watch and listen to their nonverbal and verbal reactions to it to see whether they support the idea and also follow up on their use of the information in a later session.

Example of information-giving response: You know, Mary and Gus, I sense that you are in agreement on the fact that you love your child and want what is best for him. So what I'm going to say next is based on this idea that you are both trying to find a way to do what is best for Timmy. In discussing how you feel about Timmy and his behavior, I think it is important to remember that all children need discipline or limits. Kids ask for limits in all kinds of ways and don't get along very well without them. So when I talk about discipline for Timmy, I mean the idea of setting some limits the two of you agree on and sticking to them. I don't mean spanking or getting revenge, or giving in to him and letting him have his own way. But discipline does involve taking charge, being in control —and doing so in a nurturing way that can help Timmy feel good rather than bad about himself.

Client Practice Situations

Client 1 is a young adolescent, sexually active female. She has already been pregnant three times and has had three abortions. She says she is not too worried about getting pregnant again because either she and her partners abstain on certain days or her partner withdraws "before anything happens." She also indicates that if she did happen to get pregnant again, she would just get another abortion, because it's an easy solution with no physical or emotional aftereffects.

Self-question 1: What information does this client lack about this problem or issue?

Self-question 2: What are the most important parts of this information to include in my presentation?

Self-question 3: How can I best sequence this information?

Self-question 4: How can I deliver this information so that the client is likely to comprehend it?

Self-question 5: What emotional impact is this information likely to have on this client?

Client 2 is a high school girl who is expressing her desire to be a nurse because it's an "easy curriculum, and in a field where lots of jobs are available." The client has very good grades in English and history and very poor grades in math and science.

Self-question 1: What information does this client lack about this problem or issue?

Self-question 2: What are the most important parts of this information to include in my presentation?

Self-question 3: How can I best sequence this information?

Self-question 4: How can I deliver this information so that the client is likely to comprehend it?

Self-question 5: What emotional impact is this information likely to have on this client?

Client 3 is a 35-year-old woman with two teenage daughters. She is employed as an executive secretary in a large engineering firm. Her husband is a department store manager. She and her husband have had a stormy relationship for several years. She wants to get a divorce but is hesitant to do so for fear that she will be labeled a troublemaker and will lose her job. She is also afraid that she will not be able to support her daughters financially on her limited income. However, she indicates that she believes getting a divorce will make her happy and will essentially solve all her own internal conflicts.

Self-question 1: What information does this client lack about this problem or issue?

Self-question 2: What are the most important parts of this information to include in my presentation?

Self-question 3: How can I best sequence this information?

Self-question 4: How can I deliver this information so that the client is likely to comprehend it?

Self-question 5: What emotional impact is this information likely to have on this client?

☐ SUMMARY

Listening responses reflect clients' perceptions of their world. Action responses provide alternative ways for clients to view themselves and their world. A change in the client's way of viewing and explaining things may be one indication of positive movement in counseling. According to Egan (1975, p. 132), counselor statements that move beyond the client's frame of reference are a "bridge" between listening responses and concrete change programs. To be used effectively, action responses require a great deal of counselor concern and judgment. Effective use of action responses presupposes high levels of relationship conditions and enhancers such as those described in Chapters 2 and 3. In an actual interview, these responses must be used flexibly, sensitively, and in the context of a client's nonverbal cues as well as verbal messages.

☐ SKILL INTEGRATION

In Chapters 2 and 3 you learned about important relationship conditions and variables such as empathy, genuineness, positive regard, competence, trustworthiness, and interpersonal attractiveness. In Chapter 4 you discovered valuable reasons for atending to and working with client nonverbal behavior as well as important aspects of your own nonverbal behavior, including kinesics, paralinguistics, proxemics, environment, and time variables. Synchrony, or matching, between counselor and client nonverbal behavior and congruence between your verbal and nonverbal messages were also emphasized. In Chapters 5 and 6 you acquired a base of various verbal responses to use in counseling interactions to facilitate client exploration, understanding, and action. These responses included clarification, paraphrase, reflection, summarization, probes, confrontation, interpretation, and information giving. You have also had various types of practice in which you have demonstrated each set of skills in role-play interactions. In actual counseling, these skills are blended together and used in complementary fashion. In Part Five of the postevaluation, we structure a practice opportunity designed to simulate an actual initial helping interview with a client. The purpose of this activity is to help you "put the skills together"—that is, integrate them for yourself in some meaningful, coherent fashion. It is analogous to learning anything else that requires a set of skills for successful performance. To swim, for example, you have to learn first to put your face in the water, then to float, then to kick, then to move your arms in strokes, and finally to do it all at once. Initial attempts feel awkward, but out of such first steps evolve championship swimmers.

POSTEVALUATION

PART ONE

This part is designed for you to assess your performance on Objective One. Using the written list of client statements and counselor responses below, take a sheet of paper and identify the type of action response—probe, confrontation, interpretation, or information giving—reflected in each counselor message. If you can accurately identify six out of eight responses, you have met this objective. You can check your answers against those provided in the feedback that follows the postevaluation.

1. *Client:* "The pressure from my job is starting to get to me. I'm always in a constant rush, trying to hurry and get several things done at the same time. There's never enough time."
   a. "What is it about your job that is causing you to feel so stressed?"
   b. "It's important you are aware of this. Continued anxiety and stress like this can lead to health problems if they go unchecked."
2. *Client:* "I'm tired of sitting home alone, but I feel so uptight when I ask a girl for a date."
   a. "You seem to be saying that you feel lonely and also that you're not willing to risk asking a girl to go out with you."
   b. "What makes you so anxious when you speak with girls?"
3. *Client:* "I don't know why I tolerate his abuse. I really don't love him."
   a. "On the one hand, you say that you don't love him, and on the other hand, you remain in the house and allow him to beat you. How do you put these two things together?"
   b. "You may be caught up in a vicious cycle about whether your feelings for him, even though they're not love, outweigh your regard for yourself. It might be helpful for you to know the process other women in your shoes go through before they finally get enough courage to leave for good."
4. *Client:* "I don't know why we ever got married in the first place."
   a. "What qualities attracted you to each other originally?"
   b. "You're having a difficult time right now,

(continued)

POSTEVALUATION (continued)

which has led you to question the entire marriage. I wonder whether you would react this way if this present problem weren't causing such distress."

PART TWO

Match the four action responses, listed below, with the appropriate intended purposes of these responses (Chapter Objective Two). Feedback follows the postevaluation.

Action Response

(a) Probe
(b) Confrontation
(c) Interpretation
(d) Information giving

Intended purpose of response

_____1. To identify mixed (incongruent) messages and behavior
_____2. To begin an interview
_____3. To examine client behavior or issues from an alternative frame of reference
_____4. To identify alternatives/options available to clients
_____5. To obtain information
_____6. To broaden or narrow the topic of discussion
_____7. To identify implicit messages
_____8. To dispel myths

PART THREE

For each of the following three client statements, Objective Three asks you to verbalize or write an example of each of the four action responses. In developing these responses, it may be helpful to use the cognitive learning strategy you practiced earlier for each response. Example responses are given in the Postevaluation Feedback.

Client 1, a frustrated parent: My house looks like a mess. I can't seem to get anything done with these kids always under my feet. I'm afraid that I may lose my temper and hit them one of these days.
Probe:
Confrontation:
Interpretation:
Information giving:

Client 2, a graduate student: I feel so overwhelmed. I've got books to read, papers to write. My money is running low and I don't even have a job. Plus my roommate is thinking of moving out.

Probe:
Confrontation:
Interpretation:
Information giving:

Client 3, a nurse: These doctors drive me crazy. They tell me whenever I make a mistake but never say a word when I do a good job. I'm getting tired of hearing them order me around the way they do. At my salary, who needs the aggravation?
Probe:
Confrontation:
Interpretation:
Information giving:

PART FOUR

This part of the evaluation gives you an opportunity to develop your observation skills of key aspects of client behavior that must be attended to in order to develop effective and accurate action responses:

1. Issues and messages that need more elaboration, information, or examples
2. Discrepancies and incongruities
3. Implicit messages and themes
4. Distorted perceptions and ideas
5. Myths and inaccurate information

Objective Four asks you to observe these five aspects of client behavior during a 30-minute interview. Record your observations on the Client Observation Checklist that follows. You can obtain feedback for this activity by having two or more persons observe and rate the same session—then compare your responses.

CLIENT OBSERVATION CHECKLIST

Name of counselor _____
Name of observer(s) _____
_____

Instructions: Given the five categories of client behavior (left column), use the right column to record separate occurrences of behaviors within these categories as they occur during a 30-minute counseling interview.*

* If observers are not available, audiotape or videotape your session and complete the checklist while reviewing the tape.

(continued)

Observed category	Selected key client words and behavior
1. Issues and messages that need more elaboration, information, or examples	1. _____ 2. _____ 3. _____ 4. _____
2. Discrepancies and incongruities	1. _____ 2. _____ 3. _____ 4. _____
3. Implicit messages and themes	1. _____ 2. _____ 3. _____ 4. _____
4. Distorted perceptions and ideas	1. _____ 2. _____ 3. _____ 4. _____
5. Myths or inaccurate information	1. _____ 2. _____ 3. _____ 4. _____

Observer impressions and comments _____

PART FIVE

In order to have an opportunity to integrate your skills (Chapter Objective Five), conduct at least one role-play interview that is approximately 20 minutes long. You may want to consider this an initial helping interview. Your objective is to use as many of the verbal responses (listening, action) and the nonverbal behaviors as seem appropriate within this time span. Also give some attention to the quality of your relationship with the client. Try to regard this interview as an opportunity to get involved with the person in front of you, not as just another practice. If you feel some discomfort in using your verbal and nonverbal skills, you may wish to do several more interviews with different clients with this goal in mind. To assess your interview, use the Interview Inventory that follows. You may wish to copy the inventory or superimpose a piece of paper over it for your ratings. After all the ratings are completed, look at your ratings in the light of these questions:

1. Which relationship variables were easiest for you to demonstrate? Hardest?
2. Examine the total number of the verbal responses you used in each category. Did you use responses from each category with the same frequency? Did most of your responses come from one category? Did you seem to avoid using responses from one category? If so, for what reason?
3. Was it easier to integrate the verbal responses or the nonverbal skills?
4. Which nonverbal skills were easiest for you to demonstrate? Which ones did you find most difficult to use in the interview?
5. What do you see that you have learned about your counseling interview behavior so far? What do you think you need to improve?

INTERVIEW INVENTORY

Interview No. _____ Counselor _____
Client _____ Rater _____ Date _____

Instructions for rating: This rating form has three parts. Part One (Relationship Variables) measures aspects of establishing and enhancing a therapeutic relationship. Part Two (Verbal Behavior) assesses listening and action responses. Part Three (Nonverbal Behavior) evaluates your use of various nonverbal behaviors. To use the Interview Inventory for rating, follow the instructions found on each part of the inventory.

PART ONE: RELATIONSHIP VARIABLES

Instructions: Using the 5-point scale, indicate which number on the scale best represents the counselor's behavior during the observed interaction. Circle the appropriate number on the chart on p. 138.

PART TWO: VERBAL BEHAVIOR

Instructions: Check (✓) the *type* of verbal response represented by each counselor statement in the corresponding category on the rating form. At the end of the observation period, tally the total number of checks associated with each verbal response on the chart on p. 139.

PART THREE: NONVERBAL BEHAVIOR

Instructions: This part of the inventory lists a number of significant dimensions of nonverbal behavior. Check (✓) any that you observe and provide a brief description of the key aspects and appropriateness of the behavior. An example is given on the chart on p. 140.

(continued)

POSTEVALUATION (continued)

PART ONE: RELATIONSHIP VARIABLES

1. Conveyed accurate understanding of the client.

1	2	3	4	5
Not at all	Minimally	Somewhat	A great deal	Almost always

2. Conveyed support and warmth without approving or disapproving of the client.

1	2	3	4	5
Not at all	Minimally	Somewhat	A great deal	Almost always

3. Focused on the person rather than on the procedure or on counselor's "professional role."

1	2	3	4	5
Not at all	Minimally	Somewhat	A great deal	Almost always

4. Conveyed spontaneity, was not "mechanical" when responding to client.

1	2	3	4	5
Not at all	Minimally	Somewhat	A great deal	Almost always

5. Responded to feelings and issues as they occurred within the session (that is, "here and now").

1	2	3	4	5
Not at all	Minimally	Somewhat	A great deal	Almost always

6. Displayed comfort and confidence in working with the client.

1	2	3	4	5
Not at all	Minimally	Somewhat	A great deal	Almost always

7. Responded with dynamism and frequency; was not "passive."

1	2	3	4	5
Not at all	Minimally	Somewhat	A great deal	Almost always

8. Displayed sincerity in intentions and responses.

1	2	3	4	5
Not at all	Minimally	Somewhat	A great deal	Almost always

9. Conveyed friendliness and "good will" in interacting with client.

1	2	3	4	5
Not at all	Minimally	Somewhat	A great deal	Almost always

10. Informed client about expectations and what would or would not happen in session (that is, structuring).

1	2	3	4	5
Not at all	Minimally	Somewhat	A great deal	Almost always

11. Shared similar attitudes, opinions, and experiences about oneself with client when appropriate (that is, when such sharing added to, not detracted from, client focus).

1	2	3	4	5
Not at all	Minimally	Somewhat	A great deal	Almost always

12. Other significant relationship aspects _____
_____
_____
_____

PART TWO: VERBAL BEHAVIOR

	Listening responses				Action responses					
	Clarification	Paraphrase	Reflecting feeling	Summarization	Open question	Closed question	Focused question	Confrontation	Interpretation	Information giving
1										
2										
3										
.										
.										
.										
.										
.										
.										
20										
Total										

POSTEVALUATION (continued)

PART THREE: NONVERBAL BEHAVIOR

Behavior	Check (✔) if observed	Key aspects of behavior	Behavior	Check (✔) if observed	Key aspects of behavior
Example Body posture	✔	Tense, rigid until last part of session, then relaxed	*Example* Body posture	✔	Tense, rigid until last part of session, then relaxed
1. Eye contact			19. Time in responding to messages		
2. Facial expression			20. Time in ending session		
3. Head nodding			21. Autonomic response (for example, breathing, sweat, skin flush, rash)		
4. Body posture			22. Congruence/ incongruence between counselor verbal and nonverbal behavior		
5. Body movements					
6. Body orientation					
7. Gestures					
8. Nonverbal adaptors					
9. Voice level and pitch			23. Synchrony/ dissynchrony between counselor/client nonverbal behavior		
10. Rate of speech					
11. Verbal underlining (voice emphasis)					
12. Speech errors					
13. Pauses, silence					
14. Distance					
15. Touch					
16. Position in room					
17. Environmental arousal			24. Other		
18. Time in starting session					

FEEDBACK #21: INFORMATION GIVING

Client 1

Question 1: The client seems to lack information about effective birth control and about possible effects of multiple abortions.

Question 2: a. Rhythm is not a foolproof pregnancy prevention method.

b. Withdrawal also may not prevent pregnancy, particularly if semen is around the vaginal opening.

c. Multiple abortions can have physical and/or emotional complications, depending on the individual.

Question 3: Present the problems of withdrawal and rhythm first, since this could result in another pregnancy; followed by information about effects of multiple abortions.

Question 4: Be very specific, accurate, and factual. Avoid making any value judgments. May want to use paper and pencil to draw how withdrawal could result in pregnancy.

Question 5: Probably a lot, as she is using lack of information to avoid the issue. She may initially be upset or angry.

Examples of information-giving response: Marie, since you've said you're not worried about getting pregnant again because you and your partner practice rhythm and withdrawal, let me share some information about these methods with you.

(continued)

I'm not telling you these things to say "Do this" — or "Don't do this" —but more to give you some facts that you can use to decide what might be best for you with this issue. First, withdrawal can and often does result in pregnancy, because in withdrawing, sometimes some semen is left around this vaginal opening [draws a diagram]. What can happen then is that the semen can travel up the opening and reach these tubes [continues drawing] and can fertilize an egg and result in pregnancy, just as if you had had a complete act of intercourse. Rhythm is also something that doesn't have a very high rate of preventing pregnancy — about half the time it works, half it doesn't. That's because it can get awfully difficult and tedious to know for sure when to have sex and when not to and also because women can ovulate at any time in their menstrual cycle. I mention this because depending on the person, having several abortions can result in physical or emotional complications. Since you seem to be interested in preventing another pregnancy at this time, you may want to consider other, more foolproof methods.

Client 2

Question 1: The client seems to lack information about the type of curriculum found in a nursing program, about the present job market for nurses, and about her own academic abilities and achievements as well as limitations.

Question 2: a. The nursing curriculum may or may not be easy, depending on a person's strengths. It requires ability and facility with science and math.

b. In some areas of the country, nursing jobs are now very scarce.

c. Since your record of achievement has been consistently good in English and history and consistently poor in math and science, you may find nursing to be a hard curriculum.

Question 3: Perhaps begin with the fact that jobs are not always readily available, since this is so important to her, followed by information about the amount of math and science required in a nursing curriculum and how this fits with her past record of achievement.

Question 4: Be specific and objective—dig out some statistics of the nursing job market for her in different areas of the country. Perhaps have her look through catalogues of nursing programs and assess her interest and ability in each individual course.

Question 5: Depending on her motivation to be a nurse, she may feel relieved or upset and frustrated by the information.

Example of information-giving response: Renee, you mentioned you are interested in getting into nursing because it is an easy curriculum and because there are so many nursing jobs always available. I'd like to share some facts and figures with you about the nursing field you may not be aware of. I'm not trying to say "Pursue nursing" or "Don't pursue it" —just look at the information and then at yourself in making this important decision. First, it was true at one time that nurses were always in short supply. During the last few years, however, this has changed. In some parts of the country, there are many more nurses than there are jobs. If you take a look at these figures for these five geographical areas, you'll see what I mean. So, depending on where you live, it could be easy or very difficult to get the kind of job you want in the nursing field. Second, whether nursing is easy or hard as a curriculum depends on you and your interests and abilities. I've pulled out several catalogues listing courses in typical nursing programs. Nursing involves a lot of math and science course work, which, as you know, has not seemed to be as easy for you as English and history. It may be helpful for you to look at these courses individually and see whether you think you have the interest and inclination to achieve in them.

Client 3

Question 1: Client seems to lack certain legal information about possible management and consequences of divorce. Also seems to lack information about possible psychological effects of divorce.

Question 2: a. Getting a divorce rarely results in loss of job.

b. In most situations, the husband would be legally required to give financial support for the children.

c. Although divorce may make a person feel happy and relieved, it can also be unsettling, can result in temporary feelings of loss and depression, and is not an antidote for all other life issues.

Question 3: Present the need for legal information about her job status and child support, followed by other possible effects of divorce.

Question 4: Be factual and concrete. Possibly ask her to list pros and cons of divorce on paper.

Question 5: Her feelings could range from relief about the legal issues to disappointment that divorce is not a panacea.

FEEDBACK #21: (continued)

Example of information-giving response: Leslie, in discussing your situation with you, there are a couple of things I want to mention. First, it might be useful for you to consider seeing a competent lawyer who specializes in divorce mediation. This person could give you detailed information about the legal effects and processes of a divorce. Usually, however, a person does not lose a job because of a divorce. Besides, in most instances, the husband is required to make support payments as long as the children are of minor age. I would encourage you to express these same concerns to the lawyer. The other thing I'd like to spend some time discussing is your belief that you will feel very happy after the divorce. That might be very true. It is also important to remember, though, that just the process of ending a relationship — even a bad relationship — can be very unsettling and can bring not only relief but often some temporary feelings of loss and maybe sadness.

□ SUGGESTED READINGS

Beck, J. T., & Strong, S. R. (1982). Stimulating therapeutic change with interpretations: A comparison of positive and negative connotation. *Journal of Counseling Psychology, 29,* 551–559.

Borck, L. E., & Fawcett, S. B. (1982). *Learning counseling and problem-solving skills.* New York: Haworth Press. Chapter 7, "How to Ask a Client Questions."

Brammer, L. M., Shostrom, E. L., & Abrego, P. J. (1989). *Therapeutic psychology: Fundamentals of counseling and psychotherapy* (5th ed.). Englewood Cliffs. N.J.: Prentice-Hall. Chapter 9, "Interpretation and Body Awareness Strategies."

Claiborn, C. D. (1982). Interpretation and change in counseling. *Journal of Counseling Psychology, 29,* 439–453.

Claiborn, C. D., Ward, S. R., & Strong, S. R. (1981). Effects of congruence between counselor interpretations and client beliefs. *Journal of Counseling Psychology, 28,* 101–109.

Elliott, R., Barker, C. B., Caskey, N., & Pistrang, N. (1982). Differential helpfulness of counselor verbal response modes. *Journal of Counseling Psychology, 29,* 354–361.

Gazda, G. M., Asbury, F. S., Balzer, F. J., Childers, W. C., & Walters, R. P. (1984). *Human relations development: A manual for educators.* Boston: Allyn & Bacon. Chapter 18, "Perceiving and Responding with Confrontation."

Hudson, J., & Danish, S. (1980). The acquisition of information: An important life skill. *Personnel and Guidance Journal, 59,* 164–167.

Ivey, A. E. (1988). *International interviewing and counseling* (2nd ed.). Pacific Grove, CA: Brooks/Cole. Chapter 3, "Questions: Opening Communication."

Johnson, D. W. (1986) (3rd ed.). *Reaching out: Interpersonal effectiveness and self-actualization.* Englewood Cliffs, NJ: Prentice-Hall. Chapter 11, "Confrontation and Negotiation."

Jones, A. S., & Gelso, C. (1988). Differential effects of style interpretation: Another look. *Journal of Counseling Psychology, 35,* 363–369.

Leaman, D. R. (1978). Confrontation in counseling. *Personnel and Guidance Journal, 56,* 630–633.

Long, L., Paradise, L., & Long, T. (1981). *Questioning: Skills for the helping process.* Pacific Grove, CA: Brooks/Cole.

Milne, C. R., & Dowd, E. T. (1983). Effect of interpretation style on counselor social influence. *Journal of Counseling Psychology, 30,* 603–606.

Selby, J. W., & Calhoun, L. G. (1980). Psychodidactics: An undervalued and underdeveloped treatment tool for psychological intervention. *Professional Psychology, 11,* 236–241.

Strong, S. R., Wambach, C. A., Lopez, F. G., & Cooper, R. K. (1979). Motivational and equipping functions of interpretation in counseling. *Journal of Counseling Psychology, 26,* 98–107.

FEEDBACK: POSTEVALUATION

PART ONE
1. a. Probe
   b. Information giving
2. a. Confrontation
   b. Probe
3. a. Confrontation
   b. Information giving
4. a. Probe
   b. Interpretation

PART TWO
1. b. Confrontation
2. a. Probe
3. c. Interpretation
4. d. Information giving
5. a. Probe
6. a. Probe
7. c. Interpretation
8. d. Information giving

PART THREE
Here are some examples of action responses. Are yours similar?

(continued)

Client statement 1

Probe: What exactly would you like to be able to accomplish during the day?

or

How could you keep the kids occupied while you did some of your housework?

or

When do you feel most like striking the children?

or

How could you control your anger?

Confrontation: On the one hand, you seem to be saying the kids are responsible for your difficulties, and at the same time it appears as if you feel you are the one who is out of control.

Interpretation: I wonder whether you would be able to accomplish what seems important to you even if the kids weren't always underfoot — perhaps it's easy to use their presence to account for your lack of accomplishment.

Information giving: If you believe your problem would be solved by having more time alone, we could discuss some options that seemed to help other women in this situation — things to give you more time alone as well as ways to cope with your anger.

Client statement 2

Probe: How could you organize yourself better so that you wouldn't feel so overcome by your studies?

or

What kind of work might you do that would fit in with your class schedule?

or

How might you cope with these feelings of being so overwhelmed?

Confrontation: You've mentioned several reasons that you feel so overwhelmed now, and at the same time I don't think you mentioned anything you're doing to relieve these feelings.

Interpretation: You seem to feel so discouraged with everything that I imagine it would be easy now to feel justified in giving it all up, quitting grad school altogether.

Information giving: It might be helpful if we discussed some time-management strategies to help you better organize your limited time. For example, ...

Client statement 3

Probe: What is it, specifically, about your job that bothers you?

or

Is there anything about your job you enjoy?

or

How would you manage if you didn't have your job?

Confrontation: It sounds as if you are pretty dissatisfied right now with your present job, and at the same time, I don't think I heard you mention any other job options you've considered.

Interpretation: It sounds as if you believe others are responsible for your discontent with your present job. Is it possible that you say things at work that encourage the doctors to talk to you as they do?

Information giving: Nursing can be a very stressful occupation. It sounds as if you're on the threshold of burnout now. Let's talk about some ways you might cope with this burnout. For instance, ...

CONCEPTUALIZING CLIENT PROBLEMS

SEVEN

Institutionalized patient: Why are people always out to get me?

Student: I can't even talk to my mom. What a hassle!

Disabled person: Ever since I've had this automobile accident and had to change jobs, I don't seem to be able to get it together.

Older person: I never feel like I can do anything well anymore. And I feel so depressed all the time.

These client statements are representative of the types of concerns that clients bring to counselors every day. One thing these clients and others have in common is that their initial problem presentation is often vague. A counselor can translate vague client problems into specific problem statements by using certain skills associated with problem assessment. This chapter presents a conceptual framework that a counselor can use to assess client problems. Chapter 8 demonstrates a way for the counselor to implement this framework in the interview setting.

☐ OBJECTIVES

After completing this chapter, you will be able to identify, in writing, using two client case descriptions:

1. The client's problem behaviors
2. Whether the problem behaviors are overt or covert
3. The antecedent contributing conditions
4. The consequences and secondary gains
5. The way each consequence influences the problem behaviors

☐ WHAT IS ASSESSMENT?

Problem assessment consists of procedures and tools used to collect and process information from which the entire counseling program is developed. Assessment has six purposes:

1. To obtain information on the client's presenting problem and on other, related problems.

2. To identify the controlling or contributing variables associated with the problem.
3. To determine the client's goals/expectations for counseling outcomes.
4. To gather baseline data that will be compared with subsequent data to assess and evaluate client progress and the effects of treatment strategies. This evaluation helps the practitioner decide whether to continue or modify the treatment plan or intervention strategy.
5. To educate and motivate the client by sharing your views of the problem with the client, increasing the client's receptivity to treatment, and contributing to therapeutic change through reactivity (that is, when behavior changes as a consequence of the assessment interview or procedure rather than as a result of a particular action or change strategy).
6. To use the information obtained from the client to plan effective treatment interventions and strategies. The information obtained during the assessment process should help to answer this well-thought-out question: "*What* treatment, by *whom,* is most effective for *this* individual with *that* specific problem and under *which* set of circumstances?" (Paul, 1967, p. 111).

This chapter focuses primarily on the first two purposes of assessment mentioned above: defining the problem and identifying the controlling variables associated with the problem. The next section presents several ways to conceptualize client problems.

☐ METHODS OF CONCEPTUALIZING CLIENT PROBLEMS

Interviewing the client and having the client engage in other assessment procedures are only part of the overall assessment process in counseling and therapy. Equally important is the therapist's own mental, or covert, activity that goes on during the process. The therapist typically gathers a great amount of information from clients during this stage of counseling. Unless the therapist can integrate and synthesize the data, they are of little value and use. The *counselor's* tasks during the assessment process include knowing what information to obtain and how to obtain it, putting it together in some meaningful way, and using it to generate clinical hunches, or hypotheses, about client problems, hunches that lead to tentative ideas for treatment planning. This mental activity

of the counselor's is called "conceptualization"—which simply means the way the counselor thinks about the client's problem configuration.

The assessment methods we describe later in this chapter and in Chapter 8, and our interview assessment model particularly, are based on a model of conceptualization we have used over the years in our teaching and in clinical practice. The origins of this model were first described by Kanfer and Saslow (1969). Before describing our model in detail, we would first like to describe three other current models of client or case conceptualization proposed by Swensen (1968), Seay (1978), and Lazarus (1976, 1981) that have influenced the development of our own clinical model of problem conceptualization.

The four models of problem conceptualization we present in this chapter have some distinct differences but are also similar in several respects. First, they represent a framework the therapist can use to develop hunches (educated guesses) about the client's presenting problem. Second, they recognize that problem behavior is usually multifaceted and affects how people think and feel as well as behave. Finally, they provide information about the problem that the therapist can use in selecting and planning relevant treatments. Although the major focus of the chapter is on the model we use for case conceptualization, we present three others because they are important historically in the development of case conceptualization models and because they enable the reader to look at client problems from more than one perspective.

Swensen's Model of Problem Conceptualization:
Drawing on the works of Lewin (1951) and Pascal (1959), Swensen has developed a model of case conceptualization based on the following formula:

| Deviant behavior (symptomatology; undesired result or outcome) | = | function of the degree of stress, maladaptive behaviors, habits, and defenses versus supports, strengths, and adaptive habits and defenses |

Deviant behavior. Deviant behavior is any behavior that is different from what is typical or ordinary and would be expected of a person in a similar role and may include symptomatology such as feeling anxious or depressed or more unusual (in the negative sense) behavior such as overeating and vomiting or hearing voices.

Stress.   Stress includes situations that are pressure-packed or tense or uncomfortable for the client, usually resulting in noticeable physiological sensations such as rapid heartbeat, dizziness, sweating, or stomach upset.

Maladaptive behaviors, habits, and defenses.   Maladaptive behaviors, habits, and defenses are habitual behaviors and defenses that are negative or destructive in the sense that they prevent clients from achieving their goal of a satisfying life. In other words, maladaptive habits and defenses are things that contribute to deviant behavior. For example, an adolescent is removed from a normal classroom and placed in a behavior-disorders classroom because of continued and repetitive behavioral problems, including starting fights with other kids, stealing their personal property, and swearing at teachers. In discussion with his parents, you find that this 15-year-old boy has almost never received any parental-enforced consequences for irresponsible behavior. The parents also indicate that their son's behavior has resulted in a constant strain on their own marital relationship. They say as well that this boy's behavior is especially hard for them to tolerate because of the excellent behavior of their older son, who is a "model child." They don't understand why the younger son can't act more responsibly, as his brother does. Interviews with the boy suggest that he feels very inferior to his older brother and many of his peers. The client also states that, if his parents didn't have him to fight about, they would "split" because they argue about him constantly. In this case, the undesirable result, or deviant behavior, is represented by the boy's learned and inappropriate behaviors that get him into trouble at school, such as fighting, stealing, and swearing. Maladaptive defenses/behavioral habits would be his lack of responsibility at home and his possible belief that his "problem" provides a good reason for his parents to stay together.

Supports and strengths.   Supports include resources that currently exist for the client — namely, persons or situations in the client's environment who are supportive or helpful. Strengths include accomplishments or positive performance of the client in some area. Strengths are indicators of the client's "basic abilities or talents" and "suggest areas in which the psychotherapist may work with some prospect of success. . . . [However], strengths are impossible to assess without successful performance of some kind. Strength is evidenced by prior success at some endeavor" (Swensen, 1968, p. 57).

Adaptive behaviors, habits, and defenses.   Adaptive behaviors, habits, and defenses include constructive defenses or habitual behaviors which help clients achieve their goals and which contribute to a satisfying life. Adaptive behaviors are those that are learned, are appropriate given the context, and ultimately result in success or reinforcement for the client. For example, in the case of the adolescent mentioned earlier, the client also is a member of the school's swim team. Successful performance in swimming is a strength for the client. Behaviors that contribute to this accomplishment, such as attending practices daily, being on time, and following instructions from the coach, are adaptive behavior habits or patterns that ultimately contribute to success or reinforcement for this client in this one area.

Swensen's case conceptualization model can be used by practitioners in several ways. First, it is a tool to help counselors see, hear, or grasp what is going on with a client in order to develop some hypotheses or hunches about the client's concerns. For example, consider the case analysis depicted in Figure 7-1 of the adolescent boy described earlier. In studying the figure, we get a picture of a boy who exhibits a lot of school-related "behavioral problems" and who feels a lot of pressure on him from his older brother and his parents as well as pressure to help keep together his parents' disintegrating marital relationship. This same boy has learned to respond to these stresses or pressures with maladaptive defenses and behavioral patterns, including constant unfavorable comparisons with his older brother, lack of responsibility at home, and anxiety in unstructured situations, especially at school. He does, however, have two persons in school willing to work with him — the counselor and the swim coach. He also has several other positive things in his favor, including good health, intelligence, and membership on the school swim team. And he has demonstrated adaptive defenses and behavioral patterns in certain situations, such as swim meet competitions and test-taking situations. We can use this information to generate some hunches about the client's presenting behavioral symptomatology — including (but not limited to) the following:

Deviant Behaviors	Stresses	Maladaptive Defenses and Behavioral Habits
Starts fights with other kids Steals personal property from other kids Swears at teachers Has received low grades (Cs and Ds) in four out of five classes	Older brother who is smart, well behaved, well liked at school and elsewhere Parents' relationship—constant tension Unstructured classes in school	Compares self unfavorably with older brother Lack of responsibility/tasks at home Feels anxious in unstructured situations, especially school-related

Supports	Strengths	Adaptive Habits and Defenses
School counselor is willing to work with him and with family Swim coach wants to help so he can remain on swim team	Member of swim club—performs well in competitions Good health—good appetite and sleep patterns Received high scores on intelligence tests	Attends daily practice promptly for swim club practices Follows instructions of swim club coach Applies himself to a test-taking (intelligence) situation; follows instructions on the test Generally feels comfortable and handles himself well in structured and competitive situations

Figure 7-1. *Case analysis using Swensen's case conceptualization model*

1. There is a lot of competition between himself and his older brother for his parents' attention. Most of the time, the client feels his older brother wins this one.
2. The client has never really had to be responsible for himself or his behavior.
3. The client may feel his problems provide a reason for his parents to stay together.
4. The client feels uncomfortable in unstructured situations and shows evidence of adaptive responses in situations that are structured and somewhat competitive. In fact, the client seems to thrive on competition so that he can demonstrate that he is capable of winning.

Second, this model provides ways for therapists to decide which treatment approach (or combination of strategies) they will use to help a particular client. Often this decision will be made according to theoretical models, biases, and related strengths. For example, a client-centered therapist might focus on the lack of awareness, congruence, and self-actualization of this client, who doesn't seem to have generated his own ideas about how to live his life. The reality therapist might focus on the client's prevalent irresponsible behavior and how he could learn to take responsibility for his actions. The Adlerian therapist would want to deal more with the competition between the client and his brother as well as with helping the client acquire social interest or a better sense of belonging at

home and at school. The TA therapist would view the client as relating to others out of his "adapted child" ego state and might focus on how he could use other ego states to produce different results. The Gestalt therapist would focus on the splits, or incongruence, displayed in some of the client's feelings and actions and also on ideas the client has introjected and/or projected. The cognitive or RET therapist would look at the cognitions, or internal thoughts or self-statements, behind some of the client's maladaptive behavior habits and help him learn to dispute them. The family therapist would focus on the roles and boundaries of the client's family and on the marital relationship between his parents. The behavioral therapist would focus on changing the contributing causes (maladaptive behavioral habits) and on strengthening the client's adaptive behavioral habits in order to produce change in the presenting symptoms. Ideally, the decision about which approaches to use should be based on a number of factors, not just on the therapist's particular allegiance to or preference for a particular counseling theory (see also Chapter 11). It is particularly important to select intervention approaches that are related to the identified problems and goals and have the best chance of helping the client resolve those problems.

A third, more general way in which Swensen's case conceptualization model can be used is to examine the ratio of factors in the numerator of the formula to factors present in the denominator. According to Swensen (1968, p. 31), "Any *decrease* in the factors listed in the numerator of the formula (stress, maladaptive habits, and defenses) should reduce psychological deficit, as will any *increase* in the factors listed in the denominator (supports, adaptive habits and defenses, strengths)."

Seay's Model of Problem Conceptualization

Seay's model of case conceptualization (1978) integrates thematic content and therapy techniques. It is based on major life themes (and lifestyles) drawn from the three primary modalities for human functioning: cognition, affect, and behavior (CAB).

Seay (1978) proposes the following categories to describe the client problems:

1. Major environmental contingencies — includes environmental setting events, consequences, history.
2. Cognitive themes — consists of both misconceptions and irrationalities held by the client.
3. Affective themes — consists of barriers or emotional conflicts and felt or expressed emotions that are barriers or are interfering and counterproductive.
4. Behavioral patterns — consists of overt, observable behaviors. May include verbal and nonverbal behaviors exhibited during counseling, such as rapid speech and frequent gestures, as well as behavioral patterns exhibited outside counseling and often in problem-related situations, such as overeating, periodic drug and alcohol use, or poor study skills.

As an example of Seay's conceptualization model, consider a client who reports having limited options because she is afraid to drive; she also reports depression caused by constant criticism from her husband of some 20 years. She is having difficulty sleeping (wakes up and can't go back to sleep) and also has lost weight recently. History reveals that she grew up in a home with an abusive father. The client is also approaching 40 years of age and is unsure whether she wants to spend her next 20 years as she has spent the last 20 years. The client states that she has been moderately successful in getting some people to drive her here and there but is unable to leave town on her own or do things at her convenience. She also states that, as a child, she tolerated the abuse from her father. With her husband, she listens to his criticism and then

withdraws either by leaving the room or by saying nothing. Even though she reports feeling "fed up" and "upset" with her husband's constant badgering, she also reports believing that she is a failure and not capable of making good decisions independently, despite the facts that test data reveal she is of superior intelligence and that she has had a very responsible position in a business company for the last 15 years. During the initial interview, she cries often and speaks slowly and softly in a very halting style. Figure 7-2 shows an analysis of this case according to Seay's case conceptualization model.

Information revealed from Seay's case conceptualization model can also be used to generate hypotheses, or educated guesses, about the client and to plan a comprehensive treatment program. For example, in the case given, one of the major themes is cognitive and involves the client's negative perceptions about herself, especially in relationship to men. This theme probably originated with her father's abuse and is maintained by her husband's constant criticism. One could speculate that she may have sought out a particular type of male for a spouse who reinforces her negative image of herself. Although constant verbal abuse may seem punitive to her, it may also serve a purpose in confirming her self-perceptions as dependent and as a failure and help her to avoid anxiety-producing situations such as driving alone. The affective barriers of anxiety and depression represent anger/dissatisfaction turned inward. These emotions, like the cognitive theme, underscore her lack of confidence or the way she deprecates herself. These emotions are produced both by environmental contingencies and by her cognitive misperceptions. Observed behaviors such as crying, speech patterns, sleep difficulties, and weight loss corroborate her self-report of depression. Both the cognitive misperceptions and the affective barriers are contributing conditions to her withdrawal from her husband's criticism and her not driving by herself.

For treatment planning, initial focus areas might deal with the environmental contingencies and cognitive misconceptions that produce the maladaptive emotional and behavioral patterns. For example, the client might benefit from such things as Gestalt and TA strategies and/or assertion training to explore her feelings related to being abused and to help her change her reactions to her husband's criticism. Both rational-emotive and cognitive-behavioral techniques might be useful as treatment interventions for the cognitive

Environmental Contingencies	Cognitive Misconceptions	Affective Barriers	Behavioral Patterns
E_1 Abuse from father	C_1 Thoughts of failure	A_1 Anxiety/emotional dependence	B_1 Does not drive by herself
E_2 Constant criticism from husband	C_2 Negative or self-deprecating talk and perception	A_2 Depression	B_2 Withdraws from husband's criticism
E_3 Approaching 40: midlife assessment period	C_3 Lack of trust in her decisions	A_3 Anger—directed toward self and husband	B_3 Periodic crying during session
E_4 Successful and responsible job with stable work pattern	C_4 Superior intelligence		B_4 Slow, halting soft speech pattern
			B_5 Interrupted sleep pattern
			B_6 Appetite and weight loss

Figure 7-2. *Case analysis using Seay's case conceptualization model*

misperceptions. It would also be important to deal with some of the problematic behavioral patterns she exhibits, such as not driving by herself. Taking driving lessons and engaging in various driving tasks with the therapist (see also participant modeling, Chapter 13) are two ways to deal with this particular behavior pattern.

Seay's model is similar to other recent case conceptualizations proposed by Hutchins (1979—the TFA, or "thought, feelings, action," model) and by L'Abate (1981—the ERA, or "emotionality, rationality, activity," model). Both these models also stress the interrelatedness of thoughts, feelings, and actions (overt behaviors) and the importance of choosing interventions designed to focus on one or more of these elements that will maximize the probability of desired outcomes for the client and will "increase the likelihood of an optimum match between the behavior and the method used to improve that behavior" (L'Abate, 1981, p. 263).

Lazarus' Model of Problem Conceptualization: The BASIC ID

According to Arnold Lazarus, who is associated with broad-spectrum behavior therapy and with "technical eclecticism" (1971), people "are beings who move, feel, sense, imagine, think, and relate" (1976, p. 4).* Whenever stress or psychological disturbance exists, these functions are affected. According to Lazarus (1976, 1981), there are seven modalities to explore in assessment and intervention. To refer to these seven areas of assessment and treatment in abbreviated fashion, Lazarus uses the acronym "BASIC ID." A brief discussion

* From Arnold A. Lazarus, *Multimodal Behavior Therapy,* pp. 4, 33, 34. Copyright © 1976 by Arnold A. Lazarus. Published by Springer Publishing Company, Inc., New York. Used by permission of the publisher.

of each component of the BASIC ID follows. In using this model of conceptualization, it is important to remember that each modality described by Lazarus interacts with the other modalities and should not be treated in isolation.

B: Behavior. Behavior includes simple and more complex psychomotor skills and activities such as smiling, talking, writing, eating, smoking, and having sex. In most clinical interviewing, the therapist has to infer what the client does or does not do on the basis of client self-report, although occasionally other measures of behavior can corroborate client verbal report. Lazarus (1976) notes that it is especially important to be alert to behavioral excesses and deficits—things the client does too much or too little.

A: Affect. Affect includes felt or reported feelings and emotions. According to Lazarus, it is perhaps classically the most "overworked" area in psychotherapy and also one of the least understood (p. 33). Included in this category would be presence or absence of particular feelings as well as hidden or distorted feelings.

S: Sensation. Sensation includes the five major senses mentioned in Chapter 2 with respect to sensory processing of information: visual (sight), kinesthetic (touch), auditory (hearing), olfactory (smell), and gustation (taste). Focus on sensory elements of experience is important in order to develop personal fulfillment. Sometimes, too, presenting complaints are presented by way of felt body sensations such as stomach distress or dizziness (Lazarus, 1976). Therapists need to be alert to pleasant and unpleasant reported sensations as well as sensations of which clients seem unaware.

I: Imagery. According to Lazarus, imagery comprises various "mental pictures" that exert influence on a client's life (1976, p. 37). For example, a husband who was nagged by what he called repetitive ideas about his wife having an affair (apparently with no realistic basis) actually was troubled because he generated constant pictures or images of his wife in bed with another man. Lazarus (1976) believes that this modality is especially useful with clients who tend to overuse the cognitive modality and intellectualize their feelings.

C: Cognition. Cognitions are thoughts and beliefs, and Lazarus is most interested in exploring the client's mistaken beliefs — the illogical or irrational ones. He usually looks for three faulty assumptions that he believes are common and also potentially more damaging than others:

1. The tyranny of the SHOULD (Horney, 1950). Often this belief can be inferred from the client's actions and behaviors as well as from self-report.
2. Perfectionism — understanding ways in which clients expect perfectionism or infallibility, often not only of themselves but of others as well.
3. External attributions — the myths that clients verbalize when they feel they are the victims of outside persons or circumstances and have no control over or responsibility for what is happening to them.

I: Interpersonal relationships. Many therapists (including Sullivan, Horney, and Fromm) have stressed the importance of interpersonal relationships, or "social interest" (Adler, 1964). Lazarus (1976) notes that problems in the way clients relate to others can be detected not only through self-report and role playing but also by observation of the therapist/client relationship. Assessment of this modality includes observing the way clients express and accept feelings communicated to them by others as well as the way they behave and react to others.

D: Drugs. Lazarus asserts that this is an important nonpsychological modality to assess (and potentially treat), because neurological and biochemical factors can affect behavior, affective responses, cognitions, sensations, and so on. In addition to specific inquiries about psychotropic medications, assessment of this modality includes the following:

1. Overall appearance — attire, skin or speech disturbances, tics, psychomotor disorders.
2. Physiological complaints or diagnosed illnesses.
3. General health and well-being — physical fitness, exercise, diet and nutrition, avocational interests and hobbies, and leisure time pursuits.

This modality may often require consultation with or examination by a physician or other type of health professional.

Lazarus (1976) asserts that most therapists, including eclectic ones, fail to assess and treat these seven basic modalities. Instead, they deal with only one or two modalities, depending on their personal preferences and theoretical orientation, even though "durable results are in direct proportion to the number of specific modalities deliberately invoked by any therapeutic system" (p. 13).

The BASIC ID model of case conceptualization is applied to the following case and summarized in the modality profile (Lazarus, 1976, 1981) shown in Figure 7-3.

The client is a 35-year-old female who looks about 50–75 pounds overweight, though well groomed, well dressed, and articulate. The client states that she is in generally good health, does little exercise, and works either on the job or at home and has little free time. Free time is spent mainly in sedentary activities such as reading or watching TV. The client is divorced and has two school-age daughters. She does report occasional stomach distress — often as much as once or twice weekly. The client's presenting problem is overall "dissatisfaction with myself and my life." The client notes that she lives in a small town and has been unable to meet many available partners. She would like to have a good relationship with a male. She was divorced four years ago and states that her husband became interested in another woman and "took off." She says that she also has poor relationships with her two daughters, whom she describes as "irresponsible and lazy." On inquiry, it appears that the client is easily exploited and rather submissive in most of her relationships with significant others. In her job, she agrees to take work home with her even though she receives no overtime pay. She describes herself as feeling alone, lonely, and sometimes unloved or unlovable. She

Modality	Observations
B: Behavior	Passive responding; some withdrawal from conversation
	Slow rate of speech
	Frequent shrugging of shoulders
	Overeating
A: Affect	Alone—loneliness
	Unloved
	Denies concern or upset over weight
S: Sensation	Muscular tension—upper torso particularly
I: Imagery	Frequent fantasies of a move and different lifestyle
	Persistent dreams of being rescued
C: Cognition	Negative self-verbalizations and perceptions
	Self-perfectionistic standards
	Attributes problems to forces outside herself
I: Interpersonal relationships	Is exploited by ex-husband, daughters, boss
	Submissive in interactions with others
D: Drugs	Well groomed
	Well dressed
	50–75 pounds overweight
	Articulate
	Stomach distress—weekly
	Good health—mostly sedentary activity
	Little leisure time

Figure 7-3. *Modality profile of client case using BASIC ID (Lazarus, 1976, 1981)*

also reports that she often has thoughts that her life has been a failure and that she is not the kind of person she could be, although she portrays herself as a victim of circumstances (divorce, job, small town) beyond her control. However, she also reports rather frequent fantasies of moving and living in a different town and having a different job. She also describes repetitive dreams in which she can recall vividly the image of being rescued. She behaves very passively in the session—talks slowly, shrugs her shoulders, and occasionally withdraws from the conversation. Some muscular tension is apparent during the interview, particularly in her upper body. She states that overeating is a major problem, one that she attributes to not having her life go the way she wants it to and being unable to do much about it. At the same time, she appears to deny any concern about her weight, stating that if she's not worried about it, then it shouldn't matter to anyone else either.

In treatment planning, the first areas of focus would be the two modalities about which the client is most concerned—affective and interpersonal. If the interpersonal modality is selected as the initial area of change, it is likely that changes in this modality will lead to changes in the affective one also, since the client's feelings of loneliness are a direct result of lack of effective interpersonal relationships. Skill training programs (see Chapter 12) such as assertion training and social skills training are likely to be most effective in helping the client establish new relationships and avoid further exploitation in her present ones. Such skill training could also be directed toward some of her overt behaviors that may interfere with establishing new relationships, such as her speech rate and her style of responding in conversations. Although the client denies any concern about her weight, she may also allow her weight to prevent her from engaging in the very kind of social interactions and relationships she finds absent from her life. Strategies such as Gestalt dialoguing, TA redecision work, and NLP reframing may help her to examine her conflicting feelings about being overweight. If and when she decides to make weight reduction a goal, cognitive strategies (such as cognitive restructuring, Chapter 16) aimed at modifying any problem-related cognitive misperceptions would be useful, as would behavioral strategies (such as self-management, Chapter 16) targeted toward helping her modify her overeating behavior and supporting environmental contingencies.

LEARNING ACTIVITY #22: METHODS OF CASE CONCEPTUALIZATION

Using the case of Mrs. X, described later in this Learning Activity, conceptualize the case according to the three models previously described: Swensen's, Seay's, and Lazarus'. We provide specific questions below to consider for each model. You can do this exercise by yourself, although it may be a better learning experience if you work with it in small groups. You can then share your ideas with your group or your instructor or supervisor. For additional work with these three models, you may also wish to apply the questions below to actual cases of your own or to the cases presented in the postevaluation at the end of this chapter.

1. Swensen's model
   a. Identify the client's deviant behavior or presenting symptomatology.
   b. Identify the client's stressors.
   c. Identify the client's maladaptive behaviors, habits, and defenses.
   d. Identify the client's supports and strengths.
   e. Identify the client's adaptive behaviors, habits, and defenses.
   f. Speculate on which of the above would need to be targets of change in order to resolve the presenting symptoms.

2. Seay's model
   a. Identify environmental contingencies present in the client's situation.
   b. Identify cognitive misperceptions held by the client.
   c. Identify emotions or affective barriers.
   d. Identify behavioral patterns exhibited by the client.
   e. Speculate on which of the above would be appropriate targets of change in order to resolve the major issues.

3. Lazarus' model
   a. Identify the behavior exhibited by the client, particularly excesses and deficits.
   b. Identify the primary affect (feelings and emotions) reported by the client.
   c. Identify any major sensations or sensory experiences/processing reported by the client. Speculate on the client's primary sensory system.
   d. Identify the imagery or mental pictures that exert influence on the client.
   e. Identify the apparent cognitions (thoughts, beliefs) reported by the client.

f. Assess the nature of the client's interpersonal relationships.
g. Identify any physiological factors/complaints apparent in the problem.
h. Speculate on which of these seven areas would be *primary* targets of change and which might be *secondary* targets in order to resolve the problems and issues this client presents.

The Case of Mrs. X

Mrs. X is a 28-year-old married woman who reports that an excessive fear of having her husband die has led her to seek therapy. She further states that because this is her second marriage, it is important for her to work out her problem so that it doesn't ultimately interfere with her relationship with her husband. However, her husband is a sales representative and occasionally has to attend out-of-town meetings. According to Mrs. X, whenever he has gone away on a trip during the two years of their marriage, she "goes to pieces" and feels "utterly devastated" because of recurring thoughts that he will die and not return. She states that this is a very intense fear and occurs even when he is gone on short trips, such as a half day or a day. She is not aware of any coping thoughts or behaviors she uses at these times. She indicates that she feels great as soon as her husband does get home. She states that this was also a problem for her in her first marriage, which ended in divorce five years ago. She believes this happens because her father died unexpectedly when she was 11 years old. She states that whenever her husband tells her he has to leave, or actually does leave, she reexperiences the pain of being told her father has died. She feels plagued with thoughts that her husband will not return and then feels intense anxiety. She states that she is constantly thinking about never seeing her husband again during these anxiety episodes. According to Mrs. X, her husband has been very supportive and patient and has spent a considerable amount of time trying to reassure her and to convince her, through reasoning, that he will return from a trip. She states that this has not helped her to stop worrying excessively that he will die and not return. She also states that in the past few months her husband has canceled several business trips just to avoid putting her through all this pain.

Mrs. X also reports that this anxiety has resulted in some insomnia during the past two years. She states

(continued)

that as soon as her husband informs her that he must leave town, she has difficulty going to sleep that evening. When he has to be gone on an overnight trip, she reports, she doesn't sleep at all. She simply lies in bed and worries about her husband dying and also feels very frustrated that it is getting later and later and that she is still awake. She reports sleeping fairly well as long as her husband is home and a trip is not impending.

Mrs. X reports that she feels very satisfied with her present marriage except for some occasional times when she finds herself thinking that her husband does not fulfill all her expectations. She is not sure exactly what her expectations are, but she is aware of feeling anger toward him after this happens. When she gets angry, she just "explodes" and feels as though she lashes out at her husband for no apparent reason. She reports that she doesn't like to explode at her husband like this but feels relieved after it happens. She indicates that her husband continues to

be very supportive and protective in spite of her occasional outbursts. She suspects the anger may be her way of getting back at him for going away on a trip and leaving her alone. She also expresses feelings of hurt and anger since her father's death in being unable to find a "father substitute." She also reports feeling intense anger toward her ex-husband after the divorce — anger she still sometimes experiences.

Mrs. X has no children. She is employed in a responsible position as an executive secretary and makes $18,500 a year. She reports that she enjoys her work, although she constantly worries that her boss might not be pleased with her and that she could lose her job, even though her work evaluations have been satisfactory. She reports that another event she has been worried about is the health of her brother, who was injured in a car accident this past year. She further reports that she has an excellent relationship with her brother and strong ties to her church.

☐ OUR ASSUMPTIONS ABOUT ASSESSMENT AND COGNITIVE BEHAVIOR THERAPY

Like the previously described case conceptualization models, our model of assessment in counseling and therapy is based on several assumptions about clients, problems, and behavior. These assumptions are drawn from the cognitive-behavioral approach to counseling. Cognitive behavior therapy includes a variety of techniques and strategies that are based on principles of learning and designed to produce constructive change in human behaviors. This approach was first developed in the 1950s under the term *behavior therapy* by, among others, Skinner, Wolpe, Lazarus, and Krumboltz. Early behavior therapists focused on the importance of changing clients' observable behavior. Since the 1950s, there have been significant developments in behavior therapy. Among the most important is the emergence of cognitive behavior therapy, which arose in the 1970s as a result of the work of such persons as Meichenbaum and Beck. Cognitive behavior therapy emphasizes the effects of private events such as cognitions, beliefs, and internal dialogue on resulting feelings and performance. This orientation to counseling now recognizes that both overt responding (observed behavior) and covert respond-

ing (feelings and thoughts) are important targets of change as long as they can be clearly specified (Rimm & Masters, 1979, p. 1).

Most Problem Behavior Is Learned

Problem (maladaptive) behavior is developed, maintained, and subject to alteration or modification in the same manner as normal (adaptive) behavior. Both prosocial and maladaptive, or self-defeating, behaviors are assumed to be developed and maintained either by external situational events or cues, by external reinforcers, or by internal processes such as cognition, mediation, and problem solving. For the most part, maladaptive behavior is not thought to be a function of physical disease or of underlying intrapsychic conflict. This fundamental assumption means that we do not spend a great deal of time sorting out or focusing on possible unresolved early conflicts or underlying pathological states. It does not mean, however, that we rule out or overlook possible organic and physiological causes of problem behavior. For example, clients who complain of "anxiety" and report primarily somatic (body-related) symptoms such as heart palpitations, stomach upset, chest pains, and breathlessness may be chronic hyperventilators (Lum, 1976), although this can be considered only after the client has had a physical examination to rule out cardiopathy. Physical examinations also may reveal the presence of mitral valve heart dysfunction for some individuals who complain of "panic attacks." Other somatic symptoms suggesting anxiety, such as sweating, tachycardia, lightheadedness, and dizziness, could also result from organic disorders such as hypoglycemia, hyperthyroidism or other endocrine disorders, or a low-grade infection.

Physiological variables should always be explored, particularly when the results of the assessment do not suggest the presence of other specific stimuli eliciting the problem behavior. It is also important to recognize the need for occasional physiological management of psychological problems—for example, in the kinds of disorders mentioned above. Medications may be necessary in addition to psychological intervention. Antidepressants are typically recommended for some forms of depression, particularly the endogenous type as distinct from the more reactive (situational) type. They have been found helpful as a supplement to psychological treatment for some instances of agoraphobia, a disorder typified by a marked fear of being alone or in public places. Anxiety or panic attacks often are also managed with antidepressants but additionally with beta blockers and/or other antianxiety agents. Furthermore, a biological element, such as biochemical imbalance, seems to be present in many of the psychoses, such as schizophrenia, and these conditions usually require antipsychotic drugs to improve the client's overall level of functioning.

Causes of Problems and Therefore Treatments/ Interventions Are Multidimensional

Rarely is a problem caused by only one factor, and rarely does a single, unidimensional treatment program work in actual practice. For example, with a client who reports depression, we may find evidence of organic contributing factors such as Addison's disease (dysfunction of the adrenal gland), of environmental contributing conditions such as being left by his wife after moving to a new town, and of internal contributing factors such as self-deprecatory thoughts and images. Causes and contributing conditions of most client problems are multiple and include overt behavior, environmental events and relationships with others, covert behavior such as beliefs, images, and cognitions, feelings and bodily sensations, and possibly physiological/organic conditions. Intervention is usually more effective when directed toward all these multiple factors. For the client described

above, his endocrine balance must be restored and maintained, he must be helped to deal with his feelings of rejection and anger about his wife's departure, he needs to develop alternative resources and supports, including self-support, and he needs help in learning how to modify his self-deprecating thoughts and images. Additionally, he may benefit from problem-solving skills in order to decide the direction he wants his life to take. The more complete and comprehensive the treatment, the more successful the therapy tends to be, and also the less chance of relapse. According to Lazarus (1976, pp. 13–14),

Comprehensive treament at the very least calls for the correction of irrational beliefs, deviant behaviors, unpleasant feelings, intrusive images, stressful relationships, negative sensations, and possible biochemical imbalance. To the extent that problem identification (diagnosis) systematically explores each of these modalities, whereupon therapeutic intervention remedies whatever deficits and maladaptive patterns emerge, treatment outcomes will be positive and long-lasting. To ignore any of these modalities is to practice a brand of therapy that is incomplete.

Problems Are to Be Viewed Operationally

We suggest a way to view client problems that defines the client's present problem behaviors and some contributing problem conditions. This approach is called defining the problem "operationally," or "concretely." An operational problem definition functions like a measure, a barometer, or a "behavioral anchor." Operational definitions indicate some very specific problem behaviors; they do not infer vague traits or labels from the client's problem statement. Mischel (1968, p. 10) has contrasted these two approaches to problem conceptualization: "The emphasis is on what a person *does* in situations rather than on inferences about what attributes he *has* more globally."

Consider the following example of a way to view a client's problem operationally. In working with the "depressed" client, we would try to define precisely what the client means by "depressed" in order to avoid any misinterpretation of this self-report feeling statement. Instead of viewing the client's problem as "depression," we would try to specify some problem thoughts, feelings, actions, situations, and persons that are associated with the client's depression. We would find out whether the client experiences certain physiological changes during depression, what the client is thinking about while depressed, and what activities and behaviors occur during the depressed periods.

In other words, the therapist, in conjunction with the client, identifies a series of referents that are indicative of the state of being depressed, anxious, withdrawn, lonely, and so on. The advantage of viewing the problem this way is that vague phenomena are translated into specific and observable experiences. When this occurs, we not only have a better idea of what is happening with the client, we also have made the problem potentially measurable, allowing us to assess therapy progress and outcome (see also Chapter 10).

Most Problems Occur in a Social Context and Are Functionally Related to Internal and External Antecedents and Consequences

Problems do not usually occur in a vacuum but are related to observable events (verbal, nonverbal, and motoric responses) and to less visible covert or indirect events (thoughts, images, moods and feelings, body sensations) that precipitate and maintain the problem. These internal and external events are called "antecedents" or "consequences." They are functionally related to the problem in that they exert control over it, so that a change in one of these variables often brings about a change in related variables. For example, a child's inability to behave assertively with his teacher may be a function of learned fears, lack of social skills, and the fact that he has moved, is in a new school, and also has his first male teacher. Changing one part of this overall problem—for example, helping him reduce and manage his fears—will exert an effect on all other variables in the situation.

As we discuss in Chapter 9, on goals, the therapist must be alert not only to the way different parts of the problem are related but also to the impact that change in one variable may have on the others. Occasionally a symptom may perform a very useful function for the client, and removing it could make things worse. For example, in the above illustration, add to the case the fact that the child had on one occasion been sexually abused by a male house intruder. The symptom of fear may be serving the function of protection in his relationships with unknown males. Removal of the fear without consideration of the other parts of the problem could make the presenting problem worse or could bring about the onset of other issues. We describe the functional relationship between behavior and antecedents and consequences in greater detail in the next section.

☐ THE ABC MODEL OF BEHAVIOR

One way to identify the relationship between problem behavior and environmental events is by the ABC model (Goldiamond, 1965; Goodwin, 1969; Kanfer & Saslow, 1969; Mahoney & Thoresen, 1974; Thoresen & Mahoney, 1974). The ABC model of behavior suggests that the behavior (B) is influenced by events that precede it, called "antecedents" (A), and by some types of events that follow behavior, called "consequences" (C). An antecedent (A) event is a cue or signal that can tell a person how to behave in a situation. A consequence (C) is defined as an event that strengthens or weakens a behavior. Note that these definitions of antecedents and consequences suggest that an individual's behavior is directly related to or influenced by certain events. For example, a behavior that appears to be caused by antecedent events such as anger may also be maintained or strengthened by consequences such as reactions from other people. Assessment interviews focus on identifying the particular antecedent and consequent events that influence or are functionally related to the client's defined problem behavior.

As a very simple example of the ABC model, consider a behavior (B) that most of us engage in frequently—talking. Our talking behavior is usually occasioned by certain cues, such as starting a conversation with another person, being asked a question, or the presence of a friend. Antecedents that might decrease the likelihood that we will talk may include worry about getting approval for what we say or how we answer the question or being in a hurry to get somewhere. Our talking behavior may be maintained by the verbal and nonverbal attention we receive from another person, which is a very powerful consequence, or reinforcer. Other positive consequences that might maintain our talking behavior may be feeling good or happy and engaging in positive self-statements or evaluations about the usefulness or relevance of what we are saying. We may talk less when the person's eye contact wanders or when he or she tells us more explicitly that we've talked enough. These are negative consequences (C) that decrease our talking behavior. Other negative consequences that may decrease our talking behavior could include bodily sensations of fatigue or vocal hoarseness that occur after talking for a while or thoughts and images that what we are saying is of little value to attract the interest of others. As you will see in the next three sections, not only do the components of problem behavior often vary among clients, but what functions as an antecedent or consequence for one person is often very different for someone else.

Behavior

Behavior includes things a client does as well as things a client thinks about. *Overt* behavior is behavior that is visible or could be detected by an observer, such as verbal behavior (talking), nonverbal behavior (for example, gesturing or smiling), or motoric behavior (engaging in some action such as betting, walking, or drinking). *Covert* behavior includes events that are usually internal — inside the client — and are not so readily visible to an observer, who must rely on client self-report and nonverbal behavior to detect such events. Examples of covert behavior include thoughts, beliefs, images, feelings, moods, and body sensations.

As we indicated earlier, problem behavior that clients report rarely occurs in isolated fashion. Most reported problems typically are part of a larger chain or set of behaviors. Moreover, each problem behavior mentioned usually has more than one component. For example, a client who complains of "anxiety" or "depression" is most likely using the label to refer to an experience consisting of an *affective* component (feelings, mood states), a *somatic* component (physiological and body-related sensation), a *behavioral* component (what the client does or doesn't do), and a *cognitive* component (thoughts, beliefs, images, or internal dialogue). Additionally, the experience of anxiety or depression may vary for the client, depending on *contextual* factors (time, place, concurrent events) and on *relational* factors such as presence or absence of other people. All these components may or may not be related to a particular reported problem. For example, suppose that our client who reports "anxiety" is afraid to venture out in public places except for home and work because of heightened anxiety and/or "panic attacks." Her reported concern of anxiety seems to be part of a chain that starts with a cognitive component in which she thinks worried thoughts and produces images in which she sees herself alone and unable to cope or to get the assistance of others if necessary. The cognitive component leads to somatic discomfort and tension and to feelings of apprehension and dread. These three components work together to influence her overt behavior — for the last few years, she has successfully avoided almost all public places and functions like the grocery store, theater, or church, and she functions well only at home or at work. She consequently depends on the support of family and friends to help her function adequately in the home and at work and particularly on the few occasions when she attends public functions or uses public transportation.

It is important to determine the relative importance of each component of the reported problem behavior in order to select appropriate intervention strategies (see also Chapter 11). In Chapter 8 we describe ways to obtain descriptions of these various components of problem behavior with an interview assessment method. It is often valuable to list, in writing, the various components identified for any given problem behavior.

Antecedents

According to Mischel (1968), behavior is situationally determined. This means that given behaviors tend to occur only in certain situations. For example, most of us brush our teeth in a public or private bathroom rather than during a concert or a church service. Antecedents may elicit emotional and physiological reactions such as anger, fear, joy, headaches, or elevated blood pressure. Antecedents influence behavior by either increasing or decreasing its likelihood of occurrence. For example, a child in a first-grade class may behave differently at school than at home or differently with a substitute than with the regular teacher.

Antecedent events that occur immediately before a problem behavior exert influence on it. Events that are not in temporal proximity to the problem behavior can similarly increase or decrease the probability that the behavior will occur. Antecedents that occur in immediate temporal proximity to the problem behavior are technically called *stimulus events* (Bijou & Baer, 1961) and include any external or internal event or condition that either cues the behavior or makes it more or less likely to occur under that condition. Antecedents that are temporally distant from the problem are called *setting events* (Kantor, 1970) and include behavioral circumstances that the person has recently or previously passed through. Setting events may end well before the problem and yet, like stimulus events, still facilitate or inhibit its occurrence. Examples of setting events to consider in assessing client problems are age, developmental stage, physiological state of the client, characteristics of the client's work, home, or school setting, and behaviors that emerge to affect subsequent behaviors (Wahler & Fox, 1981). Both stimulus and setting antecedent conditions must be identified and defined individually for each client.

Antecedents also usually involve more than one source or type of event. Sources of antecedents may be *affective* (feelings, mood states), *somatic* (physiological and body-related sensations), *behavioral* (verbal, nonverbal, and motoric responses), *cognitive* (thoughts, beliefs, images, internal dialogue), *contextual* (time, place, concurrent events), and *relational* (presence or absence of other people). For example, with our client who reported "anxiety," there may be a variety of antecedent sources that cue or occasion each aspect of the problem behavior, such as fear of losing control (cognitive/affective), negative self-statements and misperceptions of self and others (cognitive), awareness of apprehension-related body sensations, fatigue, and hypoglycemic tendencies (somatic), staying up late and skipping meals (behavioral), presence of public places or need to attend public functions (contextual), and absence of significant others such as friends and family (relational).

There are also a variety of antecedent sources that make components of the client's anxiety problem less likely to occur. These include feeling relaxed (affective), being rested (somatic), eating regularly (behavioral), decreasing the client's dependent behavior on her husband (behavioral), decreased fear of separation from spouse (affective), positive appraisal of self and others (cognitive), expectation of being able to handle situations (cognitive), absence of need to go to public places or functions (contextual), and being accompanied to a public place by a significant other (relational).

The influence that antecedents have on our behavior may vary with each of us, depending on our learning history. It is also important to keep in mind that antecedents are overt or covert events that in some way influence the problem behavior either by cuing it or by increasing or decreasing the likelihood that it will occur under certain conditions. In other words, not everything that precedes a behavior is automatically considered an antecedent—only those things that influence a behavioral response in some manner. Problem behavior may, however, also be affected by other situational factors (props) that are usually present in the problem situation but do not directly influ-

ence the behavior. This is especially true if any of these situational factors changes dramatically (Goldiamond & Dyrud, 1967). For instance, a child's behavior in school may be at least temporarily affected if the child's only sibling is hospitalized for injuries received in an automobile accident or if the child's father, who has been a household spouse for ten years, starts to work full-time outside the home.

During the assessment phase of counseling, it is important to identify those antecedent sources that facilitate desirable behaviors and those that are related to inappropriate responses. The reason is that, during the intervention (treatment) phase, it is important to select strategies that not only facilitate the occurrence of desirable behavior but also decrease the presence of cues for unwanted behavior. In Chapter 8 we describe and model ways to elicit information about antecedent sources and their effects on problem behavior with an interview assessment approach.

Consequences

The consequences of a behavior are events that follow a behavior and exert some influence on the behavior or are functionally related to the behavior. In other words, not everything that follows a behavior is automatically considered a consequence. For example, suppose you are counseling an overweight woman who tends occasionally to go on eating binges. She reports that, after a binge, she feels guilty, regards herself as even more unattractive, and tends to suffer from insomnia. Although these events are *results* of her eating-binge behavior, they are not consequences unless in some way they directly influence her binges, either by maintaining or by decreasing them. In this case, other events that follow the eating binges may be the real consequences. For instance, perhaps the client's binges are maintained by the enjoyment she gets from eating; perhaps they are temporarily decreased when someone else, such as her husband, notices her behavior and reprimands her for it or refuses to go out with her on their regular weekend splurge.

Consequences are categorized as positive or negative. Positive consequences can be referred to technically as *rewards* or *reinforcers;* negative ones can be labeled *punishers.* Like antecedents, the things that function as consequences will always vary with clients. By definition, positive consequences (rewarding events) will maintain or increase the behavior. Positive consequences often maintain or strengthen behavior by positive reinforcement, which involves the presentation of an overt or covert event following the behavior which increases the likelihood that the behavior will occur again in the future. People tend to repeat behaviors that result in pleasurable effects.

People also tend to engage in behaviors that have some "payoffs," or value, even if the behavior is very dysfunctional (such payoffs are called *secondary gains*). For example, a client may abuse alcohol and continue to do so even after she loses her job or her family because she likes the feelings she gets after drinking and because the drinking helps her to avoid responsibility. Another client may continue to verbally abuse his wife despite the strain it causes in their relationship because the abusive behavior gives him a feeling of power and control. In these two examples, the problem behavior is often hard to change, because the immediate consequences make the person feel better in some way. As a result, the problem behavior is reinforced, even if its delayed or long-term effects are unpleasant. In other words, in these examples, the client "values" the behavior that he or she is trying to eliminate. Often the secondary gain, the payoff derived from a manifest problem, is a cover for more severe problems that are not always readily presented by the client. According to Fishman and Lubetkin (1983), it is important for therapists to be alert to this fact in order to focus on the core problem that, when ameliorated, will generalize to other problem areas as well. For example, consider a client who is overweight and wants to "lose weight" as her goal for therapy. Yet assessment of this presenting problem reveals that the client's obesity allows her to avoid social interaction with others, particularly men. Successful therapy would need to be targeted not only to the manifest problem (weight and overeating) but also to the core, or underlying, problem that the weight masks — namely, avoidance of social interactions, particularly with the other sex. Otherwise, attempts to maintain weight reduction programs are likely to be unsuccessful. Similarly, the client described above who uses alcohol to avoid responsibility will need a treatment program targeted not only toward eliminating alcohol abuse but also toward changing her pattern of avoiding responsibility. As Fishman and Lubetkin note, many cognitive behavior therapists "are too wedded to the 'prima facie' problems that clients bring to therapy. We have observed from our own clinical experience

that 'under material' may often be responsible for maintaining the manifest behavior" (1983, p. 27). Clients may not always know the reasons they engage in problem behavior. Part of therapy involves making reasons or secondary gains more explicit.

Positive consequences can also maintain behavior by negative reinforcement — removal of an unpleasant event following the behavior, increasing the likelihood that the behavior will occur again. People tend to repeat behaviors that get rid of annoying or painful events or effects. They also use negative reinforcement to establish *avoidance* and *escape* behavior. Avoidance behavior is maintained when an *expected* unpleasant event is removed. For example, staying at home stops agoraphobia fears. Avoidance of public places is maintained by removal of these expected fears. Escape behavior is maintained when a negative (unpleasant) event *already occurring* is removed or terminated. For example, abusive behavior toward a child temporarily stops the child's annoying or aversive behaviors. Termination of the unpleasant child behaviors maintains the parental escape behavior.

Negative consequences weaken or eliminate the behavior. A behavior is typically decreased or weakened (at least temporarily) if it is followed by an unpleasant stimulus or event (punishment), if a positive, or reinforcing, event is removed or terminated (response cost), or if the behavior is no longer followed by reinforcing events (operant extinction). As an example, the overweight woman may maintain her eating binges because of the feelings of pleasure she receives from eating (a positive reinforcing consequence). Or her binges could be maintained because they allow her to escape from a boring work situation (negative reinforcing consequence). In contrast, her husband's reprimands or sarcasm or refusal to go out with her may, at least temporarily, reduce her binges (punishing consequence). Although using negative contingencies to modify behavior has many disadvantages, in real-life settings such as home, work, and school, punishment is widely used to influence the behavior of others. Therapists must be alert to the presence of negative consequences in a client's life and its effects on the client. Therapists must also be careful to avoid the use of any verbal or nonverbal behavior that may seem punitive to a client, because such behavior may contribute to unnecessary problems in the therapeutic relationship and subsequent client termination of (escape from) therapy.

Consequences also usually involve more than one source or type of event. Like antecedents, sources of consequences may be *affective, somatic, behavioral, cognitive, contextual,* and/or *relational.* For example, with our client who reports "anxiety," her avoidance of public places and functions is maintained because it results in a reduction of anxious feelings (affective), body tension (somatic), and worry (cognitive). Additional consequences that may help to maintain the problem may include avoidance of routine chores (behavioral) and increased attention from family and friends (relational).

It would be inaccurate to simply ask about whatever follows the problem behavior and automatically classify it as a consequence without determining its particular effect on the behavior. As Cullen (1983, p. 137) notes, "If variables are supposed to be functionally related to behavior when, in fact, they are not, then manipulation of those variables by the client or therapist will, at best, have no effect on the presenting difficulties or, at worst, create even more difficulties."

Occasionally students seem to confuse consequences as we present the concept in this chapter with the kind of consequences that are often the results of problem behavior—for example, Julie frequently procrastinates on studying and, as a consequence, receives poor grades. Although poor grades are the result of frequent procrastination, they are not a consequence in the way we are defining it unless the poor grades in some way increase, decrease, or maintain the procrastination behavior. Otherwise, poor grades are simply the result of studying too little. One way to distinguish consequences from mere effects of problem behavior is to remember a rule of thumb termed "gradient of reinforcement." This term refers to the belief that consequences that occur soon after the behavior are likely to have a stronger impact than consequences that occur after a long time has elapsed (Hull, 1952). Poor grades are so far removed in time from daily studying (or lack of it) that they are unlikely to exert much influence on the student's daily study behavior.

During the assessment phase of counseling, it is important to identify those consequences that maintain, increase, or decrease both desirable and undesirable behaviors related to the client's problem. In the intervention (treatment) phase, this information will help you to select strategies and approaches that will maintain and increase desirable behaviors and will weaken and decrease undesirable behaviors such as behavioral excesses and deficits. Information about consequences is also useful in planning treatment approaches that rely directly on the use of consequences to facilitate behavior change, such as self-reward (see also Chapter 19). In Chapter 8 we describe and model ways to elicit information about consequences and their effects on problem behavior with an interview assessment approach.

It is important to reiterate that antecedents, consequences, and components of the problem must be assessed and identified for each particular client. Two clients might complain of anxiety or "nerves," and the assessments might reveal very different components of the problem behavior and different antecedents and consequences. It is also important to keep in mind that there is often some overlap among antecedents, components of problem behavior, and consequences. For example, negative self-statements or irrational beliefs might function in some instances as both antecedents and consequences for a given component of the identified problem. Consider a college student who reports depression after situations with less than desired outcomes, such as asking a girl out and being turned down, getting a test back with a B or C on it, and interviewing for a job and not receiving a subsequent offer of employment. Irrational beliefs in the form of perfectionistic standards may function as an antecedent by cuing, or setting off, the resulting feelings of depression—for example, "Here is a solution that didn't turn out the way I wanted; it's awful; now I feel lousy." Irrational beliefs in the form of self-deprecatory thoughts may function as a consequence by maintaining the feelings of depression for some time even after the situation itself is over—for example, "When things don't turn out the way they should, I'm a failure."

☐ DIAGNOSTIC CLASSIFICATION OF CLIENT PROBLEMS

Our emphasis throughout this chapter is on the need to conduct a thorough and precise assessment with each client in order to be able to define client problems in very concrete ways. In addition, counselors need to be aware that client problems can be organized in some form of diagnostic taxonomy (classification).

The official classification system used currently is found in the American Psychiatric Association's *Diagnostic and Statistical Manual of Mental Dis-*

orders, third edition, revised *(DSM-III-R)* (1987). The reader is urged to consult the manual as well as the *DSM-III-R Casebook* (Spitzer, Gibbon, Skodol, Williams, & First, 1989). Our interest is simply to summarize the basic diagnostic codes and categories found in *DSM-III-R* so that the reader will not be caught off guard if a colleague or supervisor begins talking about "Axis I, II," and so on.

DSM-III-R consists largely of descriptions of various mental and psychological disorders broken down into 16 major diagnostic classes, with additional subcategories within these major categories. Specific diagnostic criteria are provided for each category. These criteria are supposed to provide the practitioner with a way to evaluate and classify the client's problems. The particular evaluation system used by *DSM-III-R* is called "multiaxial" because it consists of an assessment on five codes, or "axes":

Axis I, clinical syndromes and V codes
Axis II, developmental disorders and personality disorders
Axis III, physical disorders or conditions
Axis IV, severity of psychosocial stressors
Axis V, global assessment of functioning currently and during past year.

Axes I and II comprise the entire classification of mental disorders and V codes (conditions not attributable to a mental disorder that are a focus of attention or treatment). On Axis III the practitioner indicates any current physical disorder or condition of the client. Axis IV provides a 6-point rating scale for overall severity of stress ranging from 1 — no stressful event to 6 — a catastrophic event, and 0 meaning inadequate information or no change in condition. The stressor can be acute events such as death, divorce, or enduring circumstances such as being a single parent. Each scale level is anchored with examples for children, adolescents, and adults. The information on this axis is important because the person's prognosis may be better when a disorder develops as a consequence of marked stress than when it develops after minimal or no stress. This information may also be important in developing a treatment plan to reduce the severity and frequency of "stressors" in the client's life. Axis V permits the interviewer to indicate his or her judgment of the person's global assessment of functioning currently and

during the past year. The scale ranges from 90 — absent or minimal symptoms to 1 — expectations of death and 0 — inadequate information. It is also anchored with examples for children, adolescents, and adults. Global assessment of functioning is defined psychologically and as a composite of two areas: social relations and occupational functioning. Examples of this multiaxial evaluation system can be found following the analyses of the client cases in this chapter. Table 7-1 describes the 16 major diagnostic categories of *DSM-III-R* that are classified on Axis I and Axis II.

Taylor (1983) observes that, in spite of apparent conceptual and practical limitations of diagnosis, the process can aid therapists in assessing problem behaviors and in selecting appropriate interventions for treatment. For instance, knowledge about selected features of various types of clinical pathology, such as the usual age of the onset of some disorder or whether the disorder is more common in men or in women, can aid in assessment.

Nelson and Barlow (1981) note that selected features of *DSM-III-R* are useful for suggesting additional information about the problem behaviors and the controlling variables. For example, the operational criteria found in *DSM-III-R* often indicate further target behaviors associated with a particular disorder that should be assessed, and the associated features of a disorder often suggest controlling or contributing variables to be assessed. For instance, if a client describes behaviors related to depression, the therapist can use the operational criteria for major depressive episodes to ask about other target behaviors related to depression that the client may not mention. Therapists can also be guided by the associated features of this disorder to question the client about possible controlling variables typically associated with the disorder (for example, for depression, events such as life changes, loss of reinforcers, and family history of depression).

Nelson and Barlow (1981) also observe that diagnoses may be useful in suggesting treatments that have been found effective with similar problems. For example, clients with phobias typically benefit from modeling (see Chapters 13 and 14) or from fear-reduction approaches such as systematic desensitization (see Chapter 18) and may also require antianxiety medication (see also Chapter 11).

Diagnostic classification presents certain limita-

TABLE 7-1. The 16 major diagnostic classes of *DSM-III-R*

Disorders usually first evident in infancy, childhood, or adolescence—behavioral, intellectual, emotional, physical, and developmental disturbances that usually are first observed during infancy, childhood, or adolescence

Organic mental syndromes and disorders—behavioral or psychological disturbances related to temporary or permanent brain dysfunction

Psychoactive substance use disorders—disorders of abuse and/or dependence caused by taking substances such as alcohol, drugs, and tobacco that affect the central nervous system

Schizophrenia—five subtypes of schizophrenia; all emphasize the presence of one of the following: delusions, hallucinations, or certain thought disturbances

Delusional (paranoid) disorders—five types of disorders, features of which are persistent persecutory delusions and delusions of jealousy not attributable to some other psychotic disorder

Psychotic disorders not elsewhere classified—includes three other categories that do not fit into any of the other categories

Mood disorders—includes two classes of disorders in which there is a disturbance of mood accompanied by related symptoms

Anxiety disorders—includes four categories in which the predominant symptom is some form of anxiety

Somatoform disorders—disorders in which physical symptoms are involved but with no evidence of organic disease

Disassociative disorders—includes a variety of disorders in which there is a sudden and usually temporary alteration in the person's identity and/or consciousness

Sexual disorders—disorders involving some disturbance or disruption of psychosexual identity and/or function

Sleep disorders—disorders of sleep that are chronic (of more than one month's duration); includes two major subgroups: dyssomnias, with seven types, and parasomnias, with four types.

Factitious disorders—disorders in which physical or psychological symptoms are present that are produced by the client and under the client's voluntary control

Impulse control disorders not elsewhere classified—disorders that do not fit elsewhere and are characterized by failure to resist an impulse to perform an act potentially harmful to oneself and/or others

Adjustment disorders—eight disorders characterized by a maladaptive reaction to an identifiable psychosocial stressor, occurring within three months of the onset of the stressor and resulting in other impairment in social or occupational functioning or symptoms that are in excess of a normal reaction to such a stressor.

Psychological factors affecting physical condition—although physical conditions are noted on Axis III, this category is available to describe psychological factors that have some temporal proximity to the physical condition and appear to precipitate or exacerbate it

Personality disorders—includes three classes of personality disorders; all reflect features of maladaptive patterns of perception and relationships that are severe enough to create either subjectively felt distress or impairment in overall level of functioning

V codes—conditions that are included in treatment/intervention but not attributable to any of the previously described disorders can be noted here; this code often includes problems not involving a mental disorder or other problems (in addition to a specific disorder) that warrant attention

---

tions, and these are most apparent when a client is given a diagnostic classification without the benefit of a thorough and complete assessment. The most common criticisms of diagnosis are that it places labels on clients, often meaningless ones, and that the labels themselves are not well defined and do not describe what the clients do or don't do that makes them "histrionic" or "a conduct disorder" and so on. Despite the apparent disadvantages of diagnosis, many counselors and therapists find themselves in field placement and work settings in which they are required to make a diagnostic classification of the client's problems. Often even clients request this in order to receive reimbursement from their health insurance carrier for payment made for therapeutic services. We feel comfortable with the *DSM-III-R* system of classification as long as it is applied within the context of a complete assessment approach and is not used as a substitute for more idiographic assessment of the specified problem events and behaviors. This latter kind of assessment is illustrated in the following example case.

An ABC Model Case

To assist you in conceptualizing client problems from an ABC model, we provide a case illustration followed by two practice cases for you to complete. The conceptual understanding you should acquire from this chapter will help you actually define client problems and contributing variables with an interview assessment, described in Chapter 8. The following hypothetical case will assist you in identifying the overt and covert ABCs of a client problem. Extensions of this case will be used as illustrations in remaining chapters of the book.

The Case of Joan

Joan is a 15-year-old student completing her sophomore year of high school and presently taking a college preparatory curriculum. Her initial statement in the first counseling session is that she is "unhappy" and feels "dissatisfied" with this school experience but feels unable to do anything about it. On further clarification, Joan reveals that she is unhappy because she doesn't think she is measuring up to her classmates and that she dislikes being with these "top" kids in some of her classes, which are very competitive. She reports particular concern in one math class, which she says is composed largely of "guys" who are much smarter than she is. She states that she thinks about the fact that "girls are so dumb in math" rather frequently during the class. She reports that as soon as she is in this class, she gets anxious and "withdraws." She states that she sometimes gets anxious just thinking about the class, and when this happens, she gets "butterflies" in her stomach, her palms get sweaty and cold, and her heart beats faster. When asked what she means by "withdrawing," she says she sits by herself, doesn't talk to her classmates, and doesn't volunteer answers or go to the board. Often, when called on, she says nothing. As a result, she reports, her grades are dropping. She also states that her math teacher has spoken to her several times about her behavior and has tried to help her do better. However, Joan's nervousness in the class has resulted in her cutting the class whenever she can find any reason, and she has almost used up her number of excused absences

from school. She states that her fear of competitive academic situations has been a problem since junior high, when her parents started to compare her with other students and put "pressure" on her to do well in school so she could go to college. When asked how they "pressure" her, she says they constantly talk to her about getting good grades, and whenever she doesn't, they lash out at her and withdraw privileges, like her allowance. She reports that, during this year, since the classes are tougher and more competitive, school is more of a problem to her and she feels increasingly anxious in certain classes, especially math. Joan also states that sometimes she thinks she is almost failing on purpose to get back at her parents for their pressure. Joan reports that all this has made her dissatisfied with school and she has questioned whether she wants to stay in a college prep curriculum. She states that she has considered switching to a work-study curriculum so she can learn some skills and get a job after high school. However, she says she is a very indecisive person and does not know what she should do. In addition, she is afraid to decide this because if she changed curriculums, her parents' response would be very negative. Joan states that she cannot recall ever having made a decision without her parents' assistance. She feels they have often made decisions for her. She says her parents have never encouraged her to make decisions on her own, because they say she might not make the right decision without their help. Joan is an only child. She indicates that she is constantly afraid of making a bad or wrong choice.

Analysis of Case

Problem situations. First of all, there are two related but distinct problem situations for Joan. Her "presenting" problem is that she feels anxious in certain competitive classes in school. She identifies math class as the primary problem class. Second, she is having difficulty making a decision about the type of curriculum she should pursue. More generally, another problem is that she considers herself indecisive in most situations. The analysis of this case will explore Joan's problem behaviors and the antecedents and consequences for each of these two problem areas.

Analysis of School Problem

1. *Problem Behaviors*
   Joan's problem behaviors at school include

a. Self-defeating labeling of her math class as "competitive" and of herself as "not as smart as the guys."

b. Sitting alone, not volunteering answers in math class, not answering the teacher's questions or going to the board, and cutting class.

Her self-defeating labels are a covert behavior; her sitting alone, not volunteering answers, and cutting class are overt behaviors.

2. *Antecedent Conditions*

Joan's problem behaviors at school are elicited by anxiety about certain "competitive" classes, particularly math. Previous antecedent conditions would include verbal comparisons about Joan and her peers made by her parents and verbal pressure for good grades and withholding of privileges for bad grades by her parents. Note that these antecedent conditions do not occur at the same time. The antecedent of the anxiety in the "competitive" class occurs in close proximity to Joan's problem behaviors and is a "stimulus event." However, the verbal comparisons and parental pressure began several years ago and probably function as a "setting event."

3. *Consequences*

Joan's problem behaviors at school are maintained by

a. An increased level of attention to her problems by her math teacher.

b. Feeling relieved of anxiety through avoidance of the situation that elicits anxiety. By not participating in class and by cutting class, she can avoid putting herself in an anxiety-provoking situation.

c. Her poorer grades, possibly because of two "payoffs," or secondary gains. (1) If her grades get too low, she may not qualify to continue in the college prep curriculum. This would be the "ultimate" way to avoid putting herself in competitive academic situations that elicit anxiety. (2) The lowered grades could also be maintaining her problem behaviors because she labels the poor grades as a way to "get back at" her parents for their pressure.

Analysis of Decision-Making Problem

1. *Problem Behaviors*

Joan's problem behavior can be described as not making a decision for herself—in this case, about a curriculum change. Depending on the client, problems in making decisions can be either a covert or an overt problem. In people who have the skills to make a decision but are blocking themselves because of their "labels" or "internal dialogue" about the decision, the problem behavior would be designated as covert. In Joan's case, her indecisive behavior seems based on her past learning history of having many decisions either made for her or made with parental assistance. The lack of opportunities she has had to make choices suggests she has not acquired the skills involved in decision making. This would be classified as an overt problem.

2. *Antecedent Conditions*

Joan's previous decision-making history is the primary antecedent condition. This consists of (1) having decisions made for her and (2) a lack of opportunities to acquire and use the skills of decision making.

3. *Consequences*

The consequences that seem to be maintaining her problem behavior of not deciding include:

a. Getting help with her decisions, thereby avoiding the responsibility of making a choice.

b. Anticipation of parental negative reactions (punishment) to her decisions through her "self-talk."

c. Absence of positive consequences or lack of encouragement for any efforts at decision making in the past.

d. In the specific decision of a curriculum change, her low grades, which, if they get too bad, may help her avoid making a curriculum decision by automatically disqualifying her from the college prep curriculum.

DSM-III-R Diagnosis

Axis I: V62.89, phase-of-life problem

Axis II: none.

Axis III: none.

Axis IV: 3, *moderate* severity of psychosocial stressors (school, parents).

Axis V: current GAF 70, anxiety about competition. Past year GAF 75, poor grades, skipping school, parental negative reactions.

LEARNING ACTIVITY #23: ABCs OF PROBLEM ASSESSMENT

To help you in conceptualizing a client's problem from the ABC model, the following two cases are provided. We suggest that you work through the first case completely before going on to the second one. After reading each case, by yourself or with a partner, respond to the questions following the case. Then check your responses with the feedback.

The Case of Ms. Weare and Freddie

Ms. Weare and her 10-year-old son, Freddie, have come to counseling at the referral of Family Services. Their initial complaint is that they don't get along with each other. Ms. Weare complains that Freddie doesn't dress by himself in the morning and this makes her mad. Freddie complains that his mother yells and screams at him frequently. Ms. Weare agrees she does, especially when it is time for Freddie to leave for school and he isn't dressed yet. Freddie agrees that he doesn't dress himself and points out that he does this just to "get mom mad." Ms. Weare says this has been going on as long as she can remember. She states that Freddie gets up and usually comes down to breakfast not dressed. After breakfast, Ms. Weare always reminds him to dress and threatens him that she'll yell or hit him if he doesn't. Freddie usually goes back to his room, where, he reports, he just sits around until his mother comes up. Ms. Weare waits until five minutes before the bus comes and then calls Freddie. After he doesn't come down, she goes upstairs and sees that he's not dressed. She reports that she gets very mad and yells "You're dumb. Why do you just sit there? Why can't you dress yourself? You're going to be late for school. Your teacher will blame me, since I'm your mother." She also helps Freddie dress. So far, he has not been late, but Ms. Weare says she "knows" he will be if she doesn't "nag" him and help him dress. On further questioning, Ms. Weare says this does not occur on weekends, only on school days. She states that, as a result of this situation, she feels very nervous and edgy after Freddie leaves for school, often not doing some necessary work because of this. Asked what she means by "nervous" and "edgy," she reports that her body feels tense and jittery all over. She reports that since Freddie's father is not living at home, all the child rearing is on her shoulders. Ms. Weare also states that she doesn't spend much time with Freddie at night after school.

DSM-III-R Diagnosis for Ms. Weare

Axis I: V61.20, parent/child problem.

Axis II: none.

Axis III: none.

Axis IV: 3, *moderate* severity of psychosocial stressors (age of child, single-parent status of mother).

Axis V: current GAF 70, anxiety dealing with child. Past year GAF 75, single parent status, improved functioning at work and with son.

Respond to these questions. Feedback follows the Learning Activity.

1. What problem behavior(s) does Freddie demonstrate in this situation?
2. Is each problem behavior you have listed overt or covert?
3. What problem behavior(s) does Ms. Weare exhibit in this situation?
4. Is each problem behavior you have listed overt or covert?
5. List one or more antecedent conditions that seem to bring about each of Freddie's problem behavior(s).
6. List one or more antecedent conditions that seem to bring about each of Ms. Weare's problem behavior(s).
7. List one or more consequences (including any secondary gains) that influence each of Freddie's problem behavior(s). After each consequence listed, identify how the consequence seems to influence his behavior.
8. List one or more consequences that seem to influence each of Ms. Weare's behaviors. After each consequence listed, identify how the consequence seems to influence her behavior.

The Case of Mrs. Turner

Mrs. Turner is a 34-year-old mother of two sons: Jason, age 5, and Andrew, age 2. She was brought to the emergency room by the police after her bizarre behavior in a local supermarket. According to the police report, Mrs. Turner became very aggressive toward another shopper, accusing the man of "following me around and spying on me." When confronted by employees of the store about her charges, she stated "God speaks to me. I can hear His voice guiding me in my mission." On mental-status exami-
(continued)

nation, the counselor initially notes Mrs. Turner's unkempt appearance. She appears unclean. Her clothing is somewhat disheveled. She seems underweight and looks older than her stated age. Her tense posture seems indicative of her anxious state, and she smiles inappropriately throughout the interview. Her speech is loud and fast, and she constantly glances suspiciously around the room. Her affect is labile, fluctuating from anger to euphoria. On occasion, she looks at the ceiling and spontaneously starts talking. When the counselor asks to whom she was speaking, she replies, "Can't you hear Him? He's come to save me!" Mrs. Turner is alert and appears to be of average general intelligence. Her attention span is short. She reports no suicidal ideation and denies any past attempts. She does, however, express some homicidal feelings for those who "continue to secretly follow me around." When the family members arrive, the counselor is able to ascertain that Mrs. Turner has been in psychiatric treatment on and off for the last ten years. She has been hospitalized several times in the past ten years during similar episodes of unusual behavior. In addition, she has been treated with several antipsychotic medicines for her problem. There is no evidence of organic pathology or any indication of alcohol or drug abuse. Her husband indicates that she recently stopped taking her medicine after the death of her sister and up until then had been functioning adequately during the past year with not much impairment.

DSM-III-R Diagnosis

> Axis I: 295.3x, paranoid schizophrenia, chronic with acute exacerbation.
> Axis II: none.
> Axis III: none.
> Axis IV: 5, *extreme* severity of psychosocial stressors (death of sister).
> Axis V: current GAF 30, God speaks to her, men spying on her. Past year GAF 65, adequate functioning.

Respond to these questions. Feedback follows.

1. List several of the problem behaviors that Mrs. Turner demonstrates.
2. Is each problem behavior you have listed overt or covert?
3. List one or more antecedents that seem to elicit Mrs. Turner's problem behaviors.
4. List one or more consequences that appear to influence the problem behavior(s), including any secondary gains. Describe how each consequence seems to influence the behavior.

□ SUMMARY

Assessment is the basis for development of the entire counseling program. Assessment has important informational, educational, and motivational functions in therapy. Although the major part of assessment occurs early in the counseling process, to some extent assessment, or identification of client concerns, goes on constantly during therapy.

An important part of assessment is the counselor's ability to conceptualize client problems. In this chapter we described the models of case or problem conceptualizations proposed by Swensen (1968), Seay (1978), and Lazarus (1976, 1981). Conceptualization models help the counselor think clearly about the complexity of client problems.

The ABC model of assessment described in this chapter is based on several assumptions, including these:

1. Most problem behavior is learned, although this does not rule out organic (biological) causes of psychological problems.
2. Causes of problems are multidimensional.
3. Problems need to be viewed operationally, or concretely.
4. Problems occur in a social context and are affected by internal and external antecedents that are functionally related to or exert influence on the problem in various ways.
5. Components of the problem as well as sources of antecedents and consequences can be affective, somatic, behavioral, cognitive, contextual, and relational.

In addition to the need to identify components of the problem behavior and sources of antecedents and consequences, another part of assessment may involve a multiaxial diagnosis of the client. Current diagnosis is based on the *Diagnostic and Statistical Manual,* third edition, revised, and involves classifying the problems and assessing the severity of psychosocial stressors and the client's highest level of adaptive functioning during the past year. Diagnosis can be a useful part of assessment. For example, knowledge about selected features of various types of clinical syndromes can add to understanding of the client's concern. Diagnosis, however, is not an adequate *substitute* for other assessment approaches and is not an effective basis for specifying goals and selecting intervention strategies unless it is part of a comprehensive treatment approach in which components of the problem are identified in a concrete, or operational, manner.

FEEDBACK #23: ABCs OF PROBLEM ASSESSMENT

The Case of Ms. Weare and Freddie

1. Freddie's problem behavior is sitting in his room and not dressing for school.
2. This is an overt behavior, since it is visible to someone else.
3. Ms. Weare's problem behaviors are (a) feeling mad and (b) yelling at Freddie.
4. (a) Feeling mad is a covert behavior, since feelings can only be inferred. (b) Yelling is an overt behavior that is visible to someone else.
5. Receiving a verbal reminder and threat from his mother at breakfast elicits Freddie's behavior.
6. Ms. Weare's behavior seems to be cued by a five-minute period before the bus arrives on school days.
7. Two consequences seem to influence Freddie's problem behavior of not dressing for school. (a) He gets help in dressing himself; this influences his behavior by providing special benefits. (b) He gets some satisfaction from seeing that his mother is upset and is attending to him. This seems to maintain his behavior because of the attention he gets

from her in these instances. A possible secondary gain is the control he exerts over his mother at these times. According to the case description, he doesn't seem to get much attention at other times from his mother.

8. The major consequence that influences Ms. Weare's behavior is that she gets Freddie ready on time and he is not late. This appears to influence her behavior by helping her avoid being considered a poor mother by herself or someone else.

The Case of Mrs. Turner

1. There are various problem behaviors for Mrs. Turner: (a) disheveled appearance, (b) inappropriate affect, (c) delusional beliefs, (d) auditory hallucinations, (e) homicidal ideation, (f) noncompliance with treatment (medicine).
2. Disheveled appearance, inappropriate affect, and noncompliance with treatment are overt behaviors—they are observable by others. Delusions, hallucinations, and homicidal ideation are covert behaviors as long as they are not expressed by the client and therefore not visible to someone else. However, when expressed or demonstrated by the client, they become overt behaviors as well.
3. In this case, Mrs. Turner's problem behaviors appear to be elicited by the cessation of her medicine, which is the major antecedent. Apparently, when she stops taking her medication, an acute psychotic episode results.
4. This periodic discontinuation of her medicine and subsequent psychotic reaction may be influenced by the attention she receives from the mental health profession, her family, and even strangers when she behaves in a psychotic, helpless fashion. Additional possible secondary gains include avoidance of responsiblity and of being in control.

POSTEVALUATION

Read the case descriptions of Mr. Brown and of John that follow and then answer the following questions:

1. What are the client's problem behaviors?
2. Are the problem behaviors overt or covert?
3. What are the antecedent conditions of the client's concern?
4. What are the consequences of the problem behaviors? Secondary gains?

5. In what way do the consequences influence the problem behaviors?

Answers to these questions are provided in the Feedback section that follows the Postevaluation.

The Case of Mr. Brown

A 69-year-old man, Mr. Brown, came to counseling because he felt his performance on his job was "slip-
(continued)

ping." Mr. Brown had a job in a large automobile company. He was responsible for producing new car designs. Mr. Brown revealed that he noticed he had started having trouble about six months before, when the personnel director came in to ask him to fill out retirement papers. Mr. Brown, at the time he sought counseling, was due to retire in nine months. (The company's policy made it mandatory to retire at age 70.) Until this incident with the personnel director and the completion of the papers, Mr. Brown reported, everything seemed to be "OK." He also reported that nothing seemed to be changed in his relationship with his family. However, on some days at work, he reported having a great deal of trouble completing any work on his car designs. When asked what he did instead of working on designs, he said "Worrying." The "worrying" turned out to mean that he was engaging in constant repetitive thoughts about his approaching retirement, such as "I won't be here when this car comes out" and "What will I be without having this job?" Mr. Brown stated that there were times when he spent almost an entire morning or afternoon "dwelling" on these things and that this seemed to occur mostly when he was alone in his office actually working on a car design. As a result, he was not turning in his designs by the specified deadlines. Not meeting his deadlines made him feel more worried. He was especially concerned that he would "blow" his previously established reputation in the eyes of his colleagues and superiors, who, he felt, always could have counted on him "to get the job done." He was afraid that his present behavior would jeopardize the opinion others had of him, although he didn't report any other possible "costs" to him. In fact, Mr. Brown said that it was his immediate boss who had suggested, after several talks and after-work drinks, that he see a counselor. The boss also indicated the company would pay for Mr. Brown's counseling. Mr. Brown said that his boss had not had any noticeable reactions to his missing deadlines, other than reminding him and being solicitous, as evidenced in the talks and after-work drinks. Mr. Brown reported that he enjoyed this interaction with his boss and often wished he could ask his boss to go out to lunch with him. However, he stated that these meetings had all been at his boss's request. Mr. Brown felt somewhat hesitant about making the request himself. In the last six months, Mr. Brown had never received any sort of reprimand for missing deadlines on his drawings. Still, he was concerned with maintaining his own sense of pride about his work, which he felt might be jeopardized since he's been having this trouble.

DSM-III-R Diagnosis

> Axis I: 309.23, adjustment disorder with work inhibition.
> Axis II: none.
> Axis III: none.
> Axis IV: 3, *moderate* psychosocial stressors (impending retirement).
> Axis V: current GAF 65, repetitive thoughts, worrying. Past year GAF 90, affected some social interations with boss, family interactions were good.

The Case of John

This is a complicated case with three presenting problems: (1) work, (2) sexual, and (3) alcohol. We suggest that you complete the analysis of ABCs (Questions 1–5 listed at the beginning of this postevaluation) *separately* for each of these three problems.

John, a 30-year-old business manager, has been employed by the same large corporation for two years, since his completion of graduate school. During the first counseling session, he reports a chronic feeling of "depression" with his present job. In addition, he mentions a recent loss of interest and pleasure in sexual activity, which he describes as "frustrating." He also relates a dramatic increase in his use of alcohol as a remedy for the current difficulties he is experiencing.

John has never before been in counseling and admits to feeling "slightly anxious" about this new endeavor. He appears to be having trouble concentrating when asked a question. He traces the beginning of his problems to the completion of his master's degree a little over two years ago. At that time, he states, "everything was fine." He was working part-time during the day for a local firm and attending college during the evenings. He had been dating the same woman for a year and a half and reports a great deal of satisfaction in their relationship. Drinking occurred infrequently, usually only during social occasions or a quiet evening alone. On completion of his degree, John relates, "things changed. I guess maybe I expected too much too soon." He quit his job in the expectation of finding employment with a larger company. At first there were few offers, and he was beginning to wonder whether he had made a mistake. After several interviews, he was finally offered a job with a business firm that specialized in computer technology, an area in which John was intensely

(continued)

POSTEVALUATION (continued)

interested. He accepted and was immediately placed in a managerial position. Initially, John was comfortable and felt confident in his new occupation; however, as the weeks and months passed, the competitive nature of the job began to wear him down. He relates that he began to doubt his abilities as a supervisor and began to tell himself that he wasn't as good as the other executives. He began to notice that he was given fewer responsibilities than the other bosses, as well as fewer employees to oversee. He slowly withdrew socially from his colleagues, refusing all social invitations. He states that he began staying awake at night obsessing about what he might be doing wrong. Of course, this lack of sleep decreased his energy level even further and produced a chronic tiredness and lessening of effectiveness and productivity at work. At the same time, his relationship with his girlfriend began to deteriorate slowly. He relates that "she didn't understand what I was going through." Her insistence that his sexual performance was not satisfying her made him even more apprehensive and lowered his self-esteem even further. After a time, his inhibition of sexual desire resulted in inconsistency in maintaining an erection throughout the sexual act. This resulted in an even greater strain on their relationship, so that she threatened to "call it quits" if he did not seek treatment for his problem. He reports that it was at this time that he began to drink more heavily. At first it was just a few beers at home alone after a day at the office. Gradually, he began to

drink during lunch, even though, he states, "I could have stopped if I had wanted to." However, his repeated efforts to reduce his excessive drinking by "going on the wagon" met with little success. He began to need a drink every day in order to function adequately. He was losing days at work, was becoming more argumentative with his friends, and had been involved in several minor traffic accidents. He states, "I think I'm becoming an alcoholic." John points out that he has never felt this low before in his life. He reports feeling very pessimistic about his future and doesn't see any way out of his current difficulties. He's fearful that he might make the wrong decisions, and that's why he's come to see a counselor at this time in his life.

DSM-III-R Diagnosis

Axis I: 300.40, dysthymic disorder (depressive neurosis).

305.00, alcohol abuse, continuous.

302.72, male erectile disorder.

Axis II: none.

Axis III: none.

Axis IV: 4, *severe* psychosocial stressors (new type of job position; deterioration in relationship with girlfriend).

Axis V: current GAF 65, slightly anxious, new job. Past year GAF 70, difficulty in social and occupational functioning.

□ SUGGESTED READINGS

American Psychiatric Association. (1987). *Diagnostic and statistical manual of mental disorders* (3rd ed. revised). Washington, DC: Author.

Barlow, D. H. (Ed.). (1981). *Behavioral assessment of adult disorders.* New York: Guilford Press.

Barlow, D. H., Hayes, S. C., & Nelson, R. O. (1984). *The scientist practitioner.* New York: Pergamon Press.

Bellack, A. S., & Hersen, M. (Eds.). (1988). *Behavioral assessment: A practical handbook* (3rd ed.). New York: Pergamon Press.

Celotta, B., & Telasi-Golubscow, H. (1982). A problem taxonomy for classifying clients' problems. *Personnel and Guidance Journal, 61,* 73–76.

Fishman, S. T., & Lubetkin, B. S. (1983). Office practice of behavior therapy. In M. Hersen (Ed.), *Outpatient behav-*

ior therapy: A clinical guide. New York: Grune & Stratton.

Hutchins, D. E. (1979). Systematic counseling: The T-F-A model for counselor intervention. *Personnel and Guidance Journal, 57,* 529–531.

Kendall, P. C., & Hollon, S. D. (Eds.). (1981). *Assessment strategies for cognitive-behavioral interventions.* New York: Academic Press.

L'Abate, L. (1981). Toward a systematic classification of counseling and therapy theorists, methods, processes, and goals: The E-R-A model. *Personnel and Guidance Journal, 59,* 263–266.

Lazarus, A. A. (1981). *The practice of multimodal therapy.* New York: McGraw-Hill.

Meyer, V., & Turkat, I. (1979). Behavioral analysis of clinical cases. *Journal of Behavioral Assessment, 1,* 259–270.

Nelson, R. O. (1983). Behavioral assessment: Past, present, and future. *Behavioral Assessment, 5,* 195–206.

Owens, R. G., & Ashcroft, J. B. (1982). Functional analysis in applied psychology. *British Journal of Clinical Psychology, 21,* 181–189.

Seay, T. A. (1978). *Systematic electic therapy.* Jonesboro, TN: Pilgrimage Press.

Slade, P. (1982). Towards a functional analysis of anorexia nervosa and bulimia nervosa. *British Journal of Clinical Psychology, 21,* 167–179.

Spitzer, R. L., Gibbon, M., Skodol, A. E., Williams, J. B., & First, M. B. (1989). *DSM-III-R Casebook.* Washington, DC: American Psychiatric Association.

Swensen, C. H., Jr. (1968). *An approach to case conceptualization.* Boston: Houghton Mifflin.

Taylor, C. B. (1983). DSM-III and behavioral assessment. *Behavioral Assessment, 5,* 5–14.

Wahler, R. G., & Fox, J. J. (1981). Setting events in applied behavior analysis: Toward a conceptual and methodological expansion. *Journal of Applied Behavior Analysis, 14,* 327–338.

FEEDBACK: POSTEVALUATION

The Case of Mr. Brown

1. Mr. Brown's self-reported problem behaviors include worry about retirement and not doing work on his automobile designs.

2. Worrying about retirement is a covert behavior. Not doing work on designs is an overt behavior.

3. One antecedent condition occurred six months ago, when the personnel director conferred with Mr. Brown about retirement and papers were filled out. This is an overt antecedent in the form of a setting event. The personnel director's visit seemed to elicit Mr. Brown's worry about retirement and his not doing his designs. A covert antecedent is Mr. Brown's repetitive thoughts about retirement, getting older, and so on. This is a stimulus event.

4. The consequences include Mr. Brown's being excused from meeting his deadlines and receiving extra attention from his boss.

5. Mr. Brown's problem behaviors appear to be maintained by the consequence of being excused from not meeting his deadlines, with only a "reminder." He is receiving some extra attention and concern from his boss, whom he values highly. He may also be missing deadlines and therefore not completing required car designs as a way to avoid or postpone retirement; that is, he may expect that if his designs aren't done, he'll be asked to stay longer until they are completed.

The Case of John
Analysis of Work Problem

1. John's problem behaviors at work include (a) overemphasis on the rivalry that he assumes exists with his fellow administrators and resulting self-doubts about his competence compared with his peers and (b) missing days at work because of his feelings of depression as well as his alcohol abuse.

2. His discrediting of his skills is a covert behavior, as is much of his current dejection. Avoiding his job is an overt behavior.

3. The antecedent conditions of John's difficulties at work are his apparent misperceptions surrounding the competitiveness with his co-workers. These misperceptions constitute a stimulus event. This apprehension has led him to feel inadequate and fosters his depressive symptomatology. It should be recognized that John's occupational difficulties arose only after he obtained his present job, one that requires more responsibility than any of his previous positions. Acquisition of this job and its accompanying managerial position is a setting event.

4. The consequences that maintain John's difficulties at work are (a) failing to show up for work each day and (b) alcohol abuse.

5. Failing to show up for work each day amounts to a variable-interval schedule of reinforcement, which is quite powerful in maintaining John's evasion of the workplace. A possible secondary gain of his absenteeism is the resulting decrease in his feelings of incompetence and depression. His abuse of alcohol provides him with a ready-made excuse to miss work whenever necessary or whenever he feels too depressed to go. It should be noted that alcohol as a drug is a central nervous system depressant as well. Alcohol abuse is also a common complication of depressive episodes.

Analysis of Sexual Problem

1. John's problem behavior is an apparent loss of interest in or desire for sexual activity, which is a significant change from his previous behavior. His feelings of excitement have been inhibited so that he is unable to attain or maintain an erection throughout the sexual act.

2. The inability to achieve and/or sustain an erection is an overt problem. We may also assume that
(continued)

whatever John is telling himself is somehow influencing his observable behavior. His self-talk is a covert problem.

3. There are apparently no organic factors contributing to the disturbance. Therefore, it appears likely that the antecedent conditions of John's current sexual problem are the anxiety and depression associated with the work situation.

4. The consequences maintaining John's sexual problem appear to be (a) the lack of reassurance from his girlfriend and (b) his current alcohol abuse. The girlfriend's ultimatum that he begin to regain his normal sexual functioning is creating psychological stress that will continue to prevent adequate sexual response. Although alcohol may serve as a relaxant, it also acts to physiologically depress the usual sexual response.

Analysis of Alcohol Problem

1. Problem behavior is frequent consumption of alcoholic beverages during the day as well as at night.

2. Although alcohol abuse is certainly an overt problem behavior, we might also assume that John is engaging in some self-defeating covert behaviors to sustain his alcohol abuse.

3. It is quite apparent that John's maladaptive use of alcohol occurred only after his difficulties with his job became overwhelming. It also appears to be linked to the onset of his sexual disorder. There is no history of previous abuse of alcohol or other drugs.

4. Consequences include the payoffs of avoidance of tension, responsibility, and depression related to his job as well as possible increased attention from others.

5. By abusing alcohol, John has been missing days at work and thus avoids the tension he feels with his job. Alcohol abuse is serving as a negative reinforcer. Moreover, his use of alcohol, which is a depressant, allows him to maintain his self-pitying behavior, which, owing to the attention he derives from this, may also be maintaining the alcohol abuse. Finally, alcohol may also provide a ready-made excuse for his poor sexual functioning with his girlfriend.

DEFINING CLIENT PROBLEMS
WITH AN INTERVIEW ASSESSMENT

EIGHT

In Chapter 7 we described a number of important functions of the assessment process in therapy and noted that assessment is a way of identifying and defining a client's problems in order to make decisions about therapeutic treatment. A variety of tools or methods are available to the therapist that can help identify and define the range and parameters of client problems. These methods include standardized tests, such as interest and personality inventories; psychophysiological assessment, such as monitoring of muscle tension for chronic headaches with an electromyograph (EMG) machine; self-report checklists, such as assertiveness scales or anxiety inventories; observation by others, including observation by the therapist or by a significant person in the client's environment; self-observation, in which the client observes and records some aspect of the problem; imagery, in which the client uses fantasy and directed imagery to vicariously experience some aspect of the problem; role playing, in which the client may demonstrate some part of the problem in an *in vivo* yet simulated enactment; and direct interviewing, in which the client and counselor identify the problem through verbal and nonverbal exchanges. All these methods are also used to evaluate client progress during therapy, in addition to their use in assessment for the purpose of collecting information about client problems. Specific uses, advantages, and limitations of each of these methods as an evaluation tool are described in greater detail in Chapter 10. In this chapter we concentrate on direct interviewing, not only because it is the focus of the book but also because it is the one method readily available to all therapists without additional cost in time or money. We also, however, will mention ancillary use of some of the other methods of assessment named above. In actual practice, it is very important not to rely solely on the interview for assessment data but to use several methods of obtaining information about client problems.

☐ OBJECTIVES

1. Given a written description of a selected client problem, outline in writing at least two questions for each of the 11 problem assessment categories that you would ask during an assessment interview with this person.
2. In a 30-minute role-play interview, demonstrate leads and responses associated with 9 out of 11 categories for assessing the problem. An observer can rate you, or you can rate your performance from a tape, using the Problem Assessment Interview Checklist at the end of the chapter. After the interview, identify orally or in writing some hypotheses about antecedent sources that cue the problem, consequences that maintain it, secondary gains, or "payoffs," and client resources, skills, and assets that might be used during intervention.
3. Given a written client case description, construct in writing a self-monitoring assessment plan for the client and an example of a log to use for self-recording the data.
4. Conduct a role-play interview in which you explain at least three parts of a self-monitoring assessment plan to a client (rationale, instructions, follow-up).

☐ DIRECT ASSESSMENT INTERVIEWING

According to cognitive-behavioral literature, the interview is the most common behavioral assessment instrument (Haynes & Jensen, 1979; Nelson, 1983). "While elaborate behavioral and psychophysiological assessment procedures have been developed and evaluated, the assessment instrument most frequently employed in the clinical setting remains the behavioral interview" (Keane, Black, Collins, & Venson, 1982, p. 53). Nelson (1983) observes that the interview is the one assessment strategy used more consistently than any other procedure—perhaps because of its practicality in applied settings and its potential efficiency. Despite the overwhelming evidence confirming the popularity of the interview as an assessment tool, some persons believe it is the most difficult assessment approach for the therapist to enact. Successful assessment interviews require specific guidelines and training in order to obtain accurate and valid information from clients that will make a difference in treatment planning (Duley, Cancelli, Kratochwill, Bergan, & Meredith, 1983).

In this chapter we describe a structure and some guidelines to apply in assessment interviews in order to identify and define client problems. This chapter and other chapters in this book describe interview leads that, in applied settings, are likely to elicit certain kinds of client information. However, as Morganstern (1986) observes, little research on the effects of interview procedures has been conducted. The leads suggested in this chapter are supported more by practical considerations than by empirical data. As a result, you will need to be very attentive to the effects of using these questions with each client.

☐ INTAKE INTERVIEWS AND HISTORY

Part of assessment involves eliciting information about the client's background, especially as it may relate to *current* problems or complaints. Past, or historical, information is not sought as an end in itself or because the therapist is necessarily interested in exploring or focusing on the client's "past" during treatment. Rather, it is used as a part of the overall assessment process that helps the therapist fit the pieces of the puzzle together concerning the client's presenting problems and current life difficulties. Often a client's current problems are precipitated and maintained by events found in the client's history. For example, with one middle-aged client who felt conflicted between the demands of her job and the demands of her family, it became apparent that she carried around with her an ever-present image of the way her now-deceased mother had functioned in her own family when the client was growing up—totally nurturing, self-sacrificing, expecting her daughter to do the same, and reinforcing her for doing so. Although the client hadn't lived in her family of origin for over 25 years, this image and all the beliefs and feelings associated with it were having a very strong influence on her present complaint. The complaint was exacerbated by the client's age and stage in the life cycle: she was feeling a strong need to ascend the job ladder, to be productive, and to establish herself as an individual in her own right. At the same time, the learnings from her family of origin, particularly her mother, were holding her back and were also interfering with successful completion of an important developmental life task. In cases such as this one, history may serve as a retrospective baseline measure for the client and may help to identify cognitive or historical antecedent conditions that still exert influence on the problem behavior and might otherwise be overlooked.

The process of gathering this type of information is called "history taking." In many agency settings, history taking occurs during an initial interview called an "intake interview." An intake interview is viewed as informational rather than therapeutic and, to underscore this point, is often conducted by someone other than the therapist assigned to see the client. In these situations, someone else, such as an intake worker, sees the client for an hour interview (shorter for children and adolescents), summarizes the information in writing, and passes the information along to the therapist. In other places, the therapists conduct their own intakes. For therapists who work either in private practice or in a school or agency in which intakes are not required, it is still a good idea to do some history taking with the client.

Various kinds of information can be solicited during history taking, but the most important areas are the following:

1. Identifying information about the client
2. General appearance and demeanor
3. History related to the presenting problem(s)
4. Past psychiatric and/or counseling history
5. Educational and job history
6. Health (medical) history
7. Social/developmental history (including religious and cultural background and affiliations, predominant values, description of past problems, chronological/developmental events, military background, social/leisure activities, present social situation)
8. Family, marital, sexual history
9. Assessment of client communication patterns
10. Results of mental status; diagnostic summary

Table 8-1 presents specific questions or content areas to cover for each of these ten areas.

TABLE 8-1. History-taking interview content

I. *Identifying information*
Client's name, address, home and work telephone numbers
Age
Sex
Ethnic/cultural affiliation
Marital status
Occupation

II. *General appearance*
Approximate height
Approximate weight
Brief description of client's dress, grooming, overall demeanor

III. *Presenting problems* (do for *each* problem or complaint that client presents)
Note the presenting complaint (quote client directly):
When did it start? What other events were occurring at that time?
How often does it occur?
What are thoughts, feelings, and observable behaviors associated with it?
Where and when does it occur most? least?
Are there any events or persons that precipitate it? make it better? make it worse?
How much does it interfere with the client's daily functioning?
What previous solutions/plans have been tried for the problem and with what result?
What made the client decide to seek help at this time (or, if referred, what influenced the referring party to refer the client at this time)?

IV. *Past psychiatric/counseling history*
Previous counseling and/or psychological/psychiatric treatment:
    Type of treatment
    Length of treatment
    Treatment place or person
    Presenting complaint
    Outcome of treatment and reason for termination
    Previous hospitalization and/or prescription drugs for emotional/psychological problems

(continued)

TABLE 8-1. History-taking interview content (continued)

V. *Educational/job history*

Trace academic progress (strengths and weaknesses) from grade school through last level of education completed
Relationships with teachers and peers
Types of jobs held by client
Length of jobs
Reason for termination or change
Relationships with co-workers
Training/education received for jobs
Aspects of work that are most stressful or anxiety-producing
Aspects of work that are least stressful or most enjoyable
Overall degree of current job satisfaction

VI. *Health/medical history*

Childhood diseases, prior significant illnesses, previous surgery
Current health-related complaints or illnesses (for example, headache, hypertension)
Treatment received for current complaints: what type and by whom
Date of last physical examination and results
Significant health problems in client's family of origin (parents, grandparents, siblings)
Client's sleep patterns
Client's appetite level
Current medications (including such things as aspirin, vitamins, birth control pills, recreational drug use)
Drug and nondrug allergies
Client's typical daily diet, including caffeine-containing beverages/food; alcoholic beverages
Exercise patterns

VII. *Social/developmental history*

Current life situation (typical day/week, living arrangements, occupation and economic situation, contact
    with other people)
Social/leisure time activities, hobbies
Religious affiliation
Military background/history
Predominant values, priorities, and beliefs expressed by client
Significant chronological/developmental events noted by client:
    Earliest recollections
Significant events reported for the following developmental periods:
    Preschool (0–6 years)
    Middle childhood (6–13 years)
    Adolescence (13–21 years)
    Young adulthood (21–30 years)
    Middle adulthood (30–65 years)
    Late adulthood (65 years and over)

VIII. *Family, marital, sexual history*

Identifying data for client's mother and father
Ways in which mother rewarded and punished client
Ways in which father rewarded and punished client
Significant "parent tapes"
Activities client typically did with mother
How well client got along with mother
Activities client typically did with father
How well client got along with father
How well parents got along with each other
Identifying information for client's siblings (including those older and younger and client's birth order, or
    position in family)
Which sibling was most like client? least like client?

TABLE 8-1. History-taking interview content (continued)

Which sibling was most favored by mother? father? least favored by mother? father?
Which sibling did client get along with best? worst?
History of previous psychiatric illness/hospitalization among members of client's family of origin
Dating history
Engagement/marital history—reason for termination of relationship
Current relationship with spouse (how well they get along, problems, stresses, enjoyment, satisfaction, and so on)
Number and ages of client's children
Other people living with or visiting family frequently
Description of previous sexual experience, including first one
(note whether heterosexual, homosexual, or bisexual experiences are reported)
Present sexual activity—masturbation, intercourse, and so on; note frequency
Any present concerns or complaints about sexual attitudes or behaviors
For female clients: obtain menstrual history (onset of first period, regularity of current ones, degree of stress
and comfort before and during period)

IX. *Assessment of client's communication patterns*
(Typically completed by interviewer after the intake or initial interview)
Client's predominant representational (sensory) system
Nonverbal behavior during session:
Kinesics (eye contact, body movements, gestures)
Paralinguistics (voice level, pitch, fluency, vocal errors)
Proxemics (personal space, territoriality)

X. *Diagnostic summary* (if applicable)

Axis I. Clinical syndromes   *DSM-III-R* Code

_____

_____

_____

Axis II. Personality and specific developmental disorders

_____

_____

_____

Axis III. Physical disorders

_____

_____

_____

Avis IV. Psychological stressors (include relevant occupational, educational, legal, recreational, financial, and
social problems):
A. Ranked list:
1._____
2._____
3._____
4._____
B. Overall stressor severity:

1	2	3	4	5	6	7	0
None	Minimal	Mild	Moderate	Severe	Extreme	Catastrophic	Unspecified

Axis V. Adaptive Functioning:
A. Highest level during the past year:

1	2	3	4	5	6	7	0
Superior	Very good	Good	Fair	Poor	Very poor	Grossly impaired	Unspecified

B. Current functioning:

Work/school:	___satisfactory	___marginal	___unsatisfactory
Family:	___satisfactory	___marginal	___unsatisfactory
Other individuals and groups	___satisfactory	___marginal	___unsatisfactory

The sequence of obtaining this information in a history or intake interview is important. Generally, the interviewer begins with the least threatening topics and saves more sensitive topics (such as #6, #7, and #8) until near the end of the session, when a greater degree of rapport has been established and the client feels more at ease about revealing personal information to a total stranger.

In addition to or even in lieu of asking the client to give the history *during* the session, the therapist may give the client a written history questionnaire or form to complete as homework before another scheduled session. Two very useful forms developed for this purpose are the Life History Questionnaire (Lazarus, 1976) and the History Questionnaire (Cautela, 1976). These appear in Appendixes E and F.

☐ MENTAL-STATUS EXAMINATION

If, after conducting an initial interview, you are in doubt about the client's psychiatric status or suspicious about the possibility of an organic brain disorder, you may wish to conduct (or refer the client for) a mental-status examination. According to Kaplan and Sadock (1981), the mental-status exam is one that classifies and describes the areas and components of mental functioning involved in making diagnostic impressions and classifications. The major categories covered in a mental-status exam are general description and appearance of the client, mood and affect, perception, thought processes, level of consciousness, orientation to time, place, and people, memory, and im-

pulse control. Additionally, the examiner may note the degree to which the client appeared to report the information accurately and reliably. Of these categories, disturbances in consciousness (which involves ability to perform mental tasks, degree of effort, degree of fluency/hesitation in task performance) and orientation (whether or not clients know when, where, and who they are and who other people are) are usually indicative of organic brain impairment or disorders and require neurological assessment and follow-up as well. It is important for counselors and therapists to know enough about the functions and content of a mental-status exam in order to refer an occasional client who might benefit from this additional assessment procedure. For additional information about mental-status examinations and neurophysiological assessment, see Kaplan and Sadock (1981) and Meyer (1983). A standardized extension of the mental-status exam, called the "Present State Exam," has been developed by Wing, Cooper, and Sartorius (1974). This published version also includes reliability data and sample questions.

History taking (and mental-status exams, if applicable) usually occur near the very beginning of counseling. After obtaining this sort of preliminary information about the client as well as an idea of the range of presenting complaints, you are ready to do some direct assessment interviewing with the client in order to define the parameters of problems and concerns more specifically. We present guidelines for assessment interviews in the next section, after Learning Activity #24.

LEARNING ACTIVITY #24: INTAKE INTERVIEWS AND HISTORY

To give you a sense of the process involved in doing an intake or history interview (if you don't already do lots of these on your job!), we suggest you pair up with someone else in your class and complete intake/history interviews with each other. Conduct a 30–45 minute session with one person serving as the counselor and the other taking the client's role; then switch roles. As the counselor, you can use the format in Table 8-1 as a guide. You may wish to jot down some notes. After the session, it might be helpful to write a brief summary of the session, also using the major categories listed in Table 8-1 as a way to organize your report. As the client, in this particular activity, rather than "playing a role," it will be more helpful to be yourself so that you can respond easily and openly to the counselor's questions and also so that both of you can more readily identify the way in which your particular history has influenced the current issues in your life.

☐ ELEVEN CATEGORIES FOR ASSESSING CLIENT PROBLEMS

To help you acquire the skills associated with problem assessment interviews, we will describe 11 categories of information you need to seek from each client. Most of this information is based on the case conceptualization models presented in Chapter 7. These 11 categories are illustrated and defined in the following list and subsections. They are also summarized in the Interview Checklist at the end of the chapter.

1. Explanation of *purpose* of assessment—presenting rationale for assessment interview to the client.
2. Identification of *range* of problems—using leads to help the client identify all the relevant primary and secondary issues in order to get the "big picture."
3. *Prioritization* and *selection* of issues and problems—using leads to help the client prioritize problems and select the initial area of focus.
4. Identification of *present problem behaviors*—using leads to help the client identify the six components of problem behavior(s): affective, somatic, behavioral, cognitive, contextual, and relational.
5. Identification of *antecedents*—using leads to help the client identify sources of antecedents and their effect on the problem behavior.
6. Identification of *consequences*—using leads to help the client identify sources of consequences and their influence on the problem behavior.
7. Identification of *secondary gains*—using leads to help the client identify underlying controlling variables that serve as "payoffs" to maintain the problem behavior.
8. Identification of *previous solutions*—using leads to help the client identify previous solutions or attempts to solve the problem and their subsequent effect on the problem.
9. Identification of *client coping skills*—using leads to help client identify past and present coping or adaptive behavior and how such skills might be used in working with the present issue.
10. Identification of the *client's perceptions* of the problem—using leads to help the client de-

scribe her or his understanding of the problem.
11. Identification of *problem intensity*—using leads and/or client self-monitoring to identify impact of problem on client's life, including (a) degree of problem severity and (b) frequency or duration of problem behaviors.

The first three categories—explanation of the purpose of assessment, identification of the range of problems, and prioritization and selection of problem concerns—are a logical starting place. First, it is helpful to give the client a rationale, a reason for conducting an assessment interview, before gathering information. Next, some time must be spent in helping the client explore all the relevant issues and prioritize problems to work on in order of importance, annoyance, and so on.

The other eight categories follow problem prioritization and selection. After the counselor and client have identified and selected the problem(s) to work on, these eight categories of counselor leads are used to define and analyze parameters of the problem. The counselor will find that the order of the problem assessment leads varies among clients. A natural sequence will evolve in each interview, and the counselor will want to use the leads associated with these content categories in a pattern that fits the flow of the interview and follows the lead of the client. It is very important in assessment interviews not to impose your structure at the expense of the client. The amount of time and number of sessions required to obtain this information will vary with problems and with clients. It is possible to complete the assessment in one session, but with some clients, three or four assessment interviews may be necessary. Although the counselor may devote several interviews to assessment, the information gathering and hypothesis testing that go on do not automatically stop after these few sessions. Some degree of problem assessment continues throughout the entire therapy process (Linehan, 1977).

Explaining the Purpose of Assessment

In explaining the purpose of problem assessment, the counselor gives the client a rationale for doing an assessment interview. The intent of this first category of problem assessment is to give the client a "set," or an expectation, of what will occur during the interview and why assessment is important to both client and counselor. We also usually tell clients that we may be asking more questions during this session than we have before or will in the future so that clients are not caught off guard if our interviewing style changes. One way the counselor can communicate the purpose of the assessment interview is "Today I'd like to focus on some concerns that are bothering you most. In order to find out exactly what you're concerned about, I'll be asking you for some specific kinds of information. This information will help both of us identify what you'd like to work on in counseling. How does this sound [or appear] to you?" After presenting the rationale, the counselor looks for some confirmation or indication that the client understands the importance of assessing problems. If client confirmation or understanding is not forthcoming, the counselor may need to provide more explanation before proceeding to other areas. It is also important in initial interviews with clients to create expectations that inspire hope (Lazarus, 1981). Most clients are so focused on their pain that they are unable to see, hear, or grasp much beyond it. So you need to be in touch not only with their pain but also with their potential, their possibilities, and their future.

Identifying the Range of Problems

In this category, the counselor uses open-ended leads to help clients identify all the major issues and concerns in their life now. Often clients will initially describe only one problem, and on further inquiry and discussion, the counselor discovers a host of other problems, some of which may be more severe or stressful or have greater significance than the one the client originally described. If the counselor does not try to get the "big picture," the client may reveal additional concerns either much later in the therapy process or not at all.

These are examples of range-of-problem leads:

"What are your concerns in your life now?"
"Could you describe some of the things that seem to be bothering you?"
"What are some present stresses in your life?"
"What situations are not going well for you?"
"Is there anything else that concerns you now?"

After using range-of-problem leads, the counselor should look for the client's indication of some general areas of concern or things that are troublesome for the client or difficult to manage. An occasional client may not respond affirmatively to these leads. Krumboltz and Thoresen

(1976, p. 29) point out that sometimes a client may have a "vested interest" in not identifying a problem or may come in with a "hidden agenda" that is not readily disclosed. Other clients may be uncertain about what information to share with the counselor. In such cases, the counselor may need to use a different approach from verbal questioning to elicit problem statements. For example, Lazarus (1981, p. 55) has recommended the use of an "Inner Circle" strategy to help a client disclose problem areas.* The client is given a picture like this:

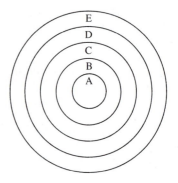

The counselor points out that topics in circle A are very personal, whereas topics in circle E are more or less public information. The counselor can provide examples of types of topics likely to be in the A circle, such as sexual concerns, feelings of hostility, marriage problems, and dishonesty. These examples may encourage the client to disclose personal concerns more readily. The counselor also emphasizes that good therapy takes place in the A and B circles and may say things like "I feel we are staying in Circle C" or "Do you think you've let me into Circle A or B yet?" (Lazarus, 1981, p. 56). Sometimes the counselor may be able to obtain more specific problem descriptions from a client by having the client role-play a typical problem situation. Another client might provide more information by describing a fantasy or visualization about the problem. This last method has been used by Meichenbaum (1976), who asks the client "to run a movie through your head" in order to recall various aspects of the problem (p. 151).

Exploring the range of problems is also a way to

* This and all other quotations from this source are from *The Practice of Multimodal Therapy* by A. A. Lazarus. Copyright © 1981 by McGraw-Hill. Reprinted by permission.

establish who is the appropriate client. A client may attribute the problem or the undesired behavior to an event or to another person. For instance, a student may say "That teacher always picks on me. I can never do anything right in her class." Since most clients seem to have trouble initially "owning" their role in their problem or tend to describe it in a way that minimizes their own contribution (Watzwalick, Beavin, & Jackson, 1967), the counselor will need to determine who is most invested in having the problem resolved and who is the real person requesting assistance. Often it is helpful to ask clients who it is that feels it is most important for the problem to be resolved— themselves or someone else. It is important for therapists not to assume that the person who arrives at their office is always the client. As Fay (1980) observes, the client is the person who wants a change and who seeks assistance for it. In the example above, if the student had desired a change and had requested assistance, the student would be the client; if it were the teacher who wanted a change and requested assistance, the teacher would be the client. (Sometimes, however, the therapist gets "stuck" in a situation in which a family or a client wants a change and the person whose behavior is to be changed is "sent" to counseling as the client. In Chapter 20 we discuss strategies for handling these "involuntary" clients.)

The question of who is the appropriate client is also tricky when the problem involves two or more persons, such as a relationship, marital, or family problem. Many family therapists view family problems as devices for maintaining the status quo of the family and recommend that either the couple or the entire family be involved in counseling, rather than one individual. Although this is a great concept in theory, in practice it is sometimes difficult to implement. Further, as Lazarus notes, "It should not be a question of *whether* to treat the individual or the family but *when* to concentrate on one or both" (1981, p. 41).

Prioritizing and Selecting Problems

Rarely do clients or the results of assessment suggest only one area or problem that needs modification or resolution. Typically, a presenting problem turns out to be one of several unresolved issues in the client's life. For example, the assessment of a client who reports depression may also reveal that the client is troubled by her relationship with her teenage daughter and her obesity. After the client describes all of her or his concerns, the counselor

and client will need to select the problems that best represent the client's purpose for seeking counseling. The primary question to be answered by these leads is "What is the specific problem situation the client chooses to start working on?"

Prioritizing problems is an important part of assessment and goal setting. If clients try to tackle too many issues simultaneously, they are likely to soon feel overwhelmed and anxious and may not experience enough success to stay in therapy. Karoly (1975) points out that the selected target for change is sometimes difficult for a client to identify. Generally, a selected problem area represents something that is "harmful" to the person's safety, "disruptive" of the person's emotions, or "damaging" to the person's effectiveness (p. 205). Selection of the problem is the client's responsibility, although the counselor may help with the client's choice. If the client selects a problem that severely conflicts with the counselor's values, a referral to another counselor may be necessary. Otherwise, the counselor may inadvertently or purposely block the discussion of certain client problem areas by listening selectively to only those problems that the counselor can or wants to work with (Kanfer & Grimm, 1977).

The following guidelines form a framework to help clients select and prioritize problems to work on:

1. Start with the presenting problem, the one that best represents the reason the client sought help. Fensterheim (1983, p. 63) observes that relief of the presenting problem often improves the client's level of functioning and may then make other, related problems more accessible to treatment. Leads to use to help determine the initial or presenting problem include "Which issue best represents the reason you are here?" and "Out of all these problems you've mentioned, identify the one that best reflects your need for assistance."

2. Start with the problem that is primary or most important to the client to resolve. Often this is the one that causes the client the most pain or discomfort or annoyance or is most interfering to the client. Modifying the more important issues seems to lead to lasting change in that area, which may then generalize to other areas (Fensterheim, 1983). Responses to determine the client's most important priority include "How much happiness or relief would you experience if this issue were resolved?," "Of these concerns, which is the most stressful or painful for you?," "Rank-order these

concerns, starting with the one that is most important for you to resolve to the one least important," and "How much sorrow or loss would you experience if you were unable to resolve this issue?"

3. Start with the problem or behavior that has the best chance of being resolved successfully and with the least effort. Some problems/behaviors are more resistant to change than others and require more time and energy to modify. Initially, it is important for the client to get reinforced for seeking help. One significant way to do this is to help the client resolve something that makes a difference without much cost to the client.

Responses to determine what problems might be resolved most successfully include "Do you believe there would be any unhappiness or discomfort if you were successful at resolving this concern?," "How likely do you think we are to succeed in resolving this issue or that one?," and "Tell me which of these problems you believe you could learn to manage most easily with the greatest success."

4. Start with the problem that needs resolution before other problems can be resolved or mastered. Sometimes the presence of one problem sets off a chain of other ones; when this problem is resolved or eliminated, the other issues either improve or at least move into a position to be explored and modified. Often this problem is one that, in the range of elicited problems, is central or prominent.

Questions to ask to help determine the most central problem include "Out of all the problems we've discussed, which is the most predominant one?" and "Out of all the problems we've discussed, describe the one that, when resolved, would have the greatest impact on the rest of the issues."

If, after this process, the counselor and client still have difficulty prioritizing problems and selecting the initial area of focus, try the procedure recommended by Goldfried (1976a). The client asks the following question about each identified problem: "What are the consequences of my *not* doing anything therapeutically to handle this particular problem?" As Goldfried notes, "Depending on the severity of the consequences associated with ignoring—at least temporarily—each of the different presenting problems, one can obtain a clearer picture as to what is most important" (p. 319).

Understanding the Problem Behaviors

After selecting the initial area of focus, it is important to determine the components of the problem behavior. For example, if the identified problem is "not getting along very well with people at work," with an expected outcome of "improving my relationships with people at work," we would want to identify the client's *feelings* (affect), *body sensations* (somatic phenomena), *actions* (overt behavior), and *thoughts and beliefs* (cognitions) that occur during the problem situations at work. We would also explore whether these problematic feelings, sensations, actions, and thoughts occurred with all *people* at work or only some *people* (relationships) and whether they occurred only at work or in other *situations,* at what *times,* and under what *conditions* or *concurrent events* (context). Without this sort of exploration, it is impossible to define the problem operationally (concretely). Furthermore, it is difficult to know whether the client's work problems result from the client's actions or observable behaviors, from covert responses such as feelings of anger or jealousy, from cognitions and irrational beliefs such as "When I make a mistake at work, it's terrible" from the client's transactions with significant others that suggest an "I'm not OK—they're OK" position, or from particular events that occur in certain times or situations during work, as during a team meeting or when working under a supervisor.

Without this kind of information about when and how the problem behavior is manifested, it would be very difficult and even presumptuous to select intervention strategies or approaches. The end result of this kind of specificity is that the problem is defined or stated in terms such that two or more persons can agree on when it exists (Brown & Brown, 1977, p. 7). In the following sections, we describe specific things to explore for each of these six components and suggest some leads and responses to facilitate this exploration with clients.

Affect and mood states. Affective components of problem behavior include self-reported feelings or mood states, such as "depression," "anxiety," and "happiness." Feelings are generally the result of complex interactions among behavioral, physiological, and cognitive systems rather than unitary experiential processes (Woolfolk, 1976, p. 49). Clients often seek therapy because of this component of the problem—that is, they feel bad, uptight, sad, angry, confused, and so on and want to get rid of such unpleasant feelings. Hence, the affective component is often "overworked" in therapy. As Lazarus observes, "It is within the domain of 'emotional disturbance' that we labor, and we consider our therapeutic interventions successful or worthwhile to the extent that we are able to alleviate suffering while also promoting new adaptive responses" (1976, p. 33).

One category of things to ask the client about to get a handle on feelings or mood states is feelings about the problem behavior. After eliciting them, note the content (pleasant/unpleasant) and level of intensity. Example leads for this are the following:

"How do you feel about this?"
"What kinds of feelings do you have when you do this or when this happens?"

A second category is concealed or distorted feelings — that is, feelings that the client seems to be hiding from, such as anger, or a feeling like anger that has been distorted into hurt. Example responses for this:

"You seem to get headaches every time your husband criticizes you. What feelings are these headaches masking?"
"When you talk about your son, you raise your voice and get a very serious look on your face. What feelings do you have — deep down — about him?"
"You've said you feel hurt and you cry whenever you think about your family. What other feelings do you have besides hurt?"
"You've indicated you feel a little guilty whenever your friends ask you to do something and you don't agree to do it. Try on resentment instead of guilt. Try to get in touch with those feelings now."

The practitioner can always be on the lookout for concealed anger, which is the one emotion that tends to get "shoved under the rug" more easily than most. Lazarus observes that "it is often easy to deny, displace, conceal, and suppress anger. It is less easy to conceal anxiety or misery, especially from oneself" (1976, p. 34). Distorted feelings that are common include reporting the feeling of hurt or anxiety for anger, guilt for resentment, and sometimes anxiety for depression, or vice versa. It is also important to be aware that exploration of the affective component may be very productive

initially for clients who process information easily in a kinesthetic manner. For clients who do not, however, asking "How do you feel?" can draw a blank, uncomprehending look accompanied by an "I don't know what you mean" statement. Like any other response, "How do you feel?" is not equally productive with all clients and tends to be a tremendously overused lead in counseling sessions.

Somatic sensations. Closely tied to feelings are body sensations. Some clients are very aware of these "internal experiencings"; others are not. Some persons are so "tuned into" each and every body sensation that they become hypochondriacal, while others seem to be switched off "below the head" (Lazarus, 1976, p. 35). Neither extreme is desirable. Somatic reactions are quite evident in problems such as sexual dysfunction, depression, and anxiety. Some persons may describe complaints in terms of body sensations rather than as feelings or thoughts — that is, as headaches, dizzy spells, back pain, and so on. Problem behavior can also be affected by other physiological processes, such as nutrition and diet, exercise and lifestyle, substance use, hormone levels, and physical illness. Usually, when this is the case, some form of physiological treatment is warranted as well as psychological intervention. The therapist will want to elicit information about physiological complaints, about lifestyle and nutrition, exercise, substance use, and so on and about other body sensations relating to the problem. Some of this information is gathered routinely during the health history portion of the intake interview.

Useful leads to elicit this component of the problem behavior include these:

"What goes on inside you when you do this or when this happens?"
"What are you aware of when this occurs?"
"What sensations do you experience in your body when this happens?"
"When this happens, are you aware of anything that feels bad or uncomfortable inside you — aches, pains, dizziness, and so on?"

Overt behaviors or motoric responses. Clients often describe a problem "behavior" in very nonbehavioral terms. In other words, they describe a situation or a process without describing their actions or specific behaviors within that event or process. For example, clients may say "I'm not getting along with my wife" or "I feel lousy" or "I have a hard time relating to authority figures" without specifying what they do to get along or not get along or to relate or not relate. In this part of the assessment interview, you are interested in finding out precisely what the client does and doesn't do related to the problem. Examples of overt behaviors might be compulsive handwashing, crying, excessive eating, stealing, and making deprecatory or critical comments about self or others.

When inquiring about the behavioral domain, the therapist will want to elicit descriptions of both the presence and absence of concrete overt behaviors connected to the problem—that is, what the client does and doesn't do. The therapist also needs to be alert to the presence of behavioral *excesses* and *deficits*. Excesses are things that the person does too much or too often or that are too extreme, such as binge eating, excessive crying, or assaultive behavior. Deficits are responses that occur too infrequently or are not in the client's repertory or do not occur in the expected context or conditions, such as failure to initiate requests on one's behalf, inability to talk to one's partner about sexual concerns and desires, or lack of physical exercise and body conditioning programs. The therapist may also wish to inquire about "behavioral opposites" (Lazarus, 1976) by asking about times when the person does *not* behave that way.

These are examples of leads to elicit information about overt behaviors and actions:

"Describe what happens in this situation."
"What do you mean when you say you're 'having trouble at work'?"
"What are you doing when this occurs?"
"What do you do when this happens?"
"What effect does this situation have on your behavior?"
"Describe what you did the last few times this occurred."
"If I were photographing this scene, what actions and dialogue would the camera pick up?"

Occasionally the counselor may want to supplement the information gleaned about behavior from the client's oral self-report with more objective assessment approaches, such as using role plays that approximate the problem or accompanying clients into their environments. These additional assessment devices will help therapists improve their knowledge of how the client does and doesn't act in the problematic situation. Additionally, when such observations are coupled with the interview data, the therapist can develop more reliable hunches about how the problem manifests itself and how the problem and the client may respond to treatment.

Cognitions, beliefs, and internal dialogue. In the last few years, therapists of almost all orientations have emphasized the relative importance of cognitions or symbolic processes (Bandura, 1969; Ellis, 1984) in contributing to, exacerbating, or improving problematic situations that clients bring to therapy. Irrational expectations of oneself and of others are often related to presenting problems, as are disturbing images, self-labeling and self-statements, and cognitive distortions. Gambrill (1977, pp. 112–113) elucidates various ways in which cognitions and symbolic processes influence problems:

Fear of elevators may be associated with vivid images of the elevator plunging to the ground. Anger may be fueled by the vivid reliving of perceived slights. Self-labeling may be involved in problematic reactions. A client may experience an unusual feeling state and consider it indicative of mental illness. He may become unduly attentive to the possible occurrence of such states, and may label ones that are only similar as also being indicators that he is "going crazy." A depressed client may engage in very few positive self-evaluative statements and a great number of punishing self-statements. Cognitive distortions may include arbitrary inference, in which conclusions are drawn in the absence of supporting evidence or in direct contradiction to such evidence; magnification, in which the meaning of an event is exaggerated; overgeneralization, in which a single incident is considered indicative of total incompetence; and dichotomous reasoning, in which polar differences are emphasized (Beck, 1970) . . . . [In addition], it is assumed that there is a close relationship between the nature of self-statements and overt behavior, in that someone who copes well in a given situation has an internal dialog that is different from that of someone who does not cope well. Clients who complain of anxiety and depression often have an internal dialog consisting of anticipated bad consequences.*

* This and all other quotations from this source are from *Behavior Modification: Handbook of Assessment, Intervention, and Evaluation* by E. Gambrill. Copyright © 1977 by Jossey-Bass. Reprinted by permission.

When the cognitive component is a very strong element of the problem, part of the resulting treatment is usually directed toward this component and involves altering irrational ideas and beliefs and cognitive distortions and misconceptions.

Not all clients process cognitions or symbolic processes in the same way. Therefore, the therapist has to be sensitive to how this component may manifest itself with each client and respond accordingly. For example, some clients can easily relate to the term *irrational ideas;* others, particularly adolescents, seem to be offended by such terminology and prefer phrases like "clean up your thinking" (Baker, 1981). Clients who process information kinesthetically may have a great deal of difficulty exploring the cognitive component because they typically don't "think" this way. In contrast, people who process visually may report cognitions as images or pictures. For example, if you ask "What do you *think* about when this happens?," the client may say "I *see* my wife getting into bed with someone else." Imagery may be a very useful supplemental assessment device with such clients. Clients who process in an auditory modality may report cognitions as "talking to myself" or "telling myself" and can probably verbalize aloud for you a chain of internal dialogue connected to the problem.

Assessment of the cognitive component is accordingly directed toward exploring the presence of both irrational and rational beliefs and images related to the identified problem. Irrational beliefs will later need to be altered. Rational beliefs are also useful during intervention. Although irrational beliefs take many forms, the most damaging ones seem to be related to "shoulds" about oneself, others, relationships, work, and so on, "awfulizing" or "catastrophizing" about things that don't turn out as we expect, "perfectionistic standards" about ourselves and often projected onto others, and "externalization," the tendency to think that outside events are responsible for our feelings and problems. The therapist will also want to be alert for the presence of cognitive distortions and misperceptions, such as overgeneralization, exaggeration, and drawing conclusions without supporting data. Finally, it is important to note what clients do and do not "say" or "think" to themselves and how that relates to the identified problem.

Leads to use to assess these aspects of the cognitive component of the identified problem include the following:

"What beliefs [or images] do you hold that contribute to this problem? make it worse? make it better?

"Complete the following sentences for me—
I should . . .
People should . . .
My husband [or mother, and so on] should . . .
Work [or school] should . . .
Sex should . . ."

"When something doesn't turn out the way you want or expect, how do you usually feel?"

"What data do you have to support these beliefs or assumptions?"

"What are you thinking about or dwelling on when this [problem] happens?"

"Can you describe what kinds of thoughts or images go through your mind when this occurs?"

"What do you say to yourself when this happens?"

"What do you say to yourself when it doesn't happen [or when you feel better, and so on]?"

"Let's set up a scene. You imagine that you're starting to feel a little upset with yourself. Now run through the scene and relate the images or pictures that come through your mind. Tell me how the scene changes [or relate the thoughts or dialogue—what you say to yourself as the scene ensues]."

Context: Time, place, and concurrent events. Problem behaviors occur in a social context, not in a vacuum. Indeed, what often makes a behavior a "problem" is the context surrounding it or the way it is linked to various situations, places, and events. For example, it is not a problem to undress in your home, but the same behavior on a public street in Western culture would be called "exhibitionism." In some other cultures, this same behavior might be more commonplace and would not be considered abnormal or maladaptive. Lazarus asserts that "if a therapist is genuinely interested in promoting constructive changes in a client . . . it is essential that he or she first obtain a comprehensive understanding of the total context in which the behaviors occur" (1976, p. 25). Looking at the context surrounding the problem has implications not only for assessment but also for intervention, because a client's cultural background, lifestyle, and values can affect how the client views the problem and also the treatment approach to resolve it. As Gambrill observes, "The norms present in given racial and cultural subgroups may expand or limit the possibilities for change" (1977, p. 118).

Assessing the context surrounding the problem is also important because most problems are "situation-specific"—that is, they are linked to certain events and situations, and they occur at certain times and places. For example, clients who say "I'm uptight" or "I'm not assertive" usually do not mean they are *always* uptight or nonassertive but, rather, in particular situations or at particular times. It is important that the therapist not reinforce the notion or belief in the client that the feeling, cognition, or behavior is pervasive. Otherwise, clients are even more likely to adopt the identity of the problem and begin to regard themselves as possessing a particular trait such as "nervousness," "social anxiety," or "nonassertiveness." They are also more likely to incorporate the problem into their lifestyle and daily functioning.

In assessing contextual factors associated with the problem, you are interested in discovering—

1. Any *cultural, ethnic, and racial affiliations,* any particular *values* associated with these affiliations, and how these values affect the client's perception of the problem and of change.
2. *Situations* or *places* in which the problem usually occurs and situations in which it does not occur (*where* the problem occurs and where it does not).
3. *Times* during which the problem usually occurs and times during which it does not occur (*when* the problem occurs and when it does not).
4. *Concurrent events*—events that typically occur at or near the same time as the problem. This information is important because sometimes it suggests a pattern or a significant chain of events related to the problem that clients might not be aware of or may not report on their own.

These are example responses to elicit information about contextual components of the problem:

"Do you have [or feel] an affiliation with any particular culture or ethnic group? [In addition to the more apparent ones, don't overlook ones such as Italian American, French Canadian, Polish American, and so on.] If so, how do the values of this group affect the way you [think about, grasp] the problem? How do these values affect what you want to do about this problem?"

"Describe some recent situations in which this problem occurred. What are the similarities in these situations? In what situations does this usually occur? Where does this usually occur?"

"Describe some situations when this problem does not occur."

"In what situations does this not occur?"

"When does this usually occur? not occur?"

"Can you identify certain times of the day [week, month, year] when this is more likely to happen? less likely?"

"Does the same thing happen at other times or in other places?"

"What else is going on when this problem occurs?"

"Describe a typical day for me when you feel 'uptight.'"

"Are you aware of any other events that normally occur at the same time as this problem?"

In addition to the information obtained from the client's oral self-report during the assessment interviews, often both counselor and client can obtain a better idea of the context of the problem by having the client self-monitor such things as when and where the problem occurs and concurrent events.

Relationships and significant others. Just as problems are often linked to particular times, places, and events, they are also often connected to the presence or absence of other people. People around the client can bring about or exacerbate a problem. Someone temporarily or permanently absent from the client's life can have the same effect. Assessing the client's relationships with others is a significant part of many theoretical orientations to counseling, including dynamic theories, Adlerian theory, family systems theory, and behavioral theory.

Interpersonal problems may occur because of a lack of significant others in the client's life or because of the way the client relates to others or because of the way significant others respond to the client. Gambrill (1977, p. 109) observes that "social reinforcement from significant others may become an important maintaining factor [in a problem], even though it was not involved in the initial occurrence of a problematic reaction." Negative reactions from others or lack of social reinforcement can also discourage a client from seeking help or from trying to change.

Other persons involved in the problem often tend to discount their role in it. It is helpful if the therapist can get a handle on what other persons are involved in the problem, how they perceive the problem, and what they might have to gain or lose from a change in the problem or the client. As Gambrill (1977) observes, such persons may anticipate negative effects of improvement in a problem and covertly try to sabotage the client's best efforts. For example, a husband may preach "equal pay and opportunity" yet secretly sabotage his wife's efforts to move up the career ladder for fear that she will make more money than he does or that she will find her new job opportunities more interesting and rewarding than her relationship with him. Other people can also influence a client's behavior by serving as role models (Bandura, 1969). People whom clients view as significant to them can often have a great motivational effect on clients in this respect.

Example leads to use to assess the relational component of the problem include the following:

"How many significant close relationships or friendships do you have in your life now?"

"What effects does this problem have on your relationships with significant others in your life?"

"What effects do these significant others have on this problem?"

"Who else is involved in this problem besides yourself? How are these persons involved? What would their reaction be if you resolved this issue?"

"From whom do you think you learned to act or think this way?"

"What persons *present* in your life now have the greatest positive impact on you? negative impact?"

"What persons *absent* from your life have the greatest positive impact on you? negative impact?"

"Whom do you know and respect who handles this issue in a way that you like?"

Identifying Antecedents

You may recall from Chapter 7 that there are usually certain things that happen before or after a problem that contribute to it. In other words, people are not born feeling depressed or thinking of themselves as inadequate. Other events may contribute to the problem by maintaining, strengthening, or weakening the problem behaviors, thoughts, or feelings. Much of the assessment process consists in exploring contributing variables that precede and cue the problem (antecedents) and things that happen after the problem (consequences) that, in some way, influence or maintain it.

To review our previous discussion of the ABC model, remember that, like problem behaviors, the sources of antecedents and consequences are varied and may be affective, somatic, behavioral, cognitive, contextual, or relational. Further, antecedents and consequences are likely to differ for each client. Antecedents are external or internal events that occasion or cue the problem behaviors and make them more or less likely to occur. Some antecedents occur immediately before the problem; other antecedents (setting events) may have taken place a long time ago.

In helping clients explore antecedents of the problem, you are particularly interested in discovering (1) what *current* conditions (covert and overt) exist *before* the problem that make it *more likely* to occur, (2) what *current* conditions (covert and overt) exist that occur *before* the problem that make it *less likely* to occur, and (3) what *previous* conditions, or setting events, exist that *still* influence the problem.

Example leads to identify antecedents follow and are categorized according to the six possible sources of antecedents, described in Chapter 7:

Affective

"What are you usually feeling before this happens?"

"When do you recall the first time you felt this way?"

"What are the feelings that occur before the problem and make it stronger or more constant?"

"What are the feelings that occur before the problem that make it weaker or less intense?"

"Are there any holdover feelings or unfinished feelings from past events in your life that still affect this problem?"

Somatic

"What goes on inside you just before this happens?"

"Are you aware of any particular sensations in your body before this happens?"

"Are there any body sensations that occur right before this problem that make it weaker or less intense?"

"Is there anything going on with you physically —an illness or physical condition—or anything about the way you eat, smoke, exercise, and so on that affects or leads to this problem?"

Behavioral

"If I were photographing this, what actions and dialogue would I pick up before this happens?"

"Can you identify any particular behavior patterns that occur right before this happens?"

"What do you typically do before this happens?"

"Can you think of anything you do that makes this problem more likely to occur? less likely to occur?"

Cognitive

"What kinds of pictures or images do you have before this happens?"

"What are your thoughts before this happens?"

"What are you telling yourself before this happens?"

"Can you identify any particular beliefs that seem to set the problem off?"

"What do you think about [see or tell yourself] before the problem occurs that makes it stronger or more likely to occur? weaker or less likely to occur?"

Contextual

"Has this ever occurred at any other time in your life? If so, describe that."

"How long ago did this happen?"

"Where and when did this occur the first time?"

"How do you see those events related to your problem?"

"What things happened that seemed to lead up to this?"

"When did the problem start—what else was going on in your life at that time?"

"What were the circumstances under which the problem first occurred?"

"What was happening in your life when you first noticed this?"

"Are there any ways in which your cultural affil-iation and values set off this problem? make it more likely to occur? less likely?"

"Are you aware of any events that occurred before this problem that in some way still influence it or set it off?"

Relational

"Can you identify any particular people that seem to bring on this problem?"

"Are you usually with certain people right before or when this occurs?"

"Whom are you usually with right before this problem occurs?"

"Can you think of any person—or of any particular reaction from a person—that makes this problem more likely to occur? less likely?"

"Are there any people or relationships from the past that still influence or set off or lead to this problem in some way?"

Identifying Consequences

Recall from Chapter 7 that consequences are external or internal events that influence the problem behavior by maintaining it, strengthening or increasing it, or weakening or decreasing it. Consequences occur after the problem behavior and are distinguished from results or effects of the problem behavior by the fact that they have direct influence on the problem by either maintaining or decreasing the problem in some way.

In helping clients explore consequences, you are interested in discovering both internal and external events that maintain and strengthen the problem behavior and also events that weaken or decrease it.

Example leads to identify consequences follow and are categorized according to the six sources of consequences described in Chapter 7.

Affective

"How do you feel after _____?"

"How does this feeling affect the problem (for example, keep it going, stop it)?"

"Are you aware of any particular feelings or emotions that you have after the problem that strengthen or weaken it?"

Somatic

"What are you aware of inside you just after this happens? How does this affect the problem?"

"Are there any body sensations that seem to occur after the problem that strengthen or weaken it?"

"Is there anything you can think of about yourself physically—illness, diet, exercise, and so on—that seems to occur after this problem? How does this affect the problem?"

Behavioral

"What do you do after this happens, and how does this make the problem worse? better?"

"How do you usually react after this is over? In what ways does your reaction keep the problem going? weaken it or stop it?"

"Can you identify any particular behavior patterns that occur after this? How do these patterns keep the problem going? stop the problem?"

Cognitive

"What do you usually think about afterward? How does this affect the problem?"

"What do you picture after this happens?"

"What do you tell yourself after this occurs?"

"Can you identify any particular thoughts [or beliefs or self-talk] during or after the problem that make the problem better? worse?"

"Are there certain thoughts or images you have afterward that either strengthen or weaken the problem?"

Contextual

"What happened after this?"

"When does the problem usually stop or go away? get worse? get better?"

"Where are you when the problem stops? gets worse? gets better?"

"Can you identify any particular times, places, or events that seem to keep the problem going? make it worse or better?"

"Are there any ways in which your cultural affiliation and values seem to keep this problem going? stop it or weaken it?"

Relational

"Are you usually with certain people during and after the problem? when the problem gets worse? better?"

"Can you identify any particular people who can make the problem worse? better? stop it? keep it going?"

"Can you identify any particular reactions from other people that occur after the problem? In

what ways do these reactions affect the issue?"

Identifying Secondary Gains: A Special Case of Consequences

As we mentioned in Chapter 7, occasionally clients have a "vested interest" in maintaining the status quo of the problem because of the "payoffs" that the problem produces. For example, a client who is overweight may find it difficult to lose weight, not because of unalterable eating and exercise habits, but because the extra weight has allowed her to avoid or escape such things as new social situations or sexual relationships and has produced a safe and secure lifestyle that she is reluctant to give up (Fishman & Lubetkin, 1983). A child who is constantly disrupting his school classroom may be similarly reluctant to give up such disruptive behavior even though it results in loss of privileges, because it has given him the status of "class clown," resulting in a great deal of peer attention and support.

It is always extremely important to explore with clients the "payoffs," or secondary gains, they may be getting from having the problem, because often during the intervention phase such clients seem "resistant." In these cases, the resistance is a sign the payoffs are being threatened (see also Chapter 20). The most common payoffs include money, attention from significant others, immediate gratification of needs, avoidance of responsibility, security, and control.

Questions you can use to help clients identify possible secondary gains include these:

"The good thing about _____ is . . . ."

"What happened afterward that was pleasant?"

"What was unpleasant about what happened?"

"Has your concern or problem ever produced any special advantages or considerations for you?"

"As a consequence of your concern, have you got out of or avoided things or events?"

"What are the reactions of others when you do this?"

"How does this problem help you?"

"What do you get out of this situation that you don't get out of other situations?"

"Do you notice anything that happens afterward that you try to prolong or to produce?"

"Do you notice anything that occurs afterward that you try to stop or avoid?"

"Are there certain feelings or thoughts that go on afterwards that you try to prolong?"

"Are there certain feelings or thoughts that go on afterwards that you try to stop or avoid?"

Exploring Previous Solutions

Another important part of the assessment interview is to explore what things the client has already tried to resolve the problem and with what effect. This information is important for two reasons. First, it helps you to avoid recommendations for problem resolution that amount to "more of the same." Second, in many instances, solutions attempted by the client either create new problems or make the existing one worse (see also Chapter 20).

Fisch, Weakland, and Segal (1982, pp. 13–14) explain how clients' attempted solutions are often responsible for the origin or persistence of problems:

Problems begin from some ordinary life difficulty, of which there is never any shortage. This difficulty may stem from an unusual or fortuitous event. More often, though, the beginning is likely to be a common difficulty associated with one of the transitions regularly experienced in the course of life—marriage, the birth of a child, going to school, and so on. . . . Most people handle most such difficulties reasonably adequately—perfect handling is neither usual nor necessary—and thus we do not see them in our offices. But for a difficulty to turn into a problem, only two conditions need to be fulfilled: (1) the difficulty is mishandled, and (2) when the difficulty is not resolved, more of the same "solution" is applied. Then the original difficulty will be escalated, by a vicious-circle process, into a problem—whose eventual size and nature may have little apparent similarity to the original difficulty.*

Leads to help the client identify previous "solutions" include the following:

"How have you dealt with this or other problems before? What was the effect? What made it work or not work?"

"How have you tried to resolve this problem?"

"What kinds of things have you done to improve this situation?"

* From *The Tactics of Change* by R. Fisch, J. H. Weakland, and L. Segal. Copyright © 1982 by Jossey-Bass. Reprinted by permission.

"What have you done that has made the problem better? worse? kept it the same?"

"What have others done to help you with this?"

Identifying the Client's Coping Skills, Strengths, and Resources

When clients come to therapists, they usually are in touch with their pain and often only with their pain. Consequently, they are shortsighted and find it hard to believe that they have any internal or external resources that can help them deal with the pain more effectively. In the assessment interview, it is useful to focus not solely on the problems and pains but also on the person's positive assets and resources (which the pain may mask). This achieves several purposes. First, it helps to convey to clients that, in spite of the psychological pain, they do have at least internal resources available that they can muster to produce a different outcome. Second, it emphasizes wholeness—the client is *more* than just his or her "problem." Third, it gives you information on potential problems that may crop up during an intervention. Finally, information about the client's past "success stories" may be applicable to current problems. Such information is extremely useful in planning intervention strategies that are geared to using the kind of problem-solving and coping skills already available in the client's repertoire.

Information to be obtained in this area includes the following:

1. Behavioral assets and problem-solving skills—at what times does the client display adaptive behavior instead of problematic behavior? Often this information can be obtained by inquiring about "opposites"—for example, "When don't you act that way?" (Lazarus, 1981).
2. Cognitive coping skills—such as rational appraisal of a situation, ability to discriminate between rational and irrational thinking, selective attention and feedback from distractions, and the presence of coping or calming "self-talk" (Meichenbaum & Cameron, 1983).
3. Self-control and self-management skills—including the client's overall ability to withstand frustration, to assume responsibility for self, to be self-directed, to control problematic behavior by either self-reinforcing or self-punishing consequences, and to perceive the self as being in control rather than being a victim of

external circumstances (Gambrill, 1977; Lazarus, 1981).

The following leads are useful in identifying these kinds of client resources and assets:

"What skills or things do you have going for you that might help you with this concern?"

"Describe a situation when this concern or problem is not interfering."

"What strengths or assets can you use to help resolve this problem?"

"When don't you act this way?"

"What kinds of thoughts or self-talk help you handle this better?"

"When don't you think in self-defeating ways?"

"What do you say to yourself to cope with a difficult situation?"

"Identify the steps you take in a situation you handle well. What do you think about and what do you do? How could these steps be applied to the present issue?"

"In what situations is it fairly easy for you to manage or control this reaction or behavior?"

"Describe any times you have been able to avoid situations in which these problems have occurred."

"To what extent can you do something for yourself in a self-directed way without relying on someone else to prod you to do it?"

"How often do you get things done by rewarding yourself in some way?"

"How often do you get things done by punishing yourself in some way?"

Exploring the Client's Perception of the Problem

Most clients have their own perception of and explanation for their problem. It is important to elicit this information during an assessment session for several reasons. First, it adds to your understanding of the problem. The therapist can note which aspects of the problem are stressed and which are ignored during the client's assessment of the issue. Second, this process gives you valuable information about "patient position," a concept we describe in greater detail in Chapter 20. Briefly stated, *patient position* refers to the client's strongly held beliefs and values — in this case, about the nature of the issue or problem (Fisch et al., 1982). Usually clients allude to such "positions" in the course of presenting their perception of the problem. Ignoring the client's position may cause the therapist to "blunder into a strategy that

will be met with resistance" (Fisch et al., 1982, p. 92). You can get clients to describe their view of the problem very concisely simply by asking them to give the problem a one-line title as if it were a movie, play, or book. Another way to elicit the client's perception of the problem that Lazarus (1981) recommends is to describe the problem in only one word and then to use the selected word in a sentence. For example, a client may say "guilt" and then "I have a lot of guilt about having an affair." The same client might title the problem "Caught between Two Lovers." This technique also works extremely well with children, who typically are quick to think of titles and words without a lot of deliberation.

Leads to use to help clients identify and describe their view of the problem include these:

"What is your understanding of this issue?"

"How do you explain this problem to yourself?"

"What does the problem mean to you?"

"What is your interpretation [analysis] of this problem?"

"What else is important to you about the problem that we haven't mentioned?"

"Give the problem a title."

"Describe the issue with just one word."

Ascertaining the Frequency, Duration, and Severity of the Problem

It is also useful to determine the intensity of the problem. In other words, you want to check out how much the problem is affecting the client and the client's daily functioning. If, for example, a client says "I feel anxious," does the client mean a little anxious or very anxious? Is this person anxious all the time or only some of the time? And does this anxiety affect any of the person's daily activities, such as eating, sleeping, or working? There are two kinds of intensity to assess: the degree of problem intensity or severity and the frequency (how often) or duration (how long) of the problem.

Degree of problem intensity. Often it is useful to obtain a client's subjective rating of the degree of discomfort, stress, or intensity of the problem. The counselor can use this information to determine how much the problem affects the client and whether the client seems to be incapacitated or immobilized by it. As you may recall from Chapter 7, assessing the severity of the stressors in the client's life is also part of the multiaxial system of diagnostic classification of problems. To assess the degree of problem intensity, the counselor can use leads similar to these:

> "You say you feel anxious. On a scale from 1 to 10, with 1 being very calm and 10 being extremely anxious, where would you be now?"
> "How strong is your feeling when this happens?"
> "How has this interfered with your daily activities?"
> "How would your life be affected if this issue were not resolved in a year?"

In assessing degree of intensity, you are looking for a client response that indicates how strong, interfering, or pervasive the problem seems to be.

Frequency or duration of problem behaviors. In asking about frequency and duration, your purpose is to have the client identify how long (duration) or how often (frequency) the problem behaviors occur. Data about how long or how often the problem occurs *before* a counseling strategy is applied are called "baseline data." Baseline data provide information about the *present* extent of the problem. They can also be used later to compare the extent of the problem before and after a counseling strategy has been used (also see our discussion of evaluation in Chapter 10).

Leads to assess the frequency and duration of the problem behavior include the following:

> "How often does this happen?"
> "How many times does this occur?"
> "How long does this feeling usually stay with you?"
> "How much does this go on, say, in an average day?"

Some clients can discuss the severity, frequency, or duration of the problem behavior during the interview rather easily. However, many clients may be unaware of the number of times the problem occurs, how much time it occupies, or how intense it is. Most clients can give the counselor more accurate information about frequency and duration by engaging in self-monitoring of the problem behaviors with a written log. Use of logs to supplement the interview data is discussed later in this chapter.

Table 8-2 provides a review of the 11 categories of problem assessment. This table may help you

TABLE 8-2. Review of 11 problem assessment categories

I. *Purpose* of assessment		
II. *Range* of problems		
III. *Prioritization* of problems		
IV, V, VI, VII. Identification of:		

Antecedents	Problem behaviors	Consequences and secondary gains (payoffs)
Affective	Affective	Affective
Somatic	Somatic	Somatic
Behavioral	Behavioral	Behavioral
Cognitive	Cognitive	Cognitive
Contextual	Contextual	Contextual
Relational	Relational	Relational

VIII. *Previous solutions*
IX. *Coping skills*
X. *Client perceptions* of problem
XI. *Frequency, duration, severity* of problem

conceptualize and summarize the types of data you will seek during assessment interviews.

☐ LIMITATIONS OF INTERVIEW LEADS IN PROBLEM ASSESSMENT

According to Lazarus (1973, p. 407), "Faulty problem identification . . . is probably the greatest impediment to successful therapy." As we mentioned earlier in this chapter, the ABC model for viewing client problems is reflected in the problem assessment leads presented in this chapter. The leads are simply tools that the counselor can use to elicit certain kinds of client information. They are designed to be used as a "road map" to provide some direction for assessment interviews. However, the leads alone are an insufficient basis for problem assessment, because they represent only about half of the process at most—the counselor responses. The other part of the process is reflected by the responses these leads generate from the client. A complete problem assessment includes not only asking the right questions but also synthesizing and integrating the client responses.

A useful way to synthesize client responses during assessment interviews is to continue to build on and use all the fundamental helping skills presented earlier in this book. Think of it this way: In an assessment interview, you are simply *supplementing* your basic skills with some specific leads designed to obtain certain kinds of information. Many of your leads will consist of open-ended questions or probes. However, even assessment interviews should not disintegrate into a question-and-answer or interrogation session. You can obtain information and give the information some meaning through other verbal responses, such as summarization, clarification, confrontation, and reflection. It is extremely important to clarify and reflect the information the client gives you before jumping ahead to another question. The model dialogue that follows will illustrate this process.

☐ MODEL DIALOGUE FOR PROBLEM ASSESSMENT: THE CASE OF JOAN

To help you identify how these problem assessment leads are used in an interview, a dialogue of the case of Joan (from Chapter 7) is given. An explanation of the counselor's response and the counselor's rationale for using it appear in italics before the responses.

Counselor response 1 is a **rationale** *to explain to the client the* **purpose** *of the assessment interview.*

1. *Counselor:* Joan, last week you dropped by to schedule today's appointment, and you mentioned you were feeling unhappy and dissatisfied with school. It might be helpful today to take some time just to explore exactly what is going on with you and school and anything else that concerns you. I'm sure there are ways we can work with this dissatisfaction, but first I think it would be helpful to both of us to get a better idea of what all the issues are for you now. Does this fit with where you want to start today?
   Client: Yeah. I guess school is the main problem. It's really bugging me.

Counselor response 2 is a lead to help Joan identify the **range** *of her concerns.*

2. *Counselor:* OK, you just said school is the *main* problem. From the way you said that and the way you look right now, I have the feeling school isn't the *only* thing you're concerned about in your life.
   Client: Well, you're right about that. I'm also kind of not getting along too well with my folks. But that's kind of related to this school thing, too.

In the next response, the counselor will simply **listen** *to Joan and synthesize what she's saying by using a* **paraphrase** *response.*

3. *Counselor:* So from your point of view, the school thing and the issue with your parents are connected.
   Client: Yeah, because I'm having trouble in

some of my classes. There's too much competition. I feel the other kids are better than I am. I've thought about changing from this college prep program to the work-study program, but I don't know what to do. I don't like to make decisions anyway. At the same time, my folks put a lot of pressure on me to perform well, to make top grades. They have a lot of influence with me. I used to want to do well, but now I'm kind of tired of it all.

In the next response, the counselor continues to listen to Joan and **reflect her feelings.**

4. *Counselor:* It seems like you're feeling pretty overwhelmed and discouraged right now.
   Client: Yeah, I am. [Lowers head, eyes, and voice tone]

Counselor senses Joan has strong feelings about these issues and doesn't want to cut them off initially. **Instructs** *Joan to continue focusing on the feelings.*

5. *Counselor:* [Pause] Let's stay with these feelings for a few minutes and see where they take you.
   Client: [Pause; eyes fill with tears] I guess I just feel like all this stuff is coming down on me at once. I'd like to work something out, but I don't know how — or where, even — to start.

Counselor continues to **attend,** *to* **listen,** *and to* **reflect** *the client's current experience:*

6. *Counselor:* It seems like you feel you're carrying a big load on your shoulders —
   Client: Yeah.

In response 7, the counselor **summarizes** *Joan's concerns, followed by a lead to determine whether Joan has* **prioritized** *her problems.*

7. *Counselor:* I think before we're finished I'd like to come back to these feelings, which seem pretty strong for you now. Before we do, it might help you to think about not having to tackle everything all at once. You know you mentioned three different things that are bothering you — your competitive classes, having trouble making decisions, and not getting along with your parents. Which of these problems bothers you most?
   Client: I'm not really sure. I'm concerned right now about having trouble in my classes. But sometimes I think if I were in another type of curriculum, I wouldn't be so tense about these classes. But I'm sort of worried about deciding to do this.

Counselor response 8 is a **clarification.** *The counselor wants to see whether the client's interest in work-study is real or is a way to avoid the present problem.*

8. *Counselor:* Do you see getting in the work-study

program as a way to get out of your present problem classes, or is it a program that really interests you?

Client: It's a program that interests me. I think sometimes I'd like to get a job after high school instead of going to college. *But* I've been thinking about this for a year and I can't decide what to do. I'm not very good at making decisions on my own.

Counselor response 9 is a **summarization** *and* **instruction.** *The counselor goes back to the three problem areas mentioned in "Identifying the Range of Problems." Note that the counselor does not draw explicit attention to the client's last self-deprecating statement.*

9. *Counselor:* Well, your concerns of your present class problems and of making this and other decisions are somewhat related. Your parents tie into this, too. Maybe you could explore all concerns and then decide later about what you want to work on first.

Client: That's fine with me.

Counselor response 10 is a lead to **identify some present problem behaviors** *related to Joan's concern about competitive classes. Asking the client for examples can elicit specificity about what does or does not occur during the problem situation.*

10. *Counselor:* OK, what is an example of some trouble you've been having in your most competitive class?

Client: Well, I withdraw in these classes. I've been cutting my math classes. It's the worst. My grades are dropping, especially in math class.

Counselor response 11 is a **problem behavior** *lead regarding the* **context** *of the problem to see whether the client's concern occurs at other* **times** *or other* **places.**

11. Counselor: Where else do you have trouble — in any other classes, or at other times or places outside school?

Client: No, not outside school. And, to some degree, I always feel anxious in any class because of the pressures my parents put on me to get good grades. But my math class is really the worst.

Counselor response 12 is a lead to help the client identify **overt problem behaviors** *in math class (***behavioral** *component of problem).*

12. *Counselor:* Describe what happens in your math class that makes it troublesome for you. [could also use imagery assessment at this point]

Client: Well, to start with, it's a harder class for me. I have to work harder to do OK. In this class I get nervous whenever I go in it. So I withdraw.

Client's statement "I withdraw" is vague. So counselor response 12 is another **overt problem behavior** *lead to help the client specify what she means by "withdrawing." Note that since the counselor did not get a complete answer to this after response 8, the same type of lead is used again.*

13. *Counselor:* What do you do when you withdraw? [This is also an ideal place for a role-play assessment.]

Client: Well, I sit by myself, I don't talk or volunteer answers. Sometimes I don't go to the board or answer when the teacher calls on me.

Now that the client has identified certain overt behaviors associated with the problem, the counselor will use a **covert problem behavior** *lead to find out whether there are any predominant* **thoughts** *the client has during the math class (***cognitive** *component of problem).*

14. *Counselor:* What are you generally thinking about in this class?

Client: What do you mean — am I thinking about math?

The client's response indicated some confusion. The counselor will have to use a more specific **covert problem behavior** *lead to assess cognition, along with some* **self-disclosure,** *to help the client respond more specifically.*

15. *Counselor:* Well, sometimes when I'm in a situation like a class, there are times when my mind is in the class and other times I'm thinking about myself or about something else I'm going to do. So I'm wondering whether you've noticed anything you're thinking about during the class?

Client: Well, some of the time I'm thinking about the math problems. Other times I'm thinking about the fact that I'd rather not be in the class and that I'm not as good as the other kids.

The client has started to be more specific, and the counselor thinks perhaps there are still other thoughts going on. To explore this possibility, the counselor uses another **covert problem behavior** *lead in response 16 to assess* **cognition.**

16. *Counselor:* What else do you recall that you tell yourself when you're thinking you're not as good as other people?

Client: Well, I think that I don't get grades that are as good as some other students'. My parents have been pointing this out to me since junior high. And in the math class I'm one of four girls. The guys in there are really smart. I just keep thinking how can a girl ever be as smart as a guy in math class? No way. It just doesn't happen.

The client identifies more specific problem-related

thoughts and also suggests two possible antecedents — parental comparison of her grades and cultural stereotyping (girls shouldn't be as good in math as boys). The counselor's records show that the client's test scores and previous grades indicate that she is definitely not "dumb" in math. The counselor will **summarize** *this and then, in the next few responses, will focus on these and on other possible* **antecedents,** *such as the nervousness the client mentioned earlier.*

17. *Counselor:* So what you're telling me is that you believe most of what you've heard from others about yourself and about the fact that girls automatically are not supposed to do too well in math.
   Client: Yeah, I guess so, now that you put it like that. I've never given it much thought.

18. *Counselor:* Yes. It doesn't sound like you've ever thought about whether *you, Joan,* really feel this way or whether these feelings are just adopted from things you've heard others tell you.
   Client: No, I never have.

19. *Counselor:* That's something we'll also probably want to come back to later.
   Client: OK.

20. *Counselor:* You know, Joan, earlier you mentioned that you get nervous about this class. When do you notice that you feel this way — before the class, during the class, or at other times?
   Client: Well, right before the class is the worst. About ten minutes before my English class ends — it's right before math — I start thinking about the math class. Then I get nervous and feel like I wish I didn't have to go. Recently, I've tried to find ways to cut math class.

The counselor still needs more information about how and when the nervousness affects the client, so 21 is another **antecedent** *lead.*

21. *Counselor:* Could you tell me more about when you feel most nervous and when you don't feel nervous about this class?
   Client: Well, I feel worst when I'm actually walking to the class and the class is starting. Once the class starts, I feel better. I don't feel nervous about it when I cut it or at other times. However, once in a while, if someone talks about it or I think about it, I feel a little nervous.

The client has indicated that the nervousness seems to be more of an antecedent than a problem behavior. She has also suggested that cutting class is a consequence that maintains the problem, because she uses this to avoid the math class that brings on the nervousness. The counselor realizes at this point that the word **nervous** *has not been defined and goes back in the*

next response to a **covert problem behavior** *lead to find out what Joan means by* **nervous** *(affective component).*

22. *Counselor:* Tell me what you mean by the word *nervous* — what goes on with you when you're nervous?
   Client: Well, I get sort of a sick feeling in my stomach, and my hands get all sweaty. My heart starts to pound.

In the next response, the counselor continues to **listen** *and* **paraphrase** *to clarify whether the nervousness is experienced somatically.*

23. *Counselor:* So your nervousness really consists of things you feel going on inside you.
   Client: Yeah.

Next the counselor will use an **intensity** *lead to determine the* **severity** *of nervousness.*

24. *Counselor:* How strong is this feeling — a little or very?
   Client: Before class, very strong — at other times, just a little.

The client has established that the nervousness seems mainly to be exhibited in somatic forms and is more intense before class. The counselor will pursue the relationship between the client's nervousness and overt and covert problem behaviors described earlier to verify that the nervousness is an **antecedent.** *Another* **antecedent** *lead is used next.*

25. *Counselor:* Which seems to come first — feeling nervous, not speaking up in class, or thinking about other people being smarter than you?
   Client: Well, the nervousness. Because that starts before I get in the class.

The counselor will **summarize** *this pattern and confirm it with the client in the next response.*

26. *Counselor:* Let's see. So you feel nervous — like in your stomach and hands — before class and when math class starts. Then during class, on days you go, you start thinking about not being as smart in math as the guys and you don't volunteer answers or don't respond sometimes when called on. But after the class is over, you don't notice the nervousness so much. Is that right?
   Client: That's pretty much what happens.

The counselor has a clue from the client's previous comments that there are other antecedents in addition to nervousness that have to do with the client's problem behavior — such as the role of her parents. The counselor will pursue this in the next response, using an **antecedent** *lead.*

27. *Counselor:* Joan, you mentioned earlier that you have been thinking about not being as smart

as some of your friends ever since junior high. When do you recall you really started to dwell on this?

Client: Well, probably in seventh grade.

The counselor didn't get sufficient information about what happened to the client in the seventh grade, so another **antecedent** *lead will be used to identify this possible* **setting event.**

28. *Counselor:* Well, what things seemed to happen then when you began to compare yourself with others?

    Client: Well, my parents said when you start junior high, your grades become really important in order to go to college. So for the last three or four years they have been telling me some of my grades aren't as good as other students'. Also, if I get a B, they will withhold a privilege, like my allowance.

The counselor has no evidence of actual parental reaction but will work with the client's report at this time, since this is how the client perceives parental input. If possible, a parent conference could be arranged later with the client's permission. The parents **seem** *to be using negative rather than positive consequences with Joan to influence her behavior. The counselor wants to pursue the relationship between the parents' input and the client's present behavior to determine whether parental reaction is eliciting part of Joan's present concerns and will use a lead to identify this as a possible* **antecedent.**

29. *Counselor:* How do you think this reaction of your parents' relates to your present problems in your math class?

    Client: Well, since I started high school, they have talked more about needing to get better grades for college. And I have to work harder in math class to do this. I guess I feel a lot of pressure to perform—which makes me withdraw and just want to hang it up. Now, of course, my grades are getting worse, not better.

The counselor, in the next lead, will **paraphrase** *Joan's previous comment.*

30. *Counselor:* So the expectations you feel from your parents seem to draw out pressure in you.

    Client: Yes, that happens.

In response 31, the counselor will explore another possible **antecedent** *that Joan mentioned before— thinking that girls aren't as good as boys in math.*

31. *Counselor:* Joan, I'd like to ask you about something else you mentioned earlier that I said we would come back to. You said one thing that you think about in your math class is that you're only

one of four girls and that, as a girl, you're not as smart in math as a boy. Do you know what makes you think this way?

Client: I'm not sure. Everyone knows or says that girls have more trouble in math than boys. Even my teacher. He's gone out of his way to try to help me because he knows it's tough for me.

The client has identified a possible consequence of her problem behavior as teacher attention. The counselor will return to this later. First, the counselor is going to respond to the client's response that "everyone" has told her this thought. Counselors have a responsibility to point out things that clients have learned from stereotypes or irrational beliefs rather than actual data, as is evident in this case from Joan's academic record. Counselor will use **confrontation** *in the next response.*

32. *Counselor:* We can deal more with this later, but it's evident to me from your records that you have a lot of potential for math. Yet you've learned to think of yourself as less capable, especially less capable than guys. This is a popular idea that people throw around in our culture. But in your case I don't see any evidence for it.

    Client: You mean I really could do as well in math as the guys?

Counselor reponse 33 is an **interpretation** *to help the client see the relation between overt and covert behaviors.*

33. *Counselor:* I don't see why not. But lots of times the way someone acts or performs in a situation is affected by how the person thinks about the situation. I think some of the reason you're having more trouble in your math class is that your performance is hindered a little by your nervousness and by the way you put yourself down.

In the next response, the counselor **checks out** *and* **clarifies** *the client's reaction to the previous interpretation.*

34. *Counselor:* I'm wondering now from the way you're looking at me whether this makes any sense or whether what I just said "muddies the waters" more for you?

    Client: No, I guess I was just thinking about things. You mentioned the word *expectations.* But I guess it's not just that my parents expect too much of me. I guess in a way I expect too little of myself. I've never really thought of that before.

35. *Counselor:* That's a great observation. In a way the two sets of expectations are probably connected. These are some of the kinds of issues we may want to work on in counseling if this track we're on seems to fit for you.

    Client: Yeah. OK, it's a problem.

The counselor is going to go back now to pursue possible consequences that are influencing the client's problem behavior. The next response is a lead to identify **consequences.**

36. *Counselor:* Joan, I'd like to go back to some things you mentioned earlier. For one thing, you said your teacher has gone out of his way to help you. Would you say that your behavior in his class has got you any extra attention or special consideration from him?

    Client: Well, certainly extra attention. He's talked to me more frequently. And he doesn't get upset when I don't go to the board.

Counselor response 37 will continue to explore the teacher's behavior as a possible **consequence.**

37. *Counselor:* Do you mean he may excuse you from board work?

    Client: For sure, and I think he, too, almost expects me *not* to come up with the answer. Just like I don't expect myself to.

The teacher's behavior may be maintaining the client's overt problem behaviors in class by giving extra attention to her for her problems and by excusing her from some kinds of work. A teacher conference may be necessary at some later point. The counselor, in the next two responses, will continue to use other leads to identify possible **consequences.**

38. *Counselor:* What do you see you're doing right now that helps you get out of putting yourself through the stress of going to math class?

    Client: Do you mean something like cutting class?

39. *Counselor:* I think that's perhaps one thing you do to get out of the class. What else?

    Client: Nothing I can think of.

The client has identified cutting class as one way to avoid the math class. The counselor, in the next response, will suggest another **consequence** *that the client mentioned earlier, though not as a way to get out of the stress associated with the class. The counselor will suggest that this consequence functions as a* **secondary gain,** *or* **payoff,** *in a tentative* **interpretation** *that is "checked out" with the client in the next three responses:*

40. *Counselor:* Well, Joan, you told me earlier that your grades were dropping in math class. Is it possible that if these grades—and others—drop too much, you'll automatically be dropped from these college prep classes?

    Client: That's right.

41. *Counselor:* I'm wondering whether one possible reason for letting your grades slide is that it is almost an automatic way for you to get out of

these competitive classes.

    Client: How so?

42. *Counselor:* Well, if you became ineligible for these classes because of your grades, you'd automatically be out of this class and others that you consider competitive and feel nervous about. What do you think about that?

    Client: I guess that's true. And then my dilemma is whether I want to stay in this or switch to the work-study program.

In the next response, the counselor uses **summarization** *and ties together the effects of "dropping grades" to math class and to the earlier-expressed concern of a curriculum-change decision.*

43. *Counselor:* Right. And letting your grades get too bad will automatically mean that decision is made for you, so you can take yourself off the hook for making that choice. In other words, it's sort of a way that part of you has rather creatively come up with to get yourself out of the hassle of having to decide something you don't really want to be responsible for deciding about.

    Client: Wow! Gosh, I guess that might be happening.

44. *Counselor:* That's something you can think about. We didn't really spend that much time today exploring the issue of having to make decisions for yourself, so that will probably be something to discuss the next time we get together. I know you have a class coming up in about ten minutes, so there's just a couple more things we might look at.

    Client: OK—what next?

In the next few responses (45–52), the counselor continues to demonstrate **listening responses** *and to help Joan explore* **solutions** *she's tried already to resolve the problem. They look together at the* **effects** *of the use of the solutions Joan identifies.*

45. *Counselor:* OK, starting with the nervousness and pressure you feel in math class—is there anything you've attempted to do to get a handle on this problem?

    Client: Not really—other than talking to you about it and, of course, cutting class.

46. *Counselor:* So cutting class is the only solution you've tried.

    Client: Yeah.

47. *Counselor:* How do you think this solution has helped?

    Client: Well, like I said before—it helps mainly because on the days I don't go, I don't feel uptight.

48. *Counselor:* So you see it as a way to get rid of these feelings you don't like.
    Client: Yeah, I guess that's it.
49. *Counselor:* Can you think of any ways in which this solution has not helped?
    Client: Gee, I don't know. Maybe I'm not sure what you're asking.
50. *Counselor:* OK, good point! Sometimes when I try to do something to resolve a problem, it can make the issue better or worse. So I guess what I'm really asking is whether you've noticed that your "solution" of cutting class has in any way made the problem worse or in any way has even contributed to the whole issue?
    Client: [Pause] I suppose maybe in a way. [Pause] In that, by cutting class, I miss out on the work, and then I don't have all the input I need for tests and homework, and that doesn't help my poor grades.
51. *Counselor:* OK. That's an interesting idea. You're saying that when you look deeper, your solution also has had some negative effects on one of the problems you're trying to deal with and eliminate.
    Client: Yeah. But I guess I'm not sure what else I could do.
52. *Counselor:* At this point, you probably are feeling a little bit stuck, like you don't know which other direction or road to take.
    Client: Yeah, kind of like a broken record.

At this point, the counselor shifts the focus a little to exploration of Joan's **assets, strengths, and resources.**

53. *Counselor:* Well, one thing I sense is that your feelings of being so overwhelmed are sort of covering up the resources and assets you have within you to handle the issue and work it out. For example, can you identify any particular skills or things you have going for you that might help you deal with this issue?
    Client: [Pause] Well, are you asking me to brag about myself?

Clients often talk about their pain or limitations freely but feel reluctant to reveal their strengths, so in the next response, the counselor gives Joan a specific **directive** *and* **permission** *to talk about her* **assets.**

54. *Counselor:* Sure. Give yourself permission. That's certainly fine in here.
    Client: Well, I am pretty responsible. I'm usually fairly loyal and dependable. It's hard to make decisions for myself, but when I say I'm going to do something, I usually do it.
55. *Counselor:* OK, great. So what you're telling me is you're good on follow-through once you decide something is important to you.

Client: Yeah. Mm-hmm. Also, although I'm usually uptight in my math class, I don't have the same feeling in my English class. I'm really doing well in there.

In response 56, the counselor will pick up on these "pluses" and use another **coping skills** *lead to have the client identify particular ways in which she handles positive situations, especially her English class. If she can demonstrate the steps to succeed in one class, this is useful information that can be applied in a different and problematic area. This topic is continued in response 57.*

56. *Counselor:* So there are some things about school that are going OK for you. You say you're doing well in your English class. What can you think of that you do or don't do to help you perform well in this class?
    Client: Well, I go to class, of course, regularly. And I guess I feel like I do well in reading and writing. I don't have the hangup in there about being one of the few girls.
57. *Counselor:* So maybe you can see some of the differences between your English and math classes—and how you handle these. This information is useful because if you can start to identify the things you do and think about in English that make it go so well for you, then you potentially can apply the same process or steps to a more difficult situation, like math class.
    Client: That sounds hopeful!

In the next few responses, the counselor tries to elicit **Joan's perception and assessment of the main issue.**

58. *Counselor:* Right. It is. I feel hopeful, too. Just a couple more things. Changing the focus a little now, could you think about the issues that you came in with today—and describe the main issue in one word?
    Client: Ooh—that's a hard question!
59. *Counselor:* I guess it could be. Take your time. You don't have to rush.
    Client: [Pause] Well, how about "can't?"
60. *Counselor:* OK, now, to help me get an idea of what that word means to you, use it in a sentence.
    Client: Any sentence?
61. *Counselor:* Yeah. Make one up. Maybe the first thing that comes in your head.
    Client: Well, "I can't do a lot of things I think I want to or should be able to do."

In response 62, the counselor uses a **confrontation** *to depict the incongruity revealed in the sentence Joan made up about her problem. This theme is continued in response 63.*

62. *Counselor:* OK, that's interesting too, because

on the one hand, you're saying there are some things you *want* to do that aren't happening, and on the other hand, you're also saying there are some things that aren't happening that you think you *should* be doing. Now, these are two pretty different things mixed together in the same sentence.

Client: Yeah. [Clarifies] I think the wanting stuff to happen is from me and the should things are from my folks and my teachers.

63. *Counselor:* OK, so you're identifying part of the whole issue as wanting to please yourself and others at the same time.

Client: M-m-hmm.

In response 64, the counselor identifies this issue as an extension of the **secondary gain** *mentioned earlier— avoiding deliberate decisions.*

64. *Counselor:* I can see how after a while that would start to feel like so much trouble that it would be easier to try to let situations or decisions get made for you rather than making a conscious or deliberate choice.

In the next two responses, the counselor explores the **context** *related to these issues and sets up some* **self-monitoring** *homework to obtain additional information. Note that this is a task likely to appeal to the client's dependability, which she revealed during exploration of* **coping skills.**

65. *Counselor:* That's something else we'll be coming back to, I'm sure. One last thing before you have to go. Earlier we talked about some specific times and places connected to some of these issues — like where and when you get in the rut of putting yourself down and thinking you're not as smart as other people. What I'd like to do is give you sort of a diary to write in this week to collect some more information about these kinds of problems. Sometimes writing these kinds of things down can help you start making changes and sorting out the issues. You've said that you're pretty dependable. Would doing this appeal to your dependability?

Client: Sure. That's something that wouldn't be too hard for me to do.

66. *Counselor:* OK, let me tell you specifically what to keep track of, and then I'll see you next week — bring this back with you. [Goes over instructions for Joan's log sheet — see Figure 8-2, p. 203].

At this time, the counselor also has the option of giving Joan a history questionnaire to complete and/or a brief self-report inventory to complete, such as an anxiety inventory or checklist.

☐ FORMING HYPOTHESES ABOUT PROBLEMS

During and after the assessment process, the therapist is constantly developing hunches, guesses, or hypotheses about what is going on with the client and about the client's problem. Hypotheses about functional relationships among the problem, antecedents, and consequences and about "patient position" and coping skills are also generated, since these "educated guesses" provide important clues for making valid treatment decisions. The counselor relies on all the assessment information available, including that obtained from interviews, history, self-monitoring, inventories, and so on. This is also a time when the therapist's intuition is useful to help put the pieces together. To provide you with an illustration of this process, we might generate the following ideas about "the case of Joan," based on the case description given in Chapter 7 and on the interview dialogue and self-monitoring log presented in this chapter on page 203.

Joan's presenting problem of having trouble in competitive classes such as math is cued by nervousness, by pressure she has felt from her parents to perform, by being female and by the cultural stereotyping she has bought into, and by her general tendency to put herself down. The problem is maintained by the attention she receives from her math teacher, who also excuses her from doing required work, and by her low expectations and irrational beliefs and misconceptions about herself. A secondary gain at stake is that by continuing to perform poorly in her college prep classes, she will automatically be disqualified from this curriculum, thereby effectively eliminating her need to make a deliberate choice about her curriculum, which is another presenting problem. This second problem (difficulty in making independent decisions) is also cued by her low expectations for herself and by her lack of confidence in her decision-making ability. It is maintained by a desire to please her parents, a lack of opportunities to make decisions, and perhaps by negative parental reactions when she made independent decisions in the past. Another secondary gain may be that this problem keeps her from taking too many risks and from becoming self-reliant and allows her to continue to be rather dependent on others for security and protection. (A way to look at this from an alternative treatment orientation would be that having the problem allows her to stay in her Child ego state, which is also heavily reinforced by her parents, who transact with her from Parental rather than Adult ego states. Another alternative interpretation is that she has never learned or has never been challenged to assume *self* rather than environmental support until recently, which is creating a push/pull conflict for her.) Information gleaned from the interview suggests that she views the problem as an extension of the decision-making issue — as something she can't do rather than something she chooses not to do. At the same time, she seems to be somewhat dependable and has demonstrated the steps and processes required to handle one class successfully. This information can be helpful for selecting strategies that appeal to

her dependability and also capitalize on the behavioral and cognitive coping skills she has been able to use in successful situations. Her tenacity and coping skills will be assets during intervention. A major difficulty will be devising and implementing strategies that challenge her to rely on herself and assume more responsibility and self-direction without unduly threatening her present "payoffs" for dependence and support from others.

In the chapter Postevaluation you will have an opportunity to develop hunches about the client based on information obtained in an assessment interview.

LEARNING ACTIVITIES #25: INTERVIEW ASSESSMENT

I. The following activity is designed to assist you in identifying problem assessment leads in an interview. You are given a counselor/client dialogue of the case of Ms. Weare and Freddie (Chapter 7). This dialogue consists of an interview with the mother, Ms. Weare. For each counselor response, your task is to identify and write down the type of problem assessment lead used by the counselor. You may find it helpful to use the Interview Checklist at the end of the chapter as a guide for this learning activity. There may be more than one example of any given lead in the dialogue. Also, responses from previous chapters (listening and action) may be used. Other basic verbal interview responses are also included. Feedback follows the Learning Activities (on page 204).

Dialogue with Ms. Weare and Counselor

1. *Counselor:* Hello, Ms. Weare. Could you tell me about some things going on now that are concerning you?
   Client: Not too much. Family Services sent me here.
2. *Counselor:* So you're here just because they sent you — or is there something bothering you?
   Client: Well, they don't think my kid and I get along too well. My kid is Freddie.
3. *Counselor:* What do you think about the way you and Freddie get along?
   Client: Well, I yell at him a lot. I don't like to do that but sometimes he gets me so mad. I don't like to, but he needs to learn.
4. *Counselor:* So there are times when you get real mad at Freddie and then you yell at him. You don't like to do this, but you see it as a way to help him learn right and wrong.
   Client: That's it. I don't like to, but there are

times when he needs to know something. Like yesterday, I bought him new pants and he came home from school with a big hole in them. Now I just don't have money to keep buying him new pants.

5. *Counselor:* You just mentioned the incident with Freddie's pants. What are some other times that you get mad at Freddie?
   Client: Every morning. Freddie's in fifth grade now. But he still doesn't dress himself in the morning. I want to be a good mother and get him to school on time, and he tries to be late. He waits around not getting dressed.
6. *Counselor:* Any other times you can remember getting mad?
   Client: Well, not too long ago he was playing outside and broke a window. I got mad then. But that doesn't happen every day like his not getting dressed does.
7. *Counselor:* So one thing that really bothers you is what goes on in the mornings. Could you tell me exactly what does happen each morning at your house?
   Client: Well, I call Freddie to get up and tell him to dress before he comes down for breakfast. He comes down all right — in his pajamas. I warn him after breakfast to get ready. Usually about five minutes before the bus comes, I'll go up. He'll just be sitting in his room! He's still not dressed. I'll yell at him and then dress him so he's not late.
8. *Counselor:* And your main feeling at this point is that you're mad. Anything else you feel?
   Client: No, just very mad.
9. *Counselor:* And what exactly do you do when you go upstairs and he's not dressed?
   Client: I yell at him. Then I help dress him.
   (continued)

10. *Counselor:* What kinds of things do you usually say to him?

    Client: I tell him he's dumb and he's going to be late for school, and that I have to make sure he won't be.

11. *Counselor:* You mentioned this happens in the morning. Does this situation go on every morning or only some mornings?

    Client: Just about every morning except weekends.

12. *Counselor:* When did these incidents seem to begin?

    Client: Ever since Freddie started going to school.

13. *Counselor:* So it appears that this has been going on for about five or six years, then?

    Client: Yes, I guess so.

14. *Counselor:* OK, now let's go back over this situation. You told me you remind Freddie every morning to get dressed. He never dresses by breakfast. You remind him again. Then, about five minutes before the bus comes, you go upstairs to check on him. When do you notice that you start to feel mad?

    Client: I think about it as soon as I realize it's almost time for the bus to come and Freddie isn't down yet. Then I feel mad.

15. *Counselor:* And what exactly do you think about right then?

    Client: Well, that he's probably not dressed and that if I don't go up and help him, he'll be late. Then I'll look like a bad mother if I can't get my son to school on time.

16. *Counselor:* So in a sense you actually go help him out so he won't be late. How many times has Freddie ever been late?

    Client: Never.

17. *Counselor:* You believe that helping Freddie may prevent him from being late. However, your help also excuses Freddie from having to help himself. What do you think would happen if you stopped going upstairs to check on Freddie in the morning?

    Client: Well, I don't know, but I'm his only parent. Freddie's father isn't around. It's up to me, all by myself, to keep Freddie in line. If I didn't go up and if Freddie was late all the time, his teachers might blame me. I wouldn't be a good mother.

18. *Counselor:* Of course, we don't *really* know what would happen if you didn't go up and yell at him or help him dress. It might be so different for Freddie after the first day or two he would dress himself. It could be that he thinks it's easier to wait and get your help than to dress himself.

He might think that by sitting up there and waiting for you to help, he's getting a special advantage or attention from you.

    Client: You mean like he's getting a favor from me?

19. *Counselor:* Sure. And when we find a way to get a favor from someone, we usually do as much as we can to keep getting the favor. Ms. Weare, I'd like to ask you about something else. Do you think maybe that you see helping Freddie out as a way to avoid having Freddie be late and then not having someone blame you for this?

    Client: Sure. I'd rather help him than get myself in hot water.

20. *Counselor:* OK, so you're concerned about what you think might happen to you if he's late. You see getting him ready on time as a way to prevent you from getting the heat for him.

    Client: Yes.

21. *Counselor:* How do you usually feel after these incidents in the morning are over?

    Client: Well, it upsets me.

22. *Counselor:* OK, you feel upset. Do these feelings seem to make you want to continue or to stop helping Freddie?

    Client: Probably to stop. I get worn out. Also, sometimes I don't get my work done then.

23. *Counselor:* So helping Freddie so he won't be late and you won't be blamed sort of makes you want to keep on helping him. Yet when you feel upset and worn out afterward, you're tempted to stop helping. Is this right?

    Client: I guess that could be true.

24. *Counselor:* Gee, I imagine that all the responsibility for a 10-year-old boy would start to feel like a pretty heavy burden after a while. Would it be right to say that it seems like you feel very responsible for Freddie and his behavior?

    Client: Yeah. I guess a lot of the time I do.

25. *Counselor:* Those may be feelings we'll want to talk about more. I'm also wondering whether there are any other things in your life causing you any difficulty now?

    Client: No, this is about it.

26. *Counselor:* Ms. Weare, we've been talking a lot about some problem situations you've had with Freddie. Could you tell me about some times when the two of you get along OK?

    Client: Well, on weekends we do. Freddie dresses himself whenever he gets up. I sleep later.

27. *Counselor:* What happens on weekends when the two of you get along better?

    Client: Sometimes I'll take him to a movie or a

(continued)

LEARNING ACTIVITIES #25: INTERVIEW ASSESSMENT (continued)

game. And we eat all our meals together. Usually weekends are pleasant. He can be a good boy and I don't scream all the time at him.

28. *Counselor:* So you realize it is possible for the two of you to get along. How do you feel about my talking with Freddie and then with both of you together?
Client: That's OK.

II. To incorporate the interview leads into your verbal repertoire. We suggest that you try a role-play interview of the case of Ms. Weare (Chapter 7) or the case of Mr. Brown (Chapter 7) with a triad. One person can take the role of the client (Ms. Weare or Mr. Brown), another can be the counselor. Your task is to assess the client's concerns using the interview leads described in this chapter. The third person can be the observer, providing feedback to the counselor during

or following the role-play, using the Interview Checklist at the end of the chapter as a guide.

III. A 40-year-old married woman with two young children complains of listlessness, fatigue, and depression. You also discover that she has become dependent on sleeping pills in order to go to sleep at night. She says that if she does not take the pills, she lies awake at night and so many thoughts and worries run through her head that she cannot go to sleep for several hours. Outline in writing the kinds of information you would seek from her during an assessment interview. An example is given to start with.

Example
Range of problems: Are there any other problems not reported, such as problems with her children, marital stress, or boredom?

◾

☐ NOTES AND RECORD KEEPING

Generally, some form of written record is started from the time the client requests an appointment. Identifying data about the client are recorded initially, as well as appointment times, cancellations, and so on. The intake or initial history-taking session is recorded next. In writing up an intake or history, it is important to avoid labels, jargon, and inferences. If records were subpoenaed, such statements could appear inflammatory or slanderous. Be as specific as possible. Don't make evaluative statements or clinical judgments without supporting documentation. For example, instead of writing "This client is homicidal," you might write "This client reports engaging in frequent (at least twice daily) fantasies of killing an unidentified or anonymous victim," or instead of "The client is disoriented," consider "The client could not remember where he was, why he was here, what day it was, and how old he was."

It is also important to keep notes of subsequent treatment sessions and of client progress. These can be recorded on a standardized form such as the Individualized Client Treatment Plan (Table 8.3) or in narrative form. Generally, treatment notes are brief and highlight only the major activities of each session and client progress and improvement (or lack of it). These notes are usually started during intakes, with additional information added from the assessment interview(s). As therapy progresses, notations about goals, intervention strategies, and client progress are also included. Again,

TABLE 8-3. Individualized client treatment plan

Client's name _____

Date _____

DSM-III-R diagnosis
   Axis I _____
   Axis II _____
   Axis III _____
   Axis IV _____
   Axis V _____

Identified problems
   1. _____
   2. _____
   3. _____
   4. _____
   5. _____

Problem antecedents
   P1[a] _____
   P2 _____
   P3 _____
   P4 _____
   P5 _____

Problem consequences
   P1 _____
   P2 _____
   P3 _____
   P4 _____
   P5 _____

Treatment goals
   P1 _____
   P2 _____
   P3 _____
   P4 _____
   P5 _____

TABLE 8-3. (continued)

Intervention strategies and treatment modalities
    P1 _____
    P2 _____
    P3 _____
    P4 _____
    P5 _____
Evaluation
    A. Expected length of treatment _____
    B. Method of assessing treatment process _____
    _____
    C. Method of assessing goals or treatment outcomes
    _____
    _____

[a] *P* stands for problem; *P1* refers to #1 under "Identified problems," *P2* to #2, and so on.
Adapted from a form developed by Albert Scott and Karen Scott. Reprinted by permission of authors.

labels and inferences should always be avoided in written notes and records.

It is also important to document in detail anything that has ethical or legal implications, particularly facts about case management. For example, with a client who reports depression and suicidal fantasies, it would be important to note that you conducted a suicide assessment and what its results were, that you consulted with your supervisor, and whether you did anything else to manage the case differently, such as seeing the client more frequently or setting up a contract with the client.

☐ CLIENT SELF-MONITORING ASSESSMENT

The data given by the client in the interview can be supplemented by client self-monitoring outside the interview. Self-monitoring can be defined as the process of observing specific things about oneself and one's interaction with others and the environment. In using self-monitoring as a problem assessment tool, the client is asked to record her or his observations in writing. These written recordings can be entered on a log (Schwartz & Goldiamond, 1975) or a daily record sheet.

One purpose of client self-monitoring is to help the counselor and client gain information about what actually occurs with respect to the problem in real-life settings. Another purpose is to validate the accuracy of the client's oral reports during the interviews. As Linehan (1977, p. 45) points out, sometimes the client's interview description is not a complete report of the events that occur, or the

way the client describes the events differs from the way the client actually experiences them. Client self-monitoring of problem situations and behaviors outside the interview should add more accuracy and specificity to the information discussed in the interview. As a result, client self-monitoring may accelerate treatment and enhance the client's expectations for change (Shelton & Ackerman, 1974, p. 7). Self-monitoring is also a useful way to test out hunches about the problem and to identify relations between classes of events such as thoughts, feelings, and behaviors (Hollon & Kendall, 1981).

As we mentioned earlier, a client can record observations on some type of written record, or log. Two types of logs can be used for different observations a client might make during problem definition. A *descriptive log* can be used to record data about identification and selection of problem concerns. A *behavior log* can be used to record information about the problem behaviors and their antecedents and consequences or the relation between these classes of events related to the problem.

Descriptive Logs

In an initial session with a client, a simple descriptive or exploratory log can be introduced to find out what is going on with the client, where, and when (Schwartz & Goldiamond, 1975). Such a descriptive log could be set up as shown in Figure 8-1. The descriptive log is extremely useful when the client has difficulty identifying problem concerns or pinpointing problem situations. However, once the problem concerns have been identified and selected, a counselor and client may find that a behavior log is helpful as an interview adjunct for defining the ABCs of the problem.

Behavior Logs

The ABCs of a problem situation and the intensity of the problem can be clarified with client self-monitoring of the problem behaviors, the contributing conditions, and the frequency or duration of the problem behavior. All this information can be recorded in a behavior log, which is simply an extension of the descriptive log. Figure 8-2 is an example of a behavior log for our client Joan.

The client is also asked to observe and record how long (duration) or how often (frequency) the problem behaviors occur. Determining the level of the present problem serves as a baseline—that is, the rate or level of the problem *before* any counsel-

Page _____ of _____

DAILY RECORD SHEET

Date	Time	Place	Activity	People	Observed behavior

Figure 8-1. A descriptive log

ing interventions have been started. The baseline is useful initially in helping establish the direction and level of change desired by the client. This information, as you will see in Chapter 9, is essential in establishing client goals. And as counseling progresses, these baseline data may help the client compare progress during and near the end of counseling with progress at the beginning of counseling (see Chapter 10).

In a behavior log, the defined problem behaviors are listed at the left. The client records the date, time, and place when these behaviors occur. To record contributing conditions, the client is asked to write down the behaviors and events that occur before and after the problem behaviors. This information helps to establish a pattern among the problem behaviors, things that cue or elicit the problem behaviors, and activities that maintain, strengthen, or weaken those behaviors.

Uses of Logs

The success of written logs may depend on the client's motivation to keep a log as well as on the instructions and training given to the client about the log. Five guidelines may increase the client's motivation to engage in self-monitoring:

1. Establish a rationale for the log, such as "We need a written record in order to find out what is going on. This will help us make some decisions about the best way to handle your problem." A client is more likely to keep a log if he or she is aware of a purpose for doing so.

2. Provide specific, detailed instructions regarding how to keep the log. The client should be told *what, how, when,* and for *how long* to record. The client should be given an example of a model log to see how it may look. Providing adequate instructions may increase the likelihood that the client will record data consistently and accurately.

3. Adapt the type of log to the client's ability to do self-monitoring. At first, you may need to start with a very simple log that does not require a great deal of recording. Gradually, you can increase the amount of information the client observes and records. If a client has trouble keeping a written log, a substitute can be used, such as a tape recorder, golf wrist counter, or, for children, gold stars or pictures. Schwartz and Goldiamond (1975, p. 106) point out that even clients who seem "out of contact" with themselves are able to keep a log if they are not overwhelmed with entries and if attention to their entries is given promptly.

4. Adapt the log and the instructions to the client's problem and degree and type of pathology, if present. Recent evidence suggests that clients exhibiting certain types of problems appear to experience predictable types of problems in implementing self-monitoring, particularly of covert, or cognitive, events (Bemis, 1980). Hollon and Kendall (1981, pp. 350–351) summarize some of these reactions:

> Depressed clients either frequently report being overwhelmed by what seems to be an unmanageable task and/or fail to initiate or maintain monitoring because they do not anticipate that it can provide any help. Anxious clients (e.g., Beck & Emery, 1979) frequently avoid attending to cognitions because doing so seems to increase distress. Anorexic clients rarely report effects, per se. Rather, they list strings of inferential descriptions when asked to record how they feel. If asked to evaluate the validity of their beliefs, they are likely to respond with moralistic prescriptions, reminiscent of "New Year's resolutions" (Bemis, 1980). Obsessive clients, as might be expected, rarely get beyond listing their thoughts—frequently working long and hard to get it just "right."*

* From "*In vivo* assessment techniques for cognitive-behavioral processes" by S. D. Hollon and P. C. Kendall. In *Assessment Strategies for Cognitive-Behavioral Interventions* by P. C. Kendall and S. D. Hollon (Eds.). Copyright © 1981 by Academic Press. Reprinted by permission.

For Joan _____

Week of Nov. 6–13 _____

(Problem behaviors) Behavior observing	Date	Time	Place	(Frequency/ duration) Number or amount	(Antecedents) What precedes behavior	(Consequences) What follows behavior
1. Thinking of self as not as smart as other students	Mon., Nov. 6	10:00 A.M.	Math class	IIII	Going into class, know have to take test in class	Leaving class, being with friends
	Tues., Nov. 7	10:15 A.M.	Math class	IIII IIII	Got test back with a B	Teacher consoled me
	Tues., Nov. 7	5:30 P.M.	Home	IIII II	Parents asked about test. Told me to stay home this weekend	Went to bed
	Thurs., Nov. 9	9:30 A.M.	English class	II	Thought about having to go to math class	Got to math class. Had substitute teacher
	Sun., Nov. 12	8:30 P.M.	Home	III	Thought about school tomorrow	Went to bed
2. a. Not volunteering answers	Tues., Nov. 7	10:05 A.M. 10:20	Math class	II	Felt dumb	Nothing
b. Not answering teacher questions	Thurs., Nov. 9	10:10 A.M. 10:20 10:40	Math class	III	Felt dumb	Nothing
c. Not going to board	Thurs., Nov. 9	10:30 A.M.	Math class	I	Teacher called on me	Nothing
	Fri., Nov. 10	10:10 A.M. 10:35 A.M.	Math class	II	Teacher called on me	Nothing
	Thurs., Nov. 9	10:45 A.M.	Math class	I	Didn't have a substitute teacher	Nothing
	Fri., Nov. 10	10:15 A.M.	Math class	I	Teacher asked girls to go up to board	Teacher talked to me after class
3. Cutting class	Wed., Nov. 8	9:55 A.M.	School	1 hour	Didn't want to hassle class or think about test	Cut class. Played sick. Went to nurse's office for an hour

Figure 8-2. *Example of behavior log*

FEEDBACK #25: INTERVIEW ASSESSMENT

I. Identifications of the responses in the dialogue between Ms. Weare and the counselor are as follows:

1. Open-ended question (probe)
2. Clarification response
3. Open-ended question (probe)
4. Summarization response
5. Paraphrase response and problem behavior lead: exploration of context
6. Problem behavior lead: exploration of context
7. Paraphrase response and problem behavior lead: exploration of overt behavior
8. Reflection-of-feeling response and problem behavior lead: exploration of affect
9. Problem behavior lead: exploration of overt behavior
10. Problem behavior lead: exploration of overt behavior
11. Paraphrase and problem behavior lead: exploration of context
12. Antecedent lead: context
13. Clarification response
14. Summarization response and antecedent lead: affect
15. Problem behavior lead: exploration of cognitions
16. Paraphrase and probe responses
17. Consequences: overt behavior
18. Consequences: secondary gains for Freddie
19. Consequences: secondary gains for Ms. Weare
20. Summarization response and exploration of secondary gains for Ms. Weare
21. Consequences: affect
22. Consequences: affect
23. Summarization (of consequences)
24. Reflection-of-feeling and interpretation responses
25. Range-of-problems lead
26. Coping skills
27. Coping skills
28. Paraphrase and open-ended question

III. In addition to range and prioritization of problems, pertinent information to seek includes the following:

1. *Description of problem behaviors* — listlessness, fatigue, depression, insomnia:
   a. *Feelings* associated with each
   b. *Body sensations* and/or *physiological responses*, illness, and so on associated with each
   c. *Behavioral reactions/patterns* associated with each
   d. *Cognitions* — thoughts, self-talk, belief systems associated with each
   e. *Times and places* when these problems occur
   f. *People* connected with these problems
2. *Antecedent sources* that set off the listlessness, fatigue, depression, insomnia — including feelings, body sensations, and physiological responses, behavioral reactions and patterns, cognitions, self-talk, times and places, and people.
3. *Consequences* that influence the listlessness, fatigue, depression, and insomnia — and ways in which they influence these behaviors. Potential sources of consequences to "check out" include feelings, body sensations and physiological responses, behavioral reactions/patterns, thoughts, beliefs, self-talk, times, situations, and reactions from other people.
4. *Secondary gains* that client may be receiving from reported symptoms, such as undivided attention from spouse and avoidance of child care or household duties.
5. *Previous solutions* — explore what, if anything, client has done to solve these concerns and the effects the solutions have had on the symptoms.
6. *Coping skills* — times when the client does not feel fatigued and depressed and what is different at these times. In addition, behavioral and cognitive assets and coping skills of client that might be applied to problems — that is, things client does or thinks about that are effective rather than self-defeating. Also explore degree to which client typically engages in self-reliant and self-directed behavior.
7. *Client's perceptions of problems* — find out how client explains these symptoms to herself; ask her to summarize her main issue in one word.
8. *Intensity of problem* — frequency, duration, severity; explore how often these symptoms occur, how long they last, and how severe they are. Determine to what degree they affect the client's level of daily functioning.

5. Involve the client in discussing and analyzing the log within the interview. At first, the counselor can begin by putting together "hunches" about

patterns of problem behavior and contributing conditions. As counseling progresses, the client can take a more active role in analyzing the log. Increasing the client's involvement in analyzing the log should serve as an incentive to the client to continue the time and effort required to collect the data.

The counselor should remember that the process of client self-monitoring can be reactive. In other words, the very act of observing oneself can influence that which is being observed. This reactivity may affect the data reflected in the log. Reactivity can be helpful in the overall counseling program when it changes the behavior in the desired direction. There are times when self-monitoring is used deliberately as a change strategy to increase or decrease a particular behavior (see Chapter 19).

Occasionally, when self-monitoring is used as an assessment tool, reactivity may cause an aspect of the problem behavior to get worse. This seems especially true when the client is monitoring negative affect, such as anxiety, anger, or depression (Hollon & Kendall, 1981). In such instances, sometimes the self-monitoring becomes a signal for the mood state, causing it to increase in frequency or intensity. If this happens, the use of self-monitoring as an *assessment* device should be discontinued, although using it as a change strategy and changing what and how the client self-records may create reactivity in the desired direction (see also Chapter 19).

The data obtained from client self-monitoring are used not only during the assessment process but also in establishing client goals. During assessment sessions, the self-monitoring data will help the client and counselor to determine the ABCs of the problem. The baseline data will be the starting place for the discussion of desired counseling outcomes (see Chapter 9).

for clients in crisis or for practitioners in high-demand, high-caseload work settings. Regardless of the type of clients with whom you work or your work setting, we encourage you to view the assessment phase of counseling with healthy respect. Skipping or glossing over assessment can actually result in longer treatment and end up costing more of your time and of the client's money. Epstein and Bishop (1981) observe that a thorough assessment usually results in a more active and shorter course of treatment by eliminating a lot of guesswork. Epstein and Bishop (1981) also observe that thorough assessment seems to prevent client dropout from therapy.

Occasionally, even after a thorough assessment period, you may still feel that there are chunks of missing information or pieces to the puzzle. It is difficult to know whether additional assessment strategies are warranted in terms of time and cost and, most important, whether they will contribute to the effectiveness of treatment for this client. At this point, the counselor must make a deliberate therapeutic decision—to conduct additional assessments or to begin intervention strategies and work on what is known about the client. Fensterheim (1983) suggests three key questions to consider before making this decision:

1. Is enough information present to make a start on treatment?
2. How urgent is the need for immediate relief?
3. How pessimistic and despondent is the patient?

We would like to conclude this chapter with one caution: above all, remember that assessment is not an end in itself! The time, structure, and tools you use for assessment are of little value unless assessment has sufficient "treatment validity" (Nelson, 1983) or contributes to greater effectiveness of therapy treatment and outcome for clients.

□ WHEN IS "ENOUGH" ASSESSMENT ENOUGH?

Occasionally people will wonder whether assessment goes on forever—or when it stops! As we mentioned earlier, assessment is something of a continuous process during therapy, in that clients are people and can't—or shouldn't—be pigeonholed, and occasionally problems are shifted and redefined.

Shorter assessment periods are often necessary

□ SUMMARY

This chapter focused on the use of direct interviewing to assess client concerns. In many settings, initial assessment interviews often begin with an intake interview to gather information about the client's presenting problems and primary symptoms as well as information about such areas as previous counseling, social/developmental history, educational/vocational history, health history, and family, marital, and sexual history. This interview often yields information that the counselor can use to develop hypotheses about the nature of the client's problems. History interviews also serve as a retrospective baseline of how the client was functioning before and what events contributed to the present difficulties and coping styles. For occasional clients, intakes or history interviews may be followed by a mental-status exam, which aids the therapist in assessing the client's psychiatric status.

The model presented in this chapter for direct assessment interviewing is based on the ABC model described in Chapter 7. Specifically, counselors are interested in defining six components of problem behavior—affective, somatic, behavioral, cognitive, contextual, and relational. They also seek to identify antecedent events that occur before the problem and cue it and consequent events that follow the problem and in some way influence it or maintain it. Consequences may include "payoffs," or secondary gains, which give value to the dysfunctional behavior and thus keep the problem going. Antecedent and consequent sources may also be affective, somatic, behavioral, cognitive, contextual, and relational. Other important components of direct assessment interviewing include identifying previous solutions the client has tried for resolving the problem, exploring client coping skills and assets, exploring the client's perceptions of the issue, and identifying the frequency, duration, or severity of the problem.

In addition to direct assessment interviewing, other assessment tools include role playing, imagery, self-report measures, and self-monitoring. All these techniques can be useful for obtaining more specific information about the identified problems.

POSTEVALUATION

PART ONE

A client is referred to you with a presenting problem of "free-floating," or generalized (pervasive), anxiety. Outline the questions you would ask during an assessment interview with this client that pertain directly to her presenting component. Your objective (Objective One) is to identify at least 2 questions for each of the 11 problem assessment categories described in this chapter and summarized in Table 8-2. Feedback follows the postevaluation.

PART TWO

Using the description of the above client, conduct a 30-minute role-play assessment interview in which your objective is to demonstrate leads and responses associated with at least 9 out of the 11 categories described for problem assessment (Chapter Objective Two). You can do this activity in triads in which one person assumes the role of counselor, another the "anxious" client, and the third person the role of observer; trade roles two times. If groups are not available, audiotape or videotape your interview. Use the Interview Checklist at the end of the chapter as a guide to assess your performance and to obtain feedback.

After completing your interview, develop some hypotheses, or hunches, about the client. In particular, try to develop "guesses" about—

1. Antecedent sources that cue or set off the anxiety, making its occurrence more likely.

2. Consequences that maintain the anxiety, keep it going, or make it worse.

3. Consequences that diminish or weaken the anxiety.

4. Secondary gains, or "payoffs," attached to the anxiety.

5. Ways in which the client's "previous solutions" may contribute to the anxiety or make it worse.

6. Particular strengths, resources, and coping skills of the client and how these might be best used during treatment/intervention.

You may wish to continue this part of the activity in triads or to do it alone, jotting down ideas as you proceed. At some point, it may be helpful to share your ideas with your group or your instructor.

PART THREE

Devise a self-monitoring assessment procedure you could give to this client for homework, to obtain information about the time, place, frequency, duration, and severity of her anxious feelings. Write an example of a log you could give to her to obtain this information (Chapter Objective Three).

PART FOUR

Conduct a role-play interview with this client in which you assign the self-monitoring plan you devised as homework (Chapter Objective Four).

(continued)

1. Provide a *rationale* to the client about the usefulness of the assignment.
2. Provide the client with detailed *instructions* about *what, how, when,* and for *how long* to monitor.
3. Follow-up — clarify and check out the client's understanding of your assignment.

If possible, continue with this activity in your triads and obtain feedback from the observer on the specificity and clarity of your instructions. If an observer is not available, tape your interview for self-assessment of its playback.

INTERVIEW CHECKLIST FOR ASSESSING CLIENT PROBLEMS

Scoring		Category of information	Examples of counselor leads or responses	Client response
Yes	No			
____	____	1. Explain purpose of assessment interview	"I am going to be asking you more questions than usual so that we can get an idea of what is going on. Getting an accurate picture about your concern (or problem) will help us to decide what we can do about it. Your input is important."	____(check if client confirmed understanding of purpose)
____	____	2. Identify range of concerns and/or problems (if you don't have this information from history)	"What would you like to talk about today?" "How would you describe the things that are really bothering you now?" "What are some things that bug you?" "What specifically led you to come to see someone now?" "What things are not going well for you?" "Are there any other issues you haven't mentioned?"	____(check if client described additional concerns)
____	____	3. Prioritize and select primary or most immediate problem to work on	"What issue best represents the reason you are here?" "Of all these concerns, which one is most stressful (or painful) for you?" "Rank-order these concerns, starting with the one that is most important for you to resolve to the one least important." "Tell me which of these problems you believe you could learn to deal with most easily and with the most success." "Which one of the things we discussed do you see as having the best chance of being solved?" "Out of all the problems we've discussed, describe the one that, when resolved, would have the greatest impact on the rest of the issues."	____(check if client selected problem to focus on)
____	____	4.0. Present problem-behavior		____(check if client identified the following components of problem)
		4.1. Affective aspects of problem: feelings, emotions, mood states	"What are you feeling when this happens?" "How does this make you feel when this occurs?" "What other feelings do you have when this occurs?" "What feelings is this problem hiding or covering up?"	____(check if client identified feelings) (continued)

POSTEVALUATION (continued)

Scoring	Category of information	Examples of counselor leads or responses	Client response
____ ____	4.2. *Somatic* aspects of problem: body sensations, physiological responses, organic dysfunction and illness, medications	"What goes on inside you then?" "What do you notice in your body when this happens?" "What are you aware of when this happens?" "When this happens, are you aware of anything that goes on in your body that feels bad or uncomfortable—aches, pains, and so on?"	____(check if client identified body sensations)
____ ____	4.3. *Behavioral* aspects of problem: overt behaviors/actions (excesses and deficits)	"In photographing this scene, what actions and dialogue would the camera pick up?" "What are you doing when this occurs?" "What do you mean by 'not communicating'?" "Describe what you did the last few times this occurred."	____(check if client identified overt behavior)
____ ____	4.4. *Cognitive* aspects of problem: automatic, helpful, unhelpful, rational, irrational thoughts and beliefs; internal dialogue; perceptions and misperceptions	"What do you say to yourself when this happens?" "What are you usually thinking about during this problem?" "What was going through your mind then?" "What kinds of thoughts can make you feel ____ ?" "What beliefs [or images] do you hold that affect this issue?" Sentence completions: I should ____, people should ____, it would be awful if ____, ____ makes me feel bad.	____(check if client identified thoughts, beliefs)
____ ____	4.5. *Contextual* aspects of problem: time, place, or setting events	"Describe some recent situations in which the problem occurred. Where were you? When was it?" "When does this usually occur?" "Where does this usually occur?" "Does this go on all the time or only sometimes?" "Does the same thing happen at other times or places?" "At what time does this *not* occur? places? situations?" "Do you have any affiliation with a cultural or ethnic group, and if so, how do the values of this group affect this issue?"	____(check if client identified time, places, other events)
____ ____	4.6. *Relational* aspects of problem: other people	"What effects does this problem have on significant others in your life?" "What effects do significant others have on this problem?" "Who else is involved in the problem? How?"	____(check if client identified people)

(continued)

Scoring	Category of information	Examples of counselor leads or responses	Client response
		"From whom do you think you learned to act or react this way?" "How many significant close relationships do you have in your life now?" "Whom do you know and respect who handles the issue the way you would like to?" "What persons *present* in your life now have the greatest positive impact on this problem? negative impact?" "What about persons *absent* from your life?"	
___ ___	5.0. Antecedents—past or current conditions that cue, or set off, the problem		___(check if client identified following antecedent sources)
___ ___	5.1. *Affective* antecedents	"What are you usually feeling before this?" "When do you recall the first time you felt this way?" "What are the feelings that occur before the problem and make it more likely to happen? less likely?" "Are there any holdover or unfinished feelings from past events in your life that still affect this problem? How?"	___(feelings, mood states)
___ ___	5.2. *Somatic* antecedents	"What goes on inside you just before this happens?" "Are you aware of any particular sensations or discomfort just before the problem occurs or gets worse?" "Are there any body sensations that seem to occur before the problem or when it starts that make it more likely to occur? less likely?" "Is there anything going on with you physically—like illness or a physical condition or in the way you eat or drink—that leads up to this problem?"	___(body sensations, physiological responses)
___ ___	5.3. *Behavioral* antecedents	"If I were photographing this, what actions and dialogue would I pick up before this happens?" "Can you identify any particular behavior patterns that occur right before this happens?" "What do you typically do before this happens?"	___(overt behavior)
___ ___	5.4. *Cognitive* antecedents	"What kinds of pictures do you have before this happens?" "What are your thoughts before this happens?"	___(thoughts, beliefs, internal dialogue)

(continued)

POSTEVALUATION (continued)

Scoring	Category of information	Examples of counselor leads or responses	Client response
		"What are you telling yourself before this happens?" "Can you identify any particular beliefs that seem to set the problem off?" "What do you think about [or tell yourself] before the problem occurs that makes it more likely to happen? less likely?"	
___ ___	5.5. *Contextual* antecedents	"How long ago did this happen?" "Has this ever occurred at any other time in your life? If so, describe that." "Where and when did this occur the first time?" "How do you see those events as related to your problem?" "What things happened that seemed to lead up to this?" "What was happening in your life when you first noticed the problem?" "Are there any ways in which your cultural values and affiliations set off this problem? make it more likely to occur? less likely?" "How were things different before you had this concern?" "What do you mean, this started 'recently'?"	___(time, places, other events)
___ ___	5.6. *Relational* antecedents	"Are there any people or relationships from past events in your life that still affect this problem? How?" "Can you identify any particular people that seem to bring on this problem?" "Are you usually with certain people right before or when this problem starts?" "Are there any people or relationships from the past that trigger this issue in some way? Who? How?"	___(other people)
___ ___	6.0. Identify consequences— conditions that maintain and strengthen problem or weaken or diminish it		___(check if client identified following sources of consequences)
___ ___	6.1. *Affective* consequences	"How do you feel after this happens?" "How does this affect the problem?" "When did you stop feeling this way?" "Are you aware of any particular feelings or reactions you have after the problem that strengthen it? weaken it?"	___(feelings, mood states)

(continued)

Scoring	Category of information	Examples of counselor leads or responses	Client response
—— ——	6.2. *Somatic* consequences	"What are you aware of inside you — sensations in your body — just after this happens?" "How does this affect the problem?" "Are there any sensations inside you that seem to occur after the problem that strengthen or weaken it?" "Is there any physical condition, illness, and so on about yourself that seems to occur after this problem? If so, how does it affect the problem?"	——(body or internal sensations)
—— ——	6.3. *Behavioral* consequences	"What do you do after this happens, and how does this make the problem better? worse?" "How do you usually react after this is over?" "In what ways does your reaction keep the problem going? weaken it or stop it?" "Can you identify any particular behavior patterns that occur after this?" "How do these patterns keep the problem going? stop it?"	——(overt responses)
—— ——	6.4. *Cognitive* consequences	"What do you usually think about afterward?" "How does this affect the problem?" "What do you picture after this happens?" "What do you tell yourself after this occurs?" "Can you identify any particular thoughts [beliefs, self-talk] that make the problem better? worse?" "Are there certain thoughts or images you have afterward that either strengthen or weaken the problem?"	——(thoughts, beliefs, internal dialogue)
—— ——	6.5. *Contextual* consequences	"When does this problem usually stop or go away? get worse? get better?" "Where are you when the problem stops? gets worse? gets better?" "Can you identify any particular times, places, or events that seem to keep the problem going? make it worse or better?" "Are there any ways in which your cultural affiliation and values seem to keep this problem going? stop it or weaken it?"	——(time, places, other events)
—— ——	6.6. *Relational* consequences	"Can you identify any particular reactions from other people that occur following the problem?" "In what ways do their reactions affect the problem?" "Are you usually with certain people when the problem gets worse? better?"	——(other people)

(continued)

POSTEVALUATION (continued)

Scoring	Category of information	Examples of counselor leads or responses	Client response
		"Can you identify any particular people who can make the problem worse? better? stop it? keep it going?"	
___ ___	7. Identify possible secondary gains from problem	"What happened afterward that was pleasant?" "What was unpleasant about what happened?" "Has your concern or problem ever produced any special advantages or considerations for you?" "As a consequence of your concern, have you got out of or avoided things or events?" "How does this problem help you?" "What do you get out of this situation that you don't get out of other situations?" "Do you notice anything that happens afterward that you try to prolong or to produce?" "Do you notice anything that occurs after the problem that you try to stop or avoid?" "Are there certain feelings or thoughts that go on after the problem that you try to prolong?" "Are there certain feelings or thoughts that go on after the problem that you try to stop or avoid?" "The good thing about ____ [problem] is . . . ."	___(check if client identified payoffs)
___ ___	8. Identify solutions already tried to solve the problem	"How have you dealt with this or other problems before? What was the effect? What made it work or not work?" "How have you tried to resolve this problem?" "What kinds of things have you done to improve this situation?" "What have you done that has made the problem better? worse? kept it the same?" "What have others done to help you with this?"	___(check if client identified prior solutions)
___ ___	9. Identify client coping skills, strengths, resources	"What skills or things do you have going for you that might help you with this concern?" "Describe a situation when this concern or problem is not interfering." "What strengths or assets can you use to help resolve this problem?" "When don't you act this way?" "What kinds of thoughts or self-talk help you handle this better?"	___(check if client identified assets, coping skills)

(continued)

Scoring	Category of information	Examples of counselor leads or responses	Client response
		"When don't you think in self-defeating ways?" "What do you say to yourself to cope with a difficult situation?" "Identify the steps you take in a situation you handle well—what do you think about and what do you do? How could these steps be applied to the present problem?" "To what extent can you do something for yourself without relying on someone else to push you or prod you to do it?" "How often do you get things done by rewarding yourself in some way? by punishing yourself?"	
___ ___	10. Identify client's description/assessment of the problem (note which aspects of problem are stressed and which are ignored)	"What is your understanding of this issue?" "How do you explain this problem to yourself?" "What does the problem mean to you?" "What is your interpretation [analysis] of the problem?" "What else is important to you about the problem that we haven't mentioned?" "Sum up the problem in just one word." "Give the problem a title."	___(check if client explained problem)
___ ___	11. Estimate frequency, duration, or severity of problem behavior/symptoms (assign monitoring homework, if useful)	"How often [how much] does this occur during a day—a week?" "How long does this feeling stay with you?" "How many times do you ___ a day? a week?" "To what extent has this problem interfered with your life? How?" "You say sometimes you feel very anxious. On a scale from 1 to 10, with 1 being very calm and 10 being very anxious, where would you put your feelings?" "How has this interfered with other areas of your life?" "What would happen if the problem were not resolved in a year?"	___(check if client estimated amount or severity of problem)

Yes	No	Other skills
___	___	12. The counselor listened attentively and recalled accurately the information given by the client.
___	___	13. The counselor used basic listening responses to clarify and synthesize the information shared by the client.
___	___	14. The counselor followed the client's lead in determining the sequence or order of the information obtained.

Observer comments _____

_____
_____
_____
_____ ■

□ SUGGESTED READINGS

Cautela, J. R. (1977). *Behavior analysis forms for clinical intervention.* Champaign, IL: Research Press.

Cautela, J. R. (1981). *Behavior analysis forms for clinical intervention* (Vol. 2). Champaign, IL: Research Press.

Duley, S. M., Cancelli, A. A., Kratochwill, T. R., Bergan, J. R., & Meredith, K. E. (1983). Training and generalization of motivational analysis interview assessment skills. *Behavioral Assessment, 5,* 281–293.

Epstein, N. B., & Bishop, D. S. (1981). Problem-centered systems therapy of the family. *Journal of Marital and Family Therapy, 7,* 23–31.

Goldfried, M. R. (1982). Behavioral assessment: An overview. In A. S. Bellack, M. Hersen, & A. E. Kazdin (Eds.), *International handbook of behavior modification and therapy.* New York: Plenum.

Haynes, S. N., Jensen, B. J., Wise, E., & Sherman, D. (1981). The marital intake interview: A multimethod criterion validity assessment. *Journal of Consulting and Clinical Psychology, 49,* 379–387.

Haynes, S. N., & Wilson, C. C. (1979). *Behavioral assessment.* San Francisco: Jossey-Bass.

Keane, T. M., Black, J. L., Collins, F. L., Jr., & Vensen, M. C. (1982). A skills training program for teaching the behavioral interview. *Behavioral Assessment, 4,* 53–62.

Lazarus, A. A. (1978). Multimodal behavior therapy (Part 3). In E. Shostrom (Ed.), *Three approaches to psychotherapy II* [16-mm film or ¾" videocassette]. Orange, CA: Psychological Films.

Morganstern, K. P. (1988). Behavioral interviewing. In A. S. Bellack & M. Hersen (Eds.). *Behavioral assessment: A practical handbook* (3rd ed.) (pp. 86–118). New York: Pergamon Press.

Nay, W. R. (1979). *Multimethod clinical assessment.* New York: Gardner Press.

Nelson, R. O., & Barlow, D. H. (1981). Behavioral assessment: Basic strategies and initial procedures. In D. H. Barlow (Ed.), *Behavioral assessment of adult disorders.* New York: Guilford Press.

FEEDBACK: POSTEVALUATION

PART ONE

See whether the questions you generated are similar to the following ones:

Is this the only issue you're concerned about now in your life, or are there other issues you haven't mentioned yet? (Range of problems)

When you say you feel anxious, what exactly do you mean? (Problem behavior—affective component)

When you feel anxious, what do you experience inside your body? (problem behavior—somatic component)

When you feel anxious, what exactly are you usually doing? (problem behavior—behavioral component)

When you feel anxious, what are you typically thinking about [or saying to yourself]? (Problem behavior—cognitive component)

Try to pinpoint exactly what times the anxiety occurs or when it is worse. (Problem behavior—contextual component)

Describe where you are or in what situations you find yourself when you get anxious. (Problem behavior—contextual component)

Describe what other things are usually going on when you have these feelings. (Problem behavior—contextual component)

Can you tell me what persons are usually around when you feel this way? (Problem behavior—relational component)

Are there any feelings that lead up to this? (Antecedent source—affective)

What about body sensations that might occur right before these feelings? (Antecedent source—somatic)

Have you noticed any particular behavioral reactions or patterns that seem to occur right before these feelings? (Antecedent source—behavioral)

Are there any kinds of thoughts—things you're dwelling on—that seem to lead up to these feelings? (Antecedent source—cognitive)

When was the first time you noticed these feelings? where were you? (Antecedent source—contextual)

Can you recall any other events or times that seem to be related to these feelings? (Antecedent source—contextual)

Does the presence of any particular people in any way set these feelings off? (Antecedent source—relational)

Are you aware of any particular other feelings that make the anxiety better or worse? (Consequence source—affective)

Are you aware of any body sensations or physiological responses that make these feelings better or worse? (Consequence source—somatic)

Is there anything you can do specifically to make these feelings stronger or weaker? (Consequence source—behavioral)

Can you identify anything you can think about or

focus on that seems to make these feelings better or worse? (Consequence source — cognitive)

At what times do these feelings diminish or go away? get worse? in what places? in what situations? (Consequence source — contextual)

Do certain people you know seem to react in ways that keep these feelings going or make them less intense? If so, how? (Consequence source — relational)

As a result of this anxiety, have you ever gotten out of or avoided things you dislike? (Consequence — secondary gain)

Has this problem with your nerves ever resulted in any special advantages or considerations for you? (Consequence — secondary gain)

What have you tried to do to resolve this issue? How have your attempted solutions worked out? (Previous solutions)

Describe some times and situations when you don't have these feelings or you feel calm and relaxed. What goes on that is different in these instances? (Coping skills)

How have you typically coped with other difficult situations or feelings in your life before? (Coping skills)

If you could give this problem a title — as if it were a movie or a book — what would that title be? (Client perceptions of problem)

How do you explain these feelings to yourself? (Client perceptions of problem)

How many times do these feelings crop up during a given day? (Frequency of problem)

How long do these feelings stay with you? (Duration of problem)

On a scale from 1 to 10, with 1 being not intense and 10 being very intense, how strong would you say these feelings usually are? (Severity of problem)

PART THREE

To start with, you may want to obtain information directly related to time and place of anxiety occurrence. The log might look something like this:

Date   Time   Place   Activity

The client would be asked to record anxious feelings daily. Later, you may wish to add recording of information about direction and severity. You could add these two columns to the log:

How long   Intensity (1 to 10)

Although it might be valuable to ask the client to also observe and record cognitions (thoughts, beliefs), there is some evidence that many anxious clients fail to complete this part of self-monitoring because attending to cognitions is reactive and may cue, or increase, rather than decrease, the anxiety (Hollon & Kendall, 1981).

SELECTING AND DEFINING OUTCOME GOALS

NINE

Pause for a few minutes to answer the following questions to yourself or with someone else.

1. What is one thing you would like to change about yourself?
2. Suppose you succeeded in accomplishing this change. How would things be different for you?
3. Does this outcome represent a change in yourself or for someone else?
4. How feasible is this change?
5. What are some of the risks — to you or others — of this change?
6. What would be your payoffs for making this change?
7. What would you be doing, thinking, or feeling as a result of this change you would like to make for yourself?
8. In what situations do you want to be able to do this?
9. How much or how often would you like to be able to do this?
10. Looking at where you are now and where you'd like to be, are there some steps along the way to get from here to there? If so, rank them in an ordered list from "easiest to do now" to "hardest to do."
11. Identify any obstacles (people, feelings, ideas, situations) that might interfere with attainment of your goal.
12. Identify any resources (skills, people, knowledge) that you need to use or acquire to attain your goal.
13. How could you monitor and review progress toward this outcome?

These steps reflect the process of selecting and defining goals for counseling. Goals represent desired results or outcomes and function as milestones of client progress. In this chapter we describe and model concrete guidelines you can use to help clients select and define outcome goals for counseling.

☐ OBJECTIVES

1. Identify a situation about you or your life that you would like to change. Select and define one desired outcome for this issue, using the Goal-Setting Worksheet in the postevaluation as a guide.
2. Given a list of ten hypothetical client outcome goals, discriminate, with an 80% accuracy rate, those goals that are statements of changes owned by the client, are based on realistic ideas, and are behaviorally defined from those that are not.
3. Given a written client case description, describe the steps you would use with this client to explore, select, and define desired outcome goals, with at least 11 of the 15 categories for selecting and defining goals represented in your description.
4. Demonstrate at least 11 of the 15 categories associated with selecting and defining outcome goals, given a role-play interview.

☐ PURPOSES OF GOALS

Goals have six important purposes in counseling. First, they provide some directions for counseling. Clearly defined goals reflect the areas of client concern that need most immediate attention (Hill, 1975). Establishing goals can also clarify the client's initial expectations of counseling (Smith, 1976). Goals may help both counselor and client anticipate more precisely what can and cannot be accomplished through counseling (Krumboltz, 1966).

Although each theoretical orientation has its own direction for counseling (Frey & Raming, 1979), specifying goals individually for each client helps to ensure that counseling is structured specifically to meet the needs of *that* client. Clients are much more likely to support and commit themselves to changes that they create than changes imposed by someone else. Without goals, counseling may be "directionless" or may be based more on the theoretical biases and personal preferences of the counselor (Bandura, 1969, p. 70). Some clients may go through counseling without realizing that the sessions are devoid of direction or are more consistent with the counselor's preferences than the client's needs and aims. In other aspects of our lives, however, most of us would be quite aware of analogous situations. If we boarded an airplane destined for a place of our choice, and the airplane went around in circles or the pilots announced a change of destination that they desired, we would be upset and indignant.

Second, goals permit counselors to determine whether or not they have the skills, competencies, and interest for working with a particular client toward a particular outcome. Depending on the client's choice of goals and the counselor's values and level of expertise, the counselor decides whether to continue working with the client or to refer the client to someone else who may be in a better position to give services.

Another often overlooked purpose of goals is their role in human cognition and problem solving. Taussig (1987) found that Mexican-Americans and Anglo-Americans respond similarly and positively to goal setting, even when problems must be discussed and goal setting must occur very early in the counseling process. Goals facilitate successful performance and problem resolution because they are usually rehearsed in our working memory and because they direct our attention to the resources and components in our environment that are most likely to facilitate the solution of a problem (Dixon & Glover, 1984, pp. 128–129). This purpose of goals is quite evident in the performance of successful athletes who set goals for themselves and then use the goals not only as motivating devices but also as standards against which they rehearse their performance over and over, often cognitively or with imagery. Running backs, for example, constantly "see themselves" getting the ball and running downfield, over and past the goal line. Champion skiers are often seen closing their eyes and bobbing their heads in the direction of the course before the race.

A fourth purpose of goals is to have some basis for selecting and using particular counseling strategies and interventions. The changes the client desires will, to some degree, determine the kinds of action plans and treatment strategies that can be used with some likelihood of success. Without an explicit identification of what the client wants from counseling, it is almost impossible to explain and defend one's choice to move in a certain direction or to use one or more counseling strategies. Without goals, the counselor may use a particular approach without any "rational basis" (Bandura, 1969, p. 70). Whether the approach will be helpful is left to chance rather than choice.

A fifth and most important purpose of goals is

their role in an outcome evaluation of counseling. Goals can indicate the difference between what and how much the client is able to do now and what and how much the client would like to do in the future. With the ultimate goal in mind, the counselor and client can monitor progress toward the goal and compare progress before and after a counseling intervention. These data provide continuous feedback to both counselor and client (Smith, 1976). The feedback can be used to assess the feasibility of the goal and the effectiveness of the intervention. Bandura (1969, p. 74) has summarized very aptly the role of well-defined outcomes in evaluation of counseling:

> When desired outcomes are designated in observable and measurable terms, it becomes readily apparent when the methods have succeeded, when they have failed, and when they need further development to increase their potency. This self-corrective feature is a safeguard against perpetuation of ineffective approaches, which are difficult to retire if the changes they are supposed to produce remain ambiguous.

Finally, goal-planning systems are useful because, like assessment procedures, they are often reactive; that is, clients make progress in change as a result of the goal-planning process itself. Lloyd (1983, p. 60) explains how reactivity in goal setting seems to work:

> It seems likely that therapists who help their clients set objectives may find a clearer focus for case planning and treatment and that therapists who are aware of their own goal attainment statistics may be more motivated to have their clients do well. It is also possible that clients who are aware of their own specific objectives may do better in therapy than those who are not. The more involved both therapists and clients are in the details of goal attainment procedures, the more likely is the system to be reactive.*

☐ AN OVERVIEW OF SELECTING AND DEFINING GOALS

The sequence of selecting and defining goals is shown in Figure 9-1, which represents the following steps in this process.

* This and all other quotations from this source are from "Selecting systems to measure client outcome in human service agencies" by M. E. Lloyd. *Behavioral Assessment, 5,* 55–70. Copyright © 1983 by Association for Advancement of Behavior Therapy. Reprinted by permission.

Selecting Goals

1. Explain the *purpose* of goals.
2. Ask the client to specify *positive change(s)* desired as a result of counseling.
3. Determine whether the goal selected represents changes *owned by the client.*
4. Explore whether the goal is *realistic.*
5. Identify possible *advantages* of goal attainment.
6. Identify possible *disadvantages* of goal attainment.
7. Make a *decision.* Using the information obtained about client-stated goals, select one of the following alternatives: to adopt these goals as the direction for counseling, to reconsider the client's goals, or to seek a referral.

The process of selecting goals may also involve values clarification between the client and the counselor.

Defining Goals

As illustrated in Figure 9-1, defining goals occurs after the goals have been selected and *agreed to* by both counselor and client. Defining goals includes eight steps.

1. Define the overt and covert *behaviors* associated with the goal.
2. Determine the circumstances or *conditions* of change.
3. Establish the *level* of the goal behavior or the extent to which it is to occur.
4. Identify *subgoals* or intermediate action steps.
5. *Sequence* the action steps by immediacy and degree of difficulty.
6. Identify *obstacles* that prevent goal attainment.
7. Identify necessary *resources.*
8. Review *progress.*

The counselor can facilitate the development of counseling goals by using leads in the interview that are directed toward selection and definition of goals. In this chapter we offer examples of leads for selecting and defining goals, and more can be found in the Interview Checklist at the end of the chapter. These leads are merely suggested examples. You can provide examples that are equally good or better for each category.

The areas illustrated in Figure 9-1 reflect the process of selecting and defining goals in counseling. In one of the first articles to describe counseling goals, Krumboltz (1966) suggested two basic guidelines for the goal-setting process. First, the goal should be stated for each client individually. Second, the goal should be stated in terms of visible outcomes. These two guidelines help to ensure that the process of developing counseling goals is highly individualized and that the goals will be observable.

Selecting and defining goals is a highly interactive process between the counselor and the client. The client usually determines the outcome of goals of counseling. However, the counselor's input is essential in helping the client identify the desired results of counseling in clearly defined, visible goal statements. The following section describes interview leads you can use to help clients identify and select desired outcomes for counseling.

□ INTERVIEW LEADS FOR SELECTING GOALS

Purpose of Goals

The first step in selecting goals is to give the client a *rationale* about goals. This statement should describe goals, the purpose of having them, and the client's participation in the goal-setting process. The counselor's intent is to convey the importance of having goals, as well as the importance of the client's participation in developing them. An example of what the counselor might say about the purpose of goals is "We've been talking about these two areas that bother you. It might be helpful now to discuss how you would like things to be different. We can develop some goals to work

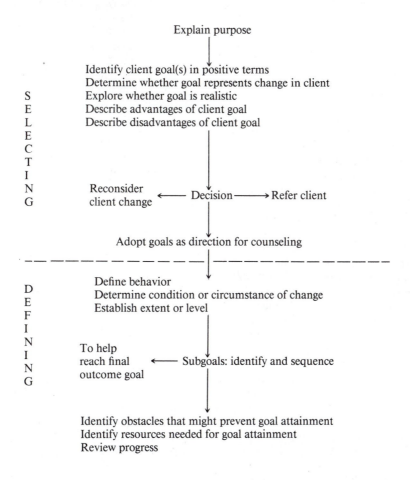

Figure 9-1. Selecting and defining goals

toward during our sessions. These goals will tell us what you want as a result of counseling. So today, let's talk about some things *you* would like to work on."

The counselor might also emphasize the role that goals play in resolving problems through attention and rehearsal. "Dean, you've been saying how stuck you feel in your marriage and yet how hopeful you feel, too. If we can identify specifically the ways that you want to relate differently, this can help you attend to the things you do that cause difficulty as well as the things you know you want to handle differently." Occasionally, offering examples of how other persons, such as athletes or dancers, use goal setting to facilitate performance may be useful to clients.

After this explanation, the counselor will look for a client response that indicates understanding. If the client seems confused, the counselor will need to explain further the purposes of goals and their benefits to the client or to clarify and explore the client's confusion.

Identifying Client Goals

What does an outcome goal represent? At the simplest level, an outcome goal represents what the client wants to happen as a result of the counseling process. Stated another way, outcome goals are an extension of the type of problem(s) the client experiences. Outcome goals represent two major classifications of problems: *choice* and *change* (Dixon & Glover, 1984). In choice problems, the client has the requisite skills and resources for problem resolution but is caught between two or more choices, often conflicting ones. In these instances, the outcome goal represents a choice or a decision the client needs to make, such as "to decide between College A and College B" or "to choose either giving up my job and having lots of free time or keeping my job and having money and stability."

In change issues, the outcome goal is a change the client wants to make. In such instances the client does not have the requisite skills and resources to solve the problem. Additionally, clients faced with change issues enter counseling with what Gottman and Leiblum (1974) call a "performance discrepancy"; in some way or in some situation, the client is performing in a manner that needs to be changed. The performance discrepancy is represented by the difference between the client's perception of current functioning and the

client's expectations of alternative ways of functioning (p. 25). The desired changes may be in overt behaviors or situations, covert behaviors, or combinations of the two. These outcome goals may be directed at eliminating something, increasing something, developing something, or restructuring something, but in all cases the change is expected to be an improvement over what currently exists (Srebalus, 1975, p. 415). Client goals based on a performance discrepancy reflect a typical definition of change cited by Srebalus as movement from one state of being to another (p. 416). This concept of change indicates a discrepancy between what the client is doing now and what the client wants to accomplish. These changes may result from developmental changes, counseling interventions, or both.

Occasionally, in addition to choice or change goals, clients want to maintain certain aspects of their life or certain behaviors at the same rate or in the same way. For example, a client may want to continue his sexual relationship with his wife (maintaining a behavior) the way it is even though he may wish to change other aspects of the relationship.

Interview leads to identify client goals. These are examples of leads the counselor can use to elicit goal statements from the client:

> "Suppose some distant relative you haven't seen for a while sees you after counseling. What would be different then from the way things are now?"
> "Assuming we are successful, what would you be doing or how would these situations change?"
> "What do you expect to accomplish as a result of counseling? Is this a choice or a change?"
> "How would you like counseling to benefit you?"
> "What do you *want* to be doing, thinking, or feeling?"

The counselor's purpose in using these sorts of leads is to have the client identify some desired outcomes of counseling. The counselor is looking for some verbal indication of the results the client expects. If the client does not know of desired changes or cannot specify a purpose for engaging in counseling, some time should be spent in exploring this area before moving on. The counselor can assist the client in selecting goals in several ways: by assigning homework ("Make a list of what you can do now and what you want to do one year from now"), by using imagery ("Imagine being someone you admire. Who would you be? What would you be doing? How would you be different?"), by additional questioning ("If you could wave a magic wand and have three wishes, what would they be?"), or by self-report questionnaires or inventories such as the Behavioral Self-Rating Checklist (BSRC) developed by Cautela and Upper (1975). This checklist asks the client which of 73 adaptive overt and covert behaviors the client needs to learn in order to function more effectively (Cautela & Upper, 1976, p. 91).

Stating the goal in positive terms.   An effective outcome goal is stated in *positive* rather than negative terms — as what the client *does* want to do, not what the client does not want to do. This is very important because of the role that goal setting plays in human cognition and performance, as mentioned earlier. When the goal is stated positively, clients are more likely to encode and rehearse the things they want to be able to *do* rather than the things they want to avoid or stop. For example, it is fairly easy to generate an image of yourself sitting down and watching TV. However, picturing yourself *not* watching TV is difficult. Instead of forming an image of not watching TV, you are likely to form images (or sounds) related to performing other activities instead, such as reading a book, talking to someone, or being in the TV room and doing something else. Maultsby (1984) explains the implications for goal setting and change as follows:

> Resolutions not to keep doing something are behavioral resolutions. To keep such behavioral resolutions, people must get rid of the undesirable habit of doing the act they have resolved not to do anymore. But in psychological science as in physical science nature seems to abhor a vacuum. Therefore, people can *not* just get rid of a habit; people have to replace every old habit with a new habit.
>
> Now, what do people have to do to form a new habit? They have to have the same mental image of themselves acting out the same new behavior, in the same way, every time they normally would act out the old, undesirable, but habitual behavior. . . . To learn a new behavioral habit, people must have the same specific, mental images, or behavioral picture-maps of themselves acting out the new behavior in the same way, every time. In addition, the people must be willing to act in the new

way every time they have a cue for the old behavior. [p. 45]*

The counselor will have to help clients "turn around" their initial goal statements, which are usually stated as something the person doesn't want to do, can't do, or wants to stop doing. Such statements reveal the "dead man's error" (Lindsley, 1968), in that these objectives are ones that could be realized by a dead person. Stating goals positively represents a self-affirming position. If the client responds to the counselor's initial leads with a negative answer, the counselor can help turn this around by saying something like "That is what you *don't* want to do. Describe what you *do* want to do [think, feel]" or "What will you do instead, and can you see [hear, feel] yourself doing it every time?"

Who Owns the Goal?

As we mentioned in Chapter 8, clients often describe problems in a way that minimizes their own contribution. The likely result is that the client projects the blame or responsibility for the problem onto someone else — for example, "I didn't do this," "It's all her fault," "If it weren't for them." Similarly, in stating goals, some clients display the same tendency and initially want to select goals that call for someone else to change rather than themselves — a teenager who says "I want my mom to stop yelling at me," a teacher who says "I want this kid to shut up so I can get some teaching done," or a husband who says "I want my wife to stop bitching." The tendency to project the desired change onto someone else is particularly evident in change problems that involve relationships with two or more persons.

Without discounting the client's feelings, the counselor needs to help get this tendency turned around. The client is the identified person seeking help and services and is the only person who can make a change. When two or more clients are involved simultaneously in counseling, such as a couple or a family, all identified clients need to contribute to the desired choice or change, not just one party or one "identified patient." More specifically, any persons directly affected by a choice or change need some involvement in selection and implementation of the desired outcomes (Gam-

---

* From *Rational behavior therapy* by M. C. Maultsby, Jr. Copyright © 1984 by Prentice-Hall. Reprinted by permission.

brill, 1977). The counselor may have a special responsibility to protect the rights of clients in "low power" positions, such as children and the elderly, to ensure that this happens, because their rights are so often easily overlooked (Gambrill, 1977).

Who owns the change is usually directly related to the degree of *control* or *responsibility* that the client has in the situation and over the choice or change. For example, suppose you are counseling an 8-year-old girl whose parents are getting a divorce. The child says she wants you to help her persuade her parents to stay married. This goal would be very difficult for the child to attain, since she has no responsibility for her parents' relationship.

The counselor will need to use leads to help clients determine whether they or someone else owns the change and whether anyone else needs to be involved in the goal selection process. If the client steers toward a goal that requires a change by someone else, the counselor will need to point this out and help the client identify his or her role in the change process.

Interview leads to determine who owns the change. To help the client explore who owns the change, the counselor can use leads similar to the following ones:

"How much control do you have over making this happen?"
"What changes will this goal require of you?"
"What changes will this goal require someone else to make?"
"Can this goal be achieved without the help of anyone else?"
"To whom is this goal most important?"
"Who, specifically, is responsible for making this happen?"

The intent of these leads is to have the client identify a goal that represents choice or change for the client, not for others unless they are directly affected. If the client persists in selecting a goal that represents change for others rather than oneself, the counselor and client will have to decide whether to pursue this goal, to negotiate a reconsidered goal, or to refer the client to another helper, as we shall discuss shortly.

Is the Goal Realistic?

Realistic goals are ones that are *feasible* and within the client's control and capabilities to achieve. Realistic goals also represent outcomes that are based on realistic expectations rather than unrealistic, irrational, or perfectionistic ideas, standards, or self-demands.

When clients select goals, the counselor needs to be on the lookout for goals that are unrealistic either because they are too high to be reached or because they are too low and either inconsequential or likely to be attained anyway during the natural course of events. Clients who set goals that are too high usually operate from perfectionistic standards and self-demands. Dixon and Glover (1984) note that often these clients also fear failure, and the selection of unrealistically high goals removes the possibility of failure in their eyes because they do not feel anyone would blame them for not reaching such a lofty objective. For example, a client who states "I want to get all As during my four years of college" knows that no one will hold her to this goal because it is so "ideal" and difficult to reach. Setting high goals is also a way to avoid trying or taking any risk, thus preventing the possibility of failing at one risk or attempt.

Clients who set goals that are inconsequential or too low also usually fear failure and select such goals because they know they can be attained. Unfortunately, the result is usually as inconsequential as the goal itself and often feels like a "hollow victory" with no sense of accomplishment (Dixon & Glover, 1984, p. 133). A client who states "I just want to maintain a C average in college" is likely to do so successfully but may feel little or no pride when the goal has been reached or even surpassed. Challenging goals are more likely to lead to higher performance than "easy" goals (Locke, Shaw, Saari, & Latham, 1981).

The counselor can help clients explore the degree to which the identified goals are realistic and are based on potential for change and on rational standards, as well as any anxiety that may be reflected by the client's choice of unrealistic goals. Counselors can also help clients examine any inappropriate attributions or notions about who is responsible for success or failure to attain the goals. Inappropriate attributions would be those in which the client attributes success or failure to factors outside the client's control (Dixon & Glover, 1984). In selecting goals that are realistic, both the counselor and the client should be careful not to overestimate or underestimate the client's potential.

Interview leads to explore feasibility. To help the client determine the realism of the identified goal(s), the counselor can use any of the following example leads:

"How feasible is it for you to do _____?"

"Is it reasonable to effect a change in _____?"

"How are you likely to feel after you have reached this goal?"

"To what extent are you leaning toward this goal because you know it's something you can achieve with little effort and/or little risk?"

"To what extent are you leaning toward this goal because it's out of your reach and may excuse you from blame if you don't try or don't make it?"

"To what extent do you want to achieve this goal?"

"To what extent do you feel you should achieve this goal?"

"To what degree is this goal based on realistic expectations?"

"To what degree does this goal represent wishful thinking?"

"Does this goal alleviate in any way a possible fear of failure on your part?"

"When you reach this goal, how will you explain your success [or if you don't reach it, how will you explain failure to reach it]?"

The intent of these leads is to have the *client* assess the degree to which a goal can be attained in a realistic way and within a practical amount of time. The counselor is looking for a response that indicates the client has some evidence that the goal is realistic and can be attained in a reasonable time and manner. If the client selects a goal and considers it feasible but the counselor does not agree, renegotiation and/or referral are options.

Advantages and Disadvantages of the Goal

It is important to explore the *cost/benefit* effect of all identified goals—that is, what is being given up (cost) versus what is being gained (benefit) from goal attainment (Dixon & Glover, 1984). We think of this step as exploration of *advantages,* or positive effects, and *disadvantages,* or negative effects, of goal attainment. Clients are unlikely to commit themselves to a goal or are likely to give up working toward a goal when the stakes become too high and the payoffs too low. Exploration of advantages and disadvantages helps the client anticipate what price will be paid to achieve the goal and then decide whether the change is worth the cost to oneself or to significant others. Many clients tend

to jump into change without considering that attainment of a desired goal may also involve a cost. Costs are usually less obvious than the benefits of change. If the counselor and client fail to explore possible costs, the client may reach the goal and solve the original problem but create new problems in the process (Dixon & Glover, 1984). Sometimes removal of or change in a symptom creates adverse effects or new problems that the client did not bargain for and the counselor did not anticipate. For example, a client may choose to give up his job to get more free time and, after doing so, become despondent because of lack of money and security and loss of an important social network and feeling of "community." Advantages and disadvantages of particular goals may be emotional and cognitive as well as behavioral (Gambrill, 1977): goal attainment may result in desirable or undesirable feelings and mood states; self-enhancing or self-defeating thoughts, images, and internal dialogue; and appropriate or inappropriate reactions and motoric responses.

Generally, the goals selected by clients should lead to benefits rather than losses. Gambrill (1977, p. 169) notes that making such a selection "calls for careful identification of the situations in which new behaviors will be displayed and anticipation of the possible consequences that might occur." Advantages and disadvantages may be both short-term and long-term. The counselor helps the client identify various kinds of short- and long-term advantages and disadvantages associated with goal attainment and offers options to expand the client's range of possibilities (Gambrill, 1977). Sometimes it is helpful to write these down in the form of a list, which can be expanded or modified at any time, such as the one found in Figure 9-2 (see also Goldfried & Goldfried, 1980).

Interview leads for advantages. Most clients can readily identify some positive consequences associated with their desired changes. Nevertheless, it is still a good idea with all clients to explore positive consequences of the change, for at least four reasons: to determine whether the advantages the client perceives are indicative of actual benefits; to point out other possible advantages for the client or for others that have been overlooked; to strengthen the client's incentive to change; and to determine to what degree the identified goal is relevant and worthwhile, given the client's overall functioning. These are examples of leads to explore advantages of client change:

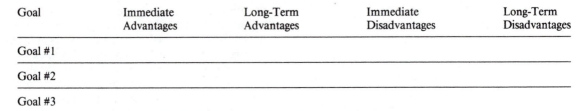

Goal	Immediate Advantages	Long-Term Advantages	Immediate Disadvantages	Long-Term Disadvantages
Goal #1				
Goal #2				
Goal #3				

Figure 9-2. List for recording advantages and disadvantages of identified goals

"In what ways is it worthwhile to pursue this goal?"
"What do you see as the benefits of this change?"
"Who would benefit from this change and how?"
"What are some positive consequences that may result from this change?"
"What are some advantages of attaining this goal?"
"Will attainment of this goal lead to solution of the issue?"

In using these leads, the counselor is looking for some indication that the client is selecting a goal on the basis of the positive consequences the goal may produce. If the client overlooks some advantages, the counselor can describe them to add to the client's incentive to change.

If the client is unable to identify any benefits of change for herself or himself, this may be viewed as a signal for caution. Failure to identify advantages of change for oneself may indicate that the client is attempting to change at someone else's request or that the identified goal is not very relevant, given the "total picture." For instance, if a client wants to find a new job while she is also fighting off a life-threatening illness, the acquisition of a new job at this time may not be in the best interests of her desire to regain her health. Further exploration may indicate that another person is a more appropriate client or that other goals should be selected.

Interview leads for disadvantages. The counselor can also use leads to have the client consider some risks or side effects that might accompany the desired change. Some examples of leads the counselor might use to explore the risks or disadvantages of change are the following:

"Will pursuing this goal affect your life in any adverse ways?"
"What might be some possible risks of doing this?"
"How would your life be changed if this happened?"
"What are some possible disadvantages of going in this direction? How willing are you to pay this price?"

"What are some negative consequences this change might have for you—or for others?"
"How will this change limit or constrain you?"
"What new problems in living might pursuing this goal create for you?"

The counselor is looking for some indication that the client has considered the possible costs associated with the goal. If the client discounts the risks or cannot identify any, the counselor can use immediacy or confrontation to point out some disadvantages. However, the counselor should be careful not to persuade or coerce the client to pursue another alternative simply because the counselor believes it is better. As Eisenberg and Delaney (1977) note, "It is one thing to help a person be aware of the consequences of the choice he or she has made and another thing to persuade the client to prefer another alternative" (p. 202).

Decision Point

The process of developing goals to this point has involved the client as the primary agent in choosing goals. The counselor's role has been secondary, confined mainly to helping the client explore the feasibility, risks, and disadvantages of change. At this point in the process, the primary issue for the counselor is whether she or he can help the client attain the selected goals. Most people agree that this is one of the biggest ethical and, to some extent, legal questions the counselor faces during the helping process (Bandura, 1969; Gottman & Leiblum, 1974; Krumboltz, 1966; Morganstern, 1986).

According to Gambrill (1977, p. 1035),

There *is* an obligation to help the client obtain desired goals, within the limits of the counselor's personal value system and theoretical orientation and the likely short- and long-term effects on the client and society. However, both the counselor's personal value system and his theoretical orientation may place unethical restrictions on the help that he or she can offer the client. In such instances, the counselor has an ethical obligation to refer the client to someone else who can view the client's desired outcomes more objectively.

The counselor and client will need to choose whether to continue with counseling and pursue the selected goals, to continue with counseling but reevaluate the client's initial goals, or to seek the services of another counselor. The particular decision is always made on an individual basis and is based on two factors: *willingness* and *competence* to help the client pursue the selected goals (Brown & Brown, 1977). Willingness involves your interest in working with the client toward identified goals and issues, your values, and your acceptance of the goals as worthwhile and important, given the overall functioning of the client. Competence involves your skills and "know-how" and whether you are familiar with alternative intervention strategies and multiple ways to work with particular problems.

We offer the following ideas as food for thought in this area. First of all, as much as possible, be responsive to the *client's* requests for change (Gottman & Leiblum, 1974, p. 64) even if these goals do not reflect your theoretical biases or personal preferences. This sort of responsiveness has been described by Gottman and Leiblum (1974, p. 64): "If [the client] wants help in accepting his homosexuality, do not set up a treatment program designed to help him find rewards in heterosexuality. Respect for your client implies respect for his diagnosis of his needs and wishes."

Too often, either knowingly or unwittingly, counselors may lead a client toward a goal they are personally comfortable with or feel more competent to treat. As Gambrill observes, "Personal values and theoretical assumptions with no empirical basis have caused profound distress to many clients over the years" (1977, p. 1035).

Second, if you have a *major* reservation about pursuing selected goals, a referral might be more helpful to the client (Gottman & Leiblum, p. 43).

Major reservations of a counselor. A counselor might have several reservations or limitations that would affect this decision point. One possible major reservation for you, the counselor, is any previous difficulty you have had in working with similar clients. Your own unresolved conflicts in the area the client wants to pursue may block successful counseling. Other reservations may surface when your values are not compatible with those reflected in the client's choice of goals. When goals

pose harm to the client or others, you may decide it would be ethically irresponsible to help the client pursue them. Some clients may select "self-defeating" goals. Self-defeating goals may constrict freedom of activity, may be impractical to achieve, or may be chosen because of political pressure or demands from others (Gambrill, 1977). Brown and Brown (1977, p. 100) observe that "sanctioning such goals reinforces a client's avoidance of the problem or reinforces the selection of inappropriate means of handling a problem situation." You also might have some reservations if the client insists that you use a technique that data suggest is ineffective or harmful or if the client insists on a treatment approach that is beyond your skill level or the realm of counseling. Finally, you may feel counseling would not help when the contributing problem conditions are outside the client's control or when the client is unwilling to change these factors.

Making the decision. If the client selects goals and neither you nor the client has any major reservations, you will probably decide to continue with counseling to help the client attain her or his goal. You might summarize this to the client as in the following example: "You stated that you want to do _____ as a result of counseling. You seem to be willing and able to change the factors that are part of this problem. The benefits of this change for you seem to outweigh the disadvantages." After this point, assuming the client confirms this statement, the counselor and client will move on to defining the goal.

In other cases, you may decide to continue with the client on the basis of some reevaluation of the client's selected goals. Morganstern (1986) observes that there may be times when it would be difficult to accept the client's goals without offering "reeducation." For example, if the client wants to have a child and cannot identify any risks or disadvantages posed by this choice, the counselor may point out some constraints. Or if a client chooses as his goal "I want to be just exactly like my best friend," the counselor might point out the difficulty in achieving this goal. In reconsidering the client's goal, the counselor might say something like "I can't help you be just like your best friend, because each of us is a little different from everyone else. Our differences are what make us unique. If there is something about yourself you'd like to work on, I can help with that."

Reevaluation of the client's goals is a very sticky

issue. Bandura (1969) observes that a redefinition of the client's goal by the counselor, especially "unilateral redefinition," is a prevailing but "largely ignored ethical issue" (p. 103). Bandura recommends that, when initiating reevaluation or redefinition of the client's goals, the counselor should make this path explicit to the client. Moreover, the counselor should inform the client that such comments are based on information *and* on the counselor's own belief system (p. 103). Reevaluation of client goals should be pursued only "with the understanding and consent of the client," who is "free to exert 'counter-control'—that is, to challenge, refute, or refuse to comply with the therapist's suggestions" (Gottman & Leiblum, 1974, p. 68). The counselor's influence in reconsideration should be explicit, not implicit, open rather than disguised.

Referral may be appropriate in any of the following cases: if the client wants to pursue a goal that is incompatible with your value system; if you are unable to be objective about the client's concern; if you are unfamiliar with or unable to use a treatment requested by the client; if you would be exceeding your level of competence in working with the client; or if more than one person is involved and, because of your emotions or biases, you favor one person instead of another. Referral may be a better choice than continuing to work with the client in the midst of serious limitations or reservation. Referral is a way to provide an alternative counseling experience and, we hope, one that will leave the client with a positive impression of counseling.

In deciding to refer a client, the counselor does have certain responsibilities. From the initial counseling contacts, the counselor and client have entered into at least an unwritten contract. Once the counselor agrees to counsel a client, he or she "assumes a degree of loyalty and responsibility for the outcomes of therapy" (Van Hoose & Kottler, 1977, p. 82). In deciding to terminate this "contract" by a referral, the referring counselor can be considered legally liable if the referral is not handled with due care (Dawidoff, 1973). Due care implies that

> when referral is undertaken the referring therapist has the responsibility for ascertaining the appropriateness of the referral, including the skill of the receiving therapist. Furthermore, he should provide the receiving therapist with information sufficient to enable him to give proper help to the client. It is also important that the therapist attempt to follow up on the status of his client's well-being. [Van Hoose & Kottler, p. 83]

Therapists are also responsible for giving clients choices of referral therapists (when available) and for ensuring that referred therapists are considered competent and do not have a reputation for poor service or unethical practices (M. Boston, personal communication, December 1980).

LEARNING ACTIVITY #26: DECISION POINT

For practice in thinking through the kinds of decisions you may face in the goal-setting process, you may want to use this learning activity. The exercise consists of three hypothetical situations. In each case, assume that you are the counselor. Read through the case. Then sit back, close your eyes, and try to imagine being in the room with the client and being faced with this dilemma. How would you feel? What would you say? What would you decide to do and why?

There are no "right" or "wrong" answers to these cases. You may wish to discuss your responses with another classmate, a co-worker, or your instructor.

Case 1

You are counseling a family with two teenage daughters. The parents and the younger daughter seem closely aligned; the elder daughter is on the periphery of the family. The parents and the younger daughter report that the older daughter's recent behavior is upsetting and embarrassing to them because she has been caught cheating in school and is hanging out with a "fast crowd." They state that they want you to help them get this girl "back in line" with the rest of the family and get her to adopt their values and socially acceptable behavior. What do you do?

Case 2

You are counseling a fourth-grader. You are the only counselor in this school. One day you notice that this boy seems to be all bruised. You inquire about this. After much hesitation, the child blurts out that he is often singled out on his way home by two big sixth-grade "bullies" who pick a fight, beat him up for a while, and then leave him alone until another time.

(continued)

Your client asks you to forget this information. He begs you not to say or do anything for fear of reprisal from these two bullies. He states he doesn't want to deal with this in counseling, since he has come to see you about something else. What do you do?

Case 3

You are working with an elderly man whose relatives are dead. After his wife died six months ago, he moved from their family home to a retirement home. Although the client is relatively young (70) and is in good health and alert, the staff has requested your help because he seems to have become increasingly morbid and discouraged. In talking with you, he indicates that he has sort of given up on everything, including himself, because he doesn't feel he has anything to live for. Consequently, he has stopped going to activities, isolates himself in his room, and has even stopped engaging in self-care activities such as personal hygiene and grooming, leaving such things up to the staff. He indicates that he doesn't care to talk with you if these are the kinds of things you are going to want to talk about. What do you do?

☐ MODEL DIALOGUE: THE CASE OF JOAN

To help you see how the leads for selecting goals are used with a client, the case of Joan, introduced in Chapter 7, is continued here as a dialogue in a counseling session directed toward goal selection. Counselor responses are prefaced by an explanation (in italics).

*In response 1, the counselor starts out with a **review** of the last session.*

1. *Counselor:* Joan, last week we talked about some of the things that are going on with you right now that you're concerned about. What do you remember that we talked about?

   Client: Well, we talked a lot about my problems in school—like my trouble in my math class. Also about the fact that I can't decide whether or not to switch over to a vocational curriculum—and if I did my parents would be upset.

2. *Counselor:* Yes, that's a good summary. We did talk about a lot of things—such as the pressure and anxiety you feel in competitive situations like your math class and your difficulty in making decisions. I believe we mentioned also that you tend to go out of your way to please others, like your parents, or to avoid making a decision they might not like.

   Client: Mm-hmm. I tend to not want to create a hassle. I also just have never made many decisions by myself.

*In response 3, the counselor will move from problem definition to goal selection. Response 3 will consist of an **explanation** about goals and their **purpose**.*

3. *Counselor:* Yes, I remember you said that last week. I've been thinking that since we've kind of got a handle on the main issues you're concerned about, today it might be helpful to talk about things you might want to happen—or how you'd like things to be different. This way we know

exactly what we can be talking about and working on that will be most helpful to you. How does that sound?

   Client: That's OK with me. I mean, do you really think there are some things I can do about these problems?

*The client has indicated some uncertainty about possible change. The counselor will pursue this in response 4 and indicate more about the **purpose** of goals and possible effects of counseling for this person.*

4. *Counselor:* You seem a little uncertain about how much things can be different. To the extent that you have some control over a situation, it is possible to make some changes. Depending on what kind of changes you want to make, there are some ways we can work together on this. It will take some work on your part, too. How do you feel about this?

   Client: OK. I'd like to get out of the rut I'm in.

*In response 5, the counselor will explore the ways in which the client would like to change. The counselor will use a lead to **identify client goals**.*

5. *Counselor:* So you're saying that you don't want to continue to feel stuck. Exactly how would you like things to be different—say, in three months from now—from the way things are now?

   Client: Well, I'd like to feel less pressured in school, especially in my math class.

*The client has identified one possible goal, although it is stated in negative terms. In response 6, the counselor will help the client identify the goal in **positive terms**.*

6. *Counselor:* OK, that's something you *don't* want to do. Can you think of another way to say it that would describe what you *do* want to do?

   Client: Well, I guess I'd like to feel confident about my ability to handle tough situations like math class.

*In the next response, the counselor **paraphrases** Joan's goal and "checks" it out to see whether she has restated it accurately.*

7. *Counselor:* So you're saying you'd like to feel more positively about yourself in different situations—is that it?

   Client: Yeah, I don't know if that is possible, but that's what I would like to have happen.

*In responses 8–14, the counselor continues to help Joan **explore and identify desired outcomes.***

8. *Counselor:* Well, in a little while we'll take some time to explore just how feasible that might be. Before we do that, let's make sure we don't over-look anything else you'd like to work on—in what other areas is it important to you to make a change or to turn things around for yourself?

   Client: Well, I'd like to start making some deci-sions for myself for a change, but I don't know exactly how to start.

9. *Counselor:* OK, that's part of what we'll do together—we'll look at how you can get started on some of these things. So far, then, you've mentioned two things you'd like to work toward—increasing your confidence in your ability to handle tough situations like math and starting to make some decisions by yourself without relying on help from someone else. Is that about it, or can you think of any other things you'd like to work on?

   Client: Well, I guess it's related to making my own decisions, but I'd like to decide whether to stay in this curriculum or switch to the voca-tional one.

10. *Counselor:* So you're concerned also about making a special type of decision about school that affects you now.

    Client: That's right. But I'm sort of afraid to, because I know if I decided to switch, my parents would have a terrible reaction when they found out about it.

11. *Counselor:* It seems that you're mentioning an-other situation that we might need to try to get a different handle on. As you mentioned last week, in certain situations, like math class or with your parents, you tend to back off and kind of let other people take over for you.

    Client: That's true, and I guess this curriculum thing is an example of it. It's like a lot of things I do know what I want to do or say, but I just don't follow through. Like not telling my folks about my opinion about this college prep curriculum. Or not telling them how their harping at me about grades makes me feel. Or even in math class, just sitting there and sort of letting the teacher do a lot of the work for me when I really

do probably know the answer or could go to the board.

12. *Counselor:* So what you're saying is that in cer-tain situations with your folks or in math class, you may have an idea or an opinion or a feeling, yet you usually don't express it.

    Client: Mm-hmm. Usually I don't because sometimes I'm afraid it might be wrong or I'm afraid my folks would get upset.

13. *Counselor:* So the anticipation that you might make a mistake or that your folks might not like it keeps you from expressing yourself in these situations?

    Client: Yup, I believe so.

14. *Counselor:* Then is this another thing that you would like to work on?

    Client: Yes, because I realize I can't go on with-drawing forever.

*Since Joan has again stated the outcome in negative terms, in the next four responses (15, 16, 17, 18), the counselor helps Joan **restate the goal in positive terms.***

15. *Counselor:* OK, now again you're sort of sug-gesting a way that you don't want to handle the situation. You don't want to withdraw. Can you describe something you *do* want to do in these situations in a way that you could see, hear, or grasp yourself doing it each time the situation occurs?

    Client: I'm not exactly sure what you mean.

16. *Counselor:* Well, for instance, suppose I want to lose weight. I could say "I don't want to eat so much, and I don't want to be fat." But that just describes not doing what I've been doing. So it would be more helpful to describe something I'm going to do instead, like "Instead of eating be-tween meals, I'm going to go out for a walk, or talk on the phone, or create a picture of myself in my head as a thinner person."

    Client: Oh, yeah, I do see what you mean. So I guess instead of withdrawing, I—well, what is the opposite of that? I guess I think it would be more helpful if I volunteered the answers or gave my ideas or opinions—things like that.

17. *Counselor:* OK, so you're saying that you want to express yourself instead of holding back. Things like expressing opinions, feelings, things like that.

    Client: Yeah.

18. *Counselor:* OK, now we've mentioned three things you want to work on—anything else?

    Client: No, I can't think of anything.

*In the next response, the counselor asks Joan to **select one of the goals** to work on initially. Tackling all three* *outcomes simultaneously could be overwhelming to a client.*

19. *Counselor:* OK, as time goes on and we start working on some of these things, you may think of something else — or something we've talked about today may change. What might be helpful now is to decide which of these three things you'd like to work on first.
Client: Gee, that's a hard decision.

In the previous response, Joan demonstrated in vivo one of her problems — difficulty in making decisions. In the next response, the counselor **provides guidelines** *to help Joan make a choice but is careful not to make the decision for her.*

20. *Counselor:* Well, it's one decision I don't want to make for you. I'd encourage you to start with the area you think is most important to you now — and also maybe one that you feel you could work with successfully.
Client: [Long pause] Can this change, too?

21. *Counselor:* Sure — we'll start with one thing, and if later on it doesn't feel right, we'll move on.
Client: OK, well, I guess it would be the last thing we talked about — starting to express myself in situations where I usually don't.

In the next response, the counselor will discuss the degree to which Joan believes the **change represents something she will do** *rather than someone else.*

22. *Counselor:* OK, sticking with this one area, it seems like these are things that you could make happen without the help of anyone else or without requiring anyone else to change too. Can you think about that for a minute and see whether that's the way it feels to you?
Client: [Pause] I guess so. You're saying that I don't need to depend on someone else; it's something I can start doing.

In the next three responses (23, 24, 25), this counselor helps Joan explore the **feasibility and realistic nature of the goal.**

23. *Counselor:* Yes, it's a case where you are in the driver's seat. You know, too, earlier you mentioned this was something you wanted to do if it was possible, and I said we'd come back to this. Do you feel this change is realistic?
Client: I think so. In what way?

24. *Counselor:* Well, assuming you have some help from me, how feasible do you think it will be to start expressing yourself in these difficult situations?
Client: Well, I think it's feasible in the long run. I guess at first it will be hard because it's something I'm not used to doing and also because I get pretty uptight in some of these situations.

25. *Counselor:* So it feels possible for you to pursue this. At the same time, you realize your lack of skills and your nervousness are roadblocks that may make it difficult. Once we remove the roadblocks, I imagine your journey will be lot faster and a lot smoother. What do you think?
Client: Yeah. If I can just get past these initial hurdles.

In the next response, the counselor shifts to exploring **possible advantages** *of goal achievement. Note that the counselor asks the client first to express her opinion about advantages; the counselor is giving her in vivo practice of one of the skills related to her goal.*

26. *Counselor:* We're going to remember these hurdles and come back to them later. Then we can develop a plan to cope with and master them, so they don't get the best of you. One thing I'm wondering about — and this will probably sound silly because in a way it's obvious — but exactly how will making this change help you or benefit you?
Client: Mm — [Pause] — I'm thinking — well, what do you think?

In the previous response, the client shifted responsibility to the counselor and "withdrew," as she does in other anxiety-producing situations, such as math class and interactions with her parents. In the next response, the counselor **confronts** *this behavior pattern.*

27. *Counselor:* You know, it's interesting, I just asked you for your opinion about something, and instead of sharing it, you asked me to sort of handle it instead. Are you aware of this?
Client: Now that you mention it, I am. But I guess that's what I do so often it's sort of automatic.

In the next three responses (28, 29, 30), the counselor does some in vivo **assessment of Joan's problems,** *which results in information that can be used later for* **planning of subgoals and action steps.**

28. *Counselor:* Can you run through exactly what you were thinking and feeling just then?
Client: Well, just that I had a couple of ideas, but then I didn't think they were important enough to mention.

29. *Counselor:* I'm wondering if you also may have felt a little concerned about what I would think of your ideas.
Client: [Face flushes] Well, yeah. I guess it's silly, but yeah.

30. *Counselor:* So is this sort of the same thing that happens to you in math class or around your parents?
Client: Yeah — only in those two situations, I feel much more uptight than I do here.

In the next four responses, the counselor continues to explore **potential advantages** *for Joan of attaining this goal.*

31. *Counselor:* OK, that's real helpful because that information gives us some clues on what we'll need to do first in order to help you reach this result. Before we explore that, let's go back and see whether you can think of any ways in which making this change will help you.

    Client: Well, I think sometimes I'm like a doormat. I just sit there and let people impose on me. Sometimes I get taken advantage of.

32. *Counselor:* So you're saying that at times you feel used as a result?

    Client: Yeah. That's a good way to put it.

33. *Counselor:* OK, other advantages or benefits to you?

    Client: Well, I'd become less dependent and more self-reliant. If I do decide to go to college, that's only two years away, and I will need to be a whole lot more independent then.

34. *Counselor:* OK, that's a good thought. Any other ways that this change would be worthwhile for you, Joan?

    Client: Mm — I can't think of any. That's honest. But if I do, I'll mention them.

In the next responses (35 – 38), the counselor initiates exploration of **possible disadvantages** *of this goal.*

35. *Counselor:* OK, great! And the ones you've mentioned I think are really important ones. Now, I'd like you to flip the coin, so to speak, and see whether you can think of any disadvantages that could result from moving in this direction?

    Client: Well, I can't think of any in math. Well, no, in a way I can. I guess it's sort of the thing to do there to act like a dumb broad. If I start expressing myself more, people might wonder what is going on.

36. *Counselor:* So you're concerned about the reaction from some of the other students?

    Client: Yeah, in a way. Although there are a couple of girls in there who are pretty popular and also made the honor roll. So I don't think it's like I'd be a social outcast.

37. *Counselor:* It sounds, then, like you believe that is one disadvantage you could live with. Any other ways in which doing this could affect your life in a negative way — or could create another problem for you?

    Client: Well, I think a real issue there is how my parents would react if I started to do some of these things. I don't know. Maybe they would welcome it. But I sort of think they would consider it a revolt or something on my part and would want to squelch it right away.

38. *Counselor:* You seem to be saying you believe your parents have a stake in keeping you somewhat dependent on them.

    Client: Yeah, I do.

This is a difficult issue. Without observing her family, it would be impossible to say whether this is Joan's perception (and a distorted one) or whether the parents do play a role in this problem — and, indeed, from a diagnostic standpoint, family members are often significantly involved when one family member has a dependent personality. The counselor will thus **reflect both possibilities** *in the next response.*

39. *Counselor:* That may or may not be true. It could be that you see the situation that way and an outsider like myself might not see it the same way. On the other hand, it is possible your parents might subtly wish to keep you from growing up too quickly. This might be a potentially serious enough disadvantage for us to consider whether it would be useful for all four of us to sit down and talk together.

    Client: Do you think that would help?

In the next two responses, the counselor and Joan continue to discuss potential **negative effects or disadvantages** *related to this goal. Note that in the next response, instead of answering the client's previous question directly, the counselor shifts the responsibility to Joan and solicits her opinion, again giving her in vivo opportunities to demonstrate one skill related to the goal.*

40. *Counselor:* What do you think?

    Client: I'm not sure. They are sometimes hard to talk to.

41. *Counselor:* How would you feel about having a joint session — assuming they were agreeable?

    Client: Right now it seems OK. How could it help exactly?

In the following response, the counselor changes from an **individual to a systemic focus,** *since the parents may have an investment in keeping Joan dependent on them or may have given Joan an injunction "Don't grow up." The systemic focus avoids blaming any one person.*

42. *Counselor:* I think you mentioned it earlier. Sometimes when one person in a family changes the way she or he reacts to the rest of the family, it has a boomerang effect, causing ripples throughout the rest of the family. If that's going to happen in your case, it might be helpful to sit down and talk about it and anticipate the effects, rather than letting you get in the middle of a situation that starts to feel too hard to handle. It could be

helpful to your parents, too, to explore their role in this whole issue.

Client: I see. Well, where do we go from here?

43. *Counselor:* Our time is about up today. Let's get together in a week and map out a plan of action. (*Note:* The same process of goal selection would also be carried out in subsequent sessions for the other two outcome goals Joan identified earlier in this session.)

□ INTERVIEW LEADS FOR DEFINING GOALS

Most clients will select more than one goal. Ultimately, it may be more realistic for the client to work toward "attainment of a variety of specific objectives rather than a single, omnibus outcome" (Bandura, 1969, p. 104). For example, in our model case, Joan has selected three terminal outcome goals: acquiring and demonstrating at least four initiating skills, increasing positive self-talk about her ability to function adequately in competitive situations, and acquiring and using five decision-making skills (see Joan's goal chart on pp. 244–245). These three outcomes reflect the three core problems revealed by the assessment interview (Chapter 8). Selection of one goal may also imply the existence of other goals. For example, if a client states "I want to get involved in a relationship with a man that is emotionally and sexually satisfying," the client may also need to work on meeting men and her approach behaviors, developing communications skills designed to foster intimacy, and learning about what responses might be sexually satisfying for her.

At first, it is useful to have the client specify one or more desired goals for each separate problem. However, to tackle several outcome goals at one time would be unrealistic. The counselor should ask the client to choose one of the outcome goals to pursue first. After selecting an initial outcome goal to work toward, the counselor and client can define the three parts of the goal and identify subgoals. The next section of this chapter will introduce some counselor leads used to help the client define the outcome goals of counseling and will present some probable responses that indicate client responsiveness to the leads.

Defining Behaviors Related to Goals

Carkhuff and Anthony (1979, pp. 136–137) assert that "to achieve any goal, a helper must *act*. And to ensure that the goal to be achieved is both functional and real, the helper must begin his or her

sequence of activity by defining this goal. . . . This is a step that all too many people overlook entirely."* Defining goals involves specifying in operational or behavioral terms what the client (whether an individual, group member, or organization) is to *do* as a result of counseling. This part of an outcome goal defines the particular behavior the client is to perform and answers the question "*What* will the client do, think, or feel differently?" Examples of behavior outcome goals include exercising more frequently, asking for help from a teacher, verbal sharing of positive feelings about oneself, and thinking about oneself in positive ways. As you can see, both overt and covert behaviors, including thoughts and feelings, can be included in this part of the outcome goal as long as the behavior is defined by what it means for each client. Defining goals behaviorally makes the goalsetting process specific, and specifically defined goals are more likely to create incentives and guide performance than vaguely stated intentions (Bandura & Simon, 1977, p. 178). When goals are behaviorally or operationally defined, it is easier to evaluate the effects of counseling (see also Chapter 10). Further, "clearly stated goals tend to make problems seem more manageable and solutions more attainable" (Dixon & Glover, 1984, p. 133).

Interview leads for defining goal behavior. The following are some leads a counselor can use to identify the behavior part of a goal:

"When you say you want to _____, what do you see yourself doing?"

"What could I see you doing, thinking, or feeling as a result of this change?"

"You say you want to be more self-confident. What things would you be thinking and doing as a self-confident person?"

"Describe a good (and a poor) example of this goal."

It is important for the counselor to continue to pursue these leads until the client can define the overt and covert behaviors associated with the goal. This is not an easy task, for most clients talk about changes in vague or abstract terms. If the client has trouble specifying behaviors, the counselor can help with further instructions, informa-

---

* This and all other quotations from this source are from *The Skills of Helping* by R. R. Carkhuff and W. A. Anthony. Copyright © 1979 by Human Resource Development Press. Reprinted by permission.

tion giving, or self-disclosing a personal goal. The counselor can also facilitate behavioral definitions of the goal by encouraging the client to use action verbs to describe what will be happening when the goal is attained (Dixon & Glover, 1984). As we mentioned earlier, it is important to get clients to specify what they *want* to do, not what they don't want or what they want to stop. The goal is usually defined sufficiently when the counselor can accurately repeat and paraphrase the client's definition.

Another way to obtain behavioral goal descriptions, suggested by Hill (1975), is to use the Counseling Outcome Inventory (COI). In using the COI, the client is asked to list some characteristics, qualities, or descriptions that are important to the client to acquire or to demonstrate. Then, for each of these descriptors, the client is asked to list one or more actual behaviors of this quality, which Hill calls "behavioral anchors" (p. 573). For instance, the vague descriptor "self-confidence" might be translated into a behavioral anchor of "making fewer negative self-statements"; the descriptor "be more attractive" might be translated into the behavioral anchors of "lose 10 pounds" and "smile more often." The COI procedure helps to make the outcome goals observable and also helps to develop goals that are stated meaningfully for different clients.

Defining the Conditions of an Outcome Goal

The second part of an outcome goal specifies the conditions—that is, the *context* or *circumstances*—where the behavior will occur. This is an important element of an outcome goal for both the client and the counselor. The conditions suggest a particular *person* with whom the client may perform the desired behaviors or a particular *setting* and answers the question "*Where, when,* and *with whom* is the behavior to occur?*" Specifying the conditions of a behavior sets boundaries and helps to ensure that the behavior will occur only in desired settings or with desired people and will not generalize to undesired settings. This idea can be illustrated vividly. For example, a woman may wish to increase the number of positive verbal and nonverbal responses she makes toward her husband. In this case, time spent with her husband would be the condition or circumstances in which the behavior occurs. However, if this behavior generalized to include all men, it might have negative effects on the very relationship she is trying to improve.

Interview leads for the conditions of a goal. Leads used to determine the conditions of the outcome goal include these:

> "Where would you like to do this?"
> "In what situations do you want to be able to do this?"
> "When do you want to do this?"
> "Whom would you be with when you do this?"
> "In what situations is what you're doing now not meeting your expectations?"

The counselor is looking for a response that indicates where or with whom the client will make the change or perform the desired behavior. If the client gives a noncommittal response, the counselor may suggest client self-monitoring to obtain these data. The counselor can also use self-disclosure and personal examples to demonstrate that a desired behavior may not be appropriate in all situations or with all people.

Defining a Level of Change

The third element of an outcome goal specifies the level or *amount* of the behavioral change. In other words, this part answers "*How much* is the client to do or to complete in order to reach the desired goal?" The level of an outcome goal serves as a barometer that measures the extent to which the client will be able to perform the desired behavior. For example, a man may state that he wishes to decrease cigarette smoking. The following week, he may report that he did a better job of cutting down on cigarettes. However, unless he can specify how much he actually decreased smoking, both he and the counselor will have difficulty determining how much the client really completed toward the goal. In this case, the client's level of performance is ambiguous. In contrast, if he had reported that he reduced cigarette smoking by two cigarettes per day in one week, his level of performance could be determined easily. If his goal were to decrease cigarette smoking by eight cigarettes per day, this information would help to determine progress toward the goal.

Like the behavior and condition parts of an outcome goal, the level of change should always be established individually for each client. The amount of satisfaction derived from goal attainment often depends on the level of performance established (Bandura & Simon, 1977, p. 178). A suitable level of change will depend on such factors as the present level of the problem behavior, the present level of the desired behavior, the resources available for change, the client's readiness to change, and the degree to which other conditions or people are maintaining the present level of problem behavior. Hosford and de Visser (1974) point out that such factors often make the level of a goal the most difficult part to define.

As an example, suppose a client wants to increase the number of assertive opinions she expresses orally with her husband. If she now withholds all her opinions, her level of change might be stated at a lower level than that defined for another client who already expresses some opinions. And if the client's husband is accustomed to her refraining from giving opinions, this might affect the degree of change made, at least initially. The counselor's and client's primary concern is to establish a level that is manageable, that the client can attain with some success. Occasionally the counselor may encounter a client who always wants to achieve more change than is desirable or even possible. As Krumboltz and Thoresen (1976) note, progressively raising levels of change has a limit (p. 105). These authors suggest that, in such cases, the counselor must avoid reinforcing the client's perfectionistic goal statements (p. 104). In addition, if the level is set too high, the desired behavior may not occur, thus ruling out chances for success and subsequent progress and rewards. Brown and Brown (1977) recommend that, as a general rule of thumb, it is better to err by moving too slowly and thus set the level too low rather than too high.

One way to avoid setting the level of a goal too high or making it too restrictive is to use a scale that identifies a series of *increasingly desired* outcomes for each given problem area. This concept, introduced by Kiresuk and Sherman (1968), is called "goal-attainment scaling" (GAS) and has been used increasingly in agencies that must demonstrate certain levels of client goal achievement in order to receive or maintain funding. In goal-attainment scaling, the counselor and client devise five outcomes for a given problem and arrange these by level or extent of change on a scale in the following order (each outcome is assigned a numerical value): most unfavorable outcome (−2), less than likely expected outcome (−1), most likely or expected outcome (0), more than likely expected outcome (+1), most favorable outcome (+2). Table 9-1 shows an example of the use of GAS for a client with ulcerative colitis.

A review of this GAS model and four similar models is presented by Lloyd (1983).

TABLE 9-1. Goal-attainment scale for client with ulcerative colitis

Date: 10/24/73	Frequency of colitis attacks	Cognitive hypothesis testing
Most unfavorable outcome thought likely	One per day	Every stress transaction per week seen as attack on self
Less than expected success with treatment	One every other day	One out of four times per week considers that a stress transaction might not be attack on self
Expected level of treatment success	One per week	Completes Treatment Steps 4 and 5 *after* every stress transaction
More than expected success with treatment	One every two weeks	Completes Treatment Steps 4 and 5 *during* stress transactions some of the time
Best expected success with treatment	None per month	Completes Treatment Steps 4 and 5 *during* stress transactions all the time

Adapted From "Behavioral treatment of mucous colitis" by K. J. Youell & J. P. McCullough. *Journal of Consulting and Clinical Psychology, 43,* 740–745. Copyright © 1975 by American Psychological Association. Reprinted by permission.

Leads to identify the level of change.   Here are some leads you can use to help identify the client's desired extent or level of change:

"How much would you like to be able to do this, compared with how much you're doing it now?"

"How often do you want to do this?"

"From the information you obtained during self-monitoring, you seem to be studying only about an hour a week now. What is a reasonable amount for you to increase this without getting bogged down?"

"You say you'd like to lose 40 pounds. Let's talk about a reasonable amount of time this might take and, to start with, what amount would be easy for you to lose just in the next 3 weeks."

"What amount of change is realistic, considering where you are right now?"

The counselor is looking for some indication of the present and future levels of the desired behavior. This level can be expressed by either the number of times or the amount the client wants to be able to do something. In some cases, an appropriate level may be only one, as when a client's outcome goal is to make one decision about a job change. The counselor can help the client establish an appropriate level of change by referring to the self-monitoring data collected during problem assessment. If the client has not engaged in monitoring, this is another point where it is almost imperative to have the client observe and record the present amounts of the problem behavior and the goal behavior. This information will give some idea of the present level of behavior, referred to as the "base-rate" or "baseline" level. This information is important because in setting the desired level, it should be contrasted with the present level of the overt or covert behavior(s). As you may recall from Chapter 8, a client's data gathering is very useful for defining problems and goals and for monitoring progress toward the goals.

Level as an indicator of type of problem and goal. The level reflected in an outcome goal reflects both the type of problem and the type of goal. From our earlier discussion about what outcome goals represent, recall that problems can be classified as either choice or change. In a choice problem, the level of the goal reflects a conflict to be resolved or a choice or decision to be made—for example, the client needs to decide on one of three options or decide between two different directions. In a change problem, the level reflected in the goal specifies both the direction and the type of change desired. In the example of the client who wants to be more assertive, if the client's present level of a specified assertive response is zero, then the goal would be to acquire the assertive skill. When the base rate of a behavior is zero, or when the client does not seem to have certain skills in her or his repertoire, the goal is stated as acquiring a behavior. If, however, the client wants to improve or increase something that she or he can already do (but at a low level), the goal is stated as increasing a behavior. Increas-

ing or acquiring overt and/or covert behaviors is a goal when the client's problem is a *response deficit,* meaning that the desired response occurs with insufficient intensity or frequency or in inappropriate form (Gambrill, 1977). Sometimes a client has an overt behavioral response in his or her repertoire, but it is masked or inhibited by the presence of certain feelings—in which case the goal would be directed toward the feelings rather than the overt behavior. In this instance, the problem stems from *response inhibition,* and the resulting goal is a disinhibition of the response, usually by the working through of the emotional reactions standing in the way.

In contrast, if the client is doing too much of something and wants to lower the present level, the goal is stated as decreasing a behavior and possibly, later on, eliminating it from the client's repertoire. Decreasing or eliminating overt and/or covert behaviors is a goal when the client's problem is a *response excess,* meaning that a response occurs so often, so long, with such excessive intensity, or in socially inappropriate contexts that it is often annoying to the client and to others (Gambrill, 1977). In problems of response excesses, it is usually the frequency or amount of the response, rather than its form, that is problematic. It is almost always easier to work on developing or increasing a behavior (response increment or acquisition) than on stopping or decreasing a response (response decrement or elimination). This is another reason to encourage clients to state their goals in positive terms, working toward doing something or doing it more, rather than stopping something or doing it less.

Sometimes, when the client wants to eliminate something, she or he wishes to replace whatever is eliminated with a more appropriate or self-enhancing behavior. For instance, a client trying to lose weight may desire to replace junk-food snacks with low-calorie snacks. This client's goal is stated in terms of "restructuring" something about her or his environment—in this case, the type of snack eaten. Although this is an example of restructuring an overt behavior, restructuring can be cognitive as well. For example, a client may want to eliminate negative, self-defeating thoughts about difficulty in taking tests and replace these with positive, self-enhancing thoughts about the capacity to perform adequately in test-taking situations. Restructuring also often takes place during family counseling when boundaries and alliances between and among family members are shifted so that, for instance, a member on the periphery is pulled into the family, or triangles are broken up, or overinvolved alliances between two persons are rearranged. Restructuring overt or covert behaviors is a goal when the problem is *inadequate, inappropriate, or defective stimulus control,* meaning that the necessary supporting environmental conditions either are missing or are arranged in such a way as to make it impossible or difficult for the desired behavior to occur.

In some instances, the level of a goal reflects maintenance of a particular overt or covert response at the current rate or frequency or under existing conditions. As you recall from our earlier discussion of client change in this chapter, not all goals will reflect a discrepancy between the client's present and future behavior. Some goals may be directed toward maintaining a desired or satisfying situation or response. Such goals may be stated as, for example, "to maintain my present amount (three hours daily) of studying," "to maintain the present balance in my life between work on weekdays and play on weekends," "to maintain the positive communication I have with my spouse in our daily talks," or "to maintain my present level (two a day) of engaging in relaxation sessions." A maintenance goal suggests that the client's present level of behavior is satisfying and sufficient, at least at this particular time. A maintenance goal may

help to put things in perspective by acknowledging the areas of the client's life that are going well. Maintenance goals are also useful and necessary when one of the change goals has been achieved. For example, if a client wanted to lose weight and has done so successfully, then the counselor and client need to be concerned about how the client can maintain the weight loss. Often maintenance goals and programs are harder to achieve and take greater effort and planning than initial change attempts.

To summarize, the level stated by the outcome goal will usually reflect one of the categories of problems and goals summarized in Table 9-2. Since most clients have more than one outcome goal, a client's objectives may reflect more than one of these directions of change. Knowledge of the direction and level of change defined in the client's goals is important in selecting counseling strategies. For example, self-monitoring (see Chapter 19) is used differently depending on whether it is applied to increase or to decrease a response. One counseling strategy might be used appropriately to help a client acquire responses; yet another strategy may be needed to help a client restructure some responses. It is very important for the counselor and client to spend sufficient time on specifying the level of the goal, even if this process seems elusive and difficult.

LEARNING ACTIVITY #27: DEFINING OUTCOME GOALS

We have found that the most difficult part of developing goals with a client is specifying the three parts of the outcome goal. We believe the reason is that the concept is foreign to most of us and difficult to internalize. This is probably because, in our own lives, we think about small, very mundane goals. With more complex goals, we still don't assess the individual overt and covert behaviors to be changed, where and with whom change will occur, and the extent of the change. This learning activity is intended to help you create some *personal* meaning from these three parts of an outcome goal. If you feel comfortable with this, you are more likely to help a client define her or his goals.

1. During the next week, keep a log of any concerns, issues, or problems you're experiencing.
2. At the end of the week, go over your log and label each problem according to type: choice or change. If change, describe the problem as re-

sponse deficit, response inhibition, response excess, or inadequate/inappropriate stimulus control (refer also to Table 9-2).

3. Select one problem you are interested in resolving and specify the corresponding type of goal (as listed in Table 9-2): decision or resolution of conflict, response increment, response acquisition, disinhibition or working through a response, response decrement, response elimination, or response restructuring.

4. Define the goal by identifying—
   a. What you'll be doing (overt behavior) and thinking and feeling (covert behavior) as a result of this goal—make sure you state this in positive terms.
   b. Where, when, and with whom you want to do this (conditions).
   c. How much or how often you want to do this (level).

(continued)

LEARNING ACTIVITY #27: DEFINING OUTCOME GOALS (continued)

Your goal is probably defined sufficiently if an objective observer can paraphrase it accurately, stating exactly what, when, where, with whom, and how much you will be doing.

5. In addition to your definition above, create a goal-attainment scale for your outcome, using the example given in Table 9-1. Your scale should specify

the following five levels of possible outcomes: most unfavorable outcome (-2), less than likely expected outcome (-1), most likely or expected outcome (0), more than likely expected outcome $(+1)$, and most favorable outcome $(+2)$.

6. Review your responses to this activity with a colleague, instructor, supervisor, or partner.

TABLE 9-2. Categories of types of client problems and related goals

Type of problem	Type of goal
1. Choice	Decision between two or more alternatives
	Resolution of at least two conflicting issues
2. Change	
A. Response deficit	Response increment
	Response acquisition
B. Response inhibition	Disinhibition of response
	Working through of emotional reactions
C. Response excess	Response decrement
	Response elimination
D. Inadequate or inappropriate stimulus control	Response restructuring
3. Maintenance	Response maintenance at current frequency or amount or in current context

Identifying and Sequencing Subgoals or Action Steps

All of us can probably recall times when we were expected to learn something so fast that the learning experience was overwhelming and produced feelings of frustration, irritation, and discouragement. The change represented by counseling goals can be achieved best if the process is gradual. Any change program should be organized into an "orderly learning sequence" that guides the client through small steps toward the ultimate desired behaviors (Bandura, 1969, p. 74). In defining goals, this gradual learning sequence is achieved by breaking down the ultimate goal into a series of smaller goals called *subgoals* or *action steps*. Subgoals help clients move toward the solution of problems in a "planful way" (Dixon & Glover, 1984, p. 136). The subgoals are usually arranged

in a hierarchy, so that the client completes subgoals at the bottom of the ranked list before the ones near the top. Although an overall outcome goal can provide a "general directive" for change, the specific subgoals may determine a person's immediate activities and degree of effort in making changes (Bandura & Simon, 1977, p. 178). As these authors note, "By focusing on the distant future, it is easy to put off efforts at change in the present. . . . Exercising control over behaviors in the present increases the likelihood that desired futures will be realized" (p. 170). In a study reported by Seidner and Kirschenbaum (1980), commitment to identified goals was enhanced more when individuals agreed to participate fully in key aspects of a change program than when they agreed to pursue distant, long-range goals.

Bandura (1969) suggests that sequencing goals into smaller subgoals is more likely to produce the desired results for two reasons. First, completion of subgoals may keep failure experiences to a minimum. Completing subgoals successfully will encourage the client and will help maintain the client's motivation to change (p. 75). Jeffery (1977) found that progressively increasing subgoals sustained a high level of client motivation even when the overall outcomes were difficult to attain. Second, arranging the ultimate goal into subgoals indicates that immediate, daily subgoals may be more potent than distant, weekly subgoals.

Subgoals identified may represent covert as well as overt behavior, since a comprehensive change program usually involves changes in the client's thoughts and feelings as well as in overt behaviors and environmental situations. Subgoals may arise out of treatment approaches or recommended ways to resolve a particular problem or, when formal procedures are not available, from more informal and common-sense ideas. In any event, they are always actions that move the client in the direction of the desired outcome goal (Carkhuff & Anthony, 1979).

After subgoals are identified and selected, they

are rank-ordered in a series of tasks—a hierarchy —according to *complexity and degree of difficulty and immediacy.* Since some clients are put off by the word *hierarchy,* we use the term *goal pyramid* instead and pull out an 8½″ × 11″ sheet of paper that has a drawing of a blank pyramid on it, such as the one in Figure 9-3 (p. 238). A series of subgoal tasks may represent either increasing requirements of the same (overt or covert) behavior or demonstrations of different behaviors, with simpler and easier responses sequenced before more complex and difficult ones (Gambrill, 1977). The second criterion for ranking is immediacy. For this criterion, subgoals are ranked according to prerequisite tasks—that is, what tasks must be done before others can be achieved.

The sequencing of subgoals in order of complexity is based on learning principles called *shaping* and *successive approximations.* Shaping helps someone learn a small amount at a time, with reinforcement or encouragement for each task completed successfully. Gradually, the person learns the entire amount or achieves the overall result through these day-to-day learning experiences that successively approximate the overall outcome.

Steps in identifying and sequencing subgoals. Identification and arrangement of subgoals are critical to the client's success with the outcome goal. The following steps are involved in this process.

First, the client identifies the *first* step he or she must take—that is, the first things that need to be done to move in the desired direction. The first step will be some action that is both comfortable and achievable (Gambrill, 1977). As Carkhuff and Anthony (1979) note, "The great majority of people who abandon [change] programs do so because they find they are unable to complete the first step successfully. . . . Conversely, successful completion of the first step invariably reinforces a helpee's determination to go on by promoting self-confidence" (pp. 185–186). If the client identifies an action as the initial step but cannot answer affirmatively the following two questions suggested by Carkhuff and Anthony, then selecting that action as the initial step is not a good idea, and the choice needs further exploration and consideration. The two questions are "Will [the client] be able to take this first step successfully?" and "Does this first step lead directly toward the goal?" (Carkhuff & Anthony, 1979, p. 185).

Second, if the client progresses satisfactorily on the first step, additional intermediate steps that bridge the gap between the first step and the terminal goal are identified and ranked. (If the client does not progress on the first step, discuss this issue and consider revising the initial step.) Effective intermediate steps are ones that build on existing client assets and resources, do not conflict with the client's value system, are decided on and owned by the client, and represent immediate, daily, or short-term actions rather than weekly, distant, long-term actions (see also Bandura & Simon, 1977; Carkhuff & Anthony, 1979; Gambrill, 1977).

There is no hard and fast rule concerning the number of intermediate steps identified, other than ensuring that the gap between adjacent steps is not too great. Each successive step gradually begins where the last step left off. Clients can consider two questions in ranking successive intermediate steps: "Where will I be when I have completed this step?" and "What should my next major step be?" (Carkhuff & Anthony, 1979, p. 184). The counselor also needs to make sure that each intermediate step requires only one basic action or activity by the client; if two or more activities are involved, it is usually better to make this two separate steps (Carkhuff & Anthony, 1979).

As we mentioned earlier, intermediate steps are ranked on two aspects:

1. Degree of difficulty and complexity—"Which is easier; which is harder?" Less complex and demanding tasks are ranked ahead of others.
2. Immediacy—"What do I need to do before I can do this?" Prerequisite tasks are ranked before others.

Ranked steps are then filled in on the goal pyramid—usually in pencil, because in the process of moving through the hierarchy, the subgoals may need to be modified or rearranged. As Dixon and Glover observe, "Subgoals represent an early representation of the problem and may well be revised by the client and counselor as strategies are tested" (1984, p. 136).

Third, after all the steps have been identified and sequenced, the client starts to carry out the actions represented by the subgoals, beginning with the initial step and moving on. Usually, it is wise not to attempt a new subgoal until the client has successfully completed the previous one on the pyramid. Progress made on initial and subsequent steps provides useful information about whether the gaps between steps are too large or just right and whether the sequencing of steps is appropriate. As the subgoals are met, they become part of the client's current repertory that can be used in additional change efforts toward the terminal goals (Schwartz & Goldiamond, 1975, p. 117).

An example may clarify the process of identifying and sequencing subgoals for a client. Suppose you are working with a person who wishes to lose 40 pounds. Losing 40 pounds is not a goal that anyone can accomplish overnight or without small requisite changes along the way. First of all, the person will need to determine a reasonable weekly level of weight loss, such as 1 to 2 pounds. Next, you and the client will have to determine the tasks the client will need to complete in order to lose weight. These tasks can be stated as subgoals that the client can strive to carry out each day, starting with the initial subgoal, the one that feels most comfortable and easy to achieve, and working the way up the pyramid as each previous step is successfully completed and maintained in the client's repertory.

Although weight loss generally may include action steps such as alteration of eating levels, increase in physical activity, restructuring of cognitions and belief systems, and development of additional social skills, the exact tasks chosen by two or more clients who want to lose weight may be quite different. The therapist should be sensitive to such differences and not impose his or her method for solving the problem (such as weight loss) on the client. Similarly, each client will have a different idea of how subgoals will be best sequenced. In Figure 9-3 we illustrate how one particular client sequenced her identified subgoals on the goal pyramid. This client's rationale was that if she increased exercise and relaxation *first,* it would be easier to alter eating habits. For her, more difficult and also less immediate goals included restructuring her thoughts about herself and her body image and developing social skills necessary to initiate new relationships. This last subgoal she viewed as the most difficult one because her weight served partly to protect her from social distress situations. After all six subgoals are achieved, the

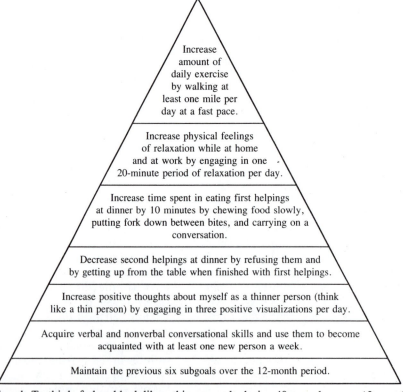

Increase amount of daily exercise by walking at least one mile per day at a fast pace.

Increase physical feelings of relaxation while at home and at work by engaging in one 20-minute period of relaxation per day.

Increase time spent in eating first helpings at dinner by 10 minutes by chewing food slowly, putting fork down between bites, and carrying on a conversation.

Decrease second helpings at dinner by refusing them and by getting up from the table when finished with first helpings.

Increase positive thoughts about myself as a thinner person (think like a thin person) by engaging in three positive visualizations per day.

Acquire verbal and nonverbal conversational skills and use them to become acquainted with at least one new person a week.

Maintain the previous six subgoals over the 12-month period.

Terminal goal: To think, feel and look like a thin person by losing 40 pounds over a 12-month period
Weekly goal: To think, feel, and look like a thin person by losing 1 pound per week

Figure 9-3. *Goal pyramid subgoals for example client*

final subgoal is simply to keep these actions going for at least a 12-month period. At the bottom of the pyramid, it would be important to discuss with her ways in which she can maintain the subgoals over an extended period of time. Note, too, in this example that her terminal goal is stated in positive terms — not "I don't want to be fat" but "I do want to feel, think, and look like a thin person." The subgoals represent actions she will take to support this desired outcome. Also note that all the subgoals are stated in the same way as the terminal outcome goal — with the definition of the behaviors to be changed, the level of change, and the conditions or circumstances of change so that the client knows what to do, where, when, with whom, and how much or how often.

Interview leads for identifying subgoals. In identifying subgoals, the counselor uses leads similar to the following to help the client determine appropriate subgoals or action steps:

"How will you go about doing [or thinking, feeling] this?"

"What exactly do you need to do to make this happen?"

"Let's brainstorm some actions you'll need to take to make your goal work for you."

"What have you done in the past to work toward this goal? How did it help?"

"Let's think of the steps you need to take to get from where you are now to where you want to be."

The counselor is always trying to encourage and support client participation and responsibility in goal setting, remembering that clients are more likely to carry out changes that they originate. Occasionally, however, after using leads like the ones above, some clients are unable to specify any desirable or necessary action steps or subgoals. The counselor may then have to prompt the client either by asking the client to think of other people who have similar problems and to identify their strategies for action or by providing a statement illustrating an example or model of an action step or subgoal (Dixon & Glover, 1984). Counselors do not prompt in these instances to give clients the answer but to "demonstrate that there are always alternatives" (Dixon & Glover, p. 97).

Interview leads for sequencing subgoals. General leads to use to sequence and rank subgoals include the following:

"What is your first step?"

"What would you be able to do most easily?"

"What would be most difficult?"

"What is most important for you to do now? least important?"

"How could we order these steps to maximize your success in reaching your goal?"

"Let's think of steps you need to take to get from where you are now to where you want to be — and arrange them in an order from what seems easiest to you to the ones that seem hardest for you."

"Can you think of some things you need to do before some other things as you make progress toward your goal?"

LEARNING ACTIVITY #28: IDENTIFYING AND SEQUENCING SUBGOALS

This learning activity is an extension of Learning Activity #27. Continue to work with the same goal you selected and defined in that activity. In this activity, we suggest the following steps:

1. First, identify the initial step you need to take to move toward your goal. Ask yourself:
   a. Does this step move directly toward the goal?
   b. Will I be able to take this step comfortably and successfully?
   Unless the answer to both questions is yes, redefine your initial step. Your initial step then becomes your first subgoal.
2. Generate a list of intermediate steps that bridge the gap between this initial step and your desired outcome. Consider where you will be after completing each step and what comes next. These intermediate steps become remaining subgoals. For each step in your list, consider:
   a. Does the step represent only one major activity?
   b. Is the step based on my existing assets and resources?
   c. Does the step support most of my major values and beliefs?
   d. Is the step something I want for myself?
   e. Does the step represent immediate, short-term activities rather than distant, long-term ones?
   If the answer to any of these questions for any particular step is no, rework that step.

(continued)

LEARNING ACTIVITY #28: IDENTIFYING AND SEQUENCING SUBGOALS (continued)

3. Write each step on a 3 X 5 index card. Then assign a numerical rating to each card for degree of difficulty, using a 0 to 100 scale: 0 = least complex, least difficult; 100 = most complex, most difficult.

4. Rank-order your steps or subgoals by arranging your cards in order, starting with the one closest to zero and ending with the one closest to 100. This represents the sequence in which you will complete your subgoals.

■

Identifying Obstacles

To ensure that the client can complete each subgoal step successfully, it is helpful to identify any *obstacles* that could interfere. Obstacles may include overt and/or covert behavior. *Potential* obstacles to "check out" with the client include the presence or absence of certain feelings or mood states, thoughts, beliefs and perceptions, other people, and situations or events. Another obstacle could be lack of knowledge or skill. As Gambrill (1977) points out, identification of lack of knowledge or skill is important because the client probably needs information or training before the subgoal action can be attempted.

Interview leads to identify obstacles. Clients are often not very aware of any factors that might interfere with completing a subgoal and may need prompts from the counselor, such as the following ones, to identify obstacles:

> "What are some obstacles you may encounter in trying to take this action?"
> "What people [feelings, ideas, situations] might get in the way of getting this done?"
> "What or who might prevent you from working on this activity?"
> "In what ways might you have difficulty completing this task successfully?"
> "What information or skills do you need in order to complete this action effectively?"

Occasionally the counselor may need to point out apparent obstacles that the client overlooks. If significant obstacles are identified, a plan to deal with or counteract the effects of these factors needs to be developed. Often this is similar to an "anti-sabotage plan" (see Chapter 20), in which the counselor and client try to predict ways in which the client might not do the desired activity and then work around the possible barriers. For example, suppose you explore obstacles with the client we described in the earlier section who wants to lose weight and become thin. Perhaps in exploring

the first subgoal, walking at least one mile a day, she identifies two things that might keep her from doing this: rain and being alone. Ways to prevent these two factors from interfering with her walking might be using an indoor facility and walking with an exercise partner.

Identifying Resources

The next step is to identify *resources* — factors that will help the client complete the subgoal task effectively. Like obstacles, resources include overt and covert behaviors. *Potential* resources to explore include feelings, thoughts and belief systems, people, situations, information, and skills. In this step, the counselor tries to help clients identify already present or developed resources that, if used, can make completion of the subgoal task(s) more likely and more successful.

Interview leads for identifying resources. Possible leads include the following:

> "Which resources do you have available to help you as you go through this activity [or action]?"
> "What specific feelings [or thoughts] are you aware of that might make it easier for you to _____?"
> "What kind of support system do you have from others that you can use to make it easier to _____?"
> "What skills [or information] do you possess that will help you do _____ more successfully?"

For example, the weight-loss client might identify a friend or other social support as a resource she could use for daily exercise, as well as her belief that exercise promotes wellness and good feelings.

Review of Progress

As any one subgoal is completed, it is helpful for the counselor and the client to review it together to assess *progress* and to determine whether the next-ranked subgoal is still relevant to the appropriate place on the goal pyramid. In any case where a subgoal is not met, the counselor and client should discuss what went wrong and what can be done more successfully in the future. According to Gambrill (1977), the most common reason for failure to carry out a subgoal is that the gaps between steps are too big. In this instance, the "failure" is a useful indication, letting the counselor know that smaller approximations are needed. Other areas to explore when subgoals are not met include whether the subgoal was really selected and owned by the client to begin with, whether it was carried out as specified, and whether the client had the resources to achieve it. If this exploration turns up nothing, then consider what the maladaptive behavior is trying to preserve and protect. Perhaps additional secondary gains yet to be identified are operating.

Counselors need to support, encourage, and reinforce the client for completion of subgoal tasks in order to help maintain client enthusiasm and commitment. It is also important to realize that goal setting has broader implications for clients than simply reaching a target objective. It is helpful to explore with clients what they are learning from this process and how this can be applied to other areas of their life as well. As Carkhuff and Anthony observe, clients "should gain more from the helping process itself than the limited ability to reach a single, isolated goal" (1979, p. 231).

Interviewing leads for reviewing progress. Leads to use during the review process include the following:

> "Can you describe how you carried out the plan [action] we worked out last week?"
> "What problems, if any, did you encounter in taking this action?"
> "What have you learned from doing this? Is it sufficient to move on now or do we need to work on this some more?"

☐ MODEL DIALOGUE: THE CASE OF JOAN

The dialogue for the case of Joan is continued to help you see how the leads for defining goals are used with a client. The session for selecting goals was presented earlier in this chapter. We pick up with the next session. As in the previous dialogue, each counselor response is prefaced by an explanation of what the counselor is doing.

The counselor will start by **summarizing** *the previous session and by checking out whether Joan's goals have changed in any way. Goal setting is a flexible process, subject to revisions along the way.*

1. *Counselor:* OK, Joan, last week when we talked, just to recap, you mentioned three areas you'd like to work on. Is this still accurate, or have you added anything or modified your thinking in any way about these since we last met?
   Client: No, that's still where I want to go right now. And I still want to start with this whole issue of expressing myself and not worrying so much about what other people think. I've been doing a lot of thinking about that this week, and I think I'm really starting to see how much I let other people use me as a doormat and also control my reactions in a lot of ways.

2. *Counselor:* Yes, you mentioned some of those things last week. They seem to be giving you some incentive to work on this.
   Client: Yeah. I guess I'm finally waking up and starting to feel a little fed up about it.

In the next response, the counselor explains the **purpose** *of the session and solicits Joan's opinion, again giving her another opportunity to express her opinions.*

3. *Counselor:* Last week I mentioned it might be helpful to map out a plan of action. How does that sound to you? If it isn't where you want to start, let me know.
   Client: No, I do. I've been kind of gearing up for this all week.

In the next two responses, the counselor helps Joan define the **behaviors** *associated with the goal—what she will be doing, thinking, or feeling.*

4. *Counselor:* OK, last week when we talked about this area of change, you described it as wanting to express yourself more without worrying so much about the reactions of other people. Could you tell me what you mean by expressing yourself—to make sure we're on the same wavelength?
   Client: Well, like in math class, I need to volunteer the answers when I know them, and volunteer to go to the board. Also, I hesitate to ask questions. I need to be able to ask a question without worrying if it sounds foolish.

5. *Counselor:* OK, you've mentioned three specific ways in math class you want to express yourself. [makes a note] I'm going to jot these down on this paper in case we want to refer to these later. Anything else you can think of in math class?
   Client: No, not really. The other situation I have trouble with is with my folks.

*"Trouble" is not very specific. Again, a **behavioral definition** of the goal is sought in the next two responses.*

6. *Counselor:* OK, "trouble." Again, can you describe exactly how you'd like to express yourself when interacting with them?

   Client: Well, kind of the same stuff. Sometimes I would like to ask them a question. Or ask for help or something. But I don't. I almost never express my ideas or opinions to them, especially if I don't agree with their ideas. I just keep things to myself.

7. *Counselor:* So you'd like to be able to make a request, ask a question, talk about your ideas with them, and express disagreement.

   Client: Yeah. Wow—sounds hard.

*In the following response, the counselor prepares Joan for the idea of working in **small steps** and also explores **conditions (situations, people)** associated with the goal.*

8. *Counselor:* It will take some time, and we won't try to do everything at once. Just one step at a time. Now, you've mentioned two different situations where these things are important to you—math class and with your parents. I noticed last week there was one time when you were reluctant to express your opinion with me. Is this something you want to do in any other situations or with any other people?

   Client: Well, sure—in that it does crop up occasionally at different times or with different people, even friends. But it's worse in math and at home. I think if I could do it there, I could do it anywhere.

*In the next response, the counselor starts to explore the **level** or **desired extent of change**. The counselor is attempting to establish a **current base rate** in order to know how much the client is doing now.*

9. *Counselor:* OK, I'm making a note of this, too. Now could you estimate how often you express yourself in the ways you've described above *right now,* either in math class or with your folks, during the course of an average week?

   Client: You mean how many times do I do these things during the week?

10. *Counselor:* Yes.

    Client: Probably almost never—at least not in math class or at home. Maybe once or twice at the most.

*The counselor continues to help Joan identify a **practical** and **realistic level of change**.*

11. *Counselor:* OK, if you express yourself in one of these ways once or twice a week now, how often

would you like to be doing this? Think of something that is also practical or realistic.

Client: Mm. Well, I don't really know. Offhand, I'd guess about four or five times—that's about once a day, and that would take a lot of energy for me to be able to do that in these situations.

*At this point, the **behavior, conditions, and level of change** for this terminal goal are defined. The counselor asks Joan whether this definition is the way she wants it.*

12. *Counselor:* OK, I'll make a note of this. Check what I have written down—does it seem accurate? [Joan reads what is listed as the first terminal goal on her goal chart at the end of this dialogue.]

    Client: Yeah. Boy, that sort of makes it official, doesn't it?

*This is the second time Joan has expressed a little hesitation. So the counselor will check out **her feelings** about the process in the next response.*

13. *Counselor:* Yes. What kinds of feelings are you having about what we're doing now?

    Client: Kind of good and a little scared too. Like do I really have what it takes to do this?

*In the next response, the counselor responds to Joan's concern. Joan has already selected this goal, yet if she has difficulty later on moving toward it, they will need to explore **what her present behavior is trying to protect.***

14. *Counselor:* One thing I am sure of is that you do have the resources inside you to move in this direction as long as this is a direction that is important to you and one that is not necessary to protect any parts of you. If we move along and you feel stuck, we'll come back to this and see how you keep getting stuck at this point.

    Client: OK.

*In the next response, the counselor introduces the idea of **subgoals** that represent small action steps toward the terminal goal and asks Joan to identify the **initial step**.*

15. *Counselor:* Another thing that I think might help with your apprehension is to map out a plan of action. What we've just done is to identify exactly where you want to get to—maybe over the course of the next few months. Instead of trying to get there all at once, let's look at different steps you could take to get there, with the idea of taking just one step at a time, just like climbing a staircase. For instance, what do you think would be your first step—the first thing you would need to do to get started in a direction that moves directly to this end result?

Client: Well, the first thing that comes to my mind is needing to be less uptight. I worry about what other people's reactions will be when I do say something.

In the next two responses, the counselor helps Joan define the **behavior and conditions associated with this initial subgoal,** *just as she did previously for the terminal goal.*

16. *Counselor:* OK, so you want to be less uptight and worry less about what other people might think. When you say other people, do you have any particular persons in mind?
    Client: Well, my folks, of course, and to some degree almost anyone that I don't know too well or anyone like my math teacher, who is in a position to evaluate me.
17. *Counselor:* So you're talking mainly about lessening these feelings when you're around your folks, your math teacher, or other people who you think are evaluating you.
    Client: Yes, I think that's it.

In response 18, the counselor is trying to establish the **current level of intensity** *associated with Joan's feelings of being uptight. She does this by using an* **imagery assessment.** *If Joan had trouble engaging in imagery,* **role-play assessment** *could be used.* **Self-reported ratings of intensity** *are used in conjunction with the imagery.*

18. *Counselor:* OK, now I'm going to ask you to close your eyes and imagine a couple of situations that I'll describe to you. Try to really get involved in the situation — put yourself there. If you feel any nervousness, signal by raising this finger. [Counselor shows Joan the index finger of her right hand and describes three situations — one related to parents, one related to math class, and one related to a job interview with a prospective employer. In all three situations, Joan raises her finger. After each situation, the counselor stops and asks Joan to rate the intensity of her anxiety on a 100-point scale, 0 being complete calm and relaxation and 100 being total panic.]

After the imagery assessment for base rate, the counselor asks Joan to **specify a desired level of change for this subgoal.**

19. *Counselor:* OK. Now, just taking a look at what happened here in terms of the intensity of your feelings, you rated the situation with your folks about 75, the one in math class 70, and the one with the employer 65. Where would you like to see this drop down to during the next couple of weeks?
    Client: Oh, I guess about a 10.

It is understandable that someone with fairly intense anxiety wants to get rid of it, and it is possible to achieve that within the next few months. However, such goals are more effective when they are **immediate rather than distant.** *In the next two responses, the counselor asks Joan to* **specify a realistic level of change** *for the immediate future.*

20. *Counselor:* OK, that may be a number to shoot for in the next few months, but I'm thinking that in the next three or four weeks the jump from, say, 70 to 10 is pretty big. Does that gap feel realistic or feasible?
    Client: Mm. I guess I was getting ahead of myself.
21. *Counselor:* Well, it's important to think about where you want to be in the long run. I'm suggesting three or four weeks mainly so you can start to see some progress and lessening of intensity of these feelings in a fairly short time. What number seems reasonable to you to shoot for in the short run?
    Client: Well, maybe a 45 or 50.

At this point, the counselor and Joan continue to **identify other subgoals or intermediate steps** *between the initial goal and the terminal outcome.*

22. *Counselor:* OK, that seems real workable. Now, we've sort of mapped out the first step. Let's think of other steps between this first one and this end result we've written down here. [Counselor and client continue to generate possible action steps. Eventually they select and define the remaining three shown on Joan's goal chart.]

Assuming the remaining subgoals are selected and defined, the next step is to **rank-order** *or* **sequence** *the subgoals and* **list them in order on the goal pyramid.**

23. *Counselor:* OK, we've got the first step, and now we've mapped out three more. Consider where you will be after this first step is completed — which one of these remaining steps comes next? Let's discuss it, and then we'll fill it in, along with this first step, on this goal pyramid, which you can keep so you know exactly what part of the pyramid you're on and when. [Counselor and Joan continue to rank-order subgoals, and Joan lists them in sequenced order on a goal pyramid.]

In response 24, the counselor points out that **subgoals may change in type or sequence.** *The counselor then shifts the focus to exploration of potential* **obstacles for the initial subgoal.**

24. *Counselor:* OK, now we've got our overall plan mapped out. This can change, too. You might find later on you may want to add a step or reorder the steps. Now, let's go back to your first

step—decreasing these feelings of nervousness and worrying less about the reactions of other people. Since this is what you want to start working on this week, can you think of anything or anybody that might get in your way or would make it difficult to work on this?

Client: Not really, because it is mostly something inside me. In this instance, I guess I am my own worst enemy.

25. *Counselor:* So you're saying there don't seem to be any people or situations outside yourself that may be obstacles. If anyone sets up an obstacle course, it will be you.

Client: Yeah. Mostly because I feel I have so little control of those feelings.

The client has identified herself and her perceived lack of control over her feelings as **obstacles.** *Later on, the counselor will need to help Joan select and work with one or two* **intervention strategies.**

26. *Counselor:* So one thing we need to do is to look at ways you can develop skills and know-how to manage these feelings so they don't get the best of you.

Client: Yup. I think that would help.

In the next response, the counselor explores **existing resources and support systems** *that Joan might use to help her work effectively with the subgoal.*

27. *Counselor:* OK, that's where I'd like to start in just a minute. Before we do, can you identify any people who could help you with these feelings—

or anything else you could think of that might help instead of hinder you?

Client: Well, coming to see you. It helps to know I can count on that. And I have a real good friend who is sort of the opposite of me, and she's real encouraging.

"Social allies" *are an important principle in effecting change, and the counselor uses this word in response 28 to underscore this point.*

28. *Counselor:* OK, so you've got at least two allies.
Client: Yeah.

In response 29, the counselor helps Joan develop a way to continue the **self-ratings of the intensity** *of her nervous feelings. This gives both of them a* **benchmark to use in assessing progress and reviewing** *the adequacy of the first subgoal selected.*

29. *Counselor:* The other thing I'd like to mention is a way for you to keep track of any progress you're making. You know how you related these situations I described today? You could continue to do this by keeping track of situations in which you feel uptight and worry about the reactions of others—jot down a brief note about what happened and then a number on this 0 to 100 scale that best represents how intense your feelings are at that time. As you do this and bring it back, it will help both of us see exactly what's happening for you on this first step. Does that sound like something you would find agreeable?

Client: Yeah—do I need to do it during the situation or after?

Joan's goal chart

Terminal goal	Related subgoals
Goal 1 (B) to acquire and demonstrate a minimum of four different initiating skills (asking a question or making a reasonable request, expressing differences of opinion, expressing positive feelings, expressing negative feelings, volunteering answers or opinions, going to the board in class) (C) in her math class and with her parents (L) in at least 4 situations a week	1. (B) to decrease anxiety associated with anticipation of failure (C) in math class or rejection by parents (L) from a self-rated intensity of 70 to 50 on a 100-point scale during the next 2 weeks 2. (B) to restructure thoughts or self-talk by replacing thoughts that "girls are dumb" with "girls are capable" (C) in math class and in other threatening or competitive situations (L) from 0–2 per day to 4–5 per day 3. (B) to increase attendance (C) at math class (L) from 2–3 times per week to 4–5 times per week 4. (B) to increase verbal participation skills (asking and answering questions, volunteering answers or offering opinions) (C) in math class and with her parents (L) from 0–1 times per day to 3–4 times per day

(continued)

Terminal goal	Related subgoals
Goal 2 (B) to increase positive perceptions about herself and her ability to function effectively (C) in competitive situations such as math class (L) by 50% over the next 3 months	1. (B) to eliminate conversations (C) with others in which she discusses her lack of ability (L) from 2–3 per week to 0 per week 2. (B) to increase self-visualizations in which she sees herself as competent and adequate to function independently (C) in competitive situations or with persons in authority (L) from 0 per day to 1–2 per day 3. (B) to identify negative thoughts and increase positive thoughts (C) about herself (L) by 25% in the next 2 weeks
Goal 3 (B) to acquire and use five different decision-making skills (identifying an issue, generating alternatives, evaluating alternatives, selecting the best alternative, and implementing action) (C) at least one of which represents a situation in which significant others have given her their opinion or advice on how to handle it (L) in at least two different situations during a month	1. (B) to decrease thoughts and worry about making a bad choice or poor decision (C) in any decision-making situation (L) by 25% in the next 2 weeks 2. (B) to choose a course of action and implement it (C) in any decision-making situation (L) at least once during the next 2 weeks

Key: B = behavior; C = condition; L = level.

Clients are more likely to do **self-ratings or self-monitoring if it falls into their daily routine,** *so this is explored in the next response.*

30. *Counselor:* What would be most practical for you?

    Client: Probably after, because it's hard to write in the middle of it.

The counselor encourages Joan to make her notes soon after the situation is over. **The longer the gap, the less accurate or reliable** *the data might be.*

31. *Counselor:* That's fine; try to write it down as soon as it ends or shortly thereafter, because the longer you wait, the harder it will be to remember.

Before the session ends, they have to work on the **obstacle** *Joan identified earlier—that she is her own worst enemy because her feelings are in control of her. At this point, some of the real nuts and bolts of counseling begin. The counselor will need to select an intervention strategy or theoretical approach to use with Joan in this instance. (Two such options, thought stopping and cognitive restructuring, are described and modeled in Chapters 15 and 16.)*

32. *Counselor:* Now, let's go back to that obstacle you mentioned earlier—that your feelings are in control of you. . . .

□ SUMMARY

The primary purpose of selecting goals is to convey to the client the responsibility and participation she or he has in contributing to the results of counseling. Without active client participation, counseling may be doomed to failure, resembling little more than a benevolent dictatorship. The selection of goals should reflect client choices. The counselor's role is mainly to use leads that facilitate the client's goal selection. Together, the counselor and client explore whether the goal is owned by the client, whether it is realistic, and what advantages and disadvantages are associated with it. However, some value judgments by both counselor and client may be inevitable during this process. If the client selects goals that severely conflict with the counselor's values or exceed the counselor's level of competence, the counselor may decide to refer the client or to renegotiate this goal. If counselor and client agree to pursue the selected goals, these goals must be defined clearly and specifically.

Well-defined goals make it easier to note and assess progress and also aid in guiding the client toward the desired goal(s). Goals are defined when you are able to specify the overt and covert behaviors associated with the goal, the conditions or context in which the goal is to be carried out or achieved, and the level of change. After the outcome goal(s) is defined, the counselor and client work jointly to identify and sequence subgoals that represent intermediate action steps and lead directly to the goal. Obstacles that might hinder goal attainment and resources that may facilitate goal attainment are also explored.

As you go through the process of helping clients develop goals, remember that goal setting is a dynamic and flexible process. "Decisions about objectives are not irrevocable" (Bandura, 1969, p. 103). Goals may change or may be redefined substantially as counseling progresses (Thompson & Wise, 1976). Once the person begins to change in a certain direction, the actual consequences of the change may lead to modification of the initial goals. Changes that the client originally perceived as feasible may turn out to be unrealistic. Moreover, as Bandura points out, at different points during the counseling process, some "previously ignored areas of behavioral functioning may become more important" (p. 104).

For these reasons, the outcome goals should always be viewed as temporary and subject to change. Client "resistance" at later stages in counseling may be the client's way of saying that the original goals need to be modified or redefined. The counselor who is committed to counseling to meet the client's needs will remember that, at any stage, the client always has the prerogative of changing or modifying directions. If the counselor is "highly sensitive to feedback from resultant changes," any or all parts of the original goal may be reevaluated and modified (Bandura, 1969, p. 104).

The flexibility required in modifying outcome goals should also be a part of the interview process for defining goals. Do not get so bogged down in checking off the interview categories that you lose touch with the client. As you become more comfortable in defining outcome goals, we hope you will not become encapsulated by the procedure. Remember, there is much more to counseling than carrying out a procedure in an assembly-line fashion.

POSTEVALUATION

PART ONE

Objective one asks you to identify a problem for which you select and define an outcome goal. Use the Goal-Setting Worksheet below for this process. You can obtain feedback by sharing your worksheet with a colleague, supervisor, or instructor.

Goal-Setting Worksheet

1. Identify a concern or problem.
2. State the desired outcome of the problem.
3. Assess the desired outcome (#2 above):
   a. Does it specify what you want to do? (If not, reword it so that you state what you want to do instead of what you don't want to do.)
   b. Is this something you can see (hear, grasp) yourself doing every time?
4. In what ways is achievement of this goal important to you? to others?
5. What will achieving this goal require of you? of others?
6. To what extent is this goal something you want to do? something you feel you should do or are expected to do?
7. Is this goal based on:
   _____ rational, logical ideas?

   _____ realistic expectations, ideas?
   _____ irrational ideas and beliefs?
   _____ logical thinking?
   _____ perfectionistic standards (for self or others)?
8. How will achieving this goal help *you*? help significant others in your life?
9. What problems could achieving this goal create for you? for others?
10. If the goal requires someone else to change, is not realistic or feasible, is not worthwhile, or poses more disadvantages than advantages, rework the goal. Then move on to #11.
11. Specify exactly *what* you will be
    a. doing_____
    b. thinking_____
    c. feeling_____
    as a result of goal achievement. Be specific.
12. Specify your goal definition in #11 by indicating:
    a. *where* this will occur: _____
    b. *when* this will occur: _____
    c. *with whom* this will occur: _____
    d. *how much or how often* this will occur: _____
13. Develop a plan that specifies *how* you will attain your goal by identifying action steps included in the plan.

(continued)

a. _____

b. _____

c. _____

d. _____

e. _____

f. _____

g. _____

h. _____

i. _____

j. _____

k. _____

l. _____

14. *Check* your list of action steps:

    a. Are the gaps between steps small? If not, add a step or two.

    b. Does each step represent only one major activity? If not, separate this one step into two or more steps.

    c. Does each step specify what, where, when, with whom, and how much or how often? If not, go back and define your action steps more concretely.

15. Use the goal pyramid below to sequence your list of action steps, starting with the easiest, most immediate step on the top and proceeding to the bottom of the pyramid by degree of difficulty and immediacy or proximity to the goal.

16. For each action step (starting with the first), brainstorm what could make it difficult to carry out or could interfere with doing it successfully. Consider feelings, thoughts, places, people, and lack of knowledge or skills. Write down the obstacles in the space provided on page 248.

17. For each action step (starting with the first), identify existing resources such as feelings, thoughts, situations, people and support systems, information, and skills that would make it more likely for you to carry out the action or complete it more successfully. Write down the resources in the space provided on page 248.

18. Identify a way to monitor and reinforce yourself for completion of each action step.

19. Develop a plan to help yourself maintain the action steps once you have attained them.

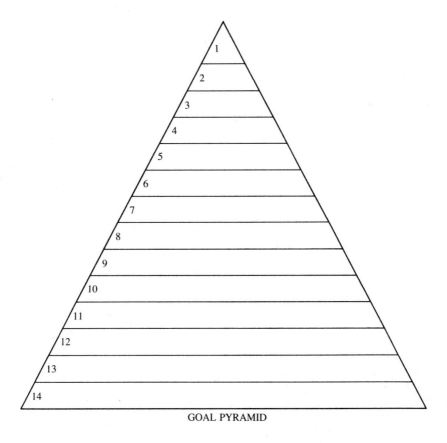

GOAL PYRAMID

(continued)

POSTEVALUATION (continued)

Obstacles		Action Steps	Resources
	1.		
	2.		
	3.		
	4.		
	5.		
	6.		
	7.		
	8.		
	9.		
	10.		
	11.		
	12.		

PART TWO

In this section of the postevaluation, you are to identify, from among 10 examples of client outcome goals, those that represent changes owned by the client, are based on realistic ideas, and are behaviorally defined, with an 80% accuracy rate (Chapter Objective Two). Examine carefully the following list of goals, and note in writing whether each goal is OK or not OK. If you decide a goal is not OK, identify which of the following are apparent problems with the goal (there may be more than one):

a. Change not owned by client
b. Goal based on irrational or magical thinking
c. Goal not behaviorally defined

Check your responses against those given in the feedback following the postevaluation.

1. I'd feel content if I could have a good sexual experience with my husband where I experience orgasm at least once a week.
2. I want him to like me.
3. I want to be more loving toward my child.
4. I wish she would see it my way.
5. I just want my dad to stop yelling at me for at least once a day.
6. I'd like to be able to get up at least in front of people I know and be able to role-play or talk without having this terrible knot in my stomach.
7. I don't ever want to get in trouble at school.
8. I'd like to get 100s on all my homework.
9. I wish my girlfriend would agree to have sex with me at least four or five times every day.
10. I want to be able to say no to any request my family makes of me that I feel is unreasonable.

PART THREE

In this part of the postevaluation, we describe a client case, the case of Jerry. Assuming that Jerry is your client, describe the steps you would go through to help him explore, select, and define desired actions, given his stated problem (Chapter Objective Three). Try to include at least 11 of the 15 steps or categories we described in this chapter for selecting and defining outcome goals. You can do this orally with a partner, in small groups, or by yourself. If you do it by yourself, you may want to jot down your ideas in writing for someone else to look at. Feedback follows the postevaluation.

The Case of Jerry

Jerry Bolwin is a 52-year-old manager of an advertising firm. He has been with the firm for 17 years and has another 12–15 years to go before drawing a rather lucrative retirement package. Over the last three years, however, Jerry has become increasingly dissatisfied with his job specifically and with the work world in general. He says he feels as if he would want nothing better than to quit and go hop on a steamer and sail off to China. Jerry is divorced and no longer has any financial obligations to his ex-wife and his only son. He does state, however, that he'd like to build up a "nest egg" for his son's two young children, as his grandchildren are very important to him. He realizes that if he left the firm now, he would lose many of his retirement benefits. Jerry defines his problem as feeling burned out with the "nine to five" job routine.

PART FOUR

According to Objective Four, you will be able to demonstrate, in an interview setting, at least 11 of the 15

(continued)

categories identified for selecting and defining client outcome goals. We suggest you complete this part of the postevaluation in triads. One person assumes the role of the counselor and demonstrates helping the client with the goal-setting process in a 20- or 30-minute interview. The second person takes the role of the client. You may wish to portray the role and problem described for Jerry Bolwin in Part Three. (If you choose to present something unfamiliar to the counselor, be sure to inform the counselor of your identi-fied problem or concern before you begin.) The third person assumes the role of the observer. The observer may act as the counselor's alter ego and cue the counselor during the role play if necessary. The observer also provides feedback to the counselor after the interview, using the Interview Checklist for Selecting and Defining Goals that follows below as a guide. If you do not have access to an observer, tape-record your interview so you can assess it yourself.

INTERVIEW CHECKLIST FOR SETTING AND DEFINING GOALS

Instructions: Determine which of the following leads or questions the counselor demonstrated. Check each counselor question or lead demonstrated. Also check whether the client answered the content of the counselor's question. Example counselor leads and questions are provided next to each item of the checklist. These are only suggestions — be alert to other responses used by the counselor.

Scoring	Category of information	Examples of counselor leads or questions	Client response
____Yes____No	1. Explain the purpose and importance of having goals or positive outcomes to the client.	"Let's talk about some areas you would like to work on during counseling. This will help us to do things that are related to what you want to accomplish."	__indicates understanding
____Yes____No	2. Determine *positive* changes desired by client ("I would like" versus "I can't").	"What would you like to be doing [thinking, feeling] differently?" "Suppose some distant relative you haven't seen for a while comes here in several months. What would be different then from the way things are now?" "Assuming we are successful, what do you want to be doing, or how would this change for you?" "In what ways do you want to benefit from counseling?"	__identifies goal in positive terms
____Yes____No	3. Determine whether the goal selected represents changes owned by the client rather than someone else ("I want to talk to my mom without yelling at her," rather than "I want my mom to stop yelling at me").	"How much control do you have to make this happen?" "What changes will this goal require of you?" "What changes will this goal require someone else to make?" "Can this goal be achieved without the help of anyone else?" "To whom is this goal most important?"	__identifies who owns the goal
____Yes____No	4. Determine whether the goal is based on realistic expectations rather than unrealistic or irra-tional ideas or self-de-mands ("I want to have more friends," rather than "I want to be liked by everyone").	"To what extent do you want to achieve this goal?" "To what extent do you feel you should achieve this goal?" "To what degree is this goal based on realistic expectations?" "To what degree does this goal represent wishful thinking?" "How feasible is it for you to _____?"	__identifies underlying expectations

(continued)

POSTEVALUATION (continued)

Scoring	Category of information	Examples of counselor leads or questions	Client response
		"Is it reasonable to expect to effect a change in this area?" "To what extent are you leaning toward this goal because you know it's something you can achieve with little effort or little risk?" "To what extent are you leaning toward this goal because it's out of your reach and you'll be excused if you don't make it?"	
____Yes____No	5. Identify advantages (positive consequences) to client and others of goal achievement.	"In what ways is it worthwhile to you and others to achieve this goal?" "How will achieving this goal help you?" "What problems will continue for you if you don't pursue this goal?" "What are the advantages of achieving this goal—for you? others?" "Who will benefit from this change—and how?"	―identifies advantages
____Yes____No	6. Identify disadvantages (negative consequences) of goal achievement to client and others.	"What new problems in living might achieving this goal pose for you?" "Are there any disadvantages to going in this direction?" "How will achieving this goal affect your life in adverse ways?" "How might this change limit or constrain you?"	―identifies disadvantages
____Yes____No	7. Identify whether, as the helper, you are willing and competent to help the client with the stated goals (decision point).	"These are things I am able to help you work with." "I feel uncomfortable working with you on this issue because of my own personal values [or lack of knowledge]. I'd like to give you the names of several other counselors . . . ." "This would be hard for me to help you with because it seems as if you're choosing something that will restrict you and not give you any options. Let's talk more about this."	―responds to counselor's decision
____Yes____No	8. Identify what the client will be doing, thinking, or feeling in a concrete, observable way as a result of goal achievement ("I want to be able to talk to my mom without yelling at her," rather than "I want to get along with my mom").	"What do you want to be able to do [think, feel] differently?" "What would I see you doing [thinking, feeling] after this change?" "Describe a good and a poor example of this goal."	―specifies overt and covert behaviors
____Yes____No	9. Specify under what conditions and what situations goals will be achieved: when, where, and with whom ("I want to be able to	"When do you want to accomplish this goal?" "Where do you want to do this?" "With whom?" "In what situations?"	―specifies people and places

(continued)

Scoring	Category of information	Examples of counselor leads or questions	Client response

	talk to my mom at home during the next month without yelling at her").		
——Yes——No	10. Specify how often or how much client will do something to achieve goal ("I want to be able to talk to my mom at home during the next month without yelling at her at least once a day").	"How much [or how often] are you doing this [or feeling this way] now?" "What is a realistic increase or decrease?" "How much [or how often] do you want to be doing this to be successful at your goal?" "What amount of change is realistic, considering where you are right now?"	——specifies amount
——Yes——No	11. Identify and list small action steps the client will need to take to reach the goal (that is, break the big goal down into little subgoals). *List of Action Steps* 1. 2. 3. 4. 5. 6. 7. 8. 9. 10.	"How will you go about doing [thinking, feeling] this?" "What exactly do you need to do to make this happen?" "Let's brainstorm some actions you'll need to take to make your goal work for you." "What have you done in the past to work toward this goal?" "How did it help?" "Let's think of the steps you need to take to get from where you are now to where you want to be."	——lists possible action steps
——Yes——No	12. Sequence the action steps on the goal pyramid (a hierarchy) in terms of a. degree of difficulty (least to most) b. immediacy (most to least immediate)	"What is your first step?" "What would you be able to do most easily?" "What would be most difficult?" "What is your foremost priority?" "What is most important for you to do soon? least important?" "How could we order these steps to maximize your success in reaching your goal?" "Let's think of the steps you need to take to get from where you are now to where you want to be and arrange them in an order from what seems easiest to you to the ones that seem hardest." "Can you think of some things you need to do before some other things as you make progress toward this outcome?"	——assists in rank-ordering

Least difficult, most immediate
1
2
3
4
5
6
7
8
9
10
Most difficult, least immediate

(continued)

POSTEVALUATION (continued)

Scoring	Category of information	Examples of counselor leads or questions	Client response
____Yes____No	13. Identify any people, feelings, or situations that could prevent the client from taking action to reach the goal.	"What are some obstacles you may encounter in trying to take this action?" "What people [feelings, ideas, situations] might get in the way of getting this done?" "In what ways could you have difficulty completing this task successfully?" "What do you need to know to take this action?" or "What skills do you need to have?"	___identifies possible obstacles
____Yes____No	14. Identify any resources (skill, knowledge, support) that client needs to take action to meet the goal.	"What resources do you have available to help you as you complete this activity?" "What particular thoughts or feelings are you aware of that might make it easier for you to ____?" "What kind of support system do you have from others that you can use to make it easier to ____?" "What skills [or information] do you possess that will help you do this more successfully?"	___identifies existing resources and supports
____Yes____No	15. Develop a plan to monitor and review progress toward the goal.	"Would it be practical for you to rate these feelings [count the times you do this] during the next two weeks? This information will help us determine the progress you are making." "Let's discuss a way you can keep track of how easy or hard it is for you to take these steps this week."	___agrees to monitor in some fashion

Observer Comments: _____

_____

☐ SUGGESTED READINGS

Carkhuff, R. R., & Anthony, W. A. (1979). *The skills of helping.* Amherst, MA: Human Resource Development Press. Chapter 5, "Helping People Define Goals and Select Courses of Action"; Chapter 6, "Helping People Develop Programs to Reach Goals"; Chapter 7, "Helping People Take Steps to Reach Their Goals."

Dixon, D. N., & Glover, J. A. (1984). *Counseling: A problem-solving approach.* New York: Wiley. Chapter 8, "Goal Selection."

Frey, D. H., & Raming, H. E. (1979). A taxonomy of counseling goals and methods. *Personnel and Guidance Journal, 58,* 26–33.

Lloyd, M. E. (1983). Selecting systems to measure client outcome in human service agencies. *Behavioral Assessment, 5,* 55–70.

Locke, E. A., Shaw, K. N., Saari, L. M., & Latham, G. P. (1981). Goal-setting and task performance; 1969–1980. *Psychological Bulletin, 90,* 125–152.

Rosen, A., & Proctor, E. (1981). Distinctions between treatment outcomes and their implications for treatment evaluation. *Journal of Consulting and Clinical Psychology, 49,* 418–425.

Seidner, M. L., & Kirschenbaum, D. S. (1980). Behavioral contracts: Effects of pretreatment information and intervention statements. *Behavior Therapy, 11,* 689–698.

FEEDBACK: POSTEVALUATION

PART TWO
1. Goal OK.
2. Goal not OK:
   a. Change is not owned by this client.
   b. Goal may represent wishful and magical thinking.
   c. Goal is not behaviorally defined.

3. Goal not OK.
   c. Goal is not behaviorally defined.
4. Goal not OK.
   a. Change is not owned by this client.
   b. Goal represents wishful and irrational thinking.
   c. Goal is not behaviorally defined.
5. Goal not OK.
   a. Change is not owned by this client.
6. Goal OK.
7. Goal not OK.
   b. Goal is based on negative and irrational thinking.
   c. Goal is not behaviorally defined.
8. Goal not OK.
   d. Goal is based on wishful thinking.
9. Goal not OK.
   a. Change is not owned by this client.
   b. Goal is *probably* not realistic or is based on wishful thinking, given the stated frequency —at least neither person would get much else done!
10. Goal OK.

PART THREE

1. First, explain to Jerry the *purpose and importance* of developing goals.
2. Help Jerry state the goal or desired change in *positive terms*.
3. Help Jerry determine whether the goal he is moving toward represents *changes owned by him* and whether such factors are under his control. Probably, deciding to give up his job and/or take a leave of absence would be changes under his control.
4. Determine whether Jerry's ideas about change are *realistic*. There seems to be a little bit of an element of wishful thinking (sail off to China). However, the degree to which his goal reflects *realistic expectations* would need to be explored with him.
5. Help Jerry identify *advantages* or *benefits* to be realized by achieving his goal. He seems to be thinking about increased leisure time as a major benefit—are there others?
6. Help Jerry identify *disadvantages* or *possible costs* of making the desired change. He has mentioned loss of retirement benefits as one cost. Are there others? Do the perceived benefits outweigh the costs?
7. If Jerry's goal is not realistic or if it looks as if it will have too many costs, explore other options with him, leaving the final decision about goals up to him. At this point, you will need to *decide whether you are able to help* him pursue his goal.
8. Assuming you will continue to work with Jerry, help him *define his goal behaviorally* by specifying exactly *what* he will be doing, thinking, and feeling as a result of goal achievement.
9. Further specification of the goal includes *where, when,* and *with whom* this will occur and
10. *how much* or *how often* it will occur. An option that might be useful for Jerry is to develop and scale five possible outcomes, ranging from the most unfavorable one to the most expected one to the best possible one.
11. Help Jerry explore and *identify action steps or subgoals* that represent small approximations toward the overall goal. Help him choose action steps that are practical, are based on his resources, and support his values.
12. Help Jerry *sequence the action steps* according to *immediacy and difficulty* so he knows what step he will take first and what step will be his last one.
13. Explore any *obstacles* that could impede progress toward the goal, such as the presence or absence of certain feelings, ideas, thoughts, situations, responses, people, and knowledge and skills.
14. Explore existing *resources* that could help Jerry complete the action steps more successfully. Like obstacles, exploration of resources also includes the presence or absence of certain feelings, ideas, thoughts, situations, responses, people, and knowledge and skills.
15. Help Jerry develop a *plan to review completion of the action steps* and *progress toward the goal,* including a way to monitor and reward himself for progress and a plan to help him maintain changes.

EVALUATING PROCESSES AND OUTCOMES IN HELPING

A primary part of helping involves monitoring and evaluating the effects of the helping process. We view evaluation as a major component of helping that is just as vital to the conduct of therapy as all the other components. An evaluation of helping provides encouragement to both counselor and client and also indicates the extent to which counseling goals have been achieved. As Egan points out,

> Tangible results form the backbone of the reinforcement process in counseling. If the client is to be encouraged to move forward, he must see results. Therefore, both counselor and client should be able to judge whether the action program is or is not being implemented, and to what degree, and the results of this implementation [1975, p. 225].

The remaining chapters contain many references to analogue and clinical research studies that have demonstrated "effective" outcomes resulting from a particular therapeutic strategy applied to certain clinical problems. These studies are examples of experimental research. The experimental designs used in research studies have been described in a variety of sources (Barlow, Hayes, & Nelson, 1984; Hersen & Barlow, 1976; Huck, Cormier, & Bounds, 1974; Kazdin, 1973b, 1976d, 1980a, 1981). It is not the purpose of this chapter to describe the potential use and relevance of experimental designs. Our objective is to present some practical techniques that a counselor can use to evaluate the process and outcomes of therapy.

Although some of the methodology and schemes for evaluation presented in this chapter are the same as some research designs, the purpose of counseling evaluation is often different from the objectives of experimental research. Empirical research can be considered a quest for causality or "truth." In contrast, a counseling evaluation is more of a hypothesis-testing process (Shapiro, 1966). The data collected in a helping evaluation are used to make decisions about selection of treatment strategies and about the extent to which a client's stated goals were achieved. Mahoney has summarized the use of data collection in making decisions about helping processes and outcomes:

The most efficient therapist is sensitively tuned to the personal data of the client. He is not collecting data for the sake of scientific appearances or because that is what is considered proper. . . . The effective therapist uses data to guide his or her own efforts at having an impact, and—regardless of theoretical bias or procedural preference—he adjusts therapeutic strategies in tune with that feedback [1977b, p. 241].

□ OBJECTIVES

1. Given a client case description and a description of data-collection and evaluation procedures, identify:
   a. Response dimensions used with this client.
   b. Methods of measurement used with this client.
   c. Times of measurement.
2. Given examples of client self-monitoring data during baseline, treatment, and posttreatment assessment periods, graph these data and identify trends reflected in the graphs.
3. With yourself, another person, or a client, conduct an outcome evaluation of one real or hypothetical outcome goal, specifying the response dimensions, methods, and times of measurement.

□ DEFINITION AND PURPOSE OF HELPING EVALUATION

In evaluation of helping, the counselor and client monitor and assess change. There are two purposes for conducting an evaluation of helping. The primary purpose is to assess therapeutic outcomes. The evaluation helps the counselor and client to determine the type, direction, and amount of change in behavior (overt or covert) shown by the client during and after therapy. Stated another way:

Individual measures of change fall within three categories. First, most measures are simply designed to find out whether a client changed during the course of treatment, e.g. pre-post global ratings of the client's overall level of functioning or pre-post multiple ratings of client symptoms. Second, and much less frequently, measures are designed to find out whether a client changed as a *result* of treatment as in single subject designs. Third, measures have been designed to find out if a client changed *enough* during treatment to produce an improvement in his or her everyday functioning [Lloyd, 1983, p. 56].

A second purpose is to evaluate the helping process. Specifically, the data collected during counseling can be used to monitor whether a strategy is helping a client in the designated way and whether a client is using the strategy accurately and systematically. Hosford and de Visser (1974) define the evaluation process in helping this way:

Observations of the client's behavior near the termination point of counseling can easily be compared with the base rate data if the counselor records the same target behavior, in the same way, and for the same period of time as was done during the initial observations. This provides the counselor with an objective measure of the success of his learning interventions. If the data indicate that little or no behavioral change occurred, the learning strategies should be reevaluated and perhaps changed [p. 81].

Although an evaluation of helping can yield valuable information about the process and outcome of therapy, it is naturally not so rigorous as an evaluation conducted under carefully controlled experimental conditions. In other words, a counseling evaluation cannot establish that the client's change resulted *solely* from this or that strategy. The results of counseling may be influenced by factors other than the particular counseling intervention used. These factors, often called "nonspecific" or "nontreatment" conditions, may contribute to the client's change. In the final analysis, it is difficult to rule out the possible effects of other sources of influence in counseling. Some of the primary nontreatment sources of influence are described in the next section.

□ NONTREATMENT FACTORS IN COUNSELING

A variety of factors occur in counseling, either independently of or in conjunction with the application of a helping strategy, that may affect counseling outcomes. Important nontreatment factors include the influence of the counselor and the counseling relationship, demand characteristics, instructions and expectancy set, and the potential reactivity of measurement.

Influence of the Counselor and the Relationship
The chemistry of the client/counselor relationship is reciprocal: client and counselor are mutual sources of influence. Client changes in counseling can result from "nonspecific aspects of attention, suggestion and faith (in the therapist or his tech-

niques) that are common to most interpersonal situations" (Paul, 1966, p. 5). As Mahoney (1977a) observes, a counselor engages in a great deal of persuasive communication to encourage the client to behave, think, or feel differently. To the extent that the client regards the counselor with trust, respect, and regard, the counselor's "power of suggestion" is greatly enhanced. In other words, the reinforcing value of the counselor is increased. As we discussed in Chapters 2 and 3, certain relationship conditions and social influence variables initiated and displayed by the counselor can motivate the client to change or to behave in certain ways.

Demand Characteristics

According to Orne (1969), demand characteristics include any cues that influence a person's perception of his or her role in a particular setting. In counseling, these cues not only may influence a client's perception of his or her role but also may affect the client's behavior during and between sessions. For example, perceiving that it is very important to complete therapy assignments systematically will probably motivate the client to complete assignments regularly and conscientiously. In this example, the demand characteristic prompts the client to use therapy in a certain way —which may affect the degree and direction of change. Another demand characteristic that may influence counseling outcomes is the client's desire to please the therapist. This may affect the client's behavior in a number of ways, ranging from the degree of improvement the client reports to the investment and "work" she or he conducts during the counseling process. Other factors that can influence counseling outcomes by communicating certain "demands" include instructions and expectancies.

Instructions and Expectancy Set

A client's motivation to change and to work at the change process is also influenced by instructions and belief factors. Clients who receive specific and detailed instructions about counseling or about a treatment strategy may be more likely to use the strategy accurately and to offer unbiased self-reports (Bootzin, 1972; Nicassio & Bootzin, 1974). In addition, clients who are given high-demand instructions emphasizing the critical importance of a task or behavior may respond to counseling differently than people who receive low-demand instructions (Jacobson, 1981). Martinez and Edel-

stein (1977) indicate that clients' behavior may fluctuate, depending on the instructions they receive and on the context or situation in which they are seen or evaluated.

Clients who receive suggestions of therapeutic improvement without "formal" treatment may demonstrate a great deal of clinical progress (Kazdin, 1973b). Client expectations about the helpfulness of therapy can significantly affect both the course and the outcomes of counseling (see Kazdin & Krouse, 1983; Southworth & Kirch, 1988). As Frank (1961, pp. 70–71) has indicated, "Part of the success of all forms of psychotherapy may be attributed to the therapist's ability to mobilize the patient's expectation of help." If the client views the counselor and the treatment as highly credible, the client's change efforts may be enhanced. Some research has indicated that therapy outcomes are improved after a positive expectancy set has been established for the client (Woy & Efran, 1972).

Reactivity of Measurement

Some of the procedures used to measure client change in counseling may be reactive; that is, the process of collecting data may itself contribute to client change. Reactivity can be defined as the changes in behavior that occur as a consequence of observing and recording the behavior despite, or in addition to, treatment intervention.

A great deal of reactivity is associated with client self-monitoring measurement techniques (Barlow et al., 1984; Nelson, Lipinski, & Black, 1976b). For example, a client may be instructed to observe and record instances of smoking cigarettes or of self-defeating thoughts for two weeks at the beginning of counseling, before any treatment strategy is used. At the end of the two weeks, decreases in the client's smoking or self-defeating thoughts may be apparent even though the counselor has not yet implemented any strategies to help the client reduce these behaviors. Other types of measures of client change, such as standardized tests, questionnaires, and simulated laboratory or role-play measures, may also have reactive qualities (Hughes & Haynes, 1978; Lick & Unger, 1977). In assessing change, the counselor should be aware of possible reactive properties of the measures used to monitor change.

Practically speaking, the influence of the counselor, the demand characteristics associated with counseling, the client's expectancy set, and the reactivity of certain types of measures can be assets for maximizing desired therapeutic changes. However, from an empirical perspective, these factors are potentially confounding sources of influence when one wishes to infer that the selected counseling strategy was the only cause of therapeutic change. In evaluating the effects of counseling, it is important to recognize the potential impact of some of the nontreatment sources of influence we have just described.

☐ CONDUCTING AN OUTCOME EVALUATION OF HELPING

The client's problem must be clearly defined and the goal behaviors specified before the therapist can conduct an outcome evaluation. There may be occasions when the client's problem is redefined and the goals changed. In such cases, the method of assessment, the target behavior, and the response dimensions may have to be altered to reflect the redefined problem. If the method of assessment of outcome is not altered when the problem has been redefined, the reliability and validity of the assessment methods may be limited. Reliability is the consistency or generalizability of the target behavior. For example, counselors want to know whether a particular assessment method will produce consistent client reponses if no intervention occurs and if the natural environment remains stable (R. O. Nelson, 1981). They also want to know, for example, whether the data recorded by the client in the natural environment will be comparable with observational data recorded at the same time by a significant other (R. O. Nelson, 1981, p. 178).

The essential question of validity for assessment methods is how well a method does the job it is employed to do (Cureton, 1951). There are four types of validity: content, concurrent, predictive, and construct. Content validity answers the question whether the method of assessment being used describes a person's present behavior (Livingston, 1977, p. 323) or adequately assesses the response of interest to the therapist and client (R. O. Nelson, 1981, p. 178). Predictive validity answers the question whether the current assessment method predicts the client's future behavior. Concurrent validity refers to whether client responses on assessment measures in the clinic are the same as those responses recorded in the natural environment. Construct validity refers to the client's status on some unobservable variable or construct such as intelligence, shyness, or introversion. Multitrait (two or more categories of behavior) assessment and multiple methods of assessment can enhance reliability and validity for evaluating client outcomes.

Figure 10-1 summarizes the major components of an evaluation procedure for monitoring and evaluating the outcomes of therapy. These components comprise five response dimensions for the target behaviors, seven methods of measurement, and four time periods for measuring the response

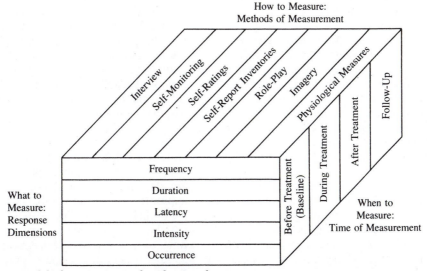

Figure 10-1. A model of monitoring and evaluating therapy outcomes

dimensions. The therapist is responsible for arranging the evaluation procedures and explaining them to the client, who is an active participant in the data-collection process. The model pictured in Figure 10-1 is not intended to connote that evaluation of therapy is easy or simple. Evaluation can be a very complex process; however, we do not believe its complexity should discourage our attempts as therapists to assess therapeutic change.

☐ WHAT TO MEASURE: RESPONSE DIMENSIONS

The therapist and client are interested in assessing the degree to which the defined outcome goal or goal behavior has been achieved (R. O. Nelson, 1981). Because the client typically monitors the covert and overt goal behaviors, evaluation of therapy outcomes depends on a clear specification of the behavior, level, and conditions of the client's goals of therapy (see Chapter 9). A therapist and client may assess one or several goals or target behaviors, depending on the number of changes they have agreed to during the goal definition process. Multiple measures of the goal behaviors are desirable for each client. The same goal behaviors should be assessed repeatedly before, during, and after treatment. Further, measures of goal behavior should be made under similar stimulus conditions (R. O. Nelson, 1981). For example, if a client records the degree of intensity of muscle tension three times a day, the intensity should be rated at about the same time each day so that comparisons can be made daily for each of the three time periods.

The goal behaviors are evaluated by having the client assess the amount or level of the defined behaviors. Five dimensions commonly used to measure the direction and level of change in goal behaviors are frequency, duration, latency, magnitude (intensity), and occurrence. A client may use one or a combination of these response dimensions, depending on the nature of the goal, the method of assessment, and the feasibility of obtaining particular data. R. O. Nelson (1981) recommends that behaviors that are inconvenient to record be assessed less frequently. For example, sexual arousal to diverse stimuli could be assessed only at each treatment session (Nelson, p. 169). The response dimensions should be individualized, particularly because they vary in the time and effort they cost the client.

Frequency

Frequency reflects the number (how many, how often) of overt or covert behaviors and is determined by obtaining measures of each occurrence of the goal behavior. Frequency counts are typically used when the goal behavior is discrete and of short duration. Panic episodes and headaches are examples of behaviors that can be monitored with frequency counts. Frequency data can also be obtained from comments written in a diary or daily journal. For example, the number of positive (or negative) self-statements before and after each snack or binging episode, reported in a daily diary, can be tabulated.

Sometimes frequency counts should be obtained as percentage data. For example, knowing the number of times a behavior occurred may not be meaningful unless data are also available on the number of *possible* occurrences of the behavior. Ciminero, Nelson, and Lipinski (1977) recommend that percentage measures be obtained when it is important to determine the number of opportunities to perform the target behavior as well as the number of times the behavior actually occurs. For example, data about the number of times an overweight client consumes snacks might be more informative if expressed as a percentage. In this example, the denominator would reflect the number of opportunities the person had to eat snacks; the numerator would indicate the number of times the person actually did snack. The advantage of percentage scores is that they indicate whether the change is a function of an actual increase or decrease in the number of times the response occurs or merely a function of an increase or decrease in the number of opportunities to perform the behavior. Thus, a percentage score may give more accurate and more complete information than a simple frequency count. However, when it is hard to detect the available opportunities, or when it is difficult for the client to collect data, percentage scores may not be useful.

Duration

Duration reflects the length of time a particular response or collection of responses occurs. Ciminero et al. indicate that duration measurement is appropriate whenever the goal behavior is not discrete and lasts for varying periods (p. 198). Thinking about one's strengths for a certain period of time, the amount of time spent on a task or with another person, the period of time for depressive thoughts, and the amount of time that anxious feelings lasted are examples of behaviors that can be measured with duration counts.

Latency

Another type of duration measure involves observing the latency of a particular response. Latency refers to the amount of time that elapses before a response or behavior occurs. The number of minutes before falling asleep is an example of a latency response. Another is the amount of time that elapsed before self-disclosing to another person or in a group. Duration and latency measures can be used in combination. For example, a client can record both the latency of self-disclosing responses and the duration of those responses in a group situation. Observing the latency of a response provides useful information about the target behavior even though the data may not always be precise. For example, clients often overestimate sleep latency. If the client can obtain information about response latency using a timer or a clock, the data are likely to be more accurate.

Frequency counts, percentage scores, duration, and latencies can be obtained in one of two ways: continuous recording or time sampling. If the client can obtain data *each time* he or she engages in the goal behavior, then the client is collecting data continuously. Sometimes continuous recording is impossible, particularly when the goal behavior occurs very often or when its onset and termination are hard to detect. In such cases, a time-sampling procedure may be more practical. In time sampling, a day is divided into equal time intervals—90 minutes, 2 hours, or 3 hours, for example. The client keeps track of the frequency or duration of the goal behavior only during randomly selected intervals. In using time sampling, data should be collected during at least three time intervals each day and during *different* time intervals each day, so that representative and unbiased data are recorded. One variation of time sampling is to divide time into intervals and indicate the presence or absence of the target behavior for each interval in an "all or none" manner (Mahoney & Thoresen, 1974, p. 31). If the behavior occurred during the interval, a *yes* would be recorded; if it did not occur, a *no* would be noted. Time sampling is less precise than continuous recordings of frequency or duration of a behavior. Yet it does provide an estimate of the behavior and may be a useful substitute in monitoring high-frequency or nondiscrete target responses (Mahoney & Thoresen, 1974).

Intensity

The intensity or degree of the goal behavior can be assessed with a rating scale. For example, intensity of anxious feelings can be measured with ratings of 1 (not anxious) to 5 (panic). Cronbach (1984) suggests three ways of decreasing sources of error frequently associated with rating scales. First, the therapist should be certain that what is to be rated is well defined and specified in the client's language. For example, if a client is to rate depressed thoughts, the counselor and client specify, with examples, what constitutes depressed thoughts (such as "Nothing is going right for me," "I can't do anything right"). These definitions should be tailored to each client, on the basis of an analysis of the client's problem behavior and contributing conditions. Second, rating scales should be designed that include a description for each point on the scale. For example, episodes of anxious feelings in a particular setting can be rated on a 5-point scale, with 1 representing little or no anxiety, 2 equal to some anxiety, 3 being moderately anxious, 4 representing strong anxious feelings, and 5 indicating very intense anxiety. Third, rating scales should be unidirectional, starting with 0 or 1. Negative points (points below 0) should not be included. In addition, the therapist should consider the range of points in constructing the scale. There should be at least 4 points and no more than 7. A scale of less than 4 points may limit a person's ability to discriminate, whereas a scale that includes more than 7 points may not produce reliable ratings by the client because too many discriminations are required.

Occurrence

Occurrence refers to presence or absence of target behaviors. Checklists can be used to rate the occurrence of behaviors. They are similar to rating scales. The basic difference is the type of judgment one makes. On a rating scale, a person can indicate the degree to which a behavior is present; a checklist simply measures the presence or absence of a behavior. Checklists describe a cluster or collection of behaviors that a client may demonstrate. A checklist assesses the client's *capability* "to emit a particular behavior to a given standard under a given condition" (Walls, Werner, Bacon, & Zane, 1977, pp. 79–80). For example, suppose a counselor is using either covert or participant modeling as a treatment strategy for teaching a person job-interview skills. The nonverbal and verbal behaviors associated with demonstrating appropriate job-interview skills can be listed on a checklist. If the client demonstrates a particular behavior in a naturalistic or simulated situation, he or she will receive a check on a list for that behavior. A checklist can also be used in conjunction with frequency and duration counts and rating scales.

As evaluative tools, checklists may be very useful, particularly when the reference points on the list are clearly defined and are representative of the particular performance domain being assessed. In the example just given, a checklist of observable job-interview skills could be a useful tool. Walls et al. (1977, pp. 90–146) provide a list and review of 166 behavior checklists.

Any or all of these five response dimensions can be used to assess the magnitude and direction of change reflected in the goal behaviors. The next section explores how the therapist and client can go about actually collecting data to be used in evaluating helping outcomes.

LEARNING ACTIVITY #29: RESPONSE DIMENSIONS

Read the following client case description and decide which response dimensions of the target behavior would be most appropriate for the client to monitor. As a review, there are five response dimensions:

1. Frequency: (a) how often the behavior occurs or (b) how often the behavior occurs in proportion to the number of opportunities available (percentage score).
2. Duration: how long the behavior lasts.
3. Latency: amount of time elapsed before the behavior occurs.
4. Intensity: ratings of intensity, severity, or degree of the behavior.
5. Occurrence: presence or absence of the behavior.

Case Description

The client is a 38-year-old single female who referred herself for counseling because of recurring fears about having cancer. Although the client is in excellent health, over the last two years she has had re-peated ruminations about the possibility that she will contract cancer. She reports that this concern began after a close friend died suddenly from an undiagnosed cancer. The client reports that she has several anxiety attacks a day about this. These occur both at work and at home. She also reports that some of the attacks are mild, but others are more severe and result in headaches and nausea. Her attacks are centered on thoughts of "worrying that I have or will get cancer and it will be too late to do anything about it." Her goal is to reduce these anxiety-producing ruminations and the concurrent feelings of anxiety and panic.

Assume that the client is going to evaluate her anxiety attacks as the outcome measure. If you were her counselor, what response dimensions would you have her use to collect data about these attacks? List your choices on a sheet of paper and briefly describe a rationale for each type you suggest. Feedback follows.

☐ HOW TO MEASURE: METHODS OF MEASUREMENT

There are at least seven methods a therapist and client can use to measure progress toward desired outcomes: interviews, self-monitoring, self-ratings, self-report inventories, role playing, imagery, and physiological measures. Any one of these methods or a combination can be used to provide indications of whether the desired goal behaviors are being achieved.

Interviews

As we have described in previous chapters, the interview is very useful for gathering data about the client's problems and for defining client goals. The interview can also be used to evaluate informally the degree to which the goal behaviors are achieved. There are at least two ways a therapist can use the interview as a measurement method. First, the helper can use open-ended verbal leads to elicit client self-report data about progress toward the desired goals. Specifically, the helper can draw on some of the leads we suggested for problem and goal definition later in counseling to find out whether progress has been made. The interview leads for determining the intensity of the problem (Chapter 8) and for specifying desired changes (Chapter 9) are particularly appropriate for eliciting client verbal descriptions of therapeutic progress. Presumably, if changes are occurring, the client will indicate that the extent and severity of the problem have decreased as helping strategies are introduced and implemented.

A second way the interview can be used in data collection is to audiotape randomly selected interview sessions at the beginning, middle, and end points of the helping process. Segments of these tapes or entire sessions can be rated independently by the therapist or by other raters on dimensions of client verbal responses that may be representative of the counseling goals. For example, if the client's goal is to reduce depressed thoughts, defined as thoughts such as "Life is rotten," "I'm no good," or "Nothing is going well for me," these operationally defined client verbalizations can be scored and rated across taped interviews. Positive statements such as "I'm getting more out of life now," "I'm realizing I'm a worthwhile person," or "Good things are starting to happen for me now" can also be scored. As counseling continues, if the client is making progress toward the goal, there should be a decrease across the interview sessions in the negative statements and an increase in the positive statements.

Advantages. The interview is perhaps the easiest and most convenient method of data collection available (Haynes & Jensen, 1979). It is a relatively "low cost" measurement method, requiring very little extra time and effort from either counselor or client. It is also a good way to elicit the client's perceptions about the value of the helping process. These perceptions may be especially important in cases where the client believes that therapy is helping (or hurting) but these beliefs are not supported by quantified data. Interviews can also provide greater flexibility and more information than self-report inventories or questionnaires. The interview can facilitate obtaining accurate and complete information from illiterate and less educated clients (Jayaratne & Levy, 1979).

Limitations. The interview is the least systematic and standardized way to collect data, however, and the resulting information is often not very precise or specific. For example, the client may be able to report the duration of change (increase or decrease, positive or negative) but not the exact level of change (increase or decrease by two per day, three hours per week, and so on). Another disadvantage involves the reliability of client verbalizations, since the information obtained in the interview is based on recall and is retrospective (Kendall & Hollon, 1981). If the interview is the only measurement method used, the helper must rely totally on the client's reports of progress. There is always a danger that some clients will report that they feel good or are making desired changes simply to please the counselor (Okun, 1987).

Haynes and Jensen (1979) enumerate several possible sources of error and bias in interviews. These sources are likely to be of more consequence in *unstructured* interviews and include such variables as differences in race, sex, or social class between interviewer and client, interviewer knowledge about or classification of the client, type of information being requested, and the nature of the interviewee (age, population group, and so on).

Guidelines for use. The interview method may be more effective as an evaluation tool when used in the following ways:

1. The helper should determine in advance some *structured,* open-ended leads to elicit client descriptions of progress. These leads should include client indications of the present extent of the problem, the present severity of the problem, and how things are different than they were at the beginning of counseling.
2. These interview leads should be used at several points during the helping process; the helper should use the same leads at each of these "sampling points."
3. Where feasible, the helper should supplement the use of interview leads with ratings of various audiotaped interview segments on dimensions of client goal-related verbal behavior.

Self-Monitoring

Self-monitoring is a process of observing and recording aspects of one's own covert or overt behavior (Kazdin, 1974f). Self-monitoring can be used in the helping process in three ways: to define client problems (see Chapter 8), to increase or decrease desired target behaviors (see Chapter 19), and to evaluate the effects of helping. The discussion of self-monitoring in this chapter is limited to its role as an evaluation method. For the purpose of evaluating goal behaviors, a client uses self-monitoring to collect data about the amount (frequency, latency, duration, or intensity) of the goal

---

FEEDBACK #29: RESPONSE DIMENSIONS

At least three types of responses could be used very appropriately with this client to collect data about dimensions of the goal behavior:

1. Frequency of attacks. The counselor and client need to know how many times these attacks occur and, ultimately, whether counseling is helping the client reduce their number.
2. Duration of attacks. If each attack lasted as long as 30 minutes, this could impede the client's overall functioning.
3. Intensity or severity of attacks. Using, perhaps, a 5- or 7-point scale, the client could rate each attack according to its severity. This information would be a clue to the overall intensity of the attacks. These data also might suggest whether more severe attacks were linked to any particular antecedent conditions.

---

behaviors. The monitoring involves not only noticing occurrences of the goal behavior but also recording them with paper and pencil, mechanical counters, timers, or electronic devices (Ciminero et al., 1977).

Advantages. This method has a number of advantages as a way to collect data about client progress toward goal behaviors. Self-monitoring, or an ongoing account of what happens in a person's daily environment, can have more concurrent validity than some other data-collection procedures (Lick & Unger, 1977). In other words, self-monitoring may produce data that more closely approximate the goals of counseling than such measures as inventories or standardized instruments. Moreover, the predictive validity of self-monitoring may be superior to that of other measurement methods, with the exception of direct observation (Mischel, 1968). As McFall (1977b) explains, "The best way to predict an individual's future behavior in a particular situation is to observe his past behavior in that same situation, but the next best way is to simply ask the person how he typically behaves in that situation" (p. 199).* Self-monitoring can also provide a thorough and repre-

---

* This and all other quotations from this source are from "Parameters of Self-Monitoring," by R. McFall. In R. B. Stuart (Ed.), *Behavioral self-management: Strategies, techniques and outcomes.* Copyright 1977 by Brunner/Mazel, Inc. Reprinted by permission.

---

sentative sample of the ongoing behaviors in the client's environment. And self-monitoring is relatively objective. McFall notes that it is more objective than informal or verbal self-reports, mainly because "it prompts subjects to use a formal structure for their self-observation and reporting" (p. 199). Finally, self-monitoring is flexible. It can be used to collect data on covert and physiological indexes of change as well as more observable behaviors (Lick & Katkin, 1976, p. 183).

Limitations. Self-monitoring should not be used by clients who cannot engage in observation because of the intensity or diagnostic nature of their problems or because of medication. Kazdin (1974f) points out that some clients may not monitor as accurately as others. In addition, not all clients will agree to engage in self-monitoring (Ciminero et al., 1977). Some clients may resist continual or quantifiable data collection. Self-monitoring can be a "high cost" method for the client because of the time and effort required to make such frequent records of the goal behavior. Finally, as an evaluation tool, self-monitoring data are subject to two potential problems: reactivity and reliability.

As we suggested earlier in this chapter, the major problem associated with any self-report measure is its potential reactivity. Simply observing oneself and one's behavior may produce a change in the behavior. However, one can argue that other methods of data collection, such as standardized tests, questionnaires, and role-play assessments, are subject to as much reactivity and invalidity as self-report procedures (Lick & Unger, 1977). And as Mahoney (1977b, p. 243) notes, the reactive effects of self-monitoring are often "variable" and "short-lived."

Another problem associated with self-monitoring is its reliability, the consistency and accuracy with which the client collects and reports the data. Some have argued that individuals do not collect and report data about themselves in a reliable manner, particularly when they know that no one else will check on their observations (Barlow et al., 1984; Lipinski & Nelson, 1974). The reliability of self-report data seems to be a problem mainly when the target behaviors are subtle or not easily discriminable.

Both reactivity and reliability can affect the use of self-monitoring as a measurement method. As Nelson (1977) notes, the potential reactivity of self-monitoring should be maximized for therapeutic change yet minimized for evaluation. In using self-monitoring solely as a helping strategy (Chapter 19), the need for reliability is not as critical as when self-monitoring is as a measurement method or for assessment and evaluation. However, for use as a measurement method, accurate reporting of self-monitored data is essential. The next section describes some guidelines that may enhance the accuracy of client self-monitoring as a data-collection method.

Guidelines for use. There are eight guidelines a counselor and client can use to increase the accuracy of self-monitoring as a data-collection procedure. Many of these have been reviewed by McFall (1977b).

1. The behaviors to be observed should be defined clearly so that there is no ambiguity about what is to be observed and reported. Reliability of self-monitoring can be increased if the behaviors to be observed are well defined and easy to discriminate (Lick & Unger, 1977; Simkins, 1971). Hawkins and Dobes (1977) suggest three criteria for an adequate response definition: objectivity, clarity, and completeness. For example, a client should be instructed to observe particular responses associated with aggressiveness instead of just recording "aggressive behavior." In this case, the client might observe and record instances of raising one's voice above a conversational tone, hitting another person, or using verbal expressions of hostility. Usually any definition of the target behavior should be accompanied by examples so the client can discriminate instances of the observed behavior from instances of other behaviors.

2. Obtaining from the client an oral and written commitment to engage in self-monitoring activity may increase compliance with the self-monitoring task (Levy, 1977).

3. The accuracy of a client's report may be increased by having the client record the target behaviors immediately rather than after a delay (Frederiksen, Epstein, & Kosevsky, 1975).

4. Bootzin (1972) and Nicassio and Bootzin (1974) suggest that increasing the specificity of self-monitoring may offset any potential client biases arising from self-report. The counselor should spell out clearly the procedures for *what, where, when, how,* and *how long* to report the behaviors. McFall (1977b, p. 200) points out that "the more systematic the [self-monitoring] method used, the more reliable and accurate it is likely to be."

5. Reliability of recording can be increased when clients are trained to make *accurate* recordings (Nelson, Lipinski, & Boykin, 1978). Mahoney (1977b, p. 252) recalls that, following his instructions to a client to record her intake of sweets, the client asked: "But what if I get three pieces of candy in my mouth at once, is that one or three responses?" Mahoney accordingly recommends that clients practice self-monitoring before leaving the session. He advocates the following training sequence:

1. Give explicit definitions and examples of the behavior(s).
2. Give explicit self-monitoring instructions.
3. Illustrate data collection with a sample (model) form — possibly one of your own.
4. Ask the client to repeat the definitions and instructions.
5. Have the client practice or monitor several trial instances you describe [p. 252].

6. Self-monitoring should not be too much of a chore for the client. Sometimes a reluctant client can be encouraged to self-monitor if the demands are minimal (Mahoney, 1977b). A client may be discouraged from self-monitoring or may record inaccurately if required to record many behaviors. The client should self-monitor at least one response dimension associated with the major goal behavior; other response dimensions can be added at the counselor's discretion. If possible, clients should be instructed to self-monitor *in vivo* when the behavior occurs, rather than self-recording at the end of the day, when the client is dependent on retrospective recall.

7. Accuracy of the data from self-monitoring increases if the client is aware that accuracy of the data could be substantiated with his or her permission. For example, a parent or spouse can monitor aspects of the target behavior to be evaluated against the concurrent self-monitored data collected by the client (R. O. Nelson, 1981).

8. The counselor may need to "sell" the client on the importance of the self-recording process and its accuracy, for the client must be motivated to use it. The counselor can point out that accurate self-recording may provide the counselor and client with an awareness of varying parameters of the problem, the possible strategies for treatment, and the extent to which the therapeutic goals are reached. Accuracy of reporting may also be increased if the counselor positively reinforces the client for producing accurate self-monitored data

(McFall, 1977b; R. O. Nelson, 1981) and if the counselor stresses the personal honesty and integrity of the client in reporting these data (Bornstein, Hamilton, Carmody, Rychtarik, & Veraldi, 1977).

Self-Ratings

Self-ratings are used to assess the magnitude, or intensity, of the client's subjective state. The rating scales may use a variety of gradations (for example, 1–5, 0–100). Self-ratings have been used to measure client mood on a 5-point scale before and after eating (Fremouw & Heyneman, 1983), severity of headaches on a 6-point scale (Blanchard, Theobald, Williamson, Silver, & Brown, 1978), and general mood states on a 0–100 scale (Kendall & Hollon, 1981). Sherman and Cormier (1972) have used the Subjective Units of Irritation (SUI) scale, with points from 0 to 100, for self-ratings of interpersonal interactions with teachers, students, and family members. Self-ratings may be used in therapy sessions or in the natural environment. Ratings may be made with particular persons or at particular times or at random intervals during the day or during a 24-hour period.

Table 10-1 illustrates two examples of self-ratings. The self-rating of headache severity (Blanchard et al., 1978) can be used to rate headaches each time they occur during the day. Orlinsky and Howard's (1965) ratings of the therapy session include the client's ratings about progress made in the session and about what the client felt he or she got from the session.

Advantages. Self-ratings are useful in at least three ways: (1) they collect data about a client's subjective mood, feelings, tension, or behavior, (2) they are individualized for the particular client problem, and (3) they are easy to administer and interpret and can help the therapist and client to focus on the specific client concern.

Limitations. Some problems with self-rating scales are that responses from self-ratings are susceptible to selectivity, demand or expectancy, and social desirability. Additionally, self-ratings are unstandardized and have undetermined norms, reliability, and validity.

Guidelines for use. Three guidelines should be considered if a therapist wishes to use self-ratings to collect data about goal behaviors.

1. The therapist and client should define and specify in the client's language what is to be rated. Ratings of feelings, thoughts, tension, or behavior should be based on the target behavior for each client.
2. Each point on the rating scale should be described so that there is no ambiguity about any point to be rated.
3. Use the individualized self-rating consistently at each point in the evaluation process. Specify where and when the client is to use the self-ratings.

Self-Report Inventories

Self-report inventories can focus on the client's reports of particular overt behaviors, on fear, on anxiety, or on perceptions of the environment (Goldfried, 1976a). Inventories range from a global focus, such as those of the Minnesota Multiphasic Personality Inventory (Butcher, Dahlstrom, Graham, Tellegen, & Kaemmer, 1989) and the Symptom Checklist (SCL-90) (Derogatis, Rickels, & Rock, 1976), to a more specific focus, such as those of the Rathus Assertiveness Scale (Rathus, 1973), the College Self-Expression Scale (Galassi, Delo, Galassi, & Bastien, 1974), and the Assertion Inventory (Gambrill & Richey, 1975). Another example of an inventory with a specific focus is the Fear Survey Schedule (Wolpe & Lang, 1964). Watson and Friend (1969) have developed two anxiety inventories—the Social Avoidance and Distress Scale and the Fear of Negative Evaluation Scale. Locke and Wallace (1957) have developed the Marital Adjustment Test for couples in counseling, LoPiccolo and Steger (1974) have created the Sexual Interaction Inventory to assess sexual dysfunction between couples, and the Beck Depression Inventory (Beck, Ward, Mendelson, Mock, & Erbaugh, 1961) was developed to assess depressed clients. Moos (1972) has devised inventories assessing a person's social environment. Cautela (1977, 1981) has developed inventories and surveys for a variety of client problems. These self-report inventories are used to measure reports of covert and overt behaviors and global traits (Cautela, 1977, 1981). Descriptive lists and summarizations of self-report instruments in these and related areas are reported by Bellack and Hersen (1977), Cautela and Upper (1976), Haynes (1978), Haynes and Wilson (1979), Nelson and Hayes (1979), and Tasto (1977). Self-report inventories can be used to assess the client's progress (outcome) before, during, and after therapy.

TABLE 10-1. Examples of self-ratings: headache severity and therapy session

---

Headache severity*

0 = No headache
1 = Aware of headache only when attention is devoted to it
2 = Mild headache, could be ignored at times
3 = Headache is painful but person can do his or her job
4 = Very severe headache, difficult to concentrate, can do only undemanding task
5 = Intense, incapacitating headache

Therapy session**

How much progress do you feel you made in dealing with your problems this session? (Circle one.)

1. A great deal of progress
2. Considerable progress
3. Moderate progress
4. Some progress
5. Didn't get anywhere this session
6. In some ways my problems seem to have gotten worse this session

What do you feel that you got out of this session? (For each item, circle the answer that best applies.)

	No	*A little*	*Some*	*A lot*
I feel that I got:				
Help in talking about what was really troubling me	0	1	2	3
Relief from tension or unpleasant feelings	0	1	2	3
More understanding of the reasons behind my behavior and feelings	0	1	2	3
Reassurance and encouragement about how I'm doing	0	1	2	3
Confidence to try to do things differently	0	1	2	3
More ability to feel my feelings to know what I really want	0	1	2	3
Ideas for better ways of dealing with people and problems	0	1	2	3

---

* Blanchard, Theobald, Williamson, Silver, & Brown, 1978
** From Orlinsky, D. E. & Howard, K. I. (1965). *Therapy session report.* Chicago: Institute for Juvenile Research.

Advantages. Bellack and Hersen (1977, p. 55) note that self-report inventories are useful in at least two ways: to collect data about a client's overt and covert behaviors and to obtain data about the person's subjective evaluation of these behaviors. As Lick and Katkin (1976, p. 179) note, inventories are relatively easy to administer, take little time to complete, and can help the therapist and client identify important clinical material. Self-report inventories generally have norms, have determined reliability and validity, and are easy to interpret.

Limitations. One problem of self-report inventories is that they may not measure *particular* client behaviors. For example, the items in an inventory may not represent the behaviors of interest in relation to fear, assertion, depression, or anxiety. Another drawback is that the wording of items may be subject to a variety of interpretations (Cronbach, 1984). Inventory responses may be biased because of the practice effect, reactivity, demand characteristics, and client faking (R. O. Nelson, 1981). The psychometric properties of self-report inventories, such as reliability, content validity and concurrent validity, and norms may not be established for all client groups or problems (Jayaratne & Levy, 1979; Nelson, 1981; Nelson & Hayes, 1979). Finally, the readability of some self-report inventories may be too difficult for clients having a limited educational background (Dentch, O'Farrell, & Cutter, 1980).

Guidelines for use. In selecting self-report inventories, the therapist might be aided by the following guidelines.

1. Select instruments that have been used and validated with more than one population. As Bellack and Hersen note, "Although data derived from studies with the college volunteer subjects are of academic interest, they frequently are of limited value when the assessor is confronted with the clinical situation in an applied setting" (1977, p. 75). However, self-report inventories used in evaluating goal behaviors may not have to be validated beyond the agreement between what a client says he or she does and what actually occurs. For example, selected individual items from the Beck Depression Scale (Beck, 1972), administered daily, provide continuous data about how the individual responds to items related to depression. One does not have to "interpret" or "score" the answers on the scale for comparison with norms.

2. Select inventories in which the wording of the items or questions is objective and is related specifically to the client's concerns. An inventory may have more meaning when the terms reflected in the items are defined explicitly (Bellack & Hersen, 1977, p. 58).

3. Select inventories in which the response choices are, in some way, quantifiable and unambiguous. Words such as *always, seldom,* or *hardly* or points along a continuum such as "1 to 7" should be clearly defined (Cronbach, 1984).

Role Play

Role play can be a valuable tool to assess the client's behavior. The procedure consists of scenarios designed by the therapist to prompt the occurrence of behaviors and to evaluate the client's performance of the goal behaviors. Role play can easily be video- or audiotape-recorded in interview situations. It can occur in the therapist's office or in the client's natural environment with the presence of other stimuli or persons. For example, role play with stimuli or "contrived situations" (Barlow et al., 1984) can be used with clients who are phobic or fearful about some particular situation or object, such as dental chairs, physicians' exam-

ining tables, automobiles, water, elevators, spiders, and darkness. Role-play scenes can also be created to evaluate interpersonal behaviors, such as those between parent and child, distressed couples, employer and potential employee, or colleagues.

Self-ratings and checklists can be used to assess the client's behavior during the role play. The particular self-ratings and checklists used should specify the major response dimensions of each outcome goal or target behavior. For example, clients could rate their degree of felt apprehension during the role plays on a 1-to-10 scale. Concurrently, the therapist may be evaluating the presence or absence of particular verbal and nonverbal behaviors associated with anxiety (or lack of it). The therapist can have the client take part in role plays before, during, and after a therapeutic intervention. Role-play evaluations of the goal behavior may be especially useful as an adjunct to self-monitoring, imagery, or self-report inventories.

Advantages. Role-play assessments have some advantages. First, direct observation of clients' verbal and nonverbal behaviors requires little inference (Barlow et al., 1984). Second, role-play assessments of target behaviors are easily conducted in the therapist's presence either in a clinic setting or in the client's natural and often stressful situation. Thus, as Lick and Unger (1977) note, role-play assessment is an "ideal context" for making "precise, multichannel assessments" of client responses to problem stimuli and provides a rich record of client responses (p. 301).

Limitations. Role play as an assessment procedure has several drawbacks. The role–play scenes must be carefully designed in order to have external validity—that is, to provide accurate data about how the client actually functions in his or her natural environment. Role–play assessments may impose "artificial constraints" on a client (McFall, 1977a, p. 162). The therapist must be aware that a client's performance, even in a well-constructed role–play test with a variety of scenarios or stimulus situations, may not correspond to how the client might behave in the actual environment. Kazdin, Matson, and Esveldt-Dawson (1984) found that role play of social skills among children did not have concurrent validity. Further, the client's performance on a role–play test may be affected by the presence of the therapist (or someone else) and by the client's knowledge that he or she is being observed (Lick & Katkin, 1976;

Lick & Unger, 1977). Small variations in the role-play scenes, the demand characteristics, the instructions, and the rationale given to the client have implications for the validity of the responses obtained (Galassi & Galassi, 1976; Higgins, Frisch, & Smith, 1983; Hopkins, Krawitz, & Bellack, 1981; Kern, 1982; Kern, Miller, & Eggers, 1983; Lick & Unger, 1977; Mahaney & Kern, 1983; Martinez & Edelstein, 1977; Orne, 1969).

Guidelines for use. Three guidelines should be considered if a therapist wishes to use role play to collect data about goal behaviors.

1. A variety of role–play scenes should be developed as vividly as possible in order to approximate a number of situations in the client's actual environment. The scenes should approximate the real-life situations to which the goal behavior is directed. This is important because, in reality, clients have to deal with a variety of stimulus situations requiring responses across different dimensions.

2. The scenes used for the role play should be developed on the basis of an individual analysis of problematic situations encountered by each client. Lick and Unger (1977, p. 302) recommend that the counselor have the client identify a series of problem situations that have "maximum relevance" for the client's everyday life. The role–play assessments can replicate some of these scenes. Basing the role-play test on an individual analysis helps to ensure that this assessment does not misrepresent or underrepresent the most important dimensions to which the client will respond in the "real world" (Lick & Unger, 1977).

3. There should be some standardization of instructions on how to role-play and of the role-play scenarios used across time. For example, suppose a counselor has developed a variety of scenes to assess a client's assertive behavior of making refusals. The nature of the scene and the responses of the other person in the scene should be standardized—that is, consistent across repeated role-play measures. This ensures that evaluation of the client's behavior is not based on changes in the nature of the scene or in the behavior of the other person in the scene.

A client's performance in role-play scenarios can be assessed with frequency counts, duration counts, rating scales, or checklists. For example, a therapist may record the number of times the client expresses opinions during the role play or the amount of time the client spends in verbal expression of opinions. The client's behavior in role plays could also be rated on a scale according to the degree of effectiveness or competence. Finally, the presence or absence of a collection of responses can be checked using a behavior checklist.

Imagery

Imagery can be used to assess the client's perception of problem situations before, during, and after treatment. Clients are instructed to relax, to close their eyes, to imagine the problem situation or problem event with detailed instructions, and to focus on as many of the sensations associated with the particular problem situation as possible (for example, sounds, visual features and colors, temperature, and smell). The purpose of focusing on the sensations is to heighten the client's awareness or vividness of recalling specific details associated with the problems.

There are three ways a therapist can use imagery as an outcome measure or a measure of progress toward the goal behaviors. First, the therapist can do a *content analysis* of the client's description of the problem after the client has imagined the problem situation. The therapist performs the content analysis by tape-recording the client's imagined description of the problem or by writing down what and how the client describes the problem. Ratings of the content can reflect changes in the way the client describes the problem situation. For example, the adjectives connoting anxiety in the client's description may decrease in frequency.

The second technique is to have the client *rate the intensity or severity* of the imagined problem situation. The client can rate descriptions of imagined problem scenes on a 0-to-4 or 0-to-100 scale, where the highest number represents the greatest degree of intensity. Another variation of rating the intensity of the imagined problem situation is the *card-sort* procedure (Barlow et al., 1984; R. O. Nelson, 1981). The card-sort procedure can be used when there are several (five to ten) variations of the problem situation, such as phobic or social situations. A scene is developed for each problem situation. A brief description of each scene is typed on an index card. After the client imagines the scene described on one card, it is placed in one of five envelopes or piles. The five envelopes or piles represent the degree of intensity or aversiveness for the particular scene: 0 equals not aversive, 1 equals a little, 2 a fair amount, 3 very aversive, and 4 extremely aversive.

A third technique is to develop a *hierarchy of imagery scenes* individualized for the client's problem. The range of intensity for the hierarchy of scenes is from neutral (0) to extremely aversive (100). The therapist helps the client to develop five to ten scenes. One or two scenes associated with the problem situation are neutral and are rated 0. The rest of the scenes reflect varying degrees of aversiveness up to extremely aversive (100). The client imagines each scene and places the scene in the hierarchy or assigns a value to the scene from 0 to 100. Presumably, therapeutic intervention is successful when the client gives lower point values to aversive scenes.

Advantages.   There are several advantages associated with imagery assessments. They are easy to administer within the interview setting, they take little time to complete, and they can be individualized for the client. Imagery assessments also can be used to reflect the degree of change in the client's perception of the problem over time.

Limitations.   Imagery assessment should not be used by clients who cannot relax because of the intensity of the problem or who are on medications that might distort imagery. Additionally, because the imagery process is retrospective, reliability and validity about the client's perception of the problem are undetermined. The demand characteristics or expectations created by instructions to engage in imagery may influence what the client imagines or may distort the vividness of the recalled problem.

Guidelines for use.   There are several guidelines to consider in using imagery evaluation methods with clients.
1. Assess the client's potential to construct believable scenes in her or his imagination.
2. Individualize the scenes to be used for each client so that they reflect the major response dimensions of the target behavior.
3. Standardize the selected scenes for each client; that is, be sure to use the same scenes at each point in the overall measurement process.
4. Select one of the three methods described earlier for imagery evaluation to use with each client. Use this method consistently at each point in the measurement process.

Physiological Measures
Another method for assessing outcome is to measure directly the client's psychophysiological responses. Barlow et al. (1984) indicate that psycho-physiological measures have been most frequently used to assess outcome of three types of disorders: (1) anxiety or phobic behavior (heart rate, pulse rate, and skin conductance), (2) psychophysiological disorders (blood pressure, headaches), and (3) sexual disorders (male or female genital arousal). A variety of instruments are used to obtain physiological measures. For example, to measure heart rate, a portable electrocardiogram machine can be used. A common device for measuring blood pressure includes a sphygmomanometer and a stethoscope. A popular technique for recording muscular activity is the electromyogram (EMG). The EMG has been used to assess tension in the frontalis muscle for clients who suffer from tension headaches. A thermistor is used to measure digital skin temperature. Instruments are also available in treatment of sexual disorders to measure male genital arousal (penile circumference and volume) and female genital arousal (vaginal photoplethysmograph).

Advantages.   Psychophysiological measures are easy to administer in an interview setting. Some devices, such as the sphygmomanometer to measure blood pressure and the manual recording of pulse rate to measure heart rate, are not so expensive and require less expertise to apply (R. O. Nelson, 1981). Furthermore, direct measurement of the client's physiological responses can minimize therapist-introduced bias about problem behavior (Jayaratne & Levy, 1979).

Limitations.   Possible disadvantages of some psychophysiological measures are the expense and expertise required for suitable instrumentation (R. O. Nelson, 1981). These disadvantages may limit the availability of such instrumentation in some clinical settings. The complex instrumentation may also exert demand characteristics and reactive effects on the person being assessed (Sturgis & Gramling, 1988).

Guidelines for use.   Three guidelines are applicable to the use of physiological measures:
1. Make every effort to obtain the most reliable equipment possible.
2. Make sure you are trained to use the equipment selected. Obtain supervision for your initial attempts.
3. Establish a fairly lengthy baseline to minimize any reactive effects of the procedure.

In the previous sections, we discussed use of the evaluation methods by the therapist (or a staff member) and/or the client to collect outcome data. Some of these methods for assessing outcomes can be used in the clinic or the natural environment. Data collected from these procedures can be verified with direct observations made by others about the client in his or her environment. For example, a spouse or parent can observe the behavior of the other spouse or child in the home environment (Margolin, 1981; Prinz, Foster, Kent, & O'Leary, 1979). Observation by others may be especially helpful when clients have altered "negative" behaviors but are still mislabeled by others in their environment. As Kazdin (1977) indicates,

The evaluation of behavior by others is important independently of the behaviors that the clients perform after treatment. The problem with many deviant populations is not merely their behavior but how they are perceived by others and perceive themselves. . . . Thus, it is possible that changing behavior of clients will not necessarily alter the evaluation of individuals with whom the target clients have interacted [pp. 446–447].

Outside observation does, however, pose ethical problems. Before contacting any other person, the counselor must obtain the client's permission, and in contacting observers or significant others, problems of confidentiality may arise. Another major drawback of using observers or of contacting other people is the possibility of communicating mistrust of the client. This could damage the counseling relationship and interventions. An alternative might be to have the client bring in representative tape-recorded samples of his or her behavior in the environment. These samples would have to be drawn from situations in which the client could use a tape recorder unobtrusively and without violating the rights of others. The client might be unable to tape-record all the clinically important situations encountered in the environment. Still, this method provides data about the client's functioning in the environment and does not pose a threat to the confidentiality and trust necessary for an effective therapeutic relationship. Another alternative is to have the therapist accompany the client into various environmental situations. Although this is very time-consuming, it does lend objectivity and reliability to client self-report data.

Selecting Methods of Evaluation

Four guidelines should be considered when selecting methods of evaluation to assess the client's progress toward the target behavior.

1. The client's problems must be clearly defined and the goal behaviors of therapy specified. If a problem is redefined, the goal behaviors and methods of outcome measurement may have to change to reflect the redefined problem. Once the problems have been defined for the client, appropriate evaluation methods can be selected and developed.

2. Methods of evaluation and outcome measures should be developed idiographically for the client. Standardized self-report inventories can be used as global measures. Interview, self-ratings, self-monitoring, role plays, and/or imagery should be developed to reflect the client's unique concerns or problems. Not all seven methods of assessment have to be used for each client. Therapists should select a global method (for example, self-report inventories) to be used at baseline, at treatment, after treatment, and as a follow-up several months or a year later. More specific methods can be used weekly (for example, interview, role play, imagery, or physiological measures) or can be recorded daily (for example, self-monitoring or self-ratings). The specific method should be designed to measure the particular client problem. However, as Nelson, Hayes, Felton, and Jarrett (1985) caution, different measurement techniques can produce different results, even when the same client and the same behavior are being assessed.

3. The therapist should provide a rationale to the client for evaluating client outcomes, stressing the importance of sufficient feedback about the degree of success of the treatment. The therapist should also explain that if the treatment is not successful, the therapist can make whatever adjustments are needed to increase its effectiveness. Otherwise, the helping process is incomplete or unfinished (Egan, 1990).

4. Once the treatment strategy or intervention has started, the therapist should monitor its application. Monitoring involves recording four aspects of treatment: (a) What treatment or variation was used? (b) When and how often was the treatment applied? (c) Where was the treatment applied? (d) Who applied the treatment?

Regardless of which of these methods is used to collect outcome data, it is important to remember that none of the methods is perfect—and all may suffer from what we refer to as "the validity of external validity." In other words, any outcome measure is effective only to the degree that it is tied directly to the clinical criterion or goal behaviors. This point was well stated by Lick and Katkin (1976, p. 182):

> Clients do not, in our estimation, seek therapy to change responses on questionnaires, physiological and behavioral reactions to imagined animals, or unassertive responses to videotaped unreasonable requests. Regardless of the reliability of such mea-

sures or the thoroughness with which they assess behavioral, cognitive, and physiological reactions, they have little *clinical value* as outcome measures unless they correlate highly with a client's reactions to problematic stimuli encountered in the natural environment.

Generally, these procedures can be used to collect data on the goal behavior at four times—before counseling (baseline), during counseling, after counseling, and at follow-up. The next section explores the ways data are collected at these four times.

LEARNING ACTIVITY #30: METHODS OF MEASUREMENT

Read the client case description in Learning Activity #29 again. Assuming you are the therapist for this client:

1. On a sheet of paper write the measurement method you believe to be most appropriate for

this case.
2. Provide a brief rationale for your choice.
3. Write sample instructions you would give to this client about how to use this method. Feedback follows.

☐ WHEN TO MEASURE: TIME OF MEASUREMENT

There are several times during which a counselor and client can log progress toward the goal behaviors. Generally, it is important to assess the client's performance before counseling (baseline), during counseling or during application of a counseling strategy, immediately after counseling, and some time after counseling at a follow-up. Repeated measurements of client change may provide more precise data than only two measurement times, such as before and after counseling (Barlow et al., 1984; Hersen & Barlow, 1976; Jayaratne & Levy, 1979; Kazdin, 1980b, 1981). Limited measurements often reflect "random fluctuation," whereas "frequent and repeated" measurements indicate stability of client change (Chassan, 1962, p. 615).

Baseline (Pretreatment) Assessment

Baseline assessment measures the goal behaviors before treatment. The baseline period is a reference point against which therapeutic change in the client's goal behavior can be compared during and after treatment. The length of the baseline period can be three days, a week, two weeks, or longer. One criterion for the length of the baseline period is that it should be long enough or contain enough data points to serve as a *representative sample* of

the client's behavior. Usually a minimum of three data points for the baseline are necessary—for example, three interviews, three role plays, three instances of self-ratings or self-monitoring. The length should also be sufficient to establish estimates of level, trend, and stability (Barlow et al., 1984). *Level* refers to the number of a particular behavior, such as number of self-critical thoughts. *Trend* refers to whether the behavior is increasing, decreasing, or remaining constant over a period of time. *Stability* is the variability or fluctuation of the behavior. Regularity or stability in behavior can be quite variable; that is, if variability in the data reflects a representative sample of the client's behavior, then these data may be considered stable.

Collecting interview, self-monitoring, and self-ratings data during baseline. Typically, during the baseline period, the client is asked to self-monitor instances of the problem and goal behaviors. All the guidelines for using self-monitoring described earlier should be followed at this time. The behaviors to be observed should be defined clearly, and the client should rehearse the process of self-observing and recording. The client will self-monitor the frequency or duration of a behavior and, in some cases, both. For example, suppose a client wants to decrease the number of self-critical thoughts. During the baseline period, the client would be instructed to observe and record (with some device) each time she or he noticed the onset of a self-critical thought. The client would be counting the number, or frequency, of self-critical thoughts.

Typically, the frequency or duration of the observed behavior during baseline can be seen more clearly if it is displayed visually. This pictorial display can be accomplished with a graph. Usually, the counselor will be responsible for taking the client's data and displaying them graphically; however, the graph should be shared with the client because of its informational value. To make a graph for our example of self-critical thoughts, a counselor would plot the number of self-critical thoughts (one to ten) along the vertical axis (the ordinate) as a function of the number of days the behavior was observed. The number of days (1 to 14) would be plotted along the horizontal axis (the abscissa). Generally, in graphing baseline data, the observed behavior is plotted along the vertical line, and the time (or days) is plotted along the horizontal line.

Graphic display of self-monitored data is very important in evaluation. The client can continue to self-monitor instances of the goal behavior during and after the application of counseling strategies. The baseline graph can be compared with the graphs of data collected at these later points to see whether there is evidence of change in the observed behavior. Graphic display of data is also of informational value to the counselor and client, particularly the graph of the baseline data. Self-monitored baseline data can give clues about the nature and intensity of problem and goal behaviors and contributing problem conditions.

A graph can also provide information about the *relative* stability or instability of the observed behavior. The observed behavior may be stable or unstable over time. If the observed behavior occurs consistently over time — even with increasing or decreasing trends or fluctuations in frequency or duration — it is usually considered stable. Unstable baseline data present more of a problem in evaluation because the irregular fluctuations in the data make comparisons more difficult. However, instability can be an important source of information for problem assessment (Chapters 7 and 8) and definition of goal behaviors (Chapter 9). For example, unstable baseline data may be a clue that different contexts (perhaps times, places, or situations) in which the behavior occurs may have been overlooked during assess-

ment (Gambrill, 1977). The instability of baseline data may add new dimensions to the defined problem or may help to refine the goal behaviors.

To demonstrate some of the ways self-monitored baseline data may look pictorially, Figure 10-2 presents five hypothetical baseline graphs for the client who observed the daily number of self-critical thoughts. Graph A illustrates relatively unvarying data. The level is about six per day, the thoughts are relatively stable, and there is no increasing or decreasing trend. Graph B illustrates an increase in the behavior over the baseline period: the level of the thoughts increases from three on the first day to nine on day 14. The increase might have been caused by the reactivity of the self-recording of self-critical thoughts. Another possibility is that greater job or home demands were imposed on the client, causing more self-critical thoughts. The counselor and client should discuss the increasing trend in these thoughts to discover possible contributing factors. Graph C depicts a decreasing trend, from nine thoughts on day 1 to three on day 14. As in Graph B, reactivity or situational demands could have contributed to the decreasing trend. Again, the counselor would query the client about what might have contributed to decreases in these thoughts. It is also possible for baseline data to reflect a combination of an increasing trend or a decreasing and increasing trend. Graph D reveals such variable data. An explanation for these fluctuations in self-critical thoughts might be that more of these thoughts occurred during days on which the client had unsuccessful experiences in his or her environment or context. A counselor might also discover that, on days in which relatively low numbers of self-critical thoughts occurred (days, 1, 2, 4, 7, and 11), the client was at home, faced fewer demands, or reported more "successful" activities.

Graphs A through D could all be considered stable if the data reflected a consistent pattern in each case. In other words, stability of data and trends in data are not mutually exclusive. In contrast, Graph E can be described as unstable because there is no indication of consistent variability, level, or trend in the goal behavior. As with the previous graph patterns, the counselor could use the hypothetical data in Graph E to determine contributing factors that might account for the varying number of self-critical thoughts. Such discussion can help define the antecedents and consequences of the problem behavior. In some cases, irregular fluctuations in the baseline data may

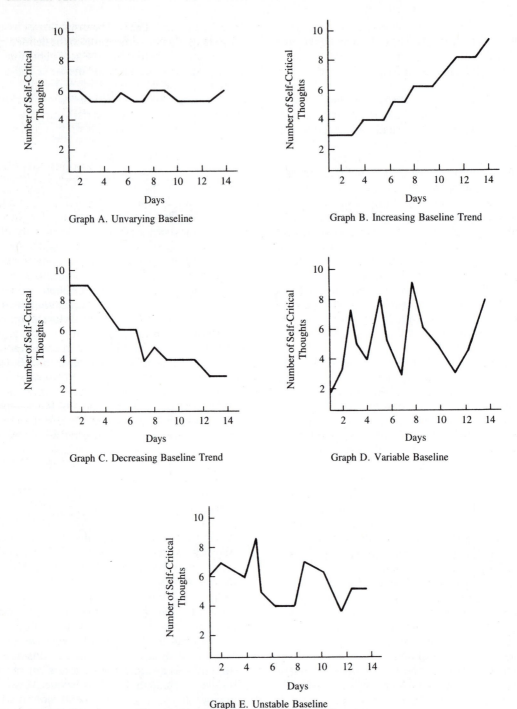

Graph A. Unvarying Baseline

Graph B. Increasing Baseline Trend

Graph C. Decreasing Baseline Trend

Graph D. Variable Baseline

Graph E. Unstable Baseline

Figure 10-2. *Graphs of unvarying, increasing, decreasing, variable, and unstable baselines*

mean that the client is not self-monitoring accurately or regularly—or that another, more important goal behavior has been overlooked. In addition to context, it is also important to note that stability in goal behavior can be affected by the *unit of time* in which data are collected and

FEEDBACK #30: METHODS OF MEASUREMENT

The method of measurement that would be most useful for this client is self-monitoring. Note that the way the therapist instructs the client to self-monitor (see below) also includes *self-ratings* of intensity of feelings. The behavior to be assessed is primarily covert, and self-monitoring lends itself to assessment of covert behavior more readily than role plays or therapist observation. In addition, because this client is concerned about a very specific anxiety-provoking situation, most of the self-report inventories typically used for fear assessment are too general to be helpful.

The client would be instructed to self-monitor the frequency and intensity of the anxiety attacks. Your instructions for this method might go something like this:

"I would like you to get some very specific information this week about these anxiety attacks. I am going to ask you to carry this note card and pencil with you during the week. Whenever you have an anxiety attack—that is, whenever you are thinking about or feeling anxious about the idea of getting cancer—I want you to mark this down with a check mark on the note card, like this:

Mon	Tues	Wed	Thurs	Fri	Sat	Sun
✔						

"Be sure you note even the slightest bit of anxiety. Sometimes the thoughts will lead up to an attack. Also, as you do this, write down the intensity or severity of your attacks, using a 5-point scale: 1 would be complete calm and 5 would be complete panic. If, for example, you feel just a little anxious, your number would be 2. If you feel very, very anxious, you would select a higher number, such as 4 or 5. See—after the check mark, indicate your rating of the intensity of the attack with a number, like this:

Mon	Tues	Wed	Thurs	Fri	Sat	Sun
✔ - 4						
✔ - 2						
✔ - 3						
✔ - 4						

"Now, to make sure we're clear on this, could you tell me what you're going to do on this note card this week? . . . OK, let's practice this. Assume you're having an anxiety attack now. You're thinking about having cancer and not knowing it until it's too late. Use the card now to mark these things down." The self-monitoring data collected by the client during *in vivo* situations can also be supplemented by the therapist's ratings of the client's self-reported anxiety in the interviews, either in response to structured leads or during imagery assessments.

graphed. If the unit of time is expanded, instability in the data will decrease.

Graphs can also be used to display client self-ratings of problem intensity during the baseline period. Remember that, in addition to self-monitoring the frequency or duration of a behavior, the client can record self-ratings of the intensity of the behavior. For example, a client might rate the level of anxiety on a 5-point scale in addition to noting the number of times anxious feelings occur. When self-rating intensity, one should try to provide anchor points that are not directly related to the problem. If anxious about public speaking, for example, one can use anxiety experienced while climbing stairs or approaching a busy intersection as an anchor point. The rationale for providing neutral anchor points is that the client's ratings can be confounded by overall reductions in anxiety, thus altering the rating scale. The self-ratings of the anxiety level can be displayed pictorially in the same way that frequency or duration counts are displayed. The time (days) would be plotted along the horizontal line and the client's ratings plotted along the vertical line (see Figure 10-3).

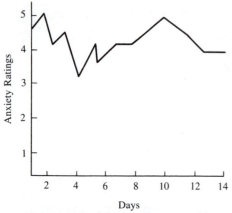

Figure 10-3. *Graph of client self-ratings of anxiety level during baseline period*

Graphs can also be used to display data obtained from the interview. For example, suppose you wanted to use the interview as a method of obtaining baseline data on the number of self-deprecatory comments a client makes. You would need to use at least three interviews as data points; you could audiotape the interviews and then, in listening to the tapes, count the self-critical comments during each session. These numbers would be plotted on the vertical axis of the graph, with the interview sessions plotted on the horizontal axis (see Figure 10-4 for an example).

Collecting role-play, imagery, and physiological data during baseline. The counselor may wish to obtain corroborative measures of the client's progress in therapy in addition to data collected from interviews, self-monitoring, or self-ratings. Moreover, self-monitoring or self-ratings may not always be feasible. In such cases, other procedures must be used. For example, consider a male client who lacks social confidence, defined as feelings of anxiety and lack of verbal skills in being able to approach and ask females for dates. It may not be possible to have this client self-report or self-rate feelings, thoughts, or behaviors in actual situations, because his reported anxiety is so high that he cannot focus on his own behavior.

In this case, the counselor might create several situations in which the client would role-play asking someone for a date. Several (at least three) role-play scenarios could be used during the baseline period. A checklist used during the role plays could indicate whether the client demonstrated a particular collection of behaviors associated with asking for a date. This topography, or collection, of behaviors is defined in the interview session in which the goals for counseling are established. As you may remember from our discussion of the role-play evaluation method, the behaviors and scenarios that make up the role play should be defined on the basis of a situational problem analysis for each client. A checklist or a rating list can be used for each role-play session during the baseline period, and the collection of behaviors the client demonstrates during role play can be scored. For example, 0 = demonstrated none of the desired

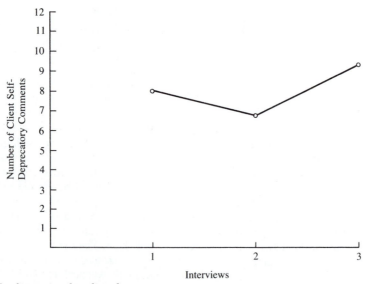

Figure 10-4. *Graph of interview baseline data*

behaviors associated with asking a female for a date, 10 (or more) = exhibited all the goal behaviors. If the client consistently demonstrates the same behaviors across all the role plays, these behaviors may reflect skills already in the client's repertory. Then the focus of counseling should be the skills that were *not* exhibited during the role plays.

The data could be plotted on a graph. Assuming that the range for the role-play checklist is 0 to 10, Figure 10-5 illustrates how data from three hypothetical role-play sessions might be graphed. The observed behaviors are plotted on the vertical axis; the three role-play occasions are plotted on the horizontal axis. Note from the graph that the client demonstrated two of the desired behaviors in the first role play and three in the second and third ones.

Data collected from imagery methods of evaluation and physiological measures can also be graphically displayed. For example, frequency of words connoting anxiety while describing an imagery scene, ratings of intensity for different scenes (card sorts), and placing of imagined scenes on a hierarchy can all be plotted on the ordinate (vertical axis) of a graph. Physiological measures taken during baseline such as heart rate, blood pressure, and digital temperature can be depicted graphically as well.

Collecting self-report inventory data during baseline. The counselor can also administer a self-report schedule or an inventory to a client during the baseline period. For example, with our male client, the Fear of Negative Evaluation (FNE) Scale or the Social Avoidance and Distress (SAD) Scale (Watson & Friend, 1969) could be used. The scores obtained on each scale each time it was adminis-

tered during the baseline period can be recorded and graphed. Figure 10-6 shows hypothetical graphs in which this client's scores on the questionnaires are plotted on the vertical axes and the two scale administrations are plotted on the horizontal axes.

It is not always necessary to plot all the baseline data graphically. The counselor can simply keep a record of the client's self-monitored data, role-play checklists, and scores on self-report schedules or inventories. However, the graphic display of data has more practical use to the client and also may make progress toward the goal behavior more observable.

A baseline measurement may not be possible with all clients. The client's problem concern may be too urgent or intense to take time to gather baseline data. For example, if a client reports "exam panic" and is faced with an immediate and very important test, the counselor and client will need to start working on reducing the test anxiety at once. In such cases, the treatment or counseling strategy must be applied immediately. Baseline measurement is also often omitted in crisis counseling.

Assessment during Treatment Strategies

According to Cronbach (1975, p. 126), any evaluator is engaged in monitoring an ongoing operation. In therapy, the therapist and client monitor the effects of a designated treatment on the goal behaviors after collecting baseline data and selecting a counseling treatment strategy. The monitoring during the treatment phase of counseling is conducted by continuing to collect data about the client's performance of the goal behavior. The same types of data collected during the baseline period are collected during treatment. For example, if the client self-monitored the frequency and duration of self-critical thoughts during the baseline period, this self-monitoring would continue during the application of a helping strategy. Or if inventories and role-play assessments of the client's social skills were used during the baseline period, these same methods would be used to collect data during treatment. Data collection during treatment is a feedback loop that gives both the counselor and the client important information about the usefulness of the selected treatment strategy and the client's demonstration of the goal behavior. Monitoring the goal behavior during treatment is analogous to what Cronbach (1975) calls "short-run empiricism," the idea of taking

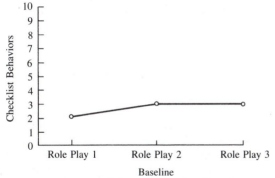

Figure 10-5. A graph for role-play baseline data

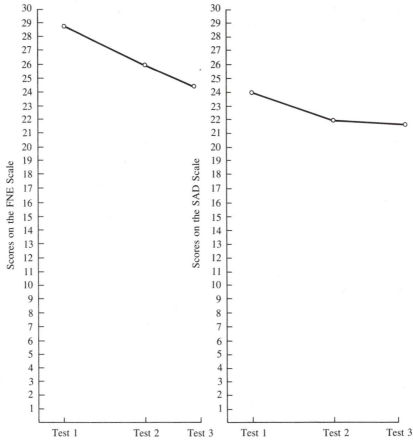

Figure 10-6. *Graphs for baseline administration of self-report inventories*

depth soundings as one moves into unknown waters (p. 126). The data collected during treatment can indicate the need for adjustments in the client's goals or in the treatment plan.

As an example, consider the client who was instructed to self-monitor instances of self-critical thoughts during a baseline period. Before working with any treatment strategies, this client and the therapist would have spent several sessions assessing the problem and establishing and defining desired outcome goals. During portions of this time, the client would have been self-monitoring instances of self-critical thoughts; data from the interviews, role plays, and self-report inventories might also have been obtained. After defining the problem and goal behaviors and collecting baseline data, the therapist and client would select and use one or several counseling (treatment) strategies to help the client achieve the designated goal behaviors. For instance, with the client who wanted to decrease self-critical thoughts, the counselor and client might decide to use a thought-stopping

procedure (Chapter 15). During the first treatment session, suppose the therapist helped this client learn how to stop instances of these thoughts. Following this session, the client would monitor application of this part of thought stopping by continuing to observe and record instances of self-critical thoughts. If role-play assessments and self-report inventories had been used during the baseline period, these sources of data would also be used at one or several points during application of the thought-stopping procedure.

Effects of treatment measures. Measures of the effects of treatment on the goal behavior can have the same degree of stability or instability as baseline measures (see Figure 10-2). For example, suppose our client continued to monitor instances of self-critical thoughts during and after thought stopping. Graphs of the effects of the treatment on this behavior might show decreasing, increasing, or variable trends, as depicted in Figure 10-7.

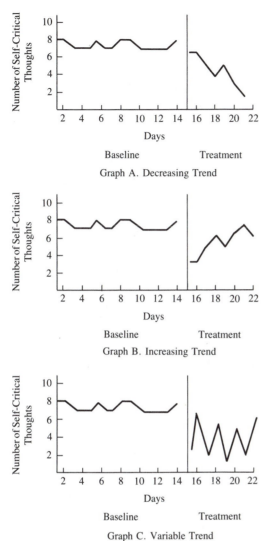

Figure 10-7. *Graphs of decreasing, increasing, and variable trends in behavior during treatment application*

The counselor and client can discuss the client's reaction to the treatment strategies used (in this case, thought stopping) and to additional factors contributing to the desired change.

In an occasional case, the opposite of the desired effect seems to occur when treatment is applied. In Graph B of Figure 10-7, for example, the client's number of self-critical thoughts increases from the beginning of treatment (day 15) to the last day data were collected (day 22). In this example, the increasing trend does not reflect the desired direction of change in the goal behavior.

When treatment has an unintended effect, several factors may be involved, and the counselor and client should discuss these to determine what might be going on. First of all, the reactivity of the measurement may be creating change in an unintended direction. For example, self-monitoring these thoughts may increase the client's attention to them. Occasionally, a heightened awareness or attention to an undesired behavior may result in an increase (although usually a temporary one) in the behavior. Another possible explanation for a behavior change in an undesired direction concerns the way the data are being collected. Perhaps the client is recording inaccurately or is monitoring the wrong behavior. An undesired effect of treatment may also be a function of time. In this case, the client's self-critical thoughts increased during the first week of treatment. A longer time period may achieve a different effect—perhaps these thoughts may increase initially and then decrease two to three weeks later. It is also possible that the nature of the client's problem behavior is contributing to a temporary setback or movement away from the desired goals. For instance, it is not uncommon for clients trying to decrease addictive behaviors to reduce their level of addiction initially—but later during treatment to increase it. Another reason for undesired effects of treatment or variability of goal behaviors may be the inappropriate application of treatment. For example, perhaps, in using the thought-stopping strategy outside therapy, the client does not regularly use a signal such as a covert or overt "Stop!" to terminate the thoughts or does not replace the thoughts with more adaptive alternatives, or the client may be practicing the strategy at home infrequently. As mentioned earlier under "Selecting Methods of Evaluation," the therapist should monitor the what, when, where, and who of the application of treatment to ensure its proper application and to make whatever adjustments to the treatment strategy are needed.

In Graph A, the client's self-observed instances of self-critical thoughts decreased after thought stopping was applied. Note the decreasing trend in the self-reported thoughts from the end of the baseline, or beginning of treatment (day 15), to the last day of treatment (day 22). In this example, the client's goal behavior is changing in the desired direction (a decrease in self-critical thoughts). Such a graph indicates that treatment is having the desired effect. It is likely that the treatment is contributing to the desired change, although nontreatment factors such as the relationship, reactivity, and demand characteristics may also be at work.

Obtaining an unintended effect of treatment may require that some adjustments be made in the way the client monitors or what the client monitors. Or the counselor may decide to extend the time period during which the treatment is applied. If such adjustments are made and the trend still continues in the undesired direction, the counselor may conclude that the selected treatment strategy is inappropriate for this client or for the target behavior. Changes in the particular counseling strategy being applied may be warranted. However, the counselor should be careful not to jump to quick conclusions about the ineffectiveness of a strategy and to terminate its use before exploring possible contributing factors.

Sometimes the effects of treatment are not so clear-cut as those depicted in Graphs A and B. Graph C in Figure 10-7 depicts variability in the goal behavior during treatment application (days 15–22). Such variability may indicate that the client is not using the treatment regularly or accurately or that more time is required for the treatment to have an effect. In some cases, a second procedure or strategy may be needed to contribute to changes in the desired level of the goal behavior. Variability in the goal behavior during treatment may also indicate a need to reexamine and possibly revise the client's goals.

Treatment without a baseline. Some client problems are so intense that treatment or a counseling strategy must be applied immediately, without obtaining baseline measures of the goal behavior. In such cases, the client can be instructed to self-monitor during treatment, and inventories or role-play assessments of the goal behavior can be made. For instance, a depressed client might be instructed to report the number of depressed thoughts per day while the counselor is applying treatment and the client is practicing the procedure. Figure 10-8 is a graph of how this client's self-monitored data of depressed thoughts would appear when treatment is applied without a baseline. Note that the average number of depressed thoughts for this client remained constant during the first five weeks of treatment and then decreased during weeks 6 through 10. The counselor and client might have used something like a cognitive restructuring counseling strategy (Chapter 16) that required some time before the client's depressed thoughts were reduced.

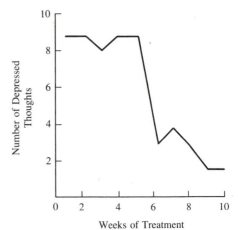

Figure 10-8. *Graph of self-monitoring data during treatment without a baseline*

Posttreatment: Assessment after Counseling

At the conclusion of a counseling treatment strategy or at the conclusion of counseling, the counselor and client should conduct a posttreatment assessment to indicate in what ways and how much counseling has helped the client achieve the desired results. Specifically, the data collected during a posttreatment assessment are used to compare the client's demonstration and level of the goal behavior after treatment with the data collected during the baseline period (before counseling) and during treatment.

The posttreatment assessment may occur at the conclusion of a counseling strategy or at the point when counseling is terminated—or both. For instance, if a counselor is using cognitive restructuring (Chapter 16) to help a client reduce depressed thoughts, the counselor and client could collect data on the client's level of depressed thoughts after they have finished working with the thought-stopping strategy. This assessment may or may not coincide with counseling termination. If the counselor plans to use a second treatment strategy, then data would be collected at the conclusion of the cognitive restructuring strategy and prior to the use of another strategy. This example is depicted in Figure 10-9. Note that the client continued to self-monitor the number of depressed thoughts for two weeks between cognitive restructuring and stimulus control and for four weeks after stimulus control, when counseling was terminated. In some cases, the final data point of treatment can serve as the posttreatment assessment.

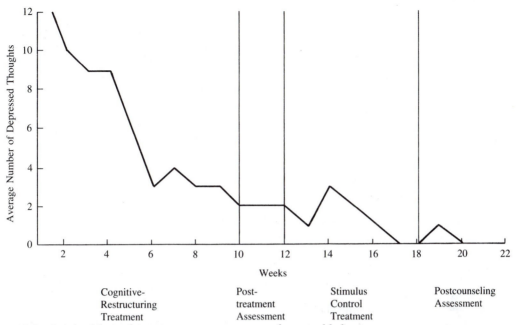

Figure 10-9. *Graph of data of posttreatment assessments of one goal behavior*

Ideally, the same types of measures used to collect data before and during counseling should be employed in the posttreatment assessment. For instance, if the client self-monitored depressed thoughts before and during treatment, then, as Figure 10-9 illustrates, self-monitoring data would also be collected during posttreatment assessment. If the counselor had also employed questionnaires or structured role-play assessments during the baseline period and treatment, these measures would be used during posttreatment data collection as well.

Follow-up Assessment

After the counseling relationship has terminated, some type of follow-up assessment should be conducted. A counselor can conduct both a short-term and a long-term follow-up. A short-term follow-up can occur three to six months after therapy. A long-term follow-up would occur six months to a year (or more) after counseling has been terminated. Generally the counselor should allow sufficient time to elapse before conducting a follow-up in order to determine to what extent the client is maintaining desired changes without the counselor's assistance.

There are several reasons for conducting follow-up assessments. First, a follow-up can indicate the counselor's continued interest in the client's welfare. As Okun observes, follow-up "is a form of recognition that both parties can appreciate in that it can communicate genuine caring and interest" (1987, p. 206). Second, a follow-up provides information that can be used to compare the client's performance of the goal behavior before and after counseling. Another important reason for conducting a follow-up is to determine to what extent the client is able to perform the goal behaviors in his or her environment without relying on the support and assistance of counseling. In other words, a follow-up can give some clues about the degree to which the counseling treatment has been effective or has generalized to the client's actual environment. This reflects one of the most important evaluative questions to be asked: Has counseling helped the client to maintain desired behaviors and to prevent the occurrence of undesired ones in some self-directed fashion?

Many practitioners are legitimately concerned about the long-term effects of therapy. Although a short-term follow-up may reflect significant gains, all too often, 6, 9, or 12 months after counseling, the client is back where he or she started. As Bandura (1976a) asserts, the value of a counseling approach must be judged not only in terms of successful "initial elimination" of a problem behavior but also in terms of the client's "vulnerability to defensive" or maladaptive "re-learning" after counseling is over (p. 261).

Both short-term and long-term follow-ups can take several forms. The kind of follow-up a counselor conducts often depends on the client's availability to participate in a follow-up and the time demands of each situation. Here are some ways a follow-up can be conducted:

1. Invite the client in for a follow-up interview. The purpose of the interview is to evaluate how the client is coping with respect to his or her "former" concern or problem. The interview may also involve client demonstrations of the goal behavior in simulated role plays.
2. Mail an inventory or questionnaire to the client, seeking information about her or his current status in relation to the original problem or concern. Be sure to include a stamped, self-addressed envelope.
3. Send a letter to the client asking about the current status of the problem.

4. Telephone the client for an oral report.

These examples represent one-shot follow-up procedures that take the form of a single interview, letter, or telephone call. A more extensive (and sometimes more difficult to obtain) kind of follow-up involves the client's engaging in self-monitoring or self-rating of the goal behavior for a designated time period, such as two or three weeks. Figure 10-10 shows the level of depressed thoughts

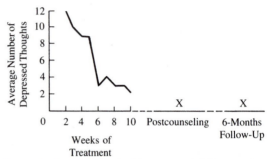

Figure 10-10. *Graph of self-monitored follow-up data*

LEARNING ACTIVITY #31: TIME OF MEASUREMENT

Continue with the client case description found in Learning Activity #29 and work through the following questions and instructions. Feedback is provided after the learning activity.

1. Assume that you asked the client to rate and self-monitor the frequency and severity of the anxiety attacks for a two-week (14-day) baseline period. Here are the client's self-recorded baseline data:

Day	Frequency	Average severity rating
1	3	1
2	2	5
3	4	2
4	3	3
5	3	5
6	4	1
7	3	2
8	4	5
9	3	1
10	3	4
11	4	3
12	3	2
13	3	4
14	3	2

On paper, plot these data on two graphs. Both should have days as the horizontal axis. The first graph should show the number of attacks on the vertical axis; the second, the average daily ratings of the severity of attacks.

a. Does the baseline for the number of attacks reflect unvarying, variable, decreasing, or increasing trends? Do the data seem to reflect a regular (stable) or irregular (unstable) pattern?

b. Does the baseline for the severity of attacks indicate unvarying, variable, decreasing, or increasing trends? Are consistent or irregular patterns reflected?

c. What hunches or clues do the baseline data give you about the client or about things to explore with the client?

2. Assume that, after two weeks of baseline data collection and four sessions of problem and goal definition, you teach the client, in session 5, the thought-stopping strategy. You work on thought stopping during sessions 5 through 8. During this time (days 15–42), you ask the client to continue to self-observe and record the frequency and severity of the anxiety attacks. Here are the client's data collected during treatment (thought stopping):

(continued)

Day	Frequency	Average severity rating
15	3	1
16	4	5
17	3	4
18	4	3
19	5	1
20	4	4
21	3	3
22	2	1
23	2	2
24	1	4
25	2	5
26	1	1
27	1	2
28	1	4
29	2	3
30	2	2
31	3	4
32	1	1
33	1	5
34	0	1
35	0	1
36	1	2
37	0	1
38	1	5
39	0	1
40	0	1
41	0	1
42	0	1

Plot these data on the same sorts of graphs you used in question 1.

a. What do the data for the number of attacks suggest about the effects of the thought-stopping strategy? Is this an intended or unintended effect?

b. What do the data for the severity of attacks indicate about the effects of the thought-stopping strategy? Is this an intended or unintended effect?

c. As the counselor, what hunches might you draw from these data? What directions would you pursue with this client in counseling?

3. Imagine that, after four weeks of thought stopping, you terminate this strategy and ask the client to continue to self-monitor the frequency and severity of attacks for two more weeks (days 43–56). Here are the client's data for this postassessment period:

Day	Frequency	Average severity rating
43	0	1
44	0	1
45	1	5
46	0	1
47	0	1
48	1	4
49	0	1
50	1	5
51	0	1
52	0	1
53	1	3
54	2	1
55	0	1
56	0	1

Plot these data on the same sorts of graphs you used in questions 1 and 2.

a. Compare these data with the data shown on your baseline graphs. To what extent have the client's counseling goals been achieved?

b. On the basis of these data, would you, at this point, suggest continuing or terminating counseling? If you continue, what direction or plan would you pursue?

c. What factors in your counseling might have contributed to the positive effects of counseling other than your treatment strategy?

d. What kind of one-shot follow-up assessment might you use with this client? When would you initiate follow-up?

a client self-monitored in a follow-up six months after counseling. Note in this graph that the client's level of depressed thoughts six months after counseling had remained at the same low level indicated by the posttreatment assessment. These data suggest that the client had been able to control his or her level of depressed thoughts while functioning in the environment without the counselor's assistance. If the number of depressed thoughts had risen substantially from the postcounseling assessment to the follow-up assessment, this might indicate a need for some additional counseling or a booster treatment. It also could be an indication that, at the end of counseling, the counselor had

FEEDBACK #31: TIME OF MEASUREMENT

1. Here are graphs for the client's baseline data:

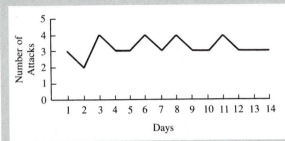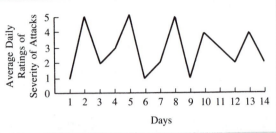

a. These data indicate a relatively stable baseline for the reported frequency of the anxiety attacks. These data might suggest that the attacks are occurring pretty consistently and seem to occur both at work and at home, as the client originally reported.

b. These data indicate a relatively variable baseline for the client's average daily ratings of the severity of the attacks. It could be that, with a longer baseline, this variability would be consistent, although it is difficult to determine the relative stability from what you see here. The data do suggest that some of the attacks are very mild but others are very severe.

c. The therapist and client would need to determine the exact conditions or problem behaviors reflected in the more intense attacks. The counselor may also need to determine whether the client understands the 5-point rating scale and is using it accurately.

2. Here are the graphs of the client's data collected during treatment:

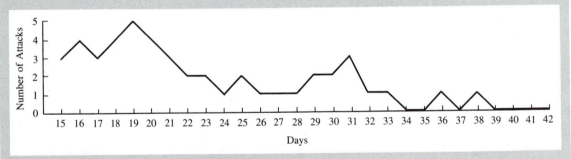

a. These data indicate that, during application of the thought-stopping strategy, the client's number of anxiety attacks did decrease, particularly after the first week of treatment (days 22–42). Clearly, the intended effect was obtained, suggesting that this approach was useful in decreasing and possibly eliminating the anxiety attacks.

(continued)

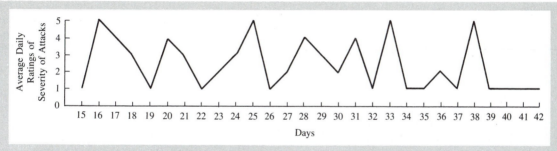

b. These data are variable, indicating that the client's ratings of severity of attacks still range from very mild to very intense. It does not appear that the thought stopping is reducing the severity of the attacks—at least during this time period. Even though the number of attacks is being reduced, the client still rates an attack occurring at the end of this period as pretty severe.

c. This may suggest that another strategy, directed more at the client's felt or experienced distress, is necessary. It also may indicate that there are times in the natural setting when the client does not stop the anxiety-producing thoughts but continues to ruminate about them. It may also be a cue that some other, unidentified thoughts are occurring that are very distressful to the client.

3. Here are the graphs for the client's post-strategy-assessment data:

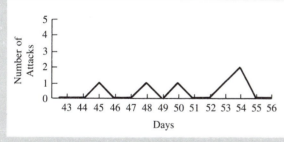

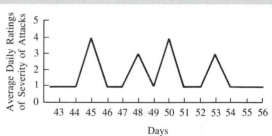

a. These data indicate that the client's goal of decreasing anxiety attacks has been achieved, although when an attack occurs, it is still rated as moderately severe or severe.

b. Because the severity of the attacks is still moderate, therapy might be continued to explore this variable. The counselor and client might focus directly on reducing the client's physiological or cognitive index of severity or stress. Or they might determine whether certain factors that could be resolved or eliminated are contributing to the severity.

c. In addition to the usefulness of thought stopping, it is possible that nontreatment variables might have contributed to the reduction of the anxiety attacks. The nature of the relationship and such therapist-initiated relationship conditions as empathy and positive regard might have helped to extinguish some of the client's anxiety, particularly in the therapy sessions. If the counselor had provided a positive expectancy set about the thought-stopping strategy, this could have enhanced the client's belief in the possibility of change. Finally, the client's self-monitoring of the anxiety attacks could have had some reactive properties that contributed to the decrease in the attacks.

d. A one-shot follow-up would occur about three months after counseling had been terminated. The follow-up could take the form of an interview, telephone call, or letter asking the client to report the general incidence and severity of anxiety attacks during this three-month period.

failed to incorporate some treatment or strategy to help the client apply coping skills to manage depressed thoughts in a self-directed manner.

A follow-up in the form of client self-monitoring has some advantages over an interview or telephone call because the data collected are more specific. However, some clients may not be willing or able to collect such data at this point. In lieu of client self-monitoring or self-ratings, an interview, letter, or telephone call is better than no follow-up at all. In addition, if possible, the counselor can incorporate structured role plays and self-report inventories into the follow-up if these measures were used during the previous assessments. Now go back to page 280 and complete Learning Activity 31.

☐ CONDUCTING A PROCESS
EVALUATION OF HELPING

The data collected from evaluation of helping outcomes should be of practical value to both counselor and client. The evaluation data serve as a feedback loop to help confirm or redefine the selected problem area and the established goals. They also aid the counselor in selecting and using strategies that are likely to help the client. The primary benefit to be realized from an outcome evaluation is the information about the extent to which the client's goals are being achieved.

In addition to the ongoing data collection about outcomes, an evaluation of helping involves some ongoing monitoring of processes. Such a *process evaluation* provides information about the means used to achieve the results—that is, about the particular counseling treatments and any nontreatment factors that may contribute to the outcomes. Both outcome and process evaluation involve continual data collection during the helping process. The primary difference between these two types of evaluation is in what is monitored. An outcome evaluation assesses the goals, or the dependent variables; a process evaluation monitors the treatment and action strategies, or the independent variables.

A process evaluation helps a counselor answer the question "What happened, or what did I do, that helped the client achieve the desired outcomes?" Answers to this question—though speculative and tentative—can help the counselor plan future cases and determine what important factors might be reproduced in future helping sessions and how. As Rinn and Vernon (1975) note,

"Outcome measures generally are not useful for further planning *unless* the intervention technique is quantifiable and its consistent application insured. Thus, the inclusion of process evaluation is mandatory for interpretation of outcome data" (p. 11).

Table 10-2 presents one example of a process measure. The example provides questions that the client answers about the therapy session. The client rates any change that occurred during the session. Questions A and B describe the positive changes that occurred, and Question C specifies particular things that happened in the session that contributed to these changes.

TABLE 10-2. An example of a process instrument

Therapy Session Report*

Significantly Helpful Events: (to be completed by the client)

A. Now take a minute to think back over the session. Do you feel that anything really *significantly positive* happened? In other words, did anything about you or your concern really *change* or *shift positively* for you during the session? (Circle one).

No	Maybe	Probably	Definitely
0	1	2	3

B. Describe briefly the positive change(s) that occurred.

C. What specific thing(s) happened in the session that helped to bring about the positive change(s) (for example, thing(s) your therapist or you said or did, including particular therapist responses)?

---

* Adapted from Elliott, R. (1980). *Therapy session report: Short-forms for client and therapist,* unpublished instrument, University of Toledo, Client form, p. 6. Reprinted by permission of author.

Sometimes process evaluations of therapy are at variance with outcome measures (Dixon & Glover, 1984). For example, clients may give very positive ratings about therapy although, at the same time, the outcome measures do not suggest much progress is being made. There may be at least three reasons for this difference. First, the outcome measures may be insensitive to the actual progress that is occurring. Second, the intervention strategy may require more time before its effects are reflected in the outcome measure(s). Finally, the client may be reporting high process evaluations of the session in order to please the therapist or to justify being in therapy. For whatever reasons the process evaluation differs from the outcome measures, the therapist should examine the monitored treatment data, assess the validity and sensitivity of the outcome measures, or discuss the disparity with the client.

These forms of process evaluation or others can be used to collect data on each session or at different times during baseline, during treatment, and after treatment. Descriptions of treatment strategies used can also be recorded and monitored on standardized forms such as the one shown in Chapter 8 (Table 8-3).

☐ MODEL EXAMPLE: THE CASE OF JOAN

Throughout this book, we provide model illustrations of processes and strategies with our hypothetical client, Joan. We now provide sample illustrations of how a counselor could use the process and outcome evaluation procedures described in this chapter with Joan.

Description of Problem and Goal Definition Sessions

In Chapters 8 and 9, three sessions with Joan were illustrated: session 1 (Chapter 8) was used to assess the problem; session 2 (Chapter 9) was devoted to selecting goals; and session 3 (Chapter 9) was used to define Joan's outcome goals for counseling. After each of these sessions, the counselor recorded the description of the session and the defined problems and goals on the Individualized Client Treatment Plan (reproduced in Chapter 8).

Selection of Treatment Strategies

In session 4, Joan and the counselor decide to work on Joan's goals in the order reflected on Joan's goal chart (from p. 244, Chapter 9) and selected corresponding treatment strategies (see Chapter 11).

Baseline Data Collection for Goal 1

Joan's first outcome goal has been defined as "to acquire and demonstrate a minimum of four initiating skills, including four of the following: (1) asking questions and making reasonable requests, (2) expressing differences of opinion, (3) expressing positive feelings, (4) expressing negative feelings, and (5) volunteering answers or opinions in at least four situations a week with her parents and in math class" (see Chapter 9). Four subgoals are associated with the first goal:

1. To decrease anxiety associated with anticipation of failure in math class and rejection by parents from self-ratings of intensity of 70 to 50 on a 100-point scale during the next two weeks of treatment.
2. To increase positive self-talk and thoughts that "girls are capable" in math class and other competitive situations from zero or two times a week to four or five times a week over the next two weeks during treatment.
3. To increase attendance in math class from two or three times a week to four or five times a week during treatment.
4. To increase verbal participation and initiation in math class and with her parents from none or once a week to three or four times a week over the next two weeks during treatment. Verbal participation is defined as asking and answering questions with teacher or parents, volunteering answers or offering opinions, or going to the chalkboard.

The therapist and Joan need to establish the method of evaluating progress on each of the four subgoals and to determine the response dimension for each subgoal. We would recommend that a global self-report assessment inventory of anxiety (Lehrer & Woolfolk, 1982) be used to measure reductions in anxiety (subgoal 1). For subgoal 1, Joan could also use self-ratings of intensity of anxiety associated with anticipated failure in math class and rejection from parents, on a scale ranging from 0 to 100. For subgoal 2, we recommend that Joan self-monitor her self-talk during math class and other competitive situations. She could be instructed to write *(in vivo)* her self-talk on note cards during baseline and treatment. Subgoal 3 is to increase her attendance in math class. Joan could keep a record of the days she attended class, and these data could be verified from the teacher's attendance records, with Joan's permission. For subgoal 4, verbal participation and initiation in math class and with her parents could be self-monitored *(in vivo)* by recording each time Joan performed these verbal responses. (Additionally, these data could be corroborated by imagery and role-play assessments within the interviews.)

Let's assume that Joan collected two weeks of baseline data on the behavior associated with the first subgoal (anxiety). Global measures of cognitive, somatic, and behavioral anxiety from the self-report inventory indicated that, at three administrations, the somatic anxiety was higher than the cognitive or behavioral anxiety, but all three anxieties were relatively high for each of the three baseline measures. In addition, Joan's daily self-ratings of the intensity of her anxiety averaged about 70, with a range of 60 to 80 during the two-week baseline. The self-rating data are shown in Figure 10-11.

Treatment Strategies and Data Collection for Goal 1

We illustrate several treatment strategies used as possible ways to help Joan with each of her four subgoals. To help Joan with her anxiety of anticipation of failure in math class and rejection by her parents (subgoal 1), muscle relaxation (Chapter 17) and stress inoculation (Chapter 16) could be used. Joan would continue to self-rate her anxiety during the application of treatment. Joan is taught muscle relaxation during the therapy session on day 15. She is instructed to practice the relaxation exercise twice a day with the help of audiotape-recorded instructions given to her by the therapist. Verification of Joan's home practice session can be obtained (see Chapter 17). Figure 10-11 reflects a decrease in Joan's ratings of anxiety between days 15 and 24; the range of self-ratings is 40 to 60, with an average of about 50. In the therapy session on day 25, a stress inoculation strategy is applied (see Chapter 16). The graph in Figure 10-11 shows a decline in the self-ratings of the intensity of anxiety to 20 on days 25 through 28.

For subgoal 2, thought stopping (Chapter 15) and cognitive restructuring (Chapter 16) could be used conjointly to help Joan increase positive self-talk. These strategies would be applied only after Joan had made sufficient progress toward subgoal 1. The treatments to help Joan with her attendance (subgoal 3) could be self-monitoring and self-reward (Chapter 19). These strategies would not be used until the treatments for subgoal 2 were concluded. Again, we would assume that the applica-

tion of self-monitoring and self-reward would increase her attendance but only after Joan's anxiety had decreased and her positive self-talk increased.

Perhaps the most difficult subgoal is the fourth. The therapist could apply two modeling strategies: participant modeling (Chapter 13) and cognitive modeling (Chapter 15). It might not be necessary to terminate self-monitoring and self-reward in subgoal 3 before applying the strategies for subgoal 4. Self-monitoring and self-reward would probably not interfere with the application of the modeling strategies used for subgoal 4. After applying the modeling strategies, we would expect the frequency of participation to increase. Again, all four measures of the subgoals could be graphed during and after treatments and the graphed data kept in Joan's file. The therapist could compare data for all measures for the subgoals with baseline during and after treatment applied to each subgoal. These comparisons would help the therapist and client determine the effectiveness of treatment and/or adjustments needed in the treatment strategies.

Follow-up Data Collection

About three to six months after this (or earlier, if school will be over for the year), the counselor would initiate a follow-up with Joan to discuss her maintenance of change for this goal. The counselor could ask Joan to report orally or to self-monitor frequency of absences from math class. Follow-up could be conducted with any of the methods described on page 280.

☐ SUMMARY

Evaluation of therapy is designed to assess the degree to which treatment has helped the client achieve the desired goals. There are a variety of

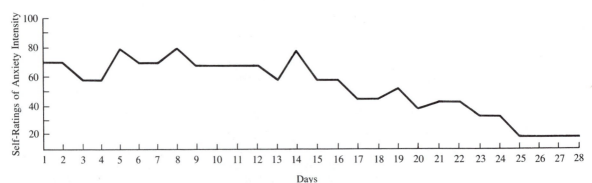

Figure 10-11. *Graph of data for subgoal 1 — intensity of anxiety*

methods for measuring outcome goals: client responses in the interview, self-monitoring, self-ratings, self-report inventories, role play, imagery, and physiological measures. The particular method for measuring outcomes should reflect the response dimension associated with the client's goal—frequency, duration, latency, intensity, or occurrence. Outcome data can be verified with direct observations made by the therapist and others in the client's natural environment. It is important that outcome data be collected at four time periods: before treatment (baseline), during treatment, after treatment, and at follow-up 3 to 12 months after therapy.

There are some sources of influence in therapy in addition to the treatment: the influence of the therapist, demand characteristics, instructions and expectancy set, and reactivity of measurement. Process evaluation of sessions provides information about the means used to achieve outcome goals, including nontreatment factors and particular intervention strategies that contribute to success of outcomes.

We believe that most therapists feel committed to making the necessary efforts to provide the best possible service they can for each of their clients. To do so, we believe, each therapist must feel personally dependent on the collection and availability of data during her or his therapy efforts. As an integral part of the entire therapy process, evaluation should occur for one primary reason—to promote the welfare of the client.

POSTEVALUATION

PART ONE

Objective One asks you to use a client case description to identify appropriate response dimensions, methods of measurement, and times of measurement.

Recall that *response dimensions* include (1) frequency, (2) duration, (3) latency, (4) intensity, and (5) occurrence. *Methods of measurement* include (1) interview, (2) self-monitoring, (3) self-ratings, (4) self-report inventories, (5) role play, (6) imagery, and (7) physiological measures. *Times* include (1) before treatment, (2) during treatment, (3) immediately after treatment, and (4) follow-up, three months to a year after treatment. Now read over the following client case description and respond in writing or covertly to the questions after the case. Feedback follows the Postevaluation.

The Case of Joe

Joe is 36 years old, is married, and has two children. Joe is a production manager for a large steel-fabrication plant in a large city and is active in several community and church organizations. He comes to a counselor concerned about his "uptightness" in crowds. After several initial sessions of problem assessment and goal definition, Joe and the counselor define the problem and goals in the following way:

Problem:

Setting—Small groups or crowds of people such as meetings at work, church services, waiting in line for a movie or restaurant, or sporting events such as swim meets or baseball games.

Thoughts—Thoughts are generally negative when in these settings. For example, "Wish I didn't have to stand in line—there are too many people," "I have to present this stuff in front of this group—boy, I'll screw up if I'm not careful," "These people are making too much noise."

Feelings—General feelings of tension in these settings—hands sweat, butterflies in stomach, heart beating faster.

Behaviors—Performance before groups generally OK, although at times his speech may be faulty (stuttering), but generally no real or obvious anxious behaviors in crowds or small groups other than stuttering occasionally.

Goals:

1. To reduce feelings of tension and discomfort and increase feelings of relaxation in group and crowd situations.
2. To reduce self-defeating thoughts and to increase positive or coping thoughts in group and crowd situations.
3. To speak without any evident stuttering when speaking in front of groups of more than two persons.

After the problem and goal definition sessions, Joe was instructed to self-monitor his level of tension on a 7-point scale (what), each time (when) he is in a crowd or in a small group, (where) on a note card he can carry in his pocket, and to self-record this tension level for the next two weeks (baseline). Joe was also instructed to make a note or count of each time he

(continued)

POSTEVALUATION   (continued)

was aware of a negative or self-defeating thought and of a positive or coping thought about his ability to speak in front of groups. He was instructed to make these tallies also on the note card during the next two weeks.

Before deciding on any treatment strategies, the counselor was interested in obtaining a general index of Joe's anxiety over receiving negative evaluations. For this purpose, Joe completed the Fear of Negative Evaluation Scale (FNE), developed by Watson and Friend (1969). The counselor also structured several role plays in which Joe was asked to talk informally to six persons. These role plays were audiotaped so that any evidence of Joe's stuttering could be rated.

During role playing, a thermistor was used to measure Joe's skin conductance. These digital temperature measures were to assess Joe's level of anxiety (for example, highly anxious, low temperature; low anxiety, normal temperature).

The therapist used imagery (the card-sort procedure) to have Joe rate on a 0-to-5 scale six situations that provoked stuttering. The six situations were typed on index cards, and Joe was instructed to imagine each situation (scene). After imagining one scene, Joe rated the intensity of tension and discomfort for that scene. The total of all six ratings was also used as a measure.

After these data were collected for two weeks, in consultation with Joe, the counselor used stress inoculation for six weeks. During these six weeks and for two weeks following, Joe continued to collect data on ratings of his tension level and frequency of self-defeating and coping thoughts in group or crowd situations. After three weeks of using stress inoculation and again following the use of this strategy, the counselor readministered the FNE Scale and the structured role-play assessments with the thermistor and the imagery card-sort procedure. According to the data collected, Joe's tension level and number of self-defeating thoughts had decreased substantially, and his coping thoughts had increased. However, Joe's level of stuttering exhibited in the role plays and imagery scenes remained at about the same level. Therefore, the counselor introduced the self-as-a-model strategy to help Joe speak in public-speaking situations without any evidence of stuttering. This strategy was used for four weeks. After two weeks and at the end of these four weeks, additional role-play assessments were made. At the end of four weeks in these role-play assessments and the imagery scenes, Joe was able to speak without any evi-

dence of stuttering in more than 50% of these assessments.

Six months after counseling, the counselor contacted Joe by telephone to see how things were going — specifically, to see how Joe felt now in talking in front of groups. The counselor also asked Joe to complete the FNE Scale again and sent it to him in the mail with a stamped, self-addressed envelope.

Now respond to these questions.

1. What response dimensions were used?
2. What methods of data collection were used?
3. At what specific times were data collected?

PART TWO

Objective Two asks you to graph examples of Joe's self-monitored data and to explain the trends reflected in the graphs. Make a graph of the data that appears in the table on p. 289 and explain what the trends for the baseline period, for the treatment period, and for the posttreatment period might mean. Feedback follows the Postevaluation. The tension rating runs from 1 (no tension) to 7 (maximum tension).

PART THREE

Objective Three asks you to conduct an outcome evaluation with yourself, another person, or a client, specifying response dimensions, methods, and times of measurement. You may wish to do so using the following guidelines.

1. Define and give examples of a desired goal behavior.
2. Specify what type of data you or the other person will collect (for example, verbal reports, frequency, duration, ratings, or occurrence of the behavior).
3. a. Identify the methods to be used to collect these data (such as interview, self-monitoring, inventories, self-ratings, role plays, or imagery).
   b. For *each* method to be used, describe very specifically the instructions you or the client would need to use this method.
4. Collect baseline data on the goal behavior for one to four weeks; graph these data.
5. Following baseline data collection, implement some treatment strategy for a designated time period. Continue to have data collected during treatment; graph these data.

(continued)

6. Collect data for one to four weeks after treatment; graph these data.

7. Compare the three graphs and note what changes have occurred in the goal behavior.

Baseline data		Data collected during four weeks of stress inoculation treatment				Data collected for two weeks after stress inoculation treatment	
Day	Tension rating	Day	Tension rating	Day	Tension rating	Day	Tension rating
1	7	15	4	29	3	43	2
2	2	16	5	30	2	44	1
3	4	17	6	31	3	45	2
4	5	18	7	32	2	46	1
5	6	19	5	33	2	47	1
6	6	20	4	34	1	48	2
7	7	21	3	35	1	49	1
8	4	22	4	36	2	50	2
9	7	23	3	37	1	51	1
10	7	24	3	38	1	52	1
11	3	25	4	39	2	53	1
12	5	26	5	40	2	54	1
13	3	27	4	41	2	55	2
14	6	28	3	42	1	56	1

◻ SUGGESTED READINGS

Barlow, D. H., Hayes, S. C., & Nelson, R. O. (1984). *The scientist practitioner*. New York: Pergamon Press.

Beck, A. T., Ward, C. H., Mendelson, M., Mock, J., & Erbaugh, J. (1961). An inventory for measuring depression. *Archives of General Psychiatry, 4,* 561–571.

Bellack, A. S., & Hersen, M. (Eds.). (1988). *Behavioral assessment* (3rd ed.). New York: Pergamon.

Blanchard, E. B., Theobald, D. E., Williamson, D. A., Silver, B. V., & Brown, D. A. (1978). Temperature biofeedback in the treatment of migraine headaches. *Archives of General Psychiatry, 35,* 581–588.

Cautela, J. R. (1977). *Behavior analysis forms for clinical intervention* (Vol. 1). Champaign, IL: Research Press.

Cautela, J. R. (1981). *Behavior analysis forms for clinical intervention* (Vol. 2). Champaign, IL: Research Press.

Ciminero, A. R., Nelson, R., & Lipinski, D. (1977). Self-monitoring procedures. In A. R. Ciminero, K. S. Calhoun, & H. E. Adams (Eds.), *Handbook of behavioral assessment.* New York: Wiley.

Cureton, E. E. (1951). Validity. In E. F. Lindquist (Ed.), *Educational measurement.* Washington, DC: American Council on Education.

Dentch, G. E., O'Farrell, T. J., & Cutter, H. S. G. (1980). Readability of mental assessment measures used by behavioral marriage therapists. *Journal of Consulting and Clinical Psychology, 48,* 790–792.

Derogatis, L. R., Rickels, K., & Rock, A. F. (1976). The SCL-90 and the MMPI: A step in the validation of a new self-report scale. *British Journal of Psychiatry, 128,* 280–289.

Jayarantne, S., & Levy, R. L. (1979). *Empirical clinical practice.* New York: Columbia University Press.

Hay, W. M., Hay, L. R., Angle, H. V., & Nelson, R. O. (1979). The reliability of problem identification in the behavioral interview. *Behavioral Assessment, 1,* 107–118.

Haynes, S. N. (1978). *Principles of behavioral assessment.* New York: Gardner Press.

Haynes, S. N., & Jensen, B. J. (1979). The interview as a behavioral assessment instrument. *Behavioral Assessment, 1,* 97–106.

Haynes, S. N., & Wilson, C. C. (1979). *Behavioral assessment.* San Francisco: Jossey-Bass.

Hersen, M., & Barlow, D. (1976). *Single case experimental designs: Strategies for studying behavioral change.* New York: Pergamon Press.

Higgins, R. L., Frisch, M. B., & Smith, D. (1983). A comparison of role-played and natural responses to identical circumstances. *Behavior Therapy, 14,* 148–169.

Hopkins, J., Krawitz, G., & Bellack, A. S. (1981). The effects of situational variations in role-play scenes on assertive behavior. *Journal of Behavioral Assessment, 3,* 271–280.

Kanfer, F. H., & Schefft, B. K. (1988). *Guiding the process of therapeutic change.* Champaign, IL: Research Press.

Kazdin, A. E. (1980). *Research design in clinical psychology.* New York: Harper & Row.

Kazdin, A. E. (1981). Drawing valid inferences from case studies. *Journal of Consulting and Clinical Psychology, 49,* 183–192.

Kazdin, A. E., Matson, J. L., & Esveldt-Dawson, K. (1984). The relationship of role-play assessment of children's social skills to multiple measures of social competence. *Behaviour Research and Therapy, 22,* 129–139.

Kern, J. M. (1982). The comparative external and concurrent validity of three role-plays for assessing heterosocial performance. *Behavior Therapy, 13,* 666–680.

Kern, J. M., Miller, C., & Eggers, J. (1983). Enhancing the validity of role-play tests: A comparison of three role-play methodologies. *Behavior Therapy, 14,* 482–492.

Lehrer, P. M., & Woolfolk, R. L. (1982). Self-report assessment of anxiety: Somatic, cognitive, and behavioral modalities. *Behavioral Assessment, 4,* 167–177.

Levy, R. L. (1977). Relationship of an overt commitment to task compliance in behavior therapy. *Journal of Behavior Therapy and Experimental Psychiatry, 8,* 25–29.

Livingston, S. A. (1977). Psychometric techniques for criterion-referenced testing and behavioral assessment. In J. D. Cone & R. P. Hawkins (Eds.), *Behavioral assessment: New directions in clinical psychology.* New York: Brunner/Mazel.

Locke, H. J., & Wallace, K. N. (1957). Short marital adjustment and prediction tests: Their reliability and validity. *Marriage and Family Living, 21,* 251–255.

LoPiccolo, J., & Steger, J. C. (1974). The Sexual Interaction Inventory: A new instrument for assessment of sexual dysfunction. *Archives of Sexual Behavior, 6,* 585–595.

Margolin, G. (1981). Behavior exchange in happy and unhappy marriages: A family cycle perspective. *Behavior Therapy, 12,* 329–343.

Nelson, R. O. (1981). Realistic dependent measures for clinical use. *Journal of Consulting and Clinical Psychology, 49,* 168–182.

Nelson, R. O., & Hayes, S. C. (1979). Some current dimensions of behavioral assessment. *Behavioral Assessment, 1,* 1–16.

Nietzel, M. T., Bernstein, D. A., & Russell, R. L. (1988). Assessment of anxiety and fear. In A. S. Bellack & M. Hersen (Eds.), *Behavioral assessment: A practical handbook* (3rd ed.) (280–312). New York: Pergamon Press.

Orne, M. T. (1969). Demand characteristics and the concept of quasi-controls. In R. Rosenthal & R. Rosnow (Eds.), *Artifact in behavioral research.* New York: Academic Press.

Prinz, R. J., Foster, S., Kent, R. N., & O'Leary, K. D. (1979). Multivariate assessment of conflict in distressed and nondistressed mother-adolescent dyads. *Journal of Applied Behavior Analysis, 12,* 691–700.

Sturgis, E. T., & Gramling, S. (1988). Psychophysiological assessment. In A. S. Bellack & M. Hersen (Eds.), *Behavioral assessment: A practical handbook* (3rd ed.) (213–251). New York: Pergamon Press.

Stiles, W. B. (1980). Measurement of the impact of psychotherapy sessions. *Journal of Consulting and Clinical Psychology, 48,* 176–185.

Walls, R. T., Werner, T. J., Bacon, A., & Zane, T. (1977). Behavior checklists. In J. D. Cone & R. P. Hawkins (Eds.), *Behavioral assessment: New directions in clinical psychology.* New York: Brunner/Mazel.

Wolf, M. M. (1978). Social validity: The case for subjective measurement, or how applied behavior analysis is finding its heart. *Journal of Applied Behavior Analysis, 11,* 203–214.

■

FEEDBACK: POSTEVALUATION

PART ONE

1. For the case of Joe, the following response dimensions were collected:
   a. Intensity ratings of Joe's level of tension
   b. Frequency counts of self-defeating and coping thoughts about Joe's speaking ability
   c. Occurrence of Joe's fear of negative evaluation
   d. Checklist of presence or absence of Joe's stuttering behavior in public-speaking situations (occurrence)
   e. Intensity of skin conductance and temperature
   f. Intensity ratings of anxiety on imagery scenes

2. The methods used to collect these data were:
   a. Self-monitoring for tension ratings (a above) and for thoughts (b above)
   b. Completion of a self-report inventory (Fear of Negative Evaluation Scale) (c above)
   c. Structured role-play assessments simulating public-speaking situations (d above)
   d. Digital temperature with a thermistor (or physiological measure; e above)
   e. Imagery ratings of six imagined scenes (f above)

3. These data were collected at the following times:
   a. Two-week baseline (before treatment)
   b. During stress inoculation treatment
   c. After stress inoculation treatment
   d. During self-as-a-model treatment
   e. After self-as-a-model treatment
   f. At a six-month follow-up

PART TWO

Figure 10-12 shows Joe's baseline, treatment, and posttreatment self-recorded data of tension levels. According to these data, Joe's tension level before treatment is variable. During the first two weeks of

(continued)

treatment (days 15–28), some variability persists; however, during the last two weeks of treatment (days 29–42), there is a decreasing trend in his re-

ported tension level. This trend is maintained in the posttreatment data, which also reflect less variability than the baseline data.

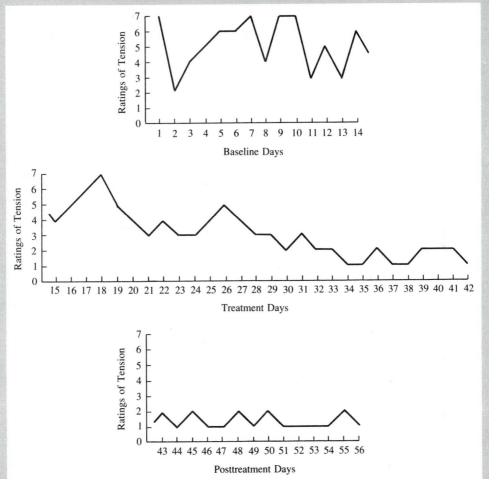

Figure 10-12. *Graphs for Joe's self-recorded data of tension ratings*

SELECTING HELPING STRATEGIES

ELEVEN

Helping strategies are "modi operandi," or plans of action, tailored to meet the particular goals of each client (Hackney & Cormier, 1988, p. 119). Strategies, along with an effective counseling relationship, "can expedite the helpee's emotional, cognitive, or behavioral changes" (Okun, 1987, p. 199). In a nutshell, helping strategies represent the procedural plan to help the client get from point A to point B. And, as in traveling from one place to another, no single means of transportation is suitable for all travelers. Hosford and de Visser (1974, p. 97) explain the emphasis on the variety of counseling strategies this way: "Just as there is no one perfect way to understand the client's problem, so there is no single perfect counseling strategy that fits all situations. Different techniques work differently for different individuals, for different problems, and for different goals."

Tailoring the treatment plan to the client is a move away from the "all-purpose single-method" therapies (Bandura, 1969, p. 89) or the "uniformity myth" (Kiesler, 1966). Goldstein and Stein (1976) charge that, all too often, helpers counsel according to the "one true light" assumption; that is, they assume that their preferred approach is "equally and widely applicable" to most or all clients (p. 3). As a result, these helpers fail to develop treatment plans on the basis of assessment and fail to orient the plan to the desired outcomes (Bandura, 1969; Goldstein & Stein, 1976). Instead, such helpers manage to mold their clients' problems to fit their "brand" of therapy and encourage clients to behave in ways that meet the assumptions of this brand (Lazarus, 1981).

In contrast to the all-purpose counseling approach, we advocate the judicious selection of treatment strategies tailored to the individual client. We believe that counselors need to ask themselves constantly "Which treatment strategy, or combination of strategies, will be most effective for this client with these desired outcomes?" (Paul,

We are extremely appreciative of the invaluable assistance of Warren Shaffer in developing the revision of this chapter.

1967, p. 111). We realize that this concept is easy to discuss but difficult to practice. Our purpose in this chapter is twofold: to propose some criteria a counselor can use to select treatment strategies and to describe an interview process in which both counselor and client can be involved in strategy selection.

□ OBJECTIVES

1. For at least four out of six written client situations, identify the corresponding guideline(s) for the timing of helping strategies.
2. For at least two out of three written client descriptions, identify accurately which of the seven criteria for strategy selection would be used.

□ TIMING OF HELPING STRATEGIES: FIVE GUIDELINES

Many counselors wonder when a helping strategy should be introduced. There is no easy answer, and the answer varies with clients. As Goldfried (1983) observes,

> Quite often, the rules for selecting the technique that is "appropriate" are poorly spelled out. In order to make such difficult clinical decisions, one needs to depend on the sensitivity of the therapist to pick upon subtle cues within the clinical interaction, the understanding of how various behavior patterns and life styles interrelate, and a keen appreciation of the environmental forces and contingencies that direct people's lives. Much of this knowledge and the rules that follow from it are not readily found in the literature, but instead come from clinicians' earlier social learning experiences, their personal experiences as human beings, and the accumulation of actual clinical experience [p. 45].

Sometimes beginning helpers tend to use intervention strategies too quickly and offer premature recommendations or action steps because of their own need to be "helpful." It is impossible (and, in our judgment, inappropriate) to state that "the time" for a strategy is the third, fifth, or eighth session. Nor do we wish to convey the erroneous idea that a treatment procedure will *always* be used with every client. We do believe that a counselor should always try to have a plan or a rationale for whatever route is taken. The transition from building a strong relationship and from problem and goal definition to selecting and implementing a counseling procedure is crucial. Eisenberg and Delaney (1977) point out that the timing of this transition is vital to the successful use of a strategy. These authors note that premature use of a procedure may have a "disastrous impact" (p. 145). Although it is hard to define what "premature use" might be in every case, we think there are a few guidelines to help you make this transition more effectively. The five guidelines you can use to help yourself judge the timing for a strategy involve the quality of the relationship, the assessment of the problem, the development of desired counseling goals, client cues of readiness and commitment, and collection of baseline measures.

Quality of the Relationship

Hackney and Cormier (1988) and Okun (1987) indicate that a counseling strategy may not be effective unless it is used with a strong counseling relationship. When the client begins working with a plan or a procedure, the counselor's support remains vital. A strong therapeutic relationship helps the client make the transition from environmental, or external, support to self-support.

How do you know when the relationship is strong enough to provide the support the client will need? Again, this may vary with clients, but here are a few indicators of "quality" in the relationship:

1. The client has given you verbal feedback that you are understanding his or her feelings or concerns accurately.
2. The client has demonstrated a willing (as opposed to reluctant) involvement in counseling through such behaviors as being on time, coming to sessions, completing homework, self-disclosing personal concerns, and sharing feelings with you.
3. The client and the counselor have discussed anything that might impede open communication.
4. You, the counselor, feel comfortable in confronting, disclosing, and using immediacy with this person.

If you sense these conditions in your relationship, it is probably sufficiently well developed to introduce a helping strategy.

Assessment of the Problem

It is always premature to suggest a plan of action unless the client's problem has been assessed adequately. Otherwise, inappropriate or irrelevant strategies may be selected. As soon as you find yourself wanting to suggest some steps the client should take, ask yourself mentally some of these questions:

1. Do I know why the client is here?
2. Is the client's presenting concern all or only part of the entire problem?
3. Do I know the problem behaviors and situations for this person?
4. Can I describe the conditions contributing to the client's problem?
5. Am I aware of the present severity and intensity of the problem?

If you can answer these questions affirmatively, then follow through on your plan. If not, maybe you should check your impulse to move into an action plan until a more thorough assessment has been completed. In some instances, the client should also be given an opportunity to respond to these questions in order to have a role in deciding the appropriate time for introducing action strategies.

Development of Counseling Goals

If you introduce a strategy before establishing counseling goals, you may be barking up the wrong tree. Because a strategy is a way to promote the goals, clearly specified outcomes are a prerequisite for strategy selection. Be sure that you and the client can describe the desired behavioral outcomes of counseling before you suggest a way to reach them. This information helps you determine whether the selected intervention(s) point toward the targeted results.

Client Readiness and Commitment

The client's readiness for and commitment to action is the fourth guideline you can use to judge the timing of strategy selection. It is always easier to move slowly and then speed up the process than to move into action plans too quickly and possibly scare clients or discourage them from taking further steps. Egan (1975) cautions counselors to "take the client where he is. Never put demands on a client for which he is not sufficiently prepared" (p. 194). For example, clients who are seeking some advice, a panacea, or a quick way to solve their problems probably are not ready for the slow and sometimes painful growth that may be involved in working toward their goals. Clients who have a history of avoidance behaviors may need

extra time before being ready to put aside their typical escape or denial patterns. Clients' motivation and incentive to change affect their use of a procedure. A client might indicate readiness to "work" by giving verbal permission, by demonstrating awareness of the positive consequences of change, and by doing at least some covert work or hard thinking between sessions. Sometimes a client's readiness to pursue the outcomes is indicated by a shift in one part of his or her behavior. For example, the client may become more disclosive or may do more initiating in the interview. Another client may demonstrate readiness for action by starting to assert his or her right to begin the session on time.

Collection of Baseline Measures

As we mentioned in the previous chapter, problem and goal definition are usually accompanied by some baseline data collection, unless the client's concerns are so urgent that immediate intervention is required. Baseline measures can provide valuable information about the nature of the client's concerns and desired goals. Collecting baseline data before implementing strategies is essential in order to determine to what extent the strategies are helping the client.

To summarize, there are no hard and fast rules about moving into the strategy phase of helping. Introduction of a strategy will depend on the quality of the helping relationship, accurate assessment of the client's problem, establishment of observable counseling goals, client behaviors that indicate readiness for action, and collection of baseline measures.

☐ CRITERIA FOR SELECTING STRATEGIES

Once you believe that the prerequisites for appropriate timing of a strategy have been met, you may be ready to move into the strategy phase of counseling. In our own counseling endeavors, in consultation with our clients, we use some criteria for selecting strategies. Our description of these criteria reflects our own preferences; however, we have been aided by the thoughtful work of Gambrill (1977), Goldfried and Davison (1976), Okun (1987), and Shaffer (1976). Seven important criteria to consider in selecting helping strategies involve counselor characteristics and preferences, the documentation for strategies, environmental factors, the nature of the client's problem behavior, type of desired outcomes, client characteristics and preferences, and diagnostic cues and patterns.

In selecting strategies, all seven of these criteria should be considered, although perhaps the most important ones are the nature of the client's problems and diagnostic cues and patterns. Counseling strategies should be used that have the best chance of helping clients resolve their particular concerns most effectively. To a lesser degree, the other five parameters will affect the choice of strategies made by the counselor and client.

Generally speaking, effective intervention strategies meet the following twelve criteria:

Are easy to carry out

Match the unique characteristics and preferences of the client

Match the characteristics of the problem and related factors

Are positive rather than punitive

Encourage the development of self-management skills

Strengthen the client's expectations of personal effectiveness or self-efficacy

Are supported by the literature

Are feasible and practical to implement

Do not create additional problems for the client or significant others

Do not burden the client or significant others with too many things to do

Do not require more of the counselor than the counselor is able to give or responsible for giving

Do not repeat or build on previous unsuccessful solutions

Counselor Characteristics and Preferences

"The best helper is the one who has the widest repertory of helping skills and who can readily call upon any of these skills to meet the different needs of any client" (Egan, 1975, p. 187). We value the counselor who keeps abreast of new procedures and is adept at using a variety of procedures in the counseling process. We question whether a counselor will be able to function adequately with many clients with only a limited range of skills. To paraphrase Maslow (1966, pp. 15–16), if your only tool is a hammer, you will probably treat everything as if it were a nail. However, our enthusiasm for a multiplicity of treatment strategies does not mean that a helper should abandon principles of human behavior just to offer "the latest thing." Nor do we believe that you should propose a strat-

egy that you know little or nothing about. As Okun (1987, p. 199) points out, "Pretending to be an expert when you're not can backfire and even if it doesn't, it is ethically questionable." Misrepresenting yourself and your qualifications to a client may also have serious legal consequences (Van Hoose & Kottler, 1977).

We are suggesting that you use *your* skills, comfort level, and values as criteria for judging which strategy may be most appropriate. Your previous use of a procedure and your attitude about it are major factors affecting your preferences. At the same time, don't restrict yourself to your old stand-bys. Be open to using different techniques —but be aware of when you need supervision or consultation to accompany your testing out a new approach. Don't hesitate to share your preferences with a client. In addition, your preferences for strategies may reflect your particular orientation to therapy; this, too, should be shared with the client at the beginning of therapy.

Documentation about Strategies

Varying amounts of data exist for different counseling procedures. These data can help you determine the ways in which the strategy has been used successfully and with what types of client problems. All the strategies presented in the remainder of this book have some empirical support. Whether a strategy has been documented should be one, but not the only, criterion to consider in deciding whether to use it. As Gambrill (1977) observes, the best strategy is not always the one the literature suggests, particularly if it poses operational problems or if the client favors another one instead. However, don't restrict yourself to past use. Participant modeling (Chapter 13), for example, has been documented most extensively for reduction of fears. We have used it also in helping clients acquire new skills. When using strategies based on documentation in the literature, it is often useful to point out to the client that procedure X and Y both have been documented to some extent and have worked for clients who had similar concerns or shared characteristics related to the problem.

Environmental Factors

Factors within the counseling environment or the client's environment may affect whether a strategy is practical or impractical. These include time, cost, equipment, role of significant others, and availability of reinforcing consequences in the natural environment (Gambrill, 1977). The amount of time you can spend with a client for each session and for the totality of counseling affects the strategies you propose. In time-limited counseling, specific, concrete procedures that are easy to work with are more practical. Your counseling setting may also limit the choice of procedures. For example, it would be difficult to train a client in deep relaxation (Chapter 17) without a comfortable chair.

The client's environment is also important. Egan (1975, pp. 221–222) points out that an action plan that may occur in an unbending environment or may meet with a lot of resistance is not a practical strategy. The availability of role models and reinforcers in the client's environment may also bear on what strategies are possible (Goldfried & Davison, 1976). It is not helpful to depend on a procedure that requires a great deal of encouragement from significant others if the client has very few close relationships.

Nature of Client Problem and Response Systems Involved

The counselor must assume some responsibility for generating suggestions of strategies that are based on the previous assessment of the client's problem. The strategies should reflect the nature of the problem behaviors. Of course, this requires a thorough problem assessment and definition, as well as knowledge about the purpose of particular procedures. As an example, if a client wanted to improve test grades and the assessment revealed the student didn't study, the counselor would have a basis for suggesting some type of study skills training. But if the assessment revealed that the client studied frequently but panicked on tests, the counselor would have a basis for suggesting an approach for managing test anxiety, such as systematic desensitization (Chapter 18), cognitive restructuring (Chapter 16), or both.

Furthermore, the counselor will need to know the nature of the response systems, or components, associated with the problem — thoughts, feelings, somatic expressions, overt behavior, and so on — in order to match the treatment strategies accordingly. For example, a client such as the one described above with test anxiety or some other kind of focal anxiety may experience anxiety in at least three response systems: *cognitive, somatic* (physiological), and *behavioral* (avoidance behavior) (Lehrer & Woolfolk, 1982). One client may report that anxiety is manifested in all three of these response systems during the problem situa-

tion; another may react behaviorally with no physiological arousal or vice versa; and still another may report only the cognitive component of anxiety. Depending on which response systems are involved, the counselor would present different treatment options (Lehrer & Woolfolk, 1984). Cognitive reactors would benefit most from cognitive-therapeutic strategies, such as reframing, cognitive restructuring, and rational-emotive approaches, and from coping skills desensitization. Somatic reactors would benefit more from anxiety-lessening techniques, such as muscle relaxation training, systematic desensitization, biofeedback, and some of the body approaches that work with chronic muscle tension. Behavioral reactors seem to benefit more from skills training, participant modeling (graduated exposure), and contact desensitization. Persons reacting in both cognitive and somatic ways may benefit from meditation, while those who are troubled by all three of these response systems may do better with a multiform treatment package such as stress inoculation training.

In contrast to these cognitive-behavioral approaches for focal anxiety and phobias (highly situation-specific forms of anxiety), client-centered therapy is often the initial treatment of choice for persons with generalized or free-floating anxiety (Mitchell, Bozarth, & Krauft, 1977; Shaffer, 1976). As Meyer (1983) observes, "The focus on empathy and warmth, combined with the initial low demand for specific discussion material, proves helpful here" (p. 120). It is also presumed that consistently high levels of the three facilitative conditions associated with this approach (empathy, positive regard, respect) gradually extinguish some of the generalized anxiety.

Data in which response components of various problems are matched to corresponding treatments are just beginning to appear. Preliminary evidence does suggest that best results are achieved when clients are treated with methods that fit their particular response pattern (Lehrer & Woolfolk, 1984; Öst, Jerremalm, & Johannson, 1981). In the absence of additional available data, the therapist will need to assess carefully the components, or response systems, associated with the client's problem(s) (as we illustrated in Chapters 7 and 8) and scrutinize the relevant parameters of possible treatment approaches in order to determine a good fit or a good match. As Lazarus notes, "This is the point at which clinical experience and a degree of artistry" are both terribly important (1981, p. 55).

Nature of Outcome Goals

The choice of strategies also depends on the nature of the identified goal and what the goal represents. As we mentioned in Chapter 9, outcome goals may reflect choice or change issues (Dixon & Glover, 1984). This is an important distinction because each kind of issue requires different intervention strategies. Choice issues are usually best served by such strategies or approaches as educational and vocational counseling, decision making and conflict resolution, role playing and role reversal, Gestalt dialoguing, and TA redecision work.

Recall that, for change issues, the outcome goal will be a response acquisition, response increment, response decrement, or response restructuring (*response* includes both overt and covert behaviors). For goals that reflect response acquisition, the skill training components described in Chapter 12 and the modeling approaches described in Chapters 13, 14, and 15 are often most helpful. Usually, the greater the deficit, the more modeling, practice, and feedback are required. For goals that reflect response increments, modeling approaches, imagery, stress inoculation, meditation, muscle relaxation, self-monitoring, self-reward, and paradoxical intention may all be applied idiosyncratically to work toward increasing desired behaviors. For goals that reflect response decrements, imagery, reframing, stress inoculation, meditation, muscle relaxation, systematic desensitization, self-monitoring, self-reward, and paradoxical intention may be used to work toward decreasing undesired responses. For goals that reflect response restructuring, thought stopping with covert assertion, cognitive restructuring, stress inoculation, coping skills or self-control desensitization, stimulus control, and reframing or relabeling may be particularly useful.

Client Characteristics and Preferences

In our opinion, the choice of appropriate counseling strategies is a joint decision in which both counselor and client are actively involved. We believe it is a misuse of the inherent influence of the helping process for the counselor to select a strategy or to implement a treatment plan independent of the client's input. We believe, as Frey (1975) does, that the client should be a coproducer of the therapy process.

The client's preference for a treatment plan is important, and most clients do have definite preferences of therapist style and therapy orientation (Manthei, 1983). Attempts to meet client expectations and preferences often yield more positive therapy results (Devine & Fernald, 1973). Exceptions to this general rule might include working with highly manipulative clients or with "emotional saboteurs," in which cases it is difficult to take their often self-serving interests at face value without further exploration and clarification (Lazarus, 1981, pp. 159–160).

During the last decade, we have also witnessed an increasing consumerism movement in counseling and therapy. This movement has at least four implications (Sue, 1977):

1. The client needs to be an active, rather than passive, participant in therapy.
2. The client's rights need to be made explicit.
3. The counseling process needs to be demystified. This demystification can occur by having the counselor explain what will take place during counseling and/or when a particular treatment approach is used.
4. The client must consent to treatment.

These implications are important for all clients, regardless of the setting in which they are helped. Counselors also must usually take special precautions with clients of "low power," such as minors and institutionalized persons, to ensure that their rights are not violated and that treatment programs are not implemented without their participation and consent. Occasionally, some therapists argue that they are withholding information about treatment in order to base a therapeutic strategy on "confusion." Limited data, however, as well as ethical and legal principles, suggest that each client has the right to choose services and strategies appropriate to his or her needs. Unfortunately, this choice means little "unless accurate, prior information about available alternatives is readily accessible" (Manthei, 1983, p. 339).

We believe the counselor is acting in good faith to protect clients' rights and welfare by providing the following kinds of information to clients about strategies:

1. A description of *all* relevant and potentially useful treatment approaches for this particular client with this particular problem.
2. A rationale for each procedure.
3. A description of the therapist's role in each procedure.
4. A description of the client's role in each procedure.
5. Discomforts or risks that may occur as a result of the procedure.

6. Benefits expected to result from the procedure.
7. The estimated time and cost of each procedure.

The therapist also needs to state that he or she will try to answer any questions the client has now or later about the procedure and that the client is always free to discontinue participation in the procedure at any time. If the client is a minor, consent must be obtained from a parent or legal guardian, just as consent must be obtained from a guardian or legal representative if the client has been declared mentally incompetent to give consent.

For the therapist's protection, it is a good idea to have some record of the session(s) in which informed consent is given, in either written or taped form. For example, the treatment contract we describe in Chapter 12 contains a paragraph summarizing the main elements of informed consent. This contract is signed and dated by both therapist and client. As we mentioned before, informed consent is extremely important with minors and institutionalized clients and also when the therapist wants to use experimental "nonstandard" procedures.

In addition to explaining and considering client preferences for treatment strategies, it is helpful to consider any client characteristics that might affect the use of a strategy. Goldfried and Davison (1976, p. 27) point out that, in some techniques, a client's ability to report specific examples is very important. In other procedures, such as covert modeling (Chapter 14) and systematic desensitization (Chapter 18), the client's ability to generate and sustain mental images is crucial. The counselor will need to determine whether the client can generate clear and vivid images before using such strategies.

Other client characteristics to consider include the client's social and self-control skills that may facilitate the use of a particular strategy. A physical condition or strongly held attitudes may preclude the use of a particular strategy (Gambrill, 1977). In Chapter 20, for instance, we describe the notion of "patient position"—the strongly held values and beliefs that are likely to support or reject the use of a particular approach. If the therapist is insensitive to the client's beliefs and values and forges ahead with a strategy that runs counter to them, the client is likely either to resist the procedure or to fail to really invest herself or himself in working with it. Occasionally, a client will reject a proposed strategy quite openly: "That sounds pretty silly to me!", "How in the world would that help?", or "I didn't even try it." Other clients convey their disapproval far more subtly, requiring the counselor from the very beginning to be alert to the client's cues, often nonverbal, for "yes" and "no." For instance, some clients' lack of acceptance of a proposed procedure may be communicated by a change in face color, eye or mouth movements, or breathing patterns.

Proposed strategies also need to take into account prior successes and failures of the client (Dixon & Glover, 1984). As we indicated in Chapter 8, the assessment interview includes identifying any previous solutions the client has used to resolve the problem and with what effect. This information is particularly useful at the strategy solution juncture in counseling. According to Watzlawick (1978), by identifying clients' previous unsuccessful attempts to resolve problems, the counselor can avoid using strategies that build on or duplicate those prior attempts, thus avoiding "problem-engendering pseudo-solutions" (Lazarus, 1981, p. 147). We discuss this concept in greater detail in Chapter 20.

Diagnostic Cues and Patterns

According to Shaffer (1976), an important category to use in selecting and ordering particular treatment interventions involves diagnostic cues and patterns that are readily observable and exhibited by the client during interviews. These diagnostic cues and patterns (or "templates") are the basis of what Shaffer (1976) calls "decision rules" —ways to select and sequence the kind of interventions most useful for a given client with a given problem and related goal. A decision rule is a series of mental questions or heuristics that the counselor constantly asks himself or herself during interviews in order to match techniques to clients and their identified concerns. In Shaffer's model, the first guideline, or heuristic, is the client-centered, or relationship, approach. According to Shaffer, it is useful to start with the Rogerian modality because listening and reflecting elicit a vast amount of client information without interrogation and because it is easier to exit from this modality than to reenter it. In subsequent sessions, the therapist's task is to observe and process certain diagnostic cues and patterns and, on the basis of these patterns, to decide to stay in the client-centered modality or to move out of it and use a different approach that is likely to be more effective. *Which* approach is selected again depends on the particular pattern of diagnostic cues exhibited by the client.

Table 11.1 describes eight major diagnostic criteria and corresponding treatment approaches delineated by Shaffer (1976). These eight diagnostic categories as well as the corresponding treatments are derived from existing empirical literature. Shaffer (1984) has also developed lists of corresponding measures to assess the effects of these treatment approaches.

It is important to note that the strategies we present in the remainder of this book reflect primarily a cognitive-behavioral approach and are most useful when the following conditions exist:

1. The client's defined problem and goal represent *change* rather than choice. As we mentioned earlier, choice issues are better served by other approaches, such as educational and vocational information and counseling, decision making, TA redecision work, and Gestalt dialoguing.
2. The client is generally intact (is not so disoriented that he or she cannot respond to treatment), is not suffering from organic impairment or dysfunction, and wants to work on a limited number of overt and/or covert behaviors.
3. The client or the client's behavior rather than the system is responsible for the problem. If not, system interventions (marriage, family, organizational development) are warranted.
4. The client is not terribly rigid and has not found successive attempts to change behavior, either alone or with a therapist, unsuccessful. Otherwise, the client may benefit more from group rather than individual treatment modalities.
5. The counselor has the expertise, resources, and interest for working with the client. If not, a referral option is warranted.

Additionally, in Table 11-2 we present examples of some particular kinds of client problems and associated treatment strategies. This list is not exhaustive, but it does represent the general kinds of problems presented by individual clients for which the strategies in this book are used frequently as primary intervention strategies. The table also includes references to other useful treatment approaches not covered in this book in order to give you some idea of the various alternative

TABLE 11-1. Eight categories of diagnostic and corresponding treatment modalities

Diagnostic cues	Corresponding treatment
1. Low self-esteem High generalized anxiety No acting out	Rogerian/relationship approach
2. Focal anxiety Intact client Gradient of anxiety	Desensitization, other counterconditioning and anxiety reduction approaches
3. Client needs to increase or decrease three or fewer specific behaviors	Operant treatment and traditional noncognitive behavioral techniques
4. Role discrepancy Lack of information about self in relation to educational or vocational environments	Educational/vocational counseling, decision making and problem solving, other "choice" strategies such as Gestalt dialogue, NLP reframing, TA redecision work
5. Client cannot introduce change System rather than client is causing the problem Therapist can get entry into the system	Organizational or systems interventions
6. "Rigidity" More than three behaviors to change Prior attempts to change behavior have failed Nonpsychotic client	"Group work"
7. Lack of cognitive sophistication Errors in cognitive conceptualizations or appraisals High degree of cognitive involvement	Interpretive and cognitive therapies and problem-solving therapy
8. Therapist's belief that someone else can handle the case better owing to training, skills, values, time, cost, or convenience or availability	Referral

Adapted from *Heuristics for the initial diagnostic interview* by Warren F. Shaffer, 1976. Reprinted by permission of the author.

TABLE 11-2. Examples of client problems and corresponding treatment approaches and strategies

DEPRESSION	ANXIETY DISORDERS
(neurotic or reactive rather than major or endogenous; also adjustment disorder with depressed mood)	*Phobias and focal anxiety disorders*
Cognitive therapy (cognitive restructuring and reframing, rational-emotive therapy, personal construct therapy)	Systematic desensitization
Self-monitoring	Participant modeling (graduated exposure)
Imagery	Stress inoculation
Reframing	Problem-solving therapy
Stimulus control	Self-help groups

DEPRESSION

(neurotic or reactive rather than major or endogenous; also adjustment disorder with depressed mood)
    Cognitive therapy (cognitive restructuring and reframing, rational-emotive therapy, personal construct therapy)
    Self-monitoring
    Imagery
    Reframing
    Stimulus control
    Supportive measures
    Problem-solving therapy
    (Anti-depressants may or may not be required)

ANGER CONTROL AND MANAGEMENT

    Cognitive restructuring
    Reframing
    Relaxation training
    Meditation
    Stress inoculation
    Skills training
    Problem-solving therapy

SKILL DEFICITS

(for example, social skills, assertive skills, job-interview skills)
    Skills training
    Modeling approaches
    Problem-solving therapy

BEHAVIORAL EXCESSES

(for example, weight, procrastination, smoking)
    Self-management techniques
    Paradoxical intention
    Imagery

ANXIETY DISORDERS

Phobias and focal anxiety disorders
    Systematic desensitization
    Participant modeling (graduated exposure)
    Stress inoculation
    Problem-solving therapy
    Self-help groups
    (Antianxiety medication — or antidepressants in the case of agoraphobias — may or may not be required)

Anxiety disorders with panic attacks
    Muscle relaxation
    Meditation
    Participant modeling and graduated exposure
    (Antianxiety medication will probably be required initially)

Generalized (free-floating, or nonspecific) anxiety
    Client-centered therapy
    Biofeedback
    Meditation
    Muscle relaxation
    (Mild tranquilizers may or may not be required)

Obsessive-compulsive disorders
    Reframing
    Problem-solving therapy
    Paradoxical intention
    Participant modeling
    Cognitive modeling with self-instructional training
    Systematic desensitization — if there is an anxiety component
    Gestalt approaches
    Group work

PERSONALITY DISORDERS

Avoidant personality disorders
    Skills training (assertiveness)
    Cognitive restructuring and rational-emotive approaches
    Paradoxical intention
    Adlerian therapy
    Existential approaches
    Gestalt approaches

Dependent personality disorders
    Assertive (skill) training
    Covert modeling
    Group work
    Marriage and family counseling

treatment options for a given problem area. Problems for which these strategies are often used as secondary components, such as sexual dysfunction and alcohol abuse, are not included. The table is intended to be used as a resource, not as a cookbook. From our earlier discussion of criteria for selecting strategies, remember that it is extremely important to match the strategies used to the response components of the defined problem. For additional information on treatment considerations, see Meyer (1983), Reid (1983), and Lehrer and Woolfolk (1984).

☐ SELECTING COMBINATIONS OF STRATEGIES

Helping strategies are rarely used in isolation. Although the counseling strategies in the remainder of this book are presented one at a time for instructional purposes, in the "real world" these strategies are often used in combination. Further, there can be a great deal of overlap among strategies in the actual implementation.

It is necessary to select and sequence a variety of strategies in order to treat the complexity and range of problems presented by a single client. It is uncommon to encounter a client with only one very straightforward concern (such as fear of flying in airplanes) that can be treated successfully with only one strategy (such as systematic desensitization). As M. J. Mahoney (1974, p. 273) asserts, "Unidimensional presenting problems appear to be a myth propagated by research conventions. The average client is not simply snake phobic — he often expresses desires to improve personal adjustment along a wide range of foci."

Because most client problems are multidimensional and are controlled by diverse variables, the targets of change and corresponding treatment strategies usually need to be multiple. Furthermore, increasing evidence indicates a strong correlation between performance changes and cognitive changes. Performance accomplishments in the form of personal mastery experiences can strengthen clients' expectations of personal effectiveness or self-efficacy (Bandura & Adams, 1977; Bandura, Adams, & Beyer, 1977). A well-integrated helping program will employ all the necessary strategies to work with a client's performance skills, cognitive skills, emotional responses, body processes, and environmental factors.

☐ MODEL DIALOGUE: THE CASE OF JOAN

In this dialogue, the counselor will explore with Joan some of the strategies they could use to work with the first subgoal on Joan's goal chart (Chapter 9) for Terminal Outcome Goal #1. This dialogue is a continuation of the ones described in Chapters 8 and 9. In this session Joan and the counselor will explore strategies that could help Joan decrease her nervousness about math class and anticipation of rejection from her parents. Note that all three strategies suggested are based on Joan's diagnostic pattern of specific, or focal, anxiety, as opposed to generalized anxiety.

In the initial part of the interview, the counselor will summarize the previous session and will introduce Joan to the idea of **exploring** *strategies.*

1. *Counselor:* Last week, Joan, we talked about some of the things you would like to see happen as a result of counseling. One of the things you indicated was pretty important to you was being able to be more initiating. You had mentioned things like wanting to be able to ask questions or make responses, express your opinions, and express your feelings. We had identified the fact that one thing that keeps you from doing these things more often is the apprehension you feel in certain situations with your parents or in math class. There are several ways we might deal with your apprehension. I thought today we might explore some of the procedures that may help. These procedures are things we can do together to help you get where you want to be. How does that sound?
   Client: It's OK. So we'll find a way, maybe, that I could be less nervous and more comfortable at these times.

In the second response, the counselor tries to explain to Joan what strategy selection involves and the importance of **Joan's input.**

2. *Counselor:* Yes. One thing to keep in mind is that there are no easy answers and there is not necessarily one right way. What we can do today is explore some ways that are typically used to help people be less nervous in specific situations and try to come up with a way that *you* think is most workable for you. I'll be giving you some information about these procedures for your input in this decision.
   Client: OK.

In responses 3 and 4, the counselor suggests possible strategies for Joan to consider. The counselor also explains how one strategy, relaxation, **is related to Joan's concerns and can help her achieve her goal.**

3. *Counselor:* From my experience, I believe that there are a couple of things that might help you manage your nervousness to the point where you don't feel as if you have to avoid the situation. First of all, when you're nervous, you're tense. Sometimes when you're tense, you feel bad or sick or just out of control. One thing we could do is to teach you some relaxation methods [Chapter 17]. The relaxation can help you learn to identify when you're starting to feel nervous, and it can help you manage this before it gets so strong you just skip class or refuse to speak up. Does this make sense?

Client: Yes, because when I really let myself get nervous, I don't want to say anything. Sometimes I force myself to, but I'm still nervous and I don't feel like it.

4. *Counselor:* That's a good point. You don't have the energy or desire to do something you're apprehensive about. Sometimes, for some people, just learning to relax and control your nervousness might be enough. If you want to try this first and it helps you be less nervous to the point where you can be more initiating, then that's fine. However, there are some other things we might do also, so I'd like you to know about these action plans, too.

Client: Like what?

The counselor proposes an additional strategy in response 5 and indicates how this procedure can help Joan decrease her nervousness by **describing how it is also related to Joan's problem and goal.**

5. *Counselor:* Well, one procedure has a very interesting name—it's called "stress inoculation" [Chapter 16]. You know when you get a shot like a polio inoculation, the shot helps to prevent you from getting polio. Well, this procedure helps you to prevent yourself from getting so overwhelmed in a stressful situation, such as your math class or with your folks, that you want to avoid the situation or don't want to say anything.

Client: Is it painful like a shot?

The counselor provides more information about what stress inoculation would involve from Joan in terms of the **time, advantages, and risks of the procedure;** *this information should help Joan assess her preferences.*

6. *Counselor:* No, not like that, although it would involve some work on your part. In addition to learning the relaxation training I mentioned earlier, you would learn how to cope with stressful situations—through relaxing your body and thinking some thoughts that would help you handle these difficult or competitive situations. When you are able to do this successfully with me, you would start to do it in your math class and with your folks. Once you learned the relaxation, it would take several sessions to learn the other parts. The advantage of stress inoculation is that it helps you learn how to cope with rather than avoid a stressful situation. Of course, it does require you to practice the relaxation and the coping thoughts on your own, and this takes some time each day. Without this sort of daily practice, this procedure may not be that helpful.

Client: It does sound interesting. Have you used it a lot?

The counselor indicates some **information and advantages** *about the strategy based on the* **counselor's experience** *and use of it with others.*

7. *Counselor:* I believe I tend to use it, or portions of it, whenever I think people could benefit from learning to manage nervousness and not let stressful situations control them. I know other counselors have used it and found that people with different stresses can benefit from it. It has a lot of potential if you're in a situation where your nervousness is getting the best of you and where you can learn to cope with the stress. Another advantage of this procedure is that it is pretty comprehensive. By that I mean it deals with different parts of a nervous reaction—like the part of you that gets sweaty palms and butterflies in your stomach, the part of you that thinks girls are dumb in math or girls don't have much to say, and then the part of you that goes out of your way to avoid these sticky situations. It's kind of like going shopping and getting a whole outfit—skirt, blouse, and shoes—rather than just the shoes or just the skirt.

Client: Well, it sounds OK to me. I also like the idea of the relaxation that you mentioned earlier.

The counselor moves on in response 8 to describe another possible strategy, explains what this involves and how it might help Joan manage her nervousness, and **relates the use of the procedure to her problem and goal.**

8. *Counselor:* There's also another procedure called "desensitization" that is a pretty standard one to help a person decrease anxiety about situations [Chapter 18]. It is a way to help you desensitize yourself to the stress of your math class.

Client: Well, how exactly does that work—to desensitize yourself to something?

The counselor explains how this strategy helps Joan decrease her nervousness and **explains elements, advantages, and risks of this strategy.**

9. *Counselor:* It works on the principle that you can't be relaxed and nervous at the same time. So, after teaching you how to relax, then you imagine situations involving your math class—or with your folks. However, you imagine a situation only when you're relaxed. You practice this way to the point where you can speak up in class or with your folks without feeling all the nervousness you do now. In other words, you become desensitized. Most of this process is something we would do together in these sessions and is an advantage over something requiring a lot of outside work on your part.

Client: Does that take a long time?

The counselor gives Joan some information about the **time** *involved in the desensitization procedure.*

10. *Counselor:* This may take a little longer than the other two procedures. This procedure has helped a great many people decrease their nervousness about specific situations—like taking a test or flying. Of course, keep in mind that any change plan takes some time.

    Client: It sounds helpful.

The counselor points out some of the **environmental factors** *involved in these procedures.*

11. *Counselor:* Another thing I should point out is that all these procedures will require you to practice on your own once or twice a day in a quiet place. Is that possible?

    Client: Sure, as long as it's something I can do at home. I don't know—what do you think will help me most?

In response 12, the counselor indicates **his or her preferences** *and provides information about* **documentation.**

12. *Counselor:* I'd like us to make the decision together. I feel comfortable with all of these things I've mentioned. Also, all three of these procedures have been found to be pretty effective in dealing with the different fears of many people who are concerned about working on their nervousness in situations so it isn't a handicap.

    Client: I'm wondering exactly how to decide where to go from here.

In responses 13 and 14, the counselor elicits information about **client preferences.**

13. *Counselor:* Well, perhaps if we reviewed the action plans I've mentioned and go over them, you can see which one you feel might work best for

you, at least now. We can always change at a later point. How does that sound?

    Client: Good. There's a lot of information and I don't know if I remember everything you mentioned.

14. *Counselor:* OK. Well, we talked first about relaxation as something you could learn here and then do on your own to help you control the feelings and physical sensations of nervousness. Then we discussed stress inoculation, which involves giving you a lot of different skills to use to cope with the stressful situations in your math class. The third plan, desensitization, involves using relaxation first but also involves having you imagine the scenes related to your math class and to interactions with your parents. This procedure is something we would work on together, although the relaxation requires daily practice from you. What do you think would be most helpful to you at this point?

    Client: I think maybe the relaxation might help, since I can practice with it on my own. It also sounds like the simplest to do, not so much in time but just in what is involved.

In the last response, the counselor pursues the option that Joan has been leaning toward during the session, thus building on **client preferences.**

15. *Counselor:* That's a good point. Of the three procedures I mentioned, relaxation training is probably the easiest and simplest to learn to use. You have also mentioned once or twice before in our session that you were intrigued with this idea, so it looks as if you've been mulling it over for a little while and it still sounds appealing and workable to you. If so, we can start working with it today.

LEARNING ACTIVITIES #32: STRATEGY SELECTION

I. Using the case of Mr. Brown, presented in Chapter 7 (p. 166), select and define an outcome goal for the client, based on the assessed problem described in that chapter. In small groups, brainstorm to generate as many action plans or strategies as possible that might be most workable for this client, given the identified problem and goal. List these strategies on paper. After the brainstorming, assess the usefulness and potential efficacy of each strategy by applying the 12 criteria for effective strategies listed earlier in this chapter on page 295.

II. This activity provides practice in eliciting informed consent from a client. If possible, use role-play triads

in which one person assumes the role of the client, another the counselor, and the third the observer. This activity will work best if you continue to use the case of Mr. Brown. The counselor's task is to select two or three strategies that your group judged effective and to describe them to the client. Be sure to include information about the activities involved, the rationale for the strategy, the client's role or expected participation, your role, possible discomforts or risks, and expected benefits. The observer can use the Checklist for Informed Consent that follows as a guide for observation and feedback.

(continued)

LEARNING ACTIVITIES #32: STRATEGY SELECTION (continued)

CHECKLIST FOR INFORMED CONSENT

Instructions: Determine whether the counselor did or did not convey the following elements of information to the client about proposed procedures.

Yes	No	Item
——	——	1. Description of each strategy, including activities involved
——	——	2. Rationale for or purpose of the strategy
——	——	3. Description of the therapist's role
——	——	4. Description of the client's role
——	——	5. Description of possible risks or discomforts

Yes	No	Item
——	——	6. Description of expected benefits
——	——	7. Estimated time and cost of each strategy
——	——	8. Offer made to answer client's questions about strategy
——	——	9. Client advised of the right to discontinue strategy at any time
——	——	10. Explanations given in clear and nontechnical language
——	——	11. Summary and/or clarifications used to explore and understand client reactions

☐ SUMMARY

Most clients will present complex problems with a diverse set of counseling goals. This will require a set of interventions and combinations of strategies designed to work with all the major target areas of a person's functioning. Both counselor and client should be active participants in choosing counseling treatment strategies that are appropriate for the client's problem and desired outcomes. The strategies reflected by the overall treatment plan should be sufficient to deal with all the important target areas of change and matched, as well as possible, to the response components of the defined problem. After the strategies have been selected, the counselor and client will continue to work together to implement the procedures. Some common elements of strategy implementation are considered in the next chapter.

POSTEVALUATION

PART ONE

Instructions: Listed below in the left column are six client situations. Listed in the right column are the five guidelines for appropriate timing of strategy introduction and selection. Decide which of these five guidelines is represented in each of the six client situations (Chapter Objective One). There may be more than one guideline that "fits" for any given situation. Feedback follows the postevaluation.

Situations

——1. The client has been late the last few weeks and on one occasion "forgot" the appointment.

——2. You asked the client to complete a self-report inventory during the week. The client started it but says he

Guidelines

a. Quality of the relationship

b. Assessment of the problem

c. Development of counseling goals

d. Client readiness and

Situations

needs another week to finish it.

——3. The client shifts the focus during the third session from not being able to decide on a major to the concern that she is "going crazy."

——4. The clients keep changing their minds about how they want their relationship to be different.

——5. The client repeatedly asks you to solve issues for him.

——6. The client has left the session early the last two times.

Guidelines

commitment

e. Collection of baseline measures

(continued)

PART TWO

In this part of the postevaluation, we present three descriptions of client cases. Read each case carefully and then determine and list in writing which among the seven criteria for strategy selection (listed below) would be the predominant or primary criteria for selecting strategies *for this particular client case* (Chapter Objective Two). Provide a rationale for your choice. You may also want to speculate on a choice of suitable intervention strategies, given the primary criteria you have identified. Feedback is provided after the postevaluation.

Criteria for Strategy Selection

1. Counselor characteristics and preferences
2. Documentation about strategies
3. Environmental factors
4. Nature of client problem and response systems
5. Nature of outcome goals
6. Client characteristics and preferences
7. Diagnostic cues and patterns

Case 1

The client, a college student, reports failing grades because of what he calls "procrastination." He says he puts off everything related to classes until the last possible moment. As a result, his work is often sloppy and/or late, and he has insufficient time to prepare adequately for tests. He says he has tried to deal with this in two ways: (1) by depriving himself of things he enjoys doing until the work is completed and (2) by forcing himself to sit at his desk for a certain amount of time. He reports that neither solution has helped at all. He also reports that he has sought therapy for this problem before and that it was unsuccessful. He states that it is difficult to study in his room because of

noise but that he is too lazy to get up and walk to the library all the time. He describes himself as a slow starter, as someone who needs a lot of pushing and prodding to get things done.

Case 2

The client, in her midtwenties, has just returned from two years of travel in Europe, which she completed after earning a college degree in art. Her funds have run out, and her traveling companion has come back to school. She would like to return to Europe to live but needs first to find work and build up her funds. Despite this realization, she says she is reluctant to "buckle down" and work, preferring the more creative life of a roving artist. She states that she read in a national newsmagazine about an approach called "CP"—creative processing—which she would like you to try with her to see whether she can start to work full-time without losing touch with the creative part of herself that she discovered during her recent travels.

Case 3

The client, a middle-aged married woman, has become increasingly anxious over a variety of things during the past year. Her anxiety began when she was shopping. Now she also can no longer drive without having panic attacks. During the last two months, she has confined herself to her house because of increasing anxiety over being out of the house. She indicates that her anxiety mainly takes the form of a terrible feeling in her stomach, rapid heart rate, shortness of breath, dizziness, and thoughts that she is going crazy or is going to die. She wants help in getting control of these feelings and not being such a bundle of nerves.

☐ SUGGESTED READINGS

Dixon, D., & Glover, J. (1984). *Counseling: A problem-solving approach.* New York: Wiley. Chapter 9, "Selecting an Intervention Strategy."

Lazarus, A. A. (1981). *The practice of multimodal therapy.* New York: McGraw-Hill. Chapter 8, "The Selection of Techniques."

Lehrer, P. M., & Woolfolk, R. L. (1984). Are stress-reduction techniques interchangeable, or do they have specific effects? A review of the comparative empirical literature. In R. L. Woolfolk & P. N. Lehrer (Eds.), *Principles and practice of stress management.* New York: Guilford Press.

Lidz, C. W., Meisel, A., Zerbavel, G. E., Carter, M., Sestak, R., & Roth, L. (1984). *Informed consent.* New York: Guilford Press.

Manthei, R. J. (1983). Client choice of therapist in therapy. *Personnel and Guidance Journal, 61,* 339–340.

Meyer, R. G. (1983). *The clinician's handbook.* Boston: Allyn & Bacon.

Öst, L. G., Jerremalm, A., & Johannson, J. (1981). Individual response patterns and the effects of different behavioral methods in the treatment of social phobia. *Behaviour Research and Therapy, 19,* 1–16.

Reid, W. H. (1983). *Treatment of the DSM-III psychiatric disorders.* New York: Brunner/Mazel.

Shaffer, W. F. (1976). *Heuristics for the initial diagnostic interview.* Paper presented at the annual meeting of the American Psychological Association, Washington, DC.

Widiger, T. A., & Rorer, L. G. (1984). The responsible psychotherapist. *American Psychologist, 39,* 503–515.

Yeaton, W. H., & Sechrest, L. (1981). Critical dimensions in the choice and maintenance of successful treatments: Strength, integrity, and effectiveness. *Journal of Consulting and Clinical Psychology, 49,* 156–167.

FEEDBACK: POSTEVALUATION

PART ONE

1. a, d
2. a, d, e
3. b
4. c
5. d
6. a, d

PART TWO

Case 1

Nature of client problem — procrastination, avoidance behavior.

Client characteristics — a slow starter; uses punitive means to manage his own behavior, and these have perhaps made problem worse.

Environmental factors — difficulty in finding quiet place to study.

Diagnostic cues — previous attempts by self and another therapist to change the pattern have been unsuccessful.

Possible treatment strategies — paradoxical intervention; group counseling/therapy.

Case 2

Counselor characteristics — counselor may not feel comfortable using the "CP" approach requested by the client.

Documentation — there is a hint that the "CP procedure" is a novel and somewhat experimental one, without much supporting demonstration of its clinical effectiveness.

Diagnostic cues — client seems to lack realistic information about herself and her environment.

Possible treatment strategies — ones related to choice issues such as vocational counseling; Gestalt dialoguing; TA redecision work.

Case 3

Nature of client problem and response systems — phobia (agoraphobia) with panic attacks; anxiety involves both somatic and cognitive components.

Nature of goal — client wants to learn to manage anxiety and control panic attacks.

Diagnostic cues — anxiety is focal rather than generalized.

Possible treatment strategies — specific anxiety management procedures such as desensitization; presence of panic attacks may indicate initial need for medication.

COMMON ELEMENTS OF
STRATEGY IMPLEMENTATION

TWELVE

Many helping strategies share four elements when used with clients: the rationale for the strategy, modeling of goal behaviors, rehearsal of goal behaviors, and *in vivo* homework and transfer of learning. Each strategy is described to the client with a treatment rationale in which the counselor explains the purpose of the procedure and provides an overview of it. Some strategies also involve some form of modeling, in which the goal behaviors are demonstrated, live or symbolically. And typically the modeling is followed by some form of rehearsal within the interview, often accompanied by coaching and feedback from the helper. Finally, most strategies include a transfer-of-learning element in which the client engages in homework or self-directed practice in the environment. For example, the four elements were used in social skills training in groups for alcoholics (Eriksen, Björnstad, & Götestan, 1986). These four elements of strategy implementation, when used in combination, comprise a variety of skill training programs, such as assertive behavior (Galassi & Galassi, 1977), social skills (Eisler & Frederiksen, 1980), and job-interview skills (Azrin & Besalel, 1980), and for some self-help therapy programs (Glasgow & Rosen, 1979). This chapter will describe the major ways in which these elements are used in implementing helping strategies. We also describe components of written treatment contracts.

☐ OBJECTIVES

1. Given a simulated client case, describe how you would apply the four elements of strategy implementation with this client.
2. With a partner, demonstrate the four elements of strategy implementation in a skill-building program.
3. Given a written client case, design a written treatment contract including the five components of such contracts.

☐ RATIONALE FOR TREATMENT STRATEGIES

Before implementing any strategy, the therapist should give the client a rationale about the treatment. Wilson and Evans (1977, p. 555) suggest what a rationale should be in order to foster realistic expectations about a particular treatment:

> Essentially the strategy is . . . to provide clients with information which will produce a cognitive structure whereby they can organize their experience in therapy. Structuring would include an explanation of the development, maintenance, and modification of the client's problems, a persuasive rationale for the specific treatment methods to be employed, a description of the procedural steps involved and the client's own responsibilities in actively participating in the treatment."

An adequate rationale about treatment consists of a *reason* for the procedure and a brief *overview* of its components (Kazdin & Krouse, 1983). After providing the rationale, you should seek the client's willingness to try out the strategy. As with any part of the counseling process, clients should never be forced or coerced to use something without their express commitment.

In the remaining chapters, examples of a rationale that might be used to explain each particular strategy to a client are modeled. Here is an example of a counselor providing a rationale about using modeling and role play as part of a skill-building program for a young girl who would like to talk more honestly with her best friend.

Counselor: Kathy, you've said you'd like to be able to learn to tell your friend Tammy when she has hurt your feelings, but you aren't sure how to do this. I think I can show you a way to talk to Tammy, and then you can pretend that I am Tammy and talk to me about how I have hurt your feelings. [overview] I believe if you can pretend I'm your friend and talk to me about this, then later on you will be able to talk to Tammy the way you want to. [rationale] How does this sound to you? [client's willingness]

Client: OK. We pretend in my class sometimes.

Counselor: So would you like for us to go ahead and try this out?

Client: Sure. It's fine with me.

To summarize, there are two things a counselor can explain in giving the client an adequate rationale about any counseling strategy: a reason, or

purpose, for the strategy and an overview of the strategy.

☐ MODELING

Modeling is a procedure by which a person can learn through observing the behavior of another person. In some instances, modeling alone is used as a therapy strategy to help a client acquire responses or extinguish fears (see Chapter 13). In other cases, modeling is a component of a strategy in which the counselor provides demonstrations of the goal behaviors. Models can be live or symbolic. Live models are people: the therapist, a teacher, a friend, or a peer. As Nye (1973) points out, a counselor can be a live model "by demonstrating a desired behavior and arranging optimal conditions for the client to do the same" (p. 381). Symbolic models can be provided through written materials such as manuals or handbooks, films, audio- or videotapes, slide tapes, or photographs. Modeling can also take place by having the client imagine someone performing the target behaviors, as is done in covert modeling (see Chapter 14).

Processes Involved in Modeling

Bandura and Jeffery (1973) claim that there are four processes involved in modeling: attention, retention, reproduction, and motivation. *Attention* refers to the activity of the observer in focusing on what is modeled. For example, it might be very difficult for a client to attend to a model when feeling anxious. In such cases, the counselor may have to introduce relaxation procedures (Chapter 17) before modeling can be used. One way the counselor can facilitate client attention is to cue or instruct the client about what to look for before the model is presented.

Retention refers to symbolic or linguistic coding, cognitive organization, or covert rehearsal of what has been modeled or demonstrated. A counselor can enhance the retention processes by sequencing the presentation of the model in a series of brief modeled scenarios. After the model has been presented, a summarization of what has been demonstrated by the counselor or client may also aid retention.

The third process involved in modeling is *reproduction,* which refers to the ability of the observer to reproduce, rehearse, or practice the modeled behavior.

The last process common to all modeling procedures is *motivation.* A counselor can encourage motivation by giving the client a rationale for using modeling. For example, a counselor might explain how the procedure is applied and the benefits the client might derive from its use. Motivation can also be increased if the client successfully performs the modeled behavior. This can be arranged by practice of small, successful steps. These four processes of attention, retention, reproduction, and motivation overlap. For example, client motivation can be enhanced by successful reproduction of the modeled behavior. These processes may be enhanced by the characteristics of the model and by the presentation of the modeling procedure.

Characteristics of the Model

The characteristics of the model can be important factors contributing to the success of modeling. The model characteristics described in this section represent the ideal. However, it may not be practical or feasible for the counselor to apply all the ideal characteristics, particularly when the counselor has to be the model or when other live models are used. It is perhaps easier to incorporate these model characteristics into symbolic models (see Chapter 13).

Research indicates that the effects of modeling may be enhanced when there is a great deal of similarity between the model and the client (Bandura, 1971a; Rosenthal & Bandura, 1978). The model selected should be like the client in age and sex. The prestige of the model and similarity in cultural and ethnic background and racial origin may also have important effects for some clients (Cormier & Cormier, 1975).

A coping model is perhaps better than a mastery model (Kazdin, 1973a, 1974a, 1974b; Meichenbaum, 1971). That is, a model who shows some fear or anxiety, makes errors in performance, and shows some degree of struggle or coping while performing the behavior or activity may be less threatening than a model who comes across as flawless. A client may be able to identify more easily with a coping model or with what Marlatt and Perry (1975) call a "slider" model, who displays gradual improvement during a complex series of modeled behaviors. For example, a phobic client may improve more quickly if timid models gradually attain calmness than if they perform fearlessly at once. Model displays should be tuned to the perspective of the clients and not be beyond their

reach. In addition, models who have concerns similar to those of the client may contribute a great deal to the success of a modeling procedure. Models who share yet overcome handicaps are therapeutically beneficial when seen by clients as having similar concerns and similar histories (Rosenthal, 1976).

Repeated demonstrations of the same response are often necessary. As Bandura (1976a, p. 250) indicates, multiple modeling demonstrations show the client how something can be performed best and also that any feared consequences do not occur. Multiple demonstrations can be arranged by having a single model repeat the demonstration or by having several models demonstrate the same response. For example, one model could demonstrate several times how our client Kathy could talk to her friend, or several models could demonstrate this same activity. The multiple models would be portrayed as possessing characteristics and concerns similar to those of the client (Perry & Furukawa, 1980). The use of multiple models may also increase the generalizability and efficacy of modeling. Multiple models may give more cues to the client and can have greater impact than a single model, because clients can draw on the strengths of each model.

Remember that, in some cases, a therapist may not be able to use multiple models in an interview setting. The selection of particular model characteristics will be dictated by the parameters of the client's problem and goals and the individual characteristics of the client. Sometimes the client is the best model (see "Self-as-a-Model," Chapter 13).

Presentation of Live Modeling

When using live modeling in the interview, the model first engages in role reversal; that is, the model plays the part of the client while the client plays the part of a significant other person in the client's environment. It is important to instruct the client to portray this person as realistically as possible. This provides an opportunity for the behaviors to be modeled under conditions that closely resemble the client's extratherapeutic environment. At the same time, it enables the model to identify the kind of person who should be portrayed later in the client's practice sequences. When using live modeling, try to remember that the modeling is a suggestion—not a decision for the client. Encourage the client to adapt the modeling to his or her own style.

Here is an example of a live modeling sequence with the counselor modeling the goal behavior for Kathy:

Counselor: We're going to pretend for a bit. I'd like you to pretend to be Tammy. Just be the way she is and tell me what she says about your clothes. I'm going to pretend to be you. Only instead of biting my lip and being quiet like you tell me you are, I'm going to tell her my feelings are hurt. OK. Now you start as Tammy.

Client (as Tammy, in a jeering voice): You know, Kathy, that dress looks funny on you today. Are those clothes yours or are they hand-me-downs from your sister?

Counselor (as Kathy, silent for a moment, starts to bite lip, then stops herself): No, they're mine. Hey, Tammy, what's the big deal about clothes? We only have so much money. . . . I have hurt feelings when you say something about my clothes like that.

Client (as Tammy): Oh, let's forget it. I'm sorry. Can you come over after school today?

After the demonstration, the client can summarize the main points of the modeled presentation. At this time, general principles that the client should remember during later practice attempts can be reviewed. These guidelines may help the client code the modeled input in a way that facilitates recall. If the client has trouble summarizing or reviewing, additional modeling may be required before practice attempts are initiated. The client should be encouraged to select for practice only those parts of the modeled demonstration that he or she finds comfortable. For example:

Counselor: OK, Kathy, let's talk about our pretending. Did you feel like you acted the way Tammy does?

Client: Yes. I believe she did feel sorry, too. I don't think she wants to be mean.

Counselor: That's probably right. But as long as you don't say anything, she doesn't know how you feel. What did you see me do?

Client: Well, you started to bite your lip. But it looked like you got brave then and told her your feelings were hurt.

Counselor: Do you think you could say something like I did to Tammy?

Client: Sure, I think so.

Counselor: Well, we can try another pretend, only this time I'll be Tammy and you be yourself. If you see that you forget to say something and start to bite your lip, just stop, take your time, and then tell me in your own words that your feelings are hurt.

To summarize, the counselor should implement modeling with the following guidelines in mind:

1. Instruct the client in what to look for before the modeled demonstration.
2. Select a model who is similar to the client and who can demonstrate the goal behaviors in a coping manner.
3. Present the modeled demonstration in a sequence of scenarios that minimize stress for the client.
4. Ask the client to summarize or review what he or she saw after the demonstration.

Typically, modeling of goal behaviors will be followed by practice or rehearsal of these responses. Modeling is used as a necessary precondition for rehearsal when the client's behavioral repertory is deficient or defective and when the goal of rehearsal is *response acquisition*. The rationale for this is very simple: if a person wants to do something but doesn't know how, without a modeled demonstration it would be very difficult to practice the desired behavior. Modeling provides the client with some response choices he or she can use during practices of the goal behaviors.

☐ REHEARSAL, OR PRACTICE

Most strategies involve some form of response practice in which the client rehearses the goal behaviors. Usually these rehearsal attempts follow the sequence in which the goal behaviors have been arranged. The actual practice of each response should be very similar to the situations that occur in the client's environment. As Mischel (1971) asserts, "Generalization is enhanced to the degree that the stimulus conditions sampled in treatment are similar to those in the life situation in which the new behaviors will be used" (p. 468). To simulate these situations realistically, the practice attempts should include any necessary props and should portray any other people involved with the client as accurately as possible. This portrayal should include acting out the probable responses of these other persons to the client's goal behavior.

Overt and Covert Rehearsal

The actual rehearsal attempts may be covert or overt. A client can rehearse covertly by imagining and reflecting about the desired response. In overt rehearsal, the client can verbalize and act out the desired behaviors in a role-play scene. Both overt and covert rehearsal have some empirical support (McFall & Twentyman, 1973). The combined effects of overt and covert rehearsal may be better than the effects of either alone (Kazdin, 1982; Kazdin & Mascitelli, 1982b). When the target response consists in sexual behaviors or acquisition or discrimination of covert responses, covert rehearsal may be more appropriate. For clients who have difficulty generating and maintaining real-life images, overt rehearsal may be more helpful. With many clients, both covert and overt practice can be used. Initially, it may be useful to have the client engage in covert rehearsal, because it is less visible and may decrease the client's concern about being observed by the counselor. Gradually, the client can approximate overt rehearsals, first by verbalizing while practicing covertly and then by acting out the situation in a role play.

Coaching and Induction Aids

Immediately before a goal behavior is rehearsed, it may help to have the client review covertly or aloud what he or she is going to do and say during the practice. In addition, the client's fear of "fouling up" may be decreased if the counselor stops to prompt, or coach, when the client gets stuck. Coaching consists in giving the client instructions about the general principles for performing the desired behavior effectively. Coaching can provide the cues for the person to make discriminations about the appropriate use of the target responses. The counselor can coach by giving verbal suggestions or by flashing cue cards to the client during practice. If a client has repeated difficulty in rehearsing one particular response, it may be necessary to go back to the previous response. In some cases, additional modeling and coaching may be required, or the order of the rehearsed responses may need rearrangement.

Sometimes a client has difficulty practicing the desired responses unless the practice attempts are supplemented with *induction aids,* performance or supportive aids arranged by the counselor to assist a client in performing a feared or difficult response. Induction aids are safeguards that are introduced temporarily during initial practice attempts to help clients do what they are too frightened to think about or too hesitant to initiate on their own (Bandura, 1976a, p. 250). Bandura describes the use of induction aids as follows: "During the early phases of treatment, therapists use whatever supplementary aids are necessary to initiate behavioral changes. As treatment progresses,

however, the supportive aids and practice controls are gradually removed until clients function effectively without assistance" (p. 251).

These are examples of induction aids, adapted from Bandura (pp. 250–251), to be used with practice attempts:

1. Practice with the counselor's (or model's) assistance.
2. Verbal or physical guidance, support, or coaching by the counselor.
3. Repeated practice of only one activity or response.
4. Use of graduated time intervals for practice, such as a shorter to a longer duration.
5. Graduated levels of severity, risk, or threat in a practice situation (low risk to high risk).
6. Any arrangement of protective practice conditions to reduce the likelihood of feared or undesired consequences.

Induction aids are useful to help clients who cannot perform an activity or behavior by themselves or to assist a client through difficult performances. A client should never be coerced to perform a behavior or engage in a particular activity. However, a client's refusal to practice might indicate a need for help in the form of induction aids, not necessarily a desire to stop trying (R. W. Jeffery, 1976, p. 304). If the counselor has difficulty thinking of suitable induction aids, she or he should ask the client to recommend induction aids that would help the client to practice or engage in the desired activity or behavior in either the interview or the natural setting. The counselor and client can use any induction aids that are necessary to initiate behavioral change and to ensure successful performance. The more aids the counselor can use, the greater the probability of success for treatment. The importance of a wide array of induction aids was demonstrated with phobic, incapacitated clients (Bandura, Jeffery, & Wright, 1974). Bandura (1976a) suggests that the number of supportive aids should be a function of the severity of the client's disabilities or deficits.

Client Self-Directed Practice

As the client becomes able to master the activity or behavior with aids, support, and guidance from the counselor, the coaching or induction aids should be *gradually* withdrawn so that the client performs the activities or behaviors unassisted. Dispense with aids and coaching when clients can perform the desired activities. But remember, encourage the client to practice only what is clearly within the client's *immediate capabilities* and what the client is *willing* to do. The counselor can decide when and how to decrease the amount of coaching and induction aids by relying on such indicators as client performance and verbal feedback. Gradually, clients should be able to rehearse a response, directing themselves with self-cuing.

Criteria for Effective Practice

One response in the sequence should be covered adequately before moving on to the next task. The therapist can use three criteria proposed by Lazarus (1966, p. 210) to determine when a practice attempt has been rehearsed satisfactorily:

1. The client is able to enact the response without feeling anxious.
2. The client's general demeanor supports his or her words.
3. The client's words and actions would seem fair and reasonable to an objective onlooker.

In addition, as Goldfried and Davison (1976, p. 147) suggest, the client should take an active role in deciding when a scene has been rehearsed sufficiently.

In the following dialogue, Kathy and the counselor are starting the practice attempts of the first response on their ordered list:

Counselor: Kathy, let's try another pretending. This time you just be yourself and I'll pretend to be Tammy. Let's just be walking home from school together. Nothing touchy has come up. Now can you tell me what you think you could say if I said something to hurt your feelings—like about your clothes? [review of target response]
Client: Well, I'd think I could just say "Tammy, I don't think my clothes should matter. But when you say they do, my feelings are hurt."
Counselor: That's great. I think it would help if you could just go over that for a few minutes, using your imagination. Just pretend Tammy makes a remark about your clothes and imagine telling her your feelings are hurt. Then imagine what she would say to you. [covert rehearsal]
[Pause]
Counselor: OK, tell me what happened in your imagination.
Client? Well, it was after school. She brought up the Girl Scout banquet and told me she thought I should borrow her dress, since our troop decided not to wear our uniforms. I told her I had a dress I

wanted to wear and it bothered me when she said something like that. [Pauses]
Counselor: And then what happened?
Client: Tammy was surprised. She said she was sorry.
Counselor: OK, let's try this out again. This time I'll be Tammy and you be yourself. [overt rehearsal]
Counselor (as Tammy): You know, Kathy, I've been noticing that your clothes look like, well, I mean don't you think you should get a new dress for the banquet—or borrow one of mine?
Client: Tammy, we don't have a lot of money right now for clothes. Besides, I'd rather spend my allowance on my bike. [somewhat defensively]
Counselor: Let's stop there. Did you say to Tammy what you really wanted to tell her? [counselor coaching]
Client: No, not really. I left out the part about my hurt feelings, didn't I?
Counselor: Yes. You got off to a good start, but you did leave it out. Sometimes you can remember that part by the words *I feel,* like "I feel hurt or upset when you talk about my clothes." Let's go over it again. [counselor coaching and repeated practice of same response]

After several successful practices, the counselor would encourage Kathy to practice the scene without any assistance from the counselor. Then practice with the next response would begin. The rehearsal attempts would continue until each response in the sequence had been completed satisfactorily. At this point, Kathy should be able to demonstrate the desired behaviors in appropriate ways, and any anxiety that was present should be decreased. However, the rehearsal efforts might be of limited value unless accompanied by some form of feedback or analysis of performance.

Feedback

Feedback is a way to observe and evaluate oneself and one's behavior and, under the right circumstances, to initiate corrective action (Melnick, 1973). Feedback that follows rehearsal provides a basis for recognizing successful performance and for recognizing and correcting any problems encountered during practice (Geis & Chapman, 1971, p. 40). Feedback should be designed to help the client improve performance and to recognize desirable and undesirable aspects of her or his rehearsal. For feedback to have a positive effect, it must be used cautiously and with some guidelines. Too much feedback, particularly if it comes from an external source, can be threatening or punishing. Thomas (1977, p. 95) summarizes the role of feedback in a behavior-change program as follows: "The problem with feedback . . . is that while it generally informs the recipient and sometimes changes his behavior favorably, its behavioral function is uncertain."

According to McKeachie (1976, p. 824), feedback is most likely to be facilitative if three conditions are met:

1. The person receiving the feedback is motivated to improve.
2. The feedback provides an adequate, but not an excessive, dose of information.
3. The feedback helps the person to identify or implement other response alternatives.

The extent to which these conditions of effective feedback are met will depend on the type, timing, and amount of feedback used in conjunction with a client's practice sessions.

The following three guidelines can be used to apply feedback in conjunction with a practice effort.

1. Give the client the first opportunity to assess his or her own performance. As Rose (1973) points out, if the client is responsible for a great deal of the feedback, this sensitizes the client to his or her behavior and helps the client to monitor performance between sessions.

2. Verbal assessment (by either the counselor or the client) should be supplemented with a periodic objective assessment, such as a playback of a video- or audiotape. Initially a taped playback may seem threatening to a client. But as a client becomes accustomed to being on tape, the playback will not be viewed with apprehension. At first, the counselor and client can go over the playback together. Eventually, the client should be able to take the tape home and evaluate progress alone. The advantage of the taped feedback is that it allows the client to see or hear objective evidence of successive rehearsals with greater refinement of the desired skills. Moreover, the knowledge of being taped may itself bring about change by activating the client's self-monitoring system (Melnick & Stocker, 1977). If it is impossible to tape-record any rehearsal sessions, a substitute playback using role reversal can be used. In this method, the counselor takes the part of the client and tries to mirror exactly the way in which the client completed the previous rehearsal attempt.

This may be more accurate than verbal analysis, which is subject to more distortions and biases.

3. Verbal assessment by the counselor should contain encouragement for some part of the client's practice attempt and some suggestions for how the client might improve or do something differently. Krumboltz and Thoresen (1976) suggest the use of Homme's "sandwiching" technique for counselor feedback. In this technique, the first part (a slice of bread) is a positive stroke, followed by a suggestion or a criticism (the filling), followed by another positive stroke (the other slice of bread). It is important to give some positive feedback for *each* rehearsal attempt. Don't wait for a perfect performance before giving encouragement. Each successive attempt should be reinforced by the counselor. Gradually, the counselor can reduce the amount of praise given and help clients learn to reinforce themselves for successes. This will help clients learn how to praise themselves after a rehearsal effort. Clients are usually able to do this after a sufficient amount of modeling or coaching has provided a basis for discriminating improved performance.

Here is an example of the counselor and Kathy using feedback after a practice attempt.

Counselor: OK, Kathy, let's stop for a minute. What do you think just happened in our practice?
Client: Well, I did tell Tammy my feelings were hurt. It wasn't as hard as I thought. Uh, well, it's harder to talk to her than to you.
Counselor: So maybe you think a little more practice might be needed. Would you like to listen to the way we sound on this tape?
Client (giggles): Sure.
[Tape is turned on and replayed. Immediately after Kathy has responded with the desired behavior, counselor adds feedback.]
Counselor: Right there, Kathy. I can play this part back again. Notice how you just told Tammy your feelings were hurt—you didn't hem and haw around. [stroke] You may want to speak up a little the next time—hear how soft your voice is. [suggestion] That was a good effort [stroke].
Client: Yeah, I didn't realize I talked softly.
Counselor: You don't seem to usually. Perhaps it was because you're learning something new. What did you hear on the tape that you liked about the way you handled the situation? [cuing Kathy for self-reinforcement]
Client: Well, I liked saying "Tammy, I have hurt feelings." As my older brother says, "Tell it like it is."

Counselor: Yes, you were being honest, and yet you were doing it in a way that was not putting down your friend, either.

To summarize, rehearsal of the goal behaviors involves the following steps:

1. A review of the target responses to practice.
2. Covert and/or overt rehearsal attempts of sequenced responses.
3. Therapist coaching and induction aids during initial practice attempts.
4. Reduction of coaching and induction aids.
5. Client self-directed practice of response.
6. Adequate practice of one response before moving on to another.
7. Therapist and client feedback, oral and taped.

After the client is able to demonstrate the goal behaviors during practice attempts in the interview, *in vivo* practice opportunities can be arranged. Typically these take the form of homework tasks that make up a transfer-of-training program.

☐ HOMEWORK AND TRANSFER OF LEARNING

Facilitating the transfer of behavior from the counseling or training session to the "natural" environment *(in vivo)* should be an integral part of the helping process. Generalization of desired changes can be achieved by homework assignments that are part of a transfer-of-training program. Martin and Worthington (1982) indicate that homework can increase the client's self-awareness about the problem and can improve the acquisition of new behavior or the elimination of old responses because the homework is to be completed between therapy sessions. Shelton and Levy (1981, pp. 12–14) suggest that homework can result in a number of benefits, including the following:

1. Provides access to private behaviors.
2. Allows treatment to continue after therapy sessions.
3. Increases the efficiency of treatment.
4. Increases client's perceptions of self-control.
5. Facilitates transfer of learning.

Homework experiences are arranged by tailoring a transfer-of-training program for each client. In an adequate program, the client's new skills are used first in low-risk situations in the client's natural environment *(in vivo)* or in any situation in which the client will probably experience success or favorable outcomes. Gradually, the client extends the application of the skills to natural situations that are more unpredictable and involve a greater threat. The particular homework developed and assigned will vary with each client and with the client's desired goal. If the client is learning to express feelings, then the homework would be structured to assist the client in that goal. For a very thorough description of various homework activities, see Shelton and Levy's *Behavioral Assignments and Treatment Compliance* (1981).

Components of Effective Homework

Whatever the homework assignment is, it should be something clients can instigate by themselves that is likely to meet with some success. Initially, the homework should involve a fairly simple task; gradually, more complex situations can be added. Kazdin and Mascitelli (1982a) found that homework is necessary to maintain desired behavior change after the treatment intervention has ended.

Homework assignments should start with a *rationale* for the homework. Jacobson and Margolin (1979, p. 127) give couples the following rationale for homework tasks for marital counseling:

"Now I'm going to assign a task which may be the most important task which you will do from now until the end of therapy. As part of our evaluation procedure, you will begin to record some of the events that take place between the two of you every day. This will give us some information that we can't get in any other way, namely, the patterns of interactions and exchanges that go on at home. You will be doing this from now until the end of therapy, if we should decide to pursue that. So, later we will be using this information to begin working on some of the problems. We'll look at it every week and see how we're doing. So, we'll be making a lot of use of this information, and I find that it functions like a seeing eye dog for me. I am blind without it. So, it is necessary that you do the work every day and do it carefully."*

In addition to the rationale, homework assignments should contain six other components: *what* the client is to do, *when* the behavior should occur,

* From *Marital Therapy: Strategies Based on Social Learning and Behavior Exchange Principles* by N. S. Jacobson and G. Margolin. Copyright © 1979 Brunner/Mazel. Reprinted by permission.

where the behavior is to be performed, *how much* or *how often* the behavior is to occur, *how* the behavior is to be recorded, and a *reminder* to bring the homework log to the next therapy session (Shelton & Levy, 1981).

To increase the probability that the client will carry out the assignment accurately, Rose (1973) suggests that self-directed prompts in the form of cue cards be made up for the client. The client can go over the cue cards just before carrying out the assignment. Both the type of homework assignment and the prompts on the cue cards should be developed in conjunction with the client. A client who has had a major role in selecting and developing the assignment is more likely to complete the homework. In lieu of using cue cards, sometimes the counselor or another person can accompany the client on a homework assignment. Ascher and Phillips (1975) suggest that a trained aide who functions in this capacity can model for the client and also can reinforce the client's progress in the *in vivo* setting.

Self-Monitoring of Homework

The client should be encouraged to self-monitor certain aspects of the completed homework. Specifically, the client should record both the use or application of the strategy and some measure of the goal behaviors. Goldfried and Davison (1976, p. 150) suggest that giving the client a daily log sheet to monitor homework completion has certain demand characteristics that may facilitate the client's written observations. Log sheets can be developed that enable the client to gather data germane to each therapy strategy. For example, a log sheet used to record homework associated with muscle relaxation is presented in Chapter 17, and one used for cognitive restructuring can be found in Chapter 16. The data the client collects during homework completion may be used as part of evaluating the overall effects of the counseling strategy, as described in Chapter 10. The counselor should also arrange for an interview or a telephone follow-up after the client has completed some part of the homework.

Here is an example of a homework assignment the counselor developed with Kathy.

Purpose: to help Kathy think about expressing her feelings to Tammy outside the counselor's office (task 1, a simple situation that Kathy can initiate).

Instructions:

Rationale:

1. "Kathy, I'm going to assign a task for you to do during the week outside our weekly sessions. The homework assignment is really important because it will help you later express your feelings to Tammy. You will keep a 'Daily Log' and check it each time you feel OK *thinking* about telling Tammy about your hurt feelings. At the next session, bring the log so that we can look it over and discuss it. How does that sound?

"What" to do:

2. "Read over the card that says 'Feelings' on it [cue card; see Figure 12-1]. Then sit back, close your eyes, and think about telling Tammy about your hurt feelings."

"When" to do the behavior:

3. "*Each day,* (1) before school, (2) after school, and (3) before bed, take out the cue card."

Kathy's Cue Card

FEELINGS "Tammy, I feel hurt when . . . "

Kathy's Homework Log

DAILY LOG					
Time	Mon	Tue	Wed	Thur	Fri
Before school					
During school					
After school					

Figure 12-1. Homework cue card and log

"How often" to do the behavior:

4. "Three times a day for one week."

"Where" the behavior is performed (context):

5. "At home."

"How" the behavior is to be recorded:

6. "Each time you are able to do this and feel OK with it, check this on this 'Daily Log'" (see Figure 12-1).

"Follow-up":

7. "At the end of the week, bring the log in to discuss and to review with me."

In vivo homework in the form of client self-directed practice or independent mastery results in more generalization of behavioral changes, more evidence of coping skills, and enhancement of self-competence levels (Bandura, Jeffery, & Gajdos, 1975). Self-competence, or confidence, is enhanced more by independent practice, because a client is more likely to attribute the stress to his or her own capabilities than to external aids or supports (Bandura et al., p. 142).

□ MODEL DIALOGUE: THE CASE OF JOAN

Recall from Chapter 9 that one of Joan's three outcome goals was to acquire and utilize various decision-making skills in situations in which she typically relies on the advice of others. In this dialogue we illustrate how these four components of various helping strategies can be used in combination as a decision-making skill training program for you.

First, the counselor gives Joan a **rationale** *about the strategies being used.*

1. *Counselor:* I believe today we can start working on some of the skills involved in making a decision. I think there is a way we could go about doing this that you might find helpful. It involves talking about the skills and practicing the skills in some role plays. It gives you a chance to practice making decisions without having to worry about what happens. As you feel more skillful about making decisions in this way, it will be easier for you to do so on your own. How does this sound to you?
Client: Pretty good. It sounds like it might be fun. We act out things in my English class.

The counselor gives an **overview** *of how they will proceed.*

2. *Counselor:* Well, what we'll do is go over one situation at a time. We'll work on the first one until you feel comfortable with it and then move on.
Client: OK.

The counselor introduces both **symbolic and live modeling** *of the first target response and situation and gives* **instructions** *about what to look for.*

3. *Counselor:* Since there are a couple of skills to work on, let's work on one at a time, and then we can practice putting all the skills together later on. I believe that it might be a good idea if you read over this book, *Deciding,** before our next session. It will give you a good overview of the decision-making skills. Or, if you prefer, you can come in and watch a filmstrip. We'll be starting with how you learn to find all the alternatives in a situation, so perhaps you can pay close attention to that area in the book or the filmstrip. Also, we could go over this today. Let's take a decision about how you spend your time. This time why don't you be your friend, Barbara, and I'll be you? As we do this, notice how many options I can find in this decision. I'll start out. (as Joan) Say, Barbara, what are you planning to do after school today?
Client (as Barbara): Oh, I've got to go to the store for Mom. Want to come along?
4. *Counselor* (as Joan): Well, that's a possibility. Actually, I don't have anything I really have to do today after school. I've been thinking all day about what I'm going to do.
Client (as Barbara): Well, what else do you need to do?
Counselor (as Joan): Well, I guess I should go home and work on my English theme. If I don't, I'll have to do it all tomorrow night. But it's so nice outside, I'd rather either go out with you or just go shopping.
Client (as Barbara): Well, make up your mind.
Counselor (as Joan): Well, I've got three choices —go with you, go shopping alone, or go home and do my English theme. Of course, those are all things I usually do. I also could go play tennis, go down and watch my little brother's baseball game, stay after school and work on the newspaper, or go see that movie the French Club is showing.
Client (as Barbara): You never usually do those things.

---

* Gelatt, H., Varenhorst, B., & Carey, R. *Deciding.* Princeton, N. J.: College Entrance Examination Board, 1972.

Counselor (as Joan): I know, but I'm trying to think of all my possible options.

Client (as Barbara): Well, why stay after school anyway? If you're going to do that, you might as well go home and work on your English theme — that's the safest thing to do.

Counselor (as Joan): Yeah, but I'm not concerned right now about whether my choices are good or bad. I'm just trying to think of all my possible choices.

The counselor stops live modeling and **coaches** *Joan on a way to generate different alternatives in a situation.*

5. *Counselor:* OK, Joan, let's stop here. What I was trying to do was to come up with all the ways I could spend my free time that day, if I were you. The idea of generating options is like brainstorming — the more ideas, the better. And you're only trying to *find* options right now, not evaluate them.

The counselor asks Joan **to review** *what she saw during the modeled demonstration.*

6. *Counselor:* What did you notice about what went on in this role play?

Client: Well, at first you sounded just like me — doing what is easy or necessary. I usually would either just let Barbara talk me into going with her, or I would probably study. When you started listing all those other ideas, it made me realize how automatic my decisions really are.

The counselor asks Joan **to review** *what she is going to try to do during* **her practice** *of this situation.*

7. *Counselor:* OK, let's switch roles now. This time let's give you a chance to practice this for yourself. You be yourself and I'll be Barbara. Could you briefly review what it is you're going to try to do during the practice?

Client: Well, I'm not going to make a snap decision. I'm going to hold out and try to come up with as many options as possible. Also, I'm not going to worry whether the ideas sound good or bad.

The counselor asks Joan **to practice the scene covertly** *at first.*

8. *Counselor:* OK, that's great. Sounds like you've got this well in mind. You know, I think before we practice this in a role play, it might be helpful if you went over this situation first in your imagination. Just put yourself in the situation and rehearse thinking about all your options. Do you understand?

Client: Yeah. How long should I do this?

9. *Counselor:* Spend as much time as you like.

Client: OK. [Closes eyes, pauses for several minutes]

The counselor **cues Joan to report** *what went on during* **covert rehearsal.**

10. *Counselor:* Now, tell me what happened.

Client: Well, I didn't tell Barbara right away I'd go with her. I could feel myself holding out longer. But it was still hard to think of some things I don't usually do after school. I did think of going to the library and reading some magazines.

The counselor **initiates overt practice** *with audiotape recording.*

11. *Counselor:* Well, let's try this in a role-play practice. If it's OK with you, I'll audiotape this and then we can both listen to a playback.

Client: That's fine. I've never heard myself on tape before, so it will be a surprise.

12. *Counselor:* OK, let's begin. I'll be Barbara and you be yourself now. (as Barbara) Hey, Joan, want to go to the store with me after school?

Client: Well, I'm not sure. I was thinking I should go home and study.

Counselor (as Barbara): Do you have a big test?

Client: No, I just didn't want to get behind. You know, though, Barbara, have you ever felt like doing something different?

Counselor (as Barbara): What do you mean?

Client: Well, I was thinking I usually just make snap judgments like this. I usually either go with you or go study. I was trying to think of something different to do.

[Note the counselor's use of the friend's **possible response** *next.]*

Counselor (as Barbara): Don't you like to go places with me?

Client: Sure, I do. But I was only trying to think of some things we could do together that we don't usually do.

Counselor (as Barbara): Like what?

Client: I'm not sure. Can you think of anything?

Joan has just gotten "stuck" in trying to get her friend to think of options. Counselor **stops and asks Joan to report** *what happened.*

13. *Counselor:* What did you just do there?

Client: I guess I sort of tried to get you to come up with the ideas.

The counselor **coaches** *Joan and* **initiates overt practice** *again.*

14. *Counselor:* Right. And I remember you said earlier that you haven't always been happy with

having Barbara make the decisions. Let's pick up there again. (as Barbara) Well, Joan, what kinds of things could we do together?

Client: Well, we could go to the library and read magazines. Or maybe go play some video games.

Counselor (as Barbara): That's sort of neat.

Client: Or we could go down to the record shop and look at records and tapes.

Counselor (as Barbara): You know, that sounds like fun. I guess we just usually do the same things. Maybe it would be fun to try something different.

The counselor asks Joan **to give herself feedback.**

15. *Counselor:* OK, let's stop here, Joan. What do you think about what just happened?

    Client: Well, it seemed to go better than when I tried to imagine it. I realize I did sort of do my same old trick when you stopped me. After I realized it was up to me, it didn't seem too hard to think of some ideas.

The counselor gives **verbal feedback.** *Note* **use of "sandwiching"** — *positive feedback, followed by suggestion, followed by positive feedback. Then the counselor initiates playback feedback.*

16. *Counselor:* You know, you were able to come up with three good ideas of things that you and Barbara don't usually do together. At first you did want to shift the decision to her. That's something to work on. But after that it seemed like you were able to think of some alternatives pretty easily. How about listening to the playback?

Counselor plays back the tape and asks Joan **to assess herself** *from the playback.*

17. *Counselor:* What did you notice from the playback that you liked about this practice?

    Client: Well, I seemed pretty persistent. I wasn't too put off by your comments, and I didn't make a snap judgment.

Note that the counselor **reinforces Joan's own positive assessment.**

18. *Counselor:* That's right. Even by the end of our practice you had successfully managed not to make an automatic decision.

The counselor assesses the extent to which the scene has been **practiced sufficiently.**

19. *Counselor:* What kinds of feelings did you have during this role play?

    Client: I felt pretty comfortable. It wasn't as hard as I thought.

The counselor points out a way in which the target response might need more work and **initiates another practice** *of the same scene.*

20. *Counselor:* You seem pretty comfortable. I think the main area where you got bogged down was just getting started. Once you got past that point, you really got going. How would you feel about practicing a similar situation again?

    Client: I think that would be good.

During the second practice, the counselor instructs Joan **to direct herself** *during practice* **(withdraws coaching).**

21. *Counselor:* OK, let's go over it again. This time try to direct yourself. If you feel like you're getting stuck, stop and talk yourself through the problem. I'll keep a low profile now.

After the second practice, the counselor **encourages Joan to direct herself and initiates playback feedback.**

22. *Counselor:* OK, let's stop. I think it would be a good idea for you to hear the playback. That practice really went smoothly and you didn't need much help from me.

    Client: You know, this is sort of fun. Let's hear the tape.

The counselor plays the tape and **points out the way Joan was able to get herself out of being "stuck."**

23. *Counselor:* Did you notice the way you stopped and got yourself back on the track?

    Client: Yeah. I was also able to come up with more ideas that time.

The counselor initiates possible in vivo **homework.**

24. *Counselor:* Right I'm wondering if this situation is something that you could initiate with Barbara this week?

    Client: Sure. We do a lot of things together after school at least a couple of days a week.

The counselor provides a **rationale for the homework.**

25. *Counselor:* OK, I'd like to give you a homework assignment. It will be very similar to what we did today, only you'll be carrying it out with Barbara. You'll initiate a conversation with Barbara where you discuss different ways you could spend your time. You can record these on a daily log sheet and write down the number of ideas you've found during the discussion. Next, we'll discuss your log sheet for each day. The homework assignment will help you become more skillful in making decisions. How does this sound to you?

    Client: OK. What exactly will I do?

In responses 26 and 27, the counselor gives **instructions** *about homework and specifies* **what** *and* **how much** *Joan is to do.*

26. *Counselor:* Well, I'd like you to initiate a situation with Barbara where you try to discuss different ways you could spend your time. Don't worry about actually deciding what to do. Your main goal is to come up with as many alternatives as possible—let's say at least three options. Does that sound reasonable to you?

Client: Sure. We did that today.

27. *Counselor:* Right. I'll write this down for you on this card—"To initiate a conversation with Barbara in which I identify at least three different ways we could spend our after-school time together."

Counselor and client work out **cue cards** *to help Joan carry out the homework successfully.*

28. *Counselor:* Now, maybe we could list some guidelines for you that we discussed today to help you carry out the homework. We'll call them cue cards—just like they use in the movies to help them remember. What cues would help you carry this out?

Client: Well, the one thing would be for me to come up with some ideas rather than asking Barbara.

29. *Counselor:* OK, I'll put down here—"I'll find ideas." What else?

Client: Mm [thinking]

30. *Counselor:* What about coming up with as many ideas as possible without evaluating them for now.

Client: Yes. You mean, don't worry if the idea is good or bad.

31. *Counselor:* Right. So your second cue can be "Think of many ideas. Don't evaluate now."

The counselor instructs Joan in **how to record use of the homework** *during the week, using log sheets.*

32. *Counselor:* OK, Joan. On these daily record sheets here, take a blank sheet for each day of the week. Every time you complete this assignment, make a check. Also, write the number of ideas *you* found during the discussion. Does that seem clear?

Client: Yes. Do I bring it back?

The counselor initiates **a follow-up.**

33. *Counselor:* Yes. Bring it with you next week at this time and we can see how your assignment worked out. Also, feel free to call me and report on your progress, all right? Next week, we'll go over the next situation on our list that we put together.

Client: OK, I'll probably call or stop in later on this week.

LEARNING ACTIVITY #33: STRATEGY IMPLEMENTATION

This activity consists of examples of counselor responses associated with the four components of strategy implementation for the case of John (from Chapter 7). Identify in writing which of the four components of strategy implementation (rationale, modeling, rehearsal, homework) is represented by each response. Feedback follows.

1. "John, your thinking gets in the way of what you're doing at work. It's possible to learn to control such thinking and to make it less interfering. You can control your thinking by first becoming aware of when you are producing negative self-statements and by identifying the negative self-talk. You can replace your negative self-talk with coping statements."

2. "I'm going to show you some coping statements you can use to replace your negative statements. Then, I'll show you how I replace the negative statements with positive coping statements."

3. "Now I'd like you to imagine that you are experiencing negative self-talk. Then imagine that you are replacing this talk with positive coping statements."

4. "Replacing your negative self-talk with positive coping statements can influence your attitude and how you feel about your job responsibilities. Positive coping statements can create positive attitudes and feelings about your work."

5. "Think of the negative self-talk or statements and then try to replace it with the three positive coping statements we developed."

6. "During this week I'd like you to replace your negative self-talk with positive coping statements every time you start thinking these thoughts throughout the day."

7. "At the end of the first day, call me and we can see how you are working with this procedure."

☐ WRITTEN TREATMENT CONTRACTS

The four elements of strategy implementation described in the previous sections of this chapter imply a contract between the therapist and the client. The therapist may wish to use an explicit or written treatment contract with some clients. The written contract can facilitate the therapeutic process and decrease ambiguity about the therapeutic relationship. A written treatment contract is an agreement between the therapist and the client. Contracts can be made with an individual client, a couple, or an entire family. Treatment contracts can have two forms: (1) contingency contract or (2) informational contract. A contingency contract is usually *quid pro quo,* in which bonuses are given for performing behaviors agreed to in the contract or sanctions are imposed on an individual for failure to perform behaviors as specified in the contract (Framer & Sanders, 1980; Stuart, 1971; Taylor, Pfenninger, & Candelaria, 1980; Wysocki, Hall, Iwata, & Riordan, 1979). The form of contract we present in this section is the informational treatment contract.

The informational contract has five elements: (1) information about the treatment strategies, (2) statements about goal (outcome) expectations, (3) client intention statements stipulating agreement to participate fully in a key aspect of the treatment, (4) duration (weeks or sessions) of the contract, and (5) an informed consent statement (Seidner & Kirschenbaum, 1980). A treatment contract has several advantages (Goodyear & Bradley, 1980, pp. 513–514). The contract reduces game playing because client and therapist are working toward clearly stated goal(s). The contract provides a standard for evaluating progress toward the outcome goal. It protects the client and therapist by specifying parameters of the treatment relationship. Finally, the contracting process provides a facilitative means for client self-exploration.

☐ MODEL TREATMENT CONTRACT: THE CASE OF JOAN

We illustrate a treatment contract for Joan. Recall the defined goals and the proposed treatments for Joan. In Chapter 9, we described Joan's overall goals for therapy. Four subgoals were specified for the first terminal outcome goal. Suppose we design a treatment contract for subgoal 1 of the first goal. This subgoal was to decrease Joan's anxiety associated with anticipation of failure in math class and rejection by parents. The level for the goal was to reduce the self-ratings of intensity from about 70 to 50 on a 100-point scale during the next two weeks. In Chapter 9, deep muscle relaxation (Chapter 17) and stress inoculation (Chapter 16) were mentioned as the two treatment strategies used to help Joan reduce her anxiety (subgoal 1).

Elements of a Treatment Contract for Joan

We model the five elements of the contract with the case of Joan. Figure 12-2 illustrates the five elements of a treatment contract. The first element is to provide information about the two treatment strategies used with Joan: muscle relaxation and stress inoculation.

Information about treatment strategies. Two strategies are listed in the contract (Figure 12-2). The counselor would describe *muscle relaxation* to Joan in the interview, somewhat as follows:

> "This process, if you practice it regularly, can help you become relaxed. The relaxation benefits can help you recognize better when you feel tension in your body because of stress or anxiety. This procedure involves learning to tense and relax 16 different muscle groups in your body. By doing this, you can contrast the difference between tenseness and relaxation. This will help you to recognize tension so you can instruct yourself to relax. Muscle relaxation is a skill, and the learning process will be gradual and will require regular practice."

Stress inoculation might be explained like this:

> "You find yourself confronted with situations in which your stress gets out of hand. It is difficult to manage your anxiety when you are confronted with these stressful situations. Stress inoculation can help you learn to cope with these situations and can help inoculate you when you are in these situations so the anxiety does not overwhelm you. I will help you understand the nature of your anxious feelings. Next, you will learn some ways to manage

TREATMENT CONTRACT

Treatment strategies: Muscle relaxation and stress inoculation

Goal: My self-ratings of anxiety intensity on a 0-to-100-point scale will decrease from 70 to 50 points in math class and in situations with my parents.

Intention statements: Muscle relaxation—I will practice tensing and relaxing all 16 muscle groups at home once after getting up in the morning and once after school or before dinner each day.

Stress inoculation—I will use the coping statements developed by the counselor and me for my math class and when confronted with situations with my parents. I will also use relaxation techniques and coping statements every time I am confronted with a stressful situation.

Duration of treatment: Treatment procedures will be used at least six weeks but no longer than ten weeks.

Informed consent: I agree that the counselor has explained the nature and purpose of muscle relaxation and stress inoculation and other alternative treatment options available to me. I understand the reasonable benefits and the potential disadvantages involved as well as the estimated length of these procedures. I understand that I am free to discontinue participation in these procedures at any time.

Signature of client	Signature of counselor

Date	Date

Figure 12-2. *Sample treatment contract*

your anxious feelings and to cope with these two stressful situations."

Goal statement. The counselor might say to Joan:

"Your self-ratings of anxiety intensity on a 0-to-100 point scale will decrease from about 70 to 50 in math class and in situations with your parents."

Client intention statements. The next portion of the contract consists of client intention statements indicating agreement to participate fully in a key aspect of the treatment. The contract in Figure 12-2 shows intention statements for the two treatment strategies (muscle relaxation and stress inoculation).

Information about duration. The next section of the contract specifies the duration of the terms of the contract:

You understand that the duration of the contract will be at least six weeks and not to exceed ten weeks. During the first two weeks, we will work on muscle relaxation treatment. Stress inoculation will be used during the next four weeks. It is important for you to continue to practice muscle relaxation exercises at home twice daily while using stress inoculation.

Informed consent statement. One final element of the contract is an informed consent paragraph and

a place for the date and the client's and counselor's signatures, as shown in Figure 12-2.

□ SUMMARY

Most counseling strategies or action plans involve similar components. The use of any strategy should be prefaced by a rationale about the procedure. Modeling, rehearsal, feedback, and homework tasks are important ingredients in any therapeutic change program. In addition, the four elements described in this chapter are the components used in all skill-building programs. For example, assertion training consists of modeling assertive skills, practicing assertive skills in simulated conditions with feedback, and practicing these responses in the actual environment. Written treatment contracts can also facilitate client change and reduce ambiguity about the action phase of counseling. In the following chapters, which present various treatment strategies, you will discover the importance of these components for strategy implementation.

As Lazarus (1981) cautions, however, the effectiveness of a particular intervention strategy depends not only on the components of the strategy but also on the skill of the therapist. Lazarus states:

I have been impressed by the fact that skillful therapists, especially great psychotherapeutic artists, share certain features regardless of their backgrounds, school affiliations, or professional identifications. They are responsible and flexible individuals with a high degree of respect for people. They are essentially nonjudgmental and firmly committed to the view that infringement on the rights and satisfactions of others is to be strongly discouraged. They will not compromise human interests, values, and dignity. . . . They bring warmth, wit, and wisdom to the therapeutic situation, and, when appropriate, they introduce humor and fun. They seem to have an endless store of relevant anecdotes and narratives. They are good role models (they practice what they preach) and are authentic, con-gruent, and willing to self-disclose. . . . The final orchestration of successful therapy depends on what techniques are selected, how they are implemented, and by whom they are delivered. As surgeons are apt to point out, it is the person behind the scalpel who can wield it as an instrument of destruction or of healing. In psychotherapy, it is even more difficult to separate the specific technique from the person who administers it [pp. 155–156].

■

POSTEVALUATION

PART ONE

Objective One asks you to take a simulated client case and describe how you would apply the four common elements of strategy implementation (rationale, modeling, rehearsal, homework) with this client.

As you may recall with our client Mr. Brown (from Chapter 7), one of his desired counseling goals was to be able to initiate social contacts with his boss. Although Mr. Brown had acquired some reasonably useful social skills, he was hesitant to initiate requests with his boss. In other words, his social skills were inhibited in his boss's presence. Mr. Brown stated that he felt awkward about initiating a social contact with his boss, although he did initiate such contacts with other people apparently quite successfully and without any discomfort. On the basis of Mr. Brown's desired goal, as well as this description, describe how you would use the four components of strategy implementation to help Mr. Brown demonstrate social skills with his boss. Feedback follows the Postevaluation.

PART TWO

Objective Two asks you to demonstrate the four components of strategy implementation in a skill-building program. Here's how you might do this:

1. Ask a partner to select a skill or skills he or she would like to learn. The person might wish to learn to give compliments to others, to initiate a conversation with strangers, or to give constructive feedback, for example.
2. Use modeling, rehearsal, and homework to teach the person the skill. Provide a rationale to the person about this process.
3. Tape your teaching and rate it using the Checklist for Strategy Implementation, or have an observer sit in and observe you. This checklist can be found at the end of the chapter.

PART THREE

For the third objective of this chapter, you are to design a written contract, given a hypothetical client case. Again use the case of Mr. Brown (from Chapter 7). Using the description in Part One of the postevaluation and the description of a skills training program to use with him in Part One of the feedback, design a treatment contract that you could use in conjunction with this skills training program. (Assume that you will be working with him for six to ten weeks.) Make sure your contract includes a description of the five components:

1. Treatment strategies
2. Goal
3. Intention statement
4. Duration of the skills training program
5. Informed consent statement

Feedback follows the Postevaluation.

CHECKLIST FOR STRATEGY IMPLEMENTATION

Check to see which of the following steps the counselor used.

I. Rationale for treatment
_____ 1. Did the counselor provide a rationale to the client about the strategy?
_____ 2. Did the counselor provide an overview of the strategy?
_____ 3. Did the counselor obtain the client's willingness to try the strategy?

II. Modeling of goal behaviors
_____ 4. Were instructions about what to look for in the modeled demonstration given to the client?

(continued)

_____ 5. Did the model demonstrate the goal behaviors in a coping manner?

_____ 6. Was the modeled demonstration presented in a series of sequential scenarios?

_____ 7. Did the client review or summarize the goal behaviors after the modeled demonstration?

III. Rehearsal of goal behaviors

_____ 8. Did the counselor ask the client to review the target responses before the practice attempts?

_____ 9. Did the client engage in:
_____ Covert rehearsal
_____ Overt rehearsal
_____ Both

_____ 10. During initial rehearsal attempts, did the counselor provide:
_____ Coaching
_____ Induction aids
_____ Both

_____ 11. Were the amount of coaching and the number of induction aids decreased with successive practice attempts?

_____ 12. Did the client engage in self-directed practice of each goal behavior?

_____ 13. Was each practice attempt covered satisfactorily before moving on to another goal behavior? (Check which criteria were used in this decision.)
_____ The decision to move on was a joint one (counselor and client)
_____ The client was able to enact the scene without feeling anxious
_____ The client was able to demonstrate the target responses, as evidenced by demeanor and words
_____ The client's words and actions during the scene would seem realistic to an objective onlooker

_____ 14. Did the counselor and client go over or arrange for a taped playback of the rehearsal?

_____ 15. Did the counselor provide feedback to the client about the rehearsal? (Check if the counselor's feedback included these elements.)
_____ Counselor's feedback contained a positive reinforcer statement, a suggestion for improvement, and another positive reinforcer
_____ Counselor encouraged each successive rehearsal attempt

IV. Homework and transfer of training

_____ 16. After successful practices in the interview, did the counselor assign rehearsal homework in the client's environment?

_____ 17. Did the homework assignment include (check any that apply):
_____ Situations the client could easily initiate
_____ Graduated tasks in which the client could gradually demonstrate the target response
_____ A rationale for the task
_____ Specification of what the client was to do
_____ Specification of when the task would be performed
_____ Specification of where the task would be performed
_____ Specification of how much or how often the client would perform or engage in the task

_____ 18. Was the client given self- or other-directed assistance in carrying out the homework through:
_____ Written cue cards
_____ A trained counselor's aide

_____ 19. Did the counselor instruct the client to make written self-recordings (how to record) of both the strategy (homework) and the goal behaviors?

_____ 20. Did the counselor arrange for a face-to-face or telephone follow-up after the client's completion of some of the homework?

☐ SUGGESTED READINGS

Bandura, A., & Jeffery, R. W. (1973). Roles of symbolic coding and rehearsal processes in observational learning. *Journal of Personality and Social Psychology, 26,* 122–130.

Bourque, P., & Ladouceur, R. (1980). An investigation of various performance-based treatments with acrophobics. *Behaviour Research and Therapy, 18,* 161–170.

Coe, W. C. (1980). Expectation, hypnosis, and suggestion methods. In F. H. Kanfer & A. P. Goldstein (Eds.), *Helping people change* (2nd ed.). New York: Pergamon Press.

Flowers, J. V., & Booraem, C. D. (1980). Simulation and role-playing methods. In F. A. Kanfer & A. P. Goldstein (Eds.), *Helping people change (2nd ed.).* New York: Pergamon Press.

Goldfried, M. R., & Davison, G. C. (1976). *Clinical behavior therapy.* New York: Holt, Rinehart and Winston. Chapter 7, "Behavior Rehearsal."

Goodyear, R. K., & Bradley, F. O. (1980). The helping process as contractual. *Personnel and Guidance Journal, 58,* 512–515.

Kazdin, A. E. (1982). The separate and combined effects of covert and overt rehearsal in developing assertive behavior. *Behaviour Research and Therapy, 20,* 17–25.

Kazdin, A. E., & Krouse, R. (1983). The impact of variations in treatment rationales on expectations for therapeutic change. *Behavior Therapy, 14,* 657–671.

Kazdin, A. E., & Mascitelli, S. (1982a). Behavioral rehearsal, self-instructions, and homework practice in developing assertiveness. *Behavior Therapy, 13,* 346–360.

Kazdin, A. E., & Mascitelli, S. (1982b). Covert and overt rehearsal and homework practice in developing assertiveness. *Journal of Consulting and Clinical Psychology, 50,* 250–258.

Martin, G. A., & Worthington, E. L. (1982). Behavioral homework. In M. Hersen, R. M. Eisler, & P. M. Miller (Eds.), *Progress in behavior modification* (Vol. 13). New York: Academic Press.

Perry, M. A., & Furukawa, M. J. (1986). Modeling methods. In F. H. Kanfer & A. P. Goldstein (Eds.), *Helping people change (2nd ed.),* (pp. 66–110). New York: Pergamon Press.

Sarason, I. G., & Sarason, B. R. (1981). Teaching cognitive and social skills to high school students. *Journal of Consulting and Clinical Psychology, 49,* 908–918.

Shelton, J. L., & Levy, R. L. (1981). *Behavioral assignments and treatment compliance.* Champaign, IL: Research Press.

Stuart, R. B. (1971). Behavioral contracting within the families of delinquents. *Journal of Behavior Therapy and Experimental Psychiatry, 2,* 1–11.

FEEDBACK: POSTEVALUATION

PART ONE

1. *Rationale for treatment*

   You might explain to Mr. Brown that this strategy will help him practice the skills he needs in approaching his boss in low-threat situations. You can tell him this involves seeing someone else (like yourself) demonstrate these skills and then having him practice them—first in the interview and then actually with the boss. You might emphasize that this method can help him gain confidence in the skills he needs to approach his boss.

2. *Modeling*

   Beginning with the easiest goal behavior (social skill), you or someone else could model this for Mr. Brown, taking his part while he assumes the role of his boss. You would instruct him about what to look for before the demonstration—which would be portrayed in a coping manner. After the modeled presentation, you would ask Mr. Brown to summarize what he saw.

3. *Rehearsal*

   Beginning with the easiest goal behavior, you would use a role play to help Mr. Brown practice this. The enactment of this scene should be as similar to Mr. Brown's actual environment as possible, in order to help Mr. Brown see how his behavior might affect others and to give him practice under conditions that will approximate those he will find outside counseling. You might ask Mr. Brown to practice the response covertly (in his head) at first, especially if he seems nervous about going over it with you. The reason is to reduce some of his concern about having you observe this initial performance. Gradually, though, you would ask Mr. Brown to shift into an overt rehearsal or an actual enactment of the response. If Mr. Brown tends to get stuck during the scene, you can prompt him or use cue cards; or you can go back to the previous scene. Consistent trouble in Mr. Brown's rehearsals may call for more coaching or for some introduction of induction aids, such as joint practice. You would make sure that each response was rehearsed satisfactorily before going on to another one. The decision to move on should be made jointly. Mr. Brown should be able to practice the response without feeling anxious and also be able to demonstrate the target response adequately before moving on. After each practice attempt, you should provide feedback that will help Mr. Brown assess his prior performance. First, you may want to give Mr. Brown an opportunity to assess his own practice. Periodically, a taped playback of the practice would be helpful to provide objective feedback. As the counselor, you want to be sure to encourage Mr. Brown for small indications of improvement as well as to give suggestions for the next practice. Gradually, you should encourage Mr. Brown to direct his own practice attempts and to assess and reinforce himself for a successful rehearsal.

4. *Homework*

   Finally, you should assign homework to Mr. Brown that will help him practice the target re-

(continued)

sponse outside the sessions. The homework, at first, may consist simply of mental rehearsal. Gradually, Mr. Brown might be assigned tasks in which he initiates a simple social contact with his boss, such as going on a coffee break. The nature of the tasks can be changed as Mr. Brown successfully and comfortably completes requisite tasks. Cue cards might be given to Mr. Brown to help him remember any guidelines for carrying out the homework. Mr. Brown should be instructed to observe his performance while carrying out the homework and to monitor his completion of the homework on log sheets. You should follow up the homework assignments with a face-to-face or telephone check-in.

PART TWO

Use the Checklist for Strategy Implementation on pages 322–323 as a guide to assess your teaching of a skill to a partner.

PART THREE

Here is a sample treatment contract for Mr. Brown:

Treatment strategy: Skills training (social skills)

Goal: To initiate social contacts with my boss (at least one a week).

Intention statements: I understand that I will be practicing situations involving social contacts with my boss with the counselor initially and later on by myself.

Duration of treatment: The skills training program will last between six and ten weeks.

Informed consent: I agree that the counselor has explained to me the nature and purpose of the skills training program we will be using as well as alternative treatment options available. I understand the reasonable benefits and potential disadvantages associated with this program and its expected length. I also understand that I am free to discontinue participation at any time.

_____ _____
Signature of client   Signature of counselor

_____ _____
Date   Date

SYMBOLIC MODELING, SELF-AS-A-MODEL, AND PARTICIPANT MODELING

THIRTEEN

Picture the following series of events. A young girl is asked what she wants to be when she grows up. Her reply: "A doctor, just like my mom." Think of a child who points a toy gun and says "Bang, bang, you're dead" after watching a police program on television. Think of people flocking to stores to buy clothes that reflect the "outdoor" or "leisure look," or "warm-up suit look," which has been described and featured in some magazines. All these events are examples of a process called imitation, copying, mimicry, vicarious learning, identification, observational learning, or modeling. Perry and Furukawa (1986, p. 66) define modeling as "the process of observational learning in which the behavior of an individual or a group — the model — acts as a stimulus for the thoughts, attitudes, or behaviors on the part of another individual who observes the model's performance."

There are several ways people can learn through modeling. A person can acquire new behaviors from live or symbolic modeling. Modeling can help a person perform an already acquired behavior in more appropriate ways or at more desirable times. Modeling can also extinguish client fears. Modeling procedures have been used to help clients acquire social skills, modify verbal behavior, acquire emotional responses, modify study behaviors, modify phobic responses, and treat drug addiction (Perry & Furukawa, 1980). According to Rachman (1972, p. 393), the clinical significance of modeling lies in the strength of the procedure to eliminate fearful and undesired behavior and to promote acquisition of desired responses.

In this chapter, we present three modeling procedures: symbolic modeling, self-as-a-model, and participant modeling. The steps we present for each procedure should be viewed only as guidelines for application. The creative variation of or departure from a particular procedure is a decision based on the counselor, the client, the nature of the assessed concern or problem, the goals for counseling, and the setting in which the problem behavior occurs.

□ OBJECTIVES

1. Develop and try out a script for one symbolic model with a client or a group of clients of your choice. After completing the script, evaluate it on the Checklist for Developing Symbolic Models at the end of the chapter.
2. Given a case description of a client and a counseling goal, describe how the five components of the self-as-a-model strategy could be used with this client.
3. Demonstrate at least 13 out of 16 steps of the self-as-a-model strategy in a role-play interview with a client.
4. Describe how you would apply the four components of participant modeling in a simulated client case.
5. Demonstrate at least 14 out of 17 steps associated with participant modeling with a role-play client.

□ SYMBOLIC MODELING

In symbolic modeling, the model is presented through written materials, audio- or videotapes, films, or slide tapes. Symbolic models can be developed for an individual client or can be standardized for a group of clients. For example, M. L. Russell (1974) used cartoon characters as models to teach decision-making skills to children. These characters were presented in a self-contained set of written materials and a cassette audiotape. Counselors may find that developing a standardized model is more cost-effective because it can reach a greater number of clients. For instance, a school counselor who sees many students with deficits in information-seeking skills could develop one tape that could be used by many of these students.

In this section, we present some suggestions for developing self-instructional symbolic modeling procedures. A self-instructional model contains demonstrations of the target behavior, opportunities for client practice, and feedback. In developing a self-instructional symbolic modeling procedure, the counselor will have to consider the following elements: the characteristics of the consumers who will use the model; the goal behaviors to be modeled or demonstrated; the media to be used; the content of the script; and the field testing of the model. These five steps are summarized in the Checklist for Developing Symbolic Models at the end of the chapter.

Characteristics of Consumers

The first consideration in developing a symbolic model is to determine the characteristics of the people for whom the model is designed. For example, the age, sex, cultural practices, racial characteristics, and problems of the people who will use the procedure should be assessed. For example, to determine problem situations, Sarason and Sarason (1981) conducted extensive interviews to assess what social skills are needed for low-achieving high school students. The authors interviewed teachers, counselors, students attending the school, former students who had dropped out, and employers who typically hired the students (Sarason & Sarason, 1981, p. 910).

The characteristics of the symbolic model should be similar to those of the people for whom the procedure is designed, as described in Chapter 12. The counselor should also consider the degree of variation that may exist in these characteristics among the users of the symbolic model. Including several persons as models (using multiple models) can make a symbolic model more useful for a variety of clients. For example, Sarason and Sarason's models were high school students who "represented several racial/ethnic groups — Western European, Mexican-American, Filipino, and black" (1981, p. 911). Gilbert, Johnson, Spillar, McCallum, Silverstein, & Rosenbloom (1982) used as peer models two children aged 6 and 8 — a Black male and White female — who were trained for self-injection of insulin. One model may be satisfactory in some situations. Peterson and Shigetomi (1981) presented a film, *Ethan Has an Operation* (produced by Melamed & Siegel, 1975), that showed a 7-year-old White male as a model. Also, an 8-year-old Caucasian boy was used as a coping and a mastery model with children who were pedodontic patients (Klorman, Hilpert, Michael, LaGana, & Sveen, 1980). Finally, a six-year-old leukemia patient who came to an oncology clinic for bone marrow aspiration and a spinal tap was used as a model for positive coping behavior and to describe her thoughts and feelings (Jay, Elliot, Ozolins, Olson, & Pruitt, 1985).

In some instances, former clients may serve as appropriate symbolic models on audio- and videotapes. Reeder and Kunce (1976) used ex-addict paraprofessional staff members and "advanced" residents of a drug-abuse treatment program as the models for their six video-model scenarios. The models in each scenario displayed a coping attitude while performing the various skills required for achieving the goal behaviors associated with one of six problem areas. For example:

> The model was initially shown as being pessimistic and ineffective in the given problem area. The model would then reflect upon his problem and discuss it with a peer or staff member. Following reflection and discussion, the model would try out new problem-solving behaviors. As the scenarios progressed, the model would progressively display more independence in solving problems, becoming less dependent upon the advice of the others [p. 561].

Goal Behaviors to Be Modeled

The goal behavior, or what is to be modeled, should be specified. A counselor can develop a series of symbolic models to focus on different behaviors, or a complicated pattern of behavior can be divided into less complex skills. For instance, Reeder and Kunce (1976) developed scenarios for their video models for six problem areas: accepting help from others, capitalizing on street skills, job interviewing, employer relations, free-time management, and new lifestyle adjustment. Craigie and Ross (1980) employed actors who modeled appropriate and inappropriate target behaviors for pretherapy training programs to encourage alcohol detoxification patients to seek treatment. Webster-Stratton (1981a, 1981b) used videotaped vignettes of parent models who displayed appropriate parent behaviors (nurturant, playful) and inappropriate behaviors (rigid and controlling) to train mothers. Webster-Stratton, Kolpacoff, and Hollinsworth (1988) used self-administered videotape therapy for families with conduct-problem children. Gilbert et al. (1982) used videotaped models who gave information about self-injection of insulin, described feelings about the procedure, modeled appropriate coping statements, and used self-instructions and self-praise statements (p. 189). Gresham and Nagle (1980) had female and male 9- and 10-year-olds model on videotape such social skills as participation, cooperation, communication, friendship making, and initiating and receiving positive and negative peer interaction. Sarason and Sarason (1981) used models who displayed social and cognitive skills for the following situations: "job interview, resisting peer pressure, asking for help in school, asking questions in class, getting along with the boss, dealing with frustration on the job, cutting class, asking for help at work, and getting along with parents" (p. 911).

Whether one model or a series of models is developed, the counselor should structure the model around three questions: What behaviors are to be acquired? Should these behaviors or activities be divided into a sequence of less complex skills? How should the sequence of skills be arranged?

Media

In an attempt to help you acquire counseling skills, we have presented written symbolic models throughout the book in the form of modeled examples, practice exercises, and feedback. Any of these modeled examples could be filmed, audio- or videotaped, or presented on slide tape. The choice of the medium will depend on where, with whom, and how symbolic modeling will be used. Written, filmed, audiotaped, and videotaped symbolic models can be checked out for the client and used independently in a school, in an agency, or at home. We have found that audiotaped models (cassettes) are economical and extremely versatile. However, in some instances, audiotapes may not be as effective because they are not visual. Written models can serve as a bibliotherapeutic procedure (reading) by portraying a person or situation similar to the client and the desired goal (Nye, 1973). However, a self-instructional written symbolic model differs from traditional bibliotherapy procedures by including additional components of self-directed practice and feedback. In other words, self-instructional symbolic models can be administered by the client without therapist contact (Glasgow & Rosen, 1978, 1979; Webster-Stratton, Kolpacoff, & Hollinsworth, 1988).

Content of the Presentation

Regardless of the medium used to portray the modeled presentation, the counselor should develop a script to reflect the content of the modeling presentations. The script should include five parts: instructions, modeling, practice, feedback, and a summarization.

Instructions. Instructions should be included for each behavior or sequence of behaviors to be demonstrated. Brief but explicit and detailed instructions presented before the model will help the client identify the necessary components of the modeled display (McGuire, Thelen, & Amolsch, 1975). Instructions provide a rationale for the modeling and cues to facilitate attention to the model. The instructions can also describe the type of model portrayed, such as "The person you are going to see or hear is similar to yourself."

Modeling. The next part of the script should include a description of the behavior or activity to be modeled and possible dialogues of the model engaging in the goal behavior or activity. This part of the script should present complex patterns of behavior in planned sequences of skills.

Practice. The effects of modeling are likely to be greater when presentation of the modeled behavior is followed by opportunities to practice. In symbolic modeling, there should be opportunities for clients to practice what they have just read, heard, or seen the model do.

Feedback. After the client has been instructed to practice and sufficient time is allowed, feedback in the form of a description of the behavior or activity should be included. The client should be instructed to repeat the modeling and practice portions again if the feedback indicates some trouble spots.

Summarization. At the conclusion of a particular scenario or series, the script should include a summary of what has been modeled and the importance for the client of acquiring these behaviors.

Field Testing of the Model

It is a good idea to check out the script before you actually construct the symbolic model from it. You can field-test the script with some colleagues or some people from the target or client group. The language, the sequencing, the model, practice time, and feedback should be examined by the potential consumer before the final symbolic model is designated as ready for use. If at all possible, a pilot program should be designed for the initial use of the symbolic model. For example, M. L. Russell

and C. E. Thoresen (1976) validated a written symbolic model on decision-making skills for children by comparing the performance of children who completed the workbook (the model) with children who did not (controls). The resulting data enabled the authors to validate the effectiveness of their written model for teaching decision-making skills to children. As another example, Sarason and Sarason (1981) conducted a series of pilot studies after identifying social skills in a variety of situations. For example, students critiqued the role-play scripts, and the language was changed or the situation was altered to enhance credibility of the scene and script. Data from the field testing can be used to make any necessary revisions before the finished product is used with a client.

☐ SELF-AS-A-MODEL

The self-as-a-model procedure uses the client as the model. The procedure as we present it in this chapter has been developed primarily by Hosford. Hosford and de Visser (1974) have described self-modeling as a procedure in which the client sees himself or herself as the model—performing the goal behavior in the desired manner. The client also practices with a tape. Successful practices are rewarded and errors are corrected. Note that this procedure involves not only modeling but also practice and feedback.

Why have the client serve as the model? As we mentioned in Chapter 12, the literature indicates that such model characteristics as prestige, status, age, sex, and ethnic identification have differential influence on clients (Bandura, 1969, 1971a). For some people, observing another person—even one with similar characteristics—may produce negative reactions (McDonald, 1973). Some peo-

---

LEARNING ACTIVITY #34: SYMBOLIC MODELING

You are working with a Caucasian client in her late twenties who is employed as a salesperson in a local department store. The client's goal at this point is to lose 20 pounds. The client has previously tried unsuccessfully to lose weight and is now seeking your assistance. One approach you believe might help the client is to portray someone like herself who models some weight reduction procedures. You decide to select an appropriate person as the model and use this person in an audiotaped symbolic model of weight reduction procedures.

1. Describe the type of model you would select, including age, sex, race, a coping or mastery model, and concerns presented by the model.
2. Develop an outline for a script you would use for the audiotaped model. Include in the script instructions to the client; a description of the model; a brief example of one modeled scenario, perhaps about one weight reduction procedure; an example of a practice opportunity; feedback about the practice; and a summarization of the script. Feedback follows.

FEEDBACK #34: SYMBOLIC MODELING

1. You would probably select a female, Caucasian model in her late twenties. Since your client has tried unsuccessfully to lose weight before, a mastery model may be too discouraging, and a coping model would be preferable. The concern presented by the model would be similar to that of your client — weight reduction. If possible, a model who has overcome a weight problem would be best.

2. After you have developed your script, check it with guideline 4 on the Checklist for Developing Symbolic Models on page 343.

---

ple may attend and listen better when they see or hear themselves on a tape or in a movie (Hosford, Moss, & Morrell, 1976). For example, when we perform in front of a video camera or a tape recorder, we have to admit there is a little exhibitionism and "ham" in each of us.

Several studies have explored the effects of self-as-a-model with different populations. Miklich, Chida, and Danker-Brown (1977) used the procedure to promote bedmaking for hospitalized children. Hosford (1980) found self-as-a-model a good instructional procedure for training counselors. Davis (1979) used the strategy to decrease problem behavior of three children in an elementary school setting. Finally, Dowrick and Dove (1980) used self-modeling to improve the swimming performance of children with spina bifida.

We have adopted five steps associated with the self-as-a-model procedure from Hosford and de Visser (1974). These five components, which are illustrated in the Interview Checklist for Self-as-a-Model at the end of the chapter, are the following:

1. Rationale about the strategy
2. Recording the desired behavior on tape
3. Editing the tape
4. Demonstrating with the edited tape
5. Homework: client self-observation and practice

Treatment Rationale

After the client and counselor have reviewed the problem behaviors and the goal behaviors for counseling, the counselor presents a treatment rationale for the self-as-a-model procedure to the client. The counselor might say something like this:

"The procedure we are going to use is based on the idea that people learn new habits or skills by observing other people in various situations. [reason] The way this is done is that people watch other people doing things or they observe a film or tape of people doing things. What we are going to do is vary this procedure a little by having you observe yourself rather than someone else. The way we can do this is to videotape [or audiotape] your desired behavior, and then you can see [hear] yourself on the tape performing the behavior. After that, you will practice the behavior that you saw [heard] on the tape, and I will give you feedback about your practice performance. I think that seeing yourself perform and practice these behaviors will help you acquire these skills. [overview] How does this sound to you?" [client's willingness]

Of course, this is only one version of the rationale for the self-as-a-model procedure a counselor might use. A counselor could add "Seeing yourself perform these behaviors will give you confidence in acquiring these skills." This statement emphasizes the cognitive component of the self-as-a-model strategy: by using oneself as the model, one sees oneself coping with a formerly anxiety-arousing or difficult situation.

Recording the Desired Behaviors

The desired goal behaviors are recorded on audio- or videotape first. For example, one particular client may need to acquire several assertion skills, such as expression of personal opinions using a firm and strong voice tone, delivery of opinions without errors in speech, and delivery of the assertive message without response latency (within five seconds after the other person's message). For this example, the counselor and client might start with voice tone and record the client expressing opinions to another person in a firm, strong voice. The counselor might have to coach the client so that at least some portion of the taped message reflects this desired response. The tape should be long enough that the client will later be able to hear himself or herself expressing opinions in a firm voice throughout several verbal exchanges with the other person. The counselor might have to spend a great deal of time staging the recording sessions in order to obtain tapes of the client's goal behavior. A dry run might be helpful before the actual tape is made.

Sometimes the counselor can instruct clients to obtain recordings of their behavior *in vivo*. For example, clients who stutter could be asked to audiotape their interactions with others during designated times of the week. We have also suggested such recordings to people who felt incompetent in talking with those of the other sex. The advantage of *in vivo* recordings is that examples of the client's actual behavior in real-life situations are obtained. However, it is not always possible or desirable to do this, particularly if the client's baseline level of performing the desired skill is very low. Whether tapes are made *in vivo* or in the session, the recording is usually repeated until a sample of the desired behavior is obtained.

Editing the Tape

Next, the counselor will edit the audio- or videotape recordings so that the client will see or hear *only* the appropriate (goal) behavior. Hosford et al. (1976) recommend that the "inappropriate" behaviors be deleted from the tape, leaving a tape of only the desired responses. The purpose in editing out the inappropriate behaviors is to provide the client with a positive, or self-enhancing, model. It is analogous to weeding out the dandelions in a garden and leaving the daffodils. In our example, we would edit out portions of the tape when the client did not express opinions in a strong voice and leave in all the times when the client did use a firm voice tone. For the stutterer, the stuttering portions of the tape would be deleted so that the edited tape included only portions of conversations in which stuttering did not occur.

Demonstrating with the Edited Tape

After the tape has been edited, the counselor plays it for the client. First, the client is told what to observe on the tape. For our examples of stuttering and assertion training, the counselor might say "Listen to the tape and notice that, in these conversations you have had, you are able to talk without stuttering," or "Note that you are maintaining eye contact when you are delivering a message to the other person."

After these instructions, the counselor and client play back the tape. If the tape is long, it can be stopped at various points to obtain the client's reaction. At these points, or after the tape playback, it is important for the counselor to give encouragement or positive feedback to the client for demonstrating the desired behavior.

After the tape playback, the client should practice behaviors that were demonstrated on the tape. The counselor can facilitate successful practice by coaching, rewarding successes, and correcting errors. This component of self-as-a-model relies heavily on practice and feedback.

Homework: Client Self-Observation and Practice

The client may benefit more from the self-as-a-model strategy when the edited tape is used in conjunction with practice outside the interview. The counselor can instruct the client to use a self-model audiotape as a homework aid by listening to it daily. (For homework purposes, the use of a videotape may not be practical.) After each daily use of the taped playback, the client should practice the target behavior covertly or overtly. The client could also be instructed to practice the behavior without the tape. Gradually, the client should be instructed to use the desired responses in actual instances outside the interview setting. In addition, the client should record the number of practice sessions and the measurement of the goal behaviors on a log sheet. And, as with any homework assignment, the counselor should arrange for a follow-up after the client completes some portion of the homework.

☐ MODEL DIALOGUE: SELF-AS-A-MODEL

To assist you in identifying the steps of a self-as-a-model strategy, the following dialogue is presented with our client Joan. In this dialogue, the strategy is used to help Joan achieve one of her counseling goals described in Chapter 9, increasing her initiating skills in her math class.

Session 1

*In response 1, the counselor provides Joan with a **rationale** for the self-as-a-model strategy. One initiating skill, that of volunteering answers to questions, will be worked with using this strategy. Note that the counselor presents a **rationale** and also confirms the **client's willingness** to try the strategy.*

1. *Counselor:* One of the things we discussed that is a problem for you now in your math class is that you rarely volunteer answers or make comments during class. As we talked about before, you feel awkward doing this and unsure about how to do it in a way that makes you feel confident. One thing we might try that will help you build up your skills for doing this is called "self-as-a-model." It's sort of a fun thing because it involves not only you but also this tape recorder. It's a way for you to actually hear how you come across when volunteering answers. It can help you do this the way you want to and also can build up your confidence about this. What do you think about trying this?
   Client: Well, I've never heard myself on tape too much before. Other than that, it sounds OK.

In response 2, the counselor **responds to Joan's concern** *about the tape recorder and initiates a period of using it so it doesn't interfere with the strategy.*

2. *Counselor:* Sometimes the tape recorder does take a little time to get used to, so we'll work with it first so you are accustomed to hearing your voice on it. We might spend some time doing that now. [Joan and the counselor spend about 15 minutes recording and playing back their conversation.]

In response 3, the counselor gives Joan an **overview** *of what is involved in the self-as-a-model strategy.*

3. *Counselor:* You seem to feel more comfortable with the recorder now. Let me tell you what this involves so you'll have an idea of what to expect. After we work out the way you want to volunteer answers, you'll practice this and we'll tape several practice sessions. Then I'll give you feedback, and we'll use the tape as feedback. We'll take the one practice that really sounds good to you, and you can take that and the recorder home so you can listen to it each day. Does that seem pretty clear?
Client: I think so. I guess the tape is a way for me to find out how I really sound.

In response 4, the counselor emphasizes the cognitive or **coping part** *of self-as-a-model.*

4. *Counselor:* That's right. The tape often indicates you can do something better than you think, which is the reason it does help.
Client: I can see that. Just hearing myself a little while ago helped. My voice doesn't sound as squeaky as I thought.

In this case, the client's verbal participation has already been defined by three behaviors. One behavior, volunteering answers, will be worked with at this point. The other two can be added later. In response 5, the counselor will **coach** *Joan on ways to perform this skill.*

5. *Counselor:* OK, Joan, let's talk about what you might do to volunteer answers in a way that you would feel good about. What comes to your mind about this?
Client: Well, I just hardly ever volunteer in the class now. I just wait until Mr. _____ calls on me. It's not that I don't know the answer, because lots of times I do. I guess I just need to raise my hand and give out the answer. See, usually he'll say, "OK, who has the answer to this problem?" So all I need to do is raise my hand and give the answer, like 25 or 40 or whatever. I don't know why I don't do it. I guess I'm afraid I will sound silly or maybe my voice will sound funny.

In the next response, the counselor uses a **clarification**

to determine Joan's particular concern about this skill.

6. *Counselor:* So are you more concerned with the way you sound than with what you have to say?
Client: I think so.

In response 7, the counselor continues to **coach** *Joan about ways to perform the desired skill, volunteering answers, and also initiates a* **trial practice.**

7. *Counselor:* Well, let's try this. Why don't I pretend to be Mr. _____ and then you raise your hand and give me an answer? Just try to speak in a firm voice that I can easily hear. Maybe even take a deep breath at first. OK? [Counselor turns on tape recorder.] (as Mr. _____) Who has the answer to this problem?
[Joan raises her hand.]
Counselor (as Mr. _____, looks around room, pauses): Joan?
Client (in a pretty audible voice): 25.

After the dry run, the counselor, in responses 8, 9, and 10, gives **feedback** *(using tape playback) about Joan's performance of the target behavior.*

8. *Counselor:* OK, let's stop. What did you think about that?
Client: Well, it wasn't really that hard. I took a deep breath.

9. *Counselor:* Your voice came across pretty clear. Maybe it could be just a little stronger. OK. Let's hear this on tape. [Playback of tape]

10. *Counselor:* How do you feel about what you just heard?
Client: Well, I sound fine. I mean my voice didn't squeak.

In response 11, the counselor initiates **tape recordings** *of Joan's demonstration of the skill (volunteering answers). This tape will be edited and used as a modeling tape.*

11. *Counselor:* No, it was pretty strong. Let's do this several times now. Just take a deep breath and speak firmly. [Practice ensues and is recorded.]

In response 12, the counselor explains the **tape-editing process;** *the tape is edited before their next session.*

12. *Counselor:* OK, I'm going to need to go over this tape before we use it for feedback. So maybe that's enough for today. We can get together next week, and I'll have this tape ready by then. Basically, I'm just going to edit it so you can hear the practice examples in which your voice sounded clear and firm. [Before the next session, the counselor erases any portions of the tape in which Joan's answers were inaudible or high-pitched, leaving only audible, firm, level-pitched answers.]

Session 2

After a brief warm-up period in this session, the counselor **instructs** *Joan about what to listen for in the* **demonstration with the edited tape playback.**

1. *Counselor:* Well, Joan, I've got your tape ready. I'd like to play back the tape. When I do, I'd like you to note how clearly and firmly you are able to give the answers. [Tape is played.]

2. *Counselor:* What did you think?
   Client: You're right. I guess I don't sound silly, at least not on that tape.

In response 3, the counselor gives **positive feedback** *to Joan about demonstrating the skill.*

3. *Counselor:* You really sounded like you felt very confident about the answers. It was very easy to hear you.
   Client: But will I be able to sound like that in class?

In response 4, the counselor instructs Joan on how to use the tape as **daily** *homework in conjunction with practice. Note that the homework assignment specifies* **what** *and* **how much** *Joan will do.*

4. *Counselor:* Yes, and we'll be working on that as our next step. In the meantime, I'd like you to work with this tape during the week. Could you set aside a certain time each day when you could listen to the tape, just like we did today? Then after you listen to the tape, practice again. Imagine Mr. _____ is asking for the answer. Just raise your hand, take a deep breath, and speak firmly. Do you understand how to use this now?

Client: Yes, just listen to it once a day and then do another round of practice.

In response 5, the counselor asks Joan to **record her use of homework on log sheets.**

5. *Counselor:* As you do this, I'd like you to use these log sheets and mark down each time you do this homework. Also, rate on this 5-point scale how comfortable you feel in doing this before and each time you practice.
   Client: That doesn't sound too difficult, I guess.

In response 6, the counselor encourages Joan to **reinforce herself** *for progress and* **arranges for follow-up** *on homework at their next session.*

6. *Counselor:* Well, this recording on your log sheet will help you see your progress. You've made a lot of progress, so give yourself a pat on the back after you hear the tape this week. Next week we can talk about how this worked out and then we'll see whether we can do the same type of thing in your classes.

The next step would be to obtain some tape-recorded samples of Joan's volunteering in a class situation. A nonthreatening class in which Joan presently does volunteer might be used first, followed by her trying this out in math class. The biggest problem in this step is to arrange for tape-recorded samples in a way that is not embarrassing to Joan in the presence of her classmates.

LEARNING ACTIVITY #35: SELF-AS-A-MODEL

You may recall from the case of Ms. Weare and Freddie that Ms. Weare wanted to eliminate the assistance she gave Freddie in getting ready for school in the morning. One of Ms. Weare's concerns is to find a way to instruct Freddie about the new ground rules —mainly that she will not help him get dressed and will not remind him when the bus is five minutes away. Ms. Weare is afraid that after she delivers her instructions, Freddie will either pout or talk back to her. She is concerned that she will not be able to follow through with her plan or else will not be firm in the way she delivers the ground rules to him.

Describe how you could use the five components of the self-as-a-model strategy to help Ms. Weare accomplish these four things:

1. Deliver clear instructions to Freddie.
2. Talk in a firm voice.
3. Maintain eye contact while talking.
4. Avoid talking down, giving in, or changing her original instructions.

Feedback follows.

☐ PARTICIPANT MODELING

Participant modeling consists of modeled demonstration, guided practice, and successful experiences (Bandura, 1976a). Participant modeling assumes that a person's successful performance is an effective means of producing change. Bandura, Jeffery, and Gajdos (1975) indicate that participant modeling is an effective way to provide "rapid reality testing, which provides the correc-

FEEDBACK #35: SELF-AS-A-MODEL

1. *Rationale for strategy*

   First, you would explain to Ms. Weare how the self-as-a-model procedure could help her (rationale) and what is involved in the procedure (overview). Then, ask Ms. Weare how she feels about trying this procedure (client's willingness).

2. *Recording the desired behavior*

   According to the case description, there are four things Ms. Weare wants to learn to do in delivering her instructions to Freddie. It would be useful to work on one thing at a time, starting with the one subskill that may be easiest for her, such as maintaining eye contact when she talks to Freddie. After each subskill is worked with separately, she can work on doing all four skills in combination.

   The counselor will probably need to coach Ms. Weare on a successful way to perform the skill before recording her demonstration of it, and a dry run may be necessary.

   When the counselor believes Ms. Weare can demonstrate the skill at least sometimes, a video or audio recording will be made. (For eye contact, a videotape would be necessary.) Since Ms. Weare presently is not engaging in these behaviors with Freddie, an in-session tape would be more useful than an *in vivo* tape at this point. The counselor can role play the part of Freddie during the taping. The taping should continue until an adequate sample of each of the four skills is obtained.

3. *Editing the tape*

   After the tape has been recorded, the counselor will edit it. Only inappropriate examples of the skill would be deleted. For example, instances when Ms. Weare looks away would be erased from the tape. The edited tape would consist only of times when she maintains eye contact. A final tape in which she uses all four skills would consist only of times when she was using the desired skills.

4. *Demonstrating with the edited tape*

   After the edited tape is ready, it would be used for demonstration and practice with Ms. Weare. The counselor would instruct Ms. Weare about what to look for and then play back the tape. The counselor would give positive feedback to Ms. Weare for instances of demonstrating eye contact and the other three skills. After the playback, Ms. Weare would practice the skill and receive feedback from the counselor about the practice performance.

5. *Homework: Client self-observation and practice*

   After Ms. Weare was able to practice the skills with the counselor, she would use the self-modeling tape as homework. Specifically, the counselor would instruct her to listen to or view the tape on her own if possible. She could also practice the skills—first covertly and later overtly—with Freddie. This practice could occur with or without the tape. A follow-up should be arranged to check on her progress.

tive experiences for change" (p. 141). By successfully performing a formerly difficult or fearful response, a person can achieve potentially enduring changes in behavior. For example, Etringer, Cash, and Rimm (1982) found that participant modeling quickly achieved very high levels of change on behavioral, attitudinal, and perceived self-efficacy measures in dealing with a feared stimulus; Ladouceur (1983) found that participant modeling and self-verbalizations (thinking aloud) reduced cat and dog phobias for adults. Participant modeling has been used to reduce avoidance behavior and the person's associated feelings about fearful activities or situations (Bandura, Blanchard, & Ritter, 1969; Bandura, Jeffery, & Gajdos, 1975; Bandura, Jeffery, & Wright, 1974; Smith & Coleman, 1977). For example, imagine an outside house painter who develops acrophobia. Participant modeling could be used to help the painter gradually climb "scary" heights by dealing directly with the anxiety associated with being in high places. In participant modeling with phobic clients, successful performance in fearful activities or situations helps the person learn to cope with the feared situation. For example, Osborn (1986) used participant modeling with a child who had warm water phobia, and participant modeling was used successfully in sexual abuse programs (Wurtele, Marro, & Miller-Perrin, 1987). There is probably nothing more persuasive than successful performance in feared situations (Bandura, 1969).

Another application of participant modeling is with people who have behavioral deficits or who lack such skills as social communication, assertiveness, child management, or physical fitness. Some of these skills might be taught as preventive measures in schools or community agencies. For example, parents can be taught child-management skills by modeling and practicing effective ways of dealing with and communicating with their children.

There are four major components of participant modeling: rationale, modeling, guided participation, and successful experiences (homework). These components are essentially the same whether participant modeling is used to reduce fearful avoidance behavior or to increase some behavior or skill. As you can see from the Interview Checklist for Participant Modeling at the end of the chapter, each component includes several parts. We present a description for each component, followed by a hypothetical counselor/client dialogue illustrating the implementation and use of the participant modeling strategy. We are indebted to the work of Bandura (1969, 1976a) in our description of this strategy.

Treatment Rationale

Here is an example of a rationale the counselor might give for participant modeling:

"This procedure has been used to help other people overcome fears or acquire new behaviors. [rationale] There are three primary things we will do. First, you will see some people demonstrating _____. Next, you will practice this with my assistance in the interview. Then we'll arrange for you to do this outside the interview in situations likely to be successful for you. This type of practice will help you perform what is now difficult for you to do [overview] Are you willing to try this now?" [client's willingness]

Modeling

The modeling component of participant modeling consists of five parts:

1. The goal behaviors, if complex, are divided into a series of subtasks or subskills.
2. The series of subskills is arranged in a hierarchy.
3. Models are selected.
4. Instructions are given to the client before the modeled demonstration.
5. The model demonstrates each successive subtask with as many repetitions as necessary.

Dividing the goal behaviors. Before the counselor (or someone else) models the behavior to be acquired by the client, it should be determined whether the behavior should be divided. Complex patterns of behavior should be divided into subskills or tasks and arranged by small steps or by a graduated series of tasks in a hierarchy. Dividing patterns of behavior and arranging them in order of difficulty may ensure that the client can perform initial behaviors or tasks. This is a very important step in the participant modeling strategy, because you want the client to experience success in performing what is modeled. Start with a response or a behavior the client can perform.

One example of dividing behaviors involved in competence training into subskills is assertion behaviors. A counselor and client might decide to divide assertive behavior into three categories: (1) eye contact with the person who is receiving the assertive message, (2) delivery of the assertive message without errors in speech, and (3) delivery of the assertive message without latency (time between the end of the other person's message and the beginning of the client's assertive response).

For our acrophobic house painter, the target behavior might be engaging in house painting at a height of 30 feet off the ground. This response could be divided into subtasks of painting at varying heights. Each task might be elevated by several feet at a time.

Arranging the subskills or tasks in a hierarchy. The counselor and client then arrange the subskills or subtasks in a hierarchy. The first situation in the hierarchy is the least difficult or threatening; other skills or situations of greater complexity or threat follow. Usually, the first behavior or response in the hierarchy is worked with first. After each of the subtasks has been successfully practiced one at a time, the client can practice all the subskills or tasks. With a nonassertive client, the counselor and client may decide it would be most helpful to work on eye contact first, then speech errors, then response latency, and finally all these behaviors at once.

In phobic cases, the content and arrangement of each session can be a hierarchical list of feared activities or objects. According to Bandura (1976a), you would first work with the situation that poses the least threat or provokes the least fear for the client. For our acrophobic house painter, we would begin with a situation involving little height and gradually progress to painting at greater heights.

Selecting a model. Before implementing the modeling component, an appropriate model should be selected. At times, it may be most efficient to use the therapist as the model. However, as you may recall from Chapter 13, therapeutic gains may be greater when multiple models are used who are somewhat similar to the client. For example, phobia clinics have successfully employed participant modeling to extinguish phobias by using several formerly phobic clients as the multiple models.

Prior instructions to the client. Immediately before the modeled demonstration, to draw the client's attention to the model, the counselor should instruct the client about what will be modeled. The client should be told to note that the model will be engaging in certain responses without experiencing any adverse consequences. With our nonassertive client, the counselor might say something like "Notice the way this person looks at you directly when refusing to type your paper." With the house painter, the counselor might say "Look to see how the model moves about the scaffolding easily at a height of five feet."

Modeled demonstrations. In participant modeling, a live model demonstrates one subskill at a time. Often, repeated demonstrations of the same response are necessary. As Bandura (1976a) indicates, multiple modeling demonstrations show the client how something can be performed best and also that any feared consequences do not occur (p. 250). Multiple demonstrations can be arranged by having a single model repeat the demonstration or by having several models demonstrate the same activity or response. For example, one model could show moving about on the scaffolding without falling several times, or several models could demonstrate this same activity. When it is feasible to use several models, you should do so. Multiple models lend variety to the way the activity is performed and believability to the idea that adverse consequences will not occur.

Guided Participation

After the demonstration of the behavior or activity, the client is given opportunities and necessary guidance to perform the modeled behaviors. Guided participation or performance is one of the most important components of learning to cope, to reduce avoidance of fearful situations, and to acquire new behaviors. People must experience success in using what has been modeled. The client's participation in the counseling session should be structured in a nonthreatening manner

aimed at "fostering new competencies and confidence, rather than at exposing deficiencies" (Bandura, 1976a, p. 262).

Guided participation consists of the following five steps:

1. Client practice of the response or activity with counselor assistance.
2. Counselor feedback.
3. Use of various induction aids for initial practice attempts.
4. Fading of induction aids.
5. Client self-directed practice.

Each of these steps will be described and illustrated.

Client practice. After the model has demonstrated the activity or behavior, the client is asked to do what has been modeled. The counselor has the client perform each activity or behavior in the hierarchy. The client performs each activity or behavior, starting with the first one in the hierarchy, until he or she can do this skillfully and confidently. It is quite possible that, for an occasional client, there does not need to be a breakdown of the behaviors or activities. For these clients, guided practice of the entire ultimate goal behavior may be sufficient without a series of graduated tasks.

Our nonassertive client would first practice delivering an assertive message using direct eye contact. When the client was able to do this easily, she or he would practice delivering a message using eye contact while concentrating on making as few speech errors as possible. When the client was able to do this successfully, the next practices would focus on decreasing response latency. Finally, the client would practice delivering assertive messages and simultaneously using direct eye contact, limiting speech errors, and shortening the amount of time between others' responses and his or her replies.

Our house painter would practice moving about on a ladder or scaffolding at a low height. Practices would continue at this height until the painter could move about easily and comfortably; then practices at the next height would ensue.

Counselor feedback. After each client practice attempt, the counselor provides verbal feedback to the client about his or her performance. There are two parts to the feedback: (1) praise or encouragement for successful practice and (2) suggestions for correcting or modifying errors. For example, after the nonassertive client delivered a message while attempting to use direct eye contact, the counselor might say "That time you were able to look at me while you were talking. You looked away after you finished talking, which did reduce the impact of your message. Your eye contact is definitely improving; let's try it again." Or, with the painter, the counselor might say "You seem comfortable at this height. You were able to go up and down the ladder very easily. Even looking down didn't seem to bother you. That's really terrific."

Use of induction aids. As you may recall from Chapter 12, induction aids are supportive aids arranged by the counselor to assist a client in performing a feared or difficult response. Many people consider successful performance a good way to reduce anxiety. However, most people are just not going to participate in something they dread simply because they are told to do so. For instance, can you think of something you really fear, such as holding a snake, riding in an airplane or a boat, climbing a high mountain, or getting in a car after a severe accident? If so, you probably realize you would be very reluctant to engage in this activity just because at this moment you read the words *do it.* However, suppose we were to be there and hold the snake first, and hold the snake while you touch it, and then hold its head and tail while you hold the middle, then hold its head while you hold the tail, and so on. You might be more willing to do this or something else you fear under conditions that incorporate some supportive aids. (However, as Bourque and Ladouceur [1980, p. 167] indicate, induction aids such as physical contact or therapist proximity may have a greater impact for people with animal phobias than for clients with territorial phobias.)

With our nonassertive client, the counselor might assist the client in initial practice attempts with verbal cues about the desired performance. Repeated practice of one type of assertive behavior could also be used. Graduated time intervals might be another feasible aid: the counselor could arrange for the client to practice short intervals of direct eye contact, followed by longer durations.

To help our acrophobic painter reduce fear of heights, an initial induction aid might be joint practice. If actual practice with a ladder or scaffold is possible, nothing may be more supportive than having the counselor up on the scaffold with the painter or standing directly behind or in front of the painter on a ladder. This also functions as a type of protective aid. Of course, this assumes that the counselor is not afraid of heights. In our own experience, the one of us who is the nonacrophobic induces the other (no names mentioned) to climb lighthouses, landmarks, hills, and other such "scenic views" by going first and extending a hand. This type of induction aid enables both of us to enjoy the experience together. As a result, the fears of one person have never interfered with the pleasures of the other, because continued practice efforts with some support have reduced the fear level substantially.

Induction aids can be used in the counseling session, but they should also be applied in settings that closely approximate the natural setting. If at all possible, the counselor or a model should accompany the client into the "field," where the client can witness further demonstrations and can participate in the desired settings. For example, teaching assertive behavior to a client in the interview must be supplemented with modeling and guided participation in the natural setting in which the final goal behavior is to occur. It is doubtful that a counselor would be equipped with scaffolds so that our acrophobic house painter could practice the modeled activities at different heights. The counselor could use covert rehearsal instead of overt practice. Our point is that the counselor who uses live participant modeling procedures must be prepared to provide aids and supports that help the client practice as closely as possible the desired goal behavior. If this is not possible, the next best alternative is to simulate those activities as closely as possible in the client's real situation.

Fading of induction aids. Induction aids can be withdrawn gradually. With our nonassertive client, the use of four induction aids initially might be gradually reduced to three, two, and one. Or, with the painter, a very supportive aid, such as joint practice, could be replaced by a less supportive aid, such as verbal coaching. The gradual withdrawal of induction aids bridges the gap between counselor-assisted and client-directed practice.

Client self-directed practice. At some point, the client should be able to perform the desired activities or responses without any induction aids or assistance. A period of client self-directed practice may reinforce changes in the client's beliefs and self-evaluation and may lead to improved behavioral functioning. Therefore, the counselor should arrange for the client to engage in successful performance of the desired responses independently unassisted. Ideally, client self-directed practice would occur both within the interview and in the client's natural setting. Our nonassertive client would practice the three desired assertion responses unassisted. The house painter would practice moving on the ladder or scaffold alone. Client self-directed practice is likely to be superior to therapist-directed practice (Smith & Coleman, 1977).

In addition to application of the participant modeling procedures in the counseling sessions, facilitating the transfer of behavior from the training session to the natural environment should be an integral part of counseling. Generalization of desired changes can be achieved by success or by reinforcing experiences that occur as part of a transfer-of-training program.

Success, or Reinforcing, Experiences

The last component of the participant modeling procedure is success (reinforcing) experiences. Clients must experience success in using what they are learning. Further, as Bandura points out, psychological changes "are unlikely to endure unless they prove effective when put into practice in everyday life" (1976a, p. 248). Success experiences are arranged by tailoring a transfer-of-training program for each client. In an adequate transfer-of-training program, the client's new skills are used first in low-risk situations in the client's natural environment or in any situation in which the client will probably experience success or favorable outcomes. Gradually, the client extends the application of the skills to natural situations that are more unpredictable and involve a greater threat.

Bandura (1976a) describes a possible transfer-of-training program for nonassertive clients:

After the clients have perfected their social skills and overcome their timidity, they accompany the therapist on excursions into the field where they witness further demonstrations of how to handle situations calling for assertive action. The therapist then reduces the level of participation to background support and guidance as the clients try their skills in situations likely to produce favorable results. By means of careful selection of encounters of increasing difficulty, the assertion requirements can be adjusted to the clients' momentary capabilities to bolster their sense of confidence. As a final step in the program, the clients are assigned a series of assertive performance tasks to carry out on their own [pp. 262–263].

To summarize, success experiences are ar-

ranged through a program that transfers skill acquisition from the interview to the natural setting. This transfer-of-training program involves the following steps:

1. The counselor and client identify situations in the client's environment in which the client desires to perform the target responses.
2. These situations are arranged in a hierarchy, starting with easy, safe situations in which the client is likely to be successful and ending with more unpredictable and risky situations.
3. The counselor accompanies the client into the environment and works with each situation on the list by modeling and guided participation. Gradually the counselor's level of participation is decreased.
4. The client is given a series of tasks to perform in a self-directed manner.

Bandura (1976a) concludes that participant modeling achieves results, given adequate demonstration, guided practice, and positive experiences. One advantage of participant modeling is that "a broad range of resource persons," such as peers or former clients, can serve as therapeutic models (p. 249). Bandura also points out that participant modeling helps clients to learn new responses under "lifelike conditions." As a result, the problems of transfer of learning from the interview to the client's real-life environment are minimized.

□ MODEL DIALOGUE: PARTICIPANT MODELING

Here is an example of the use of participant modeling with our client Joan. The participant modeling will be used to help Joan perform the four behaviors in math class that she typically avoids. The rationale for the counselor responses is set off by the italicized comments that precede the responses.

Session 1

In the first response, the counselor will provide a **rationale** *about the strategy and a brief* **overview** *of the procedure.*

1. *Counselor:* This procedure has been of help to other people who have trouble in classroom participation. We'll take each of the ways you would like to participate, and either I myself or maybe one of your classmates will show you a way to do this, then help you practice it. At first we'll just practice

here. Then gradually you'll try this out in your other classes and, of course, finally in your math class. What do you think about this?

Client: It's OK with me. It's just something I know I can do but I don't because I'm a little nervous.

*The counselor will pick up on Joan's previous response and use it to provide an **additional rationale** for the participant modeling strategy.*

2. *Counselor:* And nervousness can keep you from doing something you want. This procedure helps you to learn to do something in small steps. As you accomplish each step, your confidence in yourself will increase and your nervousness will decrease.

Client: I think that will definitely help. Sometimes I just don't believe in myself.

*In response 3, the counselor ignores Joan's previous self-effacing comment. The counselor instead begins with the **modeling component** by reviewing the ways Joan wanted to increase selected initiating skills in math class.*

3. *Counselor:* You know, last week I believe we found some ways that you would like to increase your participation in math class. And I think we arranged these in an order, starting with the one that you thought was easiest for you now, to the one that was hardest for you. Can you recall these things and this order?

Client: Yes, I believe it was like this: answering questions, going to the board, volunteering answers, and then volunteering opinions or ideas.

*The counselor asks the client **whether additional activities** need to be added or **whether the hierarchy order** needs to be rearranged.*

4. *Counselor:* OK, after thinking about it for a week, have you thought of any other ways you'd like to participate — or do you think this order needs to be rearranged at all?

Client: Well, one more thing — I would like to be able to work the problems on my own after I ask Mr. _____ for help. That's where I want to begin. He usually takes over and works the problems for me.

*In response 5, the counselor will explore **a potential model** for Joan and obtain Joan's input about this decision.*

5. *Counselor:* OK, one thing we need to do now is to consider who might model and help you with these activities. I can do it, although if you can think of a classmate in math who participates the way you want to, this person could assist you when you try this out in your class. What do you think?

Client: Is it necessary to have someone in the class

with me? If so, I think it would be less obvious if it were someone already in the class.

*The counselor picks up on Joan's discomfort about the counselor's presence in her class and **suggests another classmate as the model.***

6. *Counselor:* Well, there are ways to get around it, but it would be more helpful if someone could be there in your class, at least initially. I think you would feel more comfortable if this person were another classmate rather than me. If there is someone you could pick who already does a good job of participating, I'd like to talk to this person and have him or her help during our next sessions. So try to think of someone you like and respect and feel comfortable around.

Client: Well, there's Debbie. She's a friend of mine, and she hardly ever gets bothered by answering Mr. _____'s questions or going to the board. I could ask her. She'd probably like to do something like this. She works independently, too, on her math problems.

*The counselor provides **a rationale** for how Joan's friend will be used as the model so that Joan understands how her friend will be involved. Note that Joan's reaction to this is solicited. If Joan were uncomfortable with this, another option would be explored.*

7. *Counselor:* OK, if you could ask her and she agrees, ask her to drop by my office. If that doesn't work out, stop back and we'll think of something else. If Debbie wants to do this, I'll train her to help demonstrate the ways you'd like to participate. At our session next week, she can start modeling these things for you. How does that sound?

Client: OK. It might be kind of fun. I've helped her with her English themes before, so now maybe she can help with this.

*The counselor encourages the idea of these two friends' providing **mutual help** in the next response.*

8. *Counselor:* That's a good idea. Good friends help each other. Let me know what happens after you talk to Debbie.

After session 1, Joan stopped in to verify that Debbie would be glad to work with them. The counselor then arranged a meeting with Debbie to explain her role in the participant modeling strategy. Specifically, Debbie practiced modeling the other four participation goals Joan had identified. The counselor gave Debbie instructions and feedback so that each behavior was modeled clearly and in a coping manner. The counselor also trained Debbie in ways to assist Joan during the guided-participation phase. Debbie practiced this, with the counselor taking the role of Joan. In these practice attempts, Debbie also practiced using various induction aids that she might use with Joan, such as joint practice, verbal coaching, and graduated time intervals and difficulty of task. Debbie also practiced having the counselor (as Joan) engage in self-directed practice. Classroom simulations of success experiences were also rehearsed so Debbie could learn her role in arranging for actual success experiences with Joan. When Debbie felt comfortable with her part in the strategy, the next session with Joan was scheduled.

Session 2

In response 1, the counselor gives **instructions to Joan about what to look for** *during the modeled demonstration. Note that the counselor also points out the* **lack of adverse consequences** *in the modeling situation.*

1. *Counselor:* It's good to see you today, Joan. I have been working with Debbie, and she is here today to do some modeling for you. What we'll do first is to work with one thing you mentioned last week, telling Mr. _____ you want to work the problems yourself after you ask him for an explanation. Debbie will demonstrate this first. So I'll play the part of Mr. _____ and Debbie will come up to me and ask me for help. Note that she tells me what she needs explained, then firmly tells Mr. _____ she wants to try to finish it herself. Notice that this works out well for Debbie — Mr. _____ doesn't jump at her or anything like that. Do you have any questions?
   Client: No, I'm ready to begin. [Modeling ensues.]
   Debbie (as model): Mr. _____, I would like some explanation about this problem. I need you to explain it again so I can work it out all right.
   Counselor (as Mr. _____): OK, well, here is the answer . . .
   Debbie (as model, interrupts): Well, I'd like to find the answer myself, but I'd like you to explain this formula again.
   Counselor (as Mr. _____): OK, well, here's how you do this formula . . .
   Debbie (as model): That really helps. Thanks a lot I can take it from here. [Goes back to seat.]

After the modeling, the counselor **asks Joan to react** *to what she saw.*

2. *Counselor:* What reactions did you have to that, Joan?
   Client: Well, it looked fairly easy. I guess when I do ask him for help, I have a tendency just to let him take over. I am not really firm about telling him to let me finish the problem myself.

The counselor picks up on Joan's concern and **initiates a second modeled demonstration.**

3. *Counselor:* That's an important part of it — first being able to ask for an additional explanation and then being able to let him know you want to apply the information and go back to your seat and try that out. It might be a good idea to have Debbie do this again — see how she initiates finishing the problem so Mr. _____ doesn't take over.
   Client: OK.
   [Second modeled demonstration ensues.]

In response 4, the counselor asks Joan for her opinion about **engaging in a practice.**

4. *Counselor:* How ready do you feel now to try this out yourself in a practice here?
   Client: I believe I could.

Before the first practice attempt, the counselor will introduce **one induction aid, verbal coaching,** *from Debbie.*

5. *Counselor:* OK. Now I believe one thing that might help you is to have Debbie sort of coach you. For instance, if you get stuck or start to back down, Debbie can step in and give you a cue or a reminder about something you can do. How does that sound?
   Client: Fine. That makes it a little easier.

The first practice attempt begins.

6. *Counselor:* OK, let's begin. Now I'll be Mr. _____ and you get up out of your seat with the problem.
   Client: Mr. _____, I don't quite understand this problem.
   Counselor (as Mr. _____): Well, let me just give you the answer; you'll have one less problem to do then.
   Client: Well, uh, I'm not sure the answer is what I need.
   Counselor (as Mr. _____): Well, what do you mean?
   Debbie (intervenes to prompt): Joan, you might want to indicate you would prefer to work out the answer yourself, but you do need another explanation of the formula.
   Client: Well, I'd like to find the answer myself. I do need another explanation of the formula.
   Counselor (as Mr. _____): OK. Well, it goes like this . . .
   Client: OK, thanks.
   Debbie: Now be sure you end the conversation there and go back to your seat.

The counselor will **assess Joan's reactions** *to the practice.*

7. *Counselor:* OK, what did you think about that, Joan?

Client: It went pretty well. It *was* a help to have Debbie here. That is a good idea.

In the next response, the counselor **provides positive feedback** *to Debbie and to Joan.* **Another practice is initiated;** *this also serves as an* **induction aid.**

8. *Counselor:* I think she helps, too. You seemed to be able to start the conversation very well. You did need a little help in explaining to him what you wanted and didn't want. Once Debbie cued you, you were able to use her cue very effectively. Perhaps it would be a good idea to try this again. Debbie will only prompt this time if she really needs to.

[Second practice ensues; Debbie's amount of prompting is decreased.]

The counselor explores the idea of **a self-directed practice.**

9. *Counselor:* That seemed to go very smoothly. I think you are ready to do this again without any assistance. How does that sound?

Client: I think so, too.

After obtaining an affirmative response from Joan, the counselor asks Debbie to leave the room. Just Debbie's physical presence could be a protective condition for Joan, which is another induction aid, so Debbie leaves to make sure the **self-directed practice occurs.**

10. *Counselor:* I'm going to ask Debbie to leave the room so you'll be completely on your own this time.

[Self-directed practice ensues.]

Next the counselor cues Joan to provide herself with **feedback** *about her self-directed practice.*

11. *Counselor:* How did you feel about that practice, Joan?

Client: Well, I realized I was relying a little on Debbie. So I think it was good to do it by myself.

The counselor notes the link between self-directed performance and confidence and starts to work on **success experiences** *outside counseling.*

12. *Counselor:* Right. At first it does help to have someone there. Then it builds your confidence to do it by yourself. At this point, I think we're ready to discuss ways you might actually use this in your class. How does that sound?

Client: Fine. A little scary, but fine.

The counselor introduces the idea of **Debbie's assistance as an initial aid in Joan's practice outside the session.**

13. *Counselor:* It's natural to feel a little apprehensive at first, but one thing we will do to help you get started on the right foot is to use Debbie again at first.

Client: Oh, good. How will that work?

In response 14, the counselor **identifies a hierarchy of situations** *in Joan's math class. Joan's first attempts will be assisted by Debbie to ensure success at each step.*

14. *Counselor:* Well, apparently math is the only class where you have difficulty doing this, so we want to work on your using this in math class successfully. Since Debbie is in the class with you, instead of going up to Mr. _____ initially by yourself, first you can go with her. In fact, she could initiate the request for help the first time. The next time you could both go up and you could initiate it. She could prompt you or fill in. Gradually, you would get to the point where you would go up by yourself. But we will take one step at a time.

Client: That really does help. I know the first time it would turn out better if she was there, too.

15. *Counselor:* Right. Usually in doing anything new, it helps to start slowly and feel good each step of the way. So maybe Debbie can come in now and we can plan the first step.

Debbie will model and guide Joan in using these responses in their math class. Next, the entire procedure will be repeated to work with the other initiating skills Joan wants to work on.

LEARNING ACTIVITY #36: PARTICIPANT MODELING

This activity is designed to be completed for a behavior of yours that you wish to change. You will need a partner to complete this activity.

1. Select a skill that you wish to acquire, such as a social or assertive skill or a particular counseling skill.

2. Define the skill by describing what you would be doing, thinking, and/or feeling differently. Decide whether the skill is so broad that it needs to be divided into a series of subskills. If so, identify

(continued)

LEARNING ACTIVITY #36: PARTICIPANT MODELING (continued)

these and arrange them on a hierarchy in order of difficulty.

3. Ask your partner to model or demonstrate the skill for you. (You can also arrange to observe other people you know and respect who might be likely to use similar skills in naturally occurring circumstances.)

4. With the help of your partner, prepare for your own initial practice of the skill or of the first subskill on the hierarchy. Your partner should facilitate your initial practice attempts with at least one or two induction aids, such as joint practice or verbal coaching. With successive practice attempts,

these induction aids will gradually be removed. Your partner also needs to provide feedback after each practice.

5. With your partner, identify actual situations in which you want to apply your newly acquired skill. Rehearse such attempts and identify any induction aids that may be necessary in your initial efforts at skill application in these situations.

6. Call or see your partner to report on how you handled rehearsal efforts in step 5. Identify whether you need additional modeling, practice, or induction aids.

□ SUMMARY

The three modeling strategies presented in this chapter can be used to help clients acquire new responses or extinguish fears. These modeling strategies promote learning by providing a model to demonstrate the goal behaviors for the client. The way the model is presented differs slightly among the modeling procedures. Symbolic modeling and self-modeling use media for modeled presentations; participant modeling usually employs a live modeling demonstration. Modeling can also be carried out by means of the client's imagination. Two therapeutic strategies based on imagery, emotive imagery and covert modeling, are described in the next chapter.

POSTEVALUATION

PART ONE

Objective One asks you to develop a script for a symbolic model. Your script should contain—

1. Examples of the modeled dialogue
2. Opportunities for practice
3. Feedback
4. Summarization

Use the Checklist for Symbolic Models (p. 343) as a guide.

PART TWO

Objective Two asks you to describe how you would use the five components of the self-as-a-model procedure with a client case. Recall from the case of Mr. Brown (Chapter 7) that one of his concerns was not being able to initiate social contacts with his boss. Describe how you would use the five components of the self-as-a-model procedure to help Mr. Brown initiate social contacts with his boss (Objective Two). The five components are: (1) rationale, (2) recording the desired behavior, (3) editing the tape, (4) demonstrating with the edited tape, and (5) homework: client self-observation and practice.

PART THREE

Objective Three asks you to demonstrate at least 13 out of 16 steps associated with the self-as-a-model strategy with a role-play interview. Assess yourself or have someone else assess you, using the Interview Checklist for Self-as-a-Model on pages 343–344.

PART FOUR

Objective Four asks you to describe how you would apply the four components of participant modeling with a hypothetical client case. Using the case of Mr. Brown, describe how you would use the four components of participant modeling (rationale, modeling, guided practice, and success experiences) to help Mr. Brown acquire verbal and nonverbal skills necessary to initiate social contacts with his boss.

PART FIVE

Objective Five asks you to demonstrate 14 out of 17 steps of participant modeling with a role-play client. The client might take the role of someone who is
(continued)

afraid to perform certain responses or activities in certain situations. You can assess yourself, using the Interview Checklist for Participant Modeling on pages 345–346. Feedback for the postevaluation follows on page 347.

CHECKLIST FOR DEVELOPING SYMBOLIC MODELS

Instructions: Determine whether the following guidelines have been incorporated into the construction of your symbolic model.

Check if completed:

_____1. Determine what consumers will use the symbolic modeling procedure and identify their characteristics.
  _____Age
  _____Sex

  _____Ethnic origin, cultural practices, and/or race
  _____Coping or mastery model portrayed
  _____Possesses similar concern or problem to that of client group or population
_____2. Goal behaviors to be modeled by client have been enumerated.
_____3. Medium is selected (for example, written script, audiotape, videotape, film, slide tape).
_____4. Script includes the following ingredients:
  _____Instructions
  _____Modeled dialogue
  _____Practice
  _____Written feedback
  _____Written summarization of what has been modeled, with its importance for client
_____5. Written script has been field-tested.

INTERVIEW CHECKLIST FOR SELF-AS-A-MODEL

Instructions: Indicate with a check which of the following leads were used by the counselor in the interview. Some examples of possible leads are provided in the right column; however, these are only suggestions.

Item	Examples of counselor leads
I. Rationale about Strategy	
_____ 1. Counselor provides rationale about strategy.	"This procedure can help you improve your communication with each other, using yourselves. We'll use your own examples of good interactions to help you learn these skills."
_____ 2. Counselor provides overview of strategy.	"We'll have you practice communicating with each other and we'll tape-record your interactions. Then I'll edit the tape. You'll have a tape that consists of only positive examples of communication. You'll use the tape for homework and practice."
_____ 3. Counselor checks client's willingness to try strategy.	"How willing would you be to try this process to help you learn these communication skills?"
II. Recording the Desired Behavior	
_____ 4. Counselor and client break down desired behaviors into subskills.	"There are several things we can work on to improve your communication with each other. One thing we might start with is to help you learn to express your feelings to each other about the other person and his or her behavior."
_____ 5. For each subskill, counselor coaches client about ways to perform skill successfully.	"The basic idea here is to use an 'I' message, coupled with a word that describes how you feel, such as 'I feel angry' or 'I feel happy,' instead of 'You made me angry.'"
_____ 6. Client performs a dry run of skill, using counselor or tape for feedback.	"Let's try this out in a short role play. Just try to express a feeling you have right now to your spouse, using an 'I' message."

(continued)

POSTEVALUATION (continued)

_____ 7. Client demonstrates skill while being recorded on video- or audiotape.

_____ a. Recording took place in the interview.

"This time while you're practicing this with each other, I'm going to tape it."

_____ b. Recording took place in *in vivo* situations outside the session.

"In addition to the tape we made today, I'd like you to tape some of your interactions you have at home with each other."

_____ c. Recording is repeated until sample of desired behavior is obtained.

"Remember, start with 'I feel.' Let's try this again."

III. Editing the Tape

_____ 8. Counselor edits tape so that a clear picture of client's desired behavior is evident and instances of undesired behavior are deleted.

"I'm going to take the tape we made in our session and the one you made at home and edit them before our next session. Basically, I'm going to edit the tape so only your best interactions are left. This gives you a chance to hear yourselves communicating with each other the way you'd like to."

IV. Demonstrating with the Edited Tape

_____ 9. Counselor instructs client about what to look or listen for during tape playback.

"While we play this tape, listen to all the times you were able to say 'I feel _____' to each other."

_____ 10. Counselor initiates playback of edited tape for client observation.

"OK, we'll spend some time now listening to these tapes."

_____ 11. Counselor provides positive feedback to client for demonstration of desired behavior on tape.

"The tapes show clearly that you are both able to express your feelings to each other in this constructive way."

_____ 12. Counselor initiates client practice of taped behaviors; successes are rewarded and errors corrected.

"Now that you've heard yourselves do this on the tape, let's work on it here."

V. Homework: Client Self-Observation and Practice

_____ 13. Using model tape, counselor assigns homework:

_____ a. By asking client to observe or listen to model tape and to practice goal responses overtly or covertly.

_____ b. Daily for a designated period of time.

"I'd like you to take these tapes home and set aside a period of time each day when you can go over and listen to them. After you listen to the tapes, I'd like you to practice this with each other."

_____ 14. Counselor provides some sort of self-directed prompts, such as cue cards.

"To help you remember this, I'll give you this card. The card tells you to start each expression of feeling with 'I feel,' then to stop and listen for the other person's response."

_____ 15. Counselor asks client to record number of practice sessions and to rate performance of goal behaviors on a homework log sheet.

"I'd like you to use these log sheets and mark down each time you practice these skills — with or without the tape. Also, try to rate how well you think you demonstrated these skills at each practice on a 1-to-5 scale, 1 being very poor and 5 being excellent."

_____ 16. Counselor initiates a face-to-face or telephone follow-up to assess client's use of homework and to provide encouragement.

"Why don't you give me a call in three or four days and check in?"

Observer Comments: _____

INTERVIEW CHECKLIST FOR PARTICIPANT MODELING

Instructions: Determine which of the following leads the counselor used in the interview. Check the leads used.

Item	*Examples of counselor leads*
I. Rationale about Strategy	
____ 1. Counselor provides rationale about participant modeling strategy.	"This procedure has been used with other people who have concerns similar to yours. It is a way to help you overcome your fear of _____ or to help you acquire these skills."
____ 2. Counselor provides brief description of components of participant modeling.	"It involves three things. I'll model what you want to do, you'll practice this with my assistance, and then you'll try this out in situations that at first will be pretty easy for you so you can be successful."
____ 3. Counselor asks for client's willingness to use strategy.	"Would you be willing to try this now?"
II. Modeling	
____ 4. Counselor and client decide whether to divide goal behaviors into a series of subtasks or skills.	"Well, let's see . . . Right now you hardly ever go out of the house. You say it bothers you even to go out in the yard. Let's see whether we can identify different activities in which you would gradually increase the distance away from the house, like going to the front door, going out on the porch, out in the yard, out to the sidewalk, to the neighbor's house, and so on."
____ 5. If goal behaviors were divided (step 4), these subskills are arranged by counselor and client in a hierarchy according to order of difficulty.	"Perhaps we can take our list and arrange it in an order. Start with the activity that is easiest for you now, such as going to the door. Arrange each activity in order of increasing difficulty."
____ 6. Counselor and client determine and select appropriate model.	"I could help you learn to do this, or we could pick someone whom you know or someone similar to yourself to guide you through this. What are your preferences?"
____ 7. Counselor provides instructions to client before demonstration about what to look for.	"Notice that when the doorbell rings, I will go to the door calmly and quickly and open it without hesitation. Also notice that after I go to the door, I'm still calm; nothing has happened to me."
____ 8. Model demonstrates target response at least once; more demonstrations are repeated if necessary.	"OK, let me show this to you again."
____ If hierarchy is used, first skill is modeled, followed successively by all others, concluding with demonstration combining all subskills.	"Now that I've done the first scene, next I'll show you stepping out on the porch. Then we'll combine these two scenes."
III. Guided Participation	
____ 9. Client is asked to perform target response. If a hierarchy is used, first skill in hierarchy is practiced first, successfully followed by second, third, and so on.	"This time you try going to the door when the doorbell rings. I will assist you as you need help."
____ 10. After each practice, model or counselor provides feedback consisting of positive feedback and error corrections.	"That was quite smooth. You were able to go to the door quickly. You still hesitated a little once you got there. Try to open the door as soon as you see who is there."

(continued)

POSTEVALUATION (continued)

Item	Examples of counselor leads
___11. Initial practice attempts of each skill by client include a number of induction aids, such as —	"I'm going to assist you in your first few practices."
___a. Joint practice with model or counselor.	"Let's do it together. I will walk with you to the door."
___b. Verbal and/or physical coaching or guiding by model or counselor.	"Let me give you a suggestion here. When you open the door, greet the person there. Find out what the person wants."
___c. Repeated practice of one subtask until client is ready to move on to another.	"Let's work on this a few more times until you feel really comfortable."
___d. Graduated time intervals for practice (short to long duration).	"This time we'll increase the distance you have to walk to the door. Let's start back in the kitchen."
___e. Arrangement of protective conditions for practice to reduce likelihood of feared or undesired consequences.	"We'll make sure someone else is in the house with you."
___f. Graduated levels of severity of threat or complexity of situation.	"OK, now we've worked with opening the door when a good friend is there. This time let's pretend it's someone you are used to seeing but don't know as a friend, like the person who delivers your mail."
___12. In later practice attempts, number of induction aids is gradually reduced.	"I believe now that you can do this without my giving you so many prompts."
___13. Before moving on, client is able to engage in self-directed practice of all desired responses.	"This time I'm going to leave. I want you to do this by yourself."
IV. Success Experiences (Homework)	
___14. Counselor and client identify situations in client's environment in which client desires to perform target responses.	"Let's list all the actual times and places where you want to do this."
___15. Situations are arranged in hierarchy from easy with least risk to difficult with greater risk.	"We can arrange these in an order. Put the easiest one first, and follow it by ones that are successively harder or more threatening for you."
___16. Starting with easiest and least risky situation, counselor (or model) and client use live or symbolic modeling and guided practice in client's real-life environment. Steps 4–11 are repeated outside session until gradually counselor (or model) reduces level of assistance.	"Starting with the first situation, we're going to work with this when it actually occurs. At first I'll assist you until you can do it on your own."
___17. Client is assigned a series of related tasks to carry out in a self-directed manner.	"Now you're ready to tackle this situation without my help. You have shown both of us you are ready to do this on your own."

□ SUGGESTED READINGS

Bandura, A. (1976). Effecting change through participant modeling. In J. D. Krumboltz & C. E. Thoresen (Eds.), *Counseling methods*. New York: Holt, Rinehart and Winston.

Bandura, A., Jeffery, R. W., & Gajdos, E. (1975). Generalizing change through participant modeling with self-directed mastery. *Behaviour Research and Therapy, 13,* 141–152.

Bandura, A., Jeffery, R. W., & Wright, C. (1974). Efficacy of participant modeling as a function of response induction aids. *Journal of Abnormal Psychology, 83,* 56–64.

Bourque, P., & Ladouceur, R. (1980). An investigation of various performance-based treatments with acrophobics. *Behaviour Research and Therapy, 18,* 161–170.

Craigie, F. C., Jr., & Ross, S. M. (1980). The case of a videotape pretherapy training program to encourage treatment-seeking among alcohol detoxification patients. *Behavior Therapy, 11,* 141–147.

Davis, A., Rosenthal, T. L., & Kelley, J. E. (1981). Actual fear cues, prompt therapy, and rationale enhance participant modeling with adolescents. *Behavior Therapy, 12,* 536–542.

Davis, R. (1979). The impact of self-modeling on problem behaviors in school-age children. *School Psychology Digest, 8,* 128–132.

Dowrick, P. W., & Dove, C. (1980). The use of self-modeling to improve the swimming performance of spina bifida children. *Journal of Applied Behavior Analysis, 13,* 51–56.

Edelstein, B., & Eisler, R. (1976). Effects of modeling and modeling with instructions and feedback on the behavioral components of social skills. *Behavior Therapy, 7,* 382–389.

Etringer, B. D., Cash, T. F., & Rimm, D. C. (1982). Behavioral, affective, and cognitive effects of participant modeling and an equally credible placebo. *Behavior Therapy, 13,* 476–485.

Gilbert, B. O., Johnson, S. B., Spillar, R., McCallum, M., Silverstein, J. H., & Rosenbloom, A. (1982). The effects of a peer-modeling film on children learning to self-inject insulin. *Behavior Therapy, 13,* 186–193.

Glasgow, R. E., & Rosen, G. M. (1979). Self-help behavior therapy manuals: Recent developments and clinical usage. *Clinical Behavior Therapy Review, 1,* 1–20.

Gresham, F. M., & Nagle, R. J. (1980). Social skills training with children: Responsiveness to modeling and coaching as a function of peer orientation. *Journal of Consulting and Clinical Psychology, 48,* 718–729.

Hosford, R. (1974). *Counseling techniques: Self-as-a-model film.* Washington, DC: American Personnel and Guidance Press.

Ladouceur, R. (1983). Participant modeling with or without cognitive treatment for phobias. *Journal of Consulting and Clinical Psychology, 51,* 930–932.

Miklich, D., Chida, T., & Danker-Brown, P. (1977). Behavior modification by self-modeling without subject awareness. *Journal of Behavior Therapy and Experimental Psychiatry, 8,* 125–130.

Perry, M. A., & Furukawa, M. J. (1986). Modeling methods. In F. A. Kanfer & A. P. Goldstein (Eds.), *Helping people change* (3rd ed.) (66–110). New York: Pergamon Press.

Peterson, L., & Shigetomi, C. (1981). The use of coping techniques to minimize anxiety in hospitalized children. *Behavior Therapy, 12,* 1–14.

Sarason, I. G., & Sarason, B. R. (1981). Teaching cognitive and social skills to high school students. *Journal of Consulting and Clinical Psychology, 49,* 908–918.

Webster-Stratton, C. (1981a). Modification of mothers' behaviors and attitudes through a videotape modeling group discussion program. *Behavior Therapy, 12,* 634–642.

Webster-Stratton, C. (1981b). Videotape modeling: A method of parent education. *Journal of Clinical Child Psychology, 10,* 93–98.

FEEDBACK: POSTEVALUATION

PART ONE

Check the contents of your script outline with item 4 on the Checklist for Developing Symbolic Models on page 343.

PART TWO

1. *Rationale*

   First, you explain to Mr. Brown what the self-as-a-model procedure consists of and how it could help him practice and gain confidence in his skills of initiating social contacts with his boss.

2. *Recording of behavior*

   After a practice attempt and some coaching of the behaviors required in initiating a contact, have Mr. Brown practice initiating a social contact with you role-playing the part of his boss. Record these practices until you have obtained an adequate sample of his behavior.

3. *Editing the tape*

   After the practice tape has been made, you would edit the tape so that any inappropriate behaviors are deleted; only appropriate behaviors are left on the tape.

4. *Demonstrating with the tape*

   The edited tape would be used as the model for Mr. Brown, who would hear it replayed. After the playback, you might suggest additional practice.

5. *Homework*

   Mr. Brown would arrange to listen to or view the tape daily, followed by role play or covert (mental) practice of the behaviors involved in initiating social contacts with his boss.

PART THREE

Rate your taped interview or have someone else rate you, using the Interview Checklist for Self-as-a-Model.

PART FOUR

Here is a brief description of how you might use participant modeling to help Mr. Brown.

Rationale

First, you would explain to Mr. Brown that the procedure can help him acquire the kinds of skills he will need to initiate social contacts with his boss. You

(continued)

FEEDBACK: POSTEVALUATION (continued)

would also tell him that the procedure involves modeling, guided practice, and success experiences. You might emphasize that the procedure is based on the idea that change can occur when the desired activities are learned in small steps with successful performance emphasized at each step. This successful performance will help Mr. Brown do what he wants to do but presently avoids.

Modeling

You and Mr. Brown would explore the verbal and nonverbal responses that might be involved in Mr. Brown's approaching his boss and asking him out to lunch, for a drink, and so on. For example, these skills might be divided into direct eye contact, making a verbal request, speaking without hesitation or errors, and speaking in a firm, strong voice. After specifying all the components of the desired response, you and Mr. Brown would arrange them in a hierarchy according to order of difficulty for him. If there are any other situations in which he has trouble making a request, these could also be included.

You and Mr. Brown would select the appropriate model—yourself, an aide, or possibly one of Mr. Brown's colleagues. The model selected would demonstrate the first response in the hierarchy (followed by all the others) to Mr. Brown. Repeated demonstrations of any response might be necessary.

Guided participation

After the modeled demonstration of a response, you would ask Mr. Brown to perform it. His first attempts would be assisted with induction aids administered by you or the model. For example, you might verbally coach him or start with a short message and gradually increase it. After each practice, you would give Mr. Brown feedback, being sure to encourage his positive performance and make suggestions for improvement. Generally, Mr. Brown would practice each response several times, and the number of induction aids would be reduced gradually. Before moving on to practice a *different* response, Mr. Brown should be able to perform the response in a self-directed manner without your presence or support.

Success experiences

You and Mr. Brown would identify situations in his environment in which he would like to use the skills he has learned. In his case, most of the situations would center on social situations with his boss. For example, the situations for Mr. Brown might include

visiting his boss in his boss's office, going over to speak to his boss during a break or at lunch, asking his boss to accompany him on a coffee break, asking his boss out for lunch, and inviting his boss to his home for dinner or drinks. As you may note, some of these situations involve more risk than others. The situations should be arranged in order, from the least to the most risky. Mr. Brown would work on the least risky situation until he was able to do that easily and successfully before going on. Ideally, it would help to have the counselor or model go along with Mr. Brown to model and guide. If the model was one of his colleagues, this would be possible. If this was not possible, Mr. Brown could telephone the counselor just before his "contact" to rehearse and to receive coaching and encouragement.

PART FIVE

Use the Interview Checklist for Participant Modeling to assess your performance or to have someone else rate you.

EMOTIVE IMAGERY
AND COVERT MODELING

FOURTEEN

With some client problems, a counselor may find that it is impossible or unrealistic to provide live or symbolic models or to have the client engage in overt practice of the goal behaviors. In these cases, it may be more practical to employ strategies that use the client's imagination for the modeling or rehearsal. This chapter describes two therapeutic procedures that rely heavily on client imagery: emotive imagery and covert modeling. In both these strategies, scenes are developed that the client visualizes or rehearses by imagination. It has been assumed that the client must be able to generate strong, vivid images to use these procedures, but we do not know at present to what extent the intensity of the client's imagery correlates with therapeutic outcomes (M. J. Mahoney, 1974).

☐ OBJECTIVES

1. Given seven examples of counselor leads, identify which of the five steps of the emotive imagery procedure are presented in each counselor lead. You should be able to identify accurately at least six out of seven examples.
2. Demonstrate 10 out of 13 steps of emotive imagery with a role-play client, using the Interview Checklist for Emotive Imagery at the end of the chapter to assess your performance.
3. Describe how you would apply the five components of covert modeling, given a simulated client case.
4. Demonstrate at least 22 out of 28 steps associated with covert modeling with a role-play client, using the Interview Checklist for Covert Modeling at the end of the chapter to assess your use of this strategy.

☐ ASSESSMENT OF CLIENT IMAGERY

In both emotive imagery and covert modeling, it is essential to assess the client's potential for engaging in imagery or fantasy. To some extent, the success of these two strategies may depend on the client's capacity to generate vivid images. As Kazdin points out, "Presumably, the effect of treatment is influenced by the extent to which the client is imagining the material presented by the therapist" (1976b, p. 480). Some clients may be "turned off" by imagery; others may find it difficult to picture vivid scenes in their minds.

There are several ways the counselor can assess the intensity and clarity of client images. First, the client's level of imagery could be assessed before using emotive imagery or covert modeling with a self-report questionnaire such as the Visual and Auditory Imagery parts of the Imaginal Processes Inventory (Singer & Antrobus, 1972), the Betts QMI (Sheehan, 1967), the Imagery Survey Schedule (Cautela, 1977), or other such measures as reviewed by White, Sheehan, and Ashton (1977). The counselor and client can also develop practice scenes that the client can use to generate images. For example, the counselor might instruct the client to "visualize a scene or event that makes you feel relaxed and pleasant. Select a scenario that you really enjoy and feel good about—try to be aware of all your sensations while in the scene." Kazdin (1976b) suggests that the client can narrate aloud the events in the practice scene as they are imagined. Or, after 30 seconds to a minute of imagery, the counselor can ask the client to describe the scene in detail. After the client's description, the counselor might probe about the colors, sounds, movement, temperature, or smell reflected in the scene. The idea is to ascertain how vividly the client imagined the scene. (Additionally, the counselor might ask how the client was feeling during the imagined scene. This question helps the counselor get an impression of how much the client can "get into," or become involved in, the scene.)

If a client has some difficulty imagining specific details, the counselor can train the client to engage in more detailed imagery (Lazarus, 1982; Phillips, 1971). If this seems too time-consuming or if the client is reluctant to use or uninterested in using imagery, a strategy that does not involve imagery may be more appropriate. If a client has good feelings about imagery and can "get into" the practice scene, then the counselor and client may decide to continue with either emotive imagery or covert modeling, depending on the client's problem and goal behavior.

☐ EMOTIVE IMAGERY

In using the emotive imagery procedure, a person focuses on positive thoughts or images while imagining a discomforting or anxiety-arousing activity or situation. By focusing on positive and pleasant images, the person is able to "block" the painful, fearful, or anxiety-provoking situation. One can think of blocking in emotive imagery as a process that takes advantage of the difficulty of focusing on pleasant thoughts and on anxiety, pain, or tension at the same time. This is difficult because these emotions are incompatible.

Self-initiated imagery has been used to alter unpleasant moods (Means, Wilson, & Deugokinski, 1987) and with children coping with stress (Lamontagne, Mason, & Hepworth, 1985). Imagery is very frequently used as an induction procedure for hypnosis (Clarke & Jackson, 1983), and several studies have reported the use of emotive imagery as a therapeutic strategy. Lazarus and Abramovitz (1962) were among the first to report such a study. Children with phobias were instructed to engage in enjoyable fantasies while experiencing phobic stimuli. For example, a child's school phobia was eliminated by introducing imagery scenes about school centered on a fictional character, Noddy. As these authors point out, "The essence of this procedure was to create imagined situations where Noddy played the role of a truant and responded fearfully to the school setting. The patient (child) would then protect him, either by active reassurance or by 'setting a good example'" (pp. 191–195). Lazarus (1968) has used relaxing images to enhance muscle relaxation. The client selects any imagined scene that she or he finds relaxing and focuses on the scene while engaging in deep muscle relaxation. Lazarus claims that he can obtain deeper and more satisfying levels of relaxation with the use of relaxing images. Horan (1973) has used emotive imagery with pregnant women to reduce the discomfort and anxiety associated with childbirth. Stone, Demchik-Stone, and Horan (1977) found that emotive imagery was as effective as the Lamaze method of prophylactic childbirth in controlling pain-tolerance levels of pregnant women. In an analogue study, Horan and Dellinger (1974) found that people who listened to tape-recorded relaxation-producing images were able to hold their hands immersed in ice water more than twice as long as people who did not use relaxing images. Horan, Layng, and Pursell (1976) reported that heart rates of women who experienced discomfort while having their teeth cleaned declined, on the average, from 77 beats per minute to 65 beats after five minutes of tape-recorded relaxation-producing emotive images. Worthington and Shumate (1981) and Varni (1981) found that imagery was an effective method of pain control. Progressive muscle-relaxation training plus emotive imagery was used effectively to reduce the aversiveness of chemotherapy for cancer patients (Lyles, Burish, Krozely, & Oldham, 1982). Pickett and Cloum (1982) found that patients who had had gall-bladder surgery were able to reduce postsurgical anxiety by imagining a pleasant situation. Three types of imagery scenes — neutral (going to the library), positive (jogging on a beautiful, clear, sunny day), and self-generated scenes — were found to be equally effective in reducing depression (Jarvinen & Gold, 1981). Imagery also was applied to relieve acute pain (Raft, Smith, & Warren, 1986). A novel use of imagery has been applied to cancer patients (Simonton & Simonton, 1975). These researchers found that some terminal cancer patients instructed to imagine their disease and their body's own immune mechanisms (white blood cells) attacking the diseased and weakened cancer cells extended their lives past the predicted life expectancy.

Emotive imagery can be applied to a variety of client concerns and problems. Situations in which positive images can be used concurrently to reduce discomfort include "receiving injections, minor surgery and chronic recurring pain" (Horan, 1976, p. 318). Emotive imagery is also applicable to situations in which people experience boredom or tension created by daily routine. This use of the procedure can be viewed as a cognitive "time-out" or a "rest-and-recuperation" (R-and-R) strategy. In vivo emotive imagery can be applied as a single strategy or used with other procedures to increase relaxation and to reduce discomfort or tension. Lazarus (1982) has developed a series of audiotapes instructing the listener to use imagery to help cope with fears, phobias, and daily problems, to overcome sadness, to maintain achievement goals, and to achieve habit control.

Emotive imagery involves five steps: a rationale, assessment of the client's imagery potential, development of imagery scenes, practice of scenes, and homework. See the Interview Checklist for Emotive Imagery at the end of the chapter for some examples of counselor leads associated with these steps.

Treatment Rationale

The following illustration of the purpose and overview of emotive imagery has been given to pregnant women about the procedure for reducing childbirth anxiety and for relieving discomfort during labor (Horan, 1976):

Here is how in vivo emotive imagery works: In this culture women often learn to expect excruciating pain in childbirth. Even intelligent sophisticated women have a hard time shaking this belief. Consequently, the prospect of childbirth is often fraught with considerable anxiety. In the labor room, early contractions are seen as signals for unbearable pain to follow. The result is that even more anxiety occurs.

Now, since anxiety has a magnifying effect on childbirth discomfort, the more anxious you become the more actual pain you will probably experience. This "vicious circle" happens all too frequently.

The process of in vivo emotive imagery involves having you focus on scenes or events which please you or make you feel relaxed, while the contractions are occurring. You simply cannot feel calm, happy, secure — or whatever other emotion the scenes engender — and anxious at the same time. These opposing emotions are incompatible with each other.

So, in vivo emotive imagery blocks the anxiety which leads to increased childbirth discomfort. There is also some evidence which suggests that the holding of certain images can raise your pain threshold. Thus, in vivo emotive imagery not only eliminates anxiety-related discomfort, but it also has a dulling effect on what might be called real pain! [pp. 317–318]*

The rationale ends with a request for the client's willingness to try the strategy.

Assessment of Client's Imagery Potential

Because the success of the emotive imagery procedure may depend on the amount of positive feelings and calmness a client can derive from visualizing a particular scene, it is important for the counselor to get a feeling for the client's potential for engaging in imagery. The counselor can assess the client's imagery potential by the methods discussed at the beginning of this chapter: a self-report questionnaire, a practice scene with client narration, or counselor "probes" for details.

Development of Imagery Scenes

If the decision is made to continue with the emotive imagery procedure, the client and counselor

* From "Coping with Inescapable Discomfort Through In Vivo Emotive Imagery," by John J. Horan, in Counseling Methods, edited by John D. Krumboltz and Carl E. Thoresen, copyright © 1976 by Holt, Rinehart, and Winston, Inc., reprinted by permission of the publisher.

will then develop imagery scenes. They should develop at least two, although one scene might be satisfactory for some clients. The exact number and type of scenes developed will depend on the nature of the concern and the individual client.

Two basic ingredients should be included in the selection and development of the scene. First, the scenario should promote calmness, tranquility, or enjoyment for the client. Examples of such client scenes might include skiing on a beautiful slope, hiking on a trail in a large forest, sailing on a sunny lake, walking on a secluded beach, listening to and watching a symphony orchestra perform a favorite composition, or watching an athletic event. The scenes can involve the client as an active participant or as a participant observer or spectator. For some clients, the more active they are in the scene, the greater the degree of their involvement.

The second ingredient of the scene should be as much sensory detail as possible, such as sounds, colors, temperature, smell, touch, and motion. There may be a high positive correlation between the degree and number of sensations a scene elicits for the client and the amount or intensity of pleasant and enjoyable sensations the client experiences in a particular imagery scene. The counselor and client should decide on the particular senses that will be incorporated into the imagery scenes.

As an example, the following imagery scene was used by Horan (1976) for people who experience discomfort having their teeth cleaned. Note the sensations described in the scene instructions:

Now close your eyes, sit back, and relax. Eyes closed, sitting back in the chair, relaxing. Now visualize yourself standing by the shore of a large lake, looking out across an expanse of blue water and beyond to the far shore. Immediately in front of you stretches a small beach, and behind you a grassy meadow. The sun is bright and warm. The air is fresh and clean. It's a gorgeous summer day. The sky is pale blue with great billowy clouds drifting by. The wind is blowing gently, just enough to make the trees sway and make gentle ripples in the grass. It's a perfect day. And you have it entirely to yourself, with nothing to do, nowhere to go. You take from your car a blanket, towel, and swim-suit, and walk off through the meadow. You find a spot, spread the blanket, and lie down on it. It's so warm and quiet. It's such a treat to have the day to yourself to just relax and take it easy. Keep your eyes closed, thinking about the warm, beautiful day. You're in your suit now, walking toward the water, feeling the soft, lush grass under your feet. You reach the beach and start across it. Now you can feel the warm sand underfoot. Very warm and very nice. Now visualize yourself walking out into the water up to your ankles; out farther, up to your knees. The water's so warm it's almost like a bath. Now you're moving faster out into the lake, up to your waist, up to your chest. The water's so warm, so comfortable. You take a deep breath and glide a few feet forward down into the water. You surface and feel the water run down your back. You look around; you're still all alone. You still have this lovely spot to yourself. Far across the lake you can see a sailboat, tiny in the distance. It's so far away you can just make out the white sail jutting up from the blue water. You take another breath and kick off this time toward the shore swimming with long easy strokes. Kicking with your feet, pulling through with your arms and hands. You swim so far that when you stop and stand the water's only up to your waist, and you begin walking toward the beach, across the warm sand to the grass. Now you're feeling again the grass beneath your feet. Deep, soft, lush. You reach your blanket and pick up the towel, and begin to dry yourself. You dry your hair, your face, your neck. You stretch the towel across your shoulders, dry your back, your legs. You can feel the warm sun on your skin. It must be ninety degrees, but it's clear and dry. The heat isn't oppressive; it's just nice and warm and comfortable. You lie down on the blanket and feel the deep, soft grass under your head. You're looking up at the sky, seeing those great billowy clouds floating by, far, far, above [p. 319].*

Practice of Imagery Scenes

After the imagery scenes have been developed, the client is instructed to practice using them. There are two types of practice. In the first type, the client is instructed to focus on one of the scenes for about 30 seconds and to picture as much detail as was developed for that scene and feel all the sensations associated with it. The counselor cues the client after the time has elapsed. After the client uses the scene, the counselor obtains an impression of the imagery experience — the client's feelings and sensory details of the scene. If other scenes are developed, the client can be instructed to practice imagining them. Variations on this type of practice might be to have the client use or hold a scene for varying lengths of time.

The second type of practice is to have the client

use the scenes in simulated anxious, tense, fearful, or painful situations. The counselor and client should simulate the problem situations while using the imagery scenes. Practice under simulated conditions permits the counselor and client to assess the effectiveness of the scenes for blocking out the discomfort or for reducing the anxiety or phobic reaction. Simulated situations can be created by describing vividly the details of an anxiety-provoking situation while the client uses a scene. For example, the counselor can describe the pleasant scene while interweaving a description of the discomforting situation (Lazarus & Abramovitz, 1962). The counselor can simulate painful situations by squeezing the client's arm while the client focuses on one of the scenes. Or, to simulate labor contractions, the labor coach squeezes the woman's thigh while she focuses on a pleasant image. Another simulation technique is to have clients hold their hands in ice water for a certain length of time. Simulated practice may facilitate generalization of the scene application to the actual problem situation. After the simulated practices, the counselor should assess the client's reactions to using the scene in conjunction with the simulated discomfort or anxiety.

Homework and Follow-Up

The client is instructed to apply the emotive imagery *in vivo*—that is, to use the scenes in the fearful, painful, tense, or anxious situation. The client can use a homework log to record the day, time, and situation in which emotive imagery was used. The client can also note reactions before and after using emotive imagery with a 5-point scale, 1 representing minimum discomfort and 5 indicating maximum discomfort. The client should be told to bring the homework log to the next session or to a follow-up session.

☐ MODEL EXAMPLE: EMOTIVE IMAGERY

In this model example, we are going to deviate from our usual illustrations of hypothetical cases and present a narrative account of how the two of us used emotive imagery before and during labor for the birth of our two children.

1. *Rationale*

   First, we discussed a rationale for using emotive imagery during labor in conjunction with the breathing and relaxation techniques (see Chapter 17) we had learned in our prepared-childbirth class. We decided before labor started that

we would try emotive imagery at a point during labor when the breathing needed to be supplemented with something else. We also worked out a finger-signaling system to use during contractions so Sherry could inform Bill whether to continue or stop with the imagery scenes, depending on their effectiveness.

2. *Assessment of imagery potential*

   We also discussed whether Sherry was able to use fantasy effectively enough to concentrate during a labor contraction. We tested this out by having Bill describe imagery stimuli and having Sherry imagine these and try to increase use of all sensations to make the imagery scenes as vivid as possible.

3. *Development of imagery scenes*

   Together we selected two scenes to practice with before labor and to use during labor. One scene involved being on a sailboat on a sunny, warm day and sailing quite fast with a good breeze. We felt this scene would be effective because it produced enjoyment and also because it seemed to evoke a lot of sensory experience. The second scene involved being anchored at night on the boat with a full moon, a soft breeze, and some wine. Since both these scenes represented actual experiences, we felt they might work better than sheer fantasy.

4. *Practice of imagery scenes*

   We knew that much of the success of using emotive imagery during labor would depend on the degree to which we worked with it before labor. We practiced with our imagery scenes in two ways. First, Sherry imagined these scenes on her own, sometimes in conjunction with her self-directed practice in breathing and relaxation, and sometimes just as something to do —for instance, in a boring situation. Second, Sherry evoked the scenes deliberately while Bill simulated a contraction by tightly squeezing her upper arm.

5. *Homework: In vivo*

   We had a chance to apply emotive imagery during labor itself. We started to use it during the active phase of labor—about midway through the time of labor, when the contractions were coming about every 2 minutes. In looking back, we felt it was a useful supplement to the breathing and relaxation typically taught in the Lamaze childbirth method. Sherry felt that a lot of the effectiveness had to do with the soothing effect of hearing Bill's vocal descriptions of the scenes—in addition to the images she produced during the scene descriptions.

LEARNING ACTIVITY #37: EMOTIVE IMAGERY

This learning activity is designed to help you learn the process of emotive imagery. It will be easier to do this with a partner, although you can do it alone if a partner is not available. You may wish to try it with a partner first and then by yourself.

Instructions for Dyadic Activity

1. In dyads, one of you can take the helper role; the other takes the part of the helpee. Switch roles after the first practice with the strategy.
2. The helper should give an explanation about the emotive imagery procedure.
3. The helper should determine the helpee's potential for imagination: ask the helpee to imagine several pleasant scenes and then probe for details.
4. The helper and helpee together should develop two imagery scenes the helpee can vividly imagine. Imagination of these scenes should produce pleasant, positive feelings.
5. The helpee should practice imagining these scenes—as vividly and as intensely as possible.
6. The helpee should practice imagining a scene while the helper simulates a problem situation. For

example, the helper can simulate an anxiety-provoking situation by describing it while the helpee engages in imagery, or the helper can stimulate pain by squeezing the helpee's arm during the imagination.

Instructions for Self-Activity

1. Think of two scenes you can imagine very vividly. These scenes should produce positive or pleasant feelings for you. Supply as many details to these scenes as you can.
2. Practice imagining these scenes as intensely as you can.
3. Next, practice imagining one of these scenes while simulating a problem (discomforting) situation such as holding a piece of ice in your hands or running your hands under cold water. Concentrate very hard on the imagery as you do so.
4. Practice this twice daily for the next three days. See how much you can increase your tolerance for the cold temperature with daily practice of the imagery scene.

☐ COVERT MODELING

Covert modeling is a procedure developed by Cautela (1971) in which the client imagines a model performing behaviors by means of instructions. The covert modeling procedure assumes that a live or symbolic performance by a model is not necessary. Instead, the client is directed to imagine someone demonstrating the desired behavior. Flannery (1972) used covert modeling as part of a treatment strategy with a college dropout. Cautela, Flannery, and Hanley (1974) compared covert and overt (live) modeling in reducing avoidance behaviors of college students; both procedures were effective. In the last decade, most of the supportive data for the covert modeling procedure have resulted from studies conducted by Kazdin (1973a, 1974a, 1974b, 1974c, 1974d, 1975, 1976a, 1976b, 1976c, 1979a, 1979b, 1980a, 1982). Rosenthal and Reese (1976) explored the effectiveness of covert modeling in developing assertive behaviors. The procedure has also been used to treat alcoholism and obsessive-compulsive behaviors (Hay, Hay, & Nelson, 1977) and to decrease smoking (Nesse & Nelson, 1977). L. Watson (1976)

found that covert modeling was effective in helping prison inmates acquire job-interview skills. Covert modeling has also been used to decrease test anxiety (Gallagher & Arkowitz, 1978) and has been used with hypnosis in the treatment of obesity (Bornstein & Devine, 1980).

Covert modeling has several advantages: the procedure does not require elaborate therapeutic or induction aids; scenes can be developed to deal with a variety of problems; the scenes can be individualized to fit the unique concerns of the client; the client can practice the imagery scenes alone; the client can use the imagery scenes as a self-control procedure in problem situations; and covert modeling may be a good alternative when live or filmed models cannot be used or when it is difficult to use overt rehearsal in the interview.

Some questions about certain aspects of covert modeling remain unanswered, such as the importance of the identity of the model, the role of reinforcing consequences, and the type and duration of imagery scenes best used in the procedure. We have tried to point out the possible alternatives in our description of the components of the covert modeling strategy. Our description is based not only on our own experience with it but also on the pioneering efforts of Cautela (1971) and Kazdin (1976b). The five major components of covert modeling are rationale about the strategy, practice scenes, developing treatment scenes, applying treatment scenes, and homework. Within each of these five components are several substeps. If you would like an overview of the procedure, see the Interview Checklist for Covert Modeling at the end of the chapter.

Treatment Rationale

After the counselor and client have reviewed the problem behaviors and the goal behaviors for counseling, the counselor presents the rationale for covert modeling. Here is Kazdin's (1976b) explanation of a treatment rationale for using covert modeling in assertiveness training:

> In developing behavior such as assertive skills, it is essential to rehearse or practice elements of the skills. Specifically, it is important to rehearse the situations in which assertiveness is the appropriate response. Numerous situations in life require an assertive response of some sort. Learning what these situations are and being able to discriminate appropriate responses are important. People can rehearse situations in their imagination. Imagining certain selected situations can alter one's behavior in those actual situations. For example, to get rid of one's fear, one can imagine carefully selected scenes related to fear and remove the fear. So imagination can strongly influence behavior [p. 477].

The rationale should also provide a brief description of the process of covert modeling. Cautela (1976) provides an illustration of the way he describes the covert modeling process to a client:

> In a minute, I'll ask you to close your eyes and try to imagine, as clearly as possible, that you are observing a certain situation. Try to use all the senses needed for the particular situation, e.g., try to actually hear a voice or see a person very clearly. After I describe the scene, I will ask you some questions concerning your feelings about the scene and how clearly you imagined it [p. 324].

Practice Scenes

After providing a rationale to the client, the counselor may decide to try out the imagery process with several practice scenes. For most clients, imagining a scene may be a new experience and may seem foreign. Kazdin (1976b, p. 478) suggests that practice scenes may help to familiarize clients

with the procedure and sensitize them to focus on specific details of the imagery. Use of practice scenes also helps the counselor to assess the client's potential for carrying out instructions in the imagination.

The practice scenes usually consist of simple, straightforward situations that are unrelated to the goal behaviors. For example, if you are using covert modeling to help a client acquire job-interview skills, the practice scenes would be unrelated to job-seeking responses. You might use some of the following as practice scenes:

1. Imagine a person in a library checking out a book.
2. Imagine someone lying on the beach in the hot sun.
3. Imagine someone eating a gourmet meal at an elegant restaurant.
4. Imagine someone being entertained at a night spot.

In using practice scenes with a client, the counselor usually follows six steps.

1. The counselor instructs the client to close his or her eyes and to sit back and relax. The client is instructed to tell the counselor when he or she feels relaxed. If the client does not feel relaxed, the counselor may need to decide whether relaxation procedures (Chapter 17) should be introduced. The effect of relaxation on the quality of imagery in covert modeling has not been evaluated. However, research on live and symbolic modeling suggests that modeling may be facilitated when the client is relaxed (Bandura, Blanchard, & Ritter, 1969).

2. The counselor describes a practice scene and instructs the client to imagine the scene and to raise an index finger when the scene has been imagined vividly. The practice scenes are similar to the four previous examples. The counselor reads the scene or instructs the client about what to imagine.

3. The counselor asks the client to open his or her eyes after the scene is vividly imagined (signal of index finger) and to describe the scene or to narrate the imagined events.

4. The counselor probes for greater details about the scene—the clothes or physical features of a person in the imagery, the physical setting of the situation, the amount of light, colors of the furniture, decorative features, noises, or smells. This probing may encourage the client to focus on details of the imagery scene.

5. The counselor may suggest additional details for the client to imagine during a subsequent practice. Working with practice scenes first can facilitate the development of the details in the actual treatment scenes.

6. Usually each practice scene is presented several times. The number of practice scenes used before moving on to developing and applying treatment scenes will depend on several factors. If the client feels comfortable with the novelty of the imagined scenes after several presentations, the counselor might consider this a cue to stop using the practice scenes. Additionally, if the client can provide a fairly detailed description of the imagery after several practice scenes, this may be a good time to start developing treatment scenes. If a client reports difficulty in relaxing, the counselor may need to introduce relaxation training before continuing. For a client who cannot generate images during the practice scenes, another modeling strategy may be needed in lieu of covert modeling.

Developing Treatment Scenes

The treatment scenes used in covert modeling are developed in conjunction with the client and grow out of the desired client outcomes or goals. The scenes consist of a variety of situations in which the client wants to perform the target response in the real-life environment. If the client wants to develop assertion skills, the treatment scenes represent different situations requiring assertive responses. If a client wants to acquire effective job-interview skills, the treatment scenes are developed around job-interview situations.

Five things should be considered in the development of treatment scenes: the model characteristics, whether to use individualized or standardized scenes, whether to use vague or specific scenes, the ingredients of the scenes, and the number of scenes. It is important for the client to help in the development of treatment scenes because client participation can provide many specifics about situations in which the goal behavior is to be performed.

Model characteristics. As you may recall from Chapter 12, research about model characteristics in live and symbolic modeling indicates that similarity between the model and the client contributes to client change (Bandura, 1971a). Kazdin (1974b) found that, in covert modeling, a same-

sex and similar-age model produced greater avoidance reduction with college students than an older model or a model of the other sex. Further, clients who imagined several models showed more change than clients who imagined only one model (Kazdin, 1974a, 1976c). Coping models also seemed to be generally more effective in covert modeling than mastery models (Bornstein & Devine, 1980; Kazdin, 1973a; Meichenbaum, 1971). A coping model who self-verbalizes his or her anxiety and uses covert self-talk for dealing with fear may enhance and facilitate the behaviors to be acquired (Tearnan, Lahey, Thompson, & Hammer, 1982, p. 180).

One of the most interesting questions about the covert model is the identity of the model. Kazdin (1974a) found no differences between college-age subjects who imagined *themselves* as the model and subjects who imagined *another person* as the model. Using a somewhat different population, incarcerated youth offenders, Watson (1976) found that covert self-modeling (imagining oneself) was superior to covert modeling (imagining someone else) on some measures. As Krumboltz and Thoresen (1976, p. 484) point out, no one is more similar to the client than the client! At present there are not sufficient data to indicate who the model should be in the covert modeling procedure. We suspect that the answer varies with clients and suggest that you give clients the option of deciding whether to imagine themselves or another person as the model. One key factor may involve the particular identity the client can imagine most easily and comfortably. For clients who feel some stress at first in imagining themselves as models, imagining someone else might be introduced first and later replaced with self-modeling.

Individualized versus standardized scenes. The treatment scenes used in covert modeling can be either standardized or individualized. Standardized scenes cover different situations in everyday life and are presented to a group of clients or to all clients with the same target responses. For example, Kazdin (1976b) used a series of standardized scenes describing situations requiring assertive responses for nonassertive clients. Individualized scenes represent situations specifically tailored to suit an individual client. For example, one nonassertive client may need scenes developed around situations with strangers; another may need scenes that involve close friends. Generally, treatment scenes should be individualized for those who have unique concerns and who are counseled individually, since some standardized scenes may not be relevant for a particular client.

Kazdin (1979b, 1980a) found that clients who were instructed to individualize (elaborate) scenes increased their assertive behavior. In these two studies, clients were permitted to change (elaborate or improvise) the "scene in any way as long as the model engaged in an assertive response" (1979b, p. 727). (See also "Verbal Summary Codes and Personalization" a few pages ahead.)

Degree of specificity of scenes. Another consideration in developing treatment scenes is the degree of specificity of instruction that should be included. Some clients may benefit from very explicit instructions about the details of what to imagine. Other clients may derive more gains from covert modeling if the treatment scenes are more general, allowing the client to supply the specific features. A risk of not having detailed instructions is that some clients will introduce scene material that is irrelevant or detracts from the desired outcomes. Kazdin (1976b) has explored clients' imagery during the treatment scenes and found that clients do make some changes. However, he indicates that such changes appear to be infrequent and that there do not seem to be any particular features of a scene introduced by a client that are consistently related to treatment outcome (p. 481). At this point, the data on the necessary degree of specificity of a treatment scene are limited. Again, we suggest this decision should consider the client's preferences.

Here is an example of a fairly general treatment scene for a prison inmate about to be released on parole who is seeking employment:

"Picture yourself (or someone else like you) in a job interview. The employer asks why you didn't complete high school. You tell the employer you got in some trouble, and the employer asks what kind of trouble. You feel a little uptight but tell her you have a prison record. The employer asks why you were in prison and for how long. The employer then asks what makes you think you can stay out of trouble and what you have been doing while on parole. Imagine yourself saying that you have been looking for work while on parole and have been thinking about your life and what you want to do with it."

The generality of the treatment scene in this example assumes that the client knows what type of response to make and what details to supply in the scene.

A more detailed treatment scene would specify more of the actual responses. For example:

"Picture yourself (or someone else) in a job interview and imagine the following dialogue. The employer says, 'I see that you have only finished three years of high school. You don't intend to graduate?' Picture yourself saying (showing some anxiety): 'Well, no, I want to go to vocational school while I'm working.' The employer asks: 'What happened? How did you get so far behind in school?' Imagine yourself (or someone else) replying: 'I've been out of school for awhile because I've been in some trouble.' Now imagine the employer is showing some alarm and asks: 'What kind of trouble?' You decide to be up front as you imagine yourself saying: 'I want you to know that I have a prison record.' As the employer asks: 'Why were you in prison?' imagine yourself feeling a little nervous but staying calm and saying something like: 'I guess I was pretty immature. Some friends and I got involved with drugs. I'm on parole now. I'm staying away from drugs and I'm looking hard for a job. I really want to work'" [L. Watson, 1976].

Remember, the degree of specificity of each scene will depend largely on the client, the problem or concern, and the goals for counseling.

Ingredients for the scene. Three ingredients are required for a treatment scene in the covert modeling procedure: a description of the situation or context in which the behavior is to occur, a description of the model demonstrating the behavior to be acquired, and a depiction of some favorable outcome of the goal behavior. Kazdin (1976b) gives an example of a covert modeling scene for assertive behavior in which the situation and the goal behavior are illustrated:

Situation: Imagine the person (model) is staying at a hotel. After one night there, he (she) notices that the bed springs must be broken. The bed sags miserably and was very uncomfortable during the night.

Model demonstrating the behavior: In the morning, the person goes to the clerk at the desk and says: "The bed in my room is quite uncomfortable. I believe it is broken. I wish you would replace the bed or change my room" [p. 485].

Hay et al. (1977) developed covert modeling scenes that included a favorable outcome for an adult male alcoholic. This is an example of one of the scenes for their client:

> Imagine yourself walking in town and running into a group of your old drinking buddies. They have already been drinking heavily and ask you to join them. They are drinking white lightning. They look happy and you are alone. In the past you would have taken a drink and probably have become drunk. Now cope with the situation. Imagine yourself feeling the "urge" to drink, but refusing and slowly turning and walking down the street [p. 71].

Here the model (the client) is depicted as coping with a situation and then refusing to drink and walking away, which is a favorable outcome.

Inclusion of a favorable consequence as a scene ingredient is based on research indicating that if a client sees a model rewarded for the behavior, the client is more likely to perform the response (Bandura, 1976b). Moreover, specifying a possible favorable outcome to imagine may prevent a client from inadvertently imagining an unfavorable one. Kazdin (1974c, 1976c) found that clients who received covert modeling treatment scenes that were resolved favorably were more assertive than clients who imagined scenes without any positive consequences.

We believe that the favorable outcome in the scene should take the form of some action initiated by the client or of covert self-reinforcement or praise. For example, the favorable outcome illustrated in the scene for the alcoholic client was the client's self-initiated action of walking away from the alcohol (Hay et al., 1977). We prefer that the action be initiated by the client or model instead of someone else in the scene because, in a real situation, it may be too risky to have the client rely on someone else to deliver a favorable outcome in the form of a certain response. We cannot guarantee that clients will always receive favorable responses from someone else in the actual situation.

In some previous reports of covert modeling, nonassertive clients experienced a favorable response by another person through the person's compliance. But as Nietzel, Martorano, and Melnick (1977) point out, using compliance of someone else as a favorable outcome might reinforce inaccurate client expectations and also could fail to help a client learn how to respond to noncompliance. These authors compared the effectiveness of covert modeling with and without "reply training." In other words, some clients were trained to visualize (1) an initial assertive response by the model, (2) another person's noncomplying response, and (3) a second assertive counterreply by the model. The clients who received the extra "reply training" were more assertive and more persevering in their assertions than the clients who were trained only to make an initial assertive response that was followed by compliance from the other person. Reply training to noncompliance may be more realistic and provide more response alternatives than training someone to receive automatic compliance as a positive consequence.

Another way to incorporate a favorable outcome into a treatment scene is to include an example of client (or model) self-reinforcement or praise. For instance, models might congratulate themselves by saying "That is terrific. I am proud of myself for what I said to the hotel clerk." A favorable consequence in the form of model or client self-praise is self-administered. Again, in a real-life situation, it may be better for clients to learn to reward themselves than to expect external encouragement that might not be forthcoming.

The person who experiences the favorable outcomes will be the same person the client imagines as the model. If the client imagines someone else as the model, then the client would also imagine that person initiating a favorable outcome or reinforcing himself or herself. Clients who imagine themselves as the models would imagine themselves receiving the positive consequences. There is very little actual evidence on the role of reinforcement in covert modeling. Some of the effectiveness of adding favorable consequences to the treatment scene may depend on the identity of the covert model and the particular value of the consequences for the client (Watson, 1976).

Number of scenes. The counselor and client can develop different scenes that portray the situation in which the client experiences difficulty or wants to use the newly acquired behavior. Multiple scenes can depict different situations in which assertive behavior is generally appropriate. In a series of studies, Kazdin (1979a, 1979b, 1982) and Kazdin and Mascitelli (1982b) presented 5 scenes during the first session and 10 in each of the next three sessions, for a total of 35 scenes. Thirty-five is perhaps too many for use in therapy. The number of scenes the therapist and client develop will depend on the client and his or her problem. Although there is no set number of scenes that should be developed, certainly several scenes provide more variety than only one or two.

Applying Treatment Scenes

After all the scenes have been developed, the counselor can apply the treatment scenes by having the client imagine each scene. The basic steps in applying the treatment scenes are these:

1. Arranging the scenes in a hierarchy.
2. Instructing the client before scene presentation.
3. Presenting one scene at a time from the hierarchy.
4. Presenting a scene for a specified duration.
5. Obtaining the client's reactions to the imagined scene.
6. Instructing the client to develop verbal summary codes and/or to personalize each treatment scene.
7. Presenting each scene at least twice with the aid of the counselor or tape recorder.
8. Having the client imagine each scene at least twice while directing himself or herself.
9. Selecting and presenting scenes from the hierarchy in a random order.

Hierarchy. The scenes developed by the counselor and client should be arranged in a hierarchy for scene presentation (Rosenthal & Reese, 1976). The hierarchy is an order of scenes beginning with one that is relatively easy for the client to imagine with little stress. More difficult or stressful scenes would be ranked by the client.

Instructions. It may be necessary to repeat instructions about imagery to the client if a great amount of time has elapsed since using the practice scenes. The counselor might say:

> In a minute I will ask you to close your eyes and to sit back and relax. I want you to try to imagine as vividly and clearly as possible that you are observing a certain scene. Try to use *all* the senses needed for the particular situation—for example, try to actually hear the voice(s), see the colors, and picture features of a person (or people). After I describe the scene. I will ask you some questions concerning your feelings about the scene and how clearly you imagined it [Cautela et al., 1974].

If a person other than the client is the model, the client is instructed to picture someone his or her own age and sex whom he or she knows. The client

is told that the person who is pictured as the model will be used in all the treatment scenes. The counselor also instructs the client to signal by raising an index finger as soon as the scene is pictured clearly and to hold the scene in imagery until the counselor signals to stop.

Sequence of scene presentation. Initially, the first scene in the hierarchy is presented to the client. Each scene is presented alone. When one scene has been covered sufficiently, the next scene in the hierarchy is presented. This process continues until all scenes in the hierarchy have been covered.

Duration of scenes. There are no general ground rules for the amount of time to hold the scene in imagery once the client signals. In Kazdin's (1976c) research, the client held the imagery for 15 seconds after signaling; in two other studies the scene duration was 30 seconds (Bornstein & Devine, 1980; Nesse & Nelson, 1977). More recently, Kazdin (1979b, 1980b) and Kazdin and Mascitelli (1982b) have instructed clients to hold the scene for 40 seconds. We do not know whether this duration is optimal. For some clients, a longer duration may be more beneficial; for others, a shorter duration may be. We feel that the choice will depend on the counselor's personal preference and experience with the covert modeling procedure, the nature of the client's problem, the goal behavior for counseling, and—perhaps most important—the client's input about the scene duration. After one or two scenes have been presented, the counselor can query the client about the suitability of the scene duration. Generally, a scene should be held long enough for the client to imagine the three scene ingredients vividly without rushing.

Client reactions to the scene. After the client has imagined a particular scene, the counselor queries the client about how clearly it was imagined. The client is asked to describe feelings during particular parts of the scene. The counselor should also ask whether the scene was described too rapidly or the duration of the scene was adequate for the client to imagine the scene ingredients clearly. These questions enable the counselor and client to modify aspects of a scene before it is presented the second time. Client input about possible scene revision can be very helpful. If particular episodes of the scene elicit intense feelings of anxiety, the content of the scene or the manner of presentation can be revised. Perhaps the order of the scenes in the hierarchy needs rearrangement.

Another way to deal with the client's unpleasant feelings or discomfort with a scene is to talk it over. If the client feels stressful when the model (or the self) is engaging in the behavior or activity in the scene, examine with the client what episode in the scene is producing the discomfort. In addition, if the client is the model and has difficulty performing the behavior or activity, discuss and examine the block. Focus on the adaptive behavior or the coping with the situational ingredient of the scene, rather than on the anxiety or discomfort.

After each scene presentation, the counselor should assess the rate of delivery for the scene description, the clarity of the imagery, and the degree of unpleasantness of the scene for the client. Perhaps if the client has a great deal of input in developing the scenes, the level of discomfort produced will be minimized. In addition, the intensity of the imagined scene can be enhanced by using verbal summary codes or by personalizing the scene.

Verbal summary codes and personalization. Kazdin (1979a, 1979b, 1980a) found that clients who were instructed to use verbal summary codes and/or to elaborate, or personalize, each treatment scene showed higher levels of assertiveness than clients who received only covert modeling. You may wish to use either or both of these techniques with covert modeling.

Verbal summary codes are brief descriptions about the behavior to be acquired and the context in which the behavior is to occur *in the client's own words* (Kazdin, 1979a). Verbal coding of the modeling cues can facilitate acquisition and retention of the behaviors to be modeled and may maintain client performance during and after treatment by helping clients encode desired responses in their working memory. The verbalizations (or verbal summary codes) of the scene provide an alternative representational process to imagery or covert modeling (Kazdin, 1979a). The therapist instructs the client to use his or her descriptions of the behavior and the situation. Kazdin (1979a) recommends that clients rehearse using verbal summary codes with *practice* scenes and receive feedback from the therapist about the descriptions of the practice scenes. The practice should occur before presentation of the *treatment* scenes. Then the treatment scenes are presented and the client is instructed to develop his or her own verbal summary codes (descriptions of behavior and situa-

tion) for the scene. Have the client "try out" the treatment scene on the first presentation *without* the use of the summary code. On the second presentation of the scene, instruct the client to use the summary code and to say aloud exactly what it is.

Personalization of treatment scenes is another technique that can enhance covert modeling. Kazdin (1979b) calls this procedure "imagery elaboration." After the scene has been presented once as developed, then the client is instructed *to change the treatment scene in any way as long as the model responses to be acquired are represented in the scene* (Kazdin, 1979b, p. 727). As with verbal summary codes, the client is asked to rehearse personalizing (individualizing) or elaborating a scene using a practice scene and receives feedback about the elaboration. The counselor should encourage the client to use variations within the context of the situation presented by the scene. Variations include more details about the model responses and the situation in which the responses are to occur. The client is asked to elaborate the scene the second time the treatment scene is presented. Elaboration may lead to more client involvement because the scenes are individualized.

Remember to have the client experience imagining a scene first without instructions to use verbal summary codes or to personalize the scene. Then, on the second presentation of the treatment scene, the client is instructed to use one of these techniques. To verify that the client is complying with the instructions, the therapist can instruct the client to say aloud the verbal summary code or elaboration being used.

Counselor-directed scene repetition. In the analogue studies of Kazdin (1976b, 1976c), each scene is presented twice by the counselor or on a tape recording. However, Cautela (1976) recommends that after presenting the first scene and making any necessary revisions, the counselor repeat the scene four times. The number of scene repetitions may be dictated by the degree of comfort the client experiences while imagining the scene and the complexity of the activities or behaviors the client is to acquire. A complex series of motor skills, for example, may require more repetitions; and engaging in some situations may require more repetition until the client feels reasonably comfortable. Again, make the decision about the number of scene repetitions on the basis of client input: ask the client. If you use the verbal summary codes or personalization of the scene, remember to instruct the client to use the technique during later repetitions of each scene.

Client-directed scene repetition. In addition to counselor-directed scene practice, the client should engage in self-directed scene practice. Again, the number of client practices is somewhat arbitrary, although perhaps two is a minimum. Generally, the client can repeat imagining the scenes alone until he or she feels comfortable in doing so. The client can either use the verbal summary codes without saying the codes aloud or can personalize the scenes. Overt rehearsal of the scene can facilitate acquisition and retention of the imagined behaviors. The client should be instructed to overtly enact (rehearse) the scene with the therapist after the second or third time each scene is presented (Kazdin, 1980a, 1982; Kazdin & Mascitelli, 1982b).

Random presentation of scenes. After all the scenes in the hierarchy have been presented adequately, the counselor can check out the client's readiness for self-directed homework practice by presenting some of the scenes in random order. This random presentation guards against any "ordering" effect that the hierarchy arrangement may have had in the scene presentation.

Homework and Follow-Up

Self-directed practice in the form of homework is perhaps the most important therapeutic ingredient for generalization. If a person can apply or practice the procedure outside the counseling session, the probability of using the "new" behavior or of coping in the actual situation is greatly enhanced. Kazdin and Mascitelli (1982a, 1982b) found that homework enhanced performance, possibly because clients were instructed to use the newly acquired behaviors *in vivo* between therapy sessions. Homework can consist in having clients identify several situations in their everyday lives in which they could use the desired responses (Kazdin & Mascitelli, 1982b, p. 252). Cautela (1976) recommends that the counselor instruct the client to practice each scene at home *at least* ten times a day. Nesse and Nelson (1977) also recommend to their clients that they rehearse the scenes ten times daily. They found that most clients did rehearse scenes about eight times a day.

Some clients may find it difficult to practice the scenes at home this frequently. The counselor might encourage more frequent and more reliable home practice by providing the client with a "phone-mate" on a clinic phone. With a phone-mate, clients can call and verbalize their practice imagery over the phone. This procedure not only creates a demand characteristic to facilitate client practice but also enables the helper to assess the quality of the client's use of the homework. A client could also rehearse the treatment scenes at home with the aid of a tape recorder (Hay et al., 1977). In arranging the homework tasks, the counselor and client should specify how often, how long, what times during the day, and where practice should occur. The counselor should also instruct the client to record the daily use of the modeling scenes on log sheets. The counselor should verify whether the client understands the homework and should arrange for a follow-up after some portion of the homework is completed.

☐ MODEL DIALOGUE: COVERT MODELING

Here is an example of a covert modeling dialogue with our client Joan to help her increase initiating skills in her math class.

In response 1, the counselor briefly describes the **rationale** *and gives an* **overview** *of the strategy.*

1. *Counselor:* Joan, one way we can help you work on your initiating skills in math class is to help you learn the skills you want through practice. In this procedure, you will practice using your imagination. I will describe situations to you and ask you to imagine yourself or someone else participating in the way described in a situation. How does that sound?
   Client: OK. You mean I imagine things like daydreaming?

Further **instructions** *about the strategy are provided in counselor response 2.*

2. *Counselor:* It has some similarities. Only instead of just letting your mind wander, you will imagine some of the skills you want to use to improve your participation in your math class.
   Client: Well, I'm a pretty good daydreamer, so if this is similar, I will probably learn from it.

In response 3, the counselor initiates the idea of using **practice scenes** *to determine Joan's level and style of imagery.*

3. *Counselor:* Well, let's see. I think it might help to see how easy or hard it is for you to actually imagine a specific situation as I describe it to you. So maybe we could do this on a try-out basis to see what it feels like for you.
   Client: OK, what happens?

In response 4, the counselor instructs Joan to **sit back and relax before imagining the practice scene.**

4. *Counselor:* First of all, just sit back, close your eyes, and relax. [Gives Joan a few minutes to do this.] You look pretty comfortable. How do you feel?

    Client: Fine. It's never too hard for me to relax.

In response 5, the counselor instructs Joan **to imagine the scene vividly and to indicate this by raising her finger.**

5. *Counselor:* OK, now, Joan, I'm going to describe a scene to you. As I do so, I want you to imagine the scene as vividly as possible. When you feel you have a very strong picture, then raise your index finger. Does that seem clear?

    Client: Yes.

The counselor will offer a practice scene next. Note that the **practice scene** *is simple and relatively mundane. It asks Joan only to imagine another person.*

6. *Counselor:* OK, imagine that someone is about to offer you a summer job. Just picture a person who might offer you a job like this. [Gives Joan time until Joan raises her index finger.]

In response 7, the counselor asks Joan **to describe what she imagined.**

7. *Counselor:* OK, Joan, now open your eyes. Can you tell me what you just imagined?

    Client: Well, I pictured myself with a middle-aged man who asked me if I wanted to lifeguard this summer. Naturally I told him yes.

Joan's imagery report was specific in terms of the actions and dialogue, but she didn't describe much about the man, so the counselor **will probe for more details.**

8. *Counselor:* OK, fine. What else did you imagine about the man? You mentioned his age. What was he wearing? Any physical characteristics you can recall?

    Client: Well, he was about 35 [a 16-year-old's impression of "middle age" is different from a 30-, 40-, or 50-year-old person's definition], he was wearing shorts and a golf shirt—you see, we were by the pool. That's about it.

Joan was able to describe the setting and the man's dress but no other physical characteristics, so the counselor **will suggest that Joan add this to the next practice attempt.**

9. *Counselor:* OK, so you were able to see what he was wearing and also the setting where he was talking to you. I'd like to try another practice

with this same scene. Just imagine everything you did before, only this time try to imagine even more details about how this man actually looks. [Counselor presents the same scene, which goes on until Joan raises her finger.]

In response 10, the counselor will again **query Joan about the details of her imagery.**

10. *Counselor:* OK, let's stop. What else did you imagine this time about this person or the situation?

    Client: Well, he was wearing white shorts and a blue shirt. He was a tall man and very tanned. He had dark hair, blue eyes, and had sunglasses on. He was also barefoot. We were standing on the pool edge. The water was blue and the sun was out and it felt hot.

In response 11, the counselor will **try to determine how comfortable Joan is with imagery** *and whether more practice scenes are necessary.*

11. *Counselor:* OK, that's great. Looks like you were able to imagine colors and temperature—like the sun feeling hot. How comfortable do you feel now with this process?

    Client: Oh, I like it. It was easier the second time you described the scene. I put more into it. I like to imagine this anyway.

In response 12, the counselor decides Joan can move ahead and **initiates development of treatment scenes.**

12. *Counselor:* Well, I believe we can go on now. Our next step is to come up with some scenes that describe the situations you find yourself in now with respect to participation in math class.

    Client: And then I'll imagine them in the same way?

The counselor sets the stage to **obtain all the necessary information to develop treatment scenes.** *Note the emphasis in response 13 on Joan's* **participation** *in this process.*

13. *Counselor:* That's right. Once we work out the details of these scenes, you'll imagine each scene as you just did. Now we have sort of a series of things we need to discuss in setting up the scenes in a way that makes it easiest for you to imagine, so I'll be asking you some questions. Your input is very valuable here to both of us.

    Client: OK, shoot.

In response 14, the counselor **asks Joan whether she would rather imagine herself or someone else** *as the model.*

14. *Counselor:* Well, first of all, in that practice

scene I asked you to imagine someone else. Now, you did that, but you were also able to picture yourself from the report you gave me. In using your class scenes, which do you feel would be easiest and least stressful for you to imagine—yourself going through the scene or someone else, maybe someone similar to you, but another person? [Gives Joan time to think.]

Client (pauses): Well, that's hard to say. I think it would be easier for me to imagine myself, but it might be a little less stressful to imagine someone else . . . . [Pauses again.] I think I'd like to try using myself.

In the next response, the counselor **reinforces Joan's choice and also points out the flexibility of implementing the procedure.**

15. *Counselor:* That's fine. And besides, as you know, nothing is that fixed. If we get into this and that doesn't feel right and you want to imagine someone else, we'll change.

Client: Okey-dokey.

In response 16, the counselor **introduces the idea of a coping model.**

16. *Counselor:* Also, sometimes it's hard to imagine yourself doing something perfectly to start with, so when we get into this, I might describe a situation where you might have a little trouble but not much. That may seem more realistic to you. What do you think?

Client: That seems reasonable. I know what you mean. It's like learning to drive a car. In Driver's Ed, we take one step at a time.

In response 17, the counselor **will pose the option of individualizing the scenes** *or using* **standardized scenes.**

17. *Counselor:* You've got the idea. Now we have another choice also in the scenes we use. We can work out scenes just for you that are tailored to your situation, or we can use scenes on a cassette tape I have that have been standardized for many students who want to improve their class-participation skills. Which sounds like the best option to you?

Client: I really don't know. Does it really make a difference?

It is not that uncommon for a client not to know which route to pursue. In the next response, the counselor will **indicate a preference** *and check it out with Joan.*

18. *Counselor:* Probably not, Joan. If you don't have a choice at this point, you might later. My preference would be to tailor-make the scenes we use here in the session. Then, if you like, you could use the taped scenes to practice with at home later on. How does that sound to you?

Client: It sounds good, like maybe we could use both.

In responses 19 and 20, the counselor asks Joan to **identify situations in which Joan desires to increase these skills.** *This is somewhat a review of goal behavior described in Chapter 9.*

19. *Counselor:* Yes, I think we can. Now let's concentrate on getting some of the details we need to make up the scenes we'll use in our sessions. First of all, let's go over the situations in math class in which you want to work on these skills.

Client: Well, it's some of those things we talked about earlier, like being called on, going to the board, and so on.

Next the counselor **explores whether Joan prefers a very general description or a very specific one.** *Sometimes this makes a difference in how the person imagines.*

20. *Counselor:* OK, Joan, how much detail would you like me to give you when I describe a scene—a little detail, to let you fill in the rest, or do you want me to describe pretty completely what you should imagine?

Client: Maybe somewhere in between. I can fill in a lot, but I need to know what to fill in.

In response 21, the counselor **is asking about the specific situations** *in which Joan has trouble participating in her math class.*

21. *Counselor:* OK, let's fill out our description a little more. We're talking about situations you confront in your math class. I remember four situations in which you wanted to increase these skills—you want to answer more when Mr. _____ calls on you, volunteer more answers, go to the board, and tell Mr. _____ you want to work the problems yourself after you ask for an explanation. Any others, Joan?

Client: I can't think of any offhand.

In responses 22 through 27, the counselor asks Joan to **identify the desired behaviors for these situations.** *Again, much of this is a review of identifying outcome goals (Chapter 9).*

22. *Counselor:* OK, so we've got about four different situations. Let's take each of these separately. For each situation, can we think of what you would like to do in the situation—like when Mr. _____ calls on you, for instance?

Client: Well, I'd like to give him the answer instead of saying nothing or saying "I don't know."

23. *Counselor:* OK, good. And if you did give him

the answer—especially when you do know it—how would you feel?

Client: Good, probably relieved.

24. *Counselor:* OK. Now what about volunteering answers?

Client: Well, Mr. _____ usually asks who has the answer to this; then he calls on people who raise their hand. I usually never raise my hand even when I do know the answer, so I need to just raise my hand and, when he calls on me, give the answer. I need to speak clearly, too. I think sometimes my voice is too soft to hear.

25. *Counselor:* OK, now, how could you tell Mr. _____ to let you work out the problems yourself?

Client: Well, just go up to him when we have a work period and tell him the part I'm having trouble with and ask him to explain it.

26. *Counselor:* So you need to ask him for just an explanation and let him know you want to do the work.

Client: Yup.

27. *Counselor:* OK, now, what about going to the board?

Client: Well, I do go up. But I always feel like a fool. I get distracted by the rest of the class so I hardly ever finish the problem. Then he lets me go back to my seat even though I didn't finish it. I need to concentrate more so I can get through the entire problem on the board.

Now that the content of the scenes has been developed, the counselor asks Joan to **arrange the four scenes in a hierarchy.**

28. *Counselor:* OK, so we've got four different situations in your math class where you want to improve your participation in some way. Let's take these four situations and arrange them in an order. Could you select the situation that right now is easiest for you and least stressful to you and rank the rest in terms of difficulty and degree of stress?

Client: Sure, let me think. . . . Well, the easiest thing to do out of all of these would be to tell Mr. _____ I want to work out the problems myself. Then I guess it would be answering when he calls on me and then going to the board. I have a lot of trouble with volunteering answers, so that would be hardest for me.

The counselor emphasizes the **flexibility of the hierarchy** *and provides* **general instructions to Joan about how they will work with these scenes.**

29. *Counselor:* OK. Now, this order can change. At any point if you feel it isn't right, we can reorder these situations. What we will do is to take one situation at a time, starting with the easiest one,

and I'll describe it to you in terms of the way you want to handle it and ask you to imagine it. So the first scene will involve you telling Mr. _____ what you need explained in order to work the problems yourself.

Client: So we do this just like we did at the beginning?

The counselor will **precede the scene presentation with very specific instructions** *to Joan.*

30. *Counselor:* Right. Just sit back, close your eyes, and relax . . . . [Gives Joan a few minutes to do so.] Now remember, as I describe the scene, you are going to imagine yourself in the situation. Try to use all your senses in your imagination—in other words, get into it. When you have a very vivid picture, raise your index finger. Keep imagining the scene until I give a signal to stop. OK?

Client: Yeah.

The counselor **presents the first scene in Joan's hierarchy slowly** *and with ample pauses to give Joan time to generate the images.*

31. *Counselor:* OK, Joan, picture yourself in math class . . . . [Pause] Mr. _____ has just finished explaining how to solve for x and y. . . . Now he has assigned problems to you and has given you a work period. . . . You are starting to do the problems and you realize there is some part of the equation you can't figure out. You take your worksheet and get up out of your seat and go to Mr. _____'s desk. You are telling Mr. _____ what part of the equation you're having trouble with. You explain to him you don't want him to solve the problem, just to explain the missing part. Now you're feeling good that you were able to go up and ask him for an explanation. [The counselor waits for about 10 seconds after Joan signals with her finger.]

The counselor **signals Joan to stop** *and in responses 32 through 35* **solicits Joan's reactions** *about the imagery.*

32. *Counselor:* OK, Joan, open your eyes now. What did you imagine?

Client: Well, it was pretty easy. I just imagined myself going up to Mr. _____ and telling him I needed more explanation but that I wanted to find the answers myself.

33. *Counselor:* OK, so you were able to get a pretty vivid picture?

Client: Yes, very much so.

34. *Counselor:* What were your feelings during this —particularly as you imagined yourself?

Client: I felt pretty calm. It didn't really bother me.

35. *Counselor:* OK, so imagining yourself wasn't too stressful. Did I give you enough time before I signaled to stop?
Client: Well, probably. Although I think I could have gone on a little longer.

On the basis of Joan's response about the length of the first scene, the counselor **will modify the length during the next presentation.**

36. *Counselor:* OK, I'll give you a little more time the next time.

Before the counselor presents the treatment scenes the second time, the counselor explores whether the client would like to use **verbal summary codes** *or to* **personalize the treatment scenes.**

37. *Counselor:* Joan, there are two techniques that you can use to enhance your imagery scene of Mr. _____'s math class. One technique is to describe briefly the behavior you want to do and the situation in Mr. _____'s class when you will perform the behavior. All that you are doing is just describing the scene in your own words. This process can help you remember what to do. With the other technique, you can change the scene or elaborate on the scene in any way as long as you still imagine engaging in the behaviors you want to do. Do you have any questions about these two techniques?
Client: You think these techniques might help me imagine the scene better?

38. *Counselor:* That's right. Is there one technique you think might be more helpful to you?
Client: Yes, I think that for me to describe the scene in my own words might work better for me. It might help me to remember better what to do.

39. *Counselor:* OK, for the first scene, what verbal summary or description would you use?
Client: Well—after Mr. _____ explains how to solve for *x* and *y* and assigns problems, I might find something I can't figure out. I get out of my seat and go up to Mr. _____ and tell him I need more explanation but I want to find the answer myself.

40. *Counselor:* That's great, Joan!

The counselor **presents the same scene again.** *Usually each scene is presented* **a minimum of two times** *by the counselor or on a tape recorder. If the client has chosen one or both treatment-scene enhancement techniques, instruct the client on the technique with each scene.*

41. *Counselor:* Let's try it again. I'll present the same scene, and I'll give you more time after you signal to me you have a strong picture. [Presents the same scene again and checks out Joan's reactions after the second presentation.]

After the counselor-presented scenes, the counselor **asks Joan to self-direct her own practice.** *This also occurs a minimum of two times on each scene.*

42. *Counselor:* You seem pretty comfortable now in carrying out this situation the way you want to. This time instead of my describing the scene orally to you, I'd like you just to go through the scene on your own—sort of a mental practice without my assistance.
Client: OK. [Pauses to do this for several minutes.]

43. *Counselor:* OK, how did that feel?
Client: It was pretty easy even without your instructions, and I think I can see where I can actually do this now with Mr. _____.

The other scenes in the hierarchy are worked through in the same manner.

44. *Counselor:* Good. Now we will work through the other three scenes in the same manner, sticking with each one until you can perform your desired behaviors in your imagination pretty easily. [The other three situations in the hierarchy are worked through.]

45. *Counselor:* Well, how do you feel now that we've gone over every scene?
Client: Pretty good. I never thought that my imagination would help me in math class!

After the hierarchy has been completed, the counselor **picks scenes to practice at random.** *This is a way to see how easily the client can perform the scene when it is not presented in the order of the hierarchy.*

46. *Counselor:* Well, sometimes imagining yourself doing something helps you learn how to do it in the actual situation. Now I'd like to just pick a scene here at random and present it to you and have you imagine it again. [Selects a scene from the hierarchy at random and describes it.]
Client: That was pretty easy, too.

The counselor **initiates homework practice** *for Joan.*

47. *Counselor:* OK, I just wanted to give you a chance to imagine a scene when I took something out of the order we worked with today. I believe you are ready to carry out this imagination practice on your own during the week.
Client: Is this where I use the tapes?

The **purpose of homework** *is explained to Joan.*

48. *Counselor:* Sure. This tape has a series of scenes dealing with verbal class participation. So instead of needing me to describe a scene, the tape can do this. I'd like you to practice with this daily, because daily practice will help you learn to participate more quickly and easily.
Client: So I just go over a scene the way we did today?

The counselor instructs Joan on **how to complete the homework practice.**

49. *Counselor:* Go over the scenes one at a time—maybe about four times for each scene. Make your imagination as vivid as possible. Also, each time you go over a scene, make a check on your log sheets. Indicate the time of day and place where you use this—also, the length of each practice. And after each practice session, rate the vividness of your imagery on this scale: 1 is not vivid and 5 is very vivid. How about summarizing what you will do for your homework?

Client: Yes. I just do what we did today and check the number of times I practice each scene and assign a number to the practice according to how strongly I imagined the scene.

At the termination of the session, the counselor **indicates that a follow-up on the homework** *will occur at their next meeting.*

50. *Counselor:* Right. And bring your log sheets in at our next meeting and we'll go over this homework then. OK? We had a really good session today. You worked hard. I'll see you next Tuesday.

LEARNING ACTIVITY #38: COVERT MODELING

As you may recall from reading the goals and subgoals of Ms. Weare (Chapter 9), one of her subgoals was to arrange a school conference with Freddie's teacher. Ms. Weare was going to use the conference to explain her new strategy in dealing with Freddie and request help and cooperation from the school. Specifically, Ms. Weare might point out that one of the initial consequences of her strategy might be an increase in Freddie's tardiness at school. Assume that Ms. Weare is hesitant to initiate the conference be-cause she is unsure about what to say during the meeting. Describe how you could use covert modeling to help Ms. Weare achieve this subgoal. Describe specifically how you would use (1) a rationale, (2) practice scenes, (3) development of treatment scenes, (4) application of treatment scenes, and (5) homework to help Ms. Weare in this objective. Feedback is provided; see whether some of your ideas are similar.

Feedback follows on page 373.

□ SUMMARY

Emotive imagery and covert modeling are procedures that may be useful when media modeling and live modeling are not feasible. These two strategies can be used without elaborate therapeutic aids or expensive equipment. Both strategies involve imagery, which makes the procedures quite easy for a client to practice in a self-directed manner. The capacity of clients to generate vivid images may be important for the overall effectiveness of emotive imagery and covert modeling. Assessment of client potential to engage in imagery is a necessary prerequisite before using either of these procedures. Assuming that clients can produce clear images, counselors may use emotive imagery to deal with fears or discomfort or covert modeling to promote desired responses.

POSTEVALUATION

PART ONE

According to Objective One, you should be able to identify accurately six of the seven steps of emotive imagery represented in written examples of counselor leads. For each of the following seven counselor leads, write down which part of emotive imagery the counselor is implementing. More than one counselor lead may be associated with any part of the procedure, and the leads given here are not in any particu-lar order. The five major parts of emotive imagery are as follows:

1. Rationale
2. Determining the client's potential to use imagery
3. Developing imagery scenes
4. Imagery-scene practice training
5. Homework and follow-up

Feedback follows the Postevaluation on page 374.
(continued)

1. "Can you think of several scenes you could imagine that give you calm and positive feelings? Supply as many details as you can. You can use these scenes later to focus on instead of the anxiety."
2. "It's important that you practice with this. Try to imagine these scenes at least several times each day."
3. "This procedure can help you control your anxiety. By imagining very pleasurable scenes, you can block out some of the fear."
4. "Let's see whether you feel that it's easy to imagine something. Close your eyes, sit back, and visualize anything that makes you feel relaxed."
5. "Now, select one of these scenes you've practiced. Imagine this very intensely. I'm going to apply pressure to your arm, but just focus on your imaginary scene."
6. "What we will do, if you feel that imagination is easy for you, is to develop some scenes that are easy for you to visualize and that make you feel relaxed. Then we'll practice having you focus on these scenes while also trying to block out fear."
7. "Now I'd like you just to practice these scenes we've developed. Take one scene at a time, sit back, and relax. Practice imagining this scene for about 30 seconds. I will tell you when the time is up."

PART TWO

Objective Two asks you to demonstrate 10 out of 13 steps of emotive imagery with a role-play client. You or an observer can rate your performance, assisted by the Interview Checklist for Emotive Imagery following this Postevaluation.

PART THREE

Objective Three asks you to describe how you would use the five components of covert modeling with a simulated client case. Use the case of Mr. Brown (Chapter 7) and his stated goal of wanting to decrease his worrying about retirement and increase his positive thoughts about retiring, particularly in his work setting. Describe how you would use a rationale, practice scenes, developing treatment scenes, applying treatment scenes, and homework to help Mr. Brown do this. Feedback follows the Postevaluation.

PART FOUR

Objective Four asks you to demonstrate at least 22 out of 28 steps associated with covert modeling with a role-play client. The client might take the part of someone who wants to acquire certain skills or to perform certain activities. Use the Interview Checklist for Covert Modeling on page 369 to help you assess your interview.

INTERVIEW CHECKLIST FOR EMOTIVE IMAGERY

Instructions: In a role-play counselor/client interview, determine which of the following counselor leads or questions were demonstrated. Indicate by a check the leads used by the counselor. A few examples of counselor leads are presented in the right column.

Item	Examples of counselor leads
I. Rationale	
_____ 1. Counselor describes purpose of emotive imagery.	"The procedure is called emotive imagery because you can emote pleasant thoughts or images in situations that evoke fear, pain, tension, anxiety, or routine boredom. The procedure helps you block your discomfort or reduce the anxiety that you experience in the problem situation. The technique involves focusing on imaginary scenes that please you and make you feel relaxed while in the uncomfortable situation. This procedure works because it is extremely difficult for you to feel pleasant, calm, happy, secure, or whatever other emotion is involved in the scene and anxious (tense, fearful, stressed) at the same time. These emotions are incompatible."
_____ 2. Counselor gives an overview of procedure.	"What we will do is, first, see how you feel about engaging in imagery and look at the details of the scene you used. Then, we will decide whether emotive imagery is a procedure we want to use. If we decide to use it,

(continued)

POSTEVALUATION (continued)

Item	Examples of counselor leads
	we will develop scenes that make you feel calm and good and generate positive feelings for you. We will practice using the scenes we have developed and try to rehearse using those scenes in a simulated fashion. Later, you will apply and practice using the scene in the real situation. Do you have any questions about my explanation?''
_____ 3. Counselor assesses client's willingness to try strategy.	''Would you like to go ahead and give this a try now?''

II. Assessment of Client's Imagery Potential

_____ 4. Counselor instructs client to engage in imagery that elicits good feelings and calmness.	''Close your eyes, sit back, and relax. Visualize a scene or event that makes you feel relaxed and pleasant. Select something you really enjoy and feel good about. Try to be aware of all your sensations in the scene.''
_____ 5. After 30 seconds to a minute, the counselor probes to ascertain the sensory vividness of the client's imagined scene (colors, sounds, movement, temperature, smell). Counselor asks client's feelings about imagery and about ''getting into'' the scene (feeling good with imaginal process).	''Describe the scene to me.'' ''What sensations did you experience while picturing the scene?'' ''What temperature, colors, sounds, smells, and motions did you experience in the scene?'' ''How do you feel about the imagery?'' ''How involved could you get with the scene?''
_____ 6. Counselor discusses with client the decision to continue or discontinue emotive imagery. Decision is based on client's attitude (feelings about imagery) and imaginal vividness.	''You seem to feel good with the imagery and are able to picture a scene vividly. We can go ahead now and develop some scenes just for you.'' ''Perhaps another strategy that would reduce tension without imagery would be better, since it is hard for you to 'get into' a scene.''

III. Development of Imagery Scenes

| _____ 7. Counselor and client develop at least two scenes that promote positive feelings for client and involve many sensations (sound, color, temperature, motion, and smell). | ''What I would like to do now is to develop an inventory of scenes or situations that promote calmness, tranquility, and enjoyment for you. We want to have scenes that will have as much sensory detail as possible for you, so that you can experience color, smell, temperature, touch, sound, and motion. Later, we will use the scenes to focus on instead of anxiety. What sort of scenes can you really get into?'' |

IV. Practice of Imagery Scene

_____ 8. Counselor instructs client to practice focusing on the scene for about 30 seconds.	''Take one of the scenes, close your eyes, sit back, and relax. Practice or hold this scene for about 30 seconds, picturing as much sensory detail as possible. I will cue you when the time is up.''
_____ 9. Counselor instructs client to practice focusing on scene with simulated discomfort or anxiety.	''Let us attempt to simulate or create the problem situation and to use the scenes. While I squeeze your arm to have you feel pain, focus on one of the imagery scenes we have developed.'' ''While I describe the feared situation or scene to you, focus on the scene.''
_____10. Counselor assesses client's reaction after simulated practice.	''How did that feel?'' ''What effects did my describing the discomforting situation'' (continued)

Item	Examples of counselor leads
	ation [my application of pain] have on your relaxation?" "Rate your ability to focus on the scene with the discomfort." "How comfortable did you feel when you imagined this fearful situation then?"

V. Homework and Follow-up

Item	Examples of counselor leads
____11. Counselor instructs client to apply emotive imagery *in vivo*.	"For homework, apply the emotive imagery scenes to the discomforting situation. Focus on the scene as vividly as possible while you are experiencing the activity or situation."
____12. Counselor instructs client to record use of emotive imagery and to record level of discomfort or anxiety on log sheets.	"After each time you use emotive imagery, record the situation, the day, the time, and your general reaction on this log. For each occasion that you use imagery, record also your level of discomfort or anxiety, using a 5-point scale, with 5 equal to maximum discomfort and 1 equal to minimum discomfort."
____13. Counselor arranges a follow-up session.	"Let's get together again in two weeks to see how your practice is going and to go over your homework log."

Observer comments: _____

INTERVIEW CHECKLIST FOR COVERT MODELING

Instructions: Determine which of the following leads the counselor used in the interview. Check the leads used.

Item	Examples of counselor leads
I. Rationale	
____ 1. Counselor describes purpose of strategy.	"This strategy can help you learn how to discuss your prison record in a job interview. I will coach you on some things you could say. As we go over this, gradually you will feel as if you can handle this situation when it comes up in an actual interview."
____ 2. Counselor provides overview of strategy.	"We will be relying on your imagination a lot in this process. I'll be describing certain scenes and asking you to close your eyes and imagine that you are observing the situation I describe to you as vividly as you can."
____ 3. Counselor confirms client's willingness to use strategy.	"Would you like to give this a try now?"
II. Practice Scenes	
____ 4. Counselor instructs client to sit back, close eyes, and relax in preparation for imagining practice scenes.	"Just sit back, relax, and close your eyes."
____ 5. Counselor describes a practice scene unrelated to goal and instructs client to imagine scene as counselor describes it and to raise index finger when scene is vividly imagined.	"As I describe this scene, try to imagine it very intensely. Imagine the situation as vividly as possible. When you feel you have a vivid picture, raise your index finger."
____ 6. After client indicates vivid imagery, counselor instructs client to open eyes and describe what was imagined during scene.	"OK, now let's stop—you can open your eyes. Tell me as much as you can about what you just imagined."

(continued)

POSTEVALUATION (continued)

Item	Examples of counselor leads
____ 7. Counselor probes for additional details about scene to obtain a very specific description from client.	"Did you imagine the color of the room? What did the people look like? Were there any noticeable odors around you? How were you feeling?"
____ 8. Counselor suggests ways for client to attend to additional details during subsequent practice.	"Let's do another scene. This time try to imagine not only what you see but what you hear, smell, feel, and touch."
____ 9. Counselor initiates additional practices of one scene or introduces practice of new scene until client is comfortable with the novelty and is able to provide a detailed description of imagery.	"Let go over another scene. We'll do this for a while until you feel pretty comfortable with this."
____10. After practice scenes, counselor:	
____a. Decides to move on to developing treatment scenes.	"OK, this seems to be going pretty easily for you, so we will go on now."
____b. Decides that relaxation or additional imagery training is necessary.	"I believe before we go on it might be useful to try to help you relax a little more. We can use muscle relaxation for this purpose."
____c. Decides to terminate covert modeling because of inadequate client imagery.	"Judging from this practice, I believe another approach would be more helpful where you can actually see someone do this."

III. Developing Treatment Scenes

____11. Counselor and client decide on appropriate characteristics of model to be used in treatment scenes, including:	
____a. Identity of model (client or someone else).	"As you imagine this scene, you can imagine either yourself or someone else in this situation. Which would be easier for you to imagine?"
____b. Coping or mastery model.	"Sometimes it's easier to imagine someone who doesn't do this perfectly. What do you think?"
____c. Single or multiple models.	"We can have you imagine just one other person— someone like yourself—or several other people."
____d. Specific characteristics of model to maximize client/model similarity.	"Let's talk over the specific type of person you will imagine."
____12. Counselor and client specify:	"We have two options in developing the scenes you will imagine. We can discuss different situations and develop the scenes just to fit you, or else we can use some standardized scenes that might apply to anyone going through a job interview with a prison record. What is your preference?"
____a. Individualized scenes.	
____b. Standardized scenes.	
____13. Counselor and client decide to use either:	"On the basis of these situations you've just described, I can present them to you in one of two ways. One way is to give you a general description and leave it up to you to fill in the details. Or I can be very detailed and tell you specifically what to imagine. Which approach do you think would be best for you?"
____a. General descriptions of scenes.	
____b. Specific, detailed descriptions of scenes.	
____14. Counselor and client develop specific ingredients to be used in scenes. Ingredients include:	"Let's decide the kinds of things that will go in each scene."
____a. Situations or context in which behaviors should occur.	"In the scene in which you are interviewing for a job, go over the type of job you might seek and the kind of employer who would be hard to talk to."
____b. Behaviors and coping methods to be demonstrated by model.	"Now, what you want to do in this situation is to discuss your record calmly, explaining what happened and (continued)

Item	Examples of counselor leads
	emphasizing that your record won't interfere with your job performance."
____c. Favorable outcome of scene, such as:	
____1. Favorable client self-initiated action.	"At the end of the scene you might want to imagine you have discussed your record calmly without getting defensive."
____2. Client self-reinforcement.	"At the end of the scene, congratulate yourself or encourage yourself for being able to discuss your record."
____15. Counselor and client generate descriptions of multiple scenes.	"OK, now, the job interview is one scene. Let's develop other scenes where you feel it's important to be able to discuss your record—for example, in establishing a closer relationship with a friend."

IV. Applying Treatment Scenes

Item	Examples of counselor leads
____16. Counselor and client arrange multiple scenes in a hierarchy for scene presentation according to:	"Now I'd like you to take these six scenes we've developed and arrange them in an order. Start with the situation that you feel most comfortable with and that is easiest for you to discuss your record in now. End with the situation that is most difficult and gives you the most discomfort or tension."
____a. Client degree of discomfort in situation.	
____b. Degree of difficulty or complexity of situation.	
____17. Counselor precedes scene presentation with instructions to client, including:	"I'm going to tell you now what to do when the scene is presented."
____a. Instructions to sit back, relax, close eyes.	"First, just sit back, close your eyes, and relax."
____b. Instructions on whom to imagine.	"Now come up with an image of the person you're going to imagine."
____c. Instructions to imagine intensely, using as many senses as possible.	"As I describe the scene, imagine it as vividly as possible. Use all your senses—sight, smell, touch, and so on."
____d. Instructions to raise index finger when vivid imagery occurs.	"When you start to imagine very vividly, raise your finger."
____e. Instructions to hold imagery until counselor signals to stop.	"And hold that vivid image until I tell you when to stop."
____18. Counselor presents one scene at a time, by describing the scene orally to client or with a tape recorder.	"Here is the first scene. . . . Imagine the employer is now asking you why you got so far behind in school. Imagine that you are explaining what happened in a calm voice."
____19. Duration of each scene is determined individually for client and is held until client imagines model performing desired behavior as completely as possible (perhaps 20–30 seconds).	"You should be able to imagine yourself saying all you want to about your record before I stop you."
____20. After first scene presentation, counselor solicits client reactions about:	
____a. Rate of delivery and duration of scene.	"How did the length of the scene seem to you?"
____b. Clearness and vividness of client imagery.	"How intense were your images? What did you imagine?"
____c. Degree of discomfort or pleasantness of scene.	"How did you feel while doing this?"
____21. On basis of client reactions to first scene presentation:	
____a. Scene is presented again as is.	"I'm going to present this same scene again."
____b. Scene or manner of presentation is revised before second presentation.	"Based on what you've said. let's change the type of employer. Also, I'll give you more time to imagine this the next time."

(continued)

POSTEVALUATION (continued)

Item	Examples of counselor leads
____c. Scene order in hierarchy is changed and another scene is presented next.	"Perhaps we need to switch the order of this scene and use this other one first."
____d. Relaxation or discussion of client discomfort precedes another presentation of scene.	"Let's talk about your discomfort."
____22. Imagery enhancement techniques explained to client:	
____a. Verbal summary codes.	"You can briefly describe the scene in your own words, which can help you remember the behaviors to perform in the situation."
____b. Personalization or elaboration of treatment scene.	"You can change or elaborate on the scene in any way as long as you still imagine the behavior you want to do."
____23. Each scene is presented a minimum of two times by counselor or on tape recorder.	"Ok, now I'm going to present the same scene one or two more times."
____24. Following counselor presentations of scene, client repeats scene at least twice in a self-directed manner.	"This time I'd like you to present the scene to yourself while imagining it, without relying on me to describe it."
____25. After each scene in hierarchy is presented and imagined satisfactorily, counselor presents some scenes to client in a random order, following steps 18–20.	"Now I'm just going to pick a scene at random and describe it while you imagine it."

V. Homework

____26. Counselor instructs client to practice scenes daily outside session and explains purpose of daily practice.	"During the week, I'd like you to take these cards where we've made a written description of these scenes and practice the scenes on your own. This will help you acquire this behavior more easily and quickly."
____27. Instructions for homework include:	
____a. What to do.	"Just go over one scene at a time — make your imagination as vivid as possible."
____b. How often to do it.	"Go over this five times daily."
____c. When and where to do it.	"Go over this two times at home and three times at school."
____d. A method for self-observation of homework completion.	"Each time you go over the scene, make a tally on your log sheet. Also, after each practice session, rate the intensity of your imagery on this scale."
____28. Counselor arranges for a follow-up after completion of some amount of homework.	"Bring these sheets next week so we can discuss your practices and see what we need to do as the next step."

Observer comments: _____

FEEDBACK #38: COVERT MODELING

1. *Rationale*

First, you would explain that covert modeling could help Ms. Weare find ways to express herself and could help her practice expressing herself before initiating the actual conference. Second, you would briefly describe the strategy, emphasizing that she will be practicing her role and responses in the school conference, using her imagination.

2. *Practice Scenes*

You would explain that it is helpful to see how she feels about practicing through her imagination. You would select several unrelated scenes, such as imagining someone coming to her home, imagining an old friend calling her, or imagining a new television show about a policewoman. You would present one practice scene and instruct Ms. Weare first to close her eyes, imagine the scene intensely, and signal to you with her finger when she has a strong picture in her mind. After this point, you could tell her to open her eyes and to describe the details of what she imagined. You might suggest additional details and present the same scene again or present a different scene. If Ms. Weare is able to use imagery easily and comfortably, you could move on to developing the actual treatment scenes.

3. *Developing Treatment Scenes*

At this point, you would seek Ms. Weare's input about certain aspects of the scenes to be used as treatment scenes. Specifically, you would decide who would be used as the model, whether individualized or standardized scenes would be used, and whether Ms. Weare felt she could benefit from general or specific scenes. Our preference would be to use pretty specific, individualized scenes in which Ms. Weare imagines herself as the model, since she will ultimately be carrying out the action. Next, you should specify the three ingredients of the scenes: (1) the situation in which the behaviors should occur, (2) the behaviors to be demonstrated, and (3) a favorable outcome. For example, the scenes could include Ms. Weare calling the teacher to set up the conference, beginning the conference, explaining her strategy in the conference, and ending the conference. Specific examples of things she could say would be included in each scene. Favorable outcomes might take the form of covert self-praise or of relief from stressful, anxious feelings.

4. *Applying Treatment Scenes*

After all the treatment scenes have been developed, Ms. Weare would arrange them in a hierarchy from least to most difficult. Starting with the first scene in the hierarchy, you would again instruct Ms. Weare about how to imagine. After the first scene presentation, you would obtain Ms. Weare's reactions to the clearness of her imagery, the duration of the scene, and so on. Any needed revisions could be incorporated before a second presentation of the same scene. You would also encourage Ms. Weare to develop a verbal summary code for each scene after the initial presentation of that scene. You would present each scene to Ms. Weare several times; then have her self-direct her own scene-imagining several times. After all the scenes in the hierarchy had been covered adequately, Ms. Weare would be ready for homework.

5. *Homework*

You would instruct Ms. Weare to continue to practice the scenes in her imagination outside the session. A follow-up should be arranged. You should be sure that Ms. Weare understands how many times to practice and how such practice can benefit her. Ms. Weare might record her practice sessions on log sheets. She could also call in and verbalize the scenes, using a phone-mate.

☐ SUGGESTED READINGS

Bornstein, P. H., & Devine, D. A. (1980). Covert modeling-hypnosis in the treatment of obesity. *Psychotherapy: Theory, Research and Practice, 17,* 272–275.

Bry, A., & Bair, M. (1979). *Visualization: Directing the movies of your mind.* New York: Barnes & Noble.

Cautela, J. R. (1976). The present status of covert modeling. *Journal of Behavior Therapy and Experimental Psychiatry, 6,* 323–326.

Cautela, J. R. (1977). *Behavior analysis forms for clinical intervention.* Champaign, IL: Research Press.

Clarke, J. C., & Jackson, J. A. (1983). *Hypnosis and behavior therapy.* New York: Springer.

Horan, J. J. (1976). Coping with inescapable discomfort through in vivo emotive imagery. In J. D. Krumboltz & C. E. Thoresen (Eds.), *Counseling methods.* New York: Holt, Rinehart and Winston.

Jarvinen, P. J., & Gold, S. R. (1981). Imagery as an aid in reducing depression. *Journal of Clinical Psychology, 37,* 523–529.

Kazdin, A. E. (1979a). Effects of covert modeling and coding of modeled stimuli on assertive behavior. *Behaviour Research and Therapy, 17,* 53–61.

Kazdin, A. E. (1979b). Imagery elaboration and self-efficacy in covert modeling treatment of unassertive behavior. *Journal of Consulting and Clinical Psychology, 47,* 725–733.

Kazdin, A. E. (1980). Covert and overt rehearsal and elaboration during treatment in development of assertive behavior. *Behaviour Research and Therapy, 18,* 191–201.

Kazdin, A. E., & Mascitelli, S. (1982b). Covert and overt rehearsal and homework practice in developing assertiveness. *Journal of Consulting and Clinical Psychology, 50,* 250–258.

Lazarus, A. A. (1982). *Personal enrichment through imagery,* Workbook [Audiotape]. New York: BMA Audio Cassettes.

Lyles, J. N., Burish, T. G., Krozely, M. G., & Oldham, R. K. (1982). Efficacy of relaxation training and guided imagery in reducing the aversiveness of cancer chemotherapy. *Journal of Consulting and Clinical Psychology, 50,* 509–524.

Pickett, C., & Cloum, G. A. (1982). Comparative treatment strategies and their interaction with locus of control in the reduction of post surgical pain and anxiety. *Journal of Consulting and Clinical Psychology, 50,* 439–441.

Sheikh, A. A. (Ed.). (1983). *Imagery: Current theory, research and application.* New York: Wiley.

Shorr, J. E., Sobel-Whittington, G., Robin, P., & Connella, J. A. (Eds.). (1984). *Imagery.* Vol. 3: *Theoretical and clinical applications.* New York: Plenum.

Tearnan, B. H., Lahey, B. B., Thompson, J. R., & Hammer, D. (1982). The role of coping self-instructions combined with covert modeling in specific fear reduction. *Cognitive Therapy & Research, 6,* 185–190.

Varni, J. W. (1981). Self-regulation techniques in the management of chronic arthritic pain in hemophilia. *Behavior Therapy, 12,* 185–194.

FEEDBACK: POSTEVALUATION

PART ONE

1. Instructing the client to *develop imagery scenes.* These are used as the scenes to focus on to block the unpleasant sensation.
2. Part of *homework*—in vivo application of imagery.
3. *Rationale*—giving the client a reason for emotive imagery.
4. The counselor is determining *the client's potential to use imagery.*
5. *Imagery-scene practice*—with a pain-provoking situation.
6. *Rationale*—the counselor is giving an overview of the procedure.
7. *Imagery-scene practice*—the client is trained to imagine the scenes very vividly before using them in simulation of anxiety-provoking situations.

PART TWO

Rate your performance with the Interview Checklist for Emotive Imagery found after the Postevaluation.

PART THREE

Rationale

First you would give Mr. Brown an explanation of covert modeling. You would briefly describe the process to him and explain how using his imagination to "see" someone doing something could help him perform his desired responses.

(continued)

Practice Scenes

Next you would present a couple of unrelated practice scenes. You would instruct Mr. Brown to close his eyes, relax, and imagine the scene as you describe it. When Mr. Brown signals he is imagining the scene, you would stop and query him about what he imagined. You might suggest additional details for him to imagine during another practice scene. Assuming Mr. Brown feels relaxed and can generate vivid images, you would go on to develop treatment scenes.

Developing Treatment Scenes

You and Mr. Brown would specify certain components to be included in the treatment scenes, including the identity of the model (Mr. Brown or someone else), type of model (coping or mastery), single or multiple models, and specific characteristics of the model to maximize client/model similarity. Next you would decide whether to use individualized or standardized scenes; perhaps in Mr. Brown's case, his own scenes might work best. You would also need to decide how detailed the scene should be. In Mr. Brown's case, a scene might include some examples of positive thoughts and allow room for him to add his own. You and Mr. Brown would generate a list of scenes to be used, specifying:

1. The situation (which, for him, would be at work when the negative thoughts crop up).
2. The behavior and coping methods he would acquire (stopping interfering thoughts, generating positive thoughts about retirement, and getting back to his project at work).
3. Favorable outcomes (for Mr. Brown, this might be being able to get his work done on time).

Applying Treatment Scenes

You and Mr. Brown would arrange the scenes in order—starting with a work situation in which his thoughts are not as interfering and proceeding to situations in which they are most interfering. Starting with the first scene, you would give Mr. Brown specific instructions on imagining. Then you would present the scene to him and have him hold the scene in imagination for a few seconds after he signaled a strong image. After the scene presentation, you would get Mr. Brown's reactions to the scene and make any necessary revisions in duration, scene content, order in the hierarchy, and so on. At this time Mr. Brown could either develop a verbal summary code or personalize the scene by changing or elaborating on it in some way. The same scene would be presented to Mr. Brown at least one more time, followed by several practices in which he goes through the scene without your assistance. After you had worked through all scenes in the hierarchy, you would present scenes to him in a random order.

Homework

After each scene presentation in the session, you would instruct Mr. Brown to practice the scenes daily outside the session. A follow-up on this homework should be arranged.

PART FOUR

Assess your interview or have someone else assess it, using the Interview Checklist for Covert Modeling on pages 369–372.

COGNITIVE MODELING
AND PROBLEM SOLVING

FIFTEEN

Most systems of therapy recognize the importance of overt behavior change *and* cognitive and affective, or covert, behavior change. In recent years, more attention and effort have been directed toward developing and evaluating procedures aimed at modifying thoughts, attitudes, and beliefs. These procedures come under the broad umbrella of cognitive therapy (Beck, 1970) or cognitive behavior modification (M. J. Mahoney, 1974; Meichenbaum, 1977). Several assumptions are made about cognitive-change procedures. One of the basic assumptions is that a person's thoughts and beliefs can contribute to maladaptive behavior. Another is that maladaptive behaviors can be altered by dealing directly with the person's beliefs, attitudes, or thoughts (Beck, 1970). Krumboltz and Thoresen (1976) point out that, in many instances, a client's unreasonable self-standards and negative self-thoughts can diminish the power of a treatment program. Attention to the client's beliefs and expectations may be necessary in order for other therapeutic strategies to be successful.

Four cognitive-change procedures are presented in this chapter and in Chapter 16. This chapter describes cognitive modeling and thought stopping, and Chapter 16 describes cognitive restructuring and stress inoculation. All four of these procedures are efforts to eliminate "cognitive pollution."

☐ OBJECTIVES

1. Using a simulated client case, describe how you would apply the seven components of cognitive modeling and self-instructional training.
2. Demonstrate 16 out of 21 steps of cognitive self-instructional modeling with a role-play client, using the Interview Checklist for Cognitive Modeling at the end of the chapter to rate your performance.
3. Identify which step of the problem-solving strategy is reflected in each of ten counselor responses accurately identifying at least eight of the ten examples.

4. Demonstrate 16 out of 19 steps of problem solving in a role-play interview, using the Interview Checklist for Problem Solving at the end of the chapter to assess your performance.

□ COGNITIVE MODELING WITH COGNITIVE SELF-INSTRUCTIONAL TRAINING

Cognitive modeling is a procedure in which counselors show people what to say to themselves while performing a task. Sarason (1973), who used cognitive modeling to decrease test anxiety in college students, views the procedure as "efforts by the model to make explicit for observers the process by which he arrives at the overt responses he makes" (p. 58). Sarason points out that the uniqueness of cognitive modeling is that "the implicit or covert responses related to performance" are modeled (p. 58). These implicit factors may be just as important as the overt responses of a modeled display.

Meichenbaum and Goodman (1971) used cognitive modeling to develop self-control in young, impulsive children. The children saw a person model a set of verbalizations and behaviors that characterized a strategy they could use in performing a task. For example, the model verbalized:

I have to remember to go slowly to get it right. Look carefully at this one (the standard), now look at these carefully (the variants). Is this one different? Yes, it has an extra leaf. Good, I can eliminate this one. Now, let's look at this one (another variant). I think it's this one, but let me first check the others. Good. I'm going slow and carefully. Okay, I think it's this one [p. 121].

The performance of the children exposed to this cognitive model was compared with that of a group in which the children received cognitive modeling plus self-instructional training (Meichenbaum & Goodman, 1971). In the latter group, in addition to viewing the model, the children were trained to produce the self-instructions the model emitted while performing the task. The children performed the task while instructing themselves as the model had done. Over the course of the practice trials, the children's self-verbalizations were faded from an overt to a covert level (p. 122). This group not only decreased decision time but also significantly reduced performance errors.

Kendall and Braswell (1982) found that problem children aged 8–12 years who received cognitive modeling with cognitive self-instructional training improved on teachers' ratings of self-control. Copeland (1981) recommends that client variables should be examined when designing self-instructional programs for impulsive children. For example, indexes of cognitive maturity such as age, IQ, cognitive style, and internal versus external attributions should be considered.

Cognitive self-instruction used in combination with rehearsal and homework practice was effective in developing assertive skills (Kazdin & Mascitelli, 1982a). Written symbolic models of self-instructional statements were designed to "help the person adopt a set to facilitate the assertive response, to identify the situation as one requiring action, and to prompt a specific response (e.g., 'This person always says things to me and I must answer them now to put an end to this,' or 'This is unfair, and I have to speak up for my rights')" (Kazdin & Mascitelli, 1982a, p. 350). Also, Kirby and Grimley (1986) have described how to use cognitive modeling and cognitive self-instructional training with attention deficit disorders.

Cognitive modeling plus self-instructional training was also used effectively to train hospitalized schizophrenics to alter their thinking, attention, and language behaviors (self-talk) while performing tasks (Meichenbaum & Cameron, 1973b). According to these authors, cognitive modeling with a self-instructional training strategy consists of five steps:

1. The counselor serves as the model (or a symbolic model can be used) and first performs the task while talking aloud to himself or herself.
2. The client performs the same task (as modeled by the counselor) while the counselor instructs the client aloud.
3. The client is instructed to perform the same task again while instructing himself or herself aloud.
4. The client whispers the instructions while performing the task.
5. Finally, the client performs the task while instructing himself or herself covertly.

Note that cognitive modeling is reflected in step 1, whereas steps 2 through 5 consist of client practice of self-verbalizations while performing a task or behavior. The client's verbalizations are faded from an overt to a covert level.

We propose that cognitive modeling and self-instructional training should be implemented with seven steps as guidelines:

1. A rationale about the procedure
2. Cognitive modeling of the task and of the self-verbalizations

Client practice in the form of:

3. Overt external guidance
4. Overt self-guidance
5. Faded overt self-guidance
6. Covert self-guidance
7. Homework and follow-up

Each of these steps will be explained in the following section. Illustrations are also provided in the Interview Checklist for Cognitive Modeling at the end of the chapter.

Treatment Rationale

Here is an example of a rationale for cognitive modeling:

"It has been found that some people have difficulty in performing certain kinds of tasks. Often the difficulty is not because they don't have the ability to do it but because of what they say or think to themselves while doing it. In other words, a person's 'self-talk' can get in the way or interfere with performance. For instance, if you get up to give a speech and you're thinking 'What a flop I'll be,' this sort of thought may affect how you deliver your talk. This procedure can help you perform something the way you want to by examining and coming up with some helpful planning or self-talk to use while performing [rationale]. I'll show what I am saying to myself while performing the task. Then I'll ask you to do the task while I guide or direct you through it. Next, you will do the task again and guide yourself aloud while doing it. The end result should be your performing the task while thinking and planning about the task to yourself [overview]. How does this sound to you? [client willingness]"

After the rationale has been presented and any questions have been clarified, the counselor begins by presenting the cognitive model.

Model of Task and Self-Guidance

First, the counselor instructs the client to listen to what the counselor says to herself or himself while performing the task. Next, the counselor models performing a task while talking aloud. Meichenbaum and Goodman (1971, p. 8) describe an example of the modeled self-instructions that were given to train impulsive children to copy line patterns:

Questions
1. What has to be done?
2. Answers question in form of planning what to do.
3. Self-guidance and focused attention.
4. Self-reinforcement.
5. Coping self-evaluative statements with error correction options.

Dialogue
1. "Okay, what is it I have to do?"
2. "You want me to copy the picture with different lines."
3. "I have to go slow and be careful. Okay, draw the line down, down, good; then to the right, that's it; now down some more and to the left."
4. "Good. Even if I make an error I can go on slowly and carefully. Okay, I have to go down now."
   "Finished. I did it."
5. "Now back up again. No, I was supposed to go down. That's okay. Just erase the line carefully."

As this example indicates, the counselor's modeled self-guidance should include five parts. The first part of the verbalization asks a question about the nature and demands of the task to be performed. The purposes of the question are to compensate for a possible deficiency in comprehending what to do, to provide a general orientation, and to create a cognitive set. The second part of the modeled verbalization answers the question about what to do. The answer is designed to model cognitive rehearsal and planning in order to focus the client's attention on relevant task requirements. Self-instruction in the form of self-guidance while performing the task is the third part of the modeled verbalization. The purpose of self-guidance is to facilitate attention to the task and to inhibit any possible overt or covert distractions or task irrelevancies. In the example, modeled self-reinforcement is the fourth part and is designed to maintain task perseverance and to reinforce success. The last part in the modeled verbalization contains coping self-statements to handle errors and frustration, with an option for correcting errors. The example of the modeled verbalization used by Meichenbaum and Goodman depicts a coping model. In other words, the model does make an error in performance but corrects it and does not give up at that point. See whether you can identify these five parts of modeled self-guidance in Learning Activity #39.

LEARNING ACTIVITY #39: MODELED SELF-GUIDANCE

The following counselor verbalization is a cognitive model for a rehabilitation client who is learning how to use a wheelchair. Identify the five parts of the message: (1) questions of what to do, (2) answers to the question in the form of planning, (3) self-guidance and focused attention, (4) coping self-evaluative statements, and (5) self-reinforcement. Feedback for this activity follows.

"What is it that I have to do to get from the parking lot over the curb onto the sidewalk and then to the building? I have to wheel my chair from the car to the curb, get over the curb and onto the sidewalk, and then wheel over to the building entrance. Okay, wheeling the chair over to the curb is no problem. I have to be careful now that I am at the curb. Okay, now I've just got to get my front wheels up first. They're up now. So now I'll pull up hard to get my back wheels up. Whoops, didn't quite make it. No big deal—I'll just pull up very hard again. Good. That's better, I've got my chair on the sidewalk now. I did it! I've got it made now."

Overt External Guidance

After the counselor models the verbalizations, the client is instructed to perform the task (as modeled by the counselor) while the counselor instructs or coaches. The counselor coaches the client through the task or activity, substituting the personal pronoun *you* for *I* (for example, "What is it that *you* . . . , *you* have to wheel your chair . . . , *you* have to be careful"). The counselor should make sure that the coaching contains the same five parts of self-guidance that were previously modeled: question, planning, focused attention, coping self-evaluation, and self-reinforcement. Sometimes in the client's real-life situation, other people may be watching when the client performs the task—as could be the case whenever the wheelchair client appears in public. If the presence of other people appears to interfere with the client's performance, the counselor might say "Those people may be distracting you. Just pay attention to what you are doing." This type of coping statement can be included in the counselor's verbalizations when using overt external guidance in order to make this part of the procedure resemble what the client will actually encounter.

Overt Self-Guidance

The counselor next instructs the client to perform the task while instructing or guiding himself or herself aloud. The purpose of this step is to have the client practice the kind of self-talk that will strengthen attention to the demands of the task and will minimize outside distractions. The counselor should attend carefully to the content of the client's self-verbalizations. Again, as in the two preceding steps, these verbalizations should include the five component parts, and the client should be encouraged to use his or her own words. If the client's self-guidance is incomplete or if the client gets stuck, the counselor can intervene and coach. If necessary, the counselor can return to the previous steps—either modeling again or coaching the client while the client performs the task (overt external guidance). After the client completes this step, the counselor should provide feedback about parts of the practice the client completed adequately and about any errors or omissions. Another practice might be necessary before moving on to the next step, faded overt self-guidance.

Faded Overt Self-Guidance

The client next performs the task while whispering (lip movements). This part of cognitive modeling serves as an intermediate step between having the client verbalize aloud, as in overt self-guidance, and having the client verbalize silently, as in the next step, covert self-guidance. In other words, whispering the self-guidance is a way for the client to approximate successively the end result of the procedure: thinking to oneself while performing. In our own experience with this step, we have found that it is necessary to explain this to an occasional client who seems hesitant or concerned about whispering. If a client finds the whispering too foreign or aversive, it might be more beneficial to repeat overt self-guidance several times and finally move directly to covert self-guidance. If the client has difficulty in performing this step or leaves out any of the five parts, an additional practice may be required before moving on.

FEEDBACK #39: MODELED SELF-GUIDANCE

Question: "What is it that I have to do to get from the parking lot over the curb onto the sidewalk and then to the building?"

Answers with planning: "I have to wheel my chair from the car to the curb, get onto the curb and onto the sidewalk, and then wheel over to the building entrance."

Self-guidance and focused attention: "Okay, wheeling the chair over to the curb is no problem. I have to be careful now that I am at the curb. Okay, now I've just got to get my front wheels up first. They're up now. So now I'll pull up hard to get my back wheels up."

Coping self-evaluation and error-correction option: "Whoops, didn't quite make it. No big deal—I'll just pull up very hard again."

Self-reinforcement: "Good. That's better, I've got my chair on the sidewalk now. I did it! I've got it made now."

Covert Self-Guidance

Finally, the client performs the task while guiding or instructing covertly, or "in one's head." It is very important for clients to instruct themselves covertly after practicing the self-instructions overtly. After the client does this, the counselor might ask for a description of the covert self-instructions. If distracting or inhibiting self-talk has occurred, the counselor can offer suggestions for more appropriate verbalizations or self-talk and can initiate additional practice. Otherwise, the client is ready to use the procedure outside the session.

Homework and Follow-up

Assigning the client homework is essential for generalization to occur from the interview to the client's environment. The therapist should instruct the client to use the covert verbalizations while performing the desired behaviors alone, outside the counseling session. The homework assignment should specify what the client will do, how much or how often, and when and where the homework is to be done. The counselor should also provide a way for the client to monitor and reward himself or herself for completion of homework. A follow-up on the homework task should also be scheduled.

These seven components of cognitive modeling are modeled for you in the following dialogue with

our client Joan. Again, this strategy is used as one way to help Joan achieve her goal of increasing her verbal participation in math class.

☐ MODEL DIALOGUE: COGNITIVE MODELING WITH COGNITIVE SELF-INSTRUCTIONAL TRAINING

In response 1, the counselor introduces the possible use of cognitive modeling to help Joan achieve the goal of increasing initiating skills in her math class. The counselor is giving a **rationale** *about the strategy.*

1. *Counselor:* One of the goals we developed was to help you increase your participation level in your math class. One of the ways we might help you do that is to use a procedure in which I demonstrate the kinds of things you want to do—and also I will demonstrate a way to think or talk to yourself about these tasks. So this procedure will help you develop a plan for carrying out these tasks, as well as showing you a way to participate. How does that sound?

   Client: OK. Is it hard to do?

In response 2, the counselor provides an **overview** *of the procedure, which is also a part of the rationale.*

2. *Counselor:* No, not really, because I'll go through it before you do. And I'll sort of guide you along. The procedure involves my showing you a participation method and, while I'm doing that, I'm going to talk out loud to myself to sort of guide myself. Then you'll do that. Gradually, we'll go over the same participation method until you do it on you own and can think to yourself how to do it. We'll take one step at a time. Does that seem clear to you?

   Client: Well, pretty much. I've never done anything like this, though.

In response 3, the counselor determines **Joan's willingness** *to try out the procedure.*

3. *Counselor:* Would you like to give it a try?

   Client: Sure—I'm willing.

In responses 4 and 5, the counselor sets the stage for **modeling of the task** *and accompanying* **self-guidance** *and* **instructs the client in what will be done and what to look for in this step.**

4. *Counselor:* We mentioned there were at least four things you could do to increase your initiating skills—asking Mr. _____ for an explanation only, answering more of Mr. _____'s questions, going to the board to do problems, and volunteering answers. Let's just pick one of these to start with. Which one would you like to work with first?

Client: Going to the board to work algebra problems. If I make a mistake there, it's visible to all the class.

5. *Counselor:* Probably you're a little nervous when you do go to the board. This procedure will help you concentrate more on the task than on yourself. Now, in the first step, I'm going to pretend I'm going to the board. As I move out of my chair and up to the board, I'm going to tell you what I'm thinking that might help me do the problems. Just listen carefully to what I say, because I'm going to ask you to do the same type of things afterwards. Any questions?

Client: No, I'm just waiting to see how you handle this. I'll look like Mr. _____. His glasses are always down on his nose and he stares right at you. It's unnerving.

In responses 6 and 7, the counselor **initiates and demonstrates** *the task with accompanying* **self-guidance.** *Note, in the modeled part of response 7, the* **five components of the self-guidance process.** *Also note that a simple problem has been chosen for illustration.*

6. *Counselor:* OK, you do that. That will help set the scene. Why don't you start by calling on me to go to the board?

Client (as teacher): Joan, go to the board now and work this problem.

7. *Counselor* (gets out of seat, moves to imaginary board on the wall, picks up the chalk, verbalizing aloud): What is it I need to do? He wants me to find y. OK, I need to just go slowly, be careful, and take my time. OK, the problem here reads $4x + y = 10$, and x is 2.8. OK, I can use x to find y. [Counselor asks *question* about task.] OK, I'm doing fine so far. Just remember to go slowly. OK, y has to be $10 - 4x$. If x is 2.8, then y will be $10 - 4$ multiplied by 2.8. [Counselor focuses *attention* and uses *self-guidance.*] Let's see, 4×2.8 is 10.2. Oops, is this right? I hear someone laughing. Just keep on going. Let me refigure it. No, it's 11.2. Just erase 10.2 and put in $y = 10 - 11.2$. OK, good. If I keep on going slowly, I can catch any error and redo it. [Counselor uses *coping self-evaluation* and makes *error correction.*] Now it's simple. $10 - 11.2$ is -1.2 and y is -1.2. Good, I did it, I'm done now and I can go back to my seat. [Counselor *reinforces self.*]

In responses 8 and 9, the counselor initiates **overt external guidance:** *the client performs the task while the counselor continues to verbalize aloud the self-guidance, substituting* **you** *for* **I** *as used in the previous sequence.*

8. *Counselor:* OK, that's it. Now let's reverse roles. This time I'd like you to get up out of your seat, go to the board, and work through the problem. I will coach you about what to plan during the process. OK?

Client: Do I say anything?

9. *Counselor:* Not this time. You just concentrate on carrying out the task and thinking about the planning I give you. In other words, I'm just going to talk you through this the first time.

Client: OK, I see.

In response 10, the counselor **verbalizes self-guidance while the client performs** *the problem.*

10. *Counselor:* OK, I'll be Mr. _____. I'll ask you to go to the board, and then you go and I'll start coaching you. (as teacher): Joan, I want you to go to the board now and work out this problem: If $2x + y = 8$ and $x = 2$, what does y equal? [Joan gets up from chair, walks to imaginary board, and picks up chalk.] (as counselor): OK, first you write the problem on the board. $2x + y = 8$ and $x = 2$. Now ask yourself "What is it I have to do with this problem?" OK, now answer yourself [question].

You need to find the value of y [answer to question]. OK, just go slowly, be careful, and concentrate on what you're doing. You know $x = 2$, so you can use x to find y. Your first step is to subtract $8 - 2x$. You've got that up there. OK, you're doing fine—just keep going slowly [focuses attention and uses self-guidance].

$8 - 2$ multiplied by 2, you know is $8 - 4$. Someone is laughing at you. But you're doing fine, just keep thinking about what you're doing. $8 - 4$ is 4, so $y = 4$ [coping self-evaluation].

Now you've got y. That's great. You did it. Now you can go back to your seat [self-reinforcement].

In response 11, the counselor **assesses the client's reaction** *before moving on to the next step.*

11. *Counselor:* OK, let's stop. How did you feel about that?

Client: Well, it's such a new thing for me. I can see how it can help. See, usually when I go up to the board I don't think about the problem. I'm usually thinking about feeling nervous or about Mr. _____ or the other kids watching me.

In response 12, the counselor reiterates the **rationale** *for the cognitive modeling procedure.*

12. *Counselor:* Yes, well, those kinds of thoughts distract you from concentrating on your math problems. That's why this kind of practice may help. It gives you a chance to work on concentrating on what you want to do.

Client: I can see that.

In responses 13 and 14, the counselor instructs the client to perform the task while verbalizing to herself (**overt self-guidance**).

13. *Counselor:* This time I'd like you to go through what we just did—only on your own. In other words, you should get up, go to the board, work out the math problem, and as you're doing that, plan what you're going to do and how you're going to do it. Tell yourself to take your time, concentrate on seeing what you're doing, and give yourself a pat on the back when you're done. How does that sound?

    Client: OK, I'm just going to say something similar to what you said the last time—is that it?

14. *Counselor:* That's it. You don't have to use the same words. Just try to plan what you're doing. If you get stuck, I'll step in and give you a cue. Remember, you start by asking yourself what you're going to do in this situation and then answering yourself. This time let's take the problem $5x + y = 10$; with $x = 2.5$, solve for y.

    Client (gets out of seat, goes to board, writes problem): What do I need to do? I need to solve for y. I know $x = 2.5$. Just think about this problem. My first step is to subtract $10 - 5x$. 5 multiplied by 2.5 is 12.5. So I'll subtract $10 - 12.5$. [Counselor laughs; Joan turns around.] Is that wrong?

    Counselor: Check yourself but stay focused on the problem, not on my laughter.

    Client: Well, $10 - 12.5$ is -2.5. $y = -2.5$. Let's see if that's right. $5 \times 2.5 = 12.5 - 2.5 = 10$. I've got it. Yeah.

In response 15, the counselor **gives feedback** *to Joan about her practice. Note the use of "sandwich" feedback, discussed in Chapter 12—a positive comment, followed by a suggestion or criticism, followed by a positive comment.*

15. *Counselor:* That was really great. You only stumbled one time—when I laughed. I did that to see whether you would still concentrate. But after that, you went right back to your work and finished the problem. It seemed pretty easy for you to do this. How did you feel?

    Client: It really was easier than I thought. I was surprised when you laughed. But then, like you said, I just tried to keep going.

In responses 16, 17, and 18, the counselor instructs Joan on how to **perform the problem while whispering instructions** *to herself* (**faded overt self-guidance**).

16. *Counselor:* This time we'll do another practice. It will be just like you did the last time, with one change. Instead of talking out your plan aloud, I

just want you to whisper it. Now you probably aren't used to whispering to yourself, so it might be a little awkward at first.

    Client (laughs): Whispering to myself? That seems sort of funny.

17. *Counselor:* I can see how it does. But it is just another step in helping you practice this to the point where it becomes a part of you—something you can do naturally and easily.

    Client: Well, OK. I guess I can see that.

18. *Counselor:* Well, let's try it. This time let's take a problem with more decimals, since you get those, too. If it seems harder, just take more time to think and go slowly. Let's take $10.5x + y = 25$, with $x = 5.5$.

    Client (gets out of seat, goes to board, writes on board, whispers): OK, what do I need to do with this problem? I need to find y. This has more decimals, so I'm just going to go slowly. Let's see, $25 - 10.5x$ is what I do first. I need to multiply 10.5 by 5.5. I think it's 52.75. [Counselor laughs.] Let's see, just think about what I'm doing. I'll redo it. No, it's 57.75. Is that right? I'd better check it again. Yes, it's OK. Keep going. $25 - 57.75$ is equal to -32.75, so $y = -32.75$. I can check it—yes, 10.5×5.5 is $57.75 - 32.75 = 25$. I got it!

Counselor **gives feedback** *in response 19.*

19. *Counselor:* That was great, Joan—very smooth. When I laughed, you just redid your arithmetic rather than turning around or letting your thoughts wander off the problem.

    Client: It seems like it gets a little easier each time. Actually, this is a good way to practice math, too.

In responses 20 and 21, the counselor gives Joan instructions on how to **perform the problem while instructing herself covertly (covert self-guidance).**

20. *Counselor:* That's right. Not only for what we do in here, but even when you do your math homework. Now, let's just go through one more practice today. You're really doing this very well. This time I'd like you to do the same thing as before—only this time I'd like you to just think about the problem. In other words, instead of talking out these instructions, just go over them mentally. Is that clear?

    Client: You just want me to think to myself what I've been saying?

21. *Counselor:* Yes—just instruct yourself in your head. Let's take the problem $12x - y = 36$, with $x = 4$. Solve for y. [Joan gets up, goes to the board, and takes several minutes to work through this.]

In response 22, the counselor **asks the client to describe what happened during covert self-guidance** *practice.*

22. *Counselor:* Can you tell me what you thought about while you did that?

    Client: Well, I thought about what I had to do, then what my first step in solving the problem would be. Then I just went through each step of the problem, and then after I checked it, I thought I was right.

In response 23, the counselor **checks to see whether another practice is needed** *or whether they can move on to homework.*

23. *Counselor:* So it seemed pretty easy. That is what we want you to be able to do in class—to instruct youself mentally like this while you're working at the board. Would you like to go through this type of practice one more time, or would you rather do this on your own during the week?

    Client: I think on my own would help right now.

In response 24, the counselor sets up Joan's **homework assignment** *for the following week.*

24. *Counselor:* OK. I think it would be helpful if you could do this type of practice on your own this week—where you instruct yourself as you work through math problems.

    Client: You mean my math homework?

In response 25, the counselor **instructs Joan on how to do homework,** *including what to do, where, and how much to do.*

25. *Counselor:* Well, that would be a good way to start. Perhaps you could take seven problems a day. As you work through each problem, go through these self-instructions mentally. (Do this at home.) Does that seem clear?

    Client: Yes, I'll just work out seven problems a day the way we did here for the last practice.

In response 26, the counselor instructs Joan **to observe her homework completion on log sheets** *and* **arranges for a follow-up** *of homework at their next session.*

26. *Counselor:* Right. One more thing. On these blank log sheets, keep a tally of the number of times you actually do this type of practice on math problems during the day. This will help you keep track of your practice. And then next week bring your log sheets with you and we can go over your homework.

LEARNING ACTIVITY #40: COGNITIVE MODELING WITH COGNITIVE SELF-INSTRUCTIONAL TRAINING

You may recall from the case of Ms. Weare and Freddie (Chapter 7) that Ms. Weare wanted to eliminate the assistance she gave Freddie in getting ready for school in the morning. One of Ms. Weare's concerns is to find a successful way to instruct Freddie about the new ground rules—mainly that she will not help him get dressed and will not remind him when the bus is five minutes away. Ms. Weare is afraid that after she delivers her instructions, Freddie will either pout or talk back to her. She is concerned that she will not be able to follow through with her plan or else will not be firm in the way she delivers the ground rules to him. (a) Describe how you would use the seven major components of cognitive modeling and self-instructional training to help Ms. Weare to do this, and (b) write out an example of a cognitive modeling dialogue that Ms. Weare could use to accomplish this task. Make sure this dialogue contains the five necessary parts of the self-guidance process: question, answer, focused attention, self-evaluation, and self-reinforcement. Feedback follows.

☐ PROBLEM-SOLVING THERAPY

Problem-solving therapy or problem-solving training emerged in the late 1960s and early 1970s as a trend in the development of intervention and prevention strategies for enhancing competence in specific situations. D'Zurilla (1988) defines problem solving as a "cognitive-affective-behavioral process through which an individual (or group) attempts to identify, discover, or invent effective means of coping with problems encountered in every day living" (p. 86). Rose (1986) describes problem solving as a strategy whereby "the client learns to systematically work through a set of steps for analyzing a problem, discovering new approaches, evaluating those approaches, and developing strategies for implementing those approaches in the real world" (p. 440). Problem-solving therapy or training has been used with

FEEDBACK #40: COGNITIVE MODELING WITH COGNITIVE SELF-INSTRUCTIONAL TRAINING

a. Description of the seven components:

1. *Rationale.* First, you would explain to Ms. Weare how cognitive modeling could help her in instructing Freddie and what the procedure would involve. You might emphasize that the procedure would be helpful to her in both prior planning and practice.

2. *Model of task and self-guidance.* In this step, you would model a way Ms. Weare could talk to Freddie. Your modeling would include both the task (what Ms. Weare could say to Freddie) and the five parts of the self-guidance process.

3. *Overt external guidance.* Ms. Weare would practice giving her instructions to Freddie while you coach her on the self-guidance process.

4. *Overt self-guidance.* Ms. Weare would perform the instructions while verbalizing aloud the five parts of the self-guidance process. If she gets stuck or if she leaves out any of the five parts, you can cue her. This step also may need to be repeated before moving on.

5. *Faded overt self-guidance.* Assuming Ms. Weare is willing to complete this step, she would perform the instructions to give Freddie while whispering the self-guidance to herself.

6. *Covert self-guidance.* Ms. Weare would practice giving the instructions to Freddie while covertly guiding herself. When she is able to do this comfortably, you would assign homework.

7. *Homework.* You would assign homework by asking Ms. Weare to practice the covert self-guidance daily and arranging for a follow-up after some portion had been completed.

b. Example of a model dialogue:

"OK, what is it I want to do in this situation [question]? I want to tell Freddie that he is to get up and dress himself without my help, that I will no longer come up and help him even when it's time for the bus to come [answer]. OK, just remember to take a deep breath and talk firmly and slowly. Look at Freddie. Say "Freddie, I am not going to help you in the morning. I've got my own work to do. If you want to get to school on time, you'll need to decide to get yourself ready" [focused attention and self-guidance]. Now, if he gives me flak, just stay calm and firm. I won't back down [coping self-evaluation]. That should be fine. I can handle it [self-reinforcement]."

children, adolescents, and adults as a treatment strategy, a treatment-maintenance strategy, or a prevention strategy. As a treatment strategy, problem solving has been used alone or in conjunction with other treatment strategies presented in this book.

Problem-solving therapy has been effectively used to treat social skills deficits (Bedell, Archer, & Marlow, 1980; Edelstein, Couture, Cray, Dickens, & Lusebrink, 1980), agoraphobia (Jannoun, Munby, Catalan, & Gelder, 1980), alcohol abuse (Chaney, O'Leary, & Marlatt, 1978), depression (Nezu, 1986), shy adolescents (Christoff, Scott, Kelley, Schlundt, Baer, & Kelly, 1985; Tisdelle & St. Laurence, 1988), relapse prevention after smoking cessation treatment stops (Davis & Glaros, 1986), marital and family problems (Foster, Prinz, & O'Leary, 1983; Jacobson, 1984; Jacobson & Follette, 1985), stress and anxiety (Ewart, Taylor, Kraemer, & Agras, 1984) and weight control (Black & Threlfall, 1986). Also, Heppner (1988) has developed a problem-solving inventory: the scales of the inventory include problem-solving confidence (or self-assurance while engaging in problem activities), tendency to approach or avoid problem-solving activities, and the extent individuals believe that they are in control of their behaviors and emotions while solving problems.

Perceptions and attitudes about problem solving can play either a facilitative or disruptive role. If perceptions and attitudes have a facilitative role, the client is motivated to learn and engage in problem-solving behaviors. Clients who are unmotivated or avoid dealing with problems because of their perception about problems will not want to learn the problem-solving strategy. In these cases, the therapist will have to first help the client deal with these perceptions and attitudes. The therapist also can help the client engage in some effective coping activities or behaviors that can facilitate the problem-solving process. If the perceptual, attitudinal, and emotional components of behavior are dealt with, problem-solving training or therapy will be more than an intellectual exercise (D'Zurilla, 1988, pp. 116–117).

Many clients feel that it is easier to ignore or avoid a problem because the problem will probably go away by itself. Although some problems may simply go away, some problems will *not* go away if ignored or avoided. In fact, some problems may get worse and can become antecedents to more problems if the client does not solve the initial problem. The role of the therapist is to help the client take responsibility for solving problems and commit to spending the time and energy needed to solve them by changing the client's attitudes and perceptions about the problems. The six stages for problem-solving therapy may take several sessions, depending on the nature of the problem and the number of problem-solving obstacles.

We propose the following stages enumerated by D'Zurilla (1986):

1. *Treatment rationale:* to provide the purpose and overview of problem-solving strategy.
2. *Problem orientation:* to assess the client's problem-solving coping style; to educate clients about maladaptive and facilitative problem-solving coping skills; to determine and then to train the client to overcome cognitive and emotional obstacles to problem solving, attacking the problem from many different vantage points and assessing the time, energy, and commitment to solving the problem.
3. *Problem definition and formulation:* to help the client gather relevant and factual information for understanding the problems, to identify problem-focused and/or emotional-focused components of the problems, and to identify problem-solving goals for each problem.
4. *Generation of alternative solutions:* to instruct the client to think about different ways to handle each problem goal and to use the deferment of judgment, quantity, and variety principles.
5. *Decision making:* to instruct the client to screen the list of alternative solutions, to evaluate (judge and compare) solution outcomes for each problem goal, and to select solution plans.
6. *Solution implementation and verification:* to encourage the client to carry out several alternative solutions simultaneously; to have the client self-monitor, evaluate, and reinforce the implementation of the solutions; and to help the client troubleshoot and recycle the problem-solving strategy if the solutions do not work.

Each of these parts will be described in this section. A detailed description of these six components can be found in the Interview Checklist for Problem Solving at the end of the chapter.

Treatment Rationale

The rationale used in problem-solving therapy is that it attempt to strengthen the client's belief that problem solving can be an important coping skill for dealing with a variety of concerns that require effective functioning. The following is an example of the rationale for problem-solving treatment.

"Each of us is faced with both minor and important problems. Some problems are routine, such as trying to decide what to wear or what movie to see. Other problems are more stressful, such as dealing with a difficult relationship. One way to enhance responsibility and self-control is to learn techniques for solving our problems. To take the time, energy, and commitment necessary to solve or deal with problems immediately may relieve future frustration and pain created by a problem."

Here is an example of an overview of the procedure.

"You will learn how to become aware of how you see a problem. You will look at how much control, time and effort, and commitment you feel you have for solving the problem. We will need to gather information to understand and define the problems. Also, we'll need to look at what might prevent you from solving the problem. It is important that we explore a variety of solutions for solving the problem. After obtaining several solutions, you will decide which solutions feel most reasonable to implement simultaneously. Finally, you will implement the solution plans. (Pause) I'm wondering what your thoughts and feelings are regarding what I have described. Do you have any questions?"

Problem Orientation

After giving a rationale to the client, the counselor asks the client to describe how she or he typically solves problems. The counselor determines whether the client has a maladaptive or facilitative problem-solving style and then helps the client distinguish between these two coping styles. People with maladaptive coping styles blame themselves or others for the problem. These people often feel that something is wrong with them and may feel abnormal, hopeless, depressed, stupid, or unlucky (D'Zurilla, 1988). Maladaptive coping styles are often exhibited in persons who either minimize the benefits of problem solving or who maximize or exaggerate the losses that may occur from failure to successfully solve the problem. Individuals with poor problem-solving skills often perceive the problem as insolvable and so avoid dealing with the problem. Also, poor problem solvers may feel inadequate or incompetent and they prefer having someone else solve the problem (D'Zurilla, 1988). Some people have difficulty solving problems because they either never learned how to solve them or they feel the problem is too overwhelming.

The role of the counselor is to help the client engaging in a maladaptive problem-solving style to change his or her perception about problem solving. The counselor helps the client to see that problems are a part of daily living. Instead of viewing problems as a threat or a personal inadequacy, the counselor helps the client to view the problem as an opportunity for personal growth, self-control, and self-improvement (D'Zurilla, 1988). Clients may feel that it is easier not to solve the problem and wait for things to get better. Counselors need to help these clients to realize that if a problem is not solved, the problem may very well come to haunt them later (Peck, 1978). Clients need to believe that there is a solution to the problem and that they have the capacity and self-control to find the solution independently and successfully (D'Zurilla, 1988). An expectation that one can cope with and solve a problem successfully will produce an ability and capacity to cope with problems.

Problem solving takes time and energy. It is sometimes easier to avoid dealing with problems when they are influenced more by feelings than by reason. People often respond to problems impulsively and do not take time and effort to think about viable solutions. Problem solving requires time, energy, and commitment—a delay of gratification (Peck, 1978). The counselor needs to assess the client's willingness to spend time and energy, to be committed, and to delay gratification and the counselor may have to motivate the client to make the necessary commitment to solve the problem.

Another component of problem orientation is to discuss how the client's cognitions and emotions affect problem solving. Clients may be unmotivated to work on the problem because of how they think about it. Also, poor cognitions or self-talk such as, "it is their fault," "it will go away," or "I can't work on it" inhibits the motivation to work on a problem. The purpose of the therapy is to instruct and to train the client in positive coping methods, with the intent to overcome cognitive

and/or emotional obstacles to problem solving (D'Zurilla, 1986, 1988). Strategies such as rational-emotive therapy, cognitive restructuring, reframing, stress inoculation, meditation, muscle relaxation or systematic desensitization (see Chapters 16, 17, and 18) may help a client deal with cognitive and/or emotional barriers to problem solving. Once the sources of the client's disruptions to problem solving have been minimized, the client is ready for the next phase of the problem-solving strategy.

Problem Definition and Formulation

The purpose of this step in problem solving is for the counselor to help the client to gather as much objective information about the problem as possible. In cases where a client has a distorted cognitive view or perception of the problem, the counselor may have to use rational-emotive therapy or cognitive restructuring to help the client (see Chapter 16). The counselor explains that problem-solving strategy is a skill and practical approach whereby a person attempts to identify, explore, or create effective and adaptive ways of coping with everyday problems (D'Zurilla, 1986). A problem can be viewed as a discrepancy between how a present situation is being experienced and how that situation should or could be experienced (D'Zurilla, 1988). The client needs to obtain relevant information about the problem by identifying the obstacles that are creating the discrepancy or are preventing effective responses for reducing the discrepancy. It is also important to examine antecedent conditions or unresolved problems that may be contributing to or causing the present problem or concern. Counselors may want to use the techniques presented in Chapter 8 for this step of problem definition.

Some therapists make an important distinction between problem-focused and emotion-focused problem definition (D'Zurilla, 1988; Lazarus & Falkman, 1984). Problems that have problem-focused definitions center on problem-solving goals, with the purpose of changing the problem situation for the better. Problems with an emotional-focused definition concentrate on changing the client's personal reactions to the problem (D'Zurilla, 1988). Alternatively, D'Zurilla (1988) suggests that if the problem situation is assessed as *changeable,* the problem-focused definition should be emphasized in therapy. If problem-focused problems are *unchangeable,* the counselor helps the client deal with the client's reaction to the problem (D'Zurilla, 1988). In some cases, the client's problem may be first assessed as problem-focused but later the counselor and client discover the problem is unchangeable and the therapeutic focus then becomes changing the personal reaction. It has been our experience that it is best to include both problem-focused and emotion-focused goals in defining the client's problem.

After the problem has been identified and defined (see Chapter 8), the counselor and the client set realistic emotion-focused and/or problem-focused goals (see Chapter 9). A goal is defined as what the client would like to have happen as a consequence of solving the problem. The goals should be realistic, attainable, and should specify the type of behavior, level of behavior, and the conditions under which the goal will facilitate solving the problem. The counselor should help the client identify obstacles that might interfere with problem-solving goals. Finally, the counselor should help the client to understand that the complexities involved in most problem situations usually require attacking the problem from many different vantage points (Nezu & Nezu, 1989). Establishing problem-solving goals will help the client with the next step in the therapy; creating alternative solutions.

Generation of Alternative Solutions

The purpose of this stage of problem solving is to have the client generate as many alternative solutions to the problem as possible. The counselor instructs the client to think of *what* she or he could do, or *ways* to handle the problem. The counselor also instructs the client not to worry about *how* to go about making a plan work or how to put the solution into effect—that will come later. The client is instructed to allow her or his imagination to think of a great variety of new and original solutions, no matter how ridiculous the solution may seem. According to D'Zurilla (1986, 1988), the greater the quantity of alternative solutions that the client produces, the greater will be the quality of the solutions available for the client to choose. Similarly, when the client defers judgment or critical evaluation of the solutions, solutions of greater quality will be produced by the client.

After generating this list of alternative solutions to the problem, the client is asked to identify the number of different strategies represented. If too few strategies are represented, the client is instructed to generate more strategy solutions or

more solutions for a specific strategy. This "free-wheeling" or brainstorming process is intended to filter out functional fixity, practicality, and feasibility in generating solutions. If there are several goals for the problem, the counselor encourages the client to generate several alternative solutions for each problem goal, the rationale being that most problems are complicated and a simple alternative is often inadequate.

Decision Making

The purpose of this step is to help the client evaluate the best solution to use to solve the problem by judging and comparing all the alternatives. The client is first instructed to screen the list of available alternatives and to eliminate any solution that may be a risk or is not feasible (D'Zurilla, 1988). The best solutions are the ones that maximize benefits and minimize costs for the client's personal, immediate, and long-term welfare. The client is instructed to anticipate outcomes for each alternative (D'Zurilla, 1988) and then is asked to evaluate each solution using the following four criteria: (1) will the problem be solved, (2) what will be the status of the client's emotional well-being, (3) how much time and effort will be needed to solve the problem, and (4) what effect will it have on the client's overall personal and social well-being? (D'Zurilla, 1988).

After the client selects and evaluates all of the alternative solutions, D'Zurilla (1988) recommends that the client be instructed to answer the following three questions: (1) can the problem be solved, (2) is more information needed before a solution can be selected and implemented, and (3) what solution or combination of solutions should be used to solve the problem? If the problem cannot be solved with one of the existing solutions, the counselor may have to help the client redefine the problem and/or gather more information about the problem. If the previous three questions have been satisfactorily answered, the client is ready to implement the solution, as long as the chosen solution is consistent with the goal for solving the problem.

During the first five stages of the problem-solving strategy, the counselor assumes a directive role with the client in order to ensure a thorough application of the following steps: the problem orientation, problem definition, generation of alternatives, and decision making. The counselor assumes a less directive role with the client during the solution implementation stage. The therapeutic goal during the last stage of the strategy is to have the client become more responsible and independent.

Solution Implementation and Verification

The purpose of this step of problem solving is to test the chosen solutions to the problem-solving goals and to verify whether these solutions solve the problem. The client simultaneously implements as many solutions as possible. According to D'Zurilla (1988), there are four parts to verifying whether the solution plan is working. The first part is to implement the chosen solution. If there are obstacles (behavioral deficits, emotional concerns, or dysfunctional cognitions) to implementing the solution, the client can acquire performance skills, defuse affective concerns, and restructure cognition to remove the obstacles.

Second, the client can use self-monitoring techniques (see Chapter 19) to assess the effects of the chosen solutions for solving the problem: the counselor instructs the client to keep a daily log or journal of the self-talk or emotional reactions to the chosen solutions. The self-talk or statements recorded in the journal can be rated on a scale where 5 = extremely negative, 0 = neutral, and −5 = extremely positive and the accompanying affect state also can be recorded, such as loved, depressed, frustrated, guilty, happy, or neutral— which can increase the level of emotional awareness.

Third, the client assesses whether the chosen solutions achieve the desired goals for solving the problem. This self-evaluation process is assessed in relationship to the solution in the following areas: (1) problem resolution; (2) emotional well-being; (3) time and effort exerted; and (4) the ratio of total benefit to cost (D'Zurilla, 1988).

Finally, if the chosen solution meets all the criteria, the client engages in some form of self-reward (see Chapter 19) for having successfully solved the problem. However, if the chosen solutions do not solve the problem, the counselor and client try to pinpoint trouble areas and retrace the problem-solving steps. Some common trouble areas that clients have are emotional reaction to the problem, inadequate definition of the problem, unresolved antecedent issues to the problem, problem-focused instead of emotion-focused definition, and unsatisfactory solution choices.

D'Zurilla (1988) offers three cautions about the problem-solving strategy. One concern is the possible failure of the counselor to recognize when other strategies are more appropriate. A client with a serious concern or severe maladaptive behavior will require other strategies. For example, a depressed person may require intensive cognitive restructuring (see Chapter 16) before problem-solving therapy could be considered an appropriate strategy (D'Zurilla, 1988). The second caution is the danger of viewing problem-solving therapy as a "rational," "intellectual," or "head-trip therapy or exercise" rather than as a coping strategy that involves all three components of behavior, cognition, and affect (D'Zurilla, 1988). The problem-solving strategy should be viewed as an overall or general system for therapy that must include the emotional, behavioral, and cognitive modes of a person. The third caution is the potential failure of counselors to recognize that rapport with the client or a positive therapeutic relationship is a necessary condition for successful therapy (D'Zurilla, 1988). The ingredients of effective therapy (see Chapter 2) and the variables that enhance the therapeutic relationship (see Chapter 3) are important for successful application of any strategy; the problem-solving strategy is no exception.

Finally, Nezu, Nezu, and Perri (1989) (pp. 133–136) offer some guidelines for implementing the problem-solving strategy.

1. Training in problem solving should *not* be presented in a mechanistic manner.
2. The therapist should attempt to individualize the strategy and make it relevant to the specific client concern.
3. Homework and *in vivo* practice (see Chapter 12) of the problem-solving components are crucial.
4. The therapist should be caring and sensitive to the client's concerns and feelings.
5. The judicious use of humor by the therapist can be an effective therapeutic tool.
6. The therapist needs continuously to ensure that an accurate assessment of the problem has been obtained.
7. The therapist should encourage the client to implement as many solutions as possible during treatment.
8. The therapist must make a thorough evaluation of the patient's abilities and limitations in order to implement a solution alternative. The evaluation would also include how much control the client has over the problem situation.

9. The therapist must determine whether the client's problem deals with problem-focused coping or emotion-focused coping or both.

The role of the counselor throughout the problem-solving process is to educate the client about the problem-solving strategy and to guide the client through the problem-solving steps. As we mentioned before, the counselor is less directive with the client during the last stage of the problem-solving process in order to help the client become more independent and take responsibility for applying the chosen problem solutions and verifying the effectiveness of the chosen solutions. The counselor can help the client to maintain these problem-solving skills and to generalize them to other concerns. The counselor also can assist the client in anticipating obstacles to solving strategies and can prepare the client for coping with them. The client should be able to cope fairly well if he or she takes the time to *examine objectively* her or his orientation to the problem, to carefully define the problem, to generate a variety of alternative solutions, and to make a decision about solution alternatives that are compatible with goals or desired outcomes. Solution implementation may be easier if the first four stages of the problem-solving process have been thoroughly and objectively processed.

□ MODEL EXAMPLE: PROBLEM-SOLVING THERAPY

In this model example, we present a narrative account of how problem-solving therapy might be used with a 49-year-old male client. Nick, an air traffic controller, has reported that he would like to decrease the stress he experiences in his job. He believes that decreasing this stress will help his ulcer and help him cope better with his job. In addition to the physical signs of stress (hypertension), Nick also reports that he worries constantly about making mistakes in his job. He has also thought about taking early retirement, which would relieve him of the stress and worry.

Rationale

First, we explain to Nick that all of us face problems and sometimes we feel stuck because we don't know how to handle a problem. We tell Nick that solving problems as they occur can prevent future discomfort. We provide Nick with an overview of problem-solving therapy, telling him that we'll need to look at how he sees the problem and what obstacles there are to solving the problem. We tell him that we will need to define the problem, think of many different solutions for solving the problem, select several solutions to solve the problem, and try out the solutions and see how well the solutions solve the problem. Finally, we confirm Nick's willingness to use problem-solving therapy and answer any questions he may have about the procedure.

Problem Orientation

We determine how Nick typically solves problems. We ask him to give an example of a problem he has had in the past and how and what he did to solve it. Then we describe for Nick the difference between maladaptive and facilitative problem solving. We explain to Nick that most people inherently have problem-solving ability but something blocks the use of it. We tell Nick that problem-solving therapy removes the blocks or obstacles that are maladaptive for good problem solving. We explain that healthy problem solving is the capacity to view problems as an opportunity for personal growth and control. If Nick is encountering cognitive or emotional obstacles in his problem-solving attempts, we would introduce appropriate strategies to help remove them. Finally, we assess how much time, energy, and commitment Nick has for solving the problem.

Problem Definition and Formulation

We briefly describe the problem-solving strategy for Nick. We explain to Nick that we need to gather information about the problem, such as his thoughts and feelings about the problem, what unresolved issues contribute to the problem, how intense the problem is, what has been done to solve the problem, and when and where the problem occurs. We ask Nick what other information is needed to define the problem. If Nick has distorted views or perceptions of the problem, we would have to help him reframe his perception of the problem. We have to determine if Nick's problem is problem-focused or emotion-focused or both. For example, we can probably change his emotional and cognitive reaction to the work situation and help him reduce the stress but he cannot change the job requirements unless he leaves or retires. We help Nick identify problem-solving goals or what Nick would like to have happen so that the problem would be solved. For Nick, one of the most attainable and realistic goals might be to reduce job stress.

Generation of Alternative Solutions

Nick is instructed to generate as many alternative solutions as possible for solving the problem. We inform Nick not to worry about how to go about making the alternatives work or how to put the solution into effect. Also, Nick is instructed to defer judgment about how good or feasible his ideas or solutions are until later, to generate as many alternatives he can think of (because quantity produces quality), and to be creative and to think of nontraditional and unconventional solutions as well.

Decision Making

We instruct Nick to screen the list of alternatives and to use the following criteria for evaluating each solution: will the problem be solved with this solution; what will be the status of Nick's emotional well-being; how much time and effort will be needed to use the alternative solutions; and what will be Nick's overall personal and social well-being using each of these alternative solutions. Nick is reminded that it is important to evaluate each solution by answering these four criteria questions. Finally, Nick is instructed to select the best solutions that are compatible with the problem-solving goals.

Solution Implementation and Verification

We instruct Nick to try his chosen solutions for solving the problem. We also instruct Nick to self-monitor the alternative solutions he chose to solve the problem to determine their effectiveness. Suppose Nick chose to reduce his stress in the work place by using meditation as one solution. We instruct Nick to self-monitor by keeping a written log or journal of the effectiveness of meditation using the following criteria questions: How effective is meditation in reducing job stress? How well does he feel emotionally about the meditative experience; is the time and effort spent with daily meditations worth it? Were there more benefits for using meditation than costs and what are your thoughts, feelings, and behavior in relationship to the solution implementation? He is instructed to complete the self-monitoring or journal each day just before bed time. Nick is instructed to rate each of the criteria questions on a 5-point scale with descriptive words for each point on the scale. We tell Nick that he needs to reward himself after successfully solving the problem (reducing the stress) by selecting rewarding things or activities. Also, we tell Nick to determine the best time to receive something or to engage in rewarding activity. If, for example, the meditation did not contribute to solving the problem, we instruct Nick to look at trouble areas that might be obstacles to solving the problem, such as his emotional reactions to the problem, the fact that the problem may not be well defined, or unresolved issues that may be contributing to the problem.

LEARNING ACTIVITY #41: PROBLEM SOLVING

This learning activity provides an opportunity to try out problem solving. Think of a problem that you have, and apply the steps to problem solving to your problem. Do this in a quiet place when you will not be interrupted.

1. Determine how you solve problems.
2. Assess whether you have a maladaptive or facilitative problem-solving style.
3. What cognitive and/or emotional obstacles do you have that might be barriers to solving problems.
4. How much time, energy, and commitment do you have for solving the problem?
5. Define your problem and determine if your problem is problem-focused or emotion-focused or both.
6. Generate solutions for solving the problem. Be sure to think of a variety of solutions.
7. Select the best solutions using the criteria in the checklist.
8. Implement your solutions to the problem or at least think about how to implement the solutions and think of a method for verifying the effectiveness of each solution.

□ SUMMARY

Cognitive modeling is a procedure designed to help people learn how to use self-talk to enhance performance. In this strategy, implicit or covert responses as well as overt responses are modeled. Problem-solving therapy or training provides clients with a formalized system for viewing problems more constructively. As a treatment strategy, problem solving can be used alone or in conjunction with other treatment strategies presented in this book.

In the next chapter we will see how clients can be taught to stop self-defeating thoughts and to replace these with incompatible coping thoughts and skills. Both the strategies of cognitive restructuring and stress inoculation, presented in Chapter 16, are directed toward *replacement,* not merely elimination, of self-defeating cognitions.

■
POSTEVALUATION

PART ONE

Describe how you would use the seven components of cognitive modeling and self-instructional training to help Mr. Brown (from Chapter 7) initiate social contacts with his boss (Objective One). These are the seven components:

1. Rationale
2. Model of task and self-guidance
3. Overt external guidance
4. Overt self-guidance
5. Faded overt self-guidance
6. Covert self-guidance
7. Homework and follow-up

Feedback follows the evaluation.

PART TWO

Objective Two asks you to demonstrate at least 16 out of 21 steps of the cognitive self-instructional modeling procedure with a role-play client. You can audiotape your interview or have an observer assess your performance, using the Interview Checklist for Cognitive Modeling that follows the Postevaluation.

PART THREE

Objective Three asks you to identify accurately the steps of the problem-solving therapy represented by at least eight out of ten examples of counselor instructure responses. For each of the following counselor responses, identify on paper which step of the problem-solving procedure is being used. There may be more than one counselor response associated with a step. The six major steps of problem solving are as follows:

1. Rationale for problem solving
2. Problem orientation
3. Problem definition and formulation
4. Generation of alternative solutions

5. Decision making
6. Solution implementation and verification

Feedback for the Postevaluation follows on page 400.

1. "Self-monitoring involves keeping a diary or log about your thoughts, feelings, and behaviors."
2. "To help you assess each solution, you can answer several questions about how effective the solution will be in solving the problem."
3. "Be creative and free-wheeling. Let your imagination go. Whatever comes into your mind write it down."
4. "What goals do you want to set for your emotional or personal reaction to the problem?"
5. "When you have concerns or problems, give me an example of the problem and describe how you typically solve it."
6. "Solving problems as they occur can prevent future discomfort."
7. "Most people have an ability to solve problems but often they block the use of it and become poor problem solvers."
8. "What unresolved issues may be contributing to the problem? When does the problem occur? Where does it occur?
9. "Look over your list of solutions and see how much variety is on your list; think of new and original ones."
10. "You need to think about what you can reward yourself with after you complete this step."

PART FOUR

Objective Four asks you to demostrate 16 out of 19 steps associated with the problem-solving strategy in a role-play interview. You can audiotape your interview or have an observer rate it, using the Interview Checklist for Problem Solving at the end of the chapter. (continued)

POSTEVALUATION   (continued)

INTERVIEW CHECKLIST FOR COGNITIVE MODELING

Instructions: Determine which of the following leads the counselor used in the interview. Check each of the leads used. Some examples of counselor leads are provided in the right column; however, these are only suggestions.

Item	*Examples of counselor leads*
I. Rationale about Strategy	
____ 1. Counselor provides a rationale for the strategy.	"This strategy is a way to help you do this task and also plan how to do it. The planning will help you perform better and more easily."
____ 2. Counselor provides overview of strategy.	"We will take it step by step. First, I'll show you how to do it and I'll talk to myself aloud while I'm doing it so you can hear my planning. Then you'll do that. Gradually, you'll be able to perform the task while thinking through the planning to yourself at the same time."
____ 3. Counselor checks client's willingness to use strategy.	"Would you like to go ahead with this now?"
II. Model of Task and Self-Guidance	
____ 4. Counselor instructs client in what to listen and look for during modeling.	"While I do this, I'm going to tell you orally my plans for doing it. Just listen closely to what I say as I go through this."
____ 5. Counselor engages in modeling of task, verbalizing self-guidance aloud.	"OK, I'm walking in for the interview. [Counselor walks in.] I'm getting ready to greet the interviewer and then wait for his cue to sit down [sits down]."
____ 6. Self-guidance demonstrated by counselor includes five components:	
____a. *Question* about demands of task.	"Now what is it I should be doing in this situation?"
____b. *Answers* question by planning what to do.	"I just need to greet the person, sit down on cue, and answer the questions. I need to be sure to point out why they should take me."
____c. *Focused attention* to task and *self-guidance* during task.	"OK, just remember to take a deep breath, relax, and concentrate on the interview. Just remember to discuss my particular qualifications and experiences and try to answer questions completely and directly."
____d. *Coping self-evaluation* and, if necessary, *error correction.*	"OK, now, if I get a little nervous, just take a deep breath. Stay focused on the interview. If I don't respond too well to one question, I can always come back to it."
____e. *Self-reinforcement* for completion of task.	"OK, doing fine. Things are going pretty smoothly."
III. Overt External Guidance	
____ 7. Counselor instructs client to perform task while counselor coaches.	"This time you go through the interview yourself. I'll be coaching you on what to do and on your planning."
____ 8. Client performs task while counselor coaches by verbalizing self-guidance, changing *I* to *you.* Counselor's verbalization includes the five components of self-guidance:	"Now just remember you're going to walk in for the interview. When the interview begins, I'll coach you through it."

(continued)

Item	Examples of counselor leads
____a. Question about task.	"OK, you're walking into the interview room. Now ask yourself what it is you're going to do."
____b. Answer to question.	"OK, you're going to greet the interviewer. [Client does so.] Now he's cuing you to sit down. [Client sits.]
____c. Focused attention to task and self-guidance during task.	"Just concentrate on how you want to handle this situation. He's asking you about your background. You're going to respond directly and completely."
____d. Coping self-evaluation and error correction.	"If you feel a little nervous while you're being questioned, just take a deep breath. If you don't respond to a question completely, you can initiate a second response. Try that now."
____e. Self-reinforcement.	"That's good. Now remember you want to convey why you should be chosen. Take your time to do that. [Client does so.] Great. Very thorough job."

IV. Overt Self-Guidance

____ 9. Counselor instructs client to perform task and instruct self aloud.

"This time I'd like you to do both things. Talk to yourself as you go through the interview in the same way we have done before. Remember, there are five parts to your planning. If you get stuck, I'll help you."

____10. Client performs task while simultaneously verbalizing aloud self-guidance process. Client's verbalization includes five components of self-guidance:

    ____a. Question about task. — "Now what is it I need to do?"

    ____b. Answer to question. — "I'm going to greet the interviewer, wait for the cue to sit down, then answer the questions directly and as completely as possible."

    ____c. Focused attention and self-guidance. — "Just concentrate on how I'm going to handle this situation. I'm going to describe why I should be chosen."

    ____d. Coping self-evaluation and error correction. — "If I get a little nervous, just take a deep breath. If I have trouble with one question, I can always come back to it."

    ____e. Self-reinforcement. — "OK, things are going smoothly. I'm doing fine."

____11. If client's self-guidance is incomplete or if client gets stuck, counselor either—

    ____a. Intervenes and cues client or — "Let's stop here for a minute. You seem to be having trouble. Let's start again and try to. . . ."

    ____b. Recycles client back through step 10. — "That seemed pretty hard, so let's try it again. This time you go through the interview and I'll coach you through it."

____12. Counselor gives feedback to client about overt practice.

"That seemed pretty easy for you. You were able to go through the interview and coach yourself. The one place you seemed a little stuck was in the middle, when you had trouble describing yourself. But overall, it was something you handled well. What do you think?"

(continued)

POSTEVALUATION (continued)

Item	Examples of counselor leads
V. Faded Overt Self-Guidance	
____13. Counselor instructs client on how to perform task while whispering.	"This time I'd like you to go through the interview and whisper the instructions to yourself as you go along. The whispering may be a new thing for you, but I believe it will help you learn to do this."
____14. Client performs task and whispers simultaneously.	"I'm going into the room now, waiting for the interviewer to greet me and to sit down. I'm going to answer the questions as completely as possible. Now I'm going to talk about my background."
____15. Counselor checks to determine how well client performed.	
____a. If client stumbled or left out some of the five parts, client engages in faded overt practice again.	"You had some difficulty with ____. Let's try this type of practice again."
____b. If client performed practice smoothly, counselor moves on to next step.	"You seemed to do this easily and comfortably. The next thing is . . . ."
VI. Covert Self-Guidance	
____16. Counselor instructs client to perform task while covertly (thinking only) instructing self.	"This time while you practice, simply *think* about these instructions. In other words, instruct yourself mentally or in your head as you go along."
____17. Client performs task while covertly instructing.	Only client's actions are visible at this point.
____18. After practice (step 17), counselor asks client to describe covert instructions.	"Can you tell me what you thought about as you were doing this?"
____19. On basis of client report (step 18):	
____a. Counselor asks client to repeat covert self-guidance.	"It's hard sometimes to begin rehearsing instructions mentally. Let's try it again so you feel more comfortable with it."
____b. Counselor moves on to homework.	"OK, you seemed to do this very easily. I believe it would help if you could apply this to some things that you do on your own this week. For instance. . . ."
VII. Homework	
____20. Counselor instructs client on how to carry out homework. Instructions include:	"What I'd like you to do this week is to go through this type of mental practice on your own."
____a. What to do.	"Specifically, go through a simulated interview where you mentally plan your responses as we've done today."
____b. How much or how often to do the task.	"I believe it would help if you could do this two times each day."
____c. When and where to do it.	"I believe it would be helpful to practice at home first, then practice at school [or work]."
____d. A method for self-monitoring during completion of homework.	"Each time you do this, make a check on this log sheet. Also, write down the five parts of the self-instructions you used."

(continued)

Item	Examples of counselor leads
____21. Counselor arranges for a face-to-face or telephone follow-up after completion of homework assignment.	"Bring in your log sheets next week or give me a call at the end of the week and we'll go over your homework then."

Observer Comments: _____

INTERVIEW CHECKLIST FOR PROBLEM SOLVING

Instructions: Determine whether the counselor demonstrated each of the leads listed in the checklist. Check which leads were used.

Item	Examples of counselor leads
I. Rationale for Problem Solving	
____ 1. Counselor explains purpose of problem-solving therapy.	"All of us are faced with little and big concerns or problems. Sometimes we feel stuck because we don't know how to handle a problem. This procedure can help you identify and define a problem and examine ways of solving the problem. You can be in charge of the problem instead of the problem being in charge of you. Solving problems as they occur can prevent future discomfort."
____ 2. Counselor provides brief overview of procedure.	"There are five steps we'll do in using this procedure. Most problems are complex and to solve the problem we'll need to handle the problem from many different perspectives. First, we'll need to look at how you see the problem. We'll examine what are unhelpful and helpful problem-solving skills. Another part of this step is to explore how to overcome thoughts and feelings that could be obstacles to solving the problem. We'll also need to see how much time and energy you are willing to use to solve the problem. Second, we will define the problem by gathering information about it. Third, we'll want to see how many different solutions we can come up with for solving the problem. Next, we'll examine the solutions and decide which one to use. Finally, you will try out the chosen solutions and see how well they solve the problem. (Pause.) What are your thoughts about what I have described? Do you have any questions?"
II. Problem Orientation	
____ 3. Counselor determines how the client solves problems.	"When you have concerns or problems, give me an example of the problem and describe how you typically solve it."
____ 4. Counselor describes the difference between maladaptive and facilitative problem solving.	"Most people have ability to solve problems but often they block the use of it. Problem-solving therapy helps to remove blocks or obstacles and helps bring important issues into focus. Problem-solving therapy provides a formalized system for viewing problems differently. People who don't solve problems very well may feel inadequate or incompetent

(continued)

POSTEVALUATION   (continued)

Item	Examples of counselor leads
	to solve their problem. Often these people want to avoid the problem or want someone else to solve it. People sometimes feel it is easier not to solve the problem and things will get better. At times poor problem solvers feel hopeless, depressed, stupid, or unlucky. These people exaggerate the losses that may occur because of unsuccessful attempts to solve a problem. If you feel like a poor problem solver, we'll have to consider ways that make you feel like you are in charge and have control. You can solve problems; they are a part of daily living. There are usually a variety of solutions to every problem and you have the capacity and the control to find the solution by yourself. It can be helpful to think of problems as an opportunity for personal growth and being in control of yourself.''
_____ 5. Counselor determines what cognitive and emotional obstacles the client might have as barriers to solving the problem.	''When you think about your problem, what thoughts do you have concerning the problem? What are you usually thinking about during this problem? Do you have any 'shoulds' or beliefs concerning the problem? What feelings do you experience when thinking about the problem? Are there any holdover or unfinished feelings from past events in your life that still affect the problem? How do your thoughts and feelings affect the problem and your ability to solve it? You may not be aware of it, but think about some past issues or unfinished business you may have as we do problem solving.''

(If there are any obstacles, the counselor introduces a strategy or strategies (for example, RET, cognitive restructuring, reframing, meditation, muscle relaxation, etc.) to help the client remove cognitive or emotional obstacles to problem solving.)

Item	Examples of counselor leads
_____ 6. Counselor assesses the client's time, energy, and commitment to solving the problem.	''Any problem usually takes time, effort, and commitment to solve it. But it is often important to solve the problem now rather than wait and solve it later — or not at all. It is important to know how committed you are to solving the problem. (Wait for the answer.) Also, solving a problem takes time; do you feel you have enough time to work on the problem? (Pause, wait for answer.) Thinking about and working on a problem can take a lot of energy. How energized do you feel about working on this problem?'' (Pause for answer.)

III. Problem Definition and Formulation

Item	Examples of counselor leads
_____ 7. Counselor describes the problem-solving strategy for the client.	''People have problems or concerns. Some problems are minor and some are major. Problem-solving strategy is a skill and practical approach. People use problem solving to identify, explore, or create effective ways of dealing with everyday problems.''
_____ 8. Counselor helps the client gather information about the problem. (The steps of problem identification presented in Chapter 8 can be used for this step of problem solving.)	''We want to gather as much information about what the problem is as we can. What type of problem is it? What thoughts do you have when the problem occurs? What feelings do you experience

(continued)

Item	Examples of counselor leads

with the problem? How often does the problem occur or is it ongoing? What unresolved issues may be contributing to the problem? Who or what other people are involved with the problem? When does the problem occur? Where does it occur? How long has the problem been going on? How intense is the problem? What have you done to solve the problem? What obstacles can you identify that prevent you from solving the problem? Tell me, how do you see the problem?"

"What other information do we need to define the problem? What is your definition of the problem?"

(If the client has a distorted view or perception of the problem, the counselor may have to use rational-emotive therapy, reframing, or cognitive restructuring to help the client.)

_____ 9. Counselor determines if the client's problem is problem-focused or emotion-focused or both.

"From the way you have defined the problem, how can the problem be changed? What aspects of the problem can be changed? What emotional reactions do you have about the problem? How would you like to change your personal/emotional reaction to the problem? There may be some things about the problem you cannot change. Some problem situations are unchangeable. If there are aspects of the problem that are changeable, we will work on those things that can be changed. One thing we can change is your emotional or personal reaction to the problem."

_____10. Counselor helps the client identify problem-solving goals. (The steps in goal setting presented in Chapter 9 can be used for this step.)

"Now that we have identified and defined the problem, we need to set some goals. A goal is what you would like to have happen so that the problem would be solved. The goals should be things you can do or are attainable and realistic."

"How many obstacles are there that prevent you from setting problem-solving goals? How can you remove these obstacles? What goals do you want to set for your emotional or personal reaction to the problem? What behaviors do you want to change? How much or what level of behavior are going to change? Under what condition or circumstance will the behavior change occur? What goals do you want to set for things that are changeable in the problem situation? What behaviors or goals do you want to set for yourself, the frequency of these behaviors, and in what problem conditions? These goals will help us in the next step of problem solving."

IV. Generation of Alternative Solutions

_____11. Counselor presents the guidelines for generating alternative solutions.

"We want to generate as many alternative solutions for solving the problem as possible. We do this because problems are often complicated and a single alternative is often inadequate. We need to generate several alternative solutions for each problem-solving goal."

_____a. What

"Think of what you could do or ways to handle the problem. Don't worry about how to go about making your plan work or how to put the solution into effect—you'll do that later."

(continued)

POSTEVALUATION (continued)

Item	Examples of counselor leads
____b. Defer judgment	"Defer judgment about your ideas or solutions until later. Be loose and open to any idea or solution. You can evaluate and criticize your solutions later."
____c. Quantity	"Quantity breeds quality. The more alternative solutions or ideas you can think of, the better. The more alternatives you produce, the more quality solutions you'll discover."
____d, Variety	"Be creative and free-wheeling. Let your imagination go. Whatever comes into your mind write it down. Allow yourself to think of a variety of unusual or unconventional solutions as well as more traditional or typical ones. Look over your list of solutions and see how much variety there is. If there is little variety on your list, generate more and think of new and original solutions."

V. Decision Making

Item	Examples of counselor leads
____12. Counselor instructs the client to screen the list of alternative solutions.	"Now you need to screen and look over your list of alternative solutions for solving the problem. You want to look for the *best* solutions. The best solutions are the ones that maximize benefits and minimize costs for your personal, social, immediate, and long-term welfare."
____13. Counselor provides criteria evaluating each solution.	"To help you assess *each* solution, you answer the following four questions: 1. Will the problem be solved with this particular solution? 2. By using this solution, what will be the status of my emotional well-being? 3. If I use this solution, how much time and effort will be needed to solve the problem? 4. What will be my overall personal and social well-being if I use this solution? Remember it is important to evaluate *each* solution by answering these four questions."
____14. Counselor instructs the client to make a decision and select the best solutions compatible with problem-solving goals.	"Select as many solutions that you think will work or solve the problem. Answer these questions: 1. Can the problem be solved reasonably well with these solutions? 2. Is more information about the problem needed before these solutions can be selected and implemented? See if the solutions fit with the problem-solving goals.

(If the answer to questions one and two are Yes and No, respectively, move on to the next step. Answers of No to question one and Yes to question two may require recycling by redefining the problem, gathering more information, and determining problem obstacles.)

(continued)

Item	Examples of counselor leads
VI. Solution Implementation and Verification	
_____15. Counselor instructs the client to carry out chosen solutions.	"For the last stage of problem solving, try out the solutions you have chosen. If there are obstacles to trying out the solutions, we'll have to remove them. You can use several alternative solutions at the same time. Use as many solutions as you can."
_____16. Counselor informs client about self-monitoring strategy (described in Chapter 19).	"We'll need to develop a technique for you to see if the solution solves the problem. Self-monitoring involves keeping a diary or log about your thoughts, feelings, and behavior. You can record these behaviors as you implement your chosen solutions. We'll need to discuss what responses you'll record, when you'll record, and method of recording."
_____17. Counselor instructs the client to use these criteria to assess whether the solution achieves the desired goal for solving the problem.	"You'll need to assess if your solution solves the problem. One way to do this is to ask yourself the following:
_____a. Problem resolved.	"Did the solutions solve the problem?"
_____b. Emotional well-being.	"How is your emotional well-being after you used the solutions?"
_____c. Time and effort exerted.	"Was the time and effort you exerted worth it?"
_____d. Ratio of total benefits to total costs.	"Were there more benefits for using the solutions than costs?"
_____18. Counselor instructs the client about self-reward (see Chapter 19 for a description of the self-reward strategy).	"You need to think about what you can reward yourself with after successfully solving the problem. What type of things or activities are rewarding to you? When would be the best time to receive something or to engage in a rewarding activity?"
_____19. Counselor instructs the client what to do if solutions do not solve the problem.	"When the solutions do not solve the problem, we need to look at some trouble areas that might be obstacles to solving the problem. What is your emotional reaction to the problem? The problem may not be defined well. There may be old unresolved problems contributing to the present problem."

☐ SUGGESTED READINGS

Beck, A. T. (1976). _Cognitive therapy and the emotional disorders._ New York: International Universities Press.

Copeland, A. P. (1981). The relevance of subject variables in cognitive self-instructional programs for impulsive children. _Behavior Therapy, 12,_ 520–529.

D'Zurilla, T. J. (1986). _Problem-solving therapy: A social competence approach to clinical intervention._ New York: Springer.

D'Zurilla, T. J. (1988). _Problem-solving therapies._ In K. S. Dobson (Ed.), _Handbook of cognitive-behavioral therapies_ (pp. 85–135). New York: Guilford.

Kazdin, A. E., & Mascitelli, S. (1982). Behavioral rehearsal, self-instructions, and homework practice in developing assertiveness. _Behavior Therapy, 13,_ 346–360.

Kendall, P. C., & Braswell, L. (1982). Cognitive-behavioral self-control therapy for children: A component analysis. _Journal of Consulting and Clinical Psychology, 50,_ 672–689.

Kirby, E. A., & Grimley, L. K. (1986). _Understanding and treating attention deficit disorders._ New York: Pergamon.

Mahoney, M. J. (1974). _Cognition and behavior modification._ Cambridge, MA: Ballinger.

Meichenbaum, D. (1977). _Cognitive behavior modification: An integrative approach._ New York: Plenum.

Meichenbaum, D., & Cameron, R. (1973). Training schizophrenics to talk to themselves: A means of developing attentional controls. _Behavior Therapy, 4,_ 515–534.

Meichenbaum, D., & Goodman, J. (1971). Training impulsive children to talk to themselves: A means of developing self-control. _Journal of Abnormal Psychology, 77,_ 115–126.

Nezu, A. M., & Nezu, C. M. (Eds.). (1989). *Clinical decision making in behavior therapy: A problem-solving perspective.* Champaign, IL: Research Press.

Nezu, A. M., Nezu, C. M., & Perri, M. G. (1989). *Problem-solving therapy for depression: Theory, research, and clinical guidelines.* New York: Wiley.

Rimm, D. C., & Masters, J. C. (1979). *Behavior therapy: Techniques and empirical findings* (2nd ed.). New York: Academic Press.

Sarason, I. G. (1973). Test anxiety and cognitive modeling. *Journal of Personality and Social Psychology, 28,* 58–61.

Tryon, G. S. (1979). A review and critique of thought stopping research. *Journal of Behavior Therapy and Experimental Psychiatry, 10,* 189–192.

Tryon, G. S., & Pallandino, J. J. (1979). Thought stopping: A case study and observation. *Journal of Behavior Therapy and Experimental Psychiatry, 10,* 151–154.

FEEDBACK: POSTEVALUATION

PART ONE

1. *Rationale*

   First, you would explain the steps of cognitive modeling and self-instructional training to Mr. Brown. Then you would explain how this procedure could help him practice and plan the way he might approach his boss.

2. *Model of task and self-guidance*

   You would model for Mr. Brown a way he could approach his boss to request a social contact. You would model the five parts of the self-guidance process: (1) the question about what he wants to do, (2) the answer to the question in the form of planning, (3) focused attention on the task and guiding himself through it, (4) evaluating himself and correcting errors or making adjustments in his behavior in a coping manner, and (5) reinforcing himself for adequate performance.

3. *Overt external guidance*

   Mr. Brown would practice making an approach or contact while you coach him through the five parts of self-guidance as just described.

4. *Overt self-guidance*

   Mr. Brown would practice making a social contact while verbalizing aloud the five parts of the self-guidance process. If he got stuck, you could prompt him, or else you could have him repeat this step or recycle step 3.

5. *Faded overt self-guidance*

   Mr. Brown would engage in another practice attempt, only this time he would whisper the five parts of the self-guidance process.

6. *Covert self-guidance*

   Mr. Brown would make another practice attempt while using the five parts of the self-guidance process covertly. You would ask him afterward to describe what happened. Additional practice with covert self-guidance or recycling to step 4 or 5 might be necessary.

7. *Homework*

   You would instruct Mr. Brown to practice the self-guidance process daily before actually making a social contact with his boss.

PART TWO

Rate an audiotape of your interview or have an observer rate you, using the Interview Checklist for Cognitive Modeling on pages 392–395.

PART THREE

1. Solution Implementation and Verification
2. Decision Making
3. Generation of Alternative Solutions
4. Problem Definition and Formulation
5. Problem Orientation
6. Rationale for Problem Solving
7. Problem Orientation
8. Problem Definition and Formulation
9. Generation of Alternative Solutions
10. Solution Implementation and Verification

PART FOUR

Rate an audiotape of your interview or have someone else rate it, using the Interview Checklist for Problem Solving on pages 395–399.

COGNITIVE RESTRUCTURING, REFRAMING, AND STRESS INOCULATION

SIXTEEN

Risley and Hart (1968, p. 267) suggest that "much of psychotherapy ... is based on the assumption that reorganizing and restructuring a patient's verbal statements about himself and his world will result in a corresponding reorganization of the patient's behavior with respect to that world." Cognitive restructuring, reframing, and stress inoculation assume that maladaptive emotions and overt responses are influenced or mediated by one's beliefs, attitudes, and perceptions —one's "cognitions." These procedures help clients to determine the relation between their perceptions and cognitions and the resulting emotions and behaviors, to identify faulty or self-defeating cognitions, or perceptions, and to replace these cognitions with self-enhancing perceptions. In all strategies, clients learn how to cope; indirect benefits may include an increase in feelings of resourcefulness, greater ability to handle a problem, and enhancement of self-concept.

Although the procedures described in this chapter reflect a behavioral perspective, no description of these strategies would be complete without some discussion of a major historical antecedent —rational-emotive therapy, or RET. RET, which was developed by Ellis (1975), assumes that most problems are the result of "magical" thinking or irrational beliefs. According to Morris and Kanitz (1975), some of the irrational ideas discussed by Ellis lead to self-condemnation or anger, and others lead to a low tolerance for frustration. The RET therapist helps clients identify which of the irrational ideas are evidenced by their belief systems and emotional reactions.

Ten major irrational ideas cited by Ellis are the following:

1. The idea that it is a dire necessity for an adult to be loved or approved by virtually every significant person in his or her community.
2. The idea that one should be thoroughly competent, adequate, and achieving in all possible respects if one is to consider oneself worthwhile.

3. The idea that human unhappiness is externally caused and that people have little or no ability to control their sorrows and disturbances.
4. The idea that one's past history is an all-important determinant of one's present behavior and that because something once strongly affected one's life, it should indefinitely have a similar effect.
5. The idea that there is invariably a right, precise, and perfect solution to human problems and that it is catastrophic if this perfect solution is not found.
6. The idea that if something is or may be dangerous or fearsome, one should be terribly concerned about it and should keep dwelling on the possibility of its occurring.
7. The idea that certain people are bad, wicked, or villainous and that they should be severely blamed and punished for their villainy.
8. The idea that it is awful and catastrophic when things are not the way one would very much like them to be.
9. The idea that it is easier to avoid than to face certain life difficulties and self-responsibilities.
10. The idea that one should become quite upset over other people's problems and disturbances [Ellis, 1974, pp. 152–153].*

According to RET, it is possible to resolve a client's problems by "cognitive control of illogical emotional responses" (Morris & Kanitz, 1975, p. 8). In RET, such control is achieved primarily by reeducating the client through the use of what Ellis (1975) calls the "ABCDE model." This model involves showing the client how irrational beliefs (B) about an activity or action (A) result in irrational or inappropriate consequences (C). The client is then taught to dispute (D) the irrational beliefs (B), which are not facts and have no supporting evidence, and then to recognize the effects (E). Usually, the effects (E) are either cognitive effects (cE) or behavioral effects (bE).

As you may realize, one of the major assumptions that RET and these three cognitive change strategies share is that a person's beliefs, thoughts, and perceptions can create emotional distress and maladaptive responding. Another shared assumption is that a person's cognitive system can be

* From *Humanistic psychotherapy,* by A. Ellis. Copyright 1974 by McGraw-Hill, Inc. Reprinted by permission of the publisher, McGraw-Hill Book Company, and the author.

changed directly and that such change results in different, and presumably more appropriate, consequences. Ullmann and Krasner (1969) note that any cognitive change approach involves punishing a client's emotional labels and reinforcing more appropriate evaluations of a situation.

As you will note in this chapter's discussion of cognitive restructuring, reframing, and stress inoculation, there are some differences between RET and cognitive behavior modification procedures. One difference is that cognitive-behavior procedures do not assume that certain irrational ideas are generally held by all. In cognitive restructuring and stress inoculation, each client's *particular* irrational thoughts or perceptions are identified and are assumed to be idiosyncratic, although some elements may be shared by others as well. A second difference involves the method of change. In RET the therapist tries to help the client alter irrational beliefs by verbal persuasion and teaching. Emphasis is placed on helping the client discriminate between irrational beliefs, which have no evidence, and rational beliefs, which can be supported by data. In cognitive restructuring, reframing, and stress inoculation, in addition to these kinds of discriminations, the client is taught the skill of using alternative cognitions or perceptions in stressful or distressing situations. These strategies are efforts to eliminate "cognitive pollution."

☐ OBJECTIVES

1. Identify and describe the six components of cognitive restructuring from a written case description.
2. Teach the six major components of cognitive restructuring to another person, or demonstrate these components in a role-play interview.
3. Demonstrate 8 out of 11 steps of reframing in a role-play interview.
4. Using a simulated client case, describe how the five components of stress inoculation would be used with a client.
5. Demonstrate 17 out of 21 steps of stress inoculation in a role-play interview.

☐ COGNITIVE RESTRUCTURING

Although cognitive restructuring was described earlier by Lazarus (1971) and has its roots in rational-emotive therapy (Ellis, 1975), it has been developed by Meichenbaum (1972) under the name *cognitive behavior modification* and by Goldfried, Decenteceo, and Weinberg (1974) under the name *systematic rational restructuring.* Cognitive restructuring focuses on identifying and altering clients' irrational beliefs and negative self-statements or thoughts. Much of the supporting evidence for cognitive restructuring has come from a series of studies conducted by Fremouw and associates (Fremouw & Harmatz, 1975; Fremouw & Zitter, 1978; Glogower, Fremouw, & McCroskey, 1978). Cognitive restructuring has been used to help clients with test anxiety (Cooley & Spiegler, 1980; McCordick, Kaplan, Smith, & Finn, 1981), social anxiety (Elder, Edelstein, & Fremouw, 1981; Gormally, Varvil-Weld, Raphael, & Sipps, 1981), assertive behaviors (Jacobs & Cochran, 1982; Kaplan, 1982; Safran, Alden, & Davidson, 1980; Valerio & Stone, 1982), and musical performance anxiety (Sweeney & Horan, 1982). Baker (1981) and associates (Baker & Butler, in press; Baker, Thomas, & Munson, 1983); have developed a primary prevention unit entitled "Cleaning Up Our Thinking" for junior and senior high students. Hamilton and Fremouw (1985) implemented a cognitive restructuring procedure to improve the foul-shooting performance of male Division II college basketball players. Forman (1980) used cognitive restructuring to modify aggressive behavior of elementary school children. Dush, Hirt, and Schroeder (1983) performed a meta-analysis of controlled studies incorporating direct modification of covert self-statements. They found that self-statement modification made considerable gains beyond no-treatment controls. Finally, in a review of 48 studies, Miller and Berman (1983) found that sex, age, or experience of therapist, duration of treatment, and group or individual presentation of treatment did not affect the efficacy of cognitive behavior therapies.

More recently, cognitive restructuring has been used to increase low self-esteem (Warren, McLellarn, & Ponzoha, 1988); to influence career indecision (Mitchell & Krumboltz, 1987); to treat severe social phobia (Mattick & Peters, 1988); to change eating habits, cognitions, and feelings concerned with food for bulimia nervosa patients (Wilson, Rossiter, Kleifield, & Lindholm, 1986); and to reduce the magnitude of binge behavior (Pecsok & Fremouw, 1988). Also, cognitive restructuring was used in marital therapy to change unrealistic expectations (Baucom & Lester, 1986) and to change beliefs about relationships held by couples who fear they are bad parents (Chadez & Nurius,

1987). Finally, several books have been published about cognitive therapy applied to children and adolescents with depression (Matson, 1989), to enhance self-esteem of children and adolescents (Pope, McHale, & Craighead, 1988), to treat panic and hypochrondriasis (Clark & Salkovskis, 1989), and in groups to treat older depressed adults (Yost, Beutler, Corbishley, & Allender, 1986).

Several factors can limit or enhance the value of cognitive restructuring. Elder et al. (1981) found cognitive restructuring to be more effective for highly socially anxious clients and found negligible effects for clients reporting relatively low levels of social anxiety. In contrast, Safran et al. (1980) found that cognitive restructuring used to train nonassertive clients was not as effective as skill training for clients with high levels of anxiety. Highly anxious clients may be focusing on the "negative" features or details of the problem situation (Greenberg & Safran, 1981). Bruch, Juster, and Heisler (1982) suggest that individuals with a high degree of conceptual complexity may report more internal attributions and fewer negative task statements. For these types of clients, emphasis should be placed on internal rather than external causal factors when designing coping statements (Bruch et al., 1982). Another factor that can inhibit the use of cognitive restructuring may be the complexity of the treatment (Baker & Butler, in press; Woodward & Jones, 1980); however, the issue of complexity may be related to how well clients understand the presentation of the procedure. For this reason, it is important that counselors carefully explain the rationale for cognitive restructuring to clients.

Our presentation of cognitive restructuring reflects these sources and our own adaptations of it based on clinical usage. We present cognitive restructuring in six major parts:

1. Rationale: purpose and overview of the procedure.
2. Identification of client thoughts during problem situations.
3. Introduction and practice of coping thoughts.
4. Shifting from self-defeating to coping thoughts.
5. Introduction and practice of positive or reinforcing self-statements.
6. Homework and follow-up.

Each of these parts will be described in this section. A detailed description of these six components can be found in the Interview Checklist for Cognitive Restructuring at the end of the chapter.

Treatment Rationale

The rationale used in cognitive restructuring attempts to strengthen the client's belief that "self-talk" can influence performance and particularly that self-defeating thoughts or negative self-statements can cause emotional distress and can interfere with performance.

Rationale. Meichenbaum (1974) has provided a *rationale* he used in training test-anxious and speech-anxious college students to use cognitive restructuring. His example of the purpose for treatment follows; the language can be adapted.

> One goal of treatment is for each member to become aware of the factors which are maintaining his test (speech) anxiety. Once we can determine what these factors are, then we can change or combat them. One of the surprising things is that the factors contributing to anxiety are not something secretive, but seem to be the thinking processes you go through in evaluative situations. Simply, there seems to be a correlation between how anxious and tense people feel and the kinds of thoughts they are experiencing. For example, the anxiety you experienced in the test (speech) situation may be tied to the kinds of thoughts you had, what you chose to think about, or how you chose to focus your attention. Somehow your thinking gets all tied up with how you are feeling [pp. 9–10].

Overview. Here is an example of an overview of the procedure:

> We will learn how to control our thinking processes and attention. The control of our thinking, or what we say to ourselves, comes about by first becoming aware of when we are producing negative self-statements, catastrophizing, being task-irrelevant, etc. (Once again, give examples of the clients' thinking styles.) The recognition that we are in fact doing this will be a step forward in changing. This recognition will also act as a reminder, a cue, a bell-ringer for us to produce different thoughts and self-instructions, to challenge our thinking styles and to produce incompatible, task-relevant self-instructions and incompatible behaviors. We will learn how to control our thinking processes in our group discussion, by some specific techniques which I will describe a bit later on. (Pause.) I'm wondering about your reactions to what I have described. Do you have any questions? [pp. 11–12].*

* From *Therapist manual for cognitive behavior modification,* by D. Meichenbaum. Unpublished manuscript, 1974. Reprinted by permission of the author.

Contrast of self-defeating and self-enhancing thoughts. In addition to providing a standard rationale such as the one just illustrated, the cognitive restructuring procedure should be prefaced by some contrast between self-enhancing, or rational, thoughts and self-defeating, or irrational, thoughts. This explanation may help clients discriminate between their own self-enhancing and self-defeating thoughts during treatment. Many clients who could benefit from cognitive restructuring are all too aware of their self-defeating thoughts and are unaware of or unable to generate self-enhancing thoughts. Providing a contrast may help them see that more realistic thinking styles can be developed.

Although some therapists describe beliefs as either rational or irrational (Ellis, 1975; Goldfried et al., 1974), we prefer to label them positive, self-enhancing thoughts or negative, self-defeating ones. In our opinion, this description is less likely to confuse clients who have trouble distinguishing between their *thoughts* as irrational and *themselves* as irrational or "crazy." Besides, as Thorpe (1973) points out, the aim of cognitive restructuring is to show clients how negative thoughts are unproductive, how they defeat purposes or goals, rather than that clients' ideas are irrational and wrong.

One way to contrast these two types of thinking is to model some examples of both positive, enhancing self-talk and negative, defeating self-talk. These examples can come out of your personal experiences or can relate to the client's problem situations. The examples might occur *before, during,* or *after* a problem situation (Fremouw, 1977). For example, you might say to the client that in a situation that makes you a little uptight, such as meeting a person for the first time, you could get caught up in very negative thoughts:

Before meeting:
"What if I don't come across very well?"
"What if this person doesn't like me?"
"I'll just blow this chance to establish a good relationship."

During meeting:
"I'm not making a good impression on this person."
"This person is probably wishing our meeting were over."
"I'd just like to leave and get this over with."
"I'm sure this person won't want to see me after this."

After meeting:
"Well, that's a lost cause."
"I can never talk intelligently with a stranger."

"I might as well never bother to set up this kind of meeting again."

"How stupid I must have sounded!"

In contrast, you might demonstrate some examples of positive, self-enhancing thoughts about the same situation:

Before meeting:
"I'm just going to try to get to know this person."

"I'm just going to be myself when I meet this person."

"I'll find something to talk about that I enjoy."

"This is only an initial meeting. We'll have to get together more to see how the relationship develops."

During meeting:
"I'm going to try to get something out of this conversation."

"This is a subject I know something about."

"This meeting is giving me a chance to talk about _____."

"It will take some time for me to get to know this person, and vice versa."

After meeting:
"That went OK; it certainly wasn't a flop."

"I can remember how easy it was for me to discuss topics of interest to me."

"Each meeting with a new person gives me a chance to see someone else and explore new interests."

"I was able just to be myself then."

Influence of self-defeating thoughts on performance. The last part of the rationale for cognitive restructuring should be an *explicit* attempt to point out how self-defeating thoughts or negative self-statements are unproductive and can influence emotions and behavior. You are trying to convey to the client that, whatever we tell ourselves, we are likely to believe it and to act on that belief. However, it is also useful to point out that, in some situations, people don't *literally* tell themselves something. In many situations, our thoughts are so well learned that they are automatic (Goldfried et al., 1974, p. 250). For this reason, you might indicate that you will often ask the client to monitor or log what happens during actual situations between counseling sessions.

Thorpe (1973) has provided an example of a description for nonassertive clients about how unproductive thinking can influence emotions and behavior:

Many difficulties in social situations are simply based on the way in which we think about them. In other words, it is not that a certain situation is really, in itself, difficult, anxiety-provoking, or uncomfortable, but that we simply look on it that way. What usually happens is that we spend so much time telling ourselves negative things, that we are bound to fail, that we are no good, etc., that we cannot possibly handle the situation well. What we will be doing in therapy is to examine some of the unproductive trains of thought that we have when in a demanding situation. Research has shown that if we can only learn to get rid of such unproductive, self-defeating thoughts, and replace them with realistic, sensible ones, then difficult situations become much easier, simply by looking on them in a more positive way [p. 3].

The importance of providing an adequate rationale for cognitive restructuring cannot be over-emphasized. If one begins implementing the procedure too quickly, or without the client's agreement, the process can backfire. Some research indicates that people may be more resistant to changing beliefs if they are pushed or coerced to abandon them and adopt someone else's (Brehm, 1966; Watts, Powell, & Austin, 1973). As Goldfried and associates (1974) point out, the procedure should be implemented slowly "by having clients gradually agree to the underlying rationale" (p. 249). The counselor should not move ahead until the client's commitment to work with the strategy is obtained.

Identification of Client Thoughts in Problem Situations

Assuming that the client accepts the rationale provided about cognitive restructuring, the next step involves an analysis of the client's thoughts in anxiety-provoking or distressing situations. Both the range of situations and the content of the client's thoughts in these situations should be explored (Meichenbaum, 1974).

Description of thoughts in problem situations. Within the interview, the counselor should query the client about the particular distressing situations encountered and the things the client thinks about before, during, and after these situations. The counselor might say something like "Sit back and think about the situations that are really upsetting to you. What are they?" and then "Can you identify exactly what you are thinking about or telling yourself before you go to _____? What are you thinking during the situation? And afterward?"

In identifying negative or self-defeating thoughts, the client might be aided by a description of possible cues that compose a self-defeating thought. The counselor can point out that a negative thought may have a "worry quality" such as "I'm afraid . . . ," or a "self-oriented quality" such as "I won't do well" (Meichenbaum, 1974, p. 16). Negative thoughts may also include elements of catastrophizing ("If I fail, it will be awful") or exaggerating ("I *never* do well" or "I *always* blow it"). Goldfried (1976b) suggests that clients can identify the extent to which unrealistic thinking contributes to situational anxiety by answering three questions about each anxiety-provoking situation:

Do I make unreasonable demands of myself?
Do I feel that others are approving or disapproving of my actions?
Do I often forget that this situation is only one part of my life?

Modeling of links between events and emotions. If the client has trouble identifying negative thoughts, Meichenbaum (1974) suggests asking the client to recall the situation as if running a movie through his or her head. The counselor may need to point out that the thoughts are the link between the situation and the resulting emotion and ask the client to notice explicitly what this link seems to be. If the client is still unable to identify thoughts, the counselor can model this link, using either the client's situations or situations from the counselor's life. For example, the counselor might say

"Here is one example that happened to me. I was a music major in college, and several times a year I had to present piano recitals that were graded by several faculty members and attended by faculty, friends, and strangers. Each approaching recital got worse—I got more nervous and more preoccupied with failure. Although I didn't realize it at the time, the link between the event of the recital and my resulting feelings of nervousness was things I was thinking that I can remember now—like "What if I get out there and blank out?" or "What if my arms get so stiff I can't perform the piece?" or "What if my shaking knees are visible?" Now can you try to recall the specific thoughts you had when you felt so upset about _____?"

Client modeling of thoughts. The counselor can also have the client identify situations and thoughts by monitoring and recording events and thoughts outside the interview in the form of homework. For example, Fremouw (1977, p. 3) suggests that an initial homework assignment

might be to have the client observe and record at least three negative self-statements a day in the stressful situation for a week. For each day of the week, the client could record on a daily log the negative self-statements and the situations in which these statements were noted (see Figure 16-1).

Using the client's data, the counselor and client can determine which of the thoughts were self-enhancing and productive and which were self-defeating and unproductive. The counselor should try to have the *client* discriminate between the two types of statements and identify why the negative ones are unproductive. The identification serves several purposes. First, it is a way to determine whether the client's present repertory consists of both positive and negative self-statements or whether the client is generating or recalling only negative thoughts. These data may also provide information about the degree of distress in a particular situation. If some self-enhancing thoughts are identified, the client becomes aware that alternatives are already present in his or her thinking style. If no self-enhancing thoughts are reported, this is a cue that some specific attention may be needed in this area. The counselor can demonstrate how the client's unproductive thoughts can be changed by showing how self-defeating thoughts can be restated more constructively (Fremouw, 1977, p. 3).

Introduction and Practice of Coping Thoughts

At this point in the procedure, there is a shift in focus from the client's self-defeating thoughts to other kinds of thoughts that are incompatible with the self-defeating ones. These incompatible thoughts may be called coping thoughts, coping statements, or coping self-instructions. They are developed for each client. There is no attempt to have all clients accept a common core of rational beliefs, as is often done in rational-emotive therapy (Meichenbaum, 1974).

Introduction and practice of coping statements is, as far as we know, crucial to the overall success of the cognitive restructuring procedure. As Meichenbaum observes, "It appears that the awareness of one's self-statements is a necessary but *not* sufficient condition to cause behavior change. One needs to produce incompatible self-instructions and incompatible behaviors" (1974, p. 51). A well-controlled investigation of the components of cognitive restructuring conducted by Glogower et al. (1978) seems to support Meichenbaum's contention. These authors found that,

Name: _____   Week: _____
Date: _____

Negative Self-Statements: *Situations:*

1. _____   1. _____
2. _____   2. _____
3. _____   3. _____

Figure 16-1. *Example of daily log. From* A Client Manual for Integrated Behavior Treatment of Speech Anxiety, *by W. Fremouw, 1977. Reprinted by permission of the author.*

with communication-anxious college students, simply identifying negative self-statements was no more effective than extinction (repeated exposure to anxious feelings). The crucial component appeared to be the learning and rehearsal of coping statements, which, by itself, was almost as effective as the combination of identifying negative statements and replacing these with incompatible coping thoughts.

Explanation and examples of coping thoughts. The purpose of coping thoughts should be explained clearly. The client should understand that it is difficult to think of failing at an experience (a self-defeating thought) while concentrating on just doing one's best, regardless of the outcome (a coping thought). The counselor could explain the purpose and use of coping thoughts like this:

"So far we've worked at identifying some of the self-defeating things you think during _____. As long as you're thinking about those kinds of things, they can make you feel anxious. But as soon as you replace these with coping thoughts, then the coping thoughts take over, because it is almost impossible to concentrate on both failing at something and coping with the situation at the same time. The coping thoughts help you to manage the situation and to cope if you start to feel overwhelmed."

The counselor should also model some examples of coping thoughts so that the client can clearly differentiate between a self-defeating and a coping thought. Some examples of coping thoughts to use *before* a situation might be—

"I've done this before, and it is never as bad as I think."
"Stay calm in anticipating this."
"Do the best I can. I'm not going to worry how people will react."
"This is a situation that can be a challenge."
"It won't be bad—only a few people will be there."

Examples of coping thoughts to use *during* a situation include—

"Focus on the task."
"Just think about what I want to do or say."
"What is it I want to accomplish now?"
"Relax so I can focus on the situation."
"Step back a minute, take a deep breath."
"Take one step at a time."
"Slow down, take my time, don't rush."
"OK, don't get out of control. It's a signal to cope."

If you go back and read over these lists of coping examples, you may note some subtle differences among them. Some of them refer to the nature of the situation itself, such as "It won't be too bad," "It can be a challenge," or "Only a few people will be watching me." Fremouw (1977) refers to these as *context-* or *situation-oriented coping statements.* These coping statements help the client reduce the potential level of threat or severity of the anticipated situation. Other coping statements refer more to the plans, steps, or behaviors the person will need to demonstrate during the stressful situation, such as "Concentrate on what I want to say or do," "Think about the task," or "What do I want to accomplish?" These may be called *task-oriented coping statements* (Fremouw, 1977). Another set of coping thoughts can be used to help the client stay calm and relaxed at tense moments. Meichenbaum (1974) refers to these as *coping with being overwhelmed.* These statements include such self-instructions as "Keep cool," "Stay calm," or "Relax, take a deep breath." A fourth type of coping statement, which we call *positive self-statements,* is used to have clients reinforce or encourage themselves for having coped. These include such self-instructions as "Great, I did it," or "I managed to get through that alright." Positive self-statements can be used during a stressful situation and especially after the situation. The use of positive self-statements in cognitive restructuring is described in more detail later in this chapter.

In explaining about and modeling potential coping thoughts, the counselor may want to note the difference between *coping* and *mastery* thoughts. Coping thoughts are ones that help a client deal with or manage a situation, event, or person adequately. Mastery thoughts are ones that are directed toward helping a person "conquer" or master a situation in almost a flawless manner. For some clients, mastery self-instructions may function as perfectionistic standards that are, in reality, too difficult to attain. For these clients, use of mastery thoughts can make them feel more pressured rather than more relieved. For these reasons we recommend that counselors avoid modeling the use of mastery self-statements and also remain alert to clients who may spontaneously use mastery self-instructions in subsequent practice sessions during the cognitive restructuring procedure.

Client examples of coping thoughts. After providing some examples, the counselor should ask the client to think of additional coping statements. The client may come up with self-enhancing or positive statements she or he has used in other situations. The client should be encouraged to select coping statements that feel most natural. Goldfried (1976b) recommends that clients identify coping thoughts by discovering convincing counterarguments for their unrealistic thoughts.

Client practice. Using these client-selected coping statements, the counselor should ask the client to practice verbalizing coping statements aloud. This is very important, because most clients are not accustomed to using coping statements. Such practice may reduce some of the client's initial discomfort and can strengthen confidence in being able to produce different "self-talk." In addition, clients who are "formally" trained to practice coping statements systematically may use a greater variety of coping thoughts, may use more specific coping thoughts, and may report more consistent use of coping thoughts *in vivo* (Glogower et al., 1978).

At first, the client can practice verbalizing the individual coping statements she or he selected to use before and during the situation. Gradually, as the client gets accustomed to coping statements, the coping thoughts should be practiced in the natural sequence in which they will be used. First, the client would anticipate the situation and practice coping statements before the situation to prepare for it, followed by practice of coping thoughts during the situation—focusing on the task and coping with feeling overwhelmed.

It is important for the client to become actively involved in these practice sessions. The counselor should try to ensure that the client does not simply rehearse the coping statements by rote. Instead, the client should use these practices to try to internalize the meaning of the coping statements (Meichenbaum, 1977, p. 89). One way to encourage more client involvement and self-assertion in these practice attempts is to suggest that the client pretend that he or she is talking to an audience or a group of persons and needs to talk in a persuasive, convincing manner in order to get his or her point across.

Shifting from Self-Defeating to Coping Thoughts

After the client has identified negative thoughts and has practiced alternative coping thoughts, the counselor introduces rehearsal of shift from self-defeating to coping thoughts during stressful situations. Practice of this shift helps the client use a self-defeating thought as a cue for an immediate switch to coping thoughts.

Counselor demonstration of shift. The counselor should model this process before asking the client to try it. This gives the client an accurate idea of how to practice this shift. Here is an example of a counselor modeling for a high school student who constantly "freezes up" in competitive situations.

"OK, I'm sitting here waiting for my turn to try out for cheerleader. Ooh, I can feel myself getting very nervous. [anxious feeling] Now, wait, what am I so nervous about? I'm afraid I'm going to make a fool of myself. [self-defeating thought] Hey, that doesn't help. [cue to cope] It will take only a few minutes, and it will be over with before I know it. Besides, only the faculty sponsors are watching. It's not like the whole school. [situation-oriented coping thoughts]

Well, the person before me is just about finished. Oh, they're calling my name. Boy, do I feel tense. [anxious feelings] What if I don't execute my jumps? [self-defeating thought] OK, don't think about what I'm not going to do. OK, start out, it's my turn. Just think about my routine—the way I want it to go." [task-oriented coping thoughts]

Client practice of the shift. After the counselor demonstration, the client should practice identifying and stopping self-defeating thoughts and replacing them with coping thoughts. The counselor can monitor the client's progress and coach if necessary. Rehearsal of this shift involves four steps:

1. The client imagines the stressful situation or carries out his or her part in the situation by means of a role play.
2. The client is instructed to recognize the onset of any self-defeating thoughts and to signal this by raising a hand or finger.
3. Next, the client is told to stop these thoughts, or reframe these thoughts.
4. After the self-defeating thought is stopped, the client immediately replaces it with the coping thoughts. The client should be given some time to concentrate on the coping thoughts. Initially, it may be helpful for the client to verbalize coping thoughts; later, this can occur covertly.

As the client seems able to identify, stop, and replace the self-defeating thoughts, the counselor can gradually decrease the amount of assistance. Before homework is assigned, the client should be able to practice and carry out this shift in the interview setting in a completely self-directed manner.

Introduction and Practice of Reinforcing Self-Statements

The last part of cognitive restructuring involves teaching clients how to reinforce themselves for having coped. This is accomplished by counselor modeling and client practice of positive, or reinforcing, self-statements. Many clients who could benefit from cognitive restructuring report not only frequent self-defeating thoughts but also few or no positive or rewarding self-evaluations. Some clients may learn to replace self-defeating thoughts with task-oriented coping ones and feel better but not satisfied with their progress (Mahoney & Mahoney, 1976). The purpose of including positive self-statements in cognitive restructuring is to help clients learn to praise or congratulate themselves for signs of progress. Although the counselor can provide social reinforcement in the interview, the client cannot always be dependent on encouragement from someone else when confronted with a stressful situation.

Purpose and examples of positive self-statements. The counselor should explain the purpose of reinforcing self-statements to the client and provide some examples. An explanation might sound like this:

"You know, Joan, you've really done very well in handling these situations and learning to stop those self-defeating ideas and to use some coping thoughts. Now it's time to give yourself credit for your progress. I will help you learn to encourage

yourself by using rewarding thoughts, so that each time you're in this situation and you cope, you also give yourself a pat on the back for handling the situation and not getting overwhelmed by it. This kind of self-encouragement helps you to note your progress and prevents you from getting discouraged."

Then the counselor can give some examples of reinforcing self-statements:

"Gee, I did it."
"Hey, I handled that OK."
"I didn't let my emotions get the best of me."
"I made some progress, and that feels good."
"See, it went pretty well after all."

Client selection of positive self-statements. After providing examples, the counselor should ask the client for additional positive statements. The client should select those statements that feel suitable. This is particularly important in using reinforcing statements, because the reinforcing value of a statement may be very idiosyncratic.

Counselor demonstration of positive self-statements. The counselor should demonstrate how the client can use a positive self-statement after coping with a situation. Here is an example of a counselor modeling the use of positive self-statements during and after a stressful situation. In this case, the client was an institutionalized adolescent who was confronting her parents in a face-to-face meeting.

"OK, I can feel them putting pressure on me. They want me to talk. I don't want to talk. I just want to get the hell out of here. [self-defeating thought] Slow down, wait a minute. Don't pressure yourself. Stay cool. [coping with being overwhelmed] Good. That's better. [positive self-statement]
Well, it's over. It wasn't too bad. I stuck it out. That's progress." [positive self-statement]

Client practice of positive self-statements. The client should be instructed to practice using positive self-statements during and after the stressful situation. The practice occurs first within the interview and gradually outside the interview with *in vivo* assignments. Mahoney and Mahoney (1976) reported an ingenious type of daily self-directed practice to help increase the frequency of a client's positive self-evaluations. The client was taught to cue positive self-statements, to practice these by calling a telephone-answering device, and to verbalize self-praise for her efforts to modify and cope with negative thoughts. These recordings were reviewed by both the client and her counselor. This review served as another way to strengthen the client's positive self-evaluative thoughts (p. 104).

Homework and Follow-up

Although homework is an integral part of every step of the cognitive restructuring procedure, the client ultimately should be able to use cognitive restructuring whenever it is needed in actual distressing situations. The client should be instructed to use cognitive restructuring *in vivo* but cautioned not to expect instant success (Goldfried & Davison, 1976). As with thought stopping, clients can be reminded of the time they have spent playing the old tape over and over in their heads and of the need to make frequent and lengthy substitutions with the new tape. The client can monitor and record the instances in which cognitive restructuring was used over several weeks.

The counselor can facilitate the written recording by providing a homework log sheet that might look something like Figure 16-2. The client's log data can be reviewed at a follow-up session to determine the number of times the client is using cognitive restructuring and the amount of progress that has occurred. The counselor can also use the follow-up session to encourage the client to apply the procedure to stressful situations that could arise in the future. This may encourage the client to generalize the use of cognitive restructuring to situations other than those that are presently considered problematic.

Occasionally, a client's level of distress may not diminish even after repeated practice of restructuring self-defeating thoughts. In some cases, negative self-statements do not precede or contribute to the person's strong feelings. Some emotions may be classically conditioned and therefore treated more appropriately by a counterconditioning procedure, such as systematic desensitization (see Chapter 18). However, even in classically conditioned fears, cognitive processes may also play some role in maintaining or reducing the fear (Davison & Wilson, 1973).

When cognitive restructuring does not reduce a client's level of distress, depression, or anxiety, the counselor and client may need to redefine the problem and goals. As Goldfried and Davison (1976, p. 174) observe, the therapist should "consider the possibility that his assessment has been inaccurate, and that there are, in fact, no internal sentences which are functionally tied to this partic-

ular client's problem." Remember that assessment of initial problems may not always turn out to be valid or accurate.

Assuming that the original problem assessment is accurate, perhaps a change in parts of the cognitive restructuring procedure is necessary. Here are some possible revisions:

1. The amount of time the client uses to shift from self-defeating to coping thoughts and to imagine coping thoughts can be increased.
2. The particular coping statements selected by the client may not be very helpful; a change in the type of coping statements may be beneficial.
3. Cognitive restructuring may need to be supplemented either with additional coping skills, such as deep breathing or relaxation, or with skill training [Goldfried & Davison, 1976, p. 174].

Another reason for failure of cognitive restructuring may be that the client's problem behaviors result from errors in encoding rather than errors in reasoning. We describe a strategy designed to alter encoding or perceptual errors in the next section, after the dialogue and learning activity.

☐ MODEL DIALOGUE: COGNITIVE RESTRUCTURING

Session 2

In session 2, the counselor will follow up and review the thought stopping Joan learned the previous week (see Chapter 15). The rest of the interview will be directed toward helping Joan replace self-defeating thoughts with coping thoughts. This is the "nuts and bolts" of cognitive restructuring; it is similar to the substitution of assertive or positive thoughts in thought stopping and is also a major part of stress inoculation, described later in this chapter.

1. *Counselor:* Good to see you again, Joan. How did your week go?
   Client: Pretty good. I did a lot of practice. I also tried to do this in math class. It helped some, but I still felt nervous. Here are my logs.

In response 2, the counselor **reinforces Joan for completing her logs** *and her daily practice. Joan is usually good at completing these; nevertheless, such work on the client's part should not go unnoticed.*

2. *Counselor:* OK, these look good. Let's go over

Daily record of dysfunctional thoughts

Date	Situation	Emotion(s)	Automatic thought(s)	Rational response	Outcome
	Describe: 1. Actual event leading to unpleasant emotion or 2. Stream of thoughts, daydream, or recollection leading to unpleasant emotion.	1. Specify sad-anxious, etc. 2. Rate degree of emotion, 1–100%.	1. Write automatic thought(s) that preceded emotion(s). 2. Rate belief in automatic thought(s), 0–100%.	1. Write rational response to automatic thought(s). 2. Rate belief in rational response, 0–100%.	1. Rerate belief in automatic thought(s), 0–100%. 2. Specify and rate subsequent emotions, 0–100%.
EXAMPLE 2/5	Not getting filing and lots of other stuff done.	Anxious-sad-angry 85%	A failure again, I can never get my work done, I'm no good. 85%	I have got filing and other work done in the past, but usually in smaller bites, not all at once. 80%	1. 45% 2. Anxious-sad 50%

Explanation of rating categories: When you experience an unpleasant emotion, note the situation that seemed to stimulate the emotion. (If the emotion occurred while you were thinking, daydreaming, etc., please note this.) Then note the automatic thought associated with the emotion. Record the degree to which you believe this thought: 0% = not at all; 100% = completely. In rating degree of emotion: 1 = a trace; 100 = the most intense possible.

*"In vivo assessment techniques for cognitive-behavioral processes" by S. D. Hollon & P. C. Kendall. In *Assessment strategies for cognitive-behavioral interventions* by P. C. Kendall and S. D. Hollon (Eds.). Copyright © 1981 by Academic Press. Reprinted by permission.

Figure 16-2. *Example of homework log sheet**

them. Looks like you did a lot of daily practice. This is terrific. Now, according to your log, you needed to use the thought stopping before your class and several times during the class.
Client: Right. Especially when we had a test or I had to go to the board. You know how that makes me feel — nervous.

The counselor uses this opportunity **to reiterate how Joan's negative thoughts can, to some extent, contribute to her nervous feelings** *and explains that the physical sensations of nervousness will be dealt with later and cautions Joan not to expect too much change all at once.*

3. *Counselor:* Yes, and some of the nervousness is created by the negative thoughts. However, you've indicated you feel nervous physically, so we'll work with this in another way later on. So it's understandable if you still feel nervous this week. It won't be an overnight change — just one step at a time. (Shows Joan a cassette tape recorder.) Remember this tape recorder. You've been playing the old tape in your head for a long time and it will take some practice to eject it and put a new one in.
Client: Yes. Well, I could definitely tell that I cut off these thoughts sooner than I used to.

In response 4, the counselor gives a **rationale** *for cognitive restructuring,* **explains the purpose of "coping" thoughts to Joan,** *and gives an* **overview** *of the strategy.*

4. *Counselor:* That's great. And I bet your daily practice helped you do that when you needed to. Today we're going to go one step further. In addition to having you stop the negative thoughts, we're going to work on having you learn to use some more constructive thoughts. I call these *"coping thoughts."* You can replace the negative thoughts with coping thoughts that will help you when you're anticipating your class, in your class itself, and when things happen in your class that are especially hard for you — like taking a test or going to the board. What questions do you have about this?
Client: I don't think any — although I don't know if I know exactly what you mean by a coping thought.

The counselor, in response 5, will **explain and give some examples of coping thoughts** *and particular times or phases when Joan might need to use them.*

5. *Counselor:* OK, let me explain about these and give you some examples. Then perhaps you can think of your own examples. The first thing is

that there are probably different times when you could use coping thoughts — like before math class when you're anticipating it. Only, instead of worrying about it, you can use this time to prepare to handle it. For example, some coping thoughts you might use before math class are "No need to get nervous. Just think about doing OK" or "You can manage this situation" or "Don't worry so much — you've got the ability to do OK." Then, during math class, you can use coping thoughts to get through the class and to concentrate on what you're doing, such as "Just psych yourself up to get through this" or "Look at this class as a challenge, not a threat" or "Keep your cool, you can control your nervousness." Then, if there are certain times during math class that are especially hard for you, like taking a test or going to the board, there are coping thoughts you can use to help you deal with really hard things, like "Think about staying very calm now" or "Relax, take a deep breath" or "Stay as relaxed as possible. This will be over shortly." After math class, or after you cope with a hard situation, then you can learn to encourage yourself for having coped by thinking things like "You did it" or "You were able to control your negative thoughts" or "You're making progress." Do you get the idea?
Client: Yes, I think so.

Next, in responses 6 through 9, the counselor will instruct Joan **to select and practice coping thoughts at each critical phase,** *starting with* **preparing for class.**

6. *Counselor:* Joan, let's take one thing at a time. Let's work just with what you might think before your math class. Can you come up with some coping thoughts you could use when you're anticipating your class?
Client: Well. [Pauses] I could think about just working on my problems and not worrying about myself. I could think that when I work at it, I usually get it even if I'm slow.

7. *Counselor:* OK, good. Now just to get the feel for these, practice using them. Perhaps you could imagine you are anticipating your class — just say these thoughts aloud as you do.
Client: Well, I'm thinking that I could look at my class as a challenge. I can think about just doing my work. When I concentrate on my work, I usually do get the answers.

8. *Counselor:* OK — good! How did that feel?
Client: Well, OK. I can see how this might help. Of course, I don't usually think these kinds of things.

9. *Counselor:* I realize that, and later on today we will practice actually having you use these

thoughts after you use the thought stopping that you learned last week. You'll get to the point where you can use your nervousness as a signal to cope. You can stop the self-defeating thoughts and use these coping thoughts instead. Let's practice this some more. [Additional practice ensues.]

In responses 10, 11, and 12, the counselor asks Joan **to select and practice verbalizing coping thoughts** *she can use* **during class.**

10. *Counselor:* OK, Joan, now you seem to have several kinds of coping thoughts that might help you when you're anticipating math class. What about some coping thoughts you could use during the class? Perhaps some of these could help you concentrate on your work instead of your tenseness.

    Client: Well, I could tell myself to think about what I need to do—like to get the problems. Or I could think—just take one situation at a time. Just psych myself up 'cause I know I really can do well in math if I believe that.

11. *Counselor:* OK, it sounds like you've already thought of several coping things to use during class. This time, why don't you pretend you're sitting in your class? Try out some of these coping thoughts. Just say them aloud.

    Client: OK. Well, I'm sitting at my desk, my work is in front of me. What steps do I need to take now? Well, I could just think about one problem at a time, not worry about all of them. If I take it slowly, I can do OK.

12. *Counselor:* OK, that seemed pretty easy for you. Let's do some more practice like this just so these thoughts don't seem unfamiliar to you. As you practice, try hard to think about the meaning of what you're saying to yourself. [More practice occurs.]

Next, Joan **selects and practices coping thoughts** *to help her deal with especially* **stressful or critical situations** *that come up in math class (responses 13, 14, and 15).*

13. *Counselor:* This time, let's think of some particular coping statements that might help you if you come up against some touchy situations in your math class—things that are really hard for you to deal with, like taking a test, going to the board, or being called on. What might you think at these times that would keep the lid on your nervousness?

    Client: Well, I could think about just doing what is required of me—maybe, as you said earlier taking a deep breath and just thinking about

staying calm, not letting my anxiety get the best of me.

14. *Counselor:* OK, great. Let's see—can you practice some of these aloud as if you were taking a test or had just been asked a question or were at the board in front of the class?

    Client: OK. Well, I'm at the board, I'm just going to think about doing this problem. If I start to get really nervous, I'm going to take a deep breath and just concentrate on being calm as I do this.

15. *Counselor:* OK, let's practice this several times. Maybe this time you might use another tense moment, like being called on by your teacher. [Further practice goes on.]

Next, the counselor **points out how Joan may discourage or punish herself after class** *(responses 16 and 17). Joan selects and* **practices encouraging or self-rewarding thoughts** *(responses 18, 19, and 20).*

16. *Counselor:* OK, Joan, there's one more thing I'd like you to practice. After math class, what do you usually think?

    Client: I feel relieved. I think about how glad I am it's over. Sometimes I think about the fact that I didn't do well.

17. *Counselor:* Well, those thoughts are sort of discouraging, too. What I believe might help is if you could learn to encourage yourself as you start to use these coping thoughts. In other words, instead of thinking about not doing well, focus on your progress in coping. You can do this during class or after class is over. Can you find some more positive things you could think about to encourage yourself—like giving yourself a pat on the back?

    Client: You mean like I didn't do as bad as I thought?

18. *Counselor:* Yes, anything like that.

    Client: Well, it's over, it didn't go too badly. Actually I handled things OK. I can do this if I believe it. I can see progress.

19. *Counselor:* OK, now, let's assume you've just been at the board. You're back at your seat. Practice saying what you might think in that situation that would be encouraging to you.

    Client: Well, I've just sat down. I might think that it went fast and I did concentrate on the problem, so that was good.

20. *Counselor:* OK. Now let's assume class is over. What would you say would be positive, self-encouraging thoughts after class?

    Client: Well, I've just gotten out. Class wasn't that bad. I got something out of it. If I put my mind to it, I can do it. [More practice of positive self-statements occurs.]

In response 21, the counselor instructs Joan **to practice the entire sequence** *of stopping a self-defeating thought and using a coping thought before, during, and after class. Usually the client practices this by* **imagining the situation.**

21. *Counselor:* So far we've been practicing these coping thoughts at the different times you might use them so you can get used to these. Now let's practice this in the sequence that it might actually occur—like before your class, during the class, coping with a tough situation, and encouraging yourself after class. We can also practice this with your thought stopping. If you imagine the situation and start to notice any self-defeating thoughts, you can practice stopping these. Then switch immediately to the types of coping thoughts that you believe will help you most at that time. Concentrate on the coping thoughts. How does this sound?
    Client: OK, I think I know what you mean. [Looks a little confused.]

Sometimes long instructions are confusing. Modeling may be better. In responses 22 and 23, the counselor **demonstrates how Joan can apply thought stopping and coping thoughts in practice.**

22. *Counselor:* Well, I just said a lot, and it might make more sense if I showed this to you. First, I'm going to imagine I'm in English class. It's almost time for the bell, then it's math class. Wish I could get out of it. It's embarrassing. *Stop!* That's a signal to use my coping thoughts. I need to think about math class as a challenge. Something I can do OK if I work at it. [Pauses.] Joan, do you get the idea?
    Client: Yes, now I do.

23. *Counselor:* OK, I'll go on and imagine now I'm actually in the class. He's given us a worksheet to do in 30 minutes. Whew! How will dumb me ever do that! *Stop!* I know I can do it, but I need to go slowly and concentrate on the work, not on me. Just take one problem at a time.
    Well, now he wants us to read our answers. What if he calls on me? I can feel my heart pounding. *Stop!* If I get called on, just take a deep breath and answer. If it turns out to be wrong, it's not the end of the world.
    Well, the bell rang. I am walking out. I'm glad it's over. Now, wait a minute—it didn't go that badly. Actually I handled it pretty well.
    Client: I'm seeing now how this fits together with thought stopping. After you stop a negative thought, you go to a coping thought.

Next, the counselor encourages Joan **to try this out in practice attempts.**

24. *Counselor:* That's it. The idea is to stop the negative thoughts and use more constructive ones. Now, why don't you try this? [Joan practices the sequence of thought stopping and shifting to coping thoughts several times, first with the counselor's assistance, gradually in a completely self-directed manner.]

Before terminating the session, the counselor **assigns daily homework practice.**

25. *Counselor:* This week I'd like you to practice this several times each day—just like you did now. Keep track of your practices on your log. And you can use this whenever you feel it would be helpful—such as before, during, or after math class. Jot these times down too, and we'll go over this next week.

LEARNING ACTIVITIES #42: COGNITIVE RESTRUCTURING

I. Listed below are eight statements. Read each statement carefully and decide whether it is a self-defeating or a self-enhancing statement. Remember, a self-defeating thought is a negative, unproductive way to view a situation; a self-enhancing thought is a realistic, productive interpretation of a situation or of oneself. Write down your answers. Feedback is given after the learning activities on page 416.

1. "I'll never be able to pass this test."
2. "How can I ever give a good speech when I don't know what I want to say?"
3. "What I can do is to take one thing at a time."
4. "I know I'm going to blow it with all those people looking at me."
5. "What I need to think about is what I *want* to say, not what I think I *should* say."
6. "What if I'm imposing? Maybe I'm just wasting their time."
7. "Why bother? She probably wouldn't want to go out with me anyway."
8. "I may not win, but I'll do my best."

II. This learning activity is designed to help you personalize cognitive restructuring in some way by using it yourself.

1. Identify a problem situation for yourself—a situation in which you don't do what you want to, not

(continued)

because you don't have the skills, but because of your negative, self-defeating thoughts. Some examples:

   a. You need to approach your boss about a raise, promotion, or change in duties. You know what to say, but you are keeping yourself from doing it because you aren't sure it would have any effect and you aren't sure how the person might respond.

   b. You have the skills to be an effective helper, yet you constantly think that you aren't.

   c. You continue to get positive feedback about the way you handle a certain situation, yet you are constantly thinking you don't do this very well.

2. For about a week, every time this situation comes up, monitor all the thoughts you have *before, during,* and *after* the situation. Write these thoughts in a log. At the end of the week:

   a. Identify which of the thoughts are self-defeating.

   b. Identify which of the thoughts are self-enhancing.

   c. Determine whether the greatest number of self-defeating thoughts occur before, during, or after the situation.

3. In contrast to the self-defeating thoughts you have, identify some possible coping or self-enhancing thoughts you could use. On paper, list some you could use before, during, and after the situation, with particular attention to the time period when you tend to use almost all self-defeating thoughts. Make sure that you include in your list some positive or self-rewarding thoughts, too — for coping.

4. Imagine the situation — before, during, and after it. As you do this, stop any self-defeating thoughts and replace them with coping and self-rewarding thoughts. You can even practice this in role play. This step should be practiced until you can feel your coping and self-rewarding thoughts taking hold.

5. Construct a homework assignment for yourself that encourages you to apply this as needed when the self-defeating thoughts occur.

□ REFRAMING

Recall that the focus of cognitive restructuring is on faulty reasoning and illogical or irrational inferences and beliefs. The goal is to alter irrational beliefs or negative self-statements. Some clients, however, may exhibit maladaptive response patterns because of errors in encoding and/or encoding bias. For example:

A parent who explodes in anger at [a] child's demands for help does so because s/he focuses on cues related to his/her dependence and inability to do anything for herself/himself. S/he might selectively attend to his/her statement "I can't do it" and to the pleading look in his/her eyes or tone in his/her voice and automatically thinks "I can't stand this child. I wish I were free of her/him." S/he feels overwhelmed by his/her demands and inadequate as a parent. However, a focus on the child's tired eyes and partial achievement of the task in which the child is asking for help results in a different encoding, one of an overtired child who attempts to do things independently. This encoding would produce a different response to the child and no subsequent thoughts of personal inadequacy for the parent [Greenberg & Safran, 1981, p. 165].*

As this example illustrates, typical dysfunctional encoding activity consists of a series of discrete peripheral responses that are "linked together in a cyclical and self-perpetuating fashion" (Greenberg & Safran, 1981, p. 165). For clients who are making mistakes in encoding, identifying and modifying their perceptions — what they attend to — may be useful. This is the goal of a strategy we call "reframing." This strategy is based on the work of Greenberg and Safran (1981), Safran et al. (1980), Safran and Greenberg (1982), Bandler and Grinder (1982) and Watzlawick, Weakland, and Fisch (1974). Occasionally, *both* cognitive restructuring and reframing are useful for a client.

Reframing (sometimes also called relabeling) is an approach that modifies or restructures a client's perceptions or views of a problem or a behavior. Reframing is used frequently in family therapy as a way to redefine presenting problems in order to

* This and other quotations from this source and from "Encoding and cognitive therapy: Changing what clients attend to" by L. S. Greenberg and J. D. Safran. *Psychotherapy: Theory, Research and Practice, 18,* 163–169. Copyright © 1981 by the American Psychological Association. Reprinted by permission.

FEEDBACK #42: COGNITIVE RESTRUCTURING

I. 1. Self-defeating: the word *never* indicates the person is not giving himself or herself any chance for passing.

   2. Self-defeating: the person is doubting both the ability to give a good speech and knowledge of the subject.

   3. Self-enhancing: the person is realistically focusing on one step at a time.

   4. Self-defeating: the person is saying with certainty, as evidenced by the word *know*, that there is no chance to do well; this is said without supporting data or evidence.

   5. Self-enhancing: the client is realistically focusing on his or her own opinion, not on the assessment of others.

   6. Self-defeating: the person is viewing the situation only from a negative perspective, as if rejection were expected and deserved.

   7. Self-defeating: the person predicts a negative reaction without any supporting evidence.

   8. Self-enhancing: the person recognizes a win may not occur yet still concentrates on doing the best job.

shift the focus off of an "identified patient" or "scapegoat" and onto the family as a whole, as a system in which each member is an interdependent part (Watzlawick et al., 1974). When used in this way, reframing changes the way a family encodes an issue or a conflict.

With individual clients, reframing has a number of uses as well. By changing or restructuring what clients encode and perceive, reframing can reduce defensiveness and mobilize the client's resources and forces for change. Secondly, it can shift the focus from overly simplistic trait attributions of behavior that clients are inclined to make ("I am lazy." or "I am not assertive.") to analyses of important contextual and situational cues associated with the behavior (Alexander & Parsons, 1982). Finally, reframing can be a useful strategy for dealing with client "resistance" (see also positive connotation in Chapter 20).

Meaning Reframes

Counselors reframe whenever they ask or encourage clients to see an issue from a different perspective. In this chapter, we propose a more systematic way for counselors to help clients reframe a prob-

lem behavior. The most common method of reframing—and the one that we illustrate in this chapter—is to reframe the *meaning* of a problem situation or behavior. When you reframe meaning, you are challenging the meaning that the client (or someone else) has assigned to a given problem behavior. Usually, the longer a particular meaning (or label) is attached to a client's behavior, the more necessary the behavior itself becomes in maintaining predictability and equilibrium in the client's functioning. Also, when meanings are attached to client behavior over a long period of time, clients are more likely to develop "functional fixity"—that is, seeing things in only one way or from one perspective or being fixated on the idea that this particular situation or attribute is *the* issue. Reframing helps clients by providing alternative ways to view a problem behavior without directly challenging the behavior itself and by loosening a client's perceptual frame, thus setting the stage for other kinds of therapeutic work. Once the *meaning* of a behavior or a situation changes, the person's response to the situation or the person's typical behavior usually also changes, providing the reframe is valid and acceptable to the client. The essence of a meaning reframe is to give a situation or a behavior a new label or a new name that has a different meaning. This new meaning always has a different connotation, and usually it is a positive one. For example, client "stubbornness" might be reframed as "independence" or "greediness" might be reframed as "ambitiousness." Meaning reframes are based on two assumptions: (1) that it is possible to reframe whatever a person does (or doesn't do) as a success (Erickson, in Watzlawick et al., 1974); and (2) that persons will be cooperative if positive aspects of their behavior are stressed.

Reframing involves six steps:

1. Rationale: purpose and overview of the procedure.
2. Identification of client perceptions and feelings in problem situations.
3. Deliberate enactment of selected perceptual features.
4. Identification of alternative perceptions.
5. Modification of perceptions in problem situations.
6. Homework and follow-up.

A detailed description of the steps associated with these components can be found in the Interview Checklist for Reframing at the end of this chapter.

Treatment Rationale

The rationale used to present reframing attempts to strengthen the client's belief that perceptions or attributions about the problem situation can cause emotional distress. Here is a rationale that can be used to introduce reframing:

"When we think about or when we are in a problem situation, we automatically attend to selected features of the situation. As time goes on, we tend to get fixated on these same features of the situation and ignore other aspects of it. This can lead to some uncomfortable emotions, such as the ones you're feeling now. In this procedure, I will help you identify what you are usually aware of during these problem situations. Then we'll work on increasing your awareness of other aspects of the situation that you usually don't notice. As this happens, you will notice that your feelings about and responses to this problem will start to change. Do you have any questions?"

Identification of Client Perceptions and Feelings

Assuming that the client accepts the rationale the counselor provides, the next step is to help clients become aware of what they automatically attend to in problem situations. Clients are often unaware of what features or details they attend to in a problem situation and what information about these situations they encode. For example, one person may attend to a long hospital corridor and encode it as cold and impersonal, while someone else may attend to the people on the corridor and encode the feature as healthy, caring, and clean (Greenberg & Safran, 1981). Or clients who have a fear of water may attend to how deep the water is because they cannot see the bottom and encode the perception that they might drown. Clients who experience test anxiety might attend to the large size of the room or how quickly the other people seem to be working. These features are encoded and lead to feeling overwhelmed, anxious, and lacking in confidence. In turn, these feelings can lead to impaired performance in or avoidance of the situation.

Within the interview, the therapist helps clients discover what they typically attend to in problem situations. The therapist can use imagery or role play to help clients reenact the situation(s) in order to become aware of what they notice and encode. While engaging in role play or in imagining the problem situation, the therapist can help the client become more aware of typical encoding patterns by asking questions like these:

"What are you attending to now?"
"What are you aware of now?"

"What are you noticing about the situation?"

In order to link feelings to individual perceptions, these questions can be followed with further inquiries like

"What are you feeling at this moment?" or
"What do you experience?" (Greenberg & Safran, 1981).

The counselor may have to help clients engage in role play or imagery several times so that they can reconstruct the situation and become more aware of salient encoded features. The therapist may also suggest what the client might have felt and what the experience appears to mean to the client in order to bring these automatic perceptions into awareness (Greenberg & Safran, 1981). The therapist also helps clients notice "marginal impressions"—fleeting images, sounds, feelings, and sensations that were passively rather than deliberately processed by the client yet affect the client's reaction to the situation (Greenberg & Safran, 1981).

Deliberate Enactment of Selected Perceptual Features

After clients become aware of their rather automatic attending, they are asked to reenact the situation and intentionally attend to the selected features that they have been processing automatically. For example, the water-phobic client reenacts (through role play or imagery) approach situations with the water and deliberately attends to the salient features such as the depth of the water and inability to see the bottom of the pool. By deliberately attending to these encoded features, clients are able to bring these habitual attentional processes fully into awareness and under direct control (Greenberg & Safran, 1981, p. 165). This sort of "dramatization" seems to sharpen the client's awareness of existing perceptions. When these perceptions are uncovered and made more visible through this deliberate re-enactment, it is harder for the client to maintain old illusions (Andolfi, 1979). This step may need to be repeated several times during the session or assigned as a homework task.

Identification of Alternative Perceptions

The counselor can help the client change his or her attentional focus by selecting other features of the problem situation to attend to rather than ignore. For example, the water-phobic client who focuses on the depth of the water might be instructed to focus on how clear, clean, and wet the water appears. For the test-anxious client who attends to the size of the room, the counselor can redirect the client's attention to how roomy the testing place is or how comfortable the seats are. Both clients and counselors can suggest other features of the problem situation or person to utilize that have a positive or at least a neutral connotation. The following kinds of questions may help both counselor and client identify new meanings: "Is there a larger or different frame in which this behavior would have a positive value?" "What else could this behavior mean?" "How else could this same situation be described?" "What other aspect of this same situation that isn't apparent to the client could provide a different meaning frame?" (Bandler & Grinder, 1982, p. 15).

For reframing to be effective, the alternative perceptions you identify must be acceptable to the client. The best reframes are the ones that are accurate and are "*as* valid a way of looking at the world as the way the person sees things now. Reframes don't necessarily need to be more valid, but they really can't be less valid" (Bandler & Grinder, 1982, p. 42). Thus, all reframes or alternative perceptions have to be tailored to the clients' values, style, sociocultural context, and have to fit the clients' experience and model of their world. The alternative perceptions or reframes you suggest obviously also need to match the external reality of the situation enough to be plausible. If, for example, a husband is feeling very angry with his wife because of her extramarital affair, reframing his anger as "loving concern" is probably not representative enough of the external situation to be plausible to the client. A more plausible reframe might be something like "frustration over not being able to control your wife's behavior" or "frustration from not being able to protect the (marital) relationship."

The delivery of a reframe is also important. When suggesting alternative perceptions to clients, it is essential that the counselor's nonverbal behavior be congruent with the tone and content of the reframe. It is also important to use your voice effectively in delivering the reframe by emphasizing key words or phrases.

Modification of Perceptions in Problem Situations

Modifying what clients attend to can be facilitated with role play or imagery. The therapist instructs the client to attend to other features of the problem situations during the role play or imagery enact-

ment. This step may need to be repeated several times. According to Greenberg and Safran (1981, p. 166), these attempts to create new perceptual responses "are explicitly designed to break old encoding patterns and lay the blueprint for new, more effective patterns."

Homework and Follow-up

The therapist can suggest that the client follow during *in vivo* situations the same format used in therapy. The client is instructed to become more aware of salient encoded features of a stressful or arousing situation, to link these to uncomfortable feelings, to engage in deliberate enactments or practice activities, and to try to make "perceptual shifts" during these situations to other features of the situation previously ignored.

As the client becomes more adept at this process, the therapist will need to be alert to slight perceptual shifts and point these out to clients. Typically, clients are unskilled at detecting these shifts in encoding (Greenberg & Safran, 1981). Helping the client discriminate between old and new encodings of a problem situation can be very useful in promoting the overall goal of the reframing strategy—to alleviate and modify encoding or perceptual errors and bias.

Context Reframes

Although the steps we propose for reframing involve reframing of meaning, another way you can also reframe is to reframe the *context* of a problem behavior. Reframing the context helps a client to explore and decide *when, where,* and *with whom* a given problem behavior is *useful* or appropriate. Context reframing helps clients answer the question "In what place in your life is behavior X useful and appropriate?" (Bandler & Grinder, 1982). Context reframing is based on the assumption that every behavior is useful in *some* but not all contexts or conditions. Thus, when a client states "I'm too lazy," a context reframe would be "In what situations (or with what people) is it useful or even helpful to be lazy?" The client may respond by noting that it is useful to be lazy whenever she wants to play with the children. At this point the counselor can help the client sort out and contextualize a given problem behavior so that clients can see where and when they do and do not want the behavior to occur. Context reframes are most useful when dealing with client generalizations—for example "I'm *never* assertive," "I'm *always* late," and so on.

☐ MODEL DIALOGUE: REFRAMING

Session 3

In this session, the counselor continues to help Joan work on the anxiety she feels in math class. In the previous session, they focused on her negative self-statements. In this session, they will work with reframing the meaning associated with Joan's math class.

1. *Counselor:* Good to see you again, Joan. How did things go for you this week?
   Client: Not too bad. I did cut math class once. I still have some nervousness there, although it seems to be getting a little bit more under control.

In response 2, the counselor introduces the idea of **how perceptions can create distressing feelings.**

2. *Counselor:* Great. As we talked about last week, some of the nervousness is created by those negative thoughts. Some of it is also created by how you see math class, which is what I'd like to focus on today if that's OK.
   Client: All right.

In response 3, the counselor gives a **rationale** *for reframing.*

3. *Counselor:* OK, today we're going to go one step further. In addition to having you stop the negative thoughts, we're going to work on having you look at how you perceive the math class. Right now, if I asked you to think about math class, you would probably think about negative features of the class. By attending only to these negative features, you exclude positive or neutral aspects of math class. Just seeing the negative features of the class contributes to your nervous feelings about the class. Today, I'll help you identify what things you notice in math class. Once we become aware of this, we will modify what you attend to by focusing on the ignored positive or neutral attributes of the math class. What questions do you have about this?
   Client: I don't have any — but I'm not sure what you mean by my "perception" and "features."

The counselor, in response 4, will help Joan **identify what she attends to** *when she thinks of math class.*

4. *Counselor:* Yes, those terms are confusing! Let's work with math class and see whether this becomes more clear to you. Let's try to see what it is you are attending to in math class. For example, when you think of math class, try to identify what comes into your mind.
   Client: Well, some of the time I think about math problems and how difficult they are. And I

don't get grades that are as good as some others in the class. I get nervous and I wish I didn't have to go.

The client has identified some of her thoughts and reactions related to math class. However, the counselor wants to identify some specific features the client attends to **initially when she thinks of math class.** *In response 5, the counselor instructs the client to* **engage in imagery** *to help Joan* **increase her awareness of what she initially thinks about** *when she starts to think of math class.*

5. *Counselor:* OK, that's a good start. Now, what I want us to focus on is specific things you first think about when you start to think about math class. What are the specific features that come to your mind when I say "math class?" To help you identify these initial features, I want you to close your eyes, and I'll instruct you to imagine being in math class and being aware of all the reactions you experience. After you imagine being in class for a while, I'll ask you to identify what specific things about your math class you're focusing on. Ok, now close your eyes and imagine you are in math class. Experience all the sensations you have. After a few minutes, I'll tell you to open your eyes. [Twenty seconds elapse.] Now open your eyes and tell me what you saw in this situation.
   Client: Well, I think that math is really not important for women. I think that math won't help me and girls shouldn't be as good in math as boys.

Joan is now describing an irrational belief. The counselor provides an **example** *to show Joan what kinds of things to attend to during the imagery.*

6. *Counselor:* OK, that's an example of something you *think* about. I'm interested now in what you *notice* about the situation when you're there. For instance, right now I'm noticing that it is hot in this room, that you have a perplexed look on your face, that I have a gurgling sensation in my stomach. Let's try it again, and this time I'll ask you some questions as you imagine this. [Instructs Joan to engage in another imagery scene of math.]

In response 7, the counselor queries Joan about **present awareness of selected features.**

7. *Counselor:* OK, now, Joan, what are you aware of as you do this? Just describe whatever comes into your mind.
   Client: Well — the teacher. He is there with a smirk on his face, like he thinks I'm stupid. And all the other guys in the room. They are all look-

ing at me, especially when I get called on or have to go to the board—like I'm dumb.

This time, Joan did identify significant perceptual features she encodes in math class. The counselor **clarifies** *this in response 8.*

8. *Counselor:* OK, great. So you attend mostly to the teacher, to the guys, and to their faces. Is that accurate?
   Client: Well, I never really gave it much thought, but yes, I guess I do.

In response 9 the counselor suggests **how these perceptual features are linked to Joan's anxious feelings.**

9. *Counselor:* So you feel nervous whenever you see these guys looking at you and when you see your teacher with this smirk on his face.
   Client: Well, I guess I do because they are all guys and they all seem so smart in math.

In the next responses, the counselor instructs Joan to reenact the situation in imagery by **deliberately attending to or focusing on these identified features.**

10. *Counselor:* Well, again that is one of your beliefs that isn't necessarily true. What I was thinking was that by noticing just *them,* you might fail to notice other things that might create different feelings for you, like the other female students or other facial expressions of these people. Now this may seem a little strange, but I'd like you to imagine this situation again and this time deliberately pay attention to the teacher and to the guys. Even exaggerate the smirk and frowns and stares on their faces. [Gives instructions for imagery.]

11. *Counselor:* OK, what was that like?
    Client: Well, OK. Actually, it almost made me laugh. Like I was silly to see them like that. Because they don't look *that* bad!

In response 12, the counselor starts to help Joan **identify alternative perceptions about math class by reframing the meaning.**

12. *Counselor:* OK, that's a good point. Actually, what you see as a smirk on the teacher's face may just be what the teacher thinks is an encouraging smile. Now, along these lines, what else could you pay attention to about math class that you usually overlook or don't notice? Try to think of

things that are more positive or at least neutral.
Client: [Pauses] Well, there are times when the teacher and the guys do offer to help, and they look encouraging or sincere. Plus the fact, as you mentioned, I'm not the only girl there. There are three others, and I don't usually notice them.

The counselor **suggests another alternative feature or a new reframe** *to focus on in the next response.*

13. *Counselor:* Great. Another thing I might add is being aware of times when other people in the class also have trouble with the answers or working at the board.
    Client: That's true. I tend to only see myself like that. But sometimes even some of the guys have difficulty.

In responses 14 through 16, the counselor helps Joan **modify the original perceptions** *by setting up a practice opportunity in imagery.*

14. *Counselor:* OK, now I'm going to ask you to imagine this situation in math class again. This time, I want you to deliberately focus on these other things—the other girls, the times when the teacher offers help, the times when other guys can't get the answer. Is that clear?
    Client: You mean try to notice these things instead of their smirks?

15. Counselor: Exactly. [Gives instructions for imagery.]

16. *Counselor:* OK, what happened?
    Client: Well, it was interesting. I could do it, but I kept shifting back to the smirks at times.

In response 17, the counselor provides information about **successive practice attempts,** *in the session and as* **homework.**

17. *Counselor:* Well, it takes practice! Again remember the tape recorder. You've been playing the tape that has the teacher smirking and the guys laughing at you for a long time. Now it is time to insert a tape with new pictures and sounds on it. We'll keep working on it today, and then I'll show you a way to use it in math class during the week.
    Client: OK, I think I can see how it might prove to be helpful if I can do it.

LEARNING ACTIVITY #43: REFRAMING

This activity is designed to help you use the reframing procedure with yourself.

1. Identify a situation that typically produces uncomfortable or distressing feelings for you. Examples:

a. You are about to initiate a new relationship with someone of the other sex.

b. You are presenting a speech in front of a large audience.

(continued)

2. Try to become aware of what you rather automatically attend to or focus on during this situation. Role-play it with another person or pretend you're sitting in a movie theater and project the situation onto the screen in front of you. As you do so, ask yourself:

"What am I aware of now?"

"What am I focusing on now?"

Be sure to notice fleeting sounds, feelings, images, and sensations.

3. Establish a link between these encoded features of the situation and your resulting feelings. As you reenact the situation, ask yourself: "What am I feeling at this moment?" "What am I experiencing now?"

4. After you have become aware of the most salient features of this situation, reenact it either in role play or in imagination. This time, deliberately attend to these selected features during the reenactment. Repeat this process until you feel that you have awareness and control of the perceptual process you engage in during this situation.

5. Next, select other features of the session (previously ignored) that you focus could on or attend to during this situation which would allow you to view and handle the situation differently. Consider images, sounds, and feelings as well as people and objects. Ask yourself questions like: "What other aspects of this same situation aren't readily apparent to me that would provide me with a different way to view the situation?" You may wish to query another person for ideas. After you have identified alternative features, again reenact the situation in role play or imagination— several times if necessary—in order to break old encoding patterns.

6. Construct a homework assignment for yourself that encourages you to apply this process as needed for use during actual situations.

☐ STRESS INOCULATION

Stress inoculation is an approach to teaching both physical and cognitive coping skills. The procedure was developed by Meichenbaum and Cameron (1973a), who use it to help clients with severe phobic reactions to manage anxiety in stressful situations. Meichenbaum and Turk (1976) describe stress inoculation as a type of psychological protection that functions in the same way as a medical inoculation that provides protection from disease. According to these authors, stress inoculation gives the person "a prospective defense or set of skills to deal with future stressful situations. As in medical inoculations, a person's resistance is enhanced by exposure to a stimulus strong enough to arouse defenses without being so powerful that it overcomes them" (p. 3). Although the procedure has been used as remediation, as the name implies, it can also be used for prevention.

Stress inoculation has three major components: educating the client about the nature of stressful reactions, having the client rehearse various physical and cognitive coping skills, and helping the client apply these skills during exposure to stressful situations. Of these three components, the second, which provides training in coping skills, seems to be the most important (Horan, Hackett, Buchanan, Stone, & Demchik-Stone, 1977). Stress inoculation has been used to help manage anxiety reactions (Altmaier, Ross, Leary, & Thornbrough, 1982; Meichenbaum & Cameron, 1973a), to help people with chronic headaches, bronchial asthma, and essential hypertension (Holroyd, Appel, & Andrasik, 1983), to help patients undergoing cardiac catheterization (Kendall, 1983), to help people learn how to tolerate and cope with physiological pain (Hackett & Horan, 1980; Klepac, Hauge, Dowling, & McDonald, 1981; Turk & Genest, 1979; Wernick, 1983), to help people deal with dental anxiety (Nelson, 1981), to help juvenile delinquents control anger (Feindler & Fremouw, 1983; Schlichter & Horan, 1981), to help nurses on an acute care unit deal with occupational stress (West, Horan, & Games, 1984), with Type A people (Roskies, 1983), with dating anxiety (Jaremko, 1983), and with rape victims (Veronen & Kilpatrick, 1983). Meichenbaum and Cameron (1973a) found that stress inoculation was superior to systematic desensitization and two other anxiety-relief treatments in reducing avoidance behavior and in promoting treatment generalization of multiphobic clients. Novaco (1975) found that, for anger control, the entire stress inoculation procedure was more effective than the use of only coping thoughts or physical relaxation. One of the advantages of stress inoculation, compared with either cognitive restructuring or relaxation (Chapter 17), is that both relaxation and cognitive coping skills are learned and applied as part of the stress inoculation procedure.

We wish to acknowledge the work of Meichenbaum and Cameron (1973a), Novaco (1975), and Meichenbaum and Turk (1976) in our presentation of stress inoculation. The process of modification of perceptions described under "Reframing" can also be used in conjunction with stress inoculation (Leventhal & Nerenz, 1983). We describe the procedure in seven major components:

1. Rationale.
2. Information giving.
3. Acquisition and practice of direct-action coping skills.
4. Acquisition and practice of cognitive coping skills.
5. Application of all coping skills to problem-related situations.
6. Application of all coping skills to potential problem situations.
7. Homework and follow-up.

A detailed description of each step associated with these seven parts can be found in the Interview Checklist for Stress Inoculation at the end of this chapter.

Treatment Rationale

Here is an example of a rationale that a counselor might use for stress inoculation.

Purpose. The counselor might explain as follows the purpose of stress inoculation for a client having trouble with anger control:

"You find yourself confronted with situations in which your temper gets out of hand. You have trouble managing your anger, especially when you feel provoked. This procedure can help you learn to cope with provoking situations and can help you manage the intensity of your anger when you're in these situations so it doesn't control you."

Overview. Then the counselor can give the client a brief overview of the procedure:

"First, we will try to help you understand the nature of your feelings and how certain situations may provoke your feelings. Next you will learn some ways to manage your anger and to cope with situations in which you feel angry. After you learn these coping skills, we will set up situations where you can practice using these skills to help you control your anger. How does this sound to you?"

Information Giving

In this procedure, before learning and applying various coping strategies, it is important that the client be given some information about the nature of a stress reaction and the possible coping strategies that might be used. Most clients view a stress reaction as something that is automatic and difficult to overcome. It is helpful for the client to understand the nature of a stress reaction and how various coping strategies can help manage the stress. It appears that this education phase of stress inoculation is "necessary but insufficient for improvement" (Horan et al., 1977, p. 219). As these authors indicate, "The other components of stress inoculation are built on the education framework and cannot be logically examined or clinically administered in isolation" (p. 219).

Three things should be explained to the client: a framework for the client's emotional reaction, information about the phases of reacting to stress, and examples of types of coping skills and strategies.

Framework for client's reaction. First, the counselor should explain the nature of the client's reaction to a stressful situation. Although understanding one's reaction may not be sufficient for changing it, the conceptual framework lays some groundwork for beginning the change process. Usually an explanation of some kind of stress (anxiety, anger, pain) involves describing the stress as having two components: physiological arousal and covert self-statements or thoughts that provoke anxiety, anger, or pain. This explanation may help the client realize that coping strategies must be directed toward the arousal behaviors *and* the cognitive processes. For example, to describe this framework to a client who has trouble controlling anger, the counselor could say something like

"Perhaps you could think about what happens when you get very angry. You might notice that certain things happen to you physically—perhaps your body feels tight, your face may feel warm, you may experience more rapid breathing, or your heart may pound. This is the physical part of your anger. However, there is another thing that probably goes on while you're very angry—that is, what you're thinking. You might be thinking such things as 'He had no right to attack me; I'll get back at him; Boy, I'll show him who's boss; I'll teach her to keep her mouth shut,' and so on. These kinds of thoughts only intensify your anger. So the way you interpret and think about an anger-provoking situation also contributes to arousing hostile feelings."

Phases of stress reactions. After explaining a framework for emotional arousal, it is helpful to describe the kinds of times or phases when the client's arousal level may be heightened. Meichenbaum and Turk (1976, p. 4) point out that anxious or phobic clients tend to view their anxiety as one "massive panic reaction." Similarly, clients who are angry, depressed, or in pain may interpret their feelings as one large, continuous reaction that has a certain beginning and end. Clients who interpret their reactions this way may perceive the reaction as too difficult to change because it is so massive and overwhelming.

One way to help the client see the potential for coping with feelings is to describe the feelings by individual stages or phases of reacting to a situation. Meichenbaum and Cameron (1973a), Novaco (1975), and Turk (1975) all used four similar stages to help the client conceptualize the various critical points of a reaction: (1) preparing for a stressful, painful, or provoking situation, (2) confronting and handling the situation or the provocation, (3) coping with critical moments or with feelings of being overwhelmed or agitated during the situation, and (4) rewarding oneself after the stress for using coping skills in the first three phases. Explanation of these stages in the preliminary part of stress inoculation helps the client understand the sequence of coping strategies to be learned. To explain the client's reaction as a series of phases, the counselor might say

"When you think of being angry, you probably just think of being angry for a continuous period of time. However, you might find that your anger is probably not just one big reaction but comes and goes at different points during a provoking situation. The first critical point is when you anticipate the situation and start to get angry. At this point you can learn to prepare yourself for handling the situation in a manageable way. The next point may come when you're in the middle of the situation and you're very angry. Here you can learn how to confront a provoking situation in a constructive way. There might also be times when your anger really gets intense and you can feel it starting to control you — and perhaps feel yourself losing control. At this time, you can learn how to cope with intense feelings of agitation. Then, after the situation is over, instead of getting angry with yourself for the way you handled it, you can learn to encourage yourself for trying to cope with it. In this procedure, we'll practice using the coping skills at these especially stressful or arousing times."

Information about coping skills and strategies. Finally, the counselor should provide some information about the kinds of coping skills and strategies that can be used at these critical points. The counselor should emphasize that there are a *variety* of useful coping skills; clients' input in selecting and tailoring these for themselves is *most* important. Some research has indicated that coping strategies are more effective when clients choose those that reflect their own preferences (Chaves & Barber, 1974). In using stress inoculation, both "direct action" and "cognitive" coping skills are taught (Meichenbaum & Turk, 1976). *Direct-action* coping strategies are designed to help the client use coping behaviors to handle the stress; *cognitive* coping skills are used to give the client coping thoughts (self-statements) to handle the stress. The client should understand that *both* kinds of coping skills are important and that the two serve different functions. To provide the client with information about the usefulness of these coping skills, the counselor might explain

"In the next phase of this procedure, you'll be learning a lot of different ways to prepare for and handle a provoking situation. Some of these coping skills will help you learn to cope with provoking situations by your actions and behaviors; others will help you handle these situations by the way you interpret and think about the situation. Not all the strategies you learn may be useful or necessary for you, so your input in selecting the ones you prefer to use is important."

Acquisition and Practice of Direct-Action Coping Skills

In this phase of stress inoculation, the client acquires and practices some direct-action coping skills. Horan et al. (1977) found that coping skills training was highly effective in helping people deal with the type of pain they were trained to cope with. The counselor first discusses and models possible action strategies; the client selects some to use and practices them with the counselor's encouragement and assistance. As you may recall, direct-action coping skills are designed to help the client acquire and apply coping behaviors in stressful situations. The most commonly used direct-action coping strategies are —

1. Collecting objective or factual information about the stressful situation.
2. Identifying short-circuit or escape routes or ways to decrease the stress.

3. Palliative coping strategies.
4. Mental relaxation methods.
5. Physical relaxation methods.

Information collection.   Collecting objective or factual information about a stressful situation may help the client evaluate the situation more realistically. Moreover, information about a situation may reduce the ambiguity for the client and indirectly reduce the level of threat. For example, for a client who may be confronted with physical pain, information about the source and expected timing of pain can reduce stress. This coping method is widely used in childbirth classes. The women and their "labor coaches" are taught and shown that the experienced pain is actually a uterine contraction. They are given information about the timing and stages of labor and the timing and intensity of contractions so that when labor occurs, their anxiety will not be increased by misunderstanding or lack of information about what is happening in their bodies.

Collecting information about an anxiety- or anger-engendering situation serves the same purpose. For example, in using stress inoculation to help clients control anger, collecting information about the people who typically provoke them may help. Clients can collect information that can help them view provocation as a *task* or a problem to be solved, rather than as a *threat* or a personal attack (Novaco, 1975).

Identification of escape routes.   Identifying escape routes is a way to help the client cope with stress before it gets out of hand. The idea of an escape route is to short-circuit the explosive or stressful situation or to deescalate the stress before the client behaves in a way that may "blow it." This coping strategy may help abusive clients learn to identify cues that elicit their physical or verbal abuse and to take some preventive action before "striking out." This is similar to the stimulus-control self-management strategy discussed in Chapter 19. These escape or prevention routes can be very simple things that the client can *do* to prevent losing control or losing face in the situation. An abusive client could perhaps avoid striking out by counting to 60, leaving the room, or talking about something humorous.

Palliative coping strategies.   Meichenbaum and Cameron (1983, pp. 135–138) describe three pal-

liative coping strategies that may be particularly useful for aversive or stressful situations that cannot be substantially altered or avoided, such as chronic or life-threatening illnesses:

1. Perspective taking—thinking about or examining positive, alternative, or useful features in the stressful situation. (This is similar to the perceptual restructuring strategy.)
2. Creation of a social support network.
3. Appropriate expression of affect, such as "ventilation of feelings" or "getting things off one's chest."

Mental relaxation.   Mental relaxation can also help clients cope with stress. This technique may involve attention-diversion tactics: angry clients can control their anger by concentrating on a problem to solve, counting floor tiles in the room, thinking about a funny or erotic joke, or thinking about something positive about themselves. Attention-diversion tactics are commonly used to help people control pain. Instead of focusing on the pain, the person may concentrate very hard on an object in the room or on the repetition of a word (a mantra) or a number. Again, in the Lamaze method of childbirth, the women are taught to concentrate on a "focal point" such as an object in the room or, as the authors used, a picture of a sailboat. In this way, the woman's attention is directed to an object instead of to the tightening sensations in her lower abdomen.

Some people find that mental relaxation is more successful when they use imagery or fantasy. People who enjoy daydreaming or who report a vivid imagination may find imagery a particularly useful way to promote mental relaxation. Generally, imagery as a coping method helps the client go on a fantasy trip instead of focusing on the stress, the provocation, or the pain. For example, instead of thinking about how anxious or angry he feels, the client might learn to fantasize about lying on a warm beach, being on a sailboat, making love, or eating a favorite food (see "Emotive Imagery" in Chapter 14). For pain control, the person can imagine different things about the pain. A woman in labor can picture the uterus contracting like a wave instead of thinking about pain. Or a person who experiences pain from a routine source, such as extraction of a wisdom tooth, can use imagery to change the circumstances producing the pain. Instead of thinking about how terrible and painful it is to have a tooth pulled, the person can imagine that the pain is only the aftermath of intense training for a marathon race or is from being the underdog who was hit in the jaw during a fight with the world champion (Knox, 1972).

Physical relaxation. Physical relaxation methods are particularly useful for clients who report physiological components of anxiety and anger, such as sweaty palms, rapid breathing or heartbeat, or nausea. Physical relaxation is also a very helpful coping strategy for pain control, because body tension will heighten the sensation of pain. Physical relaxation may consist of muscle relaxation or breathing techniques. Chapter 17 describes these procedures in more detail.

Each direct-action strategy should first be explained to the client with discussion of its purpose and procedure. Several sessions may be required to discuss and model all the possible direct-action coping methods. After the strategies have been described and modeled, the clients should select the particular methods to be used. The number of direct-action strategies used by a client will depend on the intensity of the reaction, the nature of the stress, and the client's preferences. With the counselor's assistance, the client should practice using each skill in order to be able to apply it in simulated and *in vivo* situations.

Acquisition and Practice of Cognitive Coping Skills

This part of stress inoculation is very similar to the cognitive restructuring strategy described earlier in this chapter. The counselor models some examples of coping thoughts the client can use during stressful phases of problem situations, and then the client selects and practices substituting coping thoughts for negative or self-defeating thoughts.

Description of four phases of cognitive coping. As you remember from our discussion of information giving, the counselor helps the client understand the nature of an emotional reaction by conceptualizing the reaction by phases. In helping the client acquire cognitive coping skills, the counselor may first wish to review the importance of learning to cope at crucial times. The counselor can point out that the client can learn a set of cognitive coping skills for each important phase: preparing for the situation, confronting and handling the situation, coping with critical moments in the situation, and

stroking oneself after the situation. Note that the first phase concerns coping skills *before* the situation; the second and third phases, coping *during* the situation; and the fourth phase, coping *after* the situation. The counselor can describe these four phases to the client with an explanation similar to this:

"Earlier we talked about how your anger is not just one giant reaction but something that peaks at certain stressful points when you feel provoked or attacked. Now you will learn a method of cognitive control that will help you control any negative thoughts that may make you more angry and also help you use coping thoughts at stressful points. There are four times that are important in your learning to use coping thoughts, and we'll work on each of these four phases. First is how you interpret the situation initially, and how you think about responding or preparing to respond. Second is actually dealing with the situation. Third is coping with anything that happens during the situation that *really* provokes you. After the situation, you learn to encourage yourself for keeping your anger in control."

Modeling coping thoughts. After explaining the four phases of using cognitive coping skills to the client, the counselor would model examples of coping statements that are especially useful for each of the four phases.

Meichenbaum and Turk (1976) have provided an excellent summary of the coping statements used by Meichenbaum and Cameron (1973a) for anxiety control, by Novaco (1975) for anger control, and by Turk (1975) for pain control. These statements, presented in Table 16-1, are summarized for each of the four coping phases: preparing for the situation, confronting the situation, coping with critical moments, and reinforcing oneself for coping. The counselor would present examples of coping statements for each of the four phases of a stress reaction.

Client selection of coping thoughts. After the counselor models some possible coping thoughts for each phase, the client should add some or select those that fit. The counselor should encourage the client to "try on" and adapt the thoughts in whatever way feels most natural. The client might look for coping statements he or she has used in other stress-related situations. At this point in the procedure, the counselor should be helping to tailor a coping program *specifically* for this client. If the

TABLE 16-1. Examples of coping thoughts used in stress inoculation

Anxiety	Anger	Pain
I. *Preparing for a stressor* (Meichenbaum & Cameron, 1973a)	*Preparing for a provocation* (Novaco, 1975)	*Preparing for the painful stressor* (Turk, 1975)
What is it you have to do?	What is it that you have to do?	What is it you have to do?
You can develop a plan to deal with it.	You can work out a plan to handle it.	You can develop a plan to deal with it.
Just think about what you can do about it. That's better than getting anxious.	You can manage this situation. You know how to regulate your anger.	Just think about what you have to do.
No negative self-statements; just think rationally.	If you find yourself getting upset, you'll know what to do.	Just think about what you can do about it.
Don't worry; worry won't help anything.	There won't be any need for an argument.	Don't worry; worrying won't help anything.
Maybe what you think is anxiety is eagerness to confront it.	Time for a few deep breaths of relaxation. Feel comfortable, relaxed and at ease.	You have lots of different strategies you can call upon.
	This could be a testy situation, but you believe in yourself.	
II. *Confronting and handling a stressor* (Meichenbaum & Cameron, 1973a)	*Confronting the provocation* (Novaco, 1975)	*Confronting and handling the pain* (Turk, 1975)
Just "psych" yourself up—you can meet this challenge.	Stay calm. Just continue to relax.	You can meet the challenge.
One step at a time; you can handle the situation.	As long as you keep your cool, you're in control here.	One step at a time; you can handle the situation.
Don't think about fear; just think about what you have to do. Stay relevant.	Don't take it personally.	Just relax, breathe deeply and use one of the strategies.
This anxiety is what the doctor said you would feel. It's a reminder to use your coping exercises.	Don't get all bent out of shape; just think of what to do here.	Don't think about the pain, just what you have to do.
This tenseness can be an ally, a cue to cope.	You don't need to prove yourself. There is no point in getting mad.	This tenseness can be an ally, a cue to cope.
Relax; you're in control. Take a slow deep breath. Ah, good.	You're not going to let him get to you.	Relax. You're in control; take a slow deep breath. Ah. Good.
	Don't assume the worst or jump to conclusions. Look for the positives.	This anxiety is what the trainer said you might feel. That's right; it's the reminder to use your coping skills.
	It's really a shame that this person is acting the way she is.	
	For a person to be that irritable, he must be awfully unhappy.	
	If you start to get mad, you'll just be banging your head against the wall. So you might as well just relax.	
	There's no need to doubt yourself. What he says doesn't matter.	

(continued)

client's self-statements are too general, they may lead only to "rote repetition" and not function as effective self-instructions (Meichenbaum, 1977, p. 160). The counselor might explain this to the client in this way:

"You know, your input in finding coping thoughts that work for you is very important. I've given you some examples. Some of these you might feel comfortable with, and there may be others you can think of too. What we want to do now is to come up with some specific coping thoughts you can and will use during these four times that fit for *you,* not me or someone else."

TABLE 16-1. Examples of coping thoughts used in stress inoculation (continued)

Anxiety	Anger	Pain
III. *Coping with the feeling of being overwhelmed* (Meichenbaum & Cameron, 1973a)	*Coping with arousal and agitation* (Novaco, 1975)	*Coping with feelings at critical moments* (Turk, 1975)
When fear comes, just pause.	Your muscles are starting to feel tight. Time to relax and slow things down.	When pain comes just pause; keep focusing on what you have to do.
Keep the focus on the present; what is it you have to do?	Getting upset won't help.	What is it you have to do?
Label your fear from 0 to 10 and watch it change.	It's just not worth it to get so angry.	Don't try to eliminate the pain totally; just keep it manageable.
You should expect your fear to rise.	You'll let him make a fool of himself.	You were supposed to expect the pain to rise; just keep it under control.
Don't try to eliminate fear totally; just keep it manageable.	It's reasonable to get annoyed, but let's keep the lid on.	Just remember, there are different strategies; they'll help you stay in control.
You can convince yourself to do it. You can reason your fear away.	Time to take a deep breath.	When the pain mounts you can switch to a different strategy; you're in control.
It will be over shortly.	Your anger is a signal of what you need to do. Time to talk to yourself.	
It's not the worst thing that can happen.	You're not going to get pushed around, but you're not going haywire either.	
Just think about something else.	Try a cooperative approach. Maybe you are both right.	
Do something that will prevent you from thinking about fear.	He'd probably like you to get really angry. Well, you're going to disappoint him.	
Describe what is around you. That way you won't think about worrying.	You can't expect people to act the way you want them to.	
IV. *Reinforcing self-statements* (Meichenbaum & Cameron, 1973a)	*Self-reward* (Novaco, 1975)	*Reinforcing self-statements* (Turk, 1975)
It worked; you did it.	It worked!	Good, you did it.
Wait until you tell your therapist about this.	That wasn't as hard as you thought.	You handled it pretty well.
It wasn't as bad as you expected.	You could have gotten more upset than it was worth.	You knew you could do it!
You made more out of the fear than it was worth.	Your ego can sure get you in trouble, but when you watch that ego stuff you're better off.	Wait until you tell the trainer about which procedures worked best.
Your damn ideas—that's the problem. When you control them, you control your fear.	You're doing better at this all the time.	
It's getting better each time you use the procedures.	You actually got through that without getting angry.	
You can be pleased with the progress you're making.	Guess you've been getting upset for too long when it wasn't even necessary.	
You did it!		

From "The Cognitive-Behavioral Management of Anxiety, Anger, and Pain," by D. Meichenbaum and D. Turk. In P. O. Davidson (Ed.), *The behavioral management of anxiety, depression and pain.* Copyright 1976 by Brunner/Mazel, Inc. Reprinted by permission.

Client practice of coping thoughts. After the client selects coping thoughts to use for each phase, the counselor will instruct the client to practice these self-statements by saying them aloud. This verbal practice is designed to help the client become familiar with the coping thoughts and accustomed to the words. After this practice, the client should also practice the selected coping thoughts in the sequence of the four phases. This practice helps the client learn the timing of the coping thoughts in the application phase of stress inoculation.

The counselor can say something like

"First I'd like you to practice using these coping thoughts just by saying them aloud to me. This will help you get used to the words and ideas of coping. Next, let's practice these coping thoughts in the sequence in which you would use them when applying them to a real situation. Here, I'll show you. OK, first I'm anticipating the situation, so I'm going to use coping statements that help me prepare for the situation, like 'I know this type of situation usually upsets me, but I have a plan now to handle it' or 'I'm going to be able to control my anger even if this situation is rough.' Next, I'll pretend I'm actually into the situation. I'm going to cope so I can handle it. I might say something to myself like 'Just stay calm. Remember who I'm dealing with. This is her style. Don't take it personally' or 'Don't overreact. Just relax.'

OK, now the person's harassment is continuing. I am going to cope with feeling more angry. I might think 'I can feel myself getting more upset. Just keep relaxed. Concentrate on this' or 'This is a challenging situation. How can *I* handle myself in a way I don't have to apologize for?' OK, now afterwards I realize I haven't got abusive or revengeful. So I'll think something to encourage myself, like 'I did it' or 'Gee, I really kept my cool.'

Now you try it. Just verbalize your coping thoughts in the sequence of preparing for the situation, handling it, coping with getting really agitated, and then encouraging yourself."

Application of All Coping Skills to Problem-Related Situations

The next part of stress inoculation involves having the client apply both the direct-action and the cognitive coping skills in the face of stressful, provoking, or painful situations. Before the client is instructed to apply the coping skills *in vivo*, she or he practices applying coping skills under simulated conditions with the counselor's assistance. The application phase of stress inoculation apears to be important for the overall efficacy of the procedure. As Meichenbaum and Cameron (1973a) point out, simply having a client rehearse coping skills *without* opportunities to apply them in stressful situations seems to result in an improved but limited ability to cope.

The application phase involves modeling and rehearsal to provide the client with exposure to simulations of problem-related situations. For example, the client who wanted to control anger would have opportunities to practice coping in a variety of anger-provoking situations. During this application practice, it is important that the client be faced with a stressful situation and also that the client practice the skills in a coping manner. In other words, the application should be arranged and conducted as realistically as possible. The angry client can be encouraged to practice feeling very agitated and to rehearse even starting to lose control—but then applying the coping skills to gain control (Novaco, 1975). This type of application practice is viewed as the client's providing a self-model of how to behave in a stressful situation. By imagining faltering or losing control, experiencing anxiety, and then coping with this, the person practices the thoughts and feelings as they are likely to occur in a real-life situation (Meichenbaum, 1977, p. 178). In the application phase of stress inoculation, the client's anxiety, anger, or distressful emotions is used as a cue or reminder to cope.

Modeling of application of coping skills. The counselor should first model how the client can apply the newly acquired skills in a coping manner when faced with a stressful situation. Here is an example of a counselor demonstration of this process with a client who is working toward anger control (in this case, with his family):

"I'm going to imagine that the police have just called and told me that my 16-year-old son was just picked up again for breaking and entering. I can feel myself start to get really hot. Whoops, wait a minute. That's a signal [arousal cue for coping]. I'd better start thinking about using my relaxation methods to stay calm and using my coping thoughts to prepare myself for handling this situation constructively.

OK, first of all, sit down and relax. Let those muscles loosen up. Count to ten. Breathe deeply [direct-action coping methods]. OK, now I'll be seeing my son shortly. What is it I have to do? I know it won't help to lash out or to hit him. That won't solve anything. So I'll work out another plan. Let him do most of the talking. Give him the chance to make amends or find a solution [cognitive coping: preparing for the situation]. OK, now I can see him walking in the door. I feel sort of choked up. I can feel my fists getting tight. He's starting to explain. I want to interrupt and let him have it. But wait [arousal cue for coping]. Concentrate on counting and on breathing slowly [direct-action coping]. Now just tell myself—keep cool.

Let him talk. It won't help now to blow up [cognitive coping: confronting situation]. Now I can imagine myself thinking back to the last time he got arrested. Why in the hell doesn't he learn? No son of mine is going to be a troublemaker [arousal]. Whew! I'm pretty damn angry. I've got to stay in control, especially now [cue for coping]. Just relax, muscles! Stay loose [direct-action coping]. I can't expect him to live up to my expectations. I can tell him I'm disappointed, but I'm not going to blow up and shout and hit [cognitive coping: feelings of greater agitation]. OK, I'm doing a good job of keeping my lid on [cognitive coping: self-reinforcement]."

Client application of coping skills in imaginary and role-play practice. After the counselor modeling, the client should practice a similar sequence of both direct-action and cognitive coping skills. The practice can occur in two ways: imagination and role play. We find it is often useful to have the client first practice the coping skills while imagining problem-related situations. This practice can be repeated until the client feels very comfortable in applying the coping strategies to imagined situations. Then the client can practice the coping skills with the counselor's aid in a role play of a problem situation. The role-play practice should be similar to the *in vivo* situations the client encounters. For instance, our angry client could identify particular situations and people with whom he or she is most likely to blow up or lose control. The client can imagine each situation (starting with the most manageable one) and imagine using the coping skills. Then, with the counselor taking the part of someone else such as a provoker, the client can practice the coping skills in role play.

Application of All Coping Skills to Potential Problem Situations

Any therapeutic procedure should be designed not only to help clients deal with current problems but also to help them anticipate constructive handling of potential problems. In other words, an adequate therapeutic strategy should prevent future problems as well as resolve current ones. The prevention aspect of stress inoculation is achieved by having clients apply the newly learned coping strategies to situations that are not problematic now but could be in the future. If this phase of stress inoculation is ignored, the effects of the inoculation may be very short-lived. In other words, if clients do not have an opportunity to apply the

coping skills to situations other than the current problem-related ones, their coping skills may not generalize beyond the present problem situations.

Application of coping skills to other potentially stressful situations is accomplished in the same way as application to the present problem areas. First, after explaining the usefulness of coping skills in other areas of the client's life, the counselor demonstrates the application of coping strategies to a potential, hypothetical stressor. The counselor might select a situation the client has not yet encountered, one that would require active coping of anyone who might encounter it, such as not receiving a desired job promotion or raise, facing a family crisis, moving to a new place, anticipating retirement, or being very ill. After the counselor has modeled application of coping skills to these sorts of situations, the client would practice applying the skills in these situations or in similar ones that she or he identifies. The practice can occur in imagination or in role-play enactments. Turk (1975) used a novel method of role play to give clients opportunities to apply coping skills. The counselor or trainee role-played a novice, while the client took the part of a trainer or helper. The client's task in the role play was to train the novice in how to cope with stress — in this case, the stress of experiencing pain. Although Turk did not specifically assess the effects of this particular type of application practice, Fremouw and Harmatz (1975) found that speech-anxious students who acted as helpers and taught anxiety-reduction procedures to other speech-anxious students showed more improvement than other speech-anxious students who learned how to help but were not given an opportunity to do so (latent helpers). Putting the client in the role of a helper or a trainer may provide another kind of application opportunity that may also have benefits for the client's acquisition of coping strategies.

Homework and Follow-up

When the client has learned and used stress inoculation within the interviews, she or he is ready to use coping skills *in vivo*. The counselor and client should discuss the potential application of coping strategies to actual situations. The counselor might caution the client not to expect to cope beautifully with every problematic situation initially. The client should be encouraged to use a daily log to record the particular situations and the number of times the coping strategies are used.

The log data can be used in a later follow-up as one way to determine the client's progress.

In our opinion, stress inoculation training is one of the most comprehensive therapeutic treatments presently in use. Teaching clients both direct-action and cognitive coping skills that can be used in current and potential problematic situations provides skills that are under the clients' own control and are applicable to future as well as current situations. Stress inoculation deserves much more empirical investigation than it has yet received, but the results of the limited previous investigations point to its clinical potential.

□ MODEL DIALOGUE: STRESS INOCULATION

Session 1

In this session, the counselor will teach Joan some direct-action coping skills for mental and physical relaxation to help her cope with her physical sensations of nervousness about her math class. Imagery manipulations and slow, deep breathing will be used.

1. *Counselor:* Hi, Joan. How was your week?
Client: Pretty good. You know, this, well, whatever you call it, it's starting to help. I took a test this week and got an 85—I usually get a 70 or 75.

The counselor introduces the **idea of other coping skills to deal with Joan's nervousness.**

2. *Counselor:* That really is encouraging. And that's where the effects of this count—on how you do in class. Since what we did last week went well for you, I believe today we might work with some other coping skills that might help you decrease your nervous feelings.
Client: What would this be?

In responses 3 and 4, the counselor explains and **models possible direct-action coping skills.**

3. *Counselor:* Well, one thing we might do is to help you learn how to imagine something that gives you very calm feelings, and while you're doing this to take some slow, deep breaths—like this [counselor models closing eyes, breathing slowly and deeply]. When I was doing that, I thought about curling up in a chair with my favorite book—but there are many different things you could think of. For instance, to use this in your math class, you might imagine that you are doing work for which you will receive some prize or award. Or you might imagine that you are learning problems so you'll be in a

position to be a helper for someone else. Do you get the idea?
Client: I think so. I guess it's like trying to imagine or think about math in a pretend kind of way.

4. *Counselor:* Yes—and in a way that reduces rather than increases the stress of it for you.
Client: I think I get the idea. It's sort of like when I imagine that I'm doing housework for some famous person instead of just at my house—it makes it more tolerable.

In response 5, the counselor asks Joan to **find some helpful imagery manipulations to promote calm feelings.**

5. *Counselor:* That's a good example. You imagine that situation to prevent yourself from getting too bored. Here, you find a scene or scenes to think about to prevent yourself from getting too nervous. Can you take a few minutes to think about one or two things you could imagine—perhaps about math—that would help you to feel calm instead of nervous?
Client: (Pauses) Well, maybe I could pretend that the math class is part of some training I need in order to do something exciting, like being one of the females in the space program.

In responses 6 and 7, the counselor instructs Joan to **practice these direct-action coping skills.**

6. *Counselor:* OK, good. We can work with that, and if it doesn't help, we can come up with something else. Why don't you try first to practice imagining this while you also breathe slowly and deeply, as I did a few minutes ago? [Joan practices.]

7. *Counselor:* OK. How did that feel?
Client: OK—it was sort of fun.

In response 8, the counselor gives **homework**—*asks Joan to engage in* **self-directed practice** *of these coping skills before the next session.*

8. *Counselor:* Good. Now this week I'd like you to practice this in a quiet place two or three times each day. Keep track of your practice sessions in your log and also rate your tension level before and after you practice. Next week we will go over this log and then work on a way you can apply what we did today—and the thought stopping and coping thoughts we learned in our two previous sessions. So I'll see you next week.

Session 2

In this session, the counselor helps Joan integrate the strategies of some previous sessions (thought stopping, coping thoughts, and imagery and breathing coping skills). Specifically, Joan learns to apply all these coping skills in imagery and role-play practices of some stressful situations related to math class. Application of coping skills to problem-related situations is a part of stress inoculation and helps the client to generalize the newly acquired coping skills to *in vivo* situations as they occur.

In responses 1 and 2, the counselor will **review Joan's use of the direct-action skills homework.**

1. *Counselor:* How are things going, Joan?

   Client: OK. I've had a hard week—one test and two pop quizzes in math. But I got 80s. I also did my imagination and breathing practice. You know, that takes a while to learn.

2. *Counselor:* That's natural. It does take a lot of practice before you really get the feel of it. So it would be a good idea if you continued the daily practice again this week. How did it feel when you practiced?

   Client: OK—I think I felt less nervous than before.

The counselor introduces the idea of **applying all the coping skills in practice situations** *and* **presents a rationale for this application phase.**

3. *Counselor:* That's good. As time goes on, you will notice more effects from it. Up to this point, we've worked on some things to help you in your math class—stopping self-defeating thoughts and using imagination and slow breathing to help you cope and control your nervousness. What I think might help now is to give you a chance to use all these skills in practices of some of the stressful situations related to your math class. This will help you use the skills when you need to during the class or related situations. Then we will soon be at a point where we can go through some of these same procedures for the other situations in which you want to express yourself differently and more frequently, such as with your folks. Does this sound OK?

   Client: Yes.

Next, the counselor **demonstrates (models) how Joan can practice her skills in an imaginary practice.**

4. *Counselor:* What I'd like you to do is to imagine some of the situations related to your math class and try to use your coping thoughts *and* the imagination scene and deep breathing to control your nervousness. Let me show you how you might do this. OK, I'm imagining that it's almost time for math class. I'm going to concentrate on thinking about how this class will help me train for the space program. If I catch myself thinking I wish I didn't have to go, I'm going to use some coping thoughts. Let's see—class will go pretty fast. I've been doing better. It can be a challenge. Now, as I'm in class,

I'm going to stop thinking about not being able to do the work. I'm going to just take one problem at a time. One step at a time. Oops! Mr. _____ just called on me. Boy, I can feel myself getting nervous. Just take a deep breath. . . . Do the best I can. It's only one moment anyway. Well, it went pretty well. I can feel myself starting to cope when I need to. OK, Joan, why don't you try this several times now? [Joan practices applying coping thoughts and direct action with different practice situations in imagination.]

In response 5, the counselor **checks Joan's reaction** *to applying the skills in practice through imagination.*

5. *Counselor:* Are you able to really get into the situation as you practice this way?

   Client: Yes, although I believe I have to work harder to use this when it really happens.

Sometimes **role play makes the practice more real.** *The counselor introduces this next. Note that the counselor will add a stress element by calling on Joan at unannounced times.*

6. *Counselor:* That's right. This kind of practice doesn't always have the same amount of stress as the "real thing." Maybe it would help if we did some role-play practice. I'll be your teacher this time. Just pretend to be in class. I'll be talking, but at an unannounced time, I'm going to call on you to answer a question. Just use your coping thoughts and your slow breathing as you need to when this happens. [Role-play practice of this and related scenarios occurs.]

The counselor **assesses Joan's reaction** *to role-play practice and* **asks Joan to rate her level of nervousness** *during the practice.*

7. *Counselor:* How comfortable do you feel with these practices? Could you rate the nervousness you feel as you do this on a 1-to-5 scale, with 1 being not nervous and 5 being very nervous?

   Client: Well, about a 2.

The counselor encourages Joan to **apply coping statements in the math-related problem situations** *as they occur, assigns* **homework,** *and schedules a* **follow-up.**

8. *Counselor:* Well, I think you are ready to use this as you need to during the week. Remember, any self-defeating thought or body tenseness is a cue to cope, using your coping thoughts and imagination and breathing skills. I'd like you to keep track of the number of times you use this on your log sheets. Also rate your level of nervousness before, during, and after math class on the log sheet. How about coming back in two weeks to see how things are going?

   Client: Fine.

LEARNING ACTIVITIES #44: STRESS INOCULATION

I. Listed below are 12 examples of various direct-action coping skills. Using the coding system that precedes the examples, identify on paper the *type* of direct-action coping skill displayed in each example. Feedback follows on page 442.

Code
Information (I)
Escape route (ER)
Social support network (SSN)
Ventilation (V)
Perspective taking (PT)
Attention diversion (AD)
Imagery manipulations (IM)
Muscle relaxation (MR)
Breathing techniques (B)

Examples

1. "Learn to take slow, deep breaths when you feel especially tense."
2. "Instead of thinking just about the pain, try to concentrate very hard on one spot on the wall."
3. "Imagine that it's a very warm day and the warmth makes you feel relaxed."
4. "If it really gets to be too much, just do the first part only — leave the rest for a while."
5. "You can expect some pain, but it is really only the result of the stitches. It doesn't mean that something is wrong."
6. "Just tighten your left fist. Hold it and notice the tension. Now relax it — feel the difference."
7. "Try to imagine a strong, normal cell attacking the weak, confused cancer cells when you feel the discomfort of your treatment."
8. "When it gets very strong, distract yourself — listen hard to the music or study the picture on the wall."

9. "If you talk about it and express your feelings about the pain, you might feel better."
10. "Your initial or intuitive reaction might cause you to see only selected features of the situation. There are also some positive aspects we need to focus on."
11. "It would be helpful to have your family and neighbors involved to provide you feedback and another perspective."
12. "Social skills are important for you to learn in order to develop the support you need from other people. Others can lessen the effects of the aversive situation."

II. Listed below are eight examples of cognitive coping skills used at four phases: preparing for a situation, confronting or handling the situation, dealing with critical moments in the situation, and self-encouragement for coping. On paper, identify which phase is represented by each example. Feedback follows.

1. "By golly, I did it."
2. "What will I need to do?"
3. "Don't lose your cool even though it's tough now. Take a deep breath."
4. "Think about what you want to say — not how people are reacting to you now."
5. "Relax, it will be over shortly. Just concentrate on getting through this rough moment now."
6. "Can you feel this — the coping worked!"
7. "When you get in there, just think about the situation, not your anxiety."
8. "That's a signal to cope now. Just keep your mind on what you're doing."

☐ SUMMARY

The five cognitive change procedures of cognitive modeling, problem solving, cognitive restructuring, reframing, and stress inoculation are being used more frequently in counseling and therapy — even to the point of achieving acceptance, notoriety, and "best seller" status (Dyer, 1976). Yet thorough investigative efforts into the components and effects of these strategies have only just begun. We wholeheartedly agree with the plea of Mahoney and Mahoney (1976, p. 105): "As clinical scientists, our research has only recently begun to examine the functional role of cognitive processes in maladjustment and therapeutic behavior change. Our understanding of the 'inside story' needs rigorous cultivation."

POSTEVALUATION

PART ONE

Objective One asks you to identify and describe the six major components of cognitive restructuring in a client case. Using the case described here, explain briefly how you would use the steps and compo-
(continued)

nents of cognitive restructuring with *this* client. You can use the six questions following the client case to describe your use of this procedure. Feedback follows on pages 444–445.

Description of client: The client is a junior in college, majoring in education and getting very good grades. She reports that she has an active social life and has some good close friendships with both males and females. Despite obvious "plusses," the client reports constant feelings of being worthless and inadequate. Her standards for herself seem to be unrealistically high: although she has almost a straight-A average, she still chides herself that she does not have all As. Although she is attractive and has an active social life, she thinks that she should be more attractive and more talented.

1. How would you explain the rationale for cognitive restructuring to this client?
2. Give an example you might use with this client to point out the difference between a self-defeating and a self-enhancing thought. Try to base your example on the client's description.
3. How would you have the client identify her thoughts about herself—her grades, appearance, social life, and so on?
4. What are some coping thoughts this client might use?
5. Explain how, in the session, you would help the client practice shifting from self-defeating to coping thoughts.
6. What kind of homework assignment would you use to help the client increase her use of coping thoughts about herself?

PART TWO

Objective Two asks you to teach the six components of cognitive restructuring to someone else or to demonstrate these components with a role-play client. Use the Interview Checklist for Cognitive Restructuring on pages 434–437 as a teaching and evaluation guide.

PART THREE

Objective Three asks you to demonstrate at least 8 out of 11 steps of the reframing procedure with a role-play client. Assess this activity using the Interview Checklist for Reframing on pages 437–439.

PART FOUR

Objective Four asks you to describe how you would apply the five major components of stress inoculation with a client case. Using the client description below, respond to the five questions following the case de-

scription as if you were using stress inoculation with this client. Feedback follows.

Description of client: The client has been referred to you by Family Services. He is unemployed, is receiving welfare support, and has three children. He is married to his second wife; the oldest child is hers by another marriage. He has been referred because of school complaints that the oldest child, a seventh-grader, has arrived at school several times with obvious facial bruises and cuts. The child has implicated the stepfather in this matter. After a long period of talking, the client reports that he has little patience with this boy and sometimes does strike him in the face as his way of disciplining the child. He realizes that maybe, on occasion, he has gone too far. Still, he gets fed up with the boy's "irresponsibility" and "lack of initiative" for his age. At these times, he reports, his impatience and anger get the best of him.

1. Explain the purpose of stress inoculation as you would to this client.
2. Briefly give an overview of the stress inoculation procedure.
3. Describe and explain one example of each of the following kinds of direct-action coping skills that might be useful to this client.
   a. Information about the situation
   b. An escape route
   c. An attention-diversion tactic
   d. An imagery manipulation
   e. Physical relaxation
   f. A palliative coping strategy (perspective taking, social support, or ventilation)
4. Explain, as you might to this client, the four phases of an emotional reaction and of times for coping. For each of the four phases, give two examples of cognitive coping skills (thoughts) that you would give to this client. The four phases are preparing for a disagreement or argument with the boy; confronting the situation; dealing with critical, very provoking times; and encouraging himself for coping.
5. Describe how you would set up practice opportunities in the interview with this client to help him practice applying the direct-action and cognitive coping skills in simulated practices of the provoking situations.

PART FIVE

Objective Five asks you to demonstrate 17 out of 21 steps of the stress inoculation procedure with a role-play client. Assess this activity using the Interview Checklist for Stress Inoculation on pages 439–442.

(continued)

POSTEVALUATION (continued)

INTERVIEW CHECKLIST FOR COGNITIVE RESTRUCTURING

Instructions to observer: Determine whether the counselor demonstrated the lead listed in the checklist. Check which leads the counselor used.

Item	Examples of counselor leads
I. Rationale and Overview	
_____ 1. Counselor explains purpose and rationale of cognitive restructuring.	"You've reported that you find yourself getting anxious and depressed during and after these conversations with the people who have to evaluate your work. This procedure can help you identify some things you might be thinking in this situation that are just beliefs, not facts, and are unproductive. You can learn more realistic ways to think about this situation that will help you cope with it in a way that you want to."
_____ 2. Counselor provides brief overview of procedure.	"There are three things we'll do in using this procedure. *First,* this will help you identify the kinds of things you're thinking before, during, and after these situations that are self-defeating. *Second,* this will teach you how to stop a self-defeating thought and replace it with a coping thought. *Third,* this will help you learn how to give yourself credit for changing these self-defeating thoughts."
_____ 3. Counselor explains difference between rational, or self-enhancing, thoughts (facts) and irrational, or self-defeating, thoughts (beliefs) and provides examples of each.	"A self-defeating thought is one way to interpret the situation, but it is usually negative and unproductive, like thinking that the other person doesn't value you or what you say. In contrast, a self-enhancing thought is a more constructive and realistic way to interpret the situation—like thinking that what you are talking about has value to you."
_____ 4. Counselor explains influence of irrational and self-defeating thoughts on emotions and performance.	"When you're constantly preoccupied with yourself and worried about how the situation will turn out, this can affect your feelings and your behavior. Worrying about the situation can make you feel anxious and upset. Concentrating on the situation and not worrying about its outcome can help you feel more relaxed, which helps you handle the situation more easily."
_____ 5. Counselor confirms client's willingness to use strategy.	"Are you ready to try this now?"
II. Identifying Client Thoughts in Problem Situations	
_____ 6. Counselor asks client to describe problem situations and identify examples of rational, self-enhancing thoughts and of irrational, self-defeating thoughts client typically experiences in these situations.	"Think of the last time you were in this situation. Describe for me what you think before you have a conversation with your evaluator. . . . What are you usually thinking during the conversation? . . . What thoughts go through your mind after the conversation is over? Now, let's see which of those thoughts are actual facts about the situation or are constructive ways to interpret the situation. Which ones are your beliefs about the situation that are unproductive or self-defeating?"
_____ 7. If client is unable to complete step 6, counselor models examples of thoughts or "links" between event and client's emotional response.	"OK, think of the thoughts that you have while you're in this conversation as a link between this event and your feelings afterward of being upset and depressed. What is the middle part? For instance, it might be something like 'I'll never have a good evaluation, and I'll lose this position' or 'I always blow this conversation and never make a good impression.' Can you recall thinking anything like this?"
_____ 8. Counselor instructs client to monitor and record content of thoughts *before, during,*	"One way to help you identify this link or your thoughts is to keep track of what you're thinking in these situations as they happen. This week I'd like you to use this log each day. Try to identify and write down at least three specific

(continued)

Item	Examples of counselor leads
and *after* stressful or upsetting situations before next session.	thoughts you have in these situations each day and bring this in with you next week."
____ 9. Using client's monitoring, counselor and client identify client's self-defeating thoughts.	"Let's look at your log and go over the kinds of negative thoughts that seem to be predominant in these situations. We can explore how these thoughts affect your feelings and performance in this situation — and whether you feel there is any evidence or rational basis for these."

III. Introduction and Practice of Coping Thoughts

____10. Counselor explains purpose and potential use of "coping thoughts" and gives some examples of coping thoughts to be used: ____a. Before the situation —preparing for it ____b. During the situation ____1. Focusing on task ____2. Dealing with feeling over-whelmed	"Up to this point, we've talked about the negative or unproductive thoughts you have in these situations and how they contribute to your feeling uncomfortable, upset, and depressed. Now we're going to look at some alternative, more constructive ways to think about the situation — using coping thoughts. These thoughts can help you prepare for the situation, handle the situation, and deal with feeling upset or overwhelmed in the situation. As long as you're using some coping thoughts, you avoid giving up control and letting the old self-defeating thoughts take over. Here are some examples of coping thoughts."
____11. Counselor instructs client to think of additional coping thoughts client could use or has used before.	"Try to think of your own coping thoughts — perhaps ones you can remember using successfully in other situations, ones that seem to fit for you."
____12. Counselor instructs client to practice verbalizing selected coping statements. ____a. Counselor instructs client first to practice coping statements individually. Coping statements to use before a situation are practiced, then coping statements to use during a situation.	"At first you will feel a little awkward using coping statements. It's like learning to drive a stick shift after you've been used to driving an automatic. So one way to help you get used to this is for you to practice these statements aloud." "First just practice each coping statement separately. After you feel comfortable with saying these aloud, practice the ones you could use before this conversation. OK, now practice the ones you could use during this conversation with your evaluator."
____b. Counselor instructs client to practice sequence of coping statements as they would be used in actual situation.	"Now let's put it all together. Imagine it's an hour before your meeting. Practice the coping statements you could use then. We'll role-play the meeting. As you feel aroused or overwhelmed, stop and practice coping thoughts during the situation."
____c. Counselor instructs client to become actively involved and to internalize meaning of coping statements during practice.	"Try to really put yourself into this practice. As you say these new things to yourself, try to think of what these thoughts really mean."

(continued)

POSTEVALUATION (continued)

Item	Examples of counselor leads

IV. Shifting from Self-Defeating to Coping Thoughts

_____13. Counselor models shift from recognizing a self-defeating thought and stopping it to replacing it with a coping thought.

"Let me show you what we will practice today. First, I'm in this conversation. Everything is going OK. All of a sudden I can feel myself starting to tense up. I realize I'm starting to get overwhelmed about this whole evaluation process. I'm thinking that I'm going to blow it. No, I stop that thought at once. Now, I'm just going to concentrate on calming down, taking a deep breath, and thinking only about what I have to say."

_____14. Counselor helps client practice shift from self-defeating to coping thoughts. Practice consists of four steps:

"Now let's practice this. You will imagine the situation. As soon as you start to recognize the onset of a self-defeating thought, stop it. Verbalize the thought aloud, and tell yourself to stop. Then verbalize a coping thought in place of it and imagine carrying on with the situation."

    _____a. Having client imagine situation or carry it out in a role play (behavior rehearsal).

    _____b. Recognizing self-defeating thought (which could be signaled by a hand or finger).

    _____c. Stopping self-defeating thought (which could be supplemented with a hand clap).

    _____d. Replacing thought with coping thought (possibly supplemented with deep breathing).

_____15. Counselor helps client practice using shift for each problem situation until anxiety or stress felt by client while practicing situation is decreased to a reasonable or negligible level and client can carry out practice and use coping thoughts in self-directed manner.

"Let's keep working with this situation until you feel pretty comfortable with it and can shift from self-defeating to coping thoughts without my help."

V. Introduction and Practice of Positive, or Reinforcing, Self-Statements

_____16. Counselor explains purpose and use of positive self-statements and gives some examples of these to client.

"You have really made a lot of progress in learning to use coping statements before and during these situations. Now it's time to learn to reward or encourage yourself. After you've coped with a situation, you can pat yourself on the back for having done so by thinking a positive or rewarding thought like 'I did it' or 'I really managed that pretty well.'"

_____17. Counselor instructs client to think of additional positive

"Can you think of some things like this that you think of when you feel good about something or when you feel like you've accomplished something? Try

(continued)

Item	Examples of counselor leads
self-statements and to select some to try out.	to come up with some of these thoughts that seem to fit for you."
____18. Counselor models application of positive self-statements as self-reinforcement for shift from self-defeating to coping thoughts.	"OK, here is the way you reward yourself for having coped. You recognize the self-defeating thought. Now you're in the situation using coping thoughts, and you're thinking things like 'Take a deep breath' or 'Just concentrate on this task.' Now the conversation is finished. You know you were able to use coping thoughts, and you reward yourself by thinking 'Yes, I did it' or 'I really was able to manage that.'"
____19. Counselor instructs client to practice use of positive self-statements in interview following practice of shift from self-defeating to coping thoughts. This should be practiced in sequence (coping *before* and *during* situation and reinforcing oneself *after* situation).	"OK, let's try this out. As you imagine the conversation, you're using the coping thoughts you will verbalize. . . . Now, imagine the situation is over, and verbalize several reinforcing thoughts for having coped."

VI. Homework and Follow-Up

____20. Counselor instructs client to use cognitive restructuring procedure (identifying self-defeating thought, stopping it, shifting to coping thought, reinforcing with positive self-statement) in situations outside the interview.	"OK, now you're ready to use the entire procedure whenever you have these conversations in which you're being evaluated—or any *other* situation in which you recognize your negative interpretation of the event is affecting you. In these cases, you recognize and stop any self-defeating thoughts, use the coping thoughts before the situation to prepare for it, and use the coping thoughts during the situation to help focus on the task and deal with being overwhelmed. After the situation is over, use the positive self-thoughts to reward your efforts."
____21. Counselor instructs client to monitor and record on log sheet number of times client uses cognitive restructuring outside the interview.	"I'd like you to use this log to keep track of the number of times you use this procedure and to jot down the situation in which you're using it. Also rate your tension level on a 1-to-5 scale before and after each time you use this."
____22. Counselor arranges for follow-up.	"Do this recording for the next two weeks. Then let's get together for a follow-up session."

Observer comments: _____

_____

_____

INTERVIEW CHECKLIST FOR REFRAMING

Instructions to observer: Determine whether the counselor demonstrated the lead listed in the checklist. Check which leads were used.

Item	Examples of counselor leads
I. Rationale for Reframing	
____ 1. Counselor explains purpose of reframing.	"Often when we think about a problem situation, our initial or intuitive reaction can lead to emotional distress. For example, we focus only on the nega- (continued)

POSTEVALUATION (continued)

Item	Examples of counselor leads
	tive features of the situation and overlook other details. By focusing only on the selected negative features of a situation, we can become nervous or anxious about the situation."
____ 2. Counselor provides overview of reframing.	"What we'll do is to identify what features you attend to when you think of the problem situation. Once you become aware of these features, we will look for other neutral or positive aspects of the situation that you may ignore or overlook. Then we will work on incorporating these other things into your perceptions of the problem situation."
____ 3. Counselor confirms client's willingness to use the strategy.	"How does this all sound? Are you ready to try this?"

II. Identification of Client Perceptions and Feelings in Problem Situations

____ 4. Counselor has client identify features typically attended to during problem situation. (May have to use imagery with some clients.)	"When you think of the problem situation or one like it, what features do you notice or attend to? What is the first thing that pops into your head?"
____ 5. Counselor has client identify typical feelings during problem situation.	"How do you usually feel?" "What do you experience [or are you experiencing] during this situation?"

III. Deliberate Enactment of Selected Perceptual Features

____ 6. Counselor asks client to reenact situation (by role play or imagery) and to deliberately attend to selected features. (This step may need to be repeated several times.)	"Let's set up a role play [or imagery] in which we act out this situation. This time I want you to deliberately focus on these aspects of the situation we just identified. Notice how you attend to _____."

IV. Identification of Alternative Perceptions

____ 7. Counselor instructs client to identify positive or neutral features of problem situation. The new reframes are plausible and acceptable to the client and fit the client's values and experiences.	"Now, I want us to identify other features of the problem situation that are neutral or positive. These are things you have forgotten about or ignored. Think of other features." "What other aspects of this situation that aren't readily apparent to you could provide a different way to view the situation?"

V. Modification of Perceptions in Problem Situations

____ 8. Counselor instructs client to modify perceptions of problem situation by focusing on or attending to the neutral or positive features. (Use of role play or imagery can facilitate this process for some clients.) (This step may need to be repeated several times.)	"When we act out the problem situation, I want you to change what you attend to in the situation by thinking of the neutral or positive features we just identified. Just focus on these features."

(continued)

Item	Examples of counselor leads

VI. Homework and Follow-Up

_____ 9. Counselor encourages client to practice modifying perceptions during *in vivo* situations.

"Practice is very important for modifying your perceptions. Every time you think about or encounter the problem situation, focus on the neutral or positive features of the situation."

_____ 10. Counselor instructs client to monitor aspects of the strategy on homework log sheet.

"I'd like you to use this log to keep track of the number of times you practice or use this. Also record your initial and resulting feelings before and after these kinds of situations."

_____ 11. Counselor arranges for a follow-up. (During follow-up, counselor comments on client's log and points out small perceptual shifts.)

"Let's get together in two weeks. Bring your log sheet with you. Then we can see how this is working for you."

Observer comments: _____

_____

_____

INTERVIEW CHECKLIST FOR STRESS INOCULATION

Instructions to observer: Determine which of the following steps the counselor demonstrated in using stress inoculation with a client or in teaching stress inoculation to another person. Check any step the counselor demonstrated in the application of the procedure.

Item	Examples of counselor leads

I. Rationale

_____ 1. Counselor explains purpose of stress inoculation.

"Stress inoculation is a way to help you cope with feeling anxious so that you can manage your reactions when you're confronted with these situations."

_____ 2. Counselor provides brief overview of stress inoculation procedure.

"First we'll try to understand how your anxious feelings affect you now. Then you'll learn some coping skills that will help you relax physically — and help you use coping thoughts instead of self-defeating thoughts. Then you'll have a chance to test out your coping skills in stressful situations we'll set up."

_____ 3. Counselor checks to see whether client is willing to use strategy.

"How do you feel now about working with this procedure?"

II. Information Giving

_____ 4. Counselor explains nature of client's emotional reaction to a stressful situation.

"Probably you realize that when you feel anxious, you are physically tense. Also, you may be thinking in a worried way — worrying about the situation and how to handle it. Both the physical tenseness and the negative or worry thoughts create stress for you."

_____ 5. Counselor explains possible *phases* of reacting to a stressful situation.

"When you feel anxious, you probably tend to think of it as one giant reaction. Actually, you're probably anxious at certain times or phases. For example, you might feel very uptight just anticipating the situation. Then you might feel uptight during the situation, especially if it starts to overwhelm you. After the situation is over, you may feel relieved — but down on yourself, too."

_____ 6. Counselor explains specific kinds of coping skills to be learned in stress inoculation

"We'll be learning some action kinds of coping strategies — like physical or muscle relaxation, mental relaxation, and just common-sense ways to minimize the stress of the situation. Then also you'll learn some different ways to

(continued)

POSTEVALUATION (continued)

Item	Examples of counselor leads
and importance of client's input in tailoring coping strategies.	view and think about the situation. Not all of these coping strategies may seem best for you, so your input in selecting the ones you feel are best for you is important."

III. Acquisition and Practice of Direct-Action Coping Skills

Item	Examples of counselor leads
____ 7. Counselor discusses and models direct-action coping strategies (or uses a symbolic model):	"First, I'll explain and we can talk about each coping method. Then I'll demonstrate how you can apply it when you're provoked."
____a. Collecting objective or factual information about stressful situation	"Sometimes it helps to get any information you can about things that provoke and anger you. Let's find out the types of situations and people that can do this to you. Then we can see whether there are other ways to view the provocation. For example, what if you looked at it as a situation to challenge your problem-solving ability rather than as a personal attack?"
____b. Identifying short-circuit or escape routes — alternative ways to deescalate stress of situation	"Suppose you're caught in a situation. You feel it's going to get out of hand. What are some ways to get out of it or to deescalate it *before* you strike out? For example, little things like counting to 60, leaving the room, using humor, or something like that."
Mental relaxation:	
____c. Attention diversion	"OK, one way to control your anger is to distract yourself — take your attention away from the person you feel angry with. If you have to stay in the same room, concentrate very hard on an object in the room. Think of all the questions about this object you can."
____d. Imagery manipulations	"OK, another way you can prevent yourself from striking out is to use your imagination. Think of something very calming and very pleasurable, like your favorite record or like being on the beach with the hot sun."
Physical relaxation:	
____e. Muscle relaxation	"Muscle relaxation can help you cope whenever you start to feel aroused and feel your face getting flushed or your body tightening up. It can help you learn to relax your body, which can, in turn, help you control your anger."
____f. Breathing techniques	"Breathing is also important in learning to relax physically. Sometimes, in a tight spot, taking slow, deep breaths can give you time to get yourself together before saying or doing something you don't want to."
Palliative coping strategies:	
____g. Perspective taking	"Let's try to look at this situation from a different perspective — what else about the situation might you be overlooking?"
____h. Social support network	"Let's put together some people and resources you could use as a support system."
____ i. Ventilation of feelings	"Perhaps it would be helpful just to spend some time getting your feelings out in the open." [You could use Gestalt dialoging as one ventilation tool in addition to discussion.]
____ 8. Client selects most useful coping strategies and practices each under counselor's direction.	"We've gone over a lot of possible methods to help you control your anger so it doesn't result in abusive behavior. I'm sure that you have some preferences. Why don't you pick the methods that you think will work best for you, and we'll practice with these so you can get a feel for them?"

IV. Acquisition and Practice of Cognitive Coping Skills

Item	Examples of counselor leads
____ 9. Counselor describes four phases of using cognitive	"As you may remember from our earlier discussion, we talked about learning to use coping procedures at important points during a stressful or provoking

(continued)

Item	Examples of counselor leads
coping skills to deal with a stressful situation.	situation. Now we will work on helping you learn to use coping thoughts during these four important times — preparing for the situation, handling the situation, dealing with critical moments during the situation, and encouraging yourself after the situation."
_____10. For each phase, counselor models examples of coping statements.	"I'd like to give you some ideas of some possible coping thoughts you could use during each of these four important times. For instance, when I'm trying to psych myself up for a stressful situation, here are some things I think about."
_____11. For each phase, client selects most natural coping statements.	"The examples I gave may not feel natural for you. What I'd like you to do is to pick or add ones that you could use comfortably, that wouldn't seem foreign to you."
_____12. Counselor instructs client to practice using these coping statements for each phase.	"Sometimes, because you aren't used to concentrating on coping thoughts at these important times, it feels a little awkward at first. So I'd like you to get a feel for these just by practicing aloud the ones you selected. Let's work first on the ones for preparing for a provoking situation."
_____13. Counselor models and instructs client to practice sequence of all four phases and verbalize accompanying coping statements.	"OK, next I'd like you to practice verbalizing the coping thoughts aloud in the sequence that you'll be using when you're in provoking situations. For example, [counselor models]. Now you try it."

V. Application of All Coping Skills to Problem-Related Situations

_____14. Using coping strategies and skills selected by client, counselor models how to apply these in a coping manner while imagining a stressful (problem-related) situation.	"Now you can practice using all these coping strategies when confronted with a problem situation. For example, suppose I'm you and my boss comes up to me and gives me criticism based on misinformation. Here is how I might use my coping skills in that situation."
_____15. Client practices coping strategies while imagining problem-related stressful situations. (This step is repeated as necessary.)	"OK, this time why don't you try it? Just imagine this situation — and imagine that each time you start to lose control, that is a signal to use some of your coping skills."
_____16. Client practices coping strategies in role play of problem-related situation. (This step is repeated as necessary.)	"We could practice this in role play. I could take the part of your boss and initiate a meeting with you. Just be yourself and use your coping skills to prepare for the meeting. Then, during our meeting, practice your skills whenever you get tense or start to blow up."

VI. Application of All Coping Skills to Potential Problem Situations (Generalization)

_____17. Counselor models application of client-selected coping strategies to non-problem-related or other potentially stressful situations.	"Let's work on some situations now that aren't problems for you but could arise in the future. This will give you a chance to see how you can apply these coping skills to other situations you encounter in the future. For instance, suppose I just found out I didn't get a promotion that I believe I really deserved. Here is how I might cope with this."
_____18. Client practices, as often as needed, applying coping	"OK, you try this now."

(continued)

POSTEVALUATION (continued)

Item	Examples of counselor leads
strategies to potentially stressful situations by:	
____a. Imagining a potentially stressful situation.	"Why don't you imagine you've just found out you're being transferred to a new place? You are surprised by this. Imagine how you would cope."
____b. Taking part in a role-play practice.	"This time let's role-play a situation. I'll be your husband and tell you I've just found out I am very ill. You practice your coping skills as we talk."
____c. Taking part of a teacher in a role play and teaching a novice how to use coping strategies for stressful situations.	"This time I'm going to pretend that I have chronic arthritis and am in constant pain. It's really getting to me. I'd like you to be my trainer or helper and teach me how I could learn to use some coping skills to deal with this chronic discomfort."

VII. Homework and Follow-Up

____19. Counselor and client discuss application of coping strategies to *in vivo* situations.	"I believe now you could apply these coping skills to problem situations you encounter during a typical day or week. You may not find that these work as quickly as you'd like, but you should find yourself coping more and not losing control as much."
____20. Counselor instructs client how to use log to record uses of stress inoculation for *in vivo* situations.	"Each time you use the coping skills, mark it down on the log and briefly describe the situation in which you used them."
____21. Counselor arranges for a follow-up.	"We could get together next week and go over your logs and see how you're doing."

Observer comments: _____
_____
_____
_____
_____
_____
_____
_____
_____
_____
_____
_____
_____

FEEDBACK #44: STRESS INOCULATION

I.
1. B
2. AD
3. IM
4. ER
5. I
6. MR
7. IM
8. AD
9. V
10. PT
11. SSN
12. SSN

If this was difficult for you, you might review the information presented in the text on direct-action coping skills.

II.
1. Encouraging phase
2. Preparing for the situation
3. Dealing with a critical moment
4. Confronting the situation

(continued)

5. Dealing with a critical moment
6. Encouragement for coping
7. Preparing for the situation
8. Confronting the situation

If you had trouble identifying the four phases of cognitive coping skills, you may want to review Table 16-1.

□ SUGGESTED READINGS

Baker, S. B., & Butler, J. N. (1984). Effects of preventive cognitive self-instruction training on adolescent attitudes, experiences and state anxiety. *Journal of Prevention, 5,* 10–14.

Bandler, R., & Grinder, J. (1982). *Reframing.* Moab, Utah: Real People Press.

Bruch, M. A., Juster, H. R., & Heisler, B. D. (1982). Conceptual complexity as a mediator of thought content and negative affect: Implications for cognitive restructuring interventions. *Journal of Counseling Psychology, 29,* 343–353.

Clark, D. M., & Salkovskis, P. M. (1989). *Cognitive therapy for panic and hypochondriasis.* New York: Pergamon.

Dobson, K. S. (Ed.). (1988). *Handbook of cognitive-behavioral therapies.* New York: Guilford Press.

Dush, D. M., Hirt, M. L., & Schroeder, H. (1983). Self-statement modification with adults: A meta-analysis. *Psychological Bulletin, 94,* 408–422.

Elder, J. P., Edelstein, B. A., & Fremouw, W. J. (1981). Client by treatment interactions in response acquisition and cognitive restructuring approaches. *Cognitive Therapy and Research, 5,* 203–210.

Feindler, E. L., & Ecton, R. B. (1986). *Adolescent anger control.* New York: Pergamon.

Feindler, E. L., & Fremouw, W. J. (1983). Stress inoculation training for adolescent anger problems. In D. H. Meichenbaum & M. E. Jaremko (Eds.), *Stress reduction and prevention.* New York: Plenum.

Greenberg, L. S., & Safran, J. D. (1981). Encoding and cognitive therapy: Changing what clients attend to. *Psychotherapy: Theory, Research and Practice, 18,* 163–169.

Hamilton, S. A., & Fremouw, W. J. (1985). Cognitive-behavioral training for college basketball foul-shooting performance. *Cognitive Therapy and Research, 9,* 479–483.

Janis, I. L. (1983). Stress inoculation in health care: Theory and research. In D. H. Meichenbaum & M. E. Jaremko (Eds.), *Stress reduction and prevention.* New York: Plenum.

Kendall, P. C. (1983). Stressful medical procedures: Cognitive-behavioral strategies for stress management and prevention. In D. H. Meichenbaum & M. E. Jaremko (Eds.), *Stress reduction and prevention.* New York: Plenum.

Kirby, E. A., & Grimley, L. K. (1986). *Understanding and treating attention deficit and disorder.* New York: Pergamon.

Klepac, R. K., Hauge, G., Dowling, J., & McDonald, M. (1981). Direct and generalized effects of three components of stress inoculation for increased pain tolerance. *Behavior Therapy, 12,* 417–424.

Leventhal, H., & Nerenz, D. R. (1983). A model for stress research with some implications for the control of stress disorders. In D. H. Meichenbaum & M. E. Jaremko (Eds.), *Stress reduction and prevention.* New York: Plenum.

Matson, J. L. (1989). *Treating depression in children and adolescents.* New York: Pergamon.

McCordick, S. M., Kaplan, R. M., Smith, S., & Finn, M. E. (1981). Variations in cognitive behavior modification for test anxiety. *Psychotherapy: Theory, Research and Practice, 18,* 170–178.

Meichenbaum, D. (1985). *Stress-inoculation training.* Elmsford, New York: Pergamon Press.

Meichenbaum, D., & Cameron, R. (1983). Stress inoculation training: Toward a general paradigm for training coping skills. In D. H. Meichenbaum & M. E. Jaremko (Eds.), *Stress reduction and prevention.* New York: Plenum.

Miller, R. C., & Berman, J. S. (1983). The efficacy of cognitive behavior therapies: A quantitative review of the research evidence. *Psychological Bulletin, 94,* 39–53.

Novaco, R. W. (1975). *Anger control: The development and evaluation of an experimental treatment.* Lexington, MA: Heath.

Pope, A. W., McHale, S. M., & Craighead, W. E. (1988). *Self-esteem enhancement with children and adolescents.* New York: Pergamon.

Roskies, E. (1983). Stress management for Type A individuals. In D. H. Meichenbaum & M. E. Jaremko (Eds.), *Stress reduction and prevention.* New York: Plenum.

Safran, J. D., Alden, L. E., & Davidson, P. O. (1980). Client anxiety level as a moderator variable in assertion training. *Cognitive Therapy and Research, 4,* 189–200.

Safran, J. D., & Greenberg, L. S. (1982). Cognitive appraisal and reappraisal: Implications for clinical practice. *Cognitive Therapy and Research, 6,* 251–258.

Sweeney, G. A., & Horan, J. J. (1982). Separate and combined effects of cue-controlled relaxation and cognitive restructuring in the treatment of musical performance anxiety. *Journal of Counseling Psychology, 29,* 486–497.

Turk, D., & Genest, M. (1979). Regulation of pain: The application of cognitive and behavioral techniques for prevention and remediation. In P. Kendall & S. Hollon (Eds.), *Cognitive-behavioral intervention: Theory, research, and procedures.* New York: Academic Press.

Veronen, L. J., & Kilpatrick, D. G. (1983). Stress management for rape victims. In D. H. Meichenbaum & M. E. Jaremko (Eds.), *Stress reduction and prevention.* New York: Plenum.

Wernick, R. L. (1983). Stress inoculation in the management of clinical pain: Application to burn pain. In D. H. Meichenbaum & M. E. Jaremko (Eds.), *Stress reduction and prevention.* New York: Plenum.

West, D. J., Jr., Horan, J. J., & Games, P. A. (1984). Component analysis of occupational stress inoculation applied to registered nurses in an acute care hospital setting. *Journal of Counseling Psychology, 31,* 209–218.

Wilson, G. T., Rossiter, E., Kleifield, E. I., & Lindholm, L. (1986). Cognitive-behavioral treatment of bulimia nervosa: A controlled evaluation. *Behaviour Research and Therapy, 24,* 277–288.

Yost, E. B., Beutler, L. E., Corbishley, M. A., & Allender, J. R. (1986). *Group cognitive therapy: A treatment method for depressed older adults.* New York: Pergamon.

■
FEEDBACK: POSTEVALUATION

PART ONE

1. You might emphasize that the client thinks of herself as inadequate although there are, in actuality, many indications of adequacy. You can explain that CR would help her identify some of her thoughts about herself that are beliefs, not facts, and are unrealistic thoughts, leading to feelings of depression and worthlessness. In addition, CR would help her learn to think about herself in more realistic, self-enhancing ways. See the Interview Checklist for Cognitive Restructuring on pages 434–437 for another example of the CR rationale.

2. Self-enhancing or realistic thoughts for this client would be thinking that an almost straight-A average is good. A self-defeating thought is that this average is not good enough. In this case, almost any self-degrading thought is self-defeating because, for this client, these thoughts are only beliefs. Thinking that she is not good enough is self-defeating. Self-enhancing or positive thoughts about herself are more realistic interpretations of her experiences—good grades, close friends, active social life, and so on. Recognition that she is intelligent and attractive is a self-enhancing thought.

3. You could ask the client to describe different situations and the thoughts she has about herself in them. She could also observe this during the week. You could model some possible thoughts she might be having. See leads 6, 7, 8, and 9 in the Interview Checklist for Cognitive Restructuring.

4. There are many possible coping thoughts she could use. Here are some examples: "Hey, I'm doing pretty well as it is." "Don't be so hard on myself. I don't have to be perfect." "That worthless feeling is a sign to cope—recognize my assets." "What's more attractive anyway? I am attractive." "Don't let that one B get me down. It's not the end of the world."

5. See leads 13 through 16 on the Interview Checklist for Cognitive Restructuring.

6. Many possible homework assignments might help. Here are a few examples:
   a. Every time the client uses a coping thought, she could record it on her log.
   b. She could cue herself to use a coping thought by writing these down on note cards and reading a note before doing something else, like getting a drink or making a phone call, or by using a phone-answering device to report and verbalize coping thoughts.
   c. She could enlist the aid of a close friend or roommate. If the roommate notices that the client starts to "put herself down," she could interrupt her. The client could then verbalize a coping statement.

PART TWO

Use the Interview Checklist for Cognitive Restructuring on pages 434–437 to assess your teaching or counseling demonstration of this procedure.

PART THREE

Use the Interview Checklist for Reframing to assess your interview.

PART FOUR

1. Your rationale to this client might sound something like this:

   "You realize that there are times when your anger and impatience do get the best of you. This procedure can help you learn to control your feelings at especially hard times—when you're very upset with this child—so that you don't do something you will regret later."

2. Here is a brief overview of stress inoculation:

   "First, we'll look at the things the child can do that really upset you. When you realize you're in this type of situation, you can learn to control how upset you are—through keeping yourself calm. This procedure will help you learn different ways to keep calm and not let these situations get out of hand."

(continued)

3. Information—See lead 7, part a, on the Interview Checklist for Stress Inoculation for some examples.
   Escape route—See lead 7, part b.
   Attention diversion—See lead 7, part c.
   Imagery manipulations—See lead 7, part d.
   Physical relaxation—See lead 7, parts e and f.
   Palliative coping—See lead 7, parts g, h, and i.
4. Here are some examples of a possible explanation of the four coping phases and of cognitive coping skills you might present to this client.

Phase	Explanation	Cognitive coping
Preparing for a provoking situation	Before you have a disagreement or discussion, you can plan how you want to handle it.	"What do I want to say to him that gets my point across?" "I can tell him how I feel without shouting."
Confronting a provoking situation	When you're talking to him, you can think about how to stay in control.	"Just keep talking in a normal voice, no yelling." "Let him talk, too. Don't yell a lot; it doesn't help."
Dealing with a very provoking moment	If you feel very angry, you really need to think of some things to keep you from blowing your cool.	"Wait a minute. Slow down. Don't let the lid off." "Keep those hands down. Stay calm now."
Encouraging self for coping	Recognize when you do keep your cool. It's important to do this, to give yourself a pat on the back for this.	"I kept my cool that time!" "I could feel myself getting angry, but I kept in control then."

5. Practice opportunities can be carried out by the client in imagination or by you and the client in role play. In a role-play practice, you could take the part of the child. See leads 14, 15, and 16 on the Interview Checklist for Stress Inoculation for some examples of this type of practice.

PART FIVE
Use the Interview Checklist for Stress Inoculation to assess your role-play interview.

MEDITATION AND MUSCLE RELAXATION

SEVENTEEN

Feeling uptight? stressful? anxious?

Does your blood pressure zoom up at certain times or in certain situations?

Having trouble sleeping?

Does your head pound and ache at the end of the day?

A great number of people would respond affirmatively to one or more of these four questions. Anxiety is one of the most common problems reported by clients; stress is related to physiological discomfort such as headaches and indigestion. Stress is also correlated with heart disease, cancer, and other serious diseases. Perhaps as a consequence of the "stress syndrome," the last few years have produced an explosion in procedures for stress or anxiety management, originally introduced in 1929 as "progressive relaxation" (Jacobson, 1929). Related books have appeared on nonfiction best-seller lists (Benson, 1976; Bloomfield, Cain, Jaffe, & Kory, 1975; Denniston & McWilliams, 1975), and a flurry of research endeavors has explored the relative strengths and weaknesses of stress-management approaches (Nicassio & Bootzin, 1974; Lehrer & Woolfolk, 1984; Shoemaker & Tasto, 1975; Smith, 1975).

This chapter presents three stress-management or relaxation strategies. Two meditation procedures are described—Benson's (1974, 1976) relaxation response and Carrington's (1978a, 1978b) clinically standardized meditation—as well as muscle-relaxation training. These three strategies are typically used to treat both cognitive and physiological indexes of stress, including anxiety, anger, pain, and hypertension. The strategies differ somewhat in that both meditation strategies are primarily cognitive relaxation procedures, whereas muscle relaxation focuses on physical, or somatic, sensations (Marlatt & Marques, 1977, p. 131). The benefits of both procedures may not be realized unless they are used to prevent, as well as to remediate, stress-related symptoms. Lehrer, Woolfolk, Rooney, McCann, and Carrington (1983) suggest that meditation might be preferable if client motivation is a problem; the clients may enjoy practice more because cognitive absorption of attention may be greater. In contrast, clients who experience skeletal-muscle tension or tension headaches might benefit more from progressive muscle relaxation (Lehrer et al., 1983). A combination of one form of meditation and muscle relaxation may be better than one strategy alone.

☐ OBJECTIVES

1. Identify which step of the relaxation response is reflected by each of ten counselor responses, accurately identifying at least eight of the ten examples.
2. Identify which step of the clinically standardized meditation procedure is reflected by at least six of eight counselor responses.
3. Select either the relaxation response or clinically standardized meditation and teach the procedure to another person. Audiotape your teaching and assess your steps with the Interview Checklist for Muscle Relaxation or the Interview Checklist for Clinically Standardized Meditation, or have an observer evaluate your teaching, using the checklist.
4. Describe how you would apply the seven major components of the muscle-relaxation procedure, given a simulated client case.
5. Demonstrate 13 out of 15 steps of muscle relaxation with a role-play client, using the Interview Checklist for Muscle Relaxation to assess your performance.

☐ MEDITATION

"Meditation refers to a family of techniques which have in common a conscious attempt to focus attention in a nonanalytical way and an attempt not to dwell on discursive ruminating thought" (Shapiro, 1982, p. 268). The word *meditation* is associated with the mystical traditions of the East. For example, Zen (Zazen) breath meditation was developed many centuries ago as a technique for attaining religious insight (Shapiro & Zifferblatt, 1976). Transcendental Meditation (TM) is another procedure used to turn one's attention inward toward more subtle levels of thought. In a review of meditation as psychotherapy, Smith (1975, p. 558) states that "such exercises vary widely and can involve sitting still and counting breaths, attending to a repeated thought, or focusing on virtually any simple external or internal stimulus." Carrington (1978a) defines *clinically*

standardized meditation (CSM) as a Western version of the Indian practice called "mantra meditation." CSM uses a soothing sound that the client repeats mentally without conscious effort or concentration. Benson (1974, 1976) refers to meditation as the *relaxation response.*

Several studies have reported on the effectiveness of meditation as a therapeutic strategy. Smith's (1975) review of research about meditation as a therapeutic procedure yielded three general findings. First, experienced meditators who volunteer without pay for meditation research appear "healthier" than nonmeditators. Second, people who are beginners and who practice meditation for four to ten weeks show more "improvement" on a variety of tests than nonmeditators measured for the same period of time. Third, four to ten weeks of regular practice of meditation is associated with greater decrements in "psychopathology" than those experienced by control nonmeditators. However, Smith points out that none of the studies reviewed had controlled for the expectation of relief ("I want to and will get better") or the regular practice of sitting quietly.

In other studies, Boudreau (1972) found that TM relieved symptoms associated with claustrophobia in one case and excessive perspiration in another. Girodo (1974) found that people with a short history of anxiety neurosis effectively reduced their anxiety symptoms with meditation. Zen breath meditation and self-management techniques were applied to reduce methadone dosage of two drug addicts (Shapiro & Zifferblatt, 1976), to treat anxiety (Lehrer et al., 1983), and to reduce nonattending behaviors of children (Redfering & Bowman, 1981). Attention-focusing techniques derived from meditation procedures were as effective as progressive relaxation in treating 24 insomniacs to reduce latency of sleep onset (Woolfolk, Carr-Kaffashan, McNulty, & Lehrer, 1976). Breath meditation was effective in reducing systolic and diastolic blood pressure of a 71-year-old hypertensive from 170/105 before treatment to 135/90 several months after treatment (Rappaport & Cammer, 1977). Both the relaxation response and muscle relaxation significantly decreased alcohol consumption of many clients (Marlatt & Marques, 1977) and decreased daily manifestations of cognitive and somatic stress (Woolfolk, Lehrer, McCann, & Rooney, 1982). More recently, meditation has been used with children with recurrent headaches (Waranch & Keenan, 1985), for treatment of post-Vietnam adjustment (Brooks & Scarano, 1985), with heavy alcohol drinkers (Murphy, Pagano, & Marlatt, 1986), and for the self-regulation of chronic pain (Kabat-Zinn, 1982; Kabat-Zinn, Lipworth, & Burney, 1985). Delmonte and Kenny (1987) in their review found that meditation is a useful skill for focused attention, physiologically relaxing, decreasing anxiety and insomnia, decreasing drug usage, and for increasing self-actualization. Meditation appears to be most effective for mild disorders (Delmonte & Kenny, 1987).

Shapiro and Zifferblatt (1976, p. 522) have described the process of Zen meditation in five overlapping steps:

1. There is a reactive effect when a person begins to focus on breathing. For example, breathing may be faster.
2. Later, the person's attention wanders from the breathing and he or she becomes habituated in the exercise.
3. The person is taught to catch himself or herself whenever attention wanders and return to breathing. Either this process may cause another reactive effect or, with practice, one may learn to breathe effortlessly.
4. The person is able to continue to focus on breathing and at the same time passively observe new thoughts as they come into awareness.
5. The last process (step 4) may have two functions: (a) the person becomes desensitized to distracting thoughts, and (b) the person eventually removes thoughts by focusing on breathing.

Barber (1980) and Clarke and Jackson (1983) indicate that there is a great deal of commonality between meditation and hypnosis, particularly with respect to the central role of attentional focusing in both procedures. Barber noted the similarity of the two procedures:

> The overlap between self-hypnosis and meditation is tremendous. In fact it seems to me that the variability within self-hypnosis and meditation is almost as large as the variability between these procedures. There seems to me to be so many parallels so that it appears possible to at least conceptualize self-hypnosis as one type of meditation, or vice versa, meditation as one type of self-hypnosis [quoted in Shapiro, 1980, p. 57).

Benson (1974, 1976) has described meditation, or the relaxation response, as a counterbalancing technique for alleviating the environmental effects of stress. Often, when people feel stress, "fight or flight" is the coping response used. Regular practice of the relaxation response can stimulate the area of the hypothalamus in the brain that can decrease systolic and diastolic blood pressure, heart rate, respiratory rate, and oxygen consumption. The fight-or-flight response to stress can raise these physiological rates (Benson, 1976). According to Benson (1974, 1976), four basic elements are needed to elicit the relaxation response: a quiet environment, a mental device, a passive attitude, and a comfortable position. The components of clinically standardized meditation are similar: a mantra, or sound, a quiet environment free of distractions, a passive attitude in which the client flows with the process, and a comfortable and relaxed sitting position.

Shapiro (1980, p. 33) has described several characteristics of people who are successful at meditation. Some of the characteristics are high level of internal locus of control ("I'm in control of my behavior"), a great deal of enthusiasm, high interest in subjective experiences (Lehrer et al., 1983), and good ability to maintain attentional focus.

Meditation can be used alone or in conjunction with other procedures (see D. H. Shapiro & S. M. Zifferblatt, 1976). The elements listed by Benson (1976) for eliciting the relaxation response and the processes described by Shapiro and Zifferblatt have been interwoven into the following description of the steps for the relaxation response (RR) and Zen meditation (ZM).

□ STEPS FOR RELAXATION RESPONSE AND ZEN MEDITATION

We describe the relaxation response (RR) and Zen meditation (ZM) combined in one eight-step procedure (see Table 17-1).

1. The counselor gives the client a rationale for the procedure.
2. The counselor and client select a mental device.
3. The counselor instructs the client about body comfort.
4. The counselor instructs the client about breathing and use of a mental device.
5. The counselor instructs the client about a passive attitude.
6. The client tries to meditate for 10 to 20 minutes.

TABLE 17-1. Steps for relaxation response (RR) and Zen meditation (ZM) combined and clinically standardized meditation (CSM)

RR and ZM combined	*Clinically standardized meditation (CSM)*

1. Rationale
  a. Describe purpose of procedure.
  b. Give overview of procedure.
	1. Rationale
	  a. Describe purpose of procedure.
	  b. Give overview of procedure.

2. Selection of a mental device
  a. Provide rationale for mental device.
  b. Provide examples of mental device.
	2. Selection of mantra or sound
	  a. Instruct client to select a mantra.
	  b. Choose or make up a meaningless sound or word that has few associations and is not emotionally charged.

3. Instructions to patient
  a. Get in quiet environment.
  b. Relax all muscles in body and keep them relaxed.
  c. Close eyes and assume comfortable body position.
	3. Preparation for meditation
	  a. Select a quiet environment free from distractions (such as the telephone).
	  b. Should not be interrupted while meditating.
	  c. Should not take any alcoholic beverages or nonprescription drugs at least 24 hours before meditation.
	  d. Should not drink any beverages containing caffeine one hour before meditation.

4. Instructions about breathing and use of mental device: Breathe through your nose and focus on your breathing. Let the air come to you. As you do this, say the mental device for each inhalation and exhalation: "Breathe in . . . out 'one,' in . . . out, 'one.'" Breathe in and out while saying your mental device silently to yourself. Try to achieve effortless breathing.	e. Should not eat for one hour before meditation. No smoking for half an hour before. No chewing gum while meditating.
	  f. Select a comfortable straight-backed chair in a room free of clutter. Face away from direct light in dimly lit room.
	  g. Loosen tight clothing and shoes.

5. Instructions about passive attitude: When distracting thoughts occur, let them pass. Keep your mind open and return to your mental device.	4. Instructions to meditate
	  a. Sit quietly for about a half minute before you say your mantra or sound. Be relaxed and quiet.
	  b. First, close your eyes and say your mantra or sound aloud, say it softly, whisper, think the sound to yourself without moving your lips or tongue. After the first session, hear or think your sound.

6. Meditate for 10 to 20 minutes. Instruct the client to meditate 10 minutes at first. Later, the time can be extended.	c. CSM is not an exercise in discipline—it is a quiet, peaceful time with yourself. It requires no effort.

7. Probe about meditation experience
  a. How does it feel?
  b. How did you handle distracting thoughts?
	d. Allow distracting thoughts to flow. Flow with the process—allow memories, images, thoughts to occur. Don't try to influence these. Your mantra will return to you.

8. Instruct client to meditate daily
  a. Don't meditate within one hour after eating.
  b. Meditate in quiet environment.
  c. Meditate several hours before bedtime.
  d. Meditate twice daily.
	e. Meditate for five to ten minutes. You can open your eyes to look at watch periodically.
	  f. Come out of meditation slowly. Sit with your eyes closed for two minutes—take time to absorb what is happening. Get up slowly and open eyes slowly.

	5. Discuss client's reaction to first meditation.

	6. Homework
	  a. Meditate for three weeks, twice a day.
	  b. Meditate first thing in the morning after arising and during the afternoon or early evening.

* Reprinted with permission from Deane H. Shapiro, Jr., *Meditation: Self-regulation strategy and altered state of consciousness* (New York: Aldine de Gruyter). Copyright © 1980 by Deane H. Shapiro.

7. The counselor probes the client about the meditative experience.
8. Finally, the client is assigned homework and is instructed to keep a daily log of meditative experiences.

The Interview Checklist for Relaxation Response and Zen Meditation at the end of the chapter summarizes these steps.

Treatment Rationale

Here is an example of a *rationale* for meditation used by Shapiro (1978b):

. . . Meditation is nothing magical. It takes patience and practice; you have to work at it; and, just by meditating, all life's problems will not be solved. On the other hand, meditation is potentially a very powerful tool, and it is equally important to suggest what you might be able to expect from meditation the first month you practice it. Studies have shown that Zen meditation can have a strong effect within the first two to four weeks. Some of these effects can be measured physiologically—e.g., brain wave states, slower breathing, slower heart rate. These all contribute to a state of relaxation and inner calm. Meditation may help you become more aware, both of what is going on outside you, and what is happening within you—your thoughts, feelings, hopes, fears. Thus, although meditation won't solve all your problems, it can give you the calmness, the awareness, and the self-control to actively work on solving those problems (p. 71).*

Here is an illustration of an *overview* of the strategy:

"What we will do first is select a focusing or mental device. You will then get in a relaxed and comfortable position. Afterward, I will instruct you about focusing on your breathing and using your mental device. We will talk about a passive attitude while meditating. You will meditate about 10 to 20 minutes. Then we will talk about the experience."

Selection of a Mental Device

Most forms of meditation can be classified as "concentrative" meditation, in which one tries to clear one's mind of intruding thoughts by focusing

* This and all other quotations from this source are from "Instructions for a Training Package Combining Formal and Informal Zen Meditation with Behavioral Self-Control Strategies," by D. H. Shapiro. From *Psychologia.* Copyright 1978 by Kyoto University. Reprinted by permission of the publisher.

for a time on a single stimulus (Ornstein, 1972). Often this stimulus takes the form of a mental device. A mental device, or "mantra," is usually a single-syllable sound or word such as *in, out, one,* or *zum,* although concentration on a mental riddle is also possible. The client repeats the syllable or word silently or in a low tone while meditating. The rationale for the repetition of the syllable or word is to free the client from focusing on logical and externally oriented thought. Instead, the client focuses on a constant stimulus—the word, sound, syllable, or phrase. Repetition of the word assists in breaking the stream of distracting thoughts (Benson, 1976). The mental device is used to help the client focus on breathing. The counselor should describe the rationale for the mental device to the client and give examples of possible options for a mental device. Benson (1974) suggests use of the word *one* "because of its simplicity and neutrality" (p. 54). The client then selects his or her own mental device to use while meditating.

Instructions about Body Comfort

The first prerequisite for body comfort is a quiet environment in which to meditate. The counselor should create a quiet, calm environment that is as free of distractions as possible. Benson (1976) claims that some background noise may prevent the relaxation response. A quiet environment is less distracting and may facilitate elimination of intrusive thoughts. The counselor tells the client that there are several ways to meditate or to elicit the relaxation response and says that he or she will show the client one way. Then the counselor instructs the client to get into a comfortable position. This may be sitting in a comfortable chair with the head and arms supported, or the person might wish to sit on the floor, assuming a semilotus position (this is particularly good for "private" practice sessions). As in muscle relaxation, the client should wear comfortable clothing. Getting into a comfortable position minimizes muscular effort. When in a comfortable position, the client is instructed to close her or his eyes and to relax all muscles deeply. The counselor might name a few muscle groups—"Relax your face, your neck, your head, shoulders, chest, your lower torso, your thighs, going to your calves, and to your feet." The muscle groups described in Table 17-2, later in this chapter, can be used at this point. After the client is relaxed, the counselor gives instructions about breathing and using the mental device.

Instructions about Breathing and Use of the Mental Device

The counselor instructs the client to breathe through the nose and to focus on or become aware of breathing. It is believed that the focused-breathing component of meditation helps a person learn to relax and to manage tension (Shapiro, 1978a). At first, it may be difficult for some people to be natural when focusing on breathing. The counselor should encourage the client to breathe easily and naturally with a suggestion to "allow the air to come to you" on each inhalation. For each exhalation, the client is instructed to exhale slowly, letting all the air out of the lungs. While focusing on breathing, the client uses the mental device by saying it silently. Clients are instructed to repeat the mental device silently for each inhalation and each exhalation and are encouraged to keep their attention on the breathing and the mental device.

Instructions about a Passive Attitude

The counselor instructs the client to maintain a passive attitude and to allow relaxation to occur at its own pace. In addition, the client is instructed, if attention wanders and distracting images or thoughts occur, not to dwell on them and to return to repeating the mental device or word. The client should allow the distracting thoughts to pass through the mind and just be passive. If distracting thoughts occur for several minutes, instruct the client not to be evaluative and to return to repeating the mental device. As Benson states, "The purpose of the response is to help one rest and relax, and this requires a completely passive attitude. One should not scrutinize his performance or try to force the response, because this may well prevent the response from occurring. When distracting thoughts enter the mind, they should simply be disregarded" (1974, p. 54). The relaxation response is not an occasion for thinking things over or for problem solving. Shapiro (1978a) hypothesizes that this emphasis in meditation on the "ongoing present" may alert people to notice when they become distracted from tasks and also may represent a way to return to the present, or the "here and now."

Meditation for 10 to 20 Minutes

The client is instructed to meditate for about 10 to 20 minutes. The counselor tells the client to open her or his eyes to check the time if desired. A clock or watch that the client can see easily should be provided. The counselor also instructs the client in what to do after the meditative session. For example, some clients may wish to keep their eyes closed for a couple of minutes after meditating — or just to sit quietly for several minutes.

Probe about the Meditative Experience

The counselor asks the client about the experience with meditation. For example, the counselor should ask how the client felt, how the mental device was used, what happened to any distracting thoughts, and whether the client was able to maintain a passive attitude.

Homework and Follow-up

As homework, the counselor asks the client to practice the relaxation response once or twice a day at home or at work. Each practice session may last 10 to 15 minutes. Practice should not occur within two hours after any meal, because the digestive processes appear to interfere with relaxation. Practice should occur in a quiet environment free from distractions or interruptions. For some people, practice several hours before bedtime can interfere with going to sleep. The client should be instructed to keep a daily log of each time the relaxation response is used. The log might include the time of day meditation was used, the setting, the period of time spent in practice, and the client's reaction to the experience or the level of relaxation as rated on a 5-point scale. Individualize the homework for the client. Some clients may feel that they cannot practice twice daily. In such cases, encourage the client to practice several times weekly.

Another homework assignment proposed by Shapiro and Zifferblatt (1976) is *informal meditation*. This requires that a person be conscious and aware and observe or attend very closely to ordinary daily activities (pp. 521–522). A client could be instructed simply to observe all events and behaviors that occur throughout the day. This type of informal meditation is similar to what Ornstein (1972) describes as "opening up" — meditative exercises in which the person simply focuses on whatever is happening as it occurs, in the "here and now." Informal meditation may be used more frequently as homework than formal meditation because it is somewhat easier, is less structured, and takes less time.

Another way to use informal meditation as homework is to ask the client to observe some selected problem or stress-related environmental event in a detached, nonevaluative fashion. For such events that might produce tension, anxiety, anger, fear, or pain, the client could be instructed to focus on breathing and to initiate calmness and relaxation. Here is an example of this type of assignment developed by Shapiro (1980, pp. 128 – 130), which he refers to as "contingent informal meditation":

Awareness: List below current problems, difficulties, or concerns which you are having or have had that cause you to become tense and anxious:

a. _____

b. _____

c. _____

Let's pick a situation *a*, now, and see if you can make it as specific as possible. Who is present; where are you; what kinds of things are you doing, saying, thinking. Now close your eyes and imagine yourself in that situation, and allow yourself to experience the tension that you normally feel.

Interruption of sequence and competing response. Once you have observed these thoughts and actions, say to yourself "Stop!" as you clench your fist and your jaw. Then relax your fingers and your jaw and imagine yourself beginning informal breath meditation: you are closing your eyes and beginning to focus on your breathing. Now, actually take two deep breaths through your nose, and as you exhale let your "center" sink into your stomach. Say to yourself:

1. Your name: "I am _____."
2. "I am breath" (and take another deep breath).
3. "I am calm and relaxed and am in control" (and take two more deep breaths, letting your "center" sink to your stomach as you exhale).

Now imagine yourself becoming more and more relaxed; imagine yourself meditating, feeling calm, and in control. At the count of ten you may open your eyes, and you will feel calm, relaxed, and wide awake. [Repeat this process for situations *b* and *c*.]*

In addition to the formal practice of the relaxation response, informal meditation can be assigned as an *in vivo* application of the procedure.

* Reprinted with permission from Deane H. Shapiro, Jr., *Meditation: Self-regulation strategy and altered state of consciousness* (New York: Aldine de Gruyter). Copyright © 1980 by Deane H. Shapiro.

The client can also be instructed to keep a log of informal meditation applied *in vivo* to stressful situations. After the client has used the meditation homework for about a month, a follow-up session should be scheduled. This session can use the client's log data to check on the frequency of use of the homework, the client's reactions to the homework, and the client's recorded stress level.

☐ STEPS FOR CLINICALLY STANDARDIZED MEDITATION

We divide the clinically standardized meditation (CSM) procedure, based on Carrington's (1978a) descriptions, into six steps:

1. Rationale.
2. Selection of a mantra, or sound.
3. Preparation for meditation.
4. Instructions to meditate.
5. Discussion of client's reaction to first meditation.
6. Homework and follow-up.

Table 17-1 summarizes these steps, and the Interview Checklist for Clinically Standardized Meditation at the end of the chapter models the steps.

Treatment Rationale

Here is one version of a rationale and overview (adapted from Carrington, 1978b) that a counselor might give:

"The procedure called 'clinically standardized meditation' is a simple relaxation exercise. A variety of positive effects can come from meditating. For example, meditation has benefited people by reducing tension, stress, headaches, anxiety, and the time it takes to fall asleep. It has also been reported to increase athletic performance and energy. People who meditate report that they are more alert, are closer to their feelings, and have clearer thinking. Meditation may be an alternative to tranquilizers and other drugs. If you choose to try meditation as a relaxation technique, you will be asked to select a sound, or mantra, that you will use while you are relaxed and comfortable in a quiet environment. You can allow images and thoughts to flow freely. You will not have to concentrate, and meditation will require no effort. Let your thoughts or feelings come and go. Your mantra will come back to you. We will meditate for five or ten minutes at first. Then we will talk about your reaction to this quiet and peaceful experience" [after Cormier & Cormier, & Weisser, 1984, p. 270].

Selection of a Mantra

Carrington's course workbook (*Learning to Meditate,* 1978b) contains a list of 16 Sanskrit words from which a client may choose (p. 10). Alternatively, we have found that clients can create a meaningless sound or word that has few associations and is not emotionally charged. *Grik, shalom,* and *rava* are examples of sounds or words. Whatever sound is chosen, it should be soothing to the client.

Preparation for Meditation

Carrington (1978b) provides extensive instructions on preparing to meditate (see Table 17-1). First, clients should be instructed to select a quiet, uncluttered environment, free from interruptions and distractions such as ringing telephones or people talking. The idea is for people not to be interrupted or externally distracted while meditating. Clients should not consume any alcoholic beverages or nonprescription drugs for at least 24 hours before meditation. They should not meditate within one hour after consuming solid food or beverages containing caffeine. Smoking is discouraged for at least a half hour before meditation.

Clients should be instructed to loosen tight-fitting clothing or shoes and select a comfortable straight-backed chair away from direct light. These instructions are provided to enhance the quality of the meditation. The instructions can also serve as stimulus controls, or cues to increase the probability of meditating (see "Stimulus Control," in Chapter 19).

Instructions to Meditate

It is important that clients know to relax their muscles before beginning to meditate (see the next section of this chapter). Carrington (1978b) recommends sitting quietly for about half a minute before saying the mantra, or sound. After this brief period of quiet relaxation, clients are to close their eyes and focus on the mantra. At first, they pronounce the mantra aloud. Gradually, they begin to say it more softly, then to whisper it, and finally to think or hear the sound without moving their lips or tongue. It is important that clients be reminded that meditation is not an exercise in discipline but a quiet, peaceful time alone, requiring no effort or concentration. Clients should allow distracting thoughts or feelings to flow, as if they were clouds floating by. They should not actively try to influence distracting thoughts or feelings but should

merely allow their mantra to return to them. Clients should be instructed to meditate for five to ten minutes, opening their eyes occasionally to peek at a watch or clock. Finally, they should end each meditative session slowly. Carrington (1978b) advises that clients sit with closed eyes for about two minutes and take time to absorb what is happening at that moment.

Client's Reaction to First Meditation

Discuss or probe the client's reaction to meditation. People experience a variety of reactions to meditation; no two meditative experiences are alike. Clients may feel unsure of themselves when meditating, possibly because *there are no rules* for the process.

Homework and Follow-up

The therapist should tell the client when and how often to meditate. Novices should practice twice daily for at least the initial three-week period. Carrington (1978b) recommends that people regularly meditate in the morning after arising and in the late afternoon or early evening.

☐ MINDFULNESS OR AWARENESS

A third type or variation of meditation is mindfulness or awareness meditation. There are two major types of meditation: concentration meditation and mindfulness or awareness meditation. Concentration methods involve the initial restriction of attention to a single point or object, using a mental sound (mantra) to focus on the breathing experience, or fixing on a visual object, and holding the point or object in the mind for a designated period of time (Kabat-Zinn, 1982).

Mindfulness or awareness meditation involves concentrating to maintain steady attention instead of restricting attention to one point or object. The flexibility of attention is achieved by concentrating on one primary object (inhales and exhales) until attention is relatively stable. Then the focus of attention is allowed to enlarge or expand to include all body sensations, thoughts, memories, emotions, perceptions, institutions, or fantasies as they occur in time (Kabat-Zinn, 1982). The process of expanding attention is taught gradually over several sessions. The meditator is instructed to make the observation with detachment and to avoid judgment or interpretation. If the meditator's mind wanders and becomes preoccupied with thoughts and emotions, the meditator is instructed to focus all attention on breathing so as to "re-anchor" the attention to the present (Kabat-Zinn, 1982). An outline of mindfulness meditation is described by Kabat-Zinn:

"A. Sweeping: a gradual sweeping through the body from feet to head with the attentional faculty, focusing on proprioception, and with periodic suggestions of breath awareness and relaxation. This was usually practiced in the supine position.

B. Mindfulness of breath and other perceptions. This form was practiced sitting in a chair or on a cushion on the floor.

C. Hatha Yoga postures. The yoga introduced a dimension of meditative exercise designed to reverse disuse atrophy of the musculoskeletal system while developing mindfulness during movement. Although hatha yoga per se is not a traditional mindfulness technique, it was taught emphasizing mindfulness.

As in traditional monastic teaching, mindfulness meditation is also taught using the activities of walking, standing, and eating. The use of a range of objects of meditation helps to develop an ability to bring mindfulness into the varied circumstances of daily living.

Meditation instructions are as follows:

1. Bring your attention to the primary object of observation.

2. Be aware of it from moment to moment.

3. When you notice that the mind has drifted into thought, revery, and so forth, bring it back to awareness of the present moment, to the observation of what is dominant in the moment. In the sweeping meditation, the primary object is that region of the body through which one is moving at any moment.

4. When a strong feeling or emotion arises (i.e., a state of fear, pain, anger, anxiety), direct your attention to the feeling as it occurs and just be with it, observing it. When it subsides, return to the primary object of observation. Distinguish between observation of the experience itself and thoughts and interpretations of the experience.

5. Observe the thinking process itself. Avoid becoming involved in the content of individual thoughts. Observe them as impermanent mind events and not necessarily accurate. Treat all thoughts as equal in value and neither pursue them nor reject them" [1982, p. 36].

□ CONTRAINDICATIONS AND ADVERSE EFFECTS OF MEDITATION

Carrington (1978a) and Shapiro (1980, 1982) have recommended that meditation not be used with some patients unless *closely* supervised by the therapist. Meditation for some clients may not be a useful therapeutic procedure, and some clients may experience adverse effects.

Carrington (1978a) has indicated that severely disturbed or psychotic patients should not meditate unless supervised by a therapist competent in the use of meditation. Shapiro (1980) suggests that meditation may not be useful for chronically depressed clients or for people with somatic anxiety but low cognitive anxiety, for those with high external locus of control, or for those with chronic headaches or Raynaud's disease. Patients suffering from physical or emotional symptoms should be informed that meditation is not a substitute for treatment by a competent health professional (Carrington, 1978a, p. 11). Carrington advises that patients under medical treatment, particularly those who are receiving medication for endocrine or metabolic control, for pain, or for psychiatric symptoms, should have their meditation experience supervised by a therapist familiar with the effects of profound relaxation on medical conditions and on drug therapy (1978a, p. 11). Persons using insulin, thyroxin, or antihypertensive drugs *may* need to have their dosages decreased while they are regularly practicing meditation; at the very least, dosages of drugs such as these need to be monitored.

Particular types of clients may experience adverse effects from meditation. For example, Shapiro (1980) indicates that some clients may be attracted to meditation for inappropriate reasons, such as to use meditation as a strong cognitive avoidance strategy or to use it as a technique to block out most of the unpleasant events in their lives. In addition, Shapiro (1980, 1982) suggests that self-critical, perfectionistic, goal-oriented Type A people may bring this same orientation to meditation. Finally, people who meditate too long may have such adverse effects as increased anxiety, boredom, confusion, depression, restlessness, and impaired reality testing (Shapiro, 1980, p. 47).

Carrington (1978a) recommends that, to decrease the probability of adverse effects, the therapist should have the client meditate initially with and under the supervision of the therapist. As we suggested in Chapter 10, the therapist should monitor the instruction, training, and use of meditation. Monitoring the meditative process may reveal that clients need to decrease the length of time they meditate, decrease the frequency of daily sessions of meditation, or select another treatment strategy.

☐ MODEL EXAMPLE: MEDITATION (CSM)

In this model example, we present a narrative account of how meditation (CSM) might be used with a 49-year-old male client. Nick, an air traffic controller, has reported that he would like to decrease the stress he experiences in his job. He believes that decreasing this stress will help his ulcer and help him cope better with his job. In addition to the physical signs of stress (hypertension), Nick also reports that he worries constantly about making mistakes in his job.

1. Rationale

First, we explain to Nick that CSM has been used to help people cope with job-related stress. We tell Nick that the procedure has also been used to help people with high blood pressure, anxiety, and those who want to feel more alert. We provide Nick with an overview of CSM, telling him that the procedure is a technique in which a sound is selected and said while in a quiet place, with eyes closed, while allowing thoughts to flow freely, for a period of about five to ten minutes. Finally, we confirm Nick's willingness to use meditation and answer any questions he may have about the procedure.

2. Selection of a Mantra

We explain to Nick that he needs to select a mantra—a word or sound that has few associations and is not emotionally charged. We discuss the purpose of the sound as a device that helps him avoid becoming distracted by other thoughts. We give examples of sounds, such as *gome, rance,* and *shalom.* We help Nick think of a sound that is neutral and soothing. Nick selects his own sound.

3. Instructions about Preparation for Meditation

We inform Nick about how to prepare for meditation—for example, arranging a quiet environment free of distraction and interruption. We instruct him not to meditate within 24 hours of taking alcoholic beverages or nonprescription drugs or right after eating or after drinking beverages containing caffeine and not to chew gum while meditating. We discuss how all these might interfere with meditation. We also inform Nick that it is important to wear comfortable clothing and sit in a comfortable chair while meditating.

4. Instructions to Meditate

We instruct Nick to sit quietly and get relaxed for about a minute. Then he is to close his eyes and say his sound aloud, to say it softly, then to whisper the sound several times, and finally to think the sound without moving his lips or tongue. We tell Nick that meditation is not an exercise or discipline and requires no effort—don't force it. We mention that if distracting thoughts occur, he should allow them to come and not try to influence these thoughts—the sound will return. We tell Nick that he will meditate for about five to ten minutes. We will keep time. When Nick meditates alone, he can open his eyes to check the time. When the time is up, we ask Nick to come out of meditation slowly by sitting there with his eyes closed for about two minutes. We instruct Nick to try to absorb what he is experiencing and then to open his eyes slowly.

5. Discussion of Nick's Reaction to Meditation

We ask Nick a series of questions about his experience with meditation: "How did your sound work for you? How did you feel about the CSM experience? What thoughts or images occurred? How did your sound return to you?"

6. Homework and Follow-up

We instruct Nick to meditate twice a day, once after getting up in the morning and later in the late afternoon or early evening. We remind him of the things to do to prepare—quiet environment, no alcoholic beverages or nonprescription drugs at least 24 hours before meditating, wait for an hour after taking solid foods or caffeine, do not smoke half an hour before meditating, select a comfortable place, and do meditation at the same time and place each day.

Nick is instructed to keep a weekly log of each meditative experience: where he used it, time of day used, and each use rated on a 5-point scale: 5 = great, 4 = good, 3 = fair, 2 = not smooth, 1 = poor. We instruct Nick about the use of informal meditation at work and schedule an appointment the following week to talk about the meditative experiences and discuss his log.

LEARNING ACTIVITIES #45: MEDITATION (RELAXATION RESPONSE AND ZEN MEDITATION OR CLINICALLY STANDARDIZED MEDITATION)

I. Teaching relaxation response/Zen meditation or clinically standardized meditation to a client is an informational process. The counselor provides the instructions, and the client engages in meditation in a self-directed manner. To practice giving instructions to someone about meditation, select a partner or a role-play client and give instructions as described in the Interview Checklist for Relaxation Response and Zen Meditation or the Interview Checklist for Clinically Standardized Meditation at the end of the chapter. Then assess how well your partner was able to implement your instructions. If you wish, reverse roles so that you can experience being instructed by another person.

II. This learning activity provides an opportunity to try out formal meditation. Do this in a quiet, restful place when you will not be interrupted for 20 minutes. Do *not* do this within two hours *after* a meal or within two hours of going to sleep.

1. Get in a comfortable sitting position and close your eyes.
2. Relax your entire body. Think about all the tension draining out of your body.
3. Meditate for about 15 to 20 minutes.
   a. Breathe easily and naturally through your nose.
   b. Focus on your breathing with the thought of a number (one) or a word. Say (think) your word silently each time you inhale and exhale.
   c. If other thoughts or images appear, don't dwell on them but don't force them away. Just relax and focus on your word or breathing.
4. Try to assess your reactions to your meditative experience:
   How do you feel about it?
   How do you feel afterward?
   What sorts of thoughts or images come into your mind?
   How much difficulty did you have with distractions?
5. Practice the relaxation response systematically — twice daily for a week, if possible.

III. To experience "informal meditation," we suggest you follow the homework assignment developed by Shapiro described on pp. 451–452. Try to do this daily for at least a week.

☐ MUSCLE RELAXATION

In muscle relaxation, a person is taught to relax by becoming aware of the sensations of tensing and relaxing major muscle groups. Take a few moments to feel and to become aware of some of these sensations. Make a fist with your preferred (dominant) hand. Clench your fist of that hand. Clench it tightly and study the tension in your hand and forearm. Become aware and feel those sensations of tension. Now let the tension go in your fist, hand, and forearm. Relax your hand and rest it. Note the difference between the tension and the relaxation. Do the exercise once more, only this time close your eyes. Clench your fist tightly; become aware of the tension in your hand and forearm; then relax your hand and let the tension flow out. Note the different sensations of relaxing and tensing your fist. Try it.

If you did this exercise, you may have noticed that your hand and forearm *cannot* be tense and relaxed at the same time. In other words, relaxation is incompatible with tension. You may also have noted that you instructed your hand to tense up and then to relax. You sent messages from your head to your hand to impose tension and then to create relaxation. You can cue a muscle group (the hand and forearm, in this case) to perform or respond in a particular manner (tense up and relax). This exercise was perhaps too brief for you to notice changes in other bodily functions. For example, tension and relaxation can affect one's blood pressure, heart rate, and respiration rate and can also influence covert processes and the way one performs or responds overtly. The long-range goal of muscle relaxation is "for the body to monitor instantaneously all of its numerous control signals, and automatically to relieve tensions that are not desired" (McGuigan, 1984, p. 15).

Relaxation training is not new, but it has recently become a popular technique to deal with a variety of client concerns. Jacobson (1929, 1964) developed an extensive procedure called "progressive relaxation." Later, Wolpe (1958) described muscle relaxation as an anxiety-inhibiting procedure with his systematic desensitization strategy (see Chapter 18). Bernstein and Borkovec (1973) wrote a thorough relaxation manual entitled *Pro-*

gressive Relaxation Training. Goldfried and Davison (1976) have described relaxation training in their book about behavior therapy.

In a procedural analysis and review of 80 relaxation training studies, Hillenberg and Collins (1982) found that relaxation training has been used with clients who have sleep disturbance, headache, hypertension, test anxiety, speech anxiety, general anxiety, asthma, excessive drinking, hyperactivity, and problems with anger control (p. 252). Also, relaxation training has been used with dental phobia (Jerremalm, Jansson, & Öst, 1986) panic disorder (Öst, 1988) with thermal biofeedback for hypertension (Whittrock, Blanchard, & McCoy, 1988), with guided imagery for cancer chemotherapy patients (Burish, Carey, Krozely, & Greco, 1987; Carey & Burish, 1987), for reducing psychophysiological reactivity in post-myocardial infarction patients (Gatchel, Gaffney, & Smith, 1986), and as a coping strategy for working women (Long & Haney, 1988). Relaxation training was found to reduce subjective arousal (Peveler & Johnston, 1986) and, more recently, Öst (1987) described applied relaxation in which clients are trained to use relaxation in practically any phobic or anxiety-provoking situation. The Lamaze (1958) method of childbirth uses relaxation training to facilitate a more relaxed and less painful labor and delivery. Cautela and Groden (1978) have developed a relaxation training manual for children.

Studies have also compared the effectiveness of relaxation training instructions administered in person (live) and by a tape recording. Hillenberg and Collins (1982) and Lehrer (1982) indicate that live presentation of relaxation instructions is probably better than taped instructions. Our preference is to have a counselor administer relaxation training within the interview. Tape-recorded instructions can be used for homework or outside practice sessions.

The effects of muscle relaxation, like those of any other strategy, are related to satisfactory problem assessment, client characteristics, and the therapist's ability to apply the procedure competently and confidently. There are also precautions therapists should heed — one should not apply relaxation training indiscriminately.

Some Cautions in Using Muscle Relaxation

There are two areas the counselor should assess before applying muscle relaxation (Bernstein & Borkovec, 1973). First, make sure the client is medically cleared to engage in muscle relaxation (p. 12). For example, a person who suffers headaches or lower-back pain may have an organic basis for these complaints, or a person may be taking a drug that is incompatible with the purposes of muscle relaxation. For some clients, tensing certain muscle groups may have detrimental effects. The counselor should obtain a medical clearance from the client's physician or encourage the client to have a physical examination if there is a complaint that might be organically caused. Relaxation exercises may have to be adjusted for handicapped clients or for clients who cannot perform exercises for particular muscle groups.

The next caution is to discover the causes of the client's reported tension (Bernstein & Borkovec, 1973, p. 12). The counselor would probably have achieved this during problem assessment (see Chapters 7 and 8). For example, is muscle relaxation a reasonable strategy for alleviating the client's problem? If the client is experiencing tension in a job situation, the counselor and client may prefer to deal first with the client's external situation (the job). Bernstein and Borkovec point out that there is a difference between dealing with the tension of daily problems and handling the tension of someone who is on the verge of financial disaster. In the latter case, combinations of therapeutic strategies may be necessary. As Goldfried (1977, p. 84) notes, relaxation training may be more effective on a short-term basis and when supplemented with other therapeutic strategies, and the clinical potential of relaxation may be enhanced when the procedure is presented to clients as a coping skill.

Steps of Muscle Relaxation

Muscle relaxation consists of the following seven steps:

1. Rationale.
2. Instructions about dress.
3. Creation of a comfortable environment.
4. Counselor modeling of the relaxation exercises.
5. Instructions for muscle relaxation.
6. Posttraining assessment.
7. Homework and follow-up.

These steps are described in detail in the Interview Checklist for Muscle Relaxation at the end of the chapter.

Treatment rationale. Here is an example of one way a counselor might explain the *purpose* of relaxation: "This process, if you practice it regularly, can help you become relaxed. The relaxation benefits you derived can help you sleep better at night." An *overview* of the procedure might be "This procedure involves learning to tense and relax different muscle groups in your body. By doing this, you can contrast the difference between tenseness and relaxation. This will help you to recognize tension so you can instruct yourself to relax."

In addition, the counselor should explain that muscle relaxation is a *skill*. The process of learning will be gradual and will require regular practice. Finally, the counselor might explain that some discomfort may occur during the relaxation process. If so, the client can just move his or her body to a more comfortable position. Finally, the client may experience some floating, warming, or heavy sensations typical for some people learning muscle relaxation. The counselor should inform the client about these possible sensations. The rationale for muscle relaxation should be concluded by asking the client about willingness to try the procedure.

Instructions about dress.   Before the actual training session, the client should be instructed about appropriate clothing. The client should wear comfortable clothes such as slacks, a loose-fitting blouse or shirt, or any apparel that will not be distracting during the exercises. Clients who wear contact lenses should be told to wear their regular glasses for the training. They can take off the glasses while going through the exercises. It is uncomfortable to wear contact lenses when your eyes are closed.

Creation of a comfortable environment.   A comfortable environment is necessary for effective muscle-relaxation training. The training environment should be quiet and free of distracting noises such as telephone rings, workers outside breaking up the street, and airplane sounds. A padded recliner chair should be used if possible. If the counseling facility cannot afford one, an aluminum lawn chair or recliner covered with a foam pad may be satisfactory. If relaxation training is to be applied to groups, pads or blankets can be placed on the floor, with pillows used to support the head (Gershman & Clouser, 1974). The clients can lie on the floor on their backs, with their legs stretched out and their arms along their sides with palms down.

Counselor modeling of the relaxation exercises.
Just before the relaxation training begins, the counselor should model briefly at least a few of the muscle exercises that will be used in training. The counselor can start with either the right or the left hand (make a fist, then relax the hand, opening the fingers; tense and relax the other hand; bend the wrists of both arms and relax them; shrug the shoulders and relax them) and continue demonstrating some of the rest of the exercises. The counselor should tell the client that the demonstration is going much faster than the speed at which the client will perform the exercises. The counselor should also punctuate the demonstration with comments like "When I clench my biceps like this, I feel the tension in my biceps muscles, and now, when I relax and drop my arms to my side, I notice the difference between the tension that was in my biceps and the relative relaxation I feel now." These comments are used to model discriminating the contrast between tension and relaxation.

Instructions for muscle relaxation.   Muscle-relaxation training can start after the counselor has given the client the rationale for the procedure, answered any questions about relaxation training, instructed the client about what to wear, created a comfortable environment for the training, and modeled some of the various muscle-group exercises. In delivering (or reading) the instructions for the relaxation training exercises, the counselor's voice should be conversational, not dramatic. Goldfried and Davison (1976) recommend that the counselor practice along with the client during the beginning exercises. Practicing initial relaxation exercises with the client can give the counselor a sense of timing for delivering the verbalizations of relaxing and tension and may decrease any awkwardness the client feels about doing "body type" exercises.

In instructing the client to tense and relax muscles, remember that you do *not* want to instruct the client to tense up as hard as possible. You do not want the client to strain a muscle. Be careful of your vocabulary when giving instructions. Do not use phrases like "as hard as you can," "sagging or drooping muscles," or "tense the muscles until they feel like they could snap." Sometimes you can supplement instructions to tense and relax with comments about the client's breathing or the experiencing of warm or heavy sensations. These comments may help the client to relax.

The various muscle groups used for client training can be categorized into 17 groups, 7 groups, or 4 groups. These sets of muscle groups, adapted from Bernstein and Borkovec (1973), are listed in Table 17-2. Generally, in initial training sessions, the counselor instructs the client to go through all 17 muscle groups. When the client can alternately tense and relax any of the 17 muscle groups on command, you can abbreviate this somewhat long procedure and train the client in relaxation using 7 muscle groups. After this process, the client can practice relaxation using only four major muscle groups. Start with either 17 or 7 muscle groups. This may help the client to discriminate sensations of tension and relaxation in different parts of the body. Then the number of muscle groups involved in the relaxation can be reduced gradually. When the client gets to the point of using the relaxation *in vivo,* 4 muscle groups are much less unwieldy than 17!

The following section illustrates how the counselor can instruct the client in relaxation using all 17 muscle groups. First, the counselor instructs the client to settle back as comfortably as possible—either in the recliner chair or on the floor with the head on a pillow. The arms can be alongside the body, resting on the arms of the chair or on the floor with the palms of the hands down. The counselor then instructs the client to close her or his eyes. In some instances, a client may not wish to do this; at other times, the counselor and the client may decide that it might be more therapeutic to keep the eyes open during the training. In such cases, the client can focus on some object in the room or on the ceiling. Tell the client to *listen* and to *focus* on your instructions. When presenting instructions for each muscle group, direct the client's attention to the tension, which is held for five to seven seconds, and then to the feelings of relaxation that follow when the client is instructed to relax. Allow about ten seconds for the client to enjoy the relaxation associated with each muscle group before delivering another instruction. Intermittently throughout the instructions, make muscle-group comparisons—for example, "Is your forehead as relaxed as your biceps?" While delivering the instructions, gradually lower your voice and slow the pace of delivery. Usually in initial training sessions, each muscle group is presented twice.

Here is a way the counselor might proceed with initial training in muscle relaxation, using the list of 17 muscle groups in Table 17-2 (adapted from a relaxation tape recording by Lazarus, 1970):

1. *Fist of dominant hand.* "First think about your right arm, your right hand in particular. Clench your right fist. Clench it tightly and study the tension in the hand and in the forearm. Study those sensations of tension. [Pause.] Now let go. Just relax the right hand and let it rest on the arm of the chair [or floor]. [Pause.] And note the difference between the tension and the relaxation." [Ten-second pause.]

2. *Fist of nondominant hand.* "Now we'll do the same with your left hand. Clench your left fist. Notice the tension [five-second pause] and now relax. Enjoy the difference between the tension and the relaxation." [Ten-second pause.]

3. *Wrist of one or both arms.* The counselor can instruct the client to bend the wrists of both arms at the same time or to bend each separately. You might start with the dominant arm if you instruct the client to bend the wrists one at a time. "Now bend both hands back at the wrists so that you tense the muscles in the back of the hand and in the forearm. Point your fingers toward the ceiling. Study the tension, and now relax. [Pause.] Study the difference between tension and relaxation." [Ten-second pause.]

4. *Biceps.* The counselor can instruct the client to work with both biceps or just one at a time. If you train the client to do one at a time, start with the dominant biceps. The instructions for this exercise are "Now clench both your hands into fists and bring them toward your shoulders. As you do this, tighten your biceps muscles, the ones in the upper part of your arm. Feel the tension in these muscles. [Pause.] Now relax. Let your arms drop down to your sides. See the difference between the tension and the relaxation." [Ten-second pause.]

5. *Shoulders.* Usually the client is instructed to shrug both shoulders. However, the client could be instructed to shrug one shoulder at a time. "Now we'll move to the shoulder area. Shrug your shoulders. Bring them up to your ears. Feel and hold the tension in your shoulders. [Pause.] Now, let both shoulders relax. Note the contrast between the tension

TABLE 17-2. Relaxation exercises for 17, 7, and 4 muscle groups (from *Progressive relaxation training,* by D. Bernstein and T. Borkovec. Copyright 1973 by Research Press. Used by permission.)

17 muscle groups	7 muscle groups	4 muscle groups
1. Clenching *fist* of dominant *hand.* 2. Clenching *fist* of nondominant *hand.* 3. Bending *wrist* of one or both arms. 4. Clenching *biceps* (one at a time or together). 5. Shrugging *shoulders* (one at a time or together). 6. Wrinkling *forehead.* 7. Closing *eyes* tightly. 8. Pressing *tongue* or clenching *jaws.* 9. Pressing *lips* together. 10. Pressing *head* back (on chair or pillow). 11. Pushing *chin* into chest. 12. Arching *back.* 13. Inhaling and holding *chest muscles.* 14. Tightening *stomach* muscles. 15. Contracting *buttocks.*[a] 16. Stretching *legs.* 17. Pointing *toes* toward head.	1. Hold *dominant arm* in front with elbow bent at about 45-degree angle while making a *fist* (hand, lower arm, and biceps muscles). 2. Same exercise with *nondominant arm.* 3. Facial muscle groups. Wrinkle *forehead* (or frown), squint *eyes* wrinkle up *nose,* clench *jaws* or press *tongue* on roof of mouth, press *lips* or pull corners of mouth back. 4. Press or bury *chin* in chest (neck and throat). 5. *Chest, shoulders, upper back,* and *abdomen.* Take deep breath, hold it, pull shoulder blades back and together, while making stomach hard (pulling in). 6. *Dominant thigh, calf,* and *foot.* Lift foot off chair or floor slightly while pointing toes and turning foot inward. 7. Same as 6, with *nondominant thigh, calf,* and *foot.*	1. Right and left *arms, hands,* and *biceps* (same as 1 and 2 in 7-muscle group). 2. *Face* and *neck* muscles. Tense all *face* muscles (same as 3 and 4 in 7-muscle group) 3. *Chest, shoulders, back* and *stomach* muscles (same as 5 in 7-muscle group). 4. Both left and right upper *leg, calf,* and *foot* (combines 6 and 7 in 7-muscle group).

[a] This muscle group can be eliminated; its use is optional.

and the relaxation that's now in your shoulders." [Ten-second pause.]

6. *Forehead.* This and the next three exercises are for the facial muscles. The instructions for the forehead are "Now we'll work on relaxing the various muscles of the face. First, wrinkle up your forehead and brow. Do this until you feel your brow furrow. [Pause.] Now relax. Smooth out the forehead. Let it loosen up." [Ten-second pause.]

7. *Eyes.* The purpose of this exercise is for the client to contrast the difference between tension and relaxation for the muscles that control the movements of the eyes. "Now close your eyes tightly. Can you feel tension all around your eyes? [Five-second pause.] Now relax those muscles, noting the difference between the tension and the relaxation." [Ten-second pause.]

8. *Tongue or jaws.* You can instruct some clients to clench their jaws: "Now clench your jaws by biting your teeth together. Pull the corners of your mouth back. Study the tension in the

jaws. [Five-second pause.] Relax your jaws now. Can you tell the difference between tension and relaxation in your jaw area?" [Ten-second pause.] This exercise may be difficult for some clients who wear dentures. An alternative exercise is to instruct them: "Press your tongue into the roof of your mouth. Note the tension within your mouth. [Five-second pause.] Relax your mouth and tongue now. Just concentrate on the relaxation." [Ten-second pause.]

9. *Pressing the lips together.* The last facial exercise involves the mouth and chin muscles. "Now press your lips together tightly. As you do this, notice the tension all around the mouth. [Pause.] Now relax those muscles around the mouth. Enjoy this relaxation in your mouth area and your entire face. [Pause.] Is your face as relaxed as your biceps [intermuscle-group comparison]?"

10. *The head.* "Now we'll move to the neck muscles. Press your head back against your chair. Can you feel the tension in the back of your

neck and in your upper back? Hold the tension. [Pause.] Now let your head rest comfortably. Notice the difference. Keep on relaxing." [Pause.]

11. *Chin in chest.* This exercise focuses on the muscles in the neck, particularly the front of the neck. "Now continue to concentrate on the neck area. Bring your head forward. See whether you can bury your chin into your chest. Note the tension in the front of your neck. Now relax and let go." [Ten-second pause.]

12. *The back.* Be careful here—you don't want the client to get a sore back. "Now direct your attention to your upper back area. Arch your back as if you were sticking out your chest and stomach. Can you feel tension in your back? Study that tension. [Pause.] Now relax. Note the difference between the tension and the relaxation." [Ten-second pause.]

13. *Chest muscles.* Inhaling (filling the lungs) and holding the breath focuses the client's attention on the muscles in the chest and down into the stomach area. "Now take a deep breath, filling your lungs, and hold it. Feel the tension all through your chest and into your stomach area. Hold that tension. [Pause.] Now relax and let go. Let your breath out naturally. Enjoy the pleasant sensations." [Ten-second pause.]

14. *Stomach muscles.* "Now think about your stomach. Tighten up the muscles in your abdomen. Hold this. Make the stomach like a knot. Now relax. Loosen those muscles now. [Ten-second pause.] Is your stomach as relaxed as your back and chest [muscle-group comparison]?" An alternative instruction is to tell the client to "pull in your stomach" or "suck in your stomach."

15. *The buttocks.* Moving down to other areas of the body, the counselor instructs or coaches the client to tighten the buttocks. This muscle group is optional; with some clients, the counselor may delete it and move on to the legs. The model instructions are "Now tighten [tense or contract] your buttocks by pulling them together and pushing them into the floor [or chair]. Note the tension. And now relax. Let go and relax." [Ten-second pause.]

16. *Legs.* "I'd like you now to focus on your legs. Stretch both legs. Feel tension in the thighs. [Five-second pause.] Now relax. Study the difference again between tension in the thighs

and the relaxation you feel now." [Ten-second pause.]

17. *Toes.* "Now concentrate on your lower legs and feet. Tighten both calf muscles by pointing your toes toward your head. Pretend a string is pulling your toes up. Can you feel the pulling and the tension? Note that tension. [Pause.] Now relax. Let your legs relax deeply. Enjoy the difference between tension and relaxation." [Ten-second pause.]

After each muscle group has been tensed and relaxed twice, the counselor usually concludes relaxation training with a summary and review. The counselor goes through the review by listing each muscle group and asking the client to dispel any tension that is noted as the counselor names the muscle area. Here is an example:

"Now, I'm going to go over once more the muscle groups that we've covered. As I name each group, try to notice whether there is any tension in those muscles. If there is any, try to concentrate on those muscles and tell them to relax. Think of draining the tension completely out of your body as we do this. Now relax the muscles in your feet, ankles, and calves. [Pause.] Get rid of tension in your knees and thighs. [Five-second pause.] Loosen your hips. [Pause.] Let the muscles of your lower body go. [Pause.] Relax your abdomen, waist, lower back. [Pause.] Drain the tension from your upper back, chest, and shoulders. [Pause.] Relax your upper arms, forearms, and hands. Loosen the muscles of your throat and neck. [Pause.] Relax your face. [Pause.] Let all the tension drain out of your body. [Pause.] Now just sit quietly with your eyes closed."

The therapist can conclude the training session by evaluating the client's level of relaxation on a scale from 0 to 5 or by counting aloud to the client to instruct him or her to become successively more alert. For example:

"Now I'd like you to think of a scale from 0 to 5, where 0 is complete relaxation and 5 is extreme tension. Tell me where you would place yourself on that scale now."

"I'm going to count from 5 to 1. When I reach the count of 1, open your eyes. 5 . . . 4 . . . 3 . . . 2 . . . 1. Open your eyes now."

Posttraining assessment. After the session of relaxation training has been completed, the counselor asks the client about the experience. The counselor can ask "What is your reaction to the procedure?", "How do you feel?", "What reaction did you have when you focused on the tension?", "What about relaxation?", or "How did the contrast between the tension and relaxation feel?" The counselor should be encouraging about the client's performance, praise the client, and build a positive expectancy set about the training and practice.

People experiencing relaxation training may have several problems (Bernstein & Borkovec, 1973). Some of these potential problem areas are cramps, excessive laughter or talking, spasms or tics, intrusive thoughts, falling asleep, inability to relax individual muscle groups, and unfamiliar sensations. If the client experiences muscle cramps, possibly too much tension is being created in the particular muscle group. In this case, the counselor can instruct the client to decrease the amount of tension. If spasms and tics occur in certain muscle groups, the counselor can mention that these occur commonly, as in one's sleep, and possibly the reason the client is aware of them now is that he or she is awake. Excessive laughter or talking would most likely occur in group-administered relaxation training. Possibly the best solution is to ignore it or to discuss how such behavior can be distracting.

The most common problem is for the client to fall asleep during relaxation training. The client should be informed that continually falling asleep can impede learning the skills associated with muscle relaxation. By watching the client throughout training, the counselor can confirm whether the client is awake.

If the client has difficulty or is unable to relax a particular muscle group, the counselor and client might work out an alternative exercise for that muscle group. If intrusive client thoughts become too distracting, the counselor might suggest changing the focus of the thought to something less distracting or to more positive or pleasant thoughts. It might be better for some clients to gaze at a picture of their choosing placed on the wall or ceiling throughout the training. Another strategy for dealing with interfering or distracting thoughts is to help the client use task-oriented coping statements or thoughts (see Chapter 16), which would facilitate focusing on the relaxation training.

The last potential problem is the occurrence of unfamiliar sensations, such as floating, warmth, and headiness. The counselor should point out that these sensations are common and that the client should not fear them. Bernstein and Borkovec (1973) provide a more detailed discussion of these potential problems and their possible solutions. The counselor need not focus on these problems unless they are reported by the client or noted by the counselor during a training session.

Homework and follow-up. The last step in muscle relaxation is assigning homework. Four or five therapist training sessions with two daily home practice sessions between therapy sessions are probably sufficient. Some therapists found that a minimal therapist contract with the client (2½ hours) and home-based relaxation training using manuals and audiotapes with telephone consultation (two times, ten minutes each) were just as effective in reducing tension headaches as six hours of therapist training (Teders et al., 1984). Regardless of the amount of time or number of therapist training sessions with the client, the therapist should inform the client that relaxation training, like learning any skill, requires a great deal of practice.

The more the client practices the procedure, the more proficient he or she will become in gaining control over tension, anxiety, or stress. The client should be instructed to select a quiet place for practice, free from distracting noise. The client should be encouraged to practice the muscle-relaxation exercises about 15 to 20 minutes twice a day. The exercises should be done when there is no time pressure. Some clients may not be willing to practice twice a day. The therapist can encourage these clients to practice several times or as often as they can during the week. The exercises can be done in a recliner chair or on the floor with a pillow supporting the head.

The client should be encouraged to complete a homework log after each practice. Figure 17-1 is an example of a homework log. Clients can rate their reactions on a scale from 1 (little or no tension) to 5 (extremely tense) before and after each practice. They can practice the relaxation exercises using a tape recording of the relaxation instructions or from memory. After client homework practices, a follow-up session should be scheduled.

There are several techniques a therapist can use to promote client compliance with relaxation homework assignments. One technique is to ask the client to demonstrate during the therapy session how the exercises for the muscles in the neck or the calf, for example, were done during last week's home practice. The counselor can select randomly from four or five muscle groups for the client to demonstrate. If the exercises are demonstrated accurately, the client probably practiced. The "cue-tone compliance procedure" (Martin,

		HOMEWORK LOG SHEET				
DATE	TAPE NUMBER	ALL MUSCLE GROUPS EXERCISED. TONE PRESENT FOR WHICH MUSCLE GROUP	PRACTICE SESSION NUMBER	LOCATION OF SESSION	LEVEL OF TENSION (1–5)	
					BEFORE SESSION	AFTER SESSION

Note: 1 = slightly or not tense; 2 = somewhat tense; 3 = moderately tense; 4 = very tense; 5 = extremely tense.

Figure 17-1. *Example of homework log sheet for relaxation training*

Collins, Hillenberg, Zabin, & Katell, 1981) is an objective measure of client compliance. The technique involves recording cue tones on some audiotaped relaxation exercises and not on other tapes. The cue tones can be recorded for randomly selected exercises on the tape and not for others. The tapes are numbered, and the client is instructed to listen to different tapes for the two daily practice sessions. The client is instructed to listen to a different tape during each practice session and to record on the homework log sheet whether she or he heard the tone and for which exercises. The cue-tone compliance technique does not appear to interfere with relaxation (Collins, Martin, & Hillenberg, 1982). After client homework practices, a follow-up session should be scheduled. Agras, Schneider, and Taylor (1984) found that routine booster sessions may be more effective than retraining when a client relapse occurs after initial relaxation training.

Variations of the Muscle-Relaxation Procedure

There are several variations of the muscle-relaxation training procedure as we've described it. These variations, which include recall, counting, and differential relaxation, are arranged and designed in successive approximations from the counselor assisting the client to acquire the skills to the client applying the relaxation skills in real-life situations. The four-muscle-group exercises listed in Table 17-2 can be used in combination with the recall and counting procedures described by Bernstein and Borkovec (1973).

Recall. Recall proceeds according to the relaxation exercises for the four muscle groups (Table 17-2) without muscular tension. The counselor first instructs the client about the rationale for using this variation of relaxation training: "to increase your relaxation skills without the need to tense up the muscles." The client is asked to focus on each muscle group. Then the counselor instructs the client to focus on one of the four muscle groups (arms; face and neck; chest, shoulders, back, and stomach; legs and feet) and to relax and just recall what it was like when the client released the tension (in the previous session) for that particular muscle group. The counselor might suggest that if there is tension in a particular muscle group, the client should just relax or send a message for the muscle to relax and should allow what tension there is to "flow out." The counselor gives similar instructions for all four muscle groups. Again, the client is to recall what the relaxation felt like for each muscle group. Recall can generally be used after first using the tension/relaxation-contrast procedure for the four muscle groups. Gradually, the client can use recall to induce relaxation in self-directed practices. Recall can also be used in combination with counting.

An example of a recall procedure follows. This procedure can also be used as an induction aid in hypnosis.

"I'm going to help you relax even more deeply now. Just go along with the things I suggest . . . and you will experience a much deeper sense of relaxation . . . you will enjoy the experience . . . just listen to what I say . . . and let things happen. Now feel this relaxation coming into the small muscles around the eyes . . . they are feeling so relaxed that presently . . . the eyelids will feel heavy . . . very heavy . . . like lead shutters . . . almost too heavy to move . . . feeling as though they are glued together . . . and you feel this relaxation spreading outward . . . just as ripples spread out on a still pool when the water is disturbed . . . spreading out into the muscles of the face . . . so that your jaw feels relaxed and your lips part a little . . . into the forehead and scalp . . . the neck . . . notice how your head feels so heavy and relaxed . . . so comfortable against the back of the chair . . . the shoulders feel quite limp and relaxed . . . the arms are relaxing . . . heavy . . . loose and floppy by your side . . . from your shoulders right through to the tips of your fingers. Your back, too, is becoming more and more relaxed . . . sinking deeply into the chair . . . especially the small of your back . . . your muscles in your stomach and your chest are relaxing more and more . . . notice that each time you breathe out . . . you go deeper and deeper into this pleasant relaxed state . . . notice this, just let yourself be aware of this . . . don't try to do anything . . . and now your legs are gradually letting go of all the tension as well . . . all through your hips . . . your thighs . . . your knees . . . calf muscles . . . even the ankles and feet are relaxing. You feel as though all the tension within you . . . is flowing out through your toes . . . and being replaced by this very pleasant feeling of relaxation. As this grows you'll also become more aware of how fleeting and unimportant all of your thoughts are . . . aware of the quiet deep within you . . . the quiet" [Clarke & Jackson, 1983, pp. 83–84].*

* From J. Christopher Clarke and J. Arthur Jackson, *Hypnosis and behavior therapy: The treatment of anxiety and phobias,* pp. 83–84. Copyright © 1983 by Springer Publishing Company, Inc., New York. Used by permission.

Counting. The rationale for counting is that it helps the client become very deeply relaxed. Again, the counselor explains the rationale for using counting. The counselor says that she or he will count from one to ten and that this will help the client to become more relaxed after each number. The counselor might say slowly:

"One—you are becoming more relaxed; two—notice that your arms and hands are becoming more and more relaxed; three—feel your face and neck becoming more relaxed; four, five—more and more relaxed are your chest and shoulders; six—further and further relaxed; seven—back and stomach feel deeply relaxed; eight—further and further relaxed; nine—your legs and feet are more and more relaxed; ten—just continue to relax as you are—relax more and more."

The counselor can use this counting procedure with recall. The client can also be instructed to use counting in real situations that provoke tension. For a more detailed presentation of counting, see Bernstein and Borkovec (1973) and Goldfried and Davison (1976). As you may remember from Chapter 16, counting is one type of direct-action coping skill used in stress inoculation. Counting can increase relaxation and decrease tension, and the client should be encouraged to practice it outside the session.

Differential relaxation. This variation may contribute to generalization of the relaxation training from the treatment session to the client's world. The purpose of differential relaxation is to help the client recognize what muscles are needed in various situations, body positions, and activities in order to differentiate which muscle groups are used and which are not. Table 17-3 illustrates some possible levels for the differential-relaxation procedure.

As an example of differential relaxation, the counselor might have the client sit in a regular chair (not a recliner) and ask the client to identify which muscles are used and which are not when

TABLE 17-3. Levels of differential-relaxation procedure

Situation	Body position	Activity level
Quiet	Sitting	Low—inactive
Noisy	Standing	High—routine movements

sitting. If tension is felt in muscles that are not used (face, legs, and stomach), the client is instructed to induce and to maintain relaxation in the muscles not required for what the client is doing (sitting). The counselor can instruct the client to engage in different levels of the differential-relaxation procedure—for example, sitting down in a quiet place while inactive, or standing up. After several practice sessions, the client can be assigned homework to engage in various levels of these activities. Examples might be sitting in a quiet cafeteria, sitting in a noisy cafeteria while eating, standing in line for a ticket to some event, or walking in a busy shopping center. In practicing differential relaxation, the client tries to recognize whether any tension exists in the nonessential muscle groups. If there is tension in the nonengaged muscles, the client concentrates on dispelling it.

□ MODEL DIALOGUE: MUSCLE RELAXATION

In this dialogue, the counselor demonstrates relaxation training to help Joan deal with her physical sensations of nervousness.

First, the counselor gives Joan a **rationale** *for relaxation. The counselor explains the* **purpose** *of muscle relaxation and gives Joan a brief* **overview** *of the procedure.*

1. *Counselor:* Basically, we all learn to carry around some body tension. Some is OK. But in a tense spot, usually your body is even more tense, although you may not realize this. If you can learn to recognize muscle tension and relax your muscles, this state of relaxation can help to decrease your nervousness or anxiety. What we'll do is to help you recognize when your body is relaxed and when it is tense, by deliberately tensing and relaxing different muscle groups in your body. We should get to the point where, later on, you can recognize the sensations that mean tension and use these as a signal to yourself to relax. Does this make sense?
   Client: I think so. You'll sort of tell me how to do this?

Next, the counselor will **"set up" the relaxation by attending to details about the room** *and the client's comfort.*

2. *Counselor:* Yes. At first I'll show you so you can get the idea of it. One thing we need to do before we start is for you to get as comfortable as possi-

ble. So that you won't be distracted by light, I'm going to turn off the light. If you are wearing your contact lenses, take them out if they're uncomfortable, because you may feel more comfortable if you go through this with your eyes closed. Also, I use a special chair for this. You know the straight-backed chair you're sitting on can seem like a rock after a time. That might distract, too. So I have a padded chaise you can use for this. [Gets lounge chair out.]
   Client (sits in chaise): Umm. This really is comfortable.

Next the counselor begins **to model the muscle relaxation** *for Joan. This shows Joan how to do it and may alleviate any embarrassment on her part.*

3. *Counselor:* Good. That really helps. Now I'm going to show you how you can tense and then relax your muscles. I'll start first with my right arm. [Clenches right fist, pauses and notes tension, relaxes fist, pauses and notes relaxation; models several other muscle groups.] Does this give you an idea?
   Client: Yes. You don't do your whole body?

The counselor provides **further information about muscle relaxation, describes sensations** *Joan might feel, and checks to see whether Joan is completely clear on the procedure before going ahead.*

4. *Counselor:* Yes, you do. But we'll take each muscle group separately. By the time you tense and relax each muscle group, your whole body will feel relaxed. You will feel like you are "letting go," which is very important when you tense up—to let go rather than to tense even more. Now, you might not notice a lot of difference right away—but you might. You might even feel like you're floating. This really depends on the person. The most important thing is to remain as comfortable as possible while I'm instructing you. Do you have any questions before we begin, anything you don't quite understand?
   Client: I don't think so. I think that this is maybe a little like yoga.

The counselor proceeds with **instructions to alternately tense and relax** *each of 17 muscle groups.*

5. *Counselor:* Right. It's based on the same idea—learning to soothe away body tension. OK, get very comfortable in your chair and we'll begin. [Gives Joan several minutes to get comfortable, then uses the relaxation instructions. Most of the session is spent in instructing Joan in muscle relaxation as illustrated on pp. 458–461.]

After the relaxation, the counselor **queries Joan** *about her feelings during and after the relaxation. It is important to find out how the relaxation affected the client.*

6. *Counselor:* OK, Joan, how do you feel now?
   Client: Pretty relaxed.
7. *Counselor:* How did the contrast between the tensed and relaxed muscles feel?
   Client: It was pretty easy to tell. I guess sometimes my body is pretty tense and I don't think about it.

The counselor assigns **relaxation practice** *to Joan as* **daily homework.**

8. *Counselor:* As I mentioned before, this takes regular practice in order for you to use it when you need it — and to really notice the effects. I have put these instructions on this audiotape, and I'd like you to practice with this tape two times each day during the next week. Do the practice in a quiet place at a time when you don't feel pres-sured, and use a comfortable place when you do practice. Do you have any questions about the practice?
   Client: No, I think I understand.

Counselor **explains the use of the log.**

9. *Counselor:* Also, I'd like you to use a log sheet with your practice. Mark down where you practice, how long you practice, what muscle groups you use, and your tension level before and after each practice on this 5-point scale. Remember, 0 is complete relaxation and 5 is complete or extreme tension. Let's go over an example of how you use the log. . . . Now, any questions?
   Client: No. I can see this will take some practice.

Finally, the counselor arranges a **follow-up.**

10. *Counselor:* Right, it really is like learning any other skill — it doesn't just come automatically. Why don't you try this on your own for two weeks and then come back, OK?

LEARNING ACTIVITY #46: MUSCLE RELAXATION

Because muscle relaxation involves the alternate tensing and relaxing of a variety of muscle groups, it is sometimes hard to learn the procedure well enough to use it with a client. We have found that the easiest way to learn this is to do muscle relaxation yourself. Using it not only helps you learn what is involved but also may have some indirect benefits for you — increased relaxation!

This learning activity is designed for you to apply the muscle-relaxation procedure you've just read about to yourself. You can do this by yourself or with a partner. You may wish to try it out alone and then with someone else.

By Yourself

1. Get in a comfortable position, wear loose clothing, and remove your glasses or contact lenses.
2. Use the written instructions in this chapter to practice muscle relaxation. This can be done by putting the instructions on tape or by reading the instructions to yourself. Go through the procedure quickly to get a feel for the process; then do it again slowly without trying to rely too much on having to read the instructions. As you go through the relaxation, study the differences between tension and relaxation.
3. Try to assess your reactions after the relaxation.

On a scale from 0 to 5 (0 being very relaxed and 5 being very tense), how relaxed do you feel? Were there any particular muscle groups that were hard for you to contract or relax?

4. One or two times through muscle relaxation is not enough to learn it or to notice any effects. Try to practice this procedure on yourself once or twice daily over the next several weeks.

With a Partner

One of you can take the role of a helper; the other can be the person learning relaxation. Switch roles so you can practice helping someone else through the procedure and trying it out on yourself.

1. The helper should begin by giving an explanation and a rationale for muscle relaxation and any instructions about it before you begin.
2. The helper can read the instructions on muscle relaxation to you. The helper should give you ample time to tense and relax each muscle group and should encourage you to note the different sensations associated with tension and relaxation.
3. After going through the process, the helper should query you about your relaxation level and your reactions to the process.

☐ SUMMARY

In this chapter we described two meditation strategies and a procedure for muscle relaxation. A combination of the relaxation response and the Zen meditation strategies or the clinically standardized meditation strategy presented in this chapter can be used as an informal meditation procedure applied in one's natural environment. There are contraindications and adverse effects of meditation for some clients. The muscle-relaxation strategy can be used with 17, 7, or 4 muscle groups. Three variations of muscle relaxation were presented: recall, counting, and differential relaxation. All these strategies are often used as a single treatment to prevent stress and to deal with stress-related situations. In addition, these strategies may be used to countercondition anxiety as part of another therapeutic procedure called "systematic desensitization," which is presented in the next chapter.

■

POSTEVALUATION

PART ONE

For Objective One, you will be able to identify accurately the steps of the relaxation response/Zen meditation procedure represented by at least eight out of ten examples of counselor instructive responses. On paper, for each of the following counselor responses, identify which part of the meditation procedure is being implemented. There may be more than one counselor response associated with a part. These examples are not in any particular order. The eight major parts of meditation are as follows:

1. Rationale.
2. Selection of a mental device.
3. Instructions for body comfort.
4. Breathing and word instruction.
5. Instruction about passive attitude.
6. Meditating for 10 to 20 minutes.
7. Probing about the meditative experience.
8. Homework and practice.

Feedback for the Postevaluation follows on pages 477–478.

1. "It is very important that you practice this at home regularly. Usually there are no effects without regular practice—about twice daily."
2. "One position you may want to use is to sit on the floor Indian-style—crossing your legs and keeping your back straight. If this feels uncomfortable, then just assume any sitting position that is comfortable for you."
3. "This procedure has been used to help people with high blood pressure and people who have trouble sleeping and just as a general stress-reduction process."
4. "Breathe through your nose and focus on your breathing. If you can concentrate on one word as you do this, it may be easier."
5. "Be sure to practice at a quiet time when you don't think you'll be interrupted. And do not practice within two hours after a meal or within two hours before going to bed."
6. "Just continue now to meditate like this for 10 or 15 minutes. Sit quietly then for several minutes after you're finished."
7. "The procedure involves learning to focus on your breathing while sitting in a quiet place. Sometimes concentrating on just one word may help you do this. You continue to do this for about 15 minutes each time."
8. "How easy or hard was this for you to do?"
9. "There may be times when other images or thoughts come into your mind. Try to just maintain a passive attitude. If you're bothered by other thoughts, don't dwell on them, but don't force them away. Just focus on your breathing and your word."
10. "Pick a word like *one* or *zum* that you can focus on—something neutral to you."

PART TWO

Objective Two asks you to identify accurately the steps for the clinically standardized meditation procedure represented by at least six out of eight counselor instructive responses. Do this on paper. There may be more than one response for a given step. The counselor examples are not in order. The six major steps of CSM are as follows:

1. Rationale.
2. Selection of a mantra or sound.
3. Preparation for meditation.
4. Instructions to meditate.
5. Discussion of client's reaction to first meditation.
6. Homework and practice.

Feedback follows.

(continued)

POSTEVALUATION (continued)

1. "Meditation has benefited people by reducing tension, anxiety, stress, and headaches."
2. "Meditate for three weeks and at the same times twice a day."
3. "Allow distracting thoughts to flow. Allow memories, images, and thoughts to occur. Don't try to influence them."
4. "Do not take any alcoholic beverages or nonprescription drugs for at least 24 hours before meditating."
5. "Think of a meaningless sound or word that has few associations and is not emotionally charged."
6. "Come out of meditation slowly. Sit with your eyes closed for two minutes — take time to absorb what is happening. Slowly open your eyes."
7. "First, close your eyes and say your mantra aloud, say it softly, then whisper it, and then think the sound to yourself without moving your lips."
8. "Do not chew gum while meditating. Face away from direct light in a dimly lit room."

PART THREE

Objective Three asks you to teach the process of meditation to another person. Select either relaxation response/Zen meditation or clinically standardized meditation to teach. You can have an observer evaluate you, or you can audiotape your teaching session and rate yourself. You can use the Interview Checklist for Relaxation Response and Zen Meditation or the Interview Checklist for Clinically Standardized Meditation that follows as a teaching guide and evaluation tool.

PART FOUR

Objective Four asks you to describe how you would apply the seven major parts of the muscle-relaxation procedure. Using this client description and the seven questions following it, describe how you would use certain parts of the procedure with this person. You can check your responses with the feedback that follows.

Description of client: The client is a middle-aged man who is concerned about his inability to sleep at night. He has tried sleeping pills but does not want to rely on medication.

1. Give an example of a rationale you could use about the procedure. Include the purpose and an overview of the strategy.
2. Give a brief example of instructions you might give this client about appropriate dress for relaxation training.
3. List any special environmental factors that may affect the client's use of muscle relaxation.
4. Describe how you might model some of the relaxation exercises for the client.
5. Describe some of the important muscle groups that you would instruct the client to tense and relax alternately.
6. Give two examples of probes you might use with the client after relaxation to assess his use of and reactions to the process.
7. What instructions about a homework assignment (practice of relaxation) would you give to this client?

PART FIVE

Objective Five asks you to demonstrate 13 out of 15 steps of muscle relaxation with a role-play client. An observer or the client can assess your performance, or you can assess yourself, using the Interview Checklist for Muscle Relaxation on pages 472–476.

INTERVIEW CHECKLIST FOR RELAXATION RESPONSE AND ZEN MEDITATION

Instructions: Determine which of the following counselor leads or questions were demonstrated in the interview. Check each of the leads used by the counselor. Some examples of counselor leads are provided in the right column.

Item	*Examples of counselor leads*
I. Rationale	
———— 1. Counselor describes purpose of procedure.	"I would like to teach you a mental exercise called the relaxation response, or meditation. The relaxation response has been used to relieve fatigue caused by anxiety, to decrease stress that can lead to high blood pressure, and to help people who have difficulty getting to sleep at night. It can be used to (continued)

Item	Examples of counselor leads

	have you become more relaxed. The procedure helps you become more relaxed and deal more effectively with your tension and stress. It may give you a new awareness."
____ 2. Counselor gives client an overview.	"What we will do first is select a focusing device, or mental device. You will then get into a relaxed and comfortable position. Afterward, I will instruct you about focusing on your breathing and using your mental device. We will talk about a passive attitude while meditating. You will meditate about 10 to 20 minutes. Then, we will talk about the experience."
____ 3. Counselor confirms client's willingness to use strategy.	"How do you feel now about working with meditation?"

II. Selecting a Mental Device

| ____ 4. Counselor provides rationale for mental device. | "First, we want to select a mental device. It is a word, syllable, or phrase that helps you focus on breathing, and by repeating it you can become free of distracting thoughts or images." |
| ____ 5. Counselor gives examples of mental devices. | "Examples of a mental device are one, zum, in, Rama. Think of something you can say to yourself that is easy and will be fairly neutral to you." |

III. Instructions about Body Comfort

____ 6. Counselor conducts meditation training in quiet environment.	"We want to meditate in a quiet environment, free of distractions and interruption."
____ 7. Counselor tells client to close eyes and get into comfortable position.	"There are several ways to meditate. I'll show you one. I want you to get into a comfortable position while you are sitting there. Now, close your eyes."
____ 8. Counselor instructs client to relax major muscle groups.	"Relax all the muscles in your body—relax [said slowly] your head, face, neck, shoulders, chest, your torso, thighs, calves, and your feet. Keep all your muscles relaxed."

IV. Instructions about Breathing and Use of Mental Device

| ____ 9. Counselor instructs client to focus on breathing and to use mental device with each inhalation and exhalation. | "Breathe through your nose and focus on [or become aware of] your breathing. It is sometimes difficult to be natural when you are doing this. Just let the air come to you. Breathe easily and naturally. As you do this, say your mental device for each inhalation and exhalation. Say your mental device silently to yourself each time you breathe in and out." |

V. Instructions about Passive Attitude

| ____10. Counselor instructs client to maintain passive attitude and to allow relaxation to occur at its own pace. Client is also instructed, if attention wanders and unrelated images and thoughts occur that take away from breathing, not to dwell on them but return to repeating mental device. | "Be calm and passive. If distracting thoughts or images occur, attempt to be passive about them by not dwelling on them. Return to repeating the mental device. Try to achieve effortless breathing. After more practice, you will be able to examine these thoughts or images with greater detachment." |
| | "After a while, you may become aware that you were busy with distracting thoughts or images and you have not said your mental device for a couple of minutes. When this happens, just return to saying your word. Do not attempt to keep the thoughts out of your mind; just let them pass through. Keep your mind open—don't try to solve problems or think things over. Allow the thoughts to flow smoothly into your mind and then drift out. Say your mental device and relax. Don't get upset with distracting thoughts. Just return to your mental device." |

(continued)

POSTEVALUATION (continued)

Item	Examples of counselor leads
VI. Instructions to Meditate for 10 to 20 Minutes	
_____11. Counselor is instructed to meditate for 10 to 20 minutes. Counselor instructs client on what to do after meditative session.	"Continue to meditate for about 10 [15 or 20] minutes. You can open your eyes to check on the time. After you have finished, sit quietly for several minutes. You may wish to keep your eyes closed for a couple of minutes and later open them. You may not want to stand up for a few minutes."
VII. Probe about the Meditative Experience	
_____12. Counselor asks client about experience with meditation.	"How do you feel about the experience?" "What sort of thoughts or images flowed through your mind?" "What did you do when the distracting thoughts drifted in?" "How did you feel about your mental device?"
VIII. Homework and Follow-up	
_____13. Formal meditation: Counselor instructs client to practice formal meditation (relaxation response) once or twice a day at home or at work. Counselor cautions client not to meditate within two hours after a meal or within a couple of hours before bedtime.	"Practice meditation [relaxation response] two times a day. Like anything else we are trying to learn, you will become better with practice. You can do it at work or at home. Get comfortable in your meditative [relaxation-response] position. Practice in a quiet place away from noise and interruptions. Do not use meditation [relaxation response] as a substitute for sleep. Usually, meditation before sleep might make you feel very awake. Also, do not meditate within two hours after a meal or within a couple of hours before bedtime. Keep a log for each meditative experience, including where it was used and time of day used, and rate each use on a 5-point scale."
_____14. Informal meditation: Counselor instructs client to apply informal meditation _in vivo_.	"Also, I think it would be helpful for you to apply an informal meditation in problem or stressful situations that may occur daily. The way you can do this is, when in the situation, be detached and passive. Observe yourself and focus on being calm and on your breathing. Be relaxed in the situations that evoke stress. How does that sound?"
_____15. Counselor schedules follow-up session.	"After you have practiced the homework daily for the next two weeks, bring in your logs and we'll see what has happened."

Observer comments: _____

_____

_____

INTERVIEW CHECKLIST FOR CLINICALLY STANDARDIZED MEDITATION (CSM)

Instructions: Indicate by a check mark each counselor lead demonstrated in the interview. Example leads are provided in the right column.

Item	Examples of counselor leads
I. Rationale	
_____ 1. Counselor describes purpose of procedure.	"I would like to teach you a simple relaxation exercise. People who have used this procedure have reduced tension and stress, headaches, anxiety, and the time it takes to fall asleep. Meditation has been reported to increase athletic performance (continued)

Item	Examples of counselor leads
	and energy. People have also reported that they are more alert and closer to their feelings and have clearer thinking when they use meditation."
_____ 2. Counselor gives client an overview of procedure.	"If you want to use meditation as a relaxation method, you will select a soothing sound (mantra) that you will use. You will close your eyes, say the sound, and be in a quiet environment, and you will allow your images and thoughts to flow freely. You will meditate for about five to ten minutes. Then we will talk about the experience."
_____ 3. Counselor confirms client's willingness to use strategy.	"How do you feel about using this strategy?"

II. Selection of a Mantra, or Sound

Item	Examples of counselor leads
_____ 4. Counselor helps client select a sound and gives the reason for using the sound.	"Before we begin, we want to select a sound. The type of sound or word we want is one that has few associations and is not emotionally charged for you. The sound should be soothing to you. The mantra, or sound, helps you not to become distracted by other thoughts."
_____ 5. Counselor gives examples of sounds.	"Some examples of a sound are *shaham, rama,* and *gome.* Think of a sound you can say to yourself that is neutral and soothing."

III. Instructions about Preparation for Meditation

Item	Examples of counselor leads
_____ 6. Counselor conducts meditation training in quiet environment free from distractions and interruptions.	"We want to meditate in a quiet environment free of distractions and interruptions. If you decide to use meditation, you want to select a quiet place at home."
_____ 7. Counselor instructs client about alcoholic beverages, nonprescription drugs, beverages with caffeine, eating, smoking, and chewing gum.	"When you meditate, you don't want to do things that might interfere with meditation. For example, you should not take any alcoholic beverages or nonprescription drugs at least 24 hours before meditation. And you should not meditate right after you consume solid food or beverages containing caffeine. If you do these things, wait an hour before you meditate. Finally, do not chew gum while meditating."
_____ 8. Counselor instructs client about sitting, focusing away from light, and loosening tight shoes.	"Before we meditate, get comfortable in the chair, and if your shoes feel tight, loosen them. If you decide to meditate at home, you will want to wear comfortable clothing."

IV. Instructions to Meditate

Item	Examples of counselor leads
_____ 9. Counselor instructs client about sitting quietly and relaxed for a minute.	"Sit quietly for a while—just relax—don't say your sound yet."
_____10. Counselor instructs client to close eyes, to say aloud the sound, to say it softly, to whisper, and then to think the sound without moving lips or tongue.	"Close your eyes and say your sound aloud. Then say it softly. Now whisper your sound. [Allow the client to say aloud, say softly, and whisper several times for each.] Think your sound without moving your lips or tongue."
_____11. Counselor tells client that CSM is not a discipline and to allow distracting thoughts to flow.	"Remember that meditation is not an exercise in discipline—it is a quiet, peaceful time with yourself. It does not require effort. Don't force it. If distracting thoughts, memories, or images occur, allow them to come. Don't try to influence them. Your sound will return to you."
_____12. Counselor tells client that she or he will meditate for about five to ten minutes.	"I will keep time and have you meditate for about five to ten minutes. I will tell you when to stop. When you meditate alone, you can open your eyes to check the time periodically."

(continued)

POSTEVALUATION (continued)

Item	Examples of counselor leads
____13. Counselor instructs client to come out of meditation slowly.	"Our time is about up. I want you to come out of meditation slowly. Sit with your eyes closed for two minutes — take time to experience and absorb what is happening. Open your eyes slowly."

V. Discussion of Client's Reaction to Meditation

Item	Examples of counselor leads
____14. Counselor asks client about experience with meditation.	"How did you feel about your sound?" "How did you feel about CSM?" "What thoughts, images, or memories flowed through your mind?" "How did your sound return to you?"

VI. Homework and Follow-up

Item	Examples of counselor leads
____15. Counselor instructs client to meditate at home two times a day, once after getting up in the morning and once during late afternoon or early evening. Reminds client about preparations for meditation.	"Practice meditation two times a day, once after getting up in the morning and later in late afternoon or early evening. Remember the things to do to prepare for meditation. Select a quiet environment without distractions. Do not take any alcoholic beverages or nonprescription drugs at least 24 hours before meditating. Wait for an hour before meditating after eating solid foods or drinking beverages containing caffeine. Do not smoke half an hour before meditating. Select a comfortable chair away from direct light. Meditate in the same place and the same time each day. Keep a log of each meditative experience — where you used it, time of day, and rating on a 5-point scale."
____16. Informal meditation: counselor instructs client about informal meditation in stressful situations.	"You can meditate informally when you are in stressful situations that may occur daily. Just relax and say the sound to yourself, and you'll find how peaceful the situation will become."
____17. Counselor schedules follow-up session.	"After you have practiced a couple of times a day at home for a week, bring your log in and we'll discuss your home meditative experiences."

Observer comments: _____

_____

_____

INTERVIEW CHECKLIST FOR MUSCLE RELAXATION

Instructions: Indicate with a check mark each counselor lead demonstrated in the interview. Some example leads are provided in the right column.

Item	Examples of counselor leads
I. Rationale	
____ 1. Counselor explains purpose of muscle relaxation.	"The name of the strategy that I believe will be helpful is *muscle relaxation.* Muscle relaxation has been used very effectively to benefit people who have a variety of concerns like insomnia, high blood pressure, anxiety, or stress or for people who are bothered by everyday tension. Muscle relaxation will be helpful in decreasing your tension. It will benefit you because you will be able to control and to dispel tension that interferes with your daily activities."

(continued)

Item	Examples of counselor leads
_____ 2. Counselor gives overview of how muscle relaxation works.	"What we will do is that I will ask you to tense up and relax various muscle groups. All of us have some tensions in our bodies—otherwise we could not stand, sit, or move around. Sometimes we have too much tension. By tensing and relaxing, you will become aware of and contrast the feelings of tension and relaxation. Later we will train you to send a message to a particular muscle group to relax when nonessential tension creeps in. You will learn to control your tension and relax when you feel tension."
_____ 3. Counselor describes muscle relaxation as a skill.	"Muscle relaxation is a skill. And, as in learning any skill, it will take a lot of practice to learn it well—a lot of repetition and training are needed to acquire the muscle-relaxation skill."
_____ 4. Counselor instructs client about moving around if uncomfortable and informs client of sensations that may feel unusual.	"At times during the training and muscle exercises, you may want to move while you are on your back on the floor [or on the recliner]. Just feel free to do this so that you can get more comfortable. You may also feel heady sensations as we go through the exercise. These sensations are not unusual. Do you have any questions concerning what I just talked about? If not, do you want to try this now?"

II. Client Dress

_____ 5. Counselor instructs client about what to wear for training session.	"For the next session, wear comfortable clothing." "Wear regular glasses instead of your contact lenses."

III. Comfortable Environment

_____ 6. Counselor uses quiet environment, padded recliner chair, or floor with a pillow under client's head.	"During training, I'd like you to sit in this recliner chair. It will be more comfortable and less distracting than this wooden chair."

IV. Modeling the Exercises

_____ 7. Counselor models some exercises for muscle groups.	"I would like to show you [some of] the exercises we will use in muscle relaxation. First, I make a fist to create tension in my right hand and forearm and then relax it. . . ."

V. Instructions for Muscle Relaxation

_____ 8. Counselor reads or recites instructions from memory in conversational tone and practices along with client.	
_____ 9. Counselor instructs client to get comfortable, close eyes, and listen to instructions.	"Now, get as comfortable as you can, close your eyes, and listen to what I'm going to be telling you. I'm going to make you aware of certain sensations in your body and then show you how you can reduce these sensations to increase feelings of relaxation."
_____10. Counselor instructs client to tense and relax alternately each of the 17 muscle groups (*two* times for each muscle group in initial training). Also occasionally makes muscle-group comparisons.	

(continued)

POSTEVALUATION (continued)

Item	Examples of counselor leads
____a. Fist of dominant hand	"First study your right arm, your right hand in particular. Clench your right fist. Clench it tightly and study the tension in the hand and in the forearm. Study those sensations of tension. [Pause.] And now let go. Just relax the right hand and let it rest on the arm of the chair. [Pause.] And note the difference between the tension and the relaxation." [Ten-second pause.]
____b. Fist of nondominant hand	"Now we'll do the same with your left hand. Clench your left fist. Notice the tension [five-second pause] and now relax. Enjoy the difference between the tension and the relaxation." [Ten-second pause.]
____c. One or both wrists	"Now bend both hands back at the wrists so that you tense the muscles in the back of the hand and in the forearm. Point your fingers toward the ceiling. Study the tension, and now relax. [Pause.] Study the difference between tension and relaxation." [Ten-second pause.]
____d. Biceps of one or both arms	"Now, clench both your hands into fists and bring them toward your shoulders. As you do this, tighten your bicep muscles, the ones in the upper part of your arm. Feel the tension in these muscles. [Pause.] Now relax. Let your arms drop down again to your sides. See the difference between the tension and the relaxation." [Ten-second pause.]
____e. Shoulders	"Now we'll move to the shoulder area. Shrug your shoulders. Bring them up to your ears. Feel and hold the tension in your shoulders. Now, let both shoulders relax. Note the contrast between the tension and the relaxation that's now in your shoulders. [Ten-second pause.] Are your shoulders as relaxed as your arms?"
____f. Forehead	"Now we'll work on relaxing the various muscles of the face. First, wrinkle up your forehead and brow. Do this until you feel your brow furrow. [Pause.] Now relax. Smooth out the forehead. Let it loosen up." [Ten-second pause.]
____g. Eyes	"Now close your eyes tightly. Can you feel tension all around your eyes? [Five-second pause.] Now relax those muscles, noting the difference between the tension and the relaxation." [Ten-second pause.]
____h. Tongue or jaw	"Now clench your jaw by biting your teeth together. Pull the corners of your mouth back. Study the tension in the jaws. [Five-second pause.] Relax your jaws now. Can you tell the difference between tension and relaxation in your jaw area?" [Ten-second pause.]
____i. Lips	"Now, press your lips together tightly. As you do this, notice the tension all around the mouth. [Pause.] Now relax those muscles around the mouth. Just enjoy the relaxation in your mouth area and your entire face." [Pause.]
____j. Head backward	"Now we'll move to the neck muscles. Press your head back against your chair. Can you feel the tension in the back of your neck and in the upper back? Hold the tension. Now let your head rest comfortably. Notice the difference. Keep on relaxing." [Pause.]

(continued)

Item	Examples of counselor leads
____k. Chin in chest	"Now continue to concentrate on the neck area. See whether you can bury your chin into your chest. Note the tension in the front of your neck. Now relax and let go." [Ten-second pause.]
____l. Back	"Now direct your attention to your upper back area. Arch your back as if you were sticking out your chest and stomach. Can you feel tension in your back? Study that tension. [Pause.] Now relax. Note the difference between the tension and the relaxation."
____m. Chest muscles	"Now take a deep breath, filling your lungs, and hold it. See the tension all through your chest and into your stomach area. Hold that tension. [Pause.] Now relax and let go. Let your breath out naturally. Enjoy the pleasant sensations. Is your chest as relaxed as your back and shoulders?" [Ten-second pause.]
____n. Stomach muscles	"Now think about your stomach. Tighten the abdomen muscles. Hold this tension. Make your stomach like a knot. Now relax. Loosen these muscles now." [Ten-second pause.]
____o. Buttocks	"Focus now on your buttocks. Tense your buttocks by pulling them in or contracting them. Note the tension that is there. Now relax — let go." [Ten-second pause.]
____p. Legs	"I'd like you now to focus on your legs. Stretch both legs. Feel tension in the thighs. [Five-second pause.] Now relax. Study the difference again between the tension in the thighs and the relaxation you feel now." [Ten-second pause.]
____q. Toes	"Now concentrate on your lower legs and feet. Tighten both calf muscles by pointing your toes toward your head. Pretend a string is pulling your toes up. Can you feel the pulling and the tension? Note that tension. [Pause.] Now relax. Let your legs relax deeply. Enjoy the difference between tension and relaxation." [Ten-second pause.]
____11. Counselor instructs client to review and relax all muscle groups.	"Now, I'm going to go over again the different muscle groups that we've covered. As I name each group, try to notice whether there is any tension in those muscles. If there is any, try to concentrate on those muscles and tell them to relax. Think of draining any residual tension out of your body. Relax the muscles in your feet, ankles, and calves. [Pause.] Let go of your knee and thigh muscles. [Pause.] Loosen your hips. [Pause.] Loosen the muscles of your lower body. [Pause.] Relax all the muscles of your stomach, waist, lower back. [Pause.] Drain any tension from your upper back, chest, and shoulders. [Pause.] Relax your upper arms, forearms, and hands. [Pause.] Let go of the muscles in your throat and neck. [Pause.] Relax your face. [Pause.] Let all the muscles of your body become loose. Drain all the tension from your body. [Pause.] Now sit quietly with your eyes closed."
____12. Counselor asks client to rate relaxation level following training session.	"Now I'd like you to think of a scale from 0 to 5, where 0 is complete relaxation and 5 extreme tension. Tell me where you would place yourself on that scale now."

(continued)

POSTEVALUATION (continued)

Item	Examples of counselor leads
VI. Posttraining Assessment	
____13. Counselor asks client about first session of relaxation training, discusses problems with training if client has any.	"How do you feel?" "What is your overall reaction to the procedure?" "Think back about what we did — did you have problems with any muscle group?" "What reaction did you have when you focused on the tension? What about relaxation?" "How did the contrast between the tension and relaxation feel?"
VII. Homework and Follow-up	
____14. Counselor assigns homework and requests that client complete homework log for practice sessions.	"Relaxation training, like any skill, takes a lot of practice. I would like you to practice what we've done today. Do the exercises twice a day for about 15 to 20 minutes each time. Do them in a quiet place in a reclining chair, on the floor with a pillow, or on your bed with a head pillow. Also, try to do the relaxation at a time when there is no time pressure — like arising, after school or work, or before dinner. Try to avoid any interruptions, like telephone calls and people wanting to see you. Complete the homework log I have given you. Make sure you fill it in for each practice session. Do you have any questions?"
____15. Counselor arranges for follow-up session.	"Why don't you practice with this over the next two weeks and come back then?"

Notations for problems encountered or variations used: _____

□ SUGGESTED READINGS

Benson, H. (1974 July – August). Your innate asset for combating stress. *Harvard Business Review, 52,* 49 – 60.

Benson, H. (1976). *The relaxation response.* New York: Avon Books.

Benson, H. (1984). *Beyond the relaxation response.* New York: Berkley Books.

Bernstein, D. A., & Borkovec, T. D. (1973). *Progressive relaxation training: A manual for the helping professions.* Champaign, IL: Research Press.

Carrington, P. (1978a). *Clinically standardized meditation (CSM). Instructor's manual.* Kendall Park, NJ: Pace Educational Systems.

Carrington, P. (1978b). *Learning to meditate: Clinically standardized meditation (CSM). Course workbook.* Kendall Park, NJ: Pace Educational Systems.

Carrington, P., Collings, G. H., Benson, H., Robinson, H., Wood, L. W., Lehrer, P. M., Woolfolk, R. L., & Cole, J. W. (1980). The use of meditation-relaxation techniques for the management of stress in a working population. *Journal of Occupational Medicine, 22,* 221 – 231.

Cautela, J. R., & Groden, J. (1978). *Relaxation: A comprehensive manual for adults, children, and children with special needs.* Champaign, IL: Research Press.

Credidio, S. G. (1982). Comparative effectiveness of patterned biofeedback vs. meditation training on EMG and skin temperature changes. *Behaviour Research and Therapy, 20,* 233 – 241.

Ferguson, J. M., Marquis, J. N., & Taylor, C. B. (1977). A script for deep muscle relaxation. *Diseases of the Nervous System, 38,* 703 – 708.

Hillenberg, J. B., & Collins, F. L., Jr. (1982). A procedural analysis and review of relaxation training research. *Behaviour Research and Therapy, 20,* 251 – 260.

Kabat-Zinn, J. (1982). An outpatient program in behavioral medicine for chronic pain patients based on the practice of mindfulness meditation: Theoretical considerations and preliminary results. *General Hospital Psychiatry, 4,* 33 – 47.

Kabat-Zinn, J., Lipworth, L., & Burney, R. (1985). The clinical use of mindfulness meditation for the self-regulation of chronic pain. *Journal of Behavioral Medicine, 8,* 163 – 190.

Lehrer, P. M. (1982). How to relax and how not to relax: A reevaluation of the work of Edmund Jacobson—I. *Behaviour Research and Therapy, 20,* 417–428.

Lehrer, P. M., Woolfolk, R. L., Rooney, A. J., McCann, B., & Carrington, P. (1983). Progressive relaxation and meditation: A study of psychophysiological and therapeutic differences between two techniques. *Behaviour Research and Therapy, 21,* 651–662.

Öst, L-G. (1987). Applied relaxation: Description of a coping technique and review of controlled studies. *Behaviour Research & Therapy, 25,* 397–409.

Poppen, R. (1988). *Behavioral relaxation training and assessment.* New York: Pergamon.

Redfering, D. L., & Bowman, M. J. (1981). Effects of a meditative relaxation exercise on non-attending behaviors of behaviorally disturbed children. *Journal of Clinical Child Psychology, 10,* 126–127.

Shapiro, D. H. (1980). *Meditation: Self-regulation strategy and altered state of consciousness.* New York: Aldine.

Shapiro, D. H. (1982). Overview: Clinical and physiological comparison of meditation with other self-control strategies. *American Journal of Psychiatry, 139,* 267–274.

Southam, M. A., Agras, W. S., Taylor, C. B., & Kraemer, H. C. (1982). Relaxation training: Blood pressure lowering during the working day. *Archives of General Psychiatry, 39,* 715–717.

Throll, D. A. (1982). Transcendental meditation and progressive relaxation: Their physiological effects. *Journal of Clinical Psychology, 38,* 522–530.

Woolfolk, R. L., & Lehrer, P. M. (Eds.). (1984). *Principles and practice of stress management.* New York: Guilford Press.

Woolfolk, R. L., Lehrer, P. M., McCann, B. S., & Rooney, A. J. (1982). Effects of progressive relaxation and meditation on cognitive and somatic manifestations of daily stress. *Behaviour Research and Therapy, 20,* 461–467.

◼ FEEDBACK: POSTEVALUATION

PART ONE

1. *Homework* (practice).
2. *Instruction* about body comfort.
3. *Rationale*—telling the client how the procedure is used.
4. *Instruction* about breathing.
5. *Homework*—giving the client instructions about how to carry out the practice.
6. *Instructing* the client to meditate for 10 to 20 minutes.
7. *Rationale*—providing a brief overview of the procedure.

8. *Probing* about the meditative experience—assessing the client's reactions.
9. *Instruction* about a passive attitude.
10. *Selection* of a mental device such as a syllable or a number.

PART TWO

1. *Rationale*—reason.
2. *Homework*—when to practice.
3. *Instructions* about distracting thoughts.
4. *Preparation* about drinks and drugs.
5. *Selection* of a mantra, or sound.
6. *Instructions* about coming out of meditation.
7. *Instructions* about the use of mantra.
8. *Preparation* about chewing gum and about lighting in the room.

PART THREE

Use the Interview Checklist for Relaxation Response and Zen Meditation or the Interview Checklist for Clinically Standardized Meditation as a guide to assess your teaching.

PART FOUR

1. Rationale for client:
   a. Purpose: "This procedure, if you practice it regularly, can help you become relaxed. The relaxation benefits you derive can help you sleep better."
   b. Overview: "This procedure involves learning to tense and relax different muscle groups in your body. By doing this, you can contrast the difference between tenseness and relaxation. This will help you to recognize tension so you can instruct yourself to relax."
2. Instructions about dress: "You don't want anything to distract you, so wear comfortable, loose clothes for training. You may want to remove your glasses or contact lenses."
3. Environmental factors:
   a. Quiet room with reclining chair
   b. No obvious distractions or interruptions
4. Modeling of exercises: "Let me show you exactly what you'll be doing. Watch my right arm closely. I'm going to clench my fist and tighten my forearm, studying the tension as I do this. Now I'm going to relax it like this [hand goes limp], letting all the tension just drain out of the arm and hand and fingertips."

(continued)

5. Muscle groups used in the procedure include:
   a. fist of each arm
   b. wrist of each arm
   c. biceps of each arm
   d. shoulders
   e. facial muscles—forehead, eyes, nose, jaws, lips
   f. head, chin, and neck muscles
   g. back
   h. chest
   i. stomach
   j. legs and feet
6. Some possible probes are:
   a. "On a scale from 0 to 100, 0 being very relaxed and 100 very tense, how do you feel now?"
   b. "What is your overall reaction to what you just did?"
   c. "How did the contrast between the tensed and relaxed muscles feel?"
   d. "How easy or hard was it for you to do this?"
7. Homework instructions should include:
   a. practice twice daily
   b. practice in a quiet place; avoid interruptions
   c. use a reclining chair, the floor, or a bed with pillow support for your head

PART FIVE

Use the Interview Checklist for Muscle Relaxation to assess your performance.

SYSTEMATIC DESENSITIZATION

EIGHTEEN

Consider the following cases:

A man has been a successful high school teacher. He is teaching while plagued with a personal problem: he is married yet is in love with another person. One day at school he is overcome with anxiety. He leaves school to go home; the next day, the thought of school elicits so much anxiety he feels sick. For the last few months, he has not returned to school. Because of this, he is convinced he is "going crazy."

A high school student gets good grades on homework and self-study assignments. Whenever he takes a test, he "freezes." Some days, if he can, he avoids or leaves the class because he feels so anxious about the test even the day before. When he takes a test, he feels overcome with anxiety, he cannot remember very much, and his resulting test grades are quite low.

These two case descriptions reflect instances in which a person learned an anxiety response to a situation. According to Bandura (1969), anxiety is a persistent, learned maladaptive response resulting from stimuli that have acquired the capacity to elicit very intense emotional reactions. In addition, both persons described in these cases felt fear in situations where there was no obvious external danger (sometimes called a *phobia;* Morris, 1980, p. 248). Further, to some degree, each person managed to avoid the nondangerous feared situation (sometimes called a *phobic reaction;* Morris, p. 248). These persons will probably require counseling or therapy.

In contrast, in the next two cases, a person is prevented from learning an anxiety response to a certain situation.

A child is afraid to learn to swim because of a prior bad experience with water. The child's parent or teacher gradually introduces the child to swimming, first by visiting the pool, dabbling hands and feet in the water, getting in up to the knees, and so on. Each approach to swimming is accompanied by a pleasure — being with a parent, having a toy or an inner tube, or playing water games.

A person has been in a very bad car accident. The person recovers and learns to get back in a car by sitting in it, going for short distances first, often accompanied by a friend or the music on the radio.

In the two descriptions you just read, the situation never got out of hand; that is, it never acquired the capacity to elicit a persistent anxiety response, nor did the persons learn to avoid the situation continually. Why? See whether you can identify common elements in these situations that prevented these two persons from becoming therapy candidates. Go over these last two cases again. Do you notice that, in each case, some type of stimulus or emotion was present that counteracted the fear or anxiety? The parent used pleasurable activities to create enjoyment for the child while swimming; the person in the car took a friend or listened to music. In addition, these persons learned to become more comfortable with a potentially fearful situation gradually. Each step of the way represented a larger or more intense dose of the feared situation.

In a simplified manner, these elements reflect some of the processes that seem to occur in the procedure of *systematic desensitization,* a widely used anxiety-reduction strategy. According to Wolpe (1982, p. 133),

> Systematic desensitization is one of a variety of methods for breaking down neurotic anxiety-response habits in piecemeal fashion . . . a physiological state inhibitory of anxiety is induced in the patient by means of muscle relaxation, and he is then exposed to a weak anxiety-evoking stimulus for a few seconds. If the exposure is repeated several times, the stimulus progressively loses its ability to evoke anxiety. Successively "stronger" stimuli are then introduced and similarly treated.

☐ OBJECTIVES

1. Using written examples of four sample hierarchies, identify at least three hierarchies by type (spatiotemporal, thematic, personal).
2. Given a written client case description, identify and describe at least 9 of the following 11 procedural steps of desensitization:
   a. A rationale.
   b. An overview.
   c. A method for identifying client emotion-provoking situations.
   d. A type of hierarchy appropriate for this client.
   e. A method of ranking hierarchy items the client could use.
   f. An appropriate counterconditioning or coping response.
   g. A method of imagery assessment.
   h. A method of scene presentation.
   i. A method of client signaling during scene presentation.
   j. A written notation method to record scene-presentation progress.
   k. An example of a desensitization homework task.
3. Demonstrate at least 22 out of 28 steps of systematic desensitization in several role-play interviews.

☐ REPORTED USES OF DESENSITIZATION

Systematic desensitization was used widely as early as 1958 by Wolpe. In 1961 Wolpe reported its effectiveness in numerous case reports, which were substantiated by successful case reports cited by Lazarus (1967). Since 1963, when Lang and Lazovik conducted the first controlled study of systematic desensitization, its use as a therapy procedure has been the subject of numerous empirical investigations and case reports.

Desensitization has been used to treat speech anxiety (Kirsch & Henry, 1979; Lent, Russell, & Zamostny, 1981), cases of multiple phobias in children (Van Hasselt, Hersen, Bellack, Rosenblum, & Lamparski, 1979), chronic vomiting (Redd, 1980), blood phobia (Elmore, Wildman, & Westefeld, 1980), nightmares (Schindler, 1980), driving phobia (Levine & Wolpe, 1980), fear of water (Ultee, Griffioen, & Schellekens, 1982), rape trauma (Frank, Anderson, Stewart, Dancu, Hughes, & West, 1988), and to explore the role that the endogenous opiate system plays in the effectiveness of systematic desensitization (Egan, Carr, Hunt, & Adamson, 1988). It has also been used extensively with common phobias, including acrophobia (fear of heights), agoraphobia (fear of open places), and claustrophobia (fear of enclosed places). It has been used to treat fear of flying, fear of death, fear of criticism or rejection — and, after the stimulus movie *Jaws III,* fear of sharks. Of course, one should not apply desensitization automatically whenever a client reports "anxiety." In some cases, the anxiety may be the logical result of another problem. For example, a person who continually procrastinates on work deadlines may feel anxious. Using this procedure would only help the person become desensitized or numb to the possible consequences of continued procrastination. A more logical approach might be to help the client reduce the procrastination behavior that is clearly the antecedent for the experienced anxiety. This illustration reiterates the importance of thorough problem assessment (Chapters 7 and 8) as a prerequisite for selecting and implementing counseling strategies.

Generally, desensitization is appropriate when a client has the capability or the skills to handle a situation or perform an activity but avoids the situation or performs less than adequately because of anxiety. For example, in the two cases described at the beginning of this chapter, the teacher had a history of successful teaching yet persistently avoided school (or related thoughts) because of the associated anxiety. The high school student had the ability to do well and adequate study skills, yet his performance on tests was not up to par because of his response. In contrast, if a person avoids a situation because of skill deficits, then desensitization is inadequate and probably inappropriate (Rimm & Masters, 1979). As you may recall from Chapter 13, modeling procedures work very well with many kinds of skill-deficit problems. People with many fears or with general, pervasive anxiety may benefit more from cognitive change strategies (Chapters 15 and 16) or from combinations of strategies in which desensitization may play some role. In addition, some anxiety may be maintained by the client's maladaptive self-verbalizations. In such instances, cognitive restructuring, reframing, or stress inoculation (Chapter 16) may be a first treatment choice or may be used in conjunction with desensitization (see Berman, Miller, & Massman, 1985). Densensitization should not be used when the client's anxiety is nonspecific, or free-floating (Foa, Stekette, & Ascher, 1980). As you may recall from Chapter 11, generalized anxiety is often treated initially with client-centered therapy. Biofeedback, meditation, and muscle relaxation may also be useful supplemental strategies (Meyer, 1983).

At the same time, desensitization should not be overlooked as a possible treatment strategy for client problems that do not involve anxiety. Marquis, Morgan, and Piaget (1973) suggest that desensitization can be used with any conditioned emotion. It has been used to reduce anger (Hearn & Evans, 1972) and to increase tolerance of White students toward Black peers (Cotharin & Mikulas, 1975). Dengrove (1966) reports the use of desensitization to treat situations of loss and grief, such as separation from a loved one or loss of a valued job or object.

☐ COMPARISON WITH OTHER TREATMENT APPROACHES

A great many studies have compared desensitization with other therapy methods on certain dependent measures. In the treatment of test anxiety, desensitization has been compared with covert positive reinforcement (Kostka & Galassi, 1974), hypnosis (Melnick & Russell, 1976), cognitive therapy (Holroyd, 1976; Leal, Baxter, Martin, & Marx, 1981), cue-controlled relaxation (Russell, Wise & Stratoudakis, 1976), and modeling, flooding, and study skills training (Horne & Matson, 1977). In treating speech anxiety, desensitization has been compared with an insight treatment focusing on maladaptive self-verbalizations (Meichenbaum, Gilmore, & Fedoravicius, 1971), with cue-controlled relaxation (Lent et al., 1981; Russell & Wise, 1976), and with meditation (Kirsch & Henry, 1979). Shaw and Thoresen (1974) compared desensitization with modeling in treating dental phobia; Curran (1975) compared it with skills training consisting of modeling and behavior rehearsal on social-anxiety measures. Rudestam and Bedrosian (1977) compared flooding and desensitization in anxiety reduction of animal phobias and social phobias of college students. *In vitro* and *in vivo* systematic desensitization were compared in reducing the fear of water for children aged 5–10 years (Ultee et al., 1982).

Although desensitization has enjoyed substantial empirical support, a great deal of controversy surrounds its current status. There is general agreement that desensitization is effective in reducing fears and neurotic behavior. The controversy centers on how and why the procedure works, or what processes surrounding densensitization are responsible for its results (Kazdin & Wilcoxon, 1976). After a critical review of the literature, Kazdin and Wilcoxon (1976) concluded that nonspecific factors such as the rationale presented to the client and client expectancy may account for some of the therapeutic effects of desensitization. For example, Kirsch, Tennen, Wickless, Saccone, and Cody (1983) found that a credible expectancy modification procedure was just as effective as desensitization in reducing experienced fear.

☐ EXPLANATIONS OF DESENSITIZATION

We will briefly summarize some of the possible theoretical explanations of the desensitization procedure. This will help you understand both the counterconditioning and the self-control models for implementing desensitization.

Desensitization by Reciprocal Inhibition

In 1958 Wolpe explained the way in which desensitization ostensibly works with the principle of *reciprocal inhibition.* When reciprocal inhibition occurs, a response such as fear is inhibited by another response or activity that is stronger than and incompatible with the fear response (or any other response to be inhibited). In other words, if an incompatible response occurs in the presence of fear of a stimulus situation, and if the incompatible response is stronger than the fear, desensitization occurs, and the stimulus situation loses its capacity to evoke fear. The reciprocal inhibition theory is based on principles of classical conditioning. In order for desensitization to occur, according to the reciprocal inhibition principle, three processes are required:

1. A strong anxiety-competing or counterconditioning, response must be present. Usually this competing or inhibiting response is deep muscle relaxation. Although other responses (such as eating, assertion, and sexual ones) can be used, Wolpe (1982) believes relaxation is most helpful.
2. A graded series of anxiety-provoking stimuli is presented to the client. These stimulus situations are typically arranged in a hierarchy with low-intensity situations at the bottom and high-intensity situations at the top.
3. Contiguous pairing of one of these aversive stimulus situations and the competing, or counterconditioning, response (relaxation) must occur. This is usually accomplished by having the client achieve a state of deep relaxation and then imagine an aversive stimulus (presented as a hierarchy item) while relaxing. The client stops imagining the situation whenever anxiety (or any other emotion to be inhibited) occurs. After additional relaxation, the situation is represented several times.

In recent years, some parts of the reciprocal inhibition principle have been challenged, both by personal opinion and by empirical explorations. There is some doubt that relaxation functions in the manner suggested by Wolpe—as a response that is inherently antagonistic to anxiety (Lang, 1969). As Kazdin and Wilcoxon (1976) observe, some research indicates that desensitization is not dependent on muscle relaxation or a hierarchical arrangement of anxiety-provoking stimuli or the pairing of these stimuli with relaxation as an incompatible response (p. 731). These research results have led some people to abandon a reciprocal inhibition explanation for desensitization.

Desensitization by Extinction

Lomont (1965) proposed that extinction processes account for the results of desensitization. In other words, anxiety responses diminish as a result of presenting conditioned stimuli without reinforcement. This theory is based on principles of operant conditioning. Wolpe (1976) agrees that desensitization falls within this operational definition of extinction and that extinction may play a role in desensitization. Similarly, Wilson and Davison (1971) have argued that desensitization reduces a client's anxiety level sufficiently that the client gradually approaches the feared stimuli and the fear is then extinguished.

Some studies indicate that other factors, including habituation (Mathews, 1971; van Egeren, 1971), gender of the counselor and the client (Geer & Hurst, 1976), and reinforcement and instructions (Leitenberg, Agras, Barlow, & Oliveau, 1969) may be at least partly responsible for the results of desensitization.

Desensitization as Self-Control Training

In 1971 Goldfried challenged the idea that desensitization was a relatively passive process of deconditioning. Goldfried proposed that desensitization involved learning a general anxiety-reducing skill, rather than mere desensitization to some specific aversive stimulus (p. 228). According to this self-control explanation, the client learns to use relaxation as a way to cope with anxiety or to bring anxiety under control, not simply to replace anxiety. Eventually the client learns to identify the cues for muscular tension, to respond by relaxing away the tension, and to relabel the resulting emotion (p. 229). As learning occurs, Goldfried hypothesized, the relaxation responses may become "anticipatory," having the effect of partly or completely "short-circuiting" the anxiety or fear (p. 229).

Goldfried (1971) suggested certain modifications in the desensitization procedure that are more consistent with his view of the process. The client is told that desensitization involves learning the skill of relaxation as a way to cope with anxiety. During relaxation training, emphasis is placed on having the client become aware of sensations associated with tension and learning to use these sensations as a cue to relax. Since emphasis is placed on training the client to cope with anxiety cues and responses, the situations that elicit the anxiety are less important. Therefore, a single hierarchy can be used that reflects a variety of stimulus situations, not just those involving one theme (the latter is the procedure advocated by Wolpe, 1982). According to the reciprocal inhibition theory, the relaxation response must be stronger than the anxiety response. Therefore, the client is taught to stop visualizing the anxiety-provoking situation when anxious and to relax. In Goldfried's model, the client is instructed to maintain the image even though anxious and to relax away the tension. Finally, the client is taught to apply the skill to *in vivo* situations (pp. 231–232).

These procedural aspects of the self-control desensitization model were compared with the traditional (reciprocal inhibition) procedure of desensitization for the treatment of speech and test anxiety in college students (Zemore, 1975). Both methods produced improvements in treated *and* untreated fears of clients. Another study comparing these two methods of desensitization as a test-anxiety treatment found that they were comparable on the dependent measures; the self-control model showed significantly greater anxiety reduction on one test-anxiety self-report measure (Spiegler et al., 1976). These authors noted that, in the self-control model, only 4 of the 21 hierarchy items used dealt specifically with test-anxiety situations, supporting Goldfried's (1971) assumption that not all situations in the problem area need be included in the hierarchy for desensitization to occur (Spiegler et al., 1976). Further support for this position was reported by Goldfried and Goldfried (1977), who found no difference between speech-anxious subjects desensitized with a hierarchy relevant to speech anxiety and other speech-anxious people desensitized with a totally unrelated hierarchy. In another study, test-anxious students treated by self-control desensitization did better on both self-report and performance measures than students receiving standardized desensitization from a reciprocal inhibition framework (Denney & Rupert, 1977). More recent evidence of the efficacy of self-control desensitization was

provided in the treatment of a multiphobic child (Bornstein & Knapp, 1981) and in the treatment of fear of flying (Rebman, 1983).

Given the controversy surrounding the process of desensitization, what conclusions can be drawn about the possible ways to implement the procedure? First of all, perhaps there is no single right way to proceed with desensitization. A variety of procedural steps may be effective. Second, the specific ways in which desensitization is used will reflect the counselor's biases and preferences. To the extent that you believe a particular way of using desensitization works, this belief will only enhance the outcomes. Third, the details of the desensitization procedure should be adapted to each client. Very few studies have explored possible interactions between procedural variations in desensitization and client characteristics. Individual clients may respond differently to the particular rationale they receive or to the particular way a hierarchy is used. The counselor should always try to implement desensitization in a way that is likely to produce the best results for each client. Finally, perhaps the overall procedure of desensitization should integrate a variety of components from several theoretical explanations to ensure that no important contributing variable is overlooked. We have tried to do this in our presentation of the procedural aspects of desensitization in the following section. Figure 18-1 shows the seven major components of systematic desensitization. A summary of the procedural steps associated with each component is found in the Interview Checklist for Systematic Desensitization at the end of the chapter.

☐ COMPONENTS OF DESENSITIZATION

Treatment Rationale

The purpose and overview given to the client about desensitization are very important for several reasons. First, the rationale and overview establish the particular model or way in which the counselor plans to implement the procedure. The client is therefore informed of the principles of desensitization. Second, the outcomes of desensitization may be enhanced when the client is given very clear instructions and a positive expectancy set (Leitenberg et al., 1969). The *particular* rationale and overview you present to the client depend on the actual way you plan to implement desensitization.

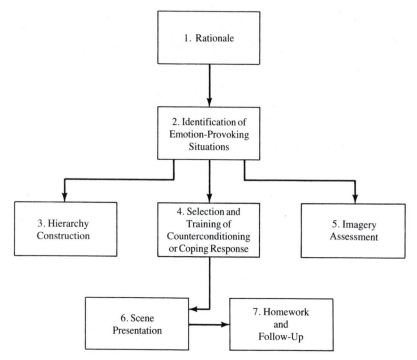

Figure 18-1. Components of systematic desensitization procedure

Rationale and overview of counterconditioning model. If you plan to use a counterconditioning model, you would present a rationale that explains how the client's fear or other conditioned emotion can be counterconditioned using desensitization. Your overview of the procedure would emphasize the use of an anxiety-free response to replace the conditioned emotion, the construction of a hierarchy consisting of a graduated series of items representing the emotion-provoking situations, and the pairing of these hierarchy items with the anxiety-free response (such as relaxation).

One rationale and overview based on a counterconditioning model has been used by Osterhouse (1976) in group-administered desensitization for test anxiety. Portions of this rationale are reprinted below:

The procedure we will use to help you overcome any unusually strong fears of examinations is called desensitization. . . . This approach is based upon the fact that it is impossible to be afraid and relaxed at the same time. For example, a student might want to ask a professor a question, or perhaps criticize something the professor has said. He may find, however, when he starts to speak that he experi-

ences shortness of breath, his heart pounds, or his hands perspire. He is unable to make his point. These are anxiety reactions and don't occur when the student is relaxed. Therefore, an important part of the method involves teaching you to relax as completely as possible. You may think that you don't have to be taught how to relax, but the fact is that most people are frequently unaware of their tensions.

Once you have learned how to relax, then this group will develop a list of situations in which the anxiety occurs. This list will be made up so that it contains items representing many different degrees of anxiety. . . . This list is called a hierarchy. . . .

One of the most interesting aspects of this procedure is that it tends to generalize to real life situations. Even though the procedure only requires you to imagine yourself in situations related to fear of examinations, there is a strong tendency for fear to decrease in the actual situation [p. 270].*

* From "Group Systematic Desensitization of Test Anxiety," by Robert A. Osterhouse, in *Counseling Methods,* edited by John D. Krumboltz and Carl E. Thoresen, copyright © 1976 by Holt, Rinehart and Winston, Inc., reprinted by permission of the publisher.

Rationale and overview of self-control model. If you plan to implement desensitization by emphasizing coping and self-control skills for tension management, your rationale and overview should reflect this emphasis. Goldfried (1971) suggests the following rationale and overview for explaining desensitization as training in self-control:

There are various situations where, on the basis of your past experience, you have learned to react by becoming tense (anxious, nervous, fearful). What I plan to do is help you to learn how to cope with these situations more successfully, so that they do not make you as upset. This will be done by taking note of a number of those situations which upset you to varying degrees, and then having you learn to cope with the less stressful situations before moving on to the more difficult ones. Part of the treatment involves learning how to relax so that in situations where you feel yourself getting nervous you will be better able to eliminate this tenseness. Learning to relax is much like learning any other skill. When a person learns to drive, he initially has difficulty in coordinating everything, and often finds himself very much aware of what he is doing. With more and more practice, however, the procedures involved in driving become easier and more automatic. You may find the same thing occurring to you when you try to relax in those situations where you feel yourself starting to become tense. You will find that as you persist, however, it will become easier and easier [p. 231].*

In one study, test-anxious students who received this sort of active coping rationale for desensitization achieved significantly better grade-point averages than students who received a rationale explaining desensitization according to the principle of classical conditioning (Denney & Rupert, 1977).

□ MODEL DIALOGUE: RATIONALE

Here is an example of a rationale the counselor could use to explain to Joan how desensitization can help her with her fear and avoidance of math class:

"Joan, we've talked about how you get very nervous before and during your math class. Some-

* From "Systematic Desensitization as Training in Self-Control" by M. R. Goldfried. *Journal of Consulting and Clinical Psychology, 37,* 228–234. Copyright © 1971 by the American Psychological Association. Reprinted by permission.

times you try to skip it. But you realize you haven't always felt this way about math. You've *learned* to feel this way. There is a procedure called desensitization that can help you replace your tension with relaxation. Eventually, the things about math class you now fear will not be tense situations for you. This procedure has been used very successfully to help other people reduce their fear of a certain situation.

"In desensitization, you will learn how to relax. After you're relaxed, I'll ask you to imagine some things about your math class—starting with not too stressful things and gradually working with more stressful things. As we go along, the relaxation will start to replace the anxiety. These stressful situations then will no longer seem so stressful to you.

"What questions do you have about this?"

Identification of Emotion-Provoking Situations

If the counselor and client have defined the problem thoroughly, there will already be some indications about the dimensions or situations that provoke anxiety (or any other emotional arousal) in the client. However, the counselor and client must be sure to isolate the most crucial situations in which the client should become less anxious or upset (Goldfried & Davison, 1976, p. 114). This is not always an easy task, as first appearances can be deceiving. Wolpe (1973) cites cases in which the initial problem seemed to indicate fear of open places (agoraphobia), yet the complaint was related to difficult unresolved situations in the client's marriage. Goldfried and Davison recommend that counselors ask themselves and their clients what the consequences may be of desensitization to one thing or another (p. 115).

The emotion-provoking situations must be defined idiosyncratically for each client. Marquis, Ferguson, and Taylor (1973) observe that, even among clients who have the same type of fear or phobia, the specific anxiety-provoking situations associated with the fear can vary greatly.

There are at least three ways in which the counselor can try to identify past and present situations that are anxiety-provoking to the client. These three methods are the interview assessment, client self-monitoring, and client completion of related self-report questionnaires.

Interview assessment. The interview assessment will be similar to the interview assessment we proposed in Chapters 7 and 8 on problem assessment. The counselor should use leads that will establish the particular circumstances and situations that elicit the conditioned emotion. For instance, does the client feel anxious in all social situations or only those with strangers present? Does the client's anxiety vary with the number of people present? with whether the client is accompanied or alone? Does the client experience more anxiety with people of the same or the other sex? These are examples of the kinds of information the interview assessment could provide about a client's anxiety in certain social situations.

Client self-monitoring. In addition to the information obtained during the session, the counselor may obtain even more data by having the client observe and record on a log the emotion-provoking situations as they occur during the week. The client would observe and note what was going on, where, with whom, and when the emotion, such as anxiety, was detected. The client also might rate the level of anxiety felt during the situation on a scale of 1 (low) to 10 (high) or on a scale of 0 (no anxiety) to 100 (panic).*

Self-report questionnaires. Some counselors find that additional data about particular emotion-provoking situations can be gained by having the client complete one or more self-report questionnaires. A commonly used questionnaire is the Wolpe-Lang (1964) Fear Survey Schedule (FSS). Lick and Katkin (1976) present descriptions of other self-report measures of fear and anxiety.

The counselor should persist in this identification process until specific emotion-provoking situations are identified. Marquis et al. (1973, p. 2) indicate that information gathering is not complete until the counselor knows the factors related to the onset and maintenance of the client's problem and until the client believes that all pertinent information has been shared with the counselor. At this point, the counselor and client are ready to construct a hierarchy.

☐ MODEL DIALOGUE: IDENTIFYING EMOTION-PROVOKING SITUATIONS

Counselor: Joan, we've already discussed some of the situations about your math class that make you feel anxious. What are some of these?

---

* Although 1–5 and 1–7 rating scales are recommended in Chapter 10, the 0–100 rating scale is typically used in desensitization because it corresponds to the suds scaling method described later in this chapter.

Client: Well, before class, just thinking about having to go bothers me. Sometimes at night I get anxious —not so much doing math homework but studying for tests.

Counselor: OK. Can you list some of the things that happen during your math class that you feel anxious about?

Client: Well, always when I take a test. Sometimes when I am doing problems and don't know the answers—having to ask Mr. _____ for help. And, of course, when he calls on me or asks me to go to the board.

Counselor: OK, good. And I believe you said before that you feel nervous about volunteering answers, too.

Client: Right—that, too.

Counselor: And yet these sorts of situations don't seem to upset you in your other classes?

Client: No. And really math class has never been as bad as it is this year. I guess part of it is the pressure of getting closer to graduating and, well, my teacher makes me feel dumb. I felt scared of him the first day of class. Yet I've always felt somewhat nervous about working with numbers.

Counselor: So some of your fear centers on your teacher, too—and then perhaps there's some worry about doing well enough to graduate.

Client: Right. Although I know I won't do *that* badly.

Counselor: OK, good. You realize that, even with not liking math and worrying about it, you won't get a bad grade.

Client: Not worse than a C.

Counselor: There's one thing I'd like you to do this week. Could you make a list of anything about the subject of math—and your math class—that has happened and has made you nervous? Also, write down anything about math or your class that *could* happen that you would feel anxious about. Then, if you think it's a situation that makes you a little anxious, mark *L* by it. If it's average, mark *A*. If it does or could make you very nervous, mark *V*.

Client: OK.

Counselor: Earlier, too, you had mentioned that sometimes these same feelings occur in situations with your parents, so after we work with math class, we'll come back and work on the situations with you and your parents.

Hierarchy Construction

A hierarchy is a list of stimulus situations to which the client reacts with graded amounts of anxiety or some other emotional response (Wolpe, 1958). Hierarchy construction can consume a good deal of interview time because of the various factors involved in constructing an adequate hierarchy.

These factors include selection of a type of hierarchy, the number of hierarchies (single or multiple), identification of hierarchy items, identification of control items, and ranking and spacing of items.

Types of hierarchies. On the basis of the stimulus situations that evoke anxiety (or any emotion to be counterconditioned), the counselor should select an appropriate type of hierarchy in which to cast individual items or descriptions of the aversive situations. Marquis et al. (1973, pp. 3–4) describe three kinds of hierarchies: spatiotemporal, thematic, and personal. Spatiotemporal and thematic hierarchies are used more commonly than personal ones, and an occasional hierarchy may be a combination of any of these three types. The particular type used will depend on the client's problem, the counselor's preferences, and the client's preferences.

A spatiotemporal hierarchy is developed by using items that represent physical or time dimensions, such as distance from one's house or time before taking an exam. In either case, anxiety, for example, seems to vary with proximity to the feared object or situation. Someone who is afraid to leave the house will get more anxious as the distance from home increases. A client who has "exam panic" will get more anxious as the exam draws closer. Therefore, in developing a spatiotemporal hierarchy, usually more items are put at the high end of the scale than at the low end, so the space or time differences at the high end of the scale are smaller.

Here is an example of a *spatiotemporal hierarchy* used with a client who was very fearful of taking tests. The items are arranged in terms of time:

1. Your instructor announces on the first day of class that the first exam will be held in one month. You know that the month will go quickly.
2. A week before the exam, you are sitting in class and the instructor reminds the class of the exam date. You realize you have a lot of studying to do during the week.
3. You are sitting in the class and the instructor mentions the exam, scheduled for the next class session, two days away. You realize you still have a lot of pages to read.
4. Now it is one day before the exam. You are studying in the library. You wonder whether you have studied as much as everyone else in the class.

5. It is the night before the test. You are in your room studying. You think about the fact that this exam grade is one-third of your final grade.
6. It is the night before the exam—late evening. You have just finished studying and have gone to bed. You're lying awake going over your reading in your mind.
7. You wake up the next morning and your mind flashes to this being exam day. You wonder how much you will remember of what you read the night and day before.
8. It is later in the day, one hour before the exam. You do some last-minute scanning of your lecture notes. You start to feel a little hassled—even a little sick. You wish you had more time to prepare.
9. It is 15 minutes before the class—time to walk over to the classroom. As you're walking over, you realize how important this grade will be. You hope you don't "blank out."
10. You go into the building, stop to get a drink of water, and then enter the classroom. You look around and see people laughing. You think that they are more confident and better prepared than you.
11. The instructor is a little late. You are sitting in class waiting for the teacher to come and pass out the tests. You wonder what will be on the test.
12. The instructor has just passed out tests. You receive your copy. Your first thought is that the test is so long—will you finish in time?
13. You start to work on the first portion of the test. There are some questions you aren't sure of. You spend time thinking and then see that people around you are writing. You skip these questions and go on.
14. You look at your watch. The class is half over—only 25 minutes left. You feel you have dawdled on the first part of the test. You wonder how much your grade will be pulled down if you don't finish.
15. You continue to work as fast as you can; occasionally you worry about the time. You glance at your watch—five minutes left. You still have a lot of unanswered questions.
16. Time is just about up. There are some questions you had to leave blank. You worry again about this test being one-third of your grade.

A *thematic hierarchy* consists of items exposing the client to various components or parameters of feared objects, activities, or situations. For example, a client who is afraid of criticism or disapproval may find that the fear varies depending on who criticizes, what is criticized, and how the criticism is delivered. Here is an example of a thematic hierarchy used with a person who found criticism very stressful:

1. A classmate whom you don't especially respect tells you you're too quiet and asks "What's the matter with you?"
2. A casual friend tells you that you looked tired today.
3. A good friend points out that the color of your attire isn't really "your best color."
4. Your tennis date, a person you consider to be just "OK," tells you that you need to improve your tennis game.
5. You're in class and the teacher assigns a group project. Your group is meeting and you offer an idea for the project — no one responds to it.
6. You run into a person you used to date regularly; he or she avoids speaking to you.
7. Your sister comes in and complains you've been too busy to pay much attention to her.
8. Your best friend comments that you seem moody today and aren't too much fun to be around.
9. Your mother suggests you're putting on a little weight and need to exercise more.
10. You meet someone you like and ask him or her to go to a game with you. The person turns down your invitation.
11. You get a paper back that you worked hard on. You only get a C. The teacher writes across the top "Some good ideas, but you didn't develop them at all."
12. You are in front of the class making an individual presentation. Several people in the class are talking and laughing as you speak.
13. Your father complains that your grades aren't as good as they should be and implies that you're lazy.
14. You're in your honors class. The class is engaged in a big discussion. You offer one idea. Someone responds with "That's dumb."

A *personal hierarchy* is not used as often as the other two types, but it is very useful with clients who are persistently bothered by thoughts or memories of a certain individual. Dengrove (1966) recommends the use of a personal hierarchy to desensitize anxiety related to the separation or termination of a relationship. Items at the bottom of

the hierarchy may consist of blissful or pleasant scenes or memories, progressing toward items at the top of the hierarchy representing painful or anxiety-provoking memories or thoughts (Marquis et al., 1973).

Here is an example of a personal hierarchy used with a male client who was bothered by painful memories of the termination of a close relationship:

1. You have been with Susie every day for the last month. You're sitting holding her in your arms and feeling like she's the only woman you'll ever love like this.
2. You and Susie are sitting on the floor in your apartment, drinking wine and listening to records.
3. You've just returned from taking Susie to her first race. She's ecstatic about the experience.
4. You and Susie are studying together in the library.
5. You and Susie are drinking beer at the local pub.
6. You and Susie aren't spending every day together. Sometimes she wants to study alone now. You're in the library by yourself studying.
7. You call Susie up late at night. The phone rings continuously without any answer. You wonder where she is.
8. You call Susie to ask her out for dinner and she turns you down — says she doesn't feel well.
9. You're walking down the street by the tennis court. You see Susie playing there with another person. You wonder why she hasn't told you about him.
10. You go over to Susie's. She isn't there. You wait until she comes. She sees you, goes back to her car, and drives away.
11. You call Susie on the phone. She says she doesn't want to see you anymore, that she never has really loved you, and hangs up on you.

Number of hierarchies. Whether you use one or several hierarchies also depends on the client's problem and preferences and on your preferences. Some therapists believe separate hierarchies should be constructed for different themes or different parameters of one theme (Marquis et al., 1973; Wolpe & Lazarus, 1966). Using multiple hierarchies may be less confusing but can require more time for hierarchy construction and presentation. Goldfried (1971) asserts that establishing separate hierarchies for carefully determined themes is not essential. He recommends constructing a single hierarchy composed of situations eliciting increasing amounts of tension, regardless of whether the hierarchy items represent any particular theme (p. 232). According to Goldfried, construction of a single hierarchy with items reflecting a variety of anxiety-provoking situations may facilitate generalization of the desensitization process from the session to the client's environment. Whether to use one or several hierarchies is a choice you will need to make during the process of hierarchy construction.

Identification of hierarchy items. The counselor must initiate a method of generating the items for the hierarchy. The client's role in this process is extremely important. Generally, the counselor can ask the client to aid in identifying hierarchy items by interview questions or by a homework assignment. The counselor can question the client about particular emotion-provoking scenes during the interview. Goldfried and Davison (1976) instruct clients to think of a large balloon and to draw items from different parts of the balloon that represent all the elements in the balloon. However, questioning the client about the scenes should not occur simultaneously with relaxation training. If the client is queried about hierarchy items after engaging in a period of deep relaxation, her or his responses may be altered.

If the client has difficulty responding concretely to interview questions, the counselor can assign homework for item identification. The counselor can give the client a stack of blank 3 × 5 index cards. The client is asked to generate items during the week and to write down each item on a separate note card. Often this homework assignment is useful even with clients who respond very thoroughly to the interview questions. During the week, the client has time to add items that were not apparent during the session.

The counselor should continue to explore and generate hierarchy items until a number have been identified that represent a range of aversive situations and varying degress of emotional arousal. A hierarchy typically contains 10 to 20 items but occasionally may have more or fewer. Goldfried and Davison (1976) and Marquis et al. (1973) suggest some criteria to use to construct adequate hierarchy items:

1. Some of the items should represent situations that, if carried out by the client *in vivo,* are under the client's control (do not require instigation from others).
2. An item must be concrete and specific. Embellishing the item description with sufficient details may help the client obtain a clear and vivid visualization of the item during scene presentation. As an example, an item that reads "Your best friend disapproves of you" is too general. A more concrete item would be "Your best friend disapproves of your boyfriend and tells you that you are stupid for going out with him."
3. Items should be similar to or represent actual situations the client has faced or may have to face in the future. If dialogue is written into an item, the language used should be adapted to the client.
4. Items selected should reflect a broad range of situations in which the client's fear (or other emotion) does or could occur.
5. Items should be included that reflect all different levels of the emotion, ranging from low to high intensity.

After the hierarchy items are identified, the client and counselor can identify several control items.

Identification of control items. A control item consists of a relaxing or neutral scene to which the client is not expected to have any strong emotional reaction. Control scenes are placed at the bottom of the hierarchy and represent a zero or "no anxiety" ranking. Some examples of control items are to "imagine a colored object," "imagine you're sitting in the sun on a day with a completely blue sky," or "imagine you're looking at a field of vivid yellow daffodils." A control item is often used to test the client's ability to visualize anxiety-free material and to give the client a relaxing or pleasant scene to imagine during scene presentation in order to enhance the level of relaxation. After all the hierarchy and control items have been identified, the client can arrange the items in order of increasing emotional arousal through a ranking method.

Ranking and spacing of hierarchy items. The counselor and client work together to identify an appropriate order for the items in the hierarchy. Generally, the client plays the major role in ranking, but the counselor must ensure that the spacing between items is satisfactory. The hierarchy items are ranked in order of increasing difficulty, stress, or emotional arousal. The control items are placed at the bottom of the hierarchy, and each item that represents more difficulty or greater anxiety is placed in a successively higher position in the hierarchy. Items at the top of the hierarchy represent the situations that are most stressful or anxiety-producing for the client.

The counselor should explain how the hierarchy items are arranged before asking the client to rank them. The counselor should also explain the purpose of this type of hierarchy arrangement so that the client fully understands the necessity of spending time to rank the items. The counselor can point out that desensitization occurs gradually and that the function of a hierarchy is to identify low-stress items to which the client will be desensitized before higher-stress items. The client's learning to face or cope with a feared situation will begin with more manageable situations first and gradually extend to more difficult situations. The counselor may emphasize that at no point will the client be asked to imagine or cope with a scene or situation that is very stressful before learning to deal successfully with less stressful scenes. This point is often reassuring to an occasional client whose anxiety is so great that the desensitization procedure itself is viewed with great trepidation.

There are several methods the client can use to order the hierarchy items. Three commonly used methods are rank-ordering; "suds" scaling; and low, medium, and high ordering. Rank-ordering is the simplest method. Each hierarchy item is written on a 3 × 5 note card (this note card is also useful later for the counselor to make notations about the item presentation). The client takes the stack of note cards and rank-orders the cards, with the least stressful situations at the bottom and successively more stressful items in an ascending order. The bottom item, a control item, can be assigned a 1; each successive item can be assigned one higher number. These numbers can be written at the top of each card in pencil, since the order of the items may change. After the client has rank-ordered the cards, the counselor can go over the order to determine whether there are too many or too few gaps between items. Items should be graduated evenly, with a fairly equal amount of difference between them. If items are bunched together, a few can be deleted. If there are large spaces between items, new ones can be added.

In the "suds" scaling method, items are arranged according to a point system in which the various points represent levels of the emotion referred to as "suds," or "subjective units of disturbance" (Wolpe & Lazarus, 1966). The most common scale is 100 points, where 0 suds represents complete relaxation and 100 suds indicates panic or an extremely stressful reaction. However, occasionally a 10-point suds scale is used, with 0 representing relaxation and 10 indicating panic. We think the 100-point scale is simpler to use, because the greater range of points makes adequate spacing between items easier. If a client uses the suds scale to arrange items, each item is assigned a number representing the amount of stress it generates for the client. If the item doesn't generate much stress, the client may assign it 10, 15, or 20 suds. Average amounts of stress might be assigned 35, 40, 45, or 50; whereas 85, 90, 95, and 100 suds represent situations that produce much anxiety or stress.

After the items are arranged according to the assigned suds, the counselor should make sure that no item is separated from the previous item by more than 10 suds; at the high end of the scale, spacing of no more than 5 suds between items is often necessary (Marquis et al., 1973). If there are large gaps (greater than 10 or 5 suds), the counselor and client should write additional, intermediate items to fill in. If there are too many items around the same level, particularly at the lower end of the hierarchy, some may be deleted. The suds system may require more explanation to the client and more time for item arrangement. However, it has advantages. First, the point system makes it easy to determine whether there is too much or too little space between items. Second, the use of the suds scale at this point in desensitization introduces the client to a way to discriminate and label varying degrees of relaxation and tension. Often this kind of labeling system is useful during relaxation training and scene presentation.

If the client has difficulty assigning exact suds ratings, a "low, medium, high" ranking method can be used instead. In this method, suggested by Goldfried and Davison (1976), the client rates items that produce little anxiety, which represent the bottom one-third of the hierarchy, or 0 to 33 suds; then rates average anxiety-producing items, which make up the middle of the hierarchy, or 34 to 66 suds; and finally the items that produce much anxiety, which compose the top end of the hierarchy, or 67 to 100 suds. The client can rank-order items within each group, after which the counselor can go over the items to make sure the spacing is reasonable.

Whichever ranking method is used, the counselor should emphasize that it is flexible and subject to change. Any type of hierarchy or order of items is useful only to the degree that it helps desensitize the emotion or helps the client to cope. Many times, a carefully constructed hierarchy will require some change during scene presentations.

Although we have described how to construct a hierarchy for an individual client, hierarchy construction can also be adapted for groups of clients. For some clients standardized hierarchies may work as well as individualized ones (Emery & Krumboltz, 1967; Howard, Murphy, & Clarke, 1983; McGlynn, Wilson, & Linder, 1970; Nawas, Fishman, & Pucel, 1970). For a description of hierarchy construction with a group of clients, see Osterhouse (1976).

□ MODEL DIALOGUE: HIERARCHY CONSTRUCTION

Counselor: Hi, Joan. I see you brought your list with you. That's great, because today we're going to work on a list that's called a hierarchy, which is like a staircase or a ladder. In your case, it will center on the theme or the idea of math anxiety. It's a list of all the situations about math that are anxiety-producing for you. We'll list these situations and then I'll ask you to rank them, starting with the less stressful ones. Does this seem clear?

Client: Yes. Actually I did something like that this week in making my list, didn't I?

Counselor: Right, you did. Now what we want to do is take your list, add any other situations that are stressful that aren't on here, and make sure each item on this list is specific. We may need to add some details to some of the items. The idea is to get a close description of the way the situation actually is or actually does or could happen. Let's take a look at your list now.

1. Sitting in English think about math class (L)
2. On way to math class (L)
3. At home, doing math homework (L)
4. At home, studying for a math test (A)
5. In math class, teacher giving out test (V)
6. In math class, taking test (V)
7. In math class, teacher asks me question (V)
8. In math class, at board, having trouble (V)
9. In math class, working problems at desk, don't know some answers (A)
10. Asking teacher for help (A)
11. Volunteering an answer (V)
12. Getting test or assignment back with low grade (V)
13. Teacher telling me I'll flunk or barely pass (V)
14. Doing anything with numbers, even outside math class, like adding up a list of numbers (A)
15. Talking about math with someone (A)

Counselor: Well, it looks like you've really worked hard at putting down some math situations that are stressful for you and indicating just how stressful they are. OK, let's go over this list and fill in some details. For each item here, can you write in one or two more details about the situation? What exactly happens that you feel nervous about? For instance, when you're sitting in English, what is it you're thinking that makes you nervous?

Client: OK, I see what you mean.

Counselor: Let's go over each item here, and as you tell me the details, I'll jot these down. [This step proceeds until a concrete description is obtained for each item. Counselor checks them to see whether items meet necessary criteria, which, with added details, these do. The criteria are: some items are under client's control; items are concrete; items represent past, present, or future anxiety-provoking scenes; items sample a broad range of situations; items represent varying levels of anxiety.]

Counselor: What else can you think of about math that is or could be stressful?

Client: Nothing right now. Not everything on my list has happened, but like if my teacher did tell me I was going to flunk, that would be very tense.

Counselor: You've got the idea. Now can you think of something not related to math that would be pleasant or relaxing for you to think about—like skiing down a slope or lying on the beach?

Client: Well, what about sitting in front of a campfire roasting marshmallows?

Counselor: Good. Now later on, as we proceed, I might ask you to relax by imagining a pleasant scene. Then you could imagine something like that.

Client: OK.

Counselor: I'd like you now to take these items we've listed on these cards and rank-order each item. We're going to put this pleasant item having to do with the campfire at the bottom of the list. Then go through the cards and put each card in an order from the least stressful to the most stressful situation. Is that clear?

Client: You mean the thing that bothers me least to the thing that makes me most nervous?

Counselor: Exactly. Each item as you go up the stack of cards should be a little more stressful than the previous item.

Client: OK. [Takes about ten minutes to rank-order the 16 cards.]

Counselor: OK. I'm going to lay each card out to see what you've got here, starting at the bottom.

Card 1: Sitting in front of a campfire on a cool night with friends, singing songs and roasting marshmallows [control item].

Card 2: Sitting in my room at my desk doing routine math homework over fairly easy material.

Card 3: Sitting in English about ten minutes before the bell. Thinking about going to math class next and wondering if I can hide or if I'll get called on.

Card 4: Walking down the hall with a couple of classmates to math class. Walking in the door and seeing the teacher looking over our homework. Wondering how I did.

Card 5: A girlfriend calls up and talks about our upcoming test in math — wonder if I'll pass it.

Card 6: Seeing a big list of numbers, like on a store receipt, and having to check the total to make sure it's OK.

Card 7: In math class, sitting at my desk; having to work on problems and coming across some that are confusing. Don't have much time to finish.

Card 8: Working on problems at my desk. I'm stumped on a couple. Nothing I try works. Having to go up and ask Mr. _____ for help. He tries to do it for me; I feel dumb.

Card 9: Sitting in my room at home the night before a big math test; studying for the test and wondering if I'll blank out on it.

Card 10: In math class taking a test and coming across some problems I don't know how to do.

Card 11: Waiting to get a test or an assignment back and worrying about a low grade.

Card 12: Sitting in math class and the teacher asks for the answer; raising my hand to volunteer it; wonder if it's right.

Card 13: Sitting in math class waiting for a big test to be passed out. Wondering what's on it and if I'll be able to remember things.

Card 14: Sitting in math class and suddenly the teacher calls on me and asks me for an answer. I feel unprepared.

Card 15: Sitting in math class and the teacher sends me to the board. I'm at the board trying to work a problem in front of the class. I'm getting stuck.

Card 16: The teacher calls me in for a conference after school. Mr. _____ is telling me I'm in big trouble and barely passing. There's a good chance I could flunk math.

Counselor: OK, now it seems like each of these items represents a somewhat more stressful situation. Do you feel that there are any large jumps between items — like going from a very low-stress situation to a higher-stress one suddenly?

Client (looks over list): No, I don't think so.

Counselor: OK, we'll stick with this list and this order for now. Of course, this is tentative. Later on, if we feel something needs to be moved around or added, we will do so.

LEARNING ACTIVITY #47: HIERARCHY CONSTRUCTION

This learning activity is designed to give you some practice in constructing different kinds of hierarchies. You can do this activity by yourself or with another person.

Part One: Spatiotemporal Hierarchy

Think of for yourself, or have your partner identify, a situation you fear and avoid. This situation should be something where the fear increases as the distance or time proximity toward the feared object or situation gets closer. For example, you might fear and avoid approaching certain kinds of animals or high places (distance). Or you might get increasingly anxious as the time before an exam, a speech, or an interview diminishes (time). For this situation, identify the specific situations that are anxiety-provoking. Try to identify all the relevant parameters of the situation.

For example, does your anxiety vary if you're alone or with another person, if you're taking a midterm or a quiz, if you're speaking before a large or a small group? List each anxiety-provoking situation that could be a hierarchy item on a separate index card. Also list one control (pleasant) item on a card. After you or your partner believes all the relevant items are listed, take the cards and rank-order them. The control item will be at the bottom, followed by items that evoke successively greater anxiety. Check the rank order to make sure items are equally spaced. Add or delete items as necessary.

Part Two: Thematic Hierarchy

This time, you or your partner should identify a situation you fear and avoid that is related to a certain

(continued)

theme: fear of being rejected or criticized, fear of engaging in risk-taking situations, fear of failure, fear of losing control, fear of getting ill or of death, and so on. Identify the particular anxiety-provoking situations associated with this theme, ones that have made or could make you anxious. Identify all the relevant parameters: does your fear vary with what you do? who is with you? List each anxiety-provoking situation that could represent a hierarchy item on a card or a piece of paper. After all the relevant items are listed, rank-order them, using the suds scale. Assign each item a number from 0 (no anxiety) to 100 (panic), depending on the intensity and amount of anxiety it provokes. Then arrange the items in order of increasing suds. Check to make sure there are no more than 10 suds between adjacent items and 5 suds between high-intensity items. Add or delete items as necessary.

Part Three: Personal Hierarchy

See whether you or your partner can identify a situation about which you have painful or unpleasant memories. Such situations might include loss of a prized object, loss of a job or friend, or termination of a close relationship. Generate emotion-provoking situations associated with pleasant memories and unpleasant memories. List each situation on a separate card. When all items are identified and listed, rank-order the cards into low, medium, and high groupings. Pleasant memories would constitute the low grouping, less pleasant the middle grouping, and very unpleasant the high grouping. Then, within each group, you can arrange the cards in another order from most pleasant at the bottom of the hierarchy to most painful at the top.

Selection and Training of Counterconditioning or Coping Response

According to the principles of reciprocal inhibition and counterconditioning, for desensitization to take place, the client must respond in a way that inhibits (or counterconditions) the anxiety or other conditioned emotion. A self-control model of desensitization emphasizes the client's learning of a skill to use to cope with the anxiety. In either model, the counselor selects, and trains the client to use, a response that can be considered either an alternative to anxiety or incompatible with anxiety.

Selection of a response. The counselor's first task is to select an appropriate counterconditioning or coping response for the client to use. Typically, the anxiety-inhibiting or counterconditioning response used in desensitization is deep muscle relaxation (Marquis et al., 1973; Wolpe, 1982). Goldfried (1971) also recommends muscle relaxation for use as the coping response. Muscle relaxation has some advantages. Levin and Gross (1985) found that relaxation heightens the vividness of imagery. Also, as you may remember from Chapter 17, its use in anxiety reduction and management is well documented. Wolpe (1982) prefers muscle relaxation because it doesn't require any sort of motor activity to be directed from the client toward the sources of anxiety (p. 135). Muscle relaxation is easily learned by most clients and easily

taught in the interview. It is also adaptable for daily client practice. However, an occasional client may have difficulty engaging in relaxation. Further, relaxation is not always applicable to *in vivo* desensitization, in which the client carries out rather than imagines the hierarchy items (Marquis et al., 1973).

When deep muscle relaxation cannot be used as the counterconditioning or coping response, the counselor may decide to proceed without this sort of response or to substitute an alternative response. In some cases, clients have been desensitized without relaxation (Daniels, 1974; Rachman, 1968). However, with a client who is very anxious, it may be risky to proceed without any response to counteract the anxiety. Many other examples of counterconditioning and coping responses have been used in desensitization, including emotive imagery and meditation (Boudreau, 1972), assertion responses, feeding responses, ginger ale (Mogan & O'Brien, 1972), music (Lowe, 1973), laughter (Ventis, 1973), sexual responses (Bass, 1974), anger (Goldstein, Serber, & Piaget, 1970), kung fu (Gershman & Stedman, 1976), and coping thoughts (Weissberg, 1975). Some of these responses quite obviously are less easily applied in an office setting but may be suitable for certain cases of *in vivo* or self-administered desensitization.

If muscle relaxation is not suitable for a client, emotive imagery (Chapter 14), meditation (Chapter 17), and coping thoughts (Chapter 16) may be reasonable substitutes that are practical to use in the interview and easy to teach. For example, if the counselor selects emotive imagery, the client can focus on pleasant scenes during desensitization. If meditation is selected, the client can focus on breathing and counting. In the case of coping thoughts, the client can whisper or subvocalize coping statements.

Explanation of response to the client. Whatever counterconditioning or coping response is selected, its use and purpose in desensitization should be explained to the client. The client will be required to spend a great deal of time in the session and at home learning the response. Usually a large amount of client time will result in more payoffs if the client understands how and why this sort of response should be learned.

In emphasizing that the response is for counterconditioning, the counselor can explain that one of the ways desensitization can help the client is by providing a substitute for anxiety (or other emotions). The counselor should emphasize that this substitute response is incompatible with anxiety and will minimize the felt anxiety so that the client does not continue to avoid the anxiety-provoking situations.

Goldfried (1971) recommends that explanations of relaxation as a coping response should inform clients that they will be made aware of sensations associated with tension and will learn to use these sensations as a signal to cope and to relax away the tension. After the client indicates understanding of the need for learning another response, the counselor can begin to teach the client how to use the selected response.

Training in the response. The counselor will need to provide training for the client in the particular response to be used. The training in muscle relaxation or any other response may require at least portions of several sessions to complete. The training in a counterconditioning or coping response can occur simultaneously with hierarchy construction. Half of the interview can be used for training; the rest can be used for hierarchy construction. Remember, though, that identifying hierarchy items should not occur simultaneously with relaxation. The counselor can follow portions of the interview protocol for cognitive restructuring (Chapter 16) for training in coping statements; the interview checklists for emotive imagery

(Chapter 14), muscle relaxation, and meditation (Chapter 17) can be used to provide training in these responses.

Before and after each training session, the counselor should ask the client to rate the felt level of stress or anxiety. This is another time when the suds scale is very useful. The client can use the 0-to-100 scale and assign a numerical rating to the level of anxiety. Generally, training in the counterconditioning or coping response should be continued until the client can discriminate different levels of anxiety and can achieve a state of relaxation after a training session equivalent to 10 or less on the 100-point suds scale (Marquis et al., 1973). If, after successive training sessions, the client has difficulty using the response in a nonanxious manner, another response may need to be selected.

After the client has practiced the response with the counselor's direction, daily homework practice should be assigned. An adequate client demonstration of the counterconditioning or coping response is one prerequisite for actual scene presentation. A second prerequisite involves a determination of the client's capacity to use imagery.

☐ MODEL DIALOGUE: SELECTION OF AND TRAINING IN COUNTERCONDITIONING OR COPING RESPONSE

Counselor: Joan, perhaps you remember that when I explained desensitization to you, I talked about replacing anxiety with something else, like relaxation. What I'd like to do today is show you a relaxation method you can learn. How does that sound?

Client: OK, is it like yoga?

Counselor: Well, it's carried out differently than yoga, but it is a skill you can learn with practice and it has effects similar to yoga. This is a process of body relaxation. It involves learning to tense and relax different muscle groups in your body. Eventually you will learn to recognize when a part of you starts to get tense, and you can signal to yourself to relax.

Client: Then how do we use it in desensitization?

Counselor: After you learn this, I will ask you to imagine the items on your hierarchy—but only when you're relaxed, like after we have a relaxation session. What happens is that you're imagining something stressful, only you're relaxed. After you keep working with this, the stressful situations become less and less anxiety-provoking for you.

Client: That makes sense to me, I think. The relaxation can help the situation to be less tense.

Counselor: Yes, it plays a big role — which is why I consider the time we'll spend on learning the relaxation skill so important. Now, one more thing, Joan. Before and after each relaxation session, I'll ask you to tell me how tense or how relaxed you feel at that moment. You can do this by using a number from 0 to 100 — 0 would be total relaxation and 100 would be total anxiety or tenseness. How do you feel right now, on that scale?

Client: Well, not totally relaxed, but not real tense. Maybe around a 30.

Counselor: OK. Would you like to begin with a relaxation-training session now?

Client: Sure. [Training in muscle relaxation following the interview checklist presented in Chapter 17 is given to Joan. An abbreviated version of this is also presented in the model dialogue on scene presentation, later in this chapter.]

Imagery Assessment

The typical administration of desensitization relies heavily on client imagery. The relearning (counterconditioning) achieved in desensitization occurs during the client's visualization of the hierarchy items. This, of course, assumes that imagination of a situation is equivalent to a real situation and that the learning that occurs in the imagined situation generalizes to the real situation (Goldfried & Davison, 1976, p. 113). M. J. Mahoney (1974) points out that recent evidence indicates there may be considerable variability in the degree to which these assumptions about imagery really operate. Still, if desensitization is implemented, the client's capacity to generate images is vital to the way this procedure typically is used.

Explanation to the client. The counselor can explain that the client will be asked to imagine the hierarchy items as if the client were a participant in the situation. The counselor might say that imagining a feared situation can be very similar to actually being in the situation. If the client becomes desensitized while imagining the aversive situation, then the client will also experience less anxiety when actually in the situation. The counselor can suggest that because people respond differently to using their imagination, it is a good idea to practice visualizing several situations.

Assessment of client imagery. The client's capacity to generate clear and vivid images can be assessed by use of practice (control) scenes or by a questionnaire, as described in Chapter 14. Generally, it is a good idea to assess the client's imagery for desensitization at two times — when the client is deliberately relaxed and when the client is not deliberately relaxed. According to Wolpe (1982), imagery assessment of a scene under relaxation conditions serves two purposes. First, it gives the therapist information about the client's ability to generate anxiety-free images. Second, it suggests whether any factors are present that may inhibit the client's capacity to imagine anxiety-free material. For example, a client who is concerned about losing self-control may have trouble generating images of a control item (Wolpe, 1982, p. 158). After each visualization, the counselor can ask the client to describe the details of the imagined scene aloud. Clients who cannot visualize scenes may have to be treated with an alternative strategy for fear reduction that does not use imagery, such as participant modeling or *in vivo* desensitization (see also page 506).

Criteria for effective imagery. Remember that, in the typical administration of desensitization, the client's use of imagery plays a major role. A client who is unable to use imagery may not benefit from a hierarchy that is presented in imagination. From the results of the client's imagery assessment, the counselor should determine whether the client's images meet the criteria for effective therapeutic imagery. These four criteria have been proposed by Marquis et al. (1973, p. 10):

1. The client must be able to imagine a scene concretely, with sufficient detail and evidence of touch, sound, smell, and sight sensations.
2. The scene should be imagined in such a way that the client is a participant, not an observer.
3. The client should be able to switch a scene image on and off upon instruction.
4. The client should be able to hold a particular scene as instructed without drifting off or changing the scene.

If these or other difficulties are encountered during imagery assessment, the counselor may decide to continue to use imagery and provide imagery training or to add a dialogue or a script; to present the hierarchy in another manner (slides, role plays, or *in vivo*); or to terminate desensitization and use an alternative therapeutic strategy. Whenever the client is able to report clear, vivid images that meet most of the necessary criteria, the counselor can initiate the "nuts and bolts" of desensitization—presentation of the hierarchy items.

☐ MODEL DIALOGUE: IMAGERY ASSESSMENT

The following assessment should be completed two times: once after a relaxation session and once when Joan is not deliberately relaxed.

Counselor: Joan, I will be asking you in the procedure to imagine the items we've listed in your hierarchy. Sometimes people use their imagination differently, so it's a good idea to see how you react to imagining something. Could you just sit back and close your eyes and relax? Now get a picture of a winter snow scene in your mind. Put yourself in the picture, doing something. [Pauses.] Now, can you describe exactly what you imagined?

Client: Well, it was a cold day, but the sun was shining. There was about a foot of snow on the ground. I was on a toboggan with two friends going down a big hill very fast. At the bottom of the hill we rolled off and fell in the snow. That was cold!

Counselor: So you were able to imagine sensations of coldness. What colors do you remember?

Client: Well, the hill, of course, was real white and the sky was blue. The sun kind of blinded you. I had on a bright red snow parka.

Counselor: OK, good. Let's try another one. I'll describe a scene and ask you to imagine it for a certain amount of time. Try to get a clear image as soon as I've described the scene. Then, when I say "Stop the image," try to erase it from your mind. OK, here's the scene. It's a warm, sunny day with a good breeze. You're out on a boat on a crystal-clear lake. OK—now imagine this—put in your own details. [Pauses.] OK, Joan, stop the image. Can you tell me what you pictured? [Joan describes the images.] How soon did you get a clear image of the scene after I described it?

Client: Oh, not long. Maybe a couple of seconds.

Counselor: Were you able to erase it when you heard me say *stop?*

Client: Pretty much. It took me a couple of seconds to get completely out of it.

Counselor: Did you always visualize being on a boat, or did you find your imagination wandering or revising the scene?

Client: No, I was on the boat the entire time.

Counselor: How do you feel about imagining a scene now?

Client: These are fun. I don't think imagination is hard for me anyway.

Counselor: Well, you do seem pretty comfortable with it, so we can go ahead.

Joan's images meet the criteria for effective imagery: the scenes are imagined concretely; she sees herself in a scene as a participant; she is able to turn the image on and off fairly well on instruction; she holds a scene constant; there is no evidence of any other difficulties.

Hierarchy Scene Presentation

Scenes in the hierarchy are presented after the client has been given training in a counterconditioning or coping response and after the client's imagery capacity has been assessed. Each scene presentation is paired with the counterconditioning or coping response so that the client's anxiety (or other emotion) is counterconditioned, or decreased. There are different ways to present scenes to the client. Our discussion of this component of desensitization reflects some of the possible variations of scene presentation. The counselor must select a method for presenting scenes and a method for client signaling before progressing with actual scene presentation. Scene presentations follow a certain format and usually are concluded after 15 to 20 minutes.

Identify and explain a method of scene presentation. The counselor will first need to decide on the method of scene presentation to use and explain it in detail to the client before proceeding. There are three methods of scene presentation; the alphabetical labels for these methods (R, H, and A) were coined by Evans (1974).

Method R is used mainly when implementing desensitization according to a traditional model based on the principles of reciprocal inhibition, or counterconditioning. In method R, when the client visualizes an item and reports anxiety associated with the visualization, the client is instructed to *remove* or stop the image, then to relax. According to Wolpe (1982), the timing of scene presentation should maximize the amount of time the client imagines a situation without anxiety and minimize the amount of time the client imagines a scene eliciting anxiety.

There are several reasons for having the client remove the image when anxiety occurs. First, the principle of reciprocal inhibition assumes that, for a response such as anxiety to be successfully counterconditioned, the relaxation (or other counterconditioning) response must be stronger than the anxiety response. This principle is applied to scene presentation, so that the reaction any given item elicits from the client is never stronger than the nonanxiety response being used. In the presence of anxiety, the client is told to stop the image to prevent the anxiety from escalating to the point where it might be stronger than the client's state of relaxation. According to Wolpe (1982), continued exposure to a disturbing scene may even increase the client's sensitivity to it. This is an added reason to terminate the scene when it evokes a strong client reaction. However, some studies have found that sensitivity to a scene does not increase when clients are asked to hold the image in spite of tension (Spiegler et al., 1976; Zemore, 1975). These findings have lent some credence to a method of scene presentation based on a self-control model of desensitization. This has been identified by Evans (1974) as method H.

In method H, when the client indicates anxiety associated with any given scene, the counselor asks the client to *hold* the image, to continue with the visualization, and to relax away the tension. Goldfried (1971) asserts that this is a more realistic method of scene presentation, since in real life the client can't "eliminate" a situation on becoming tense. This method of scene presentation was used successfully in three studies (Denney & Rupert, 1977; Spiegler et al., 1976; Zemore, 1975).

A third method of scene presentation is called method A (Evans, 1974). In method A, when the client indicates tension, he or she is instructed to switch the image to an "*adaptive alternative*" (p. 45). This might consist in an appropriate response in the feared situation or a coping response, similar to the coping thoughts taught to clients in cognitive restructuring and stress inoculation (Chapter 16). For example, a client who feared losing control of his temper with his children might be presented with the hierarchy item: "It is 5:00 at night. You are trying to fix dinner. Your three children are running underfoot and screaming. The telephone and doorbell both ring at the same time." If this item is tension-producing for the client (what parent wouldn't be tense!), he would be instructed to switch off this image and to visualize an adaptive coping response, something he can do that is under his control, such as "Think of staying calm and collected. Ask one child to get the door, the other to answer the phone. Make sure things in the oven are under control before going to the phone or to the door." These coping scenes should be worked out with the client before the hierarchy items are actually presented. This method also has some empirical support (Meichenbaum, 1972).

According to Meichenbaum, client use of coping imagery is based on the premise that when clients imagine hierarchy items, they provide themselves with "a model for their own behavior" (p. 372).

Identify and explain a signaling system. After explaining the scene-presentation method, the counselor will need to explain the use of a signaling process. During the presentation of hierarchy items, there are several times when the counselor and client need to communicate. In order not to interrupt the client's achievement of a relaxed state, it is useful to work out a signaling system the client can use in a relatively nondistracting manner. To prevent the signals from "getting crossed," it is a good idea to identify and explain a signaling system to the client before actually starting to present the hierarchy items.

There is no one right signaling method, and several can be used. You should select one that is clear to both you and the client to prevent any confusion. One signaling method advocated by Wolpe (1982) is to instruct the client to raise the left index finger one inch as soon as a clear image of the item is formed. Wolpe presents the item for a specified time (usually about seven seconds) and then asks the client to stop the image and to rate the level of anxiety felt during the visualization with a number on the 0-to-100 suds scale. This signaling method allows the counselor to determine whether and when the visualization begins. It also provides immediate feedback about the client's suds level of disturbance.

An alternative signaling method is to ask the client to imagine the scene and to indicate whether any anxiety is felt by raising an index finger. This signaling system has the advantage of letting the counselor know the time when the client started to notice the tension. However, with this method, the counselor cannot be sure when the visualization began, nor does the counselor obtain an exact rating of the client's anxiety.

Another signaling method used to indicate quantitative changes in anxiety is to instruct the client to raise a hand as the anxiety goes up (say, above 10 suds) and to lower it as the anxiety decreases (Marquis et al., 1973). This signaling method might be advantageous when the counselor asks the client to hold a scene image and to relax away the tension. The counselor can determine when the client does successfully lower the tension level.

A fourth method of signaling involves use of the words *tense* and *calm* in lieu of hand or finger signals. The client is instructed to say "tense" when anxiety is noticed and "calm" when relaxation is achieved. Marquis et al. (1973, p. 9) point out that this method may be slightly more disruptive of relaxation than hand or finger signals, but it may be clearer and prevent misunderstanding of signals.

None of these methods needs to be used arbitrarily. The counselor may wish to discuss possible signaling methods and encourage the client to choose one. Such choices strengthen the client's belief that she or he is an active, responsible participant in the treatment process. If one signaling method is used initially and seems distracting or confusing, it can be changed.

Format of a scene-presentation session. As soon as the scene-presentation and signaling methods are determined, the counselor can initiate scene presentation. Scene presentation follows a fairly standardized format. Each scene-presentation session should be preceded by a training session involving the designated counterconditioning or coping response. As you will recall, the idea is to present the hierarchy items concurrently with some counterconditioning or coping response. For example, the counselor can inform the client that they will go through a period of relaxation, after which the counselor will ask the client to imagine a scene from the hierarchy. Depending on the particular counterconditioning or coping response to be used, the client should engage in a brief period of muscle relaxation, meditation, or emotive imagery. The client's relaxation rating following this period should be 10 or less on the 100-point suds scale before the counselor presents a hierarchy item.

At this point, the counselor begins by describing a hierarchy item to the client and instructing the client to evoke the scene in imagination. The initial session begins with the first (least anxiety-provoking) item in the hierarchy. Successive scene presentations always begin with the last item successfully completed at the preceding session. This helps to make a smooth transition from one session to the next and checks on learning retention. Starting with the last successfully completed item may also prevent spontaneous recovery of the anxiety response (Marquis et al., 1973, p. 11). Sometimes relapse between two scene-presentation sessions does occur (Agras, 1965; Rachman, 1966), and this procedure is a way to check for it.

In presenting the item, the counselor should describe it and ask the client to imagine it. Usually the counselor presents an item for a specified amount of time before asking the client to stop the image. There is no set duration for scene presentation. Marquis et al. (1973) point out that typically the client is asked to visualize the scene for 20 seconds. Even clients who signal anxiety before 20 seconds are up may be asked to continue to picture the scene for the full time. Clients are then asked to remove the image and relax (the R method), or to switch to an adaptive alternative (the A method).

There are several reasons that a visualization period of at least 20 (and perhaps up to 40) seconds may be important. First, if the client signals anxiety before this time and the counselor immediately instructs the client to stop the image, some avoidance responses may be inadvertently reinforced (Miller & Nawas, 1970). Second, some evidence indicates that both physiological and self-report indexes of anxiety show greater reduction with a longer scene duration, such as 30 seconds per scene (Eberle, Rehm, & McBurney, 1975; Ross & Proctor, 1973; Rudestam & Bedrosian, 1977). Longer scene presentation may result in even greater anxiety reduction for high-intensity items (Eberle et al., 1975) and faster desensitization of high-intensity items (Watts, 1971, 1974). Watts also found that a longer scene presentation of 30 to 45 seconds tended to prevent spontaneous recovery of previously desensitized items.

If the client holds the scene for the specified duration and does not report any tension, the counselor can instruct the client to stop the scene and to take a little time to relax. This relaxation time serves as a breather between item presentations. During this time, the counselor can cue the onset of relaxation with descriptive words such as "let all your muscles relax" or with the presentation of a control item. There is no set time for a pause between items. Generally a pause of 30 to 60 seconds is sufficient, although some clients may need as much as two or three minutes (Marquis et al., 1973).

If the client indicates that anxiety was experienced during the visualization, the counselor will instruct the client to remove the image and relax (method R), hold the image and relax away the tension (method H), or switch the image to an adaptive or coping alternative (method A). Generally, the counselor will pause for 30 to 60 seconds and then present the same item again. Successful coping or anxiety reduction with one item is required before presenting the next hierarchy item. Marquis et al. (1973, p. 11) indicate that an item can be considered successfully completed with two successive no-anxiety presentations. However, items that are very anxiety-arousing, such as those at the high end of the hierarchy, may require three or four successive no-anxiety repetitions or altering items in the hierarchy (Foa et al., 1980).

If an item continues to elicit anxiety after three presentations, this may indicate some trouble and a need for adjustment. Continued anxiety for one item may indicate a problem in the hierarchy or in the client's visualization. There are at least three things a counselor can try to alleviate continual anxiety resulting from the same item: a new, less anxiety-provoking item can be added to the hierarchy; the same item can be presented to the client more briefly; or the client's visualization can be assessed to determine whether the client is drifting from or revising the scene.

The counselor should be careful to use standardized instructions at all times during scene-presentation sessions. Standardized instructions are important regardless of whether the client signals anxiety or reports a high or a low anxiety rating on the suds scale. Rimm and Masters (1979) observe that a counselor can inadvertently reinforce a client for not signaling anxiety by saying "Good." The client, often eager to please the counselor, may learn to avoid giving reports of anxiety because these are not similarly reinforced.

Each scene-presentation session should end with an item that evokes no anxiety or receives a low suds rating, since the last item of a series is well remembered (Lazarus & Rachman, 1957). At times, the counselor may need to return to a lower item on the hierarchy so that a non-anxiety-provoking scene can end the session. Generally, any scene-presentation session should be terminated

Subject's Name: Jane Doe

Theme of Hierarchy: Criticism

Time needed to relax at the beginning of the session: 15 minutes

Time needed to visualize the scene presented: 10 sec./8 sec./9 sec./5 sec.

Date and Total Time Spent in Session	Item Hierarchy Number	Anxiety + or − or Suds Rating		Time between Items	Comments, Observations, Changes in Procedure, or Other Special Treatment
7-14-84 45 minutes	4	+8 +20	−15 +30	60 sec./ 60 sec./ 30 sec./ 60 sec./	

Figure 18-2. Desensitization record sheet (from *A guidebook for systematic desensitization* (3rd ed.), by J. Marquis, W. Morgan, and G. Piaget. 1973, Veterans' Workshop, Palo Alto, California. Reprinted by permission.)

when three to five hierarchy items have been completed successfully or at the end of 15 to 30 minutes, whichever comes first. A session may be terminated sooner if the client seems restless. Desensitization requires a great deal of client concentration, and the counselor should not try to extend a session beyond the client's concentration limits.

Identify notation method. Desensitization also requires some concentration and attention on the counselor's part. Just think about the idea of conducting perhaps four or five scene-presentation sessions with one client and working with one or more hierarchies with 10 to 20 items per hierarchy! The counselor has a great deal of information to note and recall. Most counselors use some written recording method during the scene-presentation sessions. There are several ways to make notations of the client's progress in each scene-presentation session. We will describe three. These methods are only suggestions; you may discover a notation system that parallels more closely your own procedural style of desensitization.

Marquis et al. (1973) use a "Desensitization Record Sheet" to record the hierarchy item numbers and the anxiety or suds rating associated with each item presentation. Their record sheet is shown in Figure 18-2, with a sample notation provided at the top of the sheet.

Goldfried and Davison (1976) use a notation system written on the 3 × 5 index card that contains the description of the hierarchy item and the item number. Under the item description is space for the counselor to note the duration of the item presentations and whether item presentation elicited anxiety. An example is presented in Figure 18-3. In this example, the numbers refer to the time in seconds that the client visualized each presentation of the item. The plus sign indicates a no-anxiety or low-suds visualization, and the minus sign indicates an anxiety or high-suds visualization. Note that there were two successive no-anxiety visualizations (+30 and +40) before the item was terminated.

One of the most comprehensive notation methods has been developed by Evans (1974), using the front and back of a preprinted 4 × 6 index card. Notations about the client's progress in scene presentation are made on categories listed on the back of the card.

The front of this record is shown in Figure 18-4. On this side of the card, the hierarchy scene itself is

---

Item No. 6
Date 7-14-84

ITEM DESCRIPTION

You are walking to class thinking about the
upcoming exam. Your head feels crammed full of details.
You are wondering whether you've studied the right
material.

+5 −9 +10 −15 +20 −25 +30 +40

Figure 18-3. Adaptation of figure "Sample Hierarchy Card in Traditional Desensitization," from *Clinical Behavior Therapy* by Marvin R. Goldfried and Gerald C. Davison. Copyright © 1976 by Holt, Rinehart and Winston, Inc., reprinted by permission of the publisher.

HIERARCHY SCENE
  1. You are walking to class thinking about the
upcoming exam. Your head feels crammed full of
details. You are wondering whether you've studied the
right material.

VARIATIONS
  2.

  3.

  4.

Figure 18-4. *Front of record card* (from "A handy record-card for systematic desensitization hierarchy items," by I. M. Evans, *Journal of Behavior Therapy and Experimental Psychiatry,* 1974, *5,* 43–46. Copyright 1974 by Pergamon Press, Inc. Reprinted by permission.)

Item: 6   Theme: Test anxiety   Anxiety Rating: 70 Suds   Rank Order: 6
Adaptive Alternative: Concentrate on what you've studied, not
                        whether it is right or wrong.

PRESENTATION:	1	2	3	4	5	
Version	#1					Starting Suds: 5
Image Latency	8 sec.					Difficulties:
Duration Held	15 sec.					
Image Clarity	08					
Anxiety Latency	10 sec.					Physiological:
Strategy: R/H/A/	A					Some flushing of
Anxiety Decrease	25 sec.					neck.
Duration Held	5 sec.					Date Completed:
Anxiety Suds	45 suds					7-14-84
						Success *In Vivo:*
						7-28-84

Figure 18-5. *Back of record card* (from "A handy record-card for systematic desensitization hierarchy items," by I. M. Evans, *Journal of Behavior Therapy and Experimental Psychiatry,* 1974, *5,* 43–46. Copyright 1974 by Pergamon Press, Inc. Reprinted by permission.)

described. If, during scene presentation, any variations or revisions are made, these can be recorded below the scene description. A sample hierarchy item has been completed.

The back of the card, used to complete details about the scene-presentation session, is shown in Figure 18-5. Sample descriptions have been completed on this card. The back includes a place at the top of the card for the client's anxiety or suds rating of the item (Anxiety Rating) and the order of the item in the hierarchy (Rank Order). Each item can also be numbered (Item) and identified by the theme of the hierarchy (Theme). If the counselor plans to incorporate coping images into the scene presentation, these can be discussed and noted next to "Adaptive Alternative."

In the right-hand column of this card, there is a place to indicate the client's suds rating after relaxation at the beginning of the session (this should be 10 or less). Any problems encountered in the session can be recorded under "Difficulties." Signs of client anxiety can be noted under "Physiological." The date each hierarchy item is successfully completed is noted under "Date Completed," and the date the client reports an anxiety-free experience of the item in real life can be noted with "Success *In Vivo.*"

The items in the left-hand column of the card under "Presentation" refer to methods of scene presentation and, as Evans (1974) points out, were designed to reflect the major variations in this part of the procedure. The counselor can record the version of the hierarchy item used (from the front of the card), the time required for the client to obtain a clear image (Image Latency), the duration of the scene held by the client (Duration Held), and, if necessary, a rating of the image clarity from 1 (not clear) to 10 (very clear). If the client reports anxiety during the scene visualization, the time at which this is reported after the image is obtained can be noted (Anxiety Latency). Once the client indicates anxiety, the counselor can instruct the client to remove the scene (method R), hold the scene (method H), or switch to the adaptive alternative (method A). The particular method used can be recorded next to "Strategy: R/H/A." If you ask the client to indicate when the anxiety diminishes, the length of time this takes is noted after "Anxiety Decrease." If you ask the client to continue to hold an image despite anxiety, this duration can be noted after "Duration Held." A report of the client's suds level of anxiety during the scene presentation can be noted after "Anxiety Suds."

Although this recording system does take more time to complete, its comprehensiveness can aid the progress of a given session and can pinpoint trouble spots as they occur.

☐ MODEL DIALOGUE: SCENE PRESENTATION

Counselor: Joan, after our relaxation session today, we're going to start working with your hierarchy. I'd like to explain how this goes. After you've relaxed, I'll ask you to imagine the first item on the low end of your hierarchy—that is, the pleasant one. It will help you relax even more. Then I'll describe the next item. I will show you a way to let me know if you feel any anxiety while you're imagining it. If you do, I'll ask you to stop or erase the image and to relax. You'll have some time to relax before I give you an item again. Does this seem clear?

Client: I believe so.

Counselor: One more thing. If at any point during the time you're imagining a scene you feel nervous or anxious about it, just raise your finger. This will signal that to me. OK?

Client: OK.

Counselor: Just to make sure we're on the same track, could you tell me what you believe will go on during this part of desensitization?

Client: Well, after relaxation you'll ask me to imagine an item at the bottom of the hierarchy. If I feel any anxiety, I'll raise my finger and you'll ask me to erase the scene and relax.

Counselor: Good. And even if you don't signal anxiety after a little time of imagining an item, I'll tell you to stop and relax. This gives you a sort of breather. Ready to begin?

Client: Yep.

Counselor: OK, first we'll begin with some relaxation. Just get in a comfortable position and close your eyes and relax. . . . Let the tension drain out of your body. . . . Now, to the word *relax,* just let your arms go limp. . . . Now relax your face. . . . Loosen up your face and neck muscles. . . . As I name each muscle group, just use the word *relax* as the signal to let go of all the tension. . . . Now, Joan, you'll feel even more relaxed by thinking about a pleasant situation. . . . Just imagine you're sitting around a campfire on a cool winter night. . . . You're with some good friends, singing songs and roasting marshmallows. [Presentation of item 1, or control item]. [Gives Joan about 40 seconds for this image.] Now I'd like you to imagine you're sitting in your room at your desk doing math homework that's pretty routine and is fairly easy. [Presentation of item 2 in hierarchy]. [Counselor notes duration of presentation on stopwatch. At 25 seconds Joan has not signaled. Counselor records "+25" for item 2.] OK, Joan, stop that image and erase it from your mind. Just concentrate on feeling very relaxed. [Pauses 30 to 60 seconds.] Now I'd like you to again imagine you're in your room sitting at your desk doing math homework that is routine and fairly simple. [Second presentation of item 2]. [Counselor notes 35 seconds and no signal. Records "+35" on card for item 2.] OK, Joan, now just erase the image from your mind and relax. Let go of all your muscles. [Pause of 40 seconds. Since two successive presentations of this item did not elicit any anxiety, the counselor will move on to item 3.]

Now I'd like you to imagine you're sitting in English class. It's about ten minutes before the bell. Your mind drifts to math class. You wonder if anything will happen like getting called on. [Presentation of item 3 in hierarchy]. [Counselor notes duration of presentation with stopwatch. At 12 seconds, Joan's finger goes up. Counselor records "−12" on card for item 3. Waits 3 more seconds.] OK, Joan, just erase that image from your mind. . . . Now relax. Let relaxation flood your body. . . . Think again about being in front of a campfire. [Pauses for about 40 seconds for relaxation.]

Now I'd like you to again imagine you're sitting in English class. It's almost time for the bell. You think about math class and wonder if you'll be called on. [Second presentation of item 3 in the hierarchy]. [Counselor notes duration with stopwatch. At 30 seconds, Joan has not signaled. Counselor notes "+30" on card.] OK, Joan, now just erase that image and concentrate on relaxing. [Pauses about 40 seconds.] OK, again imagine yourself sitting in English class. It's just a few minutes before the bell. You think about math class and wonder if you'll be called on. [Third presentation of item 3]. [At 30 seconds, no signal. Notation of "+30" recorded on card. Since the last two presentations of this item did not evoke anxiety, the counselor can move on to item 4 or can terminate this scene-presentation session on this successfully completed item if time is up or if Joan is restless.]

Ok, Joan, stop imagining that scene. Think about a campfire. . . . Just relax. [Another control item can be used for variation. After about 30 to 40 seconds, item 4 is presented or session is terminated.]

If this session had been terminated after the successful completion of item 3, the next scene-presentation session would begin with item 3. Other hierarchy items would be presented in the same manner as in this session. If Joan reported anxiety for three successive presentations of one item, the session would be interrupted, and an adjustment in the hierarchy would be made.

LEARNING ACTIVITY #48: SCENE PRESENTATION

This learning activity is designed to familiarize you with some of the procedural aspects of scene presentation. You can complete this activity by yourself or with a partner who can serve as your client.

PART ONE

1. Select one of the hierarchies you or your partner developed in Learning Activity #47 on hierarchy construction.
2. Select a counterconditioning or coping response to use, such as muscle relaxation or imagery.
3. Administer relaxation or imagery to yourself or to your partner.
4. If you have a partner, explain the use of method R of scene presentation and the signaling system in which the person raises a finger when anxiety is noticed or reports a suds rating after the scene is terminated.

5. By yourself or with your partner, start by presenting the lowest item in the hierarchy. If no anxiety is signaled after a specified duration, instruct your partner to remove the image and relax; then re-present the same scene. Remember, two successive no-anxiety presentations are required before presenting the next item. If anxiety is signaled, instruct yourself or your partner to remove the image and relax. After about 30 to 60 seconds, re-present the same item.
6. Select a notation system to use. Record at least the number of times each item was presented, the duration of each presentation, and whether each presentation did or did not evoke anxiety (or the anxiety rating if suds is used).

(continued)

LEARNING ACTIVITY #48: SCENE PRESENTATION (continued)

PART TWO

1. Complete the activity again. This time, for step 4, substitute the following: Explain the use of method H of scene presentation and the signaling method in which the client raises a finger when anxiety is increased and lowers it when anxiety is decreased.

2. For step 5: Present the next item in the hierarchy. If no anxiety is indicated by a raised finger after about a 30-second presentation, instruct the person to relax; then present the same item again before moving on.

3. If anxiety is indicated, instruct yourself or the person to hold the scene and try to relax away the tension, indicating decreased tension by a lowered finger.

PART THREE

1. Again, with yourself or a partner, complete Part One. This time, for step 4, do the following. In-struct the person in method A of scene presenta-tion. Identify one or two coping images you or the person could use. Instruct the person in the signal-ing method in which the word *tense* is used to indicate anxiety and *calm* is used to indicate relax-ation.

2. For step 5: Present an item. When you or the person says "tense," instruct yourself or the per-son to switch to the adaptive alternative (the cop-ing image) and to report relaxation by saying "calm."

PART FOUR

Reflect on or discuss with your partner the different methods of scene presentation and signaling used in this activity. Which ones did you or your partner feel comfortable or uncomfortable using? Did any method seem less confusing or easier than another? If so, why?

Homework and Follow-Up

Homework is essential to the successful comple-tion of desensitization! Homework may include daily practice of the selected relaxation procedure, visualization of the items completed in the pre-vious session, and exposure to *in vivo* situations.

Assignment of homework tasks. Most counselors instruct clients to practice the relaxation method being used once or twice daily. This is especially critical in the early sessions, in which training in the counterconditioning or coping response occurs. In addition, a counselor can assign the client to practice visualizing the items covered in the last session after the relaxation session. Gold-fried and Davison (1976) record three to five items on a cassette tape so that clients can administer this assignment themselves. Gradually, *in vivo* homework tasks can be added. As desensitization progresses, the client should be encouraged to par-ticipate in real-life situations that correspond to the situations covered in hierarchy-item visualiza-tion during the sessions. This is very important in order to facilitate generalization from imagined to real anxiety-producing situations. However, there may be some risk in the client's engaging in a real situation corresponding to a hierarchy item that has not yet been covered in the scene-presentation sessions (Rimm & Masters, 1979).

Homework log sheets and follow-up. The client should record completion of all homework assign-ments on daily log sheets. After all desensitization sessions are completed, a follow-up session or con-tact should be arranged.

☐ MODEL DIALOGUE: HOMEWORK AND FOLLOW-UP

Counselor: Joan, you've been progressing through the items on your list very well in our session. I'd like you to try some practice on your own similar to what we've been doing.

Client: OK, what is it?

Counselor: Well, I'm thinking of an item that's near the middle of your list. It's something you've been able to imagine last week and this week without reporting any nervousness. It's the one on your volunteering an answer in class.

Client: You think I should do that?

Counselor: Yes, although there is something I'd like to do first. I will put this item and the two before it on tape. Each day after you practice your relax-ation, I'd like you to use the tape and go over these three items just as we do here. If this goes well for you, then next week we can talk about your actu-ally starting to volunteer a bit more in class.

Client: OK with me.

Counselor: One more thing. Each time you use the tape this week, write it down on a blank log sheet.

Also note your tension level before and after the practice with the tape on the 0-to-100 scale. Then I'll see you next week.

Figure 18-6 summarizes all the components of systematic desensitization. You may find this to be a useful review of procedural aspects of this strategy.

□ PROBLEMS ENCOUNTERED DURING DESENSITIZATION

Although desensitization can be a very effective therapeutic procedure, occasionally problems are encountered that make it difficult or impossible to administer. Sometimes these problems can be minimized or alleviated. At other times, a problem may require the counselor to adopt an alternative strategy.

Wolpe (1982) and Marquis et al. (1973) discuss some of the barriers to effective implementation of desensitization. Some of the more common difficulties include problems in relaxation, imagery, and hierarchy arrangement and presentation. An occasional client may not be able to relax. Sometimes relaxation can be enhanced with additional training or with a gradual shaping process (Morris, 1980). An alternative method of relaxation can be used, or a different type of counterconditioning response can be selected. Another source of difficulty may be the client's inability to generate vivid, clear images. Marquis et al. report that a counselor may be able to strengthen a client's imagery by adding dialogue or a script to the item descriptions. Phillips (1971) has proposed a method of imagery training used to heighten a person's ability to imagine scenes. If imagery continues to be a problem, then *in vivo* desensitization that does not require imagery may be used. Or the hierarchy may be presented by other means, such as slides (O'Neil & Howell, 1969), videocassette tapes

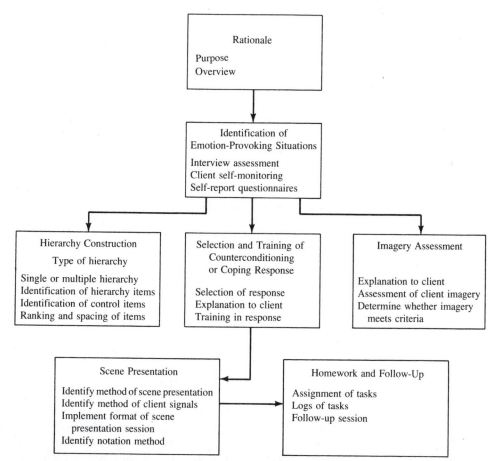

Figure 18-6. Components of systematic desensitization

(Caird & Wincze, 1974), or role play (Hosford, 1969).

An inaccurate hierarchy arrangement, selection of the wrong theme, and inadequacies in the method of hierarchy presentation can also be trouble spots. Sometimes these problems can be alleviated by reordering the hierarchy, reanalyzing the client's fear, or varying the method of scene presentation. Occasionally clients will benefit from a different form of desensitization. Some of the possible variations of desensitization are discussed in the next section.

□ VARIATIONS OF SYSTEMATIC DESENSITIZATION

The desensitization procedure described in this chapter reflects the traditional procedure applied over a series of sessions to an individual client by a counselor, using an individualized hierarchy imagined by the client. This section briefly describes the many possible variations of this method of desensitization. For more detailed information, we encourage you to consult the references mentioned in this section and those listed in the suggested readings at the end of the chapter.

Group-Administered Desensitization

Administration of desensitization to a group of clients who share similar concerns or fears is effective and is more efficient than individual administration. For example, Osterhouse (1976) and Altmaier and Woodward (1981) administered desensitization to a group of test-anxious college students. Other examples of group-administered desensitization have been reported by Paul and Shannon (1966) and Denholtz and Mann (1974). Group-administered desensitization often follows a specific treatment protocol. Standardized relaxation instructions are given to the entire group, and a standardized hierarchy is administered to the group en masse.

Self-Administered Desensitization

Some studies of desensitization have indicated that the presence of a therapist is not critical to the effectiveness of the strategy (Cornish & Dilley, 1973; Nawas et al., 1970; Rebman, 1983). Rosen, Glasgow, and Barrera (1976) found that clients who administered desensitization to themselves continued to improve after posttesting more than clients who were administered desensitization by a counselor. In self-administered desensitization, the client administers the procedure with the assistance of written instructions, audiotapes (Cornish & Dilley, 1973), or a treatment manual such as the one developed by Dawley and Wenrich (1973). Recent evidence has suggested that self-administered desensitization may incur more dropouts than therapist-administered desensitization (Marshall, Presse, & Andrews, (1976). However, this problem seems to be eliminated by even minimal counselor contact, such as a weekly telephone call to the client.

In Vivo Desensitization

In vivo desensitization involves actual client exposure to the situations in the hierarchy. The client engages in the graded series of situations instead of imagining each item. This variation is used when a client has difficulty using imagery or does not experience anxiety during imagery or when a client's actual exposure to the situations will have more therapeutic effects. If the client can actually be exposed to the feared stimuli, then *in vivo* desensitization is preferable to imagined exposure because it will produce more rapid results and will foster greater generalization. At times the counselor may accompany the client to the feared situation (Sherman, 1972). *In vivo* desensitization resembles participant modeling (Chapter 13), in which the client performs a graduated series of difficult tasks with the help of induction aids. MacDonald and Bernstein (1974) and Turnage and Logan (1974) have reported clinical cases involving *in vivo* desensitization. O'Neil and Howell (1969) found that snake-phobic clients who were exposed to *in vivo* desensitization achieved greater anxiety reduction at follow-up than clients who imagined hierarchy items or clients who saw the items portrayed on color slides. *In vivo* desensitization was effective in reducing children's fear of water (Ultee et al., 1982). Finally, Rovetto (1983) used *in vivo* desensitization to treat driving phobia with the aid of radio contact and telemonitoring of neurophysiological reactions.

The main procedural problem associated with *in vivo* desensitization involves adequate use and control of a counterconditioning response (Marquis et al., 1973). Sometimes it is difficult for a client to achieve a state of deep relaxation while simultaneously performing an activity. However, it is not always necessary to use a counterconditioning response to decrease the client's anxiety in threatening situations. Often exposure alone will result in sufficient anxiety reduction, particularly if the exposure occurs in graduated amounts and with induction aids.

☐ SUMMARY

Historically, desensitization probably has the longest track record of any of the therapeutic strategies presented in this book. Its results are well and frequently documented. Yet there is far more controversy surrounding its use than existed 15 years ago, mainly because of alternative explanations to account for its results. We do not believe that desensitization has outlived its usefulness as a method for reducing extreme anxiety or conditioned emotional reactions. But today, desensitization does not occupy a singular place in many practitioners' repertoires of possible anxiety-reduction methods. As an anxiety-management strategy, it currently may be supplemented with or replaced by a variety of other methods for reducing and coping with fears and tension. And, as Krumboltz and Thoresen (1976) assert, the aim of *any* anxiety-reduction strategy should be to teach a client self-control skills so that future stress does not push the client's anxiety beyond "tolerable limits" (p. 247).

POSTEVALUATION

PART ONE

Objective One states that you should be able to identify accurately at least three out of four hierarchies by type. Read each hierarchy carefully and then identify on a piece of paper whether the hierarchy is spatiotemporal, thematic, or personal. Feedback is provided at the end of the postevaluation.

Hierarchy 1 (fear of heights)

1. You are walking along the sidewalk. It is on a completely level street.
2. You are walking along the sidewalk, ascending. At the top of the street, you look down and realize you've climbed a hill.
3. You are climbing a ladder up to a second-story window.
4. You are riding in a car, and the road curves higher and higher.
5. You are riding in a car and you look outside. You notice you are driving on the edge of a good-sized hill.
6. You are starting to climb to the top of a fire tower. You are halfway up. You look down and see how far you've climbed.
7. You are climbing a ladder to the roof of a three-story house.
8. You have climbed to the top of a fire tower and look down.
9. You are riding in a car and are at the edge of a cliff on a mountain.
10. You are at the very top of a mountain, looking down into the surrounding valley.

Hierarchy 2 (fear of being rejected)

1. You speak to a stranger on the street. He doesn't hear you.
2. You go into a department store and request some information from one of the clerks. The clerk snaps at you in response.
3. You ask a stranger to give you change. She gives you a sarcastic reply.
4. You ask a casual acquaintance to lend you a book. He refuses.
5. You ask a friend over to dinner. The friend is too busy to come.
6. You apply for a membership in a social club, and your application is denied.
7. You are competing for a job. You and another person are interviewed. The other person is hired; you are not chosen.
8. You have an argument with your best friend. She leaves suddenly. You don't hear from her for a while.
9. You have an argument with your husband. Your husband says he would rather do things alone than with you.
10. Your husband asks you for a divorce and says he doesn't love you any more.

Hierarchy 3 (loss of a close relationship)

1. You remember a warm, starry night. You ask this woman you love to marry you. She accepts. You are very happy.
2. The two of you are traveling together soon after your marriage, camping out and traveling around in a van.
3. The two of you are running in the water together at the beach and having a good time being together.
4. You and this person are eating dinner together at home.
5. The two of you are disagreeing over how to spend money. She wants to save it; you are arguing to use some of it for camping supplies.
6. The two of you are arguing over your child. She wants the child to go with you on all trips; you want a babysitter occasionally.

(continued)

POSTEVALUATION (continued)

7. The two of you are starting to eat some meals apart. You are working late to avoid coming home for dinner.
8. She is wrapped up in her social activities; you, in your work. On the weekends you go your separate ways.
9. You have a discussion about your relationship and separate activities. You start sleeping on the couch.
10. The two of you go to see a lawyer to initiate discussion about a separation.

Hierarchy 4 (fear of giving speeches)
1. Your instructor casually mentions a required speech to be given by the end of the course.
2. Your instructor passes around a sign-up sheet for the speeches. You sign up.
3. You talk about the speech with some of your classmates. You aren't sure what to say.
4. You go to the library to look up some resource material for your speech. You don't find too much.
5. Some of your classmates start to give speeches. You think about how good their speeches are and wonder how yours will be.
6. It is a week before the speech. You're spending a lot of time working on it.
7. It is the day before the speech. You're going over your notes religiously.
8. It is the night before the speech. You lie awake thinking about it.
9. It is the next morning. You wake up and remember it is speech day. You don't feel hungry at breakfast.
10. Later that morning you're walking to speech class. A classmate comes up and says "Well, I guess you're on today."
11. You're sitting in speech class. The instructor will call on you any moment. You keep going over your major points.

PART TWO

Objective Two asks you to identify and describe at least 9 out of 11 procedural steps of desensitization, using a written client case description. Read this case description carefully; then respond by identifying and describing the 11 items listed after the description.

Your client is a fifth-grade boy at a local elementary school. This year, the client's younger sister has entered first grade at the same school. After a few weeks at school, your client, Ricky, began to complain about school to his teacher and parents. He would come to school and get sick. His parents would come and take him home. After a medical check-up, the doctor can find nothing physically wrong with Ricky. Yet Ricky continues either to get sick at school or to wake up sick in the morning. He appears to be better on weekends. He says he hates school and it makes him sick to his stomach to have to go. On occasion, he has vomited in the morning. The parents report that it is getting harder and harder to get Ricky to attend school. Suppose you were to use desensitization as one strategy in this case to help Ricky overcome his tension and avoidance of school. Identify and describe how you would implement the following 11 steps of desensitization with Ricky. Adapt your language to words that a 10-year-old could understand.

1. Your rationale of desensitization.
2. Your description of an overview of desensitization.
3. A method for helping Ricky identify the anxiety-provoking situations about school.
4. The type of hierarchy that would be used with Ricky.
5. A ranking method Ricky could use to arrange the hierarchy items.
6. An appropriate counterconditioning or coping response you could train Ricky to use.
7. A method of assessing Ricky's imagery capacity.
8. A method of scene presentation you would use with Ricky.
9. A method Ricky could use for signaling during scene presentation.
10. A notation method you might use to keep track of hierarchy presentation.
11. An example of one homework task associated with desensitization that you might assign to Ricky to complete.

Feedback follows the Postevaluation.

PART THREE

Objective Three asks you to demonstrate at least 22 out of 28 steps of systematic desensitization with a role-play client. Several role-play interviews may be required in order for you to include all the major procedural components of desensitization. Use the Interview Checklist for Systematic Desensitization on pages 511–517 as an assessment tool.

☐ SUGGESTED READINGS

Altmaier, E. M., & Woodward, M. (1981). Group vicarious desensitization of test anxiety. *Journal of Counseling Psychology, 28,* 467–469.

Berman, J. S., Miller, K. C., & Massman, P. J. (1985). Cognitive therapy versus systematic desensitization: Is one treatment superior? *Psychological Bulletin, 97,* 451–461.

Bornstein, P. H., & Knapp, M. (1981). Self-control desensitization with a multi-phobic boy: A multiple baseline design. *Journal of Behavior Therapy and Experimental Psychiatry, 12,* 281–285.

Elmore, R. T., Wildman, R. W., & Westefeld, J. S. (1980). The use of systematic desensitization in the treatment of blood phobia. *Journal of Behavior Therapy and Experimental Psychiatry, 11,* 277–279.

Foa, E. B., Stekette, G. S., & Ascher, L. M. (1980). Systematic desensitization. In A. Goldstein & E. B. Foa (Eds.), *Handbook of behavioral interventions: A clinical guide.* New York: Wiley.

Howard, W. A., Murphy, S. M., & Clarke, J. C. (1983). The nature and treatment of fear of flying: A controlled investigation. *Behavior Therapy, 14,* 557–567.

Kirsch, I., & Henry, D. (1979). Self-desensitization and meditation in the reduction of public speaking anxiety. *Journal of Consulting and Clinical Psychology, 47,* 536–541.

Kirsch, I., Tennen, H., Wickless, C., Saccone, A. J., & Cody, S. (1983). The role of expectancy in fear reduction. *Behavior Therapy, 14,* 520–533.

Leal, L., Baxter, E. G., Martin, J., & Marx, R. W. (1981). Cognitive modification and systematic desensitization with test anxious high school students. *Journal of Counseling Psychology, 28,* 525–528.

Lent, R. W., Russell, R. K., & Zamostny, K. P. (1981). Comparison of cue-controlled desensitization, rational structuring and credible placebo in the treatment of speech anxiety. *Journal of Consulting and Clinical Psychology, 49,* 608–610.

Levine, B. A., & Wolpe, J. (1980). *In vivo* desensitization of a severe driving phobia through radio contact. *Journal of Behavior Therapy and Experimental Psychiatry, 11,* 281–282.

Marquis, J., Morgan, W., & Piaget, G. (1973). *A guidebook for systematic desensitization* (3rd ed.). Palo Alto, CA: Veterans' Workshop.

Miller, W. R., & DiPilato, M. (1983). Treatment of nightmares via relaxation and desensitization: A controlled evaluation. *Journal of Consulting and Clinical Psychology, 51,* 870–877.

Morris, R. J. (1986). Fear reduction methods. In F. H. Kanfer & A. P. Goldstein (Eds.), *Helping people change* (3rd ed.) (pp. 145–190). New York: Pergamon Press.

Rebman, V. L. (1983). Self-control desensitization with cue controlled relaxation for treatment of a conditioned vomiting response to air travel. *Journal of Behavior Therapy and Experimental Psychiatry, 14,* 161–164.

Redd, W. H. (1980). *In vivo* desensitization in the treatment of chronic emesis following gastrointestinal surgery. *Behavior Therapy, 11,* 421–427.

Rimm, D. C., & Masters, J. C. (1979). *Behavior therapy: Techniques and empirical findings* (2nd ed.). New York: Academic Press.

Rovetto, F. M. (1983). *In vivo* desensitization of a severe driving phobia through radio contact with telemonitoring of neurophysiological reactions. *Journal of Behavior Therapy and Experimental Psychiatry, 14,* 49–54.

Schindler, F. E. (1980). Treatment by systematic desensitization of a recurring nightmare of a real life trauma. *Journal of Behavior Therapy and Experimental Psychiatry, 11,* 53–54.

Ultee, C. A., Griffioen, D., & Schellekens, J. (1982). The reduction of anxiety in children: A comparison of the effects of "systematic desensitization *in vitro*" and "systematic desensitization *in vivo.*" *Behaviour Research and Therapy, 20,* 61–67.

Van Hasselt, V. B., Hersen, M., Bellack, A. S., Rosenblum, N. D., & Lamparski, D. (1979). Tripartite assessment of the effects of systematic desensitization in a multi-phobic child: An experimental analysis. *Journal of Behavior Therapy and Experimental Psychiatry, 10,* 51–55.

Wolpe, J. (1958). *Psychotherapy by reciprocal inhibition.* Stanford, CA: Stanford University Press.

Wolpe, J. (1976). *Theme and variations: A behavior therapy casebook.* New York: Pergamon Press. Chapter 2, "The Reciprocal Inhibition Theme and the Emergence of Its Role in Psychotherapy."

Wolpe, J. (1982). *The practice of behavior therapy* (3rd ed.). New York: Pergamon Press.

FEEDBACK: POSTEVALUATION

PART ONE

1. Spatiotemporal. Items are arranged by increasing height off the ground.
2. Thematic. Items are arranged around the theme of rejection.
3. Personal. Items are arranged from pleasant to unpleasant memories of an ex-spouse.
4. Spatiotemporal. Items are arranged by time; as the time approaching the situation diminishes, the fear intensifies.

PART TWO

Here are some possible descriptions of the 11 procedural steps of desensitization you were asked to identify and describe. See whether your responses are in some way similar to these.

(continued)

FEEDBACK: POSTEVALUATION (continued)

1. Rationale: "Ricky, it seems that it's very hard for you to go to school now or even think about school without feeling sick. There are some things about school that upset you this much. We can work together to find out what bothers you, and I can help you learn to be able to go to school without feeling so upset or sick to your stomach, so you can go to school again and feel OK about it. How does that sound?"

2. Overview: "There are several things you and I will do together. First we'll talk about the things about school that upset you. I'll ask you to think about these situations, only instead of feeling upset when you do, I'll show you a way to stay calm and keep the butterflies out of your stomach. It will take a lot of practice in this room, but after a while you will be able to go back to your class and feel calm and OK about it!"

3. Method for identifying the anxiety-provoking situations:
   a. Use of interview leads such as "Ricky, what do you do in school that makes you feel sick? What about school makes you want to stay at home? What happens at school that bothers you? When do you feel most upset about school?"
   b. Use of client self-monitoring: "Ricky, could you keep a chart for me this week? Each time you feel upset about school, mark down what has happened or what you're thinking about that makes you feel upset or sick."

4. Type of hierachy: A thematic hierarchy would be used. One hierarchy might consist of school-related anxiety-provoking situations. Depending on the anxiety-provoking situations identified, another thematic hierarchy may emerge, dealing with jealousy. It is possible that the avoidance of school is a signal that Ricky really fears being upstaged by his younger sister.

5. Ranking method: Because of Ricky's age, an easy ranking method should be used. Probably it would be easiest to start with the low, medium, high method. You would ask Ricky to sort the cards of the hierarchy items into three piles: a low pile (things that upset him only a little), a medium pile (things that upset him somewhat), and a high pile (things that really upset him). You might give him a pictorial or visual "anchor point" to describe the three piles: "The low pile is like going to the dentist to have your teeth

examined. The middle pile is like going to the dentist to have your teeth cleaned. The high pile is going to the dentist to have a cavity in your tooth filled."

6. Counterconditioning or coping response: Muscle relaxation can be used easily with a child Ricky's age as long as you just show him (by modeling) the different muscle groups and the way to tighten and let go of a muscle.

7. Method of imagery assessment: Ask Ricky to tell you some daydreams he has or some things he loves to do. Before and after a relaxation-training session, ask him to imagine or pretend he is doing one of these things. Then have him describe the details of his imagined scene. Children often have a capacity for more vivid and descriptive imagery than adults.

8. Method of scene presentation: We would probably try method R or method A. Method R is simple to use and easily understood (stop imagining _____; now relax). Method A could be useful, since Ricky is legally required to attend school and does need to learn to cope with it. Method H may be less easily understood by a child, who might find it difficult to know what is meant by "hold the image and relax away the tension."

9. Signaling method: Again, you want to suggest something that is easily understood and used by Ricky. Perhaps the use of *word* signals might minimize any confusion. You would instruct him to say "tense" when he's upset or anxious and "calm" when he's less bothered or more relaxed.

10. Notation method: The easiest notation method might be to use each hierarchy card and note the number of times each item is presented, the duration of each presentation, and an indication of whether Ricky did or did not report being "tense" during or after the item. This notation system looks like this:

Item No. _____ Date _____
Item description
$+10 - 15 + 15 + 20$

The item was presented four times; the numbers 10, 15, 15, and 20 refer to the duration of each presentation; the $+$ indicates no anxiety report; the $-$ indicates a "tense" signal.

11. Examples of possible homework tasks:
    a. A list of anxiety-related situations.

(continued)

b. Practice of muscle relaxation.
c. Practice of items covered in the interview, possibly with the use of coping imagery.
d. Exposure to certain school-related *in vivo* situations.

PART THREE

You or an observer can rate your desensitization interviews using the Interview Checklist for Systematic Desensitization that follows.

INTERVIEW CHECKLIST FOR SYSTEMATIC DESENSITIZATION

Instructions to observer: Listed below are some procedural steps of systematic desensitization. Check which of these steps were used by the counselor in implementing this procedure. Some possible examples of these leads are described in the right column of the checklist.

Item	Examples of counselor leads
I. Rationale	
_____ 1. Counselor gives client rationale for desensitization, clearly explaining how it works.	"This procedure is based on the idea that you can learn to replace your fear (or other conditioned emotion) in certain situations with a better or more desirable response, such as relaxation or general feelings of comfort." "You have described some situations in which you have learned to react with fear (or some other emotion). This procedure will give you skills to help you cope with these situations so they don't continue to be so stressful."
_____ 2. Counselor describes brief overview of desensitization procedure.	"There are three basic things that will happen—first, training you to relax, next, constructing a list of situations in which you feel anxious, and finally, having you imagine scenes from this list, starting with low-anxiety scenes, while you are deeply relaxed." "First you will learn how to relax and how to notice tension so you can use it as a signal to relax. Then we'll identify situations that, to varying degrees, upset you or make you anxious. Starting with the least discomforting situations, you will practice the skill of relaxation as a way to cope with the stress."
_____ 3. Counselor checks to see whether client is willing to use strategy.	"Are you ready to try this now?"
II. Identification of Emotion-Provoking Situations	
_____ 4. Counselor initiates at least one of the following means of identifying anxiety-provoking stimulus situations:	
_____a. Interview assessment through problem leads.	"When do you notice that you feel most _____?" "Where are you when this happens?" "What are you usually doing when you feel _____?" "What types of situations seem to bring on this feeling?"
_____b. Client self-monitoring.	"This week I'd like you to keep track of any situation that seems to bring on these feelings. On your log, write down where you are, what you're doing, whom you're with, and the intensity of these feelings."
_____c. Self-report questionnaires.	"One way that we might learn more about some of the specific situations that you find stressful is for you to complete this short questionnaire. There are no right or wrong answers— just describe how you usually feel or react in the situations presented."

(continued)

FEEDBACK: POSTEVALUATION (continued)

Item	Examples of counselor leads
_____ 5. Counselor continues to assess anxiety-provoking situations until client identifies some specific situations.	"Let's continue with this exploration until we get a handle on some things. Right now you've said that you get nervous and upset around certain kinds of people. Can you tell me some types or characteristics of people that bother you or make you anxious almost always?" "OK, good, so you notice you're always very anxious around people who can evaluate or criticize you, like a boss or teacher."

III. Hierarchy Construction

Item	Examples of counselor leads
_____ 6. Counselor identifies a type of hierarchy to be constructed with client:	Now we're going to make a list of these anxiety-provoking situations and fill in some details and arrange these in an order, starting with the least anxiety-provoking situation all the way to the most anxiety-provoking one."
_____a. Spatiotemporal.	"Since you get more and more anxious as the time for the speech gets closer and closer, we'll construct these items by closer and closer times to the speech."
_____b. Thematic.	"We'll arrange these items according to the different kinds of situations in which people criticize you—depending on who does it, what it's about, and so on."
_____c. Personal.	"We'll construct a hierarchy of items that represent your memories about her, starting with pleasant memories and proceeding to unpleasant or painful memories."
_____d. Combination.	
_____ 7. Counselor identifies the number of hierarchies to be developed: _____a. Single hierarchy.	"We will take all these items that reflect different situations that are anxiety-producing for you and arrange them in one list."
_____b. Multiple hierarchies.	"Since there are a number of types of situations you find stressful, we'll construct one list for situations involving criticism and another list for situations involving social events."
_____ 8. Counselor initiates identification of hierarchy items through one or more methods: _____a. Interview questions (_not_ when client is engaged in relaxation).	"I'd like us to write down some items that describe each of these anxiety-provoking scenes with quite a bit of detail." "Describe for me what your mother could say that would bother you most. How would she say it? Now who, other than your mother, could criticize you and make you feel worse? What things are you most sensitive to being criticized about?"
_____b. Client completion of note cards (homework).	"This week I'd like you to add to this list of items. I'm going to give you some blank index cards. Each time you think of another item that makes you get anxious or upset about criticism, write it down on one card."
_____ 9. Counselor continues to explore hierarchy items until items are identified that meet the following criteria: _____a. Some items, if carried out _in vivo_, are under client's control (do not require instigation from others). _____b. Items are concrete and specific.	"Can you think of some items that, if you actually were to carry them out, would be things you could initiate without having to depend on someone else to make the situation happen?" "OK, now just to say that you get nervous at social functions is a little vague. Give me some details about a social function in

(continued)

Item	Examples of counselor leads
	which you might feel pretty comfortable and one that could make you feel extremely nervous."
____c. Items are similar to or represent past, present, or future situations that *have* provoked or *could* provoke the emotional response from client.	"Think of items that represent things that have made you anxious before or currently — and things that could make you anxious if you encountered them in the future."
____d. Items have sampled broad range of situations in which emotional response occurs.	"Can you identify items representing different types of situations that seem to bring on these feelings?"
____e. Items represent different levels of emotion aroused by representative stimulus situations.	"Let's see if we have items here that reflect different amounts of the anxiety you feel. Here are some items that don't make you too anxious. What about ones that are a little more anxiety-provoking, up to ones where you feel panicky?"
____10. Counselor asks client to identify several control items (neutral, non-emotion-arousing).	"Sometimes it's helpful to imagine some scenes that aren't related to things that make you feel anxious. Could you describe something you could imagine that would be pleasant and relaxing?"
____11. Counselor explains purpose of ranking and spacing items according to increasing levels of arousal.	"It may take a little time, but you will rank these hierarchy items from least anxiety-producing to most anxiety-producing. This gives us an order to the hierarchy that is gradual, so we can work just with more manageable situations before moving on to more stressful ones."
____12. Counselor asks client to arrange hierarchy items in order of increasing arousal, using one of the following ranking methods, and explains method to client:	"Now I would like you to take the items and arrange them in order of increasing anxiety, using the following method."
____a. Rank-ordering.	"We have each hierarchy item written on a separate note card. Go through the cards and rank-order them according to increasing levels of anxiety. Items that don't provoke much anxiety go on the bottom, followed by items that are successively more anxiety-producing."
____b. "Suds."	"I'd like you to arrange these items using a 0-to-100 scale. 0 represents total relaxation and 100 is comparable to complete panic. If an item doesn't give you any anxiety, give it a 0. If it is just a little stressful, may be a 15 or 20. Very stressful items would get a higher number, depending on how stressful."
____c. Low/medium/high ordering.	"Take the items written on these cards and sort them into one of three groups. One group, small amounts of anxiety. The second group would consist of items provoking an average amount of anxiety. The third group would consist of items that are very anxiety-producing for you."
____13. Counselor adds or deletes items if necessary in order to achieve reasonable spacing of items in hierarchy.	"Let's see, at the lower end of the hierarchy you have many items. We might drop out a few of these. But you have only three items at the upper end, so we have some big gaps here. Can you think of a situation provoking a little bit more anxiety than this item but not quite as much as this next one? We can add that in here."

IV. Selection and Training of Counterconditioning or Coping Response

____14. Counselor selects appropriate counterconditioning or coping response to use to countercondition or cope with anxiety (or other conditioned emotion):

(continued)

FEEDBACK: POSTEVALUATION (continued)

Item	Examples of counselor leads
____a. Deep muscle relaxation.	(contrasting tensed and relaxed muscles)
____b. Emotive imagery.	(evoking pleasurable scenes in imagination)
____c. Meditation.	(focusing on breathing and counting)
____d. Coping thoughts or statements.	(concentrating on coping or productive thoughts incompatible with self-defeating ones)
____15. Counselor explains purpose of particular response selected and describes its role in desensitization.	"This response is like a substitute for anxiety. It will take time to learn it, but it will help to decrease your anxiety so that you can face rather than avoid these feared situations." "This training will help you recognize the onset of tension. You can use these cues you learn as a signal to relax away the tension."
____16. Counselor trains client in use of counterconditioning or coping response and suggests daily practice of this response.	"We will spend several sessions learning this so you can use it as a way to relax. This relaxation on your part is a very important part of this procedure. After you practice this here, I'd like you to do this at home two times each day over the next few weeks. Each practice will make it easier for you to relax."
____17. Counselor asks client before and after each training session to rate felt level of anxiety or arousal.	"Using a scale from 0 to 100, with 0 being complete relaxation and 100 being intense anxiety, where would you rate yourself now?"
____18. Counselor continues with training until client can discriminate different levels of anxiety and can use nonanxiety response to achieve 10 or less rating on 0-to-100 scale.	"Let's continue with this until you feel this training really has an effect on your relaxation state after you use it."

V. Imagery Assessment

____19. Counselor explains use of imagery in desensitization.	"In this procedure, I'll ask you to imagine each hierarchy item as if you were actually there. We have found that imagining a situation can be very similar to actually being in the situation. Becoming desensitized to anxiety you feel while imagining an unpleasant situation will transfer to real situations, too."
____20. Counselor assesses client's capacity to generate vivid images by:	"It might be helpful to see how you react to using your imagination."
____a. Presenting control items when client is using a relaxation response.	"Now that you're relaxed, get a picture in your mind of sitting in the sun on a warm day. The sky is very blue, not a cloud in it. The grass and trees are green. You can feel the warmth of the sun on your body."
____b. Presenting hierarchy items when client is not using a relaxation response.	"OK, just imagine that you're at this party. You don't know anyone. Get a picture of yourself and the other people there. It's a very large room."
____c. Asking client to describe imagery evoked in a and b.	"Can you describe what you imagined? What were the colors you saw? What did you hear or smell?"
____21. Counselor, with client's assistance, determines whether client's imagery meets the following criteria and, if so, decides to continue with desensitization:	
____a. Client is able to imagine scene concretely with details.	"Were you able to imagine the scene clearly? How many details can you remember?"

(continued)

Item	Examples of counselor leads

_____b. Client is able to imagine scene as participant, not onlooker.

_____c. Client is able to switch scene on and off when instructed to.

_____d. Client is able to hold scene without drifting off or revising it.

_____e. Client shows no evidence of other difficulties.

"When you imagined the scene, did you feel as if you were actually there and involved—or did it seem as if you were just an observer, perhaps watching it happen to someone else?"

"How soon were you able to get an image after I gave it to you? When did you stop the image after I said _Stop?_"

"Did you ever feel as if you couldn't concentrate on the scene and started to drift off?"

"Did you ever change anything about the scene during the time you imagined it?"

"What else did you notice that interfered with getting a good picture of this in your mind?"

VI. Hierarchy Scene Presentation

_____22. Counselor identifies and explains method of scene presentation to be used:

_____a. Method R—client will be instructed to stop image when anxiety is felt and to relax.

_____b. Method H—client will be instructed to hold image when anxiety is felt and to relax away tension.

_____c. Method A—client will be instructed to switch image to coping image when anxiety is felt.

"I'd like to explain exactly how we will proceed. I'm going to present an item in the hierarchy to you after we go through relaxation. Here is what I'll instruct you to do."

"When you tell me that you feel some anxiety while imagining the scene, I'll ask you to stop or remove the scene from your mind. Then I'll instruct you to relax. You'll have some time to relax before I ask you to imagine the scene another time."

"When you indicate you're imagining a scene, I'll ask you to continue to visualize the scene but to relax away the tension as you do so."

"When you indicate that you feel some anxiety while you're imagining the scene, I'll ask you to switch the scene to a type of coping scene and to concentrate for a few minutes on the coping image."

_____23. Counselor identifies and explains method of signaling to be used:

_____a. Client is instructed to raise index finger when clear image is visualized.

_____b. Client is instructed to raise index finger when anxiety is noticed while visualizing.

_____c. Client is instructed to raise finger to signal increased anxiety and to lower finger to indicate decreased anxiety.

_____d. Client is instructed to indicate anxiety with the word _tense_ and to signal relaxation with the word _calm._

"It's very important that we work out a signaling system for you to use when I present the hierarchy items to you. I'll explain how you can signal. Make sure to tell me if it doesn't seem clear."

"When I present an item, I'd like you to raise your index finger slightly at the point when you obtain a clear picture of the scene in your mind."

"I'll ask you to imagine an item. If at any point during this imagination, you feel tension, signal this by raising your index finger."

"When you feel anxiety building up as you imagine the item, signal this by raising your finger. As the anxiety decreases and calmness takes over, signal this by lowering your finger."

"When, during the visualization of an item, you notice anxiety, say 'tense.' When you feel calmer and more relaxed, say 'calm.'"

_____24. For each session of scene presentation:

_____a. Counselor precedes scene presentation with muscle relaxation or other procedures to help client achieve relaxation before scenes are presented.

_____b. Counselor begins initial session with lowest (least anxiety-provok-

"Let your whole body become heavier and heavier as all your muscles relax. . . . Feel the tension draining out of your body. . . . Relax the muscles of your hands and arms. . . ."

"I'm going to start this first session with the item that is at the bottom of the hierarchy."

(continued)

FEEDBACK: POSTEVALUATION (continued)

Item	Examples of counselor leads
ing) item in hierarchy and for successive sessions begins with last item successfully completed at previous session.	"Today we'll begin with the item we ended on last week for a review."
_____ c. Counselor describes item and asks client to imagine it for 20 to 40 seconds.	"Just imagine you are sitting in the classroom waiting for the test to be passed to you, wondering how much you can remember." [Counts 20 to 40 seconds, then instructs client in either R, H, or A method.]
_____ (1) If client held image and did not signal anxiety, counselor instructs client to stop image and relax for 30 to 60 seconds.	"Now, stop visualizing this scene and just take a little time to relax. Think of sitting in the sun on a warm day, with blue sky all around you."
_____ (2) If client indicated anxiety during or after visualizing scene, counselor uses method R, H, or A, selected in no. 22.	(R) "Now remove the image and just relax." (H) "Now hold the image but relax away the tension." (A) "Switch the image to the coping one we discussed earlier."
_____ d. After pause of 30 to 60 seconds between items, counselor presents each item to client a second time.	"Now I want you to imagine the same thing. Concentrate on being very relaxed, then imagine that you are sitting in the classroom waiting for the test to be passed to you, wondering how much you can remember."
_____ e. Each item is successfully completed (with no anxiety) at least two successive times (more for items at top of hierarchy) before new item is presented.	"I'm going to present this scene to you once more now. Just relax, then imagine that. . . ."
_____ f. If an item elicits anxiety after three presentations, counselor makes some adjustments in hierarchy or in client's visualization process.	"Let's see what might be bogging us down here. Do you notice that you are drifting away from the scene while you're imagining it — or revising it in any way? Can you think of a situation we might add here that is just a little bit less stressful for you than this one?"
_____ g. Standardized instructions are used for each phase of scene presentation; reinforcement of *just* the no-anxiety items is avoided.	"OK, I see that was not stressful for you. Just concentrate on relaxing a minute." "What was your feeling of anxiety on the 0-to-100 scale? 20. OK, I want you to just relax for a minute, then I'll give you the same scene."
_____ h. Each scene-presentation session ends with a successfully completed item (no anxiety for at least two successive presentations).	"OK, let's end today with this item we've just been working on, since you reported 5 suds during the last two presentations."
_____ i. Each session is terminated:	"We've done quite a bit of work today. Just spend a few minutes relaxing, and then we will stop."
_____ (1) When three to five items are completed.	
_____ (2) After 15 to 20 minutes of scene presentation.	
_____ (3) After indications of client restlessness or distractibility.	

(continued)

Item	Examples of counselor leads
____25. Counselor uses written recording method during scene presentation to note client's progress through hierarchy.	"As we go through this session, I'm going to make some notes about the number of times we work with each item and your anxiety rating of each presentation."

VII. Homework and Follow-Up

Item	Examples of counselor leads
____26. Counselor assigns homework tasks that correspond to treatment progress of desensitization procedure:	"There is something I'd like you to do this week on a daily basis at home."
____a. Daily practice of selected relaxation procedure.	"Practice this relaxation procedure two times each day in a quiet place."
____b. Visualization of items successfully completed at previous session.	"On this tape there are three items we covered this week. Next week at home, after your relaxation sessions, practice imagining each of these three items."
____c. Exposure to *in vivo* situations corresponding to successfully completed hierarchy items.	"You are ready now to actually go to a party by yourself. We have gotten to a point where you can imagine doing this without any stress."
____27. Counselor instructs client to record completion of homework on daily log sheets.	"Each time you complete a homework practice, record it on your log sheets."
____28. Counselor arranges for follow-up session or check-in.	"Check in with me in two weeks to give me a progress report."

Observer comments: _____
_____

SELF-MANAGEMENT STRATEGIES: SELF-MONITORING, STIMULUS CONTROL, AND SELF-REWARD

NINETEEN

Self-management is a process in which clients direct their own behavior change with any one therapeutic strategy or a combination of strategies. For self-management to occur, the client must take charge of manipulating either internal or external variables to effect a desired change. Although a counselor may instigate self-management procedures and train the client in them, the client assumes the control for carrying out the process. Kanfer (1975, p. 310) distinguishes between therapist-managed procedures, in which a majority of the "therapeutic work" occurs *during* the interviews, and self-managed (or client-managed) procedures, in which most of the work takes place *between* sessions.

Self-management is a relatively recent phenomenon in counseling, and reports of clinical applications and theoretical descriptions have mushroomed since 1970. During this time, definitions of self-management have remained unclear, partly because of terminological confusion. Self-change methods have been referred to as self-control (Cautela, 1969; Thoresen & Mahoney, 1974), self-regulation (Kanfer, 1970, 1975), and self-management (M. J. Mahoney, 1971, 1972). We prefer the label *self-management* because it suggests conducting and handling one's life in a somewhat skilled manner. The term *self-management* also avoids the concepts of inhibition and restraint often associated with the words *control* and *regulation* (Thoresen & Mahoney).

In using self-management procedures, a client directs change efforts by modifying aspects of the environment or by manipulating and administering consequences (Jones, Nelson & Kazdin, 1977, p. 151). This chapter describes three self-management strategies:

Self-monitoring—self-observing and self-recording particular behaviors (thoughts, feelings, and actions) about oneself and the interactions with environmental events.
Stimulus control—the prearrangement of ante-

cedents or cues to increase or decrease a target behavior.

Self-reward—self-presentation of a self-determined positive stimulus following a desired response.

These three strategies are typically classified as self-management because in each procedure the client, in a self-directed fashion, prompts, alters, or controls antecedents and consequences to produce the desired behavioral changes. However, none of these strategies is entirely independent of environmental variables and external sources of influence (Jones et al., 1977).

In addition to these three self-management procedures, it should be noted that a client can use virtually any helping strategy in a self-directed manner. For example, a client could apply relaxation training to manage anxiety by using a relaxation-training audiotape without the assistance of a counselor. In fact, some degree of client self-management may be a necessary component of every successful therapy case. For example, in all the other helping strategies described in this book, some elements of self-management are suggested in the procedural guidelines for strategy implementation. These self-managed aspects of any therapy procedure typically include—

1. Client self-directed practice in the interview.
2. Client self-directed practice in the *in vivo* setting (often through homework tasks).
3. Client self-observation and recording of target behaviors or of homework.
4. Client self-reward (verbal or material) for successful completion of action steps and homework assignments.

□ OBJECTIVES

1. Given a written client case description, describe the use of the six components of self-monitoring for this client.
2. Teach another person how to engage in self-monitoring as a self-change strategy.
3. Given a client case description, describe how the client could use stimulus-control methods to reduce or increase the rate of a behavior.
4. Given a written client case description, be able to describe the use of the four components of self-reward for this client.
5. Teach another person how to use self-reward.

□ CHARACTERISTICS OF AN EFFECTIVE SELF-MANAGEMENT PROGRAM

Well-constructed and well-executed self-management programs have some advantages that are not so apparent in counselor-administered procedures. For instance, use of a self-management procedure may increase a person's perceived control over the environment and decrease dependence on the counselor or others. Perceived control over the environment often motivates a person to take some action (Rotter, Chance, & Phares, 1972). Second, self-management approaches are practical—inexpensive and portable (Thoresen & Mahoney, 1974, p. 7). Third, such strategies are usable. By this we mean that occasionally a person will refuse to go "into therapy" to stop drinking or to lose weight (for example) but will agree to use the self-administered instructions that a self-management program provides. In fact, one study found that people who had never received counseling were more agreeable than clients to the idea of using self-management (Williams, Canale, & Edgerly, 1976). Finally, self-management strategies may enhance generalization of learning—both from the interview to the environment and from problematic to nonproblematic situations (Thoresen & Mahoney, 1974, p. 7). These are some of the possible advantages of self-management that have spurred both researchers and practitioners to apply and explore some of the components and effects of successful self-management programs. Although many questions remain unanswered, we can say tentatively that the following factors may be important in an effective self-management program:

1. A combination of strategies, some focusing on antecedents of behavior and others on consequences.
2. Consistent use of strategies over a period of time.
3. Evidence of client self-evaluation, goal setting with fairly high standards.
4. Use of covert, verbal, or material self-reinforcement.
5. Some degree of external, or environmental, support.

Combination of Strategies

A combination of self-management strategies is usually more useful than a single strategy. In a weight-control study, Mahoney, Moura, and

Wade (1973) found that the addition of self-reward significantly enhanced the procedures of self-monitoring and stimulus control. Further, people who combined self-reward and self-punishment lost more weight than those who used just one of the procedures. Greiner and Karoly (1976) found that students who used self-monitoring, self-reward, and planning strategies improved their study behavior and academic performance more than students who used only one strategy. Mitchell and White (1977) found that the frequency of clients' reported migraine headaches was reduced in direct proportion to the number of self-management skills they used. Similarly, Perri and Richards (1977) and Heffernan and Richards (1981) discovered that successful self-controllers reported using a greater number of techniques for a longer time than unsuccessful self-controllers. (In these studies, successful self-controllers were defined as persons who had increased or decreased the target behavior at least 50% and had maintained this level for several months.) Problem areas for which comprehensive self-management programs have been developed include weight control (Fremouw & Heyneman, 1983; Mahoney & Mahoney, 1976), interpersonal skills training (McFall & Dodge, 1982), developmental disabilities (Litrownik, 1982), anxiety (Deffenbacher & Suinn, 1982), addictive disorders (Marlatt & Parks, 1982), depression (Rehm, 1982), insomnia (Bootzin, 1977), and academic performance (Neilans & Israel, 1981). Finally, self-reinforcement, stimulus control, and self-monitoring were used as maintenance programs on the long-term management of obesity (Perri, McAllister, Gange, Jordan, McAdoo, & Nezu, 1987).

Consistent Use of Strategies

Consistent, regular use of the strategies is a very important component of effective self-management. Seeming ineffectiveness may be due not to the impotence of the strategy but to its inconsistent or sporadic application (Thoresen & Mahoney, 1974, p. 107). Perri and Richards (1977) and Heffernan and Richards (1981) found that successful self-controllers reported using methods more frequently and more consistently than unsuccessful self-controllers. Similarly, another investigation noted that the "failures" in a self-management smoking-reduction program cheated in using the procedures and their contracts, whereas the "successes" did not (Hackett et al., 1976). In a case

study of self-management, Greenberg and Altman (1976) found that smoking decrements occurred quite slowly (two to four months). If self-management efforts are not used over a certain period of time, their effectiveness may be too limited to produce any change.

Self-Evaluation and Standard Setting

Self-evaluation in the form of standard setting (or goal setting) and intention statements seems to be an important component of a self-management program. Spates and Kanfer (1977) found that children's performance on a learning task was enhanced only after the children had been trained to set standards or performance criteria. Greiner and Karoly (1976) also reported the importance of standard setting in a self-management program designed to improve the study behavior of college students. Some evidence also suggests that self-selected stringent standards affect performance more positively than lenient standards (Bandura, 1971b; Brownell, Colletti, Ersner-Hershfield, Hershfield, & Wilson, 1977). Perri and Richards (1977) described successful self-controllers as setting higher goals and criteria for change than unsuccessful self-controllers. However, the standards set should be realistic and within reach, or it is unlikely that self-reinforcement will ever occur.

Use of Self-Reinforcement

Self-reinforcement, either covert, verbal, or material, appears to be an important ingredient of an effective self-management program. Being able to praise oneself covertly or to note positive improvement seems to be correlated with self-change (Perri & Richards, 1977; Heffernan & Richards, 1981). In contrast, self-criticism (covert and verbal) seems to militate against change (Hackett et al., 1976; Mahoney & Mahoney, 1976). Mahoney, Moura, and Wade (1973) found that a material self-reward (such as money) was more effective than either self-monitoring or self-punishment in a weight reduction program. And across four problem areas of college students (eating, smoking, studying, and dating), successful self-controllers reported using self-reward far more frequently (67%) than unsuccessful self-controllers (19%) (Perri & Richards, 1977).

Environmental Support

Some degree of external support is necessary to effect and maintain the changes resulting from a self-management program. For éxample, public display of self-monitoring data and the help of another person provide opportunities for social reinforcement that often augment behavior change (Rutner & Bugle, 1969; Van Houten, Hill, & Parsons, 1975). Successful participants in a smoking-reduction program reported effective use of environmental contracts, whereas "failures" reported sabotage of the contracts by significant others (Hackett et al., 1976). Similarly, Perri and Richards (1977) observed that successful self-controllers reported receiving more positive feedback from others about their change efforts than unsuccessful self-controllers. To maintain any self-managed change, there must be some support from the social and physical environment (Kanfer, 1980; Thoresen & Mahoney, 1974).

☐ STEPS IN DEVELOPING A CLIENT SELF-MANAGEMENT PROGRAM

We have incorporated these five characteristics of effective self-management into a description of the steps associated with a self-management program. These steps are applicable to any program in which the client uses stimulus control, self-monitoring, or self-reward. Figure 19-1 summarizes the steps associated with developing a self-management program; the characteristics of effective self-management reflected in the steps are noted in the left column of the figure.

In developing a self-management program, steps 1 and 2 both involve aspects of standard setting and self-evaluation. In step 1, the client identifies and records the target behavior and its antecedents and consequences. This step involves self-monitoring in which the client collects baseline data about the behavior to be changed. If baseline data have not been collected as part of problem assessment (Chapter 8), it is imperative that such data be collected now, before using any self-management strategies. In step 2, the client explicitly identifies the desired behavior, conditions, and level of change. As you may remember from Chapter 9, the behavior, conditions, and level of change are the three parts of a counseling outcome goal. Defining the goal is an important part of self-management because of the possible motivating effects of standard setting. Establishing goals may interact with some of the self-management procedures and contribute to the desired effects (Jones et al., 1977).

Steps 3 and 4 are directed toward helping the client select a combination of self-management strategies to use. The counselor will need to explain all the possible self-management strategies to the client (step 3). The counselor should emphasize that the client should select some strategies that involve prearrangement of the antecedents and some that involve manipulation and self-administration of consequences. Ultimately, the client is responsible for selecting which self-management strategies should be used (step 4). Client selection of the strategies is an important part of the overall *self-directed* nature of self-management.

Steps 5 through 9 all involve procedural considerations that may strengthen client commitment and may encourage consistent use of the strategies over time. First, the client commits himself or herself verbally by specifying what and how much change is desired and the action steps (strategies) the client will take to produce the change (step 5). Next, the counselor will instruct the client in how to carry out the selected strategies (step 6). (The counselor can follow the guidelines listed in Table 19-1 for self-monitoring, those listed in Table 19-2 for stimulus control, and the ones presented for self-reward on p. 540.) Explicit instructions and modeling by the counselor may encourage the client to use a procedure more accurately and effectively. The instructional set given by a counselor may contribute to some degree to the overall treatment outcomes (Jones et al., 1977). The client also may use the strategies more effectively if there is an opportunity to rehearse the procedures in the interview under the counselor's direction (step 7). Finally, the client applies the strategies *in vivo* (step 8) and records (monitors) the frequency of use of each strategy and the level of the target behavior (step 9). Some of the treatment effects of self-management may also be a function of the client's self-recording (Jones et al.).

Steps 10 and 11 involve aspects of self-evaluation, self-reinforcement, and environmental support. The client has an opportunity to evaluate progress toward the goal by reviewing the self-recorded data collected during strategy implementation (step 10). Review of the data may indicate that the program is progressing smoothly or that some adjustments are needed. When the data suggest that some progress toward the goal is being made, the client's self-evaluation may set the occasion for self-reinforcement. Charting or posting the data

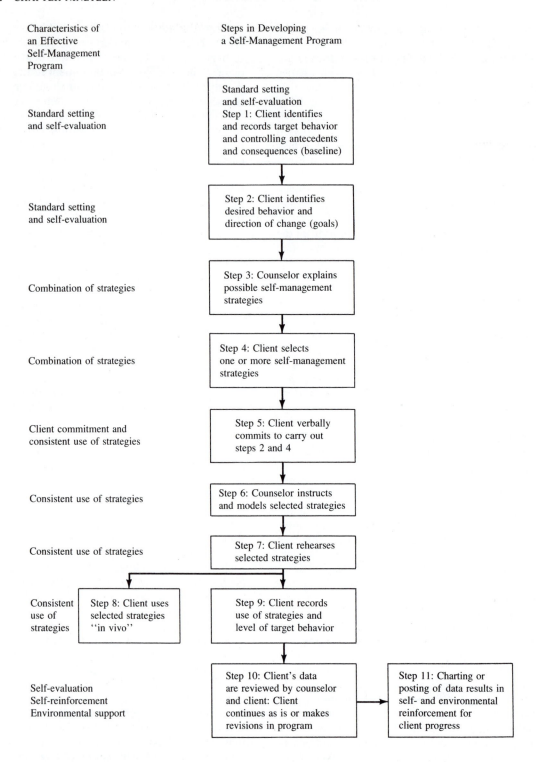

Characteristics of an Effective Self-Management Program

Standard setting and self-evaluation

Standard setting and self-evaluation

Combination of strategies

Combination of strategies

Client commitment and consistent use of strategies

Consistent use of strategies

Consistent use of strategies

Consistent use of strategies

Self-evaluation
Self-reinforcement
Environmental support

Steps in Developing a Self-Management Program

Standard setting and self-evaluation
Step 1: Client identifies and records target behavior and controlling antecedents and consequences (baseline)

Step 2: Client identifies desired behavior and direction of change (goals)

Step 3: Counselor explains possible self-management strategies

Step 4: Client selects one or more self-management strategies

Step 5: Client verbally commits to carry out steps 2 and 4

Step 6: Counselor instructs and models selected strategies

Step 7: Client rehearses selected strategies

Step 8: Client uses selected strategies "in vivo"

Step 9: Client records use of strategies and level of target behavior

Step 10: Client's data are reviewed by counselor and client: Client continues as is or makes revisions in program

Step 11: Charting or posting of data results in self- and environmental reinforcement for client progress

***Figure 19-1.** Developing an effective self-management program*

(step 11) can enhance self-reinforcement and can elicit important environmental support for long-term maintenance of client change.

The following section describes how self-monitoring can be used to record the target behavior. Such recording can occur initially for problem assessment and goal setting, or it can be introduced later as a self-change strategy. We will discuss specifically how self-monitoring can be used to promote behavior change.

□ SELF-MONITORING

Purposes of Self-Monitoring

In Chapter 8 we defined self-monitoring as a process in which clients observe and record things about themselves and their interactions with environmental situations. Self-monitoring is a useful adjunct to problem assessment because the observational data can verify or change the client's verbal report about the problem behavior. We recommend that clients record their daily self-observations over a designated time period on a behavior log. Usually the client observes and records the problem behavior, controlling antecedents, and resulting consequences. Thoresen and Mahoney (1974) assert that self-monitoring is a major *first* step in any self-change program (as in any change program!). The client must be able to discover what is happening *before* implementing a self-change strategy, just as the counselor must know what is going on before using any other therapeutic procedure. In other words, any self-management strategy, like any other strategy, should be preceded by a baseline period of self-observation and recording. During this period, the client collects and records data about the behavior to be changed (B), the antecedents (A) of the behavior, and the consequences (C) of the behavior. In addition, the client may wish to note how much or how often the behavior occurs. For example, a client might record the daily amount of study time or the number of times he or she left the study time and place to do something else. The behavior log presented in Chapter 8 for problem-assessment data can also be used by a client to collect baseline data before implementing a self-management program. If the counselor introduces self-management strategies *after* problem assessment, these self-observation data should be already available.

As we discussed in Chapter 10, self-monitoring is also very useful for evaluation. When a client self-monitors the target behavior either before or during a treatment program, "the primary utility of self-monitoring lies in its assessment or data collection function" (Ciminero et al., 1977, p. 196). In recent years, however, practitioners and researchers have realized that the mere act of self-observation can produce change. As one collects data about oneself, the data collection may influence the behavior being observed. We now know that self-monitoring is useful not only to collect data but also to promote client change. If properly structured and executed, self-monitoring can be used as one type of self-management strategy.

Clinical Uses of Self-Monitoring

A number of research reports and clinical studies have explored self-monitoring as the major treatment strategy. In many cases, a self-monitoring procedure alone has been sufficient to produce at least short-term changes in the behavior being observed. McFall (1970), one of the first to investigate self-monitoring, found that college students who monitored their urge to smoke decreased the number of cigarettes smoked and the time spent smoking per cigarette. More recently, Abrams and Wilson (1979) found that self-monitoring of nicotine content resulted in significantly greater reductions in smoking than self-monitoring of the number of cigarettes smoked. Gormally and Rardin (1981) had overweight women monitor their daily caloric intake, activity levels, and minutes of calisthenics. Coates and Thoresen (1981) had three overweight female adolescents keep a "daily energy diary" that included duration in minutes and number of meals eaten, number of places at home where food was eaten, number of times food was eaten, number of activities while eating, and minutes of exercise (p. 388). Self-monitoring plus self-reward was effective in increasing academic behaviors and grades and in decreasing procrastination behaviors (Green, 1982). Fremouw and Heyneman (1983) used self-monitoring of behaviors and cognitions (mood and self-statements) to assess and treat obesity.

Self-monitoring has been used to record the degree of headache pain a person experiences four times a day (breakfast, lunch, dinner, and bedtime), using a 6-point scale (Blanchard, Andrasik, Neff, Jurish, & O'Keefe, 1981). Hiebert and Fox (1981) found that self-monitoring decreased the perceived level of anxiety. Hollon and Kendall (1981) have reported the use of self-monitoring client moods throughout the day. Frederiksen (1975) found that self-monitoring of antecedents, consequences, and frequency of episodes of ruminative thinking of a 25-year-old woman decreased these episodes significantly. Finally, Coates and Thoresen (1984) had two clients keep a daily sleep diary that included ratings of tension and mood, mental activity, and energy level on a 9-point scale before retiring and on arising in the morning.

Factors Influencing the Reactivity of Self-Monitoring

As you may recall from Chapter 10, two issues involved in self-monitoring are the reliability of the self-recording and its reactivity. Reliability, the accuracy of the self-recorded data, is important when self-monitoring is used to evaluate the goal behaviors. However, when self-monitoring is used as a change strategy, the accuracy of the data is less crucial. From a counseling perspective, the reactivity of self-monitoring makes it suitable for a change strategy. McFall (1970, p. 140) explains the potential reactivity of self-monitoring this way: "When an individual begins paying unusually close attention to one aspect of his behavior, that behavior is likely to change, even though no change may be intended or desired." As an example of reactivity, Kanfer (1980) noted that a married couple using self-monitoring to observe their frequent arguments reported that whenever the monitoring device (a taperecorder) was turned on, the argument was avoided.

Although the reactivity of self-monitoring can be a problem in data collection, it can be an asset when self-monitoring is used intentionally as a helping strategy. In using self-monitoring as a change strategy, it is important to try to maximize the reactive effects of self-monitoring—at least to the point of producing desired behavioral changes. Self-monitoring for *long* periods of time maintains reactivity. Nelson, Boykin, and Hayes (1982) found self-monitoring to be accurate over a long period of time. Reactivity persisted over a long period but discontinued when self-monitoring ceased.

A number of factors seem to influence the reactivity of self-monitoring. A summary of these factors suggests that self-monitoring "is most likely to produce positive behavioral changes when change-motivated subjects continuously monitor a limited number of discrete, positively-valued target behaviors; when performance feedback and goals or standards are made available and are unambiguous; and when the monitoring act is both salient and closely related in time to the target behaviors" (McFall, 1977b, p. 208).

Nelson (1977) has identified eight variables that seem to be related to the occurrence, intensity, and direction of the reactive effects of self-monitoring:

1. Motivation. Clients who are interested in changing the self-monitored behavior are more likely to show reactive effects when they self-monitor.
2. Valence of target behaviors. Behaviors a person values positively are likely to increase with self-monitoring; negative behaviors are likely to decrease; neutral behaviors may not change.
3. Type of target behaviors. The nature of the behavior that is being monitored may affect the degree to which self-monitoring procedures effect change.
4. Standard setting (goals), reinforcement, and feedback. Reactivity is enhanced for people who self-monitor in conjunction with goals and the availability of performance reinforcement or feedback.
5. Timing of self-monitoring. The time when the person self-records can influence the reactivity of self-monitoring. Results may differ depending on whether self-monitoring occurs before or after the target response.
6. Devices used for self-monitoring. More obtrusive or visible recording devices seem to be more reactive than unobtrusive devices.
7. Number of target responses monitored. Self-monitoring of only one response increases reactivity. As more responses are concurrently monitored, reactivity decreases.
8. Schedule for self-monitoring. The frequency with which a person self-monitors can affect reactivity. Continuous self-monitoring may result in more behavior change than intermittent self-recording.

Fremouw and Brown (1980) suggest three factors that can contribute to the reactive effects of self-monitoring:

1. Client characteristics. Client intellectual and physical abilities may be associated with greater reactivity when self-monitoring.
2. Expectations. Clients seeking help may have

some expectations for desirable behavior changes. However, it is probably impossible to separate client expectations from implicit or explicit therapeutic "demands" to change the target behavior.

3. Behavior change skills. Reactivity may be influenced by the client's knowledge and skills associated with behavior change. For example, the reactivity of addictive behaviors may be affected by the client's knowledge of "simple, short-term strategies such as fasting or abstinence" (Fremouw & Brown, 1980, p. 213).

□ STEPS OF SELF-MONITORING

Self-monitoring has been used to record pain intensity (Kerns, Finn, Haythornthwaite, 1988), for self-regulation in the treatment of Type II diabetes (Wing, Epstein, Norwalk, & Scott, 1988), to graph caloric intake (Buxton, Williamson, Absher, & Warner, 1985), to record drinking and blood-alcohol levels (Alden, 1988), with depression (Jar-

rett & Nelson, 1987), and with cognitive restructuring for controlling binging among restrained eaters (Pecsok & Fremouw, 1988).

The effectiveness of self-monitoring seems to vary with several parameters, including the characteristics of the client and of the target behavior (Lipinski, Black, Nelson, & Ciminero, 1975; Nelson, Lipinski, & Black, 1976a), the demand characteristics of the situation (Kazdin, 1974e), and the various components of the monitoring procedure (Bellack, Rozensky, & Schwartz, 1974; Kanfer, 1980; Mahoney & Thoresen, 1974). Some of the important steps of self-monitoring will be explored in this section.

Self-monitoring involves at least six important steps: *rationale* for the strategy, *discrimination* of a response, *recording* of a response, *charting* of a response, *display* of data, and *analysis* of data (Thoresen & Mahoney, 1974, pp. 43–44). Each of these six steps and guidelines for their use will be discussed, and they are summarized in Table 19-1. However, remember that the steps are all interac-

TABLE 19-1. Steps of self-monitoring

1. *Rationale* for self-monitoring	A. Purpose B. Overview of procedure

2. *Discrimination* of a response	A. Selection of target response to monitor
	  1. Type of response
	  2. Valence of response
	  3. Number of responses

3. *Recording* of a response	A. Timing of recording
	  1. Prebehavior recording to decrease a response; postbehavior recording to increase a response
	  2. Immediate recording
	  3. Recording when no competing responses distract recorder
	B. Method of recording
	  1. Frequency counts
	  2. Duration measures
	    a. Continuous recording
	    b. Time sampling
	C. Devices for recording
	  1. Portable
	  2. Accessible
	  3. Economical
	  4. Somewhat obtrusive

4. *Charting* of a response	A. Charting and graphing of daily totals of recorded behavior
5. *Displaying* of data	A. Public display of chart for environmental support
6. *Analysis* of data	A. Accuracy of data interpretation B. Knowledge of results for self-evaluation and self-reinforcement

tive, and the presence of all of them may be required for a person to use self-monitoring effectively.

Treatment Rationale

First, the therapist explains the rationale for self-monitoring. Before using the strategy, the client should be aware of what the self-monitoring procedure will involve and how the procedure will help with the client's problem. Fremouw and Heyneman (1983) offer this rationale (overview) to treat obese clients:

"A critical part of this program is keeping the self-monitoring diaries. On these two diaries (one for meals and one for between meal eating), you will keep track of everything you eat, the situation you eat in, and your thoughts and feelings associated with eating. This will require a good deal of effort. However, it has been our experience that although people find this recording difficult at first, it soon becomes more automatic—and it certainly is well worth the effort" [p. 182].

You could conclude the above rationale for self-monitoring with a statement about the purpose of self-monitoring, such as "The self-monitoring diaries will increase your awareness of your eating episodes, help to assess specific behaviors associated with your eating episodes, and help to formulate treatment strategies and plans for desired target behaviors. Are you willing to keep the diaries?"

Discrimination of a Response

When a client engages in self-monitoring, first an observation, or discrimination, of a response is required. For example, a client who is monitoring fingernail biting must be able to discriminate instances of nail biting from instances of other behavior. Discrimination of a response occurs whenever the client is able to identify the presence or absence of the behavior, whether overt, like nail biting, or covert, like a positive self-thought. Thoresen and Mahoney (1974, p. 43) point out that making behavioral discriminations can be thought of as the "awareness" facet of self-monitoring.

Discrimination of a response involves helping the client identify *what* to monitor. Often this decision will require counselor assistance. There is some evidence that the type of the monitored response affects the results of self-monitoring. For example, Romanczyk (1974) found that self-mon-

itoring produced greater weight loss for people who recorded their daily weight and daily caloric intake than for those who recorded only daily weight. As McFall (1977b) has observed, it is not very clear why some target responses seem to be better ones to self-monitor than others; at this point, the selection of target responses remains a pragmatic choice. Mahoney (1977b, pp. 244–245) points out that there may be times when self-monitoring of certain responses could detract from therapeutic effectiveness, as in asking a suicidal client to monitor depressive thoughts.

The effects of self-monitoring also vary with the valence of the target response. There are always "two sides" of a behavior that could be monitored —the positive and the negative (Mahoney & Thoresen, 1974, p. 37). There seem to be times when one side is more important for self-monitoring than the other (Kanfer, 1970; Mahoney & Thoresen, p. 37).

Most of the evidence indicates that self-monitoring of positive responses increases these responses. In contrast, self-monitoring decreases the frequency of negative behaviors (Broden, Hall, & Mitts, 1971; Cavior & Marabotto, 1976; Kirschenbaum, Ordman, Tomarken, & Holtzbauer, 1982; Nelson, Lipinski, & Black, 1976a). Unfortunately, there are very few data to guide a decision about the exact type and valence of responses to monitor. Because the reactivity of self-monitoring is affected by the value assigned to a behavior (Watson & Tharp, 1981), one guideline might be to have the client monitor the behavior that she or he cares *most* about changing. Generally, it is a good idea to encourage the client to limit monitoring to one response, at least initially. If the client engages in self-monitoring of one behavior with no problems, then more items can be added.

Recording of a Response

After the client has learned to make discriminations about a response, the counselor can provide instructions and examples about the method for recording the observed response. Most clients have probably never recorded their behavior *systematically.* Systematic recording is crucial to the success of self-monitoring, so it is imperative that the client understand the importance and methods of recording. The client needs instructions in when and how to record and devices for recording. The timing, method, and recording devices all can influence the effectiveness of self-monitoring.

Timing of self-monitoring: When to record. One of the least understood processes of self-monitoring involves timing, or the point when the client actually records the target behavior. Instances have been reported of both prebehavior and postbehavior monitoring. In prebehavior monitoring, the client records the intention or urge to engage in the behavior *before* doing so. In postbehavior monitoring, the client records each completed instance of the target behavior — *after* the behavior has occurred. Kazdin (1974f, p. 239) points out that the precise effects of self-monitoring may depend on the point at which monitoring occurs in the chain of responses relative to the response being recorded. Kanfer (1980) concludes that existing data are insufficient to judge whether pre- or postbehavior monitoring will have maximal effects. Nelson (1977) indicates that the effects of the timing of self-monitoring may depend partly on whether other responses are competing for the person's attention at the time the response is recorded. Another factor influencing the timing of self-monitoring is the amount of time between the response and the actual recording. Most people agree that delayed recording of the behavior weakens the efficacy of the monitoring process (Kanfer, 1980; Kazdin, 1974f).

We suggest four guidelines that may help the counselor and client decide when to record. First, if the client is using monitoring as a way to *decrease* an undesired behavior, prebehavior monitoring may be more effective, as this seems to interrupt the response chain early in the process. An example of the rule of thumb for self-monitoring an undesired response would be "Record whenever you have the urge to smoke or to eat." McFall (1970) found that prebehavior monitoring did reduce smoking behavior. Similarly, Bellack et al. (1974) found that prebehavior monitoring resulted in more weight loss than postbehavior monitoring. If the client is using self-monitoring to *increase* a desired response, then postbehavior monitoring may be more helpful. As Bellack et al. observe, postbehavior monitoring can make a person more aware of a "low frequency, desirable behavior" (p. 529). Third, recording instances of a desired behavior as it occurs or immediately after it occurs may be most helpful. The rule of thumb is to "record *immediately* after you have the urge to smoke — or *immediately* after you have covertly praised yourself; do not wait even for 15 or 20 minutes, as the impact of recording may be lost."

Fourth, the client should be encouraged to self-record the response when not distracted by the situation or by other competing responses. However, as mentioned in Chapter 10, the client should be instructed to record the behavior *in vivo* as it occurs, if possible, rather than at the end of the day, when he or she is dependent on retrospective recall. *In vivo* recording may not always be feasible, and in some cases the client's self-recording may have to be performed later.

Method of self-monitoring: How to record. The counselor also needs to instruct the client in a *method* for recording the target responses. McFall (1977b) points out that the method of recording can vary in a number of ways:

> It can range from a very informal and unstructured operation, as when subjects are asked to make mental notes of any event that seems related to mood changes, to something fairly formal and structured, as when subjects are asked to fill out a mood-rating sheet according to a time-sampling schedule. It can be fairly simple, as when subjects are asked to keep track of how many cigarettes they smoke in a given time period; or it can be complex and time-consuming, as when they are asked to record not only how many cigarettes they smoke, but also the time, place, circumstances, and affective response associated with lighting each cigarette. It can be a relatively objective matter, as when counting the calories consumed each day; or it can be a very subjective matter, as when recording the number of instances each day when they successfully resist the temptation to eat sweets [p. 197].

Ciminero et al. (1977, p. 198) suggest that the recording method should be "easy to implement, must produce a representative sample of the target behavior, and must be sensitive to changes in the occurrence of the target behavior."

As you may remember from our description of outcome evaluation in Chapter 10, frequency, latency, duration, and intensity can be recorded with either a continuous recording or a time-sampling method. Selection of one of these methods will depend mainly on the type of target response and the frequency of its occurrence. To record the *number* of target responses, the client can use a frequency count. Frequency counts are most useful for monitoring responses that are discrete, do not occur all the time, and are of short duration (Ciminero et al., 1977, p. 190). For instance, clients might record the number of times they have an urge to smoke or the number of times they praise or compliment themselves covertly.

Other kinds of target responses are recorded more easily and accurately by latency or duration. Any time a client wants to record the amount or length of a response, a duration count can be used. Ciminero et al. (1977, p. 198) recommend the use of a duration measure whenever the target response is not discrete and varies in length. For example, a client might use a duration count to note the amount of time spent reading textbooks or practicing a competitive sport. Or a client might want to keep track of the length of time spent in a "happy mood." Latency would be used to self-record the amount of time that elapses before the onset of a response, such as the number of minutes elapsed between feeling angry and subsequently losing one's temper.

Sometimes a client may want to record two different responses and use both the frequency and duration methods. For example, a client might use a frequency count to record each urge to smoke and a duration count to monitor the time spent smoking a cigarette. Watson and Tharp (1981) suggest that the counselor can recommend frequency counts whenever it is easy to record clearly separate occurrences of the behavior and duration counts whenever the behavior continues for long periods.

Clients can also self-record intensity of responses whenever data are desired about the relative severity of a response. For example, a client might record the intensity of happy, anxious, or depressed feelings or moods.

Format of self-monitoring instruments. There are many formats of self-monitoring instruments a client can use to record frequency, duration, or severity of the target response as well as information about contributing variables. The particular format of the instrument can affect reactivity and can increase client compliance with self-monitoring. The format of the instrument should be tailored to the client problem. Figure 19-2 (pp. 530–531) shows examples of four formats for self-monitoring instruments. Example 1 in the figure illustrates a variety of response dimensions that Fremouw and Heyneman (1983) used in the cognitive-behavioral diary for their weight reduction program: duration of snacks or binges, types of situations, recordings and self-ratings of self-state-

ments, number of calories, and self-ratings of stress, control over eating or binging, and mood states. Example 2 illustrates a self-monitoring format used for assertive situations. The client is to record the situation, time and date, thoughts, behavior, self-rated satisfaction about the situation, and what behaviors should have been performed (Barlow et al., 1983, p. 103). Example 3 shows a format we use with couples in marital therapy for self-monitoring of content and quality of marital interactions. In this format, adapted from Williams (1979), each person records the content of the interaction with the spouse (for example, having dinner together, talking about finances, discussing work, going to movies) and self-rates the quality of that interaction. Example 4 shows a format we use with clients to self-record aspects of anxiety responses. This format can be adapted to other covert (internal) responses. Each of these formats can use a variety of self-recording devices.

Devices for self-monitoring. Often clients report that one of the most intriguing aspects of self-monitoring involves the device or mechanism used for recording. In order for recording to occur systematically and accurately, the client must have access to some recording device. A variety of devices have been used to help clients keep accurate records. Note cards, daily log sheets, and diaries can be used to make written notations. A popular self-recording device is a wrist counter, such as a golf counter. Lindsley (1968) adapted the golf counter for self-recording in different settings. If several behaviors are being counted simultaneously, the client can wear several wrist counters or use knitting tallies. K. Mahoney (1974) describes a wrist counter with rows of beads that permits the recording of several behaviors. Audio- and videotapes, toothpicks, or small plastic tokens can also be used as recording devices. Watson and Tharp (1981) report the use of pennies to count: a client can carry pennies in one pocket and transfer one penny to another pocket each time a behavior occurs. Children can record frequencies by pasting stars on a chart or by using a "countoon" (Kunzelmann, 1970), which has pictures and numbers for three recording columns: "What do I do," "My count," and "What happens." Clocks, watches, and kitchen timers can be used for duration counts.

The counselor and client select a recording device. Here is an opportunity to be inventive! There are several practical criteria to consider in helping a client select a recording device. The device should be portable and accessible so that it is present whenever the behavior occurs (Watson & Tharp, 1981). It should be easy and convenient to use and economical. The obtrusiveness of the device should also be considered. The recording device can function as a cue (discriminative stimulus) for the client to self-monitor, so it should be noticeable enough to remind the client to engage in self-monitoring. However, a device that is too obtrusive may draw attention from others who could reward or punish the client for self-monitoring (Ciminero et al., 1977, p. 202). Finally, the device should be capable of giving cumulative frequency data so that the client can chart daily totals of the behavior (Thoresen & Mahoney, 1974).

After the client has been instructed in the timing and method of recording, and after a recording device has been selected, the client should practice using the recording system. Breakdowns in self-monitoring often occur because a client did not understand the recording process clearly. Rehearsal of the recording procedures may ensure that the client will record accurately. Generally, a client should engage in self-recording for three to four weeks. Usually the effects of self-monitoring are not apparent in only one or two weeks' time.

Charting of a Response

The data recorded by the client should be translated onto a more permanent storage record such as a chart or graph that enables the client to inspect the self-monitored data visually. This type of visual guide may provide the occasion for client self-reinforcement (Kanfer, 1980), which, in turn, can influence the reactivity of self-monitoring. The data can be charted by days, using a simple line graph. For example, a client counting the number of urges to smoke a cigarette could chart these by days, as in Figure 19-3 (p. 532). A client recording the amount of time spent studying daily could use the same sort of line graph to chart duration of study time. The vertical axis would be divided into time intervals such as 15 minutes, 30 minutes, 45 minutes, or 1 hour.

The client should receive either oral or written instructions on a way to chart and graph the daily totals of the recorded response. The counselor can assist the client in interpreting the chart in the sessions on data review and analysis. If a client is using self-monitoring to increase a behavior, the line on the graph should go up gradually if the self-monitoring is having the desired effect; if self-monitoring is influencing an undesired response to decrease, the line on the graph should go down gradually.

Display of Data

After the graph has been made, the counselor should encourage the client to display the completed chart. If the chart is displayed in a "public" area, this display may prompt environmental reinforcement, a necessary part of an effective self-management program. Several studies have found that the effects of self-monitoring are augmented when the data chart is displayed as a public record (McKenzie & Rushall, 1974; Rutner & Bugle, 1969; Van Houten et al., 1975).

Analysis of Data

If the client's recording data are not reviewed and analyzed, the client may soon feel as if he or she was told to make a graph just for practice in drawing straight lines! A very important facet of self-monitoring is the information it can provide to the client. There is some evidence that people who receive feedback about their self-recording change more than those who do not (Kazdin, 1974e). The recording and charting of data should be used *explicitly* to provide the client with knowledge of results about behavior or performance. Specifically, the client should bring the data to weekly counseling sessions for review and analysis. In these sessions, the counselor can encourage the client to compare the data with the desired goals and standards. The client can use the recorded data for self-evaluation and determine whether the data indicate that the behavior is within or outside the desired limits. The counselor can also aid in data analysis by helping the client interpret the data correctly. As Thoresen and Mahoney observe, "Errors about what the charted data represent can seriously hinder success in self-control" (1974, p. 44).

□ MODEL EXAMPLE: SELF-MONITORING

As you may recall from Joan's goal chart in Chapter 9, one of Joan's goals was to increase her positive thoughts (and simultaneously decrease her negative thoughts) about her ability to do well with math. This goal lends itself well to application of self-management strategies for several reasons.

Date_____

1. Cognitive-behavioral diary (Fremouw & Heyneman, 1983, p. 176)*

Prior to eating

Day & time start/stop (duration)	Snacks/ binges	Situation	Stress	Mood	Self-statements	Rate −5 +5

Following eating

Food + quantity +calories	Mood	Self-statement	Rate −5 +5	Control

Stress: 0 = none, 7 = extreme
Mood: *B*ored, *D*epressed, *F*rustrated, *G*uilty, *H*appy, *N*eutral
Rate self-statements: −5 = extremely negative, 0 = neutral, +5 = extremely positive
Control over eating or binge: 0 = none, 7 = extreme
* From "Obesity" by W. J. Fremouw and N. Heyneman. In M. Herson (Ed.), *Outpatient behavior therapy*. Copyright © 1983 by Grune & Stratton. Reprinted by permission of Grune & Stratton, Inc. and the author.

2. Assertiveness situations (Barlow, Hayes, & Nelson, 1984, p. 103)**

Date and time	Situation	What did you do?	What were you thinking?

How did situation end?	How did you feel about the outcome? (0 = very dissatisfied, 10 = very satisfied)	What could you have done differently?

** From *The scientist practitioner* by D. H. Barlow, S. C. Hayes, & R. O. Nelson. Copyright © 1984 by Pergamon Press.

3. Content and quality of marital interactions

Record the type of interaction under "Contents." For *each* interaction circle one category that best represents the quality of that interaction.

Time	Content of interaction	Quality of interaction				
		Very pleasant	Pleasant	Neutral	Unpleasant	Very unpleasant
6:30 A.M.		++	+	0	–	– –
7:00		++	+	0	–	– –
7:30		++	+	0	–	– –
8:00		++	+	0	–	– –

4. Self-monitoring log for recording anxiety responses

	Date and time	Frequency of anxiety response	External events	Internal dialogue (self-statements)	Behavioral factors	Degree of arousal	Skill in handling situation
Instructions for recording:	Record day and time of incident	Describe each situation in which anxiety occurred	Note what triggered the anxiety	Note your thoughts or things you said to yourself when this occurred	Note how you responded —what you did	Rate the intensity of the anxiety: (1) a little intense, (2) somewhat intense, (3) very intense, (4) extremely intense	Rate the degree to which you handled the situation effectively: (1) a little, (2) somewhat, (3) very, (4) extremely

Figure 19-2. Four examples of formats for self-monitoring instruments

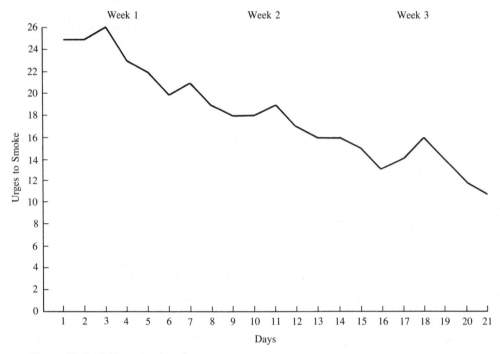

Figure 19-3. Self-monitoring chart

First, the goal represents a covert behavior (positive thoughts), which is observable only by Joan. Second, the "flip side" of the goal (the negative thoughts) represents a very well-learned habit. Probably most of these negative thoughts occur *outside* the counseling sessions. To change this thought pattern, Joan will need to use strategies she can apply frequently (as needed) *in vivo,* and she will need to use strategies she can administer to herself.

Here is a description of the way self-monitoring could be used to help Joan achieve this goal.

1. *Treatment rationale.* The counselor would provide an explanation of what Joan will self-monitor and why, emphasizing that this is a strategy she can apply herself, can use with a "private" behavior, and can use as frequently as possible in the actual setting.

2. *Discrimination of a response.* The counselor would need to help Joan define the target response explicitly. One definition could be "Any time I think about myself doing math or working with numbers successfully." The counselor should pro-

vide some possible examples of this response, such as "Gee, I did well on my math homework today" or "I was able to balance the checkbook today." Joan should also be encouraged to identify some examples of the target response. Since Joan wants to increase this behavior, the target response would be stated in the "positive."

3. *Recording of a response.* The counselor should instruct Joan in timing, a method, and a device for recording. In this case, because Joan is using self-monitoring to increase a desired behavior, she would use postbehavior monitoring. Joan should be instructed to record *immediately* after a target thought has occurred. She is interested in recording the *number* of such thoughts, so she could use a frequency count. A tally on a note card or a wrist counter could be selected as the device for recording. After these instructions, Joan should practice recording before actually doing it. She should be instructed to engage in self-monitoring for about four consecutive weeks.

4. *Charting of a response.* After each week of self-monitoring, Joan can add her daily frequency totals and chart them by days on a simple line graph.

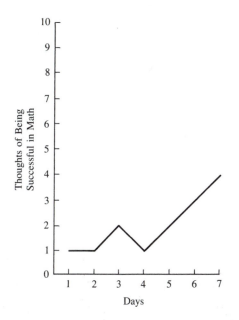

Days

Joan is using self-monitoring to increase a behavior; as a result, if the monitoring has the desired effect, the line on her graph should gradually rise. It is just starting to do so here; additional data for the next few weeks should show a greater increase if the self-monitoring is influencing the target behavior in the desired direction.

5. *Display of data.* After Joan has made a data chart, she may wish to post it in a place such as her room, where her friends could see it and encourage her for progress. Public posting may also cue Joan to reinforce herself for progress.

6. *Analysis of data.* During the period of self-monitoring, Joan should bring in her data for weekly review sessions with the counselor. The counselor can provide reinforcement and help Joan interpret the data accurately. Joan can use the data for self-evaluation by comparing the "story" of the data with her stated desired behavior and level of change.

LEARNING ACTIVITY #49: SELF-MONITORING

This learning activity is designed to help you use self-monitoring yourself. The instructions describe a self-monitoring plan for you to try out.

1. Discrimination of a target response:
   a. Specify one target behavior you would like to change. Pick either the positive or the negative side of the behavior to monitor — depending on which you value more and whether you want to increase or decrease this response.
   b. Write down a definition of this behavior. How clear is your definition?
   c. Can you write some examples of this behavior? If you had trouble with these, try to "tighten up" your definition — or else contrast positive and negative instances of the behavior.
2. Recording of the response:
   a. Specify the *timing* of your self-recording. Remember the "rules of thumb":
      1. Prebehavior monitoring to decrease an undesired response.
      2. Postbehavior monitoring to increase a desired response.
      3. Record immediately — don't wait.
      4. Record when there are no competing responses.

Write down the timing you choose.
   b. Select a *method* of recording (frequency, duration, and so on). Remember:
      1. Frequency counts for clearly separate occurrences of the response.
      2. Duration or latency measures for responses that occur for a period of time.
      3. Intensity measures to determine the severity of a response.
   c. Select a *device* to assist you in recording. Remember that the device should be —
      1. Portable.
      2. Accessible.
      3. Economical.
      4. Obtrusive enough to serve as a reminder to self-record.
   d. After you have made these determinations, engage in self-monitoring for at least a week (preferably two). Then complete steps 3, 4, and 5.
3. Charting of response: Take your daily self-recording data and chart them on a simple line graph for each day that you self-monitored.
4. Displaying of data: Arrange a place to display your chart where it may elicit strokes from others.
5. Analysis of data: Compare your chart with your stated desired behavior change. What has happened to the behavior?

☐ STIMULUS CONTROL: PREARRANGEMENT OF ANTECEDENTS

Kanfer (1980, p. 361) defines stimulus control as the predetermined arrangement of environmental conditions that makes it impossible or unfavorable for an undesired behavior to occur. Stimulus-control methods emphasize rearranging or modifying environmental conditions that serve as cues or antecedents of a particular response. As you may recall from the discussion of the ABC model of behavior in Chapter 7, a behavior often is guided by certain things that precede it (antecedents) and is maintained by positive or negative events that follow it (consequences). You may also remember that both antecedents and consequences can be external (overt) or internal (covert). For example, an antecedent could be a situation, an emotion, a cognition, or an overt or covert verbal instruction.

Clinical Uses of Stimulus Control

Stimulus-control procedures have been used for behavior change and weight loss (Carroll & Yates, 1981; Fremouw, Callahan, Zitter, & Katell, 1981), to decrease nocturnal awakenings (Norton & DeLuca, 1979; Lacks, 1987), to decrease insomnia (Lacks, Bertelson, Sugerman, & Kunkel, 1983; Turner & Ascher, 1982; Zwart & Lisman, 1979), with thought stopping to decrease persistent disturbing thoughts (Martin, 1982), to increase exercise (Keefe & Blumenthal, 1980), to decrease worry (Borkovec, Wilkinson, Folensbee, & Lerman, 1983), and to enhance social interaction and activity among elderly nursing-home residents (Quattrochi-Turbin & Jason, 1980). According to Gambrill (1977), stimulus-control procedures are most useful when the client's behavior exists but occurs in the wrong context or does not occur frequently enough in the same context. Finally, stimulus control was used with imagery to control insomnia (Morin & Azrin, 1987) and to decrease vomiting (Long, Simone, & Tucher, 1986). Herby, Ozaki, & Campos (1984) found that training in self-reinforcement and reward has implications for treating depression.

How Antecedents Acquire Stimulus Control

When antecedents are consistently associated with a behavior that is reinforced in the *presence* (not the absence) of these antecedent stimuli, they gain control over the behavior. You might think of this as "stimulus control," since an antecedent is a stimulus for a certain response. When an antecedent gains stimulus control over the response, there is a high probability that the response will be emitted in the presence of these particular antecedent events. For example, most of us "automatically" slow down, put our foot on the brake, and stop the car when we see a red traffic light. The red light is a stimulus that has gained control over our stopping-the-car behavior. Generally, the fact that antecedents exert stimulus control is helpful, as it is in driving when we go ahead with a green light and stop at the sight of a red light.

Inappropriate Stimulus Control in Problem Behavior

Client problem behaviors may occur because of *inappropriate* stimulus control. For example, Ferster, Nurnberger, and Levitt (1962) were perhaps the first to note that inappropriate stimulus control was related to obesity. They found that eating responses of overweight people tended to be associated with many environmental cues. If a person eats something not only at the dining table but also when working in the kitchen, watching television, walking by the refrigerator, and stopping at a Dairy Queen, the sheer number of eating responses could soon result in obesity. Too many environmental cues often are related to other client problems, particularly "excesses" such as smoking and drinking. In these cases, the primary aim of a self-management stimulus-control method is to reduce the number of cues associated with the undesired response, such as eating or smoking.

Other problem behaviors have been observed that seem to involve excessively narrow stimulus control. At the opposite pole from obesity are people who eat so little that their physical and psychological health suffers (a condition called "anorexia nervosa"). For these people, there are too few eating cues. Lack of exercise can be a function of too narrow stimulus control. For some people, the paucity of environmental cues associated with exercise results in very little physical activity. In these cases, the primary aim of a stimulus-control strategy is to establish or increase the number of cues that will elicit the desired behavior.

To summarize, stimulus-control self-management involves reducing the number of antecedent stimuli associated with an undesirable behavior and simultaneously increasing the antecedent cues associated with a desirable response (Mahoney & Thoresen, 1974; Thoresen & Mahoney, 1974). Table 19-2 shows the principal methods of stimulus control and some examples.

Using Stimulus Control to Decrease Behavior

To decrease the rate of a behavior, the antecedent cues associated with the behavior should be reduced in frequency or prearranged or altered in terms of time and place of occurrence. When cues are separated from the habitual behavior by alteration or elimination, the old, undesired habit can be terminated (Mahoney & Thoresen, 1974, p. 42). Many behavioral "excesses," such as eating,

smoking, drinking, or self-criticism, are tied to a great number of antecedent situations. Reducing these cues can restrict the occurrence of the undesired behavior. For instance, Nolan (1968) and Roberts (1969) reported case studies in which smoking was restricted to one special "smoking chair." Existing cues can be prearranged to make the target behavior so hard to execute that the person is unlikely to do it. An example would be altering the place of smoking by moving one's smoking chair to an inconvenient place like the basement. The smoker would have to go downstairs each time she or he wanted a cigarette. Cues can also be prearranged by placing their control in the hands of another person. Giving your pack of cigarettes

TABLE 19-2. Principles and examples of stimulus-control strategies

Principle of change	Example
To decrease a behavior: Reduce or narrow the frequency of cues associated with the behavior.	
1. Prearrange or alter cues associated with the place of the behavior:	
a. Prearrange cues that make it hard to execute the behavior.	Place fattening foods in high, hard-to-reach places.
b. Prearrange cues so that they are controlled by others.	Ask friends or family to serve you only one helping of food and to avoid serving fattening foods to you.
2. Alter the time or sequence (chain) between the antecedents cues and the resulting behaviors:	
a. Break up the sequence.	Buy and prepare food only on a full stomach.
b. Change the sequence.	Substitute and engage in nonfood activities when you start to move toward snacking (toward refrigerator, cupboard, or candy machine).
c. Build pauses into the sequence.	Delay second helpings of food or snacks for a predetermined amount of time.
To increase a behavior: Increase or prearrange the cues associated with the response.	
1. Seek out these cues deliberately to perform the desired behavior.	Initially arrange only one room with a desk to study. When you need to study, go to this place.
2. Concentrate on the behavior when in the situation.	Concentrate only on studying in the room. If you get distracted, get up and leave. Don't mix study with other activities, such as listening to records or talking.
3. Gradually extend the behavior to other situations.	When you have control over studying in one room, extend the behavior to another conducive room or place.
4. Promote the occurrence of helpful cues by other people or by self-generated reminders.	Ask your roommate to remind you to leave the desk when talking or when distracted; remind yourself of good study procedures by posting a list over your study desk or by using verbal or covert self-instructions.

to a friend is an example of this method. The friend should agree to help you reduce smoking and should agree not to reinforce or punish any instances of your smoking behavior (the undesired response).

A behavior can also be reduced through stimulus control by interrupting the learned pattern or sequence that begins with one or more antecedent cues and results in the undesired response. This sequence may be called a *chain*. A problem behavior is often the result of a long chain of events. For example, a variety of behaviors make up the sequence of smoking. Before puffing on a cigarette, a person has to go to a cigarette machine, put money in the machine, take out a pack of cigarettes, take out one cigarette from the pack, and light the cigarette.

This chain might be interrupted in one of three ways: breaking up the chain of events, changing the chain, or building pauses into the chain (Watson & Tharp, 1981, pp. 113–115). All these methods involve prearranging or altering the time of occurrence of the behavior. A chain of events can be broken up by discovering and interrupting an event early in the sequence or by scrambling the typical order of events. For example, the smoker could break up the chain by not carrying the change required for a cigarette machine. Or, if the smoker typically smokes at certain times, the usual order of events leading up to smoking could be mixed up. The smoker could also change the typical chain of events. A person who starts to light up a cigarette whenever bored, tense, or lacking something to do with his or her hands could perform a different activity at this point, such as calling a friend when bored, relaxing when tense, or knitting or playing cards to provide hand activity. Finally, the smoker could interrupt the chain by deliberately building pauses into it. As you may recall, when antecedents exert control over a behavior, the behavior occurs almost automatically. As Watson and Tharp point out, one way to deal with this automatic quality is to pause before responding to a cue (p. 114). For instance, whenever the smoker has an urge to light up in response to a stress cue, a deliberate pause of ten minutes can be built in before the person actually does light up. Gradually this time interval can be increased. Sometimes you can even strengthen the pause procedure by covertly instructing yourself on what you want to do or by thinking about the benefits of not smoking. The pause itself can then become a

new antecedent "for a more desirable link in the chain of events" (Watson & Tharp, p. 114).*

Two studies illustrate the use of stimulus-control procedures to decrease worry (Borkovec et al., 1983) and to change eating patterns to decrease weight (Fremouw et al., 1981). In the first study, worriers were instructed "(1) to learn to identify and to distinguish worrisome thoughts that were unnecessary or unpleasant and thoughts that were necessary or pleasant, (2) to establish a half-hour worry period to take place at the same time and in the same location each day, (3) when worrying, to postpone worrying to a worry period and replace it with attending to present-moment experience, and (4) to make use of the half-hour worry period to worry about concerns and to engage in problem solving to eliminate those concerns" (Borkovec et al., p. 248).

Fremouw et al. (1981) used instructions in stimulus control to promote behavior change and weight loss. Clients were instructed to use the following procedures to change the antecedents for eating:

(a) Designate one place to eat all meals and snacks; (b) avoid all other activities, such as reading, when eating; (c) buy nonfattening foods; (d) rearrange the cupboards and refrigerator to make snack foods less accessible and visible; (e) store foods in opaque containers; (f) shop from a prepared list when not hungry; (g) serve food on plates in the kitchen, do not leave serving bowls on the table; (h) use smaller plates, bowls, and glasses to make food appear larger; and (i) buy and prepare a variety of low calorie snacks such as vegetables or fruits [p. 292].

Using Stimulus Control to Increase Behavior

Stimulus-control methods can also be used to increase a desired response. As noted in Table 19-2, to increase the rate of a response, a person increases or prearranges the antecedent cues associated with the desired behavior. The person deliberately seeks out these cues to perform the behavior and concentrates only on this behavior when in the situation. Competing or distracting

---

* This and all other quotations from this source are from *Self-directed behavior: Self-modification for personal adjustment* (3rd ed.), by D. L. Watson and R. G. Tharp. Copyright © 1981, 1977, 1974 by Wadsworth Publishing Company, Inc. Reprinted by permission of the publisher, Brooks/Cole Publishing Company, Pacific Grove, California.

responses must be avoided. Gradually, as stimulus control over the behavior in one situation is achieved, the person can extend the behavior by performing it in another, similar situation. This process of stimulus generalization means that a behavior learned in one situation can be performed in different but similar situations (Watson & Tharp, 1981, p. 126). The person can promote the occurrence of new antecedent cues by using reminders from others, self-reminders, or overt or covert self-instructions (Watson & Tharp). The rate of a desired response is increased by increasing the times and places in which the person performs the response.

As an example, suppose you are working with a client who wants to increase his or her amount of daily exercise. First, more cues would be established to which the person would respond with isometric or physical activity. For example, the person might perform isometric activities whenever sitting in a chair or waiting for a traffic light. Or the person might perform physical exercises each morning and evening on a special exercise mat. The client would seek out these prearranged cues and concentrate on performing the activity while in the situation. Other behaviors should not be performed while in these situations, since a competing response could interfere with the exercise activity (Watson & Tharp, 1981, p. 125). Gradually, the client could extend the exercise activities to new but similar situations—for example, doing isometrics while sitting on the floor or waiting for a meeting to start. The person could also promote exercise behavior in these situations by reminders—posting an exercise chart on the wall or carrying it around in a pocket or wallet, displaying an exercise list, and so forth.

As an illustration of the use of stimulus-control procedures to increase behavior, Keefe and Blumenthal (1980) used stimulus control and self-reinforcement to enhance maintenance of an exercise program. Clients were asked to use the following stimulus-control procedures: (1) exercise at the same time and in a similar place each day, (2) engage in a warm-up consisting of stretching exercises for a minimum of ten minutes before beginning exercise, (3) set an exercise goal not greater than 10% of the distance previously covered in walking during the preceding week (p. 32).

Stimulus-control instructions also have been used to increase sleep. For example, clients were instructed: (1) Go to bed or lie down to sleep only when sleepy. (2) Do not read, watch TV, or eat in bed—use the bed only for sleeping and/or sexual activities. (3) If unable to fall asleep after 10 to 20 minutes, get out of bed and engage in some activity. Return to bed only when sleepy—and continue this procedure throughout the night as necessary. (4) Set the alarm clock and get up at the same time every morning regardless of the amount of sleep obtained during the night. (5) Do not take naps during the day (Turner & Ascher, 1982, pp. 35–36; Zwart & Lisman, 1979, p. 114).

According to Kanfer (1980, p. 361), one advantage of stimulus control is that only minimal self-initiated steps are required to trigger environmental changes that effect desired or undesired responses. Blechman, Olson, and Hellman (1976) found that one exposure to a family contract game was sufficient to achieve stimulus control over the family's discussion behavior. The participation in the game accelerated family problem-solving behavior and decreased their antagonistic, off-task discussion. However, stimulus-control methods often are insufficient to modify behavior without the support of other strategies. As Mahoney and Thoresen (1974) observe, stimulus-control methods are not usually sufficient for long-term self-change unless accompanied by other self-management methods that exert control over the *consequences* of the target behavior. One self-management method that involves self-presented consequences is discussed in the following section.

☐ MODEL EXAMPLE: STIMULUS CONTROL

This model example will illustrate how stimulus control can be used as *one way* to help Joan achieve her goal of increasing positive thoughts about her math ability. Recall that the principle of change in using stimulus control to increase a behavior is to increase the cues associated with the behavior. Here's how we would implement this principle with Joan.

1. Establish at least one cue that Joan could use as an antecedent for positive thoughts. We might suggest something like putting a piece of tape over her watch.
2. Develop a list of several positive thoughts about math. Each thought could be written on a blank card that Joan could carry with her.
3. Instruct Joan to read or think about a thought on one card *each* time she looks at her watch.

Instruct her to seek out the opportunity deliberately by looking at her watch frequently and then concentrating on one of these positive thoughts.

4. When Joan gets to the point where she automatically thinks of a positive thought after looking at her watch, other cues can be established that she can use in the same way. For instance, she can put a ☺ on her math book. Each time she gets out her math book and sees the "smily face," she can use this cue to concentrate on another positive thought.

5. She can promote more stimulus control over these thoughts by using reminders. For instance, Joan could put a list of positive thoughts on the mirror or the closet door in her room. Each time she sees the list, it serves as a reminder. Or she can ask a friend or classmate to remind her to "think positively" whenever the subject of math or math class is being discussed.

LEARNING ACTIVITY #50: STIMULUS CONTROL

Since the emphasis in this chapter is on self-management, the learning activities in this chapter are designed to help you use these strategies yourself! The purpose of this learning activity is to help you reduce an unwanted behavior, using stimulus-control methods.

1. Specify a behavior that you find undesirable and you wish to decrease. It can be an overt one, such as smoking, eating, biting your nails, or making sarcastic comments, or it can be a covert behavior, such as thinking about yourself in negative ways or thinking how great food or smoking tastes.

2. Select one or more stimulus-control methods to use for behavior reduction from the list and examples given in Table 19-2. Remember, you will be reducing the number of cues or antecedent events associated with this behavior by altering the times and places the undesired response occurs.

3. Implement these stimulus-control methods daily for two weeks.

4. During the two weeks, engage in self-monitoring of your target response. Record the type and use of your method and amount of your target behavior, using frequency or duration methods of recording.

5. At the end of two weeks, review your recording data. Did you use your selected method consistently? If not, what contributed to your infrequent use? If you used it consistently, did you notice any gradual reduction in the target behavior by the end of two weeks? What problems did you encounter in applying a stimulus-control method with yourself? What did you learn about stimulus control that might help you when using it with clients?

☐ SELF-REWARD

Self-reward procedures are used to help clients regulate and strengthen their behavior with the aid of self-produced consequences. Many actions of an individual are controlled by self-produced consequences as much as by external consequences (Bandura, 1974, 1976b). As Bandura (1974) explains, "People typically set themselves certain standards of behavior and self-administer rewarding or punishing consequences depending on whether their performances fall short of, match, or exceed their self-prescribed demands" (p. 87). There is evidence that most patterns of self-reinforcement and self-punishment are acquired and modified by learning (Bandura, 1971b).

According to Bandura (1971b), there are several necessary conditions of self-reinforcement, or self-reward:

1. The individual (rather than someone else) determines the criteria for adequacy of her or his performance and for resulting reinforcement.

2. The individual (rather than someone else) controls access to the reward.

3. The individual (rather than someone else) is his or her own reinforcing agent and administers the rewards.

Note that self-reward involves *both* the self-determination and the self-administration of a reward. This distinction has, at times, been overlooked in self-reinforcement research and application. The characteristics of self-reward proposed by Bandura (1971b, 1981) suggest that the person has free access to the rewards; this is considered an essential feature of self-reward procedures. Nelson, Hayes, Spong, Jarrett, and McKnight (1983, p. 565) propose that "self-reinforcement is effective primarily because of its stimulus properties in cuing natural environmental consequences."

As a self-management procedure, self-reward is used to strengthen or increase a desired response. It is assumed that the operations involved in self-reward parallel those that occur in external reinforcement. In other words, a self-presented reward, like an externally administered reward, is defined by the function it exerts on the target behavior. A reinforcer (self- or external) is something that, when administered following a target response, tends to maintain or increase the probability of that response in the future. A major advantage of self-reward over external reward is that a person can use and apply this strategy independently.

Self-rewards can be classified into two categories: positive and negative. In positive self-reward, one presents onself with a positive stimulus (to which one has free access) *after* engaging in a specified behavior. Examples of positive reward include praising yourself after you have completed a long and difficult term paper, buying yourself a new record after you have engaged in a specified amount of piano practice, or imagining that you are resting on your favorite beach after you have completed your daily exercises. Negative self-reward involves the removal of a negative stimulus after execution of a target response. For example, obese clients removed portions of suet from their refrigerators after certain amounts of weight loss (Penick, Filion, Fox, & Stunkard, 1971). Taking down an uncomplimentary picture or chart from your wall after performing the target response is another example of negative self-reward.

Our discussion of self-reward as a therapeutic strategy is limited to the use of positive self-reward for several reasons. First, there has been very little research to validate the negative self-reward procedure. Second, by definition, negative self-reward involves an aversive activity. It is usually unpleasant for a person to keep suet in the refrigerator or to put an ugly picture on the wall. Many people will not use a strategy that is aversive. Second, we

do not recommend that counselors suggest strategies that seem aversive, because the client may feel that terminating the counseling is preferable to engaging in an unpleasant change process.

Clinical Uses of Self-Reward

Self-reward has been explored as a convenient and effective classroom-management procedure (Bolstad & Johnson, 1972; McLaughlin, 1976; Neilans & Israel, 1981). It has been used as a major component in comprehensive self-change programs involving weight control (Mahoney & Mahoney, 1976; Polly, Turner, & Sherman, 1976) and exercise programming (Turner, Polly, & Sherman, 1976). Jackson (1972) used self-reward to treat a woman who was depressed and very critical of herself. Self-reinforcement decreased the client's depressive moods, as indicated by daily self-ratings. Herby, Ozaki, and Campos (1984) found that training in self-reinforcement and reward has implications for treating depression. Finally, self-reinforcement has been effective when goals and contingencies were made public (Hayes, 1985).

Self-reward has been investigated in several controlled studies that have presented evidence for the utility of self-reinforcement as a clinical treatment strategy. For example, Mahoney et al. (1973) found that self-reward was a more effective weight reduction strategy than self-monitoring, self-punishment, or stimulus control. In this study, self-reward consisted in having the people give themselves money to buy desired items after certain amounts of weight loss. M. J. Mahoney (1974) also found that self-reward strategies resulted in more weight loss than self-monitoring, especially when the clients made the rewards contingent on improved eating habits rather than weekly weight losses. Bellack (1976) reported that self-reward was more effective than self-monitoring in producing weight reduction, even without therapist contacts. He concluded that self-reward may substantially augment the role of self-monitoring in effecting behavior change.

Both the case studies and controlled investigations of self-reward indicate that this strategy has a promising place in clinical treatment programs. In a review of self-reinforcement, Jones et al. (1977, p. 160) note that "overall, self-reinforcement has been shown to be a viable technique in treating a plethora of both clinical and educational problems." However, these authors point out that some of the clinical effects typically attributed to the self-reinforcement procedure may also be due to certain external factors, including a client's previous reinforcement history, client goal setting, the role of client self-monitoring, surveillance by another person, external contingencies in the client's environment, and the instructional set given to the client about the self-reward procedure. The exact role these external variables may play in self-reward is still relatively little known. However, a counselor should acknowledge and perhaps try to capitalize on some of these factors to heighten the clinical effects of a self-reward strategy.

Components of Self-Reward

Self-reward involves planning by the client of appropriate rewards and of the conditions in which they will be used. Self-reward can be described by four major components: (1) selection of appropriate self-rewards, (2) delivery of self-rewards, (3) timing of self-rewards, and (4) planning for self-change maintenance. These components are described in this portion of the chapter and are summarized in the following list. Although these components are discussed separately, remember that all of them are integral parts of an effective self-reward procedure.

1. Selection of appropriate rewards
   a. Individualize the reward.
   b. Use accessible rewards.
   c. Use several rewards.
   d. Use different types of rewards (verbal/symbolic, material, imaginal, current, potential).
   e. Use potent rewards.
   f. Use rewards that are not punishing to others.
   g. Match rewards to target response.
2. Delivery of self-rewards
   a. Self-monitor for data of target response.
   b. Specify what and how much is to be done for a reward.
   c. Specify frequent reinforcement in small amounts for different levels of target response.
3. Timing of self-reward
   a. Reward should come after, not before, behavior.
   b. Rewards should be immediate.
   c. Rewards should follow performance, not promises.
4. Planning for self-change maintenance.
   a. Enlist help of others in sharing or dispensing rewards.
   b. Review data with counselor.

Selection of Appropriate Rewards

In helping a client to use self-reward effectively, some time and planning must be devoted to selecting rewards that are appropriate for the client and the desired target behavior. Selecting rewards can be time-consuming. However, effective use of self-reward is somewhat dependent on the availability of events that are truly reinforcing to the client. The counselor can assist the client in selecting appropriate self-rewards; however, the client should have the major role in determining the specific contingencies.

Rewards can take many different forms. A self-reward may be verbal/symbolic, material, or imaginal. One verbal/symbolic reward is self-praise, such as thinking or telling oneself "I did a good job." A material reward is something tangible—an event (such as a movie), a purchase (such as a banana split), or a token or point that can be exchanged for a reinforcing event or purchase. An imaginal reinforcer is the covert visualization of a scene or situation that is pleasurable and produces good feelings. Imaginal reinforcers might include picturing yourself as a thin person after losing weight or imagining that you are water-skiing on a lake you have all to yourself.

Self-rewards can also be classified as current or potential. A current reward is something pleasurable that happens routinely or occurs daily, such as eating, talking to a friend, or reading a newspaper. A potential reward is something that would be new and different if it happened, something a person does infrequently or anticipates doing in the future. Examples of potential rewards include going on a vacation or buying a "luxury" item (something you love but rarely buy for yourself, not necessarily something expensive). Engaging in a "luxury" activity—something you rarely do—can be a potential reinforcer. For a person who is very busy and constantly working, "doing nothing" might be a luxury activity that is a potential reinforcer.

In selecting appropriate self-rewards, a client should consider the availability of these various kinds of rewards. We believe that a well-balanced self-reward program involves a *variety* of types of self-rewards. A counselor might encourage a client to select *both* verbal/symbolic and material rewards. Relying only on material rewards may ignore the important role of positive self-evaluations in a self-change program. Further, material rewards have been criticized for overuse and misuse (O'Leary, Poulos, & Devine, 1972). Imaginal reinforcers may not be so powerful as verbal/symbolic and material ones. However, they are completely portable and can be used to supplement verbal/symbolic and material rewards when it is impossible for an individual to use these other types (Watson & Tharp, 1981).

In selecting self-rewards, a client should also consider the use of both current and potential rewards. One of the easiest ways for a client to use current rewards is to observe what daily thoughts or activities are reinforcing and then to rearrange these so that they are used in contingent rather than noncontingent ways (Kanfer, 1975; Watson & Tharp, 1981). However, whenever a client uses a current reward, some deprivation or self-denial is involved. For example, agreeing to read the newspaper only after cleaning the kitchen involves initially denying oneself some pleasant, everyday event in order to use it to reward a desired behavior. As Thoresen and Mahoney (1974) point out, this initial self-denial introduces an aversive element into the self-reward strategy. Some people do not respond well to any aversiveness associated with self-change or self-directed behavior. One of the authors, in fact, consistently "abuses" the self-reward principle by doing the reward before the response (reading the paper before cleaning the kitchen)—precisely as a reaction against the aversiveness of this "programmed" self-denial. One way to prevent self-reward from becoming too much like programmed abstinence is to have the client select novel or potential reinforcers to use in addition to current ones.

There are several ways a counselor can help a client identify and select various kinds of self-rewards. One way is simply with verbal report. The counselor and client can discuss current self-reward practices and desired luxury items and activities (Kanfer, 1980). The client can also identify rewards by using *in vivo* observation. The client should be instructed to observe and list current consequences that seem to maintain some behaviors. Finally, the client can identify and select rewards by completing preference and reinforcement surveys. A preference survey is designed to help the client identify preferred and valued activi-

ties. Here is an example of one that Watson and Tharp (1981, p. 170) recommend:

1. What will be the rewards of achieving your goal?
2. What kind of praise do you like to receive, from yourself or from others?
3. What kinds of things do you like to have?
4. What are your major interests?
5. What are your hobbies?
6. What people do you like to be with?
7. What do you like to do with those people?
8. What do you do for fun?
9. What do you do to relax?
10. What do you do to get away from it all?
11. What makes you feel good?
12. What would be a nice present to receive?
13. What kinds of things are important to you?
14. What would you buy if you had an extra $20? $50? $100?
15. On what do you spend your money each week?
16. What behaviors do you perform every day? (Don't overlook the obvious or the commonplace.)
17. Are there any behaviors that you usually perform instead of the target behavior?
18. What would you hate to lose?
19. Of the things you do every day, which would you hate to give up?
20. What are your favorite daydreams and fantasies?
21. What are the most relaxing scenes you can imagine?

The client can complete this sort of preference survey in writing or in a discussion. Clients who find it difficult to identify rewarding events might also benefit from completing a more formalized reinforcement survey, such as the Reinforcement Survey Schedule or the Children's Reinforcement Survey Schedule, written by Cautela (1977). The client can be given homework assignments to identify possible verbal/symbolic and imaginal reinforcers. For instance, the client might be asked to make a daily list for a week of positive self-thoughts or of the positive consequences of desired change. Or the client could make a list of all the things about which she or he likes to daydream or of some imagined scenes that would be pleasurable (Watson & Tharp, 1981).

Sometimes a client may seem thwarted in initial attempts to use self-reward because of difficulties in identifying rewards. Watson and Tharp (1981) note that people whose behavior consumes the reinforcer (such as smoking or eating), whose behavior is reinforced intermittently, or whose avoidance behavior is maintained by negative reinforcement may not be able to identify reinforcing consequences readily. Individuals who are "locked into" demanding schedules cannot find daily examples of reinforcers. Sometimes depressed people have trouble identifying reinforcing events. In these cases, the counselor and client have several options that can be used to overcome difficulties in selecting effective self-rewards.

A client who does not have the time or money for material rewards might use imaginal rewards. Imagining pleasant scenes following a target response has been described by Cautela (1970) as *covert positive reinforcement* (CPR). In the CPR procedure, the client usually imagines performing a desired behavior, followed by imagination of a reinforcing scene. In one example, dieters imagined more positive body images as their reinforcing scene (Horan, Baker, Hoffman, & Shute, 1975). Watson and Tharp (1981) recommend that a client use imaginal reinforcers only when other kinds are not available, since some of the research on the CPR procedure has produced very mixed results. As an example, in at least one study (Bajtelsmit & Gershman, 1976), having the person imagine the reinforcer *before* the desired behavior was just as effective in reducing test anxiety as having the person imagine the reinforcer *after* the desired behavior. For these reasons, some people have questioned the exact method by which CPR really operates (Ladouceur, 1974).

A second available option for problem cases is to use a client's everyday activity as a self-reward. Some clinical cases have used a mundane activity such as answering the phone (Lawson & May, 1970) or opening the daily mail (Spinelli & Packard, 1975) as the self-reward. (Actually, such an activity may work more as a cuing device than a reinforcer; see Thoresen and Mahoney, 1974). If a frequently occurring behavior is used as a self-reward, it should be a desirable or at least a neutral activity. As Watson and Tharp (1981) note, clients should not use as a self-reward any high-frequency behavior that they would stop immediately if they could. Using a negative high-frequency activity as a reward may seem more like punishment than reinforcement.

With depressed clients, selecting self-rewards is often difficult, because many events lose their reinforcing value for someone who is depressed. Before using self-reward with a depressed client, it might be necessary to increase the reinforcing value of certain events. Anton, Dunbar, and Friedman (1976) describe the procedure of "anticipation training" designed to increase depressed clients' positive anticipations of events. In anticipation training, a client identifies and schedules several pleasant events to perform and then constructs three positive anticipation statements for each activity. The client imagines engaging in an activity and imagines the anticipation statements associated with the activity. An example adapted from Anton et al. of some anticipation statements for one activity might be:

Activity planned: *Spending an afternoon at the lake*
Date to be carried out: *Tuesday; Wednesday if it rains Tuesday*
I will enjoy: *sitting on the beach reading a book*
I will enjoy: *getting in the water on a hot day*
I will enjoy: *getting a suntan*

No thought, event, or imagined scene is reinforcing for everyone. Often what one person finds rewarding is very different from the rewards selected by someone else. In using self-reward, it is important to help clients choose rewards that will work well for *them*—not for the counselor, a friend, or a spouse. Kanfer notes that "it is crucial that the selected reinforcers relate to the client's personal history. They must be acceptable to him as something he wants, could easily acquire or do, and that would make him feel good" (1980, p. 369).

The counselor should use the following guidelines to help the client determine some self-rewards that might be used effectively.

1. *Individualize* the reward to the client (Homme, Csanyi, Gonzales, & Rechs, 1969).
2. The reward should be *accessible* and *convenient* to use after the behavior is performed.
3. *Several* rewards should be used interchangeably to prevent satiation (a reward can lose its reinforcing value because of repeated presentations).
4. Different *types* of rewards should be selected (verbal/symbolic, material, imaginal, current, potential).
5. The rewards should be *potent* but not so valuable that an individual will not use them contingently.

6. The rewards should not be *punishing* to others. Watson and Tharp (1981) suggest that if a reward involves someone else, the other person's agreement should be obtained.
7. The reward should be *compatible* with the desired response (Kanfer, 1980). For instance, a person losing weight might use new clothing as a reward or thoughts of a new body image after weight loss. Using eating as a reward is not a good match for a weight-loss target response.

Delivery of Self-Reward

The second part of working out a self-reward strategy with a client involves specifying the conditions and method of delivering the self-rewards. First of all, a client cannot deliver or administer a self-reward without some data base. Self-reward delivery is dependent on systematic data gathering; self-monitoring is an essential first step.

Second, the client should determine the precise conditions under which a reward will be delivered. The client should, in other words, state the rules of the game. The client should know *what* and *how much* has to be done before administering a self-reward. Usually self-reward is more effective when clients reward themselves for small steps of progress (Homme et al., 1969). In other words, performance of a subgoal should be rewarded. Waiting to reward oneself for demonstration of the overall goal usually introduces too much of a delay between responses and rewards.

Finally, the client should indicate how much and what kind of reward will be given for performing various responses or different levels of the goals. The client should specify that doing so much of the response results in one type of reward and how much of it. Usually reinforcement is more effective when broken down into smaller units that are self-administered more frequently (Homme et al., 1969). The use of tokens or points provides for frequent, small units of reinforcement; these can be exchanged for a "larger" reinforcer after a certain number of points or tokens are accumulated.

Timing of Self-Reward

The counselor also needs to instruct the client about the timing of self-reward—when a self-reward should be administered. There are three ground rules for the timing of a self-reward suggested by Homme et al. (1969):

1. A self-reward should be administered *after* performing the specified response, not before.
2. A self-reward should be administered *immediately* after the response. Long delays may render the procedure ineffective.
3. A self-reward should follow *actual performance,* not promises to perform.

Planning for Self-Change Maintenance

Self-reward, like any self-change strategy, needs environmental support for long-term maintenance of change (Kanfer, 1980; M. J. Mahoney, 1974). The last part of using self-reward involves helping the client find ways to plan for self-change maintenance. First, the counselor can encourage the client to enlist the help of others in a self-reward program. Other people can share in or dispense some of the reinforcement (Watson & Tharp, 1981). Some evidence indicates that people who receive rewards from others at least initially may benefit more from self-reward (Mahoney & Thoresen, 1974). Second, the client should plan to review the data collected during self-reward with the counselor. The review sessions give the counselor a chance to reinforce the client and to help the client make any necessary revisions in the use of the strategy. Therapist expectations and approval for client progress may add to the overall effects of the self-reward strategy (Jones et al., 1977).

Some Cautions in Using Rewards

The use of rewards as a motivational and informational device is a controversial issue. Using rewards, especially material ones, as incentives has been criticized on the grounds that tangible rewards are overused, are misused, and often discourage rather than encourage the "rewardee" (Levine & Fasnacht, 1974; O'Leary et al., 1972). Furthermore, McKeachie (1974, 1976) observes high levels of reward (or punishment) are not necessarily optimal for performance (1976, p. 823).

As a therapy technique, self-reward should not be used indiscriminately. Before suggesting self-reward, the counselor should carefully consider the individual client, the client's previous reinforcement history, and the client's desired change. When a counselor and client do decide to use self-reward, two cautionary guidelines should be followed. First, material rewards should not be used solely or promiscuously. Levine and Fasnacht (1974) recommend that the therapist seek ways to increase a person's intrinsic satisfaction in performance before automatically resorting to extrinsic rewards as a motivational technique. Second, the counselor's role in self-reward should be limited to providing instructions about the procedure and encouragement for progress. The client should be the one who selects the rewards and determines the criteria for delivery and timing of reinforcement. As Jones et al. (1977) observe, when the target behaviors and the contingencies are specified by someone other than the person using self-reward, the procedure can hardly be described accurately as a self-change operation (p. 174).

☐ MODEL EXAMPLE: SELF-REWARD

This example will illustrate how self-reward could be used to help Joan increase her positive thoughts about her ability to do well in math.

1. *Selection of rewards:* First the counselor would help Joan select some appropriate rewards to use for reaching her predetermined goal. The counselor would encourage Joan to identify some self-praise she could use to reward herself symbolically or verbally ("I did it"; "I can gradually see my attitude about math changing"). Joan could give herself points for daily positive thoughts. She could accumulate and exchange the points for material rewards, including current rewards (such as engaging in a favorite daily event) and potential rewards (such as a purchase of a desired item). These are suggestions; Joan should be responsible for the actual selection. The counselor could suggest that Joan identify possible rewards through observation or completion of a preference survey. The counselor should make sure that the rewards Joan selects are accessible and easy to use. Several rewards should be selected to prevent satiation. The counselor should also make sure that the rewards selected are potent, compatible with Joan's goal, and not punishing to anyone else.

2. *Delivery of rewards:* The counselor would help Joan determine guidelines for delivery of the rewards selected. Joan might decide to give herself a point for each positive thought. This allows for reinforcement of small steps toward the overall goal. A predetermined number of daily points, such as 5, might result in delivery of a current reward, such as watching TV or going over to her friend's house. A predetermined number of weekly points could mean delivery of a potential self-reward, such as going to a movie or purchasing a new item. Joan's demonstration of her goal beyond the specified level could result in delivery of a bonus self-reward.

3. *Timing of rewards:* The counselor would instruct Joan to administer the reward *after* the positive thoughts or after the specified number of points is accumulated. The counselor can emphasize that the rewards follow performance, not promises. The counselor should encourage Joan to engage in the rewards as soon as possible after the daily and weekly target goals have been met.

4. *Planning for self-change maintenance:* The counselor can help Joan find ways to plan for self-change maintenance. One way is to schedule periodic "check-ins" with the counselor. In addition, Joan might select a friend who could help her share in the reward by watching TV or going shopping with her or by praising Joan for her goal achievement.

LEARNING ACTIVITY #51: SELF-REWARD

This learning activity is designed to have you engage in self-reward.

1. Select a target behavior you want to increase. Write down your goal (the behavior to increase, desired level of increase, and conditions in which behavior will be demonstrated).
2. Select several types of self-rewards to use and write them down. The types to use are verbal/symbolic, material (both current and potential), and imaginal. See whether your selected self-rewards meet the following criteria:
   a. Individually tailored to you?
   b. Accessible and convenient to use?
   c. Several self-rewards?
   d. Different types of self-rewards?
   e. Are rewards potent?
   f. Are rewards not punishing to others?
   g. Are rewards compatible with your desired goal?
3. Set up a plan for delivery of your self-reward: What type of reinforcement and how much will be administered? How much and what demonstration of the target behavior are required?
4. When do you plan to administer a self-reward?
5. How could you enlist the aid of another person?
6. Apply self-reward for a specified time period. Did your target response increase? To what extent?
7. What did you learn about self-reward that might help you in suggesting this to a client?

☐ PROMOTING CLIENT COMMITMENT TO USE SELF-MANAGEMENT STRATEGIES

A critical issue in any self-management strategy that is still unresolved has been termed "the contract problem" (Mahoney, 1970). Finding ways to strengthen a client's stated commitment to using a self-management strategy consistently is a major challenge to any helper (Kanfer, 1980; Thoresen & Mahoney, 1974). There are several things a counselor might do to increase the probability that a client will use self-management strategies consistently. First, some clients seem to be more hesitant about self-management methods on first entering therapy (Williams et al., 1976). Perhaps clients who decide to seek the assistance of a helper are discouraged with their own self-change efforts. For this reason, therapists may want to avoid introducing self-management strategies in early counseling sessions (Williams et al., p. 234).

Second, clients' regular use of self-management may depend partly on their motivation to change. People who are very motivated to change a behavior seem to benefit more from self-management than those who aren't interested in modifying the target response (Ciminero et al., 1977). In view of the importance of the client's desire to change the goal behavior, the counselor might precede initiating a self-management strategy with some assessment of the client's motivation level. Brown (1978) recommends that the following questions be answered orally or in writing by the client:

1. How much money would you be willing to spend to do _____? (Put any maximum dollar amount between 0 and 10,000.)
2. If unpleasant activity—real, unpaid, work— were required instead of money, how many *minutes* each day would you be willing to spend to reach your goal? (Put in any maximum number of *minutes* between 0 and 480.)
3. On the following scale, please circle the number that best indicates how motivated you are to make this change.

   4—Extremely motivated. . . . Nothing is more important to me.
   3—Very motivated. . . .
   2—Moderately motivated. . . .
   1—Not motivated [p. 127].*

* From *An analysis of self-monitoring-provided feedback in a behavioral weight reduction program*, by J. Brown. Unpublished doctoral dissertation, West Virginia University, 1978. Reprinted by permission.

Third, in using self-management programs, the help and support of other people should not be ignored. The use of significant others to aid the client in the use of a strategy may greatly enhance the behavior change. Self-help groups are one example: clients' self-directed change programs are supported by friends or by other clients working toward similar goals (Stuart, 1977).

The helper, too, should maintain at least minimal contact with the client while the self-management strategies are being used. These strategies are an excellent way to bridge the gap from regular weekly counseling sessions to termination of counseling. Use of self-management procedures at this point may promote generalization of client changes from the interview setting to the client's environment. However, the counselor should maintain some contact with the client during this period, even if it involves only informal telephone calls. Using self-management strategies in the concluding sessions can also help the counselor and client achieve a gradual and successful termination.

☐ SUMMARY

Self-management is a process in which clients direct their own behavior change with any one therapeutic strategy or a combination of strategies. The self-monitoring strategy provides a method by which a client can become more aware of his or her overt behavior or internal responses such as thoughts or feelings. Self-monitoring may also provide information about the social and environmental context that influences these behaviors. Stimulus-control procedures require predetermined arrangement of environmental conditions that are antecedents of a target behavior, or cues to increase or decrease that behavior. As a self-management strategy, self-reward involves presenting oneself with a positive stimulus *after* engaging in a specified behavior. These three strategies typically are classified as self-management because in each procedure the client prompts, alters, or controls antecedents and consequences to produce desired changes in behavior in a self-directed fashion. Promoting client commitment to use self-management strategies can be achieved by introducing these strategies later in therapy, assessing the client's motivation for change, creating a social support system to aid the client in the use of the strategy, and maintaining contact with the client while self-management strategies are being used.

POSTEVALUATION

PART ONE

Objective One asks you to describe the application of the six components of self-monitoring to a written client case. Read the following case carefully. Then respond in writing to the questions listed.

Client Case Description

The client is a 30-year-old woman who has been married for ten years. Over the last two years she has been troubled by constant thoughts that her husband will die young and she will be left alone. She realizes there is no basis for these thoughts. Her baseline data indicate that these episodes of ruminative thinking occur anywhere from five to ten times daily. Suppose you were to use self-monitoring to help this client *decrease* these thoughts.

1. Provide an example *rationale* that you could give this client about this strategy.
2. Explain the process of *response discrimination* as it would be used with this client.
3. Give brief examples of the instructions you would give to this client about *response recording*. Include instructions about (a) *timing* of the recording, (b) *method* of recording, and (c) a *device* for recording.
4. Provide an example of a *chart* the client could use to plot the daily totals of the monitored behavior.
5. What are some examples of places where you would instruct this client to *display* the charted data?
6. Describe at least one way the client could engage in *data analysis*.

Feedback follows the Postevaluation on page 548.

PART TWO

Objective Two asks you to teach someone else how to engage in self-monitoring. Your teaching should follow the six guidelines listed in Table 19-1: rationale, response discrimination, self-recording, data charting, data display, and data analysis. Feedback follows.

PART THREE

Objective Three asks you to describe how stimulus-control methods could be used to increase or reduce a behavior for a given client. Using the following case description, describe in writing how you would use stimulus control to reduce the client's eating behavior and to increase her control over her study behavior. Feedback follows.

Case Description

The client is a freshman in college, living at home. She is concerned because she is under more pressure and has gained 25 pounds recently. She is having trouble keeping up with her course work because she lacks discipline to study. She wants help in reducing her weight and increasing her studying.

1. Describe how the client could use stimulus control to reduce her eating behavior:
   a. How could she reduce or narrow the cues associated with eating?
   b. How could she prearrange cues that make overeating or eating snacks or fattening foods difficult?
   c. How could she prearrange some cues to be controlled by other people?
   d. How could she break up the sequence, or chain, of eating behavior?
   e. How could she change the typical chain resulting in eating?
   f. How could she build pauses into the eating chain?
2. Describe how she could increase control of her study behavior, using stimulus control, by—
   a. Prearranging the cues associated with studying.
   b. Concentrating on the behavior while in the prearranged situations.
   c. Promoting the occurrence of helpful cues by reminders.

PART FOUR

Objective Four asks you to describe the application of the four components of self-reward for a written client case. Read the following case; then respond in writing to the questions that follow it. Feedback follows.

Case Description

The client is a young man who wants to increase the number of women he asks out for dates; he has set a goal of asking at least three different women out per week. You have instructed the client about how to self-monitor this target behavior. In addition, you plan to instruct the client to use self-reward. He will count and chart the number of women he actually invites, then administer a self-reward if he meets his weekly goal.

(continued)

Selection of Rewards

1. What would be two examples of a verbal/symbolic reward the client could use? Two examples of a material reward? Two examples of an imaginal reward?

2. List at least three characteristics of an effective self-reward.

3. If the client had trouble identifying material reinforcers, what is one alternative that could be used?

Delivery of Rewards

4. Given an example of how you would instruct the client to administer and deliver a self-reward (for example, what type and how much reinforcement for levels of goal achievement).

Timing of Self-Rewards

5. List at least two instructions you would give the client about *when* to administer the reward.

Planning for Self-Change Maintenance

6. Write at least one thing the client could do to plan for self-change maintenance.

PART FIVE

Objective Five asks you to teach someone else how to use a self-reward procedure to increase or strengthen a behavior. You can use the list on page 541 as a guide. You should teach the person how to select appropriate self-rewards, how to deliver self-reinforcement, when to administer self-rewards, and how to plan for self-change maintenance.

□ SUGGESTED READINGS

Bandura, A. (1981). In search of pure unidirectional determinants. *Behavior Therapy, 12,* 30–40.

Barlow, D. H., Hayes, S. C., & Nelson, R. O. (1984). *The scientist practitioner.* New York: Pergamon Press.

Blanchard, E. B., Andrasik, F., Neff, D. F., Jurish, S. E., & O'Keefe, C. M. (1981). Social validation of the headache diary. *Behavior Therapy, 12,* 711–715.

Borkovec, T. D., Wilkinson, L., Folensbee, R., & Lerman, C. (1983). Stimulus control applications to the treatment of worry. *Behavior Research and Therapy, 21,* 247–251.

Carroll, L. J., & Yates, B. T. (1981). Further evidence for the role of stimulus control training in facilitating weight reduction after behavioral therapy. *Behavior Therapy, 12,* 287–291.

Coates, T. J., & Thoresen, C. E. (1984). Assessing daytime thoughts and behavior associated with good and poor sleep: Two exploratory case studies. *Behavioral Assessment, 6,* 153–167.

Fremouw, W. J., & Brown, J. P., Jr. (1980). The reactivity of addictive behaviors to self-monitoring: A functional analysis. *Addictive Behaviors, 5,* 209–217.

Fremouw, W. J., Callahan, E. J., Zitter, R. E., & Katell, A. (1981). Stimulus control and contingency contracting for behavior change and weight loss. *Addictive Behaviors, 6,* 289–300.

Fremouw, W. J., & Heyneman, N. (1983). Obesity. In M. Hersen (Ed.), *Outpatient behavior therapy.* New York: Grune & Stratton.

Heffernan, T., & Richards, C. S. (1981). Self-control of study behavior: Identification and evaluation of natural methods. *Journal of Counseling Psychology, 28,* 361–364.

Hollon, S. D., & Kendall, P. C. (1981). *In vivo* assessment techniques for cognitive-behavioral processes. In P. C. Kendall & S. D. Hollon (Eds.). *Assessment strategies for cognitive-behavioral interventions.* New York: Academic Press.

Jones, J. E. (1981). Self-monitoring of stuttering: Reactivity and accuracy. *Behaviour Research and Therapy, 19,* 291–296.

Karoly, P., & Kanfer, F. A. (Eds.). (1982). *Self-management and behavior change.* New York: Pergamon Press.

Keefe, F. J., & Blumenthal, J. A. (1980). The life fitness program: A behavioral approach to making exercise a habit. *Journal of Behavior Therapy and Experimental Psychiatry, 11,* 31–34.

Litrownik, A. J. (1982). Special considerations in the self-management training of the developmentally disabled. In P. Karoly & F. H. Kanfer (Eds.), *Self-management and behavior change.* New York: Pergamon Press.

Lacks, P. (1987). *Behavioral treatment for persistent insomnia.* New York: Pergamon Press.

Marlatt, G. A., & Parks, G. A. (1982). Self-management of addictive behaviors. In P. Karoly & F. H. Kanfer (Eds.). *Self-management and behavior change.* New York: Pergamon Press.

McFall, R. M., & Dodge, K. A. (1982). Self-management and interpersonal skills learning. In P. Karoly & F. H. Kanfer (Eds.), *Self-management and behavior change.* New York: Pergamon Press.

Nelson, R. O., Boykin, R. A., & Hayes, S. C. (1982). Long-term effects of self-monitoring on reactivity and on accuracy. *Behaviour Research and Therapy, 20,* 357–363.

Nelson, R. O., Hayes, S. C., Spong, R. T., Jarrett, R. B., & McKnight, D. L. (1983). Self-reinforcement: Appealing misnomer or effective mechanism. *Behaviour Research and Therapy, 21,* 557–566.

Quattrochi-Turbin, S., & Jason, L. A. (1980). Enhancing social interaction and activity among the elderly through stimulus control. *Journal of Applied Behavior Analysis, 13,* 159, 163.

Rehm, L. P. (1982). Self-management in depression. In P.

Karoly & F. H. Kanfer (Eds.), *Self-management and behavior change.* New York: Pergamon Press.

Watson, D. L., & Tharp, R. G. (1981). *Self-directed behavior: Self-modification for personal adjustment* (3rd ed.). Pacific Grove, CA: Brooks/Cole.

Zwart, C. A., & Lisman, S. A. (1979). Analysis of stimulus control treatment of sleep-onset insomnia. *Journal of Consulting and Clinical Psychology, 47,* 113–118.

FEEDBACK: POSTEVALUATION

PART ONE

1. In the rationale you would emphasize how this strategy could help obtain information about the client's thoughts as well as modify them in the desired direction. You would also explain that she would be recording defined thoughts *in vivo* on a daily basis for several weeks.

2. Response-discrimination training would involve selecting, defining, and giving examples of the response to be monitored. The counselor should model some examples of the defined behavior and elicit some others from the client. Specifically, you would help the client define the nature and content of the thoughts she would be recording, such as "being alone."

3. *Timing of the recording:* Since this client is using self-monitoring to decrease an undesired behavior, she would engage in prebehavior monitoring; each time she had the urge or started to think about being left alone, she would record.

Method of recording: The client would be instructed to use a frequency count and record the number of times she started to think about being left alone. If she was unable to discern when these thoughts started and ended, she could record with time sampling. For example, she could divide a day into equal time intervals and use the "all or none" method. If such thoughts occurred during an interval, she would record *yes;* if they did not, she would record *no.* Or, during each interval, she could rate the approximate frequency of these thoughts on a numerical scale, such as 0 for "never occurring," 1 for "occasionally," 2 for "often," and 3 for "very frequently."

Device for recording: There is no one right device to assist this client in recording. She could count the frequency using a tally on a note card or a golf wrist counter. Or she could use a daily log sheet to keep track of interval occurrences.

4. A simple chart might have days along the horizontal axis and frequency of thought urges along the vertical axis.

5. This client may or may not wish to display the data in a public place at home. If not, she could carry the data in her purse or knapsack.

6. The client could engage in data analysis by reviewing the data with the counselor or by comparing the data with the baseline or with her goal (desired level of behavior change). The latter involves self-evaluation and may set the stage for self-reinforcement.

PART TWO

Use Table 19-1 as a guide to assist your teaching. You might also determine whether the person you taught implemented self-monitoring accurately.

PART THREE

Refer to Table 19-2 for examples of stimulus control to reduce eating behavior and to increase study behavior.

PART FOUR

1. The *verbal symbolic rewards* used by this client could consist in self-praise for inviting a woman or covert verbalizations about the positive consequences of his behavior. Here are some examples:

"I did it! I asked her out."
"I did just what I wanted to do."
"Now that I called her, I've got a great date."
"Wow! What a good time I'll have with _____."

Material rewards would be things or events the client indicates he prefers or enjoys. These might include buying a record, eating a snack, smoking, listening to music, or playing ball. Both current and potential rewards should be used. Of course, these activities are only possibilities; the client has to decide whether they are reinforcing.

Examples of an *imaginal* reward may include either pleasant scenes or scenes related to going out:
a. Imagining oneself on a raft on a lake.
b. Imagining oneself on a football field.
c. Imagining oneself with one's date at a movie.
d. Imagining oneself with one's date lying on a warm beach.

2. See whether you identified at least three of the following seven characteristics of an effective self-reward:

(continued)

a. The rewards should be individualized for the client.
b. The rewards should be accessible and easy to use.
c. There should be several rewards.
d. Different types of rewards should be selected.
e. The rewards should be potent.
f. The rewards should not be punishing to others.
g. The rewards should be compatible with the client's desired goal.

3. If the client had trouble identifying some material reinforcers, here are some possible options:
a. The client could use high-frequency behaviors as rewards as long as these behaviors were desirable, not aversive.
b. The client could use imagery to reinforce himself covertly in lieu of material rewards.
c. Perhaps the client could increase the potency of certain material events or activities with the use of "anticipation training." In anticipation training, a client preselects several activities in which to engage and rehearses anticipation statements about each activity.

4. Each woman this client asks out is a step in the desired direction. After the client asks out one woman, he might administer a verbal/symbolic or imaginal reward. When he reaches his desired weekly level of asking out three, he could administer a larger material reward.

5. See whether your instructions about the timing of self-reward included at least two of the following:
a. The reward should be administered after, not before, the target behavior is carried out.
b. The reward should be administered immediately and without delay.
c. The reward should be administered for actual behavior, not promises.

6. The client could plan for self-change maintenance by holding review sessions with the counselor and by enlisting the aid of another person to share in or dispense the rewards.

PART FIVE

Use the list on page 540 as a guide to evaluate your teaching of the self-reward strategy. You also may wish to have your "student" keep data on the use of the procedure and the change in the target behavior.

STRATEGIES FOR MANAGING RESISTANCE

TWENTY

Resistance. The word itself is enough to make many therapists shudder. Yet many practitioners acknowledge that most clients, even self-referred ones, behave in resistive ways during the therapeutic process. For example, a client may be overtly resistant by refusing or sabotaging homework assignments or covertly resistant by using overcompliance or excessive cooperation to avoid dealing with an important issue. This chapter defines resistance, describes the most common sources of resistance, and identifies therapeutic techniques to manage resistance.

□ OBJECTIVES

After completing this chapter, you will be able to—

1. Respond to client pessimism with listening responses that match, or pace, the client's feelings, given a role-play situation.
2. Identify dysfunctional behaviors and their reinforcers, or "payoffs," and ways in which the client can achieve the same reinforcement with more adaptive behaviors, given two written descriptions of client cases.
3. Identify four aspects of "patient position," given two written descriptions of clients and their presenting problems, and describe the implications of these positions for the management of therapy.
4. Select the most appropriate type of paradoxical intervention and write a description of a corresponding task and rationale, given two written descriptions of clients.
5. Deliver a compliance-based paradoxical intervention and a defiance-based paradoxical intervention, given a role-play interview.

□ DEFINITION OF RESISTANCE

The concept of resistance originated with psychoanalysis. Freud (1900;1952) viewed resistance as a defensive reaction that served to protect the client against awareness of anxiety due to unresolved psychic conflicts or unacceptable thoughts and impulses. Freud speculated that, in spite of an expressed request for help, clients were resistant to giving up their symptoms because the symptoms were used to maintain internal equilibrium and avoid intrapsychic conflict. Bringing these sources of conflict into the client's awareness and working through the resistance are important goals of psychoanalytically oriented therapists.

Family systems literature views resistance as resulting from a need to keep a system homeostatic, or stable (Jackson, 1968). Efforts to change are resisted because such change implies too much deviation from "the way things are." According to Anderson and Stewart (1983, p. 29), "the need for stability in family systems is so strong that it is usually not the desire for change that leads families to seek therapy, but rather it is the *failure* to accommodate to change. Most families come to therapy *in response to changes* which they do not like or have not adjusted to."* From this perspective, clients tend to cling to the way things are and respond ambivalently to the threat of loss of control that seems to accompany change. In other words, clients often behave as if they wanted only more of what they already have (Gottman & Leiblum, 1974).

Although psychoanalysis and family therapy have contributed a great deal of literature about resistance, very little has been written about it from a cognitive-behavioral perspective. Some of the behavioral literature has minimized the concept of resistance by arguing that people will continue to behave in certain ways only as long as these behaviors are maintained by controlling consequences. Change will occur given the proper set of contingencies. Lack of change is attributed to failure to identify correctly the controlling contingencies or consequences rather than to "resistant behavior." An absence of available reinforcers and inability of the therapist to identify reinforcers are common reasons used to "explain away" client resistance.

In one of the first articles on the subject, Hersen (1971) acknowledged the presence of resistance in behavior therapy and asserted that it cannot always be explained away on the basis of operant

conditioning (a learning paradigm in which learning occurs because of positive, negative, or neutral consequences that follow a response). In a more recent article, Jahn and Lichstein (1980) noted that a resistive client directly defies the contingencies set by the therapist. They observed that it is impossible to blame incorrect contingency identification for all forms of client resistance or failure to change.

Other behavioral therapists tend to equate client resistance with noncompliance, or failure to achieve the desired behavior change because the client did not complete a prescribed task or assignment. Shelton and Levy (1981, p. 37) define compliance as "the client's carrying out an assignment in the way originally planned, discussed, and agreed upon by both him or herself and the therapist." As Anderson and Stewart (1983, p. 8) observe, "Most of the techniques described by behavioral therapists to increase compliance are ones which would serve to avoid the emergence of resistance." These techniques include such things as using relevant and appropriate tasks, giving the client choices, presenting tasks in a form acceptable to the client, keeping tasks small, concrete, and simple, and actively involving the client in devising the tasks.

Lewis and Evans (1986) suggest that the concept of resistance be replaced by recognizing the fears a client may have about the process. Ritchie (1986) argues that clients are resistant because they do not admit to having a problem. Either they do not want to change or they do not know how to change. Ellis (1985) illustrates how rational-emotive therapy and cognitive behavior therapy can deal with resistance for a variety of clients. Meichenbaum and Turk (1987) describe procedures for facilitating treatment adherence that may reduce client resistance.

We believe that resistance can be defined simply as any client *or* therapist behavior that interferes with or reduces the likelihood of a successful therapeutic process and outcome. Although the focus of this chapter is on client resistance, therapists also engage in resistive behavior. (This concept will be addressed in a later section of this chapter.) We also believe that most if not all clients engage in resistive behavior at some time during therapy. Perhaps most resistive are those clients who might be called "reluctant" or "involuntary"—that is, persons who would not be in the presence of a counselor and would prefer not to talk about themselves, given a choice (Patterson & Eisenberg,

---

* This and all other quotations from this source are from *Mastering resistance* by C. M. Anderson and S. Stewart. Copyright © 1983 by The Guilford Press. Reprinted by permission.

1983). Often, involuntary clients are "required" to be counseled by a referring source such as the courts, a teacher, or a parent. However, even many voluntary and self-referred clients engage in some resistive behaviors during therapy, often in initial counseling contacts or when the need for change becomes apparent.

Resistance in therapy can stem from a variety of sources, including client variables, environmental variables, and therapist variables (Gottman & Leiblum, 1974; Munjack & Oziel, 1978). The particular sources of resistance can be identified by a careful assessment of the problem. For instance, questions asked during the problem assessment process can be directed to discovery of reinforcing and punishing contingencies, secondary gains, environmental competing stimuli, past attempts to resolve the problem, and so on. (See also Chapters 7 and 8.)

In the following three sections of the chapter, we elaborate on these three sources of resistance and suggest strategies for managing resistance effectively.

□ RESISTANCE DUE TO CLIENT VARIABLES

When Clients Lack Necessary Skills or Knowledge

Some clients may seem resistant but simply don't understand what to do or how to go about doing a task or activity. In some instances, the client is too preoccupied to understand the therapist's instructions or feels inept at carrying out the instructions. Other clients may not understand the counselor's instructions or the rationale for a particular strategy or task. Resistance that occurs when the client lacks necessary skills or knowledge can be managed with the following strategies.

Provide detailed instructions. Instructions are defined as one or more verbal statements in which the therapist instructs or directs a client to do something, either in the counseling session or as take-home instructions. Instructions have both influencing and informative effects. Instructions encourage a client to respond in a certain way and also provide information to help a client complete a particular task or activity. Effective instructions increase the likelihood of client compliance. Instructions are most effective if they are (1) specific rather than general (inform the client *what* to do and *how* to do it), (2) brief and concise rather than

lengthy, and (3) delivered in a friendly rather than dogmatic manner.

To ensure that clients understand instructions, ask them to repeat the instructions to you. Written or typed summaries that clients can take home and display in a prominent place are useful adjuncts. Instructions may need to be supplemented with modeled demonstrations of the task or activity to be performed. Finally, it is important to follow up the instructions by asking about the client's experience at a later session.

Give direct skill training. Clients who are accustomed to refusing unreasonable requests are unlikely to "become more assertive" or comply with assertion homework tasks simply because the therapist exhorts them to do so. These clients need assurance that they can exercise the skill without humiliating themselves or important others. Compliance is enhanced when the counselor provides opportunities for skill acquisition that include breaking the behaviors into small steps or actions of increasing difficulty, modeling, role playing and imaginary rehearsal, feedback, and reinforcement (see also Chapter 12).

When Clients Have Pessimistic Expectations

Often therapists view some clients as "unmotivated." Usually this means these clients have minimal or even negative expectations about therapy and successful problem resolution. Resistance that occurs when clients present pessimistic expectations can be managed with the following strategies.

Acknowledge the client's pessimism. If the client expresses pessimistic ideas or expectations, a natural tendency is to counter these with expressions of optimism. Rather than encouraging the client to become less pessimistic, such comments may engender more resistance because they sound inflammatory and "preachy" or moralistic to the client. According to Fisch et al. (1982, p. 100), such comments "run counter to the client's position of pessimism, and one might predict that they will impede the client's cooperation and a successful outcome in treatment, especially if the client has already been discouraged by previous therapists who began treatment on a positive, optimistic note, only to terminate with no improvement."

What is likely to be more useful with these clients *initially* is to match your comments to those of the clients. This can be accomplished by the use of listening responses (Chapter 5) such as paraphrase and reflection that pace, or are in synchrony with, the client. Thus, instead of saying "You don't sound very hopeful about what we might accomplish, but I can assure you we can work this out successfully" the therapist might say "I can understand your wish to have this thing resolved, but after what has happened before, perhaps it would be better to start off being a little uncertain or doubtful about how this might turn out." According to Fisch et al. (1982, p. 100), "By stating this position, the therapist can, paradoxically, lessen the patient's pessimism, since he will be implying that he recognizes the patient's discouragement and its validity and that he will not patronize him through false hope." An alternative way of dealing with initial pessimism is to ask clients to recall any changes they may have experienced in the past that were preceded by an initial period of pessimism (Goldfried, 1982, p. 107). This is also more likely to bring about attitude change than trying to convince clients that their pessimistic attitudes are useless and unwarranted.

When Clients Have Negative or Anxious Thoughts

Other clients engage in resistive behaviors because of negative self-statements or cognitions about change. These clients often imagine the consequences of change as worse than the consequences of the problem. Resistance that occurs when the client's self-statements and cognitions are negative or anxiety-arousing can be managed with the following strategies.

Explore client fantasies, expectations, and fears in detail. Encourage clients to share their fears and anticipated reactions to change with you. Detailed and explicit expressions of anxious thoughts and feelings may actually help the client gain control of these feelings. Sometimes clients are reluctant to express such fears, believing that "talking about them will make them come true." On the contrary, clients are usually pleasantly surprised to find that expressing anxious feelings in the presence of a warm, nonjudgmental person actually reduces the intensity of such feelings. Having clients share aloud or role play their fantasies and fears about change also enables the counselor to correct any misperceptions. Some clients, for example, may resist change because of inaccurate or illogical beliefs such as "If I choose to get a divorce, I'll lose my job or everyone will think I'm a terrible person." The counselor can help the client sort out realistic and irrational anticipated results of change. Catastrophic expectations can be diffused in this process.

Provide support. Clients' avoidance of change may be reduced if you are highly supportive of their change efforts. Clients also benefit from hearing that their concerns are natural and that change often occurs slowly over a long period. At the same time, the counselor can challenge the client to change by suggesting that one way to discover whether fears of change are valid is to experiment with change and see what happens.

Set up what seems to be a small alteration in handling the problem. Clients who are pessimistic or fearful about change are more likely to engage in a small task than an overwhelming one. To clients, a small change in the way they handle a problem is more acceptable and is resisted less because it seems minor and inconsequential and does not require a great change in routine (Fisch et al., 1982). Therapeutic change is often like a kaleidoscope: change one small piece and the whole pattern changes.

Use a force-field analysis. The force-field analysis technique was developed by Lewin (1951) as a strategy for managing resistance to change. In this technique, the counselor assists the client in listing all possible avoidance behaviors (called "resisting forces") and all possible approach behaviors ("driving forces"). Next, the counselor and client plan ways to reduce the number and impact of the avoidance behaviors and increase the number and impact of the approach behaviors. An alternative strategy is to have the client "play out the polarity," or identify the self-talk associated with both sides of the conflict (approach and avoidance). Notice which side feels stronger. If it is the avoidance side, work on strengthening the approach side.

Give the suggestions when the client is most relaxed. A basic principle of hypnosis is to offer suggestions during the time a client is in a trance and therefore is most relaxed. The therapist can note when the client is most relaxed — or use imagery, relaxation, or focused breathing to reduce the client's tension — and offer a suggestion at this time.

Use rehearsal to practice new behaviors and to anticipate reactions from others. Very often clients are reluctant to implement a counselor's suggestion because they feel unable to do it or are unsure how it will turn out. Compliance can be increased if the counselor arranges for client practice of desired behaviors *before* having the client try these out in the real environment. Sometimes, too, clients are afraid to "handle" a situation because of anticipated responses from others. For example, a female client states "I'd really like to tell my mother I'm going to move, but I just can't, because of her reaction. She'll just go to pieces." Once you have determined that the client's perception of her mother's reaction is realistic (often it is just "mind reading"), then have the client rehearse how she will handle such a reaction. Anticipating and preparing for negative reactions helps clients comply with the task and carry it out more effectively.

Interpret the client's resistance. At some point it may be useful to provide an interpretation of the client's resistance. Tentative hypotheses, or guesses, about the source and functions of the resistance can be offered. An effective interpretation (Chapter 6) can provide the client with greater self-understanding and can decrease some expressions of resistance. Interpretations may also show the client that the counselor does not skirt behavior or issues just because they make people feel uncomfortable (Dyer & Vriend, 1975).

The overall objective of interpreting resistance is for the client to identify and discuss unspoken feelings or issues. The interpretation focuses on what the client is doing to resist and provides an alternative explanation of the underlying issue, or "hidden agenda." For example, a counselor may interpret a very hostile client's resistance as follows:

> "I'm aware that every time I mention anything that has to do with "cutting the strings" from your parents, you become very upset and change the subject or deny it. You keep insisting that your parents are very dependent on you; could it be that you are the one who is more emotionally and financially dependent on them?"

As we mentioned in Chapter 6, it is important to be tentative rather than dogmatic when interpreting. It is also helpful to be accepting of clients and their resistance even while interpreting about it. Since interpretation is an action-oriented technique, it may work best with clients who are somewhat aware of their resistance. With other clients, a listening response such as reflection may be more helpful.

LEARNING ACTIVITY #52: CLIENT SOURCES OF RESISTANCE

In this activity, we present five statements that clients may make to a therapist at the beginning of or during therapy. Your task is to discriminate whether the statement suggests client *optimism* or *pessimism* about therapy and then construct a listening response (see also Chapter 5) that *matches*, or *paces*, the client's optimistic or pessimistic feelings. The first one is completed as an example. Feedback follows on page 556.

Example

Client, a middle-aged man: "I'm here only because my wife insisted I come in or else she would leave me and take my kids with her. I don't really think this will do much good."

    ____Optimism   ✓ Pessimism

Matching response(s):

"Given the pressure you feel to be here, I can understand your skepticism."

or

"You may be right. It's awfully difficult to make changes when someone insists that you do so."

Client Practice Messages

1. *Client,* a teenager: "I just have to talk to someone. I'm in trouble. I thought I could handle it, but I've gotten in over my head."

    ____Optimism   ____Pessimism

Matching response:

2. *Client,* an older retired man: "Yes, I've been having some trouble sleeping, but all I really need is some sleeping pills. My doctor doesn't seem to agree. He thinks it's my nerves and I need to see you instead."

    ____Optimism   ____Pessimism

Matching response:

3. *Client,* a graduate student: "I just can't stand this feeling of pressure. I'm desperate. I've got to have some immediate relief."

    ____Optimism   ____Pessimism

Matching response:

4. *Client,* a young woman: "I just don't feel very comfortable talking to other people about myself.

(continued)

How can talking like this help me with my problems anyway?"

_____Optimism _____Pessimism

Matching response:

5. *Client,* a teenager: "Of course I don't want to be

here. But my parents gave me an ultimatum—shape up or ship out. They see this as a way to get me to behave. Ha!"

_____Optimism _____Pessimism

Matching response:

☐ RESISTANCE DUE TO ENVIRONMENTAL VARIABLES

Some clients resist treatment or fail to comply because of environmental variables that interfere with compliance. The client's environment may be arranged in a way that makes it difficult to engage in desired responding or in performing a desired activity. For example, the behavior may not be performed because of low visibility, competing stimuli, interactional variables, or differing norms of client's system. As Goldfried (1982, p.111) notes, "In cases where environmental determinants undermine therapeutic progress, it is clear that such variables must be the target of change."

When Environmental Variables Are Incompatible with Change

Resistance that occurs when environmental variables are incompatible with change can be managed with the following strategies.

Arrange cues that make the target response more visible. Environmental variables can contribute to client resistance when the environment is arranged in such a way that the cues or stimuli to set off and follow a particular response are not visible. For example, a student may find it difficult to study if her room is so crowded that it is hard to find space to work or if her books and school papers get lost easily. Rearranging the room to make it a less dense environment and posting reminders to study in highly visible places are ways to make the target response more visible and therefore more likely to occur. (See also "Stimulus Control" in Chapter 19.)

Reduce competing stimuli. Environmental variables can also produce resistance if the environment is arranged so that competing or distracting stimuli interfete with completion of the desired behavior or task. For example, students may find it difficult to study if the norms of their peer group are "to party." These norms competing with or distract the person from completing the desired response of studying. Students may also be less likely

to study if there is so much conflict in their families that it is distracting and interfering with their ability to sustain a concentrated focus over a period of time. Finally, students may find it difficult to study if they are involved in a great many other time-consuming activities, such as sports, band, and work, that interfere with study behavior. Finding an alternative peer group, reducing family conflicts, and reducing participation in extracurricular activities would be ways to diminish competing stimuli that prevent the occurrence of desired study behavior. For other kinds of problems, an actual shift in environmental setting (for example, change of job) or involvement in a different support system that will reinforce desired change may be warranted (Goldfried, 1982).

Change the client's pattern and routine; avoid doing what has already been attempted. Some clients find it difficult to study because good study habits have never been incorporated into their daily routine. Simply having the client continue the same routine and pattern with the addition of inserting a time and a place for studying is not likely to work, because the new behavior doesn't fit with or is not supported by the old pattern. It would be more effective to scramble the client's typical pattern and routine and incorporate studying into an entirely different and new way of doing things each day.

Another reason to avoid simply inserting some study time into the client's old pattern is that that is probably the way the client tried to resolve the problem—and did so unsuccessfully. Although it seems obvious, people are often not sensitive to whether a particular solution is successful or not. When a solution is not working, instead of simply discarding it, most people do more of it or do it more frequently, thus increasing the problem. In this way, ordinary life difficulties are turned into more severe problems because the typical difficulty has been mishandled and remains unresolved (Fisch et al., 1982).

Remember that often the very ways clients try to alter problems—the "attempted solutions"—can

FEEDBACK #52: CLIENT SOURCES OF RESISTANCE

Client 1

a. Optimism

b. Examples of matching responses: "You're feeling pretty overwhelmed right now and want someone to help pull you out of the deep."

or

"You've tried for a while to do it alone—now it's time to reach out and have someone there with you."

Client 2

a. Pessimism

b. Examples of matching responses: "It's irritating and upsetting that you are not to be able to just solve this problem immediately in a real, concrete way."

or

"It's pretty difficult to make sense of having to talk to me when taking a pill seems so easy and workable."

Client 3

a. Optimism

b. Examples of matching responses: "You've been feeling desperate long enough—like a cork on a bottle ready to pop. Now you need something to make an instant difference."

or

"This tremendous pressure has gone on long enough—too long. Now it's time for a change."

Client 4

a. Pessimism

b. Examples of matching responses: "It may or may not help. There's certainly no guarantee that talking like this will be the right avenue for you. Maybe it isn't.

or

"Yes. How can talk—just talk—really do anything concrete for anyone anyway?"

Client 5

a. Pessimism

b. Examples of matching responses: "I can certainly understand your skepticism, especially considering the fact that you're here mainly to avoid getting put out of your home."

or

"I can see where those feelings of disillusionment are coming from. How could someone think about making honest changes when feeling forced to do so?"

maintain the problem or make it even worse (Fisch et al., 1982). It is much more helpful to get the client to abandon any previous unsuccessful solutions and to implement different solutions. Scrambling one's daily pattern to increase studying is likely to be a solution that the client has not yet attempted. Of course, this needs to be checked out during the assessment interviews (see also Chapters 7 and 8).

When Problem Behavior Is Maintained by Environmental Events

Some clients are resistant because environmental variables called "consequences" are primary factors maintaining the problem. In Chapter 7 we discussed the concept of consequences in detail. Simply stated, consequences include environmental variables that maintain or exacerbate a problem—things that keep a problem going or make it worse. Although consequences may also include internal, covert events such as irrational or self-defeating thoughts, in this section we are concerned with overt variables such as situations or people in the client's environment.

Resistance that occurs when the problem behavior is maintained by environmental events and persons can be managed with the following strategies.

Find effective reinforcement for new or replacement behaviors. Behavior is followed by negative, neutral, or positive consequences (see also Chapter 7). Recall that new behaviors are more likely to be maintained when they are linked to positive, or rewarding, consequences. Melamed and Siegel (1980, p. 115) explain as follows the use of positive consequences to promote compliance:

> Consequences that immediately follow the desired behavior also affect the probable occurrence of that behavior. If the consequences are pleasant or reinforcing, the [desired] behavior is more likely to occur, whereas compliance with the therapist regimen is less likely to occur if the compliance behavior results in either no reinforcing consequences or aversive events.

To use this principle most effectively, begin with changes that are likely to make the client feel better in a short time or are likely to result in dramatic or at least visible improvement. When clients notice the benefits achieved from these initial steps, they will be more likely to engage in behaviors that make greater demands on them and take longer to effect the desired results.

Change can also be augmented by arranging for positive consequences to follow the desired behavior, in the form of either positively reinforcing activities or social reinforcement. For example, a client might engage in a daily desirable activity, such as watching television or reading, only after engaging in desired behavior or after completing some portion of assigned homework (see also "Self-Reward," in Chapter 19). Make sure the consequences selected are relevant and rewarding to the client.

Clients who receive strong doses of social reinforcement—"strokes," or encouragement and support, from counselors and significant others—are more motivated to change. The use of "social allies," persons who have frequent contact with the client and can assist the client in carrying out desired strategies and behaviors, is often very helpful (Stuart & Davis, 1972). Having a phobic client paired with a former phobic and using exercise partners to engage in daily aerobics are examples of this principle. Social allies also form the keystone of successful programs such as Alcoholics Anonymous and Weight Watchers International.

Find alternative or additional sources of rewards.
In some instances, significant others in the client's environment may react negatively to client change, causing the client to experience punitive or aversive rather than positive consequences. For example, consider the case of a woman who is very dependent on her husband and behaves very nonassertively in his presence. Simply persuading the client to be less dependent and more assertive because that is better for her own mental health is unlikely to be helpful. Even providing her with overt skill training in assertive behavior may not work if, when she is assertive, her husband yells at her. As another example, consider the case of a college-aged female with the eating disorder of "anorexia." In spite of her parents' expressed concern for her, she becomes the object of strong criticism from her parents when she begins to eat again. In all probability, the client's defined problem (anorexia), though tragic, was serving an important function in her family environment. (The exact function could be determined during the assessment interviews.) When her problem got better, the family got worse and had difficulty coping with the loss of this function. This client is a likely candidate for a relapse, which would be a way for her to avoid further punishment from the family.

In such cases, the client is unlikely to want to give up the problem unless alternative sources of positive consequences can be found. Although the counselor can provide strong doses of encouragement, the client should develop his or her own sources of rewards as well. For example, clients might learn how to arrange for positive events in their environment that do not depend strongly on the reactions of significant others such as family members. The client could engage in rewarding activities, imagine rewarding activities, or learn to use positive self-talk or self-praise ("I did a great job") following completion of the desired response. (See also "Self-Reward," Chapter 19.) Eventually, however, the new behavior itself will need to *feel* rewarding for the client in this kind of situation—for example, "It feels good to be less dependent, and I want to continue expressing more of my opinions because I like to—even though I get yelled at or punished for it."

An alternative approach when significant others punish rather than reinforce behavior change is to try to include them in counseling and use a systems approach to intervention (Minuchin, 1974).

Teach adaptive means of attaining "payoffs." As we mentioned in Chapters 7 and 8, "payoffs" (secondary gains) for dysfunctional, maladaptive behavior can have a powerful influence in maintaining that behavior, no matter how painful or uncomfortable it is for the client. Such payoffs may include—but are not limited to—money, attention from significant others, immediate (rather than delayed) gratification of needs and wants, or avoidance of work and stress.

An important and often overlooked secondary gain is security. Clients gain security in their present behavior patterns, no matter how dysfunctional or painful they may be. Maintaining problematic behavior enhances security by retaining predictability and helps the client avoid undue anxiety elicited by changing one's behavior. As Gottman & Leiblum (1974) observe, "Symptoms may be subjectively distressful, but they may produce a certain degree of consistency . . . in an otherwise unpredictable world" (p. 108).

Another important payoff is the control value, or relationship gains, that the problem behavior represents for the client. Haley (1963, p. 15) explains relationship gain this way: "The crucial aspect of a symptom is the advantage it gives the patient in gaining control of what is to happen in a relationship with someone else." When the client's problem behavior is maintained by reinforcing or useful payoffs, the client is not likely to eliminate the undesired behavior unless such benefits can be found in other ways. The counselor needs to help the client determine how such benefits could be met in other, more adaptive ways that do not jeopardize the welfare of the client or of other people. For example, if a child is using "aggressive behav-iors" at school to have other kids notice him, the child needs to learn more adaptive ways of getting his peers to include him and pay attention to him. Similarly, if a wife is constantly criticizing her husband, which makes her feel better about herself, she needs to learn more productive ways of improving her self-esteem that do not threaten to disrupt her marriage.

LEARNING ACTIVITY #53: ENVIRONMENTAL SOURCES OF RESISTANCE

In this learning activity, we present two examples of behaviors that are partially maintained by environmental variables and that you or a client may wish to modify. For each behavior, your task is to generate as many suggestions/alternatives you can think of to (1) make the target response more visible in the person's environment and (2) reduce competing environmental stimuli. We have provided several suggestions as examples, and additional suggestions are found in the feedback section following the learning activity on page 560.

Behavior One:

Decrease amount of overeating done each week (leading to weight loss)

1. Ways to make the target response (overeating) more visible in your (or someone else's) environment:
   a. Post reminders.
   b. Contract for weight loss with spouse or friend.
   c.
   d.
   e.
   (see feedback for other ideas)
2. Ways to reduce environmental stimuli that compete with eating control:
   a. Don't socialize with overeaters.

b. Put locks on cupboards or refrigerator.
c.
d.
e.
(see feedback for other ideas)

Behavior Two:

Increase number of positive thoughts about oneself (leading to a good mood)

1. Ways to make the target response more visible in your (or someone else's) environment:
   a. Post reminders to think positively or rationally.
   b. Make a list of strengths or attributes.
   c.
   d.
   e.
   (see feedback for other ideas)
2. Ways to reduce environmental stimuli that compete with thinking positively about oneself:
   a. Avoid engaging in depressing or failure-oriented activities.
   b. Avoid being around people who get down on you.
   c.
   d.
   e.
   (see feedback for other ideas)

☐ RESISTANCE DUE TO THERAPIST OR THERAPEUTIC VARIABLES

According to Lazarus and Fay (1982, p. 115), resistance "is probably the most elaborate rationalization that therapists employ to explain their treatment failures." They assert that what appears to be client resistance often has its source within the therapist. Therapist resistance can be defined as those thoughts, feelings, and actions that contribute to failure to engage with or treat a client successfully (Anderson & Stewart, 1983, p. 210). When resistance is engendered by therapist or relationship variables, the following strategies may be helpful.

Avoiding Personalizing Client Resistance

It is important for therapists to be accepting of themselves and of resistive client behavior when working with pessimistic or discouraged clients. Some therapists may personalize client resistance and feel as if they are the target of the client's resistive behavior. In such instances, acceptance of the client and of *yourself* is important. Dyer and Vriend (1975, pp. 98–99) note that when a counselor is unable or unwilling to accept a reluctant client and contracounseling behaviors, either the client, the counselor, or both are often declared *persona non grata,* and the counselor will experience failure in efforts to be helpful. Because therapists often experience client resistance as irritating, they may either give up on the client or subtly retaliate. Attempts to detach yourself from therapeutic and client outcomes may help you to be more accepting of yourself and of clients, especially when your own expectations are not met.

Encouraging Client Participation in Therapy

According to the theory of psychological reactance (J. W. Brehm, 1966; S. S. Brehm, 1976), individuals are likely to resist attempts by others to change them whenever their perception of freedom has been diminished or eliminated. Encouraging active client participation in the therapy process has a number of important benefits, all of which serve to counteract the effects of psychological reactance. First, active participation increases the client's sense of control, or perception of choice. Second, clients are in a better position to select strategies and tasks that work in *their* world (Shelton & Levy, 1981). Third, clients may be more likely to comply and be less resistant in a cooperative rather than controlling counseling environment. Oppositional behavior is less likely to occur if clients are *asked* to do something instead of *told* to (Lazarus & Fay, 1982).

There are a number of ways to encourage greater participation by clients. First, deemphasize your role in any changes made by the client. Focus on the client contributions instead. Avoid taking credit for success. Self-attributed change is more likely to be maintained than change attributed by the client to someone else, such as the therapist (Kopel & Arkowitz, 1975).

Second, actively attempt to reduce the visibility of your influence efforts. Take a low profile, speak softly, and carry a tiny stick. The distinction between constructive influence, such as genuine efforts to help, and destructive influence, such as exploitation and coercion, is often blurred (Lazarus & Fay, 1982). Although a few clients respond positively to the use of authority or active influence, the majority of clients are either intimidated by or resistant to a great deal of therapeutic influence. Since the therapeutic relationship implies a

position of presumed therapist power, the therapist must take deliberate actions to engage in what Fisch et al. (1982) call "one-downsmanship." Kiesler (1971, pp. 164–165) suggests that "if you want someone not only to behave in a particular way, but also to believe accordingly, then induce the behavior under conditions of very little apparent external pressure. Give the person the feeling that he was free to do otherwise if he wished." For example, instead of always directing a client when to do something, give some options. Say something like "Wouldn't it be interesting if sometime in the next week, you . . . ?" Most persons resist if they feel any pressure to do something *now.*

Third, solicit client input. Clients often are the best source of information about their intentions, problems, and proposed solutions. Take advantage of this resource in front of you!

Use of Timing and Pacing

Timing and pacing have to do with the speed with which a counselor moves through an interview. If the counselor proceeds too fast or paces too far ahead of the client, resistance may be engendered. Ways to decrease the resistance produced by timing and pacing include changing the pace, leaving a sensitive topic temporarily and returning to it later, or lessening the emotional intensity of the session (Brammer, Shostrom, & Abrego, 1989).

Timing and pacing also have to do with the process of taking small steps throughout therapy and assessing the client's reactions to each step before proceeding further or starting on a new task (Fisch et al., 1982, p. 27). The therapist times and paces his or her comments and actions in accordance with client responses. If the client responds in any way other than a definite verbal or nonverbal acceptance of the therapist's lead, the therapist should change the pace or strategy. If the therapist persists in using an approach or a strategy that is not working, there is a risk of increased resistance or reduced credibility (Fisch et al., 1982).

Another aspect of appropriate use of timing and pacing is to avoid taking a stand prematurely. The therapist must first assess the client's views about problems, treatment, and outcome and then offer suggestions that are likely to fit the client.

Offering Strategies and Homework Tasks That Are Relevant to the Client

The therapist needs to present alternative strategies and homework tasks that are relevant to each client. For example, assertion training may be in-

FEEDBACK #53: ENVIRONMENTAL SOURCES OF RESISTANCE

Behavior One: Overeating

Here are some ideas. Are some of yours similar? What can you add to this list?

1. *Ways to make target response more visible:*
   a. Post reminders (preferably on refrigerator or in kitchen).
   b. Contract for weight loss with spouse or friend.
   c. Keep a daily record of everything you eat.
   d. Post a picture of yourself (or someone else) when you have been slim.
   e. Keep a chart of weight loss and post it.
   Others:
2. *Ways to reduce competing environmental stimuli:*
   a. Don't socialize with overeaters.
   b. Put locks on cupboards or refrigerators.
   c. Put snacks in hard-to-reach places.
   d. Shop for food on a full stomach.
   e. Confine eating to certain times and places.
   Others:

Behavior Two: Positive Thoughts about Self

1. Ways to make target response more visible:
   a. Post reminders to think positively or rationally.
   b. Make a list of strengths or attributes.
   c. Carry a stack of note cards around with one strength or attribute listed on each card — plus a blank card. At different times during the day, examine and reflect on one card. Use the next card the next time. Each time you come to the blank card, write down another strength or something about yourself you value.
   d. Use an alarm to cue you to think positively.
   e. Make positive or rational thoughts contingent on rewarding things you do each day.
   Others:
2. *Ways to reduce competing environmental stimuli:*
   a. Avoid engaging in depressing or failure-oriented activities.
   b. Avoid being around people who get down on you.
   c. Practice thought stopping for negative or irrational thoughts about yourself.
   d. Put a timer on negative thinking; "wallow" in it for 15 minutes; stop when the buzzer goes off.
   e. Confine negative thinking to a certain place such as one room or one chair.
   Others:

compatible with a client whose strongly held religious beliefs emphasize compliant behavior toward other people. Similarly, a client from a culture with a relatively unstructured concept of time may be mortified at the idea of using a kitchen timer to monitor study time or depressed thoughts. Strategies and homework should be individually tailored for each client. Haley (1978, p. 56) writes:

> The therapist must fit the task to the people. As he interviews a family, he will observe what sort of people the members are and can fit the task to the family style. If the family members emphasize doing things in an orderly, logical manner, the task offered to them should be an orderly, logical task — they will be more likely to do it. If they form a casual, disorderly household, a casual framework for the task may be more appropriate. If they are concerned about money, the therapist emphasizes that the task costs nothing. . . . The way they go about doing [tasks in therapy] will give the therapist information on how to frame the outside task more acceptably for them.

One way to ensure that a strategy is appropriate for a given client is to ask the client to spend a few minutes imagining what it would be like to spend time on such a task (Anderson & Stewart, 1983). If the client is not enthusiastic about actually using the strategy or engaging in the task, it is not suitable for this particular client.

Assessing and Utilizing Patient Position

Fisch et al. (1982) have made a major contribution to the literature on change with the concept of patient position. *Patient position* refers to clients'

> strongly held beliefs, values, and priorities, which determine how they will act or not act. Thus, the importance of "position" is that it represents an inclination within patients which can be utilized to enhance the acceptance and carrying out of therapist directives. . . . Knowing what the client's position is allows one to formulate guidelines on how to couch — or frame — a suggestion in a way that the client is most likely to accept [p. 90].

The therapist must first listen carefully to what the client says in order to assess the client's important position statements. It is important to listen to the words clients select and use, since clients indicate their positions in specific wording. The most useful positions are those strongly held by the client and, hence, repeated over and over during the sessions. For example, Tom, a 30-year-old male client, sought help from a counselor about career choice. During the initial interview, the client said things about himself like "It is difficult for me to decide whether to go for a graduate degree or to get a good job and start earning some money. *I don't know how much you'll be able to help me* because I'm a very *complex* person. I've had an *unusual* background for someone my age. I've always been *on top* or *achieved* more than what was expected of me in school and in jobs I've held, and all at a young age. I now consider myself very *mature* and *experienced* about life. I've done a lot of things I wasn't supposed to have the ability to do. *I always rise to a challenge.* If someone says 'Tom, you can't do this,' *I set out to prove the person wrong. I guess I'm sort of a rebel.*"

In this brief example, Tom has revealed several "patient positions," such as the following:

1. He is somewhat pessimistic about whether the counselor can help him or whether counseling will benefit him ("I don't know how much you'll be able to help me").
2. He regards himself as someone special, unique, and complicated ("I'm a very complex person. I've had an unusual background. Mature and experienced, I've been on top and achieved.").
3. He functions best when told he can't do something; he may be likely to display oppositional behavior when told or asked to do something ("I rise to a challenge. I set out to prove the person wrong. I guess I'm sort of a rebel").

"Patient positions" that have most bearing on the course of therapy include the client's notions about the nature of the problem and its assumed cause, about who is responsible for the problem, about how the problem can be resolved, and about the therapy process itself and the client's role during therapy.

If the therapist cannot detect these types of positions from listening to the client's words, use of selective questions such as the following can be an additional assessment tool:

"What is your interpretation of the problem?"
"If someone described your problem this way: _____, would you agree, or would that description be all wrong?"
"What is your best guess about why this problem exists?"
"Whom do you see as creating the problem?"
"How do you explain the fact that this problem has been so persistent [or gotten better or worse]?"

"Who do you feel needs to solve the problem?"
"This may or may not work for your problem, but have you tried _____?"
"How do you feel therapy will help you?"
"What is your thinking about my role [or your role] during therapy?"
"How would you describe yourself?"

After assessment, the therapist can use client position advantageously in several ways. First, the therapist can avoid making any comments that might create resistance—that is, comments that might be inflammatory to the client or might reduce your credibility because they are too discrepant from the client's values and beliefs. For example, with Tom, the counselor would need to *avoid* inflammatory comments such as—

1. "You have a very *simple* decision to make." (The word *simple* is likely to be inflammatory because it contradicts Tom's perception of himself and his problem as difficult and complex.)
2. "*Lots of people* find it hard to make this kind of career choice." (The phrase *lots of people* may be inflammatory because it is discrepant from Tom's view that he and his problem are unique.)
3. "It would be a good idea to make this decision in the next few months so you don't end up without a job or without a degree." (This statement is likely to be too "preachy" and may elicit oppositional behavior from Tom.)

Similarly, statements that might reduce the counselor's credibility with Tom include—

4. "I'm sure I can help you."
5. "If you work at it, counseling can be of great help to you." (These two statements do not match Tom's pessimistic view of the counselor and of the value of counseling.)

or

6. "Let's discuss the pros and cons of graduate school or employment and you can find a solution *fairly easily.*" (This statement does not match Tom's view that his decision is a hard one that cannot easily be reached.)

It would be more helpful to make comments that match the views and positions of this client, such as the following ones:

1. "Since this is a *difficult* and *unique* problem, it will be important to *go slowly* and *take time* to work it through."

2. "Perhaps considering your *unusual back-ground,* it would be best to start off by being a *little more skeptical* about counseling than the *average person* might be."

3. "This is an *important* and *weighty* dilemma. It is worthy of *careful analysis* and *attention.*"

The counselor also needs to present suggestions and tasks in such a way that the client is likely to cooperate. To accomplish this, present tasks or actions in a way consistent with the client's position (Fisch et al., 1982, p. 101). Talk the client's language and suggest ideas that match the client's values and beliefs. As Erickson (quoted in Haley, 1973, p. 206) has observed, "People come for help, but they also come to be substantiated in their attitudes and they come to have face saved. I pay attention to this and I'm likely to speak in a fashion that makes them think I'm on their side." Restating or reframing ideas in such a way that the client is likely to accept them. For example, with Tom, the way the purpose or objective of therapy is framed can enlist or discourage his cooperation in working toward the purpose. Saying something like "It would be important to work toward a choice that will be satisfactory to you now and in the future, considering your background, achievements, and maturity" is likely to have more appeal to Tom than stating "You need to choose between school and a job." The strategies and actions suggested to Tom should also consider his perception of the problem and of himself. He is more likely to comply with strategies and tasks seen as unusual, grandiose, challenging, and risk-taking, because they appeal more to his perception of himself as extraordinary and uncommon, than tasks that are relatively mundane, routine, and unobtrusive.

Acknowledging Anxiety/Discomfort about Your Competence

Therapist resistance is greater with inexperienced therapists who are concerned about their competence and effectiveness with clients. Competence anxiety has to do with commitment and is worsened, in fact, by the sense of overwhelming responsibility that beginning therapists take for their clients (Anderson & Stewart, 1983). An initial step useful for dealing with competence anxiety is to acknowledge it. Expressing your anxiety with a peer, colleague, or supervisor often diminishes it and reduces your preoccupation with yourself. Seeking consultation and supervision from supportive and knowledgeable persons is another

strategy for dealing with concern about your effectiveness (Anderson & Stewart, 1983).

A third strategy is to establish your own limits in counseling. Distinguish between things that you are legitimately responsible for and things that the client must be responsible for. Avoid doing work for the client! Weeks and L'Abate (1982) observe that a common myth surrounding counseling and therapy is that a therapist is always responsible for producing change. They note:

> The therapist is expected to be optimistic about the future. Therapists are expected to be supportive. When therapy is not proceeding smoothly, then the therapist works harder. The therapist may even work on one problem more as the client works on it less. This kind of approach may eventually lead to a dependency relationship, with the therapist assuming a rescuing role [pp. 125–126].

Taking Care of Yourself

The axiom "Charity begins at home" has important implications for therapists. Therapist resistance is worse with therapists who are fatigued and overworked, who are so busy trying to take care of the lives of other people that they neglect their own needs. Eventually, what we refer to as "burnout" occurs. Signs of burnout include feeling relieved when a client cancels or postpones a session, having little energy available for sessions, lacking interest in client outcomes, and having persistent, recurring thoughts about whether you are in the right profession or about changing jobs (Anderson & Stewart, 1983). In severe cases of burnout, health problems may develop and work may be missed. Tired and overworked therapists tend to show resistance by being slow to return a client's phone call or to reschedule a canceled session, by showing pessimism about outcomes, and by displaying less enthusiasm and intensity toward clients. Clients are very sensitive about whether the therapist wants to see them, and such resistive behaviors are easily transmitted to clients, even over the telephone. Thus clients who show up late or postpone or cancel appointments may be reacting to therapist resistance rather than their own (Anderson & Stewart, 1983).

The best way to avoid resistance due to fatigue, overwork, and burnout is to prevent it. Arrange working and environmental conditions so that fatigue and burnout are not likely to occur. For example, schedule short "breathing spaces" between clients, always take a lunch break, develop a support system with other colleagues, consult frequently with your supervisor, arrange your office in a pleasing manner. When you're not working, learn to engage in relaxing activities, and don't bring your work home with you or dwell on what happened at work during leisure time.

If you are beyond this point and fatigue and burnout have already set in, start taking better care of yourself. Let off steam about your feelings to an empathic listener. Change the size or type of case-load you carry. Use vacation days or sick leave to take time off from work. Arrange for time-out periods when you are at work. Develop an ongoing support system for yourself. Do something each day that in some way is pleasing to you and meets your needs. Otherwise you are likely to feel bad about yourself and increasingly resentful of clients. Above all, remember—don't jeopardize the needs of your clients because you haven't learned or cared enough to take care of your own.

LEARNING ACTIVITY #54: THERAPIST SOURCES OF RESISTANCE

PART ONE

This activity is to be done in triads; one person assumes the role of client, another the counselor, and the third is the observer. Roles can then be switched twice so each person has an opportunity to function once in each of the three roles. As the client, decide on an issue you want to work on from the following list and tell the counselor what it is:

Assertiveness behavior
Marital (or relationship) communication
Weight control
Study skills
Rational thinking

As the counselor, give several *direct* suggestions to the client about things he or she could do to resolve this issue. Direct suggestions are framed as "I want you to," "You need to," and so on. After delivering each suggestion, watch and listen to the client's verbal and nonverbal behavior for "yes" and "no" clues that suggest receptivity or lack of interest in your suggestion. On the basis of the client's reactions, either stick with your suggestion if you get "yes" cues or modify it if you get "no" cues. As the observer, observe and monitor the client's reactions to the counselor's suggestions and note whether the counselor accurately discriminated the client's reactions by continuing with or changing the original suggestion.

PART TWO

The first part of this activity is done in writing; the second occurs in role play. First, recall the direct suggestions you gave to your client in the previous activity. Jot them down. Now reframe each direct suggestion into an *indirect* suggestion that presents an illusion of choice. For example, instead of "I want you to study two hours each day this week," try "How much do you want to study—one hour, two hours, or three hours a day?" Write down your indirect suggestions. Second, assuming the same roles you did in the previous activity, this time deliver the *indirect* suggestion and do it in a *one-down manner*. Then observe the client's reactions. The observer can also give input about the client's "yes" and "no" cues. In which activity was the client more receptive to your ideas and suggestions?

PART THREE

In dyads or small groups, discuss the problem of therapist resistance due to fatigue and burnout. Identify your own cognitive and behavioral signs of burnout and fatigue. Describe how you may communicate being resistant to clients. Identify ways to manage burnout or prevent it from occurring for yourself.

□ WHEN ALL ELSE FAILS: LAST-RESORT STRATEGIES

Occasionally the strategies mentioned so far in this chapter to manage resistance seem to have no effect. The client becomes increasingly resistant, and the counselor becomes more frustrated. In this section we describe some strategies that can be tried when all else fails.

Contracting to Change for One Week

If the client seems extremely reluctant to try out new behavior, contract to change for only one week. (This is based on the principle of successive approximations, described in Chapter 9.) Point out that change is not irreversible. Try to have the client agree to change for just one week (or any other specified time period) with the stipulation that the client can resort to the old behavior at the end of the week. At the end of the week, most clients are pleasantly surprised and desire to continue the new behavior or some variation of it. A few, however, continue to sabotage this brief plan, especially if they have a vested interest in defeating the therapist (Anderson & Stewart, 1983).

Antisabotage Procedures

"Antisabotage procedures are 'designed' to anticipate, identify and modify those interactional tendencies to resist progress" (Spinks & Birchler, 1982, p. 180). They are used with clients who tend to sabotage plans and tasks that they have agreed to carry out. There are four steps in creating antisabotage procedures (Spinks & Birchler, 1982):

1. Have the client brainstorm all the possible reasons for and ways of being noncompliant with the accepted plan or task.
2. Identify high-risk sabotage behaviors—that is, what the client is likely to do *instead* of carrying out the task or plan (watching TV instead of talking to spouse after dinner).
3. Develop ways for the client to deal with the high-risk sabotage behaviors so that they do not interfere with completion of the plan (talk to my spouse first and then watch TV).
4. Reinforce the client for follow-through and completion of the plan.

Although the therapist could easily list possible sabotage procedures, it is more effective to encourage *clients* to think of ways they might avoid the plan (Haley, 1978).

Metaphors

A metaphor is a word or phrase that implies a comparison. In therapy, metaphors are used as cognitive cues to suggest a likeness between the client and the object or person referred to in the metaphor. A classic metaphor used by Erickson (in Haley, 1967) with a cancer patient in great pain is that of a tomato plant growing from a seed. In the metaphor, Erickson described how the seed is planted and carefully nurtured, with special emphasis on the good, comfortable, peaceful feelings the plant has as it grows. What Erickson was doing was embedding within the story a number of suggestions for the client about relaxation, comfort, and disassociation from pain.

A metaphor is a useful way to tell a story that relates to a particular problem the client will recognize as his or her own without raising the client's anxiety level to the point where the client cannot assimilate the idea. A metaphor can function as an indirect confrontation or interpretation and is especially useful with denial. Metaphors also "are handy for saving face in that they often provide a vehicle for people to change without having to admit that they've been mistaken or that their ways of coping haven't worked" (Anderson & Stewart, 1983, p. 194).

For example, a counselor was working with a young man who had recently married a medical intern. The client was having difficulty accepting his wife's frequent absences while she was on call at the hospital. The client believed that his wife did not care for him as much as she should because occasionally, while on call, the wife did not telephone and check in with him. The client disputed the counselor's suggestion that a more rational interpretation might be that the wife had too many admissions or very ill patients that night in order to call him. At this point, the counselor offered the following metaphor:

"By the way, I am reminded of this story about a man and his neighbor. Now, it might seem curious to you that we are going to talk about a man and his neighbor. But perhaps this story will be interesting.

A man was enjoying a relaxing time at home one evening. There was a sudden knock on his door. His neighbor's husband was standing there. His wife had stopped breathing. He wanted his neighbor to come help him revive her. The man felt a pang; he had not been able to keep in touch with his neighbors as frequently as he wanted, because after a period of unemployment, he had started to work as a telephone switchboard operator. After finding the woman lying on the floor, he began to administer CPR. She started to breathe again. In the middle of the process, the phone began to ring. He started to stop the massage as if he felt he would answer it. The woman stopped breathing. Then he continued the massage and worked feverishly to try to get his neighbor to breathe again, which she did as he ignored the phone and continued the CPR."

Six steps are involved in creating a suitable metaphor:

1. Examine the nature of the client's problem. Identify any metaphoric themes within the problem (for example, intimacy, role behavior, self-image) and construct a metaphor that parallels the theme.
2. Select a representative "character" for the metaphor (person, animal, object, and so on).

3. Use words in the metaphor that match the client's visual, auditory, or kinesthetic representational system or frame of reference.
4. Create a process in the metaphor for each process in the problem. However, the actual content of the metaphor should be different enough from the client's problem so that the client does not overtly recognize it as her or his own story.
5. In order to use metaphors to promote behavior change, specify and elaborate on the character's behaviors. The intent is to detail "particular behaviors at specific choice points with sufficient precision and elaboration that the prescribed acts can be approximated by the listener" (Lankton & Lankton, 1983, p. 82).
6. Design the story line to provide a solution or a desired response that includes some element of suspense or mystery for attention holding (Lankton, 1980; Lankton & Lankton, 1983). The solution usually portrays the consequences of the behaviors specified in the story.

In the CPR example, a person was selected to use in the metaphor, and kinesthetic words *(feel, touch, experience)* were selected to match the client's primary representational system. The story reflected processes found in the client's problem:

1. Recent marriage = sudden knock on door; recent job.
2. Wife's frequent absences = man's absence from contact with neighbors.
3. Wife's not calling him on phone because of patient demands = ringing phone — man does not answer phone because of life-threatening situation.

The story also contained several descriptions of the character's actions or behaviors — starting CPR, stopping CPR as if he were going to answer the phone, but ignoring it and continuing the CPR.

The end of the story provided the desired response and consequences of the character's behavior: the man chose to ignore the phone, even though answering phones was his job, in order to continue CPR and to avoid his friend's death. The story provides an alternative explanation of the failure of the client's wife to call that is less threatening than a direct interpretation.

To be most effective, deliver metaphors as "stories" and offer them casually at times when telling a story seems appropriate, such as at the beginning or end of a session or during a natural break or change in focus. Since metaphors are more effective if they are told with conviction and congruence, draw on your own personal experiences and convey true stories if possible.

An object can also be used to confront clients metaphorically or to illustrate a point. A pocket calculator can be used to calculate percentages of time with clients who tend to catastrophize and generalize about the amount of time a problem or symptom occurs (Harvill, Jacobs, & Masson, 1984). We have found the use of a collapsible camping cup to be useful with some clients whose self-esteem goes up (pull cup up) or down (push cup down) depending on the reactions of other people to them or to their environment.

For further information about and examples of clinical metaphors, we suggest you peruse *Advanced Techniques of Hypnosis and Therapy: Selected Papers of Milton H. Erickson, M.D.* (Haley, 1967), *Therapeutic Metaphors* (Gordon, 1978), and *The Answer Within* (Lankton & Lankton, 1983).

Shortening Sessions or Terminating

As a final resort, the therapist always has the option of shortening the sessions, reducing their frequency, or terminating treatment until the client makes some attempt to fulfill the therapeutic agreement. According to Fisch et al. (1982, p. 23), "The therapist cannot deal effectively with patient resistance unless he is prepared to exercise this ultimate option should it become necessary."

There are many times in therapy when this option may need to be discussed explicitly with the client. Exercise of this option, however, occurs infrequently. Before exercising this option, the counselor must first understand the nature of the client's resistance. Furthermore, this option should be used only after *several* unfulfilled promises or uncompleted tasks. Finally, the therapist should not terminate as punishment but rather "to demonstrate to the client the therapist's concern and unwillingness" to have the client waste his or her time and money (Gottman & Leiblum, 1974, p. 113).

Some clients display resistance only near the termination phase of therapy. In other words, the clients become anxious and concerned about how they will do without the therapist and resist termination. With panicky clients, one option is to *insist* on one more appointment (Fisch et al., 1982).

Another option is to treat termination paradoxically, by prescribing or predicting a relapse (see also "A Taxonomy of Paradoxical Interventions," later in this chapter).

Clients are less likely to resist termination if it is done gradually and slowly. One way to do this is to gradually increase the time between sessions. Sessions can occur less and less frequently over a period of several months. It is also important to focus explicitly on the client's resources, strengths, and coping skills. According to Anderson and Stewart

(1983, p. 117), "Placing an emphasis on [client's] strengths and abilities while providing some sort of cognitive distance on the experience of therapy helps to provide the closure needed to leave therapy comfortably."

A final option that is often useful either for approaching termination or as a "last resort" strategy is paradoxical intervention. Because this strategy requires great skill to implement, we discuss it in some detail in the next section.

LEARNING ACTIVITIES #55: LAST-RESORT STRATEGIES

Part One: Antisabotage Procedures

This activity can be done by yourself or in a dyad. It is designed to assist you in creating an antisabotage plan for a behavior that you (or a partner) wish to change but are likely to sabotage instead. Some examples are procrastination and meeting deadlines, weight control, smoking cessation, and exercise. These are just examples—pick a behavior relevant to yourself. An example of what one of us did for such a behavior follows the instructions.

Instructions for yourself or your partner:

1. Identify the behavior you wish to change. State the desired change in positive terms—that is, what you want to be able to do, think, or feel differently.

2. Describe (or have the partner describe) an action plan/steps to meet this desired goal. Make sure the plan is reasonable for you (or your partner) and is consistent with your (or your partner's) values.

3. Identify (or have the partner identify) all the possible reasons you might not comply with the plan (for example, too much time, too much trouble or energy).

4. Identify (or have the partner identify) "high-risk sabotage behaviors"—that is, what you are likely to do, think, or feel *instead* of carrying out the agreed-on plan (for example, watching TV, eating, talking on phone, partying, and so on, and so on!).

5. Develop ways for yourself (or have the partner develop ways) to deal with these high-risk sabotage behaviors so that they are less likely to interfere with completion of the action plan (comply with plan first, then watch TV or party).

6. Identify (or have the partner identify) ways to get different kinds of reinforcement such as those described under "Self-Reward," in Chapter 19, for compliance with the action plan and progress toward the goal.

Example

1. Desired behavior: Wish to exercise three times a week for 40 minutes each time.

2. Action plan:
   a. Set aside three times each week, every other day, for exercise.
   b. Build exercise into my daily routine—exercise at same time each week.
   c. Use music to make it more pleasant.

3. Possible reasons I might not comply:
   a. Not enough time to exercise—should be doing housework, job work, writing, or being with family.
   b. Don't feel as if I have the energy to exercise.

4. High-risk sabotage behaviors: Sleep late instead of exercise; stay at work longer to avoid exercise time.

5. Ways to deal with sabotage behaviors: Schedule exercise sessions in late afternoon or evening instead of morning on arising: exercise with a friend (exercise partner) so I won't "cop out."

6. Reinforcement:
   a. Social—obtain praise from spouse and friend.
   b. Self—feel better after exercising, also keep weight at desired level, body looks better.

End result: Went from 0 exercise a week to 2–3 exercise sessions a week over a nine-month period.

Part Two: Metaphors, Stories

Listed below are four descriptions of various client situations. Try to pick at least one or two situations that seem personally relevant to you. For each situation, construct a metaphor you could use with this client. Try to use a real story if possible or at least one that arises out of your personal experiences. The metaphor you construct will be more effective if it parallels themes or issues reflected in the client problem.

(continued)

Design the story line to provide a solution or indication of a desired response. Also include an element of mystery or suspense to hold the client's attention. The first situation is used as an example. After you construct your metaphors, discuss them with a colleague or instructor.

Example
Situation One
The client is a child who gets down on herself very easily. After making one mistake in school or at home, she tends to become very frustrated and wants to give up rather than completing the task or following through in the situation. The metaphor below, a true story, was offered to her by one of the authors who is a "closet pianist."

"Jane, would you be interested in hearing about something that happened to me when I was about your age? If so, I'd like to share this story with you. Listen and watch and see what you get out of it.

When I was 6 years old, I started taking piano lessons every week. My teacher was very good, and every year she rented a huge auditorium for all her students to have their yearly piano recital in. It was a big deal! There was a story written up about it in the newspaper and programs printed up with the students' names on them and the titles of the songs you would play. Then there was a big stage with lights and two big pianos and a beautiful bouquet of red roses. For a couple of years, I went to these recitals and did my thing and played my song and never thought twice about it. Really enjoyed myself. Then when I was about 9 or 10, something happened. Want to know what it was? I was supposed to play a duet with my sister, who also took lessons. We had practiced and practiced together. We had learned how to start playing at the same time — which was important — by my lifting my chin up and then, as my head came down, our fingers would start touching the keys simultaneously. Well, guess what? That day I started play-

ing. I played for about a half a minute — although it seemed like an eternity — and then I stopped. Something was wrong! I was playing, but my sister was not. I realized I had forgotten to give her the "chins up" signal and she wasn't at all ready to start. I had just jumped in. So I stopped playing and felt horrified. I was ready to quit and walk off the stage and end my piano career right there, even though I loved music very much. But I didn't. Because I looked and saw my piano teacher in the wings. She had a smile on her face and whispered to me — "The show goes on. Forget about it and just start over." That's exactly what we did. And after we finished, the applause was just as loud as it would have been if I hadn't made that one mistake. After that, I never got through a recital in which I didn't make at least one mistake or play one wrong note. But it never really mattered, because for that one wrong note there were always ten thousand other notes that were just right."

Situation Two
A female client feels very dependent on her husband. When she is alone at work or attends a social function alone, she functions well and feels comfortable and confident. When she is with her husband, she feels insecure and anxious and doesn't trust herself or her decisions.

Situation Three
A male client wants his wife to depend on him to make him feel important. When she gets too close, however, he gets upset and angry and finds something about her to criticize.

Situation Four
A male client behaves very appropriately and assertively with other men but feels unable to refuse almost any request made to him by a woman, even if the request is inappropriate or costly to him in terms of time or money.

☐ PARADOXICAL INTERVENTIONS

Paradoxical interventions have been used in various ways for many years. Dunlap's (1928) negative, or massed, practice is a form of paradoxical intervention. In this strategy, the behavior decreases or stops because of *satiation;* as a result of cumulative, or massed, repetition, the behavior loses its reinforcing properties and stops.

Another form of therapy, logotherapy (developed by Frankl, 1960), also uses paradoxical intervention. In this technique clients reach a certain goal by exaggerating an undesirable response. Implied in this directive is the assumption that by engaging in the problem behavior, the client will eventually be able to eliminate it.

An important hallmark of paradoxical intervention is the therapist's *acceptance* of the client's noncompliant behavior (Haley, 1973). Therapists must avoid becoming frustrated, defensive, or counteroppositional. Perhaps the most important principle to remember in dealing with highly resistant clients is *never* to fight with them. Haley (1973) likens resistance to a river. If a therapist opposes the river by blocking it, the river simply goes over and around her or him. If, however, the therapist accepts the force of the river and diverts it in a new direction, the force of the river will create a new channel. As Shelton and Levy (1981) observe, "When the therapist accepts the resistance, the client is caught in a position where resistance becomes cooperation" (p. 72). Acceptance of clients' resistant behavior is synonymous with respecting their polarity and pacing (matching) it (Lankton, 1980). Accepting, or pacing, turns a resistant client into a potentially very cooperative client.

Regardless of the origins of paradoxical interventions, all forms have one similar feature. The client is encouraged either to produce symptomatic behavior at will or to avoid trying to get better (Omer, 1981). The paradox in these messages is that the client can change by remaining unchanged. Further, in all paradoxical treatments, the context surrounding the symptomatic behavior is changed. In paradoxical interventions, the affective, cognitive, and/or interpersonal context of the symptom may be changed. The client may be instructed to exaggerate the symptom, do it more often or with more intensity, or carry it out at different times or places. Omer (1981) asserts that, in paradoxical treatments, change may result more from the change in context than from the type of directive. Because the context is changed, the "symptom loses its function and meaning" (p. 322). Similarly, Raskin and Klein (1976) note that instructions to engage in a problem behavior *voluntarily* change the stimuli that elicit the behavior so that the client is then less likely to engage in the problem behavior in the original setting. The effectiveness of paradoxical interventions in therapy has been evaluated and overall, paradoxical interventions were as effective as typical modes of treatment (Shoham-Salomon & Rosenthal, 1987; Strong, 1984). Dowd & Milne (1986) have provided an excellent overview of paradoxical interventions in counseling psychology.

Uses of Paradoxical Interventions

Ascher has reported the effective use of paradoxical interventions with insomnia (Ascher & Efran,

1978; Ascher & Turner, 1979), urinary retention (Ascher, 1979), and agoraphobia (Ascher, 1981; Mavissakalian, Michelson, Greenwald, Kornblith, & Greenwald, 1983). Paradoxical interventions have also been used effectively in reducing procrastination of college students (Lopez & Wambach, 1982; Wright & Strong, 1982). Birchler (1981) cites the effectiveness of this strategy in promoting change in behavioral marital therapy.

Paradoxical interventions are useful for clients who are disturbed by the frequency of a response. Clients may be concerned that an undesirable behavior occurs too often or that a desired response occurs rarely (Ascher, 1979). Lopez (1983) notes that paradoxical interventions are highly useful for facilitating voluntary control over specific, habitual, or reportedly 'involuntary' behaviors. Ascher (1980) asserts that paradoxical interventions may be used as the primary treatment whenever the designated change program fails to produce desired results: "When progress is impeded in the context of an appropriate behavioral analysis and a currently administered behavioral program, then enhancing the client's ability to cooperate may become the focus of attention" (p. 268).

Paradoxical interventions should be avoided with clients who have strong self-doubts, homicidal or suicidal tendencies, or are very dependent and in situations of crisis or extreme instability (Shelton & Levy, 1981; Rohrbaugh, Tennen, Press, & White, 1981). Weeks and L'Abate (1982) observe that paradoxical interventions will not work well with sociopathic personalities, who will change the task to fit their own needs, or paranoid personalities, who may become more suspicious.

Cautions in Using Paradoxical Interventions

One caution in using paradoxical interventions has to do with the timing of the directive. Use of paradoxical interventions in *initial* therapy sessions is usually *not* advised, for several reasons. First, in order for paradoxical interventions to be effective, the therapist must formulate an accurate functional analysis that explains in a plausible way the functions of the major presenting symptoms. This formulation is not always readily achieved. Second, paradoxical interventions should be reserved only for situations of *major* noncompliance (Papp, 1980). Before using a paradoxical intervention, the therapist should first use more direct interventions. Even then, some resistance is to be expected. As Gurman (1981, p. 120) observes, "The crucial issue that the therapist must address is, thus, not whether noncompliance exists, but whether and how readily it can be overcome, especially by the use of more direct interventions, such as further development of the therapeutic alliance [and] confrontation or interpretation."

Birchler (1981, p. 125) cites three criteria to be met before paradoxical intervention should be used:

1. The client's resistant behaviors are repetitive and persistent.
2. The resistant behaviors significantly obstruct the progress of therapy.
3. The resistant behaviors are not modified by more usual direct interventions.

A second issue has to do with the ethics of using a strategy such as paradoxical intervention, which appears to violate the behavioral principle of explicitly informing clients of the treatment rationale and technique. Shelton and Levy (1981) assert that, on occasion, the therapist may use a change strategy that is not explicitly agreed on, as long as the therapist is pursuing the client's choice of treatment goals. According to Birchler (1981), if paradoxical intervention is based on an accurate functional analysis, it is possible to tell the client quite openly why an assignment is being given. Birchler asserts:

It is tempting and all too easy to make isolated paradoxical prescriptions without preparing the [client] by providing a plausible, airtight rationale for the particular assignment. The necessity for the assignment should also be explained in the context of past failure of the [client] to make the expected progress, using whatever previous techniques. . . . Obviously, the therapist does not indicate that the assignment is meant to be a paradox or have a paradoxical effect [pp. 124–126].

A final caution is to remember that paradoxical interventions are complex and require great skill and energy to implement effectively. A paradoxical intervention can be difficult to administer properly, particularly by persons who have had little training or experience in the use of this technique. We strongly recommend that no one attempt to use a paradoxical intervention with real clients from reading about it in this or any other book without first practicing it in role-play situations and obtaining feedback on your use of the strategy. Additionally, it would be important to seek supervision for your initial attempts in using paradoxical intervention with clients.

Counselors should be aware that directives of any type can have important ethical and legal implications. In a recent case in California, for example, a counselor was found negligent because she instructed the client to "sit on the client's unruly son." The client, who happened to be rather obese, took the counselor's instruction literally and went home and sat on her son for two hours. The son subsequently died by asphyxiation. In a similar vein, a jury might have a difficult time understanding why a therapist would tell an insomniac to "try to stay awake at night" or another client to deliberately engage in the problematic behavior. A therapist should consider the ethical implications when using paradoxical strategies with a client (Brown & Slee, 1986; Ridley & Tan, 1986).

A Taxonomy of Paradoxical Interventions

There are a variety of ways in which paradoxical interventions can be organized. In this section we present a taxonomy to assist you in conceptualizing the various forms of this technique.

Focus of paradoxical interventions: Individual, dyadic, systemic. The focus of paradoxical interventions can be on individuals, couples (dyadic), or groups and families (transactional or systemic). The focus of the intervention chosen depends on the therapist's theoretical orientation, the number of clients present, and the results of the problem assessment. Dyadic and systemic interventions are the most difficult because they require understanding of the relationship and/or system as well as experience in working with couples and families. Individually oriented interventions are the easiest to prescribe and the most prevalent in the literature. Some of these interventions can be carried out alone by the client; some require the involvement of other people (Weeks & L'Abate, 1982). Examples of tasks that focus on the individual client are instructing a client who can't sleep to get up and do obnoxious household chores such as cleaning the oven, instructing a client who puts off studying to schedule 30 minutes nightly to practice procrastination, or directing a client who is plagued with negative, self-defeating thoughts to dwell on and exaggerate the thoughts as they occur. Our discussion deals with individually oriented interventions. We believe that effective dyadic and systemic interventions require some additional training and supervision in marriage and family therapy, which is beyond the scope of this book.

Purpose of interventions: Compliance or defiance. Paradoxical interventions can be divided into two categories, depending on whether the purpose of the intervention is to have the client carry out (comply with) or reject (defy) the task (Rohrbaugh et al., 1981: Tennen, Rohrbaugh, Press, & White, 1981). In compliance-based prescriptions the client's attempt to comply with the therapist's request "interrupts or short-circuits the process that perpetuates the problem" (Rohrbaugh et al., 1981, p. 457).* Tennen et al. (1981) note that compliance-based interventions emphasize the *intrapersonal* domain. Compliance-based interventions are most likely

> to work with symptoms such as obsessions, anxiety attacks, and various somatic complaints that are maintained to some extent by the patient's attempts to stave them off. By attempting to bring on such a symptom deliberately, one cannot continue in the usual ways of trying to prevent it, and under these conditions, the symptom often dissolves or comes more under voluntary control [Rohrbaugh et al., 1981, p. 457].

For further descriptions of compliance-based paradoxes, see the work of Watzlawick, Weakland, and Fisch (1974).

Defiance-based interventions assume that the client will oppose carrying out the directive. This directive is meant to influence the client to change by resisting or rebelling. Defiance-based interventions emphasize the *interpersonal* domain by reflecting the client's need to oppose, defeat, or be one-up on the therapist (Tennen et al., 1981). Defiance-based interventions include predicting that something will happen when you know the client will oppose it and asking for even more extreme behavior than the client has shown. In both cases, the client is likely to rebel and decrease or eliminate the problem behavior. Defiance-based interventions work well with many relationship issues. For futher descriptions of defiance-based paradoxes, consult Haley (1976).

The therapist must decide when to use compliance- or defiance-based interventions. As Rohrbaugh et al. (1981, p. 458) observe, "In order to

enhance the power of a given intervention, it is important for the therapist to decide when paradox is being used with the expectation of compliance, and when it is being used with the expectation of defiance." Rohrbaugh et al. (1981) suggest two parameters for therapists to use in deciding whether the purpose of the paradox should be compliance or defiance. The first parameter is the *reactance potential* of the client (J. W. Brehm, 1966, 1972; S. S. Brehm, 1976). Psychological reactance is the need to preserve one's freedom. Clients who are high in reactance are typically oppositional and often find ways to say or do the opposite of what the therapist suggests. Clients who are low on reactance potential are typically cooperative and comply with what the therapist suggests. Therapists can assess this dimension by noticing early whether the client consistently takes positions opposite or complementary to the therapist's views and/or by assigning a straightforward task and noticing whether the client carries out or forgets the task (Rohrbaugh et al., 1981).

The second parameter to assess is the client's *perceived freedom* of his or her symptoms. An "unfree" symptom is one that the client believes is out of his or her control — one that occurs *spontaneously.* A "free" symptom is one that the patient defines as something that can be done *voluntarily* — either now or in the future. Therapists can assess this dimension by asking the client or by "reading" cues from the client's verbal and nonverbal behavior (Rohrbaugh et al., 1981).

In general, *compliance-based* interventions are used for clients with *low* reactance potential and with *unfree,* or spontaneous, symptoms. *Defiance-based* interventions work better when reactance is *high* and the symptom is perceived as *free,* or voluntary. Paradoxical interventions are usually not necessary in cases of *low* reactance potential and *free,* or voluntary, behavior. The most difficult combination to treat is high reactance potential coupled with an unfree symptom. In such instances, the therapist's first task is to shift the focus of intervention temporarily away from the symptom, until reactance potential lowers (Rohrbaugh et al., 1981).

Types of intervention: Prescribing and restraining. The most common forms of paradoxical interventions are labeled as prescribing or restraining. Rohrbaugh et al. (1981) define prescriptions as follows:

---

* This and all other quotations from this source are reprinted with permission, from "Compliance, Defiance, and Therapeutic Paradox" by M. Rohrbaugh, H. Tennen, S. Press, and L. White. *American Journal of Orthopsychiatry, 51,* 454–467. Copyright © 1981 by the American Orthopsychiatric Association Inc.

When using a paradoxical *prescribing* strategy, the therapist encourages or instructs someone to engage in the specific piece of behavior to be eliminated. For example, a patient may be asked to practice an obsessional thought or bring on an anxiety attack, a rebellious adolescent may be encouraged to rebel, or an overinvolved mother to be more protective of her child [p. 456].

Prescribing tactics are used for *compliance*-based interventions and are based on the assumption that engaging in the problem behavior or exaggerating the symptom will eliminate it. When using restraining interventions, the therapist discourages change or may even deny it is possible. The therapist may instruct the client to go slow or may gently suggest that change may not be feasible (Rohrbaugh et al., 1981). Restraining tactics are reserved for *defiance*-based interventions and are based on the assumption that the client will change by rebelling against the therapist's directive. The decision to use compliance- or defiance-based interventions depends on the level of the client's resistance, the nature of the problem, and the therapist's assessment of what and who constitute the problem.

A *symptom prescription* is the most common compliance-based paradoxical intervention used. The underlying rationale of a prescriptive paradox is (1) in order to ease your symptom, keep it, and (2) will your uncontrollable symptom to occur voluntarily (Tennen et al., 1981). Symptom prescription is not meant to trick clients but instead to help clients change under their own power, with their own resources, and to their own credit (Zeig, 1980a). As Lankton and Lankton (1983, p. 74) observe, "If a client can purposefully alter a symptom previously considered involuntary, a new measure of hope is realized." In all forms of symptom prescription, the therapist is introducing a small modification of the target behavior. Sometimes one small change is sufficient to disrupt a self-defeating behavior pattern. In other cases, this small change can be built on and added to with other changes.

In using a prescriptive paradox, the therapist first selects one or more elements of the symptom to prescribe such as thoughts, feelings, or behaviors. Next, the therapist decides how to prescribe the symptom. One type of prescriptive paradox is simply to ask the client to engage in or perform some element of the symptom—for example, "This week I'd like you to be aware of and keep track of all these times when you feel nervous [act nervous, have nervous thoughts, and so on]" or "This week you might try to bring on an anxiety attack deliberately." A variation is to ask the client to increase, decrease, or exaggerate some element of the symptom, such as intensity (this is similar to what occurs in implosion, or flooding). For example: "This week I'd like you to act [think, feel] even more nervous than before. Now, you said your nervousness is about a 5 on a 1-to-10 scale. Shoot for doubling its intensity this week." Or "When you realize you are blushing, exaggerate it. Get even hotter and redder in your face."

It is also important to offer the client a rationale for the prescription in order to increase the likelihood of compliance. For these forms of symptom prescription, one believable rationale is to emphasize *control.* You might tell the client that learning to turn on the symptom or do it more will help the client later to turn it off or do it less. Another useful rationale is based on *understanding.* Depending on the client's views about the problem, you could note that carrying out the directive "would help you to gain awareness" (Gestalt therapy), "would help us to get concrete data" (behavioral therapy), or "would help to get at the underlying causes of the problem" (psychodynamic therapy).

A second type of symptom prescription involves adding a positive or negative connotation to some part of the symptom. The most common way of adding a *negative* aspect to the symptom is by making its performance an *ordeal.* For example, with a client who wants to stop smoking or eating high-calorie foods, the therapist could instruct the client to put cigarettes or snacks in a hard-to-reach, locked cupboard accessible only with a footstool and a certain key, or could recommend that the client smoke or snack only in a straight-backed chair in his damp basement or in his cold garage. A client who has difficulty going to sleep at night might be instructed to get up and clean the oven if still awake after lying in bed for 30 minutes. When the symptom is scheduled as an ordeal, it is made too cumbersome and unpleasant to continue in the same way or at the same rate as before.

Positive connotations in the form of reframing can also be added to aspects of symptoms. Recall from Chapter 16 that positive connotation involves reconceptualizing the problem by describing the problem behavior in a positive manner. For example, with a client who has few good relationships because of her "bossiness," the bossiness may be described as a need for control; a client who engages in frequent negative ruminations about himself can be shown that such ruminations can produce humorous as well as unpleasant consequences; a client who has trouble going to sleep at night might be instructed to list positive aspects of staying awake. In marital therapy, a spouse's unproductive behavior, such as criticism, may be described as something the person is doing for the welfare of someone else—such as trying to get close to the partner. A rationale for these forms of interventions is to emphasize the client's *attitude* about the symptom. The therapist might say that by locking up food or cigarettes or by using time at night to clean, the client has opportunities to examine her or his attitude about the symptom under *different* conditions.

A third type of symptom prescription has to do with time. The most common form of symptom prescription based on time is *symptom scheduling.* The problem can be experienced more or less frequently, in different durations, or at different times or locations. The client is directed to try to bring on the symptom at particular times and/or in particular places. For example, the therapist may say "This week try to bring on an anxiety attack every morning before you leave the house." Scheduling of the symptom should occur before the time of its spontaneous occurrence, provided there is a typical time of day that the symptom occurs. In lieu of scheduling the symptom at prescribed times, the enactment of the symptom can be prescribed *contingent* on certain feelings, thoughts, or activities of the client or others. For example, the therapist could instruct the client to "get into your anxious feelings whenever the thoughts about your speech crop up." Usually in such cases, the client is also instructed to stay with the feelings or thoughts for a specified time period or even to exaggerate them—for example, "Once you get these anxious feelings going, keep them there for 15 minutes and make them more intense." A variation of symptom scheduling described by Weeks and L'Abate (1982) is to instruct the client to extend the feeling state. For example, depressed clients can be told to notice when they start to feel better and then to make themselves stay depressed for another 15 minutes before allowing themselves to feel better. This type of prescription is designed to show clients how they control their moods and feelings. As Weeks and L'Abate (1982) observe,

Usually, clients following this prescription realize what they do to place themselves in an undesirable mood because they use those ideas to keep themselves in the mood longer. At the same time they are learning to keep themselves in the mood longer, they are also learning what they can do to control the mood [p. 122].

A useful rationale for all forms of symptom scheduling involves *prediction.* The client is told that since the symptom is going to occur anyway, at least the client could be in a position to predict it and therefore deal with it better when it happens.

One caution on prescription-based paradoxes — never prescribe suicidal or homicidal *behavior.* If self- or other-destructive *fantasies* are prescribed, make sure the client understands that whereas having such ideas is acceptable, acting them out is not (Zeig, 1980b).

In contrast to prescribing interventions, *restraining* interventions are those in which the therapist discourages or inhibits change. The underlying message in a restraining paradox is: In order to change, stay the same or give up (Rohrbaugh et al., 1981). *Restraining* interventions are used mainly when prescriptions have failed or when the therapist expects the client to defy the directive.

The first type of restraining strategy is *delaying change.* In "delaying change," the therapist moves more slowly than the client expects. Messages that encourage *delayed* compliance reduce resistance by decreasing threat. Fisch et al. (1982, p. 159) refer to this intervention as the injunction to "go slow." They explain this strategy as follows:

The client is not instructed to do anything, certainly nothing specific. Whatever instructions are given are general and vague: "This week, it would be very important not to do anything to bring about further improvement." More of the intervention consists in offering believable rationales for "going slow": that change, even for the better, requires adjusting to; or that one needs to determine, a step at a time, how much change would be optimal as opposed to maximal: "You might be better off with a 75 percent improvement rather than a 100 percent improvement"; or "Change occurring slowly and step by step makes for a more solid change than change which occurs too suddenly" [p. 159].

The "go slow" or "slow down" injunction works either directly, by reassuring the client, or paradoxically, by enhancing the client's sense of control and confidence in his or her ability to move more quickly (Anderson & Stewart, 1983, p. 183). This strategy is particularly useful for clients who deny problems, for clients whose main attempted solution is trying too hard, and for clients who press the therapist for urgent solutions while remaining passive and uncooperative (Anderson & Stewart, 1983; Fisch et al., 1982). Delaying changes is sometimes also called "soft restraining."

The second type of restraining intervention is *forbidding change*. Forbidding change is a slightly more extreme restraining tactic than delaying change. There are two typical ways to restrain in this way. The first way is called "giving in" (Watzlawick et al., 1974). In this intervention, the client is told to give in to the symptom (or some element of it), and then the symptom is prescribed. For example: "In order to find out how often your symptom occurs this week, just give in to it and let it happen" or "In order to get some information about your problem, I want you to do something new this week. Give up trying to stop _____ [for example, arguing] and then pay attention to what is happening before and during this time."

The second way to forbid change is just to tell the client directly not to engage in the target behavior. For instance, often in sex therapy clients are told not to engage in intercourse or not to have an erection or an orgasm. Similarly, an insomniac might be instructed "not to go to sleep this week."

The most extreme type of restraining (often called "hard restraining" for this reason) is to *declare hopelessness* and to predict that change or improvement will not be possible. Through the therapist's attitude of resignation, a challenge is issued and the stage is set for the client to prove the therapist wrong. This strategy is analogous to therapeutic impotence. In using it, it is important to accept responsibility for one's impotence without blaming the client (Selvini-Palazzoli, Cecchin, Prata, & Boscolo, 1978). In other words, the therapist owns the feelings of hopelessness and does not project them onto the client. This strategy is not needed very frequently, since with most "yes, but" clients, delaying and forbidding change are tried first and usually work. Declaring hopelessness is a last resort and is usually reserved for clients who are highly reactant and repeatedly seek help but fail to benefit (Rohrbaugh et al., 1981). In such instances, the therapist can say something like "I know I made an error in judgment in initially assessing your situation and assuming we could

work together to make some changes. It is my belief that I can't really offer you anything at this point that will improve your situation. It would be a disservice to you to continue. Probably stopping and reassessing the situation and learning to live with the situation as it is would be the best possible course."

The fourth type of restraining strategy is *predicting a relapse*. This type of intervention is used frequently and is essential to most paradoxical tasks (Weeks & L'Abate, 1982). Predicting a relapse is used mainly to nurture incipient changes that result from symptom prescription. When the prescription works, the symptom disappears — often rather suddenly. Then the therapist predicts a relapse by telling the client the symptom will suddenly reappear. Again, the therapist has issued a therapeutic double bind. If the symptom does return, the therapist has predicted it, so it is under the therapist's control. If it doesn't return, it is under the client's control. In either case, it is impossible for the client to continue to view the symptom as unfree, or spontaneous. When a symptom is defined in such a way as to be under someone's control, it is less disturbing to the client and gives the client more energy to deal with the situation or person producing the problem (Weeks & L'Abate, 1982). Predicting a relapse can also be used when it is time to terminate treatment. Inform the client that, after termination, reappearance of the problem is normal and expected and will occur in the near future. A defiant client will probably prove the therapist wrong by not relapsing, and a compliant, overly anxious client will be less anxious about getting along without therapy.

Prescribing a relapse is an extension of predicting a relapse. Erickson (quoted in Haley, 1973) recommended this approach with clients who improve too quickly. Clients are requested to experience themselves as they were before treatment "to see if there is anything from that time that they wish to recover or salvage" (p. 4). Another option is to prescribe reenactment of the symptom — for example, "This week it would be a good idea to conjure up all those old angry feelings [or thoughts]" or "At this time I'd like to see whether you can still fight by screaming at each other. Have that kind of fight each day." The relapse prescription helps clients see how they can fall back into the same patterns and find ways of preventing this from happening, particularly after therapy is over (Weeks & L'Abate, 1982).

All the restraining strategies described in this chapter require careful timing and delivery and need to be offered with warmth and empathy. Sarcasm and anger must be avoided in order for these interventions to be most helpful.

Steps in Working Paradoxically

There are seven steps in formulating and delivering paradoxical interventions with clients.

Therapeutic relationship. Before a paradoxical intervention is attempted, a therapeutic relationship in which the client is an active participant must exist. Both Weeks and L'Abate (1982) and Ascher (1980) observe that paradoxical interventions do not work well unless the client is actively involved in therapy and a supportive and therapeutic relationship exists. This is why paradoxical intervention may not work well for clients who are ordered to have counseling by experts or otherwise required to seek help. A good relationship creates the rapport necessary when instructing clients to do something that seems illogical from their current frame of reference.

Assessment. Paradoxical interventions are much more effective when they are accurate; that is, the therapist's functional analysis of the symptom or interactional system must be conceivable, if not highly probable (Birchler, 1981). Accurate paradoxical interventions are based on careful assessments that lead to a concrete understanding of the client's problem. Such an assessment includes analysis of repetitive behavior patterns, sequence of events leading up to the problem, chain of events in the problem, and interactional patterns (see also Chapters 7 and 8). Failure to base a paradoxical intervention on careful functional analysis may create difficulties because other controlling contingencies have been overlooked (Ascher, 1980).

Goals. Paradoxical interventions should be based on the direction and degree of change desired by the client. It is important that the client's reasons and hopes for treatment be carefully delineated so that the therapist is not pursuing the wrong ends.

Formulation. After the therapist has completed a functional analysis and is aware of the client's goals, the therapist may formulate a paradoxical intervention *if* he or she feels it is the treatment of choice for this particular client at this time. Paradoxical interventions are formulated as homework tasks. In formulating the directive, the therapist must first (1) be able to see the symptom in functionally positive terms (closeness, care, protection, stability, and so forth), (2) understand how the problem is perpetuated and maintained, and finally (3) hypothesize the function or purpose that the symptom serves for the client. It is extremely important to keep the prescribed task simple and to formulate an intervention that incorporates the client's language (Todd, 1980). The therapist may also formulate other (nonparadoxical) interventions to be used to complement the paradoxical task.

Assignment. Questions about the task are usually postponed until the next session. Delivery or assignment of the paradox can be the most crucial and difficult part. Often it is useful to write out the task before the session. Paradoxical interventions are usually assigned to the client as homework to be completed between sessions. To avoid assigning prematurely or for the wrong issue, reserve assigning a paradoxical intervention until the end of the session. Another important reason not to give a paradoxical instruction too early is that its effectiveness may be reduced if the client comments on it. When assigning a paradoxical intervention, it is also important to suggest a rationale that is likely to motivate the client to follow through or to resist —depending on whether you expect the client to comply with or defy the directive.

Evaluation. Once you assign a paradoxical intervention, it is important to monitor the results. Record the type of task given to the client and track its effects. In later sessions, ask about the client's response to the assigned task in detail. The effects usually occur one week to one month after assignment of the task (Weeks & L'Abate, 1982). Note whether the effects are similar to or different from the changes you predicted would occur. If the desired results did not occur, be sure to obtain information about why the task failed, because such information is critical for formulating a different task (Weeks & L'Abate, 1982).

Follow-up. If the task does succeed, the therapist must nurture and solidify the resulting changes. In addition to the use of nonparadoxical techniques, the therapist can strengthen change by tactics and comments likely to encourage continued change efforts. For example, with compliance-based paradoxical interventions, it is important to follow through with more of the same. For example, if a therapist tells a client to "dwell on the negative thoughts when they occur" and the client returns saying that there were too few that occurred on

which to dwell, the therapist should urge the client to continue to concentrate on dwelling on them, until the client believes the problem has truly disappeared (Rohrbaugh et al., 1981). Other approaches to maintaining change described earlier include predicting and prescribing a relapse.

LEARNING ACTIVITIES #56: PARADOXICAL INTERVENTIONS

PART ONE

Below we list six examples of various paradoxical interventions. Read each one carefully and then identify whether the intervention is an example of a prescribing (compliance-based) or restraining (defiance-based) intervention. The first one is completed as an example. Feedback follows on page 576.

Example

1. "This week it is important not to try to change anything about your relationship."
   ____Prescribing   ✓Restraining
   Restraining because it prohibits change this week.
2. "Whatever you decide to do about it, it would be important to do it at a very slow pace."
   ____Prescribing   ____Restraining
3. "Since you've noticed these anxiety attacks at work, you might consider trying to predict when they will occur by seeing whether you could have one at home each day before you go to work."
   ____Prescribing   ____Restraining
4. "I'm absolutely sure that you will begin to yell at each other again sometime soon."
   ____Prescribing   ____Restraining
5. "If after 30 minutes you find you're still awake, you may find it helpful to get up and clean the toilets before going back to sleep. This may help to change your attitude about sleeping."
   ____Prescribing   ____Restraining
6. "This week you may find you can gain more control of your depressed feelings by extending them

when they occur another 15 or 20 minutes."
   ____Prescribing   ____Restraining

PART TWO

In this activity we list five types of symptoms along with a description of the client's reactance potential. Using this information, match the five descriptions with the three types of interventions listed below. The first one is completed as an example. Feedback follows.

Type of Intervention

A. Compliance-based paradoxical interventions
B. Defiance-based paradoxical interventions
C. Nonparadoxical interventions

Description

Example

__B__ 1. Symptom: Marital couple has frequent fights. Reactance potential: High (Defiance-based paradoxical intervention is likely to match best because symptom is free and reactance potential is high.)
____ 2. Symptom: Mother and son argue constantly. Reactance potential: Low
____ 3. Symptom: Panic attacks. Reactance potential: Low
____ 4. Symptom: Mother is very protective of only child, even though child is 17 years old. Reactance potential: High
____ 5. Symptom: Frequent headaches for which no organic basis has been found. Reactance potential: Low

---

☐ STRATEGIES FOR INVOLUNTARY CLIENTS

As we noted earlier, involuntary clients who are under some pressure to seek counseling are likely to present more resistant behaviors than voluntary clients, at least initially. Although all of the preced-

ing strategies suggested to manage resistance also apply to involuntary clients, this section describes some special tactics that may be particularly useful for these clients.

Working with clients who are there under duress requires flexibility, creativity, and resourcefulness. Since an absent client can hardly be counseled, the

■
FEEDBACK #56: PARADOXICAL INTERVENTIONS

PART ONE

2-restraining—because it emphasizes delaying change or going slow.

3-prescribing—the symptom is prescribed through scheduling.

4-restraining—the therapist predicts a relapse or recurrence of the symptom.

5-prescribing—the connotation of the symptom is changed by making it an ordeal or too much trouble.

PART TWO

1-B (Free symptom coupled with high reactance potential)

2-C (Free symptom; low reactance potential)

3-A (Unfree symptom; low reactance potential)

4-B (Free symptom; high reactance potential)

5-A (Unfree symptom; low reactance potential)

counselor needs to engage the client somehow, at least until counseling makes a difference (Dyer & Vriend, 1975).

A useful beginning point is to start where the client is. Show interest in what the client wants to talk about. As Dyer and Vriend note, "A productive assumption in converting involuntariness into a commitment to be counseled is that any client's chief interest is himself" (p. 102). Since many involuntary clients are oriented toward self-protection, avoid demanding or even expecting that the client self-disclose or engage in other behaviors that rob him or her of any masks. Adapt your methods and style to the client's needs and style. If the client talks in a stilted and pedantic manner, a more formal approach is in order than if the client presents a casual interactional style.

Another initial strategy is to do something— anything— that is likely to be perceived as helpful by the client (Anderson & Stewart, 1983). Even a small intervention such as summarizing the situation or reflecting the client's resentment may enhance the client's expectations about therapy and may increase the helper's credibility. Sometimes a more involved intervention such as teaching the client relaxation, meditation, or a way to analyze irrational thinking may be immediately useful to this type of client.

Another strategy to use is to do anything that gives the client more control over what happens. When clients have little or no control over the process and outcome of therapy, they are more likely to view the counselor as a representative of the referring agency or person, and resistance will increase (Anderson & Stewart, 1983). Discuss openly the pressures that have resulted in the client's being referred for counseling. If the court has ordered the client to have treatment, the therapist can restore the client's control by pointing out that the client can refuse therapy and accept the consequences. As Anderson and Stewart (1983, p. 241) observe, "While the consequences are usually serious enough to mean that this is not a desirable choice, it should be made clear that refusal is an option or [the client] will continue to resist the therapist at every turn."

Another strategy useful for some involuntary clients is called "metered counseling" (M. A. Kirk, personal communication, December 1983). In this strategy, the counselor indicates that the client can choose to talk about whatever she or he wishes for about one-third of the session. During the other two-thirds of each session, the client must talk about something "interesting"; the therapist decides what issues are interesting. Or if the client is required to meet with a counselor for ten 50-minute sessions, the client can choose what to do or say for about 1500 minutes; for the remaining 3500 minutes, the client talks about something "interesting."

Another way to increase the client's control and responsibility is to renegotiate the "contract" if possible. Ask clients whether they are bothered by anything in addition to what they were sent or referred for. The object of this approach is to come up with a complaint that the *client* is interested in changing (Fisch et al., 1982). If it is impossible to do this, an alternative is to jointly negotiate an explicit treatment contract that meets the needs of the referring agency or person but also gives the client some control. It is also important not to exacerbate a client's loss of control by being vague about what you as the therapist will or won't do, what you will and won't report to the referring agency, and so on (Anderson & Stewart, 1983). If you are required to write a report to the referring agency, part of the treatment contract you develop with the client might be that the report will be shared just with the client (Anderson & Stewart, 1983).

If all else fails, and the client is not interested in renegotiating a contract that reflects his or her other interests, a final strategy is to try to get the client interested in treatment. Fisch et al. (1982) describe this strategy as follows:

> If this can be accomplished, it will *not* be done by exhorting him to take his problem seriously, to buckle down to treatment, and the like. This is the one pitfall to avoid. The therapist has some chance of success, however, if he applies a different pressure by going the other way—by taking the position with the "client" that treatment probably is inadvisable. The identified patient now has the opportunity to convince the therapist why it could be in his own best interest to do something about *his* problem [pp. 43–44].

If the identified client is still not interested in therapy, the counselor has the option of terminating treatment and working with the complainant, who is usually the person pressuring the client to seek help. Often the complainant is more interested in solving the problem and more willing to make changes than the involuntary client.

□ A FINAL NOTE

There are three thoughts we would like to leave you with as we terminate this journey with you.

First, set careful and realistic personal and professional limits for yourself as a therapist. Learn what you can and cannot do for and with clients. A critical part of effective helpgiving is to know when to back off and stop and hand some responsibility over to the person in front of you. The more you do for your clients, the less they will do for themselves.

Second, examine your expectations for yourself and your clients. Therapists often find that their expectations for change differ markedly from clients', particularly with reluctant or pessimistic clients. In such instances, therapists often are meeting more of their own needs for change and success than pursuing the needs and issues of clients. Therapy is endangered when the counselor wants more for clients than they want for themselves. In such cases, the therapist fights with the client (on the client's behalf), but the client loses an important ally.

Finally, above all, be flexible. The skills and strategies offered in this book are simply methodology that is more or less effective depending on the creativity and intuition of the user. Some of what gets labeled "client resistance" is nothing more than inflexibility of the therapist. Therapists who are flexible regard each client as unique and each helping strategy as a tool to be used or set aside depending on its effectiveness in producing client-generated outcomes.

■
POSTEVALUATION

PART ONE

In this part of the postevaluation, we give three descriptions of client roles. Use triads in which one person assumes the role of the client, another the role of the counselor, and the third person an observer. As the client, present one of the roles described below to the therapist (change the sex of the client, if necessary). As the counselor, respond to the client with listening responses that match, or pace, the client's pessimism (Chapter Objective One). As the observer, note whether the counselor successfully matches the client's pessimism and provide feedback following the role play.

Client 1: The client is a teenager who is very courteous and polite and also very stubborn. She says that she is willing to try anything you suggest to improve her school performance but that she doubts whether there is any successful solution.

Client 2: The client is an older male who has been missing work recently because of alcohol problems. The client says that he is willing to talk to you but that his alcohol problems are largely the result of job stress, for which he blames his immediate supervisor.

Client 3: Background: The clients are a mother, father and his 8-year-old son, whom the school personnel have described as "incorrigible." The father is very protective and overinvolved with the son to the point of nagging, which the son resents. The father and son have constant arguments.

Client role for purposes of role play: As the client, assume the role of the "underinvolved" mother. Inform the counselor that you are willing to come in and sit in on the sessions but you don't have much to contribute or much to learn, since the problem is basically between your husband and your son.

(continued)

POSTEVALUATION (continued)

PART TWO

Listed below are two descriptions of clients. For each situation, identify the client's dysfunctional behaviors and the identified "payoffs," or reinforcers. Also identify and describe ways the client could achieve the same kind of reinforcement with other, more adaptive and less self-defeating behaviors (Chapter Objective Two). Feedback follows the Postevaluation (on page 580).

Client 1: The client is a 40-year-old married man who reports feelings of depression largely due to dissatisfaction with his job, in which he feels he works "like a horse," yet receives no credit or notice for his accomplishments. He also states that he feels his life is "going nowhere." During the past year, to compensate for his bad feelings, he has become very argumentative with and critical toward his wife and three children. He is seeking counseling because his wife, who has a good job with an adequate salary, is threatening to leave him and take the children with her unless he stops "verbally abusing" them. He would like to "save his marriage" but admits that he doesn't really know how or what to do.
  a. Identify the client's dysfunctional or self-defeating behavior(s).
  b. For each behavior identified in #1, list the presumed reinforcer, or payoff.
  c. Describe some ways in which this client might achieve the same reinforcement through more adaptive behaviors.

Client 2: The client, a 16-year-old, has had repeated behavior problems in school over the last few years, resulting in poor grades and numerous phone calls to his parents. He has skipped school, gone to school late, and missed tests and assignments. Last month, he was caught shoplifting, and on the third incident the store pressed charges. For his sentence, he was required to do four hours of community service each week for 16 weeks and also see a counselor weekly. On talking with him, you discover that he is the younger of two boys. His brother just graduated with honors from college and has been accepted into a prestigious law school. The client states that he has always resented his parents' constant comparisons between himself and his brother and he never felt he could live up to their expectations for him, no matter what he did or how hard he tried. He describes his parents' relationship as quiet—says both are reserved and don't communicate very much with each other except for yelling and nagging at him.
  a. Identify the client's dysfunctional or self-defeating behavior(s).
  b. For each behavior identified in #1, list the prescribed reinforcers, or payoffs.
  c. Describe some ways in which this client might achieve the same reinforcement through more adaptive behaviors.

PART THREE

In this part of the Postevaluation, you are given two written descriptions of clients and their presenting complaints and problems. From these descriptions, Chapter Objective Three asks you to identify in writing four aspects of "patient position" and describe the implications of these positions for the management of therapy. Tune in carefully to the language and words used by the client in making your identifications. Feedback follows the Postevaluation.

Client 1, a teenage boy: "Actually, I'm doing OK in school. Yeah, I get stuck in detention center once in a while, mostly for lateness—showing up for class late or turning in my work late—but that's pretty normal. I'm not the only one in there. My mom thinks it's a major crime, though. She says she's at her wit's end, so maybe a counselor would help. Now, don't get me wrong, but I think I could work this out without much help from you if I just took the time to sit down and write out a schedule."

Identify:
  a. Client's notions about nature/cause of problem.
  b. Client's notions about who is responsible for the problem.
  c. Client's notions about how the problem can be resolved.
  d. Client's notions about therapy.
  e. Implications for managing therapy.

Client 2, a middle-aged woman: "My son is talking about doing himself in, and I just don't know where we went wrong. We tried to be good, loving, and understanding parents. We worked so hard at giving him a supportive environment so that he could feel good about himself and develop his own interests and abilities. Now it doesn't seem like it's done any good—so maybe you can figure out what we should do next."

(continued)

Identify:
   a. Client's notions about nature/cause of problem.
   b. Client's notions about who is responsible for the problem.
   c. Client's notions about how the problem can be resolved.
   d. Client's notions about therapy.
   e. Implications for managing therapy.

PART FOUR

In this part of the postevaluation, we give two descriptions of clients. For each client, select the most appropriate type of paradoxical intervention and write a description of a corresponding task, including a rationale (Chapter Objective Four). Then, using triads or small groups, practice delivering the paradoxical intervention in a role-play situation (Chapter Objective Five).

Client 1: The client is a college student who wants to go to med school but is having trouble making decent grades because of putting things off until the last moment. Often this results in careless or missed work or poor preparation. The client says it is very important for him to get into med school, and regardless of how hard he tries to get his work done on time, it doesn't seem to help. He just can't seem to get it done.

1. Select the most appropriate type of paradoxical intervention, based on the type of symptom and on the client's reactance level. (You may wish to check the feedback for question #1 before going on.)
2. For the type of intervention you select, write a description of a task to give this client, including a rationale for the task.
3. Deliver the task to a role-play client. In triads or small groups, one person assumes the role of the client, another the counselor, and the other(s) the observer(s). The client should take the role described above (that is, college student, procrastination, low reactance). The counselor's job is to deliver the task and the rationale for it in a way that is likely to promote client *compliance* with the task, since this situation calls for a compliance-based intervention. The observer(s) can give feedback after the role play, using the Checklist for Paradoxical Interventions at the bottom of this page as a guide. Roles can be switched several times to give each person an opportunity to assume the three roles.

Client 2: The client is a 25-year-old woman who refers herself to you to discuss her long-standing difficulties in relationships with men. She has never had a satisfactory or lengthy relationship with a man. She seems to get easily involved, becomes suspicious of the man's motives, and backs off from the relationship. After a short period of initial cooperation with you, the client becomes rather quiet, reserved, and noncommittal. Slowly this leads into a more active "yes, but" stance in which she refutes almost every idea or suggestion you have (high reactance). (By the way, note the relationship parallels between the way the client behaves with the therapist and her presenting problem.)

1. Select the most appropriate type of paradoxical intervention, given the type of symptom and the reactance level of the client. (You may wish to check the feedback for question #1 before going on.)
2. For the type of intervention you select, write a description of a task to give this client, including a rationale for the task.
3. Deliver the task to a role-play client, using triads or small groups. The client should take the role described above (young woman or man, relationship problem with opposite sex, high reactance). The counselor's job is to deliver the task and its rationale in a way that is likely to promote client *defiance* of the task, since this situation calls for a defiance-based intervention. The observer(s) can give feedback, using the Checklist for Paradoxical Interventions as a guide.

CHECKLIST FOR PARADOXICAL INTERVENTIONS

Name of Counselor_____   Date_____

   I. Type of symptom client presents (circle one):   Free   Unfree

   II. Reactance level of client (circle one):   High   Low   (continued)

CHECKLIST FOR PARADOXICAL INTERVENTIONS (continued)

III. Type of paradoxical intervention used by counselor (check ✔ appropriate category):

Compliance	Defiance
_____symptom prescription	_____delay change
_____negative connotation (ordeal)	_____prohibit change
_____positive connotation (reframing)	_____predict relapse
_____symptom scheduling	_____declare hopelessness

IV. Note rationale used by counselor to accompany intervention (check ✔ appropriate category):

Compliance	Defiance
_____control	_____change others slowly
_____understanding	_____give in to symptom; let it happen
_____gain information	_____important not to engage in symptom
_____examine attitude	_____symptom needs to reappear for control
_____prediction	_____other: _____
_____other: _____	

Observer comments: _____

☐ SUGGESTED READINGS

Anderson, C. M., & Stewart, S. (1983). *Mastering resistance: A practical guide to family therapy.* New York: Guilford Press.

Ascher, L. M. (1980). Paradoxical intention. In A. Goldstein & E. B. Foa (Eds.), *Handbook of behavioral interventions: A clinical guide.* New York: Wiley.

Cavanaugh, M. E. (1982). *The counseling experience.* Pacific Grove, CA: Brooks/Cole, Chapter 10, "Resistance in Counseling."

Chamberlain, P., Patterson, G., Reid, J., Kavanagh, K., & Forgatch, M. (1984). Observation of client resistance. *Behavior Therapy, 15,* 144–155.

Dowd, E. T., & Milne, C. R. (1986). Paradoxical interventions in counseling psychology. *The Counseling Psychologist, 14,* 237–282.

Fisch, R., Weakland, J., & Segal, L. (1982). *The tactics of change.* San Francisco: Jossey-Bass.

Haley, J. (1984). *Ordeal therapy: Unusual ways to change behavior.* San Francisco: Jossey-Bass.

Jahn, D., & Lichstein, K. (1980). The resistive client. *Behavior Modification, 4,* 303–320.

King, M., Novik, L., & Citrenbaum, C. (1983). *Irresistible communication.* Philadelphia: Saunders.

Kolko, D., & Milan, M. (1983). Reframing and paradoxical instruction to overcome "resistance" in the treatment of delinquent youths: A multiple baseline analysis. *Journal of Consulting and Clinical Psychology, 51,* 655–660.

Lopez, F. G. (1983). A paradoxical approach to vocational indecision. *Personnel and Guidance Journal, 61,* 410–412.

Martin, G., & Worthington, E. (1982). Behavioral homework. In M. Hersen, R. Eisler, & P. Miller (Eds.), *Progress in behavior modification* (Vol. 13). New York: Academic Press.

Meichenbaum, D., & Turk, D. C. (1987). *Facilitating treatment adherence.* New York: Plenum.

Munjack, D. J., & Oziel, R. J. (1978). Resistance in behavioral treatment of sexual dysfunctions. *Journal of Sex and Marital Therapy, 4,* 122–138.

Papp, P. (1984). *The process of change.* New York: Guilford Press.

Rohrbaugh, M., Tennen, H., Press, S., & White, L. (1981). Compliance, defiance, and therapeutic paradox: Guidelines for strategic use of paradoxical interventions. *American Journal of Orthopsychiatry, 51,* 454–467.

Shelton, J., & Levy, R. (1981). *Behavioral assignments and treatment compliance.* Champaign, IL: Research Press.

Spinks, S., & Birchler, G. (1982). Behavioral-systems marital therapy: Dealing with resistance. *Family Process, 21,* 169–185.

Wachtel, P. (Ed.). (1982). *Resistance: Psychodynamic and behavioral approaches.* New York: Plenum.

Weeks, G. R., & L'Abate, L. (1982). *Paradoxical psychotherapy: Theory and practice with individuals, couples, and families.* New York: Brunner/Mazel.

Zeig, J. (1980). Symptom prescription techniques: Clinical applications using elements of communication. *American Journal of Clinical Hypnosis, 23,* 23–33.

FEEDBACK: POSTEVALUATION

PART TWO

Client 1:　a. Dysfunctional, self-defeating behavior: arguing with and being critical toward wife and children

　　　　　　b. Presumed reinforcers: increases his self-esteem, gives him power and control he feels are missing in his life and job

(continued)

c. Other possible ways to increase his self-esteem and power and control:
Change jobs
Talk to his boss or supervisor
Get involved in a personally fulfilling leisure time activity
Others: (list yours)

Client 2: a. Dysfunctional, self-defeating behaviors: school-related problems such as skipping class and missing tests; shoplifting
b. Presumed reinforcers: (1) probable attention from parents and others (for both school-related problems and shoplifting); (2) possibly is helping parents avoid marital issues by creating an issue about himself they can invest their energy in (that is, negative reinforcement)
c. Other ways of getting reinforcers:
Change to a new school where he can start off differently
Get involved in sports or other activities of interest to client
Social skills training
Family counseling
Others: (list yours)

PART THREE
Client 1:
a. Notions about nature and cause of his problem: In his view, "problem" is nothing more than a typical developmental issue for someone his age.
b. Notions about who is responsible for the problem: Since he does not consider it a problem, the problem is created by his mom, according to his view.
c. Notions about how the problem can be resolved: Something very simple, concrete, and nontherapeutic, such as time management.
d. Notions about therapy: Therapy is not necessary, from this client's point of view, to resolve the "problem."
e. Implications for management of therapy:
1. Avoid communicating the idea that the client has a "big problem," since he doesn't see it this way.
2. Consider consulting with or seeing the mother (or parents), since she has a stake in the issue.
3. Avoid being overly pushy or optimistic about therapy, since the client doesn't believe it is necessary.
4. Any initial strategy/option you suggest should be one that fits with the client's values and seems concrete, specific, and not overly therapeutic to him.

Client 2:
a. Notions about nature and cause of the problem: A result of something missing from home environment.
b. Notions about who is responsible for the problem: Client feels responsible for problem (as the parent).
c. Notions about how the problem can be resolved: Therapeutically oriented strategies that focus and build on self-exploration, self-understanding, and self-esteem.
d. Notions about therapy: Therapy is necessary and important—client is looking to therapist as the "expert."
e. Implications for management of therapy:
1. Avoid implying that the son has a problem, since the parents don't see it this way; at the same time, avoid reinforcing their assumption that they are the ones who are responsible—can do this initially by ignoring this assumption so you don't make opposing statements that are inflammatory.
2. Build on their hopes and optimism about therapy, including use of "expertness" of your role without being one-up.
3. Offer strategies that fit with their value system and focus on self-exploration and understanding.

PART FOUR
Client 1:
1. The most appropriate type of paradoxical intervention would be some form of a prescription or compliance-based intervention, since the symptom is unfree and the reactance potential is low.
2. Examples of various prescribing tasks and corresponding rationales—see whether your task is similar to any of these:
a. Element of symptom is prescribed—rationale is understanding: "This week you might practice putting your studies off or trying to procrastinate deliberately. This will give us a greater understanding of what we're working with."
b. Frequency of symptom is prescribed—rationale is control. "This week you may want to consider procrastinating an extra 30 minutes each evening before you tackle your homework. This will give you more control over the problem eventually."
c. Connotation is prescribed; symptom is made an ordeal. Rationale is contrast. "This week, if
(continued)

you find you're still having trouble getting your work done on time, after about an hour or so of putting if off, it could be useful to get up and do something more physical, like jogging, exercising, doing laundry, or cleaning your room. This may help give a contrast you need between physical work and mental work, thus making the mental work easier."

d. Connotation is prescribed; symptom is reframed. Rationale is understanding of symptom. "Something you might think about this week is the idea that you may put off your studies so that your life is not overly controlled. Thinking about this may help you to understand this problem better."

e. Symptom is scheduled; rationale is prediction. "This week it may be useful to try to procrastinate, but instead of waiting until evening, do it earlier in the day—as early as possible. This will help you learn to predict better when it seems to happen most."

Client 2:

1. The most appropriate type of paradoxical intervention would be some form of delaying or prohibiting change or defiance-based intervention, since the symptom is free and the client's reactance potential is high.

2. Examples of defiance-based tasks and their corresponding rationales:

   a. Delay change or go slow. Rationale: change occurs slowly. "You know it's important not to push too hard on an issue like this because the best change usually occurs very slowly, like a snail's pace. So this week it is very important that, above all else, you don't work on this problem too much or do too much about it."

   b. Prohibit change. Rationale: stop change, gain perspective. "After you've been working on a problem hard as you have, it's usually a good idea to back off from it for a while to give you some perspective. So this week, it is very important not to do anything about this problem — just go on as you have been and don't change your relationship with these guys [gals] in any way."

(Predicting a relapse is not useful yet for this client, since change has not yet occurred. Declaring hopelessness should not be tried unless the above two interventions are unsuccessful.)

ETHICAL STANDARDS, AMERICAN ASSOCIATION OF COUNSELING AND DEVELOPMENT*

(As revised by AACD Governing Council, March 1988)

☐ PREAMBLE

The American Personnel and Guidance Association is an educational, scientific, and professional organization whose members are dedicated to the enhancement of the worth, dignity, potential, and uniqueness of each individual and thus to the service of society.

The Association recognizes that the role definitions and work settings of its members include a wide variety of academic disciplines, levels of academic preparation and agency services. This diversity reflects the breadth of the Association's interest and influence. It also poses challenging complexities in efforts to set standards for the performance of members, desired requisite preparation or practice, and supporting social, legal, and ethical controls.

The specification of ethical standards enables the Association to clarify to present and future members and to those served by members, the nature of ethical responsibilities held in common by its members.

The existence of such standards serves to stimulate greater concern by members for their own professional functioning and for the conduct of fellow professionals such as counselors, guidance and student personnel workers, and others in the helping professions. As the ethical code of the Association, this document establishes principles that define the ethical behavior of Association members. Additional ethical guidelines developed by the Association's Divisions for their speciality areas may further define a member's ethical behavior.

Section A: General

1. The member influences the development of the profession by continuous efforts to improve professional practices, teaching, services, and research. Professional growth is continuous throughout the member's career and is exemplified by the development of a philosophy that explains why and how a member functions in the helping relationship. Members must gather data on their effectiveness and be guided by the findings. Members recognize the need for continuing education to ensure competent service.

2. The member has a responsibility both to the individual who is served and to the institution within which the service is performed to maintain high standards of professional conduct. The member strives to maintain the highest levels of professional services offered to the individuals to be served. The member also strives to assist the agency, organization, or institution in providing the highest caliber of professional services. The acceptance of employment in an institution implies that the member is in agreement with the general policies and principles of the institution. Therefore the professional activities of the member are also in accord with the objectives of the institution. If, despite concerted efforts, the member cannot reach agreement with the employer as to acceptable standards of conduct that allow for changes in institutional policy conducive to the positive growth and development of clients, then terminating the affiliation should be seriously considered.

3. Ethical behavior among professional associates, both members and nonmembers, must be expected at all times. When information is possessed that raises doubt as to the ethical behavior of professional colleagues, whether Association members or not, the member must take action to attempt to rectify such a condition. Such action shall use the institution's channels first and then use procedures established by the Association.

4. The member neither claims nor implies professional qualifications exceeding those possessed and is responsible for correcting any misrepresentations of these qualifications by others.

5. In establishing fees for professional counseling services, members must consider the financial status of clients and locality. In the event that the established fee structure is inappropriate for a client, assistance must be provided in finding comparable services of acceptable cost.

6. When members provide information to the public or to subordinates, peers, or supervisors, they have a responsibility to ensure that the content is general, unidentified client information that is accurate, unbiased, and consists of objective, factual data.

7. Members recognize their boundaries of competence and provide only those services and use only those techniques for which they are qualified by training or experience. Members should only accept those positions for which they are professionally qualified.

8. In the counseling relationship, the counselor is aware of the intimacy of the relationship and maintains respect for the client and avoids engaging in activities that seek to meet the counselor's personal needs at the expense of that client.

9. Members do not condone or engage in sexual harassment which is defined as deliberate or repeated comments, gestures, or physical contacts of a sexual nature.

✓ 10. The member avoids bringing personal issues into the counseling relationship, especially if the potential for harm is present. Through awareness of the negative impact of both racial and sexual stereotyping and discrimination, the counselor guards the individual rights and personal dignity of the client in the counseling relationship.

11. Products or services provided by the member by means of classroom instruction, public lectures, demonstrations, written articles, radio or television programs, or other types of media must meet the criteria cited in these standards.

Section B: Counseling Relationship

This section refers to practices and procedures of individual and/or group counseling relationships.

The member must recognize the need for client freedom of choice. Under those circumstances where this is not possible, the member must apprise clients of restrictions that may limit their freedom of choice.

✓ 1. The member's *primary* obligation is to respect the integrity and promote the welfare of the client(s), whether the client(s) is (are) assisted individually or in a group relationship. In a group setting, the member is also responsible for taking reasonable precautions to protect individuals from physical and/or psychological trauma resulting from interaction within the group.

2. Members make provisions for maintaining confidentiality in the storage and disposal of

records and follow an established record retention and disposition policy. The counseling relationship and information resulting therefrom must be kept confidential, consistent with the obligations of the member as a professional person. In a group counseling setting, the counselor must set a norm of confidentiality regarding all group participants' disclosures.

3. If an individual is already in a counseling relationship with another professional person, the member does not enter into a counseling relationship without first contacting and receiving the approval of that other professional. If the member discovers that the client is in another counseling relationship after the counseling relationship begins, the member must gain the consent of the other professional or terminate the relationship, unless the client elects to terminate the other relationship.

4. When the client's condition indicates that there is clear and imminent danger to the client or others, the member must take reasonable personal action or inform responsible authorities. Consultation with other professionals must be used where possible. The assumption of responsibility for the client's(s') behavior must be taken only after careful deliberation. The client must be involved in the resumption of responsibility as quickly as possible.

5. Records of the counseling relationship, including interview notes, test data, correspondence, tape recordings, electronic data storage, and other documents are to be considered professional information for use in counseling and they should not be considered a part of the records of the institution or agency in which the counselor is employed unless specified by state statute or regulation. Revelation to others of counseling material must occur only upon the expressed consent of the client.

6. In view of the extensive data storage and processing capacities of the computer, the member must ensure that data maintained on a computer is: (a) limited to information that is appropriate and necessary for the services being provided; (b) destroyed after it is determined that the information is no longer of any value in providing services; and (c) restricted in terms of access to appropriate staff members involved in the provision of services by using the best computer security methods available.

7. Use of data derived from a counseling relationship for purposes of counselor training or research shall be confined to content that can be disguised to ensure full protection of the identity of the subject client.

8. The member must inform the client of the purposes, goals, techniques, rules of procedure, and limitations that may affect the relationship at or before the time that the counseling relationship is entered. When working with minors or persons who are unable to give consent, the member protects these clients' best interests.

9. In view of common misconceptions related to the perceived inherent validity of computer-generated data and narrative reports, the member must ensure that the client is provided with information as part of the counseling relationship that adequately explains the limitations of computer technology.

10. The member must screen prospective group participants, especially when the emphasis is on self-understanding and growth through self-disclosure. The member must maintain an awareness of the group participants' compatibility throughout the life of the group.

11. The member may choose to consult with any other professionally competent person about a client. In choosing a consultant, the member must avoid placing the consultant in a conflict of interest situation that would preclude the consultant's being a proper party to the member's efforts to help the client.

12. If the member determines an inability to be of professional assistance to the client, the member must either avoid initiating the counseling relationship or immediately terminate that relationship. In either event, the member must suggest appropriate alternatives. (The member must be knowledgeable about referral resources so that a satisfactory referral can be initiated.) In the event the client declines the suggested referral, the member is not obligated to continue the relationship.

13. When the member has other relationships, particularly of an administrative, supervisory, and/or evaluative nature with an individual seeking counseling services, the member must not serve as the counselor but should refer the individual to another professional. Only in instances where such an alternative is unavailable and where the individual's situation warrants counseling intervention should the member enter into and/or maintain a counseling relationship. Dual relationships with clients that might impair the member's objectivity and professional judgement (e.g., as with close friends or relatives) must be avoided

and/or the counseling relationship terminated through referral to another competent professional.

14. The member will avoid any type of sexual intimacies with clients. Sexual relationships with clients are unethical.

15. All experimental methods of treatment must be clearly indicated to prospective recipients, and safety precautions are to be adhered to by the member.

16. When computer applications are used as a component of counseling services, the member must ensure that: (a) the client is intellectually, emotionally, and physically capable of using the computer application; (b) the computer application is appropriate for the needs of the client; (c) the client understands the purpose and operation of the computer application; and (d) a follow-up of client use of a computer application is provided to both correct possible problems (misconceptions or inappropriate use) and assess subsequent needs.

17. When the member is engaged in short-term group treatment/training programs (e.g., marathons and other encounter-type or growth groups), the member ensures that there is professional assistance available during and following the group experience.

18. Should the member be engaged in a work setting that calls for any variation from the above statements, the member is obligated to consult with other professionals whenever possible to consider justifiable alternatives.

19. The member must ensure that members of various ethnic, racial, religious, disability, and socioeconomic groups have equal access to computer applications used to support counseling services and that the content of available computer applications does not discriminate against the groups described above.

20. When computer applications are developed by the member for use by the general public as self-help/stand-alone computer software, the member must ensure that: (a) self-help computer applications are designed from the beginning to function in a stand-alone manner, as opposed to modifying software that was originally designed to require support from a counselor; (b) self-help computer applications will include within the program statements regarding intended user outcomes, suggestions for using the software, a description of the conditions under which self-help computer applications might not be appropriate, and a description of when and how counseling ser-

vices might be beneficial; and (c) the manual for such applications will include the qualifications of the developer, the development process, validation data, and operating procedures.

Section C: Measurement and Evaluation

The primary purpose of educational and psychological testing is to provide descriptive measures that are objective and interpretable in either comparative or absolute terms. The member must recognize the need to interpret the statements that follow as applying to the whole range of appraisal techniques including test and nontest data. Test results constitute only one of a variety of pertinent sources of information for personnel, guidance, and counseling decisions.

1. The member must provide specific orientation or information to the examinee(s) prior to and following the test administration so that the results of testing may be placed in proper perspective with other relevant factors. In so doing, the member must recognize the effects of socioeconomic, ethnic and cultural factors on test scores. It is the member's professional responsibility to use additional unvalidated information carefully in modifying interpretation of the test results.

2. In selecting tests for use in a given situation or with a particular client, the member must consider carefully the specific validity, reliability, and appropriateness of the test(s). General validity, reliability, and related issues may be questioned legally as well as ethically when tests are used for vocational and educational selection, placement, or counseling.

3. When making any statements to the public about tests and testing, the member must give accurate information and avoid false claims or misconceptions. Special efforts are often required to avoid unwarranted connotations of such terms as IQ and grade equivalent scores.

4. Different tests demand different levels of competence for administration, scoring, and interpretation. Members must recognize the limits of their competence and perform only those functions for which they are prepared. In particular, members using computer-based test interpretations must be trained in the construct being measured and the specific instrument being used prior to using this type of computer application.

5. In situations where a computer is used for test administration and scoring, the member is responsible for ensuring that administration and

scoring programs function properly to provide clients with accurate test results.

6. Tests must be administered under the same conditions that were established in their standardization. When tests are not administered under standard conditions or when unusual behavior or irregularities occur during the testing session, those conditions must be noted and the results designated as invalid or of questionable validity. Unsupervised or inadequately supervised test-taking, such as the use of tests through the mails, is considered unethical. On the other hand, the use of instruments that are so designed or standardized to be self-administered and self-scored, such as interest inventories, is to be encouraged.

7. The meaningfulness of test results used in personnel, guidance, and counseling functions generally depends on the examinee's unfamiliarity with the specific items on the test. Any prior coaching or dissemination of the test materials can invalidate test results. Therefore, test security is one of the professional obligations of the member. Conditions that produce most favorable test results must be made known to the examinee.

8. The purpose of testing and the explicit use of the results must be made known to the examinee prior to testing. The counselor must ensure that instrument limitations are not exceeded and that periodic review and/or retesting are made to prevent client stereotyping.

9. The examinee's welfare and explicit prior understanding must be the criteria for determining the recipients of the test results. The member must see that specific interpretation accompanies any release of individual or group test data. The interpretation of test data must be related to the examinee's particular concerns.

10. Members responsible for making decisions based on test results have an understanding of educational and psychological measurement, validation criteria, and test research.

11. The member must be cautious when interpreting the results of research instruments possessing insufficient technical data. The specific purposes for the use of such instruments must be stated explicitly to examinees.

12. The member must proceed with caution when attempting to evaluate and interpret the performance of minority group members or other persons who are not represented in the norm group on which the instrument was standardized.

13. When computer-based test interpretations are developed by the member to support the as-sessment process, the member must ensure that the validity of such interpretations is established prior to the commercial distribution of such a computer application.

14. The member recognizes that test results may become obsolete. The member will avoid and prevent the misuse of obsolete test results.

15. The member must guard against the appropriation, reproduction, or modification of published tests or parts thereof without acknowledgement and permission from the previous publisher.

16. Regarding the preparation, publication, and distribution of tests, refeence should be made to:

a. "Standards for Educational and Psychological Testing," revised edition, 1985, published by the American Psychological Association on behalf of itself, the American Educational Research Association and the National Council of Measurement in Education.

b. "The Responsible Use of Tests: A Position Paper of AMEG, APGA, and NCME," *Measurement and Evaluation in Guidance,* 1972, 5, 385–388.

c. "Responsibilities of Users of Standardized Tests," APGA, *Guidepost,* October 5, 1978, pp. 5–8.

Section D: Research and Publication

1. Guidelines on research with human subjects shall be adhered to, such as:

a. *Ethical Principles in the Conduct of Research with Human Participants,* Washington, D.C.: American Psychological Association, Inc., 1982.

b. Code of Federal Regulation, Title 45, Subtitle A, Part 46, as currently issued.

c. *Ethical Principles of Psychologists,* American Psychological Association, Principle #9: Research with Human Participants.

d. Family Educational Rights and Privacy Act (the Buckley Amendment).

e. Current federal regulations and various state rights privacy acts.

2. In planning any research activity dealing with human subjects, the member must be aware of and responsive to all pertinent ethical principles and ensure that the research problem, design, and execution are in full compliance with them.

3. Responsibility for ethical research practice lies with the principal researcher, while others involved in the research activities share ethical obligation and full responsibility for their own actions.

4. In research with human subjects, researchers are responsible for the subjects' welfare throughout the experiment, and they must take all reasonable precautions to avoid causing injurious psychological, physical, or social effects on their subjects.

5. All research subjects must be informed of the purpose of the study except when withholding information or providing misinformation to them is essential to the investigation. In such research the member must be responsible for corrective action as soon as possible following completion of the research.

6. Participation in research must be voluntary. Involuntary participation is appropriate only when it can be demonstrated that participation will have no harmful effects on subjects and is essential to the investigation.

7. When reporting research results, explicit mention must be made of all variables and conditions known to the investigator that might affect the outcome of the investigation or the interpretation of the data.

8. The member must be responsible for conducting and reporting investigations in a manner that minimizes the possibility that results will be misleading.

9. The member has an obligation to make available sufficient original research data to qualified others who may wish to replicate the study.

10. When supplying data, aiding in the research of another person, reporting research results, or making original data available, due care must be taken to disguise the identity of the subjects in the absence of specific authorization from such subjects to do otherwise.

11. When conducting and reporting research, the member must be familiar with and give recognition to previous work on the topic, as well as to observe all copyright laws and follow the principles of giving full credit to all to whom credit is due.

12. The member must give due credit through joint authorship, acknowledgement, footnote statements, or other appropriate means to those who have contributed significantly to the research and/or publication, in accordance with such contributions.

13. The member must communicate to other members the results of any research judged to be of professional or scientific value. Results reflecting unfavorably on institutions, programs, services, or vested interests must not be withheld for such reasons.

14. If members agree to cooperate with another individual in research and/or publication, they incur an obligation to cooperate as promised in terms of punctuality of performance and with full regard to the completeness and accuracy of the information required.

15. Ethical practice requires that authors not submit the same manuscript or one essentially similar in content for simultaneous publication consideration by two or more journals. In addition, manuscripts published in whole or in substantial part in another journal or published work should not be submitted for publication without acknowledgement and permission from the previous publication.

Section E: Consulting

Consultation refers to a voluntary relationship between a professional helper and help-needing individual, group, or social unit in which the consultant is providing help to the client(s) in defining and solving a work-related problem or potential problem with a client or client system.

1. The member acting as consultant must have a high degree of self-awareness of his/her own values, knowledge, skills, limitations, and needs in entering a helping relationship that involves human and/or organizational change and that the focus of the relationship be on the issues to be resolved and not on the person(s) presenting the problem.

2. There must be understanding and agreement between member and client for the problem definition, change of goals, and prediction of consequences of interventions selected.

3. The member must be reasonably certain that she/he or the organization represented has the necessary competencies and resources for giving the kind of help that is needed now or may be needed later and that appropriate referral resources are available to the consultant.

4. The consulting relationship must be one in which client adaptability and growth toward self-direction are encouraged and cultivated. The member must maintain this role consistently and not become a decision maker for the client or create a future dependency on the consultant.

5. When announcing consultant availability for services, the member conscientiously adheres to the Association's Ethical Standards.

6. The member must refuse a private fee or other remuneration for consultation with persons who are entitled to these services through the member's employing institution or agency. The policies of a particular agency may make explicit provisions for private practice with agency clients by members of its staff. In such instances, the clients must be apprised of other options open to them should they seek private counseling services.

Section F: Private Practice

1. The member should assist the profession by facilitating the availability of counseling services in private as well as public settings.

2. In advertising services as a private practitioner, the member must advertise the services in a manner that accurately informs the public of professional services, expertise, and techniques of counseling available. A member who assumes an executive leadership role in the organization shall not permit his/her name to be used in professional notices during periods when he/she is not actively engaged in the private practice of counseling.

3. The member may list the following: highest relevant degree, type and level of certification and/or license, address, telephone number, office hours, type and/or description of services, and other relevant information. Such information must not contain false, inaccurate, misleading, partial, out-of-context, or deceptive material or statements.

4. Members do not present their affiliation with any organization in such a way that would imply inaccurate sponsorship or certification by that organization.

5. Members may join in partnership/corporation with other members and/or other professionals provided that each member of the partnership or corporation makes clear the separate specialties by name in compliance with the regulations of the locality.

6. A member has an obligation to withdraw from a counseling relationship if it is believed that employment will result in violation of the Ethical Standards. If the mental or physical condition of the member renders it difficult to carry out an effective professional relationship or if the member is discharged by the client because the counseling relationship is no longer productive for the client, then the member is obligated to terminate the counseling relationship.

7. A member must adhere to the regulations for private practice of the locality where the services are offered.

8. It is unethical to use one's institutional affiliation to recruit clients for one's private practice.

Section G: Personnel Administration

It is recognized that most members are employed in public or quasi-public institutions. The functioning of a member within an institution must contribute to the goals of the institution and vice versa if either is to accomplish their respective goals or objectives. It is therefore essential that the member and the institution function in ways to: (a) make the institutional goals specific; and public; (b) make the member's contribution to institutional goals specific; and (c) foster mutual accountability for goal achievement.

To accomplish these objectives, it is recognized that the member and the employer must share responsibilities in the formulation and implementation of personnel policies.

1. Members must define and describe the parameters and levels of their professional competency.

2. Members must establish interpersonal relations and working agreements with supervisors and subordinates regarding counseling or clinical relationships, confidentiality, distinction between public and private material, maintenance and dissemination of recorded information, work load, and accountability. Working agreements in each instance must be specified and made known to those concerned.

3. Members must alert their employers to conditions that may be potentially disruptive or damaging.

4. Members must inform employers of conditions that may limit their effectiveness.

5. Members must submit regularly to professional review and evaluation.

6. Members must be responsible for in-service development of self and/or staff.

7. Members must inform their staff of goals and programs.

8. Members must provide personnel practices that guarantee and enhance the rights and welfare of each recipient of their service.

9. Members must select competent persons and assign responsibilities compatible with their skills and experiences.

10. The member, at the onset of a counseling relationship, will inform the client of the mem-

ber's intended use of supervisors regarding the disclosure of information concerning this case. The member will clearly inform the client of the limits of confidentiality in the relationship.

11. Members, as either employers or employees, do not engage in or condone practices that are inhumane, illegal, or unjustifiable (such as considerations based on sex, handicap, age, race) in hiring, promotion, or training.

Section H: Preparation Standards

Members who are responsible for training others must be guided by the preparation standards of the Association and relevant Division(s). The member who functions in the capacity of trainer assumes unique ethical responsibilities that frequently go beyond that of the member who does not function in a training capacity. These ethical responsibilities are outlined as follows:

1. Members must orient students to program expectations, basic skills development, and employment prospects prior to admission to the program.

2. Members in charge of learning experiences must establish programs that integrate academic study and supervised practice.

3. Members must establish a program directed toward developing students' skills, knowledge, and self-understanding, stated whenever possible in competency or performance terms.

4. Members must identify the levels of competencies of their students in compliance with relevant Division standards. These competencies must accommodate the paraprofessional as well as the professional.

5. Members, through continual student evaluation and appraisal, must be aware of the personal limitations of the learner that might impede future performance. The instructor must not only assist the learner in securing remedial assistance but also screen from the program those individuals who are unable to provide competent services.

6. Members must provide a program that includes training in research commensurate with levels of role functioning. Paraprofessional and technician-level personnel must be trained as consumers of research. In addition, personnel must learn how to evaluate their own and their program's effectiveness. Graduate training, especially at the doctoral level, would include preparation for original research by the member.

7. Members must make students aware of the ethical responsibilities and standards of the profession.

8. Preparatory programs must encourage students to value the ideals of service to individuals and to society. In this regard, direct financial remuneration or lack thereof must not be allowed to overshadow professional and humanitarian needs.

9. Members responsible for educational programs must be skilled as teachers and practitioners.

10. Members must present thoroughly varied theoretical positions so that students may make comparisons and have the opportunity to select a position.

11. Members must develop clear policies within their educational institutions regarding field placement and the roles of the student and the instructor in such placement.

12. Members must ensure that forms of learning focusing on self-understanding or growth are voluntary, or if required as part of the educational program, are made known to prospective students prior to entering the program. When the educational program offers a growth experience with an emphasis on self-disclosure or other relatively intimate or personal involvement, the member must have no administrative, supervisory, or evaluating authority regarding the participant.

13. The member will at all times provide students with clear and equally acceptable alternatives for self-understanding or growth experiences. The member will assure students that they have a right to accept these alternatives without prejudice or penalty.

14. Members must conduct an educational program in keeping with the current relevant guidelines of the Association.

ETHICAL PRINCIPLES OF PSYCHOLOGISTS, AMERICAN PSYCHOLOGICAL ASSOCIATION*

APPENDIX B

☐ PREAMBLE

Psychologists respect the dignity and worth of the individual and strive for the preservation and protection of fundamental human rights. They are committed to increasing knowledge of human behavior and of people's understanding of themselves and others and to the utilization of such knowledge for the promotion of human welfare. While pursuing these objectives, they make every effort to protect the welfare of those who seek their services and of the research participants that may be the object of study. They use their skills only for purposes consistent with these values and do not knowingly permit their misuse by others. While demanding for themselves freedom of inquiry and communication, psychologists accept the responsibility this freedom requires: competence, objectivity in the application of skills, and concern for the best interests of clients, colleagues, students, research participants, and society. In the pursuit of these ideals, psychologists subscribe to principles in the following areas: 1. Responsibility, 2. Competence, 3. Moral and Legal Standards, 4. Public Statements, 5. Confidentiality, 6. Welfare of the Consumer, 7. Professional Relationships, 8. Assessment Techniques, 9. Research with Human Participants, and 10. Care and Use of Animals.

* *Ethical Principles of Psychologists* (revised edition), by the American Psychological Association. Copyright 1989 by the American Psychological Association. Reprinted by permission of the publisher.

This version of the *Ethical Principles of Psychologists* (formerly entitled *Ethical Standards of Psychologists*) was adopted by the American Psychological Association's Council of Representatives on January 24, 1989. On that date, the Board of Directors rescinded several sections of the Ethical Principles that had been adopted by the APA Council of Representatives on January 24, 1981. Inquiries concerning the *Ethical Principles of Psychologists* should be addressed to the Administrative Director, Office of Ethics, American Psychological Association, 1200 Seventeenth Street, N.W., Washington, D.C. 20036.

Acceptance of membership in the American Psychological Association commits the member to adherence to these principles.

Psychologists cooperate with duly constituted committees of the American Psychological Association, in particular, the Committee on Scientific and Professional Ethics and Conduct, by responding to inquiries promptly and completely. Members also respond promptly and completely to inquiries from duly constituted state association ethics committees and professional standards review committees.

Principle 1: Responsibility

In providing services, psychologists maintain the highest standards of their profession. They accept responsibility for the consequences of their acts and make every effort to ensure that their services are used appropriately.

a. As scientists, psychologists accept responsibility for the selection of their research topics and the methods used in investigation, analysis, and reporting. They plan their research in ways to minimize the possibility that their findings will be misleading. They provide thorough discussion of the limitations of their data, especially where their work touches on social policy or might be construed to the detriment of persons in specific age, sex, ethnic, socioeconomic, or other social groups. In publishing reports of their work, they never suppress disconfirming data, and they acknowledge the existence of alternative hypotheses and explanations of their findings. Psychologists take credit only for work they have actually done.

b. Psychologists clarify in advance with all appropriate persons and agencies the expectations for sharing and utilizing research data. They avoid relationships that may limit their objectivity or create a conflict of interest. Interference with the milieu in which data are collected is kept to a minimum.

c. Psychologists have the responsibility to attempt to prevent distortion, misuse, or suppression of psychological findings by the institution or agency of which they are employees.

d. As members of governmental or other organizational bodies, psychologists remain accountable as individuals to the highest standards of their profession.

e. As teachers, psychologists recognize their primary obligation to help others acquire knowledge and skill. They maintain high standards of scholarship by presenting psychological information objectively, fully, and accurately.

f. As practitioners, psychologists know that they bear a heavy social responsibility because their recommendations and professional actions may alter the lives of others. They are alert to personal, social, organizational, financial, or political situations and pressures that might lead to misuse of their influence.

Principle 2: Competence

The maintenance of high standards of competence is a responsibility shared by all psychologists in the interest of the public and the profession as a whole. Psychologists recognize the boundaries of their competence and the limitations of their techniques. They only provide services and only use techniques for which they are qualified by training and experience. In those areas in which recognized standards do not yet exist, psychologists take whatever precautions are necessary to protect the welfare of their clients. They maintain knowledge of current scientific and professional information related to the services they render.

a. Psychologists accurately represent their competence, education, training, and experience. They claim as evidence of educational qualifications only those degrees obtained from institutions acceptable under the Bylaws and Rules of the Council of the American Psychological Association.

b. As teachers, psychologists perform their duties on the basis of careful preparation so that their instruction is accurate, current, and scholarly.

c. Psychologists recognize the need for continuing education and are open to new procedures and changes in expectations and values over time.

d. Psychologists recognize differences among people, such as those that may be associated with age, sex, socioeconomic, and ethnic backgrounds. When necessary, they obtain training, experience, or counsel to assure competent service or research relating to such persons.

e. Psychologists responsible for decisions involving individuals or policies based on test results have an understanding of psychological or educational measurement, validation problems, and test research.

f. Psychologists recognize that personal problems and conflicts may interfere with professional effectiveness. Accordingly, they refrain from undertaking any activity in which their personal problems are likely to lead to inadequate performance or harm to a client, colleague, student, or research participant. If engaged in such activity when they become aware of their personal problems, they seek competent professional assistance to determine whether they should suspend, terminate, or limit the scope of their professional and/or scientific activities.

Principle 3: Moral and Legal Standards

Psychologists' moral and ethical standards of behavior are a personal matter to the same degree as they are for any other citizen, except as these may compromise the fulfillment of their professional responsibilities or reduce the public trust in psychology and psychologists. Regarding their own behavior, psychologists are sensitive to prevailing community standards and to the possible impact that conformity to or deviation from these standards may have upon the quality of their performance as psychologists. Psychologists are also aware of the possible impact of their public behavior upon the ability of colleagues to perform their professional duties.

a. As teachers, psychologists are aware of the fact that their personal values may affect the selection and presentation of instructional materials. When dealing with topics that may give offense, they recognize and respect the diverse attitudes that students may have toward such materials.

b. As employees or employers, psychologists do not engage in or condone practices that are inhumane or that result in illegal or unjustifiable actions. Such practices include, but are not limited to, those based on considerations of race, handicap, age, gender, sexual preference, religion, or national origin in hiring, promotion, or training.

c. In their professional roles, psychologists avoid any action that will violate or diminish the legal and civil rights of clients or of others who may be affected by their actions.

d. As practitioners and researchers, psychologists act in accord with Association standards and guidelines related to practice and to the conduct of research with human beings and animals. In the ordinary course of events, psychologists adhere to relevant governmental laws and institutional regulations. When federal, state, provincial, organiza-

tional, or institutional laws, regulations, or practices are in conflict with Association standards and guidelines, psychologists make known their commitment to Association standards and guidelines and, wherever possible, work toward a resolution of the conflict. Both practitioners and researchers are concerned with the development of such legal and quasi-legal regulations as best serve the public interest, and they work toward changing existing regulations that are not beneficial to the public interest.

Principle 4: Public Statements

Public statements, announcements of services, advertising, and promotional activities of psychologists serve the purpose of helping the public make informed judgments and choices. Psychologists represent accurately and objectively their professional qualifications, affiliations, and functions, as well as those of the institutions or organizations with which they or the statements may be associated. In public statements providing psychological information or professional opinions or providing information about the availability of psychological products, publications, and services, psychologists base their statements on scientifically acceptable psychological findings and techniques with full recognition of the limits and uncertainties of such evidence.

a. When announcing or advertising professional services, psychologists may list the following information to describe the provider and services provided: name, highest relevant academic degree earned from a regionally accredited institution, date, type, and level of certification or licensure, diplomate status, APA membership status, address, telephone number, office hours, a brief listing of the type of psychological services offered, an appropriate presentation of fee information, foreign languages spoken, and policy with regard to third-party payments. Additional relevant or important consumer information may be included if not prohibited by other sections of these Ethical Principles.

b. In announcing or advertising the availability of psychological products, publications, or services, psychologists do not present their affiliation with any organization in a manner that falsely implies sponsorship or certification by that organization. In particular and for example, psychologists do not state APA membership or fellow status in a way to suggest that such status implies specialized professional competence or qualifications. Public statements include, but are not limited to, communication by means of periodical, book, list, directory, television, radio, or motion picture. They do not contain (i) a false, fraudulent, misleading, deceptive, or unfair statement; (ii) a misinterpretation of fact or a statement likely to mislead or deceive because in context it makes only a partial disclosure of relevant facts; (iii) a statement intended or likely to create false or unjustified expectations of favorable results.

c. Psychologists do not compensate or give anything of value to a representative of the press, radio, television, or other communication medium in anticipation of or in return for professional publicity in a news item. A paid advertisement must be identified as such, unless it is apparent from the context that it is a paid advertisement. If communicated to the public by use of radio or television, an advertisement is prerecorded and approved for broadcast by the psychologist, and a recording of the actual transmission is retained by the psychologist.

d. Announcements or advertisements of "personal growth groups," clinics, and agencies give a clear statement of purpose and a clear description of the experiences to be provided. The education, training, and experience of the staff members are appropriately specified.

e. Psychologists associated with the development or promotion of psychological devices, books, or other products offered for commercial sale make reasonable efforts to ensure that announcements and advertisements are presented in a professional, scientifically acceptable, and factually informative manner.

f. Psychologists do not participate for personal gain in commercial announcements or advertisements recommending to the public the purchase or use of proprietary or single-source products or services when that participation is based solely upon their identification as psychologists.

g. Psychologists present the science of psychology and offer their services, products, and publications fairly and accurately, avoiding misrepresentation through sensationalism, exaggeration, or superficiality. Psychologists are guided by the primary obligation to aid the public in developing informed judgments, opinions, and choices.

h. As teachers, psychologists ensure that statements in catalogs and course outlines are accurate and not misleading, particularly in terms of subject matter to be covered, bases for evaluating progress, and the nature of course experiences. Announcements, brochures, or advertisements describing workshops, seminars, or other educational programs accurately describe the audience for which the program is intended as well as eligibility requirements, educational objectives, and nature of the materials to be covered. These announcements also accurately represent the education, training, and experience of the psychologists presenting the programs and any fees involved.

i. Public announcements or advertisements soliciting research participants in which clinical services or other professional services are offered as an inducement make clear the nature of the services as well as the costs and other obligations to be accepted by participants in the research.

j. A psychologist accepts the obligation to correct others who represent the psychologist's professional qualifications, or associations with products or services, in a manner incompatible with these guidelines.

k. Individual diagnostic and therapeutic services are provided only in the context of a professional psychological relationship. When personal advice is given by means of public lectures or demonstrations, newspaper or magazine articles, radio or television programs, mail, or similar media, the psychologist utilizes the most current relevant data and exercises the highest level of professional judgment.

l. Products that are described or presented by means of public lectures or demonstrations, newspaper or magazine articles, radio or television programs, or similar media meet the same recognized standards as exist for products used in the context of a professional relationship.

Principle 5: Confidentiality

Psychologists have a primary obligation to respect the confidentiality of information obtained from persons in the course of their work as psychologists. They reveal such information to others only with the consent of the person or the person's legal representative, except in those unusual circumstances in which not to do so would result in clear danger to the person or to others. Where appropriate, psychologists inform their clients of the legal limits of confidentiality.

a. Information obtained in clinical or consulting relationships, or evaluative data concerning children, students, employees, and others, is discussed only for professional purposes and only with persons clearly concerned with the case. Written and oral reports present only data germane to the purposes of the evaluation, and every effort is made to avoid undue invasion of privacy.

b. Psychologists who present personal information obtained during the course of professional work in writings, lectures, or other public forums either obtain adequate prior consent to do so or adequately disguise all identifying information.

c. Psychologists make provisions for maintaining confidentiality in the storage and disposal of records.

d. When working with minors or other persons who are unable to give voluntary, informed consent, psychologists take special care to protect these persons' best interests.

Principle 6: Welfare of the Consumer

Psychologists respect the integrity and protect the welfare of the people and groups with whom they work. When conflicts of interest arise between clients and psychologists' employing institutions, psychologists clarify the nature and direction of their loyalties and responsibilities and keep all parties informed of their commitments. Psychologists fully inform consumers as to the purpose and nature of an evaluative, treatment, educational, or training procedure, and they freely acknowledge that clients, students, or participants in research have freedom of choice with regard to participation.

a. Psychologists are continually cognizant of their own needs and of their potentially influential position vis-à-vis persons such as clients, students, and subordinates. They avoid exploiting the trust and dependency of such persons. Psychologists make every effort to avoid dual relationships that could impair their professional judgment or increase the risk of exploitation. Examples of such dual relationships include, but are not limited to, research with and treatment of employees, students, supervisees, close friends, or relatives. Sexual intimacies with clients are unethical.

b. When a psychologist agrees to provide services to a client at the request of a third party, the psychologist assumes the responsibility of clarifying the nature of the relationships to all parties concerned.

c. Where the demands of an organization require psychologists to violate these Ethical Principles, psychologists clarify the nature of the conflict between the demands and these principles. They inform all parties of psychologists' ethical responsibilities and take appropriate action.

d. Psychologists make advance financial arrangements that safeguard the best interests of and are clearly understood by their clients. They contribute a portion of their services to work for which they receive little or no financial return.

e. Psychologists terminate a clinical or consulting relationship when it is reasonably clear that the consumer is not benefiting from it. They offer to help the consumer locate alternative sources of assistance.

Principle 7: Professional Relationships

Psychologists act with due regard for the needs, special competencies, and obligations of their colleagues in psychology and other professions. They respect the prerogatives and obligations of the institutions or organizations with which these other colleagues are associated.

a. Psychologists understand the areas of competence of related professions. They make full use of all the professional, technical, and administrative resources that serve the best interests of consumers. The absence of formal relationships with other professional workers does not relieve psychologists of the responsibility of securing for their clients the best possible professional service, nor does it relieve them of the obligation to exercise foresight, diligence, and tact in obtaining the complementary or alternative assistance needed by clients.

b. Psychologists know and take into account the traditions and practices of other professional groups with whom they work and cooperate fully with such groups. If a psychologist is contacted by a person who is already receiving similar services from another professional, the psychologist carefully considers that professional relationship and proceeds with caution and sensitivity to the therapeutic issues as well as the client's welfare. The psychologist discusses these issues with the client so as to minimize the risk of confusion and conflict.

c. Psychologists who employ or supervise other professionals or professionals in training accept the obligation to facilitate the further professional development of these individuals. They provide appropriate working conditions, timely evaluations, constructive consultation, and experience opportunities.

d. Psychologists do not exploit their professional relationships with clients, supervisees, students, employees, or research participants sexually or otherwise. Psychologists do not condone or engage in sexual harassment. Sexual harassment is defined as deliberate or repeated comments, gestures, or physical contacts of a sexual nature that are unwanted by the recipient.

e. In conducting research in institutions or organizations, psychologists secure appropriate authorization to conduct such research. They are aware of their obligations to future research workers and ensure that host institutions receive adequate information about the research and proper acknowledgment of their contributions.

f. Publication credit is assigned to those who have contributed to a publication in proportion to their professional contributions. Major contributions of a professional character made by several persons to a common project are recognized by joint authorship, with the individual who made the principal contribution listed first. Minor contributions of a professional character and extensive clerical or similar nonprofessional assistance may be acknowledged in footnotes or in an introductory statement. Acknowledgment through specific citations is made for unpublished as well as published material that has directly influenced the research or writing. Psychologists who compile and edit material of others for publication publish the material in the name of the originating group, if appropriate, with their own name appearing as chairperson or editor. All contributors are to be acknowledged and named.

g. When psychologists know of an ethical violation by another psychologist, and it seems appropriate, they informally attempt to resolve the issue by bringing the behavior to the attention of the psychologist. If the misconduct is of a minor nature and/or appears to be due to lack of sensitivity, knowledge, or experience, such an informal solution is usually appropriate. Such informal corrective efforts are made with sensitivity to any rights to confidentiality involved. If the violation does

not seem amenable to an informal solution, or is of a more serious nature, psychologists bring it to the attention of the appropriate local, state, and/or national committee on professional ethics and conduct.

Principle 8: Assessment Techniques

In the development, publication, and utilization of psychological assessment techniques, psychologists make every effort to promote the welfare and best interests of the client. They guard against the misuse of assessment results. They respect the client's right to know the results, the interpretations made, and the bases for their conclusions and recommendations. Psychologists make every effort to maintain the security of tests and other assessment techniques within limits of legal mandates. They strive to ensure the appropriate use of assessment techniques by others.

a. In using assessment techniques, psychologists respect the right of clients to have full explanations of the nature and purpose of the techniques in language the clients can understand, unless an explicit exception to this right has been agreed upon in advance. When the explanations are to be provided by others, psychologists establish procedures for ensuring the adequacy of these explanations.

b. Psychologists responsible for the development and standardization of psychological tests and other assessment techniques utilize established scientific procedures and observe the relevant APA standards.

c. In reporting assessment results, psychologists indicate any reservations that exist regarding validity or reliability because of the circumstances of the assessment or the inappropriateness of the norms for the person tested. Psychologists strive to ensure that the results of assessments and their interpretations are not misused by others.

d. Psychologists recognize that assessment results may become obsolete. They make every effort to avoid and prevent the misuse of obsolete measures.

e. Psychologists offering scoring and interpretation services are able to produce appropriate evidence for the validity of the programs and procedures used in arriving at interpretations. The public offering of an automated interpretation service is considered a professional-to-professional consultation. Psychologists make every effort to avoid misuse of assessment reports.

f. Psychologists do not encourage or promote the use of psychological assessment techniques by inappropriately trained or otherwise unqualified persons through teaching, sponsorship, or supervision.

Principle 9: Research with Human Participants

The decision to undertake research rests upon a considered judgment by the individual psychologist about how best to contribute to psychological science and human welfare. Having made the decision to conduct research, the psychologist considers alternative directions in which research energies and resources might be invested. On the basis of this consideration, the psychologist carries out the investigation with respect and concern for the dignity and welfare of the people who participate and with cognizance of federal and state regulations and professional standards governing the conduct of research with human participants.

a. In planning a study, the investigator has the responsibility to make a careful evaluation of its ethical acceptability. To the extent that the weighing of scientific and human values suggests a compromise of any principle, the investigator incurs a correspondingly serious obligation to seek ethical advice and to observe stringent safeguards to protect the rights of human participants.

b. Considering whether a participant in a planned study will be a "subject at risk" or a "subject at minimal risk," according to recognized standards, is of primary ethical concern to the investigator.

c. The investigator always retains the responsibility for ensuring ethical practice in research. The investigator is also responsible for the ethical treatment of research participants by collaborators, assistants, students, and employees, all of whom, however, incur similar obligations.

d. Except in minimal-risk research, the investigator establishes a clear and fair agreement with research participants, prior to their participation, that clarifies the obligations and responsibilities of each. The investigator has the obligation to honor all promises and commitments included in that agreement. The investigator informs the participants of all aspects of the research that might reasonably be expected to influence willingness to participate and explains all other aspects of the research about which the participants inquire. Failure to make full disclosure prior to obtaining informed consent requires additional safeguards to protect the welfare and dignity of the research participants. Research with children or with participants who have impairments that would limit understanding and/or communication requires special safeguarding procedures.

e. Methodological requirements of a study may make the use of concealment or deception necessary. Before conducting such a study, the investigator has a special responsibility to (i) determine whether the use of such techniques is justified by the study's prospective scientific, educational, or applied value; (ii) determine whether alternative procedures are available that do not use concealment or deception; and (iii) ensure that the participants are provided with sufficient explanation as soon as possible.

f. The investigator respects the individual's freedom to decline to participate in or to withdraw from the research at any time. The obligation to protect this freedom requires careful thought and consideration when the investigator is in a position of authority or influence over the participant. Such positions of authority include, but are not limited to, situations in which research participation is required as part of employment or in which the participant is a student, client, or employee of the investigator.

g. The investigator protects the participant from physical and mental discomfort, harm, and danger that may arise from research procedures. If risks of such consequences exist, the investigator informs the participant of that fact. Research procedures likely to cause serious or lasting harm to a participant are not used unless the failure to use these procedures might expose the participant to risk of greater harm, or unless the research has great potential benefit and fully informed and voluntary consent is obtained from each participant. The participant should be informed of procedures for contacting the investigator within a reasonable time period following participation should stress, potential harm, or related questions or concerns arise.

h. After the data are collected, the investigator provides the participant with information about the nature of the study and attempts to remove any misconceptions that may have arisen. Where scientific or humane values justify delaying or withholding this information, the investigator incurs a special responsibility to monitor the research and to ensure that there are no damaging consequences for the participant.

i. Where research procedures result in undesirable consequences for the individual participant, the investigator has the responsibility to detect and remove or correct these consequences, including long-term effects.

j. Information obtained about a research participant during the course of an investigation is confidential unless otherwise agreed upon in advance. When the possibility exists that others may obtain access to such information, this possibility, together with the plans for protecting confidentiality, is explained to the participant as part of the procedure for obtaining informed consent.

Principle 10: Care and Use of Animals

An investigator of animal behavior strives to advance understanding of basic behavioral principles and/or to contribute to the improvement of human health and welfare. In seeking these ends, the investigator ensures the welfare of animals and treats them humanely. Laws and regulations notwithstanding, an animal's immediate protection depends upon the scientist's own conscience.

a. The acquisition, care, use, and disposal of all animals are in compliance with current federal, state or provincial, and local laws and regulations.

b. A psychologist trained in research methods and experienced in the care of laboratory animals closely supervises all procedures involving animals and is responsible for ensuring appropriate consideration of their comfort, health, and humane treatment.

c. Psychologists ensure that all individuals using animals under their supervision have received explicit instruction in experimental methods and in the care, maintenance, and handling of the species being used. Responsibilities and activities of individuals participating in a research project are consistent with their respective competencies.

d. Psychologists make every effort to minimize discomfort, illness, and pain of animals. A procedure subjecting animals to pain, stress, or privation is used only when an alternative procedure is unavailable and the goal is justified by its prospective scientific, educational, or applied value. Surgical procedures are performed under appropriate anesthesia; techniques to avoid infection and minimize pain are followed during and after surgery.

e. When it is appropriate that the animal's life be terminated, it is done rapidly and painlessly.

CODE OF ETHICS, NATIONAL ASSOCIATION OF SOCIAL WORKERS*

APPENDIX C

☐ I. THE SOCIAL WORKER'S CONDUCT AND COMPORTMENT AS A SOCIAL WORKER

A. *Propriety.* The social worker should maintain high standards of personal conduct in the capacity or identity as social worker.

1. The private conduct of the social worker is a personal matter to the same degree as is any other person's, except when such conduct compromises the fulfillment of professional responsibilities.

2. The social worker should not participate in, condone, or be associated with dishonesty, fraud, deceit, or misrepresentation.

3. The social worker should distinguish clearly between statements and actions made as a private individual and as a representative of the social work profession or an organization or group.

B. *Competence and professional development.* The social worker should strive to become and remain proficient in professional practice and the performance of professional functions.

1. The social worker should accept responsibility or employment only on the basis of existing competence or the intention to acquire the necessary competence.

2. The social worker should not misrepresent professional qualifications, education, experience, or affiliations.

C. *Service.* The social worker should regard as primary the service obligation of the social work profession.

1. The social worker should retain ultimate responsibility for the quality and extent of the service that individual assumes, assigns, or performs.

2. The social worker should act to prevent practices that are inhumane or discriminatory against any person or group of persons.

* Code of Ethics of the National Association of Social Workers, as adopted by the 1979 NASW Delegate Assembly, effective July 1, 1980. Reprinted by permission.

D. *Integrity.* The social worker should act in accordance with the highest standards of professional integrity and impartiality.

1. The social worker should be alert to and resist the influences and pressures that interfere with the exercise of professional discretion and impartial judgment required for the performance of professional functions.
2. The social worker should not exploit professional relationships for personal gain.

E. *Scholarship and research.* The social worker engaged in study and research should be guided by the conventions of scholarly inquiry.

1. The social worker engaged in research should consider carefully its possible consequences for human beings.
2. The social worker engaged in research should ascertain that the consent of participants in the research is voluntary and informed, without any implied deprivation or penalty for refusal to participate, and with due regard for participants' privacy and dignity.
3. The social worker engaged in research should protect participants from unwarranted physical or mental discomfort, distress, harm, danger, or deprivation.
4. The social worker who engages in the evaluation of services or cases should discuss them only for the professional purposes and only with persons directly and professionally concerned with them.
5. Information obtained about participants in research should be treated as confidential.
6. The social worker should take credit only for work actually done in connection with scholarly and research endeavors and credit contributions made by others.

□ II. THE SOCIAL WORKER'S ETHICAL RESPONSIBILITY TO CLIENTS

F. *Primacy of clients' interests.* The social worker's primary responsibility is to clients.

1. The social worker should serve clients with devotion, loyalty, determination, and the maximum application of professional skill and competence.
2. The social worker should not exploit rela-

tionships with clients for personal advantage, or solicit the clients of one's agency for private practice.

3. The social worker should not practice, condone, facilitate, or collaborate with any form of discrimination on the basis of race, color, sex, sexual orientation, age, religion, national origin, marital status, political belief, mental or physical handicap, or any other preference or personal characteristic, condition, or status.
4. The social worker should avoid relationships or commitments that conflict with the interests of clients.
5. The social worker should under no circumstances engage in sexual activities with clients.
6. The social worker should provide clients with accurate and complete information regarding the extent and nature of the services available to them.
7. The social worker should apprise clients of their risks, rights, opportunities, and obligations associated with social service to them.
8. The social worker should seek advice and counsel of colleagues and supervisors whenever such consultation is in the best interest of clients.
9. The social worker should terminate service to clients, and professional relationships with them, when such service and relationships are no longer required or no longer serve the clients' needs or interests.
10. The social worker should withdraw services precipitously only under unusual circumstances, giving careful consideration to all factors in the situation and taking care to minimize possible adverse effects.
11. The social worker who anticipates the termination or interruption of service to clients should notify clients promptly and seek the transfer, referral, or continuation of services in relation to the clients' needs and preferences.

G. *Rights and prerogatives of clients.* The social worker should make every effort to foster maximum self-determination on the part of clients.

1. When the social worker must act on behalf of a client who has been adjudged legally

incompetent, the social worker should safeguard the interests and rights of that client.

2. When another individual has been legally authorized to act in behalf of a client, the social worker should deal with that person always with the client's best interest in mind.

3. The social worker should not engage in any action that violates or diminishes the civil or legal rights of clients.

H. *Confidentiality and privacy.* The social worker should respect the privacy of clients and hold in confidence all information obtained in the course of professional service.

1. The social worker should share with others confidences revealed by clients, without their consent, only for compelling professional reasons.

2. The social worker should inform clients fully about the limits of confidentiality in a given situation, the purposes for which information is obtained, and how it may be used.

3. The social worker should afford clients reasonable access to any official social work records concerning them.

4. When providing clients with access to records, the social worker should take due care to protect the confidences of others contained in those records.

5. The social worker should obtain informed consent of clients before taping, recording, or permitting third party observation of their activities.

I. *Fees.* When setting fees, the social worker should ensure that they are fair, reasonable, considerate, and commensurate with the service performed and with due regard for the clients' ability to pay.

1. The social worker should not divide a fee or accept or give anything of value for receiving or making a referral.

□ III. THE SOCIAL WORKER'S ETHICAL RESPONSIBILITY TO COLLEAGUES

J. *Respect, fairness, and courtesy.* The social worker should treat colleagues with respect, courtesy, fairness, and good faith.

1. The social worker should cooperate with colleagues to promote professional interests and concerns.

2. The social worker should respect confidences shared by colleagues in the course of their professional relationships and transactions.

3. The social worker should create and maintain conditions of practice that facilitate ethical and competent professional performance by colleagues.

4. The social worker should treat with respect, and represent accurately and fairly, the qualifications, views, and findings of colleagues and use appropriate channels to express judgments on these matters.

5. The social worker who replaces or is replaced by a colleague in professional practice should act with consideration for the interest, character, and reputation of that colleague.

6. The social worker should not exploit a dispute, between a colleague and employers to obtain a position or otherwise advance the social worker's interest.

7. The social worker should seek arbitration or mediation resolution for compelling professional reasons.

8. The social worker should extend to colleagues of other professions the same respect and cooperation that is extended to social work colleagues.

9. The social worker who serves as an employer, supervisor, or mentor to colleagues should make orderly and explicit arrangements regarding the conditions of their continuing professional relationship.

10. The social worker who has the responsibility for employing and evaluating the performance of other staff members should fulfill such responsibility in a fair, considerate, and equitable manner, on the basis of clearly enunciated criteria.

11. The social worker who has the responsibility for evaluating the performance of employees, supervisees, or students should share evaluations with them.

K. *Dealing with colleagues' clients.* The social worker has the responsibility to relate to the clients of colleagues with full professional consideration.

1. The social worker should not solicit the clients of colleagues.

2. The social worker should not assume pro-

fessional responsibility for the clients of another agency or a colleague without appropriate communication with that agency or colleague.

3. The social worker who serves the clients of colleagues, during a temporary absence or emergency, should serve those clients with the same consideration as that afforded any client.

☐ IV. THE SOCIAL WORKER'S ETHICAL RESPONSIBILITY TO EMPLOYERS AND EMPLOYING ORGANIZATIONS

L. *Commitments to employing organization.* The social worker should adhere to commitments made to the employing organization.

1. The social worker should work to improve the employing agency's policies and procedures, and the efficiency and effectiveness of its services.

2. The social worker should not accept employment or arrange student field placements in an organization which is currently under public sanction by NASW for violating personnel standards, or imposing limitations on or penalties for professional actions on behalf of clients.

3. The social worker should act to prevent and eliminate discrimination in the employing organization's work assignments and in its employment policies and practices.

4. The social worker should use with scrupulous regard, and only for the purpose for which they are intended, the resources of the employing organization.

☐ V. THE SOCIAL WORKER'S ETHICAL RESPONSIBILITY TO THE SOCIAL WORK PROFESSION

M. *Maintaining the integrity of the profession.* The social worker should uphold and advance the values, ethics, knowledge, and mission of the profession.

1. The social worker should protect and enhance the dignity and integrity of the profession and should be responsible and vigorous in discussion and criticism of the profession.

2. The social worker should take action through appropriate channels against unethical conduct by any other member of the profession.

3. The social worker should act to prevent the unauthorized and unqualified practice of social work.

4. The social worker should make no misrepresentation in advertising as to qualifications, competence, service, or results to be achieved.

N. *Community service.* The social worker should assist the profession in making social services available to the general public.

1. The social worker should contribute time and professional expertise to activities that promote respect for the utility, the integrity, and the competence of the social work profession.

2. The social worker should support the formulation, development, enactment, and implementation of social policies of concern to the profession.

O. *Development of knowledge.* The social worker should take responsibility for identifying, developing, and fully utilizing knowledge for professional practice.

1. The social worker should base practice upon recognized knowledge relevant to social work.

2. The social worker should critically examine and keep current with emerging knowledge relevant to social work.

3. The social worker should contribute to the knowledge base of social work and share research knowledge and practice wisdom with colleagues.

☐ VI. THE SOCIAL WORKER'S ETHICAL RESPONSIBILITY TO SOCIETY

P. *Promoting the general welfare.* The social worker should promote the general welfare of society.

1. The social worker should act to prevent and eliminate discrimination against any person or group on the basis of race, color, sex, sexual orientation, age, religion, national origin, marital status, political belief, mental or physical handicap, or any other

preference or personal characteristic, condition, or status.

2. The social worker should act to ensure that all persons have access to the resources, services, and opportunities which they require.

3. The social worker should act to expand choice and opportunity for all persons, with special regard for disadvantaged or oppressed groups and persons.

4. The social worker should promote conditions that encourage respect for the diversity of cultures which constitute American society.

5. The social worker should provide appropriate professional services in public emergencies.

6. The social worker should advocate changes in policy and legislation to improve social conditions and to promote social justice.

7. The social worker should encourage informed participation by the public in shaping social policies and institutions.

STANDARDS FOR THE PRIVATE PRACTICE OF CLINICAL SOCIAL WORK, NATIONAL ASSOCIATION OF SOCIAL WORKERS*

APPENDIX D

□ QUALIFICATIONS FOR THE CLINICAL SOCIAL WORKER IN PRIVATE PRACTICE

I. The clinical social worker in private practice shall meet the educational and practice requirements of the National Association of Social Workers, shall maintain current knowledge of scientific and professional developments, and shall obtain additional training when required for effective practice.

   A. The practitioner shall have a Master's or Doctoral degree from an accredited school of social work plus two years or 3,000 hours of postdegree direct practice experience, supervised by a Master's level clinical social worker, in a hospital, clinic, agency, or other institutional setting.

   B. The practitioner shall abide by NASW's continuing education requirements and other standards relating to competence in clinical practice which shall be established by the Association.

   C. The clinical social worker practicing privately for the first time should obtain consultation from an experienced clinical social worker.

   D. The practitioner shall limit the practice to demonstrated areas of professional competence.

   E. When using specialized methods of practice which range beyond those normally learned in a school of social work or social work practice setting, the practitioner shall obtain training or professional supervision in the modalities employed.

* *Standards for the Private Practice of Clinical Social Work,* by the National Association of Social Workers (draft of April 22, 1981). Reprinted with permission from the NASW Policy Statement Series.

LEGAL ASPECTS OF PRIVATE CLINICAL PRACTICE

II. The clinical social worker in private practice shall comply with the laws of the jurisdiction within which s/he practices. The practitioner shall adhere to the educational, experiential, and other practice requirements of law in those jurisdictions which regulate clinical social work.

PROFESSIONAL IDENTIFICATION AND COMMITMENT

III. The privately practicing clinician whose training is in social work: (a) identifies himself/herself as a member of the social work profession, regardless of clinical orientation; and (b) is committed to the profession.
  A. Commitment to the profession is demonstrated through organizational participation, teaching, writing, and other activities.
  B. The practitioner should belong to the NASW, ACSW, the NASW Register of Clinical Social Workers and shall adhere to the NASW Code of Ethics.
  C. The privately practicing clinical social worker, like all social workers, should seek modification within the client and within those societal systems and institutions which affect the client.
  D. The practitioner shall be subject to NASW standards and grievance procedures and to peer and utilization review depending upon state and local law and customary professional practice.

THE MAINTENANCE OF CONFIDENTIALITY

IV. The clinical social worker in private practice shall abide by the provisions of confidentiality in the NASW Code of Ethics. (See Appendix C.)
  A. The social worker should share with others confidences revealed by clients, without their consent, only for compelling professional reasons.
    1. The clinical social worker in private practice may find it necessary to reveal confidential information disclosed by the patient to protect the patient or the community from imminent danger.
    2. When the clinical social worker in private practice is ordered by the court to reveal the confidences entrusted by patients, the practitioner may comply or may ethically hold the right to dissent within the framework of the law.

THE MANAGEMENT ASPECTS OF A PRIVATE CLINICAL PRACTICE

V. To render the best possible service to the client, the clinical social worker shall be capable of managing the business aspects of a private practice.
  A. The clinical practitioner shall be familiar with relevant state and local laws on the conduct of a business.
  B. The practitioner should carry malpractice and premises liability insurance.
  C. The practitioner shall deal expediently and efficiently with insurance companies covering clinical social work services. This includes maintenance of records and the use of diagnostic categories in billing private and governmental carriers.
  D. The private practitioner and client shall agree to a contract during the initial visit(s). Conditions of the contract shall be clear and explicit. These shall include:
    1. Agreement about fees; insurance; length, frequency, and location of sessions; appointments missed or cancelled without adequate notice; vacation coverage during an absence; collateral contacts. (The foregoing information may be provided on a standardized form.)
    2. Agreement regarding goals of treatment.
    3. Informing the client of his/her rights.
  E. Private clinical practitioners shall keep up-to-date, accurate records on the treatment of the client. (Records should protect confidentiality while recording subjects discussed in sufficient detail to justify therapeutic action.)
  F. Offices in which services are rendered

shall be located for client safety, accessibility, and privacy.

G. A social worker in private practice may advertise. The advertisement should clearly inform a prospective client of the nature of the services to be received. Advertisements shall not misrepresent qualifications, competence, service, or results to be achieved. (See Code of Ethics V.M.4.)

H. When a clinical social worker terminates a private practice, there is a responsibility to refer clients elsewhere. If the clinical social worker chooses, s/he may carefully select a successor to whom the practice may be sold. Clients should be given the choice of transferring to the successor or to another clinician. The responsible practitioner collaborates with the successor for the maximum benefit of their mutual clients.

I. The privately practicing clinical social worker's rates shall be commensurate with services performed and with fees charged by mental health professionals practicing in the community. Clients who cannot pay the practitioner's fee should be referred to a mental health or family agency or to a private practitioner with lower rates.

J. The practitioner's bill shall reflect services actually rendered.

K. The clinical social worker shall not divide a fee or accept or give anything of value for receiving or making a referral. (See Code of Ethics II.I.1.)

L. Unpaid accounts may be collected through a collection agency [or] small claims court or through other legal action when efforts to collect directly from the client have failed.

☐ MODALITIES AND METHODS OF TREATMENT

VI. A variety of professionally acceptable and ethically sanctioned modalities and methods of treatment may be used in the private practice of clinical social work.

A. The practitioner shall be familiar with the client's physical condition, collaborating with a physician when the client is chronically ill or disabled and/or using medication. The practitioner shall refer the client to a physician for treatment or medication when necessary.

B. The privately practicing clinical social worker may certify or admit clients to institutional facilities depending upon state or local practice.

C. An appointment with a relative or collateral shall be made only when the client's permission has been obtained.

D. The privately practicing clinical social worker shall not discriminate against or refuse to treat a client because of race, sex, color, sexual orientation, religion, lifestyle, mental or physical handicap. (See Code of Ethics II.F.3.)

E. The private practice may be limited to certain specialties but clients outside the practitioner's area of expertise should be referred to appropriate resources.

F. The private practitioner shall not engage in sexual activities with clients. (See Code of Ethics II.F.5.)

G. Clients should be treated as expeditiously as possible. Consultation should be sought when there is a lack of progress in treatment.

☐ RELATIONSHIPS WITH OTHER PROFESSIONALS AND COMMUNITY AGENCIES

VII. The privately practicing clinical social worker shall maintain the highest professional and business ethics in dealing with other professionals and community agencies.

A. The practitioner shall be familiar with the network of professional and self-help systems in the community and shall link clients with relevant services and resources.

B. When the client is referred to another resource, the role of the primary provider of care and the specific responsibility of each party concerned with the client should be delineated clearly.

C. When the clinical social worker is unable to continue service to an individual(s), there is a responsibility to offer suitable referral(s).

D. The practitioner shall cooperate with

professionals who subsequently treat former clients.

E. The clinical social worker leaving an agency for private practice shall abide by that agency's explicit policy regarding transfer of clients. If the agency permits transfer of the client to a private practice, there shall be advance agreement between the agency and the practitioner before discussing options with the client.

F. The clinical social worker employing others in the private practice shall assume professional responsibility and accountability for all services provided.

□ APPENDIX I: CONFIDENTIALITY AND PRIVACY

The social worker should respect the privacy of clients and hold in confidence all information obtained in the course of professional service.

The social worker should share with others confidences revealed by clients, without consent, only for compelling professional reasons.

The social worker should inform clients fully about the limits of confidentiality in a given situation, the purposes for which information is obtained, and how it may be used.

The social worker should afford clients reasonable access to any official social work records concerning them.

When providing clients with access to records, the social worker should take due care to protect the confidences of others contained in those records.

The social worker should obtain informed consent of clients before taping, recording, or permitting third party observation of their activities.

MULTIMODAL LIFE HISTORY QUESTIONNAIRE*

APPENDIX E   □ PURPOSE OF THIS QUESTIONNAIRE:

The purpose of this questionnaire is to obtain a comprehensive picture of your background. In psychotherapy, records are necessary, since they permit a more thorough dealing with one's problems. By completing these questions as fully and as accurately as you can, you will facilitate your therapeutic program. You are requested to answer these routine questions in your own time instead of using up your actual consulting time. It is understandable that you might be concerned about what happens to the information about you because much or all of this information is highly personal. Case records are strictly confidential. **NO OUTSIDER IS PERMITTED TO SEE YOUR CASE RECORD WITHOUT YOUR PERMISSION.**

If you do not desire to answer any questions, merely write "Do Not Care to Answer."

Date: _____

1. General Information:

Name: _____

Address: _____

Telephone Numbers: (days) _____ (evenings) _____

Age: _____ Occupation _____ Sex _____

By whom were you referred? _____

Marital Status (circle one): Single Engaged Married Separated Divorced Widowed

Remarried (how many times? ____) Living with someone _____

Do you live in: house, hotel, room, apartment _____

2. Description of Presenting Problems:

State in your own words the nature of your main problems _____

_____

_____

_____

_____

_____

_____

On the scale below please estimate the severity of your problem(s):

Mildly Upsetting	Moderately Upsetting	Very Severe	Extremely Severe	Totally Incapacitating

When did your problems begin (give dates): _____

_____

_____

_____

_____

* *The Multimodal Life History Questionnaire* by Arnold Lazarus. Copyright © 1980 by the Multimodal Therapy Institute. Reprinted by permission.

Please describe significant events occurring at that time, or since then, which may relate to the development or maintenance of your problems: _____

What solutions to your problems have been most helpful? _____

Have you been in therapy before or received any prior professional assistance for your problems? If so, please give name(s), professional title(s), dates of treatments and results: _____

3. Personal and Social History

(a) Date of Birth _____ Place of Birth _____

(b) Siblings: Number of Brothers _____ Brothers' Ages: _____
   Number of Sisters _____ Sisters' Ages: _____

(c) Father: Living? _____ If alive, give father's present age _____
   Deceased? _____ If deceased, give his age at time of death _____
   How old were you at the time? _____
   Cause of Death _____
   Occupation _____ Health _____

(d) Mother: Living? _____ If alive, give mother's present age _____
   Deceased? _____ If deceased, give her age at time of her death _____
   How old were you at the time? _____
   Cause of Death _____
   Occupation _____ Health _____

(e) Religion: As a Child: _____ As an Adult: _____

(f) Education: What is the last grade completed (degree)? _____

(g) Scholastic Strengths and Weaknesses: _____

(h) Underline any of the following that applied during your childhood/adolescence:

Happy Childhood	School Problems	Medical Problems
Unhappy Childhood	Family Problems	Alcohol Abuse
Emotional/Behavior Problems	Strong Religious Convictions	Others:
Legal Trouble	Drug Abuse	

(i) What sort of work are you doing now? _____

(j) What kinds of jobs have you held in the past? _____

(k) Does your present work satisfy you? If not, please explain _____

(l) What is your annual family income? _____ How much does it cost you to live? _____

(m) What were your past ambitions? _____

(n) What are your current ambitions? _____

(o) What is your height? _____ ft. _____ inches   What is your weight? _____ lbs.

(p) Have you ever been hospitalized for psychological problems? Yes _____ No _____
If yes, when and where? _____

(q) Do you have a family physician? Yes _____ No _____ If so, please give his/her name(s) and telephone number(s) _____

(r) Have you ever attempted suicide? Yes _____ No _____

(s) Does any member of your family suffer from alcoholism, epilepsy, depression or anything else that might be considered a "mental disorder"? _____

(t) Has any relative attempted or committed suicide? _____

(u) Has any relative had serious problems with the "law"? _____

Modality Analysis of Current Problems

The following section is designed to help you describe your current problems in greater detail and to identify problems which might otherwise go unnoticed. This will enable us to design a comprehensive treatment program and tailor it to your specific needs. The following section is organized according to the seven (7) modalities of *Behavior, Feelings, Physical Sensations, Images, Thoughts, Interpersonal Relationships and Biological Factors.*

4. Behavior:

Underline any of the following behaviors that apply to you:

Overeat	Suicidal attempts	Can't keep a job
Take drugs	Compulsions	Insomnia
Vomiting	Smoke	Take too many risks
Odd behavior	Withdrawal	Lazy
Drink too much	Nervous tics	Eating problems
Work too hard	Concentration difficulties	Aggressive behavior
Procrastination	Sleep disturbance	Crying
Impulsive reactions	Phobic avoidance	Outbursts of temper
Loss of control		

Are there any specific behaviors, actions or habits that you would like to change? _____

What are some special talents or skills that you feel proud of? _____

What would you like to do more of? _____
What would you like to do less of? _____
What would you like to start doing? _____
What would you like to stop doing? _____
How is your free time spent? _____

Do you keep yourself compulsively busy doing an endless list of chores or meaningless activities? _____

Do you practice relaxation or meditation regularly? _____

5. Feelings

Underline any of the following feelings that often apply to you:

Angry	Guilty	Unhappy
Annoyed	Happy	Bored
Sad	Conflicted	Restless
Depressed	Regretful	Lonely
Anxious	Hopeless	Contented
Fearful	Hopeful	Excited
Panicky	Helpless	Optimistic
Energetic	Relaxed	Tense
Envious	Jealous	Others:

List your five main fears:
1.
2.
3.

4.

5.

What feelings would you most like to experience more often? _____

What feelings would you like to experience less often? _____

What are some positive feelings you have experienced recently? _____

When are you most likely to lose control of your feelings? _____

Describe any situations that make you feel calm or relaxed _____

Please complete the following:

If I told you what I'm feeling now _____

One of the things I feel proud of is _____

One of the things I feel guilty about is _____

I am happiest when _____

One of the things that saddens me the most is _____

If I weren't afraid to be myself, I might _____

I get so angry when _____

If I get angry with you _____

What kinds of hobbies or leisure activities do you enjoy or find relaxing? _____

Do you have trouble relaxing and enjoying weekends and vacations? (If "yes," please explain) _____

6. Physical Sensations:

Underline any of the following that often apply to you:

Headaches	Stomach trouble	Skin problems
Dizziness	Tics	Dry mouth
Palpitations	Fatigue	Burning or itchy skin
Muscle spasms	Twitches	Chest pains
Tension	Back pain	Rapid heart beat
Sexual disturbances	Tremors	Don't like being touched
Unable to relax	Fainting spells	Blackouts
Bowel disturbances	Hear things	Excessive sweating
Tingling	Watery eyes	Visual disturbances
Numbness	Flushes	Hearing problems

MENSTRUAL HISTORY:

Age of first period _____ Were you informed or did it come

as a shock? _____

Are you regular? _____ Date of last period _____

Duration _____ Do you have pain? _____

Do your periods affect your mood? _____

What sensations are especially:

Pleasant for you? _____

Unpleasant for you? _____

7. Images
Underline any of the following that apply to you:

Pleasant sexual images	Unpleasant sexual images
Unpleasant childhood images	Lonely images
Helpless images	Seduction images
Aggressive images	Images of being loved

Check which of the following applies to you:

I PICTURE MYSELF:

being hurt	hurting others
not coping	being in charge
succeeding	failing
losing control	being trapped
being followed	being laughed at
being talked about	being promiscuous
Others:	

What picture comes into your mind most often?

Describe a very pleasant image, mental picture, or fantasy.

Describe a very unpleasant image, mental picture, or fantasy.

Describe your image of a completely "safe place."

How often do you have nightmares?

8. Thoughts:
Underline each of the following thoughts that apply to you:

I am worthless, a nobody, useless and/or unlovable.
I am unattractive, incompetent, stupid and/or undesirable.
I am evil, crazy, degenerate and/or deviant.
Life is empty, a waste; there is nothing to look forward to.
I make too many mistakes, can't do anything right.

Underline each of the following words that you might use to describe yourself:

intelligent, confident, worthwhile, ambitious, sensitive, loyal, trustworthy, full of regrets, worthless, a nobody, useless, evil, crazy, morally degenerate, considerate, a deviant, unattractive, unlovable, inadequate, confused, ugly, stupid, naive, honest, incompetent, horrible thoughts, conflicted, concentration difficulties, memory problems, attractive, can't make decisions, suicidal ideas, persevering, good sense of humor, hard-working.

What do you consider to be your most irrational thought or idea?

Are you bothered by thoughts that occur over and over again?

On each of the following items, please circle the number that most accurately reflects your opinions:

	STRONGLY DISAGREE	DISAGREE	NEUTRAL	AGREE	STRONGLY AGREE
I should not make mistakes.	1	2	3	4	5
I should be good at everything I do.	1	2	3	4	5
When I do not know, I should pretend that I do.	1	2	3	4	5

I should not disclose personal information.	1	2	3	4	5
I am a victim of circumstances.	1	2	3	4	5
My life is controlled by outside forces.	1	2	3	4	5
Other people are happier than I am.	1	2	3	4	5
It is very important to please other people.	1	2	3	4	5
Play it safe; don't take any risks.	1	2	3	4	5
I don't deserve to be happy.	1	2	3	4	5
If I ignore my problems, they will disappear.	1	2	3	4	5
It is my responsibility to make other people happy.	1	2	3	4	5
I should strive for perfection.	1	2	3	4	5
Basically, there are two ways of doing things — the right way and the wrong way.	1	2	3	4	5

Expectations regarding therapy:

In a few words, what do you think therapy is all about?

How long do you think your therapy should last?

How do you think a therapist should interact with his or her clients? What personal qualities do you think the ideal therapist should possess?

(Please complete the following:)

I am a person who _____

All my life _____

Ever since I was a child _____

It's hard for me to admit _____

One of the things I can't forgive is _____

A good thing about having problems is _____

The bad thing about growing up is _____

One of the ways I could help myself but don't is _____

9. Interpersonal Relationships

A. Family of Origin

(1) If you were not brought up by your parents, who raised you and between what years?

(2) Give a description of your father's (or father substitute's) personality and his attitude toward you (past and present):

(3) Give a description of your mother's (or mother substitute's) personality and her attitude toward you (past and present):

(4) In what ways were you disciplined (punished) by your parents as a child?

(5) Give an impression of your home atmosphere (i.e., the home in which you grew up). Mention state of compatibility between parents and between children.

(6) Were you able to confide in your parents?

(7) Did your parents understand you?

(8) Basically, did you feel loved and respected by your parents?

(9) If you have a step-parent, give your age when parent remarried.

(10) Has anyone (parents, relatives, friends) ever interfered in your marriage, occupation, etc.?

(11) Who are the most important people in your life?

B. Friendships

(1) Do you make friends easily?

(2) Do you keep them?

(3) Were you ever bullied or severely teased?

(4) Describe any relationship that gives you:
(a) Joy

(b) Grief

(5) Rate the degree to which you generally feel comfortable and relaxed in social situations:
Very relaxed ____ Relatively comfortable ____ Relatively uncomfortable ____ Very anxious ____

(6) Generally, do you express your feelings, opinions, and wishes to others in an open, appropriate manner? Describe those individuals with whom (or those situations in which) you have trouble asserting yourself.

(7) Did you date much during High School? College?

(8) Do you have one or more friends with whom you feel comfortable sharing your most private thoughts and feelings?

C. Marriage:

(1) How long did you know your spouse before your engagement?

(2) How long have you been married?

(3) What is your spouse's age?

(4) What is your spouse's occupation?

(5) Describe your spouse's personality.

(6) In what areas are you compatible?

(7) In what areas are you incompatible?

(8) How do you get along with your in-laws (this includes brothers and sisters-in-law)?

(9) How many children do you have? _____ Please give their names, ages and sexes:

(10) Do any of your children present special problems?

(11) Any relevant information regarding abortions or miscarriages?

D. Sexual Relationships:

(1) Describe your parents' attitude toward sex. Was sex discussed in your home?

(2) When and how did you derive your first knowledge of sex?

(3) When did you first become aware of your own sexual impulses?

(4) Have you ever experienced any anxiety or guilt feelings arising out of sex or masturbation? If yes, please explain.

(5) Any relevant details regarding your first or subsequent sexual experiences?

(6) Is your present sex life satisfactory? If not, please explain.

(7) Provide information about any significant homosexual reactions or relationships.

(8) Please note any sexual concerns not discussed above.

E. Other Relationships

(1) Are there any problems in your relationships with people at work? If so, please describe.

(2) Please complete the following:
(a) One of the ways people hurt me is _____

(b) I could shock you by _____

(c) A mother should _____

(d) A father should _____

(e) A true friend should _____

(3) Give a brief description of yourself as you would be described by:
   (a) Your spouse (if married):

   (b) Your best friend:

   (c) Someone who dislikes you:

(4) Are you currently troubled by any past rejections or loss of a love relationship? If so, please explain.

10. Biological factors:

Do you have any current concerns about your physical health? Please specify:
_____

Please list any medicines you are currently taking, or have taken during the past 6 months (including aspirin, birth control pills, or any medicines that were prescribed or taken over the counter) _____

Do you eat three well-balanced meals each day? If not, please explain
_____

Do you get regular physical exercise? If so, what type and how often?
_____

Check any of the following that apply to you:

	NEVER	RARELY	FREQUENTLY	VERY OFTEN
Marijuana				
Tranquilizers				
Sedatives				
Aspirin				
Cocaine				
Painkillers				
Alcohol				
Coffee				
Cigarettes				
Narcotics				
Stimulants				
Hallucinogens (LSD, etc.)				
Diarrhea				
Constipation				
Allergies				
High blood pressure				
Heart problems				
Nausea				
Vomiting				
Insomnia				
Headaches				
Backache				
Early morning awakening				

Fitful sleep _____
Overeat _____
Poor appetite _____
Eat "junk foods" _____

Underline any of the following that apply to you or members of your family: thyroid disease, kidney disease, asthma, neurological disease, infectious diseases, diabetes, cancer, gastrointestinal disease, prostate problems, glaucoma, epilepsy, other:

Have you ever had any head injuries or loss of consciousness? Please give details. _____
_____

Please describe any surgery you have had (give dates) _____
_____

Please describe any accidents or injuries you have suffered (give dates)
_____

Sequential History

Please outline your most significant memories and experiences within the following ages:

0–5 _____
6–10 _____
11–15 _____
16–20 _____
21–25 _____
26–30 _____
31–35 _____
36–40 _____
41–45 _____
46–50 _____
51–55 _____
56–60 _____
61–65 _____
Over 65 _____

BEHAVIORAL ANALYSIS
HISTORY QUESTIONNAIRE (BAHQ)*

APPENDIX F

This questionnaire is used to supply us with information from your past history and present situation that will help us to change your undesirable behavior. Your answers will be strictly confidential and will not be revealed to anyone without your full consent.

Name: _____ Date _____

Address: _____

_____

Age: _____ Date of Birth: _____

Telephone Number: (Home) _____ (Work) _____

Sex: Male _____ Female _____

Height: _____ ft. _____ in.   Weight: _____ lbs.

Race: White _____ Black _____ Oriental _____ Other _____

Color of Eyes: Blue _____ Brown _____ Green _____ Black _____

Glasses: Yes _____ No _____

Complexion: Dark _____ Medium-dark _____ Medium _____ Fair _____ Very Fair _____

Distinguishing features: _____

_____

Referral

Who referred you? _____

What present complaints (maladaptive behaviors) do you have that make you feel you need help? _____

_____

_____

How often do these occur?   times per week _____   times per month _____

What do you think is presently causing these behaviors? _____

_____

Have you sought treatment before? Yes _____ No _____

If yes, please list in chronological order the therapists and dates seen.

---

* From "The behavioral inventory battery: The use of self-report measures" by J. R. Cautela and D. Upper. In *Behavioral assessment: A practical handbook*. Copyright 1976 by Pergamon Press. Reprinted by permission.

Name of therapist: Dates seen:

_____   _____

_____   _____

_____   _____

_____   _____

Have you ever been hospitalized for mental illness?   Yes _____   No _____

If so, list hospital(s) and dates

Hospital(s):   Dates:

_____   _____

_____   _____

_____   _____

Fears and Negative Thoughts

List below some of the fears that you have:

_____

_____

_____

If you have any thoughts as listed below, check the frequency of the occurrence:

	Hardly ever	*Occasionally*	*Frequently*
Life is hopeless.	____	____	____
I am lonely.	____	____	____
The future is hopeless.	____	____	____
Nobody cares about me.	____	____	____
I feel like killing myself.	____	____	____
I am a failure.	____	____	____
I am intellectually inferior to other people.	____	____	____
People usually don't like me.	____	____	____
I am going to faint.	____	____	____
I am going to have a panic attack.	____	____	____
Other negative thoughts you may have:	_____		

Marital Status

Married _____   Single _____   Divorced _____   Separated _____   Widowed _____

If married, wife's/husband's age and occupation.

Age: _____   Occupation: _____

If any children, list their names and ages:

Name   *Age*

_____   _____

_____   _____

_____   _____

_____   _____

_____   _____

If divorced or separated, for what reason: _____

_____

_____

List the people who currently live in your household, and their relationship to you.

Name   *Relationship to you* (e.g., Mother-in-law,
                                                daughter, roommate, etc.)

_____   _____

_____   _____

_____   _____

_____   _____

_____   _____

_____   _____

Family History

Mother: Name _____   Age: _____

Height: ____ ft. ____ in.   Weight: ____ lbs.   Religion _____

Occupation: _____

How did she punish you? _____

How did she reward you? _____

What did she punish? _____

What did she reward? _____

How would others describe your mother? _____

_____

How would you describe your mother? _____

_____

What activities did you do with your mother when you were a child? _____

_____

How did you get along with your mother? _____

_____

Father: Name: _____   Age: _____

Height: _____ ft. _____ in.   Weight: _____ lbs.   Religion _____

Occupation: _____

How did he punish you? _____

How did he reward you? _____

What did he punish? _____

What did he reward? _____

How would others describe your father? _____

_____

How would you describe your father? _____

_____

What activities did you do with your father when you were a child? _____

_____

How did you get along with your father? _____

_____

Names of Brothers and Sisters	*Age*	*How did you get along with him/her?*
_____	_____	_____
_____	_____	_____
_____	_____	_____
_____	_____	_____

Does (did) your mother favor any one?   Yes _____   No _____

If so, who and why? _____

_____

How do (did) your mother and father get along? _____

_____

Educational History

	Name of School	*Location*	*Dates*	*How were your grades?*
Grammar:				
Secondary:				
College:				
Post-Graduate school(s):				

How well did you adjust to school situations?   poorly _____   fairly _____   well _____   excellently _____

List any significant events relating to school that you think had a bearing on your present problem:

_____

_____

_____

Childhood interests and hobbies: _____

_____

Present interests and hobbies: _____

_____

Job History

List the jobs you have held and their dates. Then note which aspects of each job were the most pleasurable for you (e.g., working with people, type of work, etc.) and which aspects gave you the most anxiety or trouble.

Dates	Job Titles	Salaries	Liked	Disliked

How often did you miss work?

   a. As a general estimate for all your jobs: _____

   b. For the jobs you enjoyed: _____

   c. For the jobs you disliked: _____

How did you get along with your fellow employees?   not at all _____   fairly well _____   very well _____

What bothered you most about your fellow employees? _____

_____

How did you get along with your supervisors? _____

_____

What bothered you about your supervisors? _____

_____

What training or education have you had relevant to occupational skills? (List on-the-job training as well as course work.)

_____

_____

_____

What job, if any, are you presently holding? _____

_____

Does it satisfy you:　intellectually ＿＿＿　emotionally ＿＿＿　physically ＿＿＿

What ambitions do you have at the present time? ＿＿＿＿＿＿＿＿＿＿＿＿＿＿＿＿＿＿＿＿＿

＿＿

Sexual History

When and how did you first learn about sex? ＿＿＿＿＿＿＿＿＿＿＿＿＿＿＿＿＿＿＿＿＿＿＿

＿＿

Was sex ever discussed at home:

    not at all ＿＿＿　occasionally ＿＿＿　a fair amount of time ＿＿＿　frequently ＿＿＿

What was the attitude of your parents concerning sex?

    It was considered shameful to discuss ＿＿＿　Not exactly shameful, but not discussed much ＿＿＿

    A natural function to be discussed without embarrassment ＿＿＿

Describe your first sexual experience ＿＿＿＿＿＿＿＿＿＿＿＿＿＿＿＿＿＿＿＿＿＿＿＿＿＿＿

＿＿

If you masturbate, when did you first start? ＿＿＿＿＿＿＿＿＿＿＿＿＿＿＿＿＿＿＿＿＿＿＿＿

When did you have your first sexual intercourse? ＿＿＿＿＿＿＿＿＿＿＿＿＿＿＿＿＿＿＿＿＿＿

Have you ever had any homosexual experience? ＿＿＿＿＿＿＿＿＿＿＿＿＿＿＿＿＿＿＿＿＿＿＿

＿＿

What is your sexual activity at the present time?

	Times per week	*Times per month*
a. Masturbation	＿＿＿＿＿＿	＿＿＿＿＿＿

    What do you imagine when you masturbate? ＿＿＿＿＿＿＿＿＿＿＿＿＿＿＿＿＿＿＿＿＿

＿＿

b. Light petting (kissing & hugging)	＿＿＿＿＿＿	＿＿＿＿＿＿
c. Heavy petting (touching sexual organs)	＿＿＿＿＿＿	＿＿＿＿＿＿
d. Homosexual contacts	＿＿＿＿＿＿	＿＿＿＿＿＿
e. Intercourse	＿＿＿＿＿＿	＿＿＿＿＿＿

(For female clients)

When did you have your first period? ＿＿＿＿＿＿＿＿＿＿＿＿＿＿＿＿＿＿＿＿＿＿＿＿＿＿＿

Are your periods regular at the present time?　Yes ＿＿＿　No ＿＿＿

How comfortable are your periods?

    very uncomfortable ＿＿＿　uncomfortable ＿＿＿　fairly comfortable ＿＿＿　comfortable ＿＿＿

Do you often feel depressed just before your period? ＿＿＿＿＿＿＿＿＿＿＿＿＿＿＿＿＿＿＿＿

Do you use birth control devices or pills?　Yes ＿＿＿　No ＿＿＿　If so, what type? ＿＿＿

Marital History

How well do you and your wife/husband get along? Rate your relationship on a scale from 1 to 5:

    1 very poor　2 poor　3 fair　4 good　5 excellent

How often do you and your wife/husband go out socially?   per week _____   per month _____

Who is the dominant member of your relationship?   you _____   your husband/wife _____

List some of the behaviors of your husband/wife that you find disagreeable:

_____

_____

_____

List some of the behaviors of your husband/wife that you find agreeable:

_____

_____

_____

Health History

List any childhood diseases you've had: _____

_____

List any operations you've had: _____

_____

Have you had any significant illnesses in the past? _____

List present physical ailments (for example, high blood pressure, diabetes, etc.) _____

_____

When was the last time you had a complete physical exam? _____

   Results? _____

_____

Name and address of your physician:

   Name: _____   Address: _____

Do you have trouble falling asleep?   Yes _____   No _____

Do you wake up during the night? _____

If you do wake up, can you get back to sleep easily? _____

_____

How is your appetite?   poor _____   average _____   good _____   very good _____

Which drugs are you presently taking and why? _____

_____

_____

Religious History

In which religion were you raised?   Protestant _____   Catholic _____   Jewish _____   other _____

Do you presently engage in any religious activity?   Yes _____   No _____

If so, please describe: _____

_____

Personality Assessment

List any faults you think you have: _____

_____

_____

_____

List your good points: _____

_____

_____

_____

Please add anything you feel might help us understand your problem: _____

_____

_____

_____

_____

REFERENCES

Abrams, D. B., & Wilson, G. T. (1979). Self-monitoring and reactivity in the modification of cigarette smoking. *Journal of Consulting and Clinical Psychology, 47,* 243–251.

Adler, A. (1964). *Social interest: A challenge to mankind.* New York: Capricorn Books.

Agras, W. S. (1965). An investigation in the decrements of anxiety responses during systematic desensitization therapy. *Behaviour Research and Therapy, 2,* 267–270.

Agras, W. S., Schneider, J. A., & Taylor, C. B. (1984). Relaxation training in essential hypertension: A failure of retraining in relaxation procedures. *Behavior Therapy, 15,* 191–196.

Alagna, F. J., Whitcher, S. J., Fisher, J. D., & Wicas, E. A. (1979). Evaluative reaction to interpersonal touch in a counseling interview. *Journal of Counseling Psychology, 26,* 265–472.

Alden, L. E. (1988). Behavioral self-management controlled-drinking strategies in a context of secondary prevention. *Journal of Consulting and Clinical Psychology, 56,* 280–286.

Alexander, J., & Parsons, B. (1982). *Functional family therapy:* Pacific Grove, Calif: Brooks/Cole.

Altmaier, E. M., Ross, S. L., Leary, M. R., & Thornbrough, M. (1982). Matching stress inoculation's treatment components to clients' anxiety mode. *Journal of Counseling Psychology, 29,* 331–334.

Altmaier, E. M., & Woodward, M. (1981). Group vicarious desensitization of test anxiety. *Journal of Counseling Psychology, 28,* 467–469.

American Association for Counseling and Development. (1981). *Ethical standards* (Rev. ed.). Alexandria, VA: Author.

American Psychiatric Association. (1987). *Diagnostic and statistical manual of mental disorders* (3rd ed. revised). Washington, DC: Author.

American Psychological Association. (1981). *Ethical principles of psychologists* (Rev. ed.). Washington, DC: Author.

Anderson, C. M., & Stewart, S. (1983). *Mastering resistance: A practical guide to family therapy.* New York: Guilford Press.

Andolfi, M. (1979). *Family therapy: An interactional approach.* New York: Plenum.

Anton, J. L., Dunbar, J., & Friedman, L. (1976). Anticipation training in the treatment of depression. In J. D. Krumboltz & C. E. Thoresen (Eds.), *Counseling methods* (pp. 67–74). New York: Holt, Rinehart and Winston.

Ascher, L. M. (1979). Paradoxical intention in the treatment of urinary retention. *Behaviour Research and Therapy, 17,* 267–270.

Ascher, L. M. (1980). Paradoxical intention. In A. Goldstein & E. B. Foa (Eds.), *Behavioral interventions: A clinical guide.* New York: Wiley.

Ascher, L. M. (1981). Employing paradoxical intention in the treatment of agoraphobia. *Behaviour Research and Therapy, 19,* 533–547.

Ascher, L. M., & Efran, J. (1978). Use of paradoxical intention in a behavioral program for sleep onset insomnia. *Journal of Consulting and Clinical Psychology, 46,* 547–550.

Ascher, L. M., & Phillips, D. (1975). Guided behavior rehearsal. *Journal of Behavior Therapy and Experimental Psychiatry, 6,* 215–218.

Ascher, L. M., & Turner, R. (1979). Paradoxical intention and insomnia: An experimental investigation. *Behaviour Research and Therapy, 17,* 408–411.

Auerswald, M. C. (1974). Differential reinforcing power of restatement and interpretation on client production of affect. *Journal of Counseling Psychology, 21,* 9–14.

Azrin, N. H., & Besale, V. A. (1980). *Job club counselor's manual: A behavioral approach to vocational counseling.* Baltimore, MD: University Park Press.

Bain, J. A. (1928). *Thought control in everyday life.* New York: Funk & Wagnalls.

Bajtelsmit, J., & Gershman, L. (1976). Covert positive reinforcement: Efficacy and conceptualization. *Journal of Behavior Therapy and Experimental Psychiatry, 7,* 207–212.

Baker, S. B. (1981). *Cleaning up our thinking: A unit in self-improvement.* Unpublished manuscript, Division of Counseling and Educational Psychology, Pennsylvania State University, University Park.

Baker, S. B., & Butler, J. N. (1984). Effects of preventive cognitive self-instruction training on adolescent attitudes, experiences and state anxiety. *Journal of Primary Prevention, 5,* 10–14.

Baker, S. B., Thomas, R. N., & Munson, W. W. (1983). Effects of cognitive restructuring and structured group discussion as primary prevention strategies. *School Counselor, 31,* 26–33.

Bandler, R., & Grinder, J. (1975). *The structure of magic I: A book about language and therapy.* Palo Alto, CA: Science and Behavior Books.

Bandler, R., & Grinder, J. (1982). *Reframing.* Moab, Utah: Real People Press.

Bandura, A. (1969). *Principles of behavior modification.* New York: Holt, Rinehart and Winston.

Bandura, A. (1971a). Psychotherapy based upon modeling principles. In A. E. Bergin & S. L. Garfield (Eds.), *Handbook of psychotherapy and behavior change: An empirical analysis* (pp. 653–708). New York: Wiley.

Bandura, A. (1971b). Vicarious and self-reinforcement processes. In R. Glaser (Ed.), *The nature of reinforcement.* New York: Academic Press.

Bandura, A. (1974). Self-reinforcement processes. In M. J. Mahoney & C. E. Thoresen (Eds.), *Self-control: Power to the person* (pp. 86–110). Pacific Grove, CA: Brooks/Cole.

Bandura, A. (1976a). Effecting change through participant modeling. In J. D. Krumboltz & C. E. Thoresen (Eds.), *Counseling methods* (pp. 248–265). New York: Holt, Rinehart and Winston.

Bandura, A. (1976b). Self-reinforcement: Theoretical and methodological considerations. *Behaviorism, 4,* 135–155.

Bandura, A. (1981). In search of pure unidirectional determinants. *Behavior Therapy, 12,* 30–40.

Bandura, A., & Adams, N. E. (1977). Analysis of self-efficacy theory of behavioral change. *Cognitive Therapy and Research, 1,* 287–310.

Bandura, A., Adams, N. E., & Beyer, J. (1977). Cognitive processes mediating behavioral change. *Journal of Personality and Social Psychology, 35,* 125–139.

Bandura, A., Blanchard, E. B., & Ritter, B. (1969). Relative efficacy of desensitization and modeling approaches for inducing behavioral, affective, and attitudinal changes. *Journal of Personality and Social Psychology, 13,* 173–199.

Bandura, A., & Jeffery, R. W. (1973). Role of symbolic coding and rehearsal processes in observational learning. *Journal of Personality and Social Psychology, 26,* 122–130.

Bandura, A., Jeffery, R. W., & Gajdos, E. (1975). Generalizing change through participant modeling with self-directed mastery. *Behaviour Research and Therapy, 13,* 141–152.

Bandura, A., Jeffery, R. W., & Wright, C. (1974). Efficacy of participant modeling as a function of response induction aids. *Journal of Abnormal Psychology, 83,* 56–64.

Bandura, A., & Simon, K. (1977). The role of proximal intentions in self-regulation of refractory behavior. *Cognitive Therapy and Research, 1,* 177–193.

Banikiotes, P. G., Kubinski, J. A., & Pursell, S. A. (1981). Sex role orientation, self-disclosure, and gender-related perceptions. *Journal of Counseling Psychology, 28,* 140–146.

Barak, A., Patkin, J., & Dell, D. M. (1982). Effects of certain counselor behaviors in perceived expertness and attractiveness. *Journal of Counseling Psychology, 29,* 261–267.

Barber, T. (1980). Personal communication. Cited in D. H. Shapiro, Jr., *Meditation: Self-regulation strategy and altered state of consciousness.* New York: Aldine.

Barlow, D. H. (Ed.). (1981a). *Behavioral assessment of adult disorders.* New York: Guilford Press.

Barlow, D. H. (1981b). On the relation of clinical research to clinical practice: Current issues, new directions. *Journal of Consulting and Clinical Psychology, 49,* 147–155.

Barlow, D. H., Hayes, S. C., & Nelson, R. O. (1984). *The scientist practitioner.* New York: Pergamon Press.

Barrett-Lennard, G. T. (1981). The empathy cycle: Refinement of a nuclear concept. *Journal of Counseling Psychology, 28,* 91–100.

Bass, B. A. (1974). Sexual arousal as an anxiety inhibitor. *Journal of Behavior Therapy and Experimental Psychiatry, 5,* 151–152.

Bateson, G., & Jackson, D. (1964). Some varieties of pathogenic organization. In D. McK. Rioch (Ed.), *Disorders of communication* (Vol. 42) (pp. 270–283). Research Publications, Association for Research in Nervous and Mental Disease.

Battle, C. C., Imber, S. D., Hoehn-Saric, R., Stone, A. R., Nash, E. R., & Frank, J. D. (1966). Target complaints as criteria of improvement. *American Journal of Psychotherapy, 20,* 184–192.

Baucom, D. A., & Lester, G. W. (1986). The usefulness of cognitive restructuring as an adjunct to behavioral marital therapy. *Behavior Therapy, 17,* 385–403.

Beck, A. T. (1970). Cognitive therapy: Nature and relation to behavior therapy. *Behavior Therapy, 1,* 184–200.

Beck, A. T. (1972). *Depression: Causes and treatment.* Philadelphia: University of Pennsylvania Press.

Beck, A. T. (1976). *Cognitive therapy and the emotional disorders.* New York: International Universities Press.

Beck, A. T., & Emery, G. (1979). *Cognitive therapy of anxiety.* Philadelphia: Center for Cognitive Therapy.

Beck, A. T., Ward, C. H., Mendelson, M., Mock, J., & Erbaugh, J. (1961). An inventory for measuring depression. *Archives of General Psychiatry, 4,* 561–571.

Beck, J. T., & Strong, S. R. (1982). Stimulating therapeutic change with interpretations: A comparison of positive and negative connotation. *Journal of Counseling Psychology, 29,* 551–559.

Bedell, J. R., Archer, R. P., & Marlow, A. A., Jr. (1980). A description and evaluation of a problem solving skills training program. In D. Upper & S. M. Ross (Eds.), *Behavioral group therapy: An annual review.* Champaign, IL: Research Press.

Bellack, A. S. (1976). A comparison of self-reinforcement and self-monitoring in a weight reduction program. *Behavior Therapy, 7,* 68–75.

Bellack, A. S., & Hersen, M. (1977). Self-report inventories in behavioral assessment. In J. D. Cone & R. P. Hawkins (Eds.), *Behavioral assessment: New directions in clinical psychology* (pp. 52–76). New York: Brunner/Mazel.

Bellack, A. S., & Hersen, M. (Eds.). (1988). *Behavioral Assessment* (3rd ed.). New York: Pergamon.

Bellack, A. S., Rozensky, R., & Schwartz, J. (1974). A comparison of two forms of self-monitoring in a behavioral weight reduction program. *Behavior Therapy, 5,* 523–530.

Bemis, K. (1980). Personal communication. Cited in P. C. Kendall & S. D. Hollon (Eds.), *Assessment strategies for cognitive-behavioral interventions.* New York: Academic Press.

Benjamin, A. (1974). *The helping interview* (2nd ed.). Boston: Houghton Mifflin.

Benson, H. (1974). Your innate asset for combating stress. *Harvard Business Review, 52,* 49–60.

Benson, H. (1976). *The relaxation response.* New York: Avon Books.

Benson, H. (1984). *Beyond the relaxation response.* New York: Berkley Books.

Berenson, B. C., & Mitchell, K. M. (1974). *Confrontation: For better or worse.* Amherst, MA: Human Resource Development Press.

Berman, J. S., Miller, R. C., & Massman, P. J. (1985). Cognitive therapy vs. systematic desensitization: Is one treatment superior? *Psychological Bulletin, 97,* 451–461.

Berne, E. (1964). *Games people play.* New York: Grove Press.

Bernstein, D. A., & Borkovec, T. D. (1973). *Progressive relaxation training: A manual for the helping professions.* Champaign, IL: Research Press.

Bijou, S. W., & Baer, D. M. (1961). *Child development I: A systematic and empirical theory.* Englewood Cliffs, NJ: Prentice-Hall.

Birchler, G. (1981). Paradox and behavioral marital therapy. In A. S. Gurman (Ed.), *Questions and answers in the practice of family therapy* (Vol. 1) (pp. 123–127). New York: Brunner/Mazel.

Birdwhistell, R. L. (1970). *Kinesics and context.* Philadelphia: University of Pennsylvania Press.

Birholtz, L. (1981). Neurolinguistic programming: Testing some basic assumptions. *Dissertation Abstracts International, 42,* 356 SB. (University Microfilms No. 8118324)

Bixler, R. H. (1949). Limits are therapy. *Journal of Consulting Psychology, 13,* 1–11.

Black, D. R., & Threlfall, W. E. (1986). A stepped approach to weight control: A minimal intervention and a problem-solving program. *Behavior Therapy, 17,* 144–157.

Blanchard, E. B. (1982). Biofeedback and relaxation training with three kinds of headache: Treatment effects and their prediction. *Journal of Consulting and Clinical Psychology, 50,* 562–575.

Blanchard, E. B., Andrasik, F., Neff, D. F., Jurish, S. E., & O'Keefe, D. M. (1981). Social validation of the headache diary. *Behavior Therapy, 12,* 711–715.

Blanchard, E. B., Theobald, D. E., Williamson, D. A., Silver, B. V., & Brown, D. A. (1978). Temperature biofeedback in the treatment of migraine headaches. *Archives of General Psychiatry, 35,* 581–588.

Blechman, E., Olson, D., & Hellman, I. (1976). Stimulus control over family problem-solving behavior: The family contract game. *Behavior Therapy, 7,* 686–692.

Bloomfield, H. H., Cain, M. P., Jaffe, D. T., & Kory, R. B. (1975). *TM: Discovering inner energy and overcoming stress.* New York: Dell.

Bolstad, O. D., & Johnson, S. M. (1972). Self-regulation in the modification of disruptive classroom behavior. *Journal of Applied Behavior Analysis, 5,* 443–454.

Bootzin, R. R. (1972). Stimulus control treatment for insomnia. *American Psychological Association Proceedings, 395–396.*

Bootzin, R. R. (1977). Effects of self-control procedures for insomnia. In R. B. Stuart (Ed.), *Behavioral self-management: Strategies, techniques, and outcomes* (pp. 176–195). New York: Brunner/Mazel.

Borck, L. E., & Fawcett, S. B. (1982). *Learning counseling and problem-solving skills.* New York: Haworth Press.

Borkovec, T., Grayson, J. B., & Cooper, K. (1978). Treatment of general tension: Subjective and physiological effects of progressive relaxation. *Journal of Consulting and Clinical Psychology, 46,* 518–528.

Borkovec, T. D., Grayson, J. B., O'Brien, G. T., & Weerts, T. C. (1979). Relaxation treatment of pseudoinsomnia and idiopathic insomnia: An electroencephalographic evaluation. *Journal of Applied Behavior Analysis, 12,* 37–54.

Borkovec, T. D., Wilkinson, L., Folensbee, R., & Lerman, C. (1983). Stimulus control applications to the treatment of worry. *Behaviour Research and Therapy, 21,* 247–251.

Bornstein, P. H., & Devine, D. A. (1980). Covert modeling-hypnosis in the treatment of obesity. *Psychotherapy: Theory, Research and Practice, 17,* 272–275.

Bornstein, P. H., Hamilton, S. B., Carmody, T. B., Rychtarik, R. G., & Veraldi, D. M. (1977). Reliability enhancement: Increasing the accuracy of self-report through meditation-based procedures. *Cognitive Therapy and Research, 1,* 85–98.

Bornstein, P. H., & Knapp, M. (1981). Self-control desensitization with a multi-phobic boy: A multiple baseline design. *Journal of Behavior Therapy and Experimental Psychiatry, 12,* 281–285.

Boudreau, L. (1972). Transcendental meditation and yoga as reciprocal inhibitors. *Journal of Behavior Therapy and Experimental Psychiatry, 3,* 97–98.

Bourque, P., & Ladouceur, R. (1980). An investigation of various performance-based treatments with acrophobics. *Behaviour Research and Therapy, 18,* 161–170.

Brammer, L. M., Shostrom, E. L., and Abrego, P. J. (1989). *Therapeutic psychology: Fundamentals of counseling and psychotherapy* (5th ed.). Englewood Cliffs, NJ: Prentice-Hall.

Brauer, A. P., Horlick, L., Nelson, E., Farquhar, J. W., & Agras, W. S. (1979). Relaxation therapy for essential hypertension: A Veterans Administration outpatient study. *Journal of Behavioral Medicine, 2,* 21–29.

Brehm, J. W. (1966). *A theory of psychological reactance.* New York: Academic Press.

Brehm, J. W. (1972). *Response to loss of freedom: A theory of psychological resistance.* Morristown, NJ: General Learning Press.

Brehm, S. S. (1976). *The application of social psychology to clinical practice.* Washington, DC: Hemisphere.

Brockman, W. P. (1980). *Empathy revisited: The effect of representational system matching on certain counseling process and outcome variables.* Unpublished doctoral dissertation, College of William and Mary, Williamsburg, VA.

Broden, M., Hall, R., & Mitts, B. (1971). The effect of self-recording on the classroom behavior of two eighth-grade students. *Journal of Applied Behavior Analysis, 4,* 191–199.

Brooks, J., & Scarano, T. (1985). Transcendental meditation in the treatment of post-Vietnam adjustment. *Journal of Counseling and Development, 64,* 212–215.

Broverman, I., Broverman, D., Clarkson, F., Rosenkrantz, P., & Vogel, S. (1970). Sex-role stereotypes and clinical judgments of mental health. *Journal of Consulting and Clinical Psychology, 34,* 1–7.

Brown, J. E., & Slee, P. (1986). Paradoxical strategies: The ethics of intervention. *Professional Psychology: Research & Practice, 17,* 487–491.

Brown, J. H., & Brown, S. (1977). *Systematic counseling: A guide for the practitioner.* Champaign, IL: Research Press.

Brown, J. P. (1978). *An analysis of self-monitoring-provided feedback in a behavioral weight reduction program.* Unpublished doctoral dissertation, West Virginia University, Morgantown.

Brownell, K., Colletti, G., Ersner-Hershfield, R., Hershfield, S., & Wilson, G. (1977). Self-control in school children: Stringency and leniency in self-determined and externally imposed performance standards. *Behavior Therapy, 8,* 442–455.

Bruch, M. A., Juster, H. R., & Heisler, B. D. (1982). Conceptual complexity as a mediator of thought content and negative affect: Implications for cognitive restructuring interventions. *Journal of Counseling Psychology, 29,* 343–353.

Bry, A., & Bair, M. (1979). *Visualization: Directing the movies of your mind.* New York: Barnes and Noble.

Bucher, B., & Fabricatore, J. (1970). Use of patient-administered shock to suppress hallucinations. *Behavior Therapy, 1,* 382–385.

Buggs, D. C. (1975). *Your child's self-esteem.* New York: Doubleday.

Burish, T. C., Carey, M. P., Krozely, M. G., & Greco, F. A. (1987). Conditioned side effects induced by cancer chemotherapy: Prevention through behavioral treatment. *Journal of Consulting and Clinical Psychology, 55,* 42–48.

Burish, T. G., & Lyles, J. N. (1979). Effectiveness of relaxation training in reducing the aversiveness of chemotherapy in the treatment of cancer. *Journal of Behavior Therapy and Experimental Psychiatry, 10,* 357–361.

Butcher, J. N., Dahlstrom, W. G., Graham, J. R., Tellegen, A., & Kaemmer, B. (1989). *MMPI-2 manual.* Minneapolis, MN: University of Minnesota Press.

Buxton, A., Williamson, D. A., Absher, N., & Warner, M. (1985). Self-management of nutrition. *Addictive Behaviors, 10,* 383–396.

Caird, W. K., & Wincze, J. P. (1974). Videotaped desensitization of frigidity. *Journal of Behavior Therapy and Experimental Psychiatry, 5,* 175–178.

Carey, M. P., & Burish, T. G. (1987). Providing relaxation training to cancer chemotherapy patients: A comparison of three delivery techniques. *Journal of Consulting and Clinical Psychology, 55,* 732–757.

Carkhuff, R. R. (1969a). *Helping and human relations.* Vol. 1: *Selection and training.* New York: Holt, Rinehart and Winston.

Carkhuff, R. R. (1969b). *Helping and human relations.* Vol. 2: *Practice and research.* New York: Holt, Rinehart and Winston.

Carkhuff, R. R. (1987). *The art of helping* (6th ed.). Amherst, MA: Human Resource Development Press.

Carkhuff, R. R., & Anthony, W. A. (1979). *The skills of helping.* Amherst, MA: Human Resource Development Press.

Carkhuff, R. R., & Pierce, R. M. (1975). *Trainer's guide: The art of helping.* Amherst, MA: Human Resource Development Press.

Carkhuff, R. R., Pierce, R. M., & Cannon, J. R. (1977). *The art of helping III.* Amherst, MA: Human Resource Development Press.

Carrington, P. (1978a). *Clinically standardized meditation (CSM): Instructor's manual.* Kendall Park, NJ: Pace Educational Systems.

Carrington, P. (1978b). *Learning to meditate: Clinically standardized meditation (CSM) course workbook.* Kendall Park, NJ: Pace Educational Systems.

Carrington, P., Collings, G. H., Benson, H., Robinson, H., Wood, L. W., Lehrer, P. M., Woolfolk, R. L., & Cole, J. W. (1980). The use of meditation-relaxation techniques for the management of stress in a working population. *Journal of Occupational Medicine, 22,* 221–231.

Carroll, L. J., & Yates, B. T. (1981). Further evidence for the role of stimulus control training in facilitating weight reduction after behavioral therapy. *Behavior Therapy, 12,* 287–291.

Cash, T. F., & Salzbach, R. F. (1978). The reality of counseling: Effects of counselor physical attractiveness and self-disclosure on perceptions of counselor behavior. *Journal of Counseling Psychology, 25,* 283–291.

Cautela, J. R. (1969). Behavior therapy and self-control: Techniques and implications. In C. Franks (Ed.), *Behav-*

ior therapy: Appraisal and status (pp. 323–340). New York: McGraw-Hill.

Cautela, J. R. (1970). Covert reinforcement. *Behavior Therapy, 1,* 33–50.

Cautela, J. R. (1971). *Covert modeling.* Paper presented at the fifth annual meeting of the Association for Advancement of Behavior Therapy, Washington, DC.

Cautela, J. R. (1976). The present status of covert modeling. *Journal of Behavior Therapy and Experimental Psychiatry, 6,* 323–326.

Cautela, J. R. (1977). *Behavior analysis forms for clinical intervention.* Champaign, IL: Research Press.

Cautela, J. R. (1981). *Behavior analysis forms for clinical intervention* (Vol. 2). Champaign, IL: Research Press.

Cautela, J. R., Flannery, R., & Hanley, S. (1974). Covert modeling: An experimental test. *Behavior Therapy, 5,* 494–502.

Cautela, J. R., & Groden, J. (1978). *Relaxation: A comprehensive manual for adults, children, and children with special needs.* Champaign, IL: Research Press.

Cautela, J. R., & Upper, D. (1975). The process of individual behavior therapy. In M. Hersen, R. Eisler, & P. Miller (Eds.), *Progress in behavior modification I* (pp. 275–305). New York: Academic Press.

Cautela, J. R., & Upper, D. (1976). The behavioral inventory battery: The use of self-report measures in behavioral analysis and therapy. In M. Hersen & A. S. Bellack (Eds.), *Behavioral assessment: A practical handbook* (pp. 77–109). New York: Pergamon Press.

Cavanaugh, M. E. (1982). *The counseling experience.* Pacific Grove, CA: Brooks/Cole.

Cavior, N., & Marabotto, C. M. (1976). Monitoring verbal behaviors in a dyadic interaction. *Journal of Consulting and Clinical Psychology, 44,* 68–76.

Celotta, B., & Telasi-Golubscow, H. (1982). A problem taxonomy for classifying clients' problems. *Personnel and Guidance Journal, 61,* 73–76.

Chadez, L. A., & Nurius, P. S. (1987). Stopping bedtime crying: Treating the child and the parents. *Journal of Clinical Child Psychology, 16,* 212–217.

Chamberlain, P., Patterson, G., Reid, J., Kavanagh, K., & Forgatch, M. (1984). Observation of client resistance. *Behavior Therapy, 15,* 144–155.

Chaney, E. F., O'Leary, M. R., & Marlatt, G. A. (1978). Skill training with alcoholics. *Journal of Consulting and Clinical Psychology, 46,* 1092–1104.

Chassan, J. B. (1962). Probability processes in psychoanalytic psychiatry. In J. Scher (Ed.), *Theories of the mind.* New York: Free Press.

Chaves, J., & Barber, T. (1974). Cognitive strategies, experimenter modeling, and expectation in the attenuation of pain. *Journal of Abnormal Psychology, 83,* 356–363.

Christoff, K. A., Scott, N. O. N., Kelly, M. L., Schlundt, D., Baer, G., & Kelly, J. A. (1985). Social skills and social problem-solving training for shy young adolescents. *Behavior Therapy, 16,* 468–477.

Ciminero, A. R. (1977). Behavioral assessment: An overview. In A. R. Ciminero, K. S. Calhoun, & H. E. Adams (Eds.), *Handbook of behavioral assessment* (pp. 3–13). New York: Wiley.

Ciminero, A. R., Nelson, R. O., & Lipinski, D. P. (1977). Self-monitoring procedures. In A. R. Çiminero, K. S. Calhoun, & H. E. Adams (Eds.), *Handbook of behavioral assessment* (pp. 195–232). New York: Wiley.

Claiborn, C. D. (1979). Counselor verbal intervention, non-verbal behavior, and social power. *Journal of Counseling Psychology, 26,* 378–383.

Claiborn, C. D. (1982). Interpretation and change in counseling. *Journal of Counseling Psychology, 29,* 439–453.

Claiborn, C. D., Ward, S. R., & Strong, S. R. (1981). Effects of congruence between counselor interpretations and client beliefs. *Journal of Counseling Psychology, 28,* 101–109.

Clark, D. M., & Salkovskis, P. M. (1989). *Cognitive therapy for panic and hypochondriasis.* New York: Pergamon Press.

Clarke, J. C., & Jackson, J. A. (1983). *Hypnosis and behavior therapy.* New York: Springer.

Coates, T. J., & Thoresen, C. E. (1981). Behavior and weight changes in three obese adolescents. *Behavior Therapy, 12,* 383–399.

Coates, T. J., & Thoresen, C. E. (1984). Assessing daytime thoughts and behavior associated with good and poor sleep: Two exploratory case studies. *Behavioral Assessment, 6,* 153–167.

Coe, W. C. (1980). Expectation, hypnosis, and suggestion methods. In F. H. Kanfer & A. P. Goldstein (Eds.), *Helping people change* (2nd ed.) (pp. 423–469). New York: Pergamon Press.

Collins, F. L., Jr., Martin, J. E., & Hillenberg, J. B. (1982). Assessment of relaxation compliance: A pilot validation study. *Behavioral Assessment, 4,* 221–225.

Condon, W. S., & Ogston, W. D. (1966). Soundfilm analysis of normal and pathological behavior patterns. *Journal of Nervous and Mental Disease, 143,* 338–347.

Connolly, P. R. (1975). The perception of personal space among black and white Americans. *Central States Speech Journal, 26,* 21–28.

Cooley, E. J., & Spiegler, M. D. (1980). Cognitive versus emotional coping responses as alternatives to test anxiety. *Cognitive Therapy and Research, 4,* 159–166.

Copeland, A. P. (1981). The relevance of subject variables in cognitive self-instructional programs for impulsive children. *Behavior Therapy, 12,* 520–529.

Corey, G., Corey, M., & Callanan, P. (1988). *Professional and ethical issues in counseling and psychotherapy* (3rd ed.). Pacific Grove, CA: Brooks/Cole.

Cormier, L. S., & Cormier, W. H. (1975). *Behavioral counseling: Operant procedures, self-management strategies, and recent innovations.* Boston: Houghton Mifflin.

Cormier, L. S., Cormier, W. H., & Weisser, R. J., Jr. (1984). *Interviewing and helping skills for health professionals.* Monterey, CA: Wadsworth Health Sciences.

Cormier, W. H., & Cormier, L. S. (1975). *Behavioral counseling: Initial procedures, individual and group strategies.* Boston: Houghton Mifflin.

Cornish, R. D., & Dilley, J. S. (1973). Comparison of three methods of reducing test anxiety: Systematic desensitization, implosive therapy, and study counseling. *Journal of Counseling Psychology, 20,* 499–503.

Corrigan, J. D., Dell, D. M., Lewis, K. N., & Schmidt, L. D. (1980). Counseling as a social influence process: A review. *Journal of Counseling Psychology, 27,* 395–441.

Cotharin, R., & Mikulas, W. (1975). Systematic desensitization of racial emotional responses. *Journal of Behavior Therapy and Experimental Psychiatry, 6,* 347–348.

Cozby, P. C. (1973). Self-disclosure: A literature review. *Psychological Bulletin, 79,* 73–91.

Craigie, F. C., Jr., & Ross, S. M. (1980). The case of a video-tape pretherapy training program to encourage treatment-seeking among alcohol detoxification patients. *Behavior Therapy, 11,* 141–147.

Credidio, S. G. (1982). Comparative effectiveness of patterned biofeedback vs. meditation training on EMG and skin temperature changes. *Behaviour Research and Therapy, 20,* 233–241.

Cronbach, L. J. (1970). *Essentials of psychological testing* (3rd ed.). New York: Harper & Row.

Cronbach, L. J. (1975). Beyond the two disciplines of scientific psychology. *American Psychologist, 30,* 116–127.

Cronbach, L. J. (1984). *Essentials of psychological testing* (4th ed.). New York: Harper & Row.

Cullen, C. (1983). Implications of functional analysis. *British Journal of Clinical Psychology, 22,* 137–138.

Cureton, E. E. (1951). Validity. In E. F. Lindquist (Ed.), *Educational measurement* (pp. 621–694). Washington, DC: American Council on Education.

Curran, J. P. (1975). Social skills training and systematic desensitization in reducing dating anxiety. *Behaviour Research and Therapy, 13,* 65–68.

Daniels, L. K. (1974). A single session desensitization without relaxation training. *Journal of Behavior Therapy and Experimental Psychiatry, 5,* 207–208.

D'Augelli, A., D'Augelli, J., & Danish, S. (1981). *Helping others.* Pacific Grove, CA: Brooks/Cole.

Davis, A., Rosenthal, T. L., & Kelley, J. E. (1981). Actual fear cues, prompt therapy, and rationale enhance participant modeling with adolescents. *Behavior Therapy, 12,* 536–542.

Davis, J. R., & Glaros, A. G. (1986). Relapse prevention and smoking cessation. *Addictive Behaviors, 11,* 105–114.

Davis, R. (1979). The impact of self-modeling on problem behaviors in school-age children. *School Psychology Digest, 8,* 128–132.

Davison, G. C., & Wilson, G. T. (1973). Processes of fear-reduction in systematic desensitization: Cognitive and social reinforcement factors in humans. *Behavior Therapy, 4,* 1–21.

Dawidoff, D. J. (1973). *The malpractice of psychiatrists.* Springfield, IL: Charles C Thomas.

Dawley, H. H., & Wenrich, W. W. (1973). *Patient's manual for systematic desensitization.* Palo Alto, CA: Veterans' Workshop.

Day, R. W., & Sparacio, R. T. (1980). Structuring the counseling process. *Personnel and Guidance Journal, 59,* 246–250.

Deffenbacher, J. L., & Hahnloser, R. M. (1981). Cognitive and relaxation coping skills in stress inoculation. *Cognitive Therapy and Research, 5,* 211–215.

Deffenbacher, J. L., & Suinn, R. M. (1982). The self-control of anxiety. In P. Karoly & F. H. Kanfer (Eds.), *Self-management and behavior change* (pp. 393–442). New York: Pergamon Press.

Delmonte, M. M., & Kenny, V. (1987). Conceptual models and functions of meditation in psychotherapy. *Journal of Contemporary Psychotherapy, 17,* 38–59.

Dengrove, E. (1966). *Treatment of non-phobic disorders by the behavioral therapies.* Paper presented at the meeting of the Association for Advancement of Behavior Therapy, New York.

Denholtz, M., & Mann, E. (1974). An audiovisual program for group desensitization. *Journal of Behavior Therapy and Experimental Psychiatry, 5,* 27–29.

Denney, D. R., & Rupert, P. (1977). Desensitization and self-control in the treatment of test anxiety. *Journal of Counseling Psychology, 24,* 272–280.

Denniston, D., & McWilliams, P. (1975). *The TM book.* New York: Warner Books.

Dentch, G. E., O'Farrell, T. J., & Cutter, H. S. G. (1980). Readability of marital assessment measures used by behavioral marriage therapists. *Journal of Consulting and Clinical Psychology, 48,* 790–792.

Derogatis, L. R., Rickels, K., & Rock, A. F. (1976). The SCL-90 and the MMPI: A step in the validation of a new self-report scale. *British Journal of Psychiatry, 128,* 280–289.

Devine, D. A., & Fernald, P. S. (1973). Outcome effects of receiving a preferred, randomly assigned, or non-preferred therapy. *Journal of Consulting and Clinical Psychology, 41,* 104–107.

Dittmann, A. T. (1962). The relationship between body movements and moods in interviews. *Journal of Consulting Psychology, 26,* 480.

Dixon, D. N., & Glover, J. A. (1984). *Counseling: A problem-solving approach.* New York: Wiley.

Dobson, K. S. (Ed.). (1988). *Handbook of cognitive behavioral therapies.* New York: Guilford Press.

Dorn, F. J. (1984a). *Counseling as applied social psychology: An introduction to the social influence model.* Springfield, IL: Charles C Thomas.

Dorn, F. J. (1984b). The social influence model: A social psychological approach to counseling. *Personnel and Guidance Journal, 62,* 342–345.

Doster, J. A., & Nesbitt, J. G. (1979). Psychotherapy and self-disclosure. In G. J. Chelune (Ed.), *Self-disclosure: Origins, patterns, and implications of openness in interpersonal relationships.* San Francisco: Jossey-Bass.

Dowd, E. T., & Milne, C. R. (1986). Paradoxical interventions in counseling psychology. *The Counseling Psychologist, 14,* 237–282.

Dowrick, P. W., & Dove, C. (1980). The use of self-modeling to improve the swimming performance of spina bifida children. *Journal of Applied Behavior Analysis, 13,* 51–56.

Duhl, F. J., Kantor, D., & Duhl, B. S. (1973). Learning, space and action in family therapy: A primer of sculpture. In D. A. Bloch (Ed.), *Techniques of family psychotherapy.* New York: Grune & Stratton.

Duley, S. M., Cancelli, A. A., Kratochwill, T. R., Bergan, J. R., & Meredith, K. E. (1983). Training and generalization of motivational analysis interview assessment skills. *Behavioral Assessment, 5,* 281–293.

Duncan, S. P., Jr. (1972). Some signals and rules for taking speaking turns in conversations. *Journal of Personality and Social Psychology, 23,* 283–292.

Duncan, S. P., Jr. (1974). On the structure of speaker-auditor interaction during speaking turns. *Language in Society, 2,* 161–180.

Dunlap, K. (1928). A revision of the fundamental law of habit formation. *Science, 57,* 360–362.

Dush, D. M., Hirt, M. L., & Schroeder, H. (1983). Self-statement modification with adults: A meta-analysis. *Psychological Bulletin, 94,* 408–422.

Dyer, W. W. (1976). *Your erroneous zones.* New York: Funk & Wagnalls.

Dyer, W. W., & Vriend, J. (1975). *Counseling techniques that work.* Washington, DC: American Personnel and Guidance Association.

D'Zurilla, T. J. (1988). Problem-solving therapies. In K. D. Dobson (Ed.), *Handbook of cognitive-behavioral therapies* (pp. 85–135). New York: Guilford Press.

D'Zurilla, T. J. (1986). *Problem-solving therapy: A social competence approach to clinical intervention.* New York: Springer.

Eberle, T., Rehm, L., & McBurney, D. (1975). Fear decrement to anxiety hierarchy items: Effects of stimulus intensity. *Behaviour Research and Therapy, 13,* 225–261.

Edelstein, B. A., Couture, E. T., Cray, M., Dickens, P., & Lusebrink, N. (1980). Group training as problem-solving with chronic psychiatric patients. In D. Upper & S. Ross (Eds.), *Behavioral group therapy: An annual review* (Vol. 2). Champaign, IL: Research Press.

Edelstein, B. A., & Eisler, R. (1976). Effects of modeling and modeling with instructions and feedback on the behavioral components of social skills. *Behavioral Therapy, 7,* 382–389.

Egan, G. (1975). *The skilled helper: A model for systematic helping and interpersonal relating.* Pacific Grove, CA: Brooks/Cole.

Egan, G. (1976). *Interpersonal living: A skills contract approach to human-relations training in groups.* Pacific Grove, CA: Brooks/Cole.

Egan, G. (1990). *The skilled helper: Model, skills, and methods for effective helping* (4th ed.). Pacific Grove, CA.: Brooks/Cole.

Egan, K. J., Carr, J. E., Hunt, D. D., & Adamson, R. (1988). Endogenous opiate system and systematic desensitization. *Journal of Consulting and Clinical Psychology, 56,* 287–291.

Eisenberg, S., & Delaney, D. J. (1977). *The counseling process* (2nd ed.). Chicago: Rand McNally.

Eisler, R. M., & Frederiksen, L. W. (1980). *Perfecting social skills: A guide to interpersonal behavior development.* New York: Plenum.

Ekman, P. (1964). Body position, facial expression and verbal behavior during interviews. *Journal of Abnormal and Social Psychology, 68,* 295–301.

Ekman, P., & Friesen, W. V. (1967). Head and body cues in the judgment of emotion: A reformulation. *Perceptual and Motor Skills, 24,* 711–724.

Ekman, P., & Friesen, W. V. (1969a). Nonverbal leakage and clues to deception. *Psychiatry, 32,* 88–106.

Ekman, P., & Friesen, W. V. (1969b). The repertoire of nonverbal behavior: Categories, origins, usage, and coding. *Semiotica, 1,* 49–98.

Ekman, P., & Friesen, W. V. (1972). Hand movements. *Journal of Communication, 22,* 353–374.

Ekman, P., & Friesen, W. V. (1975). *Unmasking the face.* Englewood Cliffs, NJ: Prentice-Hall.

Ekman, P., Friesen, W. V., & Ellsworth, P. (1972). *Emotion and the human face: Guidelines for research and an integration of findings.* New York: Pergamon Press.

Ekman, P., Friesen, W. V., & Tomkins, S. S. (1971). Facial affect scoring technique: A first validity study. *Semiotica, 3,* 37–58.

Elder, J. P. (1978). *Comparison of cognitive restructuring and response acquisition in the enhancement of social competence in college freshmen.* Unpublished doctoral dissertation, West Virginia University, Morgantown.

Elder, J. P., Edelstein, B. A., & Fremouw, W. J. (1981). Client by treatment interactions in response acquisition and cognitive restructuring approaches. *Cognitive Therapy and Research, 5,* 203–210.

Elliott, R. (1980). *Therapy session report: Short-forms for client and therapist.* Unpublished instrument, University of Toledo, Toledo, Ohio.

Elliott, R., Barker, C. B., Caskey, N., & Pistrang, N. (1982). Differential helpfulness of counselor verbal response modes. *Journal of Counseling Psychology, 29,* 354–361.

Elliott, R., Filipovich, H., Harrigan, L., Gaynor, J., Reimschuessel, C., & Zapadka, J. (1982). Measuring response empathy: The development of a multicomponent rating scale. *Journal of Counseling Psychology, 29,* 379–389.

Ellis, A. (1974). *Humanistic psychotherapy.* New York: McGraw-Hill.

Ellis, A. (1975). *Growth through reason.* North Hollywood, CA: Wilshire Book Company.

Ellis, A. (1984). *Rational-emotive therapy and cognitive behavior therapy.* New York: Springer.

Ellis, A. (1985). Approaches to overcoming resistance: Handling special kinds of clients. *British Journal of Cognitive Psychotherapy, 3,* 26–42.

Ellis, A., & Grieger, R. (1977). *Handbook of rational-emotive therapy.* New York: Springer.

Elmore, R. T., Wildman, R. W., & Westefeld, J. S. (1980). The use of systematic desensitization in the treatment of blood phobia. *Journal of Behavior Therapy and Experimental Psychiatry, 11,* 277–279.

Emery, J. R., & Krumboltz, J. D. (1967). Standard versus individualized hierarchies in desensitization to reduce test anxiety. *Journal of Counseling Psychology, 14,* 204–209.

Epstein, N. B., & Bishop, D. S. (1981). Problem-centered systems therapy of the family. *Journal of Marital and Family Therapy, 7,* 23–31.

Eriksen, L., Björnstad, S., & Götestam, K. G. (1986). Social skills training in groups for alcoholics: One-year treatment outcome for groups and individuals. *Addictive Behaviors, 11,* 309–329.

Erickson, F. (1975). One function of proxemic shifts in face-to-face interaction. In A. Kendon, R. M. Harris, & M. R. Keys (Eds.), *Organization of behavior in face to face interactions* (pp. 175–187). Chicago: Aldine.

Erickson, M. H., Rossi, E., & Rossi, S. (1976). *Hypnotic realities.* New York: Irvington.

Etringer, B. D., Cash, T. F., & Rimm, D. C. (1982). Behavioral, affective, and cognitive effects of participant modeling and an equally credible placebo. *Behavior Therapy, 13,* 476–485.

Evans, I. M. (1974). A handy record-card for systematic desensitization hierarchy items. *Journal of Behavior Therapy and Experimental Psychiatry, 5,* 43–46.

Evans, R. (1970). Exhibitionism. In G. C. Costello (Ed.), *Symptoms of psychopathology: A handbook.* New York: Wiley.

Ewart, C. K., Taylor, C. B., Kraemer, H. C., & Agras, W. S. (1984). Reducing blood pressure reactivity during interpersonal conflict: Effects of marital communication training. *Behavior Therapy, 15,* 473–484.

Exline, R. V., & Winters, L. C. (1965). Affective relations and mutual glances in dyads. In S. S. Tompkins & C. E. Izard (Eds.), *Affect, cognition, and personality.* New York: Springer.

Falzett, W. C. (1981). Matched versus unmatched primary representational systems and their relationship to perceived trustworthiness in a counseling analogue. *Journal of Counseling Psychology, 28,* 305–308.

Fay, A. (1980). *The invisible diet.* New York: Manor Books.

Feindler, E. L., & Ecton, R. B. (1986). *Adolescent anger control.* New York: Pergamon Press.

Feindler, E. L., & Fremouw, W. J. (1983). Stress inoculation training for adolescent problems. In D. Meichenbaum & M. E. Jaremko (Eds.), *Stress reduction and prevention* (pp. 451–485). New York: Plenum.

Fensterheim, H. (1983). Basic paradigms, behavioral formulation and basic procedures. In H. Fensterheim & H. Glazer (Eds.), *Behavioral psychotherapy. Basic principles and case studies in an integrative clinical model* (pp. 40–87). New York: Brunner/Mazel.

Ferguson, J. M., Marquis, J. N., & Taylor, C. B. (1977). A script for deep muscle relaxation. *Diseases of the Nervous System, 38,* 703–708.

Ferster, C. B., Nurnberger, J. I., & Levitt, E. B. (1962). The control of eating. *Journal of Mathetics, 1,* 87–109.

Fisch, R., Weakland, J., & Segal, L. (1982). *The tactics of change: Doing therapy briefly.* San Francisco: Jossey-Bass.

Fishman, S. T., & Lubetkin, B. S. (1983). Office practice of behavior therapy. In M. Hersen (Ed.), *Outpatient behavior therapy: A clinical guide.* New York: Grune & Stratton.

Fling, S., Thomas, A., & Gallaher, M. (1981). Participant characteristics and the effects of two types of meditation vs. quiet sitting. *Journal of Clinical Psychology, 37,* 784–790.

Flowers, J. V., & Booraem, C. D. (1980). Simulation and role playing methods. In F. A. Kanfer & A. P. Goldstein (Eds.), *Helping people change* (pp. 172–209). New York: Pergamon Press.

Foa, E. B., Steketee, G. S., & Ascher, L. M. (1980). Systematic desensitization. In A. Goldstein & E. B. Foa (Eds.), *Handbook of behavioral interventions: A clinical guide* (pp. 38–91). New York: Wiley.

Fong, M. L., & Cox, B. G. (1983). Trust as an underlying dynamic in the counseling process: How clients test trust. *Personnel and Guidance Journal, 62,* 163–166.

Forman, S. G. (1980). A comparison of cognitive training and response cost procedures in modifying aggressive behavior of elementary school children. *Behavior Therapy, 11,* 594–600.

Forsyth, N. L., & Forsyth, D. R. (1982). Internality, controllability, and the effectiveness of attributional interpretations in counseling. *Journal of Counseling Psychology, 29,* 140–150.

Foster, S. L., Prinz, R. J., & O'Leary, K. D. (1983). Impact of problem-solving communication training and generalization procedures on family conflict. *Child and Family Behavior Therapy, 5,* 1–23.

Framer, E. M., & Sanders, S. H. (1980). The effects of family contingency contracting on disturbed sleeping behaviors of a male adolescent. *Journal of Behavior Therapy and Experimental Psychiatry, 11,* 235–237.

Frank, E., Anderson, B., Stewart, B. D., Dancu, C., Hughes, C., & West, D. (1988). Efficacy of cognitive behavior therapy and systematic desensitization in the treatment of rape trauma. *Behavior Therapy, 19,* 403–420.

Frank, J. D. (1961). *Persuasion and healing.* Baltimore: Johns Hopkins Press.

Frankl, V. (1960). Paradoxical intention: A logotherapeutic technique. *American Journal of Psychotherapy, 14,* 520–535.

Frederiksen, L. W. (1975). Treatment of ruminative thinking by self-monitoring. *Journal of Behavior Therapy and Experimental Psychiatry, 6,* 258–259.

Frederiksen, L. W., Epstein, L. H., & Kosevsky, B. P. (1975). Reliability and controlling effects of three procedures for self-monitoring smoking. *Psychological Record, 25,* 255–264.

Freedman, N. (1972). The analysis of movement behavior during the clinical interview. In A. W. Siegman & B. Pope (Eds.), *Studies in dyadic communication.* New York: Pergamon Press.

Freeman, A. (1981). Dreams and images in cognitive therapy. In G. Emery, S. D. Hollon, & R. C. Bedrosian (Eds.), *New directions in cognitive therapy* (pp. 224–238). New York: Guilford Press.

Fremouw, W. J. (1977). A client manual for integrated behavior treatment of speech anxiety. *JSAS Catalogue of Selected Documents in Psychology, 1,* 14.MS.1426.

Fremouw, W. J., & Brown, J. P., Jr. (1980). The reactivity of addictive behaviors to self-monitoring: A functional analysis. *Addictive Behaviors, 5,* 209–217.

Fremouw, W. J., Callahan, E. J., Zitter, R. E., & Katell, A. (1981). Stimulus control and contingency contracting for behavior change and weight loss. *Addictive Behaviors, 6,* 289–300.

Fremouw, W. J., & Harmatz, M. G. (1975). A helper model for behavioral treatment of speech anxiety. *Journal of Consulting and Clinical Psychology, 43,* 652–660.

Fremouw, W. J., & Heyneman, N. (1983). Obesity. In M. Hersen (Ed.), *Outpatient behavior therapy* (pp. 173–202). New York: Grune & Stratton.

Fremouw, W. J., & Zitter, R. E. (1978). A comparison of skills training and cognitive restructuring-relaxation for the treatment of speech anxiety. *Behavior Therapy, 9,* 248–259.

Fretz, B. R., Corn, R., Tuemmler, J. M., & Bellet, W. (1979). Counselor nonverbal behaviors and client evaluations. *Journal of Counseling Psychology, 26,* 304–311.

Freud, S. (1952). *A general introduction to psychoanalysis.* New York: Washington Square Press. (Original work published 1900)

Frey, D. H. (1975). The anatomy of an idea: Creativity in counseling. *Personnel and Guidance Journal, 54,* 22–27.

Frey, D. H., & Raming, H. E. (1979). A taxonomy of counseling goals and methods. *Personnel and Guidance Journal, 58,* 26–33.

Galassi, J. P., Delo, J. S., Galassi, M. D., & Bastien, S. (1974). The college self-expression scale: A measure of assertiveness. *Behavior Therapy, 5,* 165–171.

Galassi, M. D., & Galassi, J. P. (1976). The effects of role playing variations on the assessment of assertive behavior. *Behavior Therapy, 7,* 343–347.

Galassi, M. D., & Galassi, J. P. (1977). *Assert yourself! How to be your own person.* New York: Human Sciences.

Gallagher, J. W., & Arkowitz, H. (1978). Weak effects of covert modeling treatment of test anxiety. *Journal of Behavior Therapy and Experimental Psychiatry, 9,* 23–26.

Gambrill, E. D. (1977). *Behavior modification: Handbook of assessment, intervention, and evaluation.* San Francisco: Jossey-Bass.

Gambrill, E. D., & Richey, C. (1975). An assertion inventory for use in assessment and research. *Behavior Therapy, 6,* 550–561.

Gatchel, R. J., Gaffney, F. A., & Smith, J. E. (1986). Comparative efficacy of behavioral stress management versus propranolol in reducing psychophysiological reactivity in post-myocardial infarction patients. *Journal of Behavioral Medicine, 9,* 503–513.

Gazda, G. M., Asbury, F. S., Balzer, F. J., Childers, W. C., & Walters, R. P. (1977). *Human relations development.* (2nd ed.). Boston: Allyn & Bacon.

Gazda, G. M., Asbury, F. S., Balzer, F. J., Childers, W. C., & Walters, R. P. (1984). *Human relations development: A manual for educators* (3rd ed.). Boston: Allyn & Bacon.

Geer, C. A., & Hurst, J. C. (1976). Counselor-subject sex variables in systematic desensitization. *Journal of Counseling Psychology, 23,* 296–301.

Geis, G. L., & Chapman, R. (1971). Knowledge of results and other possible reinforcers in self-instructional systems. *Educational Technology, 11,* 38–50.

Gelatt, H., Varenhorst, B., Carey, R., & Miller, G. (1973). *Decisions and outcomes: A leader's guide.* Princeton, NJ: College Entrance Examination Board.

Gelder, M. G., Bancroft, J. H. J., Gath, D. H., Johnson, D. W., Matthews, A. M., & Shaw, P. M. (1973). Specific and non-specific factors in behavior therapy. *British Journal of Psychiatry, 123,* 445–462.

George, R., & Cristiani, T. (1981). *Theory, methods, and processes of counseling and psychotherapy.* Englewood Cliffs, NJ: Prentice-Hall.

Gershman, L., & Clouser, R. A. (1974). Treating insomnia with relaxation and desentitization in a group setting by an automated approach. *Journal of Behavior Therapy and Experimental Psychiatry, 5,* 31–35.

Gershman, L., & Stedman, J. M. (1976). Using Kung Fu to reduce anxiety in a claustrophobic male. In J. D. Krumboltz & C. E. Thoresen (Eds.), *Counseling methods* (pp. 312–316). New York: Holt, Rinehart and Winston.

Gilbert, B. O., Johnson, S. B., Spillar, R., McCallum, M., Silverstein, J. H., & Rosenbloom, A. (1982). The effects of a peer-modeling film on children learning to self-inject insulin. *Behavior Therapy, 13,* 186–193.

Gillen, R. W., & Heimberg, R. G. (1980). Social skills training for the job interview: Review and prospectus. In M. Hersen, R. M. Eisler, & P. M. Miller, *Progress in behavior modification* (Vol. 10) (pp. 183–206). New York: Academic Press.

Gilliland, B. E., James, R. K., & Bowman, J. T. (1989). *Theories and strategies in counseling and psychotherapy* (2nd ed.). Englewood Cliffs, NJ: Prentice-Hall.

Girodo, M. (1974). Yoga meditation and flooding in the treatment of anxiety neurosis. *Journal of Behavior Therapy and Experimental Psychiatry, 5,* 157–160.

Gladstein, G. (1983). Understanding empathy: Integrating counseling, developmental, and social psychology perspectives. *Journal of Counseling Psychology, 30,* 467–482.

Glaister, B. (1982). Muscle relaxation training for fear reduction of patients with psychological problems: A review of controlled studies. *Behaviour Research and Therapy, 20,* 493–504.

Glasgow, R. E. & Rosen, G. M. (1978). Behavioral bibliotherapy: A review of self-help behavior therapy manuals. *Psychological Bulletin, 85,* 1–23.

Glasgow, R. E., & Rosen, G. M. (1979). Self-help behavior therapy manuals: Recent developments and clinical usage. *Clinical Behavior Therapy Review, 1,* 1–20.

Glogower, F. D., Fremouw, W. J., & McCroskey, J. C. (1978). A component analysis of cognitive restructuring. *Cognitive Therapy and Research, 2,* 209–223.

Goldfried, M. R. (1971). Systematic desensitization as training in self-control. *Journal of Consulting and Clinical Psychology, 37,* 228–234.

Goldfried, M. R. (1976a). Behavioral assessment. In I. B. Weiner (Ed.), *Clinical methods in psychology.* New York: Wiley.

Goldfried, M. R. (1976b). *Exercise manual and log for self-modification of anxiety: To accompany audio cassette #T44B.* New York: Biomonitoring Applications.

Goldfried, M. R. (1977). The use of relaxation and cognitive relabeling as coping skills. In R. B. Stuart (Ed.), *Behavioral self-management: Strategies, techniques and outcomes* (pp. 82–116). New York: Brunner/Mazel.

Goldfried, M. R. (1982). Behavioral assessment: An overview. In A. S. Bellack, M. Hersen, & A. E. Kazdin (Eds.), *International handbook of behavior modification and therapy.* New York: Plenum.

Goldfried, M. R. (1983). The behavior therapist in clinical practice. *Behavior Therapist, 6,* 45–46.

Goldfried, M. R., & Davison, G. C. (1976). *Clinical behavior therapy.* New York: Holt, Rinehart and Winston.

Goldfried, M. R., Decenteceo, E. T., & Weinberg, L. (1974). Systematic rational restructuring as a self-control technique. *Behavior Therapy, 5,* 247–254.

Goldfried, M. R., & Goldfried, A. P. (1977). Importance of hierarchy content in the self-control of anxiety. *Journal of Consulting and Clinical Psychology, 45,* 124–134.

Goldfried, M. R., & Goldfried, A. P. (1980). Cognitive change methods. In F. H. Kanfer & A. P. Goldstein (Eds.), *Helping people change* (pp. 97–130). New York: Pergamon Press.

Goldfried, M. R., Linehan, M. M., & Smith, J. L. (1978). The reduction of test anxiety through cognitive restructuring. *Journal of Consulting and Clinical Psychology, 46,* 32–39.

Goldfried, M. R., & Padawer, W. (1982). Current status and future directions in psychotherapy. In M. R. Goldfried (Ed.), *Converging themes in the practice of psychotherapy* (pp. 3–49). New York: Springer.

Goldiamond, I. (1965). Self-control procedures in personal behavior problems. *Psychological Reports, 17,* 851–868.

Goldiamond, I., & Dyrud, J. E. (1967). Some applications and implications of behavioral analysis in psychotherapy. In J. Schlein (Ed.), *Research in psychotherapy* (Vol.

3). Washington, DC: American Psychological Association.

Goldstein, A. J., Serber, M., & Piaget, G. (1970). Induced anger as a reciprocal inhibitor of fear. *Journal of Behavior Therapy and Experimental Psychiatry, 1,* 67–70.

Goldstein, A. P. (1971). *Psychotherapeutic attraction.* New York: Pergamon Press.

Goldstein, A. P. (1986). Relationship-enhancement methods. In F. H. Kanfer & A. P. Goldstein (Eds.), *Helping people change* (3rd ed.) (pp. 19–65). New York: Pergamon Press.

Goldstein, A. P., & Stein, N. (1976). *Prescriptive psychotherapies.* New York: Pergamon Press.

Goodwin, D. L. (1969). Consulting with the classroom teacher. In J. D. Krumboltz & C. E. Thoresen (Eds.), *Behavioral counseling: Cases and techniques* (pp. 260–264). New York: Holt, Rinehart and Winston.

Goodyear, R. K., & Bradley, F. O. (1980). The helping process as contractual. *Personnel and Guidance Journal, 58,* 512–515.

Goodyear, R. K., & Robyak, J. (1981). Counseling as an interpersonal influence process: A perspective for counseling practice. *Personnel and Guidance Journal, 60,* 654–657.

Gordon, D. (1978). *Therapeutic metaphors.* Cupertino, CA: Meta Publications.

Gormally, J., & Rardin, D. (1981). Weight loss and maintenance and changes in diet and exercise for behavioral counseling and nutrition education. *Journal of Counseling Psychology, 28,* 295–304.

Gormally, J., Varvil-Weld, D., Raphael R., & Sipps, G. (1981). Treatment of socially anxious college men using cognitive counseling and skills training. *Journal of Counseling Psychology, 28,* 147–157.

Gottman, J. M., & Leiblum, S. R. (1974). *How to do psychotherapy and how to evaluate it.* New York: Holt, Rinehart and Winston.

Graves, J. R., & Robinson, J. D. (1976). Proxemic behavior as a function of inconsistent verbal and nonverbal messages. *Journal of Counseling Psychology, 23,* 333–338.

Green, K. D., Webster, J., Beeman, I., Rosmarin, D., & Holliway, P. (1981). Progressive and self-induced relaxation training: Their relative effects on subjective and autonomic arousal to fearful stimuli. *Journal of Clinical Psychology, 37,* 309–315.

Green, L. (1982). Minority students' self-control of procrastination. *Journal of Counseling Psychology, 29,* 636–644.

Greenberg, I., & Altman, J. (1976). Modifying smoking behavior through stimulus control: A case report. *Journal of Behavior Therapy and Experimental Psychiatry, 7,* 97–99.

Greenberg, L. S., & Safran, J. D. (1981). Encoding and cognitive therapy: Changing what clients attend to. *Psychotherapy: Theory, Research & Practice, 18,* 163–169.

Greiner, J., & Karoly, P. (1976). Effects of self-control training on study activity and academic performance: An analysis of self-monitoring, self-reward and systematic-planning components. *Journal of Counseling Psychology, 23,* 495–502.

Gresham, F. M., & Nagle, R. J. (1980). Social skills training with children: Responsiveness of modeling and coaching as a function of peer orientation. *Journal of Consulting and Clinical Psychology, 48,* 718–729.

Grinder, J., & Bandler, R. (1976). *The structure of magic II.* Palo Alto, CA: Science and Behavior Books.

Gurman, A. S. (1981). Using "paradox" in psychodynamic marital therapy. In A. S. Gurman (Ed.), *Questions and answers in the practice of family therapy,* Vol. 1 (pp. 119–122). New York: Brunner/Mazel.

Gurman, A. S. (Ed.) (1982). *Questions and answers in the practice of family therapy* (Vol. 2). New York: Brunner/Mazel.

Haase, R. F., & Tepper, D. (1972). Nonverbal components of empathic communication. *Journal of Counseling Psychology, 19,* 417–424.

Hackett, G., & Horan, J. J. (1980). Stress inoculation for pain: What's really going on? *Journal of Counseling Psychology, 27,* 107–116.

Hackett, G., Horan, J. J., Stone, C., Linberg, S., Nicholas, W., & Lukaski, H. (1976). *Further outcomes and tentative predictor variables from an evolving comprehensive program for the behavioral control of smoking.* Paper presented at the annual meeting of the American Educational Research Association, San Francisco.

Hackney, H., & Cormier, L. S. (1988). *Counseling strategies and interventions* (3rd ed.). Englewood Cliffs, NJ: Prentice-Hall.

Haley, J. (1963). *Strategies of psychotherapy.* New York: Grune & Stratton.

Haley, J. (1967). *Advanced techniques of hypnosis and therapy: Selected papers of Milton H. Erickson, M.D.* New York: Grune & Stratton.

Haley, J. (1973). *Uncommon therapy: The psychiatric techniques of Milton Erickson, M.D.* New York: Norton.

Haley, J. (1976). *Problem-solving therapy.* San Francisco: Jossey-Bass.

Haley, J. (1978). Ideas which handicap therapists. In M. M. Berger (Ed.), *Beyond the double bind: Communication and family systems, theories, and techniques with schizophrenics.* New York: Brunner/Mazel.

Haley, J. (1984). *Ordeal therapy.* San Francisco: Jossey-Bass.

Hall, E. T. (1963). A system for the notation of proxemic behavior. *American Anthropologist, 65,* 1003–1026.

Hall, E. T. (1966). *The hidden dimension.* Garden City, NY: Doubleday.

Hamilton, S. A., & Fremouw, W. J. (1985). Cognitive-behavioral training for college basketball foul-shooting performance. *Cognitive Therapy and Research, 9,* 479–483.

Hammer, A. (1983). Matching perceptual predicates: Effect on perceived empathy in a counseling analogue. *Journal of Counseling Psychology, 30,* 172–179.

Hansen, J. C., Stevic, R. R., & Warner, R. W., Jr. (1977). *Counseling theory and process* (2nd ed.). Boston: Allyn & Bacon.

Hare-Mustin, R. T., Maracek, J., Kaplan, A. G., & Liss-Levinson, N. (1979). Rights of clients, responsibilities of therapists. *American Psychologist, 34,* 3–16.

Harper, R. G., Wiens, A. N., & Matarazzo, J. D. (1978). *Nonverbal communication: The state of the art.* New York: Wiley.

Harris, G. M., & Johnson, S. B. (1983). Coping imagery and relaxation instructions in a covert modeling treatment for text anxiety. *Behavior Therapy, 14,* 144–157.

Harvill, R., Jacobs, E., & Masson, R. (1984). Using "props" to enhance your counseling. *Personnel and Guidance Journal, 62,* 273–275.

Hathaway, S. R., & McKinley, J. C. (1951). *MMPI manual.* New York: Psychological Corporation.

Hawkins, R. P., & Dobes, R. W. (1977). Behavioral definitions in applied behavior analysis: Explicit or implicit. In B. C. Etzel, J. M. LeBlanc, & D. M. Baer (Eds.), *New developments in behavioral research: Theory, method, and application* (pp. 167–188). Hillsdale, NJ: Erlbaum.

Hay, W. M., Hay, L. R., Angle, H. V., & Nelson, R. O. (1979). The reliability of problem identification in the behavioral interview. *Behavioral Assessment, 1,* 107–118.

Hay, W. M., Hay, L. R., & Nelson, R. O. (1977). The adaptation of covert modeling procedures to the treatment of chronic alcoholism and obsessive-compulsive behavior: Two case reports. *Behavior Therapy, 8,* 70–76.

Hayes, S. C. (1981). Single case experimental design and empirical clinical practice. *Journal of Consulting and Clinical Psychology, 49,* 193–211.

Hayes, S. C. (1985). Self-reinforcement effects: An artifact of social standard setting. *Journal of Applied Behavior Analysis, 18,* 201–214.

Haynes, S. N. (1978). *Principles of behavioral assessment.* New York: Gardner Press.

Haynes, S. N., & Jensen, B. J. (1979). The interview as a behavioral assessment instrument. *Behavioral Assessment, 1,* 97–106.

Haynes, S. N., Jensen, B. J., Wise, E., & Sherman. D. (1981). The marital intake interview: A multimethod criterion validity assessment. *Journal of Consulting and Clinical Psychology, 49,* 379–387.

Haynes, S. N., & Wilson, C. C. (1979). *Behavioral assessment.* San Francisco: Jossey-Bass.

Hays, V., & Waddell, K. J. (1976). A self-reinforcing procedure for thought stopping. *Behavior Therapy, 7,* 559.

Hearn, M., & Evans, D. (1972). Anger and reciprocal inhibition therapy. *Psychological Reports, 30,* 943–948.

Heffernan, T., & Richards, C. S. (1981). Self-control of study behavior: Identification and evaluation of natural methods. *Journal of Counseling Psychology, 28,* 361–364.

Hein, E. C. (1980). *Communication in nursing practice* (2nd ed.) Boston: Little, Brown.

Heppner, P. P. (1988). *The problem solving inventory.* Palo Alto, CA: Consulting Psychologist Press.

Heppner, P. P., & Dixon, D. N. (1981). Effects of client perceived need and counselor role in clients' behaviors. *Journal of Counseling Psychology, 59,* 542–550.

Heppner, P. P., & Heesacker, M. (1982). Interpersonal influence process in real-life counseling: Investigating client perceptions, counselor experience level, and counselor power over time. *Journal of Counseling Psychology, 29,* 215–223.

Heppner, P. P., & Heesacker, M. (1983). Perceived counselor characteristics, client expectations, and client satisfaction with counseling. *Journal of Counseling Psychology, 30,* 31–39.

Herby, E. M., Ozaki, M., & Campos, P. E. (1984). The effects of training in self-reinforcement and reward: Implications for depression. *Behavior Therapy, 15,* 544–549.

Hersen, M. (1971). Resistance to direction in behavior therapy: Some comments. *Journal of Genetic Psychology, 118,* 121–127.

Hersen, M., & Barlow, D. H. (1976). *Single-case experimental designs: Strategies for studying behavior change.* New York: Pergamon Press.

Hersen, M., & Bellack, A. S. (Eds.). (1976). *Behavioral assessment: A practical handbook.* New York: Pergamon Press.

Hersen, M., & Bellack, A. S. (Eds.). (1981). *Behavioral assessment: A practical handbook* (2nd ed.). New York: Pergamon Press.

Hess, E. H. (1975). *The tell-tale eye.* New York: Van Nostrand Reinhold.

Hiebert, B., & Fox, E. E. (1981). Reactive effects of self-monitoring anxiety. *Journal of Counseling Psychology, 28,* 187–193.

Higgins, R. L., Frisch, M. B., & Smith, D. (1983). A comparison of role-played and natural responses to identical circumstances. *Behavior Therapy, 14,* 148–169.

Highlen, P. S., & Baccus, G. K. (1977). Effect of reflection of feeling and probe on client self-referenced affect. *Journal of Counseling Psychology, 24,* 440–443.

Hill, C. E. (1975). A process approach for establishing counseling goals and outcomes. *Personnel and Guidance Journal, 53,* 571–576.

Hill, C. E., Carter, J. A., & O'Farrell, M. K. (1983). A case study of the process and outcome of time-limited counseling. *Journal of Counseling Psychology, 30,* 3–18.

Hill, C. E., & Gormally, J. (1977). Effects of reflection, restatement, probe, and nonverbal behaviors on client affect. *Journal of Counseling Psychology, 24,* 92–97.

Hill, C. E., Siegelman, L., Gronsky, B. R., Sturniolo, F., & Fretz, B. R. (1981). Nonverbal communication and counseling outcome. *Journal of Counseling Psychology, 28,* 203–212.

Hillenberg, J. B., & Collins, F. L., Jr. (1982). A procedural analysis and review of relaxation training research. *Behaviour Research and Therapy, 20,* 251–260.

Hoffman-Graff, M. A. (1977). Interviewer use of positive and negative self-disclosure and interviewer-subject sex pairing. *Journal of Counseling Psychology, 24,* 184–190.

Hollon, S. D., & Kendall, P. C. (1981). In vivo assessment techniques for cognitive-behavioral processes. In P. C. Kendall & S. D. Hollon (Eds.), *Assessment strategies for cognitive-behavioral interventions* (pp. 319–362). New York: Academic Press.

Holroyd, K. A. (1976). Cognition and desensitization in the group treatment of test anxiety. *Journal of Consulting and Clinical Psychology, 44,* 991–1001.

Holroyd, K. A., Appel, M. A., & Andrasik, F. (1983). A cognitive-behavioral approach to psychophysiological disorders. In D. Meichenbaum & M. E. Jaremko (Eds.), *Stress reduction and prevention* (pp. 219–259). New York: Plenum.

Homme, L., Csanyi, A., Gonzales, M., & Rechs, J. (1969). *How to use contingency contracting in the classroom.* Champaign, IL: Research Press.

Hopkins, J., Krawitz, G., & Bellack, A. S. (1981). The effects of situational variations in role-play scenes on assertive behavior. *Journal of Behavioral Assessment, 3,* 271–280.

Horan, J. J. (1973). "In vivo" emotive imagery: A technique for reducing childbirth anxiety and discomfort. *Psychological Reports, 32,* 1328.

Horan, J. J. (1976). Coping with inescapable discomfort through in vivo emotive imagery. In J. D. Krumboltz & C. E. Thoresen (Eds.), *Counseling methods* (pp. 316–320). New York: Holt, Rinehart and Winston.

Horan, J. J., Baker, S. B., Hoffman, A. M., & Shute, R. E. (1975). Weight loss through variations in the coverant control paradigm. *Journal of Counseling and Clinical Psychology, 43,* 68–72.

Horan, J. J., & Dellinger, J. K. (1974). "In vivo" emotive imagery: A preliminary test. *Perceptual and Motor Skills, 39,* 359–362.

Horan, J. J., Hackett, G., Buchanan, J. D., Stone, C. I., & Demchik-Stone, D. (1977). Coping with pain: A component analysis of stress inoculation. *Cognitive Therapy and Research, 1,* 211–221.

Horan, J. J., Layng, F. C., & Pursell, C. H. (1976). Preliminary study of the effects of "in vivo" emotive imagery on dental discomfort. *Perceptual and Motor Skills, 42,* 105–106.

Horne, A. M., & Matson, J. L. (1977). A comparison of modeling, desensitization, flooding, study skills, and control groups for reducing test anxiety. *Behavior Therapy, 8,* 1–8

Horney, K. (1950). *Neurosis and human growth: The struggle toward self-realization.* New York: Norton.

Hosford, R. E. (1969). Overcoming fear of speaking in a group. In J. D. Krumboltz & C. E. Thoresen (Eds.), *Behavioral counseling: Cases and techniques* (pp. 80–83). New York: Holt, Rinehart and Winston.

Hosford, R. E. (1974). *Counseling techniques: Self-as-a-model film.* Washington, DC: American Personnel and Guidance Press.

Hosford, R. E. (1980). Self-as-a-model: A cognitive social learning technique. *Counseling Psychologist, 9,* 45–62.

Hosford, R. E., & de Visser, L. (1974). *Behavioral approaches to counseling: An introduction.* Washington, DC: American Personnel and Guidance Press.

Hosford, R. E., Moss, C., & Morrell, G. (1976). The self-as-a-model technique: Helping prison inmates change. In J. D. Krumboltz & C. E. Thoresen (Eds.), *Counseling methods* (pp. 487–495). New York: Holt, Rinehart and Winston.

Howard, W. A., Murphy, S. M., & Clarke, J. C. (1983). The nature and treatment of fear of flying: A controlled investigation. *Behavior Therapy, 14,* 557–567.

Hubble, M. A., Noble, F. C., & Robinson, S. E. (1981). The effect of counselor touch in an initial counseling session. *Journal of Counseling Psychology, 28,* 533–535.

Huber, C. H., & Milstein, B. (1985). Cognitive restructuring and a collaborative set in couples' work. *American Journal of Family Therapy, 13,* 17–27.

Huck, S. W., Cormier, W. H., & Bounds, W. G. (1974). *Reading statistics and research.* New York: Harper & Row.

Hudson, J., & Danish, S. (1980). The acquisition of information: An important life skill. *Personnel and Guidance Journal, 59,* 164–167.

Hughes, H., & Haynes, S. (1978). Structured laboratory observation in the behavioral assessment of parent-child interactions: A methodological critique. *Behavior Therapy, 9,* 428–447.

Hull, C. L. (1952). *A behavior system.* New Haven, Conn.: Yale University Press.

Hutchins, D. E. (1979). Systematic counseling: The T-F-A model for counselor intervention. *Personnel and Guidance Journal, 57,* 529–531.

Ivey, A. E. (1988). *Intentional interviewing and counseling* (2nd ed.). Pacific Grove, CA: Brooks/Cole.

Ivey, A. E., & Gluckstern, N. (1974). *Basic attending skills: Participant manual.* Amherst, MA: Microtraining Associates.

Ivey, A. E., & Gluckstern, N. (1976). *Basic influencing skills: Participant manual.* Amherst, MA: Microtraining Associates.

Ivey, A. E., Ivey, M. B., & Simek-Downing, L. (1987). *Counseling and psychotherapy: Skills, theories, and practice* (2nd ed.). Englewood Cliffs, NJ: Prentice-Hall.

Jackson, B. (1972). Treatment of depression by self-reinforcement. *Behavior Therapy, 3,* 298–307.

Jackson, D. (1968). *Therapy, communication and change.* Palo Alto, CA: Science and Behavior Books.

Jacobs, M. K., & Cochran, S. D. (1982). The effects of cognitive restructuring on assertive behavior. *Cognitive Therapy and Research, 6,* 63–76.

Jacobsen, R., & Edinger, J. D. (1982). Side effects of relaxation treatment. *American Journal of Psychiatry, 139,* 952–953.

Jacobson, E. (1929). *Progressive relaxation.* Chicago: University of Chicago Press.

Jacobson, E. (1964). *Anxiety and tension control.* Philadelphia: Lippincott.

Jacobson, N. S. (1981). Marital problems. In J. L. Shelton & R. L. Levy (Eds.), *Behavioral assignments and treatment compliance* (pp. 147–166). Champaign, IL: Research Press.

Jacobson, N. S. (1984). A component analysis of marital behavior therapy: The relative effectiveness of behavior change and communication/problem-solving training. *Journal of Consulting and Clinical Psychology, 52,* 295–305.

Jacobson, N. S., & Follette, W. C. (1985). Clinical significance of improvement resulting from two behavioral marital therapy components. *Behavior Therapy, 16,* 249–262.

Jacobson, N. S., & Margolin, G. (1979). *Marital therapy: Strategies based on social learning and behavior exchange princples.* New York: Brunner/Mazel.

Jahn, D. L., & Lichstein, K. L. (1980). The resistive client. *Behavior Modification, 4,* 303–320.

James, J. E. (1981). Self-monitoring of stuttering: Reactivity and accuracy. *Behaviour Research and Therapy, 19,* 291–296.

Janis, I. L. (1983). Stress inoculation in health care: Theory and research. In D. Meichenbaum & M. E. Jaremko

(Eds.), *Stress reduction and prevention* (pp. 67–100). New York: Plenum.

Jannoun, L., Munby, M., Catalan, J., & Gelder, M. (1980). A home-based treatment program for agoraphobia: Replication and controlled evaluation. *Behavior Therapy, 11,* 294–305.

Jaremko, M. E. (1983). Stress inoculation training for social anxiety, with emphasis on dating anxiety. In D. Meichenbaum & M. E. Jaremko (Eds.), *Stress reduction and prevention* (pp. 419–450). New York: Plenum.

Jaremko, M. E. (1984). Stress inoculation training: A generic approach for the prevention of stress-related disorders. *Personnel and Guidance Journal, 62,* 544–550.

Jarrett, R. B., & Nelson, R. O. (1987). Mechanisms of change in cognitive therapy of depression. *Behavior Therapy, 18,* 227–241.

Jarvinen, P. J., & Gold, S. R. (1981). Imagery as an aid in reducing depression. *Journal of Clinical Psychology, 37,* 523–529.

Jay, S. M., Elliott, C. H., Ozolins, M., Olson, R. A., & Pruitt, S. D. (1985). Behavioral management of children's distress during painful medical procedures. *Behaviour Research & Therapy, 23,* 513–520.

Jayaratne, S., & Levy, R. L. (1979). *Empirical clinical practice.* New York: Columbia University Press.

Jeffery, K. M. (1977). *The effects of goal-setting on self-motivated persistence.* Unpublished doctoral dissertation, Stanford University, Stanford, CA.

Jeffery, R. W. (1976). Reducing fears through participant modeling and self-directed practice. In J. D. Krumboltz & C. E. Thoresen (Eds.), *Counseling methods* (pp. 301–312). New York: Holt, Rinehart and Winston.

Jerremalm, A., Jansson, L., & Öst, L-G. (1986). Individual response patterns and the effects of different behavioral methods in the treatment of dental phobia. *Behaviour Research & Therapy, 24,* 587–596.

Johnson, D. W. (1986). *Reaching out: Interpersonal effectiveness and self-actualization* (3rd ed.). Englewood Cliffs, NJ: Prentice-Hall.

Johnston, J. M., & O'Neill, G. (1973). The analysis of performance criteria defining course grades as a determinant of college student academic performance. *Journal of Applied Behavior Analysis, 6,* 261–268.

Jones, A. S., & Gelso, C. (1988). Differential effects of style of interpretation: Another look. *Journal of Counseling Psychology, 35,* 363–369.

Jones, R. T., Nelson, R. E., & Kazdin, A. E. (1977). The role of external variables in self-reinforcement: A review. *Behavior Modification, 1,* 147–178.

Kabat-Zinn, J. (1982). An outpatient program in behavioral medicine for chronic pain patients based on the practice of mindfulness meditation: Theoretical considerations and preliminary results. *General Hospital Psychiatry, 4,* 33–47.

Kabat-Zinn, J., Lipworth, L., & Burney, R. (1985). The clinical use of mindfulness meditation for the self-regulation of chronic pain. *Journal of Behavioral Medicine, 8,* 163–190.

Kanfer, F. H. (1970). Self-monitoring: Methodological limitations and clinical applications. *Journal of Consulting and Clinical Psychology, 35,* 148–152.

Kanfer, F. H. (1975). Self-management methods. In F. H. Kanfer & A. P. Goldstein (Eds.), *Helping people change* (pp. 309–355). New York: Pergamon Press.

Kanfer, F. H. (1980). Self-management methods. In F. H. Kanfer & A. P. Goldstein (Eds.), *Helping people change* (2nd ed.) (pp. 334–389). New York: Pergamon Press.

Kanfer, F. H., & Goldstein, A. P. (1975). Introduction. In F. H. Kanfer & A. P. Goldstein (Eds.), *Helping people change* (pp. 1–14). New York: Pergamon Press.

Kanfer, F. H., & Grimm, L. G. (1977). Behavioral analysis: Selecting target behaviors in the interview. *Behavior Modification, 1,* 7–28.

Kanfer, F. H., & Phillips, J. S. (1970). *Learning foundations of behavior therapy.* New York: Wiley.

Kanfer, F. H., & Saslow, G. (1969). Behavioral diagnosis. In C. M. Franks (Ed.), *Behavior therapy: Appraisal and status* (pp. 417–444). New York: McGraw-Hill.

Kanfer, F. H., & Schefft, B. K. (1988). *Guiding the process of therapeutic change.* Champaign, IL: Research Press.

Kantor, J. R. (1970). An analysis of the experimental analysis of behavior (TEAB). *Journal of the Experimental Analysis of Behavior, 13,* 101–108.

Kaplan, D. A. (1982). Behavioral, cognitive, and behavioral-cognitive approaches to group assertion training therapy. *Cognitive Therapy and Research, 6,* 301–314.

Kaplan, H. I., & Sadock, B. J. (1981). *Modern synopsis of comprehensive textbook of psychiatry III* (3rd ed.). Baltimore: Williams & Wilkins.

Karoly, P., & Harris, A. (1986). Operant methods. In F. H. Kanfer & A. P. Goldstein (Eds.), *Helping people change* (3rd ed.) (pp. 111–144). New York: Pergamon Press.

Karoly, P., & Kanfer, F. A. (Eds.). (1982). *Self-management and behavior change.* New York: Pergamon Press.

Kazdin, A. E. (1973a). Covert modeling and the reduction of avoidance behavior. *Journal of Abnormal Psychology, 81,* 89–95.

Kazdin, A. E. (1973b). Methodological and assessment considerations in evaluating reinforcement programs in applied settings. *Journal of Applied Behavior Analysis, 6,* 517–531.

Kazdin, A. E. (1974a). Comparative effects of some variations of covert modeling. *Journal of Behavior Therapy and Experimental Psychiatry, 5,* 225–231.

Kazdin, A. E. (1974b). Covert modeling, model similarity, and reduction of avoidance behavior. *Behavior Therapy, 5,* 325–340.

Kazdin, A. E. (1974c). Effects of covert modeling and model reinforcement on assertive behavior. *Journal of Abnormal Psychology, 83,* 240–252.

Kazdin, A. E. (1974d). The effect of model identity and fear-relevant similarity on covert modeling. *Behavior Therapy, 5,* 624–635.

Kazdin, A. E. (1974e). Reactive self-monitoring: The effects of response desirability, goal setting, and feedback. *Journal of Consulting and Clinical Psychology, 42,* 704–716.

Kazdin, A. E. (1974f). Self-monitoring and behavior change. In M. J. Mahoney & C. E. Thoresen (Eds.), *Self-control: Power to the person* (pp. 218–246). Pacific Grove, CA: Brooks/Cole.

Kazdin, A. E. (1975). Covert modeling, imagery assessment, and assertive behavior. *Journal of Consulting and Clinical Psychology, 43,* 716–724.

Kazdin, A. E. (1976a). Assessment of imagery during covert

modeling of assertive behavior. *Journal of Behavior Therapy and Experimental Psychiatry, 7,* 213–219.

Kazdin, A. E. (1976b). Developing assertive behavior through covert modeling. In J. D. Krumboltz & C. E. Thoresen (Eds.), *Counseling methods* (pp. 475–486). New York: Holt, Rinehart and Winston.

Kazdin, A. E. (1976c). Effects of covert modeling, multiple models, and model reinforcement on assertive behavior. *Behavior Therapy, 7,* 211–222.

Kazdin, A. E. (1976d). Statistical analyses for single-case experimental designs. In M. Hersen & D. H. Barlow, *Single-case experimental designs: Strategies for studying behavior change* (pp. 265–316). New York: Pergamon Press.

Kazdin, A. E. (1977). Assessing the clinical or applied importance of behavior change through social validation. *Behavior Modification, 1,* 427–452.

Kazdin, A. E. (1979a). Effects of covert modeling and coding of modeled stimuli on assertive behavior. *Behaviour Research and Therapy, 17,* 53–61.

Kazdin, A. E. (1979b). Imagery elaboration and self-efficacy in covert modeling treatment of unassertive behavior. *Journal of Consulting and Clinical Psychology, 47,* 725–733.

Kazdin, A. E. (1980a). Covert and overt rehearsal and elaboration during treatment in development of assertive behavior. *Behaviour Research and Therapy, 18,* 191–201.

Kazdin, A. E. (1980b). *Research design in clinical psychology.* New York: Harper & Row.

Kazdin, A. E. (1981). Drawing valid inferences from case studies. *Journal of Consulting and Clinical Psychology, 49,* 183–192.

Kazdin, A. E. (1982). The separate and combined effects of covert and overt rehearsal in developing assertive behavior. *Behaviour Research and Therapy, 20,* 17–25.

Kazdin, A. E., & Krouse, R. (1983). The impact of variations in treatment rationales on expectancies for therapeutic change. *Behavior Therapy, 14,* 657–671.

Kazdin, A. E., & Mascitelli, S. (1982a). Behavioral rehearsal, self-instructions, and homework practice in developing assertiveness. *Behavior Therapy, 13,* 346–360.

Kazdin, A. E., & Mascitelli, S. (1982b). Covert and overt rehearsal and homework practice in developing assertiveness. *Journal of Consulting and Clinical Psychology, 50,* 250–258.

Kazdin, A. E., Matson, J. L., & Esveldt-Dawson, K. (1984). The relationship of role-play assessment of children's social skills to multiple measures of social competence. *Behaviour Research and Therapy, 22,* 129–139.

Kazdin, A. E., & Wilcoxon, L. A. (1976). Systematic desensitization and nonspecific treatment effects: A methodological evaluation. *Psychological Bulletin, 83,* 729–758.

Keane, T. M., Black, J. L., Collins, F. L., Jr., & Venson, M. C. (1982). A skills training program for teaching the behavioral interview. *Behavioral Assessment, 4,* 53–62.

Keefe, F. J., & Blumenthal, J. A. (1980). The life fitness program: A behavioral approach to making exercise a habit. *Journal of Behavior Therapy and Experimental Psychiatry, 11,* 31–34.

Keefe, F. J., Surwit, R. S., & Pilon, R. N. (1980). Biofeedback, autogenic training and progressive relaxation in the treatment of Raynaud's disease: A comparative study. *Journal of Applied Behavior Analysis, 13,* 3–11.

Kendall, P. C. (1983). Stressful medical procedures: Cognitive-behavioral strategies for stress management and prevention. In D. Meichenbaum & M. E. Jaremko (Eds.), *Stress reduction and prevention* (pp. 159–180). New York: Plenum.

Kendall, P. C., & Braswell, L. (1982). Cognitive-behavioral self-control therapy for children: A component analysis. *Journal of Consulting and Clinical Psychology, 50,* 672–689.

Kendall, P. C., & Hollon, S. D. (Eds.). (1981). *Assessment strategies for cognitive-behavioral interventions.* New York: Academic Press.

Kern, J. M. (1982). The comparative external and concurrent validity of three role-plays for assessing heterosocial performance. *Behavior Therapy, 13,* 666–680.

Kern, J. M., Miller, C., & Eggers, J. (1983). Enhancing the validity of role-play tests: A comparison of three role-play methodologies. *Behavior Therapy, 14,* 482–492.

Kerns, R. D., Finn, P., & Haythornthwaite, J. (1988). Self-monitored pain intensity: Psychometric properties and clinical utility. *Journal of Behavioral Medicine, 11,* 71–82.

Kiesler, C. A. (1971). *The psychology of commitment.* New York: Academic Press.

Kiesler, D. J. (1966). Some myths of psychotherapy research and the search for a paradigm. *Psychological Bulletin, 65,* 110–136.

King, M., Novik, L., & Citrenbaum, C. (1983). *Irresistible communication: Creative skills for the health professional.* Philadelphia: Saunders.

Kirby, E. A., & Grimley, L. K. (1986). *Understanding and treating attention deficit disorder.* New York: Pergamon.

Kiresuk, T. J. & Sherman, R. E. (1968). Goal attainment scaling: A general method for evaluating comprehensive mental health programs. *Community Mental Health Journal, 4,* 443–453.

Kirsch, I., & Henry, D. (1979). Self-desensitization and meditation in the reduction of public speaking anxiety. *Journal of Consulting and Clinical Psychology, 47,* 536–541.

Kirsch, I., Tennen, H., Wickless, C., Saccone, A. J., & Cody, S. (1983). The role of expectancy in fear reduction. *Behavior Therapy, 14,* 520–533.

Kirschenbaum, D. S., Ordman, A. M., Tomarken, A. J., & Holtzbauer, R. (1982). Effects of differential self-monitoring and level of mastery of sports performance: Brain power bowling. *Cognitive Therapy and Research, 6,* 335–342.

Klepac, R. K., Hauge, G., Dowling, J., & McDonald, M. (1981). Direct and generalized effects of three components of stress inoculation for increased pain tolerance. *Behavior Therapy, 12,* 417–424.

Klorman, R., Hilpert, P. L., Michael, R., LaGana, C., & Sveen, O. B. (1980). Effects of coping and mastery modeling on experienced and inexperienced pedodontic patients' disruptiveness. *Behavior Therapy, 11,* 156–168.

Knapp, M. L. (1972). *Nonverbal communication in human interaction.* New York: Holt, Rinehart and Winston.

Knapp, M. L. (1978). *Nonverbal communication in human interaction* (2nd ed.). New York: Holt, Rinehart and Winston.

Knox, J. (1972). *Cognitive strategies for coping with pain:*

Ignoring vs. acknowledging. Unpublished doctoral dissertation, University of Waterloo, Waterloo, Ontario, Canada.

Kolko, D., & Milan, M. (1983). Reframing and paradoxical instruction to overcome "resistance" in the treatment of delinquent youths: A multiple baseline analysis. *Journal of Consulting and Clinical Psychology, 51,* 655–660.

Kopel, S., & Arkowitz, H. (1975). The role of attribution and self-perception in behavior change: Implications for behavior therapy. *Genetic Psychology Monographs, 92,* 175–212.

Kostka, M. P., & Galassi, J. P. (1974). Group systematic desensitization versus covert positive reinforcement in the reduction of test anxiety. *Journal of Counseling Psychology, 21,* 464–468.

Kothandapani, V. (1971). Validation of feeling, belief, and intention to act as three components of attitude and their contribution to prediction of contraceptive behavior. *Journal of Personality and Social Psychology, 19,* 321–333.

Krivonos, P. D., & Knapp, M. L. (1975). Initiating communication: What do you say when you say hello? *Central States Speech Journal, 26,* 115–125.

Krumboltz, J. D. (1966). Behavioral goals for counseling. *Journal of Counseling Psychology, 13,* 153–159.

Krumboltz, J. D., & Thoresen, C. E. (Eds.) (1969). *Behavioral counseling: Cases and techniques.* New York: Holt, Rinehart and Winston.

Krumboltz, J. D., & Thoresen, C. E. (Eds.) (1976). *Counseling methods.* New York: Holt, Rinehart and Winston.

Kunzelmann, H. D. (Ed.). (1970). *Precision teaching.* Seattle: Special Child Publications.

L'Abate, L. (1981). Toward a systematic classification of counseling and therapy theorists, methods, processes, and goals: The E-R-A model. *Personnel and Guidance Journal, 59,* 263–266.

Laborde, G. (1984). *Influencing with integrity.* Palo Alto, CA: Science and Behavior Books.

Lacks, P. (1987). *Behavioral treatment for persistent insomnia.* New York: Pergamon.

Lacks, P., Bertelson, A. D., Sugerman, J., & Kunkel, J. (1983). The treatment of sleep-maintenance insomnia with stimulus-control techniques. *Behaviour Research and Therapy, 21,* 291–295.

LaCrosse, M. B. (1980). Perceived counselor social influence and counseling outcomes: Validity of the counselor rating form. *Journal of Counseling Psychology, 27,* 320–327.

Ladouceur, R. (1974). An experimental test of the learning paradigm of covert positive reinforcement in deconditioning anxiety. *Journal of Behavior Therapy and Experimental Psychiatry, 5,* 3–6.

Ladouceur, R. (1983). Participant modeling with or without cognitive treatment for phobias. *Journal of Consulting and Clinical Psychology, 51,* 930–932.

LaFromboise, T. D., & Dixon, D. N. (1981). American Indian perception of trustworthiness in a counseling interview. *Journal of Counseling Psychology, 28,* 135–139.

Lamaze, F. (1958). *Painless childbirth: Psychoprophylactic method.* London: Burke.

Lamontagne, L., Mason, K. R., & Hepworth, J. T. (1985). Effects of relaxation on anxiety in children: Implications for coping with stress. *Nursing Research, 34,* 289–292.

Lang, P. J. (1969). The mechanics of desensitization and the laboratory study of human fear. In C. M. Franks (Ed.), *Behavior therapy: Appraisal and status* (pp. 160–191). New York: McGraw-Hill.

Lang, P. J., & Lazovik, A. (1963). Experimental desensitization of a phobia. *Journal of Abnormal and Social Psychology, 66,* 519–525.

Lankton, S. R. (1980). *Practical magic: A translation of basic neurolinguistic programming into clinical psychotherapy.* Cupertino, CA: Meta Publications.

Lankton, S. R., & Lankton, C. H. (1983). *The answer within: A clinical framework of Ericksonian hypnotherapy.* New York: Brunner/Mazel.

Lawson, D. M., & May, R. B. (1970). Three procedures for the extinction of smoking behavior. *Psychological Record, 20,* 151–157.

Lazarus, A. A. (1966). Behavioral rehearsal vs. non-directive therapy vs. advice in effecting behaviour change. *Behaviour Research and Therapy, 4,* 209–212.

Lazarus, A. A. (1967). In support of technical eclecticism. *Psychological Reports, 21,* 415–416.

Lazarus, A. A. (1968). Variations in desensitization therapy. *Psychotherapy: Theory, Research and Practice, 5,* 50–52.

Lazarus, A. A. (1970). *Daily living: Coping with tension and anxieties* [Tape of relaxation exercises]. Chicago: Instructional Dynamics.

Lazarus, A. A. (1971). *Behavior therapy and beyond.* New York: McGraw-Hill.

Lazarus, A. A. (1973). Multimodal behavior therapy: Treating the "basic id." *Journal of Nervous and Mental Disease, 156,* 404–411.

Lazarus, A. A. (1976). *Multimodal behavior therapy.* New York: Springer.

Lazarus, A. A. (1978). Multimodal behavior therapy. Part 3. In E. Shostrom (Ed.), *Three approaches to psychotherapy II* [16-mm film or ¾" videocassette]. Orange, CA: Psychological Films.

Lazarus, A. A. (1981). *The practice of multimodal therapy.* New York: McGraw-Hill.

Lazarus, A. A. (1982). *Personal enrichment through imagery,* Workbook [Audiotape]. New York: BMA Audio Cassettes.

Lazarus, A. A., & Abramovitz, A. (1962). The use of "emotive imagery" in the treatment of children's phobias. *Journal of Mental Science, 108,* 191–195.

Lazarus, A. A., & Fay, A. (1982). Resistance or rationalization? A cognitive-behavioral perspective. In P. L. Wachtel (Ed.), *Resistance: Psychodynamic and behavioral approaches* (pp. 115–132). New York: Plenum.

Lazarus, A. A., & Rachman, S. (1957). The use of systematic desensitization in psychotherapy. *South African Medical Journal, 32,* 934–937.

Lazarus, R. S., & Folkman, S. (1984). *Stress, appraisal, and coping.* New York: Springer.

Leal, L., Baxter, E. G., Martin, J., & Marx, R. W. (1981). Cognitive modification and systematic desensitization with test anxious high school students. *Journal of Counseling Psychology, 28,* 525–528.

Leaman, D. R. (1978). Confrontation in counseling. *Personnel and Guidance Journal, 56,* 630–633.

Lecomte, C., Bernstein, B. L., & Dumont, F. (1981). Counseling interactions as a function of spatial-environmental conditions. *Journal of Counseling Psychology, 28,* 536–539.

Lee, D. Y., Hallberg, E. T., Kocsis, M., & Haase, R. F. (1980). Decoding skills in nonverbal communication and perceived interviewer effectiveness. *Journal of Counseling Psychology, 27,* 89–92.

Lehrer, P. M. (1982). How to relax and how not to relax: A reevaluation of the work of Edmund Jacobson—I. *Behaviour Research and Therapy, 20,* 417–428.

Lehrer, P. M., & Woolfolk, R. L. (1982). Self-report assessment of anxiety: Somatic, cognitive, and behavioral modalities. *Behavioral Assessment, 4,* 167–177.

Lehrer, P. M., & Woolfolk, R. L. (1984). Are stress-reduction techniques interchangeable, or do they have specific effects? A review of the comparative empirical literature. In R. L. Woolfolk & P. M. Lehrer (Eds.), *Principles and practice of stress management* (pp. 404–477). New York: Guilford Press.

Lehrer, P. M., Woolfolk, R. L., Rooney, A. J., McCann, B., & Carrington, P. (1983). Progressive relaxation and meditation: A study of psychophysiological and therapeutic differences between two techniques. *Behaviour Research and Therapy, 21,* 651–662.

Leitenberg, H., Agras, W. S., Barlow, D. H., & Oliveau, D. (1969). Contribution of selective positive reinforcement and therapeutic instructions to systematic desensitization therapy. *Journal of Abnormal Psychology, 74,* 113–118.

Lent, R. W., Russell, R. K., & Zamostny, K. P. (1981). Comparison of cue-controlled desensitization, rational restructuring and a credible placebo in the treatment of speech anxiety. *Journal of Consulting and Clinical Psychology, 49,* 608–610.

Levendusky, P., & Pankratz, L. (1975). Self-control techniques as an alternative to pain medication. *Journal of Abnormal Psychology, 84,* 165–168.

Leventhal, H., & Nerenz, D. R. (1983). A model for stress research with some implications for the control of stress disorders. In D. Meichenbaum & M. G. Jaremko (Eds.), *Stress reduction and prevention* (pp. 67–100). New York: Plenum.

Levin, F. M., & Gergen, K. J. (1969). Revealingness, ingratiation, and the disclosure of self. *Proceedings of the 77th Annual Convention of the American Psychological Association, 4* (Pt. 1), 447–448.

Levin, R., & Gross, A. (1985). The role of relaxation in systematic desensitization. *Behaviour Research & Therapy, 23,* 187–196.

Levine, B. A., & Wolpe, J. (1980). *In vivo* desensitization of a severe driving phobia through radio contact. *Journal of Behavior Therapy and Experimental Psychiatry, 11,* 281–282.

Levine, F., & Fasnacht, G. (1974). Token rewards may lead to token learning. *American Psychologist, 29,* 816–820.

Levy, L. H. (1963). *Psychological interpretation.* New York: Holt, Rinehart and Winston.

Levy, R. L. (1977). Relationship of an overt commitment to task compliance in behavior therapy. *Journal of Behavior Therapy and Experimental Psychiatry, 8,* 25–29.

Lewin, K. (1951). *Field theory in social science.* New York: Harper & Row.

Lewis, E. C. (1970). *The psychology of counseling.* New York: Holt, Rinehart and Winston.

Lewis, G. K. (1978). *Nurse-patient communication* (3rd ed.). Dubuque, IA: William C. Brown.

Lewis, W. A., & Evans, J. W. (1986). Resistance: A reconceptualization. *Psychotherapy, 23,* 426–433.

Ley, P. (1976). Toward better doctor-patient communications. In A. E. Bennett (Ed.), *Communication between doctors and patients.* London: Oxford University Press.

Lick, J. R., & Katkin, E. S. (1976). Assessment of anxiety and fear. In M. Hersen & A. S. Bellack (Eds.), *Behavioral assessment: A practical handbook* (pp. 175–206). New York: Pergamon Press.

Lick, J. R., & Unger, T. (1977). The external validity of behavioral fear assessment: The problem of generalizing from the laboratory to the natural environment. *Behavior Modification, 1,* 283–306.

Lidz, C. W., Meisel, A., Zerbavel, G. E., Carter, M., Sestak, R., & Roth, L. (1984). *Informed consent: A study of decision-making in psychiatry.* New York: Guilford Press.

Lindsley, O. R. (1968). A reliable wrist counter for recording behavior rates. *Journal of Applied Behavior Analysis, 1,* 77–78.

Linehan, M. (1977). Issues in behavioral interviewing. In J. D. Cone & R. P. Hawkins (Eds.), *Behavioral assessment: New directions in clinical psychology* (pp. 30–51). New York: Brunner/Mazel.

Lipinski, D. P., Black, J. L., Nelson, R. O., & Ciminero, A. (1975). Influence of motivational variables on the reactivity and reliability of self-recording. *Journal of Consulting and Clinical Psychology, 43,* 637–646.

Lipinski, D. P., & Nelson, R. (1974). The reactivity and unreliability of self-recording. *Journal of Consulting and Clinical Psychology, 42,* 118–123.

Litrownik, A. J. (1982). Special considerations in the self-management training of the developmentally disabled. In P. Karoly & F. H. Kanfer (Eds.), *Self management and behavior change* (pp. 315–352). New York: Pergamon Press.

Livingston, S. A. (1977). Psychometric techniques for criterion-referenced testing and behavioral assessment. In J. D. Cone & R. P. Hawkins (Eds.), *Behavioral assessment: New directions in clinical psychology* (pp. 308–383). New York: Brunner/Mazel.

Lloyd, M. E. (1983). Selecting systems to measure client outcome in human service agencies. *Behavioral Assessment, 5,* 55–70.

Locke, E. A., Shaw, K. N., Saari, L. M., & Latham, G. P. (1981). Goal-setting and task performance, 1969–1980. *Psychological Bulletin, 90,* 125–152.

Locke, H. J., & Wallace, K. N. (1957). Short marital adjustment and prediction tests: Their reliability and validity. *Marriage and Family Living, 21,* 251–255.

Lomont, J. F. (1965). Reciprocal inhibition or extinction? *Behaviour Research and Therapy, 3,* 209–219.

Long, B. C., & Haney, C. J. (1986). Outpatient treatment of hyperemesis gravidarum with stimulus control and imagery procedures. *Journal of Behavior Therapy and Experimental Psychiatry, 17,* 105–109.

Long, B. C., & Haney, C. J. (1988). Coping strategies for working women: Aerobic exercise and relaxation intervention. *Behavior Therapy, 19,* 75–83.

Long, L., Paradise, L., & Long, T. (1981). *Questioning:*

Skills for the helping process. Pacific Grove, CA: Brooks/Cole.

Long, L., & Prophit, P. (1981). *Understanding/responding: A communication manual for nurses.* Monterey, CA: Wadsworth Health Sciences.

Long, M., Simone, S., & Tucher, J. (1986). Outpatient treatment of hyperemesis gravidarum with stimulus control and imagery procedures. *Journal of Behavioral Therapy and Experimental Psychiatry, 17,* 105–109.

Lopez, F. G. (1983). A paradoxical approach to vocational indecision. *Personnel and Guidance Journal, 61,* 410–412.

Lopez, F. G., & Wambach, C. A. (1982). Effects of paradoxical and self-control directives in counseling. *Journal of Counseling Psychology, 29,* 115–124.

LoPiccolo, J., & Steger, J. C. (1974). The sexual interaction inventory: A new instrument for assessment of sexual dysfunction. *Archives of Sexual Behavior, 6,* 585–595.

Lowe, J. C. (1973). Excitatory response to music as a reciprocal inhibitor. *Journal of Behavior Therapy and Experimental Psychiatry, 4,* 297–299.

Lum, L. C. (1976). The syndrome of habitual chronic hyperventilation. In O. Hill (Ed.), *Modern trends in psychosomatic medicine* (Vol. 3). Boston: Butterworths.

Lyles, J. N., Burish, T. G., Krozely, M. G., & Oldham, R. K. (1982). Efficacy of relaxation training and guided imagery in reducing the aversiveness of cancer chemotherapy. *Journal of Consulting and Clinical Psychology, 50,* 509–524.

MacDonald, M. L., & Bernstein, D. A. (1974). Treatment of a spider phobia by *in vivo* and imaginal desensitization. *Journal of Behavior Therapy and Experimental Psychiatry, 5,* 47–52.

Mahaney, M. M., & Kern, J. M. (1983). Variations in role-play tests of heterosocial performance. *Journal of Consulting and Clinical Psychology, 51,* 151–152.

Mahoney, K. (1974). Count on it: A simple self-monitoring device. *Behavior Therapy, 5,* 701–703.

Mahoney, K., & Mahoney, M. J. (1976). Cognitive factors in weight reduction. In J. D. Krumboltz & C. E. Thoresen (Eds.), *Counseling methods* (pp. 99–105). New York: Holt, Rinehart and Winston.

Mahoney, M. J. (1970). Toward an experimental analysis of coverant control. *Behavior Therapy, 1,* 510–521.

Mahoney, M. J. (1971). The self-management of covert behavior: A case study. *Behavior Therapy, 2,* 575–578.

Mahoney, M. J. (1972). Research issues in self-management. *Behavior Therapy, 3,* 45–63.

Mahoney, M. J. (1974). *Cognition and behavior modification.* Cambridge, MA: Ballinger.

Mahoney, M. J. (1977a). Cognitive therapy and research: A question of questions. *Cognitive Therapy and Research, 1,* 5–16.

Mahoney, M. J. (1977b). Some applied issues in self-monitoring. In J. Cone & R. Hawkins (Eds.), *Behavioral assessment: New directions in clinical psychology* (pp. 241–254). New York: Brunner/Mazel.

Mahoney, M. J., Moura, N. G., & Wade, T. C. (1973). Relative efficacy of self-reward, self-punishment, and self-monitoring techniques for weight loss. *Journal of Consulting and Clinical Psychology, 40,* 404–407.

Mahoney, M. J., & Thoresen, C. E. (Eds.). (1974). *Self-con-*

trol: Power to the person. Pacific Grove, CA: Brooks/Cole.

Manthei, R. J. (1983). Client choice of therapist or therapy. *Personnel and Guidance Journal, 61,* 334–340.

Margolin, G. (1981). Behavior exchange in happy and unhappy marriages: A family cycle perspective. *Behavior Therapy, 12,* 329–343.

Marlatt, G. A., & Marques, J. K. (1977). Meditation, self-control and alcohol use. In R. B. Stuart (Ed.), *Behavioral self-management: Strategies, techniques and outcomes* (pp. 117–153). New York: Brunner/Mazel.

Marlatt, G. A., & Parks, G. A. (1982). Self-management of addictive behaviors. In P. Karoly & F. H. Kanfer (Eds.), *Self-management and behavior change* (pp. 443–448). New York: Pergamon Press.

Marlatt, G. A., & Perry, M. A. (1975). Modeling methods. In F. H. Kanfer & A. P. Goldstein (Eds.), *Helping people change* (pp. 117–158). New York: Pergamon Press.

Marquis, J. N., Ferguson, J. M., & Taylor, C. B. (1980). Generalization of relaxation skills. *Journal of Behavior Therapy and Experimental Psychiatry, 11,* 95–99.

Marquis, J. N., Morgan, W., & Piaget, G. (1973). *A guidebook for systematic desensitization* (3rd ed.). Palo Alto, CA: Veterans' Workshop.

Marshall, W., Presse, L., & Andrews, W. A. (1976). A self-administered program for public speaking anxiety. *Behaviour Research and Therapy, 14,* 33–39.

Martin, G. A., & Worthington, E. L. (1982). Behavioral homework. In M. N. Hersen, R. M. Eisler, & P. M. Miller (Eds.), *Progress in behavior modification* Vol. 13 (pp. 197–226). New York: Academic Press.

Martin, G. L. (1982). Thought-stopping and stimulus control to decrease persistent disturbing thoughts. *Journal of Behavior Therapy and Experimental Psychiatry, 13,* 215–220.

Martin, J. E., Collins, F. L., Jr., Hillenberg, J. B., Zabin, M. A., & Katell, A. D. (1981). Assessing compliance to home relaxation: A simple technology for a critical problem. *Behavioral Assessment, 3,* 193–198.

Martinez, J. A., & Edelstein, B. (1977, December). *The effects of demand characteristics on the assessment of heterosocial competence.* Paper presented at the annual meeting of the Association for the Advancement of Behavior Therapy, Atlanta.

Maslin, A., & Davis, J. L. (1975). Sex-role stereotyping as a factor in mental health standards among counselors-in-training. *Journal of Counseling Psychology, 22,* 87–91.

Maslow, A. H. (1966). *The psychology of science: A reconnaisance.* New York: Harper & Row.

Matarazzo, J. D., & Wiens, A. N. (1972). *The interview: Research on its anatomy and structure:* Chicago: Aldine-Atherton.

Mathews, A. M. (1971). Psychophysiological approaches to the investigation of desensitization and related procedures. *Psychological Bulletin, 76,* 73–91.

Matson, J. L. (1989). *Treating depression in children and adolescents.* New York: Pergamon.

Mattick, R. P., & Peters, L. (1988). Treatment of severe social phobia: Effects of guided exposure with and without cognitive restructuring. *Journal of Consulting and Clinical Psychology, 56,* 251–260.

Maultsby, R. C. (1984). *Rational behavior therapy.* Englewood Cliffs, NJ: Prentice-Hall.

Maurer, R. E., & Tindall, J. H. (1983). Effect of postural congruence on client's perception of counselor empathy. *Journal of Counseling Psychology, 30,* 158–163.

Mavissakalian, M., Michelson, L., Greenwald, D., Kornblith, S., & Greenwald, M. (1983). Cognitive-behavioral treatment of agoraphobia: Paradoxical intention vs. self-statement training. *Behaviour Research and Therapy, 21,* 75–86.

McCarthy, P. (1982). Differential effects of counselor self-referent responses and counselor status. *Journal of Counseling Psychology, 29,* 125–131.

McCarthy, P., & Betz, N. (1978). Differential effects of self-disclosing versus self-involving counselor statements. *Journal of Counseling Psychology, 25,* 251–256.

McCordick, S. M., Kaplan, R. M., Smith, S., & Finn, M. E. (1981). Variations in cognitive behavior modification for test anxiety. *Psychotherapy: Theory, Research & Practice, 18,* 170–178.

McDonald, F. J. (1973). Behavior modification in teacher education. In *Behavior modification in education: 72nd yearbook of the National Society for the Study of Education* (Pt. 1). Chicago: University of Chicago Press.

McFall, R. M. (1970). Effects of self-monitoring on normal smoking behavior. *Journal of Consulting and Clinical Psychology, 35,* 135–142.

McFall, R. M. (1977a). Analogue methods in behavioral assessment: Issues and prospects. In J. D. Cone & R. P. Hawkins (Eds.), *Behavioral assessment: New directions in clinical psychology* (pp. 152–177). New York: Brunner/Mazel.

McFall, R. M. (1977b). Parameters of self-monitoring. In R. B. Stuart (Ed.), *Behavioral self-management: Strategies, techniques and outcomes* (pp. 196–214). New York: Brunner/Mazel.

McFall, R. M., & Dodge, K. A. (1982). Self-management and interpersonal skills learning. In P. Karoly & F. H. Kanfer (Eds.), *Self-management and behavior change* (pp. 353–392). New York: Pergamon Press.

McFall, R. M., & Twentyman, C. (1973). Four experiments on the relative contributions of rehearsal, modeling, and coaching to assertion training. *Journal of Abnormal Psychology, 81,* 199–218.

McGlynn, F. D. (1980). Successful treatment of anorexia nervosa with self-monitoring and long distance praise. *Journal of Behavior Therapy and Experimental Psychiatry, 11,* 283–286.

McGlynn, F. D., Bichajian, C., Giesen, J. M., & Rose, R. L. (1981). Effects of cue-controlled relaxation, a credible placebo treatment and no treatment on shyness among college males. *Journal of Behavior Therapy and Experimental Psychiatry, 12,* 299–306.

McGlynn, F. D., Wilson, A., & Linder, L. (1970). Systematic desensitization of snake-avoidance with individualized and non-individualized hierarchies. *Journal of Behavior Therapy and Experimental Psychiatry, 1,* 201–204.

McGuigan, F. J. (1984). Progressive relaxation: Origins, principles, and clinical applications. In R. L. Woolfolk & P. M. Lehrer (Eds.), *Principles and practice of stress management* (pp. 12–42). New York: Guilford Press.

McGuire, D., & Thelen, M. H. (1983). Modeling, assertion training, and the breadth of the target assertive behavior. *Behavior Therapy, 14,* 275–285.

McGuire, D., Thelen, M. H., & Amolsch, T. (1975). Interview self-disclosure as a function of length of modeling and descriptive instructions. *Journal of Consulting and Clinical Psychology, 43,* 356–362.

McKeachie, W. J. (1974). The decline and fall of the laws of learning. *Educational Researcher, 3,* 7–11.

McKeachie, W. J. (1976). Psychology in America's bicentennial year. *American Psychologist, 31,* 819–833.

McKenzie, T. L., & Rushall, B. S. (1974). Effects of self-recording on attendance and performance in a competitive swimming training environment. *Journal of Applied Behavior Analysis, 7,* 199–206.

McLaughlin, T. F. (1976). Self-control in the classroom. *Review of Educational Research, 46,* 631–663.

Meador, B., & Rogers, C. (1984). Person-centered therapy. In R. J. Corsini (Ed.), *Current psychotherapies* (pp. 142–195). Itasca, IL: Peacock.

Means, J. R., Wilson, G. L., & Dlugokinski, L. J. (1987). Self-initiated imaginable and cognitive components: Evaluation of differential effectiveness in altering unpleasant moods. *Imagination, Cognition & Personality, 6,* 219–229.

Mehrabian, A. (1976). *Public places and private spaces.* New York: Basic Books.

Meichenbaum, D., & Turk, D. C. (1987). *Facilitating treatment adherence.* New York: Plenum.

Meichenbaum, D. H. (1971). Examination of model characteristics in reducing avoidance behavior. *Journal of Personality and Social Psychology, 17,* 298–307.

Meichenbaum, D. H. (1972). Cognitive modification of test anxious college students. *Journal of Consulting and Clinical Psychology, 39,* 370–380.

Meichenbaum, D. H. (1974). *Therapist manual for cognitive behavior modification.* Unpublished manuscript, University of Waterloo, Waterloo, Ontario, Canada.

Meichenbaum, D. H. (1976). A cognitive-behavior modification approach to assessment. In M. Hersen & A. S. Bellack (Eds.), *Behavioral assessment: A practical handbook* (pp. 143–171). New York: Pergamon Press.

Meichenbaum, D. H. (1977). *Cognitive-behavior modification: An integrative approach.* New York: Plenum.

Meichenbaum, D. H. (1985). *Stress-inoculation training.* New York: Pergamon Press.

Meichenbaum, D. H., & Cameron, R. (1973a). *Stress inoculation: A skills training approach to anxiety management.* Unpublished manuscript, University of Waterloo, Waterloo, Ontario, Canada.

Meichenbaum, D. H., & Cameron, R. (1973b). Training schizophrenics to talk to themselves. A means of developing attentional control. *Behavior Therapy, 4,* 515–534.

Meichenbaum, D. H., & Cameron, R. (1983). Stress inoculation training: Toward a general paradigm on training coping skills. In D. H. Meichenbaum & M. E. Jaremko (Eds.), *Stress reduction and prevention* (pp. 115–157). New York: Plenum.

Meichenbaum, D. H., Gilmore, J., & Fedoravicius, A. (1971). Group insight versus group desensitization in treating speech anxiety. *Journal of Counseling and Clinical Psychology, 36,* 410–421.

Meichenbaum, D. H., & Goodman, J. (1971). Training impulsive children to talk to themselves: A means of developing self-control. *Journal of Abnormal Psychology, 77,* 115–126.

Meichenbaum, D. H., & Turk, D. (1976). The cognitive-behavioral management of anxiety, anger, and pain. In P. O. Davidson (Ed.), *The behavioral management of anxiety, depression and pain.* New York: Brunner/Mazel.

Melamed, B. G., & Siegel, L. J. (1975). Reduction of anxiety in children facing hospitalization and surgery by use of filmed modeling. *Journal of Consulting and Clinical Psychology, 43,* 511–521.

Melamed, B. G., & Siegel, L. J. (1980). *Behavioral medicine: Practical applications in health care.* New York: Springer.

Melnick, J. (1973). A comparison of replication techniques in the modification of minimal dating behavior. *Journal of Abnormal Psychology, 81,* 51–59.

Melnick, J., & Russell, R. W. (1976). Hypnosis versus systematic desensitization in the treatment of test anxiety. *Journal of Counseling Psychology, 23,* 291–295.

Melnick, J., & Stocker, R. (1977). An experimental analysis of the behavioral rehearsal with feedback technique in assertiveness training. *Behavior Therapy, 8,* 222–228.

Meyer, R. G. (1983). *The clinician's handbook: The psychopathology of adulthood and late adolescence.* Boston: Allyn & Bacon.

Meyer, V., & Turkat, I. (1979). Behavioral analysis of clinical cases. *Journal of Behavioral Assessment, 1,* 259–270.

Miklich, D., Chida, T., & Danker-Brown, P. (1977). Behavior modification by self-modeling without subject awareness. *Journal of Behavior Therapy and Experimental Psychiatry, 8,* 125–130.

Miller, H. R., & Nawas, M. M. (1970). Control of aversive stimulus termination in systematic desensitization. *Behaviour Research and Therapy, 8,* 57–61.

Miller, R. C., & Berman, J. S. (1983). The efficacy of cognitive behavior therapies: A quantitative review of the research evidence. *Psychological Bulletin, 94,* 39–53.

Miller, W. R., & DiPilato, M. (1983). Treatment of nightmares via relaxation and desensitization: A controlled evaluation. *Journal of Consulting and Clinical Psychology, 51,* 870–877.

Milne, C. R., & Dowd, E. T. (1983). Effect of interpretation style on counselor social influence. *Journal of Counseling Psychology, 30,* 603–606.

Minuchin, S. (1974). *Families and family therapy.* Cambridge, MA: Harvard University Press.

Mischel, W. (1968). *Personality and assessment.* New York: Wiley.

Mischel, W. (1971). *Introduction to personality.* New York: Holt, Rinehart and Winston.

Mitchell, K. M., Bozarth, J. D., & Krauft, C. C. (1977). A reappraisal of the therapeutic effect of accurate empathy, nonpossessive warmth, and genuineness. In A. S. Gurman & A. M. Razin (Eds.), *Effective psychotherapy: A handbook of research* (pp. 482–502). New York: Pergamon Press.

Mitchell, K. R., & White, R. G. (1977). Behavioral self-management: An application to the problem of migraine headaches. *Behavior Therapy, 8,* 213–221.

Mitchell, L. K., & Krumboltz, J. D. (1987). The effects of cognitive restructuring and decision-making training on career indecision. *Journal of Counseling and Development, 66,* 171–174.

Mogan, J., & O'Brien, J. S. (1972). The counterconditioning of a vomiting habit by sips of ginger ale. *Journal of Behavior Therapy and Experimental Psychiatry, 3,* 135–137.

Moos, R. H. (1972). Assessment of the psychosocial environments of community-oriented psychiatric treatment programs. *Journal of Abnormal Psychology, 79,* 9–18.

Morganstern, K. P. (1986). Behavioral interviewing. In A. S. Bellack & M. Hersen (Eds.), *Behavioral assessment: A practical handbook* (3rd ed.) (pp. 86–118). New York: Pergamon Press.

Morin, C. M., & Azrin, N. A. (1987). Stimulus control and imagery training in treating sleep-maintenance insomnia. *Journal of Consulting and Clinical Psychology, 55,* 260–262.

Morris, K. T., & Kanitz, H. M. (1975). *Rational emotive therapy.* Boston: Houghton Mifflin.

Morris, R. J. (1986). Fear reduction methods. In F. H. Kanfer & A. P. Goldstein (Eds.), *Helping people change* (3rd ed.) (pp. 145–190). New York: Pergamon Press.

Munjack, D. J., & Oziel, R. J. (1978). Resistance in the behavioral treatment of sexual dysfunctions. *Journal of Sex and Marital Therapy, 4,* 122–138.

Murphy, T. J., Pagano, R. R., & Marlatt, G. A. (1986). Lifestyle modification with heavy alcohol drinkers: Effects of aerobic exercise and meditation. *Addictive Behaviors, 11,* 175–186.

National Association of Social Workers (1979). *Code of ethics.* Washington, DC: Author.

Nawas, M., Fishman, S., & Pucel, J. (1970). A standardized desensitization program applicable to group and individual treatments. *Behaviour Research and Therapy, 8,* 49–56.

Nay, W. R. (1979). *Multimethod clinical assessment.* New York: Gardner Press.

Neilans, T. H., & Israel, A. C. (1981). Towards maintenance and generalization of behavior change: Teaching children self-regulation and self-instructional skills. *Cognitive Therapy and Research, 5,* 189–195.

Nelson, R. O. (1977). Methodological issues in assessment via self-monitoring. In J. D. Cone & R. P. Hawkins (Eds.), *Behavioral assessment: New directions in clinical psychology* (pp. 217–254). New York: Brunner/Mazel.

Nelson, R. O. (1981). Realistic dependent measures for clinical use. *Journal of Consulting and Clinical Psychology, 49,* 168–182.

Nelson, R. O. (1983). Behavioral assessment: Past, present, and future. *Behavioral Assessment, 5,* 195–206.

Nelson, R. O., & Barlow, D. H. (1981). Behavioral assessment: Basic strategies and initial procedures. In D. H. Barlow (Ed.), *Behavioral assessment of adult disorders* (pp. 13–43). New York: Guilford Press.

Nelson, R. O., Boykin, R. A., & Hayes, S. C. (1982). Long-term effects of self-monitoring on reactivity and on accuracy. *Behaviour Research and Therapy, 20,* 357–363.

Nelson, R. O., & Hayes, S. C. (1979). Some current dimensions of behavioral assessment. *Behavioral Assessment, 1,* 1–16.

Nelson, R. O., Hayes, S. C., Felton, J. L., & Jarrett, R. B. (1985). A comparison of data produced by different behavioral assessment techniques with implications for models of social-skills inadequacy. *Behaviour Research and Therapy, 23,* 1–11.

Nelson, R. O., Hayes, S. C., Spong, R. T., Jarrett, R. B., & McKnight, D. L. (1983). Self-reinforcement: Appealing misnomer or effective mechanism. *Behaviour Research and Therapy, 21,* 557–566.

Nelson, R. O., Lipinski, D. P., & Black, J. L. (1976a). The reactivity of adult retardates' self-monitoring: A comparison among behaviors of different valences, and a comparison with token reinforcement. *Psychological Record, 26,* 189–201.

Nelson, R. O., Lipinski, D., & Black, J. L. (1976b). The relative reactivity of external observations and self-monitoring. *Behavior Therapy, 7,* 314–321.

Nelson, R. O., Lipinski, D. P., & Boykin, R. A. (1978). The effects of self-recorders' training and the obtrusiveness of the self-recording device on the accuracy and reactivity of self-monitoring. *Behavior Therapy, 9,* 200–208.

Nelson, W. M., III. (1981). A cognitive-behavioral treatment for disproportionate dental anxiety and pain: A case study. *Journal of Clinical Child Psychology, 10,* 79–82.

Nesse, M., & Nelson, R. O. (1977). Variations of covert modeling on cigarette smoking. *Cognitive Therapy and Research, 1,* 343–354.

Nezu, A. M. (1986). Efficacy of a social problem solving therapy approach for unipolar depression. *Journal of Consulting and Clinical Psychology, 54,* 196–202.

Nezu, A. M., & Nezu, C. M. (Eds.). (1989). *Clinical decision making in behavior therapy: A problem-solving perspective.* Champaign, IL: Research Press.

Nezu, A. M., Nezu, C. M., & Perri, M. G. (1989). *Problem-solving therapy for depression: Theory, research, and clinical guidelines.* New York: Wiley.

Nicassio, P., & Bootzin, R. (1974). A comparison of progressive relaxation and autogenic training as treatment for insomnia. *Journal of Abnormal Psychology, 83,* 253–260.

Nietzel, M. T., & Bernstein, D. A. (1981). Assessment of anxiety and fear. In M. Hersen & A. S. Bellack (Eds.), *Behavioral assessment* (2nd ed.) (pp. 215–245). New York: Pergamon Press.

Nietzel, M. T., Bernstein, D. A., & Russell, R. L. (1988). Assessment of anxiety and fear. In A. S. Bellack & M. Hersen (Eds.), *Behavioral assessment: A practical handbook* (3rd ed) (pp. 280–312). New York: Pergamon Press.

Nietzel, M. T., Martorano, R., & Melnick, J. (1977). The effects of covert modeling with and without reply training on the development and generalization of assertive responses. *Behavior Therapy, 8,* 183–192.

Nilsson, D., Strassberg, D., & Bannon, J. (1979). Perceptions of counselor self-disclosure: An analogue study. *Journal of Counseling Psychology, 26,* 399–404.

Nolan, J. D. (1968). Self-control procedures in the modification of smoking behavior. *Journal of Consulting and Clinical Psychology, 32,* 92–93.

Norton, G. R., & DeLuca, R. V. (1979). The use of stimulus control procedures to eliminate persistent nocturnal awakenings. *Journal of Behavior Therapy and Experimental Psychiatry, 10,* 65–67.

Novaco, R. W. (1975). *Anger control: The development and evaluation of an experimental treatment.* Lexington, MA: Heath.

Novaco, R. W. (1977). A stress inoculation approach to anger management in the training of law enforcement officers. *American Journal of Community Psychology, 5,* 327–346.

Nye, L. S. (1973). Obtaining results through modeling. *Personnel and Guidance Journal, 51,* 380–384.

Okun, B. F. (1976). *Effective helping: interviewing and counseling techniques.* North Scituate, MA: Duxbury Press.

Okun, B. F. (1987). *Effective helping: interviewing and counseling techniques* (3rd ed.). Pacific Grove, CA: Brooks/Cole.

O'Leary, K., Poulos, R., & Devine, V. (1972). Tangible reinforcers: Bonuses or bribes. *Journal of Consulting and Clinical Psychology, 38,* 1–8.

Omer, H. (1981). Paradoxical treatments: A unified concept. *Psychotherapy: Theory, Research and Practice, 18,* 320–324.

O'Neil, D., & Howell, R. (1969). Three modes of hierarchy presentation in systematic desensitization therapy. *Behaviour Research and Therapy, 7,* 289–294.

Orne, M. T. (1969). Demand characteristics and the concept of quasi-controls. In R. Rosenthal & R. Rosnow (Eds.), *Artifact in behavioral research* (pp. 147–179). New York: Academic Press.

Ornstein, R. E. (1972). *The psychology of consciousness.* New York: Viking.

Osberg, J. W., III. (1981). The effectiveness of applied relaxation in the treatment of speech anxiety. *Behavior Therapy, 12,* 723–729.

Osborn, E. L. (1986). Effects of participant modeling and desensitization on childhood warm water phobia. *Journal of Behavior Therapy and Experimental Psychiatry, 17,* 117–119.

Öst, L.-G. (1987). Applied relaxation: Description of a coping technique and review of controlled studies. *Behaviour Research & Therapy, 25,* 397–409.

Öst, L.-G. (1988). Applied relaxation vs. progressive relaxation in the treatment of panic disorder. *Behaviour Research & Therapy, 26,* 13–22.

Öst, L.-G., Jerremalm, A., & Johannson, J. (1981). Individual response patterns and the effects of different behavioral methods in the treatment of social phobia. *Behaviour Research and Therapy, 19,* 1–16.

Öst, L.-G., Johannson, J., & Jerremalm, A. (1982). Individual response patterns and the effects of different behavioral methods in the treatment of claustrophobia. *Behaviour Research and Therapy, 20,* 445–460.

Osterhouse, R. A. (1976). Group systematic desensitization of test anxiety. In J. D. Krumboltz & C. E. Thoresen (Eds.), *Counseling methods* (pp. 269–279). New York: Holt, Rinehart and Winston.

Otter, S. B., & Guerra, J. J. (1976). *Assertion training.* Champaign, IL: Research Press.

Owens, R. G., & Ashcroft, J. B. (1982). Functional analysis in applied psychology. *British Journal of Clinical Psychology, 21,* 181–189.

Papp, P. (1976). Family choreography. In P. J. Guerin, Jr. (Ed.), *Family therapy: Theory and practice* (pp. 465–479). New York: Gardner Press.

Papp, P. (1980). The Greek chorus and other techniques of paradoxical therapy. *Family Process, 19,* 45–57.

Papp, P. (1984). *The process of change.* New York: Guilford Press.

Pascal, G. R. (1959). *Behavioral change in the clinic.* New York: Grune & Stratton.

Passons, W. R. (1975). *Gestalt approaches in counseling.* New York: Holt, Rinehart and Winston.

Patterson, L. E., & Eisenberg, S. (1983). *The counseling process* (3rd ed.). Boston: Houghton Mifflin.

Paul, G. L. (1966). *Insight versus desensitization in psychotherapy: An experiment in anxiety reduction.* Stanford, CA: Stanford University Press.

Paul, G. L. (1967). Strategy of outcome research in psychotherapy. *Journal of Consulting Psychology, 31,* 109–118.

Paul, G. L., & Shannon, D. T. (1966). Treatment of anxiety through systematic desensitization in therapy groups. *Journal of Abnormal Psychology, 71,* 124–135.

Peck, S. (1978). *The road less traveled.* New York: Simon and Schuster.

Pecsok, E. H., & Fremouw, W. J. (1988). Controlling laboratory binging among restrained eaters through self-monitoring and cognitive restructuring procedures. *Addictive Behaviors, 13,* 37–44.

Penick, S. B., Filion, R., Fox, S., & Stunkard, A. J. (1971). Behavior modification in the treatment of obesity. *Psychosomatic Medicine, 33,* 49–55.

Perls, F. S. (1973). *The Gestalt approach and eyewitness to therapy.* Palo Alto, CA: Science and Behavior Books.

Perri, M. G., McAllister, D. A., Gange, J. J., Jordan, R. C., McAdoo, N. G., & Nezu, A. M. (1987). Effects of four maintenance programs on the long-term management of obesity. *Journal of Consulting and Clinical Psychology, 55,* 615–617.

Perri, M. G., & Richards, C. S. (1977). An investigation of naturally occurring episodes of self-controlled behaviors. *Journal of Counseling Psychology, 24,* 178–183.

Perry, M. A., & Furukawa, M. J. (1980). Modeling methods. In F. H. Kanfer & A. P. Goldstein (Eds.), *Helping people change* (pp. 131–171). New York, Pergamon Press.

Peterson, L., & Shigetomi, C. (1981). The use of coping techniques to minimize anxiety in hospitalized children. *Behavior Therapy, 12,* 1–14.

Peveler, R. C., & Johnston, D. W. (1986). Subjective and cognitive effects of relaxation. *Behaviour Research and Therapy, 24,* 413–419.

Philips, C., & Hunter, M. (1981). The treatment of tension headache: II. EMG "normality" and relaxation. *Behaviour Research and Therapy, 19,* 499–507.

Phillips, L. W. (1971). Training of sensory and imaginal responses in behavior therapy. In R. D. Rubin, H. Fensterheim, A. A. Lazarus, & C. M. Franks (Eds.), *Advances in behavior therapy* (pp. 111–122). New York: Academic Press.

Pickett, C., & Cloum, G. A. (1982). Comparative treatment strategies and their interaction with locus of control in the reduction of postsurgical pain and anxiety. *Journal of Consulting and Clinical Psychology, 50,* 439–441.

Pietrofesa, J. J., Hoffman, A., Splete, H. H., & Pinto, D. V. (1978). *Counseling: Theory, research, and practice.* Chicago: Rand McNally.

Polly, S., Turner, R. D., & Sherman, A. R. (1976). A self-control program for the treatment of obesity. In J. D. Krumboltz & C. E. Thoresen (Eds.), *Counseling methods* (pp. 106–117). New York: Holt, Rinehart and Winston.

Pope, A. W., McHale, S. M., & Craighead, N. E. (1988). *Self-esteem enhancement with children and adolescents.* New York: Pergamon Press.

Pope, B. (1979). *The mental health interview.* New York: Pergamon Press.

Poppen, R. (1988). *Behavioral relaxation training and assessment.* New York: Pergamon.

Potter, S. (1965). Language and society. In P. Hazard & M. Hazard (Eds.), *Language and literacy today.* Chicago: Science Research Associates.

Prinz, R. J., Foster, S., Kent, R. N., & O'Leary, K. D. (1979). Multivariate assessment of conflict in distressed and nondistressed mother-adolescent dyads. *Journal of Applied Behavior Analysis, 12,* 691–700.

Quattrochi-Turbin, S., & Jason, L. A. (1980). Enhancing social interaction and activity among the elderly through stimulus control. *Journal of Applied Behavior Analysis, 13,* 159–163.

Rachman, A. W. (1981). Clinical meditation in groups. *Psychotherapy: Theory, Research and Practice, 18,* 250–252.

Rachman, S. (1966). Studies in desensitization—III: Speed of generalization. *Behaviour Research and Therapy, 4,* 7–15.

Rachman, S. (1968). The role of muscular relaxation in desensitization therapy. *Behaviour Research and Therapy, 6,* 159–166.

Rachman, S. (1972). Clinical applications of observational learning, imitation and modeling. *Behavior Therapy, 3,* 379–397.

Raft, D., Smith, R. H., & Warren, N. (1986). Selection of imagery in the relief of chronic and acute clinical pain. *Journal of Psychosomatic Research, 30,* 481–488.

Rappaport, A. F., & Cammer, L. (1977). Breath meditation in the treatment of essential hypertension. *Behavior Therapy, 8,* 269–270.

Raskin, D., & Klein, Z. (1976). Losing a symptom through keeping it: A review of paradoxical treatment techniques and rationale. *Archives of General Psychiatry, 33,* 548–555.

Raths, L., Harmin, M., & Simon, S. (1966). *Values and teaching.* Columbus, OH: Charles E. Merrill.

Rathus, S. A. (1973). A 30-item schedule for assessing assertive behavior. *Behavior Therapy, 4,* 398–406.

Raush, H. L., & Bordin, E. S. (1957). Warmth in personality development and in psychotherapy. *Psychiatry, 20,* 351–363.

Ray, W. J., & Raczynski, J. M. (1981). Psychophysiological assessment. In M. Hersen & A. S. Bellack (Eds.), *Behavioral assessment* (pp. 175–211). New York: Pergamon Press.

Reade, M. N., & Smouse, A. D. (1980). Effect of inconsistent verbal-nonverbal communication and counselor response mode on client estimate of counselor regard and effectiveness. *Journal of Counseling Psychology, 27,* 546–553.

Rebman, V. L. (1983). Self-control desensitization with cue controlled relaxation for treatment of a conditioned vomiting response to air travel. *Journal of Behavior Therapy and Experimental Psychiatry, 14,* 161–164.

Redd, W. H. (1980). *In vivo* desensitization in the treatment of chronic emesis following gastrointestinal surgery. *Behavior Therapy, 11,* 421–427.

Redfering, D. L., & Bowman, M. J. (1981). Effects of a meditative relaxation exercise on non-attending behaviors of behaviorally disturbed children. *Journal of Clinical Child Psychology, 10,* 126–127.

Reeder, C., & Kunce, J. (1976). Modeling techniques, drug-abstinence behavior, and heroin addicts: A pilot study. *Journal of Counseling Psychology, 23,* 560–562.

Rehm, L. P. (1982). Self-management in depression. In P. Karoly & F. H. Kanfer (Eds.), *Self-management and behavior change* (pp. 522–567). New York: Pergamon Press.

Reid, W. H. (1983). *Treatment of the DSM-III psychiatric disorders.* New York: Brunner/Mazel.

Reiser, D. E., & Schroder, A. K. (1980). *Patient interviewing.* Baltimore: Williams & Wilkins.

Richardson, B., & Stone, G. L. (1981). Effects of a cognitive adjunct procedure within a microtraining situation. *Journal of Counseling Psychology, 28,* 168–175.

Ridley, C. R., & Tan, S-Y. (1986). Unintentional paradoxes and potential pitfalls in paradoxical psychotherapy. *The Counseling Psychologist, 14,* 303–308.

Rimm, D. C. (1973). Thought stopping and covert assertion in the treatment of phobias. *Journal of Consulting and Clinical Psychology, 41,* 466–467.

Rimm, D. C., & Masters, J. C. (1979). *Behavior therapy: Techniques and empirical findings* (2nd ed.). New York: Academic Press.

Rinn, R. C., & Vernon, J. C. (1975). Process evaluation of outpatient treatment in a community mental health center. *Journal of Behavior and Experimental Psychiatry, 6,* 5–11.

Risley, T., & Hart, B. (1968). Developing correspondence between the nonverbal and verbal behavior of preschool children. *Journal of Applied Behavior Analysis, 1,* 267–281.

Ritchie, M. H. (1986). Counseling the involuntary client. *Journal of Counseling and Development, 64,* 516–518.

Roberts, A. H. (1969). Self-control procedures in modification of smoking behavior: Replication. *Psychological Reports, 24,* 675–676.

Rogers, C. (1942). *Counseling and psychotherapy.* Boston: Houghton Mifflin.

Rogers, C. (1951). *Client-centered therapy.* Boston: Houghton Mifflin.

Rogers, C. (1957). The necessary and sufficient conditions of therapeutic personality change. *Journal of Consulting Psychology, 21,* 95–103.

Rogers, C. (1977). *Carl Rogers on personal power: Inner strength and its revolutionary impact.* New York: Delacorte Press.

Rogers, C., Gendlin, E., Kiesler, D., & Truax, C. (1967). The therapeutic relationship and its impact: A study of psychotherapy with schizophrenics. Madison: University of Wisconsin Press.

Rohrbaugh, M., Tennen, H., Press, S., & White, L. (1981). Compliance, defiance and therapeutic paradox: Guidelines for strategic use of paradoxical interventions. *American Journal of Orthopsychiatry, 51,* 454–467.

Romanczyk, R. G. (1974). Self-monitoring in the treatment of obesity: Parameters of reactivity. *Behavior Therapy, 5,* 531–540.

Rose, S. D. (1973). *Treating children in groups: A behavioral approach.* San Francisco: Jossey-Bass.

Rose, S. D. (1986). Group methods. In F. H. Kanfer and A. P. Goldstein (Eds.), *Helping people change* (3rd ed.) (pp. 437–469), New York: Pergamon Press.

Rosen, A., & Proctor, E. (1981). Distinctions between treatment outcomes and their implications for treatment evaluation. *Journal of Consulting and Clinical Psychology, 49,* 418–425.

Rosen, G. M., Glasgow, R. E., & Barrera, M. (1976). A controlled study to assess the clinical efficacy of totally self-administered systematic desensitization. *Journal of Consulting and Clinical Psychology, 44,* 208–217.

Rosen, R. C., & Schnapp, B. J. (1974). The use of a specific behavioral technique (thought-stopping) in the context of conjoint couples therapy: A case report. *Behavior Therapy, 5,* 261–264.

Rosenthal, T. L. (1976). Modeling therapies. In M. Hersen, R. Eisler, & P. Miller (Eds.), *Progress in behavior modification* (Vol. 2) (pp. 53–97). New York: Academic Press.

Rosenthal, T. L., & Bandura, A. (1978). Psychological modeling: Theory and Practice. In S. L. Garfield & A. E. Bergin (Eds.), *Handbook of Psychotherapy and Behavior Change* (2nd ed.) (pp. 621–658). New York: Wiley.

Rosenthal, T. L., Hung, J. H., & Kelley, J. E. (1977). Therapist social influence: Sternly strike while the iron is hot. *Behaviour Research and Therapy, 15,* 253–259.

Rosenthal, T. L., & Reese, S. L. (1976). The effects of covert and overt modeling on assertive behavior. *Behaviour Research and Therapy, 14,* 463–469.

Roskies, E. (1983). Stress management for Type A individuals. In D. Meichenbaum & M. E. Jaremko (Eds.), *Stress reduction and prevention* (pp. 261–288). New York: Plenum.

Ross, S. M., & Proctor, S. (1973). Frequency and duration of hierarchy item exposure in a systematic desensitization technique. *Behaviour Research and Therapy, 11,* 303–312.

Rothmeier, R. C., & Dixon, D. N. (1980). Trustworthiness and influence: A reexamination in an extended counseling analogue. *Journal of Counseling Psychology, 27,* 315–319.

Rotter, J. B., Chance, J. E., & Phares, E. J. (Eds.). (1972). *Applications of a social learning theory of personality.* New York: Holt, Rinehart and Winston.

Rovetto, F. M. (1983). *In vivo* desensitization of a severe driving phobia through radio contact with telemonitoring of neurophysiological reactions. *Journal of Behavior Therapy and Experimental Psychiatry, 14,* 49–54.

Rudestam, K., & Bedrosian, R. (1977). An investigation of the effectiveness of desensitization and flooding with two types of phobias. *Behaviour Research and Therapy, 15,* 23–30.

Russell, M. L. (1974). *The decision-making book for children.* Unpublished manuscript, Stanford University, Stanford, CA.

Russell, M. L., & Thoresen, C. E. (1976). Teaching decision-making skills to children. In J. D. Krumboltz & C. E. Thoresen (Eds.), *Counseling methods* (pp. 377–383). New York: Holt, Rinehart and Winston.

Russell, R. K., & Lent, R. W. (1982). Cue-controlled relaxation and systematic desensitization versus nonspecific factors in treating test anxiety. *Journal of Counseling Psychology, 29,* 100–103.

Russell, R. K., & Wise, F. (1976). Treatment of speech anxiety by cue-controlled relaxation and desensitization with professional and paraprofessional counselors. *Journal of Counseling Psychology, 23,* 583–586.

Russell, R. K., Wise, F., & Stratoudakis, J. P. (1976). Treatment of test anxiety by cue-controlled relaxation and systematic desensitization. *Journal of Counseling Psychology, 23,* 563–566.

Rutner, I. T., & Bugle, C. (1969). An experimental procedure for the modification of psychotic behavior. *Journal of Consulting and Clinical Psychology, 33,* 651–653.

Safran, J. D., Alden, L. E., & Davidson, P. O. (1980). Client anxiety level as a moderator variable in assertion training. *Cognitive Therapy and Research, 4,* 189–200.

Safran, J. D., & Greenberg, L. S. (1982). Cognitive appraisal and reappraisal: Implications for clinical practice. *Cognitive Therapy and Research, 6,* 251–258.

Saha, G. B., Palchoudhury, S., & Mardal, M. K. (1982). A study on facial expression of emotion. *Psychologia, 25,* 255–259.

Samaan, M. (1975). Thought-stopping and flooding in a case of hallucinations, obsessions, and homicidal-suicidal behavior. *Journal of Behavior Therapy and Experimental Psychiatry, 6,* 65–67.

Sarason, I. G. (1973). Test anxiety and cognitive modeling. *Journal of Personality and Social Psychology, 28,* 58–61.

Sarason, I. G., & Sarason, B. R. (1981). Teaching cognitive and social skills to high school students. *Journal of Consulting and Clinical Psychology, 49,* 908–918.

Schindler, F. E. (1980). Treatment by systematic desensitization of a recurring nightmare of a real life trauma. *Journal of Behavior Therapy and Experimental Psychiatry, 11,* 53–54.

Schlichter, K. J., & Horan, J. J. (1981). Effects of stress inoculation on the anger and aggression management skills of institutionalized juvenile delinquents. *Cognitive Therapy and Research, 5,* 359–365.

Schulz, R., & Barefoot, J. (1974). Nonverbal responses and affiliative conflict theory. *British Journal of Social and Clinical Psychology, 13,* 237–243.

Schutz, B. (1982). *Legal liability in psychotherapy.* San Francisco: Jossey-Bass.

Schutz, W. (1967). *Joy: Expanding human awareness.* New York: Grove Press.

Schwartz, A., & Goldiamond, I. (1975). *Social casework: A behavioral approach.* New York: Columbia University Press.

Schwartz, G. E., Davidson, R. J., & Goleman, D. J. (1978). Patterning of cognitive and somatic processes in the self-regulation of anxiety: Effects of meditation versus exercise. *Psychosomatic Medicine, 40,* 321–328.

Seay, T. A. (1978). *Systematic eclectic therapy.* Jonesboro, TN: Pilgrimage Press.

Seay, T. A., & Altekruse, M. K. (1979). Verbal and nonverbal behavior in judgments of facilitative conditions. *Journal of Counseling Psychology, 26,* 108–119.

Seer, P., & Raeburn, J. M. (1980). Meditation training and essential hypertension: A methodological study. *Journal of Behavioral Medicine, 3,* 59–71.

Seidner, M. L., & Kirschenbaum, D. S. (1980). Behavioral contracts: Effects of pretreatment information and intention statements. *Behavior Therapy, 11,* 689–698.

Selby, J. W., & Calhoun, L. G. (1980). Psychodidactics: An undervalued and underdeveloped treatment tool of psychological intervention. *Professional Psychology, 11,* 236–241.

Selvini-Palazzoli, M., Cecchin, G., Prata, G., & Boscolo, L. (1978). *Paradox and counterparadox.* New York: Jason Aronson.

Semb, G., Hopkins, B. L., & Hursh, D. E. (1973). The effects of study questions and grades on student test performance in a college course. *Journal of Applied Behavior Analysis, 6,* 631–642.

Senour, M. (1982). How counselors influence clients. *Personnel and Guidance Journal, 60,* 345–350.

Shaffer, W. F. (1976). *Heuristics for the initial diagnostic interview.* Paper presented at the annual meeting of the American Psychological Association, Washington, DC.

Shaffer, W. F. (1984). Personal communication, June 1, 1984.

Shapiro, D. H. (1978a). Behavioral and attitudinal changes resulting from a "Zen experience" workshop and Zen meditation. *Journal of Humanistic Psychology, 18,* 21–29.

Shapiro, D. H. (1978b). Instructions for a training package combining formal and informal Zen meditation with behavioral self-control strategies. *Psychologia, 31,* 70–76.

Shapiro, D. H. (1980). *Meditation: Self-regulation strategy and altered state of consciousness.* New York: Aldine.

Shapiro, D. H., (1982). Overview: Clinical and physiological comparison of meditation with other self-control strategies. *American Journal of Psychiatry, 139,* 267–274.

Shapiro, D. H., & Zifferblatt, S. M. (1976). Zen meditation and behavioral self-control: Similarities, differences, and clinical applications. *American Psychologist, 31,* 519–532.

Shapiro, M. B. (1966). The single case in clinical psychology research. *Journal of General Psychology, 74,* 3–23.

Sharpley, C. F. (1984). Predicate matching in NLP: A review of research on the preferred representational system. *Journal of Counseling Psychology, 31,* 238–248.

Shaw, D. W., & Thoresen, C. E. (1974). Effects of modeling and desensitization in reducing dentist phobia. *Journal of Counseling Psychology, 21,* 415–420.

Sheehan, P. W. (1967). A shortened form of Betts' questionnaire upon mental imagery. *Journal of Clinical Psychology, 23,* 386–389.

Sheikh, A. A. (Ed.). (1983). *Imagery: Current theory, research and application.* New York: Wiley.

Shelton, J. L., & Ackerman, J. M. (1974). *Homework in counseling and psychotherapy.* Springfield, IL: Charles C Thomas.

Shelton, J. L., & Levy, R. L. (1981). *Behavioral assignments and treatment compliance.* Champaign, IL: Research Press.

Sherer, M., & Rogers, R. (1980). Effects of therapist's nonverbal communication on rated skill and effectiveness. *Journal of Clinical Psychology, 26,* 696–700.

Sherman, A. R. (1972). Real-life exposure as a primary therapeutic factor in the desensitization treatment of fear. *Journal of Abnormal Psychology, 79,* 19–28.

Sherman, T. M., & Cormier, W. H. (1972). The use of subjective scales for measuring interpersonal reactions. *Journal of Behavior Therapy and Experimental Psychiatry, 3,* 279–280.

Shoemaker, J. E., & Tasto, D. L. (1975). The effects of muscle relaxation on blood pressure of essential hypertensives. *Behaviour Research and Therapy, 13,* 29–43.

Shoham-Salomon, V., & Rosenthal, R. (1987). Paradoxical

interventions: A meta-analysis. *Journal of Consulting and Clinical Psychology, 55,* 22–28.

Shorr, J. E., Sobel-Whittington, G., Robin, P., & Connella, J. A. (Eds.). (1984). *Imagery.* Vol. 3: *Theoretical and clinical applications.* New York: Plenum.

Siegel, J. C. (1980). Effects of objective evidence of expertness, nonverbal behavior, and subject sex in client-perceived expertness. *Journal of Counseling Psychology, 27,* 117–121.

Sierra-Franco, M. (1978). *Therapeutic communication in nursing.* New York: McGraw-Hill.

Simkins, L. (1971). The reliability of self-recorded behaviors. *Behavior Therapy, 2,* 83–87.

Simonson, N. (1976). The impact of therapist disclosure on patient disclosure. *Journal of Counseling Psychology, 23,* 3–6.

Simonton, O. C., Matthews-Simonton, S., & Creighton, J. (1980). *Getting well again.* New York: Bantam Books.

Simonton, O. C., & Simonton, S. S. (1975). Belief systems and management of the emotional aspects of malignancy. *Journal of Transpersonal Psychology, 7,* 29–47.

Singer, J. L. (1975). Navigating the stream of consciousness: Research in daydreaming and related inner experience. *American Psychologist, 30,* 727–738.

Singer, J. L. & Antrobus, J. S. (1972). Daydreaming, imaginal processes, and personality: A normative study. In P. W. Sheehan (Ed.), *The function and nature of imagery* (pp. 175–202). New York: Academic Press.

Sitton, S. C., & Griffin, S. T. (1981). Detection of deception from clients' eye contact patterns. *Journal of Counseling Psychology, 28,* 269–271.

Slade, P. (1982). Towards a functional analysis of anorexia nervosa and bulimia nervosa. *British Journal of Clinical Psychology, 21,* 167–179.

Smith, D. L. (1976). Goal attainment scaling as an adjunct to counseling. *Journal of Counseling Psychology, 23,* 22–27.

Smith, E. J. (1977). Counseling black individuals: Some stereotypes. *Personnel and Guidance Journal, 55,* 390–396.

Smith, G. P., & Coleman, R. E. (1977). Processes underlying generalization through participant modeling with self-directed practice. *Behaviour Research and Therapy, 15,* 204–206.

Smith, J. C. (1975). Meditation as psychotherapy: A review of the literature. *Psychological Bulletin, 82,* 558–564.

Smith-Hanen, S. S. (1977). Effects of nonverbal behaviors on judged levels of counselor warmth and empathy. *Journal of Counseling Psychology, 24,* 87–91.

Snow, R. E. (1974). Representative and quasi-representative designs for research on teaching. *Review of Educational Research, 44,* 265–291.

Southam, M. A., Agras, W. S., Taylor, C. B., & Kraemer, H. C. (1982). Relaxation training: Blood pressure lowering during the working day. *Archives of General Psychiatry, 39,* 715–717.

Southworth, S., & Kirch, I. (1988). The role of expectancy in exposure-generated fear reduction in agoraphobia. *Behaviour Research & Therapy, 26,* 113–120.

Spates, C. R., & Kanfer, F. H. (1977). Self-monitoring, self-evaluation, and self-reinforcement in children's learning: A test of a multistage self-regulation model. *Behavior Therapy, 8,* 9–16.

Spiegler, M., Cooley, E., Marshall, G., Prince, H., Puckett, S., & Skenazy, J. (1976). A self-control versus a counter-conditioning paradigm for systematic desensitization: An experimental comparison. *Journal of Counseling Psychology, 23,* 83–86.

Spinelli, P. R., & Packard, T. (1975, February). *Behavioral self-control delivery systems.* Paper presented at the National Conference on Behavioral Self-Control, Salt Lake City.

Spinks, S., & Birchler, G. (1982). Behavioral-systems marital therapy: Dealing with resistance. *Family Process, 21,* 169–185.

Spirito, A., Finch, A. J., Smith, T. L., & Cooley, W. H. (1981). Stress inoculation for anger and anxiety control: A case study with one emotionally disturbed boy. *Journal of Clinical Child Psychology, 10,* 67–70.

Spitzer, R. L., Gibbon, M., Skodol, A. E., Williams, J. B., & First, M. B. (1989). *DSM III-R Casebook.* Washington, DC: American Psychiatric Association.

Spitzer, R. L., Skodol, A. E., Gibbon, M., & Williams, J. (1981). *DSM-III Casebook.* Washington, DC: American Psychiatric Association.

Spooner, S. E., & Stone, S. C. (1977). Maintenance of specific counseling skills over time. *Journal of Counseling Psychology, 24,* 66–71.

Srebalus, D. J. (1975). Rethinking change in counseling. *Personnel and Guidance Journal, 53,* 415–421.

Stiles, W. B. (1980). Measurement of the impact of psychotherapy sessions. *Journal of Consulting and Clinical Psychology, 48,* 176–185.

Stone, C. I., Demchik-Stone, D. A., & Horan, J. J. (1977). Coping with pain: A component analysis of Lamaze and cognitive-behavioral procedures. *Journal of Psychosomatic Research, 21,* 451–456.

Strong, S. R. (1968). Counseling: An interpersonal influence process. *Journal of Counseling Psychology, 15,* 215–224.

Strong, S. R. (1984). Experimental studies in explicitly paradoxical interventions: Results and implications. *Journal of Behavior Therapy and Experimental Psychiatry, 15,* 189–194.

Strong, S. R., & Claiborn, C. (1982). *Change through interaction: Social psychological processes of counseling and psychotherapy.* New York: Wiley-Interscience.

Strong, S. R., & Schmidt, L. (1970). Expertness and influence in counseling. *Journal of Counseling Psychology, 17,* 81–87.

Strong, S. R., Wambach, C. A., Lopez, F. G., & Cooper, R. K. (1979). Motivational and equipping functions of interpretation in counseling. *Journal of Counseling Psychology, 26,* 98–107.

Strupp, H. H. (1980). Success and failure in time-limited psychotherapy: A systematic comparison of two cases: Comparison 1. *Archives of General Psychiatry, 37,* 595–603.

Stuart, R. B. (1971). Behavioral contracting within the families of delinquents. *Journal of Behavior Therapy and Experimental Psychiatry, 2,* 1–11.

Stuart, R. B. (1977). Self-help group approach to self-management. In R. B. Stuart (Ed.), *Behavioral self-management: Strategies, techniques and outcomes* (pp. 275–305). New York: Brunner/Mazel.

Stuart, R. B., & Davis, B. (1972). *Slim chance in a fat world.* Champaign, IL: Research Press.

Sturgis, E. T., & Grambling, S. (1988). Psychophysiological assessment. In A. S. Bellack & M. Hersen (Eds.), *Behavioral assessment: A practical handbook* (3rd ed.) (pp. 213–251). New York: Pergamon Press.

Sue, D. W. (1977). Consumerism in counseling. *Personnel and Guidance Journal, 56,* 197.

Sue, D. W., & Sue, D. (1977). Barriers to effective cross-cultural counseling. *Journal of Counseling Psychology, 24,* 420–429.

Sweeney, G. A., & Horan, J. J. (1982). Separate and combined effects of cue-controlled relaxation and cognitive restructuring in the treatment of medical performance anxiety. *Journal of Counseling Psychology, 29,* 486–497.

Sweeney, M. A., Cottle, W. C., & Kobayashi, M. J. (1980). Nonverbal communication: A cross-cultural comparison of American and Japanese counseling students. *Journal of Counseling Psychology, 27,* 150–156.

Swensen, C. H. (1968). *An approach to case conceptualization.* Boston: Houghton Mifflin.

Tasto, D. L. (1977). Self-report schedules and inventories. In A. R. Ciminero, K. S. Calhoun, & H. E. Adams (Eds.), *Handbook of behavioral assessment* (pp. 153–193). New York: Wiley.

Taussig, I. M. (1987). Comparative responses of Mexican-Americans and Anglo-Americans to early goal setting in public mental health clinic. *Journal of Counseling Psychology, 34,* 214–217.

Taylor, C. B. (1983). DSM-III and behavioral assessment. *Behavioral Assessment, 5,* 5–14.

Taylor, C. B., Pfenninger, J. L., & Candelaria, T. (1980). The use of treatment contracts to reduce Medicaid costs of a difficult patient. *Journal of Behavior Therapy and Experimental Psychiatry, 11,* 77–82.

Taylor, J. G. (1963). A behavioral interpretation of obsessive-compulsive neurosis. *Behaviour Research and Therapy, 1,* 237–244.

Tearnan, B. H., Lahey, B. B., Thompson, J. R., & Hammer, D. (1982). The role of coping self-instructions combined with covert modeling in specific fear reduction. *Cognitive Therapy and Research, 6,* 185–190.

Teders, S. J., Blanchard, E. B., Andrasik, F., Jurish, S. E., Neff, D. F., & Arena, J. G. (1984). Relaxation training for tension headache: Comparative efficacy and cost-effectiveness of a minimal therapist contact versus a therapist-delivered procedure. *Behavior Therapy, 15,* 59–70.

Tennen, H., Rohrbaugh, M., Press, S., & White, L. (1981). Reactance theory and therapeutic paradox: A compliance-defiance model. *Journal of Counseling Psychology, 18,* 14–22.

Thomas, E. J. (1977). *Marital communication and decision making.* New York: Free Press.

Thompson, A., & Wise, W. (1976). Steps toward outcome criteria. *Journal of Counseling Psychology, 23,* 202–208.

Thoresen, C. E., & Mahoney, M. J. (1974). *Behavioral self-control.* New York: Holt, Rinehart and Winston.

Thorpe, G. L. (1973). *Short-term effectiveness of systematic desensitization, modeling and behavior rehearsal, and self-instructional training in facilitating assertive-refusal behavior.* Unpublished doctoral dissertation, Rutgers University, New Brunswick, NJ.

Throll, D. A. (1982). Transcendental meditation and progressive relaxation: Their physiological effects. *Journal of Clinical Psychology, 38,* 522–530.

Tisdelle, D. A., & St. Laurence, J. S. (1988). Adolescent interpersonal problem-solving skill training: Social validation and generalization. *Behavior Therapy, 19,* 171–182.

Todd, T. C. (1980). *Paradoxical prescriptions: Application of consistent paradox using a strategic team.* Paper presented at the annual meeting of the American Psychological Association, Montreal, Canada.

Trager, G. L. (1958). Paralanguage: A first approximation. *Studies in Linguistics, 13,* 1–12.

Truax, C. B., & Carkhuff, R. R. (1967). *Toward effective counseling and psychotherapy: Training and practice.* Chicago: Aldine.

Truax, C. B., & Mitchell, K. M. (1971). Research on certain therapist interpersonal skills in relation to process and outcome. In A. Bergin & S. Garfield (Eds.), *Handbook of psychotherapy and behavior change: An empirical analysis* (pp. 299–344). New York: Wiley.

Turk, D. (1975). *Cognitive control of pain: A skills training approach for the treatment of pain.* Unpublished master's thesis, University of Waterloo, Waterloo, Ontario, Canada.

Turk, D., & Genest, M. (1979). Regulation of pain: The application of cognitive and behavioral techniques for prevention and remediation. In P. Kendall & S. Hollon (Eds.), *Cognitive-behavioral interventions: Theory, research, and procedures* (pp. 287–314). New York: Academic Press.

Turnage, J. R., & Logan, D. L. (1974). Treatment of a hypodermic needle phobia by *in vivo* systematic desensitization. *Journal of Behavior Therapy and Experimental Psychiatry, 5,* 67–69.

Turner, J. A. (1982). Comparison of group progressive-relaxation training and cognitive-behavioral group therapy for chronic low back pain. *Journal of Consulting and Clinical Psychology, 50,* 757–765.

Turner, R. D., Polly, S., & Sherman, A. R. (1976). A behavioral approach to individualized exercise programming. In J. D. Krumboltz & C. E. Thoresen (Eds.), *Counseling methods.* New York: Holt, Rinehart and Winston.

Turner, R. M., & Ascher, L. M. (1982). Therapist factor in the treatment of insomnia. *Behaviour Research and Therapy, 20,* 33–40.

Turock, A. (1980). Immediacy in counseling: Recognizing clients' unspoken messages. *Personnel and Guidance Journal, 59,* 168–172.

Uhlemann, M. R., Lea, G. W., & Stone, G. L. (1976). Effect of instructions and modeling on trainees low in interpersonal-communication skills. *Journal of Counseling Psychology, 23,* 509–513.

Ullmann, L. P., & Krasner, L. (1969). *A psychological approach to abnormal behavior.* Englewood Cliffs, NJ: Prentice-Hall.

Ultee, C. A., Griffioen, D., & Schellekens, J. (1982). The reduction of anxiety in children: A comparison of the effects of "systematic desensitization *in vitro*" and "systematic desensitization *in vivo.*" *Behaviour Research and Therapy, 20,* 61–67.

Valerio, H. P., & Stone, G. L. (1982). Effects of behavioral, cognitive, and combined treatments for assertion as a function of differential deficits. *Journal of Counseling Psychology, 29,* 158–168.

van Egeren, L. F. (1971). Psychophysiological aspects of systematic desensitization: Some outstanding issues. *Behaviour Research and Therapy, 9,* 65–77.

Van Hasselt, V. B., Hersen, M., Bellack, A. S., Rosenblum, N. D., & Lamparski, D. (1979). Tripartite assessment of the effects of systematic desensitization in a multi-phobic child: An experimental analysis. *Journal of Behavior Therapy and Experimental Psychiatry, 10,* 51–55.

Van Hoose, W. H., & Kottler, J. A. (1977). *Ethical and legal issues in counseling and psychotherapy.* San Francisco: Jossey-Bass.

Van Houten, R., Hill, S., & Parsons, M. (1975). An analysis of a performance feedback system: The effects of timing and feedback, public posting, and praise upon academic performance and peer interaction. *Journal of Applied Behavior Analysis, 8,* 449–457.

Vargas, A. M., & Borkowski, J. G. (1982). Physical attractiveness and counseling skills. *Journal of Counseling Psychology, 29,* 246–255.

Varni, J. W. (1980). Behavioral treatment of disease-related chronic insomnia in a hemophiliac. *Journal of Behavior Therapy and Experimental Psychiatry, 11,* 143–145.

Varni, J. W. (1981). Self-regulation techniques in the management of chronic arthritic pain in hemophilia. *Behavior Therapy, 12,* 185–194.

Ventis, W. (1973). Case history: The use of laughter as an alternative response in systematic desensitization. *Behavior Therapy, 4,* 120–122.

Veronen, L. J., & Kilpatrick, D. G. (1983). Stress management for rape victims. In D. Meichenbaum & M. E. Jaremko (Eds.), *Stress reduction and prevention* (pp. 341–374). New York: Plenum.

Wachtel, P. L. (Ed.). (1982). *Resistance: Psychodynamic and behavioral approaches.* New York: Plenum.

Wahler, R. G., & Fox, J. J. (1981). Setting events in applied behavior analysis: Toward a conceptual and methodological expansion. *Journal of Applied Behavior Analysis, 14,* 327–338.

Walls, R. T., Werner, T. J., Bacon, A., & Zane, T. (1977). Behavior checklists. In J. D. Cone & R. P. Hawkins (Eds.), *Behavioral assessment: New directions in clinical psychology* (pp. 77–145). New York: Brunner/Mazel.

Waranch, H. R., & Keenan, D. M. (1985). Behavioral treatment of children with recurrent headaches. *Journal of Behavior Therapy and Experimental Psychiatry, 16,* 31–38.

Warren, R., McLellarn, R., & Ponzoha, C. (1988). Rational-emotive therapy vs. general cognitive behavior therapy in the treatment of low self-esteem and related emotional disturbances. *Cognitive Therapy and Research, 12,* 21–38.

Watkins, C. E., Jr. (1983). Transference phenomena in the counseling situation. *Personnel and Guidance Journal, 62,* 206–210.

Watson, D. L., & Friend, R. (1969). Measurement of social-evaluative anxiety. *Journal of Consulting and Clinical Psychology, 33,* 448–457.

Watson, D. L., & Tharp, R. G. (1981). *Self-directed behavior: Self-modification for personal adjustment* (3rd ed.). Pacific Grove, CA: Brooks/Cole.

Watson, L. (1976). *The effects of covert modeling and covert reinforcement on job-interview skills of youth offenders.* Unpublished doctoral dissertation, West Virginia University, Morgantown.

Watson, O. M. (1970). *Proxemic behavior: A cross-cultural study.* The Hague: Mouton.

Watts, F. N. (1971). Desensitization as an habituation phenomenon: I. Stimulus intensity as determinant of the effects of stimulus lengths. *Behavior and Therapy, 12,* 209–217.

Watts, F. N. (1974). The control of spontaneous recovery of anxiety in imaginal desensitization. *Behaviour Research and Therapy, 12,* 57–59.

Watzlawick, P. (1978). *The language of change: Elements of therapeutic communication.* New York: Basic Books.

Watzlawick, P. (1982). In Ard, B. Reality, reframing and resistance in therapy: Interview with P. Watzlawick. *AAMFT Family Therapy News, 13,* 1.

Watzlawick, P., Beavin, J. H., & Jackson, D. D. (1967). *Pragmatics of human communication—A study of interactional patterns, pathologies, and paradoxes.* New York: Norton.

Watzlawick, P., Weakland, J., & Fisch, R. (1974). *Change: Principles of problem formation and problem resolution.* New York: Norton.

Webb, L. J., DiClemente, C. C., Johnstone, E. E., Sanders, J. L., & Perley, R. A. (1981). *DSM-III training guide.* New York: Brunner/Mazel.

Webster-Stratton, C. (1981a). Modification of mothers' behaviors and attitudes through a videotape modeling group discussion program. *Behavior Therapy, 12,* 634–642.

Webster-Stratton, C. (1981b). Videotape modeling: A method of parent education. *Journal of Clinical Child Psychology, 10,* 93–98.

Webster-Stratton, C. (1982). The long-term effects of a videotape parent-training program: Comparison of immediate and 1-year follow-up results. *Behavior Therapy, 13,* 702–714.

Webster-Stratton, C., Kolpacoff, M., & Hollinsworth, T. (1988). Self-administered videotape therapy for families with conduct-problem children: Comparison with two cost-effective treatments and a control group. *Journal of Consulting and Clinical Psychology, 56,* 558–566.

Weeks, G. R., & L'Abate, L. (1982). *Paradoxical psychotherapy: Theory and practice with individuals, couples, and families.* New York: Brunner/Mazel.

Weissberg, M. (1975). Anxiety-inhibiting statements and relaxation combined in two cases of speech anxiety. *Journal of Behavior Therapy and Experimental Psychiatry, 6,* 163–164.

Wernick, R. L. (1983). Stress inoculation in the management of clinical pain: Application to burn pain. In D. Meichenbaum & M. E. Jaremko (Eds.), *Stress reduction and prevention* (pp. 191–217). New York: Plenum.

West, D. J., Jr., Horan, J. J., & Games, P. A. (1984). Component analysis of occupational stress inoculation applied to registered nurses in an acute care hospital setting. *Journal of Counseling Psychology, 31,* 209–218.

White, K., Sheehan, P. W., & Ashton, R. (1977). Imagery assessment: A survey of self-report measures. *Journal of Mental Imagery, 1,* 145–170.

Whittrock, D. A., Blanchard, E. B., & McCoy, G. C. (1988). Three studies on the relation of process to outcome in the treatment of essential hypertension with relaxation and thermal biofeedback. *Behaviour Research & Therapy, 26,* 53–66.

Widiger, T. A., & Rorer, L. G. (1984). The responsible psychotherapist. *American Psychologist, 39,* 503–515.

Williams, A. M. (1979). The quantity and quality of marital interaction related to marital satisfaction: A behavioral analysis. *Journal of Applied Behavior Analysis, 12,* 665–678.

Williams, R. L., Canale, J., & Edgerly, J. (1976). Affinity for self-management: A comparison between counseling clients and controls. *Journal of Behavior Therapy and Experimental Psychiatry, 7,* 231–234.

Wilson, G. T., & Davison, G. C. (1971). Processes of fear reduction in systematic desensitization: Animal studies. *Psychological Bulletin, 76,* 1–14.

Wilson, G. T., & Evans, I. M. (1977). The therapist-client relationship in behavior therapy. In A. S. Gurman & A. M. Razin (Eds), *Effective psychotherapy: A handbook of research.* New York: Pergamon Press.

Wilson, G. T., Rossiter, E., Kleifield, E. I., & Lindholm, L. (1986). Cognitive behavioral treatment of bulimia nervosa: A controlled evaluation. *Behaviour Research & Therapy, 24,* 277–288.

Wing, J. K., Cooper, J. E., & Sartorius, N. (1974). *The measurement and classification of psychiatric symptoms.* Cambridge, England: Cambridge University Press.

Wing, R. R., Epstein, L. H., Norwalk, M. P., & Scott, N. (1988). Self-regulation in the treatment of Type II diabetes. *Behavior Therapy, 19,* 11–23.

Wolf, M. M. (1978). Social validity: The case for subjective measurement; or, how applied behavior analysis is finding its heart. *Journal of Applied Behaviour Analysis, 11,* 203–214.

Wollersheim, J. P., Bordewick, M., Knapp, M., McLellarn, R., & Paul, W. (1982). The influence of therapy rationales upon perceptions of clinical problems. *Cognitive Therapy and Research, 6,* 167–172.

Wolpe, J. (1958). *Psychotherapy by reciprocal inhibition.* Stanford, CA: Stanford University Press.

Wolpe, J. (1961). The systematic desensitization treatment of neuroses. *Journal of Nervous and Mental Disease, 132,* 189–203.

Wolpe, J. (1969). *The practice of behavior therapy.* New York: Pergamon Press.

Wolpe, J. (1971). Dealing with resistance to thought-stopping: A transcript. *Journal of Behavior Therapy and Experimental Psychiatry, 2,* 121–125.

Wolpe, J. (1973). *The practice of behavior therapy* (2nd ed.). New York: Pergamon Press.

Wolpe, J. (1976). *Theme and variations: A behavior/therapy casebook.* New York: Pergamon Press.

Wolpe, J. (1982). *The practice of behavior therapy* (3rd ed.). New York: Pergamon Press.

Wolpe, J., & Lang, P. J. (1964). A fear survey schedule for use in behavior therapy. *Behaviour Research and Therapy, 2,* 27–30.

Wolpe, J., & Lazarus, A. A. (1966). *Behavior therapy techniques.* New York: Pergamon Press.

Woodward, R., & Jones, R. B. (1980). Cognitive restructuring treatment: A controlled trial with anxious patients. *Behaviour Research and Therapy, 18,* 401–407.

Woolfolk, R. L. (1976). The multimodal model as a framework for decision-making in psychotherapy. In A. A. Lazarus (Ed.), *Multimodal behavior therapy* (pp. 20–24). New York: Springer.

Woolfolk, R. L., Carr-Kaffashan, L., McNulty, T. F., & Lehrer, P. M. (1976). Meditation training as a treatment for insomnia. *Behavior Therapy, 7,* 359–365.

Woolfolk, R. L., & Lehrer, P. M. (Eds.). (1984). *Principles and practice of stress management.* New York: Guilford Press.

Woolfolk, R. L., Lehrer, P. M., McCann, B. S., & Rooney, A. J. (1982). Effects of progressive relaxation and meditation on cognitive and somatic manifestations of daily stress. *Behaviour Research and Therapy, 20,* 461–467.

Woolfolk, R. L., & McNulty, T. F. (1983). Relaxation treatment for insomnia: A component analysis. *Journal of Consulting and Clinical Psychology, 51,* 495–503.

Woollams, S., & Brown, M. (1979). *TA: The total handbook of transactional analysis.* Englewood Cliffs, NJ: Prentice-Hall.

Worthington, E. L., & Shumate, M. (1981). Imagery and verbal counseling methods in stress inoculation training for pain control. *Journal of Counseling Psychology, 28,* 1–6.

Woy, J. R., & Efran, J. S. (1972). Systematic desensitization and expectancy in the treatment of speaking anxiety. *Behaviour Research and Therapy, 10,* 43–49.

Wright, R. M., & Strong, S. R. (1982). Stimulating therapeutic change with directives: An exploratory study. *Journal of Counseling Psychology, 29,* 199–202.

Wurtele, S. K., Marro, S. R., & Miller-Perrin, C. L. (1987). Practice makes perfect? The role of participant modeling in sexual abuse prevention programs. *Journal of Consulting & Clinical Psychology, 55,* 599–602.

Wysocki, T., Hall, G., Iwata, B., & Riordan, M. (1979). Behavioral management of exercise: Contracting for aerobic points. *Journal of Applied Behavior Analysis, 12,* 55–64.

Yamagami, T. (1971). The treatment of an obsession by thought-stopping. *Journal of Behavior Therapy and Experimental Psychiatry, 2,* 133–135.

Yeaton, W. H., & Sechrest, L. (1981). Critical dimensions in the choice and maintenance of successful treatments: Strength, integrity, and effectiveness. *Journal of Consulting and Clinical Psychology, 49,* 156–167.

Yost, E. B., Beutler, L. E., Corbishley, M. A., & Allender, J. R. (1986). *Group cognitive therapy: A treatment method for depression in older adults.* New York: Pergamon Press.

Youell, K. J., & McCullough, J. P. (1975). Behavioral treatment of mucous colitis. *Journal of Consulting and Clinical Psychology, 43,* 740–745.

Young, D. W. (1980). Meanings of counselor nonverbal gestures: Fixed or interpretive? *Journal of Counseling Psychology, 27,* 447–452.

Zamostny, K. P., Corrigan, J. D., & Eggert, M. A. (1981). Replication and extension of social influence processes in counseling: A field study. *Journal of Counseling Psychology, 28,* 481–489.

Zeig, J. (1980a). Symptom prescription and Ericksonian principles of hypnosis and psychotherapy. *American Journal of Clinical Hypnosis, 23,* 16–22.

Zeig, J. (1980b). Symptom prescription techniques: Clinical applications using elements of communication. *American Journal of Clinical Hypnosis, 23,* 22–33.

Zemore, R. (1975). Systematic desensitization as a method of teaching a general anxiety-reducing skill. *Journal of Counseling and Clinical Psychology, 43,* 157–161.

Zlotlow, S. F., & Allen, G. J. (1981). Comparison of analogue strategies for investigating the influence of counselors' physical attractiveness. *Journal of Counseling Psychology, 28,* 194–202.

Zwart, C. A., & Lisman, S. A. (1979). Analysis of stimulus control treatment of sleep-onset insomnia. *Journal of Consulting and Clinical Psychology, 47,* 113–118.

AUTHOR INDEX

SUBJECT INDEX

TO THE OWNER OF THIS BOOK:

We have attempted to provide a useful learning tool and are interested in receiving feedback from you about how well we have achieved our goals. We encourage you to share your reactions with us so that we may improve future editions of *Interviewing Strategies for Helpers*.

School _____ Instructor's name _____

City _____ State _____ Zip _____

1. In what class did you use this book? _____

2. What did you like *most* about this book? _____

_____

_____

3. What did you like *least* about this book? _____

_____

_____

4. How useful were the learning activities? _____

_____

5. How useful were the postevaluation sections? _____

_____

6. How valuable were the feedback sections? _____

_____

7. What topics do you think should be expanded or added to this book in future editions?

_____

_____

8. What is your reaction to the layout of the text? _____

_____

_____

9. In the space below or in a separate letter, please write any other comments about the book you'd like to make. We welcome your suggestions! Thank you for taking the time to write to us.

Optional:

Your name: _____   Date: _____

May Brooks/Cole quote you, either in promotion for *Interviewing Strategies for Helpers* or in future publishing ventures?

Yes: _____   No: _____

Sincerely,
William H. Cormier
L. Sherilyn Cormier

FOLD HERE

‖‖‖‖

BUSINESS REPLY MAIL

FIRST CLASS   PERMIT NO. 358   PACIFIC GROVE, CA

POSTAGE WILL BE PAID BY ADDRESSEE

ATT: _____ *Cormier & Cormier* _____

Brooks/Cole Publishing Company
511 Forest Lodge Road
Pacific Grove, California 93950-9968

FOLD HERE